Street by Street

LONDON

GW00602837

6th edition April 2010
© AA Media Limited 2010

Original edition printed May 2001

This product includes map data licensed from Ordnance Survey® with the permission of the Controller of Her Majesty's Stationery Office. © Crown copyright 2010. All rights reserved. Licence number 100021153.

The copyright in all PAF is owned by Royal Mail Group plc.

Information on fixed speed camera locations provided by RoadPilot © 2010 RoadPilot® Driving Technology.

All rights reserved. No part of this publication may be reproduced, stored in a retrieval system, or transmitted in any form or by any means – electronic, mechanical, photocopying, recording or otherwise – unless the permission of the publisher has been given beforehand.

Published by AA Publishing (a trading name of AA Media Limited, whose registered office is Fanum House, Basing View, Basingstoke, Hampshire RG21 4EA. Registered number 06112600).

Produced by the Mapping Services Department of The Automobile Association. (A03956)

A CIP Catalogue record for this book is available from the British Library.

Printed by Oriental Press in Dubai

The contents of this atlas are believed to be correct at the time of the latest revision. However, the publishers cannot be held responsible or liable for any loss or damage occasioned to any person acting or refraining from action as a result of any use or reliance on any material in this atlas, nor for any errors, omissions or changes in such material. This does not affect your statutory rights. The publishers would welcome information to correct any errors or omissions and to keep this atlas up to date. Please write to Mapping Services, The Automobile Association, Fanum House, Basing View, Basingstoke, Hampshire, RG21 4EA.
E-mail: *streetbystreet@theaa.com*

Ref: ML038v

Key to map pages	ii–iii
Key to map symbols	iv–1
Enlarged map pages	2–19
Main map pages	20–217
Index – towns & villages	218
Index – streets	220–306
Index – featured places	306–329
Acknowledgements	330

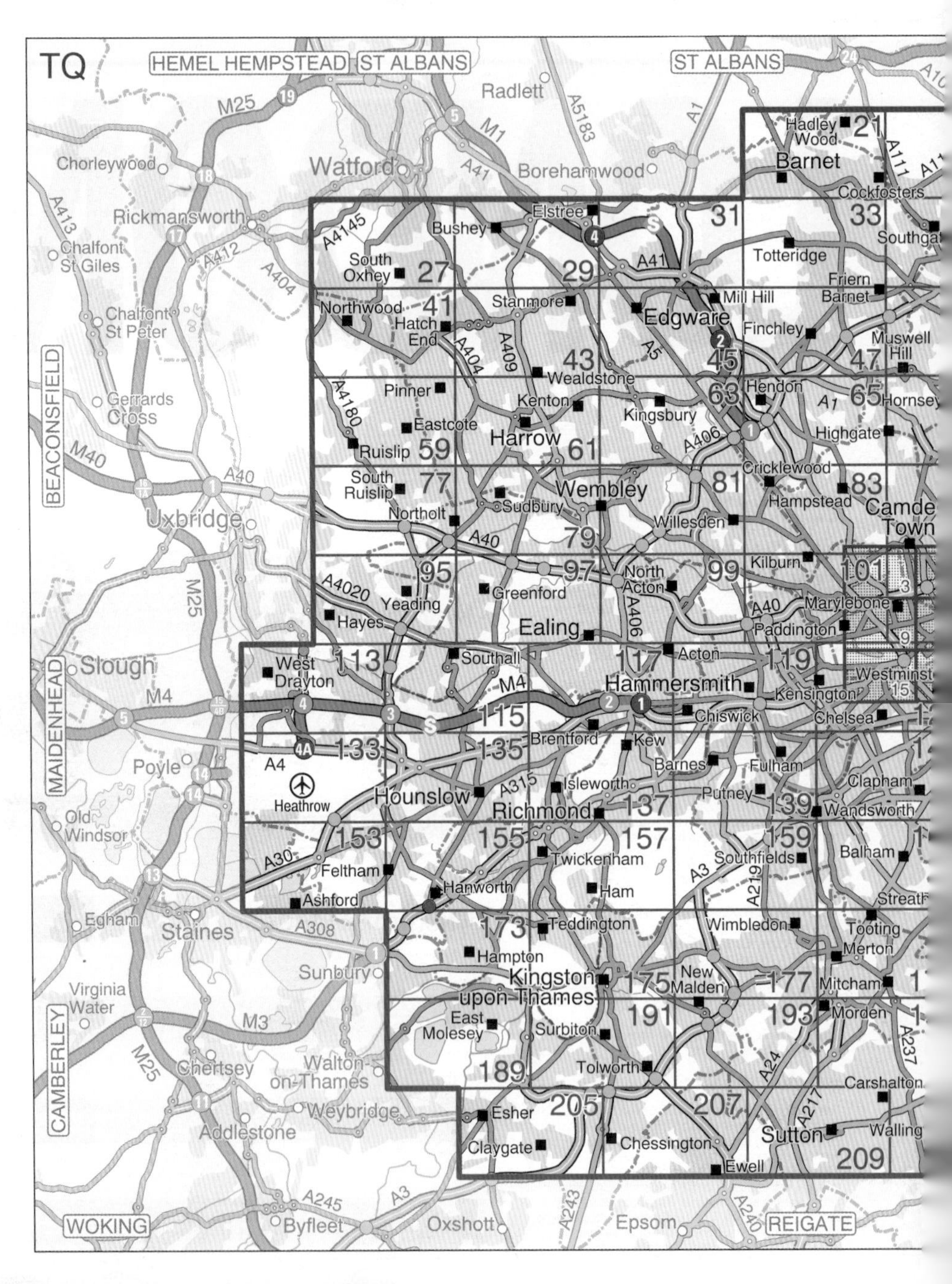

ii

TQ

HEMEL HEMPSTEAD | ST ALBANS | ST ALBANS

Scale of enlarged map pages 1:10,000 6.3 inches to 1 mile

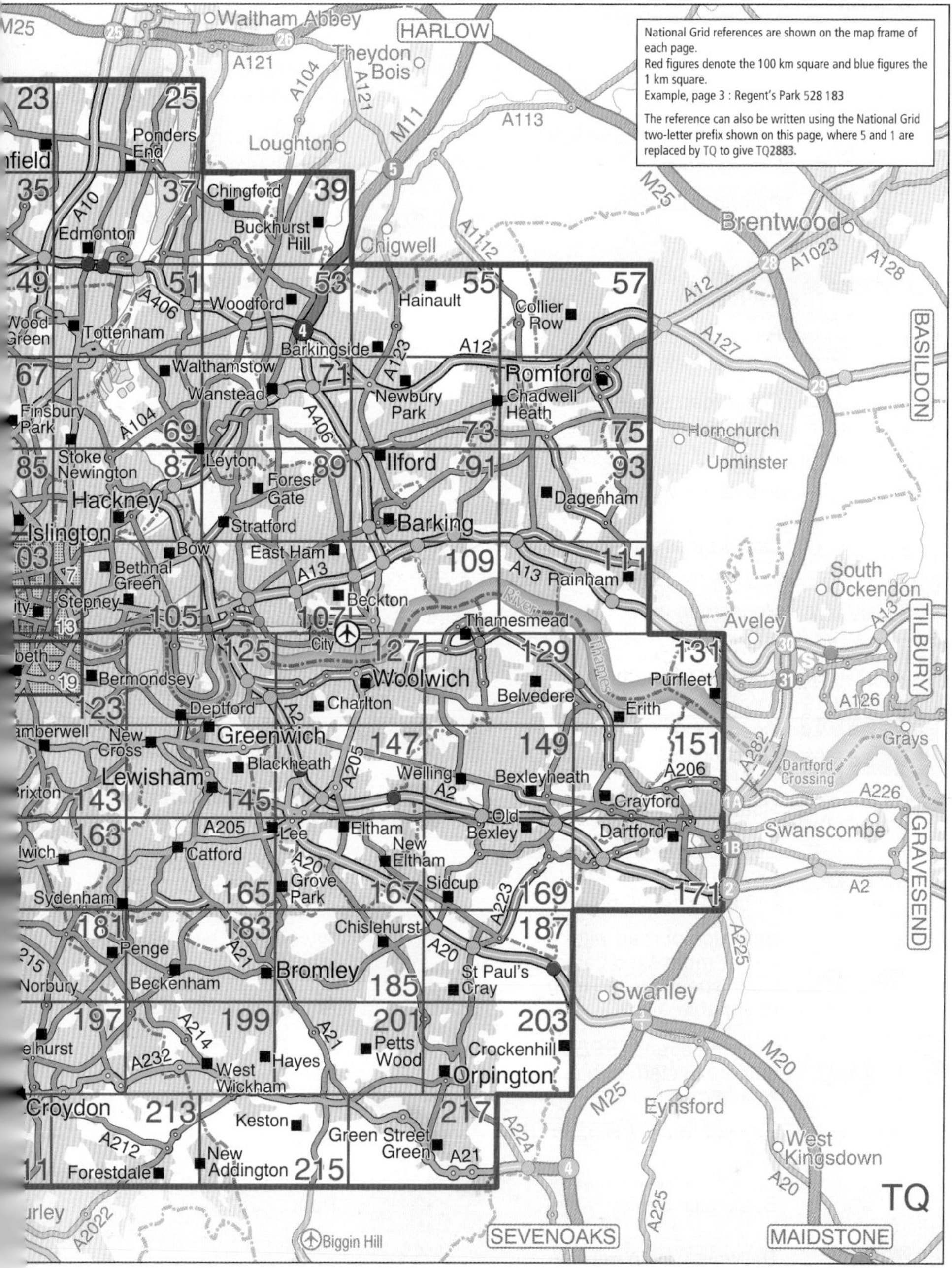

National Grid references are shown on the map frame of each page.
Red figures denote the 100 km square and blue figures the 1 km square.
Example, page 3 : Regent's Park 528 183

The reference can also be written using the National Grid two-letter prefix shown on this page, where 5 and 1 are replaced by TQ to give TQ2883.

M25
Waltham Abbey
HARLOW
M25
A121
Theydon Bois
A104
A113
M11
23   25
Ponders End
field
Loughton
Brentwood
A10
35   37
Chingford   39
Buckhurst Hill
Edmonton
Chigwell
A1023   A128
BASILDON
A406
A12
A127
49   51   53   55   57
Woodford
Hainault
Collier Row
Wood Green
Tottenham
Barkingside
A12
A123
67   71   Romford
Walthamstow
Wanstead
Newbury Park
Chadwell Heath
Hornchurch
Upminster
A104
69   73   75
Finsbury Park
Leyton
Forest Gate
Ilford
85   87   89   91   93
Stoke Newington
Hackney
Stratford
Dagenham
Islington
Bow
East Ham
Barking
03
Bethnal Green
A13   109   111
Stepney
105   107   Beckton   Rainham
ity
City
Thamesmead
Aveley
South Ockendon
A13
TILBURY
eth
123   125   127   129   131   Purfleet
Bermondsey   Woolwich   Belvedere   Erith
Deptford   Charlton
Grays
amberwell   Greenwich   147   149   151   Dartford Crossing   A226
New Cross   Blackheath   Welling   Bexleyheath   A206
Lewisham   145   A2   Crayford   Swanscombe   GRAVESEND
rixton   143   Eltham   Old Bexley   Dartford   A2
163   Lee   New Eltham   169   171
wich   Catford   Sidcup
Sydenham   165   Grove Park   167   187
181   183   Chislehurst   St Paul's Cray   Swanley
Penge   Bromley   185   M20
Norbury   Beckenham   Crockenhill   203
197   199   201   Petts Wood   M20
elhurst   West Wickham   Orpington   Eynsford
Croydon   213   Keston   217   West Kingsdown
Forestdale   New Addington   215   Green Street Green   A20   A225
urley   Biggin Hill   SEVENOAKS   MAIDSTONE   TQ

0   1/2   miles   1
0   1/2   1   kilometres   1 1/2

Junction 9	Motorway & junction	⊖	Underground station
Services	Motorway service area	⊖	Docklands Light Railway (DLR) station
	Primary road single/dual carriageway	⊖	London Overground station
Services	Primary road service area	⊖	Light railway & station
	A road single/dual carriageway	*LC*	Level crossing
	B road single/dual carriageway	●—●—●—●	Tramway
	Other road single/dual carriageway	- - - - - -	Ferry route
	Minor/private road, access may be restricted	··········	Airport runway
← ←	One-way street	— · — · —	County, administrative boundary
	Pedestrian area		Congestion Charging Zone *
- - - - - -	Track or footpath		Charge-free routes through the Charging Zone
■■■■■■	Road under construction		Low Emission Zone (LEZ) (visit **theaa.com** for further information)
⌐- - - =⌐	Road tunnel	**17**	Page continuation 1:17,500
30 **V**	Speed camera site (fixed location) with speed limit in mph or variable	**3**	Page continuation to enlarged scale 1:10,000
40 **V**	Selection of road with two or more fixed camera sites; speed limit in mph or variable		River/canal, lake, pier
50→ ←**50**	Average speed (SPECS™) camera system with speed limit in mph		Aqueduct, lock, weir
P **P+**	Parking, Park & Ride		Beach
🚌	Bus/coach station		Woodland
	Railway & main railway station		Park
	Railway & minor railway station		Cemetery
			Built-up area

* The AA central London Congestion Charging map is also available

Symbol	Description
	Industrial / business building
	Leisure building
	Retail building
	Other building
	City wall
A&E	Hospital with 24-hour A&E department
PO	Post Office, public library
i	Tourist Information Centre, seasonal
	Petrol station, 24 hour — Major suppliers only
†	Church/chapel
	Public toilets, with facilities for the less able
PH	Public house — AA recommended
	Restaurant — AA inspected
Madeira Hotel	Hotel — AA inspected
	Theatre or performing arts centre, cinema
	Golf course
▲	Camping — AA inspected
	Caravan site — AA inspected
	Camping & caravan site — AA inspected
	Theme park
	Abbey, cathedral or priory

Symbol	Description
	Castle
	Historic house or building
Wakehurst Place (NT)	National Trust property
M	Museum or art gallery
	Roman antiquity
	Ancient site, battlefield or monument
	Industrial interest
	Garden
	Garden Centre — Garden Centre Association Member
	Garden Centre — Wyevale Garden Centre
	Arboretum
	Farm or animal centre
	Zoological or wildlife collection
	Bird collection
	Nature reserve
	Aquarium
V	Visitor or heritage centre
	Country park
	Cave
	Windmill
	Distillery, brewery or vineyard

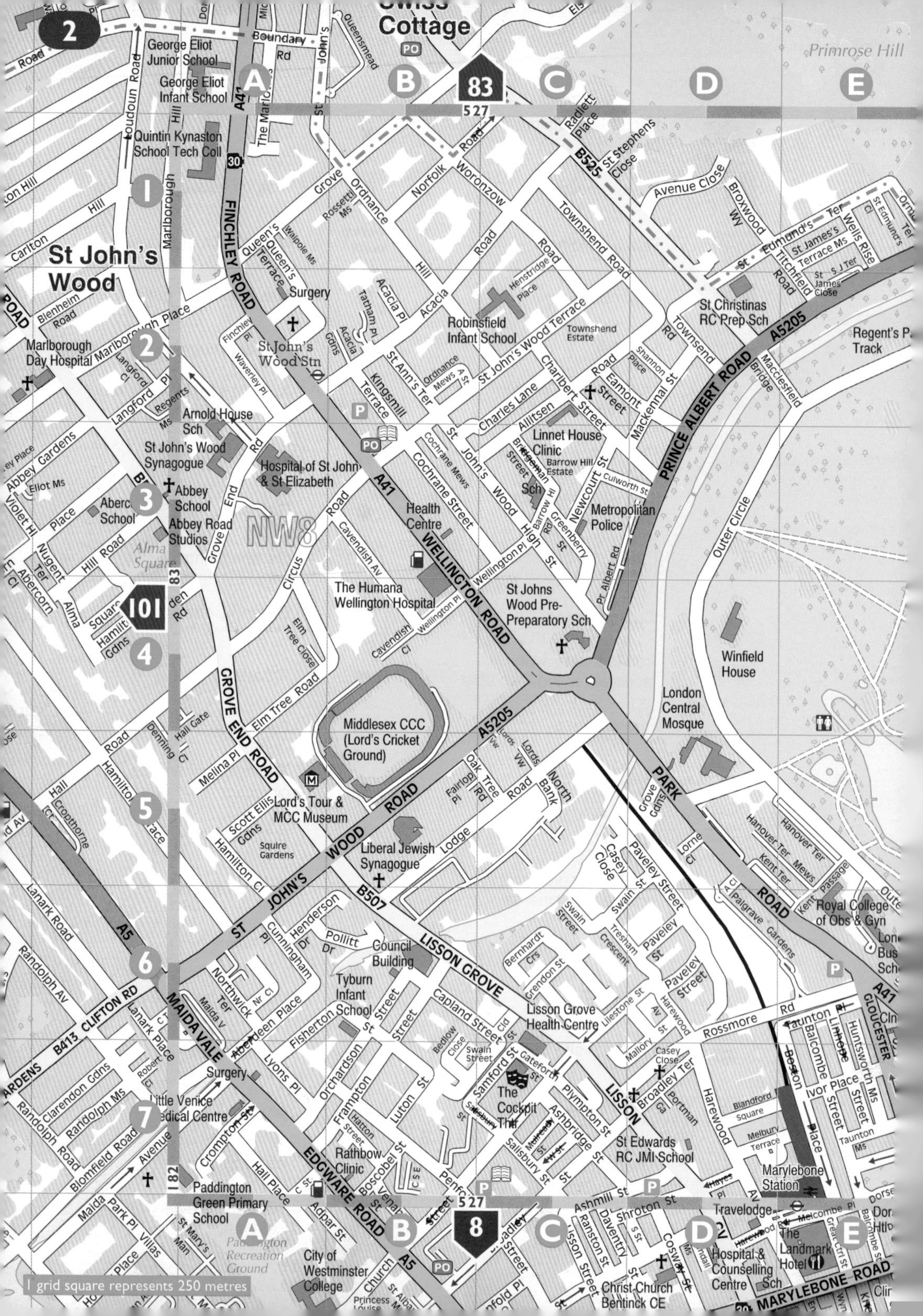

2
Swiss Cottage
Primrose Hill
A
B
C
D
E
83
527
1
2
3
4
5
6
7
8
101
St John's Wood
NW8
George Eliot Junior School
George Eliot Infant School
Quintin Kynaston School Tech Coll
Boundary Rd
Loudoun Road
Marlborough Hill
Carlton Hill
Blenheim Road
Marlborough Day Hospital
Marlborough Place
Langford Cl
Langford Pl
Regents Ms
Arnold House Sch
St John's Wood Synagogue
Abbey Gardens
Eliot Ms
Violet Hl
Abercorn School
Abbey School
Abbey Road Studios
Alma Square
Nugent Ter
Hill Road
Abercorn Pl
Alma Sq
Hamilton Gdns
Hamilton Terrace
Hall Gate
Denning Cl
Melina Pl
Grove End Road
Elm Tree Road
Elm Tree Close
Cavendish Cl
Cavendish Av
Circus Road
Hospital of St John & St Elizabeth
Health Centre
The Humana Wellington Hospital
Wellington Pl
Wellington Road
A41
Finchley Road
Queen's Grove
Queen's Terrace
Walpole Ms
Surgery
Finchley Pl
Waverley Pl
St John's Wood Stn
Kingsmill Terrace
St Ann's Ter
Ordnance Mews
Ordnance Hill
Rossetti Ms
Acacia Road
Acacia Pl
Acacia Gdns
Tatham Pl
Norfolk Road
Woronzow Road
Robinsfield Infant School
Henstridge Place
St John's Wood Terrace
Townshend Estate
Townshend Road
Charles Lane
Allitsen Rd
Charlbert Street
Eamont Street
Shannon Place
Mackennal St
Cochrane Mews
Cochrane Street
St John's Wood High St
Bridgeman Street
Linnet House Clinic
Barrow Hill Estate
Barrow Hill Rd
Newcourt St
Culworth St
Greenberry St
Metropolitan Police
Pr Albert Rd
St Johns Wood Pre-Preparatory Sch
Radlett Place
B525
St Stephens Close
Avenue Close
Broxwood Wy
St Edmund's Ter
St James's Terrace Ms
Wells Rise
St Edmund's Cl
SJ Ter
St James' Close
Titchfield Road
St Christinas RC Prep Sch
Townsend Rd
A5205
Prince Albert Road
Macclesfield Bridge
Regent's Park Track
Outer Circle
Winfield House
London Central Mosque
Middlesex CCC (Lord's Cricket Ground)
Lord's Tour & MCC Museum
Lords Vw
Oak Tree Rd
Fairlop Pl
North Bank
Lodge Road
Liberal Jewish Synagogue
St John's Wood Road
Scott Ellis Gdns
Squire Gardens
Hamilton Cl
B507
Lisson Grove
Henderson Dr
Pollitt Dr
Council Building
Cunningham Pl
Tyburn Infant School
Casey Close
Paveley Street
Swain St
Swain Street
Tresham Crescent
Bernhardt Crs
Grendon St
Lilestone St
Harewood Av
Mallory St
Rossmore Rd
Grove Gdns
Lorne Cl
Park Road
Hanover Ter
Hanover Ter Mews
Kent Ter
Kent Passage
Palgrave Gardens
Royal College of Obs & Gyn
Gloucester Pl
Taunton Pl
Balcombe St
Linhope St
Huntsworth Ms
Boston Place
Ivor Place
Blandford Square
Melbury Terrace
Taunton Ms
Marylebone Station
Hayes Pl
Harewood Row
Great Ctrl St
Melcombe Pl
Dorset Sq
The Landmark Hotel
Marylebone Road
Travelodge
Hospital & Counselling Centre
Christ Church Bentinck CE Sch
Cosway St
St Edwards RC JMI School
Broadley Ter
Portman Ga
Harewood
Lisson Grove Health Centre
Capland Street
Bedlow Close
Swain Street
Cid
Gateforth St
Samford St
The Cockpit Thtr
Salisbury St
Plympton St
Ashbridge St
Lisson
Ashmill St
Ranston St
Daventry St
Shroton St
Lisson Street
Bradley Street
Penfold St
Frampton Street
Hatton Street
Luton St
Boscobel St
Rathbone Clinic
Orchardson St
Fisherton Street
Lyons Pl
Aberdeen Place
Northwick Ter
Nr Cl
Maida Vale
Maida Av
Surgery
Little Venice Medical Centre
Crompton St
Hall Place
Edgware Road
A5
Paddington Green Primary School
Paddington Recreation Ground
City of Westminster College
Church St
Adpar St
Princess Louise
Clifton Rd
B413
Lanark Road
Lanark Place
Robert Cl
Randolph Av
Randolph Ms
Randolph Road
Clarendon Gdns
Blomfield Road
Cropthorne Ct
Hall Rd
Maida Park Pl
St Mary's Man
1 grid square represents 250 metres

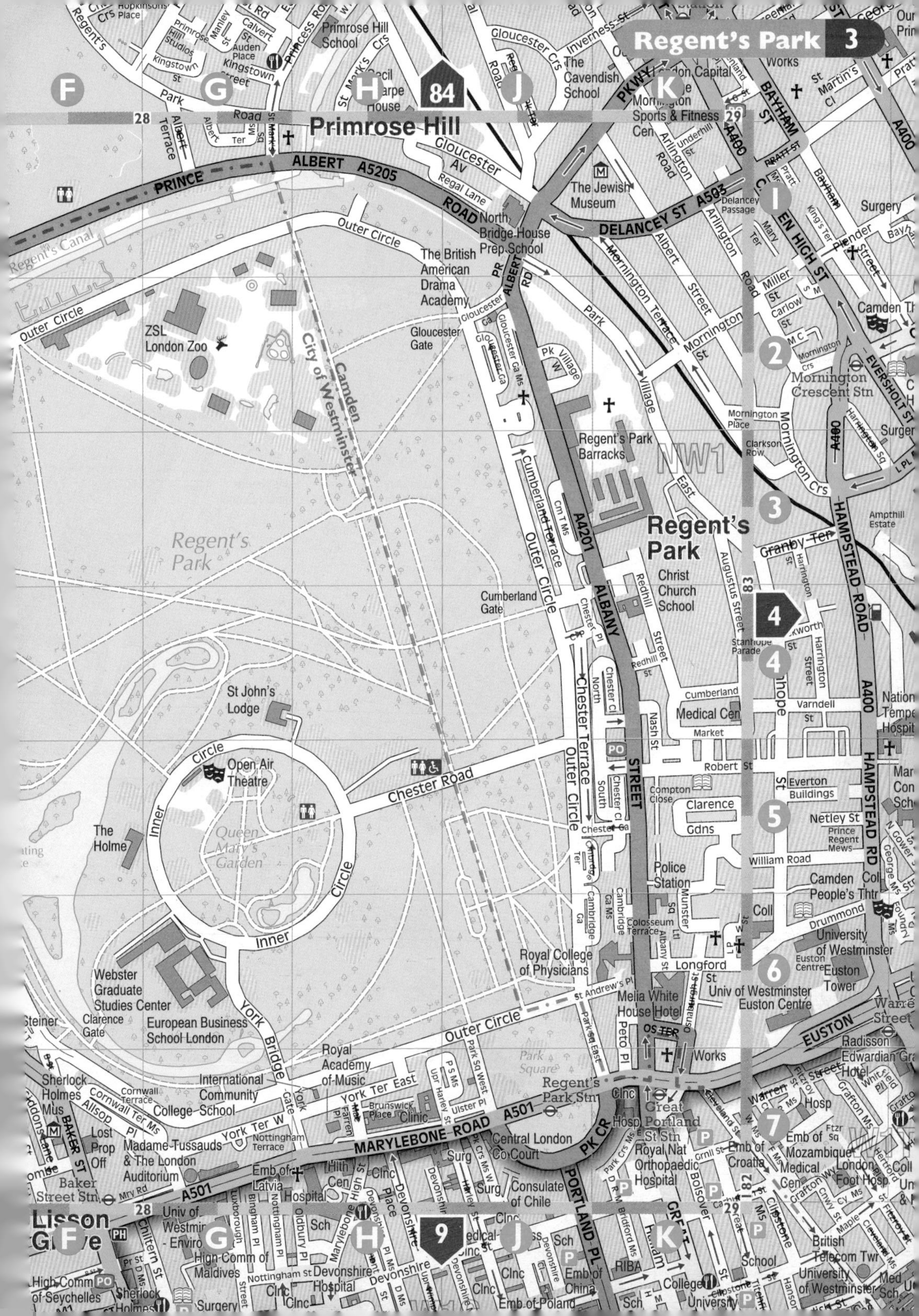
Primrose Hill
Primrose Hill School
Prince Albert Road A5205
Regent's Canal
Outer Circle
ZSL London Zoo
City of Westminster
Camden
Gloucester Gate
The British American Drama Academy
North Bridge House Prep School
The Jewish Museum
Delancey St A503
Mornington Crescent Stn
Regent's Park Barracks
NW1
Regent's Park
Christ Church School
Cumberland Gate
Cumberland Terrace
Chester Terrace
Albany Street
A4201
Hampstead Road
A400
St John's Lodge
Open Air Theatre
Queen Mary's Garden
Inner Circle
Chester Road
The Holme
Webster Graduate Studies Center
European Business School London
Clarence Gate
York Bridge
Royal Academy of Music
Royal College of Physicians
Melia White House Hotel
Camden People's Thtr
University of Westminster
Euston Tower
Regent's Park Stn
Great Portland St Stn
Royal Nat Orthopaedic Hospital
Marylebone Road A501
Madame Tussauds & The London Auditorium
Sherlock Holmes Mus
Baker Street Stn
Lisson Grove
Central London Co Court
Consulate of Chile
British Telecom Twr
Euston
Portland Pl
Great Portland St
Camden High St
Mornington Crescent
Harrington Sq
Park Square
International Community School
College School
Lost Prop Off
Baker St
Marylebone High St
Devonshire Place

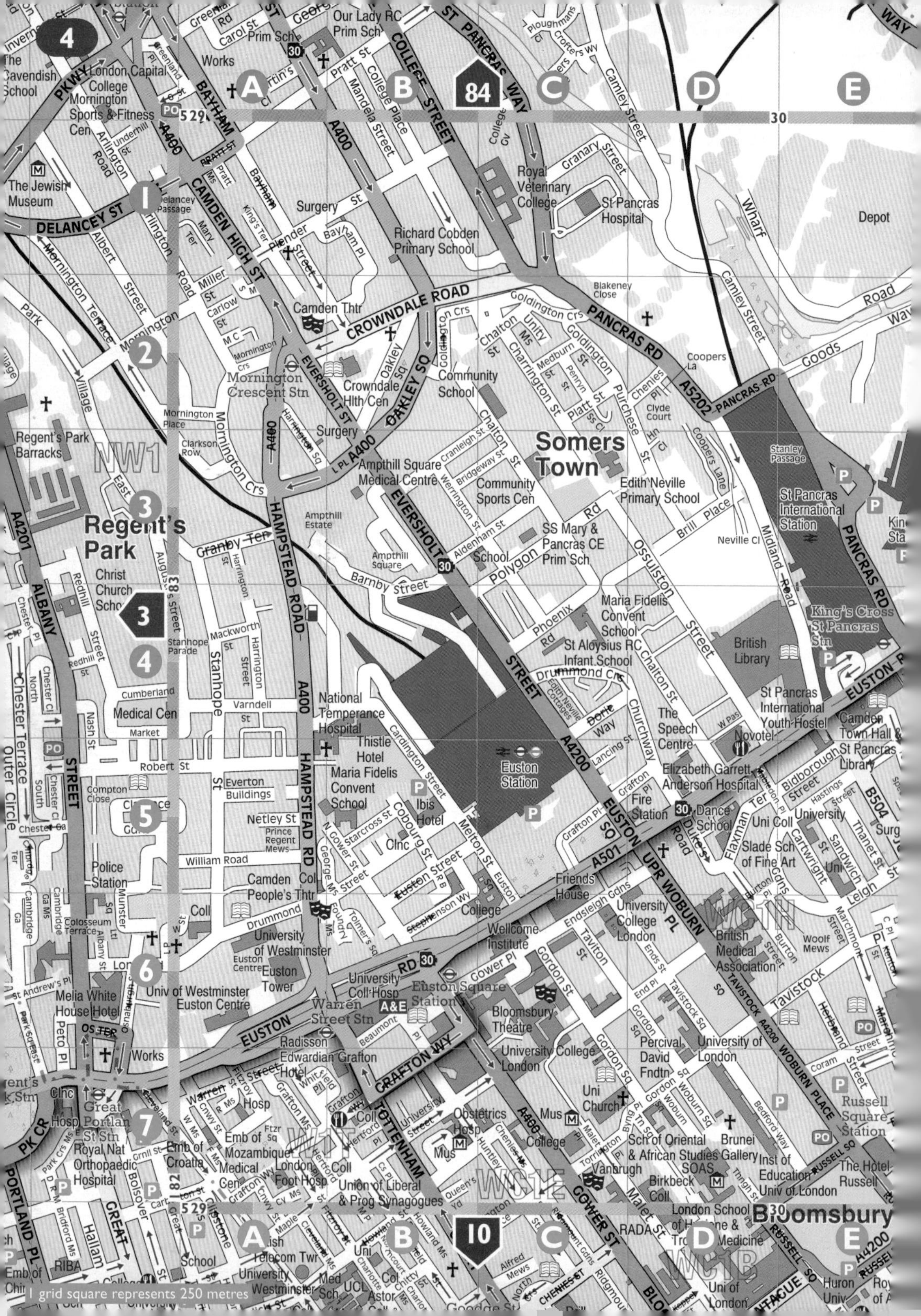

4
A
B
C
D
E
84
30
529
The Cavendish School
London Capital College
Mornington Sports & Fitness Cen
PKWY
BAYHAM
A400
Arlington Road
Underhill St
The Jewish Museum
DELANCEY ST
Delancey Passage
1
Carol St
Greenland Rd
Works
Prim Sch
Our Lady RC Prim Sch
Pratt St
College Place
Mandela Street
Bayham Street
COLLEGE STREET
ST PANCRAS WAY
College Gv
Camley Street
Granary Street
Royal Veterinary College
St Pancras Hospital
Wharf
Depot
Surgery
Plender Street
Bayham Pl
Richard Cobden Primary School
CAMDEN HIGH ST
King's Ter
Mary Ter
Albert Street
Arlington Road
Mornington Terrace
Miller St
Carlow St
Camden Thtr
CROWNDALE ROAD
Blakeney Close
PANCRAS RD
Goods Way
Road
Park Village
Mornington
2
Mornington Crs
Mornington Crescent Stn
EVERSHOLT ST
Oakley Sq
OAKLEY SQ
Crowndale Hlth Cen
Goldington Crs
Community School
Chalton St
Unity Ms
Charrington St
Medburn St
Penryn St
Goldington St
Platt St
Purchese St
Chenies Pl
Clyde Court
Coopers La
A5202
PANCRAS RD
Regent's Park Barracks
NW1
Mornington Place
Clarkson Row
Mornington Crs
Harrington Sq
Surgery
Ampthill Square Medical Centre
Cranleigh St
Bridgeway St
Somers Town
Community Sports Cen
Edith Neville Primary School
Coopers Lane
Stanley Passage
St Pancras International Station
3
Regent's Park
A4201
East
HAMPSTEAD ROAD
Ampthill Estate
EVERSHOLT
Werrington St
Aldenham St
SS Mary & Pancras CE Prim Sch
Rd
Brill Place
Neville Cl
Midland Road
Christ Church Sch
Granby Ter
Harrington
Augustus Street
Ampthill Square
Barnby Street
School
Polygon
Ossulston Street
Maria Fidelis Convent School
King's Cross St Pancras Stn
ALBANY
Redhill Street
Chester Pl
Stanhope Parade
Mackworth St
Harrington Street
Phoenix Rd
St Aloysius RC Infant School
British Library
4
Chester Cl North
Stanhope
Cumberland
Varndell St
A400
National Temperance Hospital
STREET
Drummond Crs
Chalton St
Churchway
Euston Road
Medical Cen
Market
Nash St
Chester Terrace
Outer Circle
PO
Robert St
Thistle Hotel
Maria Fidelis Convent School
Cardington Street
Euston Station
A4200
Dorie Way
Lancing St
The Speech Centre
St Pancras International Youth Hostel
Camden Town Hall & St Pancras Library
Compton Close
Everton Buildings
Ibis Hotel
Grafton Pl
Fire Station
Elizabeth Garrett Anderson Hospital
Bidborough Street
Hastings Street
B504
HAMPSTEAD RD
Netley St
Prince Regent Mews
Starcross St
Cobourg St
Clnc
Melton St
Euston Sq
EUSTON
Dance School
Flaxman Ter
Uni Coll
University
Thanet St
Surg
5
Chester Ga
William Road
N Gower St
Euston Street
Grafton Pl
A501
UPR WOBURN PL
Dukes Road
Slade Sch of Fine Art
Cartwright
Sandwich St
Police Station
Camden People's Thtr
Coll
Stephenson Wy
College
Friends House
University College London
Leigh St
Cambridge Ga Ms
Munster Sq
Coll
Drummond
University of Westminster
Tolmer's Sq
Wellcome Institute
Endsleigh Gdns
Taviton St
WC1H
British Medical Association
Burton Street
Marchmont Street
Woolf Mews
Colosseum Terrace
Albany St
Euston Centre
Euston Tower
RD
Gower Pl
Gordon St
Ends St
Tavistock
6
St Andrew's Pl
Melia White House Hotel
Univ of Westminster Euston Centre
University Coll Hosp
A&E
Euston Square Station
Warren Street Stn
Bloomsbury Theatre
End Pl
Tavistock Sq
TAVISTOCK
A4200 WOBURN PLACE
Herbrand Street
Peto Pl
OS TER
Works
EUSTON
Radisson Edwardian Grafton Hotel
Beaumont Pl
GRAFTON WY
University College London
Gordon Sq
Percival David Fndtn
University of London
Coram Street
Warren Street
Fitzroy St
Hosp
Whitfield Pl
Uni Church
Gordon Sq
Woburn Sq
Bedford Way
Russell Square Station
Great Portland St Stn
Hosp
Clnc
7
Cleveland St
Emb of Mozambique
Ftzr Sq
Coll
TOTTENHAM
University Street
Obstetrics Hosp
Mus
Huntley St
Chenies Ms
A400
College
Mus
Byng Pl
Malet Pl
Torrington Pl
Sch of Oriental & African Studies
Brunei Gallery
SOAS
Inst of Education Univ of London
The Hotel Russell
PK CR
Royal Nat Orthopaedic Hospital
Emb of Croatia
Medical Cen
London Foot Hosp
Union of Liberal & Prog Synagogues
W1T
WC1E
Vanbrugh
Birkbeck Coll
London School of Hygiene & Tropical Medicine
Bloomsbury
RUSSELL SQ
Grafton Wy
Queen's Yd
10
PORTLAND PL
Hallam Street
GREAT
Bolsover
RIBA
School
Telecom Twr
University of Westminster
Med Sch
UCL
Col
Alfred Mews
CHENIES ST
Ridgmount Gdns
GOWER ST
RADA
Malet St
Uni of London
Huron Univ
I grid square represents 250 metres

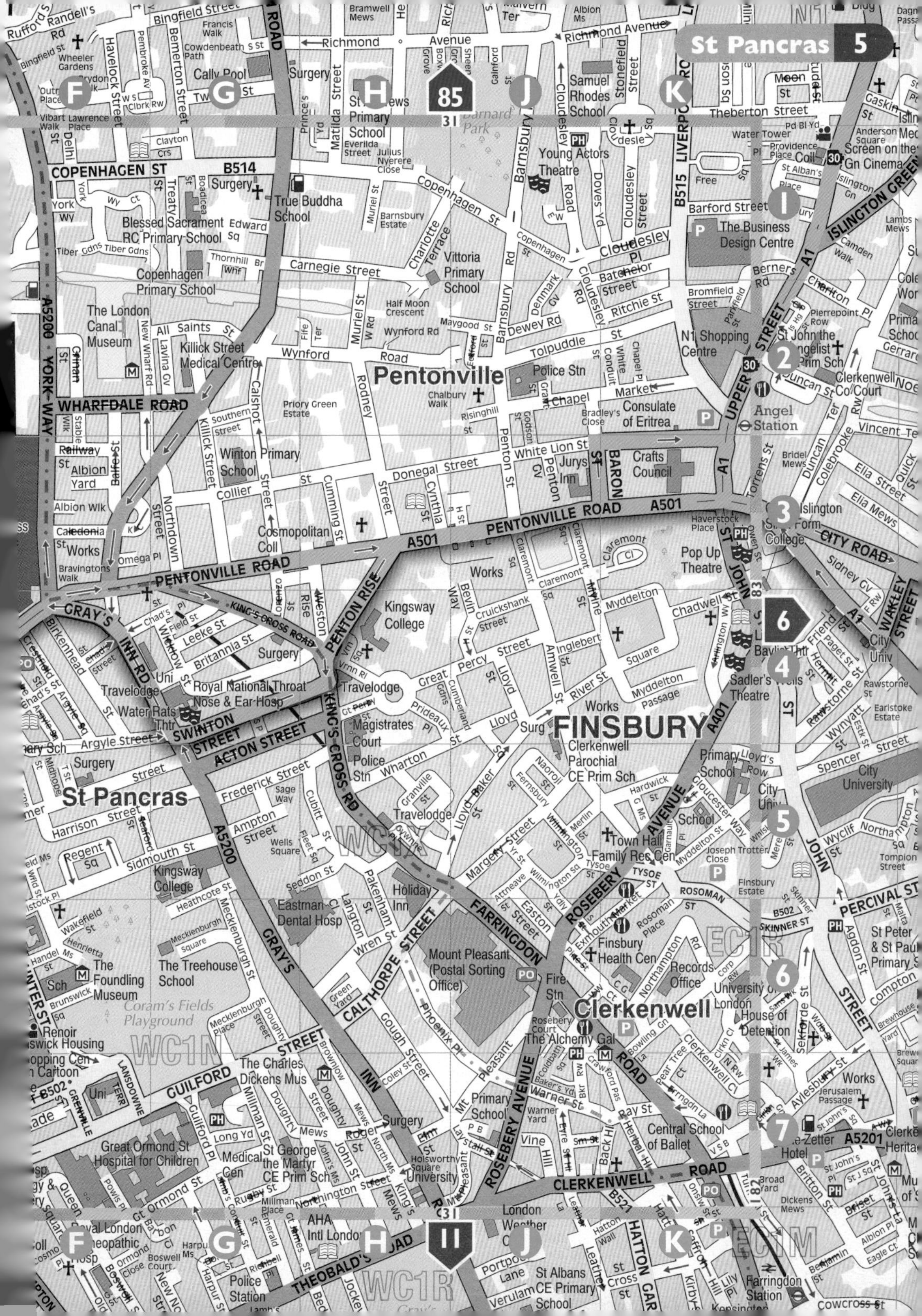
St Pancras
5
85
Pentonville
FINSBURY
St Pancras
Clerkenwell
Richmond Avenue
Copenhagen St
Copenhagen Street
Caledonian Road
York Way
A5200
Wharfdale Road
Pentonville Road
A501
Gray's Inn Rd
King's Cross Road
Swinton Street
Acton Street
Penton Rise
Rosebery Avenue
Farringdon Road
Calthorpe Street
Gray's Inn Road
Guilford Street
Clerkenwell Road
Theobald's Road
Upper Street
St John Street
City Road
Islington Green
Liverpool Road
B515
B514
A1
A401
A5201
B502
B521
Barnsbury Rd
Cloudesley Road
Chapel Market
White Lion St
Donegal Street
Baron St
Amwell St
Lloyd Baker St
Margery Street
Exmouth Market
Percival St
Skinner St
Rosoman St
Tysoe St
Sidmouth St
Argyle Street
Regent Sq
Mecklenburgh Square
Doughty Street
Lamb's Conduit St
Great Ormond St
Old Gloucester St
Hatton Garden
Cowcross St
Turnmill St
Farringdon Road
Caledonian Road
Samuel Rhodes School
Young Actors Theatre
The Business Design Centre
N1 Shopping Centre
Angel Station
Screen on the Gn Cinema
Vittoria Primary School
True Buddha School
Blessed Sacrament RC Primary School
Copenhagen Primary School
The London Canal Museum
Killick Street Medical Centre
Winton Primary School
Cosmopolitan Coll
Police Stn
Consulate of Eritrea
Jurys Inn
Crafts Council
Islington Sixth Form College
Pop Up Theatre
Sadler's Wells Theatre
Kingsway College
Royal National Throat Nose & Ear Hosp
Travelodge
Water Rats Thtr
Magistrates Court
Clerkenwell Parochial CE Prim Sch
Town Hall
Family Rec Cen
Finsbury Health Cen
Records Office
City University
Eastman Dental Hosp
Holiday Inn
Mount Pleasant (Postal Sorting Office)
The Foundling Museum
The Treehouse School
Coram's Fields Playground
The Charles Dickens Mus
Great Ormond St Hospital for Children
St George the Martyr CE Prim Sch
Central School of Ballet
The Alchemy Gal
House of Detention
Royal London Homeopathic Hosp
St Albans CE Primary School
Farringdon Station
WC1X
WC1N
WC1R
EC1R
EC1M
Angel
Finsbury Estate
Priory Green Estate
Barnsbury Estate

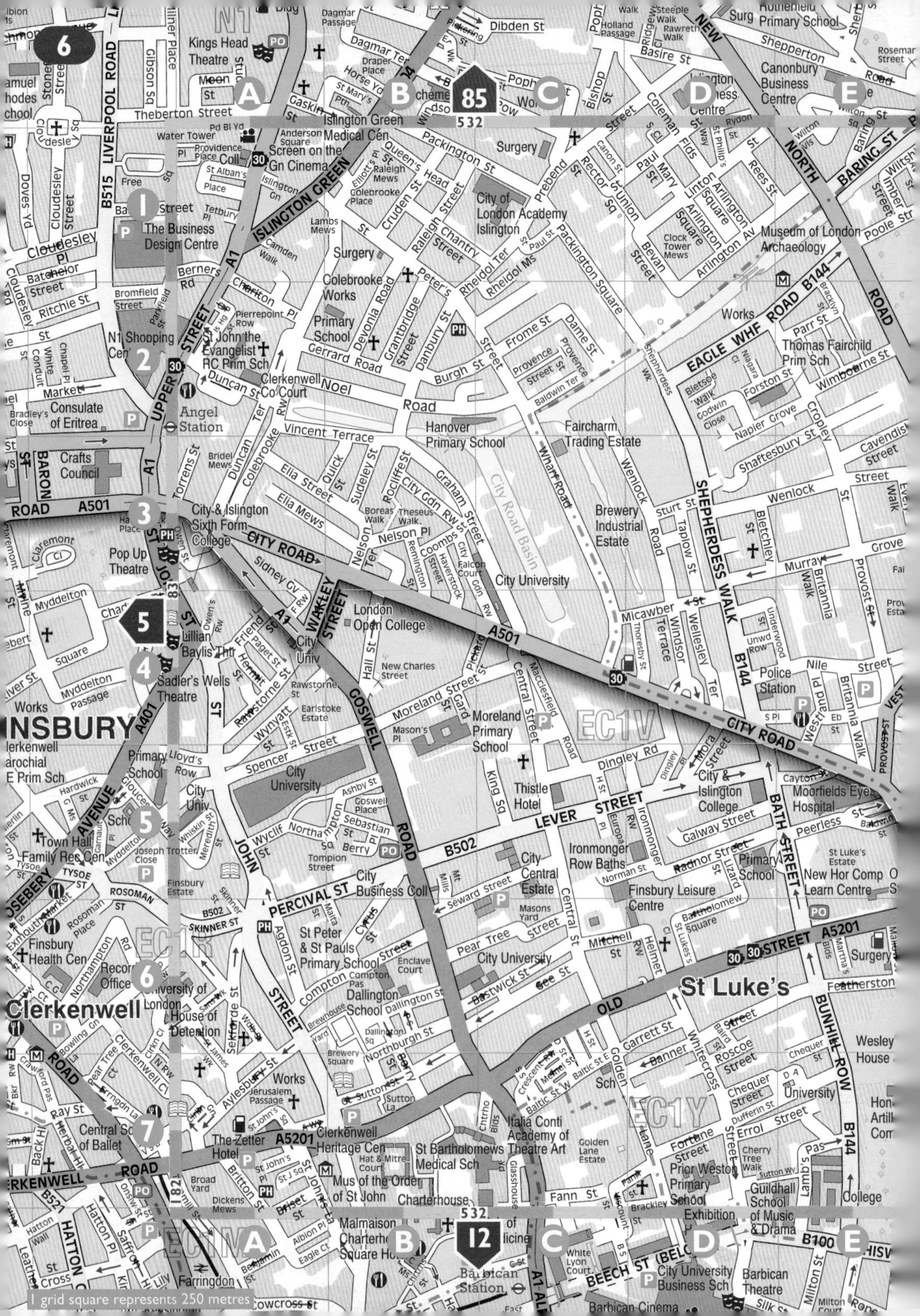

6
N1
Kings Head Theatre
Gibson Sq
Theberton Street
LIVERPOOL ROAD
B515
Moon St
Dagmar Passage
Dagmar Ter
Draper Place
Horse Yd
Gaskin St
St Mary's Pth
Dibden St
Pickering St
Popham St
Holland Passage
Steeple Walk
Rawreth Walk
Basire St
NEW NORTH ROAD
Rotherfield Primary School
Shepperton Road
Canonbury Business Centre
Rosemary Street
Wilton Sq
BARING ST
85
532
A
B
C
D
E
Islington Green Medical Cen
Screen on the Gn Cinema
Anderson Square
Water Tower
Providence Place
Coll
St Alban's Place
Islington Gn
ISLINGTON GREEN
Packington St
Queen's Head St
Raleigh Mews
Colebrooke Place
Cruden St
Surgery
City of London Academy Islington
Prebend St
Rector St
Canon St
Union Sq
Paul St
Mary St
Linton St
Arlington Square
Arlington Av
Rees St
Clock Tower Mews
Bevan Street
Museum of London Archaeology
Poole Str
Cloudesley Sq
Doves Yd
Cloudesley Street
Cloudesley Pl
Batchelor Street
Ritchie St
Barford Street
The Business Design Centre
Tetbury Pl
Berners Rd
Bromfield Street
Parkfield St
N1 Shopping Centre
White Conduit St
Chapel Pl
Market
Bradley's Close
Consulate of Eritrea
Angel Station
UPPER STREET
A1
Camden Walk
Lambs Mews
Charlton Pl
Pierrepoint Row
St John the Evangelist RC Prim Sch
Duncan St
Clerkenwell Co Court
Colebrooke Works
Primary School
Devonia Road
Grantbridge Street
Danbury St
Raleigh Street
Chantry Street
St Peter's Street
Rheidol Ter
Rheidol Ms
Packington Square
Gerrard Road
Noel Road
Burgh St
Frome St
Dame St
Provence Street
Baldwin Ter
Hanover Primary School
Faircharm Trading Estate
Shepherdess Wk
Works
EAGLE WHF ROAD B144
Parr St
Thomas Fairchild Prim Sch
Niagara Cl
Bletsoe Walk
Godwin Close
Forston St
Wimbourne St
Napier Grove
Cropley St
Shaftesbury St
Cavendish Street
Crafts Council
BARON ST
ROAD A501
Torrens St
Bridel Mews
Duncan Ter
Colebrooke Rw
Vincent Terrace
Elia Street
Elia Mews
Quick St
Sudeley St
Rocliffe St
City Gdn Rw
Graham Street
City Road Basin
Wharf Road
Wenlock Road
Brewery Industrial Estate
Sturt St
Taplow St
SHEPHERDESS WALK
Wenlock St
Bletchley St
Grove
Murray Walk
Britannia Walk
Provost St
City & Islington Sixth Form College
CITY ROAD
Sidney Gv
Nelson Ter
Nelson Pl
Boreas Walk
Theseus Walk
Remington Street
Coombs St
Haverstock St
Falcon Court
City University
Micawber St
Thoresby St
Windsor Terrace
Wellesley Ter
B144
Underwood Row
Nile Street
Police Station
Westland Pl
Britannia Walk
Claremont Cl
Pop Up Theatre
Myddelton Square
Chadwell St
5
Lillian Baylis Thtr
Sadler's Wells Theatre
Myddelton Passage
Owen's Rw
Friend St
Paget St
Hermit St
Rawstorne St
WAKLEY STREET
City Univ
London Open College
Hall St
New Charles Street
GOSWELL ROAD
Earlstoke Estate
Moreland Street
Pickard St
Central Street
Macclesfield Road
EC1V
CITY ROAD
Mora Street
Dingley Pl
Dingley Rd
Moreland Primary School
Mason's Pl
King Sq
Thistle Hotel
LEVER STREET
Europa Pl
Ironmonger Rw
City & Islington College
BATH STREET
Cayton St
Moorfields Eye Hospital
Peerless St
Baldwin St
INSBURY
Clerkenwell Parochial CE Prim Sch
Primary School
Lloyd's Row
A401
Wynyatt St
Spencer Street
City University
Ashby St
Goswell Place
Sebastian St
Berry Pl
Northampton Sq
Wyclif St
Tompion Street
JOHN STREET
Whiskin St
Meredith St
Joseph Trotter Close
Finsbury Estate
B502
City Central Estate
Ironmonger Row Baths
Galway Street
Radnor Street
Norman St
Lizard St
Primary School
St Luke's Estate
New Hor Comp Learn Centre
Finsbury Leisure Centre
Bartholomew Square
St Luke's Cl
AVENUE
ROSEBERY
Town Hall
Family Rec Cen
Tysoe St
ROSOMAN ST
Exmouth Market
Rosoman Place
Finsbury Health Cen
Northampton Rd
Record Office
EC1R
SKINNER ST
Skinner St
PERCIVAL ST
City Business Coll
Malta St
Cyrus St
Agdon St
St Peter & St Pauls Primary School
Compton Street
Compton Pas
Enclave Court
Dallington School
Dallington St
Seward Street
Masons Yard
Pear Tree Street
City University
Bastwick St
Gee St
Mitchell St
Helmet Rw
A5201
STREET
Surgery
Featherston
St Luke's
OLD
BUNHILL ROW
Wesley House
Clerkenwell
University of London House of Detention
Sekforde St
Woodbridge St
Bowling Gn
Pear Tree Ct
Clerkenwell Cl
Ray St
Central School of Ballet
Back Hill
Herbal Hill
7
Jerusalem Passage
Aylesbury St
Works
Brewhouse Yard
Brewery Square
Northburgh St
Sutton La
The Zetter Hotel
Clerkenwell Heritage Cen
St Bartholomews Medical Sch
Chtrho Blds
Italia Conti Academy of Theatre Art
Golden Lane Estate
Garrett St
Banner St
Roscoe Street
Whitecross Street
Chequer Street
Dufferin St
Errol Street
University
Fortune Street
Prior Weston Primary School
Cherry Tree Walk
Sutton Wy
Lamb's Pas
B144
College
Guildhall School of Music & Drama
Crescent Rw
Baltic St W
Baltic St E
Golden Lane
EC1Y
Sch
Hat & Mitre Court
Mus of the Order of St John
Charterhouse
St John's Sq
Britton St
Broad Yard
Dickens Mews
CLERKENWELL ROAD
B521
HATTON
Onslow St
Saffron Hill
Hatton Wall
Cross St
Farringdon
Briset St
Albion Pl
Eagle Ct
Malmaison Charterhouse Square Hotel
Barbican Station
12
White Lyon Court
BEECH ST
Fann St
Brackley St
City University Business Sch
Barbican Theatre
Milton St
Exhibition
B100
Glasshouse Yd
Cowcross St
Barbican Cinema
1 grid square represents 250 metres

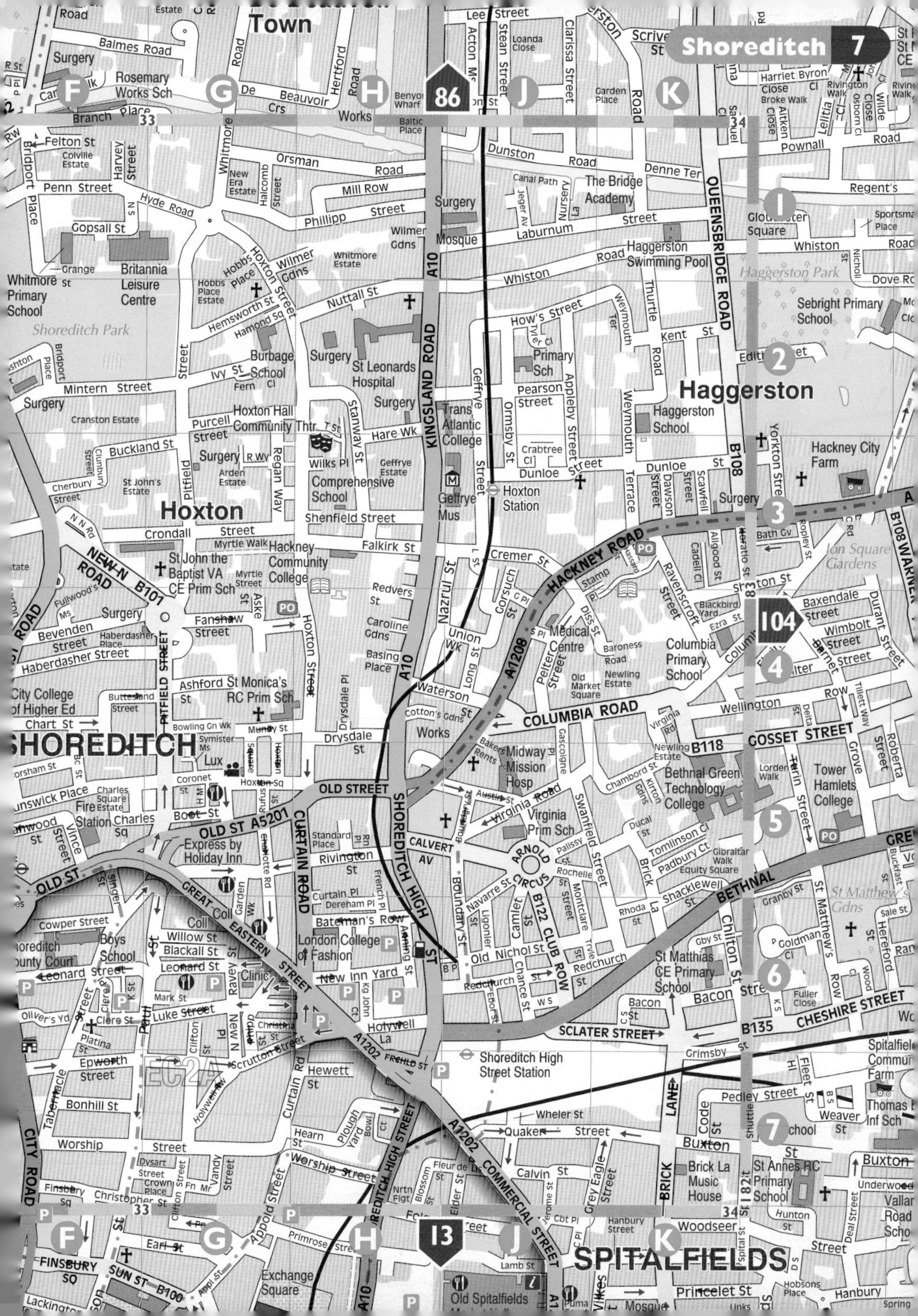
Shoreditch
7
Town
86
104
13
33
34
F
G
H
J
K
1
2
3
4
5
6
7
Balmes Road
Rosemary Works Sch
De Beauvoir Crs
Hertford Road
Whitmore Road
Branch Place
Works
Baltic Place
Benyon Wharf
Lee Street
Acton Ms
Stean Street
Loanda Close
Clarissa Street
Garden Place
Scriven St
Harriet Byron Cl
Rivington Walk
Broke Walk
Aitken Close
Pownall Road
Surgery
Felton St
Colville Estate
Bridport Place
Harvey Street
Penn Street
Hyde Road
New Era Estate
Halcomb Street
Orsman Road
Mill Row
Phillipp Street
Dunston Road
Canal Path
Jeger Av
Nursery La
The Bridge Academy
Denne Ter
QUEENSBRIDGE ROAD
Regent's
Gloucester Square
Sportsman Place
Gopsall St
Grange St
Whitmore Primary School
Britannia Leisure Centre
Hobbs Place
Hobbs Place Estate
Hoxton Street
Wilmer Gdns
Whitmore Estate
Mosque
Laburnum Street
Haggerston Swimming Pool
Whiston Road
Nicholl St
Dove Ro
Haggerston Park
Sebright Primary School
Shoreditch Park
Hemsworth St
Hamond Sq
Nuttall St
KINGSLAND ROAD
A10
How's Street
Tyler Cl
Weymouth Ter
Thurtle Road
Kent St
Edith St
Bridport Place
Mintern Street
Ivy St
Burbage School
Fern Cl
St Leonards Hospital
Primary Sch
Geffrye Street
Ormsby St
Pearson Street
Appleby Street
Weymouth Terrace
Haggerston
Haggerston School
Yorkton Street
Hackney City Farm
Cranston Estate
Hoxton Hall Community Thtr
Purcell Street
Buckland St
Surgery
Arden Estate
R Wy
Regan Way
Stanway St
Hare Wk
T St
Trans Atlantic College
Crabtree Cl
Dunloe Street
Dunloe St
Dawson Street
Scawfell Street
B108
Clunbury Street
Cherbury Street
St John's Estate
Pitfield Street
Hoxton
Wilks Pl
Comprehensive School
Geffrye Estate
Geffrye Mus
Hoxton Station
Shenfield Street
Crondall Street
Myrtle Walk
Hackney Community College
Falkirk St
Cremer St
L St
HACKNEY ROAD
Bath Gv
Cadell Cl
Allgood St
Horatio St
Ropley St
Ion Square Gardens
B108 WARNER
N N Rd
NEW N ROAD
B101
St John the Baptist VA CE Prim Sch
Myrtle Street
Aske St
Redvers St
Nazrul St
Gorsuch St
G Pl
Stamp Pl
Hassard St
Ravenscroft Street
Blackbird Yard
Ezra St
Baxendale Street
Durant Street
Fullwood's Ms
Surgery
Fanshaw Street
Bevenden Street
Haberdasher Place
Haberdasher Street
Caroline Gdns
Union Wk
Long St
A1208
S Pl
Diss St
Medical Centre
Baroness Road
Columbia Primary School
Wimbolt Street
Barnet Street
Basing Place
Hoxton Street
Pelter Street
Old Market Square
Newling Estate
Columbia Road
Alter
City College of Higher Ed
Buttesland Street
Ashford St
St Monica's RC Prim Sch
Drysdale Pl
Waterson St
COLUMBIA ROAD
Wellington Row
Delta St
Tillett Way
Chart St
Bowling Gn Wk
Mundy St
Drysdale St
Cotton's Gdns
Works
Virginia Rd
Newling Estate
B118
GOSSET STREET
Grove
Roberta Street
SHOREDITCH
Symister Ms
Lux
Hoxton Sq
Bc St
Midway Mission Hosp
Bakers Rents
Gascoigne Pl
Chambord St
Kirton Gdns
Bethnal Green Technology College
Lorden Walk
Turin Street
Tower Hamlets College
Coronet St
H M
Fairchild Pl
OLD STREET
Austin St
Virginia Road
Virginia Prim Sch
Swanfield Street
Ducal St
Tomlinson Cl
Brunswick Place
Charles Square Estate
Fire Station
Charles Sq
Boot St
OLD ST A5201
Vince Street
Express by Holiday Inn
Standard Place
Rn Pl
CALVERT AV
Boundary St
ARNOLD CIRCUS
Palissy St
Rochelle St
Padbury Ct
Gibraltar Walk
Equity Square
Brick La
Shacklewell St
BETHNAL
Granby St
St Matthew's Gdns
Buckfast St
Sale St
Charlotte Rd
Rivington St
CURTAIN ROAD
SHOREDITCH HIGH ST
OLD ST
Singer St
GREAT EASTERN STREET
Garden Wk
Curtain Pl
Dereham Pl
French Pl
Navarre St
Ligonier St
Camlet St
B122 CLUB ROW
Montclare Street
Rhoda St
Cowper Street
Coll
Boys School
Willow St
Blackall St
Leonard St
Leonard Street
Shoreditch County Court
Bateman's Row
London College of Fashion
Anning St
Old Nichol St
Redchurch St
Tryle St
Gby St
Chilton St
St Matthias CE Primary School
Bacon Street
Goldman Cl
St Matthew's Row
Hereford St
Wood St
Fuller Close
K S
Clinic
Ravey St
New Inn Yard
Kg John Ct
Redchurch Street
Chance St
Ebor St
W S
Bacon St
C S
CHESHIRE STREET
Paul St
Mark St
Luke Street
Clere Pl
Clere St
Oliver's Yd
Platina St
Christina St
Holywell La
SCLATER STREET
B135
Epworth Street
Tabernacle Street
Clifton St
New N Pl
Scrutton Street
A1202
Hewett St
Shoreditch High Street Station
Grimsby St
Fleet St
Spitalfields Community Farm
EC2A
Curtain Rd
Bonhill St
Holywell Row
Pedley Street
LANE
Code St
Thomas Buxton Inf Sch
Weaver St
School
Hearn St
Plough Yard
Bowl Ct
Wheler St
Quaker Street
Shuttle St
SHOREDITCH HIGH STREET
A1202 COMMERCIAL STREET
Buxton St
Worship Street
Dysart Street
Crown Place
Vandy Street
Worship Street
Fleur de Lis St
Calvin St
Grey Eagle Street
BRICK
Brick La Music House
St Annes RC Primary School
Underwood
Vallance Road
CITY ROAD
Finsbury Sq
Christopher St
Fn Mr
Appold Street
Blossom St
Nrtn Flgt
Elder St
Jerome St
Cbt Pl
C Pl
Hanbury Street
Woodseer
Hunton St
Deal Street
D S
Street
Earl St
Primrose Street
Folgate Street
SPITALFIELDS
Spital St
Finsbury SQ
SUN ST
B100
Appl St
Exchange Square
Lamb St
Old Spitalfields
Wilkes St
Puma Ct
Princelet St
Hobsons Place
Hanbury
Mosque
Spring
Lackington

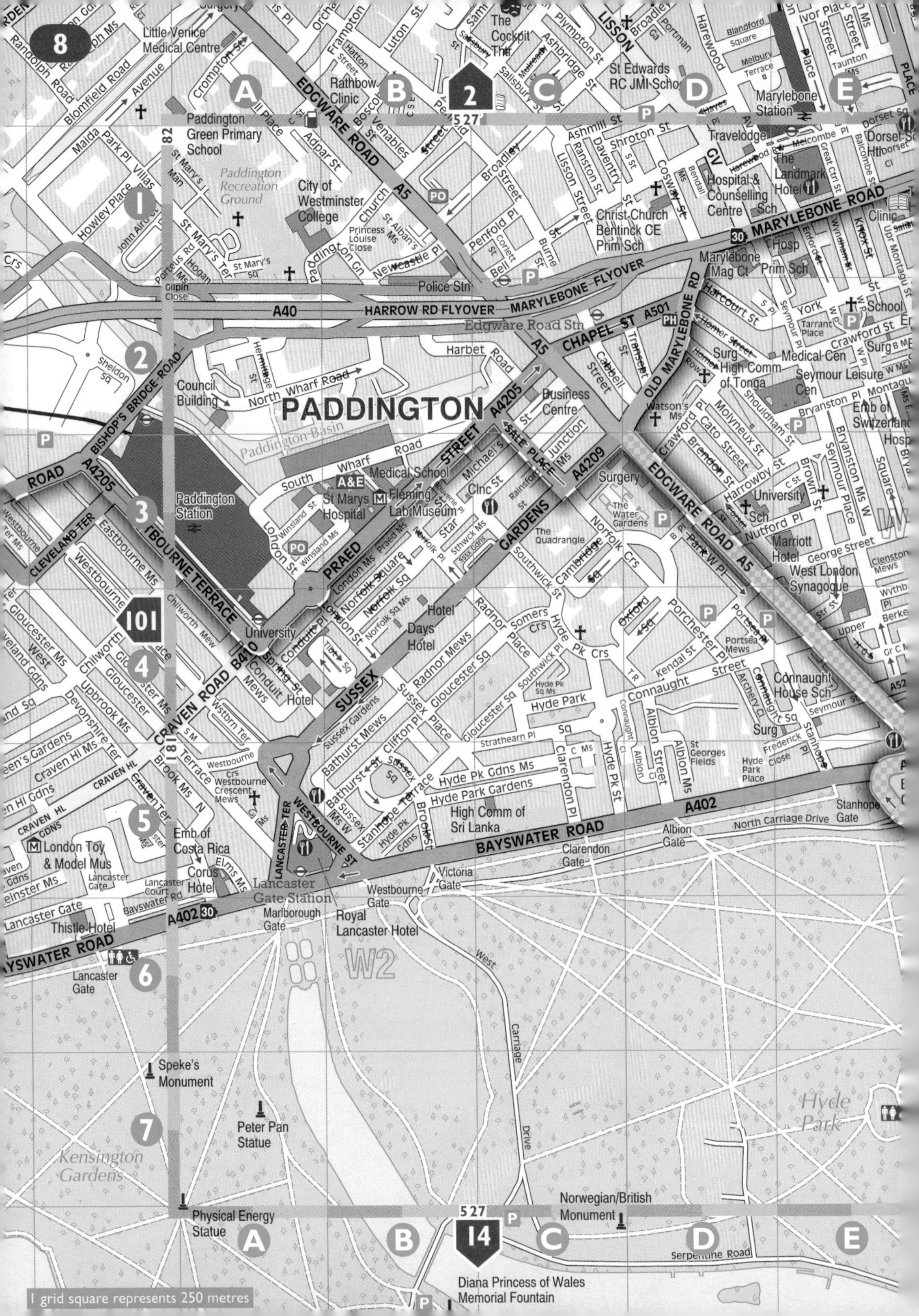
8
Little Venice Medical Centre
Randolph Road
Blomfield Road
Maida Avenue
Crompton St
Frampton
Luton St
Hatton Street
Rathbow Clinic
The Cockpit Thtr
Salisbury St
Plympton St
Ashbridge St
LISSON
Broadley
Portman
Harewood
Blandford Square
Melbury Terrace
Ivor Place
Taunton Ms
A
B
2
C
D
E
EDGWARE ROAD
Boscobel St
Penfold St
St Edwards RC JMI Sch
Marylebone Station
Paddington Green Primary School
527
Hayes Pl
Dorset Sq
Dorset Sq Htl
Ashmill St
Shroton St
Travelodge
Melcombe Pl
Maida Park Pl
St Mary's Man
Paddington Recreation Ground
City of Westminster College
Venables St
Adpar St
Broadley Street
Lisson Street
Daventry St
Ranston St
Cosway St
Bendall Ms
Hospital & Counselling Centre
Harewood Rw
The Landmark Hotel
Great Ctrl St
Balcombe St
Howley Place
Villas
1
John Aird Ct
St Mary's Ter
Porteus Rd
Hogan Ms
St Mary's Sq
Church St
St Alban's Ms
Princess Louise Close
Paddington Gn
Newcastle Pl
Penfold Pl
Corlett St
Bell St
Christ Church Bentinck CE Prim Sch
Burne St
Sch
MARYLEBONE ROAD
30
Clinic
Hosp
Prim Sch
Knox St
Upr Montagu St
Marylebone Mag Ct
Gilpin Close
Police Stn
MARYLEBONE FLYOVER
A40
HARROW RD FLYOVER
Harcourt St
York St
School
Edgware Road Stn
CHAPEL ST
A501
Tarrant Place
Crawford St
Sheldon Sq
2
Hermitage St
Harbet Road
Transept St
Cabbell Street
OLD MARYLEBONE RD
Homer Street
Homer Row
Surg
High Comm of Tonga
Medical Cen
Seymour Leisure Cen
Council Building
North Wharf Road
BISHOP'S BRIDGE ROAD
PADDINGTON
A4205
Business Centre
Watson's Ms
Crawford Pl
Molyneux St
Shouldham St
Bryanston Pl
Montagu
Emb of Switzerland
Hosp
Paddington Basin
SALE PLACE
Junction Ms
Cato Street
Brendon St
ROAD
A4205
South Wharf Road
STREET
Michael's St
A4209
Surgery
EDGWARE ROAD
Harrowby St
Seymour Place
Bryanston Ms W
Square
A&E
Medical School
3
Paddington Station
St Marys Hospital
Fleming Lab Museum
Clnc St
Rainsford St
The Water Gardens
University
Brown St
Sch
Nutford Pl
CLEVELAND TER
Westbourne Ter Ms
Eastbourne Ms
Winsland St
Winsland Ms
PO
London St
PRAED
London Ms
Praed Ms
Norfolk Square
Norfolk Pl
Star St
Sthwck Ms
Sussex Gdns
GARDENS
The Quadrangle
Southwick St
Cambridge Sq
Norfolk Crs
Park W Pl
A5
Marriott Hotel
George Street
West London Synagogue
Clenston Mews
Westbourne
TERRACE
101
Chilworth Mew
Norfolk Sq
Norfolk Sq Ms
Hotel
Days Hotel
Radnor Place
Somers Crs
Hyde Pk Crs
Oxford Sq
Porchester Pl
Portsea Pl
Portsea Mews
Upper
Gloucester Ms
Chilworth
Gloucester
Terrace
4
University
Conduit Pl
Conduit Mews
Spring St
Radnor Mews
Gloucester Sq
Kendal St
Connaught Street
Archery Cl
Connaught House Sch
Seymour St
A52
West
CRAVEN ROAD
B410
Westbourne Ter
Hotel
SUSSEX
Sussex Gardens
Bathurst Mews
Clifton Pl
Sussex Place
Gloucester Sq
Southwick Pl
Hyde Pk Sq Ms
Hyde Park Sq
Connaught Cl
Albion Street
Albion Cl
Albion Ms
Connaught Sq
Surg
Frederick Close
Stanhope Pl
Upbrook Ms
Devonshire Ter
Craven Hl Ms
CRAVEN HL
Brook Ms N
Terrace
Westbourne Crs
Westbourne Crescent Mews
Strathearn Pl
C Ms
Clarendon Pl
Hyde Pk St
St Georges Fields
Hyde Park Place
Bathurst St
Sussex Sq
Hyde Pk Gdns Ms
Hyde Park Gardens
CRAVEN GDNS
London Toy & Model Mus
5
Craven Ter
Emb of Costa Rica
LANCASTER TER
WESTBOURNE ST
Stanhope Terrace
Sussex Ms W
Hyde Pk Gdns
Brook St
High Comm of Sri Lanka
BAYSWATER ROAD
A402
North Carriage Drive
Albion Gate
Stanhope Gate
Clarendon Gate
Corus Hotel
Elms Ms
Lancaster Gate Station
Victoria Gate
Leinster Ms
Lancaster Gate
Lancaster Court
Bayswater Rd
Westbourne Gate
Lancaster Gate
A402
30
Thistle Hotel
Marlborough Gate
Royal Lancaster Hotel
BAYSWATER ROAD
W2
West
6
Lancaster Gate
Carriage
Drive
Speke's Monument
Hyde Park
7
Peter Pan Statue
Kensington Gardens
Physical Energy Statue
527
14
Norwegian/British Monument
A
B
C
D
E
Serpentine Road
Diana Princess of Wales Memorial Fountain
1 grid square represents 250 metres

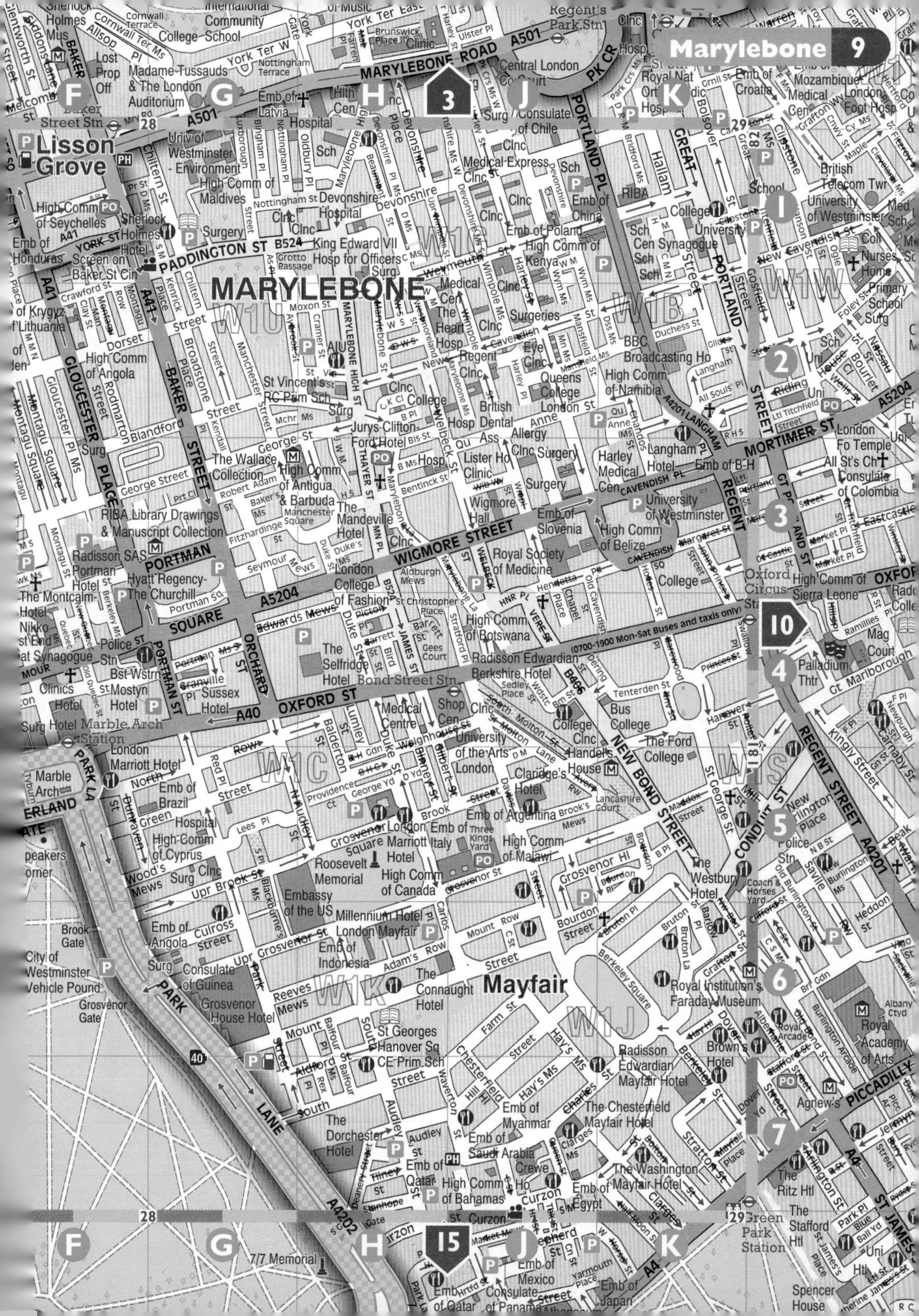
MARYLEBONE
Mayfair
Lisson Grove
MARYLEBONE ROAD
A501
Regent's Park Stn
Baker Street Stn
Madame Tussauds & The London Auditorium
Lost Prop Off
Sherlock Holmes Mus
Univ of Westminster - Environment
Central London Co Court
Consulate of Chile
Medical Express
Devonshire Hospital
King Edward VII Hosp for Officers
PADDINGTON ST
B524
YORK ST
High Comm of Seychelles
Screen on Baker St Cin
Emb of Honduras
Emb of China
Emb of Poland
High Comm of Kenya
RIBA
College
University
Cen Synagogue
PORTLAND PL
GREAT PORTLAND STREET
BBC Broadcasting Ho
High Comm of Namibia
Queens College
British Telecom Twr
University of Westminster
Langham Hotel
LANGHAM PL
A4201
MORTIMER ST
REGENT STREET
MARYLEBONE HIGH ST
BAKER STREET
GLOUCESTER PLACE
High Comm of Angola
St Vincent's RC Prim Sch
The Wallace Collection
High Comm of Antigua & Barbuda
Manchester Square
The Mandeville Hotel
Jurys Clifton-Ford Hotel
Lister Ho Clinic
Wigmore Hall
WIGMORE STREET
Royal Society of Medicine
Emb of Slovenia
High Comm of Belize
University of Westminster
RIBA Library Drawings & Manuscript Collection
PORTMAN SQUARE
Radisson SAS Portman Hotel
Hyatt Regency-The Churchill
A5204
London College of Fashion
High Comm of Botswana
Radisson Edwardian Berkshire Hotel
Oxford Circus Sta
High Comm of Sierra Leone
The Selfridge Hotel
Bond Street Stn
OXFORD ST
A40
Marble Arch Station
Marble Arch
PARK LA
London Marriott Hotel
Emb of Brazil
High Comm of Cyprus
Roosevelt Memorial
Embassy of the US
High Comm of Canada
Millennium Hotel London Mayfair
Emb of Indonesia
Emb of Argentina
Emb of Italy
High Comm of Malawi
London Marriott Hotel
GROSVENOR SQUARE
Claridge's Hotel
Handel's House
NEW BOND STREET
The Westbury Hotel
CONDUIT ST
Palladium Thtr
Royal Institution's Faraday Museum
Berkeley Square
The Connaught Hotel
Grosvenor House Hotel
Consulate of Guinea
Emb of Angola
City of Westminster Vehicle Pound
St Georges Hanover Sq CE Prim Sch
Radisson Edwardian Mayfair Hotel
The Chesterfield Mayfair Hotel
Emb of Myanmar
Emb of Saudi Arabia
The Dorchester Hotel
Emb of Qatar
High Comm of Bahamas
The Washington Mayfair Hotel
Emb of Egypt
Royal Academy of Arts
PICCADILLY
A4
The Ritz Htl
Green Park Station
The Stafford Htl
Spencer House
7/7 Memorial
Emb of Mexico
Consulate of Panama
Emb of Japan
PARK LANE
A4202
Curzon St
Mount St
South Audley St
Brook St
Upr Brook St
Upr Grosvenor St
Oxford Circus
Hanover Sq
Cavendish Sq
Regent St A4201
F
G
H
J
K
28
29
3
10
15
1
2
3
4
5
6
7
(0700-1900 Mon-Sat Buses and taxis only)

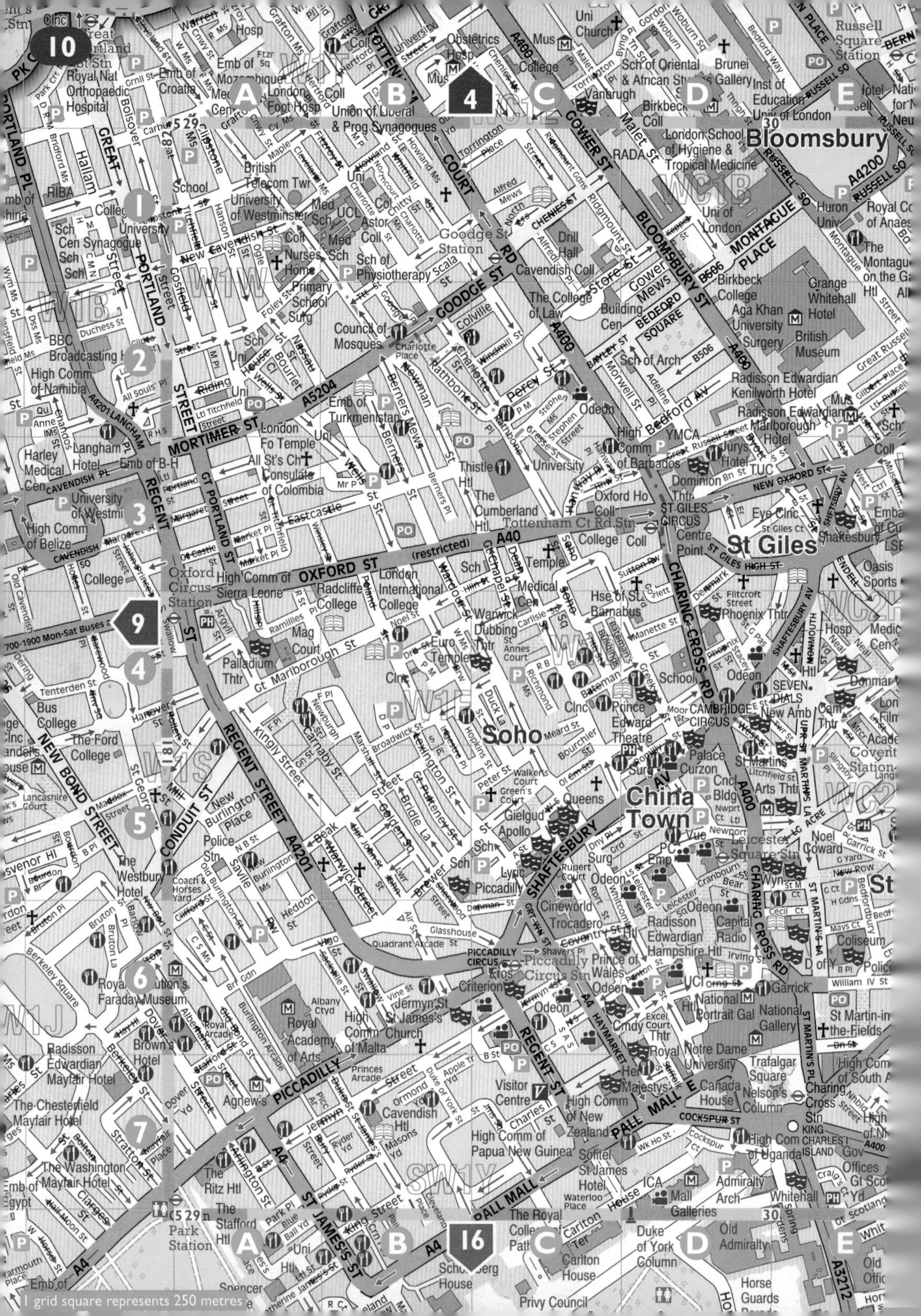

10
A
B
C
D
E
4
Bloomsbury
Russell Square Station
RUSSELL SQ
A4200
Brunei Gallery
Sch of Oriental & African Studies
Inst of Education Univ of London
London School of Hygiene & Tropical Medicine
RADA
Birkbeck Coll
GOWER ST
Malet St
Uni Church
Mus
College
Vanbrugh
Obstetrics Hosp
Union of Liberal & Prog Synagogues
TOTTENHAM COURT RD
Torrington Place
Great Portland St
Royal Nat Orthopaedic Hospital
Emb of Mozambique
London Foot Hosp
Emb of Croatia
Warren
Hosp
PORTLAND PL
GREAT PORTLAND STREET
Hallam
RIBA
Bolsover
Clipstone
School
British Telecom Twr
University of Westminster
UCL
Med Sch
Astor Coll
Nurses Home
Goodge St Station
Sch of Physiotherapy
Primary School
Surg
Cavendish Coll
Drill Hall
CHENIES ST
Alfred Mews
BLOOMSBURY ST
MONTAGUE PLACE
Uni of London
Huron Univ
Royal Coll of Anaes
The Montague on the Gardens Htl
Birkbeck College
Aga Khan University
Surgery
Grange Whitehall Hotel
British Museum
Gower Mews
BEDFORD SQUARE
The College of Law
Building Cen
Sch of Arch
GOODGE ST
Council of Mosques
Charlotte Place
Rathbone St
Percy St
Odeon
Windmill St
Radisson Edwardian Kenilworth Hotel
Radisson Edwardian Marlborough Hotel
Bedford Av
YMCA
High Comm of Barbados
Jurys Hotel
TUC
Dominion Thtr
NEW OXFORD ST
Cen Synagogue
University
W1B
W1W
BBC Broadcasting House
High Comm of Namibia
All Souls' Pl
A4201 LANGHAM PL
Langham Hotel
Harley Medical Cen
Emb of B-H
CAVENDISH PL
University of Westminster
High Comm of Belize
CAVENDISH SQ
MORTIMER ST
Riding House St
Uni
Ltl Titchfield St
PO
A5204
Emb of Turkmenistan
Berners Mews
Newman St
London Fo Temple
All St's Ch
Consulate of Colombia
Eastcastle St
Wells St
Thistle Htl
University
The Cumberland Htl
Oxford Ho Coll
Tottenham Ct Rd Stn
ST GILES CIRCUS
Centre Point
St Giles
ST GILES HIGH ST
Oasis Sports
Eye Clnc
Shakesbury
SHAFTESBURY AV
Hanway St
REGENT ST
GT PORTLAND ST
Margaret St
Market Pl
Oxford Circus Station
High Comm of Sierra Leone
OXFORD ST (restricted)
A40
London International College
Radcliffe College
Sch
Dean St
Temple
College
Coll
Soho Sq
Medical Cen
Hse of St Barnabus
CHARING CROSS RD
Flitcroft Street
Phoenix Thtr
Denmark St
Manette St
Hosp
Medic Cen
Neal St
SHAFTESBURY AV
Odeon
School
SEVEN DIALS
Donmar
New Amb
Cam Thtr
UPR ST MARTIN'S LA
Lon Film Acade
Covent Garden Station
9
700-1900 Mon-Sat Buses
Argyll St
Ramillies St
Mag Court
Palladium Thtr
Gt Marlborough St
Noel St
Euro Temple
Dubbing Thtr
St Annes Court
Richmond Ms
Bateman St
Greek St
Prince Edward Theatre
Moor St
CAMBRIDGE CIRCUS
Palace
Curzon
4
Tenterden St
Harewood Pl
Bus College
The Ford College
Hanover St
NEW BOND STREET
W1S
W1F
REGENT STREET
Kingly Street
Carnaby St
Newburgh
Broadwick St
Marshall St
Lexington St
Ingestre Pl
Hopkins St
Duck La
Clnc
Soho
Meard St
Bourchier
Peter St
Walker's Court
Green's Court
Queens
China Town
Gielgud
Apollo
Lyric
Cncl Bldg
Vue
Newport
Leicester Square Stn
Wyn
St Martins
Arts Thtr
Noel Coward
LG ACRE
WC2
Lancashire Court
St George St
CONDUIT ST
New Burlington Place
Police Stn
Savile Row
5
Maddox Street
Bourdon St
The Westbury Hotel
Coach & Horses Yard
Clifford St
Old Burlington St
New Burlington Ms
Heddon St
Beak St
Warwick Street
Golden Sq
Bridle La
Gt Pulteney St
Brewer St
Sch
Piccadilly
SHAFTESBURY AV
Rupert Court
Odeon
Surg
PC
Emp
Cranbourn St
Leicester St
Cineworld Trocadero
Coventry St
Htl
Radisson Edwardian Hampshire Htl
Odeon
Capital Radio
Irving St
CHARING CROSS RD
ST MARTIN'S LA
Coliseum
D of Y
Police
William IV St
Bruton Pl
Bruton St
Bruton La
Berkeley Square
6
Royal Institution's Faraday Museum
Albemarle St
Royal Arcade
Old Bond St
Burlington Arcade
Dover St
Vigo St
Sackville St
Albany Ctyd
Royal Academy of Arts
Glasshouse St
Quadrant Arcade
PICCADILLY CIRCUS
Piccadilly Circus Stn
Eros
Criterion
Jermyn St
St James's Church
High Comm of Malta
Vine St
Shavers Pl
Prince of Wales
Odeon
UCI
National Portrait Gal
National Gallery
Garrick
St Martin-in-the-Fields
W1J
Hay Hill
Radisson Edwardian Mayfair Hotel
Brown's Hotel
Berkeley St
The Chesterfield Mayfair Hotel
Stafford St
Agnew's
PICCADILLY
Princes Arcade
Ormond Yd
Duke of York St
Cavendish Htl
Masons Yd
Visitor Centre
REGENT ST
HAYMARKET
A4
Cmdy
Excel Court
Royal Thtr
Her Majesty's
Notre Dame University
Trafalgar Square
Nelson's Column
Canada House
Charing Cross Stn
High Comm of South Africa
7
Stratton St
The Washington Mayfair Hotel
Bolton St
Clarges St
Half Moon St
The Ritz Htl
Arlington St
Jermyn St
Bury St
Ryder St
High Comm of Papua New Guinea
Charles II St
High Comm of New Zealand
PALL MALL
PALL MALL E
COCKSPUR ST
Wk Ho St
Sofitel St James Hotel
High Com of Uganda
KING CHARLES I ISLAND
Gov Offices
Gt Scotland Yd
Whitehall
Admiralty Arch
A400
Emb of Egypt
Green Park Station
The Stafford Htl
Park Pl
Blue Ball Yd
Uni
Htl
ST JAMES'S ST
King Street
A4
16
Schomberg House
The Royal Coll of Path
Carlton Ter
Carlton House
Waterloo Place
ICA
Mall Galleries
Duke of York Column
Old Admiralty
Horse Guards
A3212
Old Offic
Spencer
Privy Council
1 grid square represents 250 metres

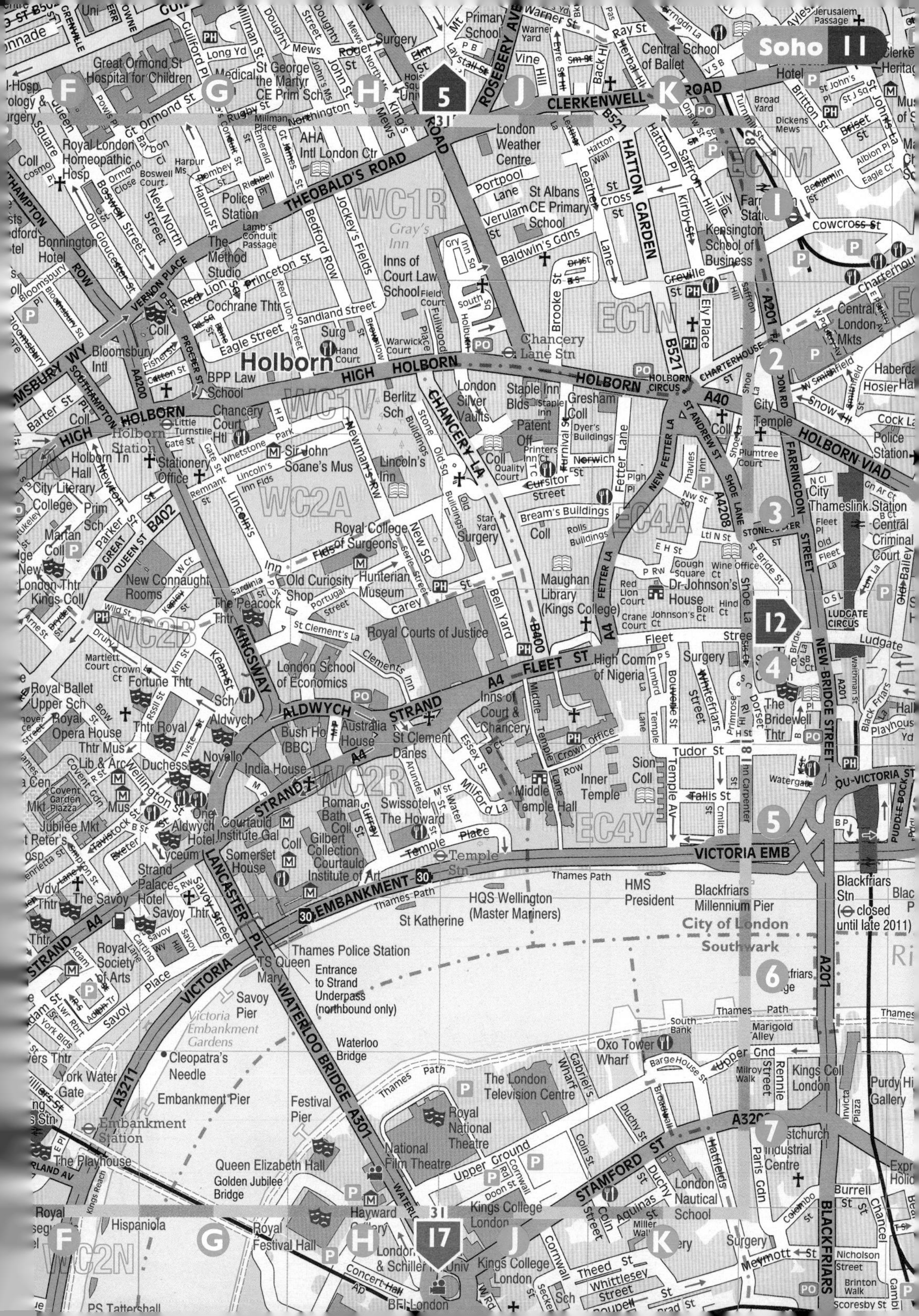
Great Ormond St Hospital for Children
Royal London Homeopathic Hosp
THEOBALD'S ROAD
CLERKENWELL ROAD
ROSEBERY AVE
London Weather Centre
Central School of Ballet
HATTON GARDEN
St Albans CE Primary School
Farringdon Station
Kensington School of Business
WC1R
Gray's Inn
Inns of Court Law School
EC1N
EC1M
Chancery Lane Stn
Holborn
HIGH HOLBORN
HOLBORN CIRCUS
CHARTERHOUSE
Central London Mkts
Holborn Station
BPP Law School
Chancery Court Htl
Sir John Soane's Mus
Lincoln's Inn
London Silver Vaults
Staple Inn Blds
Gresham Coll
HOLBORN VIAD
City Temple
Police Station
City Thameslink Station
Central Criminal Court
WC1V
WC2A
Royal College of Surgeons
Hunterian Museum
Old Curiosity Shop
New Connaught Rooms
The Peacock Thtr
Maughan Library (Kings College)
EC4A
Dr Johnson's House
FETTER LA
SHOE LANE
FARRINGDON STREET
NEW BRIDGE STREET
LUDGATE CIRCUS
Royal Courts of Justice
London School of Economics
KINGSWAY
ALDWYCH
STRAND
FLEET ST
High Comm of Nigeria
Inns of Court & Chancery
Royal Opera House
Fortune Thtr
Novello
Duchess
Bush Ho (BBC)
Australia House
St Clement Danes
India House
WC2R
Courtauld Institute Gal
Somerset House
Swissotel The Howard
Temple Stn
Middle Temple Hall
Inner Temple
EC4Y
Sion Coll
Tudor St
VICTORIA EMB
The Bridewell Thtr
Blackfriars Stn (closed until late 2011)
EMBANKMENT
HQS Wellington (Master Mariners)
HMS President
Blackfriars Millennium Pier
City of London
Southwark
Strand Palace Hotel
The Savoy
Savoy Thtr
Royal Society of Arts
LANCASTER PL
Thames Police Station
Entrance to Strand Underpass (northbound only)
Savoy Pier
Victoria Embankment Gardens
WATERLOO BRIDGE
Cleopatra's Needle
Embankment Pier
Embankment Station
York Water Gate
Festival Pier
Oxo Tower Wharf
The London Television Centre
Gabriel's Wharf
Royal National Theatre
National Film Theatre
Queen Elizabeth Hall
Golden Jubilee Bridge
Hayward Gallery
Royal Festival Hall
STAMFORD ST
Kings College London
London Nautical School
Christchurch Industrial Centre
BLACKFRIARS
Kings Coll London
The Playhouse
Hispaniola
WC2N
BFI London

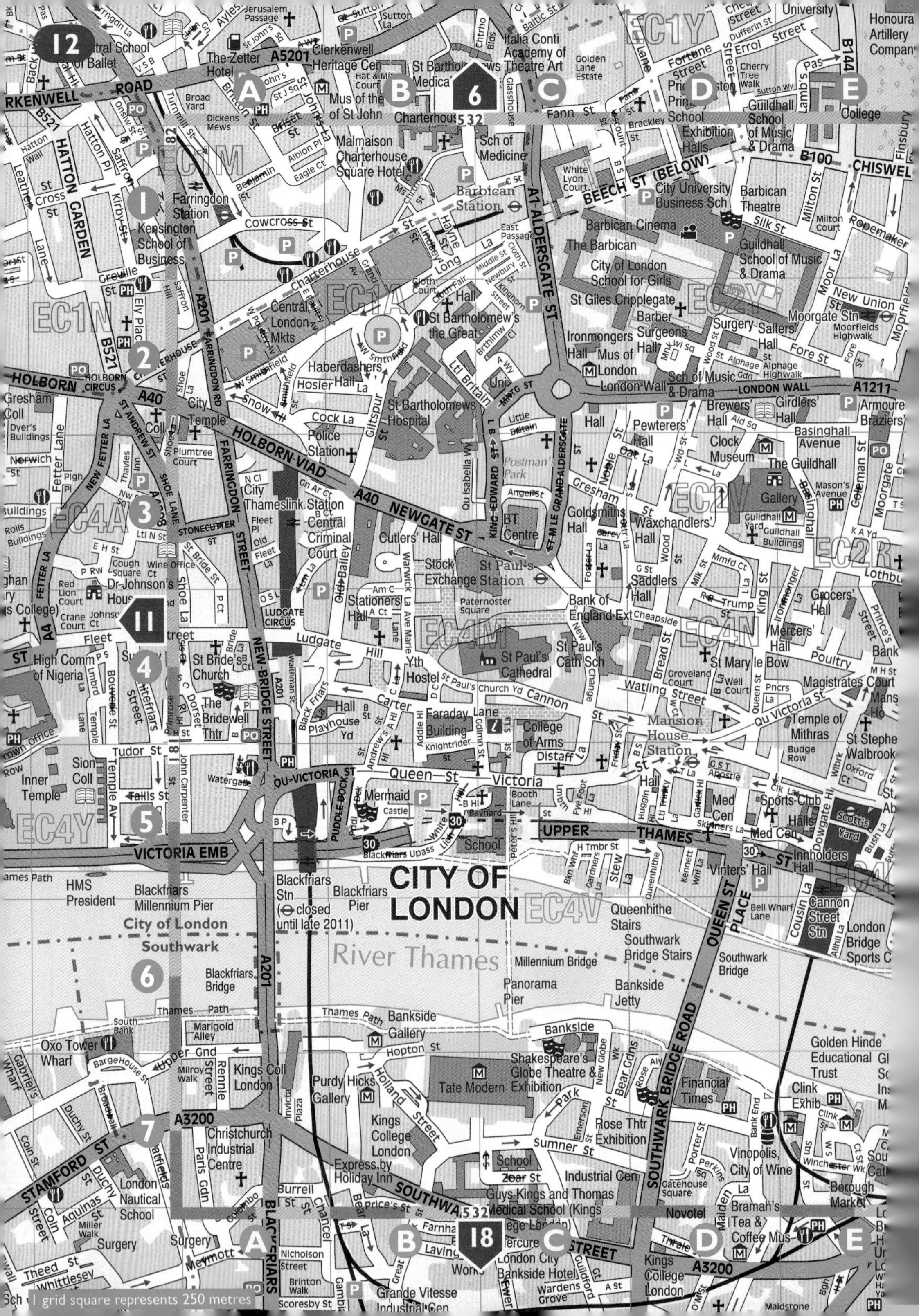

12
6
11
18
A
B
C
D
E
1
2
3
4
5
6
7
EC1M
EC1N
EC1A
EC1Y
EC2Y
EC2V
EC2R
EC4A
EC4M
EC4N
EC4Y
EC4V
CITY OF
LONDON
River Thames
City of London
Southwark
Central School of Ballet
The Zetter Hotel
Clerkenwell Heritage Cen
Mus of the of St John
Charterhouse
Italia Conti Academy of Theatre Art
Golden Lane Estate
Malmaison Charterhouse Square Hotel
Sch of Medicine
Barbican Station
Farringdon Station
Kensington School of Business
Central London Mkts
St Bartholomew's the Great
Haberdashers' Hall
St Bartholomews Hospital
Police Station
City Temple
City Thameslink Station
Central Criminal Court
Cutlers' Hall
Stock Exchange
St Paul's Station
Paternoster Square
St Paul's Cathedral
St Paul's Cath Sch
Stationers' Hall
Yth Hostel
Faraday Building
College of Arms
Mansion House Station
Temple of Mithras
Magistrates Court
Dr Johnson's House
St Bride's Church
The Bridewell Thtr
High Comm of Nigeria
Sion Coll
Inner Temple
Mermaid
HMS President
Blackfriars Millennium Pier
Blackfriars Stn
(closed until late 2011)
Blackfriars Pier
Blackfriars Bridge
Millennium Bridge
Panorama Pier
Bankside Jetty
Southwark Bridge
Southwark Bridge Stairs
Queenhithe Stairs
Bankside Gallery
Tate Modern
Shakespeare's Globe Theatre & Exhibition
Oxo Tower Wharf
Kings Coll London
Purdy Hicks Gallery
Kings College London
Christchurch Industrial Centre
London Nautical School
Express by Holiday Inn
Guys Kings and Thomas Medical School (Kings College London)
Mercure London City Bankside Hotel
Rose Thtr Exhibition
Financial Times
Vinopolis, City of Wine
Clink Exhib
Golden Hinde Educational Trust
Borough Market
Novotel
Bramah's Tea & Coffee Mus
Cannon Street Stn
London Bridge Sports C
Vinters' Hall
Innholders Hall
Scott's Yard
The Barbican
Barbican Cinema
Barbican Theatre
City of London School for Girls
St Giles Cripplegate
Guildhall School of Music & Drama
City University Business Sch
Barber Surgeons' Hall
Ironmongers Hall
Mus of London
Moorgate Stn
Salters' Hall
Girdlers' Hall
Brewers' Hall
Pewterers' Hall
Clock Museum
The Guildhall
Gallery
Goldsmiths Hall
Waxchandlers' Hall
Saddlers Hall
BT Centre
Postman's Park
Bank of England Ext
St Mary le Bow
Mercers' Hall
Grocers' Hall
Armourers Braziers'
CLERKENWELL ROAD
HOLBORN
HOLBORN VIAD
NEWGATE ST
ALDERSGATE ST
LONDON WALL
BEECH ST (BELOW)
CHISWELL
FARRINGDON RD
FARRINGDON STREET
NEW BRIDGE STREET
QU VICTORIA ST
UPPER THAMES ST
VICTORIA EMB
SOUTHWARK BRIDGE ROAD
SOUTHWARK ST
STAMFORD ST
BLACKFRIARS
HATTON GARDEN
SHOE LANE
FETTER LA
Cheapside
Poultry
Ludgate Hill
Fleet Street
Cannon St
Watling Street
Queen St
A40
A201
A1211
A3200
A5201
1 grid square represents 250 metres

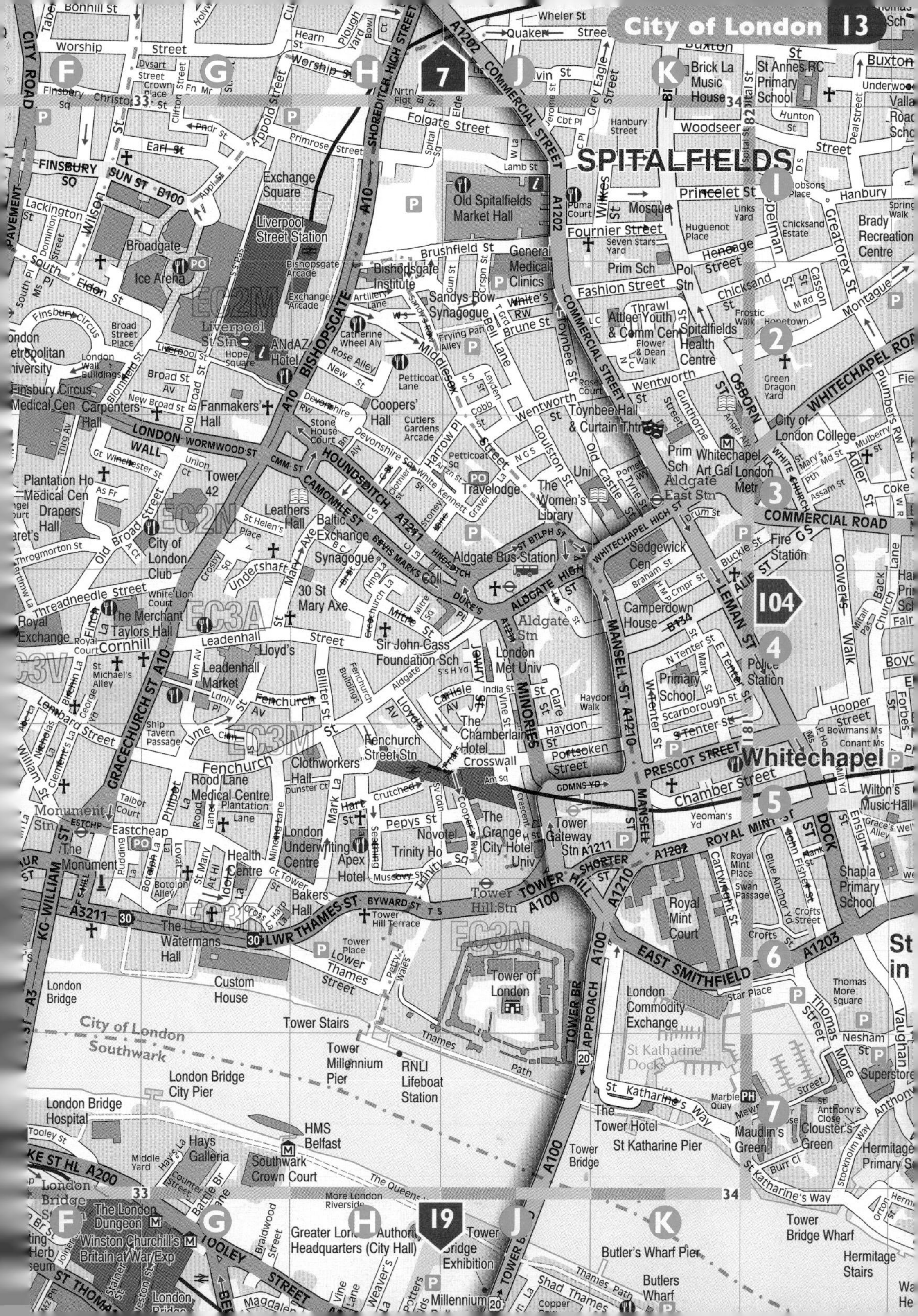
City of London
13
SPITALFIELDS
Whitechapel
City Road
Worship Street
Finsbury Sq
Christopher St
Earl St
Finsbury Sq
Sun St
Lackington St
Wilson St
Dominion Street
Broadgate
Ice Arena
Eldon St
South Pl
Finsbury Circus
London Metropolitan University
London Wall Buildings
Finsbury Circus Medical Cen
Carpenters' Hall
London Wall
Wormwood St
Gt Winchester St
Plantation Ho Medical Cen
Drapers Hall
Throgmorton St
Old Broad Street
City of London Club
Tower 42
Threadneedle Street
Royal Exchange
Cornhill
St Michael's Alley
Lombard Street
The Merchant Taylors Hall
Gracechurch St A10
Leadenhall Market
Leadenhall Street
Lloyd's
30 St Mary Axe
Undershaft
St Helen's Place
Leathers Hall
Baltic Exchange
Synagogue
Bevis Marks
Camomile St
Houndsditch A1211
Bishopsgate A10
Liverpool St Stn
ANdAZ Hotel
Liverpool Street Station
Exchange Square
Appold Street
Primrose Street
Shoreditch High Street
Folgate Street
Spital Sq
Old Spitalfields Market Hall
Lamb St
Commercial Street A1202
Brushfield St
Bishopsgate Institute
Artillery Lane
Sandys Row Synagogue
Frying Pan Alley
Bell Lane
Brune St
Catherine Wheel Aly
Rose Alley
Middlesex Street
Petticoat Lane
Devonshire Sq
Coopers' Hall
Cutlers Gardens Arcade
Stone House Court
Harrow Pl
Wentworth St
Goulston St
Toynbee Hall & Curtain Thtr
Old Castle St
The Women's Library
Travelodge
Aldgate Bus Station
Aldgate High St
Duke's Pl
Mitre St
Sir John Cass Foundation Sch
Aldgate Stn
London Met Univ
Minories
Jewry St
Fenchurch Av
Fenchurch St
Billiter St
Lime St
Ship Tavern Passage
Fenchurch Street Stn
Clothworkers' Hall
Rood Lane Medical Centre
Plantation Lane
Philpot La
Mincing Lane
Mark La
Crutched Friars
Hart St
Pepys St
Novotel
Trinity Ho
Trinity Sq
Crosswall
The Grange City Hotel
The Chamberlain Hotel
Haydon St
Portsoken Street
Mansell St A1210
Prescot Street
Chamber Street
Tower Gateway Stn
London Underwriting Centre
Apex Hotel
Monument Stn
Eastcheap
The Monument
Health Centre
St Mary At Hl
Botolph Alley
Bakers Hall
Byward St
Tower Hill Terrace
Lwr Thames St
A3211
The Watermans Hall
Custom House
Lower Thames Street
Tower Hill Stn
Tower Hill
Shorter St
Royal Mint St
East Smithfield
Tower of London
Tower Br Approach
Tower Bridge
London Bridge
Tower Stairs
Tower Millennium Pier
RNLI Lifeboat Station
City of London
Southwark
London Bridge City Pier
London Bridge Hospital
HMS Belfast
Hays Galleria
Southwark Crown Court
Tooley St
The Queen's Walk
More London Riverside
Greater London Authority Headquarters (City Hall)
Tower Bridge Exhibition
Butler's Wharf Pier
The London Dungeon
Winston Churchill's Britain at War Exp
Tooley Street
London Commodity Exchange
St Katharine Docks
St Katharine's Way
The Tower Hotel
St Katharine Pier
Marble Quay
Maudlin's Green
Clouster's Green
Hermitage Primary Sch
Tower Bridge Wharf
Hermitage Stairs
Thomas More Square
Thomas More Street
Nesham St
Superstore
Royal Mint Court
Cartwright St
Swan Passage
Blue Anchor Yd
John Fisher St
Shapla Primary School
Dock St
Wilton's Music Hall
Leman St
Police Station
Camperdown House
Primary School
Scarborough St
Aldgate East Stn
Whitechapel High St
Sedgewick Cen
Whitechapel Art Gal
London Metr
City of London College
Whitechapel Road
Commercial Road
Fire Station
Gowers Walk
Back Church Lane
Hooper Street
Osborn St
Wentworth St
Fashion Street
Thrawl St
Attlee Youth & Comm Cen
Spitalfields Health Centre
Flower & Dean Walk
Fournier Street
Princelet St
Mosque
Brick La Music House
Hanbury Street
Woodseer St
Huguenot Place
Chicksand Estate
Chicksand St
Greatorex St
Brady Recreation Centre
Hanbury St
St Annes RC Primary School
Buxton St
Green Dragon Yard
Wheler St
Quaker Street
Commercial Street
Wilkes St
Puma Court
Seven Stars Yard
General Medical Clinics
Prim Sch
Pol Stn
Fanmakers' Hall
Broad St Av
EC2M
EC2N
EC3A
EC3M
EC3N
EC3R
EC3V
7
19
104
33
34
F
G
H
J
K
1
2
3
4
5
6
7

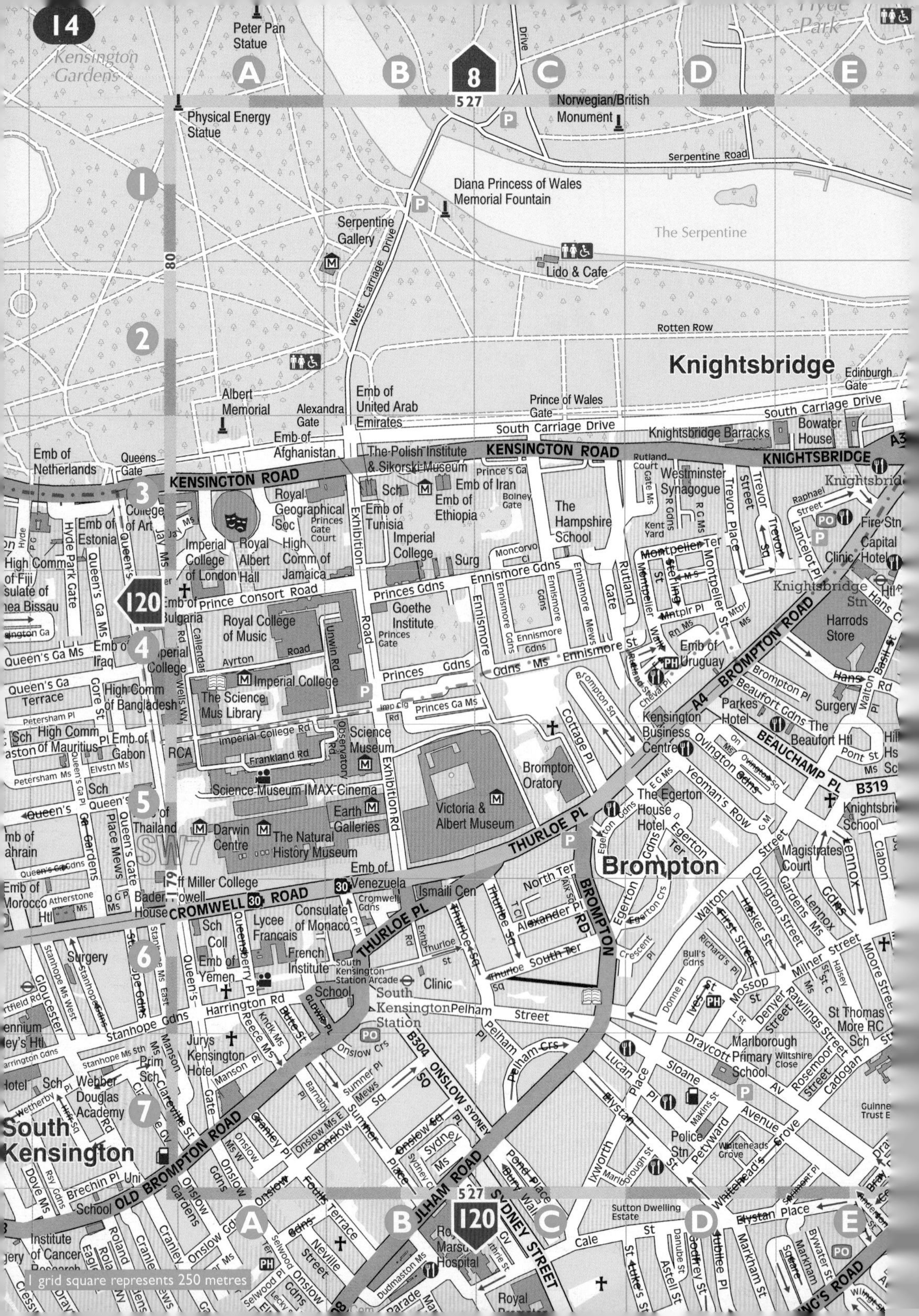
Peter Pan Statue
Kensington Gardens
Hyde Park
Physical Energy Statue
Norwegian/British Monument
Serpentine Road
Diana Princess of Wales Memorial Fountain
Serpentine Gallery
West Carriage Drive
The Serpentine
Lido & Cafe
Rotten Row
Knightsbridge
Edinburgh Gate
Albert Memorial
Alexandra Gate
Emb of United Arab Emirates
Prince of Wales Gate
South Carriage Drive
Knightsbridge Barracks
Bowater House
Emb of Afghanistan
The Polish Institute & Sikorski Museum
KENSINGTON ROAD
KNIGHTSBRIDGE
Emb of Netherlands
Queens Gate
Rutland Court
Westminster Synagogue
Trevor Street
Trevor Place
Royal College of Art
Royal Geographical Soc
Emb of Iran
Emb of Tunisia
Emb of Ethiopia
The Hampshire School
Raphael Street
Fire Stn
Capital Hotel
Emb of Estonia
Imperial College of London
Royal Albert Hall
High Comm of Jamaica
Imperial College
Surg
Ennismore Gdns
Montpelier Ter
Montpelier Place
Clinic
High Comm of Fiji
Prince Consort Road
Princes Gdns
Goethe Institute
Knightsbridge Stn
Harrods Store
Emb of Bulgaria
Royal College of Music
Emb of Iraq
Emb of Uruguay
BROMPTON ROAD
Queen's Ga Ms
Imperial College
Ayrton
Exhibition Road
Brompton Sq
Brompton Pl
Beaufort Gdns
Queen's Ga Terrace
High Comm of Bangladesh
The Science Mus Library
Princes Ga Ms
Kensington Business Centre
Parkes Hotel
The Beaufort Htl
High Comm of Mauritius
Emb of Gabon
Imperial College Rd
Science Museum
Cottage Pl
Ovington Gdns
BEAUCHAMP PL
Frankland Rd
Brompton Oratory
B319
Science Museum IMAX Cinema
Yeoman's Row
The Egerton House Hotel
Knightsbridge School
Emb of Thailand
Darwin Centre
The Natural History Museum
Earth Galleries
Victoria & Albert Museum
THURLOE PL
SW7
Emb of Bahrain
Brompton
Magistrates Court
Emb of Morocco
Emb of Venezuela
Ismaili Cen
North Ter
Alexander Pl
BROMPTON RD
Walton Street
Ovington Street
Lennox Gdns
Baden Powell House
CROMWELL ROAD
Consulate of Monaco
Lycee Francais
Egerton Crs
Milner Street
Moore Street
Surgery
French Institute
South Kensington Station Arcade
Clinic
South Ter
Hasker St
Mossop St
Stanhope Gdns
Harrington Rd
Pelham Street
South Kensington Station
Rawlings Street
St Thomas More RC Sch
Jurys Kensington Hotel
Onslow Crs
Draycott Av
Marlborough Primary School
Webber Douglas Academy
ONSLOW SQ
Pelham Crs
Lucan Place
Sloane Avenue
Police Stn
South Kensington
OLD BROMPTON ROAD
FULHAM ROAD
SYDNEY STREET
Elystan Pl
Cadogan
Sutton Dwelling Estate
Elystan Place
Cale St
Royal Marsden Hospital
Institute of Cancer Research
KING'S ROAD
1 grid square represents 250 metres

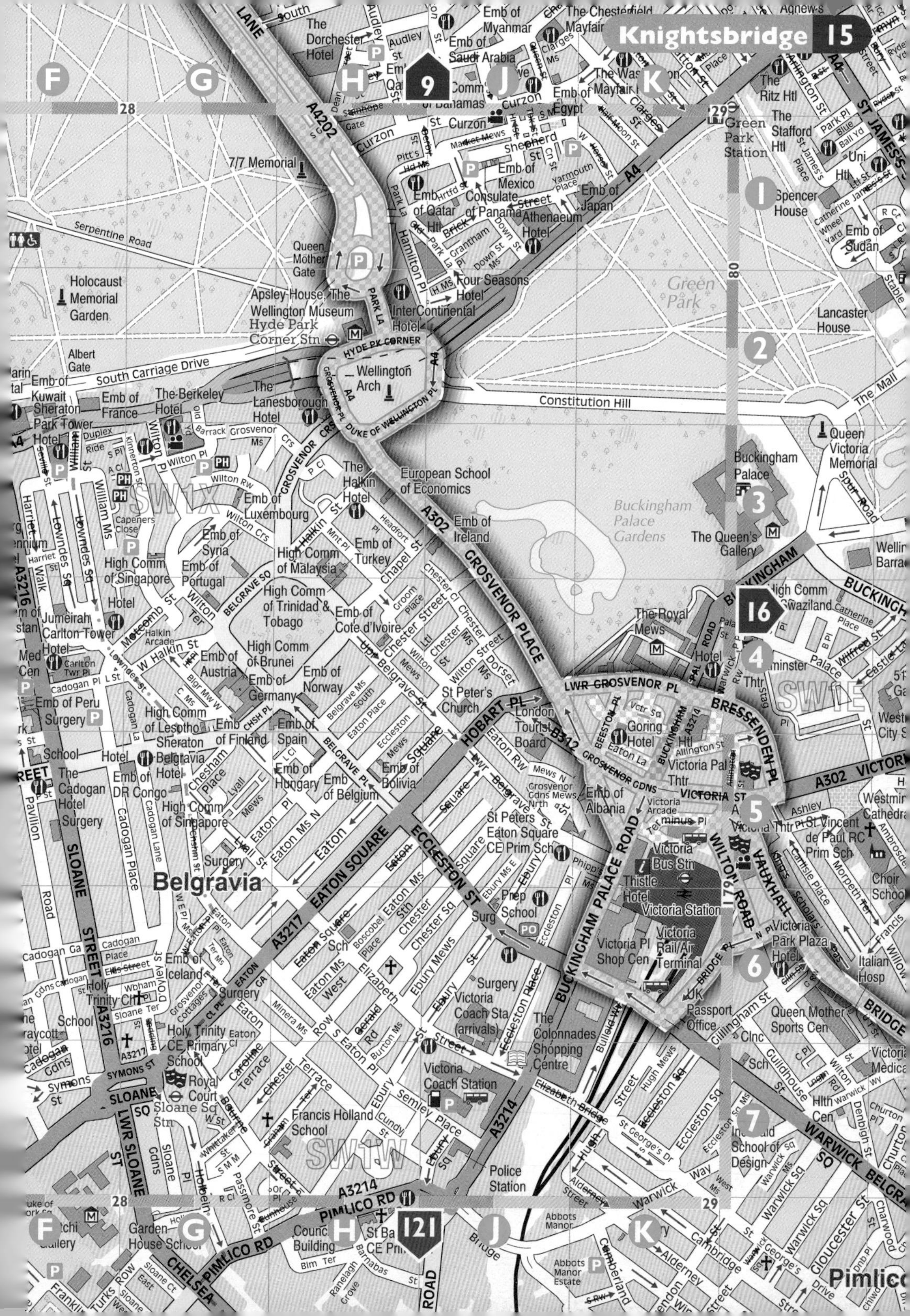

Knightsbridge 15
The Dorchester Hotel
Emb of Myanmar
The Chesterfield Mayfair
Emb of Saudi Arabia
Emb of Egypt
Curzon St
Curzon
Shepherd Market
Green Park Station
The Ritz Htl
The Stafford Htl
Uni Htl
Spencer House
Emb of Qatar
Emb of Mexico
Consulate of Panama
Emb of Japan
Athenaeum Hotel
Four Seasons Hotel
InterContinental Hotel
Emb of Sudan
7/7 Memorial
Serpentine Road
Queen Mother Gate
Holocaust Memorial Garden
Apsley House, The Wellington Museum
Hyde Park Corner Stn
HYDE PK CORNER
Wellington Arch
Green Park
Lancaster House
Constitution Hill
The Mall
Albert Gate
South Carriage Drive
Emb of Kuwait
Emb of France
The Berkeley Hotel
The Lanesborough Hotel
Sheraton Park Tower Hotel
Queen Victoria Memorial
Buckingham Palace
European School of Economics
The Halkin Hotel
Emb of Luxembourg
Emb of Ireland
Buckingham Palace Gardens
The Queen's Gallery
Emb of Syria
High Comm of Malaysia
Emb of Turkey
High Comm of Singapore
Emb of Portugal
High Comm of Trinidad & Tobago
Emb of Cote d'Ivoire
GROSVENOR PLACE
The Royal Mews
High Comm Swaziland
Jumeirah Carlton Tower Hotel
High Comm of Brunei
Emb of Austria
Emb of Germany
Emb of Norway
St Peter's Church
LWR GROSVENOR PL
BRESSENDEN PL
Goring Hotel
Victoria Pal Thtr
Emb of Peru
High Comm of Lesotho
Emb of Finland
Emb of Spain
Sheraton Belgravia Hotel
London Tourist Board
Emb of Hungary
Emb of Belgium
Emb of Bolivia
Emb of Albania
The Cadogan Hotel
Emb of DR Congo
High Comm of Singapore
St Peters Eaton Square CE Prim Sch
Victoria Bus Stn
Thistle Hotel
Victoria Station
Westminster Cathedral
St Vincent de Paul RC Prim Sch
Belgravia
EATON SQUARE
ECCLESTON ST
BUCKINGHAM PALACE ROAD
WILTON ROAD
VAUXHALL BRIDGE
Victoria Park Plaza Hotel
Italian Hosp
Emb of Iceland
Victoria Pl Shop Cen
Victoria Rail/Air Terminal
UK Passport Office
Queen Mother Sports Cen
Holy Trinity CE Primary School
Victoria Coach Sta (arrivals)
The Colonnades Shopping Centre
Royal Court
Sloane Sq Stn
Victoria Coach Station
Francis Holland School
SW1W
Police Station
Westminster Kingsway College School of Design
WARWICK SQ
PIMLICO RD
Abbots Manor Estate
Pimlico
SW1X
SW1E
SLOANE STREET
LWR SLOANE ST

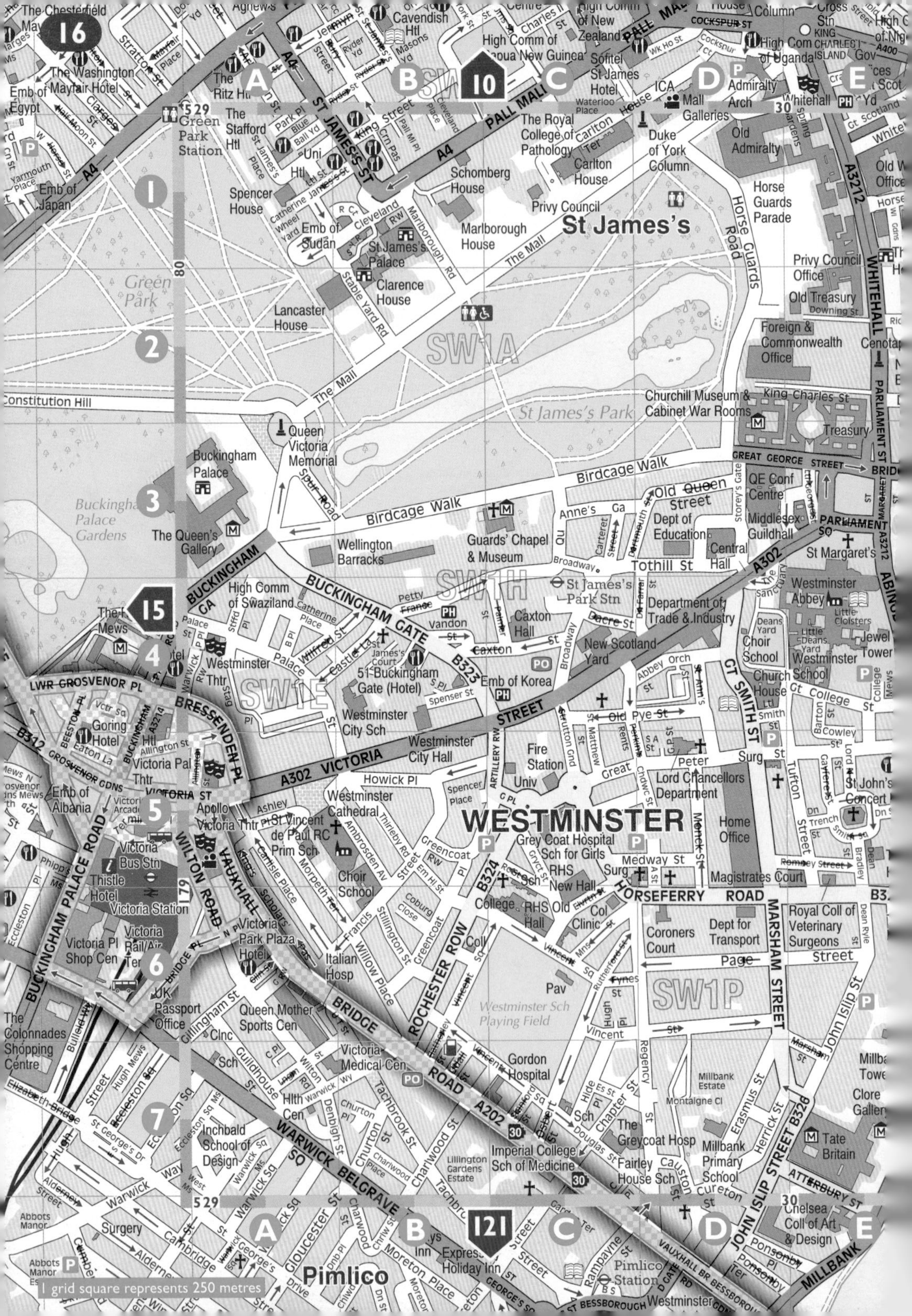
16
10
15
121
A
B
C
D
E
1
2
3
4
5
6
7
529
30
80
79
1 grid square represents 250 metres
St James's
WESTMINSTER
Pimlico
SW1A
SW1H
SW1E
SW1P
Green Park
St James's Park
Buckingham Palace Gardens
Westminster Sch Playing Field
The Chesterfield
The Washington Mayfair Hotel
Emb of Egypt
Emb of Japan
The Ritz Htl
The Stafford Htl
Green Park Station
Spencer House
Cavendish Htl
Masons Yd
High Comm of Papua New Guinea
High Comm of New Zealand
Sofitel St James Hotel
ICA
Mall Galleries
Admiralty Arch
Whitehall
Old Admiralty
The Royal College of Pathology
Carlton House
Duke of York Column
Schomberg House
Privy Council
Marlborough House
Emb of Sudan
St James's Palace
Clarence House
Lancaster House
Horse Guards Parade
Privy Council Office
Old Treasury
Foreign & Commonwealth Office
Cenotaph
Churchill Museum & Cabinet War Rooms
Treasury
Queen Victoria Memorial
Buckingham Palace
The Queen's Gallery
Wellington Barracks
Guards' Chapel & Museum
Dept of Education
Central Hall
QE Conf Centre
Middlesex Guildhall
St Margaret's
Westminster Abbey
Little Cloisters
Jewel Tower
Choir School
Westminster School
Church House
High Comm of Swaziland
St James's Park Stn
Caxton Hall
Department of Trade & Industry
New Scotland Yard
51 Buckingham Gate (Hotel)
Emb of Korea
Westminster Thtr
Goring Hotel
Victoria Pal Thtr
Emb of Albania
Apollo Victoria Thtr
Victoria Bus Stn
Thistle Hotel
Victoria Station
Victoria Pl Shop Cen
UK Passport Office
Westminster City Sch
Westminster City Hall
Westminster Cathedral
St Vincent de Paul RC Prim Sch
Choir School
Fire Station
Grey Coat Hospital Sch for Girls
RHS New Hall
RHS Old Hall
Lord Chancellors Department
Home Office
Magistrates Court
St John's Concert Hall
Royal Coll of Veterinary Surgeons
Coroners Court
Dept for Transport
Victoria Park Plaza Hotel
Italian Hosp
Queen Mother Sports Cen
Victoria Medical Cen
Gordon Hospital
The Greycoat Hosp
Millbank Primary School
Imperial College Sch of Medicine
Fairley House Sch
Inchbald School of Design
The Colonnades Shopping Centre
Tate Britain
Chelsea Coll of Art & Design
Millbank Tower
Clore Gallery
Pimlico Station
Express Holiday Inn
Lillington Gardens Estate
Millbank Estate
Abbots Manor
Surgery
PALL MALL
ST JAMES'S ST
The Mall
Constitution Hill
Birdcage Walk
Horse Guards Road
WHITEHALL
PARLIAMENT ST
GREAT GEORGE STREET
PARLIAMENT SQ
BUCKINGHAM GATE
VICTORIA STREET
BRESSENDEN PL
BUCKINGHAM PALACE ROAD
VAUXHALL BRIDGE ROAD
WILTON ROAD
ROCHESTER ROW
HORSEFERRY ROAD
MARSHAM STREET
JOHN ISLIP STREET
MILLBANK
WARWICK SQ
BELGRAVE ROAD
Tothill St
Broadway
Petty France
Old Queen Street
Victoria St
Page Street
Great Peter St
Howick Pl
Francis Street
Greencoat Pl
Tachbrook St
Charlwood St
Moreton Place
Gloucester St
Rampayne St
Vincent Sq
Eccleston Sq
Warwick Way
Hugh Street
Cambridge St
Guildhouse St

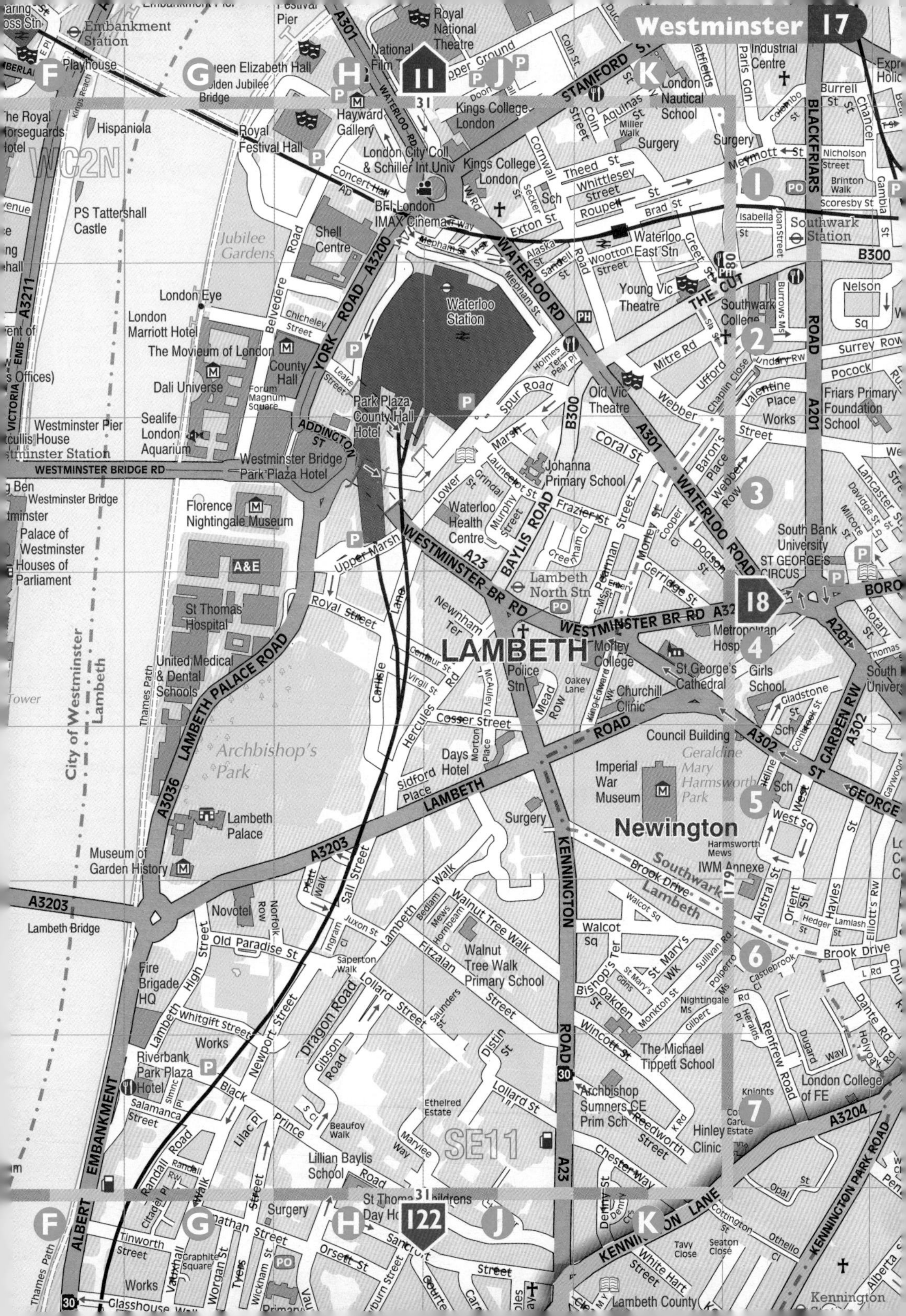
Embankment Station
Playhouse
Queen Elizabeth Hall
Golden Jubilee Bridge
Royal National Theatre
National Film Theatre
11
31
Kings College London
STAMFORD ST
London Nautical School
Industrial Centre
Paris Gdn
BLACKFRIARS ROAD
Burrell St
Chancel St
Hispaniola
Royal Festival Hall
Hayward Gallery
WATERLOO RD
London City Coll & Schiller Int Univ
Kings College London
Cornwall Rd
Aquinas St
Miller Walk
Surgery
Meymott St
Nicholson Street
Brinton Walk
Scoresby St
Gambia St
WC2N
PS Tattershall Castle
Concert Hall Ap
BFI London IMAX Cinema
Theed St
Whittlesey Street
Roupell St
Brad St
Exton St
Southwark Station
B300
Jubilee Gardens
Shell Centre
Waterloo East Stn
Wootton Street
Young Vic Theatre
THE CUT
Southwark College
Burrows Ms
Nelson Sq
Belvedere Road
Chicheley Street
London Eye
London Marriott Hotel
The Movieum of London
County Hall
YORK ROAD A3200
Waterloo Station
Mepham St
Mitre Rd
Surrey Row
Pocock St
Dali Universe
Forum Magnum Square
Leake Street
Park Plaza County Hall Hotel
Spur Road
Old Vic Theatre
Webber Street
Valentine Place
Friars Primary Foundation School
A201
Sealife London Aquarium
Westminster Pier
ADDINGTON ST
Westminster Bridge Park Plaza Hotel
WESTMINSTER BRIDGE RD
Coral St
A301
Baron's Place
Webber Row
Lancaster St
Big Ben
Westminster Bridge
Palace of Westminster Houses of Parliament
Florence Nightingale Museum
Johanna Primary School
Lower Marsh
Waterloo Health Centre
Frazier St
WATERLOO ROAD
A&E
Upper Marsh
WESTMINSTER BR RD
A23
BAYLIS ROAD
Pearman Street
Morley St
Cooper Cl
Dodson St
South Bank University
ST GEORGE'S CIRCUS
18
Royal Street
Lambeth North Stn
Cerridge St
St Thomas' Hospital
Newnham Ter
LAMBETH
WESTMINSTER BR RD A23
Metropolitan Hosp
Rotary St
Morley College
St George's Cathedral
Girls School
United Medical & Dental Schools
LAMBETH PALACE ROAD
Carlisle Lane
Centaur St
Virgil St
Hercules Rd
Police Stn
Oakey Lane
Mead Row
Churchill Clinic
Gladstone St
South Univers
City of Westminster
Lambeth
Thames Path
Cosser Street
ROAD
Council Building
A302
ST GEORGE'S RD
GARDEN RW
Archbishop's Park
Days Hotel
Morton Place
Imperial War Museum
Geraldine Mary Harmsworth Park
A3036
Sidford Place
LAMBETH
Newington
West Sq
Lambeth Palace
A3203
Surgery
KENNINGTON ROAD
Harmsworth Mews
IWM Annexe
Museum of Garden History
Brook Drive
Southwark
Lambeth
A3203
Lambeth Bridge
Novotel
Norfolk Row
Sail Street
Lambeth Walk
Walnut Tree Walk
Walcot Sq
Hedger St
Hayles St
Old Paradise St
Juxon St
Walnut Tree Walk Primary School
Bishop's Ter
St Mary's Wk
Fire Brigade HQ
High Street
Saperton Walk
Lollard Street
Fitzalan Street
Oakden St
Nightingale Ms
Renfrew Road
Dante Rd
Whitgift Street
Works
Dragon Road
Saunders St
Distin St
Wincott St
The Michael Tippett School
Dugard Way
Holyoak Rd
Riverbank Park Plaza Hotel
Newport Street
Gibson Road
Lollard St
Archbishop Sumners CE Prim Sch
London College of FE
EMBANKMENT
Black Prince Road
Salamanca Street
Lilac Pl
Beaufoy Walk
Ethelred Estate
Marylee Way
SE11
Reedworth Street
Hinley Clinic
A3204
Lillian Baylis School
Chester Way
KENNINGTON PARK ROAD
ALBERT
Randall Road
Surgery
St Thomas Childrens Day H
122
KENNINGTON LANE
Othello Cl
Tinworth Street
Graphite Square
Orsett St
Sancroft
Tavy Close
Seaton Close
White Hart Street
Works
Vauxhall Walk
Worgan St
Tyers
Wickham St
Lambeth County
Kennington
30
Glasshouse Walk

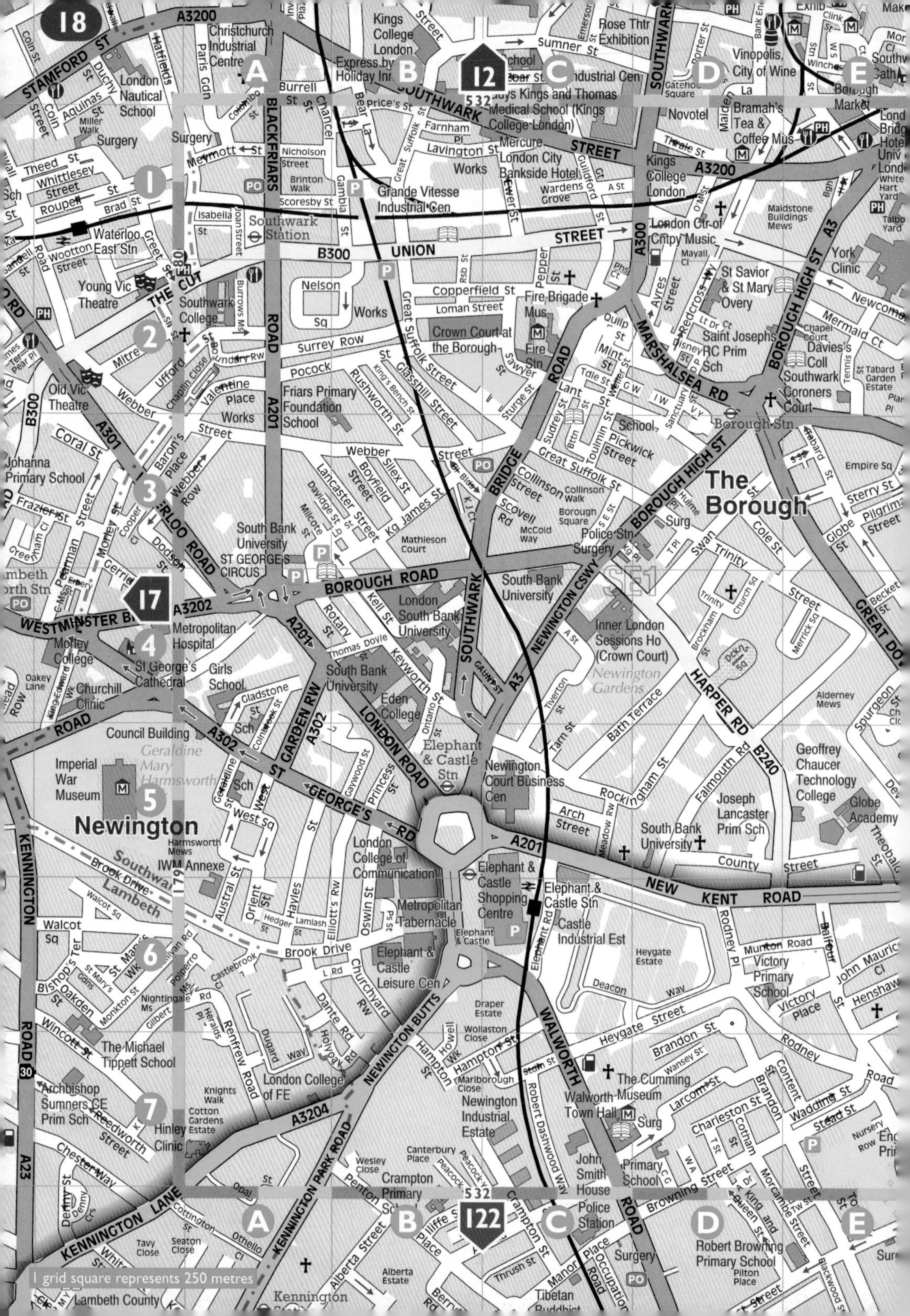

18
A3200
STAMFORD ST
Christchurch Industrial Centre
Hatfields
Paris Gdn
Kings College London
Express by Holiday Inn
12
532
Sumner St
Rose Thtr Exhibition
SOUTHWARK
Porter St
Vinopolis, City of Wine
Clink
Winchester
Southwark Cath
Borough Market
Coin Street
Duchy St
Aquinas St
London Nautical School
Miller Walk
Surgery
Burrell St
BLACKFRIARS ROAD
Chancel St
Bear La
Price's St
SOUTHWARK STREET
Guys Kings and Thomas Medical School (Kings College London)
Industrial Cen
Gatehouse Square
Novotel
Maiden La
Bramah's Tea & Coffee Mus
Farnham Pl
Mercure London City Bankside Hotel
Thrale St
Theed St
Whittlesey Street
Roupell St
Brad St
Meymott St
Nicholson Street
Brinton Walk
Lavington St
Works
Grande Vitesse Industrial Cen
Ewer St
Guildford St
Wardens Grove
A St
Kings College London
A3200
Maidstone Buildings Mews
White Hart Yard
Talbot Yard
Waterloo East Stn
Isabella St
Joan Street
Southwark Station
Scoresby St
Gambia St
London Ctr of Cntpy Music
Wootton Street
Greet St
THE CUT
B300
UNION STREET
Mayall Cl
York Clinic
Young Vic Theatre
Southwark College
Burrows Ms
Nelson Sq
Works
Rsb St
Copperfield St
Loman Street
Pepper St
Fire Brigade Mus
Phs Ct
Ayres Street
Redcross Wy
St Savior & St Mary Overy
Newcomen
Mermaid Ct
Chapel Court
Davies's Coll Southwark
Saint Josephs RC Prim Sch
Mitre
Boundary Rw
Surrey Row
Great Suffolk St
Crown Court at the Borough
Fire Stn
Quilp St
Mint St
MARSHALSEA RD
BOROUGH HIGH ST
Tabard Garden Estate
Coroners Court
Old Vic Theatre
B300
Ufford
Chaplin Close
Valentine Place
Webber Street
Works
Pocock St
King's Bench St
Glasshill Street
Rushworth St
Friars Primary Foundation School
Sawyer St
Sturge St
ROAD
Tdle St
Lant St
Weller St
Sudrey St
Toulmin St
School
Pickwick Street
Sanctuary St
Borough Stn
Tabard St
Coral St
A301
Baron's Place
Webber Row
A201
Webber Street
Boyfield Street
Silex St
Lancaster Street
Davidge St
Milcote St
Kg James St
Street
Collinson Street
Collinson Walk
Great Suffolk St
Scovell Rd
McCoid Way
Borough Square
Empire Sq
The Borough
Sterry St
Pilgrimage Street
Johanna Primary School
Frazier St
Pearman Street
Morley St
Cooper Cl
Dodson St
WATERLOO ROAD
South Bank University
ST GEORGE'S CIRCUS
Mathieson Court
BRIDGE
Police Stn
Surgery
Hulme Pl
Surg
Swan St
Trinity
Cole St
Globe St
Lambeth North Stn
Gerridge St
17
A3202
WESTMINSTER BR RD
BOROUGH ROAD
South Bank University
SE1
Trinity Church Sq
Street
Becket St
GREAT DOVER
Metropolitan Hospital
Morley College
St George's Cathedral
Rotary St
Kell St
London South Bank University
SOUTHWARK
A3
NEWINGTON CSWY
Inner London Sessions Ho (Crown Court)
Merrick Sq
Brockham St
Dickens Sq
Oakey Lane
Churchill Clinic
Girls School
Thomas Doyle St
Keyworth St
South Bank University
Eden College
Gaunt St
Newington Gardens
HARPER RD
Alderney Mews
Spurgeon St
Gladstone St
ROAD
Council Building
Geraldine Mary Harmsworth
A302
ST GEORGE'S RD
ST GARDEN RW
LONDON ROAD
Ontario St
Tiverton St
Bath Terrace
Tarn St
Elephant & Castle Stn
Newington Court Business Cen
Rockingham St
Falmouth Rd
B240
Geoffrey Chaucer Technology College
Imperial War Museum
Gaywood St
Princess St
Arch Street
Joseph Lancaster Prim Sch
Globe Academy
Newington
Harmsworth Mews
West Sq
A201
South Bank University
Meadow Rw
County Street
IWM Annexe
London College of Communication
Elephant & Castle Shopping Centre
Elephant & Castle Stn
NEW KENT ROAD
KENNINGTON ROAD
Brook Drive
Southwark
Lambeth
Walcot Sq
Austral St
Orient St
Hayles St
Elliott's Rw
Oswin St
Metropolitan Tabernacle
Castle Industrial Est
Rodney Pl
Munton Road
Balfour St
John Maurice Cl
Walcot Sq
Hedger St
Lamlash St
Brook Drive
Elephant & Castle
Elephant Rd
Heygate Estate
Victory Primary School
Bishop's Ter
St Mary's Gdns
Castlebrook Cl
L Rd
Churchyard Rw
Elephant & Castle Leisure Cen
Deacon Way
Victory Place
Henshaw St
Oakden St
Monkton St
Nightingale Ms
Gilbert Rd
Heralds Pl
Renfrew Road
Dante Rd
Draper Estate
Wollaston Close
Heygate Street
Brandon St
Rodney Road
Wincott St
The Michael Tippett School
Dugard Way
Holyoak Rd
NEWINGTON BUTTS
Hampton St
Howell Wk
WALWORTH ROAD
Wansey St
The Cumming Museum
Content St
Wadding St
Archbishop Sumners CE Prim Sch
Knights Walk
London College of FE
Marlborough Close
Newington Industrial Estate
Robert Dashwood Way
Walworth Town Hall
Larcom St
Charleston St
Brandon St
Stead St
Reedworth Street
Cotton Gardens Estate
Hinley Clinic
A3204
Surg
Cotham St
Nursery Row
A23
Chester Way
KENNINGTON PARK ROAD
Canterbury Place
Wesley Close
Crampton Primary Sch
Peacock St
John Smith House
Primary School
Browning Street
Morecambe Street
Denny St
Denny Cres
KENNINGTON LANE
Opal St
Penton Pl
532
122
Crampton St
Police Station
King and Queen St
Robert Browning Primary School
Pilton Place
Cottington St
Tavy Close
Seaton Close
Othello Cl
Alberta Street
Iliffe St
Thrush St
Manor Place
Occupation Road
Surgery
Alberta Estate
Kennington
Tibetan Buddhist
Blackwood St
1 grid square represents 250 metres
Lambeth County

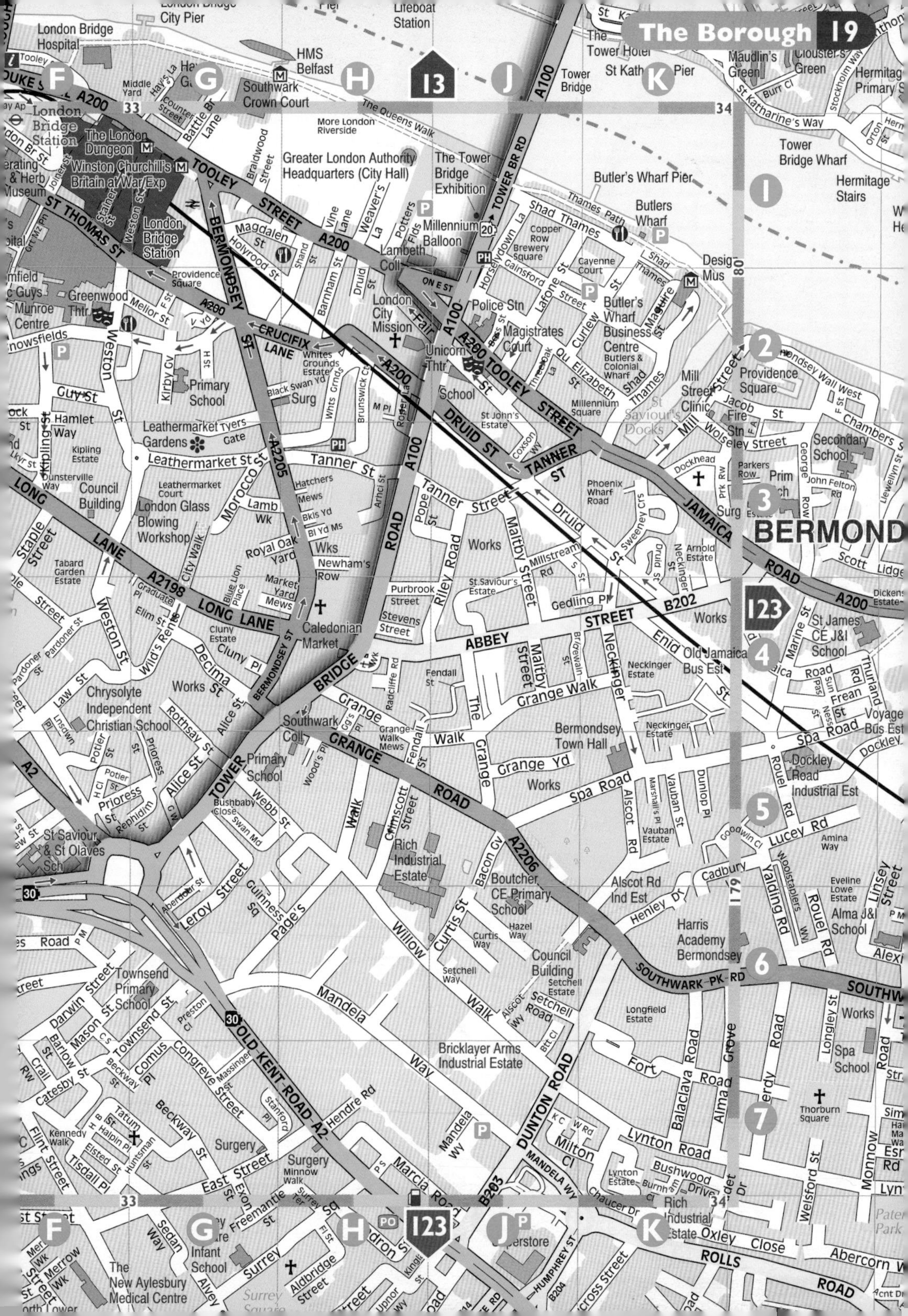
London Bridge City Pier
London Bridge Hospital
Lifeboat Station
HMS Belfast
13
The Tower Hotel
St Katharine Pier
Tower Bridge
Maudlin's Green
Clousters Green
Hermitage Primary School
F
G
H
J
K
Tooley St
Duke St Hill
A200
33
34
Middle Yard
Hay's La
Counter Street
Battle Br Lane
Southwark Crown Court
The Queens Walk
More London Riverside
London Bridge Station
The London Dungeon
Winston Churchill's Britain at War Exp
Braidwood Street
Greater London Authority Headquarters (City Hall)
The Tower Bridge Exhibition
A100
Tower Br Rd
St Katharine's Way
Burr Cl
Stockholm Way
Tower Bridge Wharf
Orton St
Butler's Wharf Pier
Hermitage Stairs
I
Joiner St
Stainer St
Weston St
London Bridge Station
St Thomas St
Tooley Street
Bermondsey St
Magdalen St
Holyrood St
Shand St
Vine Lane
Weaver's La
Potters Flds
Millennium Balloon
Lambeth Coll
Barnham St
Druid St
Horselydown La
Shad Thames
Copper Row
Brewery Square
Thames Path
Butlers Wharf
Cayenne Court
Gainsford St
Lafone St
Design Mus
80
Providence Square
Guy's
Greenwood Thtr
Munroe Centre
Melior St
F St
Snowsfields
Crucifix Lane
London City Mission
One St
Fair St
Police Stn
Magistrates Court
Curlew St
Butler's Wharf Business Centre
Maguire St
Butlers & Colonial Wharf
Bermondsey Wall West
2
Kirby Gv
Primary School
Whites Grounds Estate
Black Swan Yd
Surg
Whites Grnds
Brunswick Ct
Unicorn Thtr
Tooley Street
Three Oak La
Queen Elizabeth St
Shad Thames
Millennium Square
St Saviour's Docks
Mill Street
Mill Street Clinic
Jacob St
Fire Stn
Chambers St
Guy St
Hamlet Way
Kipling St
Kipling Estate
Leathermarket Gardens
Tyers Gate
Leathermarket St
School
M Pl
Roper La
St John's Estate
Druid St
Coxson Wy
Tanner St
Wolseley Street
Secondary School
Dockhead
Parkers Row
Prim Sch
George Row
John Felton Rd
Llewellyn St
3
Dunsterville Way
Council Building
Leathermarket Court
London Glass Blowing Workshop
Morocco St
Lamb Wk
A2205
Hatchers Mews
Bkls Yd
Bl Yd Ms
Tanner St
Arnhcl St
Pope St
Tanner Street
Phoenix Wharf Road
Sweeney Crs
Jamaica Road
BERMONDSEY
Long Lane
Staple Street
Tabard Garden Estate
City Walk
Royal Oak Yard
Wks
Newham's Row
Road
Riley Road
Works
Maltby Street
Millstream Rd
Druid St
Neckinger St
Arnold Estate
Scott Lidgett
A2198
Graduate Pl
Blue Lion Place
Market Yard Mews
Purbrook Street
Stevens Street
St Saviour's Estate
Gedling Pl
B202
Works
123
A200
Dickens Estate
Elim St
Wild's Rents
Long Lane
Caledonian Market
Abbey Street
Enid St
Old Jamaica Bus Est
St James CE J&I School
Marine St
4
Pardoner St
Cluny Estate
Cluny Pl
Decima St
Bermondsey St
Bridge
Radcliffe Rd
Fendall St
Maltby Street
Brewain St
Neckinger Estate
Jamaica Road
Frean St
Thurland Rd
Law St
Chrysolyte Independent Christian School
Works
Rothsay St
Alice St
Grange Walk
The Grange
Bermondsey Town Hall
Neckinger Estate
Voyager Bus Est
Spa Road
Dockley Road Industrial Est
Lnsdwn Pl
Potier St
Prioress St
Potier St
Tower
Southwark Coll
Grange Rd
Grange Walk Mews
Fendall St
Walk
Grange Yd
Works
Spa Road
Marshall's Pl
Vauban St
Dunlop Pl
Rouel Rd
5
A2
Prioress St
Rephidim St
Alice St
Primary School
Webb St
Wood's Pl
Grange Road
Bushbaby Close
Swan Md
Walk
Crimscott Street
Alscot Rd
Vauban Estate
Goodwin Cl
Lucey Rd
Amina Way
St Saviour & St Olaves Sch
30
Aberdour St
Leroy Street
Guinness Sq
Page's
Rich Industrial Estate
Bacon Gv
A2206
Boutcher CE Primary School
Alscot Rd Ind Est
Cadbury
179
Yalding Rd
Woolstaplers Wy
Eveline Lowe Estate
Alma J&I School
Linsey Street
Rouel Rd
Willow
Curtis St
Curtis Way
Hazel Way
Henley Dr
Harris Academy Bermondsey
6
Southwark Pk Rd
Townsend Primary School
Darwin Street
Mason St
Townsend St
Preston Cl
Mandela
Setchell Way
Council Building
Setchell Estate
Walk
Alscot Wy
Setchell Road
Longfield Estate
Works
Longley St
Barlow St
Crail Rw
Comus Pl
Congreve Street
Massinger St
Old Kent Road A2
Bricklayer Arms Industrial Estate
Way
Btt Cl
Dunton Road
Fort Road
Balaclava Road
Alma Grove
Spa School
Catesby St
Beckway St
Beckway St
Stanford Pl
Hendre Rd
Mandela Wy
Lynton Road
7
Thorburn Square
Monnow Road
Kennedy Walk
Tatum St
Halpin Pl
Elsted St
Huntsman St
Surgery
East Street
Surgery
Minnow Walk
Marcia Road
Mandela Wy
Milton Cl
Lynton Estate
Bushwood Drive
Welsford St
Flint Street
Tisdall Pl
Exon St
Freemantle St
Surrey Sq
Fl St
B203
Chaucer Dr
Rich Industrial Estate
Oxley Close
Sedan Way
Infant School
Surrey
PO
Superstore
Humphrey St
Abercorn Way
Merrow Wk
The New Aylesbury Medical Centre
Alvey
Aldbridge Street
Surrey Square
Upnor Wy
B204
Rolls Road

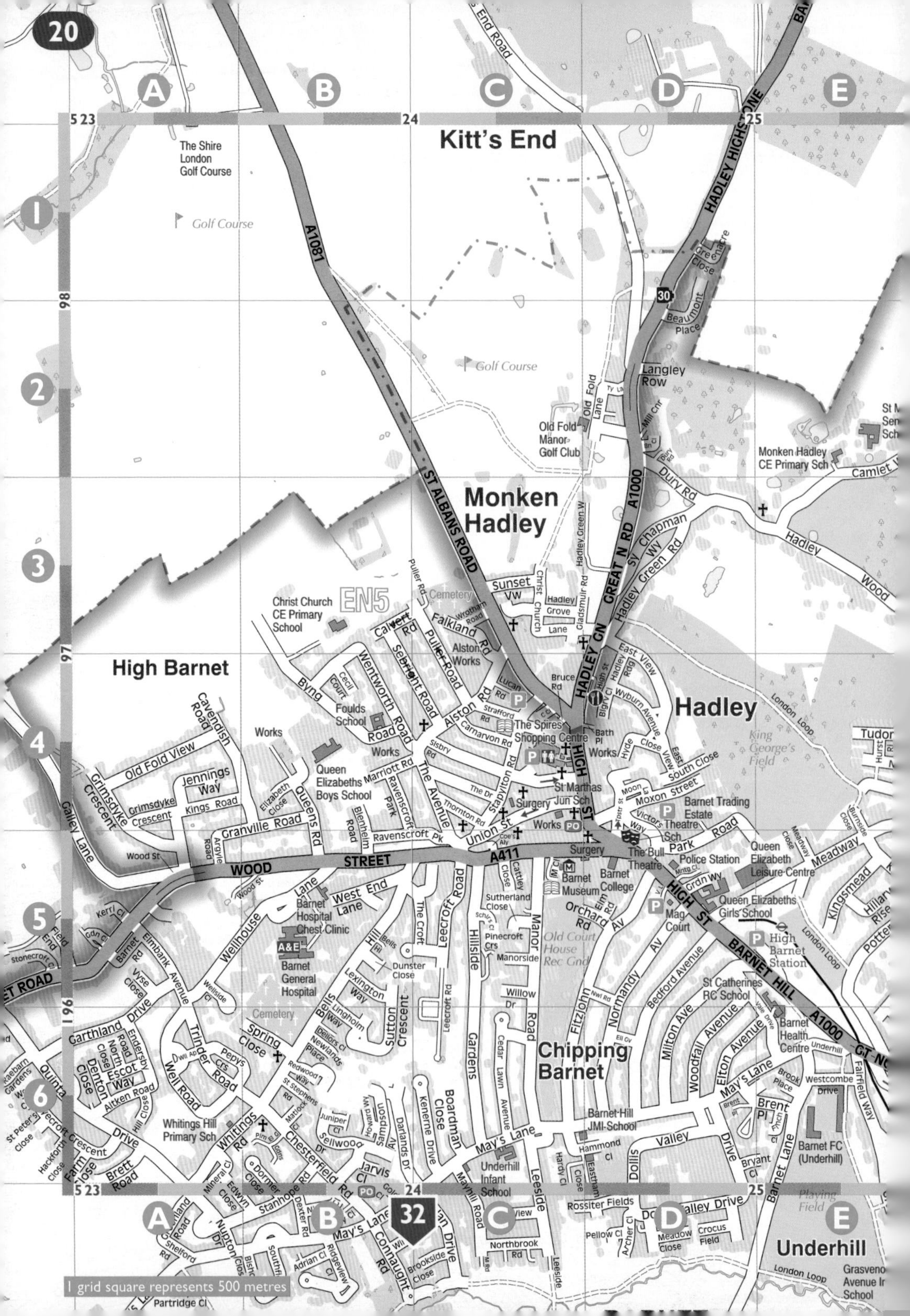

A B C D E

5 23   24   25

Kitt's End

The Shire
London
Golf Course

Golf Course

A1081

I

98

Golf Course

2

97

Old Fold
Manor
Golf Club

**Monken
Hadley**

ST ALBANS ROAD

3

EN5

Christ Church
CE Primary
School

Cemetery

Sunset
VW

Christ
Church

Hadley
Grove

Hadley
Lane

HADLEY GN

GREAT N RD

Hadley Green W

Gladsmuir Rd

A1000

Hadley Green Rd

Sy Chapman Wy

Hadley Green Rd

Hadley
Wood

Langley
Row

Beaumont
Place

30

Green
Close

Mill Crs

Dury Rd

Monken Hadley
CE Primary Sch

Camlet Way

HADLEY HIGHSTONE

St M
Sen
Sch

High Barnet

Cavendish
Road

Old Fold View

Byng
Rd

Cecil
Court

Wentworth Road

Calvert
Rd

Selbront Road

Puller
Road

Falkland
Rd

Alston
Works

Lucas
Rd

Bruce
Rd

East View

Wyburn Avenue

Bath
Pl

Hyde
Close

Moon's

Strafford Rd

Hadley

King
George's
Field

Tudor

4

Grimsdyke
Crescent

Galley Lane

Grimsdyke
Crescent

Jennings
Way

Kings Road

Elizabeth
Close

Works

Queen
Elizabeth's
Boys School

Foulds
School

Queens Rd

Road

Marriott Rd

The Avenue

Ravenscroft
Park

Sisbry

Carnarvon Rd

The Dr

Bapstone Rd

thornton Rd

Union St

St Marthas
Jun Sch

Surgery

Works

PO

Close

South Close

Moxon street

Victor's

Barnet Trading
Estate

Barnet
Theatre
Sch
Park

Queen
Elizabeth
Leisure Centre

Meadway

Kingsmead

Hillary Rise

Potte

Wood St

Blenheim
Road

Ravenscroft Pk

WOOD

STREET

A411

The Bull
Theatre.

Police Station

P

Mag
Court

Barnet
College

Gran Wy

Queen Elizabeths
Girls School

P

High
Barnet
Station

A1000

CT N

5

Kerri
Rd

Barnet
Rd

Elmbank Avenue

Vyse
Close

Wellhouse
Lane

West End
Lane

Barnet
Hospital
Chest Clinic

A&E

Barnet
General
Hospital

The Croft

Bells

Hillside

Leecroft Road

Sutherland
Close

Pinecroft
Crs

Pinecroft
Crs

Manorside

Old Court
House
Rec Gnd

Orchard Av

Fitzjohn
Ave

Normandy
Av

Milton Av

St Catherines
RC School

Bedford Avenue

Barnet
Health
Centre

Underhill

Westcombe
Drive

Fairfield Way

BARNET HILL

6

Garthland
Drive

Quinta
Drive

Stonecroft

Gardens

North
Rd

Endersby
Rd

Escot
Way

Denton
Close

Aitken Road

Well Road

Cemetery

Spring
Close

Lindholm
Way

Lexington
Way

Sutton
Crescent

Bells

Boardman
Close

Cedar
Lawn

Willow
Dr

Gardens

Kenerne Drive

**Chipping
Barnet**

May's
Close

Dollis
Valley

May's Lane

Brent
Pl

Barnet
Lane

Barnet FC
(Underhill)

Whitings Hill
Primary Sch

Whitings
Rd

Brett
Road

Chesterfield
Rd

Jarvis
Rd

Yellwood

Juniper

Darlands Dr

Mawill Road

Underhill
Infant
School

Barnet Hill
JMI School

Hammond
Cl

Bryant
Cl

Playing
Field

5 23

A B C D E

24 **32** 25

May's Lane

Connaught Rd

PO

Brookside
Close

Northbrook
Rd

Leeside

Rossiter Fields

Pellow Cl

Meadow
Close

Crocus
Field

Galley Drive

Underhill

Grasveno
Avenue In
School

London Loop

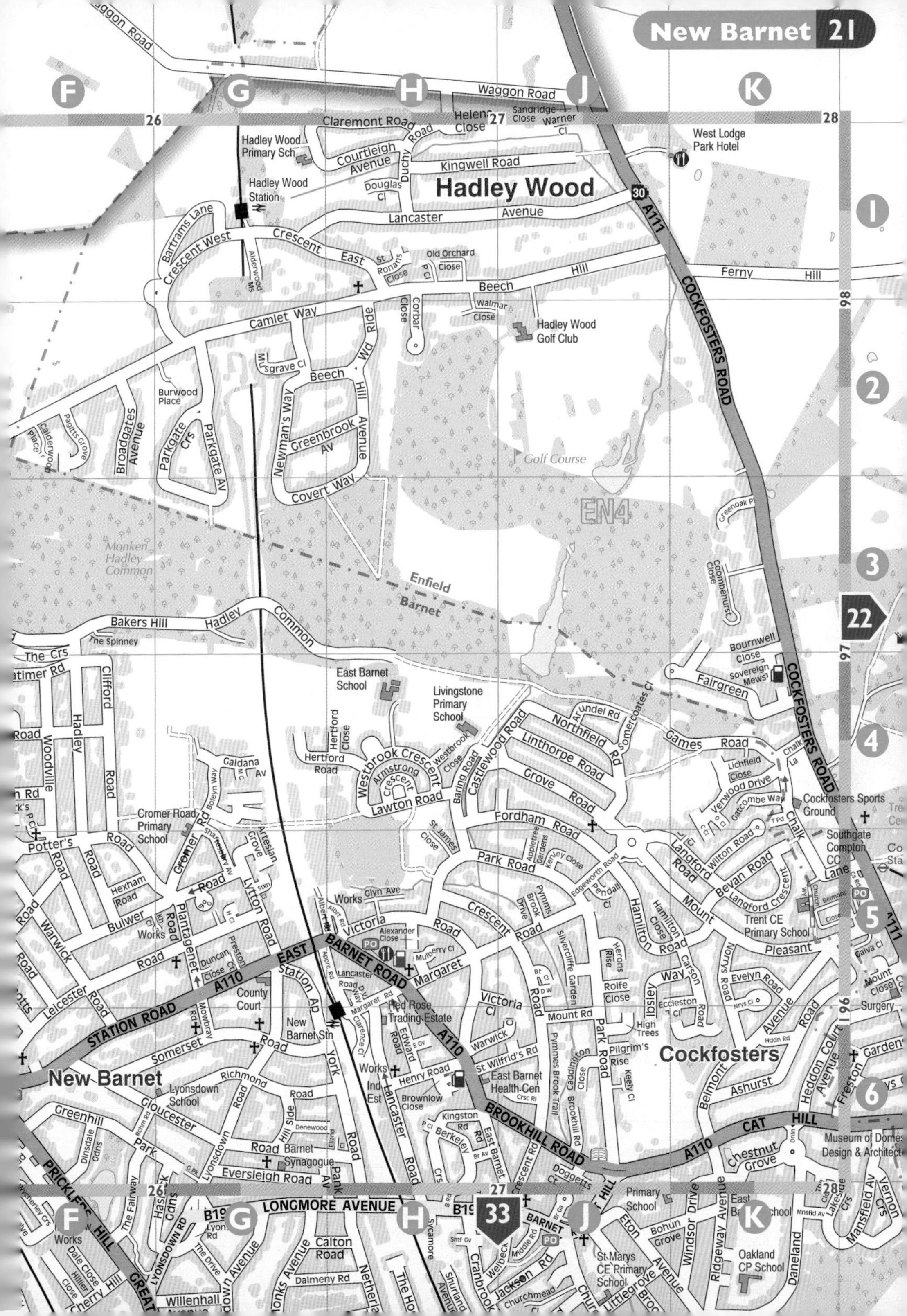
New Barnet 21
Waggon Road
Claremont Road
Helena Close
Sandridge Close
Warner Cl
Hadley Wood Primary Sch
Courtleigh Avenue
Duchy Road
Kingwell Road
West Lodge Park Hotel
Hadley Wood
Hadley Wood Station
Douglas Cl
Lancaster Avenue
A111
Bartrams Lane
Crescent West
Crescent East
Alderwood Ms
St Ronans Close
Old Orchard Close
Beech Hill
Ferny Hill
Cockfosters Road
Camlet Way
Corbar Close
Walmar Close
Hadley Wood Golf Club
Wood Ride
Musgrave Cl
Beech Hill Avenue
Newman's Way
Greenbrook Av
Burwood Place
Broadgates Avenue
Parkgate Crs
Parkgate Av
Calderwood Place
Pagitts Grove
Covert Way
Golf Course
EN4
Greenoak Pl
Coombehurst Close
Monken Hadley Common
Enfield
Barnet
Bakers Hill
Hadley Common
The Spinney
The Crs
Latimer Rd
Clifford Road
Hadley Road
Woodville Road
Bournwell Close
Sovereign Mews
Fairgreen
East Barnet School
Livingstone Primary School
Hertford Close
Hertford Road
Westbrook Crescent
Westbrook Close
Armstrong Crescent
Lawton Road
Baring Road
Castlewood Road
Arundel Rd
Northfield Rd
Somercoates Cl
Games Road
Linthorpe Road
Grove Road
Lichfield Close
Verwood Drive
Catcombe Way
Chalk La
Chalk Lane
Cockfosters Sports Ground
Galdana Av
Bolevn Way
Cromer Road Primary School
Cromer Rd
Artesian Grove
Lytton Road
St James Close
Fordham Road
Appletree Gardens
Kenley Close
Park Road
Edgeworth Road
Pendall Cl
Langford Road
Wilton Road
Bevan Road
Langford Crescent
Southgate Compton CC
Potter's Road
Hexham Road
Bulwer Road
Warwick Road
Plantagenet Road
Glyn Ave
Works
Victoria Road
Alexander Close
Mulberry Cl
Crescent Road
Pymms Brook Drive
Silvercliffe Gardens
Herons Rise
Hamilton Road
Hamilton Close
Mount Pleasant
Trent CE Primary School
Pleasant
Norrys Road
Evelyn Road
Calva Cl
Mount Close
Duncan Close
Preston Ct
East Barnet Road
Station Road
A110
Station Ap
Lancaster Road
Margaret Road
Victoria Cl
Rolfe Close
Ipsley Way
Eccleston Cl
Carson Road
Avenue Road
Surgery
County Court
Leicester Road
Mowbray Rd
Red Rose Trading Estate
Edward Road
Mount Rd
Park Road
High Trees
Pilgrim's Rise
Somerset Road
New Barnet Stn
Warwick Cl
St Wilfrid's Rd
East Barnet Health Cen
Cockfosters
Heddon Court Avenue
Ashurst
Belmont
Freston
New Barnet
Richmond Road
Lyonsdown School
Henry Road
Brownlow Close
York Road
Ind Est
Brookhill Road
Pymmes Brook Trail
Caddington Close
Brookhill Rd
Keely Cl
Cat Hill
Museum of Domestic Design & Architecture
Greenhill
Gloucester Road
Hill Side
Denewood
Kingston Rd
Berkeley Rd
East Barnet Rd
Crescent Rd
Doggetts Ct
Chestnut Grove
Dinsdale Gdns
Park Road
Barnet Synagogue
Eversleigh Road
Park Av
Primary School
Windsor Drive
Ridgeway Avenue
East Barnet School
Lakeside Crs
Mansfield Av
Vernon Crs
Prickler's Hill
The Fairway
Haslemere Gdns
Lyonsdown Rd
Longmore Avenue
B19
Lyonsdown Avenue
Calton Road
Sycamore
33
Barnet
Eton Avenue
Bohun Grove
Oakland CP School
Daneland
Works
Dale Close
Hillier Close
Cherry Hill
Great
The Drive
Monks Avenue
Dalmeny Rd
Welbeck
Middle Rd
Cranbrook
Jackson Rd
St Marys CE Primary School
Littlegrove
Churchmead
Willenhall
22
Lyonsdown Rd
F
G
H
J
K
26
27
28
1
2
3
4
5
6
98
97
96

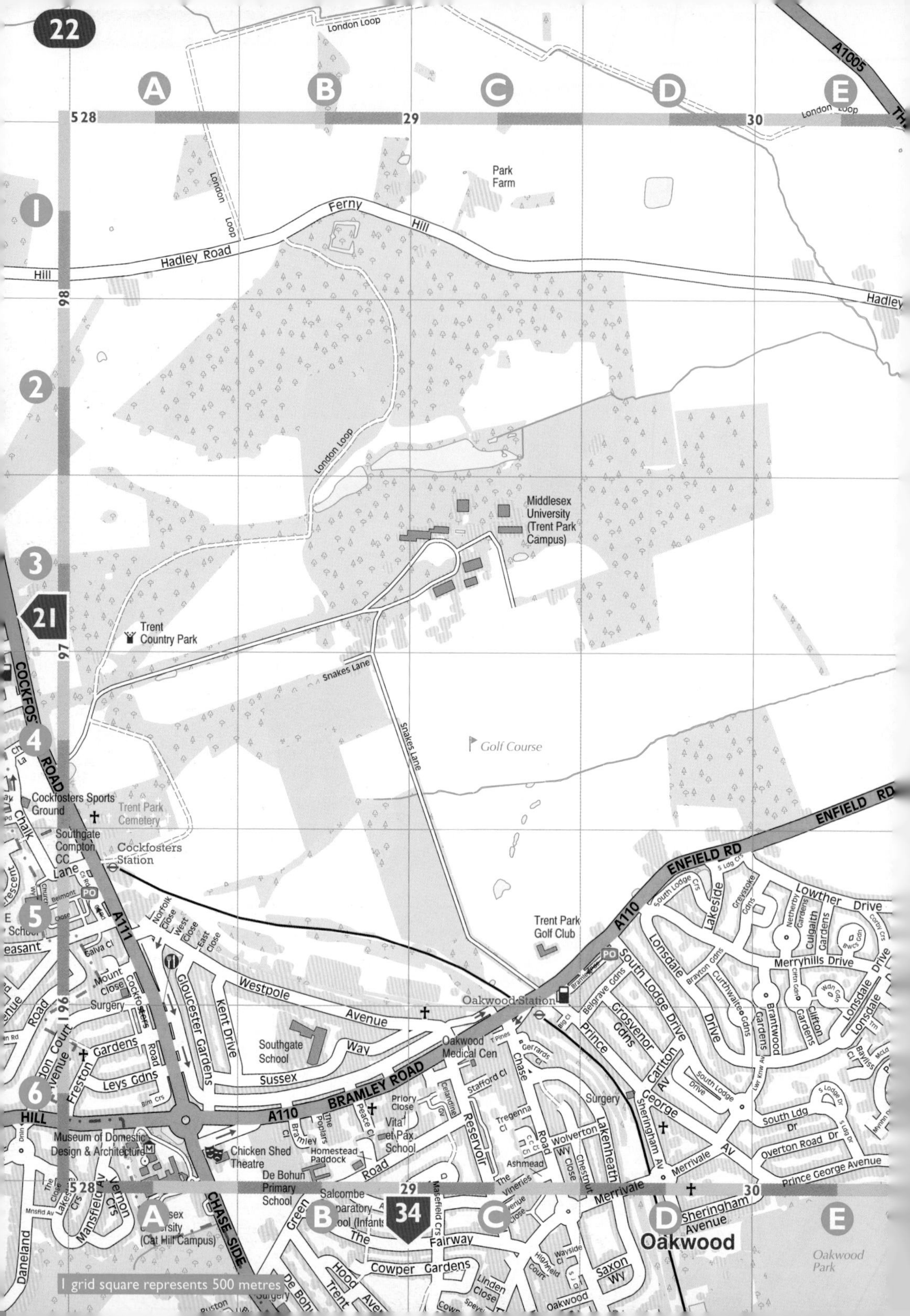

22
London Loop
A
B
C
D
E
A1005
528
29
30
Park Farm
1
Ferny
Hill
Hadley Road
Hill
Hadley
98
2
3
21
97
4
5
6
Middlesex University (Trent Park Campus)
Trent Country Park
Snakes Lane
Golf Course
COCKFOSTERS ROAD
Cockfosters Sports Ground
Trent Park Cemetery
Southgate Compton CC
Cockfosters Station
Chalk Lane
Belmont
PO
A111
Norfolk Close
West Close
East Close
Galva Cl
Mount Close
Cockfosters Road
Surgery
Westpole Avenue
Gloucester Gardens
Kent Drive
Southgate School
Sussex Way
Freston Gardens
Leys Gdns
Oakwood Station
Oakwood Medical Cen
BRAMLEY ROAD
A110
ENFIELD RD
Trent Park Golf Club
South Lodge Crs
Lakeside
Greystoke Gdns
Lowther Drive
Culgaith Gardens
Merryhills Drive
Lonsdale Drive
Brayton Gdns
Curthwaite Gdns
Brantwood Gardens
Clifton Gardens
Belgrave Gdns
Grosvenor Gdns
South Lodge Drive
Prince George Av
Carlton Av
Sheringham Av
Merrivale
South Lodge Drive
South Ldg Dr
Overton Road
Prince George Avenue
Chase Road
Gerrards Cl
Stafford Cl
Tregenna Cl
Reservoir Road
Wolverton Wy
Lakenheath
Chestnut Close
Ashmead
The Vineries
Surgery
Priory Close
Vita et Pax School
Peace Cl
The Poplars
Bramley Cl
Homestead Paddock
De Bohun Primary School
Salcombe Preparatory School (Infants)
Museum of Domestic Design & Architecture
Chicken Shed Theatre
Middlesex University (Cat Hill Campus)
CHASE SIDE
HILL
Mansfield Av
Vernon Crs
Lakeside Crs
Daneland
34
Green
The Fairway
Cowper Gardens
Masefield Crs
Linden Close
Highfield Court
Wayside Cl
Saxon Wy
Oakwood
Sheringham Avenue
Oakwood Park
1 grid square represents 500 metres

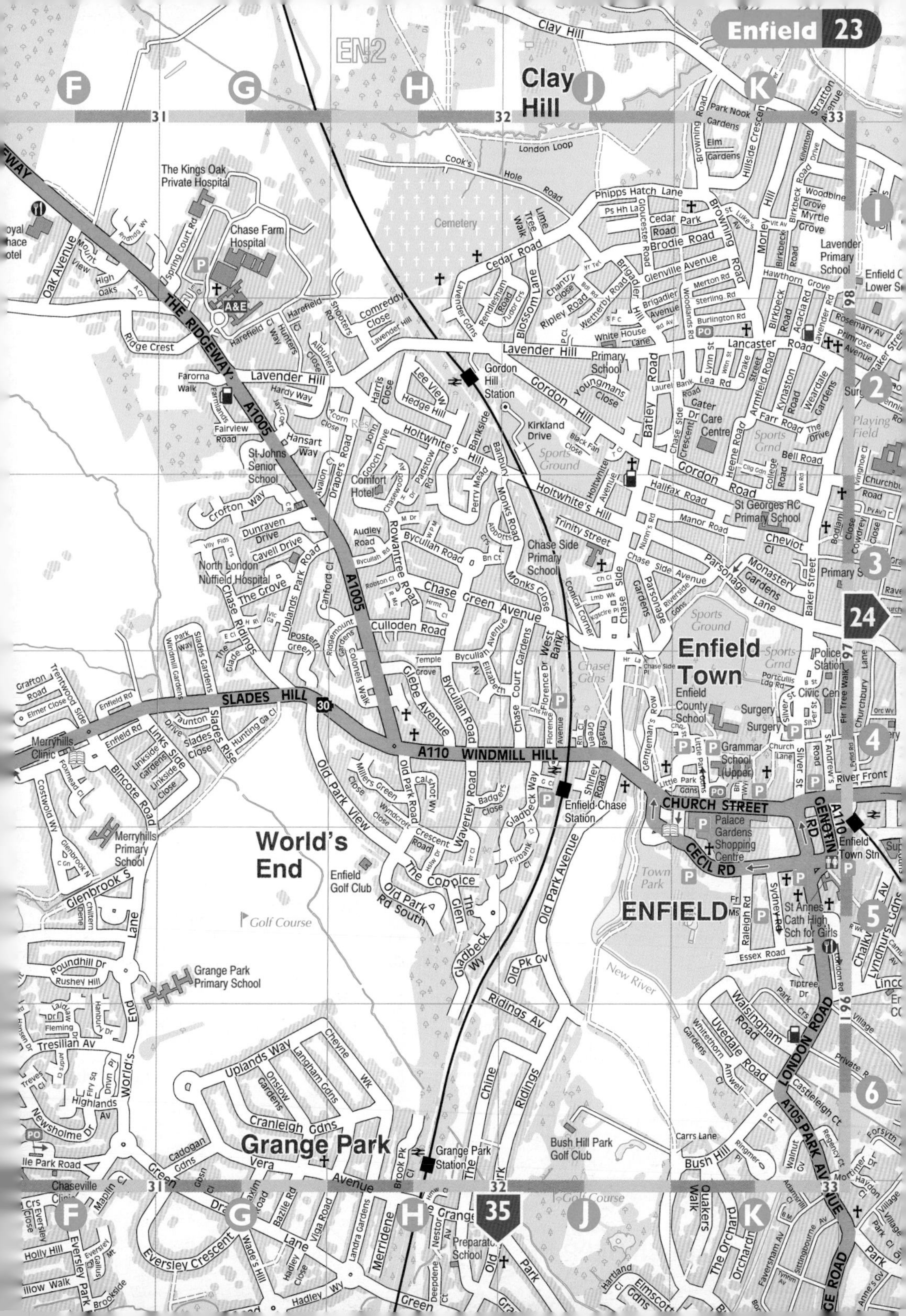
Clay Hill
EN2
Cemetery
London Loop
Cook's Hole Road
Phipps Hatch Lane
The Kings Oak Private Hospital
Chase Farm Hospital
A&E
THE RIDGEWAY A1005
Lavender Hill
Gordon Hill Station
Gordon Hill
Holtwhite's Hill
Chase Side Primary School
St Georges RC Primary School
Lavender Primary School
Enfield Town
Enfield County School
Grammar School (Upper)
Police Station
Civic Cen
CHURCH STREET
Palace Gardens Shopping Centre
CECIL RD
Enfield Town Stn
Enfield Chase Station
A110 WINDMILL HILL
SLADES HILL
World's End
Enfield Golf Club
Golf Course
ENFIELD
Town Park
New River
St Annes Cath High Sch for Girls
LONDON ROAD
A105 PARK AVENUE
Grange Park
Grange Park Station
Grange Park Primary School
Bush Hill Park Golf Club
Merryhills Primary School
Merryhills Clinic
St Johns Senior School
North London Nuffield Hospital
Comfort Hotel
Old Park Avenue
Old Park View
Ridings Av
Uplands Way
Cranleigh Gdns
Chaseville
Eversley Crescent
24
30
35
31
32
33
F
G
H
J
K
1
2
3
4
5
6

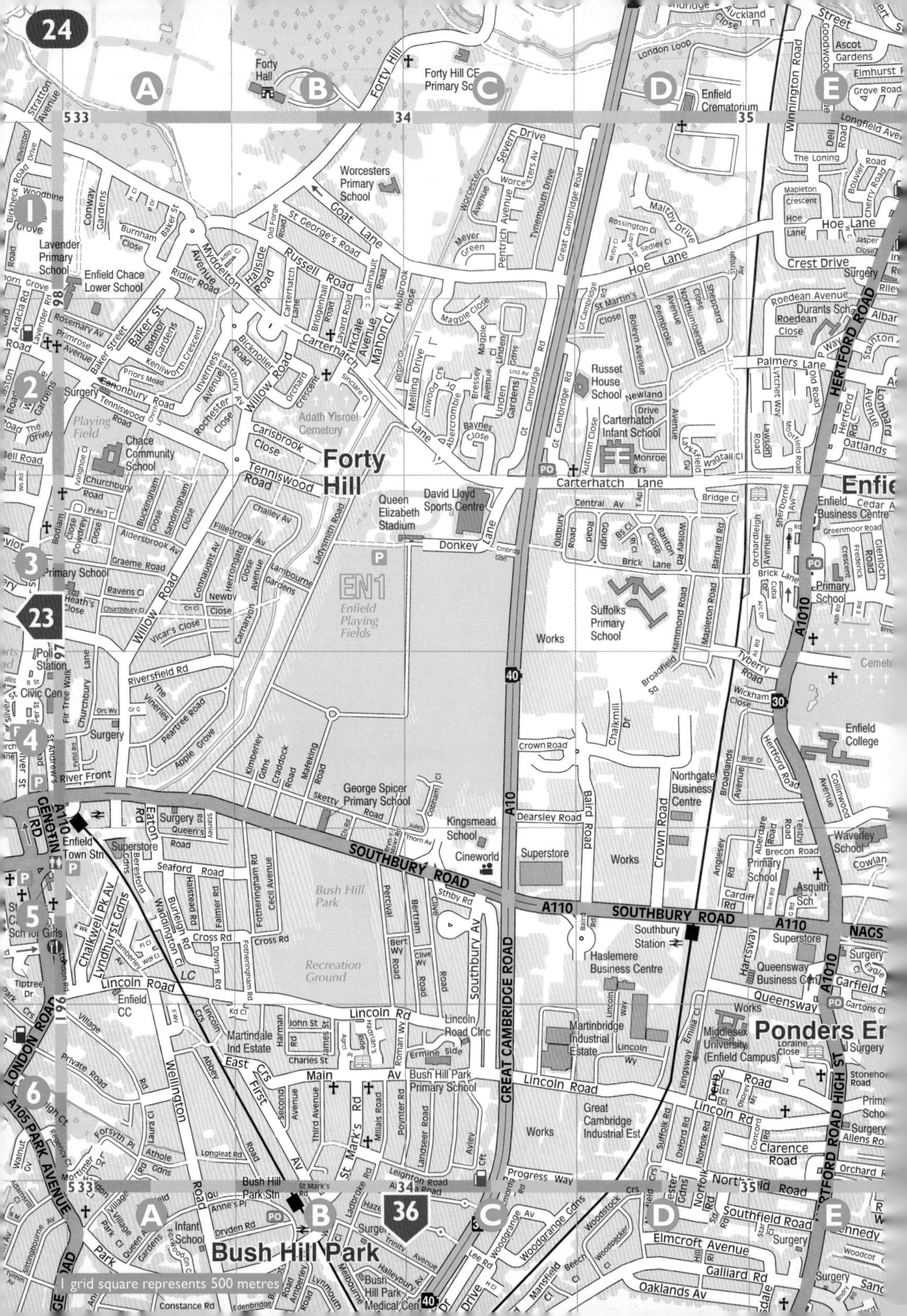
Forty Hall
Forty Hill
Forty Hill CE Primary School
Enfield Crematorium
London Loop
Auckland Close
Ascot Gardens
Elmhurst Rd
Grove Road
Longfield Av
Winnington Road
Worcesters Primary School
Goat Lane
St George's Road
Severn Drive
Worcesters Av
Tynemouth Drive
Great Cambridge Road
Maltby Drive
Hoe Lane
Crest Drive
Lavender Primary School
Enfield Chace Lower School
Myddelton Avenue
Baker Street
Carterhatch Lane
Adath Yisroel Cemetery
Chace Community School
Tenniswood Road
Carisbrook Close
Russet House School
Carterhatch Infant School
Carterhatch Lane
Queen Elizabeth Stadium
David Lloyd Sports Centre
Donkey Lane
EN1
Enfield Playing Fields
Suffolks Primary School
Works
Brick Lane
Enfield Business Centre
Enfield College
Willow Road
Riversfield Rd
Civic Cen
Police Station
Ladysmith Road
George Spicer Primary School
Kingsmead School
Cineworld
Superstore
Northgate Business Centre
Crown Road
Baird Road
Hertford Road
A1010
Enfield Town Stn
SOUTHBURY ROAD
A110
Southbury Station
Haslemere Business Centre
Queensway Business Cen
Queensway
Ponders End
Middlesex University (Enfield Campus)
Bush Hill Park
Recreation Ground
Lincoln Road
Martindale Ind Estate
Martinbridge Industrial Estate
Great Cambridge Industrial Est
Bush Hill Park Primary School
GREAT CAMBRIDGE ROAD
A10
LONDON ROAD
A105 PARK AVENUE
HERTFORD ROAD HIGH ST
Bush Hill Park Stn
Bush Hill Park
Elmcroft Avenue
Southfield Road
Oaklands Av
Galliard Rd
Bush Hill Park Medical Cen
533
34
35
23
36
40
30
1 grid square represents 500 metres

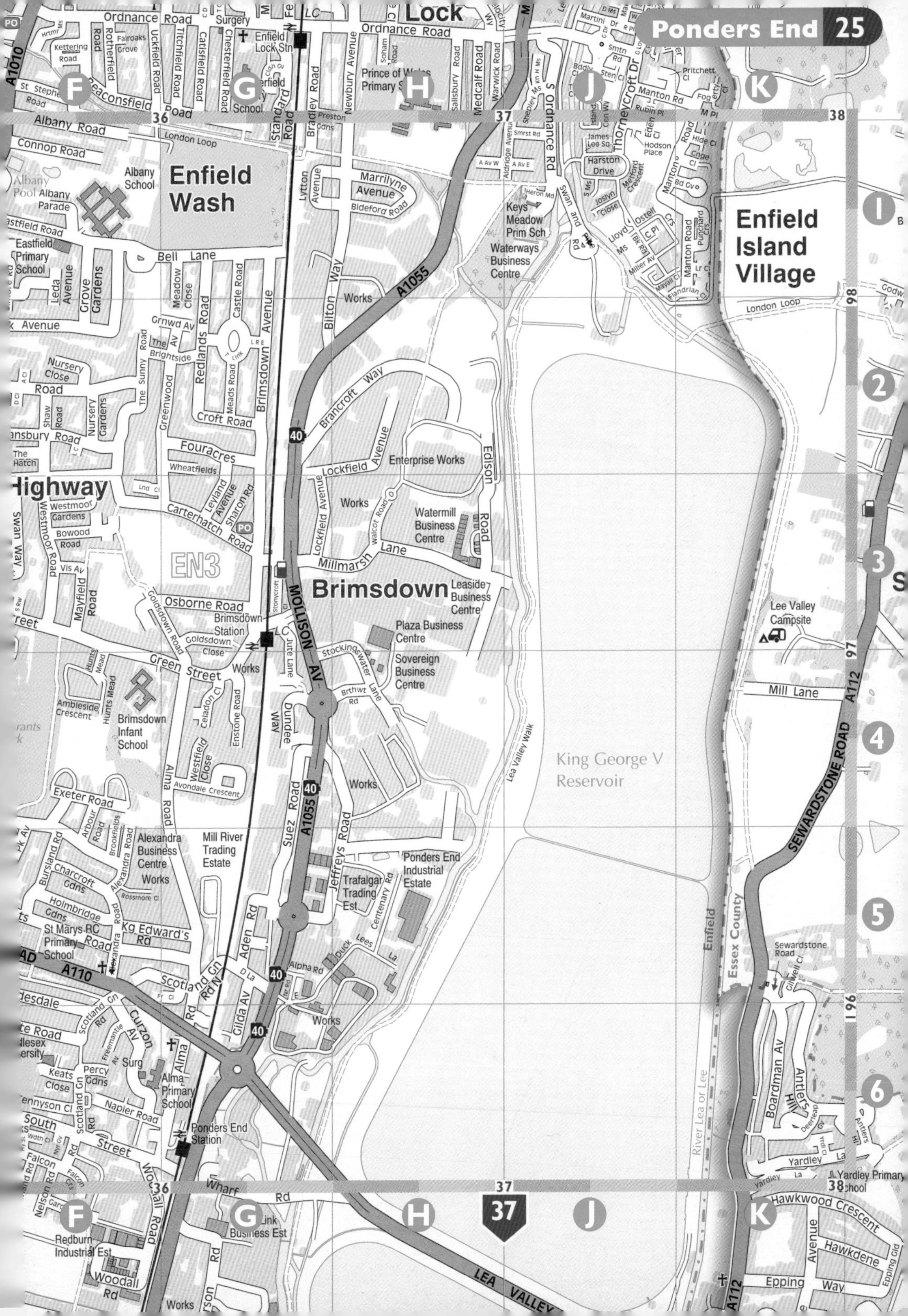
Lock
Ordnance Road
Kettering Road
Rotherfield Road
Falroaks Grove
Uckfield Road
Titchfield Road
Catisfield Road
Chesterfield Road
Surgery
Enfield Lock Stn
Prince of Wales Primary Sch
Bradley Road
Newbury Avenue
Soham Road
Salisbury Road
Medcalf Road
Warwick Road
St Stephens Road
Beaconsfield Road
School
Standard Road
Preston Gdns
Albany Road
Connop Road
London Loop
Albany School
Enfield Wash
Albany Pool
Albany Parade
Eastfield Road
Eastfield Primary School
Leda Avenue
Grove Gardens
Bell Lane
Meadow Close
Redlands Road
Castle Road
Brimsdown Avenue
Avenue
Grnwd Av
The Brightside
The Sunny Road
Nursery Close
Road
Shaw Road
Nursery Gardens
Greenwood
Meads Road
Croft Road
Ansbury Road
The Hatch
Fouracres
Wheatfields
Leyland Avenue
Sharon Rd
Highway
Westmoor Gardens
Westmoor Road
Bowood Road
Swan Way
Carterhatch Road
PO
EN3
Vis Av
Mayfield Road
Goldsdown Road
Osborne Road
Brimsdown Station
Goldsdown Close
Green Street
Street
Hunts Mead
Ambleside Crescent
Brimsdown Infant School
Celadon Cl
Enstone Road
Westfield Close
Avondale Crescent
Alma Road
Exeter Road
Arbour Road
Brookfields
Bursland Rd
Alexandra Road
Alexandra Business Centre
Works
Mill River Trading Estate
Charcroft Gdns
Holmbridge Gdns
Rossmore Cl
St Marys RC Primary School
Kg Edward's Rd
A110
Scotland Gn Rd N
Scotland Gn Rd
Curzon Av
Freemantle Av
Surg
Alma Primary School
Keats Close
Percy Gdns
Tennyson Cl
Napier Road
South Street
Scotland Gn Rd
Ponders End Station
Woodall Road
Wharf Rd
Redburn Industrial Est
Woodall Rd
Link Business Est
Works
Lytton Avenue
Marrilyne Avenue
Bideford Road
Bilton Way
A1055
Works
Brancroft Way
Lockfield Avenue
Enterprise Works
Edison Road
Works
Walcot Road
Watermill Business Centre
Millmarsh Lane
Stonycroft
Brimsdown
MOLLISON AV
Leaside Business Centre
Plaza Business Centre
Jute Lane
Stockingswater Lane
Sovereign Business Centre
Brthwt Rd
Dundee Way
Suez Road
Works
Jeffreys Road
Ponders End Industrial Estate
Trafalgar Trading Est
Centenary Rd
Aden Rd
Gilda Av
Duck Lees La
Alpha Rd
Works
LEA VALLEY
Aldridge Avenue
A Av W
A Av E
Smrst Rd
Shepley Ms
S Ordnance Rd
Keys Meadow Prim Sch
Heron Md
Waterways Business Centre
Swan and Pike Rd
Thorneycroft Dr
James Lee Sq
Harston Drive
Joslyn Close
Eden Cl
Hodson Place
Metford Crescent
Lloyd Ms
Ostell Crs
Miller Av
Mayall Cl
Flandrian Cl
Manton Road
Manton Rd
Rubin Pl
Pritchett Cl
Hide Cl
Cnge Cl
Bd Gv
Pulchard Crs
Enfield Island Village
London Loop
Lea Valley Walk
King George V Reservoir
Lee Valley Campsite
Mill Lane
A112
SEWARDSTONE ROAD
Essex County
Enfield
River Lea or Lee
Sewardstone Road
Gilwell Cl
Boardman Av
Antlers Hill
Deerleap Gv
Yardley La
Yardley Primary School
Hawkwood Crescent
Hawkdene
Avenue
Epping Way
Epping Gld
F G H J K
1 2 3 4 5 6
36 37 38
98 97 96
37

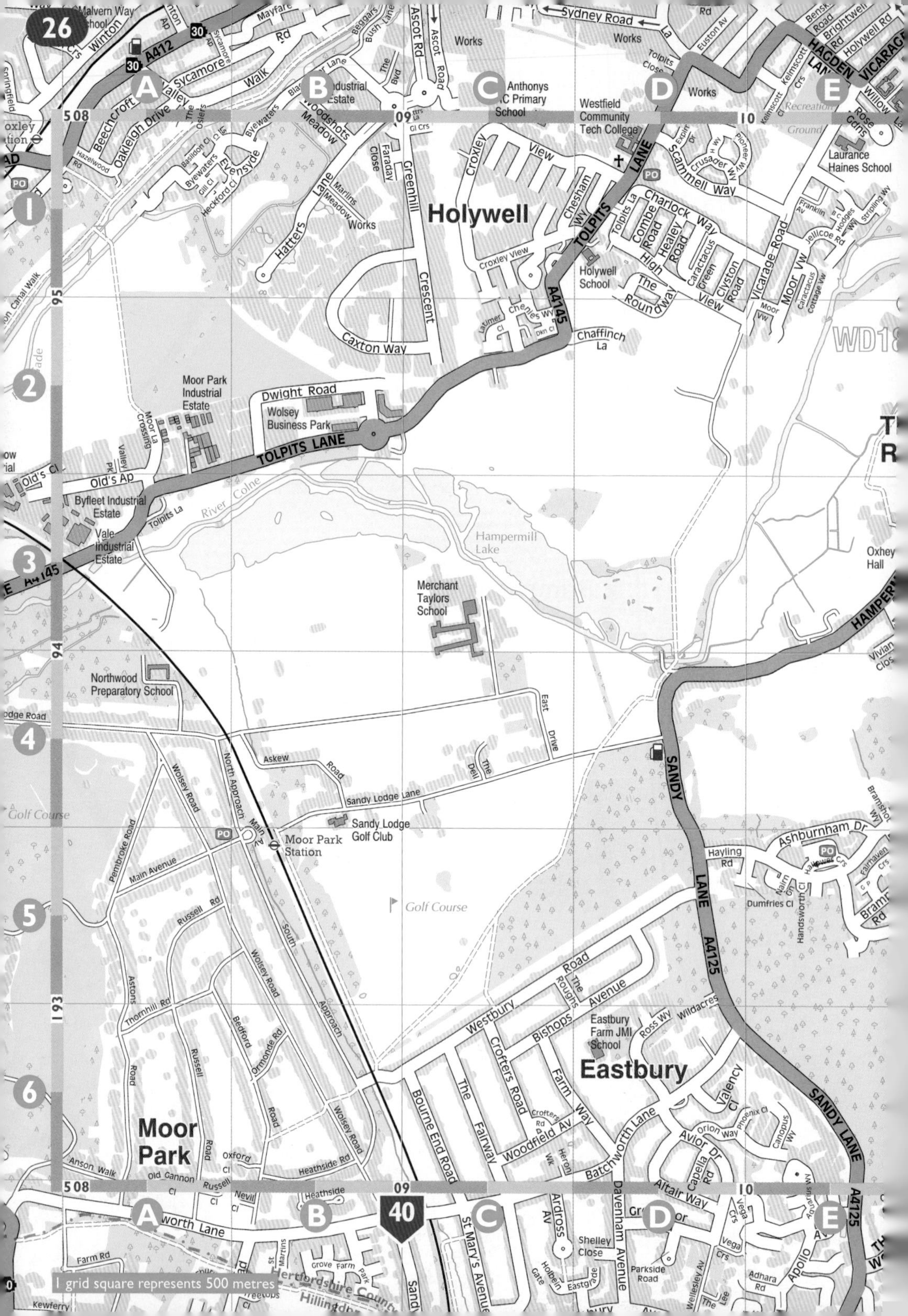
Holywell
Eastbury
Moor Park
Tolpits Lane
Sandy Lane
Moor Park Industrial Estate
Wolsey Business Park
Byfleet Industrial Estate
Vale Industrial Estate
Merchant Taylors School
Northwood Preparatory School
Sandy Lodge Golf Club
Moor Park Station
Hampermill Lake
River Colne
Holywell School
Westfield Community Tech College
Laurance Haines School
Eastbury Farm JMI School
Golf Course
Oxhey Hall
1 grid square represents 500 metres

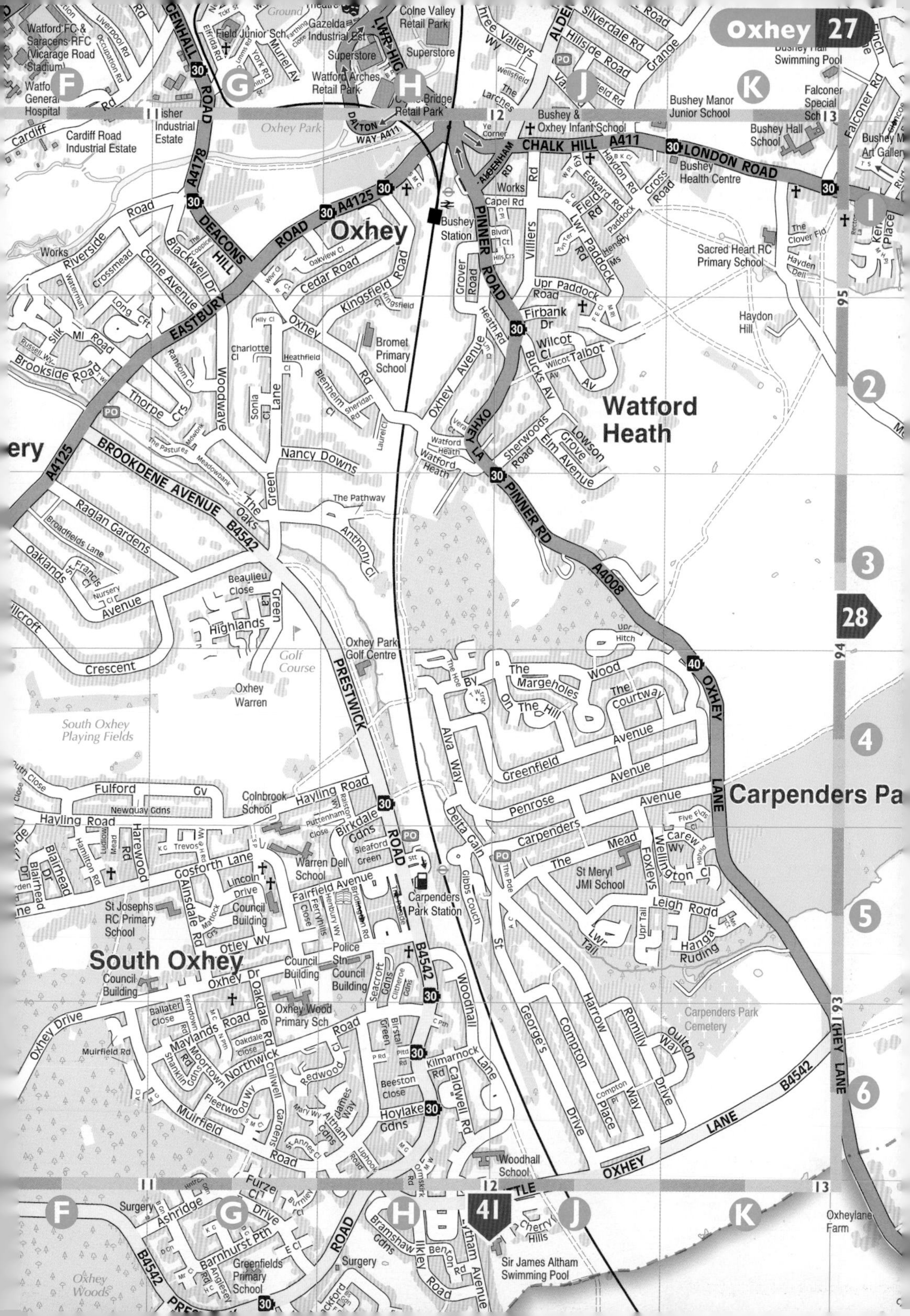
Watford FC & Saracens RFC (Vicarage Road Stadium)
Watford General Hospital
Field Junior Sch
Gazelda Industrial Est
Colne Valley Retail Park
Superstore
Superstore
Watford Arches Retail Park
Bushey Hall Swimming Pool
Falconer Special Sch
Bushey Manor Junior School
Bushey & Oxhey Infant School
Bushey Hall School
Bushey Health Centre
Fisher Industrial Estate
Cardiff Road Industrial Estate
Oxhey Park
CHALK HILL A411
LONDON ROAD
DALTON WAY A411
Ye Corner
Oxhey
Bushey Station
Sacred Heart RC Primary School
Haydon Hill
Works
DEACONS HILL
A4178
EASTBURY ROAD A4125
PINNER ROAD
Bromet Primary School
Watford Heath
Kingsfield Road
Cedar Road
Riverside Road
Coline Avenue
Brookside Road
Thorpe Crs
Woodwaye
Nancy Downs
BROOKDENE AVENUE B4542
Raglan Gardens
The Pathway
Anthony Cl
Highlands
Beaulieu Close
Crescent
Golf Course
Oxhey Warren
Oxhey Park Golf Centre
PRESTWICK ROAD
South Oxhey Playing Fields
PINNER RD A4008
OXHEY LANE
Carpenders Pa
The Margeholes
Greenfield Avenue
Penrose Avenue
Carpenders Avenue
Alva Way
Delta Gain
St Meryl JMI School
Leigh Rodd
Hangar Ruding
Carpenders Park Station
Carpenders Park Cemetery
Colnbrook School
Hayling Road
Fulford Gv
Gosforth Lane
Warren Dell School
St Josephs RC Primary School
Council Building
South Oxhey
Oxhey Drive
Oxhey Wood Primary Sch
Police Stn
Muirfield Rd
Northwick Road
Hoylake Gdns
Woodhall Lane
George's Drive
Compton Place
Harrow Way
Romilly Drive
Oulton Way
OXHEY LANE B4542
Woodhall School
Surgery
Ashridge Drive
Barnhurst Pth
Greenfields Primary School
Oxhey Woods
Bramshaw Gdns
Ilkley Road
Benton Rd
Sir James Altham Swimming Pool
Cherry Hills
Oxheylane Farm
28
41

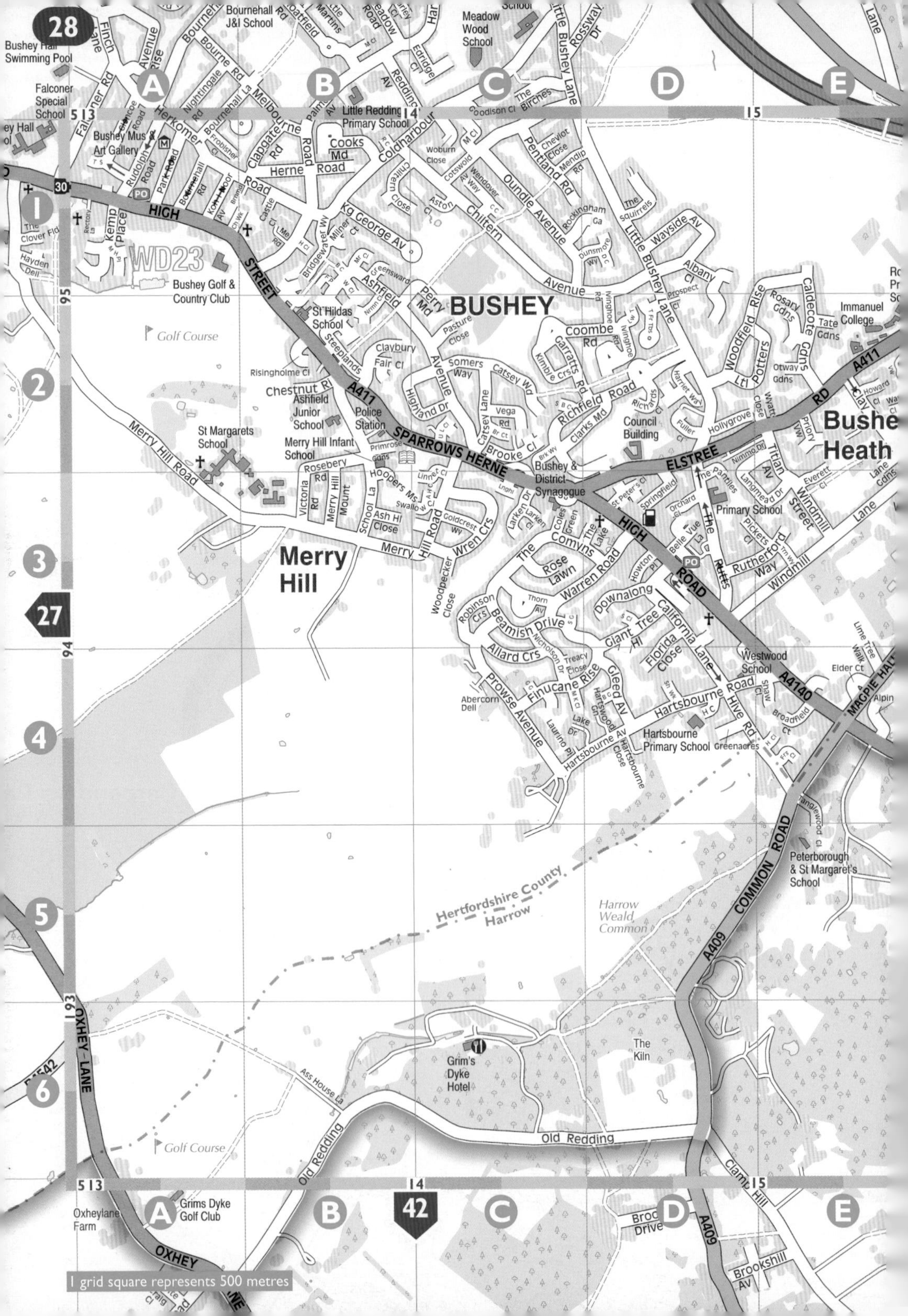

BUSHEY
Merry Hill
Bushey Heath
WD23
Bushey Golf & Country Club
Golf Course
St Margarets School
Ashfield Junior School
Merry Hill Infant School
Police Station
St Hildas School
Bushey & District Synagogue
Council Building
Primary School
Immanuel College
Westwood School
Hartsbourne Primary School
Peterborough & St Margaret's School
Hertfordshire County
Harrow
Harrow Weald Common
Grim's Dyke Hotel
The Kiln
Grims Dyke Golf Club
Oxheylane Farm
Bushey Hall Swimming Pool
Falconer Special School
Bushey Museum & Art Gallery
Little Redding Primary School
Meadow Wood School
Bournehall J&I School
HIGH STREET
SPARROWS HERNE
A411
ELSTREE RD
HIGH ROAD
A4140
COMMON ROAD
A409
OXHEY LANE
Merry Hill Road
Old Redding
Ass House La
Clamp Hill
Brookshill Av
Brod Drive
1 grid square represents 500 metres

27
30
42

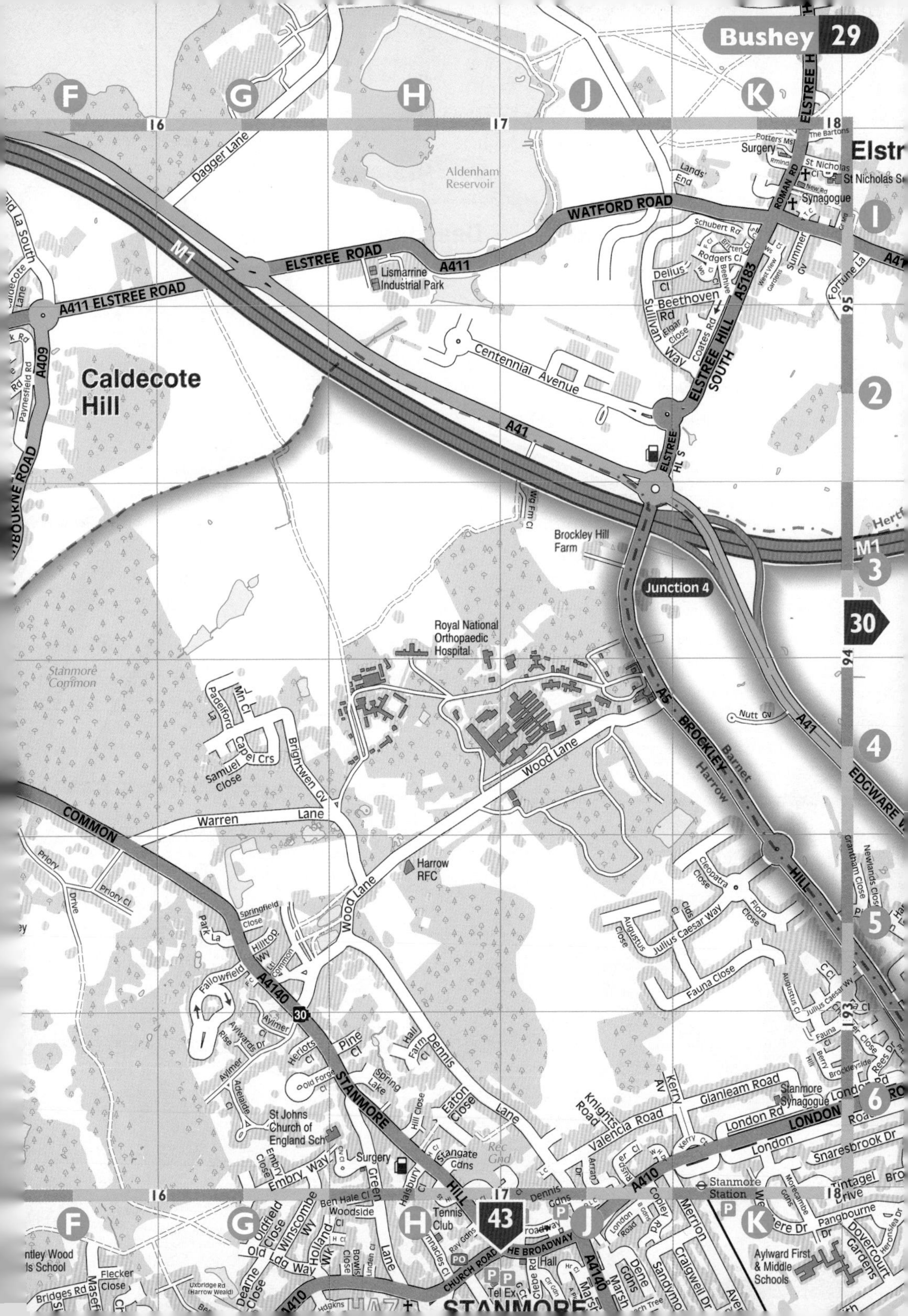
Caldecote Hill
Aldenham Reservoir
Lismarrine Industrial Park
ELSTREE ROAD
A411 ELSTREE ROAD
WATFORD ROAD
M1
A41
Centennial Avenue
Brockley Hill Farm
Junction 4
Royal National Orthopaedic Hospital
Stanmore Common
Wood Lane
Warren Lane
COMMON
Harrow RFC
A5 BROCKLEY HILL
Barnet
Harrow
STANMORE HILL
A4140
St Johns Church of England Sch
Surgery
Stanmore Station
Stanmore Synagogue
LONDON RD
Aylward First & Middle Schools
STANMORE
Elstr
Synagogue
St Nicholas
ELSTREE SOUTH
EDGWARE
30
43

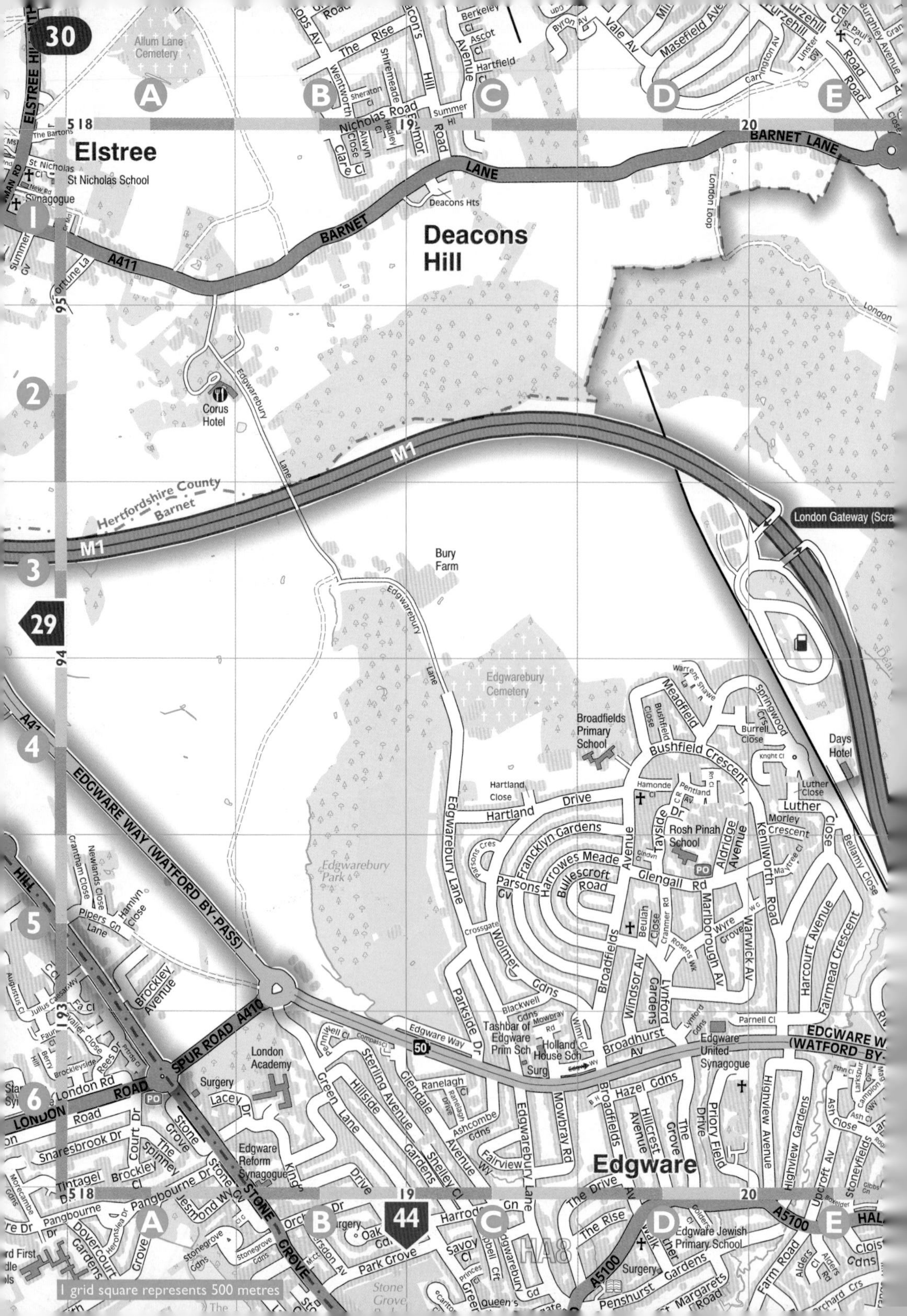
Allum Lane Cemetery
Elstree
St Nicholas School
Synagogue
ELSTREE HILL NORTH
The Barntons
The Rise
Wentworth
Shiremeade
Sheraton Cl
Nicholas Road
Alwyn Close
Hadley Cl
Clare Cl
Deacons Hill
Deacons Hts
Summer Hl
Berkeley Cl
Ascot Cl
Hartfield
Avenue
Vale Av
Masefield Ave
Carrington Av
Linster Gv
St Paul's Cl
Road
BARNET LANE
LANE
BARNET
A411
Fortune La
Summer Gv
Deacons Hill
London Loop
London
Corus Hotel
Edgwarebury Lane
M1
Hertfordshire County
Barnet
London Gateway (Scra
Bury Farm
Edgwarebury Lane
Edgwarebury Cemetery
Warrens Shawe La
Meadfield
Bushfield Close
Springwood Crs
Burrell Close
Broadfields Primary School
Bushfield Crescent
Knght Cl
Days Hotel
Hartland Close
Hartland Drive
Hamonde Cl
Pentland Av
Luther Close
Luther Close
Morley Crescent
Franklyn Gardens
Tayside Dr
Rosh Pinah School
Aldridge Avenue
Kenilworth Road
Mayfree Cl
Bellamy Close
Parsons Cres
Harrowes Meade
Bullescroft Road
Glengall Rd
Edgwarebury Park
Edgwarebury Lane
Parsons Gv
Beulah Close
Cranmer Rd
Marlborough Av
Wyre Grove
Warwick Av
Harcourt Avenue
Fairmead Crescent
Crossgate
Wolmer Gdns
Broadfields
Rosens Wk
Windsor Av
Lynford Gardens
Parkside Dr
Blackwell Gdns
Mowbray Rd
Tashbar of Edgware Prim Sch
Holland House Sch
Broadhurst Av
Parnell Cl
Edgware United Synagogue
EDGWARE W
(WATFORD BY-
Edgware Way
50
EDGWARE WAY (WATFORD BY-PASS)
A41
Grantham Close
Newlands Close
Hamlyn Close
Pipers Gn Lane
Brockley Avenue
SPUR ROAD A410
London Academy
Julius Caesar Wy
Brockleyside
Rees Dr
London Rd
LONDON ROAD
Surgery
Lacey Dr
Stone Grove
The Spinney
Court Dr
Snaresbrook Dr
Brockley Cl
Tintagel Dr
Pangbourne Dr
Jesmond Wy
Edgware Reform Synagogue
Green Lane
Hillside Drive
Sterling Avenue
Glendale Avenue
Shelley Cl
Ranelagh Cl
Ashcombe Gdns
Fairview Wy
Edgwarebury Lane
Mowbray Rd
Hazel Gdns
Broadfields Avenue
Hillcrest Avenue
The Grove
Priory Field Drive
Highview Avenue
Highview Gardens
Upcroft Av
Stoneyfields
Ash Close
Edgware
STONE GROVE
Park Grove
Harrods Gn
Savoy Cl
The Drive
The Rise
Edgware Jewish Primary School
Surgery
Penshurst Gardens
St Margarets Road
Farm Road
Alders Cl
A5100
HA8
Cloisters Gdns
44
29
518
19
20
95
94
193
A
B
C
D
E
1
2
3
4
5
6
1 grid square represents 500 metres

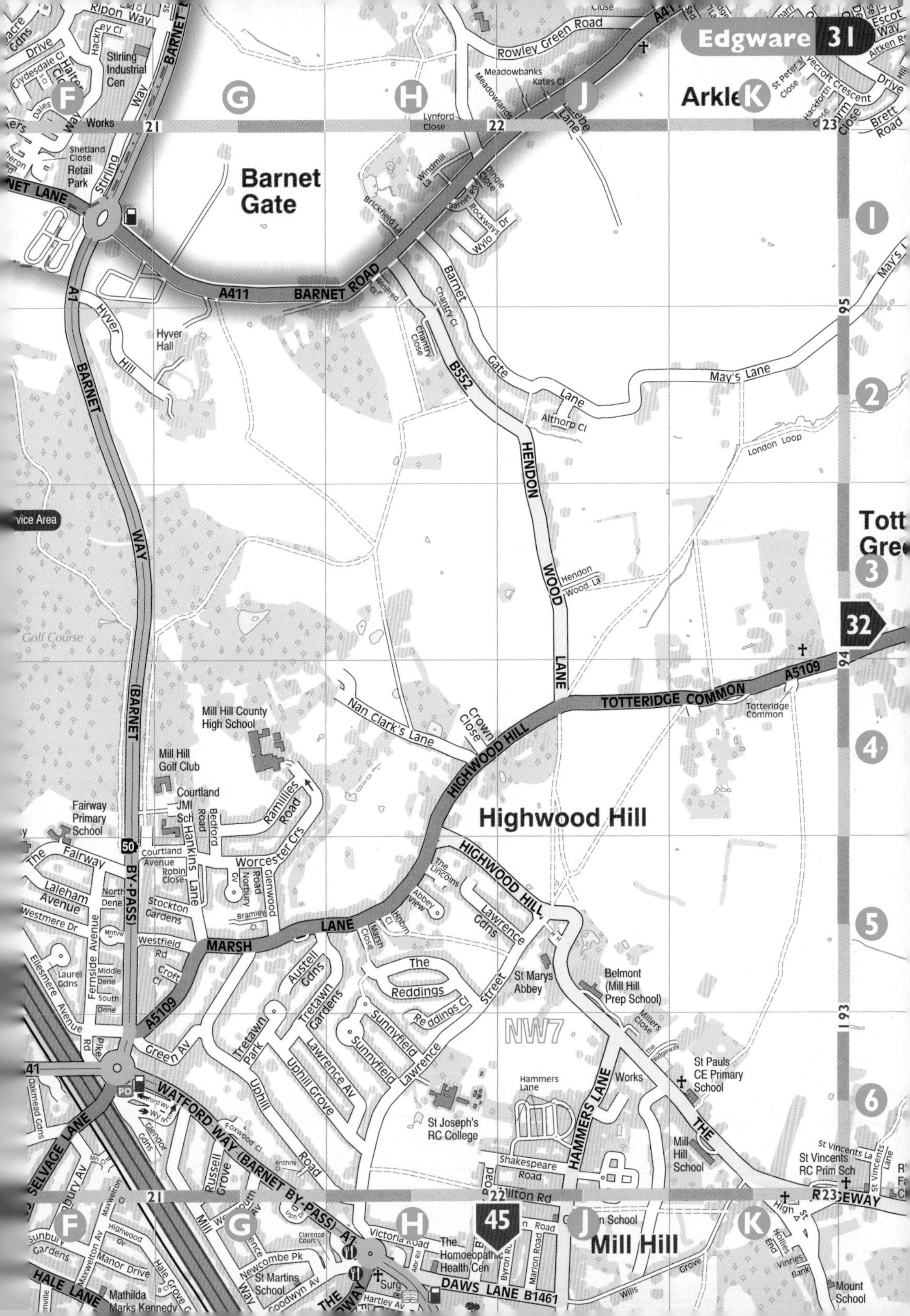
Barnet Gate
Highwood Hill
Mill Hill
Arkley
NW7
BARNET WAY (BARNET BY-PASS)
A1
A411 BARNET ROAD
B552
HENDON WOOD LANE
TOTTERIDGE COMMON
A5109
HIGHWOOD HILL
MARSH LANE
WATFORD WAY (BARNET BY-PASS) A1
SELVAGE LANE
HAMMERS LANE
DAWS LANE B1461
HALE LANE
Rowley Green Road
Mays Lane
Barnet Gate Lane
Hendon Wood La
Nan Clark's Lane
Crown Close
Mill Hill County High School
Mill Hill Golf Club
Courtland JMI Sch
Fairway Primary School
Golf Course
Hyver Hall
Hyver Hill
Stirling Industrial Cen
Retail Park
Works
St Marys Abbey
Belmont (Mill Hill Prep School)
St Pauls CE Primary School
St Joseph's RC College
Mill Hill School
St Vincents RC Prim Sch
The Homoeopathic Health Cen
St Martins School
Mount School
Totteridge Common
London Loop
Ramillies Road
Worcester Crs
Bedford Road
Hankins Lane
Glenwood Road
Stockton Gardens
Westfield Rd
Laleham Avenue
Westmere Dr
Fernside Avenue
The Fairway
Tretawn Gardens
Tretawn Park
Austell Gdns
Uphill Road
Uphill Grove
Lawrence Av
Lawrence Street
Lawrence Gdns
Sunnyfield
The Reddings
Reddings Cl
The Ridgeway
Millers Close
Shakespeare Road
Mill Hill Rd
Russell Grove
Victoria Road
Marion Road
Newcombe Pk
Sunbury Gardens
Manor Drive
Maxwelton Av
Hale Grove Gdns
Mathilda Marks Kennedy
Althorp Cl
Chantry Close
Windmill La
Brickfield La
Dingle Close
Rockways
Wylo Dr
Lynford Close
Meadowbanks
Kates Cl
Glebe Lane
Shetland Close
Ripon Way
Clydesdale Cl
Halter Close
St Peter's Close
Vecroft Crescent
Brett Road
Service Area
F G H J K
21 22 23
1 2 3 4 5 6
95 94 93
32
45
50

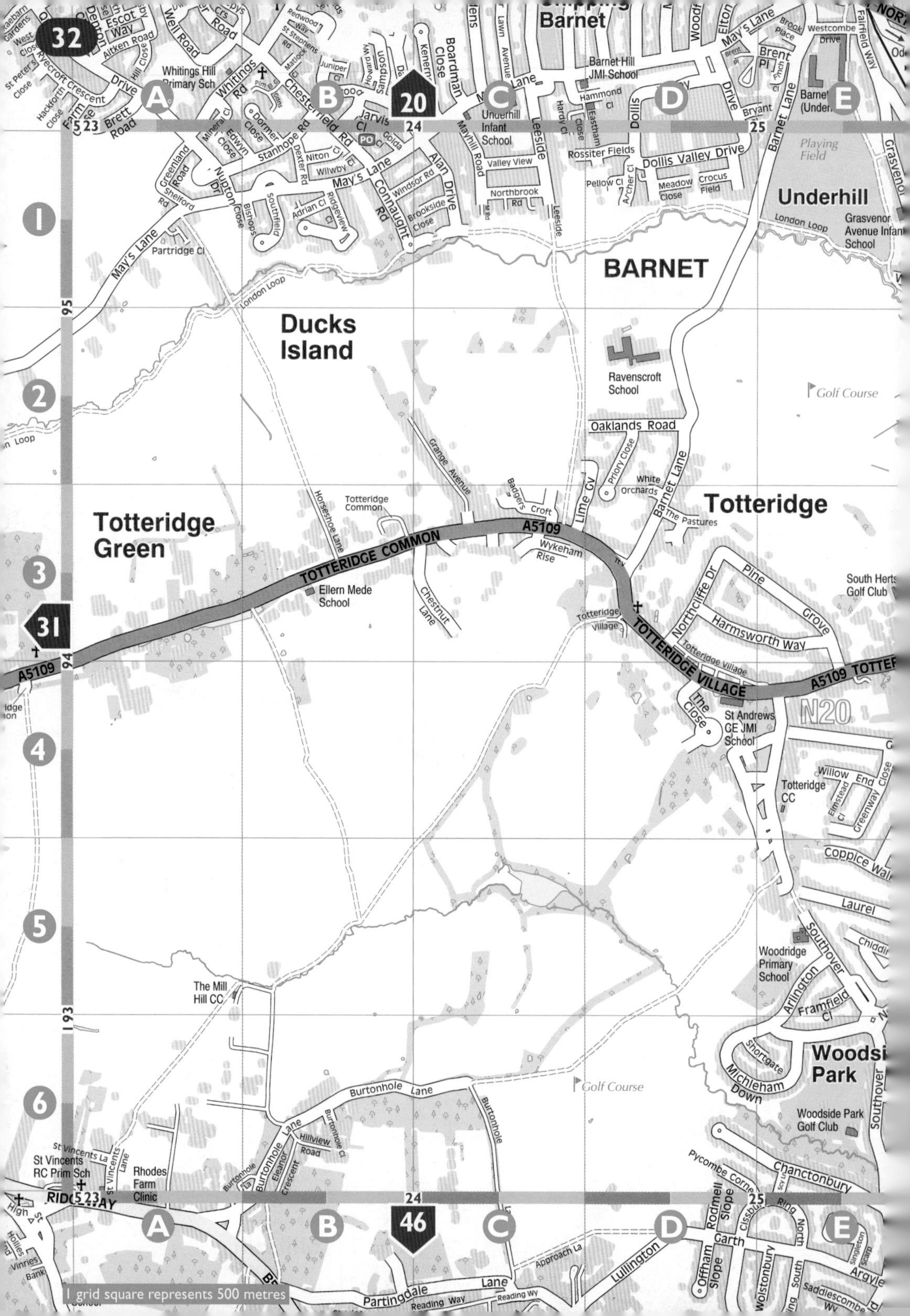

32
20
31
46
Barnet
BARNET
Ducks Island
Totteridge Green
Totteridge
Underhill
Woodside Park
N20
TOTTERIDGE COMMON
TOTTERIDGE VILLAGE
A5109
Whitings Hill Primary Sch
Barnet Hill JMI School
Underhill Infant School
Grasvenor Avenue Infant School
Ravenscroft School
Ellern Mede School
St Andrews CE JMI School
Woodridge Primary School
Woodside Park Golf Club
South Herts Golf Club
Golf Course
Totteridge CC
The Mill Hill CC
St Vincents RC Prim Sch
Rhodes Farm Clinic
Playing Field
London Loop
May's Lane
Burtonhole Lane
Barnet Lane
Oaklands Road
Dollis Valley Drive
Harmsworth Way
Pine Grove
Northcliffe Dr
Chestnut Lane
Grange Avenue
Horseshoe Lane
Southover
Chanctonbury
Partingdale Lane
Reading Way
Approach La
Lullington
1 grid square represents 500 metres

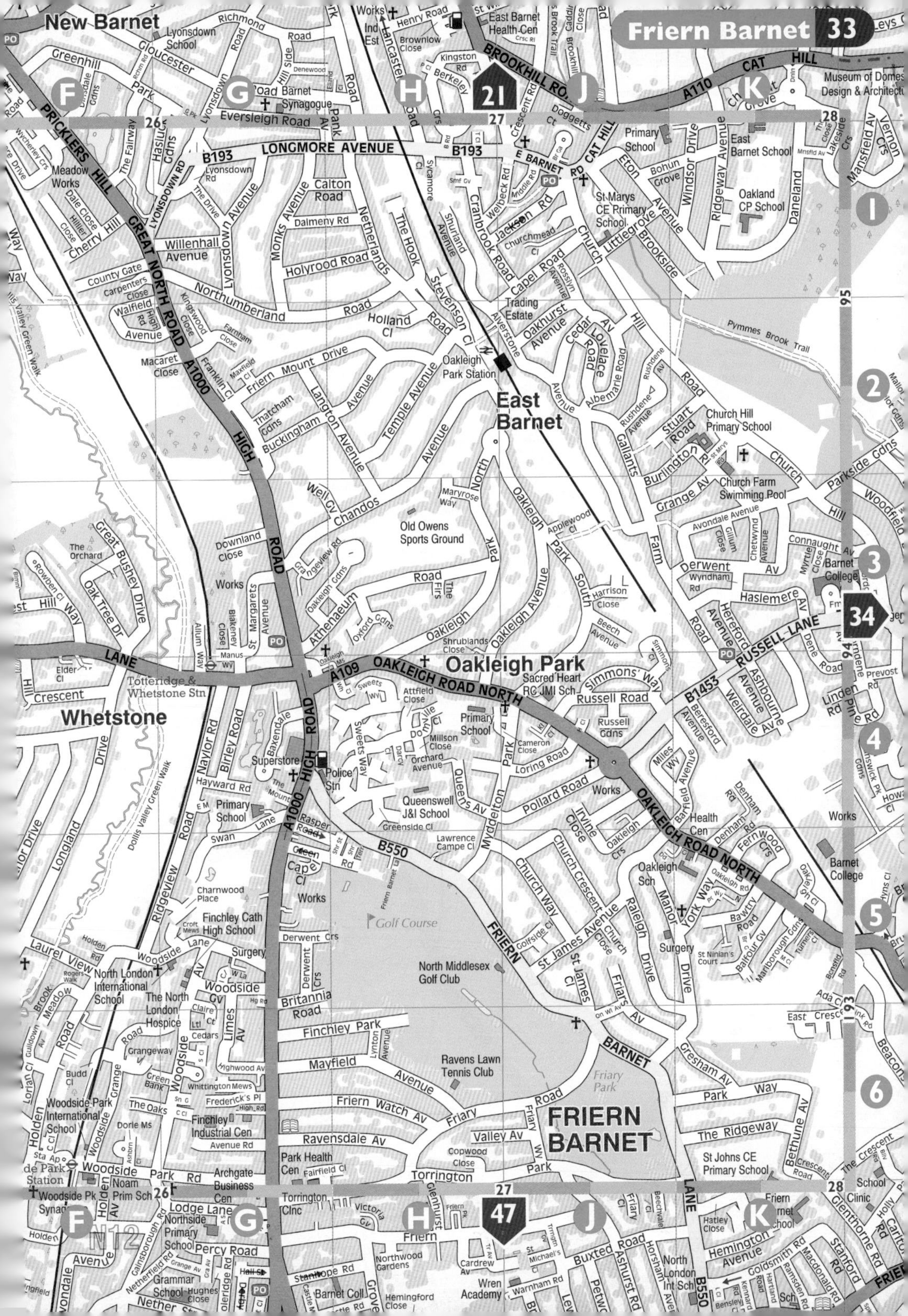
New Barnet
East Barnet
Oakleigh Park
Whetstone
FRIERN BARNET
Lyonsdown School
Richmond Road
Gloucester Road
Greenhill Park
Lyonsdown Road
Eversleigh Road
Longmore Avenue
B193
Pricklers Hill
Great North Road
A1000
High Road
Cat Hill
A110
Brookhill Road
East Barnet Health Cen
Museum of Domestic Design & Architecture
Park Road
Berkeley Crs
Lancaster Road
Crescent Rd
Doggetts Ct
East Barnet School
Oakland CP School
Primary School
St Marys CE Primary School
Church Hill Road
Littlegrove
Brookside
Windsor Drive
Ridgeway Avenue
Daneland
Meadow Works
Cherry Hill
Lyonsdown Avenue
Willenhall Avenue
Northumberland Road
Monks Avenue
Calton Road
Dalmeny Rd
Holyrood Road
Netherlands Road
The Hook
Stevenson Cl
Holland Cl
Cranbrook Road
Jackson Rd
Capel Road
Trading Estate
Averstone
Oakhurst Avenue
Cedar Road
Lovelace Road
Albemarle Road
Rushdene Avenue
Pymmes Brook Trail
Oakleigh Park Station
Friern Mount Drive
Langton Avenue
Temple Avenue
Buckingham Avenue
Thatcham Gdns
Church Hill Primary School
Stuart Road
Burlington Ri
Church Farm Swimming Pool
Grange Av
Gallants Farm Road
Parkside Gdns
Woodfield
Dollis Valley Green Walk
Great Bushey Drive
Oak Tree Dr
Chandos Avenue
Well Gv
Old Owens Sports Ground
Maryrose Way
Oakleigh Park North
Oakleigh Avenue
Oakleigh Park South
Applewood Cl
Derwent Av
Haslemere Av
Barnet College
Russell Lane
B1453
Downland Close
Works
Athenaeum Road
Oakleigh Road
The Firs
Oxford Gdns
Harrison Close
Beech Avenue
Shrublands Close
Totteridge & Whetstone Stn
Lane
Crescent
A109
Oakleigh Road North
Sacred Heart RC JMI Sch
Simmons' Way
Russell Road
Russell Gdns
Ashbourne Avenue
Beresford Avenue
Weirdale Av
Linden Rd
Pine Rd
Naylor Rd
Birley Road
Baxendale
Superstore
Police Stn
Sweets Way
Primary School
Millson Close
Orchard Avenue
Queens Av
Queenswell J&I School
Myddelton Park
Loring Road
Pollard Road
Irvine Close
Oakleigh Crs
Health Cen
Denham Rd
Fernwood Crs
Hayward Rd
Swan Lane
Ridgeview Road
Longland Drive
Rasper Road
Green Rd
Capel Cl
B550
Lawrence Campe Cl
Church Way
Church Crescent
Raleigh Drive
Manor Drive
York Way
Oakleigh Sch
Surgery
Bawtry Road
Balfour Gv
Marlborough Gdns
St Ninian's Court
Charnwood Place
Finchley Cath High School
Golf Course
Derwent Crs
Friern Barnet Lane
St James Avenue
St James Cl
Church Close
Friars Av
North Middlesex Golf Club
Britannia Road
Laurel View
Woodside Lane
North London International School
The North London Hospice
Woodside Av
Limes Av
Claire Ct
Cedars
Grangeway
Highwood Av
Whittington Mews
Frederick's Pl
Finchley Park
Mayfield Avenue
Lynton Avenue
Ravens Lawn Tennis Club
Barnet
Friary Park
Gresham Av
Park Way
Woodside Park International School
Woodside Grange Road
The Oaks
Finchley Industrial Cen
Avenue Rd
Friern Watch Av
Friary Road
Ravensdale Av
Valley Av
Copwood Close
The Ridgeway
St Johns CE Primary School
Bethune Av
Crescent Road
The Crescent
Park Health Cen
Fairfield Cl
Torrington Park
Woodside Park Station
Woodside Park Rd
Archgate Business Cen
Noam Prim Sch
Woodside Pk Synagogue
Lodge Lane
Torrington Clnc
Victoria
Glenhurst
Friern Barnet School
Hatley Close
Hemington Avenue
Goldsmith Rd
Stanford Rd
Glenthorne Rd
Clinic
School
Northside Primary School
Percy Road
N12
Grammar School
Hughes Close
Gainsborough Rd
Northwood Gardens
Stanhope Rd
Barnet Coll
Hemingford Close
Cardrew Av
Wren Academy
Warnham Rd
Buxted Road
Ashurst Rd
Horsham Av
North London Int Sch
Lane
B550
Nether St
East Crescent
Beacon
Works
Barnet College
Oakleigh Rd
F
G
H
J
K
I
2
3
4
5
6
21
34
47
26
27
28
93
94
95

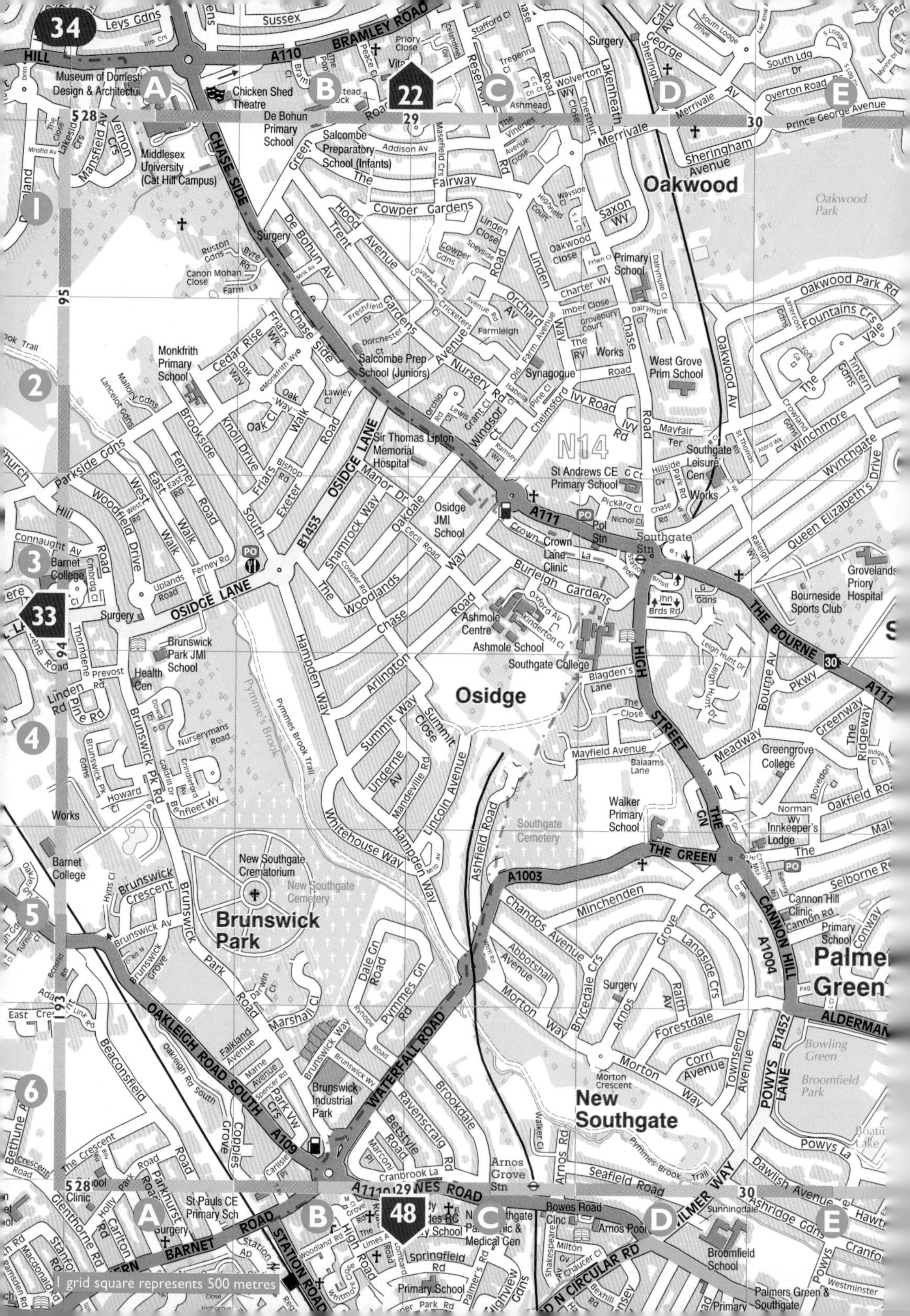
34
22
33
48
A
B
C
D
E
1
2
3
4
5
6
528
29
30
95
94
193
Leys Gdns
Sussex
Bramley Road
A110
Hill
Museum of Domestic Design & Architecture
Chicken Shed Theatre
De Bohun Primary School
Salcombe Preparatory School (Infants)
Middlesex University (Cat Hill Campus)
Chase Side
Addison Av
The Fairway
Cowper Gardens
Surgery
Oakwood
Oakwood Park
Merrivale
Sheringham Avenue
Prince George Avenue
Overton Road
South Ldg Dr
Ashmead
Wolverton Wy
Lakenheath
Chestnut
Reservoir Rd
Tregenna Cl
Saxon Wy
Oakwood Close
Linden Close
Primary School
Charter Wy
Oakwood Park Rd
Fountains Crs
Vale
Oakwood Av
Chase Road
West Grove Prim School
Monkfrith Primary School
Cedar Rise
Oak Way
Oak Cl
Friars Walk
Ferney Road
Brookside
Knoll Drive
Lancelot Gdns
Mallory Gdns
Parkside Gdns
Woodfield Drive
West Walk
East Walk
Exeter Road
South
Salcombe Prep School (Juniors)
Sir Thomas Lipton Memorial Hospital
Osidge Lane
B1453
Manor Dr
Nursery Rd
Windsor Ct
Orchard Av
Synagogue
Ivy Road
Ivy Rd
Chelmsford
Mayfair Ter
N14
St Andrews CE Primary School
Southgate Leisure Cen
Works
Winchmore
Wynchgate
Queen Elizabeth's Drive
A111
Pol Stn
Southgate Stn
Crown Lane Clinic
Burleigh Gardens
Osidge JMI School
Shamrock Way
Oakdale
The Woodlands
Chase Way
Ashmole Centre
Ashmole School
Southgate College
Grovelands Priory Hospital
Bourneside Sports Club
The Bourne
High Street
Osidge
Barnet College
Connaught Av
Uplands Road
Surgery
Brunswick Park JMI School
Health Cen
Prevost Rd
Linden Rd
Pine Rd
Thorndene
Nurserymans Road
Brunswick Pk Rd
Howard Cl
Works
Arlington
Hampden Way
Pymmes Brook Trail
Pymmes Brook
Summit Way
Summit Close
Underne Av
Mandeville Rd
Lincoln Avenue
Whitehouse Way
Mayfield Avenue
Balaams Lane
Blagden's Lane
Walker Primary School
Southgate Cemetery
The Green
The Gn
Meadway
Greengrove College
Bourne Av
Pkwy
Greenway
The Ridgeway
Oakfield Rd
Innkeeper's Lodge
Selborne Rd
Cannon Hill Clinic
Cannon Hill
A1004
Primary School
Conway
Palmers Green
Alderman
Bowling Green
Broomfield Park
Boating Lake
New Southgate Crematorium
New Southgate Cemetery
Brunswick Park
Brunswick Crescent
Brunswick Av
Brunswick Grove
Barnet College
Ashfield Road
A1003
Chandos Avenue
Minchenden Crs
Abbotshall Avenue
Morton Way
Brycedale Crs
Arnos Grove
Langside Crs
Raith Av
Forestdale
Corri Avenue
Townsend Avenue
Powys Lane
B1452
Morton Crescent
New Southgate
Powys La
Dawlish Avenue
Dale Gn Road
Pymmes Gn Rd
Marshall Cl
Darwin Cl
Park Road
Falkland Avenue
Marne Avenue
Park Vw Crs
Brunswick Way
Brunswick Industrial Park
Waterfall Road
Ravenscraig Rd
Brookdale
Betstyle Road
Oakleigh Road South
Oakleigh Rd South
A109
Beaconsfield Road
Coppies Grove
Bethune Av
The Crescent
Clinic
Parkhurst Road
Carlton Rd
Glenthorne Rd
Stanford Rd
Macdonald Rd
St Pauls CE Primary Sch
Barnet Road
Station Road
High Road
Springfield Rd
Primary School
Cranbrook La
Bowes Road
A1110
Arnos Grove Stn
Seafield Road
Bowes Road Clnc
Arnos Pool
N Circular Rd
Milton Gv
Chaucer Cl
Wilmer Way
Sunningdale
Ashridge Gdns
Broomfield School
Palmers Green & Southgate
Westminster
Cranford
Walker Cl
1 grid square represents 500 metres

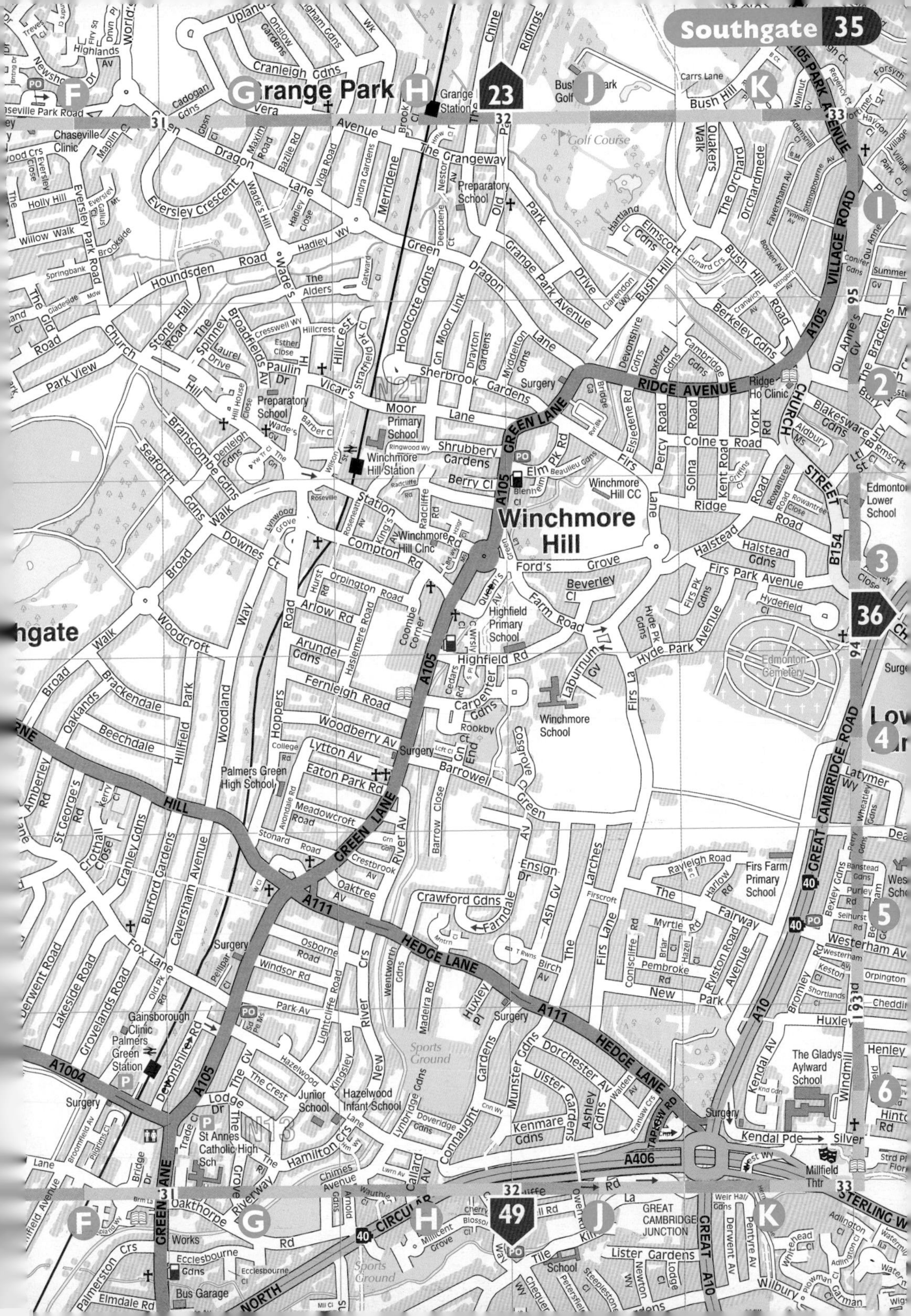
Grange Park
Winchmore Hill
Grange Station
Winchmore Hill Station
Palmers Green Station
Bush Hill Park Golf Course
Edmonton Cemetery
Winchmore School
Highfield Primary School
Palmers Green High School
Firs Farm Primary School
The Gladys Aylward School
St Annes Catholic High Sch
Hazelwood Junior School
Hazelwood Infant School
Edmonton Lower School
Sports Ground
Great Cambridge Junction
Green Lane
Ridge Avenue
Village Road
Park Avenue
Hedge Lane
North Circular
Great Cambridge Road
A105
A111
A406
A10
A1004
B154
N21
N13
23
36
49

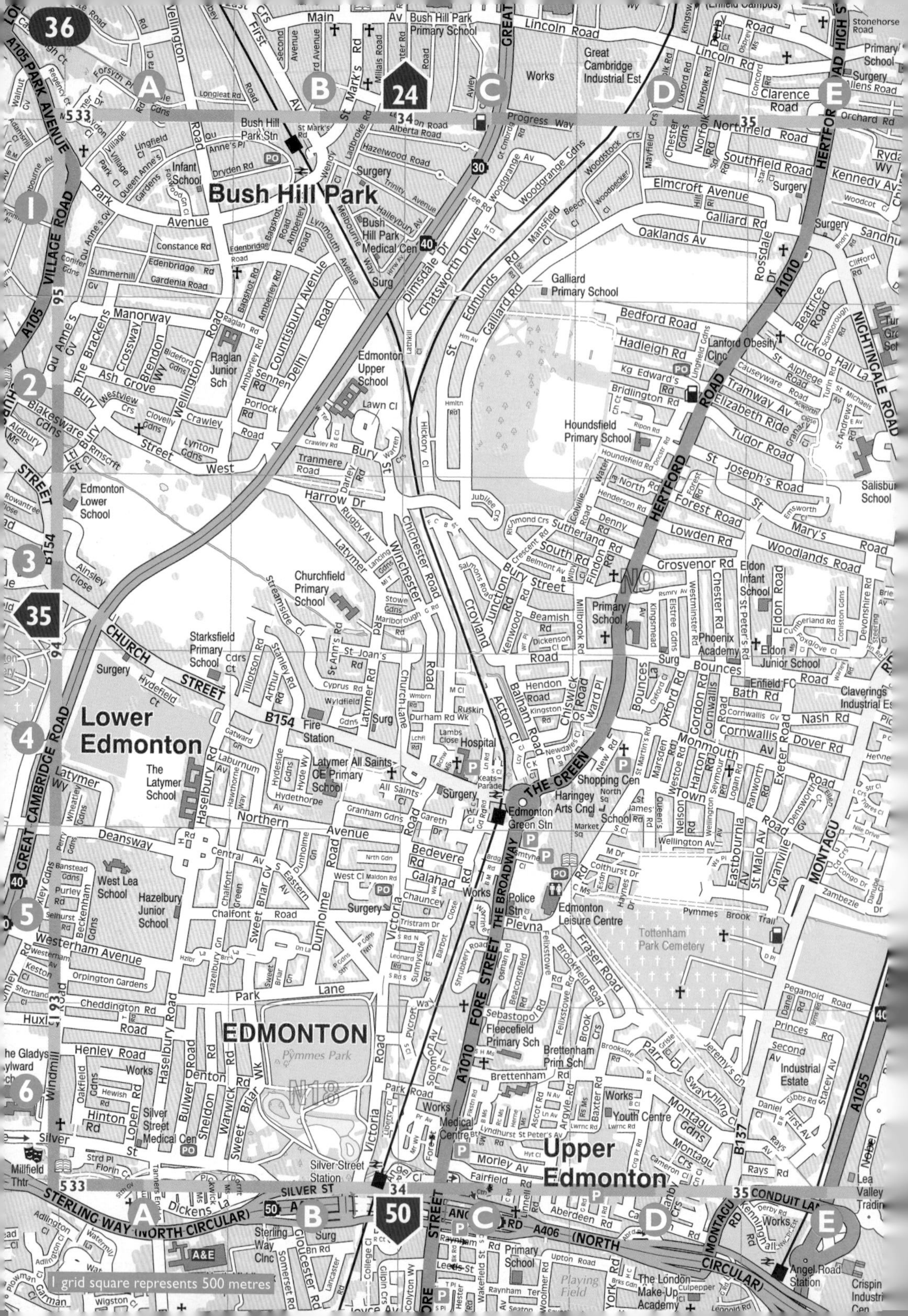

36
24
35
50
A
B
C
D
E
1
2
3
4
5
6
533
34
35
Bush Hill Park
Bush Hill Park Stn
Bush Hill Park Primary School
Bush Hill Park Medical Cen
Lower Edmonton
EDMONTON
Upper Edmonton
Pymmes Park
N18
N9
Great Cambridge Industrial Est
Galliard Primary School
Houndsfield Primary School
Edmonton Upper School
Edmonton Lower School
Raglan Junior Sch
Churchfield Primary School
Starksfield Primary School
The Latymer School
Latymer All Saints CE Primary School
West Lea School
Hazelbury Junior School
Fleecefield Primary Sch
Brettenham Prim Sch
Eldon Infant School
Eldon Junior School
Phoenix Academy
Edmonton Green Stn
Haringey Arts Cncl
Shopping Cen
Edmonton Leisure Centre
Police Stn
Tottenham Park Cemetery
Silver Street Station
Angel Road Station
Clavering Industrial Est
Industrial Estate
Lea Valley Trading
Crispin Industrial
Youth Centre
Playing Field
The London Make-Up Academy
Millfield Thtr
Lanford Obesity Clnc
Enfield FC
Salisbury School
Hospital
Fire Station
Lincoln Road
Main Av
Progress Way
Northfield Road
Southfield Road
Elmcroft Avenue
Galliard Rd
Oaklands Av
Bedford Road
Hadleigh Rd
Bridlington Rd
Hertford Road
A1010
Park Avenue
A105
Village Road
Great Cambridge Road
B154
Church Street
Bury Street
Bury St West
Manorway
Ash Grove
Dimsdale Dr
Chatsworth Drive
St Edmunds Rd
Hickory Cl
Harrow Dr
Winchester Road
Chichester Road
Croyland Rd
Junction Rd
Bury Street
Sutherland Rd
Grosvenor Rd
Woodlands Road
St Joseph's Road
St Mary's Road
Forest Road
Lowden Rd
Tudor Road
Elizabeth Ride
Tramway Av
Cuckoo Hall La
Nightingale Road
Bounces Road
Cornwallis Av
Monmouth Road
Dover Rd
Nash Rd
Montagu Road
The Green
The Broadway
Fore Street
Northern Avenue
Deansway
Central Av
Westerham Avenue
Orpington Gardens
Cheddington Rd
Henley Road
Park Lane
Silver St
Sterling Way (North Circular)
A406 (North Circular)
Conduit La
Windmill Rd
Victoria Rd
Pegamoid Road
Princes Rd
Pymmes Brook Trail
Fairfield Rd
Aberdeen Rd
Upton Road
Raynham Rd
A1055
B137
1 grid square represents 500 metres

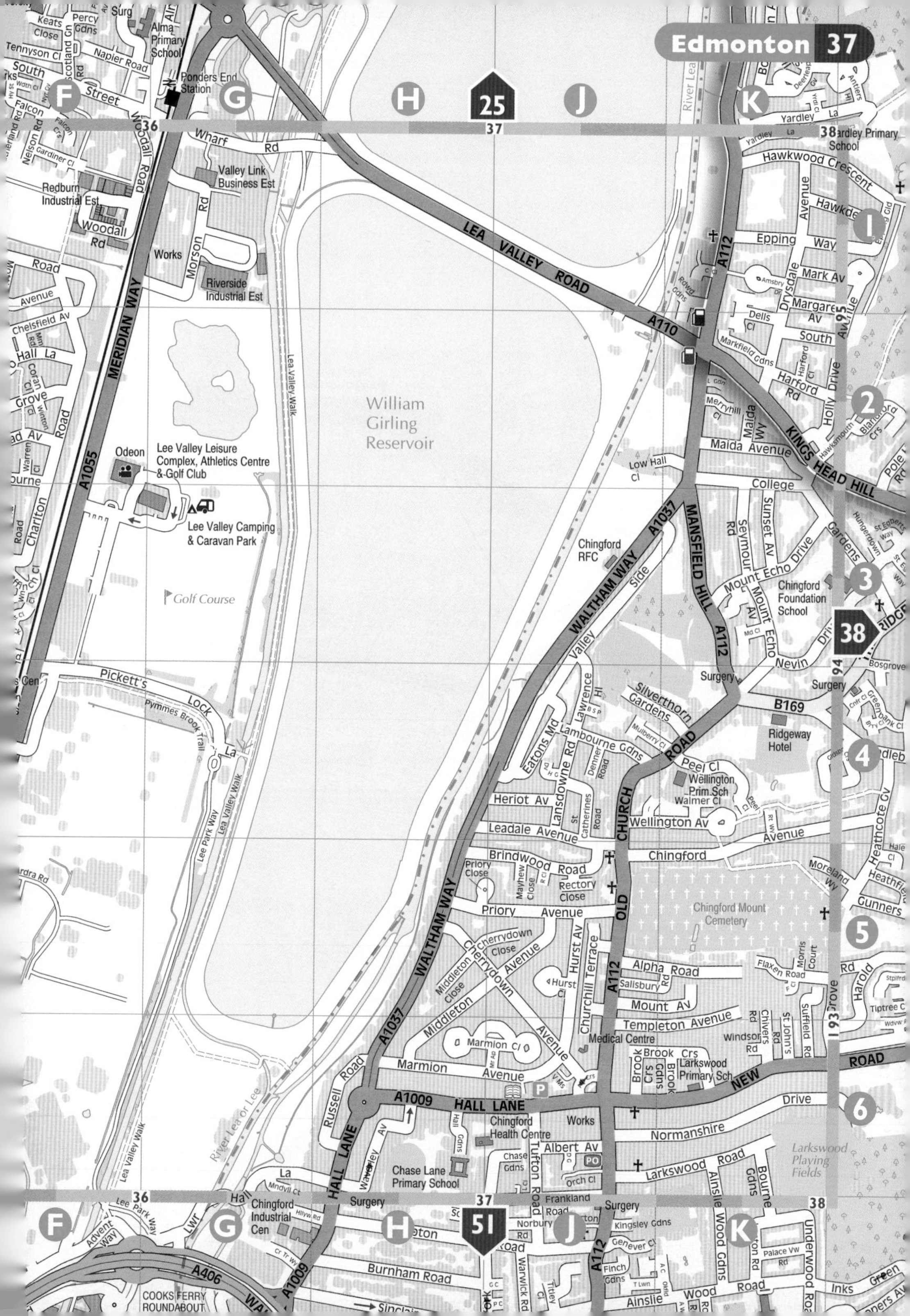

Keats Close
Percy Gdns
Surg
Alma Primary School
Tennyson Cl
Scotland Gn Rd
Napier Road
South Street
Ponders End Station
Falcon Rd
Falcon Crs
Nelson Rd
Woodall Road
Gardiner Cl
Wharf Rd
Valley Link Business Est
Redburn Industrial Est
Woodall Rd
Morson Rd
Works
Riverside Industrial Est
LEA VALLEY ROAD
A110
MERIDIAN WAY
A1055
Road
Avenue
Chelsfield Av
Hall La
Coran Cl
Grove
Winton
Road
Av
Warren Cl
Charlton Road
Odeon
Lee Valley Leisure Complex, Athletics Centre & Golf Club
Lee Valley Camping & Caravan Park
Golf Course
William Girling Reservoir
Lea Valley Walk
Pickett's Lock La
Pymmes Brook Trail
Lee Park Way
River Lea or Lee
Yardley La
Yardley Primary School
Hawkwood Crescent
Avenue
Hawkdene
Epping Way
A112
Mark Av
Amsbry Dr
Drysdale Avenue
Dells Cl
Margaret Av
South
A1009
Markfield Gdns
Harford Rd
Holly Drive
Merryhill Cl
Maida Way
Maida Avenue
KINGS HEAD HILL
Hawksmouth
Blandford Crs
Low Hall Cl
College
Sunset Av
Seymour Rd
Gardens
Mount Echo Drive
Chingford RFC
A1037
MANSFIELD HILL
WALTHAM WAY
Valley Side
Mount Echo Av
Chingford Foundation School
Nevin Dr
Surgery
Silverthorn Gardens
B169
Ridgeway Hotel
Lawrence Hill
Lambourne Gdns
Eatons Md
Lansdowne Rd
Denner Road
Peel Cl
Wellington Prim Sch
Walmer Cl
Heriot Av
St Catherines Road
Leadale Avenue
Wellington Av
Avenue
OLD CHURCH ROAD
Chingford
Brindwood Road
Priory Close
Mayhew Close
Rectory Close
Priory Avenue
Moreland Wy
Heathcote Gv
Gunners
Chingford Mount Cemetery
Cherrydown Close
Cherrydown Avenue
Middleton Close
Hurst Av
Churchill Terrace
Alpha Road
Salisbury Rd
Flaxen Road
Morris Court
Harold Rd
Hurst Cl
Middleton
Mount Av
Tiptree C
Templeton Avenue
Chivers Rd
St John's
Suffield Rd
Grove
Windsor Rd
Medical Centre
Marmion Cl
Marmion Avenue
Brook Crs
Brook Gdns
Larkswood Primary Sch
NEW ROAD
Russell Road
Avenue
A1009 HALL LANE
Drive
Works
Chingford Health Centre
Hall Gdns
Normanshire
Albert Av
Tufton Road
Chase Gdns
PO
Orch Cl
Larkswood Road
Ainslie Wood Gdns
Bourne Gdns
Larkswood Playing Fields
Chase Lane Primary School
HALL LANE
Hall La
Surgery
Frankland Road
Surgery
Kingsley Gdns
Chingford Industrial Cen
Norbury Rd
Genever Cl
Underwood Road
Palace Vw Rd
Lee Park Way
Advent Way
Lwr
A406
Burnham Road
Warwick Rd
Finch Gdns
T Lwn
Ainslie Wood Road
Inks Green
COOKS FERRY ROUNDABOUT
Sinclair

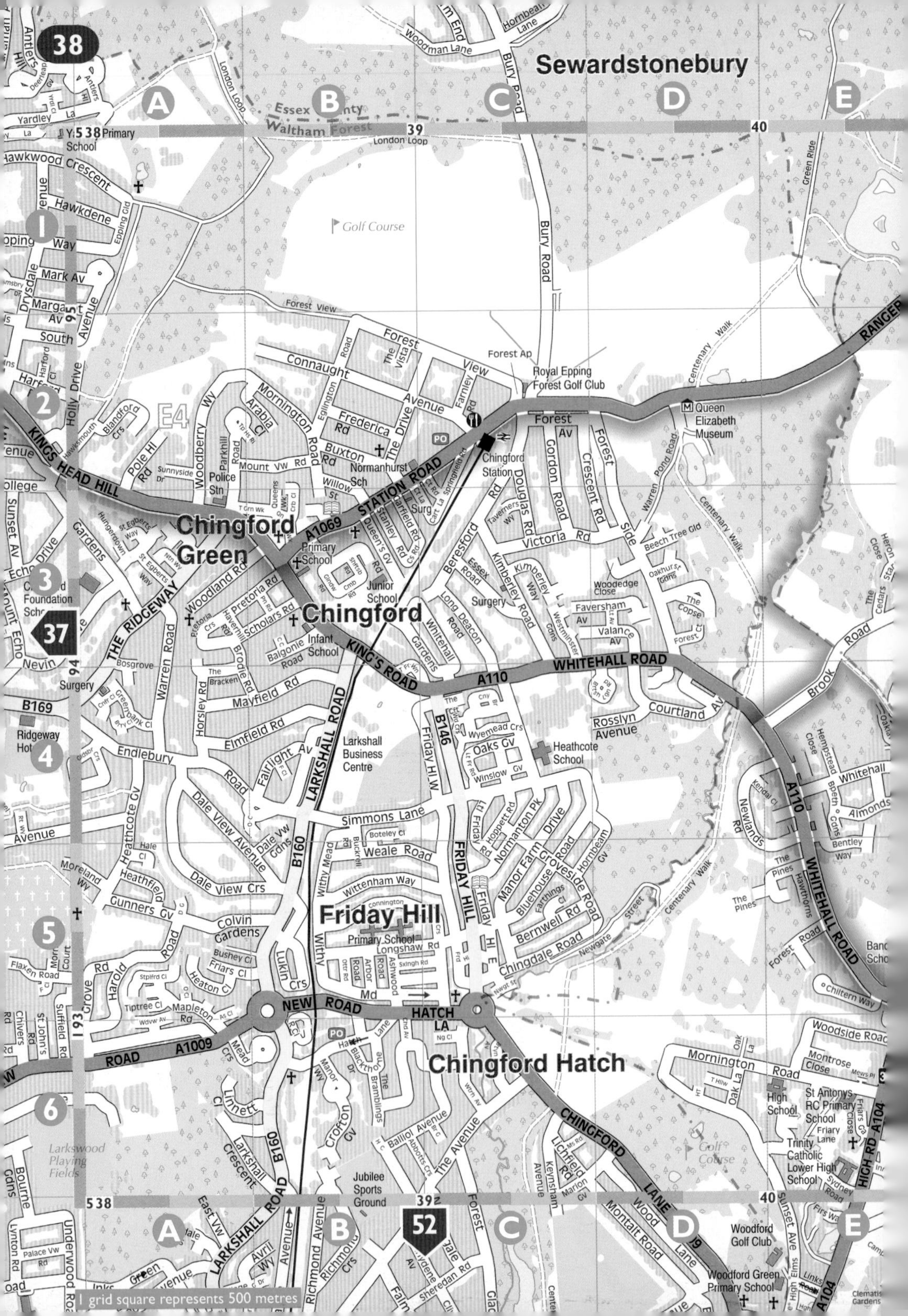

38
Sewardstonebury
Golf Course
Royal Epping Forest Golf Club
Queen Elizabeth Museum
Chingford Station
Chingford Green
Chingford
Friday Hill
Chingford Hatch
Larkshall Business Centre
Heathcote School
Jubilee Sports Ground
Woodford Golf Club
Woodford Green Primary School
Larkswood Playing Fields
Trinity Catholic Lower High School
St Antony's RC Primary School
High School
Kings Head Hill
Station Road
King's Road
Whitehall Road
Larkshall Road
Friday Hill
New Road
Hatch La
Chingford Lane
The Ridgeway
Bury Road
Forest View
Connaught Avenue
Mornington Road
Ranger's Road
Centenary Walk
Essex County
Waltham Forest
London Loop
E4
37
52
1 grid square represents 500 metres

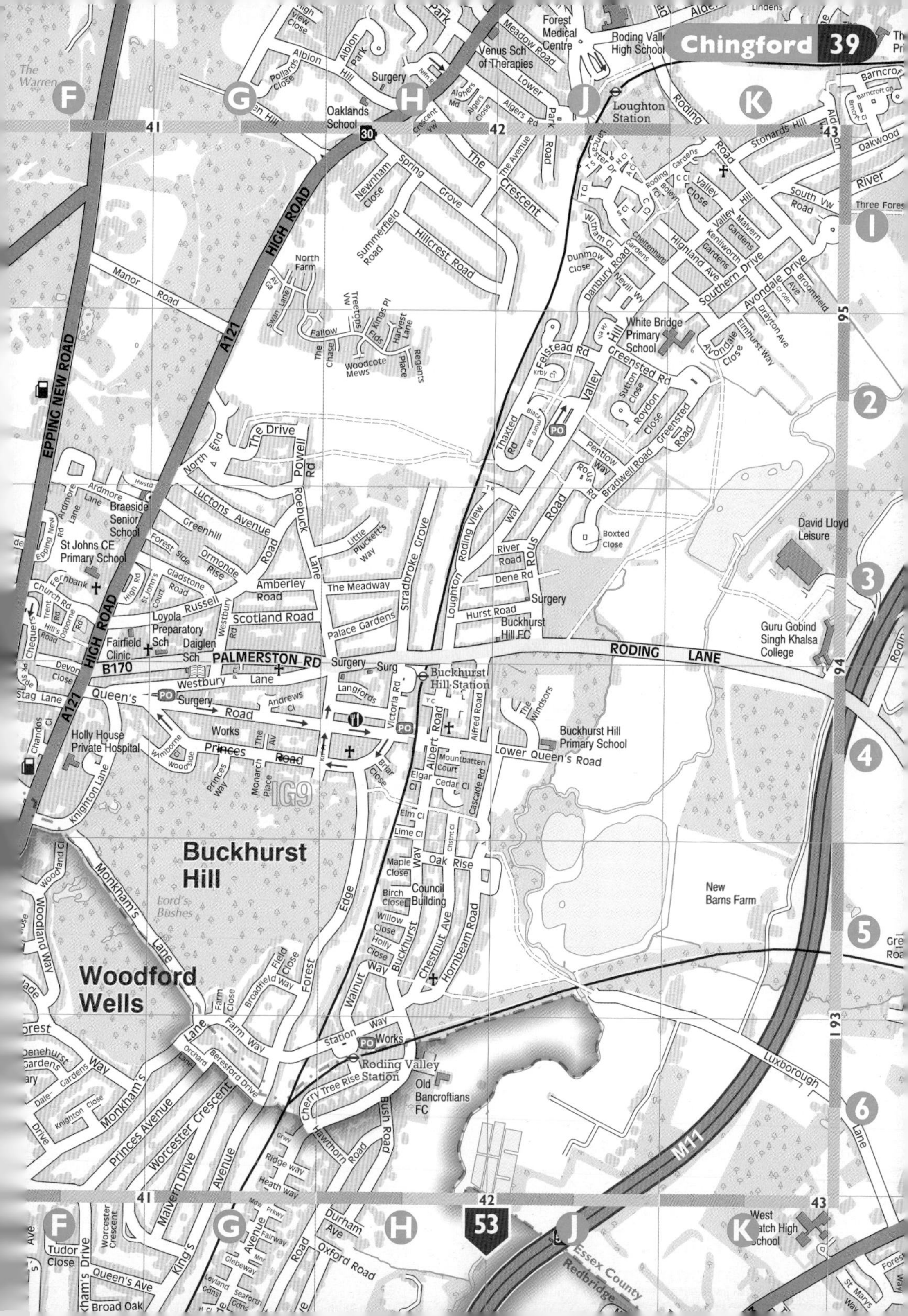
Buckhurst Hill
Woodford Wells
Lord's Bushes
IG9
Loughton Station
Buckhurst Hill Station
Roding Valley Station
EPPING NEW ROAD
HIGH ROAD
A121
B170
PALMERSTON RD
RODING LANE
M11
Manor Road
The Drive
North End
Powell Rd
Roebuck Lane
Luctons Avenue
Greenhill
Ormonde Rise
Forest Side
Gladstone Road
Amberley Road
Russell Road
Scotland Road
Westbury Rd
The Meadway
Palace Gardens
Stradbroke Grove
Little Plucketts Way
Queen's Road
Westbury Lane
Langfords
Victoria Rd
Princes Road
Princes Way
Monarch Place
Knighton Lane
Holly House Private Hospital
Loyola Preparatory Sch
Daiglen Sch
Fairfield Clinic
St Johns CE Primary School
Braeside Senior School
Church Rd
Fernbank
Ardmore Lane
Stag Lane
Devon Close
Chequers Road
Chandos Cl
Albert Road
Alfred Road
Mountbatten Court
Cedar Cl
Cascade Rd
Elm Cl
Lime Cl
Maple Close
Birch Close
Willow Close
Holly Close
Walnut Way
Buckhurst Way
Chestnut Ave
Hornbeam Road
Oak Rise
Council Building
Briar Close
Edge
Forest
Field Close
Broadfield Way
Farm Close
Farm Way
Station Way
Works
Cherry Tree Rise
Hawthorn Road
Bush Road
Ridge Way
Heath Way
Old Bancroftians FC
Monkham's Lane
Monkham's Avenue
Woodland Way
Princes Avenue
Worcester Crescent
Malvern Drive
Beresford Drive
Orchard Lane
Knighton Close
Lower Queen's Road
Buckhurst Hill Primary School
The Windsors
Loughton Way
Roding View
River Road
Rous Road
Dene Rd
Hurst Road
Buckhurst Hill FC
Surgery
Boxted Close
Bradwell Road
Pentlow Way
Greensted Road
Greensted Rd
Roydon Close
Sutton Close
Valley Hill
Felstead Rd
Thaxted Rd
White Bridge Primary School
Danbury Road
Dunmow Close
Witham Cl
Nevill Wy
Cheltenham Gardens
Highland Ave
Southern Drive
Avondale Drive
Avondale Close
Elmhurst Way
Drayton Ave
Broomfield Ave
Kenilworth Gardens
Malvern Gardens
Valley Hill
Valley Close
Roding Road
Roding Gardens
Stonards Hill
South Vw Road
Oakwood
River
Barncroft
Alderton
Three Forest
David Lloyd Leisure
Guru Gobind Singh Khalsa College
New Barns Farm
Luxborough Lane
West Hatch High School
Forest Medical Centre
Roding Valley High School
Venus Sch of Therapies
Meadow Road
Lower Park Road
Algers Rd
Algers Close
Oaklands School
Albion Hill
Albion Park
Pollards Close
High View Close
Crescent Vw
Spring Grove
Newnham Close
The Crescent
The Avenue
Summerfield Road
Hillcrest Road
North Farm
Swan Lane
Fallow
The Chase
Treetops Vw
Kings Pl
Harvest Lane
Regents Place
Woodcote Mews
The Warren
Lancaster Dr
Tudor Close
Queen's Ave
Broad Oak
King's Avenue
Durham Ave
Oxford Road
Fairway
Glebeway
Essex County
Redbridge
30
53
41
42
43
95
94
93
F
G
H
J
K
1
2
3
4
5
6

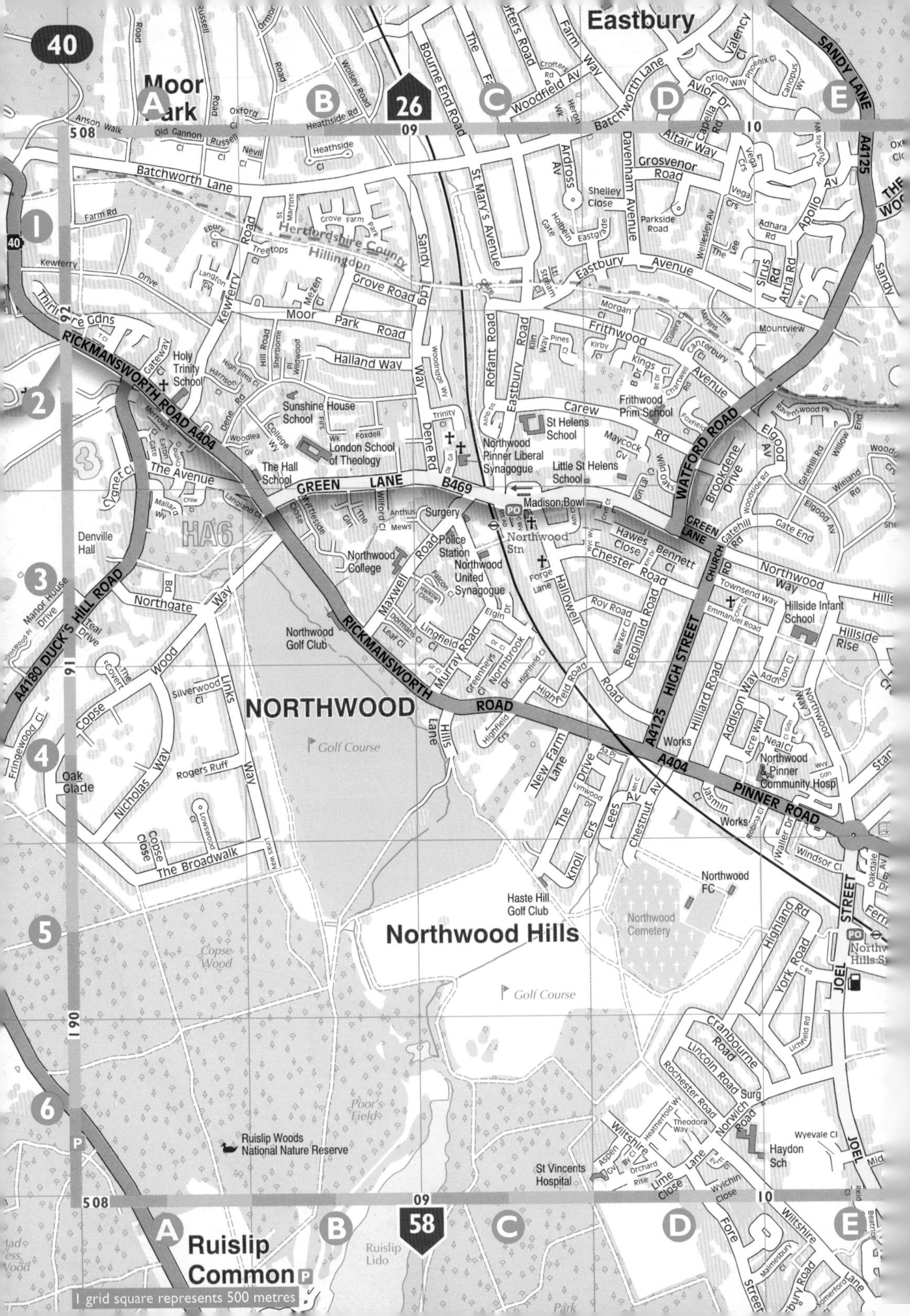

40
Moor Park
Eastbury
26
58
A
B
C
D
E
1
2
3
4
5
6
508
09
10
92
91
190
Batchworth Lane
Bourne End Road
St Mary's Avenue
Sandy Lane
A4125
Davenham Avenue
Grosvenor Road
Shelley Close
Parkside Road
Eastbury Avenue
Hertfordshire County
Hillingdon
Kewferry Road
Kewferry Drive
Grove Road
Moor Park Road
Halland Way
Sandy Lodge Way
Rofant Road
Eastbury Road
Frithwood Avenue
Mountview
RICKMANSWORTH ROAD A404
Holy Trinity School
Sunshine House School
London School of Theology
The Hall School
Frithwood Prim School
St Helens School
Little St Helens School
Carew Road
Maycock Gv
Northwood Pinner Liberal Synagogue
WATFORD ROAD
Brookdene Drive
Elgood Av
Willow End
GREEN LANE
B469
The Avenue
Cygnet Cl
Denville Hall
HA6
Surgery
Police Station
Northwood United Synagogue
Madison Bowl
Northwood Stn
Northwood College
Hawes Close
Bennett Cl
Chester Road
Hallowell Road
Roy Road
Reginald Road
Forge Lane
CHURCH RD
Northwood Way
Townsend Way
Emmanuel Road
Hillside Infant School
Hillside Rise
Gatehill Rd
Gate End
Wieland Rd
Manor House Drive
A4180 DUCK'S HILL ROAD
Teal Drive
Northgate
Way
Northwood Golf Club
RICKMANSWORTH ROAD
Maxwell Road
Lingfield Cl
Murray Road
Northbrook Dr
Highfield Road
Highfield Crs
A4125 HIGH STREET
Hilliard Road
Addison Way
Works
Northwood & Pinner Community Hosp
A404
PINNER ROAD
Windsor Cl
Waller Dr
JOEL STREET
Copse Wood Way
Silverwood Cl
Links Way
NORTHWOOD
Golf Course
Hills Lane
New Farm Lane
The Drive
Knoll Crs
Lees Av
Chestnut Av
Fringewood Cl
Oak Glade
Nicholas Way
Rogers Ruff
Lowswood Cl
Copse Close
The Broadwalk
Haste Hill Golf Club
Northwood FC
Northwood Cemetery
Northwood Hills
Northwood Hills Stn
Copse Wood
Highland Rd
York Road
Cranbourne Road
Lincoln Road
Rochester Road
Norwich Road
Surg
Lichfield Rd
Haydon Sch
Wyevale Cl
JOEL
Poor's Field
Ruislip Woods National Nature Reserve
St Vincents Hospital
Wiltshire Lane
Theodora Way
Lime Close
Wychin Close
Orchard Rise
Fore Street
Ruislip Common
Ruislip Lido
Park
I grid square represents 500 metres

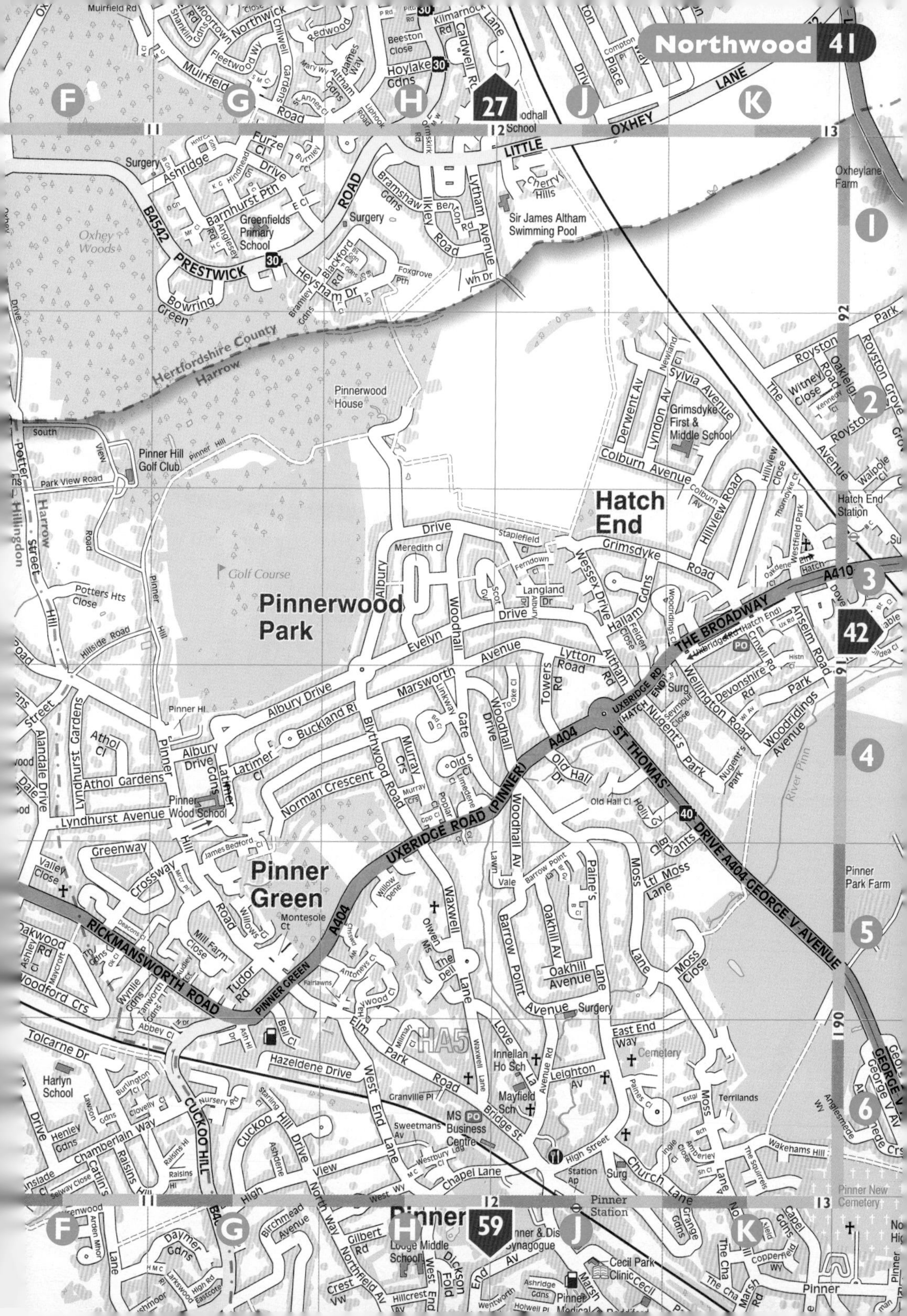
Hatch End
Pinnerwood Park
Pinner Green
Pinner
Oxhey Woods
Hertfordshire County
Harrow
Hillingdon
Pinnerwood House
Pinner Hill Golf Club
Golf Course
Greenfields Primary School
Sir James Altham Swimming Pool
Grimsdyke First & Middle School
Pinner Wood School
Harlyn School
Pinner Park Farm
Oxheylane Farm
Hatch End Station
Pinner Station
Pinner New Cemetery
Cemetery
MS Business Centre
Innellan Ho Sch
Mayfield Sch
Terrilands
HA5
Prestwick Road
Little Oxhey Lane
The Broadway
Uxbridge Road (Pinner)
Rickmansworth Road
St Thomas' Drive
George V Avenue
Cuckoo Hill
Evelyn Drive
Albury Drive
Grimsdyke Road
Colburn Avenue
Hazeldene Drive
Chamberlain Way
High Street
Chapel Lane
Church Lane
Wakehams Hill
Royston Park
Royston Grove
B4542
A404
A410
27
42
59

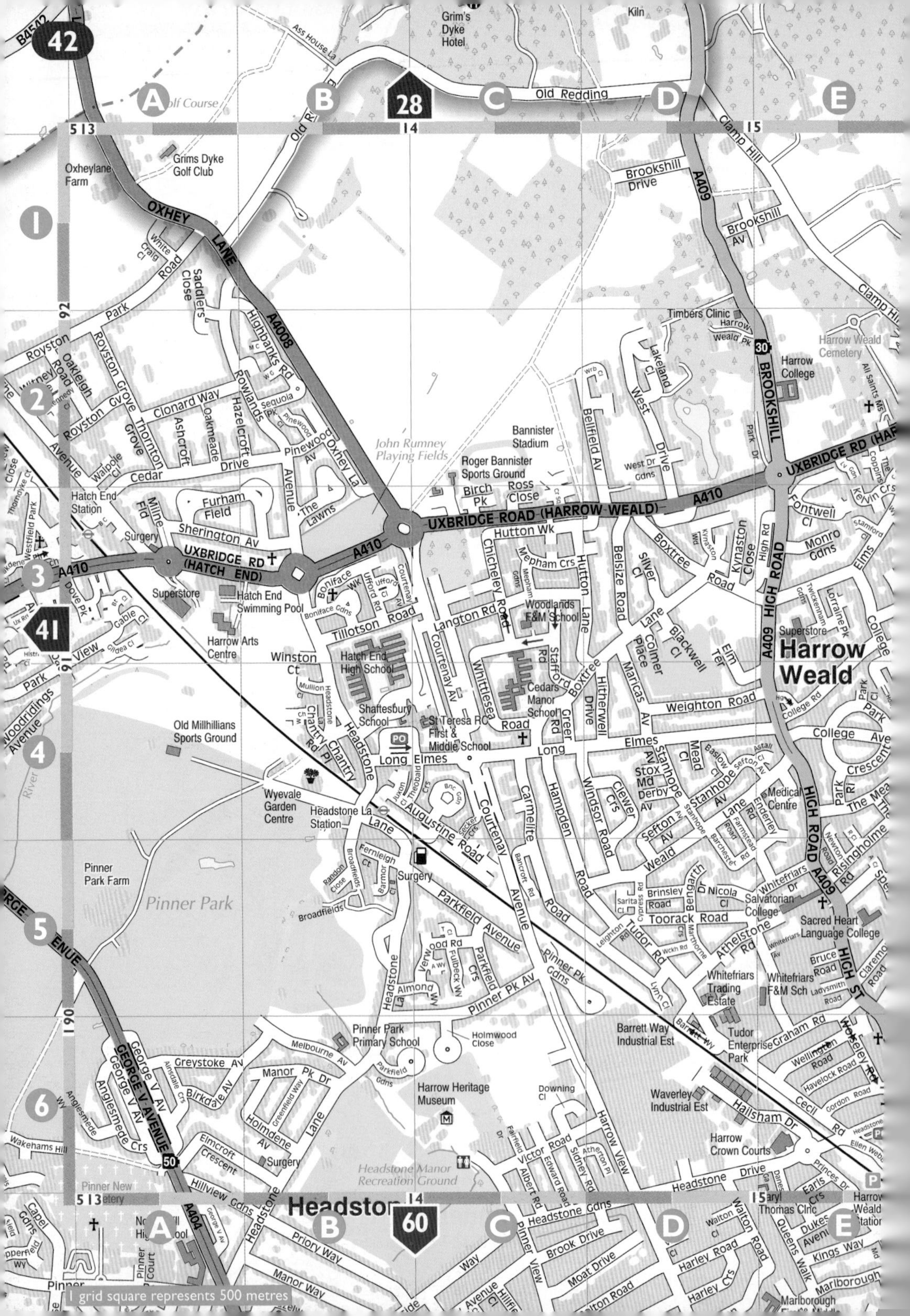
42
28
41
60
Grim's Dyke Hotel
Kiln
Golf Course
Old Redding
Ass House La
Clamp Hill
Grims Dyke Golf Club
Oxheylane Farm
Oxhey Lane
A4008
Brookshill Drive
Brookshill Av
A409
Timbers Clinic
Harrow Weald Pk
Brookshill
Harrow College
Harrow Weald Cemetery
All Saints Ms
Royston Park Road
Royston Gv
Royston Grove
Oakleigh Road
Thornton Grove
Clonard Way
Highbanks Rd
Rowlands
Hazelcroft Drive
Oakmeade
Ashcroft
Sequoia Pk
Pinewood Av
Walpole Cl
Cedar Drive
Avenue
Oxhey La
The Lawns
John Rumney Playing Fields
Bannister Stadium
Roger Bannister Sports Ground
Birch Pk
Ross Close
Lakeland Cl
West Drive
West Dr Gdns
Bellfield Av
Park Dr
Uxbridge Rd
Hatch End Station
Furham Field
Milne Fld
Sherington Av
Surgery
Uxbridge Rd (Hatch End)
A410
Uxbridge Road (Harrow Weald)
Superstore
Hatch End Swimming Pool
Harrow Arts Centre
Boniface Wk
Boniface Gdns
Ufford Rd
Courtenay Av
Tillotson Road
Hutton Wk
Mepham Crs
Chicheley Road
Langton Rd
Woodlands F&M School
Hutton Lane
Belsize Road
Silver Cl
Boxtree Road
Kynaston Close
High Rd
Fontwell Cl
Kevin Crs
Monro Gdns
Lorraine Pk
College
Twickenham Gdns
Harrow Weald
Superstore
Winston Ct
Hatch End High School
Mullion Cl
Headstone Dr
Whittlesea Road
Stafford Rd
Cedars Manor School
Boxtree Greer Rd
Hitherwell Drive
Maricas Av
Colmer Place
Blackwell Cl
Elm Ter
Weighton Road
College Rd
Park
College Ave
Shaftesbury School
St Teresa RC First & Middle School
Chantry Pl
Chantry Rd
Headstone
Long Elmes
Mead Cl
Stanhope Av
Stox Md
Derby Av
Baslow Cl
Sefton Av
Crescent
Old Millhillians Sports Ground
Wyevale Garden Centre
Headstone La Station
Lane
Augustine Road
Courtenay Avenue
Carmelite Road
Hampden Road
Windsor Road
Clewer Crs
Sefton Av
Weald Lane
Farmstead Road
Enderley
Medical Centre
The Meadow
Pinner Park Farm
Pinner Park
Fernleigh Ct
Randon Close
Broadfields
Barmor Cl
Surgery
Parkfield Avenue
Bancroft Rd
Sarita Cl
Brinsley Road
Bengarth Dr
Nicola Cl
Whitefriars Dr
Salvatorian College
Sacred Heart Language College
Risingholme Rd
Toorack Road
Tudor Rd
Athelstone Rd
Verwood Rd
Fulbeck Wy
Parkfield Crs
Almond Wy
Pinner Pk Av
Pinner Pk Gdns
Whitefriars Trading Estate
Whitefriars F&M Sch
Bruce Road
Ladysmith Road
High St
George V Avenue
George V Av
Greystoke Av
Birkdale Av
Manor Pk Dr
Melbourne Av
Pinner Park Primary School
Holmwood Close
Parkfield Gdns
Barrett Way Industrial Est
Tudor Enterprise Park
Graham Rd
Wellington Road
Havelock Road
Gordon Road
Anglesmede Crs
Holmdene Av
Lane
Harrow Heritage Museum
Downing Cl
Waverley Industrial Est
Hailsham Dr
Cecil Rd
Wakehams Hill
Elmcroft Crescent
Surgery
Headstone Manor Recreation Ground
Victor Road
Edward Road
Sidney Rd
Atherton Pl
Harrow View
Albert Rd
Harrow Crown Courts
Ellen Webb
Princes Dr
Hillview Gdns
Headstone Drive
Headstone Gdns
Pinner New Cemetery
Headstone
Priory Way
Manor Way
Pinner View
Brook Drive
Moat Drive
Walton Road
Walton Cl
Harley Road
Harley Crs
Queens Walk
Kings Way
Marlborough
Earls Crs
Dukes Avenue
Harrow Weald Station
Daryl Thomas Clnc
A404
1 grid square represents 500 metres

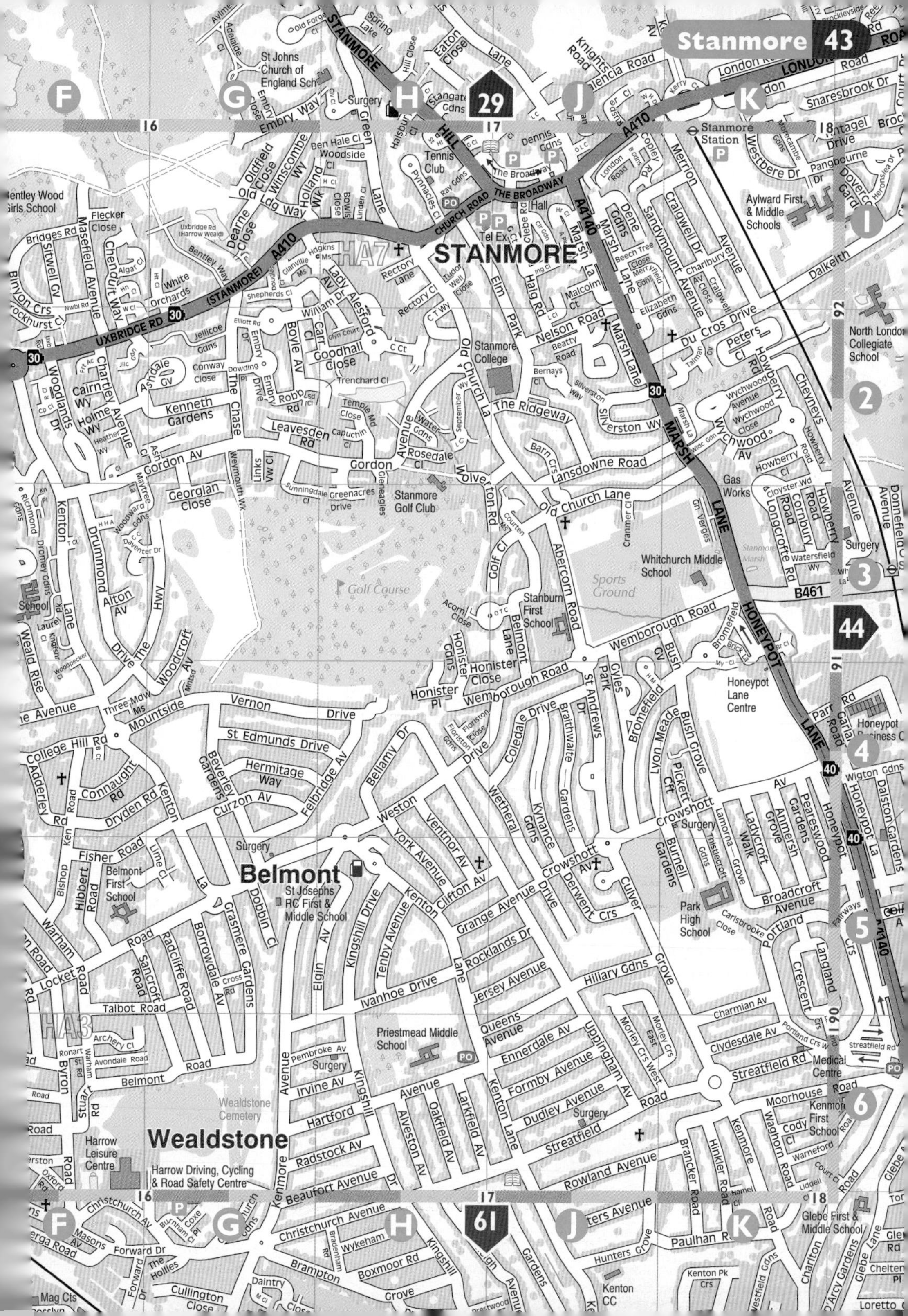
STANMORE
Belmont
Wealdstone
HA7
HA3
Stanmore Station
St Johns Church of England Sch
Surgery
Tennis Club
The Broadway
Church Road
Stanmore Hill
Uxbridge Rd
(Stanmore)
A410
A4140
B461
London Road
Marsh Lane
Honeypot Lane
Old Church La
Old Church Lane
Elm Park
Stanmore College
The Ridgeway
Silverston Wy
Lansdowne Road
Gas Works
Whitchurch Middle School
Sports Ground
Stanburn First School
Abercorn Road
Wemborough Road
Honeypot Lane Centre
Honeypot Business C
Stanmore Golf Club
Golf Course
Gordon Av
Georgian Close
Kenton Lane
Drummond Drive
Weald Rise
School
College Hill Rd
Mountside
Vernon Drive
St Edmunds Drive
Hermitage Way
Curzon Av
Kenton Rd
Belmont First School
St Josephs RC First & Middle School
Priestmead Middle School
Park High School
Wealdstone Cemetery
Harrow Leisure Centre
Harrow Driving, Cycling & Road Safety Centre
Kenmore Avenue
Kenton Lane
Streatfield Rd
Rowland Avenue
Kenmore Road
Kenmore First School
Medical Centre
Aylward First & Middle Schools
North London Collegiate School
Bentley Wood Girls School
Glebe First & Middle School
Kenton CC
Whitchurch Lane
Honister Close
Belmont Lane
Ivanhoe Drive
Talbot Road
Belmont Road
Christchurch Avenue
Beaufort Avenue
Uppingham Av
Hillary Gdns
Portland Crescent
Broadcroft Avenue
Dalkeith
29
43
44
61
30
40
16
17
18
91
92
F
G
H
J
K
1
2
3
4
5
6

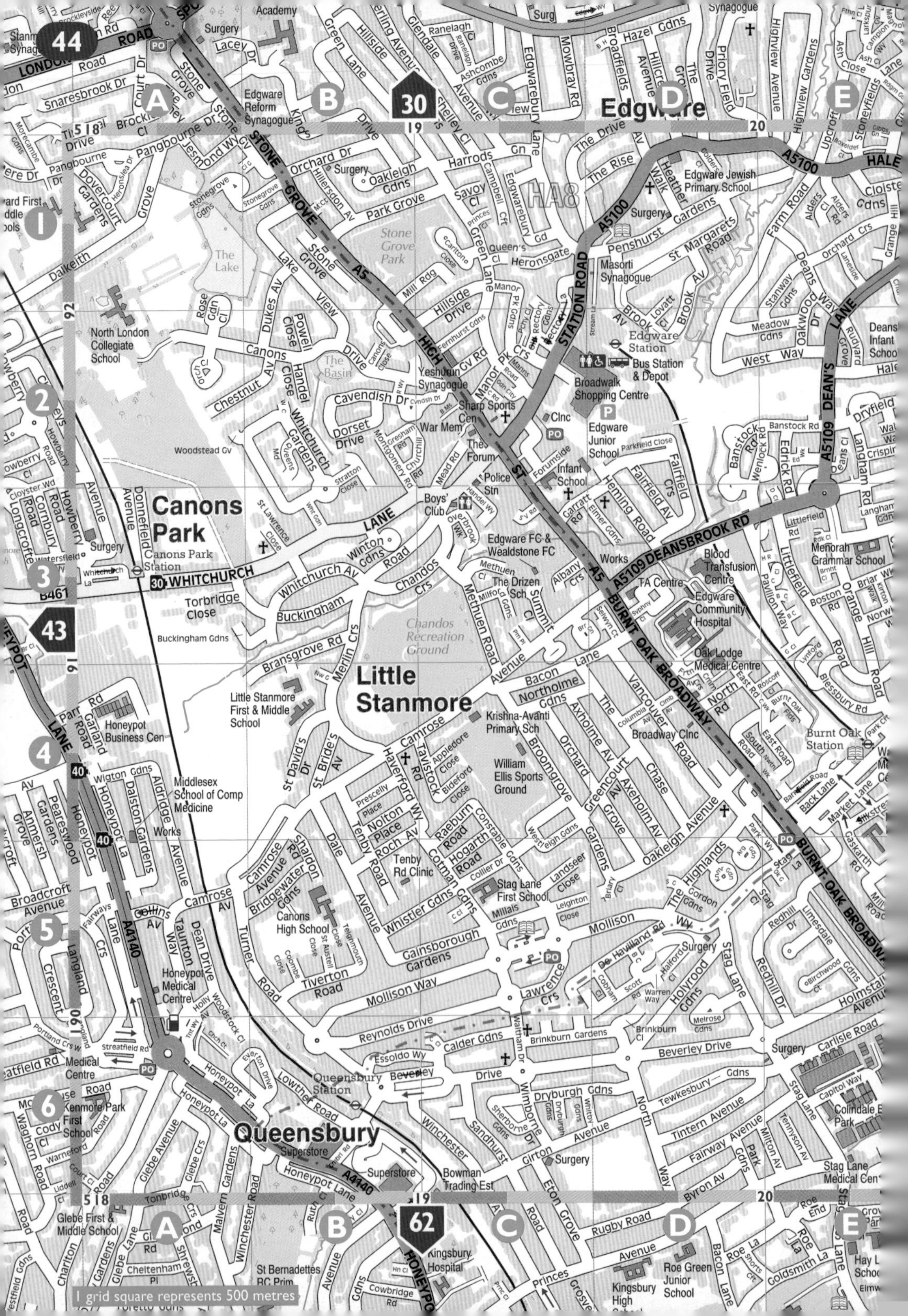
44
30
43
40
62
A
B
C
D
E
1
2
3
4
5
6
518
19
20
92
91
190
Edgware
Canons Park
Little Stanmore
Queensbury
HA8
LONDON ROAD
STONE GROVE
HIGH ST
A5
STATION ROAD
A5100
A5109 DEANSBROOK RD
BURNT OAK BROADWAY
DEAN'S LANE
A5109
WHITCHURCH LANE
B461
HONEYPOT LANE
A4140
HALE
Edgware Reform Synagogue
Academy
Surgery
Stone Grove Park
The Lake
North London Collegiate School
The Basin
Woodstead Gv
Yeshurun Synagogue
Sharp Sports Cen
War Mem
The Forum
Police Stn
Boys' Club
Edgware FC & Wealdstone FC
The Drizen Sch
Chandos Recreation Ground
Little Stanmore First & Middle School
Krishna-Avanti Primary Sch
William Ellis Sports Ground
Tenby Rd Clinic
Stag Lane First School
Canons High School
Honeypot Business Cen
Middlesex School of Comp Medicine
Works
Honeypot Medical Centre
Medical Centre
Kenmore Park First School
Glebe First & Middle School
Queensbury Station
Superstore
Bowman Trading Est
Kingsbury Hospital
St Bernadettes RC Prim
Kingsbury High
Roe Green Junior School
Stag Lane Medical Cen
Colindale Park
Surgery
Broadway Clnc
Oak Lodge Medical Centre
Edgware Community Hospital
TA Centre
Blood Transfusion Centre
Menorah Grammar School
Burnt Oak Station
Deans Infant School
Edgware Station
Bus Station & Depot
Broadwalk Shopping Centre
Edgware Junior School
Infant School
Clnc
PO
Masorti Synagogue
Edgware Jewish Primary School
Synagogue
Canons Park Station
Torbridge Close
Buckingham Gdns
Whitchurch Av
Canons Drive
Chestnut Av
Handel Close
Whitchurch Gardens
Cavendish Dr
Dorset Drive
Montgomery Rd
Merlin Crs
Bransgrove Rd
Camrose Avenue
Haverford Wy
Mollison Way
Reynolds Drive
Gainsborough Gardens
Tiverton Road
Turner Road
Dean Drive
Taunton Way
Beverley Drive
Tewkesbury Gdns
Tintern Avenue
Fairway Avenue
Byron Av
Rugby Road
Stag Lane
Holmstall Avenue
Redhill Dr
Carlisle Road
Capitol Way
Orange Hill Road
Blessbury Rd
Littlefield Rd
Pavilion Way
Heming Road
Fairfield Crs
Penshurst Gardens
St Margarets Road
Brook Av
Farm Road
Orchard Crs
Deans Way
Meadow Gdns
West Way
Rudyard Grove
Langham Rd
Heronsgate
Park Grove
Orchard Dr
Oakleigh Gdns
Hillside Drive
Manor Pk Crs
Glendale Avenue
Mowbray Rd
Hazel Gdns
Priory Field Drive
Highview Gardens
Highview Avenue
Snaresbrook Dr
Pangbourne Dr
Dalkeith Grove
Dovercourt Gardens
Howberry Road
Cornbury Road
Donnefield Avenue
Honeypot La
Pearseswood Gardens
Broadcroft Avenue
Langland Crescent
Glebe Avenue
Malvern Gardens
Winchester Road
Eton Grove
Princes Avenue
Wimborne Dr
Sandhurst Rd
Girton Avenue
Dryburgh Gdns
Brinkburn Gardens
Calder Gdns
Essoldo Wy
Lowther Road
Everton Drive
Whistler Gdns
Cotman Gdns
Hogarth Road
Raeburn Road
Constable Gdns
Broomgrove Gdns
Orchard Grove
Axholme Av
Greencourt Av
Vancouver Road
Oakleigh Avenue
The Highlands
Chase Road
Bacon Lane
Northolme Gdns
Methuen Road
Summit Cl
Albany Crs
Mill Rdg
Green Lane
Edgwarebury Lane
Harrods Gn
The Drive
The Rise
Heather Walk
Alders Rd
Grange Hill
Banstock Rd
Edrick Rd
Dryfield
Boston Rd
Briar Walk
Burnt Oak Flds
Back Lane
Market Lane
Gaskarth Rd
Limesdale Gdns
Birchwood Ct
Stag Cl
Holyrood Gdns
De Havilland Rd
Lawrence Crs
Mollison Wy
Halford Cl
Cobham Rd
Scott Rd
Warren Way
Melrose Gdns
Leighton Close
Landseer Close
Cordon Gdns
Milton Av
Tennyson Av
Roe End
Roe La
Goldsmith La
Bacon Lane
Hay L Schoo
Elmwa
Cheltenham Pl
Cowbridge Rd
Charlton Rd
Wagnorn Road
Tonbridge Crs
Glebe Crs
Streatfield Rd
Portland Crs
Woodstock Cl
Holly
Honeypot Lane
Collins Av
Fairways
Zachary
Chandos Crs
Buckingham Road
Winton Gdns
Overbrook Wk
Handel Wy
Stratton Close
St Lawrence Close
Churchill Rd
Mead Rd
Gresham Rd
Queens Md
Whitchurch La
Watersfield
Cloyster Wd
Longcroft
Rose Gdn Cl
Dukes Av
Powell Close
Lake View
Stonegrove Gdns
Jesmond Wy
Lacey Dr
Ranelagh Cl
Ashcombe Gdns
Kings Dr
Hillersdon Av
Savoy Cl
Campbell Cft
Princes Cl
Queen's Cl
Carlton Close
Manor Pk Gdns
Rectory La
Edgwarebury Gdns
Camrose Av
St David's Dr
St Bride's Av
Tenby Road
Dale Avenue
Prescelly Place
Nolton Place
Roch Av
Appledore Close
Bideford Close
Tavistock Rd
Bridgewater Gdns
Shaldon Rd
Canons Drive
1 grid square represents 500 metres

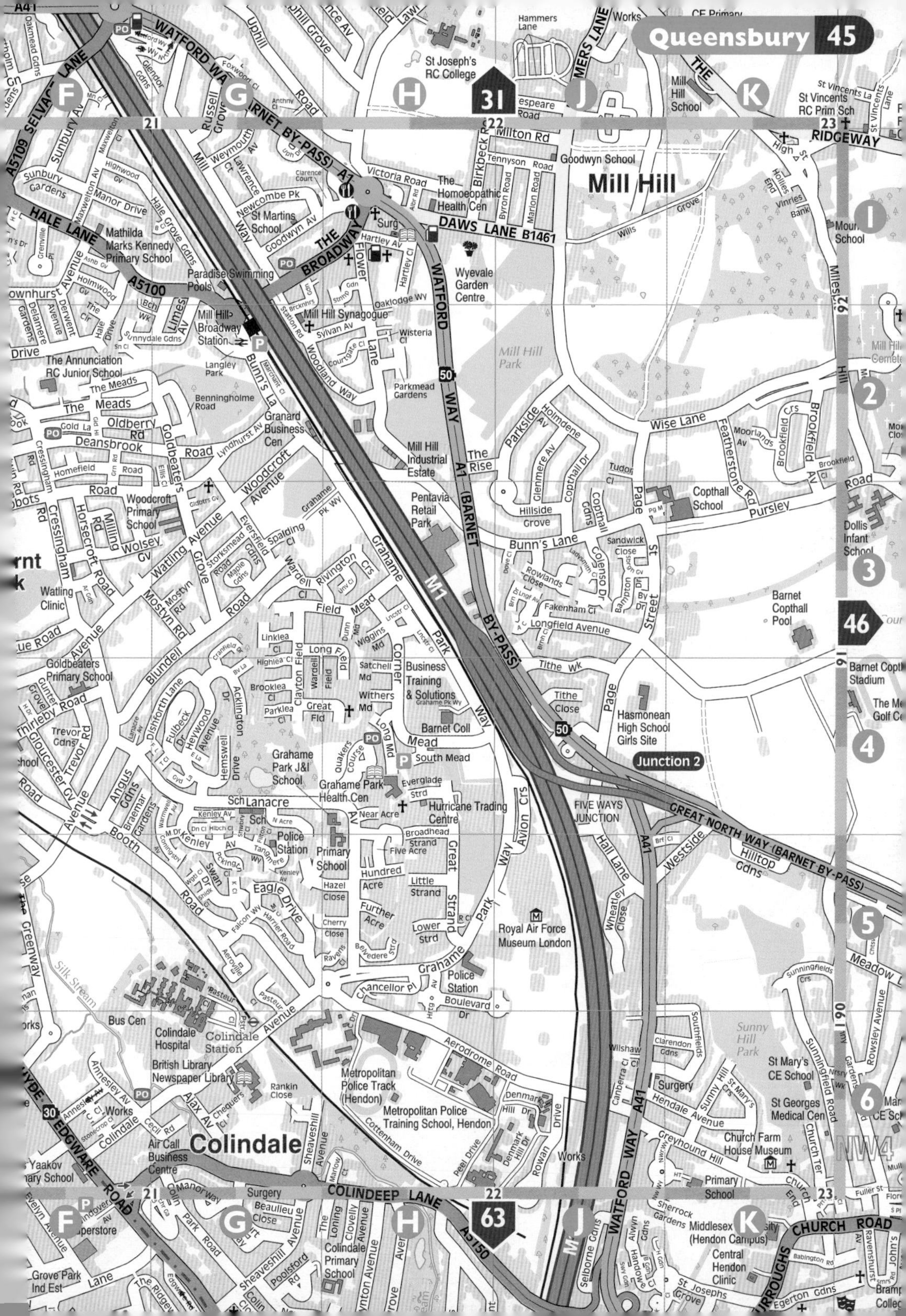
Mill Hill
Colindale
Watford Way
A1 (Barnet By-Pass)
M1
Watford Way Barnet By-Pass
A5109 Selvage Lane
Hale Lane
A5100
The Broadway
Daws Lane B1461
Victoria Road
Milton Rd
Tennyson Road
Birkbeck Rd
Byron Road
Marion Road
Goodwyn School
St Joseph's RC College
Hammers Lane
Mill Hill School
St Vincents RC Prim Sch
Ridgeway
High St
Hollies End
Vinries Bank
Wills Grove
Mount School
Milespit Hill
Mill Hill Cemetery
Wise Lane
Featherstone Rd
Brookfield Crs
Brookfield Av
Moorlands Av
Pursley Road
Copthall School
Dollis Infant School
Barnet Copthall Pool
Barnet Copthall Stadium
Tudor Cl
Page Street
Sandwick Close
Colenso Dr
Bampton Dr
Fakenham Cl
Longfield Avenue
Tithe Wk
Tithe Close
Hasmonean High School Girls Site
Junction 2
Five Ways Junction
Great North Way (Barnet By-Pass)
Hall Lane
Westside
Hilltop Gdns
Wheatley Close
Royal Air Force Museum London
Meadow
Sunningfields Crs
Sunningfield Road
Rowsley Avenue
Sunny Hill Park
St Mary's CE School
St Georges Medical Cen
Church Farm House Museum
Church Ter
Church End
Church Road
Greyhound Hill
Hendale Avenue
Sunny Hill
Primary School
Middlesex University (Hendon Campus)
Central Hendon Clinic
Sherrock Gardens
Selborne Gdns
Alwyn Gdns
St Josephs Grove
Egerton Gdns
Babington Rd
Ravenshurst Av
Burroughs
Mill Hill Park
Parkside Av
Holmdene Av
Glenmere Av
Copthall Dr
Copthall Gdns
Hillside Grove
Bunn's Lane
Rowlands Close
The Rise
Wyevale Garden Centre
The Homoeopathic Health Cen
Hartley Av
Hartley Cl
Flower Lane
Oaklodge Wy
Mill Hill Synagogue
Sylvan Av
Wisteria Cl
Courtgate Cl
Woodland Way
Parkmead Gardens
Mill Hill Industrial Estate
Pentavia Retail Park
Mill Hill Broadway Station
Paradise Swimming Pools
Langley Park
Benningholme Road
Granard Business Cen
Lyndhurst Av
Goldbeaters Road
Woodcroft Avenue
Woodcroft Primary School
Mathilda Marks Kennedy Primary School
St Martins School
Goodwyn Av
Newcombe Pk
Lawrence Ct
Weymouth Av
Russell Grove
Mill Way
Sunbury Av
Sunbury Gardens
Manor Drive
Highwood Gv
Maxwelton Av
Hale Grove Gdns
Holmwood Gv
Derwent Av
Deansbrook Rd
Oldberry Rd
The Meads
The Annunciation RC Junior School
Homefield Road
Cressingham Rd
Horsecroft Road
Milling Rd
Wolsey Gv
Watling Avenue
Watling Clinic
Grove Road
Storksmead Road
Eversfield Gdns
Spalding Cl
Grahame Pk Wy
Wardell Cl
Rivington Crs
Field Mead
Mostyn Rd
Goldbeaters Primary School
Thirleby Road
Gloucester Gv
Trevor Rd
Trevor Gdns
Blundell Road
Disforth Lane
Fulbeck Dr
Heywood Avenue
Acklington Dr
Hemswell Drive
Linklea Cl
Highlea Cl
Brooklea Cl
Parklea Cl
Clayton Field
Wardell Field
Long Field
Great Fld
Satchell Md
Withers Md
Corner Mead
Long Md
Business Training & Solutions
Barnet Coll
South Mead
Grahame Park J&I School
Grahame Park Health Cen
Everglade Strd
Hurricane Trading Centre
Near Acre
Lanacre Av
Kenley Av
Police Station
Primary School
Five Acre
Broadhead Strand
Hundred Acre
Little Strand
Great Strand
Hazel Close
Cherry Close
Further Acre
Lower Strd
Belvedere Strd
Ravens
Avion Crs
Grahame Park Way
Chancellor Pl
Boulevard Dr
Booth Road
Angus Gdns
Braemar Gardens
Eagle Drive
Swan Dr
Falcon Wy
Harrier Road
Aerodrome Road
Metropolitan Police Track (Hendon)
Metropolitan Police Training School, Hendon
Cottenham Drive
Peel Drive
Denmark Hill Dr
Rowan Drive
Works
Pasteur Cl
Colindale Hospital
Colindale Station
Colindale Avenue
Bus Cen
British Library Newspaper Library
Rankin Close
Annesley Av
Colindale Av
Cecil Rd
Ajax Av
Chequers Cl
Air Call Business Centre
Silk Stream
The Greenway
Edgware Road
Colindeep Lane
Sheaveshill Avenue
Sheaveshill Av
Beaulieu Close
Colin Park Road
Manor Way
Surgery
Colindale Primary School
Clovelly Avenue
Poolsford Rd
Grove Park Ind Est
Evelyn Avenue
Superstore
Clarendon Gdns
Southfields
Wilshaw Cl
Canberra Cl
A41
A5150
Surg
Milespit Hill
NW4

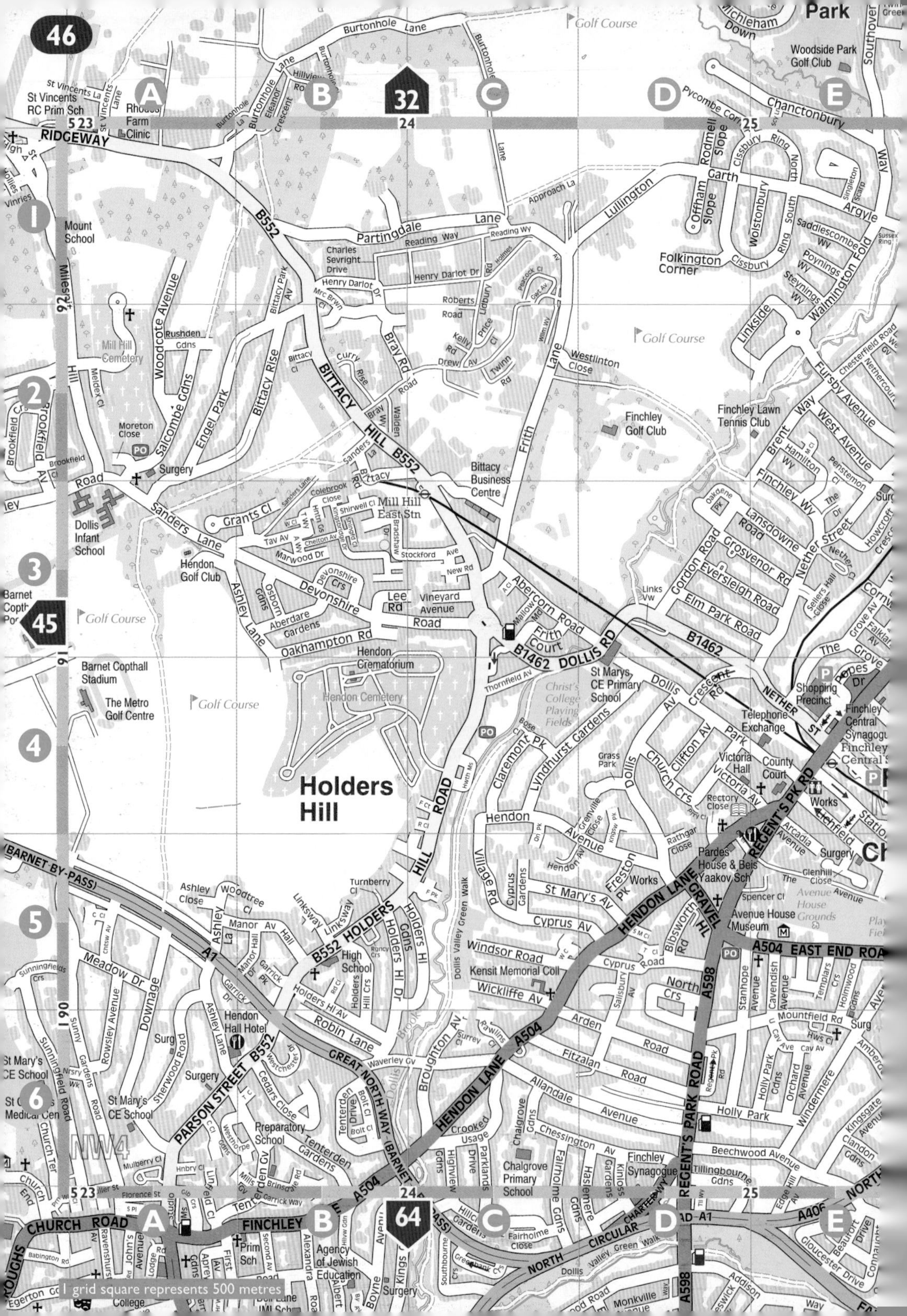

Golf Course
Park
Woodside Park Golf Club
Burtonhole Lane
RIDGEWAY
Mount School
Mill Hill Cemetery
Partingdale Lane
Lullington Garth
Folkington Corner
Golf Course
Finchley Golf Club
Finchley Lawn Tennis Club
BITTACY HILL B552
Mill Hill East Stn
Bittacy Business Centre
Dollis Infant School
Hendon Golf Club
Golf Course
Barnet Copthall Stadium
The Metro Golf Centre
Golf Course
Hendon Crematorium
Hendon Cemetery
Holders Hill
B1462 DOLLIS RD
St Marys CE Primary School
Christ's College Playing Fields
Shopping Precinct
Telephone Exchange
Finchley Central Synagogue
Victoria Hall
County Court
Pardes House & Beis Yaakov Sch
Avenue House Museum
A504 EAST END ROAD
BARNET BY-PASS
GREAT NORTH WAY
A1
Hendon Hall Hotel
High School
Kensit Memorial Coll
Preparatory School
Chalgrove Primary School
Finchley Synagogue
REGENT'S PARK ROAD
NORTH CIRCULAR
CHURCH ROAD
FINCHLEY
Agency of Jewish Education
NW4
1 grid square represents 500 metres

32
45
64

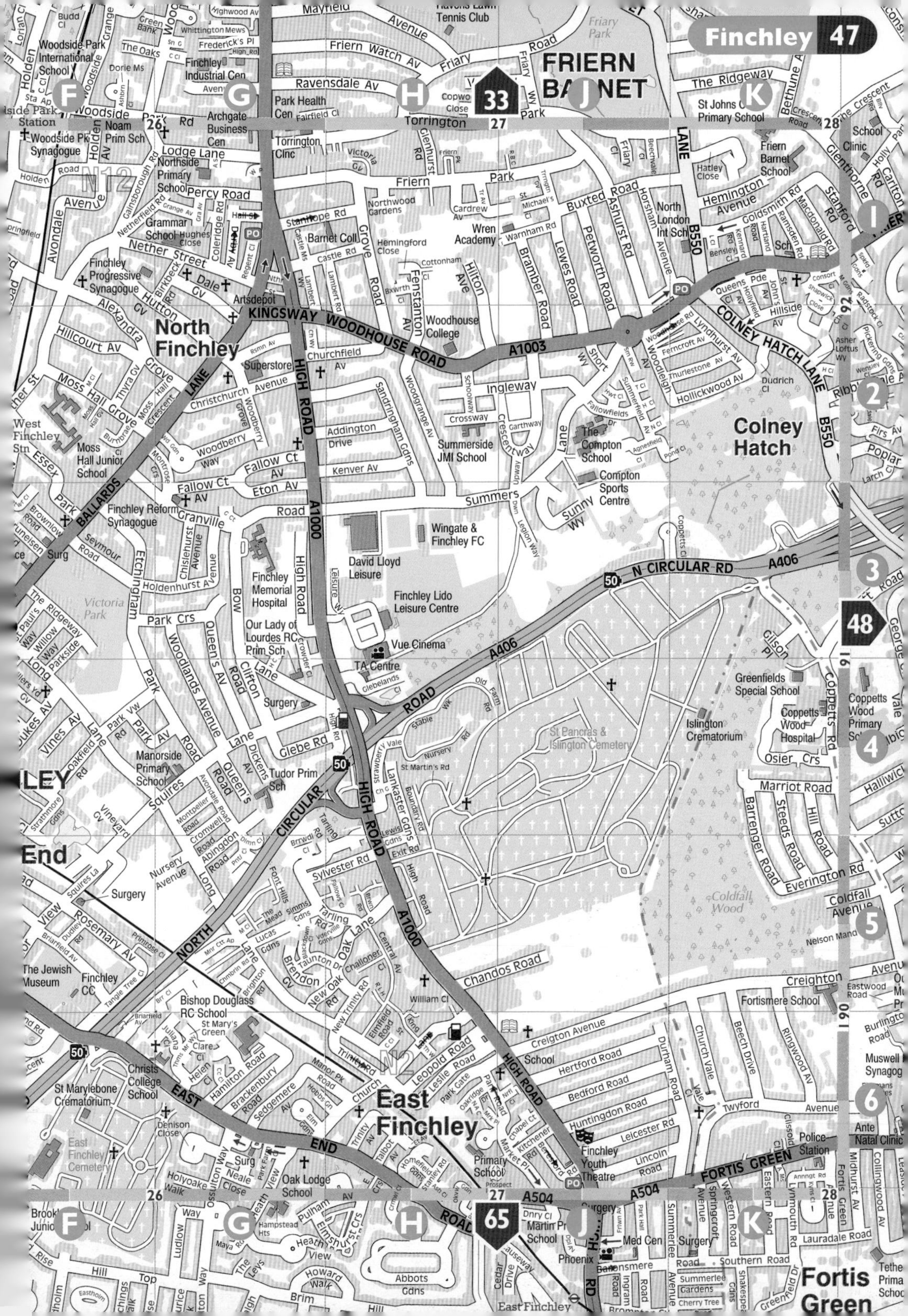

FRIERN BARNET
North Finchley
Colney Hatch
East Finchley
Fortis Green
Woodside Park International School
Woodside Park Station
Woodside Pk Synagogue
Noam Prim Sch
Archgate Business Cen
Finchley Industrial Cen
Park Health Cen
Torrington Clinc
Havens Lawn Tennis Club
Friary Park
St Johns C of E Primary School
Friern Barnet School
School
Clinic
Northside Primary School
Grammar School
Barnet Coll
Wren Academy
North London Int Sch
Finchley Progressive Synagogue
Artsdepot
Superstore
Woodhouse College
KINGSWAY
WOODHOUSE ROAD
A1003
COLNEY HATCH LANE
B550
HIGH ROAD
A1000
BALLARDS LANE
West Finchley Stn
Moss Hall Junior School
Summerside JMI School
The Compton School
Compton Sports Centre
Finchley Reform Synagogue
Wingate & Finchley FC
David Lloyd Leisure
Finchley Memorial Hospital
Finchley Lido Leisure Centre
Victoria Park
Our Lady of Lourdes RC Prim Sch
Vue Cinema
TA Centre
N CIRCULAR RD
A406
NORTH CIRCULAR
Surgery
Manorside Primary School
Tudor Prim Sch
St Pancras & Islington Cemetery
Islington Crematorium
Greenfields Special School
Coppetts Wood Hospital
Coppetts Wood Primary School
Coldfall Wood
The Jewish Museum
Finchley CC
Bishop Douglass RC School
St Mary's Green
Christs College School
St Marylebone Crematorium
East Finchley Cemetery
EAST END ROAD
Oak Lodge School
Primary School
Finchley Youth Theatre
FORTIS GREEN
A504
Police Station
Ante Natal Clinic
Fortismere School
Muswell Synagog
Martin Pr School
Med Cen
Phoenix
East Finchley
Hampstead Hts
Brookl Junio
Chandos Road
Summers Road
Friern Park
Creighton Avenue
Church Lane
N12
N2
33
48
65
26
27
28
F
G
H
J
K
1
2
3
4
5
6

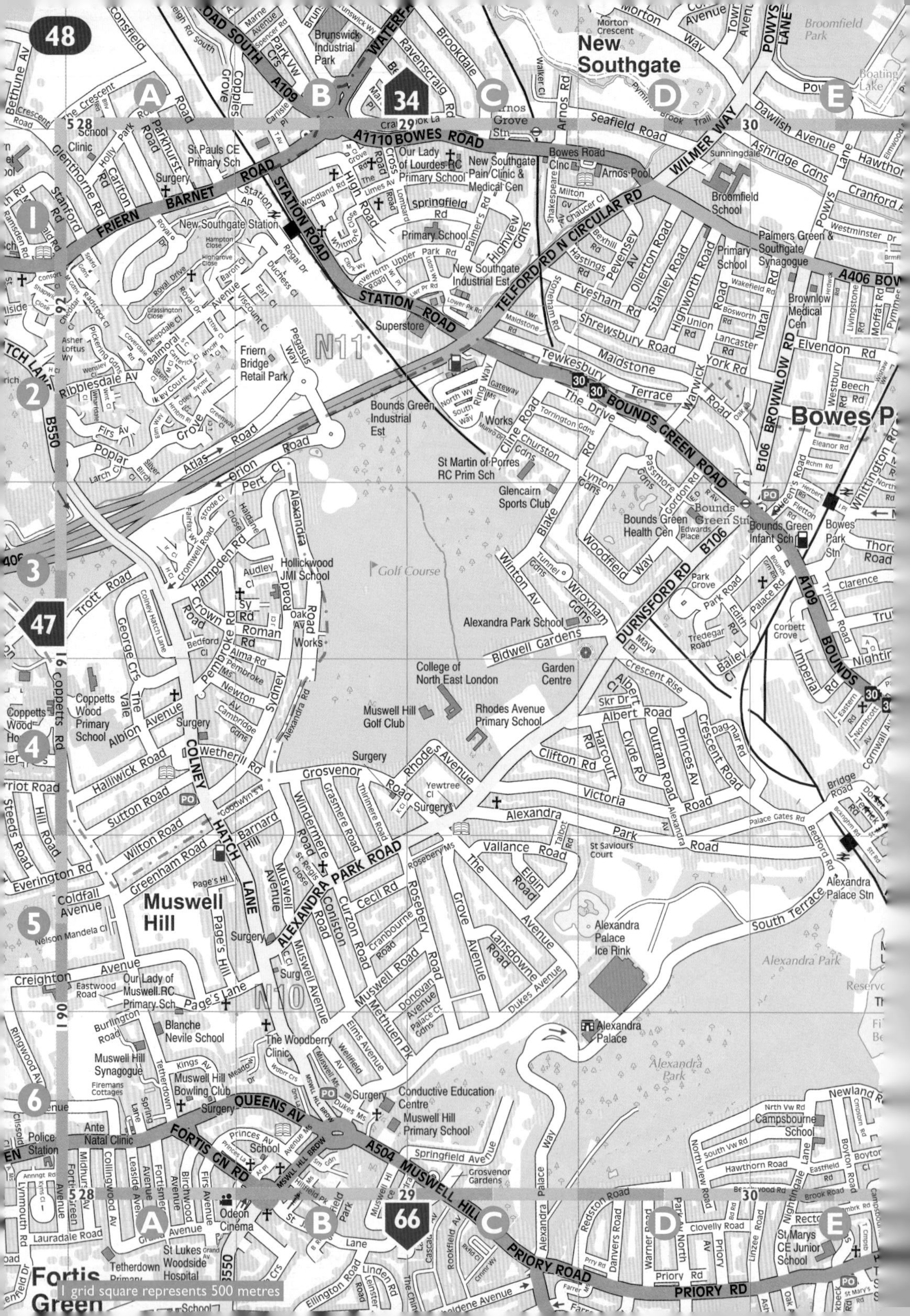
34
47
66
A
B
C
D
E
1
2
3
4
5
6
28
29
30
92
91
90
New Southgate
Bowes Park
Muswell Hill
Fortis Green
N11
N10
A1110 BOWES ROAD
FRIERN BARNET ROAD
STATION ROAD
TELFORD RD N CIRCULAR RD
WILMER WAY
BOUNDS GREEN ROAD
A406 BOWES
BROWNLOW RD
B106
B550
A109
A504 MUSWELL HILL
COLNEY HATCH LANE
ALEXANDRA PARK ROAD
QUEENS AV
FORTIS GN RD
PRIORY ROAD
PRIORY RD
DURNSFORD RD
COPPETTS Rd
Brunswick Industrial Park
St Pauls CE Primary Sch
Our Lady of Lourdes RC Primary School
New Southgate Pain Clinic & Medical Cen
Arnos Grove Stn
Arnos Pool
Broomfield School
Broomfield Park
Boating Lake
New Southgate Station
Springfield Rd Primary School
New Southgate Industrial Est
Superstore
Friern Bridge Retail Park
Bounds Green Industrial Est
Works
St Martin of Porres RC Prim Sch
Glencairn Sports Club
Primary School
Palmers Green & Southgate Synagogue
Brownlow Medical Cen
Bounds Green Health Cen
Bounds Green Stn
Bounds Green Infant Sch
Bowes Park Stn
Golf Course
Hollickwood JMI School
Alexandra Park School
College of North East London
Garden Centre
Muswell Hill Golf Club
Rhodes Avenue Primary School
Coppetts Wood Primary School
Surgery
St Saviours Court
Alexandra Palace Stn
Alexandra Palace Ice Rink
Alexandra Park
Alexandra Palace
Our Lady of Muswell RC Primary Sch
Blanche Nevile School
The Woodberry Clinic
Muswell Hill Synagogue
Muswell Hill Bowling Club
Firemans Cottages
Conductive Education Centre
Muswell Hill Primary School
Ante Natal Clinic
Police Station
Odeon Cinema
St Lukes Woodside Hospital
Campsbourne School
St Marys CE Junior School
Grosvenor Gardens
Seafield Road
Dawlish Avenue
Ashridge Gdns
Cranford
Westminster Dr
Powys Lane
Evesham Rd
Shrewsbury Road
Maidstone
Tewkesbury Terrace
The Drive
Pevensey Av
Ollerton Road
Stanley Road
Highworth Road
Warwick Road
York Rd
Natal Rd
Elvendon Rd
Beech
Whittington Rd
Woodfield Way
Lynton Gdns
Blake
Winton Av
Wroxham Gdns
Bidwell Gardens
Crescent Rise
Albert Road
Clifton Rd
Victoria
Alexandra Park Road
Vallance Road
Palace Gates Rd
Bedford Rd
South Terrace
Alexandra Rd
Grosvenor Road
Rhodes Avenue
Windermere Road
Coniston Road
Curzon Road
Cecil Rd
Rosebery Road
Grove Avenue
Lansdowne Road
Dukes Avenue
Muswell Road
Muswell Avenue
Methuen Pk
Donovan Avenue
Elms Avenue
Springfield Avenue
Alexandra Palace Way
Redston Road
Danvers Road
North View Road
Hawthorn Road
Newland Rd
Clovelly Road
Halliwick Road
Sutton Road
Wilton Road
Greenham Road
Everington Rd
Coldfall Avenue
Creighton Avenue
Page's Lane
Page's Hill
Barnard Hill
Wetherill Rd
Albion Avenue
George Crs
Trott Road
Hampden Rd
Crown Road
Roman Rd
Pembroke Rd
Sydney Road
Alexandra Road
Orion Road
Atlas Road
Poplar Grove
Ribblesdale Av
Balmoral
Royal Drive
Pegasus Way
Stanford Rd
Glenthorne Rd
Carlton Rd
Parkhurst Road
Ringwood Av
Steeds Road
Hill Road
Lauradale Road
Lynmouth Rd
Tetherdown
Grand Avenue
Linden Rd
Ellington Road
Queens Avenue
1 grid square represents 500 metres

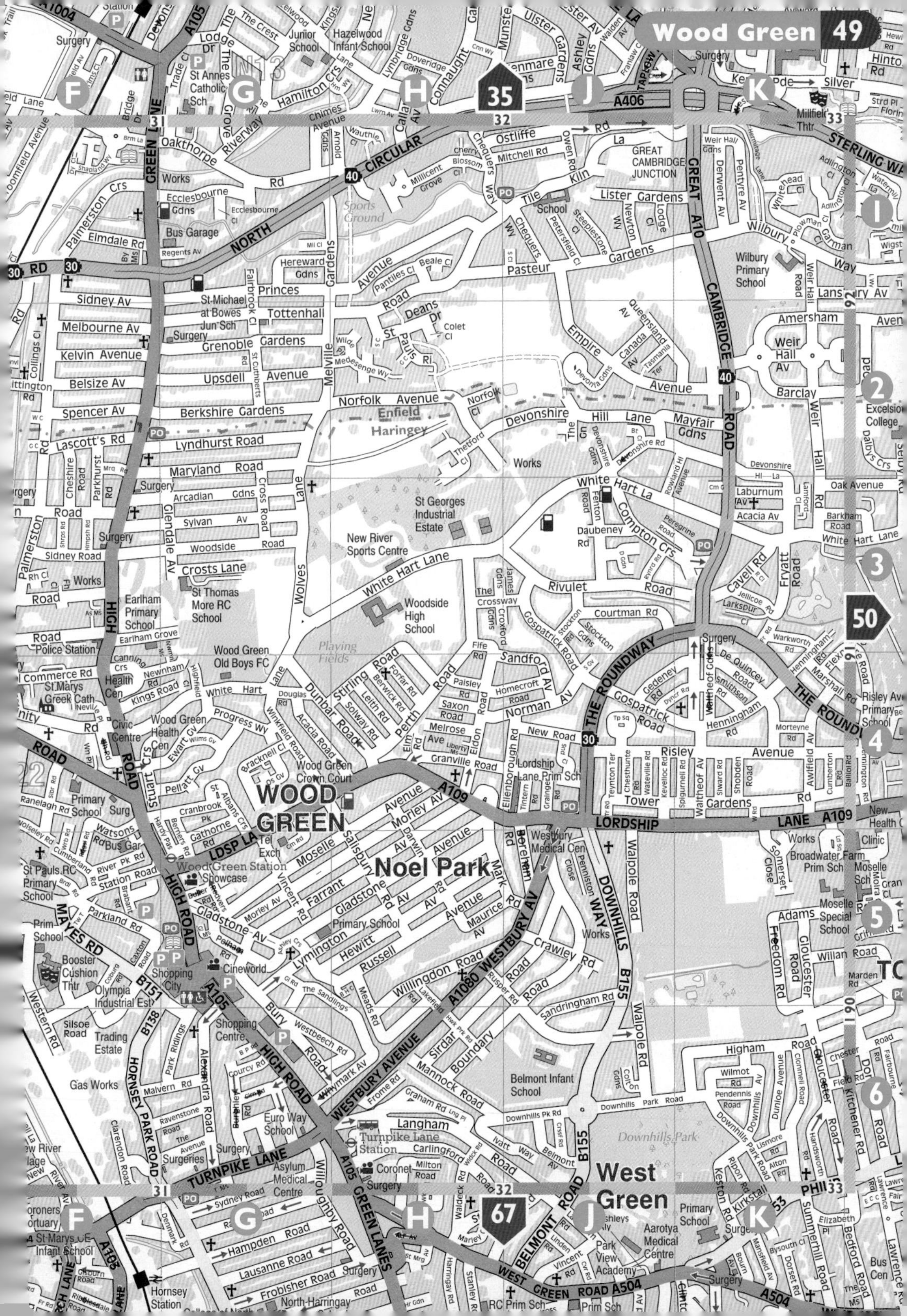
WOOD GREEN
Noel Park
West Green
NORTH CIRCULAR RD
GREAT CAMBRIDGE JUNCTION
CAMBRIDGE ROAD
GREAT A10
THE ROUNDWAY
LORDSHIP LANE A109
WESTBURY AVENUE A1080
HIGH ROAD
GREEN LANES
TURNPIKE LANE
WEST GREEN ROAD A504
HORNSEY PARK ROAD
MAYES RD
DOWNHILLS WAY
BELMONT ROAD
White Hart Lane
Devonshire Hill Lane
Enfield
Haringey
St Georges Industrial Estate
New River Sports Centre
Woodside High School
Playing Fields
Sports Ground
Wood Green Old Boys FC
Wood Green Crown Court
Wood Green Station
Turnpike Lane Station
Hornsey Station
Shopping City
Cineworld
Coronet
Asylum Medical Centre
Westbury Medical Cen
Downhills Park
Belmont Infant School
Park View Academy
Aarotya Medical Centre
Wilbury Primary School
Weir Hall Av
Excelsior College
Broadwater Farm Prim Sch
Moselle Special School
St Thomas More RC School
Earlham Primary School
St Michael at Bowes Jun Sch
St Annes Catholic Sch
Hazelwood Infant School
Junior School
Lordship Lane Prim Sch
Bus Garage
Police Station
Civic Centre
Booster Cushion Thtr
Olympia Industrial Est
Trading Estate
Gas Works
Euro Way School
Primary School
Millfield Thtr
Bus Cen
Tel Exch
STERLING WAY
F G H J K
1 2 3 4 5 6
35 50 67

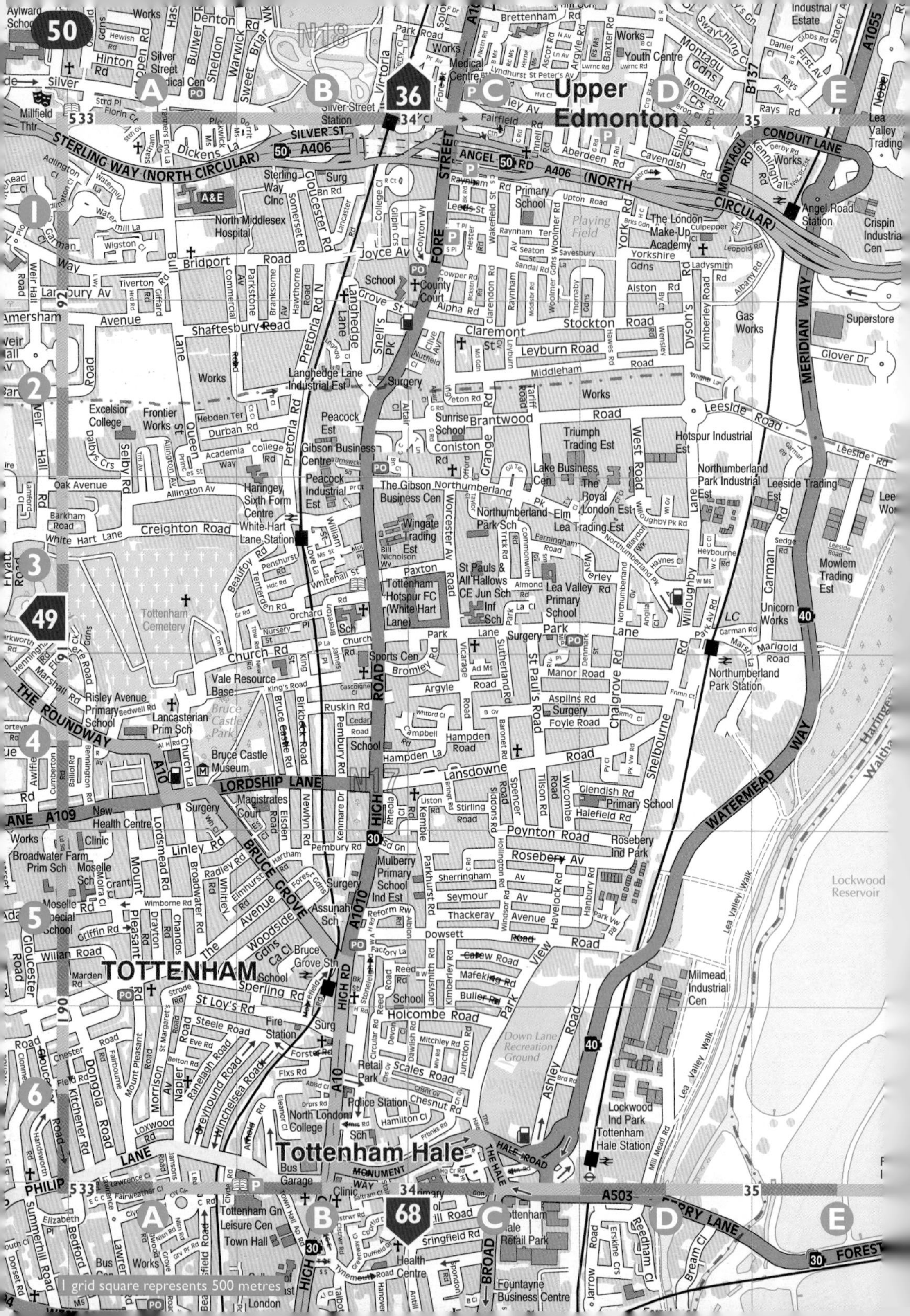
50
36
49
68
Upper Edmonton
TOTTENHAM
Tottenham Hale
N18
N17
STERLING WAY (NORTH CIRCULAR)
A406 (NORTH CIRCULAR)
SILVER ST
ANGEL RD
FORE STREET
HIGH ROAD
HIGH RD
A1010
A10
LORDSHIP LANE
A109
THE ROUNDWAY
BRUCE GROVE
MERIDIAN WAY
WATERMEAD WAY
CONDUIT LANE
MONTAGU RD
B137
A1055
A503
FERRY LANE
HALE ROAD
THE HALE
MONUMENT WAY
BROAD LANE
PHILIP LANE
Silver Street Station
White Hart Lane Station
Bruce Grove Stn
Northumberland Park Station
Tottenham Hale Station
Angel Road Station
North Middlesex Hospital
Tottenham Cemetery
Tottenham Hotspur FC (White Hart Lane)
Bruce Castle Park
Bruce Castle Museum
Haringey Sixth Form Centre
Lea Valley Primary School
Down Lane Recreation Ground
Lockwood Reservoir
Lea Valley Walk
Millfield Thtr
Police Station
North London College
Town Hall
Tottenham Gn Leisure Cen
Gas Works
Superstore
Playing Field
Lockwood Ind Park
Milmead Industrial Cen
Rosebery Ind Park
Tottenham Hale Retail Park
Fountayne Business Centre
Northumberland Park Industrial Est
Leeside Trading Est
Mowlem Trading Est
Hotspur Industrial Est
Triumph Trading Est
Lake Business Cen
Lea Trading Est
The Royal London Est
Langhedge Lane Industrial Est
Gibson Business Centre
Peacock Industrial Est
Wingate Trading Est
Lea Valley Trading
Crispin Industrial Cen
1 grid square represents 500 metres

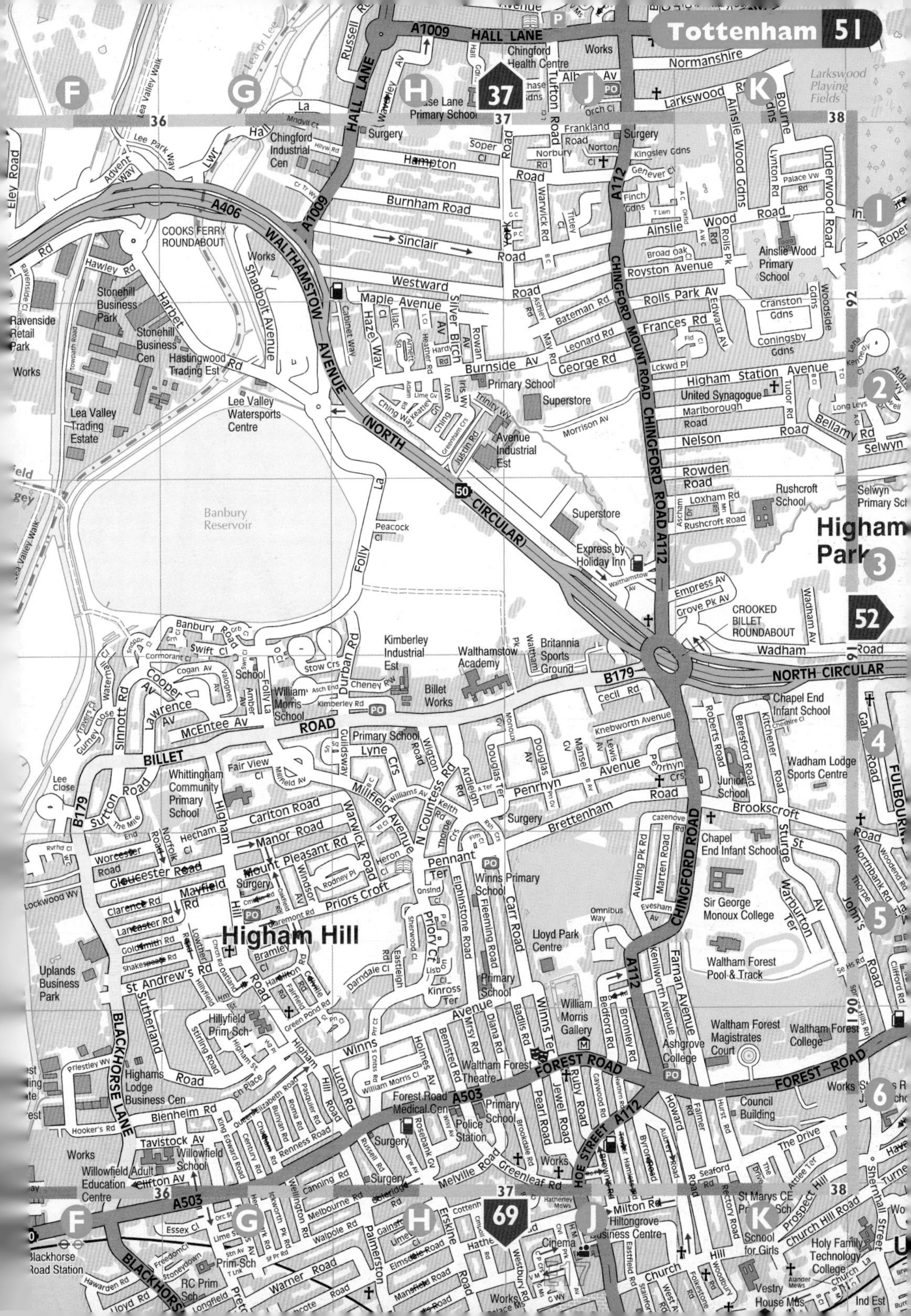
HALL LANE
A1009
Chingford Health Centre
Works
Normanshire
Larkswood Playing Fields
Albert Av
Chase Lane Primary School
37
Larkswood Rd
Bourne Gdns
36
38
Chingford Industrial Cen
Surgery
Frankland Road
Norbury Rd
Kingsley Gdns
Lee Park Way
Advent Way
Hampton Road
Soper Cl
Genever Cl
Ainslie Wood Gdns
Lynton Rd
Palace Vw Rd
Underwood Road
A406
Burnham Road
Finch Gdns
COOKS FERRY ROUNDABOUT
WALTHAMSTOW AVENUE
Sinclair Road
Warwick Rd
Titley Cl
A112
Ainslie Wood Road
Roper
Hawley Rd
Works
Shadbolt Avenue
Broad Oak Cl
Ainslie Wood Primary School
Royston Avenue
Westward Road
CHINGFORD MOUNT ROAD
Rolls Park Av
Cranston Gdns
Woodside Gdns
Stonehill Business Park
Harbet Rd
Maple Avenue
Hazel Way
Lilac Sq
Silver Birch Av
Bateman Rd
Edward Av
Ravenside Retail Park
Stonehill Business Cen
Rowan Av
Frances Rd
Coningsby Gdns
Hastingwood Trading Est
Leonard Rd
Lena Kennedy Cl
Works
Burnside Av
George Rd
Lckwd Pl
Higham Station Avenue
Primary School
United Synagogue
Tudor Rd
Lea Valley Trading Estate
Lee Valley Watersports Centre
Superstore
Marlborough Road
Long Leys
Bellamy Rd
Selwyn
Morrison Av
Nelson Road
(NORTH CIRCULAR)
Avenue Industrial Est
Justin Rd
Rowden Road
Rushcroft School
Selwyn Primary Sch
50
Banbury Reservoir
Peacock Cl
Folly La
Superstore
Loxham Rd
Rushcroft Road
Higham Park
Express by Holiday Inn
CHINGFORD ROAD A112
Empress Av
Grove Pk Av
CROOKED BILLET ROUNDABOUT
Wadham Av
52
Banbury Road
Kimberley Industrial Est
Britannia Sports Ground
Wadham Road
Swift Cl
Cormorant Cl
Stow Crs
Walthamstow Academy
NORTH CIRCULAR
Cogan Av
Cooper Av
School
Durban Rd
Cheney Rw
B179
Cecil Rd
Chapel End Infant School
William Morris School
Billet Works
Kimberley Rd
Lawrence Av
McEntee Av
ROAD
Knebworth Avenue
Roberts Road
Beresford Road
Kitchener Road
Galna Road
Primary School
Lyne Crs
BILLET
Fair View Cl
Whittingham Community Primary School
Millfield Avenue
Douglas Av
Mansel Gv
Lewis Av
Penrhyn Avenue
Wadham Lodge Sports Centre
FULBOURNE
Lee Close
Sutton Road
Higham Road
Wigton Road
Ardleigh Rd
Penrhyn Rd
Penrhyn Crs
Junior School
B179
Carlton Road
Keith Rd
N Countess Rd
Surgery
Brettenham Road
Brookscroft Road
Hecham Cl
Manor Road
Thorpe Crs
Chapel End Infant School
Sturge Av
Worcester Road
Mount Pleasant Rd
Warwick Road
Pennant Ter
Aveling Pk Rd
Marten Road
Northbank Rd
Gloucester Road
Rodney Pl
Heron Cl
Winns Primary School
Carr Road
Sir George Monoux College
Mayfield Rd
Surgery
Windsor Rd
Priors Croft
CHINGFORD ROAD
Lockwood Wy
Clarence Rd
Lancaster Rd
Priory Ct
Elphinstone Road
Fleeming Road
Omnibus Way
Evesham Av
Warburton Ter
John's Road
Higham Hill
Lloyd Park Centre
Goldsmith Rd
Shakespeare Rd
Bramley Cl
Darndale Cl
Eastleigh Rd
Kenilworth Avenue
Farnan Avenue
Waltham Forest Pool & Track
Uplands Business Park
St Andrew's Rd
Sutherland Road
Kinross Ter
Primary School
William Morris Gallery
Bedford Rd
Bromley Rd
Clifford Rd
BLACKHORSE LANE
Hillyfield Prim Sch
Higham St
Stirling Road
Green Pond Rd
Winns Avenue
Holmes Av
Diana Rd
Winns Ter
Waltham Forest Magistrates Court
Waltham Forest College
Priestley Wy
Highams Lodge Business Cen
Ch Place
Road
Hill Rd
Luton Rd
Bemsted Rd
Waltham Forest Theatre
Ashgrove College
FOREST ROAD
Blenheim Rd
William Morris Cl
A503
Forest Road Medical Cen
Primary School
Pearl Road
Jewel Road
Ruby Road
Gaywood Rd
Howard Road
Palmer Rd
Hurst Rd
Council Building
Works
Hooker's Rd
Queen Elizabeth Road
Bunyan Rd
Roma Rd
Pasquier Rd
Renness Road
Police Station
Surgery
Rosebank Gv
HOE STREET A112
Byron Road
Seaford Road
The Drive
Works
Tavistock Av
Willowfield School
Century Rd
King Edward Road
Russell Rd
Brookdale Rd
Works
Melville Road
Greenleaf Rd
Surgery
Canning Rd
Prospect Hill
Sherrall Street
Willowfield Adult Education Centre
Clifton Av
Wellington Rd
Melbourne Rd
Coleridge Rd
Hatherley Mews
Milton Rd
Rectory Road
St Marys CE Prim Sch
Church Hill Road
Essex Cl
Walpole Rd
Palmerston
Erskine Road
69
Hiltongrove Business Centre
Eastfield Rd
School for Girls
Holy Family Technology College
Blackhorse Road Station
Stonydown
Prim Sch
Warner Road
Elmsdale Road
Westbury Rd
Cinema
Church Hill
Woodbury Rd
Folkestone Rd
Hawarden Rd
BLACKHORSE
RC Prim Sch
Longfield
Lloyd Rd
Mansfield Road
Works
Vestry House Mus
Ind Est
F
G
H
J
K
I
2
3
4
5
6
91
92

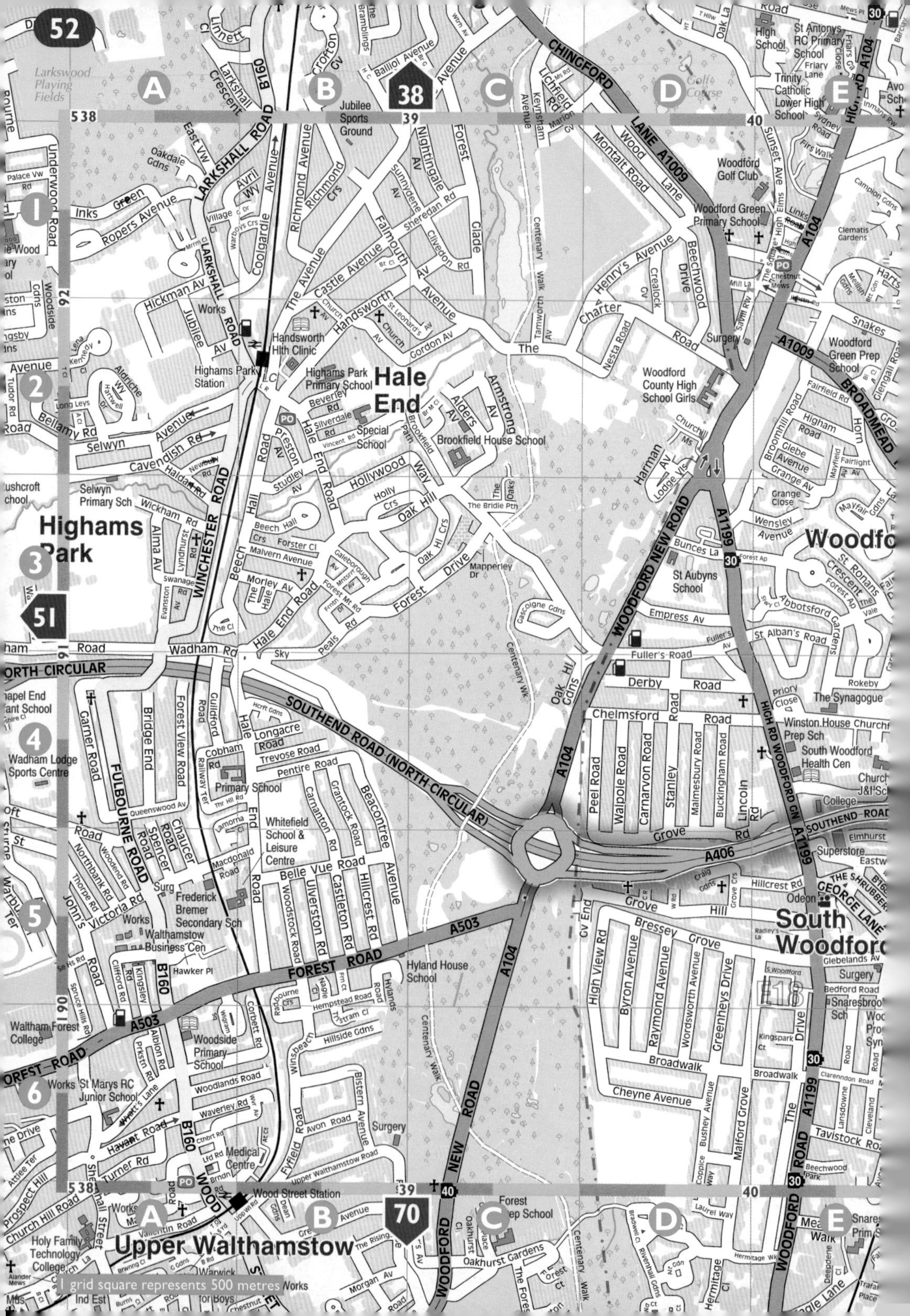
52
38
51
70
Larkswood Playing Fields
Jubilee Sports Ground
Hale End
Highams Park
Woodford
South Woodford
Upper Walthamstow
Higham Park Station
Wood Street Station
Handsworth Hlth Clinic
Highams Park Primary School
Special School
Brookfield House School
Selwyn Primary Sch
Woodford Golf Club
Woodford Green Primary School
Woodford Green Prep School
Woodford County High School Girls
St Aubyns School
Winston House Prep Sch
South Woodford Health Cen
Whitefield School & Leisure Centre
Frederick Bremer Secondary Sch
Walthamstow Business Cen
Woodside Primary School
St Marys RC Junior School
Medical Centre
Waltham Forest College
Hyland House School
Forest Prep School
Holy Family Technology College
Wadham Lodge Sports Centre
The Synagogue
Superstore
Surgery
Odeon
Trinity Catholic Lower High School
High School
St Antonys RC Primary School
CHINGFORD LANE A1009
LARKSHALL ROAD
B160
WINCHESTER ROAD
NORTH CIRCULAR
SOUTHEND ROAD (NORTH CIRCULAR)
FOREST ROAD
A503
A104
A406
A1199
WOODFORD NEW ROAD
HIGH RD WOODFORD GN
BROADMEAD
FULBOURNE ROAD
Hale End Road
Forest Drive
Wadham Rd
Ropers Avenue
Hickman Av
Selwyn Avenue
Cavendish Rd
Castle Avenue
Handsworth Avenue
Falmouth Av
The Avenue
Richmond Avenue
Nightingale Av
Forest Glade
Montalt Road
Wood Lane
Beechwood Drive
Henry's Avenue
The Charter Road
Hollywood Way
Oak Hill
Empress Av
Fuller's Road
Derby Road
Chelmsford Road
Grove Road
Bressey Grove
Broadwalk
Cheyne Avenue
Belle Vue Road
Beacontree Avenue
Pentire Road
Trevose Road
Longacre Road
Garner Road
Bridge End
Forest View Road
Centenary Walk
Oakhurst Gardens
Valentin Road
1 grid square represents 500 metres

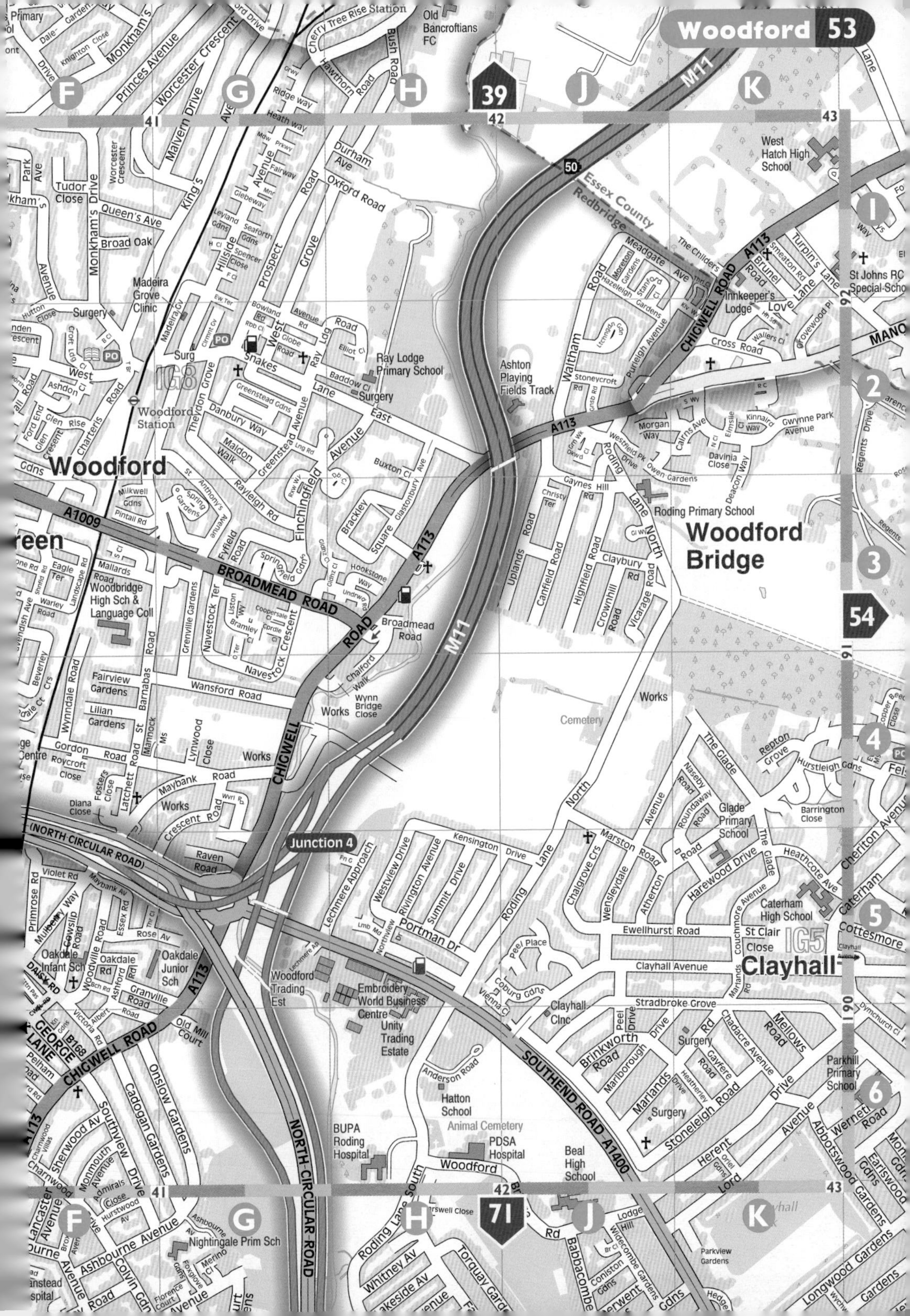
Cherry Tree Rise Station
Old Bancroftians FC
Bush Road
Hawthorn Road
Monkham's
Princes Avenue
Worcester Crescent
Knighton Close
Ridge way
Heath way
Durham Ave
Oxford Road
Malvern Drive
King's Avenue
Tudor Close
Queen's Ave
Broad Oak
Monkham's Drive
Worcester Crescent
Prospect
Grove
Road
M11
50
Essex County
Redbridge
West Hatch High School
The Childers
Meadgate Ave
Moreton Gardens
Hazeleigh Gardens
Stanford Cl
Purleigh Avenue
Waltham Road
CHIGWELL ROAD
A113
Brunel Road
Smeaton Rd
Turpin's Lane
Love Lane
Innkeeper's Lodge
St Johns RC Special School
MANOR
Cross Road
Wallers Cl
Grovewood Pl
Madeira Grove Clinic
Hillside
Spencer Close
Seaforth Gdns
Leyland Gdns
Glebeway
Surgery
Hutton Close
Croft Lodge Cl
West
Surg
IG8
Snakes
West Grove
Bowland Rd
Globe Road
Ray Lodge Road
Elliot Cl
Baddow Cl
Ray Lodge Primary School
Surgery
Lane
East
Ashton Playing Fields Track
Stoneycroft Rd
Ashdon Cl
Glen Rise
Charteris Road
Woodford Station
Theydon Grove
Greenstead Gdns
Danbury Way
Maldon Walk
Greenstead Avenue
Avenue
Buxton Cl
Glastonbury Ave
Morgan Way
Westfield Pk Drive
Owen Gardens
Cairns Ave
Kinnaird Way
Gwynne Park Avenue
Davinia Close
Deacon Way
Regents Drive
Woodford
Gdns
Milkwell Gdns
Pintail Rd
St Anthony's Avenue
Spring Gardens
Rayleigh Rd
Finchingfield
Brackley Square
Gaynes Hill Rd
Christy Ter
Roding Lane North
Roding Primary School
Woodford Bridge
A1009
reen
Eagle Ter
Mallards Road
Woodbridge High Sch & Language Coll
Landscape Rd
Warley Road
Fyfield Road
Springfield Gdns
Hookstone Way
BROADMEAD ROAD
Navestock Ter
Coopersale Cl
Bramley Cl
Navestock Crescent
Broadmead Road
Uplands Road
Canfield Road
Highfield Road
Claybury Rd
Crownhill Road
Vicarage Road
54
Beverley
Fairview Gardens
Lilian Gardens
Wynndale Road
St Barnabas Road
Grenville Gardens
Wansford Road
Chalford Walk
Wynn Bridge Close
Works
Cemetery
Works
Lynwood Close
Mannock
Gordon Road
Roycroft Close
Fosters Close
Latchett Road
Maybank Road
Diana Close
Crescent Road
Works
CHIGWELL
The Glade
Repton Grove
Hurstleigh Gdns
Naseby Road
Roundaway Road
Glade Primary School
Barrington Close
Cheriton Avenue
(NORTH CIRCULAR ROAD)
Raven Road
Junction 4
Lechmere Approach
Westview Drive
Rivington Avenue
Kensington Drive
Summit Drive
Roding Lane
Marston Road
Chalgrove Crs
Wensleydale
Atherton
Avenue
Road
Harewood Drive
Heathcote Ave
Caterham High School
Caterham
Cottesmore
Violet Rd
Maybank Av
Primrose Rd
Mulberry Way
Cowslip Road
Woodville Road
Essex Rd
Rose Av
Oakdale Infant Sch
Oakdale Rd
Oakdale Junior Sch
Ashford Road
Granville Road
Northview
Portman Dr
Woodford Trading Est
Embroidery World Business Centre
Unity Trading Estate
Peel Place
Coburg Gdns
Vienna Cl
Ewellhurst Road
St Clair Close
IG5
Couchmore Avenue
Clayhall Avenue
Clayhall
Stradbroke Grove
Marlands Rd
Clayhall Clnc
Peel Drive
Brinkworth Road
Marlborough Drive
Surgery
Chadacre Avenue
Mellows Road
Dymchurch Cl
DAISY RD
GEORGE LANE
B168
Victoria Rd
Albert Road
A113
CHIGWELL ROAD
Old Mill Court
Pelham Road
Anderson Road
Hatton School
Animal Cemetery
PDSA Hospital
BUPA Roding Hospital
Woodford
Beal High School
SOUTHEND ROAD A1400
Marlands Drive
Heatherley Drive
Gayfere Road
Stoneleigh Road
Surgery
Herent Drive
Oriel Gdns
Avenue
Abbotsford Gardens
Parkhill Primary School
Wernett Road
Earlswood Gdns
Charnwood Villas
Sherwood Av
Southview Drive
Cadogan Gardens
Onslow Gardens
Monmouth Avenue
Admirals Close
Hurstwood Av
NORTH CIRCULAR ROAD
Roding Lane South
Lodge Hill
Widecombe Gardens
Babbacombe
Lord
Longwood Gardens
Lancaster Avenue
Ashbourne Avenue
Nightingale Prim Sch
Merino Cl
Foxglove Gdns
Florence Court
Colvin Gdns
Whitney Av
Torquay Gardens
Coniston Gdns
Parkview Gardens
71
39
F
G
H
J
K
1
2
3
4
5
6
41
42
43
92
91
90

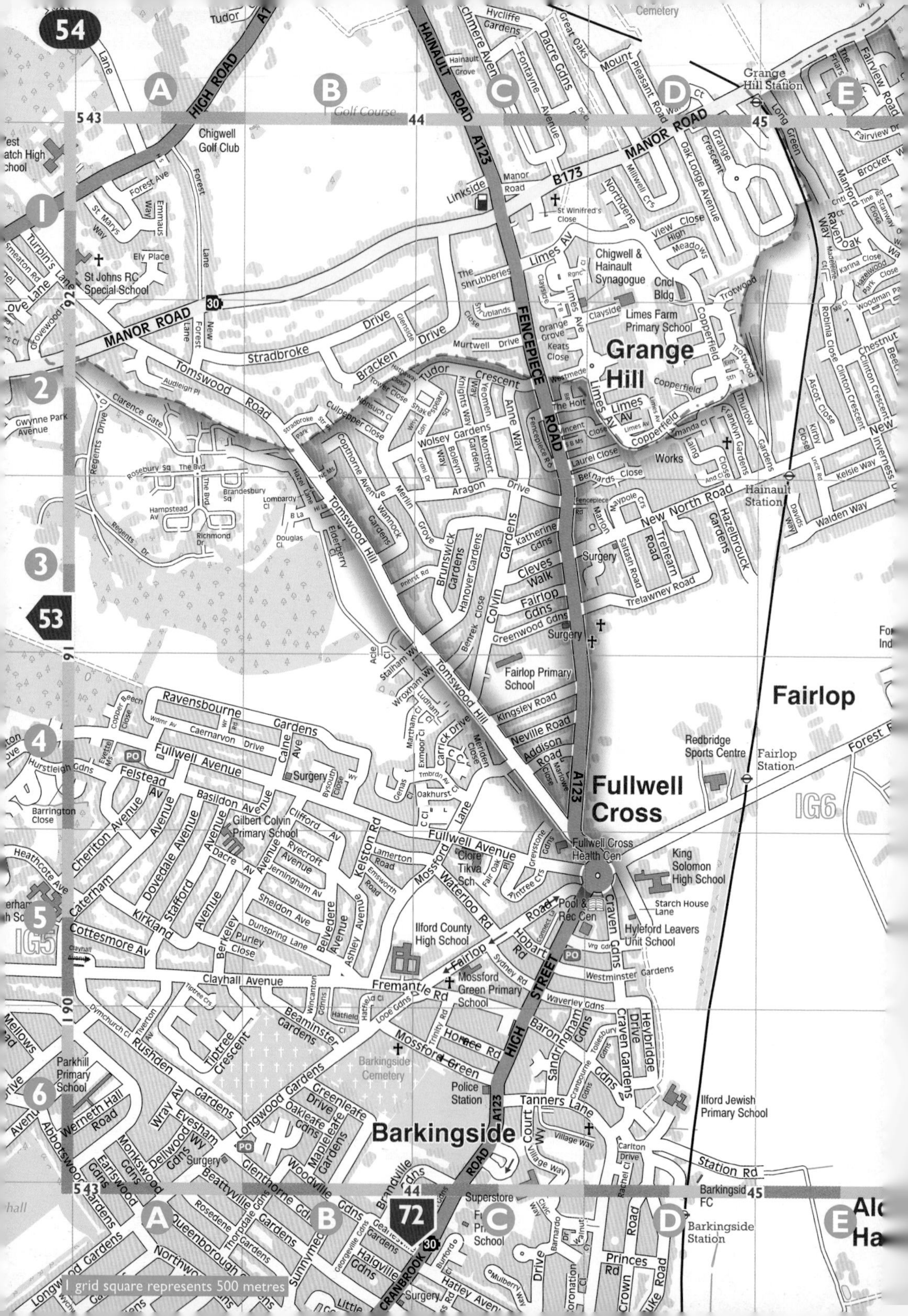
Grange Hill
Fullwell Cross
Fairlop
Barkingside
Chigwell Golf Club
Golf Course
Cemetery
HIGH ROAD
A113
HAINAULT ROAD
A123
FENCEPIECE ROAD
MANOR ROAD
B173
Manor Road
Tomswood Road
Tomswood Hill
Stradbroke Drive
Bracken Drive
Tudor Crescent
Aragon Drive
New North Road
Trelawney Road
Hazelbrouck Gardens
Colvin Gardens
Brunswick Gardens
Hanover Gardens
Cleves Walk
Fairlop Gdns
Greenwood Gdns
Kingsley Road
Neville Road
Addison Road
Ravensbourne Gardens
Caernarvon Drive
Fullwell Avenue
Basildon Avenue
Felstead Av
Cheriton Avenue
Dovedale Avenue
Stafford Avenue
Kirkland
Cottesmore Av
Clayhall Avenue
Fremantle Rd
Mossford Green
Waterloo Rd
Hobart Rd
Craven Gdns
Westminster Gardens
Waverley Gdns
Sandringham Gdns
Heybridge Drive
Craven Gardens
Tanners Lane
Station Rd
Village Way
HIGH STREET
CRANBROOK ROAD
Longwood Gardens
Beaminster Gardens
Tiptree Crescent
Rushden Gardens
Wernerh Hall Road
Abbotswood Gardens
Glenthorne Gdns
Beattyville Gardens
Woodville Gdns
Redbridge Sports Centre
Fairlop Station
Hainault Station
Grange Hill Station
Barkingside Station
Barkingside FC
King Solomon High School
Ilford County High School
Mossford Green Primary School
Ilford Jewish Primary School
Gilbert Colvin Primary School
Fairlop Primary School
Limes Farm Primary School
Chigwell & Hainault Synagogue
St Johns RC Special School
Parkhill Primary School
Hyleford Leavers Unit School
Fullwell Cross Health Cen
Pool & Rec Cen
Police Station
Barkingside Cemetery
Superstore
Surgery
PO
Works
IG5
IG6
A
B
C
D
E
1
2
3
4
5
6
543
44
45
90
91
92
30
53
72
1 grid square represents 500 metres

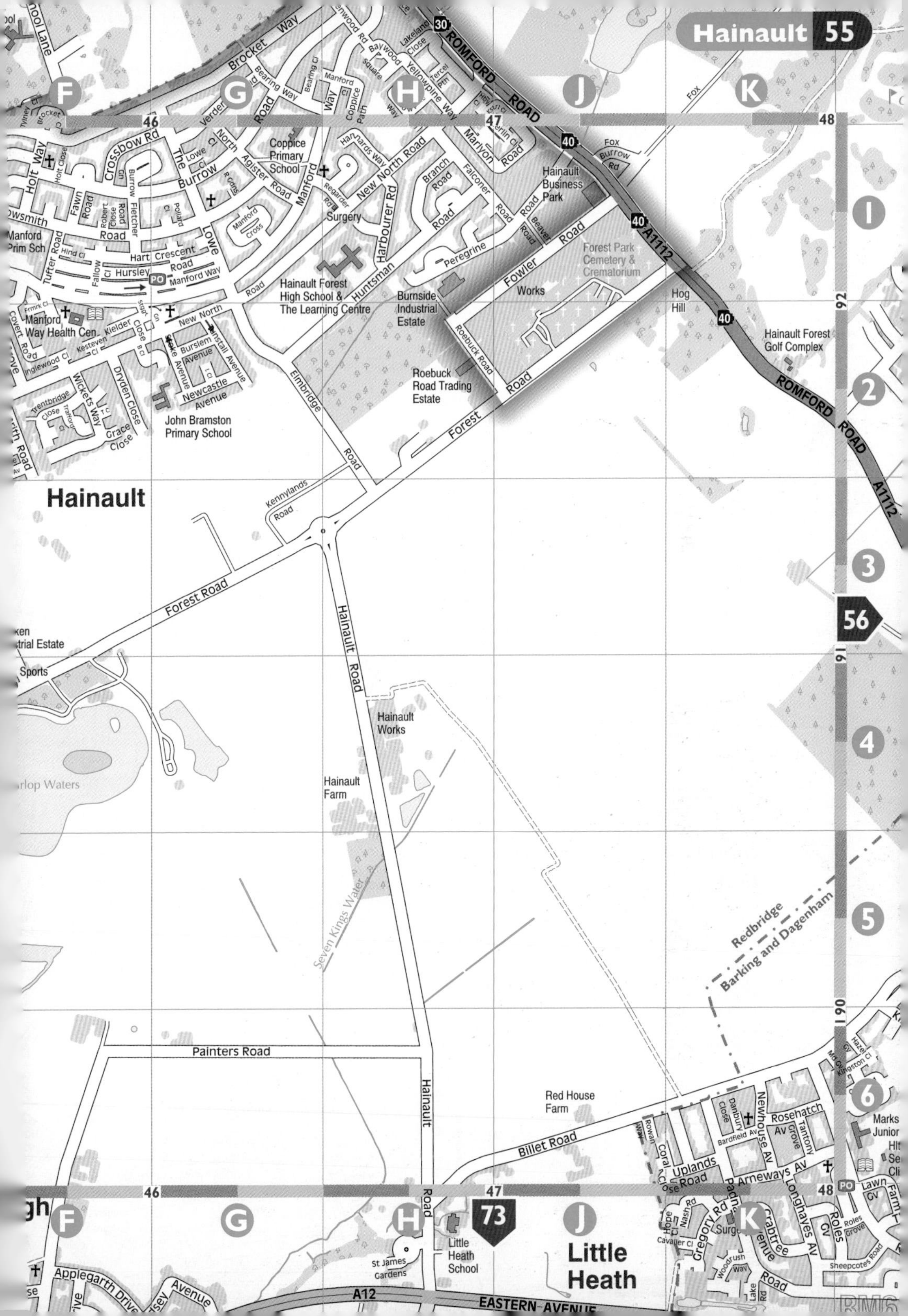
Hainault
Brocket Way
Crossbow Rd
Coppice Primary School
Romford Road
A1112
Hainault Business Park
Forest Park Cemetery & Crematorium
Fowler Road
Works
Hog Hill
Hainault Forest Golf Complex
Manford Way
Manford Prim Sch
Manford Way Health Cen.
Hainault Forest High School & The Learning Centre
Burnside Industrial Estate
Roebuck Road Trading Estate
Roebuck Road
New North Road
Huntsman Road
Harbourer Rd
Peregrine Road
Elmbridge Road
Forest Road
Kennylands Road
Surgery
John Bramston Primary School
Newcastle Avenue
Burslem Avenue
Tunstall Avenue
Dryden Close
Wickets Way
Grace Close
Hainault Road
Hainault Works
Hainault Farm
Seven Kings Water
Painters Road
Red House Farm
Billet Road
Redbridge
Barking and Dagenham
Uplands Road
Arneways Av
Longhayes Av
Newhouse Av
Rosehatch Av
Crabtree Avenue
Gregory Rd
Little Heath
Little Heath School
St James Gardens
A12
EASTERN AVENUE
Applegarth Drive
Marks Junior
56
73

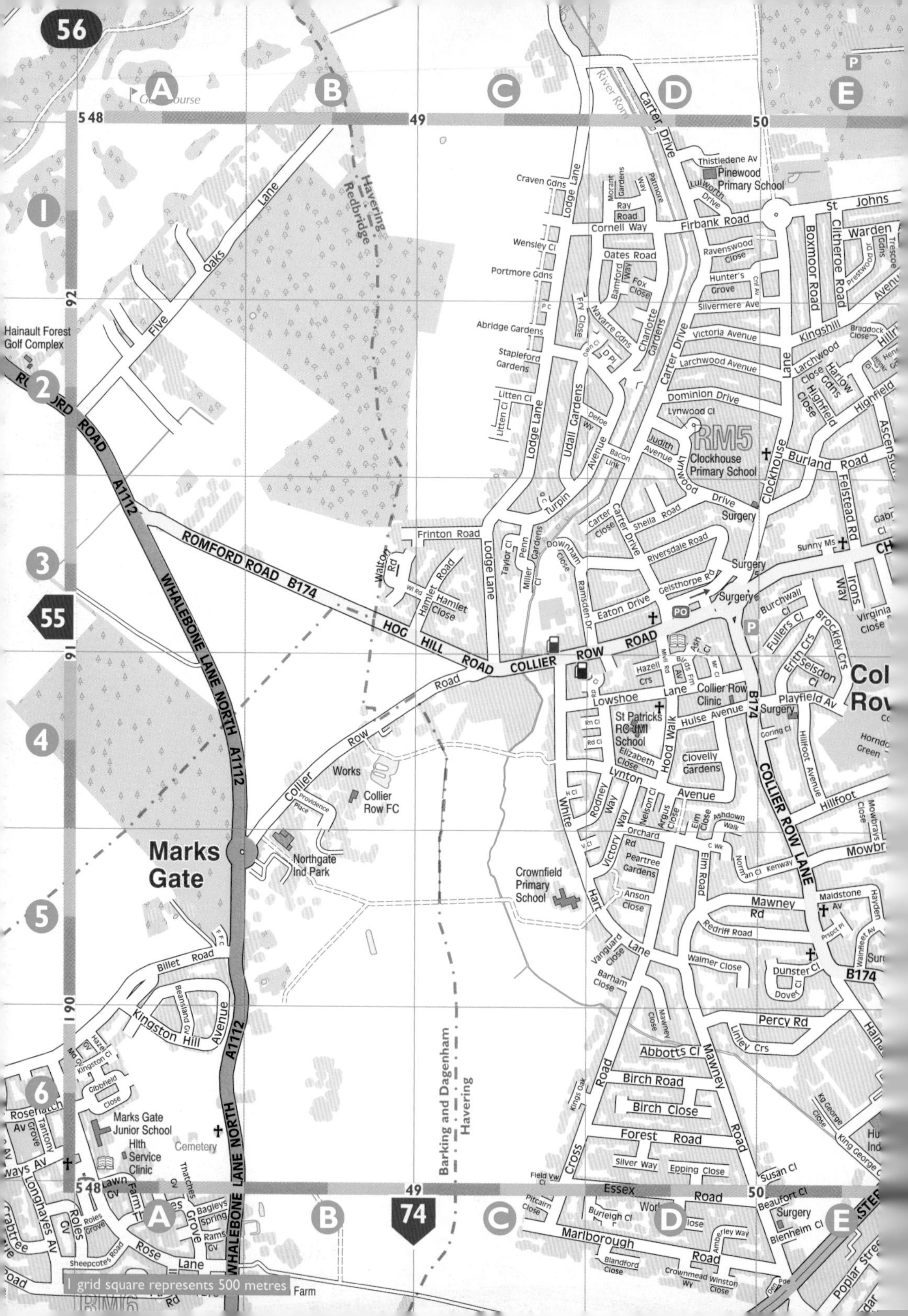

Hainault Forest Golf Complex
Five Oaks Lane
Havering
Redbridge
ROMFORD ROAD
A1112
ROMFORD ROAD B174
HOG HILL ROAD
COLLIER ROW ROAD
WHALEBONE LANE NORTH A1112
Collier Row Road
Works
Collier Row FC
Northgate Ind Park
Providence Place
Marks Gate
Billet Road
Kingston Hill Avenue
Beansland Gv
Kingston Cl
Gibbfield Close
Marks Gate Junior School
Hlth Service Clinic
Cemetery
Rosehatch Av
Tantony Grove
Longhayes Av
Roles Gv
Rose Lane
Sheepcotes Road
Lawn Farm Gv
Bagleys Spring
Rams Gv
Thatches Gv
Crabtree
Farm
RM6
Barking and Dagenham
Havering
River Rom
Carter Drive
Thistledene Av
Pinewood Primary School
Lulworth Drive
Craven Gdns
Lodge Lane
Morant Gardens
Ray Road
Patmore Way
Firbank Road
St Johns
Cornell Way
Wensley Cl
Oates Road
Portmore Gdns
Bamford Way
Fox Close
Ravenswood Close
Hunter's Grove
Silvermere Ave
Boxmoor Road
Clitheroe Road
Warden
Prestwood
Fry Close
Navarre Gdns
Charlotte Gardens
Abridge Gardens
Stapleford Gardens
Victoria Avenue
Kingshill
Braddock Close
Larchwood Avenue
Larchwood Close
Harlow Gdns
Highfield Close
Highfield
Litten Cl
Udall Gardens
Defoe Wy
Dominion Drive
Lynwood Cl
RM5
Judith Avenue
Clockhouse Primary School
Clockhouse Lane
Burland Road
Felstead Rd
Ascension
Bacon Link
Avenue
Turpin
Lynwood Drive
Surgery
Carter Close
Sheila Road
Frinton Road
Walton Rd
Hamlet Road
Hamlet Close
Taylor Cl
Penn Gardens
Miller Cl
Downham Close
Riversdale Road
Gelsthorpe Rd
Ramsden Dr
Eaton Drive
PO
Burchwall Cl
Fullers Cl
Brockley Crs
Irons Way
Virginia Close
Sunny Ms
Erith Crs
Selsdon Cl
Collier Row
Hazell Crs
Ash Cl
Lowshoe Lane
Collier Row Clinic
Playfield Av
St Patricks RC JMI School
Hulse Avenue
Goring Cl
Hood Walk
Elizabeth Close
Clovelly Gardens
Hillfoot Avenue
Hillfoot
Horndon Green
Lynton Avenue
Rodney Way
White Hart Lane
Nelson Cl
Argus Close
Elm Close
Ashdown Walk
COLLIER ROW LANE
B174
Orchard Rd
Victory Way
Peartree Gardens
Elm Road
Norman Cl
Kenway
Mowbrays Close
Mowbrays
Crownfield Primary School
Anson Close
Mawney Rd
Maidstone Av
Hayden
Redriff Road
Prospect Pl
Wainfleet Av
Vanguard Close
Lane
Walmer Close
Dunster Cl
Dover Cl
Barham Close
Mawney Close
Percy Rd
Linley Crs
Abbotts Cl
Mawney Road
Birch Road
Birch Close
Kings Oak
Cross Road
Forest Road
Kg George Close
King George
Silver Way
Epping Close
Field Vw Cl
Susan Cl
Essex Road
Pitcairn Close
Burleigh Cl
Beaufort Cl
Surgery
Blenheim Cl
Marlborough Road
Amberley Way
Blandford Close
Crownmead Wy
Winston Close
Poplar Street
1 grid square represents 500 metres

55
74

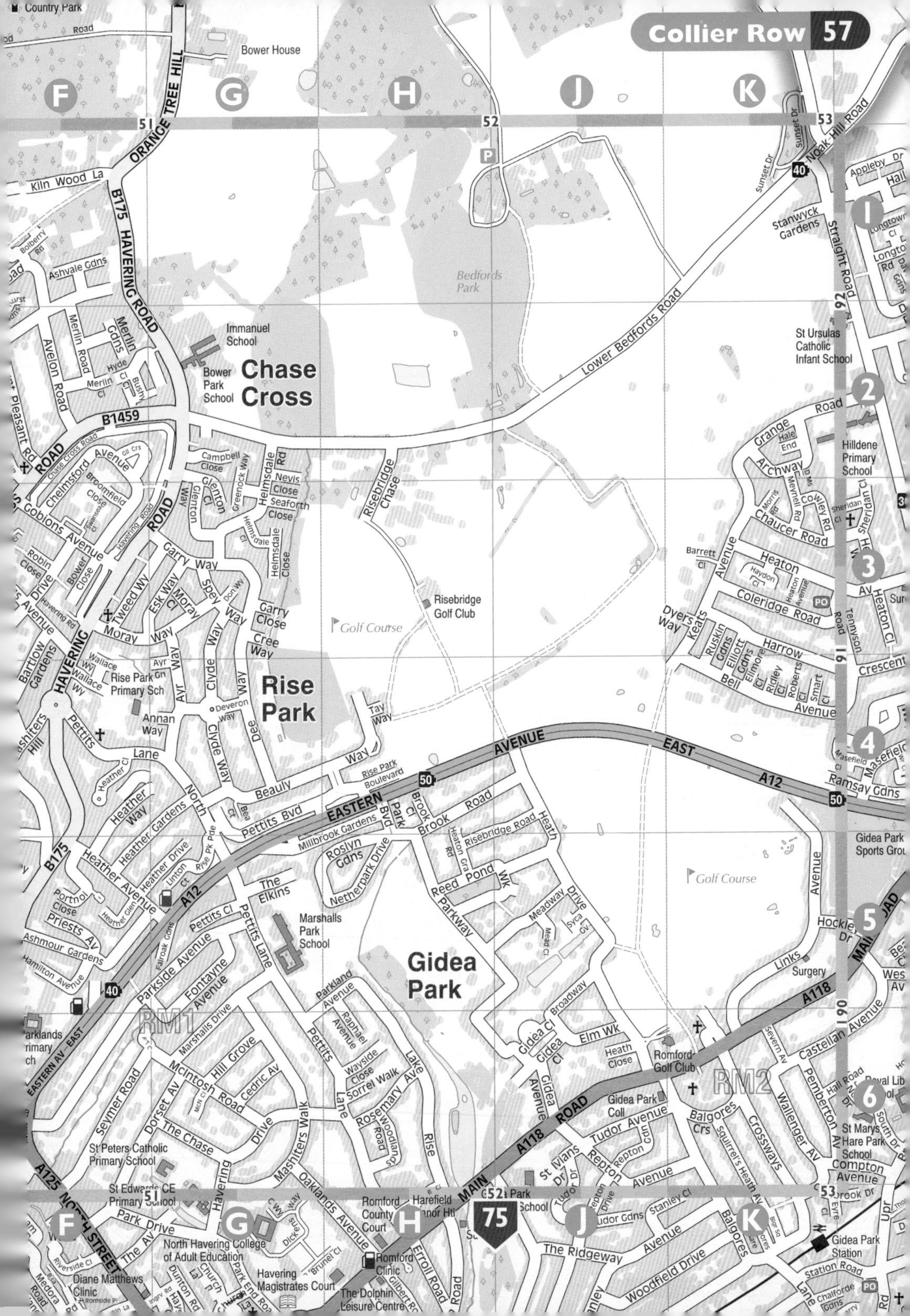

Chase Cross
Rise Park
Gidea Park
Bedfords Park
Golf Course
Immanuel School
Bower Park School
Bower House
Risebridge Golf Club
Rise Park Primary Sch
Marshalls Park School
St Ursulas Catholic Infant School
Hilldene Primary School
Gidea Park Sports Grou
Surgery
Romford Golf Club
Gidea Park Coll
St Marys Hare Park School
St Peters Catholic Primary School
St Edwards CE Primary School
North Havering College of Adult Education
Havering Magistrates Court
Romford County Court
Romford Clinic
The Dolphin Leisure Centre
Diane Matthews Clinic
Gidea Park Station
Harefield Manor Htl
Orange Tree Hill
B175 Havering Road
Lower Bedfords Road
Noak Hill Road
Straight Road
Eastern Avenue East
A12
A118 Main Road
A125 North Street
B1459
Kiln Wood La
RM1
RM2
51
52
53
75

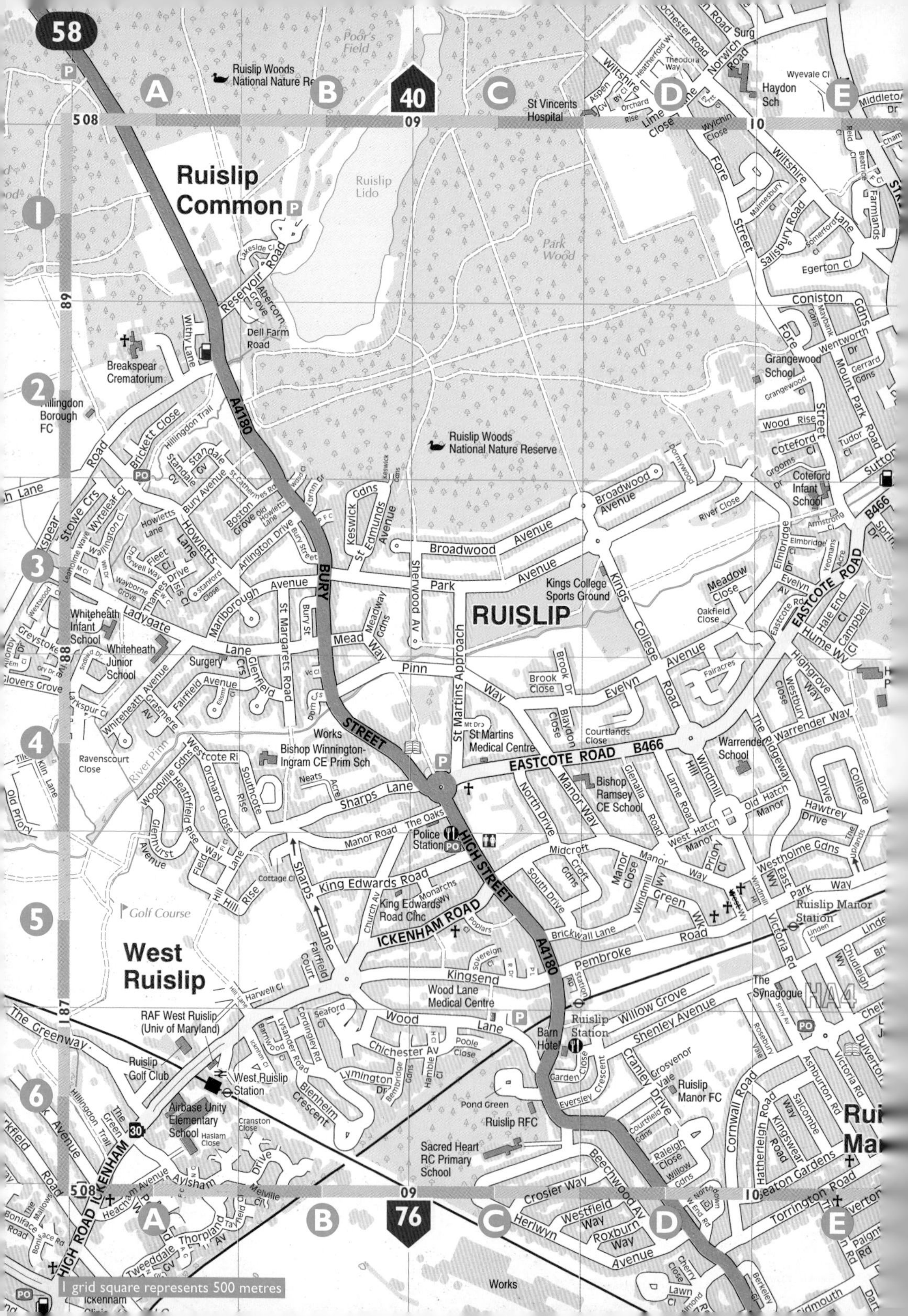
40
76
Poor's Field
Ruislip Woods National Nature Reserve
Ruislip Common
Ruislip Lido
Park Wood
St Vincents Hospital
Haydon Sch
Wyevale Cl
Middleton Dr
Norwich Road
Wiltshire Lane
Fore Street
Lime Close
Wychlin Close
Theodora Way
Heatherfold Wy
Orchard Rise
Aspen Gv
By Cl
Malmesbury Cl
Salisbury Road
Somerford Cl
Farmlands
Egerton Cl
Coniston Gdns
Maybank Gdns
Wentworth Dr
Gerrard Gdns
Mount Park Road
Grangewood School
Grangewood Cl
Wood Rise
Coteford Cl
Coteford Infant School
Grooms Dr
Tudor Cl
Sutton
Lakeside Cl
Reservoir Road
Abercorn Grove
Dell Farm Road
Withy Lane
Breakspear Crematorium
Hillingdon Borough FC
A4180
Brickett Close
Hillingdon Trail
Standale Gv
Bury Avenue
St Catherines Rd
Wood Cl
Boston Grove
Old Howletts Lane
Howletts Lane
Stowe Crs
Wyteleaf Cl
Wallington Cl
Fleet Cl
Thames Drive
Isis Cl
Stanford Close
Wayborne Grove
Arlington Drive
Bury Street
Keswick Gdns
St Edmunds Avenue
Broadwood Avenue
Dormywood
River Close
Armstrong Cl
Elmbridge Dr
Elmbridge Cl
Yeomans Acre
B466
Park Avenue
Sherwood Av
Kings College Sports Ground
Kings College Road
Meadow Close
Oakfield Close
Evelyn Av
Eastcote Rd
EASTCOTE ROAD
Hale End Cl
Campbell Cl
Hume Wy
RUISLIP
Marlborough Avenue
St Margarets Road
Bury St
Meadway Gdns
Mead Way
Whiteheath Infant School
Whiteheath Junior School
Ladygate Lane
Greystoke Dr
Glovers Grove
Larkspur Cl
Whiteheath Avenue
Grasmere Av
Fairfield Avenue
Glenfield Crs
Surgery
Pinn Way
St Martins Approach
Brook Close
Brook Dr
Blaydon Close
Evelyn Avenue
Fairacres
Highgrove Way
Westbury Close
Warrender Way
Warrender School
Courtlands Close
Works
Bishop Winnington-Ingram CE Prim Sch
St Martins Medical Centre
EASTCOTE ROAD B466
Ravenscourt Close
Kiln Lane
Old Priory
River Pinn
Westcote Ri
Woodville Gdns
Heathfield Rise
Orchard Close
Southcote Rise
Neats Acre
Sharps Lane
Manor Road
The Oaks
Police Station
HIGH STREET
North Drive
Manor Way
Bishop Ramsey CE School
Glenalla Road
Larne Road
Windmill Hill
Old Hatch Manor
West Hatch Manor
Priory Cl
The Ridgeway
Hawtrey Drive
College Drive
Westholme Gdns
The Uplands
East Wy
Park Way
Glenhurst Avenue
Field Way
Hill Rise
Cottage Cl
Sharps Lane
King Edwards Road
Monarchs Wy
King Edwards Road Clnc
Church Av
Midcroft
Croft Gdns
South Drive
Manor Close
Windmill Wy
Green Wk
Ruislip Manor Station
Linden Cl
Golf Course
West Ruislip
ICKENHAM ROAD
Poplars Cl
Brickwall Lane
Fairfield Court
Sovereign Cl
Kingsend
Pembroke Road
Victoria Rd
Chudleigh Wy
Harwell Cl
Hill Lane
Wood Lane Medical Centre
Willow Grove
Shenley Avenue
The Synagogue
HA4
Rosebury Vale
RAF West Ruislip (Univ of Maryland)
The Greenway
Ruislip Golf Club
West Ruislip Station
Seaford Cl
Cordingley Rd
Lysander Road
Barnwood Cl
Wood Lane
Chichester Av
Poole Close
Barn Hotel
Ruislip Station
Garden Close
Eversley Crescent
Cranley Drive
Grosvenor Vale
Ruislip Manor FC
Cornwall Road
Hatherleigh Road
Kingswear Road
Salcombe Way
Ashburton Rd
Victoria Rd
Dulverton
Lymington Dr
Bembridge Gdns
Hamble Cl
Blenheim Crescent
Pond Green
Ruislip RFC
Airbase Unity Elementary School
Cranston Close
Haslam Close
Hillingdon Trail
The Green
Hillingdon Avenue
HIGH ROAD ICKENHAM
Sacred Heart RC Primary School
Courtfield Gdns
Raleigh Close
Willow Gdns
Beechwood Av
Aylsham Drive
Melville Cl
Heacham Avenue
Crosier Way
Westfield Way
Herlwyn
Roxburn Way
Avenue
Heaton Gardens
Torrington Road
Ruislip Manor
Thorpland Av
Tweeddale Gv
Boniface Road
The Mallows
Cherry Close
Lawn Cl
Berkeley Cl
Sidmouth
Works
1 grid square represents 500 metres
Ickenham

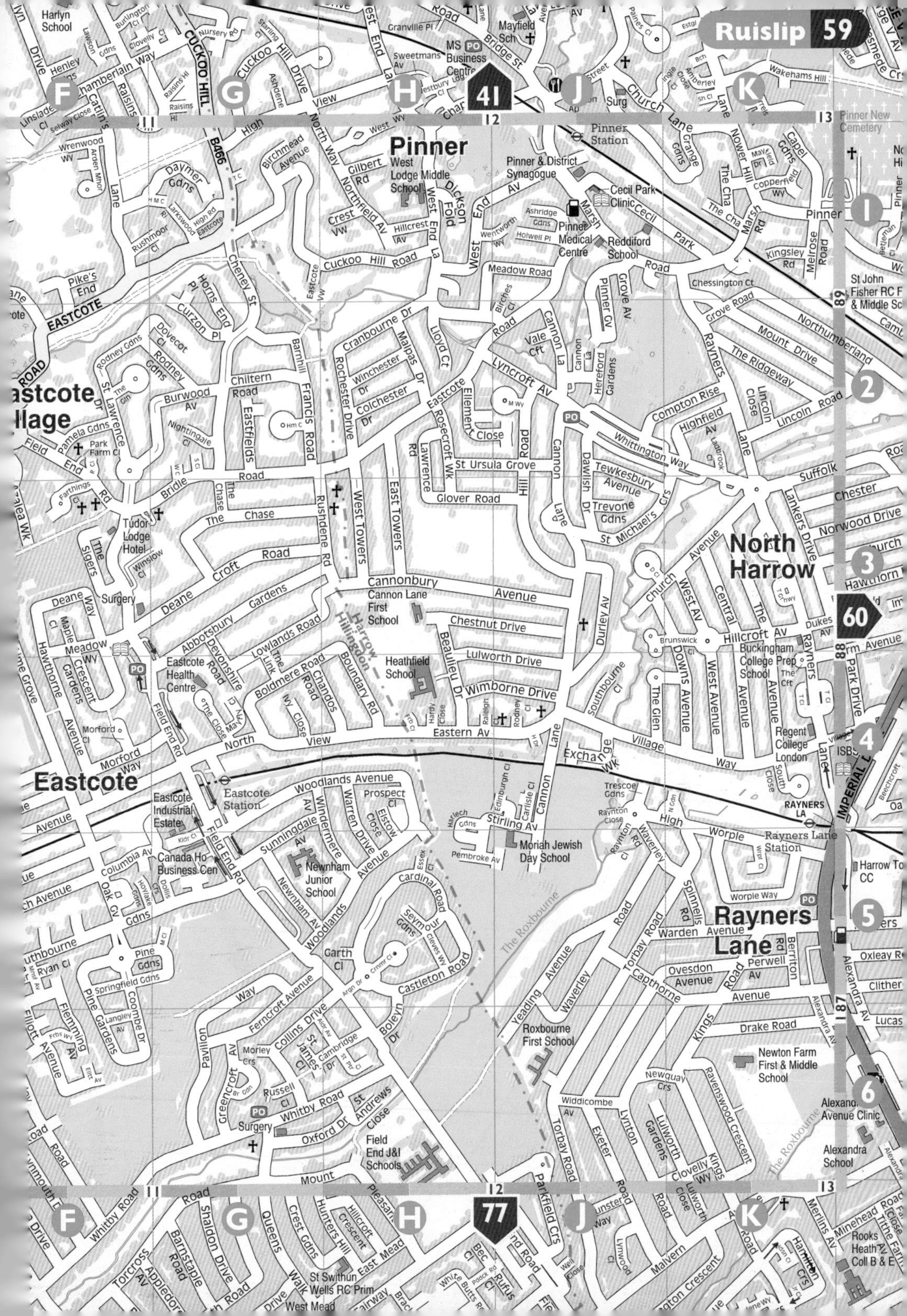
Ruislip 59
41
60
77
Pinner
North Harrow
Eastcote
Eastcote Village
Rayners Lane
Harlyn School
Chamberlain Way
Cuckoo Hill
Cuckoo Hill Drive
Cuckoo Hill Road
High Rd Eastcote
B466
Henley
Raisins Hill
Catlin's
Linslade Cl
Selway Close
Wrenwood Wy
Arden Mnr
Daymer Gdns
Larkswood Rl
Rushmoor Cl
Pike's End
Eastcote Road
Horns End Pl
Curzon Pl
Dovecot Cl
Rodney Gdns
Rodney Gdns
St Lawrence Dr
Pamela Gdns
Park Farm Cl
Field End Rd
Farthings Cl
Bridle Road
Tudor Lodge Hotel
The Sigers
Winslow Cl
Surgery
Deane Way
Deane Croft Road
Maple Cl
Meadow Wy
Hawthorne Avenue
Crescent Gardens
Morford Cl
Morford Way
Abbotsbury Gardens
Devonshire Road
Eastcote Health Centre
The Close
Eastcote Station
Eastcote Industrial Estate
Canada Ho Business Cen
Columbia Av
Oak Gv
Southbourne Gdns
Ryan Cl
Pine Gdns
Springfield Gdns
Pine Gardens
Coombe Dr
Flemming Av
Elliott Avenue
Langley Av
Cheney St
Chiltern Road
Burwood Av
Nightingale Cl
Eastfields
Francis Road
Barnhill
Rochester Drive
Cranbourne Dr
Winchester Dr
Colchester Dr
Malpas Dr
Lloyd Ct
The Chase
Rushdene Rd
West Towers
East Towers
Cannonbury Avenue
Cannon Lane First School
Chestnut Drive
Lulworth Drive
Wimborne Drive
Beaulieu Dr
Heathfield School
Lowlands Road
The Link
Boldmere Road
Chandos Road
Boundary Rd
Wy Close
North View
Eastern Av
Harrow
Hillingdon
Woodlands Avenue
Prospect Cl
Elstow Close
Warren Drive
Windermere Av
Sunningdale Av
Newnham Junior School
Newnham Av
Woodlands
Avenue
Cardinal Road
Seymour Gdns
Cleves Wy
Castleton Road
Garth Cl
Boleyn Dr
Ferncroft Avenue
Collins Drive
Cambridge Dr
St James Cl
Pavilion Way
Greencroft Av
Morley Crs
Russell Cl
Whitby Road
Oxford Dr
St Andrews Close
Field End J&I Schools
Mount Road
Pleasant
West Wy
Birchmead Avenue
Gilbert Rd
Northfield Av
Crest Vw
Hillcrest Av
West Lodge Middle School
Dickson Fold
West End La
West End Av
Eastcote Vw
Granville Pl
Sweetmans Av
MS Business Centre
Bridge St
Mayfield Sch
Church Lane
Pinner Station
Pinner & District Synagogue
Cecil Park
Cecil Park Clinic
Ashridge Gdns
Wentworth Wy
Holwell Pl
Pinner Medical Centre
Reddiford School
Marsh Road
Meadow Road
Birches Cl
Pinner Gv
Grove Av
Vale Cft
Cannon La
Hereford Gardens
Lyncroft Av
Eastcote Road
Rosecroft Wk
Ellement Close
Hill Road
Lawrence Rd
St Ursula Grove
Glover Road
Cannon Lane
Dawlish Dr
Tewkesbury Avenue
Trevone Gdns
St Michael's Crs
Whittington Way
Durley Av
Southbourne Cl
Exchange Wk
Edinburgh Cl
Carlisle Cl
Harlech Gdns
Stirling Av
Pembroke Av
Moriah Jewish Day School
Essex Cl
The Roxbourne
Grange Gdns
Nower Hill
The Cha
Capel Gdns
Copperfield Wy
Kingsley Rd
Melrose Road
Pinner
Wakehams Hill
Chessington Ct
Grove Road
Northumberland
Mount Drive
The Ridgeway
Rayners Lane
Lincoln Close
Lincoln Road
Compton Rise
Highfield Av
Ladbrook Cl
Suffolk
Chester
Norwood Drive
Lankers Drive
Church Avenue
West Av
Central
The Avenue
Hillcroft Av
Dukes Av
Buckingham College Prep School
Brunswick
Downs Avenue
West Avenue
Avenue
The Glen
Village Way
Regent College London
South Close
Park Drive
ISBS
Imperial
Rayners La
Rayners Lane Station
Trescoe Gdns
Raynton Close
Raynton Cl
Waverley
High
Worple
Worple Way
Harrow To CC
Spinnells
Torbay Road
Warden Avenue
Berriton Rd
Ovesdon Avenue
Perwell Av
Capthorne Avenue
Kings Road
Alexandra Av
Oxleay Rd
Clitheroe
Lucas
Drake Road
Newton Farm First & Middle School
Yeading Avenue
Waverley
Roxbourne First School
Newquay Crs
Ravenswood Crescent
Widdicombe Av
Exeter Road
Lynton
Lulworth Gardens
Clovelly Wy
Kings
Alexandra Avenue Clinic
Alexandra School
Parkfield Crs
Torbay Road
Pinner New Cemetery
St John Fisher RC F & Middle Sc
Whitby Road
Shaldon Drive
Barnstaple Road
Torcross
Appledore Av
Queens
Crest Gdns
Hunters Hill
Hillcroft Crescent
East Mead
St Swithun Wells RC Prim
West Mead
Walk
Bec Cl
Rufus
White Butts Rd
Padock Rd
Malvern
Lynwood Cl
Merlins Av
Minehead Road
Hamilton Crs
Rooks Heath Coll B & E
F
G
H
J
K
1
2
3
4
5
6
11
12
13
87
88
89

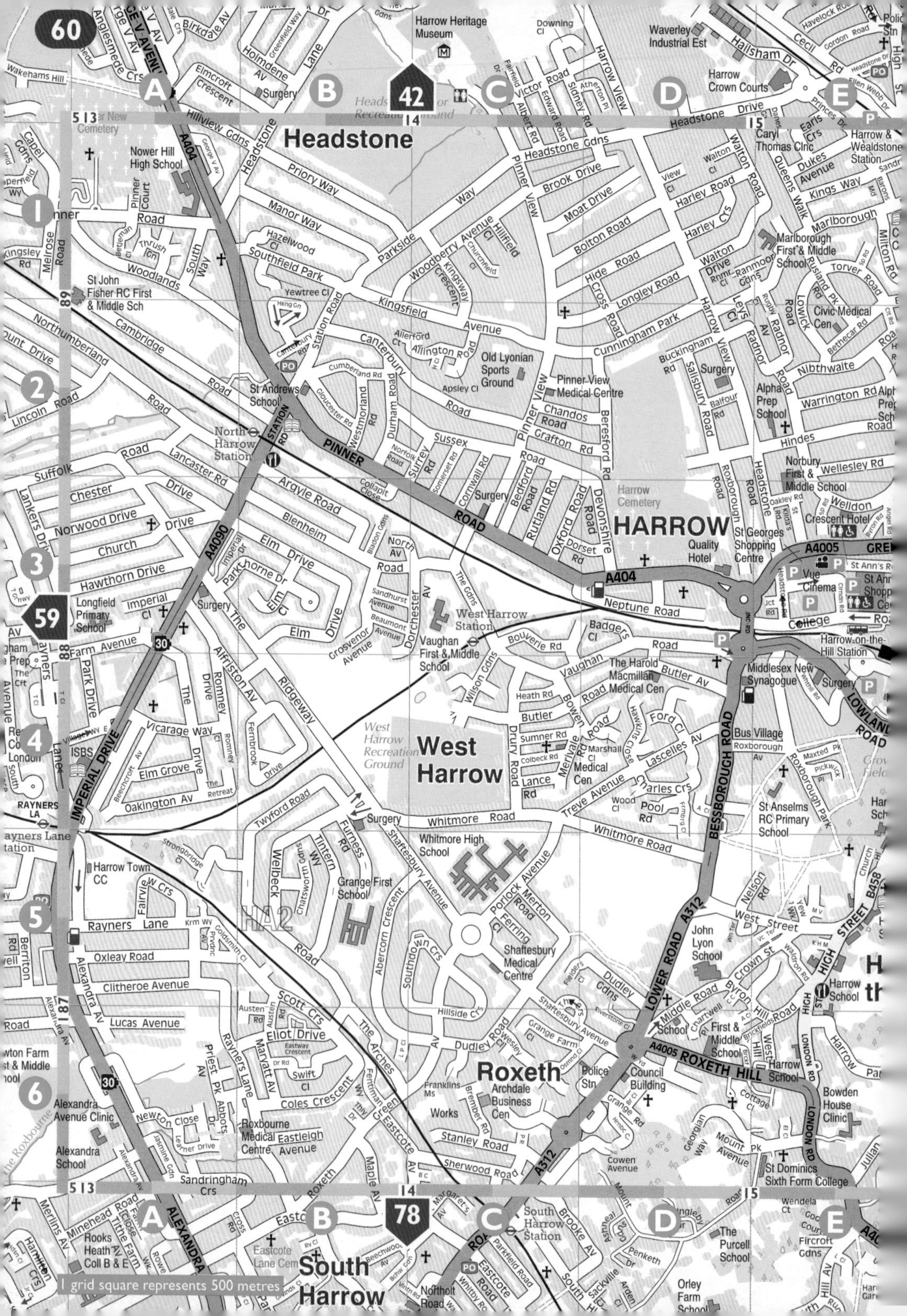

Headstone
HARROW
West Harrow
Roxeth
South Harrow
Harrow Heritage Museum
Headstone Manor Recreation Ground
West Harrow Recreation Ground
Harrow Cemetery
North Harrow Station
West Harrow Station
Harrow-on-the-Hill Station
South Harrow Station
Rayners Lane Station
Harrow & Wealdstone Station
Harrow Crown Courts
Waverley Industrial Est
Nower Hill High School
St John Fisher RC First & Middle Sch
St Andrews School
Longfield Primary School
Vaughan First & Middle School
Whitmore High School
Grange First School
John Lyon School
Harrow School
St Anselms RC Primary School
Marlborough First & Middle School
Norbury First & Middle School
Alpha Prep School
Old Lyonian Sports Ground
Pinner View Medical Centre
Civic Medical Cen
The Harold Macmillan Medical Cen
Shaftesbury Medical Centre
Roxbourne Medical Centre
Alexandra Avenue Clinic
Alexandra School
Archdale Business Cen
Council Building
Bowden House Clinic
St Dominics Sixth Form College
The Purcell School
Bus Village
Middlesex New Synagogue
St Georges Shopping Centre
Quality Hotel
Crescent Hotel
Vue Cinema
Harrow Town CC
Pinner Road
A404
A4090
A4005
A312
Bessborough Road
Lower Road
Imperial Drive
Alexandra Av
Roxeth Hill
Headstone Drive
HA2
1 grid square represents 500 metres

42
59
78

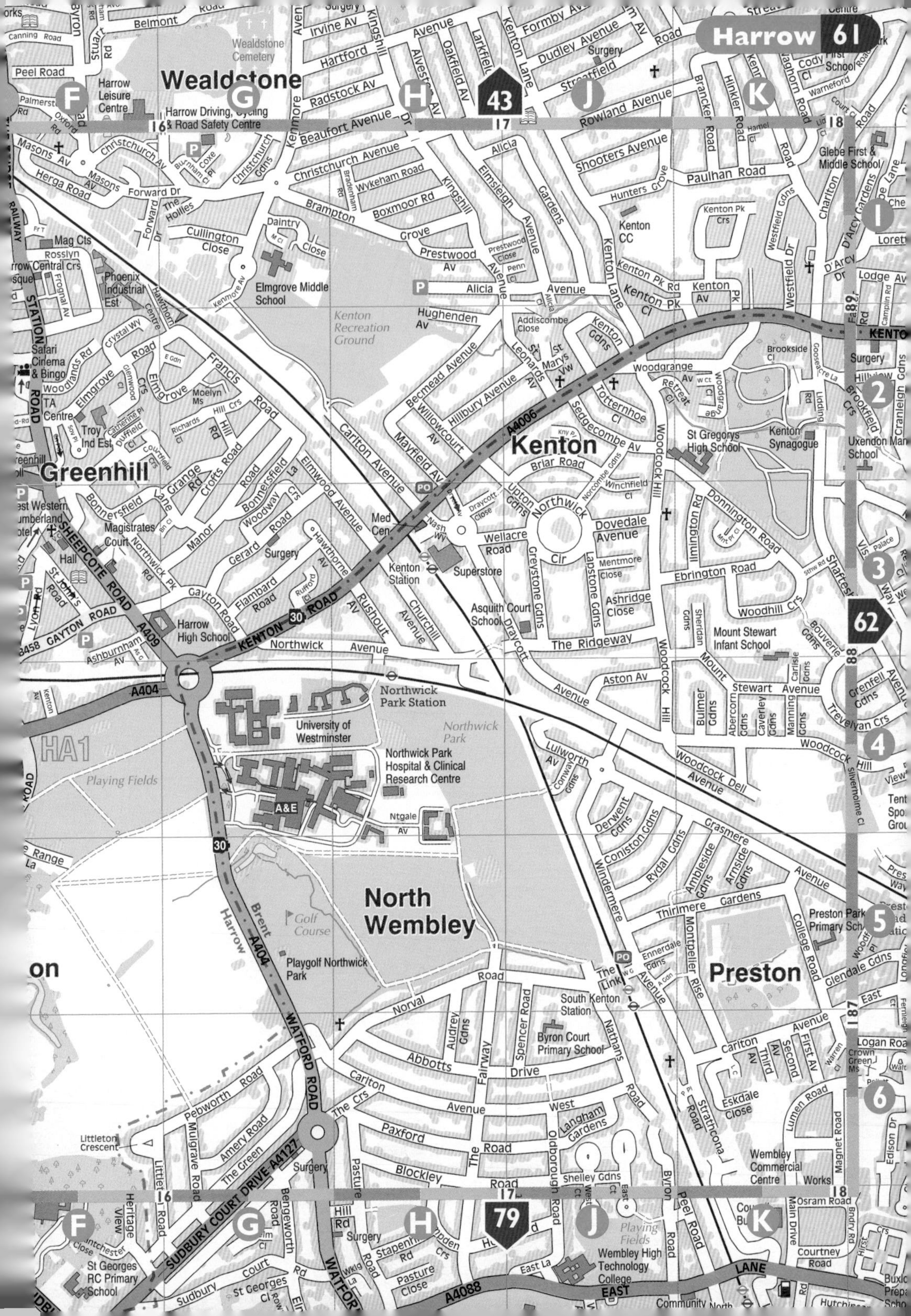
Wealdstone
Wealdstone Cemetery
Harrow Leisure Centre
Harrow Driving, Cycling & Road Safety Centre
Elmgrove Middle School
Kenton Recreation Ground
Phoenix Industrial Est
Greenhill
Safari Cinema & Bingo
Troy Ind Est
Magistrates Court
Harrow High School
Kenton
Kenton Station
Superstore
Asquith Court School
Kenton CC
St Gregorys High School
Kenton Synagogue
Glebe First & Middle School
Uxendon Manor School
Mount Stewart Infant School
Northwick Park Station
University of Westminster
Northwick Park Hospital & Clinical Research Centre
Northwick Park
Playing Fields
Golf Course
Playgolf Northwick Park
North Wembley
South Kenton Station
Byron Court Primary School
Preston
Preston Park Primary School
Wembley Commercial Centre
Wembley High Technology College
St Georges RC Primary School
HA1
A4006
A404
A409
A4088
A4127
KENTON ROAD
WATFORD ROAD
SHEEPCOTE ROAD
STATION ROAD
GAYTON ROAD
SUDBURY COURT DRIVE
EAST LANE
Kenton Lane
Northwick Avenue
Woodcock Hill
The Ridgeway
Carlton Avenue
Rushout Av
Churchill Avenue
Draycott Avenue
Northwick Cir
Windermere Avenue
Preston Road
Rowland Avenue
Shooters Avenue
Paulhan Road
Christchurch Avenue
Beaufort Avenue
Brampton Grove
Prestwood Av
Alicia Avenue
Hughenden Av
Becmead Avenue
Hillbury Avenue
Mayfield Av
Elmwood Avenue
Sedgecombe Av
Briar Road
Donnington Road
Ebrington Road
Woodhill Crs
Stewart Avenue
Woodcock Dell Avenue
Grasmere Avenue
Thirlmere Gardens
Norval Road
Abbotts Drive
Carlton Avenue West
Paxford Road
Blockley Road
Pebworth Road
Mulgrave Road
Amery Road
The Green
Littleton Crescent
43
79
62
16
17
18
F G H J K
1 2 3 4 5 6

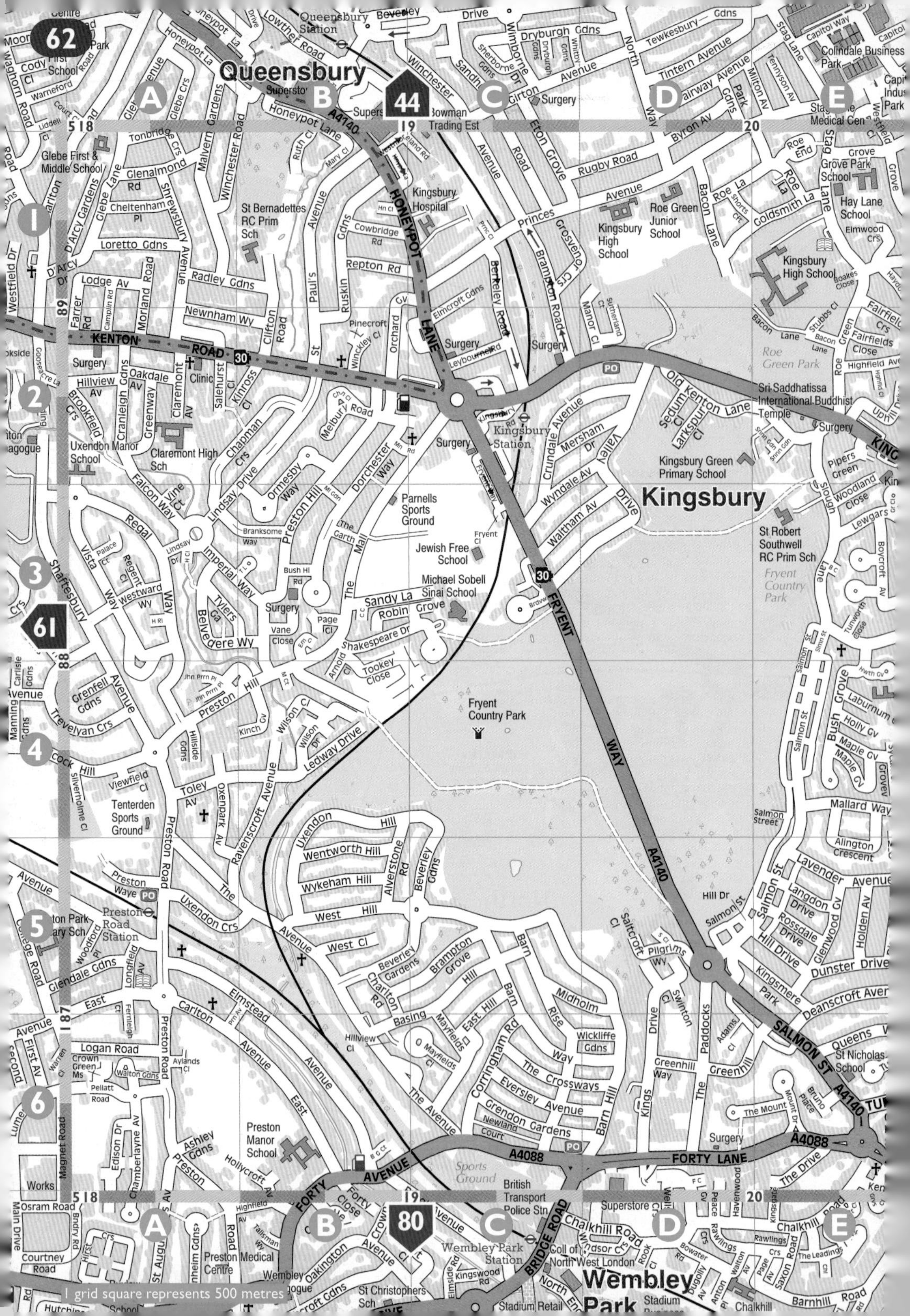
62
Queensbury
Queensbury Station
Kingsbury
Wembley Park
44
61
80
A
B
C
D
E
1
2
3
4
5
6
518
19
20
89
88
187
Honeypot Lane
Lowther Road
Winchester Road
Wimborne Dr
Dryburgh Gdns
Tewkesbury Gdns
Tintern Avenue
Fairway Avenue
Stag Lane
Capitol Way
Colindale Business Park
Girton Avenue
Surgery
Bowman Trading Est
Byron Av
Rugby Road
Eton Grove
Stag Lane Medical Cen
Glebe First & Middle School
Glebe Lane
Glenalmond Rd
Cheltenham Pl
Loretto Gdns
Shrewsbury Avenue
Malvern Gardens
St Bernadettes RC Prim Sch
Kingsbury Hospital
Cowbridge Rd
Repton Rd
Princes Avenue
Kingsbury High School
Roe Green Junior School
Bacon Lane
Roe Green
Grove Park School
Hay Lane School
Goldsmith La
Radley Gdns
Newnham Wy
Lodge Av
Morland Road
Clifton Road
Paul's Avenue
Ruskin Gdns
Pinecroft
Winckley Cl
Orchard Gv
Elmcroft Gdns
Berkeley Road
Brampton Road
Grosvenor Crs
Manor Cl
KENTON ROAD
30
Surgery
Clinic
Hillview Av
Oakdale Av
Brookfield Crs
Cranleigh Gdns
Greenway
Claremont Av
Salehurst Cl
Kinross Cl
Uxendon Manor School
Claremont High Sch
Chapman Crs
Melbury Road
Dorchester Way
HONEYPOT LANE
A4140
Kingsbury Station
Crundale Avenue
Mersham Dr
Valley Drive
Old Kenton Lane
Sedum Cl
Larkspur Cl
Roe Green Park
Sri Saddhatissa International Buddhist Temple
Kingsbury Green Primary School
Pipers Green
Woodland Close
Falcon Way
Lindsay Drive
Ormesby Way
Preston Hill
Parnells Sports Ground
Wyndale Av
Waltham Av
Regal Way
Vista Way
Imperial Way
Westward Wy
Branksome Way
The Garth
The Mall
Jewish Free School
Michael Sobell Sinai School
Sandy La
Robin Grove
FRYENT WAY
St Robert Southwell RC Prim Sch
Fryent Country Park
Shaftesbury
Tylers Ga
Belvedere Wy
Surgery
Vane Close
Page Cl
Shakespeare Dr
Tookey Close
Grenfell Gdns
Trevelyan Crs
Avenue
Preston Hill
Wilson Cl
Kinch Gv
Ledway Drive
Hillside Gdns
Salmon St
Bush Grove
Laburnum
Holly Gv
Maple Gv
Mallard Way
Cock Hill
Viewfield Cl
Silverholme Cl
Toley Av
Oxenpark Av
Ravenscroft Avenue
Tenterden Sports Ground
Uxendon Hill
Wentworth Hill
Wykeham Hill
Alverstone Rd
Beverley Gdns
West Hill
West Cl
Salmon Street
Alington Crescent
Lavender Avenue
Preston Road
Preston Waye
PO
Preston Road Station
Uxendon Crs
The Avenue
Beverley Gardens
Brampton Grove
Barn Hill
Saltcroft Cl
Pilgrims Wy
Hill Dr
Langdon Drive
Rossdale Drive
Glenwood Gv
Holden Av
Hill Drive
Dunster Drive
Kingsmere Park
Deanscroft Avenue
Woodford Pl
Glendale Gdns
Longfield Av
East Ct
Carlton Avenue
Elmstead Avenue
Charlton Rd
Basing Hill
Mayfields
East Hill
Midholm
Rise
Swinton Cl
The Paddocks
Adams Cl
SALMON ST
Queens Walk
St Nicholas School
Logan Road
Crown Green Ms
Walton Gdns
Pellatt Road
Aylands Cl
Hillview Cl
Mayfields Cl
Wickliffe Gdns
Way
The Crossways
Eversley Avenue
Corringham Rd
Grendon Gardens
Newland Court
Kings Drive
Greenhill Way
The Greenhill
The Mount
Mount Dr
Bruno Place
East Avenue
The Avenue
Edison Dr
Chamberlayne Av
Ashley Gdns
Preston Manor School
Hollycroft Av
A4088
FORTY AVENUE
FORTY LANE
Sports Ground
British Transport Police Stn
Surgery
The Drive
Magnet Road
Works
Osram Road
Main Drive
Courtney Road
Preston Medical Centre
Forty Close
Oakington Avenue
Crown Ct
Wembley Park Station
Kingswood Rd
BRIDGE ROAD
Chalkhill Road
Coll of North West London
Windsor Crs
Rook Cl
Bowater Rd
Peace Grove
Rawlings Crs
Saxon Road
The Leadings
Chalkhill
Barnhill Road
Stadium Retail
North End
St Christophers Sch
Superstore
1 grid square represents 500 metres

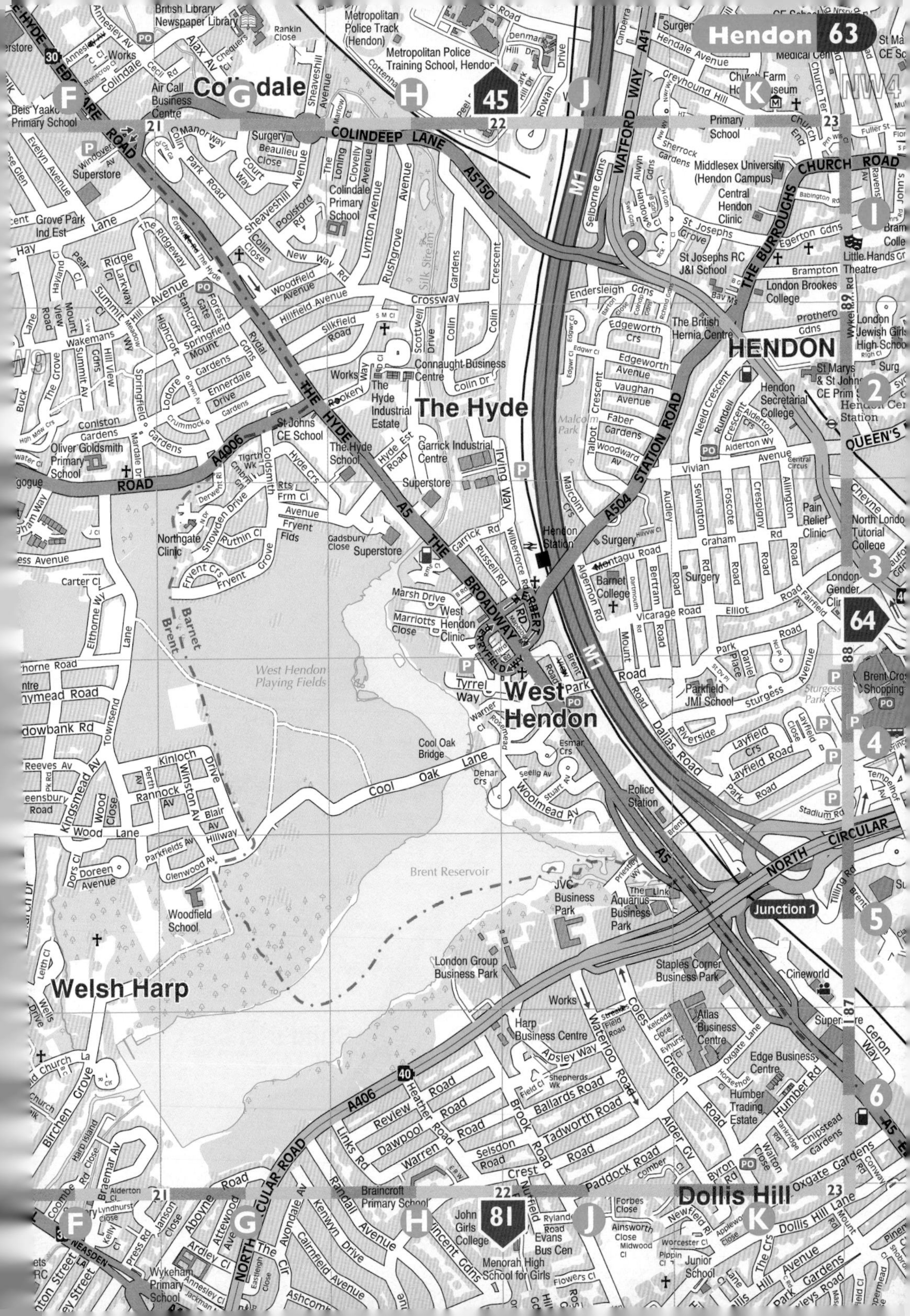
Colindale
The Hyde
HENDON
West Hendon
Welsh Harp
Dollis Hill
British Library Newspaper Library
Metropolitan Police Track (Hendon)
Metropolitan Police Training School, Hendon
Air Call Business Centre
Colindale Primary School
Beis Yaakov Primary School
Superstore
Grove Park Ind Est
Works
COLINDEEP LANE
A5150
EDGWARE ROAD
THE HYDE
THE BROADWAY
A5
M1
WATFORD WAY
A41
Middlesex University (Hendon Campus)
Central Hendon Clinic
St Josephs RC J&I School
THE BURROUGHS
CHURCH ROAD
London Brookes College
Little Hands Theatre
The British Hernia Centre
Hendon Secretarial College
Connaught Business Centre
The Hyde Industrial Estate
Garrick Industrial Centre
St Johns CE School
The Hyde School
Oliver Goldsmith Primary School
A4006
Northgate Clinic
West Hendon Playing Fields
Hendon Station
STATION ROAD
A504
Barnet College
Parkfield JMI School
West Hendon Clinic
Cool Oak Bridge
Cool Oak Lane
Police Station
NORTH CIRCULAR
Junction 1
Brent Reservoir
JVC Business Park
Aquarius Business Park
London Group Business Park
Staples Corner Business Park
Cineworld
Atlas Business Centre
Edge Business Centre
Humber Trading Estate
Harp Business Centre
Woodfield School
A406
NORTH CIRCULAR ROAD
Braincroft Primary School
John Kelly Girls College
Menorah High School for Girls
Evans Bus Cen
Wykeham Primary School
Junior School
Pain Relief Clinic
North London Tutorial College
London Jewish Girls High School
Brent Cross Shopping
Dallas Road
Woolmead Av
Kingsmead Av
Wood Lane
Townsend Lane
Dawpool Road
Heather Road
Review Road
Tadworth Road
Ballards Road
Waterloo Road
Coles Green Road
Oxgate Gardens
Dollis Hill Lane
Paddock Road

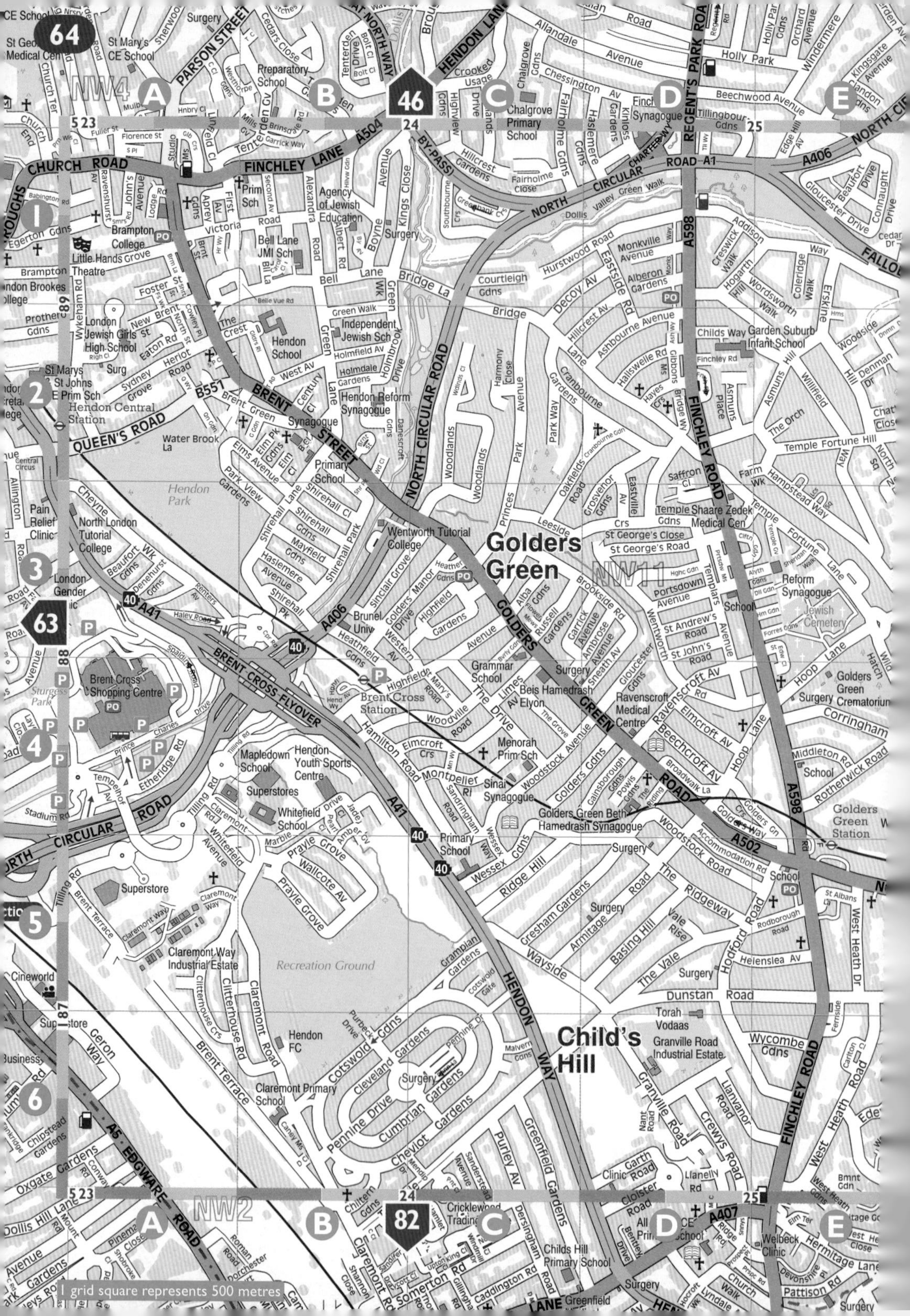
64
NW4
A
B
C
D
E
46
63
82
NW11
NW2
1
2
3
4
5
6
Golders Green
Child's Hill
Church Road
Finchley Lane
A504
Parson Street
Hendon Lane
Regent's Park Road
North Circular Road A1
A406
A598
Finchley Road
Brent Street
B551
Queen's Road
Hendon Central Station
Hendon Park
Brent Cross Shopping Centre
Brent Cross Flyover
Brent Cross Station
A41
Golders Green Road
A502
Golders Green Station
Golders Green Crematorium
Jewish Cemetery
Hendon Way
Recreation Ground
Hendon FC
Claremont Way Industrial Estate
Granville Road Industrial Estate
Cricklewood Trading
A5 Edgware Road
A407
Cineworld
Hendon School
Brampton College
London Jewish Girls High School
Hendon Reform Synagogue
Independent Jewish Sch
Agency of Jewish Education
Wentworth Tutorial College
North London Tutorial College
Brunel Univ
Menorah Prim Sch
Sinai Synagogue
Golders Green Beth Hamedrash Synagogue
Beis Hamedrash Elyon
Ravenscroft Medical Centre
Garden Suburb Infant School
Reform Synagogue
Shaare Zedek Medical Cen
Chalgrove Primary School
Claremont Primary School
Childs Hill Primary School
Mapledown School
Hendon Youth Sports Centre
Whitefield School
Torah Vodaas
Superstores
Superstore
Welbeck Clinic
1 grid square represents 500 metres

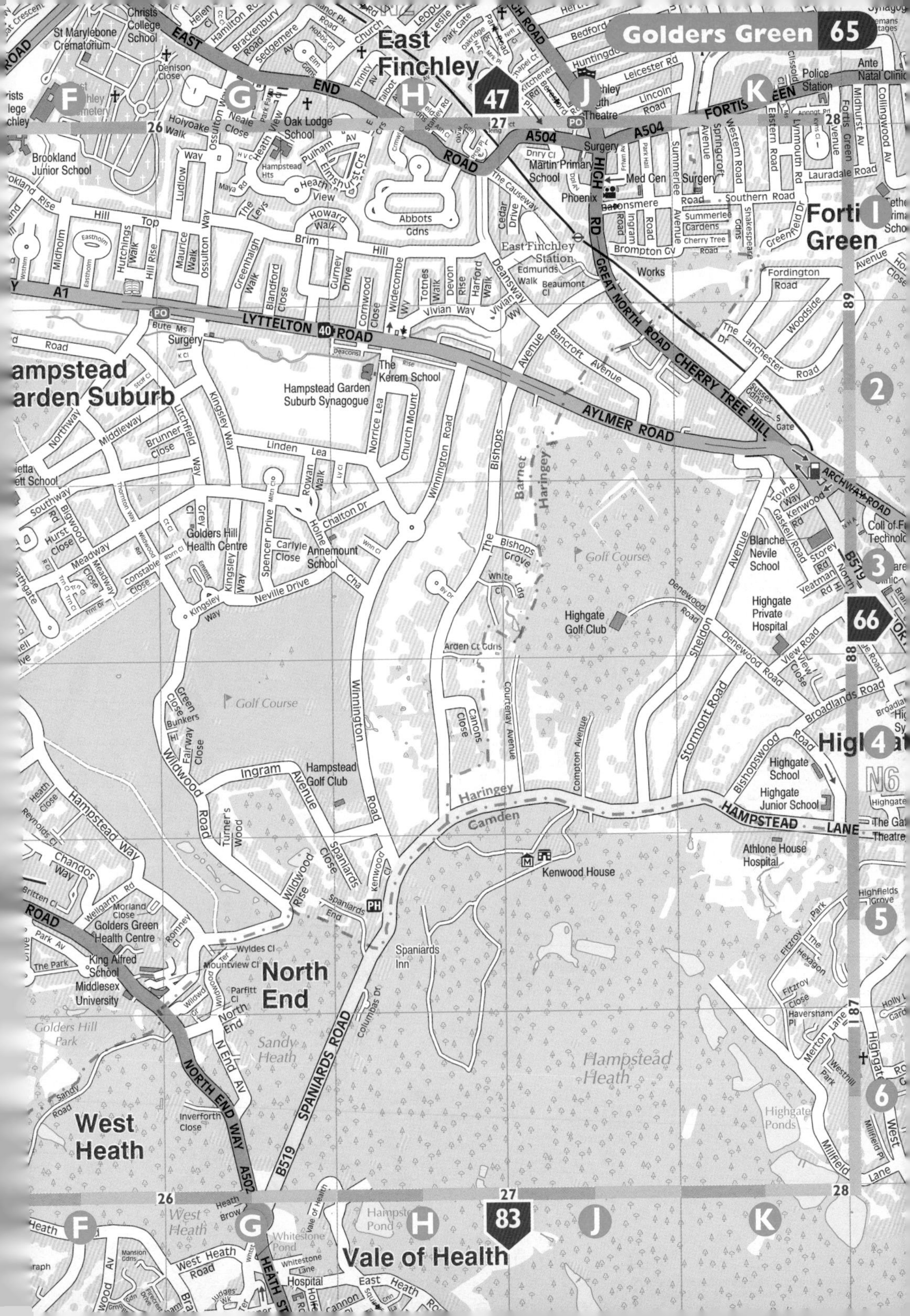
East Finchley
47
Fortis Green
Hampstead Garden Suburb
66
Highgate
N6
North End
West Heath
Vale of Health
83
Hampstead Heath
Sandy Heath
Golders Hill Park
Highgate Ponds
Kenwood House
Spaniards Inn
Golf Course
Highgate Golf Club
Hampstead Golf Club
St Marylebone Crematorium
Christs College School
Oak Lodge School
Brookland Junior School
Martin Primary School
East Finchley Station
The Kerem School
Hampstead Garden Suburb Synagogue
Golders Hill Health Centre
Annemount School
Blanche Nevile School
Highgate Private Hospital
Highgate School
Highgate Junior School
Athlone House Hospital
Golders Green Health Centre
King Alfred School
Middlesex University
EAST END ROAD
A504
A1
LYTTELTON ROAD
AYLMER ROAD
GREAT NORTH ROAD
CHERRY TREE HILL
ARCHWAY ROAD
B519
HAMPSTEAD LANE
SPANIARDS ROAD
NORTH END WAY
A502
HIGH RD
Winnington Road
Bishops Avenue
Hampstead Way
Wildwood Road
Ingram Avenue
Stormont Road
Sheldon Avenue
Denewood Road
Bishopswood Road
Courtenay Avenue
Compton Avenue
Kingsley Way
Meadway
Haringey
Camden
Barnet
F G H J K
26 27 28
2 3 4 5 6

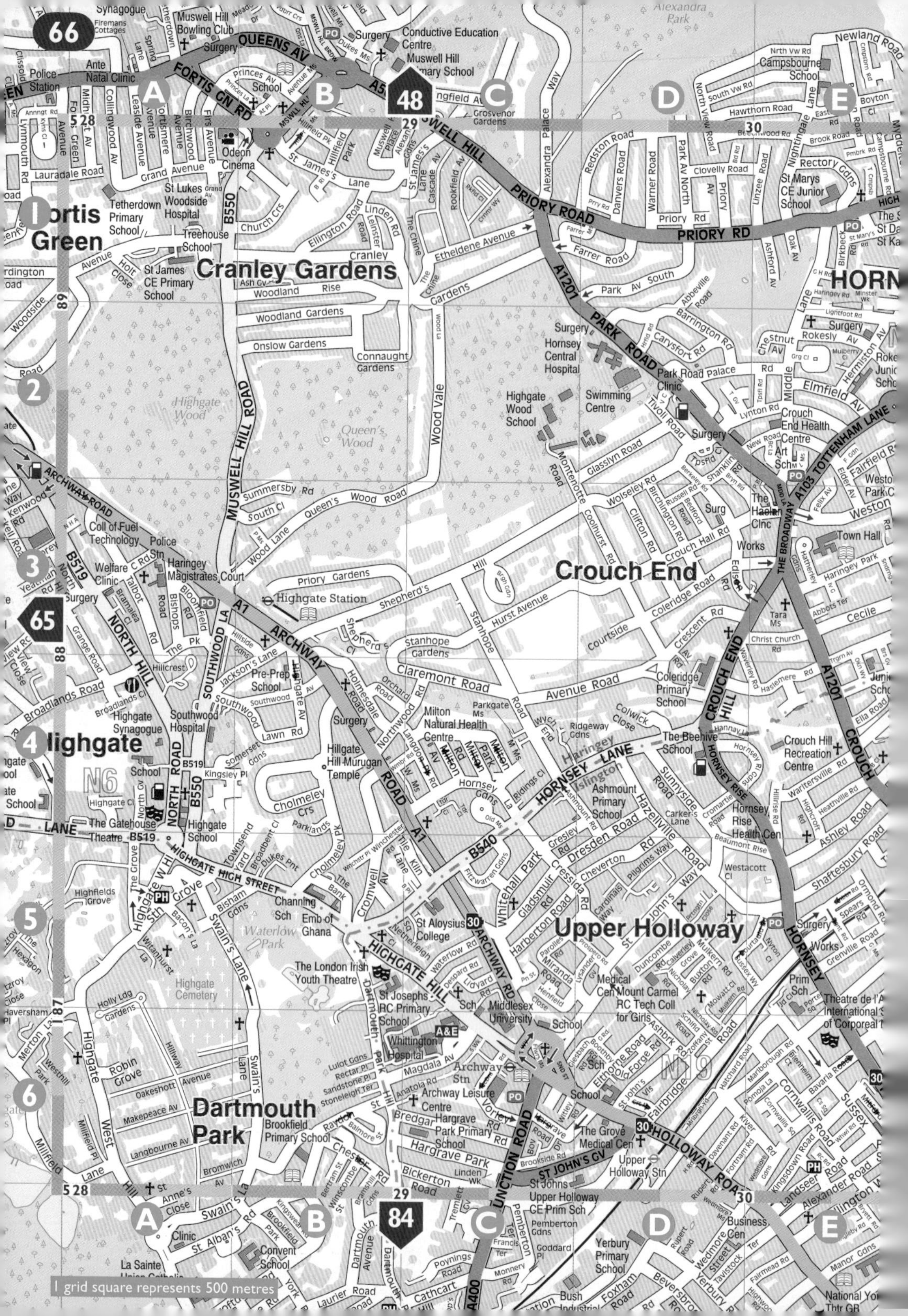
66
48
65
84
Fortis Green
Cranley Gardens
Highgate
Crouch End
Upper Holloway
Dartmouth Park
HORN
Muswell Hill Bowling Club
Conductive Education Centre
Alexandra Park
Campsbourne School
St Marys CE Junior School
Tetherdown Primary School
St Lukes Woodside Hospital
Treehouse School
St James CE Primary School
Odeon Cinema
Highgate Wood
Queen's Wood
Hornsey Central Hospital
Highgate Wood School
Swimming Centre
Park Road Palace
Crouch End Health Centre
Town Hall
Coll of Fuel Technology
Police Stn
Haringey Magistrates Court
Highgate Station
Welfare Clinic
Highgate Synagogue
Southwood Hospital
Pre-Prep School
Milton Natural Health Centre
Hillgate Hill Murugan Temple
Coleridge Primary School
The Beehive School
Ashmount Primary School
Crouch Hill Recreation Centre
Hornsey Rise Health Cen
The Gatehouse Theatre
Highgate School
Channing Sch
Emb of Ghana
Waterlow Park
Highgate Cemetery
St Aloysius College
The London Irish Youth Theatre
St Josephs RC Primary School
Whittington Hospital
Middlesex University
Archway Stn
Archway Leisure Centre
Hargrave Park Primary School
Brookfield Primary School
The Grove Medical Cen
Upper Holloway Stn
St Johns Upper Holloway CE Prim Sch
Medical Cen
Mount Carmel RC Tech Coll for Girls
Theatre de l'A International of Corporeal
Yerbury Primary School
Convent School
Business Cen
QUEENS AV
FORTIS GN RD
MUSWELL HILL
PRIORY ROAD
PRIORY RD
A1201
PARK ROAD
MUSWELL HILL ROAD
ARCHWAY ROAD
A1
NORTH HILL
NORTH ROAD
SOUTHWOOD LA
HORNSEY LANE
CROUCH END HILL
HORNSEY RISE
A103 TOTTENHAM LANE
THE BROADWAY
HIGHGATE HIGH STREET
HIGHGATE HILL
ARCHWAY RD
JUNCTION ROAD
HOLLOWAY ROAD
ST JOHN'S GV
B519
B550
B540
A400
N6
N19
1 grid square represents 500 metres

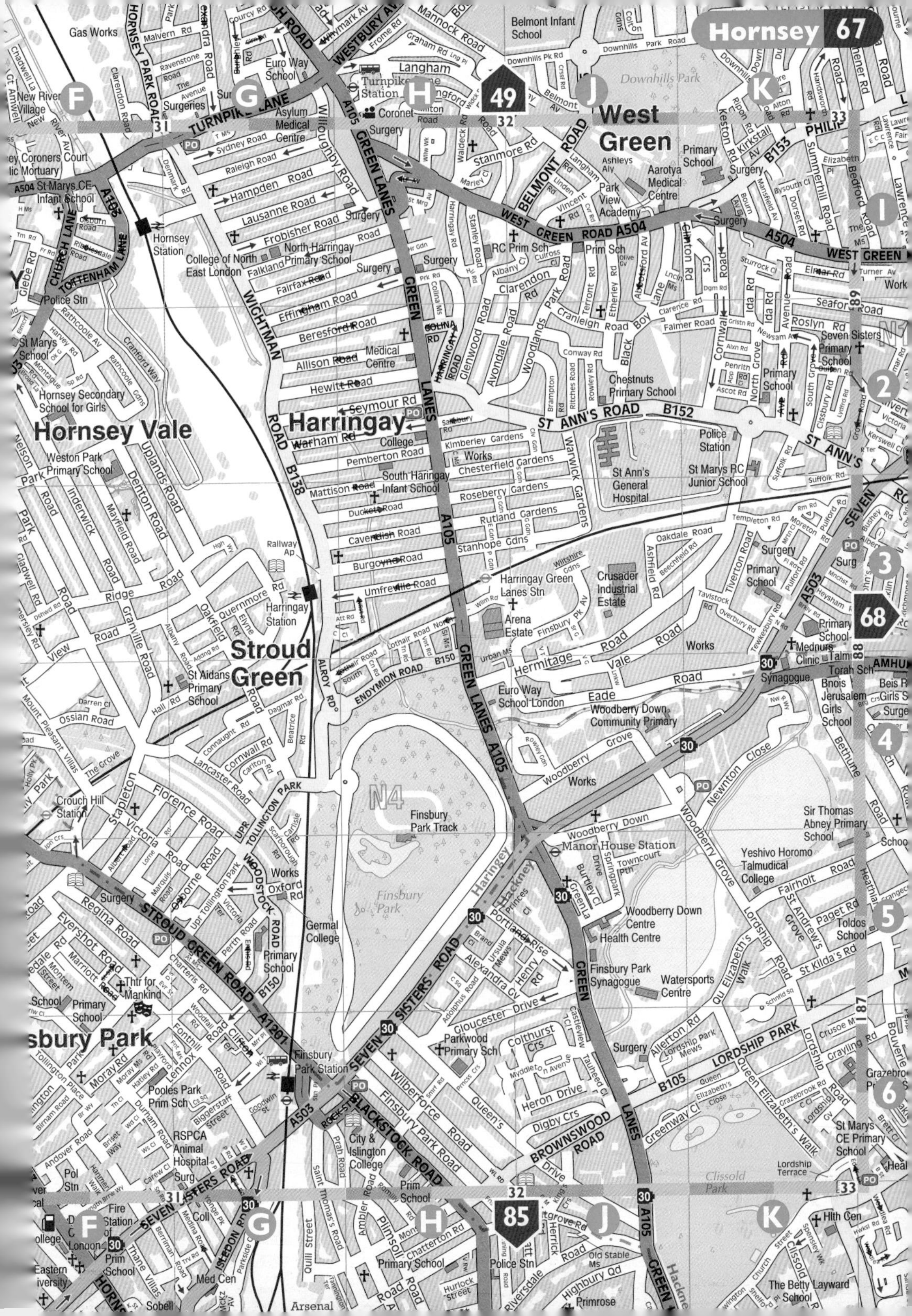
West Green
Harringay
Hornsey Vale
Stroud Green
Finsbury Park
Gas Works
Belmont Infant School
Downhills Park
Euro Way School
Turnpike Lane Station
Coronet
Asylum Medical Centre
Surgery
Coroners Court
Public Mortuary
St Marys CE Infant School
Hornsey Station
College of North East London
North Harringay Primary School
Police Stn
St Marys School
Hornsey Secondary School for Girls
Weston Park Primary School
Medical Centre
College
Works
South Haringay Infant School
RC Prim Sch
Prim Sch
Ashleys Aly
Aarotya Medical Centre
Park View Academy
Primary School
Chestnuts Primary School
Seven Sisters Primary School
Police Station
St Ann's General Hospital
St Marys RC Junior School
Crusader Industrial Estate
Harringay Green Lanes Stn
Arena Estate
Harringay Station
Railway Ap
St Aidans Primary School
Euro Way School London
Woodberry Down Community Primary
Mednurs Clinic
Synagogue
Bnois Jerusalem Girls School
Beis R Girls S
Torah Sch
Talmud
Finsbury Park Track
Finsbury Park
N4
Crouch Hill Station
Manor House Station
Sir Thomas Abney Primary School
Yeshivo Horomo Talmudical College
Toldos School
Woodberry Down Centre
Health Centre
Finsbury Park Synagogue
Watersports Centre
Germal College
Primary School
Thtr for Mankind
Poole Park Prim Sch
RSPCA Animal Hospital
Finsbury Park Station
Parkwood Primary Sch
City & Islington College
Prim School
Primary School
Police Stn
Clissold Park
St Marys CE Primary School
Lordship Terrace
Hlth Cen
The Betty Layward School
Fire Station
Pol Stn
Med Cen
Arsenal
TURNPIKE LANE
GREEN LANES
A105
WEST GREEN ROAD A504
ST ANN'S ROAD B152
SEVEN SISTERS ROAD
STROUD GREEN ROAD A1201
WICHTMAN ROAD B138
ENDYMION ROAD
BLACKSTOCK ROAD
BROWNSWOOD ROAD
LORDSHIP PARK
F G H J K
49
68
85
31 32 33

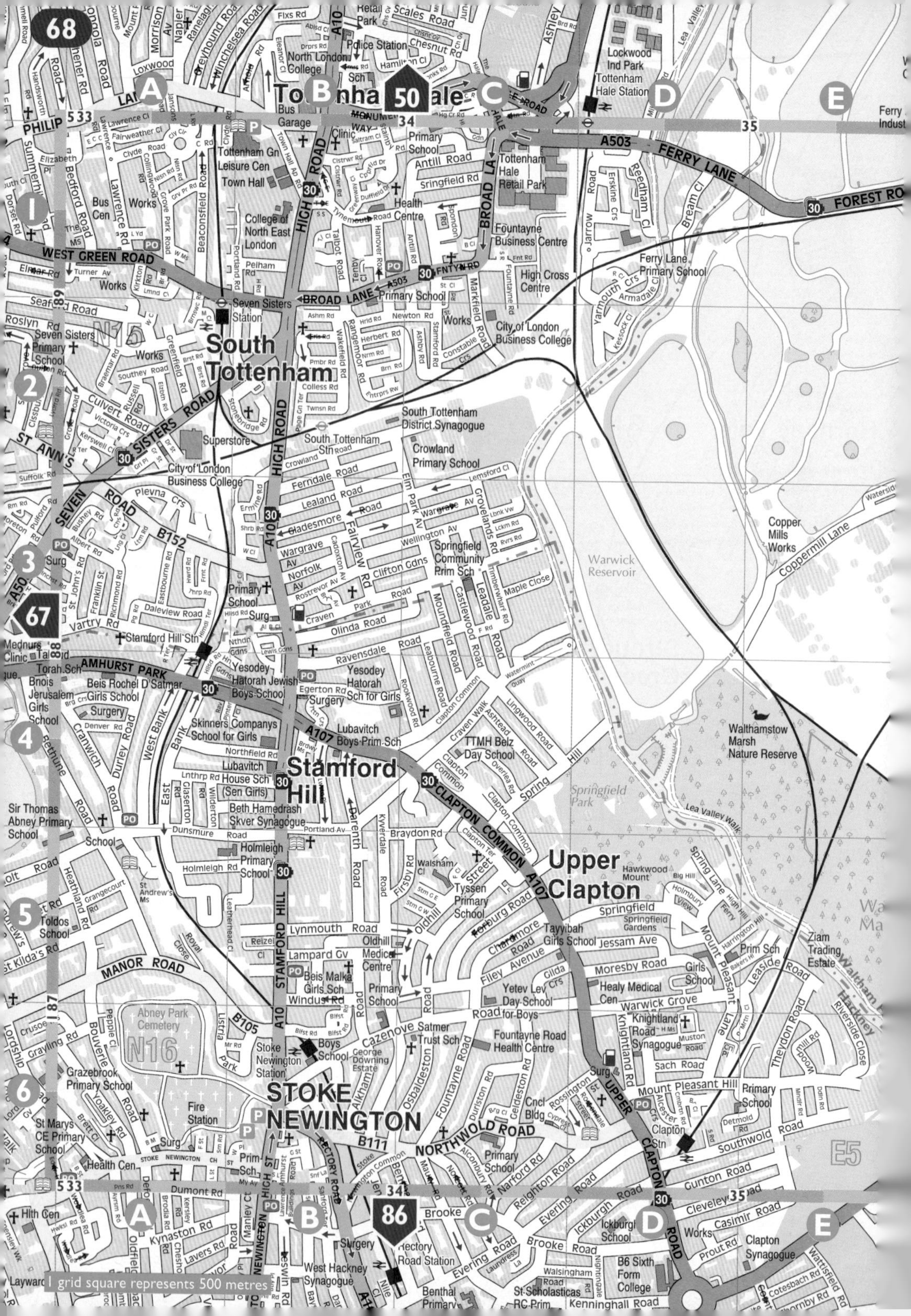

68
50
67
86
Tottenham Hale
South Tottenham
Stamford Hill
Upper Clapton
STOKE NEWINGTON
A B C D E
1 2 3 4 5 6
34
35
533
WEST GREEN ROAD
BROAD LANE
BROAD LA
FERRY LANE
A503
FOREST RD
SEVEN SISTERS ROAD
ST ANN'S
HIGH ROAD
A10
AMHURST PARK
A107
CLAPTON COMMON
STAMFORD HILL
UPPER CLAPTON ROAD
NORTHWOLD ROAD
B111
MANOR ROAD
B105
STOKE NEWINGTON HIGH ST
RECTORY ROAD
B152
Tottenham Hale Station
Lockwood Ind Park
Tottenham Hale Retail Park
Fountayne Business Centre
High Cross Centre
City of London Business College
Ferry Lane Primary School
Tottenham Gn Leisure Cen
Town Hall
College of North East London
North London College
Police Station
Bus Garage
Health Centre
Seven Sisters Station
Seven Sisters Primary School
Superstore
South Tottenham Stn
South Tottenham District Synagogue
Crowland Primary School
Springfield Community Prim Sch
Stamford Hill Stn
Yesodey Hatorah Jewish Boys School
Yesodey Hatorah Sch for Girls
Beis Rochel D'Satmar Girls School
Skinners Companys School for Girls
Lubavitch Boys Prim Sch
Lubavitch House Sch (Sen Girls)
Beth Hamedrash Skver Synagogue
TTMH Belz Day School
Holmleigh Primary School
Tyssen Primary School
Tayyibah Girls School
Yetev Lev Day School for Boys
Healy Medical Cen
Knightland Road Synagogue
Fountayne Road Health Centre
Oldhill Medical Centre
Beis Malka Girls Sch
Cazenove Satmer Trust Sch
Sir Thomas Abney Primary School
Toldos School
Abney Park Cemetery
Grazebrook Primary School
St Marys CE Primary School
Fire Station
Stoke Newington Station
Boys School
Rectory Road Station
West Hackney Synagogue
Clapton Stn
Clapton Synagogue
B6 Sixth Form College
Ickburgh School
St Scholasticas RC Prim
Warwick Reservoir
Walthamstow Marsh Nature Reserve
Springfield Park
Lea Valley Walk
Copper Mills Works
Coppermill Lane
Ziam Trading Estate
N15
N16
E5
1 grid square represents 500 metres

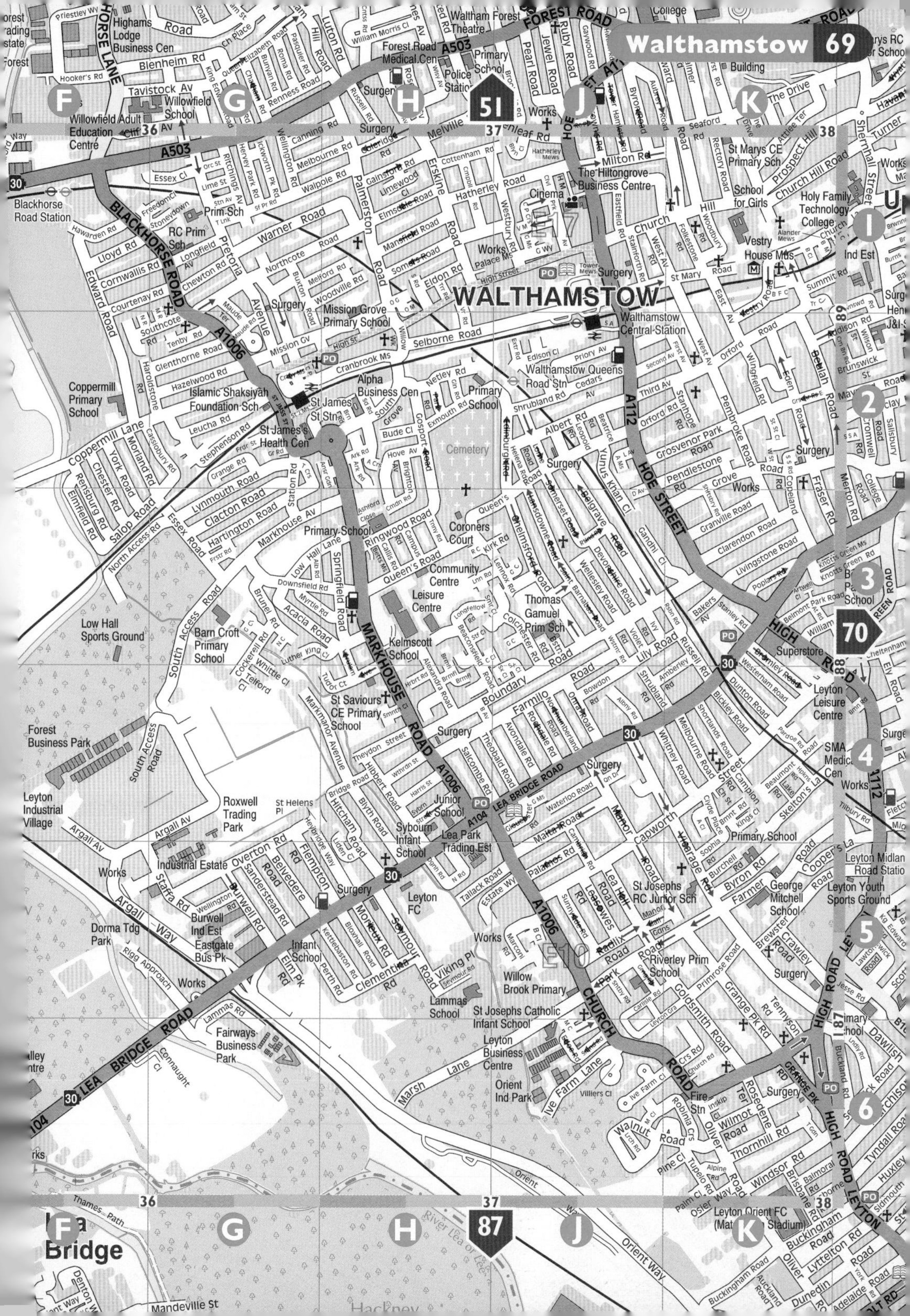
WALTHAMSTOW
E17
E10
FOREST ROAD
A503
BLACKHORSE ROAD
A1006
HOE STREET
A112
MARKHOUSE ROAD
LEA BRIDGE ROAD
A104
CHURCH ROAD
HIGH ROAD
HIGH ROAD LEYTON
Blackhorse Road Station
Walthamstow Central Station
Walthamstow Queens Road Stn
St James St Stn
Leyton Midland Road Station
Waltham Forest Theatre
Forest Road Medical Cen
Police Station
Primary School
Higham Lodge Business Cen
Willowfield Adult Education Centre
Willowfield School
Coppermill Primary School
Islamic Shaksiyah Foundation Sch
St James's Health Cen
Alpha Business Cen
Mission Grove Primary School
The Hiltongrove Business Centre
Cinema
Works Palace Ms
Vestry House Mus
Holy Family Technology College
St Marys CE Primary Sch
School for Girls
Cemetery
Coroners Court
Community Centre
Leisure Centre
Thomas Gamuel Prim Sch
Kelmscott School
St Saviours CE Primary School
Barn Croft Primary School
Low Hall Sports Ground
Forest Business Park
Leyton Industrial Village
Roxwell Trading Park
Industrial Estate
Burwell Ind Est
Eastgate Bus Pk
Dorma Tdg Park
Lea Park Trading Est
Sybourn Infant School
Junior School
Leyton FC
Infant School
Lammas School
Willow Brook Primary
St Josephs Catholic Infant School
Leyton Business Centre
Orient Ind Park
Fairways Business Park
St Josephs RC Junior Sch
Riverley Prim School
George Mitchell School
Leyton Youth Sports Ground
Leyton Leisure Centre
SMA Medical Cen
Superstore
Fire Stn
Leyton Orient FC (Matchroom Stadium)
Lea Bridge
Thames Path
River Lea or Lee
Orient Way
Hackney
51
70
87
36
37
38

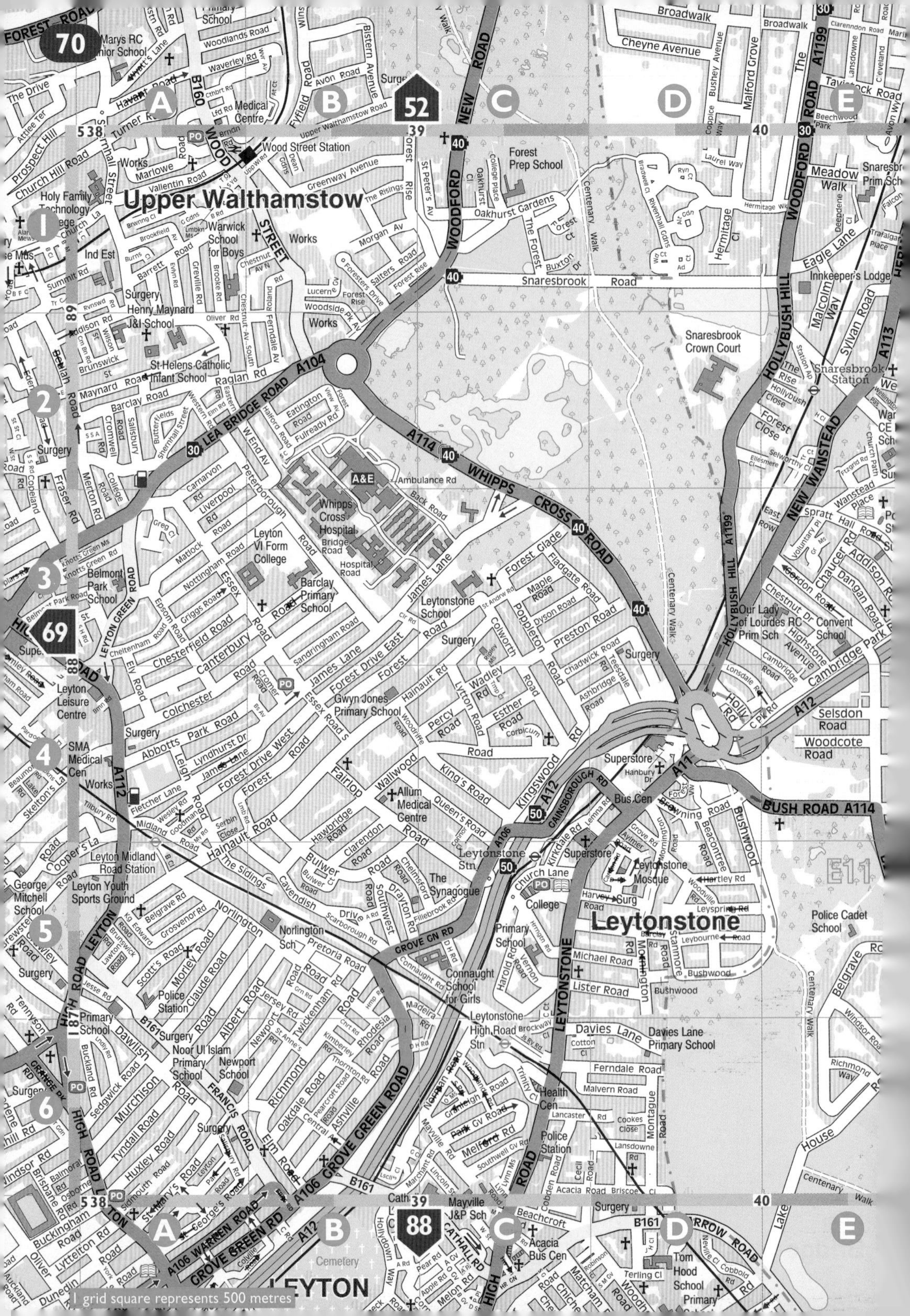
70
52
69
88
A
B
C
D
E
1
2
3
4
5
6
538
39
40
Forest Road
Marys RC
Junior School
Woodlands Road
Waverley Rd
Havant Road
B160
Avon Road
Bisterne Avenue
Fyfield Road
Surgery
Medical Centre
Turner Rd
Upper Walthamstow Road
New Road
Broadwalk
Cheyne Avenue
Bushey Avenue
Malford Grove
The Drive
Attlee Ter
Prospect Hill
Church Hill Road
Wood Street Station
Dean Gdns
Forest Rise
Works
Marlowe
Greenway Avenue
Vallentin Road
St Peter's Av
College Place
Oakhurst Cl
Forest Prep School
Centenary Walk
Laurel Way
Hermitage Wk
Meadow Walk
Snaresbrook Prim Sch
Woodford Road
A1199
Holy Family Technology College
Upper Walthamstow
The Risings
Oakhurst Gardens
The Forest
Orest Ct
Buxton Dr
Hermitage Cl
Eagle Lane
Trafalgar Place
Church La
Ind Est
Warwick School for Boys
Morgan Av
Salters Road
Forest Rise
Snaresbrook Road
Innkeeper's Lodge
Summit Rd
Barrett Road
Greville Rd
Brooke Rd
Chestnut Av N
Surgery
Henry Maynard J&I School
Addison Rd
Oliver Rd
Chestnut Av South
Ferndale Av
Lucerne
Foresters Drive
Woodside Pk Av
Works
Hollybush Hill
Malcolm Way
Sylvan Road
Snaresbrook Crown Court
Brunswick St
St Helens Catholic Infant School
Raglan Rd
A104
Lea Bridge Road
Beulah Road
Maynard Road
Barclay Road
Cromwell Road
Salisbury
Butterfields
Shernhall Street
Elm Rd
Eastern Rd
Western Rd
Halford Road
W End Av
Eatington Road
Fulready Rd
View Av
Forest
A114
Whipps Cross Road
The Rise
Hollybush Close
Forest Close
Snaresbrook Station
A113
New Wanstead
Surgery
Fraser Rd
Copeland
Merton Rd
College Rd
Carnarvon Rd
Liverpool Rd
Peterborough Road
A&E
Ambulance Rd
Back Road
Whipps Cross Hospital
Bridge Road
Hospital Road
Selworthy Cl
Ellesmere Cl
Spratt Hall Road
Wanstead Place
East Row
Knotts Green Rd
Belmont Park School
Belmont Park Road
Leyton Green Road
Greg Cl
Matlock
Nottingham Road
Leyton VI Form College
Essex Road
Barclay Primary School
James Lane
Forest Glade
Fladgate Road
Maple Road
Leytonstone School
Dyson Road
Preston Road
Poppleton
Colworth
Voluntary Pl
Chaucer Rd
Addison Road
Dangan Road
Gordon Road
Chestnut Dr
Our Lady of Lourdes RC Prim Sch
Convent School
Highstone Avenue
Cambridge Park
Cambridge Road
Lonsdale Rd
Holly Rd
C Pk Rd
A12
Selsdon Road
Woodcote Road
Griggs Road
Epsom Road
Chesterfield Road
Canterbury
Sandringham Road
Cheltenham Road
Ely Road
Colchester
Cromer Road
Forest Drive East
Forest Road
Surgery
Chadwick Road
Teesdale
Ashbridge
Leyton Leisure Centre
Abbotts Park Road
Lyndhurst Dr
Essex Road S
Gwyn Jones Primary School
Hainault Rd
Woodville
Percy Road
Lytton Road
Wadley Rd
Esther Road
Corbicum
Kingswood Rd
Surgery
SMA Medical Cen
Works
A112
Fletcher Lane
Leigh Road
James Lane
Forest Drive West
Forest Road
Fairlop
Wallwood
Allum Medical Centre
King's Road
Queen's Road
Superstore
Hanbury Dr
A11
Gainsborough Rd
Bus Cen
Browning Road
Beacontree Road
Bushwood
Bush Road A114
Skeltons La
Midland Road
Goodman Rd
Serbin Close
Hainault Road
Hawbridge Road
Clarendon Road
Leytonstone Stn
Kirkdale Rd
Superstore
Leytonstone Mosque
Hartley Rd
E11
Cooper's La
Leyton Midland Road Station
The Sidings
Cavendish
Bulwer Road
Drive
Chelmsford Road
The Synagogue
Church Lane
College
Harvey Road
Surg
Leyspring Rd
George Mitchell School
Leyton Youth Sports Ground
Belgrave Rd
Grosvenor Rd
Norlington Road
Scarborough Rd
Norlington Sch
Southwest Road
Drayton Rd
Fillebrook Rd
Grove Gn Rd
Primary School
Leytonstone
Police Cadet School
Stamford Road
Leybourne Road
Scott's Road
Morley Road
Pretoria Road
Connaught Rd
Connaught School for Girls
Harold Rd
Vernon Rd
Michael Road
Mornington Rd
Bushwood
Belgrave Rd
High Road Leyton
Jesse Rd
Claude Road
Police Station
Jersey Rd
Twickenham Rd
Madeira Rd
Lister Road
Bushwood
Tennyson Rd
Primary School
Dawlish
B161
Surgery
Albert Road
Newport Road
Rhodesia
Leytonstone High Road Stn
Brockway
Leytonstone Road
Davies Lane
Davies Lane Primary School
Cotton Cl
Windsor Rd
Richmond Way
Grange Pk Rd
Noor Ul Islam Primary School
Newport School
St Anne's
Kimberley
Thornton Rd
Ferndale Road
Trinity Cl
Malvern Road
Surgery
Sedgwick Road
Murchison
Francis Road
Richmond
Oakdale Road
Pearcroft Road
Central
Ashville
Grove Green Road
Norman Road
Granleigh Road
Park Gv Road
Melford Rd
Health Cen
Lancaster Rd
Cookes Close
Montague Road
House
Tyndall Road
Huxley Road
Surgery
Elm Road
A106
Mayville Rd
Southwell Gv Rd
Police Station
Lansdowne Rd
Centenary Walk
Windsor Rd
Brisbane Rd
Balmoral Rd
Osborne Rd
Sidmouth Road
St Mary's Road
St George's Road
Warren Road
A106 Grove Green Rd
Lincoln
Marchant Rd
Cecil Road
Cobden Road
Acacia Road
Briscoe Cl
Lake
Buckingham Road
Lyttelton Rd
Oliver Road
Dunedin
Auckland Rd
Colville
Cemetery
Leyton
Hollydown Way
Mayville J&P Sch
Cathall Rd
Pear Rd
Apple Rd
Melon Rd
Beachcroft
Acacia Bus Cen
Surgery
B161
Harrow Road
Tom Hood School
Primary
Terling Cl
Robinson
Matcham
Neville Cl
Cobbold Rd
High
1 grid square represents 500 metres

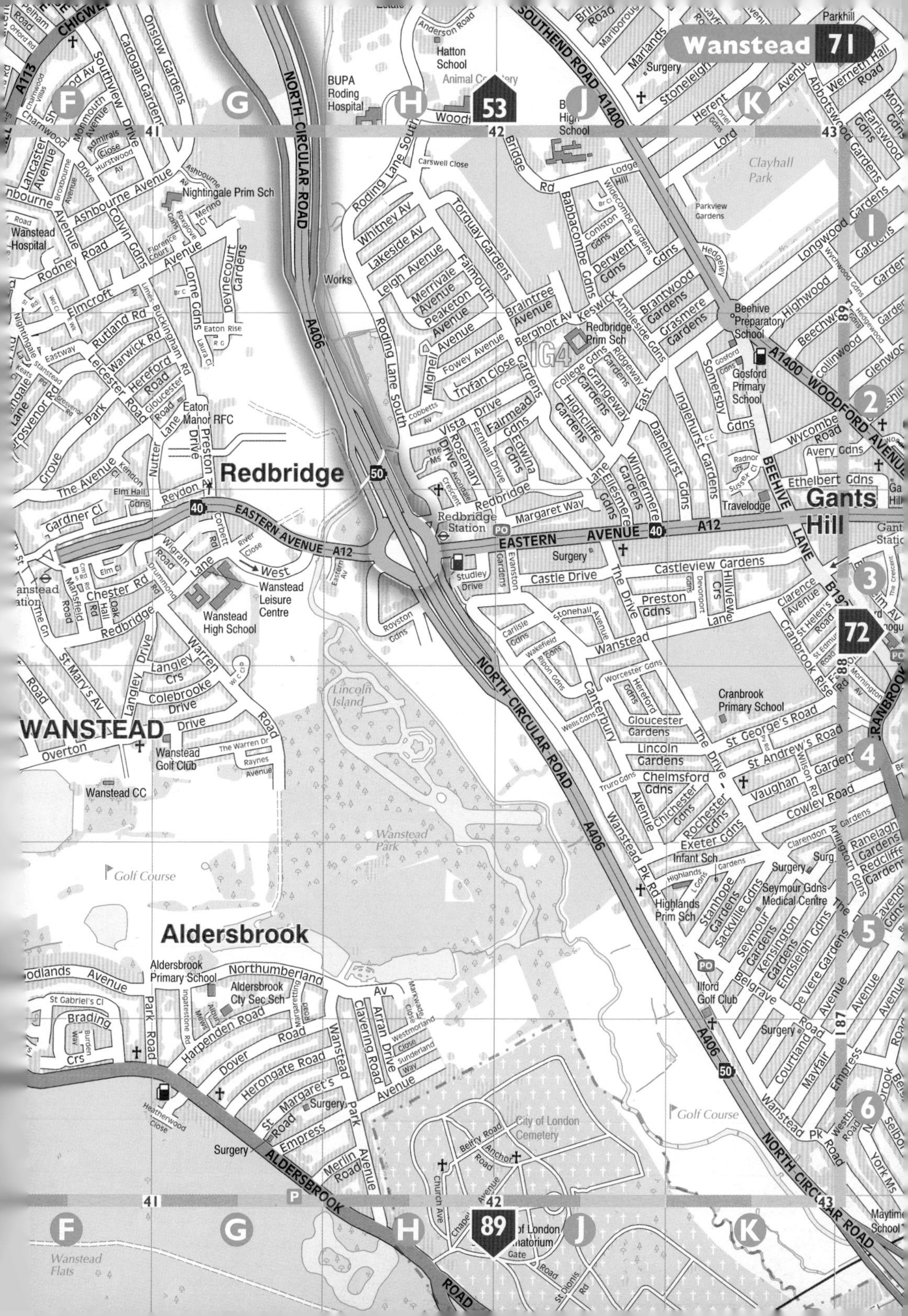
Redbridge
WANSTEAD
Aldersbrook
Gants Hill
Wanstead Park
Lincoln Island
City of London Cemetery
Wanstead Flats
Clayhall Park
Golf Course
NORTH CIRCULAR ROAD
A406
EASTERN AVENUE
A12
SOUTHEND ROAD A1400
A1400 WOODFORD AVENUE
ALDERSBROOK ROAD
BEEHIVE LANE
Hatton School
BUPA Roding Hospital
Nightingale Prim Sch
Wanstead Hospital
Eaton Manor RFC
Redbridge Station
Wanstead Leisure Centre
Wanstead High School
Wanstead Golf Club
Wanstead CC
Redbridge Prim Sch
Beehive Preparatory School
Gosford Primary School
Travelodge
Cranbrook Primary School
Infant Sch
Highlands Prim Sch
Seymour Gdns Medical Centre
Ilford Golf Club
Aldersbrook Primary School
Aldersbrook City Sec Sch
Surgery
Works
53
72
89
F
G
H
J
K
41
42
43
2
3
4
5
6

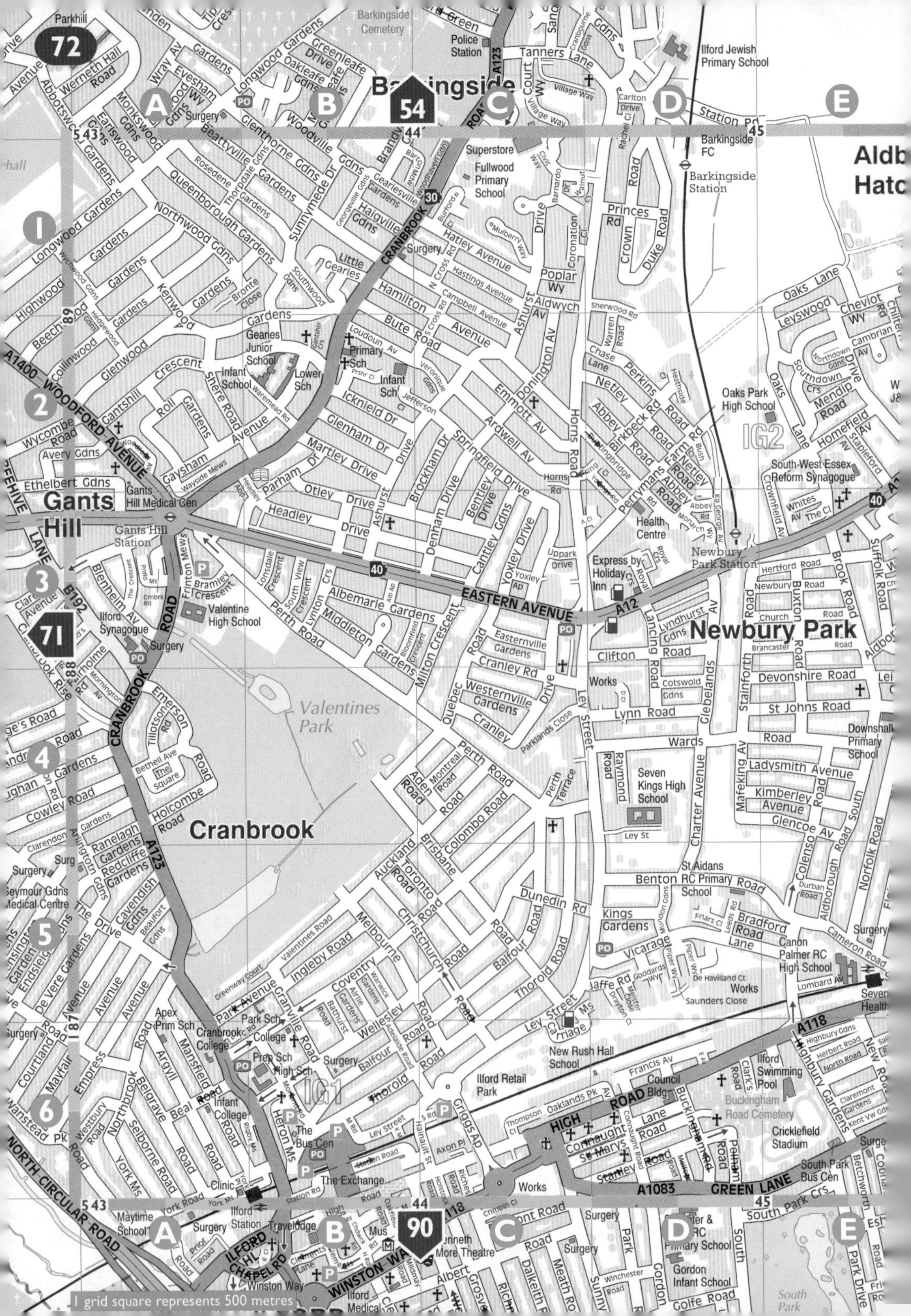

72
54
71
90
Barkingside
Gants Hill
Newbury Park
Cranbrook
Valentines Park
Aldb Hatc
IG1
IG2
A123
A12
A1400
A118
A1083
B192
EASTERN AVENUE
CRANBROOK ROAD
WOODFORD AVENUE
HIGH ROAD
GREEN LANE
NORTH CIRCULAR ROAD
Barkingside Cemetery
Police Station
Ilford Jewish Primary School
Barkingside FC
Barkingside Station
Superstore
Fullwood Primary School
Geanies Junior School
Infant School
Oaks Park High School
South West Essex Reform Synagogue
Gants Hill Medical Cen
Gants Hill Station
Newbury Park Station
Health Centre
Express by Holiday Inn
Valentine High School
Ilford Synagogue
Seven Kings High School
Downshall Primary School
St Aidans RC Primary School
Canon Palmer RC High School
New Rush Hall School
Ilford Retail Park
Ilford Swimming Pool
Council Bldg
Buckingham Road Cemetery
Cricklefield Stadium
South Park Bus Cen
Cranbrook College
The Bus Cen
The Exchange
Ilford Station
Travelodge
Kenneth More Theatre
Gordon Infant School
Maytime School
Apex Prim Sch
Seymour Gdns Medical Centre
South Park
Works
Surgery
1 grid square represents 500 metres

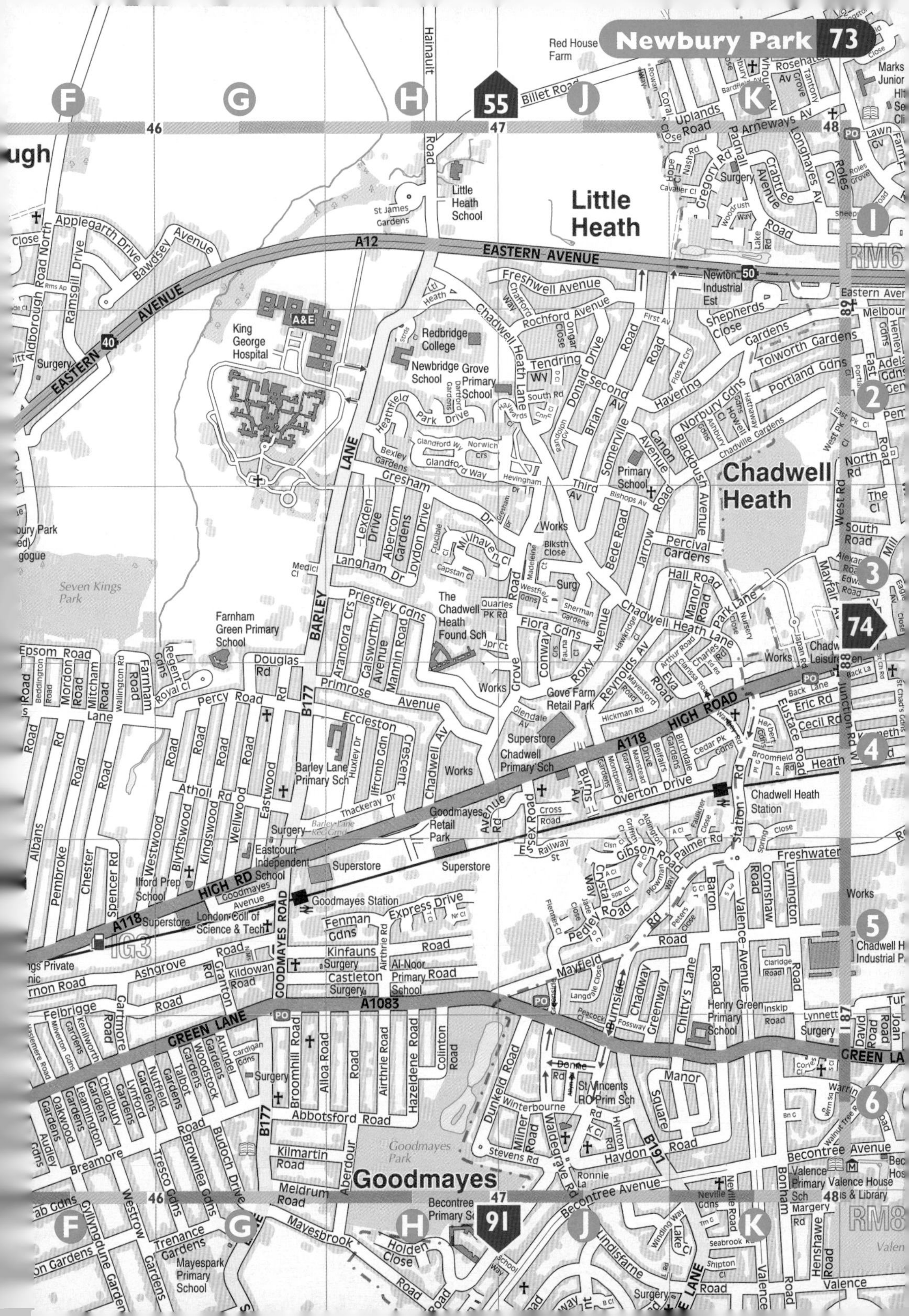
Red House Farm
55
Billet Road
Hainault Road
Little Heath School
St James Gardens
Little Heath
A12
EASTERN AVENUE
Applegarth Drive
Bawdsey Avenue
Aldborough Road North
Ramsgill Drive
Surgery
40
King George Hospital
A&E
Redbridge College
Newbridge School
Grove Primary School
Chadwell Heath Lane
Freshwell Avenue
Rochford Avenue
Ongar Close
Tendring Wy
Donald Drive
Second Av
Brian
Somerville
Third Av
First Av
Newton Industrial Est
50
Shepherds Close
Havering Gardens
Tolworth Gardens
Portland Gdns
Norbury Gdns
Chadville Gardens
Blackbush Avenue
Canon Avenue
Primary School
Chadwell Heath
Uplands Road
Arneways Av
Gregory Rd
Padnall
Crabtree Avenue
Longhayes Av
Roles Gv
Lake Rd
RM6
Eastern Avenue
Melbourne Gdns
West Rd
North Rd
The Cl
South Road
Mayfair Av
74
Heathfield Park Drive
Glandford Way
Bexley Gardens
Gresham Dr
Lexden Drive
Abercorn Gardens
Joydon Drive
Langham Dr
Millhaven Cl
Capstan Cl
Medici Cl
Works
Blksth Close
Surg
Bede Road
Jarrow Road
Percival Gardens
Hall Road
Manor Road
Park Lane
BARLEY LANE
Priestley Gdns
Arandora Crs
Galsworthy Avenue
Mannin Road
The Chadwell Heath Found Sch
Quaries Pk Rd
Flora Gdns
Conway
Roxy Avenue
Reynolds Av
Hawkridge Cl
Arthur Road
Eva Road
Chadwell Heath Lane
Nursery
Japan Rd
Chadwell Leisure Cen
Back La
Eric Rd
Cecil Rd
Junction Rd W
Eustace Road
Heath
Seven Kings Park
Farnham Green Primary School
Epsom Road
Mordon Road
Mitcham Road
Wallington Rd
Farnham Road
Regent Gdns
Royal Cl
Douglas Rd
Percy Road
B177
Primrose Avenue
Eccleston Crescent
Chadwell Av
Grove
Gove Farm Retail Park
Glendale Av
Superstore
Chadwell Primary Sch
Hickman Rd
A118
HIGH ROAD
Montpelier Gardens
Manstead Gardens
Belfairs Drive
Birchdale Gardens
Cedar Pk Gdns
Herbert Gdns
Broomfield Road
Overton Drive
Chadwell Heath Station
Station Rd
Albans Road
Pembroke Road
Chester Road
Spencer Rd
Westwood Road
Blythswood Road
Kingswood Road
Wellwood Road
Eastwood Road
Atholl Rd
Barley Lane Primary Sch
Huxley Dr
Thackeray Dr
Goodmayes Retail Park
Avenue Rd
Sussex Road
Burns Av
Cross Road
Railway St
Surgery
Barley Lane Rec Grnd
Eastcourt Independent School
Superstore
Ilford Prep School
HIGH RD
Goodmayes Avenue
Goodmayes Station
London Coll of Science & Tech
Express Drive
Fenman Gdns
Kinfauns Road
Ashgrove Road
Kildowan Road
Castleton Road
Al-Noor Primary School
Surgery
Gibson Road
Palmer Rd
Crystal Way
Pedley Road
Baron Road
Valence Avenue
Cornshaw Road
Lymington Road
Freshwater
Works
Chadwell Heath Industrial Park
IG3
Granton Rd
GOODMAYES ROAD
Felbrigge Road
Gartmore Road
Ashdon Close
Mayfield Road
Peters Close
Burnside
Chadway
Greenway
Chitty's Lane
Henry Green Primary School
Claridge Road
Inskip Road
Lynnett Road
Surgery
David Road
Joan Road
A1083
GREEN LANE
Arundel Gardens
Woodstock Gardens
Talbot Gardens
Nutfield Gardens
Lynford Gardens
Charlbury Gardens
Leamington Gardens
Oakwood Gardens
Audley Gdns
Broomhill Road
Alloa Road
Airthrie Road
Hazeldene Road
Collinton Road
Abbotsford Road
Kilmartin Road
Aberdour Road
Goodmayes Park
Goodmayes
Dunkeld Road
Winterbourne Rd
Milner Road
Waldegrave Rd
St Vincents RC Prim Sch
Hynton Rd
Manor Square
Haydon Road
Stevens Rd
Ronnie La
B191
Becontree Avenue
Valence Primary Sch
Valence House Museum & Library
Bonham Road
RM8
Breamore Road
Brownlea Gdns
Budoch Drive
Tresco Gdns
Meldrum Road
Becontree Primary Sch
91
Mayesbrook Road
Holden Close
Trenance Gardens
Westrow Gardens
Gylingdune Gardens
Mayespark Primary School
School Way
Winding Way
Lindisfarne Road
Neville Gdns
Seabrook Rd
Shipton Cl
Henshawe Road
Margery Rd
Valence
Surgery
F G H J K
46 47 48
1 2 3 4 5 6

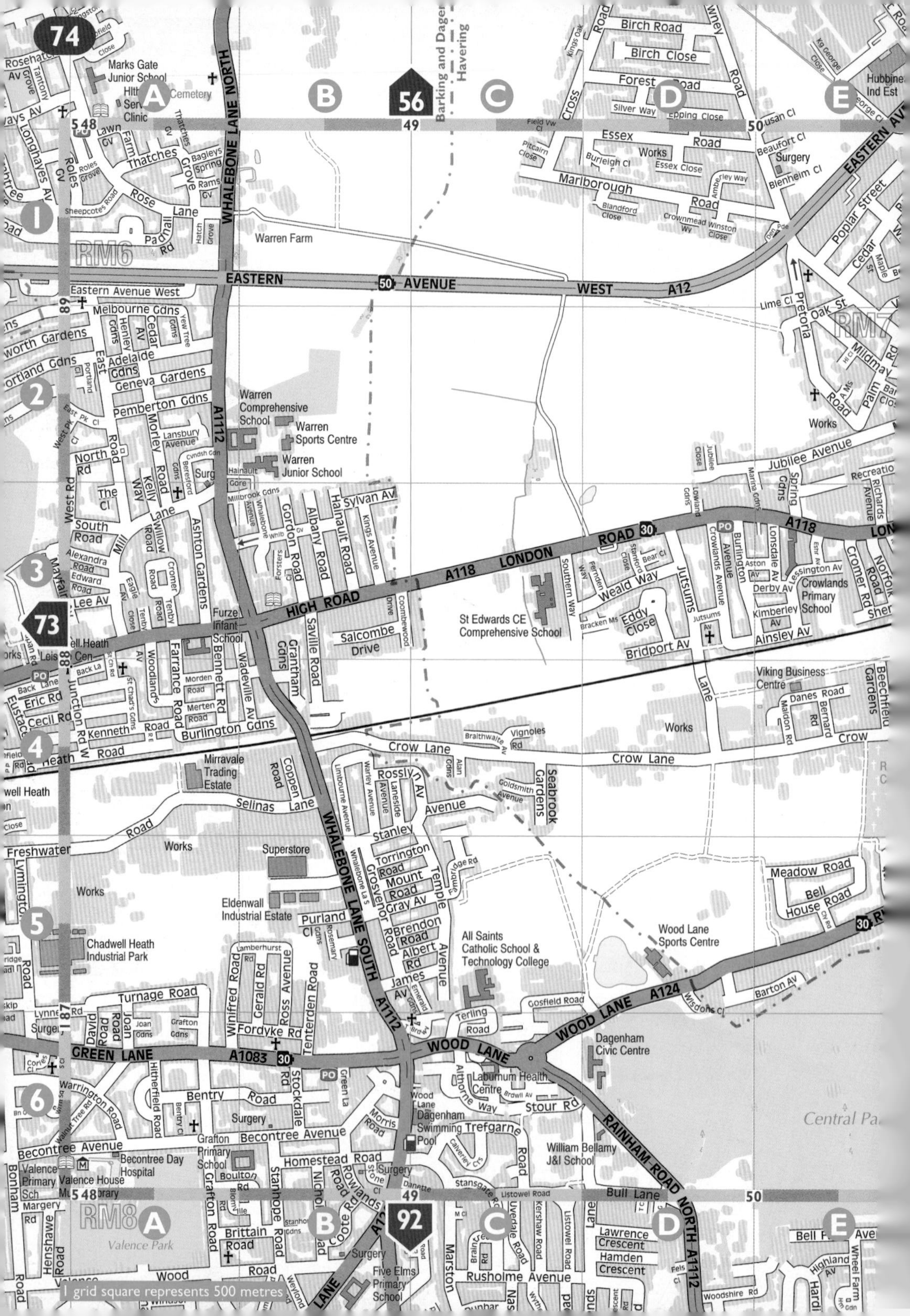

74
Marks Gate Junior School
Cemetery
Hlth Serv Clinic
A
B
56
Barking and Dagenham
Havering
C
D
E
Birch Road
Birch Close
Forest Road
Silver Way
Epping Close
Cross Road
Hubbinet Ind Est
548
49
50
Lawn Gv
Farm Gv
Thatches Grove
Bagleys Spring
Rams Gv
Roles Grove
Rose Lane
Sheepcote Rd
Padnall Rd
Hatch Grove
Longhayes Av
WHALEBONE LANE NORTH
Essex Road
Works
Burleigh Cl
Essex Close
Pitcairn Close
Marlborough Road
Blandford Close
Crownmead Wy
Winston Close
Beaufort Cl
Surgery
Blenheim Cl
EASTERN AVENUE
1
RM6
Warren Farm
EASTERN AVENUE WEST A12
50
Eastern Avenue West
Melbourne Gdns
Henley Gdns
Cedar Av
Yew Tree Gdns
Adelaide Gdns
Geneva Gardens
Pemberton Gdns
Portland Gdns
East Pk Cl
West Pk Cl
2
Lansbury Avenue
Morley Road
North Rd
Kelly Way
The Cl
South Road
West Rd
Mill Lane
Willow Road
Ashton Gardens
A1112
Warren Comprehensive School
Warren Sports Centre
Warren Junior School
Hainault Gore
Millbrook Gdns
Whalebone Avenue
Gordon Road
Albany Road
Hainault Road
Sylvan Av
Kings Avenue
Poplar Street
Cedar
Pretoria Road
Oak St
Lime Cl
RM7
Mildmay Road
Palm
Works
Jubilee Avenue
Jubilee Close
Spring Gdns
Recreation Avenue
Richards Avenue
A118 LONDON ROAD 30
A118
3
Alexandra Road
Edward Road
Lee Av
Eagle Close
Cromer Road
Tenby Road
Furze Infant School
HIGH ROAD
Saville Road
Salcombe Drive
Coombewood Drive
St Edwards CE Comprehensive School
Southern Way
Weald Way
Eddy Close
Bridport Av
Jutsums Lane
Crowlands Avenue
Burlington Avenue
Lonsdale Av
Lessington Av
Derby Av
Crowlands Primary School
Kimberley Av
Ainsley Av
Cromer Rd
Norfolk Road
73
Chadwell Heath Leis Cen
88
Back Lane
Eric Rd
Cecil Rd
Junction Rd W
Kenneth Road
Farrance Road
Bennett Rd
Wadeville Av
Grantham Gdns
Morden Road
Merten Road
Burlington Gdns
Woodlands
Viking Business Centre
Danes Road
Bernard Rd
Beechfield Gardens
4
Heath Road
Crow Lane
Vignoles Rd
Mirravale Trading Estate
Coppen Road
Selinas Lane
Rosslyn Av
Stanley Avenue
Seabrook Gardens
Goldsmith Avenue
Alan Gdns
Freshwater Road
Works
Superstore
WHALEBONE LANE SOUTH
Torrington Road
Mount Road
Gray Av
Grosvenor Road
Temple Avenue
Brendon Road
Albert Rd
James Av
Meadow Road
Bell House Road
5
Works
Eldenwall Industrial Estate
Purland Cl
Chadwell Heath Industrial Park
Lymington Road
Wood Lane Sports Centre
All Saints Catholic School & Technology College
Lamberhurst Rd
Winifred Road
Gerald Rd
Ross Avenue
Tenterden Road
Turnage Road
David Road
Joan Road
Joan Gdns
Grafton Gdns
Fordyke Rd
Surgery
Gosfield Road
Terling Road
Wood Lane A124
Barton Av
Wisdons Cl
30
187
GREEN LANE A1083 30
WOOD LANE
Dagenham Civic Centre
Laburnum Health Centre
Althorne Way
Stour Rd
6
Warrington Road
Hitherfield Road
Bentry Road
Stockdale Rd
Green La
Surgery
Morris Road
Wood Lane
Dagenham Swimming Pool
Trefgarne Road
Central Park
Becontree Avenue
Becontree Day Hospital
Valence Primary Sch
Valence House
Grafton Primary School
Homestead Road
Boulton Rd
Stanhope Road
Nichol Road
Rowlands Road
Surgery
RAINHAM ROAD NORTH A1112
William Bellamy J&I School
Stansgate Rd
Listowel Road
Bull Lane
548
49
50
Bonham Road
Margery Rd
RM8
A
Valence Park
Henshawe Road
Grafton Road
Brittain Road
Coote Rd
92
C
D
E
Marston
Uvedale Road
Kershaw Road
Listowel Road
Lawrence Crescent
Hamden Crescent
Bell Farm Ave
Highland Av
Rusholme Avenue
Five Elms Primary School
Wood Road
Woodshire Rd
1 grid square represents 500 metres

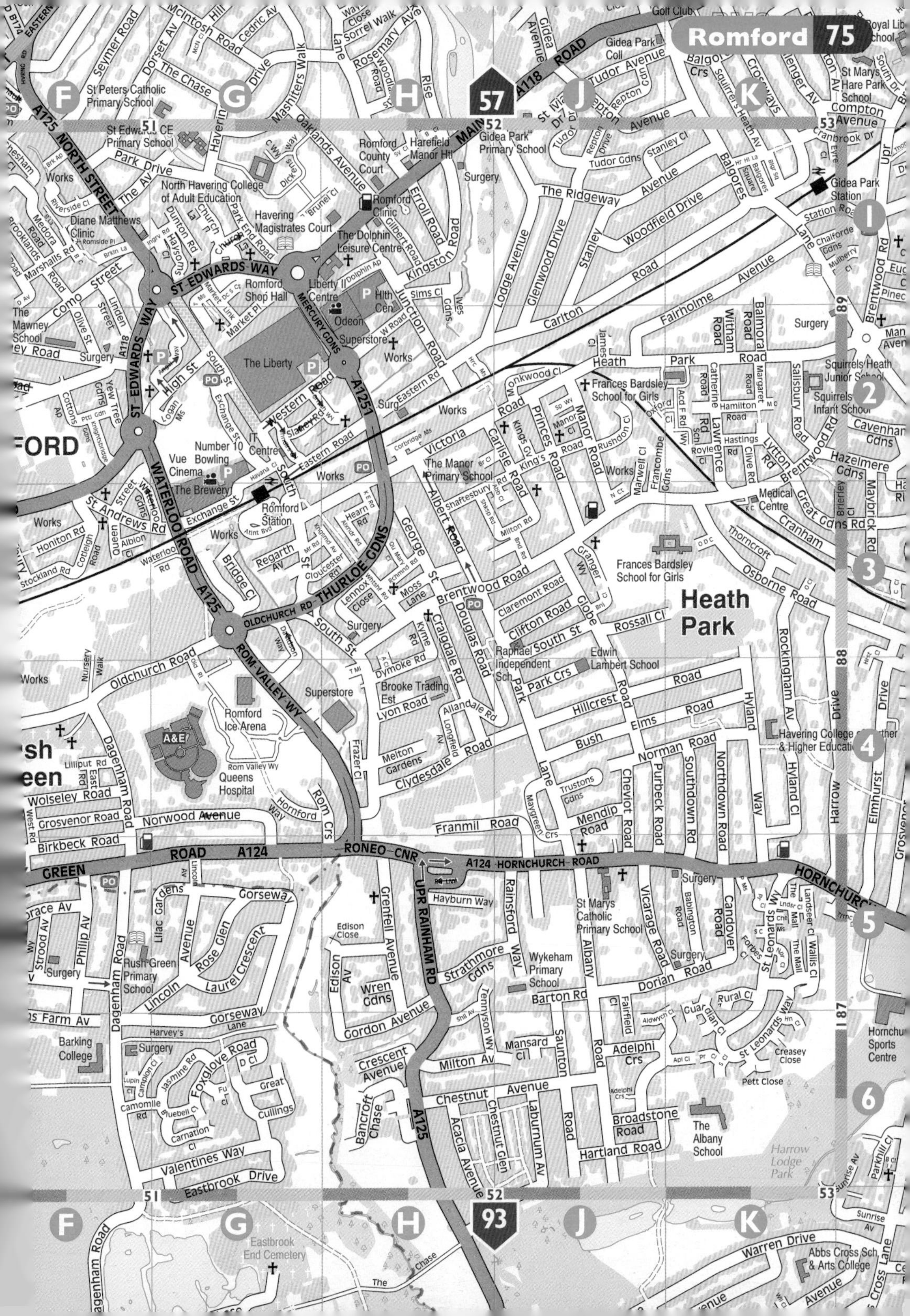

Romford
75
57
93
F
G
H
J
K
1
2
3
4
5
6
51
52
53
88
89
187
NORTH STREET
A125
A118
MAIN ROAD
ST EDWARDS WAY
WATERLOO ROAD
RONEO CNR
A124
HORNCHURCH ROAD
UPR RAINHAM RD
ROM VALLEY WY
OLDCHURCH RD
THURLOE GDNS
A1251
MERCURY GDNS
GREEN ROAD
St Peters Catholic Primary School
St Edwards CE Primary School
Park Drive
North Havering College of Adult Education
Havering Magistrates Court
Romford County Court
Harefield Manor Htl
Romford Clinic
The Dolphin Leisure Centre
Gidea Park Primary School
Gidea Park Coll
Gidea Park Station
Golf Club
Tudor Avenue
Repton Avenue
The Ridgeway
Woodfield Drive
Carlton Road
Heath Park Road
Fairholme Avenue
Squirrels Heath Junior School
Squirrels Infant School
Brentwood Road
Cranham Gdns
Osborne Road
Diane Matthews Clinic
Romford Shop Hall
Liberty II Centre
Odeon
The Liberty
Superstore
Works
Surgery
Market Pl
High St
South St
Victoria Road
Eastern Road
Western Road
Romford Station
Exchange St
Number 10 Bowling
Vue Cinema
The Brewery
The Mawney School
Como Street
Marshalls Rd
ORD
Frances Bardsley School for Girls
Heath Park
The Manor Primary School
Albert Road
Carlisle Road
Princes Road
Manor Road
King's Road
George St
Brentwood Road
Claremont Road
Clifton Road
South St
Rossall Cl
Raphael Independent Sch
Edwin Lambert School
Park Crs
Hillcrest Road
Bush Elms Road
Norman Road
Hyland Way
Havering College of Further & Higher Education
Rockingham Av
Harrow Drive
Elmhurst Drive
Oldchurch Road
Romford Ice Arena
Queens Hospital
A&E
Dagenham Road
Wolseley Road
Grosvenor Road
Norwood Avenue
Birkbeck Road
Brooke Trading Est
Lyon Road
Melton Gardens
Clydesdale Road
Craigdale Rd
Douglas Road
Franmil Road
Mendip Road
Cheviot Road
Purbeck Road
Southdown Rd
Northdown Road
St Marys Catholic Primary School
Vicarage Road
Candover Road
Dorian Road
Wykeham Primary School
Rainsford Way
Albany Road
Barton Rd
Saunton Road
Mansard Cl
Adelphi Crs
Broadstone Road
Hartland Road
The Albany School
Harrow Lodge Park
Hornchurch Sports Centre
St Leonards Way
Pett Close
Creasey Close
Grenfell Avenue
Edison Close
Wren Gdns
Gordon Avenue
Strathmore Gdns
Hayburn Way
Crescent Avenue
Milton Av
Chestnut Avenue
Acacia Avenue
Laburnum Av
Bancroft Chase
Rush Green Primary School
Lincoln Avenue
Laurel Crescent
Rose Glen
Gorseway
Lilac Gardens
Barking College
Foxglove Road
Great Cullings
Valentines Way
Eastbrook Drive
Eastbrook End Cemetery
The Chase
Warren Drive
Abbs Cross Sch & Arts College
Sunrise Av

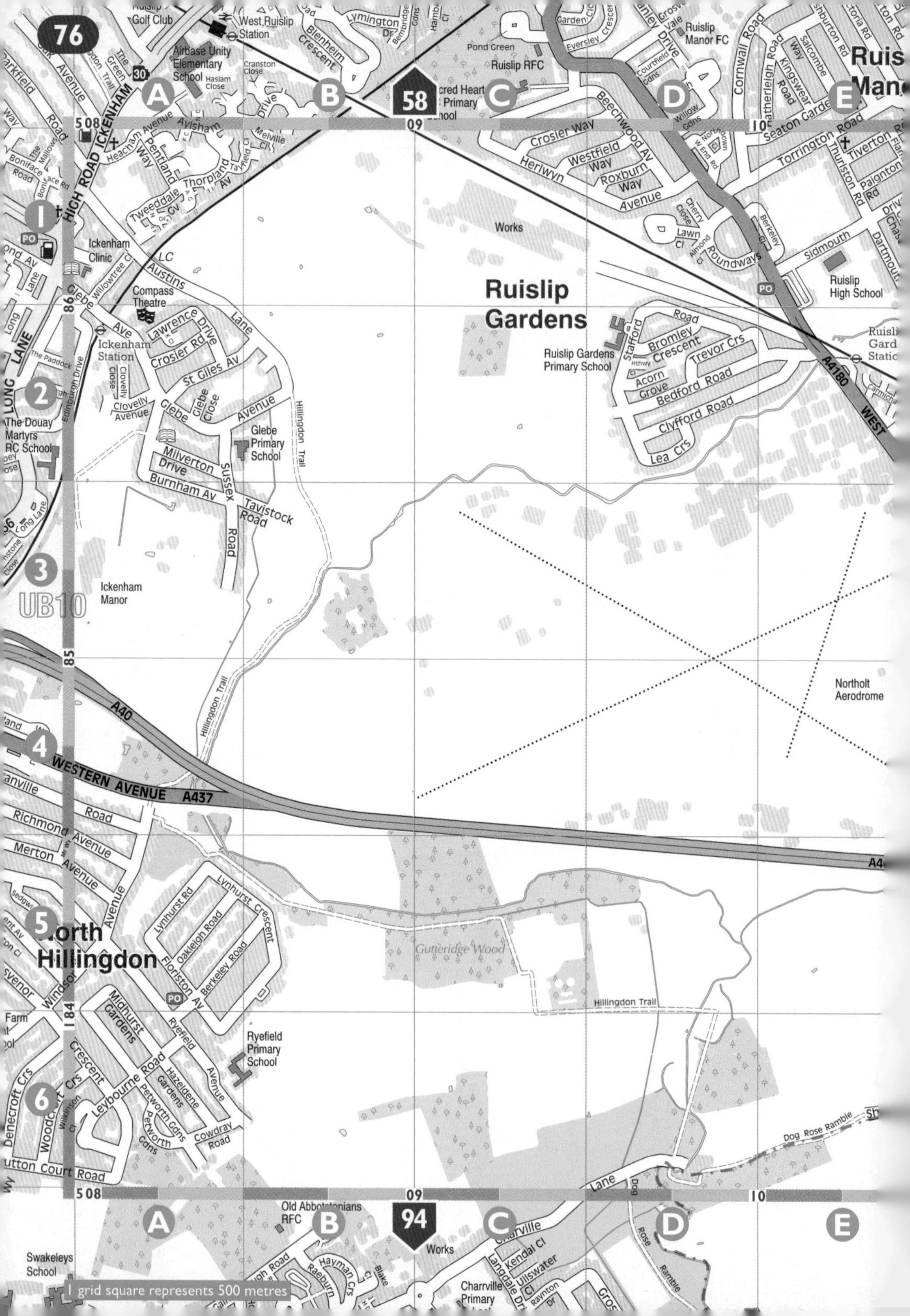

West Ruislip Station

Ruislip Golf Club

Airbase Unity Elementary School

Cranston Close

Haslam Close

Lymington Dr

Blenheim Crescent

Bembridge Gdns

Hamb

Pond Green

Garden

Eversley Crescent

Ruislip RFC

Manor Rd

Ruislip Manor FC

Cornwall Road

Kingswear

Drive

Beechwood Av

Courtfield

Gdns

Cherry

Willow Gdns

Salcombe

Wilmcote Way

netherleigh

Seaton Gardens

Victoria Rd

Kingswear

Tiverton Rd

Thurston Rd

Paignton Rd

Ruis Man

HIGH ROAD ICKENHAM

5 08

Avisham

Melville Cl

Sacred Heart RC Primary School

Crosier Way

Heriwyn

Roxburn Way

Westfield Way

Avenue

Lawn Cl

Almond

Roundways

PO

Sidmouth

Dartmouth

Ruislip High School

Ruisl Gard Stati

The Mallow

Boniface Rd

Grace Rd

I

PO

Ickenham Clinic

Heacham Avenue

Pentland Way

Thorpland Av

Tweeddale Rd

LC

Austins

Willowtree

Lane

Compass Theatre

Crosier Rd

Ruislip Gardens Primary School

Stafford Road

Bromley Crescent

Trevor Crs

Acorn Grove

Bedford Road

A4180

WEST

Ruislip Gardens

Works

2

The Douay Martyrs RC School

Ickenham Station

Glebe Close

Lawrence Drive

St Giles Av

Clovelly Close

Clovelly Avenue

Glebe Avenue

Glebe Primary School

Sussex Road

Clyfford Road

Lea Crs

LONG LANE

86

Glebe

Enfield Road

The Paddock

3

UB10

Milverton Drive

Burnham Av

Tavistock Road

Ickenham Manor

85

Hillingdon Trail

Northolt Aerodrome

4

WESTERN AVENUE A437

A40

Granville Road

Richmond Avenue

Merton Avenue

A4

Lynhurst Rd

Lynhurst Crescent

Gutteridge Wood

Hillingdon Trail

5 **orth Hillingdon**

Oakleigh Road

Berkeley Road

Windsor

Florston Av

Midhurst Gardens

PO

B184

Ryefield Avenue

Ryefield Primary School

Farm

Crescent

6 Woodcock Crs

Denecroft Crs

Willow Cr

Leybourne Road

Hazeldene Gardens

Petworth Gdns

Petworth Road

Cowdray Road

Dog Rose Ramble

utton Court Road

5 08

09

Old Abbotonians RFC

Hayman Crs

Raeburn Road

Works

Charville Cl

Kendal Cl

Charville Lane

Landgrove Dr

Ullswater Dr

Ravnton Dr

Lane

Dog

Rose

Ramble

Gros

10

Swakeleys School

Charville Primary

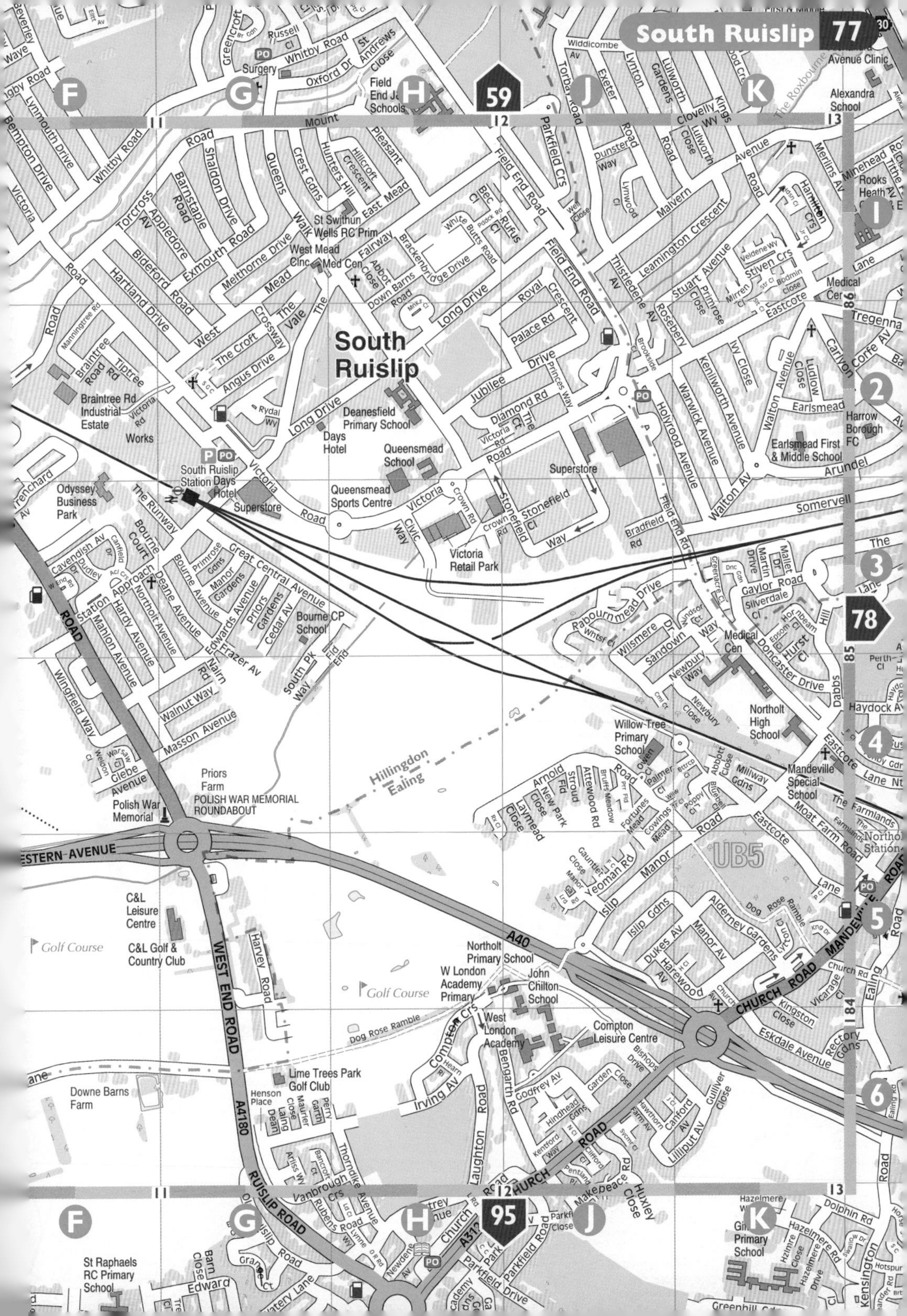
South Ruislip
Surgery
Field End Jr Schools
St Swithun Wells RC Prim
West Mead Clnc
Med Cen
Deanesfield Primary School
Days Hotel
Queensmead School
Queensmead Sports Centre
South Ruislip Station
Days Hotel
Superstore
Victoria Retail Park
Braintree Rd Industrial Estate
Works
Odyssey Business Park
Bourne CP School
Medical Cen
Northolt High School
Willow Tree Primary School
Mandeville Special School
Earlsmead First & Middle School
Harrow Borough FC
Avenue Clinic
Alexandra School
Rooks Heath
Medical Cen
Priors Farm
POLISH WAR MEMORIAL ROUNDABOUT
Polish War Memorial
WESTERN AVENUE
WEST END ROAD
A4180
RUISLIP ROAD
A40
CHURCH ROAD
MANDEVILLE ROAD
Hillingdon
Ealing
UB5
C&L Leisure Centre
C&L Golf & Country Club
Golf Course
Golf Course
Downe Barns Farm
Lime Trees Park Golf Club
Northolt Primary School
W London Academy Primary
John Chilton School
West London Academy
Compton Leisure Centre
Dog Rose Ramble
St Raphaels RC Primary School
Primary School
Northolt Station
Victoria Road
Long Drive
Queens Walk
Field End Road
Station Approach
Great Central Avenue
Eastcote Lane
Church Road
Victoria
Mount Pleasant
Malvern Avenue
Leamington Crescent
Holyrood Avenue
Warwick Avenue
Somervell
Arundel
Doncaster Drive
Rapourn mead Drive
Manor Road
Islip Manor Road
Compton Crs
Laughton Road
Bengarth Rd
Thorndike Avenue
Vanbrough Crs
Parkfield Road
Huxley Close
Makepeace Rd
Kensington
F G H J K
11 12 13
59 78 95
2 3 4 5 6
84 85 86

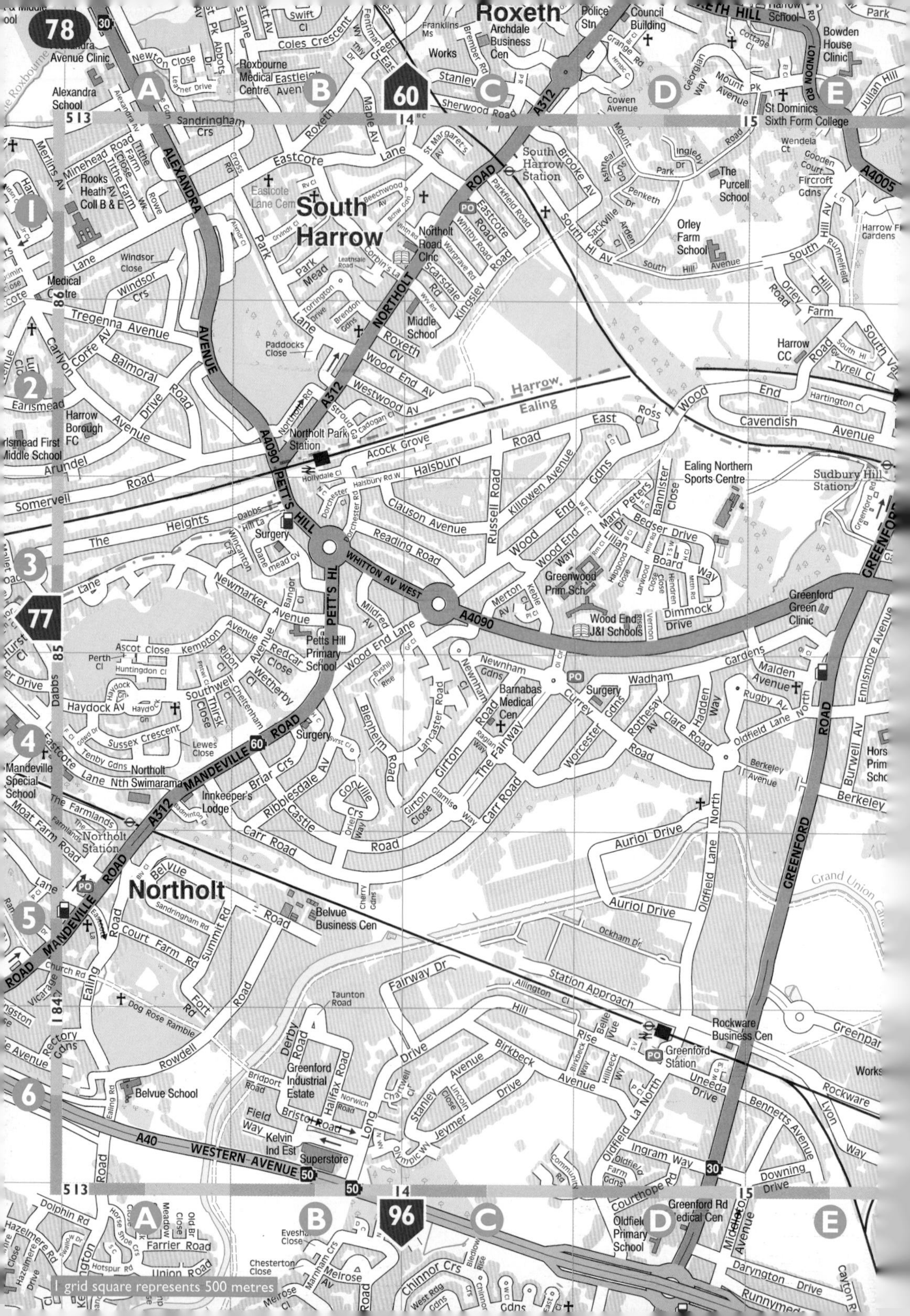

78
Roxeth
South Harrow
Northolt
Alexandra Avenue Clinic
Alexandra School
Roxbourne Medical Centre
Eastleigh Avenue
Coles Crescent
Swift Cl
Newton Close
Learner Drive
Archdale Business Cen
Franklins Ms
Works
Stanley Rd
Sherwood Road
Police Stn
Council Building
Roxeth Hill
Harrow School
Bowden House Clinic
London Rd
Georgian Way
Mount Pk Avenue
Cowen Avenue
St Dominics Sixth Form College
Wendela Ct
Gooden Court
Fircroft Gdns
Julian Hill
A4005
Harrow Fields Gardens
Sandringham Crs
Eastcote Lane
Roxeth Green Av
Maple Av
St Margaret's Av
Brooke Av
South Harrow Station
Parkfield Road
Ingleby Dr
Penketh Dr
Sackville Rd
Arden Cl
The Purcell School
Orley Farm School
South Hill Avenue
Merlins Av
Minehead Road
Farm Close
Tithe Farm Close
Rooks Heath Coll B & E
Rowe Wk
Alexandra Avenue
Eastcote Lane Cem
Beechwood Av
Northolt Road Clinic
Eastcote Road
Whitby Road
Scarsdale Rd
Kingsley Road
Windsor Close
Windsor Crs
Medical Centre
Park Mead
Torrington Drive
Brendon Gdns
Middle School
Roxeth Gv
Tregenna Avenue
Coffe Av
Balmoral Road
Carlyon Avenue
Paddocks Close
Wood End Av
Westwood Av
Harrow CC
Orley Farm Road
South Hill Cl
Tyrell Cl
Hartington Cl
Cavendish Avenue
Harrow
Ealing
Earlsmead
Harrow Borough FC
Earlsmead First & Middle School
Arundel Drive
Northolt Park Station
Acock Grove
Halsbury Road
Ross Cl
Wood End
East
Ealing Northern Sports Centre
Sudbury Hill Station
Somervell Road
Hollydale Cl
Dorchester Rd
Clauson Avenue
Russell Road
Killowen Avenue
Bannister Close
Mary Peters Dr
Bedser Drive
The Heights
A4090
Pett's Hill
Dabbs Hill La
Surgery
Wincanton Crs
Dane mead Gv
Reading Road
Whitton Av West
Wood End Gdns
Lilian Board Way
Greenwood Prim Sch
Greenford Green Clinic
Greenford Road
Newmarket Avenue
Bangor Cl
Mildred Av
Merton Av
Keble Cl
Wood End J&I Schools
Dimmock Drive
77
Ascot Close
Kempton Avenue
Perth Cl
Huntingdon Cl
Ripon Cl
Redcar Close
Petts Hill Primary School
Wood End Lane
Newnham Gdns
Barnabas Medical Cen
Currey Rd
Wadham Gardens
Malden Avenue
Ennismore Avenue
Haydock Av
Southwell Close
Thirsk Cl
Cheltenham Cl
Wetherby Cl
Mandeville Road
Blenheim Road
Lancaster Road
Girton Road
The Fairway
Worcester Gdns
Rothesay Av
Clare Road
Hadden Way
Rugby Av
Oldfield Lane North
Burwell Av
Berkeley Avenue
Sussex Crescent
Lewes Close
Tenby Gdns
Northolt Swimarama
Eastcote Lane Nth
Mandeville Special School
A312
Innkeeper's Lodge
Ribblesdale Av
Briar Crs
Castle Road
Gonville Crs
Girton Close
Glamis Way
Carr Road
Auriol Drive
The Farmlands
Moat Farm Road
Northolt Station
Belvue Rd
Belvue Business Cen
Cherry Gdns
Grand Union Canal
Court Farm Rd
Summit Rd
Sandringham Rd
Church Rd
Vicarage
Ealing Road
Fort Rd
Dog Rose Ramble
Ockham Dr
Station Approach
Allington Cl
Fairway Dr
Taunton Road
Derby Road
Rectory Gdns
Rowdell Road
Belvue School
Greenford Industrial Estate
Halifax Road
Bridport Road
Norwich Road
Bristol Road
Field Way
Kelvin Ind Est
Superstore
Long Drive
Stanley Avenue
Lincoln Close
Jevmer Drive
Birkbeck Avenue
Belle Vue Rise
Greenford Station
Rockware Business Cen
Greenpark
Uneeda Drive
Bennetts Avenue
Rockware Avenue
Lyon Way
Works
Olympic Wy
A40 Western Avenue
Ingram Way
Oldfield Farm Gdns
Courthope Rd
Downing Drive
96
Dolphin Rd
Farrier Road
Union Road
Hazelmere Rd
Evesham Close
Chesterton Close
Melrose Av
Chinnor Crs
Bledlow Rise
Greenford Rd Medical Cen
Oldfield Primary School
Middleton Avenue
Darvington Drive
Runnymede
1 grid square represents 500 metres

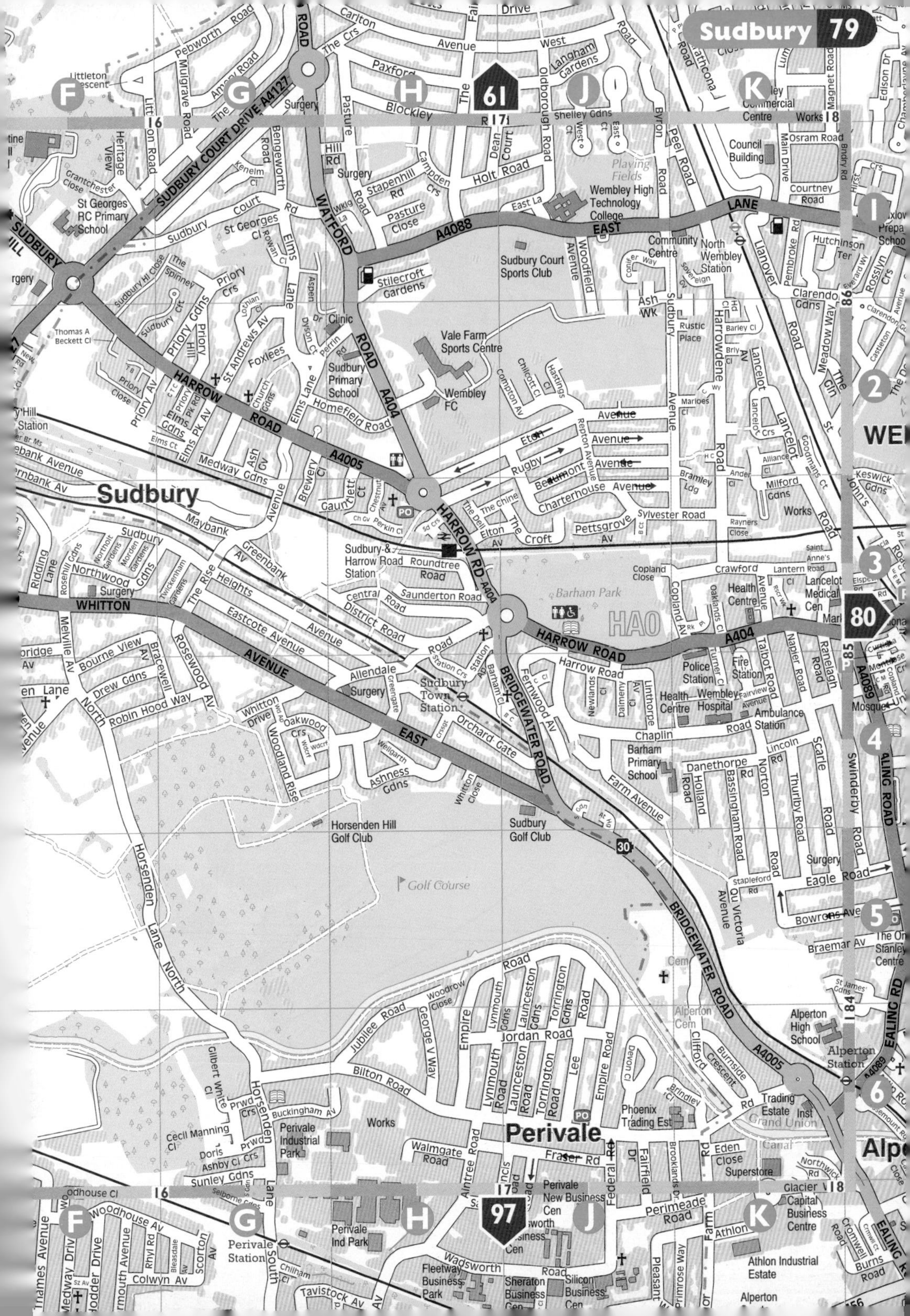
Sudbury
Perivale
Sudbury Court Drive A4127
Watford Road
A404
Harrow Road
A4005
East Lane
A4088
Whitton Avenue East
Bridgewater Road
Horsenden Lane North
Horsenden Lane South
Ealing Road
A4089
Barham Park
HA0
Horsenden Hill Golf Club
Sudbury Golf Club
Golf Course
Sudbury & Harrow Road Station
Sudbury Town Station
Sudbury Hill Station
North Wembley Station
Alperton Station
Perivale Station
Wembley High Technology College
Sudbury Court Sports Club
Vale Farm Sports Centre
Wembley FC
Sudbury Primary School
St Georges RC Primary School
Barham Primary School
Alperton High School
Wembley Hospital
Police Station
Fire Station
Ambulance Station
Health Centre
Lancelot Medical Cen
Community Centre
Council Building
Perivale Industrial Park
Perivale Ind Park
Perivale New Business Cen
Phoenix Trading Est
Trading Estate
Superstore
Capital Business Centre
Athlon Industrial Estate
Fleetway Business Park
Sheraton Business Cen
Silicon Business Cen
Grand Union Canal
Alperton Cem
Works
Surgery
Clinic
Playing Fields
61
80
97
F
G
H
J
K
16
17
18
2
3
4
5
6
30

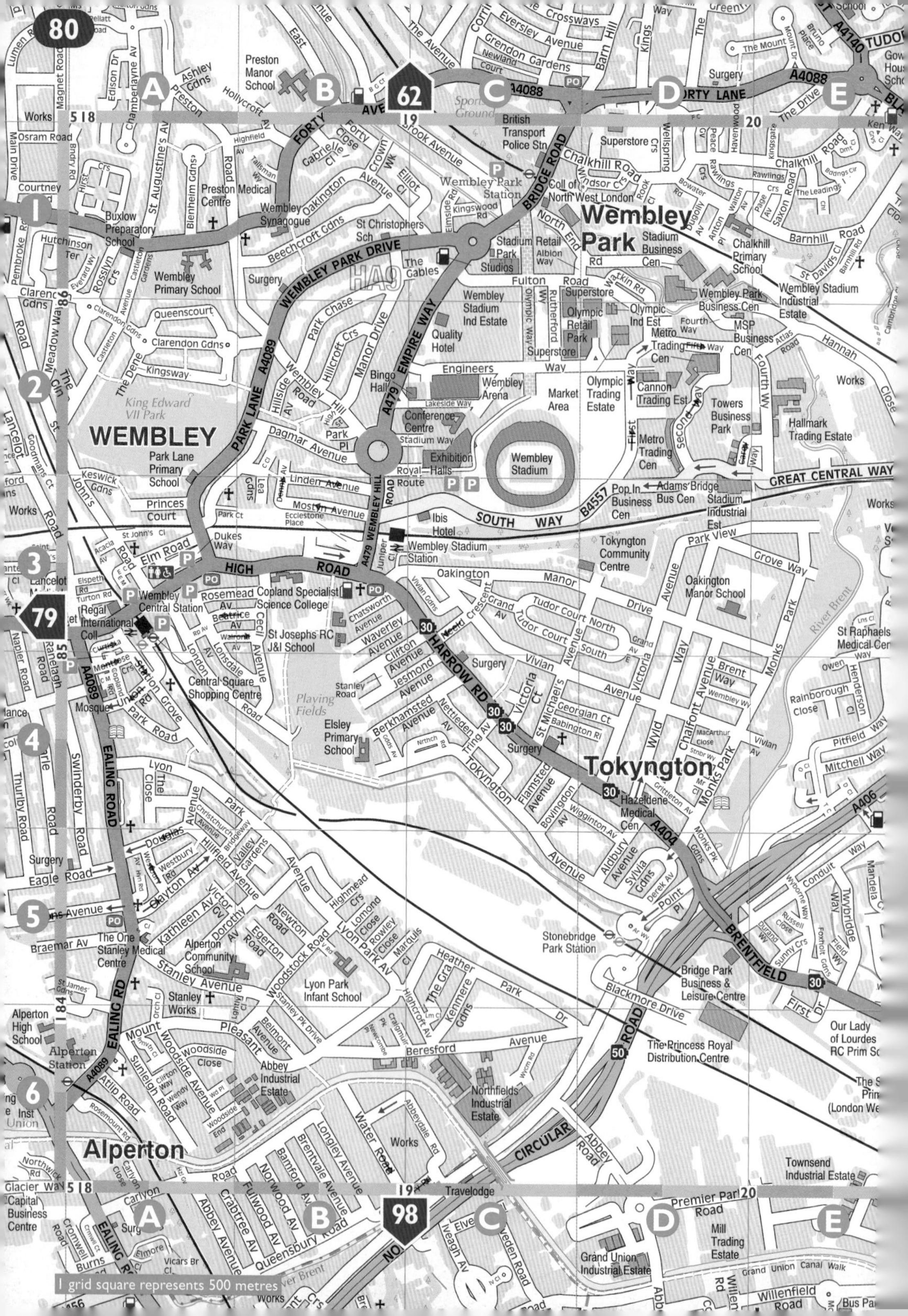

80
62
79
98
A
B
C
D
E
1
2
3
4
5
6
518
19
20
185
184
Preston Manor School
FORTY LANE
FORTY AVE
Sports Ground
British Transport Police Stn
Superstore
Chalkhill Road
Wembley Park Station
Coll of North West London
Wembley Park
BRIDGE ROAD
Crossways
Eversley Avenue
Grendon Gardens
Barn Hill
The Mount
Surgery
Preston Medical Centre
Wembley Synagogue
Buxlow Preparatory School
St Christophers Sch
WEMBLEY PARK DRIVE
Stadium Retail Park
Stadium Business Cen
Chalkhill Primary School
Barnhill Road
Wembley Stadium Industrial Estate
Wembley Park Business Cen
MSP Business Cen
Wembley Primary School
Fulton Road
Wembley Stadium Ind Estate
Quality Hotel
Olympic Retail Park
Olympic Ind Est
Metro Trading Cen
Engineers Way
Wembley Arena
Market Area
Olympic Trading Estate
Cannon Trading Est
Towers Business Park
Hallmark Trading Estate
Works
King Edward VII Park
WEMBLEY
PARK LANE A4089
A479 EMPIRE WAY
Bingo Hall
Conference Centre
Exhibition Halls
Wembley Stadium
Royal Route
GREAT CENTRAL WAY
Adams Bridge Bus Cen
Pop In Business Cen
Stadium Industrial Est
SOUTH WAY B4557
Park Lane Primary School
Princes Court
Dagmar Avenue
Linden Avenue
Mostyn Avenue
Ibis Hotel
Wembley Stadium Station
Tokyngton Community Centre
Oakington Manor School
HIGH ROAD
Wembley Central Station
Regal International Coll
Copland Specialist Science College
St Josephs RC J&I School
Central Square Shopping Centre
Playing Fields
Elsley Primary School
HARROW RD
Tudor Court North
Tudor Court South
Victoria Avenue
Monks Park
River Brent
St Raphaels Medical Cen
Rainborough Close
Tokyngton
Hazeldene Medical Cen
A404
A406
Stonebridge Park Station
BRENTFIELD
Bridge Park Business & Leisure Centre
Blackmore Drive
Our Lady of Lourdes RC Prim Sc
The Princess Royal Distribution Centre
EALING ROAD
A4089
Eagle Road
The One Stanley Medical Centre
Alperton Community School
Lyon Park Infant School
Stanley Avenue
Stanley Works
Alperton High School
Alperton Station
Abbey Industrial Estate
Northfields Industrial Estate
Beresford Avenue
Works
Water Road
CIRCULAR ROAD
Alperton
Townsend Industrial Estate
Travelodge
Capital Business Centre
Premier Park Road
Mill Trading Estate
Grand Union Industrial Estate
Grand Union Canal Walk
Willenfield Road
1 grid square represents 500 metres

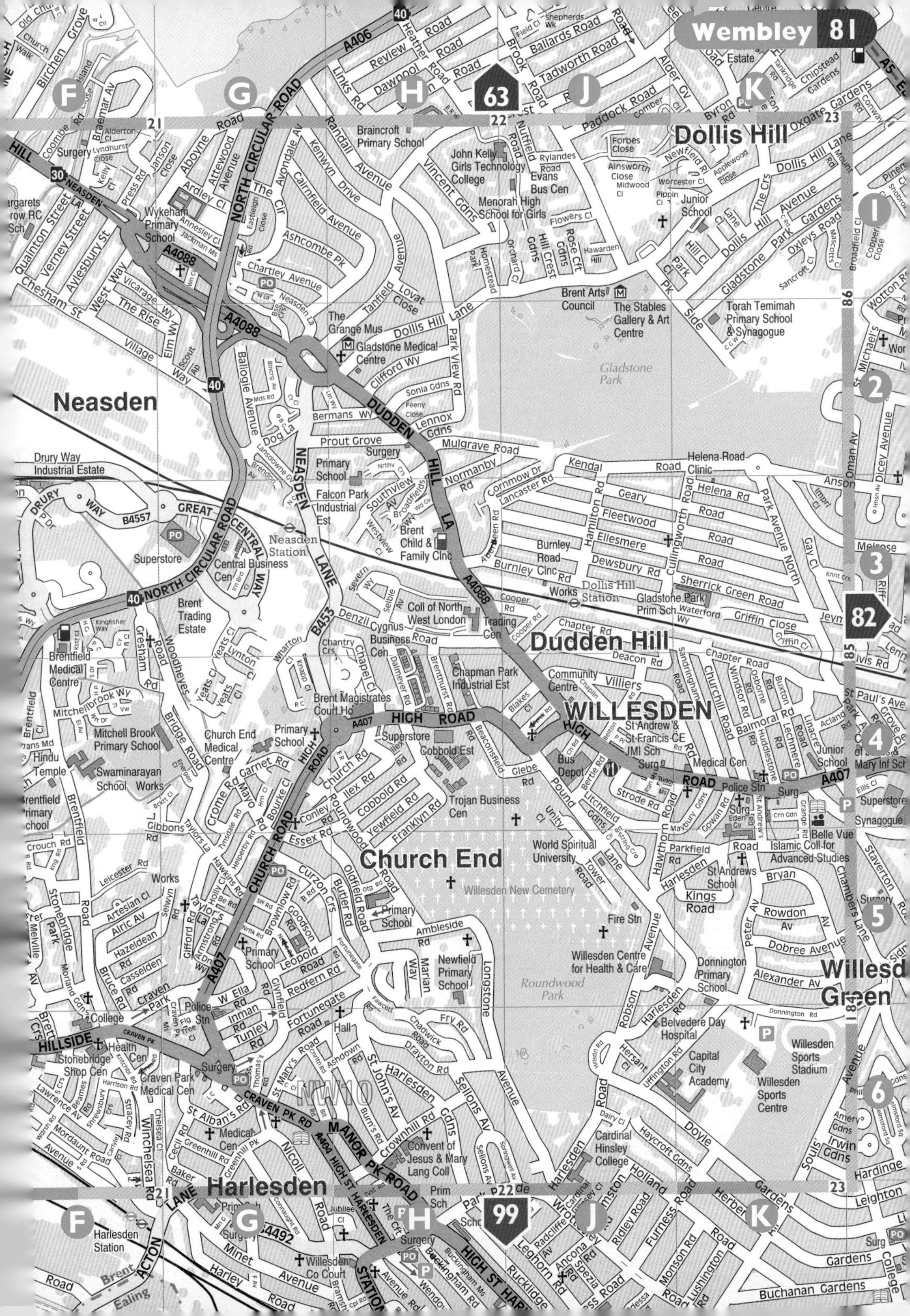

Dollis Hill

Neasden

Dudden Hill

WILLESDEN

Church End

Willesden Green

Harlesden

NW10

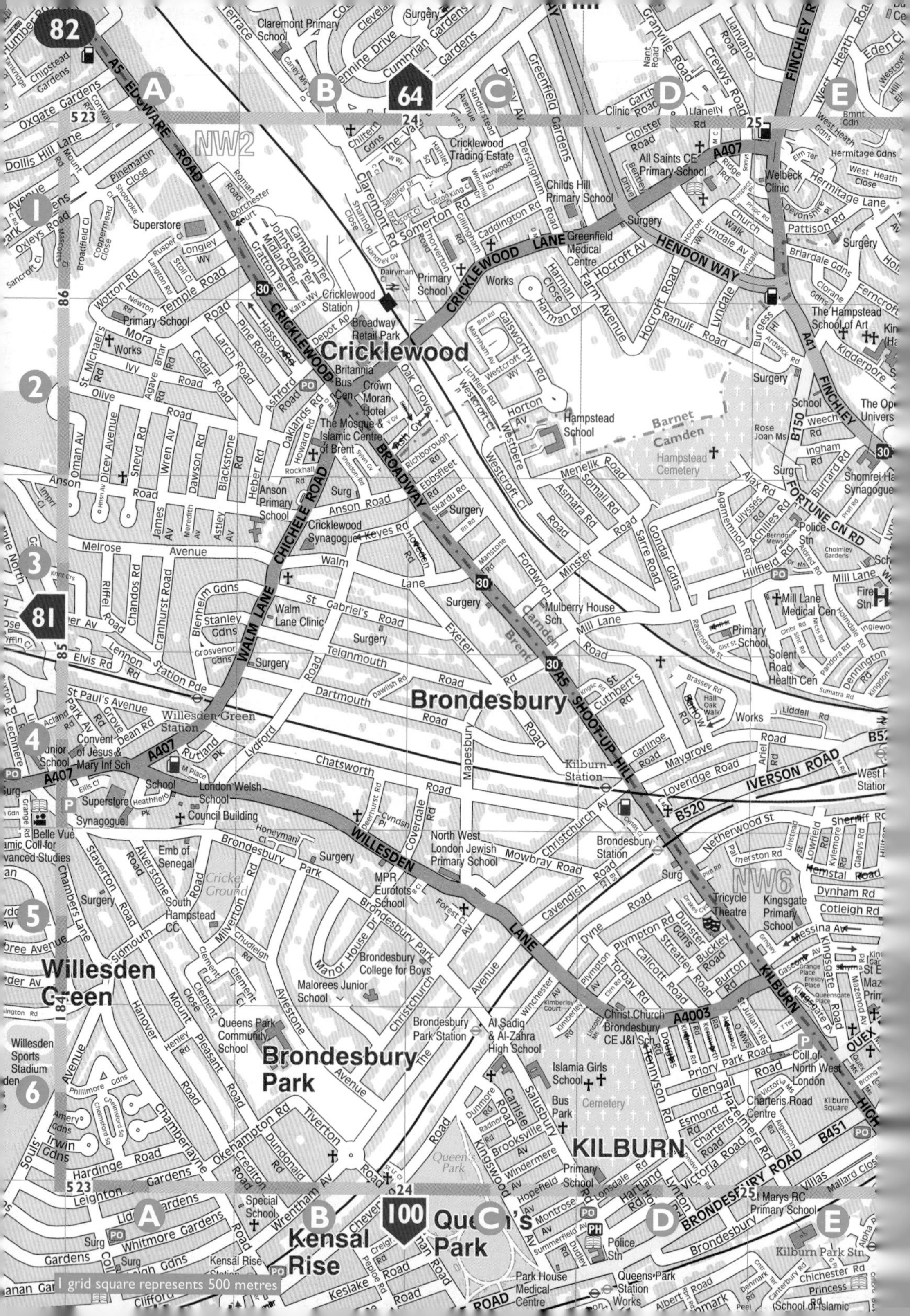
82
64
81
100
A
B
C
D
E
1
2
3
4
5
6
NW2
NW6
Cricklewood
Brondesbury
Willesden Green
Brondesbury Park
Kensal Rise
Queen's Park
KILBURN
A5 EDGWARE ROAD
CRICKLEWOOD BROADWAY
A5 SHOOT-UP HILL
KILBURN HIGH
CRICKLEWOOD LANE
HENDON WAY
FINCHLEY RD
A41 FINCHLEY
FORTUNE GN RD
WILLESDEN LANE
WALM LANE
CHICHELE ROAD
IVERSON ROAD
BRONDESBURY ROAD
A407
A4003
B520
B451
B150
Oxgate Gardens
Dollis Hill Lane
Chipstead Gardens
Claremont Primary School
Cricklewood Trading Estate
Childs Hill Primary School
All Saints CE Primary School
Welbeck Clinic
Greenfield Medical Centre
Cricklewood Station
Broadway Retail Park
Britannia Bus Cen
Crown Moran Hotel
The Mosque & Islamic Centre of Brent
Anson Primary School
Cricklewood Synagogue
Hampstead School
Hampstead Cemetery
The Hampstead School of Art
Barnet
Camden
Brent
Mulberry House Sch
Walm Lane Clinic
Mill Lane Medical Cen
Solent Road Health Cen
Police Stn
Kilburn Station
Brondesbury Station
Willesden Green Station
Convent of Jesus & Mary Inf Sch
London Welsh School
Council Building
Superstore
Synagogue
Belle Vue
North West London Jewish Primary School
MPR Eurotots School
Brondesbury College for Boys
Malorees Junior School
Queens Park Community School
Brondesbury Park Station
Al Sadiq & Al-Zahra High School
Christ Church Brondesbury CE J&I Sch
Islamia Girls School
Cemetery
Tricycle Theatre
Kingsgate Primary School
Coll of North West London
Charteris Road Centre
Kilburn Square
St Marys RC Primary School
Kilburn Park Stn
Queens Park Station
Park House Medical Centre
Kensal Rise Station
Special School
Willesden Sports Stadium
South Hampstead CC
Cricket Ground
Emb of Senegal
Queen's Park
1 grid square represents 500 metres

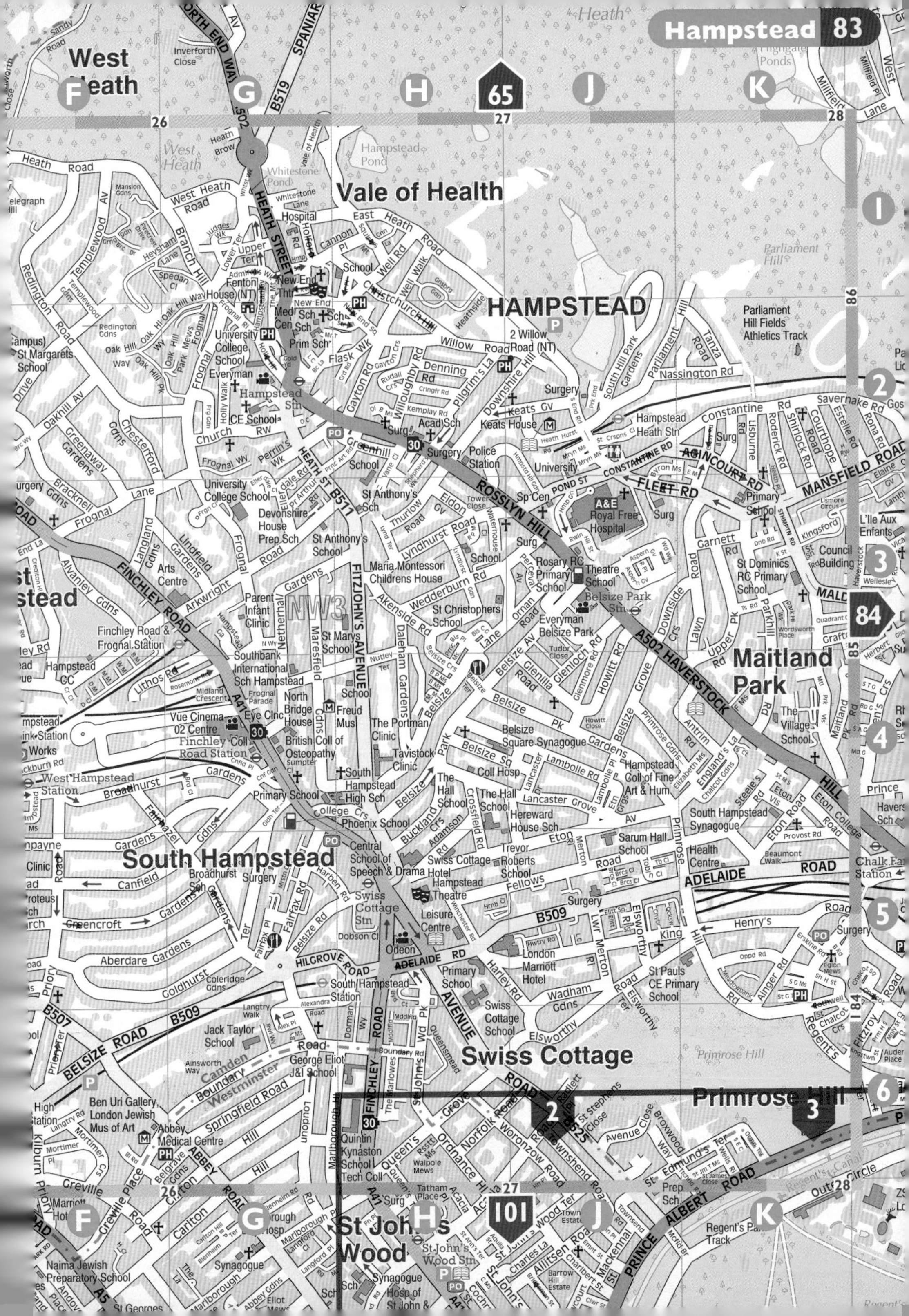
West Heath
Vale of Health
HAMPSTEAD
Parliament Hill
Parliament Hill Fields Athletics Track
Hampstead Pond
Whitestone Pond
Highgate Ponds
Maitland Park
South Hampstead
Swiss Cottage
Primrose Hill
St John's Wood
NW3
65
84
101
2
3
HEATH STREET
ROSSLYN HILL
A502 HAVERSTOCK HILL
FINCHLEY ROAD
FITZJOHN'S AVENUE
BELSIZE ROAD
ADELAIDE ROAD
PRINCE ALBERT ROAD
MANSFIELD ROAD
AGINCOURT RD
FLEET RD
CONSTANTINE RD
POND ST
HILGROVE ROAD
AVENUE
Hampstead Stn
Hampstead Heath Stn
Belsize Park Stn
Finchley Road & Frognal Station
Finchley Road Station
West Hampstead Station
South Hampstead Station
Swiss Cottage Stn
Chalk Farm Station
St John's Wood Stn
Royal Free Hospital
Keats House
2 Willow Road (NT)
Fenton House (NT)
Freud Mus
The Portman Clinic
Tavistock Clinic
Hampstead Theatre
Leisure Centre
London Marriott Hotel
Swiss Cottage Hotel
Central School of Speech & Drama
Ben Uri Gallery, London Jewish Mus of Art
Abbey Medical Centre
Vue Cinema 02 Centre
Everyman
Everyman Belsize Park
Odeon
Arts Centre
University College School
South Hampstead High Sch
Swiss Cottage School
Jack Taylor School
George Eliot J&I School
Quintin Kynaston School Tech Coll
Sarum Hall School
St Pauls CE Primary School
South Hampstead Synagogue
Belsize Square Synagogue
Hampstead Coll of Fine Art & Hum
Police Station
Council Building
Regent's Park Track
Primrose Hill

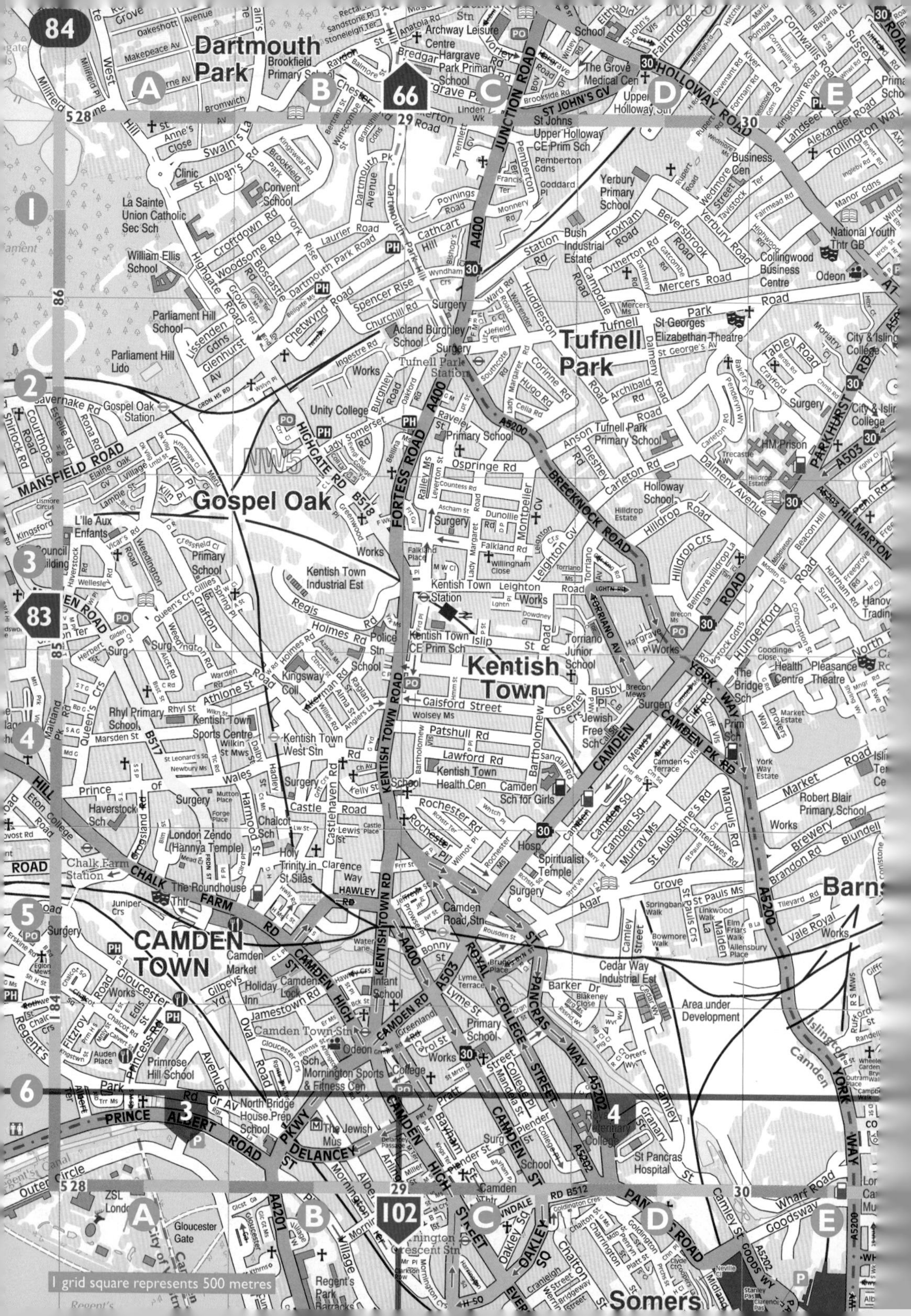

84
Dartmouth Park
Brookfield Primary School
Archway Leisure Centre
Hargrave Park Primary School
66
Junction Road
St John's Gv
St Johns Upper Holloway CE Prim Sch
The Grove Medical Cen
Upper Holloway Stn
Holloway Road
A B C D E
528
29
30
Swain's La
St Alban's Rd
Clinic
Convent School
La Sainte Union Catholic Sec Sch
William Ellis School
Croftdown Rd
Woodsome Rd
York Rise
Laurier Road
Dartmouth Park Road
Dartmouth Park Hill
Dartmouth Pk Avenue
Cathcart Hill
Highgate Road
Grove Ter
Boscastle Rd
Spencer Rise
Chetwynd Road
Churchill Rd
Surgery
Acland Burghley School
Parliament Hill School
Parliament Hill Lido
Lissenden Gdns
Glenhurst Av
Ingestre Rd
Works
Tufnell Park Station
Yerbury Primary School
Foxham Road
Beversbrook Road
Bush Industrial Estate
Station Rd
Huddleston Road
Campdale Road
Mercers Road
Tufnell Park Road
St Georges Elizabethan Theatre
Tufnell Park
Business Cen
Wedmore Street
Tavistock Ter
Yerbury Road
Collingwood Business Centre
National Youth Thtr GB
Odeon
Alexander Road
Tollington Way
Manor Gdns
City & Islington College
Tabley Road
Crayford Road
Parkhurst Rd
Surgery
HM Prison
A503
Dalmeny Avenue
Holloway School
Hillmarton Road
Hilldrop Road
Hilldrop Crs
Camden Road
Tufnell Park Primary School
Carleton Rd
Anson Rd
Plesheys Rd
Brecknock Road
A5200
Gospel Oak Station
Savernake Rd
Mansfield Road
Gospel Oak
NW5
Unity College
Lady Somerset Rd
Highgate Rd
Fortess Road
A400
B518
Raveley St
Primary School
Ospringe Rd
Countess Rd
Dunollie Rd
Montpelier Gv
Falkland Rd
Willingham Close
Kentish Town Industrial Est
Regis Rd
Kentish Town Station
Leighton Road
Torriano Av
Torriano Junior School
Islip St
Holmes Rd
Police Stn
Kentish Town CE Prim Sch
Kentish Town
School
Kingsway Coll
Gaisford Street
Wolsey Ms
Patshull Rd
Lawford Rd
Kentish Town Health Cen
Camden Sch for Girls
Sandall Rd
Bartholomew Rd
Oseney Crs
Jewish Free Sch
Busby Pl
Brecon Mews
York Way
Camden Pk Rd
Camden Mews
Camden Sq
Camden Terrace
Murray Ms
St Augustine's Rd
Marquis Rd
Cantelowes Rd
Hungerford Rd
Corporation St
Hillmarton Rd
North Rd
Health Centre
Pleasance Theatre
The Bridge Sch
Market Estate
York Way Estate
Market Road
Robert Blair Primary School
Works
Brewery Rd
Brandon Rd
Blundell
Barns
Vale Royal
Works
L'Ile Aux Enfants
Council Building
83
Primary School
Queen's Crs
Weedington Road
Grafton Rd
Warden Rd
Athlone St
Rhyl Primary School
Kentish Town Sports Centre
Kentish Town West Stn
B517
Marsden St
Wilkin St Mws
Prince of Wales Rd
Haverstock Sch
Harmood St
Chalcot Sch
London Zendo (Hannya Temple)
Castle Road
Castlehaven Rd
Kentish Town Road
Rochester Rd
Rochester Pl
Wilmot Pl
Spiritualist Temple
Hosp
Agar Grove
St Pauls Ms
Springbank Walk
Bowmore Walk
Camley Street
Cedar Way Industrial Est
Area under Development
Barker Dr
Chalk Farm Station
Chalk Farm Rd
The Roundhouse Thtr
Holy Trinity in St Silas
Clarence Way
Hawley Rd
Camden Road Stn
Royal College St
Pancras Way
Rousden St
Camden Town
Camden Market
Camden Lock
Holiday Inn
Gilbeys Yd
Jamestown Rd
Camden High St
Camden Rd
Infant School
Lyme St
Lyme Terrace
Primary School
Camden Town Stn
Odeon
Mornington Sports & Fitness Cen
College
Works
Gloucester Avenue
Oval Road
Regent's Park Rd
Fitzroy Rd
Chalcot Rd
Princess Rd
Primrose Hill School
Auden Place
Juniper Crs
Surgery
Erskine Rd
Egon Mews
Regent's Park
Prince Albert Road
3
North Bridge House Prep School
Parkway
Delancey St
The Jewish Mus
Pratt St
Bayham St
Camden St
Mandela St
College Pl
Plender St
School
A5202
4
Royal Veterinary College
St Pancras Hospital
Granary St
Camley St
Wharf Road
Goodsway
A5200
Islington
Camden
York Way
Outer Circle
ZSL London
Gloucester Gate
A4201
Mornington Crescent Stn
Regent's Park Barracks
Oakley Sq
Chalton St
Pancras Road
Somers
Camden St
1 grid square represents 500 metres

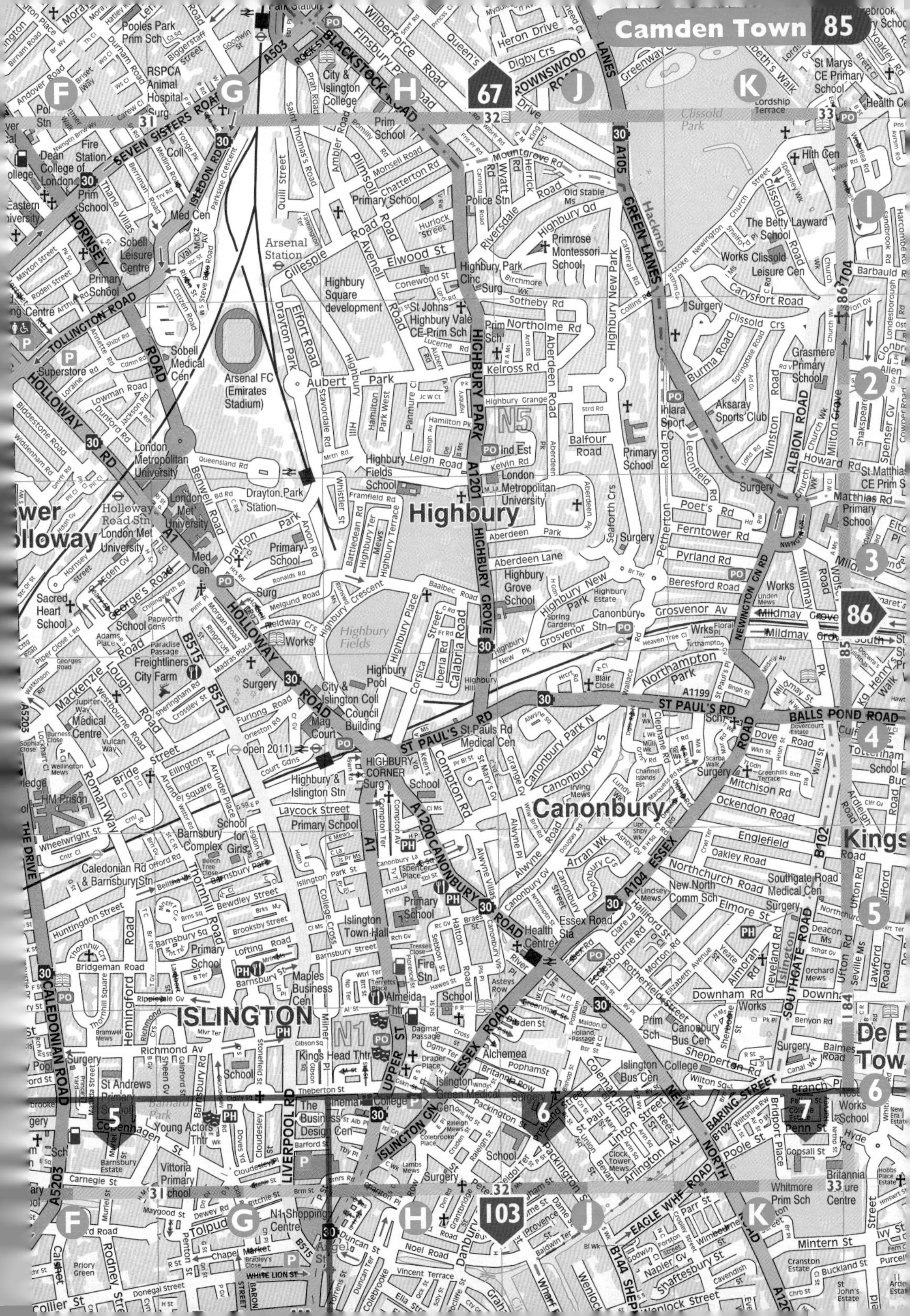
Highbury
Canonbury
ISLINGTON
Holloway
N5
N1
HOLLOWAY ROAD
SEVEN SISTERS ROAD
BLACKSTOCK ROAD
HIGHBURY PARK
HIGHBURY GROVE
GREEN LANES
ALBION ROAD
NEWINGTON GN RD
BALLS POND ROAD
ST PAUL'S RD
ESSEX ROAD
UPPER ST
LIVERPOOL RD
CALEDONIAN ROAD
CANONBURY ROAD
NEW NORTH ROAD
SOUTHGATE ROAD
TOLLINGTON ROAD
HORNSEY ROAD
ISLEDON RD
BROWNSWOOD ROAD
BARING STREET
EAGLE WHF ROAD
THE DRIVE
Arsenal FC (Emirates Stadium)
Arsenal Station
Drayton Park Station
Highbury & Islington Stn
Caledonian Rd & Barnsbury Stn
Canonbury Stn
Essex Road Sta
Holloway Road Stn
Highbury Fields
Clissold Park
HM Prison
Islington Town Hall
London Metropolitan University
City & Islington College
Freightliners City Farm
Almeida Thtr
Kings Head Thtr
Young Actors Thtr
N1 Shopping Centre
67
86
103
F
G
H
J
K
I
2
3
4
5
6
7
30
31
32
33

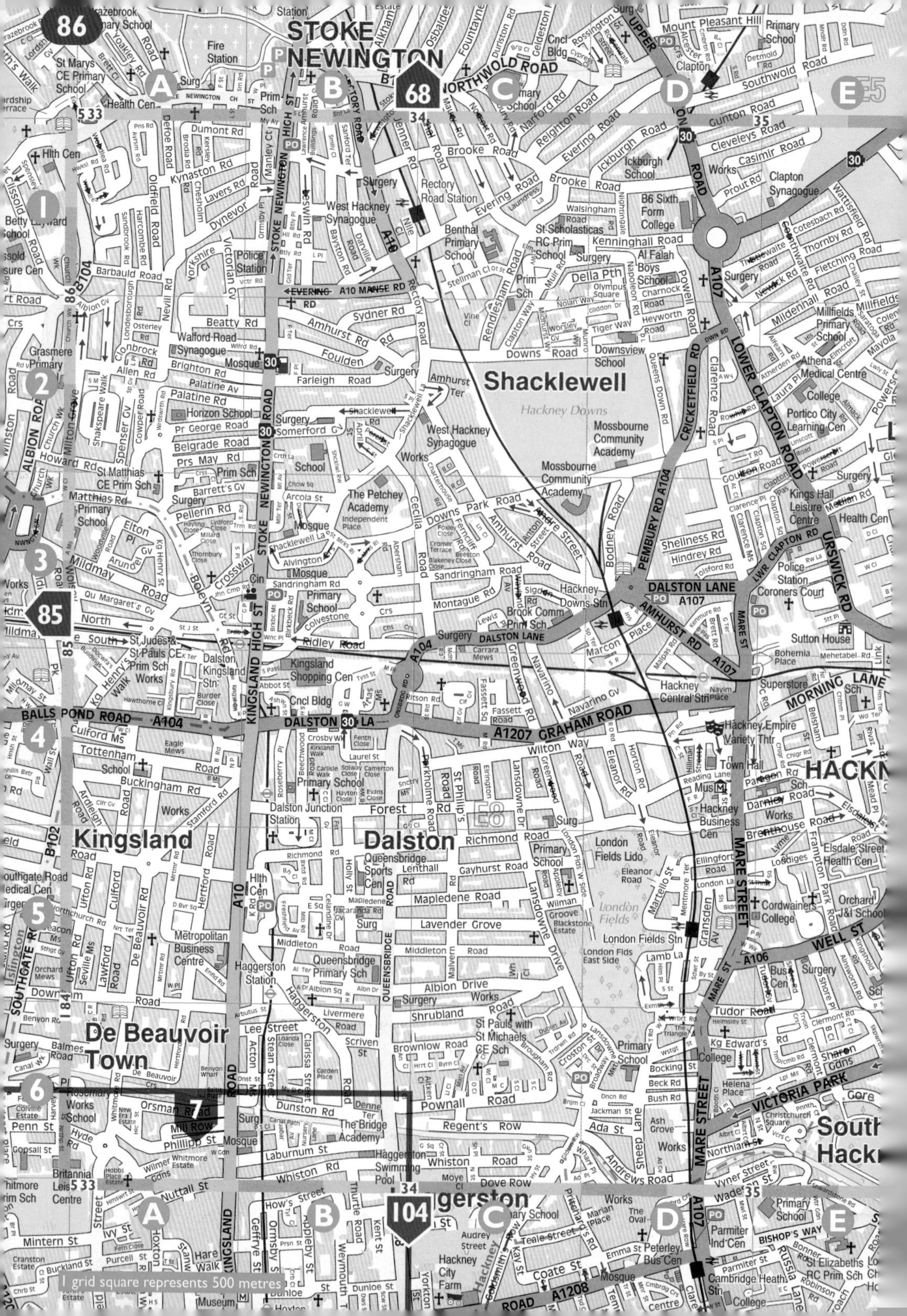

86
STOKE NEWINGTON
68
NORTHWOLD ROAD
Mount Pleasant Hill
Southwold Road
Gunton Road
Cleveleys Road
Casimir Road
Clapton Synagogue
Ickburgh School
B6 Sixth Form College
Rectory Road Station
West Hackney Synagogue
Benthal Primary School
St Scholasticas RC Prim School
Al Falah Boys School
Kenninghall Road
Brooke Road
Evering Road
Manse Rd
Shacklewell
Hackney Downs
Mossbourne Community Academy
Downsview School
Cricketfield Rd
Lower Clapton Road
Pembury Rd A104
Urswick Rd
Millfields Primary School
Athena Medical Centre
Portico City Learning Cen
Kings Hall Leisure Centre
Health Cen
Police Station
Coroners Court
Sutton House
Dalston Lane
Amhurst Rd
Hackney Downs Stn
Hackney Central Stn
Mare St
Morning Lane
Hackney Empire Variety Thtr
Town Hall
HACKNEY
Stoke Newington Road
Kingsland High St
Balls Pond Road A104
A1207 Graham Road
Dalston Junction Station
Dalston Kingsland Stn
Kingsland Shopping Cen
Dalston
Kingsland
85
Mildmay Road
Albion Road
Grasmere Primary
The Petchey Academy
St Matthias CE Prim Sch
St Judes & St Pauls CE Prim Sch
Queensbridge Sports Cen
Queensbridge Road
Queensbridge Primary Sch
London Fields
London Fields Lido
London Fields Stn
Mare Street
Well St
Cordwainers College
Haggerston Station
De Beauvoir Town
Metropolitan Business Centre
Southgate Road
Regent's Row
Whiston Road
Haggerston Swimming Pool
The Bridge Academy
Victoria Park
South Hackney
Britannia Leis Centre
104
Haggerston
Hackney City Farm
Parmiter Ind Cen
Bishop's Way
St Elizabeths RC Prim Sch
Cambridge Heath Stn
A1208
1 grid square represents 500 metres

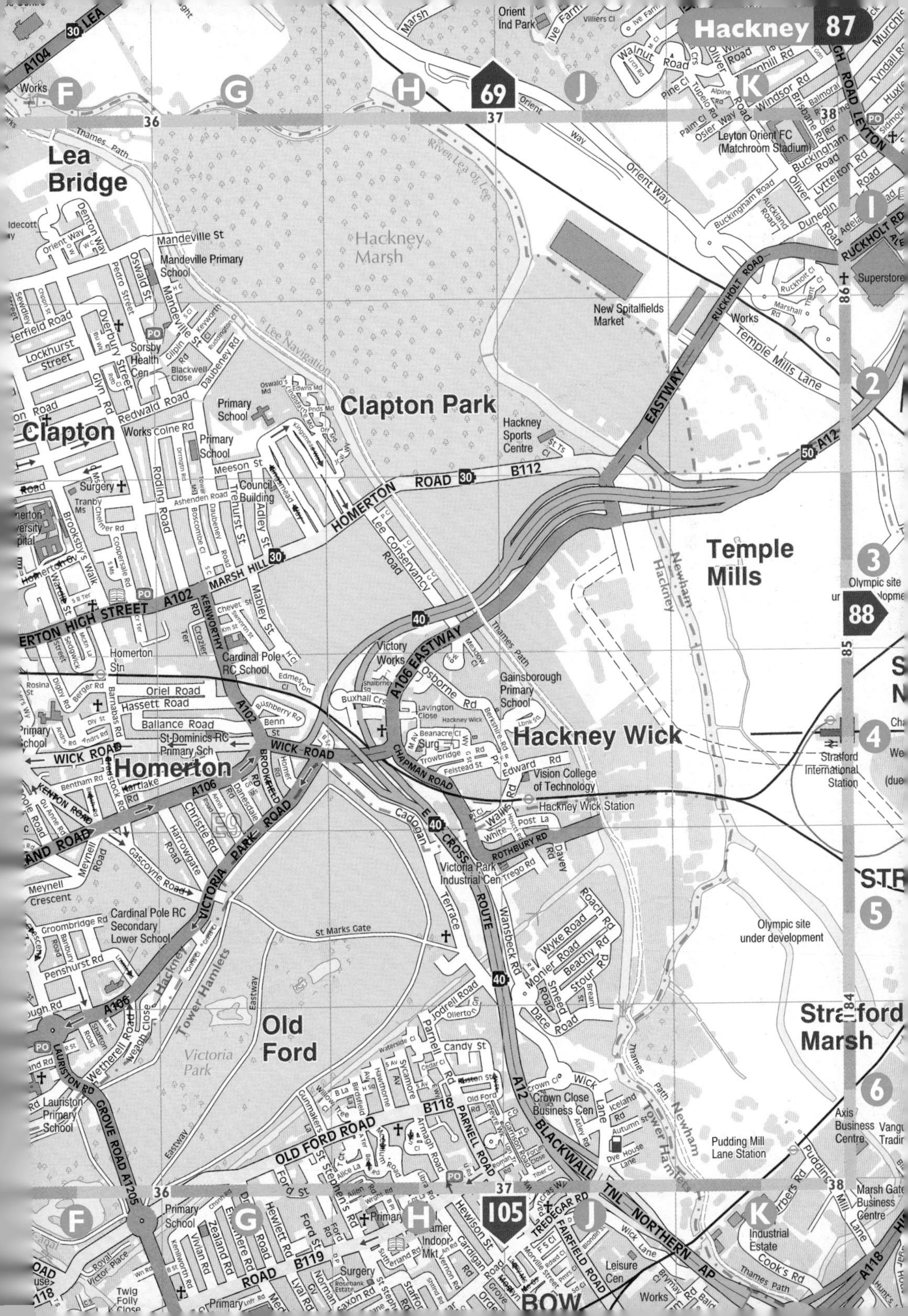
Lea Bridge
Clapton
Clapton Park
Hackney Marsh
Homerton
Hackney Wick
Temple Mills
Old Ford
Victoria Park
Stratford Marsh
BOW
New Spitalfields Market
Leyton Orient FC (Matchroom Stadium)
Superstore
Mandeville Primary School
Sorsby Health Cen
Primary School
Hackney Sports Centre
Council Building
Surgery
Homerton Stn
Cardinal Pole RC School
Victory Works
Gainsborough Primary School
St Dominics RC Primary Sch
Vision College of Technology
Hackney Wick Station
Victoria Park Industrial Cen
Stratford International Station
Olympic site under development
Cardinal Pole RC Secondary Lower School
Lauriston Primary School
Crown Close Business Cen
Pudding Mill Lane Station
Axis Business Centre
Marsh Gate Business Centre
Industrial Estate
Leisure Cen
Works
Twig Folly Close
Lee Navigation
River Lea or Lee
Thames Path
HOMERTON ROAD
HOMERTON HIGH STREET
MARSH HILL
EASTWAY
A106 EASTWAY
RUCKHOLT ROAD
Temple Mills Lane
Orient Way
WICK ROAD
VICTORIA PARK ROAD
KENWORTHY RD
CHAPMAN ROAD
EAST CROSS ROUTE
ROTHBURY RD
BLACKWALL TNL NORTHERN AP
OLD FORD ROAD
GROVE ROAD A1205
LAURISTON RD
PARNELL ROAD
TREDEGAR RD
FAIRFIELD ROAD
Wick Lane
Wansbeck Rd
Cadogan Terrace
St Marks Gate
F
G
H
J
K
36
37
38
1
2
3
4
5
6
69
86
85
84
88
105

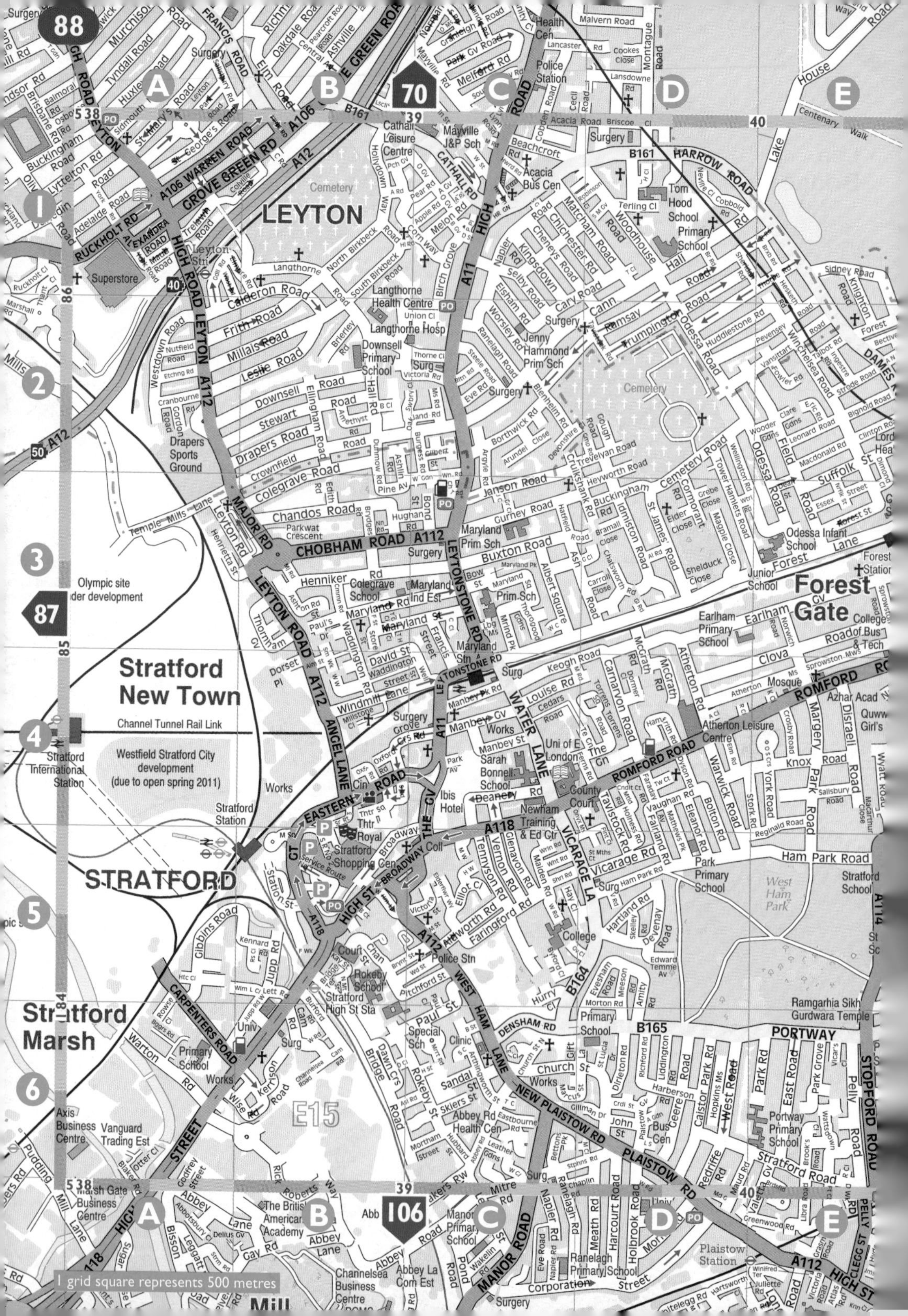

88
70
87
106
A
B
C
D
E
1
2
3
4
5
6
38
39
40
86
85
84
LEYTON
Stratford New Town
STRATFORD
Stratford Marsh
Forest Gate
E15
Cemetery
Superstore
Olympic site
Channel Tunnel Rail Link
Westfield Stratford City development (due to open spring 2011)
Stratford International Station
Stratford Station
Stratford Shopping Cen
Stratford High St Sta
Drapers Sports Ground
Cathall Leisure Centre
Langthorne Health Centre
Langthorne Hosp
Downsell Primary School
Jenny Hammond Prim Sch
Tom Hood School
Woodhouse Primary School
Maryland Prim Sch
Colegrave School
Maryland Ind Est
Maryland Stn
Odessa Infant School
Junior School
Earlham Primary School
Forest Station
College of Bus & Tech
Azhar Acad
Atherton Leisure Centre
Uni of E London
County Court
Sarah Bonnell School
Newham Training & Ed Ctr
Ibis Hotel
Royal
Thtr
West Ham Park
Park Primary School
Stratford School
Ramgarhia Sikh Gurdwara Temple
Portway Primary School
Police Stn
Rokeby School
Special Sch
Clinic
Abbey Rd Health Cen
Axis Business Centre
Vanguard Trading Est
Marsh Gate Business Centre
The British American Academy
Manor Primary School
Ranelagh Primary School
Plaistow Station
Channelsea Business Centre
Abbey La Com Est
Acacia Bus Cen
Police Station
Health Cen
Mayville J&P Sch
HIGH ROAD LEYTON
LEYTON ROAD A112
LEYTONSTONE RD
HIGH ROAD A11
CHOBHAM ROAD A112
GROVE GREEN RD
A106 WARREN ROAD
RUCKHOLT RD
MAJOR RD
ANGEL LANE
EASTERN ROAD
BROADWAY
THE GV
HIGH ST
WEST HAM LANE
NEW PLAISTOW RD
PLAISTOW RD
ROMFORD ROAD
WATER LANE
VICARAGE LA
HARROW ROAD
PORTWAY
STOPFORD ROAD
CARPENTERS ROAD
HIGH STREET
MANOR ROAD
DENSHAM RD
Temple Mills Lane
Ham Park Road
Forest Lane
1 grid square represents 500 metres

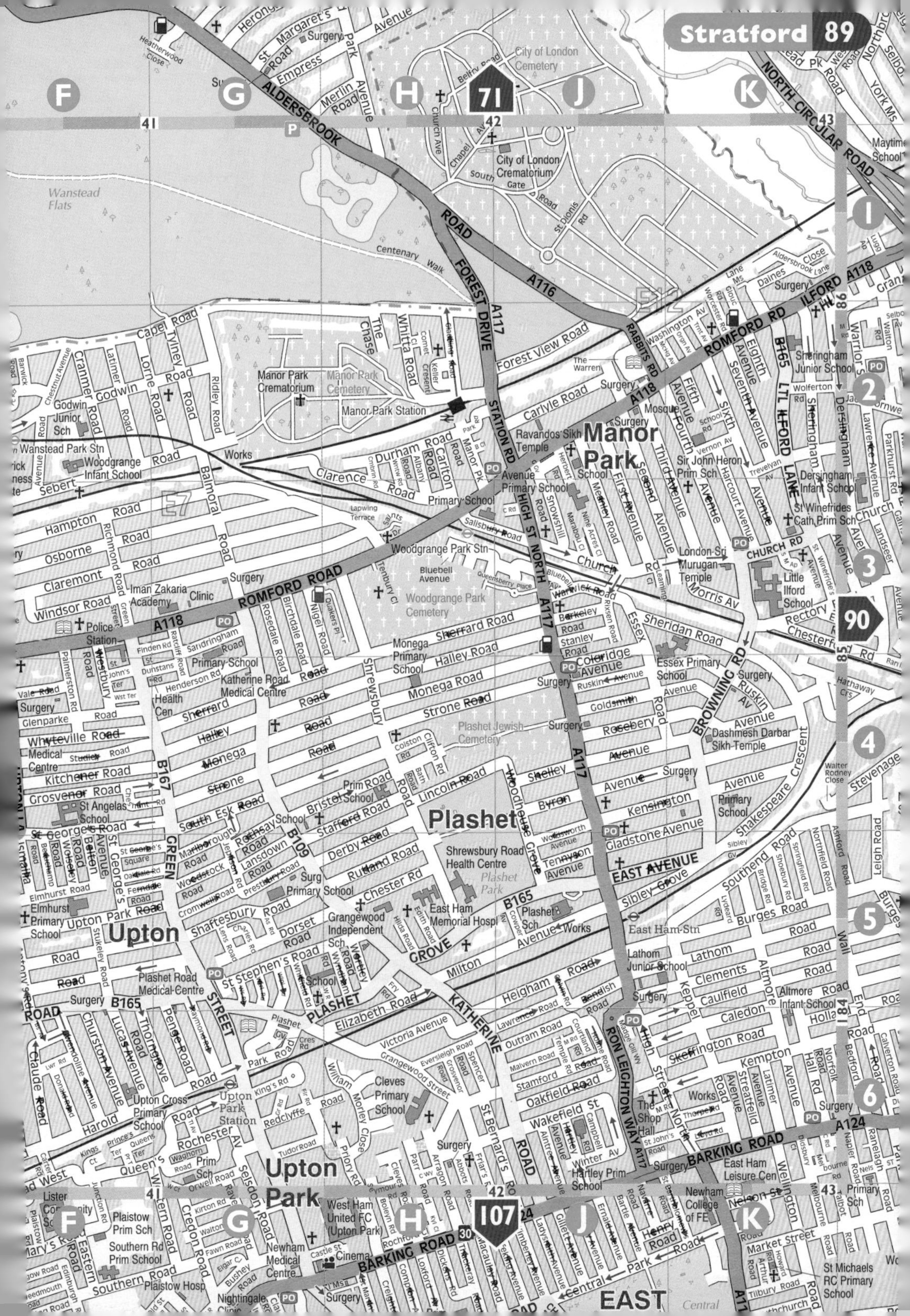

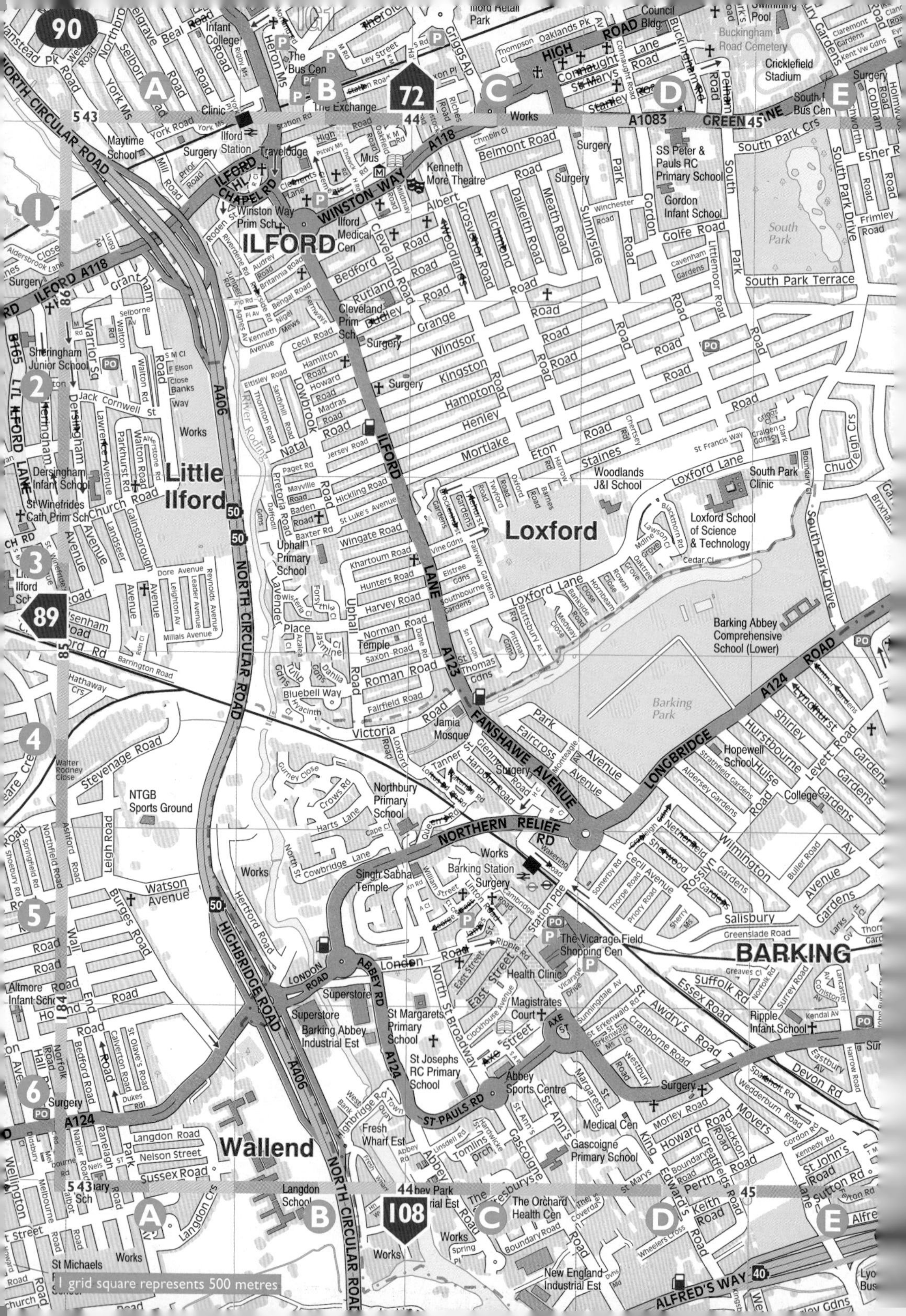
90
72
89
108
ILFORD
Little Ilford
Loxford
BARKING
Wallend
NORTH CIRCULAR ROAD
A406
ILFORD LANE
A123
FANSHAWE AVENUE
LONGBRIDGE ROAD
A124
NORTHERN RELIEF RD
HIGHBRIDGE ROAD
ABBEY RD
LONDON ROAD
ST PAULS RD
HIGH ROAD
GREEN LANE
A1083
WINSTON WAY
A118
ILFORD HILL
CHAPEL RD
ALFRED'S WAY
Ilford Station
Barking Station
The Exchange
Kenneth More Theatre
Ilford Medical Cen
Cleveland Prim Sch
Winston Way Prim Sch
Sheringham Junior School
Dersingham Infant School
St Winefrides Cath Prim Sch
Uphall Primary School
Woodlands J&I School
Loxford School of Science & Technology
South Park Clinic
South Park
Barking Park
Barking Abbey Comprehensive School (Lower)
Hopewell School
Jamia Mosque
Northbury Primary School
NTGB Sports Ground
Singh Sabha Temple
The Vicarage Field Shopping Cen
Health Clinic
Magistrates Court
Barking Abbey Industrial Est
St Margarets Primary School
St Josephs RC Primary School
Abbey Sports Centre
Gascoigne Primary School
Medical Cen
Ripple Infant School
Altmore Infant School
Langdon School
The Orchard Health Cen
New England Industrial Est
Fresh Wharf Est
SS Peter & Pauls RC Primary School
Gordon Infant School
Cricklefield Stadium
Buckingham Road Cemetery
Maytime School
Infant College
River Roding
1 grid square represents 500 metres

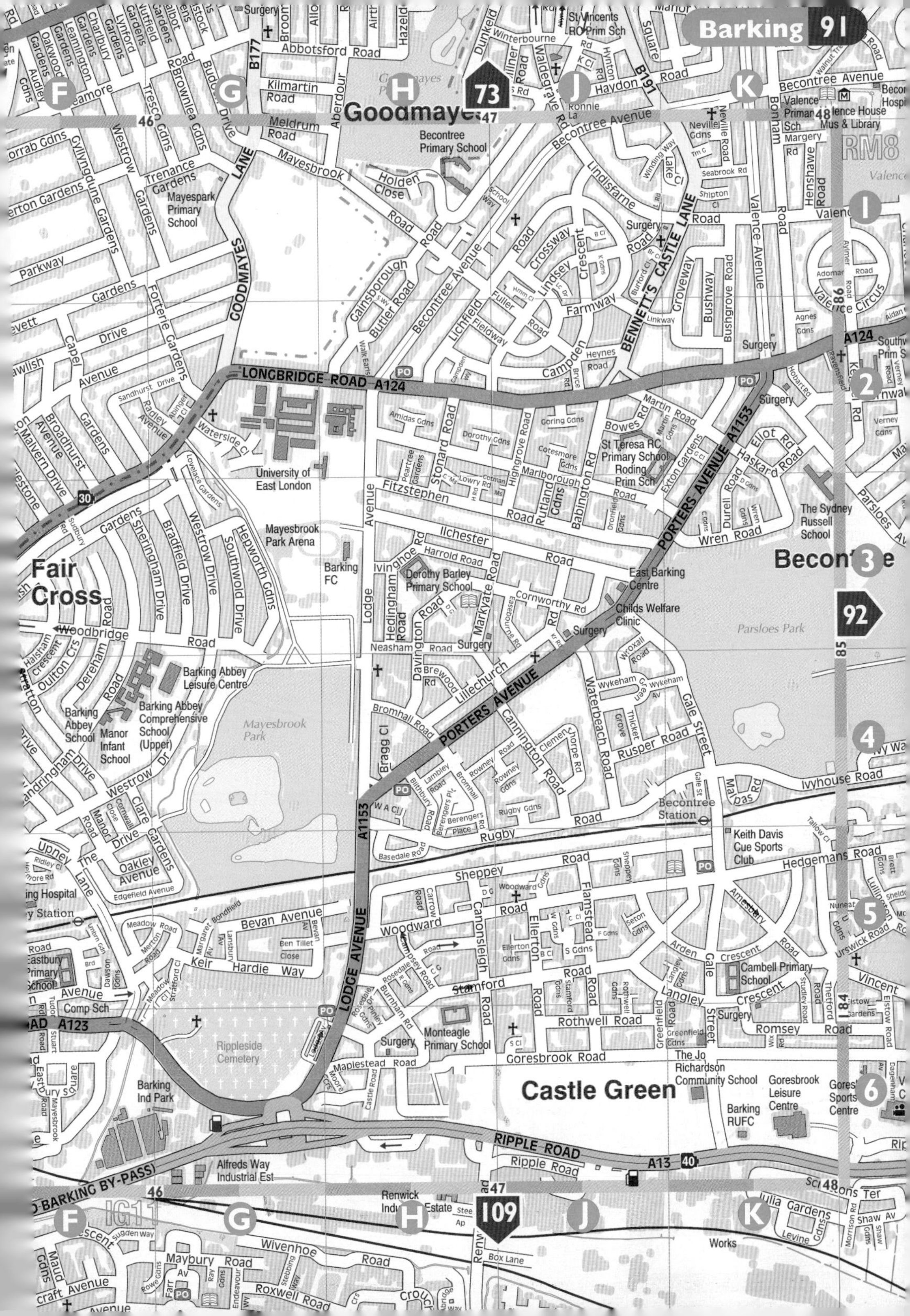
Goodmayes
Fair Cross
Becontree
Castle Green
Parsloes Park
Mayesbrook Park
Rippleside Cemetery
LONGBRIDGE ROAD A124
GOODMAYES LANE
PORTERS AVENUE A1153
LODGE AVENUE
BENNETT'S CASTLE LANE
RIPPLE ROAD
A13
BARKING BY-PASS
Becontree Avenue
Valence Avenue
Becontree Primary School
Mayespark Primary School
University of East London
Mayesbrook Park Arena
Barking FC
Dorothy Barley Primary School
St Teresa RC Primary School
Roding Prim Sch
East Barking Centre
Childs Welfare Clinic
The Sydney Russell School
Barking Abbey Leisure Centre
Barking Abbey Comprehensive School (Upper)
Barking Abbey School
Manor Infant School
Becontree Station
Keith Davis Cue Sports Club
Cambell Primary School
Monteagle Primary School
The Jo Richardson Community School
Goresbrook Leisure Centre
Barking RUFC
Barking Ind Park
Alfreds Way Industrial Est
Renwick Indu Estate
Valence House Mus & Library
St Vincents RC Prim Sch
Surgery
Works
RM8
IG11
73
92
109
F G H J K
1 2 3 4 5 6
46 47 48

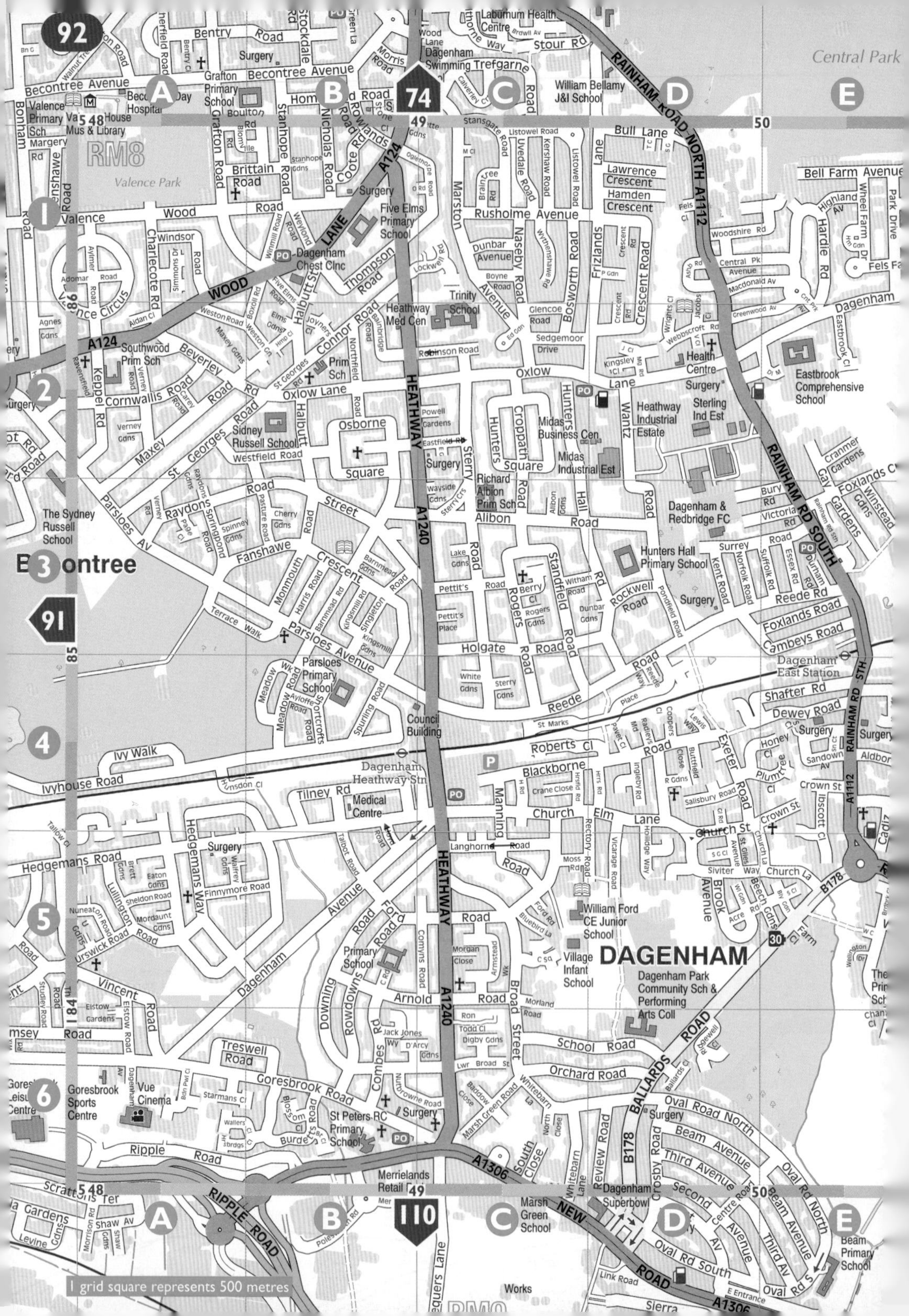

92
74
91
110
A
B
C
D
E
1
2
3
4
5
6
48
49
50
84
85
RM8
Central Park
Valence Park
Becontree Avenue
Bentry Road
Surgery
Grafton Primary School
Becontree Day Hospital
Valence Primary Sch
Valence House Mus & Library
Stockdale Road
Morris Road
Wood Lane
Dagenham Swimming
Laburnum Health Centre
Stour Rd
Trefgarne Road
William Bellamy J&I School
RAINHAM ROAD NORTH A1112
Bull Lane
Lawrence Crescent
Hamden Crescent
Bell Farm Avenue
Rusholme Avenue
Five Elms Primary School
Dagenham Chest Clnc
WOOD LANE
A124
Heathway Med Cen
Trinity School
Bosworth Road
Crescent Road
Frizlands Lane
Naseby Road
Dunbar Avenue
Glencoe Road
Sedgemoor Drive
Southwood Prim Sch
Valence Circus
Beverley Road
Connor Road
Oxlow Lane
Robinson Road
HEATHWAY A1240
Health Centre
Eastbrook Comprehensive School
Sterling Ind Est
Heathway Industrial Estate
Midas Business Cen
Midas Industrial Est
Hunters Square
Sidney Russell School
The Sydney Russell School
Osborne Square
Richard Albion Prim Sch
Alibon Road
Wantz Road
Dagenham & Redbridge FC
RAINHAM RD SOUTH
Becontree
Fanshawe Crescent
Parsloes Avenue
Parsloes Primary School
Hunters Hall Primary School
Rockwell Road
Reede Road
Foxlands Road
Cambeys Road
Dagenham East Station
Holgate Road
Council Building
Ivy Walk
Ivyhouse Road
Dagenham Heathway Stn
Roberts Cl
Blackborne Road
Medical Centre
Church Elm Lane
Exeter Road
Hedgemans Road
Hedgemans Way
Langhorne Road
William Ford CE Junior School
Village Infant School
DAGENHAM
Dagenham Park Community Sch & Performing Arts Coll
Dagenham Avenue
Primary School
Arnold Road
Broad Street
School Road
Orchard Road
BALLARDS ROAD B178
Vincent Road
Treswell Road
Goresbrook Road
Goresbrook Sports Centre
Vue Cinema
St Peters RC Primary School
Ripple Road
A1306
Merrielands Retail
RIPPLE ROAD
NEW ROAD
Marsh Green School
Dagenham Superbowl
Oval Road North
Beam Avenue
Beam Primary School
Works
1 grid square represents 500 metres

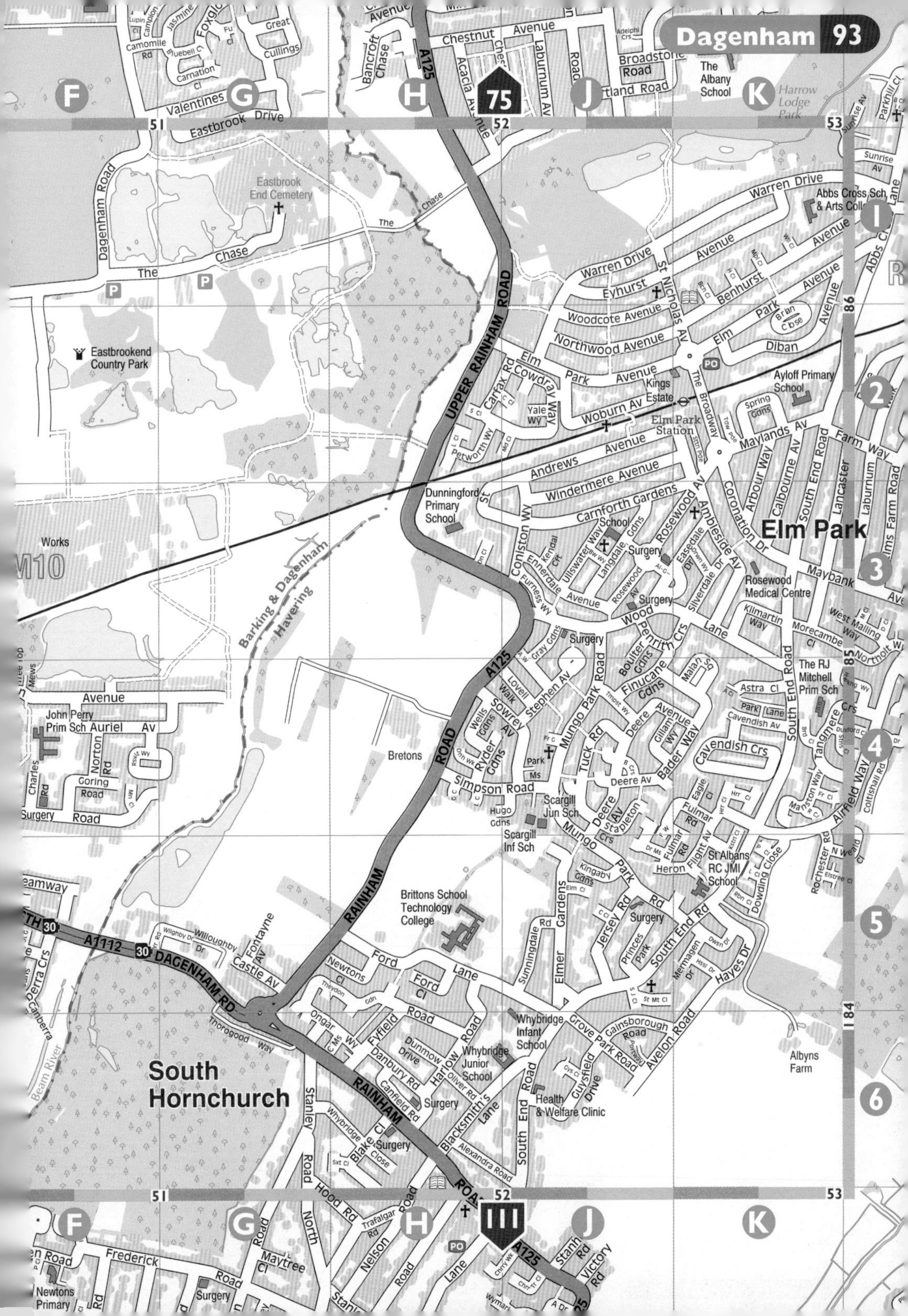
Dagenham
93
75
111
Eastbrook Drive
Valentines
Dagenham Road
Eastbrook End Cemetery
The Chase
Eastbrookend Country Park
Works
M10
Barking & Dagenham
Havering
UPPER RAINHAM ROAD
A125
Chestnut Avenue
Acacia Avenue
Laburnum Av
Broadstone Road
The Albany School
Harrow Lodge Park
Warren Drive
Abbs Cross Sch & Arts Coll
Eyhurst Avenue
Woodcote Avenue
Northwood Avenue
Benhurst Avenue
Elm Park Avenue
St Nicholas Av
Diban Avenue
Kings Estate
Woburn Av
Elm Park Station
The Broadway
Ayloff Primary School
Maylands Av
Farm Way
Andrews Avenue
Windermere Avenue
Carnforth Gardens
Dunningford Primary School
Coniston Wy
Rosewood Av
Ambleside Av
Coronation Dr
Arbour Way
Calbourne Av
South End Road
Lancaster
Laburnum
Elm Park
Rosewood Medical Centre
Maybank Av
Surgery
Wood Lane
Penrith Crs
Kilmartin Way
Morecambe Cl
West Malling Way
Northolt Way
The RJ Mitchell Prim Sch
Astra Cl
Cavendish Av
Cavendish Crs
Tangmere Crs
Airfield Way
Mungo Park Road
Finucane Gdns
Deere Avenue
Bader Way
Tuck Rd
Stephen Av
Sowrey Av
Bretons
Simpson Road
Scargill Jun Sch
Scargill Inf Sch
Hugo Gdns
Fulmar Rd
Flight Av
St Albans RC JMI School
Dowding Close
Rochester Rd
Heron
Kingaby Gdns
Jersey Rd
Princes Park
South End Rd
Hayes Dr
Sunningdale Rd
Elmer Gardens
Brittons School Technology College
RAINHAM ROAD
Avenue
John Perry Prim Sch
Auriel Av
Norton Rd
Goring Road
Surgery Road
A1112
DAGENHAM RD
30
Willoughby Dr
Fontayne Av
Castle Av
Newtons Cl
Ford Lane
Ford Cl
Ongar Wy
Fyfield Road
Dunmow Drive
Harrow Road
Danbury Rd
Whybridge Junior School
Whybridge Infant School
Grove Park Road
Gainsborough Road
Avelon Road
Guysfield Drive
Health & Welfare Clinic
Albyns Farm
Thorogood Way
South Hornchurch
Beam River
Stanley Road
Canfield Rd
Blacksmith's Lane
Surgery
Blake Cl
Whybridge Close
Alexandra Road
South End Road
Hood Rd
North Road
Trafalgar Rd
Nelson Road
Frederick Road
Maytree Cl
Newtons Primary
Victory Rd
Lane
51
52
53
84
85
86
F
G
H
J
K
1
2
3
4
5
6

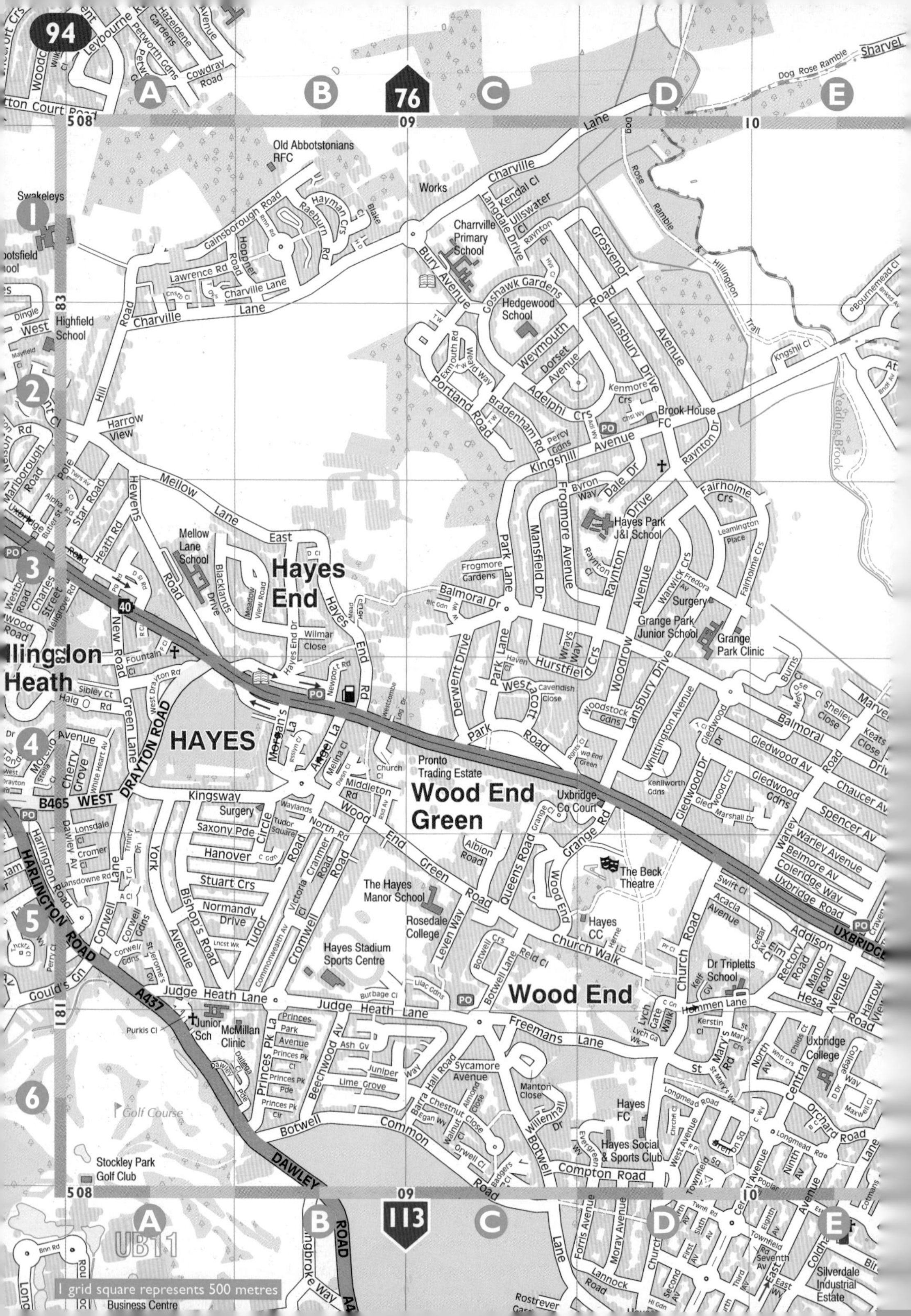
76
113
A
B
C
D
E
1
2
3
4
5
6
508
09
10
83
82
181
Old Abbotstonians RFC
Works
Charville Lane
Charville Primary School
Kendal Cl
Langdale Drive
Ullswater Cl
Raynton Dr
Grosvenor Road
Dog Rose Ramble
Hillingdon Trail
Sharvel
Swakeleys
Highfield School
Gainsborough Road
Hayman Crs
Raeburn Rd
Blake Cl
Hoppner Road
Lawrence Rd
Charville Lane
Bury Avenue
Goshawk Gardens
Hedgewood School
Weymouth Dorset Avenue
Lansbury Drive
Avenue
Kenmore Crs
Adelphi Crs
Portland Road
Bradenham Rd
Exmouth Rd
Percy Gdns
Kingshill Avenue
Brook House FC
Raynton Dr
Kngshil Cl
Bournemead Cl
Yeading Brook
Harrow View
Hill Road
Pole
Marlborough Road
Star Road
Heath Rd
Hewens Road
Mellow Lane East
Mellow Lane School
Blacklands Drive
Meadow View Road
Hayes End
Hayes End Rd
Hayes End Dr
Wilmar Close
Frogmore Gardens
Balmoral Dr
Park Lane
Mansfield Dr
Frogmore Avenue
Byron Way
Dale Dr
Hayes Park J&I School
Raynton Cl
Raynton Drive
Fairholme Crs
Leamington Place
Warwick Crs
Fredora Av
Surgery
Grange Park Junior School
Grange Park Clinic
Woodrow Avenue
Derwent Drive
Haven Cl
Wrays Way
Hurstfield Crs
West Cavendish Close
Westacott
Woodstock Gdns
Whittington Avenue
Gledwood Dr
Burns
Melrose Cl
Shelley Close
Keats Close
Marvel
Balmoral
Gledwood Av
Gledwood Gdns
Chaucer Av
Spencer Av
Warley Avenue
Belmore Av
Coleridge Way
Uxbridge Road
Kenilworth Gdns
Marshall Dr
Uxbridge Co Court
Grange Rd
Hillingdon Heath
Uxbridge
Charles Street
Nellgrove Rd
Westbourne Road
New Road
Fountain Cl
West Drayton Rd
Sibley Ct
Haig Rd
Green Lane
West Drayton Road
HAYES
Morgan's La
Angel La
Newport Rd
Westcombe Dr
Church Cl
Middleton Rd
Pronto Trading Estate
Wood End Green
Park Road
B465 West
Kingsway
Surgery
Saxony Pde
Hanover
Stuart Crs
Normandy Drive
Circle
Tudor Square
North Rd
Wood End Green Road
Victoria Road
Cranmer Road
Commonwealth Av
Cromwell Cl
Tudor
Bishop's Road
York Avenue
Albion Road
Queens Road
Wood End
The Beck Theatre
The Hayes Manor School
Rosedale College
Leven Way
Hayes Stadium Sports Centre
Hayes CC
Church Walk
Botwell Crs
Botwell Lane
Reid Cl
Herne Cl
Wood End
Church Road
Acacia Avenue
Swift Cl
Dr Tripletts School
Hemmen Lane
Kerstin Cl
St Mary's Rd
Addison
Rectory Road
Manor Road
Hesa
Avenue
Harrow View
Road
Uxbridge College
College Way
Central Avenue
Orchard Road
Lane
Maxwell Cl
North Av
Childs Crs
Lonsdale Cl
Cromer Cl
Dawley Av
Harlington Road
Lansdowne Rd
Lane
Corwell Gdns
Corwell Lane
Harlington Road
A437
Gould's Gn
Judge Heath Lane
Junior Sch
McMillan Clinic
Purkis Cl
Dawley Pde
Princes Pk La
Princes Park Avenue
Princes Pk Cl
Princes Pk Pde
Princes Pk Cir
Beechwood Av
Ash Gv
Juniper Way
Lime Grove
Barra Hall Road
Sycamore Avenue
Chestnut Close
Almond Close
Walnut Cl
Orwell Cl
Egan Wy
Manton Close
Willenhall Dr
Freemans Lane
Lych Gate Walk
St Mary's Crs
Longmead Road
Hayes FC
Hayes Social & Sports Club
West Avenue
Evergreen Wy
Botwell Common Road
Compton Road
Botwell
Stockley Park Golf Club
Golf Course
Dawley Road
UB11
Business Centre
Bolingbroke Way
Forris Avenue
Moray Avenue
Church
Lannock Road
Rostrever
Silverdale Industrial Estate
Coldharbour
Seventh Av
Townfield Rd
Townfield Sq
Eighth Av
Sixth Av
First Av
Second Av
Third Av
Ninth Av
East Av
1 grid square represents 500 metres

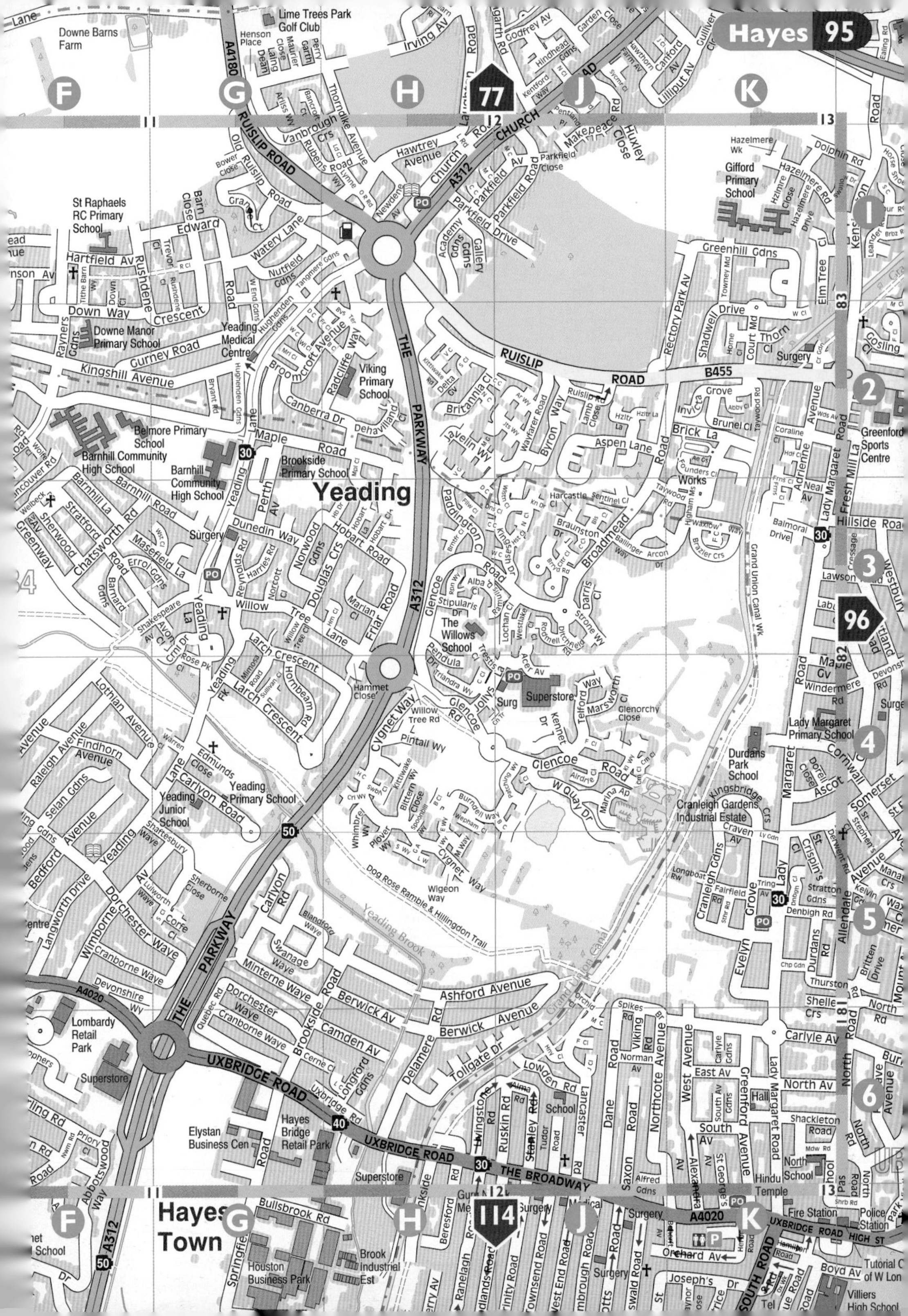

Hayes 95
Downe Barns Farm
Lime Trees Park Golf Club
Henson Place
A4180
RUISLIP ROAD
Old Ruislip Road
Irving Av
Thorndike Avenue
Vanbrough Crs
Rubens Road
Hawtrey Avenue
Church Road
A312
CHURCH ROAD
77
Godfrey Av
Hindhead Gdns
Garden Close
Kentford Way
Makepeace Rd
Huxley Close
Parkfield Av
Parkfield Road
Parkfield Close
Parkfield Drive
Academy Gdns
Gallery Gdns
Hawthorn Farm Av
Canford Av
Lilliput Av
Gulliver Cl
Hazelmere Wk
Gifford Primary School
Dolphin Rd
Hazelmere Rd
Hazelmere Drive
Greenhill Gdns
Elm Tree Cl
Rectory Park Av
Shadwell Drive
Court Md
Thorn Cl
Surgery
Gosling Cl
St Raphaels RC Primary School
Barn Close
Edward Rd
Watery Lane
Nutfield Gdns
Hartfield Av
Rushdene Crescent
Tithe Barn
Down Way
Raynes Gdns
Downe Manor Primary School
Gurney Road
Yeading Medical Centre
Kingshill Avenue
Hughenden Gdns
Broomcroft Avenue
Radcliffe Way
Viking Primary School
THE PARKWAY
RUISLIP ROAD
B455
Kittiwake Delta Gv
Britannia Cl
Wayfarer Road
Byron Way
Ruislip Rd
Lamb Close
Grove
Invicta Grove
Brunel Cl
Brick La
Aspen Lane
Taywood Rd
Founders Cl
Works
Coraline
Adrienne Avenue
Neal Av
Lady Margaret Road
Fresh Mill La
Greenford Sports Centre
Hillside Road
Balmoral Drive
Belmore Primary School
Barnhill Community High School
Maple Road
Canberra Dr
Dehavilland Cl
Javelin Wy
Brookside Primary School
Yeading
Barnhill Road
Barnhill La
Stratford
Sherwood
Greenway
Chatsworth Rd
Masefield La
Errol Gdns
Barnard Gdns
Surgery
Dunedin Way
Perth Av
Norwood Gdns
Hobart Road
Douglas Crs
Reynolds Rd
Harries Rd
Paddington Cl
Kingsash Dr
Harcastle Cl
Sentinel Cl
Braunston Dr
Broadmead
Ballinger Way
Arcon Dr
Waxlow Way
Brazier Crs
Grand Union Canal Wk
Cressage
Lawson Rd
Westbury
96
Glencoe Road
Stipularis Dr
The Willows School
Lochan Cl
Westlake Cl
Strone Wy
Darris Cl
Willow Tree Lane
Marian Cl
Friar Road
Yeading La
Shakespeare Av
Avon Cl
Rose Pk
Larch Crescent
Hornbeam Rd
Mimosa Road
Yeading Fk
Hammet Close
Pendula Dr
Triandra Wy
Acer Av
Jollys La
Superstore
Surg
Kennet Dr
Telford Way
Marsworth Cl
Glenorchy Close
Maple Gv
Windermere Rd
Devonshire
Lady Margaret Primary School
Cygnet Way
Willow Tree Rd
Pintail Wy
Glencoe Rd
Glencoe Road
W Quay Dr
Marina Ap
Durdans Park School
Kingsbridge Crs
Cranleigh Gardens Industrial Estate
Margaret Cornwall Ascot
Dorell Close
Somerset
Lothian Avenue
Raleigh Avenue
Findhorn Avenue
Selan Gdns
Edmunds Close
Carlyon Road
Yeading Primary School
Yeading Junior School
Warren Lane
Kittiwake Wy
Bittern Close
Whimbrel Wy
Plover Wy
Burnell Way
Wepham Cl
Cygnet Way
Wigeon Way
Dog Rose Ramble & Hillingdon Trail
Craven Av
Cranleigh Gdns
Longboat Rw
Fairfield Rd
Evelyn Grove
Lady Crispin's
St Stephen's
Allendale Avenue
Stratton Gdns
Denbigh Rd
Durdans Rd
Britten Drive
Thurston
Bedford Avenue
Yeading Av
Langworth Drive
Wimborne
Dorchester Waye
Shaftesbury Waye
Sherborne Close
Lulworth Waye
Corfe Cl
Carlyon Rd
Blandford Waye
Swanage Waye
Yeading Brook
Grand Union Canal
Cranborne Waye
Devonshire Wy
A4020
Minterne Waye
Brookside Road
Berwick Av
Ashford Avenue
Berwick Avenue
Delamere Rd
Camden Av
Dorchester Waye
Cranborne Waye
Quebec Rd
Lombardy Retail Park
Superstore
UXBRIDGE ROAD
Tollgate Dr
Lowden Rd
Spikes Rd
Viking Rd
Norman Av
Northcote Avenue
West Avenue
Carlyle Gdns
East Av
Greenford Avenue
Lady Margaret Road
Carlyle Av
North Av
Hall
Shackleton Road
North Road
North Avenue
Shelley Crs
Longford Gdns
Uxbridge Rd
Elystan Business Cen
Hayes Bridge Retail Park
Livingstone Rd
Ruskin Rd
Stanley Rd
Tudor Rd
School
Lancaster Rd
Dane Road
Saxon Road
Alfred Gdns
South Av
Alexandra Av
St George's
Hindu Temple
North School
UXBRIDGE ROAD
THE BROADWAY
Superstore
Hayes Town
Bullsbrook Rd
Springfield Road
Houston Business Park
Brook Industrial Est
Beresford
Ranelagh Road
Midlands Road
114
Trinity Road
Townsend Road
West End Road
Surgery
Medical
A4020
Orchard Av
Joseph's
Surgery
Fire Station
Police Station
UXBRIDGE ROAD HIGH ST
SOUTH ROAD
Boyd Av
Tutorial C of W Lon
Villiers High School
Abbotswood Way
A312
Priory Cl
F G H J K
11 12 13
1 2 3 4 5 6

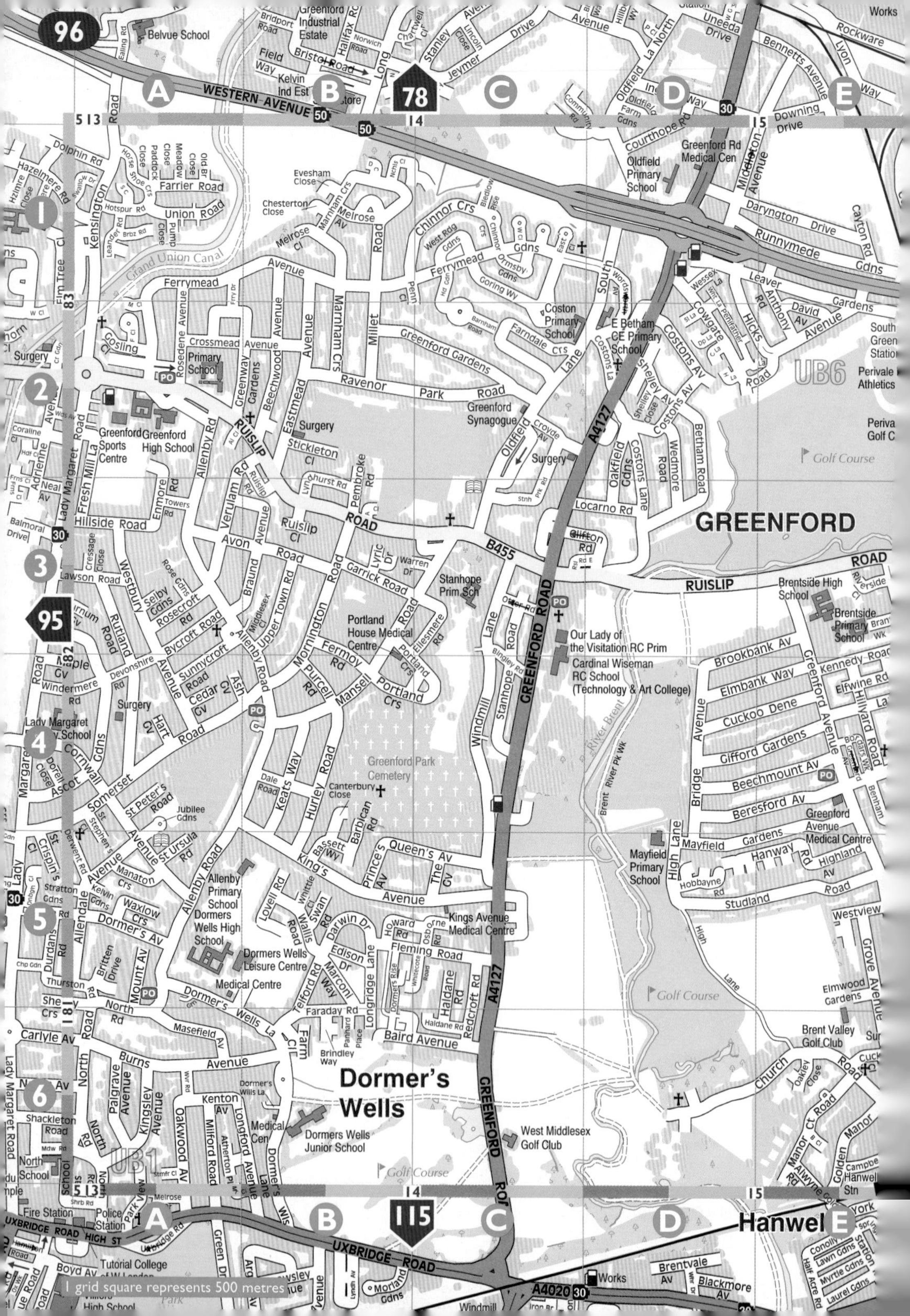

96
78
95
115
GREENFORD
Dormer's Wells
Hanwell
UB6
UB1
WESTERN AVENUE
RUISLIP ROAD
GREENFORD ROAD
UXBRIDGE ROAD
A4127
A4020
B455
Grand Union Canal
River Brent
Greenford Park Cemetery
Golf Course
Greenford Industrial Estate
Kelvin Ind Est
Belvue School
Oldfield Primary School
Greenford Rd Medical Cen
Coston Primary School
E Betham CE Primary School
Greenford Synagogue
Primary School
Greenford Sports Centre
Greenford High School
Surgery
Stanhope Prim Sch
Portland House Medical Centre
Our Lady of the Visitation RC Prim
Cardinal Wiseman RC School (Technology & Art College)
Brentside High School
Brentside Primary School
Lady Margaret School
Allenby Primary School
Dormers Wells High School
Dormers Wells Leisure Centre
Medical Centre
Kings Avenue Medical Centre
Mayfield Primary School
Greenford Avenue Medical Centre
Brent Valley Golf Club
West Middlesex Golf Club
Dormers Wells Junior School
North School
Fire Station
Police Station
Tutorial College of W London
Villiers High School
Works
Hanwell Stn
Perivale Athletics
Perivale Golf C
South Greenford Station
1 grid square represents 500 metres

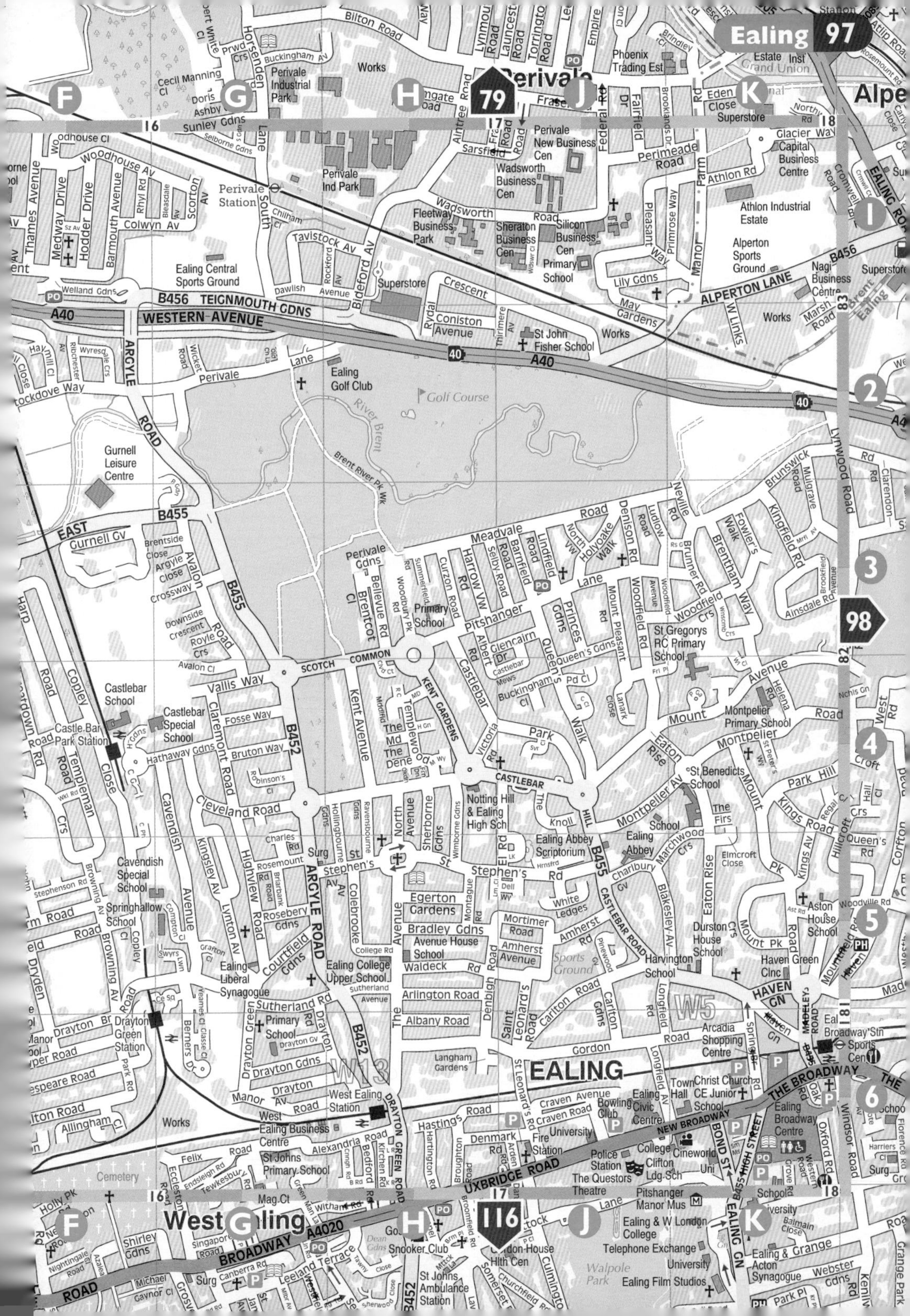
Perivale
79
Perivale Industrial Park
Works
Phoenix Trading Est
Alperton
Bilton Road
Buckingham Av
Cecil Manning Cl
Doris Ashby Cl
Sunley Gdns
Horsenden Lane South
Perivale New Business Cen
Wadsworth Business Cen
Perivale Ind Park
Perimeade Road
Eden Close
Superstore
Glacier Way
Capital Business Centre
Athlon Rd
Athlon Industrial Estate
Alperton Sports Ground
Alperton Lane
B456
Nagi Business Centre
Ealing Road
Woodhouse Cl
Woodhouse Av
Thames Avenue
Medway Drive
Hodder Drive
Barmouth Avenue
Rhyl Rd
Colwyn Av
Scorton Av
Perivale Station
Chilham Cl
Tavistock Av
Fleetway Business Park
Sheraton Business Cen
Silicon Business Cen
Primary School
Wadsworth Road
Pleasant Way
Primrose Way
Manor Farm Rd
Lily Gdns
May Gardens
W Links
Works
Marsh Road
Ealing Central Sports Ground
Welland Gdns
B456 Teignmouth Gdns
A40 Western Avenue
Dawlish Avenue
Bideford Av
Superstore
Crescent
Rydal
Coniston Avenue
Thirlmere Av
St John Fisher School
A40
Argyle Road
Perivale Lane
Ealing Golf Club
Golf Course
River Brent
Brent River Pk Wk
Stockdove Way
Gurnell Leisure Centre
East
B455
Gurnell Gv
Brentside Close
Argyle Close
Crossway
Avalon Road
Downside Crescent
Royle Crs
Avalon Cl
Lynwood Road
Brunswick Road
Mulgrave Road
Kingfield Rd
Clarendon
Meadvale Road
Harrow Vw
Selby Road
Barnfield Road
Lindfield Road
North Vw
Holyoake Walk
Denison Rd
Neville Rd
Ludlow Road
Brunner Rd
Brentham Way
Fowler's Walk
Ainsdale Rd
Brookfield Avenue
98
Perivale Gdns
Bellevue Rd
Brentcot Cl
Woodbury Pk Rd
Curzon Road
Primary School
Pitshanger Lane
Princes Gdns
Mount Pleasant Rd
Woodfield Rd
Woodfield Crs
St Gregorys RC Primary School
Scotch Common
Kent Gardens
Castlebar Rd
Albert Rd
Glencairn Dr
Queen's Walk
Queen's Gdns
Buckingham Cl
Lanark Close
Mount Avenue
Helena Rd
Montpelier Primary School
Montpelier Road
West Rd
Vallis Way
Fosse Way
Castlebar School
Castlebar Special School
Castle Bar Park Station
Hathaway Gdns
Claremont Road
Bruton Way
B452
Kent Avenue
Templewood
The Md
The Dene
Victoria Rd
Park Vw
Castlebar Hill
Eaton Rise
St Benedicts School
Mount Park
Park Hill
Croft
Kings Road
Regal Crs
Queen's Rd
Hillcroft Crs
Kings Av
Copley Road
Templeman Road
Close
Cavendish Avenue
Cleveland Road
Kingsley Av
Highview Road
Charles Rd
Rosemount Rd
Argyle Road
Hollingbourne Gdns
Ravensbourne Gdns
North Avenue
Sherborne Gdns
Wimborne Gdns
Notting Hill & Ealing High Sch
The Knoll
Montpelier Av
Ealing Abbey
Ealing Abbey Scriptorium
School
Marchwood Crs
The Firs
Elmcroft Close
St Stephen's Rd
Charlbury Gv
Blakesley Av
Eaton Rise
Mount Pk Crs
Aston House School
Woodville Rd
Cavendish Special School
Springhallow School
Browning Av
Lynton Av
Rosebery Gdns
Colebrooke Av
Egerton Gardens
Bradley Gdns
Avenue House School
Montague Rd
Mortimer Road
Amherst Avenue
Amherst Rd
White Ledges
Castlebar Road
Durston House School
Harvington School
Haven Green Clnc
Mount Pk Road
Courtfield Gdns
Ealing Liberal Synagogue
Ealing College Upper School
Sutherland Avenue
Waldeck Rd
Arlington Road
Albany Road
Denbigh Road
Saint Leonard's Road
Carlton Road
Carlton Gdns
Longfield Rd
Sports Ground
W5
Haven Gn
Madeley Road
Ealing Broadway Stn
Sports Cen
Drayton Green Station
Drayton Br Rd
Sutherland Rd
Primary School
Drayton Gv
Drayton Gdns
Berners Dr
W13
Langham Gardens
Gordon Road
Arcadia Shopping Centre
Ealing
Town Hall
Christ Church CE Junior School
The Broadway
Manor Av
Drayton Road
West Ealing Station
Drayton Green Road
Works
Allingham Cl
West Ealing Business Centre
Alexandria Road
Hastings Road
Craven Avenue
Craven Road
Bowling Club
Ealing Civic Centre
University
Fire Station
Police Station
College
Clifton Ldg Sch
Cineworld
Uni
New Broadway
Bond St
High Street
Ealing Broadway Centre
Oxford Rd
Windsor Road
Felix Road
St Johns Primary School
Bedford Rd
Kirchen Rd
Hartington Rd
Broughton Road
Denmark Rd
Arden Rd
Uxbridge Road
The Questors Theatre
Pitshanger Manor Mus
School
University
Cemetery
Mag.Ct
West Ealing
Broadway A4020
116
Holly Pk
Shirley Gdns
Leeland Terrace
Snooker Club
Gordon House Hlth Cen
St Johns Ambulance Station
Somerset Road
Culmington Road
Ealing & W London College
Telephone Exchange
University
Ealing Film Studios
Walpole Park
Ealing Gn
Ealing & Grange Acton Synagogue
Webster Gdns
Grange Park
Park Pl
Road
Surg
B452

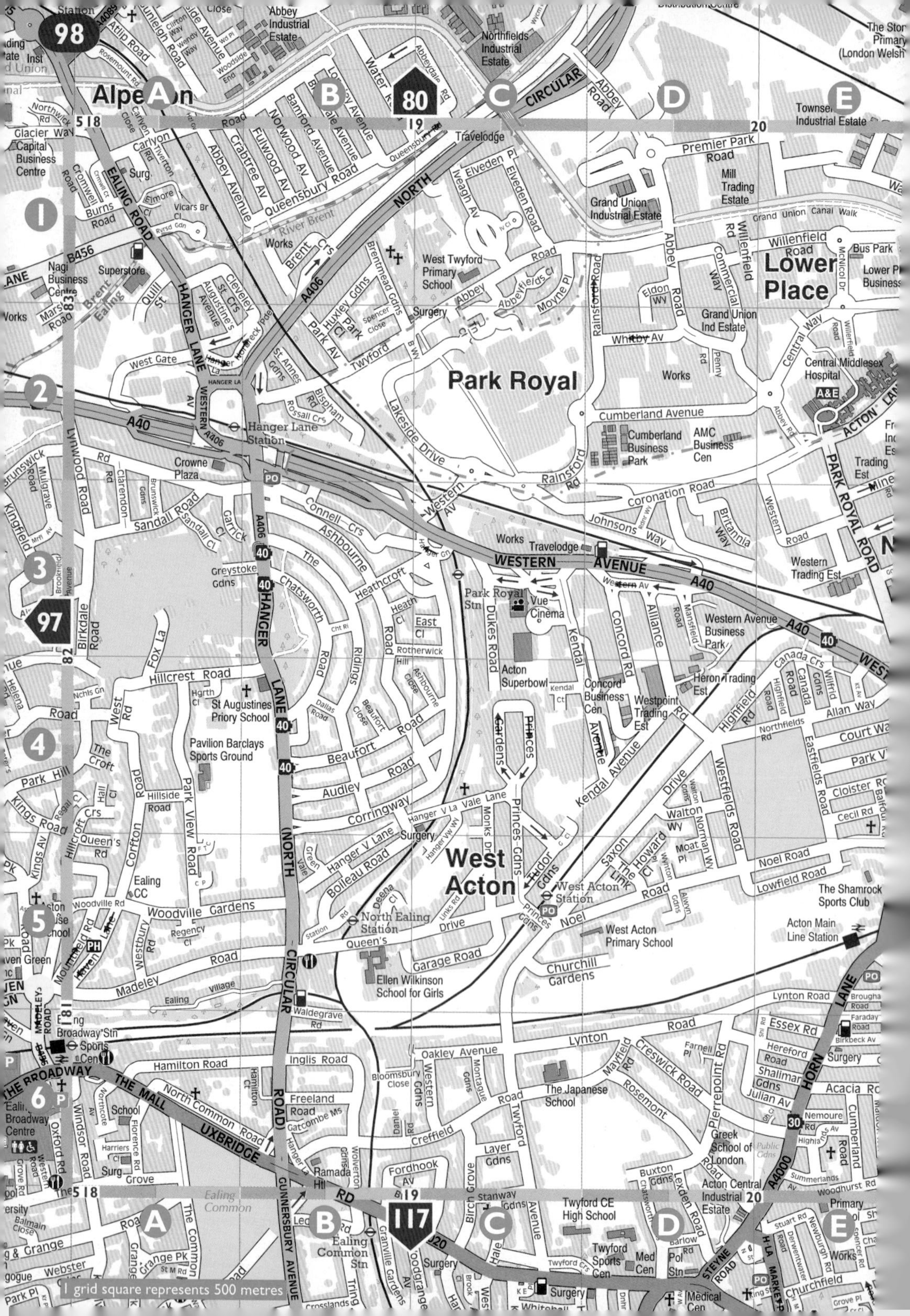
98
80
97
117
A
B
C
D
E
1
2
3
4
5
6
Alperton
Abbey Industrial Estate
Northfields Industrial Estate
The Stonebridge Primary (London Welsh)
North Circular
Townsend Industrial Estate
Glacier Way
Capital Business Centre
Ealing Road
Carlyon Rd
Abbey Avenue
Crabtree Av
Fulwood Av
Norwood Av
Bamford Avenue
Queensbury Road
Travelodge
Premier Park Road
Mill Trading Estate
Grand Union Industrial Estate
Grand Union Canal Walk
Willenfield Road
Lower Place
Bus Park
Lower Place Business
Superstore
Nagi Business Centre
Brent Crs
Works
River Brent
West Twyford Primary School
Abbeyfields Cl
Moyne Pl
Rainsford Road
Abbey Road
Commercial Way
Eldon Wy
Grand Union Ind Estate
Whitby Av
Central Way
Central Middlesex Hospital
A&E
Hanger Lane
West Gate
Twyford Abbey Rd
Park Royal
Cumberland Avenue
Cumberland Business Park
AMC Business Cen
Acton Lane
A40
Western Av
Hanger Lane Station
Crowne Plaza
Lakeside Drive
Rainsford Rd
Coronation Road
Johnsons Way
Britannia Way
Park Royal Road
Trading Est
Lynwood Road
Sandall Road
Connell Crs
Ashbourne
Western Avenue
Travelodge
Western Trading Est
Greystoke Gdns
Park Royal Stn
Vue Cinema
Dukes Road
Kendal
Concord Rd
Alliance
Western Avenue Business Park
Acton Superbowl
Heron Trading Est
Birkdale Road
Fox La
Hillcrest Road
St Augustines Priory School
Concord Business Cen
Westpoint Trading Est
Canada Crs
Allan Way
Court Way
Pavilion Barclays Sports Ground
Beaufort Road
Audley Road
Corringway
Princes Gardens
Kendal Avenue
Highfield Rd
Westfields Road
Eastfields Road
Park Hill
Kings Road
Hillcroft Crs
Corfton Road
Park View Road
Hanger V Lane
Boileau Road
West Acton
Walton Wy
Noel Road
Lowfield Road
Cloister Rd
Cecil Rd
Ealing CC
Woodville Gardens
North Ealing Station
West Acton Station
West Acton Primary School
The Shamrock Sports Club
Acton Main Line Station
Madeley Road
Queen's Drive
Garage Road
Ellen Wilkinson School for Girls
Churchill Gardens
Lynton Road
Waldegrave Rd
Ealing Broadway Stn
Sports Cen
Hamilton Road
Inglis Road
Oakley Avenue
Lynton Road
Creswick Road
Essex Rd
Hereford Road
Horn Lane
The Broadway
The Mall
North Common Road
Uxbridge Road
Freeland Road
The Japanese School
Rosemont Road
Pierrepoint Rd
Acacia Rd
Ealing Broadway Centre
Windsor Road
Oxford Rd
Greek School of London
Cumberland Road
Creffield Road
Layer Gdns
Twyford Avenue
Gunnersbury Avenue
Ramada Htl
Fordhook Av
Acton Central Industrial Estate
Ealing Common
Twyford CE High School
Ealing Common Stn
Twyford Sports Cen
Med Cen
Steyne Road
Surgery
Churchfield
1 grid square represents 500 metres

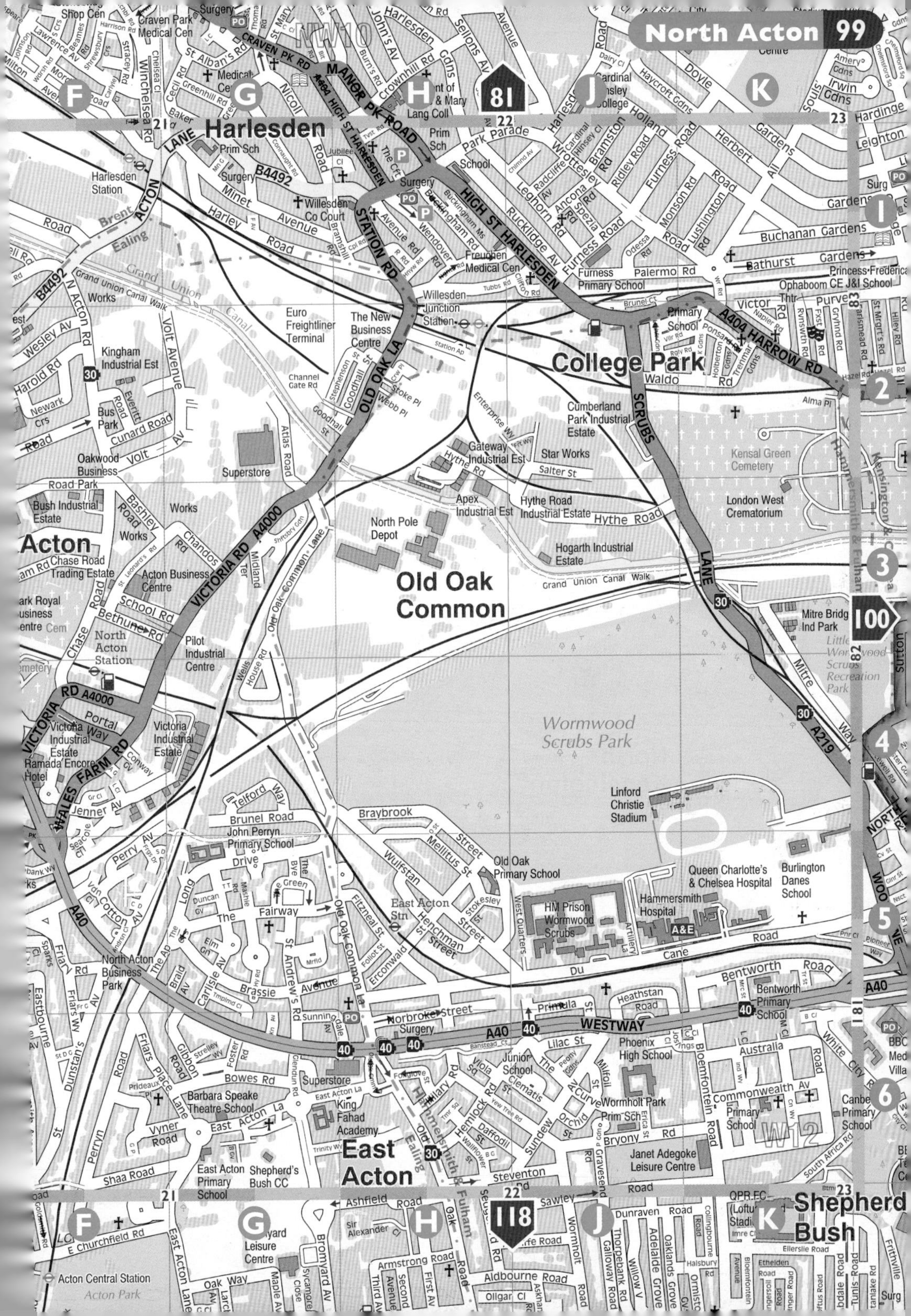

Harlesden
College Park
Old Oak Common
Acton
East Acton
Shepherd Bush
Wormwood Scrubs Park
Kensal Green Cemetery
London West Crematorium
Linford Christie Stadium
Queen Charlotte's & Chelsea Hospital
Hammersmith Hospital
HM Prison Wormwood Scrubs
Burlington Danes School
Old Oak Primary School
North Pole Depot
Willesden Junction Station
Harlesden Station
North Acton Station
East Acton Stn
Acton Central Station
Euro Freightliner Terminal
The New Business Centre
Superstore
Kingham Industrial Est
Oakwood Business Park
Bush Industrial Estate
Chase Road Trading Estate
Acton Business Centre
Pilot Industrial Centre
Victoria Industrial Estate
Ramada Encore Hotel
Cumberland Park Industrial Estate
Gateway Industrial Est
Star Works
Apex Industrial Est
Hythe Road Industrial Estate
Hogarth Industrial Estate
Mitre Bridge Ind Park
Little Wormwood Scrubs Recreation Park
John Perryn Primary School
North Acton Business Park
Barbara Speake Theatre School
East Acton Primary School
Shepherd's Bush CC
King Fahad Academy
Phoenix High School
Wormholt Park Prim Sch
Janet Adegoke Leisure Centre
Bentworth Primary School
Commonwealth Av
Furness Primary School
Willesden Co Court
Freuchen Medical Cen
Craven Park Medical Cen
VICTORIA RD A4000
OLD OAK LA
STATION RD
HIGH ST HARLESDEN
MANOR PK ROAD
A404 HARROW RD
SCRUBS LANE
A219
A40 WESTWAY
Du Cane Road
Grand Union Canal Walk
Hythe Road
Old Oak Common Lane
Wulfstan Street
Braybrook Street
Bloemfontein Road
NW10
W12
81
100
118

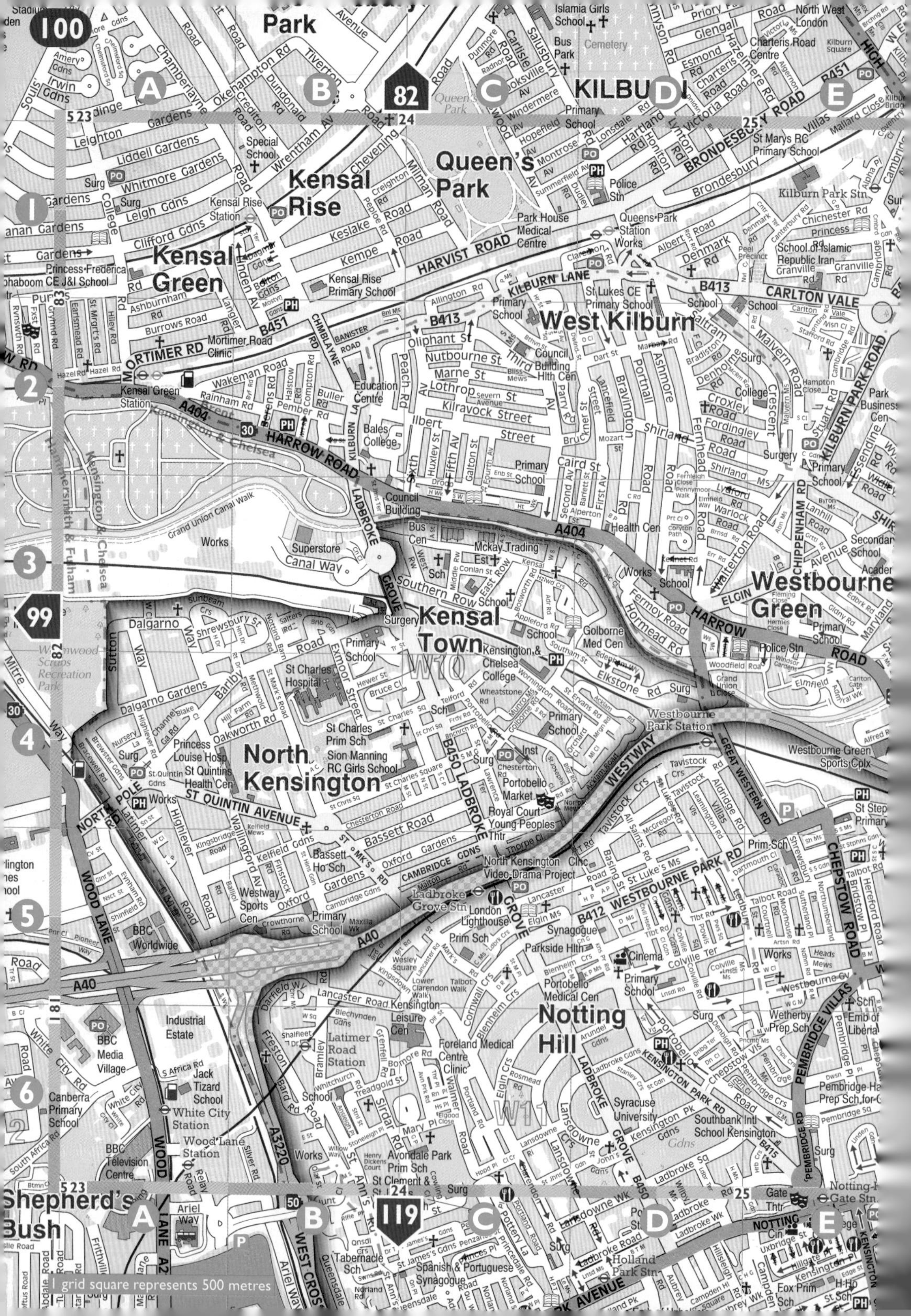
100
82
99
119
A
B
C
D
E
1
2
3
4
5
6
Park
Kensal Rise
Kensal Green
Queen's Park
KILBURN
West Kilburn
Westbourne Green
Kensal Town
North Kensington
Notting Hill
Shepherd's Bush
W10
W11
HARVIST ROAD
KILBURN LANE
HARROW ROAD
MORTIMER RD
CARLTON VALE
BRONDESBURY ROAD
KILBURN PARK ROAD
LADBROKE GROVE
B450 LADBROKE
WESTWAY
WOOD LANE
GREAT WESTERN RD
CHEPSTOW ROAD
PEMBRIDGE VILLAS
B412 WESTBOURNE PARK RD
KENSINGTON PARK RD
ST QUINTIN AVENUE
CAMBRIDGE GDNS
A404
A40
A3220
B413
B451
Kensal Rise Station
Kensal Green Station
Queens Park Station
Kilburn Park Stn
Westbourne Park Station
Ladbroke Grove Stn
Latimer Road Station
White City Station
Wood Lane Station
Holland Park Stn
Notting Hill Gate Stn
Grand Union Canal Walk
Canal Way
Superstore
Works
Kensington & Chelsea
Hammersmith & Fulham
Wormwood Scrubs Recreation Park
BBC Media Village
BBC Television Centre
BBC Worldwide
Industrial Estate
St Charles Hospital
Portobello Market
Kensington & Chelsea College
Westway Sports Cen
Westbourne Green Sports Cplx
Syracuse University
Police Stn
1 grid square represents 500 metres

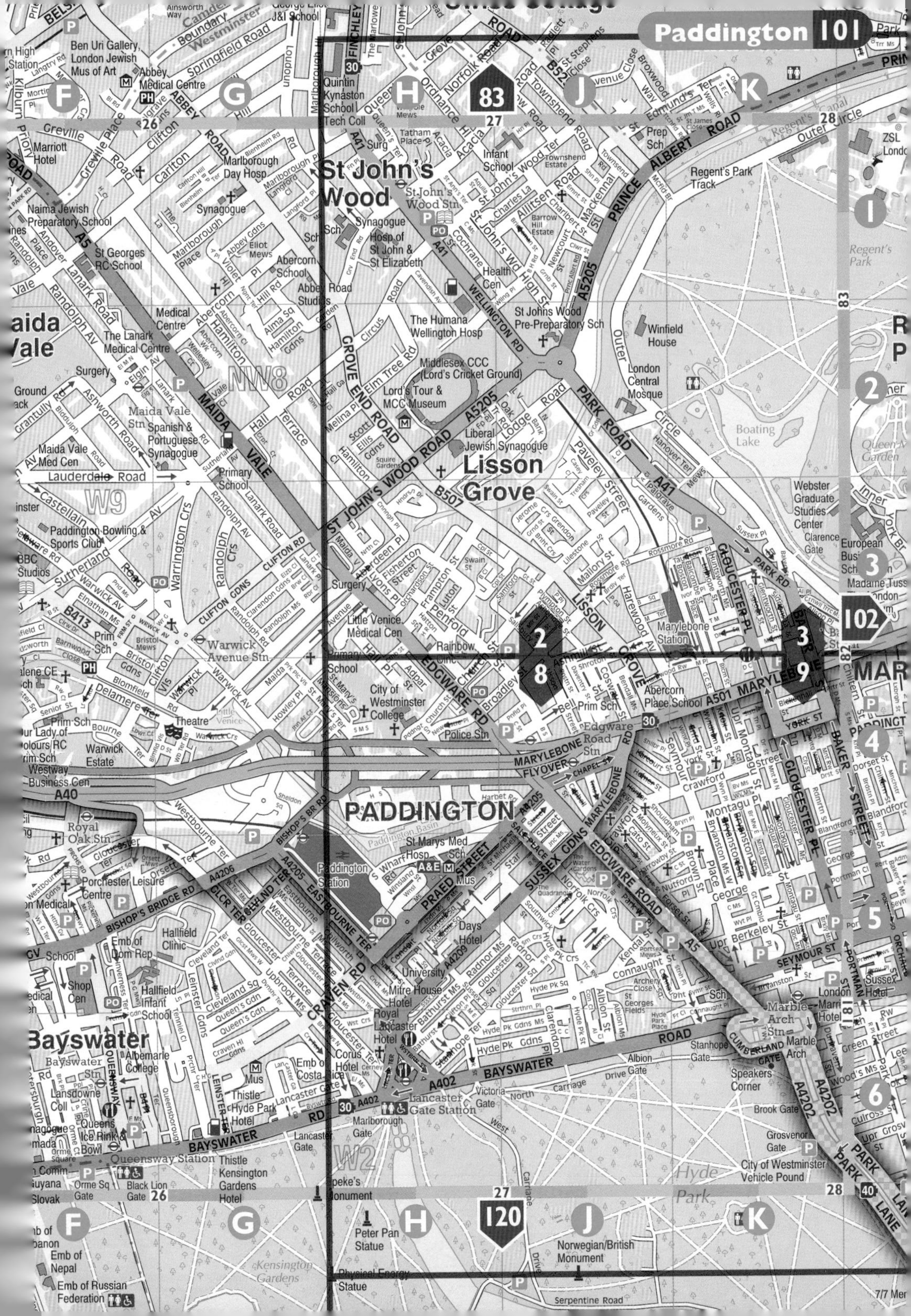
St John's Wood
Lisson Grove
PADDINGTON
Maida Vale
Bayswater
Regent's Park
Hyde Park
Kensington Gardens
Paddington Station
Marylebone Station
Lord's Tour & MCC Museum
Middlesex CCC (Lord's Cricket Ground)
London Central Mosque
Boating Lake
Marble Arch
Speakers Corner
Peter Pan Statue
Norwegian/British Monument
Physical Energy Statue
Serpentine Road
MARYLEBONE FLYOVER
EDGWARE ROAD
BAYSWATER ROAD
PRAED STREET
MAIDA VALE
NW8
W9
W2
83
102
120

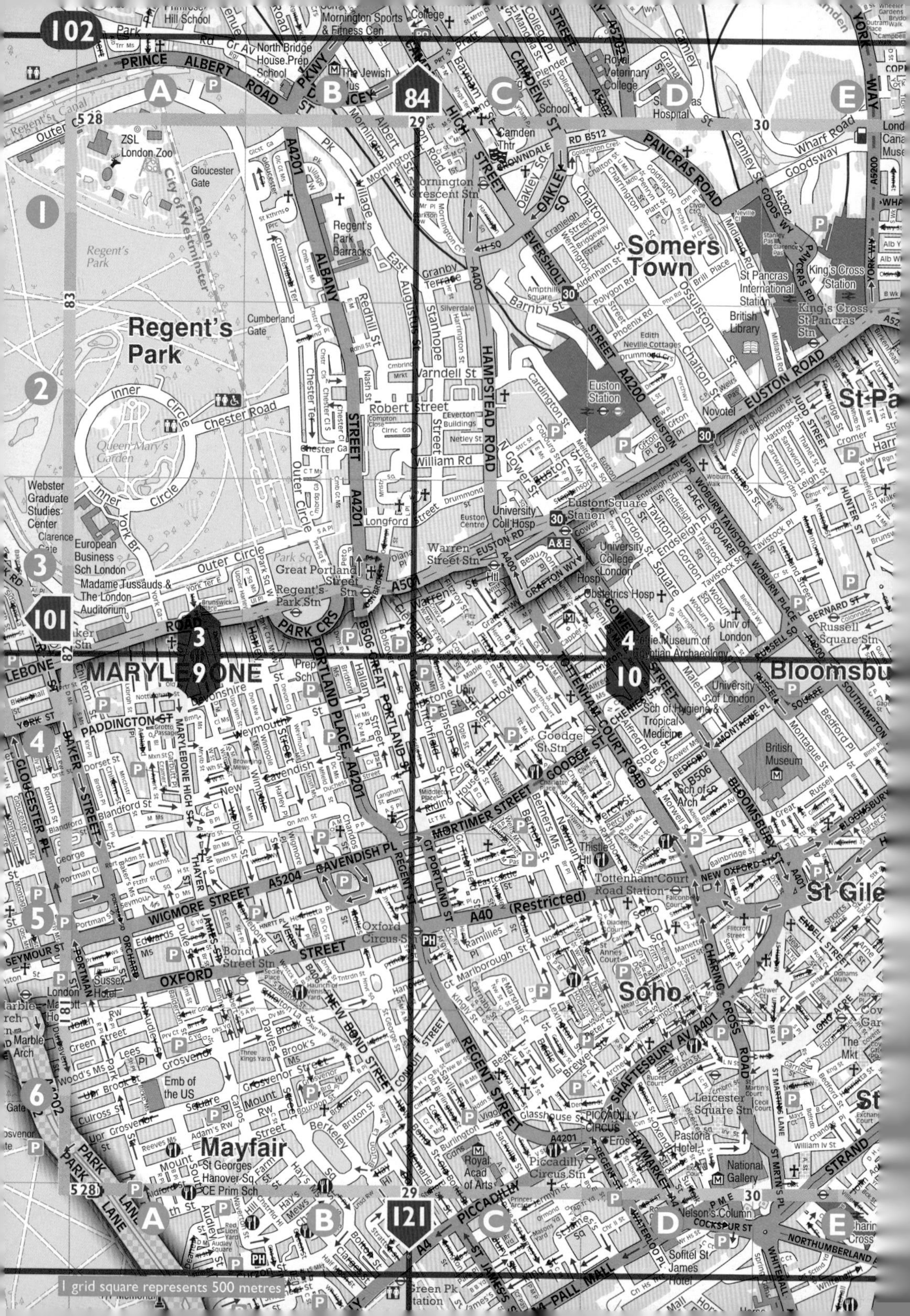

102
84
101
121
3
9
4
10
A
B
C
D
E
1
2
3
4
5
6
28
29
30
81
82
83
PRINCE ALBERT ROAD
Regent's Canal
ZSL London Zoo
Gloucester Gate
City of Westminster
Camden
Regent's Park
Cumberland Gate
Inner Circle
Chester Road
Queen Mary's Garden
Outer Circle
Webster Graduate Studies Center
Clarence Gate
European Business Sch London
Madame Tussauds & The London Auditorium
Park Sq
Great Portland Street Stn
Regent's Park Stn
PARK CRS
Mornington Crescent Stn
Regent's Park Barracks
ALBANY STREET
A4201
Camden Thtr
CAMDEN HIGH STREET
HAMPSTEAD ROAD
A400
Robert Street
William Rd
Drummond St
Varndell St
Stanhope
Granby Terrace
Euston Station
Euston Square Station
University Coll Hosp
University College London
Obstetrics Hosp
GRAFTON WY
EUSTON RD
EUSTON ROAD
Somers Town
Ossulston St
Chalton St
Polygon Rd
Phoenix Rd
Brill Place
PANCRAS ROAD
St Pancras International Station
British Library
King's Cross Station
King's Cross St Pancras Stn
Novotel
Wharf Road
Goodsway
YORK WAY
Royal Veterinary College
Hospital
Oakley Sq
Cardington St
Petrie Museum of Egyptian Archaeology
Univ of London
Russell Square Stn
Bloomsbury
MARYLEBONE
BAKER STREET
GLOUCESTER PL
PADDINGTON ST
MARYLEBONE HIGH ST
Weymouth St
Cavendish
Wigmore
PORTLAND PLACE
GT PORTLAND ST
CAVENDISH PL
WIGMORE STREET
A5204
OXFORD STREET
Oxford Circus Stn
Bond Street Stn
A40 (Restricted)
MORTIMER STREET
GOODGE ST
Goodge St Stn
TOTTENHAM COURT ROAD
Tottenham Court Road Station
Thistle Htl
Sch of Hygiene & Tropical Medicine
British Museum
BLOOMSBURY
NEW OXFORD ST
St Giles
Soho
Soho Sq
CHARING CROSS ROAD
SHAFTESBURY AV A401
Leicester Square Stn
Sussex Hotel
London Marriott Ho
Marble Arch
Emb of the US
Grosvenor Square
Mayfair
St Georges Hanover Sq CE Prim Sch
NEW BOND STREET
REGENT STREET
CONDUIT STREET
PICCADILLY CIRCUS
Piccadilly Circus Stn
Royal Acad of Arts
Glasshouse St
Eros
HAYMARKET
National Gallery
Nelson's Column
COCKSPUR ST
NORTHUMBERLAND AV
WHITEHALL
STRAND
LONG ACRE
Sofitel St James Hotel
PALL MALL
ST JAMES'S
PICCADILLY
A4
PARK LANE
Green Pk Station
1 grid square represents 500 metres

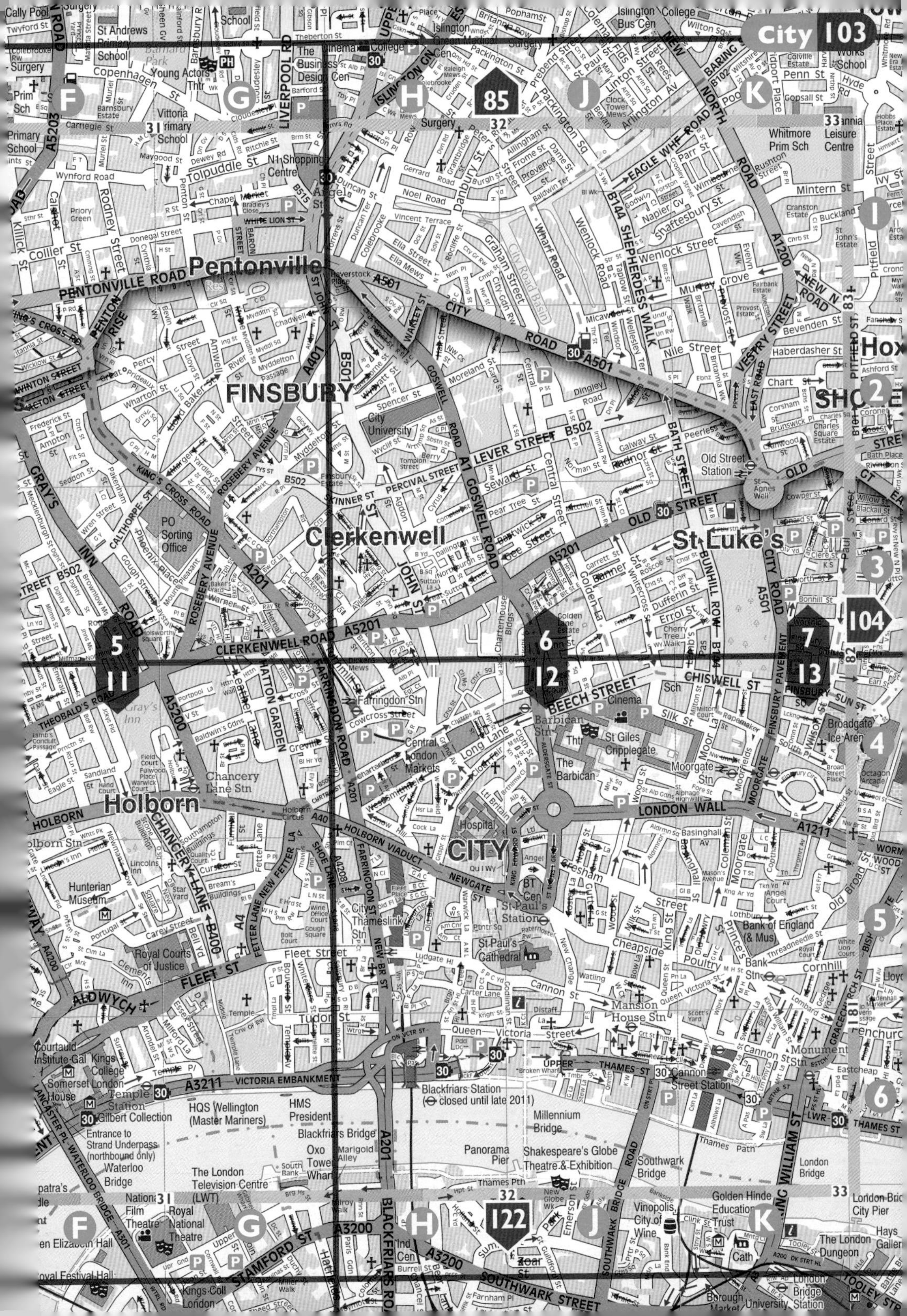

Pentonville
PENTONVILLE ROAD
FINSBURY
Clerkenwell
St Luke's
Holborn
CITY
CITY ROAD
CLERKENWELL ROAD
GOSWELL ROAD
ROSEBERY AVENUE
FARRINGDON ROAD
OLD STREET
LONDON WALL
FLEET ST
VICTORIA EMBANKMENT
SOUTHWARK STREET
CHISWELL ST
BEECH STREET
HOLBORN VIADUCT
NEWGATE
CHANCERY LANE
FETTER LANE
NEW FETTER LA
SHOE LANE
ALDWYCH
GRAY'S INN ROAD
KING'S CROSS ROAD
FINSBURY PAVEMENT
MOORGATE
BUNHILL ROW
SHEPHERDESS WALK
EAGLE WHF ROAD
NEW NORTH ROAD
UPPER THAMES ST
THAMES ST
BLACKFRIARS ROAD
SOUTHWARK BRIDGE ROAD
KING WILLIAM ST
GRACECHURCH ST
STAMFORD ST
WATERLOO BRIDGE
LIVERPOOL RD
ISLINGTON GN
City University
Central London Markets
The Barbican
Barbican
St Giles Cripplegate
Moorgate Stn
Old Street Station
Farringdon Stn
Chancery Lane Stn
Holborn Stn
St Paul's Cathedral
St Paul's Station
City Thameslink Stn
Blackfriars Station
(closed until late 2011)
Blackfriars Bridge
Millennium Bridge
Southwark Bridge
London Bridge
Cannon Street Station
Mansion House Stn
Bank of England (& Mus)
Bank Stn
Monument Stn
Royal Courts of Justice
Hunterian Museum
Temple Station
HQS Wellington (Master Mariners)
HMS President
Somerset House
Courtauld Institute Gal
Kings College London
Gilbert Collection
Entrance to Strand Underpass (northbound only)
Waterloo Bridge
The London Television Centre (LWT)
National Film Theatre
Royal National Theatre
Oxo Tower Wharf
Panorama Pier
Shakespeare's Globe Theatre & Exhibition
Vinopolis, City of Wine
Golden Hinde Education Trust
The London Dungeon
London Bridge City Pier
PO Sorting Office
Broadgate Ice Arena
Octagon Arcade
Whitmore Prim Sch
Britannia Leisure Centre
Vittoria Primary School
N1 Shopping Centre
Young Actors Thtr
The Business Design Cen
Islington Bus Cen
Islington Green Medical Cen
City Road Basin
Hoxton
F
G
H
J
K
85
104
122
5 11
6 12
7 13
31
32
33
1
2
3
4
5
6

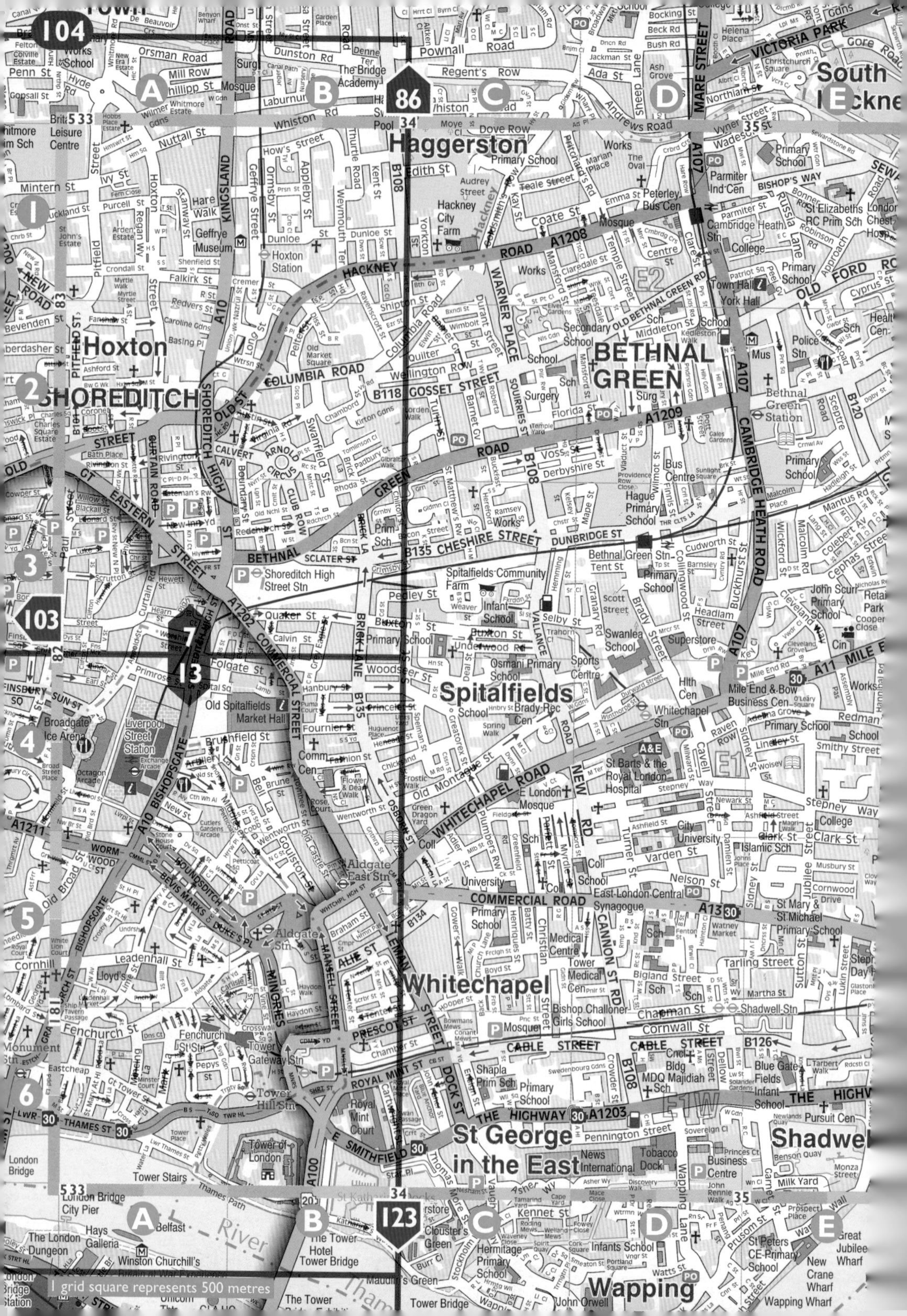

104
86
103
123
7
13
A
B
C
D
E
1
2
3
4
5
6
533
34
35
Haggerston
Hoxton
SHOREDITCH
BETHNAL GREEN
Spitalfields
Whitechapel
St George in the East
Shadwell
South Hackney
Wapping
E2
E1
E1W
HACKNEY ROAD
A1208
COLUMBIA ROAD
B118 GOSSET STREET
KINGSLAND ROAD
A10
B108
BETHNAL GREEN ROAD
A1209
CAMBRIDGE HEATH ROAD
A107
MARE STREET
VICTORIA PARK
OLD FORD ROAD
OLD BETHNAL GREEN RD
B135 CHESHIRE STREET
DUNBRIDGE ST
BRICK LANE
COMMERCIAL STREET
A1202
GT EASTERN STREET
OLD STREET
SHOREDITCH HIGH ST
BISHOPSGATE
A10 BISHOPSGATE
WHITECHAPEL ROAD
A11 MILE END
NEW RD
COMMERCIAL ROAD
A13
CANNON ST RD
CABLE STREET
THE HIGHWAY
A1203
E SMITHFIELD
ROYAL MINT ST
DOCK ST
LEMAN STREET
MANSELL STREET
MINORIES
PRESCOT ST
ALIE ST
HOUNDSDITCH
BEVIS MARKS
DUKE'S PL
WORMWOOD ST
A1211
THAMES ST
LWR
Fenchurch St
Leadenhall St
Cornhill
Eastcheap
Gt Tower St
Hackney City Farm
Geffrye Museum
Hoxton Station
Shoreditch High Street Stn
Liverpool Street Station
Old Spitalfields Market Hall
Aldgate East Stn
Aldgate Stn
Fenchurch St Stn
Tower Gateway Stn
Tower Hill Stn
Tower of London
Royal Mint Court
Bethnal Green Stn
Bethnal Green Station
Cambridge Heath Stn
Whitechapel Stn
Shadwell Stn
St Barts & the Royal London Hospital
Spitalfields Community Farm
Broadgate Ice Arena
Octagon Arcade
Monument Stn
London Bridge City Pier
London Bridge
London Bridge Station
The London Dungeon
Hays Galleria
Belfast
Winston Churchill's Britain at War Experience
The Tower Hotel Tower Bridge
Tower Bridge
River Thames
Tobacco Dock
News International
Mile End & Bow Business Cen
Britannia Leisure Centre
The Bridge Academy
Arnold Circus
Town Hall
York Hall
Hague Primary School
Osmani Primary School
Swanlea School
Bishop Challoner Girls School
East London Central Synagogue
E London Mosque
Tower Medical Cen
Blue Gate Fields Infant School
Pursuit Cen
St Peters CE Primary School
New Crane Wharf
Wapping Wharf
Great Jubilee Wharf
Hermitage Primary School
1 grid square represents 500 metres

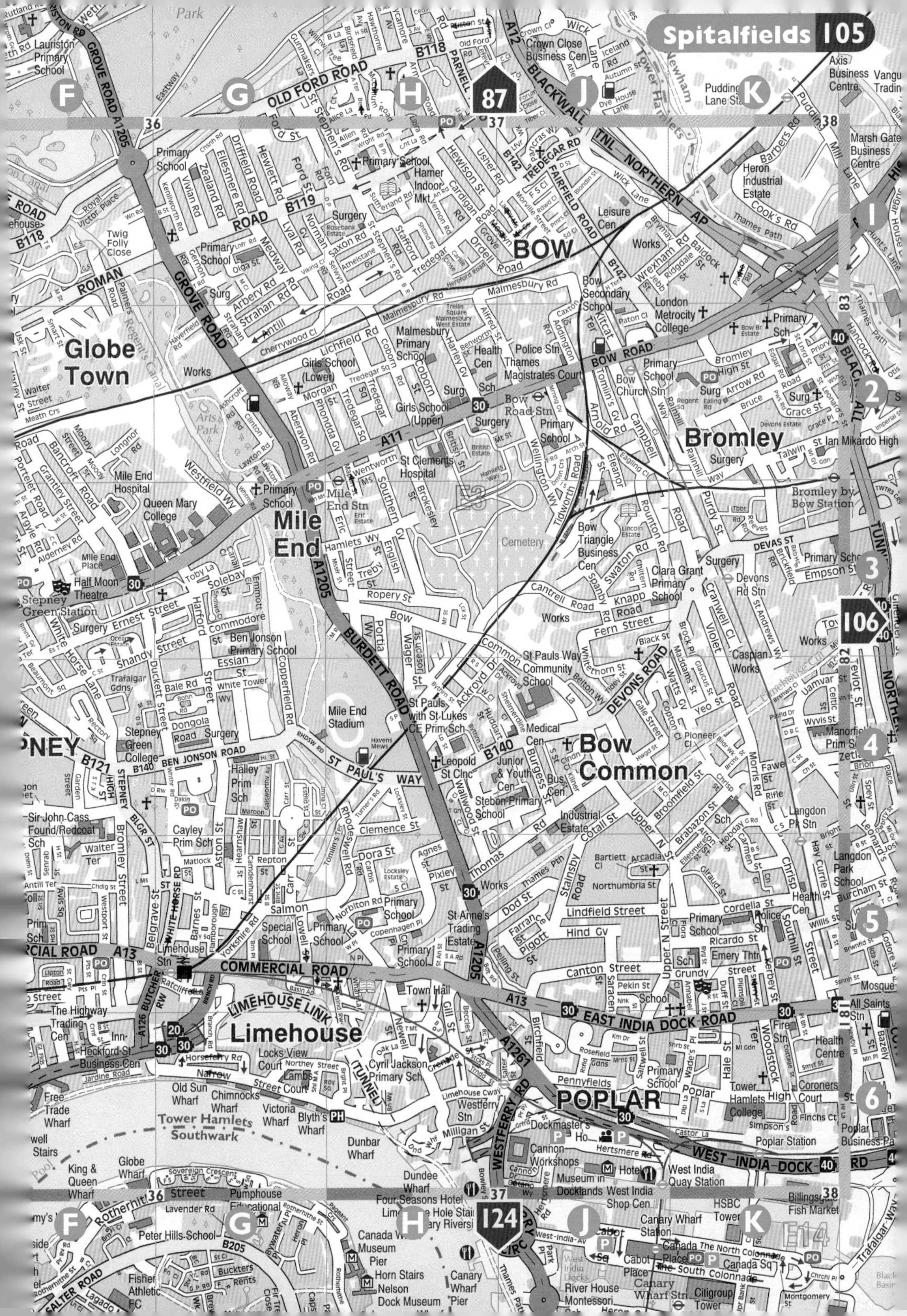
Globe Town
Mile End
BOW
Bromley
Bow Common
Limehouse
POPLAR
STEPNEY
GROVE ROAD A1205
OLD FORD ROAD
ROMAN ROAD
BOW ROAD
A11
BURDETT ROAD
A1205
ST PAUL'S WAY
DEVONS ROAD
COMMERCIAL ROAD
A13
EAST INDIA DOCK ROAD
WEST INDIA DOCK ROAD
LIMEHOUSE LINK (TUNNEL)
WESTFERRY RD
A1261
BLACKWALL TNL NORTHERN AP
TREDEGAR RD
FAIRFIELD ROAD
Regent's Canal
Mile End Hospital
Queen Mary College
Mile End Stn
Bow Road Stn
Bow Church Stn
Bromley by Bow Station
Devons Rd Stn
Langdon Pk Stn
Limehouse Stn
Westferry Stn
Poplar Station
West India Quay Station
Canary Wharf Stn
Stepney Green Station
Half Moon Theatre
Mile End Stadium
Cemetery
St Clements Hospital
Thames Magistrates Court
London Metrocity College
Heron Industrial Estate
Bow Triangle Business Cen
Tower Hamlets College
Museum in Docklands
Canary Wharf Pier
Tower Hamlets
Southwark
Newham
F G H J K
1 2 3 4 5 6
36 37 38
87
106
124

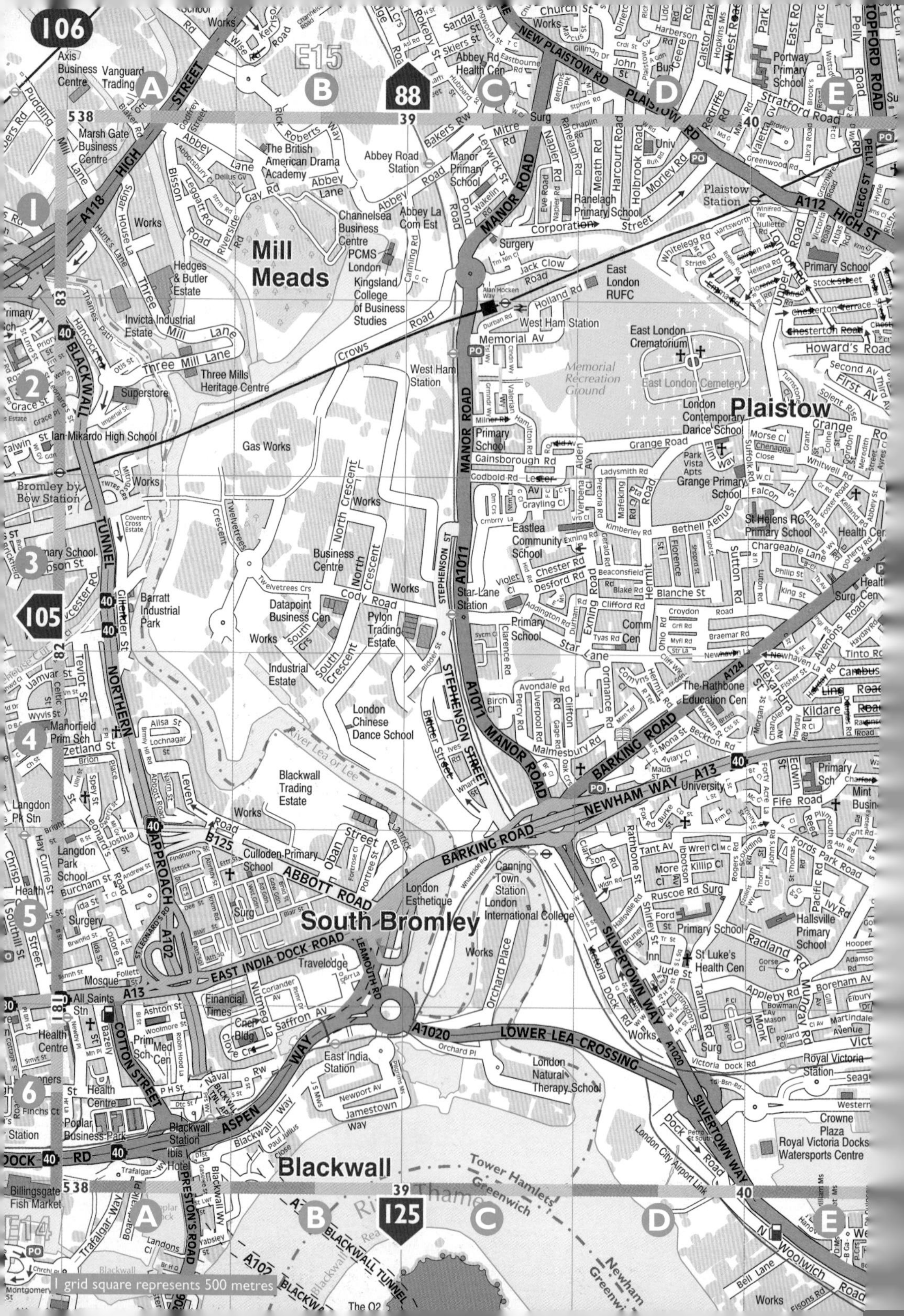
E15
88
A
B
C
D
E
538
39
40
Axis Business Centre
Vanguard Trading
Marsh Gate Business Centre
High Street
A118
Sugar House La
The British American Drama Academy
Abbey Road Station
Manor Primary School
Mill Meads
Channelsea Business Centre
PCMS London
Kingsland College of Business Studies
Abbey La Com Est
Manor Road
Hedges & Butler Estate
Invicta Industrial Estate
Three Mill Lane
Three Mills Heritage Centre
Superstore
Crows Road
West Ham Station
West Ham Station
Memorial Av
Memorial Recreation Ground
East London Crematorium
East London Cemetery
East London RUFC
Holland Rd
Jack Clow Road
Ranelagh Primary School
Corporation Street
Plaistow Station
A112
High St
New Plaistow Rd
Plaistow Rd
Portway Primary School
Stratford Road
Howard's Road
Plaistow
London Contemporary Dance School
Grange Road
Grange Primary School
St Helens RC Primary School
Chargeable Lane
Ian Mikardo High School
Gas Works
Bromley by Bow Station
Blackwall Tunnel
Northern Approach
Barratt Industrial Park
North Crescent
Business Centre
Datapoint Business Cen
Cody Road
Pylon Trading Estate
Industrial Estate
South Crescent
London Chinese Dance School
Star Lane Station
Stephenson Street
A1011
Primary School
Star Lane
Barking Road
A124
The Rathbone Education Cen
Newham Way
A13
University
Blackwall Trading Estate
River Lea or Lee
Culloden Primary School
Abbott Road
South Bromley
East India Dock Road
Travelodge
Leamouth Rd
London Esthetique
Canning Town Station
London International College
Orchard Place
Silvertown Way
Lower Lea Crossing
A1020
London Natural Therapy School
Financial Times
All Saints Stn
Cotton Street
Aspen Way
East India Station
Jamestown Way
Blackwall
Blackwall Station
Ibis Hotel
Poplar Business Park
Billingsgate Fish Market
Preston's Road
Tower Hamlets
Greenwich
Newham
Royal Victoria Station
Crowne Plaza
Royal Victoria Docks Watersports Centre
London City Airport Link
Hallsville Primary School
St Luke's Health Cen
Fife Road
Mint Business
Woolwich Road
Blackwall Tunnel
A102
The O2
105
125
E14
1 grid square represents 500 metres

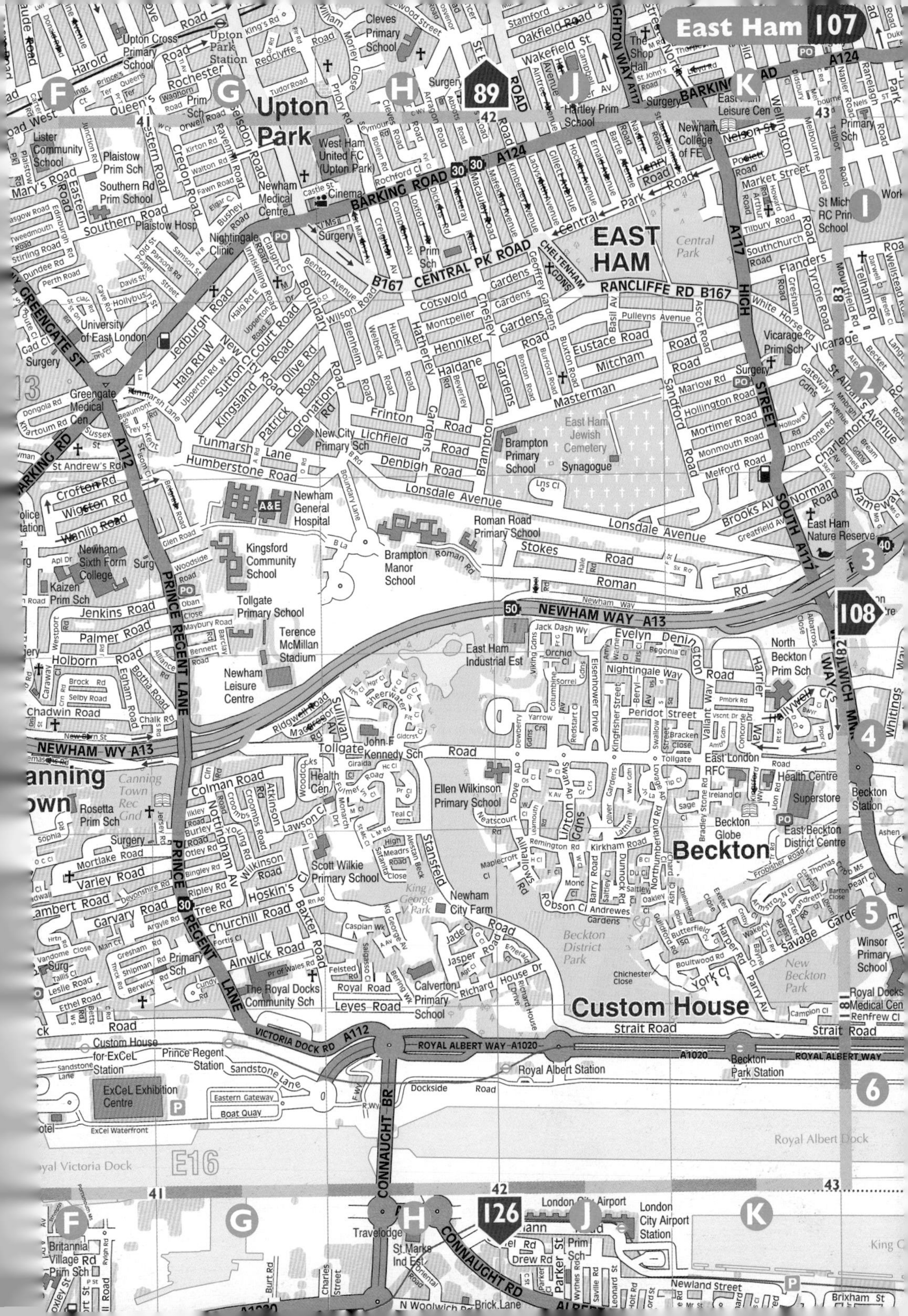

Upton Park
Upton Park Station
Upton Cross Primary School
Cleves Primary School
West Ham United FC (Upton Park)
Plaistow Prim Sch
Southern Rd Prim School
Lister Community School
Newham Medical Centre
Plaistow Hosp
Nightingale Clinic
University of East London
Greengate Medical Cen
EAST HAM
Central Park
East Ham Leisure Cen
Newham College of FE
Hartley Prim School
St Mich RC Prim School
Vicarage Prim Sch
East Ham Jewish Cemetery
Synagogue
Brampton Primary School
Newham General Hospital
Kingsford Community School
Brampton Manor School
Roman Road Primary School
East Ham Nature Reserve
Newham Sixth Form College
Kaizen Prim Sch
Tollgate Primary School
Terence McMillan Stadium
Newham Leisure Centre
East Ham Industrial Est
North Beckton Prim Sch
John F Kennedy Sch
Ellen Wilkinson Primary School
East London RFC
Health Centre
Superstore
Beckton Station
Beckton Globe
East Beckton District Centre
Beckton
Canning Town Rec Gnd
Rosetta Prim Sch
Scott Wilkie Primary School
King George V Park
Newham City Farm
Beckton District Park
New Beckton Park
Winsor Primary School
Royal Docks Medical Cen
The Royal Docks Community Sch
Calverton Primary School
Custom House
Custom House for ExCeL Station
Prince Regent Station
Royal Albert Station
Beckton Park Station
ExCeL Exhibition Centre
ExCel Waterfront
Royal Victoria Dock
Royal Albert Dock
E16
London City Airport
London City Airport Station
Travelodge
St Marks Ind Est
Britannia Village Prim Sch
BARKING ROAD A124
CENTRAL PK ROAD
RANCLIFFE RD B167
HIGH STREET SOUTH A117
NEWHAM WAY A13
NEWHAM WY A13
PRINCE REGENT LANE
A112
GREENGATE ST
VICTORIA DOCK RD A112
ROYAL ALBERT WAY A1020
CONNAUGHT BR
CONNAUGHT RD
Strait Road
Dockside Road
Sandstone Lane
Lonsdale Avenue
Humberstone Road
Tunmarsh Lane
Stokes Road
Roman Rd
Evelyn Denington Road
Tollgate Road
Mitcham Road
Masterman Road
Eustace Road
Henniker Gardens
Haldane Rd
Frinton Road
Lichfield Road
Denbigh Road
Jenkins Road
Palmer Road
Holborn Road
Chadwin Road
Colman Road
Mortlake Road
Varley Road
Lambert Road
Garvary Road
Churchill Road
Alnwick Road
Royal Road
Leyes Road
Savage Gardens
89
108
126
F G H J K
1 2 3 4 5 6
41 42 43

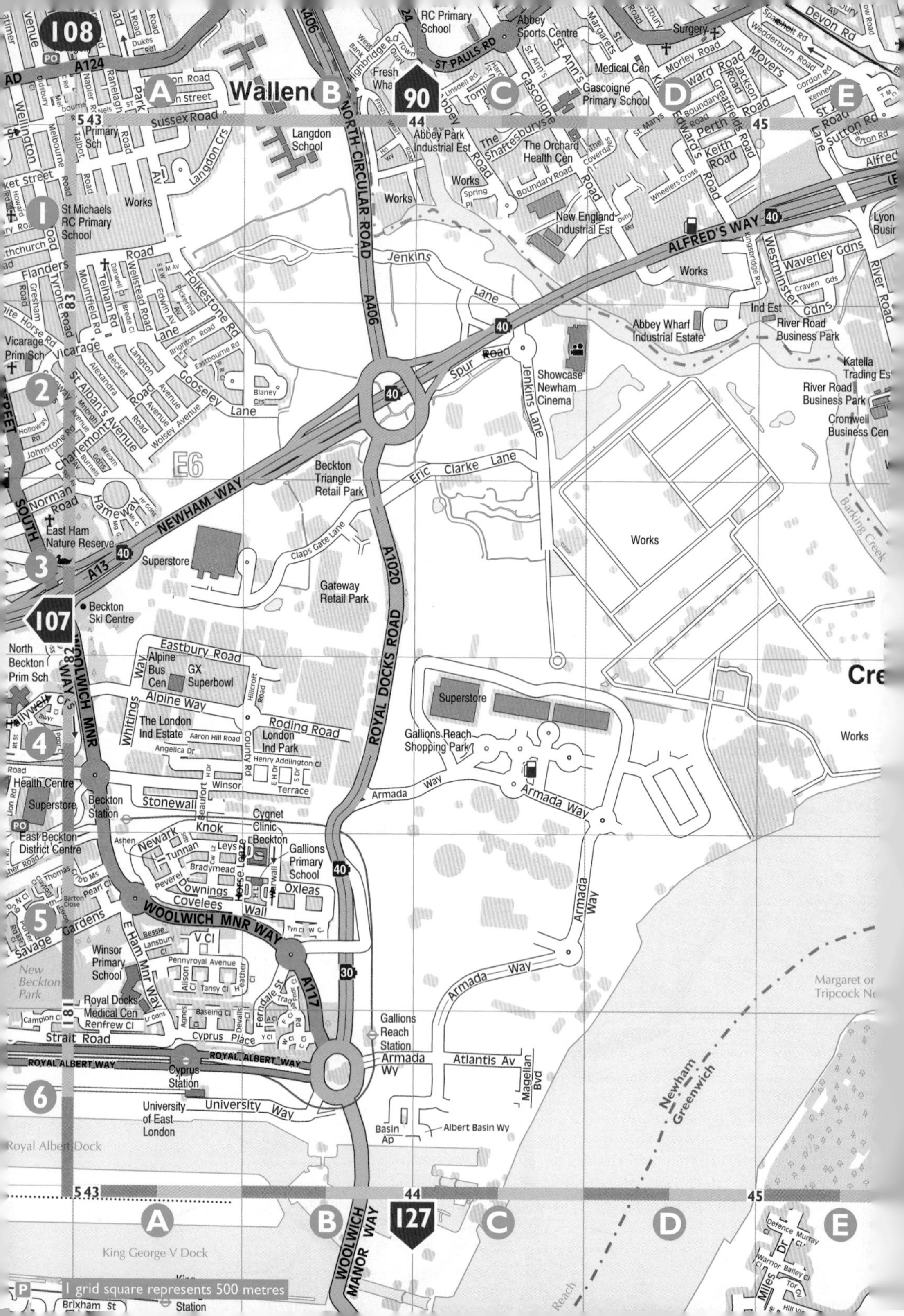

108
90
107
127
40
30
A
B
C
D
E
1
2
3
4
5
6
543
44
45
183
182
181
Wallend
A124
A406
A13
A1020
A117
Dukes Rd
Ranelagh Rd
Park
Sussex Road
Primary Sch
Langdon School
Langdon Crs
Works
St Michaels RC Primary School
Flanders
Vicarage Prim Sch
Vicarage
St Alban's Avenue
Charlemont
Norman Road
Hameway
East Ham Nature Reserve
Beckton Ski Centre
North Beckton Prim Sch
E6
NEWHAM WAY
NORTH CIRCULAR ROAD
RC Primary School
Abbey Sports Centre
ST PAULS RD
Fresh Wharf
Abbey Park Industrial Est
The Shaftesburys
Gascoigne
Gascoigne Primary School
The Orchard Health Cen
Boundary Road
New England Industrial Est
Medical Cen
Surgery
Morley Road
Devon Rd
Movers
Perth Road
Keith Road
Edward's Road
ALFRED'S WAY
Westminster Gdns
Waverley Gdns
River Road
Ind Est
Abbey Wharf Industrial Estate
River Road Business Park
Katella Trading Est
Cromwell Business Cen
Jenkins Lane
Lane
Folkestone Rd
Gooseley Lane
Spur Road
Showcase Newham Cinema
Eric Clarke Lane
Beckton Triangle Retail Park
Claps Gate Lane
Superstore
Gateway Retail Park
Barking Creek
Works
Eastbury Road
Alpine Bus Cen
GX Superbowl
Alpine Way
Whitings Way
Roding Road
The London Ind Estate
London Ind Park
County Rd
ROYAL DOCKS ROAD
Gallions Reach Shopping Park
Armada Way
Winsor Terrace
Stonewall
Beckton Station
Health Centre
East Beckton District Centre
Knok
Cygnet Clinic Beckton
Gallions Primary School
Newark
Tunnan
Leys
Bradymead
Downings
Covelees Wall
Oxleas
WOOLWICH MNR WAY
Savage Gardens
New Beckton Park
Winsor Primary School
Royal Docks Medical Cen
Renfrew Cl
Strait Road
Cyprus Place
ROYAL ALBERT WAY
Cyprus Station
Gallions Reach Station
Armada Wy
Atlantis Av
Magellan Blvd
University of East London
University Way
Basin Ap
Albert Basin Wy
Royal Albert Dock
Newham
Greenwich
Margaret or Tripcock Ness
Reach
Cre
King George V Dock
WOOLWICH MANOR WAY
Brixham St
Station
1 grid square represents 500 metres

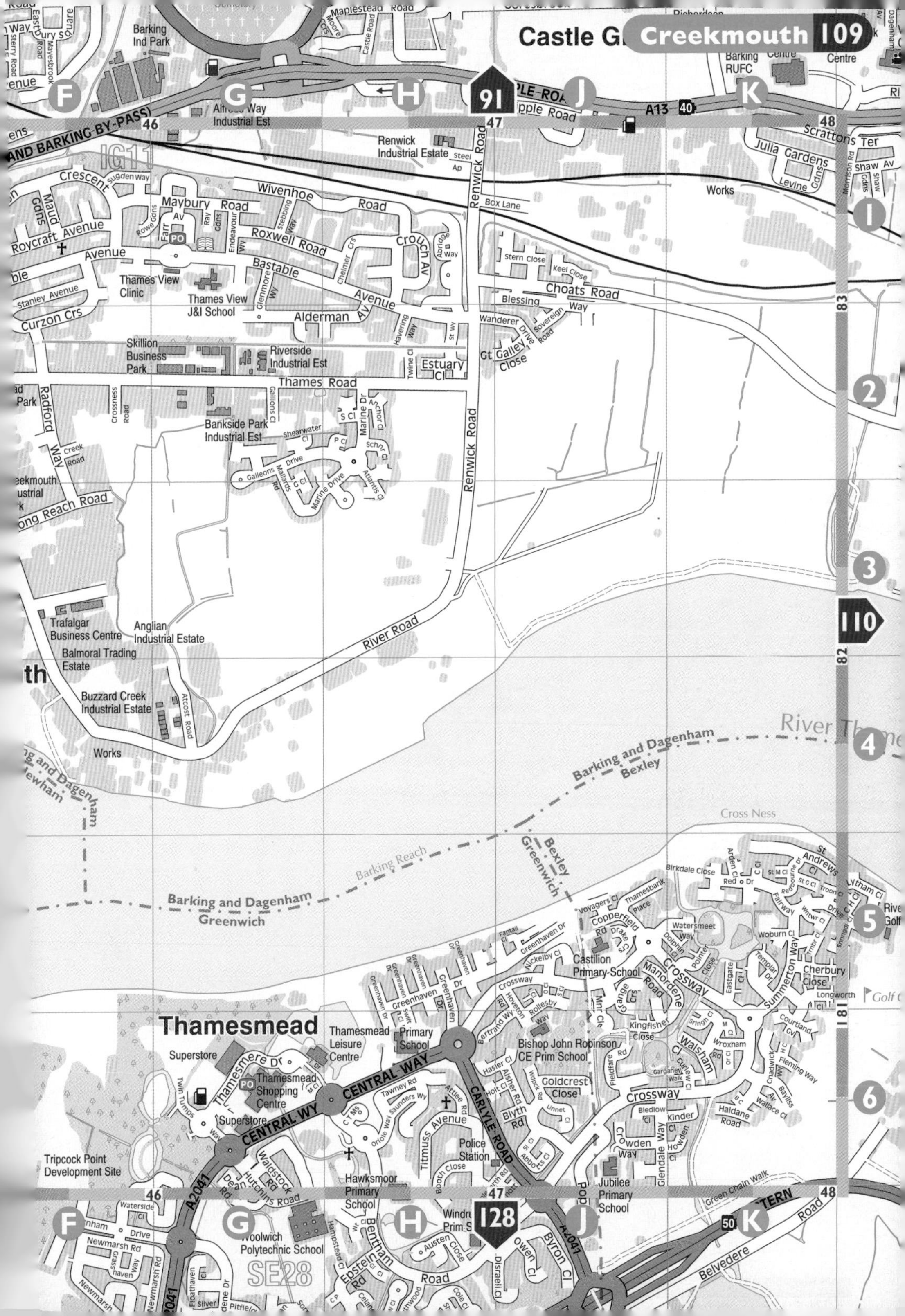
Castle Green
Barking Ind Park
Alfreds Way Industrial Est
Renwick Industrial Estate
Renwick Road
Ripple Road
A13
Barking RUFC
Julia Gardens
Scrattons Ter
Works
Maybury Road
Wivenhoe Road
Roxwell Road
Bastable Avenue
Crouch Av
Roycraft Avenue
Stanley Avenue
Curzon Crs
Thames View Clinic
Thames View J&I School
Alderman Av
Choats Road
Blessing Way
Stern Close
Keel Close
Box Lane
Skillion Business Park
Riverside Industrial Est
Thames Road
Estuary Cl
Gt Galley Close
Wanderer Drive
Radford Way
Creek Road
Long Reach Road
Bankside Park Industrial Est
Galleons Drive
Marine Drive
Trafalgar Business Centre
Anglian Industrial Estate
Balmoral Trading Estate
Buzzard Creek Industrial Estate
Atcost Road
River Road
Works
River Thames
Barking and Dagenham
Bexley
Greenwich
Newham
Cross Ness
Barking Reach
Thamesmead
Superstore
Thamesmere Dr
Thamesmead Shopping Centre
Thamesmead Leisure Centre
Primary School
Central Way
Carlyle Road
Titmuss Avenue
Police Station
Tripcock Point Development Site
Hawksmoor Primary School
Woolwich Polytechnic School
Castilion Primary School
Crossway
Manordene Road
Walsham Cl
Bishop John Robinson CE Prim School
Goldcrest Close
Jubilee Primary School
Summerton Way
Cherbury Close
Haldane Road
Birkdale Close
Copperfield Rd
Greenhaven Dr
A2041
Bentham Road
Byron Cl
Belvedere Road
Green Chain Walk
SE28
IG11
Golf

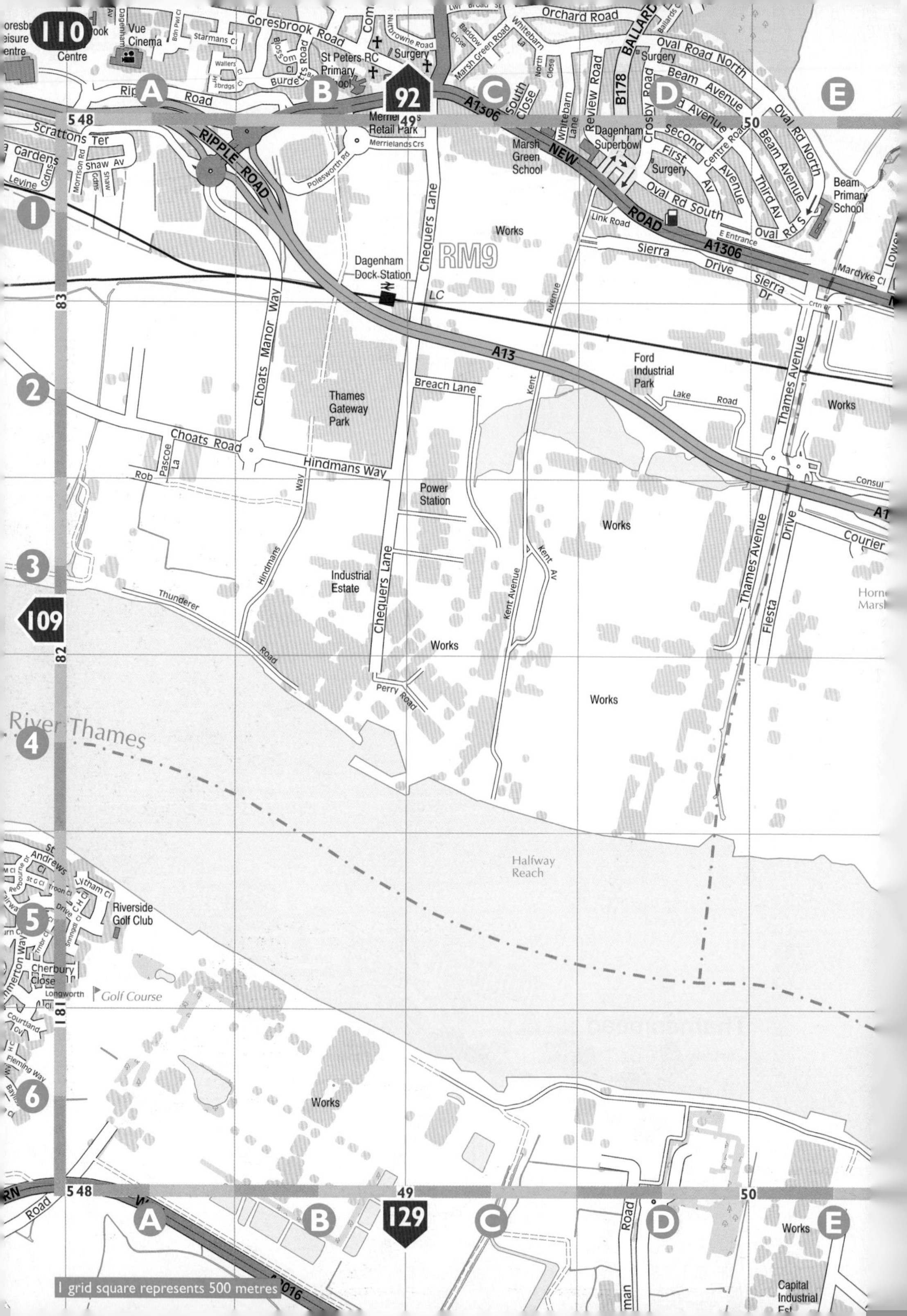
110
92
109
129
A
B
C
D
E
1
2
3
4
5
6
548
49
50
83
82
81
Goresbrook Road
Orchard Road
Vue Cinema
Starmans Cl
Surgery
St Peters RC Primary School
Ripple Road
Burdetts Road
Marsh Green Road
Whitebarn La
North Close
South Close
Review Road
Ballards
B178
Crosby Road
Oval Road North
Beam Avenue
A1306
NEW ROAD
Merrielands Retail Park
Merrielands Crs
Polesworth Rd
Scrattons Ter
Shaw Av
Morrison Rd
Levine Gdns
RIPPLE ROAD
Marsh Green School
Dagenham Superbowl
Second Avenue
First Avenue
Centre Road
Oval Rd South
Third Av
Oval Rd North
Beam Primary School
Oval Rd S
Link Road
E Entrance
Sierra Drive
Mardyke Cl
Works
RM9
Dagenham Dock Station
LC
Chequers Lane
Choats Manor Way
Kent Avenue
A13
Ford Industrial Park
Lake Road
Thames Avenue
Breach Lane
Thames Gateway Park
Choats Road
Hindmans Way
Pascoe La
Rob
Power Station
Consul
Courier
Fiesta Drive
Industrial Estate
Kent Av
Thunderer Road
Perry Road
River Thames
Halfway Reach
St Andrews Cl
Lytham Cl
Riverside Golf Club
Cherbury Close
Longworth Cl
Golf Course
Courtland Gv
Fleming Way
Road
A2016
Capital Industrial Est
1 grid square represents 500 metres

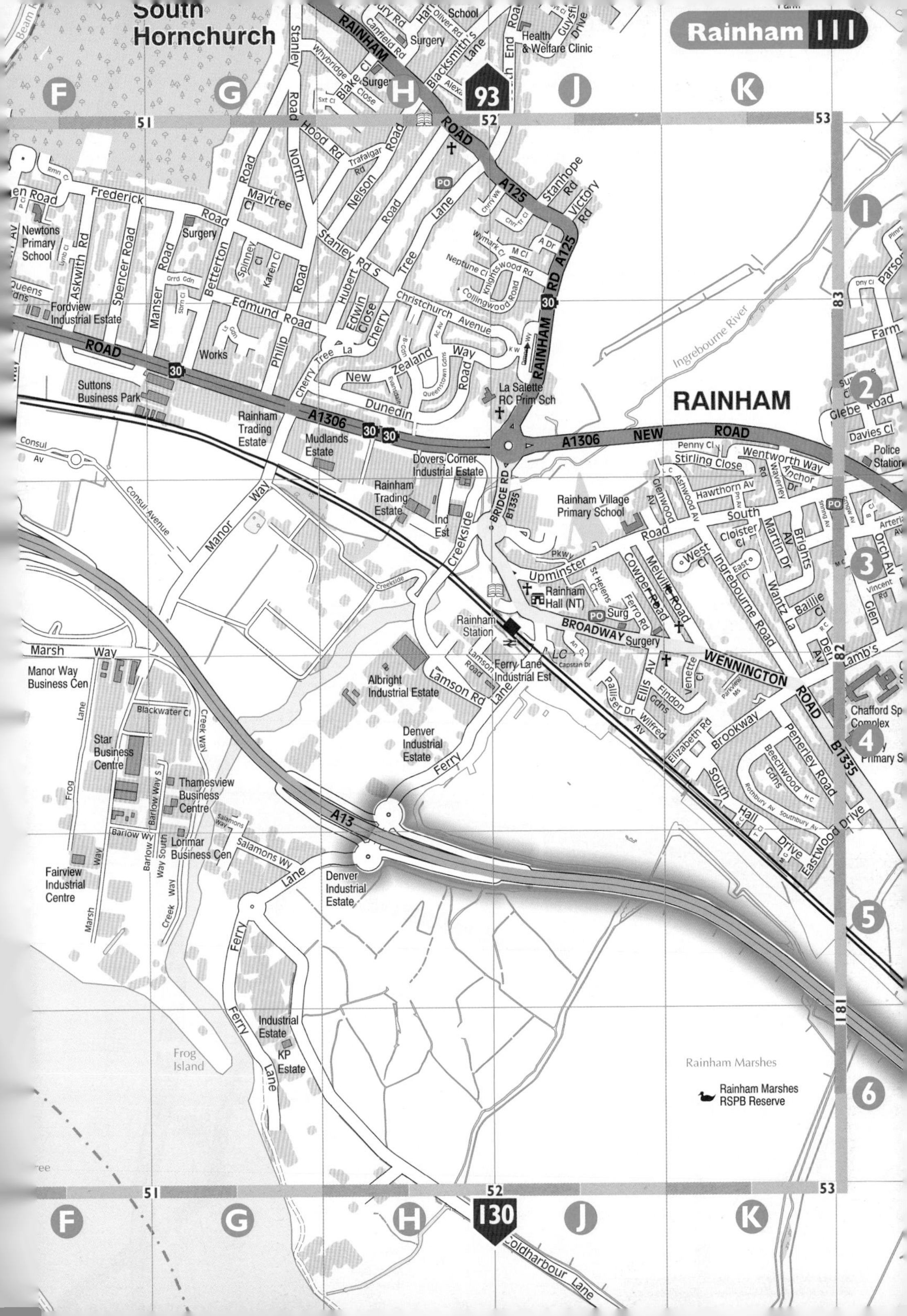
South Hornchurch
RAINHAM
Rainham Marshes
Rainham Marshes RSPB Reserve
Frog Island
Ingrebourne River
Newtons Primary School
Fordview Industrial Estate
Suttons Business Park
Rainham Trading Estate
Mudlands Estate
Dovers Corner Industrial Estate
Rainham Village Primary School
La Salette RC Prim Sch
Rainham Hall (NT)
Rainham Station
Ferry Lane Industrial Est
Albright Industrial Estate
Denver Industrial Estate
Manor Way Business Cen
Star Business Centre
Thamesview Business Centre
Lorimar Business Cen
Fairview Industrial Centre
KP Estate
Health & Welfare Clinic
Police Station
Chafford Sports Complex
A1306 NEW ROAD
RAINHAM ROAD A125
BRIDGE RD B1335
WENNINGTON ROAD B1335
BROADWAY
Upminster Road South
Ferry Lane
Coldharbour Lane
Marsh Way
Manor Way
Consul Avenue
A13

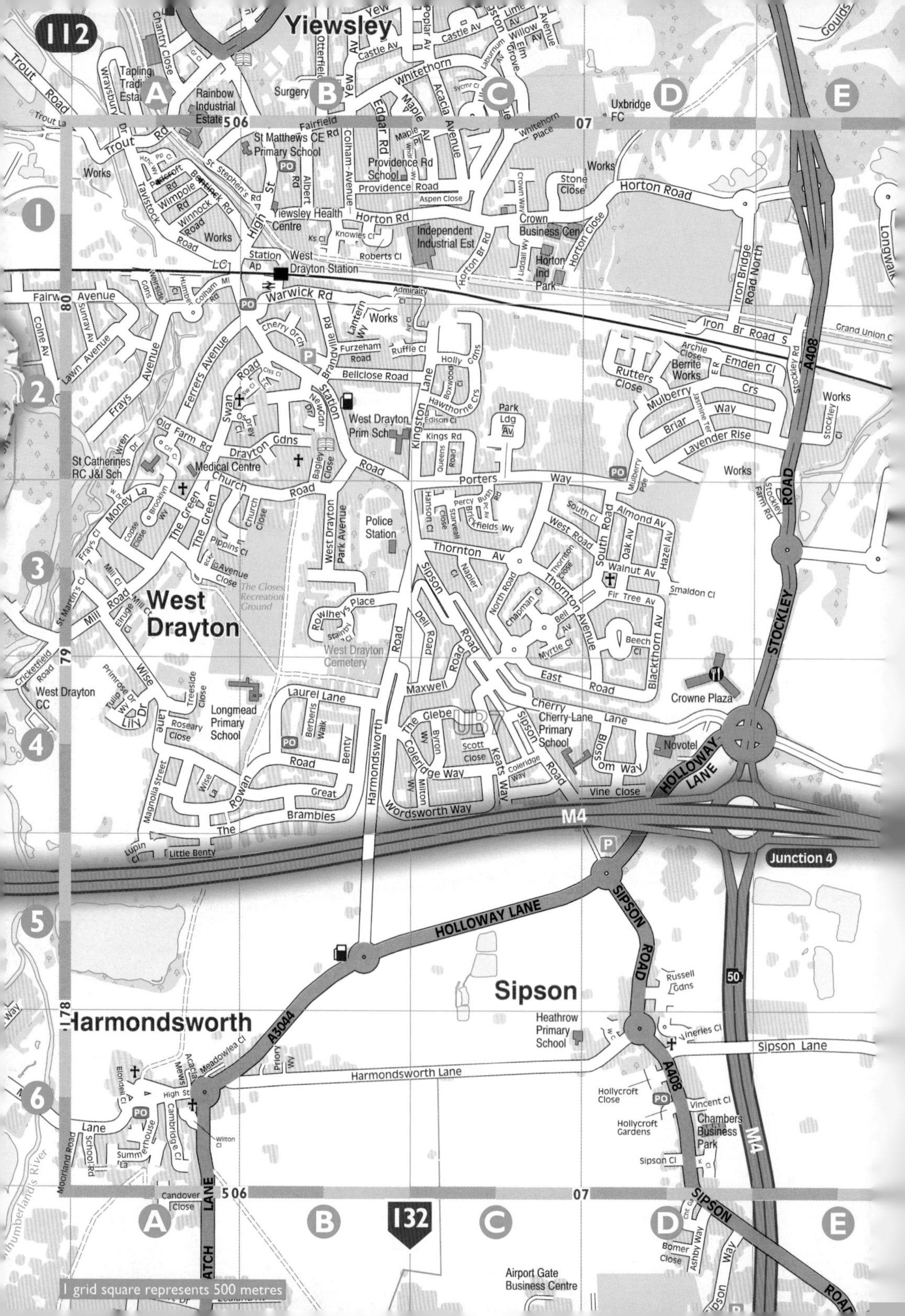

Yiewsley
West Drayton
Harmondsworth
Sipson
UB7
A
B
C
D
E
1
2
3
4
5
6
506
07
80
79
78
Trout Road
Trout Rd
Wraysbury Dr
Chantry Close
Tapling Trading Estate
Rainbow Industrial Estate
Surgery
Yew Av
Castle Av
Poplar Av
Otterfield
Whitethorn
Acacia Avenue
Edgar Rd
Maple Av
Laburnum Gr
Willow Gr
Elm Av
Lime Av
Fairfield Rd
Colham Avenue
St Matthews CE Primary School
Providence Rd School
Providence Road
Aspen Close
Whitehorn Place
Uxbridge FC
Works
Horton Road
Stone Close
Crown Way
Crown Business Cen
Horton Close
Independent Industrial Est
Horton Br Rd
Horton Ind Park
Iron Bridge Road North
Longwalk
Goulds
St Stephen's Rd
High St
Albert Rd
Tavistock Road
Wimpole Rd
Winnock Road
Bentinck Rd
Yiewsley Health Centre
Horton Rd
Knowles Cl
Roberts Cl
Station Ap
West Drayton Station
Warwick Rd
Admiralty Cl
Colham Mill Rd
Humber Cl
Fairway Avenue
Sunray Av
Colne Av
Lawn Avenue
Frays Avenue
Ferrers Avenue
Cherry Orch
Lantern Wy
Furzeham Road
Ruffle Cl
Holly Gdns
Brandville Rd
Bellclose Road
Station Road
Swan Road
Osprey Cl
Drayton Gdns
Old Farm Rd
Wren Dr
St Catherines RC J&I Sch
Medical Centre
Church Road
Money La
Brooklyn Wy
The Green
Copse Close
Church Close
Pippins Cl
Avenue Close
Bagley Close
West Drayton Prim Sch
Kingston Lane
Boxwood Cl
Hawthorne Crs
Edison Cl
Kings Rd
Queens Road
Park Lodge Av
Porters Way
Police Station
West Drayton Park Avenue
Hanson Cl
Percy Cl
Starveall Close
Bush Rd
Brickfields Wy
Thornton Av
Sipson Road
Napier Cl
North Road
West Road
South Road
Thornton Close
Almond Av
Oak Av
Hazel Av
Walnut Av
Smaldon Cl
Fir Tree Av
Chapman Cl
Bell Av
Thornton Avenue
Myrtle Cl
Beech Cl
Blackthorn Av
East Road
Cherry Lane
Cherry Lane Primary School
Blossom Way
Vine Close
Crowne Plaza
Novotel
Iron Br Road S
Grand Union Canal
Archie Close
Berrite Works
Emden Cl
Rutters Close
Mulberry Crs
Briar Way
Jasmine Ter
Lavender Rise
Mulberry Pde
Stockley Rd
Stockley Cl
Stockley Farm Rd
STOCKLEY ROAD
A408
HOLLOWAY LANE
M4
Junction 4
Frays Cl
Mill Cl
Mill Road
Elrige Cl
St Martin's Cl
The Closes Recreation Ground
Rowlheys Place
Stainby Cl
West Drayton Cemetery
Harmondsworth Road
Dell Road
Maxwell Road
Cricketfield Road
West Drayton CC
Primrose Dr
Tulip Wy
Lily Dr
Wise Lane
Treeside Close
Roseary Close
Longmead Primary School
Laurel Lane
Berberis Walk
Benty Cl
Rowan Road
Great Brambles
The Glebe
Coleridge Way
Byron Wy
Milton Wy
Scott Close
Keats Way
Wordsworth Way
Magnolia Street
Wise La
The Lupin Cl
Little Benty
Sipson Lane
Russell Gdns
Heathrow Primary School
Vineries Cl
Harmondsworth Lane
Priory Wy
Meadowlea Cl
Acacia Mews
High St
Blondell Cl
Lane
School Rd
Summerhouse La
Cambridge Cl
Wilton Cl
Moorland Road
A3044
Hollycroft Close
Hollycroft Gardens
Vincent Cl
Chambers Business Park
Sipson Cl
SIPSON ROAD
Candover Close
HATCH LANE
Airport Gate Business Centre
Bomer Close
Ashby Way
132
1 grid square represents 500 metres

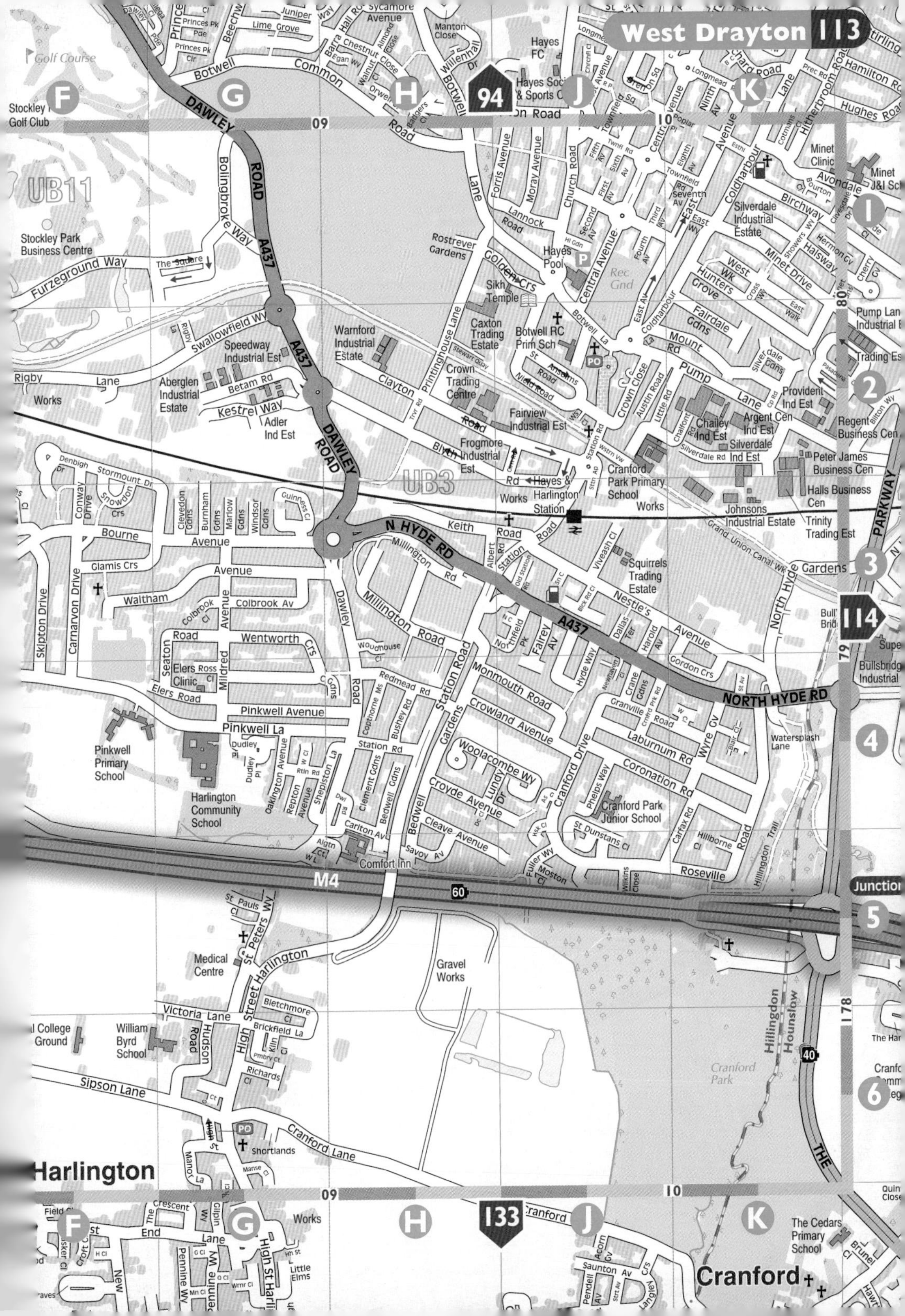
Harlington
Cranford
West Drayton
UB11
UB3
Stockley Park Business Centre
Stockley Park Golf Club
Golf Course
Dawley Road
A437
N Hyde Rd
North Hyde Rd
M4
Botwell Common Road
Furzeground Way
Rigby Lane
Pump Lane
Coldharbour Lane
Station Road
Central Avenue
Church Road
Printinghouse Lane
Clayton Road
Blyth Rd
Keith Road
Millington Road
Monmouth Road
Crowland Avenue
Cranford Drive
Coronation Rd
Laburnum Rd
Bourne Avenue
Pinkwell Avenue
Pinkwell La
Elers Road
Sipson Lane
Cranford Lane
High Street Harlington
Victoria Lane
Hayes & Harlington Station
Hayes Pool
Sikh Temple
Cranford Park Primary School
Cranford Park Junior School
Harlington Community School
Pinkwell Primary School
William Byrd School
The Cedars Primary School
Comfort Inn
Gravel Works
Cranford Park
Hillingdon Trail
Grand Union Canal Wk
Parkway
Junction
94
114
133
09
10
F G H J K
1 2 3 4 5 6

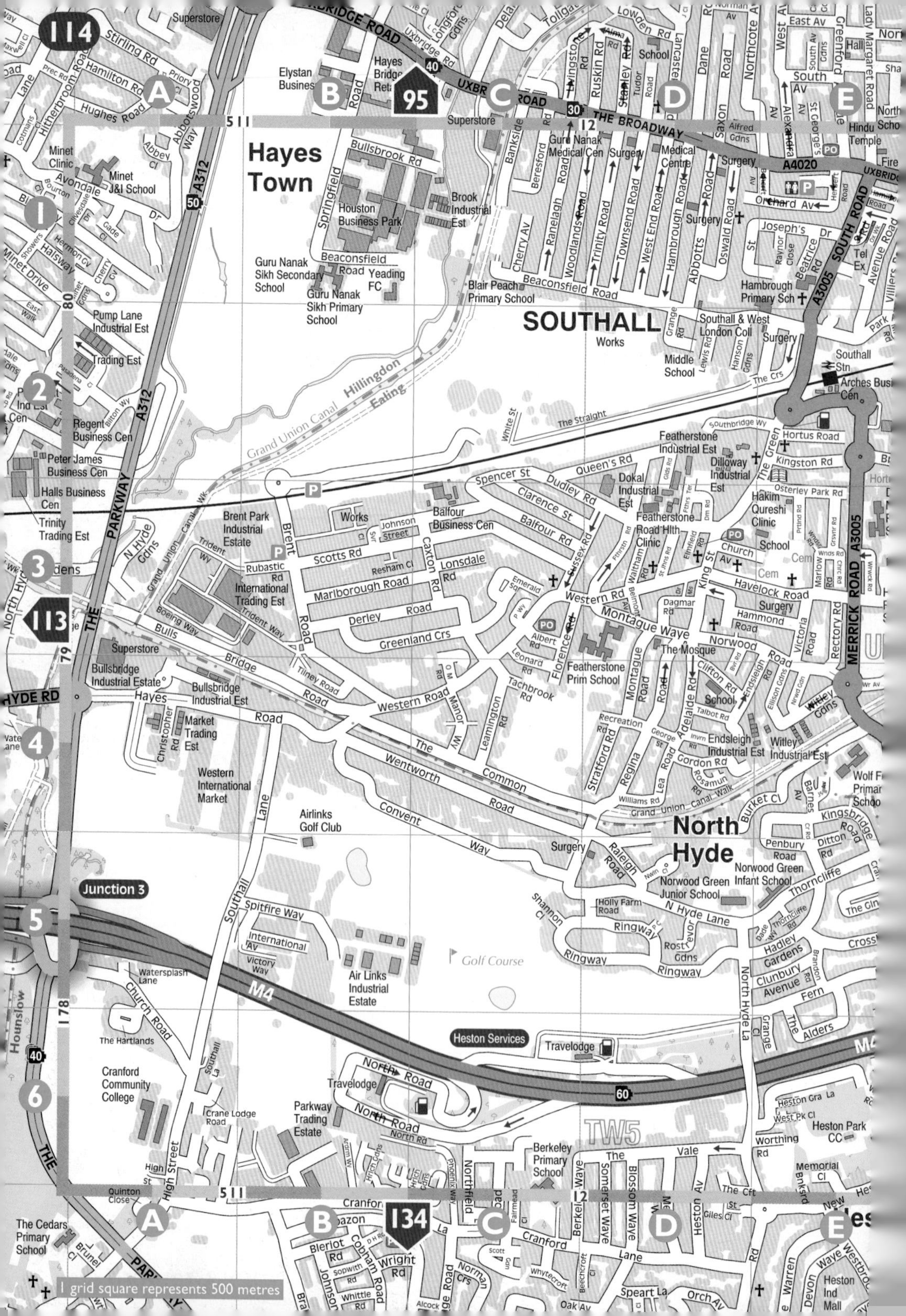
114
95
113
134
Hayes Town
SOUTHALL
North Hyde
UXBRIDGE ROAD
THE BROADWAY
A4020
A312
THE PARKWAY
A3005
SOUTH ROAD
MERRICK ROAD
M4
Junction 3
Heston Services
TW5
Stirling Rd
Hamilton Rd
Hughes Road
Hitherbroom Rd
Prec Rd
Abbotswood Way
Abbey Cl
Priory
Lane
Colmans
Minet Clinic
Minet J&I School
Avondale Dr
Bourton Cl
Clivesdale Dr
Gade Cl
Hermon Gv
Cherry Gv
Showers Wy
Halsway
Minet Drive
East Walk
Minet Gdns
Pump Lane Industrial Est
Trading Est
Pasadena Cl
Bilton Wy
Ind Est
Cen
Regent Business Cen
Peter James Business Cen
Halls Business Cen
Trinity Trading Est
N Hyde Gdns
North Hyde Gdns
HYDE RD
Vate Lane
Superstore
Elystan Business
Hayes Bridge Retail
Springfield Road
Bullsbrook Rd
Houston Business Park
Brook Industrial Est
Beaconsfield Road
Guru Nanak Sikh Secondary School
Guru Nanak Sikh Primary School
Yeading FC
Blair Peach Primary School
Congreve Gdns
Uxbridge Rd
Delamere
Tollgate
Lowden Rd
Alma Rd
Livingstone Rd
Ruskin Rd
Stanley Rd
Tudor Rd
School
Lancaster
Dane Road
Northcote Av
West Av
East Av
South Av
Greenford
Lady Margaret Road
Hall
Bankside
Beresford Rd
Guru Nanak Medical Cen
Surgery
Medical Centre
Saxon Road
Alfred Gdns
Alexandra Av
St George's
Hindu Temple
Fire
Cherry Av
Ranelagh Road
Woodlands Road
Trinity Road
Townsend Road
West End Road
Hambrough Road
Abbotts Road
Oswald Road
Orchard Av
Joseph's Dr
Raynor Close
Beatrice Rd
Avenue Road
Villiers Rd
Tel Ex
Hambrough Primary Sch
Park Av
Southall & West London Coll
Works
Grange Rd
Lewis Rd
Hanson Gdns
Middle School
The Crs
Southall Stn
Arches Business Cen
Hortus Road
Kingston Rd
Osterley Park Rd
Grand Union Canal
Hillingdon
Ealing
White St
The Straight
Southbridge Wy
Featherstone Industrial Est
Dilloway Industrial Est
The Green
Hakim Qureshi Clinic
Queen's Rd
Spencer St
Dudley Rd
Clarence St
Balfour Rd
Dokal Industrial Est
Featherstone Road Hlth Clinic
Sussex Rd
Waltham Rd
Church Av
Cem
School
Havelock Road
Hammond Road
Surgery
Victoria Road
Rectory Rd
Marlow Rd
Brent Park Industrial Estate
Brent Road
Works
Johnson Street
Balfour Business Cen
Scotts Rd
Resham Cl
Caxton Rd
Lonsdale Rd
Marlborough Road
Derley Road
Greenland Crs
Trident Wy
Rubastic Rd
International Trading Est
Trident Way
Boeing Way
Bulls Bridge Road
Tilney Road
Emerald Sq
Western Rd
Montague Waye
The Mosque
Norwood Road
Dagmar Rd
King St
Albert Rd
Leonard Rd
Florence Rd
Featherstone Prim School
Tachbrook Rd
Clifton Rd
Endsleigh Rd
School
Talbot Rd
Ellison Gdns
Witley Gdns
Superstore
Bullsbridge Industrial Estate
Bullsbridge Industrial Est
Hayes Road
Christopher Rd
Market Trading Est
Western Road
Manor Wy
Leamington Rd
Montague Road
Recreation Rd
Stratford Rd
George St
Adelaide Rd
Endsleigh Industrial Est
Witley Industrial Est
Regina Road
Lea Road
Gordon Rd
Rosamun
Williams Rd
Grand Union Canal Walk
Western International Market
The Wentworth Common Road
Convent Way
Southall Lane
Airlinks Golf Club
Surgery
Raleigh Road
Burket Cl
Barnes Av
Kingsbridge Road
Wolf Fields Primary School
Penbury Road
Ditton Rd
Norwood Green Junior School
Norwood Green Infant School
Thorncliffe
Shannon Cl
Holly Farm Road
N Hyde Lane
Ringway
Rosecroft Gdns
Hadley Gardens
Clunbury Avenue
Brandon
Cross
The Glen
Fern
The Alders
Golf Course
Spitfire Way
International Av
Victory Way
Air Links Industrial Estate
Watersplash Lane
Church Road
The Hartlands
Hounslow
Cranford Community College
Southall La
Crane Lodge Road
North Road
Travelodge
Parkway Trading Estate
North Road
North Rd
Travelodge
North Hyde La
Grange Cl
Heston Gra La
West Pk Cl
Heston Park CC
Worthing Rd
Northfield Road
Berkeley Primary School
The Vale
Berkeley Wave
Somerset Wave
Blossom Wave
Heston Av
The Cft
Memorial Cl
High Street
High St
Quinton Close
Cranford
Bazon
The Cedars Primary School
Brunel Cl
Bleriot Rd
Cobham Road
Wright Rd
Johnson
Sopwith Rd
Whittle Rd
Cranford Lane
Scott Gdn
Norman Crs
Whytecroft
Beechcroft
Speart La
Orch Av
Oak Av
Giles Cl
Heston Ind Mall
Westbrook
Devon Wave
Warren
1 grid square represents 500 metres

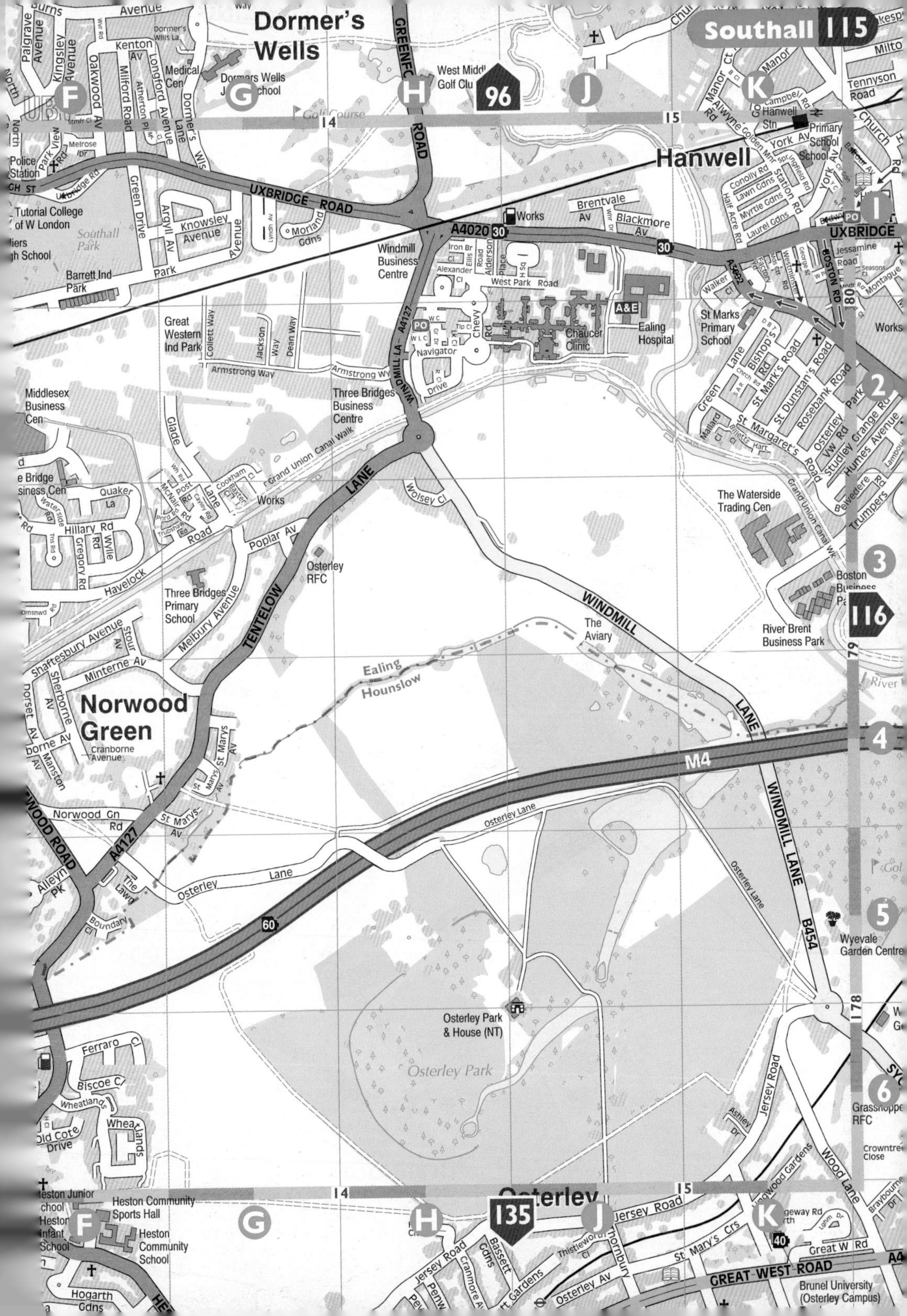

Dormer's Wells

West Middx Golf Clu   **96**

Hanwell

UB

F   G   H   J   K   I

UXBRIDGE ROAD

UXBRIDGE

Police Station

Tutorial College of W London

Southall Park

Barrett Ind Park

Great Western Ind Park

Windmill Business Centre

West Park Road

A4020   30   Works   Brentvale Av   Blackmore Av   30

Iron Br

Alexander Cl

Navigator

Chaucer Clinic

A&E   Ealing Hospital

St Marks Primary School

St Dunstan's Rd

Osterley Park

Rosebank Rd

Studley Grange Rd

Humes Avenue

Trumpers

Middlesex Business Cen

e Bridge siness Cen

Quaker La

Hillary Rd   Wylie Rd   Gregory Rd   Havelock Rd

Three Bridges Business Centre

Works

Poplar Av

Osterley RFC

Grand Union Canal Walk

Wolsey Cl

The Waterside Trading Cen

River Brent Business Park

Boston Business Pa

116

3

Three Bridges Primary School

Melbury Avenue

TENTELOW LANE

WINDMILL LA   A4127

WINDMILL LANE

The Aviary

River

4

Norwood Green

Shaftesbury Avenue

Minterne Av

Ealing Hounslow

M4

WINDMILL LANE

B454

Cranborne Avenue

Norwood Gn Rd   A4127

St Marys Av

St Marys Av

Osterley   Lane

Osterley Lane

Wyevale Garden Centre

5

Alleyn Pk

The Lawn

Osterley   Lane

60

Osterley Lane

B454

178

Grasshoppers RFC   6

Ferraro Cl

Biscoe Cl

Wheatlands

Wheatlands Dr

Old Cote Drive

Boundary Cl

Osterley Park & House (NT)

Osterley Park

Crowntree Close

Heston Junior chool   Heston Infant School

Heston Community Sports Hall

Heston Community School

Osterley   **135**

Jersey Road

Jersey Gdns

Bassett Gardens

Cranmore Av

Osterley Av

Jersey Road

Norwood Gardens

Wood Lane

Ashley

Jersey Road

Great W Rd

40

Great W Rd   A4

Hogarth Gdns

F   G   H   J   K

St Mary's Crs

GREAT WEST ROAD

Brunel University (Osterley Campus)

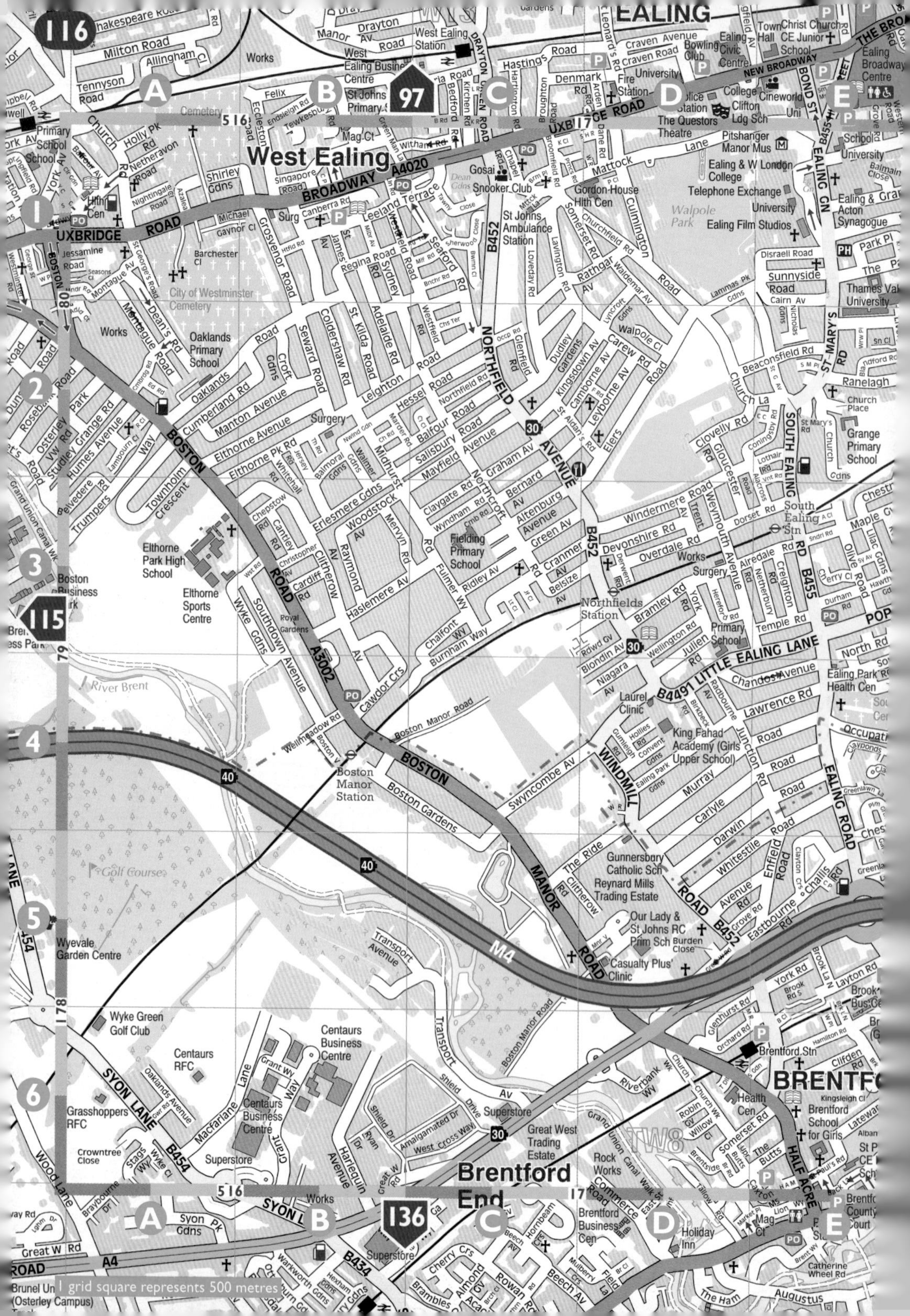
116
97
115
136
EALING
West Ealing
Brentford
End
BRENTF
UXBRIDGE ROAD
BROADWAY A4020
NEW BROADWAY
BOSTON ROAD
A3002
NORTHFIELD AVENUE
B452
LITTLE EALING LANE
B4491
SOUTH EALING RD
B455
EALING ROAD
WINDMILL ROAD
BOSTON MANOR ROAD
SYON LANE
B454
M4
A4
B434
HALF ACRE
West Ealing Station
Northfields Station
Boston Manor Station
South Ealing Stn
Brentford Stn
City of Westminster Cemetery
Walpole Park
Pitshanger Manor Mus
The Questors Theatre
Ealing Film Studios
Elthorne Park High School
Elthorne Sports Centre
Oaklands Primary School
Fielding Primary School
Grange Primary School
Gunnersbury Catholic Sch
Reynard Mills Trading Estate
Our Lady & St Johns RC Prim Sch
King Fahad Academy (Girls Upper School)
Wyevale Garden Centre
Golf Course
River Brent
Wyke Green Golf Club
Centaurs Business Centre
Centaurs RFC
Grasshoppers RFC
Great West Trading Estate
Brentford Business Cen
Holiday Inn
Brentford School for Girls
Grand Union Canal
TW8
Brunel Uni (Osterley Campus)
A
B
C
D
E
1
2
3
4
5
6
516
17
1 grid square represents 500 metres

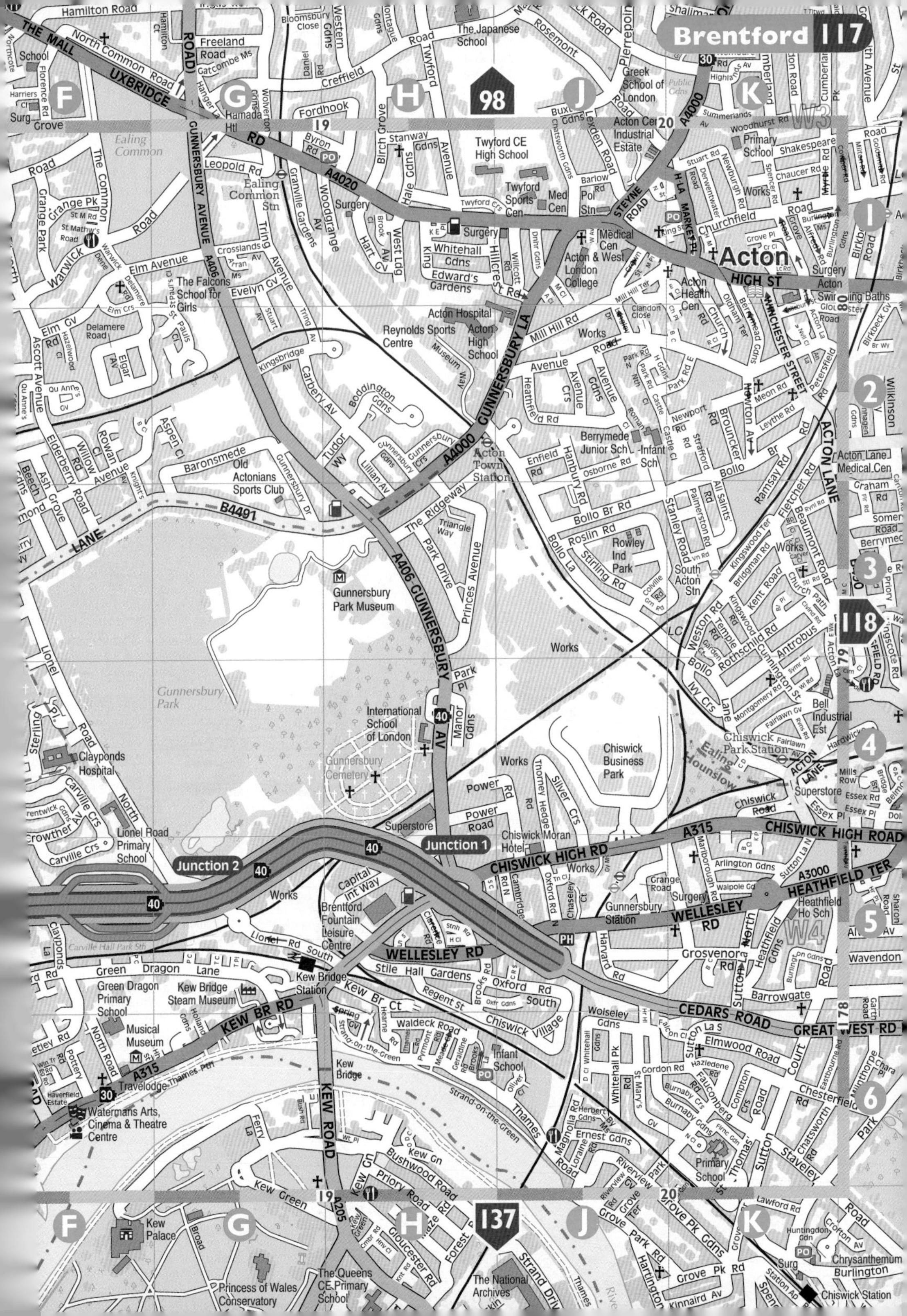

98
118
137
F
G
H
J
K
Acton
HIGH ST
Ealing Common
Ealing Common Stn
UXBRIDGE RD
A4020
GUNNERSBURY AVENUE
A406
A4000 GUNNERSBURY LA
ACTON LANE
CHISWICK HIGH ROAD
CHISWICK HIGH RD
A315
A3000
HEATHFIELD TER
WELLESLEY RD
CEDARS ROAD
GREAT WEST RD
KEW BR RD
KEW ROAD
B4491
Gunnersbury Park
Gunnersbury Park Museum
Gunnersbury Cemetery
International School of London
Acton Town Station
Chiswick Park Station
Gunnersbury Station
Kew Bridge Station
Kew Bridge Steam Museum
Musical Museum
Brentford Fountain Leisure Centre
Chiswick Business Park
Chiswick Moran Hotel
Claypond Hospital
Acton Hospital
Acton High School
Twyford CE High School
The Japanese School
Greek School of London
The Falcons School for Girls
Old Actonians Sports Club
Reynolds Sports Centre
Watermans Arts, Cinema & Theatre Centre
Travelodge
Kew Palace
Princess of Wales Conservatory
The National Archives
Chiswick Station
Junction 1
Junction 2
Superstore
Works
W3
W4

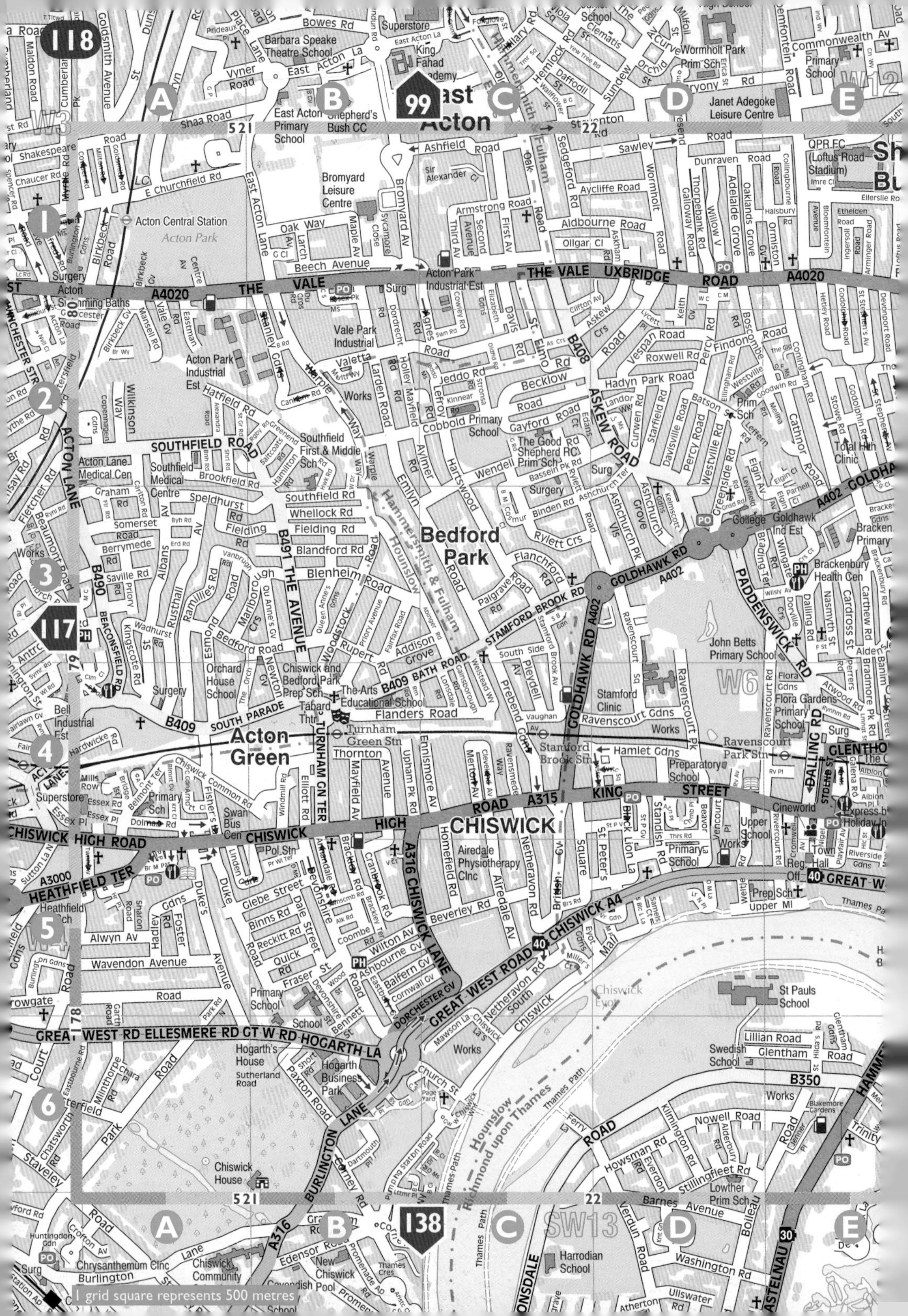

118
99
117
138
A
B
C
D
E
1
2
3
4
5
6
521
22
East Acton
W3
W12
W6
W4
SW13
Bowes Rd
Barbara Speake Theatre School
Superstore
King Fahad Academy
East Acton La
Vyner Road
Shaa Road
East Acton Primary School
Shepherd's Bush CC
Wormholt Park Prim Sch
Commonwealth Av
Primary School
Janet Adegoke Leisure Centre
QPR FC (Loftus Road Stadium)
Ashfield Road
Sawley Road
Dunraven Road
Shakespeare Road
Chaucer Rd
E Churchfield Rd
Bromyard Leisure Centre
Sir Alexander Cl
Aycliffe Road
Armstrong Road
Aldbourne Road
Ollgar Cl
Acton Central Station
Acton Park
Oak Way
Beech Avenue
Acton Park Industrial Est
THE VALE
A4020
UXBRIDGE ROAD
Acton Swimming Baths
Vale Park Industrial
Acton Park Industrial Est
Wilkinson Way
Hatfield Rd
SOUTHFIELD ROAD
Southfield First & Middle Sch
Acton Lane Medical Cen
Southfield Medical Centre
Brookfield Rd
Speldhurst Rd
Southfield Rd
Whellock Rd
Fielding Rd
Blandford Rd
Blenheim Road
Bedford Park
Cobbold Primary School
The Good Shepherd RC Prim Sch
Surgery
Wendell Park
Becklow Road
Gayford Road
Hadyn Park Road
Vespan Road
Roxwell Rd
Findon Rd
ASKEW ROAD
Askew Rd
B408
Rylett Crs
Flanchford Rd
GOLDHAWK RD
A402
A402 GOLDHAWK RD
College
Goldhawk Ind Est
Brackenbury Primary
Brackenbury Health Cen
PADDENSWICK RD
John Betts Primary School
STAMFORD BROOK RD
Stamford Clinic
Ravenscourt Gdns
Hamlet Gdns
Preparatory School
Ravenscourt Park Stn
Flora Gardens Primary School
DALLING RD
ACTON LANE
B490
BEACONSFIELD RD
B491 THE AVENUE
Bedford Road
Orchard House School
Chiswick and Bedford Park Prep Sch
The Arts Educational School
Tabard Thtr
B409 BATH ROAD
Flanders Road
SOUTH PARADE
B409
Acton Green
Turnham Green Stn
Stamford Brook Stn
TURNHAM GN TER
Thornton Avenue
Bell Industrial Est
Hardwicke Rd
Chiswick Common Rd
Superstore
Essex Rd
Swan Bus Cen
CHISWICK HIGH ROAD
CHISWICK HIGH ROAD A315
KING STREET
CHISWICK
Airedale Physiotherapy Clnc
A316 CHISWICK LANE
HEATHFIELD TER
A3000
Heathfield Sch
Pol Stn
Glebe Street
Binns Rd
Reckitt Rd
Quick Rd
Fraser St
Devonshire
Alwyn Av
Wavendon Avenue
Beverley Rd
Airedale Av
British Gv
Black Lion La
Standish Rd
Upper School
Primary School
Cineworld
Town Hall
Prep Sch
Upper Mall
GREAT WEST RD
40
CHISWICK A4
GREAT WEST ROAD
Chiswick Eyot
Chiswick Mall
DORCHESTER GV
GREAT WEST RD ELLESMERE RD GT W RD HOGARTH LA
Hogarth's House
Sutherland Road
Hogarth Business Park
Church St
Works
St Pauls School
Lillian Road
Glentham Road
Swedish School
B350
HAMMERSMITH
Hounslow
Richmond upon Thames
Thames Path
ROAD
Nowell Road
Klimington Rd
Stillingfleet Rd
Lowther Prim Sch
Howsman Rd
Barnes Avenue
Washington Rd
Verdun Road
Boileau
Harrodian School
LONSDALE
ASTELNAU
30
Trinity
BURLINGTON LANE
A316
Chiswick House
Edensor Rd
New Chiswick Pool
Promenade Ap
Chrysanthemum Clnc
Chiswick Community School
Burlington
Surg
Chatsworth
Staveley
Court
Park Road
Hammersmith & Fulham
1 grid square represents 500 metres

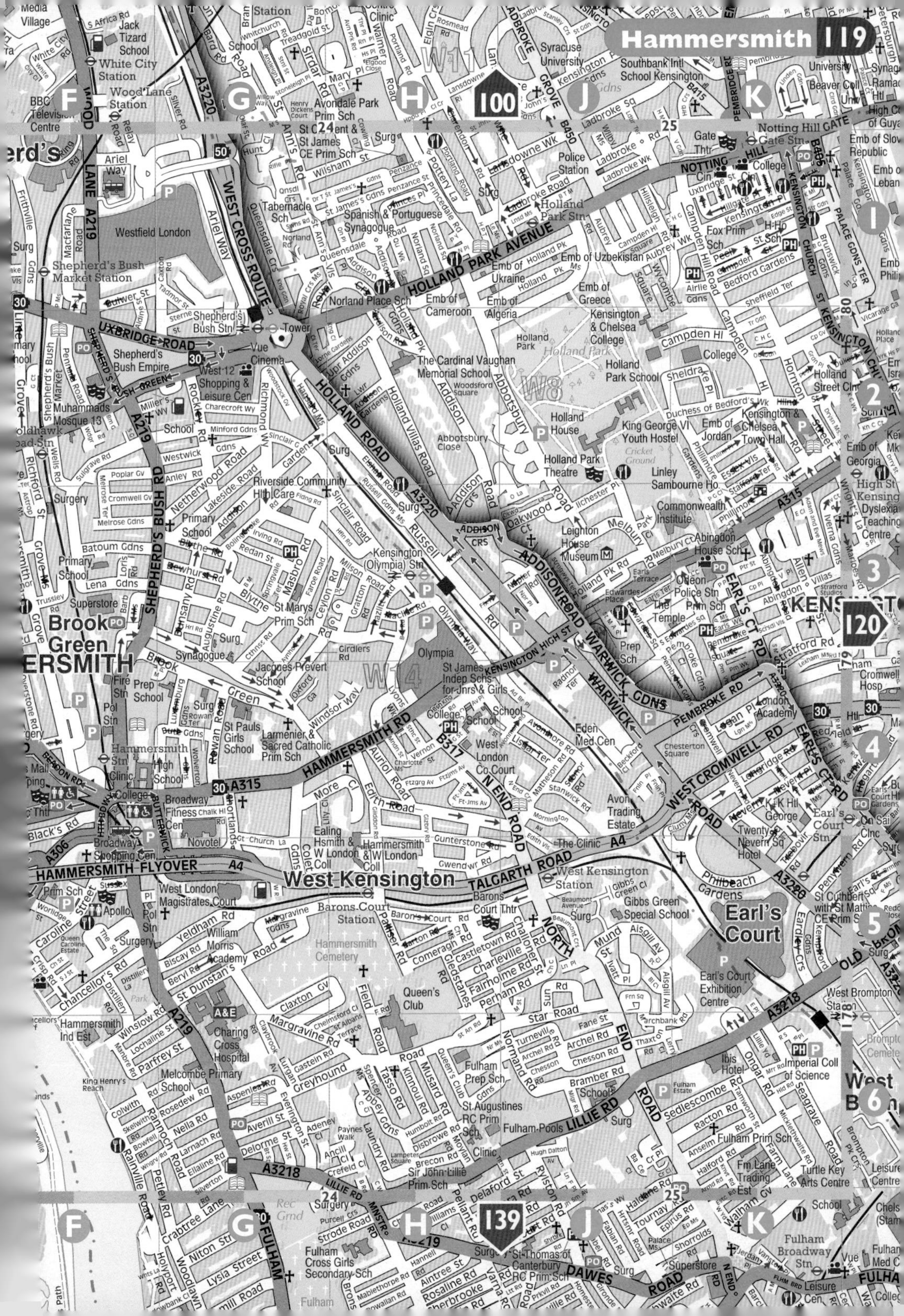

F
G
H
J
K
1
2
3
4
5
6
24
25
100
120
139
W11
W8
W14
White City Station
Wood Lane Station
BBC Television Centre
Westfield London
Shepherd's Bush Market Station
Shepherd's Bush Stn
Shepherd's Bush Empire
UXBRIDGE ROAD
WEST CROSS ROUTE
Vue Cinema
West 12 Shopping & Leisure Cen
Muhammads Mosque 13
SHEPHERD'S BUSH RD
Brook Green
HAMMERSMITH
HAMMERSMITH RD
HAMMERSMITH FLYOVER
Hammersmith Broadway Shopping Cen
Novotel
West London Magistrates Court
St Pauls Girls School
Larmenier & Sacred Catholic Prim Sch
Jacques Prevert School
Synagogue
Riverside Community Hlth Care
Kensington (Olympia) Stn
Olympia
St James Indep Schs for Jnrs & Girls
KENSINGTON HIGH ST
HOLLAND ROAD
HOLLAND PARK AVENUE
Holland Park Stn
Norland Place Sch
Tabernacle Sch
Spanish & Portuguese Synagogue
Avondale Park Prim Sch
The Cardinal Vaughan Memorial School
Holland Park
Holland House
Holland Park School
Holland Park Theatre
King George VI Youth Hostel
Linley Sambourne Ho
Commonwealth Institute
Leighton House Museum
Kensington & Chelsea College
Kensington & Chelsea Town Hall
NOTTING HILL GATE
Notting Hill Gate Stn
Gate Thtr
Syracuse University
Southbank Intl School Kensington
KENSINGTON CHURCH ST
Emb of Uzbekistan
Emb of Ukraine
Emb of Algeria
Emb of Greece
Emb of Cameroon
Emb of Jordan
Emb of Georgia
ADDISON ROAD
WARWICK GDNS
Prep Sch
Odeon
The Temple
Police Stn
Abingdon House Sch
EARL'S CT RD
PEMBROKE RD
WEST CROMWELL RD
Chesterton Square
London Academy
Earl's Court Stn
Twenty Nevern Sq Hotel
K+K Htl George
Earl's Court Exhibition Centre
Earl's Court
Philbeach Gardens
St Cuthbert with St Matthias CE Prim Sch
West Brompton Stn
West Brompton
Imperial Coll of Science
Ibis Hotel
Fulham Prim Sch
Turtle Key Arts Centre
Fulham Broadway Stn
West Kensington
West Kensington Station
TALGARTH ROAD
Barons Court Station
Barons Court Thtr
Hammersmith Cemetery
Queen's Club
Gibbs Green Special School
Avon Trading Estate
The Clinic
N END ROAD
NORTH END ROAD
West London Co Court
Ealing Hsmith & W London Coll
Hammersmith & W London Coll
William Morris Academy
Charing Cross Hospital
Melcombe Primary School
Hammersmith Ind Est
Fulham Prep Sch
St Augustines RC Prim Sch
Fulham Pools
LILLIE RD
Sir John Lillie Prim Sch
St Thomas of Canterbury RC Prim Sch
Fulham Cross Girls Secondary Sch
DAWES ROAD
FULHAM
A219
A3220
A315
A4
A306
A3218
B317
B450

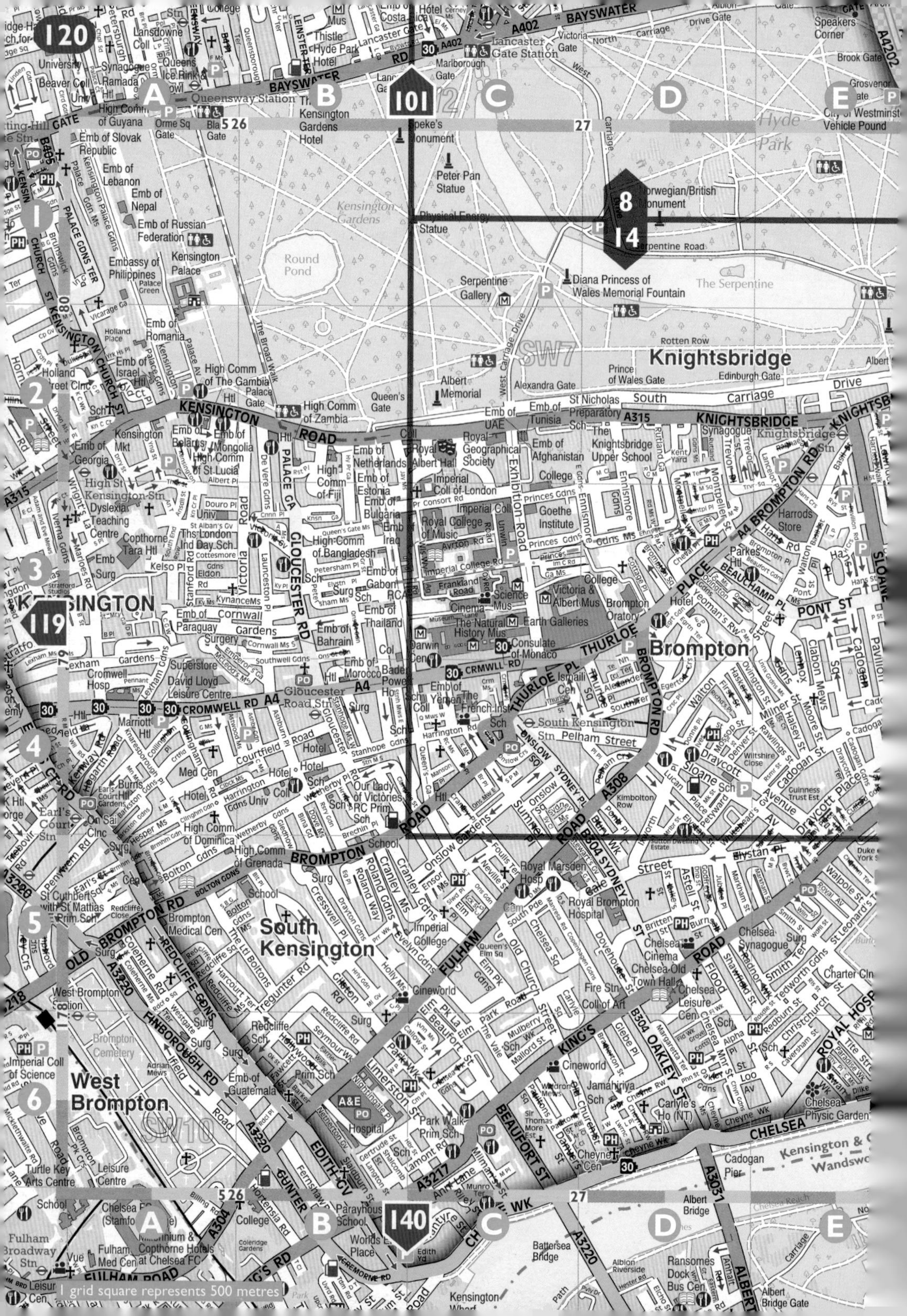

120
101
8
14
119
140
A
B
C
D
E
1
2
3
4
5
6
BAYSWATER
BAYSWATER RD
Queensway Station
Lancaster Gate Station
Speakers Corner
Brook Gate
Grosvenor Gate
City of Westminster Vehicle Pound
Hyde Park
Victoria Gate
Marlborough Gate
Kensington Gardens Hotel
Thistle Hyde Park Hotel
Speke's Monument
Peter Pan Statue
Physical Energy Statue
Norwegian/British Monument
Serpentine Road
The Serpentine
Diana Princess of Wales Memorial Fountain
Serpentine Gallery
Kensington Gardens
Round Pond
The Broad Walk
Kensington Palace
Embassy of Philippines
Emb of Russian Federation
Emb of Nepal
Emb of Lebanon
Emb of Slovak Republic
High Comm of Guyana
Rotten Row
Knightsbridge
Prince of Wales Gate
Edinburgh Gate
Alexandra Gate
South Carriage Drive
West Carriage Drive
Albert Memorial
Queen's Gate
High Comm of Zambia
High Comm of The Gambia
KENSINGTON ROAD
KNIGHTSBRIDGE
SW7
Royal Albert Hall
Royal Geographical Society
Imperial Coll of London
Royal College of Music
Emb of Afghanistan
The Knightsbridge Upper School
Goethe Institute
Harrods Store
Science Mus
Victoria & Albert Mus
The Natural History Mus
Earth Galleries
Brompton Oratory
Brompton
Consulate of Monaco
Darwin Cen
Exhibition Road
GLOUCESTER RD
CROMWELL RD
A4
KENSINGTON
High St Kensington Stn
Kensington Mkt
Dyslexia Teaching Centre
Copthorne Tara Htl
Superstore
David Lloyd Leisure Centre
Cromwell Hosp
Gloucester Road Stn
South Kensington Stn
Pelham Street
THURLOE PL
BROMPTON RD
BROMPTON ROAD
OLD BROMPTON RD
FULHAM ROAD
KING'S ROAD
South Kensington
Royal Marsden Hosp
Royal Brompton Hospital
Chelsea Cinema
Chelsea Old Town Hall
Chelsea Leisure Cen
Coll of Art
Cineworld
Carlyle's Ho (NT)
Chelsea Physic Garden
Chelsea Synagogue
Guinness Trust Est
SLOANE
PONT ST
Cadogan Pier
Albert Bridge
Battersea Bridge
Kensington & Chelsea
Wandsworth
Brompton Cemetery
West Brompton
SW10
Imperial Coll of Science
Chelsea FC
Millennium & Copthorne Hotels at Chelsea FC
Fulham Broadway Stn
Worlds End Place
Albert Bridge Gate
Ransomes Dock Bus Cen
Kensington Wharf
1 grid square represents 500 metres

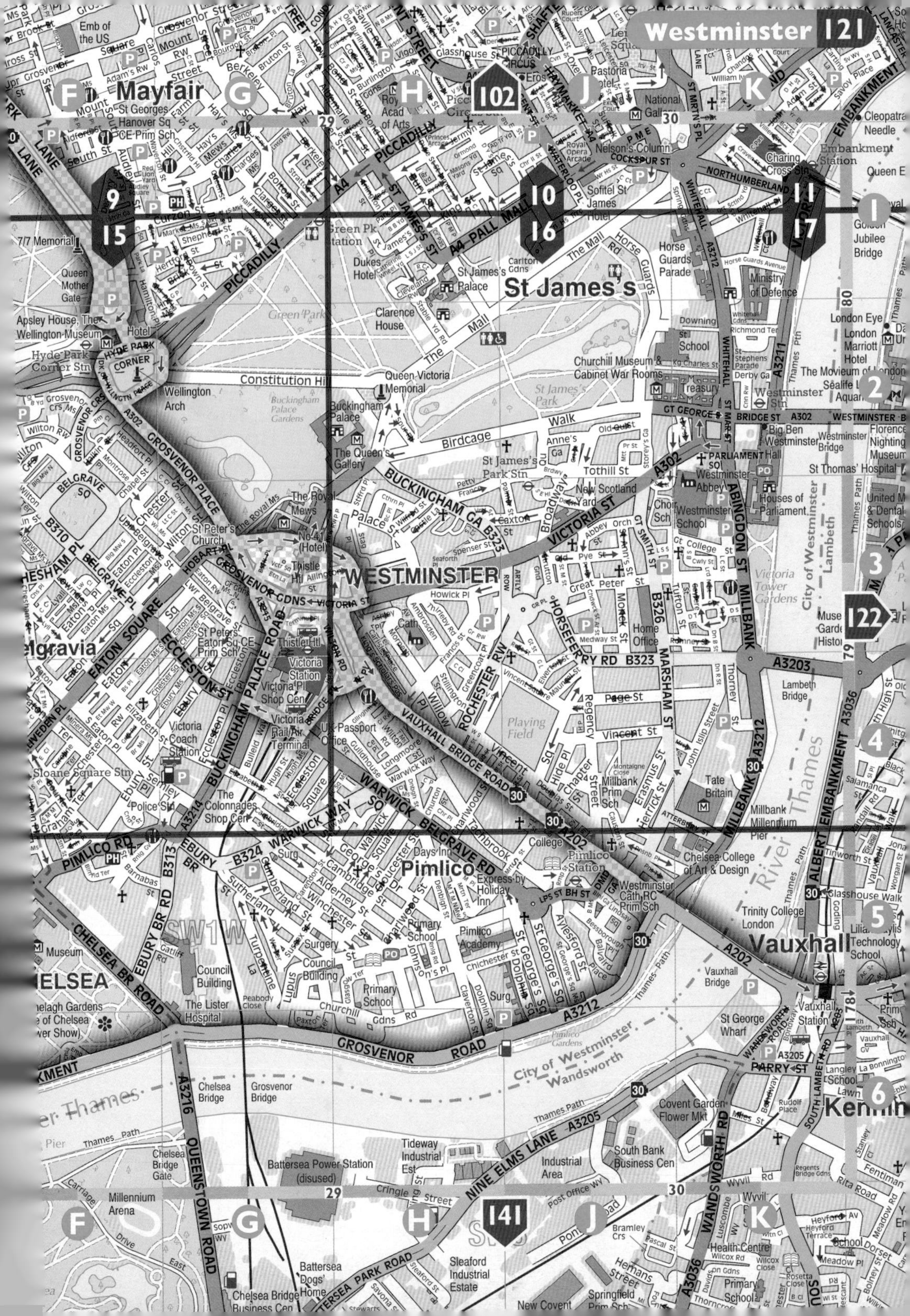

Westminster 121
Mayfair
Emb of the US
Grosvenor Square
St Georges Hanover Sq CE Prim Sch
Park Lane
Piccadilly
Piccadilly Circus
102
Royal Acad of Arts
Glasshouse St
National Gallery
Nelson's Column
Cockspur St
Royal Opera Arcade
Charing Cross Stn
Cleopatra's Needle
Embankment Station
Northumberland Av
Victoria Embankment
9
15
10
16
11
17
7/7 Memorial
Queen Mother Gate
Apsley House, The Wellington Museum
Hyde Park Corner
Hyde Park Corner Stn
Curzon St
Green Pk Station
Green Park
Dukes Hotel
A4 Pall Mall
St James's Palace
Clarence House
The Mall
St James's
Horse Guards Parade
Horse Guards Rd
Ministry of Defence
Whitehall
Downing St
Golden Jubilee Bridge
London Eye
London Marriott Hotel
Constitution Hill
Wellington Arch
Queen Victoria Memorial
Buckingham Palace
Buckingham Palace Gardens
The Queen's Gallery
Birdcage Walk
St James's Park
St James's Park Stn
Churchill Museum & Cabinet War Rooms
Treasury
Westminster Stn
Bridge St
Westminster Bridge
Big Ben
Westminster Hall
Parliament Sq
Westminster Abbey
Houses of Parliament
St Thomas' Hospital
Florence Nightingale Museum
Tothill St
New Scotland Yard
Broadway
Victoria St
Buckingham Ga
Caxton St
Belgrave Sq
Grosvenor Place
Grosvenor Crs
Wilton Crs
Chesham Pl
Eaton Pl
Belgravia
Eaton Square
Eccleston St
The Royal Mews
St Peter's Church
Hobart Pl
Grosvenor Gdns
Westminster
Thistle Htl
Victoria Station
Victoria Pl Shop Cen
Victoria Rail/Air Terminal
Victoria Coach Station
Buckingham Palace Road
UK Passport Office
Vauxhall Bridge Road
Westminster Cath
Horseferry Rd
Great Peter St
Marsham St
Home Office
Millbank
Victoria Tower Gardens
City of Westminster
Lambeth
Lambeth Bridge
Playing Field
Vincent Square
Rochester Rw
Tate Britain
Millbank Prim Sch
Millbank Millennium Pier
Chelsea College of Art & Design
River Thames
Albert Embankment
122
Sloane Square Stn
Ebury St
Warwick Way
Warwick Square
Belgrave Rd
Pimlico
Pimlico Station
Pimlico Rd
Ebury Br Rd
Chelsea Br Road
Sutherland St
Cambridge St
Alderney St
Winchester St
Lupus St
Pimlico Academy
Primary School
Trinity College London
Vauxhall
Vauxhall Bridge
Vauxhall Station
St George Wharf
Grosvenor Road
Chelsea
The Lister Hospital
Council Building
SW1W
Chelsea Bridge
Grosvenor Bridge
Queenstown Road
Battersea Power Station (disused)
Nine Elms Lane
Tideway Industrial Est
Industrial Area
South Bank Business Cen
Covent Garden Flower Mkt
Wandsworth Rd
Parry St
South Lambeth Rd
Kennington
Millennium Arena
Carriage Drive East
Cringle Street
Battersea Park Road
Battersea Dogs' Home
Chelsea Bridge Business Cen
Sleaford Industrial Estate
Health Centre
Wyvil Rd
141
New Covent
F G H J K
1 2 3 4 5 6
29 30

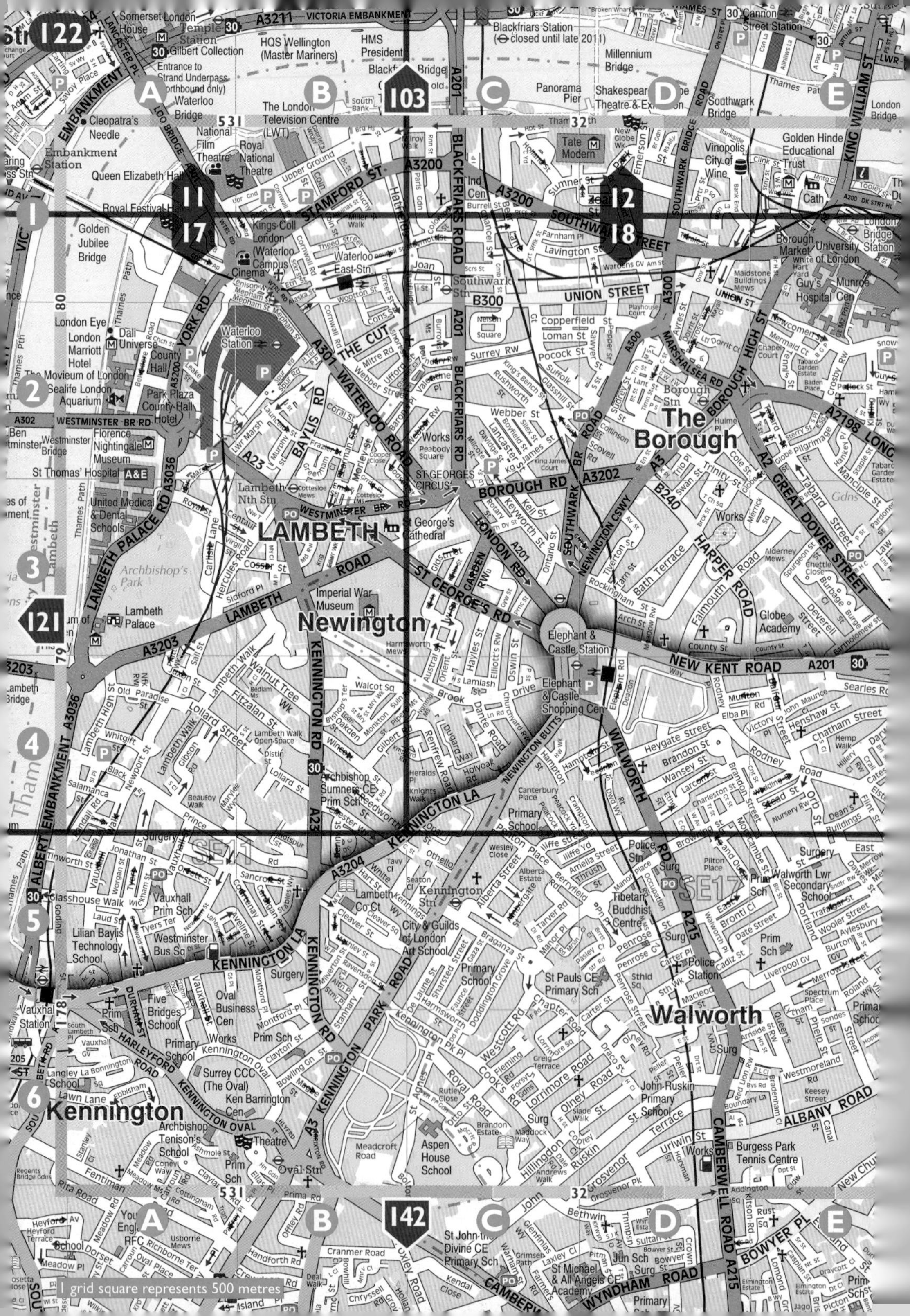

122
103
121
142
11
17
12
18
A
B
C
D
E
1
2
3
4
5
6
VICTORIA EMBANKMENT
Somerset House
Temple Station
Gilbert Collection
HQS Wellington (Master Mariners)
HMS President
Blackfriars Station
closed until late 2011
Millennium Bridge
Cannon Street Station
Entrance to Strand Underpass (northbound only)
Waterloo Bridge
Cleopatra's Needle
Embankment Station
The London Television Centre (LWT)
National Film Theatre
Royal National Theatre
Queen Elizabeth Hall
Royal Festival Hall
Panorama Pier
Shakespeare's Globe Theatre & Exhibition
Southwark Bridge
London Bridge
Tate Modern
Golden Hinde Educational Trust
Vinopolis, City of Wine
Golden Jubilee Bridge
Kings Coll London (Waterloo Campus)
Waterloo East Stn
STAMFORD ST
BLACKFRIARS ROAD
SOUTHWARK STREET
SOUTHWARK BRIDGE ROAD
KING WILLIAM ST
Borough Market
University of London
London Bridge Station
Guy's Hospital
UNION STREET
London Eye
Dali Universe
London Marriott Hotel
County Hall
Waterloo Station
THE CUT
WATERLOO ROAD
BAYLIS RD
YORK RD
The Movieum of London
Sealife London Aquarium
Park Plaza County Hall Hotel
WESTMINSTER BR RD
Westminster Bridge
Florence Nightingale Museum
St Thomas' Hospital
A&E
United Medical & Dental Schools
LAMBETH PALACE RD
Lambeth Nth Stn
LAMBETH
St George's Cathedral
ST GEORGES CIRCUS
BOROUGH RD
MARSHALSEA RD
BOROUGH HIGH ST
The Borough
GREAT DOVER STREET
Archbishop's Park
Lambeth Palace
LAMBETH ROAD
Imperial War Museum
Newington
ST GEORGE'S RD
LONDON RD
NEWINGTON CSWY
HARPER ROAD
Globe Academy
Elephant & Castle Station
Elephant & Castle Shopping Cen
NEW KENT ROAD
Lambeth Bridge
ALBERT EMBANKMENT
KENNINGTON RD
KENNINGTON LA
NEWINGTON BUTTS
WALWORTH RD
SE11
SE17
Vauxhall Station
Kennington Stn
City & Guilds of London Art School
Lilian Baylis Technology School
Westminster Bus Sq
KENNINGTON PARK ROAD
Tibetan Buddhist Centre
St Pauls CE Primary Sch
Walworth
Walworth Lwr Secondary School
HARLEYFORD ROAD
Surrey CCC (The Oval)
Ken Barrington Cen
KENNINGTON OVAL
Kennington
Archbishop Tenison's School
Theatre
Oval Stn
Aspen House School
Meadcroft Road
John Ruskin Primary School
CAMBERWELL ROAD
ALBANY ROAD
Burgess Park Tennis Centre
BOWYER PL
WYNDHAM ROAD
St John-the-Divine CE Primary Sch
St Michael & All Angels CE Academy
Usborne Mews
1 grid square represents 500 metres

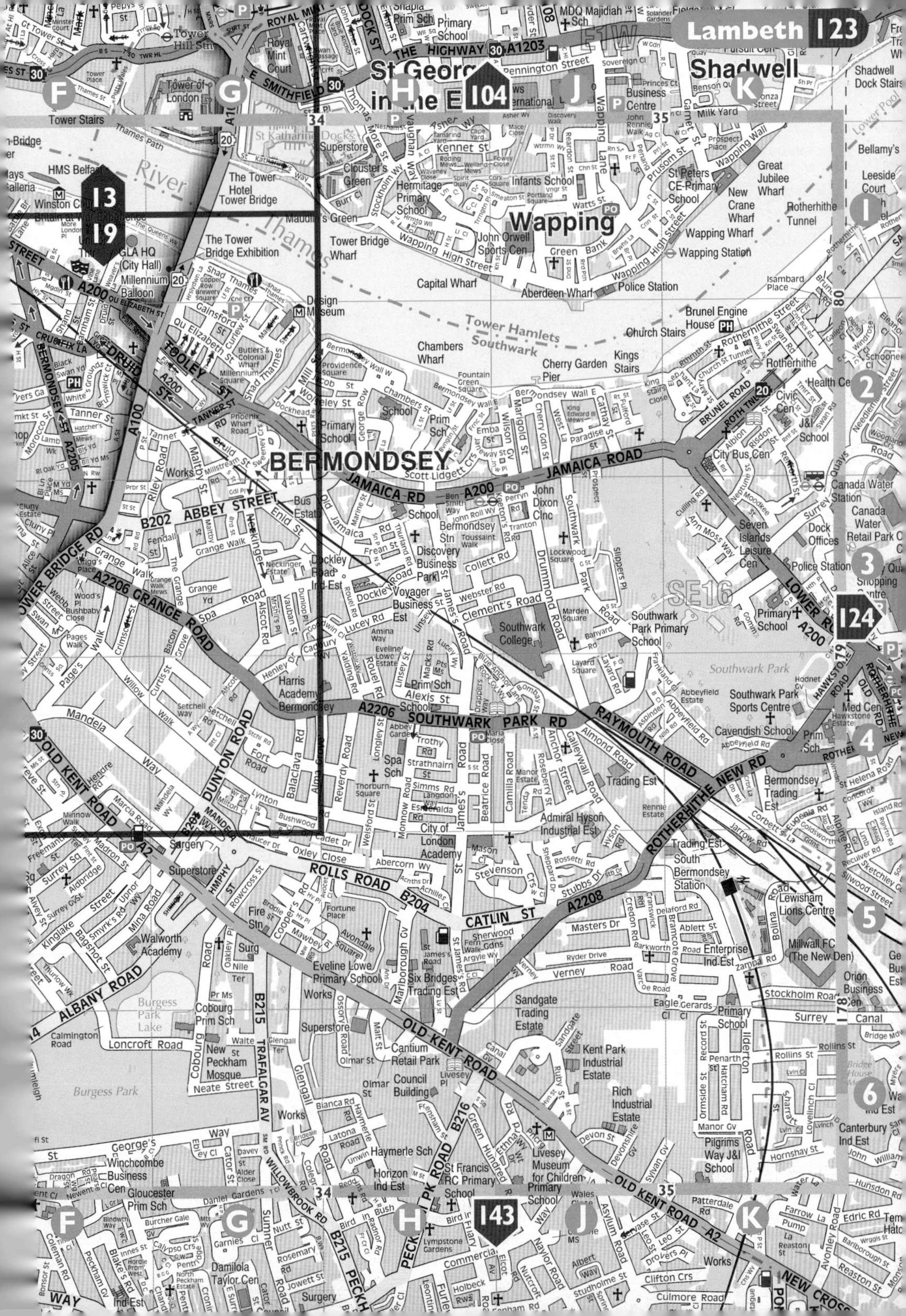

Lambeth 123
Shadwell
St George in the East
104
Wapping
Tower of London
Tower Stairs
HMS Belfast
River Thames
13
19
The Tower Hotel Tower Bridge
The Tower Bridge Exhibition
GLA HQ (City Hall)
Millennium Balloon
Design Museum
Tower Bridge Wharf
Capital Wharf
Aberdeen Wharf
Police Station
Wapping Station
Wapping Wharf
Great Jubilee Wharf
New Crane Wharf
Rotherhithe Tunnel
Shadwell Dock Stairs
Tower Hamlets
Southwark
Brunel Engine House
Church Stairs
Chambers Wharf
Cherry Garden Pier
Kings Stairs
Rotherhithe
BERMONDSEY
JAMAICA ROAD
TOOLEY ST
ABBEY STREET
TOWER BRIDGE RD
GRANGE ROAD
SOUTHWARK PARK RD
RAYMOUTH ROAD
ROTHERHITHE NEW RD
LOWER ROAD
OLD KENT ROAD
ROLLS ROAD
CATLIN ST
DUNTON ROAD
ALBANY ROAD
SE16
124
Canada Water Station
Canada Water Retail Park
Seven Islands Leisure Cen
Surrey Quays Shopping Centre
Southwark Park
Southwark Park Sports Centre
Southwark College
South Bermondsey Station
Lewisham Lions Centre
Millwall FC (The New Den)
Burgess Park
Burgess Park Lake
Walworth Academy
Harris Academy Bermondsey
City of London Academy
Livesey Museum for Children
Kent Park Industrial Estate
Rich Industrial Estate
Sandgate Trading Estate
Cantium Retail Park
Six Bridges Trading Est
New Peckham Mosque
143
F G H J K
1 2 3 4 5 6
34 35

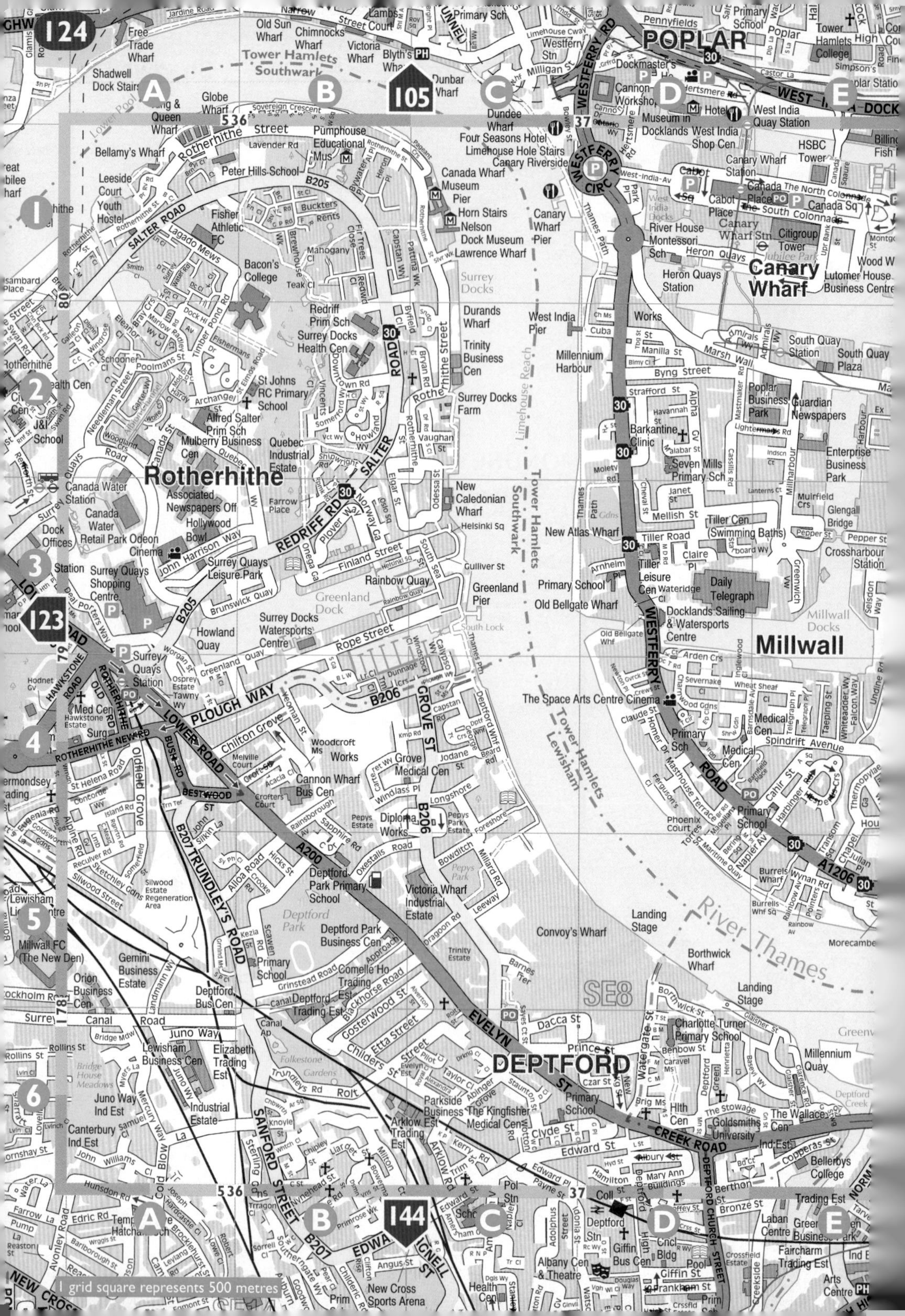
124
105
123
144
POPLAR
Rotherhithe
Canary Wharf
Millwall
DEPTFORD
SE8
River Thames
Limehouse Reach
Tower Hamlets
Southwark
Lewisham
WESTFERRY RD
WESTFERRY CIRC
WEST INDIA DOCK
SALTER ROAD
REDRIFF RD
LOWER ROAD
PLOUGH WAY
EVELYN ST
CREEK ROAD
DEPTFORD CHURCH STREET
TRUNDLEY'S ROAD
SANFORD STREET
HAWKSTONE ROAD
GROVE ST
A200
A1206
B205
B206
B207
Rotherhithe Street
Canada Water Station
Surrey Quays Station
Surrey Quays Shopping Centre
Surrey Docks
Greenland Dock
Surrey Docks Farm
Surrey Docks Watersports Centre
Canary Wharf Station
West India Quay Station
Heron Quays Station
South Quay Station
Crossharbour Station
Millwall Docks
Daily Telegraph
Millwall FC (The New Den)
Deptford Park
Deptford Stn
Convoy's Wharf
The Space Arts Centre Cinema
Museum in Docklands
Canary Wharf Pier
West India Pier
Greenland Pier
Millennium Quay
Goldsmiths University
Laban Centre
1 grid square represents 500 metres

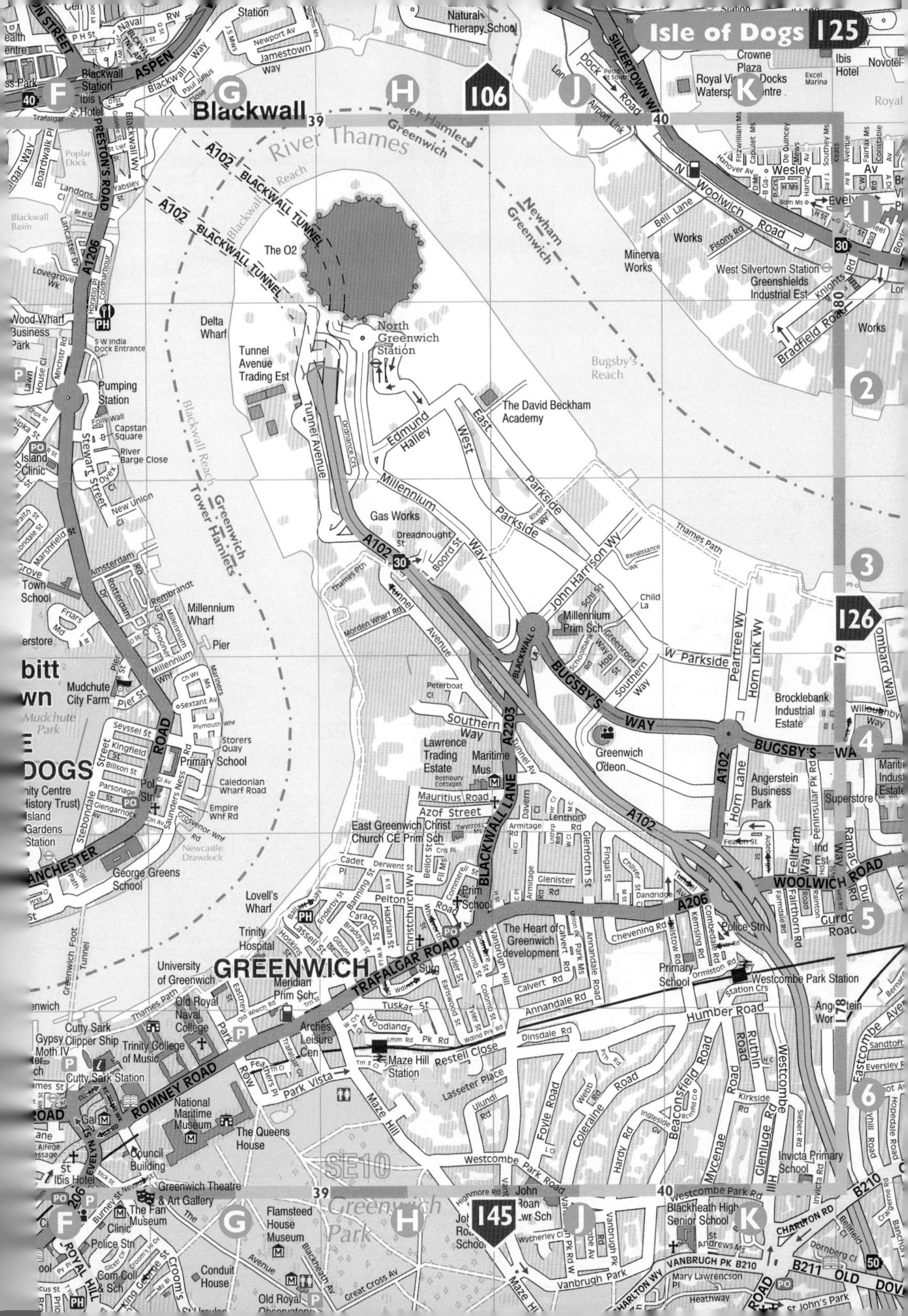
Blackwall
River Thames
The O2
North Greenwich Station
Delta Wharf
Tunnel Avenue Trading Est
The David Beckham Academy
Gas Works
Millennium Wharf
Mudchute City Farm
Millennium Prim Sch
Greenwich Odeon
Brocklebank Industrial Estate
Angerstein Business Park
Lawrence Trading Estate
Maritime Mus
East Greenwich Christ Church CE Prim Sch
GREENWICH
Trinity Hospital
University of Greenwich
Old Royal Naval College
Cutty Sark Clipper Ship
Gypsy Moth IV
Trinity College of Music
Cutty Sark Station
National Maritime Museum
The Queens House
Maze Hill Station
Westcombe Park Station
Greenwich Park
SE10
Flamsteed House Museum
Greenwich Theatre & Art Gallery
The Fan Museum
Blackheath High Senior School
ROMNEY ROAD
TRAFALGAR ROAD
BLACKWALL LANE
WOOLWICH ROAD
BUGSBY'S WAY
BLACKWALL TUNNEL
PRESTON'S ROAD
Bugsby's Reach
Blackwall Reach
Greenwich Tower Hamlets
Newham Greenwich
West Silvertown Station
Greenshields Industrial Est
Royal Victoria Docks Watersports Centre
Crowne Plaza
Ibis Hotel
Novotel
Natural Therapy School
106
126
145
39
40
F G H J K
2 3 4 5 6

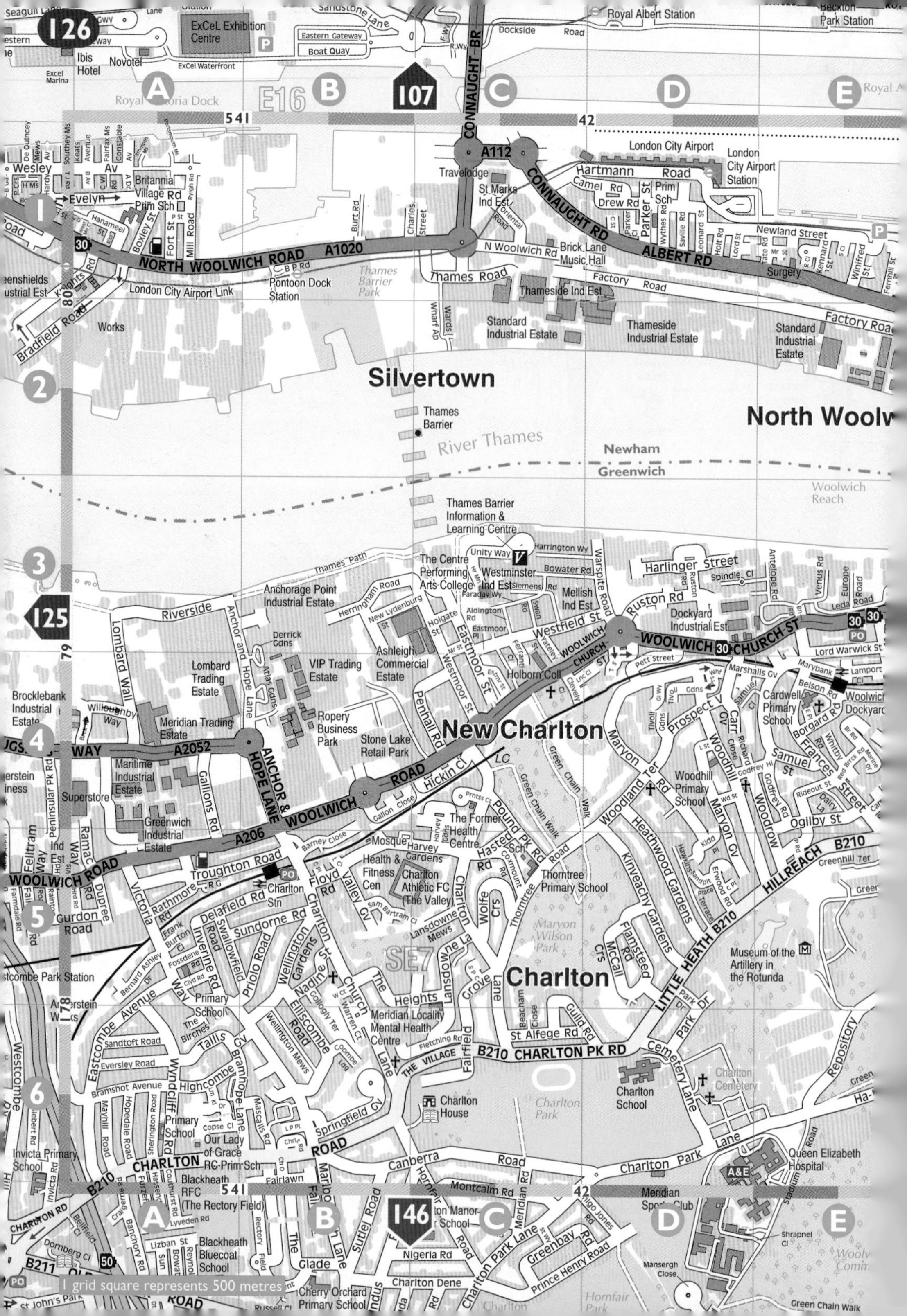
126
ExCeL Exhibition Centre
Ibis Hotel
Novotel
Excel Marina
ExCeL Waterfront
Eastern Gateway
Boat Quay
Sandstone Lane
Royal Albert Station
Dockside Road
Beckton Park Station
107
CONNAUGHT BR
A
B
C
D
E
E16
Royal Victoria Dock
541
42
A112
London City Airport
London City Airport Station
Hartmann Road
Camel Rd
Drew Rd
Parker St
Prim Sch
Travelodge
St Marks Ind Est
CONNAUGHT RD
ALBERT RD
Newland Street
Surgery
Wesley Av
Britannia Village Prim Sch
Evelyn
Hanameel St
Boxley St
Fort St
Mill Road
Burt Rd
Charles Street
Oriental Road
1
NORTH WOOLWICH ROAD
A1020
N Woolwich Rd
Brick Lane Music Hall
Thames Road
Factory Road
Thameside Ind Est
Pontoon Dock Station
Thames Barrier Park
London City Airport Link
Knights Rd
Bradfield Road
Works
Wharf Ap
Wards
Standard Industrial Estate
Thameside Industrial Estate
Silvertown
2
Thames Barrier
River Thames
North Woolw
Newham
Greenwich
Woolwich Reach
Thames Barrier Information & Learning Centre
3
Thames Path
Unity Way
Harrington Wy
Bowater Rd
Westminster Ind Est
The Centre Performing Arts College
Harlinger Street
Ruston Rd
Spindle Cl
Antelope Rd
Venus Rd
Europe Road
Leda Road
125
Riverside
Anchorage Point Industrial Estate
Herringham Road
New Lydenburg St
Holgate St
Eastmoor St
Warspite Road
Mellish Ind Est
Westfield St
Dockyard Industrial Est
WOOLWICH CHURCH ST
Lord Warwick St
Pett Street
Marshalls Gv
Lombard Wall
Derrick Gdns
VIP Trading Estate
Ashleigh Commercial Estate
Westmoor St
Holborn Coll
Lombard Trading Estate
Brocklebank Industrial Estate
Willoughby Way
Meridian Trading Estate
Ropery Business Park
Stone Lake Retail Park
Penhall Rd
New Charlton
Cardwell Primary School
Woolwich Dockyard
Borgard Rd
Frances St
Samuel St
4
WAY
A2052
ANCHOR & HOPE LANE
Maritime Industrial Estate
Superstore
Greenwich Industrial Estate
Gallions Rd
WOOLWICH ROAD
Hickin Cl
Gallon Close
Pound Pk Rd
Green Chain Walk
Maryon Rd
Woodland Ter
Woodhill
Woodhill Primary School
Maryon Gv
Woodrow
Ogilby St
Heathwood Gardens
HILLREACH
B210
Greenhill Ter
A206
Troughton Road
Charlton Stn
Barney Close
Mosque
Harvey Gardens
The Former Health Centre
Hasted Rd
Health & Fitness Cen
Charlton Athletic FC (The Valley)
Thorntree Road
Thorntree Primary School
Kinveachy Gardens
Floyd Rd
Valley Gv
Rathmore Rd
Delafield Rd
Sundorne Rd
Victoria Way
Gurdon Road
Dupree Rd
5
Lansdowne Mews
Wolfe Crs
Maryon Wilson Park
SE7
Charlton
Flamsteed Rd
McCall Crs
LITTLE HEATH B210
Museum of the Artillery in the Rotunda
Invermore Rd
Swallowfield Road
Priolo Road
Wellington Gardens
Nadine St
Charlton Church La
The Heights
Lansdowne La
Grove
Westcombe Park Station
Primary School
The Birches
Eastcombe Avenue
Sandtoft Road
Eversley Road
Tallis Gv
Wyndcliff Rd
Highcombe
Bramhope Lane
Elliscombe Road
Wellington Mews
Meridian Locality Mental Health Centre
Fletching Rd
Fairfield
St Alfege Rd
Guild Rd
Park Dr
B210 CHARLTON PK RD
THE VILLAGE
Cemetery Lane
Charlton Cemetery
Charlton School
Repository
6
Bramshot Avenue
Mayhill Road
Hopedale Road
Sherington Road
Primary School
Our Lady of Grace RC Prim Sch
Springfield Gv
Charlton House
Charlton Park
Westcombe
Invicta Primary School
CHARLTON
ROAD
Canberra Road
Charlton Park Lane
Queen Elizabeth Hospital
A&E
B210
Blackheath RFC (The Rectory Field)
Fairlawn
Montcalm Rd
Meridian Rd
Meridian Sports Club
146
Charlton Manor School
Sutlej Road
Nigeria Rd
Greenbay Rd
Prince Henry Road
Charlton Park Lane
Mansergh Close
Shrapnel Cl
Stadium Road
CHARLTON RD
Lyveden Rd
Banchory Rd
Lizban St
Blackheath Bluecoat School
The Glade
Cherry Orchard Primary School
Charlton Dene
B211
1 grid square represents 500 metres
Green Chain Walk

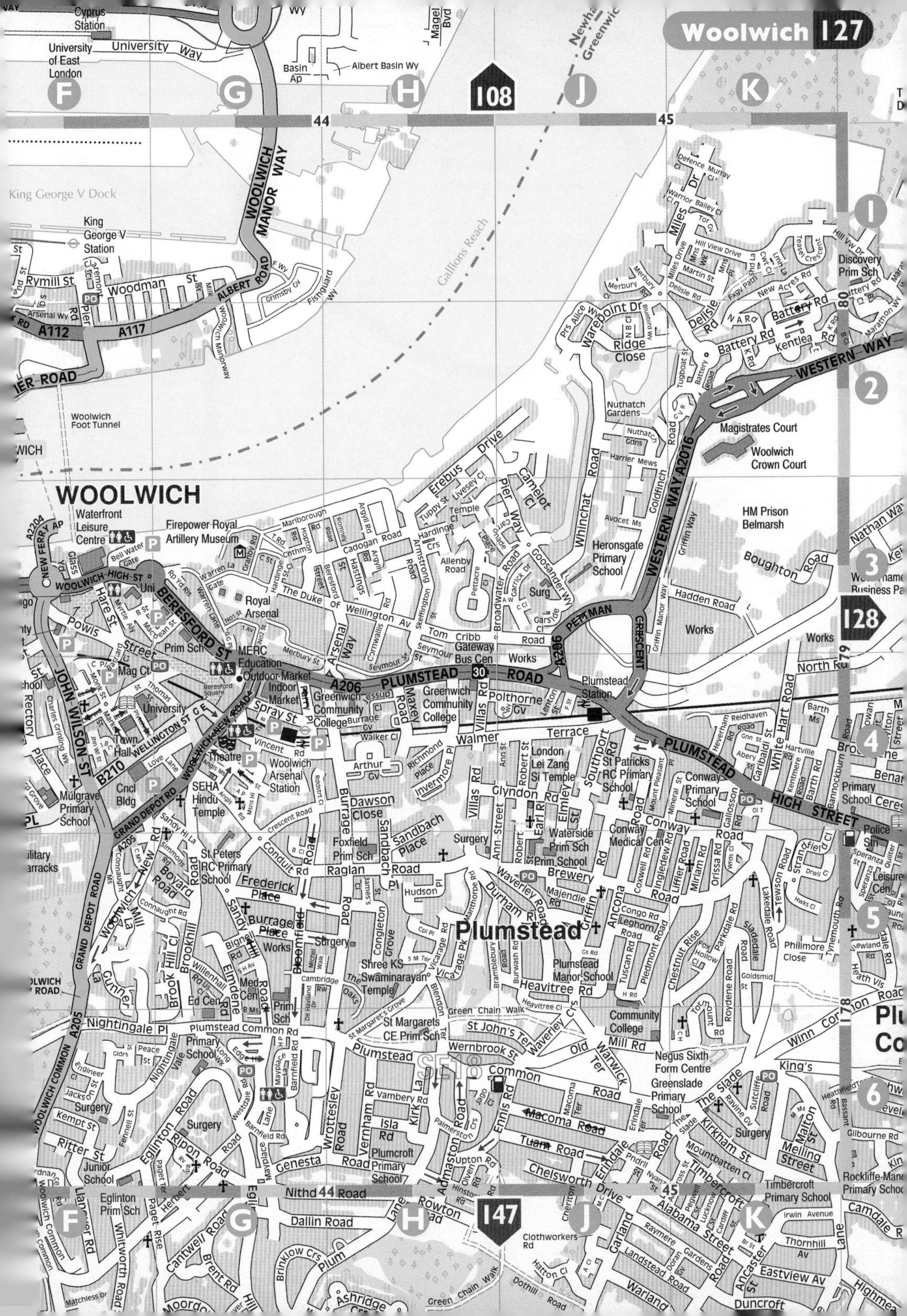

Cyprus Station
University of East London
University Way
Albert Basin Wy
Basin Ap
108
44
45
King George V Dock
King George V Station
Woolwich Manor Way
Albert Road
Rymill St
Woodman St
Pier
A112
A117
Woolwich Manorway
Fishguard Wy
Grimsby Gv
Gallions Reach
Woolwich Foot Tunnel
WOOLWICH
Waterfront Leisure Centre
Firepower Royal Artillery Museum
New Ferry Ap
A2204
Woolwich High St
Beresford St
Royal Arsenal
Prim Sch
MERC Education
Outdoor Market
Indoor Market
Greenwich Community College
Hare St
Powis Street
Mag Ct
University
Town Hall
Wellington St
John Wilson St
Rectory Place
Charles Grinling Wk
Woolwich New Road
Spray St
Vincent Rd
Woolwich Arsenal Station
Theatre
SEHA Hindu Temple
Cncl Bldg
B210
Grand Depot Rd
Mulgrave Primary School
Military Barracks
Grand Depot Road
A205
Woolwich Common
The Duke of Wellington Av
Arsenal Way
Cadogan Road
Erebus Drive
Camelot Cl
Pier Way
Armstrong Crs
Allenby Road
Broadwater Road
Tom Cribb Road
Gateway Bus Cen
Works
Seymour St
A206 Plumstead Road
30
Polthorne Gv
Villas Rd
Maxey Road
Walmer Terrace
Arthur Gv
Dawson Close
Burrage Road
Sandbach Place
Raglan Road
Foxfield Prim Sch
Frederick Place
Burrage Place
Bloomfield Road
Conduit Rd
St Peters RC Primary School
Boyard Road
Brookhill Rd
Sandy Hill Rd
Elmdene Rd
Med Cen
Ed Cen
Works
Surgery
Congleton Grove
The Oaks
Shree KS Swaminarayan Temple
Plumstead
Plumstead Common Rd
Nightingale Pl
Nightingale Vale
Primary School
St Margarets CE Prim Sch
St Margaret's Grove
Vicarage Pk
Vicarage Rd
Blendon Ter
Green Chain Walk
St John's Ter
Wernbrook St
Plumstead Common Road
SE18
Waverley Crs
Old Mill Rd
Warwick Ter
Macoma Road
Tuam Road
Chelsworth Drive
Genesta Road
Wrottesley Road
Vernham Rd
Isla Rd
Plumcroft Primary School
Admaston Road
Ennis Rd
Eglinton Road
Ripon Road
Junior School
Eglinton Prim Sch
Nithdale Road
Dallin Road
Rowton Road
147
Brinklow Crs
Ashridge Crs
Cantwell Road
Brent Rd
Whitworth Road
Llanover Rd
Kempt St
Ritter St
Jacksons Surgery
Surgery
Miles Dr
Defence Cl
Murray Cl
Warrior Cl
Bailey Cl
Hill View Drive
Martin St
Delisle Rd
Merbury Rd
Warepoint Dr
Ridge Close
Battery Rd
Kentlea Rd
New Acres Rd
Western Way
Discovery Prim Sch
Magistrates Court
Woolwich Crown Court
Nuthatch Gardens
Harrier Mews
Whinchat Road
Goldfinch Road
Avocet Ms
Heronsgate Primary School
Western Way A2016
Pettman Crescent
A206
Goosander Wy
Griffin Way
HM Prison Belmarsh
Nathan Way
Boughton Road
Hadden Road
Griffin Manor Way
Works
North Rd
Plumstead Station
Plumstead High Street
London Lei Zang Si Temple
St Patricks RC Primary School
Southport Rd
Glyndon Rd
Conway Primary School
Conway Road
Conway Medical Cen
Waterside Prim Sch
Prim School
Brewery Road
Majendie Rd
Griffin Rd
Ancona Rd
Congo Rd
Leghorn Road
Tuscan Rd
Piedmont Road
Plumstead Manor School
Heavitree Rd
Community College
Negus Sixth Form Centre
Greenslade Primary School
The Slade
Kirkham St
Timbercroft
Alabama Street
Mountbatten Cl
Surgery
Melling Street
Malton St
Timbercroft Primary School
White Hart Road
Garibaldi St
Reidhaven Road
Bannockburn Road
Barth Rd
Primary School
Police Stn
Chestnut Rise
Parkdale Rd
Sladedale Road
Lakedale Road
Tewson Road
Roydene Road
Philimore Close
Tynemouth Rd
Winn Common Road
King's
Rockliffe Manor Primary School
Irwin Avenue
Thornhill Av
Eastview Av
Ancaster St
Garland Rd
Raymere Gardens
Landstead Road
Warland Rd
Duncroft
Clothworkers Rd
Hatton Cl
Dothill Rd
Green Chain Walk
Camdale Rd
Gilbourne Rd
128
1
2
3
4
5
6
80
79
78
F
G
H
J
K

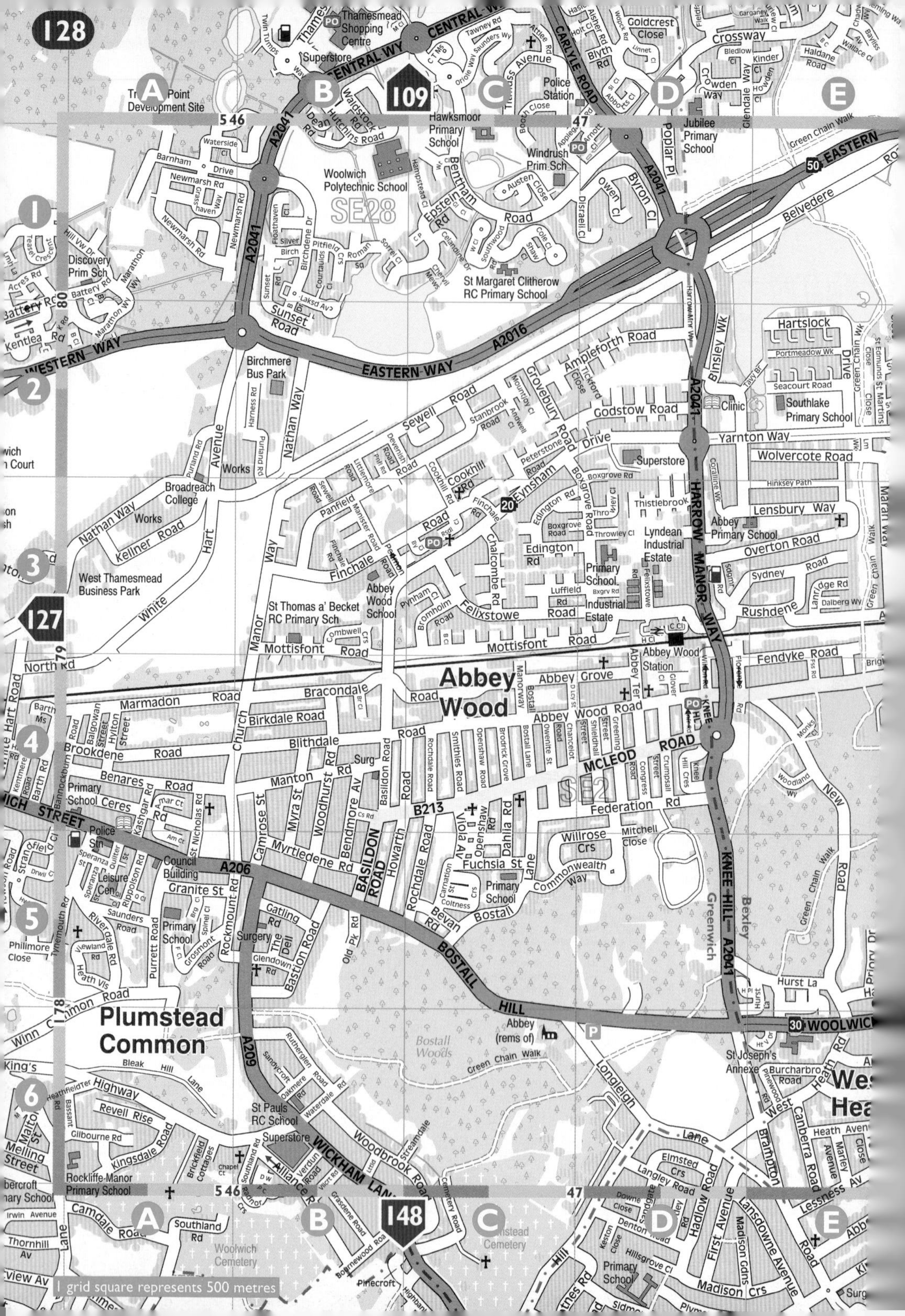

109
127
148
SE28
SE2
Abbey Wood
Plumstead Common
Thamesmead Shopping Centre
Superstore
Central Wy
Carlyle Road
Tripcock Point Development Site
Hawksmoor Primary School
Police Station
Jubilee Primary School
Windrush Prim Sch
Woolwich Polytechnic School
Discovery Prim Sch
Western Way
Eastern Way
A2016
A2041
A206
A209
B213
Birchmere Bus Park
Broadreach College
Works
West Thamesmead Business Park
Nathan Way
Kellner Road
White Hart Avenue
Harness Rd
Church Manor Way
Sewell Road
Ampleforth Road
Grovebury Road
Godstow Road
Yarnton Way
Wolvercote Road
Lensbury Way
Abbey Primary School
Overton Road
Southlake Primary School
Hartslock
Seacourt Road
Clinic
Harrow Manor Way
Lyndean Industrial Estate
Primary School
Industrial Estate
Edington Rd
Felixstowe Road
Mottisfont Road
Finchale Road
Abbey Wood School
St Thomas a' Becket RC Primary Sch
Abbey Wood Station
Fendyke Road
Abbey Grove
Abbey Wood Road
Bracondale Road
Marmadon Road
Birkdale Road
Blithdale Road
Brookdene Road
Benares Road
McLeod Road
Federation Rd
Basildon Road
Howarth Road
Rochdale Road
Bostall Hill
Bostall Lane
Knee Hill
Woolwich
High Street
Council Building
Police Stn
Leisure Cen
Primary School
Plumstead Common Road
Winn Common Road
Bostall Woods
Abbey (rems of)
Green Chain Walk
Greenwich
Bexley
New Road
Longleigh Lane
St Pauls RC School
Wickham Lane
Woodbrook Road
Rockliffe Manor Primary School
Kingsdale Road
Revell Rise
Highway
St Joseph's Annexe
West Heath
Canberra Road
Brampton Road
Lessness Av
Hurst La
Lansdowne Avenue
Madison Crs
First Avenue
Hadlow Road
Langley Road
Elmsted Crs
Woolwich Cemetery
Plumstead Cemetery
Southland Rd
Camdale Road
1 grid square represents 500 metres

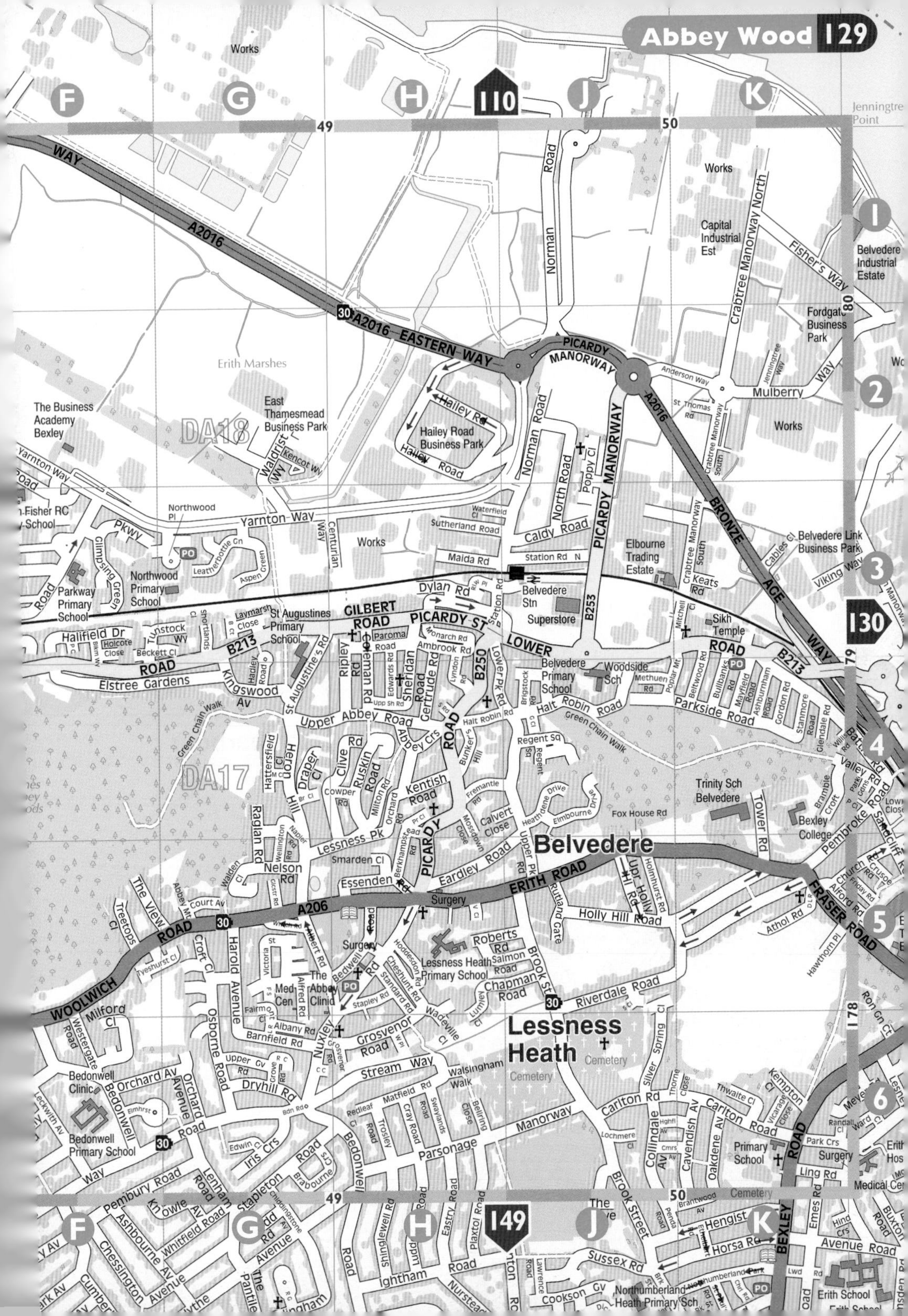

Works
F
G
H
110
J
K
49
50
Jenningtree Point
WAY
A2016
Works
Capital Industrial Est
Crabtree Manorway North
Fisher's Way
Belvedere Industrial Estate
Norman Road
30
A2016 EASTERN WAY
PICARDY MANORWAY
Fordgate Business Park
Erith Marshes
Anderson Way
Mulberry Way
The Business Academy Bexley
East Thamesmead Business Park
DA18
Hailey Rd
Hailey Road Business Park
Hailey Road
Norman Road
North Road
Poppy Cl
PICARDY MANORWAY
A2016
St Thomas Rd
Crabtree Manorway South
Works
Yarnton Way
Waldrist Wy
Kencot Wy
BRONZE AGE WAY
Northwood Pl
Yarnton Way
Centurian Way
Waterfield Cl
Sutherland Road
Caldy Road
Elbourne Trading Estate
Crabtree Manorway South
Cables Cl
Belvedere Link Business Park
Works
Maida Rd
Station Rd N
Viking Way
Northwood Primary School
Leatherbottle Gn
Aspen Green
Climpsing Green
Pkwy
Parkway Primary School
Belvedere Stn
Superstore
B253
Keats Rd
Dylan Rd
GILBERT ROAD
PICARDY ST
Station Rd
Laymarsh Close
St Augustines Primary School
Sikh Temple
130
Halifield Dr
Tunstock Wy
Shortlands Cl
Paroma Road
Monarch Rd
Ambrook Rd
LOWER ROAD
Holcote Close
Beckett Cl
B213
Hadley Road
St Augustine's Rd
Ripley Rd
Coleman Rd
Edwards Rd
Sheridan Road
Gertrude Rd
Lyndon Rd
B250
Lower Pk Rd
Brigstock Rd
Belvedere Primary School
Woodside Sch
Methuen Rd
Poplar Mt
Beltwood Rd
Bullbanks Rd
Mayfield Road
Ashburnham Road
Gordon Rd
Stanmore Road
Glendale Rd
ROAD
Elstree Gardens
Kingswood Av
Upp Sh Rd
Halt Robin Road
Parkside Road
B213
WAY
Green Chain Walk
Upper Abbey Road
Abbey Crs
ROAD
Halt Robin Rd
Bunker's Hill
Green Chain Walk
Regent Sq
Hattersfield Cl
Heron Hill
Draper Cl
Clive Rd
Ruskin Road
DA17
Cowper Rd
Milton Rd
Kentish Road
Fremantle
Heathdene Drive
Trinity Sch Belvedere
Tower Rd
Valley Rd
Bexley College
Orchard Rd
PICARDY
Mossdown Close
Calvert Close
Elmbourne Drive
Fox House Rd
Raglan Rd
Wellington Rd
Napier
Lessness Pk
Belvedere
Pembroke Road
Nelson Rd
Smarden Cl
Eardley Road
Upper Pk Rd
ERITH ROAD
Upr Holly Hill Rd
Holmhurst Rd
Church Rd
Crusoe Rd
Alford Rd
The View
Abbey Mt
Court Av
Essenden Rd
Surgery
Rutland Gate
Holly Hill Road
Athol Rd
FRASER ROAD
Treetops Cl
ROAD
30
A206
Roberts Rd
Salmon Road
Lessness Heath Primary School
Brook St
5
Harold Avenue
Croft Cl
Tyeshurst Cl
Victoria St
Albert Rd
Surgery
Bedwell Rd
Hoddesdon Rd
Cheshunt Rd
Chapman Road
30
Riverdale Road
Hawthorn Pl
WOOLWICH
Milford Cl
Osborne Road
Alfred Rd
The Abbey Clinic
Standard Rd
Wadeville Cl
Lumley Cl
Lessness Heath
Silver Spring Cl
178
Westergate Road
Albany Rd
Barnfield Rd
Nuxley
Grosvenor Road
Cemetery
Bedonwell Clinic
Orchard Av
Bedonwell
Orchard Avenue
Upper Gv Rd
Dryhill Rd
Stream Way
Walsingham Walk
Cemetery
Kempton Cl
Thwaite Cl
6
Redleaf Cl
Matfield Rd
Cray Road
Swaylands
Close
Bellring Cl
Carlton Rd
Thorne Close
Carlton Road
Vicarage Close
Bedonwell Primary School
30
Road
Edwin Cl
Iris Crs
Manorway
Collindale Av
Cavendish Av
Oakdene Av
Lochmere Cl
Primary School
Park Crs
Surgery
Way
Lenham Road
Stapleton Road
Brabourne Crs
Bedonwell Road
Parsonage
ROAD
Ling Rd
Medical Cen
Pembury Road
49
50
Cemetery
F
Ashbourne Av
Knowle Av
Whitfield Road
G
H
149
J
K
Hengist
Horsa Rd
BEXLEY
Emes Rd
Hind Crs
Avenue Road
Chessington Avenue
Ightham
Nurstead
Sussex Rd
Cookson Gv
Northumberland Heath Primary Sch
Erith School

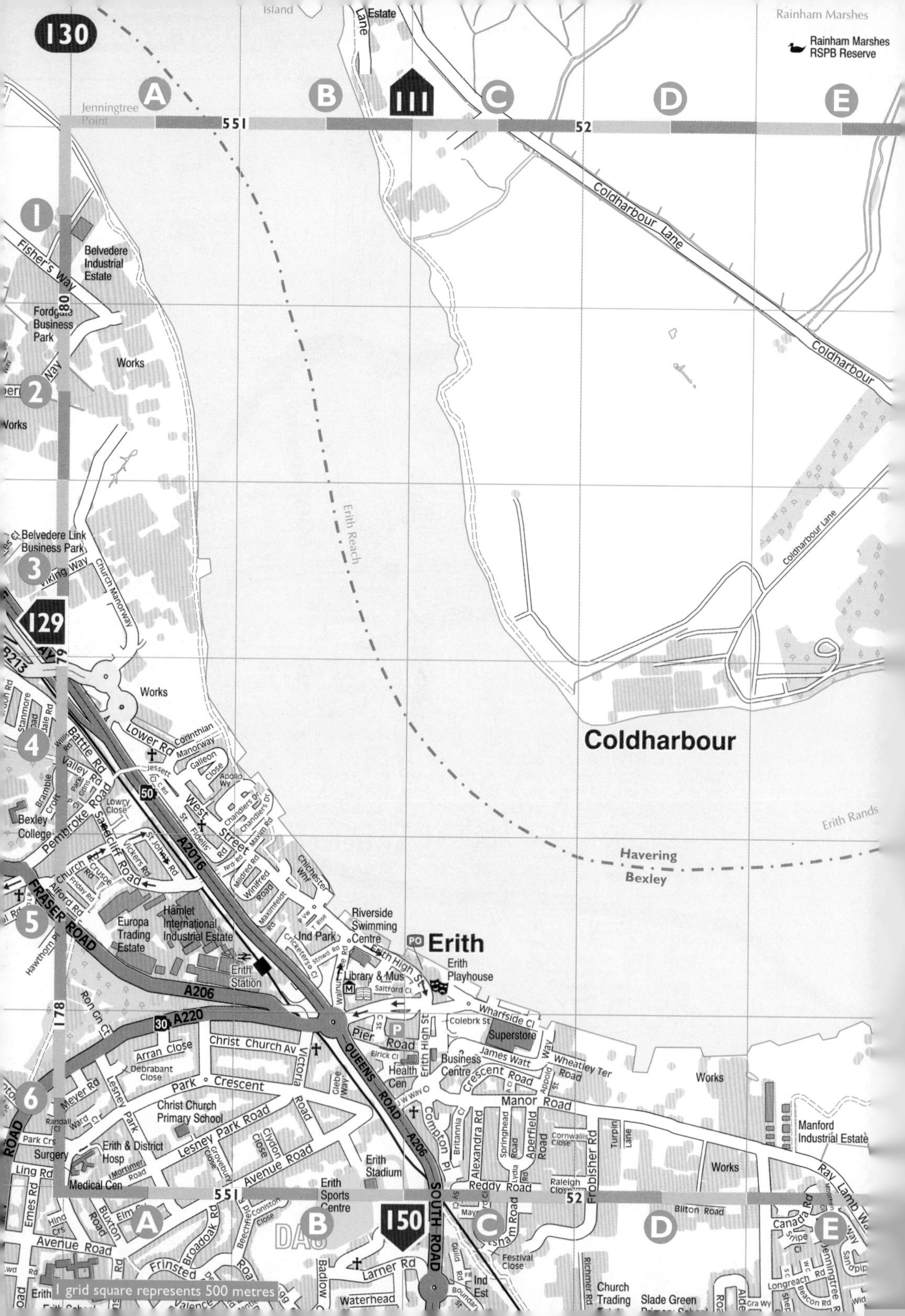

Rainham Marshes

Rainham Marshes
RSPB Reserve

A   **B**   **C**   **D**   **E**

551   52

Jenningtree
Point

Coldharbour Lane

Coldharbour

I

Belvedere Industrial
Estate

Fordgate
Business
Park

Works

Erith Reach

Belvedere Link
Business Park

Viking Way

129

A213

Works

Lower Rd

Corinthian

Manorway

Galleon
Close

Apollo

Coldharbour

Church Manorway

Erith Rands

Havering
Bexley

4

Battle Rd

Valley Road

Pembroke Road

West Street

Chandlers Dr

Chandlers Dr

Ascet Rd

Chichester Rd

Bexley
College

50

St John's Rd

St Fidelis Rd

Mildred
Winifred
Maximfield

Nrg gd

Church Rd

Alford Rd

Finlay Rd

5

FRASER ROAD

Europa
Trading
Estate

Hamlet
International
Industrial Estate

Ind Park

Riverside
Swimming
Centre

Erith High St

Erith

Erith
Playhouse

Wharfside Cl

Colebrk St

A178

Hawthorne

Ron Cn Cl

Cricketers Cl

Erith
Station

Library & Mus

Saltford Cl

Erith High St

P

Superstore

Business
Centre

James Watt
Crescent Road

Wheatley Ter
Road

Works

A206

30 A220

Pier
Road

Health
Cen

W Wy Cl

Manor Road

Aderfield
Road

Turpin
Lane

6

Meyer Rd

Lesney Rd

Arran Close

Debrabant
Close

Christ Church Av

Victoria

Park • Crescent

Glebe Way

Road

Clydon Cl

Christ Church
Primary School

Lesney Park Road

Avenue Road

Erith
Stadium

QUEENS ROAD

Compton Pl

Alexandra Rd

Britannia Cl

Springhead
Road

Cornwallis
Close

Raleigh
Close

Frobisher Rd

52

Works

Manford
Industrial
Estate

Ray Lamb Wa

ROAD

Erith & District
Hosp

Mortimer
Rd

Randall
Ward

Park Crs

Medical Cen

Elm

Buxton Rd

Broadoak Rd

Beechwood

Coniston

Reddy Road

Masham Road

Bilton Road

Canada Rd

Ling Rd

Emes Rd

Hind Cts

A   551   **B**   **C** SOUTH ROAD   **D**   **E**

Avenue Road

DA8

Frinsted

Badlow

Larner Rd

Erith Sports
Centre

150

Waterhead

Ind
Est

Festival
Close

Church
Trading

Slade Green
Primary School

Canada Rd

Longreach

Beacon Rd

grid square represents 500 metres

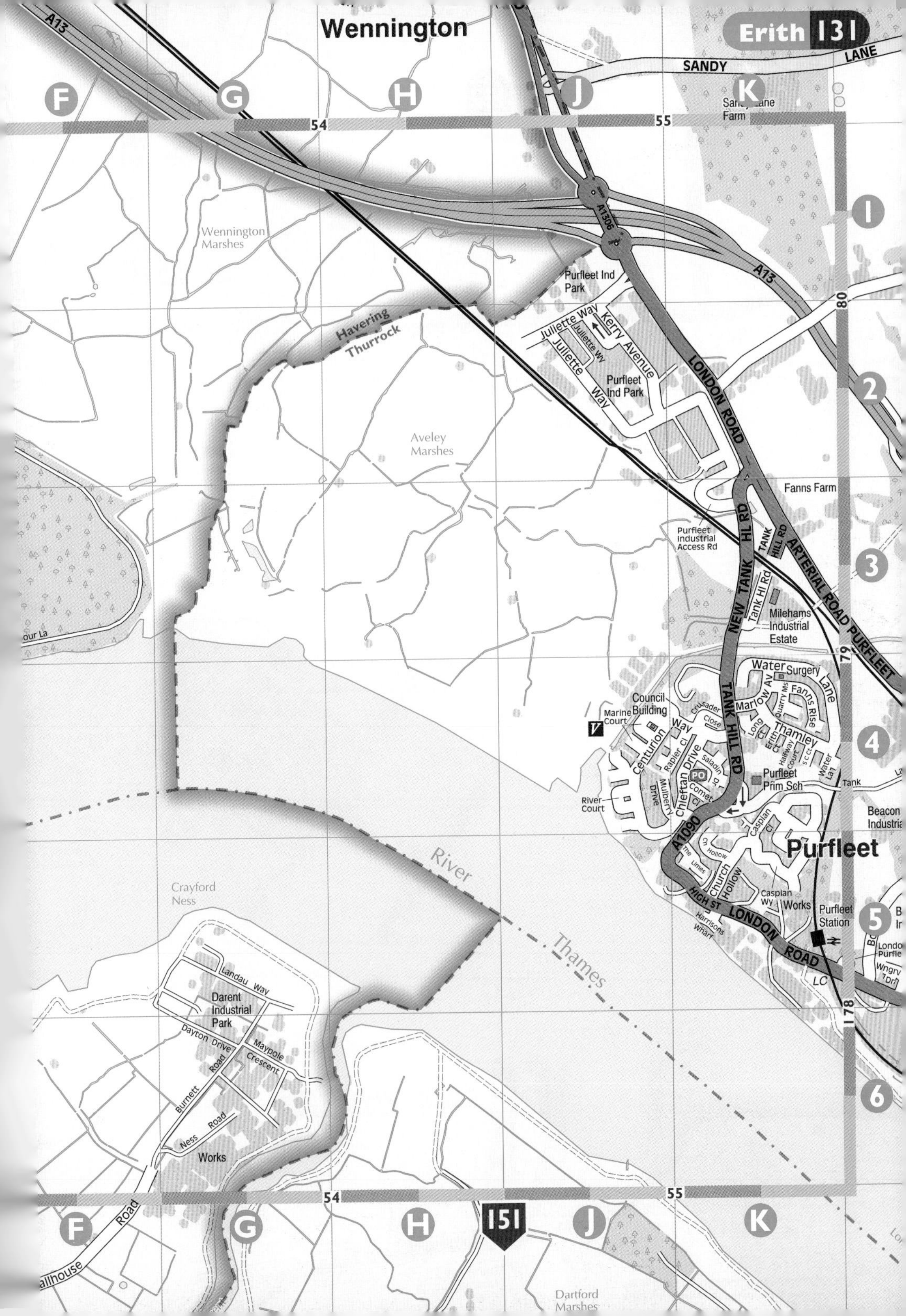

Wennington
A13
SANDY LANE
Sandy Lane Farm
F
G
H
J
K
54
55
Wennington Marshes
A1306
Purfleet Ind Park
Havering
Thurrock
Juliette Way
Kerry Avenue
Purfleet Ind Park
LONDON ROAD
Aveley Marshes
Fanns Farm
Purfleet Industrial Access Rd
NEW TANK HL RD
TANK HILL RD
ARTERIAL ROAD PURFLEET
Tank Hl Rd
Milehams Industrial Estate
Water Lane
Surgery
Marlow Av
Fanns Rise
Thamley
Council Building
Marine Court
Crusader Close
Centurion Way
Rapier Cl
Chieftan Drive
Saladin
PO
Mulberry Drive
Comet Cl
Purfleet Prim Sch
River Court
A1090
Caspian Cl
Purfleet
Church Hollow
Caspian Wy
Works
HIGH ST
LONDON ROAD
Harrisons Wharf
Purfleet Station
Crayford Ness
River
Thames
Landau Way
Darent Industrial Park
Dayton Drive
Maypole Crescent
Burnett Road
Ness Road
Works
Dartford Marshes
80
79
78
1
2
3
4
5
6

151

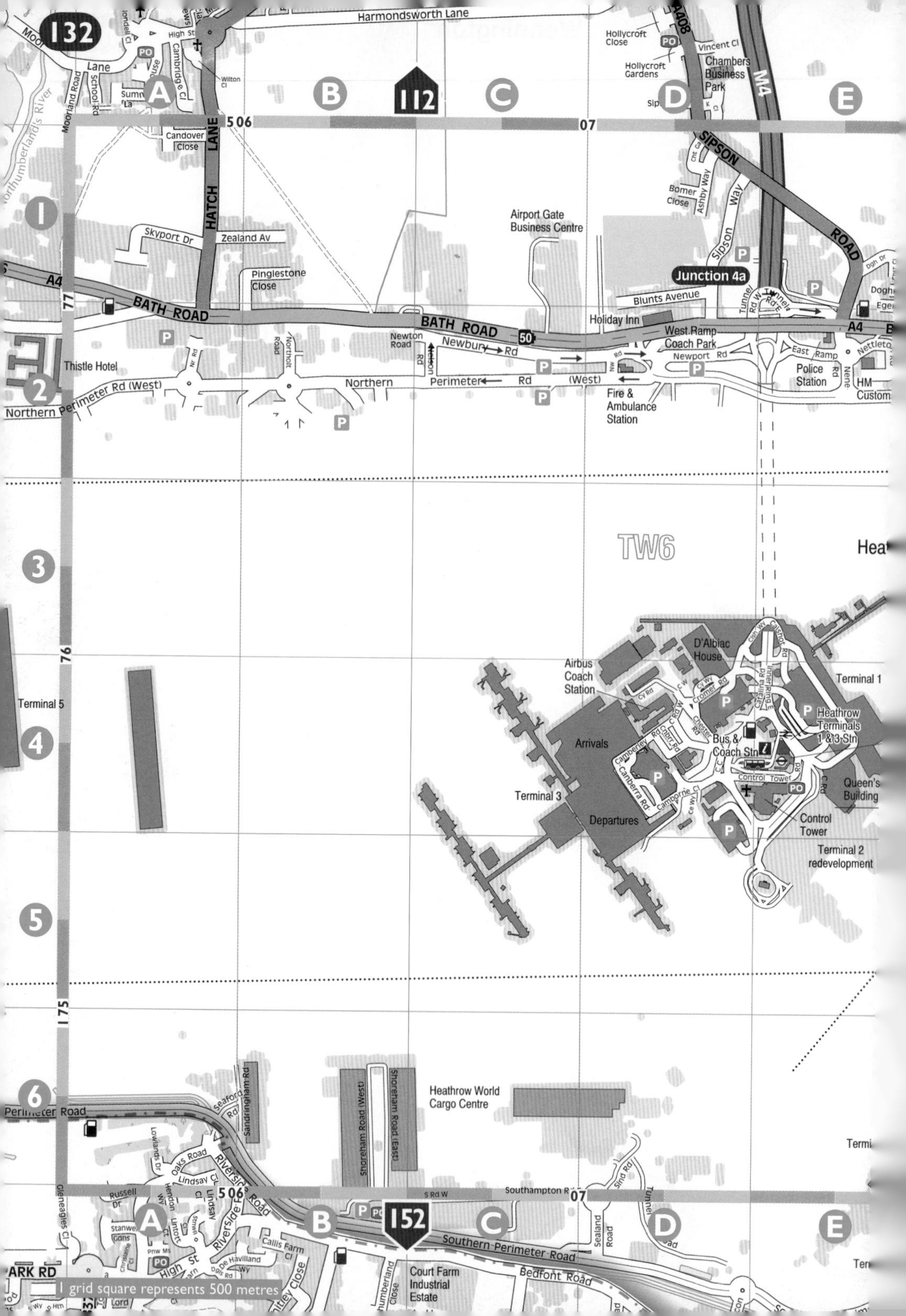
112
Harmondsworth Lane
Moor Lane
School Rd
Moorland Road
Cambridge Cl
High St
Wilton Cl
Northumberlands River
Candover Close
HATCH LANE
Hollycroft Close
Hollycroft Gardens
Vincent Cl
Chambers Business Park
A408
M4
SIPSON ROAD
Bomer Close
Ashby Way
Sipson Way
Airport Gate Business Centre
Skyport Dr
Zealand Av
Pinglestone Close
Junction 4a
Blunts Avenue
A4
BATH ROAD
Holiday Inn
West Ramp Coach Park
Newton Road
Newbury Rd
Nelson Rd
Newport Rd
East Ramp
Police Station
HM Customs
Thistle Hotel
Northern Perimeter Rd (West)
Northern Perimeter Rd (West)
Fire & Ambulance Station
TW6
Heat
D'Albiac House
Airbus Coach Station
Terminal 1
Heathrow Terminals 1 & 3 Stn
Bus & Coach Stn
Arrivals
Terminal 3
Departures
Control Tower Rd
Queen's Building
Control Tower
Terminal 2 redevelopment
Camberley Rd
Canberra Rd
Camborne Cl
Cromer Rd
Chester Rd
Terminal 5
Heathrow World Cargo Centre
Shoreham Road (West)
Shoreham Road (East)
Sandringham Rd
Seaford Rd
Perimeter Road
Lowlands Dr
Oaks Road
Lindsay Cl
Riverside Road
Russell Dr
Hendon Wy
Southampton Rd
Sealand Road
Southern Perimeter Road
Bedfont Road
Court Farm Industrial Estate
Callis Farm Cl
High St
Stanwell Gdns
De Havilland Wy
152
ARK RD
Gleneagles Cl
1 grid square represents 500 metres

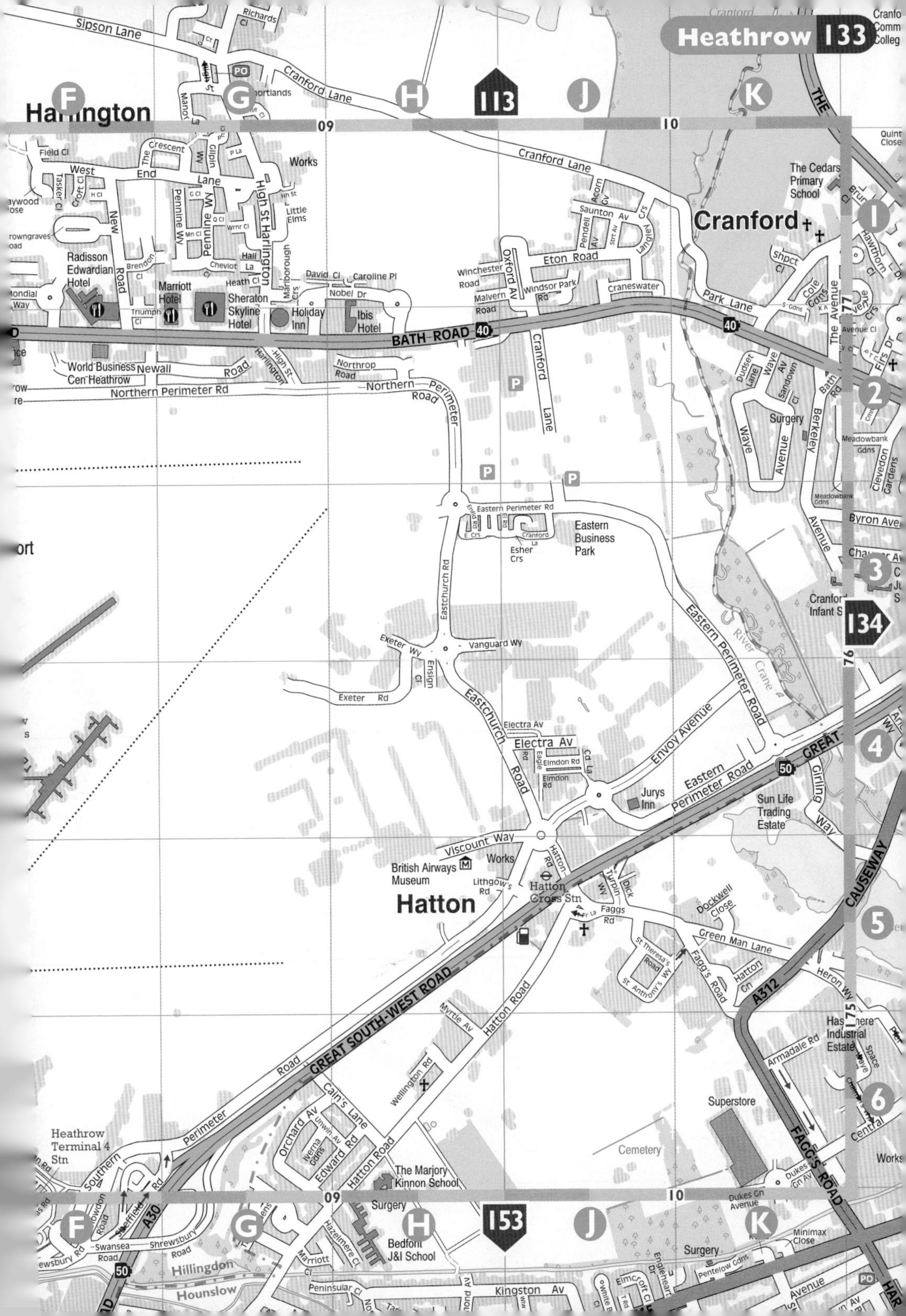
Heathrow 133
113
134
153
Harlington
Cranford
Hatton
Sipson Lane
Cranford Lane
West End Lane
High St Harlington
New Road
Radisson Edwardian Hotel
Marriott Hotel
Sheraton Skyline Hotel
Holiday Inn
Ibis Hotel
BATH ROAD
World Business Cen Heathrow
Newall Road
Northrop Road
Northern Perimeter Rd
Northern Perimeter Road
Works
Little Elms
Marlborough Crs
David Cl
Caroline Pl
Nobel Dr
Winchester Road
Malvern Road
Oxford Av
Windsor Park Rd
Eton Road
Saunton Av
Acorn Gv
Craneswater
Cranford Lane
Park Lane
The Cedars Primary School
The Avenue
Berkeley Avenue
Wave Avenue
Surgery
Meadowbank Gdns
Clevedon Gardens
Byron Ave
Cranford Infant S
Eastern Perimeter Rd
Eastern Business Park
Esher Crs
Eastchurch Rd
Eastchurch Road
Vanguard Wy
Exeter Wy
Exeter Rd
Ensign Cl
Eastern Perimeter Road
River Crane
Envoy Avenue
Electra Av
Elmdon Rd
Jurys Inn
Sun Life Trading Estate
Girling Way
Viscount Way
British Airways Museum
Hatton Cross Stn
Lithgow's Rd
Hatton Rd
Faggs Rd
Dockwell Close
Green Man Lane
St Theresa's Road
St Anthony's Wy
Fagg's Road
Hatton Gn
GREAT SOUTH-WEST ROAD
Perimeter Road
Hatton Road
Myrtle Av
Wellington Rd
Cain's Lane
Orchard Av
Edward Rd
The Marjory Kinnon School
Heathrow Terminal 4 Stn
Southern Perimeter Rd
Sheffield Rd
A30
A312
CAUSEWAY
FAGG'S ROAD
Heron Wy
Haslemere Industrial Estate
Armadale Rd
Superstore
Cemetery
Dukes Gn Av
Dukes Gn Avenue
Minimax Close
Surgery
Bedfont J&I School
Hazelmere Cl
Marriott Cl
Swansea Road
Shrewsbury Road
Hillingdon
Hounslow
Peninsular Cl
Kingston Av
Pentelow Gdns
Englehearts Dr
Works

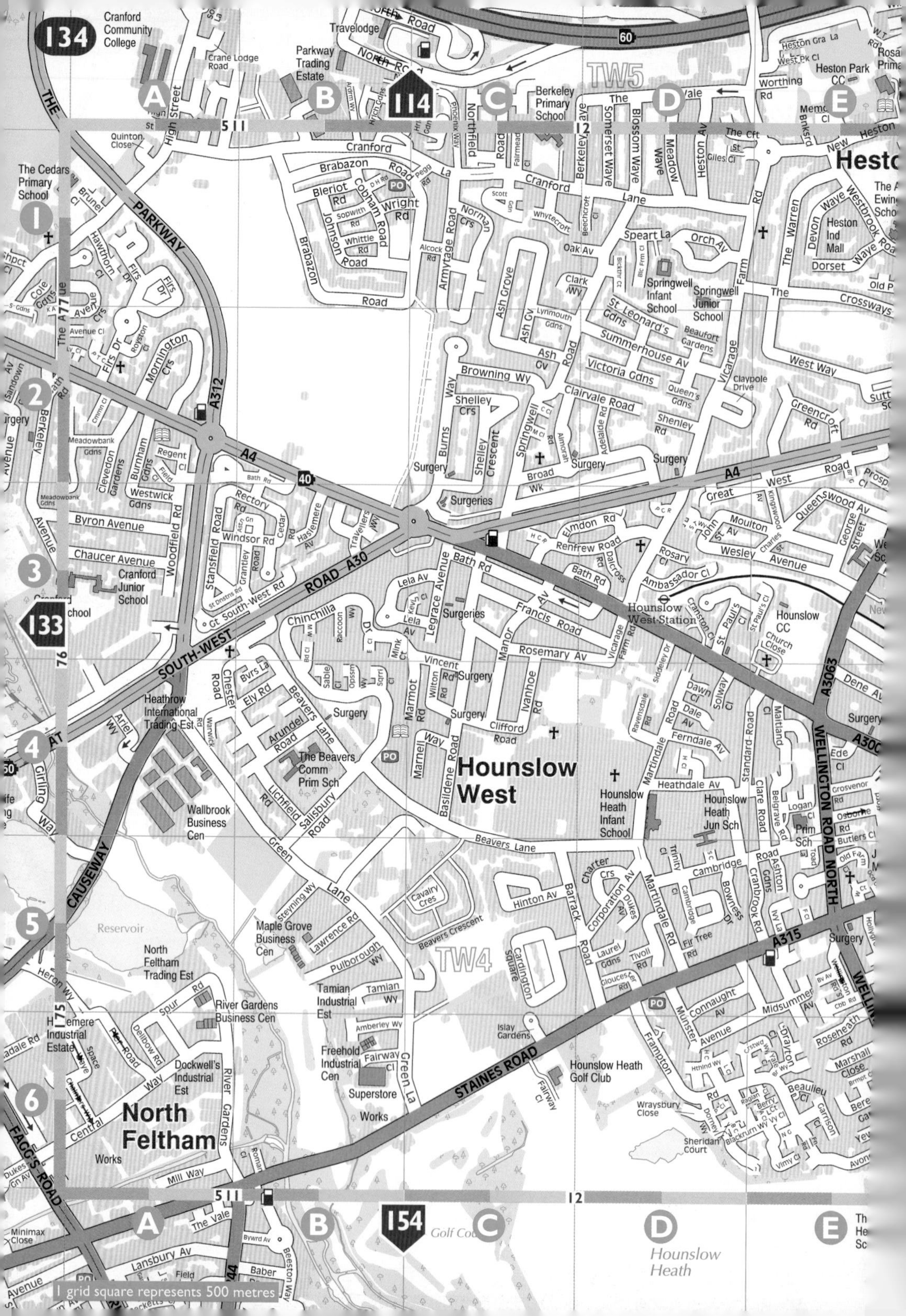
Cranford Community College
Travelodge
North Road
Crane Lodge Road
Parkway Trading Estate
114
60
TW5
Heston Gra La
West Pk Cl
Heston Park CC
Worthing Rd
Berkeley Primary School
The Somerset Wave
Blossom Wave
Meadow Wave
Heston Av
Vale
The Cft
Giles Cl
Memo Cl
New Heston
Heston
High Street
Quinton Close
Cranford
Brabazon Road
Bleriot Rd
Cobham Road
Wright Rd
Sopwith
Whittle Rd
Johnson Road
Brabazon Road
Pegg Rd
Northfield Road
Fairmead Cl
Cranford La
Cranford Lane
Scott Gdn
Whytecroft
Beechcroft Cl
Armytage Road
Norman Crs
Alcock Rd
The Cedars Primary School
Brunel
Hawthorn Cl
Firs Dr
Parkway
Cole Gdns
The A77
Avenue Cl
Royston Cl
Mornington Crs
Speart La
Orch Av
Oak Av
Clark Wy
Ash Grove
Ash Gv
Lynmouth Gdns
Ash Road
Springwell Infant School
Springwell Junior School
St Leonard's Gdns
Beaufort Gardens
Summerhouse Av
Victoria Gdns
Queen's Gdns
Vicarage Farm Rd
Claypole Drive
The Warren
Devon Waye
Westbrook Road
Heston Ind Mall
Dorset Waye
The Crossways
West Way
Old Pk
Greencroft Rd
Sutt
Browning Wy
Shelley Crs
Shelley Crescent
Burns Way
Springwell
Almorah Rd
Adelaide Rd
Clairvale Road
Shenley Rd
Surgery
Broad Wk
A4
40
Great West Road
Sandown
Berkeley Avenue
Meadowbank Gdns
Clevedon Gardens
Burnham Gdns
Regent Cl
Westwick Gdns
Woodfield Rd
A312
Byron Avenue
Chaucer Avenue
Cranford Junior School
133
Bath Rd
Rectory Rd
Windsor Rd
Cedar Rd
Haslemere Av
Travellers Wy
Stansfield Road
Grantley Road
Gt South-West Rd
Surgeries
Elmdon Rd
Renfrew Road
Dalcross Rd
Moulton Av
Kingswood Av
Queenswood Av
George Street
John St
Charles St
Wesley Avenue
Rosary Cl
Ambassador Cl
Hounslow West Station
Cranston Cl
St Paul's Cl
Hounslow CC
Church Close
Lela Av
Legrace Avenue
Bath Rd
Francis Road
Manor Av
Rosemary Av
Chinchilla Dr
Raccoon Wy
Mink Ct
Sable Cl
Vincent Rd
Wilton Rd
South-West Road A30
Chester Road
Bvrs La
Ely Rd
Beavers Lane
Heathrow International Trading Est
Ariel Wy
Warwick Rd
Arundel Road
The Beavers Comm Prim Sch
Marmot Rd
Marnell Way
Basildene Road
Clifford Road
Ivanhoe Rd
Hounslow West
Siddeley Dr
Ravensdale Rd
Martindale Road
Dawn Cl
Dale Av
Ferndale Av
Solway Cl
Standard Road
Maitland Cl
A3063
Dene Av
Wellington Road North
Surgery
A30
Ede Cl
Grosvenor Rd
Osborne Rd
Butlers Cl
Old Farm Rd
Girling Way
Wallbrook Business Cen
Lichfield Rd
Salisbury Road
Heathdale Av
Hounslow Heath Infant School
Hounslow Heath Jun Sch
Clare Road
Belgrave Rd
Logan Cl
Prim Sch
Beavers Lane
Green Lane
Causeway
Reservoir
North Feltham Trading Est
Steyning Wy
Maple Grove Business Cen
Lawrence Rd
Pulborough Wy
Cavalry Cres
Beavers Crescent
TW4
Hinton Av
Barrack Road
Charter Crs
Corporation Av
Dukes Av
Martindale Rd
Trinity Cl
Cambridge Cl
Cambridge Road
Bowness Dr
Cranbrook Rd
Ashton Gdns
Ivy La
Fir Tree Rd
Cardington Square
Laurel Gdns
Tivoli Rd
Gloucester Rd
A315
Surgery
Heron Wy
Haslemere Industrial Estate
Spur Rd
River Gardens Business Cen
Tamian Industrial Est
Tamian Wy
Amberley Wy
Islay Gardens
Munster Avenue
Connaught Av
Midsummer Av
Frampton
Drayton Cl
Roseheath Rd
Marshall Close
Dellbow Rd
Central Way
Dockwell's Industrial Est
River Gardens
Freehold Industrial Cen
Fairway Cl
Superstore
Works
Green La
Staines Road
Hounslow Heath Golf Club
Fairway Cl
Wraysbury Close
Beaulieu Cl
Garrison Cl
Raglan Cl
Berry Cl
Blackburn Wy
Vimy Cl
Sheridan Court
Dorney Wy
North Feltham
Works
Dukes Gn Av
Fagg's Road
Romaine Cl
Mill Way
511
12
A
B
C
D
E
1
2
3
4
5
6
76
175
The Vale
Bywrd Av
Minimax Close
Lansbury Av
Field
Baber
Beeston Way
Avenue
A244
154
Golf Cou
Hounslow Heath
1 grid square represents 500 metres

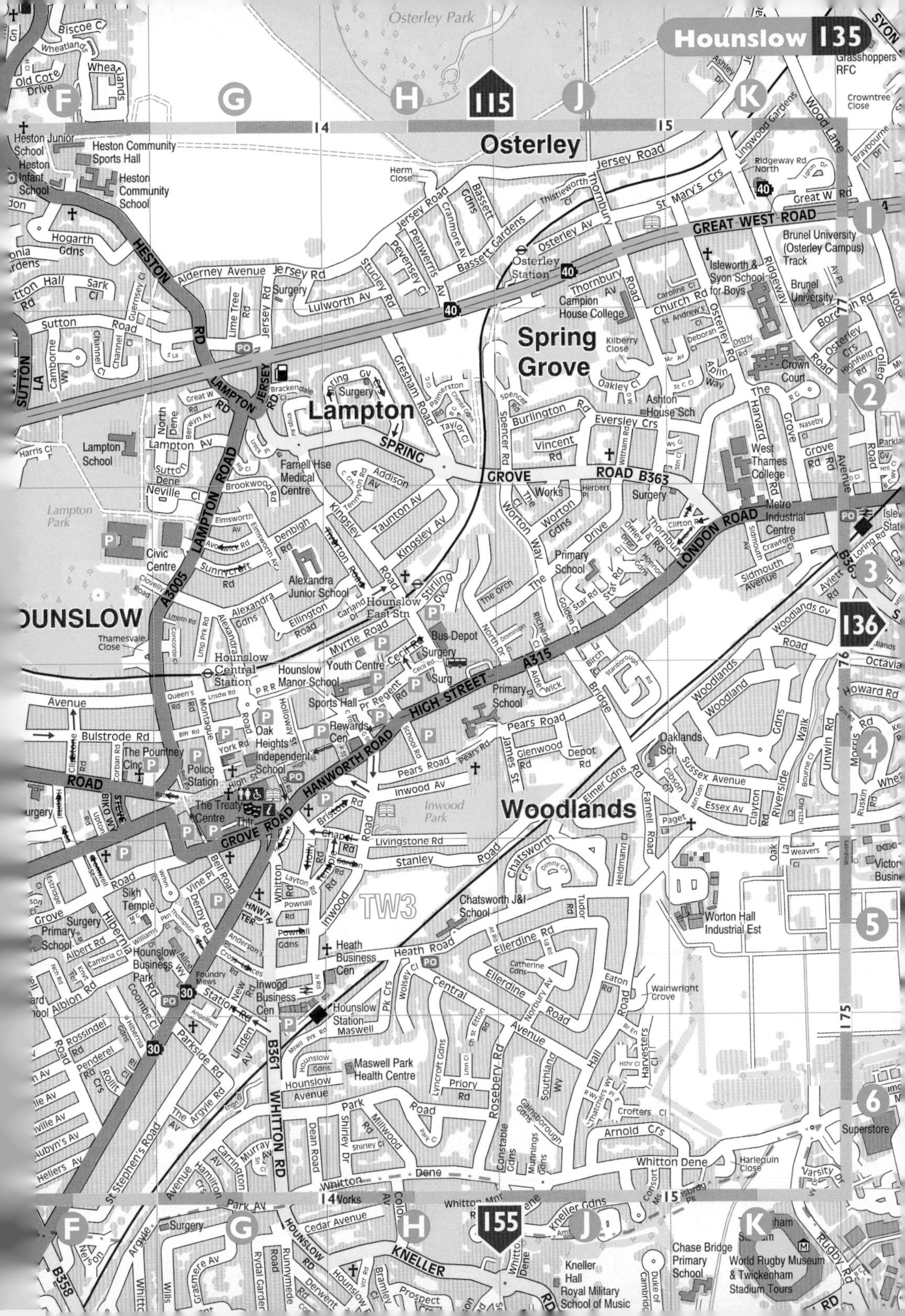
Osterley
Spring Grove
Lampton
Woodlands
HOUNSLOW
Osterley Park
Lampton Park
Inwood Park
TW3
GREAT WEST ROAD
LONDON ROAD
HIGH STREET
HANWORTH ROAD
GROVE ROAD
HESTON RD
LAMPTON ROAD
WHITTON RD
Hounslow Central Station
Hounslow East Stn
Osterley Station
Hounslow Station
Civic Centre
Brunel University (Osterley Campus) Track
West Thames College
Isleworth & Syon School for Boys
Heston Community School
Lampton School
Alexandra Junior School
Chatsworth J&I School
Maswell Park Health Centre
Worton Hall Industrial Est
World Rugby Museum & Twickenham Stadium Tours
Kneller Hall Royal Military School of Music
Chase Bridge Primary School
115
136
155

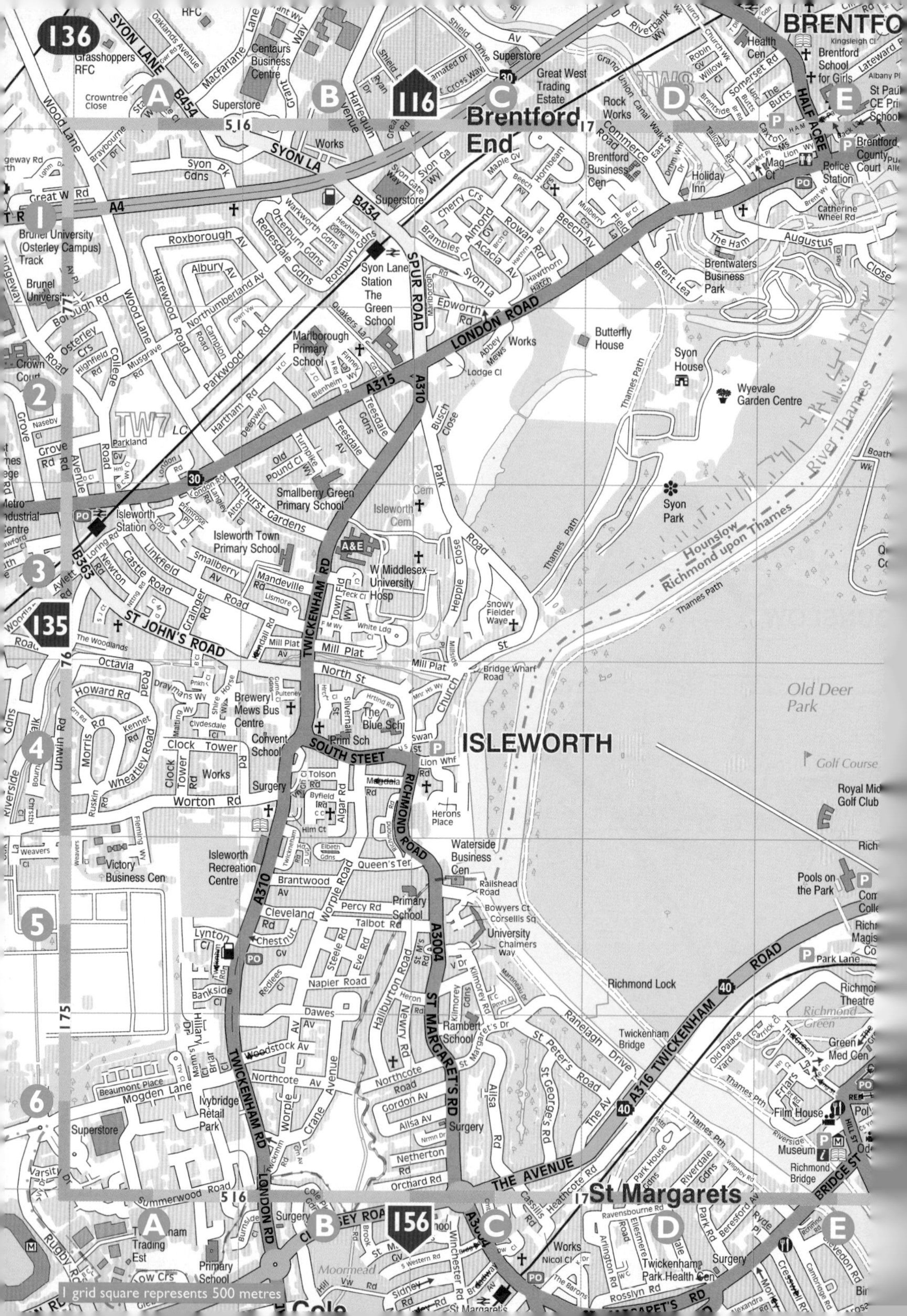
136
116
135
156
BRENTFORD
Brentford End
ISLEWORTH
St Margarets
Grasshoppers RFC
Syon Lane
Oaklands Avenue
Macfarlane Lane
Centaurs Business Centre
Grant Way
Harlequin Avenue
Shield Drive
Superstore
Great West Trading Estate
Rock Works
Commerce Road
Grand Union Canal Walk
Riverbank Wy
Health Cen
Somerset Rd
The Butts
Half Acre
Brentford School for Girls
St Paul's CE Pri School
Brentford County Court
Police Station
Catherine Wheel Rd
Holiday Inn
Brentford Business Cen
Crowntree Close
Wood Lane
Braybourne Dr
Works
Syon La
Syon Pk Gdns
Syon Gate Wy
Great W Rd
A4
B454
B434
Brunel University (Osterley Campus) Track
Brunel University
Roxborough Av
Albury Av
Harewood Road
Northumberland Av
Redesdale Gdns
Otterburn Gdns
Warkworth Gdns
Rothbury Gdns
Syon Lane Station
The Green School
Spur Road
Maple Gv
Hornbeam Cres
Cherry Crs
Almond Gv
Rowan Rd
Acacia Av
Brambles Cl
Beech Av
Mulberry Cres
Field La
Hawthorn Hatch
Edworth Rd
The Ham
Augustus Close
Brentwaters Business Park
Brent Lea
London Road
A315
Abbey Mews
Works
Butterfly House
Syon House
Wyevale Garden Centre
Lodge Cl
Osterley Crs
Borough Rd
Crown Court
Highfield Rd
College Rd
Musgrave Rd
Campion Road
Parkwood Rd
Marlborough Primary School
Quakers La
Blenheim Wy
Teesdale Gdns
Teesdale Av
A310
Busch Close
Park Road
Thames Path
River Thames
Hounslow
Richmond upon Thames
TW7
Parkland
Naseby Cl
Grove Rd
Avenue Rd
Hartham Rd
Deepwell Cl
Turnpike Wy
Old Pound Cl
Smallberry Green Primary School
Isleworth Cem
Syon Park
Metro Industrial Centre
Isleworth Station
Amhurst Gardens
Isleworth Town Primary School
Twickenham Rd
A&E
W Middlesex University Hosp
Hepple Close
Snowy Fielder Waye
B363
Loring Rd
Aylett Rd
Linkfield Road
Castle Road
Smallberry Av
Mandeville Rd
Lismore Cl
Grainger Rd
Newton Rd
St John's Road
The Woodlands
Kendall Rd
Mill Plat Av
Mill Plat
Town Fld Wy
Teck Cl
White Ldg Cl
Bridge Wharf Road
Octavia Road
Howard Rd
Draymans Wy
Brewery Mews Bus Centre
North St
Church St
Silverhall St
The Blue Sch
Prim Sch
Convent School
South Street
Swan St
Lion Whf Rd
Old Deer Park
Golf Course
Royal Mid Golf Club
Morris Rd
Kennet Rd
Wheatley Road
Clock Tower Rd
Works
Surgery
Riverside Wk
Unwin Rd
Worton Rd
Ruskin Av
Tolson Rd
Byfield Rd
Algar Rd
Richmond Road
Herons Place
Victory Business Cen
Weavers Cl
Isleworth Recreation Centre
Brantwood Av
Worple Road
Queen's Ter
Waterside Business Cen
Railshead Road
Pools on the Park
Percy Rd
Primary School
Cleveland Rd
Talbot Rd
A3004
Bowyers Ct
Corsellis Sq
University
Chalmers Way
Lynton Cl
Chestnut Gv
Steele Rd
Eve Rd
Napier Road
Redlees Cl
Bankside Cl
Halliburton Road
Newry Rd
St Margaret's Rd
Kilmorey Rd
Richmond Lock
Park Lane
A316 Twickenham Road
Richmond Theatre
Richmond Green
Hillary Dr
Dawes Av
Woodstock Av
Rambert School
St Margaret's Dr
Ranelagh Drive
Twickenham Bridge
St Peter's Road
St George's Rd
Old Palace Yard
Green Med Cen
Beaumont Place
Mogden Lane
Northcote Av
Northcote Road
Ivybridge Retail Park
Crane Avenue
Gordon Av
Ailsa Av
Ailsa Rd
Surgery
Superstore
Netherton Rd
Orchard Rd
The Avenue
Heathcote Rd
Park House Gdns
Riverdale Gdns
Thames Pth
Film House
Friars La
Museum
Richmond Bridge
Bridge St
Hill St
Summerwood Road
London Rd
Twickenham Trading Est
Surgery
Primary School
Winchester Rd
Works
Nicol Cl
Ravensbourne Rd
Arlington Rd
Ellesmere Road
Dale Rd
Park Rd
Beresford Av
Ryde Pl
Twickenham Park Health Cen
Surgery
Rosslyn Rd
Cresswell Rd
Cambridge Rd
Clevedon Rd
Moormead
1 grid square represents 500 metres

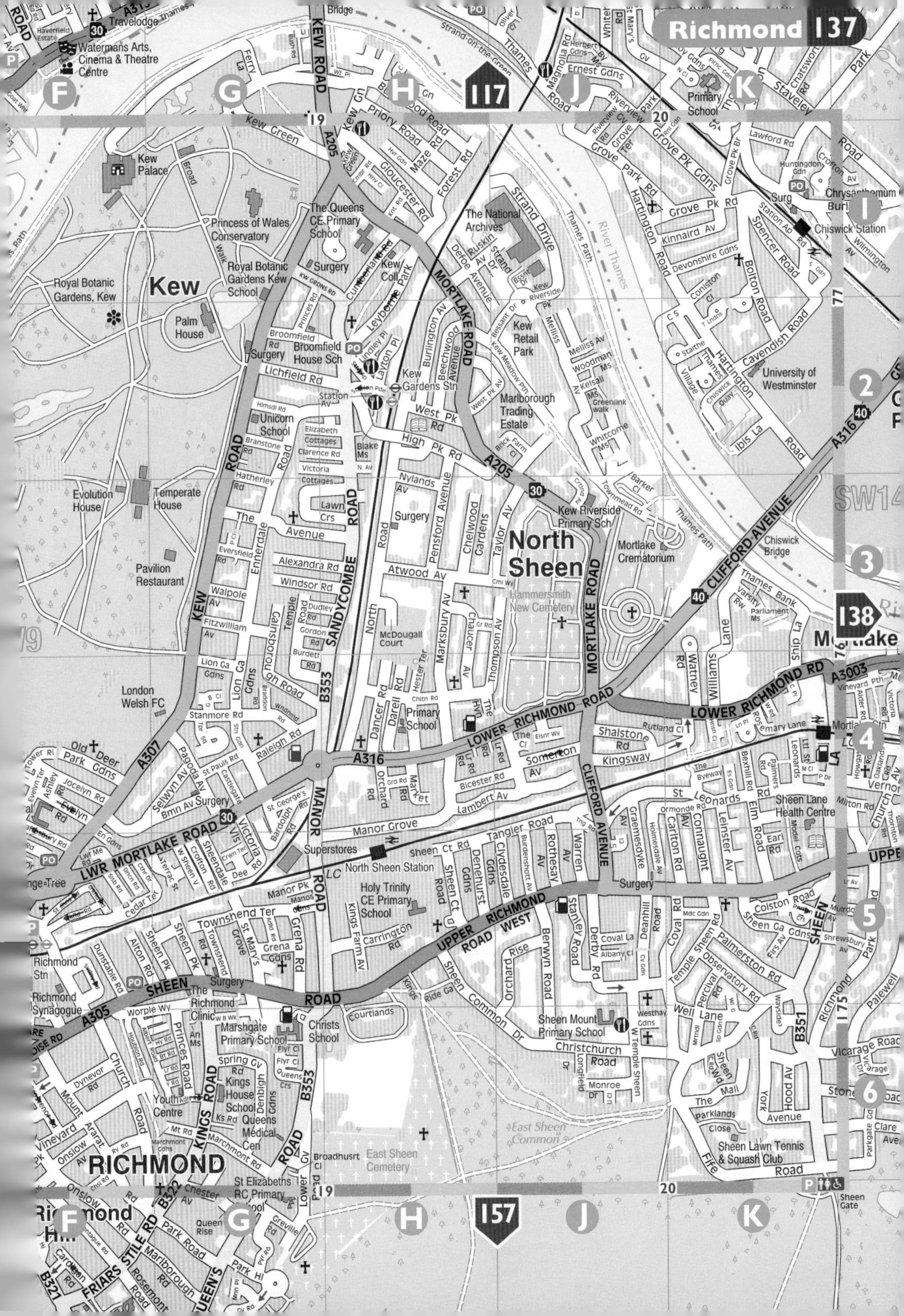
Kew
North Sheen
RICHMOND
Richmond Hill
Mortlake
Royal Botanic Gardens, Kew
Kew Palace
Princess of Wales Conservatory
Royal Botanic Gardens Kew School
Palm House
Evolution House
Temperate House
Pavilion Restaurant
London Welsh FC
Travelodge
Watermans Arts, Cinema & Theatre Centre
Haverfield Estate
The Queens CE Primary School
Surgery
Kew Coll
Broomfield House Sch
Kew Gardens Stn
Unicorn School
The National Archives
Kew Retail Park
Marlborough Trading Estate
Kew Riverside Primary Sch
Mortlake Crematorium
Hammersmith New Cemetery
McDougall Court
Primary School
Chiswick Station
Chiswick Bridge
University of Westminster
Primary School
Superstores
North Sheen Station
Holy Trinity CE Primary School
Sheen Lane Health Centre
Sheen Mount Primary School
Sheen Lawn Tennis & Squash Club
Richmond Stn
Richmond Synagogue
The Richmond Clinic
Marshgate Primary School
Christs School
Kings House School
Youth Centre
Queens Medical Cen
St Elizabeths RC Primary School
East Sheen Common
East Sheen Cemetery
Sheen Gate
Courtlands
River Thames
Thames Path
KEW ROAD
MORTLAKE ROAD
SANDYCOMBE ROAD
MANOR ROAD
CLIFFORD AVENUE
LOWER RICHMOND ROAD
LWR MORTLAKE ROAD
UPPER RICHMOND ROAD WEST
SHEEN ROAD
KINGS ROAD
A205
A316
A307
A305
A3003
B353
B351
B322
B321
SW14
117
138
157
F
G
H
J
K
I
2
3
4
5
6
19
20
30
40

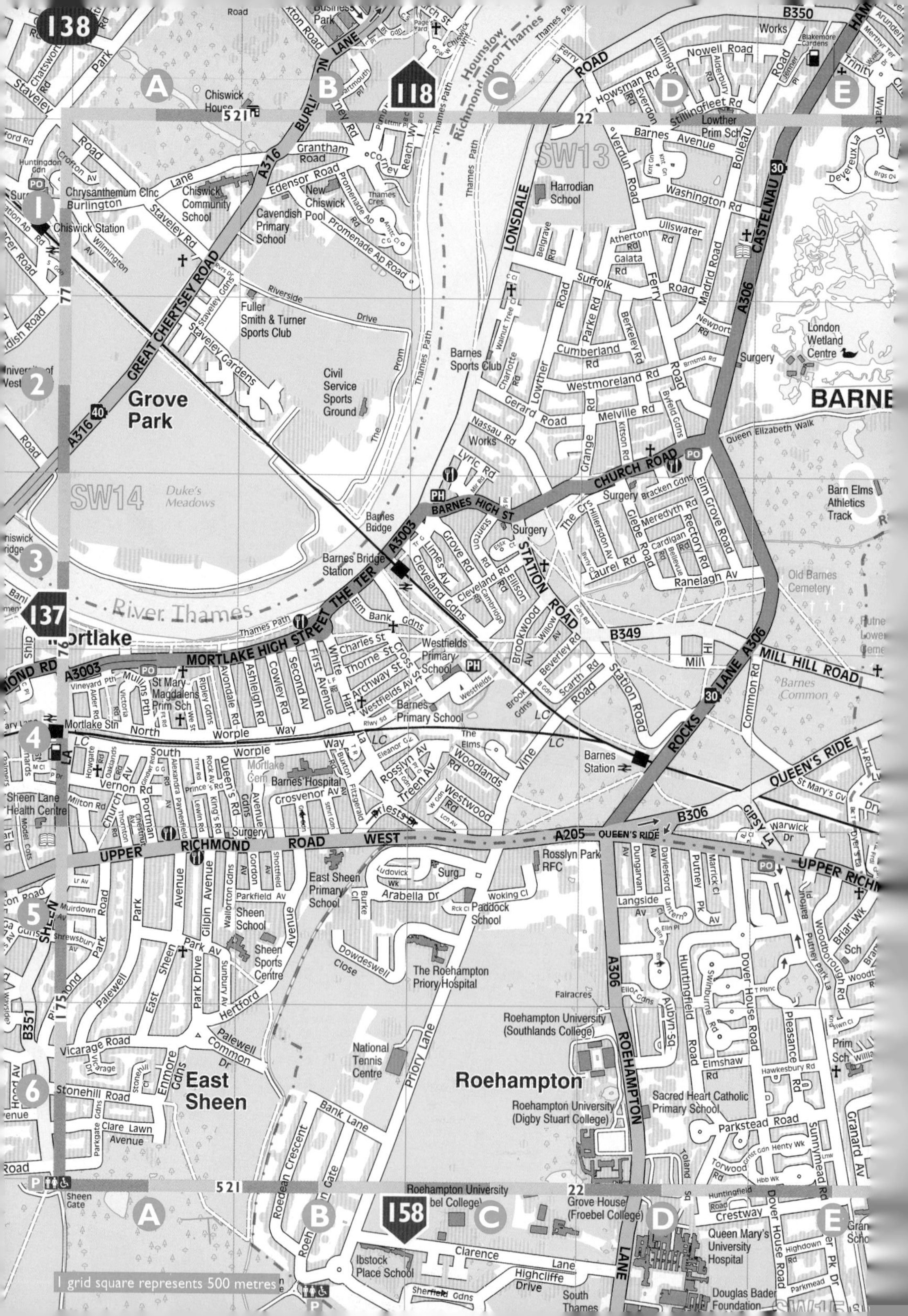
118
137
158
Grove Park
SW14
Duke's Meadows
River Thames
Mortlake
SW13
BARNES
East Sheen
Roehampton
Chiswick House
Chiswick Community School
Chiswick Station
Cavendish Primary School
Fuller Smith & Turner Sports Club
Civil Service Sports Ground
Barnes Sports Club
Harrodian School
Lowther Prim Sch
London Wetland Centre
Barn Elms Athletics Track
Old Barnes Cemetery
Barnes Common
Barnes Bridge
Barnes Bridge Station
Barnes Station
Mortlake Stn
Westfields Primary School
Barnes Primary School
St Mary Magdalens Prim Sch
Barnes Hospital
Mortlake Cem
Sheen Lane Health Centre
East Sheen Primary School
Sheen School
Sheen Sports Centre
Paddock School
Rosslyn Park RFC
The Roehampton Priory Hospital
National Tennis Centre
Roehampton University (Southlands College)
Roehampton University (Digby Stuart College)
Roehampton University Froebel College
Grove House (Froebel College)
Sacred Heart Catholic Primary School
Queen Mary's University Hospital
Douglas Bader Foundation
Ibstock Place School
GREAT CHERTSEY ROAD
BURLINGTON LANE
MORTLAKE HIGH STREET
THE TER
BARNES HIGH ST
CHURCH ROAD
STATION ROAD
LONSDALE ROAD
CASTELNAU
ROCKS LANE
MILL HILL ROAD
QUEEN'S RIDE
UPPER RICHMOND ROAD WEST
ROEHAMPTON LANE
A316
A3003
A306
A205
B349
B350
B306
B351
1 grid square represents 500 metres

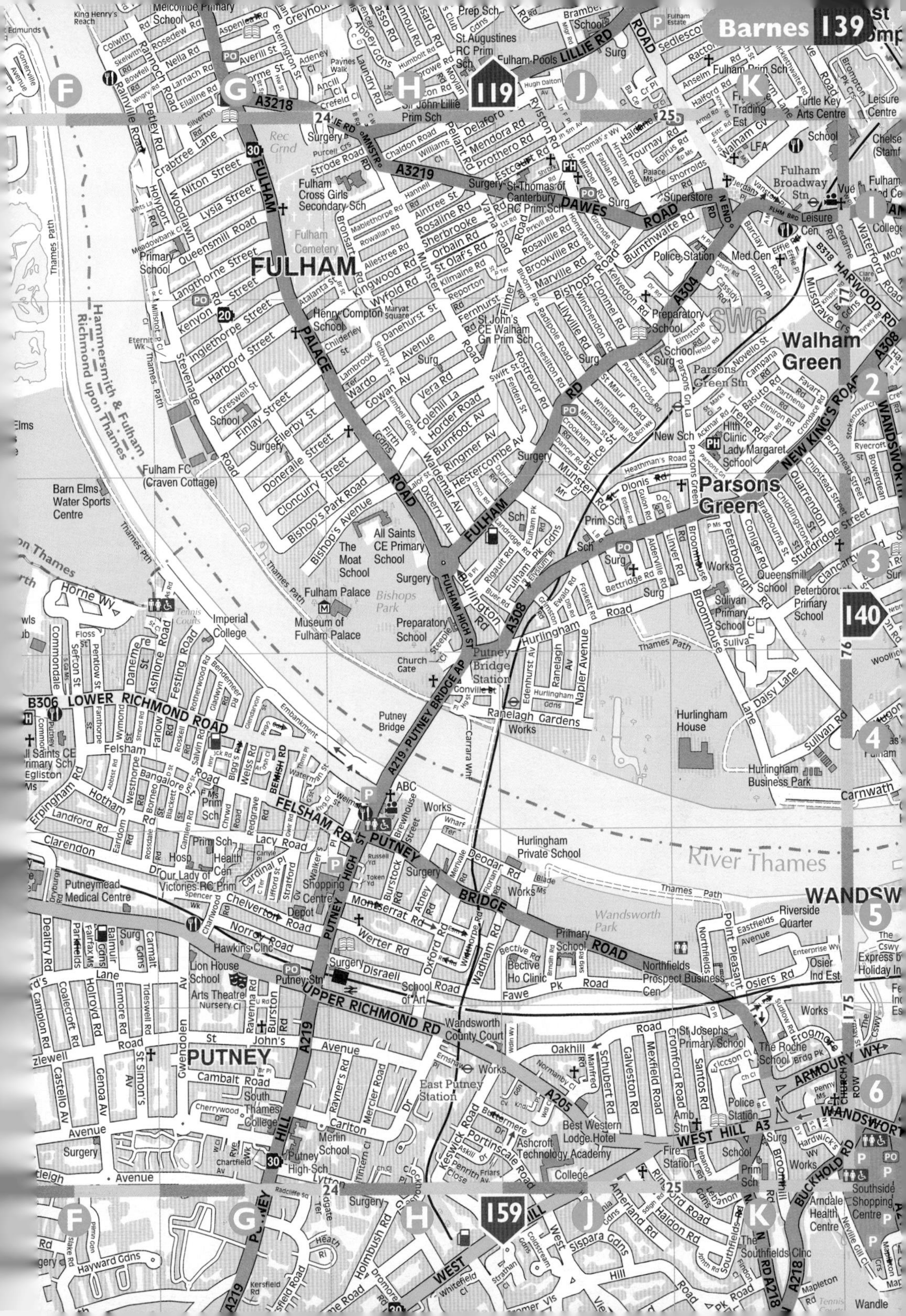
Barnes 139
119
140
159
FULHAM
PUTNEY
Walham Green
Parsons Green
WANDSWORTH
SW6
River Thames
Hammersmith & Fulham
Richmond upon Thames
Thames Path
A3218
A3219
A304
A308
A219
A205
A3
A218
B306
B318
LOWER RICHMOND ROAD
FULHAM PALACE ROAD
FULHAM HIGH ST
PUTNEY BRIDGE AP
PUTNEY BRIDGE ROAD
UPPER RICHMOND RD
PUTNEY HIGH ST
PUTNEY HILL
WEST HILL
DAWES ROAD
FULHAM RD
NEW KING'S ROAD
HARWOOD RD
LILLIE RD
NORTH END ROAD
ARMOURY WY
FELSHAM RD
BUCKHOLD RD
Hurlingham House
Hurlingham Business Park
Hurlingham Private School
Fulham Palace
Museum of Fulham Palace
Bishops Park
Fulham FC (Craven Cottage)
Barn Elms Water Sports Centre
Imperial College
Putney Bridge
Putney Bridge Station
Putney Stn
East Putney Station
Parsons Green Stn
Fulham Broadway Stn
Wandsworth Park
Ranelagh Gardens
Fulham Cemetery
Fulham Cross Girls Secondary Sch
All Saints CE Primary School
The Moat School
Henry Compton School
Sullivan Primary School
Peterborough Primary School
Queensmill School
Lady Margaret School
St Josephs Primary School
The Roche School
Ashcroft Technology Academy
Best Western Lodge Hotel
Putney High Sch
Merlin School
South Thames College
Lion House School
Arts Theatre Nursery Cl
Putneymead Medical Centre
Our Lady of Victories RC Prim
Putney Shopping Centre
Southside Shopping Centre
Arndale Health Centre
The Southfields Clnc
Riverside Quarter
Northfields Prospect Business Cen
Osier Ind Est
Wandsworth County Court
Police Station
Fire Station
Leisure Cen
Fulham Pools
Turtle Key Arts Centre
F G H J K
1 2 3 4 5 6
24 25

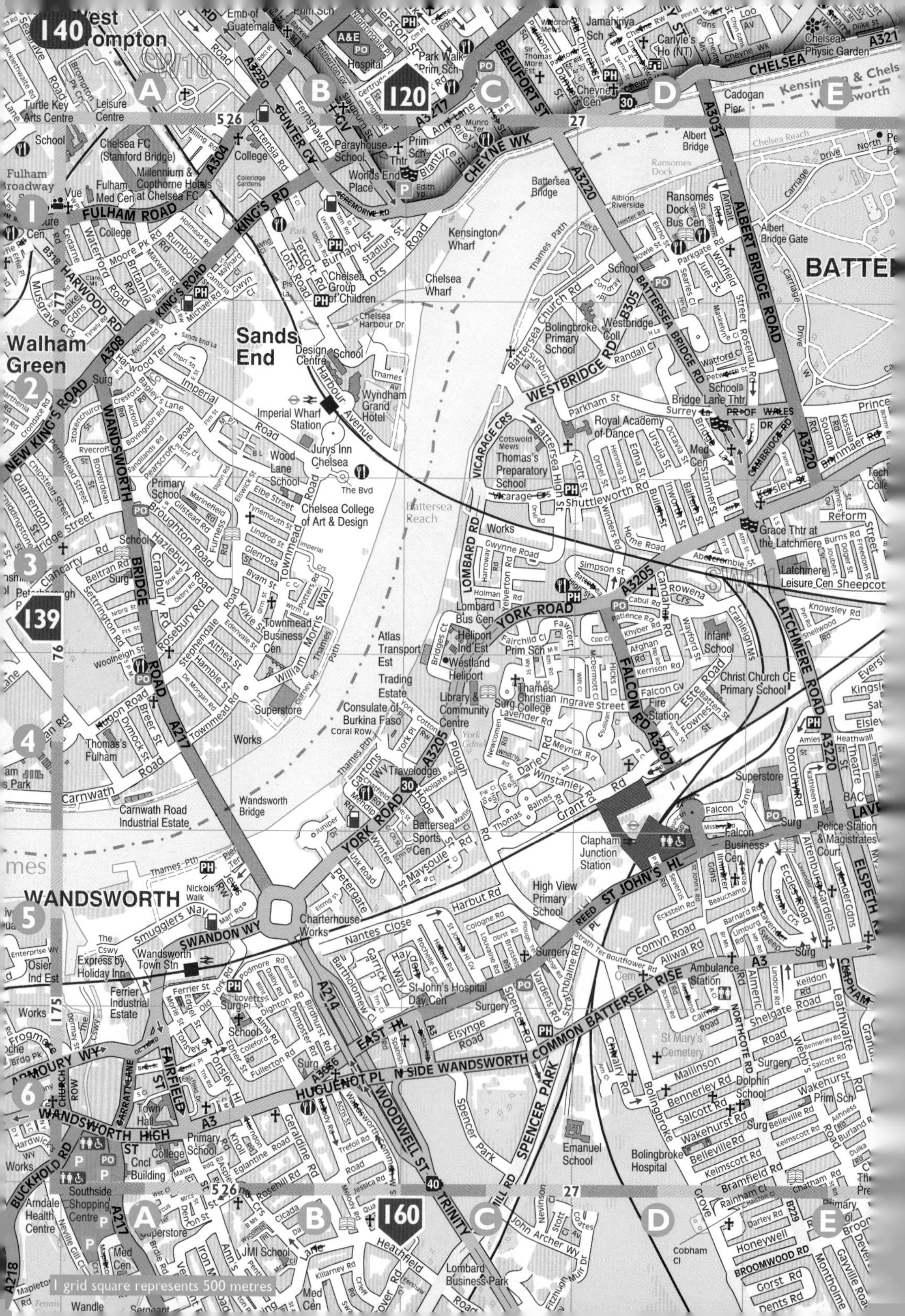

140
West Brompton
120
139
160
Chelsea FC (Stamford Bridge)
Fulham Broadway
Walham Green
Sands End
Imperial Wharf Station
Chelsea Harbour
Battersea Bridge
Albert Bridge
Chelsea Physic Garden
Kensington Wharf
Chelsea Wharf
Battersea Reach
CHEYNE WK
KING'S RD
FULHAM ROAD
NEW KING'S ROAD
WANDSWORTH BRIDGE ROAD
YORK ROAD
BATTERSEA BRIDGE RD
ALBERT BRIDGE ROAD
LATCHMERE ROAD
FALCON RD
WESTBRIDGE RD
VICARAGE CRS
LOMBARD RD
ST JOHN'S HL
SWANDON WY
Clapham Junction Station
Wandsworth Town Stn
WANDSWORTH
WANDSWORTH HIGH ST
Wandsworth Bridge
Westland Heliport
Royal Academy of Dance
Thomas's Preparatory School
Chelsea College of Art & Design
Grace Thtr at the Latchmere
Latchmere Leisure Cen
Christ Church CE Primary School
Carnwath Road Industrial Estate
Southside Shopping Centre
Emanuel School
Bolingbroke Hospital
St Mary's Cemetery
N SIDE WANDSWORTH COMMON
BATTERSEA RISE
SPENCER PARK
TRINITY RD
1 grid square represents 500 metres

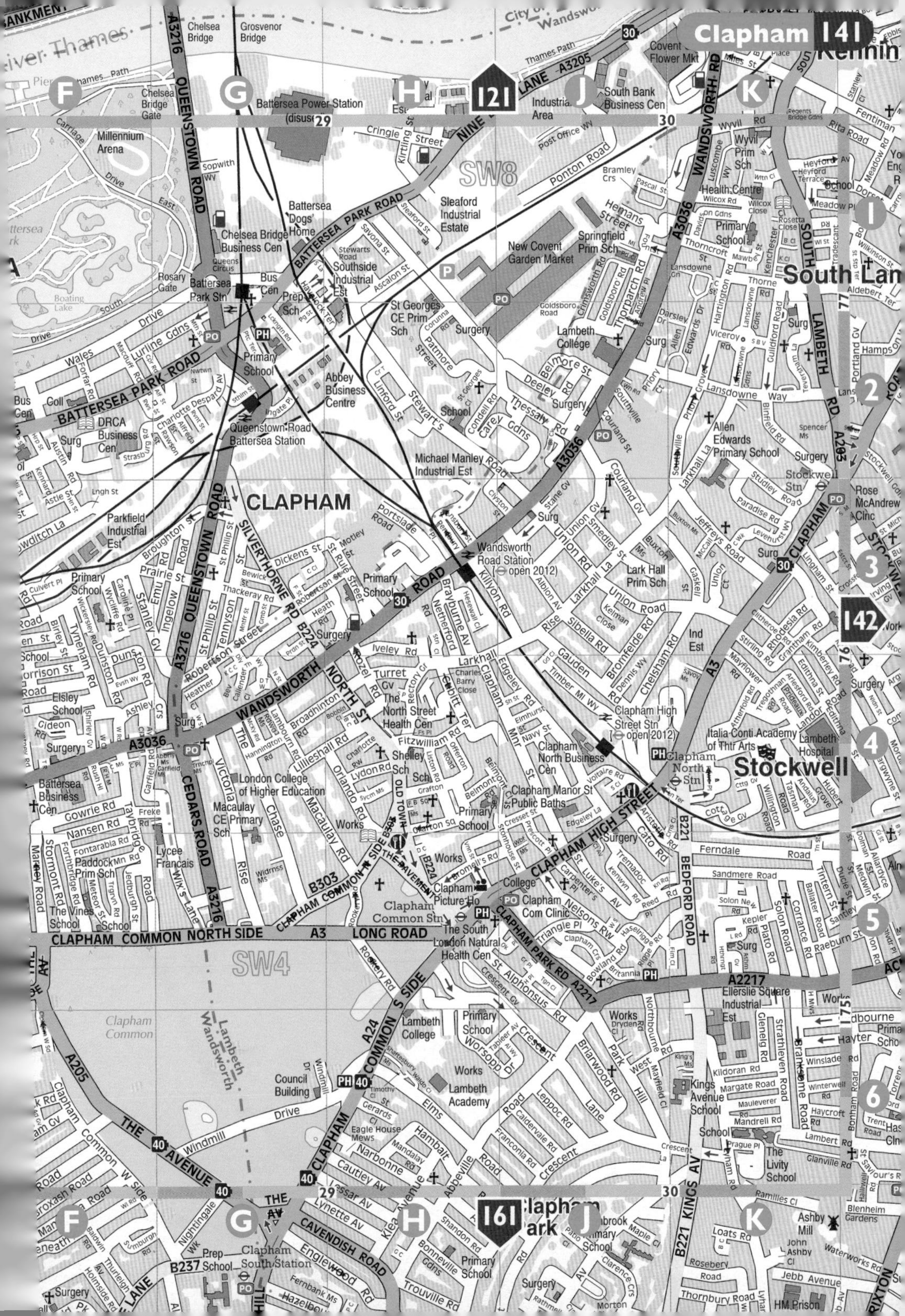
River Thames
Chelsea Bridge
Grosvenor Bridge
Battersea Power Station
Millennium Arena
Chelsea Bridge Gate
Rosary Gate
Boating Lake
Covent Garden Flower Mkt
South Bank Business Cen
Industrial Area
Thames Path
NINE ELMS LANE A3205
QUEENSTOWN ROAD
BATTERSEA PARK ROAD
Battersea Dogs' Home
Chelsea Bridge Business Cen
Battersea Park Stn
Queenstown Road Battersea Station
Southside Industrial Est
Sleaford Industrial Estate
New Covent Garden Market
Springfield Prim Sch
Ponton Road
SW8
Cringle Street
Kirtling St
Post Office Wy
Wyvil Rd
Wyvil Prim Sch
Health Centre
Primary School
WANDSWORTH RD
A3036
SOUTH LAMBETH RD
South Lambeth
Lambeth College
Abbey Business Centre
St Georges CE Prim Sch
DRCA Business Cen
Michael Manley Industrial Est
CLAPHAM
Parkfield Industrial Est
Wandsworth Road Station (open 2012)
Lark Hall Prim Sch
Allen Edwards Primary School
Stockwell Stn
Rose McAndrew Clnc
Lansdowne Way
Stockwell
Clapham High Street Stn (open 2012)
Clapham North Stn
Clapham North Business Cen
Clapham Manor St Public Baths
Italia Conti Academy of Thtr Arts
Lambeth Hospital
WANDSWORTH ROAD
SILVERTHORNE RD B224
CEDARS ROAD
A3216
Battersea Business Cen
London College of Higher Education
Macaulay CE Primary Sch
Lycee Francais
Paddock Prim Sch
The Vines School
The North Street Health Cen
CLAPHAM HIGH STREET
BEDFORD ROAD
B221
Clapham Picture Ho
Clapham Com Clinic
Clapham Common Stn
The South London Natural Health Cen
CLAPHAM COMMON NORTH SIDE
A3
LONG ROAD
SW4
Clapham Common
Lambeth
Wandsworth
CLAPHAM PARK RD A2217
A2217
Ellerslie Square Industrial Est
Kings Avenue School
The Livity School
Lambeth Academy
Council Building
Windmill Drive
THE AVENUE
A205
COMMON S SIDE
A24
CAVENDISH ROAD
Clapham South Station
B221 KINGS AV
Ashby Mill
Clapham Park
HM Prison
121
142
161

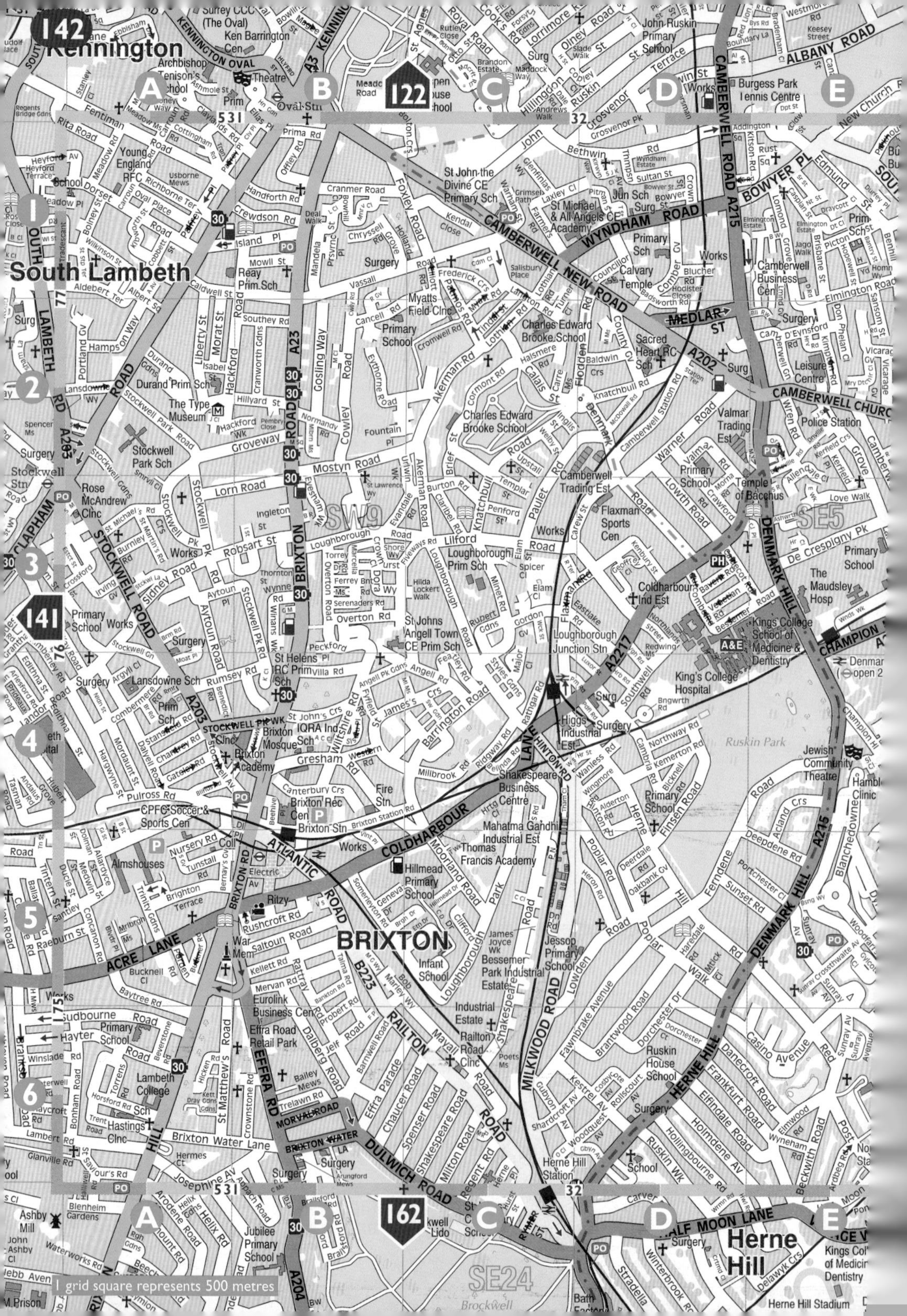
142
Kennington
Surrey CCC (The Oval)
Ken Barrington Cen
KENNINGTON OVAL
Archbishop Tenison's School
Theatre
Oval Stn
A3 KENNINGTON
122
Cook's Rd
Lorrimore Road
Olney Road
John Ruskin Primary School
CAMBERWELL ROAD A215
ALBANY ROAD
Burgess Park Tennis Centre
A B C D E
Fentiman
Rita Road
Meadow Rd
Young England RFC
Richborne Ter
Usborne Mews
Dorset Rd
Oval Place
Handforth Rd
Crewdson Rd
Cranmer Road
Foxley Road
St John the Divine CE Primary Sch
Kendal Close
CAMBERWELL NEW ROAD
WYNDHAM ROAD
BOWYER PL
St Michael & All Angels CE Academy
Jun Sch
Primary Sch
Calvary Temple
Camberwell Business Cen
South Lambeth
SOUTH LAMBETH RD A203
Island Pl
Reay Prim Sch
Vassall Road
Myatts Field Clnc
Primary School
Surgery
Charles Edward Brooke School
MEDLAR ST
Sacred Heart RC Sch
A202
Leisure Centre
Aldebert Ter
Caldwell St
Southey Rd
Liberty St
Morat St
Hackford Road
Cranworth Gdns
Gosling Way
Cowley Road
Akerman Rd
Durand Prim Sch
The Type Museum
Hillyard St
Groveway
Stockwell Park Rd
Stockwell Park Sch
Fountain Pl
CAMBERWELL CHURCH
Valmar Trading Est
Police Station
Stockwell Stn
Rose McAndrew Clnc
CLAPHAM
Lorn Road
Mostyn Road
BRIXTON ROAD A23
Camberwell Trading Est
Flaxman Sports Cen
Valmar Primary School
Temple of Bacchus
Love Walk
SW9
SE5
STOCKWELL ROAD
Robsart St
Loughborough Road
Lilford Road
Loughborough Prim Sch
Works
De Crespigny Pk
Primary School
The Maudsley Hosp
141
Primary School
Sidney Road
Aytoun Road
Stockwell Pk Rd
Overton Road
Hilda Lockert Walk
Coldharbour Ind Est
Kings College School of Medicine & Dentistry
A&E
CHAMPION
Surgery
Lansdowne Sch
Rumsey Rd
St Helens RC Prim Sch
Peckford Pl
St Johns Angell Town CE Prim Sch
Loughborough Junction Stn
A2217
King's College Hospital
Denmark Hill
Prim Sch
STOCKWELL PK WK
Brixton Mosque
IQRA Ind Sch
Barrington Road
Higgs Industrial Est
Surgery
Ruskin Park
Jewish Community Theatre
Brixton Academy
Gresham Rd
Millbrook Rd
Shakespeare Business Centre
HINTON RD
Primary School
Finsen Road
Pulross Rd
CPFC Soccer & Sports Cen
Canterbury Crs
Brixton Rec Cen
Fire Stn
Brixton Stn
Brixton Station Rd
COLDHARBOUR LANE
Mahatma Gandhi Industrial Est
Thomas Francis Academy
Nursery Rd
Almshouses
ATLANTIC ROAD
Works
Hillmead Primary School
Moorland Road
Brighton Terrace
Ritzy
Electric Av
Rushcroft Rd
BRIXTON
ACRE LANE
Saltoun Road
Infant School
Loughborough Park
James Joyce Wk
Bessemer Park Industrial Estate
Jessop Primary School
MILKWOOD ROAD
Herne Hill
DENMARK HILL A215
War Mem
Kellett Rd
Eurolink Business Cen
Effra Road Retail Park
B223
RAILTON ROAD
Industrial Estate
Railton Road Clnc
Sudbourne Road
Primary School
Lambeth College
Hastings Clnc
Brixton Water Lane
EFFRA RD
St Matthew's Road
Crownstone Rd
Trelawn Rd
MORVAL ROAD
BRIXTON WATER
Effra Parade
Chaucer Road
Spenser Road
Shakespeare Road
Milton Road
Fawnbrake Avenue
Brantwood Road
Ruskin House School
Surgery
Casino Avenue
Danecroft Road
Frankfurt Road
Elfindale Road
Holmdene Av
Hollingbourne Rd
Ruskin Wk
Herne Hill Station
School
Surgery
Surgery
Josephine Av
DULWICH ROAD
531
32
162
Blenheim Gardens
Ashby Mill
Jubilee Primary School
A204
Brockwell Lido
HALF MOON LANE
Herne Hill
Kings Coll of Medicine Dentistry
SE24
Brockwell
Herne Hill Stadium
1 grid square represents 500 metres
Stradella
Winterbrook Rd
Delawyk Crs

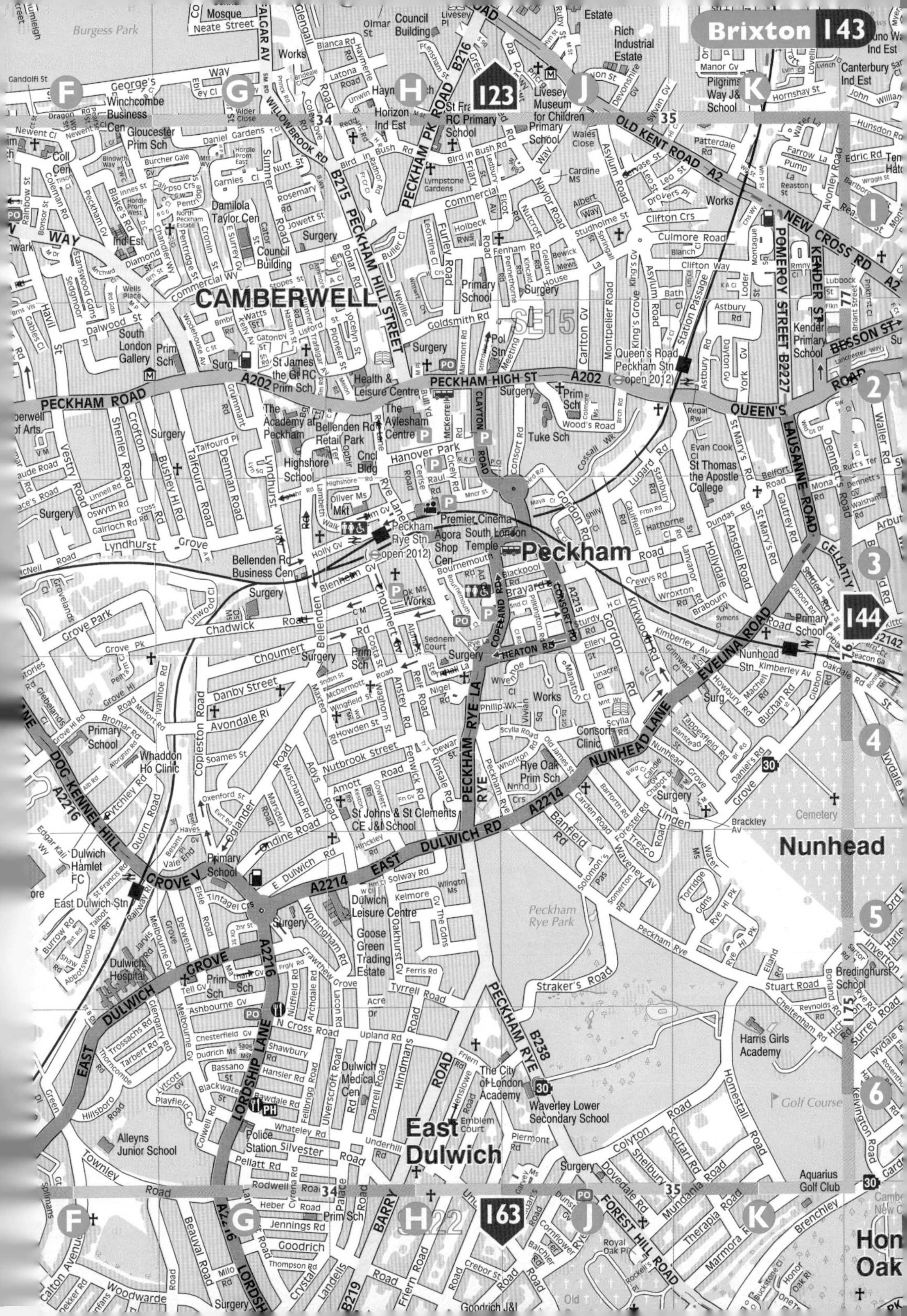
CAMBERWELL
Peckham
Nunhead
East Dulwich
SE15
SE22
Burgess Park
Peckham Rye Park
123
144
163
PECKHAM ROAD
PECKHAM HIGH ST
A202
QUEEN'S ROAD
OLD KENT ROAD A2
NEW CROSS RD
PECKHAM HILL STREET
PECKHAM PK ROAD
B215
B216
RYE LANE
PECKHAM RYE
B238
EAST DULWICH RD
A2214
NUNHEAD LANE
EVELINA ROAD
LAUSANNE ROAD
POMEROY STREET B2227
DOG KENNEL HILL
A2216
GROVE VALE
LORDSHIP LANE
DULWICH GROVE
EAST DULWICH GROVE
FOREST HILL ROAD
Peckham Rye Stn
Queen's Road Peckham Stn
Nunhead Stn
East Dulwich Stn
Livesey Museum for Children
South London Gallery
Premier Cinema
Dulwich Leisure Centre
Dulwich Hamlet FC
Dulwich Hospital
Harris Girls Academy
Aquarius Golf Club
Golf Course
Cemetery
The City of London Academy
Waverley Lower Secondary School
Alleyns Junior School
Goose Green Trading Estate
Tuke Sch
The Academy at Peckham
Highshore School
Kender Primary School
Bredinghurst School
St Thomas the Apostle College
Consort Clinic
Whaddon Ho Clinic
Rye Oak Prim Sch
St Johns & St Clements CE J&I School
Health & Leisure Centre
Bellenden Rd Retail Park
Bellenden Rd Business Cen
The Aylesham Centre
Agora Shop Cen
Damilola Taylor Cen
Dulwich Medical Cen
F
G
H
J
K
I
2
3
4
5
6
34
35

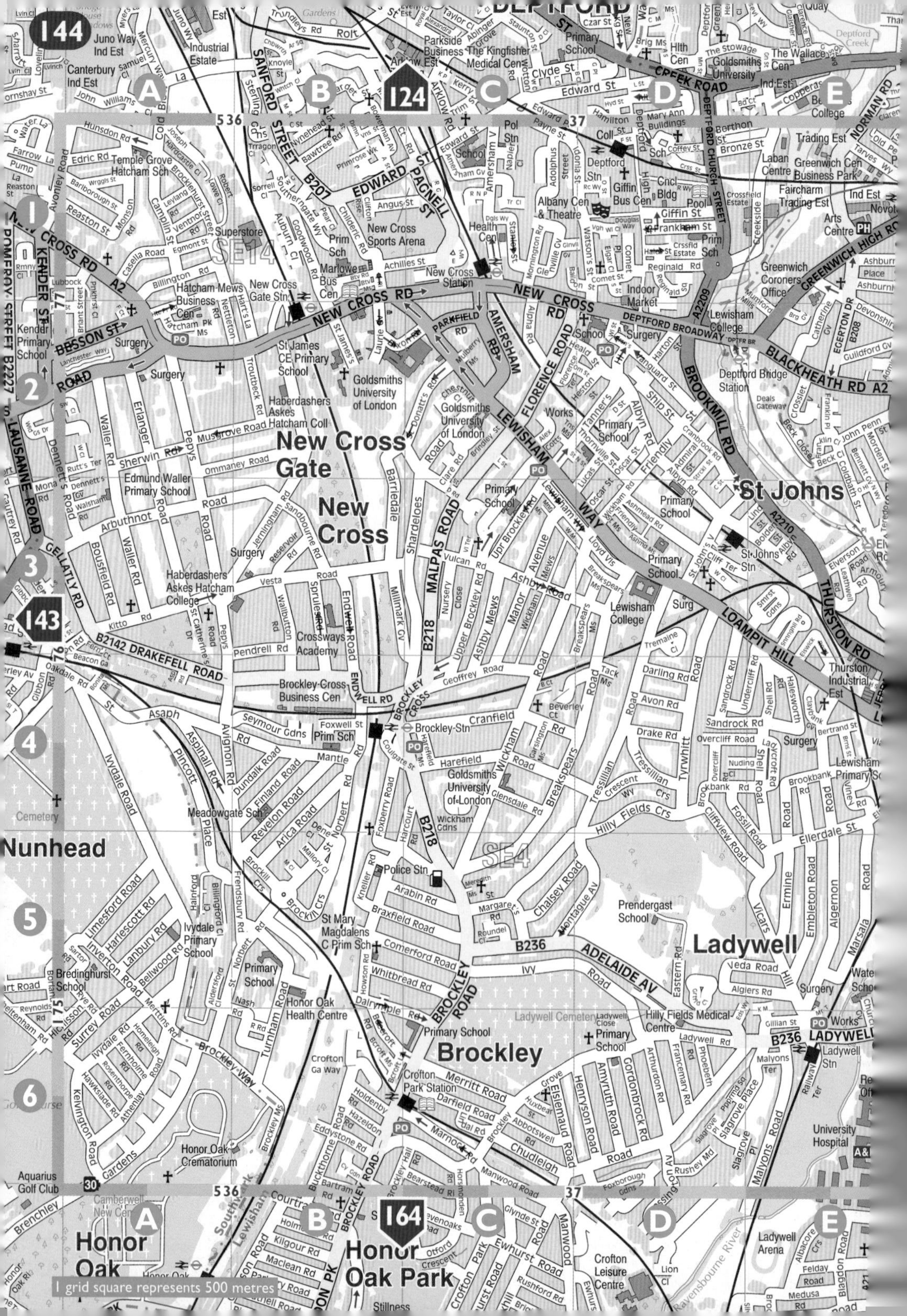
144
124
143
164
A
B
C
D
E
1
2
3
4
5
6
536
37
77
76
175
30
Juno Way Ind Est
Industrial Estate
Canterbury Ind Est
Parkside Business
The Kingfisher Medical Cen
Arklow Est
Primary School
Goldsmiths University
The Stowage
The Wallace Cen
Ind Est
College
CREEK ROAD
DEPTFORD CHURCH STREET
Edward St
Clyde St
Mary Ann Buildings
Deptford Stn
Giffin Bus Cen
Cncl Bldg
Pool
Albany Cen & Theatre
Trading Est
Laban Centre
Greenwich Cen Business Park
Faircharm Trading Est
Crossfield Estate
Arts Centre
GREENWICH HIGH ROAD
NORMAN RD
Hunsdon Rd
Edric Rd
Temple Grove Hatcham Sch
Barlborough St
Reaston St
Avonley Road
SANFORD STREET
B207
EDWARD ST
PAGNELL ST
Pol Stn
School
Amersham V
Angus St
New Cross Sports Arena
Prim Sch
Marlowe Bus Cen
Achilles St
New Cross Station
Health Cen
Superstore
SE14
NEW CROSS RD
A2
KENDER ST
POMFROY STREET B2227
Casella Road
Egmont St
Billington Rd
Hatcham Mews Business Cen
New Cross Gate Stn
BESSON ST
Kender Primary School
Surgery
ROAD
St James CE Primary School
Goldsmiths University of London
PARKFIELD RD
AMERSHAM RD
FLORENCE ROAD
LEWISHAM WAY
NEW CROSS RD
DEPTFORD BROADWAY
A2209
Lewisham College
Deptford Bridge Station
BROOKMILL RD
BLACKHEATH RD A2
Greenwich Coroners Office
B208
EGERTON DR
Haberdashers Askes Hatcham Coll
New Cross Gate
New Cross
Musgrove Road
Sherwin Rd
Ommaney Road
Edmund Waller Primary School
Arbuthnot Road
Waller Rd
Bousfield Rd
LAUSANNE ROAD
GELLATLY RD
Haberdashers Askes Hatcham College
Vesta Road
Kitto Rd
Pendrell Rd
Crossways Academy
Endwell Road
Millmark Gv
Shardeloes
Barriedale
MALPAS ROAD
B218
Primary School
Works
Tanner's Primary School
Ship St
Albyn Rd
Friendly St
St Johns
St Johns Stn
A2210
THURSTON RD
LOAMPIT HILL
Thurston Industrial Est
Lewisham College
Lewisham Primary Sch
B2142 DRAKEFELL ROAD
Brockley Cross Business Cen
ENDWELL RD
BROCKLEY CROSS
Brockley Stn
Geoffrey Road
Cranfield Rd
Harefield Rd
Goldsmiths University of London
Wickham Road
Breakspears
Tressillian Crescent
Hilly Fields Crs
Surgery
Sandrock Rd
Overcliff Road
Ellerdale St
Asaph St
Seymour Gdns
Prim Sch
Mantle Rd
Dundalk Road
Finland Road
Revelon Road
Arica Road
Meadowgate Sch
Ivydale Road
Pincott Place
Aspinall Rd
Avignon Rd
Cemetery
Nunhead
Police Stn
Arabin Rd
Braxfield Road
Comerford Road
Whitbread Rd
St Mary Magdalens C Prim Sch
SE4
Prendergast School
Ladywell
Embleton Road
Algernon Road
Marsala Road
B236
ADELAIDE AV
Ivy Road
Limesford Road
Harlescott Rd
Lanbury Rd
Ivydale Primary School
Bredinghurst School
Primary School
Honor Oak Health Centre
BROCKLEY ROAD
Primary School
Ladywell Cemetery
Hilly Fields Medical Centre
Primary School
Brockley
Veda Road
Algiers Rd
Surgery
Ladywell Stn
LADYWELL
Surrey Road
Brockley Way
Crofton Park Station
Merritt Road
Darfield Road
Henryson Road
Amyruth Road
Gordonbrock Rd
Francemary Rd
Malyons Road
Slagrove Place
University Hospital
Honor Oak Crematorium
Aquarius Golf Club
Kelvington Road
Chudleigh Road
Manwood Road
Rushey Md
Foxborough Gdns
Honor Oak
Honor Oak Park
Crofton Leisure Centre
Ladywell Arena
Ravensbourne River
BROCKLEY ROAD
1 grid square represents 500 metres

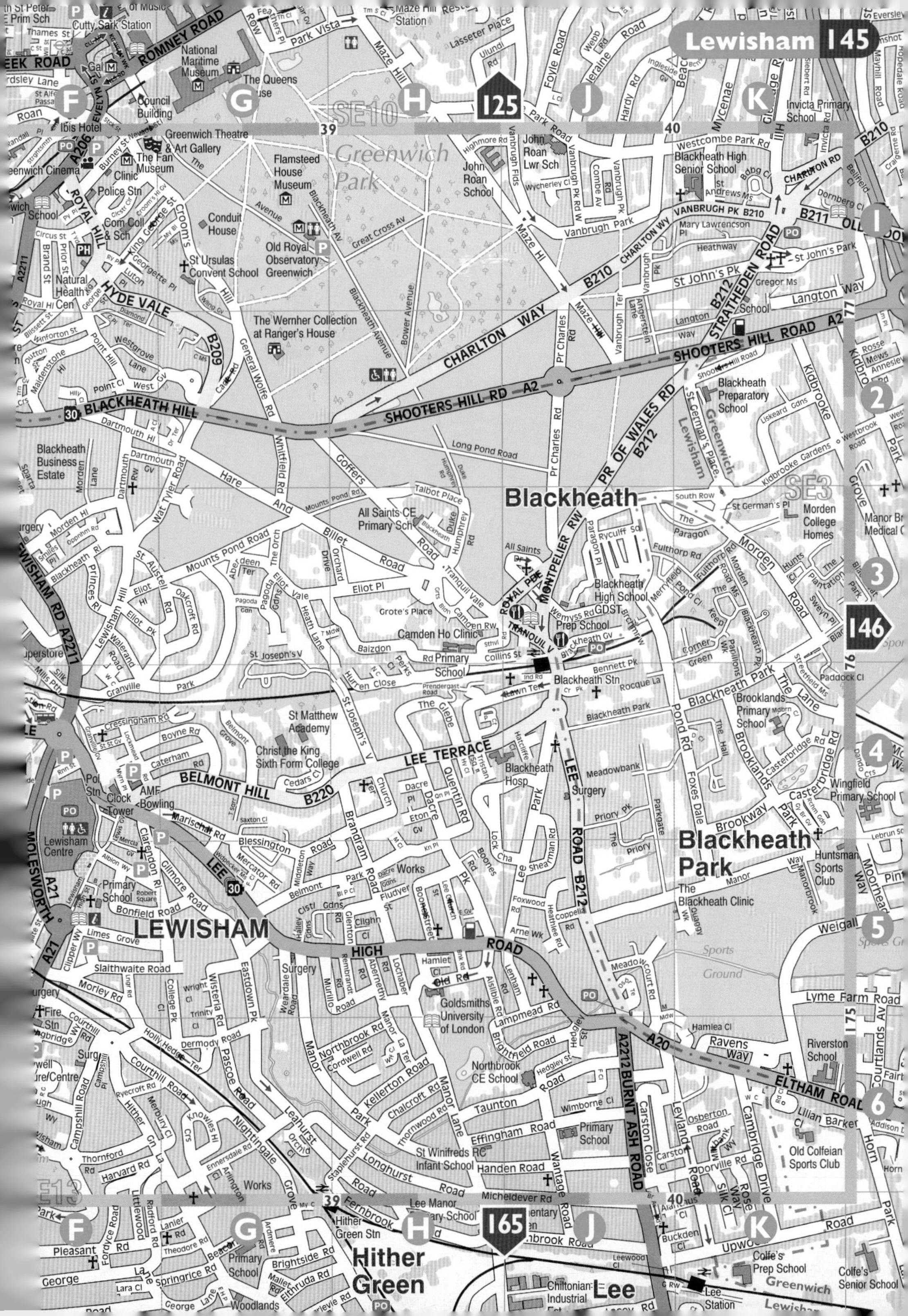

Cutty Sark Station
Romney Road
National Maritime Museum
The Queens House
Maze Hill Station
Park Vista
Lasseter Place
Maze Hill
125
SE10
Greenwich Park
Greenwich Theatre & Art Gallery
The Fan Museum
Flamsteed House Museum
Greenwich Cinema
Ibis Hotel
Council Building
Police Stn
Clinic
Com Coll & Sch
Royal Hill
Conduit House
Old Royal Observatory Greenwich
Great Cross Av
Blackheath Av
St Ursulas Convent School
Croom's Hill
Hyde Vale
Natural Health Cen
The Wernher Collection at Ranger's House
Bower Avenue
Blackheath Avenue
General Wolfe Rd
Charlton Way
Shooters Hill Rd
A2
Blackheath Hill
Westgrove Lane
Point Hill
John Roan Lwr Sch
John Roan School
Vanbrugh Park
Vanbrugh Pk Rd W
Westcombe Park Rd
Blackheath High Senior School
Invicta Primary School
Charlton Rd
St Andrews Ms
Mary Lawrencson Pl
Heathway
St John's Park
St John's Pk
Langton Way
Stratheden Road
B212
Shooters Hill Road
Blackheath Preparatory School
Kidbrooke Gardens
Pr Charles Rd
Pr of Wales Rd
Long Pond Road
St German's Place
Lewisham
Greenwich
SE3
Blackheath
South Row
St German's Pl
Morden College Homes
Manor Br Medical C
The Paragon
Paragon Pl
Morden Road
Fulthorp Rd
Blackheath High School GDST
Prep School
Montpelier Rw
Royal Pde
Tranquil Vale
All Saints
All Saints CE Primary Sch
Talbot Place
Duke Humphrey Rd
Mounts Pond Rd
Mounts Pond Road
Goffers Road
Hare And Billet Road
Orchard Drive
Eliot Pl
Eliot Vale
Heath Lane
Grote's Place
Camden Row
Camden Ho Clinic
Baizdon Rd
Primary School
Collins St
Blackheath Gv
Blackheath Stn
Bennett Pk
Rocque La
Blackheath Park
Blackheath Business Estate
Dartmouth Rd
Dartmouth Gv
Wat Tyler Road
Morden Hl
Morden Lane
Lewisham Hill
Princes Ri
Blackheath Ri
St Austell Rd
Oakcroft Rd
Eliot Pk
Walerand Road
Granville Park
Hurren Close
St Joseph's V
St Joseph's Vale
The Glebe
Lee Terrace
St Matthew Academy
Christ the King Sixth Form College
Boyne Rd
Cressingham Rd
Caterham Rd
Belmont Hill
B220
Cedars Cl
Blackheath Hosp
Lee Park
Lee Road
B212
Surgery
Meadowbank
Priory Pk
The Priory
Parkgate
Foxes Dale
Pond Rd
Brooklands
Brooklands Primary School
The Hall
Casterbridge Rd
Wingfield Primary School
Brookway
Blackheath Park
Huntsman Sports Club
Manor Way
The Blackheath Clinic
Moorhead Way
146
Paddock Cl
The Lane
Lewisham Centre
Clock Tower
AMF Bowling
Marischal Rd
Blessington Road
Mercator Rd
Lee High Road
Lewisham
Molesworth
A21
Lewisham Rd A2211
Clarendon Rl
Glimore Road
Bonfield Road
Limes Grove
Slaithwaite Road
Morley Rd
Belmont Park
Brandram Road
Dacre Pk
Quentin Rd
Eton Gv
Boones Rd
Works
Lee Church St
Weardale Road
Murillo Road
Lochaber Rd
Hamlet Cl
Old Rd
Goldsmiths University of London
Aislibie Rd
Lampmead Rd
Brightfield Road
Weigall Rd
Sports Ground
Meadowcourt Rd
Lyme Farm Road
A20
Ravens Way
Riverston School
Eltham Road
Lilian Barker Cl
Old Colfeian Sports Club
Courtlands Av
Horn Park
Wisteria Rd
Eastdown Pk
Dermody Road
Holly Hedge Ter
Courthill Road
Campshill Road
Thornford
Harvard Rd
Hither Gn La
Knowles Hl Crs
Pascoe Road
Nightingale Grove
Leahurst
Manor Park
Northbrook Rd
Cordwell Rd
Kellerton Road
Chalcroft Rd
Thornwood Rd
Manor Lane
Northbrook CE School
Hedgley St
Taunton Road
Wimborne Cl
Primary School
Effingham Road
St Winifreds RC Infant School
Handen Road
Wantage Road
A2212 Burnt Ash Road
Carston Close
Leyland Road
Osberton Road
Dorville Rd
Cambridge Drive
Staplehurst Rd
Longhurst Road
Micheldever Rd
Works
Ennersdale Rd
Fernbrook Rd
Lee Manor Primary School
Hither Green Stn
Hither Green
165
Buckden Cl
Upwood Road
Colfe's Prep School
Colfe's Senior School
Lee Station
Lee
Chiltonian Industrial Estate
Brightside Rd
Primary School
Springrice Rd
George Lane
Woodlands
Pleasant Rd
Fordyce Road
Radford Rd
Theodore Rd
F
G
H
J
K
39
40
2
3
4
5
6

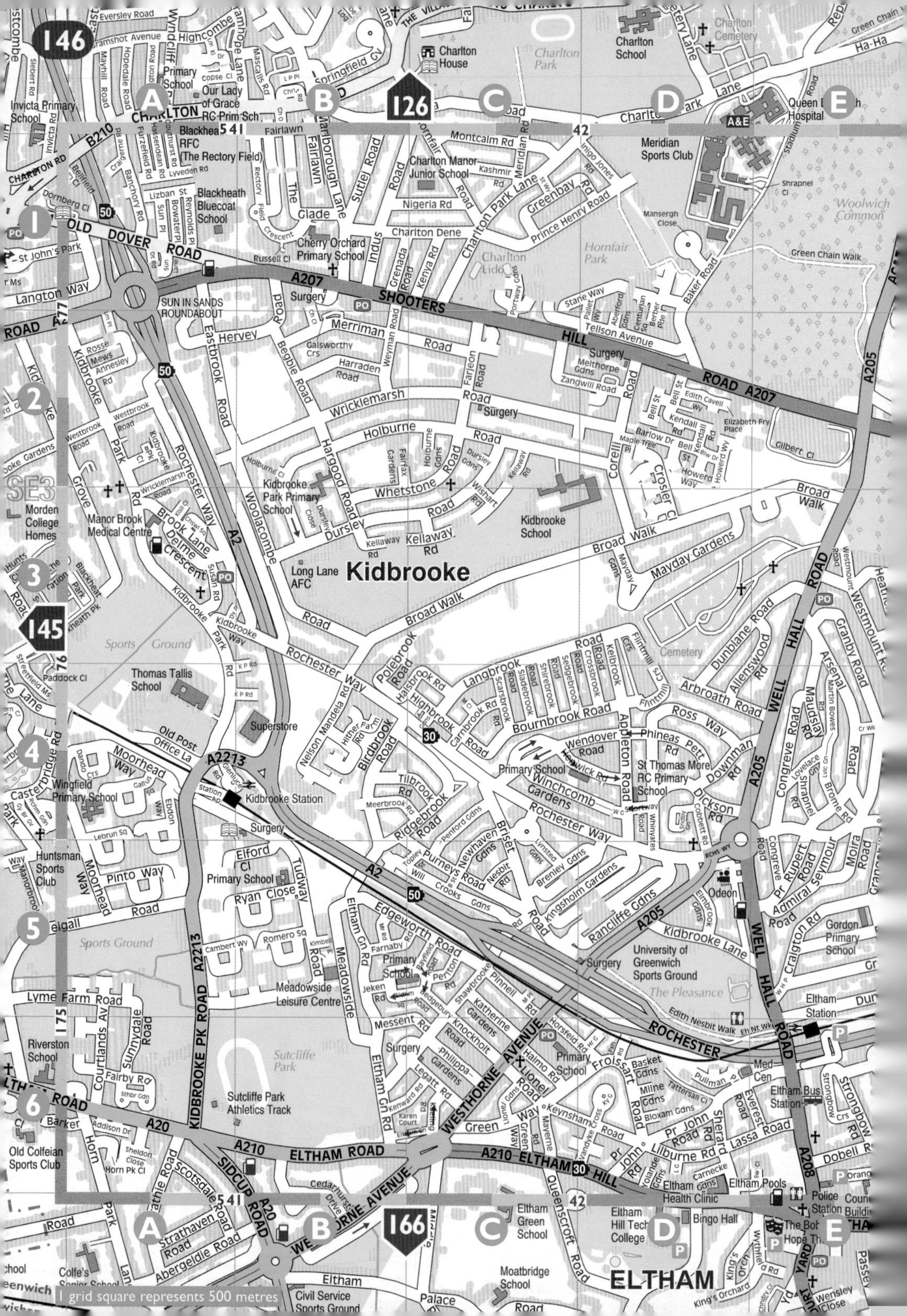
146
126
145
166
A
B
C
D
E
1
2
3
4
5
6
Eversley Road
Charlton House
Charlton Park
Charlton School
Charlton Cemetery
Green Chain Walk
Ha-Ha
Highcombe
Wyndcliff
Springfield Gv
Primary School
Our Lady of Grace RC Prim Sch
Invicta Primary School
CHARLTON ROAD
Fairlawn
Blackheath RFC (The Rectory Field)
Montcalm Rd
Meridian Rd
Charlton Park Lane
Queen Elizabeth Hospital
A&E
Meridian Sports Club
Charlton Manor Junior School
Kashmir Rd
Nigeria Rd
Charlton Dene
Greenbay Rd
Prince Henry Road
Inigo Jones Rd
Shrapnel Cl
Woolwich Common
Mansergh Close
Blackheath Bluecoat School
Marlborough Lane
Sutlej Road
Hornfair Road
The Glade
Rectory Field Crescent
Cherry Orchard Primary School
Russell Cl
Indus Road
Grenada Road
Kenya Rd
Charlton Lido
Hornfair Park
Baker Road
Green Chain Walk
OLD DOVER ROAD
St John's Park
Langton Way
SUN IN SANDS ROUNDABOUT
A207 SHOOTERS HILL ROAD A207
Surgery
Stane Way
Tellson Avenue
Melthorpe Gdns
Zangwill Road
Corelli Road
Merriman Road
Galsworthy Crs
Harraden Road
Weyman Road
Farjeon Road
Hervey Road
Eastbrook Road
Begbie Road
Wricklemarsh Road
Holburne Road
Elizabeth Fry Place
Gilbert Cl
Kendall
Bell St
Barlow Dr
Maple Tree Pl
Howerd Way
Crosier Cl
Broad Walk
A205
A2
A2213
A20
A210
A208
A177
Rosse Mews
Annesley
Westbrook Road
Kidbrooke Park Road
Kidbrooke Gardens
Rochester Way
SE3
Morden College Homes
Manor Brook Medical Centre
Brook Lane
Delme Crescent
Woolacombe Road
Hargood Road
Whetstone Road
Kidbrooke Park Primary School
Dursley Road
Kellaway Rd
Kidbrooke School
Mayday Gardens
Kidbrooke
Long Lane AFC
Broad Walk
Sports Ground
Thomas Tallis School
Paddock Cl
Superstore
Old Post Office La
Cemetery
Dunblane Road
Allenswood Road
Arbroath Road
Westmount Road
Granby Road
Arsenal Road
Well Hall Road
Langbrook Road
Bournbrook Road
Flintmill Crs
Ross Way
Phineas Pett Rd
Wendover Road
Appleton Road
Winchcomb Gardens
St Thomas More RC Primary School
Downman Rd
Dickson Rd
Congreve Road
Maudslay Rd
Brome Rd
Polebrook Road
Highbrook Rd
Birdbrook Road
Nelson Mandela Rd
Moorhead Way
Wingfield Primary School
Kidbrooke Station
Casterbridge Rd
Huntsman Sports Club
Pinto Way
Elford Cl
Primary School
Ryan Close
Tudway Road
Tilbrook Rd
Ridgebrook Road
Purneys Road
Newhaven Gdns
Briset Road
Brenley Gdns
Kingsholm Gardens
Rancliffe Gdns
Kidbrooke Lane
Odeon
Admiral Seymour Road
Moira Road
Craigton Rd
Gordon Primary School
Sports Ground
Cambert Wy
Romero Sq
Meadowside
Eltham Gn Rd
Edgeworth Road
Farnaby Rd
Pinnell Rd
Katherine Gardens
University of Greenwich Sports Ground
The Pleasance
Edith Nesbit Walk
ROCHESTER WAY
Eltham Station
Lyme Farm Road
Sunnydale Road
Courtlands Av
Fairby Rd
Riverston School
Meadowside Leisure Centre
Messent Rd
Sutcliffe Park
Sutcliffe Park Athletics Track
Knockholt Road
Philippa Gardens
Legatt Rd
Westhorne Avenue
Horsfeld Rd
Halmo Rd
Lionel Road
Froissart Road
Basket Gdns
Milne Gdns
Bloxam Gdns
Pullman
Med Cen
Eltham Bus Station
Strongbow Crs
Everest Road
Lassa Road
Dobell Rd
Keynsham Road
Pr John Rd
Sherard Rd
Lilburne Rd
Green Way
Queenscroft Road
ELTHAM ROAD
A210 ELTHAM HILL
Eltham Health Clinic
Eltham Pools
Police Station
Council Buildings
Barker
Old Colfeian Sports Club
Horn Pk Cl
Sheldon Close
Horn Park
Scotsdale Road
Strathaven Road
Abergeldie Road
SIDCUP ROAD
KIDBROOKE PK ROAD
Cedarhurst Drive
Eltham Green School
Eltham Hill Tech College
Bingo Hall
The Bob Hope Theatre
Moatbridge School
ELTHAM
King's Orchard
Wythfield Rd
Court Yard
Wensley Close
Colfe's Senior School
Eltham Palace Road
Civil Service Sports Ground
1 grid square represents 500 metres

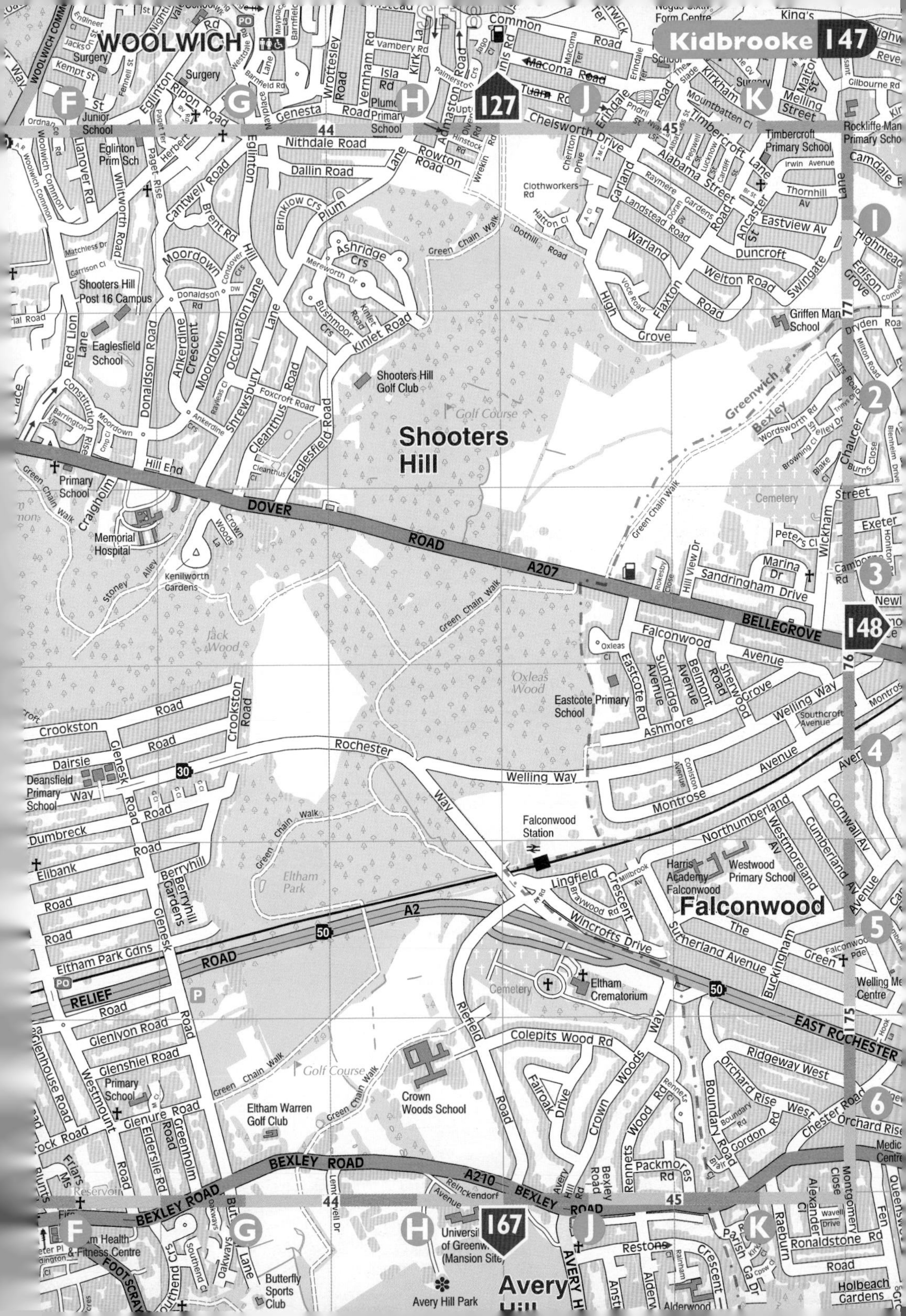
WOOLWICH
Shooters Hill
Falconwood
Avery Hill
Shooters Hill Golf Club
Golf Course
Jack Wood
Oxleas Wood
Eltham Park
Eltham Warren Golf Club
Crown Woods School
Eltham Crematorium
Cemetery
Falconwood Station
Memorial Hospital
Shooters Hill Post 16 Campus
Eaglesfield School
Eglinton Prim Sch
Timbercroft Primary School
Griffen Manor School
Eastcote Primary School
Harris Academy Falconwood
Westwood Primary School
Deansfield Primary School
Butterfly Sports Club
Avery Hill Park
University of Greenwich (Mansion Site)
DOVER ROAD
A207
BELLECROVE
ROCHESTER WAY RELIEF ROAD
A2
EAST ROCHESTER
BEXLEY ROAD
A210
127
148
167
Green Chain Walk

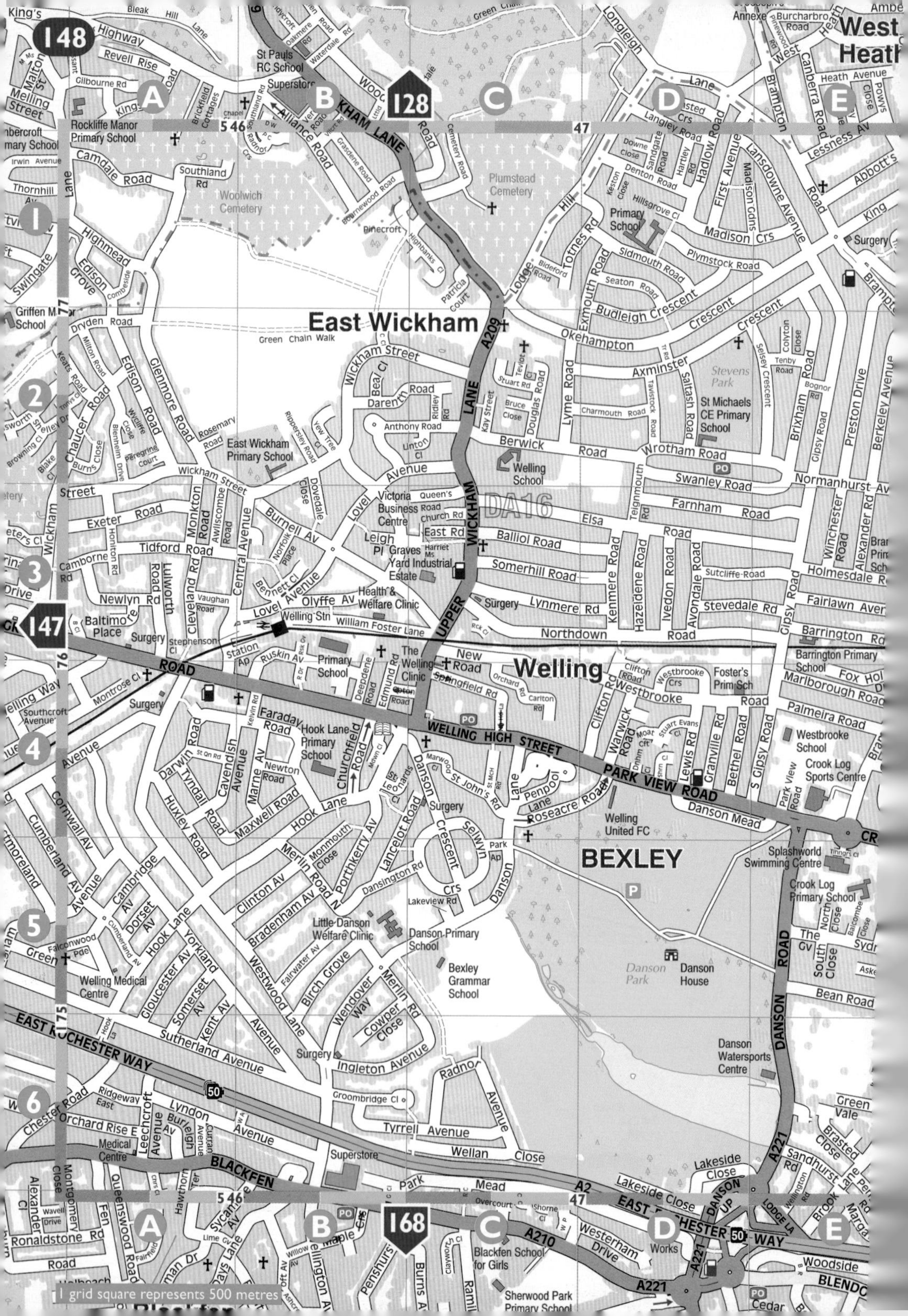
148
128
147
168
A
B
C
D
E
1
2
3
4
5
6
546
47
77
76
175
East Wickham
Welling
BEXLEY
DA16
King's Highway
Bleak Hill Lane
Revell Rise
Gilbourne Rd
Malton St
Melling Street
Rockliffe Manor Primary School
St Pauls RC School
Superstore
Wickham Lane
Alliance Road
Grasdene Road
Bournewood Road
Woolwich Cemetery
Plumstead Cemetery
Cemetery Road
Southland Rd
Camdale Road
Irwin Avenue
Thornhill Av
Highmead
Edison Grove
Swingate Lane
Griffen Manor School
Pinecroft
Highbanks Cl
Patricia Court
Green Chain Walk
Longleigh Lane
Lodge Hill
Langley Road
Downe Close
Sandgate Rd
Hartley Rd
Denton Road
Keston Close
Hadlow Road
First Avenue
Madison Gdns
Lansdowne Avenue
Hillsgrove Cl
Primary School
Madison Crs
Plymstock Road
Sidmouth Road
Seaton Road
Bideford Road
Totnes Rd
Exmouth Road
Budleigh Crescent
Okehampton Crescent
Axminster Crescent
Stevens Park
St Michaels CE Primary School
Brampton Road
West Heath
Heath Avenue
Canberra Road
Lessness Av
Abbott's
King
Surgery
Dryden Road
Milton Road
Keats Road
Edison Road
Glenmore Road
Chaucer Road
Shelley Dr
Browning Cl
Blake Cl
Burns Close
Wycliffe Close
Peregrine Court
Blenheim Drive
Rosemary Road
East Wickham Primary School
Wickham Street
Bean Cl
Darenth Road
Anthony Road
Ridley Rd
Linton Cl
Yew Tree Cl
Ripperseley Road
Dovedale Close
Avenue
Teviot Cl
Stuart Rd
Bruce Close
Kay Street
Douglas Road
Lyme Road
Charmouth Road
Tavistock Road
Saltash Road
Selsey Crescent
Colyton Close
Tenby Road
Bognor Rd
Brixham Road
Gipsy Road
Preston Drive
Berkeley Avenue
Berwick Road
Wrotham Road
Welling School
Swanley Road
Normanhurst Av
Upper Wickham Lane
A209
Victoria Business Centre
Queen's Road
Church Rd
East Rd
Lovel Avenue
Burnell Av
Exeter Road
Monkton Road
Awliscombe Road
Central Avenue
Honiton Rd
Tidford Road
Camborne Rd
Norfolk Place
Bennett Cl
Leigh Pl
Graves Yard Industrial Estate
Harriet Ms
Farnham Road
Elsa Road
Teignmouth Rd
Balliol Road
Somerhill Road
Kenmere Road
Hazeldene Road
Ivedon Road
Avondale Road
Sutcliffe Road
Stevedale Rd
Winchester Road
Alexander Rd
Holmesdale Rd
Fairlawn Aven
Newlyn Rd
Lulworth Road
Cleveland Rd
Vaughan Road
Olyffe Av
Health & Welfare Clinic
Lynmere Rd
Northdown Road
Baltimore Place
Welling Stn
William Foster Lane
Barrington Rd
Barrington Primary School
Stephenson Cl
Station Ap
Ruskin Av
Primary School
The Welling Clinic
New Road
Springfield Rd
Orchard Rd
Carlton Rd
Clifton Road
Westbrooke Crs
Westbrooke Road
Foster's Prim Sch
Marlborough Road
Fox Hol
Palmeira Road
Westbrooke School
Montrose Cl
Road
Welling Way
Southcroft Avenue
Kelvin Rd
Faraday Road
Deepdene Road
Edmund Rd
Hook Lane Primary School
Welling High Street
PO
Darwin Road
St Qn Rd
Tyndall Road
Cavendish Avenue
Marne Av
Newton Road
Maxwell Road
Churchfield Road
Huxley Road
Hook Lane
St Leonards
Danson Road
Marwood Cl
St John's Rd
Lane
Penpool Lane
Roseacre Road
Warwick Road
Moat Cft
Stuart Evans Cl
Lewis Rd
Granville Rd
Bethel Road
S Gipsy Road
Park View Road
Park View Road
Crook Log Sports Centre
Danson Mead
Welling United FC
Splashworld Swimming Centre
Crook Log Primary School
Surgery
Monmouth Close
Porthkerry Av
Lancelot Road
Danson Crescent
Selwyn Crs
Park Ap
Merlin Road N
Dansington Rd
Lakeview Rd
Cornwall Av
Cumberland Av
Westmoreland
Cambridge Avenue
Dorset Av
Clinton Av
Bradenham Av
Little Danson Welfare Clinic
Danson Primary School
Bexley Grammar School
Danson Park
Danson House
North Close
Balcombe Close
The Gv
South Close
Bean Road
Falconwood Pde
Green
Welling Medical Centre
Gloucester Av
Yorkland Av
Somerset Av
Kent Av
Westwood Lane
Westwood Avenue
Fairwater Av
Birch Grove
Wendover Way
Merlin Rd
Cowper Close
East Rochester Way
Sutherland Avenue
Surgery
Ingleton Avenue
Radnor Avenue
Danson Watersports Centre
Danson Road
Green Vale
50
Chester Road
Ridgeway East
Orchard Rise E
Leechcroft Avenue
Burleigh Av
Lyndon Avenue
Groombridge Cl
Tyrrell Avenue
Wellan Close
A221
Brasted Close
Sandhurst Rd
Brook Lane
Medical Centre
Blackfen Road
Superstore
Park Mead
A2
Lakeside Close
Lakeside Close
Danson Up
Lodge La
Montgomery Close
Alexander Cl
Wavell Drive
Ronaldstone Rd
Queenswood Road
Hawthorn Ter
Sycamore Av
Lime Gv
Maple Crs
Overcourt Cl
A210
Westerham Drive
Works
East Rochester Way
Blackfen School for Girls
Pays Lane
Pensurst
Burns A
Sherwood Park Primary School
Woodside
Blendon
Cedar
1 grid square represents 500 metres

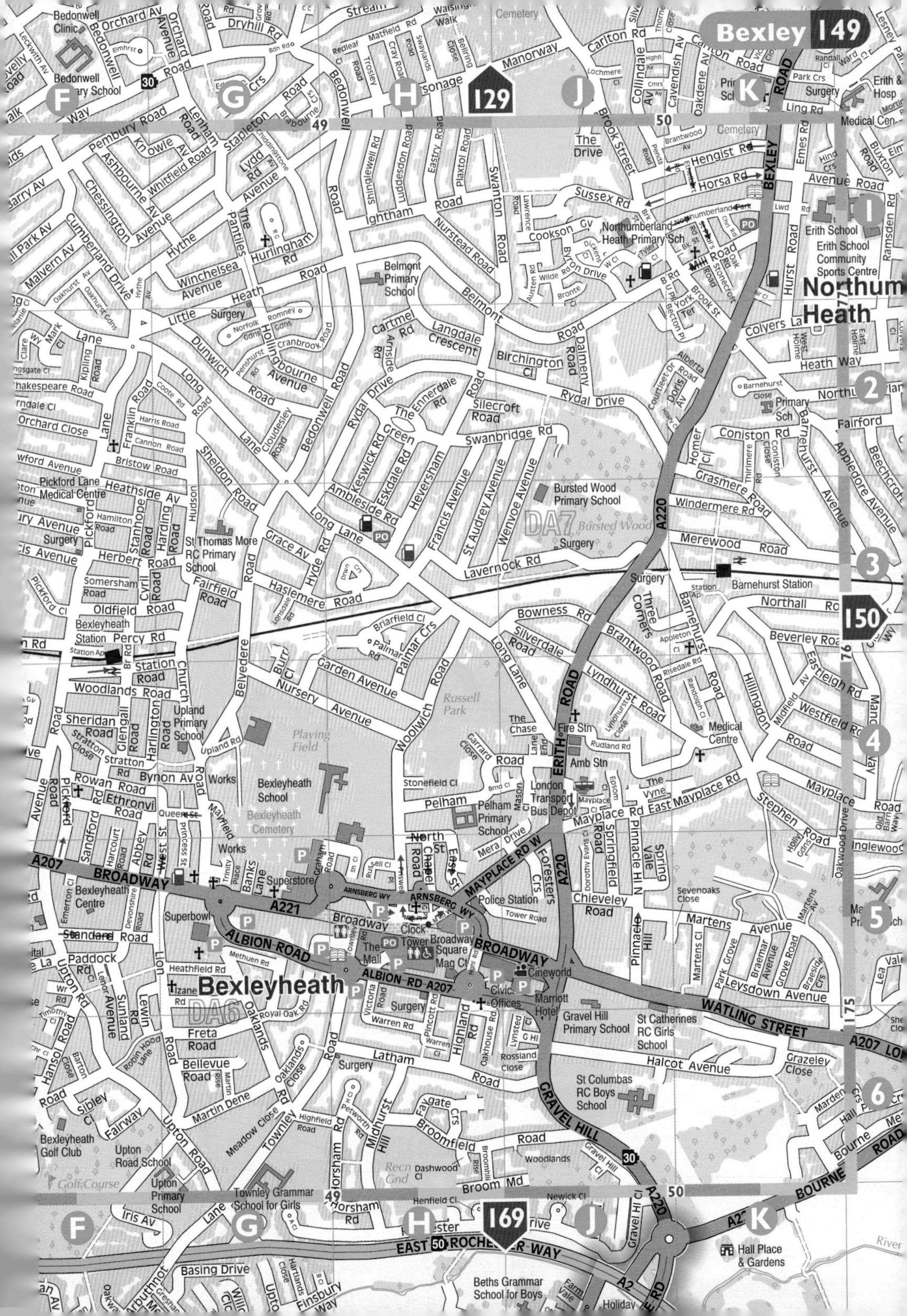
129
150
169
Bexleyheath
DA6
DA7
Northumberland Heath
Bedonwell Clinic
Bedonwell Primary School
Belmont Primary School
Northumberland Heath Primary Sch
Erith School
Erith School Community Sports Centre
Bursted Wood Primary School
Bursted Wood
Barnehurst Station
Bexleyheath Station
St Thomas More RC Primary School
Pickford Lane Medical Centre
Upland Primary School
Bexleyheath School
Bexleyheath Cemetery
Russell Park
Playing Field
Pelham Primary School
London Transport Bus Depot
Fire Stn
Amb Stn
Police Station
Medical Centre
Bexleyheath Centre
Superbowl
Superstore
The Mall
Clock Tower
Broadway Square
Civic Offices
Cineworld
Marriott Hotel
Gravel Hill Primary School
St Catherines RC Girls School
St Columbas RC Boys School
Bexleyheath Golf Club
Upton Road School
Upton Primary School
Townley Grammar School for Girls
Beths Grammar School for Boys
Hall Place & Gardens
A207 BROADWAY
A221
ALBION ROAD
ALBION RD A207
A220
ERITH ROAD
GRAVEL HILL
WATLING STREET
MAYPLACE RD W
BEXLEY ROAD
EAST ROCHESTER WAY
BOURNE ROAD
A2
Long Lane
Bedonwell Road
Brook Street
Mayplace Road East
Barnehurst Road
Woolwich Road
Belvedere Road
Pickford Lane
Upton Road
Lion Road
Latham Road
Broomfield Road
Halcot Avenue
Martens Avenue
Leysdown Avenue
Lyndhurst Road
Brantwood Road
Merewood Road
Windermere Rd
Grasmere Road
Coniston Rd
Rydal Drive
Heath Way
Colyers La
Hengist Rd
Horsa Rd
Sussex Rd
Avenue Road
Ightham Road
Nurstead Road
Swanton Road
Manorway
Carlton Rd
Lavernock Rd
Haslemere Road
Bowness Rd
Silverdale Road
Garden Avenue
Nursery Avenue
Pelham Road
Chieveley Road
Woodlands Road
Station Road
Oldfield Road
Percy Rd
Herbert Road
Fairfield Road
Church Road
Heathside Av
Franklin Road
Little Heath Road
Winchelsea Avenue
Hurlingham Rd
Hollingbourne Avenue
Dunwich Road
Sheldon Road
Stapleton Road
Pembury Road
Ashbourne Av
Chessington Avenue
Cumberland Drive
Malvern Av
Orchard Av
Dryhill Rd
Mayplace Road
Stephen Road
Westfield Rd
Eastleigh Rd
Beverley Road
Northall Road
Oakwood Drive
Basing Drive
Finsbury Way
Horsham Rd
Midhurst Hill
Townley Road
Oaklands Road
Freta Road
Bellevue Road
Martin Dene
Sunland Avenue
Hansol Road
Sibley Cl
Fairway
Meadow Close
Iris Av
Golf Course
Recn Gnd
River

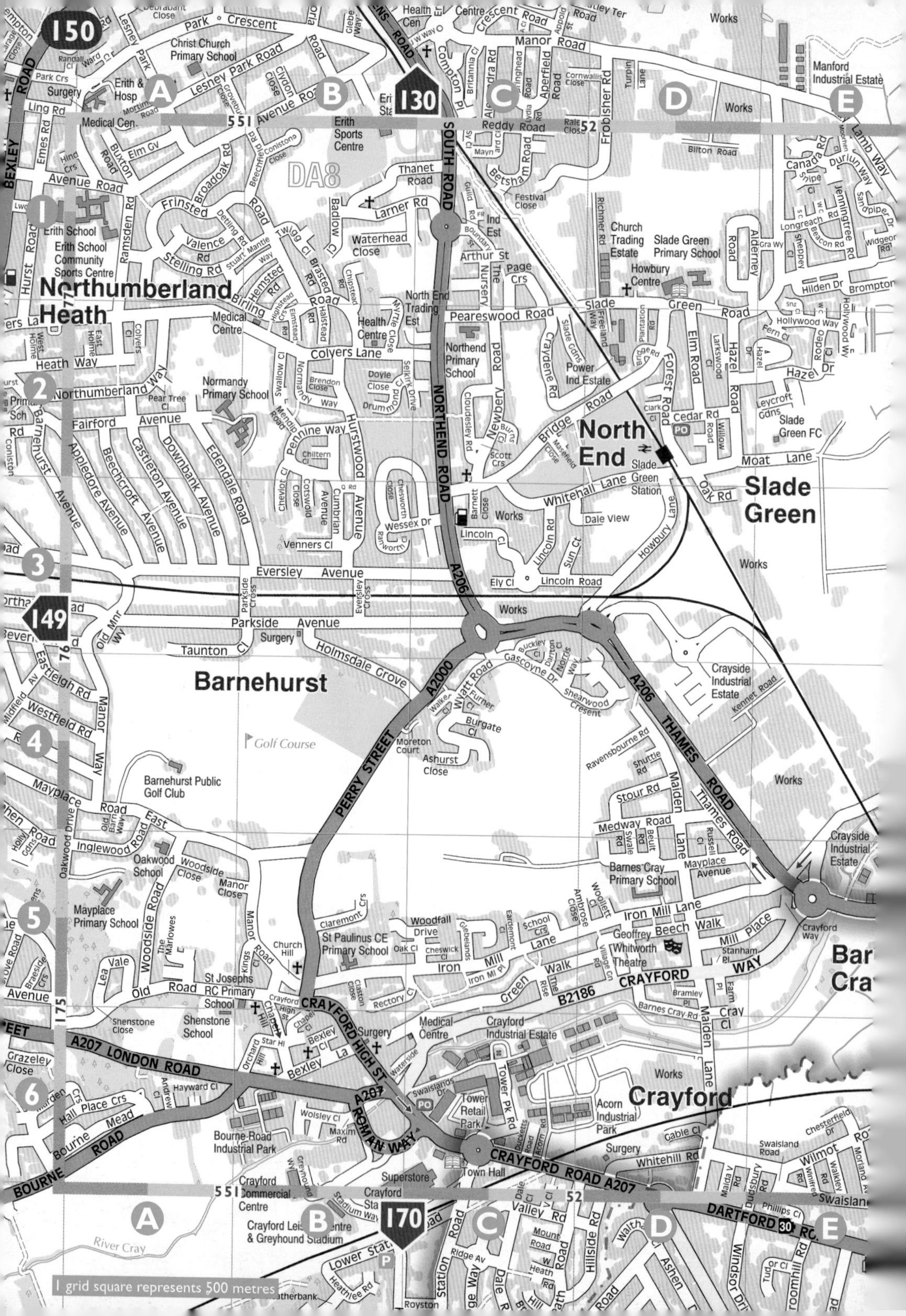

150
130
149
170
A
B
C
D
E
1
2
3
4
5
6
Park Crescent
Christ Church Primary School
Lesney Park Road
Erith & District Hosp
Surgery
Park Crs
Ling Rd
Medical Cen
551 Avenue Road
Erith Sports Centre
DA8
South Road
Crescent Road
Manor Road
Compton Pl
Alexandra Rd
Aperfield Road
Cornwallis Close
Frobisher Rd
Turpin Lane
Works
Manforth Industrial Estate
Reddy Road
52
Bilton Road
Lamb Way
Betsham Road
Festival Close
Canada Rd
Durham Way
Jenningtree Rd
Longreach Rd
Beacon Rd
Sandpiper Dr
Widgeon Rd
Bexley Road
Emes Rd
Buxton Road
Elm Gv
Avenue Road
Broadoak Rd
Beechfield Rd
Conistone Close
Thanet Road
Larner Rd
Waterhead Close
Ind Est
Arthur St
Page Crs
Erith School
Erith School Community Sports Centre
Frinsted
Valence Rd
Stelling Rd
Twigg Cl
Brasted Rd
Badlow Cl
Church Trading Estate
Slade Green Primary School
Howbury Centre
Alderney Road
Hilden Dr
Brompton
Northumberland Heath
Birling Road
Hemsted Rd
Halstead Rd
Medical Centre
North End Trading Est
Health Centre
Peareswood Road
Slade Green Road
Elm Road
Hazel Road
Hollywood Way
Fern Cl
Hazel Dr
Heath Way
Colyers Lane
Colyers Cl
Doyle Close
Selkirk Drive
Northend Primary School
Newbery Road
Craydene Rd
Power Ind Estate
Forest Road
Larkswood Cl
Northumberland Way
Pear Tree Cl
Normandy Primary School
Normandy Way
Pennine Way
Hurstwood Avenue
Northend Road
Cloudesley Rd
Bridge Road
Cedar Rd
Clark Cl
Leycroft Gdns
Slade Green FC
Fairford Avenue
Barnehurst Rd
Appledore Avenue
Beechcroft Avenue
Castleton Avenue
Downbank Avenue
Edendale Road
Cheviot Cl
Cotswold Close
Cumbrian Avenue
Chesworth Close
Wessex Dr
Barnett Close
Scott Crs
Maxfield Close
North End
Slade Green Station
Moat Lane
Oak Rd
Whitehall Lane
Slade Green
Barnehurst Avenue
Venners Cl
Lincoln Cl
Lincoln Rd
Sun Ct
Dale View
Howbury Lane
Eversley Avenue
Parkside Cross
Eversley Cross
A206
Ely Cl
Lincoln Road
Works
Old Mnr Way
Parkside Avenue
Surgery
Taunton Cl
Holmsdale Grove
Gascoyne Dr
Buckley Cl
Darton Cl
Norris Way
Barnehurst
A2000
Wyatt Road
Shearwood Cresent
A206 Thames Road
Crayside Industrial Estate
Kennet Road
Eastleigh Rd
Westfield Rd
Manor Way
Walker Cl
Furner Cl
Burgate Cl
Golf Course
Moreton Court
Ashurst Close
Perry Street
Ravensbourne Rd
Shuttle Rd
Barnehurst Public Golf Club
Mayplace Road East
Stour Rd
Maiden Lane
Medway Road
Thames Road
Inglewood Road
Oakwood Drive
Oakwood School
Woodside Close
Manor Close
Barnes Cray Primary School
Mayplace Avenue
Crayside Industrial Estate
Mayplace Primary School
Claremont Crs
Woodfall Drive
Ambrose Close
Woollett Cl
Iron Mill Lane
Beech Walk
Mill Place
Crayford Way
Woodside Road
The Marlowes
Lea Vale
Manor Road
Kings Cl
Church Hill
St Paulinus CE Primary School
Oak Cl
Cheswick Cl
Iron Mill Pl
Geoffrey Whitworth Theatre
Stanham Pl
Avenue
Old Road
St Josephs RC Primary School
Crayford High St
Rectory Cl
Green Walk
The Rise
B2186 Crayford Way
Bramley Pl
Farm Pl
Shenstone Close
Shenstone School
Chapel Hill
Barnes Cray Rd
Cray Cl
A207 London Road
Orchard Hill
Star Hl
Bexley Cl
Bexley La
Surgery
Medical Centre
Crayford Industrial Estate
Works
Grazeley Close
Hayward Cl
Crayford
Hall Place Crs
Andrew Cl
Swaislands Dr
Tower Retail Park
Tower Pk Rd
Acorn Industrial Park
Bourne Mead
Bourne Road
Wolsley Cl
Maxim Rd
A207 Roman Way
Bourne Road Industrial Park
Cable Cl
Surgery
Whitehill Rd
Crayford Road A207
Chesterfield Dr
Swaisland Road
Wilmot Rd
Morland Av
Town Hall
Superstore
Crayford Commercial Centre
551
Crayford Sta
Stadium Way
Valley Rd
52
Dartford Rd
30
Phillips Cl
Crayford Leisure Centre & Greyhound Stadium
River Cray
Lower Station Rd
Station Road
Ridge Av
Mount Road
Heath Rd
Hillside Rd
Ashen
Windsor Dr
Heathlee Rd
Royston
1 grid square represents 500 metres

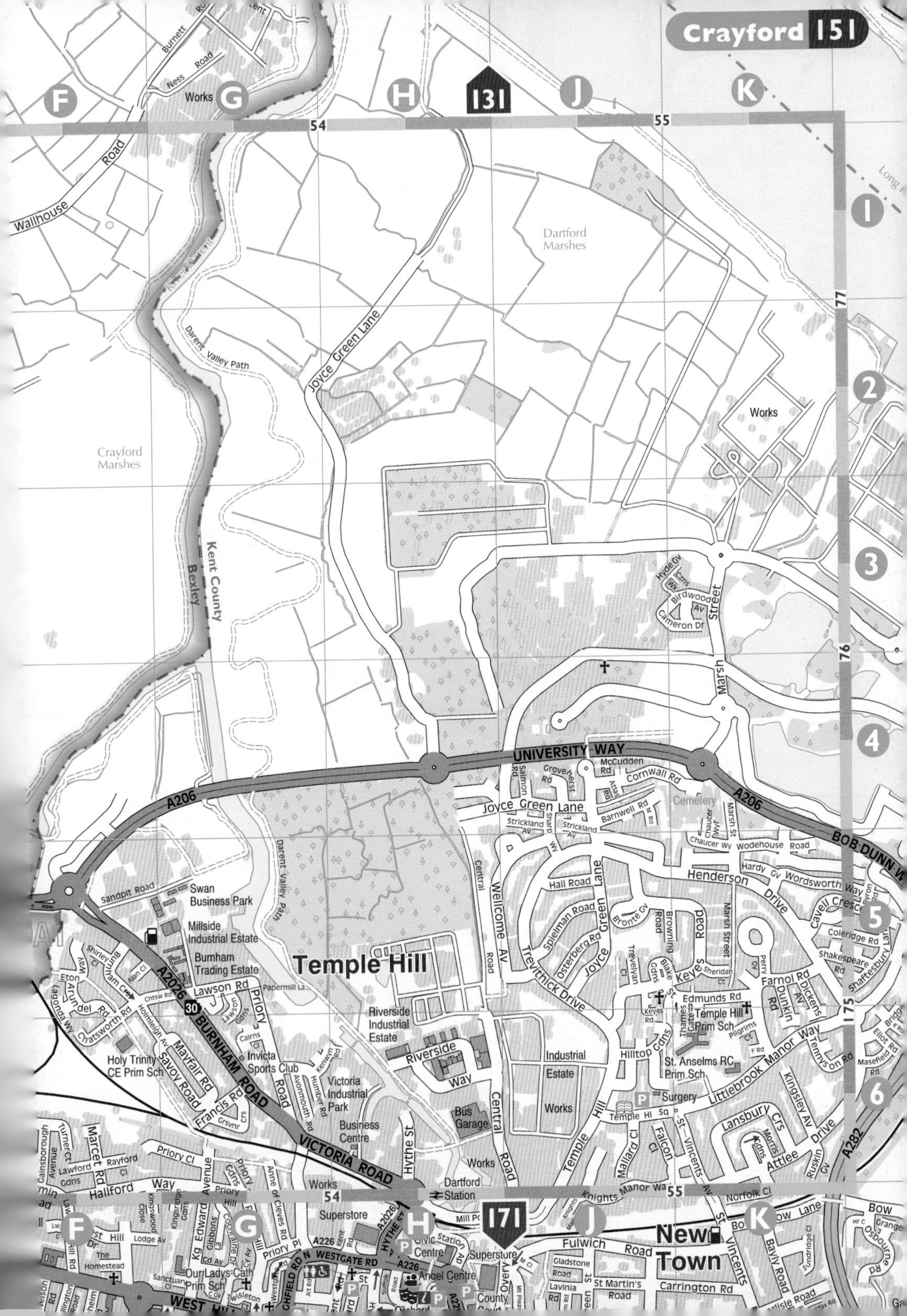

Dartford Marshes
Crayford Marshes
Joyce Green Lane
Darent Valley Path
Kent County
Bexley
River Darent
Wallhouse Road
Burnett Road
Ness Road
Works
131
171
University Way
A206
Bob Dunn Way
Temple Hill
Marsh Street
Cemetery
Henderson Drive
Wodehouse Road
Wordsworth Way
Cavell Crescent
Coleridge Rd
Shakespeare Rd
Shaftesbury La
Hall Road
Spielman Road
Osterberg Rd
Trevithick Drive
Wellcome Av
Central Road
Keyes Road
Browning Road
Edmunds Rd
Temple Hill Prim Sch
St. Anselms RC Prim Sch
Littlebrook Manor Way
Kingsley Av
Attlee Drive
Lansbury Crs
Ruskin Gv
Farnol Rd
Dickens Av
Tennyson Rd
Hilltop Gdns
Surgery
Temple Hl Sq
St Vincents Av
Mallard Cl
Falcon Cl
Knights Manor Way
Industrial Estate
Bus Garage
Riverside Way
Riverside Industrial Estate
Victoria Industrial Park
Business Centre
Hythe St
Dartford Station
Superstore
Civic Centre
Angel Centre
County Court
Swan Business Park
Millside Industrial Estate
Burnham Trading Estate
Sandpit Road
Lawson Rd
Priory Road
Invicta Sports Club
Avonmouth Rd
Humber Rd
A2026 Burnham Road
Victoria Road
Holy Trinity CE Prim Sch
Savoy Road
Mayfair Rd
Francis Rd
Arundel Rd
Chatsworth Rd
Hallford Way
Priory Cl
Marcet Rd
Rayford Cl
Lawford Gdns
Kg Edward Avenue
Anne of Cleves Rd
Priory Pl
West Hill
Our Ladys Cath Prim Sch
A226 Westgate Rd
New Town
Fulwich Road
St Martin's Road
Carrington Rd
Norfolk Cl
Bow Arrow Lane
Bayly Road
Osbourne Rd
Works
Long Reach
A282

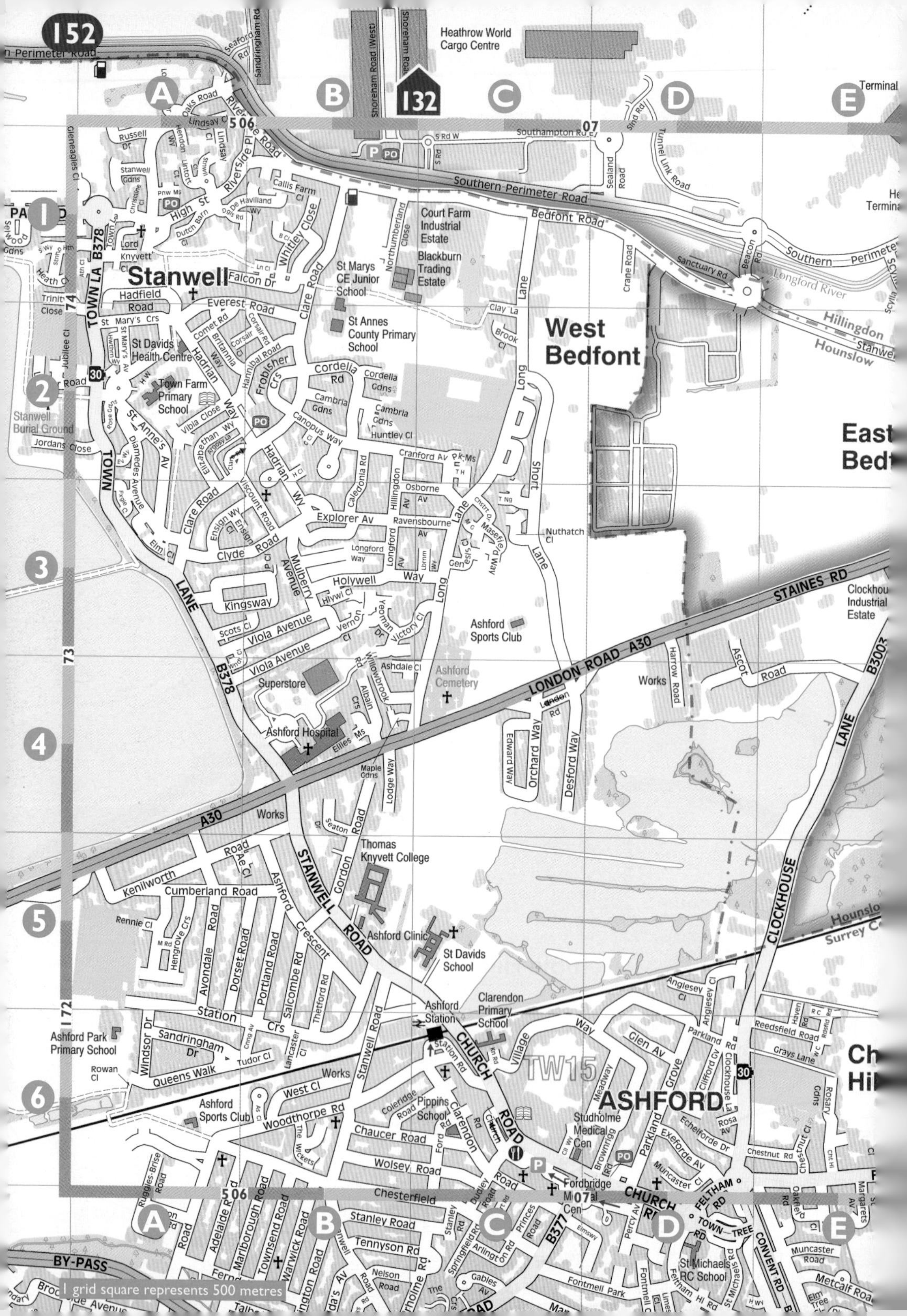

152
132
Perimeter Road
Heathrow World Cargo Centre
Shoreham Road (West)
Shoreham Road
Sandringham Rd
Seaford Rd
Terminal
Oaks Road
Lindsay Cl
Riverside Road
Southampton Rd
S Rd W
Sind Rd
Tunnel Link Road
Sealand Road
Gleneagles Cl
Russell Dr
Hendon
Lintott Ct
Lindsay Cl
Stanwell Gdns
Christine Cl
Riverside Pl
Callis Farm Cl
Southern Perimeter Road
Bedfont Road
Court Farm Industrial Estate
Blackburn Trading Estate
Northumberland Close
High St
De Havilland Wy
Dutch Barn Cl
Whitley Close
Lord Knyvett Cl
Town La
B378
Stanwell
Falcon Dr
Heath Cl
Trinity Close
Jubilee Cl
Hadfield Road
Everest Road
St Mary's Crs
St Marys CE Junior School
St Annes County Primary School
Clare Road
Clay La
Brook Cl
Crane Road
Beacon Rd
Sanctuary Rd
Southern Perimeter
Longford River
Hillingdon
Stanwell
Hounslow
West Bedfont
St Davids Health Centre
Comet Rd
Britannia Way
Corsair Cl
Corsair Rd
Hannibal Road
Frobisher Crs
Cordelia Rd
Cordelia Gdns
Cambria Gdns
Cambria Gdns
Huntley Cl
Hadrian Way
Town Farm Primary School
Stanwell Burial Ground
Jordans Close
Rose Gdns
St Anne's Av
Diamedes Avenue
Vibia Close
Elizabethan Wy
Canopus Way
Cranford Av
Long Lane
Short Lane
East Bedfont
Hadrian Wy
Viscount Road
Clare Road
Osborne Av
Caledonia Rd
Hillingdon Av
Explorer Av
Ravensbourne Av
Masefield Way
Nuthatch Cl
Ensign Wy
Clyde Road
Elm Cl
Longford Way
Longford Av
Holywell Way
Mulberry Avenue
Kingsway
Scots Cl
Viola Avenue
Viola Avenue
Vernon Cl
Yeoman Dr
Victory Cl
Ashford Sports Club
Ashford Cemetery
Ashdale Cl
Willowbrook Rd
Superstore
Albain Crs
Ashford Hospital
Ellies Ms
Maple Gdns
Lodge Way
Staines Rd
Clockhouse Industrial Estate
London Road A30
Harrow Road
Ascot Road
Works
London Rd
Edward Way
Orchard Way
Desford Way
B3003
Lane
A30
Works
Seaton Dr
Gordon Road
Thomas Knyvett College
Stanwell Road
Kenilworth Road
Ae Cl
Cumberland Road
Ashford Crescent
Rennie Cl
Hengrove Crs
Avondale Road
Dorset Road
Portland Road
Salcombe Rd
Thetford Rd
Ashford Clinic
St Davids School
Clockhouse Lane
Hounslow
Surrey
Anglesey Cl
Haven Rd
Reedsfield Road
Grays Lane
Station Crs
Ashford Station
Clarendon Primary School
Village Way
Glen Av
Parkland Rd
Clifford Gv
Grove
Sandringham Dr
Windsor Dr
Ashford Park Primary School
Tudor Cl
Lancaster Cl
Stanwell Road
Queens Walk
Rowan Cl
West Cl
Works
Station Rd
Church Road
TW15
Meadway
Ashford
Studholme Medical Cen
Brownrigg Rd
Parkland Grove
Echelforde Dr
Exeforde Av
Rosa Av
Chestnut Rd
Rosary Gdns
Ashford Sports Club
Woodthorpe Rd
Coleridge Road
Pippins School
Clarendon Road
Chaucer Road
Ford Rd
Wolsey Road
The Wickets
Ruggles-Brise Road
Chesterfield Road
Dudley Road
Fordbridge Medical Cen
Muncaster Cl
Church Rd
Feltham Rd
Town Tree Rd
Convent Rd
Oakfield Rd
Margarets Av
Adelaide Road
Marlborough Road
Townsend Road
Warwick Road
Stanley Road
Stanley Rd
Springfield Rd
Princes Road
B377
Percy Av
St Michaels RC School
Muncaster Road
Metcalf Road
Tennyson Rd
Arlington Rd
Nelson Road
Gables Av
Fontmell Park
Fontmell Cl
Feltham Hl Rd
Elm Tree
By-Pass
1 grid square represents 500 metres

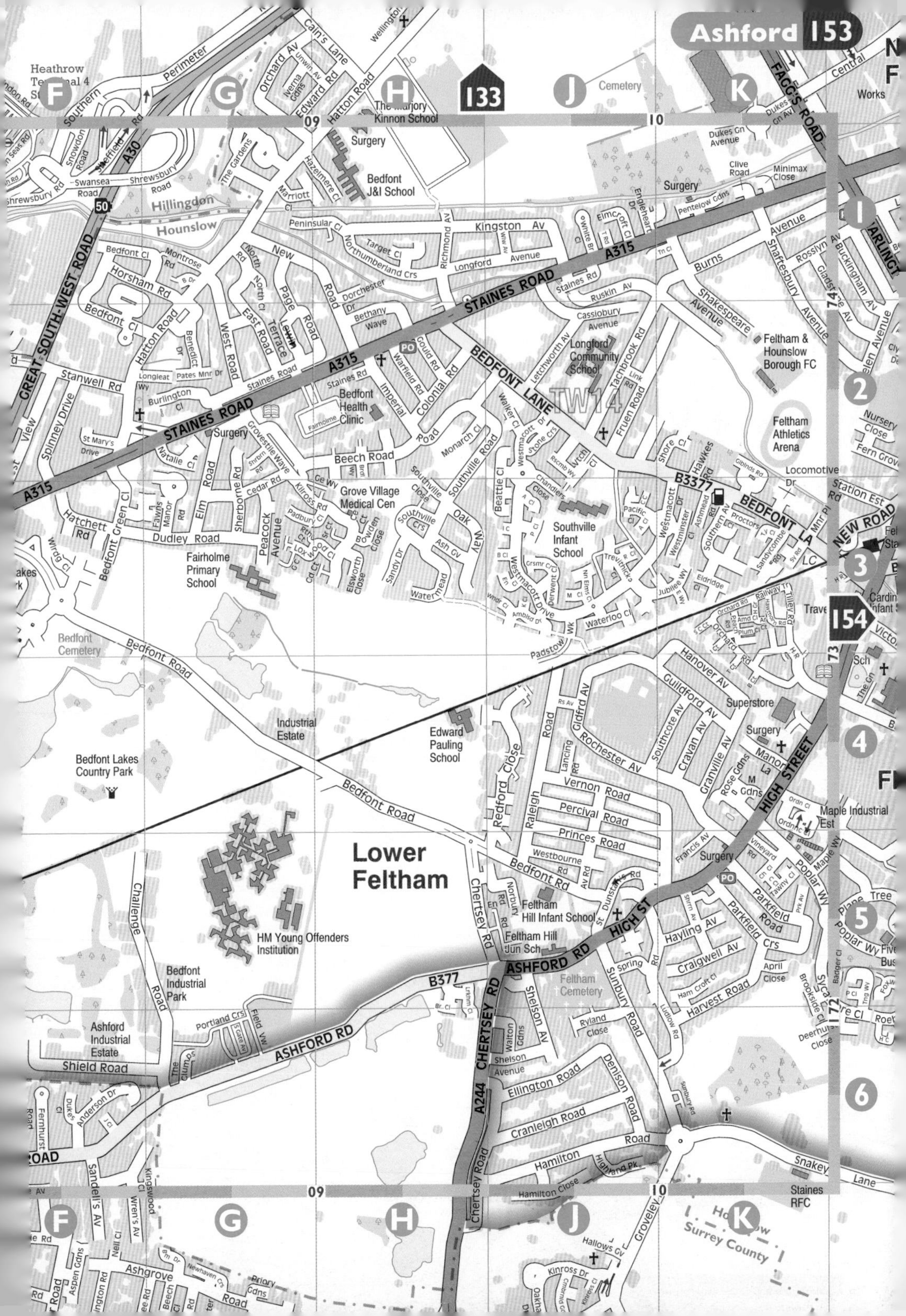
Heathrow Terminal 4
Perimeter
Southern
Cain's Lane
Orchard Av
Unwin Av
Iverna Gdns
Edward Rd
Hatton Road
Wellington
133
Cemetery
FACG'S ROAD
Central
Works
The Marjory Kinnon School
Surgery
Bedfont J&I School
Dukes Gn Avenue
Clive Road
Minimax Close
Snowdon Road
Sheffield Rd
A30
Swansea Road
Shrewsbury Road
Shrewsbury Rd
The Gardens
Hazelmere Cl
Marriott Cl
Hillingdon
Hounslow
Peninsular Cl
Kingston Av
Elmcroft Cl
Englehearts Dr
Pentelow Gdns
Avenue
GREAT SOUTH-WEST ROAD
Bedfont Cl
Montrose Rd
Horsham Rd
New Road
North Rd
North Cl
Page Road
Target Cl
Northumberland Crs
Richmond Av
Longford Avenue
A315
STAINES ROAD
Staines Rd
Ruskin Av
Burns
Shaftesbury Avenue
Rosslyn Av
Buckingham Av
Gladstone Av
Helen Avenue
Hatton Road
Benedict Dr
West Road
East Road
Terrace
Dorchester Dr
Bethany Waye
Cassiobury Avenue
Shakespeare Avenue
Feltham & Hounslow Borough FC
Longleat Wy
Pates Mnr Dr
Stanwell Rd
Burlington Cl
Staines Road
Gould Rd
Warfield Rd
Imperial Road
Colonial Rd
BEDFONT LANE
Letchworth Av
Longford Community School
Tachbrook Rd
Link Rd
Fruen Road
TW14
Spinney Drive
View
Bedfont Health Clinic
Fairholme
Surgery
Grovestile Waye
Beech Road
Monarch Cl
Southville Road
Walker Cl
Westmacott Dr
Stone Crs
Shore Cl
Hawkes Rd
Feltham Athletics Arena
Nursery Close
Fern Grove
St Mary's Drive
Natalie Cl
Elm Road
Sherborne Rd
Cedar Rd
Ge Wy
Kilross Rd
Grove Village Medical Cen
Southville Close
Oak Way
Beattie Cl
Chandlers Close
B3377
BEDFONT LA
Locomotive Dr
Station Est Rd
NEW ROAD
Hatchett Rd
Bedfont Green Cl
Fawns Manor Rd
Dudley Road
Peacock Avenue
Padbury Cl
Bowden Close
Southville Crs
Ash Gv
Sandy Dr
Southville Infant School
Pacific Cl
Westmacott Dr
Westminster Cl
Ashmead Rd
Southern Av
Proctors Cl
Sandycombe Rd
Mnr Pl
Fairholme Primary School
Elsworth Close
Watermead
Westmacott Drive
Derwent Cl
Trevithick Cl
Jubilee Wy
Eldridge
Orchard Rd
Railway Tr
Tilley Rd
Trave
Cardin Infant Sc
154
Victo
Bedfont Cemetery
Bedfont Road
Padstow Wk
Waterloo Cl
Hanover Av
Guildford Av
Sch
The Gn
Superstore
Industrial Estate
Edward Pauling School
Gldfrd Av
Rochester Av
Southcote Av
Cravan Av
Granville Av
Surgery
Manor La
Rose Gdns
M Gdns
HIGH STREET
Bedfont Lakes Country Park
Bedfont Road
Redford Close
Raleigh Road
Lancing Rd
Vernon Road
Percival Road
Princes Road
Westbourne Rd
Av Rd
Maple Industrial Est
Maple Wy
Poplar Wy
Lower Feltham
Challenge Road
Chertsey Rd
Norbury Rd
Bedfont Rd
St Dunstan's Rd
Francis Av
Surgery
Vineyard Rd
Parkfield Road
Parkfield Crs
Plane Tree
Feltham Hill Infant School
HIGH ST
Hayling Av
Craigwell Av
Poplar Wy
HM Young Offenders Institution
Feltham Hill Jun Sch
ASHFORD RD
Spring Rd
Sunbury Road
April Close
Bedfont Industrial Park
B377
Feltham Cemetery
Shelson Av
Ham Croft Cl
Harvest Road
Brookside Cl
Badger Cl
Ashford Industrial Estate
Portland Crs
Field Vw
Walton Gdns
Rylands Close
Ludlow Rd
Deerhurst Close
Shield Road
The Clumps
ASHFORD RD
A244 CHERTSEY RD
Shelson Avenue
Denison Road
Ellington Road
Fernhurst Rd
Dukes Cl
Anderson Dr
Cranleigh Road
Road
Sunbury Rd
ROAD
Sandell's Av
Kingswood Cl
Chertsey Road
Hamilton Road
Highland Pk
Snakey Lane
Staines RFC
Hamilton Close
Av
Wren's Av
Groveley Rd
Surrey County
Hallows Gv
Nell Cl
Aspen Gdns
Ashgrove Road
Newhaven Crs
Priory Gdns
Kinross Dr
F
G
H
J
K
1
2
3
4
5
6
09
10

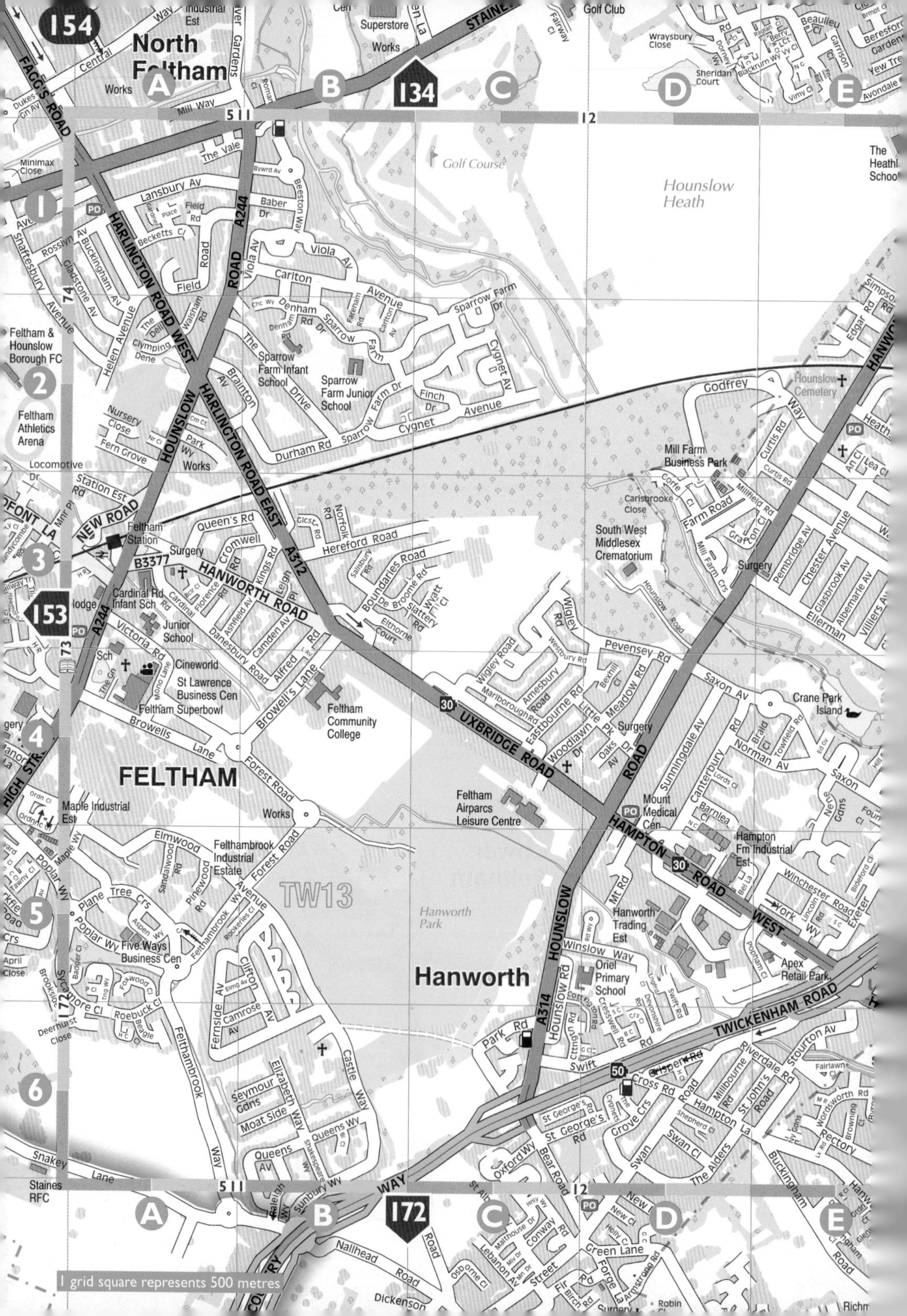
154
134
153
172
North Feltham
FELTHAM
Hanworth
Hounslow Heath
TW13
Golf Course
Golf Club
Hanworth Park
FAGG'S ROAD
HARLINGTON ROAD WEST
HARLINGTON ROAD EAST
HOUNSLOW ROAD
A244
A312
A314
B3377
HANWORTH ROAD
UXBRIDGE ROAD
HAMPTON ROAD WEST
TWICKENHAM ROAD
NEW ROAD
HIGH STREET
Feltham Station
Feltham & Hounslow Borough FC
Feltham Athletics Arena
Sparrow Farm Infant School
Sparrow Farm Junior School
Cardinal Rd Infant Sch
Junior School
Cineworld
St Lawrence Business Cen
Feltham Superbowl
Feltham Community College
Feltham Airparcs Leisure Centre
Felthambrook Industrial Estate
Five Ways Business Cen
Maple Industrial Est
South West Middlesex Crematorium
Mill Farm Business Park
Hounslow Cemetery
Crane Park Island
Mount Medical Cen
Hampton Fm Industrial Est
Hanworth Trading Est
Oriel Primary School
Apex Retail Park
Staines RFC
The Heathland School
Sheridan Court
Wraysbury Close
Superstore
Works
Surgery
Lansbury Av
Baber Dr
Beeston Way
Viola Av
Carlton Avenue
Sparrow Farm Dr
Cygnet Av
Durham Rd
Queen's Rd
Cromwell Rd
Hereford Road
Boundaries Road
Browells Lane
Forest Road
Elmwood Av
Plane Tree Crs
Poplar Wy
Godfrey Way
Saxon Av
Sunningdale Av
Chester Avenue
Pembridge Av
Glasbrook Av
Albemarle Av
Winslow Way
Castle Way
Elizabeth Way
Queens Wy
Snakey Lane
Nallhead Road
Green Lane
Bear Road
Hampton La
Buckingham Rd
Rectory
Stourton Av
Park Rd
Cross Rd
Swan Rd
The Alders
St George's Rd
Oxford Wy
Dickenson
30
50
A
B
C
D
E
1
2
3
4
5
6
11
12
72
73
74
1 grid square represents 500 metres

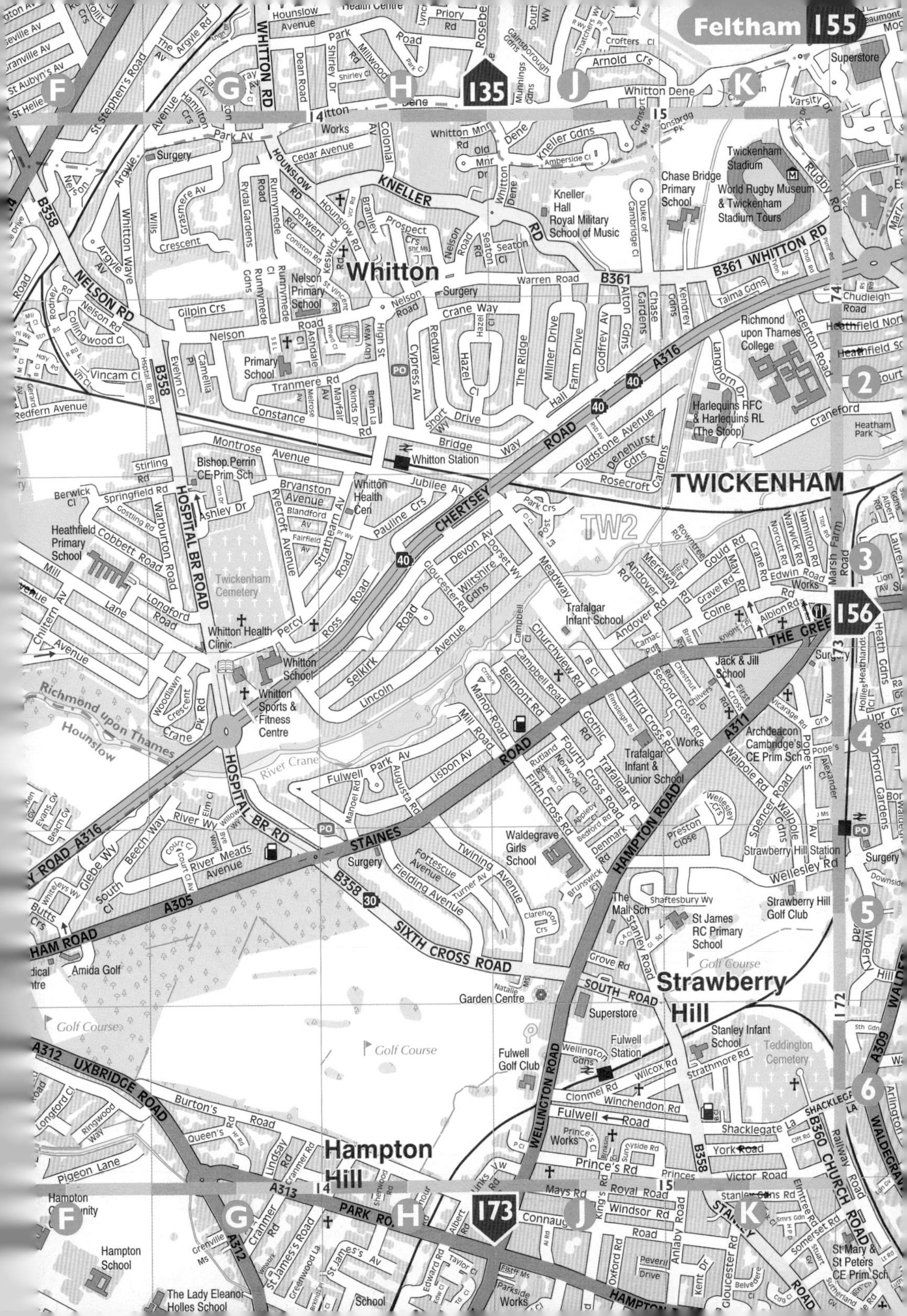
135
156
173
Whitton
TWICKENHAM
TW2
Strawberry Hill
Hampton Hill
Twickenham Stadium
World Rugby Museum & Twickenham Stadium Tours
Kneller Hall Royal Military School of Music
Chase Bridge Primary School
Richmond upon Thames College
Harlequins RFC & Harlequins RL (The Stoop)
Heatham Park
Whitton Station
Nelson Primary School
Primary School
Bishop Perrin CE Prim Sch
Heathfield Primary School
Twickenham Cemetery
Whitton Health Clinic
Whitton Health Cen
Whitton School
Whitton Sports & Fitness Centre
Trafalgar Infant School
Trafalgar Infant & Junior School
Jack & Jill School
Archdeacon Cambridge's CE Prim Sch
Waldegrave Girls School
Strawberry Hill Station
Strawberry Hill Golf Club
The Mall Sch
St James RC Primary School
Garden Centre
Superstore
Fulwell Station
Fulwell Golf Club
Stanley Infant School
Teddington Cemetery
Amida Golf
Golf Course
Hampton Community
Hampton School
The Lady Eleanor Holles School
St Mary & St Peters CE Prim Sch
Richmond upon Thames
Hounslow
River Crane
B361 WHITTON RD
CHERTSEY ROAD A316
HOSPITAL BR ROAD
STAINES ROAD
A305
SIXTH CROSS ROAD
HAMPTON ROAD A311
WELLINGTON ROAD
A312 UXBRIDGE ROAD
PARK ROAD
B360 CHURCH ROAD
NELSON RD
KNELLER RD
WHITTON RD

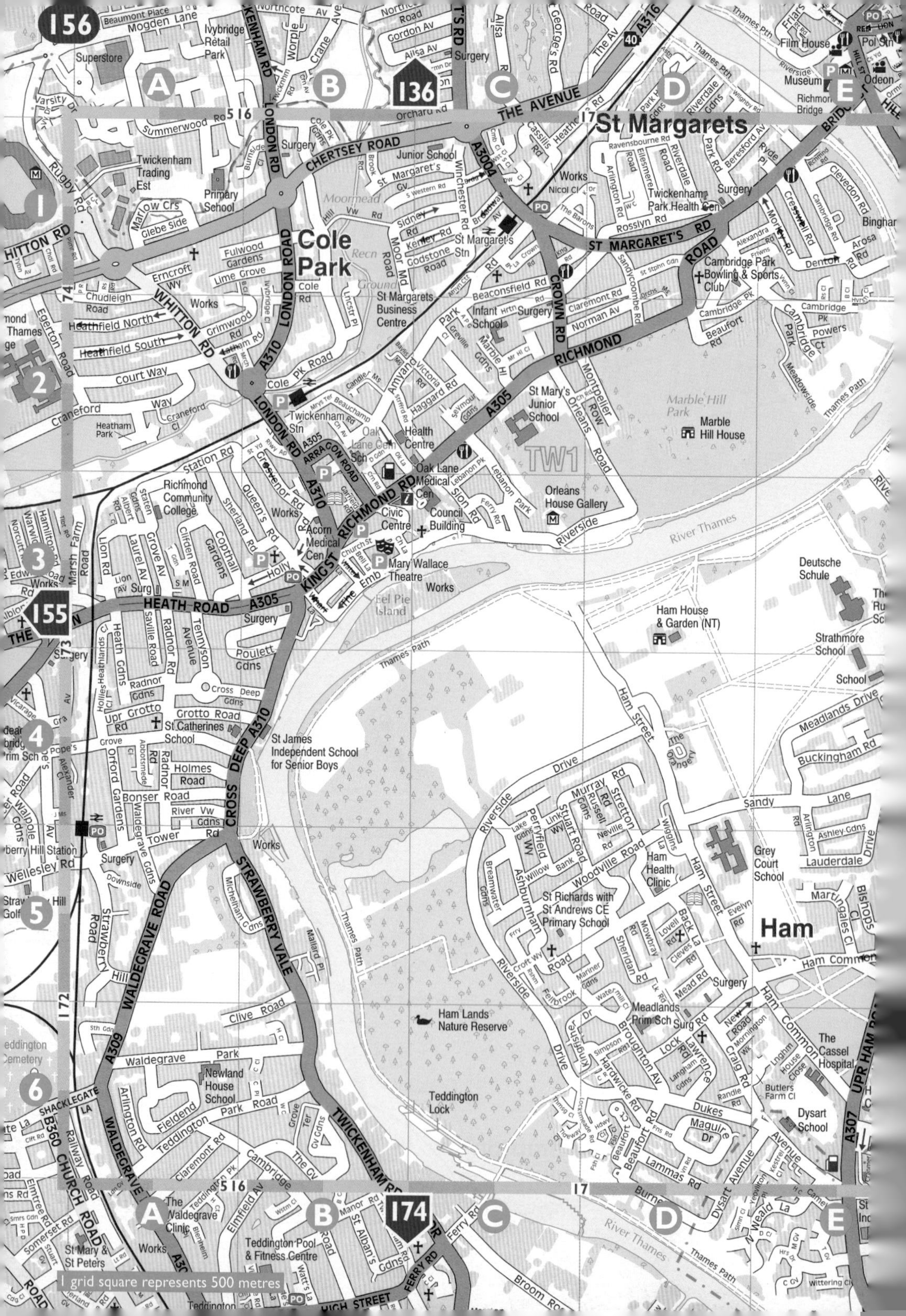
156
136
155
174
A
B
C
D
E
1
2
3
4
5
6
St Margarets
Cole Park
Ham
TW1
Mogden Lane
Beaumont Place
Ivybridge Retail Park
Superstore
Northcote Av
Gordon Av
Ailsa Av
Surgery
The Avenue
Thames Path
Film House
Museum
Richmond Bridge
Red Lion
Pol Stn
Odeon
Orchard Rd
Summerwood Rd
London Rd
Chertsey Road
Junior School
St Margaret's Gv
Twickenham Trading Est
Marlow Crs
Glebe Side
Primary School
Moormead
Winchester Rd
Sidney Rd
Kenley Rd
Godstone Road
St Margaret's Stn
Ravensbourne Rd
Arlington Rd
Ellesmere Road
Riverdale Rd
Park Rd
Beresford Av
Ryde Pl
Twickenham Park Health Cen
Rosslyn Rd
St Margaret's Rd
Cresswell Rd
Cambridge Rd
Clevedon Rd
Arosa Rd
Denton Rd
Whitton Rd
Chudleigh Road
Heathfield North
Heathfield South
Egerton Road
Court Way
Craneford Way
Heatham Park
Fulwood Gardens
Lime Grove
Erncroft Wy
Works
Grimwood Rd
Latham Rd
London Road
A310
Cole Pk Road
Cole Rd
Lncstr Pl
St Margarets Business Centre
Beaconsfield Rd
Infant School
Surgery
Crown Rd
Claremont Rd
Norman Av
Sandycoombe Rd
Cambridge Park Bowling & Sports Club
Cambridge Pk
Beaufort Rd
Powers Ct
Meadowside
Marble Hill Park
Marble Hill House
Richmond Road
A305
St Mary's Junior School
Orleans Road
Montpelier Row
Haggard Rd
Victoria Rd
Amyand
Twickenham Stn
Oak Lane Cem
Health Centre
Oak Lane Medical Cen
Lebanon Park
Sion Rd
Ferry Rd
Orleans House Gallery
Riverside
River Thames
Station Rd
Arragon Road
Richmond Community College
Queen's Rd
Sheriand Rd
Copthall Gardens
Clifden Road
Grove Av
Laurel Av
Lion Rd
Hamilton Rd
Marsh Farm Road
Acorn Medical Cen
Civic Centre
Council Building
Mary Wallace Theatre
Eel Pie Island
Heath Road
Kingst Rd
Surgery
Poulett Gdns
Tennyson Avenue
Radnor Rd
Saville Road
Heath Gdns
Radnor Gdns
Cross Deep Gdns
Grotto Road
Upr Grotto Rd
St Catherines School
Cross Deep
St James Independent School for Senior Boys
Orford Gardens
Holmes Road
Bonser Road
River Vw Gdns
Tower Rd
Waldegrave Gdns
Strawberry Hill Station
Wellesley Rd
Strawberry Road
Strawberry Vale
Waldegrave Road
A309
Clive Road
Waldegrave Park
Newland House School
Fieldend
Arlington Rd
Teddington Park Road
Claremont Rd
Cambridge
Twickenham Rd
Shacklegate La
B360 Church Road
Railway Road
Elmtree Rd
Somerset Rd
St Mary & St Peters
The Waldegrave Clinic
Elmfield Av
Teddington Pool & Fitness Centre
St Alban's Gdns
Manor Rd
Ferry Rd
High Street
Broom Rd
Thames Path
Ham House & Garden (NT)
Deutsche Schule
Strathmore School
School
Ham Street
The Orangery
Riverside Drive
Murray Rd
Stretton Rd
Stuart Road
Russell Gdns
Neville Rd
Woodville Road
Ashburnham Road
Perryfield Wy
Ham Health Clinic
St Richards with St Andrews CE Primary School
Sheridan Rd
Mowbray Rd
Back La
Mead Rd
Meadlands Prim Sch
Broughton Av
Lock Rd
Lawrence Rd
Craig Rd
New Road
Ham Lands Nature Reserve
Teddington Lock
Mallard Pl
Kingfisher Dr
Hardwicke Rd
Beaufort Rd
Lammas Rd
Dukes Av
Maguire Dr
Dysart Avenue
Grey Court School
Sandy Lane
Meadlands Drive
Buckingham Rd
Ashley Gdns
Lauderdale Drive
Martingales Cl
Bishops Cl
Ham Common
The Cassel Hospital
Butlers Farm Cl
Dysart School
Upr Ham Rd
A307
Weald La
Wittering Cl
1 grid square represents 500 metres

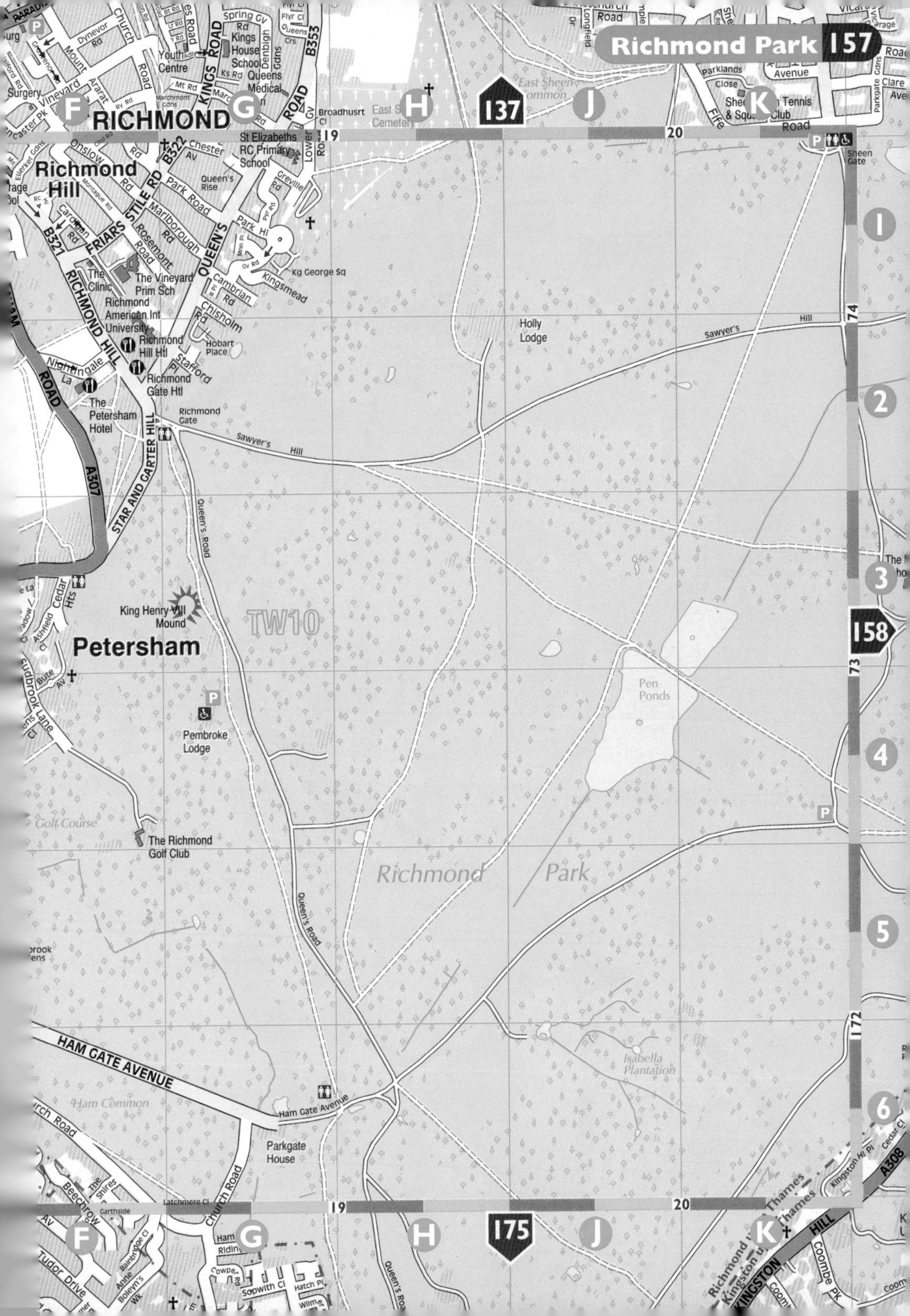

F

RICHMOND

Richmond Hill

Petersham

TW10

King Henry VIII Mound

The Clinic

The Vineyard Prim Sch

Richmond American Int University

Richmond Hill Htl

Richmond Gate Htl

The Petersham Hotel

Richmond Gate

Sawyer's Hill

Pembroke Lodge

Golf Course

The Richmond Golf Club

Ham Common

HAM GATE AVENUE

Ham Gate Avenue

Parkgate House

G

St Elizabeths RC Primary School

Kg George Sq

Kingsmead

Queen's Road

Church Road

Ham Riding

H

Broadhusrt Cl

East Sheen Cemetery

137

J

East Sheen Common

Parklands Close

Sheen Common

Fife Road

K

Sheen Tennis Club

Sheen Gate

Holly Lodge

Sawyer's Hill

Pen Ponds

Richmond Park

Isabella Plantation

175

19

20

I

2

3

158

4

5

172

6

74

73

Richmond u. Thames

Kingston u. Thames

KINGSTON HILL

A308

Coombe Pk

Coombe Cl

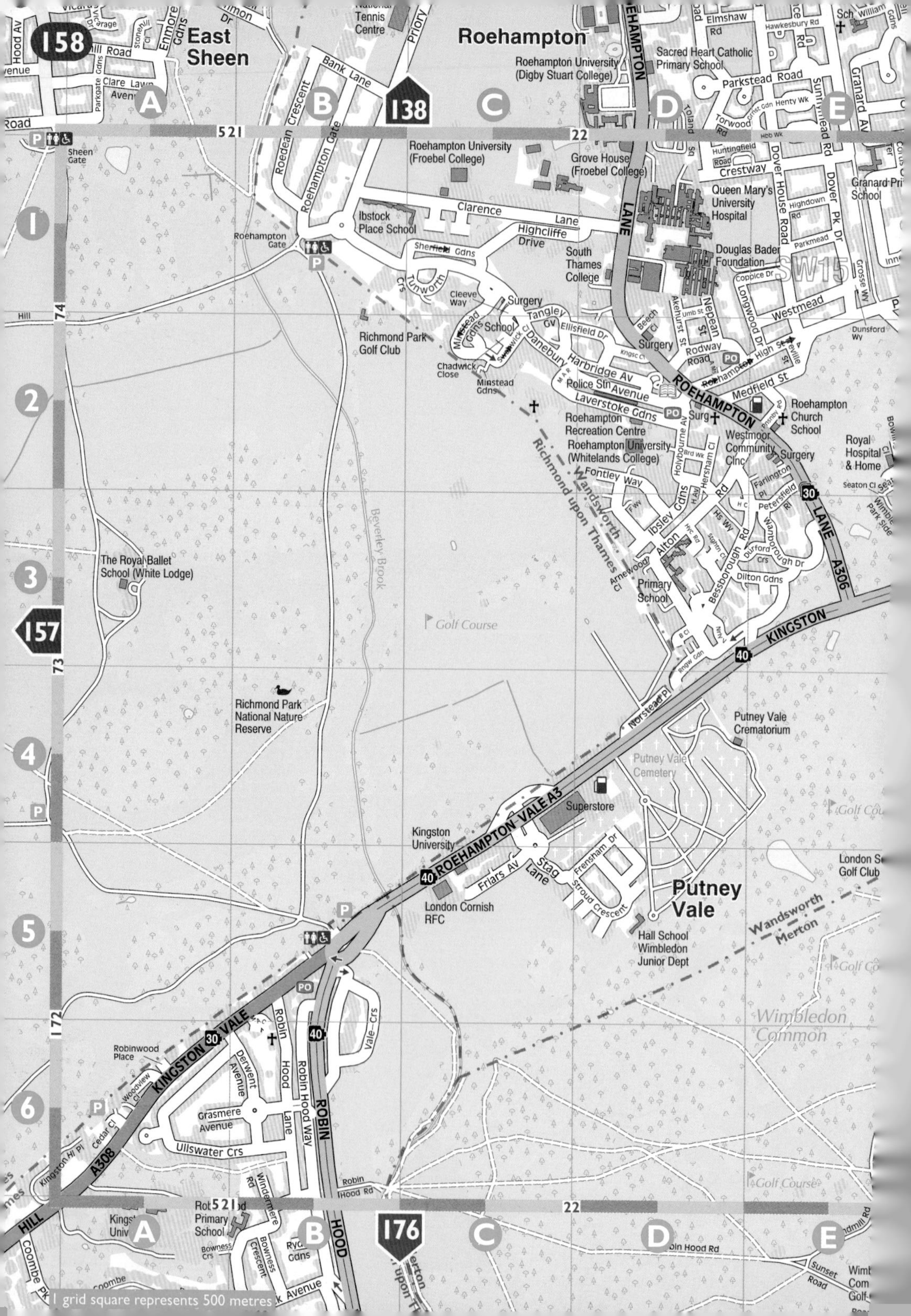
East Sheen
Roehampton
Roehampton University (Digby Stuart College)
Sacred Heart Catholic Primary School
138
Roehampton University (Froebel College)
Grove House (Froebel College)
Queen Mary's University Hospital
Ibstock Place School
Clarence Lane
Highcliffe Drive
South Thames College
Douglas Bader Foundation
SW15
Roehampton Gate
Sheen Gate
Richmond Park Golf Club
Surgery
School
Police Stn
Roehampton Recreation Centre
Roehampton University (Whitelands College)
Roehampton Church School
Westmoor Community Clinic
Royal Hospital & Home
Granard Primary School
Richmond upon Thames
Wandsworth
The Royal Ballet School (White Lodge)
157
Golf Course
Beverley Brook
Primary School
KINGSTON
A306
Richmond Park National Nature Reserve
Putney Vale Crematorium
Putney Vale Cemetery
Superstore
ROEHAMPTON VALE A3
Kingston University
London Cornish RFC
Putney Vale
Hall School Wimbledon Junior Dept
London Scottish Golf Club
Wandsworth
Merton
Wimbledon Common
KINGSTON VALE
A308
Robinwood Place
Derwent Avenue
Grasmere Avenue
Ullswater Crs
Robin Hood Lane
Robin Hood Way
ROBIN HOOD
Vale Crs
Robin Hood Rd
Golf Course
176
Primary School
Bowness Crescent
Coombe
Sunset Road
521
22
A B C D E
1 2 3 4 5 6
74
73
172
1 grid square represents 500 metres

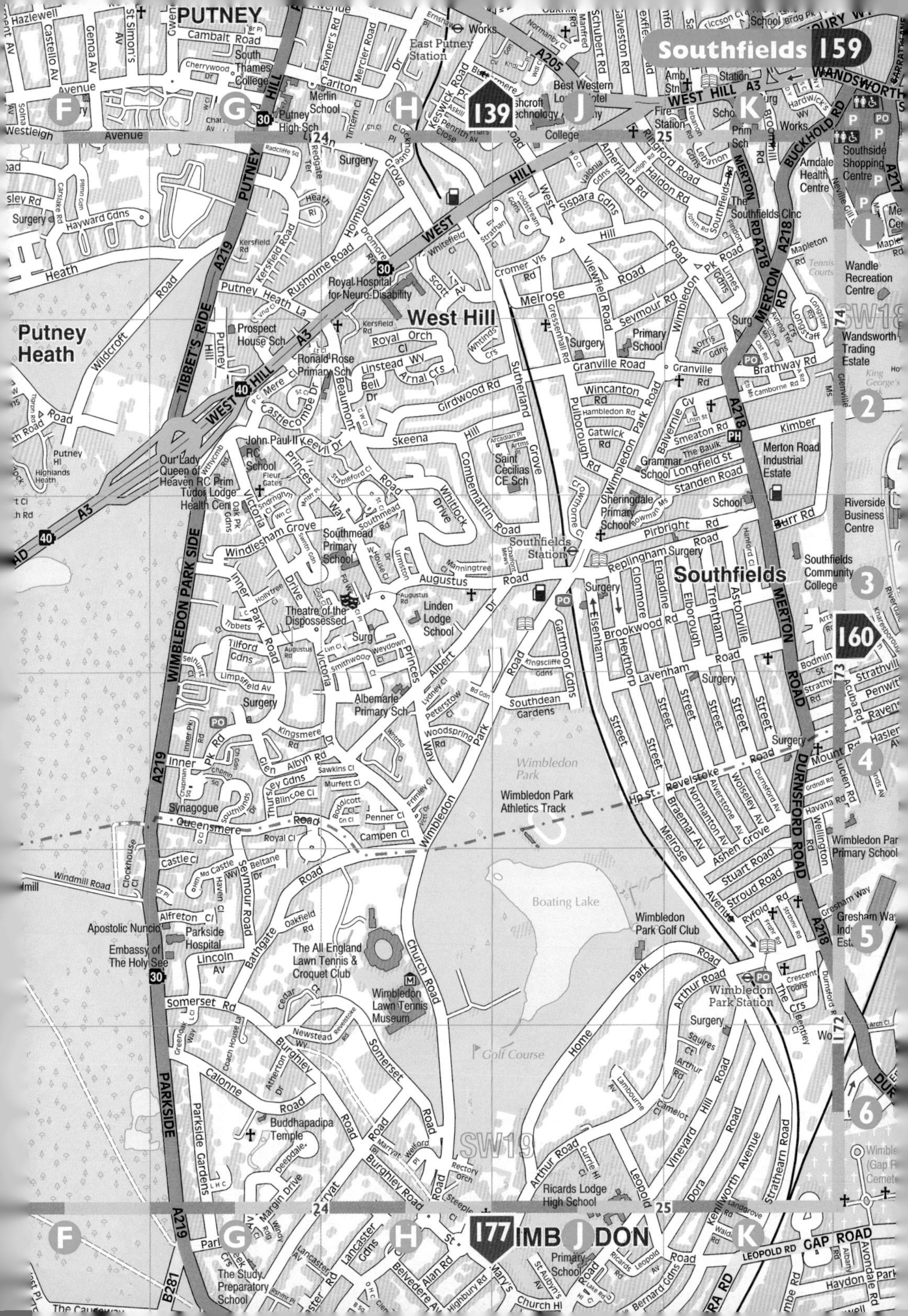
PUTNEY
Putney Heath
West Hill
Southfields
WIMBLEDON
East Putney Station
Southfields Station
Wimbledon Park Station
Wimbledon Park
Wimbledon Park Athletics Track
Boating Lake
Wimbledon Park Golf Club
Golf Course
The All England Lawn Tennis & Croquet Club
Wimbledon Lawn Tennis Museum
Buddhapadipa Temple
Royal Hospital for Neuro-Disability
Southside Shopping Centre
Arndale Health Centre
Wandle Recreation Centre
Wandsworth Trading Estate
Merton Road Industrial Estate
Riverside Business Centre
Southfields Community College
Wimbledon Park Primary School
Ricards Lodge High School
The Study Preparatory School
Parkside Hospital
Apostolic Nuncio
Embassy of The Holy See
Theatre of the Dispossessed
Linden Lodge School
Albemarle Primary Sch
Southmead Primary School
Saint Cecilias CE Sch
Sheringdale Primary School
Prospect House Sch
Ronald Rose Primary Sch
John Paul II RC School
Our Lady Queen of Heaven RC Prim
Tudor Lodge Health Cen
Merlin School
Putney High Sch
South Thames College
Synagogue
WEST HILL
PUTNEY HILL
TIBBET'S RIDE
WIMBLEDON PARK SIDE
PARKSIDE
MERTON ROAD
DURNSFORD ROAD
BUCKHOLD RD
CAP ROAD
LEOPOLD RD
A3
A205
A218
A219
A217
B281
SW18
SW19
139
160
177

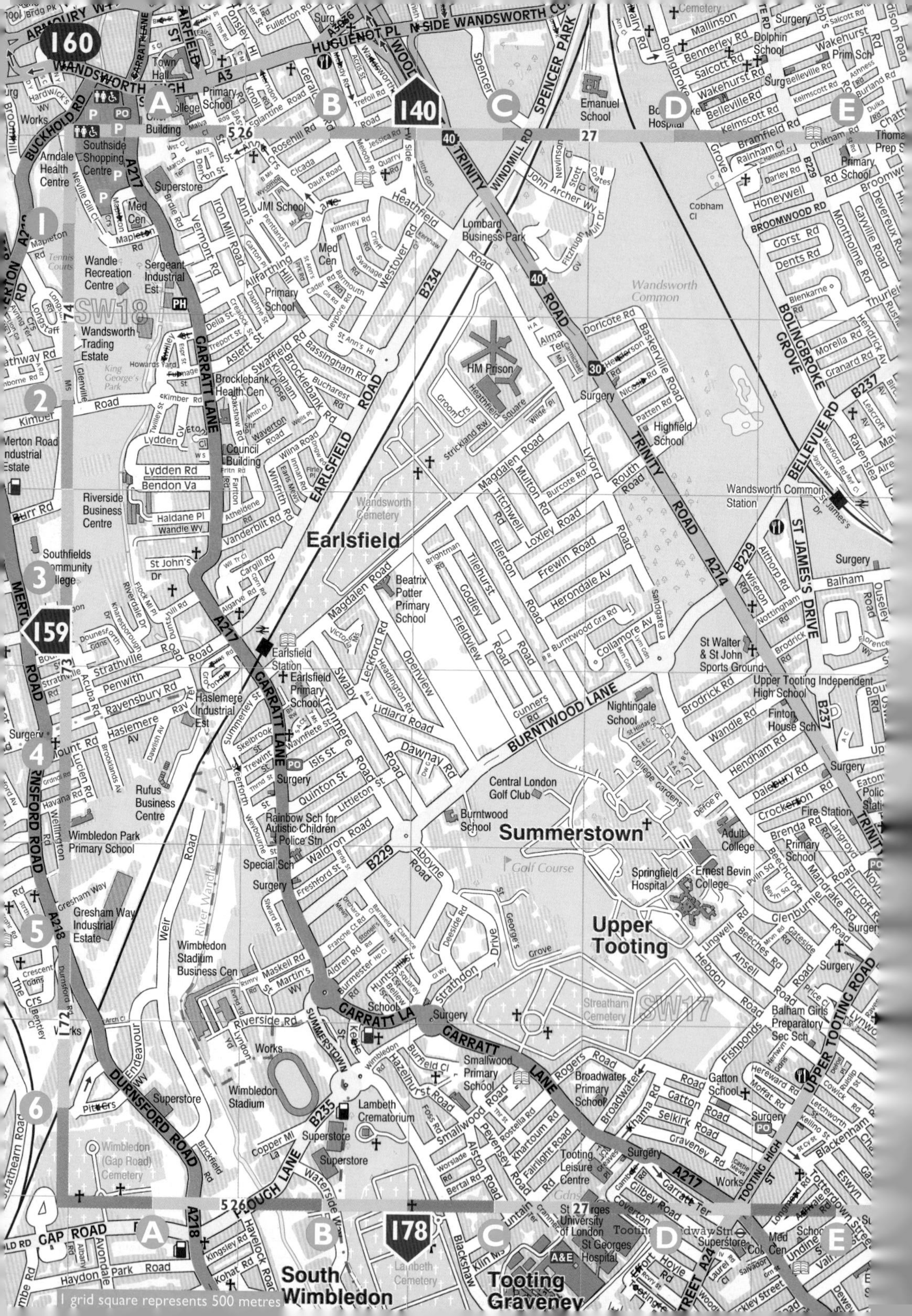

160
140
159
178
A
B
C
D
E
1
2
3
4
5
6
ARMOURY WY
WANDSWORTH HIGH
HUGUENOT PL
N SIDE WANDSWORTH CO
SPENCER PARK
AIRFIELD
GARRATT LANE
BUCKHOLD RD
Town Hall
Primary School
College
Building
Southside Shopping Centre
Arndale Health Centre
Superstore
Med Cen
JMI School
Mapleton Rd
Wandle Recreation Centre
Sergeant Industrial Est
SW18
Wandsworth Trading Estate
King George's Park
Brocklebank Health Cen
Council Building
Merton Road Industrial Estate
Riverside Business Centre
Southfields Community College
Haslemere Industrial Est
Rufus Business Centre
Wimbledon Park Primary School
Gresham Way Industrial Estate
Wimbledon Stadium Business Cen
Wimbledon Stadium
Superstore
Wimbledon (Gap Road) Cemetery
DURNSFORD ROAD
GAP ROAD
Haydon Park Road
South Wimbledon
1 grid square represents 500 metres
PLOUGH LANE
Lambeth Crematorium
Lambeth Cemetery
Earlsfield
Earlsfield Station
Earlsfield Primary School
EARLSFIELD ROAD
Wandsworth Cemetery
Beatrix Potter Primary School
Rainbow Sch for Autistic Children
Police Stn
Special Sch
Surgery
HM Prison
Lombard Business Park
Emanuel School
Bolingbroke Hospital
TRINITY ROAD
WINDMILL RD
John Archer Wy
Wandsworth Common
Highfield School
Heathfield Square
Magdalen Road
BURNTWOOD LANE
Nightingale School
Central London Golf Club
Burntwood School
Summerstown
Golf Course
Springfield Hospital
Ernest Bevin College
Adult College
Upper Tooting
Streatham Cemetery
SW17
Smallwood Primary School
Broadwater Primary School
Tooting Leisure Centre
St Georges University of London
St Georges Hospital
A&E
Tooting Graveney
Superstore
Gatton School
Balham Girls Preparatory Sec Sch
UPPER TOOTING ROAD
TOOTING HIGH ST
Upper Tooting Independent High School
Finton House Sch
St Walter & St John Sports Ground
Wandsworth Common Station
ST JAMES'S DRIVE
BOLINGBROKE GROVE
BELLEVUE RD
Dolphin School
Wakehurst Prim Sch
Thomas Prep S
Primary School
BROOMWOOD RD
Fire Station
Primary School
Works
A217
A218
A214
B229
B234
B235
B237
A3
A24

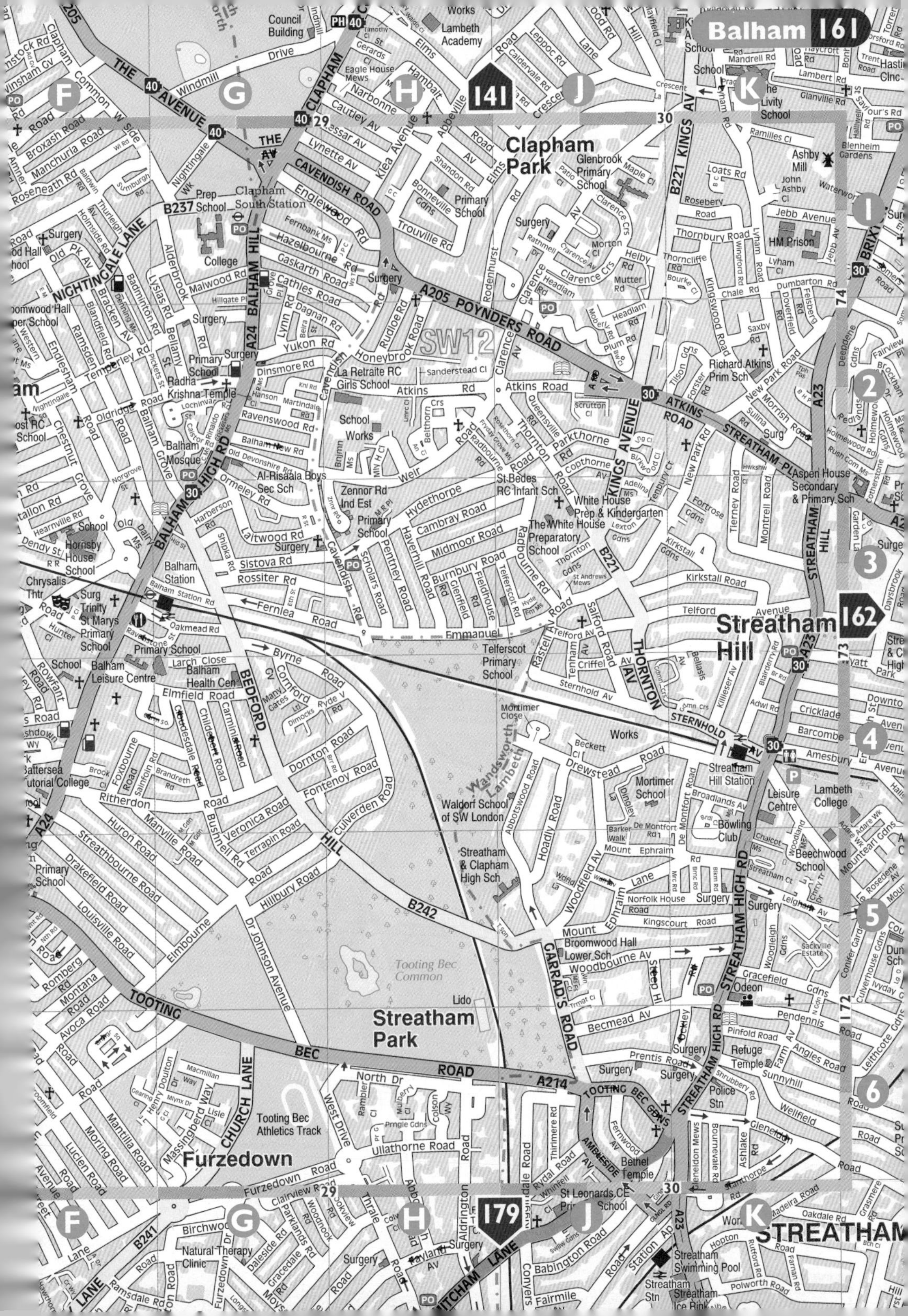
Balham
161
141
162
179
F
G
H
J
K
1
2
3
4
5
6
29
30
Clapham Park
SW12
Streatham Hill
Streatham Park
Furzedown
STREATHAM
Tooting Bec Common
Tooting Bec Athletics Track
Wandsworth
Lambeth
THE AVENUE
Windmill Drive
Council Building
Lambeth Academy
Works
CLAPHAM COMMON
Clapham Common West Side
Winsham Gv
Broxash Road
Manchuria Road
Roseneath Rd
NIGHTINGALE LANE
Nightingale Wk
Clapham South Station
Prep School
College
B237
A24 BALHAM HILL
CAVENDISH ROAD
Englewood Rd
Hazelbourne Rd
Gaskarth Road
Cathles Road
Malwood Rd
Alderbrook
Lysias Rd
Badminton Rd
Bracken Av
Blandfield Rd
Ramsden Rd
Endlesham Road
Temperley Rd
Bellamy St
Dagnan Rd
Yukon Rd
Lynn Rd
Honeybrook Road
Rudloe Rd
Trouville Rd
Bonneville Gdns
Primary School
Shandon Rd
Abbeville Road
Klea Avenue
Narbonne Av
Cautley Av
Elms Road
Hambalt Rd
A205 POYNDERS ROAD
Rodenhurst Rd
Clarence Av
Glenbrook Primary School
Clarence Crs
Headlam St
Helby Rd
Mutter Rd
B221 KINGS AV
Rosebery Road
Thornbury Road
Kingswood Road
Lyham Road
HM Prison
Jebb Avenue
Ashby Mill
Blenheim Gardens
The Livity School
Mandrell Rd
Lambert Rd
Glanville Rd
Ramilles Cl
Loats Rd
Chale Rd
Dumbarton Rd
Felsberg Rd
Deverfield Rd
Richard Atkins Prim Sch
New Park Road
ATKINS ROAD
STREATHAM PL
A23
BRIXTON HILL
Aspen House Secondary & Primary Sch
Morrish Road
Sulina Rd
Tierney Road
Montrell Road
STREATHAM HILL
Kirkstall Gdns
Kirkstall Road
Telford Avenue
Fortrose Gdns
Tenbury Ct
Atkins Road
Sanderstead Cl
La Retraite RC Girls School
Dinsmore Rd
Hanson Cl
Martindale Rd
Ravenswood Rd
Balham New Rd
Old Devonshire Rd
Al-Risaala Boys Sec Sch
Ormeley Rd
Radha Krishna Temple
Balham Mosque
Balham Grove
BALHAM HIGH RD
Weir Road
Hydethorpe Road
Cambray Road
Midmoor Road
Burnbury Road
Zennor Rd Ind Est
Primary School
Surgery
Sistova Rd
Rossiter Rd
Fernlea Road
Emmanuel Road
Scholars Road
Pentney Road
Haverhill Road
Glenfield Rd
Fieldhouse Rd
Telferscot Rd
Radbourne Rd
St Bedes RC Infant Sch
Thornton Road
Parkthorne Rd
Copthorne Av
KINGS AVENUE
White House Prep & Kindergarten
The White House Preparatory School
B221
THORNTON AV
Salford Road
Telford Av
Tenham Av
Criffel Av
Sternhold Av
Telferscot Primary School
Balham Station
Balham Station Rd
Oakmead Rd
Ravenstone St
Primary School
Larch Close
Balham Leisure Centre
Balham Health Cen
Elmfield Road
Chrysalis Thtr
St Marys Primary School
Hornsby House School
Dendy St
Hearnville Rd
Laitwood Rd
BEDFORD HILL
Byrne Road
Cornford Gv
Childebert Road
Carminia Road
Dornton Road
Fontenoy Road
Culverden Road
Veronica Road
Terrapin Road
Bushnell Rd
Manville Road
Ritherdon Road
Huron Road
Foxbourne Road
Brook Cl
Battersea Tutorial College
A24
Streathbourne Road
Drakefield Road
Louisville Road
Hillbury Road
Elmbourne Road
Dr Johnson Avenue
B242
TOOTING BEC ROAD
A214
Lido
Streatham & Clapham High Sch
Waldorf School of SW London
Abbotswood Road
Hoadly Road
Mortimer Close
Beckett Cl
Drewstead Road
Mortimer School
Works
STERNHOLD AV
Streatham Hill Station
Leisure Centre
Lambeth College
Amesbury Avenue
Barcombe Av
Cricklade Av
Broadlands Av
De Montfort Road
Bowling Club
Mount Ephraim Lane
Mount Ephraim Rd
Woodfield Av
Norfolk House Road
Kingscourt Road
Surgery
Broomwood Hall Lower Sch
Woodbourne Av
GARRAD'S ROAD
Becmead Av
Prentis Road
STREATHAM HIGH RD
Gracefield Gdns
Odeon
Pendennis Road
Pinfold Road
Refuge Temple
Sunnyhill Road
Angles Road
Wellfield Road
Beechwood School
Leigham Av
Police Stn
Streatham Ct
Woodleigh Gdns
Sackville Estate
TOOTING BEC GDNS
Fernwood Av
AMBLESIDE AV
Bethel Temple
Thirlmere Rd
Rydal Road
North Dr
West Drive
Ullathorne Road
Aldrington Road
Colson Wy
Rambler Cl
Mulberry Cl
Pringle Gdns
CHURCH LANE
Massingberd Way
Henry Doulton Dr
Lisle Cl
Macmillan Way
Furzedown Road
Clairview Road
Mantilla Road
Moring Road
Lucien Road
Avenue
Romberg Rd
Montana Road
Avoca Road
TOOTING
St Leonards CE Primary School
Glenelon Mews
Bournevale Rd
Ashlake Rd
Gleneldon Road
Streatham Swimming Pool
Streatham Stn
Station Ap
Babington Road
Conyers Road
Fairmile Av
MITCHAM LANE
Natural Therapy Clinic
Birchwood Rd
Daleside Rd
Gracedale Rd
Parklands Rd
Woodnook Rd
Thrale Rd
Faylands Av
Surgery
B241
Ramsdale Rd
Madeira Road
Oakdale Rd
Hopton Road
Rutford Rd
Polworth Road
Grasmere Rd
Leithcote Gdns
Conifer Gdns
Culverhouse Gdns
Ivyday Gv

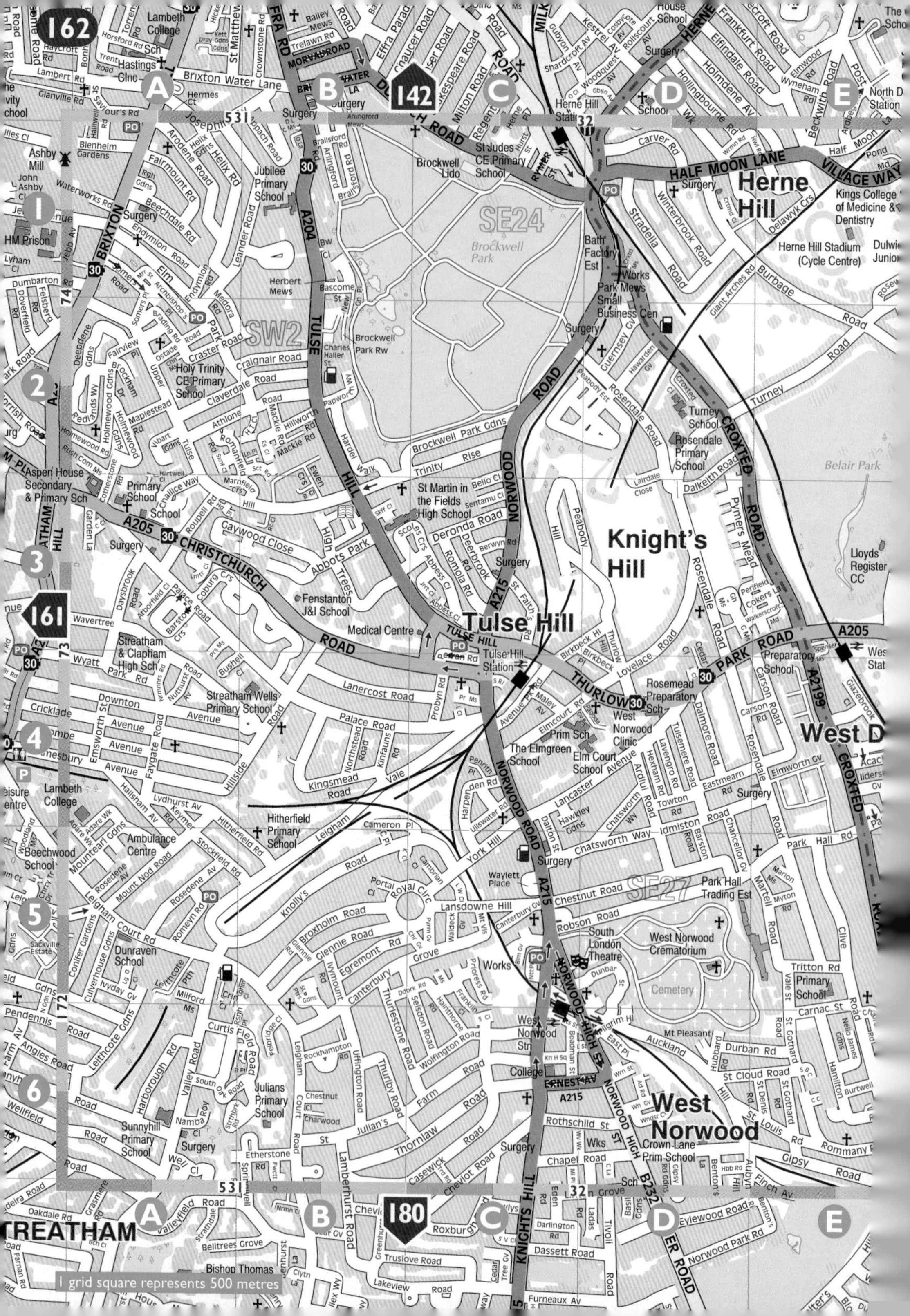

162
142
161
180
A
B
C
D
E
1
2
3
4
5
6
Lambeth College
Hastings Clinic
Brixton Water Lane
Lambert Rd
Glanville Rd
Saviour's Rd
Josephine Av
Arodene Road
Fairmount Rd
Helix Rd
Jubilee Primary School
Ashby Mill
Blenheim Gardens
Waterworks Rd
HM Prison
Jebb Av
Brixton
Surgery
Beechdale Rd
Endymion Road
Leander Road
Medora Rd
Craster Road
Cralgnair Road
Claverdale Road
Holy Trinity CE Primary School
Dumbarton Rd
Deerfield
Deepdene Gdns
Fairview Pl
Redlands Wy
Holmewood Gdns
Holmewood Rd
Brockham Dr
Maplestead Rd
Athlone
Tulse Hill
Aspen House Secondary & Primary Sch
Primary School
School
Challice Way
Roupell Rd
Caywood Close
A205
CHRISTCHURCH ROAD
Streatham Hill
Surgery
Daysbrook Road
Palace Road
Coburg Crs
Fenstanton J&I School
Wavertree
Streatham & Clapham High Sch
Wyatt Park Rd
Downton Avenue
Cricklade Avenue
Emsworth St
Faygate Road
Streatham Wells Primary School
Lambeth College
Hitherfield Rd
Hillside Road
Lydhurst Av
Hailsham Av
Beechwood School
Mountearl Gdns
Ambulance Centre
Mount Nod Road
Rosedene Av
Stockfield Rd
Hitherfield Primary School
Leigham Vale
Kingsmead Road
Palace Road
Lanercost Road
Medical Centre
Leigham Court Rd
Conifer Gardens
Culverhouse Gdns
Dunraven School
Leithcote Gdns
Pendennis Road
Angles Road
Wellfield Road
Harborough Rd
Valley Road
Curtis Field Road
Sunnyhill Primary School
Julians Primary School
Surgery
Milford Ms
Etherstone
Lamberhurst Road
Chestnut Cl
Charwood
Julian's
Thornlaw
Casewick Road
Cheviot Road
Knolly's Road
Broxholm Road
Glennie Road
Egremont Rd
Royal Circ
Lansdowne Hill
Canterbury Grove
Thurlestone Road
Uffington Road
Selsdon Road
Wolfington Road
Rockhampton Rd
Thurlby Road
Farm Road
York Hill
Cameron Pl
Waylett Place
Works
Brockwell Lido
St Judes CE Primary School
Brockwell Park
SE24
SW2
SE27
Herbert Mews
Bascome St
Charles Haller St
Brockwell Park Rw
Papworth Wy
Brockwell Park Gdns
Trinity Rise
Hardel Walk
Tulse Hill
A204
St Martin in the Fields High School
Deronda Road
Abbots Park
High Trees
Abbess Cl
Romola Rd
Deerbrook Rd
Norwood Road
A215
Tulse Hill
Tulse Hill Station
Knight's Hill
Peabody Hill
Rosendale Road
Turney School
Rosendale Primary School
Lairdale Close
Dalkeith Road
Croxted Road
Pymers Mead
Lovelace Road
Thurlow Park Road
Rosemead Preparatory Sch
West Norwood Clinic
Elmcourt Rd
Prim Sch
The Elmgreen School
Elm Court School
Lancaster Avenue
Chatsworth Way
Idmiston Road
Eastmearn Rd
Dalmore Road
Tulsemere Road
Park Hall Rd
Park Hall Trading Est
Chestnut Road
Robson Road
South London Theatre
West Norwood Crematorium
Cemetery
Norwood High St
West Norwood Stn
College
Ernest Av
Rothschild St
Chapel Road
Crown Lane Prim School
West Norwood
Auckland
Durban Rd
St Cloud Road
St Louis Rd
Gipsy Road
Tritton Rd
Primary School
Carnac St
Hamilton
Martell Road
Clive Road
Preparatory School
Carson Road
Elmworth Gv
Croxted
Lloyds Register CC
Belair Park
West Dulwich
Herne Hill
Half Moon Lane
Village Way
Kings College of Medicine & Dentistry
Herne Hill Stadium (Cycle Centre)
Stradella Road
Winterbrook Road
Burbage Road
Turney Road
Herne Hill Station
Carver Rd
Hollingbourne Rd
Holmdene Av
Frankfurt Road
Elfindale Road
Milkwood Road
Railton Road
Dulwich Road
Shakespeare Road
Milton Road
Effra Parade
Chaucer Road
Morval Road
Trelawn Rd
Brailsford Rd
Arlingford Rd
Batn Factory Est
Park Mews Small Business Cen
Guernsey Gv
Hawarden Gv
Valleyfield Road
Streatham
Oakdale Rd
Belltrees Grove
Bishop Thomas
Truslove Road
Lakeview Road
Roxburgh
Dassett Road
Darlington Rd
Knights Hill
Eden Rd
Tivoli Road
Eylewood Road
Norwood Park Rd
Furneaux Av
B232
531
32
1 grid square represents 500 metres

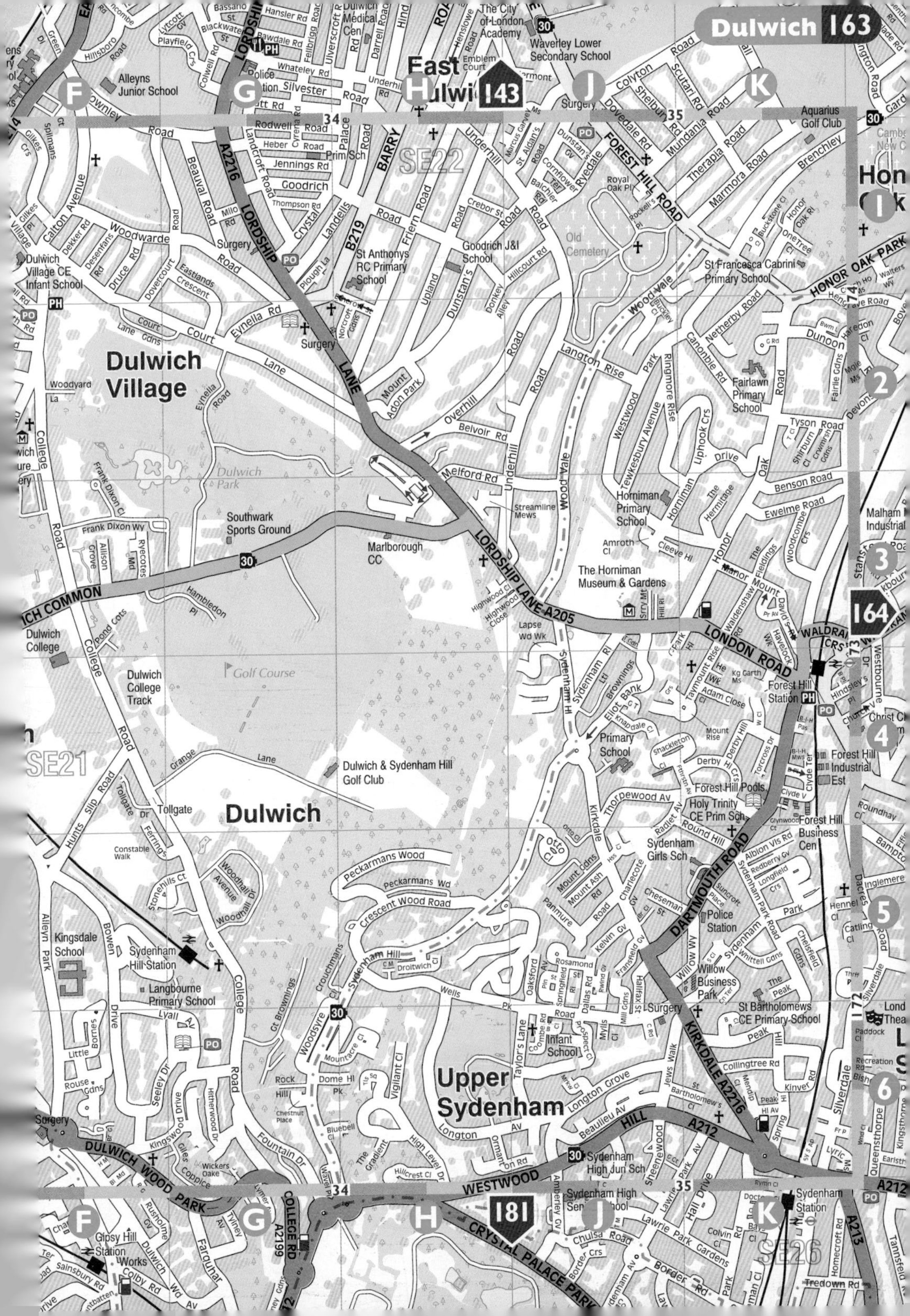
East Dulwich
143
SE22
Dulwich Village
Dulwich
SE21
Upper Sydenham
SE26
164
181
Honor Oak
Alleyns Junior School
Dulwich Village CE Infant School
The City of London Academy
Waverley Lower Secondary School
Aquarius Golf Club
St Anthonys RC Primary School
Goodrich J&I School
St Francesca Cabrini Primary School
Fairlawn Primary School
Horniman Primary School
The Horniman Museum & Gardens
Old Cemetery
Dulwich Park
Southwark Sports Ground
Marlborough CC
Dulwich College
Dulwich College Track
Golf Course
Dulwich & Sydenham Hill Golf Club
Kingsdale School
Sydenham Hill Station
Langbourne Primary School
Forest Hill Station
Forest Hill Industrial Est
Forest Hill Pools
Holy Trinity CE Prim Sch
Sydenham Girls Sch
Forest Hill Business Cen
Police Station
Willow Business Park
St Bartholomews CE Primary School
Infant School
Sydenham High Jun Sch
Sydenham High Sen School
Sydenham Station
Gipsy Hill Station
Malham Industrial
Lordship Lane
A2216
B219
A205
London Road
Dartmouth Road
Kirkdale A2216
Forest Hill Road
Honor Oak Park
Dulwich Common
College Road
Dulwich Wood Park
Westwood Hill
A212
Crystal Palace Park
College Rd
A2199
A213
Wood Vale
Sydenham Hill
Peckarmans Wood
Crescent Wood Road
Wells Pk Road
Longton Grove
Hunts Slip Road
Alleyn Park
Grange Lane
Tollgate
Eynella Rd
Overhill
Belvoir Rd
Melford Rd
Langton Rise
Westwood Park
Tewkesbury Avenue
Ringmore Rise
Canonbie Rd
Liphook Crs
Benson Road
Ewelme Road
Thorpewood Av
Round Hill
Sydenham Park Road
Kirkdale
Taylor's Lane
Jews Walk
Lawrie Park Gardens
Border Crs
Chulsa Road
F
G
H
J
K
I
2
3
4
5
6
34
35
30
172
173
174

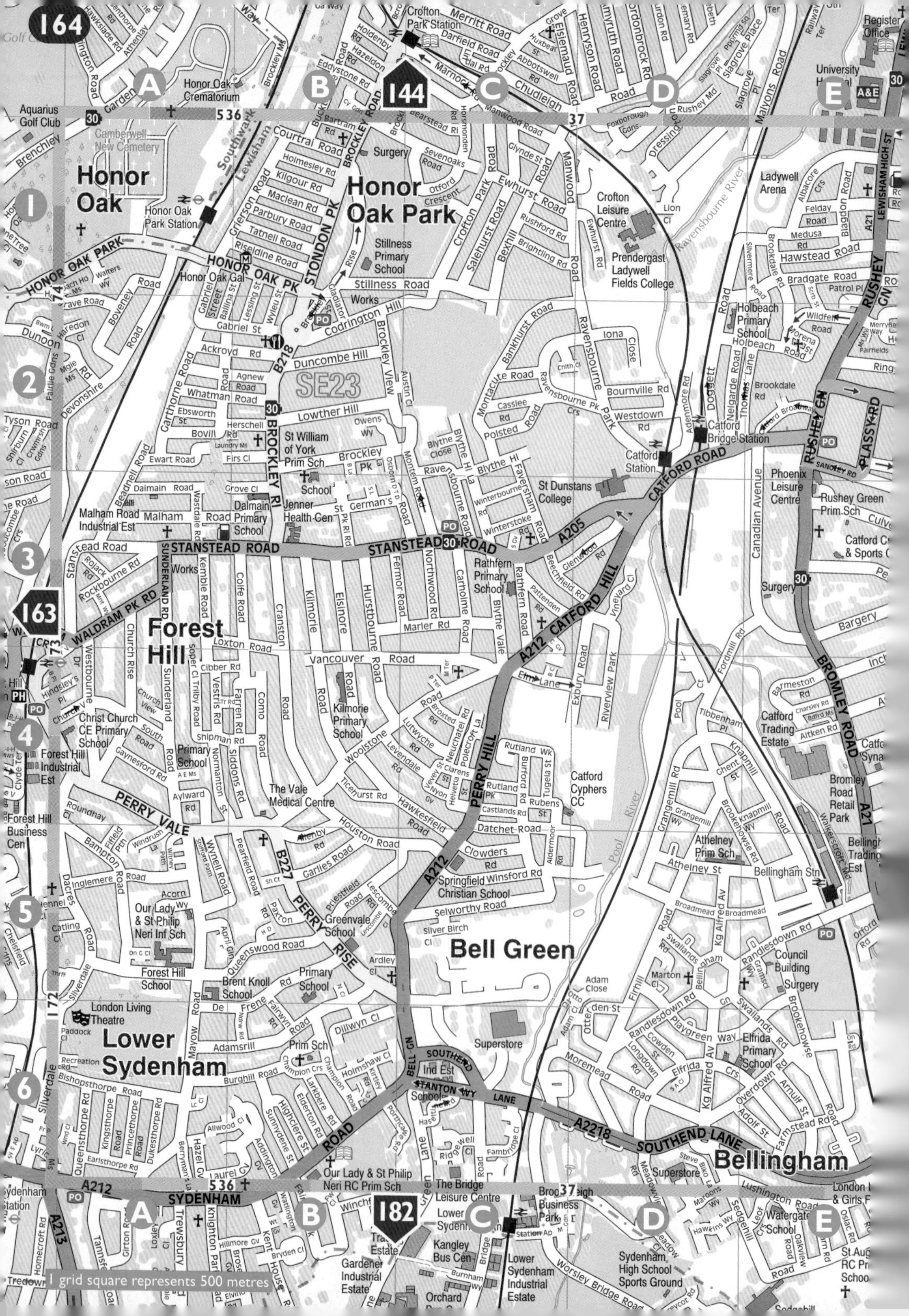
164
Crofton Park Station
Merritt Road
Holdenby Rd
Hazeldon Rd
Eddystone Rd
Darfield Road
Marnock Rd
Abbotswell Rd
Chudleigh
Huxbear
Eislemaud Road
Henryson Road
Slagrove Place
Malyons Road
Register Office
University Hospital
A&E
Honor Oak Crematorium
Aquarius Golf Club
Camberwell New Cemetery
Honor Oak
Honor Oak Park Station
Honor Oak Park
Brenchley
Southwark
Lewisham
Courtrai Road
Holmesley Rd
Kilgour Rd
Maclean Rd
Parbury Road
Tatnell Road
Riseldine Road
Grierson Road
Bartram Rd
Bearstead Ri
Manwood Road
Glynde St
Sevenoaks Road
Otford Crescent
Surgery
Stondon Pk
Brockley Road
Stillness Primary School
Stillness Road
Crofton Park Road
Salehurst Road
Bexhill
Ewhurst Road
Rushford Rd
Brightling Rd
Ewhurst Rd
Crofton Leisure Centre
Prendergast Ladywell Fields College
Ravensbourne River
Lion Cl
Ladywell Arena
Albacore Crs
Feldav Road
Medusa Rd
Hawstead Road
Blagdon Road
Bradgate Road
Patrol Pl
Lewisham High St
A21
Rushey Gn
Honor Oak Pk
Honor Oak Gal
Gabriel Street
Ballina St
Lessing St
Wyleu St
Walters Ho
Boveney Road
Haredon Cl
Dunoon
Fairlie Gdns
Devonshire Rd
Mgle Ms
Tyson Road
Shirburn Cl
Gabriel St
Codrington Hill
Works
Ackroyd Rd
Agnew Road
Duncombe Hill
Brockley View
Austin Cl
SE23
Whatman Road
Ebsworth St
Garthorne Road
Lowther Hill
Owens Wy
B218
Brockley Ri
Herschell Rd
Laundry Ms
Bovill Rd
Firs Cl
Ewart Road
St William of York Prim Sch
Brockley Pk
School
Jenner Health Cen
St German's Road
Ravensbourne Road
Montem Road
Blythe Close
Blythe Hi La
Blythe Hl
Faversham Road
Bankhurst Road
Iona Close
Ravensbourne Pk Crs
Montacute Road
Casslee Rd
Polsted Road
Bournville Rd
Westdown Rd
Ravensbourne Park
Doggett Road
Adenmore Rd
Nelgarde Road
Thomas Lane
Brookdale Rd
Holbeach Primary School
Holbeach Road
Wildfell Road
Morena St
Catford Bridge Station
Catford Station
Catford Road
St Dunstans College
Winterbourne Rd
Winterstoke Road
Dalmain Road
Dalmain Primary School
Beadnell Road
Malham Road Industrial Est
Malham Road
Wastdale Rd
Stanstead Road
A205
Rockbourne Rd
Rojack Rd
Sunderland Rd
Waldram Pk Rd
163
Kemble Road
Colfe Road
Cranston
Kilmorie
Elsinore
Hurstbourne
Fermor Road
Northwood Rd
Carholme Road
Rathfern Primary School
Rathfern Road
Blythe Vale
Beechfield Rd
Glenwood Rd
Catford Hill
A212
Vineyard Cl
Canadian Avenue
Phoenix Leisure Centre
Rushey Green Prim Sch
Catford Cr & Sports
Plassy Rd
Sangley Rd
Forest Hill
Church Rise
Loxton Road
Marler Rd
Vancouver Road
Cibber Rd
Vestris Rd
Farren Rd
Como Road
Kilmorie Primary School
Exbury Road
Riverview Park
Elm Lane
Fordmill Rd
Tibbenham Pl
Barmeston Rd
Bargery
Bromley Road
Christ Church CE Primary School
Westbourne Dr
Hindsley's Pl
Church Vale
Church View
South Road
Sunderland
Forest Hill Industrial Est
Clyde Ter
Caynesford Rd
Shipman Rd
Siddons Rd
Normanton St
Primary School
Broxted Rd
Lutwyche Rd
Woolstone
Levendale
Neuchatel Rd
Polecroft La
Perry Hill
Rutland Wk
Burford Rd
Tugela St
Rutland Pk
Rubens St
Catford Cyphers CC
Castlands Rd
Datchet Road
Aldermoor Rd
Grangemill Rd
Grangemill Wy
Knapmill Rd
Knapmill Wy
Ghent St
Brookehowse Rd
Catford Trading Estate
Aitken Rd
Bromley Road Retail Park
Walkerscroft Md
Perry Vale
Aylward Rd
Roundhay Cl
Forest Hill Business Cen
Bampton Rd
Fifield Pth
Windrush La
Wynell Road
Pearfield Road
The Vale Medical Centre
Ticehurst Rd
Hawkesfield Road
Houston Road
Allenby Rd
Garlies Road
B227
Clowders Rd
Springfield Christian School
Winsford Rd
Pool River
Athelney Prim Sch
Athelney St
Bellingham Stn
Bellingham Trading Est
Inglemere Road
Dacres Road
Acorn Wy
Our Lady & St Philip Neri Inf Sch
Perry Rise
Priestfield Road
Lescombe
Paxton Rd
Greenvale School
Selworthy Road
Silver Birch Cl
Bell Green
Broadmead
Kg Alfred Av
Randlesdown Rd
Swallands Rd
Council Building
Surgery
Catling Cl
Queenswood Road
Forest Hill School
Brent Knoll School
Frene Rd
Primary School
Ardley Cl
Adam Close
Otterden St
Marton Cl
Firhill
Bellingham Gn
Crumsci Rd
Playgreen Way
Silverdale
London Living Theatre
Paddock Cl
Lower Sydenham
Mayow Road
Adamsrill Rd
Dillwyn Cl
Prim Sch
Superstore
Longdown Rd
Cowden St
Elfrida Primary School
Elfrida Crs
Brookehowse Rd
Arnulf St
Recreation Ground
Bishopsthorpe Road
Burghill Road
Champion Crs
Holmshaw Cl
Southend Ind Est
Stanton Wy
Schools
Bell Gn
Moremead Road
Overdown Rd
Adolf St
Farmstead Rd
Queensthorpe Rd
Kingsthorpe Road
Princethorpe Road
Dukesthorpe Road
Allwood Cl
Sunnydene St
Highclere St
Elderton Rd
Larkbere Rd
Road
Lane
Ridgewell Cl
Fambridge Cl
A2218
Southend Lane
Bellingham
Superstore
Steve Biko La
Earlsthorpe Rd
Laurel Gv
Addington Gv
Our Lady & St Philip Neri RC Prim Sch
The Bridge Leisure Centre
Lushington Road
London Girls
536
37
A212
Sydenham
Sydenham Station
A213
Trewsbury
Girton Road
Knighton Park
Watlington
Kent House
Bryden Cl
Hillmore Gv
Winchfield
182
Trade Estate
Gardener Industrial Estate
Lower Sydenham
Kangley Bus Cen
Bridge
Lower Sydenham Industrial Estate
Station Ap
Business Park
Maroons Wy
Hawkins Wy
Sedgehill
Meadowview Road
Sydenham High School Sports Ground
Worsley Bridge Road
Watergate School
Oaklands Road
St Aug RC Pri School
Homecroft Rd
Tredown
1 grid square represents 500 metres
144
A B C D E
1 2 3 4 5 6
30
172
173
174

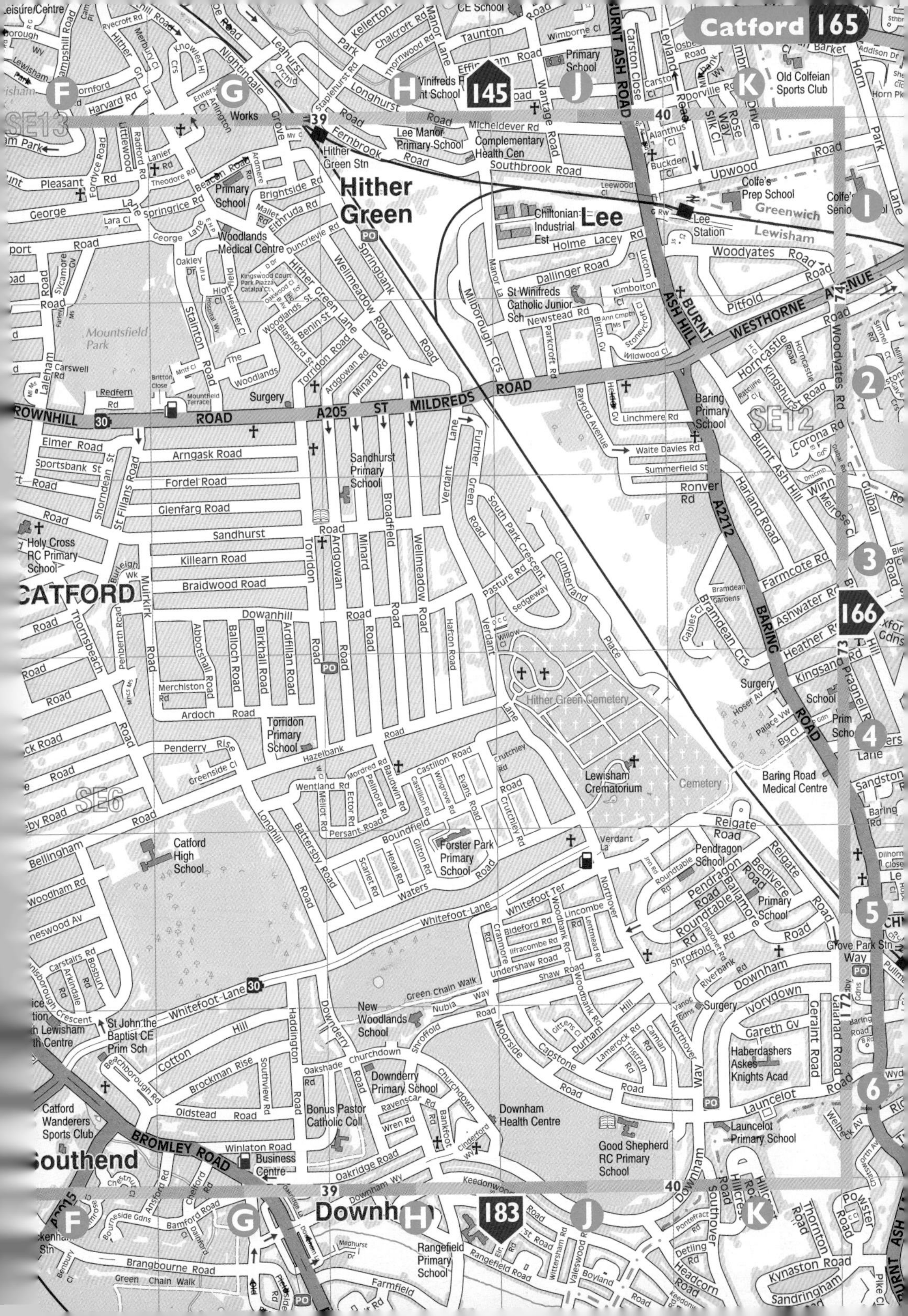
Hither Green
Lee
CATFORD
Southend
Downham
SE13
SE12
SE6
145
166
183
F
G
H
J
K
I
2
3
4
5
6
39
40
30
A205
A2212
ST MILDREDS ROAD
ROWNHILL ROAD
BURNT ASH ROAD
BURNT ASH HILL
WESTHORNE AVENUE
BARING ROAD
BROMLEY ROAD
Hither Green Stn
Lee Station
Grove Park Stn
Chiltonian Industrial Est
Mountsfield Park
Hither Green Cemetery
Lewisham Crematorium
Cemetery
Colfe's Prep School
Old Colfeian Sports Club
Lee Manor Primary School
Complementary Health Cen
St Winifreds Catholic Junior Sch
Woodlands Medical Centre
Sandhurst Primary School
Torridon Primary School
Holy Cross RC Primary School
Baring Primary School
Baring Road Medical Centre
Forster Park Primary School
Pendragon School
Catford High School
New Woodlands School
St John the Baptist CE Prim Sch
Catford Wanderers Sports Club
Downderry Primary School
Bonus Pastor Catholic Coll
Downham Health Centre
Good Shepherd RC Primary School
Haberdashers Askes Knights Acad
Launcelot Primary School
Rangefield Primary School
Business Centre
Surgery
Works
Green Chain Walk
Whitefoot Lane
Southbrook Road
Manor Lane
Leahurst Road
Nightingale Grove
Springbank Road
Hither Green Lane
Wellmeadow Road
Broadfield Road
Minard Road
Ardgowan Road
Torridon Road
Sandhurst Road
Arngask Road
Fordel Road
Glenfarg Road
Killearn Road
Braidwood Road
Dowanhill Road
Ardoch Road
Hazelbank Road
Penderry Rise
Verdant Lane
Further Green Road
South Park Crescent
Cumberland Place
Milborough Crs
Dallinger Road
Holme Lacey Rd
Woodyates Road
Pitfold Road
Harland Road
Farmcote Rd
Ashwater Rd
Heather Rd
Kingsand Rd
Reigate Road
Pendragon Road
Roundtable Road
Bedivere Road
Downham Way
Ivorydown
Launcelot Road
Geraint Road
Capstone Road
Moorside Road
Churchdown
Oakridge Road
Haddington Road
Longhill Road
Battersby Road
Cotton Hill
Brockman Rise
Oldstead Road
Winlaton Road
Brangbourne Road
Farmfield Road
Kynaston Road
Sandringham
Rangefield Road
Headcorn Road
Southover
Hillcrest Road
Thornton Road

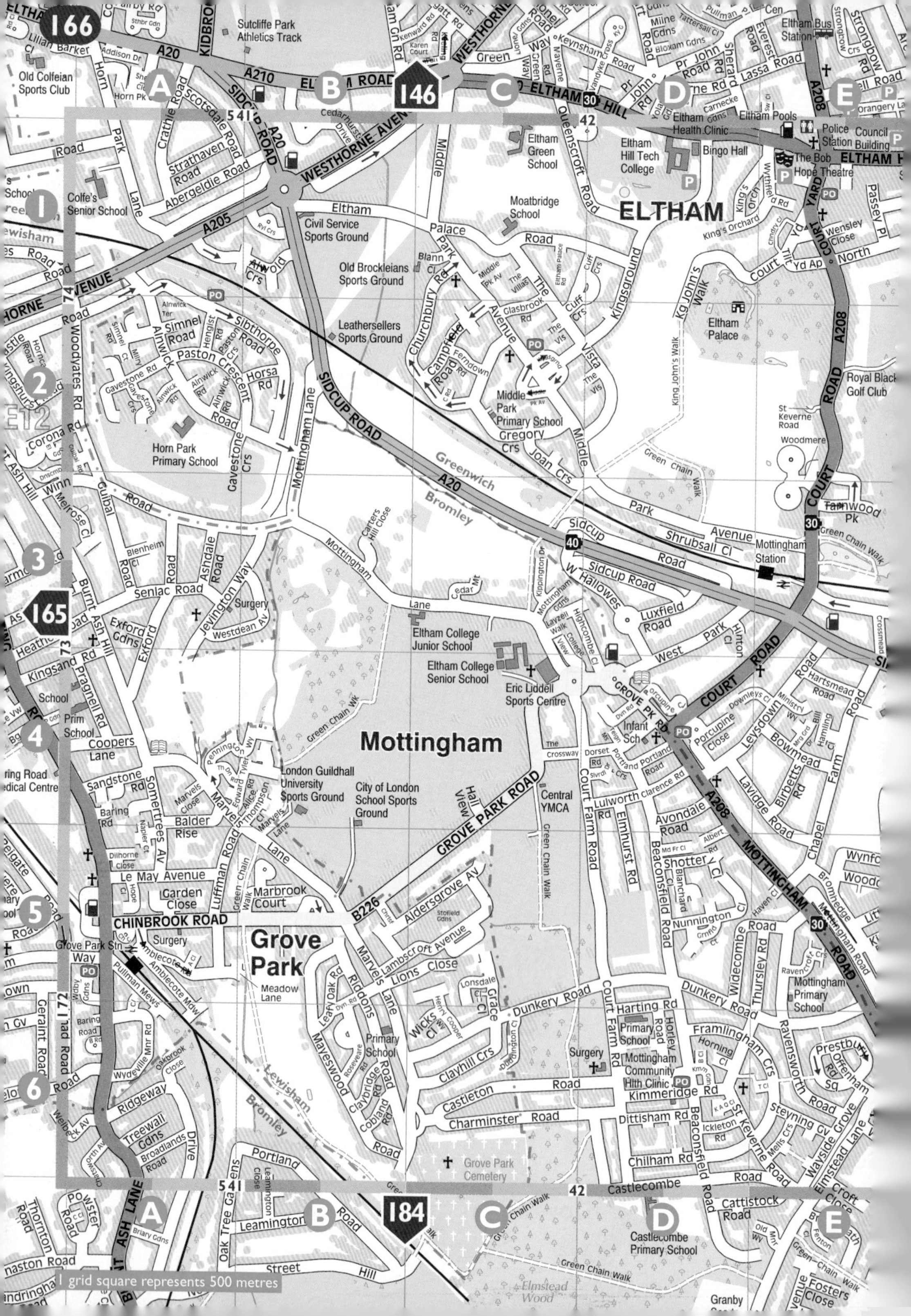

166
146
165
184
A
B
C
D
E
1
2
3
4
5
6
541
42
74
73
172
Sutcliffe Park Athletics Track
Old Colfeian Sports Club
Lilian Barker
Addison Dr
Horn
Park
Lane
A20
A210
ELTHAM ROAD
KIDBROOKE
SIDCUP ROAD
WESTHORNE AVENUE
ELTHAM HILL
Crathie Road
Scotsdale Road
Strathaven Road
Abergeldie Road
Cedarhurst Drive
Colfe's Senior School
A205
Eltham
Palace
Road
Civil Service Sports Ground
Alwold Crs
Old Brockleians Sports Ground
Leathersellers Sports Ground
Middle
Park
Avenue
Keynsham Road
Green Way
Queenscroft Road
Eltham Green School
Eltham Hill Tech College
Moatbridge School
Bingo Hall
Eltham Health Clinic
Eltham Pools
Eltham Bus Station
Police Station
Council Building
The Bob Hope Theatre
ELTHAM
Kingsground
King John's Walk
Eltham Palace
Court Yard
Court Road
A208
Royal Blackheath Golf Club
Strongbow Crs
Lassa Road
Everest
Sherard Rd
Pr John Road
Carnecke Gdns
Wythfield Rd
King's Orchard
Wensley Close
North
Passey Pl
St Keverne Road
Woodmere
Tarnwood Pk
Green Chain Walk
Mottingham Station
Shrubsall Cl
Park Avenue
Sidcup Road
Churchbury Rd
Campfield Road
Ferndown
Glasbrook Rd
Cuff Crs
The Vista
Middle Park Primary School
Gregory Crs
Joan Crs
Greenwich
Bromley
Sibthorpe Road
Simnel Road
Paston Crescent
Horsa Rd
Alnwick Road
Gavestone Rd
Gavestone Crs
Horn Park Primary School
Mottingham Lane
Woodyates Rd
Corona Rd
Winn Road
Cuibai Road
Melrose Cl
Burnt Ash Hill
Blenheim Cl
Ashdale Road
Senlac Road
Jevington Way
Surgery
Westdean Av
Exford Gdns
Exford Road
Kingsand Rd
Pragnell Rd
School
Prim School
Heathfield Road
Carters Hill Close
Mottingham
Cedar Mt
Lane
Eltham College Junior School
Eltham College Senior School
Eric Liddell Sports Centre
Kippington Dr
Mottingham Gdns
Layzell Walk
Highcombe Cl
W Hallowes
Luxfield Road
West Park
Hinton Cl
Court Road
Grove Pk Rd
Infant Sch
Porcupine Close
Leysdown Road
Hartsmead Road
Bowmead
Lavidge Road
Farm
Chapel
Birbetts Rd
Mottingham
Green Chain Wk
Coopers Lane
Sandstone Rd
Somertrees Av
Baring Rd
Balder Rise
Marvels Close
Marvels Lane
Luffman Road
Thompson Cl
London Guildhall University Sports Ground
City of London School Sports Ground
Hall View
GROVE PARK ROAD
The Crossway
Dorset Rd
Portland Rd
Central YMCA
Court Farm Road
Lulworth
Elmhurst Rd
Clarence Rd
Avondale Road
Beaconsfield Road
Shotter Cl
Blanchard
Nunnington Cl
MOTTINGHAM ROAD
Bromhedge
Wynford
Le May Avenue
Garden Close
Marbrook Court
CHINBROOK ROAD
B226
Aldersgrove Av
Lambscroft Avenue
Grove Park
Grove Park Stn
Surgery
Amblecote Rd
Amblecote Mdw
Pullman Mews
Meadow Lane
Riddons Road
Leafy Oak Rd
Lions Close
Grace Cl
Wicks Cl
Dunkery Road
Harting Rd
Primary School
Horley Road
Mottingham Community Hlth Clinic
Framlingham Crs
Widecombe Road
Thursley Rd
Ravenscroft Crs
Mottingham Primary School
Ravensworth Road
Prestbury Sq
Offenham Road
Mayeswood Road
Claybridge Rd
Cobland Rd
Clayhill Crs
Castleton Road
Charminster Road
Kimmeridge Rd
Dittisham Rd
Ickleton Rd
Chilham Rd
St Keverne Road
Steyning Gv
Wayside Grove
Elmstead Lane
Grove Park Cemetery
Castlecombe Road
Cattistock Road
Croft Close
Castlecombe Primary School
Green Chain Walk
Lewisham
Bromley
Geraint Road
Ridgeway
Treewall Gdns
Broadlands Road
Drive
Wydeville Mnr Rd
Oakbrook Close
Welbeck Av
Portland Road
Leamington Close
Leamington
Road
Oak Tree Gardens
Street
Hill
Thornton Road
Powster Road
Briary Gdns
BURNT ASH LANE
Elmstead Wood
Granby
Fosters Close
1 grid square represents 500 metres

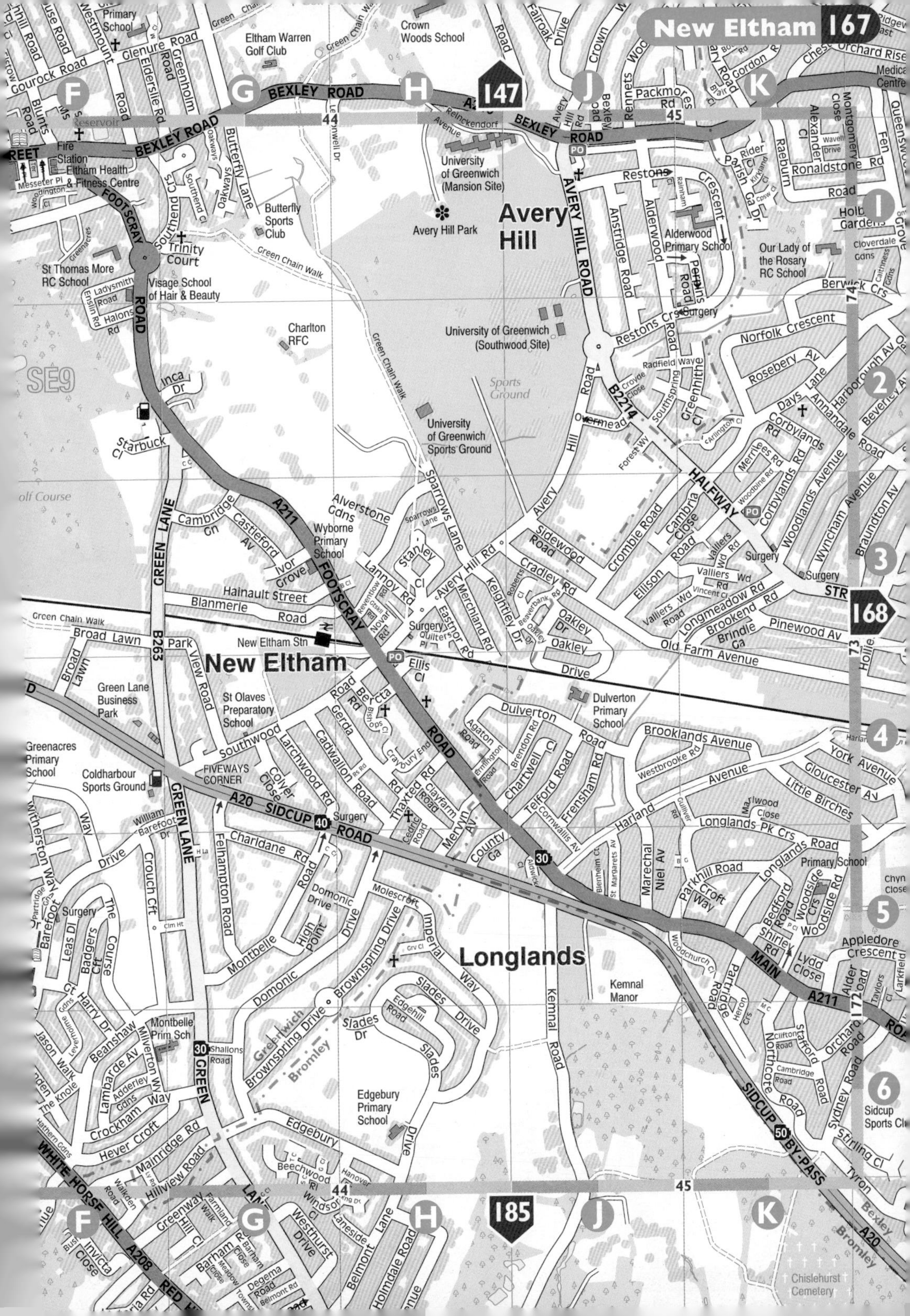
New Eltham
Avery Hill
Longlands
SE9
Bexley Road
Footscray Road
A211
Avery Hill Road
B2214
Halfway Street
Green Lane
B263
A20 Sidcup Road
Sidcup By-Pass
White Horse Hill
A208
Main Road
Kemnal Road
Eltham Warren Golf Club
Crown Woods School
University of Greenwich (Mansion Site)
Avery Hill Park
University of Greenwich (Southwood Site)
University of Greenwich Sports Ground
Sports Ground
Butterfly Sports Club
Charlton RFC
St Thomas More RC School
Visage School of Hair & Beauty
Trinity Court
Fire Station
Eltham Health & Fitness Centre
Alderwood Primary School
Our Lady of the Rosary RC School
Wyborne Primary School
New Eltham Stn
St Olaves Preparatory School
Green Lane Business Park
Greenacres Primary School
Coldharbour Sports Ground
Fiveways Corner
Dulverton Primary School
Montbelle Prim Sch
Edgebury Primary School
Kemnal Manor
Primary School
Chislehurst Cemetery
Sidcup Sports Cl
Green Chain Walk
Greenwich
Bromley
Bexley
Surgery
147
168
185
44
45
73
74
F
G
H
J
K
I
2
3
4
5
6

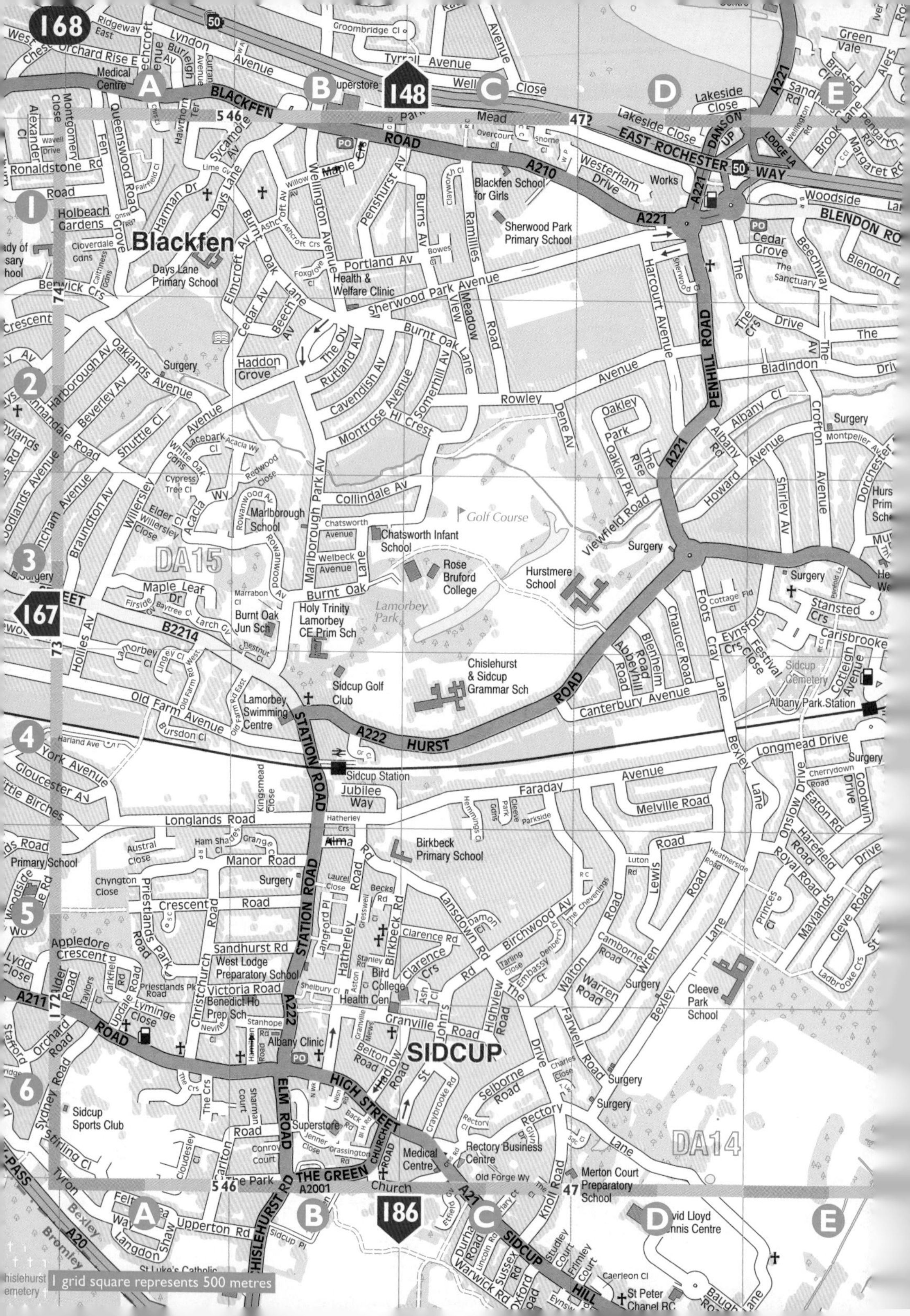
168
148
167
186
A
B
C
D
E
1
2
3
4
5
6
74
73
72
546
47
Blackfen
SIDCUP
DA15
DA14
BLACKFEN ROAD
A210
EAST ROCHESTER WAY
A221
DANSON UP
LODGE LA
PENHILL ROAD
BLENDON RO
HURST ROAD
A222
STATION ROAD
B2214
HIGH STREET
ELM ROAD
THE GREEN
A2001
A211
A20
A21
SIDCUP HILL
CHISLEHURST RD
Ridgeway East
Orchard Rise E
Lyndon Avenue
Burleigh Av
Curran Avenue
Groombridge Cl
Tyrrell Avenue
Wellcome Close
Superstore
Medical Centre
Mead
Park
Overcourt
Lakeside Close
Westerham Drive
Works
Green Vale
Brasted Cl
Sandford Rd
Brook Lane
Wellington Rd
Pengarth Rd
Margaret Rd
Woodside
Alexander Cl
Montgomery Close
Wavell Drive
Queenswood Road
Fen Gr
Ronaldstone Rd
Holbeach Gardens
Cloverdale Gdns
Caithness Gdns
Harman Dr
Days Lane
Sycamore Av
Lime Gv
Elmcroft Av
Burnt Oak Lane
Ashcroft Av
Ashcroft Crs
Willow Av
Wellington Avenue
Maple Crs
Penshurst Av
Burns Av
Bowes
Portland Av
Ramillies
Blackfen School for Girls
Sherwood Park Primary School
Sherwood Park Avenue
Harcourt Avenue
Cedar Grove
Beechway
The Sanctuary
Blendon Dr
The Crs
Drive
Days Lane Primary School
Berwick Crs
Crescent
Health & Welfare Clinic
Foxglove Cl
View
Meadow Road
Cedar Av
Beech Av
The Ov
Rutland Av
Cavendish Av
Montrose Avenue
Somerhill Av
Hill Crest
Burnt Oak Lane
Surgery
Haddon Grove
Harborough Av
Oaklands Avenue
Beverley Av
Annandale Road
Shuttle Cl
Avenue
Rowley Avenue
Bladindon
Dene Av
Oakley Park
Oakley Pk
The Rise
Albany Cl
Albany Rd
Howard Avenue
Shirley Av
Crofton Avenue
Montpelier Av
Dorchester
Lacebark Cl
Acacia Wy
White Oak Gdns
Redwood Close
Cypress Tree Cl
Willersley Av
Willersley Close
Elder Cl
Braundton Av
Marlborough School
Rowanwood Av
Marlborough Park Av
Collindale Av
Golf Course
Viewfield Road
Chatsworth Avenue
Chatsworth Infant School
Welbeck Avenue
Lane
Rose Bruford College
Hurstmere School
Foots Cray Lane
Cottage Fld Cl
Stansted Crs
Carisbrooke
Maple Leaf Dr
Firside Gv
Baytree Cl
Larch Gv
Marrabon Cl
Burnt Oak Jun Sch
Holy Trinity Lamorbey CE Prim Sch
Lamorbey Park
Chaucer Road
Blenheim Road
Abbeyhill Road
Eynsford Crs
Festival Close
Sidcup Cemetery
Cotleigh Avenue
Hollies Av
Lamorbey Cl
Lingey Cl
Old Farm Rd West
Old Farm Rd East
Chestnut Cl
Chislehurst & Sidcup Grammar Sch
Sidcup Golf Club
Old Farm Avenue
Lamorbey Swimming Centre
Canterbury Avenue
Albany Park Station
Bursdon Cl
Harland Ave
York Avenue
Gloucester Av
Little Birches
Sidcup Station
Jubilee Way
Kingsmead Close
Faraday Avenue
Longmead Drive
Cherrydown Road
Onslow Drive
Goodwin Drive
Eaton Rd
Bexley Lane
Melville Road
Longlands Road
Hatherley Crs
Hemmings Cl
Cleeve Park Gdns
Parkside
Austral Close
Ham Shades Cl
Grange Cl
Alma Rd
Manor Road
Birkbeck Primary School
Luton Rd
Lewis Road
Heatherside Road
Harefield Road
Royal Road
Primary School
Chyngton Close
Priestlands Park Road
Laurel Close
Becks Rd
Gresswell Cl
Birkbeck Rd
Lansdown Rd
Damon Cl
Birchwood Av
The Chevenings
Walton Road
Camborne Road
Wren
Princes Cl
Maylands
Cleve Road
Ladbrooke Crs
Crescent Road
Christchurch Road
Langford Pl
Hatherley Road
Clarence Rd
Clarence Crs
Tarling Close
The Embassy Ct
Denberry Dr
Warren Road
Cleeve Park School
Appledore Crescent
Lydd Close
Larkfield Rd
Sandhurst Rd
West Lodge Preparatory School
Priestlands Pk Road
Stanley Cl
Bird College
Shelbury Cl
Aston Rd
Ash Cl
St John's Rd
Highview Road
The Drive
Farwell Road
Victoria Road
Benedict Ho Prep Sch
Lymingee Close
Updale Road
Taylors Cl
Elder Road
Orchard Road
Health Cen
Granville Road
Granville Mews
Nevile Cl
Stanhope Rd
Albany Clinic
Belton Road
Hadlow Road
Stafford Cl
Sydney Road
Sidcup Sports Club
The Crs
Sharman Court
Road
Charles Close
Selborne Road
Craybrooke Rd
Superstore
Jenner Close
Grassington Rd
Back Rd
Church Road
Medical Centre
Rectory Business Centre
Rectory Cl
Rectory Lane
Glyn Dr
Stirling Cl
Cloudesley Cl
Carlton Rd
Conrov Court
The Park
Church
Old Forge Wy
Merton Court Preparatory School
Tyron Way
Felts
Langdon Shaw
Upperton Rd
Sidcup Pl
Etfield Gr
Durham Road
Lincoln Rd
Sussex Rd
Warwick Rd
Oxford Road
Knoll Road
Studley Court
Frimley Court
Caerleon Cl
St Peter Chanel RC
David Lloyd Tennis Centre
Baugh Road
Bexley
Bromley
Chislehurst Cemetery
St Luke's Catholic
1 grid square represents 500 metres

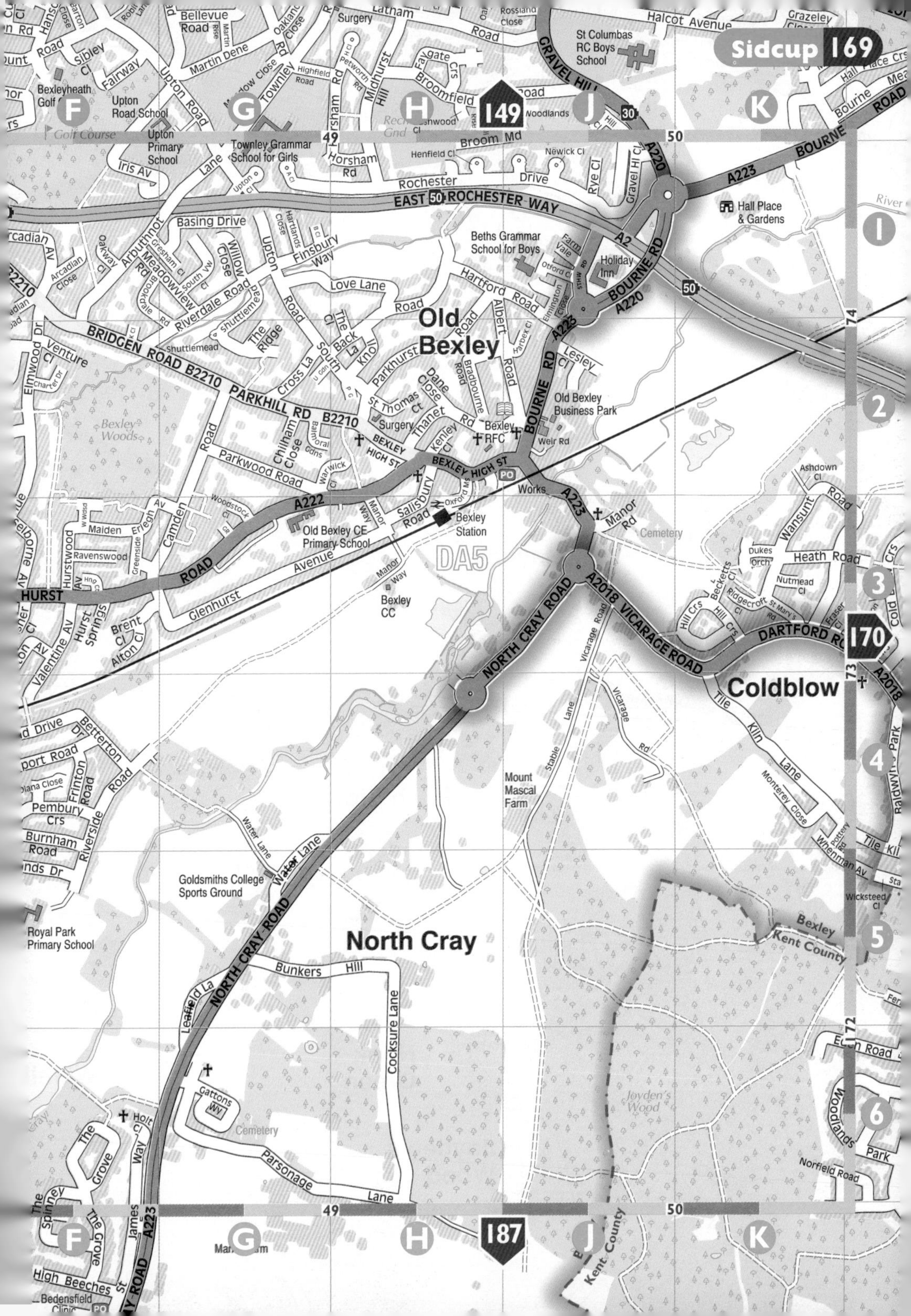
Old Bexley
North Cray
Coldblow
DA5
149
170
187
Bexley Station
Old Bexley CE Primary School
Beths Grammar School for Boys
Townley Grammar School for Girls
Upton Primary School
Upton Road School
Bexleyheath Golf Course
St Columbas RC Boys School
Hall Place & Gardens
Holiday Inn
Old Bexley Business Park
Bexley RFC
Bexley CC
Bexley Woods
Goldsmiths College Sports Ground
Royal Park Primary School
Mount Mascal Farm
Joyden's Wood
Cemetery
Surgery
Works
EAST ROCHESTER WAY
BRIDGEN ROAD B2210
PARKHILL RD B2210
BEXLEY HIGH ST
NORTH CRAY ROAD
A2018 VICARAGE ROAD
DARTFORD RD
BOURNE RD
GRAVEL HILL
Bunkers Hill
Cocksure Lane
Parsonage Lane
Tile Kiln Lane
Water Lane
Bexley
Kent County

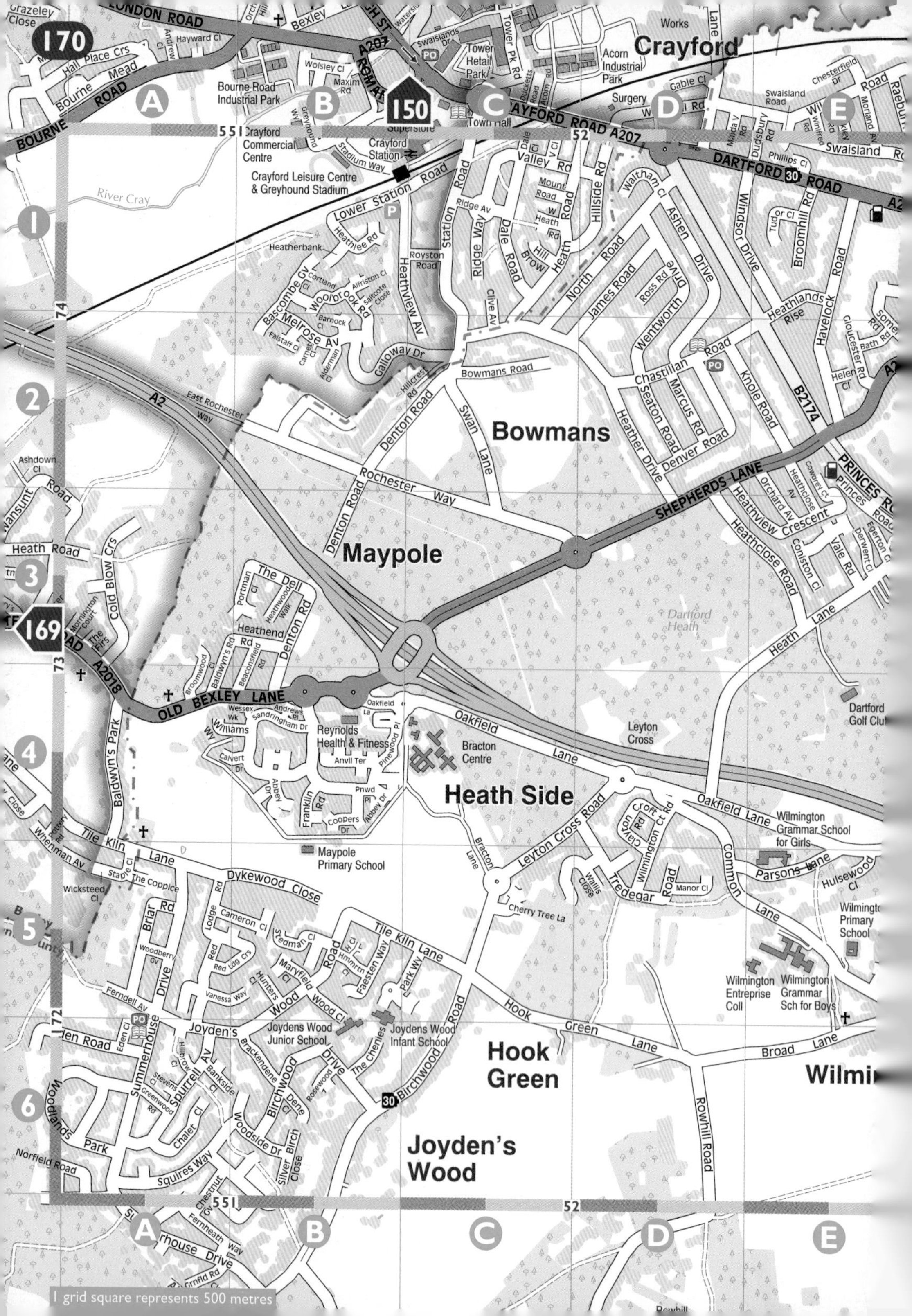
170
150
169
Crayford
Bowmans
Maypole
Heath Side
Hook Green
Joyden's Wood
Wilmi
London Road
Bourne Road
Dartford Road
Crayford Road A207
Shepherds Lane
Old Bexley Lane
A2018
A2
B2174
Princes Road
Tile Kiln Lane
Hook Green Lane
Broad Lane
Rowhill Road
Oakfield Lane
Leyton Cross Road
Rochester Way
East Rochester Way
Denton Road
Swan Lane
Heath Lane
Common Lane
Parsons Lane
Station Road
Lower Station Road
Bourne Road Industrial Park
Crayford Commercial Centre
Crayford Station
Crayford Leisure Centre & Greyhound Stadium
Acorn Industrial Park
Town Hall
Superstore
Surgery
Works
River Cray
Dartford Heath
Dartford Golf Club
Leyton Cross
Bracton Centre
Reynolds Health & Fitness
Maypole Primary School
Wilmington Grammar School for Girls
Wilmington Primary School
Wilmington Entreprise Coll
Wilmington Grammar Sch for Boys
Joydens Wood Junior School
Joydens Wood Infant School
Heatherbank
A
B
C
D
E
1
2
3
4
5
6
551
52
74
73
72
1 grid square represents 500 metres

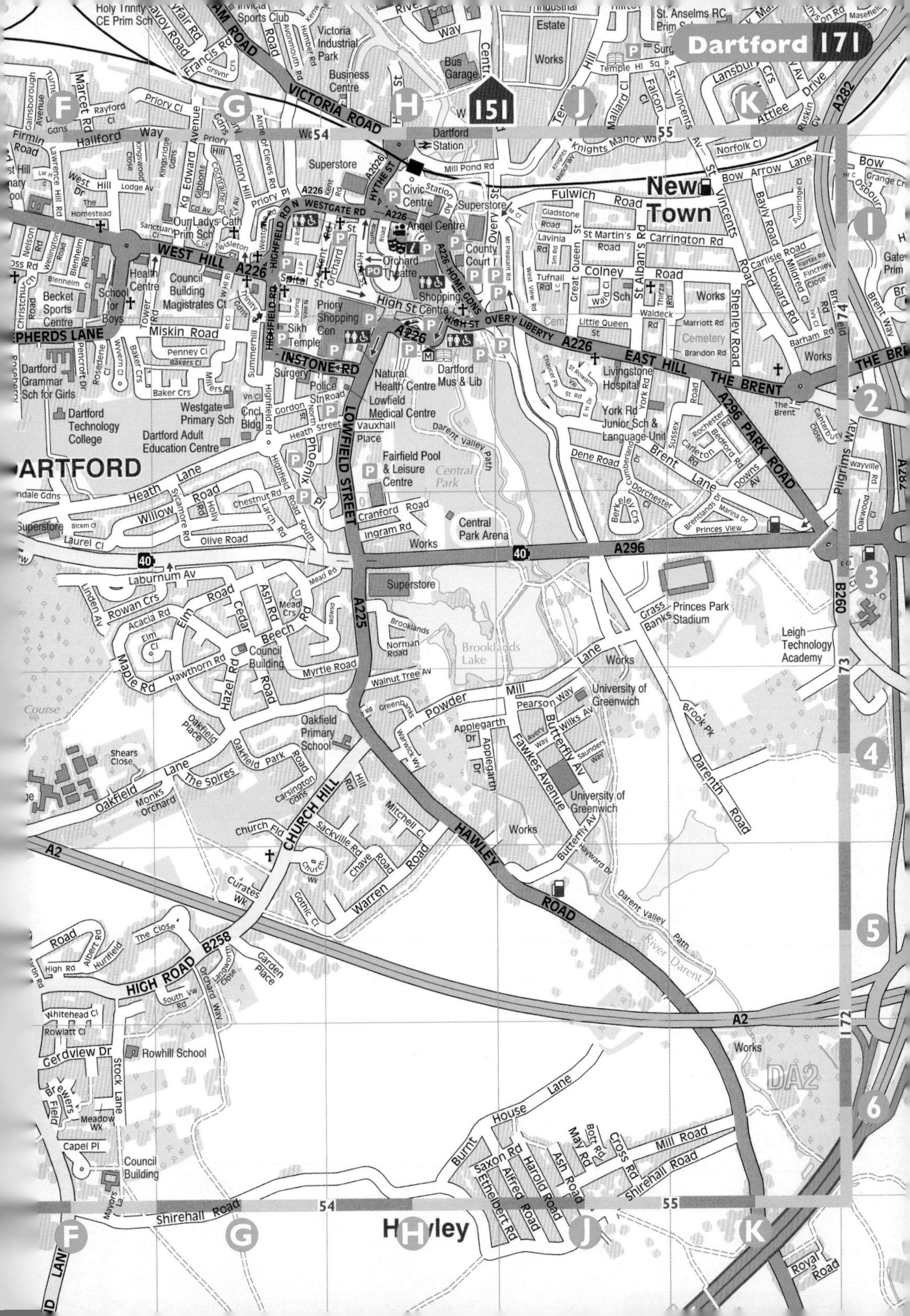

151
Victoria Road
Dartford Station
West Hill
A226
Westgate Rd
Hythe St
Highfield Rd N
Spital St
High St
Orchard Theatre
Angel Centre
Civic Centre
County Court
Shopping Centre
Priory Shopping Cen
Sikh Temple
Instone Rd
Lowfield Street
Lowfield Medical Centre
Natural Health Centre
Dartford Mus & Lib
Dartford Grammar Sch for Girls
Dartford Technology College
Dartford Adult Education Centre
Westgate Primary Sch
Miskin Road
Heath Lane
DARTFORD
Fairfield Pool & Leisure Centre
Central Park
Central Park Arena
Darent Valley Path
East Hill
The Brent
A296 Park Road
Livingstone Hospital
York Rd Junior Sch & Language Unit
New Town
Fulwich Road
St Vincents Road
Shenley Road
Cemetery
Princes Park Stadium
Leigh Technology Academy
Brooklands Lake
Powder Mill Lane
University of Greenwich
Hawley Road
A225
A296
A2
Church Hill
Oakfield Lane
Oakfield Primary School
High Road
B258
Rowhill School
Stock Lane
Council Building
Shirehall Road
Mill Road
House Lane
Hawley
Darenth Road
River Darent
B260
DA2
Works
Superstore
F
G
H
J
K
I
2
3
4
5
6
54
55
74
73
72

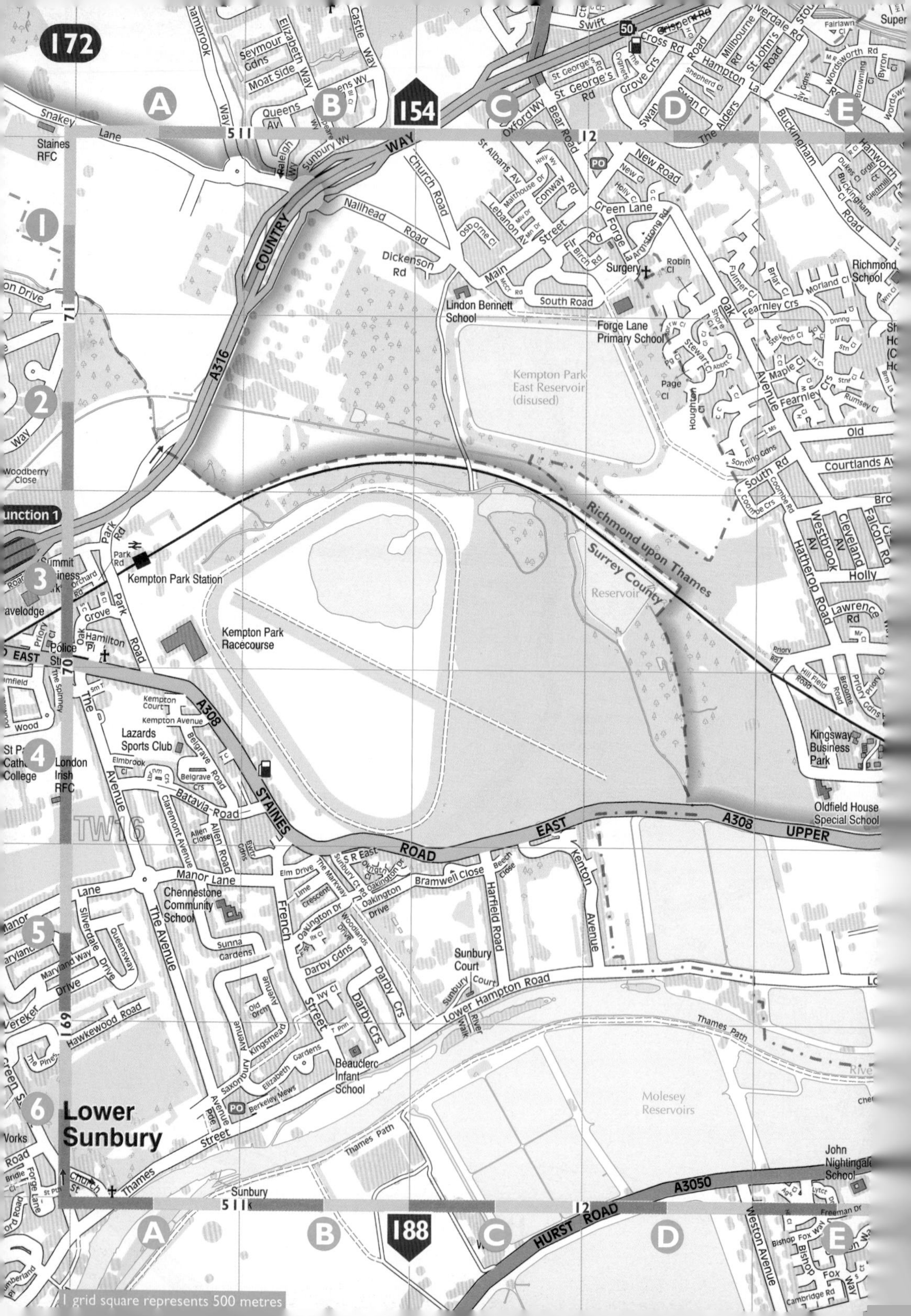
154
188
Kempton Park Station
Kempton Park Racecourse
Kempton Park East Reservoir (disused)
Reservoir
Molesey Reservoirs
Richmond upon Thames
Surrey County
Lower Sunbury
Sunbury
TW16
COUNTRY WAY
A316
A308
STAINES ROAD
EAST
UPPER
A3050
HURST ROAD
Lower Hampton Road
Thames Path
Thames Street
Church St
Snakey Lane
Staines RFC
Lindon Bennett School
Forge Lane Primary School
Surgery
Lazards Sports Club
Chennestone Community School
Beauclerc Infant School
Sunbury Court
St Paul's Catholic College
London Irish RFC
Kingsway Business Park
Oldfield House Special School
Richmond School
John Nightingale School
Junction 1
Summit Business Park
Travelodge
Police Stn
Woodberry Close
Church Road
Nallhead Road
Dickenson Rd
Main Street
South Road
Green Lane
Forge La
New Road
Oak Avenue
Hatherop Road
Westbrook Av
Cleveland Av
Fearnley Crs
Buckingham Road
Hanworth Rd
Hampton Rd
St John's Road
Millbourne Rd
Cross Rd
Swift
St George's Rd
Bear Road
Oxford Wy
St Albans Av
Lebanon Av
Conway Rd
Park Road
Park Rd
Grove
Hamilton Pl
Kempton Avenue
Belgrave Road
Batavia Road
Allen Road
Claremont Avenue
Manor Lane
The Avenue
French Street
Darby Gdns
Darby Crs
Oakington Drive
Bramwell Close
Harfield Road
Kenton Avenue
Saxonbury Avenue
Kingsmead Avenue
Elizabeth Gardens
Berkeley Mews
Hawkewood Road
Maryland Way
Silverdale Drive
Queensway
Vereker Drive
Weston Avenue
Bishop Fox Way
Cambridge Rd
Freeman Dr
Priory Rd
Hill Field Road
Broome Road
Lawrence Rd
Holly
Old Courtlands Av
Sonning Gdns
Robin Cl
Elmbrook Cl
Sunna Gardens
Lime Crescent
Woodlands Drive
Oakington Dr
Ivy Cl
A B C D E
1 2 3 4 5 6
511 12
70 71 69
1 grid square represents 500 metres

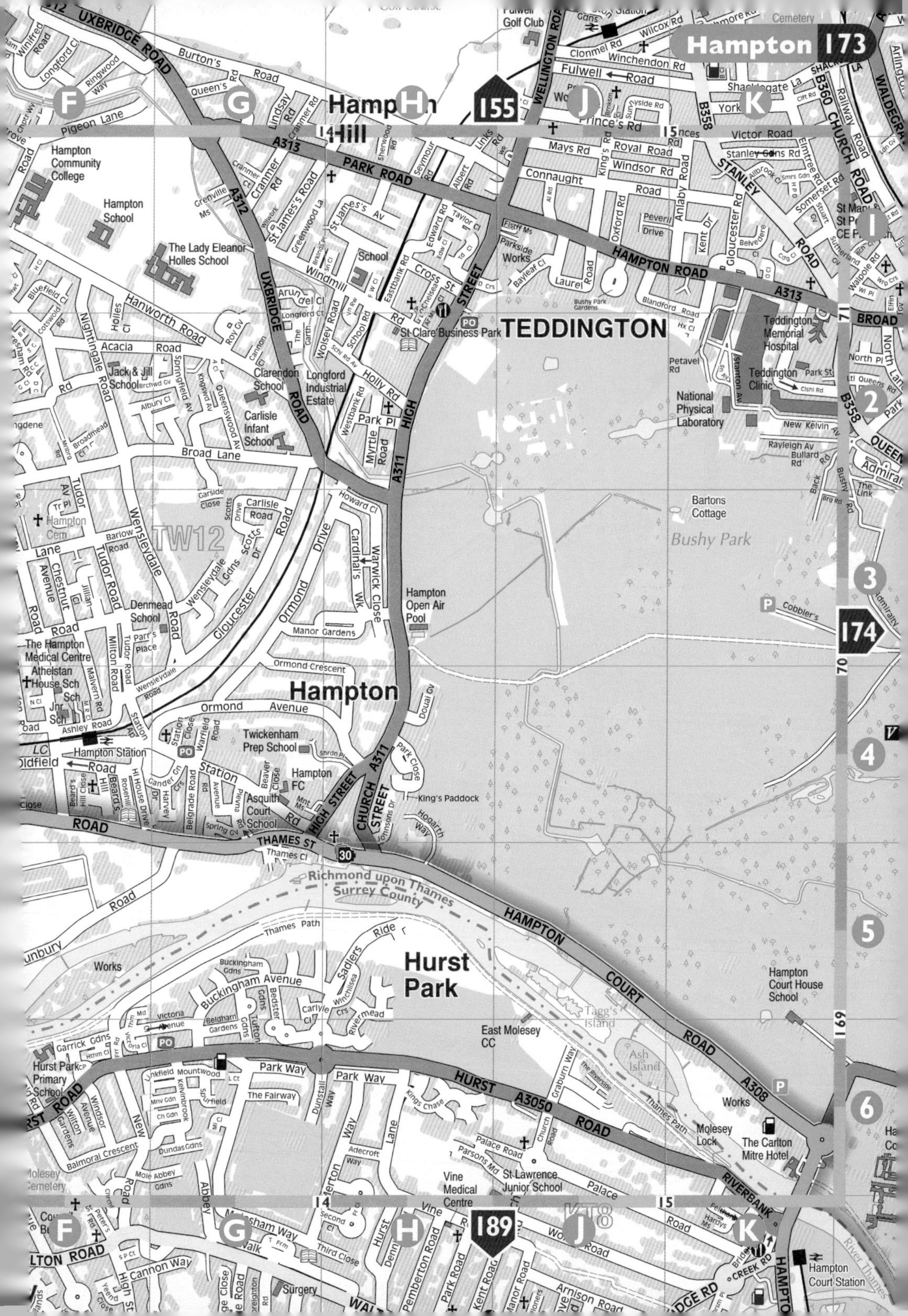
Hampton
Hampton Hill
TEDDINGTON
Bushy Park
Hurst Park
Teddington Memorial Hospital
National Physical Laboratory
Hampton Station
Hampton Court Station
Hampton Open Air Pool
Hampton School
The Lady Eleanor Holles School
Hampton Community College
Fulwell Golf Club
Uxbridge Road
Hampton Road
Hampton Court Road
Hurst Road
Park Road
High Street
TW12
KT8
155
174
189

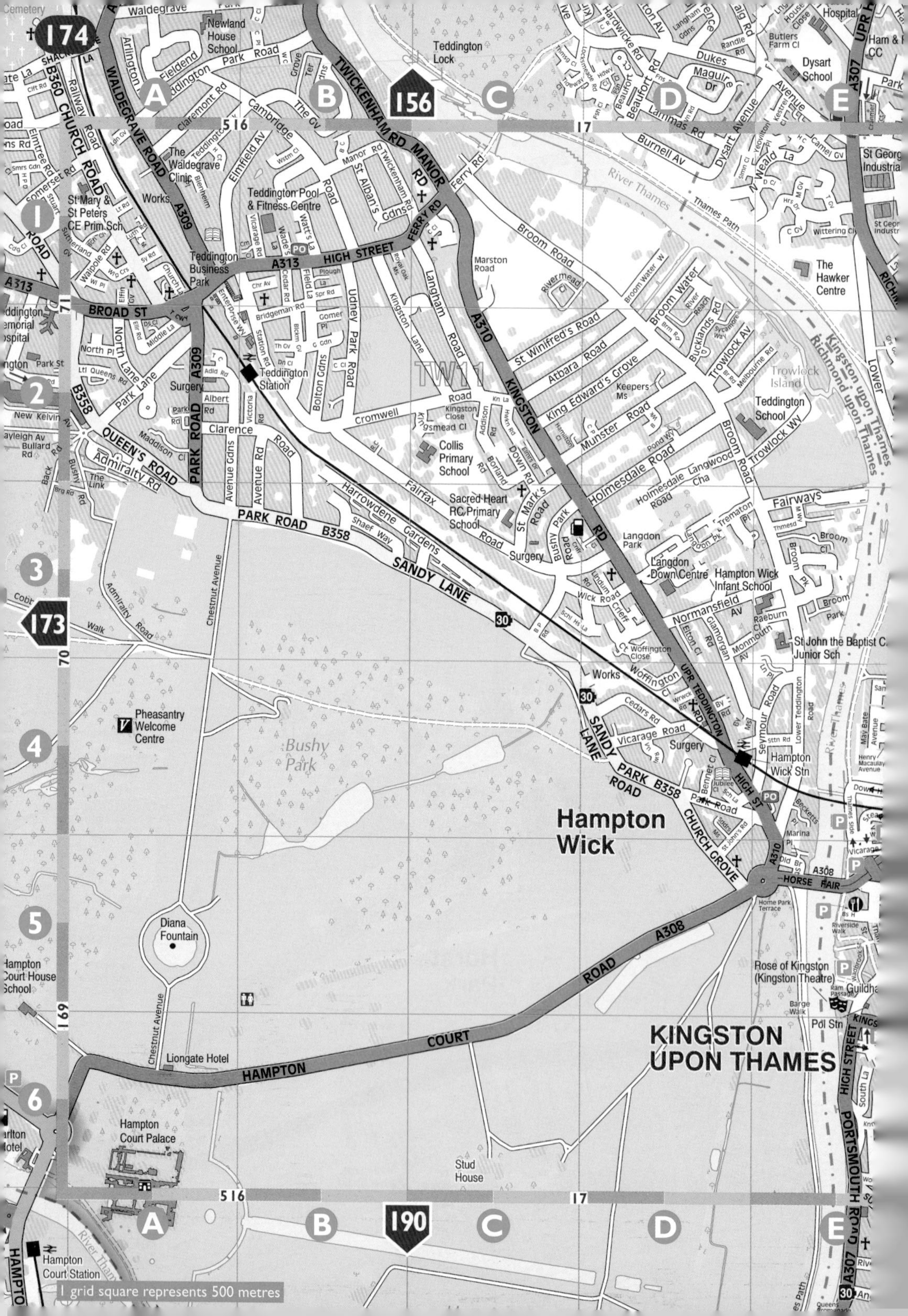

Cemetery

174

156

173

190

1 grid square represents 500 metres

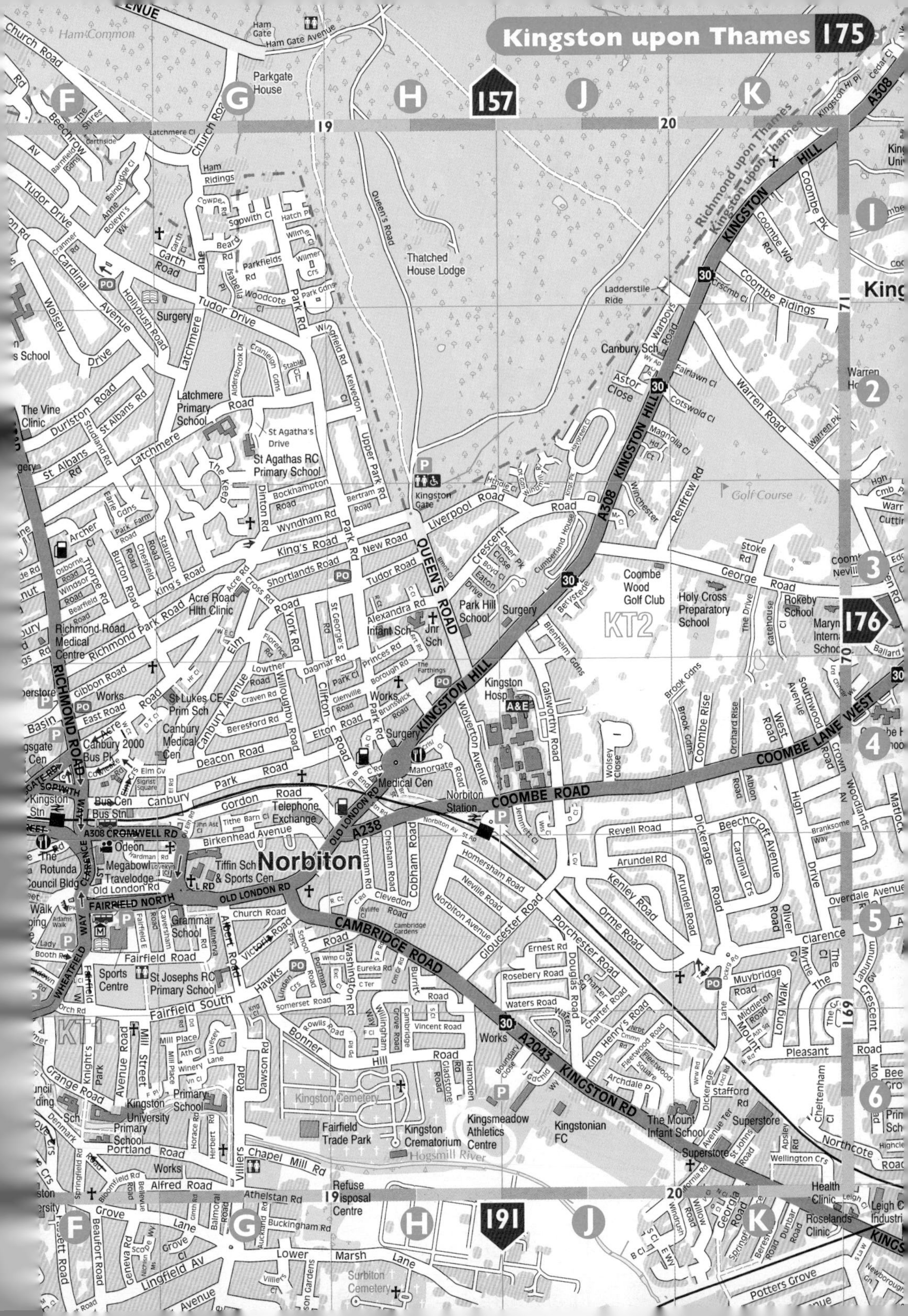
157
191
176
F
G
H
J
K
19
20
KT1
KT2
Norbiton
Ham Common
Ham Gate
Ham Gate Avenue
Parkgate House
Church Road
Latchmere Cl
Ham Ridings
Queen's Road
Thatched House Lodge
Kingston Gate
Ladderstile Ride
Richmond upon Thames
Kingston upon Thames
KINGSTON HILL
Coombe Ridings
Warren Road
Coombe Wood Golf Club
Golf Course
George Road
Holy Cross Preparatory School
Rokeby School
Canbury Sch
Astor Close
Tudor Drive
Cardinal Avenue
Wolsey Drive
Latchmere Primary School
St Agathas RC Primary School
The Vine Clinic
Durlston Road
St Albans Road
Richmond Park Road
Richmond Road Medical Centre
Acre Road Hlth Clinic
King's Road
Liverpool Road
Park Hill School
Alexandra Infant Sch
Jnr Sch
Kingston Hosp
A&E
Galsworthy Road
Coombe Road
COOMBE LANE WEST
Norbiton Station
Canbury Medical Cen
Canbury 2000 Bus Pk
Canbury Park Road
Gordon Road
Telephone Exchange
Medical Cen
Manorgate Road
Kingston Stn
Bus Stn
A308 CROMWELL RD
Odeon
Megabowl
Travelodge
The Rotunda
Council Bldg
Tiffin Sch & Sports Cen
OLD LONDON RD
FAIRFIELD NORTH
Grammar School
CAMBRIDGE ROAD
Fairfield Road
Sports Centre
St Josephs RC Primary School
Fairfield South
Kingston University
Primary School
Kingston Cemetery
Fairfield Trade Park
Kingston Crematorium
Kingsmeadow Athletics Centre
Kingstonian FC
Hogsmill River
A2043 KINGSTON RD
The Mount Infant School
Superstore
Health Clinic
Roselands Clinic
Refuse Disposal Centre
Portland Road
Alfred Road
Athelstan Rd
Lower Marsh Lane
Surbiton Cemetery
Potters Grove
Lingfield Av

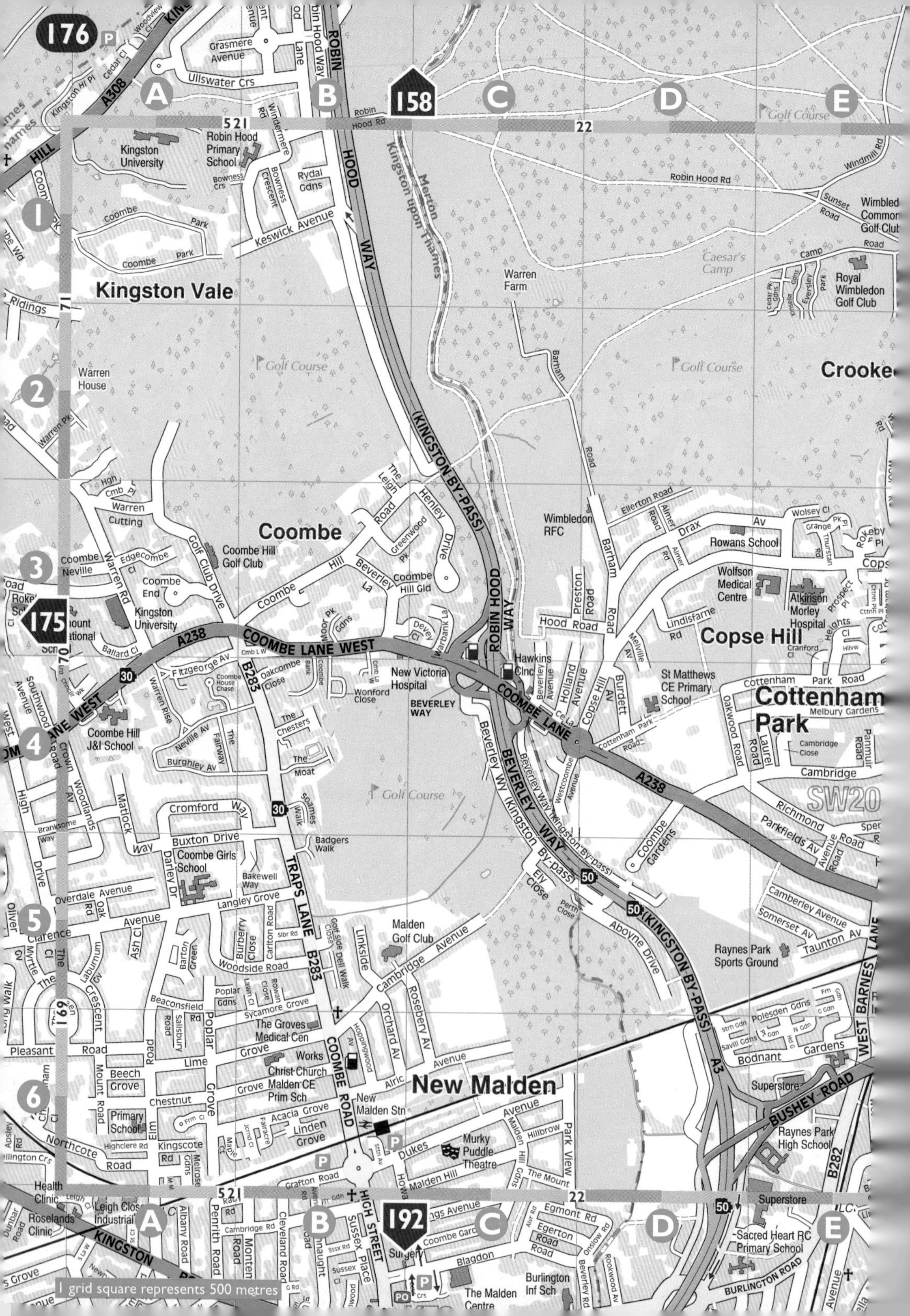

176
158
175
192
Kingston Vale
Coombe
Copse Hill
Cottenham Park
New Malden
Kingston University
Robin Hood Primary School
Warren House
Warren Farm
Caesar's Camp
Royal Wimbledon Golf Club
Coombe Hill Golf Club
Wimbledon RFC
Rowans School
Wolfson Medical Centre
Atkinson Morley Hospital
New Victoria Hospital
Hawkins Clnc
St Matthews CE Primary School
Coombe Hill J&I School
Coombe Girls School
Malden Golf Club
Raynes Park Sports Ground
The Groves Medical Cen
Christ Church Malden CE Prim Sch
New Malden Stn
Murky Puddle Theatre
Raynes Park High School
Superstore
Sacred Heart RC Primary School
Burlington Inf Sch
The Malden Centre
Roselands Clinic
Health Clinic
Golf Course
ROBIN HOOD WAY
(KINGSTON BY-PASS)
COOMBE LANE WEST
COOMBE LANE
BEVERLEY WAY
TRAPS LANE
COOMBE ROAD
HIGH STREET
BUSHEY ROAD
WEST BARNES LANE
BURLINGTON ROAD
A238
A308
A3
B283
B282
SW20
1 grid square represents 500 metres

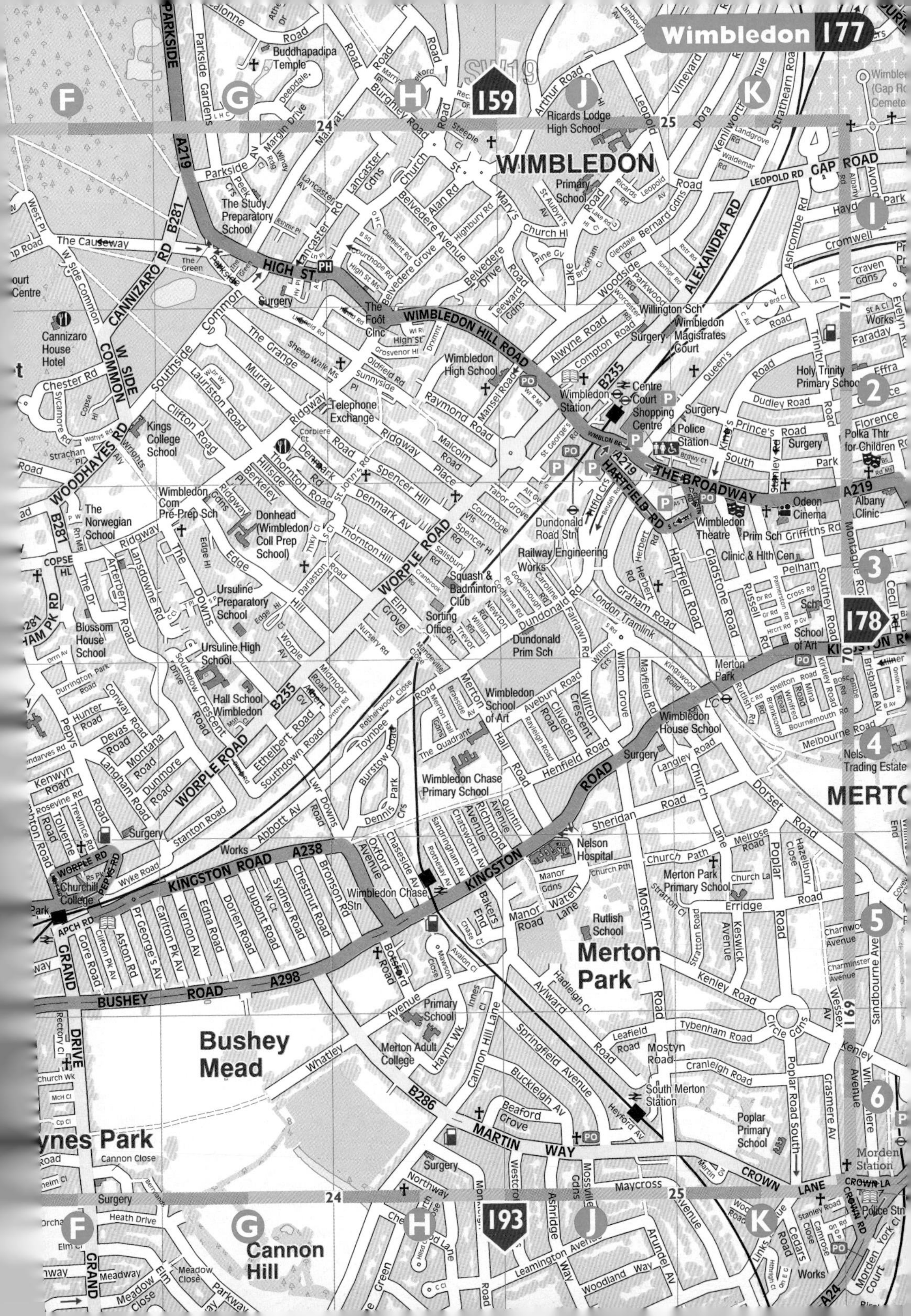
SW19
159
178
193
F
G
H
J
K
F
G
H
J
K
1
2
3
4
5
6
24
25
24
25
WIMBLEDON
Merton Park
Bushey Mead
Cannon Hill
MERTO
ynes Park
Parkside
A219
B281
Buddhapadipa Temple
Ricards Lodge High School
Primary School
The Study Preparatory School
The Causeway
Cannizaro Rd
W Side Common
Cannizaro House Hotel
High St
Wimbledon Hill Road
The Foot Clnc
Surgery
Wimbledon High School
Wimbledon Station
Centre Court Shopping Centre
Police Station
Willington Sch
Wimbledon Magistrates Court
Holy Trinity Primary School
Polka Thtr for Children
Alexandra Rd
Leopold Rd
Gap Road
The Broadway
Odeon Cinema
Albany Clinic
Wimbledon Theatre
Prim Sch
Clinic & Hlth Cen
School of Art
Kings College School
Woodhayes Rd
Telephone Exchange
Ridgway
Worple Road
Wimbledon Com Pre-Prep Sch
The Norwegian School
Donhead (Wimbledon Coll Prep School)
Ursuline Preparatory School
Ursuline High School
Blossom House School
Hall School Wimbledon
Squash & Badminton Club
Sorting Office
Railway Engineering Works
Dundonald Road Stn
Dundonald Prim Sch
London Tramlink
Hartfield Road
Gladstone Road
Merton Park
Kingston Road
Wimbledon School of Art
Wimbledon House School
Wimbledon Chase Primary School
Nelson Hospital
Merton Park Primary School
Rutlish School
Nelson Trading Estate
Wimbledon Chase Stn
Churchill College
Bushey Road
A298
A238
Merton Adult College
Primary School
B286
Martin Way
South Merton Station
Poplar Primary School
Crown Lane
Morden Station
Police Stn
Works
Cannon Close
Heath Drive
Kenley Road
Tybenham Road
Cranleigh Road
Springfield Avenue
Grand Drive
A24

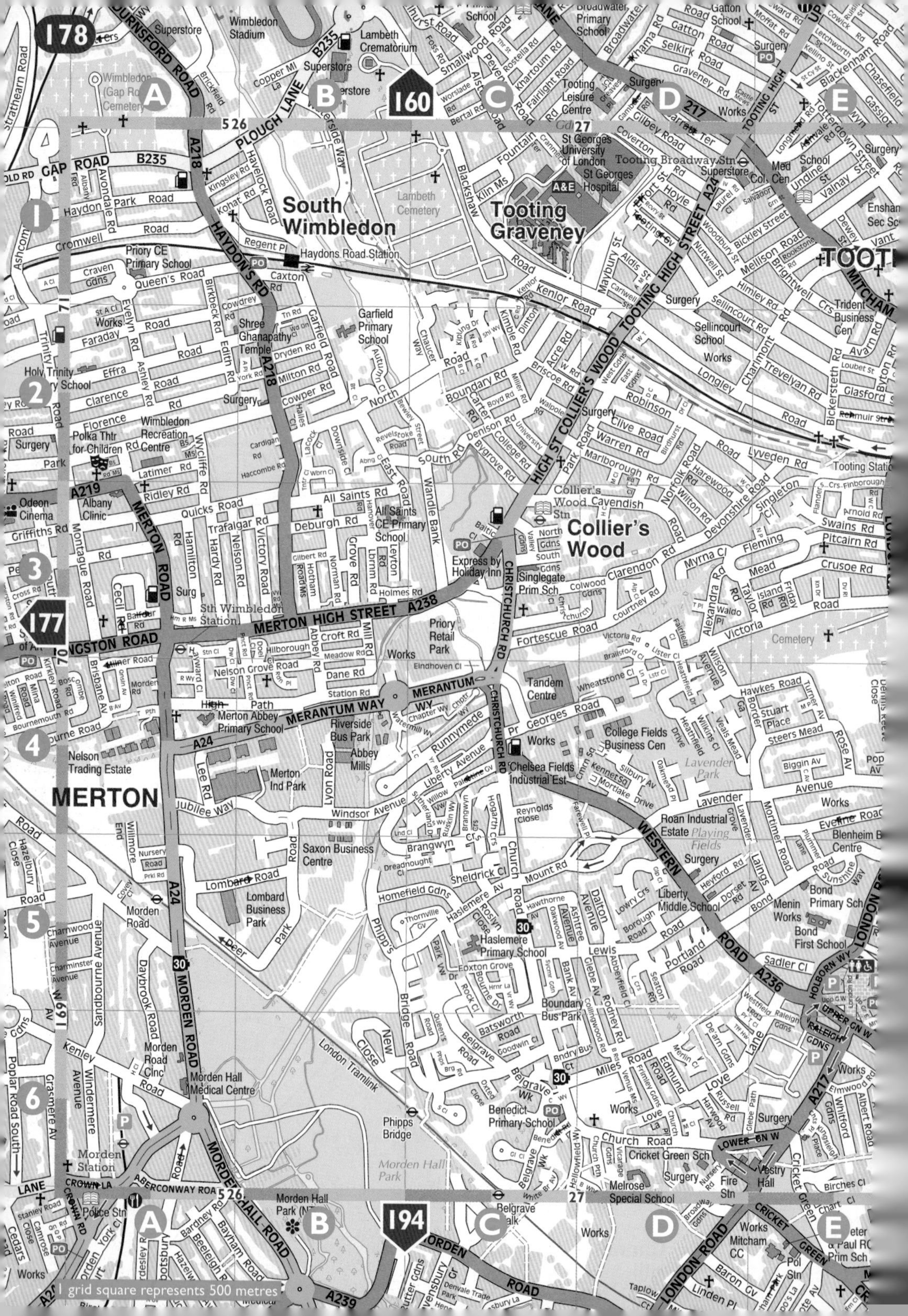

178
160
177
194
A
B
C
D
E
1
2
3
4
5
6
526
27
South Wimbledon
Tooting Graveney
Collier's Wood
MERTON
TOOT
Wimbledon Stadium
Superstore
Lambeth Crematorium
Wimbledon (Gap Rd) Cemetery
Lambeth Cemetery
Broadwater Primary School
Gatton School
Tooting Leisure Centre
St Georges University of London
St Georges Hospital
A&E
Tooting Broadway Stn
Haydons Road Station
Priory CE Primary School
Garfield Primary School
Shree Ghanapathy Temple
Holy Trinity Primary School
Wimbledon Recreation Centre
Polka Thtr for Children
Odeon Cinema
Albany Clinic
All Saints CE Primary School
Sellincourt School
Trident Business Cen
Enshan Sec Sc
Tooting Station
Collier's Wood Stn
Express by Holiday Inn
Singlegate Prim Sch
Priory Retail Park
Sth Wimbledon Station
Merton Abbey Primary School
Riverside Bus Park
Abbey Mills
Tandem Centre
College Fields Business Cen
Chelsea Fields Industrial Est
Nelson Trading Estate
Merton Ind Park
Saxon Business Centre
Lombard Business Park
Roan Industrial Estate
Playing Fields
Lavender Park
Liberty Middle School
Haslemere Primary School
Boundary Bus Park
Benedict Primary School
Cricket Green Sch
Melrose Special School
Fire Stn
Vestry Hall
Mitcham CC
Bond Primary Sch
Bond First School
Menin Works
Blenheim B Centre
Morden Hall Medical Centre
Morden Road Clinic
Morden Road
Morden Station
Morden Hall Park (NT)
Phipps Bridge
Morden Hall Park
London Tramlink
Police Stn
Cemetery
MERTON HIGH STREET A238
MERANTUM WAY
CHRISTCHURCH RD
HIGH ST COLLIER'S WOOD
TOOTING HIGH STREET A24
WESTERN ROAD A236
MERTON ROAD
MORDEN ROAD A24
MORDEN HALL ROAD
HAYDON'S RD A218
PLOUGH LANE B235
DURNSFORD ROAD
KINGSTON ROAD
GAP ROAD B235
LONDON ROAD
CRICKET GREEN
LOWER GN W
UPPER GN W
HOLBORN WY
MITCHAM
A239
A217
1 grid square represents 500 metres

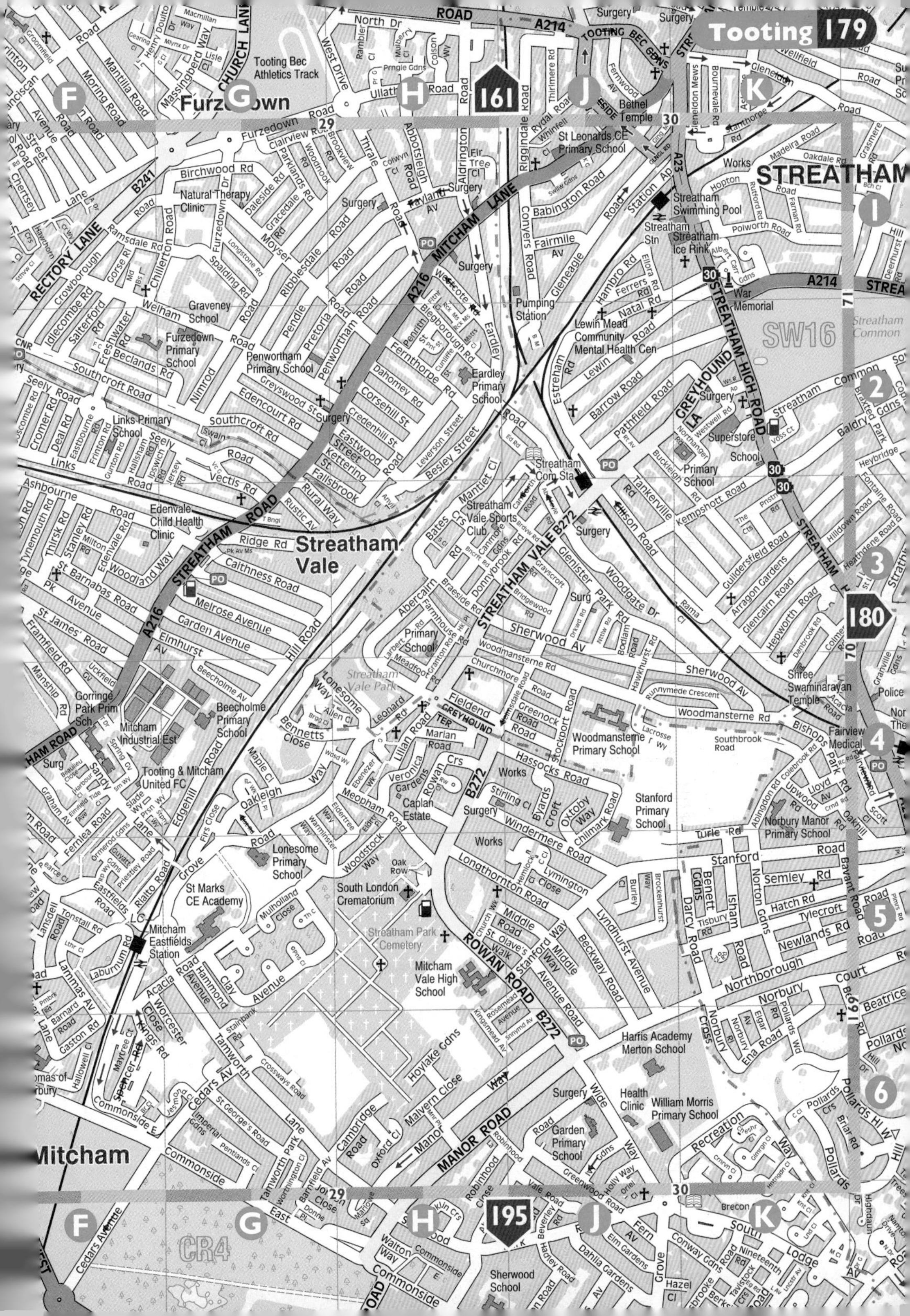

Tooting 179
161
180
195
Furzedown
Tooting Bec Athletics Track
STREATHAM
Streatham Vale
Mitcham
SW16
CR4
Streatham Common
ROAD
A214
TOOTING BEC GDNS
North Dr
West Drive
Pringle Gdns
Ullathorne Road
Furzedown Road
Church Lane
Massingberd Way
Mantilla Road
Moring Road
Rectory Lane
B241
Birchwood Rd
Natural Therapy Clinic
Graveney School
Furzedown Primary School
Penwortham Primary School
Eardley Primary School
Links Primary School
Edenvale Child Health Clinic
Streatham Vale Sports Club
Streatham Com Sta
Mitcham Lane
A216
Streatham Road
Streatham Vale B272
Streatham High Road
A23
Greyhound La
Streatham Swimming Pool
Streatham Stn
Streatham Ice Rink
War Memorial
Bethel Temple
St Leonards CE Primary School
Pumping Station
Lewin Mead Community Mental Health Cen
Northanger Primary School
Superstore
School
Surgery
Riggindale Road
Babington Road
Conyers Road
Fairmile Av
Gleneagle Road
Estreham Rd
Barrow Road
Pathfield Road
Kempshott Road
Tankerville Rd
Ellison Road
Guildersfield Road
Arragon Gardens
Gleneldon Mews
Madeira Road
Oakdale Rd
Polworth Road
Hopton Road
Southcroft Road
Seely Road
Ashbourne
Thirsk Rd
Stanley Rd
Edenvale Rd
Woodland Way
St Barnabas Road
St James' Road
Ridge Rd
Caithness Road
Melrose Avenue
Garden Avenue
Elmhurst Av
Hill Road
Beecholme Av
Beecholme Primary School
Gorringe Park Prim Sch
Mitcham Industrial Est
Tooting & Mitcham United FC
Streatham Vale Park
Primary School
Sherwood Av
Woodmansterne Rd
Woodmansterne Primary School
Stanford Primary School
Norbury Manor Primary School
Shree Swaminarayan Temple
Fairview Medical
Police
Southbrook Road
Bishops Park Rd
Lonesome Way
Lonesome Primary School
St Marks CE Academy
South London Crematorium
Streatham Park Cemetery
Mitcham Vale High School
Mitcham Eastfields Station
Oakleigh Way
Grove Road
Rowan Road B272
Windermere Road
Longthornton Road
Stanford Road
Semley Rd
Hatch Rd
Newlands Rd
Northborough Road
Norbury Cross
Harris Academy Merton School
Health Clinic
William Morris Primary School
Garden Primary School
Recreation Way
Manor Road
Malvern Close
Hoylake Gdns
Cambridge Road
Tamworth Lane
Commonside
Commonside East
Cedars Av
Cedars Avenue
Sherwood School
Conway Gdns
Dahlia Gardens
Fern Av
Beatrice
Pollards Hill
Caplan Estate
Works
29
30
F
G
H
J
K
I
2
3
4
5
6

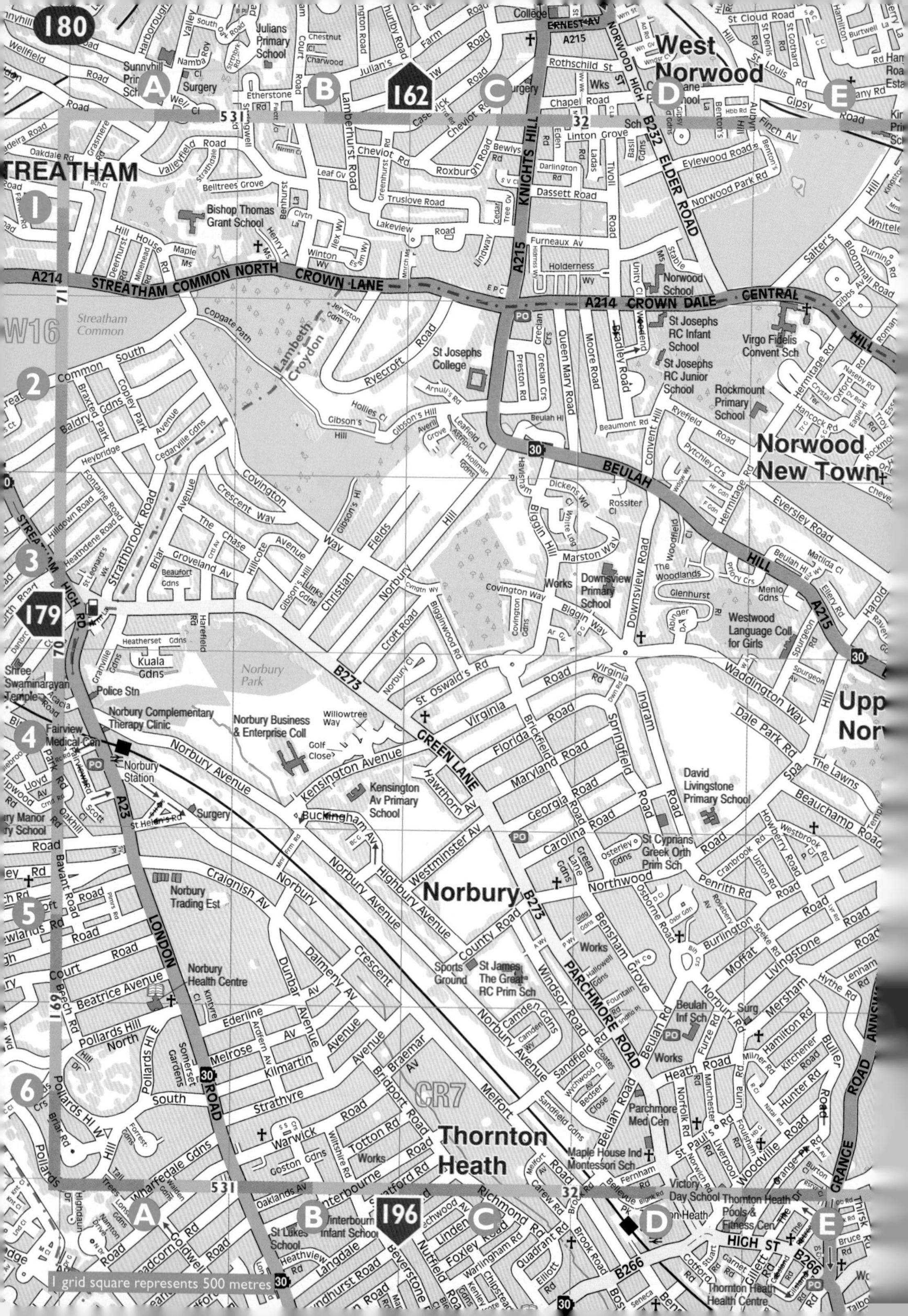
180
162
179
196
West Norwood
STREATHAM
Norwood New Town
Norbury
Thornton Heath
Upp
Nor
W16
CR7
Streatham Common
Norbury Park
A214 STREATHAM COMMON NORTH
CROWN LANE
A214 CROWN DALE
CENTRAL HILL
KNIGHTS HILL
A215
NORWOOD HIGH ST
B232 ELDER ROAD
BEULAH HILL
STREATHAM HIGH RD
LONDON ROAD
A23
B273
GREEN LANE
PARCHMORE ROAD
GRANGE ROAD
HIGH ST
B266
Julians Primary School
Sunnyhill Prim Sch
Surgery
Bishop Thomas Grant School
Norwood School
St Josephs RC Infant School
St Josephs RC Junior School
Virgo Fidelis Convent Sch
Rockmount Primary School
St Josephs College
Downsview Primary School
Westwood Language Coll for Girls
David Livingstone Primary School
Norbury Business & Enterprise Coll
Norbury Complementary Therapy Clinic
Fairview Medical Cen
Norbury Station
Police Stn
Shree Swaminarayan Temple
Kensington Av Primary School
St Cyprians Greek Orth Prim Sch
Norbury Trading Est
Norbury Health Centre
Sports Ground
St James The Great RC Prim Sch
Beulah Inf Sch
Parchmore Med Cen
Maple House Ind Montessori Sch
Victory Day School
Thornton Heath Pools & Fitness Cen
Thornton Heath Health Centre
St Lukes School
Winterbourn Infant School
Works
1 grid square represents 500 metres

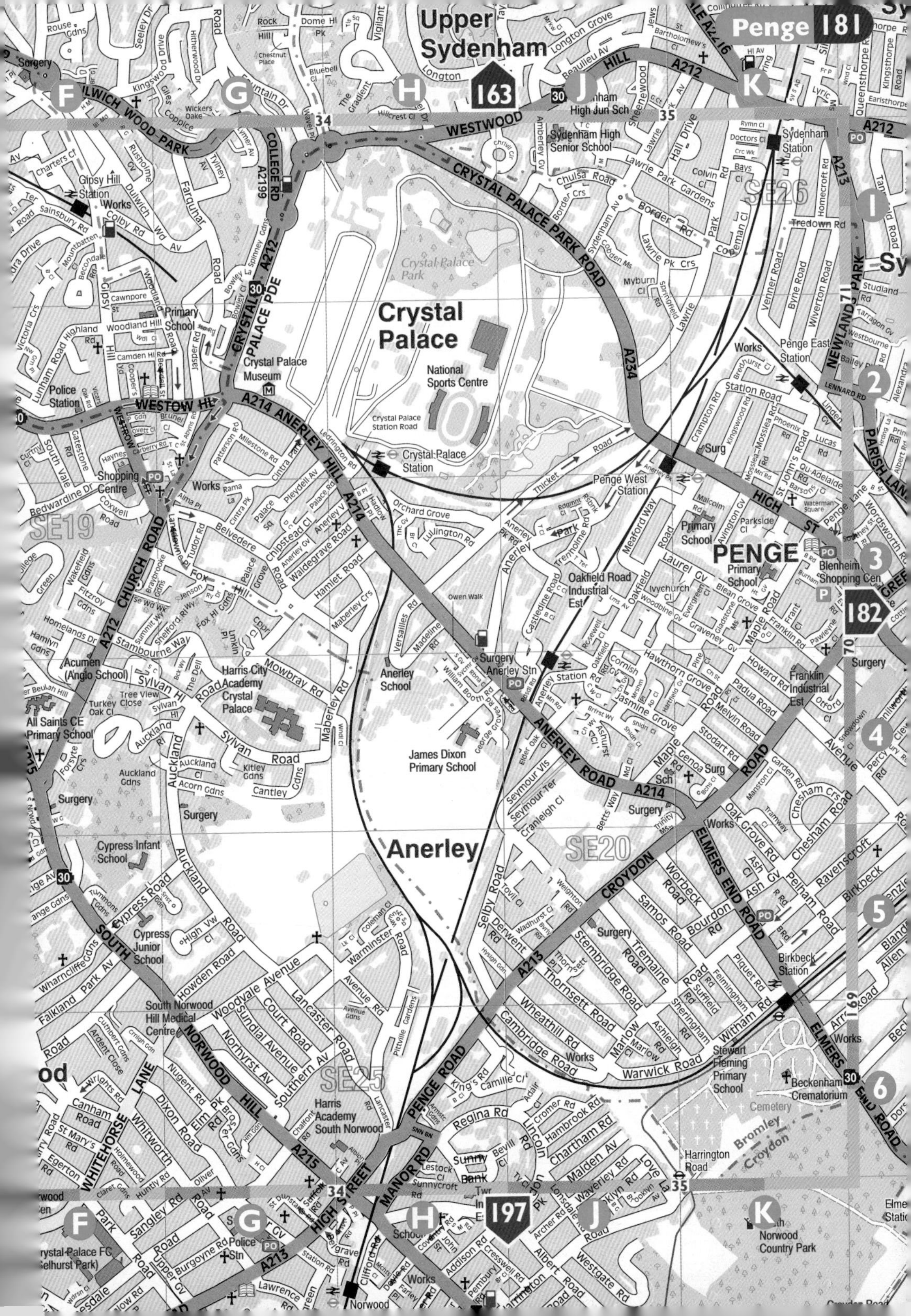

Penge 181
Upper Sydenham
163
182
197
Crystal Palace
Crystal Palace Park
National Sports Centre
Crystal Palace Museum
Crystal Palace Station
Crystal Palace Station Road
Anerley
PENGE
SE19
SE20
SE25
SE26
Gipsy Hill Station
Sydenham Station
Penge East Station
Penge West Station
Anerley Station
Birkbeck Station
Sydenham High Senior School
Harris City Academy Crystal Palace
James Dixon Primary School
Anerley School
Harris Academy South Norwood
Stewart Fleming Primary School
Beckenham Crematorium
Cemetery
South Norwood Country Park
South Norwood Hill Medical Centre
Cypress Infant School
Cypress Junior School
All Saints CE Primary School
Acumen (Anglo School)
Blenheim Shopping Cen
Franklin Industrial Est
Oakfield Road Industrial Est
Crystal Palace FC (Selhurst Park)
Police Station
Shopping Centre
Bromley
Croydon
WESTWOOD HILL
CRYSTAL PALACE PARK ROAD
CRYSTAL PALACE PDE
COLLEGE RD
WESTOW HILL
A214 ANERLEY HILL
ANERLEY ROAD
CHURCH ROAD
SOUTH NORWOOD HILL
WHITEHORSE LANE
HIGH STREET
PENGE ROAD
CROYDON ROAD
ELMERS END ROAD
HIGH ST
NEWLANDS PARK
PARISH LANE
SYDENHAM HILL
DULWICH WOOD PARK
MANOR RD
A212
A213
A214
A215
A234
A2199
F
G
H
J
K
I
2
3
4
5
6
34
35

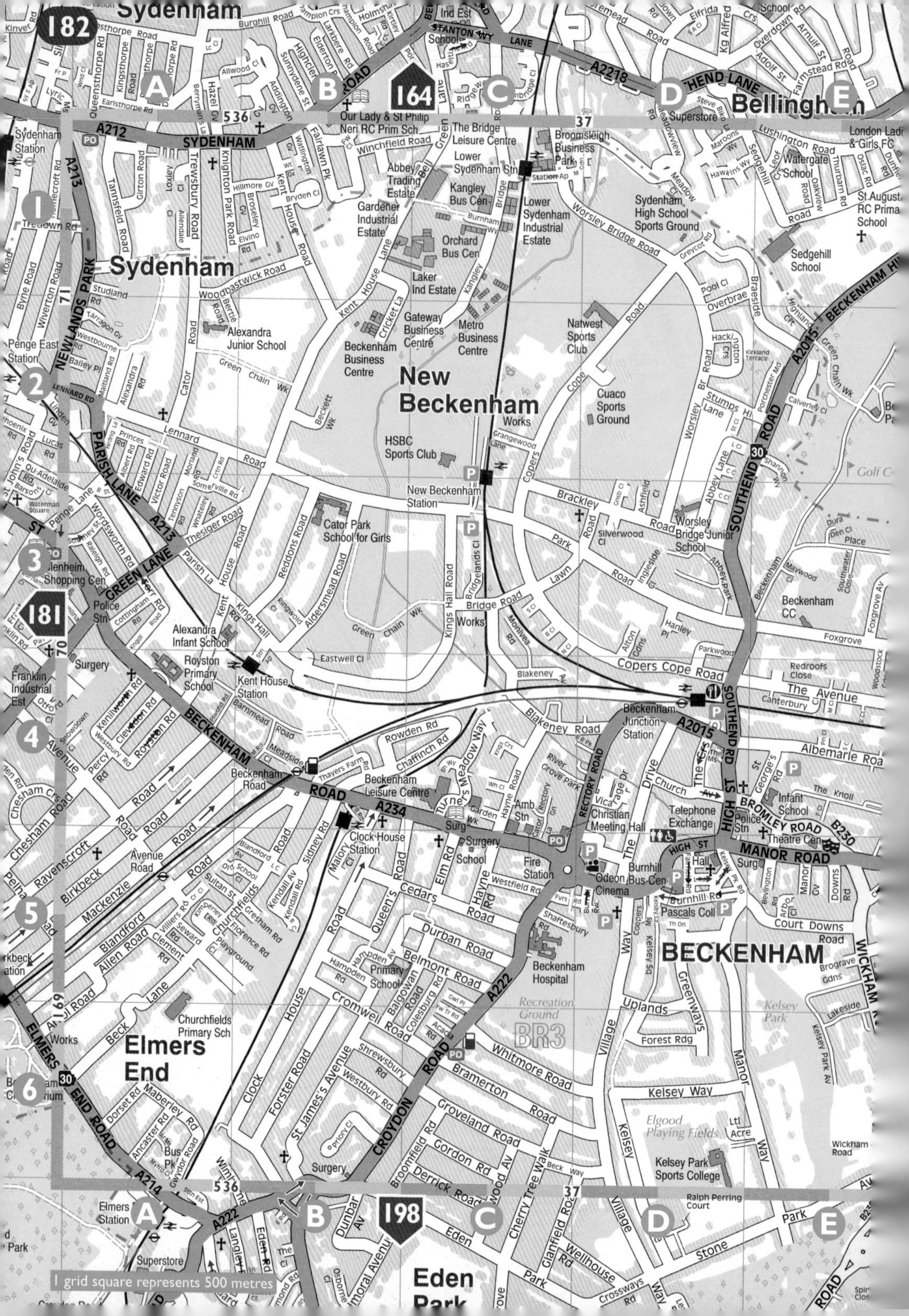
182
164
181
198
Sydenham
Bellingham
New Beckenham
BECKENHAM
Elmers End
Eden Park
A212 SYDENHAM ROAD
A213 NEWLANDS PARK
A2218
A2015
A234 BECKENHAM ROAD
A222 CROYDON ROAD
A214 ELMERS END ROAD
SOUTHEND ROAD
HIGH ST
MANOR ROAD
BROMLEY ROAD
B230
PARISH LANE
GREEN LANE
LENNARD RD
RECTORY ROAD
WICKHAM
Sydenham Station
Penge East Station
Lower Sydenham Stn
New Beckenham Station
Kent House Station
Beckenham Road
Clock House Station
Beckenham Junction Station
Elmers Station
Alexandra Junior School
Alexandra Infant School
Royston Primary School
Cator Park School for Girls
Beckenham Business Centre
Gateway Business Centre
Metro Business Centre
Laker Ind Estate
Abbey Trading Estate
Gardener Industrial Estate
Kangley Bus Cen
Orchard Bus Cen
Lower Sydenham Industrial Estate
Broomsleigh Business Park
The Bridge Leisure Centre
Our Lady & St Philip Neri RC Prim Sch
Sydenham High School Sports Ground
Natwest Sports Club
Cuaco Sports Ground
HSBC Sports Club
Worsley Bridge Junior School
Sedgehill School
Watergate School
St Augustine RC Primary School
London Ladies & Girls FC
Beckenham CC
Beckenham Leisure Centre
Christian Meeting Hall
Telephone Exchange
Infant School
Theatre Cen
Odeon Cinema
Burnhill Bus Cen
Pascals Coll
Beckenham Hospital
Fire Station
Recreation Ground
BR3
Kelsey Park
Elgood Playing Fields
Kelsey Park Sports College
Hampden Primary School
Churchfields Primary Sch
Ralph Perring Court
Superstore
Golf C
Green Chain Wk
1 grid square represents 500 metres

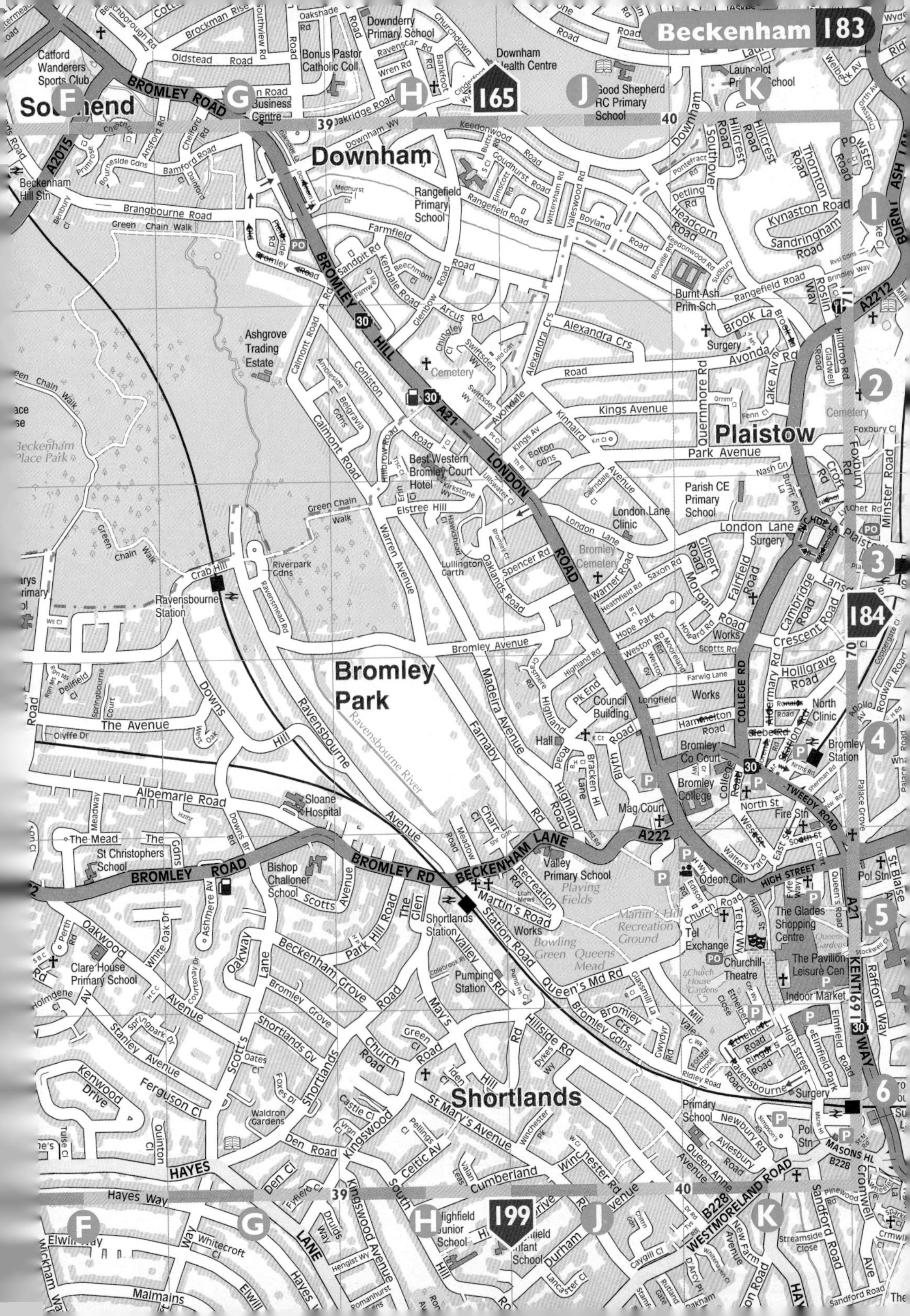
Southend
Downham
Plaistow
Bromley Park
Shortlands
Catford Wanderers Sports Club
Bromley Road
Business Centre
Bonus Pastor Catholic Coll.
Downderry Primary School
Downham Health Centre
165
Good Shepherd RC Primary School
Launcelot Prim School
Beckenham Hill Stn
Brangbourne Road
Green Chain Walk
Rangefield Primary School
Rangefield Road
Bromley Hill
London Road
Ashgrove Trading Estate
Cemetery
Burnt Ash Prim Sch
Kynaston Road
Sandringham Road
Alexandra Crs
Avondale Road
Kings Avenue
Park Avenue
Best Western Bromley Court Hotel
Beckenham Place Park
Elstree Hill
Warren Avenue
Parish CE Primary School
London Lane Clinic
London Lane
Bromley Cemetery
Ravensbourne Station
Crab Hill
Riverpark Gdns
Bromley Avenue
Ravensbourne River
Madeira Avenue
Farnaby
Council Building
Works
College Rd
Bromley Station
North Clinic
184
The Avenue
Albemarle Road
Sloane Hospital
Bromley Co Court
Bromley College
Mag Court
A222
Tweedy Road
Fire Stn
The Mead
St Christophers School
Bishop Challoner School
Bromley Rd
Beckenham Lane
Valley Primary School
Playing Fields
High Street
Odeon Cin
Shortlands Station
Martin's Road
Martin's Hill Recreation Ground
Bowling Green
Queens Mead
The Glades Shopping Centre
The Pavilion Leisure Cen
Indoor Market
Churchill Theatre
Church House Gardens
Tel Exchange
Clare House Primary School
Beckenham Grove
Pumping Station
Queen's Md Rd
Bromley Gdns
Ravensbourne Road
Kenwood Drive
Ferguson Cl
Stanley Avenue
Oakwood Avenue
Shortlands Gv
Waldron Gardens
St Mary's Avenue
Winchester Rd
Primary School
Newbury Rd
Aylesbury Road
Pol Stn
Masons Hl
Westmoreland Road
B228
Hayes
Hayes Way
Den Road
Den Cl
Cumberland
Celtic Av
Kingswood Avenue
Highfield Junior School
Infant School
199
Durham
Cavgill Cl
New Farm Avenue
Sandford Road
Streamside Close
Elwill Way
Whitecroft Cl
Malmains
Hayes Lane
Wickham Way
Kent Way
A21
A2015
A2212
39
40

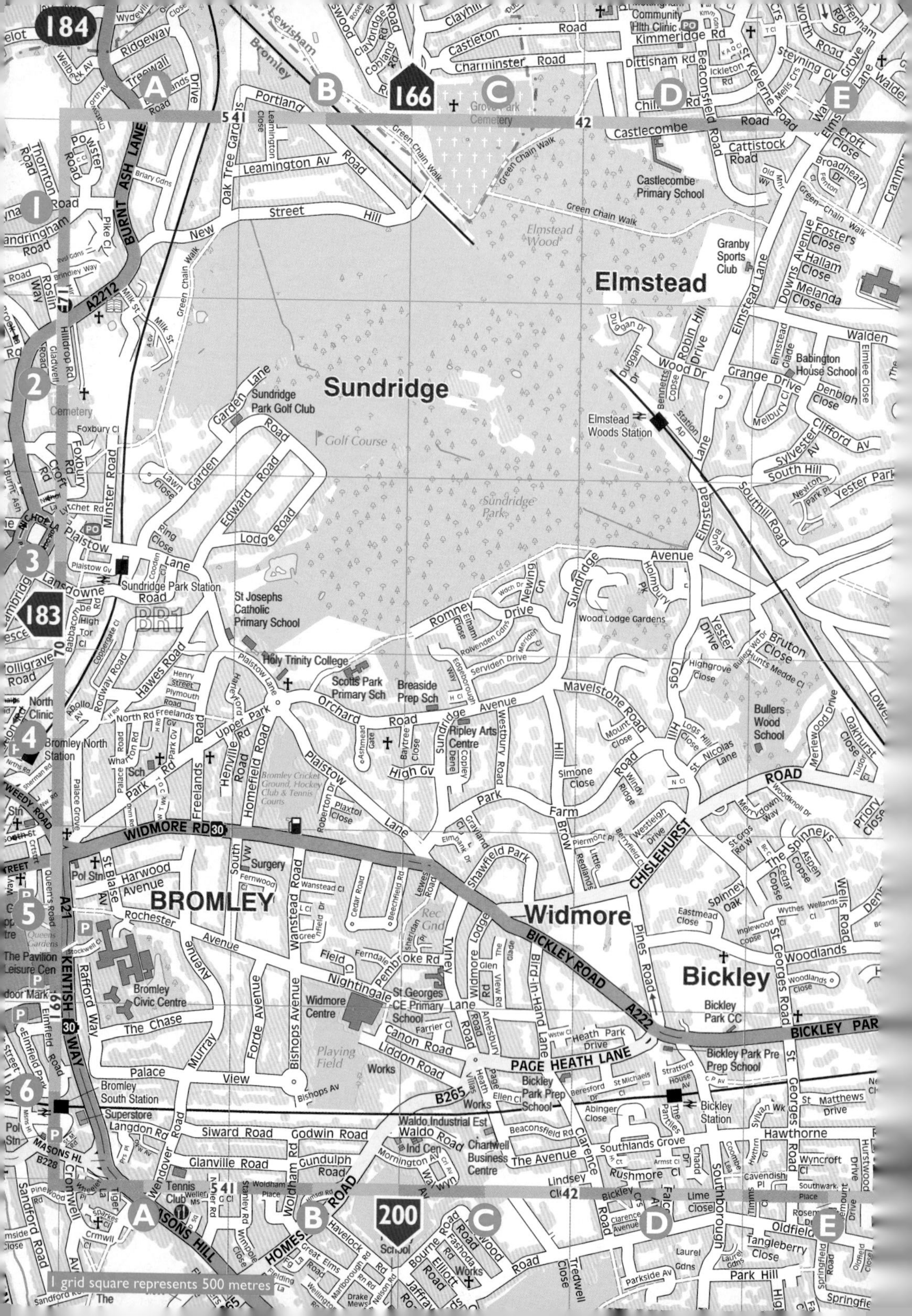
184
166
183
200
A
B
C
D
E
1
2
3
4
5
6
Sundridge
Elmstead
BROMLEY
Widmore
Bickley
BR1
Sundridge Park Golf Club
Golf Course
Sundridge Park
Elmstead Wood
Grove Park Cemetery
Green Chain Walk
Castlecombe Primary School
Granby Sports Club
Babington House School
Elmstead Woods Station
Sundridge Park Station
St Josephs Catholic Primary School
Holy Trinity College
Scotts Park Primary Sch
Breaside Prep Sch
Ripley Arts Centre
Bullers Wood School
Bromley North Station
Bromley Cricket Ground, Hockey Club & Tennis Courts
Surgery
Rec Gnd
Bromley Civic Centre
The Pavilion Leisure Cen
Queens Gardens
Widmore Centre
St Georges CE Primary School
Playing Field
Works
Bickley Park CC
Bickley Park Pre Prep School
Bickley Park Prep School
Bickley Station
Bromley South Station
Superstore
Waldo Industrial Est
Waldo Ind Cen
Chartwell Business Centre
Tennis Club
Wood Lodge Gardens
Cemetery
BURNT ASH LANE
A2212
WIDMORE RD
BICKLEY ROAD
A222
A21
KENTISH WAY
PAGE HEATH LANE
B265
MASONS HILL
HOMESDALE ROAD
CHISLEHURST ROAD
BICKLEY PARK
Plaistow Lane
Sundridge Avenue
Orchard Road
Elmstead Lane
Southill Road
Park Farm Road
Nightingale Lane
Rochester Avenue
Palace View
Siward Road
Godwin Road
Glanville Road
Southborough Lane
St Georges Road
Woodlands Road
Hawthorne Road
1 grid square represents 500 metres

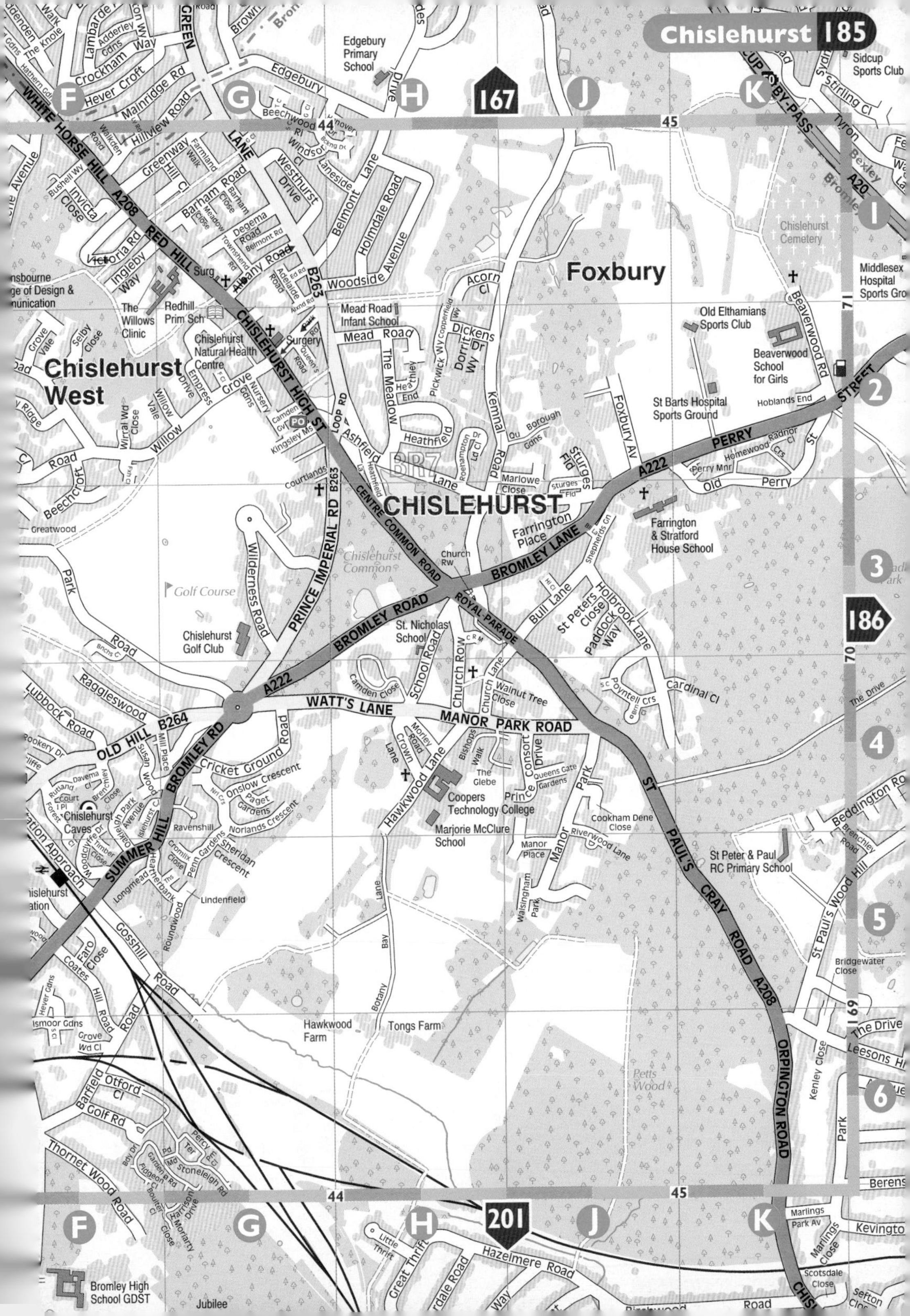

Chislehurst 185
167
186
201
Foxbury
CHISLEHURST
Chislehurst West
BR7
Edgebury Primary School
Sidcup Sports Club
Chislehurst Cemetery
Middlesex Hospital Sports Ground
Old Elthamians Sports Club
Beaverwood School for Girls
St Barts Hospital Sports Ground
Farrington & Stratford House School
Mead Road Infant School
Redhill Prim Sch
The Willows Clinic
Chislehurst Natural Health Centre
Surgery
Surg
Chislehurst Common
Golf Course
Chislehurst Golf Club
St. Nicholas School
Coopers Technology College
Marjorie McClure School
St Peter & Paul RC Primary School
Chislehurst Caves
Chislehurst Station
Hawkwood Farm
Tongs Farm
Petts Wood
Bromley High School GDST
WHITE HORSE HILL
A208
RED HILL
CHISLEHURST HIGH ST
CENTRE COMMON ROAD
ROYAL PARADE
ST PAUL'S CRAY ROAD
ORPINGTON ROAD
A222
PERRY STREET
BROMLEY LANE
BROMLEY ROAD
PRINCE IMPERIAL RD
B263
LOOP RD
WATT'S LANE
MANOR PARK ROAD
OLD HILL
B264
BROMLEY RD
SUMMER HILL
SIDCUP BY-PASS
A20
Edgebury
Beechwood Ri
Windsor Cl
Laneside
Belmont Lane
Holmdale Road
Westhurst Drive
Woodside Avenue
Hever Croft
Crockham Way
Mainridge Rd
Hillview Road
Greenway
Farmland Walk
Barham Road
Degema Road
Belmont Rd
Albany Road
Adelaide Road
Invicta Close
Victoria Rd
Ingleby Way
Acorn Cl
Dickens Dr
Dorrit Wy
Pickwick Wy
Heathley End
The Meadow
Mead Road
Heathfield Lane
Ashfield La
Kemnal Road
Roehampton Dr
Borough Gdns
Marlowe Close
Sturges Fld
Foxbury Av
Farrington Place
Hoblands End
Beaverwood Rd
Homewood Crs
Radnor Cl
Perry Mnr
Old Perry St
Church Rw
Bull Lane
St Peters Close
Holbrook Lane
Paddock Way
Cardinal Cl
Poyntell Crs
Walnut Tree Close
Church Lane
Church Row
School Road
Camden Close
Wilderness Road
Courtlands
Kingsley Ms
Camden Gro
Empress Drive
Grove Vale
Selby Close
Willow Vale
Willow Grove
Wirral Wd Close
Beechcroft Road
Greatwood
Park Road
Raggleswood
Lubbock Road
Rookery Dr
Mill Place
Susan Wood
Cricket Ground Road
Onslow Crescent
Paget Gardens
Norlands Crescent
Ravenshill
Penn Gardens
Sheridan Crescent
Lindenfield
Heatherbank
Longmead
Roundwood
Gosshill Road
Faro Close
Coates Hill Road
Hever Gdns
Grove Wd Cl
Barfield Road
Otford Cl
Golf Rd
Thornet Wood Road
Stoneleigh Rd
Percy Ter
Harrison Close
Moriarty Drive
Morley Road
Crown Lane
Hawkwood Lane
Bishops Walk
The Glebe
Consort Drive
Queens Gate Gardens
Prince Consort
Manor Park
Cookham Dene Close
Riverwood Lane
Manor Place
Walsingham Park
Botany Bay Lane
Bridgewater Close
St Paul's Wood Hill
Beddington Road
Brenchley Road
The Drive
Leesons Hill
Kenley Close
Berens
Marlings Park Av
Marlings Close
Kevington
Scotsdale Close
Sefton Close
Hazelmere Road
Little Thrift
Great Thrift
Jubilee
Stirling Cl
Tyron
Bexley
F G H J K
44 45
2 3 4 5 6
71 70 69

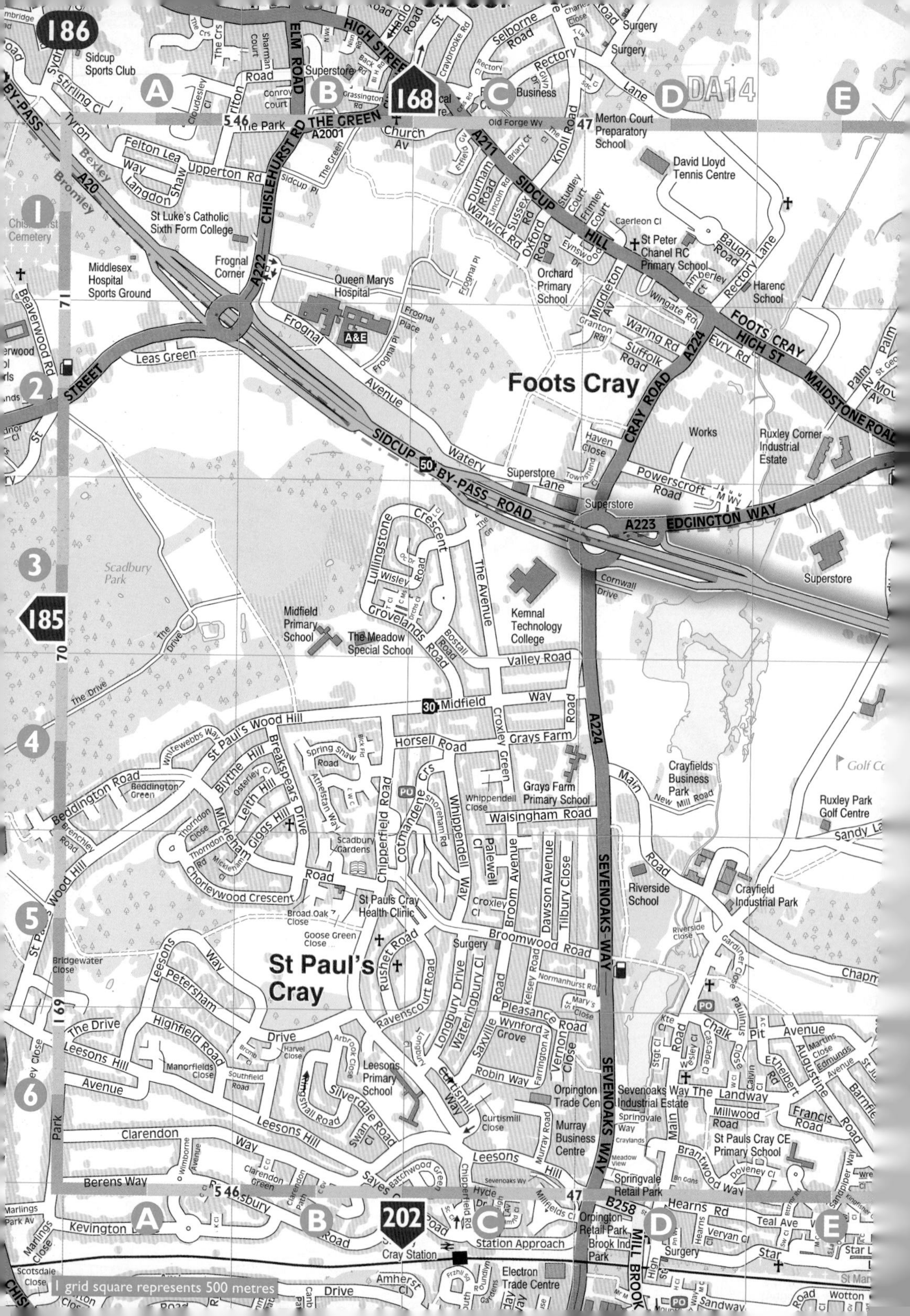

186
168
185
202
Sidcup Sports Club
Elm Road
High Street
Superstore
DA14
Merton Court Preparatory School
David Lloyd Tennis Centre
The Park
The Green
A2001
Church Av
Old Forge Wy
Felton Lea
Upperton Rd
Sidcup Pl
Chislehurst Rd
A222
A20
A211
Sidcup Hill
Bexley
Bromley
Chislehurst Cemetery
St Luke's Catholic Sixth Form College
Frognal Corner
Middlesex Hospital Sports Ground
Queen Marys Hospital
A&E
Frognal Avenue
Orchard Primary School
St Peter Chanel RC Primary School
Harenc School
Baugh Road
Rectory Lane
Foots Cray High St
Maidstone Road
Foots Cray
Cray Road
A224
Works
Ruxley Corner Industrial Estate
Leas Green
Street
Sidcup By-Pass Road
Watery Lane
Superstore
Powerscroft Road
A223
Edgington Way
Scadbury Park
The Drive
Lullingstone Crescent
Wisley Road
Grovelands Road
Midfield Primary School
The Meadow Special School
The Avenue
Kemnal Technology College
Cornwall Drive
Valley Road
Midfield Way
Crayfields Business Park
New Mill Road
Main Road
Ruxley Park Golf Centre
St Paul's Wood Hill
Horsell Road
Grays Farm Road
Grays Farm Primary School
Beddington Road
Breakspears Drive
Chipperfield Road
Cotmandene Crs
Whippendell Way
Walsingham Road
Broom Avenue
Dawson Avenue
Tilbury Close
Sevenoaks Way
Riverside School
Crayfield Industrial Park
Chorleywood Crescent
St Pauls Cray Health Clinic
Broomwood Road
St Paul's Cray
Leesons Way
Petersham
Rushet Road
Ravenscourt Road
Longbury Drive
Pleasance Road
Wynford Grove
Chalk Pit Avenue
Augustine
Highfield Road
Leesons Hill
Leesons Primary School
Silverdale Road
Robin Way
Orpington Trade Cen
Sevenoaks Way Industrial Estate
The Landway
Millwood Road
Francis Road
Murray Business Centre
St Pauls Cray CE Primary School
Clarendon Way
Berens Way
Springvale Retail Park
Orpington Retail Park
Brook Ind Park
B258
Hearns Rd
Mill Brook
Station Approach
Cray Station
Electron Trade Centre
Kevington
Star Lane
1 grid square represents 500 metres

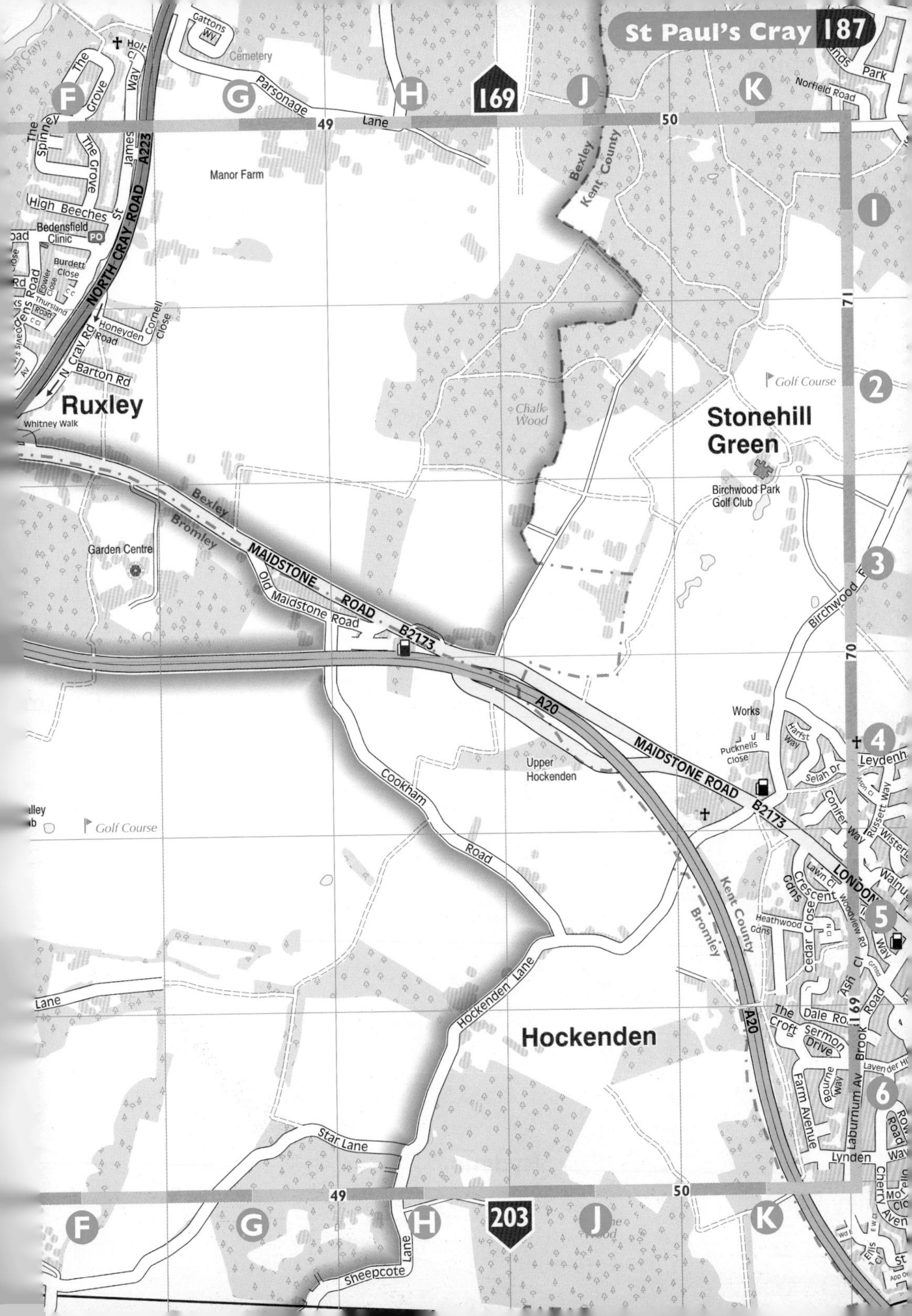
169
203
Ruxley
Stonehill Green
Hockenden
Manor Farm
Cemetery
Gattons Wy
Parsonage Lane
Holt Cl
James St
NORTH CRAY ROAD
A223
The Grove
The Spinney
High Beeches
Bedensfield Clinic
Burdett Close
Fowler Close
Thursland Road
Honeyden Road
Cornell Close
N. Cray Rd
Barton Rd
Whitney Walk
Chalk Wood
Bexley
Kent County
Bromley
Golf Course
Birchwood Park Golf Club
Garden Centre
MAIDSTONE ROAD
Old Maidstone Road
B2173
A20
Birchwood Rd
Works
Pucknells Close
Harfst Way
Selah Dr
Upper Hockenden
Cookham Road
Conifer Way
Russett Way
Leydenhatch
LONDON
Crescent Gdns
Lawn Cl
Heathwood Gdns
Cedar Close
Woodview Rd
Ash Cl
Brook Road
The Croft
The Dale Rd
Sermon Drive
Bourne Way
Farm Avenue
Laburnum Av
Lynden Way
Cherry Avenue
Hockenden Lane
Star Lane
Sheepcote Lane
Lane
Norfield Road
Park

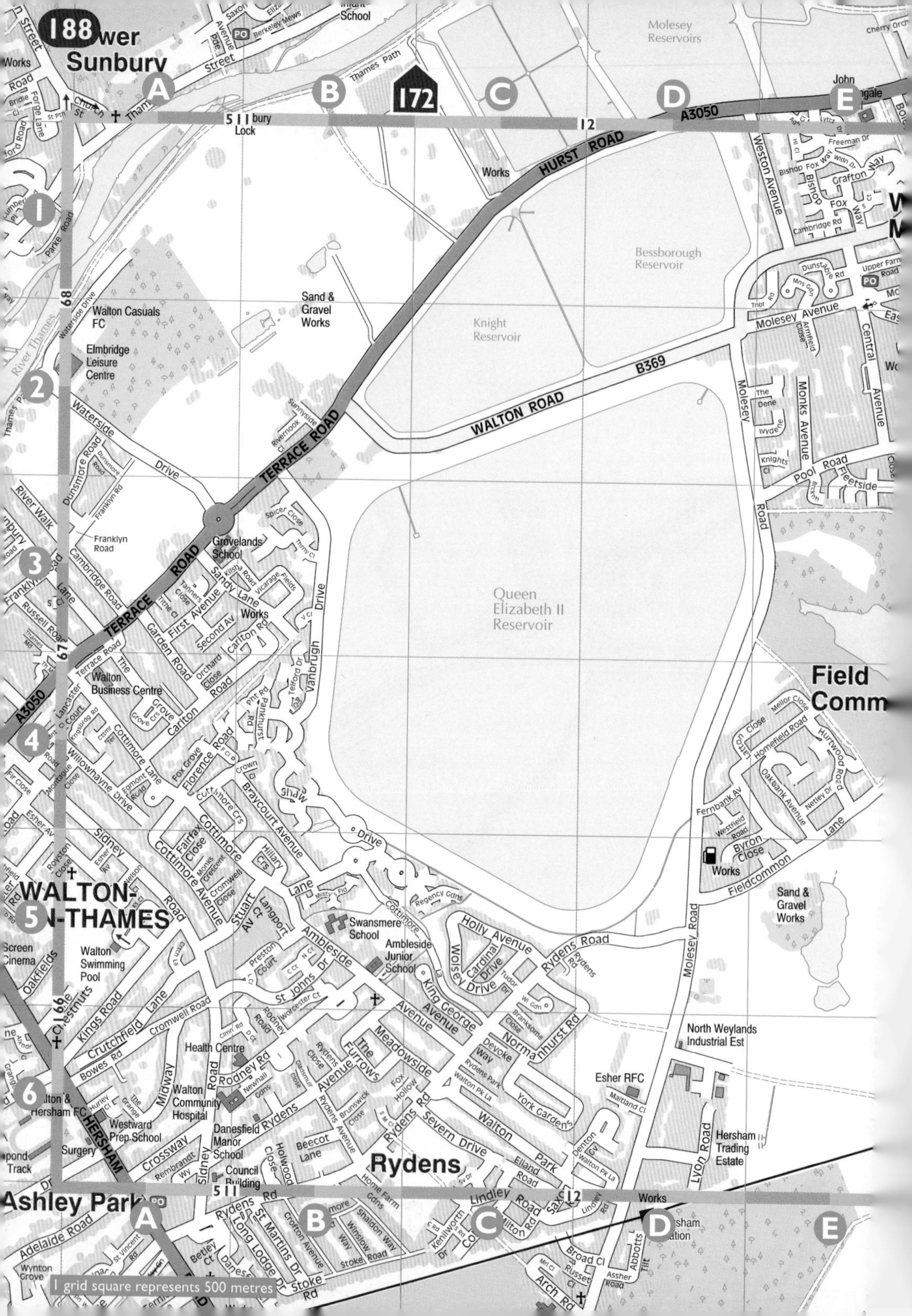

188
Lower Sunbury
172
A
B
C
D
E
1
2
3
4
5
6
Molesey Reservoirs
Thames Path
Sunbury Lock
Works
HURST ROAD
A3050
Weston Avenue
Bishop Fox Way
Grafton Way
Freeman Dr
Cambridge Rd
Bessborough Reservoir
Upper Farm Road
Molesey Avenue
Central Avenue
Knight Reservoir
Sand & Gravel Works
Walton Casuals FC
Elmbridge Leisure Centre
River Thames
Waterside Drive
B369
WALTON ROAD
TERRACE ROAD
Molesey Road
Monks Avenue
The Dene
Ivydene
Knights Cl
Pool Road
Fleetside
Dunsmore Road
Franklyn Road
River Walk
Grovelands School
Spicer Close
Sandy Lane
Vicarage Fields
Cambridge Road
First Avenue
Second Av
Carlton Rd
Queen Elizabeth II Reservoir
Field Common
Vanbrugh Drive
Walton Business Centre
Garden Road
Orchard Close
Grove Crs
Carlton Road
Telford Dr
Pankhurst Rd
Lancaster Court
Cottimore Lane
Willowhayne Drive
Florence Road
Fox Grove
Braycourt Avenue
Cottimore Crs
Shaw Drive
Mellor Close
Homefield Road
Hurtwood Road
Oakbank Avenue
Netley Dr
Fernbank Av
Westfield Road
Byron Close
Fieldcommon Lane
Montague Close
Fir Close
Esher Av
Sidney Road
Fairfax Close
Cottimore Avenue
Monks Crescent
Cromwell Close
Hillary Crs
Royston Close
Nelson Cl
WALTON-ON-THAMES
Stuart Av
Langport Ct
Lane
Regency Gdns
Swansmere School
Ambleside Junior School
Ambleside Avenue
Holly Avenue
Cardinal Drive
Wolsey Drive
Rydens Road
Works
Screen Cinema
Walton Swimming Pool
Oakfields
Chestnuts
Kings Road
Preston Court
St Johns Dr
King George Avenue
Tudor Dr
Normanhurst Rd
Branksome Close
North Weylands Industrial Est
Crutchfield Lane
Cromwell Road
Rodney Road
Worcester Ct
Meadowside
The Furrows
Devoke Way
Rydens Park
Walton Pk La
York Gardens
Bowes Rd
Health Centre
Rodney Rd
Rydens Close
Rydens Avenue
Fox Hollow
Esher RFC
Maitland Cl
Walton & Hersham FC
Westward Prep School
The Grange
Midway
Walton Community Hospital
Newhall Gdns
Danesfield Manor School
Rydens Rd
Brunswick Close
Severn Drive
Walton Park
Denton Gv
Hersham Trading Estate
Lyon Road
HERSHAM
Surgery
Crossway
Rembrandt Wy
Sidney Road
Holwood Close
Beecot Lane
Rydens
Elland Road
Council Building
Ashley Park
Rydens Rd
Home Farm Gdns
Lindley Road
Saxon
Works
Adelaide Road
Wynton Grove
Long Lodge Dr
St Martins Dr
Crofton Avenue
Winslow Way
Shaldon Way
Stoke Road
Kenilworth Dr
Milton Rd
Broad Cl
Russet Cl
Abbotts Tilt
Assher Road
Arch Rd
Stoke Rd
Track
1 grid square represents 500 metres

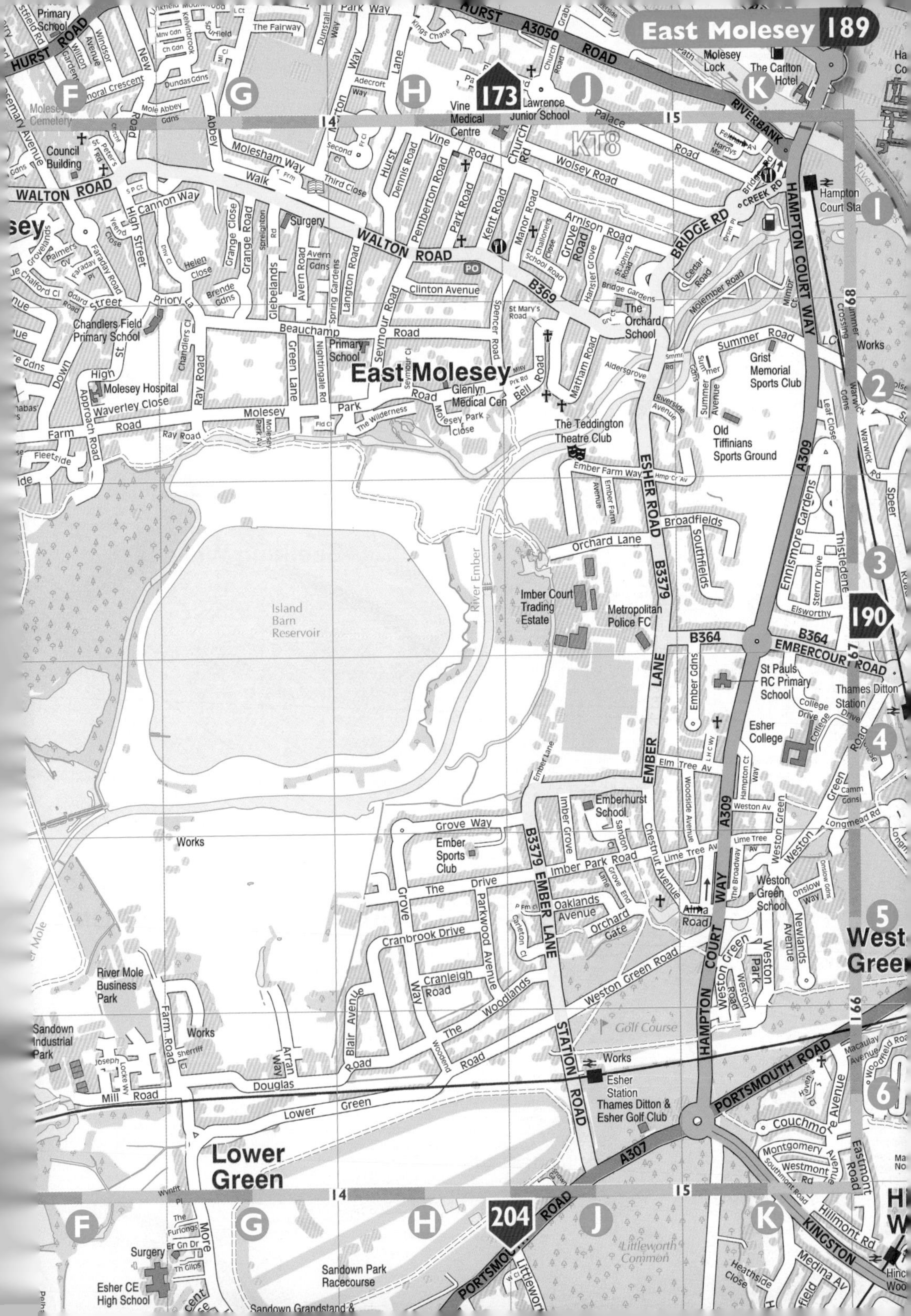
East Molesey
KT8
173
190
204
F
G
H
J
K
14
15
2
3
4
5
6
HURST ROAD
A3050
Molesey Lock
The Carlton Hotel
RIVERBANK
Hampton Court Station
HAMPTON COURT WAY
A309
CREEK RD
BRIDGE RD
Palace Road
Wolsey Road
Arnison Road
WALTON ROAD
B369
Vine Road
Vine Medical Centre
Lawrence Junior School
Church Road
Kent Road
Park Road
Pemberton Road
Dennis Road
Hurst Road
Molesham Way
Walk
Third Close
Second Cl
Adecroft Way
Molesey Cemetery
Council Building
Cannon Way
High Street
Surgery
Grange Close
Grange Road
Helen Close
Brende Gdns
Glebelands
Avern Road
Avern Gdns
Spring Gardens
Langton Road
Seymour Road
Clinton Avenue
Beauchamp Road
Spencer Road
Manor Road
Challoners Close
School Road
Grove Road
Hansler Grove
Bridge Gardens
The Orchard School
Matham Road
Aldersgrove
Chandlers Field Primary School
Priory La
Chandlers Cl
Ray Road
Green Lane
Nightingale Rd
Primary School
Seymour Cl
Park Road
Glenlyn Medical Cen
Bell Road
Molesey Park Close
The Wilderness
Molesey Hospital
Waverley Close
Approach Road
Farm Road
Molesey Road
Fleetside
The Teddington Theatre Club
Ember Farm Way
Summer Road
Grist Memorial Sports Club
Riverside Avenue
Old Tiffinians Sports Ground
ESHER ROAD
Broadfields
Southfields
Orchard Lane
River Ember
Island Barn Reservoir
Imber Court Trading Estate
Metropolitan Police FC
B3379
B364
EMBERCOURT ROAD
Ennismore Gardens
Sterry Drive
Thistledene
Elsworthy
Warwick Gdns
Summer Works
Crossing
Leaf Close
St Pauls RC Primary School
College Drive
Thames Ditton Station
Esher College
Ember Gdns
EMBER LANE
Elm Tree Av
Woodside Avenue
Hampton Ct Way
Weston Av
Weston Green
Longmead Rd
Emberhurst School
Imber Grove
Sandon Close
Grove Way
Ember Sports Club
Imber Park Road
Lime Tree Av
Chestnut Avenue
The Broadway
Weston Green School
Onslow Way
Newlands Avenue
West Green
The Drive
Parkwood Avenue
Oaklands Avenue
Orchard Gate
Alma Road
Grove
Cranbrook Drive
Cranleigh Road
Way
Weston Green Road
The Woodlands
Weston Park
Golf Course
Works
River Mole Business Park
Sandown Industrial Park
Farm Road
Mill Road
Douglas Road
Blair Avenue
Arran Way
STATION ROAD
Esher Station
Thames Ditton & Esher Golf Club
PORTSMOUTH ROAD
Couchmore Avenue
Montgomery Avenue
Westmont Rd
Eastmont Road
Lower Green
A307
Lower Green
Littleworth Common
KINGSTON
Hillmont Rd
Medina Av
Surgery
Esher CE High School
Sandown Park Racecourse
Heathside Close

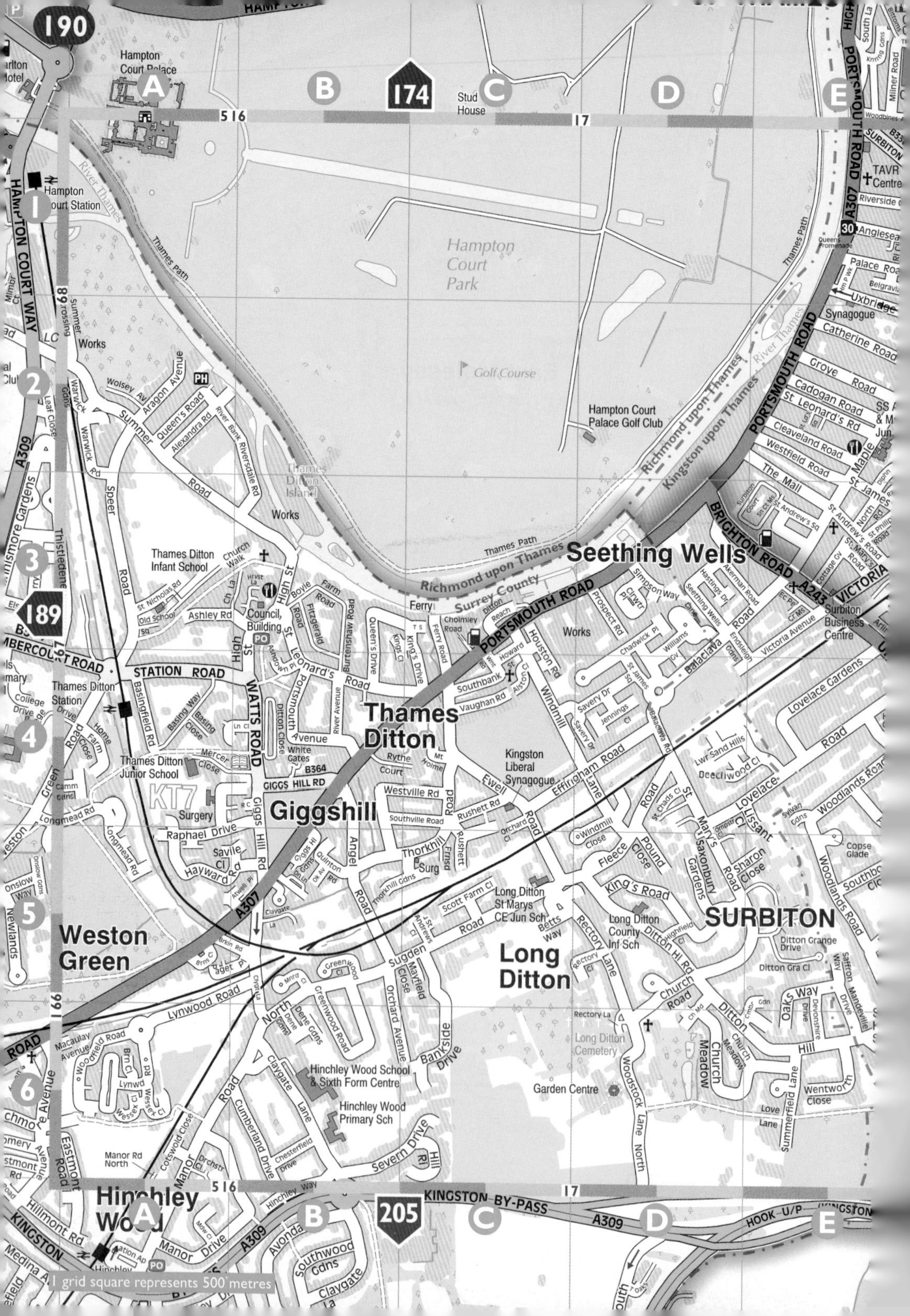

190
174
189
205
Hampton Court Palace
Hampton Court Station
HAMPTON COURT WAY
Stud House
Hampton Court Park
Golf Course
Hampton Court Palace Golf Club
River Thames
Thames Path
Thames Ditton Island
Richmond upon Thames
Kingston upon Thames
Surrey County
Seething Wells
PORTSMOUTH ROAD
BRIGHTON ROAD
A243
VICTORIA
Surbiton Business Centre
Works
Thames Ditton Infant School
Church Walk
Council Building
Ferry
Thames Ditton
Thames Ditton Station
STATION ROAD
WATTS ROAD
GIGGS HILL RD
B364
Thames Ditton Junior School
KT7
Surgery
Giggshill
Kingston Liberal Synagogue
Effingham Road
Long Ditton St Marys CE Jun Sch
Long Ditton County Inf Sch
Long Ditton
Long Ditton Cemetery
Garden Centre
SURBITON
Weston Green
Hinchley Wood School & Sixth Form Centre
Hinchley Wood Primary Sch
Hinchley Wood
KINGSTON BY-PASS
A309
A307
HOOK U/P
Synagogue
TAVR Centre
Catherine Road
Grove Road
Cadogan Road
St Leonard's Rd
Cleaveland Road
Westfield Road
The Mall
Lovelace Gardens
Woodlands Road
Copse Glade
Ditton Grange Drive
Oaks Way
Wentworth Close
Love Lane
Summerfield Lane
Church Meadow
Woodstock Lane North
Rectory Lane
Ditton Hl Rd
King's Road
Fleece Road
Windmill Lane
Sugden Road
Orchard Avenue
Mayfield Close
Bankside Drive
Greenwood Road
Claygate Lane
Cumberland Drive
Severn Drive
Manor Drive
Manor Rd North
Lynwood Road
Woodfield Road
Macaulay Avenue
Eastmont Road
Hillmont Rd
KINGSTON ROAD
Southwood Gdns
Avondale
Raphael Drive
Hayward Rd
Longmead Rd
Speer Road
Summer Road
Queen's Road
Alexandra Rd
Riversdale Rd
Aragon Avenue
Wolsey Av
Warwick Rd
Thistledene
Ennismore Gardens
A309
Portsmouth Avenue
Ditton Close
Basing Way
Basingfield Rd
Westville Rd
Southville Road
Thorkhill Road
Rushett Rd
Angel Road
Queen's Drive
King's Drive
Ferry Road
Burtenshaw Road
Fitzgerald Road
Boyle Farm Road
Ashley Rd
Houston Rd
Prospect Rd
Simpson Way
Balaclava Road
Victoria Avenue
Lovelace Road
Pound Close
St Mary's Road
Saxonbury Gardens
Sharon Close
Lissant Cl
1 grid square represents 500 metres

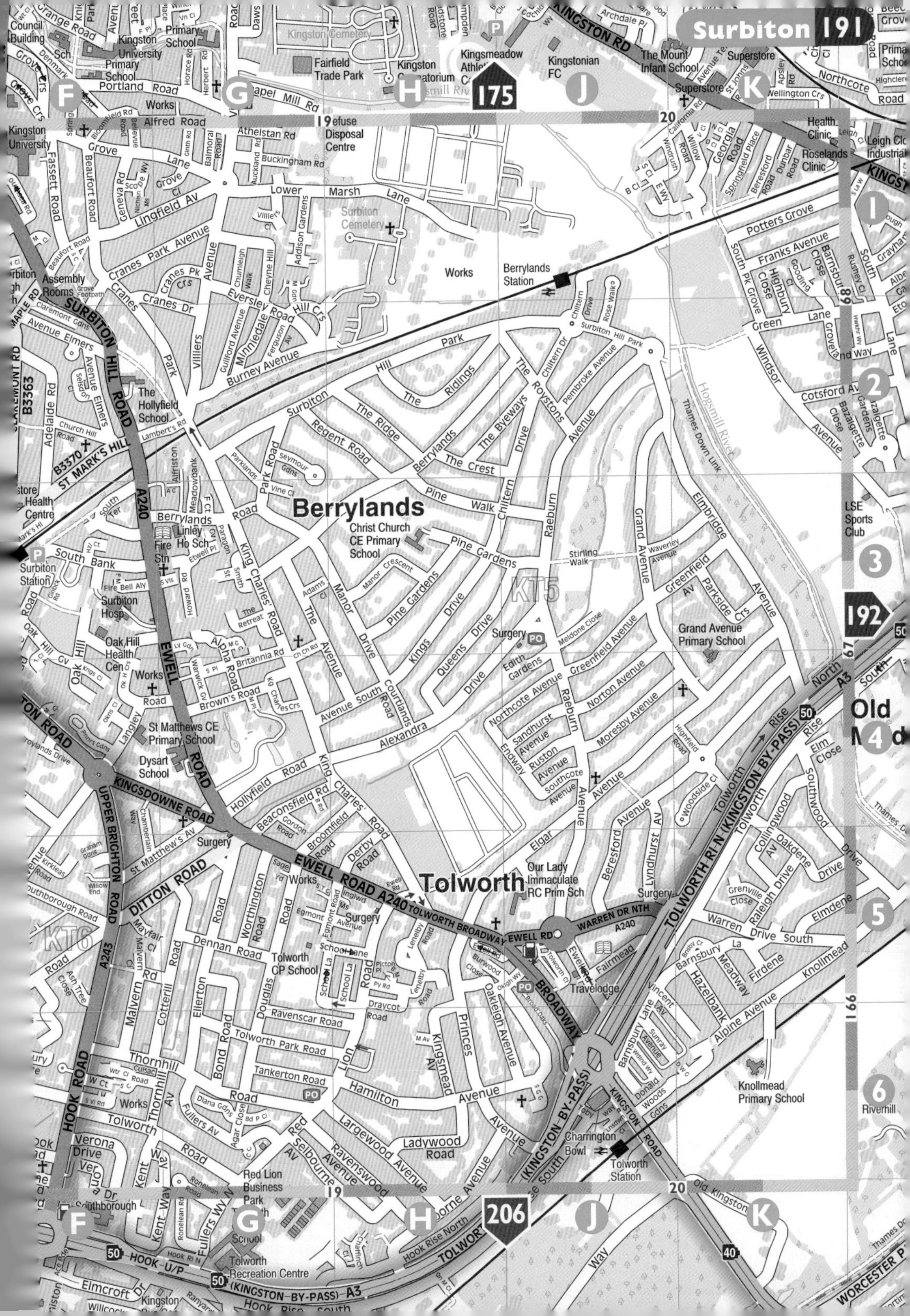

175
192
206
Berrylands
Tolworth
Old Malden
KT5
KT6
Kingston Cemetery
Fairfield Trade Park
Kingston Crematorium
Kingsmeadow Athletics Centre
Kingstonian FC
The Mount Infant School
Superstore
Kingston University
Kingston University Primary School
Council Building
Refuse Disposal Centre
Surbiton Cemetery
Works
Berrylands Station
Assembly Rooms
The Hollyfield School
Health Centre
Surbiton Station
Surbiton Hosp
Oak Hill Health Cen
Berrylands Linley Ho Sch
Fire Stn
Christ Church CE Primary School
St Matthews CE Primary School
Dysart School
Surgery
Grand Avenue Primary School
LSE Sports Club
Health Clinic
Roselands Clinic
Leigh Close Industrial
Our Lady Immaculate RC Prim Sch
Tolworth CP School
Travelodge
Knollmead Primary School
Charrington Bowl
Tolworth Station
Red Lion Business Park
Tolworth Recreation Centre
Southborough
Riverhill
SURBITON HILL ROAD
EWELL ROAD
EWELL ROAD A240
TOLWORTH BROADWAY
KINGSTON RD
KINGSDOWNE ROAD
UPPER BRIGHTON ROAD
DITTON ROAD
HOOK ROAD
ST MARK'S HILL
TOLWORTH RI N (KINGSTON BY-PASS)
(KINGSTON-BY-PASS) A3
HOOK U/P
WORCESTER PARK
Hogsmill River
Thames Down Link
Alexandra Drive
Hollyfield Road
Cranes Park Avenue
Lower Marsh Lane
Grand Avenue
Raeburn Avenue
Elmbridge Avenue
Warren Drive South
Alpine Avenue
Knollmead
Hamilton Avenue
Largewood Avenue
Ladywood Road
Tolworth Park Road
Ravenscar Road
Dennan Road
Portland Road
Alfred Road
Potters Grove
Franks Avenue

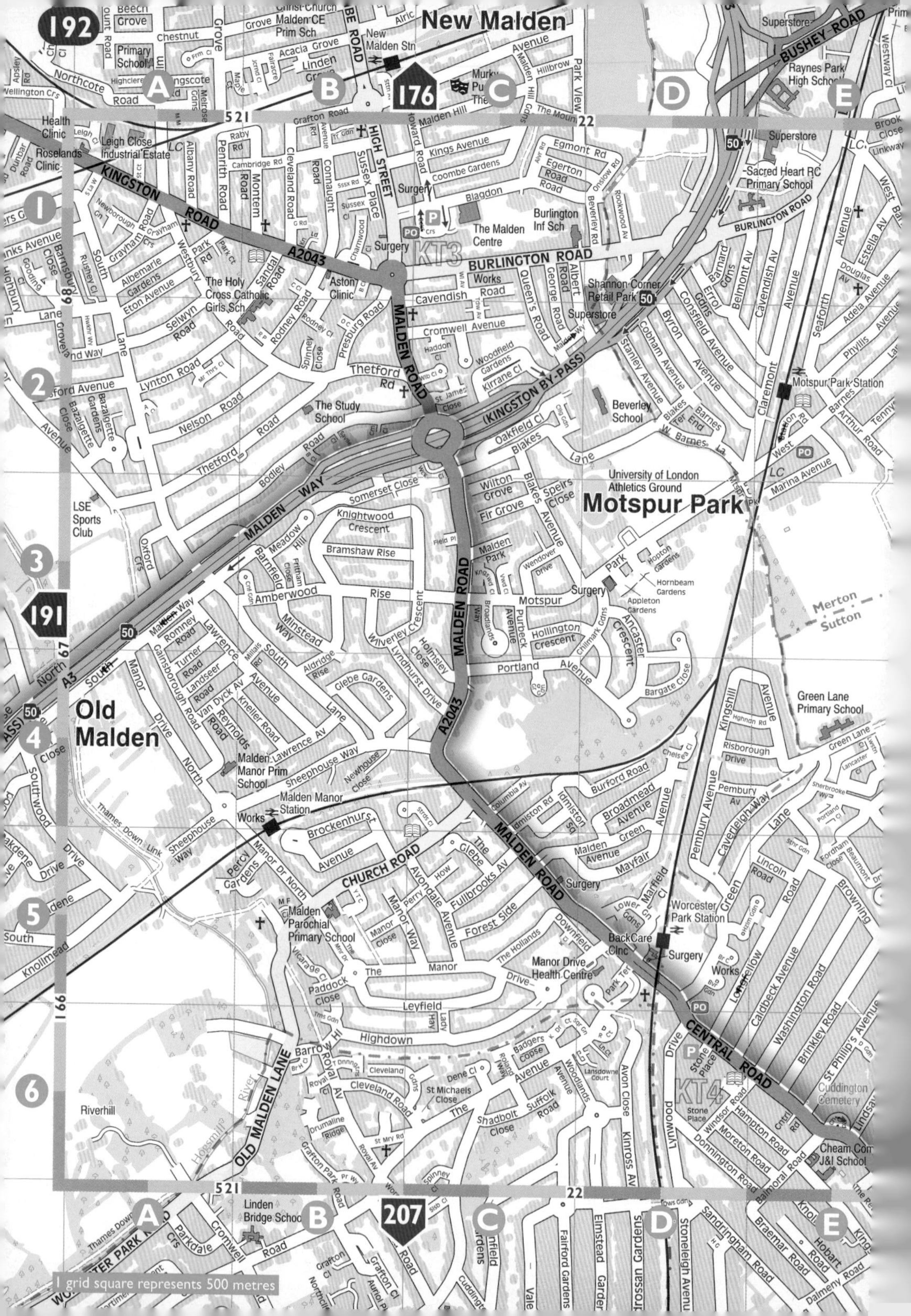
New Malden
New Malden Stn
176
A
B
C
D
E
Beech Grove
Christ Church Malden CE Prim Sch
Primary School
Chestnut
Northcote Road
Kingscote Rd
Acacia Grove
Linden Grove
Grafton Road
Malden Hill
Hillbrow
Park View
The Mount
Avenue
Bushey Road
Superstore
Raynes Park High School
Brook Close
Health Clinic
Leigh Close Industrial Estate
Roselands Clinic
Kingston Road
Albany Road
Penrith Road
Montem Road
Cambridge Rd
Cleveland Road
Connaught Road
Sussex Place
High Street
Kings Avenue
Coombe Gardens
Egmont Rd
Egerton Road
Onslow Rd
Rookwood Av
Sacred Heart RC Primary School
Burlington Road
Surgery
Blagdon
The Malden Centre
Burlington Inf Sch
KT3
A2043
Burlington Road
Works
Cavendish Road
Queen's Road
George Road
Albert Road
Beverley Rd
Shannon Corner Retail Park
Superstore
The Holy Cross Catholic Girls Sch
Aston Clinic
Malden Road
Cromwell Avenue
Woodfield Gardens
Kirrane Cl
Kingston By-Pass
Byron
Cobham Avenue
Stanley Avenue
Consfield Avenue
Cavendish Av
Belmont Av
Errol Gdns
Barnard Gdns
Claremont Avenue
Seaforth Avenue
Estella Av
Douglas Av
Adela Avenue
Phyllis Avenue
West Barnes Lane
Grayham Road
Albemarle Gardens
Eton Avenue
Selwyn Road
Westbury Park Rd
Sandal Road
Rodney Road
Presburg Road
Spinney Close
Thetford Rd
Groveland Way
Barnsbury Close
Lynton Road
Nelson Road
Thetford Road
Bodley Road
Malden Way
The Study School
Beverley School
Oakfield Cl
Blakes Lane
Blakes Ter
Barnes End
W. Barnes La
Motspur Park Station
Marina Avenue
Arthur Road
Bazalgette Gardens
Bazalgette Close
Avenue
LSE Sports Club
Oxford Crs
Somerset Close
Knightwood Crescent
Bramshaw Rise
Meadow Hill
Barnfield
Wilton Grove
Fir Grove
Spiers Close
Blakes Avenue
University of London Athletics Ground
Motspur Park
Hopton Gardens
Hornbeam Gardens
Appleton Gardens
Malden Park
Wendover Drive
Motspur Park
Surgery
Amberwood Rise
Minstead Way
Wiverley Crescent
Holmsley Close
Lyndhurst Drive
Broadlands Way
Purbeck Avenue
Hollington Crescent
Chilmark Gdns
Ancaster Crescent
Portland Avenue
Bargate Close
Merton
Sutton
191
50
67
A3
North
South
Malden Way
Romney Road
Turner Road
Landseer Road
Lawrence Avenue
Van Dyck Av
Kneller Road
Reynolds Road
Gainsborough Road
Manor Drive North
South Lane
Aldridge Rise
Glebe Gardens
Lawrence Av
Old Malden
Malden Manor Prim School
Sheephouse Way
Newhouse Close
Kingshill Avenue
Risborough Drive
Green Lane Primary School
Green Lane
Pembury Avenue
Pembury Av
Caverleigh Way
Chelsea Cl
Burford Road
Idmiston Rd
Idmiston Sq
Broadmead Avenue
Avenue
Malden Green Avenue
Mayfair
Malden Manor Station
Works
Thames Down Link
Sheephouse Way
Brockenhurst Avenue
Church Road
Percy Gardens
Manor Dr North
Avondale Avenue
Glebe
Fullbrooks Av
Forest Side
Malden Road
Surgery
Marfield Cl
Lower Gn Gdns
Worcester Park Station
Lincoln Road
Fordham Close
Beaumont Dr
Browning
Sherbrooke Way
Portland Cl
Lancaster Cl
Soutwood
Oakdene Drive
Drive
South
Knollmead
Malden Parochial Primary School
Manor Way
Manor Close
Vicarage Cl
The Manor Drive
The Hollands
Downfield
BackCare Clnc
Surgery
Manor Drive Health Centre
Works
Longfellow Road
Caldbeck Avenue
Washington Road
Brinkley Road
St Philip's Avenue
Paddock Close
Leyfield
Lady Hay
Highdown
Barrow Hi
Park Ter
PO
Central Road
166
Riverhill
Hogsmill River
Old Malden Lane
Royal Av
Cleveland
Cleveland Road
Dene Cl
St Michaels Close
Badgers Copse
Avenue
Woodlands Avenue
Lansdowne Court
Avon Close
Kinross Av
Drive
Stone Place
KT4
Lyndhurst
Windsor Road
Hampton Road
Moreton Road
Donnington Road
Cntrl Rd
Cuddington Cemetery
Cheam Com J&I School
Drumaline Ridge
The Shadbolt Close
Suffolk Road
St Mry Rd
Grafton Park Road
Spinney
521
22
207
Linden Bridge School
Thames Down
Parkdale Crs
Cromwell Road
Worcester Park Road
Grafton Cl
Fairford Gardens
Elmstead Gardens
Crossan Gardens
Stoneleigh Avenue
Sandringham Road
Balmoral Road
Braemar Road
Hobart Road
Dalmeny Road
Vale
1 grid square represents 500 metres

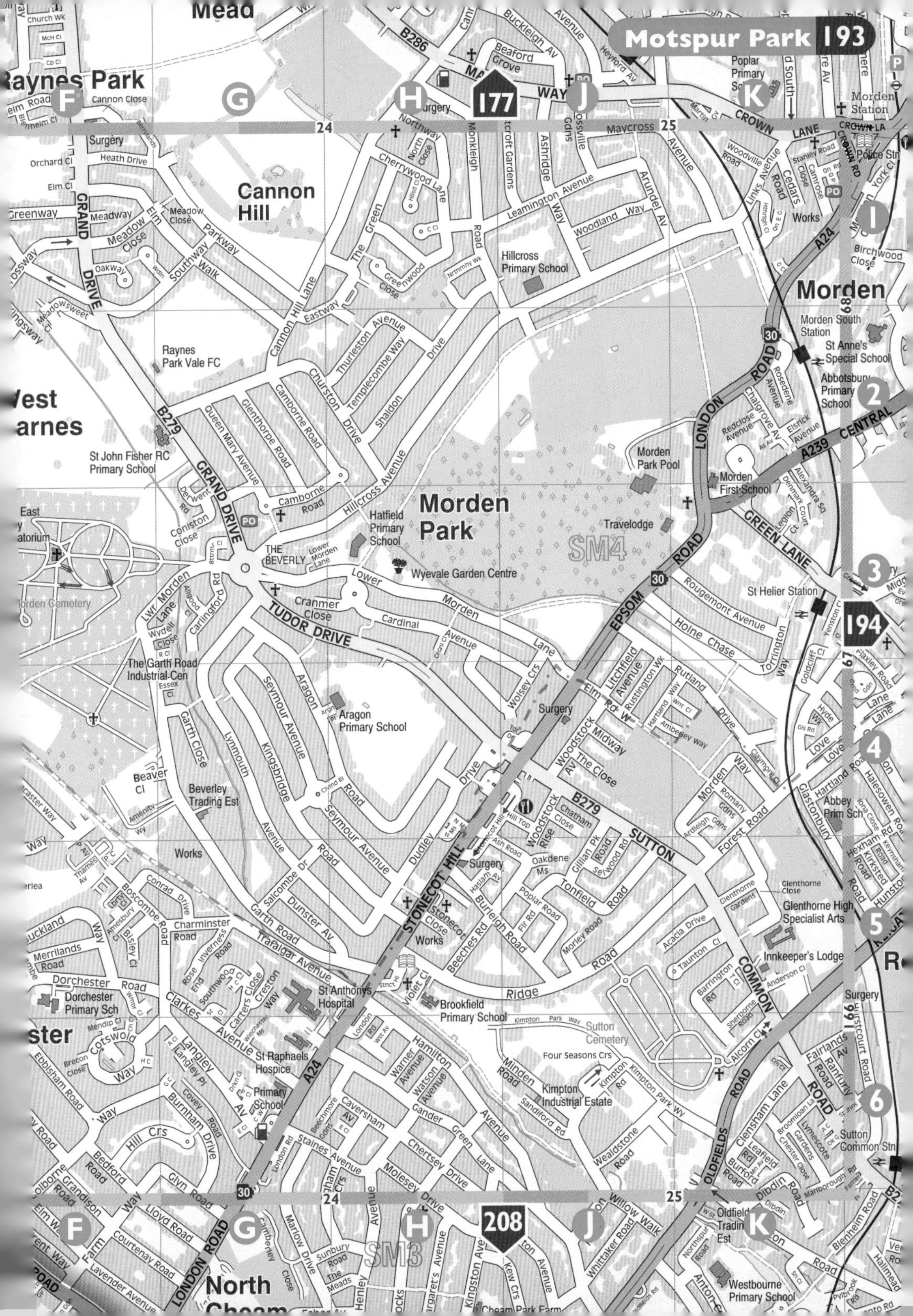
Raynes Park
Cannon Hill
West Barnes
Morden Park
Morden
North Cheam
SM4
SM3
Hillcross Primary School
Raynes Park Vale FC
St John Fisher RC Primary School
Hatfield Primary School
Wyevale Garden Centre
Morden Park Pool
Travelodge
Morden First School
Morden South Station
St Anne's Special School
Abbotsbury Primary School
St Helier Station
Aragon Primary School
The Garth Road Industrial Cen
Beverley Trading Est
Morden Cemetery
St Anthony's Hospital
St Raphaels Hospice
Brookfield Primary School
Sutton Cemetery
Kimpton Industrial Estate
Four Seasons Crs
Glenthorne High Specialist Arts
Innkeeper's Lodge
Abbey Prim Sch
Dorchester Primary Sch
Westbourne Primary School
Oldfield Tradin Est
Sutton Common Stn
Morden Station
Poplar Primary Sch
Police Stn
GRAND DRIVE
TUDOR DRIVE
LONDON ROAD
EPSOM ROAD
STONECOT HILL
SUTTON COMMON ROAD
OLDFIELDS ROAD
GREEN LANE
CROWN LANE
CENTRAL
177
194
208

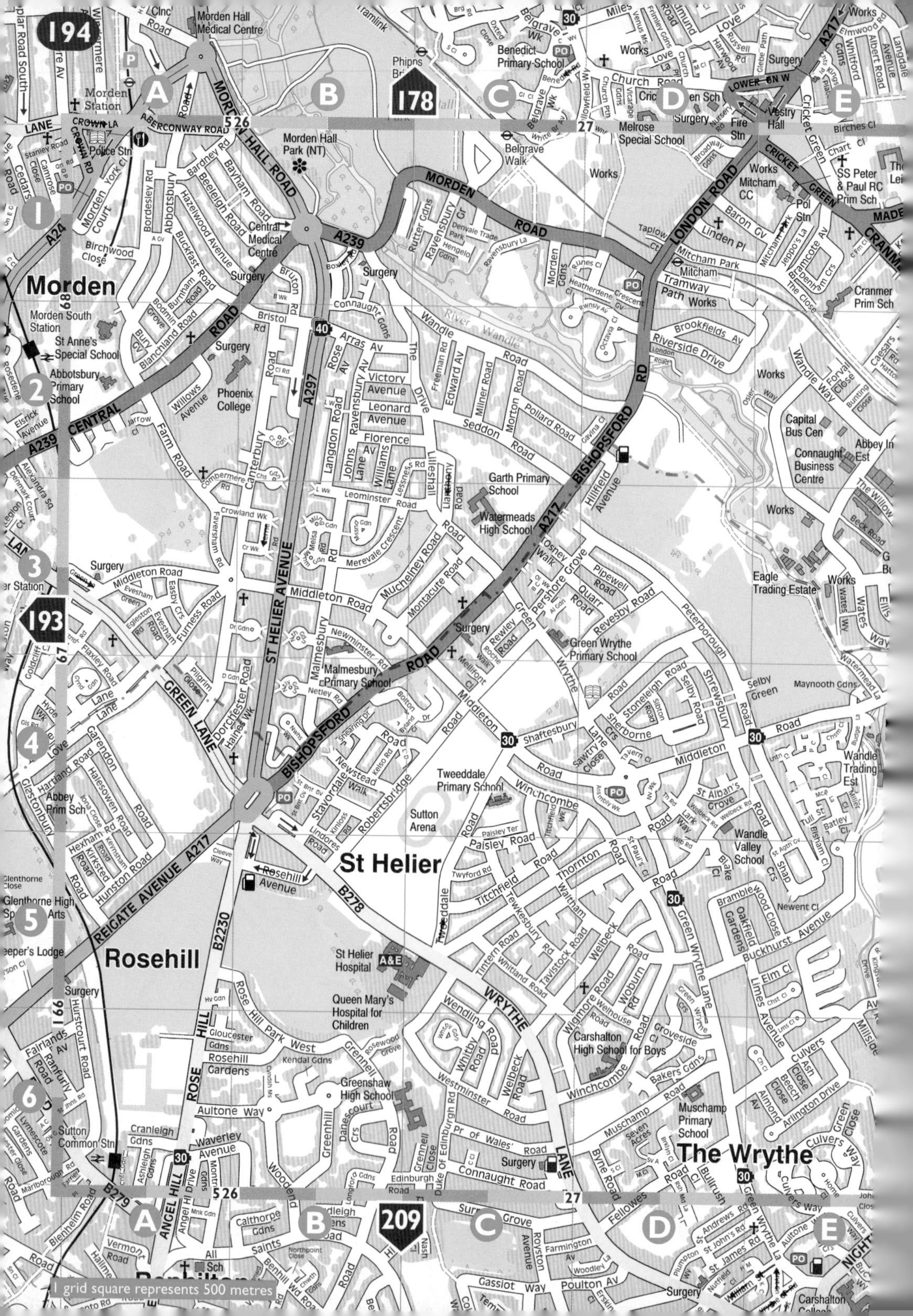
194
178
193
209
A
B
C
D
E
1
2
3
4
5
6
526
27
Morden
Morden Station
Morden South Station
Morden Hall Medical Centre
Morden Hall Park (NT)
Phipps Bridge
Tramlink
Crown La
Crown Rd
Aberconway Road
Morden Hall Road
Morden Road
Central Road
Police Stn
Morden Court
Birchwood Close
Central Medical Centre
Surgery
St Anne's Special School
Abbotsbury Primary School
Phoenix College
Benedict Primary School
Belgrave Walk
Melrose Special School
Works
Church Road
Fire Stn
Vestry Hall
Lower Gn W
Cricket Green
Mitcham CC
Pol Stn
SS Peter & Paul RC Prim Sch
Cranmer Prim Sch
Linden Pl
Baron Gv
Mitcham
Mitcham Park
Tramway Path
London Road
Riverside Drive
Brookfields Av
River Wandle
Wandle Road
Wandle Way
Capital Bus Cen
Connaught Business Centre
Abbey Ind Est
Eagle Trading Estate
Wandle Trading Est
Garth Primary School
Watermeads High School
Hillfield Avenue
Bishopsford Road
St Helier Avenue
Middleton Road
Green Wrythe Primary School
Malmesbury Primary School
Tweeddale Primary School
Sutton Arena
St Helier
Wandle Valley School
Reigate Avenue
Green Lane
Abbey Prim Sch
Glenthorne High Sports Arts
Keeper's Lodge
Rosehill
Rosehill Avenue
Rose Hill
Angel Hill
St Helier Hospital
A&E
Queen Mary's Hospital for Children
Greenshaw High School
Carshalton High School for Boys
Muschamp Primary School
The Wrythe
Wrythe Lane
Green Wrythe Lane
Buckhurst Avenue
Sutton Common Stn
Aultone Way
Connaught Road
Carshalton College
A24
A239
A297
A217
B278
B2230
B279
1 grid square represents 500 metres

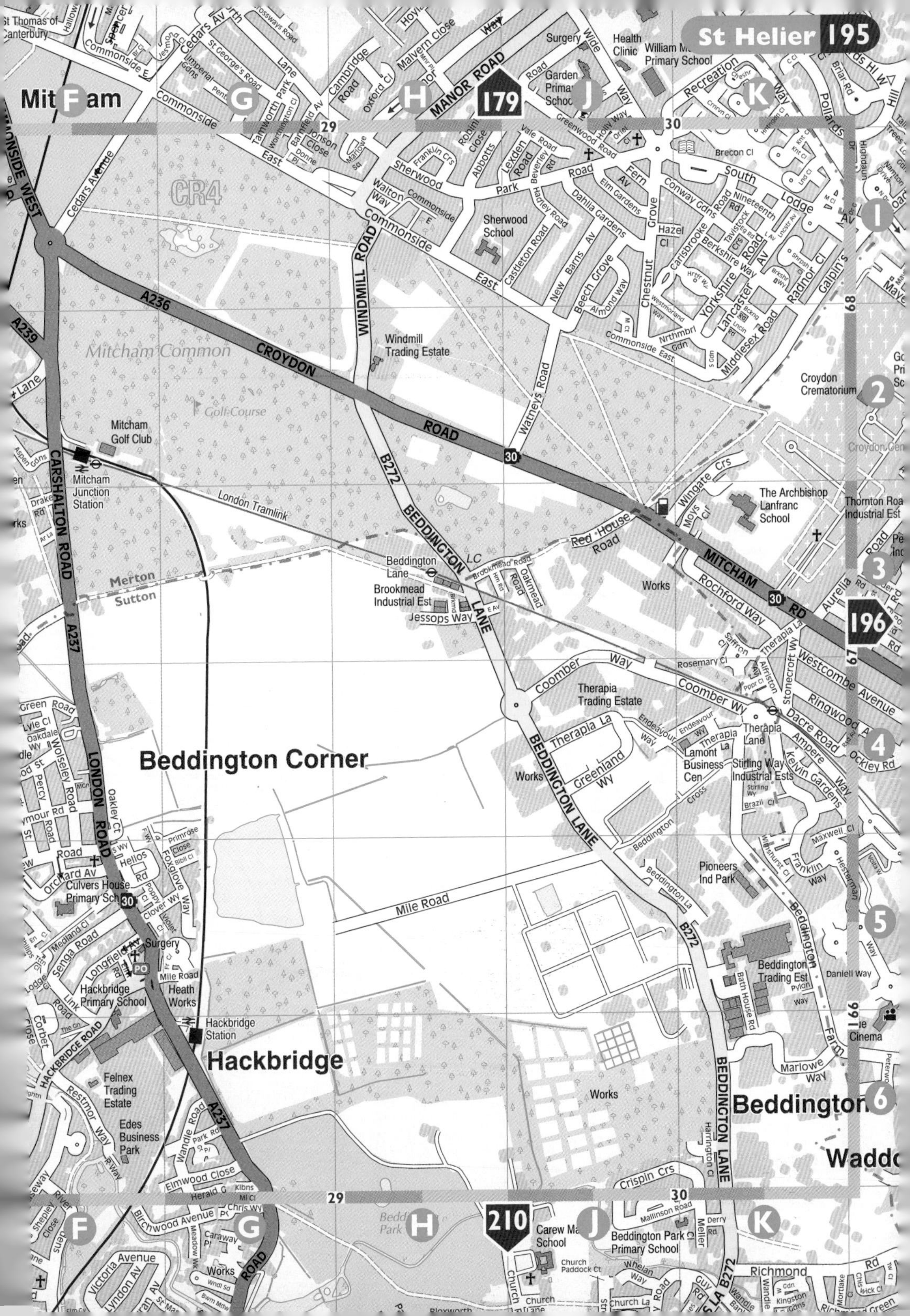

Mitcham
Beddington Corner
Hackbridge
Beddington
Mitcham Common
Golf Course
Mitcham Golf Club
Mitcham Junction Station
London Tramlink
CROYDON ROAD
A236
A239
A237
CARSHALTON ROAD
LONDON ROAD
WINDMILL ROAD
B272
BEDDINGTON LANE
MITCHAM RD
Windmill Trading Estate
Sherwood School
Croydon Crematorium
The Archbishop Lanfranc School
Thornton Road Industrial Est
Therapia Trading Estate
Lamont Business Cen
Stirling Way Industrial Ests
Pioneers Ind Park
Beddington Trading Est
Brookmead Industrial Est
Beddington Lane
Therapia Lane
Felnex Trading Estate
Edes Business Park
Hackbridge Station
Hackbridge Primary School
Culvers House Primary Sch
Beddington Park Primary School
Carew Manor School
Mile Road
Coomber Way
Red House Road
Merton
Sutton
CR4
179
196
210

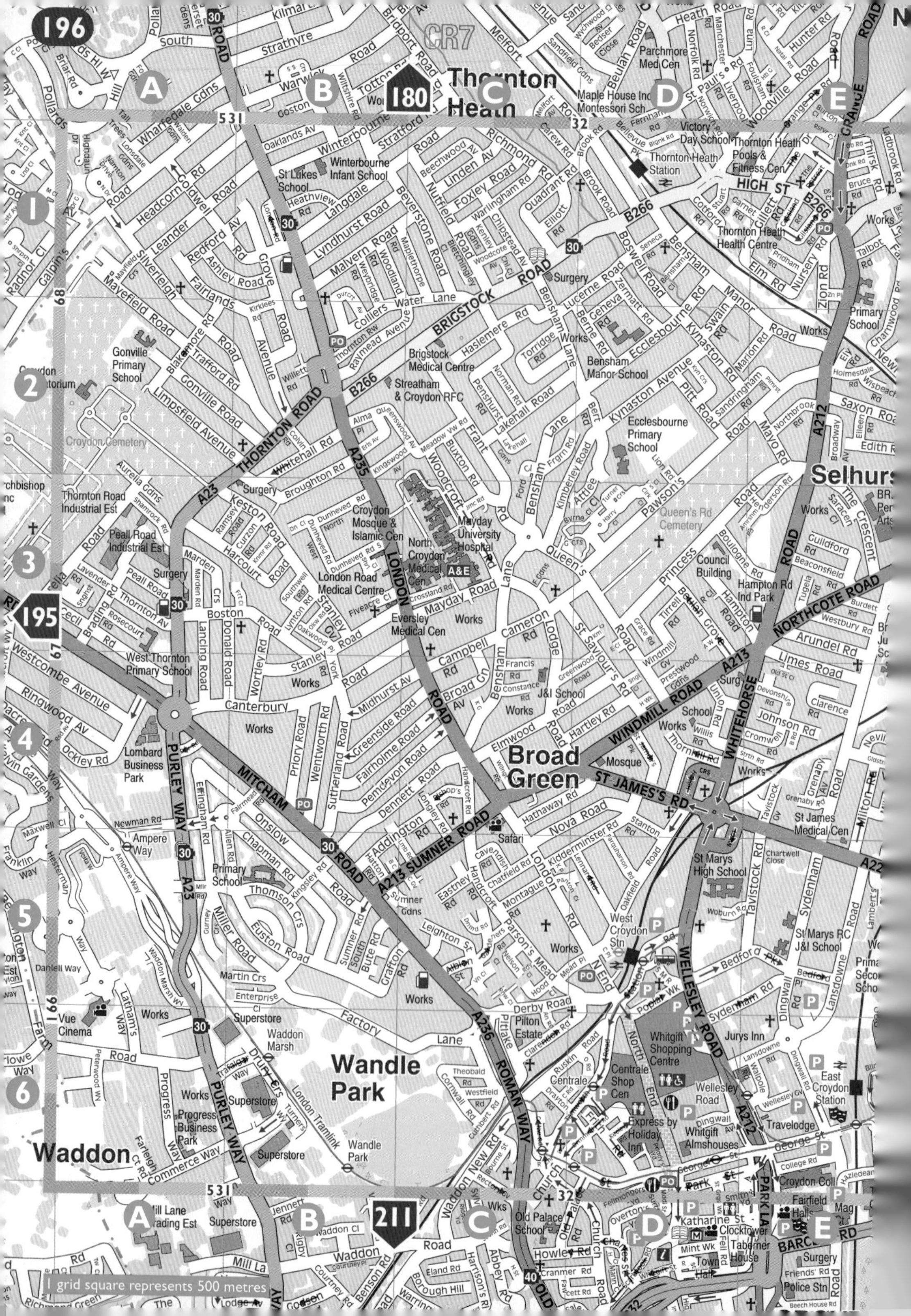
Thornton Heath
CR7
180
Broad Green
Selhurst
Wandle Park
Waddon
195
211
A
B
C
D
E
1
2
3
4
5
6
THORNTON ROAD
LONDON ROAD
BRIGSTOCK ROAD
MITCHAM ROAD
PURLEY WAY
WINDMILL ROAD
WHITEHORSE ROAD
NORTHCOTE ROAD
ST JAMES'S RD
A213 SUMNER ROAD
ROMAN WAY
WELLESLEY ROAD
PARK LA
HIGH ST
Canterbury
Factory Lane
Commerce Way
Mill Lane Trading Est
Croydon Cemetery
Queen's Rd Cemetery
Thornton Road Industrial Est
Peall Road Industrial Est
Lombard Business Park
Progress Business Park
Mayday University Hospital
A&E
Croydon Mosque & Islamic Cen
North Croydon Medical Cen
London Road Medical Centre
Eversley Medical Cen
Brigstock Medical Centre
Streatham & Croydon RFC
Gonville Primary School
West Thornton Primary School
Ecclesbourne Primary School
Bensham Manor School
St Lukes School
Winterbourne Infant School
Thornton Heath Station
Thornton Heath Pools & Fitness Cen
Thornton Heath Health Centre
Victory Day School
Parchmore Med Cen
Maple House Ind Montessori Sch
Council Building
Hampton Rd Ind Park
St Marys High School
St Marys RC J&I School
St James Medical Cen
West Croydon Stn
Whitgift Shopping Centre
Centrale Shop Cen
Express by Holiday Inn
Whitgift Almshouses
Jurys Inn
Travelodge
East Croydon Station
Croydon Coll
Fairfield Halls
Clocktower
Taberner House
Town Hall
Police Stn
Old Palace School
Vue Cinema
Superstore
Waddon Marsh
Wandle Park
London Tramlink
Ampere Way
Safari
Mosque
J&I School
Pilton Estate
Works
Surgery
1 grid square represents 500 metres

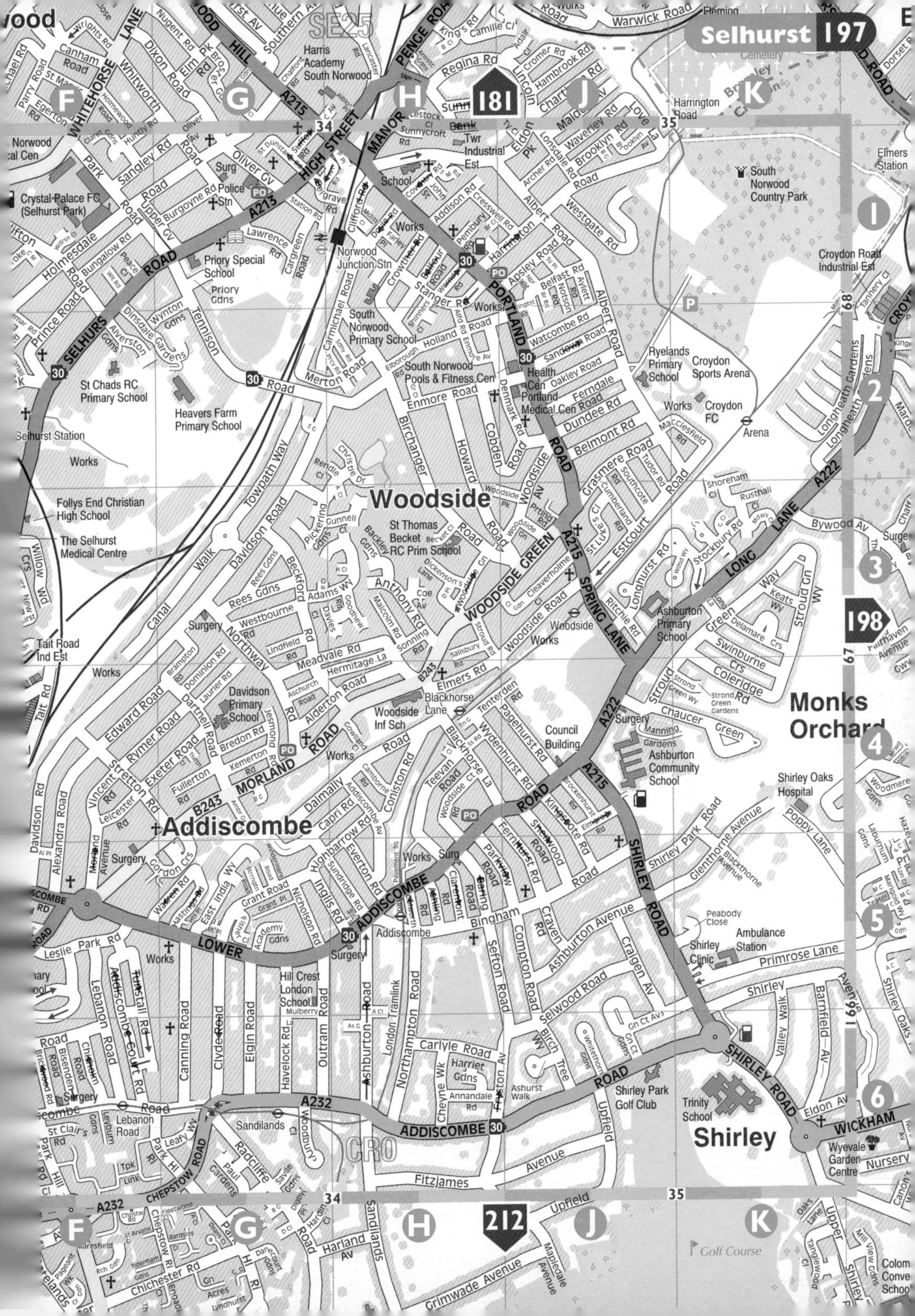
Selhurst 197
SE25
CR0
Harris Academy South Norwood
Whitehorse Lane
Penge Road
Regina Rd
Crystal Palace FC (Selhurst Park)
Holmesdale Road
Selhurst Road
High Street
Portland Road
Police Stn
Norwood Junction Stn
Priory Special School
Priory Gdns
Tennison Road
Station Road
Towpath Way
Canal Walk
Davidson Road
Selhurst Station
St Chads RC Primary School
Heavers Farm Primary School
Follys End Christian High School
The Selhurst Medical Centre
Tait Road Ind Est
South Norwood Primary School
South Norwood Pools & Fitness Cen
Health Cen
Portland Medical Cen
Enmore Road
Birchanger Road
Howard Road
Cobden Road
Woodside
Woodside Green
St Thomas Becket RC Prim School
Spring Lane
Long Lane
Woodside Road
Estcourt Road
Belmont Rd
Dundee Rd
Albert Road
South Norwood Country Park
Croydon Road Industrial Est
Elmers End Station
Ryelands Primary School
Croydon Sports Arena
Croydon FC
Arena
Ashburton Primary School
Monks Orchard
Shirley Oaks Hospital
Poppy Lane
Ashburton Community School
Council Building
Addiscombe
Addiscombe Road
Lower Addiscombe Road
Morland Road
Blackhorse Lane
Woodside Inf Sch
Davidson Primary School
Shirley Road
Shirley Park Road
Glenthorne Avenue
Ashburton Avenue
Primrose Lane
Shirley Clinic
Ambulance Station
Peabody Close
Hill Crest London School
Shirley Park Golf Club
Trinity School
Shirley
Wickham
Wyevale Garden Centre
Chepstow Road
Sandilands
Fitzjames Avenue
Golf Course
Grimwade Avenue
181
198
212

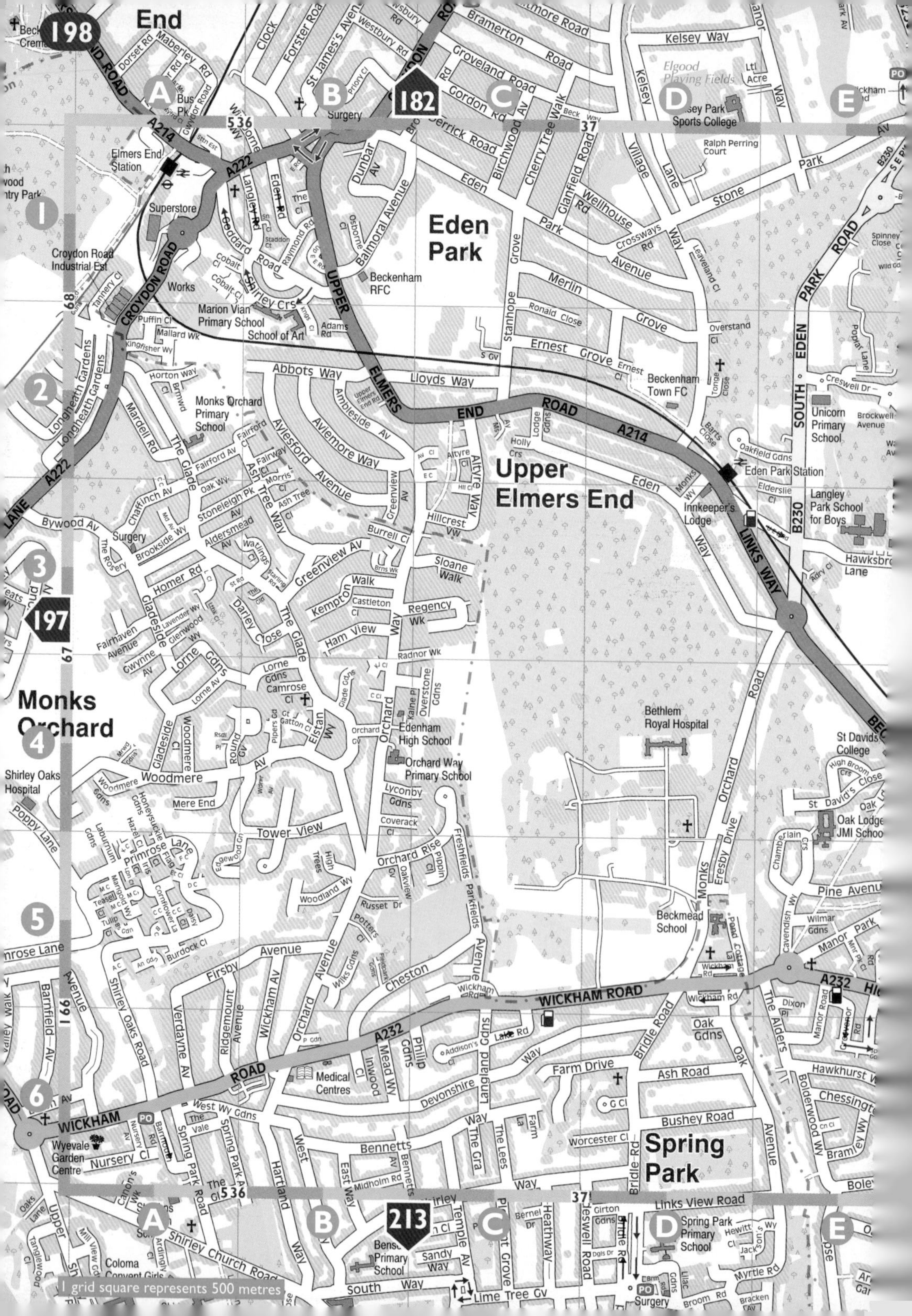

198
182
197
213
End
Eden Park
Upper Elmers End
Monks Orchard
Spring Park
A214
A222
A232
B230
Elmers End Station
Superstore
Croydon Road Industrial Est
Works
Marion Vian Primary School
School of Art
Beckenham RFC
Elgood Playing Fields
Kelsey Park Sports College
Ralph Perring Court
Beckenham Town FC
Eden Park Station
Innkeeper's Lodge
Unicorn Primary School
Langley Park School for Boys
Monks Orchard Primary School
Surgery
Edenham High School
Orchard Way Primary School
Bethlem Royal Hospital
St Davids College
Oak Lodge JMI School
Beckmead School
Shirley Oaks Hospital
Medical Centres
Wyevale Garden Centre
Spring Park Primary School
Benson Primary School
Coloma Convent Girls
Croydon Road
Upper Elmers End Road
Elmers End Road
Links Way
Wickham Road
South Eden Park Road
Eden Park Avenue
Stone Park Avenue
Bramerton Road
Groveland Road
Gordon Road
Kelsey Way
Birchwood Av
Cherry Tree Walk
Glanfield Road
Wellhouse Rd
Crossways Rd
Merlin Grove
Ernest Grove
Stanhope Grove
Abbots Way
Lloyds Way
Aylesford Avenue
Aviemore Way
Greenview Av
Altyre Way
Hillcrest Vw
Sloane Walk
Regency Wk
Orchard Way
Kempton Walk
Ham View
Radnor Wk
The Glade
Gladeside
Woodmere
Mere End
Tower View
Orchard Rise
Freshfields
Parkfields
Orchard Avenue
Monks Orchard Road
Eresby Drive
Bridle Road
Oak Avenue
Ash Road
Bushey Road
Farm Drive
Devonshire Way
Langland Gdns
Bennetts Way
Shirley Oaks Road
Verdayne Av
Ridgemount Avenue
Wickham Av
Firsby Avenue
Cheston Avenue
Primrose Lane
Woodmere Av
Barnfield Av
Longheath Gardens
Bywood Av
Chaffinch Av
Homer Rd
Lorne Gdns
Spring Park Road
Shirley Church Road
South Way
Lime Tree Gv
Links View Road
Temple Av
Pine Avenue
Manor Park
Hawkhurst Way
Bolderwood Wy
1 grid square represents 500 metres

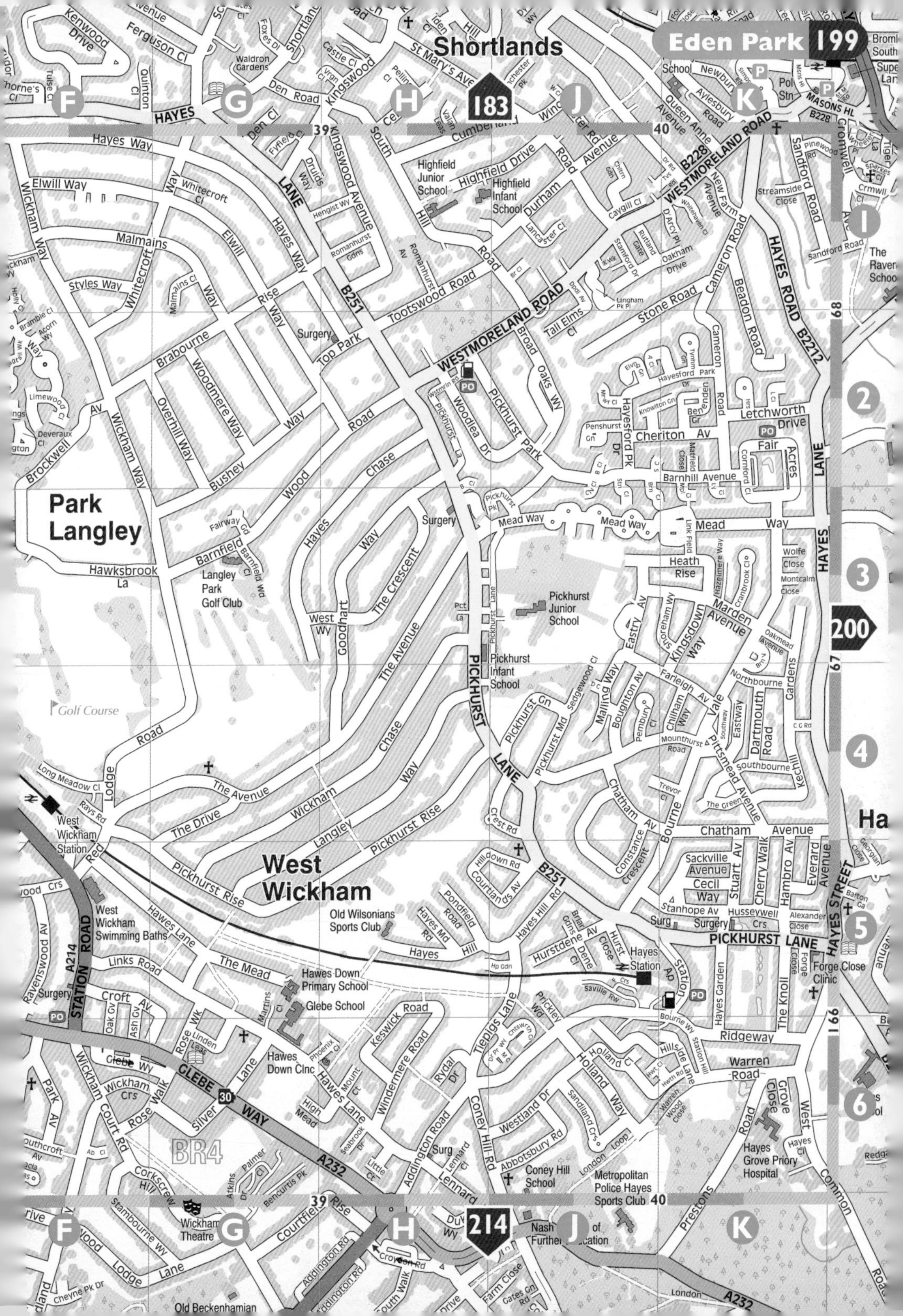

Eden Park 199
183
200
214
Shortlands
Park Langley
West Wickham
BR4
F
G
H
J
K
F
G
H
J
K
I
2
3
4
5
6
39
40
39
40
68
67
66
Kenwood Drive
Ferguson Cl
Quinton Cl
Tulse Cl
Waldron Gardens
Den Road
Den Cl
Shortlands
Kingswood
Castle Cl
St Mary's Ave
Pelling Cl
South
Cumberland
Hayes Way
HAYES
Fyfield Cl
Kingswood Avenue
Druids Way
LANE
Highfield Junior School
Highfield Infant School
Highfield Drive
Hill
Durham
Road
Avenue
Caygill Cl
Queen Anne Avenue
Aylesbury Road
Newbury
School
Pol Stn
MASONS HL
B228
WESTMORELAND ROAD
New Farm Avenue
Streamside Close
Sandford Road
Pinewood Rd
Cromwell
HAYES ROAD
B2212
Beadon Road
Cameron Road
Stone Road
Tall Elms Cl
Langham Pk Pl
Oakham Drive
Rutland Gate
Stamford Dr
Lancaster Cl
Elwill Way
Whitecroft Cl
Wickham Way
Malmains
Elwill Way
Hayes Way
Hengist Wy
Romanhurst Gdns
Romanhurst Av
Tootswood Road
B251
Styles Way
Malmains Cl
Whitecroft Way
Rise Way
Surgery
Top Park
WESTMORELAND ROAD
Broad Oaks Wy
PO
Pickhurst Park
Woodlea Dr
Pickhurst La
Brabourne
Woodmere Way
Overhill Way
Way
Road
Bramble Cl
Acorn Wy
Limewood Cl
Deveraux Cl
Brockwell Av
Wickham Way
Bushey Way
Wood
Chase
Hayes
Way
Surgery
Pickhurst Pk
Mead Way
Mead Way
Mead Way
Hayesford Park Dr
Elvington Gn
Penshurst Gn
Cheriton Av
Knowlton Gn
Letchworth Drive
PO
Fair Acres
Barnhill Avenue
Link Field
Heath Rise
Hazelmere Way
Cranbrook Cl
Wolfe Close
Montcalm Close
HAYES LANE
Fairway Gd
Barnfield
Barnfield Wd
Langley Park Golf Club
Hawksbrook La
The Crescent
West Wy
Goodhart
Pct La
Pickhurst Lane
Pickhurst Junior School
Eastry Av
Shoreham Wy
Kingsdown Way
Marden Avenue
Oakmead Avenue
Northbourne
Gardens
The Avenue
Pickhurst Infant School
PICKHURST LANE
Sedgewood Cl
Malling Way
Boughton Av
Farleigh Av
Vale
Eastway
Dartmouth Road
Golf Course
Road
Chase
Pickhurst Gn
Pickhurst Md
Pembury Cl
Chilham Way
Southway
Mounthurst Road
Pittsmead Avenue
Southbourne
Kechill
Long Meadow Cl
Lodge
The Avenue
The Drive
Wickham
Way
Langley
Pickhurst Rise
Crest Rd
Chatham Av
Trevor Cl
Bourne
The Green
Chatham Avenue
Ha
West Wickham Station
Rays Rd
Red
Pickhurst Rise
Hilldown Rd
Courtlands Av
Constance Crescent
Sackville Avenue
Cecil Way
Stuart Av
Cherry Walk
Hambro Av
Everard Avenue
Georgian Close
HAYES STREET
West Wickham Swimming Baths
Hawes Lane
Old Wilsonians Sports Club
Hayes Md Rd
Pondfield Road
Hayes Hill Rd
B251
Hayes Hill
Stanhope Av
Husseywell Crs
Surgery
Surg
Alexander Close
Barton Ga
PICKHURST LANE
Forge Close
Forge Close Clinic
Links Road
The Mead
Hurstdene Av
Briar Gdns
Dene Cl
Hurst Close
Hayes Station
Station Ap
Ravenswood Av
A214
STATION ROAD
Surgery
Croft Av
PO
Hawes Down Primary School
Glebe School
Martins Cl
Saville Rw
Hayes Garden
The Knoll
Oak Gv
Ash Gv
Rose Wk
Linden Leas
Keswick Road
Tiepigs Lane
Prickley Wd
Bourne Wy
Station Hill
Ridgeway
Glebe Wy
Hawes Down Clnc
Phoenix Cl
Mount Ct
Windermere Road
Rydal Dr
Holland Cl
Holland Way
Hillside Lane
Warren Road
Grove Close
Park Av
Wickham Court Rd
Wickham Crs
Rose Walk
Silver Lane
GLEBE WAY
30
A232
High Mead
Hawes Lane
Seabrook Dr
Coney Hill Rd
Westland Dr
Sandiland Crs
Warren Wood Close
Road
West
Southcroft Av
Ab Cl
Corkscrew Hill
Palmer Cl
Atkins Dr
Bencurtis Pk
Little Cl
Addington Road
Surg
Lennard Cl
Abbotsbury Rd
London Loop
Coney Hill School
Metropolitan Police Hayes Sports Club
Hayes Grove Priory Hospital
Hayes Cl
Common
Lennard
Prestons
Stambourne Wy
Wickham Theatre
Courtfield Rise
Addington Rd
Croydon Rd
Nash College of Further Education
Lodge Lane
Addington Rd
South Walk
Farm Close
Gates Gn Rd
Cheyne Pk Dr
Old Beckenhamian
London
A232

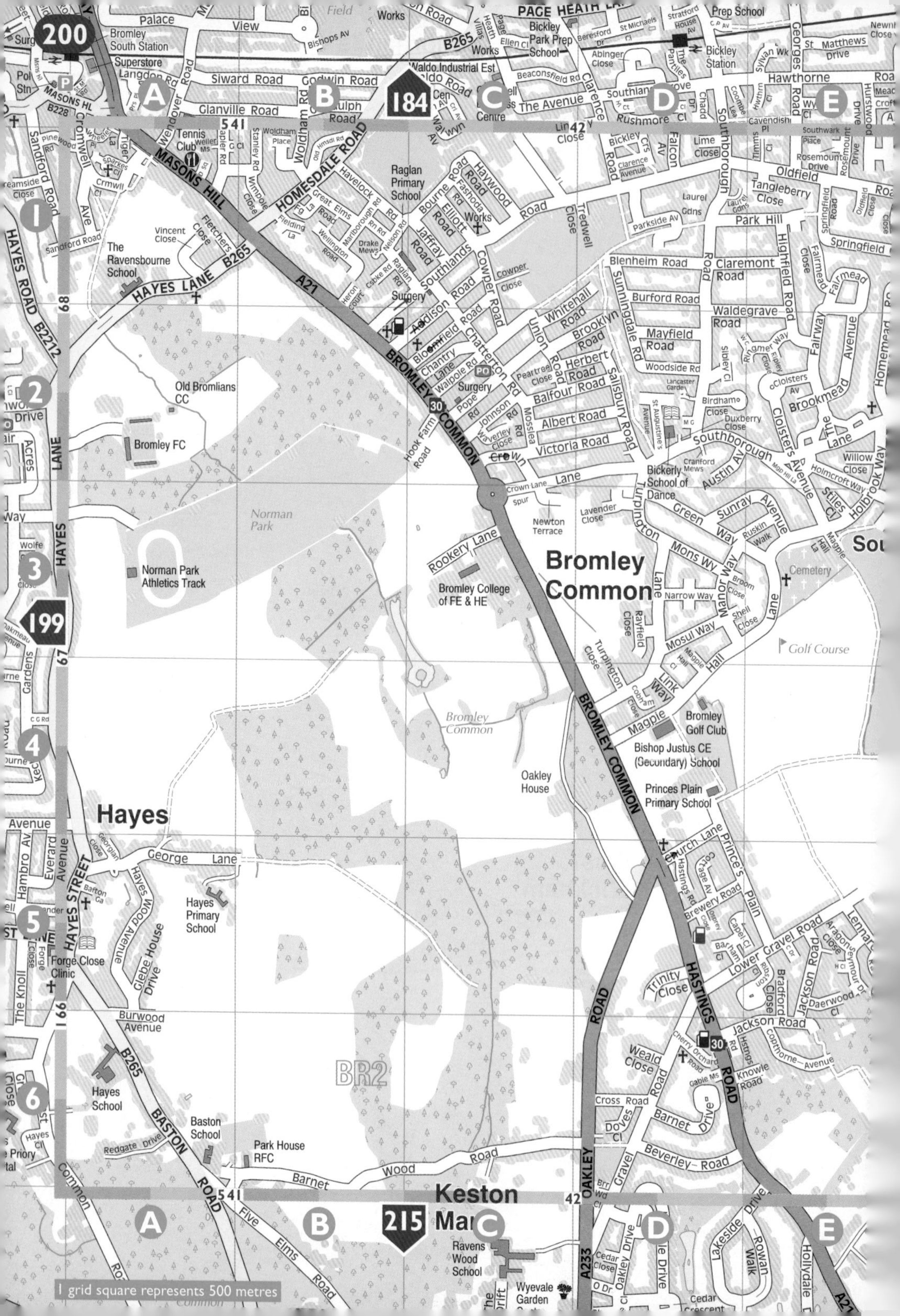
200
184
199
215
Bromley South Station
Superstore
Tennis Club
The Ravensbourne School
Old Bromlians CC
Bromley FC
Norman Park
Norman Park Athletics Track
Raglan Primary School
Works
Surgery
Bromley College of FE & HE
Bromley Common
Oakley House
Bromley Golf Club
Bishop Justus CE (Secondary) School
Princes Plain Primary School
Golf Course
Cemetery
Bickerly School of Dance
Bickley Park Prep School
Bickley Station
Prep School
Waldo Industrial Est
Hayes
Hayes Primary School
Forge Close Clinic
Hayes School
Baston School
Park House RFC
Keston
Ravens Wood School
Wyevale Garden
BR2
MASONS HILL
A21
BROMLEY COMMON
HAYES LANE
B265
HOMESDALE ROAD
HAYES ROAD B2212
HAYES LANE
HAYES STREET
BASTON ROAD
OAKLEY ROAD
A233
HASTINGS ROAD
Southborough Lane
Magpie Hall Lane
Turpington Lane
Barnet Wood Road
George Lane
Five Elms Road
Page Heath Lane
1 grid square represents 500 metres

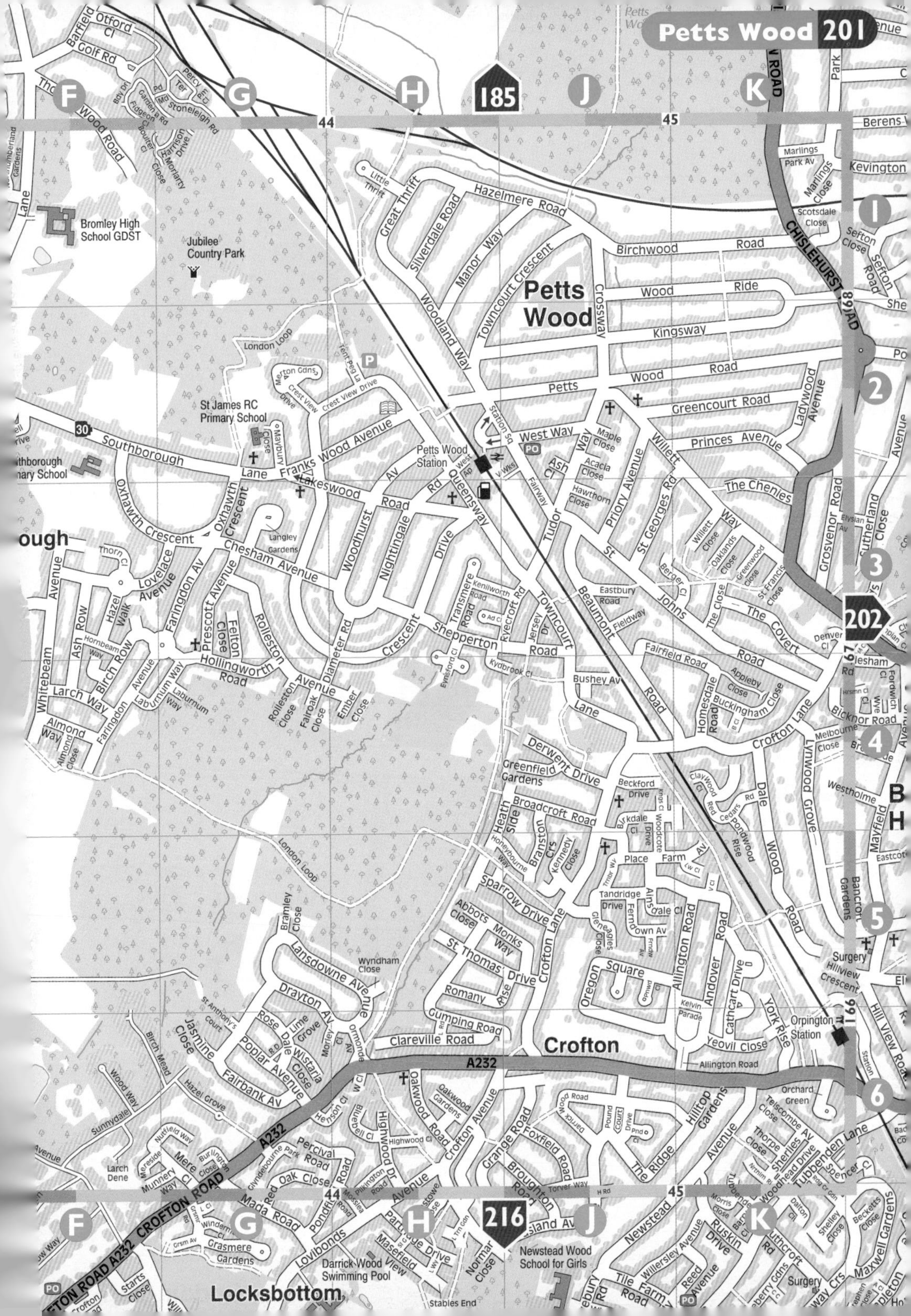
Petts Wood
Crofton
Locksbottom
Petts Wood Station
Orpington Station
Jubilee Country Park
Bromley High School GDST
St James RC Primary School
Newstead Wood School for Girls
Darrick Wood Swimming Pool
London Loop
A232
CROFTON ROAD
CHISLEHURST ROAD
185
202
216

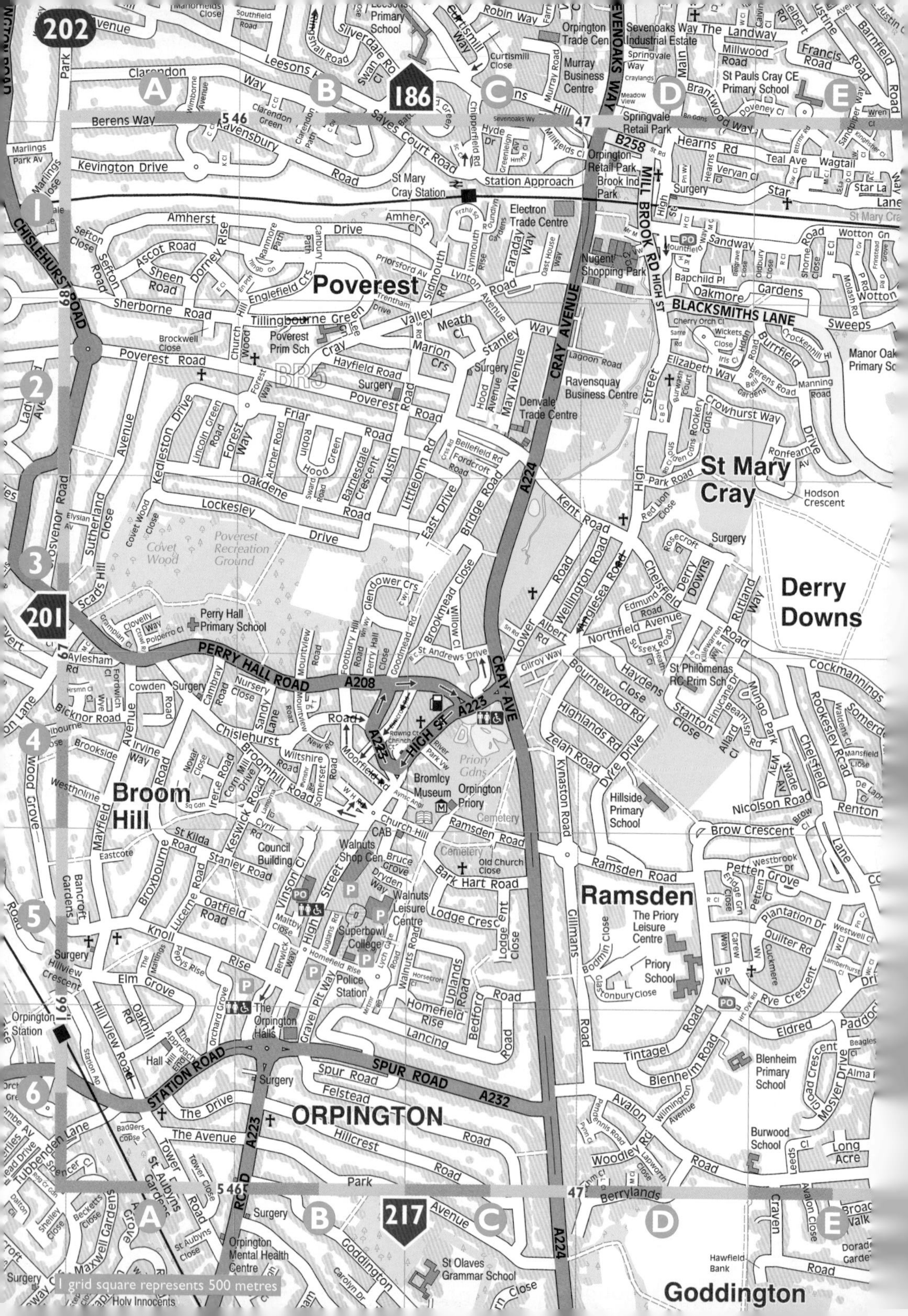

202
186
201
217
A
B
C
D
E
1
2
3
4
5
6
Poverest
St Mary Cray
Derry Downs
Broom Hill
Ramsden
ORPINGTON
Goddington
BR5
Poverest Recreation Ground
Covet Wood
St Mary Cray Station
Orpington Station
Sevenoaks Way Industrial Estate
Orpington Trade Cen
Murray Business Centre
Springvale Retail Park
Orpington Retail Park
Brook Ind Park
Electron Trade Centre
Nugent Shopping Park
Ravensquay Business Centre
Denvale Trade Centre
Leesons Primary School
St Pauls Cray CE Primary School
Manor Oak Primary Sc
Poverest Prim Sch
Perry Hall Primary School
St Philomenas RC Prim Sch
Hillside Primary School
The Priory Leisure Centre
Priory School
Blenheim Primary School
Burwood School
St Olaves Grammar School
Orpington Mental Health Centre
Bromley Museum
Orpington Priory
Priory Gdns
Cemetery
Council Building
Walnuts Shop Cen
Walnuts Leisure Centre
Superbowl College
Police Station
The Orpington Halls
Surgery
CAB
PO
CHISLEHURST ROAD
PERRY HALL ROAD
A208
CRAY AVENUE
CRAY AVE
A224
A223
HIGH ST
SPUR ROAD
A232
STATION ROAD
SEVENOAKS WAY
MILL BROOK RD
HIGH ST
B258
BLACKSMITHS LANE
Poverest Road
Sherborne Road
Station Approach
Sayes Court Road
Kevington Drive
Berens Way
Ravensbury Road
Leesons Hill
Clarendon Way
Amherst Drive
Ascot Road
Sheen Road
Dorney Rise
Tillingbourne Green
Cray Valley Road
Hayfield Road
Marion Crs
Stanley Way
Friar Road
Oakdene Road
Lockesley Drive
Kedleston Drive
Sutherland Avenue
Avenue
Grosvenor Road
Scads Hill Close
Austin Road
Littlejohn Rd
East Drive
Bridge Road
Brookmead Close
Goodmead Rd
St Andrews Drive
Kent Road
Lower Road
Wellington Road
Anglesea Road
Chelsfield Road
Derry Downs
Rutland Way
Northfield Avenue
Haydens Close
Bournewood Rd
Highlands Rd
Zelah Road
Kynaston Road
Dyke Drive
Stanton Close
Mungo Park Way
Nicolson Road
Brow Crescent
Ramsden Road
Petten Grove
Plantation Dr
Quilter Rd
Rye Crescent
Eldred
Tintagel Road
Blenheim Road
Avalon Road
Woodley Rd
Berrylands
Gillmans Road
Cockmannings
Rookesley Road
Chelsfield Lane
Renton
Crockenhill Rd
Burrfield
Manning Road
Berens Road
Crowhurst Way
Elizabeth Way
Oakmore Gardens
Sweeps
Wotton Gn
Sandway
Bapchild Pl
Hearns Rd
Teal Ave
Wagtail
Star La
Veryan Cl
Brantwood Way
Francis Road
Millwood Road
The Landway
Robin Way
Silverdale Ro
Curtismill Way
Hyde Dr
Chislehurst Road
Broomhill Road
Moorfield Rd
Church Hill
Ramsden Road
Hart Road
Lodge Cresc
Homefield Rise
Lancing
Bedford Road
Uplands Road
Walnuts Road
Gravel Pit Way
High Street
Vinson Cl
Knoll Rise
Elm Grove
Oatfield Road
Lucerne Road
Broxbourne Road
St Kilda Road
Stanley Road
Keswick Road
Irvine Way
Mayfield Avenue
Bancroft Gardens
Hill View Road
Oakhill Rd
The Drive
The Avenue
Tower Road
Hillcrest Road
Felstead Road
Park Avenue
Goddington Lane
Tubbenden Lane
Maxwell Gardens
St Aubyns Gardens
Hawfield Bank
Craven Road
Leeds Cl
Long Acre
Mosyer Drive
Alma Rd
Holy Innocents
1 grid square represents 500 metres

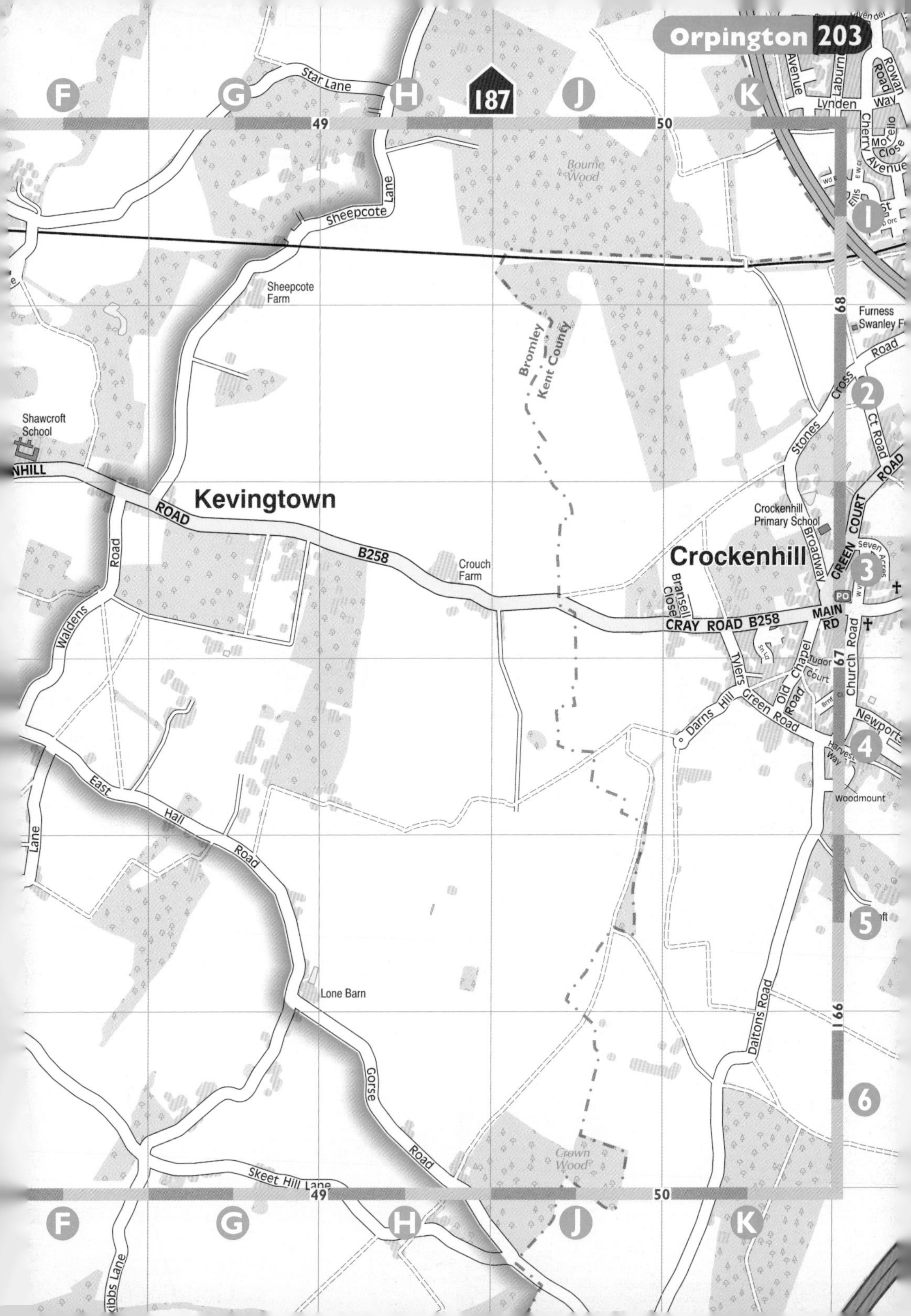

Star Lane
Sheepcote Lane
187
Bourne Wood
Sheepcote Farm
Bromley
Kent County
Shawcroft School
Kevingtown
ROAD
B258
Crouch Farm
Waldens Road
Crockenhill
Crockenhill Primary School
Broadway
GREEN COURT ROAD
Stones Cross Road
Bransell Close
CRAY ROAD B258
MAIN RD
Tylers Green Road
Old Chapel Road
Tudor Court
Church Road
Darns Hill
Newports
Harvest Way
Woodmount
Furness Swanley
Lynden Way
Cherry Avenue
Morello Close
Laburnum
Rowan Road
East Hall Road
Lane
Lone Barn
Gorse Road
Daltons Road
Crown Wood
Skeet Hill Lane
Kibbs Lane
Seven Acres
PO
F G H J K
49 50
1 2 3 4 5 6
68 67 66

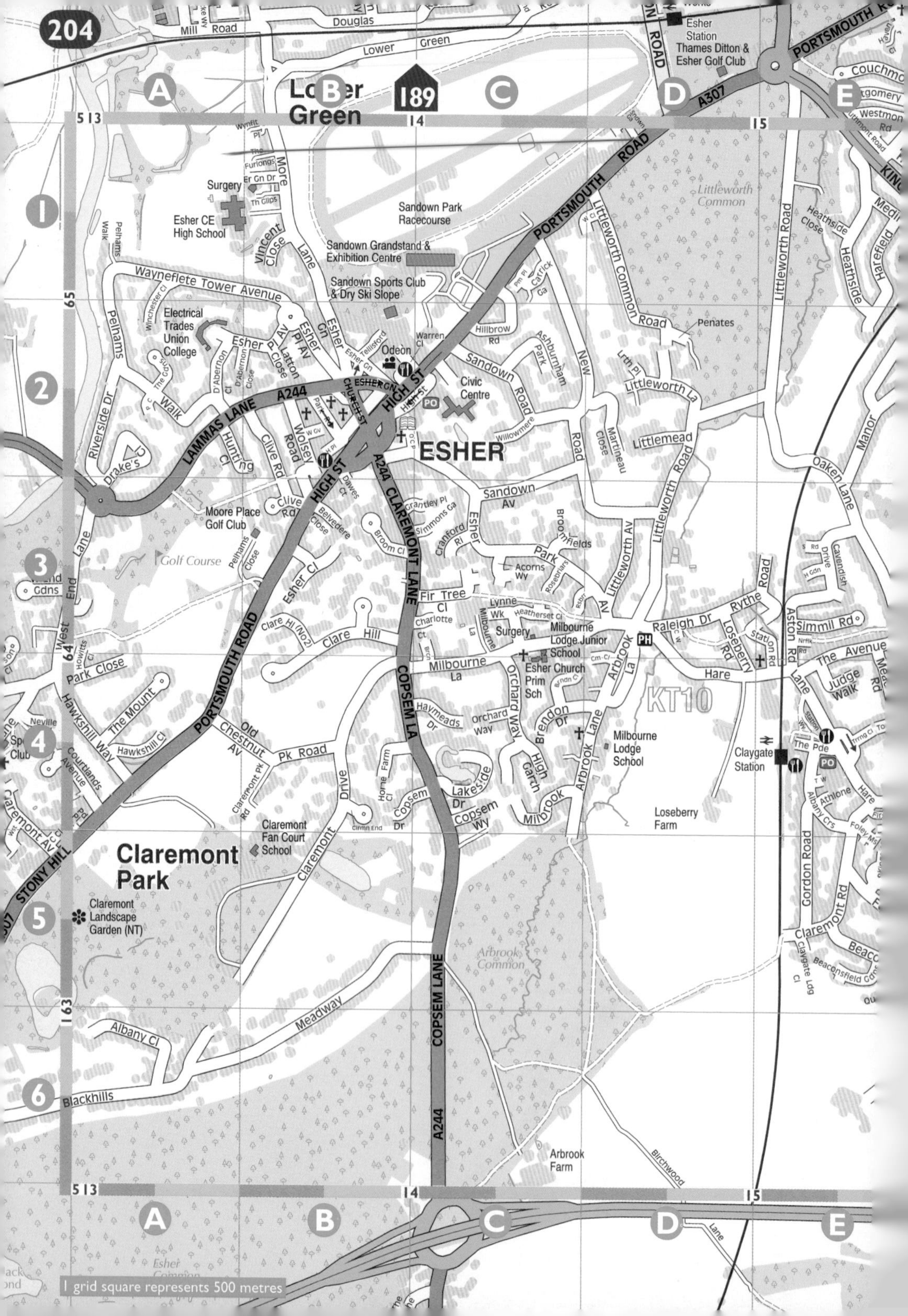

ESHER
Lower Green
189
Sandown Park Racecourse
Sandown Grandstand & Exhibition Centre
Sandown Sports Club & Dry Ski Slope
Esher Station
Thames Ditton & Esher Golf Club
Littleworth Common
Esher CE High School
Electrical Trades Union College
Civic Centre
Moore Place Golf Club
Golf Course
Claremont Park
Claremont Landscape Garden (NT)
Claremont Fan Court School
Milbourne Lodge Junior School
Esher Church Prim Sch
Milbourne Lodge School
Loseberry Farm
Arbrook Common
Arbrook Farm
Claygate Station
Penates
KT10
PORTSMOUTH ROAD
A307
LAMMAS LANE
A244
HIGH ST
CLAREMONT LANE
COPSEM LANE
STONY HILL
1 grid square represents 500 metres

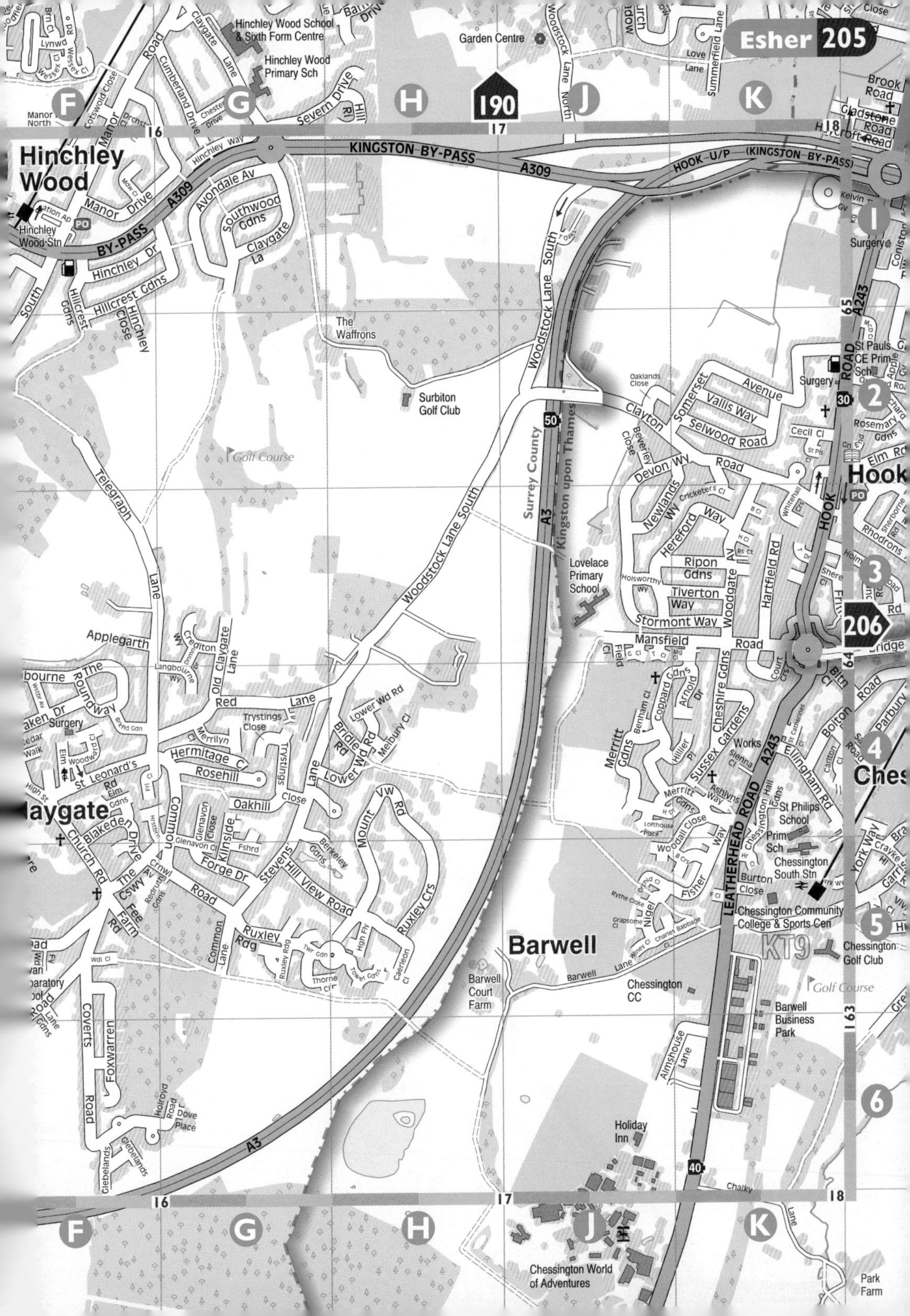
Hinchley Wood
Hinchley Wood Stn
Hinchley Wood School & Sixth Form Centre
Hinchley Wood Primary Sch
Garden Centre
190
KINGSTON BY-PASS
A309
HOOK U/P (KINGSTON BY-PASS)
Avondale Av
Southwood Gdns
Claygate La
Hinchley Dr
Hillcrest Gdns
Hinchley Close
Manor Drive
Cumberland Drive
Claygate Lane
Severn Drive
Woodstock Lane North
Woodstock Lane South
Summerfield Lane
Love Lane
Brook Road
Gladstone Road
Kelvin Gv
Surgery
The Waffrons
Surbiton Golf Club
Golf Course
Telegraph Lane
Surrey County
Kingston upon Thames
A3
Lovelace Primary School
Oaklands Close
Clayton Road
Somerset Avenue
Vallis Way
Selwood Road
Beverley Close
Devon Wy
Newlands Wy
Cricketers Cl
Hereford Way
Ripon Gdns
Tiverton Way
Stormont Way
Holsworthy Wy
Woodgate Av
Hartfield Rd
Mansfield Road
St Pauls CE Prim Sch
Cecil Cl
Rosemary Gdns
Elm Rd
Hook
HOOK ROAD
A243
Rhodrons
206
Applegarth
Crediton Wy
Langbourne Wy
Old Claygate Lane
Red Lane
Trystings Close
Merrilyn Cl
Hermitage Cl
Rosehill
Oakhill
Glenavon Close
Kilnside
Forge Dr
Common Road
Stevens' Lane
Hill View Road
Berkeley Gdns
Mount Vw Rd
Ruxley Crs
Ruxley Rdg
Thorne Cl
Caerleon Cl
Lower Wd Rd
Bridle Rd
Melbury Cl
The Roundway
Surgery
St Leonard's Rd
Claygate
Church Rd
Blakeden Drive
The Cswy
Fee Farm Rd
Common Lane
Covert Road
Foxwarren
Holroyd Road
Dove Place
Gebelands
Merritt Gdns
Coppard Gdns
Arnold Dr
Cheshire Gdns
Sussex Gardens
Hillier Pl
Merritt Way
Ashlyns Way
Woodall Close
Lofthouse Place
Fisher Way
Nigel
Rythe Close
Grapsome Cl
Charles Babbage Cl
Works
LEATHERHEAD ROAD
Chessington Hall Gdns
St Philips School
Prim Sch
Chessington South Stn
Burton Close
Ellingham Rd
Bolton Road
Parbury
York Way
Chessington Community College & Sports Cen
KT9
Chessington Golf Club
Golf Course
Barwell
Barwell Court Farm
Barwell Lane
Chessington CC
Barwell Business Park
Almshouse Lane
Holiday Inn
Chalky Lane
Chessington World of Adventures
Park Farm
F G H J K
16 17 18
1 2 3 4 5 6
63 64 65

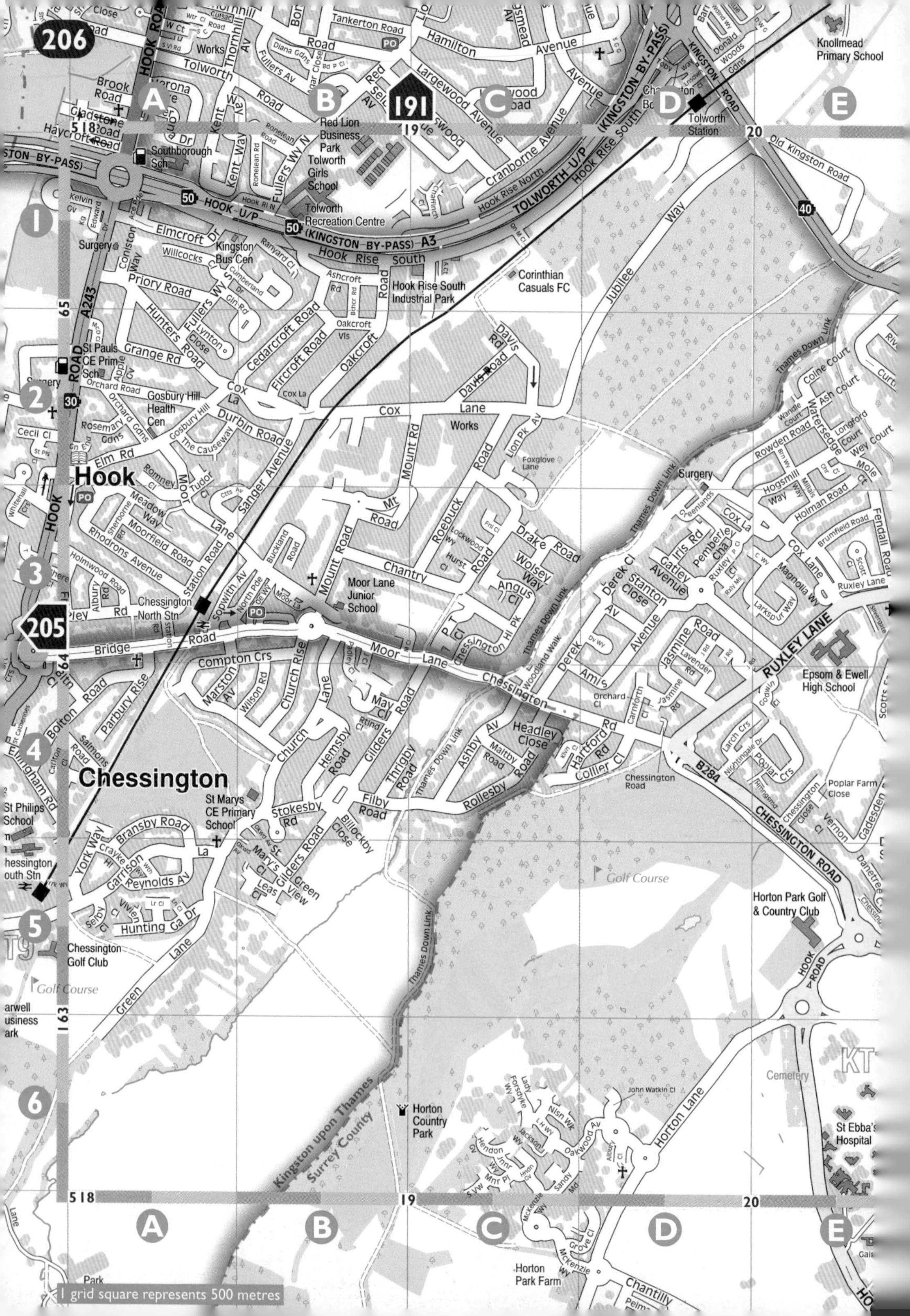
191
205
Hook
Chessington
HOOK ROAD
A243
Tolworth Road
Hamilton Avenue
Tankerton Road
Largewood Avenue
Cranborne Avenue
TOLWORTH U/P
(KINGSTON-BY-PASS) A3
HOOK U/P
Hook Rise North
Hook Rise South
Red Lion Business Park
Tolworth Girls School
Tolworth Recreation Centre
Southborough Sch
Kingston Bus Cen
Hook Rise South Industrial Park
Corinthian Casuals FC
Tolworth Station
Knollmead Primary School
Old Kingston Road
Jubilee Way
Elmcroft Dr
Priory Road
Hunters Road
Grange Rd
Cedarcroft Road
Fircroft Road
Oakcroft Road
Cox Lane
Davis Road
Works
Mount Rd
Mount Road
Gosbury Hill Health Cen
St Pauls CE Prim Sch
Surgery
Durbin Road
Elm Rd
Sanger Avenue
Moor Lane
Meadow Way
Moorfield Road
Rhodrons Avenue
Station Road
Chantry Road
Roebuck Road
Drake Road
Wolsey Way
Moor Lane Junior School
Chessington North Stn
Bridge Road
Compton Crs
Church Rise
Chessington Road
Thames Down Link
Thames Down Walk
Woodland Walk
Derek Av
Stanton Close
Catley Avenue
Jasmine Road
RUXLEY LANE
Epsom & Ewell High School
Ruxley Lane
Cox Lane
Fendall Road
Holman Road
Bolton Road
Parbury Rise
Filby Road
Gilders Road
Rollesby Road
Headley Close
Hartford Rd
Collier Cl
B284
CHESSINGTON ROAD
St Marys CE Primary School
St Philips School
Chessington South Stn
Bransby Road
Garrison La
Reynolds Av
Hunting Ga Dr
Chessington Golf Club
Golf Course
Green Lane
Horton Park Golf & Country Club
Horton Country Park
Kingston upon Thames
Surrey County
Horton Lane
Cemetery
St Ebba's Hospital
Horton Park Farm
Chantilly
518
19
20
65
64
63
A B C D E
1 2 3 4 5 6
1 grid square represents 500 metres

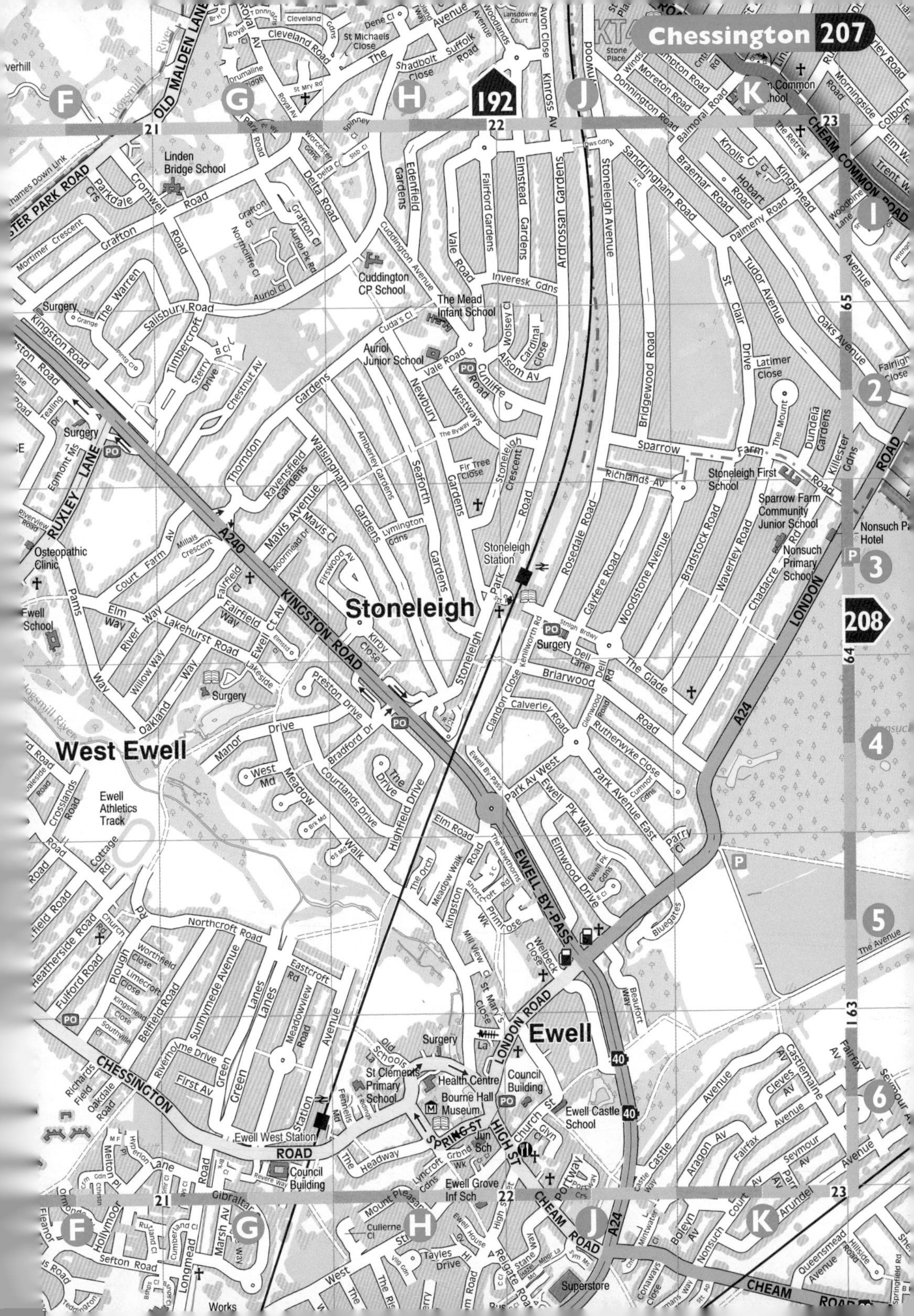
192
208
Stoneleigh
West Ewell
Ewell
Old Malden Lane
Cleveland Road
Royal Av
Dene Cl
St Michaels Close
The Avenue
Shadbolt Close
Suffolk Road
Woodlands Avenue
Lansdowne Court
Avon Close
Kinross Av
Stone Place
Moreton Road
Donnington Road
Balmoral Road
Cheam Common Road
Morningside Road
Colborne
Elm Way
Trent Way
Hogsmill River
Linden Bridge School
Cromwell Road
Parkdale Crs
Grafton Road
Mortimer Crescent
Northcliffe Cl
Auriol Cl
Delta Road
Edenfield Gardens
Fairford Gardens
Elmstead Gardens
Ardrossan Gardens
Stoneleigh Avenue
Sandringham Road
Braemar Road
Knolls Cl
Hobart Road
Kingsmead
Dalmeny Road
Woodbine Lane
Cuddington Avenue
Cuddington CP School
Vale Road
Inveresk Gdns
The Mead Infant School
Auriol Junior School
Wolsey Cl
Cardinal Close
Alsom Av
Cunliffe Road
Bridgewood Road
St Clair Drive
Tudor Avenue
Oaks Avenue
Latimer Close
The Mount
Dundela Gardens
Killester Gdns
Sparrow Farm Road
Richlands Av
Stoneleigh First School
Sparrow Farm Community Junior School
Nonsuch Park Hotel
Nonsuch Primary School
Surgery
The Warren
Salisbury Road
Timbercroft
Sterry Drive
Chestnut Av
Kingston Road
Tealing Dr
Egmont Ms
Ruxley Lane
Riverview Road
Osteopathic Clinic
Ewell School
Thorndon Gardens
Ravensfield Gardens
Walsingham Gardens
Amberley Gardens
Seaforth Gardens
Newbury Gardens
Westways
The Byway
Fir Tree Close
Stoneleigh Crescent
Stoneleigh Park Road
Stoneleigh Station
Mavis Avenue
Mavis Cl
Moormead Dr
Court Farm Av
Millais Crescent
Fairfield Cl
Fairfield Way
Elm Way
River Way
Lakehurst Road
Ewell Ct Av
Firswood Av
Lymington Gdns
Kirby Close
A240 Kingston Road
Rosedale Road
Gayfere Road
Woodstone Avenue
Bradstock Road
Waverley Road
Chadacre Rd
London Road
A24
Kenilworth Rd
Dell Lane
Dell Rd
The Glade
Briarwood Road
Clandon Close
Calverley Road
Glenwood Road
Rutherwyke Close
Cumnor Gdns
Park Av West
Park Avenue East
Parry Cl
Ewell Pk Way
Elmwood Drive
Ewell By-Pass
Willow Way
Oakland Way
Lakeside
Preston Drive
Manor Drive
West Md
Meadow Walk
Bradford Dr
Courtlands Drive
The Drive
Highfield Drive
Elm Road
The Orch
Meadow Walk
Kingston Road
The Hawthorns
Shortcroft Rd
Primrose Wk
Mill View Cl
St Mary's Close
Welbeck Close
Bluegates
Beaufort Way
The Avenue
Ewell Athletics Track
Crosslands Road
Cottage Rd
Church Rd
Northcroft Road
Heatherside Road
Fulford Road
Plough Close
Worthfield Close
Limecroft Close
Kingsmead Close
Belfield Road
Sunnymede Avenue
Green Lanes
Eastcroft Rd
Meadowview Road
Riverholme Drive
First Av
Chessington Road
Richards Field
Oakdale Road
Old Schools La
St Clements Primary School
Health Centre
Bourne Hall Museum
Council Building
Ewell Castle School
Spring St
High St
Church St
Glyn Cl
Ewell West Station
Station Avenue
Fennells Mead
The Headway
Lyncroft Gdns
Ewell Grove Inf Sch
Portway Crs
Castle Avenue
Castlemaine Av
Cleves Av
Fairfax Avenue
Aragon Av
Seymour Av
Nonsuch Court Av
Arundel Avenue
Parr Av
Boleyn Av
Hyperion Lane
Melton Pl
Gibraltar Cres
Revere Way
Council Building
Hollymoor
Eleanor
Rutland Cl
Cumberland Cl
Marsh Av
Sefton Road
Longmead Road
Mount Pleasant
Cullerne Cl
Tayles Drive
Ewell House Gv
Reigate Road
Cheam Road
Stane Way
Superstore
Conaways Close
Queensmead Avenue
Hillside Avenue
Springfield Rd
Works
Teddington

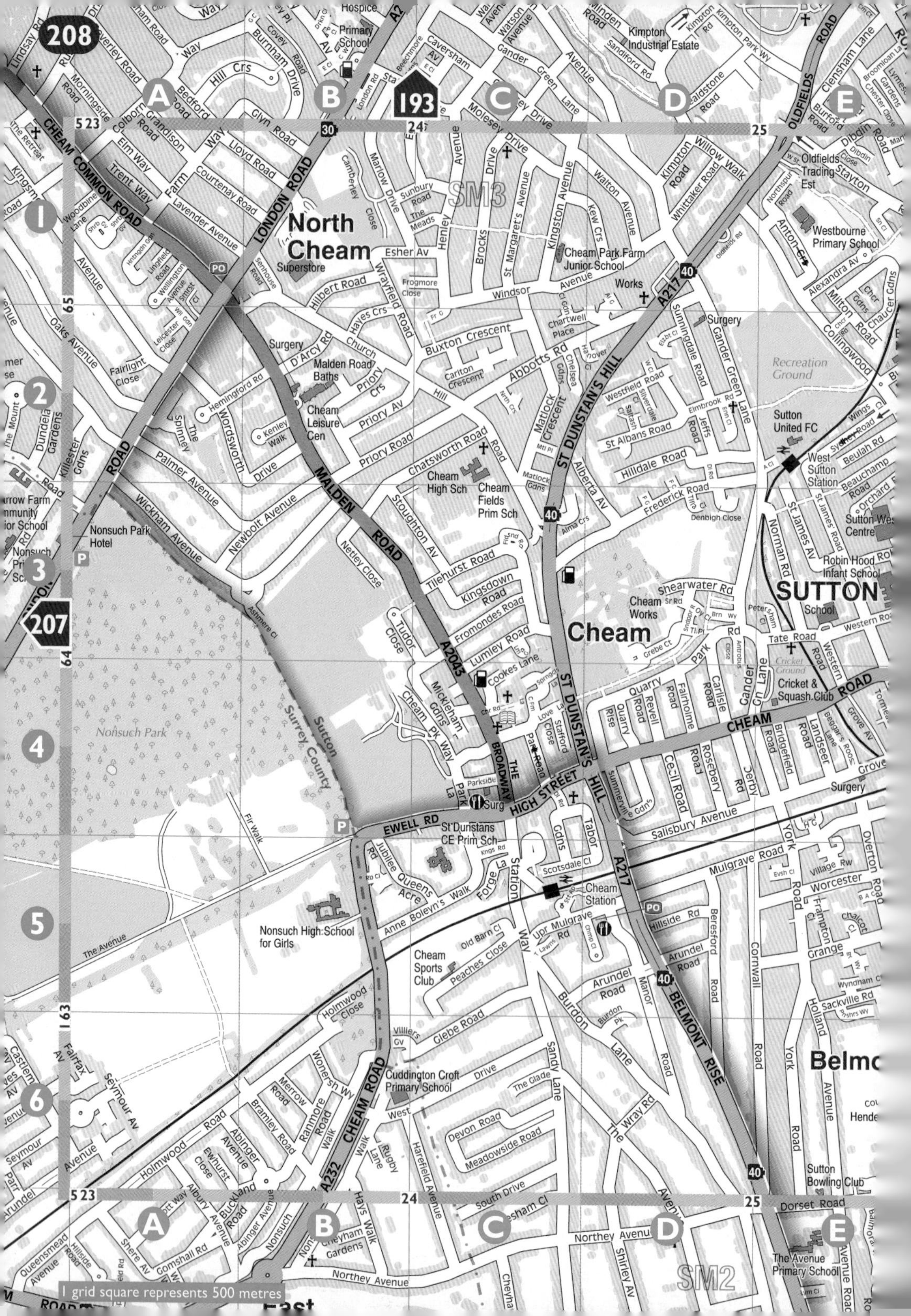
208
193
207
North Cheam
Cheam
SUTTON
Belmo
SM3
SM2
A
B
C
D
E
1
2
3
4
5
6
5 23
24
25
64
65
1 63
Cheam Common Road
London Road
Malden Road
A2043
St Dunstan's Hill
A217
Oldfields Road
Belmont Rise
Cheam Road
A232
High Street
Ewell Rd
The Broadway
Nonsuch Park
Surrey County
Sutton
Nonsuch Park Hotel
Nonsuch High School for Girls
Cuddington Croft Primary School
St Dunstans CE Prim Sch
Cheam High Sch
Cheam Fields Prim Sch
Cheam Park Farm Junior School
Westbourne Primary School
Robin Hood Infant School
The Avenue Primary School
Kimpton Industrial Estate
Oldfields Trading Est
Malden Road Baths
Cheam Leisure Cen
Cheam Sports Club
Cheam Works
Sutton United FC
Recreation Ground
West Sutton Station
Cheam Station
Sutton West Centre
Cricket Ground
Cricket & Squash Club
Sutton Bowling Club
Superstore
Surgery
Works
Hospice
Primary School
Windsor Avenue
Priory Road
Chatsworth Road
Gander Green Lane
Abbotts Rd
Tilehurst Road
Kingsdown Road
Fromondes Road
Lumley Road
Cookes Lane
Park Road
Station Way
Burdon Lane
Arundel Road
Mulgrave Road
Salisbury Avenue
Glebe Road
Sandy Lane
Northey Avenue
Dorset Road
Wickham Avenue
Palmer Avenue
Newbolt Avenue
Oaks Avenue
The Avenue
Tate Road
Western Road
Shearwater Rd
Frederick Road
Hilldale Road
St Albans Road
Westfield Road
Buxton Crescent
Carlton Crescent
Lavender Avenue
Courtenay Road
Lloyd Road
Glyn Road
Elm Way
Trent Way
Fir Walk
Holmwood Road
Seymour Av
Cornwall Road
York Road
Holland Avenue
Devon Road
Meadowside Road
The Wray Rd
Harefield Avenue
Hays Walk
Abinger Avenue
Bramley Road
Merrow Road
Ranmore Road
Anne Boleyn's Walk
Jubilee Queens Acre
Forge La
Scotsdale Cl
Tabor Gdns
Upr Mulgrave Rd
Old Barn Cl
Peaches Close
Hillside Rd
Beresford Road
Manor Road
Mickleham Gdns
Tudor Close
Netley Close
Stoughton Av
Matlock Crescent
Alberta Av
Alma Crs
Denbigh Close
Norman Rd
St James Av
Quarry Rise
Quarry Road
Revell Road
Fairholme Road
Carlisle Road
Cecil Road
Rosebery Road
Derby Rd
Bridgefield Road
Landseer Road
Beggar's Roost Lane
Grove Av
Overton Road
Worcester Road
Frampton Cl
Chalcot Cl
Grange
Sackville Rd
Hilbert Road
Wrayfield Road
Hayes Crs
D'Arcy Rd
Church Hill Road
Priory Crs
Priory Av
Hemingford Rd
Wordsworth Drive
The Spinney
Kenley Walk
Fairlight Close
Killester Gdns
Dundela Gardens
The Mount
Woodbine Lane
Grandison Road
Colborne Way
Bedford Road
Farm Way
Burnham Drive
Caversham Av
Marlow Drive
Sunbury Road
The Meads
Henley Avenue
Brocks Drive
St Margaret's Avenue
Kingston Avenue
Kew Crs
Walton Avenue
Molesey Drive
Gander Green Lane
Kimpton Road
Whittaker Road
Willow Walk
Caldstone Road
Sunningdale Road
Jeffs Road
Chelsea Gdns
Alexandra Av
Milton Gdns
Chaucer Gdns
Collingwood
Anton Crs
Stayton
Dibdin Road
Burford Road
Clensham Lane
Sydney Road
Beulah Rd
Beauchamp Road
Orchard Rd
Wings Cl
Esher Av
Frogmore Close
Chartwell Place
Summerville Gdns
Parkside
Grove
Queensmead Avenue
Hillside Road
Shere Av
Gomshall Rd
Albury Avenue
Buckland Road
Ewhurst Close
Wonersh Wy
Holmwood Close
Villiers Gv
The Glade
South Drive
Cheyham Gardens
Nonsuch Walk
Rugby Lane
Shirley Av
Fairfax Av
Castlemaine Av
1 grid square represents 500 metres

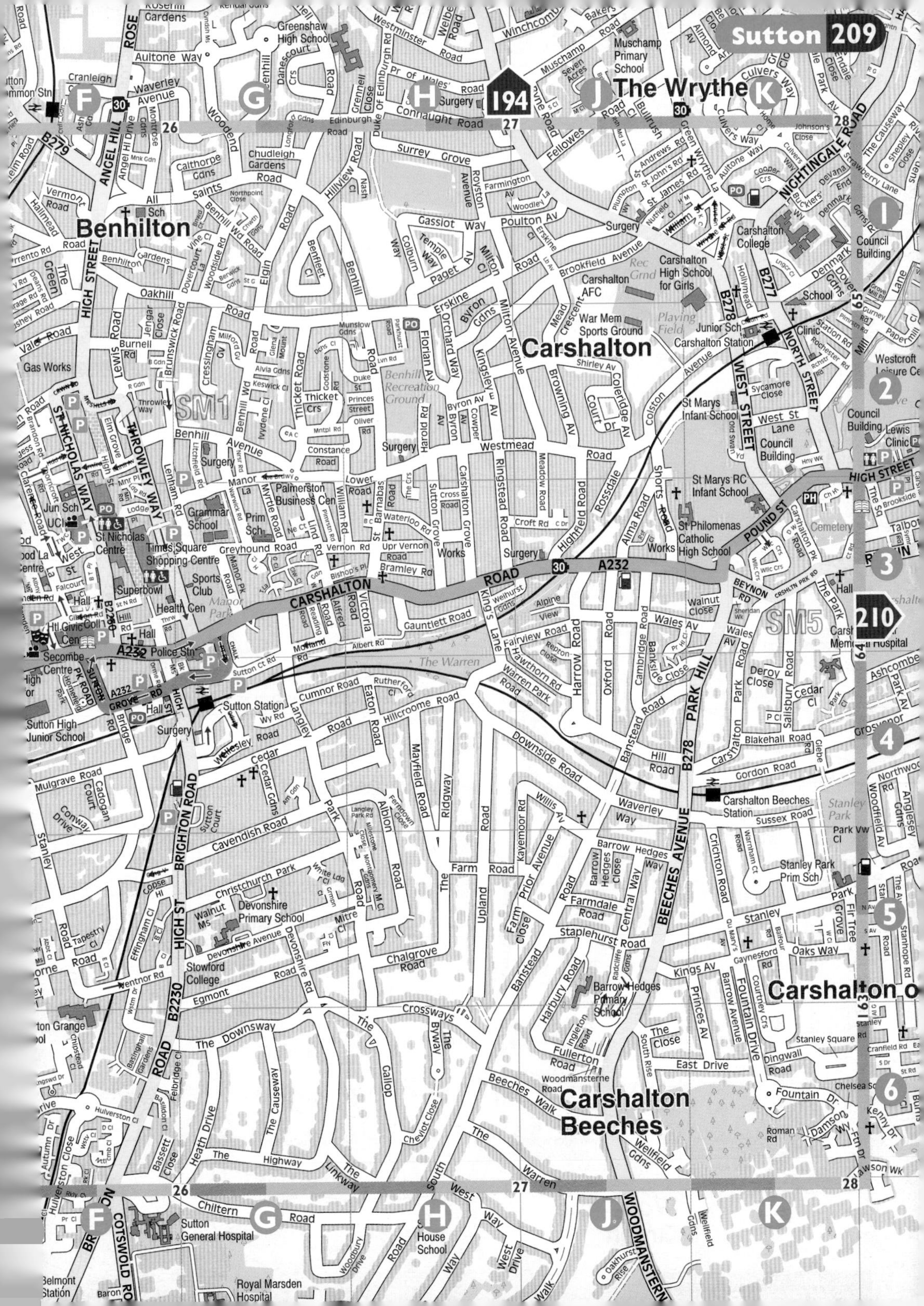

The Wrythe
Benhilton
Carshalton
Carshalton Beeches
Carshalton o
SM1
SM5
194
210
Greenshaw High School
Muschamp Primary School
Carshalton College
Carshalton High School for Girls
Carshalton AFC
War Mem Sports Ground
Carshalton Station
Council Building
Westcroft Leisure Ce
Benhill Recreation Ground
Grammar School
Times Square Shopping Centre
St Nicholas Centre
Superbowl
Sports Club
Health Cen
Palmerston Business Cen
St Marys Infant School
St Marys RC Infant School
St Philomenas Catholic High School
Sutton Station
Sutton High Junior School
Secombe Centre
Police Stn
Devonshire Primary School
Stowford College
Carshalton Beeches Station
Stanley Park Prim Sch
Barrow Hedges Primary School
Sutton General Hospital
Royal Marsden Hospital
Belmont Station
House School
Gas Works
The Warren
Manor Park
Stanley Park
Carshalton Road
High Street
Brighton Road
Beeches Avenue
Park Hill
North Street
West Street
Nightingale Road
Woodmansterne
Cotswold Road
The Downsway
Banstead Road
Westmead Road
Cavendish Road
Chiltern Road

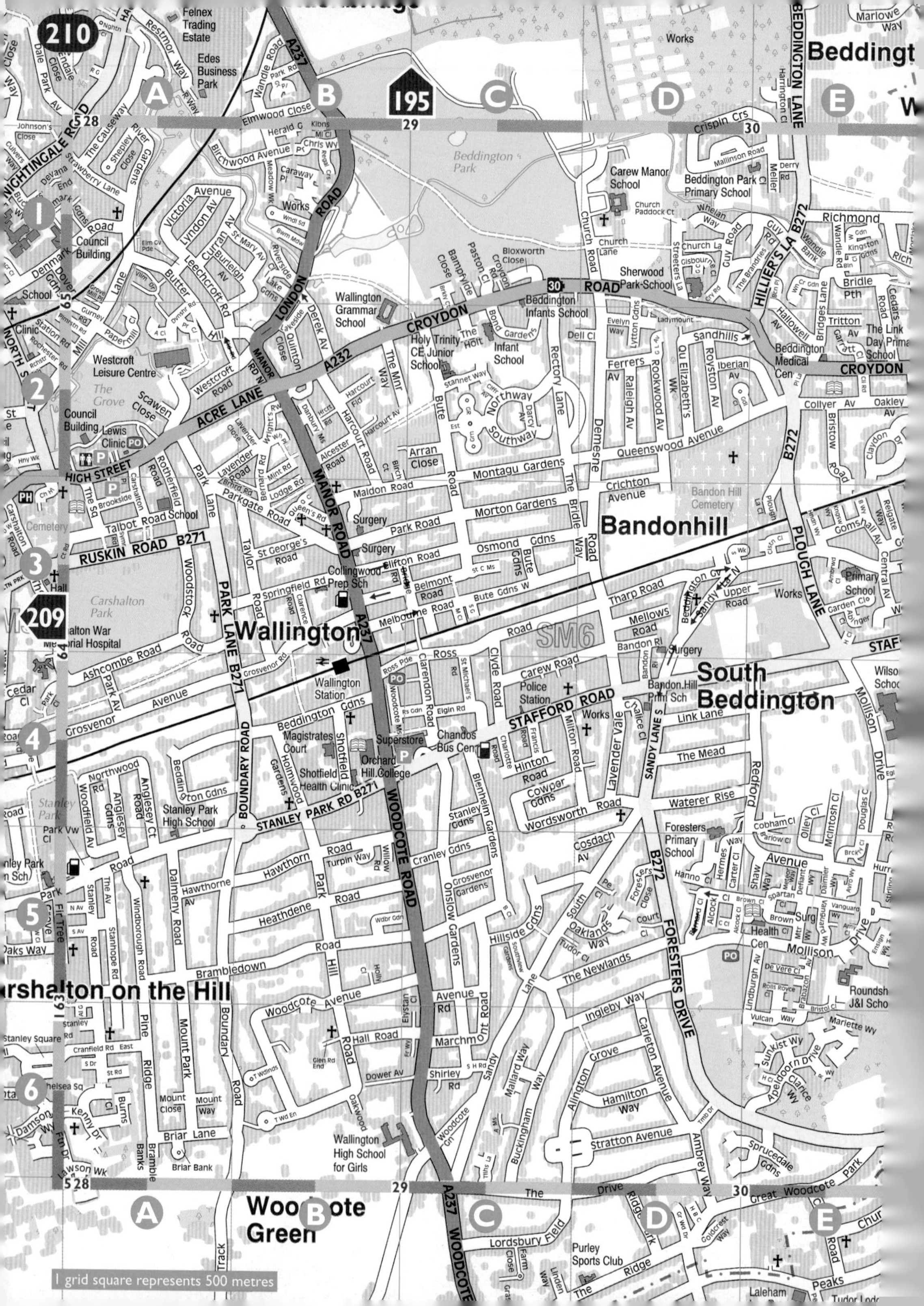
210
195
209
Felnex Trading Estate
Edes Business Park
Restmor Way
Wandle Road
Elmwood Close
Works
Beddington
BEDDINGTON LANE
Marlowe Way
Harrington Cl
Crispin Crs
NIGHTINGALE ROAD
The Causeway
River Gardens
Shepley Close
Strawberry Lane
Birchwood Avenue
Caraway Pl
Beddington Park
Carew Manor School
Mallinson Road
Beddington Park Primary School
Church Paddock Ct
Meller Cl
Derry Rd
Council Building
Victoria Avenue
Lyndon Av
Curran Av
Burleigh Av
Leechcroft Rd
Butter Hill
Riverside
Lake Gdns
LONDON ROAD
Church Road
Church Lane
Church La
Whelan Way
Guy Road
HILLIER'S LA B272
Richmond
Wandle Rd
Kingston Gdns
Bridle Pth
Cedars Road
Denmark Gdns
Dover
School
Clinic
Station Rd
Rochester Rd
Mill Lane
Papermill Cl
Bloxworth Close
Croydon Rd
Paston Cl
Bampfylde Close
Wallington Grammar School
Derek Av
Quinton Close
Lakeside
Sherwood Park School
Beddington Infants School
ROAD
CROYDON
A232
Holy Trinity CE Junior School
The Holt
Bond Gardens
Infant School
Dell Cl
Evelyn Way
Lytton Gdns
Ladymount
Sandhills
Beddington Medical Cen
Tritton Av
The Link Day Primary School
Hallowell Av
Bridges Lane
Garratt Cl
Westcroft Leisure Centre
Westcroft Road
The Grove
Scawen Close
Council Building
Lewis Clinic
PO
ACRE LANE
MANOR RD N
Harcourt Fld
Harcourt Av
Harcourt Road
The Mnr Way
Stannet Way
Northway
Southway
Darcy Av
Bute Road
Rectory Lane
Ferrers Av
Raleigh Av
Rookwood Av
Qu Elizabeth's Wk
Royston Av
Iberian Av
Collyer Av
Oakley Av
Bristow Road
Claydon Dr
HIGH STREET
The Sq
Brookside
Carshalton Pl
Rotherfield Road
Park Lane
Lavender Close
Lavender Road
Wright's Rw
Mint Rd
Bernard Rd
Lodge Rd
Alcester Road
Danbury Ms
MANOR ROAD
Arran Close
Birch Ct
Montagu Gardens
Demesne Road
Queenswood Avenue
B272
Bandon Hill Cemetery
Crichton Avenue
Cemetery
Carshalton Road
Talbot Road School
Parkgate Road
Queen's Rd
Maldon Road
Surgery
Park Road
Morton Gardens
The Bridle Way
Bandonhill
PLOUGH LANE
Plough La Cl
Gomshall Av
Reigate Av
RUSKIN ROAD B271
Woodstock Road
Taylor Road
St George's Road
Clifton Road
Osmond Gdns
Bute Gdns
Carshalton Park
Springfield Rd
Clarence Rd
Collingwood Prep Sch
Belmont Road
Bute Gdns W
Tharp Road
Upper Road
Sandy Lane N
Beddington Gv
Works
Primary School
Garden Clo
Central Av
Carshalton War Memorial Hospital
PARK LANE B271
Wallington
Melbourne Road
Mellows Road
Bandon Ri
Surgery
SM6
Ashcombe Road
Grosvenor Rd
Ross Pde
Ross Rd
Clarendon Road
St Michael's Rd
Clyde Road
Carew Road
Police Station
Bandon Hill Prim Sch
South Beddington
Wilson School
Mollison Drive
Cedar Cl
Park Av
Grosvenor Avenue
Wallington Station
Beddington Gdns
Woodcote Ms
Elgin Rd
STAFFORD ROAD
Works
Chalice Cl
Link Lane
BOUNDARY ROAD
Magistrates Court
Shotfield
Superstore
Chandos Bus Cen
Charlotte Road
Francis Road
Milton Road
Lavender Vale
SANDY LANE S
The Mead
Northwood Rd
Beddington Gdns
Holmwood Gardens
Orchard Hill College
Shotfield Health Clinic
Hinton Road
Cowper Gdns
Woodfield Av
Anglesey Gdns
Anglesey Ct Road
Stanley Park High School
STANLEY PARK RD B271
Stanley Gdns
Blenheim Gardens
Wordsworth Road
Waterer Rise
Redford Av
Stanley Park
Park Vw Cl
Foresters Primary School
Cobham Cl
Olley Cl
McIntosh Cl
Douglas Cl
Barlow Cl
Road
Turpin Way
Willow Rd
Hawthorn Road
Cranley Gdns
Cosdach Av
Hermes Way
Carter Cl
Shaw Way
Avenue
WOODCOTE ROAD
The Av
Stanley
Windborough Road
Dalmeny Road
Hawthorne Av
Grosvenor Gardens
Onslow Gardens
South Cl
Foresters Close
Court Cl
Hanno Cl
Alcock Cl
Brown Cl
Health Cen
Surg
Spartan Cl
Mollison Drive
Heathdene Road
Park Road
Hillside Gdns
Oaklands Way
Tudor Cl
FORESTERS DRIVE
Fir Tree Grove
Oaks Way
Stanhope Rd
Brambledown Road
Hill Road
Holly Cl
The Newlands
Lindburgh Av
De Vere Cl
Rolls Royce Cl
Roundshaw J&I School
Carshalton on the Hill
Pine Ridge
Mount Park
Boundary Road
Woodcote Avenue
Elvstan Cl
Avenue Rd
Lane
Ingleby Way
Vulcan Way
Bristol Cl
Marlette Wy
Stanley Square
Cranfield Rd East
Hall Road
Marchmont Road
Mallard Way
Carleton Avenue
Grove
Allington Way
Sunkist Way
Apeldoorn Drive
Clarice Way
Chelsea Sq
Kenny Dr
Damson Wy
Burns Cl
Mount Close
Mount Way
Dower Av
Shirley Rd
Sandy Lane
Buckingham Way
Hamilton Way
Oakwood Road
Woodcote Gn
Stratton Avenue
Ambrey Way
Sprucedale Gdns
Briar Lane
Banks
Bramble
Briar Bank
Lawson Wk
Wallington High School for Girls
The Drive
Great Woodcote Park
Woodcote Green
A237 WOODCOTE
Lordsbury Field
Farm Close
Purley Sports Club
The Ridge
Linden Way
Goldcrest Way
Laleham
Peaks
Tudor Lodge
Road
Track
1 grid square represents 500 metres

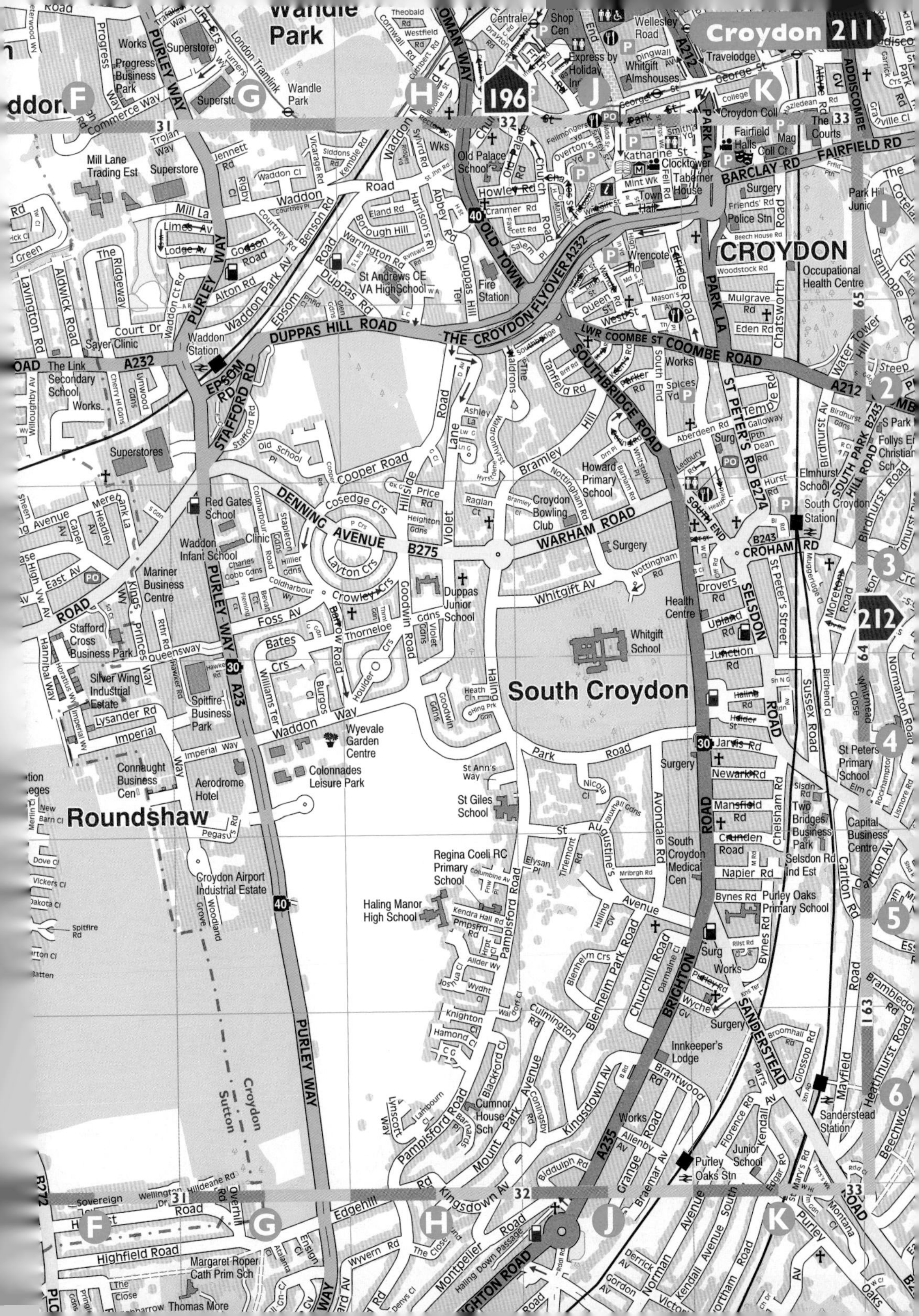

Croydon 211
Wandle Park
Purley Way
Progress Business Park
Superstore
London Tramlink
Commerce Way
Trojan Way
Mill Lane Trading Est
Waddon
Waddon Station
The Ridgeway
Aldwick Road
Lavington Rd
Court Dr
Sayer Clinic
The Link Secondary School
Works
A232
Epsom Rd
Stafford Rd
Duppas Hill Road
The Croydon Flyover A232
Old Town
Roman Way
196
Old Palace School
Howley Rd
Cranmer Rd
Church Road
Fire Station
St Andrews CE VA HighSchool
Borough Hill
Warrington Rd
Waddon Park Av
Benson Rd
Godson Road
Alton Rd
Croydon
Croydon Coll
Fairfield Halls
Katharine St
Clocktower
Taberner House
Town Hall
Barclay Rd
Fairfield Rd
Park La
George St
Wellesley Road
Whitgift Almshouses
Travelodge
Addiscombe
Park Hill Junior
Police Stn
Occupational Health Centre
Mulgrave Rd
Eden Rd
Chatsworth Road
Coombe Road
Lwr Coombe St
Southbridge Road
Tanfield Rd
Bramley Hill
Howard Primary School
St Peter's Rd B274
South End
A212
Water Tower Hill
Elmhurst School
South Park Hill Road
South Croydon Station
Croham Rd
B243
Denning Avenue
Cooper Road
Cosedge Crs
Layton Crs
Crowley Crs
B275
Warham Road
Croydon Bowling Club
Violet Lane
Duppas Junior School
Whitgift Av
Whitgift School
Drovers Rd
Health Centre
Selsdon Road
St Peter's Street
212
Red Gates School
Waddon Infant School
Mariner Business Centre
Stafford Cross Business Park
Queensway
Silver Wing Industrial Estate
Spitfire Business Park
Lysander Rd
Imperial Way
Foss Av
Bates Crs
Thorneloe Gdns
Goodwin Road
Waddon Way
Wyevale Garden Centre
Colonnades Leisure Park
South Croydon
Park Road
St Giles School
Connaught Business Cen
Aerodrome Hotel
Roundshaw
Croydon Airport Industrial Estate
A23
Woodland Grove
Regina Coeli RC Primary School
Haling Manor High School
Pampisford Road
St Augustine's Avenue
Avondale Rd
South Croydon Medical Cen
Brighton Road
Surgery
Newark Rd
Mansfield Rd
Napier Rd
Purley Oaks Primary School
Two Bridges Business Park
Selsdon Rd Ind Est
Capital Business Centre
Carlton Rd
St Peters Primary School
Sussex Road
Normanton Road
Blenheim Park Road
Churchill Road
Innkeeper's Lodge
Brantwood Rd
Kingsdown Av
Cumnor House Sch
Mount Park Avenue
A235
Allenby Road
Grange Road
Purley Oaks Stn
Junior School
Sanderstead Road
Sanderstead Station
Mayfield Road
Heathhurst Road
Croydon
Sutton
Purley Way
Sovereign
Highfield Road
Margaret Roper Cath Prim Sch
Edgehill
Montpeller Road
Haling Down Passage
Brighton Road
Norman Avenue
Kendall Avenue South
Purley
F
G
H
J
K
I
2
3
4
5
6
31
32
33
30
40

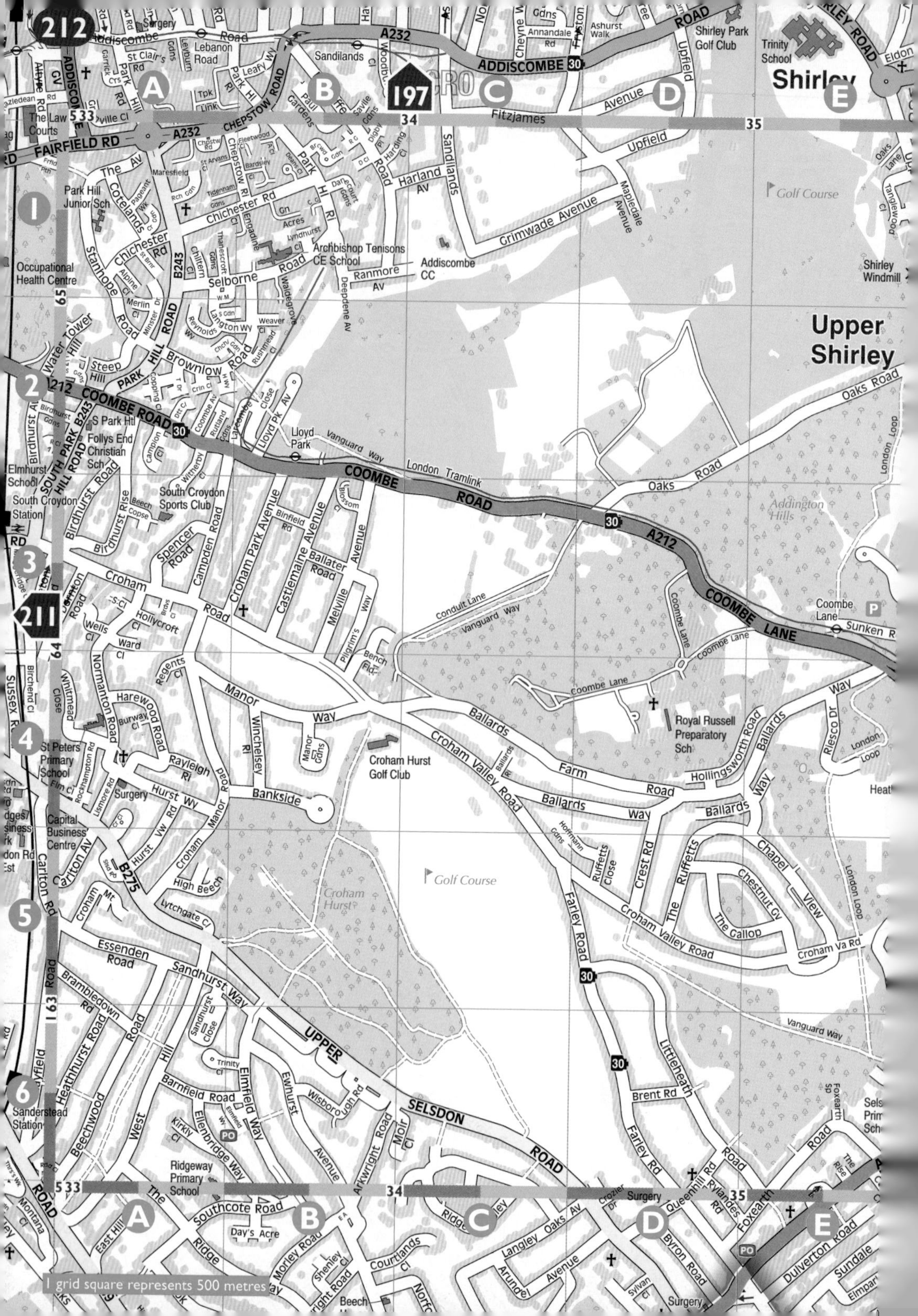

212
197
211
Addiscombe Road
ADDISCOMBE ROAD
A232
Sandilands
Shirley Park Golf Club
Trinity School
Shirley
Lebanon Road
St Clair's Rd
Park Hill Rd
Chepstow Road
Ashurst Walk
Annandale Rd
Upfield
Fitzjames Avenue
The Law Courts
FAIRFIELD RD
Park Hill Junior Sch
The Av
Cotelands
Chichester Rd
Harland Av
Grimwade Avenue
Mapledale Avenue
Golf Course
Archbishop Tenisons CE School
Addiscombe CC
Ranmore Av
Selborne Road
Deepdene Av
Occupational Health Centre
Shirley Windmill
Stanhope Road
Upper Shirley
Water Tower Hill
Steep Hill
PARK HILL ROAD
Brownlow Road
Oaks Road
COOMBE ROAD
A212
S Park Htl
Follys End Christian Sch
Lloyd Park
Vanguard Way
London Tramlink
Elmhurst School
SOUTH PARK HILL ROAD
B243
South Croydon Station
South Croydon Sports Club
Birdhurst Road
Birdhurst Rise
Spencer Road
Campden Road
Croham Park Avenue
Castlemaine Avenue
Ballater Road
Melville Avenue
Addington Hills
Croham Road
Conduit Lane
Coombe Lane
COOMBE LANE
Sunken Rd
London Loop
Hollycroft
Ward Cl
Pilgrim's Way
Bench Fld
Manor Way
Ballards Farm Road
Royal Russell Preparatory Sch
Hollingsworth Road
Ballards Way
Riesco Dr
Harewood Road
Normanton Road
Winchelsey Ri
Croham Hurst Golf Club
Croham Valley Road
St Peters Primary School
Rayleigh Ri
Surgery
Hurst Wy
Bankside
Croham Manor Road
Capital Business Centre
Hurst Vw Rd
Carlton Av
B275
High Beech
Croham Hurst
Crest Rd
The Ruffetts
Chestnut Gv
The Gallop
Chapel View
Farley Road
Lytchgate Cl
Essenden Road
Sandhurst Way
Brambledown Rd
Heathhurst Road
Beechwood Road
West Hill
UPPER SELSDON ROAD
Vanguard Way
Littleheath Road
Brent Rd
Trinity Cl
Elmfield Way
Ewhurst Avenue
Wisborough Rd
Barnfield Road
Ellenbridge Way
Arkwright Road
Moir Cl
Farley Rd
Queenhill Rd
Foxearth Road
Sanderstead Station
Ridgeway Primary School
Southcote Road
Day's Acre
Morley Road
Courtlands Cl
Langley Oaks Av
Arundel Avenue
Byron Road
Dulverton Road
Sundale
Surgery
PO
1 grid square represents 500 metres

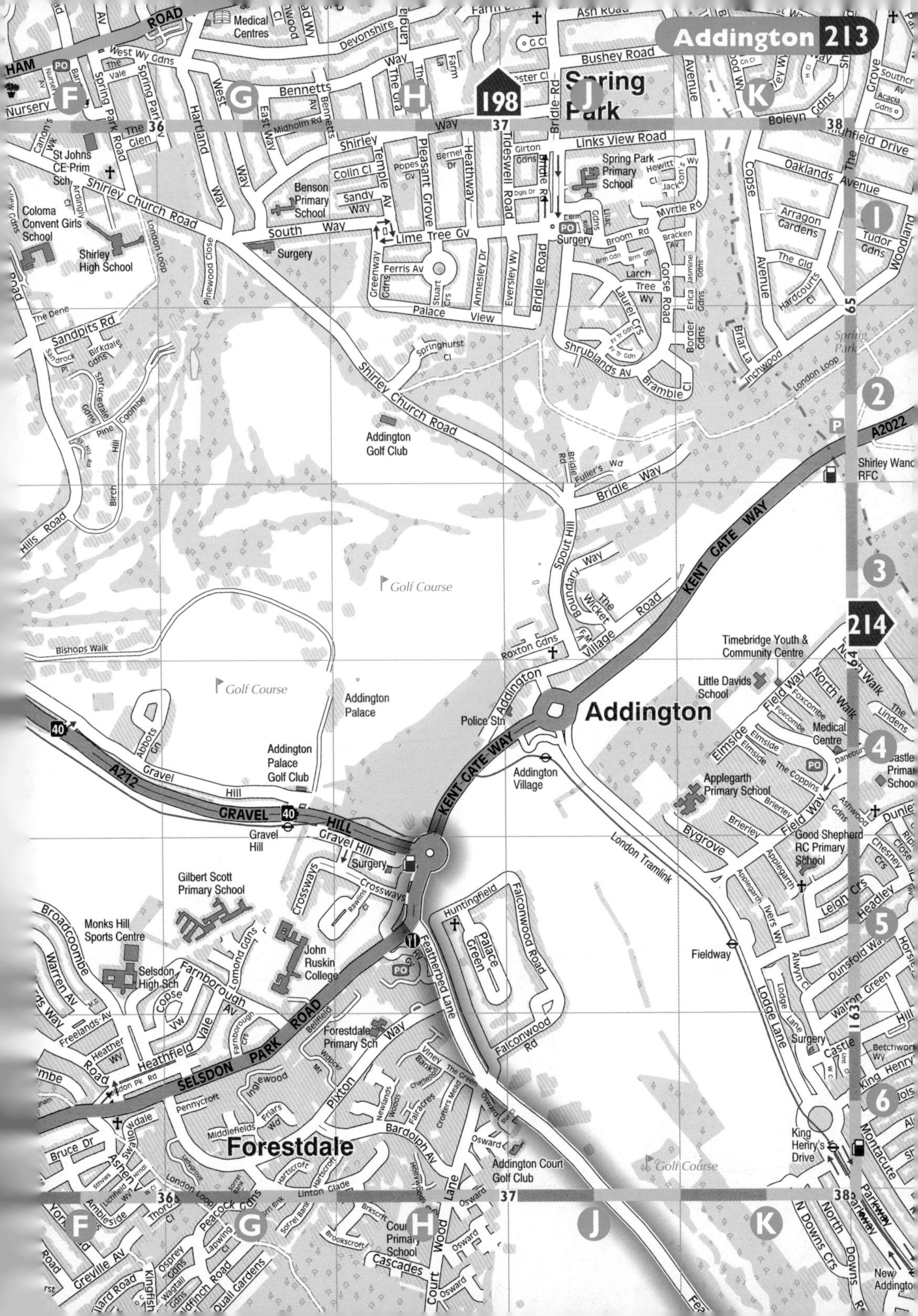

Addington 213
198
214
Spring Park
Addington
Forestdale
Medical Centres
Devonshire
Bushey Road
Ash Road
Nursery
West Wy Gdns
The Vale
Spring Park Road
Bennetts
Bennetts Av
East Way
Midholm Rd
Shirley Way
West Way
Hartland Way
The Glen
Boleyn Gdns
Links View Road
Highfield Drive
Oaklands Avenue
St Johns CE Prim Sch
Shirley Church Road
Coloma Convent Girls School
Shirley High School
London Loop
Benson Primary School
Colin Cl
Sandy Way
Temple Av
Pleasant Grove
Heathway
Tideswell Road
Bridle Rd
Spring Park Primary School
Hewitt Cl
Jackson's Wy
Myrtle Rd
South Way
Lime Tree Gv
Surgery
Ferris Av
Greenway Gdns
Stuart Crs
Annesley Dr
Eversley Wy
Bridle Road
Palace View
Broom Rd
Bracken Av
Larch Tree Wy
Laurel Crs
Gorse Road
Erica Gdns
Jasmine Gdns
Border Gdns
Briar La
Shrublands Av
Bramble Cl
Copse Avenue
Arragon Gardens
The Gld
Hardcourts Cl
Tudor Gdns
Woodland
Inchwood
Pinewood Close
The Dene
Sandpits Rd
Birkdale Gdns
Sprucedale Gdns
Pine Coombe
Birch Hill
Hills Road
Springhurst Cl
Addington Golf Club
Fuller's Wd
Bridle Way
Spout Hill
Boundary Way
The Wicket
Village Road
KENT GATE WAY
A2022
Shirley Wanderers RFC
Golf Course
Bishops Walk
Roxton Gdns
Addington Palace
Abbots Gn
A212
Gravel Hill
GRAVEL HILL
Addington Palace Golf Club
Police Stn
Addington Village
Timebridge Youth & Community Centre
Little Davids School
Field Way
North Walk
The Lindens
Foxcombe
Elmside
Medical Centre
Danebury
Castle Primary School
The Coppins
Applegarth Primary School
Brierley
Ashwood Gdns
Bygrove
London Tramlink
Good Shepherd RC Primary School
Applegarth
Ivers Wy
Leigh Crs
Headley
Chesney Crs
Crossways
Rawlins Cl
Huntingfield
Falconwood Road
Palace Green
Gilbert Scott Primary School
Monks Hill Sports Centre
Broadcoombe
Warren Av
Selsdon High Sch
Farnborough Av
John Ruskin College
Lomond Gdns
Featherbed Lane
Fieldway
Lodge Lane
Alwyn Cl
Dunsfold Way
Walton Green
Surgery
Castle
King Henry's Drive
Betchworth Wy
Montacute
Copse Vw
Freelands Av
Heather Wy
Heathfield Vale
SELSDON PARK ROAD
Selsdon Pk Rd
Forestdale Primary Sch
Falconwood Rd
Pennycroft
Inglewood
Pixton Way
Viney Bank
The Green
Newlands Woods
Fairacres
Crofters Mead
Oswald
Middlefields
Friars Wd
Bardolph Av
Addington Court Golf Club
Bruce Dr
Ashen
Swallowdale
Hartscroft
Linton Glade
London Loop
Peacock Gdns
Ambleside
Court Wood Lane
Court Primary School
Brookscroft
Cascades
North Downs Crs
Parkway
New Addington
Greville Av
Osprey Gdns
Lapwing Cl
Quail Gardens
Kingfisher
36 37 38
63 64 65
F G H J K
1 2 3 4 5 6

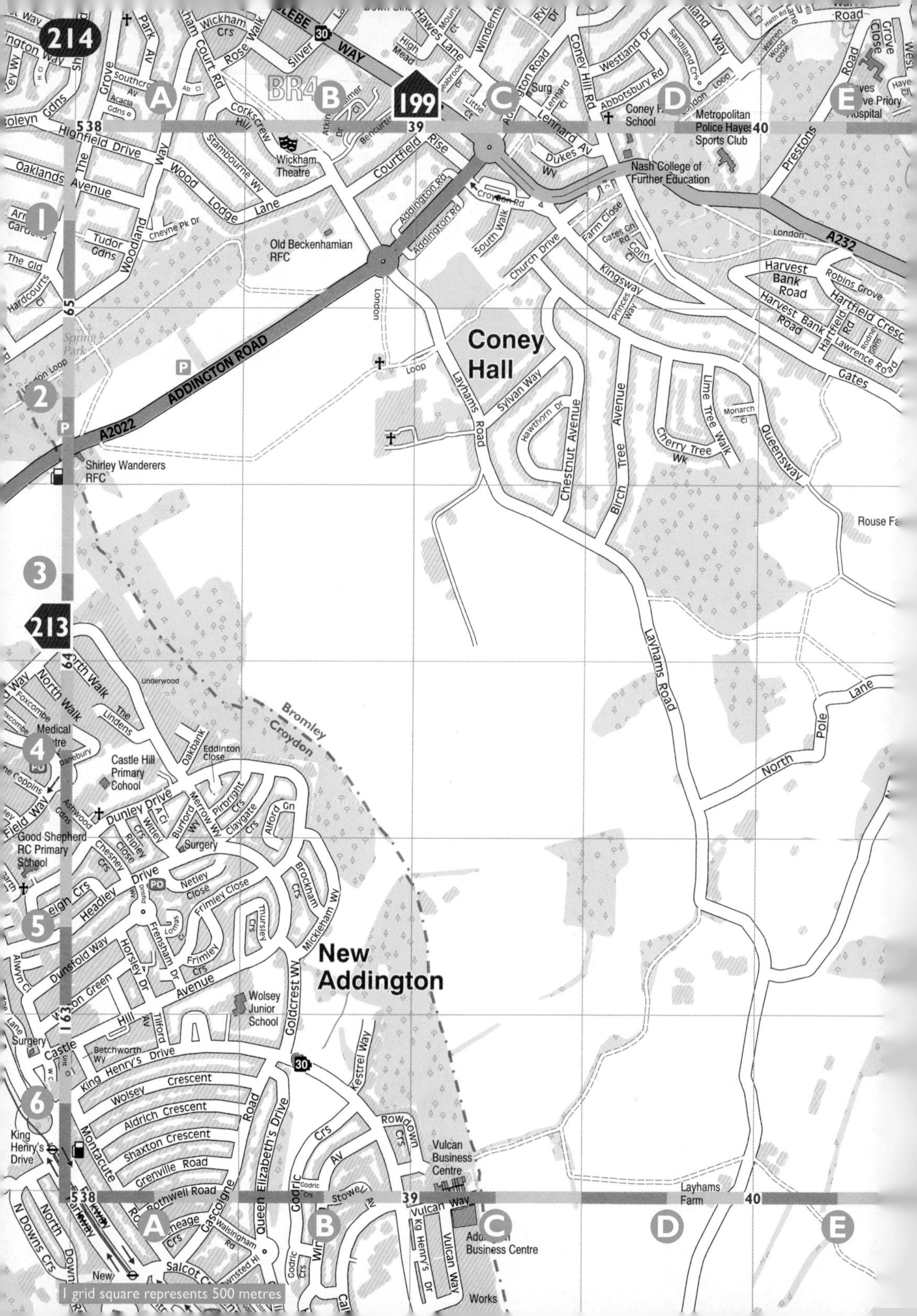

BR4

199

213

Coney Hall

New Addington

1 grid square represents 500 metres

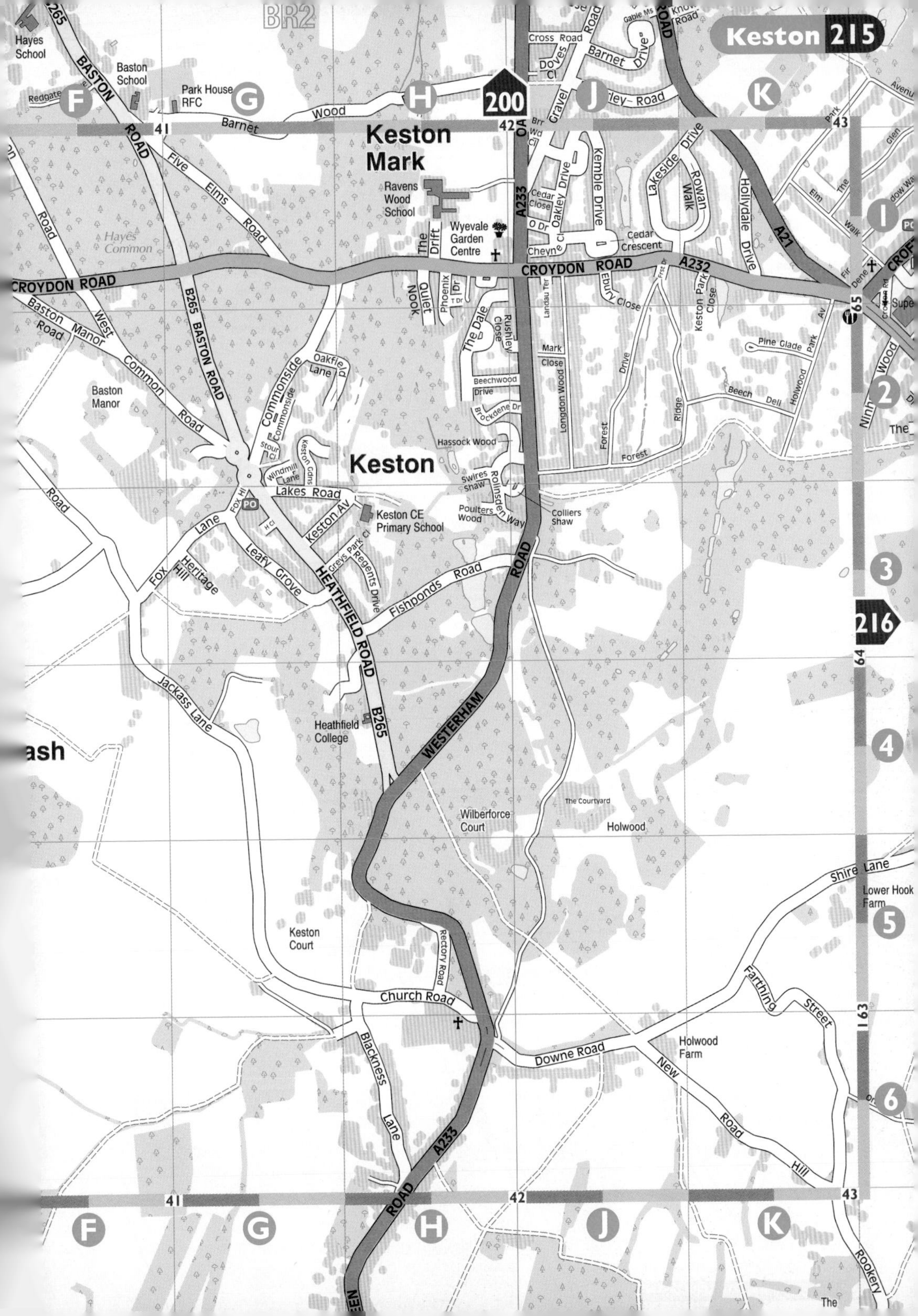
Keston Mark
Keston
Hayes School
Baston School
Park House RFC
Ravens Wood School
Wyevale Garden Centre
Hayes Common
Baston Manor
Keston CE Primary School
Heathfield College
Wilberforce Court
Holwood
The Courtyard
Keston Court
Holwood Farm
Lower Hook Farm
Hassock Wood
Swires Shaw
Poulters Wood
Colliers Shaw
CROYDON ROAD
A232
A233
A21
B265
BASTON ROAD
HEATHFIELD ROAD
WESTERHAM ROAD
Barnet Wood Road
Five Elms Road
West Common Road
Baston Manor Road
Commonside
Oakfield Lane
Lakes Road
Fox Lane
Fox Hill
Heritage Hill
Leafy Grove
Keston Av
Fishponds Road
Jackass Lane
Church Road
Rectory Road
Blackness Lane
Downe Road
New Road Hill
Farthing Street
Shire Lane
Cross Road
Doves Cl
Barnet Drive
Gravel Road
Kemble Drive
Oakley Drive
Cedar Close
Cedar Crescent
Lakeside Drive
Rowan Walk
Hollydale Drive
Ebury Close
Keston Park Close
Forest Drive
Forest Ridge
Longdon Wood
Mark Close
Beechwood Drive
Brockdene Dr
Rushley Close
The Dale
Rollinsden Way
Quiet Nook
Phoenix Dr
The Drift
Pine Glade
Beech Dell
Holwood Park Av
Windmill Lane
Keston Gdns
Stour Cl
Greys Park Cl
Regents Drive
Redgate
Gable Ms
Landau Ter
F G H J K
1 2 3 4 5 6
41 42 43
65 64 163
200
216
BR2

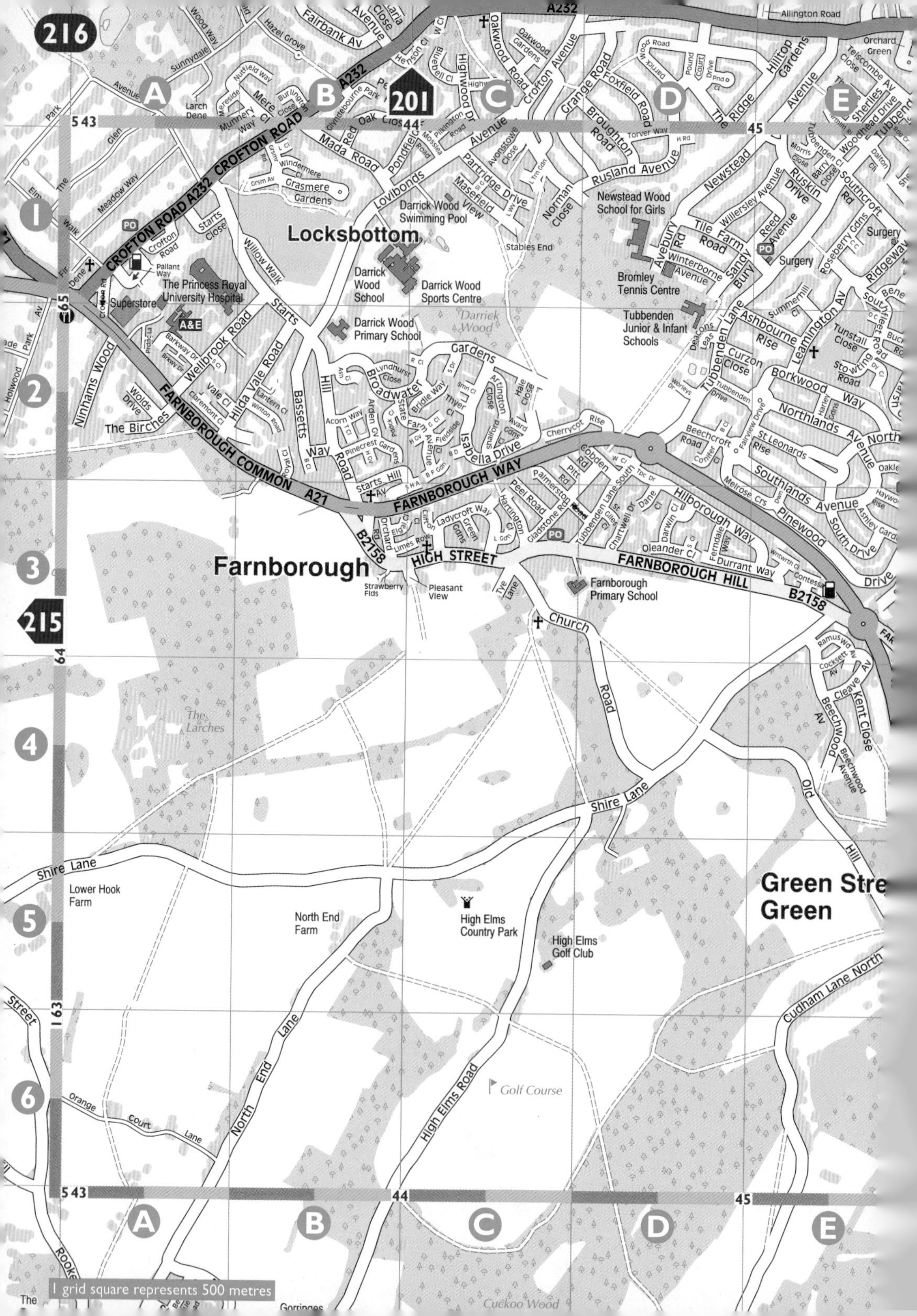
201
215
A232
Allington Road
Fairbank Av
Hazel Grove
Sunnydale
Wood Way
Orchard Green
Telscombe Av
Oakwood Gardens
Oakwood Road
Crofton Avenue
Grange Road
Foxfield Road
Broughton Road
Darrick Wood Road
Pound Court Drive
The Ridge
Hilltop Gardens
Avenue
Larch Dene
Mere Cl
Munnery Way
Burlington Close
Glyndebourne Park
Red Oak Close
Mada Road
Pondfield Road
Highwood Dr
Bluebell Cl
Pilkington Road
Mosslea Road
Torver Way
Rusland Avenue
Newstead
Tubbenden Cl
Woodhead Drive
Sherlies Av
Tubbenden
Southcroft Rd
Crofton Road A232
Meadow Way
Glen
The Walk
Elm
Park
Windermere Cl
Grasmere Gardens
Grsm Av
Starts Close
Willow Walk
Lovibonds Avenue
Avonstowe Close
Partridge Drive
Masefield View
Darrick Wood Swimming Pool
Norman Close
Stables End
Newstead Wood School for Girls
Willersley Avenue
Tile Farm Road
Avebury Rd
Reed Avenue
Ruskin Drive
Rosebery Gdns
Surgery
Ridgeway
Locksbottom
PO
Crofton Road
Pallant Way
Fir Dene
The Princess Royal University Hospital
Superstore
A&E
Darrick Wood School
Darrick Wood Sports Centre
Darrick Wood
Darrick Wood Primary School
Winterborne Avenue
Bromley Tennis Centre
Sandy Bury
Tubbenden Junior & Infant Schools
Deacons Leas
Tubbenden Lane
Ashbourne Rise
Curzon Close
Summerhill Cl
Leamington Av
Southfleet Road
Tunstall Close
Stowting Road
Borkwood Way
Northlands Avenue
Harley Gdns
Ninhams Wood
Wellbrook Road
Hilda Vale Road
Barkway Dr
Vale Cl
Claremont Cl
Lantern Cl
Winton Road
Starts Hill
Bassetts Way
Gardens
Lyndhurst Close
Broadwater
Bridle Way
Thyer Cl
Arlington Close
Hale Close
Acorn Way
Arden Gv
State Farm Avenue
Fieldside Cl
Isabella Drive
Avard Gdns
Cherrycot Rise
Pinecrest Gardens
Worlds Drive
The Birches
Holwood Park Av
Farnborough Common A21
Farnborough Way
Royal Cl
Starts Hill Av
Cobden Rd
Pitt Rd
Palmerston Rd
Peel Road
Hartington Cl
Gladstone Rd
Tubbenden Lane South
St Giles Cl
Chartwell Dr
Dane Cl
Darwin Cl
Hilborough Way
Beechcroft Road
Conifer Cl
Fairview Drive
St Leonards Rise
Melrose Crs
Southlands Avenue
Pinewood Drive
South Drive
Ladycroft Way
Green Gdns
Clifton Cl
Elgal Cl
Orchard Rd
Limes Row
B2158
High Street
Farnborough Hill
Oleander Cl
Ferndale Way
Durrant Way
Contessa
Farnborough
Strawberry Flds
Pleasant View
Tye Lane
Farnborough Primary School
Church Road
Ramus Wd Av
Cocksett Av
Cleave Av
Kent Close
Beechwood Av
Beechwood Avenue
Old Hill
Shire Lane
The Larches
Lower Hook Farm
North End Farm
High Elms Country Park
High Elms Golf Club
Green Street Green
Cudham Lane North
Street
Orange Court Lane
North End Lane
High Elms Road
Golf Course
Rookery
Cuckoo Wood
Gorringes
The
5 43
44
45
65
64
1 63
A
B
C
D
E
1
2
3
4
5
6
1 grid square represents 500 metres

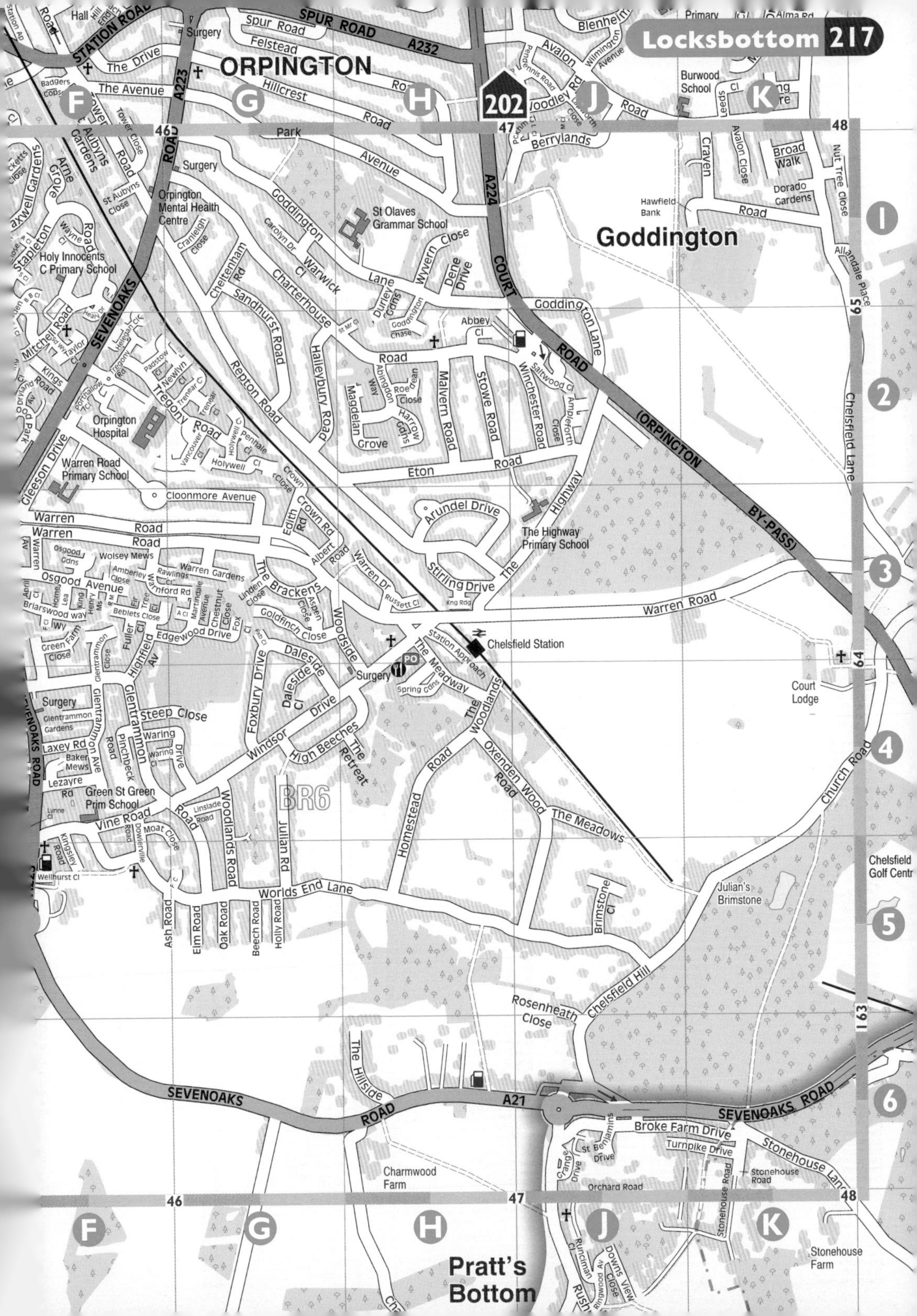
ORPINGTON
Goddington
Pratt's Bottom
202
SPUR ROAD
A232
Spur Road
Felstead
STATION ROAD
The Drive
The Avenue
Hillcrest
Road
Surgery
A223
SEVENOAKS ROAD
A224
COURT ROAD
(ORPINGTON BY-PASS)
Park Avenue
Goddington Lane
St Olaves Grammar School
Wyvern Close
Dene Drive
Warwick Cl
Charterhouse
Durley Gdns
Goddington Chase
Abbey Cl
Carolyn Dr
Road
Haileybury Road
Magdelan Grove
Abingdon Way
Roedean Close
Harrow Gdns
Malvern Road
Stowe Road
Winchester Road
Saltwood Cl
Ampleforth Close
Eton Road
Arundel Drive
The Highway
The Highway Primary School
Stirling Drive
Kng Rdg
Warren Road
Chelsfield Station
Station Approach
The Meadway
Spring Gdns
The Woodlands
Oxenden Wood Road
The Meadows
Homestead Road
Brimstone Cl
Julian's Brimstone
Chelsfield Hill
Rosenheath Close
Court Lodge
Church Road
Chelsfield Lane
Allandale Place
Nut Tree Close
Dorado Gardens
Broad Walk
Avalon Close
Craven Road
Hawfield Bank
Burwood School
Leeds Cl
Avalon Road
Blenheim
Wilmington Avenue
Pendennis Road
Woodley Rd
Berrylands
Primary
Alma Rd
Orpington Mental Health Centre
Cranleigh Close
Cheltenham Rd
Sandhurst Road
Repton Road
Holy Innocents C Primary School
Stapleton
Wayne Road
Maxwell Gardens
Arne Grove
Aubyns Gardens
Tower Close
St Aubyns Close
Badgers Copse
Station Ap
Hall Hill
Mitchell Road
Taylor
Kings Road
Orpington Hospital
Tregony Road
Padstow Cl
Newlyn Cl
Trenear Cl
Holywell Cl
Penhale Cl
Vancouver Cl
Gleeson Drive
Warren Road Primary School
Cloonmore Avenue
Crown Close
Crown Rd
Edith Rd
Albert Road
Warren Dr
Russett Cl
Woodside
The Brackens
Aspen Close
Linden Close
Goldfinch Close
Warren Gardens
Wolsey Mews
Osgood Gdns
Osgood Avenue
Amberley Close
Rawlings Cl
Warnford Rd
Martindale Avenue
Chestnut Close
Fox Cl
Beblets Close
Briarswood way
Edgewood Drive
Green Farm Close
Fuller Cl
Highfield Av
Glentrammon Close
Surgery
Glentrammon Gardens
Glentrammon Ave
Glentrammon Road
Laxey Rd
Baker Mews
Lezayre Rd
Pinchbeck Road
Steep Close
Waring Drive
Waring Cl
Green St Green Prim School
Foxbury Drive
Daleside
Daleside Cl
Drive
Windsor Drive
High Beeches
The Retreat
PO
Surgery
BR6
Vine Road
Kingsley Road
Wellhurst Cl
Moat Close
Dowlerville Road
Linslade Road
Woodlands Road
Julian Rd
Worlds End Lane
Ash Road
Elm Road
Oak Road
Beech Road
Holly Road
SEVENOAKS ROAD
A21
The Hillside
Charmwood Farm
Broke Farm Drive
St Benjamins Drive
Turnpike Drive
Grange Drive
Orchard Road
Stonehouse Road
Stonehouse Lane
Stonehouse Farm
Runciman Cl
Ringwood Av
Downs View Close
Chelsfield Golf Centr
F G H J K
46 47 48
1 2 3 4 5 6
65 64 63

Abbey Wood 128 C4
Acton 117 K1
Acton Green 118 A4
Addington 213 J4
Addiscombe 197 G4
Aldborough Hatch 72 E1
Aldersbrook 71 G5
Alperton 80 A6
Anerley 181 H5
Ashford 152 D6
Avery Hill 167 H1
Balham 160 E2
Bandonhill 210 D3
Barking 90 D5
Barkingside 54 B6
Barnehurst 150 A4
Barnes 138 E2
Barnes Cray 150 E5
Barnet 32 D1
Barnet Gate 31 G1
Barnsbury 84 E5
Barwell 205 J5
Battersea 140 E1
Bayswater 101 F6
Beckenham 182 D5
Beckton 107 K5
Becontree 91 K3
Beddington 195 K6
Beddington Corner 195 F4
Bedford Park 118 C3
Belgravia 15 G6
Bell Green 164 C5
Bellingham 164 D6
Belmont 43 G5
Belmont 208 E6
Belvedere 129 J5
Benhilton 209 F1
Berrylands 191 G3
Bethnal Green 104 D2
Bexley 148 D5
Bexleyheath 149 G5
Bickley 184 D5
Blackfen 168 A1
Blackheath 145 J3
Blackheath Park 145 K5
Blackwall 106 B6
Bloomsbury 10 D1
The Borough 18 D3
Bow 105 J1
Bow Common 105 J4
Bowes Park 48 E2
Bowmans 170 C2
Brentford 116 E6
Brentford End 116 C6
Brimsdown 25 G3
Brixton 142 B5
Broad Green 196 C4
Brockley 144 C6
Bromley 105 K2
Bromley 184 A5
Bromley Common 200 C3
Bromley Park 183 H4
Brompton 14 C5
Brondesbury 82 C4
Brondesbury Park 82 B6
Brook Green 119 F3
Broom Hill 202 A4
Brunswick Park 34 A5
Buckhurst Hill 39 G5
Burnt Oak 45 F3
Bushey 28 C2
Bushey Heath 28 E2
Bushey Mead 177 G6
Bush Hill Park 36 A1
Caldecote Hill 29 F2
Camberwell 143 G2
Camden Town 84 A5
Canary Wharf 124 D1
Canning Town 107 F4
Cannon Hill 193 G1
Canonbury 85 J4
Canons Park 44 A3
Carpenders Park 27 K4
Carshalton 209 J2
Carshalton Beeches 209 J6
Carshalton on the Hill 209 K5
Castle Green 91 J6
Catford 165 F3
Chadwell Heath 73 K2
Charlton 126 C5
Chase Cross 57 G2
Chattern Hill 152 E6
Cheam 208 C3
Chelsea 121 F5
Chessington 206 A4
Child's Hill 64 C6
China Town 10 D5
Chingford 38 B3
Chingford Green 38 A3
Chingford Hatch 38 C6
Chipping Barnet 20 C6
Chislehurst 185 H3
Chislehurst West 185 F2
Chiswick 118 C4
Church End 46 E5
Church End 81 H5
City of London 12 B5
Clapham 141 G3
Clapham Park 161 J1
Clapton Park 87 H2
Claremont Park 204 A5
Claygate 205 F4
Clayhall 53 K5
Clerkenwell 5 J6
Cockfosters 21 J6
Coldblow 169 K4
Coldharbour 130 D4
Cole Park 156 B1
Colindale 45 G6
College Park 99 J2
Collier Row 56 E4
Collier's Wood 178 C3
Colney Hatch 47 K2
Coney Hall 214 C2
Coombe 176 B3
Copse Hill 176 D3
Cottenham Park 176 E4
Cranbrook 72 A4
Cranford 133 K1
Cranley Gardens 66 A1
Crayford 150 D6
Creekmouth 108 E4
Cricklewood 82 B2
Crockenhill 203 K3
Crofton 201 J6
Crooked Billet 176 E2
Crouch End 66 C3
Croydon 211 K1
Crystal Palace 181 H2
Cubitt Town 125 F4
Custom House 107 J6
Dagenham 92 D5
Dalston 86 B5
Dartford 171 F2
Dartmouth Park 66 A6
Deacons Hill 30 C1
De Beauvoir Town 86 A6
Deptford 124 C6
Derry Downs 202 E3
Dollis Hill 81 K1
Dormer's Wells 96 B6
Downham 183 G1
Ducks Island 32 B2
Dudden Hill 81 J3
Dulwich 163 G4
Dulwich Village 163 F2
Ealing 97 J6
Earl's Court 119 K5
Earlsfield 160 B3
East Acton 99 H6
East Barnet 33 H2
East Bedfont 152 E2
Eastbury 26 D6
Eastcote 59 F4
Eastcote Village 59 F2
East Dulwich 143 H6
East Finchley 47 H6
East Ham 107 J1
East Molesey 189 H2
East Sheen 138 A6
East Wickham 148 B2
Eden Park 198 C1
Edgware 30 D6
Edmonton 36 A6
Elmers End 182 A6
Elm Park 93 K3
Elmstead 184 D1
Elstree 30 A1
Eltham 166 D1
Enfield 23 J5
Enfield Highway 24 E3
Enfield Island Village 25 K1
Enfield Town 23 K4
Enfield Wash 25 G1
Erith 130 C5
Esher 204 C2
Ewell 207 J6
Fair Cross 91 F3
Fairlop 54 E4
Falconwood 147 K5
Farnborough 216 A3
Feltham 154 A4
Field Common 188 E4
Finchley 46 E4
Finsbury 5 J4
Finsbury Park 66 E6
Foots Cray 186 C2
Forestdale 213 G6
Forest Gate 88 E3
Forest Hill 164 A3
Fortis Green 65 K1
Forty Hill 24 B2
Foxbury 185 J1
Friday Hill 38 B5
Friern Barnet 33 J6
Fulham 139 G1
Fullwell Cross 54 D4
Furzedown 161 G6
Gants Hill 71 K3
Gidea Park 57 H5
Giggshill 190 B4
Globe Town 105 F2
Goddington 217 J1
Golders Green 64 C3
Goodmayes 73 H6
Gospel Oak 84 A3
Grange Hill 54 D2
Grange Park 23 G6
Greenford 96 D3
Greenhill 61 F2
Green Street Green 216 E5
Greenwich 125 G5
Grove Park 138 A2
Grove Park 166 B5
Hackbridge 195 G6
Hackney 86 E4
Hackney Wick 87 J4
Hadley 20 D4
Hadley Wood 21 H1
Haggerston 7 K2
Hainault 55 F3
Hale End 52 B2
Ham 156 E5
Hammersmith 118 E4
Hampstead 83 H2
Hampstead Garden Suburb 65 F2
Hampton 173 G4
Hampton Hill 155 H6
Hampton Wick 174 C4
Hanwell 115 J1
Hanworth 154 C5
Harlesden 99 G1
Harlington 113 F6
Harmondsworth 112 A6
Harringay 67 G2
Harrow 60 D3
Harrow on the Hill 60 E5
Harrow Weald 42 E3
Hatch End 41 J3
Hatton 133 H5
Hayes 94 A4
Hayes 200 A4
Hayes End 94 B3
Hayes Town 114 B1
Headstone 60 B1
Heath Park 75 K3
Heath Side 170 C4
Hendon 63 K2
Herne Hill 162 D1
Heston 134 E1
Higham Hill 51 G5
Highams Park 51 K3
High Barnet 20 A4
Highbury 85 H3
Highgate 65 K4
Highwood Hill 31 H4
Hinchley Wood 205 F1
Hither Green 165 H1
Hockenden 187 J6
Holborn 11 G2
Holders Hill 46 B4
Holywell 26 C1
Homerton 87 F4
Honor Oak 164 A1
Honor Oak Park 164 B1
Hook 206 A3
Hook Green 170 C6
Hornsey 66 E1
Hornsey Vale 67 F2
Hounslow 135 F3
Hounslow West 134 C4
Hoxton 7 G3
Hurst Park 173 H5
The Hyde 63 H2
Ilford 90 B1
Isle of Dogs 125 F4
Isleworth 136 C4
Islington 85 G6
Joyden's Wood 170 C6
Kennington 121 K6
Kensal Green 100 A1
Kensal Rise 100 B1
Kensal Town 100 C3
Kensington 119 K3
Kentish Town 84 C4
Kenton 61 J2
Keston 215 H2
Keston Mark 215 H1
Kevingtown 203 G3
Kew 137 G1
Kidbrooke 146 B3
Kilburn 82 C6
Kingsbury 62 D3
Kingsland 86 A5
Kingston upon Thames 174 D6
Kingston Vale 176 A1
Kitt's End 20 C1
Knightsbridge 14 D2
Knight's Hill 162 D3
Ladywell 144 D5
Lambeth 17 J4
Lampton 135 G2
Lea Bridge 87 F1
Lee 165 J1
Lessness Heath 129 J6
Lewisham 145 F5
Leyton 88 B1
Leytonstone 70 D5
Limehouse 105 G6
Lisson Grove 9 F1
Little Heath 73 J1
Little Ilford 90 A3
Little Stanmore 44 B4
Locksbottom 216 B1
Long Ditton 190 C5
Longlands 167 H5
Lower Clapton 86 E2
Lower Edmonton 36 A4
Lower Feltham 153 H5
Lower Green 189 G6
Lower Holloway 85 F3
Lower Place 98 E1
Lower Sydenham 164 A6
Loxford 90 C3
Maida Vale 101 F2
Maitland Park 83 K4
Manor Park 89 J2
Marks Gate 56 A5
Marylebone 9 G2
Mayfair 9 J6
Maypole 170 B3
Merry Hill 28 B3
Merton 177 K4
Merton Park 177 J5
Mile End 105 G3
Mill Hill 45 J1
Mill Meads 106 B1
Millwall 124 E3
Mitcham 179 F6
Monken Hadley 20 G3
Monks Orchard 197 K4
Moor Park 26 A6
Morden 193 K1
Morden Park 193 H3
Mortlake 137 K3
Motspur Park 192 D3
Mottingham 166 B4
Muswell Hill 48 A5
Nash 215 F4
Neasden 81 F2
New Addington 214 B5
New Barnet 21 F6
New Beckenham 182 B2
Newbury Park 72 D3
New Charlton 126 C4
New Cross 144 B3
New Cross Gate 144 B2
New Eltham 167 G4
Newington 17 K5
New Malden 176 C6
New Southgate 34 C6
New Town 171 J1
Noel Park 49 H5
Norbiton 175 G5
Norbury 180 C5
North Acton 98 E3
North Cheam 208 B1
North Cray 169 H5
North End 65 G5
North End 150 C2
North Feltham 134 A6
North Finchley 47 G2
North Harrow 59 K3
North Hyde 114 D4
North Kensington 100 B4
Northolt 78 A5
North Sheen 137 J3
Northumberland Heath 149 K1
North Wembley 61 H5
Northwood 40 A4
Northwood Hills 40 B5
North Woolwich 126 D2
Norwood Green 115 F4
Norwood New Town 180 E2
Notting Hill 100 C6
Nunhead 143 K5
Oakleigh Park 33 H4
Oakwood 34 D1
Old Bexley 169 H2
Old Ford 87 G6
Old Malden 192 A4
Old Oak Common 99 H3
Orpington 202 B6
Osidge 34 C4
Osterley 135 H1
Oxhey 27 H1
Paddington 8 A2
Palmers Green 34 E5
Park Langley 199 F3
Park Royal 98 C2
Parsons Green 139 K3
Peckham 143 J3
Penge 181 K3
Pentonville 5 H2
Perivale 79 J6
Petersham 157 F3
Petts Wood 201 J1
Pimlico 121 H5
Pinner 59 H1
Pinner Green 41 G5
Pinnerwood Park 41 G3
Plaistow 106 D2
Plaistow 183 K2
Plashet 89 H4
Plumstead 127 H5
Plumstead Common 128 A6
Ponders End 24 E6
Poplar 105 J6
Poverest 202 B1
Preston 61 K5
Primrose Hill 3 H1
Purfleet 131 K5
Putney 139 G6
Putney Heath 159 F2
Putney Vale 158 D5
Queensbury 44 A6
Queen's Park 100 C1
Rainham 111 K2
Ramsden 202 D5
Rayners Lane 59 K5
Raynes Park 177 F6
Redbridge 71 G2
Regent's Park 3 K3
Richmond 137 F6
Richmond Hill 157 F1
Rise Park 57 G4
Roehampton 138 C6
Romford 74 E2
The Rookery 26 E2
Rosehill 194 A5
Rotherhithe 124 A3
Roundshaw 211 F4
Roxeth 60 C6
Ruislip 58 C3
Ruislip Common 58 A1
Ruislip Gardens 76 C1
Ruislip Manor 58 E6
Rush Green 75 F4
Ruxley 187 F2
Rydens 188 B6
St George in the East 104 C6
St Giles 10 D3
St Helier 194 B5
St James's 16 C1
St Johns 144 D3
St John's Wood 101 G1
St Luke's 6 D6
St Margarets 156 D1
St Mary Cray 202 D2
St Pancras 5 F5
St Paul's Cray 186 B5
Sands End 140 B2
Seething Wells 190 C3
Selhurst 196 E2
Seven Kings 72 E5
Shacklewell 86 C2
Shadwell 104 E6
Shepherd's Bush 118 E1
Shirley 197 K6
Shooters Hill 147 H2
Shoreditch 7 F5
Shortlands 183 H6
Sidcup 168 C6
Silvertown 126 B2
Sipson 112 C5
Slade Green 150 D3
Soho 10 C4
Somers Town 4 C3
Southall 114 C2
South Beddington 210 D4
Southborough 200 E3
South Bromley 106 B5
South Croydon 211 H4
Southend 165 F6
Southfields 159 K3
Southgate 34 E3
South Hackney 86 E6
South Hampstead 83 F5
South Harrow 78 B1
South Hornchurch 93 F6
South Kensington 120 B5
South Lambeth 141 K1
South Norwood 180 E6
South Oxhey 27 F5
South Ruislip 77 H2
South Tottenham 68 A2
South Wimbledon 178 B1
South Woodford 52 E5
Spitalfields 13 J1
Spring Grove 135 J2
Spring Park 198 D6
Stamford Hill 68 B4
Stanmore 43 H1
Stanwell 152 A1
Stepney 104 E4
Stockwell 141 K4
Stoke Newington 68 B6
Stonehill Green 187 K2
Stoneleigh 207 H3
Strand 10 E5
Stratford 88 A5
Stratford Marsh 87 K6
Stratford New Town 88 A4
Strawberry Hill 155 J5
Streatham 179 K1
Streatham Hill 161 K3
Streatham Park 161 H6
Streatham Vale 179 G3
Stroud Green 67 G3
Sudbury 79 F3
Summerstown 160 C4
Sundridge 184 B2
Surbiton 190 D5
Sutton 208 E3
Swiss Cottage 83 H6
Sydenham 182 A1
Teddington 173 J2
Temple Hill 151 G5
Temple Mills 87 K3
Thames Ditton 190 B4
Thamesmead 109 G6
Thornton Heath 180 C6
Tokyngton 80 D4
Tolworth 191 H5
Tooting 178 E1
Tooting Graveney 178 C1
Tottenham 50 A5
Tottenham Hale 50 B6
Totteridge 32 D3
Totteridge Green 32 A3
Tufnell Park 84 C2
Tulse Hill 162 C3
Twickenham 155 K3
Underhill 32 E1
Upper Clapton 68 C5
Upper Edmonton 36 C6
Upper Elmers End 198 C2
Upper Holloway 66 C5
Upper Norwood 180 E4
Upper Shirley 212 E2
Upper Sydenham 163 H6
Upper Tooting 160 D5
Upper Walthamstow 70 A1
Upton 89 F5
Upton Park 89 G6
Vale of Health 83 H1
Vauxhall 121 K5
Waddon 195 K6
Walham Green 139 K2
Wallend 90 A6
Wallington 210 A3
Walthamstow 69 H1
Walworth 122 D6
Wandle Park 196 B6
Wandsworth 139 K5
Wanstead 71 F4
Wapping 123 J
Watford Heath 27 J2
Wealdstone 43 G6
Welling 148 C4
Welsh Harp 63 F5
Wembley 80 A2
Wembley Park 80 C
West Acton 98 C5
West Barnes 193 F
West Bedfont 152 C
Westbourne Green 100 E
West Brompton 120 A
West Drayton 112 A
West Dulwich 162 E
West Ealing 116 B
West Ewell 207 F
West Green 49 J
West Hampstead 82 E
West Harrow 60 C
West Heath 65 F
West Heath 128 E
West Hendon 63
West Hill 159 H
West Kensington 119 C
West Kilburn 100 C
Westminster 16 E
West Molesey 188 E
West Norwood 162 D
Weston Green 189
West Ruislip 58 A
West Wickham 199 C
Whetstone 33
Whitechapel 13
Whitton 155 H
Widmore 184 C
Willesden 81
Willesden Green 81
Wilmington 170
Wimbledon 177
Winchmore Hill 35
Wood End 94
Wood End Green 94
Woodford 53
Woodford Bridge 53
Woodford Green 52
Woodford Wells 39
Wood Green 49
Woodlands 135
Woodside 197
Woodside Park 32
Woolwich 127
Worcester Park 192
World's End 23
The Wrythe 194
Yeading 95

USING THE STREET INDEX

Street names are listed alphabetically. Each street name is followed by its postal town or area locality, the Postcode District, the page number, and the reference to the square in which the name is found.

Standard index entries are shown as follows:

1 Av *WOOL/PLUM* SE18.............. **127** G3

Street names and selected addresses not shown on the map due to scale restrictions are shown in the index with an asterisk:

Abbeville Ms *CLAP* SW4 * **141** J6

Entries in red indicate streets located within the London Congestion Zone. Refer to the map pages for the location of the Zone boundary.

GENERAL ABBREVIATIONS

ACC	ACCESS	CTYD	COURTYARD	HLS	HILLS
ALY	ALLEY	CUTT	CUTTINGS	HO	HOUSE
AP	APPROACH	CV	COVE	HOL	HOLLOW
AR	ARCADE	CYN	CANYON	HOSP	HOSPITAL
ASS	ASSOCIATION	DEPT	DEPARTMENT	HRB	HARBOUR
AV	AVENUE	DL	DALE	HTH	HEATH
BCH	BEACH	DM	DAM	HTS	HEIGHTS
BLDS	BUILDINGS	DR	DRIVE	HVN	HAVEN
BND	BEND	DRO	DROVE	HWY	HIGHWAY
BNK	BANK	DRY	DRIVEWAY	IMP	IMPERIAL
BR	BRIDGE	DWGS	DWELLINGS	IN	INLET
BRK	BROOK	E	EAST	IND EST	INDUSTRIAL ESTATE
BTM	BOTTOM	EMB	EMBANKMENT	INF	INFIRMARY
BUS	BUSINESS	EMBY	EMBASSY	INFO	INFORMATION
BVD	BOULEVARD	ESP	ESPLANADE	INT	INTERCHANGE
BY	BYPASS	EST	ESTATE	IS	ISLAND
CATH	CATHEDRAL	EX	EXCHANGE	JCT	JUNCTION
CEM	CEMETERY	EXPY	EXPRESSWAY	JTY	JETTY
CEN	CENTRE	EXT	EXTENSION	KG	KING
CFT	CROFT	F/O	FLYOVER	KNL	KNOLL
CH	CHURCH	FC	FOOTBALL CLUB	L	LAKE
CHA	CHASE	FK	FORK	LA	LANE
CHYD	CHURCHYARD	FLD	FIELD	LDG	LODGE
CIR	CIRCLE	FLDS	FIELDS	LGT	LIGHT
CIRC	CIRCUS	FLS	FALLS	LK	LOCK
CL	CLOSE	FM	FARM	LKS	LAKES
CLFS	CLIFFS	FT	FORT	LNDG	LANDING
CMP	CAMP	FTS	FLATS	LTL	LITTLE
CNR	CORNER	FY	FERRY	LWR	LOWER
CO	COUNTY	GA	GATE	MAG	MAGISTRATES'
COLL	COLLEGE	GAL	GALLERY	MAN	MANSIONS
COM	COMMON	GDN	GARDEN	MD	MEAD
COMM	COMMISSION	GDNS	GARDENS	MDW	MEADOWS
CON	CONVENT	GLD	GLADE	MEM	MEMORIAL
COT	COTTAGE	GLN	GLEN	MI	MILL
COTS	COTTAGES	GN	GREEN	MKT	MARKET
CP	CAPE	GND	GROUND	MKTS	MARKETS
CPS	COPSE	GRA	GRANGE	ML	MALL
CR	CREEK	GRG	GARAGE	MNR	MANOR
CREM	CREMATORIUM	GT	GREAT	MS	MEWS
CRS	CRESCENT	GTWY	GATEWAY	MSN	MISSION
CSWY	CAUSEWAY	GV	GROVE	MT	MOUNT
CT	COURT	HGR	HIGHER	MTN	MOUNTAIN
CTRL	CENTRAL	HL	HILL	MTS	MOUNTAINS
CTS	COURTS			MUS	MUSEUM

MWY	MOTORWAY	SE	SOUTH EAST
N	NORTH	SER	SERVICE AREA
NE	NORTH EAST	SH	SHORE
NW	NORTH WEST	SHOP	SHOPPING
O/P	OVERPASS	SKWY	SKYWAY
OFF	OFFICE	SMT	SUMMIT
ORCH	ORCHARD	SOC	SOCIETY
OV	OVAL	SP	SPUR
PAL	PALACE	SPR	SPRING
PAS	PASSAGE	SQ	SQUARE
PAV	PAVILION	ST	STREET
PDE	PARADE	STN	STATION
PH	PUBLIC HOUSE	STR	STREAM
PK	PARK	STRD	STRAND
PKWY	PARKWAY	SW	SOUTH WEST
PL	PLACE	TDG	TRADING
PLN	PLAIN	TER	TERRACE
PLNS	PLAINS	THWY	THROUGHWAY
PLZ	PLAZA	TNL	TUNNEL
POL	POLICE STATION	TOLL	TOLLWAY
PR	PRINCE	TPK	TURNPIKE
PREC	PRECINCT	TR	TRACK
PREP	PREPARATORY	TRL	TRAIL
PRIM	PRIMARY	TWR	TOWER
PROM	PROMENADE	U/P	UNDERPASS
PRS	PRINCESS	UNI	UNIVERSITY
PRT	PORT	UPR	UPPER
PT	POINT	V	VALE
PTH	PATH	VA	VALLEY
PZ	PIAZZA	VIAD	VIADUCT
QD	QUADRANT	VIL	VILLA
QU	QUEEN	VIS	VISTA
QY	QUAY	VLG	VILLAGE
R	RIVER	VLS	VILLAS
RBT	ROUNDABOUT	VW	VIEW
RD	ROAD	W	WEST
RDG	RIDGE	WD	WOOD
REP	REPUBLIC	WHF	WHARF
RES	RESERVOIR	WK	WALK
RFC	RUGBY FOOTBALL CLUB	WKS	WALKS
RI	RISE	WLS	WELLS
RP	RAMP	WY	WAY
RW	ROW	YD	YARD
S	SOUTH	YHA	YOUTH HOSTEL
SCH	SCHOOL		

POSTCODE TOWNS AND AREA ABBREVIATIONS

AR/ST	Abridge/Stapleford Abbotts	CHCR	Charing Cross	FSBYPK	Finsbury Park	LEW	Lewisham	ROM	Romford
ABYW	Abbey Wood	CHDH	Chadwell Heath	FSBYW	Finsbury west	LEY	Leyton	ROMW/RG	Romford west/Rush Green
ACT	Acton	CHEAM	Cheam	FSTGT	Forest Gate	LINN	Lincoln's Inn		
ALP/SUD	Alperton/Sudbury	CHEL	Chelsea	FSTH	Forest Hill	LOTH	Lothbury	RSEV	Rural Sevenoaks
ARCH	Archway	CHIG	Chigwell	FUL/PGN	Fulham/Parsons Green	LOU	Loughton	RSLP	Ruislip
ASHF	Ashford (Surrey)	CHING	Chingford	GDMY/SEVK	Goodmayes/Seven Kings	LSQ/SEVD	Leicester Square/Seven Dials	RSQ	Russell Square
BAL	Balham	CHSGTN	Chessington					RYLN/HDSTN	Rayners Lane/Headstone
BANK	Bank	CHST	Chislehurst	GFD/PVL	Greenford/Perivale	LVPST	Liverpool Street		
BAR	Barnet	CHSWK	Chiswick	GINN	Gray's Inn	MANHO	Mansion House	RYNPK	Raynes Park
BARB	Barbican	CITYW	City of London west	GLDGN	Golders Green	MBLAR	Marble Arch	SAND/SEL	Sanderstead/Selsdon
BARK	Barking	CLAP	Clapham	GNTH/NBYPK	Gants Hill/Newbury Park	MHST	Marylebone High Street	SCUP	Sidcup
BARK/HLT	Barking side/Hainault	CLAY	Clayhall			MLHL	Mill Hill	SDTCH	Shoreditch
		CLKNW	Clerkenwell	GNWCH	Greenwich	MNPK	Manor Park	SEVS/STOTM	Seven Sisters/South Tottenham
BARN	Barnes	CLPT	Clapton	GPK	Gidea Park	MON	Monument		
BAY/PAD	Bayswater/Paddington	CMBW	Camberwell	GTPST	Great Portland Street	MORT/ESHN	Mortlake/East Sheen	SHB	Shepherd's Bush
BECK	Beckenham	CONDST	Conduit Street	GWRST	Gower Street	MRDN	Morden	SKENS	South Kensington
BCTR	Becontree	COVGDN	Covent Garden	HACK	Hackney	MTCM	Mitcham	SNWD	South Norwood
BELMT	Belmont	CRICK	Cricklewood	HAMP	Hampstead	MUSWH	Muswell Hill	SOCK/AV	South Ockendon/Aveley
BELV	Belvedere	CROY/NA	Croydon/New Addington	HARH	Harold Hill	MV/WKIL	Maida Vale/West Kilburn		
BERM/RHTH	Bermondsey/Rotherhithe			HAYES	Hayes			SOHO/CST	Soho/Carnaby Street
		CRW	Collier Row	HBRY	Highbury	MYFR/PICC	Mayfair/Piccadilly	SOHO/SHAV	Soho/Shaftesbury Avenue
BETH	Bethnal Green	DAGE	Dagenham east	HCH	Hornchurch	MYFR/PKLN	Mayfair/Park Lane		
BFN/LL	Blackfen/Longlands	DAGW	Dagenham west	HCIRC	Holborn Circus	NFNCH/WDSPK	North Finchley/Woodside Park	SRTFD	Stratford
BGVA	Belgravia	DART	Dartford	HDN	Hendon			STAN	Stanmore
BKHH	Buckhurst Hill	DEN/HRF	Denham/Harefield	HDTCH	Houndsditch	NKENS	North Kensington	STBT	St Bart's
BKHTH/KID	Blackheath/Kidbrooke	DEPT	Deptford	HEST	Heston	NOXST/BSQ	New Oxford Street/Bloomsbury Square	STHGT/OAK	Southgate/Oakwood
		DUL	Dulwich	HGDN/ICK	Hillingdon/Ickenham			STHL	Southall
BLFR	Blackfriars	E/WMO/HCT	East & West Molesey/Hampton Court	HGT	Highgate	NRWD	Norwood	STHWK	Southwark
BMLY	Bromley			HHOL	High Holborn	NTGHL	Notting Hill	STJS	St James's
BMSBY	Bloomsbury	EA	Ealing	HMSMTH	Hammersmith	NTHLT	Northolt	STJSPK	St James's Park
BORE	Borehamwood	EBAR	East Barnet	HNHL	Herne Hill	NTHWD	Northwood	STJWD	St John's Wood
BOW	Bow	EBED/NFELT	East Bedfont/North Feltham	HNWL	Hanwell	NWCR	New Cross	STKPK	Stockley Park
BROCKY	Brockley			HOL/ALD	Holborn/Aldwych	NWDGN	Norwood Green	STLK	St Luke's
BRXN/ST	Brixton north/Stockwell	ECT	Earl's Court	HOLWY	Holloway	NWMAL	New Malden	STMC/STPC	St Mary Cray/St Paul's Cray
		ED	Edmonton	HOM	Homerton	OBST	Old Broad Street		
BRXS/STRHM	Brixton south/Streatham Hill	EDGW	Edgware	HOR/WEW	Horton/West Ewell	ORP	Orpington	STNW/STAM	Stoke Newington/Stamford Hill
BRYLDS	Berrylands	EDUL	East Dulwich	HPTN	Hampton	OXHEY	Oxhey		
BTFD	Brentford	EFNCH	East Finchley	HRW	Harrow	OXSTW	Oxford Street west	STP	St Paul's
BTSEA	Battersea	EHAM	East Ham	HSLW	Hounslow			STPAN	St Pancras
BUSH	Bushey	ELTH/MOT	Eltham/Mottingham	HSLWW	Hounslow west	PECK	Peckham	STRHM/NOR	Streatham/Norbury
BXLY	Bexley	EMB	Embankment	HTHAIR	Heathrow Airport	PEND	Ponders End	STWL/WRAY	Stanwell/Wraysbury
BXLYHN	Bexleyheath north	EMPK	Emerson Park	HYS/HAR	Hayes/Harlington	PGE/AN	Penge/Anerley	SUN	Sunbury
BXLYHS	Bexleyheath south	EN	Enfield	IL	Ilford	PIM	Pimlico	SURB	Surbiton
CAMTN	Camden Town	ENC/FH	Enfield Chase/Forty Hill	IS	Islington	PIN	Pinner	SUT	Sutton
CAN/RD	Canning Town/Royal Docks	ERITH	Erith	ISLW	Isleworth	PLMGR	Palmers Green	SWFD	South Woodford
		ERITHM	Erith Marshes	KENS	Kensington	PLSTW	Plaistow	SWLY	Swanley
CANST	Cannon Street station	ESH/CLAY	Esher/Claygate	KIL/WHAMP	Kilburn/West Hampstead	POP/IOD	Poplar/Isle of Dogs	SYD	Sydenham
						PUR	Purfleet	TEDD	Teddington
CAR	Carshalton	EW	Ewell	KTBR	Knightsbridge	PUR/KEN	Purley/Kenley	THDIT	Thames Ditton
CAT	Catford	FARR	Farringdon	KTN/HRWW/WS	Kenton/Harrow Weald/Wealdstone	PUT/ROE	Putney/Roehampton	THHTH	Thornton Heath
CAVSQ/HST	Cavendish Square/Harley Street	FBAR/BDGN	Friern Barnet/Bounds Green			RAIN	Rainham GE Lon	THMD	Thamesmead
		FELT	Feltham	KTTN	Kentish Town	RCH/KEW	Richmond/Kew	TOOT	Tooting
CDALE/KGS	Colindale/Kingsbury	FENCHST	Fenchurch Street	KUT/HW	Kingston upon Thames/Hampton Wick	RCHPK/HAM	Richmond Park/ham	TOTM	Tottenham
CEND/HSY/T	Crouch End/Hornsey/Turnpike Lane	FITZ	Fitzrovia			RDART	Rural Dartford	TPL/STR	Temple/Strand
		FLST/FETLN	Fleet Street/Fetter Lane	KUTN/CMB	Kingston upon Thames north/Coombe	REDBR	Redbridge	TRDG/WHET	Totteridge/Whetstone
CHARL	Charlton	FNCH	Finchley	LBTH	Lambeth	REGST	Regent Street	TWK	Twickenham
		FSBYE	Finsbury east	LEE/GVPK	Lee/Grove Park	RKW/CH/CXG	Rickmansworth/Chorleywood/Croxley Green	TWRH	Tower Hill
								UED	Upper Edmonton

UX/CGN .... Uxbridge/Colham Green
VX/NE .... Vauxhall/Nine Elms
WALTH .... Walthamstow
WALW .... Walworth
WAN .... Wanstead
WAND/EARL .... Wandsworth/Earlsfield
WAP .... Wapping
WAT .... Watford
WATW .... Watford west
WBLY .... Wembley
WBPTN .... West Brompton
WCHMH .... Winchmore Hill
WCHPL .... Whitechapel
WDGN .... Wood Green
WDR/YW .... West Drayton/Yiewsley
WEA .... West Ealing
WELL .... Welling
WEST .... Westminster
WESTW .... Westminster west
WFD .... Woodford
WHALL .... Whitehall
WHTN .... Whitton
WIM/MER .... Wimbledon/Merton
WKENS .... West Kensington
WLGTN .... Wallington
WLSDN .... Willesden
WNWD .... West Norwood
WOOL/PLUM .... Woolwich/Plumstead
WOT/HER .... Walton-on-Thames/Hersham
WPK .... Worcester Park
WWKM .... West Wickham
YEAD .... Yeading

Index - streets

1

1 Av *WOOL/PLUM* SE18 127 G3

A

Aaron Hill Rd *EHAM* E6 108 A4
Abberley Ms *BTSEA* SW11 141 G4
Abbess Cl *BRXS/STRHM* SW2 162 C3
Abbeville Ms *CLAP* SW4 * 141 J6
Abbeville Rd *CEND/HSY/T* N8 66 D1
CLAP SW4 161 H1
Abbey Av *ALP/SUD* HA0 98 A1
Abbey Cl *HYS/HAR* UB3 114 A1
NTHLT UB5 95 K2
ORP BR6 217 H2
PIN HA5 41 F6
ROM RM1 75 H3
Abbey Crs *BELV* DA17 129 H4
Abbeydale Rd *ALP/SUD* HA0 80 B6
Abbey Dr *TOOT* SW17 179 F1
Abbeyfield Cl *MTCM* CR4 178 D5
Abbeyfield Est
BERM/RHTH SE16 123 K4
Abbeyfield Rd
BERM/RHTH SE16 123 K4
Abbeyfields Cl *WLSDN* NW10 98 C2
Abbey Gdns *CHST* BR7 185 F4
HMSMTH W6 119 H6
STHWK SE1 123 H4
STJWD NW8 101 G1
Abbey Gv *ABYW* SE2 128 C4
Abbeyhill Rd *BFN/LL* DA15 168 D3
Abbey La *BECK* BR3 182 D3
SRTFD E15 106 A1
Abbey Ms *ISLW* TW7 136 C2
WALTH E17 69 J2
Abbey Mt *BELV* DA17 129 G5
Abbey Orchard St
WEST SW1P 16 D4
Abbey Pk *BECK* BR3 182 D3
Abbey Pl *DART* DA1 * 151 G6
Abbey Rd *BARK* IG11 90 B6
BELV DA17 128 E4
CROY/NA CR0 211 H1
EN EN1 24 A6
GNTH/NBYPK IG2 72 D2
SRTFD E15 106 B1
STJWD NW8 83 G6
WIM/MER SW19 178 B3
WLSDN NW10 98 D1
Abbey St *PLSTW* E13 106 E3
STHWK SE1 19 J4
Abbey Vw *MLHL* NW7 31 H5
Abbey Wk *E/WMO/HCT* KT8 173 G6
Abbey Wood Rd *ABYW* SE2 128 C4
Abbot Cl *RSLP* HA4 77 H1
Abbotsbury Cl *SRTFD* E15 106 A1
WKENS W14 119 H2
Abbotsbury Gdns *PIN* HA5 59 G3
Abbotsbury Ms *PECK* SE15 143 K4
Abbotsbury Rd *MRDN* SM4 194 A1
WKENS W14 119 H2
WWKM BR4 199 J6
Abbots Cl *STMC/STPC* BR5 201 H5
Abbots Dr *RYLN/HDSTN* HA2 60 A6
Abbotsford Av
SEVS/STOTM N15 67 J1
Abbotsford Gdns *WFD* IG8 52 E3
Abbotsford Rd
GDMY/SEVK IG3 73 G6
Abbots Gdns *EFNCH* N2 65 H1
Abbots Gn *CROY/NA* CR0 213 F4
Abbotshade Rd
BERM/RHTH SE16 * 124 A1
Abbotshall Av
STHGT/OAK N14 34 C5
Abbotshall Rd *CAT* SE6 165 G3
Abbotsleigh Cl *BELMT* SM2 209 F5
Abbotsleigh Rd
STRHM/NOR SW16 161 H6
Abbots Mnr *PIM* SW1V * 121 G5
Abbotsmede Cl *TWK* TW1 156 A4
Abbots Pk *BRXS/STRHM* SW2 162 B3
Abbot's Pl *KIL/WHAMP* NW6 83 F6
Abbots Rd *EDGW* HA8 45 F3
EHAM E6 89 H6
Abbots Ter *CEND/HSY/T* N8 66 E3
Abbotstone Rd
PUT/ROE SW15 139 F4
Abbot St *HACK* E8 86 B4
Abbots Wk *KENS* W8 * 120 A3
Abbots Wy *BECK* BR3 198 B2
Abbotswell Rd *BROCKY* SE4 144 C6
Abbotswood Cl *BELV* DA17 129 F3
Abbotswood Gdns *CLAY* IG5 53 K6
Abbotswood Rd *EDUL* SE22 143 F5
STRHM/NOR SW16 161 J5
Abbotswood Wy
HYS/HAR UB3 114 A1
Abbott Av *RYNPK* SW20 177 G5
Abbott Cl *HPTN* TW12 172 D2
NTHLT UB5 77 K4
Abbott Rd *POP/IOD* E14 106 A4
Abbotts Cl *IS* N1 * 85 J5
ROMW/RG RM7 56 D6
THMD SE28 109 J6
Abbotts Crs *CHING* E4 38 B6
ENC/FH EN2 23 H3
Abbotts Dr *ALP/SUD* HA0 61 H6
Abbotts Md
RCHPK/HAM TW10 * 156 D6
Abbotts Park Rd *LEY* E10 70 A4
Abbotts Rd *BAR* EN5 21 F5
CHEAM SM3 208 C2
MTCM CR4 195 H1
STHL UB1 114 D1
Abbott's Wk *BXLYHN* DA7 148 E1
Abchurch La *MANHO* EC4N 13 F5
Abdale Rd *SHB* W12 118 E1
Aberavon Rd *BOW* E3 105 G2
Abercairn Rd
STRHM/NOR SW16 179 H3
Aberconway Rd *MRDN* SM4 178 A6
Abercorn Cl *MLHL* NW7 46 C3
STJWD NW8 101 G2
Abercorn Crs
RYLN/HDSTN HA2 60 B5
Abercorn Dell *BUSH* WD23 28 C4
Abercorn Gdns *CHDH* RM6 73 H3
KTN/HRWW/WS HA3 61 K4
Abercorn Gv *RSLP* HA4 58 B1
Abercorn Ms
RCHPK/HAM TW10 137 G6
Abercorn Pl *STJWD* NW8 101 G2
Abercorn Rd *MLHL* NW7 46 C3
STAN HA7 43 J3
Abercorn Wk *STJWD* NW8 101 G2
Abercorn Wy *STHWK* SE1 123 H5
Abercrombie Dr *EN* EN1 24 C2
Abercrombie St *BTSEA* SW11 140 D3
Aberdare Cl *WWKM* BR4 199 F6
Aberdare Gdns
KIL/WHAMP NW6 83 F5
MLHL NW7 46 B3
Aberdare Rd *PEND* EN3 24 E5
Aberdeen Cots *STAN* HA7 * 43 J3
Aberdeen La *HBRY* N5 85 H3
Aberdeen Pde *UED* N18 * 50 D1
Aberdeen Pk *HBRY* N5 85 H3
Aberdeen Pl *BAY/PAD* W2 2 A7
Aberdeen Rd *CROY/NA* CR0 211 J2
HBRY N5 85 J2
KTN/HRWW/WS HA3 43 F5
UED N18 50 C1
WLSDN NW10 81 H3
Aberdeen Ter *BKHTH/KID* SE3 145 G3
Aberdour Rd *GDMY/SEVK* IG3 91 H1
Aberdour St *STHWK* SE1 19 G6
Aberfeldy St *POP/IOD* E14 106 A5
Aberford Gdns
WOOL/PLUM SE18 146 D2
Aberfoyle Rd
STRHM/NOR SW16 179 J3
Abergeldie Rd
LEE/GVPK SE12 166 A1
Abernethy Rd *LEW* SE13 145 H5
Abersham Rd *HACK* E8 86 B3
Abery St *WOOL/PLUM* SE18 127 K4
Abingdon Cl *STHWK* SE1 * 123 G5
WIM/MER SW19 178 B2
WPK KT4 207 K1
Abingdon Rd *FNCH* N3 47 G5
KENS W8 119 K3
STRHM/NOR SW16 179 K4
Abingdon St *WEST* SW1P 16 E3
Abingdon Vls *KENS* W8 119 K3
Abingdon Wy *ORP* BR6 217 H2
Abinger Av *BELMT* SM2 208 A6
Abinger Cl *BMLY* BR1 184 D6
CROY/NA CR0 214 A4
GDMY/SEVK IG3 91 G2
WLGTN SM6 210 E3
Abinger Dr *NRWD* SE19 180 D3
Abinger Gdns *ISLW* TW7 135 K4
Abinger Gv *DEPT* SE8 124 C6
Abinger Ms *MV/WKIL* W9 100 E3
Abinger Rd *CHSWK* W4 118 C3
Ablett St *BERM/RHTH* SE16 123 K5
Abney Park Ter
STNW/STAM N16 * 68 B6
Aboyne Dr *RYNPK* SW20 176 D5
Aboyne Rd *TOOT* SW17 160 B5
WLSDN NW10 81 G1
Abraham Cl *OXHEY* WD19 27 F6
Abridge Gdns *CRW* RM5 56 C2
Abridge Wy *BARK* IG11 109 H1
Abyssinia Cl *BTSEA* SW11 140 D5
Abyssinia Rd *BTSEA* SW11 * 140 D5
Acacia Av *BTFD* TW8 136 C1
HCH RM12 75 H6
HYS/HAR UB3 94 D5
RSLP HA4 58 E5
TOTM N17 49 K3
WBLY HA9 80 A3
Acacia Cl *DEPT* SE8 124 B4
STAN HA7 42 E2
STMC/STPC BR5 201 J2
Acacia Dr *CHEAM* SM3 193 J5
Acacia Gdns *STJWD* NW8 2 B2
WWKM BR4 199 F6
Acacia Gv *DUL* SE21 162 E4
NWMAL KT3 176 B6
Acacia Ms *WDR/YW* UB7 112 A6
Acacia Pl *STJWD* NW8 2 B2
Acacia Rd *ACT* W3 98 E6
BECK BR3 182 C6
ENC/FH EN2 23 K2
HPTN TW12 173 F2
MTCM CR4 179 F5
STJWD NW8 2 B2
STRHM/NOR SW16 179 K4
WALTH E17 69 G3
WAN E11 70 C6
WDGN N22 49 G4
The Acacias *EBAR* EN4 * 21 H6
Acacia Wy *BFN/LL* DA15 168 A2
Academia Wy *TOTM* N17 50 A2
Academy Fields Rd *GPK* RM2 75 K2
Academy Gdns *CROY/NA* CR0 197 G5
NTHLT UB5 95 H1
Academy Pl *ISLW* TW7 135 K1
WOOL/PLUM SE18 146 E2
Academy Rd
WOOL/PLUM SE18 146 E1
Acanthus Dr *STHWK* SE1 123 H5
Acanthus Rd *BTSEA* SW11 141 F4
Accommodation Rd
GLDGN NW11 64 D4
Ace Pde *CHSGTN* KT9 206 A1
Acer Av *YEAD* UB4 95 J3
Acfold Rd *FUL/PGN* SW6 140 A2
Achilles Cl *STHWK* SE1 123 H5
Achilles Rd *KIL/WHAMP* NW6 82 E3
Achilles St *NWCR* SE14 144 B1
Acklam Rd *NKENS* W10 100 D4
Acklington Dr
CDALE/KGS NW9 45 G4
Ackmar Rd *FUL/PGN* SW6 139 K2
Ackroyd Dr *BOW* E3 105 H4
Ackroyd Rd *FSTH* SE23 164 A2
Acland Cl *WOOL/PLUM* SE18 147 J1
Acland Crs *CMBW* SE5 142 E5
Acland Rd *CRICK* NW2 81 K4
Acle Cl *BARK/HLT* IG6 54 B4
Acock Gv *NTHLT* UB5 78 B2
Acol Crs *RSLP* HA4 77 F3
Acol Rd *KIL/WHAMP* NW6 83 F5
Acorn Cl *CHING* E4 51 K1
CHST BR7 185 H1
ENC/FH EN2 23 G2
HPTN TW12 173 G2
STAN HA7 43 H3
Acorn Gdns *ACT* W3 99 F4
NRWD SE19 181 G4
Acorn Gv *HYS/HAR* UB3 133 J1
RSLP HA4 76 D2
Acorn Pde *PECK* SE15 * 143 J1
Acorn Rd *DART* DA1 150 C6
Acorns Wy *ESH/CLAY* KT10 204 C3
Acorn Wy *BECK* BR3 199 F2
FSTH SE23 164 A5
ORP BR6 216 B2
Acre Dr *EDUL* SE22 143 H5
Acre La *BRXS/STRHM* SW2 142 A5
CAR SM5 210 A2
Acre Rd *DAGE* RM10 92 D5
KUTN/CMB KT2 175 F4
WIM/MER SW19 178 C2
Acre Wy *NTHWD* HA6 40 D4
Acris St *WAND/EARL* SW18 140 D6
Acton Cl *ED* N9 36 C4
Acton Hill Ms *ACT* W3 * 117 J1
Acton La *CHSWK* W4 117 K3
Acton Ms *HACK* E8 86 B6
Acton St *FSBYW* WC1X 5 G5
Acuba Rd *WAND/EARL* SW18 160 A4
Acworth Cl *ED* N9 36 E2
Acworth Pl *DART* DA1 * 171 F1
Ada Cl *FBAR/BDGN* N11 33 K5
Ada Gdns *POP/IOD* E14 106 B5
SRTFD E15 88 D6
Adair Cl *SNWD* SE25 181 J6
Adair Rd *NKENS* W10 100 C3
Adam Cl *CAT* SE6 164 C6
FSTH SE23 163 K4
Adam & Eve Ms *KENS* W8 119 K3
Adam Rd *CHING* E4 51 H2
Adams Cl *BRYLDS* KT5 191 G3
FNCH N3 46 E3
WBLY HA9 62 D6
Adams Ct *OBST* EC2N 13 F3
Adams Ms *TOOT* SW17 160 E4
WDGN N22 49 F3
Adamson Rd *CAN/RD* E16 106 E5
HAMP NW3 83 H5
Adamson Wy *BECK* BR3 199 F2
Adams Pl *HOLWY* N7 85 F3
Adamsrill Cl *EN* EN1 35 K1
Adamsrill Rd *SYD* SE26 164 A6
Adams Rd *BECK* BR3 198 B2
TOTM N17 49 K5
Adam's Rw *MYFR/PKLN* W1K 9 H6
Adam St *CHCR* WC2N 11 F6
Adams Wk *KUT/HW* KT1 175 F5
Adams Wy *CROY/NA* CR0 197 G3
Adam Wk *FUL/PGN* SW6 * 139 F1
Ada Pl *BETH* E2 86 C6
Adare Wk *STRHM/NOR* SW16 161 K4
Ada Rd *ALP/SUD* HA0 * 79 J1
CMBW SE5 143 F1
Ada St *HACK* E8 86 D6
Adderley Gdns *ELTH/MOT* SE9 167 F6
Adderley Gv *BTSEA* SW11 141 F6
Adderley Rd
KTN/HRWW/WS HA3 43 F4
Adderley St *POP/IOD* E14 106 A5
Addington Dr
NFNCH/WDSPK N12 47 H2
Addington Gv *SYD* SE26 164 B6
Addington Rd *BOW* E3 105 J2
CAN/RD E16 106 C3
CROY/NA CR0 196 B5
FSBYPK N4 67 G4
WWKM BR4 199 H6
WWKM BR4 214 A2
Addington Sq *CMBW* SE5 142 D1
Addington St *STHWK* SE1 17 H3
Addington Village Rd
CROY/NA CR0 213 H4
Addis Cl *PEND* EN3 25 F2
Addiscombe Av *CROY/NA* CR0 197 H4
Addiscombe Cl
KTN/HRWW/WS HA3 61 J2
Addiscombe Court Rd
CROY/NA CR0 197 F5
Addiscombe Gv
CROY/NA CR0 196 E6
Addiscombe Rd
CROY/NA CR0 197 F6
Addison Av *HSLW* TW3 135 H2
NTGHL W11 119 H1
STHGT/OAK N14 34 B1
Addison Bridge Pl
WKENS W14 119 J4
Addison Cl *NTHWD* HA6 40 E4
STMC/STPC BR5 201 H3
Addison Crs *WKENS* W14 119 H3
Addison Dr *LEE/GVPK* SE12 146 A6
Addison Gdns *BRYLDS* KT5 191 G1
WKENS W14 119 G3
Addison Gv *CHSWK* W4 118 B3
Addison Pl *NTGHL* W11 119 H1
Addison Rd *BARK/HLT* IG6 54 C4
HAYES BR2 200 C2
PEND EN3 24 E2
SNWD SE25 197 H1
TEDD TW11 174 C2
WALTH E17 69 K2
WAN E11 70 E3
WKENS W14 119 H2
Addison's Cl *CROY/NA* CR0 198 C6
Addison Ter *CHSWK* W4 * 117 K4
Addison Wy *GLDGN* NW11 64 D1
HYS/HAR UB3 94 E5
NTHWD HA6 40 D4
Addle Hl *BLKFR* EC4V 12 B5
Addle St *CITYW* EC2V * 12 D3
Adecroft Wy
E/WMO/HCT KT8 173 H6
Adela Av *NWMAL* KT3 192 E2
Adelaide Av *BROCKY* SE4 144 D5
Adelaide Cl *EN* EN1 24 A1
STAN HA7 29 G6
Adelaide Ct *HNWL* W7 116 A2
Adelaide Gdns *CHDH* RM6 74 A2
Adelaide Gv *SHB* W12 118 D1
Adelaide Rd *CHST* BR7 185 G1
HEST TW5 134 D2
IL IG1 72 B6
LEY E10 88 A1
NWDGN UB2 114 D4
PUT/ROE SW15 139 K6
RCH/KEW TW9 137 G5
STJWD NW8 83 H5
SURB KT6 191 F2
TEDD TW11 174 A2
WEA W13 116 B2
Adelaide St *CHCR* WC2N * 10 E6
Adelaide Ter *BTFD* TW8 * 116 E5
Adela St *NKENS* W10 100 C3
Adelina Gv *WCHPL* E1 104 E4
Adelina Ms *BAL* SW12 161 J3
Adeline Pl *RSQ* WC1B 10 D2
Adeliza Cl *BARK* IG11 90 C5
Adelphi Crs *HCH* RM12 75 J6
YEAD UB4 94 C2
Adelphi Ter *CHCR* WC2N 11 F6
Adelphi Wy *YEAD* UB4 94 D2
Adeney Cl *HMSMTH* W6 119 G6
Aden Gv *STNW/STAM* N16 85 K2
Adenmore Rd *CAT* SE6 164 D2
Aden Rd *IL* IG1 72 B4
PEND EN3 25 G5
Adhara Rd *NTHWD* HA6 40 E1
Adie Rd *HMSMTH* W6 119 F3
Adine Rd *PLSTW* E13 106 E3
Adler St *WCHPL* E1 104 C4
Adley St *CLPT* E5 87 G3
Adlington Cl *UED* N18 49 K1
Admaston Rd
WOOL/PLUM SE18 147 H1
Admiral Cl *STMC/STPC* BR5 202 E1
Admiral Ms *NKENS* W10 100 B3
Admiral Pl *BERM/RHTH* SE16 124 B1
Admirals Cl *SWFD* E18 71 F1
Admiral Seymour Rd
ELTH/MOT SE9 146 E5
Admiral's Ga *GNWCH* SE10 144 E2
Admiral Sq *WBPTN* SW10 * 140 B2
Admiral St *DEPT* SE8 144 D2
Admiral's Wk *HAMP* NW3 83 G1
Admirals Wy *POP/IOD* E14 124 D2
Admiralty Cl *DEPT* SE8 * 144 D2
WDR/YW UB7 112 B1
Admiralty Rd *TEDD* TW11 174 A2
Admiralty Wy *TEDD* TW11 * 174 A2
Admiral Wk *MV/WKIL* W9 100 E4
Adnams Wk *RAIN* RM13 93 J3
Adolf St *CAT* SE6 164 D6
Adolphus Rd *FSBYPK* N4 67 H6
Adolphus St *DEPT* SE8 144 C1
Adomar Rd *BCTR* RM8 91 K1
Adpar St *BAY/PAD* W2 8 A1
Adrian Cl *BAR* EN5 32 B1
Adrian Ms *WBPTN* SW10 120 A6
Adrienne Av *STHL* UB1 95 K3
Advance Rd *WNWD* SE27 162 D6
Advent Wy *UED* N18 51 F1
Adys Lawn *CRICK* NW2 * 81 K4
Adys Rd *PECK* SE15 143 G4
Aerodrome Rd
CDALE/KGS NW9 45 H6
Aerodrome Wy *HEST* TW5 114 B6
Aeroville *CDALE/KGS* NW9 45 G5
Affleck St *IS* N1 * 5 H3
Afghan Rd *BTSEA* SW11 140 D3
Aftab Ter *WCHPL* E1 * 104 D3
Agamemnon Rd
KIL/WHAMP NW6 82 D3
Agar Cl *SURB* KT6 191 G6
Agar Gv *CAMTN* NW1 84 D5
Agar St *CHCR* WC2N 10 E6
Agate Cl *CAN/RD* E16 107 H5
Agate Rd *HMSMTH* W6 119 F3
Agatha Cl *WAP* E1W 123 J
Agaton Rd *ELTH/MOT* SE9 167 H
Agave Rd *CRICK* NW2 82 A
Agdon St *FSBYE* EC1V 6 A
Agincourt Rd *HAMP* NW3 83 K
Agister Rd *CHIG* IG7 55 G
Agnes Av *IL* IG1 90 A
Agnes Cl *EHAM* E6 108 A
Agnesfield Cl
NFNCH/WDSPK N12 47 J
Agnes Gdns *BCTR* RM8 91 K
Agnes Riley Gdns *CLAP* SW4 * 161 H
Agnes Rd *ACT* W3 118 C
Agnes St *POP/IOD* E14 105 H
Agnew Rd *FSTH* SE23 164 B
Agricola Pl *EN* EN1 24 E
Aidan Cl *BCTR* RM8 92 A
Ailsa Av *TWK* TW1 136 B
Ailsa Rd *TWK* TW1 136 C
Ailsa St *POP/IOD* E14 106
Ainger Rd *HAMP* NW3 83
Ainsdale Cl *ORP* BR6 201
Ainsdale Crs *PIN* HA5 42
Ainsdale Dr *STHWK* SE1 123
Ainsdale Rd *EA* W5 97
OXHEY WD19 27
Ainsley Av *ROMW/RG* RM7 74
Ainsley Cl *ED* N9 36
Ainslie St *BETH* E2 104
Ainslie Wood Crs *CHING* E4 51
Ainslie Wood Gdns *CHING* E4 37
Ainslie Wood Rd *CHING* E4 51
Ainsty St *BERM/RHTH* SE16 * 123
Ainsworth Cl *CMBW* SE5 * 143
CRICK NW2 81
Ainsworth Rd *CROY/NA* CR0 196
HOM E9 86
Ainsworth Wy *STJWD* NW8 83
Aintree Av *EHAM* E6 89
Aintree Crs *BARK/HLT* IG6 54
Aintree Rd *GFD/PVL* UB6 97
Aintree St *FUL/PGN* SW6 139
Airco Cl *CDALE/KGS* NW9 44
Airdrie Cl *IS* N1 * 85
YEAD UB4 95
Airedale Av *CHSWK* W4 118
Airedale Av South
CHSWK W4 * 118
Airedale Rd *BAL* SW12 160
EA W5 116
Airfield Wy *HCH* RM12 93
Airlie Gdns *IL* IG1 72
KENS W8 119
Air St *REGST* W1B 10
Airthrie Rd *GDMY/SEVK* IG3 73
Aisgill Av *WKENS* W14 119
Aisher Rd *THMD* SE28 109
Aislibie Rd *LEE/GVPK* SE12 145
Aiten Pl *HMSMTH* W6 118
Aitken Cl *HACK* E8 86
MTCM CR4 194
Aitken Rd *BAR* EN5 20
CAT SE6 164
Aitman Dr *BTFD* TW8 * 117
Ajax Av *CDALE/KGS* NW9 45
Ajax Rd *KIL/WHAMP* NW6 82
Akabusi Cl *CROY/NA* CR0 197
Akehurst St *PUT/ROE* SW15 158
Akenside Rd *HAMP* NW3 83
Akerman Rd *BRXN/ST* SW9 142
SURB KT6 190
Alabama St
WOOL/PLUM SE18 147
Alacross Rd *EA* W5 116
Alandale Dr *PIN* HA5 41
Alander Ms *WALTH* E17 69
Alan Dr *BAR* EN5 32
Alan Gdns *ROMW/RG* RM7 74
Alan Hocken Wy *SRTFD* E15 106
Alan Rd *WIM/MER* SW19 177
Alaska St *STHWK* SE1 17
Alba Cl *YEAD* UB4 95
Albacore Crs *LEW* SE13 164
Alba Gdns *GLDGN* NW11 64
Albain Crs *ASHF* TW15 15
Albany Cl *BUSH* WD23 2
BXLY DA5 16
ESH/CLAY KT10 20
MORT/ESHN SW14 13
SEVS/STOTM N15 6
Albany Cots *HNWL* W7 * 11
Albany Ctyd *MYFR/PICC* W1J 1
Albany Crs *EDGW* HA8 4
ESH/CLAY KT10 20
Albany Ms *BMLY* BR1 18

CMBW SE5 122 D6
IS N1 85 G5
KUTN/CMB KT2 * 174 E2
SUT SM1 209 F3
Albany Pde BTFD TW8 * 117 F6
PEND EN3 25 F1
Albany Pk PEND EN3 * 25 F1
Albany Park Av PEND EN3 24 E2
Albany Park Rd
KUTN/CMB KT2 174 E2
Albany Pl BTFD TW8 116 E6
Albany Rd BELV DA17 129 G6
BTFD TW8 116 E6
BXLY DA5 168 D2
CHDH RM6 74 B3
CHST BR7 185 G1
FSBYPK N4 67 F3
HCH RM12 75 J5
LEY E10 69 J4
MNPK E12 89 H2
NWMAL KT3 192 A1
RCHPK/HAM TW10 * 137 G6
UED N18 50 D1
WALTH E17 69 G3
WALW SE17 122 E6
WEA W13 97 H6
WIM/MER SW19 178 A1
Albany Rw EFNCH N2 * 65 J1
Albany St CAMTN NW1 3 K4
Albany Ter
RCHPK/HAM TW10 * 137 G6
The Albany KUTN/CMB KT2 174 E2
Albany Vw BKHH IG9 38 E3
Alba Pl NTGHL W11 100 D5
Albatross Cl EHAM E6 107 K3
Albatross St
WOOL/PLUM SE18 147 K1
Albemarle Ap
GNTH/NBYPK IG2 72 B3
Albemarle Av WHTN TW2 154 E3
Albemarle Gdns
GNTH/NBYPK IG2 72 B3
NWMAL KT3 192 A1
Albemarle Pk BECK BR3 * 182 E4
STAN HA7 43 J1
Albemarle Rd BECK BR3 182 E4
EBAR EN4 33 J2
Albemarle St CONDST W1S 10 A6
Albemarle Wy FSBYE EC1V 6 A7
Alberon Gdns GLDGN NW11 64 D1
Alberta Av SUT SM1 208 C2
Alberta Est WALW SE17 122 C5
Alberta Rd EN EN1 36 B1
Alberta St WALW SE17 122 C5
Albert Av CHING E4 37 J6
VX/NE SW8 142 A1
Albert Basin Wy CAN/RD E16 108 C6
Albert Br BTSEA SW11 140 D1
Albert Bridge Ga BTSEA SW11 140 E1
Albert Bridge Rd BTSEA SW11 140 D1
Albert Carr Gdns
STRHM/NOR SW16 179 K1
Albert Cl HOM E9 86 D6
WDGN N22 48 D4
Albert Cots WCHPL E1 * 104 C4
Albert Crs CHING E4 37 J6
Albert Dr WIM/MER SW19 159 H4
Albert Emb STHWK SE1 121 K5
Albert Gdns WCHPL E1 105 F5
Albert Ga KTBR SW1X 15 F2
Albert Gv RYNPK SW20 177 G4
Albert Ms BROCKY SE4 * 144 C5
FSBYPK N4 * 67 F5
KENS W8 120 B3
POP/IOD E14 * 105 G6
Albert Pl FNCH N3 46 E4
KENS W8 120 A2
Albert Rd BCTR RM8 74 B5
BELV DA17 129 G5
BKHH IG9 39 H4
BXLY DA5 169 H1
CAN/RD E16 126 D1
EA W5 97 H3
EBAR EN4 21 G5
ELTH/MOT SE9 166 D5
FSBYPK N4 67 F5
HAYES BR2 200 C2
HDN NW4 64 B1
HPTN TW12 173 H1
HSLW TW3 135 F5
HYS/HAR UB3 113 H3
IL IG1 90 C1
KIL/WHAMP NW6 100 D1
KUT/HW KT1 175 G5
LEY E10 70 A6
MLHL NW7 45 H1
MTCM CR4 178 E6
NWDGN UB2 114 C3
NWMAL KT3 192 C1
ORP BR6 217 G3
PGE/AN SE20 182 A3
RCHPK/HAM TW10 137 F6
ROM RM1 75 H3
RYLN/HDSTN HA2 42 C6
SEVS/STOTM N15 68 A3
SNWD SE25 197 J1
STMC/STPC BR5 202 C3
SUT SM1 209 H3
SWFD E18 53 F6
TEDD TW11 174 A2
TWK TW1 156 A3
WALTH E17 69 J2
WDGN N22 48 D4
WDR/YW UB7 112 B1
Albert Sq SRTFD E15 88 C3
VX/NE SW8 142 A1
Albert St CAMTN NW1 3 K1
NFNCH/WDSPK N12 47 G1
Albert Ter CAMTN NW1 84 A6
EA W5 * 97 H3
WLSDN NW10 * 81 F6
Albert Wy PECK SE15 143 J1
Albion Av MUSWH N10 48 A4
VX/NE SW8 141 J3
Albion Cl BAY/PAD W2 8 D5
ROMW/RG RM7 75 F3
Albion Dr HACK E8 86 B5
Albion Est BERM/RHTH SE16 * 123 K2
Albion Ga BAY/PAD W2 8 D5
Albion Gv STNW/STAM N16 86 A2
Albion Ms BAY/PAD W2 8 D4
HMSMTH W6 118 E4
IS N1 * 85 G6
Albion Pl FARR EC1M 12 A1
HMSMTH W6 118 E4
SNWD SE25 181 H6
Albion Riverside BTSEA SW11 140 D1
Albion Rd BELMT SM2 209 H4
HSLW TW3 135 F5
HYS/HAR UB3 94 C5
KUTN/CMB KT2 175 K4
STNW/STAM N16 85 K3
TOTM N17 50 B5
WALTH E17 52 A6
WHTN TW2 155 K3
Albion Sq HACK E8 86 B5
Albion St BAY/PAD W2 8 D4
BERM/RHTH SE16 123 K2
CROY/NA CR0 196 C5
Albion Ter CHING E4 * 25 K5
HACK E8 86 B5
Albion Villas Rd SYD SE26 163 K5
Albion Wk IS N1 5 F3
Albion Wy LEW SE13 145 F5
STBT EC1A 12 C2
WBLY HA9 80 C1
Albion Yd IS N1 5 F3
Albrighton Rd EDUL SE22 143 F4
Albuhera Cl ENC/FH EN2 23 G2
Albury Av BELMT SM2 208 A6
ISLW TW7 136 A1
Albury Cl HOR/WEW KT19 206 D6
HPTN TW12 173 F2
Albury Dr PIN HA5 41 G4
Albury Ms MNPK E12 71 G5
Albury Rd CHSGTN KT9 206 A3
Albury St DEPT SE8 124 D6
Albyfield BMLY BR1 184 E6
Albyn Rd DEPT SE8 144 D2
Alcester Crs CLPT E5 68 D6
Alcester Rd WLGTN SM6 210 B2
Alcock Cl WLGTN SM6 210 D5
Alcock Rd HEST TW5 134 C1
Alconbury Rd CLPT E5 68 C6
Alcorn Cl CHEAM SM3 193 K6
Alcott Cl HNWL W7 97 F4
Aldborough Rd DAGE RM10 92 E4
Aldborough Rd North
GNTH/NBYPK IG2 73 F2
Aldborough Rd South
GDMY/SEVK IG3 72 E5
Aldbourne Rd SHB W12 118 C1
Aldbridge St WALW SE17 123 F5
Aldburgh Ms MHST W1U 9 H3
Aldbury Av WBLY HA9 80 D5
Aldbury Ms ED N9 35 K2
Aldebert Ter VX/NE SW8 142 A1
Aldeburgh Pl WFD IG8 38 E6
Alden Av SRTFD E15 106 D2
Aldenham Rd OXHEY WD19 27 H1
Aldenham St CAMTN NW1 4 B3
Alden Md PIN HA5 * 42 A3
Aldensley Rd HMSMTH W6 118 E3
Alderbrook Rd BAL SW12 161 G1
Alderbury Rd BARN SW13 118 D6
Alder Cl PECK SE15 123 G6
Alder Gv CRICK NW2 63 J6
Alderholt Wy PECK SE15 * 143 F1
Alderman Av BARK IG11 109 G2
Aldermanbury CITYW EC2V * 12 D3
Aldermanbury Sq
CITYW EC2V 12 D2
Alderman Judge Ml
KUT/HW KT1 * 175 F5
Alderman's Hl PLMGR N13 34 E6
Aldermary Rd BMLY BR1 183 K4
Aldermoor Rd CAT SE6 164 C5
Alderney Av HEST TW5 135 G1
Alderney Gdns NTHLT UB5 77 K5
Alderney Ms STHWK SE1 18 E4
Alderney Rd ERITH DA8 150 D1
WCHPL E1 105 F3
Alderney St PIM SW1V 15 J7
Alder Rd MORT/ESHN SW14 138 A4
SCUP DA14 167 K5
Alders Av WFD IG8 52 C2
Aldersbrook Av EN EN1 24 A3
Aldersbrook Dr
KUTN/CMB KT2 175 G2
Aldersbrook La MNPK E12 89 K1
Aldersbrook Rd MNPK E12 71 G6
Alders Cl EA W5 116 E3
EDGW HA8 44 E1
WAN E11 71 F6
Aldersey Gdns BARK IG11 90 D4
Aldersford Cl BROCKY SE4 144 A5
Aldersgate St CITYW EC2V 12 C3
STBT EC1A 12 C1
Aldersgrove E/WMO/HCT KT8 189 J2
Aldersgrove Av
ELTH/MOT SE9 166 B5
Aldershot Rd
KIL/WHAMP NW6 82 D6
Aldershot Ter
WOOL/PLUM SE18 * 147 F1
Aldersmead Av CROY/NA CR0 198 A3
Aldersmead Rd BECK BR3 182 B3
Alderson Pl NWDGN UB2 115 H1
Alderson St NKENS W10 100 C3
Alders Rd EDGW HA8 44 E1
The Alders FELT TW13 172 D1
HEST TW5 114 E6
STRHM/NOR SW16 * 161 H6
WCHMH N21 35 G1
WWKM BR4 198 E5
Alderton Cl WLSDN NW10 81 F1
Alderton Crs HDN NW4 63 K2
Alderton Rd CROY/NA CR0 197 G4
HNHL SE24 142 D4
Alderton Wy HDN NW4 63 K2
Alderville Rd FUL/PGN SW6 139 J3
Alderwick Dr HSLW TW3 135 J4
Alderwood Ms EBAR EN4 21 G1
Alderwood Rd ELTH/MOT SE9 167 J1
Aldford St MYFR/PKLN W1K 9 G7
Aldgate FENCHST EC3M 13 H4
Aldgate Barrs WCHPL E1 * 13 K3
Aldgate High St TWRH EC3N 13 J4
Aldine St SHB W12 119 F2
Aldingham Gdns HCH RM12 93 J3
Aldington Cl CHDH RM6 73 J4
Aldington Rd CHARL SE7 126 C3
Aldis Ms TOOT SW17 178 D1
Aldis St TOOT SW17 178 D1
Aldred Rd KIL/WHAMP NW6 82 E3
Aldren Rd TOOT SW17 160 B5
Aldrich Crs CROY/NA CR0 214 A6
Aldriche Wy CHING E4 52 A2
Aldrich Gdns CHEAM SM3 208 D1
Aldrich Ter WAND/EARL SW18 160 B4
Aldridge Av EDGW HA8 30 D5
PEND EN3 25 J1
RSLP HA4 59 G6
STAN HA7 44 A4
Aldridge Ri NWMAL KT3 192 B4
Aldridge Road Vls
NTGHL W11 100 D4
Aldridge Wk STHGT/OAK N14 34 E2
Aldrington Rd
STRHM/NOR SW16 179 H1
Aldsworth Cl MV/WKIL W9 101 F3
Aldwick Cl ELTH/MOT SE9 167 J5
Aldwick Rd CROY/NA CR0 211 F1
Aldworth Gv LEW SE13 165 F1
Aldworth Rd SRTFD E15 88 C5
Aldwych HOL/ALD WC2B 11 G4
Aldwych Av BARK/HLT IG6 72 C1
Aldwych Cl HCH RM12 75 J6
Alers Rd BXLYHS DA6 148 E6
Alesia Cl WDGN N22 48 E3
Alestan Beck Rd CAN/RD E16 107 H5
Alexander Av WLSDN NW10 81 K5
Alexander Cl BFN/LL DA15 147 K6
EBAR EN4 21 H5
NWDGN UB2 115 H1
WHTN TW2 155 K4
Alexander Evans Ms
FSTH SE23 164 A4
Alexander Ms BAY/PAD W2 101 F5
Alexander Pl SKENS SW7 14 C6
Alexander Rd ARCH N19 84 E1
BXLYHN DA7 148 E3
CHST BR7 185 G2
Alexander Sq CHEL SW3 14 C6
Alexander St BAY/PAD W2 100 E5
Alexander Ter ABYW SE2 * 128 C5
Alexandra DEPT SE8 124 C6
Alexandra Av BTSEA SW11 * 141 F2
RYLN/HDSTN HA2 59 K5
STHL UB1 95 K6
SUT SM1 208 E1
WDGN N22 48 D4
Alexandra Cl
RYLN/HDSTN HA2 78 A1
Alexandra Cots NWCR SE14 144 C2
Alexandra Crs BMLY BR1 183 J2
Alexandra Dr BRYLDS KT5 191 H4
NRWD SE19 181 F1
Alexandra Gdns CAR SM5 210 A6
HSLW TW3 135 G3
MUSWH N10 66 B1
Alexandra Ga SKENS SW7 14 A2
Alexandra Gv FSBYPK N4 67 H5
NFNCH/WDSPK N12 47 F1
Alexandra Ms EFNCH N2 47 K6
Alexandra Palace Wy
CEND/HSY/T N8 66 C1
MUSWH N10 48 C6
Alexandra Pde
RYLN/HDSTN HA2 * 78 B2
Alexandra Park Rd
MUSWH N10 48 B5
Alexandra Pl SNWD SE25 196 E2
STJWD NW8 83 G6
Alexandra Rd BTFD TW8 * 116 E6
CEND/HSY/T N8 49 G6
CHDH RM6 73 K3
CHSWK W4 118 A2
CROY/NA CR0 197 F5
ED N9 * 36 D2
EHAM E6 108 A2
ERITH DA8 130 C6
HDN NW4 64 B1
HSLW TW3 135 G3
KUTN/CMB KT2 175 H3
LEY E10 88 A1
MORT/ESHN SW14 138 A4
MTCM CR4 178 D3
MUSWH N10 48 B4
PEND EN3 25 F5
PGE/AN SE20 182 A2
RAIN RM13 93 H6
RCH/KEW TW9 137 G3
ROM RM1 75 H3
SEVS/STOTM N15 67 K2
STJWD NW8 83 G5
SWFD E18 53 F6
THDIT KT7 190 A2
TWK TW1 156 D1
WALTH E17 69 H3
WIM/MER SW19 177 K1
Alexandra Sq MRDN SM4 193 K2
Alexandra St CAN/RD E16 106 E4
NWCR SE14 144 B1
Alexandria Rd WEA W13 97 G6
Alexis St BERM/RHTH SE16 123 H4
Alfearn Rd CLPT E5 86 E2
Alford Gn CROY/NA CR0 214 B4
Alford Pl IS N1 * 6 D3
Alford Rd ERITH DA8 129 K5
Alfoxton Av SEVS/STOTM N15 67 H2
Alfreda St BTSEA SW11 141 G2
Alfred Cl CHSWK W4 118 A4
Alfred Gdns STHL UB1 95 J6
Alfred Ms GWRST WC1E 10 C1
Alfred Pl GWRST WC1E 10 C1
Alfred Rd ACT W3 117 K1
BAY/PAD W2 100 E4
BELV DA17 129 G5
BKHH IG9 39 H4
FELT TW13 154 B3
KUT/HW KT1 175 F6
SNWD SE25 197 H2
SRTFD E15 88 D3
SUT SM1 209 G3
Alfred's Gdns BARK IG11 108 E1
Alfred St BOW E3 105 H2
Alfred's Way (East Ham & Barking By-Pass)
BARK IG11 108 D1
Alfred Vls WALTH E17 * 70 A1
Alfreton Cl WIM/MER SW19 159 G5
Alfriston BRYLDS KT5 191 G3
Alfriston Av CROY/NA CR0 195 K4
RYLN/HDSTN HA2 60 A3
Alfriston Cl BRYLDS KT5 191 G3
Alfriston Rd BTSEA SW11 140 E6
Algar Cl STAN HA7 43 F1
Algar Rd ISLW TW7 136 B4
Algarve Rd WAND/EARL SW18 160 A3
Algernon Rd HDN NW4 63 J3
KIL/WHAMP NW6 82 E6
LEW SE13 144 E4
Algiers Rd LEW SE13 144 D5
Alguin Ct STAN HA7 * 43 J2
Alibon Gdns DAGE RM10 92 C3
Alibon Rd DAGE RM10 92 C3
Alice La BOW E3 87 H6
Alice St STHWK SE1 19 G5
Alice Thompson Cl
LEE/GVPK SE12 166 B4
Alice Walker Cl HNHL SE24 * 142 C5
Alice Wy HSLW TW3 135 G5
Alicia Av KTN/HRWW/WS HA3 61 H1
Alicia Cl KTN/HRWW/WS HA3 61 J1
Alicia Gdns
KTN/HRWW/WS HA3 61 H1
Alie St WCHPL E1 13 K4
Alington Crs CDALE/KGS NW9 62 E5
Alington Gv WLGTN SM6 210 D6
Alison Cl CROY/NA CR0 198 A5
EHAM E6 108 A5
Aliwal Ms BTSEA SW11 * 140 D5
Aliwal Rd BTSEA SW11 140 D5
Alkerden Rd CHSWK W4 118 B5
Alkham Rd STNW/STAM N16 68 B6
Allan Barclay Cl
SEVS/STOTM N15 68 B3
Allan Cl NWMAL KT3 192 A2
Allandale Av FNCH N3 46 C6
Allandale Pl ORP BR6 217 K1
Allandale Rd EMPK RM11 75 H4
Allan Wy ACT W3 98 E4
Allard Cl STMC/STPC BR5 202 D4
Allard Crs BUSH WD23 28 C4
Allardyce St CLAP SW4 142 A5
Allbrook Cl TEDD TW11 173 K1
Allcot Cl EBED/NFELT TW14 153 J3
Allcroft Rd KTTN NW5 84 A4
Allder Wy SAND/SEL CR2 211 H5
Allenby Av SAND/SEL CR2 211 J6
Allenby Cl GFD/PVL UB6 96 A2
Allenby Rd FSTH SE23 164 B5
STHL UB1 96 A5
WOOL/PLUM SE18 127 H3
Allen Cl MTCM CR4 179 G4
SUN TW16 172 A4
Allendale Av STHL UB1 96 A5
Allendale Cl CMBW SE5 142 E3
SYD SE26 182 A1
Allendale Rd GFD/PVL UB6 79 H4
Allen Edwards Dr VX/NE SW8 141 K2
Allen Rd BECK BR3 182 A5
BOW E3 105 H1
CROY/NA CR0 196 A4
STNW/STAM N16 86 A2
SUN TW16 172 A4
Allensbury Pl CAMTN NW1 84 D5
Allens Rd PEND EN3 24 E6
Allen St KENS W8 119 K3
Allenswood Rd
ELTH/MOT SE9 146 D4
Allerford Ct HRW HA1 60 B2
Allerford Rd CAT SE6 164 E6
Allerton Rd STNW/STAM N16 67 J6
Allerton St IS N1 7 F3
Allestree Rd FUL/PGN SW6 139 H1
Alleyn Crs DUL SE21 162 E4
Alleyndale Rd BCTR RM8 73 J6
Alleyn Pk DUL SE21 162 E4
NWDGN UB2 114 E5
Alleyn Rd DUL SE21 162 E5
Allfarthing La
WAND/EARL SW18 160 B1
Allgood Cl MRDN SM4 193 G3
Allgood St BETH E2 7 K3
Allhallows La CANST EC4R 12 E6
Allhallows Rd EHAM E6 107 J5
All Hallows Rd TOTM N17 50 A4
Alliance Cl ALP/SUD HA0 79 K2
HSLWW TW4 134 E6
Alliance Rd ACT W3 98 D3
PLSTW E13 107 G3
WOOL/PLUM SE18 128 B6
Allied Wy ACT W3 * 118 B2
Allingham Cl HNWL W7 97 F6
Allingham St IS N1 * 6 C2
Allington Av TOTM N17 50 A2
Allington Cl GFD/PVL UB6 78 C5
WIM/MER SW19 177 G1
Allington Rd HDN NW4 63 K2
NKENS W10 100 C2
ORP BR6 201 K5
RYLN/HDSTN HA2 60 C2
Allington St BGVA SW1W 15 K5
WESTW SW1E 16 A5
Allison Cl GNWCH SE10 145 F2
Allison Gv DUL SE21 163 F3
Allison Rd ACT W3 98 E5
CEND/HSY/T N8 67 G2
Allitsen Rd STJWD NW8 2 C3
Allnutt Wy CLAP SW4 141 J6
Alloa Rd DEPT SE8 124 A5
GDMY/SEVK IG3 73 H6
Allonby Gdns WBLY HA9 61 J5
Alloway Rd BOW E3 105 G2
Allport Ms WCHPL E1 * 104 E4
All Saints' Cl ED N9 36 B4
All Saints Dr BKHTH/KID SE3 145 J3
All Saints Ms STAN HA7 42 E2
All Saints Pas
WAND/EARL SW18 * 139 K6
All Saints Rd SUT SM1 209 F1
WIM/MER SW19 178 B3
All Saints' Rd ACT W3 117 K3
NTGHL W11 100 D4
All Saints St IS N1 5 G2
Allsop Pl CAMTN NW1 3 F7
All Souls' Av WLSDN NW10 99 K1
All Souls' Pl REGST W1B 9 K2
Allum Wy TRDG/WHET N20 33 G3
Allwood Cl SYD SE26 164 A6
Alma Av CHING E4 52 A3
Almack Rd CLPT E5 86 E2
Alma Cl MUSWH N10 * 48 B4
Alma Ct RYLN/HDSTN HA2 * 60 D6
Alma Crs SUT SM1 208 C3
Alma Gv STHWK SE1 19 K7
Alma Pl NRWD SE19 181 G3
THHTH CR7 196 B2
WLSDN NW10 99 K2
Alma Rd BFN/LL DA15 168 B5
CAR SM5 209 J3
ESH/CLAY KT10 189 K5
MUSWH N10 48 A3
PEND EN3 25 G6
STHL UB1 95 J6
STMC/STPC BR5 202 E6
WAND/EARL SW18 140 B6
Alma Rw
KTN/HRWW/WS HA3 * 42 D4
Alma Sq STJWD NW8 101 G2
Alma St KTTN NW5 84 B4
SRTFD E15 88 B4
Alma Ter BOW E3 87 H6
KENS W8 * 119 K3
WAND/EARL SW18 160 C2
Almeida St IS N1 85 H6
Almeric Rd BTSEA SW11 140 E5
Almer Rd RYNPK SW20 176 D3
Almington St FSBYPK N4 * 66 E5
Almond Av CAR SM5 194 E6
EA W5 117 F3
WDR/YW UB7 112 D3
Almond Cl FELT TW13 153 K3
HAYES BR2 201 F4
HYS/HAR UB3 94 C6
PECK SE15 143 H3
RSLP HA4 76 D1
Almond Gv BTFD TW8 136 C1
Almond Rd BERM/RHTH SE16 123 J4
TOTM N17 50 C3
Almonds Av BKHH IG9 38 E4
Almond Wy HAYES BR2 201 F4
MTCM CR4 195 J2
RYLN/HDSTN HA2 42 B5
Almorah Rd HEST TW5 134 C2
IS N1 85 K5
Almshouse La CHSGTN KT9 205 J6
Alnwick Gv MRDN SM4 194 A1
Alnwick Rd CAN/RD E16 107 G5
LEE/GVPK SE12 166 A2
Alnwick Ter LEE/GVPK SE12 166 A2
Alperton La ALP/SUD HA0 97 K2
Alperton St NKENS W10 100 C3
Alphabet Gdns CAR SM5 194 C3
Alpha Cl CAMTN NW1 2 D6
Alpha Est HYS/HAR UB3 * 113 H2
Alpha Gv POP/IOD E14 124 D2
Alpha Pl CHEL SW3 120 D6
KIL/WHAMP NW6 100 E1
MRDN SM4 * 193 G4
Alpha Rd BRYLDS KT5 191 G3
CHING E4 37 J5
CROY/NA CR0 197 F5
NWCR SE14 144 C2
PEND EN3 25 G5
TEDD TW11 173 J1
UED N18 50 C2
Alpha St PECK SE15 143 H3
Alphea Cl WIM/MER SW19 178 D3
Alpine Av BRYLDS KT5 191 K6
Alpine Cl CROY/NA CR0 212 A1
Alpine Copse BMLY BR1 185 F5
Alpine Gv HOM E9 86 E5
Alpine Rd BERM/RHTH SE16 123 K4
LEY E10 69 K6
Alpine Vw CAR SM5 209 J3
Alpine Wk BUSH WD23 28 E4
Alpine Wy EHAM E6 108 A4
Alric Av NWMAL KT3 176 B6
WLSDN NW10 81 F5
Alroy Rd FSBYPK N4 67 G4
Alsace Rd WALW SE17 123 F5
Alscot Rd STHWK SE1 19 K5
Alscot Wy STHWK SE1 19 J6
Alsike Rd ERITHM DA18 128 E3
Alsom Av WPK KT4 207 H2
Alston Cl SURB KT6 190 C4
Alston Rd BAR EN5 20 C4
TOOT SW17 160 C6
UED N18 50 D1
Altair Cl TOTM N17 50 B2
Altair Wy NTHWD HA6 40 D1
Altash Wy ELTH/MOT SE9 166 E4
Altenburg Av WEA W13 116 C3
Altenburg Gdns BTSEA SW11 140 E5
Alt Gv WIM/MER SW19 177 J3
Altham Ct RYLN/HDSTN HA2 * 42 B4
Altham Gdns OXHEY WD19 27 H6
Altham Rd PIN HA5 41 J3
Althea St FUL/PGN SW6 140 A3
Althorne Gdns SWFD E18 70 D1
Althorne Wy DAGE RM10 74 C6
Althorp Cl BAR EN5 31 J2
Althorpe Rd HRW HA1 * 60 C2
Althorp Rd TOOT SW17 160 E3
Altmore Av EHAM E6 89 K5
Alton Av STAN HA7 43 F3
Alton Cl BXLY DA5 169 F3
ISLW TW7 136 A3
Alton Gdns BECK BR3 182 D3
WHTN TW2 155 J1
Alton Rd CROY/NA CR0 211 G1
PUT/ROE SW15 158 D3
RCH/KEW TW9 137 F5
TOTM N17 49 K6
Alton St POP/IOD E14 105 K4
Altyre Cl BECK BR3 198 C2
Altyre Rd CROY/NA CR0 196 E6
Altyre Wy BECK BR3 198 C2
Alvanley Gdns
KIL/WHAMP NW6 83 F3
Alva Wy OXHEY WD19 27 H4
Alverstone Av EBAR EN4 33 H2
WAND/EARL SW18 159 K4
Alverstone Gdns
ELTH/MOT SE9 167 G3
Alverstone Rd CRICK NW2 82 A5
MNPK E12 90 A2
NWMAL KT3 192 C1

WBLY HA9 62 B5
Alverston Gdns *SNWD* SE25 197 F2
Alverton St *DEPT* SE8 124 C5
Alveston Av
KTN/HRWW/WS HA3 43 H6
Alveston Sq *SWFD* E18 * 52 E5
Alvey St *WALW* SE17 123 F5
Alvia Gdns *SUT* SM1 209 G2
Alvington Crs *HACK* E8 86 B3
Alway Av *HOR/WEW* KT19 206 E3
Alwold Crs *LEE/GVPK* SE12 166 B5
Alwyn Av *CHSWK* W4 118 A5
Alwyn Cl *BORE* WD6 30 B1
CROY/NA CR0 213 K5
Alwyne La *IS* N1 * 85 H5
Alwyne Pl *IS* N1 85 J4
Alwyne Rd *HNWL* W7 96 E6
IS N1 85 J5
WIM/MER SW19 177 J2
Alwyne Sq *IS* N1 85 J4
Alwyne Vls *IS* N1 85 H5
Alwyn Gdns *ACT* W3 98 D5
HDN NW4 63 J1
Alyn Bank *CEND/HSY/T* N8 * 66 D3
Alyth Gdns *GLDGN* NW11 64 D3
Amalgamated Dr *BTFD* TW8 116 B6
Amanda Cl *CHIG* IG7 54 D2
Amanda Ms *ROMW/RG* RM7 74 E2
Amar Ct *WOOL/PLUM* SE18 128 A4
Amardeep Ct
WOOL/PLUM SE18 128 A5
Amazon St *WCHPL* E1 104 D5
Ambassador Cl *HSLW* TW3 134 D3
Ambassador Gdns *EHAM* E6 107 K4
Ambassador Sq *POP/IOD* E14 124 E4
Amber Av *WALTH* E17 51 G4
Amberden Av *FNCH* N3 46 E6
Ambergate St *WALW* SE17 122 C5
Amber Gv *CRICK* NW2 64 B5
Amberley Cl *ORP* BR6 217 F3
PIN HA5 41 K6
Amberley Ct *SCUP* DA14 186 D1
Amberley Gdns
HOR/WEW KT19 207 H2
Amberley Gv *CROY/NA* CR0 197 G4
SYD SE26 163 J6
Amberley Rd *ABYW* SE2 128 E6
BKHH IG9 39 G3
EN EN1 36 B2
LEY E10 69 J4
MV/WKIL W9 100 E4
PLMGR N13 35 F4
Amberley Wy *HSLWW* TW4 134 B6
MRDN SM4 193 J4
ROMW/RG RM7 74 D1
Amberside Cl *ISLW* TW7 155 J1
Amber St *SRTFD* E15 * 88 B4
Amberwood Cl *WLGTN* SM6 210 E3
Amberwood Ri *NWMAL* KT3 192 B3
Amblecote Cl *LEE/GVPK* SE12 166 A5
Amblecote Meadow
LEE/GVPK SE12 166 A5
Amblecote Mdw
LEE/GVPK SE12 * 166 A5
Amblecote Rd
LEE/GVPK SE12 166 A5
Ambler Rd *FSBYPK* N4 85 H1
Ambleside *BMLY* BR1 183 G2
Ambleside Av *BECK* BR3 198 B2
HCH RM12 93 K3
STRHM/NOR SW16 161 J6
WOT/HER KT12 188 B5
Ambleside Cl *HOM* E9 86 E3
LEY E10 69 K4
SEVS/STOTM N15 50 B6
Ambleside Crs *PEND* EN3 25 F4
Ambleside Dr
EBED/NFELT TW14 153 J3
Ambleside Gdns *BELMT* SM2 209 G4
REDBR IG4 71 J1
WBLY HA9 61 K5
Ambleside Rd *WLSDN* NW10 81 H5
Ambrey Wy *WLGTN* SM6 210 D6
Ambrook Rd *BELV* DA17 129 H3
Ambrosden Av *WEST* SW1P 16 B5
Ambrose Av *GLDGN* NW11 64 D3
Ambrose Cl *ORP* BR6 217 F1
Ambrose St *BERM/RHTH* SE16 123 J4
Ambulance Rd *WAN* E11 70 B2
Amelia Cl *ACT* W3 117 J1
Amelia St *WALW* SE17 122 C5
Amen Cnr *STP* EC4M 12 B4
TOOT SW17 179 F2
Amen Ct *STP* EC4M 12 B4
Amenity Wy *MRDN* SM4 193 F4
America Sq *TWRH* EC3N 13 J5
America St *STHWK* SE1 18 C1
Amerland Rd *PUT/ROE* SW15 159 J1
Amersham Av *UED* N18 49 K2
Amersham Gv *NWCR* SE14 144 C1
Amersham Rd *CROY/NA* CR0 196 D3
NWCR SE14 144 C2
Amersham V *NWCR* SE14 144 C1
Amery Gdns *WLSDN* NW10 81 K6
Amery Rd *HRW* HA1 61 G6
Amesbury Av
BRXS/STRHM SW2 161 K4
Amesbury Cl *WPK* KT4 193 F5
Amesbury Dr *CHING* E4 37 K1
Amesbury Rd *BMLY* BR1 184 C6
DAGW RM9 91 K5
FELT TW13 154 C4
Ames Cotts *POP/IOD* E14 * 105 G4
Amethyst Ct *ORP* BR6 216 E4
Amethyst Rd *SRTFD* E15 88 B2
Amherst Av *WEA* W13 97 J5
Amherst Cl *STMC/STPC* BR5 202 B1
Amherst Dr *STMC/STPC* BR5 202 A1
Amherst Gdns *WEA* W13 * 97 J5
Amherst Rd *WEA* W13 97 J5
Amhurst Gdns *ISLW* TW7 136 A2
Amhurst Pde
STNW/STAM N16 * 68 B4
Amhurst Pk *STNW/STAM* N16 68 A4
Amhurst Rd *STNW/STAM* N16 86 B2
Amhurst Ter *STNW/STAM* N16 86 C2
Amidas Gdns *BCTR* RM8 91 H2
Amiel St *WCHPL* E1 104 E3
Amies St *BTSEA* SW11 140 E4
Amina Wy *BERM/RHTH* SE16 123 H3
Amis Av *HOR/WEW* KT19 206 C4
Amity Gv *RYNPK* SW20 177 F4
Amity Rd *SRTFD* E15 88 D5
Ammanford Gn
CDALE/KGS NW9 * 63 G3
Amner Rd *BTSEA* SW11 161 F1
Amor Rd *HMSMTH* W6 119 F3
Amott Rd *PECK* SE15 143 H4
Ampere Wy *CROY/NA* CR0 195 K4
Ampleforth Cl *ORP* BR6 217 J2
Ampleforth Rd *ABYW* SE2 128 C2
Ampthill Est *CAMTN* NW1 4 A3
Ampthill Sq *CAMTN* NW1 4 B3
Ampton St *FSBYW* WC1X 5 G5
Amroth Cl *FSTH* SE23 163 J3
Amroth Gn *CDALE/KGS* NW9 * 63 G3
Amsterdam Rd *POP/IOD* E14 125 F3
Amwell Cl *ENC/FH* EN2 23 K6
Amwell St *CLKNW* EC1R 5 J4
Amyand Cots *TWK* TW1 156 C1
Amyand Park Gdns *TWK* TW1 156 C2
Amyand Park Rd *TWK* TW1 156 B2
Amy Cl *WLGTN* SM6 210 E5
Amyruth Rd *BROCKY* SE4 144 D6
Amy Warne Cl *EHAM* E6 107 J4
Anatola Rd *ARCH* N19 66 B6
Ancaster Crs *NWMAL* KT3 192 D3
Ancaster Ms *BECK* BR3 182 A6
Ancaster Rd *BECK* BR3 182 A6
Ancaster St
WOOL/PLUM SE18 147 K1
Anchorage Cl
WIM/MER SW19 177 K1
Anchor And Hope La
CHARL SE7 126 A3
Anchor Cl *BARK* IG11 109 H2
Anchor Dr *RAIN* RM13 111 K2
Anchor Rd *MNPK* E12 71 H6
Anchor St *BERM/RHTH* SE16 123 J4
Anchor Ter *WCHPL* E1 * 104 E3
Anchor Yd *FSBYE* EC1V * 6 D6
Ancill Cl *HMSMTH* W6 119 G6
Ancona Rd *WLSDN* NW10 99 J1
WOOL/PLUM SE18 127 J5
Andace Park Gdns
BMLY BR1 * 184 B4
Andalus Rd *BRXN/ST* SW9 141 K4
Ander Cl *ALP/SUD* HA0 79 K2
Anderson Cl *ACT* W3 99 F5
CHEAM SM3 193 K5
WCHMH N21 23 F6
Anderson Dr *ASHF* TW15 153 F6
Anderson Rd *HOM* E9 87 F4
WFD IG8 53 H6
Anderson's Pl *HSLW* TW3 135 G5
Anderson Sq *IS* N1 6 A1
Anderson St *CHEL* SW3 120 E5
Anderson Wy *BELV* DA17 129 J2
Andover Av *CAN/RD* E16 107 H5
Andover Cl *EBED/NFELT* TW14 153 J3
GFD/PVL UB6 96 B3
Andover Pl *KIL/WHAMP* NW6 101 F1
Andover Rd *HOLWY* N7 67 F6
ORP BR6 201 K5
WHTN TW2 155 J3
Andover Ter *HMSMTH* W6 * 118 E4
Andre St *HACK* E8 86 C3
Andrew Borde St
LSQ/SEVD WC2H * 10 D3
Andrew Cl *BARK/HLT* IG6 54 D3
Andrewes Gdns *EHAM* E6 107 J5
Andrew Pl *VX/NE* SW8 141 J2
Andrews Cl *BKHH* IG9 39 G4
HRW HA1 60 D4
STMC/STPC BR5 186 E6
WPK KT4 193 G6
Andrews Rd *BETH* E2 00 D0
Andrew St *POP/IOD* E14 106 A5
Andrews Wk *WALW* SE17 122 C6
Andwell Cl *ABYW* SE2 128 C2
Anerley Gv *NRWD* SE19 181 G3
Anerley Hl *NRWD* SE19 181 G2
Anerley Pk *PGE/AN* SE20 181 J2
Anerley Park Rd
PGE/AN SE20 181 J3
Anerley Rd *PGE/AN* SE20 181 H4
Anerley Station Rd
PGE/AN SE20 181 J4
Anerley V *NRWD* SE19 181 G3
Anfield Cl *BAL* SW12 161 H2
Angela Carter Cl
BRXN/ST SW9 142 B4
Angel Aly *WCHPL* E1 13 K2
Angel Cl *HPTN* TW12 173 H1
UED N18 50 B1
Angel Corner Pde *UED* N18 * 50 C1
Angel Ct *LOTH* EC2R 13 F3
Angelfield *HSLW* TW3 135 G5
Angel Hl *SUT* SM1 209 F1
Angel Hill Dr *SUT* SM1 209 F1
Angelica Dr *EHAM* E6 108 A4
Angelica Gdns *CROY/NA* CR0 198 A5
Angel La *HYS/HAR* UB3 94 B4
SRTFD E15 88 B4
Angell Park Gdns
BRXN/ST SW9 142 B4
Angell Rd *BRXN/ST* SW9 142 C4
Angell Town Est
BRXN/ST SW9 * 142 B3
Angel Ms *PUT/ROE* SW15 158 D2
WCHPL E1 104 D6
Angel Pas *CANST* EC4R 12 E6
Angel Rd *HRW* HA1 60 E3
THDIT KT7 190 B5
Angel Road (North Circular)
UED N18 50 C1
Angel Sq *FSBYE* EC1V * 6 A3
Angel St *STBT* EC1A 12 C3
Angel Wk *HMSMTH* W6 119 F4
Angel Wy *ROM* RM1 75 G2
Angerstein La *BKHTH/KID* SE3 145 J1
Anglers La *KTTN* NW5 84 B4
Anglers Reach *SURB* KT6 * 190 E2
Anglesea Ms
WOOL/PLUM SE18 127 G4
Anglesea Rd *KUT/HW* KT1 190 E1
STMC/STPC BR5 202 D3
WOOL/PLUM SE18 127 G4
Anglesey Cl *ASHF* TW15 152 D5
Anglesey Court Rd *CAR* SM5 210 A4
Anglesey Dr *RAIN* RM13 111 J3
Anglesey Gdns *CAR* SM5 210 A4
Anglesey Rd *OXHEY* WD19 41 G1
PEND EN3 24 D5
Anglesmede Crs *PIN* HA5 42 A6
Anglesmede Wy *PIN* HA5 41 K6
Angles Rd *STRHM/NOR* SW16 161 K6
Anglia Cl *TOTM* N17 50 D3
Anglian Rd *WAN* E11 88 B1
Anglo Rd *BOW* E3 105 H1
Angus Cl *CHSGTN* KT9 206 C3
Angus Dr *RSLP* HA4 77 G2
Angus Gdns *CDALE/KGS* NW9 45 F4
Angus Rd *PLSTW* E13 107 G2
Angus St *NWCR* SE14 144 B1
Anhalt Rd *BTSEA* SW11 140 D1
Ankerdine Crs
WOOL/PLUM SE18 147 G2
Anlaby Rd *TEDD* TW11 173 K1
Anley Rd *HMSMTH* W6 119 G2
Anmersh Gv *STAN* HA7 43 K4
Annabel Cl *POP/IOD* E14 105 K5
Anna Cl *HACK* E8 86 B6
Annandale Gv
HGDN/ICK UB10 76 A1
Annandale Rd *BFN/LL* DA15 167 K2
CHSWK W4 118 B4
CROY/NA CR0 197 H6
GNWCH SE10 125 J5
Anna Neagle Cl *FSTGT* E7 88 E2
Annan Wy *ROM* RM1 57 F4
Anne Boleyn's Wk
CHEAM SM3 208 B5
KUTN/CMB KT2 175 F1
Anne Case Ms *NWMAL* KT3 * 176 A6
Anne Compton Ms
LEE/GVPK SE12 165 J2
Annesley Av *CDALE/KGS* NW9 45 F6
Annesley Cl *WLSDN* NW10 81 G1
Annesley Dr *CROY/NA* CR0 213 H1
Annesley Rd *BKHTH/KID* SE3 146 A2
Annesmere Gdns
BKHTH/KID SE3 146 C4
Anne St *PLSTW* E13 106 E3
Annette Cl
KTN/HRWW/WS HA3 42 E5
Annette Rd *HOLWY* N7 85 F2
Anne Wy *BARK/HLT* IG6 54 C2
Annie Besant Cl *BOW* E3 * 87 H6
Anning St *WCHPL* E1 7 H6
Annington Rd *EFNCH* N2 47 K6
Annis Rd *HOM* E9 87 G4
Ann La *WBPTN* SW10 140 C1
Ann Moss Wy
BERM/RHTH SE16 123 K3
Ann's Cl *KTBR* SW1X 15 F3
Ann St *WOOL/PLUM* SE18 127 J4
Annsworthy Av *THHTH* CR7 180 E6
Annsworthy Crs *SNWD* SE25 180 E6
Ansar Gdns *WALTH* E17 69 G2
Ansdell Rd *PECK* SE15 143 K3
Ansdell St *KENS* W8 120 A3
Ansdell Ter *KENS* W8 120 A3
Ansell Gv *CAR* SM5 194 E5
Ansell Rd *TOOT* SW17 160 D5
Anselm Cl *CROY/NA* CR0 212 B1
Anselm Rd *FUL/PGN* SW6 119 K6
PIN HA5 41 K3
Ansford Rd *BMLY* BR1 183 F1
Ansleigh Pl *NTGHL* W11 100 B6
Anson Cl *ROMW/RG* RM7 56 D5
Anson Rd *ARCH* N19 84 C2
CRICK NW2 81 K3
Anson Wk *NTHWD* HA6 26 A6
Anstead Dr *RAIN* RM13 111 J1
Anstey Rd *PECK* SE15 143 H4
Anstice Cl *CHSWK* W4 138 B1
Anstridge Rd *ELTH/MOT* SE9 167 J1
Antelope Rd
WOOL/PLUM SE18 126 E3
Anthony Cl *MLHL* NW7 31 G6
OXHEY WD19 27 H3
Anthony Rd *GFD/PVL* UB6 96 E1
SNWD SE25 197 H3
WELL DA16 148 B2
Anthony's Cl *WAP* E1W 123 H1
Anthony St *WCHPL* E1 104 D5
Anthus Ms *NTHWD* HA6 40 B3
Antill Rd *BOW* E3 105 G2
SEVS/STOTM N15 68 C1
Antill Ter *WCHPL* E1 105 F5
Antlers Hl *CHING* E4 25 K6
Anton Crs *SUT* SM1 208 E1
Antoneys Cl *PIN* HA5 41 H5
Anton Pl *WBLY* HA9 80 D1
Anton St *HACK* E8 86 C3
Antrim Rd *HAMP* NW3 83 K4
Antrobus Cl *SUT* SM1 208 D3
Antrobus Rd *CHSWK* W4 117 K4
Anvil Cl *STRHM/NOR* SW16 179 H3
Anworth Cl *WFD* IG8 53 F2
Aostle Wy *THHTH* CR7 180 C5
Apeldoorn Dr *WLGTN* SM6 210 E6
Aperfield Rd *ERITH* DA8 130 C6
Apex Cl *BECK* BR3 182 E4
Apex Pde *MLHL* NW7 * 31 F6
Aplin Wy *ISLW* TW7 135 K2
Apollo Av *BMLY* BR1 184 A4
NTHWD HA6 40 E1
Apollo Cl *HCH* RM12 75 K6
Apollo Pl *WAN* E11 88 C1
WBPTN SW10 * 140 C1
Apollo Wy *ERITH* DA8 130 A4
THMD SE28 127 J3
Apothecary St *BLKFR* EC4V * 12 A4
Appach Rd *BRXS/STRHM* SW2 142 B6
Apple Blossom Ct
VX/NE SW8 * 141 J1
Appleby Cl *CHING* E4 52 A2
SEVS/STOTM N15 67 K2
STMC/STPC BR5 201 K4
UX/CGN UB8 94 A5
WHTN TW2 155 J4
Appleby Gdns
EBED/NFELT TW14 * 153 J3
Appleby Rd *CAN/RD* E16 106 E5
HACK E8 86 C5
Appleby St *BETH* E2 7 J2
Appledore Av *BXLYHN* DA7 149 K2
RSLP HA4 77 F1
Appledore Cl *EDGW* HA8 44 C4
HAYES BR2 199 J2
TOOT SW17 160 E4
Appledore Crs *SCUP* DA14 167 K5
Appledore Wy *MLHL* NW7 46 B3
Appleford Rd *NKENS* W10 100 C3
Apple Garth *BTFD* TW8 116 E4
Applegarth *CROY/NA* CR0 213 K5
ESH/CLAY KT10 205 F3
Applegarth Dr
GNTH/NBYPK IG2 73 F1
Applegarth Rd *THMD* SE28 128 C1
WKENS W14 * 119 G3
Apple Gv *CHSGTN* KT9 206 A2
EN EN1 24 A4
Apple Ldg *ALP/SUD* HA0 * 79 J1
Apple Market *KUT/HW* KT1 * 174 E5
Apple Rd *WAN* E11 88 C1
Appleton Gdns *NWMAL* KT3 192 D3
Appleton Rd *ELTH/MOT* SE9 146 D4
Appletree Cl *PGE/AN* SE20 181 J4
Appletree Gdns *EBAR* EN4 21 J5
Apple Tree Yd *STJS* SW1Y 10 B7
Applewood Cl *CRICK* NW2 81 K1
TRDG/WHET N20 33 J3
Applewood Dr *PLSTW* E13 107 F3
Appold St *SDTCH* EC2A 13 G1
Apprentice Gdns *NTHLT* UB5 95 K2
Apprentice Wy *CLPT* E5 86 D2
Approach La *MLHL* NW7 46 C1
Approach Rd *BETH* E2 104 E1
E/WMO/HCT KT8 189 F2
EBAR EN4 21 G5
RYNPK SW20 177 F5
The Approach *ACT* W3 99 F5
EN EN1 24 D3
HDN NW4 64 B2
ORP BR6 202 A6
Aprey Gdns *HDN* NW4 64 A1
April Cl *FELT* TW13 153 K5
HNWL W7 96 E6
ORP BR6 217 F3
April Gln *FSTH* SE23 164 A5
April St *HACK* E8 86 B2
Apsley Cl *HRW* HA1 60 C2
Apsley Rd *NWMAL* KT3 175 K6
SNWD SE25 197 J1
Apsley Wy *CRICK* NW2 63 J6
MYFR/PICC W1J * 15 J1
Aquarius *TWK* TW1 * 156 C3
Aquarius Wy *NTHWD* HA6 40 E1
Aquila St *STJWD* NW8 2 B2
Aquinas St *STHWK* SE1 17 K1
Arabella Dr *PUT/ROE* SW15 138 B5
Arabia Cl *CHING* E4 38 A2
Arabin Rd *BROCKY* SE4 144 B5
Aragon Av *EW* KT17 207 K6
THDIT KT7 190 A2
Aragon Cl *ENC/FH* EN2 23 F1
HAYES BR2 200 E5
LOU IG10 39 J1
Aragon Dr *BARK/HLT* IG6 54 C3
RSLP HA4 59 H5
Aragon Pl *MRDN* SM4 193 G4
Aragon Rd *KUTN/CMB* KT2 175 F1
MRDN SM4 193 G4
Arandora Crs *CHDH* RM6 73 H4
Arbery Rd *BOW* E3 105 G2
Arbor Cl *BECK* BR3 182 E5
Arborfield Cl
BRXS/STRHM SW2 162 A3
Arbor Rd *CHING* E4 38 B5
Arbour Rd *PEND* EN3 25 F5
Arbour Sq *WCHPL* E1 105 F5
Arbour Wy *HCH* RM12 93 K3
Arbroath Gn *OXHEY* WD19 20 C5
Arbroath Rd *ELTH/MOT* SE9 146 D4
Arbrook Cl *STMC/STPC* BR5 186 B6
Arbrook La *ESH/CLAY* KT10 204 D4
Arbuthnot La *BXLY* DA5 169 F1
Arbuthnot Rd *NWCR* SE14 144 A3
Arbutus St *HACK* E8 86 A6
Arcade Chambers
ELTH/MOT SE9 * 167 F1
Arcade Pde *CHSGTN* KT9 * 206 A2
The Arcade *ELTH/MOT* SE9 * 167 F1
LVPST EC2M * 13 G2
WALTH E17 * 69 J1
Arcadia Av *FNCH* N3 46 E4
Arcadia Cl *CAR* SM5 210 A2
Arcadian Av *BXLY* DA5 169 F1
Arcadian Cl *BXLY* DA5 169 F1
Arcadian Gdns *WDGN* N22 49 G3
Arcadian Pl
WAND/EARL SW18 159 H2
Arcadian Rd *BXLY* DA5 169 F2
Arcadia St *POP/IOD* E14 105 J5
Archangel St
BERM/RHTH SE16 124 A2
Archbishop's Pl
BRXS/STRHM SW2 162 A1
Archdale Pl *NWMAL* KT3 175 J6
Archdale Rd *EDUL* SE22 143 G6
Archel Rd *WKENS* W14 119 J6
Archer Cl *BAR* EN5 32 D1
KUTN/CMB KT2 175 F3
Archer Ct *FELT* TW13 153 K3
Archer Ms *HPTN* TW12 173 H2
Archer Rd *SNWD* SE25 197 J1
STMC/STPC BR5 202 B3
Archers Dr *PEND* EN3 24 E3
Archer Sq *NWCR* SE14 124 B6
Archer St *SOHO/SHAV* W1D 10 C5
Archery Cl *BAY/PAD* W2 8 D4
KTN/HRWW/WS HA3 43 F6
Archery Rd *ELTH/MOT* SE9 146 E6
The Arches *CHCR* WC2N * 11 F7
RYLN/HDSTN HA2 60 B6
Archibald Rd *HOLWY* N7 84 D2
Archibold St *BOW* E3 105 J2
Archie Cl *WDR/YW* UB7 112 D2
Arch St *STHWK* SE1 18 C5
Archway *HARH* RM3 57 K2
Archway Cl *ARCH* N19 * 66 C6
NKENS W10 100 B4
WIM/MER SW19 160 A6
WLGTN SM6 * 210 E1
Archway Rd *ARCH* N19 66 C5
HGT N6 65 K2
Archway St *BARN* SW13 138 B4
Arcola St *HACK* E8 86 B3
Arcon Dr *NTHLT* UB5 95 J3
Arctic St *KTTN* NW5 84 B3
Arcus Rd *BMLY* BR1 183 H2
Ardbeg Rd *HNHL* SE24 162 E1
Arden Cl *BUSH* WD23 29 F2
HRW HA1 78 D1
THMD SE28 109 K5
WHTN TW2 154 E2
Arden Court Gdns *EFNCH* N2 65 H3
Arden Crs *DAGW* RM9 91 K5
POP/IOD E14 124 D4
Arden Est *IS* N1 7 G3
Arden Gv *ORP* BR6 216 B2
Arden Mhor *PIN* HA5 59 F1
Arden Rd *FNCH* N3 46 C6
WEA W13 97 J6
Ardent Cl *SNWD* SE25 181 F6
Ardfern Av *STRHM/NOR* SW16 180 B6
Ardfillan Rd *CAT* SE6 165 G3
Ardgowan Rd *CAT* SE6 165 H2
Ardilaun Rd *HBRY* N5 85 J2
Ardingly Cl *CROY/NA* CR0 213 F1
Ardleigh Gdns *CHEAM* SM3 193 K5
Ardleigh Rd *IS* N1 85 K4
WALTH E17 51 H4
Ardleigh Ter *WALTH* E17 51 H4
Ardley Cl *CAT* SE6 164 B5
WLSDN NW10 81 G1
Ardlui Rd *WNWD* SE27 162 D4
Ardmay Gdns *SURB* KT6 * 191 F2
Ardmere Rd *LEW* SE13 165 G1
Ardmore La *BKHH* IG9 39 F3
Ardmore Pl *BKHH* IG9 * 39 F2
Ardoch Rd *CAT* SE6 165 G4
Ardra Rd *ED* N9 37 F5
Ardrossan Gdns *WPK* KT4 207 J1
Ardross Av *NTHWD* HA6 40 C1
Ardshiel Cl *PUT/ROE* SW15 139 G4
Ardwell Av *BARK/HLT* IG6 72 C2
Ardwell Rd *BRXS/STRHM* SW2 161 K4
Ardwick Rd *CRICK* NW2 82 E2
Arena Est *FSBYPK* N4 * 67 H3
The Arena *STKPK* UB11 * 113 F
Argall Av *LEY* E10 69 F
Argall Wy *LEY* E10 69 F5
Argenta Wy *WLSDN* NW10 80 D5
Argent Ct *SURB* KT6 * 191 H
SURB KT6 206 C
Argon Ms *FUL/PGN* SW6 139 K
Argon Rd *UED* N18 50 E
Argosy La *STWL/WRAY* TW19 152 A
Argus Cl *ROMW/RG* RM7 56 D
Argus Wy *NTHLT* UB5 95 J
Argyle Av *HSLW* TW3 155 F
Argyle Cl *WEA* W13 97 C
Argyle Cnr *WEA* W13 * 97 H
Argyle Pl *HMSMTH* W6 118 E
Argyle Rd *BAR* EN5 20 A
CAN/RD E16 107 F
GFD/PVL UB6 97 F
HSLW TW3 135 C
IL IG1 72 A
NFNCH/WDSPK N12 46 E
RYLN/HDSTN HA2 60 E
SRTFD E15 88 C
TOTM N17 50 C
UED N18 36 C
WCHPL E1 105
WEA W13 97
Argyle Sq *STPAN* WC1H 5
Argyle St *CAMTN* NW1 4
Argyle Wk *STPAN* WC1H * 4
Argyle Wy *BERM/RHTH* SE16 123
Argyll Av *STHL* UB1 115
Argyll Cl *BRXN/ST* SW9 142
Argyll Gdns *EDGW* HA8 44
Argyll Rd *KENS* W8 119
WOOL/PLUM SE18 127
Argyll St *SOHO/SHAV* W1D 10
Arhchie St *STHWK* SE1 19
Arica Rd *BROCKY* SE4 144
Ariel Rd *KIL/WHAMP* NW6 82
Ariel Wy *HSLWW* TW4 134
NTGHL W11 119
SHB W12 119
Aristotle Rd *CLAP* SW4 141
Arkell Gv *NRWD* SE19 180
Arkindale Rd *CAT* SE6 165
Arkley Crs *WALTH* E17 69
Arkley Rd *WALTH* E17 69
Arklow Rd *NWCR* SE14 124
Arkwright Rd *HAMP* NW3 83
Arlesford Rd *BRXN/ST* SW9 141
Arlingford Rd
BRXS/STRHM SW2 162
Arlington *NFNCH/WDSPK* N12 32
Arlington Av *IS* N1 6
Arlington Cl *BFN/LL* DA15 167
LEW SE13 145
SUT SM1 193
TWK TW1 * 156
Arlington Ct *HYS/HAR* UB3 113
Arlington Dr *CAR* SM5 194
RSLP HA4 58
Arlington Gdns *CHSWK* W4 117
IL IG1 7
Arlington Pde
BRXS/STRHM SW2 * 14
Arlington Rd *CAMTN* NW1
STHGT/OAK N14 3
SURB KT6 19
TEDD TW11 15
WEA W13 9
WFD IG8 5
Arlington Sq *IS* N1
Arlington St *MYFR/PICC* W1J 1
Arlington Wy *CLKNW* EC1R
Arliss Wy *NTHLT* UB5 7
Arlow Rd *WCHMH* N21 3
Armadale Cl *TOTM* N17 6
Armadale Rd
EBED/NFELT TW14 13
FUL/PGN SW6 13
Armada St *DEPT* SE8 12
Armada Wy *CAN/RD* E16 10
Armagh Rd *BOW* E3
Armfield Cl *E/WMO/HCT* KT8 18
Armfield Crs *MTCM* CR4 17
Armfield Rd *ENC/FH* EN2

Arminger Rd SHB W12 .... 118 E1
Armistice Gdns SNWD SE25.... 181 H6
Armitage Rd GLDGN NW11...... 64 C5
  GNWCH SE10................... 125 J4
Armour Rd IS HOLWY N7 .... 85 F4
Armoury Rd DEPT SE8............. 144 E3
Armoury Wy
  WAND/EARL SW18 .... 139 K6
Armstead Wk DAGE RM10........ 92 C7
Armstrong Av WFD IG8............. 52 C2
Armstrong CI BCTR RM8........... 73 K4
  BMLY BR1.......................... 184 D6
  EHAM E6........................... 107 K5
  RSLP HA4.......................... 58 E3
Armstrong Crs EBAR EN4........ 21 H5
Armstrong Rd ACT W3 .... 118 C1
  FELT TW13.......................... 172 D1
  WLSDN NW10....................... 81 G5
  WOOL/PLUM SE18 .... 127 H3
Armstrong Wy NWDGN UB2 .. 115 G2
Armytage Rd HEST TW5............ 134 C1
Arnal Crs WAND/EARL SW18 .. 159 H2
Arncliffe CI FBAR/BDGN N11... 48 A2
Arne Gv ORP BR6.................... 217 F1
Arne St LSQ/SEVD WC2H......... 11 H2
Arnett Sq IS N1..................... 85 F4
Arne Wk LEE/GVPK SE12.......... 145 J5
Arneways Av CHDH RM6 .... 73 K1
Arneway St WEST SW1P 16 D5
Arnewood CI PUT/ROE SW15.. 158 D3
Arngask Rd CAT SE6............... 165 G2
Arnheim PI POP/IOD E14........ 124 D3
Arnison Rd E/WMO/HCT KT8.. 189 J1
Arnold Av East PEND EN3........ 25 J1
Arnold Av West PEND EN3........ 25 H1
Arnold Circ BETH E2............... 7 J5
Arnold CI KTN/HRWW/WS HA3. 62 B4
Arnold Crs ISLW TW7............. 135 J6
Arnott CI CHSWK W4.............. 118 A4
  THMD SE28........................ 128 D1
Arnould Av CMBW SE5............ 142 E5
Arnside Gdns WBLY HA9.......... 61 K5
Arnside Rd St WALW SE17........ 122 D6
Arnulf St CAT SE6................... 164 E6
Arnulls Rd STRHM/NOR SW16. 180 C2
Arodene Rd
  BRXS/STRHM SW2............... 162 A1
Arosa Rd TWK TW1................. 156 E1
Arragon Gdns
  STRHM/NOR SW16............... 179 K3
  WWKM BR4........................ 213 K1
Arragon Rd EHAM E6.............. 89 H6
  TWK TW1........................... 156 B2
  WAND/EARL SW18 .... 159 K3
Arran CI ERITH DA8............... 150 A6
  WLGTN SM6........................ 210 C2
Arran Dr MNPK E12................. 71 H5
  STAN HA7............................ 29 J6
Arran Ms OXHEY WD19 *......... 27 H6
Arran Rd CAT SE6.................. 164 E4
Arran Wk IS N1..................... 85 J5
Arras Av MRDN SM4............... 194 B2
Arrol Rd BECK BR3................. 181 K5
Arrow Rd BOW E3.................. 105 K2
Arrowsmith Rd ELTH/MOT SE9. 55 F1
Arrowsmith Rd ELTH/MOT SE9. 146 E3
Arsenal Wy WOOL/PLUM SE18. 127 F2
Artemis PI WAND/EARL SW18. 159 J2
Arterberry Rd RYNPK SW20.... 177 F3
Artesian CI ROM RM1............. 75 H3
  WLSDN NW10....................... 81 F5
Artesian Gv BAR EN5............. 21 G5
Artesian Houses
  BAY/PAD W2 *.................... 100 E5
Artesian Rd BAY/PAD W2....... 100 E5
Arthingworth St SRTFD E15.... 88 C6
Arthurdon Rd BROCKY SE4..... 144 D6
Arthur Gv WOOL/PLUM SE18.. 127 H4
Artesian Gv BAR EN5............. 21 G5
  ED N9............................... 36 B4
  EHAM E6........................... 107 K1
  HOLWY N7.......................... 85 F2
  KUTN/CMB KT2.................. 175 H5
  NWMAL KT3........................ 192 E2
  WIM/MER SW19.................. 159 J6
Arthur St CANST EC4R............ 13 F6
  ERITH DA8.......................... 150 C1
Artichoke HI WAP E1W........... 104 D6
Artichoke PI CMBW SE5 *........ 142 E2
Artillery CI GNTH/NBYPK IG2 .. 72 C3
Artillery La LVPST EC2M......... 13 H2
  SHB W12........................... 99 J5
Artillery Pas WCHPL E1 *........ 13 H2
Artillery Rd WOOL/PLUM SE18. 127 H4
Artillery Rw WEST SW1P......... 16 C5
Artington CI ORP BR6............. 216 C2
Artisan CI EHAM E6............... 108 B6
Arvizan St WCHPL E1............. 13 H5
Arwell St LEY E10................. 193 J1
Arundel Av MRDN SM4........... 193 J1
Arundel CI BTSEA SW11........ 140 D6
  BXLY DA5.......................... 169 G1
  CROY/NA CRO *.................. 211 H1
  HPTN TW12........................ 173 G5
  WAN E11............................ 52 C7
Arundel Dr ORP BR6.............. 217 H3
  RYLN/HDSTN HA2................ 77 K2
  WFD IG8............................ 52 E3
Arundel Gdns EDGW HA8....... 45 F3
  GDMY/SEVK IG3................. 73 H1
  NTGHL W11....................... 100 D6
  SEVS/STOTM N15................ 67 J2
Arundel Gv IS N1.................. 86 A3
Arundel PI HOLWY N7 .... 85 G4
Arundel Rd BELMT SM2.......... 208 D5

Arundel Wk ROMW/RG RM7.... 56 D4
Ashdown Wy TOOT SW17....... 161 F4
Asher CI EHAM E6................ 108 A5
Ashenden Rd CLPT E5........... 87 G3
Ashen Gv WIM/MER SW19...... 159 K5
Ashen V SAND/SEL CR2......... 213 F6
Asher Loftus Wy
  FBAR/BDGN N11................ 47 K2
Asher Wy WAP E1W.............. 104 D6
Ashfield Av BUSH WD23......... 28 B1
  FELT TW13........................ 154 A3
Ashfield CI BECK BR3............ 182 D3
  RCHPK/HAM TW10............. 157 F3
Ashfield Ct EA W5 *............... 98 A6
Ashfield La CHST BR7........... 185 H2
Ashfield Rd ACT W3.............. 118 C1
  FSBYPK N4......................... 67 J3
  STHGT/OAK N14................ 34 C5
Ashfield St WCHPL E1........... 104 D4
Ashfield Yd WCHPL E1 *......... 104 E4
Ashford Av CEND/HSY/T N8.... 66 E1
  YEAD UB4.......................... 95 H5
Ashford CI ASHF TW15........... 152 B5
  WALTH E17......................... 69 H5
Ashford Crs ASHF TW15......... 152 B5
  PEND EN3.......................... 24 E3
Ashford Gn OXHEY WD19...... 41 H1
Ashford Ms TOTM N17........... 50 B2
Ashford Rd CRICK NW2......... 82 B2
  EHAM E6........................... 89 K4
  FELT TW13......................... 153 G6
  SWFD E18........................... 53 F5
Ash Gv ALP/SUD HA0............. 79 G2
  CEND/HSY/T N8................ 67 F3
  EA W5............................... 117 F2
  EBED/NFELT TW14.............. 153 H3
  EN EN1.............................. 36 A2
  HACK E8............................ 86 D6
  HEST TW5.......................... 134 C2
  HYS/HAR UB3................... 94 B6
  MUSWH N10........................ 66 B1
  PGE/AN SE20.................... 181 K5
  PLMGR N13......................... 35 J5
  STHL UB1........................... 96 A4
  WWKM BR4........................ 199 F5
Ashgrove Rd BMLY BR1........ 183 G2
  GDMY/SEVK IG3................ 73 F5
Ash Hill CI BUSH WD23......... 28 B3
Ash Hill Dr PIN HA5.............. 41 G6
Ashington Ct CHING E4.......... 38 A6
Ashington Rd FUL/PGN SW6.. 139 J3
Ashlake Rd
  STRHM/NOR SW16............. 161 K6
Ashland PI MHST W1U............ 9 G1
Ashlar PI WOOL/PLUM SE18.. 127 C4
Ashleigh Gdns SUT SM1....... 194 A6
Ashleigh Rd
  MORT/ESHN SW14............. 138 B4
  PGE/AN SE20.................... 181 H5
Ashley Av BARK/HLT IG6....... 54 B5
  MRDN SM4........................ 193 K2
Ashley CI HDN NW4.............. 46 A5
  PIN HA5............................. 41 F5
Ashley Crs BTSEA SW11........ 141 F3
  WDGN N22......................... 49 G5
Ashley Dr ISLW TW7............. 115 K6
  WHTN TW2......................... 155 F3
Ashley Gdns ORP BR6.......... 216 E3
  PLMGR N13........................ 35 K5
  RCHPK/HAM TW10............. 156 E5
  WBLY HA9.......................... 62 A1
Ashley La CROY/NA CRO........ 211 H2
  HDN NW4........................... 46 A5
Ashley PI WESTW SW1E......... 16 E5
Ashley Rd ARCH N19............. 66 E5
  CHING E4........................... 51 J1
  FSTGT E7........................... 89 G5
  HPTN TW12........................ 173 F4
  PEND EN3.......................... 24 E3
  THDIT KT7......................... 189 K3
  THHTH CR7........................ 196 A1
  TOTM N17......................... 50 C6
  WIM/MER SW19.................. 178 A2
Ashleys Ay SEVS/STOTM N15. 67 J1
Ashling Rd CROY/NA CRO...... 197 H5
Ashlin Rd SRTFD E15............ 88 B2
Ashlone Rd PUT/ROE SW15... 139 F4
Ashlyns Wy CHSGTN KT9...... 205 K4
Ashmead Rd EBED/NFELT TW14. 153 K3
Ashmead Ga BMLY BR1......... 184 B4
Ashmead Ms DEPT SE8 *....... 144 D3
Ashmead Rd DEPT SE8......... 144 D3
  EBED/NFELT TW14............. 153 K3
Ashmere Av BECK BR3.......... 183 G5
Ashmere CI CHEAM SM3........ 208 B3
Ashmere Gv
  BRXS/STRHM SW2.............. 141 K5
Ash Ms KTTN NW5............... 84 C3
Ashmill St STJWD NW8.......... 2 B7
Ashmole St VX/NE SW8......... 122 A6
Ashmore CI PECK SE15......... 143 G1
Ashmore Gv WELL DA16........ 147 J4
Ashmore Rd MV/WKIL W9..... 100 D2
Ashmount Rd ARCH N19....... 66 D3
Ashmount Ter EA W5 *.......... 116 E4
Ashmour Gdns ROM RM1...... 57 H5
Ashneal Gdns HRW HA1........ 78 D1
Ashness Gdns GFD/PVL UB6.. 79 H4
Ashness Rd BTSEA SW11...... 140 E6
Ashridge CI
  KTN/HRWW/WS HA3.......... 61 J3
Ashridge Crs
  WOOL/PLUM SE18.............. 147 H1
Ashridge Dr OXHEY WD19.... 41 H1
Ashridge Wy MRDN SM4...... 193 J2
Ash Rd CHEAM SM3.............. 193 H5
  CROY/NA CRO................... 198 D6
  SRTFD E15......................... 88 C3
Ash Rw HAYES BR2................ 201 F3
Ashstead Rd STNW/STAM N16. 68 A2
Ashton CI SUT SM1............... 208 E2
Ashton Gdns CHDH RM6........ 74 A3
  HSLWW TW4...................... 134 E5
Ashton Rd SRTFD E15............ 88 B3

Ashton St POP/IOD E14........ 106 A6
Ashtree Av MTCM CR4........... 178 C5
Ash Tree CI CROY/NA CRO.... 198 B3
Ashtree CI ORP BR6............. 216 B2
Ash Tree Dell CDALE/KGS NW9. 62 E2
Ash Tree Wy CROY/NA CRO... 198 B2
Ashurst CI DART DA1............. 150 C4
  NTHWD HA6........................ 40 C5
  PGE/AN SE20.................... 181 J3
Ashurst Gdns
  BRXS/STRHM SW2............. 162 B3
Ashurst Rd EBAR EN4........... 21 K6
  NFNCH/WDSPK N12.......... 47 J1
Ashurst Wk CROY/NA CRO.... 197 J6
Ashvale Gdns CRW RM5........ 57 F1
Ashvale Rd TOOT SW17........ 178 E1
Ashville Rd WAN E11............ 70 B6
Ash Wk ALP/SUD HA0........... 79 J2
Ashwell CI EHAM E6............. 107 K5
Ashwin St HACK E8.............. 86 B4
Ashwood Av RAIN RM13....... 111 K2
Ashwood Gdns CROY/NA CRO. 213 K4
  HYS/HAR UB3................... 113 J4
Ashwood Rd CHING E4.......... 38 B5
Ashworth CI CMBW SE5......... 142 E3
Ashworth Rd MV/WKIL W9.... 101 F2
Askern CI BXLYHS DA6......... 148 E5
Aske St IS N1........................ 7 G4
Askew Crs SHB W12.............. 118 C2
Askew Rd NTHWD HA6......... 26 B4
  SHB W12........................... 118 C2
Askew Vis PLMGR N13 *......... 35 H5
Askham Rd SHB W12............. 118 D1
Askill Dr PUT/ROE SW15....... 139 H6
Askwith Rd RAIN RM13......... 111 F1
Asland Rd SRTFD E15........... 88 B6
Aslett St WAND/EARL SW18.. 160 A2
Asmara Rd CRICK NW2......... 82 C3
Asmuns HI GLDGN NW11...... 64 E2
Asmuns PI GLDGN NW11...... 64 D2
Aspen CI EA W5.................... 117 G2
  WDR/YW UB7..................... 217 G3
Aspen Copse BMLY BR1........ 184 E5
Aspen Ct HACK E8 *.............. 86 C4
Aspen Dr ALP/SUD HA0......... 79 F4
Aspen Gdns MTCM CR4......... 195 F2
Aspen Gn ERITH DA18.......... 129 G3
Aspen Gv PIN HA5................. 40 D6
Aspen La NTHLT UB5............ 95 J2
Aspenlea Rd HMSMTH W6.... 119 G6
Aspen Wy POP/IOD E14........ 106 A6
Aspern Gv HAMP NW3........... 83 J3
Aspinall Rd BROCKY SE4....... 144 A4
Aspinden Rd
  BERM/RHTH SE16............... 123 J4
Aspley Rd WAND/EARL SW18. 140 A6
Asplins Rd TOTM N17........... 50 C4
Asplins VIs TOTM N17 *......... 50 C4
Asprey Ms BECK BR3............ 198 C2
Asquith CI BCTR RM8............ 73 J5
Assam St WCHPL E1............. 104 C5
Assata Ms IS N1.................... 85 H4
Assembly Pas WCHPL E1...... 104 E4
Assembly Wk CAR SM5......... 194 D4
Ass House La
  KTN/HRWW/WS HA3........... 28 B6
Astall CI KTN/HRWW/WS HA3. 42 D4
Astbury Rd PECK SE15......... 143 K2
Astell Rd CHEL SW3............. 15 K8
Asteys Rw IS N1................... 85 H5
Astle St BTSEA SW11........... 141 F3
Astley Av CRICK NW2............ 82 A3
Aston Av KTN/HRWW/WS HA3. 61 J4
Aston CI BUSH WD23 *.......... 28 C1
  SCUP DA14........................ 168 B5
Aston Gn HSLWW TW4.......... 134 B3
Astonplace
  STRHM/NOR SW16............. 180 C2
Aston Rd EA W5................... 97 K5
  ESH/CLAY KT10................. 204 E3
  RYNPK SW20...................... 177 F6
Aston St BOW E3................. 105 G5
Aston Ter BAL SW12 *........... 161 G1
Astonville St
  WAND/EARL SW18............. 159 K3
Astor Av ROMW/RG RM7...... 74 D3
Astor CI KUTN/CMB KT2........ 175 J2
Astoria Pde ASHF TW15 *...... 152 D6
  STRHM/NOR SW16 *........... 161 K5
Astoria Wk BRXN/ST SW9...... 142 B4
Astrop Ms HMSMTH W6........ 119 F3
Astrop Ter HMSMTH W6....... 119 F2
Astwood Ms SKENS SW7....... 120 A4
Asylum Rd PECK SE15......... 143 J1
Atalanta St FUL/PGN SW6.... 139 G2
Atbara Rd TEDD TW11.......... 174 C2
Atcham Rd HSLW TW3.......... 135 H5
Atcost Rd BARK IG11............. 109 G4
Atheldene Rd
  WAND/EARL SW18.............. 160 A3
Athelney St CAT SE6............ 164 D5
Athelstane Gv BOW E3.......... 105 H1
Athelstane Ms FSBYPK N4.... 67 G5
Athelstan Gdns
  KIL/WHAMP NW6 *.............. 82 C5
Athelstan Rd KUT/HW KT1.... 191 G1
Athelstan Wy
  STMC/STPC BR5................ 186 B4
Athelstone Rd
  KTN/HRWW/WS HA3........... 42 D5
Athena CI KUT/HW KT1......... 175 C6
  RYLN/HDSTN HA2.............. 60 D6
Athenaeum PI MUSWH N10.. 48 B6
Athenaeum Rd
  TRDG/WHET N20................ 33 G3
Athenlay Rd PECK SE15........ 144 A6
Athens Gdns MV/WKIL W9 *.. 100 E3
Atherden Rd CLPT E5........... 86 E2
Atherfold Rd BRXN/ST SW9... 141 K4
Atherley Wy HSLWW TW4..... 154 E2
Atherstone Ms SKENS SW7 *. 120 B4
Atherton CI
  STWL/WRAY TW19............. 152 A1

Atherton Dr WIM/MER SW19.. 159 C6
Atherton Hts ALP/SUD HA0... 79 J4
Atherton Ms FSTGT E7.......... 88 D4
Atherton PI RYLN/HDSTN HA2. 42 C6
  STHL UB1.......................... 96 A6
Atherton Rd BARN SW13...... 138 D1
  CLAY IG5............................ 53 J5
  FSTGT E7........................... 88 D3
Atherton St BTSEA SW11...... 140 D3
Athlone ESH/CLAY KT10....... 204 E4
Athlone CI CLPT E5............... 86 D3
  WALTH E17 *...................... 52 B6
Athlone Rd BRXS/STRHM SW2. 162 A2
Athlone St KTTN NW5........... 84 A4
Athlon Rd ALP/SUD HA0....... 97 K1
Athol CI PIN HA5.................. 41 F4
Athole Gdns EN EN1............. 24 A6
Athol Gdns PIN HA5............. 41 F4
Atholl Rd GDMY/SEVK IG3.... 73 G4
Athol Rd ERITH DA8............. 129 K5
Athol Sq POP/IOD E14.......... 106 A5
Atkins Dr WWKM BR4........... 214 B1
Atkinson CI ORP BR6............ 217 G3
Atkinson Rd CAN/RD E16..... 107 G4
Atkins Rd BAL SW12............. 161 H2
  LEY E10............................. 69 K3
Atlanta Bvd ROM RM1.......... 75 F3
Atlantic Rd BRXN/ST SW9.... 142 B5
Atlantis CI CAN/RD E16........ 108 C6
Atlantis CI BARK IG11........... 109 H2
Atlas Gdns CHARL SE7......... 126 B4
Atlas Ms HACK E8................. 86 B4
  ED N9............................... 36 C3
Atlas Rd FBAR/BDGN N11.... 48 A2
  PLSTW E13......................... 106 E1
  WBLY HA9.......................... 80 E2
  WLSDN NW10.................... 99 G2
Atley Rd BOW E3.................. 87 K6
  ALP/SUD HA0..................... 80 A6
Atney Rd PUT/ROE SW15...... 139 H5
Attenborough CI
  OXHEY WD19..................... 27 J5
Atterbury Rd FSBYPK N4...... 67 G3
Atterbury St WEST SW1P...... 16 D7
Attewood Av WLSDN NW10... 81 G1
Attewood Rd NTHLT UB5...... 77 J4
Attfield CI TRDG/WHET N20.. 33 H3
Attlee CI THHTH CR7............ 196 D3
  YEAD UB4 *........................ 95 F2
Attlee Rd THMD SE28........... 109 H6
  YEAD UB4.......................... 94 E2
Attlee Ter WALTH E17........... 51 K6
Attneave St FSBYW WC1X..... 5 J6
Atwell PI THDIT KT7............. 190 B5
Atwell Rd PECK SE15 *......... 143 H3
Atwood Av RCH/KEW TW9.... 137 H2
Atwood Rd HMSMTH W6...... 118 E4
Aubert Pk HBRY N5.............. 85 H2
Aubert Rd HBRY N5.............. 85 H2
Aubrey PI STJWD NW8.......... 2 A3
Aubrey Rd CEND/HSY/T N8 *. 66 E2
  NTGHL W11....................... 119 J1
  WALTH E17........................ 51 J6
Aubyn HI WNWD SE27.......... 162 D6
Aubyn Sq PUT/ROE SW15..... 138 D5
Auckland CI NRWD SE19...... 181 G4
Auckland Gdns NRWD SE19.. 181 F4
Auckland HI WNWD SE27..... 162 D6
Auckland Ri NRWD SE19...... 181 F4
Auckland Rd BTSEA SW11... 140 D6
  CROY/NA CRO................... 196 E3
  IL IG1............................... 72 B5
  KUT/HW KT1...................... 191 G4
  LEY E10............................. 87 K1
  NRWD SE19....................... 181 G4
Auckland St LBTH SE11........ 122 A5
Auckland Vis WELL DA16 *.... 148 C4
Audax CDALE/KGS NW9........ 45 H5
Auden PI CAMTN NW1.......... 84 A6
  CHEAM SM3 *.................... 208 A2
Audleigh PI CHIG IG7............ 54 A2
Audley CI BTSEA SW11........ 141 F4
  BORE WD6 *....................... 30 A1
  ENC/FH EN2...................... 23 H3
  HDN NW4 *........................ 63 J3
  RCHPK/HAM TW10............ 137 G6
Audley Sq MYFR/PKLN W1K *. 9 H7
Audley Ct BECK BR3............. 181 K6
Audley Gdns GDMY/SEVK IG3. 73 F6
Audley PI BELMT SM2........... 208 E6
Audley Rd EA W5................. 98 B4
  ENC/FH EN2...................... 23 H3
  HDN NW4........................... 63 J3
  RCHPK/HAM TW10............ 137 G6
Audley Sq MYFR/PKLN W1K *. 9 H7
Audrey CI BECK BR3............. 198 E3
Audrey Gdns ALP/SUD HA0.. 61 H6
Audrey Rd IL IG1.................. 72 B6
Audrey St BETH E2............... 7 K1
Audric CI KUTN/CMB KT2..... 175 H4
Augurs La PLSTW E13........... 107 F2
Augusta CI E/WMO/HCT KT8. 172 E6
Augusta Rd WHTN TW2........ 155 H4
Augustine Rd HMSMTH W6.. 119 G3
  KTN/HRWW/WS HA3............ 42 B4
  STMC/STPC BR5................ 186 D1
Augustus CI BTFD TW8......... 136 E1
  SHB W12........................... 118 E2
  STAN HA7........................... 43 H6
Augustus Rd WIM/MER SW19. 159 G3
Augustus St CAMTN NW1...... 4 A3
Aultone Wy CAR SM5........... 209 K1
  SUT SM1............................ 194 A6
Aulton PI LBTH SE11............ 122 B5
Aurelia Gdns CROY/NA CRO.. 196 A2
Aurelia Rd CROY/NA CRO..... 195 K3
Auriel Av DAGE RM10........... 93 F4
Auriga Ms IS N1................... 85 K3
Auriol CI WPK KT4................ 207 G1
Auriol Dr GFD/PVL UB6........ 78 D5
Auriol Park Rd WPK KT4....... 207 G1
Auriol Rd WKENS W14.......... 119 H4
Austell Gdns MLHL NW7....... 31 G4
Austen CI THMD SE28.......... 128 C1
Austen Rd ERITH DA8........... 149 J1
  RYLN/HDSTN HA2.............. 60 B6
Austin Av HAYES BR2........... 200 D2
Austin CI FSTH SE23............. 164 B2
  TWK TW1........................... 156 D4
Austin Friars OBST EC2N...... 13 F3

Austin Friars Sq OBST EC2N * 13 F3
Austin Rd BTSEA SW11 141 F2
HYS/HAR UB3 113 J2
STMC/STPC BR5 202 B3
Austins La HGDN/ICK UB10 76 A1
Austin St BETH E2 7 J5
Austral Cl BFN/LL DA15 168 A5
Australia Rd SHB W12 99 K6
Austral St LBTH SE11 18 A6
Austyn Gdns BRYLDS KT5 * 191 J5
Autumn Cl EN EN1 24 D3
WIM/MER SW19 178 B2
Autumn Dr BELMT SM2 209 F6
Autumn Gv BMLY BR1 184 A2
Autumn St BOW E3 87 J6
Avalon Cl ENC/FH EN2 23 G3
ORP BR6 202 E6
RYNPK SW20 177 H5
WEA W13 97 G4
Avalon Rd FUL/PGN SW6 140 A2
ORP BR6 202 D6
WEA W13 97 G3
Avard Gdns ORP BR6 216 C2
Avarn Rd TOOT SW17 178 E2
Avebury Pk SURB KT6 * 190 E3
Avebury Rd ORP BR6 216 D1
WAN E11 70 B5
WIM/MER SW19 177 J4
Avebury St IS N1 6 E1
Aveline St LBTH SE11 122 A5
Aveling Park Rd WALTH E17 51 J5
Avelon Rd CRW RM5 57 F2
RAIN RM13 93 J6
Ave Marie La STP EC4M 12 B4
Avenell Rd HBRY N5 85 H1
Avening Rd
WAND/EARL SW18 159 K2
Avening Ter
WAND/EARL SW18 159 K1
Avenons Rd PLSTW E13 106 E4
Avenue Cl HEST TW5 134 A2
STHGT/OAK N14 34 C1
STJWD NW8 2 D1
WDR/YW UB7 112 A3
Avenue Crs ACT W3 117 J2
HEST TW5 134 A2
Avenue Elmers SURB KT6 191 F2
Avenue Gdns ACT W3 117 J2
HEST TW5 * 133 K1
MORT/ESHN SW14 138 B4
SNWD SE25 181 H6
TEDD TW11 174 A3
Avenue Ga LOU IG10 39 G1
Avenue Ms MUSWH N10 48 B6
Avenue Pde SUN TW16 172 A6
WCHMH N21 * 35 K2
Avenue Park Rd WNWD SE27 162 C4
Avenue Rd ACT W3 117 J2
BTFD TW8 116 D5
CEND/HSY/T N8 66 D3
CHDH RM6 73 H4
FELT TW13 153 J5
FSTGT E7 89 F2
HGT N6 66 C4
HPTN TW12 173 G4
ISLW TW7 135 K2
KUT/HW KT1 175 F6
NFNCH/WDSPK N12 33 G6
NWMAL KT3 176 B6
PGE/AN SE20 181 K4
PIN HA5 41 J6
RYNPK SW20 176 E5
SEVS/STOTM N15 67 K2
SNWD SE25 181 H5
STHGT/OAK N14 34 C1
STHL UB1 114 E1
STJWD NW8 83 H5
STRHM/NOR SW16 179 J5
TEDD TW11 174 B3
WFD IG8 53 G2
WLGTN SM6 210 C5
WLSDN NW10 99 H1
Avenue South BRYLDS KT5 191 G4
Avenue Ter NWMAL KT3 175 K6
OXHEY WD19 27 J1
The Avenue BAR EN5 20 C4
BECK BR3 182 E4
BELMT SM2 208 D6
BKHH IG9 39 G4
BMLY BR1 184 C6
BRYLDS KT5 191 G3
BXLY DA5 168 E2
CAR SM5 210 A5
CEND/HSY/T N8 49 G6
CHING E4 52 B2
CHSWK W4 118 B3
CLAP SW4 141 F6
CROY/NA CR0 212 A1
ESH/CLAY KT10 204 E4
EW KT17 208 A5
FBAR/BDGN N11 48 B1
FNCH N3 46 E5
GNWCH SE10 145 G1
HEST TW5 133 K2
HPTN TW12 172 E2
HSLW TW3 135 G6
KIL/WHAMP NW6 82 C5
KTN/HRWW/WS HA3 43 F4
LOU IG10 39 J1
MUSWH N10 48 C5
NTHWD HA6 40 A2
ORP BR6 202 A6
PIN HA5 41 K2
PIN HA5 59 K3
RCH/KEW TW9 137 G3
ROM RM1 75 F1
STMC/STPC BR5 186 C3
SUN TW16 172 A5
TOTM N17 50 A5
TWK TW1 136 D6
WAN E11 71 F3
WBLY HA9 62 A5
WEA W13 97 H6
WPK KT4 192 C6
WWKM BR4 199 G4
Averil Gv STRHM/NOR SW16 180 C2
Averill St HMSMTH W6 119 G6
Avern Gdns E/WMO/HCT KT8 189 G1
Avern Rd E/WMO/HCT KT8 189 G1
Avery Farm Rw BGVA SW1W * 15 J7
Avery Gdns GNTH/NBYPK IG2 71 K2
Avery Hill Rd ELTH/MOT SE9 167 H3
ELTH/MOT SE9 167 J1
Avery Rw MYFR/PKLN W1K 9 J5
Aviary Cl CAN/RD E16 106 D4
Aviemore Cl BECK BR3 198 C2
Aviemore Wy BECK BR3 198 B2
Avignon Rd BROCKY SE4 144 A4
Avington Gv PGE/AN SE20 181 K3
Avington Wy PECK SE15 * 143 G1
Avion Crs CDALE/KGS NW9 45 J5
Avior Dr NTHWD HA6 26 D6
Avis Sq WCHPL E1 105 F5
Avoca Rd TOOT SW17 161 F6
Avocet Cl STHWK SE1 123 H5
Avocet Ms THMD SE28 127 J3
Avon Cl SUT SM1 209 G2
WPK KT4 192 D6
YEAD UB4 95 G3
Avon Ct PIN HA5 * 42 A3
Avondale Av CRICK NW2 81 G1
EBAR EN4 33 K3
ESH/CLAY KT10 205 G1
NFNCH/WDSPK N12 47 F1
WPK KT4 192 C5
Avondale Cl LOU IG10 39 K2
Avondale Ct SWFD E18 53 F4
Avondale Crs PEND EN3 25 G4
REDBR IG4 71 H2
Avondale Dr HYS/HAR UB3 113 K1
LOU IG10 39 K1
Avondale Gdns HSLWW TW4 134 E6
Avondale Park Gdns
NTGHL W11 * 100 C6
Avondale Park Rd
NTGHL W11 100 C6
Avondale Pavement
STHWK SE1 * 123 H5
Avondale Ri PECK SE15 143 G4
Avondale Rd ASHF TW15 152 A5
BMLY BR1 183 H2
CAN/RD E16 106 C4
ELTH/MOT SE9 166 D4
FNCH N3 47 G4
KTN/HRWW/WS HA3 43 F6
MORT/ESHN SW14 138 A4
PLMGR N13 35 G4
SAND/SEL CR2 211 J4
SEVS/STOTM N15 67 H2
WALTH E17 69 J4
WELL DA16 148 D3
WIM/MER SW19 178 A1
Avondale Sq STHWK SE1 123 H5
Avonley Rd NWCR SE14 143 K1
Avonmore Gdns
WKENS W14 * 119 J4
Avonmore Pl WKENS W14 119 H4
Avonmore Rd WKENS W14 119 J4
Avonmouth St STHWK SE1 18 C4
Avon Rd BROCKY SE4 144 D4
GFD/PVL UB6 96 A3
WALTH E17 52 B6
Avonstowe Cl ORP BR6 216 C1
Avon Wy SWFD E18 70 E1
Avonwick Rd HSLW TW3 135 G3
Avril Wy CHING E4 52 A1
Avro Wy WLGTN SM6 210 E5
Awberry Ct WATW WD18 * 26 B1
Awlfield Av TOTM N17 49 K4
Awliscombe Rd WELL DA16 148 A3
Axeholm Av EDGW HA8 44 D4
Axe St BARK IG11 90 C6
Axholme Av EDGW HA8 44 C4
Axis Ct GNWCH SE10 125 H6
Axminster Crs WELL DA16 148 D2
Axminster Rd HOLWY N7 84 E1
Axon Pl IL IG1 72 C6
Axtaine Rd STMC/STPC BR5 202 E4
Aybrook St MHST W1U 9 G2
Aycliff Ct KUT/HW KT1 * 175 H5
Aycliffe Cl BMLY BR1 200 E1
Aycliffe Rd SHB W12 118 C1
Aylands Cl WBLY HA9 62 A6
Aylesbury Cl FSTGT E7 88 D4
Aylesbury Rd HAYES BR2 183 K6
WALW SE17 122 E5
Aylesbury St CLKNW EC1R 6 A7
WLSDN NW10 81 F1
Aylesford Av BECK BR3 198 B2
Aylesford St PIM SW1V 121 J5
Aylesham Cl MLHL NW7 45 J3
Aylesham Rd ORP BR6 201 K4
Ayles Rd YEAD UB4 95 F2
Aylestone Av
KIL/WHAMP NW6 82 B5
Aylett Rd ISLW TW7 135 K3
SNWD SE25 197 J1
Ayley Cft EN EN1 24 C6
Ayliffe Cl KUT/HW KT1 175 H5
Aylmer Cl STAN HA7 29 G6
Aylmer Dr STAN HA7 29 G6
Aylmer Pde EFNCH N2 * 65 K2
Aylmer Rd BCTR RM8 92 A1
EFNCH N2 65 J2
SHB W12 118 B2
WAN E11 70 D4
Ayloffe Rd DAGW RM9 92 B4
Aylsham Dr HGDN/ICK UB10 58 A6
Aylton Est
BERM/RHTH SE16 * 123 K2
Aylward Rd FSTH SE23 164 A4
RYNPK SW20 177 J5
Aylwards Ri STAN HA7 29 G6
Aylward St WCHPL E1 105 F5
Aynhoe Rd WKENS W14 119 G4
Aynscombe Angle ORP BR6 202 B4
Ayres Cl PLSTW E13 106 E2
Ayres Crs WLSDN NW10 81 F5
Ayres St STHWK SE1 18 D2
Ayr Gn ROM RM1 57 G4
Ayrsome Rd STNW/STAM N16 86 A1
Ayrton Rd SKENS SW7 14 A4
Ayr Wy ROM RM1 57 G4
Aysgarth Rd DUL SE21 162 E1
Aytoun Pl BRXN/ST SW9 142 A3
Aytoun Rd BRXN/ST SW9 142 A3
Azalea Cl HNWL W7 116 A1
IL IG1 90 B3
Azalea Ct WFD IG8 * 52 C3
Azalea Wk PIN HA5 59 F3
Azania Ms KTTN NW5 84 B3
Azenby Rd PECK SE15 143 G3
Azof St GNWCH SE10 125 H4

B

Baalbec Rd HBRY N5 85 H3
Babbacombe Cl CHSGTN KT9 205 K3
Babbacombe Gdns
REDBR IG4 71 J1
Babbacombe Rd BMLY BR1 184 A4
Baber Bridge Pde
EBED/NFELT TW14 * 154 B1
Baber Dr EBED/NFELT TW14 154 B1
Babington Ri WBLY HA9 80 C4
Babington Rd BCTR RM8 91 J3
HCH RM12 75 K5
HDN NW4 63 K1
STRHM/NOR SW16 179 J1
Babmaes St STJS SW1Y 10 C7
Bache's St IS N1 7 F5
Back Church La WCHPL E1 104 C6
Back Hl CLKNW EC1R 5 K7
Back La BTFD TW8 136 E1
BXLY DA5 169 H2
CEND/HSY/T N8 66 E2
CHDH RM6 73 K4
EDGW HA8 44 E4
HAMP NW3 83 G2
RCHPK/HAM TW10 156 D5
Backley Gdns CROY/NA CR0 197 H3
Back Rd SCUP DA14 168 B6
TEDD TW11 173 K3
WAN E11 70 B3
Bacon Gv STHWK SE1 19 J6
Bacon La CDALE/KGS NW9 62 D1
EDGW HA8 44 C4
Bacon Link CRW RM5 56 D2
Bacon's La HGT N6 66 A5
Bacon St BETH E2 7 K6
WCHPL E1 7 K6
Bacton St BETH E2 104 E2
Baddow Cl DAGE RM10 92 C6
WFD IG8 53 H2
Baden Pl STHWK SE1 18 E2
Baden Powell Cl DAGW RM9 92 A6
SURB KT6 191 G6
Baden Rd CEND/HSY/T N8 66 D1
IL IG1 90 B3
Bader Wy RAIN RM13 93 J4
Badger Cl FELT TW13 154 A5
HSLWW TW4 134 B4
Badgers Cl ENC/FH EN2 23 H4
HRW HA1 60 D3
HYS/HAR UB3 113 H1
Badgers Copse ORP BR6 202 A6
WPK KT4 192 C6
Badgers Ct WPK KT4 * 192 C6
Badgers Cft ELTH/MOT SE9 167 F5
TRDG/WHET N20 32 C2
Badgers Wk NWMAL KT3 176 B5
Badlis Rd WALTH E17 51 J5
Badminton Cl HRW HA1 * 60 E1
NTHLT UB5 78 A4
Badminton Ms CAN/RD E16 125 K1
Badminton Rd BAL SW12 161 F1
Badsworth Rd CMBW SE5 142 D1
Bafton Ga HAYES BR2 200 A5
Bagley Cl WDR/YW UB7 112 B2
Bagley House
WOOL/PLUM SE18 * 146 D1
Bagley's La FUL/PGN SW6 140 A2
Bagleys Spring CHDH RM6 74 A1
Bagshot Ct
WOOL/PLUM SE18 * 147 F2
Bagshot Rd EN EN1 36 B1
Bagshot St WALW SE17 123 F5
Baildon St DEPT SE8 144 C1
Bailey Cl FBAR/BDGN N11 48 D4
THMD SE28 127 K1
Bailey Cots POP/IOD E14 * 105 G4
Bailey Crs CHSGTN KT9 205 K5
Bailey House
WOOL/PLUM SE18 * 146 D1
Bailey Ms BRXS/STRHM SW2 142 B6
CHSWK W4 117 J6
Bailey Pl SYD SE26 181 K2
Baillie Cl RAIN RM13 111 K3
Bainbridge Cl
RCHPK/HAM TW10 175 F1
Bainbridge Rd DAGW RM9 92 B2
Bainbridge St
NOXST/BSQ WC1A 10 D3
Baines Cl SAND/SEL CR2 211 K3
Baird Av STHL UB1 96 B6
Baird Cl BUSH WD23 28 B1
CDALE/KGS NW9 62 E3
LEY E10 69 J5
Baird Gdns NRWD SE19 163 F6
Baird Memorial Cots
STHGT/OAK N14 * 34 D4
Baird Rd EN EN1 24 D4
Baird St STLK EC1Y 6 D6
Baizdon Rd BKHTH/KID SE3 145 H3
Baker La MTCM CR4 179 F5
Baker Ms ORP BR6 217 F4
Baker Pl HOR/WEW KT19 206 E4
Baker Rd WLSDN NW10 81 G6
WOOL/PLUM SE18 146 D1
Bakers Av WALTH E17 69 K3
Bakers Cl DART DA1 171 G2
Bakers End RYNPK SW20 177 H5
Bakers Fld HOLWY N7 84 D2
Bakers Gdns CAR SM5 194 D6
Bakers Hl BAR EN5 21 F3
CLPT E5 68 D5
Baker's Ms MHST W1U 9 G3
Bakers Rents BETH E2 7 J4
Bakers Rw SRTFD E15 106 C1
Baker's Rw CLKNW EC1R 5 J7
Baker St CAMTN NW1 3 F7
EN EN1 23 K3
MHST W1U 9 G2
Baker's Yd CLKNW EC1R 5 J7
Bakery Cl BRXN/ST SW9 * 142 A1
Bakery Ms SURB KT6 191 H5
Bakewell Wy NWMAL KT3 176 B5
Balaams La STHGT/OAK N14 34 D4
Balaam St PLSTW E13 106 E2
Balaclava Rd STHWK SE1 19 K7
SURB KT6 190 D4
Bala Gn CDALE/KGS NW9 * 63 G3
Balcaskie Rd ELTH/MOT SE9 146 E6
Balchier Rd EDUL SE22 163 J1
Balcombe Cl BXLYHS DA6 148 E5
Balcombe St CAMTN NW1 2 E6
Balcorne St HOM E9 86 E5
Balder Ri LEE/GVPK SE12 166 A4
Balderton St OXSTW W1C 9 H4
Baldock St BOW E3 105 K1
Baldry Gdns
STRHM/NOR SW16 179 K2
Baldwin Crs CMBW SE5 142 D2
Baldwin Gdns HSLW TW3 135 H2
Baldwin Rd BTSEA SW11 161 F1
Baldwin's Gdns FSBYW WC1X 11 J1
Baldwin St FSBYE EC1V 6 E5
Baldwin Ter IS N1 6 C2
Baldwyn Gdns ACT W3 98 E6
Bale Rd WCHPL E1 105 G4
Bales Ter ED N9 * 36 B5
Balfern Gv CHSWK W4 118 B5
Balfern St BTSEA SW11 140 D3
Balfe St IS N1 5 F3
Balfour Av HNWL W7 116 A1
Balfour Gv TRDG/WHET N20 33 K5
Balfour Ms ED N9 36 C5
MYFR/PKLN W1K 9 H7
Balfour Pl MYFR/PKLN W1K 9 H6
PUT/ROE SW15 138 E5
Balfour Rd ACT W3 98 E4
CAR SM5 209 K5
HAYES BR2 200 C2
HBRY N5 85 J2
HRW HA1 60 D2
HSLW TW3 135 G4
IL IG1 72 B6
NWDGN UB2 114 C3
SNWD SE25 197 H1
WEA W13 116 C2
WIM/MER SW19 178 A3
Balfour St STHWK SE1 18 E6
Balgonie Rd CHING E4 38 B3
Balgores Crs GPK RM2 57 K6
Balgores La GPK RM2 75 K1
Balgores Sq GPK RM2 75 K1
Balgowan Cl NWMAL KT3 192 B1
Balgowan Rd BECK BR3 182 B6
Balgowan St
WOOL/PLUM SE18 128 A4
Balham Gv BAL SW12 161 F2
Balham High Rd BAL SW12 161 G3
Balham Hl BAL SW12 161 G2
Balham New Rd BAL SW12 161 G2
Balham Park Rd BAL SW12 160 E3
Balham Rd ED N9 36 C4
Balham Station Rd BAL SW12 161 F3
Balkan Wk WAP E1W * 104 D6
Balladier Wk POP/IOD E14 105 K4
Ballance Rd HOM E9 87 F4
Ballantine St
WAND/EARL SW18 140 B5
Ballantyne Cl ELTH/MOT SE9 166 D6
Ballard Cl KUTN/CMB KT2 176 A3
Ballards Cl DAGE RM10 92 D6
Ballards Farm Rd
SAND/SEL CR2 212 C4
Ballards La FNCH N3 47 F3
Ballards Ms EDGW HA8 44 C2
Ballards Ri SAND/SEL CR2 212 C4
Ballards Rd CRICK NW2 63 J6
DAGE RM10 92 D6
Ballards Wy SAND/SEL CR2 212 C4
Ballast Quay GNWCH SE10 125 G5
Ballater Cl OXHEY WD19 27 G6
Ballater Rd BRXS/STRHM SW2 141 K5
SAND/SEL CR2 212 B3
Ballina St FSTH SE23 164 A2
Ballingdon Rd BTSEA SW11 161 F1
Ballinger Wy NTHLT UB5 95 J3
Balliol Av CHING E4 38 B6
Balliol Rd NKENS W10 100 A5
TOTM N17 50 A4
WELL DA16 148 C3
Balloch Rd CAT SE6 165 G3
Ballogie Av WLSDN NW10 81 G2
Ballow Cl CMBW SE5 * 142 E1
Ball's Pond Pl IS N1 * 85 K4
Balls Pond Rd IS N1 85 K4
Balmain Cl EA W5 116 E1
Balmer Rd BOW E3 105 H1
Balmes Rd IS N1 85 K6
Balmoral Av BECK BR3 198 B1
FBAR/BDGN N11 48 A2
Balmoral Cl PUT/ROE SW15 * 159 G1
Balmoral Crs
E/WMO/HCT KT8 173 F6
Balmoral Dr STHL UB1 95 K3
YEAD UB4 94 C3
Balmoral Gdns BXLY DA5 169 G2
WEA W13 116 B3
Balmoral Gv HOLWY N7 85 F4
Balmoral Ms SHB W12 118 C3
Balmoral Rd CRICK NW2 81 K4
FSTGT E7 89 G2
GPK RM2 75 K1
KUT/HW KT1 191 G1
LEY E10 69 K6
RYLN/HDSTN HA2 78 A2
WPK KT4 207 K1
Balmore Crs EBAR EN4 22 A6
Balmore St ARCH N19 66 B6
Balmuir Gdns PUT/ROE SW15 139 F5
Balnacraig Av WLSDN NW10 81 G2
Balniel Ga PIM SW1V 121 J5
Baltic Cl WIM/MER SW19 178 C3
Baltic St East STLK EC1Y 6 C7
Baltic St West FARR EC1M 6 C7
Baltimore Pl WELL DA16 148 A3
Balvaird Pl PIM SW1V 121 J5
Balvernie Gv
WAND/EARL SW18 159 J2
Bamber Rd PECK SE15 143 G2
Bamborough Gdns SHB W12 119 F2
Bamford Av ALP/SUD HA0 80 B6
Bamford Rd BMLY BR1 183 G1
Bamford Wy CRW RM5 56 D1
Bampfylde Cl WLGTN SM6 210 C1
Bampton Dr MLHL NW7 45 J3
Bampton Rd FSTH SE23 164 A5
Banavie Gdns BECK BR3 182 E4
Banbury Cl ENC/FH EN2 23 H2
Banbury Ct BELMT SM2 * 208 E5
COVGDN WC2E * 10 E5
Banbury Rd HOM E9 87 F5
WALTH E17 51 G3
Banbury St BTSEA SW11 * 140 D3
Banchory Rd BKHTH/KID SE3 146 A1
Bancroft Av EFNCH N2 65 J2
Bancroft Cha HCH RM12 75 H6
Bancroft Ct NTHLT UB5 77 G6
Bancroft Gdns
KTN/HRWW/WS HA3 42 C4
ORP BR6 202 A5
Bancroft Rd
KTN/HRWW/WS HA3 42 C5
WCHPL E1 104 E3
Bandon Ri WLGTN SM6 210 D3
Banfield Rd PECK SE15 143 J4
Bangalore St PUT/ROE SW15 139 F4
Bangor Cl NTHLT UB5 78 B3
Banim St HMSMTH W6 118 E3
Banister Rd NKENS W10 100 B2
Bank Av MTCM CR4 178 C5
Bank Blds CHING E4 * 52 B2
Bank End STHWK SE1 12 D7
Bankfoot Rd BMLY BR1 165 H6
Bankhurst Rd CAT SE6 164 C2
Bank La KUTN/CMB KT2 175 F3
PUT/ROE SW15 138 B6
Bank Ms SUT SM1 209 G4
Banksia Rd UED N18 50 E1
Bankside ENC/FH EN2 23 H2
SAND/SEL CR2 212 B4
STHL UB1 114 C1
STHWK SE1 12 C6
Bankside Av LEW SE13 145 F4
NTHLT UB5 94 E1
Bankside Cl CAR SM5 209 J3
ISLW TW7 136 A5
Bankside Dr THDIT KT7 190 C6
Bankside Rd IL IG1 90 C3
Banks Wy MNPK E12 90 A2
Banksyard HEST TW5 114 E6
The Bank HGT N6 66 B5
Bankton Rd
BRXS/STRHM SW2 142 B5
Bankwell Rd LEW SE13 145 H5
Banner St STLK EC1Y 6 D7
Banning St GNWCH SE10 125 H5
Bannister Cl
BRXS/STRHM SW2 162 B3
GFD/PVL UB6 78 D3
Bannister Gdns
STMC/STPC BR5 186 D6
Bannockburn Rd
WOOL/PLUM SE18 127 K
Bannow Cl HOR/WEW KT19 207 G
Banstead Ct SHB W12 99 H
Banstead Gdns ED N9 35 K
Banstead Rd CAR SM5 209 H
Banstead St PECK SE15 143 K
Banstead Wy WLGTN SM6 210 E
Banstock Rd EDGW HA8 44 D
Banting Dr WCHMH N21 23 F
Banton Cl EN EN1 24 D
Bantry St CMBW SE5 142 E
Banwell Rd BXLY DA5 168 E
Banyard Rd
BERM/RHTH SE16 123
Bapchild Pl STMC/STPC BR5 202 D
Baptist Gdns KTTN NW5 84 A
Barandon Wk NTGHL W11 * 100 E
Barbara Castle Cl
FUL/PGN SW6 119
Barbara Hucklesbury Cl
WDGN N22 49
Barbauld Rd STNW/STAM N16 86
Barber Cl WCHMH N21 35
Barbers Rd SRTFD E15 105
Barbican Rd GFD/PVL UB6 96
Barb Ms HMSMTH W6 119
Barbon Aly LVPST EC2M 13
Barbon Cl BMSBY WC1N 11
Barbot Cl ED N9 36
Barchard St
WAND/EARL SW18 140
Barchester Cl HNWL W7 116
Barchester Rd
KTN/HRWW/WS HA3 42
Barchester St POP/IOD E14 105
Barclay Cl FUL/PGN SW6 * 139
WATW WD18 26
Barclay Ov WFD IG8 38
Barclay Rd CROY/NA CR0 211
FUL/PGN SW6 139
PLSTW E13 107
UED N18 49
WALTH E17 70
WAN E11 70
Barcombe Av
BRXS/STRHM SW2 161
Barcombe Cl STMC/STPC BR5 186
Barden St WOOL/PLUM SE18 147
Bardfield Av CHDH RM6 55
Bardney Rd MRDN SM4 194
Bardolph Av CROY/NA CR0 213
Bardolph Rd HOLWY N7 84
RCH/KEW TW9 137
Bard Rd NKENS W10 100
Bardsey Pl WCHPL E1 104
Bardsey Wk IS N1 * 85
Bardsley Cl CROY/NA CR0 212
Bardsley La GNWCH SE10 125
Barfett St NKENS W10 100
Barfield Av TRDG/WHET N20 33
Barfield Rd BMLY BR1 185
WAN E11 * 70
Barford Cl HDN NW4 45
Barford St IS N1 5
Barforth Rd PECK SE15 143
Barfreston Wy PGE/AN SE20 181
Bargate Cl NWMAL KT3 192
WOOL/PLUM SE18 128
Barge House St STHWK SE1 1
Barge La BOW E3 87
Bargery Rd CAT SE6 164

Barge Wk KUT/HW KT1 174 E5
Bargrove Cl PGE/AN SE20 181 H3
Bargrove Crs CAT SE6 164 C4
Barham Cl ALP/SUD HA0 79 H4
CHST BR7 185 G1
HAYES BR2 200 D5
ROMW/RG RM7 56 D5
Barham Ct ALP/SUD HA0 79 J4
Barham Rd CHST BR7 185 G1
RYNPK SW20 176 D3
SAND/SEL CR2 211 J2
WIM/MER SW19 176 C2
Baring Rd CROY/NA CR0 197 H5
EBAR EN4 21 H4
LEE/GVPK SE12 166 A4
LEE/GVPK SE12 166 A6
Baring St IS N1 6 E1
Barker Cl NTHWD HA6 40 D3
NWMAL KT3 191 J1
RCH/KEW TW9 137 J3
Barker Dr CAMTN NW1 84 C5
Barker St WBPTN SW10 120 B6
Barker Wk STRHM/NOR SW16 161 J5
Barkham Rd TOTM N17 49 K3
Bark Hart Rd ORP BR6 202 C5
Barking Rd EHAM E6 107 H1
POP/IOD E14 106 C5
Bark Pl BAY/PAD W2 101 F6
Barkston Gdns ECT SW5 120 A4
Barkway Dr ORP BR6 216 A2
Barkwood Cl ROMW/RG RM7 74 E2
Barkworth Rd
BERM/RHTH SE16 123 J5
Barlborough St NWCR SE14 144 A1
Barlby Gdns NKENS W10 100 B3
Barlby Rd NKENS W10 100 A4
Barley Cl ALP/SUD HA0 79 K2
Barleycorn Wy POP/IOD E14 105 H6
Barley La GDMY/SEVK IG3 73 G3
Barley Mow Pas CHSWK W4 118 A5
Barlow Cl WLGTN SM6 210 E4
Barlow Dr BKHTH/KID SE3 146 D2
WOOL/PLUM SE18 146 D2
Barlow Pl MYFR/PICC W1J 9 K6
Barlow Rd ACT W3 117 J1
HPTN TW12 173 F3
KIL/WHAMP NW6 82 D4
Barlow St WALW SE17 19 F6
Barlow Wy RAIN RM13 111 F5
Barlow Wy South RAIN RM13 111 F5
Barmeston Rd CAT SE6 164 E4
Barmor Cl RYLN/HDSTN HA2 42 B5
Barmouth Av GFD/PVL UB6 97 F1
Barmouth Rd CROY/NA CR0 198 A6
WAND/EARL SW18 160 B1
Barnabas Rd HOM E9 87 F4
Barnaby Cl RYLN/HDSTN HA2 60 C6
Barnaby Pl SKENS SW7 14 A7
Barnard Cl CHST BR7 185 J4
SUN TW16 172 A3
WLGTN SM6 210 D5
WOOL/PLUM SE18 127 F4
Barnard Gdns NWMAL KT3 192 D1
YEAD UB4 95 F3
Barnard Hl MUSWH N10 48 B5
Barnard Ms BTSEA SW11 140 D5
Barnardo Dr BARK/HLT IG6 72 C1
Barnardo Gdns WCHPL E1 * 105 F5
Barnardo St WCHPL E1 105 F5
Barnard Rd BTSEA SW11 140 D5
EN EN1 24 D3
MTCM CR4 179 F6
Barnards Pl SAND/SEL CR2 211 H6
Barnby St CAMTN NW1 4 B3
SRTFD E15 88 C6
Barn Cl KTTN NW5 * 84 D3
NTHLT UB5 95 G1
Barn Crs STAN HA7 43 J2
Barneby Cl WHTN TW2 155 K3
Barnehurst Av BXLYHN DA7 149 K2
Barnehurst Cl ERITH DA8 149 K2
Barnehurst Rd BXLYHN DA7 149 K3
Barnes Av BARN SW13 138 D1
NWDGN UB2 114 E4
Barnes Br CHSWK W4 138 B3
Barnes Cl MNPK E12 89 H2
Barnesdale Crs
STMC/STPC BR5 202 B3
Barnes End NWMAL KT3 192 D2
Barnes High St BARN SW13 138 C3
Barnes Rd IL IG1 90 C3
UED N18 36 E6
Barnes St POP/IOD E14 105 G5
Barnes Ter DEPT SE8 124 C5
Barnet Dr HAYES BR2 200 D6
Barnet Gate La BAR EN5 31 H1
Barnet Gv BETH E2 104 C2
Barnet Hl BAR EN5 20 D5
Barnet La BORE WD6 30 B1
TRDG/WHET N20 32 D3
Barnet Rd BAR EN5 31 G1
Barnett Cl ERITH DA8 150 C3
Barnetts Ct
RYLN/HDSTN HA2 * 78 B1
Barnett St WCHPL E1 104 D5
Barnet Way (Barnet By-Pass)
MLHL NW7 31 F2
Barnet Wood Rd HAYES BR2 200 B6
HAYES BR2 * 215 F1
Barney Cl CHARL SE7 126 B5
Barn Fld HAMP NW3 * 83 K3
Barnfield NWMAL KT3 192 B3
Barnfield Av CROY/NA CR0 197 K5
KUTN/CMB KT2 156 E6
MTCM CR4 195 G1
Barnfield Cl FSBYPK N4 66 E4
SWLY BR8 203 K4
TOOT SW17 160 B5
Barnfield Gdns
KUTN/CMB KT2 175 F1
WOOL/PLUM SE18 * 127 G6
Barnfield Pl POP/IOD E14 124 D4
Barnfield Rd BELV DA17 129 G6
EA W5 97 J3
EDGW HA8 44 E4
SAND/SEL CR2 212 A6
STMC/STPC BR5 186 E6
WOOL/PLUM SE18 127 G6
Barnfield Wood Cl BECK BR3 199 G3
Barnfield Wood Rd BECK BR3 199 G3
Barnham Dr THMD SE28 128 A1
Barnham Rd GFD/PVL UB6 96 C2
Barnham St STHWK SE1 19 H2
Barnhill PIN HA5 59 G2
Barn Hl WBLY HA9 62 D6
Barnhill La YEAD UB4 95 F2
Barnhill Rd WBLY HA9 80 E1
YEAD UB4 95 F3
Barnhurst Pth OXHEY WD19 41 G1
Barningham Wy
CDALE/KGS NW9 62 E3
Barnlea Cl FELT TW13 154 D4
Barnmead Gdns DAGW RM9 92 B3
Barnmead Rd BECK BR3 182 A4
DAGW RM9 92 B3
Barn Ri WBLY HA9 62 C5
Barnsbury Cl NWMAL KT3 191 K1
Barnsbury Crs BRYLDS KT5 191 K5
Barnsbury Est IS N1 5 H1
Barnsbury Gv HOLWY N7 85 F5
Barnsbury La BRYLDS KT5 191 J6
Barnsbury Pk IS N1 85 G5
Barnsbury Rd IS N1 5 J1
Barnsbury Sq IS N1 85 G5
Barnsbury St IS N1 85 G5
Barnsbury Ter IS N1 85 F5
Barnscroft RYNPK SW20 176 E6
Barnsdale Av POP/IOD E14 124 E4
Barnsdale Rd MV/WKIL W9 100 D3
Barnsley St WCHPL E1 104 D3
Barnstaple La LEW SE13 145 F5
Barnstaple Rd RSLP HA4 77 G1
Barnston Wk IS N1 * 85 J6
Barn St STNW/STAM N16 68 A6
Barn Wy WBLY HA9 62 C5
Barnwell Rd
BRXS/STRHM SW2 142 B6
Barnwood Cl MV/WKIL W9 101 F3
RSLP HA4 58 B6
Baron Cl FBAR/BDGN N11 48 A1
Baroness Rd BETH E2 7 K4
Baronet Gv TOTM N17 50 C4
Baronet Rd TOTM N17 50 C4
Baron Gdns BARK/HLT IG6 54 C6
Baron Gv MTCM CR4 194 D1
Baron Rd BCTR RM8 73 K5
Barons Cl IS N1 * 5 J2
Baron's Court Rd WKENS W14 119 H5
Baronsfield Rd TWK TW1 * 156 C1
Barons Ga EBAR EN4 33 J1
Barons Keep WKENS W14 * 119 H5
Barons Md HRW HA1 60 E1
Baronsmead Rd BARN SW13 138 D2
Baronsmede EA W5 117 G2
Baronsmere Ct BAR EN5 * 20 C5
Baronsmere Rd EFNCH N2 65 J1
Baron's Pl STHWK SE1 17 K3
The Barons TWK TW1 156 C1
Baron St IS N1 5 K3
Baron's Wk CROY/NA CR0 198 B3
Barque Ms DEPT SE8 124 D6
Barrack Rd HSLWW TW4 134 C5
Barra Hall Rd HYS/HAR UB3 94 C6
Barratt Av WDGN N22 49 F5
Barratt Wy
KTN/HRWW/WS HA3 42 D6
Barrenger Rd MUSWH N10 47 K4
Barrett Cl HARH RM3 57 K3
Barrett Rd WALTH E17 70 A1
Barrett's Green Rd
WLSDN NW10 98 E1
Barrett's Gv STNW/STAM N16 86 A3
Barrett St MHST W1U 9 H4
Barrhill Rd BRXS/STRHM SW2 161 K4
Barriedale NWCR SE14 144 B2
Barrier Point Rd CAN/RD E16 126 B1
Barringer Sq TOOT SW17 161 F6
Barrington Cl CLAY IG5 53 K4
KTTN NW5 84 A3
Barrington Rd BRXN/ST SW9 142 C4
BXLYHN DA7 148 E3
CEND/HSY/T N8 66 D2
CHEAM SM3 193 K5
MNPK E12 90 A4
Barrington Vls
WOOL/PLUM SE18 147 F2
Barrington Wk NRWD SE19 * 181 F2
Barrow Av CAR SM5 209 K5
Barrow Cl WCHMH N21 35 H5
Barrowdene Cl PIN HA5 41 J5
Barrowell Gn WCHMH N21 35 H4
Barrowgate Rd CHSWK W4 117 K5
Barrow Hedges Cl CAR SM5 209 J5
Barrow Hedges Wy CAR SM5 209 J5
Barrow Hl WPK KT4 192 B6
Barrow Hill Cl WPK KT4 192 B6
Barrow Hill Est STJWD NW8 2 C3
Barrow Hill Rd STJWD NW8 2 C3
Barrow Point Av PIN HA5 41 J5
Barrow Point La PIN HA5 41 J5
Barrow Rd CROY/NA CR0 211 G3
STRHM/NOR SW16 179 J2
Barrs Rd WLSDN NW10 81 F5
Barry Av SEVS/STOTM N15 68 B3
Barry Cl ORP BR6 216 E1
Barry Pde EDUL SE22 * 143 H5
Barry Rd EDUL SE22 163 H1
EHAM E6 107 J5
WLSDN NW10 80 E5
Barry Ter ASHF TW15 * 152 C4
Barset Rd PECK SE15 143 K4
Barsons Cl PGE/AN SE20 181 K3
Barston Rd WNWD SE27 162 D4
Barstow Crs
BRXS/STRHM SW2 162 A3
Barter St NOXST/BSQ WC1A 11 F2
Barth Ms WOOL/PLUM SE18 127 K4
Bartholomew Cl STBT EC1A 12 C2
WAND/EARL SW18 140 B5
Bartholomew La OBST EC2N 13 F3
Bartholomew Pl KTTN NW5 84 C4
Bartholomew Sq FSBYE EC1V 6 D6
Bartholomew St STHWK SE1 18 E5
Bartholomew Vls KTTN NW5 84 C4
Barth Rd WOOL/PLUM SE18 127 K4
Bartle Av EHAM E6 107 J1
Bartle Rd NTGHL W11 100 B5
Bartlett Cl POP/IOD E14 105 J5
Bartlett Ct FLST/FETLN EC4A * 11 K3
Bartlett St SAND/SEL CR2 211 K3
Bartlow Gdns CRW RM5 57 F4
Barton Av ROMW/RG RM7 74 E5
Barton Cl EHAM E6 107 K5
HDN NW4 63 J2
HOM E9 86 E3
PECK SE15 143 J4
Barton Gn NWMAL KT3 176 A5
Barton Mdw BARK/HLT IG6 72 B1
Barton Rd HCH RM12 75 J5
SCUP DA14 187 F2
WKENS W14 119 H5
The Bartons BORE WD6 29 K1
Barton St WEST SW1P 16 E5
Bartram Rd BROCKY SE4 144 B6
Bartrams La EBAR EN4 21 G1
Bartrip St HOM E9 87 G4
Barts Cl BECK BR3 198 D2
Barwell Ct CHSGTN KT9 * 205 J5
Barwell La CHSGTN KT9 205 J5
Barwick Rd FSTGT E7 89 F2
Barwood Av WWKM BR4 198 E5
Bascome St
BRXS/STRHM SW2 162 B1
Basden Gv FELT TW13 155 F4
Basedale Rd DAGW RM9 91 H5
Baseing Cl EHAM E6 108 A6
Basevi Wy DEPT SE8 124 D6
Bashley Rd WLSDN NW10 99 F3
Basil Av EHAM E6 107 J2
Basildene Rd HSLWW TW4 134 C4
Basildon Av CLAY IG5 54 A4
Basildon Cl BELMT SM2 209 F6
WATW WD18 26 A1
Basildon Rd ABYW SE2 128 B4
Basil Gdns CROY/NA CR0 198 A5
WNWD SE27 180 D1
Basil St CHEL SW3 14 E3
Basin Ap CAN/RD E16 108 B6
POP/IOD E14 105 G5
Basing Cl THDIT KT7 190 A4
Basing Ct PECK SE15 143 G2
Basingdon Wy CMBW SE5 142 E5
Basing Dr BXLY DA5 169 G1
Basingfield Rd THDIT KT7 190 A4
Basinghall Av CITYW EC2V 12 E3
Basinghall Gdns BELMT SM2 209 F6
Basinghall St CITYW EC2V 12 E3
Basing Hl GLDGN NW11 64 D5
WBLY HA9 62 B6
Basing Pl BETH E2 7 H4
Basing St NTGHL W11 100 D5
Basing Wy FNCH N3 46 E6
THDIT KT7 190 A4
Basire St IS N1 85 J6
Baskerville Gdns
WLSDN NW10 81 G2
Baskerville Rd
WAND/EARL SW18 160 D2
Basket Gdns ELTH/MOT SE9 146 D6
Baslow Cl
KTN/HRWW/WS HA3 42 D4
Baslow Wk CLPT E5 87 F2
Basnett Rd BTSEA SW11 * 141 F4
Bassano St EDUL SE22 143 G6
Bassant Rd WOOL/PLUM SE18 128 A6
Bassein Park Rd SHB W12 118 C2
Bassett Cl BELMT SM2 209 F6
Bassett Gdns ISLW TW7 135 H1
Bassett Rd NKENS W10 100 B5
Bassetts Cl ORP BR6 216 B2
Bassett St KTTN NW5 84 A4
Bassetts Wy ORP BR6 216 B2
Bassett Wy GFD/PVL UB6 96 B5
Bassingham Rd ALP/SUD HA0 79 K4
WAND/EARL SW18 160 B2
Basswood Cl PECK SE15 143 J4
Bastable Av BARK IG11 109 F1
Bastion Rd ABYW SE2 128 B5
Baston Manor Rd WWKM BR4 215 F1
Baston Rd HAYES BR2 200 A6
HAYES BR2 215 G2
Bastwick St FSBYE EC1V 6 B6
Basuto Rd FUL/PGN SW6 139 K2
Batavia Ms NWCR SE14 144 B1
Batavia Rd NWCR SE14 144 B1
SUN TW16 172 A4
Batchelor St IS N1 5 J2
Batchwood Gn
STMC/STPC BR5 202 B1
Batchworth La NTHWD HA6 40 A1
Bateman Cl BARK IG11 90 C4
Bateman Rd CHING E4 51 J2
Bateman's Blds
SOHO/SHAV W1D 10 C4
Batemans Cnr CHSWK W4 * 118 A5
Bateman's Rw SDTCH EC2A 7 H6
Bateman St SOHO/SHAV W1D 10 C4
Bates Crs CROY/NA CR0 211 G3
STRHM/NOR SW16 179 H3
Bate St POP/IOD E14 105 H6
Bath Cl PECK SE15 143 J1
Bathgate Rd WIM/MER SW19 159 G5
Bath Gv BETH E2 104 C1
Bath House Rd CROY/NA CR0 195 K5
Bath Pas KUT/HW KT1 174 E5
Bath Pl BAR EN5 20 D4
SDTCH EC2A * 7 G5
Bath Rd CHSWK W4 118 B4
ED N9 36 D4
FSTGT E7 89 H4
HSLWW TW4 134 C3
WDR/YW UB7 132 A2
Baths Ap FUL/PGN SW6 * 139 J1
Bath St FSBYE EC1V 6 D5
Bath Ter STHWK SE1 18 C5
Bathurst Av WIM/MER SW19 178 A4
Bathurst Gdns WLSDN NW10 99 K1
Bathurst Ms BAY/PAD W2 8 B5
Bathurst Rd IL IG1 72 B5
Bathurst St BAY/PAD W2 8 B5
Bathway WOOL/PLUM SE18 127 F4
Batley Cl MTCM CR4 194 E4
Batley Pl STNW/STAM N16 86 B1
Batley Rd ENC/FH EN2 23 J2
STNW/STAM N16 86 B1
Batman Cl SHB W12 118 E1
Batoum Gdns HMSMTH W6 119 F3
Batson St SHB W12 118 D2
Batsworth Rd MTCM CR4 178 C6
Batten Cl EHAM E6 107 K5
Batten Cots POP/IOD E14 * 105 G4
Batten St BTSEA SW11 140 D4
Battersby Rd CAT SE6 165 G4
Battersea Br WBPTN SW10 140 C1
Battersea Bridge Rd
BTSEA SW11 140 D1
Battersea Church Rd
BTSEA SW11 140 C2
Battersea High St
BTSEA SW11 140 C3
Battersea Park Rd
BTSEA SW11 141 F2
Battersea Ri BTSEA SW11 140 D6
Battersea Sq BTSEA SW11 * 140 D1
Battery Rd THMD SE28 127 K2
THMD SE28 128 A1
Battishill St IS N1 85 H5
Battle Bridge La STHWK SE1 19 G1
Battle Cl WIM/MER SW19 178 B2
Battledean Rd HBRY N5 85 H3
Battle Rd ERITH DA8 129 K4
Batty St WCHPL E1 104 C5
Baudwin Rd CAT SE6 165 H4
Baugh Rd SCUP DA14 186 D1
The Baulk WAND/EARL SW18 159 K2
Bavant Rd STRHM/NOR SW16 179 K5
Bavaria Rd ARCH N19 66 E6
Bavdene Ms HDN NW4 63 K1
Bavent Rd CMBW SE5 142 D3
Bawdale Rd EDUL SE22 143 G6
Bawdsey Av GNTH/NBYPK IG2 73 F1
Bawtree Rd NWCR SE14 144 B1
Bawtry Rd TRDG/WHET N20 33 K5
Baxendale TRDG/WHET N20 33 G4
Baxendale St BETH E2 104 C2
Baxter Cl NWDGN UB2 115 G3
Baxter Rd CAN/RD E16 107 G5
IL IG1 90 B3
IS N1 85 K4
UED N18 36 D6
Bay Ct EA W5 * 117 F3
Baycroft Cl PIN HA5 * 41 G6
Bayfield Rd ELTH/MOT SE9 146 C5
Bayford Ms HACK E8 * 86 D5
Bayford Rd WLSDN NW10 100 B2
Bayford St HACK E8 86 D5
Baygrove Ms KUT/HW KT1 174 D4
Bayham Pl CAMTN NW1 4 A1
Bayham Rd CHSWK W4 118 A3
MRDN SM4 194 A1
WEA W13 97 H6
Bayham St CAMTN NW1 4 A1
Bayhurst Dr NTHWD HA6 40 D2
Bayleaf Cl HPTN TW12 173 J1
Bayley St FITZ W1T 10 C2
Baylis Ms TWK TW1 156 B2
Baylis Rd STHWK SE1 17 J4
Bayliss Av THMD SE28 109 K6
Bayliss Cl ENC/FH EN2 22 E6
Bayne Cl EHAM E6 107 K5
Baynes Cl EN EN1 24 C2
Baynes Ms HAMP NW3 83 H4
Baynes St CAMTN NW1 84 C5
Baynham Cl BXLY DA5 169 G1
Bayonne Rd HMSMTH W6 119 H6
Bays Cl SYD SE26 181 K1
Bayshill Ri NTHLT UB5 78 B4
Bayston Rd STNW/STAM N16 86 B1
Bayswater Rd BAY/PAD W2 101 G6
Baythorne St BOW E3 105 H4
Baytree Cl BFN/LL DA15 168 A3
BMLY BR1 184 C4
Baytree Rd BRXS/STRHM SW2 142 A5
Bazalgette Cl NWMAL KT3 191 K2
Bazalgette Gdns NWMAL KT3 192 A2
Bazely St POP/IOD E14 106 A6
Bazile Rd WCHMH N21 35 G1
Beacham Cl CHARL SE7 126 C6
Beachborough Rd BMLY BR1 165 F6
Beachcroft Rd WAN E11 88 C1
Beach Gv FELT TW13 155 F5
Beachy Rd BOW E3 87 J5
Beacon Ga NWCR SE14 144 A4
Beacon Hl HOLWY N7 84 E3
Beacon Pl CROY/NA CR0 210 E1
Beacon Rd ERITH DA8 150 E1
HTHAIR TW6 152 D1
LEW SE13 165 G1
Beaconsfield Cl CHSWK W4 117 K5
Beaconsfield Cots
TRDG/WHET N20 * 32 E5
Beaconsfield Gdns
ESH/CLAY KT10 204 E5
Beaconsfield Rd BMLY BR1 184 C6
CAN/RD E16 106 D3
CHSWK W4 118 A3
CROY/NA CR0 196 E3
EA W5 116 D2
ED N9 36 C5
ELTH/MOT SE9 166 D5
ESH/CLAY KT10 204 E5
LEY E10 * 88 A1
NWMAL KT3 176 A5
SEVS/STOTM N15 68 A1
SURB KT6 191 G4
TRDG/WHET N20 33 K5
TWK TW1 156 C1
WALTH E17 69 H3
WALW SE17 122 E6
WLSDN NW10 81 H4
YEAD UB4 114 B1
Beaconsfield Terrace Rd
WKENS W14 119 H3
Beaconsfield Wk
FUL/PGN SW6 139 J2
Beacontree Av WALTH E17 52 B4
Beacontree Rd WAN E11 70 D4
Beadlow Cl CAR SM5 194 C3
Beadman Pl WNWD SE27 * 162 C6
Beadman St WNWD SE27 162 C6
Beadnell Rd FSTH SE23 164 A3
Beadon Rd HMSMTH W6 119 F4
Beaford Gv RYNPK SW20 177 H6
Beagle Cl FELT TW13 154 A6
Beagles Cl STMC/STPC BR5 202 E6
Beak St REGST W1B 10 A5
Beal Cl WELL DA16 148 B2
Beale Cl PLMGR N13 49 H1
Beale Pl BOW E3 105 H1
Beale Rd BOW E3 87 H6
Beal Rd IL IG1 72 A6
Beam Av DAGE RM10 92 D6
Beames Rd WLSDN NW10 81 F6
Beaminster Gdns
BARK/HLT IG6 54 B6
Beamish Dr BUSH WD23 28 C3
Beamish Rd ED N9 36 C3
STMC/STPC BR5 202 D4
Beamway DAGE RM10 93 F5
Beanacre Cl HOM E9 87 H4
Bean Rd BXLYHS DA6 148 E5
Beanshaw ELTH/MOT SE9 167 F6
Beansland Gv CHDH RM6 56 A5
Bear Cl ROMW/RG RM7 74 D3
Beardell St NRWD SE19 181 G2
Beardow Gv
STHGT/OAK N14 * 34 C1
Beard Rd KUTN/CMB KT2 175 G1
Beardsfield PLSTW E13 88 E6
Beard's Hl HPTN TW12 173 F4
Beard's Hill Cl HPTN TW12 173 F4
Beardsley Wy ACT W3 118 A2
Bearfield Rd KUTN/CMB KT2 175 F3
Bear Gdns STHWK SE1 12 C7
Bear La STHWK SE1 12 B7
Bear Rd FELT TW13 154 C6
Bearstead Ri BROCKY SE4 144 C6
Bearstead Ter BECK BR3 * 182 D4
Bear St LSQ/SEVD WC2H 10 D5
Beatrice Av
STRHM/NOR SW16 180 A6
WBLY HA9 80 A3
Beatrice Cl PIN HA5 58 E1
PLSTW E13 106 E3
Beatrice Pl KENS W8 120 A3
Beatrice Rd ED N9 36 E2
FSBYPK N4 67 G4
RCHPK/HAM TW10 137 G6
STHL UB1 114 E1
STHWK SE1 123 H4
WALTH E17 69 J2
Beattie Cl EBED/NFELT TW14 153 J2
Beattock Ri MUSWH N10 66 B1
Beatty Rd STAN HA7 43 J2
STNW/STAM N16 86 A2
Beatty St CAMTN NW1 * 4 A2
Beattyville Gdns CLAY IG5 54 A6
Beauchamp Cl CHSWK W4 117 K3
Beauchamp Pl CHEL SW3 14 D5
Beauchamp Rd BTSEA SW11 140 D5
E/WMO/HCT KT8 189 G2
FSTGT E7 89 F5
NRWD SE19 180 E4
SUT SM1 208 E3
TWK TW1 156 B2
Beauchamp St HCIRC EC1N 11 J2
Beauchamp Ter BARN SW13 138 E4
Beauclerc Rd HMSMTH W6 118 E3
Beauclerk Cl FELT TW13 154 A3
Beaufort EHAM E6 108 A4
Beaufort Av
KTN/HRWW/WS HA3 61 G1
Beaufort Cl CHING E4 51 K2
EA W5 98 B4
PUT/ROE SW15 159 F3
ROMW/RG RM7 74 E1
Beaufort Ct
RCHPK/HAM TW10 156 D6
Beaufort Dr GLDGN NW11 64 E1
Beaufort Gdns CHEL SW3 14 D4
HDN NW4 64 A3
HEST TW5 134 D2
IL IG1 72 A5
STRHM/NOR SW16 180 A3
Beaufort Rd EA W5 98 B4
KUT/HW KT1 191 F1
RCHPK/HAM TW10 156 D6
RSLP HA4 * 58 B6
Beaufort St CHEL SW3 120 C6
Beaufort Wy EW KT17 207 J5
Beaufoy Rd TOTM N17 50 A3
Beaufoy Wk LBTH SE11 17 H7
Beaulieu Av CAN/RD E16 126 A1
SYD SE26 163 J6
Beaulieu Cl CDALE/KGS NW9 63 G1
CMBW SE5 142 E4
HSLWW TW4 134 E6
MTCM CR4 179 F4
OXHEY WD19 27 G3
TWK TW1 156 E1
Beaulieu Dr PIN HA5 59 H3
Beaulieu Gdns WCHMH N21 35 J2
Beaulieu Pl CHSWK W4 117 K3
Beauly Ct ROM RM1 57 G4
Beauly Wy ROM RM1 57 G4
Beaumaris Gn
CDALE/KGS NW9 * 63 G3
Beaumont Av ALP/SUD HA0 79 J3
RCH/KEW TW9 137 G4
RYLN/HDSTN HA2 60 B3
WKENS W14 119 J5
Beaumont Cl EFNCH N2 65 J1
KUTN/CMB KT2 175 H3
Beaumont Ct ALP/SUD HA0 79 J3
Beaumont Crs RAIN RM13 93 J4
WKENS W14 119 J5
Beaumont Dr WPK KT4 192 E5
Beaumont Gdns HAMP NW3 64 E6
Beaumont Gv WCHPL E1 105 F3
Beaumont Ms MHST W1U * 9 H1
PIN HA5 * 41 J6
Beaumont Pl BAR EN5 20 D2
FITZ W1T 4 B6
ISLW TW7 136 A6
Beaumont Ri ARCH N19 66 D5
Beaumont Rd CHSWK W4 117 K3
LEY E10 69 K4
NRWD SE19 180 D2
PLSTW E13 107 F2
STMC/STPC BR5 201 J3
WIM/MER SW19 159 H2
Beaumont Sq WCHPL E1 105 F4
Beaumont St
CAVSQ/HST W1G 9 H1
Beaumont Ter LEW SE13 * 165 H2
Beaumont Wk HAMP NW3 83 K5
Beauvais Ter NTHLT UB5 95 H2
Beauval Rd EDUL SE22 163 G1
Beaverbank Rd
ELTH/MOT SE9 167 J3

Beaver Cl HPTN TW12 173 G4
MRDN SM4 193 F4
PGE/AN SE20 * 181 H3
Beaver Rd BARK/HLT IG6 55 J1
Beavers Crs HSLWW TW4 134 C5
Beavers La HSLWW TW4 134 B4
Beaverwood Rd CHST BR7 185 K1
Beavor La HMSMTH W6 118 D4
Bebbington Rd
WOOL/PLUM SE18 * 127 K4
Beblets Cl ORP BR6 217 F3
Beccles Dr BARK IG11 91 F4
Beccles St POP/IOD E14 105 H5
Bec Cl RSLP HA4 77 H1
Beck Cl GNWCH SE10 144 E2
Beckenham Gdns ED N9 36 A5
Beckenham Gv HAYES BR2 183 G5
Beckenham Hill Rd BECK BR3 182 E2
Beckenham La HAYES BR2 183 H5
Beckenham Place Pk
BECK BR3 182 E3
Beckenham Rd BECK BR3 182 B4
PGE/AN SE20 182 A4
Becket Av EHAM E6 108 A2
Becket Cl SNWD SE25 197 H3
WIM/MER SW19 * 178 A4
Becket Fold HRW HA1 * 61 F2
Becket Rd UED N18 36 E6
Becket St STHWK SE1 18 E4
Beckett Cl BELV DA17 129 F3
STRHM/NOR SW16 161 J4
WLSDN NW10 81 F4
Becketts Cl BXLY DA5 169 K3
EBED/NFELT TW14 154 A1
ORP BR6 217 F1
Becketts Pl KUT/HW KT1 174 E4
Beckett Wk BECK BR3 182 B2
Beckford Cl WKENS W14 119 J4
Beckford Dr STMC/STPC BR5 201 J4
Beckford Pl WALW SE17 * 122 D5
Beckford Rd CROY/NA CR0 197 G3
Beck La BECK BR3 182 A6
Becklow Rd SHB W12 118 C2
Beck River Pk BECK BR3 182 C4
Beck Rd HACK E8 86 D6
MTCM CR4 194 E3
Becks Rd SCUP DA14 168 B5
Beckton Rd CAN/RD E16 106 D4
Beck Wy BECK BR3 182 C6
Beckway Rd
STRHM/NOR SW16 179 J5
Beckway St WALW SE17 19 F7
Beckwith Rd HNHL SE24 162 E1
Beclands Rd TOOT SW17 179 F2
Becmead Av
KTN/HRWW/WS HA3 61 H2
STRHM/NOR SW16 161 J6
Becondale Rd NRWD SE19 181 F1
Becontree Av BCTR RM8 73 K6
BCTR RM8 91 H2
Bective Rd FSTGT E7 88 E2
PUT/ROE SW15 139 H5
Bedale Rd ENC/FH EN2 23 J1
Bedale St STHWK SE1 * 18 E1
Beddington Cross
CROY/NA CR0 195 J5
Beddington Farm Rd
CROY/NA CR0 195 K5
Beddington Gdns CAR SM5 210 A4
Beddington Gn
STMC/STPC BR5 186 A4
Beddington Gv WLGTN SM6 210 D3
Beddington La CROY/NA CR0 195 H3
Beddington Rd
GDMY/SEVK IG3 73 F4
STMC/STPC BR5 185 K4
Beddington Ter
CROY/NA CR0 * 196 A4
Bede Cl PIN HA5 41 H4
Bedens Rd SCUP DA14 187 F2
Bede Rd CHDH RM6 73 J3
Bedevere Rd ED N9 36 C5
Bedfont Cl EBED/NFELT TW14 153 F1
MTCM CR4 179 F5
Bedfont Green Cl
EBED/NFELT TW14 153 F3
Bedfont La EBED/NFELT TW14 153 H2
Bedfont Rd
STWL/WRAY TW19 152 C1
Bedford Av BAR EN5 20 D6
RSQ WC1B 10 D2
YEAD UB4 95 F5
Bedfordbury CHCR WC2N 10 E5
Bedford Cl CHSWK W4 118 B6
MUSWH N10 48 A3
Bedford Cnr CHSWK W4 * 118 B4
Bedford Ct CHCR WC2N 10 E6
Bedford Gdns KENS W8 119 K1
Bedford Hl BAL SW12 161 G4
Bedford Ms CAT SE6 164 E4
Bedford Pk CROY/NA CR0 196 D5
Bedford Pl CROY/NA CR0 196 E5
RSQ WC1B 10 E1
Bedford Rd BFN/LL DA15 167 K5
CEND/HSY/T N8 66 D3
CHSWK W4 118 A3
CLAP SW4 141 K5
ED N9 36 D2
EFNCH N2 47 J6
EHAM E6 90 A6
HRW HA1 60 C3
IL IG1 90 B1
MLHL NW7 31 G4
NTHWD HA6 26 B6
ORP BR6 202 C6
RSLP HA4 76 D2
SEVS/STOTM N15 67 K1
SWFD E18 52 E5
WALTH E17 51 J5
WDGN N22 48 E4
WEA W13 97 H6
WHTN TW2 155 J5
WPK KT4 193 F6
Bedford Rw GINN WC1R 11 H1
Bedford Sq RSQ WC1B 10 D2
Bedford St COVGDN WC2E 10 E5
Bedford Vls KUT/HW KT1 * 175 G5
Bedford Wy STPAN WC1H 4 D7
Bedgebury Gdns
WIM/MER SW19 159 H4
Bedgebury Rd ELTH/MOT SE9 146 C5
Bedlam Ms LBTH SE11 17 H6
Bedlow Cl STJWD NW8 2 B7
Bedlow Wy CROY/NA CR0 211 F2
Bedonwell Rd BELV DA17 129 F6
BXLYHN DA7 129 H6
Bedser Cl LBTH SE11 * 122 A6
THHTH CR7 180 D6
Bedser Dr GFD/PVL UB6 78 D3
Bedster Gdns
E/WMO/HCT KT8 173 G5
Bedwardine Rd NRWD SE19 181 F3
Bedwell Gdns HYS/HAR UB3 113 H4
Bedwell Rd BELV DA17 129 H5
TOTM N17 50 A4
Beeby Rd CAN/RD E16 107 F4
Beech Av ACT W3 118 B1
BFN/LL DA15 168 B2
BKHH IG9 39 F4
BTFD TW8 136 C1
RSLP HA4 59 F5
TRDG/WHET N20 33 J3
Beech Cl CAR SM5 194 E6
DEPT SE8 124 C6
ED N9 36 C1
HCH RM12 93 K1
PUT/ROE SW15 158 D2
SUN TW16 172 C5
WDR/YW UB7 112 D3
WIM/MER SW19 177 F2
Beech Copse BMLY BR1 184 E5
SAND/SEL CR2 212 A3
Beech Ct ELTH/MOT SE9 * 166 D1
Beechcroft CHST BR7 185 F3
Beechcroft Av BXLYHN DA7 150 A2
GLDGN NW11 64 D4
NWMAL KT3 175 K4
RKW/CH/CXG WD3 26 A1
RYLN/HDSTN HA2 60 A4
STHL UB1 114 E1
Beechcroft Cl HEST TW5 134 D1
ORP BR6 216 D2
STRHM/NOR SW16 180 A1
Beechcroft Gdns WBLY HA9 80 B1
Beechcroft Rd CHSGTN KT9 206 B2
MORT/ESHN SW14 * 137 K4
ORP BR6 216 D2
SWFD E18 53 F5
TOOT SW17 160 E5
Beechdale WCHMH N21 35 F4
Beechdale Rd
BRXS/STRHM SW2 162 A1
Beech Dell HAYES BR2 215 K2
Beech Dr EFNCH N2 47 K6
Beechen Cliff Wy ISLW TW7 136 A2
Beechengrove PIN HA5 41 K6
Beechen Pl FSTH SE23 163 K4
Beeches Av CAR SM5 209 J5
Beeches Cl PGE/AN SE20 181 K4
Beeches Rd CHEAM SM3 193 H5
TOOT SW17 160 D5
The Beeches CHING E4 * 38 B3
HNWL W7 * 116 A2
Beeches Wk BELMT SM2 209 H6
Beechfield Gdns
ROMW/RG RM7 74 E4
Beechfield Rd BMLY BR1 184 B5
CAT SE6 164 C3
FSBYPK N4 67 J3
Beech Gdns DAGE RM10 92 D5
EA W5 117 F2
Beech Gv BARK/HLT IG6 54 E2
MTCM CR4 195 J2
NWMAL KT3 176 A6
Beech Hall Crs CHING E4 52 B3
Beech Hall Rd CHING E4 52 A3
Beech Hl EBAR EN4 21 H1
Beech Hill Av EBAR EN4 21 G2
Beechhill Rd ELTH/MOT SE9 147 F6
Beech House Rd
CROY/NA CR0 211 K1
Beech Lawns
NFNCH/WDSPK N12 * 47 H1
Beechmont Cl BMLY BR1 183 H1
Beechmore Gdns
CHEAM SM3 193 G6
Beechmore Rd BTSEA SW11 140 E2
Beechmount Av HNWL W7 96 D4
Beecholme Av MTCM CR4 179 G4
Beecholme Est CLPT E5 * 86 E1
Beech Rd EBED/NFELT TW14 153 H2
FBAR/BDGN N11 48 E2
ORP BR6 217 G5
STRHM/NOR SW16 179 K5
Beechrow KUTN/CMB KT2 157 F6
Beech St ROMW/RG RM7 74 E1
Beech Street (Below)
BARB EC2Y 12 C1
Beech Tree Cl IS N1 85 G5
STAN HA7 43 J1
Beech Tree Gld CHING E4 38 D3
Beech Tree Pl SUT SM1 209 F3
Beechvale Cl
NFNCH/WDSPK N12 47 J1
Beech Wk DART DA1 150 D5
MLHL NW7 45 F1
Beechway BXLY DA5 168 E1
Beech Wy WHTN TW2 155 F5
WLSDN NW10 81 F5
Beechwood Av FNCH N3 46 D6
GFD/PVL UB6 96 B2
HYS/HAR UB3 94 B6
ORP BR6 216 E4
RCH/KEW TW9 137 H2
RSLP HA4 58 D6
RYLN/HDSTN HA2 78 B1
THHTH CR7 196 C1
Beechwood Cl EFNCH N2 * 65 K1
MLHL NW7 45 G1
SURB KT6 190 D4
Beechwood Crs BXLYHN DA7 148 E4
Beechwood Dr HAYES BR2 215 H2
WFD IG8 52 D1
Beechwood Gdns CLAY IG5 71 K2
RAIN RM13 111 K4
RYLN/HDSTN HA2 78 B1
Beechwood Gv ACT W3 99 G6
Beechwood Ms ED N9 36 C4
Beechwood Pk SWFD E18 52 E6
Beechwood Ri CHST BR7 167 G6
Beechwood Rd
CEND/HSY/T N8 66 D1
HACK E8 86 B4
SAND/SEL CR2 212 A6
Beechworth Cl HAMP NW3 65 F6
Beecot La WOT/HER KT12 188 B6
Beecroft La BROCKY SE4 144 B6
Beecroft Ms BROCKY SE4 144 B6
Beecroft Rd BROCKY SE4 144 B6
Beehive Cl BORE WD6 29 K1
HACK E8 86 B5
Beehive La REDBR IG4 71 K2
Beehive Pl BRXN/ST SW9 142 B4
Beeken Dene ORP BR6 216 C2
Beeleigh Rd MRDN SM4 194 A1
Beeston Cl HACK E8 86 C3
OXHEY WD19 27 H6
Beeston Pl BGVA SW1W 15 K5
Beeston Rd EBAR EN4 33 H1
Beeston Wy
EBED/NFELT TW14 154 B1
Beethoven Rd BORE WD6 29 J2
Beethoven St NKENS W10 100 C2
Beeton Cl PIN HA5 42 A3
Begbie Rd BKHTH/KID SE3 146 B2
Beggar's Roost La SUT SM1 208 E4
Begonia Cl EHAM E6 107 J4
Begonia Pl HPTN TW12 173 F2
Beira St BAL SW12 161 G2
Bekesbourne St
POP/IOD E14 * 105 G5
Belcroft Cl BMLY BR1 183 J3
Beldham Gdns
E/WMO/HCT KT8 173 G6
Belfairs Dr CHDH RM6 73 J4
Belfairs Gdn OXHEY WD19 41 H1
Belfairs Gn OXHEY WD19 41 H1
Belfast Rd SNWD SE25 197 J1
STNW/STAM N16 68 B6
Belfield Rd HOR/WEW KT19 207 F6
Belford Gv WOOL/PLUM SE18 127 F4
Belfort Rd PECK SE15 143 K3
Belfry Cl BERM/RHTH SE16 * 123 J5
Belfry Rd MNPK E12 71 H6
Belgrade Rd HPTN TW12 173 G4
STNW/STAM N16 86 A2
Belgrave Cl ACT W3 117 K2
MLHL NW7 45 F1
STHGT/OAK N14 22 C6
STMC/STPC BR5 202 D1
Belgrave Crs SUN TW16 172 A4
Belgrave Gdns STAN HA7 43 J1
STHGT/OAK N14 22 D6
STJWD NW8 83 F6
Belgrave Ms South
KTBR SW1X 15 H4
Belgrave Ms West KTBR SW1X 15 G4
Belgrave Pl KTBR SW1X 15 H5
Belgrave Rd BARN SW13 138 C1
HSLWW TW4 134 E4
IL IG1 71 K5
LEY E10 70 A5
MTCM CR4 178 C6
PIM SW1V 16 A7
PLSTW E13 107 G3
SNWD SE25 197 G1
SUN TW16 172 A4
WALTH E17 69 J3
WAN E11 70 E5
Belgrave Sq KTBR SW1X 15 G4
Belgrave St WCHPL E1 105 F4
Belgrave Wk MTCM CR4 178 C6
Belgravia Cl BAR EN5 20 D4
Belgravia Gdns BMLY BR1 183 H2
Belgravia Ms KUT/HW KT1 190 E1
Belgrove St CAMTN NW1 4 E4
Belinda Rd BRXN/ST SW9 142 C4
Belitha Vls IS N1 85 G5
Bellamaine Cl THMD SE28 128 A2
Bellamy Cl EDGW HA8 30 E5
POP/IOD E14 124 D2
WKENS W14 119 J5
Bellamy Dr STAN HA7 43 H4
Bellamy Rd CHING E4 51 K2
ENC/FH EN2 * 23 K3
Bellamy St BAL SW12 161 G2
Bel La FELT TW13 154 D5
Bellarmine Cl THMD SE28 128 A1
Bellasis Av BRXS/STRHM SW2 161 K3
Bell Av HARH RM3 57 K4
WDR/YW UB7 112 C3
Bell Cl PIN HA5 41 G6
Bellclose Rd WDR/YW UB7 112 B2
Bell Dr WAND/EARL SW18 159 H2
Bellefield Rd STMC/STPC BR5 202 C2
Bellefields Rd BRXN/ST SW9 142 A4
Bellegrove Cl WELL DA16 148 A3
Bellegrove Rd WELL DA16 147 K3
Bellenden Rd PECK SE15 143 G3
Belle Staines Pleasaunce
CHING E4 37 J4
Belleville Rd BTSEA SW11 140 D6
Belle Vue GFD/PVL UB6 78 D6
Belle Vue La BUSH WD23 28 D3
Bellevue Pk THHTH CR7 180 D6
Bellevue Pl WCHPL E1 * 104 E3
Bellevue Rd FBAR/BDGN N11 34 A6
KUT/HW KT1 175 F6
TOOT SW17 160 E2
WEA W13 97 H3
BARN SW13 138 D3
Belle Vue Rd CRW RM5 56 E2
HDN NW4 64 B1
WALTH E17 52 B5
Bellew St TOOT SW17 160 B5
Bell Farm Av DAGE RM10 92 E1
Bellfield CROY/NA CR0 213 G6
Bellfield Av
KTN/HRWW/WS HA3 42 D2
Bellfield Cl BKHTH/KID SE3 146 A1
Bell Gdns LEY E10 * 69 J5
STMC/STPC BR5 202 D2
Bellgate Ms KTTN NW5 84 B2
Bell Gn SYD SE26 164 C6
Bell Green La SYD SE26 182 C1
Bell House Rd ROMW/RG RM7 74 E5
Bellina Ms KTTN NW5 84 B2
Bellingham Gn CAT SE6 164 D5
Bellingham Rd CAT SE6 165 F5
Bell La CAN/RD E16 125 J1
HDN NW4 64 B1
PEND EN3 25 F1
TWK TW1 156 B3
WBLY HA9 * 61 K6
WCHPL E1 13 J2
Bell Meadow NRWD SE19 163 F6
Bello Cl HNHL SE24 162 C3
Bellot St GNWCH SE10 125 H5
Bell Pde HSLW TW3 * 135 G4
WWKM BR4 * 199 F6
Bellring Cl BELV DA17 129 H6
Bell Rd E/WMO/HCT KT8 189 J2
EN EN1 23 K2
HSLW TW3 135 G4
Bells Hl BAR EN5 20 B5
Bell St BAY/PAD W2 8 C1
WOOL/PLUM SE18 146 D2
Belltrees Gv
STRHM/NOR SW16 180 A1
Bell Water Ga
WOOL/PLUM SE18 127 F3
Bell Wharf La CANST EC4R 12 D6
Bellwood Rd PECK SE15 144 A5
Bell Yd LINN WC2A 11 J4
Bell Yard Ms STHWK SE1 19 H3
Belmont Av ALP/SUD HA0 80 B6
EBAR EN4 21 K6
ED N9 36 C3
NWDGN UB2 114 D3
NWMAL KT3 192 D2
PLMGR N13 48 E1
WELL DA16 147 K3
Belmont Cir
KTN/HRWW/WS HA3 * 43 H4
Belmont Cl CHING E4 52 B1
CLAP SW4 141 H4
EBAR EN4 21 K5
TRDG/WHET N20 33 F3
WFD IG8 39 F6
Belmont Gv CHSWK W4 118 A4
LEW SE13 145 G4
Belmont Hl LEW SE13 145 G4
Belmont La CHST BR7 185 H1
STAN HA7 43 J3
Belmont Pde CHST BR7 * 185 G1
GLDGN NW11 * 64 D2
Belmont Pk LEW SE13 145 G5
Belmont Park Cl LEW SE13 145 H5
Belmont Park Rd LEY E10 69 K3
Belmont Ri BELMT SM2 208 D5
Belmont Rd BECK BR3 182 B5
CHST BR7 185 G1
CLAP SW4 141 H4
IL IG1 90 C1
KTN/HRWW/WS HA3 43 F6
SEVS/STOTM N15 67 J1
SNWD SE25 197 J2
WHTN TW2 155 J4
WLGTN SM6 210 C3
Belmont St CAMTN NW1 84 A5
Belmont Ter CHSWK W4 118 A4
Belmore Av YEAD UB4 94 E5
Belmore La HOLWY N7 84 D3
Belmore St VX/NE SW8 141 J2
Beloe Cl PUT/ROE SW15 138 D5
Belsham St HOM E9 86 E4
Belsize Av HAMP NW3 83 H4
PLMGR N13 49 F2
WEA W13 116 C3
Belsize Court Gdns
HAMP NW3 83 H3
Belsize Crs HAMP NW3 83 H3
Belsize Gdns SUT SM1 209 F2
Belsize Gv HAMP NW3 83 J4
Belsize La HAMP NW3 83 H4
Belsize Ms HAMP NW3 * 83 H4
Belsize Pk HAMP NW3 83 H4
Belsize Park Gdns HAMP NW3 83 H4
Belsize Park Ms HAMP NW3 83 H4
Belsize Pl HAMP NW3 83 H3
Belsize Rd KIL/WHAMP NW6 83 F6
KTN/HRWW/WS HA3 42 D3
Belsize Sq HAMP NW3 83 H4
Belsize Ter HAMP NW3 83 H4
Belson Rd WOOL/PLUM SE18 126 E4
Beltane Dr WIM/MER SW19 159 G5
Belthorn Crs BAL SW12 161 H2
Belton Rd FSTGT E7 89 F5
SCUP DA14 168 B6
TOTM N17 50 A6
WAN E11 88 C2
WLSDN NW10 81 J4
Belton Wy BOW E3 105 J4
Beltran Rd FUL/PGN SW6 140 A3
Beltwood Rd BELV DA17 129 K4
Belvedere Av CLAY IG5 54 B5
WIM/MER SW19 177 H1
Belvedere Blds STHWK SE1 18 B3
Belvedere Cl ESH/CLAY KT10 204 B3
TEDD TW11 173 K1
Belvedere Ct BELV DA17 129 G3
OXHEY WD19 27 H1
Belvedere Dr WIM/MER SW19 177 H1
Belvedere Gdns
E/WMO/HCT KT8 188 E2
Belvedere Gv WIM/MER SW19 177 H1
Belvedere Ms PECK SE15 143 K4
Belvedere Pl
BRXS/STRHM SW2 142 A5
Belvedere Rd ABYW SE2 128 E1
HNWL W7 115 K3
LEY E10 69 G5
NRWD SE19 181 G3
STHWK SE1 17 G2
Belvedere Sq WIM/MER SW19 177 H1
Belvedere Strd
CDALE/KGS NW9 45 H5
The Belvedere WBPTN SW10 * 140 B2
Belvedere Wy
KTN/HRWW/WS HA3 62 A3
Belvoir Rd EDUL SE22 163 H2
Belvue Cl NTHLT UB5 78 A5
Belvue Rd NTHLT UB5 78 A5
Bembridge Cl
KIL/WHAMP NW6 82 C5
Bembridge Gdns RSLP HA4 58 B6
Bemerton St IS N1 85 F6
Bemish Rd PUT/ROE SW15 139 G4
Bempton Dr RSLP HA4 59 F6
Bemsted Rd WALTH E17 51 H6
Benares Rd
WOOL/PLUM SE18 128 A4
Benbow Rd HMSMTH W6 118 E3
Benbow St DEPT SE8 124 D6
Benbury Cl BMLY BR1 183 F1
Bench Fld SAND/SEL CR2 212 B4
The Bench
RCHPK/HAM TW10 * 156 D5
Bencroft Rd
STRHM/NOR SW16 179 H3
Bencurtis Pk WWKM BR4 214 B1
Bendall Ms CAMTN NW1 8 D1
Bendemeer Rd
PUT/ROE SW15 139 G4
Bendish Rd EHAM E6 89 J5
Bendmore Av ABYW SE2 128 B5
Bendon Va WAND/EARL SW18 160 A2
Benedict Cl ORP BR6 216 E1
Benedict Dr
EBED/NFELT TW14 153 G2
Benedict Rd BRXN/ST SW9 142 A4
MTCM CR4 178 C6
Benedict Wy EFNCH N2 * 47 G6
Benedict Whf MTCM CR4 178 D6
Benett Gdns
STRHM/NOR SW16 179 K5
Benfleet Cl SUT SM1 209 G1
Benfleet Wy FBAR/BDGN N11 34 A4
Bengal Rd IL IG1 90 B2
Bengarth Dr
KTN/HRWW/WS HA3 42 D5
Bengarth Rd NTHLT UB5 77 H6
Bengeworth Rd CMBW SE5 142 D4
HRW HA1 61 G6
Ben Hale Cl STAN HA7 43 G1
Benham Cl CHSGTN KT9 205 J4
Benham Gdns HSLWW TW4 134 E6
Benham Rd HNWL W7 96 E4
Benhill Av SUT SM1 209 F2
Benhill Rd CMBW SE5 142 E1
SUT SM1 209 H1
Benhill Wood Rd SUT SM1 209 G2
Benhilton Gdns SUT SM1 209 F1
Benhurst Av HCH RM12 93 K2
Benhurst La
STRHM/NOR SW16 180 B1
Benin St LEW SE13 165 G2
Benjafield Cl UED N18 36 D6
Benjamin Cl EMPK RM11 75 J3
HACK E8 86 C6
Benjamin Ms BAL SW12 161 H2
Benjamin St FARR EC1M 12 A1
Ben Jonson Rd WCHPL E1 105 G4
Benledi St POP/IOD E14 106 B5
Bennelong Cl SHB W12 99 K6
Bennerley Rd BTSEA SW11 140 D6
Bennet Cl KUT/HW KT1 174 D4
Bennetsfield Rd STKPK UB11 112 E1
Bennet's Hl BLKFR EC4V 12 B5
Bennett Cl HSLWW TW4 134 D6
NTHWD HA6 40 D3
WELL DA16 148 B3
Bennett Gv LEW SE13 144 E
Bennett Pk BKHTH/KID SE3 145 J
Bennett Rd BRXN/ST SW9 142 B
CHDH RM6 74 A
PLSTW E13 107 G
Bennetts Av CROY/NA CR0 198 B
GFD/PVL UB6 78 E
Bennett's Castle La
BCTR RM8 91
Bennetts Cl MTCM CR4 179 C
TOTM N17 50 B
Bennetts Copse CHST BR7 184 D
Bennett St CHSWK W4 118 B
WHALL SW1A 10 A
Bennetts Wy CROY/NA CR0 198 B
Benningholme Rd EDGW HA8 45 C
Bennington Rd TOTM N17 50 A
WFD IG8 * 52 C
Benn St HOM E9 87 C
Benrek Cl BARK/HLT IG6 54 C
Bensbury Cl PUT/ROE SW15 158
Bensham Cl THHTH CR7 196 D
Bensham Gv THHTH CR7 180 D
Bensham La CROY/NA CR0 196 C
Bensham Manor Rd
THHTH CR7 196
Bensley Cl FBAR/BDGN N11 47
Ben Smith Wy
BERM/RHTH SE16 123
Benson Av PLSTW E13 107
Benson Cl HSLW TW3 135
Benson Quay WAP E1W 104
Benson Rd CROY/NA CR0 211
FSTH SE23 163
Benthal Rd STNW/STAM N16 68
Bentham Rd HOM E9 87
THMD SE28 128
Ben Tillet Cl BARK IG11 91
CAN/RD E16 * 126
Bentinck Ms MHST W1U 9
Bentinck Rd WDR/YW UB7 112
Bentinck St MHST W1U 9
Bentley Cl WIM/MER SW19 159
Bentley Dr CRICK NW2 82
GNTH/NBYPK IG2 72
Bentley Ms EN EN1 35
Bentley Rd IS N1 86
Bentley Wy STAN HA7 43
WFD IG8 38
Benton Rd IL IG1 72
OXHEY WD19 41
Benton's La WNWD SE27 162
Benton's Ri WNWD SE27 180
Bentry Cl BCTR RM8 74
Bentry Rd BCTR RM8 74
Bentworth Rd SHB W12 99
Benwell Rd HOLWY N7 85
Benwick Cl BERM/RHTH SE16 123
Benwood Ct SUT SM1 209
Benworth St BOW E3 105
Benyon Rd IS N1 85
Benyon Whf IS N1 86
Berberis Wk WDR/YW UB7 112
Berber Pde WOOL/PLUM SE18 146
Berber Rd BTSEA SW11 * 140
Bercta Rd ELTH/MOT SE9 167
Berengers Pl DAGW RM9 91
Berenger Wk WBPTN SW10 * 140

Berens Rd STMC/STPC BR5 202 D2
WLSDN NW10 100 B2
Berens Wy CHST BR7 202 A1
Beresford Av ALP/SUD HA0 80 C6
BRYLDS KT5 191 J5
HNWL W7 96 D4
TRDG/WHET N20 33 K4
TWK TW1 156 D1
Beresford Dr BMLY BR1 184 C6
WFD IG8 39 G6
Beresford Gdns CHDH RM6 74 A2
EN EN1 24 A5
HSLWW TW4 134 E6
Beresford Rd BELMT SM2 208 D5
CEND/HSY/T N8 67 G2
CHING E4 38 C3
EFNCH N2 47 J6
HBRY N5 85 K3
HRW HA1 60 D2
KUTN/CMB KT2 175 G4
NWMAL KT3 191 K1
STHL UB1 95 H6
WALTH E17 51 K4
Beresford Sq
WOOL/PLUM SE18 127 G4
Beresford St
WOOL/PLUM SE18 127 G3
Beresford Ter HBRY N5 85 J3
Berestede Rd HMSMTH W6 118 C5
Bere St WAP E1W 105 F6
Berger Cl STMC/STPC BR5 201 J3
Berger Rd HOM E9 87 F4
Berghem Ms WKENS W14 119 G3
Bergholt Av REDBR IG4 71 J2
Bergholt Crs STNW/STAM N16 68 A4
Bergholt Ms CAMTN NW1 84 C5
Bering Sq POP/IOD E14 124 D5
Bering Wk CAN/RD E16 107 H5
Berisford Ms
WAND/EARL SW18 160 B1
Berkeley Av BXLYHN DA7 148 E2
CLAY IG5 54 A5
CRW RM5 56 E3
GFD/PVL UB6 78 E4
HSLWW TW4 133 K2
Berkeley Cl KUTN/CMB KT2 175 F3
RSLP HA4 76 D1
STMC/STPC BR5 201 K4
Berkeley Ct WLGTN SM6 210 C1
Berkeley Crs EBAR EN4 21 H6
Berkeley Dr E/WMO/HCT KT8 172 E6
Berkeley Gdns
ESH/CLAY KT10 205 G5
KENS W8 119 K1
WCHMH N21 35 K2
Berkeley Ms MBLAR W1H 9 F3
SUN TW16 172 B6
Berkeley Pl WIM/MER SW19 177 G2
Berkeley Rd BARN SW13 138 D2
CDALE/KGS NW9 62 C1
CEND/HSY/T N8 66 D2
HGDN/ICK UB10 76 A5
MNPK E12 89 J3
Berkeley Sq MYFR/PICC W1J 9 K6
The Berkeleys SNWD SE25 * 197 H1
Berkeley St MYFR/PICC W1J 9 K6
Berkeley Waye HEST TW5 134 D1
Berkhampstead Rd
BELV DA17 129 H5
Berkhamsted Av WBLY HA9 80 B4
Berkley Cl WHTN TW2 * 155 K5
Berkley Rd CAMTN NW1 83 K5
Berkshire Gdns PLMGR N13 49 G2
UED N18 50 D1
Berkshire Rd HOM E9 87 H4
Berkshire Wy MTCM CR4 195 K1
Bermans Wy WLSDN NW10 81 G2
Bermondsey St STHWK SE1 19 G4
Bermondsey Wall East
BERM/RHTH SE16 123 J2
Bermondsey Wall West
STHWK SE1 123 H2
Bernal Cl THMD SE28 109 K6
Bernard Ashley Dr CHARL SE7 126 A5
Bernard Av WEA W13 116 C3
Bernard Cassidy St
CAN/RD E16 106 D4
Bernard Gdns
WIM/MER SW19 177 J1
Bernard Rd ROMW/RG RM7 74 E4
SEVS/STOTM N15 68 B2
WLGTN SM6 210 A3
ernards Cl BARK/HLT IG6 54 C3
ernard St BMSBY WC1N 4 E7
ernays Cl STAN HA7 43 J2
ernay's Gv BRXN/ST SW9 142 A5
ernel Dr CROY/NA CR0 213 H1
erne Rd THHTH CR7 196 C2
erners Dr WEA W13 97 G6
erners Ms FITZ W1T 10 B2
erners Pl FITZ W1T 10 B3
erners Rd IS N1 6 A1
WDGN N22 49 G4
erners St FITZ W1T 10 B2
erner Ter WCHPL E1 * 104 C5
erney Rd CROY/NA CR0 196 E4
ernhardt Crs STJWD NW8 2 C6
ernhart Cl EDGW HA8 44 E3
ernwell Rd CHING E4 38 C5
erridge Gn EDGW HA8 44 C3
erridge Ms KIL/WHAMP NW6 82 E3
erridge Rd NRWD SE19 180 E1
erriman Rd HOLWY N7 85 F1
erriton Rd RYLN/HDSTN HA2 59 K5
errybank Cl CHING E4 38 A4
erry Cl DAGE RM10 92 C3
WCHMH N21 35 H3
erry Cots POP/IOD E14 * 105 G5
erry Ct HSLWW TW4 134 E6
errydale Rd YEAD UB4 95 J3
erryfield Cl BMLY BR1 184 D4
erry Field Cl WALTH E17 69 K1
erryfield Rd WALW SE17 122 C5
erryhill ELTH/MOT SE9 147 G5
erry Hl STAN HA7 29 K6
erryhill Gdns ELTH/MOT SE9 147 G5
errylands BRYLDS KT5 191 H2
ORP BR6 217 J1
RYNPK SW20 177 F6
errylands Rd BRYLDS KT5 191 G3
Berry La DUL SE21 162 E6
Berryman Cl BCTR RM8 91 J1
Berryman's La SYD SE26 164 A6
Berrymead Gdns ACT W3 117 K1
Berrymede Rd CHSWK W4 118 A3
Berry Pl FSBYE EC1V 6 B5
Berry St FSBYE EC1V 6 B7
Berry Wy EA W5 117 F3
Bertal Rd TOOT SW17 160 C6
Berthons Gdns WALTH E17 * 70 B2
Berthon St DEPT SE8 144 D1
Bertie Rd SYD SE26 182 A2
WLSDN NW10 81 J4
Bertram Rd EN EN1 24 C5
HDN NW4 63 J3
KUTN/CMB KT2 175 H3
Bertram St KTTN NW5 84 B1
Bertrand St LEW SE13 144 E4
Bertrand Wy THMD SE28 109 H6
Bert Rd THHTH CR7 196 D2
Bert Wy EN EN1 24 B5
Berwick Av YEAD UB4 95 H5
Berwick Cl STAN HA7 43 F2
WHTN TW2 155 F3
Berwick Crs BFN/LL DA15 167 K1
Berwick Gdns SUT SM1 209 G1
Berwick Rd CAN/RD E16 107 F5
WDGN N22 49 H4
WELL DA16 148 C2
Berwick St SOHO/CST W1F 10 B4
Berwick Wy ORP BR6 202 B5
Berwyn Av HSLW TW3 135 G2
Berwyn Rd HNHL SE24 162 C3
RCHPK/HAM TW10 137 J5
Beryl Av EHAM E6 107 J4
Beryl Rd HMSMTH W6 119 G5
Berystede KUTN/CMB KT2 175 J3
Besant Cl CRICK NW2 * 82 C1
Besant Pl EDUL SE22 143 G4
Besant Rd CRICK NW2 82 C2
Besant Wy WLSDN NW10 80 E3
Besley St STRHM/NOR SW16 179 H2
Bessant Dr RCH/KEW TW9 137 J1
Bessborough Pl PIM SW1V 121 J5
Bessborough Rd HRW HA1 60 D5
PUT/ROE SW15 158 D3
Bessborough St PIM SW1V 121 J5
Bessemer Rd CMBW SE5 142 D3
Bessie Lansbury Cl EHAM E6 108 A5
Bessingby Rd RSLP HA4 58 E6
Besson St NWCR SE14 143 K2
Bessy St BETH E2 * 104 E2
Best Ter SWLY BR8 * 203 K2
Bestwood St DEPT SE8 124 A4
Beswick Ms KIL/WHAMP NW6 83 F3
Betam Rd HYS/HAR UB3 113 G2
Betchworth Cl SUT SM1 209 H3
Betchworth Rd
GDMY/SEVK IG3 72 E6
Betchworth Wy
CROY/NA CR0 214 A6
Betham Rd GFD/PVL UB6 96 D2
Bethany Waye
EBED/NFELT TW14 153 H2
Bethecar Rd HRW HA1 60 E2
Bethel Cl HDN NW4 64 B2
Bethell Av CAN/RD E16 106 D3
IL IG1 72 A4
Bethel Rd WELL DA16 148 D4
Bethersden Cl BECK BR3 182 C3
Bethnal Green Rd BETH E2 7 K6
Bethune Av FBAR/BDGN N11 33 K6
Bethune Rd STNW/STAM N16 67 K4
WLSDN NW10 99 F3
Bethwin Rd CMBW SE5 142 C1
Betjeman Cl
RYLN/HDSTN HA2 60 A1
Betjeman Ct WDR/YW UB7 * 112 A1
Betony Cl CROY/NA CR0 198 A5
Betoyne Av CHING E4 38 C6
Betstyle Rd FBAR/BDGN N11 34 B6
Betterton Dr SCUP DA14 169 F4
Betterton Rd RAIN RM13 111 G1
Betterton St LSQ/SEVD WC2H 10 E4
Bettons Pk SRTFD E15 88 C6
Bettridge Rd FUL/PGN SW6 139 J3
Betts Cl BECK BR3 182 B5
Betts Ms WALTH E17 69 H3
Betts Rd CAN/RD E16 107 F5
Betts St WAP E1W 104 D6
Betts Wy PGE/AN SE20 181 J5
SURB KT6 190 C5
Beulah Av THHTH CR7 * 180 D5
Beulah Cl EDGW HA8 30 D5
Beulah Crs THHTH CR7 180 D5
Beulah Gv CROY/NA CR0 196 D3
Beulah Hl NRWD SE19 180 C2
Beulah Rd SUT SM1 208 E2
THHTH CR7 180 D6
WALTH E17 69 K2
WIM/MER SW19 177 J3
Bevan Av BARK IG11 91 G5
Bevan Ct CROY/NA CR0 211 G3
Bevan Rd ABYW SE2 128 C5
EBAR EN4 21 K5
Bevan St IS N1 6 D1
Bev Callender Cl VX/NE SW8 141 G4
Bevenden St IS N1 7 F4
Beveridge Rd WLSDN NW10 81 G5
Beverley Av BFN/LL DA15 168 A2
HSLWW TW4 134 E5
RYNPK SW20 176 C4
Beverley Cl BARN SW13 138 D3
BTSEA SW11 140 C5
CHSGTN KT9 205 J2
WCHMH N21 35 J3
Beverley Ct BROCKY SE4 144 C4
Beverley Crs WFD IG8 53 F4
Beverley Dr EDGW HA8 44 B6
Beverley Gdns BARN SW13 138 C4
GLDGN NW11 64 C4
STAN HA7 43 G4
WBLY HA9 62 B5
WPK KT4 192 D5
Beverley La KUTN/CMB KT2 176 B3
Beverley Rd BARN SW13 138 C4
BXLYHN DA7 149 K3
CHING E4 52 B2
CHSWK W4 118 C5
DAGW RM9 92 A2
EHAM E6 107 H2
HAYES BR2 200 D6
KUT/HW KT1 174 D4
MTCM CR4 195 J1
NWDGN UB2 114 D4
NWMAL KT3 192 D1
PGE/AN SE20 181 J5
RSLP HA4 59 F6
WPK KT4 193 F6
Beverley Wy KUTN/CMB KT2 176 C4
RYNPK SW20 176 C4
Beverley Way (Kingston
By-Pass) NWMAL KT3 176 C5
Beversbrook Rd ARCH N19 84 D1
Beverstone Rd
BRXS/STRHM SW2 142 A6
THHTH CR7 196 B1
Beverston Ms MBLAR W1H 8 E2
Bevill Allen Cl TOOT SW17 178 E2
Bevill Cl SNWD SE25 181 H6
Bevin Cl BERM/RHTH SE16 124 B1
Bevington Rd BECK BR3 182 E5
NKENS W10 * 100 C4
Bevington St
BERM/RHTH SE16 123 H2
Bevin Rd YEAD UB4 94 E2
Bevin Sq TOOT SW17 160 E5
Bevin Wy FSBYW WC1X 5 J3
Bevis Marks HDTCH EC3A 13 H3
Bewcastle Gdns ENC/FH EN2 22 E5
Bewdley St IS N1 85 G5
Bewick Ms PECK SE15 143 J1
Bewick St VX/NE SW8 141 G3
Bewley St WCHPL E1 104 E5
WIM/MER SW19 178 B2
Bewlys Rd WNWD SE27 180 C1
Bexhill Cl FELT TW13 154 D4
Bexhill Rd BROCKY SE4 164 C1
FBAR/BDGN N11 48 D1
MORT/ESHN SW14 137 K4
Bexley Gdns CHDH RM6 73 H2
ED N9 35 K5
Bexley High St BXLY DA5 169 H2
Bexley La SCUP DA14 168 D4
SCUP DA14 168 D6
Bexley Rd ELTH/MOT SE9 147 G6
ELTH/MOT SE9 147 J6
ELTH/MOT SE9 167 F1
ERITH DA8 * 130 C5
Beynon Rd CAR SM5 209 K3
Bianca Rd PECK SE15 123 G6
Bibsworth Rd FNCH N3 46 D5
Bibury Cl PECK SE15 123 F6
Bicester Rd RCH/KEW TW9 137 H4
Bickenhall St MHST W1U 9 F1
Bickersteth Rd TOOT SW17 178 E2
Bickerton Rd ARCH N19 66 B6
Bickles Yd STHWK SE1 19 H3
Bickley Crs BMLY BR1 200 D1
Bickley Park Rd BMLY BR1 184 E6
Bickley Rd BMLY BR1 184 C5
LEY E10 69 K4
Bickley St TOOT SW17 178 D1
Bicknell Rd CMBW SE5 142 D4
Bicknoller Rd EN EN1 24 B2
Bicknor Rd ORP BR6 201 K4
Bidborough Cl HAYES BR2 199 J2
Bidborough St STPAN WC1H 4 E5
Biddenden Wy ELTH/MOT SE9 167 F6
Bidder St CAN/RD E16 106 C4
Biddestone Rd HOLWY N7 85 F2
Biddulph Rd MV/WKIL W9 101 F2
SAND/SEL CR2 211 J6
Bideford Av GFD/PVL UB6 97 H2
Bideford Cl EDGW HA8 44 C4
FELT TW13 154 E5
Bideford Gdns EN EN1 36 A2
Bideford Rd BMLY BR1 165 J5
PEND EN3 25 H1
RSLP HA4 77 F1
WELL DA16 148 C1
Bidwell Gdns
FBAR/BDGN N11 48 C4
Bidwell St PECK SE15 * 143 J2
Biggerstaff Rd SRTFD E15 88 A6
Biggerstaff St FSBYPK N4 67 G6
Biggin Av MTCM CR4 178 E4
Biggin Hl NRWD SE19 180 C3
Biggin Wy NRWD SE19 180 C3
Bigginwood Rd
STRHM/NOR SW16 180 C3
Bigg's Rw PUT/ROE SW15 139 G4
Big Hl CLPT E5 68 D5
Bigland St WCHPL E1 104 D5
Bignell Rd WOOL/PLUM SE18 127 G5
Bignold Rd FSTGT E7 88 E2
Bigwood Rd GLDGN NW11 65 F3
Billet Rd CHDH RM6 55 J6
WALTH E17 51 F4
Billetts Hart Cl HNWL W7 115 K2
Bill Hamling Cl ELTH/MOT SE9 166 E4
Billingford Cl BROCKY SE4 144 A5
Billing Pl WBPTN SW10 * 140 A1
Billing Rd WBPTN SW10 140 A1
Billings Cl DAGW RM9 91 J5
Billing St WBPTN SW10 * 140 A1
Billington Hl CROY/NA CR0 196 E6
Billington Rd NWCR SE14 144 A1
Billiter Sq FENCHST EC3M * 13 H4
Billiter St FENCHST EC3M 13 H4
Bill Nicholson Wy TOTM N17 50 B3
Billockby Cl CHSGTN KT9 206 B4
Billson St POP/IOD E14 125 F4
Bilton Rd ERITH DA8 150 D1
GFD/PVL UB6 79 H6
Bilton Wy HYS/HAR UB3 114 A2
PEND EN3 25 H2
Bina Gdns ECT SW5 120 B4
Bincote Rd ENC/FH EN2 23 F4
Binden Rd SHB W12 118 C3
Binfield Rd CLAP SW4 141 K2
SAND/SEL CR2 212 B3
Bingfield St IS N1 84 E6
Bingham Ct IS N1 * 85 H5
Bingham Pl CAMTN NW1 3 G7
MHST W1U 9 G1
Bingham Rd CROY/NA CR0 197 H5
Bingham St IS N1 85 K4
Bingley Rd CAN/RD E16 107 G5
GFD/PVL UB6 96 C3
Binney St MYFR/PKLN W1K 9 H5
Binns Rd CHSWK W4 118 B5
Binstead Cl YEAD UB4 95 J4
Binyon Crs STAN HA7 43 F1
Birbetts Rd ELTH/MOT SE9 166 E4
Birchanger Rd SNWD SE25 197 H2
Birch Av PLMGR N13 35 J5
Birch Cl BKHH IG9 39 H5
BTFD TW8 136 C1
CAN/RD E16 106 C4
HSLW TW3 135 J4
ROMW/RG RM7 56 D6
TEDD TW11 174 B1
Birch Ct WLGTN SM6 210 B2
Birchdale Gdns CHDH RM6 73 K4
Birchdale Rd FSTGT E7 89 G3
Birchdene Dr THMD SE28 128 B1
Birchen Cl CDALE/KGS NW9 63 F6
Birchend Cl SAND/SEL CR2 211 K4
Birchen Gv CDALE/KGS NW9 63 F6
Birches Cl MTCM CR4 178 E6
PIN HA5 59 J2
The Birches CHARL SE7 126 A6
CMBW SE5 * 143 F4
HSLWW TW4 * 154 E2
ORP BR6 216 A2
WCHMH N21 35 F1
Birchfield St POP/IOD E14 105 J6
Birch Gdns DAGE RM10 92 E1
Birch Gv ACT W3 117 H1
LEE/GVPK SE12 165 J2
WAN E11 88 C1
WELL DA16 148 B5
Birch Hl CROY/NA CR0 213 F3
Birchington Rd BRYLDS KT5 191 G4
CEND/HSY/T N8 66 D3
KIL/WHAMP NW6 82 E6
Birchin La BANK EC3V 13 F4
Birchlands Av BAL SW12 160 E2
Birch Md ORP BR6 201 F6
Birchmead Av PIN HA5 59 G1
Birchmere Rw
BKHTH/KID SE3 145 J3
Birchmore Wk HBRY N5 85 J1
Birch Pk KTN/HRWW/WS HA3 42 C3
Birch Rd FELT TW13 172 C1
ROMW/RG RM7 56 D6
Birch Rw HAYES BR2 201 F4
Birch Tree Av WWKM BR4 214 D3
Birch Tree Wy CROY/NA CR0 197 J6
Birch Wk MTCM CR4 179 G4
Birchway HYS/HAR UB3 113 K1
Birchwood Av BECK BR3 198 C1
MUSWH N10 48 A6
SCUP DA14 168 C5
WLGTN SM6 210 A1
Birchwood Cl MRDN SM4 194 A1
Birchwood Ct EDGW HA8 44 E5
Birchwood Dr HAMP NW3 83 F1
Birchwood Gv HPTN TW12 173 F2
Birchwood La ESH/CLAY KT10 204 D6
Birchwood Rd
STMC/STPC BR5 201 J1
SWLY BR8 187 K3
TOOT SW17 179 G1
Birchwood Ter SWLY BR8 * 187 K4
Birdbrook Cl DAGE RM10 92 E5
Birdbrook Rd BKHTH/KID SE3 146 B4
Birdcage Wk WESTW SW1E 16 B3
Birdham Cl BMLY BR1 200 D2
Birdhurst Av SAND/SEL CR2 211 K2
Birdhurst Gdns
SAND/SEL CR2 211 K2
Birdhurst Ri SAND/SEL CR2 212 A3
Birdhurst Rd SAND/SEL CR2 212 A3
WAND/EARL SW18 140 B5
WIM/MER SW19 178 D2
Bird In Bush Rd PECK SE15 143 H1
Bird-In-Hand La BMLY BR1 184 C5
Bird-In-Hand Ms FSTH SE23 163 K4
Bird-In-Hand Pas FSTH SE23 163 K4
Birds Farm Av CRW RM5 56 D4
Birdsfield La BOW E3 87 H6
Bird St MHST W1U 9 H4
Bird Wk WHTN TW2 154 E3
Birdwood Av LEW SE13 165 G1
Birdwood Cl TEDD TW11 155 K6
Birkbeck Av ACT W3 98 E6
GFD/PVL UB6 78 C6
Birkbeck Gv ACT W3 118 A1
Birkbeck Hl DUL SE21 162 C4
Birkbeck Ms ACT W3 * 99 F6
HACK E8 86 B3
Birkbeck Pl DUL SE21 162 C3
Birkbeck Rd ACT W3 118 A1
BECK BR3 181 K5
CEND/HSY/T N8 66 E1
EA W5 116 D4
ENC/FH EN2 23 K1
GNTH/NBYPK IG2 72 D2
HACK E8 86 B3
MLHL NW7 45 H1
NFNCH/WDSPK N12 47 G1
ROMW/RG RM7 75 F5
SCUP DA14 168 B5
TOTM N17 50 B4
WIM/MER SW19 178 A1
Birkbeck St BETH E2 104 D2
Birkbeck Wy GFD/PVL UB6 78 D6
Birkdale Av PIN HA5 42 A6
Birkdale Cl
BERM/RHTH SE16 * 123 J5
ORP BR6 201 J4
THMD SE28 109 J5
Birkdale Gdns CROY/NA CR0 213 F2
OXHEY WD19 27 H5
Birkdale Rd ABYW SE2 128 B4
EA W5 98 A3
Birkenhead Av
KUTN/CMB KT2 175 G5
Birkenhead St CAMTN NW1 5 F4
Birkhall Rd CAT SE6 165 G3
Birkwood Cl BAL SW12 161 J2
Birley Rd TRDG/WHET N20 33 G4
Birley St BTSEA SW11 141 F3
Birnam Rd FSBYPK N4 67 F6
Birse Crs WLSDN NW10 81 G2
Birstal Gn OXHEY WD19 27 H6
Birstall Rd SEVS/STOTM N15 68 A2
Biscay Rd HMSMTH W6 119 G5
Biscoe Cl HEST TW5 115 F6
Biscoe Wy LEW SE13 * 145 G5
Bisenden Rd CROY/NA CR0 197 F6
Bisham Cl CAR SM5 194 E4
Bisham Gdns HGT N6 66 A5
Bishop Butt Cl ORP BR6 217 F1
Bishop Fox Wy
E/WMO/HCT KT8 188 E1
Bishop Ken Rd
KTN/HRWW/WS HA3 43 F5
Bishop King's Rd WKENS W14 119 H4
Bishop Rd STHGT/OAK N14 34 B2
Bishops Av BMLY BR1 184 B6
CHDH RM6 73 J3
NTHWD HA6 26 C6
PLSTW E13 89 F6
Bishop's Av FUL/PGN SW6 139 G3
The Bishops Av EFNCH N2 65 H3
Bishop's Bridge Rd
BAY/PAD W2 101 F5
Bishops Cl BAR EN5 32 B1
CHSWK W4 117 K5
ELTH/MOT SE9 167 H4
EN EN1 24 D3
RCHPK/HAM TW10 156 E5
SUT SM1 208 E1
Bishop's Cl ARCH N19 84 C1
WALTH E17 69 K1
Bishop's Ct STP EC4M 12 A3
Bishops Dr EBED/NFELT TW14 153 G1
NTHLT UB5 77 J6
Bishopsford Rd MRDN SM4 194 B4
Bishopsgate LVPST EC2M 13 H2
Bishopsgate Ar LVPST EC2M 13 G2
Bishops Gn BMLY BR1 * 184 B4
Bishops Gv EFNCH N2 65 H3
HPTN TW12 154 E6
Bishop's Hall KUT/HW KT1 174 E5
Bishops Md CMBW SE5 * 142 D1
Bishops Park Rd
STRHM/NOR SW16 179 K4
Bishop's Park Rd
FUL/PGN SW6 139 G3
Bishop's Pl SUT SM1 209 G3
Bishops Rd FUL/PGN SW6 139 J2
HGT N6 66 A3
Bishop's Rd CROY/NA CR0 196 C4
HNWL W7 115 K2
HYS/HAR UB3 94 A5
Bishop's Ter LBTH SE11 17 K6
Bishopsthorpe Rd SYD SE26 164 A6
Bishop St IS N1 85 J6
Bishops Wk CHST BR7 185 H4
CROY/NA CR0 213 F3
Bishop's Wy BETH E2 104 E1
Bishopswood Rd HGT N6 65 K4
Bisley Cl WPK KT4 193 F5
Bispham Rd WLSDN NW10 98 B2
Bisson Rd SRTFD E15 106 A1
Bistern Av WALTH E17 52 B6
Bittacy Cl MLHL NW7 46 B2
Bittacy Hl MLHL NW7 46 B2
Bittacy Park Av MLHL NW7 46 B1
Bittacy Ri MLHL NW7 46 B2
Bittacy Rd MLHL NW7 46 B2
Bittern Cl YEAD UB4 95 H4
Bittern Pl WDGN N22 * 49 F5
Bittern St STHWK SE1 18 C3
Bittoms Ct KUT/HW KT1 * 174 E6
The Bittoms KUT/HW KT1 174 E6
Bixley Cl NWDGN UB2 114 E4
Blackall St SDTCH EC2A 7 G6
Blackberry Farm Cl HEST TW5 134 D1
Blackberry Fld
STMC/STPC BR5 186 B4
Blackbird Hl WBLY HA9 62 E6
Blackbird Yd BETH E2 7 K4
Blackborne Rd DAGE RM10 92 C4
Black Boy La
SEVS/STOTM N15 67 J2
Blackbrook La HAYES BR2 201 F2
Blackburne's Ms
MYFR/PKLN W1K 9 G5
Blackburn Rd
KIL/WHAMP NW6 83 F4
Blackbush Av CHDH RM6 73 K2
Blackbush Cl BELMT SM2 209 F5
Blackdown Cl EFNCH N2 47 G5
Blackdown Ter
WOOL/PLUM SE18 * 146 E2
Blackenham Rd TOOT SW17 160 E6
Blackett St PUT/ROE SW15 139 G4
Black Fan Cl ENC/FH EN2 23 J2
Blackfen Pde BFN/LL DA15 * 168 B1
Blackfen Rd BFN/LL DA15 148 A6
Blackford Cl SAND/SEL CR2 211 H6
Blackford Rd OXHEY WD19 41 H1
Blackfriars Br STHWK SE1 12 A6
Black Friars La BLKFR EC4V 12 A4
Blackfriars Pas BLKFR EC4V 12 A5
Blackfriars Rd STHWK SE1 12 A7
Blackfriars U/P BLKFR EC4V 12 B5
Blackheath Av GNWCH SE10 145 G1
Blackheath Gv
BKHTH/KID SE3 145 J3
Blackheath Hl GNWCH SE10 145 F2
Blackheath Pk
BKHTH/KID SE3 145 J4
BKHTH/KID SE3 146 A3
Blackheath Ri LEW SE13 145 F3
Blackheath Rd GNWCH SE10 144 E2
Blackheath V BKHTH/KID SE3 145 H3
Black Horse Ct STHWK SE1 * 19 F5
Blackhorse La CROY/NA CR0 197 H4
WALTH E17 51 F6
Black Horse Pde PIN HA5 * 59 F2
Blackhorse Rd DEPT SE8 124 B6
Black Horse Rd SCUP DA14 168 B6
Blackhorse Rd WALTH E17 69 F1
Blacklands Dr YEAD UB4 94 A3
Blacklands Rd CAT SE6 165 F6
Blacklands Ter CHEL SW3 14 E7
Black Lion Ga BAY/PAD W2 101 F6
Black Lion La HMSMTH W6 118 D4
Blackmans Yd WCHPL E1 * 7 K6
Blackmore Av STHL UB1 115 J1
Blackmore Dr WLSDN NW10 80 D5
Blackmore Rd BKHH IG9 39 J2
Blackmore's Gv TEDD TW11 174 B2
Blackness Cots HAYES BR2 * 215 H6

Blackness La HAYES BR2 215 H6
Blackpool Gdns YEAD UB4 94 C3
Blackpool Rd PECK SE15 143 J3
Black Prince Rd LBTH SE11 17 G7
Black Rod Cl HYS/HAR UB3 113 J3
Blackrurn Wy HSLWW TW4 134 D6
Blackshaw Rd TOOT SW17 178 C1
Blacksmith Cl CHDH RM6 73 J3
Blacksmiths La
STMC/STPC BR5 202 D2
Blacksmith's La RAIN RM13 93 H6
Black's Rd HMSMTH W6 119 F5
Blackstock Rd FSBYPK N4 67 H6
Blackstone Est HACK E8 86 C5
Blackstone Rd CRICK NW2 82 A3
Black Swan Yd STHWK SE1 19 G2
Blackthorn Av WDR/YW UB7 112 D4
Blackthorn Ct HEST TW5 134 D1
Blackthorne Av CROY/NA CR0 197 K5
Blackthorne Dr CHING E4 38 B6
Blackthorn Rd IL IG1 90 D3
Blackthorn St BOW E3 105 J3
Blacktree Ms BRXN/ST SW9 * 142 B4
Blackwall La GNWCH SE10 125 H5
Blackwall Tnl POP/IOD E14 125 G1
Blackwall Tunnel Ap
POP/IOD E14 106 A6
Blackwall Tunnel Northern Ap
BOW E3 87 J6
Blackwall Wy POP/IOD E14 106 A6
Blackwater Cl RAIN RM13 111 F4
Blackwater St EDUL SE22 143 G6
Blackwell Cl CLPT E5 87 G2
KTN/HRWW/WS HA3 42 D3
WCHMH N21 22 E6
Blackwell Dr OXHEY WD19 27 G1
Blackwell Gdns EDGW HA8 30 C6
Blackwood St WALW SE17 122 E5
Blade Ms PUT/ROE SW15 139 J5
Bladindon Dr BXLY DA5 168 E2
Bladon Gdns
RYLN/HDSTN HA2 60 B3
Blagden's La STHGT/OAK N14 34 D4
Blagdon Rd CAT SE6 164 E1
NWMAL KT3 192 C1
Blagdon Wk TEDD TW11 174 D2
Blagrove Rd NKENS W10 100 C4
Blair Av CDALE/KGS NW9 63 G4
ESH/CLAY KT10 189 H6
Blair Cl BFN/LL DA15 147 K6
HYS/HAR UB3 113 K4
IS N1 85 J4
Blairderry Rd
BRXS/STRHM SW2 161 K4
Blairhead Dr OXHEY WD19 27 F5
Blair St POP/IOD E14 106 A5
Blake Av BARK IG11 90 E6
Blake Cl CAR SM5 194 D5
NKENS W10 100 A4
RAIN RM13 93 H6
WELL DA16 147 K2
YEAD UB4 94 B1
Blakeden Dr ESH/CLAY KT10 205 F5
Blake Gdns FUL/PGN SW6 139 K2
Blakehall Rd CAR SM5 209 K4
Blake Hall Rd WAN E11 70 E5
Blake Ms RCH/KEW TW9 137 H2
Blakemore Gdns BARN SW13 118 E6
Blakemore Rd
STRHM/NOR SW16 161 K5
THHTH CR7 196 A2
Blakemore Wy BELV DA17 129 F3
Blakeney Av BECK BR3 182 C4
Blakeney Cl CAMTN NW1 4 C2
HACK E8 86 C3
TRDG/WHET N20 33 G3
Blakeney Rd BECK BR3 182 C4
Blaker Ct CHARL SE7 * 146 B1
Blake Rd CAN/RD E16 106 D3
CROY/NA CR0 197 F6
FBAR/BDGN N11 48 C3
MTCM CR4 178 D6
Blaker Rd SRTFD E15 88 A6
Blakes Av NWMAL KT3 192 C2
Blakes Cl WLSDN NW10 81 J4
Blake's Gn WWKM BR4 199 F4
Blakes La NWMAL KT3 192 C2
Blakesley Av EA W5 97 J5
Blake's Rd PECK SE15 143 F1
Blakes Ter NWMAL KT3 192 D2
Blakesware Gdns ED N9 35 K2
Blakewood Cl FELT TW13 154 B6
Blanchard Cl ELTH/MOT SE9 166 D5
Blanchard Gv PEND EN3 25 J1
Blanchard Wy HACK E8 * 86 C4
Blanch Cl PECK SE15 143 K1
Blanchedowne CMBW SE5 142 E5
Blanche St CAN/RD E16 106 D3
Blanchland Rd MRDN SM4 194 A2
Blandfield Rd BAL SW12 161 F1
Blandford Av BECK BR3 182 B5
WHTN TW2 155 G3
Blandford Cl CROY/NA CR0 210 E1
EFNCH N2 65 G2
ROMW/RG RM7 74 D1
Blandford Crs CHING E4 38 A2
Blandford Rd BECK BR3 182 A5
CHSWK W4 118 B3
EA W5 116 E2
NWDGN UB2 115 F4
TEDD TW11 173 J1
Blandford Sq CAMTN NW1 2 D7
Blandford St MHST W1U 9 F3
Blandford Waye YEAD UB4 95 G5
Bland St ELTH/MOT SE9 146 C5
Blaney Crs EHAM E6 108 B2
Blanmerle Rd ELTH/MOT SE9 167 G3
Blann Cl ELTH/MOT SE9 166 C1
Blantyre St WBPTN SW10 140 C1
Blantyre Wk WBPTN SW10 * 140 C1
Blashford St LEW SE13 165 G2
Blawith Rd HRW HA1 60 E1
Blaydon Cl RSLP HA4 58 C4
TOTM N17 * 50 D3
Blaydon Wk TOTM N17 50 D3
Bleak Hill La
WOOL/PLUM SE18 128 A6
Blean Gv PGE/AN SE20 181 K3
Bleasdale Av GFD/PVL UB6 97 G1
Blechynden Gdns NKENS W10 100 B6
Blechynden St NKENS W10 * 100 B6
Bledlow Cl THMD SE28 109 J6
Bledlow Ri GFD/PVL UB6 96 C1
Bleeding Heart Yd
HCIRC EC1N * 11 K2
Blegborough Rd
STRHM/NOR SW16 179 H2
Blendon Dr BXLY DA5 168 E1
Blendon Rd BXLY DA5 168 E1
Blendon Ter
WOOL/PLUM SE18 127 H5
Blendworth Wy PECK SE15 143 F1
Blenheim CDALE/KGS NW9 * 45 H5
Blenheim Av
GNTH/NBYPK IG2 72 A3
Blenheim Cl GFD/PVL UB6 * 96 D1
LEE/GVPK SE12 166 A3
OXHEY WD19 27 G2
ROMW/RG RM7 74 E1
RYNPK SW20 177 F6
WCHMH N21 35 J3
WLGTN SM6 210 C5
Blenheim Ct ARCH N19 66 E6
BFN/LL DA15 167 J5
WFD IG8 53 F3
Blenheim Crs NTGHL W11 100 C5
RSLP HA4 58 B6
SAND/SEL CR2 211 J5
Blenheim Dr WELL DA16 148 A2
Blenheim Gdns
BRXS/STRHM SW2 162 A1
CRICK NW2 82 A3
KUTN/CMB KT2 175 J3
WBLY HA9 80 A1
WLGTN SM6 210 C4
Blenheim Gv PECK SE15 143 G3
Blenheim Park Rd
SAND/SEL CR2 211 J6
Blenheim Pas STJWD NW8 101 G1
Blenheim Pl TEDD TW11 174 A1
Blenheim Ri
SEVS/STOTM N15 * 68 B1
Blenheim Rd BAR EN5 20 B4
BFN/LL DA15 168 D3
BMLY BR1 200 D1
CHSWK W4 118 B3
EHAM E6 107 H2
NTHLT UB5 78 B4
ORP BR6 202 D6
PGE/AN SE20 181 K3
RYLN/HDSTN HA2 60 B3
RYNPK SW20 177 F6
STJWD NW8 101 G1
SUT SM1 208 E1
WALTH E17 51 F6
WAN E11 88 C2
Blenheim St CONDST W1S * 9 J4
Blenheim Ter STJWD NW8 101 G1
Blenheim Wy ISLW TW7 136 B2
Blenkarne Rd BTSEA SW11 160 E1
Bleriot Rd HEST TW5 134 B1
Blessbury Rd EDGW HA8 44 E4
Blessington Rd LEW SE13 145 G5
Blessing Wy BARK IG11 109 J1
Bletchingley Cl THHTH CR7 196 C1
Bletchley St IS N1 6 D3
Bletchmore Cl HYS/HAR UB3 113 G5
Bletsoe Wk IS N1 6 D2
Blincoe Cl WIM/MER SW19 159 G4
Blissett St GNWCH SE10 145 F2
Bliss Ms NKENS W10 100 C2
Blisworth Cl YEAD UB4 95 J3
Blithbury Rd DAGW RM9 91 H4
Blithdale Rd ABYW SE2 128 B4
Blithfield St KENS W8 120 A3
Blockley Rd ALP/SUD HA0 61 H6
Bloemfontein Av SHB W12 118 E1
Bloemfontein Rd SHB W12 99 K6
Blomfield Rd MV/WKIL W9 101 F4
Blomfield St LVPST EC2M 13 F2
Blomfield Vls BAY/PAD W2 101 F4
Blomville Rd BCTR RM8 74 A6
Blondell Cl WDR/YW UB7 112 A6
Blondel St BTSEA SW11 141 F3
Blondin Av EA W5 116 D4
Blondin St BOW E3 105 J1
Bloomfield Crs
GNTH/NBYPK IG2 72 B3
Bloomfield Pl
MYFR/PKLN W1K 9 K5
Bloomfield Rd HAYES BR2 200 C2
HGT N6 66 A3
KUT/HW KT1 191 F1
WOOL/PLUM SE18 127 G5
Bloomfield Ter BGVA SW1W 121 F5
Bloom Gv WNWD SE27 162 C5
Bloomhall Rd NRWD SE19 180 E1
Bloom Park Rd FUL/PGN SW6 139 J1
Bloomsbury Cl EA W5 98 B6
Bloomsbury Pl
NOXST/BSQ WC1A 11 F2
Bloomsbury Sq
NOXST/BSQ WC1A 11 F2
Bloomsbury St GWRST WC1E 10 D1
Bloomsbury Wy
NOXST/BSQ WC1A 10 E2
Blore Cl VX/NE SW8 141 J2
Blossom Cl DAGW RM9 92 B6
EA W5 117 F2
SAND/SEL CR2 212 B3
Blossom La ENC/FH EN2 23 J2
Blossom St WCHPL E1 7 H7
Blossom Wy WDR/YW UB7 112 D4
Blossom Waye HEST TW5 114 D6
Blount St POP/IOD E14 105 G5
Bloxam Gdns ELTH/MOT SE9 146 D6
Bloxhall Rd LEY E10 69 H5
Bloxham Crs HPTN TW12 172 E4
Bloxworth Cl WLGTN SM6 210 C1
Blucher Rd CMBW SE5 142 D1
Blue Anchor La
BERM/RHTH SE16 123 H4
Blue Anchor Yd WCHPL E1 104 C6
Blue Ball Yd WHALL SW1A 16 A1
Bluebell Av MNPK E12 89 H3
Bluebell Cl HOM E9 86 E6
NTHLT UB5 77 K4
ORP BR6 201 H6
ROMW/RG RM7 75 G6
SYD SE26 163 G6
WLGTN SM6 195 G5
Bluebell Wy IL IG1 90 B4
Blueberry Cl WFD IG8 52 E2
Bluebird La DAGE RM10 92 C5
Bluebird Wy THMD SE28 127 J2
Bluefield Cl HPTN TW12 173 F1
Bluegates EW KT17 207 J5
Bluehouse Rd CHING E4 38 C5
Blue Lion Pl STHWK SE1 19 G4
Blue Riband Est
CROY/NA CR0 * 196 C6
Blundell Cl HACK E8 86 C2
Blundell Rd EDGW HA8 45 F4
Blundell St HOLWY N7 84 E5
Blunden Cl BCTR RM8 73 J5
Blunt Rd SAND/SEL CR2 211 K3
Blunts Av WDR/YW UB7 132 D1
Blunts Rd ELTH/MOT SE9 147 F6
Blurton Rd CLPT E5 87 F2
Blyth Cl TWK TW1 156 A1
Blythe Cl CAT SE6 164 C2
Blythe Hl CAT SE6 164 C2
STMC/STPC BR5 186 A4
Blythe Hill La CAT SE6 164 C2
Blythe Hill Pl FSTH SE23 * 164 B2
Blythe Ms WKENS W14 * 119 G3
Blythe Rd WKENS W14 119 G3
Blythe St BETH E2 * 104 D2
Blytheswood Pl
STRHM/NOR SW16 162 A6
Blythe V CAT SE6 164 C3
Blyth Rd BMLY BR1 183 J4
HYS/HAR UB3 113 H2
THMD SE28 109 J6
WALTH E17 69 H4
Blyth's Whf POP/IOD E14 * 105 G6
Blythswood Rd
GDMY/SEVK IG3 73 G5
Blythwood Rd FSBYPK N4 66 E4
PIN HA5 41 H4
Boadicea St IS N1 5 G1
Boakes Cl CDALE/KGS NW9 62 E1
Boardman Av CHING E4 25 K6
Boardman Cl BAR EN5 20 C6
Boardwalk Pl POP/IOD E14 125 F1
Boathouse Wk PECK SE15 143 G1
RCH/KEW TW9 136 E2
Boat Lifter Wy
BERM/RHTH SE16 124 B4
Boat Quay CAN/RD E16 107 G6
Bob Anker Cl PLSTW E13 106 E2
Bobbin Cl CLAP SW4 141 H4
Bob Marley Wy HNHL SE24 142 B5
Bockhampton Rd
KUTN/CMB KT2 175 G3
Bocking St HACK E8 86 D6
Boddicott Cl WIM/MER SW19 159 H4
Boddington Gdns ACT W3 117 H2
Bodiam Cl EN EN1 23 K3
Bodiam Rd STRHM/NOR SW16 179 J4
Bodiam Wy WLSDN NW10 98 B2
Bodicea Ms HSLWW TW4 154 E1
Bodley Cl NWMAL KT3 192 B2
Bodley Rd NWMAL KT3 192 B3
Bodmin Cl RYLN/HDSTN HA2 77 K1
STMC/STPC BR5 202 D5
Bodmin Gv MRDN SM4 194 A1
Bodmin St WAND/EARL SW18 159 K3
Bodnant Gdns RYNPK SW20 176 D6
Bodney Rd CLPT E5 86 D3
Boeing Wy NWDGN UB2 114 A3
Bofors House CHARL SE7 * 146 D1
Bognor Gdns OXHEY WD19 * 41 G1
Bognor Rd WELL DA16 148 E2
Bohemia Pl HACK E8 86 E4
Bohn Rd WCHPL E1 105 G4
Bohun Gv EBAR EN4 33 J1
Boileau Rd BARN SW13 138 D1
EA W5 98 B5
Bolberry Rd CRW RM5 57 F1
Bolden St DEPT SE8 144 E3
Boldero Pl STJWD NW8 * 2 C7
Bolderwood Wy WWKM BR4 198 E6
Boldmere Rd PIN HA5 59 G4
Boleyn Av EN EN1 24 D2
Boleyn Cl LOU IG10 39 J1
WALTH E17 69 J1
Boleyn Ct BKHH IG9 38 E3
Boleyn Dr E/WMO/HCT KT8 172 E6
RSLP HA4 59 H6
Boleyn Gdns DAGE RM10 92 E5
WWKM BR4 198 E6
Boleyn Rd EHAM E6 107 H1
FSTGT E7 88 E5
STNW/STAM N16 86 A3
Boleyn Wy BAR EN5 21 G4
BARK/HLT IG6 54 C2
Bolina Rd BERM/RHTH SE16 123 K5
Bolingbroke Gv BTSEA SW11 140 D6
Bolingbroke Rd WKENS W14 119 G3
Bolingbroke Wk
BTSEA SW11 * 140 C1
Bolingbroke Wy
HYS/HAR UB3 113 G1
Bollo Bridge Rd ACT W3 117 J3
Bollo La ACT W3 117 J3
Bolney Ga SKENS SW7 14 C3
Bolney St VX/NE SW8 142 A1
Bolsover St GTPST W1W 3 K7
Bolstead Rd MTCM CR4 179 G4
Bolster Gv WDGN N22 * 48 D4
Bolt Ct FLST/FETLN EC4A 11 K4
Boltmore Cl HDN NW4 46 B6
Bolton Cl CHSGTN KT9 205 K4
Bolton Crs LBTH SE11 122 B6
Bolton Dr MRDN SM4 194 B4
Bolton Gdns BMLY BR1 183 J2
ECT SW5 120 A5
TEDD TW11 174 B2
WLSDN NW10 100 B1
Bolton Gardens Ms
WBPTN SW10 120 A5
Bolton Pl IS N1 * 85 H5
Bolton Rd CHSGTN KT9 205 K4
CHSWK W4 137 K1
HRW HA1 60 C1
SRTFD E15 88 D4
STJWD NW8 83 F6
UED N18 50 B1
WLSDN NW10 81 G6
Bolton's La HYS/HAR UB3 133 F1
Boltons Pl ECT SW5 120 B5
The Boltons ALP/SUD HA0 79 F2
WBPTN SW10 * 120 B5
WFD IG8 * 38 E6
Bolton St MYFR/PICC W1J 9 K7
Bombay St BERM/RHTH SE16 123 J4
Bomer Cl WDR/YW UB7 132 D1
Bomore Rd NTGHL W11 100 B6
Bonar Pl CHST BR7 184 D3
Bonar Rd PECK SE15 143 H1
Bonchester Cl CHST BR7 185 F3
Bonchurch Cl BELMT SM2 209 F5
Bonchurch Rd NKENS W10 100 C4
WEA W13 116 C1
Bondfield Av YEAD UB4 94 E2
Bond Gdns WLGTN SM6 210 C2
Bond Rd MTCM CR4 178 E5
SURB KT6 191 G6
Bond St EA W5 97 K6
SRTFD E15 88 C3
Bondway VX/NE SW8 121 K6
Boneta Rd WOOL/PLUM SE18 126 E3
Bonfield Rd LEW SE13 145 F5
Bonham Gdns BCTR RM8 73 K6
Bonham Rd BCTR RM8 73 K6
BRXS/STRHM SW2 142 A6
Bonheur Rd CHSWK W4 118 A2
Bonhill St SDTCH EC2A 7 F7
Boniface Gdns
KTN/HRWW/WS HA3 42 B3
Boniface Wk
KTN/HRWW/WS HA3 42 B3
Bonita Ms PECK SE15 144 A4
Bonner Hill Rd KUT/HW KT1 175 G6
Bonner Rd BETH E2 104 E1
Bonnersfield Cl HRW HA1 61 G3
Bonnersfield La HRW HA1 61 F3
Bonner St BETH E2 * 104 E1
Bonneville Gdns CLAP SW4 161 H1
Bonnington Sq VX/NE SW8 122 A6
Bonny St CAMTN NW1 84 C5
Bonser Rd TWK TW1 156 A4
Bonsor St CMBW SE5 143 F1
Bonville Gdns HDN NW4 63 J1
Bonville Rd BMLY BR1 183 J1
Booker Rd UED N18 50 C1
Boones Rd LEW SE13 145 H5
Boone St LEW SE13 145 H5
Boord St GNWCH SE10 125 H3
Boothby Rd ARCH N19 66 D6
Booth Cl HOM E9 86 D6
THMD SE28 128 C1
Booth La BLKFR EC4V 12 C5
Booth Rd CDALE/KGS NW9 45 F4
CROY/NA CR0 * 196 C6
Boot Pde EDGW HA8 * 44 C2
Boot St FSBYE EC1V 7 G5
Bordars Rd HNWL W7 96 E4
Bordars Wk HNWL W7 96 E4
Borden Av EN EN1 35 K1
Border Crs SYD SE26 181 J1
Border Gdns CROY/NA CR0 213 K2
Border Ga MTCM CR4 178 D4
Border Rd SYD SE26 181 J1
Bordesley Rd MRDN SM4 194 A1
Bordon Wk PUT/ROE SW15 158 D2
Boreas Wk IS N1 6 B3
Boreham Av CAN/RD E16 106 E5
Boreham Cl WAN E11 70 A5
Boreham Rd WDGN N22 49 J4
Borgard House CHARL SE7 * 146 D1
Borgard Rd
WOOL/PLUM SE18 126 E4
Borkwood Pk ORP BR6 217 F2
Borkwood Wy ORP BR6 216 E2
Borland Rd PECK SE15 143 K5
TEDD TW11 174 C2
Borneo St PUT/ROE SW15 139 F4
Borough High St STHWK SE1 18 D3
Borough Hl CROY/NA CR0 211 H1
Borough Rd ISLW TW7 135 K2
KUTN/CMB KT2 175 H4
MTCM CR4 178 D5
STHWK SE1 18 A4
Borough Sq STHWK SE1 18 C3
Borrett Cl WALW SE17 122 D5
Borrodaile Rd
WAND/EARL SW18 160 A1
Borrowdale Av
KTN/HRWW/WS HA3 43 G5
Borrowdale Cl EFNCH N2 47 G5
REDBR IG4 71 J1
Borthwick Ms WAN E11 * 88 C2
Borthwick Rd
CDALE/KGS NW9 63 H3
SRTFD E15 88 C2
Borthwick St DEPT SE8 124 D5
Borwick Av WALTH E17 51 H6
Bosbury Rd CAT SE6 165 F5
Boscastle Rd KTTN NW5 84 B1
Boscobel Cl BMLY BR1 184 E5
Boscobel Pl BGVA SW1W 15 H6
Boscobel St BAY/PAD W2 8 B1
Boscombe Av LEY E10 70 B4
Boscombe Cl CLPT E5 87 G3
Boscombe Rd SHB W12 118 D2
TOOT SW17 179 F2
WIM/MER SW19 177 K4
WPK KT4 193 F5
Bose Cl FNCH N3 46 C4
Bosgrove CHING E4 38 A3
Boss St STHWK SE1 19 J2
Bostall Hl ABYW SE2 128 C5
Bostall La ABYW SE2 128 C4
Bostall Manorway ABYW SE2 128 C4
Bostall Rd STMC/STPC BR5 186 C3
Boston Gdns BTFD TW8 116 B4
CHSWK W4 118 B6
Boston Gv RSLP HA4 58 A3
Boston Manor Rd BTFD TW8 116 B4
Boston Pde HNWL W7 * 116 B4
Boston Park Rd BTFD TW8 * 116 D6
Boston Pl CAMTN NW1 2 E7
Boston Rd CROY/NA CR0 196 A3
EDGW HA8 44 E3
EHAM E6 107 J2
HNWL W7 115 K1
WALTH E17 69 J3
Bostonthorpe Rd HNWL W7 * 115 K2
Boston V HNWL W7 116 B4
Boswell Cl STMC/STPC BR5 202 D3
Boswell Ct BMSBY WC1N 11 F1
Boswell Rd THHTH CR7 196 D1
Boswell St BMSBY WC1N 11 F1
Bosworth Cl WALTH E17 51 H4
Bosworth Rd BAR EN5 20 E4
DAGE RM10 92 C2
FBAR/BDGN N11 48 D2
NKENS W10 100 C3
Botany Bay La CHST BR7 185 H5
Botany Cl EBAR EN4 21 J5
Botany Ter PUR RM19 * 131 K5
Boteley Cl CHING E4 38 B4
Botham Cl EDGW HA8 44 E3
Botha Rd PLSTW E13 107 F4
Bothwell Cl CAN/RD E16 106 E4
Bothwell St HMSMTH W6 119 G6
Botolph Aly MON EC3R 13 G6
Botolph La MON EC3R 13 G6
Botsford Rd RYNPK SW20 177 H5
Bott's Ms BAY/PAD W2 100 E5
Botwell Common Rd
HYS/HAR UB3 94 B6
Botwell Crs HYS/HAR UB3 94 C5
Botwell La HYS/HAR UB3 94 C5
Boucher Cl TEDD TW11 174 A1
Boughton Av HAYES BR2 199 J4
Boughton Rd THMD SE28 127 K3
Boulcott St WCHPL E1 105 F5
Boulevard Dr
CDALE/KGS NW9 45 H5
The Boulevard FUL/PGN SW6 140 B3
WFD IG8 54 A2
Boulogne Rd CROY/NA CR0 196 D3
Boulter Cl BMLY BR1 185 F6
Boulter Gdns RAIN RM13 93 J4
Boulton Rd BCTR RM8 74 A6
Boultwood Rd EHAM E6 107 K5
Bounces La ED N9 36 D4
Bounces Rd ED N9 36 D4
Boundaries Rd BAL SW12 160 E4
FELT TW13 154 B3
Boundary Av WALTH E17 69 H4
Boundary Business Ct
MTCM CR4 178 C6
Boundary Cl BAR EN5 20 D2
GDMY/SEVK IG3 90 E2
KUT/HW KT1 175 H6
NWDGN UB2 115 F5
Boundary La CMBW SE5 122 D6
PLSTW E13 107 H2
Boundary Ms STJWD NW8 83 G6
Boundary Pass WCHPL E1 7 J6
Boundary Rd BARK IG11 108 C1
BFN/LL DA15 147 K6
CAR SM5 210 A6
ED N9 36 E1
EFNCH N2 47 H4
PIN HA5 59 H3
PLSTW E13 107 G1
ROM RM1 75 J3
STJWD NW8 83 G6
WALTH E17 69 H4
WBLY HA9 80 A1
WDGN N22 49 H6
WIM/MER SW19 178 C2
WLGTN SM6 210 B4
Boundary Rw STHWK SE1 18 A2
Boundary St BETH E2 7 J5
Boundary Wy CROY/NA CR0 213 J5
Boundfield Rd CAT SE6 165 H5
Bounds Green Rd
FBAR/BDGN N11 48 D2
Bourchier St
SOHO/SHAV W1D 10 C5
Bourdon Pl MYFR/PKLN W1K 9 K5
Bourdon Rd PGE/AN SE20 181 K5
Bourdon St MYFR/PKLN W1K 9 J6
Bourke Cl CLAP SW4 161 K1
WLSDN NW10 81 G4
Bourlet Cl GTPST W1W 10 A2
Bourn Av EBAR EN4 21 H6
SEVS/STOTM N15 67 K1
Bournbrook Rd
BKHTH/KID SE3 146 C4
Bourne Av HYS/HAR UB3 113 F3
RSLP HA4 77 G3
STHGT/OAK N14 34 E4
Bourne Cl ISLW TW7 135 K4
THDIT KT7 190 A
Bourne Ct RSLP HA4 77 F
Bourne Dr MTCM CR4 178 C
Bourne End Rd NTHWD HA6 26 C
Bourne Est HCIRC EC1N * 11 J
Bourne Gdns CHING E4 37 K
Bournehall BUSH WD23 * 28 A
Bournehall La BUSH WD23 28 A
Bournehall Rd BUSH WD23 28 A
Bourne Hl PLMGR N13 34 E
Bourne Hill Cl PLMGR N13 * 35
Bournemead BUSH WD23 28 A
Bournemead Av NTHLT UB5 94 E
Bournemead Cl NTHLT UB5 94 E
Bournemouth Cl PECK SE15 143 H
Bournemouth Rd PECK SE15 143 H
WIM/MER SW19 177 K
Bourne Pde BXLY DA5 * 169
Bourne Rd BXLY DA5 169
CEND/HSY/T N8 66
HAYES BR2 200
WAN E11 88
Bourneside Crs
STHGT/OAK N14 34
Bourneside Gdns CAT SE6 183
Bourne St BGVA SW1W 15
CROY/NA CR0 196
Bourne Ter BAY/PAD W2 101
The Bourne STHGT/OAK N14 34
Bournevale Rd
STRHM/NOR SW16 161
Bourne Vw GFD/PVL UB6 79
Bourne Wy HOR/WEW KT19 206
SUT SM1 208
SWLY BR8 187
Bournewood Rd
STMC/STPC BR5 202
WOOL/PLUM SE18 148
Bournville Rd CAT SE6 164
Bournwell Cl EBAR EN4 21

Bourton Cl HYS/HAR UB3 113 K1
Bousfield Rd NWCR SE14 144 A3
Boutflower Rd BTSEA SW11 140 D5
Boutique Hall LEW SE13 * 145 F5
Bouverie Gdns
KTN/HRWW/WS HA3 61 K3
Bouverie Ms STNW/STAM N16 68 A6
Bouverie Pl BAY/PAD W2 8 B3
Bouverie Rd HRW HA1 60 C3
STNW/STAM N16 68 A6
Bouverie St EMB EC4Y 11 K4
Bouvier Rd PEND EN3 24 E1
Boveney Rd FSTH SE23 164 A2
Bovill Rd FSTH SE23 164 A2
Bovingdon Av WBLY HA9 80 C4
Bovingdon La
CDALE/KGS NW9 45 G4
Bovingdon Rd FUL/PGN SW6 140 A2
Bovington Dr ARCH N19 66 C6
Bowater Cl BRXS/STRHM SW2 161 K1
CDALE/KGS NW9 63 F2
Bowater Gdns SUN TW16 172 B4
Bowater Pl BKHTH/KID SE3 146 A1
Bowater Rd WBLY HA9 80 D1
WOOL/PLUM SE18 126 C3
Bow Bridge Est BOW E3 105 K2
Bow Churchyard STP EC4M * 12 D4
Bow Common La BOW E3 105 H3
Bowden Cl EBED/NFELT TW14 153 H3
Bowden St LBTH SE11 122 B5
Bowditch DEPT SE8 124 C5
Bowdon Rd WALTH E17 69 J4
Bowen Dr DUL SE21 163 F5
Bowen Rd HRW HA1 60 C4
Bowen St POP/IOD E14 105 K5
Bowens Wd CROY/NA CR0 * 213 H6
Bower Av GNWCH SE10 145 H2
Bower Cl CRW RM5 57 F3
NTHLT UB5 95 G1
Bowerdean St FUL/PGN SW6 140 A2
Bowerman Av NWCR SE14 124 B6
ower St WCHPL E1 * 105 F5
owes Cl BFN/LL DA15 168 C1
owes Rd ACT W3 99 G6
BCTR RM8 91 J2
FBAR/BDGN N11 48 B1
WOT/HER KT12 188 A6
owfell Rd HMSMTH W6 119 F6
owhill Cl BRXN/ST SW9 142 B1
owie Cl CLAP SW4 161 J2
owland Rd CLAP SW4 141 J5
WFD IG8 53 G2
owland Yd KTBR SW1X * 15 F3
ow La NFNCH/WDSPK N12 47 G3
STP EC4M 12 D4
owl Ct WCHPL E1 7 H7
owley Cl NRWD SE19 181 G2
owley La NRWD SE19 181 G1
owley St POP/IOD E14 105 H6
owling Green Cl
PUT/ROE SW15 158 E2
owling Green Ct WBLY HA9 62 B6
owling Green La
CLKNW EC1R 5 K7
wling Green Pl
STHWK SE1 * 18 E2
wling Green Rw
WOOL/PLUM SE18 * 126 E4
wling Green St LBTH SE11 122 B6
wling Green Wk IS N1 7 G4
w Locks BOW E3 * 106 A3
wls Cl STAN HA7 43 H1
wman Av CAN/RD E16 106 E5
wman Ms
WAND/EARL SW18 159 J3
wmans Cl WEA W13 116 C1
wmans Lea FSTH SE23 163 K2
wman's Meadow
WLGTN SM6 210 B1
wmans Ms WCHPL E1 104 C6
wman's Ms HOLWY N7 84 E1
wman's Pl HOLWY N7 84 E1
wmead ELTH/MOT SE9 166 E4
wmore Wk CAMTN NW1 84 D5
wness Cl HACK E8 * 86 B4
wness Crs PUT/ROE SW15 176 A1
CROY/NA CR0 196 A3
wness Dr HSLWW TW4 134 D5
wness Rd CAT SE6 164 E2
wness Wy HCH RM12 93 J3
wood Rd CLAP SW4 141 F5
PEND EN3 25 F3
wring Gn OXHEY WD19 41 G1
Rd BOW E3 105 J2
wrons Av ALP/SUD HA0 79 K5
sley Ct FELT TW13 153 K4
St COVGDN WC2E 11 F4
RTFD E15 88 C3
yer Cl EHAM E6 107 K4
yer Pl CMBW SE5 142 D1
yers Ct TWK TW1 136 C5
yer St CMBW SE5 142 D1
all Rd DUL SE21 163 F1
elder Cl EDGW HA8 44 E1
grove Rd ABYW SE2 128 C2
La BARK IG11 109 H1
ey Rd MRDN SM4 194 B1
ey St CAN/RD E16 126 A1
moor Rd CRW RM5 56 E1
N/HRWW/WS HA3 61 H1
ll Rd DAGW RM9 92 B2
ed Cl BKHH IG9 39 J3
ree La
N/HRWW/WS HA3 42 C4
ee Rd
N/HRWW/WS HA3 42 D3
vood Cl WDR/YW UB7 112 C2
vorth Cl
NCH/WDSPK N12 47 H1
vorth Gv IS N1 85 F6
rd Rd WOOL/PLUM SE18 127 G5
e Wy PLSTW E13 106 E3
roft Av CDALE/KGS NW9 62 E3
Av STHL UB1 114 E1
Cl KUTN/CMB KT2 175 H3
ell Ct STJWD NW8 83 H5
Rd WIM/MER SW19 178 C2
St WCHPL E1 104 C5
eld St STHWK SE1 18 B3
nd Rd BMLY BR1 183 J1
Av STAN HA7 43 G2

Boyle Farm Rd THDIT KT7 190 B3
Boyne Av HDN NW4 64 B1
Boyne Rd DAGE RM10 92 C1
LEW SE13 145 G4
Boyne Terrace Ms
NTGHL W11 119 J1
Boyson Rd WALW SE17 122 D6
Boyton Cl CEND/HSY/T N8 48 E6
WCHPL E1 105 F3
Boyton Rd CEND/HSY/T N8 48 E6
Brabant Rd WDGN N22 49 F5
Brabazon Av WLGTN SM6 210 E5
Brabazon Rd HEST TW5 134 B1
NTHLT UB5 96 A1
Brabazon St POP/IOD E14 105 K5
Brabourne Cl NRWD SE19 181 F1
Brabourne Crs BXLYHN DA7 129 G6
Brabourne Ri BECK BR3 199 G2
Brabourn Gv PECK SE15 143 K3
Bracewell Av GFD/PVL UB6 79 F3
Bracewell Rd NKENS W10 100 A4
Bracewood Gdns
CROY/NA CR0 212 B1
Bracey St FSBYPK N4 * 66 E6
Bracken Av BAL SW12 161 F1
CROY/NA CR0 213 J1
Brackenbridge Dr RSLP HA4 77 H1
Brackenbury Gdns
HMSMTH W6 118 E3
Brackenbury Rd EFNCH N2 47 G6
HMSMTH W6 118 E3
Bracken Cl EHAM E6 107 K4
WHTN TW2 155 F1
Brackendale WCHMH N21 35 F4
Brackendale Cl HSLW TW3 135 G2
Bracken Dr CHIG IG7 54 B2
Bracken End ISLW TW7 135 J6
Bracken Gdns BARN SW13 138 D3
Brackenhill RSLP HA4 * 77 J2
Bracken Hill Cl BMLY BR1 183 J4
Bracken Hill La BMLY BR1 183 J4
Bracken Ms ROMW/RG RM7 75 F5
The Brackens EN EN1 36 A2
ORP BR6 217 G3
The Bracken CHING E4 38 A4
Brackley Av PECK SE15 143 K4
Brackley Cl WLGTN SM6 210 E5
Brackley Rd BECK BR3 182 C3
CHSWK W4 118 B4
Brackley Sq WFD IG8 53 H3
Brackley St BARB EC2Y 12 D1
Brackley Ter CHSWK W4 118 B5
Bracklyn St IS N1 6 E2
Bracknell Cl WDGN N22 49 G4
Bracknell Gdns HAMP NW3 83 F3
Bracknell Wy HAMP NW3 83 F2
Bracondale ESH/CLAY KT10 204 C3
Bracondale Rd ABYW SE2 128 B4
Bracton La RDART DA2 170 C4
Bradbourne Rd BXLY DA5 169 H2
Bradbourne St FUL/PGN SW6 139 K3
Bradbury Cl NWDGN UB2 114 E4
Bradbury St STNW/STAM N16 86 A3
Braddock Cl CRW RM5 56 E2
ISLW TW7 136 A4
Braddon Ct BAR EN5 * 20 C4
Braddon Rd RCH/KEW TW9 137 G4
Braddyll St GNWCH SE10 125 H5
Bradenham Av WELL DA16 148 B5
Bradenham Cl WALW SE17 122 E6
Bradenham Rd
KTN/HRWW/WS HA3 61 H1
YEAD UB4 94 C2
Braden St MV/WKIL W9 101 F3
Bradfield Dr BARK IG11 91 G3
Bradfield Rd RSLP HA4 77 J3
Bradford Cl HAYES BR2 200 E5
SYD SE26 163 J6
TOTM N17 50 B2
Bradford Dr HOR/WEW KT19 207 H4
Bradford Rd ACT W3 118 B2
IL IG1 72 D5
Bradgate Rd CAT SE6 164 E1
Brading Crs WAN E11 71 F6
Brading Rd BRXS/STRHM SW2 162 A2
CROY/NA CR0 196 A3
Brading Ter SHB W12 118 D3
Bradiston Rd MV/WKIL W9 100 D2
Bradley Cl HOLWY N7 84 E5
Bradley Gdns WEA W13 97 H5
Bradley Rd NRWD SE19 180 D2
PEND EN3 25 G1
WDGN N22 49 F5
Bradley's Cl IS N1 5 J2
Bradley Stone Rd EHAM E6 107 K5
Bradman Rw EDGW HA8 * 44 E3
Bradmead VX/NE SW8 * 141 G2
Bradmore Park Rd
HMSMTH W6 118 E3
Bradshaw Cl WIM/MER SW19 177 K2
Bradshaw Cots
POP/IOD E14 * 105 G5
Bradshaw Dr MLHL NW7 46 B3
Bradshaws Cl SNWD SE25 181 H6
Bradstock Rd EW KT17 207 K3
HOM E9 87 F4
Brad St STHWK SE1 17 K1
Bradwell Av DAGE RM10 74 C6
Bradwell Cl HCH RM12 93 K4
SWFD E18 70 D1
Bradwell Ms UED N18 36 C6
Bradwell Rd BKHH IG9 39 J3
Brady Dr BMLY BR1 185 F6
Bradymead EHAM E6 108 A5
Brady St WCHPL E1 104 D3
Braemar Av ALP/SUD HA0 79 K5
THHTH CR7 180 B6
WDGN N22 48 E4
WIM/MER SW19 159 K4
WLSDN NW10 81 F1
Braemar Gdns BFN/LL DA15 167 J5
CDALE/KGS NW9 45 F4
WWKM BR4 199 F5
Braemar Rd BTFD TW8 116 E6
PLSTW E13 106 D3
SEVS/STOTM N15 68 A2
WPK KT4 207 K1
Braeside BECK BR3 182 D1
Braeside Av RYNPK SW20 177 H4
Braeside Cl PIN HA5 42 A3

Braeside Crs BXLYHN DA7 149 K5
Braeside Rd
STRHM/NOR SW16 179 H3
Braes St IS N1 85 H5
Braesyde Cl BELV DA17 129 G4
Brafferton Rd CROY/NA CR0 211 J2
Braganza St WALW SE17 122 C5
Bragg Cl BCTR RM8 91 H4
Bragg Rd TEDD TW11 173 K3
Braham St WCHPL E1 13 K4
Braid Av ACT W3 99 G5
Braid Cl FELT TW13 154 E4
Braidwood Rd CAT SE6 165 G3
Braidwood St STHWK SE1 19 G1
Brailsford Cl WIM/MER SW19 178 D3
Brailsford Rd
BRXS/STRHM SW2 162 B1
Brainton Av
EBED/NFELT TW14 154 A2
Braintree Av REDBR IG4 71 J2
Braintree Rd DAGE RM10 92 C1
RSLP HA4 77 F2
Braintree St BETH E2 * 104 E2
Braithwaite Av
ROMW/RG RM7 74 C4
Braithwaite Gdns STAN HA7 43 J4
Braithwaite Rd PEND EN3 25 H4
Bramalea Cl HGT N6 66 A3
Bramall Cl SRTFD E15 88 D3
Bramber Ct EA W5 117 F4
Bramber Rd
NFNCH/WDSPK N12 47 J1
WKENS W14 119 J6
Bramble Acres Cl BELMT SM2 208 E5
Bramble Banks CAR SM5 210 A6
Bramblebury Rd
WOOL/PLUM SE18 127 J5
Bramble Cl BECK BR3 199 F2
CROY/NA CR0 213 J2
SEVS/STOTM N15 68 C1
STAN HA7 43 K3
Bramble Cft ERITH DA8 129 K4
Brambledown Cl WWKM BR4 199 H3
Brambledown Rd CAR SM5 210 A5
SAND/SEL CR2 212 A5
Bramble Gdns SHB W12 99 H6
Bramble La HPTN TW12 172 E2
Brambles Cl ISLW TW7 136 C1
The Brambles CHIG IG7 54 C2
SUT SM1 * 194 C6
WDR/YW UB7 112 A5
WIM/MER SW19 * 177 J1
Bramblewood Cl CAR SM5 194 D5
The Bramblings CHING E4 38 B6
Bramcote Av MTCM CR4 194 E1
Bramcote Gv
BERM/RHTH SE16 123 K5
Bramcote Rd PUT/ROE SW15 138 E5
Bramerton Rd BECK BR3 182 C6
Bramerton St CHEL SW3 120 D6
Bramfield Rd BTSEA SW11 160 D1
Bramford Rd
WAND/EARL SW18 140 B5
Bramham Ct NTHWD HA6 * 40 C1
Bramham Gdns CHSGTN KT9 * 205 K3
ECT SW5 120 A5
Bramhope La CHARL SE7 126 A6
Bramlands Cl BTSEA SW11 140 D4
Bramley Cl HYS/HAR UB3 94 E6
MLHL NW7 31 G5
ORP BR6 201 G5
PIN HA5 40 D6
SAND/SEL CR2 211 H3
STHGT/OAK N14 22 B6
WALTH E17 51 G5
WFD IG8 53 G3
WHTN TW2 155 H1
Bramley Crs GNTH/NBYPK IG2 72 A3
VX/NE SW8 141 J1
Bramley Gdns OXHEY WD19 41 G2
Bramley Hl SAND/SEL CR2 211 J2
Bramley Hyrst
SAND/SEL CR2 * 211 J3
Bramley Ldg ALP/SUD HA0 79 K2
Bramley Pde
STHGT/OAK N14 22 C5
Bramley Rd BELMT SM2 208 B6
EA W5 116 D3
NKENS W10 100 B6
STHGT/OAK N14 22 B6
SUT SM1 209 H3
Bramley Wy HSLWW TW4 134 E6
WWKM BR4 198 E6
Brampton Cl CLPT E5 68 D6
Brampton Gv HDN NW4 63 K1
KTN/HRWW/WS HA3 61 G1
WBLY HA9 62 C5
Brampton La HDN NW4 64 A1
Brampton Park Rd
WDGN N22 49 G6
Brampton Rd BXLYHN DA7 128 E6
BXLYHN DA7 148 E1
BXLYHN DA7 148 E4
CDALE/KGS NW9 62 C1
CROY/NA CR0 197 G4
EHAM E6 107 H3
OXHEY WD19 26 E5
SEVS/STOTM N15 67 J2
Bramshaw Gdns
OXHEY WD19 41 H1
Bramshaw Ri NWMAL KT3 192 B3
Bramshaw Rd HOM E9 87 F4
Bramshill Gdns KTTN NW5 84 B1
Bramshill Rd WLSDN NW10 99 G1
Bramshot Av CHARL SE7 126 A6
Bramshot Wy OXHEY WD19 26 E4
Bramston Cl BARK/HLT IG6 55 F2
Bramston Rd MTCM CR4 178 E3
WLSDN NW10 99 J1
Bramwell Cl SUN TW16 172 C5
Bramwell Ms IS N1 85 F6
Brancaster Dr MLHL NW7 45 J3
Brancaster Rd
GNTH/NBYPK IG2 72 D3
STRHM/NOR SW16 161 K5
Brancepeth Gdns BKHH IG9 38 E4
Branch Hl HAMP NW3 83 G1
Branch Rd BARK/HLT IG6 55 H1
POP/IOD E14 105 G5
Branch St CMBW SE5 143 F1

Brancker Rd
KTN/HRWW/WS HA3 43 K6
Brancroft Wy PEND EN3 25 G2
Brand Cl FSBYPK N4 67 H5
Brandesbury Sq WFD IG8 54 A3
Brandlehow Rd
PUT/ROE SW15 139 J5
Brandon Est WALW SE17 122 C6
Brandon Ms BARB EC2Y * 12 E1
Brandon Rd HOLWY N7 84 E5
NWDGN UB2 114 E5
SUT SM1 209 F2
WALTH E17 70 A1
Brandon St WALW SE17 18 D6
Brandram Ms LEW SE13 * 145 H5
Brandram Rd LEW SE13 145 H4
Brandreth Ct HRW HA1 * 61 F3
Brandreth Rd EHAM E6 107 K5
TOOT SW17 161 G4
The Brandries WLGTN SM6 210 D1
Brand St GNWCH SE10 145 F1
Brandville Gdns
BARK/HLT IG6 72 B1
Brandville Rd WDR/YW UB7 112 B2
Brandy Wy BELMT SM2 208 E5
Brangbourne Rd BMLY BR1 183 F1
Brangton Rd LBTH SE11 122 A5
Brangwyn Crs
WIM/MER SW19 178 C4
Branksea St FUL/PGN SW6 139 H1
Branksome Av UED N18 50 B2
Branksome Cl TEDD TW11 155 J6
WOT/HER KT12 188 C6
Branksome Rd
BRXS/STRHM SW2 141 K6
WIM/MER SW19 177 K4
Branksome Wy
KTN/HRWW/WS HA3 62 B3
NWMAL KT3 175 K5
Bransby Rd CHSGTN KT9 206 A5
Branscombe Gdns
WCHMH N21 35 G2
Branscombe St LEW SE13 144 E4
Bransdale Cl
KIL/WHAMP NW6 82 E6
Bransell Cl SWLY BR8 203 J3
Bransgrove Rd EDGW HA8 44 B4
Branston Crs STMC/STPC BR5 201 J5
Branstone Rd RCH/KEW TW9 137 G2
Brants Wk HNWL W7 96 E3
Brantwood Av ERITH DA8 149 K1
ISLW TW7 136 B5
Brantwood Cl WALTH E17 * 51 K6
Brantwood Gdns
ENC/FH EN2 22 E5
REDBR IG4 71 J2
Brantwood Rd HNHL SE24 142 D6
SAND/SEL CR2 211 J6
TOTM N17 50 C2
Brantwood Wy
STMC/STPC BR5 186 D6
Brasenose Dr BARN SW13 119 F6
Brasher Cl GFD/PVL UB6 78 D3
Brassey Cl
EBED/NFELT TW14 * 153 K3
Brassey Rd KIL/WHAMP NW6 82 D4
Brassey Sq BTSEA SW11 141 F4
Brassie Av ACT W3 99 G5
Brasted Cl BXLYHS DA6 148 E6
SYD SE26 163 K6
Brasted Rd ERITH DA8 150 B1
Brathway Rd
WAND/EARL SW18 159 K2
Bratley St WCHPL E1 104 C3
Braund Av GFD/PVL UB6 96 B3
Braundton Av BFN/LL DA15 168 A3
Braunston Dr YEAD UB4 95 J3
Bravington Pl MV/WKIL W9 100 D3
Bravington Rd MV/WKIL W9 100 D2
Bravingtons Wk IS N1 5 F3
Braxfield Rd BROCKY SE4 144 B5
Braxted Pk
STRHM/NOR SW16 180 A2
Brayard's Rd PECK SE15 143 J3
Braybourne Dr ISLW TW7 136 A1
Braybrooke Gdns NRWD SE19 181 F3
Braybrook St SHB W12 99 H4
Brayburne Av VX/NE SW8 141 H3
Braycourt Av WOT/HER KT12 188 B4
Bray Crs BERM/RHTH SE16 124 A2
Braydon Rd STNW/STAM N16 68 B5
Bray Dr CAN/RD E16 106 D6
Brayfield Ter IS N1 85 G5
Brayford Sq WCHPL E1 * 104 E5
Bray Pl CHEL SW3 120 E5
Bray Rd MLHL NW7 46 B2
Brayton Gdns ENC/FH EN2 22 D5
Braywood Rd ELTH/MOT SE9 147 J5
Brazier Crs NTHLT UB5 95 K3
Brazil Cl CROY/NA CR0 195 K4
Breach La DAGW RM9 110 C2
Bread St STP EC4M 12 D4
Breakspears Dr
STMC/STPC BR5 186 B4
Breakspears Ms BROCKY SE4 144 D3
Breakspears Rd BROCKY SE4 144 C4
Bream Cl TOTM N17 68 D1
Bream Gdns EHAM E6 108 A2
Breamore Cl PUT/ROE SW15 158 D3
Breamore Rd GDMY/SEVK IG3 73 F6
Bream's Blds LINN WC2A 11 J3
Bream St BOW E3 87 J5
Breamwater Gdns
RCHPK/HAM TW10 156 C5
Brearley Cl EDGW HA8 44 E3
Breasley Cl PUT/ROE SW15 138 E5
Breasy Pl HDN NW4 * 63 K1
Brechin Pl SKENS SW7 120 B4
Brecknock Rd ARCH N19 84 C2
Brecknock Road Est
ARCH N19 * 84 D3
Brecon Cl MTCM CR4 195 K1
WPK KT4 193 F6
Brecon Gn CDALE/KGS NW9 * 63 G3
Brecon Ms HOLWY N7 84 D3
KTTN NW5 84 D4
Brecon Rd HMSMTH W6 119 H6
PEND EN3 24 E5
Brede Cl EHAM E6 108 A2
Bredgar Rd ARCH N19 66 B6

Bredhurst Cl PGE/AN SE20 181 K2
Bredon Rd CROY/NA CR0 197 G4
Breer St FUL/PGN SW6 140 A4
Breezer's Hl WAP E1W * 104 C6
Bremans Rw
WAND/EARL SW18 160 B4
Brember Rd
RYLN/HDSTN HA2 60 C6
Bremer Ms WALTH E17 69 K1
Bremner Rd SKENS SW7 * 120 B3
Brenchley Cl CHST BR7 185 F4
HAYES BR2 199 J2
Brenchley Gdns EDUL SE22 163 K1
Brenchley Rd STMC/STPC BR5 185 K4
Brenda Rd TOOT SW17 160 E4
Brende Gdns
E/WMO/HCT KT8 189 G1
Brendon SCUP DA14 * 168 B6
Brendon Av WLSDN NW10 81 G2
Brendon Cl ESH/CLAY KT10 204 C4
HYS/HAR UB3 133 F1
Brendon Dr ESH/CLAY KT10 204 C4
Brendon Gdns
RYLN/HDSTN HA2 78 B2
Brendon Gv EFNCH N2 47 G5
Brendon Rd BCTR RM8 74 B5
ELTH/MOT SE9 167 J4
Brendon St MBLAR W1H 8 D3
Brendon Vls WCHMH N21 * 35 J3
Brendon Wy EN EN1 36 A2
Brenley Cl MTCM CR4 179 F6
Brenley Gdns ELTH/MOT SE9 146 C5
Brent Cl BXLY DA5 169 F3
Brentcot Cl WEA W13 97 H3
Brent Crs WLSDN NW10 98 B1
Brent Cross F/O HDN NW4 64 A3
Brentfield WLSDN NW10 80 D5
Brentfield Cl WLSDN NW10 81 F4
Brentfield Gdns CRICK NW2 * 64 B4
Brentfield Rd WLSDN NW10 81 F4
Brentford Cl YEAD UB4 95 H3
Brent Gn HDN NW4 64 A2
Brentham Wy EA W5 97 K3
Brenthouse Rd HACK E8 86 D5
Brenthurst Rd WLSDN NW10 81 H4
Brent Lea BTFD TW8 136 D1
Brentmead Cl HNWL W7 96 E6
Brentmead Gdns
WLSDN NW10 98 B1
Brenton St POP/IOD E14 105 G5
Brent Park Rd
CDALE/KGS NW9 63 J5
Brent Pl BAR EN5 20 D6
Brent River Park Wk
HNWL W7 96 D4
Brent Rd BTFD TW8 116 D6
CAN/RD E16 106 E5
NWDGN UB2 114 B3
SAND/SEL CR2 212 D6
WOOL/PLUM SE18 147 G1
Brentside BTFD TW8 116 D6
Brentside Cl WEA W13 97 F3
Brent St HDN NW4 64 A1
Brent Ter CRICK NW2 64 A6
The Brent DART DA1 171 K2
Brentvale Av ALP/SUD HA0 80 B6
STHL UB1 115 J1
Brent View Rd
CDALE/KGS NW9 63 J3
Brent Wy BTFD TW8 136 E1
FNCH N3 46 E2
WBLY HA9 80 D4
Brentwick Gdns BTFD TW8 117 F4
Brentwood Cl ELTH/MOT SE9 167 H3
Brentwood Rd ROM RM1 75 H3
Brereton Rd TOTM N17 50 B3
Bressay Dr MLHL NW7 45 J3
Bressenden Pl WESTW SW1E 15 K4
Bressey Av EN EN1 24 C2
Bressey Gv SWFD E18 52 D5
Brett Cl NTHLT UB5 95 H2
STNW/STAM N16 68 A6
Brett Crs WLSDN NW10 81 F6
Brettell St WALW SE17 122 E5
Brettenham Av WALTH E17 51 J4
Brettenham Rd UED N18 36 C6
WALTH E17 51 J5
Brett Gdns DAGW RM9 92 A5
Brett Pas HACK E8 86 D3
Brett Rd BAR EN5 20 A6
HACK E8 86 D3
Brett Vls ACT W3 * 99 F4
Brewer St REGST W1B 10 B5
Brewery Cl ALP/SUD HA0 79 G3
Brewery Rd HAYES BR2 200 D5
HOLWY N7 84 E5
WOOL/PLUM SE18 127 J5
Brewery Sq FSBYE EC1V 6 B7
STHWK SE1 19 J1
Brewhouse La WAP E1W 123 J1
Brewhouse Rd
WOOL/PLUM SE18 126 E4
Brewhouse St PUT/ROE SW15 139 H5
Brewhouse Wk
BERM/RHTH SE16 124 B1
Brewhouse Yd FSBYE EC1V 6 A6
Brewood Rd BCTR RM8 91 H4
Brewster Gdns NKENS W10 100 A4
Brewster Rd LEY E10 69 K5
Brian Cl HCH RM12 93 K2
Brian Rd CHDH RM6 73 J2
Briants Cl PIN HA5 41 J4
Briant St NWCR SE14 144 A2
Briar Av STRHM/NOR SW16 180 A3
Briar Bank CAR SM5 210 A6
Briarbank Rd WEA W13 97 G5
Briar Cl BKHH IG9 39 H4
EFNCH N2 47 G5
HPTN TW12 172 E1
ISLW TW7 136 A6
PLMGR N13 35 J5
Briar Crs NTHLT UB5 78 B4
Briardale Gdns HAMP NW3 82 E1
Briarfield Av EFNCH N2 47 F6
Briar Gdns HAYES BR2 199 J5
Briar La CAR SM5 210 A6
CROY/NA CR0 213 K2
Briar Rd CRICK NW2 82 A2
KTN/HRWW/WS HA3 61 J2
STRHM/NOR SW16 179 K6

WHTN TW2 155 K3
Briarswood Wy ORP BR6 217 F3
Briar Wk EDGW HA8 44 E3
NKENS W10 * 100 C3
PUT/ROE SW15 138 E5
Briar Wy WDR/YW UB7 112 D2
Briarwood Cl
CDALE/KGS NW9 * 62 E3
FELT TW13 153 H5
Briar Wood Cl HAYES BR2 200 D6
HAYES BR2 215 J1
Briarwood Ct WPK KT4 * 192 D5
Briarwood Dr NTHWD HA6 40 E5
Briarwood Rd CLAP SW4 141 J6
EW KT17 207 J4
Briary Cl EDGW HA8 44 D5
HAMP NW3 * 83 J5
Briary Ct SCUP DA14 186 C1
Briary Gdns BMLY BR1 184 A1
Briary La ED N9 36 A5
Brickbarn Cl WBPTN SW10 * 140 B1
Brick Ct EMB EC4Y * 11 J4
Brickett Cl RSLP HA4 58 A2
Brick Farm Cl RCH/KEW TW9 137 J2
Brickfield Cl BTFD TW8 136 D1
Brickfield Cots
WOOL/PLUM SE18 128 A6
Brickfield Farm Gdns
ORP BR6 216 C2
Brickfield La BAR EN5 31 H1
HYS/HAR UB3 113 G6
Brickfield Rd BOW E3 105 K3
THHTH CR7 180 C4
WIM/MER SW19 160 A6
Brickfields RYLN/HDSTN HA2 60 D6
Brickfields Wy WDR/YW UB7 112 C3
Brickfield Vls CAR SM5 * 209 J1
Brick Kiln Cl OXHEY WD19 27 J1
Brick La BETH E2 7 K5
EN EN1 24 D3
NTHLT UB5 95 K2
PEND EN3 24 E3
STAN HA7 43 K3
WCHPL E1 7 K7
Brick St MYFR/PKLN W1K 15 J1
Brickwall La RSLP HA4 58 C5
Brickwood Cl SYD SE26 163 J5
Brickwood Rd CROY/NA CR0 197 F6
Brideale Cl PECK SE15 123 G6
Bride Ct EMB EC4Y 12 A4
Bride La EMB EC4Y 12 A4
Bridel Ms FSBYE EC1V 6 A3
Bride St HOLWY N7 85 F4
Bridewain St STHWK SE1 19 J4
Bridewell Pl BLKFR EC4V 12 A4
WAP E1W 123 J1
Bridford Ms GTPST W1W 9 K1
Bridge Av HMSMTH W6 119 F5
HNWL W7 96 D4
Bridge Cl EN EN1 24 D3
NKENS W10 100 B5
ROMW/RG RM7 75 G3
Bridge Dr PLMGR N13 35 F6
Bridge End WALTH E17 52 A4
Bridge End Cl KUTN/CMB KT2 175 H4
Bridgefield Rd SUT SM1 208 E4
Bridge Gdns E/WMO/HCT KT8 189 J1
Bridge Ga WCHMH N21 35 J2
Bridge House Quay
POP/IOD E14 125 F1
Bridgeland Rd CAN/RD E16 106 E6
Bridgelands Cl BECK BR3 182 C3
Bridge La BTSEA SW11 140 D2
HDN NW4 64 B1
Bridgeman Rd IS N1 85 F5
TEDD TW11 174 B2
Bridgeman St STJWD NW8 2 C3
Bridge Mdw NWCR SE14 124 A6
Bridgenhall Rd EN EN1 24 B2
Bridgen Rd BXLY DA5 169 F2
Bridge Pde
STRHM/NOR SW16 * 179 K1
WCHMH N21 * 35 J2
Bridge Pk WAND/EARL SW18 139 K6
Bridge Pl CROY/NA CR0 196 E5
PIM SW1V 15 K6
Bridgepoint Pl HGT N6 66 B5
Bridgeport Pl WAP E1W * 123 H1
Bridge Rd BECK BR3 182 C3
CHSGTN KT9 206 A3
E/WMO/HCT KT8 189 K1
ED N9 36 C5
EHAM E6 89 K5
ERITH DA8 150 C2
HSLW TW3 135 J4
LEY E10 70 B3
NWDGN UB2 114 E2
RAIN RM13 111 J3
SRTFD E15 88 B6
STMC/STPC BR5 202 C3
SUT SM1 209 F4
TWK TW1 156 C1
WALTH E17 69 H4
WBLY HA9 80 C1
WDGN N22 48 E4
WLGTN SM6 210 B3
WLSDN NW10 81 G4
Bridge Rw CROY/NA CR0 * 196 E5
Bridges Ct BTSEA SW11 140 C4
Bridges La CROY/NA CR0 210 E2
Bridges Rd STAN HA7 43 F1
Bridges Road Ms
WIM/MER SW19 178 A2
Bridge St CHSWK W4 118 A4
PIN HA5 41 H6
TWK TW1 156 E1
WHALL SW1A 16 E3
Bridge Ter LEW SE13 * 145 G5
SRTFD E15 88 B5
The Bridge EA W5 * 117 G1
KTN/HRWW/WS HA3 43 F6
Bridgetown Cl NRWD SE19 181 F1
Bridgeview HMSMTH W6 119 F5
Bridge Vls WIM/MER SW19 * 177 K1
Bridgewater Cl
STMC/STPC BR5 185 K5
Bridgewater Gdns EDGW HA8 44 B5
Bridgewater Rd
ALP/SUD HA0 79 H4
Bridgewater Sq BARB EC2Y * 12 C1
Bridgewater St BARB EC2Y 12 C1
Bridgewater Wy BUSH WD23 28 B1
Bridgeway ALP/SUD HA0 80 A5
BARK IG11 91 F5
Bridge Wy GLDGN NW11 64 D2
WHTN TW2 155 H2
Bridgeway St CAMTN NW1 4 B3
Bridge Wharf Rd ISLW TW7 136 C4
Bridgewood Cl PGE/AN SE20 181 J3
Bridgewood Rd
STRHM/NOR SW16 179 J3
WPK KT4 207 J2
Bridgford St
WAND/EARL SW18 160 B5
Bridgman Rd CHSWK W4 117 K3
Bridgwater Rd RSLP HA4 76 E2
Bridle Cl HOR/WEW KT19 206 E2
KUT/HW KT1 190 E1
Bridle La SOHO/CST W1F 10 B5
TWK TW1 156 C1
Bridle Pth CROY/NA CR0 210 E1
The Bridle Pth WFD IG8 52 C3
Bridlepath Wy
EBED/NFELT TW14 153 H2
Bridle Rd CROY/NA CR0 198 D6
CROY/NA CR0 213 J2
ESH/CLAY KT10 205 H4
PIN HA5 59 G3
Bridle Wy CROY/NA CR0 213 J3
ORP BR6 216 C2
The Bridle Wy WLGTN SM6 210 C2
Bridlington Rd ED N9 36 D2
OXHEY WD19 27 H5
Bridport Av ROMW/RG RM7 74 D3
Bridport Pl IS N1 7 F1
Bridport Rd GFD/PVL UB6 78 B6
THHTH CR7 180 B6
UED N18 50 A1
Bridstow Pl BAY/PAD W2 100 E5
Brief St BRXN/ST SW9 142 C2
Brierley CROY/NA CR0 213 K4
Brierley Av ED N9 36 E3
Brierley Cl SNWD SE25 197 H1
Brierley Rd BAL SW12 161 H4
WAN E11 88 B2
Brierly Gdns BETH E2 * 104 E1
Brigade Cl RYLN/HDSTN HA2 60 E6
Brigade St BKHTH/KID SE3 * 145 J3
Brigadier Av ENC/FH EN2 23 J2
Brigadier Hl ENC/FH EN2 23 J1
Briggeford Cl CLPT E5 68 C6
Briggs Cl MTCM CR4 179 G4
Bright Cl BELV DA17 128 E4
Brightfield Rd LEE/GVPK SE12 145 H6
Brightling Rd BROCKY SE4 164 C1
Brightlingsea Pl POP/IOD E14 105 H6
Brightman Rd
WAND/EARL SW18 160 C3
Brighton Av WALTH E17 69 H2
Brighton Dr NTHLT UB5 * 78 A4
Brighton Rd BELMT SM2 209 G5
EFNCH N2 47 G5
EHAM E6 108 A2
SAND/SEL CR2 211 J6
STNW/STAM N16 86 A2
SURB KT6 190 D3
Brighton Ter BRXN/ST SW9 142 A5
Brights Av RAIN RM13 111 K3
Brightside Rd LEW SE13 165 G1
The Brightside PEND EN3 25 F2
Bright St POP/IOD E14 105 K5
Brightwell Cl CROY/NA CR0 196 B5
Brightwell Crs TOOT SW17 178 E1
Brightwen Gv STAN HA7 29 G4
Brig Ms DEPT SE8 124 D6
Brigstock Rd BELV DA17 129 J4
THHTH CR7 196 C2
Brill Pl CAMTN NW1 4 D3
Brim Hl EFNCH N2 65 G1
Brimpsfield Cl ABYW SE2 128 C3
Brimsdown Av PEND EN3 25 G2
Brimstone Cl ORP BR6 217 J5
Brindle Ga BFN/LL DA15 167 K3
Brindley Cl ALP/SUD HA0 79 J6
Brindley St BROCKY SE4 144 C2
Brindley Wy BMLY BR1 183 K1
STHL UB1 96 B6
Brindwood Rd CHING E4 37 J5
Brinkburn Cl ABYW SE2 128 B4
EDGW HA8 44 D6
Brinkburn Gdns EDGW HA8 44 C6
Brinkley Rd WPK KT4 192 E6
Brinklow Crs
WOOL/PLUM SE18 147 G1
Brinkworth Rd CLAY IG5 53 J6
Brinkworth Wy HOM E9 87 H4
Brinsdale Rd HDN NW4 46 B6
Brinsley Rd
KTN/HRWW/WS HA3 42 D5
Brinsley St WCHPL E1 * 104 D5
Brinsworth Cl WHTN TW2 155 J4
Brinton Wk STHWK SE1 18 A1
Brion Pl POP/IOD E14 106 A4
Brisbane Av WIM/MER SW19 178 A4
Brisbane Rd IL IG1 72 C4
LEY E10 69 K6
Brisbane St CMBW SE5 142 E1
Briscoe Cl WAN E11 70 D6
Briscoe Rd WIM/MER SW19 178 C2
Briset Rd ELTH/MOT SE9 146 C4
Briset St FARR EC1M 12 A1
Briset Wy HOLWY N7 67 F6
Bristol Cl HSLWW TW4 155 F2
STWL/WRAY TW19 152 B1
WLGTN SM6 210 E6
Bristol Gdns MV/WKIL W9 101 F3
Bristol Ms MV/WKIL W9 101 F3
Bristol Park Rd WALTH E17 * 69 G1
Bristol Rd FSTGT E7 89 G4
GFD/PVL UB6 78 B6
MRDN SM4 194 B2
Briston Gv CEND/HSY/T N8 66 E3
Bristowe Cl
BRXS/STRHM SW2 162 B1
Bristow Rd CROY/NA CR0 210 E2
HSLW TW3 135 G4
NRWD SE19 181 F1
Britannia Cl CLAP SW4 141 J5
NTHLT UB5 95 H2
Britannia Ga CAN/RD E16 125 K1
Britannia La WHTN TW2 155 H2
Britannia Rd BRYLDS KT5 191 G4
FUL/PGN SW6 140 A1
IL IG1 90 B1
NFNCH/WDSPK N12 33 G5
POP/IOD E14 124 D4
Britannia Rw IS N1 85 H6
Britannia St FSBYW WC1X 5 G4
Britannia Wk IS N1 6 E3
Britannia Wy FUL/PGN SW6 140 A1
STWL/WRAY TW19 152 A2
WLSDN NW10 98 D3
British Est BOW E3 105 H2
British Gv HMSMTH W6 118 C5
British Grove Pas
CHSWK W4 * 118 C5
British Legion Rd CHING E4 38 D4
British St BOW E3 105 H2
Brittage Rd WLSDN NW10 81 G5
Brittain Rd BCTR RM8 92 A1
Britten Cl BORE WD6 29 K1
GLDGN NW11 65 F5
Brittenden Pde ORP BR6 * 217 F4
Britten Dr STHL UB1 96 A5
Britten St CHEL SW3 120 D5
Brittidge Rd WLSDN NW10 * 81 G5
Britton Cl CAT SE6 165 G2
Britton St FARR EC1M 6 A7
Brixham Crs RSLP HA4 58 E5
Brixham Gdns
GDMY/SEVK IG3 90 E3
Brixham Rd WELL DA16 148 E2
Brixham St CAN/RD E16 126 E1
Brixton Hl BRXS/STRHM SW2 162 A1
Brixton Hill Pl
BRXS/STRHM SW2 161 K2
Brixton Ov BRXS/STRHM SW2 142 B5
Brixton Rd BRXN/ST SW9 142 B5
LBTH SE11 122 B6
Brixton Station Rd
BRXN/ST SW9 142 B4
Brixton Water La
BRXS/STRHM SW2 142 A6
Broadbent Cl HGT N6 66 B5
Broadbent St
MYFR/PKLN W1K * 9 J5
Broadberry Ct UED N18 50 D1
Broad Common Est
STNW/STAM N16 * 68 C5
Broadcoombe SAND/SEL CR2 213 F5
Broad Ct COVGDN WC2E * 11 F4
Broadcroft Av STAN HA7 43 K5
Broadcroft Rd
STMC/STPC BR5 201 J4
Broadeaves Cl SAND/SEL CR2 212 A3
Broadfield Cl CRICK NW2 82 A1
ROM RM1 75 H2
Broadfield Ct BUSH WD23 28 E4
Broadfield La CAMTN NW1 84 E5
Broadfield Pde EDGW HA8 * 30 D5
Broadfield Rd CAT SE6 165 H3
Broadfields E/WMO/HCT KT8 189 J3
RYLN/HDSTN HA2 42 B5
Broadfields Av EDGW HA8 30 D5
WCHMH N21 35 G2
Broadfields Hts EDGW HA8 30 D6
Broadfields La OXHEY WD19 27 F3
Broadfield Sq EN EN1 24 D4
Broadfields Wy WLSDN NW10 81 H3
Broadfield Wy BKHH IG9 39 G5
Broadgates Av EBAR EN4 21 F2
Broadgates Rd
WAND/EARL SW18 160 C3
Broad Green Av
CROY/NA CR0 196 C4
Broadhead Strd
CDALE/KGS NW9 45 H5
Broadheath Dr CHST BR7 184 E1
Broadhinton Rd CLAP SW4 141 G4
Broadhurst Av EDGW HA8 30 D6
GDMY/SEVK IG3 91 F2
Broadhurst Cl
KIL/WHAMP NW6 83 G4
Broadhurst Gdns
KIL/WHAMP NW6 83 F4
RSLP HA4 59 G6
Broadhurst Cl
RCHPK/HAM TW10 137 G6
Broadlands FELT TW13 154 E5
Broadlands Av PEND EN3 24 D4
STRHM/NOR SW16 161 K4
Broadlands Cl HGT N6 66 A4
PEND EN3 24 D4
STRHM/NOR SW16 161 K4
Broadlands Rd BMLY BR1 166 A6
HGT N6 65 K4
Broadlands Wy NWMAL KT3 192 C3
Broad La CEND/HSY/T N8 67 F2
HPTN TW12 172 E3
SEVS/STOTM N15 68 B2
Broad Lawn ELTH/MOT SE9 167 F3
Broadlawns Ct
KTN/HRWW/WS HA3 43 F4
Broadley St STJWD NW8 8 C1
Broadley Ter CAMTN NW1 2 D7
Broadmead CAT SE6 164 D5
Broadmead Av WPK KT4 192 D4
Broadmead Cl HPTN TW12 173 F2
PIN HA5 * 41 J3
Broadmead Rd WFD IG8 52 E2
YEAD UB4 95 J3
Broad Oak WFD IG8 53 F1
Broad Oak Cl CHING E4 51 J1
STMC/STPC BR5 186 B5
Broad Oaks SURB KT6 191 J5
Broad Oaks Wy HAYES BR2 199 J2
Broadstone Pl MHST W1U 9 G2
Broadstone Rd HCH RM12 75 J6
Broad St DAGE RM10 92 C5
TEDD TW11 174 A2
Broad Street Av LVPST EC2M 13 G2
Broad Street Pl LVPST EC2M 13 F2
Broadview CDALE/KGS NW9 62 C3
Broadview Rd
STRHM/NOR SW16 179 J3
Broad Wk WCHMH N21 35 F4
BKHTH/KID SE3 146 B3
BKHTH/KID SE3 146 D3
HEST TW5 134 C2
ORP BR6 217 K1
RCH/KEW TW9 137 G1
Broadwalk
RYLN/HDSTN HA2 * 60 B2
SWFD E18 52 D6
Broadwalk La GLDGN NW11 64 D4
The Broad Wk KENS W8 120 B2
The Broadwalk NTHWD HA6 40 A5
Broadwall STHWK SE1 11 K7
Broadwater Gdns ORP BR6 216 B2
Broadwater Rd THMD SE28 127 J3
TOOT SW17 160 D6
TOTM N17 50 A5
Broadway BARK IG11 90 C6
GPK RM2 57 J6
HNWL W7 115 K1
RAIN RM13 111 J3
SRTFD E15 88 B5
STJSPK SW1H 16 C3
SURB KT6 191 J5
SWLY BR8 203 K3
WEA W13 116 B1
Broadway Av CROY/NA CR0 196 E2
TWK TW1 156 C1
Broadway Cl WFD IG8 53 F2
Broadway Ct WIM/MER SW19 177 K2
Broadway Gdns MTCM CR4 194 D1
Broadway Market HACK E8 86 D6
Broadway Market Ms
HACK E8 * 86 C6
Broadway Ms PLMGR N13 49 F1
STNW/STAM N16 68 B4
WCHMH N21 35 H3
Broadway Pde CHING E4 * 52 A2
HYS/HAR UB3 * 113 J2
RYLN/HDSTN HA2 * 60 B2
WDR/YW UB7 * 112 B2
The Broadway ACT W3 * 117 H2
BCTR RM8 74 B6
CDALE/KGS NW9 63 H3
CEND/HSY/T N8 66 E3
CHEAM SM3 208 C4
EA W5 97 K6
ED N9 36 C5
FBAR/BDGN N11 * 47 K1
HCH RM12 93 K2
KTN/HRWW/WS HA3 42 E5
MLHL NW7 45 G1
PIN HA5 41 K3
PLSTW E13 106 E1
RYLN/HDSTN HA2 * 60 D6
STAN HA7 43 J1
SUT SM1 209 G2
THDIT KT7 189 K5
WFD IG8 53 F2
WIM/MER SW19 177 J2
Broadwell Pde
KIL/WHAMP NW6 * 83 G4
Broadwick St SOHO/CST W1F 10 B5
Broadwood Av RSLP HA4 58 C3
Broadwood Ter WKENS W14 * 119 J4
Broad Yd FARR EC1M 6 A7
Brocas Cl HAMP NW3 83 J5
Brockdene Dr HAYES BR2 215 H2
Brockdish Av BARK IG11 91 F3
Brockenhurst
E/WMO/HCT KT8 188 E2
Brockenhurst Av WPK KT4 192 B5
Brockenhurst Gdns IL IG1 90 C3
MLHL NW7 45 G1
Brockenhurst Ms UED N18 36 C6
Brockenhurst Rd
CROY/NA CR0 197 J4
Brockenhurst Wy
STRHM/NOR SW16 179 J5
Brocket Wy CHIG IG7 54 E1
Brockham Cl WIM/MER SW19 177 J1
Brockham Crs CROY/NA CR0 214 B5
Brockham Dr
BRXS/STRHM SW2 162 A2
GNTH/NBYPK IG2 72 C3
Brockham St STHWK SE1 18 D4
Brockhurst Cl STAN HA7 43 F2
Brockill Crs BROCKY SE4 144 B5
Brocklebank Rd CHARL SE7 126 A4
WAND/EARL SW18 160 B2
Brocklehurst St NWCR SE14 144 A1
Brocklesby Rd SNWD SE25 197 J1
Brockley Av STAN HA7 30 A5
Brockley Cl STAN HA7 30 A6
Brockley Crs CRW RM5 56 E3
Brockley Cross BROCKY SE4 144 B4
Brockley Gv BROCKY SE4 144 C6
Brockley Hall Rd BROCKY SE4 164 B1
Brockley Hl STAN HA7 29 K4
Brockley Ms BROCKY SE4 144 B6
Brockley Pk FSTH SE23 164 B2
Brockley Ri FSTH SE23 164 B2
Brockley Rd FSTH SE23 164 B1
Brockleyside STAN HA7 29 K6
Brockley Vw FSTH SE23 164 B2
Brockley Wy FSTH SE23 144 A6
Brockman Ri BMLY BR1 165 G6
Brock Pl BOW E3 105 K3
Brock Rd PLSTW E13 107 F4
Brocks Dr CHEAM SM3 208 C1
Brockshot Cl BTFD TW8 116 E6
Brock St PECK SE15 * 143 K4
Brockton Cl ROM RM1 75 H1
Brockway Cl WAN E11 70 C6
Brockwell Av BECK BR3 198 E2
Brockwell Cl STMC/STPC BR5 202 A2
Brockwell Park Gdns
HNHL SE24 162 C2
Brockwell Park Rw
BRXS/STRHM SW2 162 B2
Brodia Rd STNW/STAM N16 86 A1
Brodie Rd CHING E4 38 A3
ENC/FH EN2 23 J1
Brodie St STHWK SE1 123 G5
Brodlove La WAP E1W 105 F6
Brodrick Gv ABYW SE2 128 C4
Brodrick Rd TOOT SW17 160 D4
Brograve Gdns BECK BR3 182 E5
Broke Farm Dr ORP BR6 217 J6
Broken Whf BLKFR EC4V 12 C5
Brokesley St BOW E3 105 H3
Broke Wk HACK E8 * 86 C6
Bromar Rd CMBW SE5 143 F4
Bromborough Gn
OXHEY WD19 41 G1
Bromefield STAN HA7 43 J4
Bromehead St WCHPL E1 104 E5
Brome House CHARL SE7 * 146 D1
Bromell's Rd CLAP SW4 141 H5
Brome Rd ELTH/MOT SE9 146 E4
Bromfelde Rd CLAP SW4 141 J4
Bromfield St IS N1 5 K2
Bromhall Rd DAGW RM9 91 H4
Bromhedge ELTH/MOT SE9 166 E5
Bromholm Rd ABYW SE2 128 C3
Bromley Av BMLY BR1 183 H3
Bromley Common HAYES BR2 200 B2
HAYES BR2 200 D4
Bromley Ct BMLY BR1 183 H3
Bromley Crs HAYES BR2 183 J6
RSLP HA4 76 D2
Bromley Gdns HAYES BR2 183 J5
Bromley Gv HAYES BR2 183 G5
Bromley Hall Rd POP/IOD E14 106 A4
Bromley High St BOW E3 105 K2
Bromley Hl BMLY BR1 183 G1
Bromley La CHST BR7 185 H3
Bromley Rd BECK BR3 182 D4
CAT SE6 164 E5
CHST BR7 185 G4
HAYES BR2 183 H5
LEY E10 69 K3
TOTM N17 50 B4
UED N18 35 K6
WALTH E17 51 J6
Bromley St WCHPL E1 105 F
Brompton Ar CHEL SW3 * 14 E
Brompton Cl HSLWW TW4 134 E
Brompton Cots
WBPTN SW10 * 120 B
Brompton Dr ERITH DA8 150 E
Brompton Gv EFNCH N2 65 J
Brompton Park Crs
FUL/PGN SW6 120 A
Brompton Pl CHEL SW3 14 D
Brompton Rd CHEL SW3 14 C
Brompton Sq CHEL SW3 14 C
Brompton Ter
WOOL/PLUM SE18 * 147 F
Bromwich Av HGT N6 66 A
Bromyard Av ACT W3 118 B
Brondesbury Ms
KIL/WHAMP NW6 * 82 E
Brondesbury Pk
KIL/WHAMP NW6 82 A
Brondesbury Rd
KIL/WHAMP NW6 100 D
Brondesbury Vls
KIL/WHAMP NW6 100 D
Bronhill Ter TOTM N17 * 50 C
Bronsart Rd FUL/PGN SW6 139 H
Bronson Rd RYNPK SW20 177
Bronte Cl FSTGT E7 * 88
GNTH/NBYPK IG2 72
Bronti Cl WALW SE17 122
Bronze Age Wy BELV DA17 129
Bronze St DEPT SE8 144
Brook Av DAGE RM10 92
EDGW HA8 44
WBLY HA9 80
Brookbank Av HNWL W7 96
Brookbank Rd LEW SE13 144
Brook Cl ACT W3 117
GPK RM2 57
HOR/WEW KT19 207
RSLP HA4 58
RYNPK SW20 176
STWL/WRAY TW19 152
TOOT SW17 161
Brook Ct BECK BR3 * 182
Brook Crs CHING E4 37
ED N9 36
Brookdale FBAR/BDGN N11 34
Brookdale Rd BXLY DA5 169
CAT SE6 164
WALTH E17 51
Brookdene Av OXHEY WD19 27
Brookdene Dr NTHWD HA6 40
Brookdene Rd
WOOL/PLUM SE18 127
Brook Dr HRW HA1 60
LBTH SE11 17
RSLP HA4 58
Brooke Av RYLN/HDSTN HA2 78
Brooke Cl BUSH WD23 28
Brookehowse Rd CAT SE6 164
Brookend Rd BFN/LL DA15 167
Brooker Cl POP/IOD E14 10
Brooke Rd STNW/STAM N16 8
WALTH E17 7
Brooke's Market
HCIRC EC1N * 1
Brooke St HCIRC EC1N 1
Brooke Wy BUSH WD23 2
Brookfield Av EA W5 9
MLHL NW7 4
SUT SM1 20
WALTH E17 7
Brookfield Cl MLHL NW7 4
Brookfield Crs
KTN/HRWW/WS HA3 6
MLHL NW7 4
Brookfield Gdns
ESH/CLAY KT10 20
Brookfield Pk KTTN NW5 8
Brookfield Pth WFD IG8 5
Brookfield Rd CHSWK W4 1
ED N9
HOM E9
Brookfields PEND EN3
Brookfields Av MTCM CR4 1
Brook Gdns BARN SW13 1
CHING E4
KUTN/CMB KT2 1
Brook Ga MYFR/PKLN W1K
Brook Gn HMSMTH W6
Brookhill Cl EBAR EN4
Brook Hill Cl
WOOL/PLUM SE18
Brookhill Rd EBAR EN4
WOOL/PLUM SE18
Brookhouse Gdns CHING E4
Brooking Cl BCTR RM8
Brooking Rd FSTGT E7
Brookland Cl GLDGN NW11

Brookland Garth
GLDGN NW11 64 E1
Brookland Hl GLDGN NW11 64 E1
Brookland Ri GLDGN NW11 64 E1
Brooklands Ap ROM RM1 75 F1
Brooklands Av BFN/LL DA15 167 J4
WIM/MER SW19 160 A4
Brooklands Cl ROMW/RG RM7 75 F1
Brooklands Ct
KIL/WHAMP NW6 82 D5
WCHMH N21 23 K6
Brooklands Dr GFD/PVL UB6 79 J6
Brooklands La
ROMW/RG RM7 75 F1
Brooklands Pl HPTN TW12 173 G1
Brooklands Rd
ROMW/RG RM7 75 F1
THDIT KT7 190 A5
The Brooklands ISLW TW7 * 135 J2
Brook La BKHTH/KID SE3 146 A3
BMLY BR1 183 K2
BXLY DA5 168 E1
Brook La North BTFD TW8 116 E5
Brooklea Cl CDALE/KGS NW9 45 G4
Brooklyn Av SNWD SE25 197 J1
Brooklyn Cl CAR SM5 194 D6
Brooklyn Gv SNWD SE25 197 J1
Brooklyn Rd HAYES BR2 200 C2
SNWD SE25 197 J1
Brooklyn Wy WDR/YW UB7 112 A3
Brookmead CROY/NA CR0 195 H3
Brook Md HOR/WEW KT19 207 G4
Brookmead Av HAYES BR2 200 E2
Brookmead Cl
STMC/STPC BR5 202 C3
Brook Meadow
NFNCH/WDSPK N12 33 F6
Brook Meadow Cl WFD IG8 52 C2
Brookmead Rd CROY/NA CR0 195 H3
Brook Ms North BAY/PAD W2 101 G6
Brookmill Cl OXHEY WD19 * 27 F2
Brookmill Rd DEPT SE8 144 D2
Brook Park Cl WCHMH N21 23 H6
Brook Pl BAR EN5 20 E6
Brook Rd BKHH IG9 38 E3
CEND/HSY/T N8 66 E1
CRICK NW2 63 J6
GNTH/NBYPK IG2 72 E3
GPK RM2 57 H5
SURB KT6 191 F6
THHTH CR7 196 D1
TWK TW1 156 B1
WDGN N22 * 49 F5
rook Rd South BTFD TW8 116 E5
rooks Av EHAM E6 107 K3
rooksbank St HOM E9 * 87 F4
rooksby Ms IS N1 85 G5
rooksby St IS N1 85 G5
rooksby's Wk HOM E9 87 F3
rookscroft CROY/NA CR0 * 213 H6
rookscroft Rd WALTH E17 51 K4
rookshill
KTN/HRWW/WS HA3 42 E2
ookshill Av
KTN/HRWW/WS HA3 42 D1
ookshill Dr
KTN/HRWW/WS HA3 42 D1
ookside BARK/HLT IG6 54 C2
CAR SM5 210 A3
EBAR EN4 33 J1
ORP BR6 202 A4
WCHMH N21 35 F1
ookside Cl BAR EN5 32 B1
FELT TW13 153 K5
KTN/HRWW/WS HA3 61 K2
RSLP HA4 77 J2
ookside Crs WPK KT4 192 D5
ookside Rd ARCH N19 66 C6
ED N9 36 D6
GLDGN NW11 64 C3
OXHEY WD19 27 F2
YEAD UB4 95 G6
ookside South EBAR EN4 34 A2
ookside Wy CROY/NA CR0 198 A3
ooks La CHSWK W4 117 H6
ook's Ms MYFR/PKLN W1K 9 J5
ooks Rd CHSWK W4 117 H5
ook's Rd PLSTW E13 88 E6
ook St BAY/PAD W2 8 B5
BELV DA17 129 J5
ERITH DA8 129 J6
ERITH DA8 149 K1
KUT/HW KT1 175 F5
MYFR/PKLN W1K 9 H5
TOTM N17 50 B5
oksville Av
IL/WHAMP NW6 82 C6
okview Rd
TRHM/NOR SW16 179 H1
okville Rd FUL/PGN SW6 139 J1
ok Wk EDGW HA8 45 F2
FNCH N2 * 47 H4
ok Water La HDN NW4 * 64 B2
okway RAIN RM13 111 K4
okwood Av BARN SW13 138 C4
okwood Cl HAYES BR2 199 J1
okwood Rd HSLW TW3 135 G3
AND/EARL SW18 159 J3
om Av STMC/STPC BR5 186 C5
om Cl ESH/CLAY KT10 204 B3
AYES BR2 200 D3
EDD TW11 174 E3
omcroft Av NTHLT UB5 95 G2
ome Rd HPTN TW12 172 E4
ome Wy CMBW SE5 142 E1
omfield WALTH E17 69 H3
omfield Av LOU IG10 39 K1
MGR N13 35 F6
mfield Cl CRW RM5 57 F2
mfield Cots WEA W13 * 116 C1
mfield La PLMGR N13 34 E6
mfield Pl WEA W13 116 C1
mfield Rd BECK BR3 198 B1
HDH RM6 73 K4
MGR N13 48 E1
H/KEW TW9 137 G2
RB KT6 191 G5
DD TW11 174 D2
EA W13 116 C1
mfields ESH/CLAY KT10 204 C3

Broomfield St POP/IOD E14 105 J4
Broom Gdns CROY/NA CR0 213 J1
Broomgrove Gdns EDGW HA8 44 C4
Broomgrove Rd
BRXN/ST SW9 142 A3
Broomhall Rd SAND/SEL CR2 211 K6
Broomhill Rd GDMY/SEVK IG3 73 G6
ORP BR6 202 B4
WAND/EARL SW18 139 K6
WFD IG8 52 E2
Broomhouse La
FUL/PGN SW6 139 K3
Broomhouse Rd
FUL/PGN SW6 139 K3
Broomloan La SUT SM1 193 K6
Broom Lock TEDD TW11 * 174 D1
Broom Md BXLYHS DA6 169 H1
Broom Pk TEDD TW11 174 E3
Broom Rd CROY/NA CR0 213 J1
TEDD TW11 174 C1
Broomsleigh St
KIL/WHAMP NW6 * 82 E3
Broom Water TEDD TW11 174 D1
Broom Water West
TEDD TW11 174 D1
Broomwood Cl CROY/NA CR0 198 A2
Broomwood Rd BTSEA SW11 160 D1
STMC/STPC BR5 186 C5
Broseley Gv SYD SE26 182 B1
Broster Gdns SNWD SE25 181 G6
Brougham Rd ACT W3 98 E5
HACK E8 86 C6
Brougham St BTSEA SW11 140 E3
Brough Cl KUTN/CMB KT2 * 174 E1
VX/NE SW8 141 K1
Broughton Av FNCH N3 46 C6
RCHPK/HAM TW10 156 D6
Broughton Dr BRXN/ST SW9 142 B5
Broughton Gdns HGT N6 66 C3
Broughton Rd FUL/PGN SW6 140 A3
ORP BR6 201 J6
THHTH CR7 196 B3
WEA W13 97 H6
Broughton Road Ap
FUL/PGN SW6 * 140 A3
Broughton St VX/NE SW8 141 F3
Brouncker Rd ACT W3 117 K2
Brow Cl STMC/STPC BR5 202 E4
Brow Crs STMC/STPC BR5 202 D5
Browell's La FELT TW13 154 B4
Brown Cl WLGTN SM6 210 D5
Brownfield St POP/IOD E14 105 K5
Browngraves Rd
HYS/HAR UB3 133 F1
Brown Hart Gdns
MYFR/PKLN W1K 9 H5
Brownhill Rd CAT SE6 165 F2
Browning Av HNWL W7 97 F5
SUT SM1 209 J2
WPK KT4 192 E5
Browning Cl HPTN TW12 154 E6
MV/WKIL W9 101 G3
WALTH E17 70 A1
WELL DA16 147 K2
Browning Ms
CAVSQ/HST W1G * 9 H2
Browning Rd DART DA1 151 J5
ENC/FH EN2 23 K1
MNPK E12 89 K4
WAN E11 70 D4
Browning St WALW SE17 122 D5
Browning Wy HEST TW5 134 C2
Brownlea Gdns
GDMY/SEVK IG3 73 G6
Brownlow Cl EBAR EN4 21 H6
Brownlow Ms BMSBY WC1N 5 H6
Brownlow Rd CROY/NA CR0 212 A2
FBAR/BDGN N11 48 E2
FNCH N3 47 F3
FSTGT E7 88 E2
HACK E8 86 B6
WEA W13 * 116 B1
WLSDN NW10 81 G5
Brownlow St HHOL WC1V 11 H2
Brownrigg Rd ASHF TW15 152 D6
Brownspring Dr
ELTH/MOT SE9 167 G5
Brown's Rd BRYLDS KT5 191 G4
WALTH E17 51 J6
Brown St MBLAR W1H 8 E3
Brownswell Rd EFNCH N2 47 H5
Brownswood Rd FSBYPK N4 67 J6
Broxash Rd BTSEA SW11 161 F1
Broxbourne Av SWFD E18 71 F1
Broxbourne House BOW E3 105 K3
Broxbourne Rd FSTGT E7 88 E1
ORP BR6 202 A5
Broxholme Cl SNWD SE25 196 E1
Broxholm Rd WNWD SE27 162 B5
Broxted Rd FSTH SE23 164 C4
Broxwood Wy STJWD NW8 2 D1
Bruce Castle Rd TOTM N17 50 B4
Bruce Cl NKENS W10 100 B4
WELL DA16 148 C2
Bruce Dr SAND/SEL CR2 213 F6
Bruce Gdns TRDG/WHET N20 33 K5
Bruce Gv ORP BR6 202 B5
TOTM N17 50 B5
Bruce Rd BAR EN5 20 C4
BOW E3 105 K2
KTN/HRWW/WS HA3 42 E5
MTCM CR4 179 F3
SNWD SE25 196 E1
WLSDN NW10 81 F5
Bruckner St NKENS W10 100 C2
Brudenell Rd TOOT SW17 160 E5
Bruffs Meadow NTHLT UB5 77 J4
Bruford Ct DEPT SE8 124 D6
Bruges Pl CAMTN NW1 84 C5
Brumfield Rd HOR/WEW KT19 206 E3
Brunel Cl HEST TW5 134 A1
NRWD SE19 181 G2
NTHLT UB5 95 K2
ROM RM1 75 G1
Brunel Ct WLSDN NW10 99 J2
Brunel Est BAY/PAD W2 * 100 E4
Brunel House
WOOL/PLUM SE18 * 146 D1
Brunel Ms NKENS W10 100 B2
Brunel Rd ACT W3 99 G4

BERM/RHTH SE16 123 K2
WALTH E17 69 G3
WFD IG8 53 K1
Brunel St CAN/RD E16 106 D5
Brunel Wk WHTN TW2 155 F2
Brune St WCHPL E1 13 J2
Brunner Cl GLDGN NW11 65 F2
Brunner Rd EA W5 97 K3
WALTH E17 69 H2
Bruno Pl CDALE/KGS NW9 62 E6
Brunswick Av
FBAR/BDGN N11 34 A5
Brunswick Cl BXLYHS DA6 148 E5
PIN HA5 59 J3
THDIT KT7 190 A5
WHTN TW2 155 J5
WOT/HER KT12 188 B6
Brunswick Ct STHWK SE1 19 H3
Brunswick Crs
FBAR/BDGN N11 34 A5
Brunswick Gdns
BARK/HLT IG6 54 C3
EA W5 98 A2
KENS W8 119 K1
Brunswick Gv
FBAR/BDGN N11 34 A5
Brunswick Ms MBLAR W1H 9 F3
STRHM/NOR SW16 179 J2
Brunswick Pk CMBW SE5 142 E2
Brunswick Park Gdns
FBAR/BDGN N11 34 A4
Brunswick Park Rd
FBAR/BDGN N11 34 A5
Brunswick Pl CAMTN NW1 3 H7
IS N1 7 F5
NRWD SE19 181 H3
Brunswick Quay
BERM/RHTH SE16 124 A3
Brunswick Rd BXLYHS DA6 148 E5
EA W5 97 K3
KUTN/CMB KT2 175 H4
LEY E10 70 A5
PEND EN3 25 J1
SEVS/STOTM N15 68 A1
SUT SM1 209 F2
Brunswick Sq BMSBY WC1N 5 F6
TOTM N17 50 B2
Brunswick St WALTH E17 70 A2
Brunswick Vls CMBW SE5 143 F2
Brunswick Wy
FBAR/BDGN N11 34 B6
Brunton Pl POP/IOD E14 105 G5
Brushfield St WCHPL E1 13 H1
Brushwood Cl POP/IOD E14 105 K4
Brussels Rd BTSEA SW11 140 C5
Bruton Cl CHST BR7 184 E3
Bruton La MYFR/PICC W1J 9 K6
Bruton Pl MYFR/PICC W1J 9 K6
Bruton Rd MRDN SM4 194 B1
Bruton St MYFR/PICC W1J 9 K6
Bruton Wy WEA W13 97 G4
Bryan Av WLSDN NW10 81 K5
Bryan Rd BERM/RHTH SE16 124 C2
Bryanston Av WHTN TW2 155 G3
Bryanston Cl NWDGN UB2 114 E4
Bryanstone Rd
CEND/HSY/T N8 66 D2
Bryanston Ms East
MBLAR W1H 8 E2
Bryanston Ms West
MBLAR W1H 8 E2
Bryanston Pl MBLAR W1H 8 E2
Bryanston Sq MBLAR W1H 8 E3
Bryanston St MBLAR W1H 8 E4
Bryant Cl BAR EN5 20 D6
Bryant Rd NTHLT UB5 95 G2
Bryant St SRTFD E15 88 B5
Bryantwood Rd HOLWY N7 85 G3
Brycedale Crs
STHGT/OAK N14 34 D6
Bryce Rd BCTR RM8 91 J2
Bryden Cl SYD SE26 182 B1
Brydges Pl CHCR WC2N 10 E6
Brydges Rd SRTFD E15 88 B3
Brydon Wk IS N1 84 E6
Bryett Rd HOLWY N7 84 E1
Brymay Cl BOW E3 105 J1
Brynmaer Rd BTSEA SW11 140 E2
Bryn-Y-Mawr Rd EN EN1 24 B5
Bryony Rd SHB W12 99 J6
Buchanan Cl WCHMH N21 23 F6
Buchanan Gdns
WLSDN NW10 99 K1
Buchan Rd PECK SE15 143 K4
Bucharest Rd
WAND/EARL SW18 160 B2
Buckfast Rd MRDN SM4 194 A1
Buckfast St BETH E2 104 C2
Buckhold Rd
WAND/EARL SW18 159 K1
Buckhurst Av CAR SM5 194 D5
Buckhurst St WCHPL E1 104 D3
Buckhurst Wy BKHH IG9 39 H5
Buckingham Av
E/WMO/HCT KT8 173 G5
EBED/NFELT TW14 154 A1
GFD/PVL UB6 79 G6
THHTH CR7 180 B4
TRDG/WHET N20 33 G2
WELL DA16 147 K5
Buckingham Cl EA W5 97 J4
EN EN1 24 A3
HPTN TW12 172 E1
STMC/STPC BR5 201 K4
Buckingham Ct BELMT SM2 * 208 E6
Buckingham Dr CHST BR7 185 G1
Buckingham Gdns
E/WMO/HCT KT8 173 G5
STAN HA7 44 A3
THHTH CR7 180 B5
Buckingham Ga
WESTW SW1E 16 A4
Buckingham La FSTH SE23 164 B2
Buckingham Ms IS N1 86 A4
WESTW SW1E * 16 A4
WLSDN NW10 99 H1
Buckingham Palace Rd
BGVA SW1W 15 J6
Buckingham Pde STAN HA7 * 43 J1
Buckingham Pl WESTW SW1E 16 A4

Buckingham Rd EDGW HA8 44 B3
HPTN TW12 154 E6
HRW HA1 60 D2
IL IG1 72 D6
IS N1 86 A4
KUT/HW KT1 191 G1
LEY E10 87 K1
MTCM CR4 195 K2
RCHPK/HAM TW10 156 E4
SRTFD E15 88 D3
SWFD E18 52 D4
WAN E11 71 F1
WDGN N22 48 E4
Buckingham St CHCR WC2N 11 F6
Buckingham Wy WLGTN SM6 210 C6
Buckland Crs HAMP NW3 83 H5
Buckland Ri PIN HA5 41 G4
Buckland Rd CHSGTN KT9 206 B3
LEY E10 70 A6
ORP BR6 216 E2
Bucklands OXHEY WD19 * 27 H5
Bucklands Rd TEDD TW11 174 D2
Buckland St IS N1 7 F3
Bucklands Whf KUT/HW KT1 * 174 E5
Buckland Wk MRDN SM4 194 B1
Buckland Wy WPK KT4 193 F5
Buck La CDALE/KGS NW9 63 F2
Buckleigh Av RYNPK SW20 177 J6
Buckleigh Rd
STRHM/NOR SW16 179 J2
Buckleigh Wy NRWD SE19 181 G4
Bucklersbury MANHO EC4N * 12 E4
Bucklers' Wy CAR SM5 209 K1
Buckle St WCHPL E1 13 K3
Buckley Cl DART DA1 150 C3
FSTH SE23 163 J2
Buckley Rd KIL/WHAMP NW6 82 D5
Buckmaster Rd BTSEA SW11 140 D5
Bucknall St NOXST/BSQ WC1A 10 E3
Bucknall Wy BECK BR3 198 E1
Bucknell Cl BRXS/STRHM SW2 142 A5
Buckner Rd
BRXS/STRHM SW2 142 A5
Buckrell Rd CHING E4 38 B4
Bucks Av OXHEY WD19 27 J2
Buckstone Cl FSTH SE23 163 K1
Buckstone Rd UED N18 50 C2
Buck St CAMTN NW1 84 B6
Buckters Rents
BERM/RHTH SE16 124 B1
Buckthorne Rd BROCKY SE4 164 B1
Budd Cl NFNCH/WDSPK N12 33 F6
Buddings Cir WBLY HA9 80 E1
Bude Cl WALTH E17 69 H2
Budge La MTCM CR4 194 E4
Budge Rw MANHO EC4N 12 E5
Budleigh Crs WELL DA16 148 D2
Budoch Dr GDMY/SEVK IG3 73 G6
Buer Rd FUL/PGN SW6 139 H3
Bugsby's Wy GNWCH SE10 125 J4
Bulganak Rd THHTH CR7 196 D1
Bulinca St WEST SW1P * 16 E7
Bullace Rw CMBW SE5 142 E2
Bullard Rd TEDD TW11 173 K2
Bullards Pl BETH E2 105 F2
Bullbanks Rd BELV DA17 129 K4
Bulleid Wy BGVA SW1W 15 K7
Bullen St BTSEA SW11 140 D3
Buller Cl PECK SE15 143 H1
Buller Rd BARK IG11 90 E5
THHTH CR7 180 E6
TOTM N17 50 C5
WDGN N22 49 G5
WLSDN NW10 100 B2
Bullers Cl SCUP DA14 187 F1
Bullers Wood Dr CHST BR7 184 D4
Bullescroft Rd EDGW HA8 30 C5
Bullivant St POP/IOD E14 106 A6
Bull La CHST BR7 185 J3
DAGE RM10 92 D1
UED N18 50 A1
Bull Rd SRTFD E15 106 D1
Bullrush Cl CAR SM5 194 D6
CROY/NA CR0 197 F3
Bulls Aly MORT/ESHN SW14 * 138 A4
Bull's Br NWDGN UB2 113 K3
Bulls Bridge Rd NWDGN UB2 114 A3
Bullsbrook Rd YEAD UB4 114 B1
Bull's Gdns CHEL SW3 14 D6
Bull Yd PECK SE15 143 H2
Bulmer Gdns
KTN/HRWW/WS HA3 61 K4
Bulstrode Av HSLW TW3 134 E4
Bulstrode Gdns HSLW TW3 135 F4
Bulstrode Pl MHST W1U 9 H2
Bulstrode Rd HSLW TW3 135 F4
Bulstrode St MHST W1U 9 H3
Bulwer Court Rd WAN E11 70 B5
Bulwer Gdns BAR EN5 21 G5
Bulwer Rd BAR EN5 21 F5
UED N18 36 A6
WAN E11 70 B5
Bulwer St SHB W12 119 F1
Bunces La WFD IG8 52 D3
Bungalow Rd SNWD SE25 197 F1
The Bungalows
RYLN/HDSTN HA2 * 77 K1
STRHM/NOR SW16 179 G3
Bunhill Rw STLK EC1Y 6 E6
Bunhouse Pl BGVA SW1W 121 F5
Bunkers Hl GLDGN NW11 65 G4
SCUP DA14 169 G5
Bunker's Hl BELV DA17 129 H4
Bunning Wy HOLWY N7 * 84 E5
Bunn's La MLHL NW7 45 G2
Bunsen St BOW E3 105 G1
Buntingbridge Rd
BARK/HLT IG6 72 D2
Bunting Cl ED N9 37 F3
MTCM CR4 194 E2
Bunton St WOOL/PLUM SE18 127 F3
Bunyan Rd WALTH E17 51 G6
Buonaparte Ms PIM SW1V 121 J5
Burbage Cl HYS/HAR UB3 94 B5
STHWK SE1 18 E5
Burbage Rd HNHL SE24 162 E1
Burberry Cl NWMAL KT3 176 B5
Burbridge Wy TOTM N17 50 C5
Burcham St POP/IOD E14 105 K5
Burcharbro Rd ABYW SE2 128 E6

Burchell Ct BUSH WD23 28 C2
Burchell Rd LEY E10 69 K5
PECK SE15 143 J2
Burcher Gale Gv PECK SE15 143 F1
Burchwall Cl CRW RM5 56 E3
Burcote Rd WAND/EARL SW18 160 C3
Burden Cl BTFD TW8 116 D5
Burdenshott Av
RCHPK/HAM TW10 137 J5
Burden Wy WAN E11 71 F6
Burder Cl IS N1 86 A4
Burder Rd IS N1 86 A4
Burdett Av RYNPK SW20 176 D4
Burdett Cl HNWL W7 * 116 A1
SCUP DA14 187 F1
Burdett Rd CROY/NA CR0 196 E3
POP/IOD E14 105 H5
RCH/KEW TW9 137 G3
Burdetts Rd DAGW RM9 92 B6
Burdock Cl CROY/NA CR0 198 A5
Burdock Rd TOTM N17 50 C6
Burdon La BELMT SM2 208 C5
Burdon Pk BELMT SM2 208 D6
Burfield Cl TOOT SW17 160 B6
Burford Cl BARK/HLT IG6 72 C1
BCTR RM8 91 J1
Burford Gdns PLMGR N13 35 F5
Burford Rd BMLY BR1 200 D1
BTFD TW8 117 F5
CAT SE6 164 C4
EHAM E6 107 J2
SRTFD E15 88 B5
SUT SM1 193 K6
WPK KT4 192 D4
Burford Wk FUL/PGN SW6 * 140 A1
Burford Wy CROY/NA CR0 214 A4
Burgate Cl DART DA1 150 C4
Burges Gv BARN SW13 138 E1
Burges Rd EHAM E6 89 K5
Burgess Av CDALE/KGS NW9 63 F3
Burgess Cl FELT TW13 154 D6
Burgess Hl CRICK NW2 82 E2
Burgess Ms WIM/MER SW19 178 A2
Burgess Rd SRTFD E15 88 C2
SUT SM1 209 F2
Burgess St POP/IOD E14 105 J4
Burge St STHWK SE1 19 F5
Burghill Rd SYD SE26 164 A6
Burghley Av NWMAL KT3 176 A4
Burghley Hall Cl
WIM/MER SW19 * 159 H3
Burghley Pl MTCM CR4 194 E1
Burghley Rd CEND/HSY/T N8 49 G6
KTTN NW5 84 B2
WAN E11 * 70 C5
WIM/MER SW19 159 G6
Burgh St IS N1 6 B2
Burgon St BLKFR EC4V 12 B4
Burgos Cl CROY/NA CR0 211 G4
Burgos Gv GNWCH SE10 144 E2
Burgoyne Rd BRXN/ST SW9 142 A4
FSBYPK N4 67 H3
SNWD SE25 197 G1
Burham Cl PGE/AN SE20 181 K3
Burhill Gv PIN HA5 41 J5
Burke Cl PUT/ROE SW15 138 B5
Burke St CAN/RD E16 106 D4
Burket Cl NWDGN UB2 114 D4
Burland Rd BTSEA SW11 140 E6
CRW RM5 56 E2
Burleigh Av BFN/LL DA15 148 A6
WLGTN SM6 210 A1
Burleigh Cl ROMW/RG RM7 74 D1
Burleigh Gdns
STHGT/OAK N14 34 C3
Burleigh Pde
STHGT/OAK N14 * 34 D3
Burleigh Pl PUT/ROE SW15 139 G6
Burleigh Rd CHEAM SM3 193 H5
EN EN1 24 A5
Burleigh St COVGDN WC2E 11 F5
Burleigh Wk CAT SE6 165 F3
Burleigh Wy ENC/FH EN2 23 K4
Burley Cl CHING E4 51 J1
STRHM/NOR SW16 179 J5
Burley Rd CAN/RD E16 107 G5
Burlington Ar CONDST W1S 10 A6
Burlington Av RCH/KEW TW9 137 H2
ROMW/RG RM7 74 D3
Burlington Cl
EBED/NFELT TW14 153 G2
EHAM E6 107 J5
MV/WKIL W9 100 E3
ORP BR6 201 G6
PIN HA5 41 F6
Burlington Gdns CHDH RM6 74 A4
CHSWK W4 117 K5
CONDST W1S 10 A6
Burlington La CHSWK W4 137 K1
Burlington Ms ACT W3 117 K1
Burlington Pde CRICK NW2 * 82 B2
Burlington Pl FUL/PGN SW6 139 H3
WFD IG8 38 E5
Burlington Ri EBAR EN4 33 J3
Burlington Rd CHSWK W4 * 117 K5
ENC/FH EN2 23 K2
FUL/PGN SW6 139 H3
ISLW TW7 135 J2
MUSWH N10 48 A6
NWMAL KT3 192 C1
THHTH CR7 180 D5
TOTM N17 50 C4
Burma Rd STNW/STAM N16 85 K2
Burma Ter NRWD SE19 * 181 F1
Burmester Rd TOOT SW17 160 B5
Burnaby Crs CHSWK W4 117 J6
Burnaby Gdns CHSWK W4 117 J6
Burnaby St WBPTN SW10 140 B1
Burnbrae Cl
NFNCH/WDSPK N12 47 F2
Burnbury Rd BAL SW12 161 H3
Burncroft Av PEND EN3 24 E3
Burndell Wy YEAD UB4 95 H4
Burnell Av RCHPK/HAM TW10 174 D1
WELL DA16 148 B3
Burnell Gdns STAN HA7 43 K5
Burnell Rd SUT SM1 209 F2
Burnell Wk STHWK SE1 * 123 G5
Burnels Av EHAM E6 108 A2
Burness Cl HOLWY N7 85 F4

Burne St *CAMTN* NW1 8 C1
Burnet Cl *HOM* E9 86 E3
Burnett La *BARK/HLT* IG6 54 B3
Burnett Rd *ERITH* DA8 131 G6
Burney Av *BRYLDS* KT5 191 G2
Burney St *GNWCH* SE10 145 F1
Burnfoot Av *FUL/PGN* SW6 139 H2
Burnham Av *HGDN/ICK* UB10 76 A2
Burnham Cl *EN* EN1 24 A1
KTN/HRWW/WS HA3 61 G1
MLHL NW7 45 J3
STHWK SE1 19 K7
Burnham Crs *WAN* E11 71 G1
Burnham Dr *WPK* KT4 193 G6
Burnham Gdns *CROY/NA* CR0 197 G4
HSLWW TW4 134 A2
HYS/HAR UB3 113 G3
Burnham Rd *CHING* E4 51 H1
DAGW RM9 91 H5
MRDN SM4 194 A2
ROMW/RG RM7 56 E6
SCUP DA14 169 F4
Burnham St *BETH* E2 104 E2
KUTN/CMB KT2 175 H4
Burnham Ter *DART* DA1 * 151 G6
Burnham Wy *SYD* SE26 182 C1
WEA W13 116 C4
Burnhill Rd *BECK* BR3 182 D5
Burnley Cl *OXHEY* WD19 41 G1
Burnley Rd *BRXN/ST* SW9 142 A3
WLSDN NW10 81 H3
Burnsall St *CHEL* SW3 120 D5
Burns Av *BFN/LL* DA15 168 C1
CHDH RM6 73 J4
EBED/NFELT TW14 153 K1
STHL UB1 96 A6
Burns Cl *CAR* SM5 210 A6
WALTH E17 70 A1
WELL DA16 148 A2
WIM/MER SW19 178 C2
YEAD UB4 94 E4
Burnside Av *CHING* E4 51 H2
Burnside Cl *BAR* EN5 20 E4
BERM/RHTH SE16 124 A1
TWK TW1 156 B1
Burnside Crs *ALP/SUD* HA0 79 K6
Burnside Rd *BCTR* RM8 73 J6
Burns Rd *ALP/SUD* HA0 98 A1
BTSEA SW11 140 E3
WEA W13 * 116 C2
Burn's Rd *WLSDN* NW10 81 H6
Burns Wy *HEST* TW5 134 C2
Burnt Ash Hl *LEE/GVPK* SE12 166 A3
Burnt Ash La *BMLY* BR1 184 A1
Burnt Ash Rd *LEE/GVPK* SE12 145 J6
Burnthwaite Rd
FUL/PGN SW6 139 J1
Burnt Oak Broadway
EDGW HA8 44 D3
Burnt Oak Flds *EDGW* HA8 44 E4
Burnt Oak La *BFN/LL* DA15 168 B1
BFN/LL DA15 168 B3
Burntwood Cl
WAND/EARL SW18 * 160 C3
Burntwood Grange Rd
WAND/EARL SW18 160 C3
Burntwood La *TOOT* SW17 160 C4
Burntwood Vw *NRWD* SE19 * 181 G1
Buross St *WCHPL* E1 104 D5
Burpham Cl *YEAD* UB4 95 H4
Burrage Gv *WOOL/PLUM* SE18 127 H4
Burrage Pl *WOOL/PLUM* SE18 127 G5
Burrage Rd
WOOL/PLUM SE18 127 H4
Burrard Rd *CAN/RD* E16 106 E5
KIL/WHAMP NW6 82 E3
Burr Bank Ter *RDART* DA2 * 171 F6
Burr Cl *WAP* E1W 123 H1
Burrell Cl *CROY/NA* CR0 198 B3
EDGW HA8 30 D4
Burrell Rw *BECK* BR3 182 D5
Burrell St *STHWK* SE1 12 A7
Burrells Wharf Sq
POP/IOD E14 124 E5
Burrels Whf *POP/IOD* E14 124 E5
Burrfield Dr *STMC/STPC* BR5 202 E2
Burritt Rd *KUT/HW* KT1 175 H5
Burroughs Cots
POP/IOD E14 * 105 G4
Burroughs Gdns *HDN* NW4 63 K1
The Burroughs *HDN* NW4 63 K1
Burrow Gn *CHIG* IG7 55 F1
Burrow Rd *CHIG* IG7 55 G1
EDUL SE22 143 F5
Burrows Ms *STHWK* SE1 18 A2
Burrows Rd *WLSDN* NW10 100 A2
Burr Rd *WAND/EARL* SW18 159 K3
Bursar St *STHWK* SE1 * 19 G1
Bursdon Cl *BFN/LL* DA15 168 A4
Bursland Rd *PEND* EN3 25 F5
Burslem Av *BARK/HLT* IG6 55 G2
Burslem St *WCHPL* E1 * 104 D5
Burstock Rd *PUT/ROE* SW15 139 H5
Burston Rd *PUT/ROE* SW15 139 G6
Burstow Rd *RYNPK* SW20 177 H4
Burtenshaw Rd *THDIT* KT7 190 B4
Burtley Cl *FSBYPK* N4 67 J5
Burton Bank *IS* N1 * 85 K5
Burton Cl *CHSGTN* KT9 205 K5
THHTH CR7 180 E6
Burton Gdns *HEST* TW5 134 E2
Burton Gv *WALW* SE17 122 E5
Burtonhole Cl *MLHL* NW7 32 B6
Burtonhole La *MLHL* NW7 32 B6
Burton La *BRXN/ST* SW9 * 142 B3
Burton Ms *BGVA* SW1W 15 H7
Burton Pl *STPAN* WC1H 4 D6
Burton Rd *BRXN/ST* SW9 142 B3
KIL/WHAMP NW6 82 D5
KUTN/CMB KT2 175 F3
SWFD E18 53 F6
Burtons Ct *SRTFD* E15 88 B5
Burton's Rd *HPTN* TW12 155 G6
Burton St *STPAN* WC1H 4 D6
Burt Rd *CAN/RD* E16 126 B1
Burtwell La *WNWD* SE27 162 E6
Burwash Ct *STMC/STPC* BR5 202 D2
Burwash Rd
WOOL/PLUM SE18 127 J5
Burway Cl *SAND/SEL* CR2 212 A4
Burwell Av *GFD/PVL* UB6 78 E4
Burwell Cl *WCHPL* E1 104 D5
Burwell Rd *LEY* E10 69 G5
Burwood Av *HAYES* BR2 200 A6
PIN HA5 59 G2
Burwood Cl *SURB* KT6 191 H5
Burwood Gdns *RAIN* RM13 111 H2
Burwood Pl *BAY/PAD* W2 8 D3
EBAR EN4 21 G2
Bury Av *RSLP* HA4 58 A3
YEAD UB4 94 C1
Bury Cl *BERM/RHTH* SE16 124 A1
Bury Ct *HDTCH* EC3A 13 H3
Bury Gv *MRDN* SM4 194 A2
Bury Pl *NOXST/BSQ* WC1A 10 E2
Bury Rd *CHING* E4 38 C1
DAGE RM10 92 E3
WDGN N22 49 G5
Buryside Cl *GNTH/NBYPK* IG2 73 F2
Bury St *ED* N9 36 B2
HDTCH EC3A 13 H4
RSLP HA4 58 B3
STJS SW1Y 10 A7
Bury St West *ED* N9 36 A2
Bury Wk *CHEL* SW3 14 C7
Busby Pl *KTTN* NW5 84 D4
Busch Cl *ISLW* TW7 136 C2
Bushbaby Cl *STHWK* SE1 19 G5
Bushberry Rd *HOM* E9 87 G4
Bush Cl *GNTH/NBYPK* IG2 72 D2
Bush Cots *WAND/EARL* SW18 139 K6
Bushell Cl *BRXS/STRHM* SW2 162 A4
Bushell Gn *BUSH* WD23 28 D4
Bushell Wy *CHST* BR7 185 F1
Bush Elms Rd *EMPK* RM11 75 J4
Bushey Av *STMC/STPC* BR5 201 J4
SWFD E18 52 D6
Bushey Cl *CHING* E4 38 A5
Bushey Hill Rd *CMBW* SE5 143 G2
Bushey La *SUT* SM1 208 E1
Bushey Lees *BFN/LL* DA15 * 168 A1
Bushey Rd *CROY/NA* CR0 198 D6
HYS/HAR UB3 113 H4
PLSTW E13 107 G1
RYNPK SW20 176 E6
SEVS/STOTM N15 68 A3
SUT SM1 208 E2
Bushey Wy *BECK* BR3 199 G3
Bushfield Cl *EDGW* HA8 30 D4
Bushfield Crs *EDGW* HA8 30 D4
Bush Gv *CDALE/KGS* NW9 62 E4
STAN HA7 43 K3
Bushgrove Rd *BCTR* RM8 91 K2
Bush Hl *WCHMH* N21 35 J2
Bush Hill Pde *ED* N9 * 35 K2
Bush Hill Rd
KTN/HRWW/WS HA3 62 B3
WCHMH N21 35 K1
Bush House
WOOL/PLUM SE18 * 146 D1
Bush La *CANST* EC4R 12 E5
Bushmead Cl
SEVS/STOTM N15 * 68 B1
Bushmoor Crs
WOOL/PLUM SE18 147 G1
Bushnell Rd *TOOT* SW17 161 G4
Bush Rd *BKHH* IG9 39 H6
DEPT SE8 124 A4
HACK E8 86 D6
RCH/KEW TW9 117 G6
WAN E11 70 D4
Bushway *BCTR* RM8 91 K2
Bushwood *WAN* E11 70 D5
Bushwood Dr *STHWK* SE1 19 K7
Bushwood Rd *RCH/KEW* TW9 117 H6
Bushy Cl *CRW* RM5 57 F2
Bushy Park Gdns *HPTN* TW12 173 J1
Bushy Park Rd *TEDD* TW11 174 C3
Bushy Rd *TEDD* TW11 173 K2
Butcher Rw *WAP* E1W 105 F5
Butchers Rd *CAN/RD* E16 106 E5
Bute Av *RCHPK/HAM* TW10 157 F4
Bute Gdns *HMSMTH* W6 119 G4
RCHPK/HAM TW10 * 157 F3
WLGTN SM6 210 C3
Bute Gdns West *WLGTN* SM6 210 C3
Bute Ms *GLDGN* NW11 65 F2
Bute Rd *BARK/HLT* IG6 72 B2
CROY/NA CR0 196 B5
WLGTN SM6 210 C2
Bute St *SKENS* SW7 14 A6
Bute Wk *IS* N1 * 85 K4
Butler Av *HRW* HA1 60 D4
Butler Cl *EDGW* HA8 44 D5
Butler Rd *BCTR* RM8 91 H2
HRW HA1 60 C4
WLSDN NW10 81 H5
Butlers Cl *HSLWW* TW4 134 E5
Butlers & Colonial Whf
STHWK SE1 19 K2
Butlers Farm Cl
RCHPK/HAM TW10 156 E6
Butler St *BETH* E2 * 104 E2
Buttercup Cl *NTHLT* UB5 77 K4
Buttercup Sq
STWL/WRAY TW19 * 152 A3
Butterfield Cl
BERM/RHTH SE16 * 123 H2
TOTM N17 49 J2
TWK TW1 156 A1
Butterfield House
CHARL SE7 * 146 D1
Butterfield Ms
WOOL/PLUM SE18 127 G6
Butterfields *WALTH* E17 70 A2
Butterfield Sq *EHAM* E6 107 K5
Butterfly La *ELTH/MOT* SE9 167 G1
Butterfly Wk *CMBW* SE5 * 142 E2
Butter Hl *CAR* SM5 210 A1
Butteridges Cl *DAGW* RM9 92 B6
Butterly Av *DART* DA1 * 171 J4
Buttermere Cl
EBED/NFELT TW14 153 J3
MRDN SM4 193 G3
SRTFD E15 88 B2
STHWK SE1 19 J7
Buttermere Dr
PUT/ROE SW15 139 H6
Buttermere Rd
STMC/STPC BR5 202 E1
Buttermere Wk *HACK* E8 86 B4
Butterwick *HMSMTH* W6 119 F4
Butterworth Gdns *WFD* IG8 52 E2
Butterworth Ter
WALW SE17 * 122 D5
Buttery Ms *STHGT/OAK* N14 34 E5
Buttesland St *IS* N1 7 F4
Buttfield Cl *DAGE* RM10 92 D4
Buttmarsh Cl
WOOL/PLUM SE18 127 G5
Buttsbury Rd *IL* IG1 90 C3
Butts Crs *FELT* TW13 155 F5
Buttsmead *NTHWD* HA6 40 A3
Butts Piece *NTHLT* UB5 95 F1
Butts Rd *BMLY* BR1 183 H1
The Butts *BTFD* TW8 116 E6
Buxhall Crs *HOM* E9 87 H4
Buxted Rd *EDUL* SE22 143 F5
HACK E8 86 B5
NFNCH/WDSPK N12 47 J1
Buxton Cl *WFD* IG8 53 H2
Buxton Crs *CHEAM* SM3 208 C2
Buxton Dr *NWMAL* KT3 176 A5
WAN E11 70 C1
Buxton Gdns *ACT* W3 98 D6
Buxton Ms *CLAP* SW4 141 J3
Buxton Pth *OXHEY* WD19 * 27 G5
Buxton Rd *ARCH* N19 66 D5
CHING E4 38 B2
CRICK NW2 81 K4
EHAM E6 107 J2
ERITH DA8 150 A1
GNTH/NBYPK IG2 72 E3
MORT/ESHN SW14 138 B4
SRTFD E15 88 C3
THHTH CR7 196 C2
WALTH E17 69 G1
Buxton St *WCHPL* E1 7 K7
Byam St *FUL/PGN* SW6 140 B3
Byards Cft *STRHM/NOR* SW16 179 J4
Bychurch End *TEDD* TW11 * 174 A1
Bycroft Rd *STHL* UB1 96 A4
Bycroft St *PGE/AN* SE20 182 A3
Bycullah Av *ENC/FH* EN2 23 H4
Bycullah Rd *ENC/FH* EN2 23 H3
Byelands Cl *BERM/RHTH* SE16 124 A1
The Bye *ACT* W3 99 G5
Byewaters *WATW* WD18 26 A1
Bye Ways *WHTN* TW2 155 G5
The Byeways *BRYLDS* KT5 191 H2
The Bye Wy
KTN/HRWW/WS HA3 42 E4
The Byeway
MORT/ESHN SW14 137 K4
Byfeld Gdns *BARN* SW13 138 D2
Byfield Cl *BERM/RHTH* SE16 124 B2
Byfield Rd *ISLW* TW7 136 B4
Byford Cl *SRTFD* E15 88 C5
Bygrove *CROY/NA* CR0 213 K4
Bygrove Rd *WIM/MER* SW19 178 C2
Bygrove St *POP/IOD* E14 105 K5
Byland Cl *ABYW* SE2 128 C3
CAR SM5 194 B4
STHGT/OAK N14 35 F2
Byne Rd *CAR* SM5 194 D6
SYD SE26 181 K2
Bynes Rd *SAND/SEL* CR2 211 K5
Byng Pl *GWRST* WC1E 4 D7
Byng Rd *BAR* EN5 20 B4
Byng St *POP/IOD* E14 124 D2
Byre Rd *STHGT/OAK* N14 34 A1
Byrne Cl *CROY/NA* CR0 196 C3
Byrne Rd *BAL* SW12 161 G3
Byron Av *CDALE/KGS* NW9 62 D1
HSLWW TW4 134 A3
MNPK E12 89 J4
NWMAL KT3 192 D2
SUT SM1 209 H2
SWFD E18 52 D6
Byron Av East *SUT* SM1 209 H2
Byron Cl *HACK* E8 86 C6
HPTN TW12 154 E6
PGE/AN SE20 * 181 J6
SYD SE26 * 164 B6
THMD SE28 128 D1
WOT/HER KT12 188 D5
Byron Ct *ENC/FH* EN2 23 H3
Byron Dr *EFNCH* N2 65 H3
Byron Gdns *SUT* SM1 209 H2
Byron Hill Rd
RYLN/HDSTN HA2 60 D5
Byron Ms *HAMP* NW3 83 J3
MV/WKIL W9 100 E3
Byron Rd *ALP/SUD* HA0 61 J6
CRICK NW2 63 K6
EA W5 117 G1
HRW HA1 60 E3
KTN/HRWW/WS HA3 43 F5
LEY E10 69 K5
MLHL NW7 45 J1
WALTH E17 51 J6
Byron St *POP/IOD* E14 106 A5
Byron Ter *ED* N9 * 36 E2
Byron Wy *NTHLT* UB5 95 J2
WDR/YW UB7 112 C4
YEAD UB4 94 C3
Bysouth Cl *CLAY* IG5 54 B4
SEVS/STOTM N15 67 K1
By The Wood *OXHEY* WD19 27 H4
Bythorn St *BRXN/ST* SW9 142 A4
Byton Rd *TOOT* SW17 178 E2
Byward Av *EBED/NFELT* TW14 154 B1
Byward St *MON* EC3R 13 H6
Bywater Pl *BERM/RHTH* SE16 124 B1
Bywater St *CHEL* SW3 120 E5
The Byway *BELMT* SM2 209 H6
HOR/WEW KT19 207 H2
Bywell Pl *GTPST* W1W * 10 A2
Bywood Av *CROY/NA* CR0 197 K3

C

Cabbell St *CAMTN* NW1 8 C2
Cabinet Wy *CHING* E4 51 H2
Cable Pl *GNWCH* SE10 145 F2
Cables Cl *ERITH* DA8 129 K3
Cable St *WCHPL* E1 104 C6
Cabot Sq *POP/IOD* E14 124 D1
Cabot Wy *EHAM* E6 89 H6
Cabul Rd *BTSEA* SW11 140 D3
Cactus Cl *CMBW* SE5 * 143 F3
Cadbury Cl *ISLW* TW7 136 B2
Cadbury Wy
BERM/RHTH SE16 19 K5
Caddington Cl *EBAR* EN4 21 J6
Caddington Rd *CRICK* NW2 82 C1
Caddis Cl *STAN* HA7 * 43 F3
Cadell Cl *BETH* E2 7 K3
Cade Rd *GNWCH* SE10 145 G2
Cader Rd *WAND/EARL* SW18 160 B1
Cadet Dr *STHWK* SE1 123 G5
Cadet Pl *GNWCH* SE10 125 H5
Cadiz Rd *DAGE* RM10 92 E5
Cadiz St *WALW* SE17 122 D5
Cadman Cl *BRXN/ST* SW9 142 C1
Cadmer Cl *NWMAL* KT3 192 B1
Cadmus Cl *CLAP* SW4 141 J5
Cadogan Cl *HOM* E9 * 87 H5
RYLN/HDSTN HA2 78 B2
TEDD TW11 173 K1
Cadogan Ct *BELMT* SM2 209 F4
Cadogan Gdns *CHEL* SW3 15 F6
FNCH N3 * 47 F4
SWFD E18 53 F6
WCHMH N21 23 G6
Cadogan Ga *KTBR* SW1X 15 F6
Cadogan La *KTBR* SW1X 15 G4
Cadogan Pl *KTBR* SW1X 15 F4
Cadogan Rd *SURB* KT6 190 E2
WOOL/PLUM SE18 127 H3
Cadogan Sq *KTBR* SW1X 14 E5
Cadogan St *CHEL* SW3 14 E7
Cadogan Ter *HOM* E9 87 H4
Cadoxton Av
SEVS/STOTM N15 68 B3
Cadwallon Rd *ELTH/MOT* SE9 167 G4
Caedmon Rd *HOLWY* N7 85 F2
Caerleon Cl *ESH/CLAY* KT10 205 H5
SCUP DA14 186 D1
Caernarvon Cl *MTCM* CR4 179 K6
Caernarvon Dr *CLAY* IG5 54 A4
Caesars Wk *MTCM* CR4 194 E2
Cahill St *STLK* EC1Y * 6 D7
Cahir St *POP/IOD* E14 124 E4
Cain's La *EBED/NFELT* TW14 133 G6
Caird St *NKENS* W10 100 C2
Cairn Av *EA* W5 116 E1
Cairndale Cl *BMLY* BR1 183 J3
Cairnfield Av *CRICK* NW2 81 G1
Cairngorm Cl *TEDD* TW11 174 B1
Cairns Av *WFD* IG8 53 K2
Cairns Rd *BTSEA* SW11 140 D6
Cairn Wy *STAN* HA7 43 F2
Cairo New Rd *CROY/NA* CR0 196 C6
Cairo Rd *WALTH* E17 * 69 J1
Caister Ms *BAL* SW12 161 G2
Caistor Park Rd *SRTFD* E15 88 D6
Caistor Rd *BAL* SW12 161 G2
Caithness Gdns *BFN/LL* DA15 168 A1
Caithness Rd *MTCM* CR4 179 G3
WKENS W14 119 G3
Calabria Rd *HBRY* N5 85 H4
Calais St *CMBW* SE5 142 C2
Calbourne Av *HCH* RM12 93 K3
Calbourne Rd *BAL* SW12 160 E2
Caldbeck Av *WPK* KT4 192 E6
Caldecote Gdns *BUSH* WD23 28 E1
Caldecote La *BUSH* WD23 29 F2
Caldecot Rd *CMBW* SE5 142 D3
Caldecott Wy *CLPT* E5 87 F1
Calder Av *GFD/PVL* UB6 97 F1
Calder Gdns *EDGW* HA8 44 C6
Calderon Rd *WAN* E11 88 A2
Calder Rd *MRDN* SM4 194 B2
Caldervale Rd *CLAP* SW4 141 J6
Calderwood Pl *EBAR* EN4 21 F2
Calderwood St
WOOL/PLUM SE18 127 F4
Caldew St *CMBW* SE5 142 E1
Caldicote Gn
CDALE/KGS NW9 * 63 G3
Caldwell Rd *OXHEY* WD19 27 H6
Caldwell St *BRXN/ST* SW9 142 A1
Caldy Rd *BELV* DA17 129 J3
Caldy Wk *IS* N1 * 85 J4
Caledonian Cl
GDMY/SEVK IG3 * 73 H5
Caledonian Rd *HOLWY* N7 85 F3
Caledonian Sq *CAMTN* NW1 84 D4
Caledonian Wharf Rd
POP/IOD E14 125 G4
Caledonia Rd
STWL/WRAY TW19 152 B3
Caledonia St *IS* N1 5 F3
Caledon Rd *EHAM* E6 89 K6
WLGTN SM6 210 A2
Calendar Ms *SURB* KT6 190 E3
Cale St *CHEL* SW3 120 D5
Calidore Cl
BRXS/STRHM SW2 * 162 A1
California La *BUSH* WD23 28 D3
California Rd *NWMAL* KT3 191 K1
Callaby Ter *IS* N1 * 85 K4
Callaghan Cl *LEW* SE13 145 H5
Callaghan Cots *WCHPL* E1 * 104 E4
Callander Rd *CAT* SE6 164 E4
The Callanders *BUSH* WD23 * 28 E3
Callard Av *PLMGR* N13 49 H1
Callcott Rd *KIL/WHAMP* NW6 82 D5
Callcott St *KENS* W8 119 K1
Callendar Rd *SKENS* SW7 14 A4
Callingham Cl *POP/IOD* E14 105 H4
Callis Farm Cl
STWL/WRAY TW19 152 B1
Callisons Pl *GNWCH* SE10 125 H5
Callis Rd *WALTH* E17 69 H3
Callow St *WBPTN* SW10 120 B6
Calmington Rd *CMBW* SE5 123 F6
Calmont Rd *BMLY* BR1 183 G2
Calne Av *CLAY* IG5 54 B4
Calonne Rd *WIM/MER* SW19 159 G6
Calshot Rd *HTHAIR* TW6 132 E3
Calshot St *IS* N1 5 G2
Calshot Wy *ENC/FH* EN2 23 H4
HTHAIR TW6 132 D3
Calthorpe Gdns *EDGW* HA8 44 B1
SUT SM1 209 G1
Calthorpe St *FSBYW* WC1X 5 H6
Calton Av *DUL* SE21 163 F1
Calton Rd *BAR* EN5 33 G1
Calverley Cl *BECK* BR3 182 E2
Calverley Crs *DAGE* RM10 74 C6
Calverley Gv *ARCH* N19 66 D5
Calverley Rd *EW* KT17 207 J4
Calvert Av *WCHPL* E1 7 H5
Calvert Cl *BELV* DA17 129 H4
SCUP DA14 187 F2
Calverton Rd *EHAM* E6 90 A6
Calvert Rd *BAR* EN5 20 B3
GNWCH SE10 125 J5
Calvert St *CAMTN* NW1 84 A6
Calvin Cl *STMC/STPC* BR5 186 E6
Calvin St *WCHPL* E1 7 J7
Calydon Rd *CHARL* SE7 126 A5
Calypso Crs *PECK* SE15 143 F1
Calypso Wy *BERM/RHTH* SE16 124 C3
Camac Rd *WHTN* TW2 155 J3
Camarthen Gn
CDALE/KGS NW9 * 63 G3
Cambalt Rd *PUT/ROE* SW15 139 G6
Camberley Av *EN* EN1 24 A5
RYNPK SW20 176 E5
Camberley Cl *CHEAM* SM3 208 B1
Camberley Rd *HTHAIR* TW6 132 D4
Cambert Wy *BKHTH/KID* SE3 146 A5
Camberwell Church St
CMBW SE5 142 E2
Camberwell Glebe *CMBW* SE5 142 E2
Camberwell Gn *CMBW* SE5 142 E2
Camberwell Gv *CMBW* SE5 142 E2
Camberwell New Rd
CMBW SE5 142 C1
Camberwell Rd *CMBW* SE5 122 D6
Camberwell Station Rd
CMBW SE5 142 D2
Cambeys Rd *DAGE* RM10 92 E
Camborne Av *WEA* W13 116 C
Camborne Cl *HTHAIR* TW6 132 D
Camborne Crs *HTHAIR* TW6 132 D
Camborne Ms
WAND/EARL SW18 159 K
Camborne Rd *BELMT* SM2 208 E
CROY/NA CR0 197 H
MRDN SM4 193 G
SCUP DA14 168 D
WAND/EARL SW18 159 K
WELL DA16 147 K
Camborne Wy *HEST* TW5 135 F
HTHAIR TW6 132 D
Cambourne Av *ED* N9 37 F
Cambourne Ms *NTGHL* W11 100 C
Cambray Rd *BAL* SW12 161 H
ORP BR6 202 A
Cambria Cl *BFN/LL* DA15 167
HSLW TW3 135
Cambria Ct *EBED/NFELT* TW14 154
Cambria Gdns
STWL/WRAY TW19 152
Cambrian Av
GNTH/NBYPK IG2 72
Cambrian Cl *WNWD* SE27 162
Cambrian Gn *CDALE/KGS* NW9 63
Cambrian Rd *LEY* E10 69
RCHPK/HAM TW10 157
Cambria Rd *CMBW* SE5 142
Cambria St *FUL/PGN* SW6 140
Cambridge Av *GFD/PVL* UB6 79
KIL/WHAMP NW6 100
NWMAL KT3 176
WELL DA16 148
Cambridge Barracks Rd
WOOL/PLUM SE18 126
Cambridge Circ
SOHO/SHAV W1D 10
Cambridge Cl *EBAR* EN4 34
HSLWW TW4 134
RYNPK SW20 176
WALTH E17 69
WDGN N22 * 49
WDR/YW UB7 112
WLSDN NW10 80
Cambridge Crs *BETH* E2 104
TEDD TW11 * 174
Cambridge Dr *RSLP* HA4 59
Cambridge Gdns *EN* EN1 24
KIL/WHAMP NW6 100
KUT/HW KT1 175
MUSWH N10 48
NKENS W10 100
TOTM N17 49
WCHMH N21 35
Cambridge Ga *CAMTN* NW1
Cambridge Gate Ms
CAMTN NW1
Cambridge Gn *ELTH/MOT* SE9 167
Cambridge Gv *HMSMTH* W6 118
PGE/AN SE20 * 18
Cambridge Grove Rd
KUT/HW KT1 17
Cambridge Heath Rd
BETH E2 10
Cambridge Pde *EN* EN1 * 2
Cambridge Pk *TWK* TW1 15
Cambridge Park Rd *WAN* E11 7
Cambridge Pas *HOM* E9 8
Cambridge Pl *KENS* W8 * 12
Cambridge Rd *BARK* IG11 9
BARN SW13 13
BMLY BR1 18
BTSEA SW11 14
CAR SM5 20
CHING E4
E/WMO/HCT KT8 18
GDMY/SEVK IG3 7
HNWL W7 11
HPTN TW12 17
HSLWW TW4 13
KIL/WHAMP NW6 10
KUT/HW KT1 17
MTCM CR4 1
NWMAL KT3 1
PGE/AN SE20 1
RCH/KEW TW9 1
RYLN/HDSTN HA2
RYNPK SW20 1
SCUP DA14 1
STHL UB1 * 1

TEDD TW11 ... 156 B6
TWK TW1 ... 156 E1
WAN E11 ... 70 E3
WOT/HER KT12 ... 188 A3
Cambridge Rd North
　CHSWK W4 ... 117 J5
Cambridge Rd South
　CHSWK W4 ... 117 J5
Cambridge Rw
　WOOL/PLUM SE18 ... 127 G5
Cambridge Sq BAY/PAD W2 ... 8 C3
Cambridge Ter CAMTN NW1 ... 3 J5
　ED N9 * ... 36 B2
Cambridge Terrace Ms
　CAMTN NW1 * ... 3 K5
Cambridge Yd HNWL W7 * ... 116 A2
Cambus Cl YEAD UB4 ... 95 H5
Cambus Rd CAN/RD E16 ... 106 E4
Camdale Rd
　WOOL/PLUM SE18 ... 148 A1
Camden Av FELT TW13 ... 154 B4
　YEAD UB4 ... 95 G5
Camden Cl CHST BR7 ... 185 H4
Camden Gdns CAMTN NW1 * ... 84 B5
　SUT SM1 ... 209 F3
　THHTH CR7 ... 188 C2
Camden Gv CHST BR7 ... 185 G2
Camden High St CAMTN NW1 ... 4 A1
Camden Hill Rd NRWD SE19 ... 181 F2
Camdenhurst St
　POP/IOD E14 ... 105 G5
Camden Lock Pl CAMTN NW1 ... 84 B5
Camden Ms CAMTN NW1 ... 84 C5
Camden Park Rd CAMTN NW1 ... 84 D4
　CHST BR7 ... 184 E5
Camden Pas IS N1 ... 6 A1
Camden Rd BXLY DA5 ... 169 G3
　CAMTN NW1 ... 84 B6
　SUT SM1 ... 209 F3
　WALTH E17 ... 69 H3
　WAN E11 ... 71 F3
Camden Road (Permanent
　Way) CAMTN NW1 ... 4 C1
Camden Rw BKHTH/KID SE3 ... 145 H3
　PIN HA5 * ... 41 G6
Camden Sq CAMTN NW1 ... 84 D4
Camden Ter CAMTN NW1 ... 84 D4
Camden Wk IS N1 ... 6 A1
Camden Wy CHST BR7 ... 184 E6
Camelford Wk NTGHL W11 * ... 100 C5
Camel Gv KUT/HW KT2 ... 174 E1
Camellia St VX/NE SW8 ... 141 K1
Camelot Cl THMD SE28 ... 127 J2
　WIM/MER SW19 ... 159 J6
Camel Rd CAN/RD E16 ... 126 C1
　CAN/RD E16 ... 126 D1
Camera Pl WBPTN SW10 ... 120 C6
Cameron Cl TRDG/WHET N20 ... 33 J4
　UED N18 ... 36 D4
Cameron Pl
　STRHM/NOR SW16 ... 162 B4
Cameron Rd CAT SE6 ... 164 C4
　CROY/NA CR0 ... 196 C4
　GDMY/SEVK IG3 ... 72 E5
Cameron Ter
　LEE/GVPK SE12 ... 166 A5
Camerton Cl HACK E8 ... 86 B4
Camilla Rd BERM/RHTH SE16 ... 123 J4
Camille Cl SNWD SE25 ... 181 H6
Camlet St BETH E2 ... 7 J6
Camlet Wy EBAR EN5 ... 20 E3
Camley St CAMTN NW1 ... 4 D1
Camm Gdns KUT/HW KT1 * ... 175 G5
　THDIT KT7 ... 189 K4
Camomile Av MTCM CR4 ... 178 E4
Camomile St OBST EC2N ... 13 G3
Camomile Rd ROMW/RG RM7 ... 75 F6
Campana Rd FUL/PGN SW6 ... 139 K2
Campbell Av BARK/HLT IG6 ... 72 C1
Campbell Cl ROM RM1 ... 57 G2
　RSLP HA4 ... 58 D4
　STRHM/NOR SW16 * ... 179 J1
　WHTN TW2 ... 155 J3
Campbell Cft EDGW HA8 ... 44 C1
Campbell Gordon Wy
　CRICK NW2 ... 81 K2
Campbell Rd BOW E3 ... 105 J2
　CROY/NA CR0 ... 196 C4
　EHAM E6 ... 89 J6
　HNWL W7 ... 96 E6
　SRTFD E15 ... 88 D4
　WALTH E17 ... 69 H1
　WHTN TW2 ... 155 J4
Campbell Wk IS N1 ... 84 E6
Campdale Rd HOLWY N7 ... 79 H1
Campden Gv KENS W8 ... 119 K2
Campden Hl KENS W8 ... 119 J2
Campden Hill Gdns KENS W8 ... 119 J1
Campden Hill Pl NTGHL W11 * ... 119 J1
Campden Hill Rd KENS W8 ... 119 J2
Campden Hill Sq KENS W8 ... 119 J1
Campden House Cl KENS W8 * ... 119 K2
Campden House Ter
　KENS W8 * ... 119 K1
Campden St KENS W8 ... 119 J1
Campden Ter CHSWK W4 * ... 118 B5
Campen Cl WIM/MER SW19 ... 159 H5
Camperdown St WCHPL E1 ... 13 K4
Campfield Rd ELTH/MOT SE9 ... 166 C2
Campion Cl CROY/NA CR0 ... 212 A3
　EHAM E6 ... 107 K6
　KTN/HRWW/WS HA3 ... 43 K2
　ROMW/RG RM7 ... 75 F6
Campion Gdns WFD IG8 ... 52 E1
Campion Pl THMD SE28 ... 128 C1
Campion Rd ISLW TW7 ... 136 A2

LEY E10 ... 69 K4
　PUT/ROE SW15 ... 139 F5
Campion Ter CRICK NW2 ... 82 B1
Campion Wy EDGW HA8 ... 30 E6
Camplin Rd
　KTN/HRWW/WS HA3 ... 62 A2
Camplin St NWCR SE14 ... 144 A1
Camp Rd WIM/MER SW19 ... 176 E1
Campsbourne Pde
　CEND/HSY/T N8 * ... 66 E1
Campsbourne Rd
　CEND/HSY/T N8 ... 48 E6
The Campsbourne
　CEND/HSY/T N8 ... 66 E1
Campsey Gdns DAGW RM9 ... 91 H5
Campsey Rd DAGW RM9 ... 91 H5
Campshill Pl LEW SE13 ... 145 F6
Campshill Rd LEW SE13 ... 145 F6
Campus Rd WALTH E17 ... 69 H5
Camp Vw WIM/MER SW19 ... 176 E1
Cam Rd SRTFD E15 ... 88 B6
Camrose Av EDGW HA8 ... 44 B5
　ERITH DA8 * ... 129 K6
　FELT TW13 ... 154 A6
　STAN HA7 ... 43 H1
Camrose Cl CROY/NA CR0 ... 198 B4
　MRDN SM4 ... 193 K1
Camrose St
　WOOL/PLUM SE18 ... 128 B5
Canada Av UED N18 ... 49 J2
Canada Cr ACT W3 ... 98 E4
Canada Park Pde
　EDGW HA8 * ... 44 D4
Canada Rd ACT W3 ... 98 E4
　POP/IOD E14 ... 124 C1
Canada St BERM/RHTH SE16 ... 124 A2
Canada Wy SHB W12 ... 99 K6
Canadian Av CAT SE6 ... 164 E3
Canal Ap DEPT SE8 ... 124 B5
Canal Bvd KTTN NW1 ... 84 D4
Canal Cl NKENS W10 ... 100 B3
　WCHPL E1 ... 105 G3
Canal Gv PECK SE15 ... 123 H6
Canal Pth BETH E2 ... 7 J1
Canal St CMBW SE5 ... 122 E6
Canal Wk CROY/NA CR0 ... 197 F3
　IS N1 ... 85 K6
　WLSDN NW10 * ... 80 E5
Canal Wy NKENS W10 ... 100 B3
Canal Whf GFD/PVL UB6 * ... 79 G6
Canal Yd NWDGN UB2 * ... 114 A4
Canberra Cl DAGE RM10 ... 93 F5
　HDN NW4 ... 45 J6
Canberra Dr NTHLT UB5 ... 95 G2
Canberra Rd ABYW SE2 ... 128 E6
　CHARL SE7 ... 126 B6
　EHAM E6 ... 89 K6
　HTHAIR TW6 ... 132 D4
　WEA W13 ... 116 B2
Canbury Av KTBR SW1X ... 175 G4
Canbury Ms SYD SE26 ... 163 H5
Canbury Park Rd
　KUTN/CMB KT2 ... 175 F4
Canbury Pth STMC/STPC BR5 ... 202 B1
Cancell Rd BRXN/ST SW9 ... 142 B2
Candahar Rd BTSEA SW11 ... 140 D3
Candle Gv PECK SE15 ... 143 J4
Candlelight Ct SRTFD E15 * ... 88 D4
Candler Ms TWK TW1 ... 156 B2
Candler St SEVS/STOTM N15 * ... 67 K3
Candover Cl WDR/YW UB7 ... 132 A1
Candover St GTPST W1W * ... 10 A2
Candy St BOW E3 ... 87 H6
Caney Ms CRICK NW2 ... 64 B6
Canfield Dr RSLP HA4 ... 77 F3
Canfield Gdns
　KIL/WHAMP NW6 ... 83 F5
Canfield Pl KIL/WHAMP NW6 * ... 83 G4
Canfield Rd RAIN RM13 ... 93 H6
　WFD IG8 ... 53 J3
Canford Av NTHLT UB5 ... 77 J6
Canford Cl ENC/FH EN2 ... 23 G3
Canford Gdns NWMAL KT3 ... 192 B3
Canford Pl TEDD TW11 ... 174 D2
Canford Rd CLAP SW4 ... 141 F5
Canham Rd CHSWK W4 ... 118 B2
　SNWD SE25 ... 181 F6
Canmore Gdns
　STRHM/NOR SW16 ... 179 H3
Cann Hall Rd WAN E11 ... 88 D2
Canning Cross CMBW SE5 ... 143 F3
Canning Pl KENS W8 ... 120 B3
Canning Place Ms KENS W8 * ... 120 B3
Canning Rd CROY/NA CR0 ... 197 G6
　HBRY N5 ... 85 H2
　KTN/HRWW/WS HA3 ... 42 E6
　SRTFD E15 ... 106 C1
　WALTH E17 ... 51 H6
Cannington Rd DAGW RM9 ... 91 J4
Cannizaro Rd
　WIM/MER SW19 ... 177 F2
Cannonbury Av PIN HA5 ... 59 H3
Cannon Cl HPTN TW12 ... 173 G2
　RYNPK SW20 ... 177 F6
Cannon Dr POP/IOD E14 ... 105 J6
Cannon Hl KIL/WHAMP NW6 ... 83 F3
　STHGT/OAK N14 ... 34 D5
Cannon Hill La RYNPK SW20 ... 193 G2
Cannon Hill Ms
　STHGT/OAK N14 ... 34 E5
Cannon La HAMP NW3 ... 83 H1
　PIN HA5 ... 59 J4
Cannon Pl CHARL SE7 ... 126 D5
　HAMP NW3 ... 83 H1
Cannon Rd STHGT/OAK N14 ... 34 E5
　WCHMH N21 ... 35 H4
Cannon Street Rd WCHPL E1 ... 104 C5
Cannon St STP EC4N ... 12 C4
Cannon Wy E/WMO/HCT KT8 ... 189 F1
Canon Av CHDH RM6 ... 73 J2
Canon Beck Rd
　BERM/RHTH SE16 ... 123 K2
Canonbie Rd FSTH SE23 ... 163 K2
Canonbury Crs IS N1 ... 85 J5
Canonbury Gv IS N1 ... 85 J5
Canonbury La IS N1 ... 85 H5
Canonbury Pk North IS N1 ... 85 J4
Canonbury Pk South IS N1 ... 85 J4

Canonbury Pk South IS N1 ... 85 J4
Canonbury Rd EN EN1 ... 24 A2
　IS N1 ... 85 H5
Canonbury Sq IS N1 ... 85 H5
Canonbury St IS N1 ... 85 J5
Canonbury Vls IS N1 ... 85 H5
Canonbury Yd East IS N1 * ... 85 J5
Canon Mohan Cl
　STHGT/OAK N14 ... 34 A1
Canon Rw WHALL SW1A ... 16 E3
Canons Cl EDGW HA8 ... 44 B2
　EFNCH N2 ... 65 H4
Canons Cots EDGW HA8 * ... 44 B2
Canons Dr EDGW HA8 ... 44 A2
Canonsleigh Rd DAGW RM9 ... 91 H5
Canons Pk Cl EDGW HA8 * ... 44 A2
Canon's Wk CROY/NA CR0 ... 213 F1
Canopus Wy NTHWD HA6 ... 26 E6
　STWL/WRAY TW19 ... 152 B2
Canrobert St BETH E2 ... 104 D1
Cantelowes Rd CAMTN NW1 ... 84 D4
Canterbury Av BFN/LL DA15 ... 168 A4
　IL IG1 ... 71 J4
Canterbury Cl BECK BR3 ... 182 E4
　CMBW SE5 * ... 142 D3
　EHAM E6 ... 107 K5
　GFD/PVL UB6 ... 96 B4
　NTHWD HA6 ... 40 D4
Canterbury Crs BRXN/ST SW9 ... 142 B4
Canterbury Gv WNWD SE27 ... 162 B5
Canterbury Pl WALW SE17 ... 18 B7
Canterbury Rd CROY/NA CR0 ... 196 A4
　FELT TW13 ... 154 D4
　KIL/WHAMP NW6 ... 100 E1
　LEY E10 ... 70 A4
　MRDN SM4 ... 194 B3
　RYLN/HDSTN HA2 ... 60 B2
Canterbury Ter
　KIL/WHAMP NW6 ... 100 E1
Cantley Gdns IL IG2 ... 72 C3
　NRWD SE19 ... 181 G4
Cantley Rd HNWL W7 ... 116 B3
Canton St POP/IOD E14 ... 105 J5
Cantrell Rd BOW E3 ... 105 J3
Cantwell Rd
　WOOL/PLUM SE18 ... 147 G1
Canvey St STHWK SE1 ... 12 C7
Cape Cl BARK IG11 ... 90 B5
Capel Av WLGTN SM6 ... 211 F3
Capel Cl HAYES BR2 ... 200 D5
　TRDG/WHET N20 ... 33 G5
Capel Crs STAN HA7 ... 29 G4
Capel Gdns GDMY/SEVK IG3 ... 91 F1
　PIN HA5 ... 59 K1
Capella Rd NTHWD HA6 ... 40 D1
Capel Rd EBAR EN4 ... 33 J1
　FSTGT E7 ... 89 F2
　OXHEY WD19 ... 27 H1
Capeners Cl KTBR SW1X ... 15 F5
Capern Rd WAND/EARL SW18 ... 160 B3
Cape Rd TOTM N17 ... 50 C6
Cape Yd WAP E1W ... 123 H1
Capital Interchange Wy
　BTFD TW8 ... 117 H5
Capitol Wy CDALE/KGS NW9 ... 44 E6
Capland St STJWD NW8 ... 2 B6
Caple Pde WLSDN NW10 * ... 99 H1
Caple Rd WLSDN NW10 ... 99 H1
Capri Rd CROY/NA CR0 ... 197 G4
Capstan Cl CHDH RM6 ... 73 H3
Capstan Dr RAIN RM13 ... 111 J4
Capstan Ride ENC/FH EN2 ... 23 G3
Capstan Rd DEPT SE8 ... 124 C4
Capstan Sq POP/IOD E14 ... 125 F2
Capstan Wy
　BERM/RHTH SE16 ... 124 B1
Capstone Rd BMLY BR1 ... 165 J6
Capthorne Av
　RYLN/HDSTN HA2 ... 59 J5
Capuchin Cl STAN HA7 ... 43 H2
Capulet Ms CAN/RD E16 ... 125 K1
Capworth St LEY E10 ... 69 J5
Caractacus Cottage Vw
　WATW WD18 ... 26 E2
Caractacus Gn WATW WD18 ... 26 D1
Caradoc Cl BAY/PAD W2 ... 100 E5
Caradoc Evans Cl
　FBAR/BDGN N11 * ... 48 B1
Caradoc St GNWCH SE10 ... 125 H5
Caradon Cl WAN E11 ... 70 C5
Caradon Wy
　SEVS/STOTM N15 ... 67 K1
Caravel Cl POP/IOD E14 ... 124 D3
Caravel Ms DEPT SE8 ... 124 C6
Caraway Cl PLSTW E13 ... 107 F4
Caraway Pl WLGTN SM6 ... 210 B1
Carberry Rd NRWD SE19 ... 181 F2
Carbery Av ACT W3 ... 117 G2
Carbis Cl CHING E4 ... 38 B3
Carbis Rd POP/IOD E14 ... 105 H5
Carburton St GTPST W1W ... 9 K1
Cardale St POP/IOD E14 ... 125 F3
Carden Rd PECK SE15 ... 143 J4
Cardiff Cl CRW RM5 ... 57 F3
Cardiff Rd ENC/FH EN1 ... 24 C6
　HNWL W7 ... 116 A3
　PEND EN3 ... 24 D5
　WATW WD18 ... 27 F1
Cardigan Gdns
　GDMY/SEVK IG3 ... 73 G6
Cardigan Pl LEW SE13 * ... 145 G3
Cardigan Rd BARN SW13 ... 138 D3
　BOW E3 ... 105 H1
　RCHPK/HAM TW10 ... 157 F1
　WIM/MER SW19 ... 178 B2
Cardigan St LBTH SE11 ... 122 B5
Cardigan Wk IS N1 * ... 85 J5
Cardinal Av KUTN/CMB KT2 ... 175 F1
　MRDN SM4 ... 193 H3
Cardinal Bourne St
　STHWK SE1 ... 19 F5
Cardinal Cl CHST BR7 ... 185 J4
　EDGW HA8 ... 44 E3
　MRDN SM4 ... 193 H3
　WPK KT4 ... 207 J2
Cardinal Crs NWMAL KT3 ... 175 K5

Cardinal Dr BARK/HLT IG6 ... 54 C2
　WOT/HER KT12 ... 188 C5
Cardinal Hinsey Cl
　WLSDN NW10 ... 99 J1
Cardinal Pl PUT/ROE SW15 ... 139 G5
Cardinal Rd FELT TW13 ... 154 A3
　RSLP HA4 ... 59 H6
Cardinals Wk HPTN TW12 ... 173 H5
Cardinals Wy ARCH N19 ... 66 D5
Cardinal Wy
　KTN/HRWW/WS HA3 ... 42 E6
Cardine Ms PECK SE15 ... 143 J1
Cardington Sq HSLWW TW4 ... 134 C5
Cardington St CAMTN NW1 ... 4 A4
Cardozo Rd HOLWY N7 ... 84 E3
Cardrew Av
　NFNCH/WDSPK N12 ... 47 H1
Cardross St HMSMTH W6 ... 118 E3
Cardwell Rd HOLWY N7 ... 84 E2
Cardwell Ter HOLWY N7 * ... 84 E2
Carew Cl HOLWY N7 ... 67 F6
Carew Rd MTCM CR4 ... 179 F5
　NTHWD HA6 ... 40 C2
　THHTH CR7 ... 180 C6
　TOTM N17 ... 50 C5
　WEA W13 ... 116 C2
　WLGTN SM6 ... 210 C4
Carew St CMBW SE5 ... 142 D3
Carew Wy OXHEY WD19 ... 27 K5
　STMC/STPC BR5 ... 202 D5
Carey Ct DAGW RM9 ... 92 A2
Carey Gdns VX/NE SW8 ... 141 H4
Carey La CITYW EC2V ... 12 C3
Carey Pl PIM SW1V ... 16 C7
Carey Rd DAGW RM9 ... 92 A2
Carey St LINN WC2A ... 11 H4
Carey Wy WBLY HA9 ... 80 D2
Carfax Pl CLAP SW4 ... 141 J5
Carfax Rd HCH RM12 ... 93 H2
　HYS/HAR UB3 ... 113 K5
Carfree Cl IS N1 ... 85 G5
Cargill Rd WAND/EARL SW18 ... 160 B3
Cargreen Rd SNWD SE25 ... 197 G1
Carholme Rd FSTH SE23 ... 164 C3
Carisbrook Cl EN EN1 ... 24 B2
Carisbrooke Av BXLY DA5 ... 168 E3
Carisbrooke Cl HSLWW TW4 ... 154 D3
　STAN HA7 ... 43 K5
Carisbrooke Gdns
　PECK SE15 * ... 143 G1
Carisbrooke Rd HAYES BR2 ... 195 K1
　MTCM CR4 ... 195 J1
　WALTH E17 ... 69 G1
Carker's La ARCH N19 ... 66 D4
Carleton Av WLGTN SM6 ... 210 D6
Carleton Cl ESH/CLAY KT10 ... 189 J5
Carleton Gdns ARCH N19 * ... 84 C3
Carleton Rd HOLWY N7 ... 84 D2
Carleton Vls KTTN NW1 * ... 84 D5
Carlile Cl BOW E3 ... 105 H1
Carlina Gdns WFD IG8 ... 53 F1
Carlingford Gdns
　MRDN SM4 ... 193 C3
Carlingford Rd HAMP NW3 ... 83 G2
　MRDN SM4 ... 193 G3
　SEVS/STOTM N15 ... 49 K5
Carlisle Av ACT W3 ... 99 G5
　TWRH EC3N ... 13 J4
Carlisle Cl KUTN/CMB KT2 ... 175 H4
　PIN HA5 ... 59 J4
Carlisle Gdns KTN/HRWW/WS HA3 ... 61 K4
　IL IG1 ... 71 J3
Carlisle La STHWK SE1 ... 17 H4
Carlisle Ms CDALE/KGS NW9 * ... 63 F3
　MBLAR W1H ... 8 C2
Carlisle Pl FBAR/BDGN N11 ... 34 B6
　WEST SW1P ... 16 A5
Carlisle Rd CDALE/KGS NW9 ... 62 E1
　FSBYPK N4 ... 67 G5
　HPTN TW12 ... 173 G3
　KIL/WHAMP NW6 ... 82 B6
　LEY E10 ... 69 J5
　ROM RM1 ... 75 H2
　SUT SM1 ... 208 C4
Carlisle St SOHO/SHAV W1D ... 10 C4
Carlisle Wk HACK E8 ... 86 B4
Carlisle Wy TOOT SW17 ... 179 F1
Carlos Pl MYFR/PKLN W1K ... 9 H5
Carlow St CAMTN NW1 ... 4 A2
Carlton Av EBED/NFELT TW14 ... 154 A1
　HYS/HAR UB3 ... 113 H4
　KTN/HRWW/WS HA3 ... 61 H2
　SAND/SEL CR2 ... 211 K5
　STHGT/OAK N14 ... 22 D6
Carlton Av East WBLY HA9 ... 61 K6
Carlton Av West
　ALP/SUD HA0 ... 61 H6
Carlton Cl CHSGTN KT9 ... 205 K4
　EDGW HA8 ... 44 C1
　HAMP NW3 ... 82 D6
Carlton Crs CHEAM SM3 ... 208 C2
Carlton Dene BAR/HLT IG6 ... 207 K3 -- Carlton Dr BARK/HLT IG6
　PUT/ROE SW15 ... 139 G6
Carlton Gdns EA W5 ... 97 J5
　STHGT/OAK N14 ... 34 A4
Carlton Ga MV/WKIL W9 ... 100 E4
Carlton Gn SCUP DA14 * ... 168 A6
Carlton Gv PECK SE15 ... 143 J2
Carlton Hl STJWD NW8 ... 101 G1
Carlton House Ter STJS SW1Y ... 16 C1
Carlton Ms
　KIL/WHAMP NW6 ... 82 E3
Carlton Pde WBLY HA9 * ... 62 C5
Carlton Park Av RYNPK SW20 ... 177 F5
Carlton Rd CHSWK W4 ... 118 A2
　EA W5 ... 97 J6
　ERITH DA8 ... 129 J6
　ERITH DA8 ... 129 K6
　FBAR/BDGN N11 ... 48 A1
　FSBYPK N4 ... 67 G4
　GPK RM2 ... 75 J2
　MNPK E12 ... 89 H2
　MORT/ESHN SW14 ... 137 K4
　NWMAL KT3 ... 176 B5
　SAND/SEL CR2 ... 212 A5
　SCUP DA14 ... 168 B5
　WALTH E17 ... 51 F6
　WAN E11 ... 70 D5
　WELL DA16 ... 148 C4
　WOT/HER KT12 ... 188 A4
Carlton Sq WCHPL E1 * ... 105 F3
Carlton St STJS SW1Y ... 10 C6

Carlton Ter SYD SE26 ... 163 K6
　UED N18 ... 35 K6
　WAN E11 ... 71 F2
Carlton Tower Pl KTBR SW1X ... 15 F4
Carlton V KIL/WHAMP NW6 ... 100 E1
Carlwell St TOOT SW17 ... 178 D1
Carlyle Av BMLY BR1 ... 184 C6
　STHL UB1 ... 95 K6
Carlyle Cl WBPTN SW10 ... 140 B2
　EFNCH N2 ... 65 G5
　WLSDN NW10 ... 81 F6
Carlyle Gdns STHL UB1 ... 95 K6
Carlyle Pl PUT/ROE SW15 ... 139 G5
Carlyle Rd CROY/NA CR0 ... 197 H6
　EA W5 ... 116 D4
　MNPK E12 ... 89 J2
　THMD SE28 ... 109 H6
Carlyle Sq CHEL SW3 ... 120 C5
Carlyon Av RYLN/HDSTN HA2 ... 77 K2
Carlyon Cl ALP/SUD HA0 ... 80 A6
Carlyon Rd ALP/SUD HA0 ... 98 A1
　YEAD UB4 ... 95 G4
Carlys Cl BECK BR3 ... 182 A5
Carmarthen Gn PUT/ROE SW15 ... 139 F5
Carmel Ct KENS W8 * ... 120 A2
Carmelite Rd
　KTN/HRWW/WS HA3 ... 42 C4
Carmelite St EMB EC4Y ... 11 K5
Carmel Wy RCH/KEW TW9 ... 137 H5
Carmen St POP/IOD E14 ... 105 K5
Carmichael Cl BTSEA SW11 ... 140 C4
　RSLP HA4 ... 76 E2
Carmichael Ms
　WAND/EARL SW18 ... 160 C2
Carminia Rd TOOT SW17 ... 161 G4
Carnaby St SOHO/CST W1F ... 10 A4
Carnac St WNWD SE27 ... 162 E6
Carnarvon Rd WALTH E17 ... 52 B4
　BAR EN5 ... 24 B3
　SRTFD E15 ... 88 D4
Carnarvon Av EN EN1 ... 24 C4
Carnarvon Dr HYS/HAR UB3 ... 113 F3
Carnarvon Rd BAR EN5 ... 20 C4
　LEY E10 ... 70 A3
　SRTFD E15 ... 88 D4
　WFD IG8 ... 52 D4
Carnation St ABYW SE2 ... 128 C5
Carnbrook Rd BKHTH/KID SE3 ... 146 C4
Carnecke Gdns
　ELTH/MOT SE9 ... 146 D6
Carnegie Cl PEND EN3 ... 25 K1
　SURB KT6 ... 191 G6
Carnegie Pl WIM/MER SW19 ... 159 G5
Carnegie St IS N1 ... 5 G1
Carnet Cl DART DA1 ... 170 D2
Carnforth Cl HOR/WEW KT19 ... 206 D4
Carnforth Gdns HCH RM12 ... 93 J3
Carnforth Rd
　STRHM/NOR SW16 ... 179 J3
Carnoustie Dr IS N1 ... 85 F5
Carnoustie Cl THMD SE28 ... 109 K5
Carnwath Rd FUL/PGN SW6 ... 139 K4
Carol Cl HDN NW4 ... 64 B1
Carolina Cl SRTFD E15 ... 88 C3
Carolina Rd THHTH CR7 ... 180 C5
Caroline Cl CROY/NA CR0 ... 212 A2
　ISLW TW7 ... 135 J1
　MUSWH N10 ... 48 B5
　STRHM/NOR SW16 ... 162 A5
　WDR/YW UB7 ... 112 A2
Caroline Ct STAN HA7 * ... 43 G2
　PECK SE15 * ... 143 J1
Caroline Gdns BETH E2 ... 7 G4
Caroline Pl BAY/PAD W2 ... 101 F6
　BTSEA SW11 ... 141 F3
　HYS/HAR UB3 ... 133 H1
　OXHEY WD19 ... 27 J2
Caroline Rd WIM/MER SW19 ... 177 J3
Caroline St WCHPL E1 ... 105 F5
Caroline Ter BGVA SW1W ... 15 G7
Caroline Wk HMSMTH W6 ... 119 H6
Carol St CAMTN NW1 ... 84 C6
Carolyn Dr ORP BR6 ... 217 G1
Carpenders Av OXHEY WD19 ... 27 J3
Carpenter Cl HOR/WEW KT19 ... 207 H6
Carpenter Gdns WCHMH N21 ... 35 H4
Carpenter's Cl BAR EN5 ... 33 F1
Carpenters Ms HOLWY N7 ... 84 E3
Carpenters Pl CLAP SW4 ... 141 J5
Carpenters PI SRTFD E15 ... 88 A5
Carpenter St
　MYFR/PKLN W1K ... 9 J6
Carrara Ms HACK E8 ... 86 C3
Carrara Whf FUL/PGN SW6 ... 139 H4
Carr Gv WOOL/PLUM SE18 ... 126 D5
Carriage Dr East CHEL SW3 ... 121 F6
Carriage Dr North
　BTSEA SW11 ... 140 E1
Carriage Dr South
　BTSEA SW11 ... 140 E2
Carriage Dr West
　BTSEA SW11 ... 140 E1
Carriage Ms IL IG1 ... 72 C6
Carrick Cl ISLW TW7 ... 136 B4
Carrick Dr BARK/HLT IG6 ... 54 D4
Carrick Gdns TOTM N17 ... 50 A3
Carrick Ga ESH/CLAY KT10 ... 204 C1
Carrick Ms DEPT SE8 ... 124 D6
Carrill Wy BELV DA17 ... 128 E4
Carrington Av HSLW TW3 ... 135 G6
Carrington Cl CROY/NA CR0 ... 198 B4
　BAR EN5 ... 31 K1
Carrington Gdns FSTGT E7 ... 88 E2
Carrington Pl
　ESH/CLAY KT10 ... 204 B2
Carrington Rd
　RCHPK/HAM TW10 ... 137 H5
Carrington Sq
　KTN/HRWW/WS HA3 ... 42 C3
Carrington St
　MYFR/PICC W1J ... 15 J1
Carrol Cl KTTN NW5 ... 84 B2
Carroll Cl SRTFD E15 ... 88 D3
Carronade Pl THMD SE28 ... 127 H3
Carron Cl POP/IOD E14 ... 105 K5
Carroun Rd VX/NE SW8 ... 142 A1
Carroway La GFD/PVL UB6 ... 96 D2
Carrow Rd DAGW RM9 ... 91 H5

Carr Rd NTHLT UB5 78 B5
WALTH E17 51 J5
Carrs La WCHMH N21 23 K6
Carr St POP/IOD E14 105 G4
Carshalton Gv SUT SM1 209 H2
Carshalton Park Rd CAR SM5 209 K4
Carshalton Pl CAR SM5 210 A2
Carshalton Rd MTCM CR4 195 F2
SUT SM1 209 G3
Carslake Rd PUT/ROE SW15 159 F1
Carson Rd CAN/RD E16 106 E4
DUL SE21 162 D4
EBAR EN4 21 K5
Carstairs Rd CAT SE6 165 F5
Carston Cl LEE/GVPK SE12 145 J6
Carswell Cl REDBR IG4 71 H1
Carswell Rd CAT SE6 165 F2
Carter Cl CDALE/KGS NW9 63 F3
CRW RM5 56 D3
WLGTN SM6 210 D5
Carter Dr CRW RM5 56 D2
Carteret St STJSPK SW1H 16 C3
Carteret Wy DEPT SE8 124 B4
Carterhatch La EN EN1 24 B2
Carterhatch Rd PEND EN3 25 G3
Carter La BLKFR EC4V 12 B4
Carter Pl WALW SE17 122 D5
Carter Rd PLSTW E13 89 F6
WIM/MER SW19 178 C2
Carters Cl KTTN NW5 * 84 D4
WPK KT4 193 G6
Carters Hill Cl ELTH/MOT SE9 166 B3
Carter St WALW SE17 122 D6
Carters Yd
WAND/EARL SW18 * 139 K6
Carthew Rd HMSMTH W6 118 E3
Carthew Vls HMSMTH W6 118 E3
Carthusian St FARR EC1M 12 C1
Carting La TPL/STR WC2R 11 F6
Cart La CHING E4 38 B3
Cartmel Cl TOTM N17 50 D3
Cartmel Ct NTHLT UB5 77 J4
Cartmel Gdns MRDN SM4 194 B2
Cartwright Gdns
STPAN WC1H 4 D5
Cartwright St WCHPL E1 13 K5
Cartwright Wy BARN SW13 138 E1
Carver Cl CHSWK W4 117 K3
Carver Rd HNHL SE24 162 D1
Carville Crs BTFD TW8 117 F4
Cary Rd WAN E11 88 C2
Carysfort Rd CEND/HSY/T N8 66 D2
STNW/STAM N16 85 K1
Cascade Av MUSWH N10 66 C1
Cascade Cl STMC/STPC BR5 186 D6
Cascade Rd BKHH IG9 39 H4
Casella Rd NWCR SE14 144 A1
Casewick Rd WNWD SE27 180 C1
Casey Cl STJWD NW8 2 C5
Casimir Rd CLPT E5 86 D1
Casino Av HNHL SE24 142 D6
Caspian St CMBW SE5 142 E1
Caspian Wk CAN/RD E16 107 H5
Cassandra Cl NTHLT UB5 78 D2
Casselden Rd WLSDN NW10 81 F5
Cassidy Rd FUL/PGN SW6 139 K1
Cassilda Rd ABYW SE2 128 B4
Cassilis Rd POP/IOD E14 124 D2
TWK TW1 156 C1
Cassiobury Av
EBED/NFELT TW14 153 J2
Cassiobury Rd WALTH E17 69 F2
Cassland Rd HOM E9 87 F5
THHTH CR7 196 E1
Casslee Rd CAT SE6 164 C2
Casson St WCHPL E1 104 C4
Castellain Rd MV/WKIL W9 101 F3
Castellan Av GPK RM2 57 K6
Castellane Cl STAN HA7 43 F3
Castello Av PUT/ROE SW15 139 F6
Castelnau BARN SW13 138 E1
Casterton St HACK E8 86 D4
Castile Rd WOOL/PLUM SE18 127 F4
Castillon Rd CAT SE6 165 H4
Castlands Rd CAT SE6 164 C4
Castle Av CHING E4 52 B1
EW KT17 207 J6
RAIN RM13 93 G5
Castlebar Hl WEA W13 97 H4
Castlebar Ms EA W5 97 H4
Castlebar Pk EA W5 97 H4
Castlebar Rd WEA W13 97 J5
Castle Baynard St
BLKFR EC4V 12 B5
Castlebrook Cl LBTH SE11 18 A6
Castle Cl ACT W3 117 J2
BUSH WD23 28 B1
HAYES BR2 183 H6
WIM/MER SW19 159 G5
Castlecombe Dr
WIM/MER SW19 159 G2
Castlecombe Rd
ELTH/MOT SE9 184 D1
Castle Ct BANK EC3V * 13 F4
SYD SE26 164 B6
Castledine Rd PGE/AN SE20 181 J3
Castle Dr REDBR IG4 71 J3
Castleford Av ELTH/MOT SE9 167 G3
Castleford Cl TOTM N17 50 B2
Castlegate RCH/KEW TW9 137 G4
Castlehaven Rd CAMTN NW1 84 B5
Castle Hill Av CROY/NA CR0 213 K6
Castle Hill Pde WEA W13 * 97 H6
Castle La WESTW SW1E 16 A4
Castleleigh Ct ENC/FH EN2 23 K6
Castlemaine Av EW KT17 207 K6
SAND/SEL CR2 212 B3
Castlemaine St WCHPL E1 104 D4
Castle Md CMBW SE5 * 142 D1
Castle Ms CAMTN NW1 84 B4
NFNCH/WDSPK N12 47 G1
TOOT SW17 160 D6
Castle Pde EW KT17 * 207 J5
Castle Pl CAMTN NW1 84 B4
Castlereagh St MBLAR W1H 8 E3
Castle Rd CAMTN NW1 84 B4
DAGW RM9 91 H6
ISLW TW7 136 A3
NFNCH/WDSPK N12 47 G1
NTHLT UB5 78 B4
NWDGN UB2 * 114 E3
PEND EN3 25 G2
Castle Rw CHSWK W4 * 118 A5
Castle St EHAM E6 107 G1
KUT/HW KT1 * 175 F5
Castleton Av BXLYHN DA7 150 A2
WBLY HA9 80 A2
Castleton Cl CROY/NA CR0 198 B3
Castleton Gdns WBLY HA9 80 A1
Castleton Rd ELTH/MOT SE9 166 C6
GDMY/SEVK IG3 73 H5
MTCM CR4 195 J1
RSLP HA4 59 H5
WALTH E17 52 B5
Castletown Rd WKENS W14 119 H5
Castleview Cl FSBYPK N4 67 J5
Castleview Gdns IL IG1 71 J3
Castle Vls CRICK NW2 * 81 J4
Castle Wk SUN TW16 * 172 B6
Castle Wy FELT TW13 154 B6
WIM/MER SW19 159 G5
Castlewood Dr
ELTH/MOT SE9 146 E3
Castlewood Rd EBAR EN4 21 H4
STNW/STAM N16 68 C3
Castle Yd HGT N6 * 66 A4
RCH/KEW TW9 136 E6
STHWK SE1 * 12 B7
Castor La POP/IOD E14 105 K6
Catalina Rd HTHAIR TW6 132 E4
Catalpa Ct LEW SE13 165 G1
Caterham Av CLAY IG5 54 A5
Caterham Rd LEW SE13 145 F4
Catesby St WALW SE17 19 F7
Catford Broadway CAT SE6 164 E2
Catford Hl CAT SE6 164 C3
Catford Island CAT SE6 * 164 E2
Catford Rd CAT SE6 164 D3
Cathall Rd WAN E11 88 C1
Cathay St BERM/RHTH SE16 123 J2
Cathcart Dr ORP BR6 201 K6
Cathcart Hl ARCH N19 84 C1
Cathcart Rd WBPTN SW10 * 120 A6
Cathcart St KTTN NW5 84 B4
Cathedral St STHWK SE1 12 E7
Catherall Rd HBRY N5 85 J1
Catherine Cl LOU IG10 39 K1
Catherine Ct STHGT/OAK N14 22 C6
Catherine Dr RCH/KEW TW9 137 F5
Catherine Gdns HSLW TW3 135 J5
Catherine Griffiths Ct
CLKNW EC1R 5 K6
Catherine Gv GNWCH SE10 144 E2
Catherine Pl HRW HA1 61 F2
WESTW SW1E 16 A4
Catherine Rd GPK RM2 75 K2
SURB KT6 190 E2
Catherines Cl WDR/YW UB7 * 112 A2
Catherine St HOL/ALD WC2B * 11 G5
Catherine Vls RYNPK SW20 * 176 E3
Catherine Wheel Aly
LVPST EC2M 13 H2
Catherine Wheel Rd
BTFD TW8 136 E1
Catherine Wheel Yd
WHALL SW1A 16 A1
Cat Hl EBAR EN4 33 J1
Cathles Rd BAL SW12 161 G1
Cathnor Rd SHB W12 118 E2
Catling Cl FSTH SE23 163 K5
Catlin's La PIN HA5 41 F6
Catlin St BERM/RHTH SE16 123 H5
Cator La BECK BR3 182 C5
Cato Rd CLAP SW4 141 J4
Cator Rd CAR SM5 209 K3
SYD SE26 182 A2
Cator St PECK SE15 123 G6
Cato St MBLAR W1H 8 D2
Catsey La BUSH WD23 28 C2
Catsey Wd BUSH WD23 28 C2
Catterick Cl FBAR/BDGN N11 48 A2
Cattistock Rd ELTH/MOT SE9 184 D1
Cattley Cl BAR EN5 20 C5
Catton St RSQ WC1B 11 G2
Caudwell Ter
WAND/EARL SW18 * 160 C1
Caulfield Rd EHAM E6 89 K5
PECK SE15 143 J3
Causeway EBED/NFELT TW14 134 A5
The Causeway BELMT SM2 209 G6
CAR SM5 210 A1
CHSGTN KT9 206 A2
EFNCH N2 65 H1
ESH/CLAY KT10 205 F5
TEDD TW11 174 A2
WAND/EARL SW18 140 A5
WIM/MER SW19 177 F1
Causeyware Rd ED N9 36 D2
Causton Cots POP/IOD E14 * 105 G4
Causton Rd HGT N6 * 66 B4
Causton Sq DAGE RM10 92 C5
Causton St WEST SW1P 16 D7
Cautley Av CLAP SW4 141 H6
Cavalier Cl CHDH RM6 73 J1
Cavalier Gdns HYS/HAR UB3 94 B5
Cavalry Crs HSLWW TW4 134 C5
Cavalry Gdns PUT/ROE SW15 139 H6
Cavan Pl PIN HA5 * 41 K4
Cavaye Pl WBPTN SW10 120 B5
Cavell Crs DART DA1 151 K5
Cavell Dr ENC/FH EN2 23 G3
Cavell Rd TOTM N17 49 K3
Cavell St WCHPL E1 104 D4
Cavendish Av BFN/LL DA15 168 B2
ERITH DA8 129 K6
FNCH N3 46 E5
HCH RM12 93 K4
HRW HA1 78 D2
NWMAL KT3 192 E2
RSLP HA4 77 F3
STJWD NW8 2 B3
WEA W13 97 G4
WELL DA16 148 A4
WFD IG8 53 F3
Cavendish Cl
KIL/WHAMP NW6 82 D4
STJWD NW8 2 B4
UED N18 * 50 D1
YEAD UB4 94 C4
Cavendish Crs HCH RM12 93 K4
Cavendish Dr EDGW HA8 44 B2
ESH/CLAY KT10 204 E3
WAN E11 70 B5
Cavendish Gdns BARK IG11 91 F3
CHDH RM6 74 A2
CLAP SW4 * 161 H1
IL IG1 72 A5
Cavendish Ms SUT SM1 194 B6
Cavendish Ms North
GTPST W1W 9 K1
Cavendish Ms South
GTPST W1W * 9 K2
Cavendish Pde CLAP SW4 * 141 H5
HSLWW TW4 * 134 D3
Cavendish Pl BMLY BR1 184 E6
CAVSQ/HST W1G 9 K3
CRICK NW2 82 B4
Cavendish Rd BAL SW12 161 H3
BAR EN5 20 A4
BELMT SM2 209 G5
CHING E4 52 A2
CHSWK W4 137 K2
CLAP SW4 161 G1
CROY/NA CR0 196 C5
FSBYPK N4 67 H3
KIL/WHAMP NW6 82 C5
NWMAL KT3 192 C2
UED N18 50 D1
WIM/MER SW19 178 D3
Cavendish Sq
CAVSQ/HST W1G 9 K3
Cavendish St IS N1 6 E3
Cavendish Ter BOW E3 * 105 H2
FELT TW13 * 153 K4
Cavendish Wy WWKM BR4 198 E5
Cavenham Gdns IL IG1 90 D1
Caverleigh Wy WPK KT4 192 D5
Caverley Gdns
KTN/HRWW/WS HA3 61 K4
Cave Rd PLSTW E13 107 F1
RCHPK/HAM TW10 156 D6
Caversham Av CHEAM SM3 193 H6
PLMGR N13 35 G5
Caversham Flats CHEL SW3 * 120 E6
Caversham Rd KTTN NW5 * 84 C4
KUT/HW KT1 175 G5
SEVS/STOTM N15 67 J1
Caversham St CHEL SW3 120 E6
Caverswall St SHB W12 100 A5
Cawdor Crs HNWL W7 116 B4
Cawnpore St NRWD SE19 181 F1
Caxton Gv BOW E3 105 J2
Caxton Ms BTFD TW8 116 D6
Caxton Rd NWDGN UB2 114 C3
SHB W12 119 G1
WDGN N22 49 F5
WIM/MER SW19 178 B1
The Caxtons BRXN/ST SW9 * 142 C1
Caxton St STJSPK SW1H 16 B4
Caxton St North CAN/RD E16 106 D5
Caxton Wy ROM RM1 75 G1
WATW WD18 26 B2
Cayenne Ct STHWK SE1 19 J1
Caygill Cl HAYES BR2 199 J1
Cayley Rd NWDGN UB2 115 G3
Cayton Rd GFD/PVL UB6 96 E1
Cayton St FSBYE EC1V 6 E5
Cazenove Rd
STNW/STAM N16 68 B6
WALTH E17 51 J4
Cecil Av BARK IG11 90 D5
EN EN1 24 B5
WBLY HA9 80 B3
Cecil Cl CHSGTN KT9 205 K2
EA W5 * 97 K4
Cecil Ct BAR EN5 20 B4
LSQ/SEVD WC2H 10 D6
Cecile Pk CEND/HSY/T N8 66 E3
Cecilia Cl EFNCH N2 47 G6
Cecilia Rd HACK E8 86 B3
Cecil Manning Cl
GFD/PVL UB6 79 G6
Cecil Pk PIN HA5 59 J1
Cecil Pl MTCM CR4 194 E2
Cecil Rd ACT W3 98 E4
CDALE/KGS NW9 45 F6
CHDH RM6 73 K4
CROY/NA CR0 195 K3
ENC/FH EN2 23 K5
HSLW TW3 135 H4
IL IG1 90 B2
KTN/HRWW/WS HA3 42 E6
MUSWH N10 48 B5
PLSTW E13 88 E6
STHGT/OAK N14 34 B3
SUT SM1 208 D4
WALTH E17 51 J4
WAN E11 70 C6
WIM/MER SW19 178 A3
WLSDN NW10 81 G6
Cedar Av BFN/LL DA15 168 B2
CHDH RM6 74 A2
EBAR EN4 33 J2
HYS/HAR UB3 94 E5
PEND EN3 24 E3
RSLP HA4 77 G3
WDR/YW UB7 * 112 C1
WHTN TW2 155 G1
Cedar Cl BKHH IG9 39 H4
BOW E3 87 H6
CAR SM5 209 K4
DUL SE21 162 D3
HAYES BR2 215 J1
IL IG1 90 D3
KUTN/CMB KT2 158 A6
ROMW/RG RM7 74 E1
SWLY BR8 187 K5
Cedar Copse BMLY BR1 184 E5
Cedar Ct CHARL SE7 * 126 B6
ELTH/MOT SE9 * 166 D1
WIM/MER SW19 159 G5
Cedar Crs HAYES BR2 215 J1
Cedarcroft Rd CHSGTN KT9 206 B2
Cedar Dr EFNCH N2 65 J1
GLDGN NW11 64 E1
PIN HA5 42 A2
Cedar Gdns BELMT SM2 209 G4
Cedar Gv BXLY DA5 168 E1
EA W5 116 E3
STHL UB1 96 A4
Cedar Hts RCHPK/HAM TW10 157 F3
Cedarhurst BMLY BR1 * 183 H3
Cedarhurst Dr ELTH/MOT SE9 146 B6
Cedar Lawn Av BAR EN5 20 C6
Cedar Mt ELTH/MOT SE9 166 C3
Cedarne Rd FUL/PGN SW6 139 K1
Cedar Park Gdns CHDH RM6 73 K4
WIM/MER SW19 176 E1
Cedar Park Rd ENC/FH EN2 23 J1
Cedar Pl CHARL SE7 126 B5
Cedar Ri STHGT/OAK N14 34 A2
Cedar Rd BELMT SM2 209 G4
BMLY BR1 184 B5
CRICK NW2 82 A2
CROY/NA CR0 197 F6
E/WMO/HCT KT8 189 K1
EBED/NFELT TW14 153 G3
ENC/FH EN2 23 H1
ERITH DA8 150 D2
HSLWW TW4 134 B3
OXHEY WD19 27 G1
ROMW/RG RM7 74 E1
TEDD TW11 174 B1
TOTM N17 50 B4
Cedars Av MTCM CR4 195 F1
WALTH E17 69 J2
Cedars Cl HDN NW4 46 B6
LEW SE13 145 G4
Cedars Cots PUT/ROE SW15 * 158 D1
Cedars Ct ED N9 36 A4
Cedars Ms CLAP SW4 * 141 G5
Cedars Rd BARN SW13 138 C3
BECK BR3 182 B5
CHSWK W4 117 K6
CLAP SW4 141 G4
CROY/NA CR0 210 E1
ED N9 36 C4
KUT/HW KT1 174 D4
MRDN SM4 193 K1
SRTFD E15 88 C4
WCHMH N21 35 H4
The Cedars BKHH IG9 38 E3
HOM E9 * 87 F5
SRTFD E15 * 88 D6
TEDD TW11 174 A2
Cedar Ter RCH/KEW TW9 137 F5
Cedar Tree Gv WNWD SE27 180 C1
Cedarville Gdns
STRHM/NOR SW16 180 A2
Cedar Wk ESH/CLAY KT10 205 F4
Cedar Wy CAMTN NW1 84 D5
Cedric Av ROM RM1 57 G6
Cedric Rd ELTH/MOT SE9 167 H5
Celadon Cl PEND EN3 25 G4
Celandine Cl POP/IOD E14 105 J4
Celandine Dr HACK E8 86 B5
THMD SE28 128 C1
Celandine Gv STHGT/OAK N14 22 C6
Celandine Wy SRTFD E15 106 C2
Celbridge Ms BAY/PAD W2 * 101 F5
Celestial Gdns LEW SE13 145 G5
Celia Rd ARCH N19 84 C2
Celtic Av HAYES BR2 183 H6
Celtic St POP/IOD E14 105 K4
Cemetery La CHARL SE7 126 D6
Cemetery Rd ABYW SE2 128 C6
FSTGT E7 88 D3
TOTM N17 50 A3
Cenacle Cl HAMP NW3 82 E1
Centaur Ct BTFD TW8 * 117 F5
Centaur St STHWK SE1 17 H4
Centenary Rd PEND EN3 25 H5
Centenary Wk CHING E4 52 C1
LOU IG10 39 F1
MNPK E12 89 H1
WALTH E17 52 C6
WAN E11 70 C1
WFD IG8 52 C3
Centennial Av BORE WD6 29 H2
Centennial Pk BORE WD6 * 29 J2
Central Ar ASHF TW15 * 152 C6
Central Av E/WMO/HCT KT8 188 E2
ED N9 36 A5
EFNCH N2 47 H5
EN EN1 24 C3
HSLW TW3 135 H5
HYS/HAR UB3 113 J2
PIN HA5 59 K3
WAN E11 70 B6
WELL DA16 148 B3
WLGTN SM6 210 E3
Central Blds EA W5 * 97 K6
Central Circ HDN NW4 63 K2
Central Ct CHIG IG7 54 E1
Central Hall Blds ARCH N19 * 66 C6
Central Hl NRWD SE19 180 D1
Central Pde ACT W3 * 117 H2
BFN/LL DA15 * 168 B5
E/WMO/HCT KT8 * 188 E1
GFD/PVL UB6 * 97 G2
HRW HA1 61 F2
PEND EN3 * 24 E3
PGE/AN SE20 * 182 A3
STRHM/NOR SW16 * 161 K6
SURB KT6 * 191 F3
WALTH E17 * 69 J1
Central Park Av DAGE RM10 92 D1
Central Park Est
HSLWW TW4 * 134 C5
Central Park Rd EHAM E6 107 H1
Central Pl SNWD SE25 * 197 H1
Central Rd ALP/SUD HA0 79 H3
DART DA1 151 H5
MRDN SM4 194 A2
WPK KT4 192 D6
Central Sq E/WMO/HCT KT8 188 E1
GLDGN NW11 64 E3
Central St FSBYE EC1V 6 C4
Central Ter BECK BR3 * 182 A6
Central Wy CAR SM5 209 J5
EBED/NFELT TW14 134 A6
NTHWD HA6 40 C3
THMD SE28 109 G6
WLSDN NW10 98 E2
Centre Av ACT W3 118 A1
Centre Common Rd
CHST BR7 185 H3
Centre Rd DAGE RM10 110 D1
WAN E11 70 E6
Centre St BETH E2 104 D1
Centre Wy ED N9 36 E4
Centric Cl CAMTN NW1 * 84 B6
Centurian Sq
WOOL/PLUM SE18 146 D2
Centurian Wy ERITHM DA18 129 G3
Centurion Cl HOLWY N7 85 F5
Centurion Ct WLGTN SM6 * 195 G6
Centurion La BOW E3 105 H1
Centurion Sq CHARL SE7 * 146 D1
Century Cl HDN NW4 64 B2
Century Ct WATW WD18 * 26 A2
Century Ms CLPT E5 * 86 E2
Century Rd WALTH E17 51 G6
Cephas Av WCHPL E1 104 E3
Cephas St WCHPL E1 104 E3
Ceres Rd WOOL/PLUM SE18 128 A4
Cerise Rd PECK SE15 143 H2
Cerne Cl YEAD UB4 95 G6
Cerne Rd MRDN SM4 194 B3
Cerney Ms BAY/PAD W2 8 A5
Cervantes Ct BAY/PAD W2 * 101 F5
NTHWD HA6 40 D3
Ceylon Rd WKENS W14 119 G3
Chabot Dr PECK SE15 143 J4
Chadacre Av CLAY IG5 53 K6
Chadacre Rd EW KT17 207 K3
Chadbourn St POP/IOD E14 105 K4
Chad Crs ED N9 36 E5
Chadd Dr BMLY BR1 184 D6
Chadville Gdns CHDH RM6 73 K2
Chadway BCTR RM8 73 J6
Chadwell Av CHDH RM6 73 H4
Chadwell Heath La
CHDH RM6 73 H1
Chadwell La CEND/HSY/T N8 49 F6
Chadwell St CLKNW EC1R 5 K4
Chadwick Av CHING E4 38 B6
WCHMH N21 * 23 F6
WIM/MER SW19 177 K2
Chadwick Cl PUT/ROE SW15 158 C
TEDD TW11 174 B
Chadwick Pl SURB KT6 190 D
Chadwick Rd IL IG1 90 B
PECK SE15 143 G
WAN E11 70 C
WLSDN NW10 81 H
Chadwick St WEST SW1P 16 C
Chadwick Wy THMD SE28 109 K
Chadwin Rd PLSTW E13 107 F
Chadworth Wy
ESH/CLAY KT10 204 D
Chaffinch Av CROY/NA CR0 198 A
Chaffinch Cl CROY/NA CR0 198 A
ED N9 37 F
SURB KT6 206 C
Chaffinch Ct ORP BR6 202 E
Chaffinch La WATW WD18 26 D
Chaffinch Rd BECK BR3 182 E
Chafford Wy CHDH RM6 73
Chagford St CAMTN NW1 2
Chailey Av EN EN1 24
Chailey Cl HEST TW5 134
Chailey St CLPT E5 86
Chalbury Wk IS N1 5
Chalcombe Rd ABYW SE2 128
Chalcot Cl BELMT SM2 208
Chalcot Crs CAMTN NW1 83
Chalcot Gdns HAMP NW3 83
Chalcot Ms STRHM/NOR SW16 161
Chalcot Rd CAMTN NW1 84
Chalcot Sq CAMTN NW1 84
Chalcott Gdns SURB KT6 * 190
Chalcroft Rd LEW SE13 145
Chaldon Rd FUL/PGN SW6 139
Chale Rd BRXS/STRHM SW2 161
Chalet Est MLHL NW7 * 31
Chalfont Av WBLY HA9 80
Chalfont Gn ED N9 36
Chalfont Ms
WAND/EARL SW18 159
Chalfont Rd ED N9 36
HYS/HAR UB3 113
SNWD SE25 181
Chalfont Wk PIN HA5 * 41
Chalfont Wy WEA W13 116
Chalford Cl E/WMO/HCT KT8 189
Chalforde Gdns GPK RM2 75
Chalford Rd DUL SE21 162
Chalford Wk WFD IG8 53
Chalgrove Av MRDN SM4 193
Chalgrove Crs CLAY IG5 53
Chalgrove Gdns FNCH N3 46
Chalgrove Rd BELMT SM2 209
HACK E8 86
TOTM N17 50
Chalice Cl WLGTN SM6 210
Chalkenden Cl PGE/AN SE20 181
Chalk Farm Pde HAMP NW3 * 84
Chalk Farm Rd CAMTN NW1 84
Chalk Hl OXHEY WD19 27
Chalk Hill Rd HMSMTH W6 11
Chalkhill Rd WBLY HA9 8
Chalklands WBLY HA9 8
Chalk La EBAR EN4 2
Chalkley Cl MTCM CR4 17
Chalkmill Dr EN EN1 2
Chalk Pit Av STMC/STPC BR5 18
Chalk Pit Rd SUT SM1 20
Chalk Rd PLSTW E13 10
Chalkstone Cl WELL DA16 14
Chalkwell Park Av EN EN1 2
Chalky La CHSGTN KT9 20
Challenge Cl WLSDN NW10 8
Challenge Rd ASHF TW15 15
Challice Wy
BRXS/STRHM SW2 16
Challin St PGE/AN SE20 18
Challis Rd BTFD TW8 1
Challoner Cl EFNCH N2
Challoner Crs WKENS W14 1
Challoners Cl
E/WMO/HCT KT8 1
Challoner St WKENS W14 1
Chalmers Rd ASHF TW15 1
Chalmers Rd East ASHF TW15 1
Chalmers Wk WALW SE17 *
Chalmers Wy
EBED/NFELT TW14 1
TWK TW1
Chalsey Rd BROCKY SE4 1

Chalton Dr EFNCH N2 65 G3
Chalton St CAMTN NW1 4 C2
Chamberlain Cl IL IG1 90 C1
THMD SE28 127 J3
Chamberlain Cots
CMBW SE5 * 142 E2
Chamberlain Crs WWKM BR4 198 E5
Chamberlain Gdns HSLW TW3 135 H2
Chamberlain La PIN HA5 58 E1
Chamberlain Pl WALTH E17 51 G6
Chamberlain Rd EFNCH N2 47 G5
WEA W13 116 B2
Chamberlain St
CAMTN NW1 * 83 K5
Chamberlain Wy PIN HA5 41 F6
SURB KT6 191 F4
Chamberlayne Av WBLY HA9 80 A1
Chamberlayne Rd
WLSDN NW10 82 A6
Chamberlens Garages
HMSMTH W6 * 118 E4
Chambers Av SCUP DA14 187 F2
Chambers Gdns EFNCH N2 47 H4
Chambers La WLSDN NW10 81 K5
Chambers Pl SAND/SEL CR2 211 K5
Chambers Rd HOLWY N7 84 E2
Chambers St
BERM/RHTH SE16 123 H2
Chamber St WCHPL E1 13 K5
Chambon Pl HMSMTH W6 118 D4
Chambord St BETH E2 7 K5
Champa Cl TOTM N17 50 B5
Champion Crs SYD SE26 164 B6
Champion Gv CMBW SE5 142 E4
Champion Hl CMBW SE5 142 E4
Champion Pk CMBW SE5 142 E4
Champion Rd SYD SE26 164 B6
Champness Cl WNWD SE27 162 E6
Champness Rd BARK IG11 91 F5
Champneys OXHEY WD19 * 27 J4
Champneys Cl BELMT SM2 208 D5
Chancellor Gdns
SAND/SEL CR2 211 H6
Chancellor Gv DUL SE21 162 D4
hancellor Pl
CDALE/KGS NW9 45 H5
hancellor's Rd HMSMTH W6 119 F5
hancellors St HMSMTH W6 119 F5
hancellors Whf
HMSMTH W6 119 F6
hancelot Rd ABYW SE2 128 C4
hancel St STHWK SE1 12 A7
hancery La BECK BR3 182 E5
LINN WC2A 11 H2
hance St BETH E2 7 J6
hanctonbury Cl
ELTH/MOT SE9 167 G5
hanctonbury Gdns
BELMT SM2 209 F5
hanctonbury Wy
NFNCH/WDSPK N12 32 E6
handler Av CAN/RD E16 106 E4
handler Cl HPTN TW12 172 E4
handlers Cl E/WMO/HCT KT8 189 G2
EBED/NFELT TW14 153 J2
andlers Ct
LEE/GVPK SE12 * 166 A4
andlers Ms POP/IOD E14 124 D2
andler St WAP E1W 123 J1
andlers Wy ROM RM1 75 G2
andler Wy PECK SE15 143 G1
andos Av EA W5 116 D4
STHGT/OAK N14 34 C5
TRDG/WHET N20 33 H3
WALTH E17 * 51 J5
andos Cl BKHH IG9 39 F4
andos Ct STAN HA7 43 H2
andos Crs EDGW HA8 44 B3
andos Pl CHCR WC2N 10 E6
andos Rd CRICK NW2 82 A3
EFNCH N2 47 H5
HRW HA1 60 C2
PIN HA5 59 G4
SRTFD E15 88 B3
TOTM N17 50 A5
WLSDN NW10 99 G3
andos St CAVSQ/HST W1G 9 K2
andos Wy GLDGN NW11 65 F5
annel Cl HEST TW5 135 F2
annel Gate Rd NKENS W10 100 A4
WLSDN NW10 99 G2
annel Islands Est IS N1 85 J4
annelsea Rd SRTFD E15 88 B6
antress Cl DAGE RM10 92 E6
antrey Cl SCUP DA14 187 F1
antrey Rd BRXN/ST SW9 142 A4
antry Cl BAR EN5 31 H1
ENC/FH EN2 23 J1
KTN/HRWW/WS HA3 62 B2
MLHL NW7 31 H2
MV/WKIL W9 * 100 D3
ntry Crs WLSDN NW10 81 G3
ntry La HAYES BR2 200 C2
ntry Pl
KTN/HRWW/WS HA3 42 B4
ntry Rd CHSGTN KT9 206 B3
KTN/HRWW/WS HA3 42 B4
ntry Sq KENS W8 * 120 A3
ntry St IS N1 6 B1
Chantry CHING E4 * 38 A3
ntry Wy MTCM CR4 178 C6
nt Sq SRTFD E15 * 88 B5
nt St SRTFD E15 88 B5
pel Av MNPK E12 89 H1
pel Cl WLSDN NW10 81 H3
pel Ct EFNCH N2 47 J6
THWK SE1 18 E2
OOL/PLUM SE18 128 A6
pel Farm Rd
TH/MOT SE9 166 E5
pel House St
OP/IOD E14 124 E5
pel La CHDH RM6 * 73 K4
N HA5 41 H6
el Market IS N1 5 J2
el Mill Rd KUT/HW KT1 175 G6
el Pl CAVSQ/HST W1G 9 J3
N1 5 K2
TM N17 50 B3
el Rd HSLW TW3 135 G4
IL IG1 90 A1
TWK TW1 156 C2
WEA W13 116 C1
WNWD SE27 162 C6
Chapel Side BAY/PAD W2 101 F6
Chapel St BAY/PAD W2 8 C2
ENC/FH EN2 23 J4
KTBR SW1X 15 H4
Chapel Vw SAND/SEL CR2 212 E5
Chaplemount Rd WFD IG8 * 53 K2
Chaplin Cl ALP/SUD HA0 * 79 K4
STHWK SE1 17 K2
Chaplin Rd ALP/SUD HA0 79 J4
CRICK NW2 81 J4
SRTFD E15 106 C1
TOTM N17 * 50 B6
Chapman Cl WDR/YW UB7 112 C3
Chapman Crs
KTN/HRWW/WS HA3 62 A2
Chapman Rd BELV DA17 129 H5
CROY/NA CR0 196 B5
HOM E9 87 H4
Chapmans Gn WDGN N22 * 49 G4
Chapman's La
STMC/STPC BR5 186 E5
Chapman Sq WIM/MER SW19 159 G4
Chapman St WCHPL E1 104 D6
Chapman Ter WDGN N22 * 49 H4
Chapter Cl CHSWK W4 117 K3
Chapter Rd CRICK NW2 81 J3
WALW SE17 122 C5
Chapter St WEST SW1P 16 C7
Chapter Wy HPTN TW12 155 F6
WIM/MER SW19 178 C4
Chara Pl CHSWK W4 118 A6
Charcroft Gdns PEND EN3 25 F5
Chardin Rd CHSWK W4 * 118 B4
Chardmore Rd
STNW/STAM N16 68 C5
Chardwell Cl EHAM E6 107 J5
Charecroft Wy WKENS W14 119 G2
Charford Rd CAN/RD E16 106 E4
Chargeable La PLSTW E13 106 E3
Chargeable St CAN/RD E16 106 D3
Chargrove Cl
BERM/RHTH SE16 124 A2
Charing Cl ORP BR6 217 F2
Charing Cross CHCR WC2N * 10 E7
Charing Cross Rd
LSQ/SEVD WC2H 10 D5
Chariot Cl BOW E3 87 J6
Charlbert St STJWD NW8 2 C2
Charlbury Av STAN HA7 43 K1
Charlbury Gdns
GDMY/SEVK IG3 73 F6
Charlbury Gv EA W5 97 J5
Charldane Rd ELTH/MOT SE9 167 G5
Charlecote Gv SYD SE26 163 J5
Charlecote Rd BCTR RM8 92 A1
Charlemont Rd EHAM E6 107 K2
Charles Babbage Cl
CHSGTN KT9 205 J5
Charles Barry Cl CLAP SW4 141 H4
Charles Cl SCUP DA14 168 C6
Charles Cobb Gdns
CROY/NA CR0 211 G3
Charles Coveney Rd
CMBW SE5 * 143 G2
Charles Crs HRW HA1 60 D4
Charles Dickens Ter
PGE/AN SE20 * 181 K3
Charlesfield ELTH/MOT SE9 166 B5
Charles Flemwell Ms
CAN/RD E16 * 125 K1
Charles Grinling Wk
WOOL/PLUM SE18 127 F4
Charles Haller St
BRXS/STRHM SW2 162 B2
Charles II Pl CHEL SW3 * 120 E5
Charles II St STJS SW1Y 10 C7
Charles La STJWD NW8 2 C3
Charles Pl CAMTN NW1 * 4 B5
Charles Rd CHDH RM6 73 K4
DAGE RM10 93 F4
FSTGT E7 89 G5
WEA W13 97 G5
WIM/MER SW19 177 K4
Charles Sevright Dr
MLHL NW7 46 B1
Charles Sq IS N1 7 F5
Charles Square Est IS N1 7 F5
Charles St BARN SW13 138 B4
CAN/RD E16 126 B1
CROY/NA CR0 211 J1
EN EN1 24 B6
HSLW TW3 134 E3
MYFR/PICC W1J 9 J7
Charleston Cl FELT TW13 153 K5
Charleston St WALW SE17 18 D7
Charles Whincup Rd
CAN/RD E16 126 A1
Charleville Circ SYD SE26 181 H1
Charleville Rd WKENS W14 119 H5
Charlmont Rd TOOT SW17 178 D2
Charlock Wy WATW WD18 26 D1
Charlotte Cl OXHEY WD19 27 G2
Charlotte Ct ESH/CLAY KT10 204 C3
Charlotte Despard Av
BTSEA SW11 141 G2
Charlotte Gdns CRW RM5 56 D2
Charlotte Ms ESH/CLAY KT10 * 204 B2
FITZ W1T 10 B1
NKENS W10 100 B5
WKENS W14 119 H4
Charlotte Pde FSTH SE23 * 164 B4
Charlotte Park Av BMLY BR1 184 D6
Charlotte Pl FITZ W1T 10 B2
PIM SW1V 16 A7
Charlotte Rd BARN SW13 138 C2
SDTCH EC2A 7 G5
WLGTN SM6 210 C4
Charlotte Rw CLAP SW4 141 H4
Charlotte St FITZ W1T 10 B1
Charlotte Ter IS N1 5 H1
Charlow Cl FUL/PGN SW6 140 B3
Charlton Church La
CHARL SE7 126 B5
Charlton Crs BARK IG11 109 F1
Charlton Dene CHARL SE7 146 B1
Charlton King's Rd KTTN NW5 84 D3
Charlton La CHARL SE7 126 C5
Charlton Park La CHARL SE7 126 D6
CHARL SE7 146 C1
Charlton Park Rd CHARL SE7 126 C6
Charlton Pl IS N1 6 A2
Charlton Rd BKHTH/KID SE3 126 A6
CHARL SE7 126 B6
ED N9 37 F3
KTN/HRWW/WS HA3 61 K1
WLSDN NW10 81 G6
Charlton Wy GNWCH SE10 145 H2
Charlwood CROY/NA CR0 213 H6
Charlwood Cl
KTN/HRWW/WS HA3 42 E2
Charlwood Pl PIM SW1V 16 B7
Charlwood Rd
PUT/ROE SW15 139 G4
Charlwood St PIM SW1V 16 B7
Charlwood Ter
PUT/ROE SW15 139 G5
Charmian Av STAN HA7 43 K6
Charminster Av
WIM/MER SW19 177 K5
Charminster Rd
ELTH/MOT SE9 166 C6
WPK KT4 193 G5
Charmouth Rd WELL DA16 148 D2
Charnock Rd CLPT E5 86 D1
Charnwood Av
WIM/MER SW19 177 K5
Charnwood Cl NWMAL KT3 192 B1
Charnwood Dr SWFD E18 53 F6
Charnwood Gdns
POP/IOD E14 124 D4
Charnwood Pl
TRDG/WHET N20 33 G5
Charnwood Rd SNWD SE25 196 E2
Charnwood St CLPT E5 * 68 C6
Charnwood Vls SWFD E18 53 F6
Charrington Rd CROY/NA CR0 196 C6
Charrington St CAMTN NW1 4 C2
Charsley Rd CAT SE6 164 E4
Chart Cl CROY/NA CR0 197 K3
HAYES BR2 183 H4
MTCM CR4 194 E1
Charter Av GNTH/NBYPK IG2 72 D5
Charter Crs HSLWW TW4 134 D5
Charter Dr BXLY DA5 169 F2
Charterhouse Av
ALP/SUD HA0 79 J3
Charterhouse Blds
FARR EC1M 6 C7
Charterhouse Ms FARR EC1M 12 B1
Charterhouse Rd HACK E8 86 C2
ORP BR6 217 G1
Charterhouse St HCIRC EC1N 11 K2
The Charterhouse
FARR EC1M * 6 B7
Charteris Rd FSBYPK N4 67 F5
KIL/WHAMP NW6 82 D6
WFD IG8 53 F2
Charter Rd KUT/HW KT1 175 J6
The Charter Rd WFD IG8 52 C2
Charters Cl NRWD SE19 181 F1
Charter Sq KUT/HW KT1 175 J5
Charter Wy FNCH N3 64 D1
STHGT/OAK N14 34 C1
Chartfield Av PUT/ROE SW15 138 E6
Chartfield Sq
PUT/ROE SW15 * 139 G6
Chartham Gv WNWD SE27 162 B5
Chartham Rd SNWD SE25 181 J6
Chart Hills Cl THMD SE28 110 A5
Chartley Av CRICK NW2 81 G1
STAN HA7 43 F2
Chartley Pde CRICK NW2 * 81 G1
Charton Cl BELV DA17 129 G6
Chartridge OXHEY WD19 * 27 H4
Chartridge Cl BUSH WD23 28 C1
Chart St IS N1 7 F4
Chartwell Cl CROY/NA CR0 196 E5
ELTH/MOT SE9 167 J4
GFD/PVL UB6 78 B6
Chartwell Dr ORP BR6 216 D3
Chartwell Gdns CHEAM SM3 208 C1
Chartwell Pl CHEAM SM3 208 C2
RYLN/HDSTN HA2 60 D6
Chartwell Rd NTHWD HA6 40 D2
Chartwell Wy PGE/AN SE20 181 J4
Charville La HGDN/ICK UB10 94 A2
Charwood STRHM/NOR SW16 162 B6
Chase Ct RYNPK SW20 177 H5
Chase Court Gdns
ENC/FH EN2 23 J4
Chase Cross Rd CRW RM5 56 E3
Chasefield Rd TOOT SW17 160 E6
Chase Gdns CHING E4 37 J6
WHTN TW2 155 J1
Chase Gn ENC/FH EN2 23 J4
Chase Green Av ENC/FH EN2 23 H3
Chase Hl ENC/FH EN2 23 J4
Chase La BARK/HLT IG6 72 D2
Chaseley Ct CHSWK W4 117 J5
Chaseley St POP/IOD E14 * 105 G5
Chasemore Cl MTCM CR4 194 E4
Chasemore Gdns
CROY/NA CR0 211 G3
Chase Ridings ENC/FH EN2 23 G3
Chase Rd ACT W3 99 F3
STHGT/OAK N14 22 C6
Chase Side ENC/FH EN2 23 J3
STHGT/OAK N14 34 A1
Chase Side Av ENC/FH EN2 23 J3
Chaseside Av RYNPK SW20 177 H4
Chaseside Cl ROM RM1 * 57 G2
Chase Side Crs ENC/FH EN2 23 K2
Chase Side Pl ENC/FH EN2 23 J4
The Chase BMLY BR1 184 A6
CLAP SW4 141 G4
EDGW HA8 44 D4
FSTGT E7 89 H2
LOU IG10 39 G2
PIN HA5 59 G3
ROM RM1 57 G6
ROMW/RG RM7 93 F1
STAN HA7 43 G2
STRHM/NOR SW16 180 A3
SUN TW16 172 A4
WLGTN SM6 210 E3
Chaseville Pde WCHMH N21 * 23 F6
Chaseville Park Rd
WCHMH N21 23 F6
Chase Wy STHGT/OAK N14 34 B3
Chasewood Av ENC/FH EN2 23 H3
Chasewood Pk HRW HA1 * 78 E1
Chatfield Rd BTSEA SW11 140 B4
CROY/NA CR0 196 C5
Chatham Av HAYES BR2 199 J4
Chatham Cl CHEAM SM3 193 J4
GLDGN NW11 64 E2
WOOL/PLUM SE18 127 G3
Chatham Pl HOM E9 86 E4
Chatham Rd BTSEA SW11 160 E1
KUT/HW KT1 175 H5
SWFD E18 52 D5
WALTH E17 51 G6
Chatham St WALW SE17 18 E6
WOOL/PLUM SE18 127 G3
Chatsfield Pl EA W5 98 A5
Chatsworth Av BFN/LL DA15 168 B3
BMLY BR1 184 A1
HDN NW4 46 A5
RYNPK SW20 177 H4
WBLY HA9 80 B3
Chatsworth Cl CHSWK W4 * 117 K6
HDN NW4 46 A5
WWKM BR4 199 J6
Chatsworth Crs HSLW TW3 135 J5
Chatsworth Dr EN EN1 36 C2
Chatsworth Est CLPT E5 * 87 F2
Chatsworth Gdns ACT W3 98 D6
NWMAL KT3 * 192 C2
RYLN/HDSTN HA2 60 B5
Chatsworth Pl MTCM CR4 178 E6
TEDD TW11 156 B6
Chatsworth Ri EA W5 98 B3
Chatsworth Rd CHEAM SM3 208 B2
CHSWK W4 117 K6
CLPT E5 86 E1
CRICK NW2 82 B4
CROY/NA CR0 211 K2
EA W5 98 B3
SRTFD E15 88 D3
YEAD UB4 95 F3
Chatsworth Wy WNWD SE27 162 C5
Chattern Hl ASHF TW15 152 E6
Chattern Rd ASHF TW15 153 F6
Chatterton Ms FSBYPK N4 * 85 H1
Chatterton Rd FSBYPK N4 85 H1
HAYES BR2 200 C2
Chatto Rd BTSEA SW11 140 E6
Chaucer Av HSLWW TW4 134 A3
RCH/KEW TW9 137 H3
YEAD UB4 94 E4
Chaucer Cl FBAR/BDGN N11 48 C1
Chaucer Dr STHWK SE1 19 K7
Chaucer Gdns SUT SM1 208 E1
Chaucer Gn CROY/NA CR0 197 J4
Chaucer Rd ACT W3 117 K1
ASHF TW15 152 B6
BFN/LL DA15 168 D3
FSTGT E7 88 E4
HARH RM3 57 K3
HNHL SE24 142 B6
SUT SM1 208 E2
WALTH E17 52 A4
WAN E11 70 E3
WELL DA16 148 A2
Chaucer Wy WIM/MER SW19 178 C2
Chauncey Cl ED N9 36 C5
Chaundrye Cl ELTH/MOT SE9 166 E1
Chauntler Rd CAN/RD E16 107 F5
Cheam Common Rd WPK KT4 192 E6
Cheam Man CHEAM SM3 * 208 C4
Cheam Park Wy CHEAM SM3 208 B4
Cheam Rd BELMT SM2 208 B6
SUT SM1 208 D4
Cheam St PECK SE15 * 143 J4
Cheapside CITYW EC2V 12 D4
EFNCH N2 * 47 K6
PLMGR N13 35 J6
WDGN N22 * 49 G6
Cheddar Cl FBAR/BDGN N11 47 K2
Cheddar Waye YEAD UB4 95 F5
Cheddington Rd UED N18 36 A6
Cheeseman Cl HPTN TW12 172 D2
Cheesemans Ter
WKENS W14 * 119 J5
Chelford Rd BMLY BR1 183 G1
Chelmer Crs BARK IG11 109 H1
Chelmer Rd HOM E9 87 F3
Chelmsford Av CRW RM5 57 F3
Chelmsford Cl BELMT SM2 208 E6
EHAM E6 107 K5
HMSMTH W6 119 G6
Chelmsford Gdns IL IG1 71 J4
Chelmsford Rd
STHGT/OAK N14 34 C2
SWFD E18 52 D4
WALTH E17 69 J3
WAN E11 70 B5
Chelmsford Sq WLSDN NW10 82 A6
Chelsea Br VX/NE SW8 121 G6
Chelsea Bridge Ga
VX/NE SW8 121 F6
Chelsea Bridge Rd
BGVA SW1W 121 F5
Chelsea Cl EDGW HA8 44 C5
HPTN TW12 173 H1
WLSDN NW10 81 F6
WPK KT4 192 D4
Chelsea Crs CRICK NW2 * 82 D4
WBPTN SW10 * 140 B2
Chelsea Emb CHEL SW3 120 E6
Chelsea Gdns BGVA SW1W * 121 F5
CHEAM SM3 208 C2
WEA W13 97 F4
Chelsea Harbour Dr
WBPTN SW10 140 B2
Chelsea Manor Gdns
CHEL SW3 * 120 D6
Chelsea Manor St CHEL SW3 120 D5
Chelsea Ms EMPK RM11 75 K5
Chelsea Park Gdns CHEL SW3 120 C6
Chelsea Sq CAR SM5 209 K6
CHEL SW3 120 C5
Chelsea Towers CHEL SW3 * 120 D6
Chelsea Village
FUL/PGN SW6 * 140 A1
Chelsfield Av ED N9 37 F2
Chelsfield Gdns SYD SE26 163 K5
Chelsfield Hl ORP BR6 217 J6
Chelsfield La ORP BR6 217 K2
STMC/STPC BR5 202 E4
Chelsfield Rd STMC/STPC BR5 202 D3
Chelsham Rd CLAP SW4 141 J4
SAND/SEL CR2 211 K5
Chelston Rd RSLP HA4 58 E6
Chelsworth Dr
WOOL/PLUM SE18 127 J6
Cheltenham Av TWK TW1 156 B2
Cheltenham Cl NTHLT UB5 78 B4
NWMAL KT3 175 K6
Cheltenham Gdns EHAM E6 107 J1
LOU IG10 39 J1
Cheltenham Pl ACT W3 117 K2
KTN/HRWW/WS HA3 62 A1
Cheltenham Rd LEY E10 70 A3
ORP BR6 217 G1
PECK SE15 143 K5
Cheltenham Ter CHEL SW3 120 E5
Chelton Av MLHL NW7 46 B3
Chelverton Rd
PUT/ROE SW15 139 G5
Chelwood Cl CHING E4 37 K1
NTHWD HA6 40 A3
Chelwood Gdns
RCH/KEW TW9 137 H3
Chenappa Cl PLSTW E13 106 E2
Chenduit Wy STAN HA7 43 F1
Cheney Rw WALTH E17 51 H4
Cheneys Rd WAN E11 88 C1
Cheney St PIN HA5 59 G1
Chenies Ms GWRST WC1E 4 C7
Chenies Pl CAMTN NW1 4 D2
Chenies St GWRST WC1E 10 C1
The Chenies ORP BR6 201 K3
Chenies Wy WATW WD18 26 C2
Cheniston Gdns KENS W8 * 120 A3
Chepstow Cl PUT/ROE SW15 139 H6
Chepstow Cnr BAY/PAD W2 * 100 E5
Chepstow Crs
GDMY/SEVK IG3 72 E3
NTGHL W11 100 E6
Chepstow Gdns STHL UB1 95 K5
Chepstow Pl BAY/PAD W2 100 E6
Chepstow Ri CROY/NA CR0 212 A1
Chepstow Rd BAY/PAD W2 100 E5
CROY/NA CR0 212 A1
HNWL W7 116 B3
Chepstow Vls NTGHL W11 100 D6
Chequers BKHH IG9 39 F3
Chequers Cl CDALE/KGS NW9 45 G6
STMC/STPC BR5 202 A1
Chequers La DAGW RM9 110 B3
Chequers Pde PLMGR N13 * 49 J1
The Chequers PIN HA5 * 41 H6
Chequer St STLK EC1Y 6 D7
Chequers Wy PLMGR N13 49 H1
Cherbury Cl THMD SE28 109 K5
Cherbury St IS N1 7 F3
Cherimoya Gdns
E/WMO/HCT KT8 173 G6
Cherington Rd HNWL W7 * 116 A1
Cheriton Av CLAY IG5 54 A5
Cheriton Cl EA W5 97 J4
EBAR EN4 21 K4
Cheriton Ct WOT/HER KT12 188 B5
Cheriton Dr
WOOL/PLUM SE18 147 J1
Cheriton Sq TOOT SW17 161 F4
Cherry Av STHL UB1 114 C1
Cherry Blossom Cl
PLMGR N13 49 H1
Cherry Cl BRXS/STRHM SW2 * 162 B2
CAR SM5 194 E6
CDALE/KGS NW9 45 H5
EA W5 116 E3
MRDN SM4 193 H1
RSLP HA4 76 D1
Cherrycot Ri ORP BR6 216 C2
Cherry Ct PIN HA5 41 H4
Cherry Crs BTFD TW8 136 C1
Cherry Croft Gdns PIN HA5 * 41 K3
Cherrydown Av CHING E4 37 H5
Cherrydown Cl CHING E4 37 H5
Cherrydown Rd SCUP DA14 168 E4
Cherrydown Wk
ROMW/RG RM7 56 D5
Cherry Gdns DAGW RM9 92 B3
NTHLT UB5 78 B5
Cherry Garden St
BERM/RHTH SE16 123 J2
Cherry Garth BTFD TW8 116 E4
Cherry Gv HYS/HAR UB3 114 A1
UX/CGN UB8 94 A4
Cherry Hl BAR EN5 33 F1
KTN/HRWW/WS HA3 42 E2
Cherry Hill Gdns
CROY/NA CR0 211 F2
Cherry Hills OXHEY WD19 41 J1
Cherrylands Cl
CDALE/KGS NW9 * 62 E6
Cherry La WDR/YW UB7 112 C4
Cherry Orch CHARL SE7 126 B6
WDR/YW UB7 112 B2
Cherry Orchard Cl
STMC/STPC BR5 202 D2
Cherry Orchard Gdns
CROY/NA CR0 196 E5
E/WMO/HCT KT8 172 E6
Cherry Orchard Rd
CROY/NA CR0 196 E5
E/WMO/HCT KT8 173 F6
HAYES BR2 200 D6
Cherry Rd PEND EN3 24 E1
Cherry St ROMW/RG RM7 75 F2
Cherry Tree Cl ALP/SUD HA0 79 G2
HOM E9 86 E6
RAIN RM13 111 J1
Cherry Tree Ct CHARL SE7 * 126 B6
Cherry Tree Dr
STRHM/NOR SW16 161 K5
Cherry Tree Hl EFNCH N2 65 J2
Cherry Tree La RAIN RM13 111 G2
Cherry Tree Ri BKHH IG9 39 G6
Cherry Tree Rd EFNCH N2 65 K1
SRTFD E15 88 C3
Cherry Tree Wk BECK BR3 198 C1
STLK EC1Y 6 D7

WWKM BR4 214 D2
Cherry Tree Wy STAN HA7 43 H2
Cherry Wk RAIN RM13 111 H1
Cherry Wy HOR/WEW KT19 207 F4
Cherrywood Cl BOW E3 105 G2
KUTN/CMB KT2 175 H3
Cherrywood Dr
PUT/ROE SW15 139 G6
Cherrywood La RYNPK SW20 193 H1
Chertsey Dr CHEAM SM3 193 H6
Chertsey Rd FELT TW13 153 H6
IL IG1 90 D2
TWK TW1 156 B1
WAN E11 70 B6
WHTN TW2 155 H3
Chertsey St TOOT SW17 179 F1
Chervil Cl FELT TW13 153 K5
Chervil Ms THMD SE28 128 C1
Cherwell Ct HOR/WEW KT19 206 E2
Cherwell Wy RSLP HA4 58 A3
Cheryls Cl FUL/PGN SW6 140 A2
Cheseman St SYD SE26 163 J5
Chesfield Rd KUTN/CMB KT2 175 F3
Chesham Av STMC/STPC BR5 201 G3
Chesham Cl KTBR SW1X * 15 G5
ROMW/RG RM7 75 F1
Chesham Crs PGE/AN SE20 181 K4
Chesham Ms KTBR SW1X 15 G4
Chesham Pl KTBR SW1X 15 G4
Chesham Rd KUT/HW KT1 175 H5
PGE/AN SE20 181 K5
WIM/MER SW19 178 C2
Chesham St KTBR SW1X 15 G5
WLSDN NW10 81 F1
Chesham Ter WEA W13 116 C2
Chesham Wy WATW WD18 26 C1
Cheshire Cl MTCM CR4 179 K6
WALTH E17 51 K4
Cheshire Gdns CHSGTN KT9 205 K4
Cheshire Rd WDGN N22 49 F3
Cheshire St BETH E2 104 C3
Chesholm Rd
STNW/STAM N16 86 A1
Cheshunt Rd BELV DA17 129 H5
FSTGT E7 89 F4
Chesilton Rd FUL/PGN SW6 139 J2
Chesil Wy YEAD UB4 94 D2
Chesley Gdns EHAM E6 107 H1
Chesney Crs CROY/NA CR0 214 A5
Chesney St BTSEA SW11 141 F2
Chesnut Av North WALTH E17 70 A1
Chesnut Gv TOTM N17 50 B6
Chesnut Rd TOTM N17 50 C6
Chesnut Rw FNCH N3 * 46 E3
Chessell Cl THHTH CR7 196 C1
Chessington Av FNCH N3 46 C6
Chessington Cl
HOR/WEW KT19 206 E4
Chessington Ct PIN HA5 59 K1
Chessington Hall Gdns
CHSGTN KT9 205 K5
Chessington Hill Pk
CHSGTN KT9 206 C4
Chessington Pde
CHSGTN KT9 * 205 K3
Chessington Rd CHSGTN KT9 206 C4
Chessington Wy WWKM BR4 198 E6
Chesson Rd WKENS W14 119 J6
Chesswood Wy PIN HA5 41 H5
Chester Av RCHPK/HAM TW10 157 G1
WHTN TW2 154 E3
Chester Cl BARN SW13 * 138 E4
KTBR SW1X 15 H3
SUT SM1 193 K6
Chester Cl North CAMTN NW1 3 K4
Chester Cl South CAMTN NW1 3 K5
Chester Crs HACK E8 86 B3
Chester Dr RYLN/HDSTN HA2 60 A3
Chesterfield Cl
STMC/STPC BR5 202 E1
Chesterfield Dr
ESH/CLAY KT10 190 B6
Chesterfield Gdns FSBYPK N4 67 H2
GNWCH SE10 * 145 G1
MYFR/PICC W1J * 9 J7
Chesterfield Gv EDUL SE22 143 G6
Chesterfield Hl
MYFR/PKLN W1K 9 J6
Chesterfield Ms FSBYPK N4 67 H2
Chesterfield Rd BAR EN5 20 B6
CHSWK W4 117 K6
FNCH N3 46 E2
HOR/WEW KT19 207 F5
LEY E10 70 A4
Chesterfield St
MYFR/PICC W1J 9 J7
Chesterfield Wy
HYS/HAR UB3 * 113 K2
PECK SE15 143 K1
Chesterford Gdns HAMP NW3 83 F2
Chesterford Rd MNPK E12 89 K3
Chester Gdns MRDN SM4 194 B2
PEND EN3 36 D1
WEA W13 * 97 H5
Chester Ga CAMTN NW1 3 J5
Chester Ms KTBR SW1X 15 J4
Chester Pl CAMTN NW1 3 J4
NTHWD HA6 * 40 C3
Chester Rd ARCH N19 66 B6
BFN/LL DA15 147 K6
CAMTN NW1 3 H5
CAN/RD E16 106 C3
ED N9 36 D3
FSTGT E7 89 H5
GDMY/SEVK IG3 73 F5
HSLWW TW4 134 A4
HTHAIR TW6 132 D4
NTHWD HA6 40 D3
TOTM N17 49 K6
WALTH E17 69 F2
WAN E11 71 F3
WIM/MER SW19 177 F2
Chester Rw BGVA SW1W 15 G7
Chester Sq BGVA SW1W 15 H6
Chester Square Ms
BGVA SW1W * 15 J5
The Chesters NWMAL KT3 176 B4
Chester St BETH E2 104 C3
KTBR SW1X 15 H4
Chester Ter CAMTN NW1 3 J4
Chesterton Cl GFD/PVL UB6 96 B1
WAND/EARL SW18 139 K6
Chesterton Ct EA W5 * 97 K5
Chesterton Dr
STWL/WRAY TW19 152 C3
Chesterton Rd NKENS W10 100 B4
PLSTW E13 106 E2
Chesterton Sq KENS W8 119 J4
Chesterton Ter KUT/HW KT1 175 H5
PLSTW E13 106 E2
Chester Wy LBTH SE11 17 K7
Chesthunte Rd TOTM N17 49 J4
Chestnut Aly FUL/PGN SW6 * 119 J6
Chestnut Av ALP/SUD HA0 79 H3
BKHH IG9 39 H5
BTFD TW8 116 E5
CEND/HSY/T N8 66 E2
E/WMO/HCT KT8 174 A6
EDGW HA8 44 A2
ESH/CLAY KT10 189 J4
FSTGT E7 89 F2
HCH RM12 75 H6
HOR/WEW KT19 207 G2
HPTN TW12 173 F3
MORT/ESHN SW14 138 A4
NTHWD HA6 40 D5
WWKM BR4 214 C3
Chestnut Av South
WALTH E17 70 A1
Chestnut Cl ASHF TW15 152 E6
BFN/LL DA15 168 B4
BKHH IG9 39 H5
CAR SM5 194 E5
CAT SE6 165 F6
HYS/HAR UB3 94 C6
HYS/HAR UB3 132 E1
NWCR SE14 144 C2
ORP BR6 217 G3
STHGT/OAK N14 22 C6
STNW/STAM N16 67 K6
STRHM/NOR SW16 162 B6
Chestnut Cots
TRDG/WHET N20 * 32 C3
Chestnut Dr BXLYHN DA7 148 E4
KTN/HRWW/WS HA3 43 F3
PIN HA5 59 H3
WAN E11 70 E3
Chestnut Gln HCH RM12 75 H6
Chestnut Gv ALP/SUD HA0 79 H3
BAL SW12 161 F2
BARK/HLT IG6 54 E2
EA W5 116 E3
EBAR EN4 21 K6
ISLW TW7 136 B5
MTCM CR4 195 J2
NWMAL KT3 176 A6
SAND/SEL CR2 212 D5
Chestnut La TRDG/WHET N20 32 C3
Chestnut Ms WFD IG8 52 E1
Chestnut Pl SYD SE26 163 G6
Chestnut Ri BUSH WD23 28 B2
WOOL/PLUM SE18 127 K5
Chestnut Rd ASHF TW15 152 D6
KUTN/CMB KT2 175 F3
RYNPK SW20 177 G5
WHTN TW2 155 K4
WNWD SE27 162 C5
The Chestnuts BECK BR3 * 182 A6
PIN HA5 * 41 K3
Chestnut Ter SUT SM1 * 209 F2
Chestnut Wy FELT TW13 154 A5
Cheston Av CROY/NA CR0 198 B5
Chesworth Cl ERITH DA8 150 B2
Chettle Cl STHWK SE1 18 E4
Chetwode Rd TOOT SW17 160 E5
Chetwynd Av EBAR EN4 33 K3
Chetwynd Rd KTTN NW5 84 B2
Chetwynd Vls KTTN NW5 * 84 B2
Chevalier Cl STAN HA7 29 K5
Cheval Pl SKENS SW7 14 D4
Cheval St POP/IOD E14 124 D3
Cheveney Wk HAYES BR2 183 K6
Chevening Rd GNWCH SE10 125 J5
KIL/WHAMP NW6 100 B1
NRWD SE19 180 E3
The Chevenings SCUP DA14 168 C5
Cheverton Rd ARCH N19 66 D5
Chevet St HOM E9 87 G3
Chevington CRICK NW2 * 82 D4
Cheviot Cl BELMT SM2 209 H6
BUSH WD23 28 C1
ENC/FH EN2 23 K3
HYS/HAR UB3 133 G1
Cheviot Gdns CRICK NW2 64 B6
Cheviot Rd EMPK RM11 75 J4
WNWD SE27 180 B1
Cheviot Wy GNTH/NBYPK IG2 72 E2
Chevron Cl CAN/RD E16 106 E5
Chevy Rd NWDGN UB2 115 H2
Chewton Rd WALTH E17 69 G1
Cheyne Av SWFD E18 52 D6
WHTN TW2 154 E3
Cheyne Cl HAYES BR2 215 J1
Cheyne Gdns CHEL SW3 120 D6
Cheyne Hl BRYLDS KT5 191 G1
Cheyne Ms CHEL SW3 120 D6
Cheyne Park Dr WWKM BR4 214 A1
Cheyne Pth HNWL W7 97 F4
Cheyne Pl CHEL SW3 * 120 E6
Cheyne Rw CHEL SW3 120 D6
Cheyne Wk CHEL SW3 120 D6
CROY/NA CR0 197 H6
HDN NW4 64 A3
WBPTN SW10 140 C1
WCHMH N21 23 G6
Cheyneys Av EDGW HA8 43 K2
Chichele Gdns CROY/NA CR0 212 A2
Chichele Rd CRICK NW2 82 B3
Chicheley Rd
KTN/HRWW/WS HA3 42 C3
Chicheley St STHWK SE1 17 H2
Chichester Av RSLP HA4 58 B6
Chichester Cl BKHTH/KID SE3 146 B1
EHAM E6 107 J5
HPTN TW12 172 E2
Chichester Ct EW KT17 * 207 H6
STAN HA7 44 A6
Chichester Gdns IL IG1 71 J4
Chichester Rd CROY/NA CR0 212 A1
ED N9 36 B3
KIL/WHAMP NW6 100 E1
WAN E11 88 C1
Chichester St PIM SW1V 121 H5
Chichester Wy
EBED/NFELT TW14 154 B2
POP/IOD E14 125 G4
Chicksand St WCHPL E1 13 K2
Chiddingfold
NFNCH/WDSPK N12 32 E5
Chiddingstone St
FUL/PGN SW6 139 K3
Chieftan Dr PUR RM19 131 K4
Chignell Pl WEA W13 116 B1
Chigwell Hl WAP E1W 104 D6
Chigwell Rd SWFD E18 53 F6
WFD IG8 53 K2
Chilcott Cl ALP/SUD HA0 79 J2
Childebert Rd TOOT SW17 161 G4
Childeric Rd NWCR SE14 144 B1
Childerley St FUL/PGN SW6 139 H2
Childers St DEPT SE8 124 B6
The Childers WFD IG8 53 K1
Child La GNWCH SE10 125 J3
Childs Ct HYS/HAR UB3 94 E6
Childs La NRWD SE19 * 181 F2
Child's Ms ECT SW5 * 119 K4
Child's Pl ECT SW5 119 K4
Child's St ECT SW5 119 K4
Child's Wk ECT SW5 * 119 K4
Childs Wy GLDGN NW11 64 D2
Chilham Cl BXLY DA5 169 G2
GFD/PVL UB6 97 G1
Chilham Rd ELTH/MOT SE9 166 D6
Chillerton Rd TOOT SW17 179 F1
Chillington Dr BTSEA SW11 140 B5
Chillingworth Gdns
TWK TW1 * 156 A4
Chillingworth Rd HOLWY N7 85 F3
Chilmark Gdns NWMAL KT3 192 C3
Chilmark Rd
STRHM/NOR SW16 179 J5
Chiltern Av BUSH WD23 28 C1
WHTN TW2 155 F3
Chiltern Cl BUSH WD23 28 B1
BXLYHN DA7 150 B2
CROY/NA CR0 212 A1
WPK KT4 193 F6
Chiltern Dene ENC/FH EN2 23 F5
Chiltern Dr BRYLDS KT5 191 J3
Chiltern Gdns CRICK NW2 82 B1
HAYES BR2 199 J1
Chiltern Pl CLPT E5 68 D6
Chiltern Rd BOW E3 105 J3
GNTH/NBYPK IG2 72 E1
PIN HA5 59 G2
The Chilterns BELMT SM2 * 209 F6
Chiltern St MHST W1U 9 F1
Chiltern Wy WFD IG8 38 E5
Chilthorne Cl CAT SE6 164 C2
Chilton Av EA W5 116 E4
Chilton Gv DEPT SE8 124 A4
Chilton Rd EDGW HA8 44 C2
RCH/KEW TW9 137 H4
Chilton St BETH E2 7 K6
Chilvers Cl WHTN TW2 155 K4
Chilver St GNWCH SE10 125 J5
Chilwell Gdns OXHEY WD19 27 G6
Chilworth Gdns SUT SM1 209 G1
Chilworth Ms BAY/PAD W2 101 G5
Chilworth St BAY/PAD W2 101 G5
Chimes Av PLMGR N13 35 G6
China Hall Ms
BERM/RHTH SE16 123 K3
China Ms BRXS/STRHM SW2 162 A2
Chinbrook Crs LEE/GVPK SE12 166 A5
Chinbrook Rd LEE/GVPK SE12 166 A5
Chinchilla Dr HSLWW TW4 134 B3
The Chine ALP/SUD HA0 79 H3
MUSWH N10 66 B1
WCHMH N21 35 H1
Chingdale Rd CHING E4 38 C5
Chingford Av CHING E4 37 J5
Chingford La WFD IG8 38 C6
Chingford Mount Rd
CHING E4 51 J1
Chingford Rd CHING E4 51 J2
Chingley Cl BMLY BR1 183 H2
Ching Wy CHING E4 51 H2
Chinnery Cl EN EN1 24 B1
Chinnor Crs GFD/PVL UB6 96 C1
Chipka St POP/IOD E14 125 F2
Chipley St NWCR SE14 124 B6
Chippendale St CLPT E5 87 F1
Chippenham Cl PIN HA5 * 58 D1
Chippenham Gdns
KIL/WHAMP NW6 100 E2
Chippenham Ms
MV/WKIL W9 * 100 E3
Chippenham Rd MV/WKIL W9 100 E3
Chipperfield Rd
STMC/STPC BR5 186 B5
Chipping Cl BAR EN5 20 C4
Chipstead Av THHTH CR7 196 C1
Chipstead Cl BELMT SM2 209 F6
NRWD SE19 181 G3
Chipstead Gdns CRICK NW2 63 K6
Chipstead St FUL/PGN SW6 139 K2
Chirk Cl YEAD UB4 95 J3
Chisenhale Rd BOW E3 105 G1
Chisholm Rd CROY/NA CR0 197 F6
RCHPK/HAM TW10 157 G1
Chislehurst Av
NFNCH/WDSPK N12 47 G3
Chislehurst High St CHST BR7 185 G2
Chislehurst Rd BMLY BR1 184 D5
ORP BR6 202 A4
RCHPK/HAM TW10 157 F1
SCUP DA14 186 B1
STMC/STPC BR5 201 K1
Chislet Cl BECK BR3 182 D3
Chisley Rd SEVS/STOTM N15 68 A3
Chiswell Sq BKHTH/KID SE3 146 A3
Chiswell St STMBW SE5 * 142 E1
STLK EC1Y 12 E1
Chiswick Br CHSWK W4 137 K3
Chiswick Cl CROY/NA CR0 211 F1
Chiswick Common Rd
CHSWK W4 118 A4
Chiswick High Rd
CHSWK W4 117 H5
Chiswick House Grounds
CHSWK W4 * 118 A6
Chiswick La CHSWK W4 118 B5
Chiswick La South CHSWK W4 118 C6
Chiswick Ml CHSWK W4 118 C6
Chiswick Pk CHSWK W4 * 117 K3
Chiswick Pier CHSWK W4 * 138 C1
Chiswick Quay CHSWK W4 137 K2
Chiswick Rd CHSWK W4 117 K4
ED N9 36 C4
Chiswick Sq CHSWK W4 118 B6
Chiswick Staithe CHSWK W4 137 K2
Chiswick Village CHSWK W4 117 H6
Chiswick Whf CHSWK W4 118 C6
Chitterfield Ga WDR/YW UB7 132 D1
Chitty's La BCTR RM8 73 K6
Chitty St FITZ W1T 10 B1
Chivalry Rd BTSEA SW11 140 D6
Chivenor Gv KUTN/CMB KT2 174 E1
Chivers Rd CHING E4 37 K5
Choats Manor Wy DAGW RM9 110 B2
Choats Rd BARK IG11 109 J1
Chobham Gdns
WIM/MER SW19 159 G4
Chobham Rd SRTFD E15 88 B3
Cholmeley Cl HGT N6 * 66 B4
Cholmeley Crs HGT N6 66 B4
Cholmeley Pk HGT N6 66 B5
Cholmley Gdns
KIL/WHAMP NW6 82 E3
Cholmley Rd THDIT KT7 190 C3
Cholmley Ter THDIT KT7 * 190 C4
Cholmley Vls THDIT KT7 * 190 C4
Cholmondeley Av
WLSDN NW10 99 J1
Chopwell Cl SRTFD E15 * 88 B5
Chorleywood Crs
STMC/STPC BR5 186 A5
Choumert Gv PECK SE15 143 H3
Choumert Ms PECK SE15 143 H3
Choumert Rd PECK SE15 143 G4
Chow Sq HACK E8 86 B3
Chrislaine Cl
STWL/WRAY TW19 152 A1
Chrisp St POP/IOD E14 105 K4
Christabel Cl ISLW TW7 135 K4
Christ Church Av ERITH DA8 130 A6
Christchurch Av
ALP/SUD HA0 80 A4
KIL/WHAMP NW6 82 B6
KTN/HRWW/WS HA3 61 F1
NFNCH/WDSPK N12 47 G2
RAIN RM13 111 H1
TEDD TW11 174 B1
Christchurch Cl ENC/FH EN2 23 J3
NFNCH/WDSPK N12 * 47 H3
WIM/MER SW19 178 C3
Christchurch Gdns
KTN/HRWW/WS HA3 61 G1
Christchurch Hl HAMP NW3 83 H1
Christ Church La BAR EN5 20 C3
Christchurch Ldg EBAR EN4 * 21 K5
Christchurch Pk BELMT SM2 209 G5
Christ Church Rd BRYLDS KT5 191 G4
CEND/HSY/T N8 66 E3
BECK BR3 * 182 D5
Christchurch Rd BFN/LL DA15 168 A6
BRXS/STRHM SW2 162 A3
IL IG1 72 B5
MORT/ESHN SW14 137 J6
WIM/MER SW19 178 C3
Christchurch Sq HOM E9 86 E6
Christchurch St CHEL SW3 120 E6
Christchurch Ter CHEL SW3 * 120 E6
Christchurch Wy
GNWCH SE10 125 H5
Christian Flds
STRHM/NOR SW16 180 B3
Christian St WCHPL E1 104 C5
Christie Dr CROY/NA CR0 197 H2
Christie Rd HOM E9 87 G4
Christina Sq FSBYPK N4 67 H5
Christina St SDTCH EC2A 7 G6
Christine Worsley Cl
WCHMH N21 35 H3
Christopher Av HNWL W7 116 B3
Christopher Cl
BERM/RHTH SE16 124 A2
BFN/LL DA15 148 A6
Christopher Gdns DAGW RM9 91 K3
Christopher Pl CAMTN NW1 * 4 D4
Christopher Rd NWDGN UB2 114 A4
Christophers Ms
NTGHL W11 * 119 H1
Christopher St SDTCH EC2A 7 F7
Christy Ter WFD IG8 53 J3
Chryssell Rd BRXN/ST SW9 142 B1
Chubworthy St NWCR SE14 124 B6
Chudleigh Crs
GDMY/SEVK IG3 90 E2
Chudleigh Gdns SUT SM1 209 G1
Chudleigh Rd BROCKY SE4 144 C6
KIL/WHAMP NW6 82 A5
WHTN TW2 155 K1
Chudleigh St WCHPL E1 105 F5
Chudleigh Wy RSLP HA4 58 E5
Chulsa Rd SYD SE26 181 J1
Chumleigh Gdns CMBW SE5 * 123 F6
Chumleigh St CMBW SE5 123 F6
Chumleigh Wk BRYLDS KT5 191 G1
Church Ap DUL SE21 162 E5
Church Av BECK BR3 182 D4
CAMTN NW1 84 B4
CHING E4 52 B2
MNPK E12 71 H6
MORT/ESHN SW14 138 A5
NTHLT UB5 77 K5
NWDGN UB2 114 D3
PIN HA5 59 J3
RSLP HA4 58 B5
SCUP DA14 186 B1
Churchbury Cl EN EN1 24 A3
Churchbury La EN EN1 24 A4
Churchbury Rd
ELTH/MOT SE9 166 C2
EN EN1 24 A3
Church Cl EDGW HA8 44 E1
HSLW TW3 134 E3
HYS/HAR UB3 94 B4
KENS W8 * 120 A2
NTHWD HA6 40 D3
TRDG/WHET N20 33 J5
WDR/YW UB7 112 B3
Church Crs FNCH N3 46 D4
HOM E9 87 F5
MUSWH N10 66 B1
TRDG/WHET N20 33 J5
Churchcroft Cl BAL SW12 * 161 F2
Churchdown BMLY BR1 165 H6
Church Dr CDALE/KGS NW9 63 F5
RYLN/HDSTN HA2 60 A3
WWKM BR4 214 C1
Church Elm La DAGE RM10 92 C4
Church End HDN NW4 45 K6
WALTH E17 * 69 K1
Church Farm EBAR EN4 * 33 K2
Church Farm La CHEAM SM3 208 C4
Churchfield Av
NFNCH/WDSPK N12 47 G2
Churchfield Cl HYS/HAR UB3 94 D6
RYLN/HDSTN HA2 60 C1
Churchfield Rd ACT W3 117 K1
HNWL W7 115 K2
WEA W13 116 C1
WELL DA16 148 B4
Churchfields
E/WMO/HCT KT8 173 F6
GNWCH SE10 125 F6
SWFD E18 52 E4
Churchfields Av FELT TW13 154 E5
Churchfields Rd BECK BR3 182 A5
Churchfield Wy
NFNCH/WDSPK N12 47 G2
Church Gdns ALP/SUD HA0 79 G2
EA W5 116 E2
Church Garth ARCH N19 * 66 D6
Church Ga FUL/PGN SW6 139 H
Church Gn BRXN/ST SW9 * 142 B
HYS/HAR UB3 94 D
Church Gv KUT/HW KT1 174 D
LEW SE13 144 E
Church Hl CAR SM5 209 K
HRW HA1 60 E
ORP BR6 202 B
WALTH E17 69 J
WCHMH N21 35 F
WIM/MER SW19 177 J
WOOL/PLUM SE18 126 E
Church Hill Rd CHEAM SM3 208 B
EBAR EN4 33 J
SURB KT6 191 F
WALTH E17 69 K
Church Hill Wd
STMC/STPC BR5 202 A
Church Hollow PUR RM19 131 K
Church Hyde
WOOL/PLUM SE18 127 K
Churchill Av
KTN/HRWW/WS HA3 61 H
Churchill Cl
EBED/NFELT TW14 153
Churchill Gdns ACT W3 98
Churchill Gardens Rd
PIM SW1V 121
Churchill Ms WFD IG8 52
Churchill Pl POP/IOD E14 124
Churchill Rd CAN/RD E16 107
CRICK NW2 81
EDGW HA8 44
KTTN NW5 84
SAND/SEL CR2 211
Churchill Ter CHING E4 37
Churchill Wk HOM E9 86
Churchill Wy BMLY BR1 183
Churchlands Wy WPK KT4 193
Church La CDALE/KGS NW9 62
CEND/HSY/T N8 67
CHSGTN KT9 206
CHST BR7 185
DAGE RM10 92
EA W5 116
ED N9 36
EFNCH N2 47
ENC/FH EN2 23
HAYES BR2 200
KTN/HRWW/WS HA3 43
PIN HA5 41
PUR RM19 * 131
ROM RM1 75
TEDD TW11 174
THDIT KT7 190
TOOT SW17 178
TOTM N17 50
TWK TW1 156
WALTH E17 69
WAN E11 70
WIM/MER SW19 177
WLGTN SM6 210
Churchley Rd SYD SE26 163
Church Manor Wy ABYW SE2 128
Church Md CMBW SE5 * 142
Churchmead Cl EBAR EN4 33
Church Meadow SURB KT6 190
Churchmead Rd
WLSDN NW10 8
Churchmore Rd
STRHM/NOR SW16 17
Church Mt EFNCH N2 6
Church Paddock Ct
WLGTN SM6 21
Church Pde ASHF TW15 * 15
Church Pas BAR EN5 * 2
Church Pth CHSWK W4 11
MTCM CR4 17
NFNCH/WDSPK N12 * 4
RYNPK SW20 17
WAN E11 7
Church Pl EA W5 11
MTCM CR4 1
Church Rd LEY E10 6
Church Ri CHSGTN KT9 20
FSTH SE23 16
Church Rd ACT W3 11
ASHF TW15 1
BARK IG11
BARN SW13 1
BKHH IG9 3
CHEAM SM3 2
CROY/NA CR0 2
E/WMO/HCT KT8 1

ERITH DA8 129 K5
ESH/CLAY KT10 205 F4
FELT TW13 172 B1
GNTH/NBYPK IG2 72 E3
HAYES BR2 183 H6
HAYES BR2 215 H5
HAYES BR2 183 K5
HDN NW4 63 K1
HEST TW5 135 F1
HGT N6 66 A3
HNWL W7 96 E6
HOR/WEW KT19 207 F5
HYS/HAR UB3 113 J1
IS N1 85 J4
ISLW TW7 135 J2
KUT/HW KT1 175 G5
LEY E10 69 J5
MNPK E12 89 J3
MTCM CR4 178 D6
NRWD SE19 181 F3
NTHLT UB5 95 H1
NTHWD HA6 40 D3
NWDGN UB2 114 E3
ORP BR6 216 C3
ORP BR6 217 K4
PEND EN3 36 E1
RCHPK/HAM TW10 137 F6
RCHPK/HAM TW10 175 G1
SCUP DA14 168 B6
STAN HA7 43 H1
SURB KT6 190 D5
TEDD TW11 155 K6
TOTM N17 50 A4
WALTH E17 51 G5
WDR/YW UB7 112 A2
WELL DA16 148 C3
WIM/MER SW19 178 C5
WLGTN SM6 210 C1
WLSDN NW10 81 G4
WPK KT4 192 B5
Church Rw CHST BR7 185 H3
FUL/PGN SW6 * 140 A1
HAMP NW3 83 G2
WAND/EARL SW18 140 A6
Church Row Ms CHST BR7 185 H3
Church St BAY/PAD W2 8 B1
CHSWK W4 118 B6
CROY/NA CR0 211 H1
DAGE RM10 92 D5
ED N9 35 K2
ENC/FH EN2 23 J4
ESH/CLAY KT10 204 B2
EW KT17 207 J6
HPTN TW12 173 H4
HSLW TW3 135 H6
ISLW TW7 136 C4
KUT/HW KT1 174 E5
SRTFD E15 88 C6
TWK TW1 156 B3
Church Street Est
STJWD NW8 2 B7
Church St North SRTFD E15 88 C6
Church Ter BKHTH/KID SE3 145 H4
FUL/PGN SW6 * 140 A3
HDN NW4 45 K6
RCHPK/HAM TW10 136 E6
Church V EFNCH N2 47 K6
FSTH SE23 163 K4
Church Vw FSTH SE23 164 A4
Churchview Rd WHTN TW2 155 J3
Church Wk BTFD TW8 116 D6
BUSH WD23 28 A1
CDALE/KGS NW9 63 F6
CRICK NW2 82 D1
HYS/HAR UB3 94 C5
RYNPK SW20 177 F6
STNW/STAM N16 85 K2
STRHM/NOR SW16 179 H5
THDIT KT7 190 A3
Churchway CAMTN NW1 4 D4
Church Wy EBAR EN4 21 K5
TRDG/WHET N20 33 J5
Churchyard Rw LBTH SE11 18 B6
Churston Av PLSTW E13 89 F6
Churston Cl
BRXS/STRHM SW2 * 162 C3
Churston Dr MRDN SM4 193 G2
Churston Gdns
FBAR/BDGN N11 48 C2
Churton Pl CHSWK W4 * 117 J6
PIM SW1V 16 B7
Churton St PIM SW1V 16 B7
Chyngton Cl BFN/LL DA15 168 A5
bber Rd FSTH SE23 164 A4
cada Rd WAND/EARL SW18 160 B1
cely Rd PECK SE15 143 H2
nderford Wy BMLY BR1 165 H6
nema Pde EDGW HA8 * 44 C2
nnamon Cl CROY/NA CR0 * 195 K4
PECK SE15 143 G1
nnamon St WAP E1W 123 J1
ntra Pk NRWD SE19 181 G3
rcle Gdns WIM/MER SW19 177 K6
e Circle CRICK NW2 81 G1
MLHL NW7 45 F2
e Circuits PIN HA5 59 G1
rcular Rd TOTM N17 50 B6
rcular Wy
WOOL/PLUM SE18 126 E6
rcus Ms MBLAR W1H * 8 E1
rcus Pl LVPST EC2M * 13 F2
rcus Rd STJWD NW8 2 A4
rcus St GNWCH SE10 145 F1
rencester St BAY/PAD W2 101 F4
sbury Ring North
NFNCH/WDSPK N12 46 D1
sbury Ring South
NFNCH/WDSPK N12 46 D1
sbury Rd SEVS/STOTM N15 67 K2
adel Pl LBTH SE11 122 A5
izen Rd HOLWY N7 85 G1
ron Ter PECK SE15 * 143 J4
y Barracks SHB W12 * 119 F1
y Garden Rw IS N1 6 B3
y Rd FSBYE EC1V 6 A3
STLK EC1Y 7 F7
y Wk STHWK SE1 19 G4
ic Wy BARK/HLT IG6 72 C1
RSLP HA4 77 H3
bon Ms KTBR SW1X 14 E5
Clack St BERM/RHTH SE16 123 K2
Clacton Rd TOTM N17 * 50 B5
WALTH E17 69 G3
Claire Ct NFNCH/WDSPK N12 33 G5
Claire Gdns STAN HA7 43 J1
Claire Pl POP/IOD E14 124 D3
Clairvale Rd HEST TW5 134 C2
Clairview Rd
STRHM/NOR SW16 179 G1
Clairville Gdns HNWL W7 115 K1
Clamp Hl STAN HA7 42 E1
Clancarty Rd FUL/PGN SW6 139 K3
Clandon Cl ACT W3 117 J2
EW KT17 207 H4
Clandon Gdns FNCH N3 46 E6
Clandon Rd GDMY/SEVK IG3 72 E6
Clandon St DEPT SE8 144 D3
Clandon Ter RYNPK SW20 * 177 G5
Clanricarde Gdns
BAY/PAD W2 100 E6
Clapgate Rd BUSH WD23 28 B1
Clapham Common North Side
CLAP SW4 141 F5
Clapham Common South Side
CLAP SW4 141 G6
Clapham Common West Side
BTSEA SW11 140 E5
Clapham Court Ter
CLAP SW4 * 141 K6
Clapham Crs CLAP SW4 141 J5
Clapham High St CLAP SW4 141 J5
Clapham Manor St CLAP SW4 141 H4
Clapham Park Est CLAP SW4 * 161 J2
Clapham Park Rd CLAP SW4 141 H5
Clapham Park Ter
BRXS/STRHM SW2 * 141 K6
Clapham Rd BRXN/ST SW9 141 K3
Claps Gate La EHAM E6 108 B3
Clapton Common CLPT E5 68 C4
Clapton Pas CLPT E5 86 E3
Clapton Sq CLPT E5 86 D3
Clapton Ter CLPT E5 68 C4
Clapton Wy CLPT E5 86 C2
Clara Pl WOOL/PLUM SE18 127 F4
Clare Cl BORE WD6 30 B1
EFNCH N2 47 G6
Clare Cnr ELTH/MOT SE9 167 G2
Clare Ct NTHWD HA6 40 C1
Claredale St BETH E2 104 C1
Clare Gdns BARK IG11 91 F4
FSTGT E7 88 E2
NTGHL W11 * 100 C5
Clare Hl ESH/CLAY KT10 204 B3
Clare La IS N1 85 J5
Clare Lawn Av
MORT/ESHN SW14 138 A6
Clare Ms FUL/PGN SW6 140 A1
Claremont Av
KTN/HRWW/WS HA3 62 A2
NWMAL KT3 192 E2
SUN TW16 172 A4
Claremont Cl
BRXS/STRHM SW2 162 A3
CAN/RD E16 127 F1
IS N1 5 K3
ORP BR6 216 A2
Claremont Crs DART DA1 150 B5
Claremont Dr ESH/CLAY KT10 204 B5
Claremont End
ESH/CLAY KT10 204 B4
Claremont Gdns
GDMY/SEVK IG3 72 E6
SURB KT6 191 F1
Claremont Gv CHSWK W4 138 B1
WFD IG8 53 G2
Claremont House
WATW WD18 * 26 B1
Claremont La ESH/CLAY KT10 204 B3
Claremont Pk FNCH N3 46 C4
Claremont Park Rd
ESH/CLAY KT10 204 A4
Claremont Rd BMLY BR1 200 D1
CRICK NW2 64 A4
CROY/NA CR0 197 H5
EBAR EN4 21 G1
EMPK RM11 75 J3
ESH/CLAY KT10 204 E5
FSTGT E7 89 F3
GLDGN NW11 82 B1
HGT N6 66 B4
KTN/HRWW/WS HA3 42 E5
MV/WKIL W9 100 C1
SURB KT6 191 F2
TEDD TW11 174 A1
TWK TW1 156 C2
WALTH E17 51 G5
WAN E11 88 B1
WEA W13 97 G4
Claremont Sq IS N1 5 J3
Claremont St GNWCH SE10 124 E6
UED N18 50 C2
Claremont Ter THDIT KT7 * 190 C4
Claremont Vls CMBW SE5 * 142 E1
KUT/HW KT1 * 175 G5
Claremont Wy CRICK NW2 64 A5
Clarence Av BMLY BR1 200 D1
CLAP SW4 161 J1
IL IG1 71 K3
NWMAL KT3 175 K5
Clarence Cl BUSH WD23 29 F2
EBAR EN4 21 H6
Clarence Ct MLHL NW7 45 G1
Clarence Crs CLAP SW4 161 J1
SCUP DA14 168 C5
Clarence Gdns CAMTN NW1 3 K5
Clarence Ga CAMTN NW1 3 F6
CHIG IG7 54 A2
Clarence La PUT/ROE SW15 158 C1
Clarence Ms
BERM/RHTH SE16 124 A1
CLPT E5 86 D3
TOOT SW17 160 B5
Clarence Pas CAMTN NW1 * 4 E3
Clarence Pl CLPT E5 86 D3
Clarence Rd BMLY BR1 184 D6
CAN/RD E16 106 C3
CHSWK W4 117 H5
CLPT E5 86 D2
CROY/NA CR0 196 E4
DEPT SE8 124 E6
ELTH/MOT SE9 166 D4
KIL/WHAMP NW6 82 D5
MNPK E12 89 G2
PEND EN3 24 E6
RCH/KEW TW9 137 G2
SCUP DA14 168 C5
SEVS/STOTM N15 67 J2
SUT SM1 209 F2
TEDD TW11 174 A2
WALTH E17 51 F5
WDGN N22 48 E3
WIM/MER SW19 178 A2
WLGTN SM6 210 B3
Clarence St KUT/HW KT1 174 E5
NWDGN UB2 114 C3
RCH/KEW TW9 137 F5
Clarence Ter CAMTN NW1 3 F6
HSLW TW3 135 G5
Clarence Vls KUT/HW KT1 * 175 G5
Clarence Wk CLAP SW4 141 K3
Clarence Wy CAMTN NW1 84 B5
Clarendon Cl BAY/PAD W2 * 8 C5
HOM E9 86 E5
STMC/STPC BR5 186 B6
Clarendon Crs WHTN TW2 155 J5
Clarendon Cross NTGHL W11 100 C6
Clarendon Dr PUT/ROE SW15 139 F5
Clarendon Gdns HDN NW4 45 J6
IL IG1 71 K5
MV/WKIL W9 101 G3
WBLY HA9 79 K1
Clarendon Ga BAY/PAD W2 8 C5
Clarendon Gn
STMC/STPC BR5 186 B6
Clarendon Gv MTCM CR4 178 E6
STMC/STPC BR5 202 B1
Clarendon Ms BAY/PAD W2 8 C5
Clarendon Pth
STMC/STPC BR5 202 B1
Clarendon Pl BAY/PAD W2 8 C5
Clarendon Ri LEW SE13 145 F4
Clarendon Rd ASHF TW15 152 C6
CEND/HSY/T N8 49 F6
CROY/NA CR0 196 C6
EA W5 98 A2
HRW HA1 60 E3
HYS/HAR UB3 113 J2
NTGHL W11 100 C6
SEVS/STOTM N15 67 H1
SWFD E18 52 E6
UED N18 50 C1
WALTH E17 69 K3
WAN E11 70 B5
WDGN N22 * 49 F5
WIM/MER SW19 178 D3
WLGTN SM6 210 C3
Clarendon St PIM SW1V 121 G5
Clarendon Ter MV/WKIL W9 101 G3
Clarendon Wy CHST BR7 186 A6
WCHMH N21 35 J2
Clarens St CAT SE6 164 C4
Clare Pde GFD/PVL UB6 * 78 D4
Clare Rd GFD/PVL UB6 78 D4
HSLWW TW4 134 E4
NWCR SE14 144 C3
STWL/WRAY TW19 152 A2
WAN E11 70 B3
WLSDN NW10 81 J5
Clare St BETH E2 104 D1
Claret Gdns SNWD SE25 197 F1
Clareville Gv SKENS SW7 * 120 B4
Clareville Grove Ms
SKENS SW7 * 120 B4
Clareville Rd STMC/STPC BR5 201 H6
Clareville St SKENS SW7 120 B4
Clarges Ms MYFR/PICC W1J 9 J7
Clarges St MYFR/PICC W1J 9 K7
Claribel Rd BRXN/ST SW9 142 C3
Clarice Wy WLGTN SM6 210 E6
Claridge Rd BCTR RM8 73 K5
Clarissa Rd CHDH RM6 73 K3
Clarissa St HACK E8 86 B6
Clark Cl ERITH DA8 150 D2
Clarke Cl THHTH CR7 196 D3
Clarke Ms ED N9 36 D5
Clarkers La KTTN NW5 84 B3
Clarkes Av WPK KT4 193 G5
Clarkes Ms CAVSQ/HST W1G 9 H1
Clark Gv IL IG1 90 E2
Clarks Md BUSH WD23 28 C2
Clarkson Rd CAN/RD E16 106 D5
Clarkson Rw CAMTN NW1 4 A3
Clarkson St BETH E2 * 104 D2
Clark's Rd IL IG1 72 D6
Clark St WCHPL E1 104 E5
Clark Wy HEST TW5 134 C1
Classon Cl WDR/YW UB7 112 B2
Claude Monet Ct EDUL SE22 * 143 H6
Claude Rd LEY E10 70 A5
PECK SE15 143 J3
PLSTW E13 89 F6
Claude St POP/IOD E14 124 D4
Claudia Pl WIM/MER SW19 159 H3
Claudius Cl STAN HA7 29 K5
Claughton Rd PLSTW E13 107 G1
Clauson Av NTHLT UB5 78 B3
Clavell St GNWCH SE10 125 F6
Claverdale Rd
BRXS/STRHM SW2 162 A2
Clavering Av BARN SW13 118 E6
Clavering Cl TEDD TW11 156 B6
Clavering Rd MNPK E12 71 H5
Claverley Gv FNCH N3 46 E4
Claverley Vls FNCH N3 47 F3
Claverton St PIM SW1V 121 H5
Clave St WAP E1W 123 K1
Claxton Gv HMSMTH W6 119 G5
Clay Av MTCM CR4 179 G5
Claybank Gv LEW SE13 144 E4
Claybridge Rd LEE/GVPK SE12 166 B6
Claybrook Cl EFNCH N2 47 H6
Claybrook Rd HMSMTH W6 119 G6
Claybury BUSH WD23 28 B2
Claybury Rd WFD IG8 53 J3
Claydon Dr CROY/NA CR0 210 E2
Claydown Ms
WOOL/PLUM SE18 127 F5
Clayfarm Rd ELTH/MOT SE9 167 H4
Claygate Cl HCH RM12 93 J2
Claygate Crs CROY/NA CR0 214 A4
Claygate La ESH/CLAY KT10 205 G1
THDIT KT7 190 B5
Claygate Lodge Cl
ESH/CLAY KT10 204 E5
Claygate Rd WEA W13 116 C3
Clayhall Av CLAY IG5 53 J5
Clayhill Crs ELTH/MOT SE9 166 C6
Claylands Pl VX/NE SW8 142 B1
Claylands Rd VX/NE SW8 122 A6
Clay La BUSH WD23 28 E2
STWL/WRAY TW19 152 C2
Claymore Cl MRDN SM4 193 K4
Claypole Dr HEST TW5 134 D2
Claypole Rd SRTFD E15 * 106 A1
Clayponds Av BTFD TW8 117 F4
Clayponds Gdns EA W5 116 E4
Clayponds La BTFD TW8 117 F5
Clayside CHIG IG7 54 C1
Clay St MHST W1U 9 F2
Clayton Av ALP/SUD HA0 80 A5
Clayton Cl EHAM E6 107 K5
Clayton Crs BTFD TW8 116 E5
IS N1 5 G1
Clayton Dr DEPT SE8 124 B5
Clayton Fld CDALE/KGS NW9 45 G4
Clayton Ms GNWCH SE10 145 G2
Clayton Rd CHSGTN KT9 205 J2
HYS/HAR UB3 113 H2
ISLW TW7 135 K4
PECK SE15 143 H2
ROMW/RG RM7 74 E5
Clayton St LBTH SE11 122 B6
Clayton Ter YEAD UB4 95 J4
Claytonville Ter BELV DA17 * 129 K2
Clay Wood Cl ORP BR6 201 K4
Clayworth Cl BFN/LL DA15 168 C1
Cleanthus Cl
WOOL/PLUM SE18 147 G2
Cleanthus Rd
WOOL/PLUM SE18 147 G2
Clearbrook Wy WCHPL E1 104 E5
Clearwater Pl SURB KT6 190 D3
Clearwater Ter NTGHL W11 119 G2
Clearwell Dr MV/WKIL W9 101 F3
Cleave Av HYS/HAR UB3 113 H4
ORP BR6 216 E4
Cleaveland Rd SURB KT6 190 E2
Cleaverholme Cl SNWD SE25 197 J3
Cleaver Sq LBTH SE11 122 B5
Cleaver St LBTH SE11 122 B5
Cleeve Ct EBED/NFELT TW14 153 H3
Cleeve Hl FSTH SE23 163 J3
Cleeve Park Gdns SCUP DA14 168 C4
Cleeve Wy PUT/ROE SW15 158 C1
SUT SM1 194 A5
Clegg St PLSTW E13 106 E1
WAP E1W 123 J1
Clematis Cots SHB W12 * 99 J6
Clematis Gdns WFD IG8 52 E1
Clematis St SHB W12 99 H6
Clem Attlee Ct
FUL/PGN SW6 * 119 J6
Clem Attlee Pde
FUL/PGN SW6 * 119 J6
Clemence Rd DAGE RM10 92 E6
Clemence St POP/IOD E14 105 H4
Clement Av CLAP SW4 141 J5
Clement Cl CHSWK W4 118 A4
KIL/WHAMP NW6 82 A5
Clement Gdns HYS/HAR UB3 113 H4
Clementhorpe Rd DAGW RM9 91 J4
Clementina Rd LEY E10 69 H5
Clementine Cl WEA W13 116 C2
Clement Rd BECK BR3 182 A5
WIM/MER SW19 177 H1
Clements Av CAN/RD E16 106 E6
Clements Cl
NFNCH/WDSPK N12 33 F6
Clements Inn LINN WC2A 11 H4
Clements La IL IG1 90 B1
Clement's La MANHO EC4N 13 F5
Clements Pl BTFD TW8 116 E5
Clements Rd EHAM E6 89 K5
IL IG1 90 B1
WOT/HER KT12 188 A6
Clement's Rd
BERM/RHTH SE16 123 H3
Clendon Wy
WOOL/PLUM SE18 127 J4
Clennam St STHWK SE1 * 18 D2
Clensham Ct SUT SM1 193 K6
Clensham La SUT SM1 193 K6
Clenston Ms MBLAR W1H 8 E3
Cleopatra Cl STAN HA7 29 K5
Clephane Rd IS N1 85 J4
Clere Pl SDTCH EC2A 7 F6
Clere St SDTCH EC2A 7 F6
Clerkenwell Cl CLKNW EC1R 5 K6
Clerkenwell Gn CLKNW EC1R 6 A7
Clerkenwell Rd CLKNW EC1R 5 J7
Clermont Rd HOM E9 86 E6
Clevedon Gdns HEST TW5 134 A3
HYS/HAR UB3 113 G3
Clevedon Rd KUT/HW KT1 175 H5
PGE/AN SE20 182 A4
TWK TW1 156 E1
Cleveland Av CHSWK W4 118 C4
HPTN TW12 172 E3
Cleveland Gdns BARN SW13 138 C3
BAY/PAD W2 101 G5
CRICK NW2 64 B6
SEVS/STOTM N15 67 J2
WPK KT4 192 B6
Cleveland Gv WCHPL E1 104 E3
Cleveland Ms FITZ W1T 10 A1
Cleveland Park Av WALTH E17 69 J1
Cleveland Park Crs
WALTH E17 69 J1
Cleveland Pl STJS SW1Y 10 B7
Cleveland Ri MRDN SM4 193 G4
Cleveland Rd BARN SW13 138 C3
CHSWK W4 117 K3
ED N9 * 36 D2
IL IG1 90 B1
IS N1 85 K5
ISLW TW7 136 B5
NWMAL KT3 192 B1
SWFD E18 52 E6
WEA W13 97 G4
WELL DA16 148 A3
WPK KT4 192 B6
Cleveland Rw WHALL SW1A 16 B1
Cleveland Sq BAY/PAD W2 101 G6
Cleveland St CAMTN NW1 3 K7
Cleveland Ter BAY/PAD W2 101 G5
Cleveland Wy WCHPL E1 104 E3
Cleveley Crs EA W5 98 A1
Cleveleys Rd CLPT E5 86 D1
Clevely Cl CHARL SE7 126 C4
Cleverly Est SHB W12 * 118 D1
Cleve Rd KIL/WHAMP NW6 82 E5
SCUP DA14 168 E5
Cleves Av EW KT17 207 K6
Cleves Cl LOU IG10 39 J1
Cleves Rd EHAM E6 89 H6
RCHPK/HAM TW10 156 D5
Cleves Wk BARK/HLT IG6 54 C3
Cleves Wy HPTN TW12 172 E3
RSLP HA4 59 H5
Clewer Crs
KTN/HRWW/WS HA3 42 D4
Clifden Ms CLPT E5 87 F2
Clifden Rd BTFD TW8 116 E6
CLPT E5 86 E3
TWK TW1 156 A3
Cliffe Rd SAND/SEL CR2 211 K3
Clifford Av CHST BR7 184 E2
CLAY IG5 54 B4
RCH/KEW TW9 137 J4
WLGTN SM6 210 C2
Clifford Cl NTHLT UB5 77 J6
PLSTW E13 * 107 F2
Clifford Dr BRXN/ST SW9 142 C5
Clifford Gdns HYS/HAR UB3 113 G4
WLSDN NW10 100 A1
Clifford Gv ASHF TW15 152 D6
Clifford Rd ALP/SUD HA0 79 K6
BAR EN5 21 F4
CAN/RD E16 106 D3
ED N9 36 E1
HSLWW TW4 134 C4
RCHPK/HAM TW10 156 E4
SNWD SE25 197 H1
WALTH E17 52 A5
Clifford St CONDST W1S 10 A6
Clifford Wy WLSDN NW10 81 H2
Cliff Rd CAMTN NW1 84 D4
Cliff Ter DEPT SE8 144 D3
Cliffview Rd LEW SE13 144 D4
Cliff Vls CAMTN NW1 84 D4
Cliff Wk CAN/RD E16 106 D4
Clifton Av FELT TW13 154 B5
FNCH N3 46 D4
KTN/HRWW/WS HA3 43 H5
SHB W12 118 C2
WALTH E17 69 F1
WBLY HA9 80 B4
Clifton Cl ORP BR6 216 C3
Clifton Ct BECK BR3 * 182 E4
Clifton Crs PECK SE15 143 J1
Clifton Gdns CHSWK W4 118 A4
ENC/FH EN2 22 E5
GLDGN NW11 64 D3
MV/WKIL W9 101 G3
SEVS/STOTM N15 68 B3
Clifton Ga WBPTN SW10 * 120 B6
Clifton Gv HACK E8 86 C4
Clifton Hl STJWD NW8 101 G1
Clifton Ms SNWD SE25 197 F1
Clifton Pde FELT TW13 * 154 B6
Clifton Park Av RYNPK SW20 177 F5
Clifton Pl BAY/PAD W2 8 B5
BERM/RHTH SE16 123 K2
KUTN/CMB KT2 * 175 H4
WBPTN SW10 * 120 B6
Clifton Ri NWCR SE14 144 B1
Clifton Rd CAN/RD E16 106 C4
CEND/HSY/T N8 66 D3
EMPK RM11 75 J3
FNCH N3 47 G4
FSTGT E7 89 H4
GFD/PVL UB6 96 C3
GNTH/NBYPK IG2 72 D3
HTHAIR TW6 132 E4
ISLW TW7 135 K3
KTN/HRWW/WS HA3 62 B2
KUTN/CMB KT2 175 G4
MV/WKIL W9 101 G3
NWDGN UB2 114 D4
SCUP DA14 167 K6
SNWD SE25 197 F1
TEDD TW11 155 K6
WDGN N22 48 C4
WELL DA16 148 D4
WIM/MER SW19 177 G2
WLGTN SM6 210 B3
WLSDN NW10 99 J1
Clifton St SDTCH EC2A 7 G7
Clifton Ter FSBYPK N4 67 G6
Clifton Vls MV/WKIL W9 101 F4
Clifton Wy ALP/SUD HA0 80 A6
PECK SE15 143 K1
Cline Rd FBAR/BDGN N11 48 C2
Clink St STHWK SE1 12 E7
Clinton Av E/WMO/HCT KT8 189 H1
WELL DA16 148 B5
Clinton Crs BARK/HLT IG6 54 E2
Clinton Rd BOW E3 105 G2
FSTGT E7 88 E2
SEVS/STOTM N15 67 K1
Clinton Ter DEPT SE8 * 124 D6
SUT SM1 * 209 G2
Clipper Cl BERM/RHTH SE16 124 A2
Clipper Wy LEW SE13 145 F5
Clippesby Cl CHSGTN KT9 * 206 B4
Clipstone Ms GTPST W1W 10 A1
Clipstone Rd HSLW TW3 135 F4
Clipstone St GTPST W1W 9 K1
Clissold Cl EFNCH N2 47 K6
Clissold Crs STNW/STAM N16 85 K2
Clissold Rd STNW/STAM N16 85 K1
Clitheroe Av
RYLN/HDSTN HA2 60 A5
Clitheroe Gdns OXHEY WD19 27 H5
Clitheroe Rd BRXN/ST SW9 141 K3
CRW RM5 56 E1
Clitherow Av HNWL W7 116 B3
Clitherow Rd BTFD TW8 116 C5
Clitterhouse Crs CRICK NW2 64 A5
Clitterhouse Rd CRICK NW2 64 A5

Clive Av UED N18 50 C2
Clive Ct WLSDN NW10 * 81 H5
Cliveden Cl
NFNCH/WDSPK N12 33 G6
Cliveden Pl BGVA SW1W 15 G6
Cliveden Rd WIM/MER SW19 177 J4
Clivedon Ct WEA W13 97 H4
Clivedon Rd CHING E4 52 C1
Clive Rd BELV DA17 129 H4
DUL SE21 162 E5
EBED/NFELT TW14 153 K1
EN EN1 24 C5
ESH/CLAY KT10 204 B2
GPK RM2 75 K2
TWK TW1 156 A6
WIM/MER SW19 178 D2
Clivesdale Dr HYS/HAR UB3 113 K1
Clive Wy EN EN1 24 C5
Cloak La CANST EC4R 12 D5
Clockhouse Av BARK IG11 90 C6
Clockhouse Cl
WIM/MER SW19 159 F5
Clockhouse La ASHF TW15 152 D6
CRW RM5 56 E3
EBED/NFELT TW14 152 E5
Clock House Pde
PLMGR N13 * 49 G1
Clockhouse Pl PUT/ROE SW15 139 H6
Clock House Rd BECK BR3 182 B6
Clock Pde ENC/FH EN2 * 23 K6
Clocktower Ms HNWL W7 * 115 K1
Clock Tower Ms IS N1 6 D1
THMD SE28 109 H6
Clock Tower Pl HOLWY N7 * 84 E4
Clock Tower Rd ISLW TW7 136 A4
Cloister Cl RAIN RM13 111 K3
TEDD TW11 174 C1
Cloister Gdns EDGW HA8 44 E1
SNWD SE25 197 J3
Cloister Rd ACT W3 98 E4
CRICK NW2 82 D1
Cloisters Av HAYES BR2 200 E2
Clonard Wy PIN HA5 42 A2
Clonbrock Rd
STNW/STAM N16 86 A2
Cloncurry St FUL/PGN SW6 139 G3
Clonmel Cl RYLN/HDSTN HA2 60 D5
Clonmell Rd TOTM N17 49 K6
Clonmel Rd FUL/PGN SW6 139 J1
TEDD TW11 155 J6
Clonmore St
WAND/EARL SW18 159 J3
Cloonmore Av ORP BR6 217 F3
Clorane Gdns HAMP NW3 82 E1
Closemead Cl NTHWD HA6 40 A2
The Close ALP/SUD HA0 80 A4
BECK BR3 198 B1
BUSH WD23 * 28 A1
BXLY DA5 169 H1
CAR SM5 209 J6
CHDH RM6 74 A3
CHEAM SM3 193 J4
CHING E4 52 A3
EBAR EN4 33 K1
GNTH/NBYPK IG2 72 E3
ISLW TW7 135 J3
MTCM CR4 194 E1
NWMAL KT3 175 K5
PIN HA5 59 G4
RCH/KEW TW9 137 J4
SCUP DA14 186 C1
SNWD SE25 * 197 H3
STHGT/OAK N14 34 D4
STMC/STPC BR5 201 K3
SURB KT6 191 F4
TRDG/WHET N20 32 D4
WBLY HA9 80 E1
Cloth Ct STBT EC1A 12 B2
Cloth Fair STBT EC1A 12 B2
Clothier St HDTCH EC3A 13 H3
Cloth St STBT EC1A 12 C1
Clothworkers Rd
WOOL/PLUM SE18 147 J1
Cloudesdale Rd TOOT SW17 161 G4
Cloudesley Cl SCUP DA14 186 A1
Cloudesley Pl IS N1 5 K1
Cloudesley Rd IS N1 5 J1
Cloudesley St IS N1 5 K1
Clouston Cl WLGTN SM6 210 E3
Clova Rd FSTGT E7 88 E3
Clove Crs POP/IOD E14 106 A6
Clovelly Av CDALE/KGS NW9 63 H1
HGDN/ICK UB10 76 A2
Clovelly Cl HGDN/ICK UB10 76 A2
PIN HA5 41 F6
Clovelly Gdns EN EN1 36 A2
ROMW/RG RM7 56 D4
Clovelly Rd BXLYHN DA7 129 F6
CEND/HSY/T N8 66 D1
CHSWK W4 * 118 A2
EA W5 116 D2
HSLW TW3 135 F3
Clovelly Wy ORP BR6 202 A3
RYLN/HDSTN HA2 77 K1
WCHPL E1 104 E5
Clover Cl WAN E11 * 70 B6
Cloverdale Gdns BFN/LL DA15 168 A1
The Clover Fld BUSH WD23 27 K1
Clover Ms CHEL SW3 120 E6
Clover Wy WLGTN SM6 195 F5
Clove St PLSTW E13 106 E3
Clowders Rd CAT SE6 164 C5
Clowser Cl SUT SM1 209 G3
Cloysters Gn WAP E1W * 123 H1
Cloyster Wd EDGW HA8 43 K3
Club Rw BETH E2 7 J6
The Clumps ASHF TW15 153 G6
Clunbury Av NWDGN UB2 114 E5
Clunbury St IS N1 7 F3
Cluny Est STHWK SE1 19 G4
Cluny Ms ECT SW5 119 J4
Cluny Pl STHWK SE1 19 G4
Clutton St POP/IOD E14 105 K4
Clydach Rd EN EN1 24 B5
Clyde Circ SEVS/STOTM N15 68 A1
Clyde Ct CAMTN NW1 4 D2
Clyde Flats FUL/PGN SW6 * 139 J1
Clyde Pl LEY E10 69 K4
Clyde Rd CROY/NA CR0 197 G6
SEVS/STOTM N15 68 A1
STWL/WRAY TW19 152 A3
SUT SM1 208 E3
WDGN N22 48 D4
WLGTN SM6 210 C3
Clydesdale PEND EN3 25 F5
Clydesdale Av STAN HA7 43 K6
Clydesdale Cl ISLW TW7 136 A4
Clydesdale Gdns
RCHPK/HAM TW10 137 J5
Clydesdale Rd EMPK RM11 75 H4
NTGHL W11 100 D5
Clyde St DEPT SE8 124 C6
Clyde Ter FSTH SE23 163 K4
Clyde V FSTH SE23 163 K4
Clyde Wy ROM RM1 57 G4
Clydon Cl ERITH DA8 130 B6
Clyfford Rd RSLP HA4 76 D2
Clymping Dene
EBED/NFELT TW14 154 A2
Clyston Rd WATW WD18 26 D1
Clyston St VX/NE SW8 141 H3
Coach & Horses Yd
CONDST W1S 9 K5
Coach House La HBRY N5 * 85 H2
WIM/MER SW19 159 G6
Coach House Ms FSTH SE23 163 K1
NWCR SE14 * 144 A2
Coach House Yd
WAND/EARL SW18 * 140 A5
Coalecroft Rd PUT/ROE SW15 139 F5
Coal Post Cl ORP BR6 * 217 F5
Coates Av WAND/EARL SW18 160 D1
Coates Cl THHTH CR7 180 D6
Coates Hill Rd BMLY BR1 185 F5
Coates Rd BORE WD6 29 K2
Coate St BETH E2 104 C1
Cobalt Cl BECK BR3 198 A1
Cobbett Rd ELTH/MOT SE9 146 D4
WHTN TW2 155 F3
Cobbetts Av REDBR IG4 71 H2
Cobbett St VX/NE SW8 142 A1
Cobble La IS N1 85 H5
Cobble Ms HBRY N5 85 J1
Cobbler's Wk TEDD TW11 173 K3
Cobblestone Pl CROY/NA CR0 196 D5
Cobbold Ms SHB W12 * 118 C2
Cobbold Rd SHB W12 118 C2
WAN E11 88 D1
WLSDN NW10 81 H4
Cobb's Rd HSLWW TW4 134 E5
Cobb St WCHPL E1 13 J3
Cobden Ms SYD SE26 181 J1
Cobden Rd ORP BR6 216 D2
SNWD SE25 197 H2
WAN E11 88 C1
Cobham Av NWMAL KT3 192 D2
Cobham Cl BFN/LL DA15 168 C1
BTSEA SW11 160 D1
EDGW HA8 44 D5
EN EN1 24 C4
HAYES BR2 200 D4
WLGTN SM6 210 E4
Cobham Ms CAMTN NW1 84 D5
Cobham Pl BXLYHS DA6 148 E6
Cobham Rd GDMY/SEVK IG3 72 E6
HEST TW5 134 B1
KUT/HW KT1 175 H5
WALTH E17 52 A4
Cobland Rd LEE/GVPK SE12 166 B6
Coborn Rd BOW E3 105 H2
Coborn St BOW E3 105 H2
Cobourg Rd CMBW SE5 123 G5
Cobourg St CAMTN NW1 4 B5
Coburg Cl WEST SW1P 16 B6
Coburg Crs BRXS/STRHM SW2 162 A3
Coburg Dwellings
WCHPL E1 * 104 E6
Coburg Gdns CLAY IG5 53 H5
Coburg Rd WDGN N22 49 F5
Cochrane Ms STJWD NW8 2 B3
Cochrane Rd WIM/MER SW19 177 H3
Cochrane St STJWD NW8 2 B3
Cockcrow Hl SURB KT6 * 190 E5
Cockerell Rd WALTH E17 69 G4
Cockfosters Pde EBAR EN4 * 22 A5
Cockfosters Rd EBAR EN4 21 K4
Cock La STBT EC1A 12 A2
Cockmannings La
STMC/STPC BR5 202 E5
Cockmannings Rd
STMC/STPC BR5 202 E4
Cocks Crs NWMAL KT3 192 C1
Cocksett Av ORP BR6 216 E4
Cockspur Ct STJS SW1Y 10 D7
Cockspur St STJS SW1Y 10 D7
Cocksure La SCUP DA14 169 H6
Code St WCHPL E1 7 K7
Codling Cl WAP E1W 123 H1
Codling Wy ALP/SUD HA0 79 K2
Codrington Hl FSTH SE23 164 B2
Codrington Ms NTGHL W11 100 C5
Cody Cl KTN/HRWW/WS HA3 43 K6
WLGTN SM6 210 D5
Cody Rd CAN/RD E16 106 B3
Coe Av SNWD SE25 197 H3
Coe's Aly BAR EN5 20 C5
Coffey St DEPT SE8 144 D1
Cogan Av WALTH E17 51 G4
Coin St STHWK SE1 11 J7
Coity Rd KTTN NW5 84 A4
Cokers La DUL SE21 162 D3
Coke St WCHPL E1 104 C5
Colas Ms KIL/WHAMP NW6 82 E6
Colbeck Ms SKENS SW7 120 A4
Colbeck Rd HRW HA1 60 C4
Colberg Pl STNW/STAM N16 * 68 B4
Colborne Wy WPK KT4 208 A1
Colbrook Av HYS/HAR UB3 113 G3
Colbrook Cl HYS/HAR UB3 113 G3
Colburn Av PIN HA5 41 J2
Colburn Wy SUT SM1 209 H1
Colby Rd NRWD SE19 181 F1
Colchester Dr PIN HA5 59 H2
Colchester Rd EDGW HA8 44 E3
LEY E10 70 A4
NTHWD HA6 40 E5
WALTH E17 69 J3
Coldbath Sq CLKNW EC1R 5 J7
Coldbath St LEW SE13 144 E2
Cold Blow La NWCR SE14 144 A1
Coldershaw Rd WEA W13 116 B2
Coldfall Av MUSWH N10 47 K5
Coldharbour POP/IOD E14 125 F1
Coldharbour Crest
ELTH/MOT SE9 * 167 F5
Coldharbour La BRXN/ST SW9 142 B5
BUSH WD23 28 B1
HYS/HAR UB3 113 J2
RAIN RM13 130 D1
Coldharbour Pl CMBW SE5 142 D3
Coldharbour Rd
CROY/NA CR0 211 G3
Coldharbour Wy
CROY/NA CR0 211 G3
Coldstream Gdns
WAND/EARL SW18 159 J1
Colebeck Ms IS N1 85 H4
Colebert Av WCHPL E1 104 E3
Colebrook Cl MLHL NW7 46 B3
Colebrooke Av WEA W13 97 H5
Colebrooke Dr WAN E11 71 F4
Colebrooke Pl IS N1 6 B1
Colebrooke Rw IS N1 6 A3
Colebrook Ri HAYES BR2 183 H5
Colebrook Rd
STRHM/NOR SW16 179 K4
Colebrook Wy
FBAR/BDGN N11 48 B1
Coleby Pth CMBW SE5 * 142 E1
Cole Cl THMD SE28 128 C1
Coledale Dr STAN HA7 43 J4
Coleford Rd
WAND/EARL SW18 140 B6
Cole Gdns HEST TW5 133 K1
Colegrave Rd SRTFD E15 88 B3
Colegrove Rd PECK SE15 123 G6
Coleherne Ms WBPTN SW10 120 A5
Coleherne Rd ECT SW5 120 A5
Colehill Gdns FUL/PGN SW6 * 139 H2
Colehill La FUL/PGN SW6 139 H2
Coleman Cl SNWD SE25 181 H5
Coleman Flds IS N1 85 J6
Coleman Rd BELV DA17 129 H3
CMBW SE5 143 F1
Colemans Heath
ELTH/MOT SE9 167 F5
Coleman St CITYW EC2V 12 E3
Colenso Dr MLHL NW7 45 J3
Colenso Rd CLPT E5 86 E2
GNTH/NBYPK IG2 72 E5
Cole Park Gdns TWK TW1 156 B1
Cole Park Rd TWK TW1 156 B2
Colepits Wood Rd
ELTH/MOT SE9 147 J6
Coleraine Rd BKHTH/KID SE3 125 J6
CEND/HSY/T N8 49 G6
Coleridge Av MNPK E12 89 J4
SUT SM1 209 J2
Coleridge Cl VX/NE SW8 141 G3
Coleridge Gdns
KIL/WHAMP NW6 83 G5
WBPTN SW10 140 B1
Coleridge Rd ASHF TW15 152 B6
CEND/HSY/T N8 66 D3
CROY/NA CR0 197 K4
DART DA1 151 K5
FSBYPK N4 67 G6
HARH RM3 57 K3
NFNCH/WDSPK N12 47 G1
WALTH E17 69 H1
Coleridge Sq WEA W13 97 G5
Coleridge Wk GLDGN NW11 64 E1
Coleridge Wy ORP BR6 202 B3
WDR/YW UB7 112 B4
YEAD UB4 94 E5
Cole Rd TWK TW1 156 B1
Colesburg Rd BECK BR3 182 C6
Coles Crs RYLN/HDSTN HA2 60 B6
Coles Gn BUSH WD23 28 C3
Coles Green Rd CRICK NW2 63 J5
Coleshill Rd TEDD TW11 173 K2
Colestown St BTSEA SW11 140 D3
Cole St STHWK SE1 18 D3
Colet Cl PLMGR N13 49 H2
Colet Gdns WKENS W14 119 G5
Coley St FSBYW WC1X 5 H7
Colfe & Hatcliffe Glebe
LEW SE13 * 144 E6
Colfe Rd FSTH SE23 164 B3
Colham Av WDR/YW UB7 112 B1
Colham Mill Rd WDR/YW UB7 112 A1
Colina Ms SEVS/STOTM N15 67 H1
Colina Rd CEND/HSY/T N8 67 H2
Colin Cl CDALE/KGS NW9 63 G1
CROY/NA CR0 213 H1
WWKM BR4 214 D1
Colin Crs CDALE/KGS NW9 63 H2
Colindale Av CDALE/KGS NW9 45 F6
Colindeep Gdns HDN NW4 63 J2
Colindeep La CDALE/KGS NW9 63 H1
Colin Dr CDALE/KGS NW9 63 H2
Colinette Rd PUT/ROE SW15 139 F5
Colin Gdns CDALE/KGS NW9 63 H2
Colin Park Rd
CDALE/KGS NW9 45 G6
Colinton Rd GDMY/SEVK IG3 73 H6
Coliston Rd
WAND/EARL SW18 159 K2
Collamore Av
WAND/EARL SW18 160 D3
Collapit Cl HRW HA1 60 B3
Collard Pl CAMTN NW1 84 B5
College Ap GNWCH SE10 125 F6
College Av
KTN/HRWW/WS HA3 42 E4
College Cl
KTN/HRWW/WS HA3 42 E3
UED N18 50 B1
WHTN TW2 155 J3
College Ct EA W5 * 98 A6
College Crs HAMP NW3 83 G4
College Cross IS N1 85 G5
College Dr RSLP HA4 58 E4
THDIT KT7 189 K4
College East WCHPL E1 * 13 K2
College Gdns CHING E4 37 K2
ENC/FH EN2 23 K2
NWMAL KT3 192 C2
REDBR IG4 71 J2
TOOT SW17 160 D4
UED N18 * 50 B1
College Gn NRWD SE19 181 F3
College Gv CAMTN NW1 4 C1
College Hl CANST EC4R * 12 D5
College Hill Rd
KTN/HRWW/WS HA3 42 E3
College La KTTN NW5 84 B2
College Ms IS N1 85 G5
WEST SW1P 16 E4
College Pde
KIL/WHAMP NW6 * 82 C6
College Park Cl LEW SE13 145 F5
College Pl WALTH E17 70 C1
WBPTN SW10 * 140 B1
College Rd BMLY BR1 183 K4
CROY/NA CR0 196 E6
DUL SE21 163 F3
ENC/FH EN2 23 K3
HRW HA1 60 E3
ISLW TW7 136 A2
KTN/HRWW/WS HA3 42 E4
NRWD SE19 181 G1
TOTM N17 50 B2
WALTH E17 70 A2
WBLY HA9 61 K5
WCHMH N21 35 G4
WEA W13 97 H5
WIM/MER SW19 178 C2
WLSDN NW10 100 A1
College St CANST EC4R * 12 D5
College Ter FNCH N3 46 D4
College Vw ELTH/MOT SE9 166 C3
College Wy ASHF TW15 152 C6
HYS/HAR UB3 94 E6
NTHWD HA6 40 B2
College Yd KIL/WHAMP NW6 * 82 C6
KTTN NW5 84 B2
Collent St HOM E9 86 E4
Colless Rd SEVS/STOTM N15 68 B2
Collett Rd BERM/RHTH SE16 123 H3
Collett Wy NWDGN UB2 115 G2
Collier Cl EHAM E6 108 B6
HOR/WEW KT19 206 C4
Collier Dr EDGW HA8 44 C5
Collier Row La CRW RM5 56 E4
Collier Row Rd CRW RM5 56 B4
Colliers Shaw HAYES BR2 215 J3
Collier St IS N1 5 G3
Colliers Water La THHTH CR7 196 B2
Collindale Av BFN/LL DA15 168 B3
CDALE/KGS NW9 45 G6
ERITH DA8 129 J6
Collingbourne Rd SHB W12 118 E1
Collingham Gdns ECT SW5 120 A4
Collingham Pl ECT SW5 120 A4
Collingham Rd ECT SW5 120 A4
Collings Cl WDGN N22 49 F2
Collington St GNWCH SE10 * 125 G5
Collingtree Rd SYD SE26 163 K6
Collingwood Av BRYLDS KT5 191 K5
MUSWH N10 48 A6
Colling Wood Cl PGE/AN SE20 181 J4
Collingwood Cl WHTN TW2 155 F2
Collingwood Rd MTCM CR4 178 D5
RAIN RM13 111 H1
SEVS/STOTM N15 68 A1
SUT SM1 208 E2
Collingwood St WCHPL E1 104 D3
Collins Av STAN HA7 44 A5
Collins Dr RSLP HA4 59 G6
Collinson St STHWK SE1 18 C3
Collinson Wk STHWK SE1 18 C3
Collins Rd HBRY N5 85 J2
Collins Sq BKHTH/KID SE3 * 145 J4
Collins St BKHTH/KID SE3 145 H3
Collinwood Av PEND EN3 24 E4
Collinwood Gdns
GNTH/NBYPK IG2 71 K2
Collyer Av CROY/NA CR0 210 E2
Collyer Pl PECK SE15 143 H2
Collyer Rd CROY/NA CR0 210 E2
Colman Pde EN EN1 * 24 A4
Colman Rd CAN/RD E16 107 G4
Colmar Cl WCHPL E1 105 F3
Colmer Pl
KTN/HRWW/WS HA3 42 D3
Colmer Rd STRHM/NOR SW16 179 K3
Colmore Ms PECK SE15 143 J2
Colmore Rd PEND EN3 24 E5
Colnbrook St STHWK SE1 18 A5
Colne Av OXHEY WD19 27 F1
Colne Ct HOR/WEW KT19 206 E2
Colne Rd CLPT E5 87 F2
WCHMH N21 35 K2
WHTN TW2 155 K3
Colne St PLSTW E13 106 E2
Colney Hatch La
FBAR/BDGN N11 47 K2
MUSWH N10 48 A4
Cologne Rd BTSEA SW11 140 C5
Colombo Rd IL IG1 72 C5
Colombo St STHWK SE1 18 A1
Colomb St GNWCH SE10 125 H5
Colonels Wk ENC/FH EN2 23 H3
Colonial Av WHTN TW2 155 H1
Colonial Dr CHSWK W4 117 K4
Colonial Rd
EBED/NFELT TW14 153 H2
Colonnade BMSBY WC1N 4 E7
The Colonnade DEPT SE8 * 124 C4
Colosseum Ter CAMTN NW1 3 K6
Colson Rd CROY/NA CR0 196 E6
Colson Wy STRHM/NOR SW16 161 H6
Colsterworth Rd
SEVS/STOTM N15 68 B1
Colston Av CAR SM5 209 J2
Colston Rd FSTGT E7 89 H4
MORT/ESHN SW14 137 K5
Colthurst Crs FSBYPK N4 67 H6
Colthurst Dr ED N9 36 D5
Coltness Crs ABYW SE2 128 C5
Colton Gdns TOTM N17 49 J6
Colton Rd HRW HA1 60 E2
Colts Yd WAN E11 * 70 D5
Columbas Dr HAMP NW3 65 H6
Columbia Av EDGW HA8 44 D4
RSLP HA4 59 F5
WPK KT4 192 C4
Columbia Rd BETH E2 7 J4
PLSTW E13 * 106 D3
Columbia Whf PEND EN3 * 25 G6
Columbine Av EHAM E6 107 J4
SAND/SEL CR2 211 H5
Columbine Wy LEW SE13 * 145 F3
Columbus Gdns NTHWD HA6 40 E4
Colvestone Crs HACK E8 86 B3
Colville Est IS N1 7 F1
Colville Gdns NTGHL W11 100 D5
Colville Houses NTGHL W11 100 D5
Colville Ms NTGHL W11 100 D5
Colville Pl FITZ W1T 10 B2
Colville Rd ACT W3 117 J3
ED N9 36 D3
NTGHL W11 100 D5
WALTH E17 51 G5
WAN E11 88 A1
Colville Sq NTGHL W11 * 100 D5
Colville Square Ms
NTGHL W11 * 100 D5
Colville Ter NTGHL W11 100 D5
Colvin Cl SYD SE26 181 K1
Colvin Gdns BARK/HLT IG6 54 C3
CHING E4 38 A5
SWFD E18 71 F1
Colvin Rd EHAM E6 89 J5
THHTH CR7 196 B2
Colwall Gdns WFD IG8 52 E1
Colwell Rd EDUL SE22 143 G6
Colwick Cl HGT N6 66 D4
Colwith Rd HMSMTH W6 119 F6
Colwood Gdns
WIM/MER SW19 178 C3
Colworth Gv WALW SE17 18 D7
Colworth Rd CROY/NA CR0 197 H5
WAN E11 70 C3
Colwyn Av GFD/PVL UB6 97 F1
Colwyn Cl STRHM/NOR SW16 179 H1
Colwyn Crs HSLW TW3 135 H2
Colwyn Gn CDALE/KGS NW9 * 63 G3
Colwyn Rd CRICK NW2 81 K1
Colyer Cl ELTH/MOT SE9 167 G4
Colyers Cl ERITH DA8 150 A2
Colyton Cl ALP/SUD HA0 79 J4
WELL DA16 148 E2
Colyton La STRHM/NOR SW16 180 B1
Colyton Rd EDUL SE22 143 J6
Colyton Wy UED N18 50 C1
Combe Av BKHTH/KID SE3 145 J1
Combemartin Rd
WAND/EARL SW18 159 H2
Comber Cl CRICK NW2 63 J6
Comber Gv CMBW SE5 142 D1
Combermere Rd
BRXN/ST SW9 142 A
MRDN SM4 194 A3
Combe Rd WATW WD18 26 D
Comberton Rd CLPT E5 68 D6
Combeside WOOL/PLUM SE18 148 A
Combes Rd DAGW RM9 92 B
Combwell Crs ABYW SE2 128 B
Comely Bank Rd WALTH E17 70 A
Comeragh Ms WKENS W14 119 H
Comeragh Rd WKENS W14 119 H
Comerford Rd BROCKY SE4 144 B
Comet Cl MNPK E12 89 H
PUR RM19 131 K
Comet Pl DEPT SE8 144 D
Comet Rd STWL/WRAY TW19 152 A
Comet St DEPT SE8 144 D
Comfort St PECK SE15 143 F
Commerce Rd BTFD TW8 116 D
WDGN N22 49 F
Commerce Wy CROY/NA CR0 211 F
Commercial Rd POP/IOD E14 105 G
UED N18 50 A
Commercial St WCHPL E1 7 J
Commercial Wy CMBW SE5 143
WLSDN NW10 98 D
Commerell Pl GNWCH SE10 125
Commerell St GNWCH SE10 125
Commodore Pde
STRHM/NOR SW16 * 180
Commodore St WCHPL E1 105
Commondale PUT/ROE SW15 139 F
Common La ESH/CLAY KT10 205
Common Rd BARN SW13 138
ESH/CLAY KT10 205
STAN HA7 28
Commonside HAYES BR2 215
Commonside East MTCM CR4 195
Commonside West
MTCM CR4 179
The Common EA W5 117
NWDGN UB2 114
SRTFD E15 88
STAN HA7 29
Commonwealth Av
HYS/HAR UB3 94
SHB W12 99
Commonwealth Rd
TOTM N17 50
Commonwealth Wy
ABYW SE2 128
Community Cl HEST TW5 134
Community Rd GFD/PVL UB6 78
SRTFD E15 88
Como Rd FSTH SE23 164
Como St ROMW/RG RM7 75
Compass Cl EDGW HA8 30
Compass Hl
RCHPK/HAM TW10 156
Compayne Gdns
KIL/WHAMP NW6 83
Compton Av ALP/SUD HA0 79
EHAM E6 107
GPK RM2 57
HGT N6 65
IS N1 85
Compton Cl CAMTN NW1 3
EDGW HA8 44
ESH/CLAY KT10 204
GLDGN NW11 82
PECK SE15 143
WEA W13 97
Compton Crs CHSGTN KT9 206
CHSWK W4 117
NTHLT UB5 77
TOTM N17 49
Compton Pas FSBYE EC1V 6
Compton Pl ERITH DA8 130

OXHEY WD19 27 J6
STPAN WC1H 4 E6
Compton Ri PIN HA5 59 J2
Compton Rd CROY/NA CR0 197 J5
HYS/HAR UB3 94 C6
IS N1 85 H4
WCHMH N21 35 H3
WIM/MER SW19 177 J2
WLSDN NW10 100 B2
Compton St FSBYE EC1V 6 A6
Compton Ter IS N1 85 H4
WCHMH N21 * 35 G3
Comreddy Cl ENC/FH EN2 23 H2
Comus Pl WALW SE17 19 G7
Comyn Rd BTSEA SW11 140 D5
Comyns Cl CAN/RD E16 106 D4
Comyns Rd DAGW RM9 92 C5
The Comyns BUSH WD23 28 C3
Conant Ms WCHPL E1 104 C6
Concanon Rd CLAP SW4 142 A5
Concert Hall Ap STHWK SE1 17 H1
Concord Cl NTHLT UB5 95 H2
Concorde Cl HSLW TW3 135 G3
Concorde Dr EHAM E6 107 K4
Concorde Wy
BERM/RHTH SE16 124 A4
Concord Rd ACT W3 98 D3
PEND EN3 24 E6
Concord Wy
BERM/RHTH SE16 * 124 A4
Condell Rd VX/NE SW8 141 H2
Conder St POP/IOD E14 105 G5
Condover Crs
WOOL/PLUM SE18 147 G1
Condray Pl BTSEA SW11 140 D1
Conduit Ct COVGDN WC2E * 10 E5
Conduit La SAND/SEL CR2 212 C3
UED N18 50 E1
Conduit Ms BAY/PAD W2 8 A4
Conduit Pl BAY/PAD W2 8 A4
Conduit Rd WOOL/PLUM SE18 127 G5
Conduit St CONDST W1S 9 K5
Conduit Wy WLSDN NW10 80 E5
Conewood St HBRY N5 85 H1
Coney Burrows CHING E4 38 C4
Coney Hall Pde WWKM BR4 * 214 C1
Coney Hill Rd WWKM BR4 199 H6
Coney Wy VX/NE SW8 122 A6
Conference Cl CHING E4 38 A4
Congleton Gv
WOOL/PLUM SE18 127 H5
Congo Dr ED N9 36 E5
Congo Rd WOOL/PLUM SE18 127 J5
Congreve Rd ELTH/MOT SE9 146 E4
Congreve St WALW SE17 19 G7
Conical Cnr ENC/FH EN2 23 J3
Conifer Av CRW RM5 56 D1
Conifer Cl ORP BR6 216 D2
Conifer Gdns EN EN1 35 K1
STRHM/NOR SW16 162 A5
SUT SM1 194 A6
Conifers Cl TEDD TW11 174 C3
Conifer Wy ALP/SUD HA0 79 J1
HYS/HAR UB3 94 E6
SWLY BR8 187 K4
Coniger Rd FUL/PGN SW6 139 K3
Coningham Ms SHB W12 118 D1
Coningham Rd SHB W12 118 E2
Coningsby Av
CDALE/KGS NW9 45 G5
Coningsby Cots EA W5 116 E2
Coningsby Gdns CHING E4 51 K2
Coningsby Rd EA W5 116 D2
FSBYPK N4 67 H4
SAND/SEL CR2 211 J6
Conington Rd LEW SE13 144 E3
Conisbee Ct STHGT/OAK N14 22 C6
Conisborough Crs CAT SE6 165 F5
Coniscliffe Cl CHST BR7 185 F4
Coniscliffe Rd PLMGR N13 35 J5
Coniston Av BARK IG11 90 E5
GFD/PVL UB6 97 H2
WELL DA16 147 K4
Coniston Cl BARN SW13 138 C1
BXLYHN DA7 149 K2
CHSWK W4 137 K2
MRDN SM4 193 G3
Coniston Ct BAY/PAD W2 * 8 D4
Conistone Wy HOLWY N7 84 E5
Coniston Gdns BELMT SM2 * 209 H4
CDALE/KGS NW9 63 F2
ED N9 36 E3
PIN HA5 58 E1
REDBR IG4 71 J1
WBLY HA9 61 J5
Coniston Rd BMLY BR1 183 H2
BXLYHN DA7 149 K2
CROY/NA CR0 197 H4
MUSWH N10 48 B5
TOTM N17 50 C2
WHTN TW2 155 G1
Coniston Wk HOM E9 86 E3
Coniston Wy CHSGTN KT9 206 A1
HCH RM12 93 J3
Conlan St NKENS W10 100 C3
Conley Rd WLSDN NW10 81 G4
Conley St GNWCH SE10 * 125 H5
Connaught Av ASHF TW15 152 B6
CHING E4 38 B2
EBAR EN4 33 K3
EN EN1 24 A3
HSLWW TW4 134 D6
MORT/ESHN SW14 137 K4
Connaught Br CAN/RD E16 107 H6
CAN/RD E16 126 C1
Connaught Cl BAY/PAD W2 8 C4
EN EN1 24 A3
LEY E10 69 G6
SUT SM1 194 C6
UX/CGN UB8 * 94 A4
Connaught Dr GLDGN NW11 64 E1
Connaught Gdns MRDN SM4 194 B2
MUSWH N10 66 B2
PLMGR N13 35 H6
Connaught La IL IG1 72 C6
Connaught Ms
FUL/PGN SW6 * 139 H2
HAMP NW3 * 83 J3
WOOL/PLUM SE18 127 F5
Connaught Rd BAR EN5 32 B1
CAN/RD E16 126 C1
CHING E4 38 C2
FSBYPK N4 67 G4
IL IG1 72 D6
KTN/HRWW/WS HA3 43 F4
NWMAL KT3 192 B1
RCHPK/HAM TW10 * 137 G6
SUT SM1 194 C6
TEDD TW11 173 J1
WALTH E17 * 69 J2
WAN E11 70 B5
WEA W13 97 H6
WLSDN NW10 99 G1
WOOL/PLUM SE18 127 F5
Connaught Sq BAY/PAD W2 8 D4
Connaught St BAY/PAD W2 8 C4
Connaught Wy PLMGR N13 35 H6
Connect La BARK/HLT IG6 54 C5
Connell Crs EA W5 98 B3
Connemara Cl BORE WD6 * 30 E1
Connington Crs CHING E4 38 B5
Connop Rd PEND EN3 25 F1
Connor Cl BARK/HLT IG6 54 C4
WAN E11 70 C5
Connor Rd DAGW RM9 92 B2
Connor St HOM E9 * 87 F6
Conolly Rd HNWL W7 115 K1
Conrad Dr WPK KT4 193 F5
Conroy Ct SCUP DA14 168 B6
Consfield Av NWMAL KT3 192 D1
Consort Cl FBAR/BDGN N11 47 K1
Consort Ms ISLW TW7 155 J1
Consort Rd PECK SE15 143 J2
Cons St STHWK SE1 * 17 K2
Constable Av CAN/RD E16 126 A1
Constable Cl GLDGN NW11 65 F3
YEAD UB4 94 A1
Constable Crs
SEVS/STOTM N15 68 C2
Constable Gdns EDGW HA8 44 C4
ISLW TW7 135 J6
Constable Ms BCTR RM8 91 H3
Constable Wk DUL SE21 163 F5
Constance Crs HAYES BR2 199 J5
Constance Rd CROY/NA CR0 196 C4
EN EN1 36 A1
SUT SM1 209 G2
WHTN TW2 155 G2
Constance St CAN/RD E16 126 D1
Constantine Rd HAMP NW3 83 J3
Constitution Hl
MYFR/PICC W1J 15 J2
Constitution Ri
WOOL/PLUM SE18 147 F2
Consul Av DAGW RM9 110 E3
RAIN RM13 111 F2
Content St WALW SE17 18 D7
Contessa Cl ORP BR6 216 E3
Control Tower Rd
HTHAIR TW6 132 D4
Convent Cl BECK BR3 183 F3
Convent Gdns EA W5 116 D4
NTGHL W11 100 D5
Convent Hl NRWD SE19 180 D2
Convent Wy NWDGN UB2 114 B4
Conway Cl RAIN RM13 93 J5
STAN HA7 43 G2
Conway Crs CHDH RM6 73 J4
GFD/PVL UB6 96 E1
Conway Dr BELMT SM2 209 F4
HYS/HAR UB3 113 F3
Conway Gdns ENC/FH EN2 24 A1
MTCM CR4 195 J1
WBLY HA9 61 J4
Conway Gv ACT W3 99 F4
Conway Ms FITZ W1T 10 A1
Conway Rd CRICK NW2 64 A6
FELT TW13 172 C1
HSLWW TW4 154 E2
RYNPK SW20 177 F4
SEVS/STOTM N15 67 J2
STHGT/OAK N14 34 E5
WOOL/PLUM SE18 127 J4
Conway St FITZ W1T 4 A7
Conybeare HAMP NW3 83 J5
Conyers Rd
STRHM/NOR SW16 179 J1
Conyer St BOW E3 * 105 G1
Cooden Cl BMLY BR1 184 A3
Cookes Cl WAN E11 70 D6
Cookes La CHEAM SM3 208 C4
Cookham Cl NWDGN UB2 115 G3
Cookham Dene Cl CHST BR7 185 J4
Cookham Rd SCUP DA14 187 H4
Cookhill Rd ABYW SE2 128 C2
Cook's Cl CRW RM5 56 E4
Cooks Ferry Rbt UED N18 51 G1
Cook's Hole Rd ENC/FH EN2 23 H1
Cooks Md BUSH WD23 28 B1
Cook's Rd SRTFD E15 105 K1
WALW SE17 122 C6
Coolfin Rd CAN/RD E16 106 E5
Coolgardie Av CHING E4 52 B1
Coolhurst Rd HGT N6 66 D3
Cool Oak Br CDALE/KGS NW9 63 H4
Cool Oak La CDALE/KGS NW9 63 H4
Coomassie Rd MV/WKIL W9 100 D3
Coombe Av CROY/NA CR0 212 A2
Coombe Bank KUTN/CMB KT2 176 B4
Coombe Cl EDGW HA8 44 B5
HSLW TW3 135 F5
Coombe Cnr WCHMH N21 35 H3
Coombe Crs HPTN TW12 172 D3
Coombe Dr RSLP HA4 59 F5
Coombe End KUTN/CMB KT2 176 A3
Coombefield Cl NWMAL KT3 192 B2
Coombe Gdns NWMAL KT3 192 C1
RYNPK SW20 176 D5
Coombe Hill Gld
KUTN/CMB KT2 176 B3
Coombe Hill Rd
KUTN/CMB KT2 176 B3
Coombe House Cha
NWMAL KT3 176 A4
Coombehurst Cl EBAR EN4 21 K3
Coombe La CROY/NA CR0 212 C4
RYNPK SW20 176 C4
Coombe La West
KUTN/CMB KT2 175 K4
Coombe Lea BMLY BR1 184 D6
Coombe Ldg CHARL SE7 126 B6
Coombe Neville
KUTN/CMB KT2 175 K3
Coombe Pk KUTN/CMB KT2 175 K1
Coombe Ridings
KUTN/CMB KT2 175 K1
Coombe Ri KUTN/CMB KT2 175 K4
Coombe Rd BUSH WD23 28 C2
CHSWK W4 118 B5
CROY/NA CR0 211 J2
HPTN TW12 172 E2
KUTN/CMB KT2 175 H4
SAND/SEL CR2 212 A2
SYD SE26 163 J6
WDGN N22 49 G5
WEA W13 116 C3
WLSDN NW10 81 F1
Coomber Wy CROY/NA CR0 195 J4
Coombe Vls
WAND/EARL SW18 * 159 K2
Coombewood Dr CHDH RM6 74 B3
Coombe Wood Rd
KUTN/CMB KT2 175 K1
Coombs St IS N1 6 B3
Coomer Ms FUL/PGN SW6 * 119 J6
Coomer Pl FUL/PGN SW6 119 J6
Cooms Wk EDGW HA8 44 D4
Cooperage Cl TOTM N17 50 B2
Cooper Av WALTH E17 51 F4
Cooper Cl STHWK SE1 17 K3
Cooper Crs CAR SM5 209 K1
Cooperdale Cl WFD IG8 53 G3
Cooper Rd CROY/NA CR0 211 G2
HDN NW4 64 B3
WLSDN NW10 81 H3
Coopersale Cl WFD IG8 53 G3
Coopersale Rd HOM E9 87 F3
Coopers Cl DAGE RM10 92 D4
WCHPL E1 104 E3
Coopers La CAMTN NW1 4 D2
LEE/GVPK SE12 166 A4
Cooper's La LEY E10 69 K5
Coopers Ms BECK BR3 182 D5
Cooper's Rd STHWK SE1 123 G5
Cooper's Rw TWRH EC3N 13 J5
Cooper St CAN/RD E16 106 D4
Coopers Yd IS N1 * 85 H5
Cooper's Yd NRWD SE19 181 F2
Coote Rd BCTR RM8 92 B1
Copeland Rd PECK SE15 143 H3
WALTH E17 69 K2
Copeman Cl SYD SE26 181 K1
Copenhagen Gdns CHEL SW3 120 C5
CHSWK W4 118 A2
Copenhagen Pl POP/IOD E14 105 H5
Copenhagen St IS N1 5 F1
Cope Pl KENS W8 119 K3
Copers Cope Rd BECK BR3 182 C3
Cope St BERM/RHTH SE16 124 A4
Copford Wk IS N1 * 85 J6
Copgate Pth
STRHM/NOR SW16 180 A2
Copland Av ALP/SUD HA0 79 K3
Copland Cl ALP/SUD HA0 79 J3
Copland Ms ALP/SUD HA0 80 A4
Copland Rd ALP/SUD HA0 80 A4
Copleston Rd PECK SE15 143 G4
Copley Cl HNWL W7 97 F5
WALW SE17 122 C6
Copley Dene BMLY BR1 184 C4
Copley Pk STRHM/NOR SW16 180 A2
Copley Rd STAN HA7 43 J1
Coppard Gdns CHSGTN KT9 205 J4
Coppelia Rd BKHTH/KID SE3 145 J5
Coppen Rd BCTR RM8 74 B4
Copperas St DEPT SE8 124 E6
Copper Beech Cl CLAY IG5 54 A4
STMC/STPC BR5 202 D2
Copper Cl NRWD SE19 181 G3
TOTM N17 50 D3
Copperdale Rd HYS/HAR UB3 113 K2
Copperfield CHIG IG7 54 D2
Copperfield Dr
SEVS/STOTM N15 68 B1
Copperfield Rd BOW E3 105 G3
THMD SE28 109 J5
Copperfield St STHWK SE1 18 B2
Copperfield Wy CHST BR7 185 H2
PIN HA5 59 K1
Coppergate Cl BMLY BR1 184 A4
Coppermead Cl CRICK NW2 82 A1
Copper Mill Dr ISLW TW7 136 A3
Copper Mill La TOOT SW17 160 B6
Coppermill La WALTH E17 68 E3
Copper Rw STHWK SE1 19 J1
Coppetts Cl
NFNCH/WDSPK N12 47 K3
Coppetts Rd MUSWH N10 47 K4
Coppice Cl BECK BR3 198 E1
RSLP HA4 * 58 A3
RYNPK SW20 177 F6
STAN HA7 43 F2
Coppice Dr PUT/ROE SW15 158 D1
The Coppice BAR EN5 * 33 F1
ENC/FH EN2 23 H5
OXHEY WD19 27 G1
Coppice Wk TRDG/WHET N20 32 E5
Coppice Wy SWFD E18 70 D1
Coppies Gv FBAR/BDGN N11 34 B6
Copping Cl CROY/NA CR0 212 A2
The Coppins CROY/NA CR0 213 K4
KTN/HRWW/WS HA3 42 E2
Coppock Cl BTSEA SW11 140 D3
Coppsfield E/WMO/HCT KT8 173 F6
Copse Av WWKM BR4 213 K1
Copse Cl CHARL SE7 126 A5
NTHWD HA6 40 A4
WDR/YW UB7 112 A3
Copse Gld SURB KT6 190 E5
Copse Hl BELMT SM2 209 F5
RYNPK SW20 176 D4
WIM/MER SW19 177 F2
Copsem Dr ESH/CLAY KT10 204 B4
Copsem La ESH/CLAY KT10 204 B4
Copsem Wy ESH/CLAY KT10 204 C4
The Copse CHING E4 38 D3
EFNCH N2 * 47 K6
Copse Vw SAND/SEL CR2 213 F5
Copsewood Cl BFN/LL DA15 167 K1
Copse Wood Wy NTHWD HA6 40 A4
Coptefield Dr BELV DA17 128 E3
Copthall Av LOTH EC2R 13 F3
Copthall Dr MLHL NW7 45 J3
Copthall Gdns MLHL NW7 45 J3
TWK TW1 156 A3
Copthorne Av BAL SW12 161 J2
BARK/HLT IG6 54 B2
HAYES BR2 200 E6
Copthorne Ms HYS/HAR UB3 113 H4
Coptic St NOXST/BSQ WC1A 10 E2
Copton Cl BOW E3 105 J4
Copwood Cl
NFNCH/WDSPK N12 33 H6
Coral Cl CHDH RM6 55 J6
Coraline Cl STHL UB1 95 K2
Coral Rw BTSEA SW11 140 B4
Coral St STHWK SE1 17 K3
Coram St STPAN WC1H 4 E7
Coran Cl ED N9 37 F2
Corban Rd HSLW TW3 135 F4
Corbar Cl EBAR EN4 21 H1
Corbet Cl WLGTN SM6 195 F5
Corbet Pl WCHPL E1 13 J1
Corbett Gv FBAR/BDGN N11 48 E3
Corbett Rd WALTH E17 52 B5
WAN E11 71 G3
Corbett's La
BERM/RHTH SE16 123 K4
Corbicum WAN E11 70 C4
Corbiere Ct WIM/MER SW19 177 G2
Corbin's La RYLN/HDSTN HA2 78 B1
Corbridge Crs BETH E2 104 D1
Corbridge Ms ROM RM1 75 H2
Corby Crs ENC/FH EN2 22 E5
Corbylands Rd BFN/LL DA15 167 K2
Corbyn St FSBYPK N4 66 E5
Corby Rd WLSDN NW10 98 E1
Cordelia Cl HNHL SE24 142 C5
Cordelia Gdns
STWL/WRAY TW19 152 B2
Cordelia Rd
STWL/WRAY TW19 152 B2
Cordelia St POP/IOD E14 105 K5
Cordingley Rd RSLP HA4 58 B5
Cording St POP/IOD E14 105 K4
Cordwell Rd LEW SE13 145 G6
Corelli Rd BKHTH/KID SE3 146 D2
Corfe Av RYLN/HDSTN HA2 78 A2
Corfe Cl HSLWW TW4 154 D3
YEAD UB4 95 G5
Corfield Rd WCHMH N21 23 F6
Corfield St BETH E2 104 D3
Corfton Rd EA W5 98 A5
Coriander Av POP/IOD E14 106 B5
Cories Cl BCTR RM8 73 K6
Corinium Cl WBLY HA9 80 B2
Corinne Rd ARCH N19 84 C2
Corkran Rd SURB KT6 190 E4
Cork St Ms CONDST W1S 10 A6
Corkscrew Hl WWKM BR4 199 F6
Cork Sq WAP E1W 123 H1
Cork St CONDST W1S 10 A6
Cork Tree Wy CHING E4 51 G1
Corlett St CAMTN NW1 8 C1
Cormont Rd CMBW SE5 142 C2
Cormorant Cl WALTH E17 51 F4
Cormorant Rd FSTGT E7 88 D3
Cornbury Rd EDGW HA8 43 K3
Cornelia Dr YEAD UB4 95 G4
Cornelia St HOLWY N7 85 F4
Cornell Cl SCUP DA14 187 F2
Cornell Wy CRW RM5 56 D1
Corner Fielde
BRXS/STRHM SW2 * 162 A3
Corner Md CDALE/KGS NW9 45 H3
The Corner EA W5 * 117 F1
Corney Reach Wy CHSWK W4 138 B1
Corney Rd CHSWK W4 118 B6
Cornflower La CROY/NA CR0 198 A5
Cornflower Ter EDUL SE22 163 J1
Cornford Gv BAL SW12 161 G4
Cornhill BANK EC3V 13 F4
Cornish Ct ED N9 36 D2
Cornish Gv PGE/AN SE20 181 J4
Corn Mill Dr ORP BR6 202 A4
Cornmill La LEW SE13 144 E4
Cornmow Dr WLSDN NW10 81 H3
Cornshaw Rd BCTR RM8 73 K5
Cornthwaite Rd CLPT E5 86 E1
Cornwall Av BETH E2 104 E2
ESH/CLAY KT10 205 F5
FNCH N3 46 E3
STHL UB1 95 K4
WDGN N22 48 E4
WELL DA16 147 K4
Cornwall Cl BARK IG11 91 F4
Cornwall Crs NTGHL W11 100 C6
Cornwall Dr STMC/STPC BR5 186 D3
Cornwall Gdns SKENS SW7 120 A3
SNWD SE25 * 197 G1
WLSDN NW10 81 K4
Cornwall Gardens Wk
KENS W8 120 A3
Cornwall Gv CHSWK W4 118 B5
Cornwallis Av ED N9 36 D4
ELTH/MOT SE9 167 J4
Cornwallis Cl ERITH DA8 130 C6
Cornwallis Gv ED N9 36 D4
Cornwallis Rd ARCH N19 66 E6
DAGW RM9 92 A2
ED N9 36 D4
WALTH E17 69 F1
WOOL/PLUM SE18 127 H4
Cornwallis Sq ARCH N19 66 E6
Cornwallis Wk ELTH/MOT SE9 146 E4
Cornwall Ms South
SKENS SW7 120 B3
Cornwall Ms West
SKENS SW7 * 120 A3
Cornwall Rd BELMT SM2 208 D5
CROY/NA CR0 196 C6
FSBYPK N4 67 G4
HRW HA1 60 C3
PIN HA5 41 K3
RSLP HA4 58 D6
SEVS/STOTM N15 67 K2
STHWK SE1 11 J7
TWK TW1 156 B2
UED N18 50 C1
Cornwall Sq LBTH SE11 * 122 B5
Cornwall St WCHPL E1 104 D6
Cornwall Ter CAMTN NW1 3 F7
Cornwall Terrace Ms
CAMTN NW1 3 F7
Corn Wy WAN E11 88 B1
Cornwood Cl EFNCH N2 65 H2
Cornwood Dr WCHPL E1 104 E5
Cornworthy Rd BCTR RM8 91 J3
Coronation Cl BARK/HLT IG6 72 C1
BXLY DA5 168 E1
Coronation Dr HCH RM12 93 K3
Coronation Rd HYS/HAR UB3 113 J4
PLSTW E13 107 G2
WLSDN NW10 98 D3
Coronation Vls
WLSDN NW10 * 98 D3
Coronet Pde ALP/SUD HA0 * 80 A4
Coronet St IS N1 7 G5
Corporation Av HSLWW TW4 134 D5
Corporation Rw CLKNW EC1R 5 K6
Corporation St HOLWY N7 84 E3
SRTFD E15 106 C1
Corrance Rd
BRXS/STRHM SW2 141 K5
Corri Av STHGT/OAK N14 34 D6
Corrib Dr SUT SM1 209 J3
Corrigan Cl HDN NW4 46 A6
Corringham Rd GLDGN NW11 64 E4
WBLY HA9 62 C6
Corringway EA W5 98 B4
GLDGN NW11 65 F4
Corris Gn CDALE/KGS NW9 * 63 G3
Corry Dr BRXN/ST SW9 142 C5
Corsair Cl STWL/WRAY TW19 152 A2
Corsair Rd STWL/WRAY TW19 152 B2
Corscombe Cl KUTN/CMB KT2 175 K1
Corsehill St
STRHM/NOR SW16 179 H2
Corsellis Sq TWK TW1 136 C5
Corsham St IS N1 7 F5
Corsica St HBRY N5 85 H4
Cortayne Rd FUL/PGN SW6 * 139 J3
Cortina Dr DAGW RM9 110 E2
Cortis Rd PUT/ROE SW15 158 E1
Cortis Ter PUT/ROE SW15 138 E6
Corunna Rd VX/NE SW8 141 H2
Corunna Ter VX/NE SW8 141 H2
Corwell Gdns UX/CGN UB8 94 A5
Corwell La UX/CGN UB8 94 A5
Coryton Pth MV/WKIL W9 100 D3
Cosbycote Av HNHL SE24 142 D6
Cosdach Av WLGTN SM6 210 D5
Cosedge Crs CROY/NA CR0 211 G3
Cosgrove Cl WCHMH N21 35 J4
YEAD UB4 95 H3
Cosmo Pl RSQ WC1B 11 F1
Cosmur Cl SHB W12 118 C3
Cossall Wk PECK SE15 143 J2
Cossar Ms BRXS/STRHM SW2 162 B1
Cosser St STHWK SE1 17 J4
Costa St PECK SE15 143 H3
Costons Av GFD/PVL UB6 96 D2
Costons La GFD/PVL UB6 96 D2
Cosway St CAMTN NW1 8 D1
Cotall St POP/IOD E14 105 J5
Coteford Cl PIN HA5 58 E2
Coteford St TOOT SW17 160 E6
Cotelands CROY/NA CR0 212 A1
Cotesbach Rd CLPT E5 86 E1
Cotesmore Gdns BCTR RM8 91 J2
Cotford Rd THHTH CR7 196 D1
Cotham St WALW SE17 18 D7
Cotherstone HOR/WEW KT19 207 F6
Cotherstone Rd
BRXS/STRHM SW2 162 A3
Cotleigh Av BXLY DA5 168 E4
Cotleigh Rd KIL/WHAMP NW6 82 E5
ROMW/RG RM7 75 F3
Cotman Cl GLDGN NW11 65 G3
Cotmandene Crs
STMC/STPC BR5 186 C5
Cotman Ms BCTR RM8 91 H3
Cotmans Cl HYS/HAR UB3 113 K1
Coton Rd WELL DA16 148 B4
Cotsford Av NWMAL KT3 191 K2
Cotswold Av BUSH WD23 28 C1
Cotswold Cl BXLYHN DA7 150 B2
ESH/CLAY KT10 190 A6
KUTN/CMB KT2 175 K2
Cotswold Gdns CRICK NW2 64 B6
EHAM E6 107 H2
GNTH/NBYPK IG2 72 D4
Cotswold Ga CRICK NW2 64 C5
Cotswold Gn ENC/FH EN2 23 F5
Cotswold Ms BTSEA SW11 140 C2
Cotswold Ri ORP BR6 202 A3
Cotswold Rd HPTN TW12 173 F2
Cotswold St WNWD SE27 162 C6
Cotswold Wy ENC/FH EN2 23 F4
WPK KT4 193 F6
Cottage Av HAYES BR2 200 D5
Cottage Cl RSLP HA4 58 B5
RYLN/HDSTN HA2 60 D6
Cottage Field Cl SCUP DA14 168 D3
Cottage Gn CMBW SE5 142 E1
Cottage Gv BRXN/ST SW9 141 K4
SURB KT6 190 E3
Cottage Pl CHEL SW3 14 C4
Cottage Rd HOLWY N7 85 F3
HOR/WEW KT19 207 F5
The Cottages EDGW HA8 * 44 D3
Cottage St POP/IOD E14 105 K6
Cottenham Dr
CDALE/KGS NW9 45 H6
RYNPK SW20 176 E3
Cottenham Park Rd
RYNPK SW20 176 D4
Cottenham Pl RYNPK SW20 176 E3
Cottenham Rd WALTH E17 69 H1
Cotterill Rd SURB KT6 191 G6
Cottesbrook St NWCR SE14 144 B1
Cottesloe Ms STHWK SE1 17 K4
Cottesmore Av CLAY IG5 53 K5
Cottesmore Gdns KENS W8 120 A3
Cottimore Av WOT/HER KT12 188 A5
Cottimore Crs WOT/HER KT12 188 A4
Cottimore La WOT/HER KT12 188 A4
Cottimore Ter WOT/HER KT12 188 A4
Cottingham Cha RSLP HA4 76 E1
Cottingham Rd PGE/AN SE20 182 A3

VX/NE SW8 142 A1
Cottington Rd FELT TW13 154 C5
Cottington St LBTH SE11 122 B5
Cotton Av ACT W3 99 F5
Cotton Cl DAGW RM9 91 J5
WAN E11 70 C6
Cotton Gardens Est
LBTH SE11 18 A7
Cottongrass Cl CROY/NA CR0 198 A5
Cottonham Cl
NFNCH/WDSPK N12 47 H1
Cotton Hl BMLY BR1 165 G6
Cotton Rw BTSEA SW11 140 C4
Cottons Ap ROMW/RG RM7 75 F2
Cotton's Gdns BETH E2 7 H4
Cotton St POP/IOD E14 106 A6
Couchmore Av CLAY IG5 53 K5
ESH/CLAY KT10 189 K6
Coulgate St BROCKY SE4 144 B4
Coulson Cl BCTR RM8 73 J5
Coulson St CHEL SW3 120 E5
Coulter Cl YEAD UB4 95 J3
Coulter Rd HMSMTH W6 118 E3
Councillor St CMBW SE5 142 D1
Counter St STHWK SE1 13 G7
Countess Rd KTTN NW5 84 C3
Countisbury Av EN EN1 36 B2
Country Wy FELT TW13 172 B1
County Ga BAR EN5 33 F1
ELTH/MOT SE9 167 H5
County Gv CMBW SE5 142 D2
County Pde BTFD TW8 * 136 E1
County Rd EHAM E6 108 B4
THHTH CR7 180 C5
County St STHWK SE1 18 D5
Coupland Pl
WOOL/PLUM SE18 127 H5
Courcy Rd CEND/HSY/T N8 49 G6
Courier Rd DAGW RM9 110 E3
Courland Gv VX/NE SW8 141 J2
Courland St VX/NE SW8 141 J2
The Course ELTH/MOT SE9 167 F5
Courtauld Rd ARCH N19 66 D5
Courtaulds Cl THMD SE28 128 B1
Court Av BELV DA17 129 G5
Court Cl KTN/HRWW/WS HA3 48 K6
STJWD NW8 * 83 H5
WHTN TW2 155 G5
WLGTN SM6 210 D5
Court Close Av WHTN TW2 155 G5
Court Crs CHSGTN KT9 205 K4
Court Downs Rd BECK BR3 182 E5
Court Dr CROY/NA CR0 211 F2
STAN HA7 30 A6
SUT SM1 209 J2
Courtenay Av BELMT SM2 208 E6
HGT N6 65 J4
KTN/HRWW/WS HA3 42 B3
Courtenay Dr BECK BR3 183 G5
Courtenay Ms WALTH E17 69 G2
Courtenay Pl WALTH E17 69 G2
Courtenay Rd PGE/AN SE20 182 A3
WALTH E17 69 F2
WAN E11 * 88 D1
WBLY HA9 * 79 K1
WPK KT4 208 A1
Courtenay Sq LBTH SE11 * 122 B5
Courtenay St LBTH SE11 122 A5
Courten Ms STAN HA7 43 J3
Court Farm Av
HOR/WEW KT19 207 F3
Court Farm Rd
ELTH/MOT SE9 166 C4
NTHLT UB5 78 A5
Courtfield Av HRW HA1 * 61 F2
Courtfield Crs HRW HA1 61 F2
Courtfield Gdns ECT SW5 120 A4
RSLP HA4 58 D6
WEA W13 97 G5
Courtfield Ms SKENS SW7 120 B4
Courtfield Ri WWKM BR4 214 B1
Courtfield Rd ECT SW5 120 B4
Court Gdns HOLWY N7 85 G4
Courtgate Cl MLHL NW7 45 H2
Courthill Rd LEW SE13 145 F5
Courthope Rd GFD/PVL UB6 96 D1
HAMP NW3 83 K2
WIM/MER SW19 177 H1
Courthope Vls
WIM/MER SW19 177 H3
Courthouse La
STNW/STAM N16 86 B2
Court House Rd FNCH N3 47 F2
Courtland Av CHING E4 38 D4
IL IG1 71 K6
MLHL NW7 31 F5
STRHM/NOR SW16 180 A3
Courtland Gv THMD SE28 109 K6
Courtland Rd EHAM E6 89 J6
Courtlands CHST BR7 185 G3
RCHPK/HAM TW10 137 H6
Courtlands Av HAYES BR2 199 H5
HPTN TW12 172 E2
LEE/GVPK SE12 146 A6
RCH/KEW TW9 137 J3
Courtlands Cl RSLP HA4 58 D4
Courtlands Dr
HOR/WEW KT19 207 G4
Courtlands Rd BRYLDS KT5 191 H4
Court La DUL SE21 163 G2
Court Lane Gdns DUL SE21 163 F2
Courtleigh Av EBAR EN4 21 H1
Courtleigh Gdns
GLDGN NW11 64 C1
Courtman Rd TOTM N17 49 J3
Court Md NTHLT UB5 95 K2
Courtmead Cl HNHL SE24 162 D1
Courtnell St BAY/PAD W2 100 E5
Courtney Cl NRWD SE19 181 F2
Courtney Crs CAR SM5 209 K5
Courtney Pl CROY/NA CR0 211 G1
Courtney Rd CROY/NA CR0 211 G1
HOLWY N7 85 G3
HTHAIR TW6 132 D4
WBLY HA9 79 K1
WIM/MER SW19 178 D3
Courtney Wy HTHAIR TW6 132 D4
Courtrai Rd FSTH SE23 164 B1
Court Rd ELTH/MOT SE9 166 D4
NWDGN UB2 114 E4
SNWD SE25 181 G5
Court Road (Orpington
By-Pass) ORP BR6 217 H1
Courtside HGT N6 66 D3
SYD SE26 * 163 K5
The Courts STRHM/NOR SW16 179 K3
Courtstreet BMLY BR1 183 K5
Court St WCHPL E1 104 D4
The Court MUSWH N10 * 66 C1
RSLP HA4 77 J2
Court Vw HGT N6 * 66 B6
Court Wy ACT W3 98 E4
BARK/HLT IG6 54 C6
CDALE/KGS NW9 63 G1
WHTN TW2 156 A2
The Courtway OXHEY WD19 27 J4
Court Yd ELTH/MOT SE9 166 D1
Courtyard Ms RAIN RM13 93 H6
STMC/STPC BR5 186 B3
The Courtyards
WATW WD18 * 26 B2
The Courtyard IS N1 85 F5
Cousin La CANST EC4R 12 E5
Couthurst Rd BKHTH/KID SE3 126 A6
BKHTH/KID SE3 146 A1
Coutts Av CHSGTN KT9 206 A3
Coutts Crs KTTN NW5 * 84 A1
Couzins Wk DART DA1 151 J3
Coval Gdns MORT/ESHN SW14 137 J5
Coval La MORT/ESHN SW14 137 J5
Coval Rd MORT/ESHN SW14 137 K5
Covelees Wall EHAM E6 108 A5
Covent Gdn COVGDN WC2E 11 F5
Covent Garden Plazza
COVGDN WC2E 11 F5
Coventry Cl EHAM E6 107 K5
KIL/WHAMP NW6 100 E1
Coventry Cross Est BOW E3 106 A3
Coventry Rd IL IG1 72 B5
SNWD SE25 197 H1
WCHPL E1 104 D3
Coventry St SOHO/SHAV W1D 10 C6
Coverack Cl CROY/NA CR0 198 B4
STHGT/OAK N14 34 C1
Coverdale Gdns
CROY/NA CR0 212 B1
Coverdale Rd CRICK NW2 82 C5
FBAR/BDGN N11 48 A2
SHB W12 118 E1
The Coverdales BARK IG11 108 D1
Coverley Cl WCHPL E1 * 104 C4
Coverton Rd TOOT SW17 160 D6
Covert Rd BARK/HLT IG6 55 F2
Coverts Rd ESH/CLAY KT10 205 F5
The Covert NRWD SE19 * 181 G3
NTHWD HA6 40 A3
ORP BR6 201 K3
Covert Wy EBAR EN4 21 G3
Covet Wood Cl
STMC/STPC BR5 202 A3
Covey Cl WIM/MER SW19 178 A5
Covey Rd WPK KT4 193 G6
Covington Gdns
STRHM/NOR SW16 180 C3
Covington Wy
STRHM/NOR SW16 180 B3
Cowbridge La BARK IG11 90 B5
Cowbridge Rd
KTN/HRWW/WS HA3 62 B1
Cowcross St FARR EC1M 12 A1
Cowdenbeath Pth IS N1 84 E6
Cowden Rd ORP BR6 202 A4
Cowden St CAT SE6 164 D6
Cowdray Rd HGDN/ICK UB10 76 A6
Cowdray Wy HCH RM12 93 J2
Cowdrey Cl EN EN1 24 A3
Cowdrey Rd WIM/MER SW19 178 A2
Cowen Av HRW HA1 60 D6
Cowgate Rd GFD/PVL UB6 96 D2
Cowick Rd TOOT SW17 160 E6
Cowings Md NTHLT UB5 77 J5
Cowland Av PEND EN3 24 E5
Cow La BUSH WD23 * 28 A1
Cow Leaze EHAM E6 108 A5
Cowleaze Rd KUTN/CMB KT2 175 F4
Cowley Cl SAND/SEL CR2 212 E6
Cowley Ct WAN E11 * 88 C1
Cowley La WAN E11 * 88 C1
Cowley Pl HDN NW4 64 A2
Cowley Rd ACT W3 118 C1
BRXN/ST SW9 142 B2
HARH RM3 57 K3
IL IG1 71 K4
MORT/ESHN SW14 138 B4
WAN E11 71 F2
Cowley St WEST SW1P 16 E5
Cowling Cl NTGHL W11 100 C6
Cowper Av EHAM E6 89 J5
SUT SM1 209 H2
Cowper Cl HAYES BR2 200 C1
WELL DA16 148 B6
Cowper Gdns STHGT/OAK N14 34 B1
WLGTN SM6 210 C4
Cowper Rd ACT W3 118 A1
BELV DA17 129 G4
HAYES BR2 200 C1
HNWL W7 97 F6
KUTN/CMB KT2 175 G1
RAIN RM13 111 J3
STHGT/OAK N14 34 B3
STNW/STAM N16 86 A2
UED N18 50 C1
WIM/MER SW19 178 B2
Cowper St STLK EC1Y 7 F6
Cowper Ter NKENS W10 * 100 B4
Cowslip Rd SWFD E18 53 F5
Cowthorpe Rd VX/NE SW8 141 J2
Coxe Pl KTN/HRWW/WS HA3 61 G1
Cox La CHSGTN KT9 206 A2
HOR/WEW KT19 206 D3
Coxmount Rd CHARL SE7 126 C5
Coxson Wy STHWK SE1 19 J3
Coxwell Rd NRWD SE19 181 F3
WOOL/PLUM SE18 127 J5
Crabbs Croft Cl ORP BR6 * 216 C3
Crab Hl BECK BR3 183 G3
Crabtree Av ALP/SUD HA0 98 A1
CHDH RM6 73 K1
Crabtree Cl BETH E2 7 J3
Crabtree La FUL/PGN SW6 139 G1
Crabtree Manorway North
BELV DA17 129 K2
Crabtree Manorway South
BELV DA17 129 K3
Craddock Rd EN EN1 24 B4
Craddock St KTTN NW5 * 84 A4
Cradley Rd ELTH/MOT SE9 167 J3
Cragie Lea MUSWH N10 * 48 B5
Craigdale Rd EMPK RM11 75 H3
Craigen Av CROY/NA CR0 197 J5
Craigen Gdns IL IG1 90 E2
Craigerne Rd BKHTH/KID SE3 146 A1
Craig Gdns SWFD E18 52 D5
Craigholm WOOL/PLUM SE18 147 F3
Craigmuir Pk ALP/SUD HA0 80 B6
Craignair Rd
BRXS/STRHM SW2 162 A2
Craignish Av
STRHM/NOR SW16 180 A5
Craig Park Rd UED N18 36 D6
Craig Rd RCHPK/HAM TW10 156 D6
Craig's Ct WHALL SW1A 10 E7
Craigton Rd ELTH/MOT SE9 146 E5
Craigweil Cl STAN HA7 43 K1
Craigweil Dr STAN HA7 43 K1
Craigwell Av FELT TW13 153 K5
Crail Rw WALW SE17 19 F7
Cramer St MHST W1U 9 H2
Crammond Cl HMSMTH W6 119 H6
Cramond Ct
EBED/NFELT TW14 153 G3
Crampton Rd PGE/AN SE20 181 K2
Cranberry Cl NTHLT UB5 95 H1
Cranberry La CAN/RD E16 106 C3
Cranborne Av NWDGN UB2 115 F4
SURB KT6 206 C1
Cranborne Rd BARK IG11 90 D6
Cranborne Waye YEAD UB4 95 F5
Cranbourne Av WAN E11 71 F1
Cranbourne Cl
STRHM/NOR SW16 179 K6
Cranbourne Dr PIN HA5 59 H2
Cranbourne Gdns
BARK/HLT IG6 54 C6
GLDGN NW11 64 C2
Cranbourne Rd MNPK E12 89 J3
MUSWH N10 48 B5
NTHWD HA6 40 D6
SRTFD E15 88 A2
Cranbourn St
LSQ/SEVD WC2H 10 D5
Cranbrook Dr ESH/CLAY KT10 189 H5
GPK RM2 75 K1
WHTN TW2 155 G3
Cranbrook La
FBAR/BDGN N11 34 B6
Cranbrook Ms WALTH E17 69 H2
Cranbrook Pk WDGN N22 49 G4
Cranbrook Ri IL IG1 71 K3
Cranbrook Rd BARK/HLT IG6 54 C6
CHSWK W4 118 B5
DEPT SE8 144 D2
EBAR EN4 33 H1
GNTH/NBYPK IG2 72 A3
HSLWW TW4 134 E5
IL IG1 72 A6
THHTH CR7 180 D5
WIM/MER SW19 177 H3
Cranbrook St BETH E2 105 F1
Cranbury Rd FUL/PGN SW6 140 A3
Crane Av ACT W3 98 E6
ISLW TW7 136 B6
Cranebank Ms TWK TW1 * 136 C6
Cranebrook WHTN TW2 155 H4
Crane Cl DAGE RM10 92 C4
Crane Ct FLST/FETLN EC4A 11 K4
MORT/ESHN SW14 * 137 K5
Craneford Cl WHTN TW2 156 A2
Craneford Wy WHTN TW2 155 K2
Crane Gdns HYS/HAR UB3 113 J4
Crane Gv HOLWY N7 85 G4
Crane Lodge Rd HEST TW5 114 A6
Crane Md BERM/RHTH SE16 124 A4
Crane Park Rd WHTN TW2 155 G4
Crane Rd STWL/WRAY TW19 152 D1
WHTN TW2 155 K3
Cranesbill Cl CDALE/KGS NW9 45 F6
STRHM/NOR SW16 179 J5
Cranes Dr BRYLDS KT5 191 F1
Cranes Pk BRYLDS KT5 191 F1
Cranes Park Av BRYLDS KT5 191 F1
Cranes Park Crs BRYLDS KT5 191 G1
Crane St PECK SE15 143 G2
Craneswater HYS/HAR UB3 133 J1
Craneswater Pk NWDGN UB2 114 E5
Crane Wy WHTN TW2 155 H2
Cranfield Dr CDALE/KGS NW9 45 G4
Cranfield Rd BROCKY SE4 144 C4
Cranfield Rd East CAR SM5 210 A6
Cranfield Rd West CAR SM5 * 209 K6
Cranford Av PLMGR N13 48 E1
STWL/WRAY TW19 152 B2
Cranford Cl RYNPK SW20 176 E3
STWL/WRAY TW19 152 B2
Cranford Cots WAP E1W * 105 F6
Cranford Dr HYS/HAR UB3 113 J4
Cranford La HTHAIR TW6 133 J4
Cranford Ms HAYES BR2 200 D2
Cranford Park Rd
HYS/HAR UB3 113 J4
Cranford Ri ESH/CLAY KT10 204 C3
Cranford St WAP E1W 105 F6
Cranford Wy CEND/HSY/T N8 67 F2
Cranham Rd EMPK RM11 75 K3
Cranhurst Rd CRICK NW2 82 A3
Cranleigh Cl BXLY DA5 * 169 J1
ORP BR6 217 G1
PGE/AN SE20 181 J5
Cranleigh Gdns BARK IG11 90 D5
KTN/HRWW/WS HA3 62 A2
KUTN/CMB KT2 175 G2
LOU IG10 39 K1
SNWD SE25 181 F6
STHL UB1 95 K5
SUT SM1 194 A6
WCHMH N21 23 G6
Cranleigh Ms BTSEA SW11 140 D3
Cranleigh Rd ESH/CLAY KT10 189 H5
FELT TW13 153 J6
SEVS/STOTM N15 67 J2
WIM/MER SW19 177 K6
Cranleigh St CAMTN NW1 4 B3
Cranley Dr GNTH/NBYPK IG2 72 C4
RSLP HA4 58 D6
Cranley Gdns MUSWH N10 66 B1
PLMGR N13 35 F5
SKENS SW7 120 B5
WLGTN SM6 210 C5
Cranley Ms SKENS SW7 120 B5
Cranley Pl SKENS SW7 14 A7
Cranley Rd GNTH/NBYPK IG2 72 C3
PLSTW E13 107 F4
Cranley Ter HDN NW4 * 46 B5
Cranmer Av WEA W13 116 C3
Cranmer Cl MRDN SM4 193 G3
RSLP HA4 59 H5
STAN HA7 43 J3
Cranmer Ct HPTN TW12 173 G1
KUTN/CMB KT2 156 E6
Cranmer Farm Cl MTCM CR4 194 E1
Cranmer Gdns DAGE RM10 92 E2
Cranmer Rd BRXN/ST SW9 142 B1
CROY/NA CR0 211 H1
EDGW HA8 30 D5
FSTGT E7 89 F2
HPTN TW12 173 G1
HYS/HAR UB3 94 B5
KUTN/CMB KT2 175 F1
MTCM CR4 194 E1
Cranmer Ter TOOT SW17 178 C1
Cranmore Av ISLW TW7 135 H1
Cranmore Rd BMLY BR1 165 H5
CHST BR7 184 E1
Cranmore Wy MUSWH N10 66 C1
Cranston Cl HGDN/ICK UB10 58 B6
HSLW TW3 134 D3
Cranston Est IS N1 7 F2
Cranston Gdns CHING E4 51 K2
Cranston Rd FSTH SE23 164 B3
Cranswick Rd
BERM/RHTH SE16 123 J5
Crantock Rd CAT SE6 165 F4
Cranwell Cl BOW E3 105 K3
Cranwich Av WCHMH N21 35 K2
Cranwich Rd
STNW/STAM N16 68 A4
Cranwood St FSBYE EC1V 7 F5
Cranworth Crs CHING E4 38 B3
Cranworth Gdns
BRXN/ST SW9 142 B2
Craster Rd BRXS/STRHM SW2 162 A2
Crathie Rd LEE/GVPK SE12 166 A1
Cravan Av FELT TW13 153 K4
Craven Av EA W5 97 J6
STHL UB1 95 K4
Craven Cl STNW/STAM N16 * 68 C4
YEAD UB4 94 E5
Craven Gdns BARK IG11 108 E1
BARK/HLT IG6 54 D5
CRW RM5 56 C1
WIM/MER SW19 178 A1
Craven Hill Gdns BAY/PAD W2 101 G6
Craven Ms BTSEA SW11 141 F4
Craven Pk WLSDN NW10 81 F5
Craven Park Ms WLSDN NW10 81 G5
Craven Park Rd
SEVS/STOTM N15 68 B3
WLSDN NW10 81 G6
Craven Pas CHCR WC2N 10 E7
Craven Rd BAY/PAD W2 101 G6
CROY/NA CR0 197 J5
KUTN/CMB KT2 175 G4
ORP BR6 217 K1
WEA W13 97 J6
WLSDN NW10 81 F6
Craven St CHCR WC2N 10 E7
Craven Ter BAY/PAD W2 101 G6
Craven Wk CLPT E5 68 C4
Crawford Av ALP/SUD HA0 79 K3
Crawford Cl ISLW TW7 135 K3
Crawford Gdns NTHLT UB5 95 K2
PLMGR N13 35 H5
Crawford Ms MBLAR W1H * 8 E2
Crawford Pas CLKNW EC1R 5 J7
Crawford Pl MBLAR W1H 8 D3
Crawford Rd CMBW SE5 142 D3
Crawford St MBLAR W1H 8 E2
MHST W1U 9 F2
WLSDN NW10 81 F5
Crawley Rd EN EN1 36 A2
LEY E10 69 K5
WDGN N22 49 J5
Crawthew Gv EDUL SE22 143 G5
Cray Av ORP BR6 202 C4
STMC/STPC BR5 202 C2
Craybrooke Rd SCUP DA14 168 C6
Craybury End ELTH/MOT SE9 167 H4
Crayford Rd HOLWY N7 84 E2
Crayke Hl CHSGTN KT9 206 A5
Craylands STMC/STPC BR5 186 D6
Crayleigh Ter SCUP DA14 * 186 D2
Cray Rd BELV DA17 129 H6
SCUP DA14 186 D2
SWLY BR8 203 K3
Crays Pde STMC/STPC BR5 * 186 D5
Cray Valley Rd
STMC/STPC BR5 202 B2
Cray View Cl STMC/STPC BR5 202 D1
Crealock Gv WFD IG8 52 D1
Crealock St WAND/EARL SW18 160 A1
Creasey Cl EMPK RM11 75 K6
Crebor St EDUL SE22 163 H1
Credenhall Dr HAYES BR2 200 E5
Credenhill St
STRHM/NOR SW16 179 H2
Crediton Hl KIL/WHAMP NW6 83 F3
Crediton Rd WLSDN NW10 82 B6
Crediton Wy ESH/CLAY KT10 205 G3
Credon Rd BERM/RHTH SE16 123 J5
PLSTW E13 107 G1
Creechurch La HDTCH EC3A 13 H3
Creechurch Pl HDTCH EC3A * 13 H4
Creed La BLKFR EC4V 12 B4
Creek Cots E/WMO/HCT KT8 * 189 K1
Creek Rd BARK IG11 109 F2
DEPT SE8 124 D6
E/WMO/HCT KT8 189 K1
Creekside DEPT SE8 144 E1
RAIN RM13 111 H3
Creek Wy RAIN RM13 111 G5
Creeland Gv CAT SE6 164 C3
Cree Wy ROM RM1 57 G3
Crefeld Cl HMSMTH W6 119 G6
Creffield Rd EA W5 98 C6
Creighton Av EFNCH N2 47 K5
EHAM E6 107 H1
Creighton Cl SHB W12 99 K6
Creighton Rd EA W5 116 E3
KIL/WHAMP NW6 100 B1
TOTM N17 50 A3
Creigton Av EFNCH N2 47 J6
Cremer St BETH E2 7 J3
Cremorne Est WBPTN SW10 * 120 C6
Cremorne Gdns
HOR/WEW KT19 207 F6
Cremorne Rd WBPTN SW10 140 B1
Crescent TWRH EC3N 13 J5
Crescent Ar GNWCH SE10 125 F6
Crescent Av HCH RM12 75 H6
Crescent Dr STMC/STPC BR5 201 H3
Crescent East EBAR EN4 21 G1
Crescent Gdns RSLP HA4 59 F4
SWLY BR8 187 K5
WIM/MER SW19 159 K5
Crescent Gv CLAP SW4 141 H5
MTCM CR4 194 D1
Crescent La CLAP SW4 141 J6
Crescent Pl CHEL SW3 14 C6
Crescent Ri EBAR EN4 21 J6
FNCH N3 * 46 D4
WDGN N22 48 D4
Crescent Rd BECK BR3 182 E5
BFN/LL DA15 168 A5
BMLY BR1 183 K3
CEND/HSY/T N8 66 D3
CHING E4 38 C2
DAGE RM10 92 D
EBAR EN4 21 H5
ED N9 36 C
EHAM E6 89 G6
ENC/FH EN2 23 H
FBAR/BDGN N11 33 K
FNCH N3 46 D
KUTN/CMB KT2 175 H
LEY E10 69 K
PLSTW E13 88 E
RYNPK SW20 177 G
SEVS/STOTM N15 * 49 H
SWFD E18 53 G
WDGN N22 48 D
WOOL/PLUM SE18 127 G
Crescent Rw STLK EC1Y 6 C
Crescent St IS N1 * 85 F
The Crescent ACT W3 99 C
ALP/SUD HA0 61 H
BAR EN5 21 F
BARN SW13 138 C
BECK BR3 182 D
BXLY DA5 168 D
CRICK NW2 81
CROY/NA CR0 196
E/WMO/HCT KT8 188
FBAR/BDGN N11 33
GNTH/NBYPK IG2 72
HYS/HAR UB3 133
LOU IG10 39
NWMAL KT3 175
RYLN/HDSTN HA2 60
SCUP DA14 168
STHL UB1 114
SURB KT6 191
SUT SM1 209
WALTH E17 69
WIM/MER SW19 159
WWKM BR4 199
Crescent Vw LOU IG10 39
Crescent Wy BROCKY SE4 144
Crescentway
NFNCH/WDSPK N12 47
Crescent Wy ORP BR6 216
STRHM/NOR SW16 180
Crescent West EBAR EN4 21
Crescent Wood Rd SYD SE26 163
Cresford Rd FUL/PGN SW6 140
Crespigny Rd HDN NW4 63
Cressage Cl STHL UB1 96
Cresset Rd HOM E9 86
Cresset St CLAP SW4 141
Cressfield Cl KTTN NW5 84
Cressida Rd ARCH N19 66
Cressingham Gv SUT SM1 209
Cressingham Rd EDGW HA8 45
LEW SE13 145
Cressington Cl
STNW/STAM N16 86
Cresswell Pk BKHTH/KID SE3 145
Cresswell Pl WBPTN SW10 120
Cresswell Rd FELT TW13 154
SNWD SE25 197
TWK TW1 156
Cresswell Wy WCHMH N21 35
Cressy Ct HMSMTH W6 118
WCHPL E1 104
Cressy Houses WCHPL E1 * 104
Cressy Pl WCHPL E1 104
Cressy Rd HAMP NW3 83
Cressys Cnr HSLW TW3 * 135
Crestbrook Av PLMGR N13 35
Crestbrook Pl PLMGR N13 * 35
Crest Dr PEND EN3 24
Crestfield St CAMTN NW1
Crest Gdns RSLP HA4 7
Creston Wy WPK KT4 19
Crest Rd CRICK NW2 6
HAYES BR2 19
SAND/SEL CR2 21
The Crest BRYLDS KT5 19
HDN NW4 6
HOLWY N7 * 8
PLMGR N13
Crest Vw PIN HA5
Crest View Dr
STMC/STPC BR5 20
Crestway PUT/ROE SW15 15
Crestwood Wy HSLWW TW4 13
Creswell Dr BECK BR3 18
Creswick Rd ACT W3
Creswick Wk GLDGN NW11
Creukhorne Rd
WLSDN NW10 *

Crewdson Rd BRXN/ST SW9 142 A1
Crewe Pl WLSDN NW10 99 H2
Crews St POP/IOD E14 124 D4
Crewys Rd CRICK NW2 64 D6
PECK SE15 143 J3
Crichton Av WLGTN SM6 210 D3
Crichton Rd CAR SM5 209 K5
Crichton St VX/NE SW8 * 141 H3
Cricketers Arms Rd
ENC/FH EN2 * 23 J3
Cricketers Cl CHSGTN KT9 205 K3
ERITH DA8 130 B5
STHGT/OAK N14 34 C2
Cricketers Ms BAL SW12 161 G2
WAND/EARL SW18 140 A6
Cricketers Wk SYD SE26 181 K1
Cricketfield Rd CLPT E5 86 D2
Cricket Gn MTCM CR4 178 E6
Cricket Ground Rd CHST BR7 185 G4
Cricket La BECK BR3 182 B2
Cricket Rw EFNCH N2 * 47 H6
Cricklade Av
BRXS/STRHM SW2 161 K4
Cricklewood Broadway
CRICK NW2 82 B2
Cricklewood La CRICK NW2 82 C2
Cridland St SRTFD E15 88 D6
Crieff Ct TEDD TW11 174 D3
Crieff Rd WAND/EARL SW18 160 B1
Criffel Av BRXS/STRHM SW2 161 J4
Crimscott St STHWK SE1 19 H5
Crimsworth Rd VX/NE SW8 141 J1
Crinan St IS N1 5 F2
Cringle St VX/NE SW8 141 H1
Cripplegate St BARB EC2Y * 12 C1
Crispen Rd FELT TW13 154 D6
Crispian Cl WLSDN NW10 81 G2
Crispin Crs CROY/NA CR0 195 J6
Crispin Rd EDGW HA8 44 E2
Crispin St WCHPL E1 13 J2
Crisp Rd HMSMTH W6 119 F5
Cristowe Rd FUL/PGN SW6 * 139 J3
Criterion Ms ARCH N19 66 D6
Crockenhill Hl
STMC/STPC BR5 202 E2
Crockenhill Rd
STMC/STPC BR5 202 E3
Crockerton Rd TOOT SW17 160 E4
Crockham Wy ELTH/MOT SE9 167 F6
Crocus Cl CROY/NA CR0 198 A5
Crocus Fld BAR EN5 32 D1
Croft Av WWKM BR4 199 F5
Croft Cl ABYW SE2 129 G5
CHST BR7 184 E1
HYS/HAR UB3 133 F1
MLHL NW7 31 G5
Croft Ct RSLP HA4 * 58 D5
SUT SM1 * 194 C6
Croftdown Rd KTTN NW5 84 A1
Crofters Cl ISLW TW7 135 J6
Crofters Ct DEPT SE8 124 B4
Crofters Md CROY/NA CR0 213 H6
Crofters Rd NTHWD HA6 26 C6
Crofters Wy CAMTN NW1 84 D6
Croft Gdns HNWL W7 116 B2
RSLP HA4 58 C5
Croft Lodge Cl WFD IG8 53 F2
Croft Ms NFNCH/WDSPK N12 33 G5
Crofton Av BXLY DA5 168 E2
CHSWK W4 137 K1
ORP BR6 201 H6
Crofton Gate Wy BROCKY SE4 144 B6
Crofton Gv CHING E4 38 B6
Crofton La ORP BR6 201 K4
STMC/STPC BR5 201 J5
Crofton Park Rd BROCKY SE4 164 C1
Crofton Rd CMBW SE5 143 F2
ORP BR6 216 A1
PLSTW E13 107 F3
Crofton Ter RCH/KEW TW9 137 G5
Crofton Wy BAR EN5 * 33 F1
ENC/FH EN2 23 G3
Croft Rd BMLY BR1 183 K2
PEND EN3 25 G2
STRHM/NOR SW16 180 B3
SUT SM1 209 H3
WIM/MER SW19 178 B3
Crofts Rd HRW HA1 61 G3
Croft St DEPT SE8 124 B4
WCHPL E1 104 C6
The Croft ALP/SUD HA0 79 J3
BAR EN5 20 C5
CHING E4 38 C4
EA W5 98 A4
HEST TW5 134 D1
PIN HA5 59 K4
RSLP HA4 77 G2
SWLY BR8 187 K6
WLSDN NW10 99 H1
Croft Wy BFN/LL DA15 167 K5
RCHPK/HAM TW10 156 C5
Crogsland Rd CAMTN NW1 84 A5
Croham Cl SAND/SEL CR2 212 A5
Croham Manor Rd
SAND/SEL CR2 212 A5
Croham Mt SAND/SEL CR2 212 A5
Croham Park Av
SAND/SEL CR2 212 B3
Croham Rd SAND/SEL CR2 211 K3
Croham Valley Rd
SAND/SEL CR2 212 C4
Croindene Rd
STRHM/NOR SW16 179 K4
Cromartie Rd ARCH N19 66 D4
Cromarty Rd EDGW HA8 30 D4
Cromarty Vls BAY/PAD W2 * 101 G6
Crombie Cl REDBR IG4 71 K2
Crombie Ms BTSEA SW11 * 140 D3
Crombie Rd BFN/LL DA15 167 J3
Cromer Cl UX/CGN UB8 94 A5
Cromer Hyde MRDN SM4 * 194 A2
Crome Rd WLSDN NW10 81 G4
Cromer Rd BAR EN5 21 G5
CHDH RM6 74 A3
HTHAIR TW6 132 D4
LEY E10 70 B4
ROMW/RG RM7 74 E3
SNWD SE25 181 J6
TOOT SW17 179 F2
TOTM N17 50 C5
Cromer Rd West HTHAIR TW6 132 D4
Cromer St STPAN WC1H 5 F5
Cromer Ter HACK E8 86 C3
Cromer Villas Rd
WAND/EARL SW18 159 J1
Cromford Cl ORP BR6 216 E1
Cromford Rd PUT/ROE SW15 139 J6
Cromford Wy NWMAL KT3 176 A4
Cromlix Cl CHST BR7 185 G5
Crompton Pl PEND EN3 25 J1
Crompton St BAY/PAD W2 2 A7
Cromwell Av HAYES BR2 184 A6
HGT N6 66 B5
HMSMTH W6 118 E5
NWMAL KT3 192 C2
Cromwell Cl CHSWK W4 * 117 J5
EFNCH N2 65 H1
HAYES BR2 200 A1
WOT/HER KT12 188 A5
Cromwell Ct ALP/SUD HA0 98 A1
PEND EN3 25 F6
Cromwell Crs ECT SW5 119 K4
Cromwell Gdns SKENS SW7 14 B6
Cromwell Gv HMSMTH W6 119 F3
Cromwell Ms SKENS SW7 * 14 A6
Cromwell Pde ALP/SUD HA0 * 98 A1
Cromwell Pl ACT W3 117 K1
HGT N6 * 66 B5
MORT/ESHN SW14 137 K4
SKENS SW7 14 B6
Cromwell Rd ALP/SUD HA0 97 K1
BECK BR3 182 B5
BRXN/ST SW9 142 C2
CROY/NA CR0 196 E4
ECT SW5 120 A4
FELT TW13 154 A3
FNCH N3 47 G5
FSTGT E7 89 G5
HSLW TW3 135 F5
HYS/HAR UB3 94 B5
KUTN/CMB KT2 175 F4
MUSWH N10 48 A3
TEDD TW11 174 B2
WALTH E17 70 A2
WIM/MER SW19 177 K1
WOT/HER KT12 188 A6
WPK KT4 207 F1
Cromwell St HSLW TW3 135 F5
Cromwell Ter HSLW TW3 * 135 F5
Crondace Rd FUL/PGN SW6 139 K2
Crondall St IS N1 7 F3
Cronin St PECK SE15 143 G1
Crooked Billet Rbt CHING E4 51 K3
Crooked Usage FNCH N3 46 C6
Crooke Rd DEPT SE8 124 B5
Crookham Rd FUL/PGN SW6 139 J2
Crook Log BXLYHS DA6 148 E4
Crookston Rd ELTH/MOT SE9 147 F4
Croombs Rd CAN/RD E16 107 G4
Croom's Hl GNWCH SE10 145 G1
Croom's Hill Gv GNWCH SE10 145 F1
Cropley St IS N1 6 E2
Croppath Rd DAGE RM10 92 C2
Cropthorne Ct MV/WKIL W9 101 G2
Crosby Cl FELT TW13 154 D6
Crosby Rd DAGE RM10 110 D1
FSTGT E7 88 E4
Crosby Rw STHWK SE1 18 E3
Crosby Sq HDTCH EC3A 13 G4
Crosby Wk HACK E8 86 B4
Crosier Cl BKHTH/KID SE3 146 D2
Crosier Rd HGDN/ICK UB10 76 A2
Crosier Wy RSLP HA4 76 C1
Crosland Pl BTSEA SW11 141 F4
Crossbow Rd CHIG IG7 55 F1
Crossbrook Rd
BKHTH/KID SE3 146 D3
Cross Deep TWK TW1 156 A5
Cross Deep Gdns TWK TW1 156 A4
Crossfield Est DEPT SE8 144 D1
Crossfield Rd HAMP NW3 83 H4
TOTM N17 49 J6
Crossfield St DEPT SE8 144 D1
Crossford St BRXN/ST SW9 142 A3
Crossgate EDGW HA8 30 C5
GFD/PVL UB6 79 H4
Cross Keys Cl ED N9 36 C4
MHST W1U 9 H2
Cross Lances Rd HSLW TW3 135 G5
Crossland Rd THHTH CR7 196 C3
Crosslands Av EA W5 117 G1
NWDGN UB2 114 E5
Crosslands Pde NWDGN UB2 * 115 F5
Crosslands Rd
HOR/WEW KT19 207 F4
Cross La BXLY DA5 169 G2
CEND/HSY/T N8 67 F1
MON EC3R 13 G6
Crosslet St WALW SE17 19 F6
Crosslet V GNWCH SE10 144 E2
Crossley St HOLWY N7 85 G4
Crossmead ELTH/MOT SE9 166 E3
OXHEY WD19 27 F1
Crossmead Av GFD/PVL UB6 96 A2
Crossness Rd BARK IG11 109 F2
Cross Rd CHDH RM6 73 J4
CHING E4 38 B3
CMBW SE5 143 F3
CROY/NA CR0 196 E5
EN EN1 24 A5
FBAR/BDGN N11 48 B1
FELT TW13 154 D6
HAYES BR2 200 D6
HRW HA1 60 D1
KTN/HRWW/WS HA3 43 G5
KUTN/CMB KT2 175 G3
OXHEY WD19 27 J1
ROMW/RG RM7 56 C6
RYLN/HDSTN HA2 78 A1
SCUP DA14 168 C6
STMC/STPC BR5 202 C2
SUT SM1 209 H3
WDGN N22 49 G2
WFD IG8 53 K2
WIM/MER SW19 177 K3
Cross St BARN SW13 138 B3
HPTN TW12 173 H1
IS N1 85 H6
UED N18 50 C1
Crossthwaite Av HNHL SE24 142 E5
Crosswall TWRH EC3N 13 J5
Cross Wy HYS/HAR UB3 113 K2
Crossway BCTR RM8 91 J1
CDALE/KGS NW9 63 H1
EN EN1 36 A2
NFNCH/WDSPK N12 47 H2
NWMAL KT3 193 F1
PIN HA5 41 F5
RSLP HA4 77 G2
STMC/STPC BR5 201 J1
STNW/STAM N16 86 A3
THMD SE28 109 J5
WEA W13 97 F3
WOT/HER KT12 188 A6
Crossway Pde WDGN N22 * 49 H3
Crossways BELMT SM2 209 H6
GPK RM2 57 K6
SAND/SEL CR2 213 G5
Crossways Rd BECK BR3 198 D1
MTCM CR4 179 G6
Crossways Ter CLPT E5 * 86 E2
The Crossways BRYLDS KT5 * 191 J5
HEST TW5 134 E1
WBLY HA9 62 C6
The Crossway ELTH/MOT SE9 166 C4
The Cross Wy
KTN/HRWW/WS HA3 42 E5
The Crossway WDGN N22 49 H3
Croston St HACK E8 86 C6
Crosts La WDGN N22 49 G3
Crothall Cl PLMGR N13 35 F5
Crouch Av BARK IG11 109 H1
Crouch Cl BECK BR3 182 D2
Crouch Cft ELTH/MOT SE9 167 F5
Crouch End Hl
CEND/HSY/T N8 66 D4
Crouch Hall Rd
CEND/HSY/T N8 66 D3
Crouch Hl CEND/HSY/T N8 66 E4
Crouchmans Cl SYD SE26 163 G5
Crouch Rd WLSDN NW10 81 F5
Crowborough Pth
OXHEY WD19 27 H6
Crowborough Rd TOOT SW17 179 F1
Crowden Wy THMD SE28 109 J6
Crowder Cl
NFNCH/WDSPK N12 47 G3
Crowder St WCHPL E1 104 D6
Crowfoot Cl HOM E9 87 H3
THMD SE28 127 K1
Crowhurst Cl BRXN/ST SW9 142 B3
Crowhurst Wy
STMC/STPC BR5 202 D2
Crowland Av HYS/HAR UB3 113 H4
Crowland Gdns
STHGT/OAK N14 34 E2
Crowland Rd
SEVS/STOTM N15 68 B2
THHTH CR7 * 196 E1
Crowlands Av ROMW/RG RM7 74 D3
Crowland Ter IS N1 85 K5
Crowland Wk MRDN SM4 194 A3
Crow La ROMW/RG RM7 74 B4
Crowley Crs CROY/NA CR0 211 G3
Crowline Wk IS N1 * 85 J4
Crowmarsh Gdns FSTH SE23 163 K2
Crown Ar KUT/HW KT1 * 174 E5
Crownbourne Ct SUT SM1 * 209 F2
Crown Blds CHING E4 * 38 B3
Crown Cl BOW E3 87 J6
HYS/HAR UB3 113 J2
KIL/WHAMP NW6 83 F4
MLHL NW7 31 H4
ORP BR6 217 G2
WOT/HER KT12 188 B4
Crown Ct HOL/ALD WC2B 11 F4
Crown Dl NRWD SE19 180 D2
Crowndale Rd CAMTN NW1 4 B2
Crownfield Av
GNTH/NBYPK IG2 72 E2
Crownfield Rd SRTFD E15 88 B3
Crown Green Ms WBLY HA9 62 A6
Crown Hl CROY/NA CR0 * 196 D6
Crownhill Rd WFD IG8 53 J3
WLSDN NW10 81 H6
Crown La CHST BR7 185 H4
HAYES BR2 200 C2
MRDN SM4 177 K6
STHGT/OAK N14 34 C3
STRHM/NOR SW16 180 B1
Crown Lane Gdns
STRHM/NOR SW16 * 180 B1
Crown Lane Sp HAYES BR2 200 C3
Crownmead Wy
ROMW/RG RM7 74 D1
Crown Office Rw EMB EC4Y 11 J5
Crown Pde MRDN SM4 * 194 A1
STHGT/OAK N14 * 34 C3
Crown Pas STJS SW1Y 16 B1
Crown Pl KTTN NW5 84 B4
SDTCH EC2A 7 G7
Crown Rd BARK/HLT IG6 72 D1
EN EN1 24 C4
KUTN/CMB KT2 175 K4
MRDN SM4 193 K1
MUSWH N10 48 A3
ORP BR6 217 G3
RSLP HA4 77 H3
SUT SM1 208 E2
TWK TW1 156 C1
Crownstone Rd
BRXS/STRHM SW2 142 B6
Crown St ACT W3 117 J1
CMBW SE5 142 D1
DAGE RM10 92 E4
RYLN/HDSTN HA2 60 D5
Crown Ter CRICK NW2 * 82 B2
RCH/KEW TW9 137 G5
STHGT/OAK N14 * 34 D3
Crowntree Cl ISLW TW7 116 A6
Crown Vls ACT W3 * 117 K2
Crown Wk WBLY HA9 80 B1
Crown Wy WDR/YW UB7 112 C1
Crown Woods La
WOOL/PLUM SE18 147 G3
Crown Woods Wy
ELTH/MOT SE9 147 J6
Crown Yd HSLW TW3 135 H4
Crowshott Av STAN HA7 43 J4
Crows Rd BARK IG11 90 B4
BOW E3 106 B2
Crowther Av BTFD TW8 117 F5
Crowther Cl FUL/PGN SW6 119 J6
Crowther Rd SNWD SE25 197 H1
Crowthorne Cl
WAND/EARL SW18 159 J2
Crowthorne Rd NKENS W10 100 B5
Croxden Cl EDGW HA8 44 C6
Croxden Wk MRDN SM4 194 B3
Croxford Gdns WDGN N22 49 H3
Croxford Wy ROMW/RG RM7 75 F5
Croxley Cl STMC/STPC BR5 186 C5
Croxley Gn STMC/STPC BR5 186 C4
Croxley Rd MV/WKIL W9 100 D2
Croxley Vw WATW WD18 26 C1
Croxted Cl DUL SE21 162 D2
Croxted Ms HNHL SE24 162 D1
Croxted Rd DUL SE21 162 D2
Croyde Av GFD/PVL UB6 96 C2
HYS/HAR UB3 113 H4
Croyde Cl BFN/LL DA15 167 J2
The Croydon F/O
CROY/NA CR0 211 H2
Croydon Gv CROY/NA CR0 196 C5
Croydon Rd BECK BR3 198 A2
CROY/NA CR0 210 E2
HAYES BR2 215 J1
MTCM CR4 195 G2
PGE/AN SE20 181 J5
PLSTW E13 106 D3
WLGTN SM6 210 B2
WWKM BR4 214 C1
WWKM BR4 215 F1
Croyland Rd ED N9 36 C3
Croylands Dr SURB KT6 191 F4
Crozier Ter HOM E9 87 F3
Crucible Cl CHDH RM6 73 H3
Crucifix La STHWK SE1 19 G2
Cruden St IS N1 6 B1
Cruickshank St FSBYW WC1X 5 J4
Cruikshank Rd SRTFD E15 88 C2
Crummock Gdns
CDALE/KGS NW9 63 G2
Crundale Av CDALE/KGS NW9 62 C2
Crunden Rd SAND/SEL CR2 211 K5
Crusader Gdns CROY/NA CR0 212 A1
Crusader Wy WATW WD18 26 D1
Crusoe Ms STNW/STAM N16 67 K6
Crusoe Rd MTCM CR4 178 E3
Crutched Friars TWRH EC3N 13 H5
Crutchfield La WOT/HER KT12 188 A5
Crutchley Rd CAT SE6 165 H4
Crystal Palace NRWD SE19 * 181 H3
Crystal Palace Pde
NRWD SE19 181 G2
Crystal Palace Park Rd
SYD SE26 181 H1
Crystal Palace Rd EDUL SE22 163 G1
Crystal Palace Station Rd
NRWD SE19 181 H2
Crystal Ter NRWD SE19 180 E2
Crystal Wy BCTR RM8 73 J5
HRW HA1 61 F2
Cuba Dr PEND EN3 24 E3
Cuba St POP/IOD E14 124 D2
Cubitt Sq NWDGN UB2 * 115 H1
Cubitt St FSBYW WC1X 5 H5
Cubitt Ter CLAP SW4 141 H4
Cuckmere Wy
STMC/STPC BR5 202 E5
Cuckoo Av HNWL W7 96 E3
Cuckoo Dene HNWL W7 96 D4
Cuckoo Hall La ED N9 36 E2
Cuckoo Hl PIN HA5 41 G6
Cuckoo Hill Dr PIN HA5 41 G6
Cuckoo Hill Rd PIN HA5 59 H1
Cuckoo La HNWL W7 96 E6
Cuda's Cl HOR/WEW KT19 207 H2
Cuddington Av WPK KT4 207 H1
Cudham La North ORP BR6 216 E6
Cudham St CAT SE6 164 E2
Cudworth St WCHPL E1 104 D3
Cuff Crs ELTH/MOT SE9 166 C2
Culford Gdns CHEL SW3 15 F7
Culford Gv IS N1 86 A4
Culford Ms IS N1 85 K4
Culford Rd IS N1 86 A5
Culgaith Gdns ENC/FH EN2 22 E5
Cullera Cl NTHWD HA6 40 D2
Culling Rd BERM/RHTH SE16 123 K3
Cullington Cl
KTN/HRWW/WS HA3 61 G1
Cullingworth Rd
WLSDN NW10 81 K3
Culloden Cl BERM/RHTH SE16 123 H5
Culloden Rd ENC/FH EN2 23 H3
Culloden St POP/IOD E14 106 A5
Cullum St FENCHST EC3M 13 G5
Culmington Pde WEA W13 * 97 J6
Culmington Rd
SAND/SEL CR2 211 J5
WEA W13 116 D1
Culmore Rd PECK SE15 143 J1
Culmstock Rd BTSEA SW11 141 F6
Culpepper Cl CHIG IG7 54 B2
UED N18 50 D1
Culross Cl SEVS/STOTM N15 67 J1
Culross St MYFR/PKLN W1K 9 G6
Culsac Rd SURB KT6 191 F6
Culverden Rd BAL SW12 161 H5
OXHEY WD19 27 F5
Culver Gv STAN HA7 43 J5
Culverhouse Gdns
STRHM/NOR SW16 162 A6
Culverlands Cl STAN HA7 29 H6
Culverley Rd CAT SE6 164 E3
Culvers Av CAR SM5 194 E6
Culvers Retreat CAR SM5 194 E5
Culverstone Cl HAYES BR2 199 J3
Culvers Wy CAR SM5 194 E6
Culvert Pl BTSEA SW11 141 F3
Culvert Rd BTSEA SW11 140 E3
SEVS/STOTM N15 68 A2
Culworth St STJWD NW8 2 C3
Cumberland Av WELL DA16 147 K4
WLSDN NW10 98 D2
Cumberland Cl BARK/HLT IG6 54 C4
HACK E8 86 B4
RYNPK SW20 177 G3
TWK TW1 156 C1
Cumberland Crs WKENS W14 119 H4
Cumberland Dr CHSGTN KT9 206 A1
ESH/CLAY KT10 190 B6
Cumberland Gdns
FSBYW WC1X 5 H4
HDN NW4 * 46 B5
Cumberland Ga BAY/PAD W2 8 E5
CAMTN NW1 3 J4
Cumberland House
KUTN/CMB KT2 175 J3
Cumberland Market
CAMTN NW1 3 K4
Cumberland Ms LBTH SE11 122 B5
Cumberland Pk ACT W3 98 E6
Cumberland Pl CAMTN NW1 3 J4
CAT SE6 165 J3
Cumberland Rd ACT W3 98 E6
ASHF TW15 152 A5
BARN SW13 138 C2
ED N9 36 E3
HAYES BR2 199 H1
HNWL W7 116 A2
HRW HA1 60 B2
MNPK E12 89 H2
PLSTW E13 107 F4
RCH/KEW TW9 137 H2
SNWD SE25 197 J3
STAN HA7 44 B6
WALTH E17 51 G5
WDGN N22 49 F5
Cumberland St PIM SW1V 121 G5
Cumberland Ter CAMTN NW1 3 J3
PGE/AN SE20 * 181 J3
Cumberland Terrace Ms
CAMTN NW1 3 J3
Cumberlow Av SNWD SE25 181 H6
Cumberton Rd TOTM N17 49 K4
Cumbrae Gdns SURB KT6 190 E6
Cumbrian Av BXLYHN DA7 150 B3
Cumbrian Gdns CRICK NW2 64 B6
Cumming St IS N1 5 H3
Cumnor Cl BRXN/ST SW9 * 142 A3
Cumnor Gdns EW KT17 207 J4
Cumnor Rd BELMT SM2 209 G4
Cunard Crs WCHMH N21 35 K1
Cunard Rd WLSDN NW10 99 F2
Cundy Rd CAN/RD E16 107 G5
Cundy St BGVA SW1W 15 H7
Cunliffe Rd HOR/WEW KT19 207 H2
Cunliffe St STRHM/NOR SW16 179 H2
Cunningham Cl CHDH RM6 73 J2
WWKM BR4 198 E6
Cunningham Pk HRW HA1 60 D2
Cunningham Pl STJWD NW8 2 A6
Cunningham Rd
SEVS/STOTM N15 * 68 C1
Cunnington St CHSWK W4 117 K3
Cupar Rd BTSEA SW11 141 F2
Cupola Cl BMLY BR1 184 A1
Cureton St WEST SW1P * 121 J5
Curlew Cl THMD SE28 109 K6
Curlew St STHWK SE1 19 J2
Curlew Wy YEAD UB4 95 H4
Curness St LEW SE13 145 F5
Curnick's La WNWD SE27 162 D6
Curran Av BFN/LL DA15 148 A6
WLGTN SM6 210 A1
Currey Rd NTHLT UB5 78 C4
Curricle St ACT W3 118 B1
Currie Hill Cl WIM/MER SW19 159 J6
Curry Ri MLHL NW7 46 B2
Cursitor St FLST/FETLN EC4A 11 J3
Curtain Pl SDTCH EC2A 7 H5
Curtain Rd SDTCH EC2A 7 G7
Curthwaite Gdns
ENC/FH EN2 22 D5
Curtis Dr ACT W3 99 F5
Curtis Field Rd
STRHM/NOR SW16 162 A6
Curtis La ALP/SUD HA0 80 A4
Curtismill Cl STMC/STPC BR5 186 C6
Curtismill Wy STMC/STPC BR5 186 C6
Curtis Rd HOR/WEW KT19 206 E2
HSLWW TW4 154 E2
Curtis St STHWK SE1 19 J6
Curtis Wy STHWK SE1 19 J6
The Curve SHB W12 99 J6
Curwen Av FSTGT E7 89 F2
Curwen Rd SHB W12 118 D2
Curzon Av PEND EN3 25 F6
STAN HA7 43 G4
Curzon Cl ORP BR6 216 D2
Curzon Crs BARK IG11 109 F2
WLSDN NW10 81 G5
Curzon Pl PIN HA5 59 G2
Curzon Rd EA W5 97 H3
MUSWH N10 48 B5
THHTH CR7 196 B3
Curzon St MYFR/PKLN W1K 15 H1
Cusack Cl TWK TW1 * 156 A6
Custom House Reach
BERM/RHTH SE16 * 124 C3
Cutcombe Rd CMBW SE5 142 D3
Cuthberga Cl BARK IG11 90 C5
Cuthbert Gdns SNWD SE25 181 F6
Cuthbert Rd CROY/NA CR0 196 C6
UED N18 50 C1
WALTH E17 52 A6
Cuthbert St BAY/PAD W2 2 A7
Cutlers Gardens Ar
LVPST EC2M 13 H3
Cutler St HDTCH EC3A 13 H3
The Cut STHWK SE1 17 K2
Cyclamen Cl HPTN TW12 173 F2
Cyclamen Wy
HOR/WEW KT19 206 E3
Cygnet Av
EBED/NFELT TW14 154 B2
Cygnet Cl NTHWD HA6 40 A3
WLSDN NW10 81 F3
The Cygnets FELT TW13 154 D6
Cygnet St WCHPL E1 7 K6
Cygnet Wy YEAD UB4 95 H4
Cymbeline Ct HRW HA1 * 61 F3
Cynthia St IS N1 5 H3
Cypress Av WHTN TW2 155 H2
Cypress Cl CLPT E5 68 C6
Cypress Gdns BROCKY SE4 144 B6
Cypress Gv BARK/HLT IG6 54 E2
Cypress Pl FITZ W1T 4 B7

Cypress Rd
KTN/HRWW/WS HA3 42 D5
SNWD SE25 181 F5
Cypress Tree Cl BFN/LL DA15 168 A3
Cyprus Av FNCH N3 46 C5
Cyprus Cl FSBYPK N4 67 G3
Cyprus Gdns FNCH N3 46 C5
Cyprus Pl BETH E2 104 E1
EHAM E6 108 A6
Cyprus Rd ED N9 36 B4
FNCH N3 46 D5
Cyprus St BETH E2 104 E1
Cyrena Rd EDUL SE22 163 G1
Cyril Rd ORP BR6 202 B4
Cyrus St FSBYE EC1V 6 B6
Czar St DEPT SE8 124 D6

D

Dabbling Cl ERITH DA8 * 150 E1
Dabbs Hill La NTHLT UB5 77 K3
D'Abernon Cl ESH/CLAY KT10 204 A2
Dabin Crs GNWCH SE10 145 F2
Dacca St DEPT SE8 124 C6
Dace Rd BOW E3 87 J6
Dacre Av CLAY IG5 54 A5
Dacre Cl GFD/PVL UB6 96 B1
Dacre Gdns LEW SE13 145 H5
Dacre Pk LEW SE13 145 H4
Dacre Pl LEW SE13 145 H4
Dacre Rd CROY/NA CR0 195 K4
PLSTW E13 89 F6
WAN E11 70 D5
Dacres Est FSTH SE23 * 164 A5
Dacres Rd FSTH SE23 164 A5
Dacre St STJSPK SW1H 16 C4
Dade Wy NWDGN UB2 114 E5
Daerwood Cl HAYES BR2 200 E5
Daffodil Cl CROY/NA CR0 198 A5
HPTN TW12 173 F2
Daffodil Gdns IL IG1 90 B3
Daffodil St SHB W12 99 H6
Dafforne Rd TOOT SW17 160 E5
Dagenham Av DAGW RM9 92 A5
Dagenham Rd DAGE RM10 92 E2
LEY E10 69 H5
RAIN RM13 93 F5
Dagger La BORE WD6 29 G1
Dagmar Av WBLY HA9 80 B2
Dagmar Gdns WLSDN NW10 100 B1
Dagmar Ms NWDGN UB2 114 D3
Dagmar Pas IS N1 85 H6
Dagmar Rd CMBW SE5 143 F2
DAGE RM10 92 E5
FSBYPK N4 67 G4
KUTN/CMB KT2 175 G4
NWDGN UB2 114 D3
SEVS/STOTM N15 67 K1
SNWD SE25 197 F1
WDGN N22 48 D4
Dagmar Ter IS N1 85 H6
Dagnall Pk SNWD SE25 197 F2
Dagnall Rd SNWD SE25 197 F2
Dagnall St BTSEA SW11 140 E3
Dagnan Rd BAL SW12 161 G2
Dahlia Gdns IL IG1 90 B4
MTCM CR4 195 J1
Dahlia Rd ABYW SE2 128 C5
Dahomey Rd
STRHM/NOR SW16 179 H2
Daimler Wy WLGTN SM6 210 E5
Daines Cl MNPK E12 89 K1
Dainford Cl BMLY BR1 183 G1
Daintry Cl
KTN/HRWW/WS HA3 61 G1
Dairsie Rd ELTH/MOT SE9 147 F4
Dairy Cl BMLY BR1 * 184 A3
THHTH CR7 180 D5
WLSDN NW10 81 J6
Dairy La WOOL/PLUM SE18 126 E4
Dairyman Cl CRICK NW2 82 B1
Daisy Cl CROY/NA CR0 198 A5
Daisy La FUL/PGN SW6 139 K4
Daisy Rd SWFD E18 53 F5
Dakin Pl WCHPL E1 105 G4
Dakota Cl WLGTN SM6 211 F5
Dalberg Rd BRXS/STRHM SW2 142 B6
Dalberg Wy ABYW SE2 128 E3
Dalby Rd WAND/EARL SW18 140 B5
Dalbys Crs TOTM N17 50 A2
Dalby St KTTN NW5 84 B4
Dalcross Rd HSLWW TW4 134 D3
Dale Av EDGW HA8 44 B4
HSLWW TW4 134 D4
Dalebury Rd TOOT SW17 160 E4
Dale Cl BAR EN5 33 F1
PIN HA5 41 F4
Dale Dr YEAD UB4 94 D3
Dale Gdns WFD IG8 39 F6
Dale Green Rd
FBAR/BDGN N11 34 B5
Dale Gv NFNCH/WDSPK N12 47 G1
Daleham Gdns HAMP NW3 83 H3
Daleham Ms HAMP NW3 * 83 H4
Dalemain Ms CAN/RD E16 125 K1
Dale Park Av CAR SM5 194 E6
Dale Park Rd NRWD SE19 180 D4
Dale Rd KTTN NW5 84 A3
STHL UB1 96 B4
SUT SM1 208 D2
SWLY BR8 187 K6
WALW SE17 122 C6
Dale Rw NTGHL W11 100 C5
Daleside ORP BR6 217 G3
Daleside Cl ORP BR6 217 G4
Daleside Rd HOR/WEW KT19 207 F4
STRHM/NOR SW16 179 G1
Dalestone Ms HARH RM3 57 K2
Dale St CHSWK W4 118 B5
The Dale HAYES BR2 215 H2
Dale Vw BAR EN5 * 20 D4
ERITH DA8 150 D3
Dale View Av CHING E4 38 A4
Dale View Crs CHING E4 38 A5
Dale View Gdns CHING E4 38 B5
Daleview Rd
SEVS/STOTM N15 68 A3
Dalewood Gdns WPK KT4 192 E6
Dale Wood Rd ORP BR6 201 K4
Daley St HOM E9 87 F4
Daley Thompson Wy
VX/NE SW8 141 G3
Dalgarno Gdns NKENS W10 100 A4
Dalgarno Wy NKENS W10 100 A3
Dalkeith Gv STAN HA7 43 K1
Dalkeith Rd DUL SE21 162 D3
IL IG1 90 C1
Dallas Rd CHEAM SM3 208 C4
EA W5 98 B4
HDN NW4 63 J4
SYD SE26 163 J6
Dallas Ter HYS/HAR UB3 113 J3
Dallega Cl HYS/HAR UB3 94 A6
Dallinger Rd LEE/GVPK SE12 165 J1
Dalling Rd HMSMTH W6 118 E4
Dallington Sq FSBYE EC1V 6 B6
Dallington St FSBYE EC1V 6 B6
Dallin Rd BXLYHS DA6 148 E5
WOOL/PLUM SE18 147 G1
Dalmain Rd FSTH SE23 164 A3
Dalmally Rd CROY/NA CR0 197 G4
Dalmeny Av HOLWY N7 84 D2
STRHM/NOR SW16 180 B5
Dalmeny Cl ALP/SUD HA0 79 J4
Dalmeny Crs HSLW TW3 135 J5
Dalmeny Rd BAR EN5 33 G1
CAR SM5 210 A5
HOLWY N7 84 D2
WPK KT4 207 K1
Dalmeyer Rd WLSDN NW10 81 H4
Dalmore Av ESH/CLAY KT10 205 F4
Dalmore Rd DUL SE21 162 D4
Dalrymple Cl STHGT/OAK N14 34 D1
Dalrymple Rd BROCKY SE4 144 B5
Dalston Gdns STAN HA7 44 A4
Dalston La HACK E8 86 B4
Dalton Av MTCM CR4 178 D5
Dalton Cl ORP BR6 216 E1
YEAD UB4 94 B3
Daltons Rd SWLY BR8 203 K6
Dalton St WNWD SE27 162 C4
Dalwood St CMBW SE5 143 F2
Dalyell Rd BRXN/ST SW9 142 A4
Damask Crs CAN/RD E16 106 C3
Damer Ter WBPTN SW10 140 B1
Dames Rd FSTGT E7 88 E2
Dame St IS N1 6 C2
Damien St WCHPL E1 104 D4
Damon Cl SCUP DA14 168 C5
Damsel Ct BERM/RHTH SE16 * 123 H2
Damson Dr HYS/HAR UB3 94 E6
Damson Wy CAR SM5 209 K6
Damsonwood Rd
NWDGN UB2 115 F3
Danbrook Rd
STRHM/NOR SW16 179 K4
Danbury Cl CHDH RM6 55 K6
Danbury Ms WLGTN SM6 210 B2
Danbury Rd LOU IG10 39 J1
RAIN RM13 93 H6
Danbury St IS N1 6 B2
Danbury Wy WFD IG8 53 G2
Danby St PECK SE15 143 G4
Dancer Rd FUL/PGN SW6 139 J2
RCH/KEW TW9 137 H4
Dandelion Cl ROMW/RG RM7 75 G6
Dando Crs BKHTH/KID SE3 146 A4
Dandridge Cl GNWCH SE10 125 J5
Danebury CROY/NA CR0 213 K4
Danebury Av PUT/ROE SW15 158 C2
Daneby Rd CAT SE6 165 F5
Dane Cl BXLY DA5 169 H2
ORP BR6 216 D3
Danecourt Gdns
CROY/NA CR0 212 B1
Danecroft Rd HNHL SE24 142 D6
Danehurst Gdns REDBR IG4 71 J2
Danehurst St FUL/PGN SW6 139 H2
Daneland EBAR EN4 33 K1
Danemead Gv NTHLT UB5 78 B3
Danemere St PUT/ROE SW15 139 F4
Dane Pl BOW E3 105 G1
Dane Rd IL IG1 90 C3
STHL UB1 95 J6
UED N18 36 E6
WEA W13 98 C6
WIM/MER SW19 178 B4
Danesbury Rd FELT TW13 154 A3
Danescourt Crs SUT SM1 194 B6
Danescroft Av HDN NW4 * 64 B2
Danescroft Gdns HDN NW4 64 B2
Danesdale Rd HOM E9 87 G4
Danes Ga HRW HA1 42 E6
Danes Rd ROMW/RG RM7 74 E4
Dane St GINN WC1R 11 G2
Daneswood Av CAT SE6 165 F5
Danethorpe Rd ALP/SUD HA0 79 K4
Danetree Cl HOR/WEW KT19 206 E5
Danetree Rd HOR/WEW KT19 206 E5
Danette Gdns DAGE RM10 74 B6
Daneville Rd CMBW SE5 142 E2
Dangan Rd WAN E11 70 E3
Daniel Bolt Cl POP/IOD E14 105 K4
Daniel Cl HSLWW TW4 154 E2
TOOT SW17 178 D2
UED N18 36 E6
Daniel Gdns PECK SE15 143 G1
Daniell Wy CROY/NA CR0 195 K5
Daniel Pl HDN NW4 63 K3
Daniel Rd EA W5 98 B6
Daniel's Rd PECK SE15 143 K4
Dan Leno Wk FUL/PGN SW6 * 140 A1
Dansey Pl SOHO/SHAV W1D 10 C5
Dansington Rd WELL DA16 148 B5
Danson Crs WELL DA16 148 C4
Danson La WELL DA16 148 C5
Danson Md WELL DA16 148 D4
Danson Rd BXLYHS DA6 148 E6
Danson U/P BFN/LL DA15 168 D1
Dante Rd LBTH SE11 18 A6
Danube Cl ED N9 36 E5
Danube St CHEL SW3 120 D5
Danvers Rd CEND/HSY/T N8 66 D1
Danvers St CHEL SW3 120 C6
Daphne Gdns CHING E4 38 A5
Daphne St WAND/EARL SW18 160 B1
Daplyn St WCHPL E1 104 C4
D'Arblay St SOHO/CST W1F 10 B4
Darby Crs SUN TW16 172 B5
Darby Gdns SUN TW16 172 B5
Darcy Av WLGTN SM6 210 C2
Darcy Cl TRDG/WHET N20 33 H4
D'Arcy Dr
KTN/HRWW/WS HA3 61 K1
D'Arcy Gdns DAGW RM9 92 B6
KTN/HRWW/WS HA3 62 A1
Darcy Rd ISLW TW7 136 B2
STRHM/NOR SW16 179 K5
D'Arcy Rd CHEAM SM3 208 B2
Darell Rd RCH/KEW TW9 137 H4
Darenth Rd STNW/STAM N16 68 B4
WELL DA16 148 B2
Darent Valley Pth DART DA1 171 H2
ERITH DA8 151 G2
Darfield Rd BROCKY SE4 144 C6
Darfield Wy NKENS W10 100 B6
Darfur St PUT/ROE SW15 139 G4
Dargate Cl NRWD SE19 181 G3
Darien Rd BTSEA SW11 140 C4
Darlands Dr BAR EN5 20 B6
Darlan Rd FUL/PGN SW6 139 J1
Darlaston Rd WIM/MER SW19 177 G3
Darley Cl CROY/NA CR0 198 A3
Darley Dr NWMAL KT3 176 A5
Darley Gdns MRDN SM4 194 A3
Darley Rd BTSEA SW11 160 E1
ED N9 36 B3
Darling Rd BROCKY SE4 144 D4
Darling Rw WCHPL E1 104 D3
Darlington Rd WNWD SE27 180 C1
Darmaine Cl SAND/SEL CR2 211 J5
Darndale Cl WALTH E17 51 H5
Darnley Rd HACK E8 86 D4
WFD IG8 52 E4
Darnley Ter NTGHL W11 119 G1
Darns Hl SWLY BR8 203 K4
Darrell Rd EDUL SE22 143 H6
Darren Cl FSBYPK N4 67 F4
Darrick Wood Rd ORP BR6 201 J6
Darris Cl YEAD UB4 95 J3
Darsley Dr VX/NE SW8 141 J2
Dartford Av ED N9 36 E1
Dartford Gdns CHDH RM6 73 H2
Dartford Rd BXLY DA5 169 K3
Dartford St WALW SE17 122 D6
Dartmoor Wk POP/IOD E14 * 124 D4
Dartmouth Cl NTGHL W11 100 D5
Dartmouth Gv GNWCH SE10 145 F2
Dartmouth Hl GNWCH SE10 145 F2
Dartmouth Park Av
KTTN NW5 84 B1
Dartmouth Park Hl
KTTN NW5 84 B1
Dartmouth Park Rd
KTTN NW5 84 B1
Dartmouth Pl CHSWK W4 118 B6
FSTH SE23 163 K4
Dartmouth Rd CRICK NW2 82 B4
HDN NW4 63 J3
RSLP HA4 76 E1
SYD SE26 163 J5
Dartmouth Rw GNWCH SE10 145 F3
Dartmouth St STJSPK SW1H 16 C3
Dartmouth Ter GNWCH SE10 145 G2
Dartnell Rd CROY/NA CR0 197 G4
Dartrey Wk WBPTN SW10 * 140 B1
Dart St NKENS W10 100 D2
Darville Rd STNW/STAM N16 86 B1
Darwell Cl EHAM E6 108 A1
Darwin Cl FBAR/BDGN N11 34 B5
ORP BR6 216 D3
Darwin Dr STHL UB1 96 B5
Darwin Gdns OXHEY WD19 41 G1
Darwin Rd EA W5 116 D5
WDGN N22 49 H4
WELL DA16 148 A4
Darwin St WALW SE17 19 F6
Daryngton Dr GFD/PVL UB6 96 D1
Dashwood Rd
CEND/HSY/T N8 67 F3
Dassett Rd WNWD SE27 180 C1
Datchelor Pl CMBW SE5 * 142 E2
Datchet Rd CAT SE6 164 C5
Date St WALW SE17 122 D5
Daubeney Gdns TOTM N17 49 J3
Daubeney Rd CLPT E5 87 G2
TOTM N17 49 J3
Dault Rd WAND/EARL SW18 160 B1
Davema Cl CHST BR7 185 F4
Davenant Rd ARCH N19 66 D6
Davenant St WCHPL E1 104 C4
Davenham Av NTHWD HA6 26 D6
Davenport Cl TEDD TW11 * 174 B2
Davenport Rd CAT SE6 164 E1
SCUP DA14 168 E4
Daventer Dr STAN HA7 43 F3
Daventry Av WALTH E17 69 J3
Daventry St CAMTN NW1 8 C1
Davern Cl GNWCH SE10 125 J4
Davey Cl HOLWY N7 85 F4
PLMGR N13 49 F1
Davey Rd HOM E9 87 J5
Davey St PECK SE15 123 G6
David Av GFD/PVL UB6 96 E2
David Cl HYS/HAR UB3 133 G1
Davidge St STHWK SE1 18 A3
David Ms MHST W1U 9 F1
David Rd BCTR RM8 74 A6
Davidson Gdns VX/NE SW8 141 K1
Davidson Rd CROY/NA CR0 197 F5
Davidson Wy ROMW/RG RM7 75 G3
David's Rd FSTH SE23 163 K3
David St SRTFD E15 88 B4
Davids Wy BARK/HLT IG6 54 E3
David Twigg Cl
KUTN/CMB KT2 175 F4
Davies Cl CROY/NA CR0 197 G3
Davies La WAN E11 70 C6
Davies Ms MYFR/PKLN W1K 9 J5
Davies St MYFR/PKLN W1K 9 J5
Davies Wk ISLW TW7 135 J2
Davington Gdns BCTR RM8 91 H3
Davington Rd BCTR RM8 91 H4
Davinia Cl WFD IG8 53 K2
Davis Rd ACT W3 118 C1
CHSGTN KT9 206 C2
Davis St PLSTW E13 107 F1
Davisville Rd SHB W12 118 D2
Davis Wy SCUP DA14 187 F2
Dawes Av ISLW TW7 136 B6
Dawes Ct ESH/CLAY KT10 204 B2
Dawes Rd FUL/PGN SW6 139 J1
Dawes St WALW SE17 122 E5
Dawley Pde HYS/HAR UB3 94 A6
Dawley Rd HYS/HAR UB3 113 G2
Dawlish Av GFD/PVL UB6 97 G1
PLMGR N13 34 E6
WAND/EARL SW18 160 A4
Dawlish Dr GDMY/SEVK IG3 91 F2
PIN HA5 59 J2
RSLP HA4 58 E6
Dawlish Rd CRICK NW2 82 B4
LEY E10 70 A6
TOTM N17 50 C6
Dawnay Gdns
WAND/EARL SW18 160 C4
Dawnay Rd
WAND/EARL SW18 160 B4
Dawn Cl HSLWW TW4 134 D4
Dawn Crs SRTFD E15 88 B6
Dawpool Rd CRICK NW2 63 H6
Daws La MLHL NW7 45 H1
Dawson Av BARK IG11 91 F5
STMC/STPC BR5 186 C5
Dawson Cl HYS/HAR UB3 94 B4
WOOL/PLUM SE18 127 H4
Dawson Dr RAIN RM13 93 K5
Dawson Gdns BARK IG11 91 F5
Dawson Pl BAY/PAD W2 100 E6
Dawson Rd CRICK NW2 82 A3
KUT/HW KT1 175 G6
Dawson St BETH E2 7 K3
Dawson Ter ED N9 * 36 E2
Daybrook Rd WIM/MER SW19 178 A5
Daylesford Av PUT/ROE SW15 138 D5
Daymer Gdns PIN HA5 59 G1
Daysbrook Rd
BRXS/STRHM SW2 162 A3
Days La BFN/LL DA15 167 K2
BFN/LL DA15 168 A1
Dayton Dr ERITH DA8 131 G6
Dayton Gv PECK SE15 143 K2
Deacon Cl PUR/KEN CR8 210 E6
The Deacon Est CHING E4 * 51 H2
Deacon Ms IS N1 85 K5
Deacon Rd CRICK NW2 81 J4
KUTN/CMB KT2 175 G4
Deacons Cl PIN HA5 41 F5
Deacons Hts BORE WD6 30 C1
Deacons Hl OXHEY WD19 27 G1
Deacons Leas ORP BR6 216 D2
Deacons Ri EFNCH N2 65 H2
Deacons Ter IS N1 * 85 J4
Deacons Wk HPTN TW12 155 F6
Deacon Wy WALW SE17 18 C6
WFD IG8 53 K3
Deakin Cl WATW WD18 26 C2
Deakins Ter ORP BR6 202 B4
Deal Porters Wy
BERM/RHTH SE16 123 K3
Deal Rd TOOT SW17 179 F2
Deals Gtwy LEW SE13 144 E2
Deal St WCHPL E1 104 C4
Dealtry Rd PUT/ROE SW15 139 F5
Deal Wk BRXN/ST SW9 142 B1
Dean Bradley St WEST SW1P 16 E5
Dean Cl BERM/RHTH SE16 124 A1
HOM E9 86 E3
Dean Ct ALP/SUD HA0 79 H1
Deancross St WCHPL E1 104 E5
Dean Dr STAN HA7 44 A5
Deane Av RSLP HA4 77 F3
Deane Ct NTHWD HA6 * 40 C4
Deane Croft Rd PIN HA5 59 G3
Deanery Cl EFNCH N2 65 J1
Deanery Ms
MYFR/PKLN W1K * 9 H7
Deanery Rd SRTFD E15 88 C4
Deanery St MYFR/PKLN W1K 9 H7
Deane Wy RSLP HA4 59 F3
Dean Farrar St STJSPK SW1H 16 D4
Deanfield Gdns
CROY/NA CR0 * 211 K2
Dean Gdns WALTH E17 70 B1
Deanhill Ct
MORT/ESHN SW14 * 137 J5
Deanhill Rd
MORT/ESHN SW14 137 J5
Dean Rd CRICK NW2 82 A4
CROY/NA CR0 211 K2
HPTN TW12 173 F1
HSLW TW3 135 G6
THMD SE28 109 G6
Dean Ryle St WEST SW1P 16 E6
Deansbrook Cl EDGW HA8 44 E3
Deansbrook Rd EDGW HA8 44 D3
Dean's Blds WALW SE17 19 F7
Deans Cl CHSWK W4 117 J6
CROY/NA CR0 212 B1
EDGW HA8 44 E2
Dean's Ct STP EC4M 12 B4
Deanscroft Av
CDALE/KGS NW9 62 E6
Deans Dr PLMGR N13 49 H2
Dean's Dr EDGW HA8 45 F1
Deans Gate Cl FSTH SE23 164 A5
Dean's La EDGW HA8 44 E2
Dean's Ms CAVSQ/HST W1G * 9 K3
Deans Rd SUT SM1 209 F1
Dean's Rd HNWL W7 116 A2
Dean Stanley St WEST SW1P 16 E5
Dean St FSTGT E7 88 E3
SOHO/SHAV W1D 10 C3
Deans Wy EDGW HA8 44 E2
Deansway ED N9 36 A5
EFNCH N2 65 H1
Deans Yd WEST SW1P 16 D4
Dean Trench St WEST SW1P 16 E5
Dean Wy NWDGN UB2 115 G2
Dearne Cl STAN HA7 43 G1
De'Arn Gdns MTCM CR4 178 D6
Dearsley Rd EN EN1 24 C4
Deason St SRTFD E15 * 88 A6
De Barowe Ms HBRY N5 85 H2
Debden Cl CDALE/KGS NW9 45 G4
KUTN/CMB KT2 174 E1
WFD IG8 53 H3
De Beauvoir Crs IS N1 86 A6
De Beauvoir Est IS N1 * 86 A6
De Beauvoir Rd IS N1 86 A5
De Beauvoir Sq IS N1 86 A5
Debnams Rd
BERM/RHTH SE16 123 K4
De Bohun Av STHGT/OAK N14 34 B1
Deborah Cl ISLW TW7 135 K2
Deborah Crs RSLP HA4 58 B4
De Broome Rd FELT TW13 154 B3
Deburgh Rd WIM/MER SW19 178 B3
Decima St STHWK SE1 19 G4
Decimus Cl THHTH CR7 196 E1
Deck Cl BERM/RHTH SE16 124 A1
Decoy Av GLDGN NW11 64 C2
De Crespigny Pk CMBW SE5 142 E3
Deeley Rd VX/NE SW8 141 J2
Deena Cl ACT W3 98 B5
Deepdale WIM/MER SW19 159 G6
Deepdale Av HAYES BR2 199 J1
Deepdale Cl FBAR/BDGN N11 48 A2
Deepdene Av CROY/NA CR0 212 B1
Deepdene Cl WAN E11 70 E1
Deepdene Ct WCHMH N21 35 H1
Deepdene Gdns
BRXS/STRHM SW2 162 A2
Deepdene Rd HNHL SE24 142 D5
WELL DA16 148 B4
Deepwell Cl ISLW TW7 136 B2
Deepwood La GFD/PVL UB6 96 D2
Deerbrook Rd HNHL SE24 162 C3
Deerdale Rd HNHL SE24 142 D5
Deere Av RAIN RM13 93 J4
Deerfield Cl CDALE/KGS NW9 63 H2
Deerhurst Cl FELT TW13 153 K6
Deerhurst Crs HPTN TW12 173 H1
Deerhurst Rd
KIL/WHAMP NW6 82 B5
STRHM/NOR SW16 180 A1
Deerings Dr PIN HA5 58 E2
Deerleap Gv CHING E4 25 K6
Dee Rd RCH/KEW TW9 137 G5
Deer Park Cl KUTN/CMB KT2 175 J3
Deer Park Gdns MTCM CR4 * 194 C1
Deer Park Rd WIM/MER SW19 178 A5
Deer Park Wy WWKM BR4 199 J6
Deeside Rd TOOT SW17 160 C5
Dee St POP/IOD E14 106 A5
Dee Wy ROM RM1 57 G4
Defence Cl THMD SE28 127 K1
Defiant Wy WLGTN SM6 210 E
Defoe Av RCH/KEW TW9 137 H1
Defoe Cl TOOT SW17 178 D2
Defoe Pl TOOT SW17 160 D4
Defoe Rd BERM/RHTH SE16 124 C2
STNW/STAM N16 68 A6
Defoe Wy CRW RM5 56 C2
De Frene Rd SYD SE26 164 A
Degema Rd CHST BR7 185 G
Dehar Crs CDALE/KGS NW9 63 H
De Haviland Dr
WOOL/PLUM SE18 127 G
Dehavilland Cl NTHLT UB5 95 H
De Havilland Ct IL IG1 72 D
De Havilland Rd EDGW HA8 44 D
HEST TW5 134 B
De Havilland Wy
STWL/WRAY TW19 152 A
Dekker Rd DUL SE21 163 F
Delacourt Rd BKHTH/KID SE3 146 A
Delafield Rd CHARL SE7 126 A
Delaford Rd
BERM/RHTH SE16 123 J
Delaford St FUL/PGN SW6 139 H
Delamare Crs CROY/NA CR0 197 K
Delamere Gdns MLHL NW7 45 F
Delamere Rd EA W5 117 F
RYNPK SW20 177 G
YEAD UB4 95 H
Delamere St BAY/PAD W2 101 C
Delamere Ter BAY/PAD W2 101 F
Delancey Pas CAMTN NW1 3 K
Delancey St CAMTN NW1 3 K
De Lapre Cl STMC/STPC BR5 202 E
De Laune St LBTH SE11 122 C
Delaware Rd MV/WKIL W9 101 F
Delawyk Crs HNHL SE24 162 E
Delcombe Av WPK KT4 193 F
Delhi Rd EN EN1 36 E
Delhi St IS N1 5
Delia St WAND/EARL SW18 160
Delisle Rd THMD SE28 127
Delius Cl BORE WD6 29
Delius Gv SRTFD E15 106
Della Pth CLPT E5 86
Dellbow Rd
EBED/NFELT TW14 134
Dell Cl SRTFD E15 88
WFD IG8 39
WLGTN SM6 210
Dell Farm Rd RSLP HA4 58
Dellfield Cl BECK BR3 183
Dell La EW KT17 207
Dellors Cl BAR EN5 20
Dellow Cl GNTH/NBYPK IG2 72
Dellow St WCHPL E1 104
Dell Rd EW KT17 207
PEND EN3 24
WDR/YW UB7 112
Dells Cl CHING E4 37
TEDD TW11 174
Dell's Ms PIM SW1V * 16
The Dell ABYW SE2 128
ALP/SUD HA0 79
BECK BR3 * 182
BTFD TW8 116
EBED/NFELT TW14 154
NRWD SE19 181
NTHWD HA6 26
PIN HA5 41
WFD IG8 39
Dell Wk NWMAL KT3 176
Dell Wy WEA W13 97
Dellwood Gdns CLAY IG5 54
Delme Crs BKHTH/KID SE3 146
Delmey Cl CROY/NA CR0 212
Deloraine St DEPT SE8 144
Delorme St HMSMTH W6 119
Delta Cl WPK KT4 207
Delta Est BETH E2 * 104

Delta Gain *OXHEY* WD19 27 H4
Delta Gv *NTHLT* UB5 95 H2
Delta Rd *WPK* KT4 207 G1
Delta St *BETH* E2 * 104 C2
De Luci Rd *ERITH* DA8 129 K5
De Lucy St *ABYW* SE2 128 C4
Delvers Md *DAGE* RM10 92 E2
Delverton Rd *WALW* SE17 122 C5
Delvino Rd *FUL/PGN* SW6 139 K2
Demesne Rd *WLGTN* SM6 210 D2
Demeta Cl *WBLY* HA9 80 E1
De Montfort Pde
STRHM/NOR SW16 * 161 K5
De Montfort Rd
STRHM/NOR SW16 161 J4
De Morgan Rd *FUL/PGN* SW6 140 A4
Dempster Cl *SURB* KT6 190 D4
Dempster Rd
WAND/EARL SW18 140 B6
Denbar Pde *ROMW/RG* RM7 74 E1
Denberry Dr *SCUP* DA14 168 C5
Denbigh Cl *CHST* BR7 184 E2
NTGHL W11 100 D6
STHL UB1 95 K5
SUT SM1 208 D3
Denbigh Dr *HYS/HAR* UB3 113 F2
Denbigh Gdns
RCHPK/HAM TW10 137 G6
Denbigh Pl *PIM* SW1V * 121 H5
Denbigh Rd *EHAM* E6 107 H2
HSLW TW3 135 G3
NTGHL W11 100 D6
STHL UB1 95 K5
WEA W13 97 H6
Denbigh St *PIM* SW1V 16 A7
Denbigh Ter *NTGHL* W11 100 D6
Denbridge Rd *BMLY* BR1 184 E5
Den Cl *BECK* BR3 199 G1
Dendy St *BAL* SW12 161 F3
Dene Av *BFN/LL* DA15 168 C2
HSLW TW3 134 E4
Dene Cl *BROCKY* SE4 144 B4
HAYES BR2 199 J5
WPK KT4 192 C6
Dene Dr *ORP* BR6 217 H1
Dene Gdns *STAN* HA7 43 J1
THDIT KT7 190 B6
Denehurst Gdns *ACT* W3 117 J1
HDN NW4 64 A3
RCHPK/HAM TW10 137 H5
WFD IG8 39 F6
WHTN TW2 155 J2
Dene Rd *BKHH* IG9 39 J3
NTHWD HA6 40 A2
TRDG/WHET N20 33 K3
The Dene *CROY/NA* CR0 213 F2
E/WMO/HCT KT8 188 E2
WBLY HA9 80 A2
WEA W13 97 H4
Denewood *BAR* EN5 21 G6
Denewood Rd *HGT* N6 65 J3
Dengie Wk *IS* N1 * 85 J6
Denham Cl *WELL* DA16 148 D4
Denham Crs *MTCM* CR4 194 E1
Denham Dr *GNTH/NBYPK* IG2 72 C3
Denham Rd
EBED/NFELT TW14 154 B2
TRDG/WHET N20 33 K4
Denham Wy *BARK* IG11 90 E6
Denholme Rd *MV/WKIL* W9 100 D2
Denholme Wk *RAIN* RM13 93 H4
Denison Cl *EFNCH* N2 47 G6
Denison Rd *EA* W5 97 J3
FELT TW13 153 J6
WIM/MER SW19 178 C2
Deniston Av *BXLY* DA5 168 E3
Denleigh Gdns *THDIT* KT7 * 189 K3
WCHMH N21 35 G2
Denman Dr *ESH/CLAY* KT10 205 G3
GLDGN NW11 64 E2
Denman Dr North
GLDGN NW11 64 E2
Denman Dr South
GLDGN NW11 64 E2
Denman Rd *PECK* SE15 143 G2
Denman St *SOHO/SHAV* W1D 10 B6
Denmark Av *WIM/MER* SW19 177 H3
Denmark Ct *MRDN* SM4 193 K2
Denmark Gdns *CAR* SM5 209 K1
Denmark Gv *IS* N1 5 J2
Denmark Hl *HNHL* SE24 142 E1
Denmark Hill Dr
CDALE/KGS NW9 45 J6
Denmark Rd *BMLY* BR1 184 A4
CAR SM5 209 K1
CEND/HSY/T N8 67 F1
CMBW SE5 142 D2
KIL/WHAMP NW6 100 D1
KUT/HW KT1 175 F6
SNWD SE25 197 J2
WEA W13 97 H6
WHTN TW2 155 J5
WIM/MER SW19 177 G2
Denmark St *LSQ/SEVD* WC2H 10 D4
PLSTW E13 107 F4
TOTM N17 50 D4
WAN E11 88 C1
Denmark Ter *EFNCH* N2 * 47 K6
Denmead Rd *CROY/NA* CR0 196 C5
Dennan Rd *SURB* KT6 191 G5
Denner Rd *CHING* E4 37 J4
Denne Ter *HACK* E8 7 K1
Dennett Rd *CROY/NA* CR0 196 B4
Dennett's Gv *NWCR* SE14 144 A3
Dennett's Rd *NWCR* SE14 143 K2
Denning Av *CROY/NA* CR0 211 G3
Denning Cl *HPTN* TW12 172 E2
TJWD NW8 101 G2
Denning Ms *BAL* SW12 161 F1
Denning Rd *HAMP* NW3 83 H2
Dennington Park Rd
KIL/WHAMP NW6 82 E4
Denningtons *WPK* KT4 192 B6
Dennis Av *WBLY* HA9 80 B3
Dennis Gdns *STAN* HA7 43 J1
Dennis La *STAN* HA7 29 H6
Dennis Pde *STHGT/OAK* N14 * 34 D3
Dennis Park Crs *RYNPK* SW20 177 H4
Dennis Reeve Cl *MTCM* CR4 178 E4
Dennis Rd *E/WMO/HCT* KT8 189 H1
Dennis Wy *CLAP* SW4 141 J4
Denny Crs *LBTH* SE11 122 B5
Denny Gdns *DAGW* RM9 91 H5
Denny Rd *ED* N9 36 D3
Denny St *LBTH* SE11 122 B5
Den Rd *HAYES* BR2 183 G6
Densham Rd *SRTFD* E15 88 C6
Densole Cl *BECK* BR3 * 182 B4
Densworth Gv *ED* N9 36 E4
Denton Cl *BAR* EN5 20 A6
Denton Gv *WOT/HER* KT12 188 D6
Denton Rd *CEND/HSY/T* N8 67 F2
TWK TW1 156 E1
UED N18 36 A6
WELL DA16 148 D1
Denton St *WAND/EARL* SW18 160 A1
Denton Ter *BXLY* DA5 * 170 B4
Denton Wy *CLPT* E5 87 F1
Dents Rd *BTSEA* SW11 160 E1
Denvale Trade Pk *MTCM* CR4 194 C1
Denver Cl *ORP* BR6 201 K3
Denver Rd *STNW/STAM* N16 68 A4
Denyer St *CHEL* SW3 14 D6
Denzil Rd *WLSDN* NW10 81 H3
Deodar Rd *PUT/ROE* SW15 139 H5
Deodora Cl *TRDG/WHET* N20 33 J5
Depot Ap *CRICK* NW2 82 B2
Depot Rd *HSLW* TW3 135 J4
Depot St *CMBW* SE5 122 E6
Deptford Br *DEPT* SE8 144 D2
Deptford Broadway
NWCR SE14 144 D2
Deptford Church St *DEPT* SE8 124 D6
Deptford Gn *DEPT* SE8 124 D6
Deptford High St *DEPT* SE8 124 D6
Deptford Whf *DEPT* SE8 124 C4
De Quincey Ms *CAN/RD* E16 125 K1
De Quincey Rd *TOTM* N17 49 K4
Derby Av *KTN/HRWW/WS* HA3 42 D4
NFNCH/WDSPK N12 47 G1
ROMW/RG RM7 74 D3
Derby Ga *WHALL* SW1A 16 E2
Derby Hl *FSTH* SE23 163 K4
Derby Hill Crs *FSTH* SE23 163 K4
Derby Rd *BRYLDS* KT5 191 H5
CROY/NA CR0 196 C6
FSTGT E7 89 H5
GFD/PVL UB6 78 B6
HOM E9 87 F6
HSLW TW3 135 G5
MORT/ESHN SW14 137 J5
PEND EN3 24 D6
SUT SM1 208 D4
SWFD E18 52 D4
UED N18 50 E1
WIM/MER SW19 177 K3
Derbyshire St *BETH* E2 104 D2
Derby St *MYFR/PICC* W1J 15 H1
Dereham Pl *CRW* RM5 56 D2
SDTCH EC2A 7 H6
Dereham Rd *BARK* IG11 91 F4
Derek Av *HOR/WEW* KT19 206 C4
WBLY HA9 80 D5
WLGTN SM6 210 B2
Derek Cl *HOR/WEW* KT19 206 D3
Derek Walcott Cl *HNHL* SE24 * 142 C6
Deri Av *RAIN* RM13 111 K3
Dericote St *HACK* E8 86 C6
Deri Dene Cl
STWL/WRAY TW19 * 152 B1
Derifall Cl *EHAM* E6 107 K4
Dering Pl *CROY/NA* CR0 211 J2
Dering Rd *CROY/NA* CR0 211 J2
Dering St *OXSTW* W1C 9 J4
Derinton Rd *TOOT* SW17 161 F6
Derley Rd *NWDGN* UB2 114 B3
Dermody Gdns *LEW* SE13 * 145 G6
Dermody Rd *LEW* SE13 145 G6
Deronda Rd *HNHL* SE24 162 C3
Deroy Cl *CAR* SM5 209 K4
Derrick Gdns *CHARL* SE7 126 B3
Derrick Rd *BECK* BR3 182 C6
Derry Downs *STMC/STPC* BR5 202 D3
Derry Rd *CROY/NA* CR0 210 E1
Derry St *KENS* W8 120 A2
Dersingham Av *MNPK* E12 89 K2
Dersingham Rd *CRICK* NW2 82 C1
Derwent Av *CDALE/KGS* NW9 63 G2
EBAR EN4 33 K3
MLHL NW7 45 F1
PIN HA5 41 J2
PUT/ROE SW15 158 B6
UED N18 49 K1
Derwent Cl
EBED/NFELT TW14 153 J3
ESH/CLAY KT10 204 E4
Derwent Crs
NFNCH/WDSPK N12 33 G5
STAN HA7 43 J5
Derwent Dr *STMC/STPC* BR5 201 J4
YEAD UB4 94 C4
Derwent Gdns *REDBR* IG4 71 J1
WBLY HA9 61 J4
Derwent Gv *EDUL* SE22 143 G5
Derwent Ri *CDALE/KGS* NW9 63 G3
Derwent Rd *EA* W5 116 D3
PGE/AN SE20 181 H5
PLMGR N13 35 F6
RYNPK SW20 193 G3
STHL UB1 95 K5
WHTN TW2 155 G1
Derwent St *GNWCH* SE10 125 H5
Derwentwater Rd *ACT* W3 117 K1
Derwent Wy *HCH* RM12 93 K3
Derwent Yd *EA* W5 * 116 D3
De Salis Rd *HGDN/ICK* UB10 94 A3
Desenfans Rd *DUL* SE21 163 F1
Desford Rd *CAN/RD* E16 106 C3
Desford Wy *ASHF* TW15 152 C4
Desmond St *NWCR* SE14 124 B6
Desmond Tutu Dr *FSTH* SE23 164 B3
Despard Rd *ARCH* N19 66 C5
Desvignes Dr *LEW* SE13 165 G1
Detling Rd *BMLY* BR1 183 K1
ERITH DA8 150 A1
Detmold Rd *CLPT* E5 68 D6
Devalls Cl *EHAM* E6 108 A6
Devana End *CAR* SM5 209 K1
Devas Rd *RYNPK* SW20 177 F4
Devas St *BOW* E3 105 K3
Devenay Rd *SRTFD* E15 88 D5
Devenish Rd *ABYW* SE2 128 B2
Deveraux Cl *BECK* BR3 199 F2
De Vere Cl *WLGTN* SM6 210 E5
De Vere Gdns *IL* IG1 71 K5
KENS W8 120 B2
Deverell St *STHWK* SE1 18 E5
De Vere Ms *KENS* W8 * 120 B3
Devereux Ct *TPL/STR* WC2R 11 J5
Devereux La *BARN* SW13 138 E1
Devereux Rd *BTSEA* SW11 160 E1
Deveron Wy *ROM* RM1 57 G4
Devey Cl *KUTN/CMB* KT2 176 C3
Devizes St *IS* N1 * 7 F1
Devoke Wy *WOT/HER* KT12 188 C6
Devon Av *WHTN* TW2 155 H3
Devon Cl *BKHH* IG9 39 F4
GFD/PVL UB6 79 J6
TOTM N17 50 B6
Devoncroft Gdns *TWK* TW1 156 B2
Devon Gdns *FSBYPK* N4 67 H3
Devonhurst Pl *CHSWK* W4 * 118 A5
Devonia Gdns *UED* N18 49 J2
Devonia Rd *IS* N1 6 B2
Devon Man
KTN/HRWW/WS HA3 * 61 J2
Devonport Gdns *IL* IG1 71 K3
Devonport Ms *SHB* W12 * 118 E1
Devonport Rd *SHB* W12 118 E2
Devonport St *WCHPL* E1 104 E5
Devon Ri *EFNCH* N2 65 H1
Devon Rd *BARK* IG11 90 E6
BELMT SM2 208 C6
Devons Est *BOW* E3 105 K2
Devonshire Av *BELMT* SM2 209 G5
Devonshire Cl
CAVSQ/HST W1G 9 J1
SRTFD E15 88 C2
Devonshire Ct *FELT* TW13 * 154 A4
Devonshire Crs *MLHL* NW7 46 B3
Devonshire Dr *GNWCH* SE10 144 E2
SURB KT6 190 E5
Devonshire Gdns *CHSWK* W4 137 K1
TOTM N17 49 J2
WCHMH N21 35 J2
Devonshire Gv *PECK* SE15 123 J6
Devonshire Hill La *TOTM* N17 49 J2
Devonshire Ms *CHSWK* W4 118 B5
Devonshire Ms South
CAVSQ/HST W1G 9 J1
Devonshire Ms West
CAVSQ/HST W1G 3 H7
Devonshire Pl
CAVSQ/HST W1G 3 H7
CRICK NW2 82 E1
KENS W8 120 A3
Devonshire Place Ms
CAVSQ/HST W1G 3 H7
Devonshire Rd *BELMT* SM2 209 G5
CAN/RD E16 107 F5
CAR SM5 210 A2
CHSWK W4 118 B5
CROY/NA CR0 196 E4
EA W5 116 D3
ED N9 36 E3
ELTH/MOT SE9 166 D4
FELT TW13 154 D5
FSTH SE23 164 A2
GNTH/NBYPK IG2 72 D4
HRW HA1 60 D3
MLHL NW7 46 B3
ORP BR6 202 B4
PIN HA5 59 G3
PLMGR N13 35 F6
STHL UB1 96 A4
TOTM N17 49 J2
WALTH E17 69 J3
WIM/MER SW19 178 D3
Devonshire Rw *LVPST* EC2M 13 H2
Devonshire Row Ms
GTPST W1W 3 K7
Devonshire Sq *HAYES* BR2 200 A1
LVPST EC2M 13 H3
Devonshire St
CAVSQ/HST W1G 9 H1
CHSWK W4 118 B5
Devonshire Ter *BAY/PAD* W2 101 G5
EDUL SE22 * 143 H5
Devonshire Wy *CROY/NA* CR0 198 C6
YEAD UB4 95 F5
Devons Rd *BOW* E3 105 J4
Devon St *PECK* SE15 123 J6
Devon Wy *CHSGTN* KT9 205 J2
HOR/WEW KT19 206 D3
Devon Waye *HEST* TW5 134 E1
De Walden St
CAVSQ/HST W1G 9 H2
Dewar St *PECK* SE15 143 H4
Dewberry Gdns *EHAM* E6 107 J4
Dewberry St *POP/IOD* E14 106 A5
Dewey La *BRXS/STRHM* SW2 162 B1
Dewey Rd *DAGE* RM10 92 E4
IS N1 5 J2
Dewey St *TOOT* SW17 178 E1
Dewhurst Rd *HMSMTH* W6 119 G3
Dewsbury Cl *PIN* HA5 59 J3
Dewsbury Gdns *WPK* KT4 207 J1
Dewsbury Rd *WLSDN* NW10 81 J3
Dexter Rd *BAR* EN5 32 B1
Deyncourt Rd *TOTM* N17 49 J4
Deynecourt Gdns *WAN* E11 71 G1
D'Eynsford Rd *CMBW* SE5 142 E2
Diadem Ct *SOHO/CST* W1F 10 C3
Diamedes Av
STWL/WRAY TW19 152 A2
Diameter Rd *STMC/STPC* BR5 201 G4
Diamond Cl *BCTR* RM8 73 J5
Diamond Rd *RSLP* HA4 77 H2
Diamond St *CMBW* SE5 143 F1
WLSDN NW10 81 F5
Diamond Ter *GNWCH* SE10 145 F2
Diana Cl *DEPT* SE8 124 C6
SCUP DA14 169 F4
SWFD E18 53 F4
Diana Gdns *SURB* KT6 191 G6
Diana Rd *WALTH* E17 51 H6
Dianne Wy *EBAR* EN4 21 J5
Dianthus Cl *ABYW* SE2 * 128 C5
Diban Av *HCH* RM12 93 K2
Dibden St *IS* N1 85 J6
Dibdin Cl *SUT* SM1 208 E1
Dibdin Rd *SUT* SM1 208 E1
Dicey Av *CRICK* NW2 82 A3
Dickens Av *DART* DA1 151 K5
FNCH N3 47 G4
Dickens Cl *HYS/HAR* UB3 113 H4
RCHPK/HAM TW10 157 F4
Dickens Dr *CHST* BR7 185 H2
Dickens Est
BERM/RHTH SE16 * 123 H3
Dickens La *UED* N18 50 A1
Dickens Ms *FARR* EC1M 6 A7
Dickenson Cl *ED* N9 36 C3
Dickenson Rd
CEND/HSY/T N8 66 E4
FELT TW13 172 B1
Dickenson's La *SNWD* SE25 197 H3
Dickenson's Pl *SNWD* SE25 197 H3
Dickens Rd *EHAM* E6 107 H1
Dickens Sq *STHWK* SE1 18 D4
Dickens St *VX/NE* SW8 141 G3
Dickens Wy *ROM* RM1 75 G1
Dickens Wood Cl *NRWD* SE19 180 C3
Dickerage La *NWMAL* KT3 175 K6
Dickerage Rd *KUT/HW* KT1 175 K4
NWMAL KT3 175 K5
Dickson Fold *PIN* HA5 59 H1
Dickson House *CHARL* SE7 * 146 D1
Dickson Rd *ELTH/MOT* SE9 146 D4
Dick Turpin Wy
EBED/NFELT TW14 133 J5
Didsbury Cl *EHAM* E6 89 K6
Digby Crs *FSBYPK* N4 67 J6
Digby Gdns *DAGE* RM10 92 C6
Digby Pl *CROY/NA* CR0 212 B1
Digby Rd *BARK* IG11 91 F5
HOM E9 87 F4
Digby St *BETH* E2 104 E2
Diggon St *WCHPL* E1 105 F4
Dighton Rd
WAND/EARL SW18 140 B6
Dignum St *IS* N1 * 5 J2
Digswell St *HOLWY* N7 * 85 G4
Dilhorne Cl *LEE/GVPK* SE12 166 A5
Dilke St *CHEL* SW3 120 E6
Dillwyn Cl *SYD* SE26 164 B6
Dilston Cl *NTHLT* UB5 95 G2
Dilton Gdns *PUT/ROE* SW15 158 D3
Dimes Pl *HMSMTH* W6 118 E4
Dimmock Dr *GFD/PVL* UB6 78 D3
Dimond Cl *FSTGT* E7 88 E2
Dimsdale Dr *CDALE/KGS* NW9 62 E5
EN EN1 36 C2
Dimsdale Wk *PLSTW* E13 88 E6
Dimson Crs *BOW* E3 105 J3
Dingle Cl *BAR* EN5 31 H1
Dingle Gdns *POP/IOD* E14 * 105 J6
Dingley La *STRHM/NOR* SW16 161 J4
Dingley Pl *FSBYE* EC1V 6 D5
Dingley Rd *FSBYE* EC1V 6 C5
Dingwall Av *CROY/NA* CR0 196 D6
Dingwall Gdns *GLDGN* NW11 64 E3
Dingwall Rd *CAR* SM5 209 K6
CROY/NA CR0 196 E6
WAND/EARL SW18 160 B2
Dinmont St *BETH* E2 104 D1
Dinsdale Gdns *BAR* EN5 21 F6
SNWD SE25 197 F2
Dinsdale Rd *BKHTH/KID* SE3 125 J6
Dinsmore Rd *BAL* SW12 161 G2
Dinton Rd *KUTN/CMB* KT2 175 G3
WIM/MER SW19 178 C2
Diploma Av *EFNCH* N2 65 J1
Dirleton Rd *SRTFD* E15 88 D6
Disbrowe Rd *HMSMTH* W6 119 H6
Discovery Wk *WAP* E1W 104 D6
Dishforth La *CDALE/KGS* NW9 45 G4
Disney Pl *STHWK* SE1 18 D2
Disney St *STHWK* SE1 18 D2
Dison Cl *PEND* EN3 25 F2
Disraeli Cl *THMD* SE28 128 C1
Disraeli Rd *EA* W5 116 E1
FSTGT E7 88 E4
PUT/ROE SW15 139 H5
WLSDN NW10 98 E1
Diss St *BETH* E2 7 J4
Distaff La *BLKFR* EC4V 12 C5
Distillery La *HMSMTH* W6 119 F5
Distillery Rd *HMSMTH* W6 119 F5
Distin St *LBTH* SE11 17 J7
District Rd *ALP/SUD* HA0 79 H3
Ditchburn St *POP/IOD* E14 106 A6
Ditchfield Rd *YEAD* UB4 95 J3
Dittisham Rd *ELTH/MOT* SE9 166 D6
Ditton Cl *THDIT* KT7 190 B4
Dittoncroft Cl *CROY/NA* CR0 212 A2
Ditton Grange Cl *SURB* KT6 190 E5
Ditton Grange Dr *SURB* KT6 190 E5
Ditton Hl *SURB* KT6 190 D5
Ditton Hill Rd *SURB* KT6 190 D5
Ditton Lawn *THDIT* KT7 190 B5
Ditton Pl *PGE/AN* SE20 * 181 J4
Ditton Reach *THDIT* KT7 190 C3
Ditton Rd *BXLYHS* DA6 148 E6
NWDGN UB2 114 E5
SURB KT6 191 F5
Dixey Cots *EFNCH* N2 * 65 J2
Dixon Cl *EHAM* E6 107 K5
Dixon Pl *WWKM* BR4 198 E5
Dixon Rd *NWCR* SE14 144 B2
SNWD SE25 181 F6
Dixon Wy *WLSDN* NW10 81 G5
Dobbin Cl
KTN/HRWW/WS HA3 43 G5
Dobell Rd *ELTH/MOT* SE9 146 E6
Dobree Av *WLSDN* NW10 81 K5
Dobson Cl *KIL/WHAMP* NW6 83 H5
Dockers Tanner Rd
POP/IOD E14 124 D4
Dockhead *STHWK* SE1 19 K3
Dock Hill Av
BERM/RHTH SE16 124 A2
Dockland St *CAN/RD* E16 127 F1
Dockley Rd *BERM/RHTH* SE16 123 H3
Dock Rd *BTFD* TW8 * 136 E1
CAN/RD E16 106 D6
Dockside Rd *CAN/RD* E16 107 H6
Dock St *WCHPL* E1 104 C6
Dockwell Cl
EBED/NFELT TW14 133 K5
Doctors Cl *SYD* SE26 181 K1
Docwra's Blds *IS* N1 86 A4
Dodbrooke Rd *WNWD* SE27 162 B5
Doddington Gv *WALW* SE17 122 C6
Doddington Pl *LBTH* SE11 122 C6
Dodsley Pl *ED* N9 36 E5
Dodson St *STHWK* SE1 17 K3
Dod St *POP/IOD* E14 105 J5
Doebury Wk
WOOL/PLUM SE18 128 B6
Doel Cl *WIM/MER* SW19 178 B3
Doggett Rd *CAT* SE6 164 D2
Doggetts Ct *EBAR* EN4 21 J6
Doghurst Av *WDR/YW* UB7 132 E1
Doghurst Dr *WDR/YW* UB7 132 E1
Dog Kennel Hl *CMBW* SE5 143 F4
Dog La *WLSDN* NW10 81 G2
Dog Rose Ramble *YEAD* UB4 76 E6
Dog Rose Ramble & Hillingdon
Trail *YEAD* UB4 94 D1
Doherty Rd *PLSTW* E13 106 E3
Dolben Ct *DEPT* SE8 * 124 C4
Dolben St *STHWK* SE1 * 18 B1
Dolby Rd *FUL/PGN* SW6 139 J3
Dolland St *LBTH* SE11 122 A5
Dollary Pde *KUT/HW* KT1 * 175 J6
Dollis Av *FNCH* N3 46 D4
Dollis Crs *RSLP* HA4 59 G5
Dollis Hill Av *CRICK* NW2 81 K1
Dollis Hill Est *CRICK* NW2 * 81 J1
Dollis Hill La *CRICK* NW2 81 H2
Dollis Pk *FNCH* N3 46 D4
Dollis Rd *MLHL* NW7 46 C4
Dollis Valley Dr *BAR* EN5 20 D6
Dollis Valley Green Wk
FNCH N3 64 C1
TRDG/WHET N20 33 F5
Dollis Valley Wy *EBAR* EN4 21 H5
Dolman Cl *FNCH* N3 47 G5
Dolman Rd *CHSWK* W4 118 A4
Dolman St *CLAP* SW4 142 A5
Dolphin Ap *ROM* RM1 75 H1
Dolphin Cl *BERM/RHTH* SE16 124 A2
SURB KT6 190 E3
THMD SE28 109 J5
Dolphin La *POP/IOD* E14 105 K6
Dolphin Rd *NTHLT* UB5 95 K1
Dolphin Sq *CHSWK* W4 * 138 B1
PIM SW1V 121 H5
Dolphin St *KUT/HW* KT1 175 F5
Dombey St *BMSBY* WC1N 11 G1
Dome Blds *RCH/KEW* TW9 * 136 E6
Dome Hill Pk *SYD* SE26 163 G6
Domett Cl *CMBW* SE5 142 E5
Domingo St *FSBYE* EC1V 6 C6
Dominica Cl *PLSTW* E13 107 H2
Dominion Cl *HSLW* TW3 135 J3
Dominion Dr *CRW* RM5 56 D2
Dominion Pde *HRW* HA1 * 61 F2
Dominion Rd *CROY/NA* CR0 197 G4
NWDGN UB2 114 D3
Dominion St *LVPST* EC2M 13 F1
Dominion Wy *RAIN* RM13 111 J2
Domonic Dr *ELTH/MOT* SE9 167 G5
Domville Cl *TRDG/WHET* N20 33 H4
Donald Dr *CHDH* RM6 73 J2
Donald Rd *CROY/NA* CR0 196 A3
PLSTW E13 89 F6
Donaldson Rd
KIL/WHAMP NW6 82 D6
WOOL/PLUM SE18 147 F2
Donald Woods Gdns
BRYLDS KT5 191 J6
Doncaster Dr *NTHLT* UB5 77 K3
Doncaster Gdns *FSBYPK* N4 * 67 J3
NTHLT UB5 77 K3
Doncaster Gn *OXHEY* WD19 41 G1
Doncaster Rd *ED* N9 36 D2
Donegal St *IS* N1 5 H3
Doneraile St *FUL/PGN* SW6 139 G3
Dongola Rd *PLSTW* E13 107 F2
TOTM N17 50 A6
WCHPL E1 105 G4
Dongola Rd West *PLSTW* E13 107 F2
Donington Av *BARK/HLT* IG6 72 C2
Donkey Aly *EDUL* SE22 163 H2
Donkey La *EN* EN1 24 C3
Donnefield Av *EDGW* HA8 44 A2
Donne Pl *CHEL* SW3 14 D6
MTCM CR4 195 G1
Donne Rd *BCTR* RM8 73 J6
Donnington Rd
KTN/HRWW/WS HA3 61 K3
WLSDN NW10 81 K6
WPK KT4 192 D6
Donnybrook Rd
STRHM/NOR SW16 179 H3
Donoghue Cots
POP/IOD E14 * 105 G4
Donovan Av *MUSWH* N10 48 B5
Donovan Pl *WCHMH* N21 23 F6
Don Phelan Cl *CMBW* SE5 142 E2
Don Wy *ROM* RM1 57 G3
Doone Cl *TEDD* TW11 174 B2
Doon St *STHWK* SE1 11 J7
Dorado Gdns *ORP* BR6 217 K1
Doral Wy *CAR* SM5 209 K3
Dorando Cl *SHB* W12 * 99 K6
Doran Gv *WOOL/PLUM* SE18 147 K1
Dora Rd *WIM/MER* SW19 177 K1
Dora St *POP/IOD* E14 105 H5
Dora Wy *BRXN/ST* SW9 142 B3
Dorchester Av *BXLY* DA5 168 E3
PLMGR N13 35 J6
RYLN/HDSTN HA2 60 C3
Dorchester Cl *ESH/CLAY* KT10 190 A6
NTHLT UB5 78 B3
STMC/STPC BR5 186 C3
Dorchester Ct *CRICK* NW2 82 A1
HNHL SE24 142 D6
STHGT/OAK N14 34 B2
Dorchester Dr
EBED/NFELT TW14 153 H1
HNHL SE24 142 D6
Dorchester Gdns *CHING* E4 37 J6
GLDGN NW11 * 64 E1
Dorchester Gv *CHSWK* W4 118 B6
Dorchester Ms *TWK* TW1 156 D1
Dorchester Pde
STRHM/NOR SW16 * 161 K4

Dorchester Rd MRDN SM4 194 A4
NTHLT UB5 78 B3
WPK KT4 193 F5
Dorchester Ter HDN NW4 * 46 B5
Dorchester Wy
KTN/HRWW/WS HA3 62 B2
Dorchester Waye YEAD UB4 95 F5
Dordrecht Rd ACT W3 118 B1
Dore Av MNPK E12 90 A3
Doreen Av CDALE/KGS NW9 63 F5
Dore Gdns MRDN SM4 194 A4
Dorell Cl STHL UB1 95 K4
Dorian Rd HCH RM12 75 J5
Doria Rd FUL/PGN SW6 139 J3
Doric Wy CAMTN NW1 4 C4
Dorie Ms NFNCH/WDSPK N12 33 F6
Dorien Rd RYNPK SW20 177 G5
Doris Ashby Cl GFD/PVL UB6 79 G6
Doris Rd FSTGT E7 88 E5
Dorking Cl DEPT SE8 124 C6
WPK KT4 193 G6
Dorlcote Rd
WAND/EARL SW18 160 C2
Dorman Pl ED N9 36 C4
Dormans Cl NTHWD HA6 40 B3
Dorman Wy STJWD NW8 83 H6
Dormay St WAND/EARL SW18 140 A6
Dormer Cl BAR EN5 20 B6
SRTFD E15 88 D4
Dormer's Av STHL UB1 96 A5
Dormers Ri STHL UB1 96 B6
Dormer's Wells La STHL UB1 96 A5
Dormywood RSLP HA4 58 D2
Dornberg Rd
BKHTH/KID SE3 * 146 A1
Dorncliffe Rd FUL/PGN SW6 139 H3
Dorney Ri STMC/STPC BR5 202 A1
Dorney Wy HSLWW TW4 134 D6
Dornfell St KIL/WHAMP NW6 82 D3
Dornton Rd BAL SW12 161 G4
SAND/SEL CR2 212 A3
Dorothy Av ALP/SUD HA0 80 A5
Dorothy Gdns BCTR RM8 91 H2
Dorothy Rd BTSEA SW11 140 E4
Dorrell Pl BRXN/ST SW9 142 B4
Dorrington St HCIRC EC1N 11 J1
Dorrington Wy BECK BR3 199 F2
Dorrit Ms UED N18 36 B6
Dorrit St STHWK SE1 * 18 D2
Dorrit Wy CHST BR7 185 H2
Dors Cl CDALE/KGS NW9 63 F5
Dorset Av NWDGN UB2 115 F4
ROM RM1 57 F6
WELL DA16 148 A5
YEAD UB4 94 C2
Dorset Blds EMB EC4Y * 12 A4
Dorset Cl CAMTN NW1 8 E1
YEAD UB4 * 94 C2
Dorset Dr EDGW HA8 44 B2
Dorset Gdns MTCM CR4 196 A1
Dorset Ms FNCH N3 46 E4
KTBR SW1X 15 J4
Dorset Pl SRTFD E15 88 B4
Dorset Ri EMB EC4Y 12 A4
Dorset Rd ASHF TW15 152 A5
BECK BR3 182 A6
EA W5 116 D3
ELTH/MOT SE9 166 D4
FSTGT E7 89 G5
HRW HA1 60 C3
MTCM CR4 178 D5
SEVS/STOTM N15 67 K1
VX/NE SW8 142 A1
WDGN N22 48 E4
WIM/MER SW19 177 K4
Dorset Sq CAMTN NW1 2 E7
Dorset St MHST W1U 9 F2
Dorset Wy WHTN TW2 155 H3
Dorset Waye HEST TW5 134 E1
Dorton Cl PECK SE15 143 F1
Dorville Crs HMSMTH W6 118 E3
Dothill Rd WOOL/PLUM SE18 147 J1
Douai Gv HPTN TW12 173 H4
Doughty Ms BMSBY WC1N 5 G7
Doughty St BMSBY WC1N 5 G6
Douglas Av ALP/SUD HA0 80 A5
NWMAL KT3 192 E1
WALTH E17 51 J4
Douglas Cl BARK/HLT IG6 54 B3
EBAR EN4 21 H1
STAN HA7 43 G1
WLGTN SM6 210 E4
Douglas Crs YEAD UB4 95 G3
Douglas Dr CROY/NA CR0 213 J1
Douglas Est IS N1 * 85 J4
Douglas Ms CRICK NW2 82 C1
Douglas Pth POP/IOD E14 125 F5
Douglas Pl POP/IOD E14 * 125 F5
Douglas Rd CAN/RD E16 106 E4
CHING E4 38 C2
ESH/CLAY KT10 189 G6
GDMY/SEVK IG3 73 G4
HSLW TW3 135 G4
IS N1 85 J5
KIL/WHAMP NW6 82 D6
KUT/HW KT1 175 J5
ROM RM1 75 H3
STWL/WRAY TW19 152 A1
SURB KT6 191 G6
WDGN N22 49 G4
WELL DA16 148 C2
Douglas Rd North IS N1 85 J4
Douglas Rd South IS N1 * 85 J4
Douglas St WEST SW1P 16 C7
Douglas Ter WALTH E17 51 H4
Douglas Vls KUT/HW KT1 * 175 G5
Douglas Wy NWCR SE14 144 C1
Doulton Ms KIL/WHAMP NW6 83 F4
Dounesforth Gdns
WAND/EARL SW18 160 A3
Douro Pl KENS W8 120 A3
Douro St BOW E3 105 J1
Douthwaite Sq WAP E1W 123 H1
Dove Ap EHAM E6 107 J4
Dove Cl MLHL NW7 45 J3
NTHLT UB5 95 H3
WLGTN SM6 211 F5
Dovecot Cl PIN HA5 59 G2
Dove Ct LOTH EC2R * 12 E4
Dovedale Av CLAY IG5 54 A5
KTN/HRWW/WS HA3 61 J3
Dovedale Cl WELL DA16 148 B2
Dovedale Ri MTCM CR4 178 E3
Dovedale Rd EDUL SE22 143 J6
Dovedon Cl STHGT/OAK N14 34 E4
Dove House Gdns CHING E4 37 J4
Dovehouse Md BARK IG11 108 D1
Dovehouse St CHEL SW3 120 C5
Dove Ms ECT SW5 120 B4
Doveney Cl STMC/STPC BR5 186 D6
Dove Pk PIN HA5 41 K3
Dove Pl ESH/CLAY KT10 205 G6
Dover Cl CRICK NW2 64 B6
CRW RM5 56 E5
Dovercourt Av THHTH CR7 196 B1
Dovercourt Est IS N1 85 K4
Dovercourt Gdns STAN HA7 44 A1
Dovercourt La SUT SM1 209 G1
Dovercourt Rd DUL SE21 163 F1
Doverfield Rd
BRXS/STRHM SW2 161 K1
Dover Gdns CAR SM5 209 K1
Dover House Rd
PUT/ROE SW15 138 D5
Doveridge Gdns PLMGR N13 35 H6
Dove Rd IS N1 85 K4
Dove Rw BETH E2 104 C1
Dover Park Dr
PUT/ROE SW15 158 E1
Dover Patrol BKHTH/KID SE3 146 A3
Dover Rd ED N9 36 E4
MNPK E12 71 G6
NRWD SE19 180 E2
WOOL/PLUM SE18 147 G3
Dover St CONDST W1S 9 K6
Dover Ter RCH/KEW TW9 * 137 H3
Dover Yd MYFR/PICC W1J 9 K7
Doves Cl HAYES BR2 200 D6
Doves Yd IS N1 5 J1
Doveton Rd SAND/SEL CR2 211 K3
Doveton St WCHPL E1 104 E3
Dowanhill Rd CAT SE6 165 G3
Dowd Cl FBAR/BDGN N11 34 A4
Dowdeswell Cl
PUT/ROE SW15 138 B5
Dowding Cl HCH RM12 93 K5
Dowding Pl STAN HA7 43 G2
Dowdney Cl KTTN NW5 84 C3
Dower Av WLGTN SM6 210 B6
Dowgate Hl CANST EC4R 12 E5
Dowland St NKENS W10 100 C2
Dowlas St CMBW SE5 143 F1
Dowlerville Rd ORP BR6 217 F4
Dowman Cl WIM/MER SW19 178 A3
Downage HDN NW4 46 A6
Downalong BUSH WD23 28 D3
Downbank Av BXLYHN DA7 150 A2
Down Barns Rd RSLP HA4 77 H2
Down Cl NTHLT UB5 95 F2
Downderry Rd BMLY BR1 165 G5
Downe Cl WELL DA16 148 D1
Downend WOOL/PLUM SE18 147 G1
Downe Rd HAYES BR2 215 J6
MTCM CR4 178 E5
Downer's Cots CLAP SW4 141 H5
Downes Cl TWK TW1 156 C1
Downes Ct WCHMH N21 35 G3
Downfield WPK KT4 192 C5
Downfield Cl MV/WKIL W9 101 F3
Down Hall Rd KUT/HW KT1 174 E4
Downham Cl CRW RM5 56 C3
Downham La BMLY BR1 183 G1
Downham Rd IS N1 85 K5
Downham Wy BMLY BR1 183 H1
Downhills Av TOTM N17 49 K6
Downhills Park Rd TOTM N17 49 J6
Downhills Wy TOTM N17 49 J5
Downhurst Av MLHL NW7 45 F1
Downing Cl RYLN/HDSTN HA2 42 C6
Downing Dr GFD/PVL UB6 78 E6
Downing Rd DAGW RM9 92 B6
Downings EHAM E6 108 A5
Downing St WHALL SW1A 16 E2
Downland Cl
TRDG/WHET N20 33 G3
Downleys Cl ELTH/MOT SE9 166 D4
Downman Rd ELTH/MOT SE9 146 D4
Down Pl HMSMTH W6 118 E4
Down Rd TEDD TW11 174 C2
Downs Av CHST BR7 184 E1
PIN HA5 59 K3
Downs Bridge Rd BECK BR3 183 G4
Downs Court Pde HACK E8 * 86 D3
Downsell Rd SRTFD E15 88 B2
Downsfield Rd WALTH E17 69 G3
Downshall Av
GDMY/SEVK IG3 72 E3
Downs Hl BECK BR3 183 G4
Downshire Hl HAMP NW3 83 H2
Downside BECK BR3 * 182 D4
TWK TW1 156 A5
Downside Cl WIM/MER SW19 178 B2
Downside Crs HAMP NW3 83 J3
WEA W13 97 G3
Downside Rd BELMT SM2 209 H4
Downs La CLPT E5 86 D2
Downs Park Rd HACK E8 86 C3
Downs Rd BECK BR3 182 E5
CLPT E5 86 C2
EN EN1 24 A5
THHTH CR7 180 D4
The Downs RYNPK SW20 177 G3
Down St E/WMO/HCT KT8 189 F2
MYFR/PICC W1J 15 J1
Downs Vw ISLW TW7 136 A2
Downsview Gdns NRWD SE19 180 D3
Downsview Rd NRWD SE19 180 D3
Downsway ORP BR6 216 E3
The Downsway BELMT SM2 209 G6
Downton Av
BRXS/STRHM SW2 162 A4
Downtown Rd
BERM/RHTH SE16 124 B2
Downway
NFNCH/WDSPK N12 47 J3
Down Wy NTHLT UB5 95 F2
Dowrey St IS N1 85 G6
Dowsett Rd TOTM N17 50 C5
Dowson Cl CMBW SE5 * 142 E5
Doyce St STHWK SE1 * 18 C2
Doyle Cl ERITH DA8 150 B2
Doyle Gdns WLSDN NW10 81 K6
Doyle Rd SNWD SE25 197 H1
D'Oyley St BGVA SW1W 15 G6
Doynton St ARCH N19 * 66 B6
Draco Ga PUT/ROE SW15 * 139 F4
Draco St WALW SE17 122 D6
Dragonfly Cl PLSTW E13 107 F2
Dragon Rd LBTH SE11 17 H7
PECK SE15 123 F6
Dragoon Rd DEPT SE8 124 C5
Dragor Rd WLSDN NW10 98 E2
Drake Cl BERM/RHTH SE16 124 A2
Drake Crs THMD SE28 109 J5
Drakefell Rd NWCR SE14 144 A3
Drakefield Rd TOOT SW17 161 F5
Drake Ms HAYES BR2 200 B1
HCH RM12 93 J5
Drake Rd BROCKY SE4 144 D4
CHSGTN KT9 206 C3
MTCM CR4 195 F3
RYLN/HDSTN HA2 59 K6
Drake's Cl ESH/CLAY KT10 204 A3
Drakes Ctyd KIL/WHAMP NW6 82 D5
Drake St ENC/FH EN2 23 K2
FSBYW WC1X 11 G2
Drakewood Rd
STRHM/NOR SW16 179 J3
Draper Cl BELV DA17 129 G4
ISLW TW7 135 J3
Draper Est STHWK SE1 18 B6
Draper Pl IS N1 85 H6
Drapers Rd ENC/FH EN2 23 H3
SRTFD E15 88 A2
TOTM N17 50 B6
Drappers Wy
BERM/RHTH SE16 123 H4
Draven Cl HAYES BR2 199 J4
Drawell Cl WOOL/PLUM SE18 127 K5
Drax Av RYNPK SW20 176 D3
Draxmont WIM/MER SW19 177 H2
Draycot Rd SURB KT6 191 H5
WAN E11 71 F3
Draycott Av CHEL SW3 14 D7
KTN/HRWW/WS HA3 61 H3
Draycott Cl CMBW SE5 142 E1
CRICK NW2 82 B1
KTN/HRWW/WS HA3 61 H3
Draycott Pl CHEL SW3 14 E7
Draycott Ter CHEL SW3 14 E6
Dray Ct ALP/SUD HA0 * 79 J4
Drayford Cl MV/WKIL W9 * 100 D3
Dray Gdns BRXS/STRHM SW2 142 A6
Draymans Ms PECK SE15 143 G3
Draymans Wy ISLW TW7 136 A4
Drayson Ms KENS W8 119 K2
Drayton Av LOU IG10 39 K1
ORP BR6 201 G5
WEA W13 97 G6
Drayton Bridge Rd HNWL W7 97 F6
Drayton Cl HSLW TW4 134 E6
IL IG1 72 D5
Drayton Ct WDR/YW UB7 * 112 C4
Drayton Court Chambers
WEA W13 * 97 H6
Drayton Gdns WBPTN SW10 120 B5
WCHMH N21 35 H2
WDR/YW UB7 112 A2
WEA W13 97 G6
Drayton Gn WEA W13 97 G6
Drayton Green Rd WEA W13 97 H6
Drayton Gv WEA W13 97 G6
Drayton Pk HBRY N5 85 G3
Drayton Park Ms HOLWY N7 * 85 G3
Drayton Rd CROY/NA CR0 196 C6
TOTM N17 50 A5
WAN E11 70 B5
WEA W13 97 G5
WLSDN NW10 81 H6
Dreadnought Cl
WIM/MER SW19 178 B5
Dreadnought St GNWCH SE10 125 H3
Drenon Sq HYS/HAR UB3 94 D6
Dresden Cl KIL/WHAMP NW6 83 F4
Dresden Rd ARCH N19 66 C5
Dressington Av BROCKY SE4 164 D1
Drew Av MLHL NW7 46 C2
Drewery Ct BKHTH/KID SE3 * 145 H4
Drew Gdns GFD/PVL UB6 79 F4
Drew Rd CAN/RD E16 126 D1
Drews Cots
STRHM/NOR SW16 * 161 J4
Drewstead Rd
STRHM/NOR SW16 161 J4
Driffield Rd BOW E3 105 G1
The Drift HAYES BR2 215 H1
The Driftway MTCM CR4 179 F4
Drinkwater Rd
RYLN/HDSTN HA2 60 B6
Drive Ct EDGW HA8 * 44 C1
The Drive ACT W3 98 E5
BAR EN5 33 G1
BARK IG11 91 F5
BECK BR3 182 D5
BKHH IG9 39 G2
BXLY DA5 168 D1
CHING E4 38 B2
CHST BR7 186 A3
CHST BR7 186 A6
CRW RM5 57 F4
EBED/NFELT TW14 154 A2
EDGW HA8 44 C1
ENC/FH EN2 23 K2
ESH/CLAY KT10 189 H5
FBAR/BDGN N11 48 C2
FNCH N3 46 E3
GLDGN NW11 64 C4
HGT N6 65 K2
HOLWY N7 85 F4
HOR/WEW KT19 207 H4
HSLW TW3 135 J3
IL IG1 72 B3
KUTN/CMB KT2 175 K3
MRDN SM4 194 B2
NTHWD HA6 40 C4
ORP BR6 202 A6
RYLN/HDSTN HA2 60 A4
RYNPK SW20 177 F3
SCUP DA14 168 C5
SURB KT6 191 F4
SWFD E18 52 E6
THHTH CR7 196 E1
WALTH E17 51 K6
WBLY HA9 62 E6
WWKM BR4 199 G4
Dr Johnson Av TOOT SW17 161 G5
Droitwich Cl SYD SE26 163 H5
Dromey Gdns
KTN/HRWW/WS HA3 43 F3
Dromore Rd PUT/ROE SW15 159 H1
Dronfield Gdns BCTR RM8 91 J3
Droop St NKENS W10 100 C3
Drovers Pl PECK SE15 143 J1
Drovers Rd SAND/SEL CR2 211 K3
Drovers Wy HOLWY N7 84 E4
Druce Rd DUL SE21 163 F1
Druid St STHWK SE1 19 H2
Druids Wy HAYES BR2 199 G1
Drumaline Rdg WPK KT4 192 B6
Drummond Av
ROMW/RG RM7 75 F1
Drummond Cl ERITH DA8 150 B2
Drummond Crs CAMTN NW1 4 C4
Drummond Dr STAN HA7 43 F3
Drummond Ga PIM SW1V 121 J5
Drummond Rd
BERM/RHTH SE16 123 J3
CROY/NA CR0 196 D6
ROMW/RG RM7 74 E1
WAN E11 71 F3
Drummonds Pl
RCH/KEW TW9 137 F5
Drummond St CAMTN NW1 4 A6
Drum St WCHPL E1 13 K3
Drury Crs CROY/NA CR0 196 B6
Drury La HOL/ALD WC2B 10 E3
Drury Rd HRW HA1 60 C4
Drury Wy WLSDN NW10 81 F3
Dryad St PUT/ROE SW15 139 G4
Dryburgh Gdns
CDALE/KGS NW9 44 C6
Dryburgh Rd PUT/ROE SW15 138 E4
Dryden Av HNWL W7 97 F5
Dryden Cl BARK/HLT IG6 55 F2
CLAP SW4 141 J6
Dryden Rd EN EN1 36 A1
KTN/HRWW/WS HA3 43 F4
WELL DA16 148 A2
WIM/MER SW19 178 B2
Dryden St COVGDN WC2E 11 F4
Dryden Wy ORP BR6 202 B5
Dryfield Cl WLSDN NW10 80 E4
Dryfield Rd EDGW HA8 44 E2
Dryhill Rd BELV DA17 129 G6
Dryland Av ORP BR6 217 F2
Drylands Rd CEND/HSY/T N8 66 E3
Drysdale Av CHING E4 37 K1
Drysdale Cl NTHWD HA6 40 C3
Drysdale Dwellings
HACK E8 * 86 B3
Drysdale Pl IS N1 7 H4
Drysdale St IS N1 7 H5
Dublin Av HACK E8 86 C6
Du Burstow Ter HNWL W7 115 K2
Ducal St BETH E2 7 K5
Du Cane Cl SHB W12 * 100 A5
Du Cane Rd SHB W12 99 J5
Duchess Cl FBAR/BDGN N11 48 B1
SUT SM1 209 G2
Duchess Gv BKHH IG9 * 39 F4
Duchess Ms CAVSQ/HST W1G 9 K2
Duchess of Bedford's Wk
KENS W8 119 J2
Duchess St REGST W1B 9 K2
Duchy Rd EDAR EN4 21 H1
Duchy St STHWK SE1 11 K7
Ducie St CLAP SW4 141 K5
Duckett Rd FSBYPK N4 67 H3
Duckett St WCHPL E1 105 F4
Ducking Stool Ct ROM RM1 75 G1
Duck La SOHO/CST W1F 10 C4
Duck Lees La PEND EN3 25 G5
Du Cros Dr STAN HA7 43 K2
Du Cros Rd ACT W3 118 B1
Dudden Hill La WLSDN NW10 81 H2
Dudden Hill Pde
WLSDN NW10 * 81 H2
Duddington Cl ELTH/MOT SE9 166 C6
Dudley Av
KTN/HRWW/WS HA3 43 J6
Dudley Dr MRDN SM4 193 H5
RSLP HA4 77 F3
Dudley Gdns
RYLN/HDSTN HA2 60 D5
WEA W13 116 C2
Dudley Pl HYS/HAR UB3 113 G4
Dudley Rd EBED/NFELT TW14 153 G3
FNCH N3 47 F5
IL IG1 90 B2
KIL/WHAMP NW6 100 C1
KUT/HW KT1 175 G6
NWDGN UB2 114 C2
RCH/KEW TW9 137 G3
RYLN/HDSTN HA2 60 C6
WALTH E17 51 J5
WIM/MER SW19 177 K2
Dudley St BAY/PAD W2 * 8 A2
Dudlington Rd CLPT E5 68 E6
Dudmaston Ms CHEL SW3 120 C5
Dudrich Cl
NFNCH/WDSPK N12 47 K2
Dudrich Ms EDUL SE22 143 G6
Dudset La HEST TW5 133 K2
Dufferin Av STLK EC1Y 6 E7
Dufferin St STLK EC1Y 6 D7
Duffield Cl HRW HA1 61 F2
Duffield Dr SEVS/STOTM N15 68 B1
Duff St POP/IOD E14 105 K5
Dufour's Pl SOHO/CST W1F 10 B4
Dugard Wy LBTH SE11 18 A6
Duggan Dr CHST BR7 184 D2
Dugolly Av WBLY HA9 80 D1
Duke Humphrey Rd
BKHTH/KID SE3 145 H2
Duke of Cambridge Cl
WHTN TW2 155 J1
Duke of Edinburgh Rd
SUT SM1 209 H1
The Duke of Wellington Av
WOOL/PLUM SE18 127 G3
Duke of Wellington Pl
KTBR SW1X 15 H3
Duke of York Sq CHEL SW3 120 E5
Duke of York St STJS SW1Y 10 B7
Duke Rd BARK/HLT IG6 72 D1
CHSWK W4 118 A5
Dukes Av EDGW HA8 44 B2
FNCH N3 47 F4
HRW HA1 60 E1
HSLWW TW4 134 D5
MUSWH N10 48 C6
NTHLT UB5 77 J5
NWMAL KT3 176 B6
PIN HA5 59 K3
RCHPK/HAM TW10 156 D6
Duke's Av CHSWK W4 118 A5
Dukes Cl ASHF TW15 153 F6
HPTN TW12 172 E1
Dukes Ga CHSWK W4 * 117 K4
Dukes Green Av
EBED/NFELT TW14 133 K6
Dukes La KENS W8 119 K2
Dukes Lane Chambers
KENS W8 * 120 A2
Dukes Lane Man KENS W8 * 120 A2
Dukes Ms MUSWH N10 48 B6
Duke's Ms MHST W1U 9 H3
Dukes Orch BXLY DA5 169 K3
Duke's Pl HDTCH EC3A 13 J4
Dukes Point HGT N6 66 B5
Dukes Rd ACT W3 98 C3
EHAM E6 90 A6
Duke's Rd CAMTN NW1 4 D5
Dukesthorpe Rd SYD SE26 164 A6
Duke St MHST W1U 9 H3
RCH/KEW TW9 136 E5
SUT SM1 209 H2
Duke Street Hl STHWK SE1 13 F7
Duke Street St James's
MYFR/PICC W1J 10 B7
Dukes Wy WBLY HA9 80 A3
WWKM BR4 214 C1
Duke's Yd MYFR/PKLN W1K 9 H5
Dulas St FSBYPK N4 67 F5
Dulford St NTGHL W11 100 C6
Dulka Rd BTSEA SW11 140 E6
Dulverton Rd ELTH/MOT SE9 167 H4
RSLP HA4 58 E6
Dulwich Common DUL SE21 162 E3
The Dulwich Oaks DUL SE21 * 163 G5
Dulwich Rd HNHL SE24 142 B6
Dulwich Village DUL SE21 162 E
Dulwich Wood Av
NRWD SE19 181 F
Dulwich Wood Pk
NRWD SE19 163 F
Dumbarton Rd
BRXS/STRHM SW2 161 K
Dumbleton Cl KUT/HW KT1 175 J
Dumbreck Rd ELTH/MOT SE9 147 F
Dumfries Cl OXHEY WD19 26 E
Dumont Rd STNW/STAM N16 86 A
Dumpton Pl CAMTN NW1 84 A
Dunbar Av BECK BR3 198 E
DAGE RM10 92 C
STRHM/NOR SW16 180 E
Dunbar Cl YEAD UB4 94 E
Dunbar Ct WOT/HER KT12 188 E
Dunbar Gdns DAGE RM10 92 C
Dunbar Rd FSTGT E7 88 E
NWMAL KT3 191 K
WDGN N22 49 G
Dunbar St WNWD SE27 162 D
Dunblane Rd ELTH/MOT SE9 146 D
Dunboyne Rd HAMP NW3 83
Dunbridge St BETH E2 104
Duncan Cl BAR EN5 21
Duncan Gv ACT W3 99
Duncannon St CHCR WC2N 10
Duncan Rd HACK E8 86
RCH/KEW TW9 137
Duncan St IS N1 6
Duncan Ter IS N1 6
Dunch St WCHPL E1 104
Duncombe Hl FSTH SE23 164
Duncombe Rd ARCH N19 66
Duncrievie Rd LEW SE13 165
Duncroft WOOL/PLUM SE18 147
Dundalk Rd BROCKY SE4 144
Dundas Gdns
E/WMO/HCT KT8 173
Dundas Rd PECK SE15 143
Dundee Rd PLSTW E13 107
SNWD SE25 197
Dundee St WAP E1W 123
Dundee Wy PEND EN3 25
Dundee Whf POP/IOD E14 105
Dundela Gdns WPK KT4 207
Dundonald Cl EHAM E6 107
Dundonald Rd
WIM/MER SW19 177
WLSDN NW10 82
Dunedin Rd IL IG1 72
LEY E10 87
RAIN RM13 111
Dunedin Wy YEAD UB4 95
Dunelm St WCHPL E1 105
Dunfield Rd CAT SE6 182
Dunford Rd HOLWY N7 85
Dungarvan Av
PUT/ROE SW15 138
Dunheved Cl THHTH CR7 196
Dunheved Rd North
THHTH CR7 196
Dunheved Rd South
THHTH CR7 19
Dunheved Rd West
THHTH CR7 19
Dunholme Gn ED N9 3
Dunholme La ED N9 3
Dunholme Rd ED N9 3
Dunkeld Rd BCTR RM8 7
SNWD SE25 19
Dunkery Rd ELTH/MOT SE9 16
Dunkin Rd DART DA1 15
Dunkirk St WNWD SE27 * 16
Dunlace Rd CLPT E5 8
Dunleary Cl HSLWW TW4 15
Dunley Dr CROY/NA CR0 2
Dunloe Av TOTM N17 4

Dunloe St BETH E2 7 J3
Dunlop Pl BERM/RHTH SE16 19 K5
Dunmore Rd
KIL/WHAMP NW6 82 C6
RYNPK SW20 177 F4
Dunmow Cl CHDH RM6 73 J2
FELT TW13 * 154 D6
LOU IG10 39 J1
Dunmow Dr RAIN RM13 93 H6
Dunmow Rd SRTFD E15 88 B2
Dunmow Wk IS N1 * 85 J6
Dunnage Crs
BERM/RHTH SE16 124 B4
Dunningford Cl HCH RM12 93 H3
Dunn Md CDALE/KGS NW9 45 H3
Dunnock Cl ED N9 37 F3
Dunnock Rd EHAM E6 107 J5
Dunn St HACK E8 86 B3
Dunollie Pl KTTN NW5 84 C3
Dunollie Rd KTTN NW5 84 C3
Dunoon Gdns FSTH SE23 * 164 A2
Dunoon Rd FSTH SE23 163 K2
Dunraven Dr ENC/FH EN2 23 G3
Dunraven Rd SHB W12 118 D1
Dunraven St MYFR/PKLN W1K 9 F5
Dunsany Rd HMSMTH W6 119 G3
Dunsbury Cl BELMT SM2 209 F6
Dunsfold Wy CROY/NA CR0 213 K5
Dunsford Wy PUT/ROE SW15 158 E2
Dunsmore OXHEY WD19 * 27 H4
Dunsmore Cl BUSH WD23 28 D1
YEAD UB4 95 H3
Dunsmore Rd WOT/HER KT12 188 A2
Dunsmore Wy BUSH WD23 28 C1
Dunsmure Rd
STNW/STAM N16 68 A5
Dunspring La CLAY IG5 54 B5
Dunstable Ms
CAVSQ/HST W1G 9 H1
Dunstable Rd
E/WMO/HCT KT8 188 E1
RCH/KEW TW9 137 F5
Dunstall Rd RYNPK SW20 176 E2
Dunstall Wy E/WMO/HCT KT8 173 G6
Dunstall Welling Est
WELL DA16 * 148 C3
Dunstan Cl EFNCH N2 * 47 G6
Dunstan Gld
STMC/STPC BR5 * 201 J3
Dunstan Houses WCHPL E1 * 104 E4
Dunstan Rd GLDGN NW11 64 D5
Dunstan's Gv EDUL SE22 163 J1
Dunstan's Rd EDUL SE22 163 H2
Dunster Av MRDN SM4 193 G5
Dunster Cl BAR EN5 20 B5
CRW RM5 56 E5
Dunster Ct MON EC3R 13 G5
Dunster Dr CDALE/KGS NW9 62 E5
Dunster Gdns
KIL/WHAMP NW6 82 D5
Dunsterville Wy STHWK SE1 19 F3
Dunster Wy RYLN/HDSTN HA2 77 J1
Dunston Rd BTSEA SW11 141 F3
HACK E8 7 J1
Dunston St HACK E8 86 A6
Dunton Cl SURB KT6 191 F5
Dunton Rd LEY E10 69 K4
ROM RM1 75 G1
STHWK SE1 19 J7
Duntshill Rd
WAND/EARL SW18 160 A3
Dunvegan Cl
E/WMO/HCT KT8 189 G1
Dunvegan Rd ELTH/MOT SE9 146 E5
Dunworth Ms NTGHL W11 100 D5
Duplex Ride KTBR SW1X 15 F3
Dupont Rd RYNPK SW20 177 G5
Duppas Av CROY/NA CR0 211 H2
Duppas Hill Rd CROY/NA CR0 211 G2
Duppas Hill Ter CROY/NA CR0 211 H1
Duppas Rd CROY/NA CR0 211 G1
Dupree Rd CHARL SE7 126 A5
Dura Den Cl BECK BR3 182 E3
Durand Gdns BRXN/ST SW9 142 A2
Durand Wy WLSDN NW10 80 E5
Durants Park Av PEND EN3 25 F5
Durants Rd PEND EN3 24 E5
Durant St BETH E2 104 C1
Durban Gdns DAGE RM10 92 E5
Durban Rd BECK BR3 182 C5
GNTH/NBYPK IG2 72 E5
SRTFD E15 106 C2
TOTM N17 50 A2
WALTH E17 51 H4
WNWD SE27 162 D6
Durbin Rd CHSGTN KT9 206 A2
Durdans Rd STHL UB1 95 K5
Durell Gdns DAGW RM9 91 K3
Durell Rd DAGW RM9 91 K3
Durfey Pl CMBW SE5 142 E1
Durford Crs PUT/ROE SW15 158 D3
Durham Av HAYES BR2 199 J1
HEST TW5 114 E6
WFD IG8 53 H1
Durham Hl BMLY BR1 165 J6
Durham House St
CHCR WC2N * 11 F6
Durham Pl CHEL SW3 * 120 E5
Durham Ri WOOL/PLUM SE18 127 H5
Durham Rd CAN/RD E16 106 C3
DAGE RM10 92 E3
EA W5 116 E3
EBED/NFELT TW14 154 B2
ED N9 36 C4
EFNCH N2 47 J6
HOLWY N7 67 F6
HRW HA1 60 B2
MNPK E12 89 H2
RYNPK SW20 176 E4
SCUP DA14 186 C1
Durham Rw WCHPL E1 105 F4
Durham St LBTH SE11 122 A5
Durham Ter BAY/PAD W2 101 F5
PGE/AN SE20 * 181 J3
Durham Wharf Dr BTFD TW8 136 D1
Durham Yd BETH E2 * 104 D2
Durley Av PIN HA5 59 J3
Durley Gdns ORP BR6 217 H2
Durley Rd STNW/STAM N16 68 A4
Durlston Rd CLPT E5 68 C6
KUTN/CMB KT2 175 F2
Durnford St SEVS/STOTM N15 68 A2
Durning Rd NRWD SE19 180 E1
Dursford Av
WIM/MER SW19 159 K4
Dursford Rd WDGN N22 48 D3
WIM/MER SW19 159 K5
Durrant Wy ORP BR6 216 D3
Durrell Rd FUL/PGN SW6 139 H2
Durrington Av RYNPK SW20 177 F3
Durrington Park Rd
RYNPK SW20 177 F4
Durrington Rd CLPT E5 87 G2
Dursley Cl BKHTH/KID SE3 146 B3
Dursley Gdns BKHTH/KID SE3 146 C2
Dursley Rd BKHTH/KID SE3 146 B3
Durward St WCHPL E1 104 D4
Durweston Ms MHST W1U * 9 F1
Durweston St MBLAR W1H 8 E2
Dury Rd BAR EN5 20 D2
Dutch Barn Cl
STWL/WRAY TW19 152 A1
Dutch Gdns KUTN/CMB KT2 175 J2
Dutch Yd WAND/EARL SW18 139 K6
Duthie St POP/IOD E14 106 A6
Dutton St GNWCH SE10 145 F2
Duxberry Cl HAYES BR2 200 D2
Duxford Cl HCH RM12 93 K4
Dwight Rd WATW WD18 26 B2
Dye House La BOW E3 87 J6
Dyer's Blds FLST/FETLN EC4A 11 J2
Dyers Hall Rd WAN E11 70 B6
Dyer's La PUT/ROE SW15 138 E4
Dyers Wy HARH RM3 57 J3
Dyke Dr STMC/STPC BR5 202 D4
Dykes Wy HAYES BR2 183 J6
Dylan Cl BORE WD6 * 29 K2
Dylan Rd BELV DA17 129 H3
HNHL SE24 142 C5
Dylways CMBW SE5 142 E5
Dymchurch Cl CLAY IG5 54 A6
ORP BR6 216 E2
Dymock St FUL/PGN SW6 140 A4
Dymoke Rd ROM RM1 75 H4
Dyneley Rd LEE/GVPK SE12 166 B6
Dyne Rd KIL/WHAMP NW6 82 D5
Dynevor Rd
RCHPK/HAM TW10 137 F6
STNW/STAM N16 86 A1
Dynham Rd KIL/WHAMP NW6 82 E5
Dyott St RSQ WC1B 10 D2
Dysart Av KUTN/CMB KT2 174 D1
Dysart St SDTCH EC2A 7 F7
Dyson Ct ALP/SUD HA0 79 G2
Dyson Rd SRTFD E15 88 D4
WAN E11 70 C3
Dyson's Rd UED N18 50 D2

E

Eade Rd FSBYPK N4 67 J4
Eagans Cl EFNCH N2 * 47 H6
Eagle Av CHDH RM6 74 A3
Eagle Cl BERM/RHTH SE16 123 J5
HCH RM12 93 K4
PEND EN3 24 E5
WLGTN SM6 210 E4
Eagle Ct FARR EC1M 12 A1
Eagle Dr CDALE/KGS NW9 45 G5
Eagle Hl NRWD SE19 180 E2
Eagle House Ms CLAP SW4 141 H6
Eagle La WAN E11 70 E1
Eagle Ms IS N1 86 A4
Eagle Pl WBPTN SW10 120 B5
Eagle Rd ALP/SUD HA0 79 K5
HTHAIR TW6 133 J4
Eaglesfield Rd
WOOL/PLUM SE18 147 G2
Eagle St HHOL WC1V 11 G2
Eagle Ter WFD IG8 53 F3
Eagle Wharf Rd IS N1 6 D2
Eagling Cl BOW E3 105 J2
Ealdham Sq ELTH/MOT SE9 146 B5
Ealing Golf Course
GFD/PVL UB6 * 97 G2
Ealing Gn EA W5 116 E1
Ealing Park Gdns EA W5 116 D4
Ealing Rd ALP/SUD HA0 98 A1
BOW E3 105 K2
EA W5 116 E4
NTHLT UB5 78 A5
Ealing Village EA W5 98 A5
Eamont St STJWD NW8 2 C2
Eardley Crs ECT SW5 119 K5
Eardley Rd BELV DA17 129 H5
STRHM/NOR SW16 179 H2
Earl Cl FBAR/BDGN N11 48 B1
Earldom Rd PUT/ROE SW15 139 F5
Earle Gdns KUTN/CMB KT2 175 F3
Earlham Gv FSTGT E7 88 D3
WDGN N22 49 F3
Earlham St LSQ/SEVD WC2H 10 D4
Earl Ri WOOL/PLUM SE18 127 J5
Earl Rd MORT/ESHN SW14 137 K5
Earls Court Gdns ECT SW5 120 A4
Earl's Court Rd ECT SW5 119 K4
Earl's Court Sq ECT SW5 120 A5
Earls Crs HRW HA1 60 E1
Earlsferry Wy IS N1 84 E5
Earlsfield Rd
WAND/EARL SW18 160 B3
Earlshall Rd ELTH/MOT SE9 146 E5
Earlsmead RYLN/HDSTN HA2 77 K2
Earlsmead Rd
SEVS/STOTM N15 68 B2
WLSDN NW10 100 A2
Earls Ms WAND/EARL SW18 160 B2
Earls Ter KENS W8 119 J3
Earlsthorpe Ms BAL SW12 161 F1
Earlsthorpe Rd SYD SE26 164 A6
Earlstoke Est FSBYE EC1V 6 A4
Earlstoke St FSBYE EC1V 6 A4
Earlston Gv HOM E9 86 D6
Earl St SDTCH EC2A 13 G1
Earls Wk BCTR RM8 91 H2
KENS W8 119 K3
Earlswood Av THHTH CR7 196 B2
Earlswood Gdns CLAY IG5 54 A6
Earlswood St GNWCH SE10 125 H5
Early Ms CAMTN NW1 84 B6
Earnshaw St
NOXST/BSQ WC1A 10 D3
Earsby St WKENS W14 119 H4
Easby Crs MRDN SM4 194 A3
Easebourne Rd BCTR RM8 91 J3
Easedale Dr HCH RM12 93 K3
East Acton Ar ACT W3 * 99 H5
East Acton La ACT W3 99 G6
East Arbour St WCHPL E1 105 F5
East Av EHAM E6 89 J5
HYS/HAR UB3 113 J2
STHL UB1 95 K6
WALTH E17 69 K1
WLGTN SM6 211 F3
East Bank STNW/STAM N16 68 A4
Eastbank Rd HPTN TW12 173 H1
East Barnet Rd BAR EN5 21 G5
Eastbourne Av ACT W3 99 F5
Eastbourne Gdns
MORT/ESHN SW14 137 K4
Eastbourne Ms BAY/PAD W2 101 G5
Eastbourne Rd BTFD TW8 116 E5
CHSWK W4 117 K6
EHAM E6 108 A2
FELT TW13 154 C4
SEVS/STOTM N15 68 A3
SRTFD E15 88 C6
TOOT SW17 179 F2
Eastbourne Ter BAY/PAD W2 101 G5
Eastbournia Av ED N9 36 D5
Eastbrook Av ED N9 36 E2
Eastbrook Cl DAGE RM10 92 E2
Eastbrook Dr ROMW/RG RM7 93 G1
Eastbrook Rd BKHTH/KID SE3 146 A2
Eastbury Av BARK IG11 90 E6
EN EN1 24 A2
NTHWD HA6 40 C1
Eastbury Ct OXHEY WD19 * 27 G2
Eastbury Gv CHSWK W4 118 B5
Eastbury Rd EHAM E6 108 A3
KUTN/CMB KT2 175 F3
NTHWD HA6 40 C2
OXHEY WD19 27 G2
ROMW/RG RM7 75 F3
STMC/STPC BR5 201 J3
Eastbury Sq BARK IG11 91 F6
Eastbury Ter WCHPL E1 105 F3
Eastcastle St GTPST W1W 10 A3
Eastcheap FENCHST EC3M 13 F5
East Churchfield Rd ACT W3 118 A1
Eastchurch Rd HTHAIR TW6 133 H3
East Cl EA W5 98 C3
EBAR EN4 22 A5
GFD/PVL UB6 96 C1
RAIN RM13 111 K3
Eastcombe Av CHARL SE7 126 A6
Eastcote ORP BR6 202 A5
Eastcote Av E/WMO/HCT KT8 188 E2
GFD/PVL UB6 79 G3
RYLN/HDSTN HA2 60 B6
Eastcote La NTHLT UB5 77 K4
Eastcote La North NTHLT UB5 77 K4
Eastcote Rd PIN HA5 59 H2
RSLP HA4 58 C4
RYLN/HDSTN HA2 78 C1
WELL DA16 147 J3
Eastcote St BRXN/ST SW9 141 K3
Eastcote Vw PIN HA5 59 G1
East Ct ALP/SUD HA0 61 J6
East Crs EN EN1 24 A6
FBAR/BDGN N11 33 K6
Eastcroft Rd HOR/WEW KT19 207 G5
East Cross Route HOM E9 87 H4
Eastdown Pk LEW SE13 145 G5
East Dr CAR SM5 209 J6
NTHWD HA6 26 C4
STMC/STPC BR5 202 C3
East Duck Lees La PEND EN3 25 G5
East Dulwich Gv EDUL SE22 143 F6
East Dulwich Rd EDUL SE22 143 G5
East End Rd FNCH N3 46 E5
East End Wy PIN HA5 41 J6
East Entrance DAGE RM10 110 D1
Eastern Av CHDH RM6 73 H1
GNTH/NBYPK IG2 72 C3
PIN HA5 59 H4
WAN E11 71 G3
Eastern Av East ROM RM1 57 F6
Eastern Av West CHDH RM6 74 A1
Eastern Gtwy CAN/RD E16 107 G6
Eastern Perimeter Rd
HTHAIR TW6 133 H3
Eastern Rd BROCKY SE4 144 D5
EFNCH N2 47 K6
PLSTW E13 107 F1
ROM RM1 75 G2
WALTH E17 70 A2
WDGN N22 48 E4
Easternville Gdns
GNTH/NBYPK IG2 72 C3
Eastern Wy ERITHM DA18 129 H2
THMD SE28 128 B2
THMD SE28 128 E1
East Ferry Rd POP/IOD E14 124 E4
Eastfield Gdns DAGE RM10 92 C2
Eastfield Rd CEND/HSY/T N8 48 E6
DAGE RM10 92 C2
PEND EN3 25 F1
WALTH E17 69 J1
Eastfields PIN HA5 59 G2
Eastfields Av
WAND/EARL SW18 139 K5
Eastfields Rd ACT W3 98 E4
MTCM CR4 179 F5
Eastfield St POP/IOD E14 105 G4
East Gdns TOOT SW17 178 D2
Eastgate Cl THMD SE28 109 K5
Eastglade NTHWD HA6 40 C1
East Hall Rd STMC/STPC BR5 203 F4
Eastham Cl BAR EN5 20 C6
East Ham Manor Wy
EHAM E6 108 A5
East Harding St
FLST/FETLN EC4A 11 K3
East Heath Rd HAMP NW3 83 H1
East Hl WAND/EARL SW18 140 B6
WBLY HA9 62 C6
Eastholm GLDGN NW11 65 F1
East Holme ERITH DA8 150 A2
Eastholme HYS/HAR UB3 113 K1
East India Dock Rd
POP/IOD E14 105 J6
East India Wy CROY/NA CR0 197 G5
Eastlake Rd CMBW SE5 142 C3
Eastlands Crs EDUL SE22 163 G1
East La ALP/SUD HA0 79 J1
BERM/RHTH SE16 123 H2
KUT/HW KT1 174 E6
Eastlea Ms CAN/RD E16 106 C3
Eastleigh Av
RYLN/HDSTN HA2 60 B6
Eastleigh Cl BELMT SM2 209 F5
CRICK NW2 81 G1
Eastleigh Rd BXLYHN DA7 149 K3
WALTH E17 51 H5
Eastleigh Wy
EBED/NFELT TW14 153 K3
Eastman Rd ACT W3 118 A2
East Md RSLP HA4 77 H1
Eastmead Av GFD/PVL UB6 96 B2
Eastmead Cl BMLY BR1 184 D5
Eastmearn Rd WNWD SE27 162 D4
Eastmont Rd ESH/CLAY KT10 190 A6
Eastmoor Pl CHARL SE7 126 C3
Eastmoor St CHARL SE7 126 C3
WOOL/PLUM SE18 126 C4
East Mount St WCHPL E1 * 104 D4
Eastney Rd CROY/NA CR0 196 C5
Eastney St GNWCH SE10 125 G5
Eastnor Rd ELTH/MOT SE9 167 H3
Easton St FSBYW WC1X 5 J6
East Park Cl CHDH RM6 73 K2
East Parkside GNWCH SE10 125 H2
East Pas STBT EC1A 12 C1
East Pl WNWD SE27 162 D6
East Pole Cots
STHGT/OAK N14 * 22 D5
East Poultry Av FARR EC1M 12 A2
East Rp HTHAIR TW6 132 E2
East Rd CHDH RM6 74 A2
CHEL SW3 121 F5
EBAR EN4 34 A3
EBED/NFELT TW14 153 G2
EDGW HA8 44 D4
IS N1 7 F4
KUTN/CMB KT2 175 F4
PEND EN3 24 E1
ROMW/RG RM7 75 F4
SRTFD E15 88 E6
WDR/YW UB7 112 C4
WELL DA16 148 C3
WIM/MER SW19 178 B2
East Rochester Wy
BFN/LL DA15 147 K6
BFN/LL DA15 168 D1
BXLY DA5 169 H1
DART DA1 170 A2
East Rw NKENS W10 100 C3
WAN E11 70 E3
Eastry Av HAYES BR2 199 J3
East Sheen Av
MORT/ESHN SW14 138 A5
East Side SHB W12 * 119 F2
Eastside Rd GLDGN NW11 64 D1
East Smithfield WAP E1W 13 K6
East St BARK IG11 90 C5
BMLY BR1 183 K5
BTFD TW8 136 D1
WALW SE17 19 G7
East Surrey Gv PECK SE15 143 G1
East Tenter St WCHPL E1 13 K4
East Ter BFN/LL DA15 * 167 K3
East Towers PIN HA5 59 H3
East V ACT W3 * 118 C1
East Vw BAR EN5 20 D3
CHING E4 52 A1
Eastview Av
WOOL/PLUM SE18 147 K1
Eastville Av GLDGN NW11 64 D2
East Wk EBAR EN4 34 A3
HYS/HAR UB3 113 K2
East Wy CROY/NA CR0 198 B6
HYS/HAR UB3 113 K1
RSLP HA4 58 E5
Eastway BOW E3 87 G6
HOM E9 87 H4
LEY E10 87 J2
MRDN SM4 193 G2
WAN E11 71 F2
WLGTN SM6 210 C2
Eastway Crs
RYLN/HDSTN HA2 60 B6
Eastwell Cl BECK BR3 182 B4
Eastwood Cl HOLWY N7 85 G3
SWFD E18 52 E5
TOTM N17 * 50 D3
Eastwood Dr RAIN RM13 111 K5
Eastwood Rd GDMY/SEVK IG3 73 G4
MUSWH N10 48 A5
SWFD E18 52 E5
WDR/YW UB7 112 D2
Eastwood St
STRHM/NOR SW16 179 H2
Eatington Rd LEY E10 70 B2
Eaton Cl BGVA SW1W 15 G6
STAN HA7 29 H6
Eaton Dr BRXN/ST SW9 142 C5
CRW RM5 56 D3
KUTN/CMB KT2 175 H3
Eaton Gdns DAGW RM9 92 A5
Eaton Ga BGVA SW1W 15 G6
NTHWD HA6 40 A2
Eaton La BGVA SW1W 15 K5
Eaton Ms North KTBR SW1X 15 H5
Eaton Ms South BGVA SW1W 15 H6
Eaton Ms West BGVA SW1W 15 H6
Eaton Park Rd PLMGR N13 35 G4
Eaton Pl KTBR SW1X 15 G5
Eaton Ri EA W5 97 J4
WAN E11 71 G2
Eaton Rd BELMT SM2 209 H4
EN EN1 24 A4
HDN NW4 64 A2
HSLW TW3 135 J5
SCUP DA14 168 E4
Eaton Rw BGVA SW1W 15 J4
Eatons Md CHING E4 37 J4
Eaton Sq BGVA SW1W 15 H5
Eaton Ter BGVA SW1W 15 G6
BOW E3 * 105 G2
Eaton Terrace Ms
BGVA SW1W 15 G6
Eatonville Rd TOOT SW17 160 E4
Eatonville Vls TOOT SW17 160 E4
Ebbisham Dr VX/NE SW8 122 A6
Ebbisham Rd WPK KT4 193 F6
Ebbsfleet Rd CRICK NW2 82 C3
Ebdon Wy BKHTH/KID SE3 146 A4
Ebenezer St IS N1 6 E4
Ebenezer Wk
STRHM/NOR SW16 179 H4
Ebley Cl PECK SE15 123 G6
Ebner St WAND/EARL SW18 140 A6
Ebor St WCHPL E1 7 J6
Ebrington Rd
KTN/HRWW/WS HA3 61 K3
Ebsworth St FSTH SE23 164 A2
Eburne Rd HOLWY N7 84 E1
Ebury Br BGVA SW1W 121 G5
Ebury Bridge Rd
BGVA SW1W 121 F5
Ebury Cl HAYES BR2 215 J1
NTHWD HA6 40 A1
Ebury Ms BGVA SW1W 15 H6
Ebury Ms East BGVA SW1W 15 J6
Ebury Sq BGVA SW1W 15 J7
Ebury St BGVA SW1W 15 H7
Ecclesbourne Cl PLMGR N13 49 G1
Ecclesbourne Gdns
PLMGR N13 49 G1
Ecclesbourne Rd IS N1 85 J5
THHTH CR7 196 D2
Eccles Rd BTSEA SW11 140 E5
Eccleston Cl EBAR EN4 21 J6
ORP BR6 * 201 J5
Eccleston Crs CHDH RM6 73 H4
Ecclestone Ct WBLY HA9 80 A3
Ecclestone Ms WBLY HA9 80 A3
Ecclestone Pl WBLY HA9 80 B3
Eccleston Ms KTBR SW1X 15 H5
Eccleston Pl BGVA SW1W 15 J5
Eccleston Rd WEA W13 97 G6
Eccleston Sq PIM SW1V 15 K7
Eccleston Square Ms
PIM SW1V 15 K7
Eccleston St BGVA SW1W 15 H5
Echelforde Dr ASHF TW15 152 D6
Echo Hts CHING E4 * 37 K3
Eckford St IS N1 5 J2
Eckstein Rd BTSEA SW11 140 D5
Eclipse Rd PLSTW E13 107 F4
Ector Rd CAT SE6 165 H4
Edans Ct SHB W12 118 C2
Edbrooke Rd MV/WKIL W9 100 E3
Eddinton Cl CROY/NA CR0 214 A4
Eddiscombe Rd
FUL/PGN SW6 139 J3
Eddy Cl ROMW/RG RM7 74 D3
Eddystone Rd BROCKY SE4 144 B6
Ede Cl HSLW TW3 134 E4
Edenbridge Cl
BERM/RHTH SE16 * 123 J5
STMC/STPC BR5 202 E1
Edenbridge Rd EN EN1 36 A1
HOM E9 * 87 F5
Eden Cl ALP/SUD HA0 79 K6
HAMP NW3 64 E6
KENS W8 119 K3
PEND EN3 25 J1
Edencourt Rd
STRHM/NOR SW16 179 G2
Edendale Rd BXLYHN DA7 150 A2
Edenfield Gdns WPK KT4 207 H1
Eden Gv HOLWY N7 85 F3
WLSDN NW10 81 K4
Edenham Wy NKENS W10 100 D3
Edenhurst Av FUL/PGN SW6 139 J4
Eden Pde BECK BR3 * 198 B1
Eden Park Av BECK BR3 198 C1
Eden Rd BECK BR3 198 B1
BXLY DA5 169 K6
CROY/NA CR0 211 K2
WALTH E17 69 K2
WNWD SE27 180 C1
Edensor Rd CHSWK W4 138 B1
Eden St KUT/HW KT1 174 E5
Edenvale Rd MTCM CR4 179 F3
Edenvale St FUL/PGN SW6 140 A3
Eden Wk KUT/HW KT1 * 175 F5
Eden Wy BECK BR3 198 D2
BOW E3 87 H6
Ederline Av
STRHM/NOR SW16 180 A6
Edgar Kail Wy CMBW SE5 143 F4
Edgarley Ter FUL/PGN SW6 * 139 H2
Edgar Rd BOW E3 105 K2
HSLWW TW4 154 E2
Edgar Wallace Cl PECK SE15 143 F1
Edgeborough Wy BMLY BR1 184 C4
Edgebury CHST BR7 167 G6
Edgecombe Cl
KUTN/CMB KT2 176 A3
Edgecoombe SAND/SEL CR2 213 F6
Edgecote Cl ACT W3 117 K1
Edgefield Av BARK IG11 91 F5
Edge Hl WIM/MER SW19 177 G3
WOOL/PLUM SE18 127 G6
Edge Hill Av FNCH N3 64 E1
Edge Hill Ct WIM/MER SW19 177 G3
Edgehill Ct WOT/HER KT12 * 188 B5
Edgehill Gdns DAGE RM10 92 C2
Edgehill Rd CHST BR7 167 H5
MTCM CR4 179 G4
WEA W13 97 J5
Edgeley La CLAP SW4 141 J4
Edgeley Rd CLAP SW4 141 H4
Edgel St WAND/EARL SW18 140 A5
Edge Point Cl
STRHM/NOR SW16 180 C1
Edge St KENS W8 119 K1
Edgewood Dr ORP BR6 217 F3
Edgewood Gn CROY/NA CR0 198 A5
Edgeworth Av HDN NW4 63 J2
Edgeworth Cl HDN NW4 63 J2
Edgeworth Crs HDN NW4 63 J2
Edgeworth Rd EBAR EN4 21 J5
ELTH/MOT SE9 146 B5

Edgington Rd *STRHM/NOR* SW16 179 J2
Edgington Wy *SCUP* DA14 186 D3
Edgwarebury Gdns *EDGW* HA8 44 C1
Edgwarebury La *EDGW* HA8 30 B3
Edgware Rd *BAY/PAD* W2 2 A7
CDALE/KGS NW9 45 F6
CRICK NW2 64 A6
Edgware Road High St *EDGW* HA8 44 C2
Edgware Road The Hyde *CDALE/KGS* NW9 63 G1
Edgware Road Wy *CRICK* NW2 63 H6
Edgware Way (Watford By-Pass) *EDGW* HA8 30 A4
Edinburgh Cl *BETH* E2 104 E1
PIN HA5 59 J4
Edinburgh Ct *KUT/HW* KT1 * 175 F6
Edinburgh Ga *KTBR* SW1X 14 E2
Edinburgh Rd *HNWL* W7 116 A2
PLSTW E13 107 F1
SUT SM1 194 B6
UED N18 * 50 C1
WALTH E17 69 J2
Edington Rd *ABYW* SE2 128 C3
PEND EN3 24 E3
Edison Av *HCH* RM12 75 H5
Edison Cl *HCH* RM12 75 H5
WDR/YW UB7 112 C2
Edison Dr *STHL* UB1 96 B5
WBLY HA9 62 A6
Edison Gv *WOOL/PLUM* SE18 148 A1
Edison Rd *CEND/HSY/T* N8 66 D3
HAYES BR2 183 K5
PEND EN3 25 H2
WELL DA16 148 A2
Edis St *CAMTN* NW1 84 A6
Edith Cavell Wy *WOOL/PLUM* SE18 146 D2
Edith Gdns *BRYLDS* KT5 191 J4
Edith Gv *WBPTN* SW10 120 B6
Edithna St *BRXN/ST* SW9 141 K4
Edith Nesbit Wk *ELTH/MOT* SE9 146 D5
Edith Neville Cots *CAMTN* NW1 4 C4
Edith Rd *CHDH* RM6 73 K4
EHAM E6 89 H5
FBAR/BDGN N11 48 D3
ORP BR6 217 G3
SNWD SE25 196 E2
SRTFD E15 88 B3
WIM/MER SW19 178 A2
WKENS W14 119 H4
Edith Rw *FUL/PGN* SW6 140 A2
Edith St *BETH* E2 7 K2
Edith Ter *WBPTN* SW10 * 140 B1
Edith Vls *WKENS* W14 119 J4
Edith Yd *WBPTN* SW10 140 C1
Edison Cl *WALTH* E17 69 J2
Edmansons Cl *TOTM* N17 50 B5
Edmeston Cl *HOM* E9 87 G4
Edmund Gv *FELT* TW13 154 E4
Edmund Halley Wy *GNWCH* SE10 125 H2
Edmund Hurst Dr *EHAM* E6 108 B4
Edmund Rd *MTCM* CR4 178 D6
RAIN RM13 111 G2
STMC/STPC BR5 202 D3
WELL DA16 148 B4
Edmunds Av *STMC/STPC* BR5 186 E6
Edmunds Cl *YEAD* UB4 95 G4
Edmund St *CMBW* SE5 142 E1
Edmunds Wk *EFNCH* N2 65 J1
Edna Rd *RYNPK* SW20 177 G5
Edna St *BTSEA* SW11 140 D2
Edrick Rd *EDGW* HA8 44 E2
Edrick Wk *EDGW* HA8 44 E2
Edric Rd *NWCR* SE14 144 A1
Edridge Rd *CROY/NA* CR0 211 J1
Edward Av *CHING* E4 51 K1
MRDN SM4 194 C2
Edward Cl *CRICK* NW2 * 82 B2
ED N9 36 B2
HPTN TW12 173 H1
Edward Ct *CAN/RD* E16 106 E4
Edwardes Pl *WKENS* W14 119 J3
Edwardes Sq *KENS* W8 119 J3
Edward Gv *EBAR* EN4 21 H6
Edward Mann Cl East *WCHPL* E1 * 105 F5
Edward Mann Cl West *WCHPL* E1 * 105 F5
Edward Ms *CAMTN* NW1 * 3 K4
Edward Pl *DEPT* SE8 124 C6
Edward Rd *BMLY* BR1 184 A3
CHDH RM6 74 A3
CHST BR7 185 G1
CROY/NA CR0 197 F4
EBAR EN4 21 H6
EBED/NFELT TW14 133 G6
HPTN TW12 173 H1
NTHLT UB5 95 G1
PGE/AN SE20 182 A3
RYLN/HDSTN HA2 42 C6
WALTH E17 69 F1
Edwards Av *RSLP* HA4 77 G3
Edwards Cl *WPK* KT4 193 G6
Edward's Cots *IS* N1 * 85 H5
Edwards Dr *FBAR/BDGN* N11 48 D3
Edward's La *STNW/STAM* N16 67 K6
Edwards Ms *IS* N1 85 H5
MHST W1U 9 G4
Edwards Pl *FBAR/BDGN* N11 48 D3
Edward Sq *IS* N1 5 G1
Edwards Rd *BELV* DA17 129 H4
Edward St *CAN/RD* E16 106 E3
DEPT SE8 124 C6
NWCR SE14 144 B1
Edward's Wy *BROCKY* SE4 144 D6
Edward Temme Av *SRTFD* E15 88 D5
Edward Tyler Rd *LEE/GVPK* SE12 166 A4
Edward Wy *ASHF* TW15 152 C4
Edwina Gdns *REDBR* IG4 71 J2
Edwin Av *EHAM* E6 108 A1
Edwin Cl *BXLYHN* DA7 129 G6
RAIN RM13 111 H2
Edwin Hall Pl *LEW* SE13 165 G1
Edwin Pl *CROY/NA* CR0 196 E5
Edwin Rd *EDGW* HA8 45 F2
WHTN TW2 155 K3
Edwin's Md *HOM* E9 87 G2
Edwin St *CAN/RD* E16 106 E4
WCHPL E1 104 E3
Edwin Ware Ct *PIN* HA5 * 41 G5
Edwyn Cl *BAR* EN5 32 A1
Effie Pl *FUL/PGN* SW6 139 K1
Effie Rd *FUL/PGN* SW6 139 K1
Effingham Cl *BELMT* SM2 209 F5
Effingham Rd *CEND/HSY/T* N8 67 G2
CROY/NA CR0 196 A4
LEE/GVPK SE12 145 H6
SURB KT6 190 C4
Effort St *TOOT* SW17 178 D1
Effra Pde *BRXS/STRHM* SW2 142 B6
Effra Rd *BRXS/STRHM* SW2 142 B6
WIM/MER SW19 178 A2
Egan Wy *HYS/HAR* UB3 94 C6
Egbert St *CAMTN* NW1 84 A6
Egerton Cl *PIN* HA5 58 E1
Egerton Crs *CHEL* SW3 14 D6
Egerton Dr *GNWCH* SE10 144 E2
Egerton Gdns *CHEL* SW3 14 C5
GDMY/SEVK IG3 91 F1
HDN NW4 63 K1
WEA W13 97 H5
WLSDN NW10 * 82 A6
Egerton Gardens Ms *CHEL* SW3 14 D5
Egerton Pl *CHEL* SW3 * 14 D5
Egerton Rd *ALP/SUD* HA0 80 B5
NWMAL KT3 192 C1
SNWD SE25 181 F6
STNW/STAM N16 68 B4
WHTN TW2 155 K2
Egerton Ter *CHEL* SW3 14 D5
Egerton Wy *HYS/HAR* UB3 132 E1
Egham Cl *CHEAM* SM3 193 H6
Egham Crs *CHEAM* SM3 208 B1
Egham Rd *PLSTW* E13 107 F4
Eglantine Rd *WAND/EARL* SW18 140 B6
Egleston Rd *MRDN* SM4 194 A3
Eglington Rd *CHING* E4 38 B2
Eglinton Hl *WOOL/PLUM* SE18 127 G6
Eglinton Rd *WOOL/PLUM* SE18 127 F6
Egliston Ms *PUT/ROE* SW15 139 F4
Egliston Rd *PUT/ROE* SW15 139 F4
Eglon Ms *CAMTN* NW1 83 K5
Egmont Av *SURB* KT6 191 G5
Egmont Ms *HOR/WEW* KT19 207 F3
Egmont Rd *BELMT* SM2 209 G5
NWMAL KT3 192 C1
SURB KT6 191 G5
WOT/HER KT12 188 A4
Egmont St *NWCR* SE14 144 A1
Egremont Rd *WNWD* SE27 162 B5
Egret Wy *YEAD* UB4 95 H5
Eider Cl *SRTFD* E15 88 D3
Eighteenth Rd *MTCM* CR4 195 K1
Eighth Av *HYS/HAR* UB3 113 K1
MNPK E12 89 K2
Eileen Rd *SNWD* SE25 196 E2
Eindhoven Cl *CAR* SM5 195 F5
WIM/MER SW19 178 C4
Eisenhower Dr *EHAM* E6 107 J4
Elaine Gv *KTTN* NW5 84 A3
Elam Cl *CMBW* SE5 142 C3
Elam St *CMBW* SE5 142 C3
Eland Rd *BTSEA* SW11 140 E4
CROY/NA CR0 211 H1
Elba Pl *WALW* SE17 * 18 D6
Elberon Av *CROY/NA* CR0 195 H3
Elbe St *FUL/PGN* SW6 140 B3
Elborough Rd *SNWD* SE25 197 H2
Elborough St *WAND/EARL* SW18 159 K3
Elbury Dr *CAN/RD* E16 106 E5
Elcho St *BTSEA* SW11 140 D1
Elcot Av *PECK* SE15 143 J1
Elder Av *CEND/HSY/T* N8 66 E2
Elderberry Cl *BARK/HLT* IG6 54 B3
Elderberry Rd *EA* W5 117 F2
Elder Cl *BFN/LL* DA15 168 A3
TRDG/WHET N20 33 F4
Elder Ct *BUSH* WD23 28 E4
Elderfield Rd *CLPT* E5 87 F2
Elderfield Wk *WAN* E11 71 F2
Elderflower Wy *SRTFD* E15 88 C5
Elder Oak Cl *PGE/AN* SE20 181 J4
Elder Rd *WNWD* SE27 180 D1
Elderslie Cl *BECK* BR3 198 D3
Elderslie Rd *ELTH/MOT* SE9 147 F6
Elder St *WCHPL* E1 13 J1
Elderton Rd *SYD* SE26 164 B6
Eldertree Pl *MTCM* CR4 179 H4
Eldertree Wy *MTCM* CR4 179 G4
Elder Wk *IS* N1 85 H6
Eldon Av *CROY/NA* CR0 197 K6
HEST TW5 135 F1
Eldon Gv *HAMP* NW3 83 H3
Eldon Pde *WDGN* N22 * 49 H4
Eldon Pk *SNWD* SE25 197 J1
Eldon Rd *ED* N9 36 E3
KENS W8 120 A3
WALTH E17 69 H1
WDGN N22 49 H4
Eldon St *LVPST* EC2M 13 F2
Eldon Wy *WLSDN* NW10 98 D1
Eldred Dr *STMC/STPC* BR5 202 E6
Eldridge Cl *EBED/NFELT* TW14 153 K3
Eleanora Ter *SUT* SM1 * 209 G3
Eleanor Cl *BERM/RHTH* SE16 124 A2
SEVS/STOTM N15 50 B6
Eleanor Crs *MLHL* NW7 32 B6
Eleanor Gdns *BAR* EN5 20 B6
Eleanor Gv *BARN* SW13 138 B4
Eleanor Rd *FBAR/BDGN* N11 48 E2
HACK E8 86 D4
SRTFD E15 88 D4
Eleanor St *BOW* E3 105 J2
Electra Av *HTHAIR* TW6 133 J4
Electric Av *BRXN/ST* SW9 142 B5
Electric La *BRXN/ST* SW9 * 142 B5
Electric Pde *SURB* KT6 190 E3
Elephant & Castle *STHWK* SE1 18 B6
Elephant La *BERM/RHTH* SE16 123 K2
Elephant Rd *WALW* SE17 18 C6
Elers Rd *HYS/HAR* UB3 113 F4
WEA W13 116 D2
Eley Rd *UED* N18 51 F1
Elfindale Rd *HNHL* SE24 142 D6
Elfin Gv *TEDD* TW11 174 A1
Elford Cl *BKHTH/KID* SE3 146 B5
Elfort Rd *HBRY* N5 85 G2
Elfrida Crs *CAT* SE6 164 D6
Elf Rw *WAP* E1W 104 E6
Elfwine Rd *HNWL* W7 96 E4
Elgal Cl *ORP* BR6 216 B3
Elgar Av *BRYLDS* KT5 191 J5
EA W5 117 F2
STRHM/NOR SW16 179 K6
WLSDN NW10 81 F4
Elgar Cl *BKHH* IG9 39 H4
BORE WD6 29 J2
DEPT SE8 144 D1
PLSTW E13 107 G1
Elgar St *BERM/RHTH* SE16 124 B2
Elgin Av *KTN/HRWW/WS* HA3 43 H5
MV/WKIL W9 100 D3
SHB W12 118 D2
Elgin Cl *SHB* W12 118 E2
Elgin Crs *HTHAIR* TW6 133 H3
NTGHL W11 100 C6
Elgin Dr *NTHWD* HA6 40 C3
Elginmeads South *MV/WKIL* W9 101 F2
Elgin Ms *NTGHL* W11 100 C5
Elgin Ms North *MV/WKIL* W9 101 F2
Elgin Rd *CROY/NA* CR0 197 G6
GDMY/SEVK IG3 72 E5
SUT SM1 209 G1
WDGN N22 48 C5
WLGTN SM6 210 C4
Elgood Av *NTHWD* HA6 40 E2
Elgood Cl *NTGHL* W11 100 C6
Elham Cl *BMLY* BR1 184 C3
Elia Ms *IS* N1 6 A3
Elias Pl *VX/NE* SW8 122 B6
Elia St *IS* N1 6 A3
Elibank Rd *ELTH/MOT* SE9 147 F5
Elim St *STHWK* SE1 19 G4
Elim Wy *PLSTW* E13 106 D2
Eliot Bank *FSTH* SE23 163 J4
Eliot Dr *RYLN/HDSTN* HA2 60 B6
Eliot Gdns *PUT/ROE* SW15 138 D5
Eliot Hl *LEW* SE13 145 F3
Eliot Ms *STJWD* NW8 101 G1
Eliot Pk *LEW* SE13 145 F3
Eliot Pl *BKHTH/KID* SE3 145 H3
Eliot Rd *DAGW* RM9 91 K2
Eliot V *BKHTH/KID* SE3 145 G3
Elizabethan Wy *STWL/WRAY* TW19 152 A2
Elizabeth Av *ENC/FH* EN2 23 H4
IL IG1 72 D6
IS N1 85 J5
Elizabeth Barnes Ct *FUL/PGN* SW6 * 140 A3
Elizabeth Br *BGVA* SW1W 15 J7
Elizabeth Cl *BAR* EN5 20 B4
MV/WKIL W9 101 G3
ROMW/RG RM7 56 D4
SUT SM1 208 D2
Elizabeth Clyde Cl *SEVS/STOTM* N15 68 A1
Elizabeth Cots *RCH/KEW* TW9 137 G2
Elizabeth Fry Pl *WOOL/PLUM* SE18 146 D2
Elizabeth Gdns *ACT* W3 118 C1
ISLW TW7 136 B5
STAN HA7 43 J2
SUN TW16 172 B6
Elizabeth Ms *HAMP* NW3 83 J4
Elizabeth Pl *SEVS/STOTM* N15 67 K1
Elizabeth Ride *ED* N9 36 D2
Elizabeth Rd *EHAM* E6 89 H6
RAIN RM13 111 K4
SEVS/STOTM N15 68 A2
Elizabeth Sq *BERM/RHTH* SE16 105 G6
Elizabeth St *BGVA* SW1W 15 H6
Elizabeth Wy *FELT* TW13 154 B6
NRWD SE19 180 E3
STMC/STPC BR5 202 D2
Elkanette Ms *TRDG/WHET* N20 33 G4
Elkington Rd *PLSTW* E13 107 F3
The Elkins *ROM* RM1 57 G5
Elkstone Rd *NKENS* W10 100 D4
Ellaline Rd *HMSMTH* W6 119 G6
Ella Ms *HAMP* NW3 83 K2
Ellanby Crs *UED* N18 50 D1
Elland Cl *BAR* EN5 21 H6
Elland Rd *PECK* SE15 143 K5
WOT/HER KT12 188 C6
Ella Rd *CEND/HSY/T* N8 66 E4
Ellement Cl *PIN* HA5 59 H2
Ellenborough Pl *PUT/ROE* SW15 138 D5
Ellenborough Rd *SCUP* DA14 186 E2
WDGN N22 49 J4
Ellenbridge Wy *SAND/SEL* CR2 212 A6
Ellen Cl *BMLY* BR1 184 C6
Ellen Ct *ED* N9 36 E4
Ellen St *WCHPL* E1 * 104 C5
Ellen Webb Dr *KTN/HRWW/WS* HA3 42 E6
Elleray Rd *TEDD* TW11 174 A2
Ellerby St *FUL/PGN* SW6 139 G2
Ellerdale Cl *HAMP* NW3 83 G3
Ellerdale Rd *HAMP* NW3 83 G3
Ellerdale St *LEW* SE13 144 E5
Ellerdine Rd *HSLW* TW3 135 H5
Ellerker Gdns *RCHPK/HAM* TW10 157 F1
Ellerman Av *WHTN* TW2 154 E3
Ellerslie Rd *SHB* W12 118 E1
Ellerton Gdns *DAGW* RM9 91 J5
Ellerton Rd *BARN* SW13 * 138 D2
DAGW RM9 91 J5
RYNPK SW20 176 D3
SURB KT6 191 G6
WAND/EARL SW18 160 C3
Ellery Rd *NRWD* SE19 180 E3
Ellery St *PECK* SE15 143 J3
Ellesborough Cl *OXHEY* WD19 41 G1
Ellesmere Av *BECK* BR3 182 E5
MLHL NW7 31 F5
Ellesmere Cl *RSLP* HA4 58 A4
WAN E11 70 D2
Ellesmere Gdns *REDBR* IG4 71 J2
Ellesmere Gv *BAR* EN5 20 D6
Ellesmere Rd *BOW* E3 105 G1
GFD/PVL UB6 96 C3
TWK TW1 156 D1
WLSDN NW10 81 J3
Ellesmere St *POP/IOD* E14 105 K5
Ellies Ms *ASHF* TW15 152 B4
Ellingfort Rd *HACK* E8 86 D5
Ellingham Rd *CHSGTN* KT9 205 K4
SHB W12 118 D2
SRTFD E15 88 B2
Ellington Rd *FELT* TW13 153 J6
HSLW TW3 135 G3
MUSWH N10 66 B1
Ellington St *HOLWY* N7 85 G4
Elliot Cl *SRTFD* E15 88 C5
WBLY HA9 80 B1
WFD IG8 53 H2
Elliot Rd *HDN* NW4 63 K3
Elliott Av *RSLP* HA4 59 F6
Elliott Gdns *HARH* RM3 57 K4
Elliott Rd *BRXN/ST* SW9 142 C1
CHSWK W4 118 B4
HAYES BR2 200 C1
STAN HA7 43 G2
THHTH CR7 196 C1
Elliott's Pl *IS* N1 6 B1
Elliott Sq *HAMP* NW3 83 J5
Elliott's Rw *LBTH* SE11 18 B6
Ellis Av *RAIN* RM13 111 J4
Ellis Cl *EDGW* HA8 45 G2
ELTH/MOT SE9 167 H4
WLSDN NW10 82 A4
Elliscombe Mt *CHARL* SE7 * 126 B6
Elliscombe Rd *CHARL* SE7 126 B5
Ellisfield Dr *PUT/ROE* SW15 158 C2
Ellison Gdns *NWDGN* UB2 114 E4
Ellison Rd *BARN* SW13 138 C3
BFN/LL DA15 167 J3
STRHM/NOR SW16 179 J3
Ellis Rd *MTCM* CR4 194 E3
NWDGN UB2 115 H1
Ellis St *KTBR* SW1X 15 F6
Ellis Wy *DART* DA1 * 171 J4
Ellmore Cl *HARH* RM3 57 K4
Ellora Rd *STRHM/NOR* SW16 179 J1
Ellsworth St *BETH* E2 * 104 D2
Elmar Rd *SEVS/STOTM* N15 67 K1
Elm Av *EA* W5 117 F1
OXHEY WD19 27 J2
RSLP HA4 58 E5
Elmbank *STHGT/OAK* N14 34 E2
Elmbank Av *BAR* EN5 20 A5
Elmbank Dr *BMLY* BR1 184 C5
Elm Bank Gdns *BARN* SW13 138 B3
Elmbank Wy *HNWL* W7 96 D4
Elmbourne Dr *BELV* DA17 129 J4
Elmbourne Rd *TOOT* SW17 161 G5
Elmbridge Av *BRYLDS* KT5 191 K3
Elmbridge Cl *RSLP* HA4 58 E3
Elmbridge Dr *RSLP* HA4 58 E3
Elmbridge Rd *BARK/HLT* IG6 55 G2
Elmbridge Wk *HACK* E8 * 86 C5
Elmbrook Cl *SUN* TW16 172 A4
Elmbrook Gdns *ELTH/MOT* SE9 146 D5
Elmbrook Rd *SUT* SM1 208 D2
Elm Cl *BKHH* IG9 39 H4
BRYLDS KT5 191 K4
CAR SM5 194 E5
HDN NW4 64 B2
HYS/HAR UB3 94 E5
ROMW/RG RM7 56 D4
RYLN/HDSTN HA2 60 B3
RYNPK SW20 193 F1
SAND/SEL CR2 211 K4
STWL/WRAY TW19 152 A3
WAN E11 71 F3
WHTN TW2 155 G4
Elm Cots *MTCM* CR4 * 178 E5
Elmcourt Rd *WNWD* SE27 162 C4
Elm Crs *EA* W5 117 F2
KUTN/CMB KT2 175 F4
Elmcroft *CEND/HSY/T* N8 67 F2
Elmcroft Av *BFN/LL* DA15 168 A2
ED N9 36 D1
GLDGN NW11 64 D4
WAN E11 71 F2
Elmcroft Cl *CHSGTN* KT9 * 206 A1
EA W5 97 K5
EBED/NFELT TW14 153 J1
Elmcroft Crs *GLDGN* NW11 64 B4
RYLN/HDSTN HA2 42 A6
Elmcroft Dr *CHSGTN* KT9 206 A1
Elmcroft Gdns *CDALE/KGS* NW9 62 C2
Elmcroft Rd *ORP* BR6 202 B4
Elmcroft St *CLPT* E5 86 E2
Elmdale Rd *PLMGR* N13 49 F1
Elmdene *BRYLDS* KT5 191 K5
Elmdene Cl *BECK* BR3 198 C2
Elmdene Rd *WOOL/PLUM* SE18 127 G5
Elmdon Rd *HSLWW* TW4 134 C3
HTHAIR TW6 133 J4
Elm Dr *RYLN/HDSTN* HA2 60 B3
SUN TW16 172 B5
Elmer Cl *ENC/FH* EN2 23 F4
RAIN RM13 93 J5
Elmer Gdns *EDGW* HA8 44 D3
ISLW TW7 135 J4
RAIN RM13 93 J5
Elmer Rd *CAT* SE6 165 F2
Elmer's Dr *TEDD* TW11 174 C2
Elmers End Rd *BECK* BR3 181 K6
Elmerside Rd *BECK* BR3 198 B1
Elmers Rd *SNWD* SE25 197 H4
Elmfield Av *CEND/HSY/T* N8 66 E2
MTCM CR4 179 F4
TEDD TW11 174 A1
Elmfield Cl *HRW* HA1 60 E6
Elmfield Pk *BMLY* BR1 183 K6
Elmfield Rd *BMLY* BR1 183 K6
CHING E4 38 A4
EFNCH N2 47 H6
NWDGN UB2 114 D3
TOOT SW17 161 G4
WALTH E17 69 F3
Elmfield Wy *MV/WKIL* W9 100 D3
SAND/SEL CR2 212 B6
Elm Friars Wk *CAMTN* NW1 84 D5
Elm Gdns *EFNCH* N2 47 G6
ENC/FH EN2 23 K1
ESH/CLAY KT10 205 F4
MTCM CR4 195 J1
Elmgate Av *FELT* TW13 154 A5
Elmgate Gdns *EDGW* HA8 44 E1
Elm Gn *ACT* W3 99 G5
Elmgreen Cl *SRTFD* E15 88 C6
Elm Gv *CEND/HSY/T* N8 66 E3
CRICK NW2 82 B2
ERITH DA8 150 A1
KUTN/CMB KT2 175 F4
ORP BR6 202 A5
PECK SE15 143 H3
RYLN/HDSTN HA2 60 A4
SUT SM1 209 F2
WIM/MER SW19 177 H3
Elmgrove Crs *HRW* HA1 61 F2
Elmgrove Gdns *HRW* HA1 61 G2
Elm Grove Pde *CAR* SM5 210 A1
Elm Grove Rd *EA* W5 117 F2
BARN SW13 138 D3
Elmgrove Rd *CROY/NA* CR0 197 J4
HRW HA1 61 F2
Elm Hall Gdns *WAN* E11 71 F3
Elm Hatch *PIN* HA5 41 K3
Elmhurst *BELV* DA17 129 F6
Elmhurst Av *EFNCH* N2 47 H6
MTCM CR4 179 F3
Elmhurst Crs *EFNCH* N2 47 H6
Elmhurst Dr *SWFD* E18 52 E5
Elmhurst Rd *ELTH/MOT* SE9 166 D4
FSTGT E7 89 F5
TOTM N17 50 A5
Elmhurst St *CLAP* SW4 141 J4
Elmhurst Wy *LOU* IG10 39 K2
Elmington Cl *BXLY* DA5 169 J2
Elmington Est *CMBW* SE5 142 D1
Elmington Rd *CMBW* SE5 142 E2
Elmira St *LEW* SE13 144 E4
Elm La *CAT* SE6 164 C4
Elmlee Cl *CHST* BR7 184 E2
Elmley St *WOOL/PLUM* SE18 127 J4
Elmore Cl *ALP/SUD* HA0 98 A1
Elmore Rd *PEND* EN3 25 F2
WAN E11 88 A1
Elmore St *IS* N1 85 K5
Elm Pde *SCUP* DA14 * 168 B6
Elm Pk *BRXS/STRHM* SW2 162 A1
STAN HA7 43 H1
Elm Park Av *HCH* RM12 93 J2
SEVS/STOTM N15 68 B2
Elm Park Gdns *HDN* NW4 64 B2
WBPTN SW10 120 C5
Elm Park La *CHEL* SW3 120 C5
Elm Park Rd *CHEL* SW3 120 C6
FNCH N3 46 D3
LEY E10 69 G5
PIN HA5 41 H6
SNWD SE25 181 G6
WCHMH N21 35 J2
Elm Pl *SKENS* SW7 120 C5
Elm Rd *BAR* EN5 20 D5
BECK BR3 182 C5
CHSGTN KT9 206 A2
EBED/NFELT TW14 153 G3
ERITH DA8 150 D2
ESH/CLAY KT10 205 F4
EW KT17 207 H4
FSTGT E7 88 D
KUTN/CMB KT2 175 G
MORT/ESHN SW14 137 K
NWMAL KT3 176 A
ORP BR6 217 G
ROMW/RG RM7 56 D
SCUP DA14 168 B
THHTH CR7 196 D
WALTH E17 70 A
WBLY HA9 80 A
WDGN N22 49 H
WLGTN SM6 195 F
Elm Rd West *CHEAM* SM3 193
Elm Rw *HAMP* NW3 83
Elms Av *HDN* NW4 64 A
MUSWH N10 48
Elmscott Gdns *WCHMH* N21 35
Elmscott Rd *BMLY* BR1 183
Elms Ct *ALP/SUD* HA0 79
Elms Crs *CLAP* SW4 161
Elmsdale Rd *WALTH* E17 69
Elms Gdns *ALP/SUD* HA0 79
DAGW RM9 92
Elmshaw Rd *PUT/ROE* SW15 138
Elmshurst Crs *EFNCH* N2 65
Elmside *CROY/NA* CR0 213
Elmside Rd *WBLY* HA9 80
Elms La *ALP/SUD* HA0 79
Elmsleigh Av *KTN/HRWW/WS* HA3 61
Elmsleigh Rd *WHTN* TW2 155
Elmslie Cl *WFD* IG8 53
Elms Ms *BAY/PAD* W2 8
Elms Park Av *ALP/SUD* HA0 79
Elms Rd *CLAP* SW4 141
KTN/HRWW/WS HA3 42
Elmstead Av *CHST* BR7 184
WBLY HA9 62
Elmstead Cl *HOR/WEW* KT19 207
TRDG/WHET N20 32
Elmstead Gdns *WPK* KT4 207
Elmstead Gld *CHST* BR7 184
Elmstead La *CHST* BR7 184
CHST BR7 184
Elmstead Rd *ERITH* DA8 150
GDMY/SEVK IG3 72
The Elms *BARN* SW13 138
ESH/CLAY KT10 * 205
NFNCH/WDSPK N12 * 47
TOOT SW17 * 161

WLGTN SM6 * 210 C2
Elmstone Rd FUL/PGN SW6 139 K2
Elmstone Ter
STMC/STPC BR5 * 202 D1
Elm St FSBYW WC1X 5 H7
Elmsworth Av HSLW TW3 135 G3
Elm Ter CRICK NW2 82 E1
ELTH/MOT SE9 167 F1
KTN/HRWW/WS HA3 42 D3
Elmton Wy CLPT E5 86 C1
Elm Tree Av ESH/CLAY KT10 189 J4
Elm Tree Cl NTHLT UB5 95 K1
STJWD NW8 2 A4
Elm Tree Ct CHARL SE7 * 126 B6
Elm Tree Rd STJWD NW8 2 A4
Elmtree Rd TEDD TW11 173 K1
Elm Vls HNWL W7 * 96 E6
Elm Wk GPK RM2 57 J6
HAMP NW3 64 E6
ORP BR6 215 K1
RYNPK SW20 193 F1
Elm Wy FBAR/BDGN N11 48 A2
HOR/WEW KT19 207 F3
WLSDN NW10 81 G2
WPK KT4 208 A1
Elmwood CHIG IG7 54 D2
Elmwood Av FELT TW13 154 A5
KTN/HRWW/WS HA3 61 G2
PLMGR N13 48 E1
Elmwood Cl EW KT17 207 J5
WLGTN SM6 195 G6
Elmwood Crs
CDALE/KGS NW9 62 E1
Elmwood Dr BXLY DA5 169 F2
EW KT17 207 J5
Elmwood Gdns HNWL W7 96 E5
Elmwood Rd CHSWK W4 117 K6
CROY/NA CR0 196 C4
HNHL SE24 142 E6
MTCM CR4 178 E6
Elmworth Gv DUL SE21 162 E4
Elnathan Ms MV/WKIL W9 101 F3
Elphinstone Rd WALTH E17 51 H5
Elphinstone St HBRY N5 85 H2
Elrington Rd HACK E8 86 C4
WFD IG8 52 E1
Elruge Cl WDR/YW UB7 112 A3
Elsa Cots POP/IOD E14 * 105 G4
Elsa Rd WELL DA16 148 D3
Elsa St WCHPL E1 * 105 G4
Elsdale St HOM E9 86 E4
Elsden Ms BETH E2 * 104 E1
Elsden Rd TOTM N17 50 B4
Elsenham Rd MNPK E12 89 K3
Elsenham St
WAND/EARL SW18 159 J3
Elsham Rd WAN E11 88 C1
WKENS W14 119 H2
Elsham Ter WKENS W14 * 119 H2
Elsiedene Rd WCHMH N21 35 J2
Elsiemaud Rd BROCKY SE4 144 C6
Elsie Rd EDUL SE22 143 G5
Elsinore Av
STWL/WRAY TW19 * 152 B2
Elsinore Gdns CRICK NW2 * 82 C1
Elsinore Rd FSTH SE23 164 B3
Elsinore Wy RCH/KEW TW9 137 J4
Elsley Rd BTSEA SW11 140 E4
Elspeth Rd ALP/SUD HA0 80 A3
BTSEA SW11 140 E5
Elsrick Av MRDN SM4 193 K2
Elstan Wy CROY/NA CR0 198 B4
Elsted St WALW SE17 19 F7
Elstow Cl ELTH/MOT SE9 146 E6
RSLP HA4 59 H4
Elstow Gdns DAGW RM9 92 A6
Elstow Rd DAGW RM9 92 A5
Elstree Cl HCH RM12 93 K5
Elstree Gdns BELV DA17 129 F4
ED N9 36 D3
IL IG1 90 C3
Elstree Hl BMLY BR1 183 H3
Elstree Hl South BORE WD6 29 J2
Elstree Pk BORE WD6 * 31 F1
Elstree Rd BUSH WD23 28 D3
Elswick Rd LEW SE13 144 E3
Elswick St FUL/PGN SW6 140 B3
Elsworth Cl
EBED/NFELT TW14 153 H3
Elsworthy THDIT KT7 189 K3
Elsworthy Ri HAMP NW3 83 J5
Elsworthy Rd HAMP NW3 83 J6
Elsworthy Ter HAMP NW3 83 J5
Elsynge Rd WAND/EARL SW18 140 C6
Eltham Gn ELTH/MOT SE9 146 B6
Eltham Green Rd
ELTH/MOT SE9 146 B5
Eltham High St
ELTH/MOT SE9 166 E1
Eltham Hl ELTH/MOT SE9 146 C6
Eltham Palace Rd
ELTH/MOT SE9 166 B1
Eltham Park Gdns
ELTH/MOT SE9 147 F5
Eltham Rd ELTH/MOT SE9 146 B6
Elthiron Rd FUL/PGN SW6 139 K2
Elthorne Av HNWL W7 116 A2
Elthorne Ct FELT TW13 154 B3
Elthorne Park Rd HNWL W7 116 A3
Elthorne Rd ARCH N19 66 D6
CDALE/KGS NW9 63 F4
Elthorne Wy CDALE/KGS NW9 63 F3
Elthruda Rd LEW SE13 165 G1
Eltisley Rd IL IG1 90 B2
Elton Av ALP/SUD HA0 79 H3
BAR EN5 20 D6
GFD/PVL UB6 79 F4
Elton Cl KUT/HW KT1 174 D3
Elton Pl STNW/STAM N16 86 A3
Elton Rd KUTN/CMB KT2 175 G4
Eltringham St
WAND/EARL SW18 140 B5
Elvaston Ms SKENS SW7 * 120 B3
Elvaston Pl SKENS SW7 120 B3
Elvenden Pl WLSDN NW10 98 C1
Elvenden Rd WLSDN NW10 98 C1
Elvendon Rd FELT TW13 153 J5
Elverdon Rd FBAR/BDGN N11 48 E2
Elver Gdns BETH E2 104 C2
Elverson Ms DEPT SE8 * 144 C1
Elverson Rd DEPT SE8 144 E3
Elverton St WEST SW1P 16 C6
Elvington Gn HAYES BR2 199 J2
Elvington La CDALE/KGS NW9 45 G4
Elvino Rd SYD SE26 182 A1
Elvis Rd CRICK NW2 82 A4
Elwill Wy BECK BR3 199 F1
Elwin St BETH E2 104 C2
Elwood St HBRY N5 85 H1
Ely Cl ERITH DA8 150 C3
NWMAL KT3 176 C5
Ely Cots VX/NE SW8 * 142 A1
Ely Gdns DAGE RM10 92 E1
Elyne Rd FSBYPK N4 67 G3
Ely Pl HCIRC EC1N 11 K2
WFD IG8 54 A1
Ely Rd CROY/NA CR0 196 E2
HSLWW TW4 134 B4
HTHAIR TW6 133 J3
LEY E10 70 A3
Elysan Pl SAND/SEL CR2 211 J5
Elysian Av STMC/STPC BR5 201 K3
Elysium Pl FUL/PGN SW6 139 J3
Elysium St FUL/PGN SW6 139 J3
Elystan Cl WLGTN SM6 210 C6
Elystan Pl CHEL SW3 120 D5
Elystan St CHEL SW3 14 C7
Elystan Wk IS N1 5 J1
Emanuel Av ACT W3 98 E5
Embankment PUT/ROE SW15 139 G4
Embankment Gdns
CHEL SW3 120 E6
Embankment Pl CHCR WC2N 11 F7
The Embankment TWK TW1 156 B3
Embassy Ct SCUP DA14 168 C5
WLGTN SM6 * 210 B4
Emba St BERM/RHTH SE16 123 H2
Ember Cl STMC/STPC BR5 201 H4
Embercourt Rd THDIT KT7 189 K3
Ember Farm Av
E/WMO/HCT KT8 189 J3
Ember Farm Wy
E/WMO/HCT KT8 189 J2
Ember Gdns THDIT KT7 189 K4
Ember La ESH/CLAY KT10 189 J4
Emblem Ct EDUL SE22 143 H6
Embleton Rd LEW SE13 144 E5
OXHEY WD19 26 E5
Embry Cl STAN HA7 29 G6
Embry Dr STAN HA7 43 G2
Embry Wy STAN HA7 43 G1
Emden Cl WDR/YW UB7 112 D2
Emden St FUL/PGN SW6 140 A2
Emerald Cl CAN/RD E16 107 J5
Emerald Gdns BCTR RM8 74 B5
Emerald Sq NWDGN UB2 114 C3
Emerald St BMSBY WC1N 11 G1
Emerson Gdns
KTN/HRWW/WS HA3 62 B3
Emerson Rd IL IG1 72 A4
Emerson St STHWK SE1 12 C7
Emery Hill St WEST SW1P 16 B5
Emery St STHWK SE1 17 K4
Emes Rd ERITH DA8 149 K1
Emilia Cl PEND EN3 24 D6
Emily St CAN/RD E16 106 D5
Emlyn Rd SHB W12 118 B2
Emmanuel Rd BAL SW12 161 H3
NTHWD HA6 40 D3
Emma Rd PLSTW E13 106 D1
Emma St BETH E2 104 D1
Emma Ter RYNPK SW20 * 177 F3
Emmaus Wy CHIG IG7 54 A1
Emmott Av BARK/HLT IG6 72 C2
Emmott Cl GLDGN NW11 65 G3
WCHPL E1 105 G3
Emperor's Ga SKENS SW7 120 A3
Empire Av UED N18 49 J2
Empire Pde UED N18 * 49 K2
WBLY HA9 * 80 C1
Empire Rd GFD/PVL UB6 79 H6
Empire Sq STHWK SE1 18 E3
Empire Wy WBLY HA9 80 B2
Empire Wharf Rd
POP/IOD E14 125 G4
Empress Av CHING E4 51 K3
IL IG1 72 A6
MNPK E12 71 G6
WFD IG8 52 D3
Empress Dr CHST BR7 185 G2
Empress Pde CHING E4 * 51 J3
Empress Pl FUL/PGN SW6 119 K5
Empress St WALW SE17 122 D6
Empson St BOW E3 105 K3
Emsworth Cl ED N9 36 E3
Emsworth Rd BARK/HLT IG6 54 B5
Emsworth St
BRXS/STRHM SW2 162 A4
Emu Rd VX/NE SW8 141 G3
Ena Rd STRHM/NOR SW16 179 K6
Enbrook St NKENS W10 100 C2
Enclave Ct FSBYE EC1V 6 B6
Endale Cl CAR SM5 194 E6
Endeavour Wy BARK IG11 109 G1
CROY/NA CR0 195 J4
WIM/MER SW19 160 A6
Endell St LSQ/SEVD WC2H 10 E3
Enderby St GNWCH SE10 125 H5
Enderley Rd
KTN/HRWW/WS HA3 42 D4
Endersby Rd BAR EN5 20 A6
Enders Cl ENC/FH EN2 23 G1
Endersleigh Gdns HDN NW4 63 J1
Endlebury Rd CHING E4 38 A4
Endlesham Rd BAL SW12 161 F2
Endsleigh Gdns IL IG1 71 K5
STPAN WC1H 4 C6
SURB KT6 190 D3
Endsleigh Pl STPAN WC1H 4 D6
Endsleigh Rd NWDGN UB2 114 D4
WEA W13 116 B1
Endsleigh St STPAN WC1H 4 D6
Endway BRYLDS KT5 191 H4
Endwell Rd BROCKY SE4 144 B3
Endymion Rd
BRXS/STRHM SW2 162 A1
FSBYPK N4 67 H4
Energen Cl WLSDN NW10 81 G4
Enfield Rd ACT W3 117 J2
BTFD TW8 116 E5
ENC/FH EN2 22 D5
HTHAIR TW6 133 H3
IS N1 86 A5
Enford St CAMTN NW1 8 E1
Engadine Cl CROY/NA CR0 212 B1
Engadine St
WAND/EARL SW18 159 J3
Engate St LEW SE13 145 F5
Engel Pk MLHL NW7 46 A2
Engineer Cl
WOOL/PLUM SE18 127 F6
Engineers Wy WBLY HA9 80 C2
England's La HAMP NW3 83 K4
England Wy NWMAL KT3 191 J1
Englefield Cl CROY/NA CR0 196 D3
ENC/FH EN2 23 G3
STMC/STPC BR5 202 A1
Englefield Crs
STMC/STPC BR5 202 B2
Englefield Pth
STMC/STPC BR5 202 B1
Englefield Rd IS N1 85 K5
Engleheart Dr
EBED/NFELT TW14 153 J1
Engleheart Rd CAT SE6 164 E2
Englewood Rd BAL SW12 161 G1
English St BOW E3 105 H3
Enid St BERM/RHTH SE16 19 K4
Enmore Av SNWD SE25 197 H2
Enmore Gdns
MORT/ESHN SW14 138 A6
Enmore Rd PUT/ROE SW15 139 F5
SNWD SE25 197 H2
STHL UB1 96 A3
Ennerdale Av HCH RM12 93 J3
STAN HA7 43 J6
Ennerdale Cl
EBED/NFELT TW14 153 J3
SUT SM1 208 D2
Ennerdale Dr
CDALE/KGS NW9 63 G2
Ennerdale Gdns WBLY HA9 61 J5
Ennerdale Rd RCH/KEW TW9 137 G3
Ennersdale Rd LEW SE13 145 G6
Ennismore Av CHSWK W4 118 B4
GFD/PVL UB6 78 E4
Ennismore Gdns SKENS SW7 14 B4
THDIT KT7 189 K3
Ennismore Gardens Ms
SKENS SW7 14 B4
Ennismore Ms SKENS SW7 14 C3
Ennismore St SKENS SW7 14 C4
Ennis Rd FSBYPK N4 67 G5
WOOL/PLUM SE18 127 J6
Ensign Cl HTHAIR TW6 133 H3
STWL/WRAY TW19 152 A3
Ensign Dr PLMGR N13 35 J5
Ensign St WCHPL E1 104 C6
Ensign Wy STWL/WRAY TW19 152 A3
WLGTN SM6 210 E5
Enslin Rd ELTH/MOT SE9 167 F1
Ensor Ms SKENS SW7 120 C5
Enstone Rd PEND EN3 25 G4
Enterprise Cl CROY/NA CR0 196 B5
Enterprise Rw
SEVS/STOTM N15 68 B2
Enterprise Wy TEDD TW11 174 A1
WAND/EARL SW18 139 K5
WLSDN NW10 99 H2
Enterprize Wy DEPT SE8 * 124 C4
Envoy Av HTHAIR TW6 133 J4
Epcot Ms WLSDN NW10 * 100 B2
Epirus Ms FUL/PGN SW6 139 K1
Epirus Rd FUL/PGN SW6 139 J1
Epping Cl POP/IOD E14 124 D4
ROMW/RG RM7 56 D6
Epping Gld CHING E4 38 A1
Epping New Rd BKHH IG9 39 F2
Epping Pl IS N1 85 G4
Epping Wy CHING E4 37 K1
Epple Rd FUL/PGN SW6 139 J2
Epsom Cl NTHLT UB5 77 K3
Epsom Rd CHEAM SM3 * 193 J4
CROY/NA CR0 211 G2
GDMY/SEVK IG3 73 F3
LEY E10 70 A3
MRDN SM4 193 J3
Epstein Rd THMD SE28 128 C1
Epworth Rd ISLW TW7 136 C1
Epworth St SDTCH EC2A 7 F7
Equity Sq BETH E2 7 K5
Erasmus St WEST SW1P 16 D7
Erconwald St SHB W12 99 H5
Erebus Dr THMD SE28 127 H3
Eresby Dr BECK BR3 198 D5
Eresby Pl KIL/WHAMP NW6 82 E5
Erica Gdns CROY/NA CR0 213 K2
Erica St SHB W12 99 J6
Eric Clarke La EHAM E6 108 B3
Ericcson Cl WAND/EARL SW18 139 K6
Eric Est BOW E3 105 H3
Eric Rd CHDH RM6 73 K4
FSTGT E7 88 E2
WLSDN NW10 81 H4
Eric St BOW E3 105 H3
Eridge Green Cl
STMC/STPC BR5 202 D5
Eridge Rd CHSWK W4 118 A3
Erin Cl BMLY BR1 183 H3
Erindale WOOL/PLUM SE18 127 J6
Erindale Ter
WOOL/PLUM SE18 127 J6
Erin Ms WDGN N22 * 49 H4
Erith Ct PUR RM19 131 K4
Erith Crs CRW RM5 56 E4
Erith Rd BELV DA17 129 J5
Erlanger Rd NWCR SE14 144 A2
Erlesmere Gdns HNWL W7 116 B3
Erlich Cots WCHPL E1 * 104 E4
Ermine Cl HSLWW TW4 134 B3
Ermine Rd LEW SE13 144 E4
SEVS/STOTM N15 68 B3
Ermine Side EN EN1 24 C6
Ermington Rd ELTH/MOT SE9 167 H4
Ernald Av EHAM E6 107 J1
Erncroft Wy TWK TW1 156 A1
Ernest Av WNWD SE27 162 C6
Ernest Cl BECK BR3 198 D2
Ernest Gdns CHSWK W4 117 J6
Ernest Gv BECK BR3 198 C2
Ernest Rd KUT/HW KT1 175 J5
Ernest St WCHPL E1 105 F3
Ernle Rd RYNPK SW20 176 E3
Ernshaw Pl PUT/ROE SW15 139 H6
Erpingham Rd
PUT/ROE SW15 139 F4
Erridge Rd WIM/MER SW19 177 K5
Errington Rd MV/WKIL W9 100 D3
Errol Gdns NWMAL KT3 192 D1
YEAD UB4 95 F3
Erroll Rd ROM RM1 75 H1
Errol St STLK EC1Y 6 D7
Erskine Cl SUT SM1 209 J1
Erskine Crs TOTM N17 68 D1
Erskine Hl GLDGN NW11 64 E1
Erskine Ms HAMP NW3 * 83 K5
Erskine Rd HAMP NW3 83 K5
SUT SM1 209 H2
WALTH E17 69 H1
Erwood Rd CHARL SE7 126 D5
Esam Wy STRHM/NOR SW16 180 B1
Escot Wy BAR EN5 20 A6
Escreet Gv WOOL/PLUM SE18 127 F4
Esher Av CHEAM SM3 208 B1
ROMW/RG RM7 74 E3
WOT/HER KT12 188 A5
Esher Cl BXLY DA5 169 F3
ESH/CLAY KT10 204 B3
Esher Crs HTHAIR TW6 133 J3
Esher Gn ESH/CLAY KT10 204 B2
Esher Green Dr
ESH/CLAY KT10 204 A1
Esher Ms MTCM CR4 179 F6
Esher Park Av ESH/CLAY KT10 204 C3
Esher Place Av
ESH/CLAY KT10 204 A2
Esher Rd E/WMO/HCT KT8 189 J2
GDMY/SEVK IG3 90 E1
Eskdale Av NTHLT UB5 77 K6
Eskdale Cl WBLY HA9 61 K6
Eskmont Rdg NRWD SE19 181 F3
Esk Rd PLSTW E13 107 F3
Esk Wy ROM RM1 57 G3
Esmar Crs CDALE/KGS NW9 63 J4
Esmeralda Rd STHWK SE1 123 H4
Esmond Cl RAIN RM13 * 93 K5
Esmond Gdns CHSWK W4 * 118 A4
Esmond Rd CHSWK W4 118 A3
KIL/WHAMP NW6 82 D6
Esmond St PUT/ROE SW15 139 H5
Esparto St WAND/EARL SW18 160 A2
Essenden Rd BELV DA17 129 H5
SAND/SEL CR2 212 A5
Essendine Rd MV/WKIL W9 100 E2
Essex Av ISLW TW7 135 K4
Essex Cl MRDN SM4 193 G4
ROMW/RG RM7 74 D1
RSLP HA4 59 H5
WALTH E17 69 G1
Essex Ct BARN SW13 138 C3
EMB EC4Y * 11 J4
Essex Gdns FSBYPK N4 67 H3
Essex Gv NRWD SE19 180 E2
Essex Pk FNCH N3 47 F2
Essex Park Ms ACT W3 118 B1
Essex Pl CHSWK W4 117 K4
Essex Place Sq CHSWK W4 * 118 A4
Essex Rd ACT W3 98 E6
BARK IG11 90 D5
CHDH RM6 73 J5
CHING E4 38 C3
CHSWK W4 118 A4
DAGE RM10 92 E3
DART DA1 * 171 G1
ENC/FH EN2 23 K5
IS N1 85 H6
LEY E10 70 A3
MNPK E12 89 J3
ROMW/RG RM7 74 D1
SWFD E18 53 F5
WALTH E17 69 G3
WLSDN NW10 81 G5
Essex Rd South WAN E11 70 B4
Essex St FSTGT E7 88 E3
TPL/STR WC2R 11 J4
Essex Vls KENS W8 119 K2
Essex Whf CLPT E5 * 69 F6
Essian St WCHPL E1 105 G4
Essoldo Wy EDGW HA8 44 B6
Estate Wy LEY E10 69 H5
Estcourt Rd FUL/PGN SW6 139 J1
SNWD SE25 197 J3
Estella Av NWMAL KT3 192 E1
Estelle Rd HAMP NW3 83 K2
Esterbrooke St WEST SW1P 16 C7
Este Rd BTSEA SW11 140 D4
Esther Cl WCHMH N21 35 G2
Esther Rd WAN E11 70 C4
Estoria Cl BRXS/STRHM SW2 162 B2
Estreham Rd
STRHM/NOR SW16 179 J2
Estridge Cl HSLW TW3 135 F5
Estuary Cl BARK IG11 109 H2
Eswyn Rd TOOT SW17 160 E6
Etchingham Park Rd
FNCH N3 47 F3
Etchingham Rd SRTFD E15 88 A2
Eternit Wk FUL/PGN SW6 139 F2
Etfield Gv SCUP DA14 186 C1
Ethelbert Cl BMLY BR1 183 K5
Ethelbert Gdns REDBR IG4 71 K2
Ethelbert Rd BMLY BR1 183 K6
RYNPK SW20 177 G4
STMC/STPC BR5 186 E6
Ethelbert St BAL SW12 161 G3
Ethelburga St BTSEA SW11 * 140 D2
Etheldene Av MUSWH N10 66 C1
Ethelden Rd SHB W12 118 E1
Ethelred Est LBTH SE11 17 J7
Ethel Rd CAN/RD E16 107 F6
Ethel St WALW SE17 * 18 D7
Ethel Ter ORP BR6 * 217 J6
Etheridge Rd CRICK NW2 64 A4
Etherley Rd SEVS/STOTM N15 67 J2
Etherow St EDUL SE22 163 H1
Etherstone Rd
STRHM/NOR SW16 162 B6
Ethnard Rd PECK SE15 123 J6
Etloe Rd LEY E10 69 J6
Eton Av ALP/SUD HA0 79 J2
EBAR EN4 33 J1
HAMP NW3 83 J5
HEST TW5 114 E6
NFNCH/WDSPK N12 47 G3
NWMAL KT3 192 A2
Eton Cl WAND/EARL SW18 160 A2
Eton College Rd HAMP NW3 83 K4
Eton Garages HAMP NW3 83 J4
Eton Gv CDALE/KGS NW9 44 C6
LEW SE13 145 H4
Eton Pl HAMP NW3 * 84 A5
Eton Ri HAMP NW3 * 83 K4
Eton Rd HAMP NW3 83 K5
HYS/HAR UB3 133 J1
IL IG1 90 C2
ORP BR6 217 H2
Eton St RCH/KEW TW9 136 E6
Eton Vls HAMP NW3 83 K4
Etta St DEPT SE8 124 B6
Etton Rd HSLW TW3 135 H6
Ettrick St POP/IOD E14 106 A5
Etwell Pl BRYLDS KT5 191 G3
Euesdon Cl ED N9 36 D5
Eugenia Rd BERM/RHTH SE16 123 K5
Eureka Rd KUT/HW KT1 175 H5
Europa Pl FSBYE EC1V 6 C5
Europe Rd WOOL/PLUM SE18 126 E3
Eustace Pl WOOL/PLUM SE18 126 E4
Eustace Rd CHDH RM6 73 K4
EHAM E6 107 J2
FUL/PGN SW6 139 K1
Euston Centre CAMTN NW1 4 A6
Euston Rd CAMTN NW1 4 A6
CROY/NA CR0 196 B5
STPAN WC1H 4 E4
Euston Sq CAMTN NW1 4 C5
Euston St CAMTN NW1 4 B6
Evan Cook Cl PECK SE15 143 K2
Evandale Rd BRXN/ST SW9 142 B3
Evangelist Rd KTTN NW5 84 B2
Evans Cl HACK E8 86 B4
Evansdale RAIN RM13 111 H2
Evans Gv FELT TW13 155 F4
Evans Rd CAT SE6 165 H4
Evanston Av CHING E4 52 A3
Evanston Gdns REDBR IG4 71 J3
Eva Rd CHDH RM6 73 J4
Evelina Rd PECK SE15 143 K4
PGE/AN SE20 181 K3
Eveline Lowe Est
BERM/RHTH SE16 123 H3
Eveline Rd MTCM CR4 178 E4
Evelyn Av CDALE/KGS NW9 63 F1
RSLP HA4 58 D4
Evelyn Cl WHTN TW2 155 G2
Evelyn Denington Rd
EHAM E6 107 J3
Evelyn Dr PIN HA5 41 H3
Evelyn Est DEPT SE8 124 B6
Evelyn Gdns RCH/KEW TW9 137 F5
SKENS SW7 120 B5
Evelyn Gv EA W5 117 G1
STHL UB1 95 K5
Evelyn Rd CAN/RD E16 125 K1
CAN/RD E16 126 A1
EBAR EN4 21 K5
RCH/KEW TW9 137 F4
RCHPK/HAM TW10 156 D5
WALTH E17 70 A1
WIM/MER SW19 178 A1
Evelyn St DEPT SE8 124 C6
GNWCH SE10 125 F6
Evelyn Ter RCH/KEW TW9 137 F4
Evelyn Wk IS N1 6 E3
Evelyn Wy WLGTN SM6 210 D2
Evensyde WATW WD18 26 A1
Evenwood Cl
PUT/ROE SW15 * 139 H6
Everard Wy WBLY HA9 80 A1
Everatt Cl WAND/EARL SW18 * 159 J1
Everdon Rd BARN SW13 118 D6
Everest Pl POP/IOD E14 106 A4
Everest Rd ELTH/MOT SE9 146 D6
STWL/WRAY TW19 152 A2
Everett Cl BUSH WD23 28 E3
PIN HA5 40 D6
The Everglades HSLW TW3 * 135 H4
Everglade Strd
CDALE/KGS NW9 45 H4
Evergreen Cl PGE/AN SE20 181 K3
Evergreen Ct
STWL/WRAY TW19 * 152 A2
Evergreen Sq HACK E8 86 B5
Evergreen Wy HYS/HAR UB3 94 D6
STWL/WRAY TW19 152 A2
Everilda St IS N1 5 H1
Evering Rd STNW/STAM N16 86 B1
Everington Rd MUSWH N10 47 K5
Everington St HMSMTH W6 119 G6
Everitt Rd WLSDN NW10 99 F2
Everleigh St FSBYPK N4 67 F5
Eve Rd ISLW TW7 136 B5
SRTFD E15 106 C1
TOTM N17 50 A6
WAN E11 88 C2
Eversfield Gdns EDGW HA8 45 G3
Eversfield Rd RCH/KEW TW9 137 G3
Evershed Wk CHSWK W4 117 K3
Eversholt St CAMTN NW1 4 A2
Evershot Rd FSBYPK N4 67 F5
Eversleigh Rd BAR EN5 21 G6
BTSEA SW11 140 E4
EHAM E6 89 H6
FNCH N3 46 D3
Eversley Av BXLYHN DA7 150 B3
WBLY HA9 62 C6
Eversley Cl WCHMH N21 35 F1
Eversley Crs ISLW TW7 135 J2
RSLP HA4 58 C6
WCHMH N21 35 F1
Eversley Mt WCHMH N21 35 F1
Eversley Pk WIM/MER SW19 176 E1
Eversley Park Rd
WCHMH N21 35 F1
Eversley Rd BRYLDS KT5 191 G1
CHARL SE7 126 A6
NRWD SE19 180 E3
Eversley Wy CROY/NA CR0 213 J1
Everthorpe Rd PECK SE15 143 G4
Everton Blds CAMTN NW1 4 A5

Everton Dr STAN HA7 44 A6
Everton Rd CROY/NA CR0 197 H5
Evesham Av WALTH E17 51 J5
Evesham Cl BELMT SM2 208 E5
GFD/PVL UB6 96 B1
Evesham Gn MRDN SM4 194 A3
Evesham Rd FBAR/BDGN N11 48 C1
MRDN SM4 194 A3
SRTFD E15 88 D5
Evesham St NTGHL W11 100 B6
Evesham Ter SURB KT6 * 190 E3
Evesham Wk BRXN/ST SW9 142 B3
Evesham Wy BTSEA SW11 141 F4
CLAY IG5 54 A6
Evette Ms CLAY IG5 54 A4
Evry Rd SCUP DA14 186 D2
Ewald Rd FUL/PGN SW6 139 J3
Ewanrigg Ter WFD IG8 53 G1
Ewart Gv WDGN N22 49 G4
Ewart Pl BOW E3 * 105 H1
Ewart Rd FSTH SE23 164 A2
Ewe Cl HOLWY N7 84 E4
Ewell By-Pass EW KT17 207 H4
Ewell Court Av
HOR/WEW KT19 207 G3
Ewellhurst Rd CLAY IG5 53 J5
Ewell Park Gdns EW KT17 207 J5
Ewell Park Wy EW KT17 207 J4
Ewell Rd SURB KT6 191 J5
CHEAM SM3 208 B4
SURB KT6 190 C4
Ewelme Rd FSTH SE23 163 K3
Ewen Crs BRXS/STRHM SW2 162 B2
Ewer St STHWK SE1 18 C1
Ewhurst Av SAND/SEL CR2 212 B6
Ewhurst Cl BELMT SM2 208 A6
WCHPL E1 104 E4
Ewhurst Rd BROCKY SE4 164 C1
Exbury Rd CAT SE6 164 D4
Excel Ct LSQ/SEVD WC2H 10 D6
Excel Marina CAN/RD E16 106 E6
Excelsior Cl KUT/HW KT1 175 H5
Excel Waterfront
CAN/RD E16 107 F6
Exchange Ar LVPST EC2M 13 G2
Exchange Ct COVGDN WC2E * 11 F6
Exchange Sq SDTCH EC2A * 13 H1
Exchange St ROMW/RG RM7 75 G3
Exchange Wk PIN HA5 59 J4
Exeforde Av ASHF TW15 152 D6
Exeter Cl EHAM E6 107 K5
Exeter Gdns IL IG1 71 K5
Exeter Ms FUL/PGN SW6 139 K1
Exeter Pde CRICK NW2 * 82 C4
Exeter Rd CAN/RD E16 106 E4
CRICK NW2 82 C3
CROY/NA CR0 197 F4
DAGE RM10 92 D4
ED N9 36 E4
FELT TW13 154 E5
HTHAIR TW6 133 H4
PEND EN3 25 F4
RYLN/HDSTN HA2 59 J6
STHGT/OAK N14 34 B3
WALTH E17 69 J2
WELL DA16 148 A3
Exeter St COVGDN WC2E 11 F5
Exeter Wy HTHAIR TW6 133 H3
NWCR SE14 144 C1
Exford Gdns LEE/GVPK SE12 166 A3
Exford Rd LEE/GVPK SE12 166 A4
Exhibition Grounds
WBLY HA9 * 80 D2
Exhibition Rd SKENS SW7 14 B5
Exit Rd EFNCH N2 47 H5
Exmoor Cl BARK/HLT IG6 54 C4
Exmoor St NKENS W10 100 B3
Exmouth Market
CLKNW EC1R 5 J6
Exmouth Ms CAMTN NW1 * 4 B5
Exmouth Pl HACK E8 86 D6
Exmouth Rd RSLP HA4 77 G1
WALTH E17 69 H2
WELL DA16 148 D2
YEAD UB4 94 C2
Exmouth St WCHPL E1 104 E5
Exning Rd CAN/RD E16 106 C3
Exon St WALW SE17 19 G7
Explorer Av
STWL/WRAY TW19 152 B3
Explorer Dr WATW WD18 26 D1
Express Dr GDMY/SEVK IG3 73 H5
Exton Gdns BCTR RM8 91 K3
Exton Rd WLSDN NW10 80 E5
Exton St STHWK SE1 17 J1
Eyebright Cl CROY/NA CR0 198 A5
Eyhurst Av HCH RM12 93 J1
Eyhurst Cl CRICK NW2 63 J6
Eylewood Rd WNWD SE27 180 D1
Eynella Rd DUL SE21 163 G2
Eynham Rd SHB W12 100 A5
Eynsford Cl STMC/STPC BR5 201 H4
Eynsford Crs SCUP DA14 168 D3
Eynsford Rd GDMY/SEVK IG3 72 E6
Eynsham Dr ABYW SE2 128 C3
Eynswood Dr SCUP DA14 186 C1
Eyot Gdns HMSMTH W6 118 C5
Eyre Cl GPK RM2 75 K1
Eyre Street Hl CLKNW EC1R 5 J7
Eythorne Rd BRXN/ST SW9 142 B2
Ezra St BETH E2 7 K4

F

Faber Gdns HDN NW4 63 J2
Fabian Rd FUL/PGN SW6 139 J1
Fabian St EHAM E6 107 K3
The Facade FSTH SE23 * 163 K4
Factory La CROY/NA CR0 196 B6
TOTM N17 50 B5
Factory Pl POP/IOD E14 125 F5
Factory Rd CAN/RD E16 126 D1
CAN/RD E16 126 E2
Factory Yd HNWL W7 115 K1
Faggs Rd EBED/NFELT TW14 133 J5
Fairacre ISLW TW7 * 135 J2
NWMAL KT3 176 B6
Fairacres CROY/NA CR0 213 H6
PUT/ROE SW15 138 C5
RSLP HA4 58 D4
Fairbank Av ORP BR6 201 G6
Fairbank Est IS N1 6 E3
Fairbanks Rd TOTM N17 50 C6
Fairbourne Rd TOTM N17 50 A6
Fairbridge Rd ARCH N19 66 D6
Fairbrook Cl PLMGR N13 49 G1
Fairby Rd LEE/GVPK SE12 146 A6
Fairchild Cl BTSEA SW11 140 C3
Fairchild Pl SDTCH EC2A * 7 H7
Fairchild St SDTCH EC2A 7 H7
Fair Cl BUSH WD23 28 B2
Fairclough Cl NTHLT UB5 95 K3
Fairclough St WCHPL E1 104 C5
Faircross Av BARK IG11 90 C4
CRW RM5 57 F3
Fairdale Gdns HYS/HAR UB3 113 K2
PUT/ROE SW15 138 E5
Fairey CDALE/KGS NW9 * 45 H5
Fairey Av HYS/HAR UB3 113 J3
Fairfax Av EW KT17 207 K6
Fairfax Cl WOT/HER KT12 188 A5
Fairfax Gdns BKHTH/KID SE3 146 B2
Fairfax Ms CAN/RD E16 126 A1
CEND/HSY/T N8 * 67 H1
PUT/ROE SW15 139 F5
Fairfax Pl KIL/WHAMP NW6 83 G5
WKENS W14 119 H3
Fairfax Rd CEND/HSY/T N8 67 G1
CHSWK W4 118 B3
DART DA1 171 K1
KIL/WHAMP NW6 83 G5
TEDD TW11 174 B3
Fairfax Wy MUSWH N10 48 A3
Fairfield Av EDGW HA8 44 D2
HDN NW4 63 K3
OXHEY WD19 27 G5
RSLP HA4 58 A4
WHTN TW2 155 G3
Fairfield Cl BFN/LL DA15 168 A1
HCH RM12 75 J5
HOR/WEW KT19 207 G3
MTCM CR4 178 D3
NFNCH/WDSPK N12 33 G6
PEND EN3 25 F5
Fairfield Cnr KUT/HW KT1 * 175 G5
Fairfield Ct RSLP HA4 58 B5
Fairfield Crs EDGW HA8 44 D2
Fairfield Dr GFD/PVL UB6 79 J6
RYLN/HDSTN HA2 42 C6
WAND/EARL SW18 140 A6
Fairfield East KUT/HW KT1 175 F5
Fairfield Gdns
CEND/HSY/T N8 66 E2
Fairfield Gv CHARL SE7 126 C6
Fairfield North
KUTN/CMB KT2 175 F5
Fairfield Pth CROY/NA CR0 211 K1
Fairfield Pl KUT/HW KT1 175 F6
Fairfield Rd BECK BR3 182 D5
BMLY BR1 183 K3
BOW E3 105 J1
CEND/HSY/T N8 66 E2
CROY/NA CR0 211 K1
IL IG1 90 B4
KUT/HW KT1 175 F5
STHL UB1 95 K5
STMC/STPC BR5 201 J3
UED N18 36 C6
WALTH E17 51 G5
WDR/YW UB7 112 B1
WFD IG8 52 E2
Fairfields CAT SE6 164 E2
Fairfields Cl CDALE/KGS NW9 62 E2
Fairfields Crs
CDALE/KGS NW9 62 E1
Fairfield South KUT/HW KT1 175 F6
Fairfield St WAND/EARL SW18 140 A6
Fairfield Wy BAR EN5 20 E6
HOR/WEW KT19 207 G3
Fairfield West KUT/HW KT1 175 F5
Fairfoot Rd BOW E3 * 105 J3
Fairford Av BXLYHN DA7 149 K2
CROY/NA CR0 198 A2
Fairford Cl CROY/NA CR0 198 A2
Fairford Ct BELMT SM2 * 209 F5
Fairford Gdns WPK KT4 207 H1
Fairgreen EBAR EN4 21 K4
Fairgreen Ct EBAR EN4 * 21 K4
Fairgreen Rd THHTH CR7 196 C2
Fairhaven Av CROY/NA CR0 198 A3
Fairhaven Crs OXHEY WD19 26 E5
Fairhazel Gdns
KIL/WHAMP NW6 83 F4
Fairholme EBED/NFELT TW14 153 G2
Fairholme Av GPK RM2 75 J2
Fairholme Cl FNCH N3 64 C1
Fairholme Ct PIN HA5 * 42 A2
Fairholme Crs YEAD UB4 94 D3
Fairholme Gdns FNCH N3 46 C6
Fairholme Rd CROY/NA CR0 196 B4
HRW HA1 60 E2
IL IG1 71 K4
SUT SM1 208 D4
WKENS W14 119 H5
Fairholt Rd STNW/STAM N16 67 K5
Fairholt St SKENS SW7 14 D4
Fairland Rd SRTFD E15 88 D4
Fairlands Av BKHH IG9 38 E4
SUT SM1 193 K6
THHTH CR7 196 A1
Fairlawn CHARL SE7 146 B1
Fairlawn Av BXLYHN DA7 148 E3
CHSWK W4 117 K4
EFNCH N2 65 J1
Fairlawn Cl ESH/CLAY KT10 205 F4
FELT TW13 154 E6
KUTN/CMB KT2 175 K2
STHGT/OAK N14 34 D1
Fairlawn Ct CHARL SE7 * 146 B1
Fairlawn Dr WFD IG8 52 E3
Fairlawn Gdns STHL UB1 * 95 K6
Fairlawn Gv CHSWK W4 117 K4
Fairlawn Pk SYD SE26 182 B1
Fairlawn Rd WIM/MER SW19 177 J3
Fairlawns PIN HA5 41 G5
TWK TW1 156 D1
Fairlea Pl EA W5 97 J4
Fairlie Gdns FSTH SE23 163 K2
Fairlight Av CHING E4 38 B4
WFD IG8 52 E2
WLSDN NW10 99 G1
Fairlight Cl CHING E4 38 B4
WPK KT4 208 A2
Fairlight Rd TOOT SW17 160 C6
Fairlop Cl HCH RM12 93 K4
Fairlop Gdns BARK/HLT IG6 54 C3
Fairlop Pl STJWD NW8 2 B5
Fairlop Rd BARK/HLT IG6 54 C5
WAN E11 70 B4
Fairmead BMLY BR1 200 E1
BRYLDS KT5 191 J5
Fairmead Cl BMLY BR1 200 E1
HEST TW5 134 C1
NWMAL KT3 176 A6
Fairmead Crs EDGW HA8 30 E6
Fairmead Gdns REDBR IG4 71 H2
Fairmead Rd ARCH N19 84 E1
CROY/NA CR0 196 B4
Fairmile Av
STRHM/NOR SW16 179 J1
Fairmont Cl BELV DA17 129 G5
Fairmount Rd
BRXS/STRHM SW2 162 A1
Fairoak Cl STMC/STPC BR5 201 G4
Fairoak Dr ELTH/MOT SE9 147 J6
Fairoak Gdns ROM RM1 57 G5
Fair Oak Pl BARK/HLT IG6 54 C5
Fairseat Cl BUSH WD23 28 E4
Fairstead Wk IS N1 * 85 J6
Fair St HSLW TW3 135 H4
STHWK SE1 19 H2
Fairview Av ALP/SUD HA0 79 K4
Fair View Cl WALTH E17 51 G4
Fairview Cl SYD SE26 182 B1
Fairview Ct HDN NW4 * 46 B5
Fairview Crs
RYLN/HDSTN HA2 60 A5
Fairview Dr CHIG IG7 54 E1
ORP BR6 216 D2
Fairview Gdns WFD IG8 53 F4
Fairview Pl BRXS/STRHM SW2 162 A2
Fairview Rd ENC/FH EN2 23 G2
SEVS/STOTM N15 68 B3
STRHM/NOR SW16 180 A4
SUT SM1 209 H3
Fairview Vls CHING E4 * 51 J3
Fairview Wy EDGW HA8 30 C6
Fairwater Av WELL DA16 148 B5
Fairway RYNPK SW20 177 F6
STMC/STPC BR5 201 J3
WFD IG8 53 G1
Fairway Av CDALE/KGS NW9 44 D6
Fairway Cl CROY/NA CR0 198 B2
GLDGN NW11 65 G4
HOR/WEW KT19 206 E2
HSLWW TW4 134 B6
Fairway Ct MLHL NW7 * 31 F5
Fairway Dr GFD/PVL UB6 78 B5
THMD SE28 109 K5
Fairway Gdns BECK BR3 199 G3
IL IG1 90 C3
Fairways ISLW TW7 * 135 K2
STAN HA7 44 A5
TEDD TW11 174 E3
WALTH E17 * 70 A1
The Fairway ACT W3 99 G5
ALP/SUD HA0 61 H6
BAR EN5 33 F1
E/WMO/HCT KT8 173 G6
HAYES BR2 200 E2
HNWL W7 * 96 E6
MLHL NW7 31 F5
NTHLT UB5 78 C4
NTHWD HA6 26 C6
NWMAL KT3 176 A4
PLMGR N13 35 J5
RSLP HA4 77 G2
STHGT/OAK N14 34 B1
Fairweather Cl
SEVS/STOTM N15 68 A1
Fairweather Rd
STNW/STAM N16 68 C3
Fairwyn Rd SYD SE26 164 B5
Faithfield BUSH WD23 * 27 J1
Fakenham Cl MLHL NW7 45 J3
NTHLT UB5 78 A4
Fakruddin St WCHPL E1 104 C3
Falaize Av IL IG1 90 B2
Falcon Av BMLY BR1 184 D6
Falconberg Ct
SOHO/SHAV W1D * 10 C3
Falcon Cl CHSWK W4 117 J6
NTHWD HA6 40 C3
Falcon Ct IS N1 6 B3
Falcon Crs PEND EN3 25 F6
Falcon Dr STWL/WRAY TW19 152 A1
Falconer Rd BARK/HLT IG6 55 H1
BUSH WD23 28 A1
Falcon Gv BTSEA SW11 140 D4
Falcon La BTSEA SW11 140 D4
Falcon Rd BTSEA SW11 140 D4
HPTN TW12 172 E3
PEND EN3 25 F6
Falcon St PLSTW E13 106 E3
Falcon Ter BTSEA SW11 * 140 D4
Falcon Wy CDALE/KGS NW9 45 G5
KTN/HRWW/WS HA3 62 A2
POP/IOD E14 124 E4
WAN E11 70 E1
Falconwood Av WELL DA16 147 J3
Falconwood Pde WELL DA16 147 K5
Falconwood Rd
CROY/NA CR0 213 H6
Falcourt Cl SUT SM1 209 F3
Falkirk Gdns OXHEY WD19 41 H1
Falkirk St IS N1 7 H3
Falkland Av FBAR/BDGN N11 34 A6
FNCH N3 46 E3
Falkland Park Av SNWD SE25 181 F5
Falkland Pl KTTN NW5 84 C3
Falkland Rd BAR EN5 20 C3
CEND/HSY/T N8 67 G1
KTTN NW5 84 C3
Falloden Wy GLDGN NW11 64 E1
Fallow Cl CHIG IG7 55 F1
Fallow Ct
BERM/RHTH SE16 * 123 H5
Fallow Court Av
NFNCH/WDSPK N12 47 G2
Fallowfield STAN HA7 29 G5
Fallowfield Ct STAN HA7 29 G5
Fallow Flds LOU IG10 39 G2
Fallowfields Dr
NFNCH/WDSPK N12 47 J2
Fallows Cl EFNCH N2 47 H5
Fallsbrook Rd
STRHM/NOR SW16 179 G2
Falman Cl ED N9 36 C3
Falmer Rd EN EN1 24 A5
SEVS/STOTM N15 67 J2
WALTH E17 51 K6
Falmouth Av CHING E4 52 B1
Falmouth Cl LEE/GVPK SE12 145 J6
WDGN N22 49 F3
Falmouth Gdns REDBR IG4 71 H1
Falmouth Rd STHWK SE1 18 D5
Falmouth St SRTFD E15 88 B3
Falstaff Ms HPTN TW12 173 J1
Fambridge Cl SYD SE26 164 C6
Fambridge Rd BCTR RM8 74 C5
Fane St WKENS W14 119 J6
Fann St FARR EC1M 6 C7
Fanshawe Av BARK IG11 90 C4
Fanshawe Crs DAGW RM9 92 A3
Fanshawe Rd
RCHPK/HAM TW10 156 D6
Fanshaw St IS N1 7 G4
Fantail Cl THMD SE28 109 J5
Fanthorpe St PUT/ROE SW15 139 F4
Faraday Av SCUP DA14 168 C4
Faraday Cl HOLWY N7 85 F4
WATW WD18 26 B1
Faraday Pl E/WMO/HCT KT8 189 F1
Faraday Rd ACT W3 98 E6
E/WMO/HCT KT8 189 F1
NKENS W10 100 C4
SRTFD E15 88 D4
STHL UB1 96 B6
WELL DA16 148 B4
WIM/MER SW19 178 A2
Faraday Wy STMC/STPC BR5 202 C1
WOOL/PLUM SE18 126 C3
Fareham Rd
EBED/NFELT TW14 154 B2
Fareham St SOHO/CST W1F * 10 C3
Farewell Pl MTCM CR4 178 C4
Faringdon Av HAYES BR2 201 F4
Faringford Rd SRTFD E15 88 C5
Farjeon Rd BKHTH/KID SE3 146 C2
Farleigh Court Rd
CROY/NA CR0 196 A6
Farleigh Pl STNW/STAM N16 86 B2
Farleigh Rd STNW/STAM N16 86 B2
Farley Dr GDMY/SEVK IG3 72 E5
Farley Ms CAT SE6 165 F2
Farley Pl SNWD SE25 197 H1
Farley Rd CAT SE6 165 F2
SAND/SEL CR2 212 C5
Farlington Pl PUT/ROE SW15 158 E2
Farlow Rd PUT/ROE SW15 139 G4
Farlton Rd WAND/EARL SW18 160 A2
Farman Ter
KTN/HRWW/WS HA3 * 61 K1
Farm Av ALP/SUD HA0 79 J4
CRICK NW2 82 C1
RYLN/HDSTN HA2 60 A4
STRHM/NOR SW16 161 K6
SWLY BR8 187 K6
Farmborough Cl HRW HA1 60 D4
Farm Cl BELMT SM2 209 H5
BKHH IG9 39 G5
DAGE RM10 92 F5
FUL/PGN SW6 * 139 K1
STHL UB1 96 B6
WWKM BR4 214 C1
Farm Cots E/WMO/HCT KT8 * 190 B1
Farmdale Rd CAR SM5 209 J5
Farm Dr CROY/NA CR0 198 C6
Farmer Rd LEY E10 69 K5
Farmers Rd CMBW SE5 142 C1
Farmer St KENS W8 * 119 K1
Farmfield Rd BMLY BR1 183 H1
Farmhouse Rd
STRHM/NOR SW16 179 H3
Farmilo Rd WALTH E17 69 J4
Farmington Av SUT SM1 209 H1
Farmlands ENC/FH EN2 23 G2
PIN HA5 58 E1
The Farmlands NTHLT UB5 77 K4
Farmland Wk CHST BR7 185 G1
Farm La CROY/NA CR0 198 C6
FUL/PGN SW6 119 K6
STHGT/OAK N14 34 A1
Farmleigh STHGT/OAK N14 34 C2
Farm Pl KENS W8 119 K1
Farm Rd BELMT SM2 209 H5
EDGW HA8 44 E1
ESH/CLAY KT10 189 F5
HSLWW TW4 154 D3
MRDN SM4 194 A2
NTHWD HA6 40 A1
WCHMH N21 35 J3
WLSDN NW10 81 F6
Farmstead Rd CAT SE6 164 E6
KTN/HRWW/WS HA3 42 D4
Farm St MYFR/PICC W1J 9 J6
The Farm WIM/MER SW19 * 159 G2
Farm V BXLY DA5 169 J1
Farm Wk GLDGN NW11 64 D2
Farmway BCTR RM8 91 J2
Farm Wy BKHH IG9 39 G6
HCH RM12 93 K1
NTHWD HA6 26 C6
WPK KT4 208 A1
Farnaby Rd BMLY BR1 183 H4
ELTH/MOT SE9 146 B5
Farnan Av WALTH E17 51 J5
Farnan Rd STRHM/NOR SW16 179 K1
Farnborough Av
SAND/SEL CR2 213 G5
WALTH E17 * 51 G6
Farnborough Cl WBLY HA9 62 D6
Farnborough Common
ORP BR6 216 A2
Farnborough Crs HAYES BR2 199 J5
SAND/SEL CR2 213 G6
Farnborough Hl ORP BR6 216 D3
Farnborough Wy ORP BR6 216 B3
PECK SE15 * 143 F1
Farncombe St
BERM/RHTH SE16 123 H2
Farndale Av PLMGR N13 35 H5
Farndale Crs GFD/PVL UB6 96 C2
Farnell Ms ECT SW5 120 A5
Farnell Pl ACT W3 98 D6
Farnell Rd ISLW TW7 135 J4
Farnham Cl TRDG/WHET N20 33 G2
Farnham Gdns RYNPK SW20 176 E5
Farnham Pl STHWK SE1 18 B1
Farnham Rd GDMY/SEVK IG3 73 F3
WELL DA16 148 D3
Farnham Royal LBTH SE11 122 A5
Farningham Rd TOTM N17 50 C3
Farnley Rd CHING E4 38 C2
SNWD SE25 196 E1
Faro Cl BMLY BR1 185 F5
Faroe Rd WKENS W14 119 G3
Farorna Wk ENC/FH EN2 23 G2
Farquhar Rd NRWD SE19 181 G1
WIM/MER SW19 159 K5
Farquharson Rd
CROY/NA CR0 196 D4
Farrance Rd CHDH RM6 74 A3
Farrance St POP/IOD E14 105 J5
Farrant Av WDGN N22 49 G5
Farrant Cl ORP BR6 217 G5
Farr Av BARK IG11 109 G1
Farren Rd FSTH SE23 164 B4
Farrer Ms CEND/HSY/T N8 66 C1
Farrer Rd CEND/HSY/T N8 66 C1
KTN/HRWW/WS HA3 62 A2
Farrier Cl BMLY BR1 184 C6
Farrier Pl SUT SM1 209 F1
Farrier Rd NTHLT UB5 96 A1
Farrier St CAMTN NW1 84 B5
Farriers Wy BORE WD6 31 F1
Farrier Wk WBPTN SW10 120 B6
Farringdon La CLKNW EC1R 5 K7
Farringdon Rd CLKNW EC1R 5 J6
HCIRC EC1N 12 A2
Farringdon St
FLST/FETLN EC4A 12 A3
Farrington Av
STMC/STPC BR5 186 C6
Farrington Pl CHST BR7 185 J3
Farrins Rents
BERM/RHTH SE16 124 B1
Farrow La NWCR SE14 143 K
Farrow Pl BERM/RHTH SE16 124 B
Farr Rd ENC/FH EN2 23 K
Farthingale Wk SRTFD E15 88 B
Farthing Aly STHWK SE1 * 123 H
Farthing Flds WAP E1W 123 J
Farthings Cl CHING E4 38 C
PIN HA5 59 F
The Farthings KUTN/CMB KT2 175 H
Farthing St HAYES BR2 215 K
Farwell Rd SCUP DA14 168 C
Farwig La BMLY BR1 183 K
Fashion St WCHPL E1 13 J
Fashoda Rd HAYES BR2 200 C
Fassett Rd HACK E8 86 C
KUT/HW KT1 191 F
Fassett Sq HACK E8 86 C
Fauconberg Rd CHSWK W4 117 K
Faulkner Cl BCTR RM8 73 K
Faulkner St NWCR SE14 143 K
Fauna Cl CHDH RM6 73
STAN HA7 29 K
Faunce St WALW SE17 122 C
Favart Rd FUL/PGN SW6 139 K
Faversham Av CHING E4 38
EN EN1 35
Faversham Rd BECK BR3 182 C
CAT SE6 164
MRDN SM4 194
Fawcett Cl BTSEA SW11 140
STRHM/NOR SW16 162
Fawcett Est CLPT E5 * 68
Fawcett Rd CROY/NA CR0 211
WLSDN NW10 81
Fawcett St WBPTN SW10 120
Fawcus Cl ESH/CLAY KT10 204
Fawe Park Rd PUT/ROE SW15 139
Fawe St POP/IOD E14 105
Fawley Rd KIL/WHAMP NW6 83
Fawnbrake Av HNHL SE24 142
Fawn Rd CHIG IG7 55
PLSTW E13 107
Fawns Manor Rd
EBED/NFELT TW14 153
Fawood Av WLSDN NW10 81
Faygate Rd
BRXS/STRHM SW2 162
Fayland Av
STRHM/NOR SW16 179
Fearnley Crs HPTN TW12 172
Featherbed La SAND/SEL CR2 213
Feathers Pl GNWCH SE10 125
Featherstone Av FSTH SE23 163
Featherstone Rd MLHL NW7 45
NWDGN UB2 114
Featherstone St STLK EC1Y 6
Featherstone Ter
NWDGN UB2 114
Featley Rd BRXN/ST SW9 142
Federal Rd GFD/PVL UB6 97
Fee Farm Rd ESH/CLAY KT10 20
Feeny Cl WLSDN NW10 8
Felbridge Av STAN HA7 4
Felbridge Cl BELMT SM2 20
STRHM/NOR SW16 16
Felbrigge Rd GDMY/SEVK IG3 7
Felday Rd LEW SE13 16
Felden Cl PIN HA5 4
Felden St FUL/PGN SW6 13
Feldman Cl STNW/STAM N16 6
Felgate Ms HMSMTH W6 11
Felhampton Rd
ELTH/MOT SE9 16
Felix Av CEND/HSY/T N8 6
Felix Pl BRXS/STRHM SW2 14
Felix Rd WEA W13 9
Felixstowe Rd ABYW SE2 12
ED N9
SEVS/STOTM N15
WLSDN NW10

Felix St BETH E2 * 104 D1
Fellbrigg Rd EDUL SE22 143 G6
Fellbrigg St WCHPL E1 104 D3
Fellbrook RCHPK/HAM TW10 156 C5
Fellmongers Yd
CROY/NA CR0 211 J1
Fellowes Cl YEAD UB4 95 H3
Fellowes Rd CAR SM5 209 J1
Fellows Rd HAMP NW3 83 H5
Fell Rd CROY/NA CR0 211 J1
Felmersham Cl CLAP SW4 141 K5
Felmingham Rd PGE/AN SE20 181 K5
Felsberg Rd
BRXS/STRHM SW2 161 K1
Fels Cl DAGE RM10 92 D1
Fels Farm Av DAGE RM10 92 E1
Felsham Ms PUT/ROE SW15 139 G4
Felsham Rd PUT/ROE SW15 139 F4
Felspar Cl WOOL/PLUM SE18 128 A5
Felstead Av CLAY IG5 54 A4
Felstead Rd CRW RM5 56 E2
HOM E9 87 J4
LOU IG10 39 J2
ORP BR6 202 B6
WAN E11 70 E4
Felstead St HOM E9 87 H4
Felsted Rd CAN/RD E16 107 H5
Feltham Av E/WMO/HCT KT8 189 K1
Felthambrook Wy FELT TW13 154 A5
Feltham Rd ASHF TW15 152 E6
MTCM CR4 178 E5
Felton Cl STMC/STPC BR5 201 G3
Felton Lea SCUP DA14 186 A1
Felton Rd BARK IG11 108 E1
WEA W13 116 D2
Felton St IS N1 7 F1
Fencepiece Rd BARK/HLT IG6 54 C2
Fenchurch Av FENCHST EC3M 13 G4
Fenchurch Blds
FENCHST EC3M 13 H4
Fenchurch Pl
FENCHST EC3M * 13 H5
Fenchurch St FENCHST EC3M 13 G5
Fendall Rd HOR/WEW KT19 206 E3
Fendall St STHWK SE1 19 H4
Fendt Cl CAN/RD E16 106 D5
Fendyke Rd BELV DA17 128 E4
Fenelon Pl WKENS W14 119 J4
Fen Gv BFN/LL DA15 168 A1
Fenham Rd PECK SE15 143 H1
Fenman Ct TOTM N17 50 D4
Fenman Gdns
GDMY/SEVK IG3 73 H5
Fenn Cl BMLY BR1 183 K2
Fennel Cl CAN/RD E16 106 C3
CROY/NA CR0 198 A5
Fennells Md HOR/WEW KT19 207 H6
Fennell St WOOL/PLUM SE18 127 F6
Fenner Cl BERM/RHTH SE16 123 J4
Fenner Sq BTSEA SW11 * 140 C4
Fenning St STHWK SE1 19 G2
Fenn St HOM E9 87 F3
Fenstanton Av
NFNCH/WDSPK N12 47 H1
en St CAN/RD E16 106 D6
entiman Rd VX/NE SW8 122 A6
entiman Wy
RYLN/HDSTN HA2 60 B6
enton Cl BRXN/ST SW9 * 142 A3
CHST BR7 184 E1
HACK E8 86 B4
enton Rd TOTM N17 49 J3
enton's Av PLSTW E13 107 F2
enton St WCHPL E1 104 D5
enwick Gv PECK SE15 143 H4
enwick Pl BRXN/ST SW9 141 K4
SAND/SEL CR2 211 H5
enwick Rd PECK SE15 143 H4
erdinand Pl CAMTN NW1 84 A5
erdinand St CAMTN NW1 84 A5
erguson Av BRYLDS KT5 191 G2
erguson Cl BECK BR3 183 F6
erguson Dr ACT W3 99 F5
erguson's Cl POP/IOD E14 124 D4
ergus Rd HBRY N5 85 H3
erme Park Rd
CEND/HSY/T N8 66 E2
ermor Rd FSTH SE23 164 B3
ermoy Rd GFD/PVL UB6 96 B3
MV/WKIL W9 100 D3
rn Av MTCM CR4 195 J1
rnbank BKHH IG9 39 F3
rnbank Av ALP/SUD HA0 79 F2
WOT/HER KT12 188 D4
rnbank Ms BAL SW12 161 G1
rnbrook Dr
RYLN/HDSTN HA2 60 B4
rnbrook Rd LEW SE13 165 H1
rncliff Rd HACK E8 86 C3
rn Cl IS N1 7 G2
rn Ct NWCR SE14 144 A3
ncroft Av HAMP NW3 82 E1
NFNCH/WDSPK N12 47 J2
RSLP HA4 59 G6
ndale BMLY BR1 184 B5
ndale Av HSLWW TW4 134 D4
WALTH E17 70 B2
ndale Rd CLAP SW4 141 K5
CRW RM5 56 E5
FSTGT E7 89 F5
SEVS/STOTM N15 68 B3
SNWD SE25 197 J2
WAN E11 70 D6
ndale St EHAM E6 108 B6
ndale Ter HRW HA1 61 F1
ndale Wy ORP BR6 216 D3
n Dene WEA W13 97 H4
ndene Rd HNHL SE24 142 D5
nden Wy ROMW/RG RM7 74 D3
ndown NTHWD HA6 40 E5
ndown Av ORP BR6 201 J5
ndown Cl BELMT SM2 209 H4
PIN HA5 41 J3
ndown Rd ELTH/MOT SE9 166 C2
OXHEY WD19 27 G5
ney Meade Wy ISLW TW7 136 B3
ney Rd EBAR EN4 34 A2
Gv EBED/NFELT TW14 154 A2
hall Dr REDBR IG4 71 H2
ham Rd THHTH CR7 180 D6
Fernhead Rd MV/WKIL W9 100 D2
Fernhill Ct WALTH E17 52 B5
Fernhill Gdns KUTN/CMB KT2 174 E1
Fernhill St CAN/RD E16 126 E1
Fernholme Rd PECK SE15 144 A6
Fernhurst Gdns EDGW HA8 44 C2
Fernhurst Rd ASHF TW15 153 F6
CROY/NA CR0 197 H4
FUL/PGN SW6 139 H2
Fern La HEST TW5 114 E5
Fernlea Rd BAL SW12 161 G3
MTCM CR4 179 F5
Fernleigh Cl CROY/NA CR0 211 G2
MV/WKIL W9 100 D2
Fernleigh Ct
RYLN/HDSTN HA2 42 B5
WBLY HA9 62 A5
Fernleigh Rd WCHMH N21 35 G4
Fernley Cl PIN HA5 58 E1
Fernsbury St FSBYW WC1X 5 J5
Fernshaw Cl WBPTN SW10 * 120 B6
Fernshaw Rd WBPTN SW10 120 B6
Fernside BKHH IG9 39 F3
GLDGN NW11 64 E6
THDIT KT7 190 C5
Fernside Av FELT TW13 154 A6
MLHL NW7 31 F5
Fernside Rd BAL SW12 160 E3
Ferns Rd SRTFD E15 88 C4
Fern St BOW E3 105 J3
Fernthorpe Rd
STRHM/NOR SW16 179 H2
Ferntower Rd HBRY N5 85 K3
Fern Wk BERM/RHTH SE16 123 H5
Fernways IL IG1 90 B1
Fernwood Av ALP/SUD HA0 79 J4
STRHM/NOR SW16 161 J6
Fernwood Cl BMLY BR1 184 B5
Fernwood Crs
TRDG/WHET N20 33 K5
Ferny Hl EBAR EN4 21 K1
Ferranti Cl WOOL/PLUM SE18 126 C3
Ferraro Cl HEST TW5 115 F6
Ferrers Av WDR/YW UB7 112 A2
WLGTN SM6 210 D2
Ferrers Rd STRHM/NOR SW16 179 J1
Ferrestone Rd
CEND/HSY/T N8 67 F1
Ferrey Ms BRXN/ST SW9 142 B3
Ferriby Cl IS N1 85 G5
Ferrier St WAND/EARL SW18 140 A5
Ferring Cl RYLN/HDSTN HA2 60 C5
Ferrings DUL SE21 163 F4
Ferris Av CROY/NA CR0 213 H1
Ferris Rd EDUL SE22 143 H5
Ferron Rd CLPT E5 * 86 D1
Ferro Rd RAIN RM13 111 J3
Ferryhills Cl OXHEY WD19 27 G5
Ferry La BARN SW13 118 C6
BTFD TW8 117 F6
RAIN RM13 111 G5
TOTM N17 68 D1
Ferrymead Av GFD/PVL UB6 96 A1
Ferrymead Dr GFD/PVL UB6 96 A2
Ferrymead Gdns
GFD/PVL UB6 96 C1
Ferrymoor RCHPK/HAM TW10 156 C5
Ferry Rd BARN SW13 138 D1
E/WMO/HCT KT8 173 F6
TEDD TW11 174 C1
THDIT KT7 190 C3
TWK TW1 156 C3
Ferry Sq BTFD TW8 117 F6
Ferry St POP/IOD E14 125 F5
Festing Rd PUT/ROE SW15 139 G4
Festival Cl BXLY DA5 168 E3
Festoon Wy CAN/RD E16 107 H6
Fetter La FLST/FETLN EC4A 11 K3
Ffinch St DEPT SE8 144 D1
Fidgeon Cl BMLY BR1 185 F6
Fidler Pl BUSH WD23 28 B1
Field Cl BKHH IG9 39 G5
BMLY BR1 184 B5
CHING E4 51 K2
CHSGTN KT9 205 J3
CRICK NW2 63 J6
E/WMO/HCT KT8 189 G2
HSLWW TW4 134 A2
HYS/HAR UB3 133 F1
RSLP HA4 58 A5
Fieldcommon La
WOT/HER KT12 188 D5
Field Cots EFNCH N2 * 47 K6
FUL/PGN SW6 * 139 J3
Field Ct GINN WC1R 11 H2
Field End RSLP HA4 77 H4
Fieldend TEDD TW11 156 A6
Field End Cl OXHEY WD19 27 J2
Field End Rd PIN HA5 59 F2
RSLP HA4 77 H1
Fieldend Rd
STRHM/NOR SW16 179 H4
Fielders Cl EN EN1 24 A5
RYLN/HDSTN HA2 60 C5
Fieldfare Rd THMD SE28 109 J6
Fieldgate St WCHPL E1 104 C4
Fieldhouse Cl SWFD E18 53 F4
Fieldhouse Rd BAL SW12 161 H3
Fielding Av WHTN TW2 155 H5
Fielding La HAYES BR2 200 B1
Fielding Rd CHSWK W4 118 A3
WKENS W14 119 G3
The Fieldings FSTH SE23 163 K3
Fielding Ter EA W5 * 98 B6
Field La BTFD TW8 136 D1
TEDD TW11 174 B1
Field Md CDALE/KGS NW9 45 G3
Fieldpark Gdns CROY/NA CR0 198 B5
Field Pl NWMAL KT3 192 C3
Field Rd EBED/NFELT TW14 154 A1
FSTGT E7 88 E2
HMSMTH W6 119 H5
OXHEY WD19 27 J1
TOTM N17 49 K6
Fieldsend Rd CHEAM SM3 208 C3
Fields Est HACK E8 * 86 C5
Fieldside Cl ORP BR6 216 C2
Fieldside Cots
TRDG/WHET N20 * 32 D2
Fieldside Rd BMLY BR1 183 G1
Fields Park Crs CHDH RM6 73 K2
Field St FSBYW WC1X 5 G4
Field Vw FELT TW13 153 G6
Fieldview WAND/EARL SW18 160 C3
Field View Cl ROMW/RG RM7 56 C6
Fieldview Cots
STHGT/OAK N14 * 34 D4
Fieldway BCTR RM8 91 H2
Field Wy CROY/NA CR0 213 K4
GFD/PVL UB6 78 B6
RSLP HA4 58 A5
Fieldway STMC/STPC BR5 201 J3
Field Wy WLSDN NW10 80 E5
Fieldway Crs HBRY N5 85 G3
Fiennes Cl BCTR RM8 73 J5
Fiesta Dr RAIN RM13 110 E3
Fife Rd CAN/RD E16 106 E4
KUT/HW KT1 175 F5
MORT/ESHN SW14 137 K6
WDGN N22 49 H3
Fife Ter IS N1 5 H2
Fifield Pth FSTH SE23 164 A5
Fifth Av HYS/HAR UB3 113 J1
MNPK E12 89 K2
NKENS W10 100 C3
Fifth Cross Rd WHTN TW2 155 J4
Fifth Wy WBLY HA9 80 D2
Figge's Rd MTCM CR4 179 F3
Fig Tree Cl WLSDN NW10 81 G6
Filby Rd CHSGTN KT9 206 B4
Filey Av STNW/STAM N16 68 C5
Filey Cl BELMT SM2 209 G5
Filey Waye RSLP HA4 58 E6
Fillebrook Av EN EN1 24 A3
Fillebrook Rd WAN E11 70 B5
Filmer Chambers
FUL/PGN SW6 * 139 J2
Filmer Rd FUL/PGN SW6 139 J2
Filton Cl CDALE/KGS NW9 45 G5
Finborough Rd TOOT SW17 178 E3
WBPTN SW10 120 A6
Finchale Rd ABYW SE2 128 B3
Fincham Cl HGDN/ICK UB10 76 A1
Finch Av WNWD SE27 162 E6
Finch Cl BAR EN5 20 E6
Finch Dr EBED/NFELT TW14 154 C2
Finch Gdns CHING E4 51 J1
Finchingfield Av WFD IG8 53 G3
Finch La BANK EC3V 13 F4
Finchley La HDN NW4 64 B1
Finchley Pk
NFNCH/WDSPK N12 33 G6
Finchley Pl STJWD NW8 2 A2
Finchley Rd GLDGN NW11 64 D2
HAMP NW3 82 E2
STJWD NW8 2 A1
Finchley Vls
NFNCH/WDSPK N12 * 33 H6
Finchley Wy FNCH N3 46 E2
Finch Ms PECK SE15 * 143 G2
Finchs Ct POP/IOD E14 105 K6
Finden Rd FSTGT E7 89 F3
Findhorn Av YEAD UB4 95 F4
Findhorn St POP/IOD E14 106 A5
Findon Cl RYLN/HDSTN HA2 * 78 B1
WAND/EARL SW18 159 K1
Findon Gdns RAIN RM13 111 J4
Findon Rd ED N9 36 D3
SHB W12 118 D2
Fingal St GNWCH SE10 125 J5
Finglesham Cl
STMC/STPC BR5 202 E5
Finland Rd BROCKY SE4 144 B4
Finland St BERM/RHTH SE16 124 B3
Finlays Cl CHSGTN KT9 206 C3
Finlay St FUL/PGN SW6 139 G2
Finney La ISLW TW7 136 B2
Finnis St BETH E2 104 D2
Finnymore Rd DAGW RM9 92 A5
Finsbury Av LVPST EC2M * 13 F2
Finsbury Circ LVPST EC2M 13 F2
Finsbury Cots WDGN N22 48 E3
Finsbury Est CLKNW EC1R 5 K5
Finsbury Market SDTCH EC2A 7 G7
Finsbury Park Av FSBYPK N4 67 J3
Finsbury Park Rd FSBYPK N4 67 H6
Finsbury Pavement
LVPST EC2M 13 F1
Finsbury Rd WDGN N22 49 F3
Finsbury Sq SDTCH EC2A 7 F7
Finsbury St STLK EC1Y 12 E1
Finsbury Wy BXLY DA5 169 G1
Finsen Rd CMBW SE5 142 D5
Finstock Rd NKENS W10 100 B5
Finucane Dr STMC/STPC BR5 202 D4
Finucane Gdns RAIN RM13 93 J4
Finucane Ri BUSH WD23 28 C4
Fiona Ct ENC/FH EN2 * 23 H4
Firbank Cl CAN/RD E16 107 H4
ENC/FH EN2 23 J5
Firbank Dr OXHEY WD19 27 J2
Firbank Rd CRW RM5 56 D1
PECK SE15 143 J3
Fircroft Gdns HRW HA1 78 E1
Fircroft Rd CHSGTN KT9 206 B2
TOOT SW17 160 E5
Firdene BRYLDS KT5 191 K5
Fir Dene ORP BR6 215 K1
Fire Bell Aly SURB KT6 191 F3
Firebell Ms SURB KT6 191 F3
Firecrest Dr HAMP NW3 83 F1
Firefly Cl WLGTN SM6 * 210 E5
Firefly Gdns EHAM E6 107 J3
Firemans Cots EFNCH N2 48 A6
Firethorn Cl EDGW HA8 30 E6
Fir Gv NWMAL KT3 192 C3
Fir Grove Rd BRXN/ST SW9 * 142 B3
Firhill Rd CAT SE6 164 D5
Firle Pl WAND/EARL SW18 160 B2
Fir Rd CHEAM SM3 193 J5
FELT TW13 172 C1
Firs Av FBAR/BDGN N11 48 A2
MORT/ESHN SW14 137 K5
MUSWH N10 48 A6
Firsby Av CROY/NA CR0 198 A5
Firsby Rd STNW/STAM N16 68 B5
Firs Cl ESH/CLAY KT10 204 E4
FSTH SE23 164 A2
MTCM CR4 179 G5
Firscroft PLMGR N13 35 J5
Firs Dr HEST TW5 134 A1
Firside Gv BFN/LL DA15 168 A3
Firs La PLMGR N13 35 J5
Firs Park Av WCHMH N21 35 K3
Firs Park Gdns WCHMH N21 35 K3
First Av ACT W3 118 C1
BXLYHN DA7 148 D1
CHDH RM6 73 J2
DAGE RM10 110 D1
E/WMO/HCT KT8 188 E1
EN EN1 24 B6
HDN NW4 64 A1
HOR/WEW KT19 207 G6
HYS/HAR UB3 113 J1
MNPK E12 89 J2
MORT/ESHN SW14 138 B3
NKENS W10 100 D3
PLSTW E13 106 E2
UED N18 36 E6
WALTH E17 69 K2
WBLY HA9 61 K6
WOT/HER KT12 188 A3
First Cl E/WMO/HCT KT8 189 H1
First Cross Rd WHTN TW2 155 K4
First Dr WLSDN NW10 80 E5
The Firs EA W5 97 K4
EBED/NFELT TW14 * 153 H1
EDGW HA8 * 31 F6
TRDG/WHET N20 33 H3
First St CHEL SW3 14 D6
Firstway RYNPK SW20 177 F5
First Wy WBLY HA9 80 D2
Firs Wk NTHWD HA6 40 B2
WFD IG8 52 E1
Firswood Av HOR/WEW KT19 207 G3
Firth Gdns FUL/PGN SW6 139 H2
Firtree Av MTCM CR4 179 F5
Fir Tree Av WDR/YW UB7 112 D3
Fir Tree Cl EA W5 98 A5
ESH/CLAY KT10 204 C3
HOR/WEW KT19 207 H2
ORP BR6 217 F3
ROM RM1 57 F6
STRHM/NOR SW16 179 H1
Fir Tree Gdns CROY/NA CR0 213 J2
Fir Tree Gv CAR SM5 209 K5
Fir Tree Pl ASHF TW15 * 152 D6
Fir Tree Rd HSLWW TW4 134 D5
Fir Trees Cl BERM/RHTH SE16 124 B1
Fir Tree Wk EN EN1 24 A4
Fir Wk CHEAM SM3 208 B4
Fisher Cl CROY/NA CR0 197 G5
GFD/PVL UB6 96 A2
Fisherdene ESH/CLAY KT10 205 G5
Fisherman Cl
RCHPK/HAM TW10 156 D6
Fishermans Dr
BERM/RHTH SE16 124 A2
Fisher Rd
KTN/HRWW/WS HA3 43 F5
Fishers Cl STRHM/NOR SW16 161 J5
Fishers Ct NWCR SE14 144 A2
Fisher's La CHSWK W4 118 A4
Fisher St CAN/RD E16 106 E4
RSQ WC1B 11 G2
Fisher's Wy BELV DA17 129 K1
Fisherton St STJWD NW8 2 A7
Fishguard Wy CAN/RD E16 127 G1
Fishponds Rd HAYES BR2 215 H3
TOOT SW17 160 D6
Fish Street Hl MON EC3R 13 F6
Fisons Rd CAN/RD E16 125 K1
Fitzalan Rd ESH/CLAY KT10 204 E5
FNCH N3 46 C6
Fitzalan St LBTH SE11 17 H6
Fitzgeorge Av NWMAL KT3 176 A4
WKENS W14 119 H4
Fitzgerald Av
MORT/ESHN SW14 138 B4
Fitzgerald Rd
MORT/ESHN SW14 138 A4
THDIT KT7 190 B3
WAN E11 70 E2
Fitzhardinge St MBLAR W1H 9 G3
Fitzhugh Gv
WAND/EARL SW18 160 C1
Fitzjames Av CROY/NA CR0 197 H6
WKENS W14 119 H4
Fitzjohn Av BAR EN5 20 C6
Fitzjohn's Av HAMP NW3 83 H3
Fitzmaurice Pl
MYFR/PICC W1J * 9 K7
Fitzneal St SHB W12 99 H5
Fitzroy Cl HGT N6 65 K5
Fitzroy Crs CHSWK W4 * 138 A1
Fitzroy Gdns NRWD SE19 181 F3
Fitzroy Ms FITZ W1T 4 A7
Fitzroy Pk HGT N6 65 K5
Fitzroy Rd CAMTN NW1 84 A6
Fitzroy Sq FITZ W1T 4 A7
Fitzroy St FITZ W1T 10 A1
Fitzstephen Rd BCTR RM8 91 H3
Fitzwarren Gdns HGT N6 66 C5
Fitzwilliam Av RCH/KEW TW9 137 G3
Fitzwilliam Cl
TRDG/WHET N20 33 K3
Fitzwilliam Ms CAN/RD E16 106 E6
Fitzwilliam Rd CLAP SW4 141 H4
Fitz Wygram Cl HPTN TW12 173 H1
Five Acre CDALE/KGS NW9 45 H5
Fiveacre Cl CROY/NA CR0 196 B3
Five Elms Rd DAGW RM9 92 B1
HAYES BR2 215 G1
Five Fields Cl OXHEY WD19 27 K4
Five Oaks La CHIG IG7 56 A2
Fiveways Cnr ELTH/MOT SE9 167 G4
Five Ways Jct HDN NW4 45 J4
Fiveways Rd BRXN/ST SW9 142 B3
Fladbury Rd
SEVS/STOTM N15 67 K3
Fladgate Rd WAN E11 70 C3
Flag Cl CROY/NA CR0 198 A5
Flag Wk PIN HA5 58 E3
Flambard Rd HRW HA1 61 G3
Flamborough Rd RSLP HA4 76 E1
Flamborough St
POP/IOD E14 105 G5
Flamborough Wk
POP/IOD E14 * 105 G5
Flamingo Wk HCH RM12 93 J5
Flamstead Gdns DAGW RM9 91 J5
Flamstead Rd DAGW RM9 91 J5
Flamsted Av WBLY HA9 80 C4
Flamsteed Rd CHARL SE7 126 D5
Flanchford Rd SHB W12 118 C3
Flanders Crs TOOT SW17 178 E3
Flanders Rd CHSWK W4 118 B4
EHAM E6 107 K1
Flanders Wy HOM E9 87 F4
Flandrian Cl PEND EN3 25 J2
Flank St WCHPL E1 104 C6
Flask Wk HAMP NW3 83 G2
Flather Cl STRHM/NOR SW16 179 H2
Flavell Ms GNWCH SE10 125 H5
Flaxen Cl CHING E4 37 K5
Flaxen Rd CHING E4 37 K5
Flaxley Rd MRDN SM4 194 A3
Flaxman Rd CMBW SE5 142 C3
Flaxman Ter STPAN WC1H 4 D5
Flaxton Rd WOOL/PLUM SE18 147 J2
Flecker Cl STAN HA7 43 F1
Fleece Dr ED N9 36 C6
Fleece Rd SURB KT6 190 D5
Fleece Wk HOLWY N7 * 84 E4
Fleeming Cl WALTH E17 51 H5
Fleeming Rd WALTH E17 51 H5
Fleet Cl E/WMO/HCT KT8 188 E2
RSLP HA4 58 A3
Fleet Pl FLST/FETLN EC4A 12 A3
Fleet Rd HAMP NW3 83 J3
Fleetside E/WMO/HCT KT8 188 E2
Fleet Sq FSBYW WC1X 5 G5
Fleet St EMB EC4Y 11 J4
Fleet Street Hl WCHPL E1 * 104 C3
Fleet Ter CAT SE6 * 165 F2
Fleetwood Cl CAN/RD E16 107 H4
CHSGTN KT9 205 K5
CROY/NA CR0 212 B1
Fleetwood Rd KUT/HW KT1 175 J6
WLSDN NW10 81 J3
Fleetwood Sq KUT/HW KT1 175 J6
Fleetwood St
STNW/STAM N16 68 A6
Fleetwood Wy OXHEY WD19 27 G6
Fleming Cl MV/WKIL W9 100 E3
WBPTN SW10 * 120 B6
Fleming Ct CROY/NA CR0 211 G3
Fleming Dr WCHMH N21 23 F6
Fleming Md MTCM CR4 178 D3
Fleming Rd STHL UB1 96 B5
WALW SE17 122 C6
Fleming Wk
CDALE/KGS NW9 * 45 G5
Fleming Wy ISLW TW7 136 A4
THMD SE28 109 K6
Flemming Av RSLP HA4 59 F5
Flempton Rd LEY E10 69 G5
Fletcher Cl EHAM E6 108 B6
Fletcher La LEY E10 70 A4
Fletcher Rd CHIG IG7 55 F1
CHSWK W4 117 K3
Fletchers Cl HAYES BR2 200 A1
Fletcher St WCHPL E1 104 C6
Fletching Rd CHARL SE7 126 C6
CLPT E5 86 E1
Fletton Rd FBAR/BDGN N11 48 E3
Fleur De Lis St WCHPL E1 7 H7
Fleur Gates WIM/MER SW19 159 G2
Flexmere Rd TOTM N17 49 K4
Flight Ap CDALE/KGS NW9 * 45 H4
Flimwell Cl BMLY BR1 183 H1
Flint Cl ORP BR6 * 217 F4
SRTFD E15 88 D4
Flint Down Cl
STMC/STPC BR5 * 186 B4
Flintmill Crs BKHTH/KID SE3 146 D3
ELTH/MOT SE9 146 D4
Flinton St WALW SE17 123 F5
Flint St WALW SE17 19 F7
Flitcroft St LSQ/SEVD WC2H 10 D4
Floathaven Cl THMD SE28 128 B1
Flock Mill Pl
WAND/EARL SW18 160 A3
Flockton St BERM/RHTH SE16 123 H2
Flodden Rd CMBW SE5 142 D2
Flood La TWK TW1 * 156 B3
Flood St CHEL SW3 120 D5
Flood Wk CHEL SW3 120 D6
Flora Cl POP/IOD E14 105 K5
STAN HA7 29 K5
Flora Gdns CHDH RM6 73 J3
HMSMTH W6 118 E4
Floral Pl IS N1 85 K3
Floral St COVGDN WC2E 11 F5
Flora St BELV DA17 129 G5
Florence Av ENC/FH EN2 23 J4
MRDN SM4 194 B2
Florence Cl WOT/HER KT12 188 A4
Florence Ct WAN E11 71 F1
Florence Dr ENC/FH EN2 23 J4
Florence Elson Cl MNPK E12 90 A2
Florence Gdns CHSWK W4 117 K6
Florence Rd BECK BR3 182 A5
BMLY BR1 183 K4
CHSWK W4 118 A3
EA W5 98 A6
EHAM E6 89 G6
FELT TW13 154 A3
FSBYPK N4 67 F4
KUTN/CMB KT2 175 G3
NWCR SE14 144 C2
NWDGN UB2 114 C4
PLSTW E13 106 E1
SAND/SEL CR2 211 K6
WIM/MER SW19 178 A2
WOT/HER KT12 188 A4
Florence St CAN/RD E16 106 D3
HDN NW4 64 A1
IS N1 85 H5
Florence Ter NWCR SE14 144 C2
Florence Vls HGT N6 * 66 B4
Florey Wy BAL SW12 160 E3
Florey Sq WCHMH N21 23 F6
Florfield Rd HACK E8 86 D4
Florian Av SUT SM1 209 H2
Florian Rd PUT/ROE SW15 139 H5
Florida Cl BUSH WD23 28 D4
Florida Rd THHTH CR7 180 C4
Florida St BETH E2 104 C2
Florin Ct UED N18 36 A6

Floris Pl CLAP SW4 141 H4
Floriston Av HGDN/ICK UB10 76 A5
Floriston Cl STAN HA7 43 H4
Floriston Gdns STAN HA7 43 H4
Floss St PUT/ROE SW15 139 F3
Flower & Dean Wk WCHPL E1 13 K2
Flower La MLHL NW7 45 H1
Flower Ms GLDGN NW11 64 C3
Flowerpot Cl
SEVS/STOTM N15 68 B3
Flowers Cl CRICK NW2 81 J1
Flowers Ms ARCH N19 66 C6
Floyd Rd CHARL SE7 126 B5
Floyer Cl RCHPK/HAM TW10 137 G6
Fludyer St LEW SE13 145 H5
Foley Ms ESH/CLAY KT10 204 E4
Foley Rd ESH/CLAY KT10 204 E5
Foley St GTPST W1W 10 A2
Foley Wd ESH/CLAY KT10 205 F5
Folgate St WCHPL E1 13 H1
Foliot St SHB W12 99 H5
Folkestone Rd EHAM E6 108 A1
UED N18 36 C6
WALTH E17 69 K1
Folkingham La
CDALE/KGS NW9 45 F4
Folkington Cnr
NFNCH/WDSPK N12 46 D1
Follett St POP/IOD E14 106 A5
Folly La WALTH E17 51 G4
Folly Wall POP/IOD E14 125 F2
Fontaine Rd
STRHM/NOR SW16 180 A2
Fontarabia Rd BTSEA SW11 141 F5
Fontayne Av RAIN RM13 93 G5
ROM RM1 57 G5
Fontenoy Rd BAL SW12 161 G4
Fonteyne Gdns WFD IG8 53 H5
Fonthill Ms FSBYPK N4 67 F6
Fonthill Rd FSBYPK N4 67 F6
Font Hills EFNCH N2 47 G5
Fontley Wy PUT/ROE SW15 158 D2
Fontwell Cl
KTN/HRWW/WS HA3 42 E3
NTHLT UB5 78 A4
Fontwell Dr HAYES BR2 201 F2
Footbury Hill Rd ORP BR6 202 B4
The Footpath
PUT/ROE SW15 * 138 D6
Foots Cray High St
SCUP DA14 186 D2
Foots Cray La SCUP DA14 168 D3
Footscray Rd ELTH/MOT SE9 167 F1
ELTH/MOT SE9 167 G3
Forbes Cl CRICK NW2 81 J1
HCH RM12 75 K5
Forbes St WCHPL E1 104 C5
Forbes Wy RSLP HA4 59 F6
Forburg Rd STNW/STAM N16 68 C5
Ford Cl HRW HA1 60 D4
RAIN RM13 93 H5
THHTH CR7 196 C3
Fordcroft Rd STMC/STPC BR5 202 C2
Forde Av BMLY BR1 184 B6
Fordel Rd CAT SE6 165 G3
Ford End WFD IG8 53 F2
Fordham Cl WPK KT4 192 E5
Fordham Rd EBAR EN4 21 H4
Fordham St WCHPL E1 104 C5
Fordhook Av EA W5 98 B6
Fordingley Rd MV/WKIL W9 100 D2
Fordington Rd HGT N6 65 K1
Ford La RAIN RM13 93 H5
Fordmill Rd CAT SE6 164 D4
Ford Rd ASHF TW15 152 C6
BOW E3 105 G1
DAGW RM9 92 B5
Ford's Gv WCHMH N21 35 J3
Fords Park Rd CAN/RD E16 106 E5
Ford Sq WCHPL E1 104 D4
Ford St BOW E3 105 G1
Fordwich Cl ORP BR6 202 A4
Fordwych Rd CRICK NW2 82 C3
Fordyce Rd LEW SE13 165 F1
Fordyke Rd BCTR RM8 74 A6
Foreland Ct HDN NW4 46 C4
Foreland St
WOOL/PLUM SE18 127 J4
Foremark Cl BARK/HLT IG6 55 F2
Foreshore DEPT SE8 124 C5
Forest Ap CHING E4 38 C2
WFD IG8 52 D3
Forest Av CHIG IG7 54 A1
CHING E4 38 C2
Forest Cl CHST BR7 185 F4
KIL/WHAMP NW6 82 C5
WAN E11 70 D2
WFD IG8 39 F6
Forest Ct CHING E4 38 D3
WAN E11 70 C1
Forestdale STHGT/OAK N14 34 D6
Forest Dr HAYES BR2 215 J1
MNPK E12 89 H1
WFD IG8 52 B3
Forest Dr East WAN E11 70 B4
Forest Dr West WAN E11 70 A4
Forest Edge BKHH IG9 39 G5
Forester Rd PECK SE15 143 J5
Foresters Cl WLGTN SM6 210 D5
Foresters Dr WALTH E17 70 B1
WLGTN SM6 210 D5
Forest Gdns TOTM N17 50 B5
Forest Ga CDALE/KGS NW9 63 G1
Forest Gld CHING E4 52 C1
WAN E11 70 C3
Forest Gv HACK E8 86 B4
Forest Hill Rd EDUL SE22 163 J1
Forestholme Cl FSTH SE23 163 K4
SYD SE26 * 181 K1
Forest La CHIG IG7 54 A1
FSTGT E7 88 E3
Forest Mount Rd WFD IG8 52 B3
Fore St BARB EC2Y 12 E2
ED N9 36 C6
PIN HA5 58 D1
UED N18 50 C1
Forest Rdg BECK BR3 182 D6
HAYES BR2 215 J2
Forest Ri WALTH E17 70 B1
Forest Rd BARK/HLT IG6 54 E4
CHEAM SM3 193 K5
ED N9 36 D3
ERITH DA8 150 D2
FELT TW13 154 B4
FSTGT E7 88 E2
HACK E8 86 B4
RCH/KEW TW9 137 H1
ROMW/RG RM7 56 D6
TOTM N17 68 E1
WALTH E17 51 J6
WAN E11 70 A4
WFD IG8 38 E5
Forest Side CHING E4 38 D2
FSTGT E7 89 F2
WPK KT4 192 C5
Forest St FSTGT E7 88 E3
The Forest WAN E11 70 C1
Forest Vw CHING E4 38 B1
WAN E11 70 D4
Forest View Av LEY E10 70 B2
Forest View Rd MNPK E12 89 J2
WALTH E17 52 A4
Forest Wy BFN/LL DA15 167 J2
STMC/STPC BR5 202 A2
WFD IG8 39 F6
Forfar Rd BTSEA SW11 141 F2
WDGN N22 49 H4
Forge Cots EA W5 * 116 E1
Forge Dr ESH/CLAY KT10 205 G5
Forge La CHEAM SM3 208 C5
FELT TW13 172 D1
NTHWD HA6 40 C3
RCHPK/HAM TW10 157 F3
Forge Ms CROY/NA CR0 213 J3
Forge Pl CAMTN NW1 84 A4
Formby Av
KTN/HRWW/WS HA3 43 J6
Formosa St MV/WKIL W9 101 F3
Formunt Cl CAN/RD E16 106 D4
Forres Gdns GLDGN NW11 64 E3
Forrester Pth SYD SE26 163 K6
Forrest Gdns
STRHM/NOR SW16 180 A6
Forris Av HYS/HAR UB3 113 J1
Forset St MBLAR W1H 8 D3
Forstal Cl HAYES BR2 183 K6
Forster Cl CHING E4 52 B3
Forster Rd BECK BR3 182 B6
BRXS/STRHM SW2 161 K2
TOTM N17 50 B6
WALTH E17 69 G3
Forsters Cl CHDH RM6 74 B3
Forston St IS N1 6 D2
Forsyte Crs NRWD SE19 181 F4
Forsyth Gdns WALW SE17 122 C6
Forsythia Cl IL IG1 90 B3
Forsyth Pl EN EN1 24 A6
Forterie Gdns
GDMY/SEVK IG3 91 G1
Fortescue Av WHTN TW2 155 H5
Fortescue Rd EDGW HA8 45 F4
WIM/MER SW19 178 C3
Fortess Gv KTTN NW5 84 C3
Fortess Rd KTTN NW5 84 B3
Fortess Wk KTTN NW5 84 B3
Forthbridge Rd BTSEA SW11 141 F5
Fortis Cl CAN/RD E16 107 G5
Fortis Gn EFNCH N2 47 K6
Fortis Green Av EFNCH N2 48 A6
Fortis Green Rd MUSWH N10 48 A6
Fortismere Av MUSWH N10 48 A6
Fortnam Rd ARCH N19 66 D6
Fortnums Acre STAN HA7 43 F2
Fort Rd NTHLT UB5 78 A5
STHWK SE1 19 K7
Fortrose Cl POP/IOD E14 106 B5
Fortrose Gdns
BRXS/STRHM SW2 161 K3
Fort St CAN/RD E16 126 A1
WCHPL E1 * 13 H2
Fortuna Cl HOLWY N7 * 85 F4
Fortune Av EDGW HA8 44 D4
Fortunegate Rd
WLSDN NW10 81 G6
Fortune Green Rd
KIL/WHAMP NW6 82 E3
Fortune La BORE WD6 29 K1
Fortune Pl STHWK SE1 123 H5
Fortunes Md NTHLT UB5 77 J4
Fortune St STLK EC1Y 6 D7
Fortune Wy WLSDN NW10 99 J2
Forty Acre La CAN/RD E16 106 E4
Forty Av WBLY HA9 80 B1
Forty Cl WBLY HA9 80 B1
Forty La WBLY HA9 62 D6
Forum Cl BOW E3 87 J6
Forum Magnum Sq
STHWK SE1 17 G2
Forumside EDGW HA8 44 C2
The Forum E/WMO/HCT KT8 189 G1
Forval Cl MTCM CR4 194 E2
Forward Dr
KTN/HRWW/WS HA3 61 F1
Fosbury Ms BAY/PAD W2 101 F6
Foscote Ms MV/WKIL W9 100 E3
Foscote Rd HDN NW4 63 K3
Foskett Rd FUL/PGN SW6 139 J3
Foss Av CROY/NA CR0 211 G3
Fossdene Rd CHARL SE7 126 A5
Fossdyke Cl YEAD UB4 95 J4
Fosse Wy WEA W13 97 G4
Fossil Rd LEW SE13 144 D4
Fossington Rd BELV DA17 128 E4
Foss Rd TOOT SW17 160 C6
Fossway BCTR RM8 73 J6
Foster La CITYW EC2V 12 C3
Foster Rd ACT W3 99 G6
CHSWK W4 118 A5
PLSTW E13 106 E3
Fosters Cl CHST BR7 184 E1
SWFD E18 53 F4
Foster St HDN NW4 64 A1
Foster Wk HDN NW4 64 A1
Fothergill Cl PLSTW E13 88 E6
Fothergill Dr WCHMH N21 22 E6
Fotheringham Rd EN EN1 24 B5
Foubert's Pl SOHO/CST W1F 10 A4
Foulden Rd STNW/STAM N16 86 B2
Foulden Ter STNW/STAM N16 86 B2
Foulis Ter SKENS SW7 14 A7
Foulser Rd TOOT SW17 160 E5
Foulsham Rd THHTH CR7 180 D6
Foundation Pl
ELTH/MOT SE9 * 147 F6
Founder Cl EHAM E6 108 B5
Founders Cl NTHLT UB5 95 K2
Founders Gdns NRWD SE19 180 D3
Foundry Cl BERM/RHTH SE16 124 B1
Foundry Ms CAMTN NW1 4 B6
HSLW TW3 135 G5
Foundry Pl
WAND/EARL SW18 * 160 A2
Fountain Cl UX/CGN UB8 94 A4
Fountain Dr CAR SM5 209 K5
NRWD SE19 163 G6
Fountain Green Sq
BERM/RHTH SE16 123 H2
Fountain Ms HAMP NW3 83 K4
Fountain Pl BRXN/ST SW9 142 B2
Fountain Rd THHTH CR7 180 D5
TOOT SW17 178 C1
Fountains Av FELT TW13 154 E5
Fountains Cl FELT TW13 154 E4
Fountains Crs
STHGT/OAK N14 34 E2
Fountayne Rd
SEVS/STOTM N15 68 C1
STNW/STAM N16 68 C6
Fount St VX/NE SW8 141 J1
Fouracres PEND EN3 25 G2
Fourland Wk EDGW HA8 44 E2
Fournier St WCHPL E1 13 J1
Four Seasons Cl BOW E3 105 J1
Four Seasons Crs CHEAM SM3 193 J6
Fourth Av HYS/HAR UB3 113 J1
MNPK E12 89 K2
NKENS W10 100 C3
ROMW/RG RM7 74 E5
Fourth Cross Rd WHTN TW2 155 J4
Fourth Wy WBLY HA9 80 D2
The Four Tubs BUSH WD23 28 D2
The Four Wents CHING E4 38 B4
Fowey Av REDBR IG4 71 H2
Fowey Cl WAP E1W 123 J1
Fowler Cl BTSEA SW11 140 C4
SCUP DA14 187 F1
Fowler Rd BARK/HLT IG6 55 J1
FSTGT E7 88 E2
IS N1 85 H6
Fowler's Wk EA W5 97 K3
Fownes St BTSEA SW11 140 D4
Foxberry Rd BROCKY SE4 144 B5
Foxborough Gdns
BROCKY SE4 164 D1
Foxbourne Rd TOOT SW17 161 F4
Fox Burrow Rd BARK/HLT IG6 55 J1
Foxbury Av CHST BR7 185 J2
Foxbury Cl BMLY BR1 184 A2
ORP BR6 217 G3
Foxbury Dr ORP BR6 217 G4
Foxbury Rd BMLY BR1 184 A2
Fox Cl BORE WD6 29 K1
CAN/RD E16 106 E4
CRW RM5 56 D1
ORP BR6 217 G3
WCHPL E1 104 E3
Foxcombe CROY/NA CR0 213 K4
Foxcroft Rd
WOOL/PLUM SE18 147 G2
Foxdell NTHWD HA6 40 B2
Foxdene Cl SWFD E18 53 F6
Foxearth Sp SAND/SEL CR2 212 E6
Foxes Dl HAYES BR2 183 G6
Foxfield Cl NTHWD HA6 40 D2
Foxfield Rd ORP BR6 201 J6
Foxglove Cl BFN/LL DA15 168 B1
ED N9 36 E3
STHL UB1 95 J6
STWL/WRAY TW19 152 A3
Foxglove Gdns WAN E11 71 G1
Foxglove La CHSGTN KT9 206 C2
Foxglove Pth THMD SE28 127 K2
Foxglove Rd ROMW/RG RM7 75 G6
Foxglove St ACT W3 99 H6
Foxglove Wy WLGTN SM6 195 F4
Foxgrove STHGT/OAK N14 34 E5
Fox Gv WOT/HER KT12 188 A4
Foxgrove Av BECK BR3 182 E3
Foxgrove Pth OXHEY WD19 41 H1
Foxgrove Rd BECK BR3 182 E3
Foxham Rd ARCH N19 84 D1
Fox Hl HAYES BR2 215 G3
NRWD SE19 181 G3
Fox Hill Gdns NRWD SE19 181 G3
Foxhole Rd ELTH/MOT SE9 146 D6
Fox Hollow WOT/HER KT12 188 B6
Fox Hollow Cl
WOOL/PLUM SE18 127 K5
Fox Hollow Dr BXLYHN DA7 148 E4
Foxholt Gdns WLSDN NW10 80 E5
Foxhome Cl CHST BR7 185 F2
Fox House Rd BELV DA17 129 J4
Fox & Knot St FARR EC1M * 12 B1
Foxlands Crs DAGE RM10 92 E3
Foxlands Rd DAGE RM10 92 E3
Fox La EA W5 98 A4
HAYES BR2 215 F3
PLMGR N13 35 F5
Foxlees ALP/SUD HA0 79 G2
Foxley Cl HACK E8 86 C3
Foxley Rd CMBW SE5 142 B1
THHTH CR7 196 C1
Foxleys OXHEY WD19 27 J5
Foxley Sq BRXN/ST SW9 * 142 C1
Foxmead Cl ENC/FH EN2 23 F4
Foxmore St BTSEA SW11 140 E2
Fox Rd CAN/RD E16 106 D4
Foxton Gv MTCM CR4 178 C5
Foxwarren ESH/CLAY KT10 205 F6
Foxwell St BROCKY SE4 144 B4
Foxwood Cl FELT TW13 154 A5
MLHL NW7 31 G6
Foxwood Green Cl EN EN1 36 A1
Foxwood Rd BKHTH/KID SE3 145 J5
Foyle Rd BKHTH/KID SE3 125 J6
TOTM N17 50 C4
Framfield Cl
NFNCH/WDSPK N12 32 E6
Framfield Rd HBRY N5 85 H3
HNWL W7 97 F5
MTCM CR4 179 F3
Framlingham Crs
ELTH/MOT SE9 166 D6
Frampton Cl BELMT SM2 208 E5
Frampton Park Rd HOM E9 86 E4
Frampton Rd HSLWW TW4 134 D6
Frampton St STJWD NW8 2 B7
Francemary Rd LEW SE13 144 D6
Frances Rd CHING E4 51 J2
Frances St WOOL/PLUM SE18 126 E4
Franche Court Rd TOOT SW17 160 B5
Francis Av FELT TW13 153 K5
IL IG1 72 D6
Francis Barber Cl
STRHM/NOR SW16 * 162 A6
Francis Bentley Ms CLAP SW4 141 H4
Franciscan Rd TOOT SW17 161 F6
Francis Chichester Wy
BTSEA SW11 * 141 F2
Francis Cl HOR/WEW KT19 207 F2
Francis Gv WIM/MER SW19 177 J3
Francis Ms LEE/GVPK SE12 * 165 J1
Francis Rd CROY/NA CR0 196 C4
EFNCH N2 * 65 K1
GFD/PVL UB6 97 J1
HRW HA1 61 G2
HSLWW TW4 134 C3
LEY E10 70 A6
PIN HA5 59 G2
STMC/STPC BR5 186 E6
WLGTN SM6 210 C4
Francis St SRTFD E15 88 C3
WEST SW1P 16 B6
Francis Ter ARCH N19 84 C1
Francis Wk IS N1 85 F6
Francklyn Gdns EDGW HA8 30 C5
Francombe Gdns ROM RM1 75 J3
Franconia Rd CLAP SW4 141 H6
Frank Burton Cl CHARL SE7 126 A5
Frank Dixon Cl DUL SE21 163 F2
Frank Dixon Wy DUL SE21 163 F3
Frankfurt Rd HNHL SE24 142 D6
Frankham St DEPT SE8 144 D1
Frankland Cl
BERM/RHTH SE16 123 J3
WFD IG8 53 G1
Frankland Rd CHING E4 51 J1
SKENS SW7 14 A5
Franklin Av WATW WD18 26 E1
Franklin Cl KUT/HW KT1 175 H6
LEW SE13 144 E2
TRDG/WHET N20 33 G2
WNWD SE27 162 C5
Franklin Crs MTCM CR4 195 H1
Franklin Pl GNWCH SE10 144 E2
Franklin Rd PGE/AN SE20 181 K3
Franklins Ms
RYLN/HDSTN HA2 60 C6
Franklin Sq WKENS W14 119 J5
Franklins Rw CHEL SW3 * 120 E5
Franklin's Rw CHEL SW3 120 E5
Franklin St BOW E3 105 K2
SEVS/STOTM N15 68 A3
Franklin Wy CROY/NA CR0 195 K5
Franklyn Gdns BARK/HLT IG6 54 D2
Franklyn Rd WLSDN NW10 81 H5
WOT/HER KT12 188 A3
Franks Av NWMAL KT3 191 K1
Franks Wood Av
STMC/STPC BR5 201 G2
Franlaw Crs PLMGR N13 35 J6
Franmil Rd HCH RM12 75 H4
Fransfield Gv SYD SE26 163 J5
Franshams BUSH WD23 * 28 E4
Frant Cl PGE/AN SE20 181 K3
Frant Rd THHTH CR7 196 C2
Fraser Cl BXLY DA5 169 K3
EHAM E6 107 J5
Fraser Rd ED N9 36 D5
ERITH DA8 129 K5
GFD/PVL UB6 79 J6
WALTH E17 69 K2
Fraser St CHSWK W4 118 B5
Frating Crs WFD IG8 52 E2
Frays Av WDR/YW UB7 112 A2
Frays Cl WDR/YW UB7 112 A3
Frazer Av RSLP HA4 77 G3
Frazer Cl ROM RM1 75 H4
Frazier St STHWK SE1 17 J3
Frean St BERM/RHTH SE16 123 H3
Freda Corbett Cl PECK SE15 143 H1
Frederica Rd CHING E4 38 B2
Frederica St HOLWY N7 85 F5
Frederick Cl BAY/PAD W2 8 D5
SUT SM1 208 D2
Frederick Crs BRXN/ST SW9 142 C1
PEND EN3 24 E3
Frederick Gdns CROY/NA CR0 196 C3
SUT SM1 208 D3
Frederick Pl
WOOL/PLUM SE18 127 G5
Frederick Rd RAIN RM13 111 F1
SUT SM1 208 D3
WALW SE17 122 C6
Frederick's Pl LOTH EC2R * 12 E4
NFNCH/WDSPK N12 33 G6
Frederick Sq
BERM/RHTH SE16 105 G6
Frederick's Rw FSBYE EC1V 6 A4
Frederick St FSBYW WC1X 5 G5
Frederick Ter HACK E8 * 86 B5
Frederic Ms KTBR SW1X * 15 G3
Frederic St WALTH E17 69 G2
Fredora Av YEAD UB4 94 D3
Freeborne Gdns RAIN RM13 93 J4
Freedom Cl WALTH E17 69 F1
Freedom Rd TOTM N17 49 K5
Freedom St BTSEA SW11 140 E3
Freegrove Rd HOLWY N7 84 E3
Freeland Pk HDN NW4 46 C5
Freeland Rd EA W5 98 B6
Freelands Av SAND/SEL CR2 213 F6
Freelands Gv BMLY BR1 184 A4
Freelands Rd BMLY BR1 184 A4
Freeland Wy ERITH DA8 150 D2
Freeling St IS N1 85 F5
Freeman Cl NTHLT UB5 77 J5
Freeman Dr E/WMO/HCT KT8 188 E1
Freeman Rd MRDN SM4 194 C2
Freemans La HYS/HAR UB3 94 C6
Freemantle Av PEND EN3 25 F6
Freemantle St WALW SE17 123 F5
Freemasons Pl CROY/NA CR0 197 F5
Freemasons Rd CAN/RD E16 107 F4
Freemason's Rd
CROY/NA CR0 197 F5
Freesia Cl ORP BR6 217 F3
Freethorpe Cl NRWD SE19 181 F4
Freightmaster Est
RAIN RM13 * 130 D4
Freke Rd BTSEA SW11 141 F4
Fremantle Rd BARK/HLT IG6 54 B5
BELV DA17 129 H4
Fremont St HOM E9 86 D6
French Pl SDTCH EC2A 7 H5
French St SUN TW16 172 B5
Frendsbury Rd BROCKY SE4 144 B5
Frensham Cl STHL UB1 95 K3
Frensham Dr CROY/NA CR0 214 A5
PUT/ROE SW15 158 D4
Frensham Rd ELTH/MOT SE9 167 J4
Frensham St PECK SE15 123 H6
Frere St BTSEA SW11 140 D3
Freshfield Av HACK E8 86 B5
Freshfield Cl LEW SE13 145 G5
Freshfield Dr STHGT/OAK N14 34 B2
Freshfields CROY/NA CR0 198 C4
Freshford St TOOT SW17 160 B5
Fresh Mill La STHL UB1 96 A3
Freshwater Cl TOOT SW17 179 F2
Freshwater Rd BCTR RM8 73 K5
TOOT SW17 179 F2
Freshwell Av CHDH RM6 73 J1
Fresh Wharf Rd BARK IG11 90 B6
Freshwood Cl BECK BR3 182 E4
Freshwood Wy WLGTN SM6 210 C6
Freston Gdns EBAR EN4 22 A6
Freston Pk FNCH N3 46 D5
Freston Rd NKENS W10 100 B6
Frewin Rd WAND/EARL SW18 160 C3
Friar Ms WNWD SE27 162 C5
Friar Rd STMC/STPC BR5 202 B2
YEAD UB4 95 H3
Friars Av PUT/ROE SW15 158 C5
TRDG/WHET N20 33 J5
Friars Cl CHING E4 38 A5
IL IG1 72 D5
NTHLT UB5 95 G2
STHWK SE1 * 12 B7
Friars Gdns ACT W3 99 F5
Friars Gate Cl WFD IG8 38 E6
Friars La RCH/KEW TW9 136 E6
Friars Md POP/IOD E14 125 F3
Friars Ms ELTH/MOT SE9 147 F6
Friars Place La ACT W3 99 F6
Friar's Rd EHAM E6 89 H6
Friars Stile Rd
RCHPK/HAM TW10 157 F
Friars Wk ABYW SE2 128 E
STHGT/OAK N14 34 B
Friars Wy ACT W3 99 F
Friars Wd CROY/NA CR0 213 G
Friary Cl NFNCH/WDSPK N12 47 J
Friary Est PECK SE15 * 143 H
Friary La WFD IG8 38 E
Friary Pk
NFNCH/WDSPK N12 * 33 J
Friary Park Ct ACT W3 * 98 E
Friary Rd ACT W3 98 E
NFNCH/WDSPK N12 33 H
PECK SE15 143 H
Friary Wy NFNCH/WDSPK N12 33 J
Friday Hl CHING E4 38 C
Friday Hl East CHING E4 38 C
Friday Hl West CHING E4 38 C
Friday Rd ERITH DA8 130 A
MTCM CR4 178 E
Friday St STP EC4M 12 C
Frideswide Pl KTTN NW5 84 C
Friendly Pl LEW SE13 144
Friendly St DEPT SE8 144
Friendly Street Ms DEPT SE8 144
Friendship Wy SRTFD E15 * 88
Friends' Rd CROY/NA CR0 211
Friend St FSBYE EC1V 6
Friern Barnet La
TRDG/WHET N20 33
Friern Barnet Rd
FBAR/BDGN N11 48
Friern Mount Dr
TRDG/WHET N20 33
Friern Pk NFNCH/WDSPK N12 47
Friern Rd EDUL SE22 163
Friern Watch Av
NFNCH/WDSPK N12 33
Frigate Ms DEPT SE8 124
Frimley Av WLGTN SM6 210
Frimley Cl CROY/NA CR0 214
WIM/MER SW19 159
Frimley Ct SCUP DA14 186
Frimley Crs CROY/NA CR0 214
Frimley Gdns MTCM CR4 178
Frimley Rd CHSGTN KT9 205
GDMY/SEVK IG3 90
Frimley Wy WCHPL E1 * 105
Frinstead Gv STMC/STPC BR5 202
Frinsted Rd ERITH DA8 150
Frinton Cl OXHEY WD19 27
Frinton Dr WFD IG8 52
Frinton Ms GNTH/NBYPK IG2 72
Frinton Rd CRW RM5 56
EHAM E6 107
SCUP DA14 169
SEVS/STOTM N15 68
TOOT SW17 179
Friston St FUL/PGN SW6 140
Fritham Cl NWMAL KT3 192
Frith Ct MLHL NW7 46
Frith La MLHL NW7 46
Frith Manor Farm Cotts
MLHL NW7 * 4
Frith Rd CROY/NA CR0 19
WAN E11 8
Frith St SOHO/SHAV W1D 1
Frithville Gdns SHB W12 1
Frithwood Av NTHWD HA6 4
Frizlands La DAGE RM10 9
Frobisher Cl BUSH WD23 2
PIN HA5 5
Frobisher Crs BARB EC2Y * 1

STWL/WRAY TW19	152	B2
Frobisher Gdns LEY E10 *	69	K3
Frobisher Ms ENC/FH EN2	23	K5
Frobisher Rd CEND/HSY/T N8	67	G1
EHAM E6	107	K5
Frog La RAIN RM13	111	F4
Frogley Rd EDUL SE22	143	G5
Frogmore WAND/EARL SW18	139	K6
Frogmore Av YEAD UB4	94	C3
Frogmore Cl CHEAM SM3	208	B1
Frogmore Gdns CHEAM SM3	85	J2
YEAD UB4	94	C3
Frognal HAMP NW3	83	G3
Frognal Av HRW HA1	61	F1
SCUP DA14	186	B2
Frognal Cl HAMP NW3	83	G3
Frognal Gdns HAMP NW3	83	G2
Frognal La HAMP NW3	82	F3
Frognal Man HAMP NW3 *	83	G2
Frognal Pde HAMP NW3	83	G4
Frognal Pl SCUP DA14	186	B2
Frognal Ri HAMP NW3	83	G1
Frognal Wy HAMP NW3	83	G2
Froissart Rd ELTH/MOT SE9	146	D6
Frome Rd SEVS/STOTM N15	49	H6
Frome St IS N1	6	C2
Fromondes Rd CHEAM SM3	208	C3
Fromows Cnr CHSWK W4 *	117	K5
Frostic Wk WCHPL E1	13	K2
Froude St VX/NE SW8	141	G3
Fruen Rd EBED/NFELT TW14	153	J2
Fryatt Rd TOTM N17	49	K3
Fry Cl CRW RM5	56	C1
Fryday Grove Ms BAL SW12 *	161	H2
Frying Pan Al WCHPL E1	13	J3
Fry Rd EHAM E6	89	H5
WLSDN NW10	81	H6
Fryston Av CROY/NA CRO	197	G6
Fuchsia Cl ROMW/RG RM7	75	C6
Fuchsia St ABYW SE2	128	C5
Fulbeck Dr CDALE/KGS NW9	45	G4
Fulbeck Wy RYLN/HDSTN HA2	42	C5
Fulbourne Rd WALTH E17	52	A4
Fulbourne St WCHPL E1	104	D4
Fulbrook Ms ARCH N19	84	C2
Fulbrook Rd ARCH N19	84	C2
Fulford Gv OXHEY WD19	27	F4
Fulford Rd HOR/WEW KT19	207	F5
Fulford St BERM/RHTH SE16	123	J2
Fulham Broadway
FUL/PGN SW6	139	K1
Fulham High St HGDN/ICK UB10	94	A3
Fulham High St FUL/PGN SW6	139	K6
Fulham Palace Rd
FUL/PGN SW6	139	G1
Fulham Park Gdns
FUL/PGN SW6	139	J3
Fulham Park Rd
FUL/PGN SW6	139	J3
Fulham Rd FUL/PGN SW6	139	H5
WBPTN SW10	120	C5
Fullbrooks Av WPK KT4	192	C5
Fuller Cl BETH E2 *	104	C3
BUSH WD23	28	D2
ORP BR6	217	F5
Fuller Rd BCTR RM8	91	J1
Fullers Av SURB KT6	191	G6
Fullers Av WFD IG8	52	D5
Fullers Cl CRW RM5	56	E3
Fuller's Rd SWFD E18	52	C3
Fuller St HDN NW4	64	A1
Fullers Wy North SURB KT6	191	H6
Fullers Wy South CHSGTN KT9	206	A2
Fullers Wd CROY/NA CRO	213	J3
Fuller St CAR SM5	209	K6
CROY/NA CRO	197	G4
WAND/EARL SW18	140	B6
Fuller Wy HYS/HAR UB3	113	J5
Fullwell Av CLAY IG5	54	A4
Fullwood Ms ISLW TW7	11	H2
Fullwood's Ms IS N1	7	F4
Fulmar Ct BRYLDS KT5	191	G3
Fulmar Rd HCH RM12	93	J5
Fulmead St FUL/PGN SW6	140	A2
Fulmer Cl HPTN TW12	172	D1
Fulmer Rd WEA W13	116	C3
Fulmer Wy WEA W13	116	C3
Fulready Rd LEY E10	70	B2
Fulstone Cl HSLWW TW4	134	E5
Fulthorp Rd BKHTH/KID SE3	145	J3
Fulton Ms BAY/PAD W2 *	101	H6
Fulton Rd WBLY HA9	62	D6
Fulwell Park Av WHTN TW2	155	H4
Fulwell Rd TEDD TW11	155	J4
Fulwood Av ALP/SUD HA0	98	B1
Fulwood Gdns TWK TW1	156	A1
Fulwood Wk WIM/MER SW19	159	H3
Furber St HMSMTH W6	118	E3
Furham Feild PIN HA5	42	A3
Furley Rd PECK SE15	143	H1
Furlong Cl WLGTN SM6	195	C5
Furlong Rd HOLWY N7	85	G4
Furlongs HYS/HAR UB3	113	H1
Furmage St
WAND/EARL SW18	160	A2
Furneaux Av WNWD SE27	180	C1
Furness Cl DART DA1	150	D4
Furness Rd FUL/PGN SW6	140	A3
HRW HA2	60	C4
MRDN SM4	194	A3
WLSDN NW10	99	J1
Furnival St HCH RM12	75	J6
Furnival St FLST/FETLN EC4A	11	J3
Furrow La HOM E9	86	E3
Fursby Av FNCH N3	46	E2
Further Acre CDALE/KGS NW9	45	H5
Furtherfield Cl CROY/NA CRO	196	B3
Further Green Rd CAT SE6	165	H2
Furze Cl OXHEY WD19	41	G1
Furzedown Dr TOOT SW17	179	G1
Furzedown Rd TOOT SW17	179	G1
Furze Farm Cl CHDH RM6	56	A5

Furzefield Cl CHST BR7	185	C2
Furzefield Rd BKHTH/KID SE3	126	A6
Furzeground Wy STKPK UB11	113	F1
Furzeham Rd WDR/YW UB7	112	B2
Furzehill Sq STMC/STPC BR5	202	C1
Furze Rd THHTH CR7	180	D6
Furze St BOW E3	105	J4
Fye Foot La BLKFR EC4V	12	C5
Fyfe Wy BMLY BR1	183	K5
Fyfield Cl HAYES BR2	199	G1
Fyfield Rd BRXN/ST SW9	142	B4
EN EN1	24	A4
RAIN RM13	93	H6
WALTH E17	52	B6
Fynes St WEST SW1P	16	C6

G

Gable Cl PIN HA5	42	A3
Gable Ct SYD SE26	163	H4
Gable Ms HAYES BR2	200	D6
Gables Cl CMBW SE5	143	F2
The Gables NRWD SE19 *	181	F1
WBLY HA9	80	B1
Gabriel Cl CRW RM5	56	E3
FELT TW13	154	D6
Gabrielle Cl WBLY HA9	80	B1
Gabriel St FSTH SE23	164	A2
Gabriel's Whf STHWK SE1 *	11	J7
Gad Cl PLSTW E13	107	F2
Gaddesden Av WBLY HA9	80	B4
Gade Cl HYS/HAR UB3	114	A1
Gadesden Rd HOR/WEW KT19	206	E4
Gadsbury Cl CDALE/KGS NW9	63	J3
Gadwall Cl CAN/RD E16	107	F5
Gage Rd CAN/RD E16	106	C4
Gage St BMSBY WC1N	11	F1
Gainford St IS N1	85	G6
Gainsboro Gdns GFD/PVL UB6	78	E3
Gainsborough Av MNPK E12	90	A3
Gainsborough Cl BECK BR3	182	D3
ESH/CLAY KT10 *	189	J5
Gainsborough Ct SHB W12	119	F2
Gainsborough Gdns
EDGW HA8	44	B5
GLDGN NW11	64	D4
HAMP NW3	83	H1
HSLW TW5	135	J6
Gainsborough Ms DUL SE21	162	D3
SYD SE26 *	163	J5
Gainsborough Rd BCTR RM8	91	H2
CHSWK W4	118	C4
NFNCH/WDSPK N12	47	F1
NWMAL KT3	192	A3
RAIN RM13	93	J6
RCH/KEW TW9	137	G3
SRTFD E15	106	C2
WAN E11	70	C4
WFD IG8	53	J2
YEAD UB4	94	A1
Gainsborough Sq
BXLYHS DA6	148	E4
Gainsborough St HOM E9	87	H4
Gainsborough Ter
BELMT SM2 *	208	D5
Gainsford Rd WALTH E17	69	H1
Gainsford St STHWK SE1	19	J1
Gairloch Rd CMBW SE5	143	F3
Gaisford St KTTN NW5	84	C4
Gaitskell Rd ELTH/MOT SE9	167	H3
Gaitskell Wy STHWK SE1 *	18	C2
Galahad Rd ED N9	36	C4
Galata Rd BARN SW13	138	D1
Galatea Sq PECK SE15	143	J4
Galbraith St POP/IOD E14	125	F3
Galdana Av BAR EN5	21	G4
Galeborough Av WFD IG8	52	B3
Gale Cl HPTN TW12	172	D2
MTCM CR4	178	C6
Galena Rd HMSMTH W6	118	E4
Galesbury Rd
WAND/EARL SW18	160	B1
Gales Gdns BETH E2	104	D2
Gale St BOW E3	105	J4
DAGW RM9	91	K6
Gales Wy WFD IG8	53	J3
Galgate Cl WIM/MER SW19	159	G3
Gallants Farm Rd EBAR EN4	33	J2
Galleon Cl BERM/RHTH SE16	123	K2
ERITH DA8	129	G2
Galleon Wy WOOL/PLUM SE18	127	J4
The Galleries IS N1 *	6	A2
Gallery Gdns NTHLT UB5	95	H1
Gallery Rd DUL SE21	162	E3
Galleywall Rd
BERM/RHTH SE16	123	J4
Galleywood Crs CRW RM5	57	F2
Galliard Rd ED N9	36	C2
Gallia Rd HBRY N5	85	H3
Gallions Cl BARK IG11	109	G2
Gallions Rd CHARL SE7	126	A4
Gallions View Rd THMD SE28	127	J2
Gallon Cl CHARL SE7	126	B4
The Gallops ESH/CLAY KT10	204	B1
The Gallop BELMT SM2	209	H6
SAND/SEL CR2	212	D5
Gallosson Rd
WOOL/PLUM SE18	127	K4
Galloway Pth CROY/NA CRO	211	K2
Galloway Rd SHB W12	118	D1
Gallus Cl WCHMN N21	35	F1
Gallus Sq BKHTH/KID SE3	146	A4
Galpin's Rd THHTH CR7	195	K1
Galsworthy Av CHDH RM6	73	H4
POP/IOD E14	105	G4
Galsworthy Cl THMD SE28	128	C1
Galsworthy Crs
BKHTH/KID SE3	146	B2
Galsworthy Rd CRICK NW2	82	C2
KUTN/CMB KT2	175	J4
Galton St NKENS W10	100	C3
Galva Cl EBAR EN4	22	A5
Galveston Rd PUT/ROE SW15	139	J6
Galway Cl BERM/RHTH SE16 *	123	J5
Galway St FSBYE EC1V	6	D5
Gambetta St VX/NE SW8	141	G3
Gambia St STHWK SE1	18	B1
Gamble Rd TOOT SW17	160	D6

Games Rd EBAR EN4	21	J4
Gamlen Rd PUT/ROE SW15	139	G5
Gamuel Cl WALTH E17	69	J3
Gander Green Crs HPTN TW12	173	F4
Gander Green La CHEAM SM3	193	H6
SUT SM1	208	D4
Gandhi Cl WALTH E17	69	J3
Gandolfi St CMBW SE5	123	F6
Ganton St REGST W1B	10	A5
Ganton Wk OXHEY WD19 *	27	J6
Gantshill Crs GNTH/NBYPK IG2	72	A2
Gap Rd WIM/MER SW19	177	K1
Garage Rd ACT W3	98	C5
Garbrand Wk EW KT17	207	H6
Garbutt Pl MHST W1U *	9	H1
Garden Av MTCM CR4	179	G3
Garden City EDGW HA8	44	C2
Garden Cl BAR EN5	20	A5
CHING E4	51	J1
HPTN TW12	172	E1
LEE/GVPK SE12	166	A5
NTHLT UB5	77	J6
PUT/ROE SW15	158	E2
RSLP HA4	58	C6
WLGTN SM6	210	E3
Garden Ct CHSWK W4	117	K3
EMB EC4Y *	11	J5
HPTN TW12	172	E1
Gardeners Rd CROY/NA CRO	196	C5
Garden Flats HMSMTH W6 *	119	G6
Gardenia Rd BMLY BR1	185	F1
EN EN1	36	A1
Gardenia Wy WFD IG8	52	E2
Garden La BMLY BR1	184	A2
BRXS/STRHM SW2	162	A3
Garden Lodge Ct EFNCH N2 *	66	B6
Garden Pl HACK E8	86	B6
Garden Rd BMLY BR1	184	A3
PGE/AN SE20	181	K4
RCH/KEW TW9	137	H4
STJWD NW8	101	G2
WOT/HER KT12	188	A3
Garden Rw STHWK SE1	18	A5
The Gardens BECK BR3	183	F5
CEND/NFELT TW14	66	E1
CLPT E5	68	E6
EBED/NFELT TW14	153	C1
ESH/CLAY KT10	189	F5
HRW HA1	60	C3
PIN HA5 *	59	K3
Garden St WCHPL E1	105	F4
Garden Studios
BAY/PAD W2 *	101	G4
Garden Ter PIM SW1V *	121	J5
Garden Vis ESH/CLAY KT10 *	205	F5
Garden Wk BECK BR3	182	C4
SDTCH EC2A	7	G6
Garden Wy WLSDN NW10	80	E4
STJWD NW8	101	G2
Gardiner Av CRICK NW2	82	A3
Gardiner Cl BCTR RM8	91	K2
PEND EN3	25	H1
STMC/STPC BR5	186	D5
Gardiner House CHARL SE7 *	146	D1
Gardner Pl WAN E11	71	F3
Gardner Pl EBED/NFELT TW14	154	A1
Gardner Rd PLSTW E13	107	F3
Gardners La BLKFR EC4V	12	C5
Gardnor Rd HAMP NW3	83	H2
Gard St FSBYE EC1V	6	B4
Garendon Gdns MRDN SM4	194	A4
Garendon Rd MRDN SM4	194	A4
Gareth Cl WPK KT4	193	G6
Gareth Dr ED N9	36	C4
Gareth Gv BMLY BR1	165	K6
Garfield Ms BTSEA SW11	141	F4
Garfield Rd BTSEA SW11	141	F4
CHING E4	38	B3
PEND EN3	24	E5
PLSTW E13	106	D3
TWK TW1	156	B3
WIM/MER SW19	178	B2
Garganey Wk THMD SE28	109	J6
Garibaldi St
WOOL/PLUM SE18	127	K4
Garland Dr HSLW TW3	135	H3
Garland Rd STAN HA7	43	K4
WOOL/PLUM SE18	147	J1
Garlick Hl BLKFR EC4V	12	D5
Garlies Rd FSTH SE23	164	B5
Garlinge Rd CRICK NW2	82	D4
Garling Ct BAR EN5 *	20	E5
Garman Cl UED N18	49	J1
Garman Rd TOTM N17	50	D3
Garnault Ms CLKNW EC1R	5	K5
Garnault Pl CLKNW EC1R	5	K5
Garnault Rd EN EN1	24	B1
Garner Cl BCTR RM8	73	K5
Garner Rd WALTH E17	52	B4
Garner St BETH E2	104	C1
Garnet Rd THHTH CR7	180	D6
WLSDN NW10	81	G4
Garnet St WAP E1W	104	E6
Garnett Cl ELTH/MOT SE9	146	E4
Garnett Rd HAMP NW3	83	K3
Garnham St STNW/STAM N16 *	68	B1
Garnies Cl PECK SE15	143	G1
Garrad's Rd
STRHM/NOR SW16	161	J5
Garrard Cl CHST BR7	185	G1
Garrard Wk WLSDN NW10 *	81	G4
Garratt Cl CROY/NA CRO	210	E2
Garratt La TOOT SW17	160	D6
WAND/EARL SW18	160	A2
Garratt Rd EDGW HA8	44	C3
Garratts Rd BUSH WD23	28	C2
Garratt Ter TOOT SW17	160	D6
Garrett Cl ACT W3	99	F4
Garrett St STLK EC1Y	6	D7
Garrick Av GLDGN NW11	64	C3
Garrick Cl EA W5	98	A2
RCH/KEW TW9	136	E6
WAND/EARL SW18	140	B5
Garrick Crs CROY/NA CRO	197	F6
Garrick Dr HDN NW4	46	A5
THMD SE28	127	J3
Garrick Gdns
E/WMO/HCT KT8	173	F6
Garrick Pk HDN NW4	46	B5
Garrick Rd CDALE/KGS NW9	63	H3
FSTH SE23	164	A4

GFD/PVL UB6	96	B3
RCH/KEW TW9	137	H3
Garrick St COVGDN WC2E	10	E5
Garrick Wy HDN NW4	64	B1
Garrick Yd CHCR WC2N	10	E5
Garrison Cl HSLWW TW4	134	E6
WOOL/PLUM SE18	147	F1
Garrison La CHSGTN KT9	206	F1
Garrison Rd BOW E3	87	J6
Garry Cl ROM RM1	57	J3
Garry Wy ROM RM1	57	J3
Garsdale Ter WKENS W14 *	119	J5
Garside Cl HPTN TW12	173	G3
THMD SE28	127	J3
Garsington Ms BROCKY SE4	144	C4
Garter Wy BERM/RHTH SE16	124	A2
Garth Cl KUTN/CMB KT2	175	G1
MRDN SM4	193	G4
RSLP HA4	59	H5
Garth Ms EA W5 *	98	A3
Garthorne Rd FSTH SE23	164	A2
Garth Rd CHSWK W4	118	A5
CRICK NW2	64	D6
KUTN/CMB KT2	175	F1
MRDN SM4	193	G5
Garthside KUTN/CMB KT2	175	G6
The Garth HPTN TW12	173	G2
NFNCH/WDSPK N12	47	G2
Garthway
NFNCH/WDSPK N12	47	J2
Gartmoor Gdns
WIM/MER SW19	159	J3
Gartmore Rd GDMY/SEVK IG3	73	F5
Garton Pl WAND/EARL SW18	160	B1
Gartons Cl PEND EN3	24	E6
Gartons Wy BTSEA SW11	140	B4
Garvary Rd CAN/RD E16	107	F5
Garway Rd BAY/PAD W2	101	F5
Gascoigne Gdns WFD IG8	52	C3
Gascoigne Pl BETH E2	7	J4
Gascoigne Rd BARK IG11	90	C6
Gascony Av KIL/WHAMP NW6	82	E5
Gascoyne Dr DART DA1	150	C4
Gascoyne Rd HOM E9	87	F5
Gaselee St POP/IOD E14	106	A6
Gasholder Pl LBTH SE11	122	A5
Gaskarth Rd BAL SW12	161	G1
EDGW HA8	44	E4
Gaskell Rd HGT N6	65	K3
Gaskell St CLAP SW4	141	K3
Gaskin St IS N1	6	B1
Gaspar Ms ECT SW5	120	A4
Gassiot Rd TOOT SW17	160	E6
Gassiot Wy SUT SM1	209	H1
Gastein Rd HMSMTH W6	119	G6
Gaston Bridge Rd
SHPTN TW17	188	E5
Gaston Rd MTCM CR4	179	F6
Gataker St BERM/RHTH SE16	123	J3
Gatcombe Ms EA W5	98	B6
Gatcombe Rd ARCH N19	84	D1
CAN/RD E16	125	K1
Gate Cotts EDGW HA8 *	30	C4
Gate End NTHWD HA6	40	E3
Gateforth St STJWD NW8	2	C7
Gatehill Rd NTHWD HA6	40	D3
Gatehouse Cl KUTN/CMB KT2	175	K3
Gatehouse Sq STHWK SE1 *	12	D7
Gateley Rd BRXN/ST SW9	142	A4
Gate Ms SKENS SW7 *	14	E3
Gater Dr ENC/FH EN2	23	K2
Gates Green Rd WWKM BR4	214	D1
WWKM BR4	214	E2
Gateside Rd TOOT SW17	160	E5
Gatestone Rd NRWD SE19	181	F2
Gate St LINN WC2A	11	G3
Gateway WALW SE17	122	D6
Gateway Ar IS N1 *	6	A2
Gateway Cl NTHWD HA6	40	A2
Gateway Gdns EHAM E6	107	K2
Gateway Ms HACK E8 *	86	B3
The Gateways
RCH/KEW TW9	136	E5
Gatfield Gv FELT TW13	155	F4
Gathorne Rd WDGN N22	49	G5
Gathorne St BETH E2	105	F1
Gatley Av HOR/WEW KT19	206	D3
Gatliff Cl BGVA SW1W *	121	F5
Gatliff Rd BGVA SW1W	121	F5
Gatling Rd ABYW SE2	128	B5
Gatonby St PECK SE15	143	G2
Gatton Cl BELMT SM2	209	F6
Gatton Rd TOOT SW17	160	D6
Gattons Wy SCUP DA14	169	G6
Gatward Cl WCHMH N21	35	H1
Gatward Gn ED N9	36	A4
Gatwick Rd
WAND/EARL SW18	159	J2
Gauden Cl CLAP SW4	141	J4
Gauden Rd CLAP SW4	141	J3
Gaumont Ter SHB W12 *	119	F2
Gauntlet Cl NTHLT UB5	77	J6
Gauntlett Cl ALP/SUD HA0	79	G3
Gauntlett Rd SUT SM1	209	H3
Gaunt St STHWK SE1	18	B4
Gautrey Rd PECK SE15	143	K3
Gavel St WALW SE17 *	19	F6
Gaverick St POP/IOD E14	124	D4
Gavestone Crs
LEE/GVPK SE12	166	A2
Gavestone Rd LEE/GVPK SE12	166	A2
Gaviller Pl CLPT E5 *	86	D2
Gavin St WOOL/PLUM SE18	128	A4
Gawain Wk ED N9	36	D5
Gawber St BETH E2	104	E2
Gawsworth Cl SRTFD E15	88	D3
Gawthorne Av MLHL NW7	46	C1
Gawthorne Ct BOW E3 *	87	J6
Gay Cl CRICK NW2	81	K3
Gaydon La CDALE/KGS NW9	45	G4
Gayfere Rd CLAY IG5	53	K6
EW KT17	207	J3
Gayfere St WEST SW1P	16	E5
Gayford Rd SHB W12	118	C2
Gay Gdns DAGE RM10	92	E2
Gayhurst HACK E8 *	86	C5
Gaylor Rd NTHLT UB5	77	K3
Gaynesford Rd CAR SM5	209	K5
FSTH SE23	164	A4

Gaynes Hill Rd WFD IG8	53	J3
Gay Rd SRTFD E15	106	B1
Gaysham Av GNTH/NBYPK IG2	72	A2
Gay St PUT/ROE SW15	139	G4
Gayton Crs HAMP NW3	83	H2
Gayton Rd HAMP NW3	83	H2
HRW HA1	61	F3
Gayville Rd BTSEA SW11	160	E1
Gaywood Cl
BRXS/STRHM SW2	162	A3
Gaywood Rd WALTH E17	51	J6
Gaywood St STHWK SE1	18	B5
Gaza St WALW SE17	122	C5
Geariesville Gdns
BARK/HLT IG6	72	B1
Geary Cl STRHM/NOR SW16	161	F6
Gearing Cl TOOT SW17	161	F1
Geary Rd WLSDN NW10	81	J3
Geary St HOLWY N7	85	F3
Gedeney Rd TOTM N17	49	J4
Gedling Pl STHWK SE1	19	J4
Geere Rd SRTFD E15	88	D6
Geffrye Est IS N1	7	H3
Geffrye St BETH E2	7	J2
Geldart Rd PECK SE15	143	J1
Geldeston Rd CLPT E5	68	C6
Gellatly Rd NWCR SE14	143	K3
Gelsthorpe Rd CRW RM5	56	D3
Genas Cl BARK/HLT IG6	54	B4
General Gordon Pl
WOOL/PLUM SE18	127	G3
General Wolfe Rd
GNWCH SE10	145	G2
Genesis Cl STWL/WRAY TW19	152	C3
Genesta Rd
WOOL/PLUM SE18	127	G6
Geneva Dr BRXN/ST SW9	142	B5
Geneva Gdns CHDH RM6	74	A2
Geneva Rd KUT/HW KT1	191	F1
THHTH CR7	196	D2
Genever Cl CHING E4	51	J1
Genista Rd UED N18	50	D1
Genoa Av PUT/ROE SW15	139	F6
Genoa Rd PGE/AN SE20	181	K4
Genotin Rd EN EN1	23	K4
Gentleman's Rw ENC/FH EN2	23	J4
Geoffrey Cl CMBW SE5	142	D3
Geoffrey Gdns EHAM E6	107	J1
Geoffrey Rd BROCKY SE4	144	C4
George Beard Rd DEPT SE8	124	C4
George Crs MUSWH N10	48	A3
George Downing Est
STNW/STAM N16	68	B6
George Gange Wy
KTN/HRWW/WS HA3	42	E6
George Groves Rd
PGE/AN SE20	181	H4
George La HAYES BR2	200	A5
LEW SE13	165	F1
SWFD E18	52	E5
George Lowe Ct
BAY/PAD W2 *	101	F4
George Mathers Rd
LBTH SE11	18	A6
George Ms BRXN/ST SW9	142	B3
CAMTN NW1	4	A5
George Rd CHING E4	51	J2
KUTN/CMB KT2	175	K3
NWMAL KT3	192	C1
George Rw BERM/RHTH SE16	123	H2
Georges Md BORE WD6	30	A1
Georges Rd HOLWY N7	85	F2
George St BARK IG11	90	C5
CAN/RD E16	106	D5
CROY/NA CRO	196	D6
HNWL W7	115	K1
MBLAR W1H	8	E3
NWDGN UB2	114	D4
RCH/KEW TW9	136	E6
ROM RM1	75	H3
Georgetown Cl NRWD SE19	181	F1
Georgette Pl GNWCH SE10	145	F1
George V Av PIN HA5	41	K5
Georgeville Gdns
BARK/HLT IG6	72	B1
George V Wy GFD/PVL UB6	79	H5
George Wyver Cl
WIM/MER SW19	159	H2
George Yd BANK EC3V	13	F4
MYFR/PKLN W1K	9	H5
Georgiana St CAMTN NW1	84	C6
Georgian Ct HAYES BR2	200	D4
STAN HA7	43	G3
Georgian Ct WBLY HA9	80	D6
Georgia Rd NWMAL KT3	191	K1
THHTH CR7	180	C4
Georgina Gdns BETH E2 *	7	K4
Geraldine Rd CHSWK W4	117	H6
WAND/EARL SW18	140	B6
Geraldine St LBTH SE11	18	A5
Gerald Rd BGVA SW1W	15	H6
CAN/RD E16	106	C3
Gerard Av HSLWW TW4	155	F2
Gerard Gdns RAIN RM13	93	G3
Gerard Rd BARN SW13	138	C2
HRW HA1	61	G3
Gerards Cl BERM/RHTH SE16	123	K6
Gerda Rd ELTH/MOT SE9	167	G4
Germander Wy SRTFD E15	106	C2
Gernon Rd BOW E3	105	G1
Geron Wy CRICK NW2	63	K6
Gerrard Gdns PIN HA5	58	E2
Gerrard Pl SOHO/SHAV W1D *	10	D5
Gerrard Rd IS N1	6	A2
Gerrards Cl STHGT/OAK N14	22	C6
Gerrard St SOHO/SHAV W1D	10	D5
Gerridge St STHWK SE1	17	K3
Gertrude Rd BELV DA17	129	H4
Gertrude St WBPTN SW10	120	B6
Gervase Cl WBLY HA9	80	E1
Gervase Rd EDGW HA8	44	E4
Gervase St PECK SE15	143	J1
Ghent St CAT SE6	164	D4
Ghent Wy HACK E8	86	B4
Giant Arches Rd HNHL SE24	162	D2
Giant Tree Hi BUSH WD23	28	D4

Gibbfield Cl CHDH RM6 56 A6
Gibbins Rd SRTFD E15 88 A5
Gibbon Rd ACT W3 99 G6
KUTN/CMB KT2 175 F4
PECK SE15 143 K3
Gibbons Ms GLDGN NW11 64 D2
Gibbons Rd WLSDN NW10 81 F4
Gibbon Wk PUT/ROE SW15 * 138 D5
Gibbs Av NRWD SE19 180 E2
Gibbs Cl NRWD SE19 * 180 E1
Gibbs Couch OXHEY WD19 27 H5
Gibbs Gn EDGW HA8 30 E6
WKENS W14 * 119 J5
Gibbs Green Cl WKENS W14 119 J5
Gibbs Rd UED N18 36 E6
Gibbs Sq NRWD SE19 * 180 E1
Gibraltar Wk BETH E2 7 K5
Gibson Cl CHSGTN KT9 205 J3
ISLW TW7 135 J4
WCHMH N21 35 G1
WCHPL E1 104 E3
Gibson Gdns
STNW/STAM N16 * 68 B6
Gibson Rd BCTR RM8 73 J5
LBTH SE11 17 H7
SUT SM1 209 F3
Gibson's Hl STRHM/NOR SW16 180 B3
Gibson Sq IS N1 85 G6
Gibson St GNWCH SE10 125 H5
Gidea Av GPK RM2 57 J6
Gidea Cl GPK RM2 57 J6
Gideon Cl BELV DA17 129 J4
Gideon Ms EA W5 * 116 E2
Gideon Rd BTSEA SW11 141 F4
Giesbach Rd ARCH N19 66 C6
Giffard Rd UED N18 50 A1
Giffin St DEPT SE8 144 D1
Gifford Gdns HNWL W7 96 D4
Gifford Rd WLSDN NW10 81 G5
Gifford St IS N1 84 E5
Gift La SRTFD E15 88 C6
Giggs Hl STMC/STPC BR5 186 B5
Giggs Hill Gdns THDIT KT7 190 B5
Giggs Hill Rd THDIT KT7 190 B4
Gilbert Cl WIM/MER SW19 * 178 A4
WOOL/PLUM SE18 146 E2
Gilbert Gv EDGW HA8 44 E4
Gilbert Pl NOXST/BSQ WC1A 10 E2
Gilbert Rd BELV DA17 129 H3
BMLY BR1 183 K3
LBTH SE11 17 K6
PIN HA5 59 H1
ROM RM1 75 H1
WIM/MER SW19 178 B3
Gilbert St HSLW TW3 135 H4
MYFR/PKLN W1K 9 H4
SRTFD E15 88 C2
Gilbert White Cl GFD/PVL UB6 79 G6
Gilbey Rd TOOT SW17 160 D6
Gilbeys Yd CAMTN NW1 84 A5
Gilbourne Rd
WOOL/PLUM SE18 128 A6
Gilda Av PEND EN3 25 G6
Gilda Crs STNW/STAM N16 68 C5
Gildea Cl PIN HA5 42 A3
Gildea St GTPST W1W 9 K2
Gilden Crs KTTN NW5 84 A3
Gildersome St
WOOL/PLUM SE18 127 F6
Gilders Rd CHSGTN KT9 206 B4
Giles Coppice NRWD SE19 163 G6
Gilkes Crs DUL SE21 163 F1
Gilkes Pl DUL SE21 163 F1
Gillam Wy RAIN RM13 93 J4
Gillan Gn BUSH WD23 28 C4
Gillards Ms WALTH E17 69 J1
Gillards Wy WALTH E17 69 J1
Gill Av CAN/RD E16 106 E5
Gill Cl WATW WD18 26 A1
Gillender St BOW E3 106 A3
Gillespie Rd HBRY N5 85 G1
Gillett Av EHAM E6 107 J1
Gillett Pl HACK E8 86 B3
Gillett Rd THHTH CR7 196 E1
Gillett St STNW/STAM N16 86 A3
Gillham Ter TOTM N17 50 C2
Gillian Park Rd CHEAM SM3 193 J5
Gillian St LEW SE13 144 E6
Gillian Ter BRYLDS KT5 * 191 G3
Gillies St KTTN NW5 84 A3
Gillingham Rd CRICK NW2 82 C1
Gillingham Rw PIM SW1V 16 A6
Gillingham St PIM SW1V 15 K7
Gillison Wk
BERM/RHTH SE16 * 123 H3
Gillman Dr SRTFD E15 88 C6
Gillmans Rd STMC/STPC BR5 202 C5
Gill St POP/IOD E14 105 H5
Gillum Cl EBAR EN4 33 K3
Gilmore Rd LEW SE13 145 G5
Gilpin Av MORT/ESHN SW14 138 A5
Gilpin Cl MTCM CR4 178 D5
Gilpin Crs UED N18 50 B1
WHTN TW2 155 G2
Gilpin Rd CLPT E5 87 G2
Gilpin Wy HYS/HAR UB3 133 G1
Gilroy Cl RAIN RM13 93 H4
Gilroy Wy STMC/STPC BR5 202 C4
Gilsland Rd THHTH CR7 196 E1
Gilson Pl MUSWH N10 47 K3
Gilstead Rd FUL/PGN SW6 140 A3
Gilston Rd WBPTN SW10 120 B5
Gilton Rd CAT SE6 165 H5
Giltspur St STBT EC1A 12 B3
Gilwell Cl CHING E4 25 K5
Gippeswyck Cl PIN HA5 41 H4
Gipsy Hl NRWD SE19 181 F1
Gipsy La PUT/ROE SW15 138 D4
Gipsy Rd WELL DA16 148 E2
WNWD SE27 162 E6
Gipsy Road Gdns WNWD SE27 162 D6
Giralda Cl CAN/RD E16 107 H4
Giraud St POP/IOD E14 105 K5
Girdlers Rd WKENS W14 119 H3
Girdwood Rd
WAND/EARL SW18 159 H2
Girling Wy EBED/NFELT TW14 133 K4
Gironde Rd FUL/PGN SW6 139 J1
Girton Av CDALE/KGS NW9 44 C6
Girton Cl NTHLT UB5 78 C4
Girton Gdns CROY/NA CR0 213 J1
Girton Rd NTHLT UB5 78 C4
SYD SE26 182 A1
Gisbourne Cl WLGTN SM6 210 D1
Gisburn Rd CEND/HSY/T N8 67 F1
Gissing Wk IS N1 * 85 G5
Gittens Cl BMLY BR1 165 J6
Glacier Wy ALP/SUD HA0 97 K1
Gladbeck Wy ENC/FH EN2 23 H5
Gladding Rd MNPK E12 89 H2
Glade Cl SURB KT6 * 190 E6
Glade Gdns CROY/NA CR0 198 B4
Glade La NWDGN UB2 115 G2
Gladeside CROY/NA CR0 198 A4
WCHMH N21 35 F2
Gladesmore Rd
SEVS/STOTM N15 68 B3
The Glade BELMT SM2 208 C6
BMLY BR1 184 C5
CHARL SE7 146 B1
CLAY IG5 53 K4
CROY/NA CR0 198 A2
ENC/FH EN2 23 G4
EW KT17 207 J4
HACK E8 * 86 B4
NFNCH/WDSPK N12 * 33 H6
SHB W12 118 E2
WCHMH N21 35 F1
WFD IG8 39 F5
WWKM BR4 213 K1
Gladiator St FSTH SE23 164 B1
Glading Ter STNW/STAM N16 86 B1
Gladioli Cl HPTN TW12 173 F2
Gladsdale Dr PIN HA5 58 E1
Gladsmuir Cl WOT/HER KT12 188 B6
Gladsmuir Rd ARCH N19 66 C5
BAR EN5 20 C3
Gladstone Av
EBED/NFELT TW14 153 K1
MNPK E12 89 J5
WDGN N22 49 G5
WHTN TW2 155 J2
Gladstone Gdns HSLW TW3 135 H2
Gladstone Ms
KIL/WHAMP NW6 * 82 D5
PGE/AN SE20 181 K3
WDGN N22 49 G5
Gladstone Pde CRICK NW2 * 82 A1
Gladstone Park Gdns
CRICK NW2 81 K1
Gladstone Pl BAR EN5 * 20 B5
E/WMO/HCT KT8 * 189 K2
Gladstone Rd BKHH IG9 39 G3
CHSWK W4 * 118 A3
CROY/NA CR0 196 E4
KUT/HW KT1 175 H6
NWDGN UB2 114 D2
ORP BR6 216 C3
SURB KT6 190 E6
WIM/MER SW19 177 K3
Gladstone St STHWK SE1 18 A4
Gladstone Ter VX/NE SW8 * 141 G2
WNWD SE27 * 162 D6
Gladstone Wy
KTN/HRWW/WS HA3 42 E6
Gladwell Rd BMLY BR1 183 K2
CEND/HSY/T N8 67 F3
Gladwyn Rd PUT/ROE SW15 139 G4
Gladys Rd KIL/WHAMP NW6 82 E5
Glaisher St DEPT SE8 124 D6
Glamis Crs HYS/HAR UB3 113 F3
Glamis Pl WAP E1W 104 E6
Glamis Rd WAP E1W 104 E6
Glamis Wy NTHLT UB5 78 C4
Glamorgan Cl MTCM CR4 179 K6
Glamorgan Rd KUT/HW KT1 174 D3
Glandford Wy CHDH RM6 73 H2
Glanfield Rd BECK BR3 198 C1
Glanleam Rd STAN HA7 29 K6
Glanville Ms STAN HA7 43 G1
Glanville Rd
BRXS/STRHM SW2 141 K6
HAYES BR2 184 A6
Glasbrook Av WHTN TW2 154 E3
Glasbrook Rd ELTH/MOT SE9 166 C2
Glaserton Rd
STNW/STAM N16 68 A4
Glasford St TOOT SW17 178 E2
Glasgow Rd PLSTW E13 107 F1
UED N18 50 D1
Glasgow Ter PIM SW1V 121 H5
Glaskin Ms HOM E9 87 G4
Glasse Cl WEA W13 97 G6
Glasshill St STHWK SE1 18 B2
Glasshouse Flds WAP E1W 105 F6
Glasshouse St REGST W1B 10 B6
Glasshouse Wk LBTH SE11 121 K5
Glasshouse Yd FARR EC1M 6 C7
Glasslyn Rd CEND/HSY/T N8 66 D2
Glassmill La HAYES BR2 183 J5
Glass St BETH E2 * 104 D3
Glass Yd WOOL/PLUM SE18 127 F3
Glastonbury Av WFD IG8 53 H3
Glastonbury Cl
STMC/STPC BR5 202 D5
Glastonbury Pl WCHPL E1 104 E5
Glastonbury Rd ED N9 36 C3
MRDN SM4 193 K3
Glastonbury St
KIL/WHAMP NW6 82 D3
Glaston Ct EA W5 * 116 E1
Glaucus St BOW E3 105 K4
Glazbury Rd WKENS W14 119 H4
Glazebrook Cl DUL SE21 162 E4
Glebe Av ENC/FH EN2 23 H4
HGDN/ICK UB10 76 A2
KTN/HRWW/WS HA3 44 A6
MTCM CR4 178 D5
RSLP HA4 77 F4
WFD IG8 52 E2
Glebe Cl CHSWK W4 * 118 B5
HGDN/ICK UB10 76 A2
Glebe Ct BKHTH/KID SE3 * 145 H4
EA W5 * 116 E1
STAN HA7 43 J1
Glebe Crs HDN NW4 64 A1
KTN/HRWW/WS HA3 44 A6
Glebe Gdns NWMAL KT3 192 B4
Glebe House Dr HAYES BR2 200 A5
Glebelands DART DA1 150 C5
E/WMO/HCT KT8 189 G2
ESH/CLAY KT10 205 F6
Glebelands Av
GNTH/NBYPK IG2 72 D4
SWFD E18 52 E5
Glebelands Cl CMBW SE5 143 F4
NFNCH/WDSPK N12 47 H4
Glebelands Rd
EBED/NFELT TW14 153 K2
Glebe La KTN/HRWW/WS HA3 62 A1
Glebe Pth MTCM CR4 178 E6
Glebe Pl CHEL SW3 120 D6
Glebe Rd BARN SW13 138 D3
BELMT SM2 208 C6
BMLY BR1 183 K4
CAR SM5 209 K4
CEND/HSY/T N8 67 F1
DAGE RM10 92 D4
FNCH N3 47 G4
HACK E8 * 86 B5
RAIN RM13 111 K2
STAN HA7 43 J1
WLSDN NW10 81 J4
Glebe Side TWK TW1 156 A1
Glebe Sq MTCM CR4 * 178 E6
Glebe St CHSWK W4 118 A5
The Glebe BKHTH/KID SE3 145 H4
CHST BR7 185 H4
STRHM/NOR SW16 * 161 J6
WDR/YW UB7 112 B4
WPK KT4 192 C5
Glebe Wy WWKM BR4 199 F6
ERITH DA8 130 B6
FELT TW13 155 F5
Glebeway WFD IG8 53 G1
Gledhow Gdns ECT SW5 120 B4
Gledstanes Rd WKENS W14 119 H5
Gledwood Av YEAD UB4 94 E4
Gledwood Crs YEAD UB4 94 D4
Gledwood Dr YEAD UB4 94 D4
Gledwood Gdns YEAD UB4 94 E4
Gleed Av BUSH WD23 28 D4
Gleeson Dr ORP BR6 217 F3
Glegg Pl PUT/ROE SW15 * 139 G5
Glenaffric Av POP/IOD E14 125 F4
Glen Albyn Rd
WIM/MER SW19 159 G4
Glenalla Rd RSLP HA4 58 D4
Glenalmond Rd
KTN/HRWW/WS HA3 62 A1
Glenalvon Wy
WOOL/PLUM SE18 126 D4
Glena Mt SUT SM1 209 G2
Glenarm Rd CLPT E5 86 E2
Glen Av ASHF TW15 152 D6
Glenavon Cl ESH/CLAY KT10 205 G4
Glenavon Rd SRTFD E15 88 C5
Glenbarr Cl ELTH/MOT SE9 147 G4
Glenbow Rd BMLY BR1 183 H2
Glenbrook North
ENC/FH EN2 23 F5
Glenbrook Rd
KIL/WHAMP NW6 82 E3
Glenbrook South
ENC/FH EN2 23 F5
Glenbuck Rd SURB KT6 190 E3
Glenburnie Rd TOOT SW17 160 E5
Glencairn Dr EA W5 97 H3
Glencairne Cl CAN/RD E16 107 H4
Glencairn Rd
STRHM/NOR SW16 179 K3
Glencoe Av GNTH/NBYPK IG2 72 E4
Glencoe Rd BUSH WD23 28 A1
DAGE RM10 92 C2
YEAD UB4 95 H3
Glencorse Gn OXHEY WD19 * 27 H6
Glen Crs WFD IG8 53 F2
Glendale Av CHDH RM6 73 J4
EDGW HA8 30 B6
WDGN N22 49 G3
Glendale Cl ELTH/MOT SE9 147 F4
Glendale Dr WIM/MER SW19 177 J1
Glendale Gdns WBLY HA9 61 K5
Glendale Ms BECK BR3 182 E4
Glendale Rd ERITH DA8 129 K4
Glendale Wy THMD SE28 128 D1
Glendall St BRXN/ST SW9 142 A4
Glendarvon St
PUT/ROE SW15 139 G4
Glendevon Cl EDGW HA8 30 D5
Glendish Rd TOTM N17 50 C4
Glendor Gdns MLHL NW7 31 F6
Glendower Crs ORP BR6 202 B3
Glendower Gdns
MORT/ESHN SW14 138 A4
Glendower Pl SKENS SW7 14 A6
Glendower Rd CHING E4 38 B3
MORT/ESHN SW14 138 A4
Glendown Rd ABYW SE2 128 B5
Glendun Rd ACT W3 99 G6
Gleneagle Ms
STRHM/NOR SW16 179 J1
Gleneagle Rd
STRHM/NOR SW16 179 J1
Gleneagles STAN HA7 43 H2
Gleneagles Cl
BERM/RHTH SE16 * 123 J5
ORP BR6 201 J5
OXHEY WD19 * 41 H1
Gleneldon Ms
STRHM/NOR SW16 179 K1
Gleneldon Rd
STRHM/NOR SW16 161 K6
Glenelg Rd BRXS/STRHM SW2 141 K6
Glenesk Rd ELTH/MOT SE9 147 F4
Glenfarg Rd CAT SE6 165 G3
Glenfield Crs RSLP HA4 58 B4
Glenfield Rd BAL SW12 161 H3
WEA W13 116 C2
Glenfinlas Wy CMBW SE5 142 C1
Glenforth St GNWCH SE10 125 J4
Glengall Br POP/IOD E14 124 E3
Glengall Gv POP/IOD E14 124 E3
Glengall Rd EDGW HA8 30 D5
KIL/WHAMP NW6 82 D6
PECK SE15 123 G6
WFD IG8 52 E2
Glengall Ter PECK SE15 123 G6
Glen Gdns CROY/NA CR0 211 G1
Glengarnock Av POP/IOD E14 125 F4
Glengarry Rd EDUL SE22 143 F5
Glenham Dr GNTH/NBYPK IG2 72 B2
Glenhead Cl ELTH/MOT SE9 147 G4
Glenhill Cl FNCH N3 46 E5
Glenhouse Rd ELTH/MOT SE9 147 F6
Glenhurst Av BXLY DA5 169 G3
KTTN NW5 84 A2
RSLP HA4 58 A4
Glenhurst Ri NRWD SE19 180 D3
Glenhurst Rd BTFD TW8 116 D6
NFNCH/WDSPK N12 33 H6
Glenilla Rd HAMP NW3 83 J4
Glenister Park Rd
STRHM/NOR SW16 179 J3
Glenister Rd GNWCH SE10 125 J5
Glenlea Rd ELTH/MOT SE9 147 F6
Glenloch Rd HAMP NW3 83 J4
PEND EN3 24 E3
Glenluce Rd BKHTH/KID SE3 146 A4
Glenlyon Rd ELTH/MOT SE9 147 F6
Glenmere Av MLHL NW7 45 J3
Glenmere Rw LEE/GVPK SE12 165 J1
Glenmill HPTN TW12 172 E1
Glenmore Lawns WEA W13 * 97 G5
Glenmore Pde ALP/SUD HA0 * 80 A6
Glenmore Rd HAMP NW3 83 J4
WELL DA16 148 A2
Glenmore Wy BARK IG11 109 G2
Glennie Rd WNWD SE27 162 B5
Glenny Rd BARK IG11 90 C4
Glenorchy Cl YEAD UB4 95 J4
Glenparke Rd FSTGT E7 89 F4
Glen Ri WFD IG8 53 F2
Glen Rd CHSGTN KT9 206 A1
PLSTW E13 107 G3
WALTH E17 69 H2
Glen Road End WLGTN SM6 210 B6
Glenrosa St FUL/PGN SW6 140 B3
Glenroy St SHB W12 100 A5
Glensdale Rd BROCKY SE4 144 C4
Glenshiel Rd ELTH/MOT SE9 147 F6
Glenside CHIG IG7 54 B2
Glentanner Wy TOOT SW17 160 C5
Glentham Cots BARN SW13 * 118 D6
Glentham Gdns BARN SW13 118 E5
Glentham Rd BARN SW13 118 D6
The Glen BELMT SM2 * 209 G4
CROY/NA CR0 213 F1
ENC/FH EN2 23 H5
HAYES BR2 183 H5
NTHWD HA6 40 B3
NWDGN UB2 114 E5
ORP BR6 215 K1
PIN HA5 59 F2
WBLY HA9 79 K2
Glenthorne Av CROY/NA CR0 197 K5
Glenthorne Cl CHEAM SM3 193 K5
Glenthorne Gdns
BARK/HLT IG6 54 A6
CHEAM SM3 193 K5
Glenthorne Rd
FBAR/BDGN N11 47 K1
HMSMTH W6 118 E4
KUT/HW KT1 191 G1
WALTH E17 69 G2
Glenthorpe Rd MRDN SM4 193 G2
Glenton Cl ROM RM1 57 G3
Glenton Rd LEW SE13 145 H5
Glenton Wy ROM RM1 57 G3
Glentrammon Av ORP BR6 217 F4
Glentrammon Cl ORP BR6 217 F4
Glentrammon Gdns ORP BR6 217 F4
Glentrammon Rd ORP BR6 217 F4
Glentworth St CAMTN NW1 3 F7
Glenure Rd ELTH/MOT SE9 147 F6
Glenview ABYW SE2 128 E6
Glen View Rd BMLY BR1 184 C5
Glenville Av ENC/FH EN2 23 J1
Glenville Gv DEPT SE8 144 C1
Glenville Ms
WAND/EARL SW18 160 A2
Glenville Rd KUTN/CMB KT2 175 H4
Glenwood Av
CDALE/KGS NW9 63 G5
RAIN RM13 111 J3
Glenwood Cl HRW HA1 61 F2
Glenwood Dr GPK RM2 75 J2
Glenwood Gdns
GNTH/NBYPK IG2 72 A2
Glenwood Gv
CDALE/KGS NW9 62 E5
Glenwood Rd CAT SE6 164 C3
EW KT17 207 J4
HSLW TW3 135 J4
MLHL NW7 31 G5
SEVS/STOTM N15 67 H2
Glenwood Rw NRWD SE19 * 181 G4
Glenwood Wy CROY/NA CR0 198 A3
Glenworth Av POP/IOD E14 125 G4
Gliddon Dr CLPT E5 86 D2
Gliddon Rd WKENS W14 119 H4
Glimpsing Gn ERITHM DA18 129 F3
Gload Crs STMC/STPC BR5 202 E6
Globe Pond Rd
BERM/RHTH SE16 124 B1
Globe Rd BETH E2 104 E2
EMPK RM11 75 J3
SRTFD E15 88 D3
WFD IG8 53 G2
Globe St STHWK SE1 18 E3
Globe Ter BETH E2 104 E2
Glossop Rd SAND/SEL CR2 211 K6
Gloster Rd NWMAL KT3 192 B1
Gloucester Av BFN/LL DA15 167 K4
CAMTN NW1 3 H1
WELL DA16 148 A6
Gloucester Circ GNWCH SE10 145 F1
Gloucester Cl THDIT KT7 * 190 B5
WLSDN NW10 81 F5
Gloucester Ct MTCM CR4 * 195 K2
RCH/KEW TW9 * 137 H1
Gloucester Crs CAMTN NW1 84 B6
Gloucester Dr FSBYPK N4 67 H6
GLDGN NW11 64 E1
Gloucester Gdns
BAY/PAD W2 * 101 G5
EBAR EN4 22 A5
GLDGN NW11 64 D4
IL IG1 71 J4
SUT SM1 194 A6
Gloucester Ga CAMTN NW1 3 H2
Gloucester Gate Ms
CAMTN NW1 3 J2
Gloucester Gv EDGW HA8 45 F4
Gloucester Ms BAY/PAD W2 101 G5
LEY E10 69 J4
Gloucester Ms West
BAY/PAD W2 101 G5
Gloucester Pde
BFN/LL DA15 * 148 B6
HYS/HAR UB3 * 113 F3
Gloucester Pl CAMTN NW1 2 E6
MHST W1U 9 F2
Gloucester Place Ms
MHST W1U 9 F3
Gloucester Rd ACT W3 117 K2
BAR EN5 21 F6
BELV DA17 129 G5
CROY/NA CR0 196 E4
EA W5 116 D2
ENC/FH EN2 23 J1
FELT TW13 154 B3
HPTN TW12 173 G3
HRW HA1 60 B2
HSLWW TW4 134 D5
KUT/HW KT1 175 H5
LEY E10 69 J4
MNPK E12 89 K1
RCH/KEW TW9 137 H1
ROM RM1 75 G3
SKENS SW7 120 B4
TEDD TW11 173 K1
TOTM N17 49 K5
UED N18 50 B1
WALTH E17 51 F5
WAN E11 71 F2
WHTN TW2 155 H3
Gloucester Sq BAY/PAD W2 8 B4
BETH E2 86 C6
Gloucester St PIM SW1V 121 H5
Gloucester Ter BAY/PAD W2 101 F5
STHGT/OAK N14 * 34 D3
Gloucester Wk KENS W8 * 119 K2
Gloucester Wy CLKNW EC1R 5 K
Glover Dr UED N18 50 E
Glover Rd PIN HA5 59 H
Glycena Rd BTSEA SW11 140 E
Glyn Av EBAR EN4 21 H
Glyn Cl EW KT17 207 J
SNWD SE25 181 F
Glyn Ct STAN HA7 43 H
Glyndebourne Pk ORP BR6 216 B
Glynde Ms CHEL SW3 14 D
Glynde Rd BXLYHN DA7 148 E
Glynde St BROCKY SE4 164 C
Glyndon Rd
WOOL/PLUM SE18 127 H
Glyn Dr SCUP DA14 168 C
Glynfield Rd WLSDN NW10 81
Glynne Rd WDGN N22 49
Glyn Rd CLPT E5 87
PEND EN3 24
WPK KT4 193
Glyn St LBTH SE11 122
Glynwood Ct FSTH SE23 163
Goat La EN EN1 24
Goat Rd MTCM CR4 195
Goat Whf BTFD TW8 117
Gobions Av CRW RM5 57
Godalming Av WLGTN SM6 210
Godalming Rd POP/IOD E14 105
Godbold Rd SRTFD E15 106
Goddard Pl ARCH N19 84
Goddard Rd BECK BR3 198
Goddards Wy IL IG1 72
Goddington Cha ORP BR6 217
Goddington La ORP BR6 217
Godfrey Av NTHLT UB5 77
WHTN TW2 155
Godfrey Hl WOOL/PLUM SE18 126
Godfrey Rd
WOOL/PLUM SE18 126
Godfrey St CHEL SW3 120
SRTFD E15 106
Godfrey Wy HSLWW TW4 154
Goding St LBTH SE11 12
Godley Rd WAND/EARL SW18 160
Godliman St BLKFR EC4V 1
Godman Rd PECK SE15 * 14
Godolphin Cl PLMGR N13 4
Godolphin Pl ACT W3 9
Godolphin Rd SHB W12 11
Godric Crs CROY/NA CR0 21
Godson Rd CROY/NA CR0 21
Godson St IS N1
Godstone Rd SUT SM1 20
TWK TW1 15
Godwin Cl HOR/WEW KT19 20
IS N1
Godwin Rd FSTGT E7
HAYES BR2 18
Goffers Rd BKHTH/KID SE3 14
Goidel Cl WLGTN SM6 2
Golborne Gdns NKENS W10 * 1
Golborne Ms NKENS W10 1
Golborne Rd NKENS W10 1
Golda Cl BAR EN5
Goldbeaters Gv EDGW HA8
Goldcliff Cl MRDN SM4 1
Goldcrest Cl CAN/RD E16 1
THMD SE28 1
Goldcrest Ms EA W5 *
Goldcrest Wy BUSH WD23
CROY/NA CR0 2
Golden Ct HSLW TW3 1
Golden Crs HYS/HAR UB3
Golden Cross Ms
NTGHL W11 *
Golden Hind Pl DEPT SE8 *
Golden Jubilee Br STHWK SE1
Golden La STLK EC1Y
Golden Lane Est STLK EC1Y
Golden Mnr HNWL W7
Golden Pde WALTH E17 *
Golden Plover Cl
CAN/RD E16
Golden Sq SOHO/CST W1F
Golden Yd HAMP NW3
Golders Cl EDGW HA8
Golders Gdns GLDGN NW11

Golders Green Crs
GLDGN NW11 64 D4
Golders Green Rd
GLDGN NW11 64 C3
Golders Hl HAMP NW3 * 65 F6
Goldersiea GLDGN NW11 * 64 E5
Golders Manor Dr
GLDGN NW11 64 B3
Golders Park Cl GLDGN NW11 64 E5
Golders Ri HDN NW4 64 B2
Golders Wy GLDGN NW11 64 D4
Goldfinch Cl ORP BR6 217 G3
Goldfinch Rd THMD SE28 127 J3
Goldhawk Ms SHB W12 118 E2
Goldhawk Rd HMSMTH W6 118 C4
Goldhaze Cl WFD IG8 53 G3
Gold Hl EDGW HA8 45 F2
Goldhurst Ter
KIL/WHAMP NW6 83 F5
Golding St WCHPL E1 104 C5
Goldington Crs CAMTN NW1 4 B2
Goldington St CAMTN NW1 4 C2
Gold La EDGW HA8 45 F2
Goldman Cl BETH E2 104 C3
Goldney Rd MV/WKIL W9 100 E3
Goldrill Dr FBAR/BDGN N11 34 A4
Goldsboro Rd VX/NE SW8 141 J2
Goldsborough Crs CHING E4 37 K4
Goldsdown Cl PEND EN3 25 G3
Goldsdown Rd PEND EN3 25 F3
Goldsmid St
WOOL/PLUM SE18 127 K5
Goldsmith Av ACT W3 99 F6
CDALE/KGS NW9 63 G2
MNPK E12 89 J4
ROMW/RG RM7 74 C4
Goldsmith Cl
RYLN/HDSTN HA2 60 A5
Goldsmith La
CDALE/KGS NW9 62 E1
Goldsmith Pl
KIL/WHAMP NW6 * 83 F6
Goldsmith Rd ACT W3 118 A1
FBAR/BDGN N11 47 K1
LEY E10 69 K5
PECK SE15 143 H2
WALTH E17 51 F5
Goldsmiths Cl ACT W3 * 118 A1
Goldsmith's Rw BETH E2 104 C1
Goldsmith St CITYW EC2V 12 D3
oldsworthy Gdns
BERM/RHTH SE16 123 K4
oldwell Rd THHTH CR7 196 A1
oldwing Cl CAN/RD E16 106 E5
olf Cl STAN HA7 43 J3
THHTH CR7 180 B4
olf Club Dr KUTN/CMB KT2 176 A3
olfe Rd IL IG1 90 D1
olf Rd BMLY BR1 185 F6
EA W5 * 98 B5
olf Side WHTN TW2 155 J5
olf Side Cl NWMAL KT3 176 B5
olfside Cl TRDG/WHET N20 33 J5
ollogly Ter CHARL SE7 126 B5
omer Gdns TEDD TW11 174 B2
omer Pl TEDD TW11 174 B2
omm Rd BERM/RHTH SE16 123 K3
omshall Av WLGTN SM6 210 E3
ondar Gdns CRICK NW2 82 D3
onson St DEPT SE8 124 E6
onston Cl WIM/MER SW19 159 H4
onville Crs NTHLT UB5 78 B4
onville Rd THHTH CR7 196 A2
onville St FUL/PGN SW6 139 H4
oodall Rd WAN E11 88 A1
ooden Ct HRW HA1 78 E1
oodenough Rd
WIM/MER SW19 177 J3
oodey Rd BARK IG11 91 F5
oodge Pl FITZ W1T 10 B2
odge St FITZ W1T 10 B2
odhall Cl STAN HA7 43 G2
odhall St WLSDN NW10 99 G2
odhart Wy WWKM BR4 199 H3
odhew Rd CROY/NA CR0 197 H3
oding Cl NWMAL KT3 191 K1
odinge Cl HOLWY N7 84 E3
odinge Rd HOLWY N7 84 E4
odman Ct ALP/SUD HA0 * 79 K2
odman Crs
BRXS/STRHM SW2 161 J4
CROY/NA CR0 196 C3
odman Rd LEY E10 70 A4
odmans Ct ALP/SUD HA0 79 K2
odman's Yd TWRH EC3N 13 J5
odmayes Av
GDMY/SEVK IG3 73 G5
odmayes La
GDMY/SEVK IG3 91 G2
odmayes Rd
GDMY/SEVK IG3 73 G5
odmead Rd ORP BR6 202 B4
odrich Rd EDUL SE22 163 G1
dson Rd WLSDN NW10 81 G5
ds Wy CAMTN NW1 4 E2
dway Gdns POP/IOD E14 106 B5
dwin Cl BERM/RHTH SE16 19 K5
MTCM CR4 178 C6
dwin Dr SCUP DA14 168 E4
dwin Gdns CROY/NA CR0 211 H4
dwin Rd CROY/NA CR0 211 H3
D N9 36 E3
HB W12 118 D2
dwins Ct CHCR WC2N 10 E5
dwin St FSBYPK N4 67 G6
dwood Cl MRDN SM4 193 K1
dwood Dr NTHLT UB5 78 A4
dwood Pde BECK BR3 * 198 B1
dwood Rd NWCR SE14 144 B1
dwyn Av MLHL NW7 45 G1
dwyn's V MUSWH N10 48 A4
dyers Gdns HDN NW4 64 B2
sander Wy THMD SE28 127 J3
seacre La
N/HRWW/WS HA3 61 K2
e Green Cl
MC/STPC BR5 186 B5
seley La EHAM E6 108 A2
ssens Cl SUT SM1 209 G3
ir La CANST EC4R * 12 E5
Gopsall St IS N1 7 F1
Gordon Av CHING E4 52 C2
HCH RM12 75 H6
MORT/ESHN SW14 138 B5
STAN HA7 43 F2
TWK TW1 136 B6
Gordonbrock Rd BROCKY SE4 144 D6
Gordon Cl WALTH E17 69 J3
Gordon Cots KENS W8 * 119 K2
Gordon Crs CROY/NA CR0 197 F5
HYS/HAR UB3 113 K4
Gordondale Rd
WIM/MER SW19 159 K4
Gordon Gdns EDGW HA8 44 D5
Gordon Gv CMBW SE5 142 C3
Gordon Hl ENC/FH EN2 23 J2
Gordon House Rd KTTN NW5 84 A2
Gordon Pl KENS W8 119 K2
Gordon Rd ASHF TW15 152 B5
BARK IG11 90 E6
BECK BR3 182 C6
BELV DA17 129 K4
BFN/LL DA15 147 K6
BRYLDS KT5 191 G4
CAR SM5 209 K4
CHDH RM6 74 B3
CHING E4 38 C2
CHSWK W4 117 J6
EA W5 97 J6
ED N9 36 D4
ENC/FH EN2 23 K2
ESH/CLAY KT10 204 E5
FBAR/BDGN N11 48 D3
FNCH N3 46 D3
HSLW TW3 135 H5
IL IG1 90 D1
KTN/HRWW/WS HA3 42 E6
KUTN/CMB KT2 175 G4
NWDGN UB2 114 D4
PECK SE15 143 J3
RCH/KEW TW9 137 G3
SRTFD E15 88 A2
SWFD E18 53 F4
WAN E11 70 E3
Gordon Sq STPAN WC1H 4 C6
Gordon St PLSTW E13 106 E2
STPAN WC1H 4 C6
Gordon Wy BAR EN5 20 D5
BMLY BR1 183 K4
Gorefield Pl KIL/WHAMP NW6 100 E1
Gore Rd HOM E9 86 E6
RYNPK SW20 177 F5
Goresbrook Rd DAGW RM9 91 J6
Gore St SKENS SW7 120 B3
Gorham Pl NTGHL W11 100 C6
Goring Cl CRW RM5 56 E4
Goring Gdns BCTR RM8 91 J2
Goring Rd DAGE RM10 93 F4
FBAR/BDGN N11 * 48 E2
Goring St HDTCH EC3A 13 H3
Goring Wy GFD/PVL UB6 96 C1
Gorleston Rd
SEVS/STOTM N15 67 K2
Gorleston St WKENS W14 119 H4
Gorman Rd WOOL/PLUM SE18 126 E4
Gorringe Park Av MTCM CR4 179 F3
Gorse Cl CAN/RD E16 106 E5
Gorse Ri TOOT SW17 179 F1
Gorse Rd CROY/NA CR0 213 J1
STMC/STPC BR5 203 H6
Gorseway ROMW/RG RM7 75 G5
Gorst Rd BTSEA SW11 160 E1
WLSDN NW10 98 E3
Gorsuch Pl BETH E2 7 J4
Gorsuch St BETH E2 7 J4
Gosberton Rd BAL SW12 160 E3
Gosbury Hl CHSGTN KT9 206 A2
Gosfield Rd BCTR RM8 74 C5
Gosfield St GTPST W1W 9 K1
Gosford Gdns REDBR IG4 71 K2
Gosforth La OXHEY WD19 26 E5
Gosforth Pth OXHEY WD19 26 E5
Goshawk Gdns YEAD UB4 94 C2
Goslett Yd SOHO/SHAV W1D 10 D3
Gosling Cl GFD/PVL UB6 96 A2
Gosling Wy BRXN/ST SW9 142 B2
Gospatrick Rd TOTM N17 49 J3
Gosport Rd WALTH E17 69 H2
Gosport Wy PECK SE15 143 G1
Gossage Rd
WOOL/PLUM SE18 127 J5
Gosset St BETH E2 104 C2
Gosshill Rd BMLY BR1 185 F5
Gossington Cl CHST BR7 167 G6
Gosterwood St DEPT SE8 124 B6
Gostling Rd WHTN TW2 155 F3
Goston Gdns THHTH CR7 180 B6
Goswell Pl FSBYE EC1V 6 B5
Goswell Rd FSBYE EC1V 6 B4
Gothic Ct HYS/HAR UB3 113 G6
Gothic Rd WHTN TW2 155 J4
Gottfried Ms KTTN NW5 84 C2
Goudhurst Rd BMLY BR1 183 H1
Gough Rd EN EN1 24 D3
SRTFD E15 88 D2
Gough Sq FLST/FETLN EC4A 11 K3
Gough St FSBYW WC1X 5 H6
Goulding Gdns THHTH CR7 180 D5
Gould Rd EBED/NFELT TW14 153 H2
WHTN TW2 155 K3
Gould Ter HACK E8 86 D3
Goulston St WCHPL E1 13 J3
Goulton Rd CLPT E5 86 D3
Gourley Pl SEVS/STOTM N15 68 A2
Gourley St SEVS/STOTM N15 68 A2
Gourock Rd ELTH/MOT SE9 147 F6
Govan St BETH E2 86 C6
Govier Cl SRTFD E15 88 C5
Gowan Av FUL/PGN SW6 139 H2
Gowan Rd WLSDN NW10 81 K5
Gower Cl CLAP SW4 161 H1
Gower Ms GWRST WC1E 10 D2
Gower Pl GWRST WC1E 4 B6
Gower Rd FSTGT E7 88 E4
ISLW TW7 116 A6
Gower St GWRST WC1E 4 C7
Gower's Wk WCHPL E1 104 C5
Gowland Pl BECK BR3 182 C5
Gowlett Rd PECK SE15 143 H4
Gowlland Cl CROY/NA CR0 197 H4
Gowrie Rd BTSEA SW11 141 F4
Graburn Wy E/WMO/HCT KT8 173 J6
Gracechurch St BANK EC3V 13 F5
Grace Cl BARK/HLT IG6 55 F2
EDGW HA8 44 E3
ELTH/MOT SE9 166 C5
Gracedale Rd
STRHM/NOR SW16 179 G1
Gracefield Gdns
STRHM/NOR SW16 161 K5
Grace Jones Cl HACK E8 86 B4
Grace Pl BOW E3 105 K2
Grace Rd CROY/NA CR0 196 D3
Graces Aly WCHPL E1 * 104 C6
Graces Ms STJWD NW8 * 101 G1
Grace's Ms CMBW SE5 142 E3
Grace's Rd CMBW SE5 143 F3
Grace St BOW E3 105 K2
The Gradient SYD SE26 163 H6
Graduate Pl STHWK SE1 19 G4
Graeme Rd EN EN1 24 A3
Graemesdyke Av
MORT/ESHN SW14 137 J4
Grafton Cl HSLWW TW4 154 D3
WEA W13 97 G5
WPK KT4 207 G1
Grafton Ct EBED/NFELT TW14 153 G3
Grafton Crs CAMTN NW1 84 B4
Grafton Gdns BCTR RM8 74 A6
FSBYPK N4 67 J3
Grafton Ms FITZ W1T 4 A7
Grafton Park Rd WPK KT4 192 B6
Grafton Pl CAMTN NW1 4 C5
Grafton Rd ACT W3 98 E6
BCTR RM8 74 A6
CROY/NA CR0 196 B5
ENC/FH EN2 23 F4
HRW HA1 60 C2
KTTN NW5 84 A3
NWMAL KT3 192 B1
WPK KT4 207 F1
Grafton Sq CLAP SW4 141 H4
Grafton St CONDST W1S 9 K6
Grafton Ter HAMP NW3 83 K3
Grafton Wy E/WMO/HCT KT8 188 E1
FITZ W1T 10 A1
Grafton Yd KTTN NW5 84 B4
Graham Av MTCM CR4 179 F4
WEA W13 116 C2
Graham Cl CROY/NA CR0 198 D6
Grahame Park Wy MLHL NW7 45 G3
Graham Gdns SURB KT6 191 F5
Graham Rd CHSWK W4 118 A3
HACK E8 86 C4
HDN NW4 63 K3
HPTN TW12 155 F6
KTN/HRWW/WS HA3 42 E6
MTCM CR4 179 F4
PLSTW E13 106 E3
SEVS/STOTM N15 49 H6
WIM/MER SW19 177 J3
Graham St IS N1 6 B3
Graham Ter BFN/LL DA15 * 168 C1
BGVA SW1W 15 G7
Grainger Cl NTHLT UB5 78 C3
Grainger Rd ISLW TW7 136 A3
WDGN N22 49 J4
Gramer Cl WAN E11 70 B6
Grampian Cl BELMT SM2 209 G5
HYS/HAR UB3 133 G1
ORP BR6 202 A3
Grampian Gdns CRICK NW2 64 C5
Gramsci Wy CAT SE6 164 E5
Granada St TOOT SW17 178 E1
Granard Av PUT/ROE SW15 138 E6
Granard Rd BTSEA SW11 160 E2
Granary Cl ED N9 36 E2
Granary Rd WCHPL E1 104 D3
Granary Sq IS N1 85 G4
Granary St CAMTN NW1 4 C1
Granby Rd ELTH/MOT SE9 146 E3
WOOL/PLUM SE18 127 G3
Granby St BETH E2 7 K6
Granby Ter CAMTN NW1 4 A3
Grand Av BRYLDS KT5 191 J3
FARR EC1M 12 B1
MUSWH N10 66 A1
WBLY HA9 80 C3
Grand Av East WBLY HA9 80 D3
Grand Depot Rd
WOOL/PLUM SE18 127 F5
Grand Dr NWDGN UB2 115 H2
RYNPK SW20 193 F1
Granden Rd
STRHM/NOR SW16 * 179 K5
Grandison Rd BTSEA SW11 140 E6
WPK KT4 193 F6
Grand Junction Whf IS N1 * 6 C3
Grand Pde FSBYPK N4 * 67 H3
MORT/ESHN SW14 * 137 K5
SURB KT6 * 191 H5
WBLY HA9 * 62 D6
Grand Union Canal Wk
NTHLT UB5 95 K3
Grand Union Cl MV/WKIL W9 100 D4
Grand Union Crs HACK E8 * 86 C6
Grand Union Wk
CAMTN NW1 * 84 B5
Grand Wk WCHPL E1 * 105 G3
Granfield St BTSEA SW11 * 140 C2
Grange Av EBAR EN4 33 J3
KTN/HRWW/WS HA3 43 H5
NFNCH/WDSPK N12 47 G1
SNWD SE25 181 F5
TRDG/WHET N20 32 C2
WFD IG8 52 E2
WHTN TW2 155 K4
Grangecliffe Gdns
SNWD SE25 181 F5
Grange Cl BFN/LL DA15 168 B2
E/WMO/HCT KT8 189 G1
HEST TW5 114 E5
HYS/HAR UB3 94 C4
WFD IG8 52 E3
Grange Ct ALP/SUD HA0 * 79 J3
BELMT SM2 * 209 F5
HRW HA1 * 79 F1
NTHLT UB5 95 G1
PIN HA5 * 41 J6
WLGTN SM6 * 210 B1
Grangecourt Rd
STNW/STAM N16 68 A5
Grange Crs CHIG IG7 54 D1
THMD SE28 109 J5
Grangedale Cl NTHWD HA6 40 C4
Grange Dr CHST BR7 184 D2
ORP BR6 217 J6
Grange Farm Cl
RYLN/HDSTN HA2 60 C6
Grange Gdns HAMP NW3 83 F1
PIN HA5 59 K1
SNWD SE25 181 F5
STHGT/OAK N14 34 D3
Grange Gv IS N1 85 J4
Grange Hl EDGW HA8 44 E1
SNWD SE25 181 F5
Grangehill Pl ELTH/MOT SE9 146 E4
Grangehill Rd ELTH/MOT SE9 146 E5
Grange Houses HBRY N5 * 85 J2
Grange La DUL SE21 163 G4
Grange Ms FELT TW13 * 153 G5
Grangemill Rd CAT SE6 164 D5
Grangemill Wy CAT SE6 164 D4
Grange Pk EA W5 117 F1
Grange Park Av WCHMH N21 35 H1
Grange Park Pl RYNPK SW20 176 E3
Grange Park Rd LEY E10 69 K5
THHTH CR7 180 E6
Grange Pl KIL/WHAMP NW6 82 E5
Grange Rd BARN SW13 138 D2
BELMT SM2 208 E5
CHSGTN KT9 206 A2
CHSWK W4 117 J5
E/WMO/HCT KT8 189 G1
EA W5 116 E1
EDGW HA8 45 F2
HARH RM3 57 K2
HGT N6 66 A3
HRW HA1 61 G3
HYS/HAR UB3 94 C5
IL IG1 90 C2
KUT/HW KT1 175 F6
LEY E10 69 J5
ORP BR6 201 H6
PLSTW E13 106 D2
RYLN/HDSTN HA2 60 D6
SNWD SE25 196 E1
STHL UB1 114 D2
STHWK SE1 19 H5
TOTM N17 50 C2
WALTH E17 69 G2
WLSDN NW10 81 K4
Granger Wy ROM RM1 75 J3
Grange St IS N1 7 F1
The Grange ALP/SUD HA0 80 C5
CROY/NA CR0 198 C6
NWMAL KT3 * 192 D2
STHWK SE1 19 J4
WIM/MER SW19 177 G2
WKENS W14 * 119 J4
WOT/HER KT12 188 A6
WPK KT4 207 F2
Grange V BELMT SM2 209 F5
Grangeview Rd
TRDG/WHET N20 33 G3
Grange Wk STHWK SE1 19 H4
Grange Walk Ms STHWK SE1 19 H5
Grangeway KIL/WHAMP NW6 82 E5
NFNCH/WDSPK N12 33 F6
WFD IG8 39 G6
Grangeway Gdns REDBR IG4 71 J2
The Grangeway WCHMH N21 35 H1
Grangewood BXLY DA5 169 G3
Grangewood Cl PIN HA5 58 E2
Grangewood La BECK BR3 182 C2
Grangewood St EHAM E6 89 H6
Grange Yd STHWK SE1 19 J5
Granham Gdns ED N9 36 B4
Granite St WOOL/PLUM SE18 128 A5
Granleigh Rd WAN E11 70 C6
Gransden Av HACK E8 86 D5
Gransden Rd SHB W12 118 C2
Grantbridge St IS N1 6 B2
Grantchester KUT/HW KT1 * 175 H5
Grantchester Cl HRW HA1 79 F1
Grant Cl STHGT/OAK N14 34 C2
TOTM N17 50 A5
Grantham Cl EDGW HA8 30 A5
Grantham Gdns CHDH RM6 74 B3
Grantham Pl
MYFR/PKLN W1K 15 J1
Grantham Rd BRXN/ST SW9 141 K4
CHSWK W4 138 B1
MNPK E12 90 A1
Grantley Pl ESH/CLAY KT10 204 B3
Grantley Rd HSLWW TW4 134 B3
Grantley St WCHPL E1 105 F2
Grantock Rd WALTH E17 52 B4
Granton Rd GDMY/SEVK IG3 73 G5
SCUP DA14 186 C2
STRHM/NOR SW16 179 H4
Grant Pl CROY/NA CR0 197 G5
Grant Rd BTSEA SW11 140 C4
CROY/NA CR0 197 G5
KTN/HRWW/WS HA3 42 E6
Grants Cl MLHL NW7 46 A3
Grant St IS N1 5 J2
PLSTW E13 106 E2
Grant Ter STNW/STAM N16 * 68 C4
Grantully Rd MV/WKIL W9 101 F2
Grant Wy ISLW TW7 116 B6
Granville Ar BRXN/ST SW9 * 142 B5
Granville Av ED N9 36 E5
FELT TW13 153 K4
HSLW TW3 135 F6
Granville Cl CROY/NA CR0 197 F6
Granville Gdns EA W5 117 G1
STRHM/NOR SW16 180 A4
Granville Gv LEW SE13 145 F4
Granville Ms SCUP DA14 168 B6
Granville Pk LEW SE13 145 F4
Granville Pl FUL/PGN SW6 * 140 A1
MBLAR W1H 9 G4
NFNCH/WDSPK N12 * 47 G3
PIN HA5 41 H6
Granville Rd BAR EN5 20 A5
CEND/HSY/T N8 67 F3
CRICK NW2 64 D6
HYS/HAR UB3 113 J4
IL IG1 72 B5
KIL/WHAMP NW6 100 E1
NFNCH/WDSPK N12 47 G3
PLMGR N13 49 F2
SCUP DA14 168 B6
SWFD E18 53 F5
WALTH E17 69 K3
WAND/EARL SW18 159 J2
WDGN N22 49 H4
WELL DA16 148 D4
WIM/MER SW19 177 K3
Granville Sq PECK SE15 * 143 F1
Granville St FSBYW WC1X 5 H5
Grape St LSQ/SEVD WC2H 10 E3
Graphite Sq LBTH SE11 * 122 A5
Grapsome Cl CHSGTN KT9 205 J5
Grasdene Rd
WOOL/PLUM SE18 148 B1
Grasgarth Cl ACT W3 98 E6
Grasmere Av ACT W3 98 E6
HSLW TW3 155 G1
ORP BR6 216 B1
PUT/ROE SW15 158 A6
RSLP HA4 58 A4
WBLY HA9 61 K4
WIM/MER SW19 177 K6
Grasmere Cl
EBED/NFELT TW14 153 J3
Grasmere Ct WDGN N22 49 F2
Grasmere Gdns
KTN/HRWW/WS HA3 43 G5
ORP BR6 216 B1
REDBR IG4 71 J2
Grasmere Rd BMLY BR1 183 J4
BXLYHN DA7 149 K2
MUSWH N10 48 B4
ORP BR6 216 B1
PLSTW E13 106 E1
SNWD SE25 197 J3
STRHM/NOR SW16 180 A1
TOTM N17 50 C2
Grasshaven Wy THMD SE28 128 A1
Grassington Cl
FBAR/BDGN N11 48 A2
Grassington Rd SCUP DA14 168 B6
Grassmount FSTH SE23 163 J4
Grass Pk FNCH N3 46 D4
Grassway WLGTN SM6 210 C2
Grasvenor Av BAR EN5 32 E1
Grately Wy PECK SE15 * 143 F1
Gratton Rd WKENS W14 119 H3
Gratton Ter CRICK NW2 82 B1
Gravel Hl CROY/NA CR0 213 F4
FNCH N3 46 D5
Gravel Hill Cl BXLYHS DA6 169 J1
Gravel La WCHPL E1 13 J3
Gravel Pit Wy ORP BR6 202 B6
Gravel Rd HAYES BR2 200 D6
WHTN TW2 155 K3
Gravelwood Cl CHST BR7 167 H5
Gravenel Gdns TOOT SW17 * 178 D1
Graveney Gv PGE/AN SE20 181 K3
Graveney Rd TOOT SW17 160 D6
Gravesend Rd SHB W12 99 J6
Gray Av BCTR RM8 74 B5
Gray Gdns RAIN RM13 93 J4
Grayham Crs NWMAL KT3 192 A1
Grayham Rd NWMAL KT3 192 A1
Grayland Cl BMLY BR1 184 C4
Grayling Cl CAN/RD E16 106 C3
Grayling Ct EA W5 * 116 E1
Grayling Rd STNW/STAM N16 67 K6
Grayling Sq BETH E2 * 104 C2
Grays Cots STMC/STPC BR5 * 186 D4
Grayscroft Rd
STRHM/NOR SW16 179 J3
Grays Farm Rd
STMC/STPC BR5 186 C4
Grayshott Rd BTSEA SW11 141 F4
Gray's Inn Rd FSBYW WC1X 5 F4
Gray's Inn Sq GINN WC1R 11 J1
Grays La ASHF TW15 152 E6
Grayswood Gdns
RYNPK SW20 176 E5
Gray's Yd MHST W1U * 9 H4
Graywood Ct
NFNCH/WDSPK N12 47 G3
Grazebrook Rd
STNW/STAM N16 67 K6
Great Amwell La
CEND/HSY/T N8 49 F6
Great Benty WDR/YW UB7 112 B4
Great Brownings DUL SE21 163 G6
Great Bushey Dr
TRDG/WHET N20 33 F3
Great Cambridge Jct
PLMGR N13 49 J1
Great Cambridge Rd ED N9 35 K5
EN EN1 24 C2
UED N18 49 K1
Great Castle St REGST W1B 10 A3
Great Central Av RSLP HA4 77 G3
Great Central St CAMTN NW1 8 E1
Great Central Wy WBLY HA9 80 E3
Great Chapel St
SOHO/SHAV W1D 10 C3
Great Chart St BTSEA SW11 140 B4
Great Chertsey Rd
CHSWK W4 138 A2
FELT TW13 154 E5
Great Church La HMSMTH W6 119 G5
Great College St WEST SW1P 16 E4
Great Cross Av GNWCH SE10 145 H1
Great Cullings
ROMW/RG RM7 75 G6
Great Cumberland Ms
MBLAR W1H 8 E4
Great Cumberland Pl
MBLAR W1H 8 E3
Great Dover St STHWK SE1 18 E4
Greatdown Rd HNWL W7 97 F4
Great Eastern Rd SRTFD E15 88 B5
Great Eastern St SDTCH EC2A 7 G5
Great Eastern Whf
BTSEA SW11 140 D1
Great Elms Rd HAYES BR2 200 B1
Great Fld CDALE/KGS NW9 45 G4
Greatfield Av EHAM E6 107 K3
Greatfield Cl ARCH N19 84 C2
BROCKY SE4 144 D5
Greatfields Rd BARK IG11 90 D6

Great Galley Cl BARK IG11 109 H2
Great Gardens Rd
EMPK RM11 75 K3
Great Gatton Cl CROY/NA CR0 198 B4
Great George St STJSPK SW1H 16 D3
Great Guildford St
STHWK SE1 18 C1
Great Harry Dr ELTH/MOT SE9 167 F5
Great James St BMSBY WC1N 11 G1
Great Marlborough St
REGST W1B 10 A4
Great Maze Pond STHWK SE1 19 F1
Great New St
FLST/FETLN EC4A * 11 K3
Great North Rd BAR EN5 20 D3
EFNCH N2 65 J1
Great North Way (Barnet By-Pass) HDN NW4 45 K4
Greatorex St WCHPL E1 104 C4
Great Ormond St
BMSBY WC1N 11 F1
Great Percy St FSBYW WC1X 5 H4
Great Peter St WEST SW1P 16 C5
Great Portland St
GTPST W1W 9 K1
Great Pulteney St
SOHO/CST W1F 10 B5
Great Queen St
HOL/ALD WC2B 11 F3
Great Russell St RSQ WC1B 10 D3
Great St Thomas Apostle
BLKFR EC4V 12 D5
Great Scotland Yd
WHALL SW1A 16 E1
Great Smith St WEST SW1P 16 D4
Great South-West Rd
EBED/NFELT TW14 153 F2
HSLWW TW4 134 A3
Great Spilmans EDUL SE22 143 F6
Great Strd CDALE/KGS NW9 45 H5
Great Suffolk St STHWK SE1 18 B1
Great Sutton St FSBYE EC1V 6 B7
Great Swan Aly LOTH EC2R 12 E3
Great Thrift STMC/STPC BR5 201 H1
Great Titchfield St
GTPST W1W 9 K1
Great Tower St MON EC3R 13 G5
Great Trinity La BLKFR EC4V 12 D5
Great Turnstile HHOL WC1V * 11 H2
Great Western Rd
NTGHL W11 100 D4
Great West Rd BTFD TW8 136 B1
HEST TW5 134 D3
HMSMTH W6 118 E5
ISLW TW7 135 K1
Great West Road Chiswick
CHSWK W4 118 C5
Great West Road Ellesmere Rd
CHSWK W4 117 K6
Great West Road Hogarth La
CHSWK W4 118 A6
Great Winchester St
OBST EC2N 13 F3
Great Windmill St
SOHO/SHAV W1D 10 C6
Greatwood CHST BR7 185 F3
Greaves Cl BARK IG11 90 D5
Greaves Cots POP/IOD E14 * 105 G4
Greaves Pl TOOT SW17 160 D6
Grebe Av YEAD UB4 95 H5
Grebe Cl BARK IG11 109 G3
FSTGT E7 88 D3
WALTH E17 51 G3
Grebe Ct SUT SM1 208 D3
Grebe Ter KUT/HW KT1 * 175 F6
Grecian Crs NRWD SE19 180 C2
Greek St SOHO/SHAV W1D 10 D4
Greenacre Cl BAR EN5 20 D1
NTHLT UB5 77 K3
Greenacre Gdns WALTH E17 70 A1
Greenacre Pl WLGTN SM6 195 G6
Greenacres BUSH WD23 28 D4
Green Acres CROY/NA CR0 212 B1
Greenacres ELTH/MOT SE9 167 F1
Green Acres SCUP DA14 * 168 A6
Greenacres Cl ORP BR6 216 C2
Greenacres Dr STAN HA7 43 H3
Greenacre Sq
BERM/RHTH SE16 * 124 A2
Greenacre Wk
STHGT/OAK N14 34 D5
Green Arbour Ct STP EC4M 12 A3
Green Av MLHL NW7 31 F6
WEA W13 116 C3
Greenaway Av UED N18 * 51 F1
Greenaway Gdns HAMP NW3 83 F2
Green Bank
NFNCH/WDSPK N12 33 F6
WAP E1W 123 J1
Greenbank Av ALP/SUD HA0 79 G3
Greenbank Cl CHING E4 38 A4
Greenbank Crs HDN NW4 64 C1
Greenbay Rd CHARL SE7 146 C1
Greenberry St STJWD NW8 2 C3
Greenbrook Av EBAR EN4 21 G2
Green Chain Wk ABYW SE2 128 C6
BELV DA17 129 G4
BMLY BR1 184 A2
CHARL SE7 126 C4
CHST BR7 184 E1
ELTH/MOT SE9 147 G5
ELTH/MOT SE9 166 D2
ELTH/MOT SE9 167 G1
ERITHM DA18 128 E3
LEE/GVPK SE12 166 B4
SYD SE26 182 A2
WELL DA16 147 H3
WELL DA16 148 B2
WOOL/PLUM SE18 126 E6
WOOL/PLUM SE18 127 H6
WOOL/PLUM SE18 146 E1
WOOL/PLUM SE18 147 F2
Green Cl CAR SM5 194 E6
CDALE/KGS NW9 62 E3
FELT TW13 172 D1
GLDGN NW11 65 G4
HAYES BR2 183 H6
Greencoat Pl WEST SW1P 16 B6
Greencoat Rw WEST SW1P 16 B5
Green Court Av CROY/NA CR0 197 J6
Greencourt Av EDGW HA8 44 C4
Green Court Gdns
CROY/NA CR0 197 J6
Greencourt Rd
STMC/STPC BR5 201 K2
Greencroft EDGW HA8 44 E1
Greencroft Av RSLP HA4 59 G6
Greencroft Gdns EN EN1 24 A4
KIL/WHAMP NW6 83 F5
Greencroft Rd HEST TW5 134 E2
Green Dl EDUL SE22 143 F6
Green Dragon La BTFD TW8 117 F5
WCHMH N21 23 F6
Green Dragon Yd WCHPL E1 104 C4
Green Dr STHL UB1 115 F1
Green End CHSGTN KT9 205 K2
WCHMH N21 35 H4
Greenend Rd CHSWK W4 118 B2
Green Farm Cl ORP BR6 217 F3
Greenfell Man DEPT SE8 * 124 C5
Greenfield Av BRYLDS KT5 191 J3
OXHEY WD19 27 J4
Greenfield Ct ELTH/MOT SE9 166 D5
Greenfield Dr BMLY BR1 184 B5
EFNCH N2 65 K1
Greenfield Gdns CRICK NW2 64 C6
DAGW RM9 91 J6
STMC/STPC BR5 201 H4
Greenfield Rd DAGW RM9 91 J6
SEVS/STOTM N15 68 A2
WCHPL E1 104 C4
Greenfields STHL UB1 96 A6
Greenfield Wy
RYLN/HDSTN HA2 42 B6
Greenford Av HNWL W7 96 E5
STHL UB1 95 K6
Greenford Gdns
GFD/PVL UB6 96 B2
Greenford Rd STHL UB1 96 C6
SUT SM1 209 F2
Green Gdns ORP BR6 216 C3
Greengate GFD/PVL UB6 79 H4
Greengate St PLSTW E13 107 F1
Greenhalgh Wk EFNCH N2 65 G1
Greenham Cl STHWK SE1 17 J3
Greenham Crs CHING E4 51 H2
Greenham Rd MUSWH N10 48 A5
Greenhaven Dr THMD SE28 109 H5
Greenheys Cl NTHWD HA6 40 C4
Greenheys Dr SWFD E18 52 D6
Greenhill BKHH IG9 39 G3
HAMP NW3 83 H2
SUT SM1 194 B6
WBLY HA9 62 D6
Green Hl WOOL/PLUM SE18 126 E5
Greenhill Ct BAR EN5 * 21 F6
Greenhill Crs WATW WD18 26 C1
Greenhill Gdns NTHLT UB5 95 K1
Greenhill Gv MNPK E12 89 J2
Greenhill Pde BAR EN5 * 21 F6
Greenhill Pk BAR EN5 21 F6
WLSDN NW10 81 G6
Greenhill Rd HRW HA1 60 E3
WLSDN NW10 81 G6
Greenhill's Rents
FARR EC1M * 12 A1
Greenhills Ter IS N1 85 K4
Greenhill Ter NTHLT UB5 * 95 K1
WOOL/PLUM SE18 126 E5
Greenhill Wy HRW HA1 60 E3
WBLY HA9 62 D6
Greenhithe Cl BFN/LL DA15 167 K2
Greenholm Rd ELTH/MOT SE9 147 G6
Green Hundred Rd PECK SE15 123 H6
Greenhurst Rd WNWD SE27 180 B1
Greenland Crs NWDGN UB2 114 B3
Greenland Ms DEPT SE8 124 A5
Greenland Pl CAMTN NW1 * 84 B6
Greenland Quay
BERM/RHTH SE16 124 A4
Greenland Rd BAR EN5 32 A1
CAMTN NW1 84 B6
Greenlands HOR/WEW KT19 206 D3
Greenland St CAMTN NW1 * 84 B6
Greenland Wy CROY/NA CR0 195 J4
Green La BCTR RM8 74 A6
CHSGTN KT9 206 A6
E/WMO/HCT KT8 189 G2
EDGW HA8 30 B6
ELTH/MOT SE9 167 F3
ELTH/MOT SE9 167 G6
FELT TW13 172 D1
GDMY/SEVK IG3 73 G6
HDN NW4 64 B2
HNWL W7 115 K2
HSLWW TW4 134 B6
IL IG1 72 D6
MRDN SM4 193 K3
NTHWD HA6 40 B3
NWMAL KT3 191 K2
OXHEY WD19 27 G3
PGE/AN SE20 182 A3
STAN HA7 29 H6
THHTH CR7 180 C4
UX/CGN UB8 94 A4
WPK KT4 192 D5
Green Lane Cots STAN HA7 * 29 H6
Green Lane Gdns THHTH CR7 180 D5
Green Lanes FSBYPK N4 67 H3
HBRY N5 85 J1
HOR/WEW KT19 207 G6
PLMGR N13 49 F1
SEVS/STOTM N15 67 H1
WCHMH N21 35 J2
Greenlaw Ct EA W5 * 97 K5
Greenlaw Gdns NWMAL KT3 192 C4
Greenlawn La BTFD TW8 116 E4
Green Lawns
NFNCH/WDSPK N12 * 47 F2
RSLP HA4 * 59 G5
Greenlaw St
WOOL/PLUM SE18 127 F3
Green Leaf Av WLGTN SM6 210 D2
Greenleaf Cl
BRXS/STRHM SW2 * 162 B2
Greenleafe Dr BARK/HLT IG6 54 B6
Greenleaf Rd EHAM E6 89 G6
WALTH E17 51 H6
Greenleaf Wy
KTN/HRWW/WS HA3 43 F6
Greenlea Pk
WIM/MER SW19 * 178 D4
Greenleigh Av
STMC/STPC BR5 202 C1
Greenlink Wk RCH/KEW TW9 137 J2
Green Man La
EBED/NFELT TW14 133 K5
WEA W13 97 G6
Greenman St IS N1 85 J5
Greenmead Cl SNWD SE25 197 H2
Green Moor Link
WCHMH N21 35 H2
Greenmoor Rd PEND EN3 24 E3
Greenoak Pl EBAR EN4 21 K3
Green Oaks NWDGN UB2 * 114 C4
Greenoak Wy
WIM/MER SW19 159 G6
Greenock Rd ACT W3 117 J3
STRHM/NOR SW16 179 J4
Greenock Wy ROM RM1 57 G3
Green Pde HSLW TW3 * 155 G1
Greenpark Wy GFD/PVL UB6 78 E6
Green Pond Cl WALTH E17 51 G6
Green Pond Rd WALTH E17 51 G6
Green Ride CHING E4 38 E1
Green Rd TRDG/WHET N20 33 G5
Greenroof Wy GNWCH SE10 125 J3
Greens Ct NTGHL W11 * 119 J1
Green's Ct SOHO/CST W1F 10 C5
Greens End
WOOL/PLUM SE18 127 G4
Greenshank Cl WALTH E17 51 G3
Greenside BCTR RM8 73 J6
BXLY DA5 169 F3
Greenside Cl CAT SE6 165 G4
TRDG/WHET N20 33 H4
Greenside Rd CROY/NA CR0 196 B4
SHB W12 118 D3
Greenslade Rd BARK IG11 90 D5
Greenstead Av WFD IG8 53 G2
Greenstead Gdns
PUT/ROE SW15 138 D6
WFD IG8 53 G2
Greensted Rd LOU IG10 39 J2
Greenstone Ms WAN E11 70 E3
Green St FSTGT E7 89 F3
MYFR/PKLN W1K 9 F5
PEND EN3 24 E3
Greenstreet Hl NWCR SE14 * 144 A4
Greensward BUSH WD23 28 B1
Green Ter CLKNW EC1R 5 K5
The Green ACT W3 99 G5
BKHH IG9 * 39 F3
CAR SM5 * 210 A2
CROY/NA CR0 213 H6
ED N9 36 C4
FELT TW13 154 A4
HEST TW5 115 F6
HGDN/ICK UB10 58 A6
HRW HA1 61 G6
MRDN SM4 193 H1
NWDGN UB2 114 E2
NWMAL KT3 175 K6
RCH/KEW TW9 136 E6
SCUP DA14 186 B1
SRTFD E15 88 D4
STHGT/OAK N14 34 D4
STMC/STPC BR5 186 C3
SUT SM1 209 F1
TOTM N17 49 J2
WAN E11 71 F3
WCHMH N21 35 G2
WDR/YW UB7 112 A3
WELL DA16 147 K5
WHTN TW2 155 K3
WIM/MER SW19 177 G1
WLGTN SM6 195 F6
Green V BXLYHS DA6 148 E6
EA W5 98 B5
Greenvale Rd ELTH/MOT SE9 146 E5
Green Verges STAN HA7 43 K3
Green Vw CHSGTN KT9 206 B5
Greenview Av BECK BR3 198 B3
Greenview Cl ACT W3 118 B1
Green Wk HDN NW4 64 B1
NWDGN UB2 115 F5
RSLP HA4 58 D5
STHWK SE1 19 G5
WFD IG8 53 J2
The Green Wk CHING E4 38 A3
Greenway BCTR RM8 73 J6
CHST BR7 185 F1
Green Wy ELTH/MOT SE9 146 C6
HAYES BR2 200 D3
Greenway
KTN/HRWW/WS HA3 62 A2
PIN HA5 41 F5
RYNPK SW20 193 F1
STHGT/OAK N14 34 E4
TRDG/WHET N20 32 E4
WLGTN SM6 210 C2
YEAD UB4 95 F3
Greenway Av WALTH E17 70 B1
Greenway Cl
SEVS/STOTM N15 68 B1
CDALE/KGS NW9 45 F5
FBAR/BDGN N11 48 A2
FSBYPK N4 67 J6
TRDG/WHET N20 32 E4
Greenway Ct IL IG1 72 A5
SRTFD E15 106 C1
Greenway Gdns
CDALE/KGS NW9 44 E5
CROY/NA CR0 213 H1
GFD/PVL UB6 96 A2
Green Way Gdns
KTN/HRWW/WS HA3 42 E5
Greenways BECK BR3 182 D5
ESH/CLAY KT10 204 E2
NFNCH/WDSPK N12 * 47 G2
The Greenways TWK TW1 * 156 B1
The Green Wy
KTN/HRWW/WS HA3 42 E4
The Greenway
CDALE/KGS NW9 45 F5
HSLWW TW4 * 134 E5
PIN HA5 59 K3
Greenwell St GTPST W1W 3 K7
Greenwich Church St
GNWCH SE10 * 125 F6
Greenwich Crs EHAM E6 107 J4
Greenwich Foot Tnl
GNWCH SE10 125 F5
Greenwich Hts CHARL SE7 * 146 D1
Greenwich High Rd
GNWCH SE10 144 E1
Greenwich House LEW SE13 165 G1
Greenwich Park St
GNWCH SE10 * 125 G6
Greenwich Quay DEPT SE8 124 E6
Greenwich South St
GNWCH SE10 144 E2
Greenwich Vw POP/IOD E14 124 E3
Greenwood Av DAGE RM10 92 D2
PEND EN3 25 F2
Greenwood Cl BFN/LL DA15 168 B4
MRDN SM4 193 H1
STMC/STPC BR5 201 K3
THDIT KT7 190 B5
Greenwood Dr CHING E4 52 A1
Greenwood Gdns
BARK/HLT IG6 54 C3
PLMGR N13 35 H5
Greenwood La HPTN TW12 173 G1
Greenwood Pk
KUTN/CMB KT2 176 B3
Greenwood Pl KTTN NW5 84 B3
Greenwood Rd CROY/NA CR0 196 C4
HACK E8 86 C3
ISLW TW7 135 K4
MTCM CR4 179 J6
PLSTW E13 106 D1
THDIT KT7 190 B5
Greenwood Ter
WLSDN NW10 * 81 F6
Green Wrythe Crs CAR SM5 194 D5
Green Wrythe La CAR SM5 194 C3
Green Yd FSBYW WC1X 5 H6
Greer Rd KTN/HRWW/WS HA3 42 C4
Greet St STHWK SE1 17 K1
Greg Cl LEY E10 70 A3
Gregory Crs ELTH/MOT SE9 166 C2
Gregory Pl KENS W8 120 A2
Gregory Rd CHDH RM6 73 K1
NWDGN UB2 115 F3
Greig Cl CEND/HSY/T N8 66 E2
Greig Ter WALW SE17 122 C6
Grenaby Av CROY/NA CR0 196 E4
Grenaby Rd CROY/NA CR0 196 E4
Grenada Rd BKHTH/KID SE3 146 B1
Grenade St POP/IOD E14 105 H6
Grenadier St CAN/RD E16 127 F1
Grena Gdns RCH/KEW TW9 137 G5
Grenard Cl PECK SE15 * 143 H1
Grena Rd RCH/KEW TW9 137 G5
Grendon Gdns WBLY HA9 62 C6
Grendon St STJWD NW8 2 C6
Grenfell Av HCH RM12 75 H5
Grenfell Ct MLHL NW7 * 45 K2
Grenfell Gdns
KTN/HRWW/WS HA3 62 A4
Grenfell Rd NTGHL W11 100 B6
TOOT SW17 178 E2
Grennell Cl SUT SM1 194 C6
Grennell Rd SUT SM1 194 B6
Grenoble Gdns PLMGR N13 49 G2
Grenville Cl BRYLDS KT5 191 K5
FNCH N3 46 D4
Grenville Gdns WFD IG8 53 G3
Grenville Ms ARCH N19 66 E5
HPTN TW12 173 G1
Grenville Pl MLHL NW7 45 F1
SKENS SW7 * 120 B3
Grenville Rd ARCH N19 66 E5
CROY/NA CR0 214 A6
Grenville St BMSBY WC1N 5 F7
Gresham Av TRDG/WHET N20 33 K6
Gresham Cl BXLY DA5 169 F1
ENC/FH EN2 23 J4
Gresham Dr CHDH RM6 73 H2
Gresham Gdns GLDGN NW11 64 C5
Gresham Rd BECK BR3 182 B5
BRXN/ST SW9 142 B4
CAN/RD E16 107 F5
EDGW HA8 44 B2
EHAM E6 107 K1
HPTN TW12 173 F2
HSLW TW3 135 H2
SNWD SE25 * 197 H1
WLSDN NW10 81 F3
Gresham St CITYW EC2V 12 C3
Gresham Wy WIM/MER SW19 159 K5
Gresley Cl SEVS/STOTM N15 * 67 K1
WALTH E17 69 G3
Gresley Rd ARCH N19 66 C5
Gressenhall Rd
WAND/EARL SW18 159 J1
Gresse St FITZ W1T 10 C2
Gresswell Cl SCUP DA14 168 B5
Greswell St FUL/PGN SW6 139 G2
Gretton Rd TOTM N17 50 A3
Greville Cl TWK TW1 156 C2
Greville Ms KIL/WHAMP NW6 83 F6
Greville Pl KIL/WHAMP NW6 101 F1
Greville Rd KIL/WHAMP NW6 101 F1
RCHPK/HAM TW10 157 G1
WALTH E17 70 A1
Greville St HCIRC EC1N 11 K2
Grey Cl GLDGN NW11 65 G3
Greycoat Pl WEST SW1P 16 C5
Greycoat St WEST SW1P 16 C5
Greycot Rd BECK BR3 182 D1
Grey Eagle St WCHPL E1 7 K7
Greyfell Cl STAN HA7 43 H1
Greyhound Hl HDN NW4 45 J6
Greyhound La
STRHM/NOR SW16 179 K2
Greyhound Rd HMSMTH W6 119 G6
SUT SM1 209 G3
TOTM N17 50 A6
WLSDN NW10 99 K2
Greyhound Ter
STRHM/NOR SW16 179 H4
Greyladies Gdns
GNWCH SE10 * 145 F3
Greys Park Cl HAYES BR2 215 G3
Greystead Rd FSTH SE23 163 K2
Greystoke Av PIN HA5 42 A6
Greystoke Cots EA W5 * 98 A3
Greystoke Gdns EA W5 98 A3
ENC/FH EN2 22 D5
Greystone Gdns
BARK/HLT IG6 54 C5
KTN/HRWW/WS HA3 61 J3
Greyswood Av UED N18 * 51 F1
Greyswood St
STRHM/NOR SW16 179 G2
Grierson Rd FSTH SE23 164 B1
Griffin Cl WLSDN NW10 81 K3
Griffin Manor Wy THMD SE28 127 J3
Griffin Rd TOTM N17 50 A5
WOOL/PLUM SE18 127 J5
Griffins Cl WCHMH N21 35 K3
Griffin Wy THMD SE28 127 K3
Griffith Cl CHDH RM6 73 J4
Griffiths Rd WIM/MER SW19 177 K3
Griggs Ap IL IG1 72 C6
Griggs Cl IL IG1 90 E2
Grigg's Pl STHWK SE1 19 H5
Griggs Rd LEY E10 70 A3
Grimsby Gv CAN/RD E16 127 G1
Grimsby St WCHPL E1 7 K7
Grimsdyke Crs BAR EN5 20 A4
Grimsdyke Rd PIN HA5 41 J3
Grimsel Pth CMBW SE5 142 C1
Grimshaw Cl HGT N6 * 66 A4
Grimshaw Wy ROM RM1 75 G2
Grimston Rd FUL/PGN SW6 139 J3
Grimwade Av CROY/NA CR0 212 C1
Grimwade Cl PECK SE15 143 J3
Grimwood Rd TWK TW1 156 A2
Grindall Cl CROY/NA CR0 211 H2
Grindal St STHWK SE1 17 J3
Grindleford Av
FBAR/BDGN N11 34 A4
Grindley Gdns CROY/NA CR0 * 197 G3
Grinling Pl DEPT SE8 124 D6
Grinstead Rd DEPT SE8 124 B5
Grisle Cl ED N9 36 D6
Grittleton Av WBLY HA9 80 D4
Grittleton Rd MV/WKIL W9 100 E3
Grizedale Ter FSTH SE23 163 J4
Grocers' Hall Ct LOTH EC2R * 12 E4
Groombridge Cl WELL DA16 148 B6
Groombridge Rd HOM E9 87 F5
Groom Cl HAYES BR2 200 A1
Groom Crs WAND/EARL SW18 160 C2
Groomfield Cl TOOT SW17 161 F6
Groom Pl KTBR SW1X 15 H4
Grooms Dr PIN HA5 58 E2
Grosmont Rd
WOOL/PLUM SE18 128 A5
Grosse Wy PUT/ROE SW15 158 E1
Grosvenor Av CAR SM5 209 K4
HBRY N5 85 J3
MORT/ESHN SW14 138 B4
RYLN/HDSTN HA2 60 B4
YEAD UB4 94 D1
Grosvenor Br VX/NE SW8 121 G6
Grosvenor Cots KTBR SW1X 15 G6
Grosvenor Crs
CDALE/KGS NW9 62 C
KTBR SW1X 15 H3
Grosvenor Crescent Ms
KTBR SW1X 15 G3
Grosvenor Gdns BGVA SW1W 15 K5
CRICK NW2 82 A4
GLDGN NW11 64 D3
KUTN/CMB KT2 174 E
MORT/ESHN SW14 138 B4
MUSWH N10 48 C
STHGT/OAK N14 22 D
WFD IG8 52 E
WLGTN SM6 210 C
Grosvenor Gardens Ms East
BGVA SW1W * 15 K
Grosvenor Gardens Ms North
BGVA SW1W 15
Grosvenor Ga
MYFR/PKLN W1K 9 F
Grosvenor Hl
MYFR/PKLN W1K 9
WIM/MER SW19 177
Grosvenor Pde EA W5 * 117
Grosvenor Pk CMBW SE5 142
Grosvenor Park Rd
WALTH E17 69
Grosvenor Pl KTBR SW1X 15
Grosvenor Ri East WALTH E17 69
Grosvenor Rd BCTR RM8 74
BELV DA17 129
BTFD TW8 116
BXLYHS DA6 148
CHSWK W4 117
ED N9 36
EHAM E6 89
FNCH N3 46
FSTGT E7 89
HNWL W7 116
HSLWW TW4 134
IL IG1 90
LEY E10 70
MUSWH N10 48
NTHWD HA6 40
NWDGN UB2 114
PIM SW1V 121
RCHPK/HAM TW10 137
ROMW/RG RM7 75
SNWD SE25 197
STMC/STPC BR5 201
TWK TW1 156
WAN E11 71
WLGTN SM6 210
WWKM BR4 198
Grosvenor Sq
MYFR/PKLN W1K 9
Grosvenor St
MYFR/PKLN W1K 9
Grosvenor Ter CMBW SE5 142
Grosvenor V RSLP HA4 58
Grosvenor Wharf Rd
POP/IOD E14 125
Grote's Blds BKHTH/KID SE3 145
Grote's Pl BKHTH/KID SE3 145
Groton Rd WAND/EARL SW18 160
Grotto Ct STHWK SE1 * 18
Grotto Pas MHST W1U
Grotto Rd TWK TW1 15
Grove Av FNCH N3 4
HNWL W7 9

MUSWH N10 48 C5
PIN HA5 59 J1
SUT SM1 208 E4
TWK TW1 156 A3
Grove Bank OXHEY WD19 * 27 H3
Grovebury Cl ERITH DA8 130 A6
Grovebury Ct STHGT/OAK N14 34 C2
Grovebury Rd ABYW SE2 128 C2
Grove Cl FSTH SE23 164 A3
KUT/HW KT1 191 G1
STHGT/OAK N14 * 34 B2
Grove Cots CHEL SW3 120 D6
CHSWK W4 * 118 B6
Grove Ct E/WMO/HCT KT8 189 J2
EA W5 * 117 F1
Grove Crs CDALE/KGS NW9 62 E1
FELT TW13 154 D6
KUT/HW KT1 175 F6
SWFD E18 52 D5
WOT/HER KT12 188 A4
Grove Crescent Rd
SRTFD E15 88 B4
Grovedale Rd ARCH N19 66 D6
Grove Dwellings WCHPL E1 * 104 E4
Grove End KTTN NW5 84 B2
SWFD E18 52 D5
Grove End La ESH/CLAY KT10 189 J5
Grove End Rd STJWD NW8 2 A3
Grove Farm Pk NTHWD HA6 40 B1
Grove Footpath BRYLDS KT5 191 F1
Grove Gdns HDN NW4 * 63 J2
PEND EN3 25 F2
STJWD NW8 2 D5
TEDD TW11 156 B6
Grove Green Rd WAN E11 88 A1
Grove Hl HRW HA1 60 E4
SWFD E18 52 D5
Grove Hill Rd CMBW SE5 143 F4
HRW HA1 61 F4
Grove House Rd
CEND/HSY/T N8 66 E1
Groveland Av
STRHM/NOR SW16 180 A3
Groveland Ct STP EC4M 12 D4
Groveland Rd BECK BR3 182 C6
Grovelands E/WMO/HCT KT8 189 F1
Grovelands Cl CMBW SE5 143 F3
RYLN/HDSTN HA2 78 B1
Grovelands Ct
STHGT/OAK N14 34 D2
rovelands Rd PLMGR N13 35 F6
SEVS/STOTM N15 68 C3
STMC/STPC BR5 186 B3
roveland Wy NWMAL KT3 191 K2
rove La CMBW SE5 142 E2
KUT/HW KT1 191 F1
rove Market Pl
ELTH/MOT SE9 * 166 E1
rove Ms HMSMTH W6 119 F3
rove Mill Pl CAR SM5 210 A1
rove Pk CDALE/KGS NW9 62 E1
CMBW SE5 143 F3
WAN E11 71 F2
rove Park Av CHING E4 51 K3
rove Park Br CHSWK W4 137 K1
rove Park Gdns CHSWK W4 137 J1
rove Park Rd CHSWK W4 137 J1
ELTH/MOT SE9 166 D4
RAIN RM13 93 J6
SEVS/STOTM N15 68 A1
rove Park Ter CHSWK W4 137 J1
rove Pl ACT W3 117 K1
BAL SW12 161 G1
HAMP NW3 83 H1
rove Rd ACT W3 117 K1
BARN SW13 138 C3
BELV DA17 129 G6
BOW E3 105 G1
BTFD TW8 116 D5
BXLYHN DA7 149 K5
CHDH RM6 73 J4
CHING E4 38 A5
CRICK NW2 82 A4
E/WMO/HCT KT8 189 J1
EA W5 97 K6
EBAR EN4 21 J4
EDGW HA8 44 C2
FBAR/BDGN N11 48 B1
HOM E9 87 F6
HSLW TW3 135 F5
ISLW TW7 135 K2
MTCM CR4 179 G5
NFNCH/WDSPK N12 47 H1
NTHWD HA6 40 B1
PIN HA5 59 K2
RCHPK/HAM TW10 157 G1
SEVS/STOTM N15 68 A2
SURB KT6 190 E2
SUT SM1 208 E4
SWFD E18 52 D5
THHTH CR7 196 B1
WALTH E17 69 K2
WAN E11 70 D4
WHTN TW2 155 J5
WIM/MER SW19 178 B3
ver Rd OXHEY WD19 27 H1
veside Cl ACT W3 98 C5
CAR SM5 194 D6
veside Rd CHING E4 38 C5
vestile Waye
EBED/NFELT TW14 153 G2
ve St BERM/RHTH SE16 124 C4
UED N18 50 B1
ve Ter KTTN NW5 84 A1
STHL UB1 * 96 A6
TEDD TW11 156 B6
ve Terrace Ms KTTN NW5 84 B1
Grove BXLYHS DA6 148 E5
DALE/KGS NW9 63 F2
END/HSY/T N8 66 D2
A W5 116 E1
DGW HA8 30 D6
NC/FH EN2 23 G3
NCH N3 46 E3
SBYPK N4 67 F4
FD/PVL UB6 96 C5
LDGN NW11 64 C4
GT N6 66 A5
LW TW7 135 K2
LMGR N13 35 G6
SCUP DA14 169 F6
SRTFD E15 88 C5
TEDD TW11 156 B6
WOT/HER KT12 188 A4
WWKM BR4 214 A1
Grove V CHST BR7 185 F2
EDUL SE22 143 F5
Grove Wy ESH/CLAY KT10 189 H4
WBLY HA9 80 E3
Groveway BCTR RM8 91 K2
BRXN/ST SW9 142 A2
Grove Wood Cl BMLY BR1 185 F6
Grovewood Pl WFD IG8 53 K2
Grummant Rd PECK SE15 143 G2
Grundy St POP/IOD E14 105 K5
Gruneisen Rd FNCH N3 47 F3
Guardian Ct EMPK RM11 75 K6
Gubyon Av HNHL SE24 142 C6
Guernsey Cl HEST TW5 135 F2
Guernsey Gv HNHL SE24 162 D2
Guernsey Rd IS N1 85 J4
LEY E10 70 B5
Guibal Rd LEE/GVPK SE12 166 A3
Guildersfield Rd
STRHM/NOR SW16 179 K3
Guildford Av FELT TW13 153 J4
Guildford Gv GNWCH SE10 144 E2
Guildford Rd CROY/NA CR0 196 E3
EHAM E6 107 J5
GDMY/SEVK IG3 72 E6
VX/NE SW8 141 K2
WALTH E17 52 A4
Guildford Wy WLGTN SM6 210 E3
Guildhall Blds CITYW EC2V 12 D3
Guildhall Yd CITYW EC2V 12 D3
Guildhouse St PIM SW1V 16 A7
Guildown Av
NFNCH/WDSPK N12 33 F6
Guild Rd CHARL SE7 126 C5
Guildsway WALTH E17 51 H4
Guilford Av BRYLDS KT5 191 G2
Guilford Pl BMSBY WC1N 5 G7
Guilford St BMSBY WC1N 5 G7
Guillemot Pl WDGN N22 * 49 F5
Guinness Cl HOM E9 87 G5
HYS/HAR UB3 113 G3
Guinness Ct CROY/NA CR0 * 197 G6
Guinness Sq STHWK SE1 19 G5
Guinness Trust
STNW/STAM N16 * 68 B5
Guinness Trust Est CHEL SW3 14 E7
SRTFD E15 * 88 D6
Guion Rd FUL/PGN SW6 139 J3
Gulland Wk IS N1 * 85 J4
Gulliver Cl NTHLT UB5 77 K6
Gulliver Rd BFN/LL DA15 167 J4
Gulliver St BERM/RHTH SE16 124 C3
Gumleigh Rd EA W5 116 D4
Gumley Gdns ISLW TW7 136 B4
Gumping Rd
STMC/STPC BR5 201 H6
Gundulph Rd HAYES BR2 184 B6
Gunmakers La BOW E3 87 G6
Gunnell Cl CROY/NA CR0 197 G3
SYD SE26 * 163 H6
Gunner La WOOL/PLUM SE18 127 F5
Gunnersbury Ave ACT W3 117 H3
Gunnersbury Avenue (North
Circular Road) EA W5 98 B6
Gunnersbury Cl CHSWK W4 * 117 J5
Gunnersbury Crs ACT W3 117 H2
Gunnersbury Dr EA W5 117 H2
Gunnersbury Gdns ACT W3 117 H2
Gunnersbury La ACT W3 117 H2
Gunnersbury Ms CHSWK W4 117 J5
Gunners Gv CHING E4 38 A5
Gunners Rd
WAND/EARL SW18 160 C4
Gunning St
WOOL/PLUM SE18 127 K4
Gunstor Rd
STNW/STAM N16 * 86 A2
Gun St WCHPL E1 13 J2
Gunter Gv EDGW HA8 45 F4
WBPTN SW10 120 B6
Gunterstone Rd WKENS W14 119 H5
Gunthorpe St WCHPL E1 13 K2
Gunton Rd CLPT E5 86 D1
TOOT SW17 179 F2
Gunwhale Cl
BERM/RHTH SE16 124 A1
Gunyard Ms
WOOL/PLUM SE18 * 146 D1
Gurnell Gv WEA W13 97 F3
Gurney Cl BARK IG11 90 B4
SRTFD E15 88 C3
WALTH E17 51 F4
Gurney Crs CROY/NA CR0 196 A5
Gurney Dr EFNCH N2 65 H1
Gurney Rd CAR SM5 210 A2
FUL/PGN SW6 140 B4
NTHLT UB5 95 F2
SRTFD E15 88 C3
Guthrie St CHEL SW3 120 D5
Gutter La CITYW EC2V 12 C3
Guyatt Gdns MTCM CR4 179 F5
Guy Rd WLGTN SM6 210 D1
Guyscliff Rd LEW SE13 145 F6
Guysfield Cl RAIN RM13 93 J6
Guysfield Dr RAIN RM13 93 J6
Guy St STHWK SE1 19 F2
Gwalior Rd PUT/ROE SW15 139 G5
Gwendolen Av
PUT/ROE SW15 139 G6
Gwendoline Av PLSTW E13 89 F6
Gwendwr Rd WKENS W14 119 H5
Gweneth Cots EDGW HA8 * 44 C2
Gwillim Cl BFN/LL DA15 168 B1
Gwydor Rd BECK BR3 198 A1
Gwydyr Rd HAYES BR2 183 J6
Gwyn Cl FUL/PGN SW6 140 B1
Gwynne Av CROY/NA CR0 198 A4
Gwynne Park Av WFD IG8 53 K2
Gwynne Rd BTSEA SW11 140 C3
Gwynne Whf CHSWK W4 118 C6
Gylcote Cl CMBW SE5 142 E5
Gyles Pk STAN HA7 43 J4
Gyllyngdune Gdns
GDMY/SEVK IG3 91 F1
Gywnne Pl FSBYW WC1X 5 H5

H

Haarlem Rd WKENS W14 119 G3
Haberdasher Pl IS N1 7 F4
Haberdasher St IS N1 7 F4
Habington Cl CMBW SE5 * 142 E1
Habitat Cl PECK SE15 143 J3
Haccombe Rd
WIM/MER SW19 178 B2
Hackbridge Park Gdns
CAR SM5 194 E6
Hackbridge Rd CAR SM5 195 F6
Hackford Rd BRXN/ST SW9 142 A2
Hackford Wk BRXN/ST SW9 142 A2
Hackington Crs BECK BR3 182 D2
Hackney Gv HACK E8 * 86 D4
Hackney Rd BETH E2 7 J4
Hackney Wick HOM E9 87 H4
Hadar Cl TRDG/WHET N20 32 E3
Haddenham Ct
OXHEY WD19 * 27 H5
Hadden Rd THMD SE28 127 K3
Hadden Wy GFD/PVL UB6 78 D4
Haddington Rd BMLY BR1 165 G5
Haddon Cl EN EN1 36 C1
NWMAL KT3 192 C2
Haddon Gv BFN/LL DA15 168 B2
Haddon Rd STMC/STPC BR5 202 D2
SUT SM1 209 F2
Haddo St GNWCH SE10 124 E6
Hadfield Cl STHL UB1 95 K2
Hadfield Rd
STWL/WRAY TW19 152 A1
Hadleigh Cl RYNPK SW20 177 J5
WCHPL E1 104 E3
Hadleigh Dr BELMT SM2 208 E6
Hadleigh Rd ED N9 36 D2
Hadleigh St BETH E2 104 E3
Hadley Cl WCHMH N21 35 G1
Hadley Common BAR EN5 21 G3
Hadley Gdns CHSWK W4 118 A5
NWDGN UB2 114 E5
Hadley Gn BAR EN5 20 D4
Hadley Green Rd BAR EN5 20 D3
Hadley Gn West BAR EN5 20 C3
Hadley Gv BAR EN5 20 C3
Hadley Highstone BAR EN5 20 D1
Hadley Pde BAR EN5 * 20 C4
Hadley Rdg BAR EN5 20 D4
Hadley Rd BAR EN5 21 F4
BELV DA17 129 G4
MTCM CR4 195 J1
Hadley St KTTN NW5 84 B4
Hadley Wy WCHMH N21 35 G1
Hadley Wood Rd BAR EN5 20 E3
Hadlow Pl NRWD SE19 181 H3
Hadlow Rd SCUP DA14 168 B6
WELL DA16 148 D1
Hadrian Cl BOW E3 87 J6
STWL/WRAY TW19 152 B2
Hadrian Est BETH E2 * 104 C1
Hadrian's Ride EN EN1 24 B6
Hadrian St GNWCH SE10 125 H5
Hadrian Wy
STWL/WRAY TW19 152 A2
Hadyn Park Rd SHB W12 118 D2
Hafer Rd BTSEA SW11 140 E5
Hafton Rd CAT SE6 165 H3
Haggard Rd TWK TW1 156 C2
Hagger Ct WALTH E17 * 52 B6
Haggerston Rd HACK E8 86 B5
Hague St BETH E2 104 C2
Ha-Ha Rd WOOL/PLUM SE18 126 E6
Haig Rd STAN HA7 43 J1
UX/CGN UB8 94 A4
Haig Rd East PLSTW E13 107 G2
Haig Rd West PLSTW E13 107 G2
Haigville Gdns BARK/HLT IG6 72 B1
Hailes Cl WIM/MER SW19 178 B2
Haileybury Av EN EN1 36 B1
Haileybury Rd ORP BR6 217 G2
Hailey Rd ERITHM DA18 129 H2
Hailsham Av
BRXS/STRHM SW2 162 A4
Hailsham Cl SURB KT6 190 E4
Hailsham Dr HRW HA1 42 D6
Hailsham Rd TOOT SW17 179 F2
Hailsham Ter UED N18 * 49 K1
Haimo Rd ELTH/MOT SE9 146 C6
Hainault Blds LEY E10 * 70 A5
Hainault Gore CHDH RM6 74 A2
Hainault Rd BARK/HLT IG6 55 H3
CHDH RM6 55 H6
CRW RM5 55 H6
WAN E11 70 A5
Hainault St ELTH/MOT SE9 167 G3
IL IG1 72 B6
Haines Wk MRDN SM4 194 A4
Hainford Cl PECK SE15 144 A5
Haining Cl CHSWK W4 117 H5
Hainthorpe Rd WNWD SE27 162 C5
Hainton Cl WCHPL E1 104 D5
Halberd Ms CLPT E5 68 D6
Halbutt St DAGW RM9 92 B2
Halcomb St IS N1 7 G1
Halcot Av BXLYHS DA6 149 J6
Halcrow St WCHPL E1 * 104 D4
Haldane Cl MUSWH N10 48 B3
PEND EN3 25 K1
Haldane Pl WAND/EARL SW18 160 A3
Haldane Rd EHAM E6 107 H2
FUL/PGN SW6 139 J1
STHL UB1 96 C6
THMD SE28 109 K6
Haldan Rd CHING E4 52 A2
Haldon Rd
WAND/EARL SW18 159 J1
Hale Cl CHING E4 38 A5
EDGW HA8 44 E1
ORP BR6 216 C2
Hale Dr MLHL NW7 44 E2
Hale End HARH RM3 57 K2
Hale End Cl RSLP HA4 58 E3
Hale End Rd WALTH E17 52 B5
Halefield Rd TOTM N17 50 C4
Hale Gdns ACT W3 117 H1
TOTM N17 50 C6
Hale Grove Gdns MLHL NW7 45 F1
Hale House
WOOL/PLUM SE18 * 146 D1
Hale La EDGW HA8 44 E1
Hale Rd EHAM E6 107 J3
TOTM N17 50 C6
Halesowen Rd MRDN SM4 194 A4
Hales St DEPT SE8 144 D1
Hale St POP/IOD E14 105 K6
Halesworth Rd LEW SE13 144 E4
The Hale CHING E4 52 B3
TOTM N17 50 C6
Haley Rd HDN NW4 64 A3
Half Acre BTFD TW8 116 E6
Half Acre Ms BTFD TW8 136 E1
Half Acre Rd HNWL W7 115 K1
Half Moon Crs IS N1 5 H2
Half Moon La HNHL SE24 162 D1
Half Moon Pas WCHPL E1 13 K4
Half Moon St MYFR/PICC W1J 9 K7
Halford Cl EDGW HA8 44 D5
Halford Rd FUL/PGN SW6 119 K6
LEY E10 70 B2
RCHPK/HAM TW10 137 F6
Halfway Ct PUR RM19 131 K4
Halfway St BFN/LL DA15 167 K3
Haliburton Rd TWK TW1 136 B6
Haliday Wk IS N1 85 K4
Halifax Cl TEDD TW11 173 K2
Halifax Rd ENC/FH EN2 23 J3
GFD/PVL UB6 78 B6
Halifax St SYD SE26 163 J5
Halifield Dr BELV DA17 129 F3
Haling Gv SAND/SEL CR2 211 J5
Haling Park Gdns
SAND/SEL CR2 211 H4
Haling Park Rd SAND/SEL CR2 211 H4
Haling Rd SAND/SEL CR2 211 K4
Halkin Ar KTBR SW1X 15 G4
Halkin Ms KTBR SW1X * 15 G4
Halkin Pl KTBR SW1X 15 G4
Halkin St KTBR SW1X 15 H3
Hallam Cl CHST BR7 184 E1
Hallam Gdns PIN HA5 41 J3
Hallam Ms GTPST W1W 9 K1
Hallam Rd BARN SW13 138 E4
SEVS/STOTM N15 67 H1
Hallam St GTPST W1W 9 K1
Halland Wy NTHWD HA6 40 B2
Hall Cl EA W5 98 A4
Hall Ct TEDD TW11 174 A1
Hall Dr SYD SE26 181 K1
Halley Gdns LEW SE13 145 G5
Halley Rd FSTGT E7 89 G4
MNPK E12 89 H4
Halley St POP/IOD E14 105 G4
Hall Farm Cl STAN HA7 29 H6
Hall Farm Dr WHTN TW2 155 J2
Hallfield Est BAY/PAD W2 * 101 G5
Hall Gdns CHING E4 37 H6
Halliday Sq NWDGN UB2 115 J1
Halliford St IS N1 85 J5
Halliwell Rd
BRXS/STRHM SW2 162 A1
Halliwick Court Pde
NFNCH/WDSPK N12 * 47 K1
Halliwick Rd MUSWH N10 48 A4
Hall La CHING E4 37 H6
HDN NW4 45 J5
HYS/HAR UB3 133 G1
Hallmead Rd SUT SM1 209 F1
Hall Oak Wk KIL/WHAMP NW6 82 D4
Hallowell Av CROY/NA CR0 210 E2
Hallowell Cl MTCM CR4 179 F6
Hallowell Gdns THHTH CR7 180 D5
Hallowell Rd NTHWD HA6 40 C3
Hallowes Crs OXHEY WD19 26 E5
Hallowfield Wy MTCM CR4 178 C6
Hall Pl BAY/PAD W2 2 A7
Hall Rd CHDH RM6 73 J3
DART DA1 151 J5
EHAM E6 89 K6
GPK RM2 57 K6
ISLW TW7 135 J6
MV/WKIL W9 101 G2
SRTFD E15 88 B2
WLGTN SM6 210 B6
Hallside Rd EN EN1 24 B1
Hall St FSBYE EC1V 6 B4
NFNCH/WDSPK N12 47 G1
Hallsville Rd CAN/RD E16 106 D5
Hallswelle Pde
GLDGN NW11 * 64 D2
Hallswelle Rd GLDGN NW11 64 D2
Hall Vw ELTH/MOT SE9 166 C4
Hallywell Crs EHAM E6 107 K4
Halons Rd ELTH/MOT SE9 167 F2
Halpin Pl WALW SE17 19 F7
Halsbrook Rd BKHTH/KID SE3 146 B4
Halsbury Cl STAN HA7 43 H1
Halsbury Rd SHB W12 118 E1
Halsbury Rd East NTHLT UB5 78 C2
Halsbury Rd West NTHLT UB5 78 B3
Halsend HYS/HAR UB3 * 114 A1
Halsey St CHEL SW3 14 E6
Halsham Crs BARK IG11 91 F4
Halsmere Rd CMBW SE5 142 C2
Halstead Cl CROY/NA CR0 211 J1
Halstead Gdns WCHMH N21 35 K3
Halstead Rd EN EN1 24 A5
ERITH DA8 150 B2
WAN E11 71 F2
WCHMH N21 35 K3
Halston Cl BTSEA SW11 160 E1
Halstow Rd WLSDN NW10 100 B2
Halsway HYS/HAR UB3 113 K1
Halton Cl FBAR/BDGN N11 47 K2
Halton Cross St IS N1 * 85 H6
Halton Rd IS N1 85 H5
Halt Pde CDALE/KGS NW9 * 63 F1
Halt Robin Rd BELV DA17 129 H4
Hambalt Rd CLAP SW4 141 H6
Hamble Cl RSLP HA4 58 C6
Hambledon WALW SE17 * 122 E6
Hambledon Ct EA W5 * 98 A6
Hambledon Gdns SNWD SE25 181 G6
Hambledon Pl DUL SE21 163 G3
Hambledon Rd
WAND/EARL SW18 159 J2
Hambledown Rd
BFN/LL DA15 * 167 J2
Hamble St FUL/PGN SW6 140 A4
Hambleton Cl WPK KT4 193 F6
Hambrook Rd SNWD SE25 181 J6
Hambro Rd
STRHM/NOR SW16 179 J2
Hambrough Rd STHL UB1 114 D1
Ham Common
RCHPK/HAM TW10 156 E5
Ham Croft Cl FELT TW13 153 K5
Hamden Crs DAGE RM10 92 D1
Hamel Cl KTN/HRWW/WS HA3 61 K1
Hameway EHAM E6 108 A3
Ham Farm Rd
RCHPK/HAM TW10 156 E6
Hamfrith Rd SRTFD E15 88 D4
Ham Gate Av
RCHPK/HAM TW10 157 F6
Hamilton Av BARK/HLT IG6 72 B1
CHEAM SM3 193 H6
ED N9 36 C2
ROM RM1 57 F5
SURB KT6 191 H6
Hamilton Cl BERM/RHTH SE16 124 B2
EBAR EN4 21 J5
STJWD NW8 2 A5
TEDD TW11 174 C2
TOTM N17 50 B6
Hamilton Ct EA W5 98 B6
Hamilton Crs HSLW TW3 135 G6
PLMGR N13 35 G6
RYLN/HDSTN HA2 77 K1
Hamilton Gdns STJWD NW8 101 G2
Hamilton Ms MYFR/PICC W1J 15 J2
Hamilton Pde FELT TW13 * 153 K6
Hamilton Pk HBRY N5 85 H2
Hamilton Pk West HBRY N5 85 H2
Hamilton Pl MYFR/PKLN W1K 15 H1
SUN TW16 172 A3
Hamilton Rd BTFD TW8 116 E6
CHSWK W4 118 B3
EA W5 98 A6
EBAR EN4 21 J5
ED N9 36 C2
EFNCH N2 47 G6
FELT TW13 153 J6
GLDGN NW11 64 B4
GPK RM2 75 K2
HRW HA1 60 E2
HYS/HAR UB3 95 F6
IL IG1 90 B2
OXHEY WD19 27 F5
SCUP DA14 168 B6
SRTFD E15 106 C2
STHL UB1 114 E1
THHTH CR7 180 E6
WALTH E17 51 G5
WHTN TW2 155 K3
WIM/MER SW19 178 A3
WLSDN NW10 81 J3
WNWD SE27 162 E6
Hamilton Road Ms
WIM/MER SW19 178 A3
Hamilton Sq
NFNCH/WDSPK N12 * 47 G2
Hamilton St DEPT SE8 124 D6
Hamilton Ter STJWD NW8 101 G2
Hamilton Wy FNCH N3 46 E2
PLMGR N13 35 H6
WLGTN SM6 210 D6
Hamlet Cl CRW RM5 56 C3
LEW SE13 145 H5
Hamlet Gdns HMSMTH W6 118 D4
Hamlet Rd CRW RM5 56 C3
NRWD SE19 181 G3
Hamlet Sq CRICK NW2 82 C1
Hamlets Wy BOW E3 105 H3
The Hamlet CMBW SE5 142 E4
Hamlet Wy STHWK SE1 19 F3
Hamlin Crs PIN HA5 59 G2
Hamlyn Cl EDGW HA8 30 A5
Hamlyn Gdns NRWD SE19 181 F3
Hammelton Rd BMLY BR1 183 K4
Hammers La MLHL NW7 31 J6
Hammersmith Br
HMSMTH W6 118 E5
Hammersmith Bridge Rd
BARN SW13 118 E5
Hammersmith Broadway
HMSMTH W6 119 F4
Hammersmith Emb
HMSMTH W6 * 119 F6
Hammersmith F/O
HMSMTH W6 119 F5
Hammersmith Gv
HMSMTH W6 119 F3
Hammersmith Rd
HMSMTH W6 119 G4
Hammersmith Ter
HMSMTH W6 * 118 D5
Hammerton Cl BXLY DA5 170 B5
Hammet Cl YEAD UB4 95 H4
Hammett St TWRH EC3N 13 J5
Hammond Av MTCM CR4 179 G5
Hammond Cl BAR EN5 20 C6
GFD/PVL UB6 78 D3
HPTN TW12 173 F4
Hammond Rd EN EN1 24 D4
NWDGN UB2 114 D3
Hammonds Cl BCTR RM8 91 J1
Hammond St KTTN NW5 84 C4
Hamond Cl SAND/SEL CR2 211 H6
Hamonde Cl EDGW HA8 30 D4
Hamond Sq IS N1 7 G2
Ham Park Rd SRTFD E15 88 D5
Hampden Av BECK BR3 182 B5
Hampden Cl CAMTN NW1 4 D3
Hampden Gurney St
MBLAR W1H 8 E4
Hampden La TOTM N17 50 B4
Hampden Rd ARCH N19 66 D6
BECK BR3 182 B5
CEND/HSY/T N8 67 G1
KTN/HRWW/WS HA3 42 C4
KUT/HW KT1 175 H6
MUSWH N10 48 A3
TOTM N17 50 C4
Hampden Wy
STHGT/OAK N14 34 B5
Hampermill La OXHEY WD19 26 E3
Hampshire Cl UED N18 50 D1

Hampshire Hog La
HMSMTH W6 * 118 E4
Hampshire Rd WDGN N22 49 F3
Hampshire St KTTN NW5 * 84 D4
Hampson Wy VX/NE SW8 142 A2
Hampstead Av WFD IG8 54 A3
Hampstead Cl THMD SE28 128 C1
Hampstead Gdns
GLDGN NW11 64 E3
Hampstead Ga HAMP NW3 83 G3
Hampstead Gn HAMP NW3 83 J3
Hampstead Gv HAMP NW3 83 G2
Hampstead Hts EFNCH N2 65 G1
Hampstead Hill Gdns
HAMP NW3 83 J2
Hampstead La HGT N6 65 K4
Hampstead Rd CAMTN NW1 4 A3
Hampstead Sq HAMP NW3 83 G1
Hampstead Wy GLDGN NW11 64 E3
Hampton Cl FBAR/BDGN N11 48 A1
KIL/WHAMP NW6 100 E2
RYNPK SW20 * 177 F3
Hampton Ct IS N1 85 H4
Hampton Court Av
E/WMO/HCT KT8 189 J3
Hampton Court Crs
E/WMO/HCT KT8 * 173 J6
Hampton Court Est
THDIT KT7 * 189 K2
Hampton Court Rd
HPTN TW12 173 J5
Hampton Court Wy
ESH/CLAY KT10 189 K6
Hampton La FELT TW13 154 D6
Hampton Ri
KTN/HRWW/WS HA3 62 A3
Hampton Rd CHING E4 51 H1
CROY/NA CR0 196 D3
FSTGT E7 89 F3
IL IG1 90 C2
TEDD TW11 173 J1
WAN E11 70 B5
WHTN TW2 155 J5
WPK KT4 192 D6
Hampton Rd East FELT TW13 154 E5
Hampton Rd West FELT TW13 154 D4
Hampton St WALW SE17 18 B7
Ham Ridings
RCHPK/HAM TW10 175 G1
Ham Shades Cl BFN/LL DA15 168 A5
Ham St RCHPK/HAM TW10 156 D4
The Ham BTFD TW8 136 D1
Ham Vw CROY/NA CR0 198 B3
Ham Yd SOHO/SHAV W1D * 10 C5
Hanameel St CAN/RD E16 125 K1
CAN/RD E16 126 A1
Hanbury Cl HDN NW4 46 A6
Hanbury Ct HRW HA1 * 61 F3
Hanbury Dr WAN E11 70 D4
WCHMH N21 23 F5
Hanbury Rd ACT W3 117 J2
TOTM N17 50 D5
Hanbury St WCHPL E1 13 K1
Hancock Rd BOW E3 106 A2
NRWD SE19 180 E2
Handa Wk IS N1 85 J4
Hand Ct HHOL WC1V 11 H2
Handcroft Rd CROY/NA CR0 196 C4
Handel Cl EDGW HA8 44 B2
Handel Pde EDGW HA8 * 44 C2
Handel Pl WLSDN NW10 81 F4
Handel St BMSBY WC1N 4 E6
Handel Wy EDGW HA8 44 C3
Handen Rd LEE/GVPK SE12 145 H6
Handforth Rd BRXN/ST SW9 142 B1
IL IG1 90 B1
Handley Gv CRICK NW2 82 B1
Handley Page Rd WLGTN SM6 211 F5
Handley Rd HOM E9 86 E5
Handowe Cl HDN NW4 63 J1
Handside Cl WPK KT4 193 G5
Handsworth Av CHING E4 52 B2
Handsworth Cl OXHEY WD19 26 E5
Handsworth Rd TOTM N17 49 K6
Handtrough Wy BARK IG11 108 B1
Hanford Cl WAND/EARL SW18 159 K3
Hangar Lane (North Circular
Road) EA W5 98 B4
Hangar Ruding OXHEY WD19 27 K5
Hanger Gn EA W5 98 C3
Hanger La EA W5 98 A1
Hanger Vale La EA W5 98 B4
Hanger View Wy ACT W3 98 C5
Hankey Pl STHWK SE1 19 F3
Hankins La MLHL NW7 31 G4
Hanley Gdns FSBYPK N4 67 F5
Hanley Pl BECK BR3 182 D3
Hanley Rd FSBYPK N4 66 E5
Hanmer Wk HOLWY N7 67 F6
Hannah Cl BECK BR3 182 E6
WLSDN NW10 80 E2
Hannah Mary Wy
STHWK SE1 * 123 H4
Hannards Wy BARK/HLT IG6 55 H1
Hannay La ARCH N19 66 D4
Hannell Rd FUL/PGN SW6 139 H1
Hannen Rd WNWD SE27 * 162 C5
Hannibal Rd
STWL/WRAY TW19 152 B2
WCHPL E1 104 E4
Hannibal Wy CROY/NA CR0 211 F3
Hannington Rd CLAP SW4 141 G4
Hanno Cl WLGTN SM6 210 D5
Hanover Av CAN/RD E16 125 K1
FELT TW13 153 K3
Hanover Cir HYS/HAR UB3 94 A5
Hanover Cl CHEAM SM3 208 C2
RCH/KEW TW9 137 H1
Hanover Dr CHST BR7 167 H6
Hanover Gdns BARK/HLT IG6 54 C3
LBTH SE11 122 B6
Hanover Pk PECK SE15 143 H2
Hanover Pl COVGDN WC2E 11 F4
Hanover Rd SEVS/STOTM N15 68 B1
WIM/MER SW19 178 B3
WLSDN NW10 82 A5
Hanover Sq CONDST W1S 9 K4
Hanover Steps BAY/PAD W2 * 8 D4
Hanover St CONDST W1S 9 K4
CROY/NA CR0 211 H1
Hanover Ter CAMTN NW1 2 E5
Hanover Terrace Ms
CAMTN NW1 2 D5
Hanover Wy BXLYHS DA6 148 E4
Hanover Yd IS N1 * 6 B2
Hansard Ms WKENS W14 119 G2
Hansart Wy ENC/FH EN2 23 G2
Hans Crs KTBR SW1X 14 E4
Hanselin Cl STAN HA7 43 F1
Hansen Dr WCHMH N21 23 F6
Hanshaw Dr EDGW HA8 45 F4
Hansler Gv E/WMO/HCT KT8 189 J2
Hansler Rd EDUL SE22 143 G6
Hansom Ter BMLY BR1 * 184 A4
Hanson Cl BAL SW12 161 G2
BECK BR3 * 182 E2
MORT/ESHN SW14 137 K4
WDR/YW UB7 112 C3
Hanson Gdns STHL UB1 114 D2
Hanson St GTPST W1W 10 A1
Hans Pl KTBR SW1X 14 E4
Hans Rd CHEL SW3 14 E4
Hans St KTBR SW1X 15 F5
Hanway Pl FITZ W1T 10 C3
SOHO/SHAV W1D 10 C3
Hanway Rd HNWL W7 96 D5
Hanway St FITZ W1T 10 C3
Hanworth Rd FELT TW13 154 A3
HPTN TW12 154 E6
HSLW TW3 135 G4
HSLWW TW4 154 E2
Hanworth Ter HSLW TW3 135 G5
Hapgood Cl GFD/PVL UB6 78 D3
Harben Pde HAMP NW3 * 83 H5
Harben Rd KIL/WHAMP NW6 83 G5
Harberson Rd BAL SW12 161 G3
SRTFD E15 88 D6
Harberton Rd ARCH N19 66 C5
Harbet Rd BAY/PAD W2 8 B2
UED N18 51 F1
Harbex Cl BXLY DA5 169 J2
Harbinger Rd POP/IOD E14 124 E4
Harbledown Pl
STMC/STPC BR5 202 D1
Harbledown Rd
FUL/PGN SW6 139 K2
Harbord Cl CMBW SE5 142 E3
Harbord St FUL/PGN SW6 139 G2
Harborne Cl OXHEY WD19 41 G1
Harborough Av BFN/LL DA15 167 K2
Harborough Rd
STRHM/NOR SW16 162 A6
Harbour Av WBPTN SW10 140 B2
Harbour Cl MTCM CR4 179 F4
Harbourer Rd BARK/HLT IG6 55 H1
Harbour Exchange Sq
POP/IOD E14 124 E2
Harbour Rd CMBW SE5 142 D4
Harbour Yd WBPTN SW10 * 140 B2
Harbridge Av PUT/ROE SW15 158 C2
Harbury Rd CAR SM5 209 J6
Harbut Rd BTSEA SW11 140 C5
Harcastle Cl YEAD UB4 95 J3
Harcombe Rd
STNW/STAM N16 86 A1
Harcourt Av BFN/LL DA15 168 D1
EDGW HA8 30 E5
MNPK E12 89 K2
WLGTN SM6 210 B2
Harcourt Blds EMB EC4Y * 11 J5
Harcourt Cl ISLW TW7 136 B4
Harcourt Fld WLGTN SM6 210 B2
Harcourt Ms GPK RM2 75 H2
Harcourt Rd BROCKY SE4 144 C5
SRTFD E15 106 D1
THHTH CR7 196 A3
WDGN N22 48 D4
WIM/MER SW19 177 K3
WLGTN SM6 210 B2
Harcourt St MBLAR W1H 8 D2
Harcourt Ter WBPTN SW10 120 A5
Hardcastle Cl CROY/NA CR0 197 H3
Hardcourts Cl WWKM BR4 213 K2
Hardel Wk BRXS/STRHM SW2 162 B2
Hardens Manorway
WOOL/PLUM SE18 126 C3
Harders Rd PECK SE15 143 J3
Hardess St HNHL SE24 142 D4
Hardie Cl WLSDN NW10 81 F3
Hardie Rd DAGE RM10 92 E1
Harding Cl CROY/NA CR0 212 B1
KUTN/CMB KT2 175 G4
WALW SE17 122 D6
Hardinge Rd UED N18 50 A1
WLSDN NW10 82 A6
Hardinge St WCHPL E1 104 E5
WOOL/PLUM SE18 127 G3
Hardings La PGE/AN SE20 182 A2
Hardinge Crs
WOOL/PLUM SE18 127 H3
Hardman Rd CHARL SE7 126 A5
KUTN/CMB KT2 175 F5
Hardres Ter STMC/STPC BR5 * 202 E6
Hardwick Cl STAN HA7 43 J1
Hardwicke Av HEST TW5 * 135 F2
Hardwicke Ms FSBYW WC1X * 5 H5
Hardwicke Rd CHSWK W4 117 K4
PLMGR N13 48 E1
RCHPK/HAM TW10 156 D6
Hardwicke St BARK IG11 90 C6
Hardwick Gn WEA W13 97 H4
Hardwick Pl
STRHM/NOR SW16 179 H3
Hardwick St CLKNW EC1R 5 K5
Hardwick's Wy
WAND/EARL SW18 139 K6
Hardwidge St STHWK SE1 19 G2
Hardy Av CAN/RD E16 125 K1
RSLP HA4 77 F3
Hardy Cl BAR EN5 20 C6
BERM/RHTH SE16 124 A2
PIN HA5 59 H4
Hardy Cots GNWCH SE10 * 125 G6
Hardy Gv DART DA1 151 K5
Hardy Pas WDGN N22 49 F4
Hardy Rd BKHTH/KID SE3 125 J6
CHING E4 51 H2
WIM/MER SW19 178 A3
Hardys Ms E/WMO/HCT KT8 189 K1
Hardy Wy ENC/FH EN2 23 G2
Harebell Dr EHAM E6 108 A4
Hare & Billet Rd
BKHTH/KID SE3 145 G2
Hare Ct EMB EC4Y * 11 J4
Harecourt Rd IS N1 85 J4
Haredale Rd HNHL SE24 142 D5
Haredon Cl FSTH SE23 163 K2
Harefield ESH/CLAY KT10 204 E1
Harefield Av BELMT SM2 208 C6
Harefield Cl ENC/FH EN2 23 G2
Harefield Ms BROCKY SE4 144 C4
Harefield Rd BROCKY SE4 144 C4
CEND/HSY/T N8 66 D2
SCUP DA14 168 E4
STRHM/NOR SW16 180 A3
Hare Hall La GPK RM2 75 K1
Hare La ESH/CLAY KT10 204 D4
Hare Marsh BETH E2 104 C3
Harepit Cl SAND/SEL CR2 211 H5
Hare Rw BETH E2 104 D1
Haresfield Rd DAGE RM10 92 C4
Hare St WOOL/PLUM SE18 127 F3
Hare Wk IS N1 7 H3
Harewood Av CAMTN NW1 2 D7
NTHLT UB5 77 J5
STJWD NW8 2 D6
Harewood Cl NTHLT UB5 77 K5
Harewood Dr CLAY IG5 53 K5
Harewood Pl CONDST W1S 9 K4
Harewood Rd ISLW TW7 136 A1
OXHEY WD19 27 F4
SAND/SEL CR2 212 A4
WIM/MER SW19 178 D2
Harewood Rw CAMTN NW1 8 D1
Harewood Ter NWDGN UB2 114 E4
Harfield Gdns CMBW SE5 * 143 F4
Harfield Rd SUN TW16 172 C5
Harford Cl CHING E4 37 K2
Harford Rd CHING E4 37 K2
Harford St WCHPL E1 105 G3
Harford Wk EFNCH N2 65 H1
Harfst Wy SWLY BR8 187 K4
Harglaze Ter
CDALE/KGS NW9 * 45 G6
Hargood Cl
KTN/HRWW/WS HA3 62 A3
Hargood Rd BKHTH/KID SE3 146 B2
Hargrave Pk ARCH N19 66 C6
Hargrave Pl KTTN NW5 84 D3
Hargrave Rd ARCH N19 66 C6
Hargwyne St BRXN/ST SW9 142 A4
Haringey Pk CEND/HSY/T N8 66 E3
Haringey Rd CEND/HSY/T N8 66 E1
Harington Ter UED N18 * 35 K6
Harkett Cl
KTN/HRWW/WS HA3 43 F5
Harland Av BFN/LL DA15 167 J5
CROY/NA CR0 212 B1
Harland Cl WIM/MER SW19 178 A6
Harlands Gv ORP BR6 216 B2
Harlech Gdns HEST TW5 114 B6
PIN HA5 59 H4
Harlech Rd STHGT/OAK N14 34 E5
Harlequin Av BTFD TW8 116 B6
Harlequin Cl ISLW TW7 135 K6
YEAD UB4 95 H4
Harlequin Ct EA W5 * 97 J6
Harlequin Rd TEDD TW11 * 174 C3
Harlescott Rd PECK SE15 144 A5
Harlesden Gdns
WLSDN NW10 81 H6
Harlesden Rd WLSDN NW10 99 J1
Harley Cl ALP/SUD HA0 * 79 K4
Harley Crs HRW HA1 60 D1
Harleyford BMLY BR1 184 B4
Harleyford Rd LBTH SE11 122 A6
Harleyford St LBTH SE11 122 B6
Harley Gdns ORP BR6 216 E2
WBPTN SW10 120 B5
Harley Gv BOW E3 105 H2
Harley Pl CAVSQ/HST W1G 9 J2
Harley Rd HAMP NW3 83 H5
HRW HA1 60 D1
WLSDN NW10 99 G1
Harley St CAVSQ/HST W1G 3 J7
Harley Vls WLSDN NW10 * 99 G1
Harlinger St
WOOL/PLUM SE18 126 D3
Harlington Cl HYS/HAR UB3 133 F1
Harlington Rd East
EBED/NFELT TW14 154 A2
Harlington Rd West
EBED/NFELT TW14 154 A1
Harlow Gdns CRW RM5 56 E2
Harlow Rd PLMGR N13 35 K5
RAIN RM13 93 H6
Harlyn Dr PIN HA5 41 F6
Harman Av WFD IG8 52 D3
Harman Cl CHING E4 38 B6
CRICK NW2 82 C1
STHWK SE1 * 123 H5
Harman Dr BFN/LL DA15 168 A1
CRICK NW2 82 C1
Harman Rd EN EN1 24 B6
Harmondsworth La
WDR/YW UB7 112 B6
Harmondsworth Rd
WDR/YW UB7 112 B3
Harmony Cl GLDGN NW11 64 C2
WLGTN SM6 210 E6
Harmony Pl STHWK SE1 123 G5
Harmony Wy BMLY BR1 183 K5
HDN NW4 64 A1
Harmood Gv CAMTN NW1 84 B5
Harmood St CAMTN NW1 84 B4
Harmsworth Ms STHWK SE1 17 K5
Harmsworth St WALW SE17 122 C5
Harmsworth Wy
TRDG/WHET N20 32 D3
Harness Rd THMD SE28 128 B2
Harold Av BELV DA17 129 G5
HYS/HAR UB3 113 J3
Harold Rd CEND/HSY/T N8 67 F2
CHING E4 38 A5
NRWD SE19 180 E3
PLSTW E13 89 F6
SEVS/STOTM N15 68 B2
SUT SM1 209 H2
SWFD E18 52 E4
WAN E11 70 C5
WLSDN NW10 99 F2
Haroldstone Rd WALTH E17 69 F2
Harpenden Rd MNPK E12 71 G6
WNWD SE27 162 C4
Harper Rd EHAM E6 107 K5
STHWK SE1 18 D4
Harpers Yd ISLW TW7 * 136 A3
Harp Island Cl WLSDN NW10 63 F6
Harp La MON EC3R 13 G6
Harpley Sq WCHPL E1 104 E3
Harpour Rd BARK IG11 90 C4
Harp Rd HNWL W7 97 F3
Harpsden St BTSEA SW11 141 F2
Harpur Ms BMSBY WC1N 11 G1
Harpur St BMSBY WC1N 11 G1
Harraden Rd BKHTH/KID SE3 146 B2
Harrier Cl HCH RM12 93 K4
Harrier Ms THMD SE28 127 J2
Harrier Rd CDALE/KGS NW9 45 G5
Harriers Cl EA W5 98 A6
Harrier Wy EHAM E6 107 K4
Harries Rd YEAD UB4 95 G3
Harriet Cl HACK E8 86 C6
Harriet Gdns CROY/NA CR0 197 H6
Harriet Ms WELL DA16 148 C3
Harriet St KTBR SW1X 15 F3
Harriet Tubman Cl
BRXS/STRHM SW2 162 B2
Harriet Wk KTBR SW1X 15 F3
Harriet Wy BUSH WD23 28 D2
Harringay Gdns
CEND/HSY/T N8 67 H1
Harringay Rd
SEVS/STOTM N15 67 H2
Harrington Cl CROY/NA CR0 195 K6
WLSDN NW10 81 F1
Harrington Ct NKENS W10 * 100 D2
Harrington Gdns SKENS SW7 120 A4
Harrington Hl CLPT E5 68 D5
Harrington Rd SKENS SW7 14 A6
SNWD SE25 197 H1
WAN E11 70 C5
Harrington Sq CAMTN NW1 4 A2
Harrington St CAMTN NW1 4 A3
Harrington Wy
WOOL/PLUM SE18 126 C3
Harriott Cl GNWCH SE10 125 J4
Harris Cl ENC/FH EN2 23 H2
HSLW TW3 135 F2
Harrison Cl NTHWD HA6 40 A2
TRDG/WHET N20 33 J3
Harrison Dr BMLY BR1 201 G1
Harrison Rd DAGE RM10 92 D4
WLSDN NW10 81 F6
Harrison's Ri CROY/NA CR0 211 H1
Harrison St STPAN WC1H 5 F5
Harris Rd DAGW RM9 92 B3
Harris St CMBW SE5 142 E1
WALTH E17 69 H4
Harrods Gn EDGW HA8 44 C1
Harrogate Rd OXHEY WD19 27 G5
Harrold Rd BCTR RM8 91 H3
Harrow Av EN EN1 36 B1
Harroway Rd BTSEA SW11 140 C3
Harrowby St MBLAR W1H 8 D3
Harrow Cl CHSGTN KT9 205 K5
Harrow Crs HARH RM3 57 K3
Harrowdene Cl ALP/SUD HA0 79 K2
Harrowdene Gdns
TEDD TW11 174 B3
Harrowdene Rd
ALP/SUD HA0 79 K2
Harrow Dr ED N9 36 B3
Harrowes Meade EDGW HA8 30 C5
Harrow Fields Gdns HRW HA1 78 E1
Harrow Gdns ORP BR6 217 H2
Harrowgate Rd HOM E9 87 G4
Harrow Gn WAN E11 88 C1
Harrow La POP/IOD E14 106 A6
Harrow Manor Wy ABYW SE2 128 D1
Harrow Pk HRW HA1 60 E6
Harrow Pl WCHPL E1 13 H3
Harrow Rd ALP/SUD HA0 79 G2
CAR SM5 209 J4
EBED/NFELT TW14 152 D3
IL IG1 90 C2
MV/WKIL W9 100 D3
WAN E11 88 D1
WBLY HA9 80 C3
WLSDN NW10 99 K2
Harrow Road F/O
BAY/PAD W2 8 B2
Harrow St CAMTN NW1 * 8 D1
Harrow Vw HGDN/ICK UB10 94 A2
HRW HA1 60 D1
HYS/HAR UB3 94 E6
RYLN/HDSTN HA2 42 D6
Harrow View Rd EA W5 97 H3
Harrow Wy OXHEY WD19 27 J5
Harrow Weald Pk
KTN/HRWW/WS HA3 42 D2
Harry Cl THHTH CR7 196 D3
Harston Dr PEND EN3 25 J1
Hartcliff Ct HNWL W7 * 116 A2
Hart Crs CHIG IG7 55 F1
Hart Dyke Rd STMC/STPC BR5 202 D6
Harte Rd HSLW TW3 134 E3
Hartfield Av NTHLT UB5 95 F1
Hartfield Crs WIM/MER SW19 177 J3
WWKM BR4 214 E1
Hartfield Gv PGE/AN SE20 181 J4
Hartfield Rd CHSGTN KT9 205 K3
WIM/MER SW19 177 J2
WWKM BR4 214 E2
Hartfield Ter BOW E3 105 J1
Hartford Av
KTN/HRWW/WS HA3 43 G6
Hartford Rd BXLY DA5 169 H1
HOR/WEW KT19 206 C4
Hart Gv EA W5 117 H1
STHL UB1 96 A4
Hartham Cl HOLWY N7 84 E3
ISLW TW7 136 B2
Hartham Rd HOLWY N7 84 E3
ISLW TW7 136 A2
TOTM N17 50 B5
Harting Rd ELTH/MOT SE9 166 D6
Hartington Cl HRW HA1 78 E2
ORP BR6 216 C3
Hartington Rd CAN/RD E16 107 F5
CHSWK W4 137 J1
NWDGN UB2 * 114 D3
TWK TW1 156 C2
VX/NE SW8 141 K2
WALTH E17 69 G3
WEA W13 97 H6
Hartismere Rd FUL/PGN SW6 139 J1
Hartlake Rd HOM E9 87 F4
Hartland Cl EDGW HA8 30 C4
WCHMH N21 35 J1
Hartland Dr EDGW HA8 30 C4
RSLP HA4 77 F1
Hartland Rd CAMTN NW1 * 84 B5
FBAR/BDGN N11 47 K1
HCH RM12 75 J6
HPTN TW12 155 G6
ISLW TW7 136 B4
KIL/WHAMP NW6 100 D1
MRDN SM4 193 K4
SRTFD E15 88 D5
Hartland Road Arches
CAMTN NW1 * 84 A5
Hartlands Cl BXLY DA5 169 G1
The Hartlands HEST TW5 114 A6
Hartland Wy CROY/NA CR0 198 B6
MRDN SM4 193 J4
Hartley Av EHAM E6 89 J6
MLHL NW7 45 H1
Hartley Cl BMLY BR1 184 E5
MLHL NW7 45 H1
Hartley Rd CROY/NA CR0 196 D4
WAN E11 70 D5
WELL DA16 148 D1
Hartley St BETH E2 104 E2
Hartmann Rd CAN/RD E16 126 C1
Hartnoll St HOLWY N7 85 F3
Harton Cl BMLY BR1 184 C4
Harton Rd ED N9 36 D4
Harton St DEPT SE8 144 D2
Hartsbourne Av BUSH WD23 28 C4
Hartsbourne Cl BUSH WD23 28 D4
Hartsbourne Rd BUSH WD23 28 D4
Hartscroft CROY/NA CR0 213 G6
Harts Gv WFD IG8 52 E1
Hartshorn Gdns EHAM E6 108 A3
Harts La BARK IG11 90 B5
Hart's La NWCR SE14 144 B1
Hartslock Dr ABYW SE2 128 E2
Hartsmead Rd ELTH/MOT SE9 166 E4
Hart Sq MRDN SM4 * 194 A2
Hart St MON EC3R 13 H5
Hartsway PEND EN3 24 D5
Hartswood Gdns SHB W12 * 118 C3
Hartswood Gn BUSH WD23 28 D4
Hartswood Rd SHB W12 118 C2
Hartsworth Cl PLSTW E13 106 D1
Hartville Rd
WOOL/PLUM SE18 127 K4
Hartwell Cl BRXS/STRHM SW2 162 A3
Hartwell Dr CHING E4 52 A2
Hartwell St HACK E8 86 B4
Harvard Hl CHSWK W4 117 J5
Harvard Rd CHSWK W4 117 J5
ISLW TW7 135 K2
LEW SE13 145 F6
Harvel Cl CHST BR7 186 B6
Harvel Crs ABYW SE2 128 E5
Harvest Bank Rd
WWKM BR4 214 E
Harvesters Cl ISLW TW7 135 J
Harvest La LOU IG10 39 H
THDIT KT7 190 B
Harvest Rd FELT TW13 153 K
Harvest Wy SWLY BR8 203 K
Harvey Dr HPTN TW12 173 G
Harvey Gdns CHARL SE7 126 B
Harvey Rd CEND/HSY/T N8 67 F
CMBW SE5 142 E
HSLWW TW4 154 E
IL IG1 90 E
NTHLT UB5 77 C
WAN E11 70 C
Harvey's La ROMW/RG RM7 75 F
Harvey St IS N1 7 F
Harvill Rd SCUP DA14 186 E
Harvington Wk HACK E8 * 86 C
Harvist Rd KIL/WHAMP NW6 100 C
Harwell Cl RSLP HA4 58 E
Harwood Av BMLY BR1 184 A
MTCM CR4 178 D
Harwood Cl ALP/SUD HA0 79 K
NFNCH/WDSPK N12 47
Harwood Ms FUL/PGN SW6 * 140
Harwood Rd FUL/PGN SW6 139
Harwood Ter FUL/PGN SW6 140
Hascombe Ter CMBW SE5 * 142
Haselbury Rd UED N18 36
Haseley End FSTH SE23 * 163
Haselrigge Rd CLAP SW4 141
Haseltine Rd SYD SE26 164
Haselwood Dr ENC/FH EN2 23
Haskard Rd DAGW RM9 91
Hasker St CHEL SW3 14
Haslam Av CHEAM SM3 193
Haslam Cl HGDN/ICK UB10 58
IS N1 85
Haslam St PECK SE15 143
Haslemere Av EBAR EN4 33
HDN NW4 64
HEST TW5 134
HNWL W7 116
MTCM CR4 178
WAND/EARL SW18 160
Haslemere Cl HPTN TW12 172
WLGTN SM6 210
Haslemere Gdns FNCH N3 46
Haslemere Heathrow Est
HSLWW TW4 * 134
Haslemere Rd
CEND/HSY/T N8 66
GDMY/SEVK IG3 73
THHTH CR7 196
WCHMH N21 35
Hasler Cl THMD SE28 109
Hasluck Gdns BAR EN5 33
Hassard St BETH E2
Hassendean Rd
BKHTH/KID SE3 126
Hassett Rd HOM E9 87
Hassocks Cl SYD SE26 163

Hassocks Rd
STRHM/NOR SW16 179 J4
Hassock Wd HAYES BR2 215 H2
Hassop Rd CRICK NW2 82 B2
Hasted Rd CHARL SE7 126 C5
Hastings Av BARK/HLT IG6 72 C1
Hastings Cl ALP/SUD HA0 79 J2
BAR EN5 21 G5
PECK SE15 * 143 H1
Hastings Dr SURB KT6 190 D3
Hastings Pl CROY/NA CR0 197 G5
Hastings Rd CROY/NA CR0 197 G5
FBAR/BDGN N11 48 C1
GPK RM2 75 K2
HAYES BR2 200 D5
TOTM N17 * 49 K6
WEA W13 97 H6
Hastings St STPAN WC1H 4 E5
Hastings Ter
SEVS/STOTM N15 * 67 J2
Hastings St WOOL/PLUM SE18 127 H3
Hastoe Cl YEAD UB4 95 J3
Hatcham Park Ms NWCR SE14 144 A2
Hatcham Park Rd NWCR SE14 144 A2
Hatcham Rd PECK SE15 123 K6
Hatchard Rd ARCH N19 66 D6
Hatchcroft HDN NW4 45 K6
Hatchers Ms STHWK SE1 19 H3
Hatchett Rd
EBED/NFELT TW14 153 F3
Hatch Gv CHDH RM6 74 A1
Hatch La CHING E4 38 B6
WDR/YW UB7 132 A1
Hatch Pl KUTN/CMB KT2 175 G1
Hatch Rd STRHM/NOR SW16 179 K5
Hatch Side CHIG IG7 54 A1
The Hatch PEND EN3 25 F2
Hatchwoods WFD IG8 38 D6
Hatcliffe Cl BKHTH/KID SE3 145 J4
Hatcliffe St GNWCH SE10 125 J5
Hatfield Cl BARK/HLT IG6 54 B6
BELMT SM2 208 E6
MTCM CR4 * 194 C1
Hatfield Rd CHSWK W4 118 A2
HNWL W7 116 B1
SRTFD E15 88 C3
Hatfields STHWK SE1 11 K7
Hathaway Cl CHIG IG7 54 B2
HAYES BR2 200 E5
RSLP HA4 76 D2
STAN HA7 43 G1
Hathaway Crs MNPK E12 89 K4
Hathaway Gdns CHDH RM6 73 K2
WEA W13 97 F4
Hathaway Rd CROY/NA CR0 196 C4
Hatherleigh Cl CHSGTN KT9 205 K3
MRDN SM4 193 K1
Hatherleigh Rd RSLP HA4 58 E6
Hatherley Crs BFN/LL DA15 168 B4
Hatherley Gdns
CEND/HSY/T N8 66 E3
EHAM E6 107 H2
Hatherley Gv BAY/PAD W2 101 F5
Hatherley Ms WALTH E17 69 J1
Hatherley Rd RCH/KEW TW9 137 G2
SCUP DA14 168 B5
WALTH E17 69 H1
Hatherley St WEST SW1P 16 B7
Hathern Gdns ELTH/MOT SE9 167 F6
Hatherop Rd HPTN TW12 172 E3
Hathorne Cl PECK SE15 143 J3
Hathorne Ter ARCH N19 * 66 D5
Hathway St PECK SE15 143 K3
Hatley Av BARK/HLT IG6 72 C1
Hatley Cl FBAR/BDGN N11 47 K1
Hatley Rd FSBYPK N4 67 F6
Hat & Mitre Ct FARR EC1M 6 B7
Hatteraick St
BERM/RHTH SE16 123 K2
Hattersfield Cl BELV DA17 129 G4
Hatters La WATW WD18 26 B1
Hatton Cl WOOL/PLUM SE18 147 J1
Hatton Cross Est
HTHAIR TW6 * 133 J5
Hatton Gdn HCIRC EC1N 11 K1
Hatton Gdns MTCM CR4 194 E2
Hatton Gn EBED/NFELT TW14 133 K5
Hatton Gv WDR/YW UB7 * 112 A2
Hatton Pl HCIRC EC1N 5 K7
Hatton Rd CROY/NA CR0 196 B5
EBED/NFELT TW14 153 F2
HTHAIR TW6 133 J5
Hatton Rw STJWD NW8 * 2 B7
Hatton St STJWD NW8 2 B7
Hatton Wall HCIRC EC1N 11 J1
Haunch of Venison Yd
OXSTW W1C * 9 J4
Havana Cl ROM RM1 75 G2
Havana Rd WIM/MER SW19 154 E2
Havannah St POP/IOD E14 124 D2
Havant Rd WALTH E17 52 A6
Havelock Cl SHB W12 * 99 K6
Havelock Pl HRW HA1 60 E3
Havelock Rd BELV DA17 * 129 G4
CROY/NA CR0 197 G6
HAYES BR2 200 B1
KTN/HRWW/WS HA3 42 E6
NWDGN UB2 114 D3
TOTM N17 50 C5
WIM/MER SW19 178 B1
Havelock St IS N1 84 E6
Havelock Ter VX/NE SW8 141 G1
Havelock Wk FSTH SE23 163 K3
Haven Cl ELTH/MOT SE9 166 E5
ESH/CLAY KT10 189 K6
SCUP DA14 186 D2
WIM/MER SW19 159 G5
YEAD UB4 94 C4
Haven Ct BRYLDS KT5 * 191 G3
Haven Gn EA W5 97 K5
Havenhurst Ri ENC/FH EN2 23 G3
Haven La EA W5 98 A5
Haven Rd ASHF TW15 152 E6
Havens Ms BOW E3 105 H4
Haven St CAMTN NW1 84 B5
Havenswood Ct
KUTN/CMB KT2 175 J2
The Haven RCH/KEW TW9 137 H4
Havenwood WBLY HA9 80 D1
Haverfield Est BTFD TW8 117 F6
Haverfield Gdns
RCH/KEW TW9 137 H1
Haverfield Rd BOW E3 105 G2
Haverford Wy EDGW HA8 44 B4
Havergal Vls
SEVS/STOTM N15 * 67 H1
Haverhill Rd BAL SW12 161 H3
CHING E4 38 A3
Havering Dr ROM RM1 75 G1
Havering Gdns CHDH RM6 73 J2
Havering Rd ROM RM1 57 F5
Havering St WCHPL E1 105 F5
Havering Wy BARK IG11 109 H2
Haversham Cl TWK TW1 156 E2
Haversham Pl HGT N6 65 K6
Haverstock Hl HAMP NW3 83 J4
Haverstock Pl FSBYE EC1V 5 K3
Haverstock Rd KTTN NW5 84 A3
Haverstock St IS N1 6 B3
Haverthwaite Rd ORP BR6 216 D1
Havil St CMBW SE5 143 F2
Havisham Pl NRWD SE19 180 C2
Hawarden Gv HNHL SE24 162 D2
Hawarden Hl CRICK NW2 81 J1
Hawarden Rd WALTH E17 69 F1
Hawbridge Rd WAN E11 70 B5
Hawes Cl NTHWD HA6 40 D3
Hawes La WWKM BR4 199 F5
Hawes Rd BMLY BR1 184 A4
UED N18 50 D2
Hawes St IS N1 85 H5
Hawfield Bank ORP BR6 217 J1
Hawgood St BOW E3 105 J4
Hawkdene CHING E4 37 K1
Hawke Park Rd WDGN N22 49 H6
Hawke Pl BERM/RHTH SE16 * 124 A2
Hawke Rd NRWD SE19 180 E2
Hawker Pl WALTH E17 52 A5
Hawker Rd CROY/NA CR0 211 F4
Hawkesbury Rd
PUT/ROE SW15 138 E6
Hawkesfield Rd FSTH SE23 164 B4
Hawkesley Cl TWK TW1 156 B6
Hawkes Rd
EBED/NFELT TW14 153 K2
MTCM CR4 178 D4
Hawkesworth Cl NTHWD HA6 40 C3
Hawkhurst Gdns CRW RM5 57 F2
Hawkhurst Rd
STRHM/NOR SW16 179 J3
Hawkhurst Wy NWMAL KT3 192 A2
WWKM BR4 198 E6
Hawkins Cl EDGW HA8 45 F1
HRW HA1 60 D4
Hawkins Rd TEDD TW11 174 C2
WLSDN NW10 81 G5
Hawkins Ter CHARL SE7 126 D5
Hawkins Wy CAT SE6 182 D1
Hawkley Gdns WNWD SE27 162 C4
Hawkridge Cl CHDH RM6 73 J3
Hawksbrook La BECK BR3 198 E3
Hawkshaw Cl
BRXS/STRHM SW2 161 K2
Hawkshead Cl BMLY BR1 183 H3
Hawkshead Rd CHSWK W4 118 B3
WLSDN NW10 * 81 H5
Hawkshill Cl ESH/CLAY KT10 204 A4
Hawkshill Pl ESH/CLAY KT10 * 204 A4
Hawkslade Rd PECK SE15 144 A6
Hawksley Rd
STNW/STAM N16 85 K1
Hawks Ms GNWCH SE10 * 145 F1
Hawksmoor Cl EHAM E6 107 J5
WOOL/PLUM SE18 127 K5
Hawksmoor Ms WCHPL E1 104 D6
Hawksmoor St HMSMTH W6 119 G6
Hawksmouth CHING E4 37 K2
Hawks Rd KUT/HW KT1 175 G5
Hawkstone Est
BERM/RHTH SE16 123 K4
Hawkstone Rd
BERM/RHTH SE16 123 K4
Hawkwell Wk IS N1 * 85 J6
Hawkwood Crs CHING E4 37 K1
Hawkwood La CHST BR7 185 H4
Hawkwood Mt CLPT E5 68 D5
Hawlands Dr PIN HA5 59 J4
Hawley Cl HPTN TW12 172 E2
Hawley Crs CAMTN NW1 84 B5
Hawley Ms CAMTN NW1 84 B5
Hawley Rd CAMTN NW1 84 B5
UED N18 51 F1
Hawley Ter RDART DA2 * 171 K6
Hawstead Rd CAT SE6 164 E1
Hawsted BKHH IG9 39 F2
Hawthorn Av PLMGR N13 48 E1
RAIN RM13 111 K3
THHTH CR7 180 C4
Hawthorn Centre HRW HA1 61 F1
Hawthorn Cl HEST TW5 134 A1
HPTN TW12 173 F1
STMC/STPC BR5 201 J3
Hawthorn Crs TOOT SW17 179 F1
Hawthornden Cl
NFNCH/WDSPK N12 47 J2
Hawthorndene Cl HAYES BR2 199 J6
Hawthorn Dr
RYLN/HDSTN HA2 60 A3
WWKM BR4 214 C2
Hawthorne Av BOW E3 87 H6
CAR SM5 210 A5
KTN/HRWW/WS HA3 61 G3
MTCM CR4 178 C5
RSLP HA4 59 F3
Hawthorne Cl BMLY BR1 184 E6
IS N1 86 A4
Hawthorne Ct
STWL/WRAY TW19 * 152 A2
Hawthorne Crs WDR/YW UB7 112 C2
Hawthorne Gv
CDALE/KGS NW9 62 E4
Hawthorne Rd BMLY BR1 184 E6
UED N18 50 B2
WALTH E17 51 J6
Hawthorne Wy ED N9 36 B4
STWL/WRAY TW19 152 A2
Hawthorn Farm Av
NTHLT UB5 77 J6
Hawthorn Gdns EA W5 116 E3
Hawthorn Gv ENC/FH EN2 23 K1
PGE/AN SE20 181 J4
Hawthorn Hatch BTFD TW8 136 C1
Hawthorn Ms MLHL NW7 46 C4
Hawthorn Pl ERITH DA8 129 K5
HYS/HAR UB3 * 94 D6
Hawthorn Rd BTFD TW8 136 C1
CEND/HSY/T N8 48 D6
FELT TW13 153 K3
SUT SM1 209 H3
WFD IG8 39 G6
WLGTN SM6 210 B5
WLSDN NW10 81 J5
Hawthorns WFD IG8 38 E5
The Hawthorns EW KT17 207 H4
Hawthorn Ter BFN/LL DA15 168 A1
Hawthorn Wk NKENS W10 100 C3
Hawtrey Av NTHLT UB5 95 H1
Hawtrey Dr RSLP HA4 58 E4
Hawtrey Rd HAMP NW3 83 J5
Haxted Rd BMLY BR1 184 A4
Hayburn Wy HCH RM12 75 H5
Hay Cl SRTFD E15 88 C5
Haycroft Gdns WLSDN NW10 81 J6
Haycroft Rd
BRXS/STRHM SW2 141 K6
SURB KT6 190 E6
Hay Currie St POP/IOD E14 105 K5
Hayday Rd CAN/RD E16 106 E3
Hayden Dell BUSH WD23 27 K1
Haydens Cl STMC/STPC BR5 202 D4
Hayden's Pl NTGHL W11 100 D5
Hayden Wy CRW RM5 56 E5
Haydock Av NTHLT UB5 78 A4
Haydock Gn NTHLT UB5 78 A4
Haydon Cl CDALE/KGS NW9 62 E1
EN EN1 36 A1
HARH RM3 57 K3
Haydon Dell Farm
BUSH WD23 * 27 K2
Haydon Dr PIN HA5 58 E1
Haydon Park Rd
WIM/MER SW19 177 K1
Haydon Rd BCTR RM8 73 J6
OXHEY WD19 27 J1
Haydon's Rd WIM/MER SW19 178 A1
Haydon St TWRH EC3N 13 J5
Haydon Wk WCHPL E1 13 J4
Haydon Wy
WAND/EARL SW18 140 B5
Hayes Cha WWKM BR4 199 G3
Hayes Crs CHEAM SM3 208 B2
GLDGN NW11 64 D2
Hayes Dr RAIN RM13 93 K5
Hayes End Dr YEAD UB4 94 B4
Hayes End Rd YEAD UB4 94 B3
Hayesford Park Dr
HAYES BR2 199 J2
Hayes Gv EDUL SE22 143 G4
Hayes Hl HAYES BR2 199 H5
Hayes Hill Rd HAYES BR2 199 J5
Hayes La BECK BR3 183 G6
HAYES BR2 200 A1
Hayes Mead Rd HAYES BR2 199 H5
Hayes Pl CAMTN NW1 2 D7
Hayes Rd NWDGN UB2 114 A4
Hayes St HAYES BR2 200 A5
Hayes Wy BECK BR3 199 F1
Hayes Wood Av HAYES BR2 200 A5
Hayfield Pas WCHPL E1 104 E3
Hayfield Rd STMC/STPC BR5 202 B2
Haygarth Pl WIM/MER SW19 177 G1
Haygreen Cl KUTN/CMB KT2 175 J2
Hay Hl MYFR/PICC W1J 9 K6
Hayland Cl CDALE/KGS NW9 63 F1
Hay La CDALE/KGS NW9 63 F1
Hayles St LBTH SE11 18 A6
Haylett Gdns KUT/HW KT1 * 190 E1
Hayling Av FELT TW13 153 K5
Hayling Cl STNW/STAM N16 86 A3
Hayling Rd OXHEY WD19 26 D5
Hayman Crs YEAD UB4 94 B1
Haymarket STJS SW1Y 10 C6
Haymeads Dr ESH/CLAY KT10 204 C4
Haymer Gdns WPK KT4 207 J1
Haymerle Rd PECK SE15 123 H6
Haymill Cl GFD/PVL UB6 97 F2
Hayne Rd BECK BR3 182 C4
Haynes Cl BKHTH/KID SE3 145 H4
FBAR/BDGN N11 34 A5
TOTM N17 50 D3
Haynes Dr ED N9 36 D5
Haynes La NRWD SE19 181 F2
Haynes Rd ALP/SUD HA0 80 A5
Hayne St STBT EC1A 12 B1
Haynt Wk RYNPK SW20 177 H6
Hay Pl SWLY BR8 * 203 K3
Hay's La STHWK SE1 13 G7
Haysleigh Gdns PGE/AN SE20 181 H5
Hay's Ms MYFR/PICC W1J 9 J6
Haysoms Cl ROM RM1 75 G1
Haystall Cl YEAD UB4 94 C1
Hay St BETH E2 86 C6
Hayter Rd BRXS/STRHM SW2 141 K6
Hayton Cl HACK E8 86 B4
Hayward Cl WIM/MER SW19 178 A3
Hayward Dr DART DA1 * 171 J5
Hayward Gdns
PUT/ROE SW15 159 F1
Hayward Rd THDIT KT7 190 A5
TRDG/WHET N20 33 G4
Haywards Cl CHDH RM6 73 J2
Hayward's Pl CLKNW EC1R * 6 A7
Haywood Cl PIN HA5 41 H5
Haywood Ri ORP BR6 216 E3
Haywood Rd HAYES BR2 200 C1
Hazel Av WDR/YW UB7 112 D3
Hazelbank BRYLDS KT5 191 K5
Hazelbank Rd CAT SE6 165 G4
Hazelbourne Rd BAL SW12 161 G1
Hazelbrouck Gdns
BARK/HLT IG6 54 D3
Hazelbury Cl WIM/MER SW19 177 K5
Hazelbury Gn ED N9 36 A5
Hazelbury La ED N9 36 A5
Hazel Cl BTFD TW8 * 136 C1
CDALE/KGS NW9 45 H5
CROY/NA CR0 198 A4
HCH RM12 93 K1
MTCM CR4 195 J1
PLMGR N13 35 K5
WHTN TW2 155 H2
Hazelcroft PIN HA5 42 A2
Hazeldean Rd WLSDN NW10 81 F5
Hazeldene Dr PIN HA5 41 G6
Hazeldene Gdns
HGDN/ICK UB10 76 A6
Hazeldene Rd
GDMY/SEVK IG3 73 H6
WELL DA16 148 D3
Hazeldon Rd BROCKY SE4 144 B6
Hazel Dr ERITH DA8 150 D2
Hazeleigh Gdns WFD IG8 53 J1
Hazel Gdns EDGW HA8 30 D6
Hazelgreen Cl WCHMH N21 35 H3
Hazel Gv ALP/SUD HA0 80 A6
CHDH RM6 56 A6
EN EN1 * 36 C1
FELT TW13 153 K3
ORP BR6 201 G6
SYD SE26 164 A6
Hazelhurst BECK BR3 183 G4
Hazelhurst Rd TOOT SW17 160 B6
Hazel La BARK/HLT IG6 54 B2
Hazell Crs CRW RM5 56 D4
Hazellville Rd ARCH N19 66 D4
Hazelmere Cl
EBED/NFELT TW14 153 G1
NTHLT UB5 95 K1
Hazelmere Dr NTHLT UB5 95 K1
Hazelmere Gdns EMPK RM11 75 K2
Hazelmere Rd
KIL/WHAMP NW6 82 D6
NTHLT UB5 95 K1
STMC/STPC BR5 201 H1
Hazelmere Wk NTHLT UB5 95 K1
Hazel Rd SRTFD E15 * 88 C3
WLSDN NW10 99 K2
Hazel Rw
NFNCH/WDSPK N12 * 47 H1
Hazeltree La NTHLT UB5 95 J2
Hazel Wk HAYES BR2 201 F3
Hazel Wy CHING E4 51 H2
STHWK SE1 19 J6
Hazelwood Av MRDN SM4 194 A1
Hazelwood Cl CLPT E5 87 G1
EA W5 117 F2
RYLN/HDSTN HA2 60 B1
Hazelwood Ct SURB KT6 191 F3
Hazelwood Dr PIN HA5 41 F5
Hazelwood La PLMGR N13 35 G6
Hazelwood Park Cl CHIG IG7 54 E1
Hazelwood Rd EN EN1 36 B1
RKW/CH/CXG WD3 26 A1
WALTH E17 69 G2
Hazlebury Rd FUL/PGN SW6 140 A3
Hazledean Rd CROY/NA CR0 196 E6
Hazledene Rd CHSWK W4 117 K6
Hazlemere Gdns WPK KT4 192 D5
Hazlewell Rd PUT/ROE SW15 139 F6
Hazlewood Crs NKENS W10 100 C3
Hazlitt Cl FELT TW13 154 D6
Hazlitt Ms WKENS W14 * 119 H3
Hazlitt Rd WKENS W14 119 H3
Heacham Av HGDN/ICK UB10 76 A1
Headcorn Rd THHTH CR7 196 A1
TOTM N17 50 B3
Headfort Pl KTBR SW1X 15 H3
Headington Rd
WAND/EARL SW18 160 B3
Headlam Rd CLAP SW4 161 J1
Headlam St WCHPL E1 104 D3
Headley Ap GNTH/NBYPK IG2 72 A2
Headley Av WLGTN SM6 211 F3
Headley Cl CHSGTN KT9 206 C4
Headley Dr CROY/NA CR0 214 A5
GNTH/NBYPK IG2 72 B3
Heads Ms NTGHL W11 100 E5
Headstone Dr HRW HA1 60 D1
KTN/HRWW/WS HA3 42 E6
Headstone Gdns
RYLN/HDSTN HA2 60 C1
Headstone La
RYLN/HDSTN HA2 42 B5
Headstone Pde HRW HA1 * 60 D1
Headstone Rd HRW HA1 60 E2
Head St WCHPL E1 105 F5
Headway Cl
RCHPK/HAM TW10 156 D6
The Headway EW KT17 207 H6
Heald St NWCR SE14 144 C2
Healey Rd WATW WD18 26 D1
Healey St CAMTN NW1 * 84 B4
Healy Dr ORP BR6 217 F2
Hearne Rd CHSWK W4 117 H5
Hearn Ri NTHLT UB5 77 H6
Hearn Rd ROM RM1 75 H3
Hearn's Blds WALW SE17 19 F7
Hearns Cl STMC/STPC BR5 202 D1
Hearnshaw St POP/IOD E14 105 G5
Hearns Rd STMC/STPC BR5 202 D1
Hearn St SDTCH EC2A 7 H7
Hearnville Rd BAL SW12 161 F3
Heatham Pk WHTN TW2 156 A2
Heath Av BXLYHN DA7 128 E6
Heathbourne Rd BUSH WD23 28 E4
Heath Brow HAMP NW3 83 G1
Heath Cl EA W5 98 B3
GLDGN NW11 65 F4
GPK RM2 57 J6
HYS/HAR UB3 133 G1
SAND/SEL CR2 211 H4
STMC/STPC BR5 202 D3
Heathcote Av CLAY IG5 53 K5
Heathcote Gv CHING E4 38 A5
Heathcote Rd TWK TW1 156 C1
Heathcote St BMSBY WC1N 5 G6
Heathcote Wy WDR/YW UB7 112 A1
Heathcroft EA W5 98 B3
Heathcroft Gdns WALTH E17 52 B4
Heathdale Av HSLWW TW4 134 D4
Heathdene Dr BELV DA17 129 J4
Heathdene Rd
STRHM/NOR SW16 180 A3
WLGTN SM6 210 B5
Heath Dr BELMT SM2 209 G6
GPK RM2 57 J4
HAMP NW3 83 F2
RYNPK SW20 193 F1
Heathedge SYD SE26 * 163 J4
Heather Av ROM RM1 57 F5
Heatherbank CHST BR7 185 F5
ELTH/MOT SE9 146 E3
Heather Cl EHAM E6 108 A5
HPTN TW12 172 E4
ISLW TW7 135 J6
LEW SE13 165 G1
ROM RM1 57 F4
VX/NE SW8 141 G4
Heatherdale Cl
KUTN/CMB KT2 175 H2
Heatherdene Cl MTCM CR4 194 C1
NFNCH/WDSPK N12 47 G4
Heather Dr ENC/FH EN2 23 H3
ROM RM1 57 F5
Heatherfold Wy PIN HA5 40 D6
Heather Gdns BELMT SM2 208 E4
GLDGN NW11 64 C3
ROM RM1 57 F5
Heather Gln ROM RM1 57 F5
Heatherlea Gv WPK KT4 193 F5
Heatherley Dr CLAY IG5 53 K6
Heather Park Dr
ALP/SUD HA0 80 C5
Heather Park Pde
ALP/SUD HA0 * 80 B5
Heather Pl ESH/CLAY KT10 204 B2
Heather Rd CHING E4 51 H2
CRICK NW2 63 H6
Heatherset Cl ESH/CLAY KT10 204 C3
Heatherset Gdns
STRHM/NOR SW16 180 A3
Heatherside Rd
HOR/WEW KT19 207 F5
SCUP DA14 168 D5
The Heathers
STWL/WRAY TW19 152 C2
Heather Wk EDGW HA8 44 D1
NKENS W10 100 C3
Heather Wy ROM RM1 57 F4
SAND/SEL CR2 213 F6
STAN HA7 43 F2
Heatherwood Cl MNPK E12 71 F6
Heatherwood Dr YEAD UB4 94 B1
Heathfield CHING E4 38 A5
CHST BR7 185 H2
HRW HA1 * 61 F4
Heathfield Av
WAND/EARL SW18 160 C2
Heathfield Cl CAN/RD E16 107 H4
HAYES BR2 215 G3
OXHEY WD19 27 G2
Heathfield Dr MTCM CR4 178 D3
Heathfield Gdns CHSWK W4 117 K5
CROY/NA CR0 * 211 J2
GLDGN NW11 64 B3
WAND/EARL SW18 160 C1
Heathfield La CHST BR7 185 H2
Heathfield North WHTN TW2 155 K2
Heathfield Pk CRICK NW2 82 A4
Heathfield Park Dr
CHDH RM6 73 H2
Heathfield Ri RSLP HA4 58 A4
Heathfield Rd ACT W3 117 J2
BMLY BR1 183 J3
HAYES BR2 215 G3
SAND/SEL CR2 211 K3
WAND/EARL SW18 160 B1
Heathfield South WHTN TW2 156 A2
Heathfield Sq
WAND/EARL SW18 160 C2
Heathfield Ter CHSWK W4 117 K5
WOOL/PLUM SE18 127 K6
Heathfield V SAND/SEL CR2 213 F6
Heath Gdns DART DA1 * 171 F3
TWK TW1 156 A3
Heathgate GLDGN NW11 65 F3
Heathgate Pl HAMP NW3 83 K2
Heath Gv PGE/AN SE20 181 K3
Heath Hurst Rd HAMP NW3 83 J2
Heathhurst Rd SAND/SEL CR2 212 A6
Heathland Rd
STNW/STAM N16 68 A5
Heathlands Cl TWK TW1 156 A4
Heathlands Ct HSLWW TW4 134 D6
Heathlands Wy HSLWW TW4 134 D6
Heath La BKHTH/KID SE3 145 G3
Heathlee Rd BKHTH/KID SE3 145 J5
Heathley End CHST BR7 185 H2
Heath Ldg BUSH WD23 * 28 D3
Heathman's Rd FUL/PGN SW6 139 J2
Heath Md WIM/MER SW19 159 G5
Heath Park Dr BMLY BR1 184 D6
Heath Park Rd GPK RM2 75 J2
Heath Ri PUT/ROE SW15 159 G1
Heath Rd BXLY DA5 169 K3
CHDH RM6 73 K4
HGDN/ICK UB10 94 A3
HRW HA1 60 C4
HSLW TW3 135 H5
OXHEY WD19 27 H2
THHTH CR7 180 D6
TWK TW1 156 A3
VX/NE SW8 141 G3
Heath's Cl EN EN1 23 K3
Heathside ESH/CLAY KT10 204 E1
HAMP NW3 83 H2
HSLWW TW4 154 E2
Heath Side STMC/STPC BR5 201 H5
Heathside Cl ESH/CLAY KT10 204 E1
GNTH/NBYPK IG2 72 D2
NTHWD HA6 40 B1
Heathside Rd NTHWD HA6 26 B6
Heathstan Rd SHB W12 99 J5
Heath St HAMP NW3 83 G2
The Heath HNWL W7 * 115 K2
Heath Vw EFNCH N2 65 G1
Heath View Cl EFNCH N2 65 G1
Heath View Dr ABYW SE2 128 E6
Heathview Gdns
PUT/ROE SW15 159 F2
Heathview Rd THHTH CR7 196 B1
Heath Vls WAND/EARL SW18 * 160 B3
WOOL/PLUM SE18 128 A5
Heathville Rd ARCH N19 66 E4
Heathwall St BTSEA SW11 140 E4
Heathway CROY/NA CR0 213 H1
DAGW RM9 92 B2
NWDGN UB2 * 114 C4
WFD IG8 39 G6
Heathwood Gdns CHARL SE7 126 D4

SWLY BR8 187 K5
Heathwood Pde SWLY BR8 * 187 K5
Heaton Av HARH RM3 57 K3
Heaton Cl CHING E4 38 A5
Heaton Grange Rd GPK RM2 57 H4
Heaton Rd MTCM CR4 179 F3
PECK SE15 143 J4
Heaven Tree Cl IS N1 85 J3
Heaver Rd BTSEA SW11 * 140 C4
Heavitree Cl
WOOL/PLUM SE18 127 J5
Heavitree Rd
WOOL/PLUM SE18 127 J5
Hebden Ter TOTM N17 50 A2
Hebdon Rd TOOT SW17 160 D5
Heber Rd CRICK NW2 82 B3
EDUL SE22 163 G1
Hebron Rd HMSMTH W6 118 E3
Hecham Cl WALTH E17 51 G5
Heckfield Pl FUL/PGN SW6 139 K1
Heckford Cl WATW WD18 26 A1
Heckford St WAP E1W 105 F6
Hector Cl ED N9 36 C4
Hector St WOOL/PLUM SE18 * 127 K4
Heddington Gv HOLWY N7 85 F3
Heddon Cl ISLW TW7 136 B5
Heddon Court Av EBAR EN4 21 K6
Heddon Court Pde
EBAR EN4 * 22 A6
Heddon Rd EBAR EN4 21 K6
Heddon St CONDST W1S 10 A6
Hedge Hl ENC/FH EN2 23 H2
Hedge La PLMGR N13 35 H5
Hedgeley REDBR IG4 71 K1
Hedgemans Rd DAGW RM9 91 K5
Hedgemans Wy DAGW RM9 92 A4
Hedgerley Gdns
GFD/PVL UB6 96 C1
Hedger's Gv HOM E9 * 87 G4
Hedger St LBTH SE11 18 A6
Hedgewood Gdns CLAY IG5 72 A1
Hedgley St LEE/GVPK SE12 145 J6
Hedingham Cl IS N1 85 J5
Hedingham Rd BCTR RM8 91 H3
Hedley Rd WHTN TW2 155 F2
Hedley Rw HBRY N5 85 K3
Heenan Cl BARK IG11 90 C4
Heene Rd ENC/FH EN2 23 K3
Heidegger Crs BARN SW13 138 E1
Heigham Rd EHAM E6 89 J5
Heighton Gdns CROY/NA CR0 211 H3
Heights Cl RYNPK SW20 176 E3
The Heights BECK BR3 * 183 F3
CHARL SE7 126 B5
NTHLT UB5 78 A3
Heiron St WALW SE17 122 C6
Helby Rd CLAP SW4 161 J1
Helder Gv LEE/GVPK SE12 165 J2
Helder St SAND/SEL CR2 211 K4
Heldmann Cl HSLW TW3 135 J5
Helegan Cl ORP BR6 217 F2
Helena Pl HACK E8 86 D6
Helena Rd EA W5 97 K4
PLSTW E13 106 D1
WALTH E17 69 J2
WLSDN NW10 81 K3
Helena Sq BERM/RHTH SE16 105 G6
Helen Av EBED/NFELT TW14 154 A2
Helen Cl E/WMO/HCT KT8 189 G1
EFNCH N2 47 G6
Helenslea Av GLDGN NW11 64 D5
Helen's Pl BETH E2 104 E2
Helen St WOOL/PLUM SE18 * 127 G4
Helford Cl RSLP HA4 58 C6
Helios Rd WLGTN SM6 195 F5
Helix Gdns BRXS/STRHM SW2 162 A1
Helix Rd BRXS/STRHM SW2 162 A1
Hellings St WAP E1W 123 H1
Helme Cl WIM/MER SW19 177 J1
Helmet Rw FSBYE EC1V 6 D6
Helmore Rd BARK IG11 91 F5
Helmsdale Cl ROM RM1 57 G3
YEAD UB4 * 95 J3
Helmsdale Rd ROM RM1 57 G3
STRHM/NOR SW16 179 H4
Helmsley Pl HACK E8 86 D5
Helmsley St HACK E8 86 D6
Helperby Rd WLSDN NW10 81 G5
Helsinki Sq BERM/RHTH SE16 124 B3
Helston Cl PIN HA5 41 K3
Helvetia St CAT SE6 164 C4
Hemans St VX/NE SW8 141 J1
Hemery Rd GFD/PVL UB6 78 D3
Hemingford Cl
NFNCH/WDSPK N12 47 H1
Hemingford Rd CHEAM SM3 208 A2
IS N1 85 F6
Heming Rd EDGW HA8 44 D2
Hemington Av
FBAR/BDGN N11 47 K1
Hemlock Cl
STRHM/NOR SW16 179 J5
Hemlock Rd SHB W12 99 H6
Hemmen La HYS/HAR UB3 94 D6
Hemming Cl HPTN TW12 173 F4
Hemmings Cl SCUP DA14 168 C4
Hemmingsmead
HOR/WEW KT19 206 E4
Hemming St WCHPL E1 104 C3
Hemmingway Cl KTTN NW5 84 A2
Hempstead Cl BKHH IG9 38 E4
Hempstead Rd WALTH E17 52 B6
Hemp Wk WALW SE17 19 F6
Hemsby Rd CHSGTN KT9 206 B4
Hemstal Rd KIL/WHAMP NW6 82 E5
Hemsted Rd ERITH DA8 150 B2
Hemswell Dr CDALE/KGS NW9 45 G4
Hemsworth St IS N1 7 G2
Henbury Wy OXHEY WD19 27 H5
Henchman St SHB W12 99 H5
Hendale Av HDN NW4 45 J6
Henderson Cl EMPK RM11 75 K6
WLSDN NW10 80 E4
Henderson Dr DART DA1 151 K5
STJWD NW8 2 A6
Henderson Rd CROY/NA CR0 196 E3
ED N9 36 D3
FSTGT E7 89 G4
WAND/EARL SW18 160 D2
YEAD UB4 94 E2
Hendham Rd TOOT SW17 160 D4
Hendon Av FNCH N3 46 C4
Hendon Gdns CRW RM5 56 E2
Hendon Gv HOR/WEW KT19 206 C6
Hendon Hall Ct HDN NW4 * 46 B6
Hendon La FNCH N3 46 C6
Hendon Park Rw
GLDGN NW11 * 64 D3
Hendon Rd ED N9 36 C4
Hendon Wy CRICK NW2 64 B4
STWL/WRAY TW19 132 A6
Hendon Wood La MLHL NW7 31 J3
Hendren Cl GFD/PVL UB6 78 D3
Hendre Rd STHWK SE1 19 H7
Hendrick Av BAL SW12 160 E1
Heneage La HDTCH EC3A 13 H4
Heneage St WCHPL E1 13 K1
Henfield Cl ARCH N19 66 C5
BXLY DA5 169 H1
Henfield Rd WIM/MER SW19 177 J4
Hengelo Gdns MTCM CR4 194 C1
Hengist Rd ERITH DA8 149 K1
LEE/GVPK SE12 166 A2
Hengist Wy HAYES BR2 199 G1
Hengrave Rd FSTH SE23 163 K2
Hengrove Ct BXLY DA5 169 F3
Hengrove Crs ASHF TW15 152 A5
Henley Av CHEAM SM3 208 C1
Henley Cl BERM/RHTH SE16 * 123 K2
GFD/PVL UB6 * 96 C1
ISLW TW7 136 A2
Henley Dr KUTN/CMB KT2 176 C3
STHWK SE1 19 K6
Henley Gdns CHDH RM6 74 A2
PIN HA5 41 F6
Henley Rd CAN/RD E16 126 E2
IL IG1 90 C2
UED N18 36 A6
WLSDN NW10 82 A6
Henley St BTSEA SW11 141 F3
Henley Wy FELT TW13 172 C1
Henneker Cl CRW RM5 56 E2
Hennel Cl FSTH SE23 163 K5
Hennessy Rd ED N9 36 E4
Henniker Gdns EHAM E6 107 H2
Henniker Ms CHEL SW3 120 C6
Henniker Rd SRTFD E15 88 B3
Henningham Rd TOTM N17 49 K4
Henning St BTSEA SW11 140 D2
Henrietta Cl DEPT SE8 124 D6
Henrietta Ms BMSBY WC1N 5 F6
Henrietta Pl CAVSQ/HST W1G 9 J3
Henrietta St COVGDN WC2E 11 F5
SRTFD E15 88 A3
Henriques St WCHPL E1 104 C5
Henry Addlington Cl
EHAM E6 108 B4
Henry Cl ENC/FH EN2 24 A1
Henry Cooper Wy
ELTH/MOT SE9 166 C5
Henry Darlot Dr MLHL NW7 46 B1
Henry Dickens Ct NTGHL W11 100 B6
Henry Doulton Dr TOOT SW17 161 F6
Henry Jackson Rd
PUT/ROE SW15 139 G4
Henry Macaulay Av
KUTN/CMB KT2 174 E4
Henry Peters Dr TEDD TW11 173 K1
Henry Rd EBAR EN4 21 H6
EHAM E6 107 J1
FSBYPK N4 67 J5
Henry's Av WFD IG8 52 D1
Henryson Rd BROCKY SE4 144 D6
Henry St BMLY BR1 184 A4
Henry Tate Ms
STRHM/NOR SW16 180 B1
Hensby Ms OXHEY WD19 27 J1
Henshall St IS N1 85 K4
Henshawe Rd BCTR RM8 91 K1
Henshaw St WALW SE17 18 E6
Henslowe Rd EDUL SE22 143 H6
Henson Av CRICK NW2 82 A3
Henson Cl ORP BR6 201 G6
Henson Pl NTHLT UB5 77 G6
Henstridge Pl STJWD NW8 2 C2
Henty Cl BTSEA SW11 140 D1
Henty Wk PUT/ROE SW15 138 E6
Henville Rd BMLY BR1 184 A4
Henwick Rd ELTH/MOT SE9 146 C4
Henwood Side WFD IG8 53 K2
Hepburn Gdns HAYES BR2 199 J5
Hepple Cl ISLW TW7 136 C3
Hepscott Rd HOM E9 87 J4
Hepworth Gdns BARK IG11 91 G3
Hepworth Rd
STRHM/NOR SW16 179 K3
Herald Gdns WLGTN SM6 210 B1
Heralds Pl LBTH SE11 18 A6
Herald St BETH E2 104 D3
Herbal Hl CLKNW EC1R 5 K7
Herbert Crs KTBR SW1X 15 F4
Herbert Gdns CHDH RM6 73 K4
CHSWK W4 117 J6
WLSDN NW10 99 K1
Herbert Ms BRXS/STRHM SW2 162 B1
Herbert Pl ISLW TW7 135 J3
WOOL/PLUM SE18 127 G6
Herbert Rd CDALE/KGS NW9 63 J3
FBAR/BDGN N11 48 E3
GDMY/SEVK IG3 72 E6
HAYES BR2 200 C2
KUT/HW KT1 175 G6
MNPK E12 89 J2
SEVS/STOTM N15 68 B2
STHL UB1 114 E1
WALTH E17 69 H4
WIM/MER SW19 177 J3
WOOL/PLUM SE18 147 G1
Herbert St KTTN NW5 84 A4
PLSTW E13 106 E1
Herbrand St BMSBY WC1N 4 E6
Hercules Pl HOLWY N7 84 E1
Hercules Rd STHWK SE1 17 H5
Hercules St HOLWY N7 84 E1
Hereford Av EBAR EN4 33 K3
Hereford Gdns IL IG1 71 J4
PIN HA5 59 J2
WHTN TW2 * 155 H3
Hereford Ms BAY/PAD W2 * 100 E5
Hereford Pl NWCR SE14 * 144 C1
Hereford Retreat PECK SE15 143 H1
Hereford Rd ACT W3 98 E6
BAY/PAD W2 100 E5
BOW E3 105 H1
EA W5 116 D3
FELT TW13 154 B3
WAN E11 71 F2
Hereford Sq SKENS SW7 120 B4
Hereford St BETH E2 104 C3
Hereford Wy CHSGTN KT9 205 J3
Herent Dr CLAY IG5 53 K6
Heretage Cl BRXN/ST SW9 142 C4
Hereward Gdns PLMGR N13 49 G1
Hereward Rd TOOT SW17 160 D6
Herga Rd
KTN/HRWW/WS HA3 61 F1
Heriot Av CHING E4 37 J4
Heriot Rd HDN NW4 64 A2
Heriots Cl STAN HA7 29 G6
Heritage Av CDALE/KGS NW9 45 H5
Heritage Hl HAYES BR2 215 G3
Heritage Pl
WAND/EARL SW18 * 160 C1
Heritage Vw HRW HA1 79 F1
Herkomer Cl BUSH WD23 28 B1
Herlwyn Av RSLP HA4 76 C1
Herlwyn Gdns TOOT SW17 160 E6
Herm Cl ISLW TW7 135 H1
Hermes Cl MV/WKIL W9 100 E3
Hermes Ct BRXS/STRHM SW2 142 A6
Hermes St IS N1 5 J3
Hermes Wy WLGTN SM6 210 D5
Hermiston Av
CEND/HSY/T N8 66 E2
Hermitage Cl ENC/FH EN2 23 H3
ESH/CLAY KT10 205 G4
RCHPK/HAM TW10 * 136 E6
SWFD E18 70 D1
Hermitage Cots STAN HA7 * 42 E1
Hermitage Gdns CRICK NW2 82 E1
NRWD SE19 180 D3
Hermitage La CRICK NW2 82 E1
CROY/NA CR0 197 G4
STRHM/NOR SW16 180 A3
UED N18 49 K1
Hermitage Rd FSBYPK N4 67 J4
NRWD SE19 180 D3
Hermitage Rw HACK E8 * 86 C3
Hermitage St BAY/PAD W2 8 A2
The Hermitage BARN SW13 * 138 C2
FELT TW13 * 153 J5
FSTH SE23 163 K3
KUT/HW KT1 * 190 E1
LEW SE13 * 145 F3
RCHPK/HAM TW10 137 F6
Hermitage Wk SWFD E18 70 D1
Hermitage Wall WAP E1W 123 H1
Hermitage Wy STAN HA7 43 G4
Hermit Pl KIL/WHAMP NW6 83 F6
Hermit Rd CAN/RD E16 106 D3
Hermit St FSBYE EC1V 6 A4
Hermon Gv HYS/HAR UB3 113 K1
Hermon Hl WAN E11 70 E1
Herndon Rd
WAND/EARL SW18 140 B6
Herne Cl HYS/HAR UB3 94 D5
WLSDN NW10 81 F3
Herne Ct BUSH WD23 * 28 C3
Herne Hl HNHL SE24 142 D6
Herne Hill Rd HNHL SE24 142 D4
Herne Ms UED N18 36 C6
Herne Pl HNHL SE24 162 C1
Herne Rd BUSH WD23 28 B1
SURB KT6 190 E6
Heron Cl BKHH IG9 38 E3
WALTH E17 51 H5
WLSDN NW10 81 G4
Heron Ct HAYES BR2 200 B1
KUT/HW KT1 * 175 F6
Heron Crs SCUP DA14 167 K6
Herondale SAND/SEL CR2 213 F6
Herondale Av
WAND/EARL SW18 160 C3
Heron Dr FSBYPK N4 67 J6
Heron Flight Av HCH RM12 93 J5
Herongate Rd MNPK E12 71 G6
Heron Hl BELV DA17 129 G4
Heron Md PEND EN3 25 J1
Heron Ms IL IG1 72 B6
Heron Pl BERM/RHTH SE16 124 B1
Heron Quays POP/IOD E14 124 D1
Heron Rd CROY/NA CR0 * 197 F5
HNHL SE24 142 D5
TWK TW1 136 B5
Heronsforde WEA W13 97 J5
Heronsgate EDGW HA8 44 C1
Herons Lea HGT N6 * 65 K3
Heronslea Dr STAN HA7 44 A1
Herons Pl ISLW TW7 136 C4
Herons Ri EBAR EN4 21 J5
Heron Wk NTHWD HA6 26 C6
Heron Wy EBED/NFELT TW14 133 K5
Herrick Rd HBRY N5 85 J1
Herrick St WEST SW1P 16 D7
Herries St NKENS W10 100 C1
Herringham Rd CHARL SE7 126 B3
Herrongate Cl EN EN1 24 A3
Hersant Cl WLSDN NW10 81 J6
Herschell Rd FSTH SE23 164 A2
Hersham Cl PUT/ROE SW15 158 D2
Hersham Rd WOT/HER KT12 188 A6
Hershell Ct
MORT/ESHN SW14 * 137 J5
Hertford Av
MORT/ESHN SW14 138 A6
Hertford Cl EBAR EN4 21 H4
Hertford Ct STAN HA7 * 43 K3
Hertford End Ct
NTHWD HA6 * 40 C1
Hertford Pl FITZ W1T 4 A7
Hertford Rd BARK IG11 90 A5
EBAR EN4 21 G4
ED N9 36 D3
EFNCH N2 47 J6
GNTH/NBYPK IG2 72 E3
IS N1 86 A6
PEND EN3 24 E4
Hertford Road High St
PEND EN3 36 E1
Hertford St MYFR/PICC W1J 9 J7
Hertford Wy MTCM CR4 195 K1
Hertslet Rd HOLWY N7 85 F1
Hertsmere Rd POP/IOD E14 105 J6
Hertswood Ct BAR EN5 * 20 C5
Hervey Cl FNCH N3 46 E4
Hervey Park Rd WALTH E17 69 G1
Hesa Rd HYS/HAR UB3 94 E5
Hesewall Cl CLAP SW4 141 H3
Hesketh Pl NTGHL W11 100 C6
Hesketh Rd FSTGT E7 88 E1
Heslop Rd BAL SW12 160 E3
Hesper Ms ECT SW5 120 A5
Hesperus Crs POP/IOD E14 124 E4
Hessel Rd WEA W13 116 B2
Hessel St WCHPL E1 104 D5
Hesselyn Dr RAIN RM13 93 K5
Hestercombe Av
FUL/PGN SW6 139 H3
Hesterman Wy CROY/NA CR0 195 K5
Hester Rd BTSEA SW11 140 D1
UED N18 50 C1
Hester Ter RCH/KEW TW9 137 H4
Heston Av HEST TW5 134 D1
Heston Grange La HEST TW5 114 E6
Heston Rd HEST TW5 135 F1
Heston St NWCR SE14 144 C2
Heswell Gn OXHEY WD19 * 26 E5
Hetherington Rd CLAP SW4 141 K5
Hetley Rd SHB W12 118 E1
Heton Gdns HDN NW4 63 J1
Hevelius Cl GNWCH SE10 125 J5
Hever Cft ELTH/MOT SE9 167 F6
Hever Gdns BMLY BR1 185 F5
Heverham Rd
WOOL/PLUM SE18 127 K4
Hevingham Dr CHDH RM6 73 J2
Hewens Rd HGDN/ICK UB10 94 A2
Hewer St NKENS W10 100 B4
Hewett Cl STAN HA7 29 H6
Hewett St SDTCH EC2A 7 H7
Hewish Rd UED N18 36 A6
Hewison St BOW E3 105 H1
Hewitt Av WDGN N22 49 H5
Hewitt Cl CROY/NA CR0 213 J1
Hewitt Rd CEND/HSY/T N8 67 G2
Hewlett Rd BOW E3 105 G1
The Hexagon HGT N6 65 K5
Hexal Rd CAT SE6 165 H5
Hexham Gdns ISLW TW7 136 B1
Hexham Rd BAR EN5 21 F5
MRDN SM4 194 A5
WNWD SE27 162 D4
Heybourne Rd TOTM N17 50 D3
Heybridge Av
STRHM/NOR SW16 180 A2
Heybridge Dr BARK/HLT IG6 54 D6
Heybridge Wy LEY E10 69 G4
Heyford Av RYNPK SW20 177 J6
VX/NE SW8 141 K1
Heyford Rd MTCM CR4 178 D5
Heyford Ter VX/NE SW8 141 K1
Heygate Est WALW SE17 18 D6
Heygate St WALW SE17 18 C7
Heynes Rd BCTR RM8 91 J2
Heysham Dr OXHEY WD19 41 G1
Heysham La HAMP NW3 83 F1
Heysham Rd
SEVS/STOTM N15 67 K3
Heythorp St
WAND/EARL SW18 159 J4
Heywood Av CDALE/KGS NW9 45 G4
Heyworth Rd CLPT E5 86 D2
SRTFD E15 88 D2
Hibbert Rd
KTN/HRWW/WS HA3 43 F5
WALTH E17 69 H4
Hibbert St BTSEA SW11 140 B4
Hibernia Gdns HSLW TW3 135 F6
Hibernia Rd HSLW TW3 135 F5
Hichisson Rd PECK SE15 143 K6
Hicken Rd BRXS/STRHM SW2 142 A6
Hickin Cl CHARL SE7 126 C4
Hickin St POP/IOD E14 125 F3
Hickling Rd IL IG1 90 B3
Hickman Av CHING E4 52 A2
Hickman Cl CAN/RD E16 107 H4
Hickman Rd CHDH RM6 73 J4
Hickory Cl ED N9 36 C2
Hicks Av GFD/PVL UB6 96 D2
Hicks Cl BTSEA SW11 140 D4
Hicks St DEPT SE8 124 B5
Hidcote Gdns RYNPK SW20 176 E6
Hide Pl WEST SW1P 16 C7
Hide Rd HRW HA1 60 D1
Higham Hill Rd WALTH E17 51 G6
Higham Ms NTHLT UB5 95 K3
Higham Pl WALTH E17 51 G6
Higham Rd TOTM N17 49 K6
WFD IG8 52 E2
Higham Station Av CHING E4 51 K2
The Highams WALTH E17 * 52 A4
Higham St WALTH E17 51 G5
Highbank Pl
WAND/EARL SW18 * 160 A3
Highbanks Cl WELL DA16 148 B1
Highbanks Rd PIN HA5 42 B2
Highbank Wy
CEND/HSY/T N8 67 G3
Highbarrow Rd CROY/NA CR0 197 G5
High Beech SAND/SEL CR2 212 A5
High Beeches ORP BR6 217 G4
SCUP DA14 187 F1
Highbridge Rd BARK IG11 90 B6
Highbrook Rd BKHTH/KID SE3 146 C4
High Broom Crs WWKM BR4 198 E4
Highbury Av THHTH CR7 180 B5
Highbury Cl NWMAL KT3 191 K1
WWKM BR4 198 E6
Highbury Cnr IS N1 85 H4
Highbury Crs HBRY N5 85 G3
Highbury Est HBRY N5 85 J3
Highbury Gdns
GDMY/SEVK IG3 72 E6
Highbury Gra HBRY N5 85 H2
Highbury Gv HBRY N5 85 H3
Highbury Hl HBRY N5 85 H4
Highbury New Pk HBRY N5 85 H4
Highbury Pk HBRY N5 85 H2
Highbury Pl HBRY N5 85 H4
Highbury Qd HBRY N5 85 J1
Highbury Rd WIM/MER SW19 177 H1
Highbury Station Pde
HBRY N5 * 85 H4
Highbury Station Rd IS N1 * 85 G4
Highbury Ter HBRY N5 85 H3
Highbury Terrace Ms
HBRY N5 85 H3
High Cedar Dr RYNPK SW20 176 E3
Highclere Rd NWMAL KT3 176 A6
Highclere St SYD SE26 164 B6
Highcliffe Dr PUT/ROE SW15 158 C1
Highcliffe Gdns REDBR IG4 71 J2
Highcombe CHARL SE7 126 A6
Highcombe Cl ELTH/MOT SE9 166 C3
High Coombe Pl
KUTN/CMB KT2 176 A3
Highcroft CDALE/KGS NW9 63 G2
Highcroft Av ALP/SUD HA0 80 B5
Highcroft Gdns GLDGN NW11 64 D3
Highcroft Rd ARCH N19 66 E4
High Cross Rd TOTM N17 50 C6
Highcross Wy PUT/ROE SW15 158 D3
Highdaun Dr
STRHM/NOR SW16 196 A1
Highdown WPK KT4 192 B6
Highdown Rd PUT/ROE SW15 158 E1
High Dr NWMAL KT3 175 K4
High Elms WFD IG8 52 E1
High Elms Cl NTHWD HA6 40 A2
High Elms Rd ORP BR6 216 C6
Highfield OXHEY WD19 27 K5
Highfield Av CDALE/KGS NW9 62 E2
ERITH DA8 129 J6
ERITH DA8 * 129 K6
GFD/PVL UB6 78 E3
GLDGN NW11 64 B4
ORP BR6 217 F4
PIN HA5 59 K2
WBLY HA9 80 A1
Highfield Cl CDALE/KGS NW9 62 E2
CRW RM5 56 E2
LEW SE13 165 G1
NTHWD HA6 40 C4
SURB KT6 190 D5
WDGN N22 49 G4
Highfield Ct STHGT/OAK N14 34 C1
Highfield Crs NTHWD HA6 40 C4
Highfield Dr HAYES BR2 199 H
HOR/WEW KT19 207 H5
WWKM BR4 213 K
Highfield Gdns GLDGN NW11 64 C3
Highfield Hl NRWD SE19 180 E1
Highfield Link CRW RM5 56 E
Highfield Rd ACT W3 98 D
BMLY BR1 200 E
BRYLDS KT5 191 K
CHST BR7 186 A
CRW RM5 56 E
FELT TW13 153 K
GLDGN NW11 * 64 C
ISLW TW7 136 A
NTHWD HA6 40 C
SUT SM1 209
WCHMH N21 35 H
WFD IG8 53
Highfields Gv HGT N6 66
High Foleys ESH/CLAY KT10 205
High Garth ESH/CLAY KT10 204
Highgate Av HGT N6 66 E
Highgate Cl HGT N6 66
Highgate Edge EFNCH N2 * 65
Highgate High St HGT N6 66
Highgate Hl ARCH N19 66
Highgate Rd KTTN NW5 84
Highgate Spinney
CEND/HSY/T N8 * 66
Highgate Wk FSTH SE23 165
Highgate West Hl HGT N6 66
High Gv BMLY BR1 184
WOOL/PLUM SE18 147
Highgrove Cl CHST BR7 184
FBAR/BDGN N11 48
Highgrove Ms CAR SM5 209
Highgrove Rd BCTR RM8 91
Highgrove Wy RSLP HA4 58
High Hill Ferry CLPT E5 68
High Holborn HHOL WC1V 11
Highland Av DAGE RM10 92
HNWL W7 96
LOU IG10 39
Highland Cots WLGTN SM6 * 210
Highland Cft BECK BR3 182
Highland Dr BUSH WD23 28
Highland Pk FELT TW13 153
Highland Rd BMLY BR1 183
HAYES BR2 183
NRWD SE19 181
NTHWD HA6 40
Highlands OXHEY WD19 27
Highlands Av ACT W3 98
WCHMH N21 23
Highlands Cl FSBYPK N4 66
HSLW TW3 135
Highlands Gdns IL IG1 71
Highlands Heath
PUT/ROE SW15 159
Highlands Rd BAR EN5 20
STMC/STPC BR5 202
The Highlands BAR EN5 20
EDGW HA8 44
Highland Ter LEW SE13 * 144
High La HNWL W7 96
Highlea Cl CDALE/KGS NW9 45
High Level Dr SYD SE26 163
Highlever Rd NKENS W10 100
High Limes NRWD SE19 * 18
High Md HRW HA1 60
Highmead WOOL/PLUM SE18 148
High Md WWKM BR4 199
Highmead Crs ALP/SUD HA0 80
High Meadow Cl PIN HA5 59
High Meadow Crs
CDALE/KGS NW9 63
High Mdw CHIG IG7 5
High Meads Rd CAN/RD E16 10
Highmore Rd BKHTH/KID SE3 14
High Mt HDN NW4 * 6
High Oaks ENC/FH EN2 2
The High Pde
STRHM/NOR SW16 * 16

High Park Rd RCH/KEW TW9 137 H2
High Pth WIM/MER SW19 178 A4
High Point ELTH/MOT SE9 167 G5
High Rdg MUSWH N10 * 48 B4
Highridge Pl ENC/FH EN2 * 23 F1
High Rd BKHH IG9 39 F3
BUSH WD23 28 D3
CHDH RM6 73 K4
EFNCH N2 65 J1
FBAR/BDGN N11 48 B1
FNCH N3 47 H4
GDMY/SEVK IG3 73 G5
IL IG1 90 B1
KTN/HRWW/WS HA3 42 E4
LEY E10 69 K3
LOU IG10 39 G1
NFNCH/WDSPK N12 47 G3
SEVS/STOTM N15 68 B2
TOTM N17 50 B6
TRDG/WHET N20 33 F2
WBLY HA9 80 A3
WDGN N22 49 F3
WLSDN NW10 81 G4
High Road Eastcote PIN HA5 59 F2
High Road Leyton LEY E10 69 K6
High Road Leytonstone
WAN E11 88 C1
High Road Woodford Gn
SWFD E18 52 E4
WFD IG8 38 E6
Highshore Rd PECK SE15 143 G3
Highstead Crs ERITH DA8 150 B2
Highstone Av WAN E11 70 E3
High St ACT W3 117 K1
BAR EN5 20 C4
BARK/HLT IG6 54 C5
BECK BR3 182 D4
BELMT SM2 209 G5
BMLY BR1 183 K5
BTFD TW8 116 E6
BUSH WD23 28 A1
CAR SM5 209 K3
CEND/HSY/T N8 66 E1
CHEAM SM3 208 C4
CROY/NA CR0 211 J1
DART DA1 171 H1
E/WMO/HCT KT8 189 F2
EA W5 97 K6
ESH/CLAY KT10 204 B2
ESH/CLAY KT10 205 F4
EW KT17 207 H6
FBAR/BDGN N11 48 B1
FELT TW13 153 J5
HEST TW5 114 A6
HPTN TW12 173 G4
HRW HA1 60 E5
HSLW TW3 135 G4
HYS/HAR UB3 113 G6
KTN/HRWW/WS HA3 42 E6
KUT/HW KT1 174 D4
MLHL NW7 45 K1
NTHWD HA6 40 D4
NWMAL KT3 192 B1
ORP BR6 202 B5
ORP BR6 216 C3
ORP BR6 217 F3
PGE/AN SE20 181 K3
PIN HA5 41 J6
PLSTW E13 106 E1
ROM RM1 75 G2
RSLP HA4 58 C4
SCUP DA14 168 B6
SNWD SE25 197 G1
SRTFD E15 106 A1
STHGT/OAK N14 34 D3
STMC/STPC BR5 202 D1
STMC/STPC BR5 202 D3
STWL/WRAY TW19 152 A1
SUT SM1 209 F4
TEDD TW11 174 B1
THDIT KT7 190 B3
THHTH CR7 196 D1
WALTH E17 69 H1
WAN E11 71 F3
WBLY HA9 80 B2
WDR/YW UB7 112 A6
WHTN TW2 155 H2
WIM/MER SW19 177 G1
WWKM BR4 198 E5
High Street Collier's Wd
WIM/MER SW19 178 C3
High Street Harlesden
WLSDN NW10 81 G6
igh Street Harlington
HTHAIR TW6 133 G2
High Street Ms
WIM/MER SW19 177 H1
igh St North EHAM E6 89 J6
igh St South EHAM E6 107 K1
igh Timber St BLKFR EC4V 12 C5
igh Tor Cl BMLY BR1 184 A3
igh Trees BRXS/STRHM SW2 162 B3
CROY/NA CR0 198 B5
EBAR EN4 21 J6
igh Vw PIN HA5 59 G1
WATW WD18 26 D1
ighview Av EDGW HA8 30 E6
igh View Av WLGTN SM6 211 F3
igh View Cl NRWD SE19 181 G5
ighview Gdns EDGW HA8 44 E1
FBAR/BDGN N11 48 C1
FNCH N3 46 C6
igh View Rd NRWD SE19 180 E2
ighview Rd SCUP DA14 168 C6
igh View Rd SWFD E18 52 D5
ighview Rd WEA W13 97 G5
ighview Ter DART DA1 * 151 G6
ne Highway BELMT SM2 209 G6
ORP BR6 217 H3
STAN HA7 43 F4
WCHPL E1 104 C6
ighwood Av
NFNCH/WDSPK N12 33 G6
ghwood Cl EDUL SE22 163 H3
ORP BR6 201 H6
ghwood Dr ORP BR6 201 H6
ghwood Gdns CLAY IG5 71 K2
ghwood Gv MLHL NW7 45 F1
ghwood Hl MLHL NW7 31 H4
ghwood Rd ARCH N19 84 E1
High Worple
RYLN/HDSTN HA2 59 J4
Highworth Rd
FBAR/BDGN N11 48 D2
Highworth St CAMTN NW1 * 8 D1
Hilary Av MTCM CR4 179 F6
Hilary Cl FUL/PGN SW6 * 140 A1
Hilary Rd SHB W12 99 H6
Hilberry Ct BUSH WD23 * 28 B2
Hilbert Rd CHEAM SM3 208 B2
Hilborough Cl
WIM/MER SW19 178 B3
Hilborough Rd HACK E8 86 B5
Hilborough Wy ORP BR6 216 D3
Hilda Lockert Wk
BRXN/ST SW9 142 C3
Hilda Rd CAN/RD E16 106 C3
EHAM E6 89 H5
Hilda Ter BRXN/ST SW9 * 142 B3
Hilda Vale Rd ORP BR6 216 A2
Hildenborough Gdns
BMLY BR1 183 H2
Hilden Dr ERITH DA8 150 E1
Hildenlea Pl HAYES BR2 183 H5
Hildreth St BAL SW12 161 G3
Hildyard Rd FUL/PGN SW6 119 K6
Hiley Rd WLSDN NW10 100 A2
Hilgrove Rd KIL/WHAMP NW6 83 G5
Hiliary Gdns STAN HA7 43 J5
Hillary Crs WOT/HER KT12 188 B5
Hillary Dr ISLW TW7 136 A5
Hillary Ri BAR EN5 20 E5
Hillary Rd NWDGN UB2 115 F3
Hillbeck Cl PECK SE15 143 K1
Hillbeck Wy GFD/PVL UB6 78 D6
Hillborne Cl HYS/HAR UB3 113 K5
Hillborough Cl
WIM/MER SW19 * 178 B3
Hillbrook Rd TOOT SW17 160 E5
Hill Brow BMLY BR1 184 C4
Hillbrow NWMAL KT3 176 C6
Hillbrow Rd BMLY BR1 183 H3
ESH/CLAY KT10 204 C2
Hillbury Av
KTN/HRWW/WS HA3 61 H2
Hillbury Rd TOOT SW17 161 G5
Hill Cl BAR EN5 20 A6
CHST BR7 185 G1
CRICK NW2 81 K1
GLDGN NW11 64 E3
HRW HA1 78 E1
STAN HA7 29 H6
Hillcote Av STRHM/NOR SW16 180 B3
Hillcourt Av
NFNCH/WDSPK N12 47 F2
Hillcourt Rd EDUL SE22 163 J1
Hill Crs BRYLDS KT5 191 G2
BXLY DA5 169 K3
BXLY DA5 169 K3
HRW HA1 61 G2
TRDG/WHET N20 33 F4
WPK KT4 193 F6
Hill Crest BFN/LL DA15 168 B2
Hillcrest HGT N6 66 A4
HNHL SE24 * 142 E5
Hill Crest SURB KT6 * 191 F4
Hillcrest WCHMH N21 35 G2
Hillcrest Av EDGW HA8 30 D6
GLDGN NW11 64 C2
PIN HA5 59 H1
Hillcrest Cl BECK BR3 198 C3
SYD SE26 163 H6
Hill Crest Gdns CRICK NW2 81 J1
Hillcrest Gdns ESH/CLAY KT10 205 F1
FNCH N3 64 C1
Hillcrest Rd ACT W3 117 H1
DART DA1 170 B2
EA W5 98 A4
EMPK RM11 75 J4
LOU IG10 39 H1
ORP BR6 202 B6
WALTH E17 52 B5
Hillcrest Vw BECK BR3 198 C3
Hillcroft Av PIN HA5 59 K3
Hillcroft Crs EA W5 97 K5
OXHEY WD19 27 F3
RSLP HA4 77 H1
WBLY HA9 80 B2
Hillcroft Rd EHAM E6 108 B4
Hillcroome Rd BELMT SM2 209 H4
Hillcross Av MRDN SM4 193 H3
Hilldale Rd SUT SM1 208 D2
Hilldown Rd HAYES BR2 199 H5
STRHM/NOR SW16 179 K3
Hill Dr CDALE/KGS NW9 62 D5
STRHM/NOR SW16 180 A6
Hilldrop Crs HOLWY N7 84 D3
Hilldrop Est HOLWY N7 84 D3
Hilldrop La HOLWY N7 84 D3
Hilldrop Rd BMLY BR1 183 K2
HOLWY N7 84 D3
Hill End ORP BR6 202 A6
WOOL/PLUM SE18 147 F2
Hillersdon Av BARN SW13 138 D3
EDGW HA8 44 B1
Hillery Cl WALW SE17 19 F7
Hill Farm Rd NKENS W10 100 A4
Hillfield Av ALP/SUD HA0 80 A5
CDALE/KGS NW9 63 G2
CEND/HSY/T N8 67 F1
MRDN SM4 194 D3
Hillfield Cl RYLN/HDSTN HA2 60 C1
Hillfield La South BUSH WD23 28 E1
Hillfield Ms CEND/HSY/T N8 67 F1
Hillfield Pde MRDN SM4 * 194 C3
Hillfield Pk MUSWH N10 48 B6
WCHMH N21 35 G3
Hillfield Park Ms MUSWH N10 66 B1
Hill Field Rd HPTN TW12 172 E3
Hillfield Rd KIL/WHAMP NW6 82 D3
Hillfoot Av CRW RM5 56 E4
Hillfoot Rd CRW RM5 56 E4
Hillgate Pl BAL SW12 161 G1
KENS W8 119 K1
Hillgate St KENS W8 * 119 K1
Hill Gv FELT TW13 154 E4
ROM RM1 57 G6
Hill House Av STAN HA7 43 F3
Hill House Cl WCHMH N21 35 G2
Hill House Dr HPTN TW12 173 F4
Hill House Rd
STRHM/NOR SW16 180 A1
Hilliard Rd NTHWD HA6 40 D4
Hilliard's Ct WAP E1W * 123 K1
Hillier Cl BAR EN5 33 F1
Hillier Gdns CROY/NA CR0 211 G3
Hillier Pl CHSGTN KT9 205 K4
Hillier Rd BTSEA SW11 160 E1
Hillier's La CROY/NA CR0 210 E1
Hillingdon Av
STWL/WRAY TW19 152 B3
Hillingdon Rd BXLYHN DA7 149 K4
Hillingdon St WALW SE17 122 C6
Hillingdon Trail
HGDN/ICK UB10 76 A4
HYS/HAR UB3 113 K5
RSLP HA4 58 A2
Hill La RSLP HA4 58 A5
Hillman Dr NKENS W10 100 A3
Hillman St HACK E8 86 D4
Hillmarton Rd HOLWY N7 84 E3
Hillmarton Ter HOLWY N7 * 84 E3
Hillmead Dr BRXN/ST SW9 142 C5
Hillmont Rd ESH/CLAY KT10 204 E1
Hillmore Gv SYD SE26 182 A1
Hillreach WOOL/PLUM SE18 126 E5
Hill Ri ED N9 36 D1
ESH/CLAY KT10 190 C6
FSTH SE23 163 J3
GFD/PVL UB6 78 C6
GLDGN NW11 65 F1
RCHPK/HAM TW10 136 E6
RSLP HA4 58 A5
Hillrise Rd ARCH N19 66 E4
CRW RM5 56 E2
Hill Rd ALP/SUD HA0 79 H1
CAR SM5 209 J4
HRW HA1 61 G2
MTCM CR4 179 G4
MUSWH N10 47 K4
NTHWD HA6 40 B2
PIN HA5 59 J3
STJWD NW8 101 G1
SUT SM1 209 F3
Hillsboro Rd EDUL SE22 143 F6
Hillsborough Gn
OXHEY WD19 * 26 E5
Hillsgrove Cl WELL DA16 148 D1
Hill Side BAR EN5 21 G6
Hillside CDALE/KGS NW9 63 F1
ESH/CLAY KT10 * 204 B3
WIM/MER SW19 177 G2
WLSDN NW10 81 F6
Hillside Av FBAR/BDGN N11 47 K2
WBLY HA9 80 B2
WFD IG8 53 G1
Hillside Cl MRDN SM4 193 H1
STJWD NW8 101 F1
WFD IG8 53 G1
Hillside Crs ENC/FH EN2 23 K1
NTHWD HA6 40 E4
OXHEY WD19 27 H1
RYLN/HDSTN HA2 60 C6
Hillside Dr EDGW HA8 44 C2
Hillside Gdns BAR EN5 20 C5
BRXS/STRHM SW2 * 162 B4
EDGW HA8 30 B6
FBAR/BDGN N11 * 48 C2
HGT N6 66 A3
KTN/HRWW/WS HA3 62 A4
NTHWD HA6 40 E3
WALTH E17 52 B6
WLGTN SM6 210 C5
Hillside Gv MLHL NW7 45 J3
STHGT/OAK N14 34 D2
Hillside Ri NTHWD HA6 40 E3
Hillside Rd BELMT SM2 208 D5
BRXS/STRHM SW2 162 A4
CROY/NA CR0 211 H3
EA W5 98 A4
HAYES BR2 183 J6
NTHWD HA6 40 E3
SEVS/STOTM N15 68 A3
STHL UB1 96 A3
The Hillside ORP BR6 217 H6
Hills La NTHWD HA6 40 C4
Hillsleigh Rd KENS W8 119 J1
Hills Ms EA W5 * 98 A6
Hills Pl SOHO/SHAV W1D 10 A4
Hill's Rd BKHH IG9 39 F3
Hillstowe St CLPT E5 68 E6
Hill St MYFR/PICC W1J 9 J7
RCH/KEW TW9 136 E6
Hill Top CHEAM SM3 193 J4
GLDGN NW11 65 F1
Hilltop WALTH E17 * 51 K6
Hilltop Av WLSDN NW10 80 E5
Hilltop Cots SYD SE26 * 163 J6
Hilltop Gdns HDN NW4 45 K5
ORP BR6 201 K6
Hilltop Rd KIL/WHAMP NW6 82 E5
Hill Top Vw WFD IG8 * 53 K2
Hilltop Wy STAN HA7 29 G5
Hillview RYNPK SW20 176 E3
Hillview Av
KTN/HRWW/WS HA3 62 A2
Hillview Cl PIN HA5 41 K2
WBLY HA9 62 B6
Hillview Crs IL IG1 71 K3
ORP BR6 201 K5
Hill View Dr THMD SE28 127 K1
WELL DA16 147 K3
Hill View Gdns
CDALE/KGS NW9 63 F2
Hillview Gdns HDN NW4 64 B1
RYLN/HDSTN HA2 42 A6
Hill View Rd TWK TW1 156 B1
Hillview Rd CHST BR7 185 F1
Hill View Rd ESH/CLAY KT10 205 G5
Hillview Rd MLHL NW7 32 B6
Hill View Rd ORP BR6 202 A5
Hillview Rd PIN HA5 41 K3
SUT SM1 209 G1
Hillway CDALE/KGS NW9 63 G5
HGT N6 66 A6
Hillworth BECK BR3 * 182 E5
Hillworth Rd
BRXS/STRHM SW2 162 B2
Hillyard Rd HNWL W7 96 E4
Hillyard St BRXN/ST SW9 142 B2
Hillyfield WALTH E17 51 G5
Hillyfield Cl HOM E9 87 G3
Hilly Flds BROCKY SE4 * 144 D5
Hilly Fields Crs BROCKY SE4 144 D5
Hilsea St CLPT E5 86 E2
Hilton Av NFNCH/WDSPK N12 47 H1
Himalayan Wy WATW WD18 26 D1
Himley Rd TOOT SW17 178 D1
Hinchley Cl ESH/CLAY KT10 205 F1
Hinchley Dr ESH/CLAY KT10 205 F1
Hinchley Wy ESH/CLAY KT10 205 G1
Hinckley Rd PECK SE15 143 H5
Hind Cl CHIG IG7 55 F1
Hind Ct FLST/FETLN EC4A 11 K4
Hind Crs ERITH DA8 149 K1
Hinde Ms MHST W1U * 9 H3
Hindes Rd HRW HA1 60 E2
Hinde St MHST W1U 9 H3
Hind Gv POP/IOD E14 105 J5
Hindhead Gdns NTHLT UB5 77 J6
Hindhead Gn OXHEY WD19 41 G1
Hindhead Wy WLGTN SM6 210 E3
Hindmans Rd EDUL SE22 143 H6
Hindmans Wy DAGW RM9 110 B2
Hindmarsh Cl WCHPL E1 * 104 C6
Hindrey Rd CLPT E5 86 D3
Hindsley's Pl FSTH SE23 163 K4
Hinkler Rd
KTN/HRWW/WS HA3 43 K6
Hinksey Pth ABYW SE2 128 E3
Hinstock Rd
WOOL/PLUM SE18 147 H1
Hinton Av HSLWW TW4 134 C5
Hinton Cl ELTH/MOT SE9 166 D3
Hinton Rd BRXN/ST SW9 142 C4
UED N18 36 A6
WLGTN SM6 210 C4
Hippodrome Pl NTGHL W11 100 C6
Hirst Crs WBLY HA9 80 A1
Hitcham Rd WALTH E17 69 H4
Hithe Gv BERM/RHTH SE16 123 K3
Hitherbroom Rd
HYS/HAR UB3 113 K1
Hither Farm Rd
BKHTH/KID SE3 146 B4
Hitherfield Rd BCTR RM8 74 A6
STRHM/NOR SW16 162 A4
Hither Green La LEW SE13 145 F6
Hitherwell Dr
KTN/HRWW/WS HA3 42 D4
Hitherwood Dr NRWD SE19 163 G6
Hive Cl BUSH WD23 28 D4
Hive Rd BUSH WD23 28 D4
Hoadly Rd STRHM/NOR SW16 161 J5
Hobart Cl TRDG/WHET N20 33 J4
YEAD UB4 95 H3
Hobart Dr YEAD UB4 95 H3
Hobart Gdns THHTH CR7 180 E6
Hobart La YEAD UB4 95 H3
Hobart Pl BGVA SW1W 15 J5
RCHPK/HAM TW10 157 G2
Hobart Rd BARK/HLT IG6 54 C5
DAGW RM9 91 K2
WPK KT4 207 K1
YEAD UB4 95 H3
Hobbayne Rd HNWL W7 96 D5
Hobbes Wk PUT/ROE SW15 138 E6
Hobbs Gn EFNCH N2 47 G6
Hobbs Pl IS N1 7 G1
Hobbs Place Est IS N1 7 G2
Hobbs Rd WNWD SE27 162 D6
Hobby St PEND EN3 25 F6
Hobday St POP/IOD E14 105 K5
Hoblands End CHST BR7 185 K2
Hobsons Pl WCHPL E1 * 104 C4
Hobury St WBPTN SW10 120 B6
Hockenden La SWLY BR8 187 H6
Hocker St BETH E2 * 7 J5
Hockley Av EHAM E6 107 J1
Hockley Dr GPK RM2 57 K5
Hockley Ms BARK IG11 108 E1
Hocroft Av CRICK NW2 82 D1
Hocroft Rd CRICK NW2 82 D2
Hocroft Wk CRICK NW2 82 D1
Hodder Dr GFD/PVL UB6 97 F1
Hoddesdon Rd BELV DA17 129 H5
Hodes Rw HAMP NW3 83 K2
Hodford Rd GLDGN NW11 64 D5
Hodges Wy WATW WD18 26 E1
Hodgkins Cl THMD SE28 109 K6
Hodgkins Ms STAN HA7 43 G1
Hodister Cl CMBW SE5 142 D1
Hodnet Gv BERM/RHTH SE16 123 K4
Hodson Cl RYLN/HDSTN HA2 77 K1
Hodson Crs STMC/STPC BR5 202 E3
Hodson Pl PEND EN3 25 J1
Hoe La EN EN1 24 D1
Hoe St WALTH E17 69 J2
The Hoe OXHEY WD19 27 H4
Hoffmann Gdns
SAND/SEL CR2 212 C4
Hoffman Sq IS N1 * 7 F4
Hofland Rd WKENS W14 119 H3
Hogan Ms BAY/PAD W2 8 A1
Hogarth Cl CAN/RD E16 107 H4
EA W5 98 A4
Hogarth Crs CROY/NA CR0 196 D4
WIM/MER SW19 178 C4
Hogarth Gdns HEST TW5 135 F1
Hogarth Hl GLDGN NW11 64 D1
Hogarth Pl ECT SW5 * 120 A4
Hogarth Rd BCTR RM8 91 H3
ECT SW5 120 A4
EDGW HA8 44 C5
Hogarth Ter CHSWK W4 * 118 B6
Hogarth Wy HPTN TW12 173 H4
Hog Hill Rd CRW RM5 56 B3
Hogshead Pas WAP E1W * 104 D6
Hogsmill Wy HOR/WEW KT19 206 E3
Holbeach Cl CDALE/KGS NW9 45 G4
Holbeach Gdns BFN/LL DA15 167 K1
Holbeach Rd CAT SE6 164 D2
Holbeck Rw PECK SE15 143 H1
Holbein Ga NTHWD HA6 40 C1
Holbein Ms BGVA SW1W 121 F5
Holbein Pl BGVA SW1W 15 G7
Holberton Gdns
WLSDN NW10 99 K2
Holborn HCIRC EC1N 11 J2
Holborn Circ HCIRC EC1N 11 K2
Holborn Pl HHOL WC1V 11 G2
Holborn Rd PLSTW E13 107 F4
Holborn Viad STBT EC1A 12 A2
Holborn Wy MTCM CR4 178 E5
Holbrook Cl EN EN1 24 B2
Holbrooke Ct HOLWY N7 84 E1
Holbrook La CHST BR7 185 J3
Holbrook Rd SRTFD E15 106 D1
Holbrook Wy HAYES BR2 200 E3
Holburn GINN WC1R 11 J2
Holburne Cl BKHTH/KID SE3 146 B2
Holburne Gdns
BKHTH/KID SE3 146 C2
Holburne Rd BKHTH/KID SE3 146 B2
Holcombe Hl MLHL NW7 31 J5
Holcombe Rd IL IG1 72 A4
TOTM N17 50 B6
Holcombe St HMSMTH W6 118 E5
Holcote Cl BELV DA17 129 F3
Holcroft Rd HOM E9 86 E5
Holden Av CDALE/KGS NW9 62 E5
NFNCH/WDSPK N12 47 F1
Holdenby Rd BROCKY SE4 144 B6
Holden Cl BCTR RM8 91 H1
Holdenhurst Av FNCH N3 47 F3
Holden Rd
NFNCH/WDSPK N12 33 F6
Holden St BTSEA SW11 141 F3
Holdernesse Rd ISLW TW7 136 B2
TOOT SW17 160 E5
Holderness Wy WNWD SE27 180 C1
Holders Hill Av HDN NW4 46 B5
Holders Hill Crs HDN NW4 46 B5
Holders Hill Dr HDN NW4 46 B5
Holders Hill Gdns HDN NW4 46 B5
Holders Hill Pde MLHL NW7 * 46 C4
Holders Hill Rd HDN NW4 46 B5
Holford Ms FSBYW WC1X * 5 G4
Holford Rd HAMP NW3 83 G1
Holford St FSBYW WC1X 5 J4
Holford Yd FSBYW WC1X * 5 J3
Holgate Av BTSEA SW11 140 C4
Holgate Rd DAGE RM10 92 C3
Holgate St CHARL SE7 126 C3
Holland Av BELMT SM2 208 E5
RYNPK SW20 176 C4
Holland Cl BAR EN5 33 H2
HAYES BR2 199 J6
ROMW/RG RM7 74 E2
STAN HA7 43 H1
Holland Dr FSTH SE23 164 B5
Holland Gdns BTFD TW8 117 G5
WKENS W14 119 H3
Holland Gv BRXN/ST SW9 142 B1
Holland Pk NTGHL W11 119 J2
Holland Park Av
GDMY/SEVK IG3 72 E3
NTGHL W11 119 H1
Holland Park Gdns
WKENS W14 119 H2
Holland Park Ms NTGHL W11 119 J1
Holland Park Rd WKENS W14 119 J3
Holland Park Ter NTGHL W11 119 H1
Holland Pas IS N1 85 J6
Holland Pl KENS W8 120 A2
Holland Place Chambers
KENS W8 * 120 A2
Holland Rd ALP/SUD HA0 79 K4
EHAM E6 89 K6
SNWD SE25 197 H2
SRTFD E15 106 C2
WKENS W14 119 G2
WLSDN NW10 81 J6
The Hollands WPK KT4 192 C5
Holland St KENS W8 119 K2
STHWK SE1 12 B7
Holland Villas Rd WKENS W14 119 H2
Holland Wk STAN HA7 43 G1
Holland Wy HAYES BR2 199 J6
Hollar Rd STNW/STAM N16 86 B1
Hollen St SOHO/CST W1F 10 B4
Holles Cl HPTN TW12 173 F2
Holles St OXSTW W1C 9 K4
Holley Rd ACT W3 118 B2
Hollickwood Av
NFNCH/WDSPK N12 47 K2
Holliday Sq BTSEA SW11 140 C4
Hollidge Wy DAGE RM10 92 D4
Hollies Av BFN/LL DA15 168 A4
Hollies Cl STRHM/NOR SW16 180 B2
TWK TW1 156 A4
Hollies End MLHL NW7 45 K1
Hollies Rd EA W5 116 D4
The Hollies
KTN/HRWW/WS HA3 61 G1
Hollies Wy BAL SW12 * 161 F2
Holligrave Rd BMLY BR1 183 K4
Hollingbourne Gdns
WEA W13 97 G4
Hollingbourne Rd HNHL SE24 142 D6
Hollingsworth Rd
CROY/NA CR0 212 D4
Hollington Crs NWMAL KT3 192 C3
Hollington Rd EHAM E6 107 K2
TOTM N17 50 C5
Hollingworth Cl
E/WMO/HCT KT8 188 E1
Hollingworth Rd
STMC/STPC BR5 201 G4
Hollman Gdns
STRHM/NOR SW16 180 C2
Holloway La WDR/YW UB7 112 C5
Holloway Rd ARCH N19 66 D6
EHAM E6 107 K2
HOLWY N7 85 F2
WAN E11 88 B1
Holloway St HSLW TW3 135 G4
The Hollow WFD IG8 38 D6
Holly Av STAN HA7 44 A5
WOT/HER KT12 188 C5
Holly Bank MUSWH N10 * 66 C1
Hollybank Cl HPTN TW12 173 F1
Hollybrake Cl CHST BR7 185 J3
Hollybush Cl
KTN/HRWW/WS HA3 42 E4
OXHEY WD19 27 G2
WAN E11 70 E2
Hollybush Gdns BETH E2 104 D2
Hollybush Hl WAN E11 70 D3
Holly Bush La HPTN TW12 172 E3

Hollybush Pl *BETH* E2 104 D2
Hollybush Rd *KUTN/CMB* KT2 175 F1
Hollybush St *PLSTW* E13 107 F2
Hollybush Ter *NRWD* SE19 * 181 F2
Hollybush V *HAMP* NW3 * 83 G2
Holly Cl *BECK* BR3 199 F1
BKHH IG9 39 H5
FELT TW13 172 D1
WLGTN SM6 210 B5
WLSDN NW10 81 G5
Holly Crs *BECK* BR3 198 C2
WFD IG8 52 B3
Hollycroft Av *HAMP* NW3 82 E1
WBLY HA9 62 A6
Hollycroft Cl *SAND/SEL* CR2 212 A3
WDR/YW UB7 112 D6
Hollycroft Gdns
WDR/YW UB7 112 D6
Hollydale Cl *NTHLT* UB5 78 B3
Hollydale Dr *HAYES* BR2 215 K1
Hollydale Rd *PECK* SE15 143 K3
Hollydown Wy *WAN* E11 88 B1
Holly Dr *CHING* E4 37 K2
Holly Farm Rd *NWDGN* UB2 114 D5
Hollyfield Av *FBAR/BDGN* N11 47 K1
Hollyfield Rd *BRYLDS* KT5 191 G4
Holly Gdns *WDR/YW* UB7 112 C2
Hollygrove *BUSH* WD23 28 D2
Holly Gv *CDALE/KGS* NW9 62 E4
PECK SE15 143 G3
PIN HA5 41 J4
Hollygrove Cl *HSLW* TW3 134 E5
Holly Hedge Ter *LEW* SE13 145 F6
Holly Hl *HAMP* NW3 83 G2
WCHMH N21 35 F1
Holly Hill Rd *BELV* DA17 129 J5
Holly Lodge Gdns *HGT* N6 66 A6
Hollymead *CAR* SM5 209 K1
Holly Ms *WBPTN* SW10 120 B5
Holly Mt *HAMP* NW3 * 83 G2
Hollymount Cl *GNWCH* SE10 145 F2
Holly Pk *FNCH* N3 46 D6
FSBYPK N4 66 E4
Holly Park Gdns *FNCH* N3 46 E6
Holly Park Rd
FBAR/BDGN N11 48 A1
HNWL W7 116 A1
Holly Rd *CHSWK* W4 * 118 A4
HPTN TW12 173 H2
HSLW TW3 135 G5
ORP BR6 217 G5
TWK TW1 156 B3
WAN E11 70 D4
Holly St *HACK* E8 86 B5
Hollytree Cl *WIM/MER* SW19 159 G3
Hollytree Pde *SCUP* DA14 * 186 D1
Hollyview Cl *HDN* NW4 63 J3
Holly Vls *HMSMTH* W6 * 118 E3
Holly Wk *HAMP* NW3 83 G2
Holly Wy *MTCM* CR4 195 J1
Hollywood Gdns *YEAD* UB4 95 F5
Hollywood Ms *WBPTN* SW10 * 120 B6
Hollywood Rd *CHING* E4 51 G1
WBPTN SW10 120 B6
Hollywoods *CROY/NA* CR0 213 H6
Hollywood Wy *WFD* IG8 52 B3
Holman Ct *EW* KT17 * 207 J6
Holman Rd *BTSEA* SW11 140 C3
HOR/WEW KT19 206 E3
Holmbridge Gdns *PEND* EN3 25 F5
Holmbrook Dr *HDN* NW4 64 B2
Holmbury Cl *BUSH* WD23 28 E4
Holmbury Ct *WIM/MER* SW19 178 D3
Holmbury Gdns
HYS/HAR UB3 113 J1
Holmbury Gv *CROY/NA* CR0 213 H5
Holmbury Mnr *SCUP* DA14 * 168 B6
Holmbury Pk *BMLY* BR1 184 D3
Holmbury Vw *CLPT* E5 68 D5
Holmbush Rd *PUT/ROE* SW15 159 H1
Holmcote Gdns *HBRY* N5 85 J3
Holmcroft Wy *HAYES* BR2 200 E2
Holmdale Gdns *HDN* NW4 64 B2
Holmdale Rd *CHST* BR7 185 H1
KIL/WHAMP NW6 82 E3
Holmdale Ter
SEVS/STOTM N15 68 A3
Holmdene Av *HNHL* SE24 142 D6
MLHL NW7 45 J2
RYLN/HDSTN HA2 42 B6
Holmdene Cl *BECK* BR3 183 F5
Holmdene Ct *BMLY* BR1 184 D6
Holmead Rd *FUL/PGN* SW6 140 A1
Holmebury Cl *BUSH* WD23 * 28 E4
Holme Ct *ISLW* TW7 136 B4
Holme Lacey Rd
LEE/GVPK SE12 165 J1
Holme Rd *EHAM* E6 89 J6
Holmes Av *MLHL* NW7 46 C1
WALTH E17 51 H6
Holmes Cl *EDUL* SE22 143 H5
Holmesdale Av
MORT/ESHN SW14 137 J4
Holmesdale Cl *SNWD* SE25 181 G6
Holmesdale Rd *BXLYHN* DA7 148 E3
CROY/NA CR0 196 E2
HGT N6 66 B4
RCH/KEW TW9 137 G2
SNWD SE25 197 F1
TEDD TW11 174 D3
Holmesley Rd *FSTH* SE23 164 B1
Holmes Rd *KTTN* NW5 84 B3
TWK TW1 156 A4
WIM/MER SW19 178 B3
Holmes Ter *STHWK* SE1 17 J2
Holme Wy *STAN* HA7 43 F2
Holmewood Gdns
BRXS/STRHM SW2 162 A2
Holmewood Rd
BRXS/STRHM SW2 161 K2
SNWD SE25 181 F6
Holmfield Av *HDN* NW4 64 B2
Holmhurst Rd *BELV* DA17 129 J5
Holmleigh Rd
STNW/STAM N16 68 A5
Holm Oak Cl *PUT/ROE* SW15 159 J1
Holmshaw Cl *SYD* SE26 164 B6
Holmside Ri *OXHEY* WD19 27 F5
Holmside Rd *BAL* SW12 161 F1
Holmsley Cl *NWMAL* KT3 192 C3
Holmstall Av *EDGW* HA8 44 E5
Holmstall Pde *EDGW* HA8 * 44 E5
Holmwood Cl *BELMT* SM2 208 B6
NTHLT UB5 78 B4
RYLN/HDSTN HA2 42 C6
Holmwood Gdns *FNCH* N3 46 E5
WLGTN SM6 210 B4
Holmwood Gv *MLHL* NW7 45 F1
Holmwood Rd *BELMT* SM2 208 A6
CHSGTN KT9 206 A3
GDMY/SEVK IG3 72 E6
Holne Cha *EFNCH* N2 65 G3
MRDN SM4 193 K3
Holness Rd *SRTFD* E15 88 D4
Holroyd Rd *ESH/CLAY* KT10 205 F6
PUT/ROE SW15 139 F5
Holstein Wy *ERITHM* DA18 128 E3
Holstock Rd *IL* IG1 72 C6
Holsworth Cl
RYLN/HDSTN HA2 60 C2
Holsworthy Sq *FSBYW* WC1X 5 H7
Holsworthy Wy *CHSGTN* KT9 205 J3
Holt Cl *CHIG* IG7 55 F1
MUSWH N10 66 A1
SCUP DA14 169 F6
THMD SE28 109 H6
Holton St *WCHPL* E1 105 F3
Holt Rd *ALP/SUD* HA0 79 H1
CAN/RD E16 126 D1
The Holt *BARK/HLT* IG6 54 C2
MRDN SM4 * 193 K1
WLGTN SM6 210 C2
Holt Wy *CHIG* IG7 55 F1
Holtwhite Av *ENC/FH* EN2 23 J3
Holtwhite's Hl *ENC/FH* EN2 23 H2
Holwell Pl *PIN* HA5 59 J1
Holwood Cl *WOT/HER* KT12 188 B6
Holwood Park Av *ORP* BR6 215 K2
Holwood Pl *CLAP* SW4 141 J5
Holybourne Av
PUT/ROE SW15 158 D2
Holyhead Cl *BOW* E3 105 J2
Holyoake Ct
BERM/RHTH SE16 124 B2
Holyoake Wk *EA* W5 97 J3
EFNCH N2 47 G6
Holyoak Rd *LBTH* SE11 18 A6
Holyport Rd *FUL/PGN* SW6 139 F1
Holyrood Av
RYLN/HDSTN HA2 77 J2
Holyrood Gdns *EDGW* HA8 44 D5
Holyrood Ms *CAN/RD* E16 125 K1
Holyrood Rd *BAR* EN5 33 G1
Holyrood St *STHWK* SE1 19 G1
Holywell Cl
BERM/RHTH SE16 * 123 J5
ORP BR6 217 G2
STWL/WRAY TW19 152 B3
Holywell La *SDTCH* EC2A 7 H6
Holywell Rw *SDTCH* EC2A 7 G7
Holywell Wy
STWL/WRAY TW19 152 B3
Home Cl *CAR* SM5 194 E6
NTHLT UB5 95 K2
Home Ct *FELT* TW13 * 153 K3
SURB KT6 * 190 E2
Homecroft Rd *SYD* SE26 181 K1
WDGN N22 49 H4
Home Farm Cl *ESH/CLAY* KT10 204 B4
THDIT KT7 190 A4
Home Farm Gdns
WOT/HER KT12 188 B6
Homefarm Rd *HNWL* W7 96 E5
Homefield Av
GNTH/NBYPK IG2 72 E2
Homefield Cl *STMC/STPC* BR5 202 C1
WLSDN NW10 80 E4
YEAD UB4 95 H3
Homefield Gdns *EFNCH* N2 47 H6
WIM/MER SW19 178 B5
Homefield Ms *BECK* BR3 * 182 D4
Homefield Pk *SUT* SM1 209 F4
Homefield Ri *ORP* BR6 202 B5
Homefield Rd *ALP/SUD* HA0 79 G2
BMLY BR1 184 B4
CHSWK W4 118 C4
EDGW HA8 45 F2
WIM/MER SW19 177 H2
WOT/HER KT12 188 E4
Homefield St *IS* N1 * 7 G3
The Homefield *MRDN* SM4 * 193 K1
Home Gdns *DAGE* RM10 92 E1
Homeland Dr *BELMT* SM2 209 F6
Homelands Dr *NRWD* SE19 181 F3
Home Lea *ORP* BR6 217 F3
Homeleigh Rd *PECK* SE15 144 A6
Home Md *STAN* HA7 43 J4
Homemead Rd *CROY/NA* CR0 195 H3
HAYES BR2 200 E2
Home Park Ct *KUT/HW* KT1 * 190 E1
Home Park Rd
WIM/MER SW19 159 J6
Home Park Ter *KUT/HW* KT1 174 E5
Home Park Wk *KUT/HW* KT1 190 E1
Homer Dr *POP/IOD* E14 124 D4
Home Rd *BTSEA* SW11 140 D3
Homer Rd *CROY/NA* CR0 198 A3
HOM E9 87 G4
Homer Rw *CAMTN* NW1 8 D2
Homersham Rd *KUT/HW* KT1 175 H5
Homer St *MBLAR* W1H 8 D2
Homerton Gv *HOM* E9 87 F3
Homerton High St *HOM* E9 87 F3
Homerton Rd *HOM* E9 87 H3
Homerton Rw *HOM* E9 86 E3
Homerton Ter *HOM* E9 86 E4
Homesdale Cl *WAN* E11 70 E2
Homesdale Rd *HAYES* BR2 200 B1
ORP BR6 201 K4
Homesfield *GLDGN* NW11 64 E2
Homestall Rd *EDUL* SE22 143 K6
Homestead Gdns
ESH/CLAY KT10 204 E3
Homestead Paddock
STHGT/OAK N14 22 B6
Homestead Pk *CRICK* NW2 81 H1
Homestead Rd *BCTR* RM8 74 B6
FUL/PGN SW6 139 J1
ORP BR6 217 H5
Homewillow Cl *WCHMH* N21 35 H1
Homewood Cl *HPTN* TW12 172 E2
Homewood Crs *CHST* BR7 185 K2
Homewood Gdns
SNWD SE25 * 197 F2
Honduras St *FSBYE* EC1V 6 C6
Honeybourne Rd
KIL/WHAMP NW6 83 F3
Honeybourne Wy
STMC/STPC BR5 201 H5
Honeybrook Rd *BAL* SW12 161 H2
Honey Cl *DAGE* RM10 92 E4
Honeyden Rd *SCUP* DA14 187 F2
Honeyman Cl *CRICK* NW2 82 B5
Honeypot Cl *CDALE/KGS* NW9 62 B1
Honeypot La *CDALE/KGS* NW9 62 B1
KTN/HRWW/WS HA3 44 B6
STAN HA7 43 K4
Honeysett Rd *TOTM* N17 50 B5
Honeysuckle Cl *STHL* UB1 95 J6
Honeysuckle Gdns
CROY/NA CR0 198 A4
Honeywell Rd *BTSEA* SW11 160 D1
Honeywood Rd *ISLW* TW7 * 136 B5
WLSDN NW10 99 H1
Honeywood Wk *CAR* SM5 209 K2
Honister Cl *STAN* HA7 43 H4
Honister Gdns *STAN* HA7 43 H3
Honister Pl *STAN* HA7 43 H4
Honiton Gdns *MLHL* NW7 46 B3
PECK SE15 * 143 K3
Honiton Rd *KIL/WHAMP* NW6 100 D1
ROMW/RG RM7 75 F3
WELL DA16 148 A3
Honley Rd *CAT* SE6 164 E2
Honnor Gdns *ISLW* TW7 135 J3
Honor Oak Pk *FSTH* SE23 163 K2
Honor Oak Ri *FSTH* SE23 163 K1
Honor Oak Rd *FSTH* SE23 163 K3
Hood Av *MORT/ESHN* SW14 137 K6
STHGT/OAK N14 34 B1
STMC/STPC BR5 202 C2
Hood Cl *CROY/NA* CR0 196 C5
Hoodcote Gdns *WCHMH* N21 35 H2
Hood Rd *RAIN* RM13 93 G6
RYNPK SW20 176 C3
Hood Wk *ROMW/RG* RM7 56 D4
Hooker's Rd *WALTH* E17 51 F6
Hook Farm Rd *HAYES* BR2 200 C2
Hooking Gn *RYLN/HDSTN* HA2 60 B2
Hook La *WELL* DA16 148 B4
Hook Ri North *SURB* KT6 206 B1
Hook Ri South *CHSGTN* KT9 206 B1
Hook Rd *CHSGTN* KT9 205 K3
HOR/WEW KT19 206 E5
SURB KT6 191 F6
Hooks Hall Dr *DAGE* RM10 92 E1
Hookstone Wy *WFD* IG8 53 H3
The Hook *BAR* EN5 33 H1
Hook Underpass (Kingston By-Pass) *SURB* KT6 205 K1
Hook Wk *EDGW* HA8 44 E2
Hooper Rd *CAN/RD* E16 106 E5
Hoopers Ms *BUSH* WD23 28 B3
Hooper's Ms *ACT* W3 117 K1
Hooper St *WCHPL* E1 104 C6
Hoop La *GLDGN* NW11 64 D4
Hop Ct *ALP/SUD* HA0 * 79 J4
Hope Cl *BTFD* TW8 117 F5
CHDH RM6 73 K1
IS N1 85 J4
LEE/GVPK SE12 166 A5
SUT SM1 209 G3
Hopedale Rd *CHARL* SE7 126 A6
Hopefield Av
KIL/WHAMP NW6 100 C1
Hope Gdns *ACT* W3 117 J2
Hope La *ELTH/MOT* SE9 167 G5
Hope Pk *BMLY* BR1 183 J3
Hopes Cl *HEST* TW5 115 F6
Hope Sq *LVPST* EC2M 13 G2
Hope St *BTSEA* SW11 140 C4
Hopewell St *CMBW* SE5 142 E1
Hopewell Yd *CMBW* SE5 142 E1
Hop Gdns *CHCR* WC2N 10 E6
Hopgood St *SHB* W12 119 F2
Hopkins Cl *MUSWH* N10 48 A3
Hopkins Ms *SRTFD* E15 88 D6
Hopkinsons Pl *CAMTN* NW1 * 83 K6
Hopkins Rd *LEY* E10 69 K4
Hopkins St *SOHO/CST* W1F 10 B4
Hoppers Rd *WCHMH* N21 35 G4
Hoppett Rd *CHING* E4 38 C5
Hopping La *IS* N1 * 85 H4
Hoppingwood Av
NWMAL KT3 176 B6
Hoppner Rd *YEAD* UB4 94 B1
Hop St *GNWCH* SE10 125 J4
Hopton Gdns *NWMAL* KT3 192 D3
Hopton Pde
STRHM/NOR SW16 * 179 K1
Hopton Rd *STRHM/NOR* SW16 179 K1
WOOL/PLUM SE18 127 G3
Hoptons Gdns *STHWK* SE1 * 12 B7
Hopton St *STHWK* SE1 12 B6
Hoptree Cl
NFNCH/WDSPK N12 * 33 F6
Hopwood Cl *TOOT* SW17 160 B5
Hopwood Rd *WALW* SE17 122 E6
Hopwood Wk *HACK* E8 * 86 C5
Horace Av *ROMW/RG* RM7 75 F5
Horace Rd *BARK/HLT* IG6 54 C6
FSTGT E7 89 F2
KUT/HW KT1 175 G6
Horatio Pl *POP/IOD* E14 125 F2
Horatio St *BETH* E2 7 K3
Horatius Wy *CROY/NA* CR0 211 F4
Horbury Crs *NTGHL* W11 100 E6
Horbury Ms *NTGHL* W11 100 D6
Horder Rd *FUL/PGN* SW6 139 H2
Hordle Prom East *PECK* SE15 143 G1
Hordle Prom North
PECK SE15 143 G1
Hordle Prom West *PECK* SE15 143 F1
Horley Rd *ELTH/MOT* SE9 166 D6
Hormead Rd *MV/WKIL* W9 100 D3
Hornbeam Cl *IL* IG1 90 D3
LBTH SE11 17 J6
MLHL NW7 31 H5
NTHLT UB5 77 K3
Hornbeam Crs *BTFD* TW8 136 C1
Hornbeam Gdns *NWMAL* KT3 192 D3
Hornbeam Gv *CHING* E4 38 C5
Hornbeam Rd *BKHH* IG9 39 H5
YEAD UB4 95 G4
Hornbeam Sq *BOW* E3 87 H6
Hornbeams Ri
FBAR/BDGN N11 48 A2
Hornbeam Wy *HAYES* BR2 201 F3
Hornbuckle Cl
RYLN/HDSTN HA2 60 D6
Hornby Cl *HAMP* NW3 83 H5
Hornchurch Cl
KUTN/CMB KT2 174 E1
Hornchurch Rd *HCH* RM12 75 J5
Horndean Cl *PUT/ROE* SW15 158 D3
Horndon Cl *CRW* RM5 56 E4
Horndon Gn *CRW* RM5 56 E4
Horndon Rd *CRW* RM5 56 E4
Horne House *CHARL* SE7 * 146 D1
Horner La *MTCM* CR4 178 C5
Horne Wy *PUT/ROE* SW15 139 F3
Hornfair Rd *CHARL* SE7 126 C6
CHARL SE7 146 C1
Hornford Wy *ROMW/RG* RM7 75 G4
Horniman Dr *FSTH* SE23 163 J3
Horniman Gdns *FSTH* SE23 * 163 J3
Horning Cl *ELTH/MOT* SE9 166 D6
Horn La *ACT* W3 117 K1
WFD IG8 52 E2
Horn Park Cl *LEE/GVPK* SE12 146 A6
Horn Park La *LEE/GVPK* SE12 146 A6
Hornscroft Cl *BARK* IG11 90 E5
Horns End Pl *PIN* HA5 59 G1
Hornsey Chambers *CLPT* E5 * 68 D6
Hornsey La *HGT* N6 66 C4
Hornsey Lane Est *ARCH* N19 * 66 D4
Hornsey Lane Gdns *HGT* N6 66 C4
Hornsey Park Rd
CEND/HSY/T N8 49 F6
Hornsey Ri *ARCH* N19 66 D4
Hornsey Rise Gdns *ARCH* N19 66 D4
Hornsey Rd *ARCH* N19 66 E5
Hornsey St *HOLWY* N7 85 F3
Hornshay St *PECK* SE15 123 K6
Horns Rd *BARK/HLT* IG6 72 C2
Hornton Pl *KENS* W8 119 K2
Hornton St *KENS* W8 119 K2
Horsa Rd *ERITH* DA8 149 K1
LEE/GVPK SE12 166 B2
Horsebridges Cl *DAGW* RM9 92 A6
Horsecroft Cl *ORP* BR6 202 C5
Horsecroft Rd *EDGW* HA8 45 F3
Horse Fair *KUT/HW* KT1 174 E5
Horseferry Pl *GNWCH* SE10 125 F6
Horseferry Rd *POP/IOD* E14 105 G6
WEST SW1P 16 C5
Horse Guards Av
WHALL SW1A 16 E1
Horse Guards Rd
WHALL SW1A 16 D1
Horse Leaze *EHAM* E6 108 B5
Horsell Rd *HBRY* N5 85 G3
STMC/STPC BR5 186 B4
Horselydown La *STHWK* SE1 19 J2
Horsenden Av *GFD/PVL* UB6 78 E3
Horsenden Crs *GFD/PVL* UB6 79 F3
Horsenden La North
GFD/PVL UB6 78 E4
Horsenden La South
GFD/PVL UB6 79 G6
Horseshoe Cl *CRICK* NW2 63 K6
POP/IOD E14 125 F5
Horse Shoe Crs *NTHLT* UB5 96 A1
Horseshoe La *ENC/FH* EN2 23 J4
TRDG/WHET N20 32 B3
Horseshoe Ms
BRXS/STRHM SW2 141 K5
Horse Yd *IS* N1 85 H6
Horsfeld Gdns *ELTH/MOT* SE9 146 D6
Horsfeld Rd *ELTH/MOT* SE9 146 C6
Horsford Rd
BRXS/STRHM SW2 142 A6
Horsham Av
NFNCH/WDSPK N12 47 J1
Horsham Rd *BXLYHS* DA6 169 G1
EBED/NFELT TW14 153 F1
Horsley Dr *CROY/NA* CR0 214 A5
KUTN/CMB KT2 174 E1
Horsley Rd *BMLY* BR1 184 A4
CHING E4 38 A4
Horsley St *WALW* SE17 122 E6
Horsmans Pl *DART* DA1 * 171 H2
Horsman St *CMBW* SE5 122 D6
Horsmonden Cl *ORP* BR6 201 K4
Horsmonden Rd *BROCKY* SE4 144 C6
Hortensia Rd *WBPTN* SW10 140 B1
Horticultural Pl *CHSWK* W4 118 A5
Horton Av *CRICK* NW2 82 C2
Horton Bridge Rd
WDR/YW UB7 112 C1
Horton Cl *WDR/YW* UB7 112 C1
Horton La *HOR/WEW* KT19 206 D6
Horton Pde *WDR/YW* UB7 * 112 B1
Horton Rd *HACK* E8 86 D4
WDR/YW UB7 112 B1
Horton St *LEW* SE13 144 E4
Horton Wy *CROY/NA* CR0 198 A2
Hortus Rd *NWDGN* UB2 114 E2
Hosack Rd *TOOT* SW17 160 E4
Hosier La *STBT* EC1A 12 A2
Hoskins Cl *HYS/HAR* UB3 113 J5
Hoskin's Cl *CAN/RD* E16 107 G5
Hoskins St *GNWCH* SE10 125 G5
Hospital Bridge Rd
WHTN TW2 155 F2
Hospital Rd *HSLW* TW3 135 F4
LEY E10 70 B3
Hospital Wy *LEW* SE13 165 G1
Hotham Cl *E/WMO/HCT* KT8 173 F6
Hotham Rd *PUT/ROE* SW15 139 F4
Hotham Road Ms
WIM/MER SW19 178 B3
Hotham St *SRTFD* E15 88 C6
Hothfield Pl
BERM/RHTH SE16 123 K3
Hotspur Rd *NTHLT* UB5 96 A1
Hotspur St *LBTH* SE11 122 B5
Houblon Rd
RCHPK/HAM TW10 137 F6
Houghton Cl *HACK* E8 * 86 B4
HPTN TW12 172 D2
Houghton Rd
SEVS/STOTM N15 68 B1
Houghton St *LINN* WC2A * 11 H4
Houlder Crs *CROY/NA* CR0 211 H3
Houndsden Rd *WCHMH* N21 35 F1
Houndsditch *HDTCH* EC3A 13 H3
Houndsfield Rd *ED* N9 36 D2
Hounslow Av *HSLW* TW3 135 G6
Hounslow Gdns *HSLW* TW3 135 G6
Hounslow Rd
EBED/NFELT TW14 154 A2
Houseman Wy *CMBW* SE5 142 E1
Houston Rd *FSTH* SE23 164 B4
SURB KT6 190 C3
Hove Av *WALTH* E17 69 H2
Hoveden Rd *CRICK* NW2 82 B3
Hove Gdns *SUT* SM1 194 A5
Hoveton Rd *THMD* SE28 109 J5
Howard Av *BXLY* DA5 168 D3
Howard Cl *ACT* W3 98 D5
BUSH WD23 28 E2
CRICK NW2 * 82 C2
FBAR/BDGN N11 34 A4
HPTN TW12 173 H3
LOU IG10 39 J1
Howard Rd *BARK* IG11 90 D6
BMLY BR1 183 K3
CRICK NW2 82 B2
EHAM E6 107 K1
IL IG1 90 B2
ISLW TW7 136 A4
NWMAL KT3 176 B6
PGE/AN SE20 181 K4
SEVS/STOTM N15 68 A3
SNWD SE25 197 H2
STHL UB1 96 B5
STNW/STAM N16 85 K2
SURB KT6 191 G3
WALTH E17 51 J6
WAN E11 88 C1
Howards Cl *PIN* HA5 * 41 F5
Howards Crest Cl *BECK* BR3 183 F5
Howard's La *PUT/ROE* SW15 139 F5
Howard's Rd *PLSTW* E13 106 E2
Howard St *THDIT* KT7 190 C4
Howards Yd
WAND/EARL SW18 160 A2
Howard Wk *EFNCH* N2 65 G1
Howard Wy *BAR* EN5 20 B6
Howarth Rd *ABYW* SE2 128 B5
Howberry Cl *EDGW* HA8 43 K2
Howberry Rd *EDGW* HA8 43 K2
THHTH CR7 180 E4
Howbury Rd *PECK* SE15 143 K4
Howcroft Crs *FNCH* N3 46 E3
Howcroft La *GFD/PVL* UB6 96 D2
Howden Cl *THMD* SE28 109 J6
Howden Rd *SNWD* SE25 181 G5
Howden St *PECK* SE15 143 H4
Howe Cl *ROMW/RG* RM7 56 C4
Howell Cl *CHDH* RM6 73 K2
Howell Wk *STHWK* SE1 18 B7
Howerd Wy
WOOL/PLUM SE18 146 D2
Howes Cl *FNCH* N3 46 E6
Howfield Pl *TOTM* N17 * 50 B6
Howgate Rd
MORT/ESHN SW14 138 A4
Howick Pl *WESTW* SW1E 16 B5
Howie St *BTSEA* SW11 140 D1
Howitt Cl *HAMP* NW3 83 J4
Howitt Rd *HAMP* NW3 83 J4
Howitts Cl *ESH/CLAY* KT10 204 A
Howland Ct *PIN* HA5 * 42 A
Howland Ms East *FITZ* W1T 10 B
Howland St *FITZ* W1T 10 B
Howland Wy
BERM/RHTH SE16 124 B
Howletts La *RSLP* HA4 58 A
Howletts Rd *HNHL* SE24 162 D
Howley Pl *BAY/PAD* W2 101 G
Howley Rd *CROY/NA* CR0 211 H
Howsman Rd *BARN* SW13 118 D
Howson Rd *BROCKY* SE4 144 B
Howson Ter
RCHPK/HAM TW10 * 157 F
How's St *BETH* E2 7
Howton Pl *BUSH* WD23 28 D
Hoxton Market *IS* N1 7 G
Hoxton Sq *IS* N1 7 G
Hoxton St *IS* N1 7 G
Hoylake Gdns *MTCM* CR4 179
OXHEY WD19 27
RSLP HA4 59
Hoylake Rd *ACT* W3 99
Hoyland Cl *PECK* SE15 * 143
Hoyle Rd *TOOT* SW17 178
Hoy St *CAN/RD* E16 106
Hubbard Dr *CHSGTN* KT9 205
Hubbard Rd *WNWD* SE27 162
Hubbard St *SRTFD* E15 88
Hubert Cl *WIM/MER* SW19 * 178
Hubert Gv *BRXN/ST* SW9 141
Hubert Rd *EHAM* E6 107
RAIN RM13 111
Huddart St *BOW* E3 105
Huddleston Cl *BETH* E2 * 104
Huddlestone Rd *CRICK* NW2 81
FSTGT E7 88
Huddleston Rd *HOLWY* N7 84
Hudson Cl *SHB* W12 * 99
Hudson Pl *WOOL/PLUM* SE18 127
Hudson Rd *HYS/HAR* UB3 113
Huggin Hl *BLKFR* EC4V 12
Huggins Pl *BRXS/STRHM* SW2 162
Hughan Rd *SRTFD* E15 88
Hugh Dalton Av
FUL/PGN SW6 119
Hughenden Av
KTN/HRWW/WS HA3 61
Hughenden Gdns *NTHLT* UB5 95
Hughenden Rd *WPK* KT4 192
Hughes Cl
NFNCH/WDSPK N12 47
Hughes Rd *HYS/HAR* UB3 95
Hughes Ter *CAN/RD* E16 * 106
Hughes Wk *CROY/NA* CR0 196
Hugh Gaitskell Cl
FUL/PGN SW6 * 119

Hugh Ms PIM SW1V 15 K7
Hugh Pl WEST SW1P 16 C6
Hugh St PIM SW1V 15 K7
Hugo Gdns RAIN RM13 93 H4
Hugon Rd FUL/PGN SW6 140 A4
Hugo Rd ARCH N19 84 C2
Huguenot Pl
WAND/EARL SW18 140 B6
WCHPL E1 13 K1
Huitt Sq BTSEA SW11 140 C4
Hullbridge Ms IS N1 85 K6
Hull Cl BERM/RHTH SE16 * 124 A1
Hull St FSBYE EC1V 6 C5
Hulme Pl STHWK SE1 18 D3
Hulse Av BARK IG11 90 E4
ROMW/RG RM7 56 D4
Hulverston Cl BELMT SM2 209 F6
Humber Cl WDR/YW UB7 112 A1
Humber Dr NKENS W10 100 B3
Humber Rd CRICK NW2 63 K6
Humberstone Rd PLSTW E13 107 G2
Humbolt Rd HMSMTH W6 119 H6
Humes Av HNWL W7 116 A3
Hume Wy RSLP HA4 58 E3
Humphrey Cl CLAY IG5 * 53 K4
Humphrey St STHWK SE1 123 G5
Humphries Cl DAGW RM9 92 B2
Hundred Acre
CDALE/KGS NW9 45 H5
Hungerdown CHING E4 38 A3
Hungerford Rd HOLWY N7 84 D4
Hungerford St WCHPL E1 * 104 D5
Hunsdon Cl DAGW RM9 92 A3
Hunsdon Rd NWCR SE14 144 A1
Hunslett St BETH E2 * 104 E1
Hunston Rd MRDN SM4 194 A5
Hunt Cl NTGHL W11 119 G1
Hunter Cl BAL SW12 161 F3
STHWK SE1 19 F5
WLGTN SM6 210 E5
Hunter Ct CMBW SE5 * 142 E5
Huntercrombe Gdns
OXHEY WD19 41 G1
Hunter Rd RYNPK SW20 177 F4
THHTH CR7 180 E6
Hunters Ct RCH/KEW TW9 136 E6
Hunters Gv HYS/HAR UB3 113 K1
KTN/HRWW/WS HA3 61 J1
Hunter's Gv CRW RM5 56 D1
ORP BR6 216 C2
Hunters Hall Rd DAGE RM10 92 C2
Hunters Hl RSLP HA4 77 G1
Hunters Meadow NRWD SE19 163 F6
Hunters Rd CHSGTN KT9 206 A1
IL IG1 90 B3
Hunters Sq DAGE RM10 92 C2
Hunter St BMSBY WC1N 5 F6
Hunters Wy CROY/NA CR0 212 A2
ENC/FH EN2 23 G2
Hunting Cl ESH/CLAY KT10 204 A2
Huntingdon Cl MTCM CR4 195 K1
NTHLT UB5 78 A4
untingdon Gdns CHSWK W4 137 K1
WPK KT4 208 A1
untingdon Rd ED N9 36 E3
EFNCH N2 47 J6
untingdon St CAN/RD E16 106 D5
IS N1 85 F5
untingfield CROY/NA CR0 213 H5
untingfield Rd
PUT/ROE SW15 158 D1
unting Gate Cl ENC/FH EN2 23 G4
unting Gate Dr CHSGTN KT9 206 A5
unting Gate Ms
WHTN TW2 * 155 K3
untings Rd DAGE RM10 92 C4
untland Cl RAIN RM13 111 K4
untley Cl STWL/WRAY TW19 152 B2
untley St GWRST WC1E 4 B7
untley Wy RYNPK SW20 * 176 D5
untly Dr FNCH N3 46 E2
untly Rd SNWD SE25 181 F6
unton St WCHPL E1 104 C4
unt Rd NWDGN UB2 115 F3
unt's La SRTFD E15 106 A1
untsman Cl FELT TW13 154 A6
untsman Rd BARK/HLT IG6 55 H2
untsman St WALW SE17 19 G7
unts Md PEND EN3 25 F4
unts Medde Cl CHST BR7 184 D3
untsmoor Rd
HOR/WEW KT19 207 F3
ntspill St TOOT SW17 160 B5
nts Slip Rd DUL SE21 163 F4
ntsworth Ms CAMTN NW1 2 E6
rdwick Pl CAMTN NW1 * 4 A2
rley Cl WOT/HER KT12 188 A6
rley Crs BERM/RHTH SE16 124 A1
rley Rd GFD/PVL UB6 96 B4
rlingham Gdns
FUL/PGN SW6 139 J4
rlingham Pk
FUL/PGN SW6 * 139 J4
rlingham Rd FUL/PGN SW6 139 J3
rlingham Sq
FUL/PGN SW6 * 139 K4
rlock St HBRY N5 85 H1
rstone Rd SNWD SE25 196 E2
n Court Rd HSLWW TW4 134 C3
ron Cl ORP BR6 216 E4
ron Rd TOOT SW17 161 F4
rren Cl BKHTH/KID SE3 145 H4
rricane House
WOOL/PLUM SE18 * 146 D1
rricane Rd WLGTN SM6 210 E5
rry Cl SRTFD E15 88 C5
rsley Rd CHIG IG7 55 F1
rst Av CHING E4 37 J5
HGT N6 66 C3
rstbourne ESH/CLAY KT10 205 F4
rstbourne Gdns
BARK IG11 90 D4
rstbourne Rd FSTH SE23 164 B3
st Cl CHING E4 37 J5
CHSGTN KT9 206 C3
GLDGN NW11 65 F3
HAYES BR2 199 J5
NTHLT UB5 77 K4
stcourt Rd SUT SM1 194 A5
stdene Av HAYES BR2 199 J5

Hurstdene Gdns
SEVS/STOTM N15 68 A4
Hurstfield Crs YEAD UB4 94 C4
Hurstfield Rd
E/WMO/HCT KT8 173 F6
Hurst La ABYW SE2 128 E5
E/WMO/HCT KT8 189 H1
Hurstleigh Gdns CLAY IG5 53 K4
Hurst Pl DART DA1 * 171 F1
Hurst Ri BAR EN5 20 E4
Hurst Rd BFN/LL DA15 168 C4
BKHH IG9 39 H3
BXLY DA5 169 F3
CROY/NA CR0 211 K3
E/WMO/HCT KT8 173 F6
ERITH DA8 149 K1
WALTH E17 51 K6
WCHMH N21 35 G3
WOT/HER KT12 188 C1
Hurst Springs BXLY DA5 169 F3
Hurst St HNHL SE24 162 C1
Hurst View Rd SAND/SEL CR2 212 A5
Hurst Wy SAND/SEL CR2 212 A4
Hurstway Rd NTGHL W11 * 100 B6
Hurstway Wk NTGHL W11 * 100 B6
Hurstwood Av BXLY DA5 169 F3
SWFD E18 71 F1
Hurstwood Dr BMLY BR1 184 E6
Hurstwood Rd GLDGN NW11 64 C1
Hurtwood Rd WOT/HER KT12 188 E4
Huson Cl HAMP NW3 * 83 J5
Hussain Cl HRW HA1 79 F2
Hussars Cl HSLWW TW4 134 D4
Hutching's St POP/IOD E14 124 D2
Hutchings Wk GLDGN NW11 65 F1
Hutchins Cl SRTFD E15 88 A5
Hutchinson Ter WBLY HA9 79 K1
Hutchins Rd THMD SE28 109 G6
Hutton Cl GFD/PVL UB6 78 D3
WFD IG8 53 F2
Hutton Gv
NFNCH/WDSPK N12 47 F1
Hutton La
KTN/HRWW/WS HA3 42 C3
Hutton Rw EDGW HA8 44 E3
Hutton St EMB EC4Y 11 K4
Hutton Wk
KTN/HRWW/WS HA3 42 C3
Huxbear St BROCKY SE4 144 C6
Huxley UED N18 * 49 K1
Huxley Cl NTHLT UB5 95 J1
Huxley Dr CHDH RM6 73 H4
Huxley Gdns WLSDN NW10 98 B2
Huxley Pde UED N18 * 49 K1
Huxley Pl PLMGR N13 35 H6
Huxley Rd LEY E10 70 A6
UED N18 35 K6
WELL DA16 148 A4
Huxley Sayze UED N18 * 49 K1
Huxley St NKENS W10 100 C2
Hyacinth Cl HPTN TW12 173 F2
IL IG1 90 B4
Hyacinth Rd PUT/ROE SW15 158 D3
Hyde Cl BAR EN5 20 D4
CRW RM5 57 F2
PLSTW E13 106 E1
Hyde Crs CDALE/KGS NW9 63 G2
Hyde Dr STMC/STPC BR5 202 C1
Hyde Estate Rd
CDALE/KGS NW9 63 H2
Hyde Farm Ms BAL SW12 161 J3
Hydefield Cl WCHMH N21 35 K3
Hydefield Ct ED N9 36 A4
Hyde Gv DART DA1 151 J3
Hyde La BTSEA SW11 140 D2
Hyde Park Av WCHMH N21 35 J4
Hyde Park Cnr
MYFR/PICC W1J 15 H2
Hyde Park Crs BAY/PAD W2 8 C4
Hyde Park Gdns BAY/PAD W2 8 B5
WCHMH N21 35 J3
Hyde Park Gardens Ms
BAY/PAD W2 8 B5
Hyde Park Ga SKENS SW7 120 B2
Hyde Park Gate Ms
SKENS SW7 * 120 B2
Hyde Park Pl BAY/PAD W2 8 D5
Hyde Park Sq BAY/PAD W2 8 C4
Hyde Park Square Ms
BAY/PAD W2 8 C4
Hyde Park St BAY/PAD W2 8 C5
Hyderabad Wy SRTFD E15 88 C5
Hyde Rd IS N1 7 F1
RCHPK/HAM TW10 137 G6
Hydeside Gdns ED N9 36 B4
Hyde's Pl IS N1 85 H5
Hyde St DEPT SE8 124 D6
The Hyde CDALE/KGS NW9 63 G2
Hydethorpe Av ED N9 36 B4
Hydethorpe Rd BAL SW12 161 H3
Hyde V GNWCH SE10 145 F1
Hyde Wk MRDN SM4 193 K4
Hyde Wy ED N9 36 B4
HYS/HAR UB3 113 J4
Hyland Cl EMPK RM11 75 K4
Hylands Rd WALTH E17 52 B5
Hyland Wy EMPK RM11 75 K4
Hylton St WOOL/PLUM SE18 128 A4
Hyndewood FSTH SE23 * 164 A5
Hyndman St PECK SE15 123 J6
Hynton Rd BCTR RM8 73 J6
Hyperion Pl HOR/WEW KT19 207 F6
Hyrstdene SAND/SEL CR2 211 H2
Hyson Rd BERM/RHTH SE16 123 J5
Hythe Cl STMC/STPC BR5 202 D1
UED N18 36 C6
Hythe Rd THHTH CR7 180 E5
WLSDN NW10 99 H2
Hyver Hl BAR EN5 31 F1

I

Ibbotson Av CAN/RD E16 106 D5
Ibbott St WCHPL E1 104 E3
Iberian Av WLGTN SM6 210 D2
Ibis La CHSWK W4 137 K2
Ibis Wy YEAD UB4 95 H5
Ibscott Cl DAGE RM10 92 E4
Ibsley Gdns PUT/ROE SW15 158 D3
Ibsley Wy EBAR EN4 21 J6
Iceland Rd BOW E3 87 J6
Ickburgh Est CLPT E5 * 68 D6
Ickburgh Rd CLPT E5 86 D1
Ickenham Cl RSLP HA4 58 B6
Ickenham Rd RSLP HA4 58 B5
Ickleton Rd ELTH/MOT SE9 166 D6
Icknield Dr GNTH/NBYPK IG2 72 B2
Ickworth Park Rd WALTH E17 69 G1
Ida Rd SEVS/STOTM N15 67 K2
Ida St POP/IOD E14 106 A5
Iden Cl HAYES BR2 183 H6
Idlecombe Rd TOOT SW17 179 F2
Idmiston Rd SRTFD E15 88 D3
WNWD SE27 162 D5
WPK KT4 192 C4
Idmiston Sq WPK KT4 192 C4
Idol La MON EC3R 13 G6
Idonia St DEPT SE8 144 C1
Iffley Rd HMSMTH W6 118 E3
Ifield Rd WBPTN SW10 120 A6
Ilbert St NKENS W10 100 C2
Ilchester Pl WKENS W14 119 J3
Ilchester Rd BCTR RM8 91 H3
Ildersly Gv DUL SE21 162 E4
Ilderton Rd PECK SE15 123 K6
Ilex Cl SUN TW16 172 B5
Ilex Rd WLSDN NW10 81 H4
Ilex Wy STRHM/NOR SW16 180 B1
Ilford Hl MNPK E12 89 K2
Ilford La IL IG1 90 B2
Ilfracombe Gdns CHDH RM6 73 H4
Ilfracombe Rd BMLY BR1 165 J5
Iliffe St WALW SE17 122 C5
Iliffe Yd WALW SE17 122 C5
Ilkley Cl NRWD SE19 * 180 E2
Ilkley Ct FBAR/BDGN N11 48 A2
Ilkley Rd CAN/RD E16 107 G4
OXHEY WD19 41 H1
Illingworth Wy EN EN1 24 A6
Ilmington Rd
KTN/HRWW/WS HA3 61 K3
Ilminster Gdns BTSEA SW11 140 D5
Imber Cl STHGT/OAK N14 34 C2
Imber Cross THDIT KT7 * 190 A4
Imber Gv ESH/CLAY KT10 189 J4
Imber Park Rd
ESH/CLAY KT10 189 J5
Imber St IS N1 6 E1
Imperial Av
STNW/STAM N16 * 86 A2
Imperial Cl CRICK NW2 81 K3
RYLN/HDSTN HA2 60 A3
Imperial College Rd
SKENS SW7 14 A5
Imperial Crs FUL/PGN SW6 140 B3
Imperial Dr RYLN/HDSTN HA2 60 A4
Imperial Gdns MTCM CR4 179 G6
Imperial Ms EHAM E6 107 H1
Imperial Pl CHST BR7 185 F4
Imperial Rd
EBED/NFELT TW14 153 H2
FUL/PGN SW6 140 A2
WDGN N22 48 E3
Imperial Sq FUL/PGN SW6 140 A2
Imperial St BOW E3 106 A2
Imperial Wy CHST BR7 167 H5
CROY/NA CR0 211 F4
KTN/HRWW/WS HA3 62 A3
Imre Cl SHB W12 118 E1
Inca Dr ELTH/MOT SE9 167 G2
Inchmery Rd CAT SE6 164 E4
Inchwood CROY/NA CR0 213 K2
Independent Pl HACK E8 86 B3
Independents Rd
BKHTH/KID SE3 145 J4
Inderwick Rd CEND/HSY/T N8 67 F3
Indescon Ct POP/IOD E14 124 E2
India St TWRH EC3N 13 J4
India Wy SHB W12 99 K6
Indigo Ms POP/IOD E14 * 106 A6
STNW/STAM N16 85 K1
Indus Rd CHARL SE7 146 B1
Infant House
WOOL/PLUM SE18 * 146 D1
Ingal Rd PLSTW E13 106 E3
Ingate Pl VX/NE SW8 141 G2
Ingatestone Rd MNPK E12 71 G5
SNWD SE25 197 J2
WFD IG8 53 F3
Ingelow Rd VX/NE SW8 141 G3
Ingersoll Rd PEND EN3 24 E1
SHB W12 118 E1
Ingestre Pl SOHO/CST W1F 10 B4
Ingestre Rd FSTGT E7 88 E2
KTTN NW5 84 B2
Ingham Cl SAND/SEL CR2 213 F6
Ingham Rd KIL/WHAMP NW6 82 E2
SAND/SEL CR2 212 E6
Inglebert St CLKNW EC1R 5 J4
Ingleborough St
BRXN/ST SW9 142 B3
Ingleby Dr HRW HA1 78 D1
Ingleby Rd DAGE RM10 92 D4
HOLWY N7 84 E1
IL IG1 72 B5
Ingleby Wy CHST BR7 185 F1
WLGTN SM6 210 D6
Ingle Cl PIN HA5 41 K6
Ingledew Rd
WOOL/PLUM SE18 127 J5
Inglefield Sq WAP E1W * 123 J1
Inglehurst Gdns REDBR IG4 71 K2
Inglemere Rd FSTH SE23 164 A5
TOOT SW17 178 E3
Ingleside Cl BECK BR3 182 D3
Ingleside Gv BKHTH/KID SE3 125 J6
Inglethorpe St FUL/PGN SW6 139 G2
Ingleton Av WELL DA16 148 B6
Ingleton Rd CAR SM5 209 J6
UED N18 50 C2
Ingleton St BRXN/ST SW9 142 B3
Ingleway NFNCH/WDSPK N12 47 H2
Inglewood CROY/NA CR0 213 G6
Inglewood Cl BARK/HLT IG6 55 F2
POP/IOD E14 124 D4
Inglewood Copse BMLY BR1 184 D5
Inglewood Ms SURB KT6 191 H5
Inglewood Rd BXLYHN DA7 150 A5
KIL/WHAMP NW6 82 E3
Inglis Rd CROY/NA CR0 197 G5
EA W5 98 B6
Inglis St CMBW SE5 142 C2
Ingram Av GLDGN NW11 65 G4
Ingram Cl LBTH SE11 17 H6
STAN HA7 43 J1
Ingram Rd EFNCH N2 65 J1
THHTH CR7 180 D4
Ingram Wy GFD/PVL UB6 78 D6
Ingrave Rd ROM RM1 75 F1
Ingrave St BTSEA SW11 140 C4
Ingrebourne Rd RAIN RM13 111 K3
Ingress St CHSWK W4 118 B5
Inigo Jones Rd CHARL SE7 146 C1
Inkerman Rd KTTN NW5 84 B4
Inks Gn CHING E4 52 A1
Inkwell Cl NFNCH/WDSPK N12 33 G5
Inman Rd WAND/EARL SW18 160 B2
WLSDN NW10 81 G6
Inmans Rw WFD IG8 38 E6
Inner Cir CAMTN NW1 3 G5
Inner Park Rd
WIM/MER SW19 159 G4
Inner Ring East HTHAIR TW6 132 E4
Innes Cl RYNPK SW20 177 H5
Innes Gdns PUT/ROE SW15 158 E1
Innes St PECK SE15 143 F1
Innes Yd CROY/NA CR0 211 J1
Inniskilling Rd PLSTW E13 107 G1
Innovation Cl ALP/SUD HA0 80 A6
Inskip Cl LEY E10 69 K6
Inskip Rd BCTR RM8 73 K5
Institute Pl HACK E8 86 D3
Integer Gdns WAN E11 * 70 B4
International Av HEST TW5 114 B5
Inver Ct BAY/PAD W2 * 101 F5
Inveresk Gdns WPK KT4 207 H1
Inverforth Cl HAMP NW3 65 G6
Inverforth Rd
FBAR/BDGN N11 48 B1
Inverine Rd CHARL SE7 126 A5
Invermore Pl
WOOL/PLUM SE18 127 H4
Inverness Av EN EN1 24 A2
Inverness Dr BARK/HLT IG6 54 E2
Inverness Gdns KENS W8 120 A1
Inverness Pl BAY/PAD W2 * 101 F6
Inverness Rd HSLW TW3 134 E5
NWDGN UB2 114 D4
UED N18 50 D1
WPK KT4 193 G5
Inverness St CAMTN NW1 84 B6
Inverness Ter BAY/PAD W2 101 F5
WDGN N22 * 49 H4
Inverton Rd PECK SE15 144 A5
Invicta Cl CHST BR7 185 F1
EBED/NFELT TW14 153 J3
Invicta Gv NTHLT UB5 95 K2
Invicta Pde SCUP DA14 * 168 C6
Invicta Plaza STHWK SE1 12 A7
Inville Rd WALW SE17 122 E5
Inwood Av HSLW TW3 135 H4
Inwood Cl CROY/NA CR0 198 B6
Inwood Rd HSLW TW3 135 H5
Inworth St BTSEA SW11 140 D3
Inworth Wk IS N1 * 85 J6
Iona Cl CAT SE6 164 D2
MRDN SM4 194 A4
Ion Sq BETH E2 * 104 C1
Ipswich Rd TOOT SW17 179 F2
Ireland Cl EHAM E6 107 K4
Ireland Pl WDGN N22 48 E3
Irene Ms HNWL W7 * 116 A1
Irene Rd FUL/PGN SW6 139 K2
ORP BR6 202 A4
Ireton Cl MUSWH N10 48 A3
Ireton St BOW E3 105 J3
Iris Av BXLY DA5 169 F1
Iris Cl CROY/NA CR0 198 A5
EHAM E6 107 J4
STMC/STPC BR5 202 D2
SURB KT6 * 191 G4
Iris Crs BXLYHN DA7 129 G6
Iris Rd HOR/WEW KT19 206 D3
Iris Wy CHING E4 51 H2
Irkdale Av EN EN1 24 B2
Iron Bridge Cl NWDGN UB2 115 H1
WLSDN NW10 81 G3
Iron Bridge Rd STKPK UB11 * 112 E1
Iron Bridge Rd North
STKPK UB11 112 D1
Iron Bridge Rd South
WDR/YW UB7 112 D2
Iron Mill Pl
WAND/EARL SW18 * 160 A1
Iron Mill Rd WAND/EARL SW18 160 A1
Ironmonger La CITYW EC2V 12 E4
Ironmonger Rw FSBYE EC1V 6 D5
Ironmongers Pl POP/IOD E14 124 D4
Ironside Cl BERM/RHTH SE16 124 A2
Irons Wy CRW RM5 56 E3
Irvine Av KTN/HRWW/WS HA3 43 G6
Irvine Cl POP/IOD E14 105 K4
TRDG/WHET N20 33 J4
Irvine Wy ORP BR6 202 A4
Irving Av NTHLT UB5 77 H6
Irving Gv BRXN/ST SW9 142 A3
Irving Ms IS N1 85 J4
Irving Rd WKENS W14 119 G3
Irving St LSQ/SEVD WC2H 10 D6
Irving Wy CDALE/KGS NW9 63 H2
Irwell Est BERM/RHTH SE16 * 123 K2
Irwin Av WOOL/PLUM SE18 147 K1
Irwin Gdns WLSDN NW10 81 K6
Isaac Wy STHWK SE1 18 D2
Isabella Cl STHGT/OAK N14 34 C2
Isabella Ct
RCHPK/HAM TW10 * 157 G1
Isabella Dr ORP BR6 216 C2
Isabella Ms IS N1 * 86 A4
Isabella Pl KUTN/CMB KT2 175 G1
Isabella Rd HOM E9 * 86 E3
Isabella St STHWK SE1 18 A1
Isabel St BRXN/ST SW9 142 A2
Isambard Ms POP/IOD E14 125 F3
Isambard Pl
BERM/RHTH SE16 123 K1
Isham Rd STRHM/NOR SW16 179 K5
Isis Cl PUT/ROE SW15 139 F5
RSLP HA4 58 A3
Isis St WAND/EARL SW18 160 B4
Island Centre Wy PEND EN3 25 J1
Island Farm Av
E/WMO/HCT KT8 188 E2
Island Farm Rd
E/WMO/HCT KT8 188 E2
Island Rd BERM/RHTH SE16 124 A4
MTCM CR4 178 E3
Island Rw POP/IOD E14 105 H5
Isla Rd WOOL/PLUM SE18 127 H6
Islay Gdns HSLWW TW4 134 C6
Islay Wk IS N1 * 85 J4
Islay Whf POP/IOD E14 * 106 A4
Isledon Rd HOLWY N7 85 G1
Islehurst Cl CHST BR7 185 F4
Islington Gn IS N1 6 A1
Islington High St IS N1 6 A2
Islington Park Ms IS N1 85 H5
Islington Park St IS N1 85 G5
Islip Gdns EDGW HA8 45 F2
NTHLT UB5 77 J5
Islip Manor Rd NTHLT UB5 77 J5
Islip St KTTN NW5 84 C3
Ismailia Rd FSTGT E7 89 F5
Isom Cl PLSTW E13 107 F2
Issa Rd HSLW TW3 134 E5
Ivanhoe Dr
KTN/HRWW/WS HA3 43 H5
Ivanhoe Rd CMBW SE5 143 G4
HSLWW TW4 134 C4
Ivatt Pl WKENS W14 119 J5
Ivatt Wy SEVS/STOTM N15 49 H6
Iveagh Av WLSDN NW10 98 C1
Iveagh Cl HOM E9 87 F6
WLSDN NW10 98 C1
Ivedon Rd WELL DA16 148 D3
Ive Farm Cl LEY E10 69 J6
Ive Farm La LEY E10 69 J6
Iveley Rd CLAP SW4 141 H3
Ivere Dr BAR EN5 33 F1
Iverhurst Cl BXLYHS DA6 148 E6
Iverna Ct KENS W8 119 K3
Iverna Gdns
EBED/NFELT TW14 133 G6
KENS W8 119 K3
Iverson Rd KIL/WHAMP NW6 82 D4
Ivers Wy CROY/NA CR0 213 K5
Ives Gdns ROM RM1 75 H1
Ives Rd CAN/RD E16 106 C4
Ives St CHEL SW3 14 D6
Ivimey St BETH E2 * 104 C2
Ivinghoe Cl EN EN1 24 A3
Ivinghoe Rd BCTR RM8 91 H3
BUSH WD23 28 D1
Ivor Gv ELTH/MOT SE9 167 G3
Ivor Pl CAMTN NW1 2 E7
Ivor St CAMTN NW1 84 C5
Ivory Ct FELT TW13 153 K3
Ivybridge Cl TWK TW1 156 B1
Ivychurch Cl PGE/AN SE20 181 J3
Ivy Church La WALW SE17 * 123 G5
Ivy Cl PIN HA5 59 G4
RYLN/HDSTN HA2 77 K2
SUN TW16 172 B5
Ivy Ct BERM/RHTH SE16 * 123 H5
Ivy Crs CHSWK W4 117 K4
Ivydale Rd CAR SM5 194 E6
PECK SE15 144 A6
Ivyday Gv STRHM/NOR SW16 162 A5
Ivydene E/WMO/HCT KT8 188 E2
Ivydene Cl SUT SM1 209 G2
Ivy Gdns CEND/HSY/T N8 66 E3
MTCM CR4 179 J6
Ivyhouse Rd DAGW RM9 91 K4
Ivy La HSLWW TW4 134 E5
Ivymount Rd WNWD SE27 162 B5
Ivy Rd BROCKY SE4 144 C5
CAN/RD E16 106 E5
CRICK NW2 82 A2
HSLW TW3 135 G5
STHGT/OAK N14 34 C2
SURB KT6 * 191 H6
TOOT SW17 178 D1
WALTH E17 69 J3
Ivy St IS N1 7 G2
Ivy Wk DAGW RM9 92 A4
NTHWD HA6 * 40 C4
Ixworth Pl CHEL SW3 14 C7

J

Jacaranda Cl NWMAL KT3 176 B6
Jacaranda Gv HACK E8 86 B5
Jackass La HAYES BR2 215 F4
Jack Clow Rd SRTFD E15 106 C1
Jack Cornwell St MNPK E12 90 A2
Jack Dash Wy EHAM E6 107 J3
Jack Jones Wy DAGW RM9 92 B6
Jackman Ms WLSDN NW10 81 G1
Jackman St HACK E8 86 D6
Jackson Cl HOM E9 87 F5
Jackson Rd BARK IG11 90 D6
EBAR EN4 33 H1
HAYES BR2 200 D6
HOLWY N7 85 F2
Jackson's La HGT N6 66 A4
Jackson's Pl CROY/NA CR0 196 E5
Jackson St WOOL/PLUM SE18 127 F6
Jackson's Wy CROY/NA CR0 213 J1
Jackson Wy HOR/WEW KT19 206 C6
NWDGN UB2 115 G2
Jack Walker Ct HBRY N5 85 H2
Jacobs Cl DAGE RM10 92 D2
Jacob St STHWK SE1 19 K2
Jacob's Well Ms MHST W1U 9 H3
Jacqueline Cl NTHLT UB5 77 J6
Jacqueline Creft Ter
HGT N6 * 66 A3
Jacqueline Vls WALTH E17 * 70 A2
Jade Cl BCTR RM8 73 J5
CAN/RD E16 107 H5
CRICK NW2 64 B4
Jade Ter KIL/WHAMP NW6 * 83 G5
Jaffe Rd IL IG1 72 C5
Jaffray Rd HAYES BR2 200 C1

Jaggard Wy BAL SW12 .... 160 E2
Jago Cl WOOL/PLUM SE18 .... 127 H6
Jago Wk CMBW SE5. .... 142 E1
Jamaica Rd STHWK SE1 .... 19 K3
THHTH CR7 .... 196 C3
Jamaica St WCHPL E1 .... 104 E4
James Av BCTR RM8 .... 74 B5
CRICK NW2 .... 82 A3
James Bedford Cl PIN HA5 .... 41 C5
James Cl GLDGN NW11 * 64 C3
GPK RM2 .... 75 J2
PLSTW E13 .... 106 E1
James Collins Cl MV/WKIL W9. .... 100 D3
James Gdns TOTM N17 .... 49 J3
James Joyce Wk
BRXN/ST SW9 .... 142 C5
James La WALTH E17 .... 70 A4
Jameson St KENS W8 .... 119 K1
James Pl TOTM N17 .... 50 B5
James St BARK IG11 .... 90 C5
COVGDN WC2E 11 F5
EN EN1 .... 24 B6
HSLW TW3 .... 135 J4
MHST W1U 9 H3
Jamestown Rd CAMTN NW1 .... 84 B6
Jamestown Wy POP/IOD E14 .... 106 B6
James Voller Wy WCHPL E1 .... 104 E5
James Wy OXHEY WD19 .... 27 H6
James Yd CHING E4 * 52 B2
Jamuna Cl POP/IOD E14 .... 105 G4
Jane St WCHPL E1 .... 104 D5
Janet St POP/IOD E14 .... 124 D3
Janeway Pl BERM/RHTH SE16 .... 123 J2
Janeway St BERM/RHTH SE16 .... 123 H2
Janson Cl SRTFD E15 .... 88 C3
WLSDN NW10 .... 81 F1
Janson Rd SRTFD E15 .... 88 C3
Jansons Rd SEVS/STOTM N15. .... 50 A6
Japan Crs FSBYPK N4 .... 67 F5
Japan Rd CHDH RM6 .... 73 K3
Jardine Rd WAP E1W 105 F6
Jarrett Cl BRXS/STRHM SW2 .... 162 C3
Jarrow Cl MRDN SM4 .... 194 A2
Jarrow Rd BERM/RHTH SE16 .... 123 K4
CHDH RM6 .... 73 J3
TOTM N17 .... 68 D1
Jarrow Wy HOM E9 .... 87 H2
Jarvis Cl BAR EN5 .... 20 B6
BARK IG11 .... 90 C6
Jarvis Rd EDUL SE22 .... 143 F5
SAND/SEL CR2 .... 211 K4
Jasmin Cl NTHWD HA6 .... 40 D4
Jasmine Cl IL IG1 .... 90 B3
ORP BR6 .... 201 G6
STHL UB1 .... 95 J6
Jasmine Gdns CROY/NA CRO 213 K1
RYLN/HDSTN HA2 .... 60 A6
Jasmine Gv PGE/AN SE20 .... 181 J4
Jasmine Ter WDR/YW UB7 .... 112 D2
Jasmin Rd HOR/WEW KT19 .... 206 D3
Jason Wk ELTH/MOT SE9 .... 167 F6
Jasper Cl PEND EN3 .... 24 E1
Jasper Rd CAN/RD E16 .... 107 H5
NRWD SE19 .... 181 G2
Javelin Wy NTHLT UB5 .... 95 H2
Jaycroft ENC/FH EN2 .... 23 G2
Jay Ms SKENS SW7 .... 15 F3
Jean Batten Cl WLGTN SM6 .... 211 F5
Jebb Av BRXS/STRHM SW2 .... 161 K1
Jebb St BOW E3 .... 105 J1
Jedburgh Rd PLSTW E13 .... 107 G2
Jedburgh St BTSEA SW11 .... 141 F5
Jeddo Ms SHB W12 .... 118 C2
Jeddo Rd SHR W12 .... 118 C2
Jefferson Cl GNTH/NBYPK IG2. .... 72 D3
WEA W13 .... 116 C3
Jeffrey's Pl CAMTN NW1 .... 84 C5
Jeffreys Rd CLAP SW4 .... 141 K4
PEND EN3 .... 25 H5
Jeffrey's St CAMTN NW1 .... 84 B5
Jeffs Cl HPTN TW12 * 173 G2
Jeffs Rd SUT SM1 .... 208 D2
Jeger Av BETH E2 .... 7 J1
Jeken Rd ELTH/MOT SE9 .... 146 B5
Jelf Rd BRXS/STRHM SW2 .... 142 B6
Jellicoe Gdns STAN HA7 .... 43 F2
Jellicoe Rd TOTM N17 .... 49 K3
WATW WD18 .... 26 E1
Jemmett Cl KUTN/CMB KT2... .... 175 J4
Jem Paterson Ct HRW HA1 *. 78 E2
Jengar Cl SUT SM1 .... 209 F2
Jenkins La BARK IG11 .... 108 B1
Jenkins Rd PLSTW E13 .... 107 F3
Jenner Av ACT W3 .... 99 F4
Jenner Cl SCUP DA14 .... 168 B5
Jenner Pl BARN SW13 .... 118 E6
Jenner Rd STNW/STAM N16 .... 68 B1
Jennett Rd CROY/NA CRO 211 G1
Jennifer Rd BMLY BR1 .... 165 J5
Jennings Cl SURB KT6 .... 190 D4
Jennings Rd EDUL SE22 .... 143 G4
Jennings Wy BAR EN5 .... 20 A4
Jenningtree Rd ERITH DA8 .... 150 E1
Jenningtree Wy BELV DA17 .... 129 K2
Jenny Hammond Cl WAN E11.. .... 88 D1
Jenson Wy NRWD SE19 .... 181 G3
Jephson Rd FSTGT E7 .... 89 G5
Jephson St CMBW SE5 .... 142 E2
Jephtha Rd
WAND/EARL SW18 .... 159 K1
Jeppo's La MTCM CR4 .... 194 E1
Jerdan Pl FUL/PGN SW6 .... 139 K1
Jeremiah St POP/IOD E14 .... 105 K5
Jeremy's Gn UED N18 .... 36 E6
Jermyn St STJS SW1Y 10 A7
Jerningham Av CLAY IG5. .... 54 B5
Jerningham Rd NWCR SE14 .... 144 B3
Jerome St WCHPL E1 .... 13 J1
Jerrard St LEW SE13 .... 144 E4
Jerrold St IS N1 * 7 H3
Jersey Av
KTN/HRWW/WS HA3 .... 43 H3
Jersey Dr STMC/STPC BR5 .... 201 J3
Jersey Rd BARK/EDG E16 .... 107 G4
HEST TW5 .... 135 G1

HNWL W7 .... 116 B2
HSLW TW3 .... 135 G2
IL IG1 .... 90 B2
John Wilson St
WOOL/PLUM SE18 .... 127 F4
John Wooley Cl LEW SE13 * 145 H3
Joiners Arms Yd CMBW SE5 * 142 E2
Joiner St SE1 .... 19 F1
Jollys La YEAD UB4 .... 95 H4
Jonathan St LBTH SE11 .... 122 A5
Jones Rd PLSTW E13 .... 107 F3
Jonson Cl MTCM CR4 .... 195 H4
YEAD UB4 .... 94 E4
Jordan Cl RYLN/HDSTN HA2 .... 77 K1
Jordan Rd GFD/PVL UB6 .... 79 H6
Jordans Cl DAGE RM10 .... 92 D2
Jordans Ms WHTN TW2 .... 155 K4
Joseph Av ACT W3 .... 99 F5
Joseph Hardcastle Cl
NWCR SE14 .... 144 A1
Josephine Av
BRXS/STRHM SW2 .... 142 A6
Joseph Locke Wy
ESH/CLAY KT10 .... 189 F6
Joseph Powell Cl BAL SW12 .... 161 H1
Joseph Ray Rd WAN E11 .... 70 C6
Joseph St BOW E3 .... 105 H4
Joseph Trotter Cl
CLKNW EC1R 5 K5
Joshua Cl MUSWH N10 .... 48 B3
SAND/SEL CR2 .... 211 H5
Joshua St POP/IOD E14 .... 106 A5
Joslings Cl SHB W12 .... 99 J6
Joslyn Cl PEND EN3 .... 25 J1
Joubert St BTSEA SW11 .... 140 E3
Jowett St PECK SE15 .... 143 G1
Joyce Av UED N18 .... 50 B1
Joyce Green La DART DA1 .... 151 J5
Joydon Dr CHDH RM6 .... 73 H3
Joyners Cl DAGW RM9 .... 92 B2
Joyce La ELTH/MOT SE9 .... 167 F2
ROMW/RG RM7 .... 74 E2
WHTN TW2 .... 155 H3
Jubilee Cl CDALE/KGS NW9 .... 63 C1
KUT/HW KT1 .... 174 D4
ROMW/RG RM7 .... 74 D2
WLSDN NW10 .... 99 C1
Jubilee Crs ED N9 .... 36 C5
Jubilee Dr RSLP HA4 .... 77 H4
Jubilee Pl CHEL SW3 .... 120 D5
STHWK SE1 * 17 H1
Jubilee Rd CHEAM SM3 .... 208 B5
GFD/PVL UB6. .... 79 H6
Jubilee St WCHPL E1 .... 104 E5
Jubilee Ter FUL/PGN SW6 * 139 J6
The Jubilee CNWCH SE10 * 144 E1
Jubilee Vls ESH/CLAY KT10 * 189 K5
Jubilee Wy CHSGTN KT9 .... 206 E3
EBED/NFELT TW14 .... 153 K3
SCUP DA14 .... 168 B4
WIM/MER SW19 .... 178 A4
Judd St STPAN WC1H 4 E5
Jude St CAN/RD E16 .... 106 D5
Judge Heath La HYS/HAR UB3. .... 94 A5
Judges' Wk HAMP NW3 .... 83 G1
Judge Wk ESH/CLAY KT10 .... 204 E4
Judith Av CRW RM5 .... 56 D2
Juer St BTSEA SW11 .... 140 D1
Juglans Rd ORP BR6 .... 202 B5
Jules Thorn Av EN EN1 .... 24 C4
Julia Gdns BARK IG11 .... 109 K1
Juliana Cl EFNCH N2 .... 47 G6
Julian Av ACT W3 .... 98 D6
Julian Cl BAR EN5 .... 21 F4
Julian Pl POP/IOD E14 .... 124 E5
Julian Rd ORP BR6 .... 217 G4
Julian Tayler Pth
FSTH SE23 .... 163 J4
Julien Rd EA W5 .... 116 D3
Juliette Rd PLSTW E13 .... 106 E1
Julius Nyerere Cl IS N1 .... 5 H1
Junction Ap BTSEA SW11 .... 140 D4
LEW SE13 .... 145 F4
Junction Ms BAY/PAD W2 .... 8 C3
Junction Pl BAY/PAD W2 * 8 C3
Junction Rd ARCH N19 .... 84 C1
EA W5 .... 116 D3
ED N9 .... 36 C3
HRW HA1 .... 60 D3
PLSTW E13 .... 89 F6
ROM RM1 .... 75 H1
SAND/SEL CR2 .... 211 K4
TOTM N17 .... 50 C6
Junction Rd East CHDH RM6. .... 73 K4
Junction Rd West
CHDH RM6 .... 73 K4
Juniper Cl BAR EN5 .... 20 B6
CHSGTN KT9 .... 206 B3
WBLY HA9 .... 80 B3
Juniper Ct CHDH RM6. .... 73 H3
KTN/HRWW/WS HA3 * 43 H4
NTHWD HA6 * 40 E4
Juniper Crs CAMTN NW1 .... 84 A5
Juniper Dr
WAND/EARL SW18 .... 140 B5
Juniper Gdns MTCM CR4 .... 179 H4
Juniper La EHAM E6 .... 107 J4
Juniper Rd IL IG1 .... 90 A1
Juniper St WCHPL E1 * 104 E6
Juniper Wy HYS/HAR UB3 .... 94 B6
Jupiter Wy HOLWY N7 .... 85 F4
Jupp Rd SRTFD E15 .... 88 B5
Jupp Rd West SRTFD E15 .... 88 B6
Justice Wk CHEL SW3 .... 120 D6
Justin Cl BTFD TW8 .... 136 E1
Justin Rd CHING E4 .... 51 H2
Jute La PEND EN3 .... 25 G3
Jutland Cl ARCH N19 .... 66 E5
Jutland Rd CAT SE6 .... 165 F2
PLSTW E13 .... 106 E3
Jutsums Av ROMW/RG RM7 .... 74 D5
Jutsums La ROMW/RG RM7 .... 74 D5
Juxon Cl
KTN/HRWW/WS HA3 .... 42 B4
Juxon St LBTH SE11 .... 17 H6

K

Kaduna Cl PIN HA5 .... 59 F2
Kaine Pl CROY/NA CRO 198 C4
Kale Rd ERITHM DA18 .... 128 E2
Kambala Rd BTSEA SW11 .... 140 C3
Kangley Bridge Rd SYD SE26 .... 182 C1
Kaplan Dr WCHMH N21 .... 23 F6
Kara Wy CRICK NW2 .... 82 A2
Karen Ct RAIN RM13 .... 111 U1
Karen Ct BMLY BR1 .... 183 J4
Karenza Ct WBLY HA9 .... 61 J4
Karina Cl CHIG IG7 .... 54 E1
Karma Wy RYLN/HDSTN HA2 .... 60 A5
Kashgar Rd
WOOL/PLUM SE18 .... 128 A5
Kashmir Rd CHARL SE7 .... 146 C1
Kassala Rd BTSEA SW11 .... 140 E2
Katharine St CROY/NA CRO 211 J1
Katherine Cl
BERM/RHTH SE16 .... 124 A1
Katherine Gdns BARK/HLT IG6. .... 54 C3
ELTH/MOT SE9 .... 146 C1
Katherine Rd EHAM E6 .... 89 H5
Katherine Sq NTGHL W11 * 119 H1
Kathleen Av ACT W3 .... 98 E4
ALP/SUD HA0 .... 80 A5
Kathleen Rd BTSEA SW11 .... 140 E4
Kayemoor Rd BELMT SM2. .... 209 J5
Kay Rd BRXN/ST SW9 .... 141 K3
Kays Ter SWFD E18 * 52 D5
Kay St BETH E2 .... 104 C1
SRTFD E15 .... 88 B5
WELL DA16 .... 148 C2
Kean St HOL/ALD WC2B 11 G4
Keatley Gn CHING E4 .... 51 H2
Keats Av CAN/RD E16 .... 126 A1
HARH RM3 .... 57 K3
Keats Cl CHIG IG7 .... 54 E2
PEND EN3 .... 25 F6
STHWK SE1 .... 19 J7
WAN E11 .... 71 F2
WIM/MER SW19 .... 178 C2
Keats Est STNW/STAM N16 * 68 B6
Keats Gv HAMP NW3 .... 83 J2
Keats Pde ED N9 .... 36 C4
Keats Rd BELV DA17 .... 129 K3
WELL DA16 .... 147 K2
Keats Wy CROY/NA CRO 197 K3
GFD/PVL UB6. .... 96 B5
WDR/YW UB7 .... 112 C4
Keble Cl NTHLT UB5 .... 78 C5
WPK KT4 .... 192 C5
Keble Pl BARN SW13 .... 118 E6
Keble St TOOT SW17 .... 160 B6
Kedleston Dr STMC/STPC BR5. .... 202 A3
Kedleston Wk BETH E2 .... 104 D2
Keebie Cl WOOL/PLUM SE18 * 127 G6
Keedonwood Rd BMLY BR1. .... 165 H1
Keel Cl BARK IG11 .... 109 J1
BERM/RHTH SE16 .... 124 A1
Keeley Rd CROY/NA CRO 196 D6
Keeley St HOL/ALD WC2B 11 G4
Keeling Rd ELTH/MOT SE9 .... 146 C6
Keely Cl EBAR EN4 .... 21 J6
Keemor Cl
WOOL/PLUM SE18 * 147 F1
Keens Cl STRHM/NOR SW16 * 179 J1
Keen's Rd CROY/NA CRO 211 J2
Keens Yd IS N1 * 85 H4
Keepers Ms TEDD TW11 .... 174 D2
The Keep KUTN/CMB KT2 .... 175 G2
Keesey St WALW SE17 .... 122 E6
Keetons Rd
BERM/RHTH SE16 * 123 J3
Keeton's Rd
BERM/RHTH SE16 * 123 J3
Keevil Dr WIM/MER SW19 .... 159 G2
Keighley Cl HOLWY N7 .... 84 E2
Keightley Dr ELTH/MOT SE9 .... 167 H3
Keilder Cl HGDN/ICK UB10. .... 94 A2
Keir Hardie Est CLPT E5 * 68 D5
Keir Hardie Wy BARK IG11 .... 91 G5
YEAD UB4 * 94 E2
Keith Connor Cl VX/NE SW8 .... 141 G4
Keith Gv SHB W12 .... 118 D2
Keith Rd BARK IG11 .... 108 D1
HYS/HAR UB3 .... 113 H3
WALTH E17 .... 51 J4
Kelbrook Rd BKHTH/KID SE3. .... 146 C3
Kelburn Wy RAIN RM13 .... 111 J2
Kelceda Cl CRICK NW2 .... 63 J6
Kelf Gv HYS/HAR UB3 .... 94 D5
Kelfield Gdns NKENS W10. .... 100 A5
Kelfield Ms NKENS W10. .... 100 B5
Kelland Rd PLSTW E13 .... 106 E3
Kellaway Rd BKHTH/KID SE3. .... 146 B3
Keller Cresent MNPK E12 * 89 J2
Kellerton Rd LEW SE13 .... 145 H6
Kellett Rd BRXS/STRHM SW2 .... 142 B5
Kelling Gdns CROY/NA CRO 196 C4
Kellino St TOOT SW17 .... 160 E6
Kellner Rd THMD SE28 .... 128 A3
Kell St STHWK SE1 .... 18 B4
Kelly Av PECK SE15 .... 143 G1
Kelly Cl WLSDN NW10 .... 81 F1
Kelly Ms MV/WKIL W9 * 100 D4
Kelly Rd MLHL NW7 .... 46 C2
Kelly St CAMTN NW1 .... 84 B4
Kelly Wy CHDH RM6 .... 74 A2
Kelman Cl CLAP SW4 .... 141 J3
Kelmore Gv EDUL SE22 .... 143 H5
Kelmscott Cl WALTH E17 .... 51 H4
WATW WD18 .... 26 E1
Kelmscott Gdns SHB W12 .... 118 D3
Kelmscott Rd BTSEA SW11 .... 160 D1
Kelross Rd HBRY N5 .... 85 H2
Kelsall Cl BKHTH/KID SE3 .... 146 A3
Kelsall Ms RCH/KEW TW9. .... 137 J2
Kelsey La BECK BR3 .... 182 D5
Kelsey Park Av BECK BR3 .... 182 E5
Kelsey Park Rd BECK BR3 .... 182 D5
Kelsey Sq BECK BR3 .... 182 D5
Kelsey St BETH E2 .... 104 C3

Kelsey Wy BECK BR3 .... 182 D6
Kelsie Wy BARK/HLT IG6. .... 54 E2
Kelso Pl KENS W8 .... 120 A3
Kelso Rd CAR SM5 .... 194 B4
Kelston Rd BARK/HLT IG6 .... 54 B5
Kelton Vls KUT/HW KT1 * 175 G5
Kelvedon Cl KUTN/CMB KT2 .... 175 H2
Kelvedon Wy WFD IG8 .... 53 K2
Kelvin Av WDGN N22 .... 49 F2
Kelvinbrook E/WMO/HCT KT8. .... 173 F5
Kelvin Cl HOR/WEW KT19 .... 206 C4
Kelvin Crs
KTN/HRWW/WS HA3 .... 42 E3
Kelvin Dr TWK TW1 .... 156 C1
Kelvin Gdns CROY/NA CRO 195 K4
STHL UB1 .... 96 A5
Kelvin Gv CHSGTN KT9 .... 205 K1
SYD SE26 .... 163 J5
Kelvington Cl CROY/NA CRO 198 B4
Kelvington Rd PECK SE15. .... 144 B5
Kelvin Pde ORP BR6 .... 201 K5
Kelvin Rd HBRY N5 .... 85 H2
WELL DA16 .... 148 B4
Kember St IS N1. .... 85 F5
Kemble Dr HAYES BR2. .... 215 J5
Kemble Rd CROY/NA CRO 211 H1
FSTH SE23 .... 164 A3
TOTM N17 .... 50 C4
Kemble St HOL/ALD WC2B 11 G4
Kemerton Rd BECK BR3 .... 182 E5
CMBW SE5 .... 142 D4
CROY/NA CRO 197 G4
Kemey's St HOM E9 .... 87 G3
Kemnal Rd CHST BR7 .... 167 J3
CHST BR7 .... 185 H2
Kempe Rd KIL/WHAMP NW6 .... 100 B1
Kemp Gdns CROY/NA CRO 196 D4
Kemplay Rd HAMP NW3 .... 83 H2
Kemp Pl BUSH WD23 .... 28 C1
Kemps Dr NTHWD HA6 .... 40 D1
POP/IOD E14 .... 105 J6
Kempsford Gdns ECT SW5 .... 119 K5
Kempsford Rd LBTH SE11 .... 17 K7
Kempshott Rd
STRHM/NOR SW16 .... 179 K4
Kempson Rd FUL/PGN SW6 .... 139 K2
Kempthorne Rd DEPT SE8 .... 124 B4
Kempton Av NTHLT UB5 .... 78 A4
SUN TW16 .... 172 A4
Kempton Cl ERITH DA8 .... 129 K4
HGDN/ICK UB10 .... 76 A5
Kempton Ct SUN TW16 .... 172 A4
Kempton Pk SUN TW16 * 172 E2
Kempton Rd EHAM E6 .... 89 K6
Kempton Wk CROY/NA CRO 198 C3
Kempt St WOOL/PLUM SE18 .... 127 F6
Kemsing Cl BXLY DA5 .... 169 F2
THHTH CR7 .... 196 C1
Kenbury St CMBW SE5 .... 142 D3
Kenchester Cl VX/NE SW8 .... 141 K1
Kencot Wy ERITHM DA18 .... 129 H2
Kendal Av ACT W3 .... 98 A4
BARK IG11 .... 90 E5
UED N18 .... 35 K6
Kendal Cl ACT W3 .... 98 A4
EBED/NFELT TW14 .... 153 J1
TRDG/WHET N20 .... 33 J4
WFD IG8 .... 38 E3
YEAD UB4 .... 94 C3
Kendale Rd BMLY BR1 .... 165 H1
Kendal Gdns SUT SM1 .... 194 A6
UED N18 .... 35 K6
Kendall Av BECK BR3 .... 182 B5
SAND/SEL CR2 .... 211 J6
Kendall Pl MHST W1U 9 G2
Kendall Rd BECK BR3 .... 182 B5
ISLW TW7 .... 136 B3
WOOL/PLUM SE18 .... 146 D2
Kendalmere Cl MUSWH N10. .... 48 B4
Kendal Pde UED N18. .... 35 K6
Kendal Pl PUT/ROE SW15 .... 139 J6
Kendal Rd WLSDN NW10 .... 81 J2
Kendal Steps BAY/PAD W2 * 8 D4
Kender St NWCR SE14 .... 143 K1
Kendoa Rd CLAP SW4 .... 141 J5
Kendon Cl WAN E11 .... 71 F2
Kendra Hall Rd SAND/SEL CR2. .... 211 H5
Kendrey Gdns WHTN TW2 .... 155 K1
Kendrick Ms SKENS SW7 .... 14 A6
Kendrick Pl SKENS SW7 * 14 A6
Kenelm Cl HRW HA1 .... 79 G1
Kenerne Dr BAR EN5 .... 20 C6
Keniliford Rd BAL SW12 .... 161 G2
Kenilworth Av
RYLN/HDSTN HA2 .... 77 J1
WALTH E17 .... 51 J1
WIM/MER SW19 .... 177 K1
Kenilworth Crs EN EN1 .... 24 A2
Kenilworth Gdns
GDMY/SEVK IG3 .... 72 E5
LOU IG10 .... 39 J1
OXHEY WD19 .... 41 G1
STHL UB1 * 95 K3
WOOL/PLUM SE18 .... 147 G2
YEAD UB4 .... 94 E4
Kenilworth Rd ASHF TW15 .... 152 B4
BOW E3 .... 105 G1
EA W5 .... 117 F1
EDGW HA8 .... 30 E4
EW KT17 .... 207 J6
KIL/WHAMP NW6 .... 82 D6
PGE/AN SE20 .... 182 A4
STMC/STPC BR5 .... 201 G3
Kenilworth Ter BELMT SM2 * 208 E5
Kenley Av CDALE/KGS NW9 .... 45 G4
NTGHL W11 * 100 C6
Kenley Cl BXLY DA5 .... 169 H2
CHST BR7 .... 185 K4
EBAR EN4 .... 21 J6
Kenley Gdns THHTH CR7 .... 196 C1
Kenley Rd KUT/HW KT1 .... 175 J6
TWK TW1 .... 156 B1
WIM/MER SW19 .... 177 J5
Kenley Wk CHEAM SM3 .... 208 B2
NTGHL W11 * 100 C6
Kenlor Rd TOOT SW17 .... 178 C1
Kenmare Dr MTCM CR4 .... 179 F3

TOTM N17 50 B5
Kenmare Gdns PLMGR N13 35 J6
Kenmare Rd THHTH CR7 196 B3
Kenmere Gdns ALP/SUD HA0 80 C6
Kenmere Rd WELL DA16 148 D3
Kenmont Gdns WLSDN NW10 99 K2
Kenmore Av
KTN/HRWW/WS HA3 61 G2
Kenmore Crs YEAD UB4 94 D2
Kenmore Gdns EDGW HA8 44 D5
Kenmore Rd
KTN/HRWW/WS HA3 43 K6
Kenmure Rd HACK E8 86 D3
Kenmure Yd HACK E8 * 86 D3
Kennacraig Cl CAN/RD E16 126 A1
Kennard Rd FBAR/BDGN N11 47 K1
SRTFD E15 88 B5
Kennard St BTSEA SW11 141 F2
CAN/RD E16 126 E1
Kennedy Av PEND EN3 36 E1
Kennedy Cl MTCM CR4 179 F5
PIN HA5 41 K2
PLSTW E13 106 E1
STMC/STPC BR5 201 J5
Kennedy Rd BARK IG11 90 E6
HNWL W7 96 E4
Kennedy Wk WALW SE17 19 F7
Kennet Cl BTSEA SW11 140 C5
Kennet Dr YEAD UB4 95 J4
Kenneth Av IL IG1 90 B2
Kenneth Crs CRICK NW2 81 K3
Kenneth Gdns STAN HA7 43 G2
Kenneth More Rd IL IG1 90 B1
Kenneth Rd CHDH RM6 74 A4
Kennet Rd DART DA1 150 D4
ISLW TW7 136 A4
MV/WKIL W9 100 D3
Kennet Sq MTCM CR4 178 D4
Kennet St WAP E1W 123 H1
Kennett Wharf La
BLKFR EC4V 12 D5
Kenninghall Rd CLPT E5 86 D1
UED N18 50 D1
Kenning St BERM/RHTH SE16 123 K2
Kennings Wy LBTH SE11 122 B5
Kennington Gdns
KUT/HW KT1 174 E6
Kennington La LBTH SE11 122 A5
Kennington Ov LBTH SE11 122 A6
Kennington Park Gdns
LBTH SE11 122 C6
Kennington Park Pl
LBTH SE11 122 B6
Kennington Park Rd
LBTH SE11 122 B6
Kennington Rd LBTH SE11 17 J5
Kenny Dr CAR SM5 210 A6
Kennylands Rd BARK/HLT IG6 55 G3
Kenrick Pl MHST W1U 9 G1
Kensal Rd NKENS W10 100 C3
Kensal Whf NKENS W10 * 100 C3
Kensington Av MNPK E12 89 J4
THHTH CR7 180 B4
Kensington Church Ct
KENS W8 120 A2
Kensington Church St
KENS W8 119 K2
Kensington Church Wk
KENS W8 120 A2
Kensington Cl
FBAR/BDGN N11 * 48 A1
Kensington Ct KENS W8 120 A2
Kensington Court Gdns
KENS W8 * 120 A3
Kensington Court Ms
KENS W8 * 120 A3
Kensington Court Pl
KENS W8 120 A3
ensington Dr WFD IG8 53 H5
ensington Gdns IL IG1 71 K5
ensington Gardens Sq
BAY/PAD W2 * 101 F5
ensington Ga KENS W8 120 B3
ensington Hall Gdns
WKENS W14 * 119 J5
ensington High St
KENS W8 * 120 A2
WKENS W14 119 H4
ensington Ml KENS W8 119 K1
ensington Palace
KENS W8 * 120 A1
ensington Palace Gdns
KENS W8 120 A2
ensington Park Gdns
NTGHL W11 100 D6
ensington Park Ms
NTGHL W11 100 D5
ensington Park Rd
NTGHL W11 100 D5
ensington Pl KENS W8 119 K1
ensington Rd KENS W8 120 A2
NTHLT UB5 96 A1
ROMW/RG RM7 74 E3
ensington Sq KENS W8 * 120 A2
ensington Ter
SAND/SEL CR2 211 K5
nt Av DAGW RM9 110 C3
WEA W13 97 H4
WELL DA16 148 A6
nt Cl MTCM CR4 195 K1
ORP BR6 216 E4
nt Ct CDALE/KGS NW9 * 45 G5
nt Dr EBAR EN4 22 A5
TEDD TW11 173 K1
ntford Wy NTHLT UB5 77 J6
nt Gdns RSLP HA4 58 E3
WEA W13 97 H4
nt Gate Wy CROY/NA CR0 213 H4
nt House La BECK BR3 182 B2
nt House Rd BECK BR3 182 A3
ntish Rd BELV DA17 129 H4
ntish Town Rd
CAMTN NW1 84 B5
ntish Wy BMLY BR1 184 A5
ntlea Rd THMD SE28 127 K2
ntmere Rd
WOOL/PLUM SE18 127 K4
nton Av HRW HA1 61 F4
STHL UB1 96 A6
SUN TW16 172 C5
Kenton Gdns
KTN/HRWW/WS HA3 61 J2
Kenton La
KTN/HRWW/WS HA3 43 F3
Kenton Park Av
KTN/HRWW/WS HA3 61 K1
Kenton Park Cl
KTN/HRWW/WS HA3 61 J1
Kenton Park Crs
KTN/HRWW/WS HA3 61 K1
Kenton Park Pde
KTN/HRWW/WS HA3 * 61 J2
Kenton Park Rd
KTN/HRWW/WS HA3 61 J1
Kenton Rd HOM E9 87 F4
KTN/HRWW/WS HA3 61 G3
Kenton St STPAN WC1H 4 E6
Kenton Wy YEAD UB4 94 C2
Kent Pas CAMTN NW1 2 E6
Kent Rd CHSWK W4 117 K3
DAGE RM10 92 D3
E/WMO/HCT KT8 189 H1
KUT/HW KT1 174 E6
RCH/KEW TW9 137 H1
STMC/STPC BR5 202 C3
WCHMH N21 35 K3
WWKM BR4 198 E5
Kent St BETH E2 7 K2
PLSTW E13 107 F2
Kent Ter CAMTN NW1 2 D5
Kent View Gdns
GDMY/SEVK IG3 72 E6
Kent Wy SURB KT6 206 A1
Kentwell Cl BROCKY SE4 * 144 B5
Kentwode Gn BARN SW13 138 D1
Kent Yd SKENS SW7 14 D3
Kenver Av
NFNCH/WDSPK N12 47 H2
Kenward Rd ELTH/MOT SE9 146 B6
Kenway CRW RM5 56 E5
Ken Wy WBLY HA9 62 E6
Kenway Rd ECT SW5 120 A4
Kenwood Cl HAMP NW3 65 H5
WDR/YW UB7 112 D6
Kenwood Dr BECK BR3 183 F6
Kenwood Gdns CLAY IG5 72 A1
SWFD E18 53 F6
Kenwood Rd ED N9 36 C4
HGT N6 65 K3
Kenworthy Rd HOM E9 87 G3
Kenwyn Dr CRICK NW2 81 G1
Kenwyn Rd CLAP SW4 141 J5
RYNPK SW20 177 F4
Kenya Rd CHARL SE7 146 C1
Kenyngton Pl
KTN/HRWW/WS HA3 61 J2
Kenyon St FUL/PGN SW6 139 G2
Keogh Rd SRTFD E15 88 C4
Kepler Rd CLAP SW4 141 K5
Keppel Rd DAGW RM9 92 A2
EHAM E6 89 K5
Keppel St GWRST WC1E 10 D1
Kerbela St BETH E2 104 C3
Kerbey St POP/IOD E14 105 K5
Kerfield Crs CMBW SE5 142 E2
Kerfield Pl CMBW SE5 142 E2
Kerri Cl BAR EN5 20 A5
Kerrison Pl EA W5 116 E1
Kerrison Rd BTSEA SW11 140 D4
EA W5 116 E1
SRTFD E15 88 B6
Kerry Av SOCK/AV RM15 131 J2
STAN HA7 29 J6
Kerry Cl CAN/RD E16 107 F5
PLMGR N13 35 F4
Kerry Ct STAN HA7 29 K6
Kerry Pth NWCR SE14 124 C6
Kerry Rd NWCR SE14 124 C6
Kersfield Rd PUT/ROE SW15 159 G1
Kershaw Cl WAND/EARL SW18 160 C1
Kershaw Rd DAGE RM10 92 C1
Kersley Ms BTSEA SW11 * 140 E2
Kersley Rd STNW/STAM N16 86 A1
Kersley St BTSEA SW11 140 E3
Kerstin Cl HYS/HAR UB3 94 D6
Kerswell Cl SEVS/STOTM N15 68 A2
Kerwick Cl HOLWY N7 85 F5
Keslake Rd KIL/WHAMP NW6 100 B1
Kessock Cl TOTM N17 68 D2
Kesteven Cl BARK/HLT IG6 55 F2
Keston Av HAYES BR2 215 G3
Keston Cl UED N18 35 K5
WELL DA16 148 D1
Keston Gdns HAYES BR2 215 G2
Keston Park Cl HAYES BR2 215 K2
Keston Rd PECK SE15 143 H4
THHTH CR7 196 A3
TOTM N17 49 K6
Kestrel Av EHAM E6 107 J4
HNHL SE24 142 C6
Kestrel Cl CDALE/KGS NW9 45 G5
HCH RM12 93 K5
KUTN/CMB KT2 156 E6
WLSDN NW10 81 F3
Kestrel Pl NWCR SE14 * 124 B6
Kestrel Wy CROY/NA CR0 214 B6
HYS/HAR UB3 113 G2
Keswick Av PUT/ROE SW15 176 B1
WIM/MER SW19 177 K5
Keswick Cl SUT SM1 209 G2
Keswick Gdns REDBR IG4 71 J2
RSLP HA4 58 B2
WBLY HA9 80 A3
Keswick Ms EA W5 117 F1
Keswick Rd ORP BR6 202 A5
PUT/ROE SW15 139 H6
WHTN TW2 155 H1
WWKM BR4 199 H6
Kettering St
STRHM/NOR SW16 179 G2
Kett Gdns BRXS/STRHM SW2 142 A6
Kettlebaston Rd LEY E10 69 H5
Kettlewell Cl FBAR/BDGN N11 48 A2
Kevelioc Rd TOTM N17 49 J4
Kevin Cl HSLWW TW4 134 C3
Kevington Cl STMC/STPC BR5 202 A1
Kevington Dr CHST BR7 202 A1
Kew Br RCH/KEW TW9 117 H6
Kew Bridge Arches
CHSWK W4 * 117 H6
Kew Bridge Ct BTFD TW8 117 H5
Kew Bridge Rd BTFD TW8 117 G6
Kew Crs CHEAM SM3 208 D1
Kewferry Rd NTHWD HA6 40 A2
Kew Foot Rd RCH/KEW TW9 137 F5
Kew Gardens Rd
RCH/KEW TW9 137 G1
Kew Gn RCH/KEW TW9 117 G6
Kew Meadow Pth
RCH/KEW TW9 137 H2
Kew Riverside Pk
RCH/KEW TW9 137 J1
Kew Rd RCH/KEW TW9 137 F5
Key Cl WCHPL E1 104 D3
Keyes Rd CRICK NW2 82 B3
Keymer Rd BRXS/STRHM SW2 162 A4
Keynes Cl EFNCH N2 47 K6
Keynsham Av WFD IG8 38 C6
Keynsham Gdns
ELTH/MOT SE9 146 D6
Keynsham Rd ELTH/MOT SE9 146 C6
MRDN SM4 194 A5
Keysham Av HEST TW5 133 K2
Keystone Crs IS N1 5 F3
Keyworth Cl CLPT E5 87 G2
Keyworth St STHWK SE1 18 B4
Kezia St DEPT SE8 124 B5
Khama Rd TOOT SW17 160 D6
Khartoum Rd IL IG1 90 B3
PLSTW E13 107 F2
TOOT SW17 160 C6
Khyber Rd BTSEA SW11 140 D3
Kibworth St VX/NE SW8 142 A1
Kidbrooke La ELTH/MOT SE9 146 D5
Kidbrooke Park Cl
BKHTH/KID SE3 146 A2
Kidbrooke Park Rd
BKHTH/KID SE3 146 A2
LEE/GVPK SE12 146 A6
Kidbrooke Wy
BKHTH/KID SE3 146 A3
Kidderminster Pl
CROY/NA CR0 196 C5
Kidderminster Rd
CROY/NA CR0 196 C5
Kidderpore Av HAMP NW3 82 E2
Kidderpore Gdns HAMP NW3 82 E2
Kidd Pl CHARL SE7 126 D5
Kielder Cl BARK/HLT IG6 55 F2
Kiffen St SDTCH EC2A 7 F6
Kilberry Cl ISLW TW7 135 J2
Kilburn Br KIL/WHAMP NW6 82 E6
Kilburn High Rd
KIL/WHAMP NW6 82 E5
Kilburn La NKENS W10 100 B2
Kilburn Park Rd
KIL/WHAMP NW6 100 E2
Kilburn Pl KIL/WHAMP NW6 82 E6
Kilburn Priory
KIL/WHAMP NW6 83 F6
Kilburn Sq KIL/WHAMP NW6 82 E6
Kilburn V KIL/WHAMP NW6 82 E6
Kildare Cl RSLP HA4 59 G5
Kildare Rd CAN/RD E16 106 E4
Kildare Ter BAY/PAD W2 100 E5
Kildoran Rd CLAP SW4 141 K6
Kildowan Rd GDMY/SEVK IG3 73 G5
Kilgour Rd FSTH SE23 164 B1
Kilkie St FUL/PGN SW6 140 B3
Killarney Rd
WAND/EARL SW18 160 B1
Killburns Mill Cl WLGTN SM6 195 G6
Killearn Rd CAT SE6 165 G3
Killester Gdns WPK KT4 207 K2
Killewarren Wy
STMC/STPC BR5 202 D4
Killick St IS N1 5 G2
Killieser Av BRXS/STRHM SW2 161 K4
Killip Cl CAN/RD E16 106 D5
Killowen Av NTHLT UB5 78 C3
Killowen Rd HOM E9 * 87 F4
Killyon Rd VX/NE SW8 141 H3
Kilmaine Rd FUL/PGN SW6 139 H1
Kilmarnock Gdns BCTR RM8 91 J1
Kilmarnock Rd OXHEY WD19 27 H6
Kilmarsh Rd HMSMTH W6 119 F4
Kilmartin Av
STRHM/NOR SW16 180 B6
Kilmartin Rd GDMY/SEVK IG3 73 G6
Kilmartin Wy HCH RM12 93 K3
Kilmington Rd BARN SW13 118 D6
Kilmorey Gdns TWK TW1 136 C6
Kilmorey Rd TWK TW1 136 C5
Kilmorie Rd FSTH SE23 164 B3
Kiln Cl HYS/HAR UB3 113 G6
Kilner St POP/IOD E14 105 J4
Kiln Ms TOOT SW17 178 C1
Kiln Pl KTTN NW5 84 A2
Kilnside ESH/CLAY KT10 205 G5
Kiln Wy NTHWD HA6 40 C2
Kiln Wood La ABR/ST RM4 57 F1
Kilpatrick Wy YEAD UB4 95 J4
Kilravock St NKENS W10 100 C2
Kilross Rd EBED/NFELT TW14 153 G3
Kilsha Rd WOT/HER KT12 188 A3
Kilvinton Dr ENC/FH EN2 23 K1
Kimbell Gdns FUL/PGN SW6 139 H2
Kimbell Pl BKHTH/KID SE3 146 B5
Kimberley Av EHAM E6 107 J1
GNTH/NBYPK IG2 72 D4
PECK SE15 143 J3
ROMW/RG RM7 74 D3
Kimberley Ct
KIL/WHAMP NW6 82 C5
Kimberley Dr SCUP DA14 168 E4
Kimberley Gdns EN EN1 24 B4
FSBYPK N4 67 H2
Kimberley Rd BECK BR3 182 A5
BRXN/ST SW9 141 K3
CAN/RD E16 106 D3
CHING E4 38 C3
CROY/NA CR0 196 C3
KIL/WHAMP NW6 82 C6
TOTM N17 50 C5
WAN E11 70 B6
Kimberley Wy CHING E4 38 C3
Kimber Rd WAND/EARL SW18 160 A2
Kimble Cl WATW WD18 * 26 C1
Kimble Crs BUSH WD23 28 C2
Kimble Rd WIM/MER SW19 178 C2
Kimbolton Cl LEE/GVPK SE12 165 J1
Kimmeridge Gdns
ELTH/MOT SE9 166 D6
Kimmeridge Rd
ELTH/MOT SE9 166 D6
Kimpton Park Wy
CHEAM SM3 193 J6
Kimpton Rd CHEAM SM3 208 D1
CMBW SE5 142 E2
Kinburn St
BERM/RHTH SE16 * 124 A2
Kincaid Rd PECK SE15 143 J1
Kincardine Gdns
MV/WKIL W9 * 100 E3
Kinch Gv WBLY HA9 62 B4
Kinder Cl THMD SE28 109 J6
Kinder St WCHPL E1 104 D5
Kinderton Cl STHGT/OAK N14 34 C3
Kinfauns Rd
BRXS/STRHM SW2 162 B4
GDMY/SEVK IG3 73 H5
Kingaby Gdns RAIN RM13 93 J5
King Alfred Av CAT SE6 164 D6
King And Queen Cl
ELTH/MOT SE9 166 D6
King Arthur Cl PECK SE15 143 K1
King Charles Crs BRYLDS KT5 191 G4
King Charles I Island
WHALL SW1A 10 E7
King Charles' Rd BRYLDS KT5 191 G4
King Charles St WHALL SW1A 16 D2
King Charles Ter WAP E1W * 104 D6
King Charles Wk
WIM/MER SW19 * 159 H3
Kingcup Cl CROY/NA CR0 198 A5
King David La WCHPL E1 104 E6
Kingdon Rd KIL/WHAMP NW6 82 E4
King Edward Dr CHSGTN KT9 206 A1
King Edward III Ms
BERM/RHTH SE16 123 J2
King Edward Rd BAR EN5 20 E5
LEY E10 70 A5
OXHEY WD19 27 J1
ROM RM1 75 H3
WALTH E17 51 G6
King Edward's Gdns ACT W3 117 H1
King Edward's Gv TEDD TW11 174 C2
King Edwards Pl ACT W3 117 H1
King Edwards Rd RSLP HA4 58 B5
King Edward's Rd BARK IG11 90 D6
ED N9 36 D2
HACK E8 86 D6
PEND EN3 25 F5
King Edward St STBT EC1A 12 C3
King Edward Wk STHWK SE1 17 K4
Kingfield Rd EA W5 97 K3
Kingfield St POP/IOD E14 125 F4
Kingfisher Cl
KTN/HRWW/WS HA3 43 F3
STMC/STPC BR5 202 E1
THMD SE28 109 J6
Kingfisher Dr
RCHPK/HAM TW10 156 D6
Kingfisher Ms LEW SE13 144 E6
Kingfisher Pl WDGN N22 * 49 F5
Kingfisher St EHAM E6 107 J4
Kingfisher Wy BECK BR3 198 A2
WLSDN NW10 81 F3
King Gdns CROY/NA CR0 211 H3
King Garth Ms FSTH SE23 163 K4
King George Av BUSH WD23 28 B1
CAN/RD E16 107 H5
GNTH/NBYPK IG2 72 D3
WOT/HER KT12 188 C5
King George Cl
ROMW/RG RM7 56 E6
King George Sq
RCHPK/HAM TW10 157 G1
King George St GNWCH SE10 145 F1
King George VI Av MTCM CR4 194 E1
Kingham Cl NTGHL W11 119 H2
WAND/EARL SW18 160 B2
King Harolds Wy BXLYHN DA7 148 E1
King Henry Ms HRW HA1 60 E5
ORP BR6 217 F3
King Henry's Dr CROY/NA CR0 214 A6
King Henry's Reach
HMSMTH W6 119 F6
King Henry's Rd HAMP NW3 83 J5
KUT/HW KT1 175 J6
King Henry St
STNW/STAM N16 86 A3
King Henry's Wk IS N1 86 A4
King Henry Ter WAP E1W * 104 D6
Kinghorn St STBT EC1A 12 C2
King James Ct STHWK SE1 18 B3
King James St STHWK SE1 18 B3
King John Ct SDTCH EC2A 7 H6
King John St WCHPL E1 105 F4
King John's Wk
ELTH/MOT SE9 166 D2
Kinglake Est WALW SE17 * 123 F5
Kinglake St WALW SE17 123 F5
Kinglet Cl FSTGT E7 88 E4
Kingly Ct REGST W1B * 10 B5
Kingly St REGST W1B 10 A4
King & Queen Cl
ELTH/MOT SE9 * 166 D6
King & Queen St WALW SE17 122 D5
King & Queen Whf
BERM/RHTH SE16 * 124 A1
King's Arms Yd LOTH EC2R 12 E3
Kingsash Dr YEAD UB4 95 J3
Kings Av BAL SW12 161 J3
BMLY BR1 183 J2
CAR SM5 209 J5
CHDH RM6 74 B3
CLAP SW4 161 K1
EA W5 97 K5
MUSWH N10 48 A6
NWMAL KT3 192 C1
King's Av GFD/PVL UB6 96 B3
HSLW TW3 135 G2
WCHMH N21 35 H3
WFD IG8 53 G1
King's Bench St STHWK SE1 18 B2
King's Bench Wk EMB EC4Y * 11 K5
Kingsbridge Av EA W5 117 G2
Kingsbridge Ct POP/IOD E14 124 D3
Kingsbridge Crs STHL UB1 95 K4
Kingsbridge Dr MLHL NW7 46 B3
Kingsbridge Rd BARK IG11 108 D1
MRDN SM4 193 G4
NKENS W10 100 A5
NWDGN UB2 114 E4
WOT/HER KT12 188 A4
Kingsbury Gn
CDALE/KGS NW9 * 62 E2
Kingsbury Rd
CDALE/KGS NW9 62 C2
IS N1 86 A4
Kingsbury Ter IS N1 86 A4
Kings Cha E/WMO/HCT KT8 173 H6
Kingsclere Cl PUT/ROE SW15 158 D2
Kingsclere Pl ENC/FH EN2 23 J3
Kingscliffe Gdns
WIM/MER SW19 159 J3
Kings Cl HDN NW4 64 B1
LEY E10 69 K4
NTHWD HA6 40 D2
THDIT KT7 190 B3
WOT/HER KT12 188 A5
Kings College Rd RSLP HA4 58 D3
King's College Rd
HAMP NW3 * 83 H5
Kingscote Rd CHSWK W4 118 A3
CROY/NA CR0 197 J4
NWMAL KT3 176 A6
Kingscote St BLKFR EC4V 12 A5
Kings Ct PLSTW E13 89 F6
King's Ct STHWK SE1 * 18 B2
Kingscourt Rd
STRHM/NOR SW16 161 J5
King's Crs FSBYPK N4 85 J1
Kingscroft Rd CRICK NW2 82 D4
King's Cross Br IS N1 * 5 F4
King's Cross Rd FSBYW WC1X 5 G4
Kingsdale Gdns NTGHL W11 119 G1
Kingsdale Rd PGE/AN SE20 182 A3
WOOL/PLUM SE18 128 A6
Kingsdown Av ACT W3 99 G6
SAND/SEL CR2 211 J6
WEA W13 116 C2
Kingsdown Cl
BERM/RHTH SE16 * 123 J5
NKENS W10 100 B5
Kingsdowne Ct EA W5 * 98 A6
Kingsdowne Rd SURB KT6 191 F4
Kingsdown Rd ARCH N19 84 E1
CHEAM SM3 208 C3
WAN E11 88 C1
Kings Dr BRYLDS KT5 191 H4
EDGW HA8 30 B6
WBLY HA9 62 D6
King's Dr THDIT KT7 190 C3
Kingsend RSLP HA4 58 C5
Kingsend Ct RSLP HA4 * 58 C5
Kings Farm WALTH E17 * 51 K4
Kings Farm Av
RCHPK/HAM TW10 137 H5
Kingsfield Av
RYLN/HDSTN HA2 60 B2
Kingsfield Ct OXHEY WD19 27 H1
Kingsfield Rd HRW HA1 * 60 D4
OXHEY WD19 27 H2
Kingsfield Ter DART DA1 * 171 G1
Kingsford St KTTN NW5 83 K3
Kingsford Wy EHAM E6 107 K4
Kings Gdns IL IG1 72 D5
KIL/WHAMP NW6 82 E5
Kingsgate WBLY HA9 80 E1
Kingsgate Av FNCH N3 46 E6
Kingsgate Cl STMC/STPC BR5 186 D6
Kingsgate Est IS N1 * 86 A4
Kingsgate Pl
KIL/WHAMP NW6 82 E5
Kingsgate Rd
KIL/WHAMP NW6 82 E5
KUT/HW KT1 175 F4
Kingsground ELTH/MOT SE9 166 C2
Kings Gv ROM RM1 75 J2
King's Gv PECK SE15 143 J1
Kings Hall Ms LEW SE13 * 145 F4
Kings Hall Rd BECK BR3 182 A3
Kings Head Hl CHING E4 37 K2
King's Hwy WOOL/PLUM SE18 127 K6
Kingshill Av CRW RM5 56 E2
KTN/HRWW/WS HA3 61 H1
NTHLT UB5 95 F2
WPK KT4 192 D4
YEAD UB4 94 C2
Kingshill Cl YEAD UB4 94 E2
Kingshill Ct BAR EN5 * 20 C5
Kingshill Dr
KTN/HRWW/WS HA3 43 H5
Kingshold Rd HOM E9 86 E5
Kingsholm Gdns
ELTH/MOT SE9 146 C5
Kings Keep HAYES BR2 * 183 H6
KUT/HW KT1 * 191 F1
Kingsland Gn
STNW/STAM N16 86 A4
Kingsland High St HACK E8 86 B4
Kingsland Pas HACK E8 86 A4
Kingsland Rd BETH E2 7 H3
PLSTW E13 107 G2
King's La SUT SM1 209 H3
Kingslawn Cl PUT/ROE SW15 138 E6
Kingsleigh Cl BTFD TW8 116 E6
Kingsleigh Pl MTCM CR4 178 E6
Kingsleigh Wk HAYES BR2 199 J1
Kingsley Av HSLW TW3 135 H3
STHL UB1 96 A6
SUT SM1 209 H2
WEA W13 97 G5
Kingsley Cl DAGE RM10 92 D2
EFNCH N2 65 G2
Kingsley Ct EDGW HA8 * 30 D4
GPK RM2 75 K3
Kingsley Dr WPK KT4 192 C6
Kingsley Gdns CHING E4 51 J1
Kingsley Ms CHST BR7 185 G2
IL IG1 72 B6
SKENS SW7 120 A3
WAP E1W * 104 D6
Kingsley Pl HGT N6 66 A4
Kingsley Rd BARK/HLT IG6 54 C4
CROY/NA CR0 196 B5
FSTGT E7 88 E5
HSLW TW3 135 H3

KIL/WHAMP NW6 82 D6
ORP BR6 217 F4
PIN HA5 59 K1
PLMGR N13 35 G6
RYLN/HDSTN HA2 78 C2
WALTH E17 52 A5
WIM/MER SW19 178 A1
Kingsley St BTSEA SW11 140 E4
Kingsley Wy EFNCH N2 65 G3
Kingsley Wood Dr
ELTH/MOT SE9 166 E5
Kingslyn Crs NRWD SE19 181 F4
Kings Ml HMSMTH W6 * 119 F4
Kingsman St
WOOL/PLUM SE18 126 E4
Kingsmead BAR EN5 20 E5
RCHPK/HAM TW10 157 G1
Kingsmead Av
CDALE/KGS NW9 63 F4
ED N9 36 D3
MTCM CR4 179 H6
ROM RM1 75 G3
SUN TW16 172 B6
SURB KT6 191 H6
WPK KT4 207 K1
Kingsmead Cl BFN/LL DA15 168 B4
HOR/WEW KT19 207 F5
TEDD TW11 174 C2
Kingsmead Dr NTHLT UB5 77 K5
Kingsmead Pde NTHLT UB5 * 77 K5
Kings Mead Pk
ESH/CLAY KT10 204 E5
Kingsmead Rd
BRXS/STRHM SW2 162 B4
Kingsmead Wy CLPT E5 87 G2
Kingsmere Cl PUT/ROE SW15 139 G4
Kingsmere Pk
CDALE/KGS NW9 62 E5
Kingsmere Pl
STNW/STAM N16 * 67 K5
Kingsmere Rd
WIM/MER SW19 159 G4
King's Ms BMSBY WC1N 5 H7
CLAP SW4 141 K6
Kingsmill Gdns DAGW RM9 92 B3
Kingsmill Rd DAGW RM9 92 B3
Kingsmill Ter STJWD NW8 2 B2
Kingsnympton Pk
KUTN/CMB KT2 175 J3
Kings Oak ROMW/RG RM7 56 C6
King's Orch ELTH/MOT SE9 166 D1
King's Paddock HPTN TW12 173 H4
Kings Pde CAR SM5 * 209 J1
SHB W12 * 118 D3
TOTM N17 * 50 B6
WLSDN NW10 * 82 A6
Kingspark Ct SWFD E18 52 E6
Kings Pas WAN E11 * 70 C4
Kings Pl BKHH IG9 39 H4
CHSWK W4 117 K5
LOU IG10 39 H2
King's Pl STHWK SE1 18 C3
King Sq FSBYE EC1V 6 C5
King's Quay WBPTN SW10 * 140 B2
Kings Reach EMB EC4Y * 11 K5
WHALL SW1A 17 F1
Kings Ride Ga
RCHPK/HAM TW10 137 H5
Kings Rd BAR EN5 20 A4
EA W5 97 K4
FELT TW13 154 B3
MTCM CR4 179 F6
ORP BR6 217 F2
RCHPK/HAM TW10 137 G6
RYLN/HDSTN HA2 59 K6
WDGN N22 49 F4
WDR/YW UB7 112 C2
WLSDN NW10 81 K5
WOT/HER KT12 188 A6
King's Rd BARK IG11 90 C5
CHEL SW3 120 C6
CHING E4 38 B3
FUL/PGN SW6 140 A2
KUTN/CMB KT2 175 G3
MORT/ESHN SW14 138 A4
PLSTW E13 89 G6
ROM RM1 75 J2
SNWD SE25 181 H6
SURB KT6 190 D5
TEDD TW11 173 J1
TOTM N17 50 B4
TWK TW1 156 C1
WAN E11 70 C4
WIM/MER SW19 177 K2
King's Scholars' Pas
PIM SW1V 16 A5
King Stairs Cl
BERM/RHTH SE16 123 J2
King's Ter CAMTN NW1 4 A1
Kingsthorpe Rd SYD SE26 164 A6
Kingston Av CHEAM SM3 208 C1
EBED/NFELT TW14 153 H1
Kingston By-Pass
ESH/CLAY KT10 204 E1
RYNPK SW20 176 C2
Kingston Cl CHDH RM6 56 A6
NTHLT UB5 77 K5
TEDD TW11 174 C2
Kingston Crs BECK BR3 182 C4
Kingston Gdns CROY/NA CR0 210 E1
Kingston Ga KUTN/CMB KT2 175 H3
Kingston Hall Rd KUT/HW KT1 174 E6
Kingston Hl KUTN/CMB KT2 175 H4
Kingston Hill Av CHDH RM6 56 A6
Kingston Hill Pl
KUTN/CMB KT2 157 K6
Kingston House Est
SURB KT6 * 190 C3
Kingston La TEDD TW11 174 B1
WDR/YW UB7 112 C2
Kingston Ldg NWMAL KT3 192 B1
Kingston Pl
KTN/HRWW/WS HA3 43 F3
Kingston Rd BRYLDS KT5 191 J6
EBAR EN4 21 H6
ED N9 36 C4
HOR/WEW KT19 207 F2
IL IG1 90 C2
KUT/HW KT1 175 J6
NWDGN UB2 114 E2
NWMAL KT3 192 A1
PUT/ROE SW15 158 E3
ROM RM1 75 H1
RYNPK SW20 177 G5
TEDD TW11 174 C2
WIM/MER SW19 177 K3
Kingston Sq NRWD SE19 180 E1
Kingston V PUT/ROE SW15 158 A6
Kingstown St CAMTN NW1 83 K6
King St ACT W3 117 J1
CITYW EC2V 12 D4
COVGDN WC2E 10 E5
EFNCH N2 47 H6
HMSMTH W6 118 D4
NWDGN UB2 114 D3
PLSTW E13 106 E3
RCH/KEW TW9 136 E6
TOTM N17 50 B4
TWK TW1 156 B3
WHALL SW1A 16 B1
King Street Cloisters
HMSMTH W6 * 118 E4
King Street Pde TWK TW1 * 156 B3
Kingswater Pl BTSEA SW11 * 140 D1
Kings Wy CROY/NA CR0 211 F3
HRW HA1 60 E1
Kingsway HOL/ALD WC2B 11 G4
HYS/HAR UB3 94 A4
MORT/ESHN SW14 137 J4
NFNCH/WDSPK N12 47 G2
NWMAL KT3 193 F1
PEND EN3 24 D6
STMC/STPC BR5 201 J2
STWL/WRAY TW19 152 A3
WBLY HA9 80 A2
WWKM BR4 214 D1
Kingsway Av SAND/SEL CR2 212 E6
Kingsway Crs
RYLN/HDSTN HA2 60 C1
Kingsway Pde
STNW/STAM N16 * 85 K1
Kingsway Pl CLKNW EC1R * 5 K6
Kingsway Rd CHEAM SM3 208 C5
Kingswear Rd KTTN NW5 84 B1
RSLP HA4 58 E6
Kingswood Av BELV DA17 129 G4
HAYES BR2 183 H6
HPTN TW12 173 G2
HSLW TW3 134 E3
KIL/WHAMP NW6 82 C6
THHTH CR7 196 B2
Kingswood Cl ASHF TW15 153 F6
BAR EN5 33 G1
EN EN1 24 A6
NWMAL KT3 192 C3
STMC/STPC BR5 201 J4
SURB KT6 191 F4
VX/NE SW8 141 K1
Kingswood Ct LEW SE13 165 G1
Kingswood Dr BELMT SM2 209 F6
CAR SM5 194 E5
DUL SE21 163 F6
Kingswood Pk FNCH N3 46 D5
Kingswood Pl LEW SE13 145 H5
Kingswood Rd
BRXS/STRHM SW2 161 K1
CHSWK W4 117 K3
GDMY/SEVK IG3 73 G5
HAYES BR2 183 H6
PGE/AN SE20 181 K2
WAN E11 70 C4
WBLY HA9 80 C1
WIM/MER SW19 177 J4
Kingswood Ter CHSWK W4 117 K3
Kingswood Wy WLGTN SM6 210 E3
Kingsworth Cl BECK BR3 198 B2
Kingsworthy Cl KUT/HW KT1 175 G5
Kings Yd PUT/ROE SW15 * 139 G5
SRTFD E15 * 87 J4
Kingthorpe Rd WLSDN NW10 81 F5
Kingthorpe Ter
WLSDN NW10 * 81 F5
Kingwell Rd EBAR EN4 21 H1
Kingweston Cl CRICK NW2 82 C1
King William La GNWCH SE10 125 H5
King William St CANST EC4R 13 F5
King William Wk GNWCH SE10 125 F6
Kingwood Rd FUL/PGN SW6 139 H1
Kinlet Rd WOOL/PLUM SE18 147 H1
Kinloch Dr CDALE/KGS NW9 63 G4
Kinloch St HOLWY N7 85 F1
Kinloss Gdns FNCH N3 46 D6
Kinloss Rd CAR SM5 194 B4
Kinnaird Av BMLY BR1 183 J2
CHSWK W4 137 K1
Kinnaird Cl BMLY BR1 183 J2
Kinnaird Wy WFD IG8 53 K2
Kinnear Rd SHB W12 118 C2
Kinnerton Pl North
KTBR SW1X * 15 F3
Kinnerton Pl South
KTBR SW1X * 15 F3
Kinnerton St KTBR SW1X 15 G3
Kinnerton Yd KTBR SW1X * 15 G3
Kinnoul Rd HMSMTH W6 119 H6
Kinross Av WPK KT4 192 D6
Kinross Cl
KTN/HRWW/WS HA3 62 B2
Kinross Ter WALTH E17 51 H5
Kinsale Rd PECK SE15 143 H4
Kinsella Gdns WIM/MER SW19 176 E2
Kintyre Cl STRHM/NOR SW16 180 A5
Kinveachy Gdns CHARL SE7 126 D5
Kinver Rd SYD SE26 163 K6
Kipling Dr WIM/MER SW19 178 C2
Kipling Est STHWK SE1 19 F3
Kipling St STHWK SE1 19 F3
Kipling Ter ED N9 * 35 K5
Kippington Dr ELTH/MOT SE9 166 C3
Kirby Cl BARK/HLT IG6 54 E2
HOR/WEW KT19 207 H3
LOU IG10 39 J2
NTHWD HA6 40 D2
Kirby Est BERM/RHTH SE16 * 123 J3
Kirby Gv STHWK SE1 19 G2
Kirby St HCIRC EC1N 11 K1
Kirchen Rd WEA W13 97 H6
Kirkcaldy Gn OXHEY WD19 27 G5
Kirkdale SYD SE26 163 J4
Kirkdale Cnr SYD SE26 * 163 K6
Kirkdale Rd WAN E11 70 C5
Kirkfield Cl WEA W13 116 C1
Kirkham Rd EHAM E6 107 J5
Kirkham St WOOL/PLUM SE18 127 K6
Kirkland Av CLAY IG5 54 A5
Kirkland Cl BFN/LL DA15 167 K1
Kirkland Dr ENC/FH EN2 23 J2
Kirkland Ter BECK BR3 182 D2
Kirkland Wk HACK E8 86 B4
Kirk La WOOL/PLUM SE18 127 H6
Kirkleas Rd SURB KT6 191 F5
Kirklees Rd BCTR RM8 91 J3
THHTH CR7 196 B2
Kirkley Rd WIM/MER SW19 177 K4
Kirkly Cl SAND/SEL CR2 212 A6
Kirkmichael Rd POP/IOD E14 106 A5
Kirk Rd WALTH E17 69 H3
Kirkstall Av TOTM N17 67 K1
Kirkstall Gdns
BRXS/STRHM SW2 161 J3
Kirkstall Rd
BRXS/STRHM SW2 161 K3
Kirksted Rd MRDN SM4 194 A5
Kirkstone Wy BMLY BR1 183 H3
Kirkton Rd SEVS/STOTM N15 68 A1
Kirkwall Pl BETH E2 * 104 E2
Kirkwood Rd PECK SE15 143 J3
Kirn Rd WEA W13 97 H6
Kirrane Cl NWMAL KT3 192 C2
Kirtley Rd SYD SE26 164 B6
Kirtling St VX/NE SW8 141 H1
Kirton Cl CHSWK W4 118 A4
Kirton Gdns BETH E2 7 K5
Kirton Ldg
WAND/EARL SW18 * 160 A1
Kirton Rd PLSTW E13 107 G1
Kirton Wk EDGW HA8 44 E3
Kirwyn Wy CMBW SE5 142 D1
Kitcat Ter BOW E3 105 J2
Kitchener Rd EFNCH N2 47 J6
FSTGT E7 89 F4
THHTH CR7 180 E6
TOTM N17 50 A6
WALTH E17 51 K4
Kite Pl BETH E2 * 104 C2
Kite Yd BTSEA SW11 * 140 E2
Kitley Gdns NRWD SE19 181 G4
Kitson Rd BARN SW13 138 D2
CMBW SE5 142 D1
Kittiwake Rd NTHLT UB5 95 H2
Kittiwake Wy YEAD UB4 95 H4
Kitto Rd NWCR SE14 144 A3
Kiver Rd ARCH N19 66 D6
Kiwi Ter EHAM E6 108 A2
Klea Av CLAP SW4 161 H1
Knapdale Cl FSTH SE23 163 J4
Knapmill Rd CAT SE6 164 D4
Knapmill Wy CAT SE6 164 D4
Knapp Cl WLSDN NW10 81 G4
Knapp Rd ASHF TW15 152 C6
BOW E3 105 J3
Knapton Ms TOOT SW17 179 F2
Knaresborough Dr
WAND/EARL SW18 160 A3
Knaresborough Pl ECT SW5 120 A4
Knatchbull Rd CMBW SE5 142 C3
WLSDN NW10 81 F6
Knebworth Av WALTH E17 51 J4
Knebworth Cl BAR EN5 21 F5
Knebworth Rd
STNW/STAM N16 * 86 A2
Kneller Gdns ISLW TW7 155 J1
Kneller Rd BROCKY SE4 144 B5
NWMAL KT3 192 B4
WHTN TW2 155 H1
Knevett Ter HSLW TW3 135 F5
Knight Cl BCTR RM8 73 J6
Knighten St WAP E1W 123 J1
Knighthead Point
POP/IOD E14 * 124 D2
Knightland Rd CLPT E5 68 D6
Knighton Cl ROMW/RG RM7 75 F3
SAND/SEL CR2 211 H6
WFD IG8 39 F6
Knighton Dr WFD IG8 39 F6
Knighton La BKHH IG9 39 F4
Knighton Park Rd SYD SE26 182 A1
Knighton Rd FSTGT E7 88 E1
ROMW/RG RM7 74 E3
Knightrider Ct BLKFR EC4V * 12 B5
Knightrider St BLKFR EC4V 12 B5
Knight's Av EA W5 117 F2
Knightsbridge SKENS SW7 14 D3
Knightsbridge Gdns
ROMW/RG RM7 75 F2
Knightsbridge Gn
KTBR SW1X * 14 E3
Knights Chambers ED N9 * 36 C5
Knights Cl E/WMO/HCT KT8 188 E2
Knights Hl WNWD SE27 180 C1
Knight's Hill Sq WNWD SE27 162 C6
Knight's Pk KUT/HW KT1 175 F6
Knight's Pl WHTN TW2 155 K3
Knights Rdg ORP BR6 217 H3
Knights Rd CAN/RD E16 125 K1
STAN HA7 29 J6
Knights Wk LBTH SE11 18 A7
Knights Wy BARK/HLT IG6 54 C2
Knightswood Cl EDGW HA8 30 E4
Knightswood Rd RAIN RM13 111 H1
Knightwood Crs NWMAL KT3 192 B3
Knivet Rd FUL/PGN SW6 119 K6
Knockholt Rd ELTH/MOT SE9 146 C6
Knole Cl CROY/NA CR0 * 197 K3
The Knole ELTH/MOT SE9 167 F6
Knoll Crs NTHWD HA6 40 C5
Knoll Dr STHGT/OAK N14 34 A2
Knollmead BRYLDS KT5 191 K5
Knoll Ri ORP BR6 202 A5
Knoll Rd BXLY DA5 169 H2
SCUP DA14 186 C1
WAND/EARL SW18 140 A6
Knolls Cl WPK KT4 207 K1
The Knoll BECK BR3 182 E4
EA W5 97 J4
PIN HA5 * 41 H5
Knollys Cl
STRHM/NOR SW16 * 162 C5
Knolly's Cl STRHM/NOR SW16 162 B5
Knolly's Rd STRHM/NOR SW16 162 B5
Knotley Wy WWKM BR4 198 E6
Knottisford St BETH E2 105 F2
Knotts Green Ms LEY E10 69 K3
Knotts Green Rd LEY E10 69 K3
Knowle Cl BRXN/ST SW9 142 B4
Knowle Rd HAYES BR2 200 D6
WHTN TW2 155 K3
Knowles Cl WDR/YW UB7 112 B1
Knowles Hill Crs LEW SE13 145 G6
Knowlton Gn HAYES BR2 199 J2
Knowsley Av STHL UB1 115 G1
Knowsley Rd BTSEA SW11 140 E3
Knox Rd FSTGT E7 88 E4
Knox St CAMTN NW1 8 E1
Knoyle St NWCR SE14 124 B6
Kohat Rd WIM/MER SW19 178 A1
Koh-I-Noor Av BUSH WD23 28 A1
Kossuth St GNWCH SE10 125 H5
Kramer Ms ECT SW5 * 119 K5
Kreedman Wk HACK E8 * 86 C3
Kuala Gdns
STRHM/NOR SW16 180 A4
Kydbrook Cl STMC/STPC BR5 201 H4
Kylemore Cl EHAM E6 107 H1
Kylemore Rd
KIL/WHAMP NW6 82 E5
Kymberley Rd HRW HA1 * 60 E3
Kyme Rd ROM RM1 75 H3
Kynance Gdns STAN HA7 43 J4
Kynance Ms SKENS SW7 120 A3
Kynance Pl KENS W8 120 B3
Kynaston Av THHTH CR7 196 D2
Kynaston Cl
KTN/HRWW/WS HA3 42 D3
Kynaston Crs THHTH CR7 196 D2
Kynaston Rd BMLY BR1 183 K1
ENC/FH EN2 23 K2
STMC/STPC BR5 202 C4
STNW/STAM N16 86 A1
THHTH CR7 196 D2
Kynaston Wd
KTN/HRWW/WS HA3 42 D3
Kynersley Cl CAR SM5 209 K1
Kynoch Rd UED N18 50 E1
Kyrle Rd BTSEA SW11 161 F1
Kyverdale Rd
STNW/STAM N16 68 B4

L

Laburnum Av ED N9 36 A4
HCH RM12 75 J6
SUT SM1 209 J1
TOTM N17 49 K3
Laburnum Cl ALP/SUD HA0 80 C6
CHING E4 51 H2
FBAR/BDGN N11 48 A2
PECK SE15 143 K1
Laburnum Ct STAN HA7 29 J6
Laburnum Crs SUN TW16 172 A4
Laburnum Gdns
CROY/NA CR0 198 A4
Laburnum Gv
CDALE/KGS NW9 62 E4
HSLW TW3 134 E5
NWMAL KT3 176 A5
RSLP HA4 58 B3
STHL UB1 95 K3
WCHMH N21 35 J4
Laburnum Pl ELTH/MOT SE9 * 147 F6
Laburnum Rd HYS/HAR UB3 113 J4
MTCM CR4 179 F5
WIM/MER SW19 178 B3
Laburnum St BETH E2 7 J1
Laburnum Wy HAYES BR2 201 F4
STWL/WRAY TW19 152 C3
Lacebark Cl BFN/LL DA15 168 A2
Lacewing Cl PLSTW E13 106 E2
Lacey Cl ED N9 36 C4
Lacey Dr BCTR RM8 91 J1
EDGW HA8 30 A6
HPTN TW12 172 E4
Lacey Ms BOW E3 105 J1
Lackington St SDTCH EC2A 13 F1
Lacock Cl WIM/MER SW19 178 B2
Lacon Rd EDUL SE22 143 H5
Lacrosse Wy
STRHM/NOR SW16 179 J4
Lacy Rd PUT/ROE SW15 139 G5
Ladas Rd WNWD SE27 180 D1
Ladbroke Crs NTGHL W11 100 C5
Ladbroke Gdns NTGHL W11 100 D6
Ladbroke Gv NKENS W10 100 B3
NTGHL W11 100 D6
Ladbroke Ms NTGHL W11 119 H1
Ladbroke Rd EN EN1 36 B1
NTGHL W11 119 J1
Ladbroke Sq NTGHL W11 100 D6
Ladbroke Ter NTGHL W11 100 D6
Ladbroke Wk NTGHL W11 119 J1
Ladbrook Cl PIN HA5 59 K2
Ladbrooke Crs SCUP DA14 168 E5
Ladbrook Rd SNWD SE25 180 E6
Ladderstile Ride
KUTN/CMB KT2 175 J1
Ladderswood Wy
FBAR/BDGN N11 48 C1
Lady Alesford Av STAN HA7 43 H1
Lady Booth Rd KUT/HW KT1 175 F5
Ladycroft Gdns ORP BR6 216 C3
Ladycroft Rd LEW SE13 144 E4
Ladycroft Wk STAN HA7 43 K4
Ladycroft Wy ORP BR6 216 C3
Lady Forsdyke Wy
HOR/WEW KT19 206 C6
Ladygate La RSLP HA4 58 A3
Ladygrove CROY/NA CR0 213 G6
Lady Harewood Wy
HOR/WEW KT19 206 C6
Lady Hay WPK KT4 192 C6
Lady Margaret Rd KTTN NW5 84 C3
STHL UB1 96 A2
Ladymount WLGTN SM6 210 D2
Ladyship Ter EDUL SE22 * 163 J2
Ladysmith Av EHAM E6 107 J1
GNTH/NBYPK IG2 72 D4
Ladysmith Cl MLHL NW7 45 J3
Ladysmith Rd CAN/RD E16 106 D2
ELTH/MOT SE9 167 F1
EN EN1 24 B3
KTN/HRWW/WS HA3 42 E5
TOTM N17 50 C5
Lady Somerset Rd KTTN NW5 84 B2
Ladywell Cl BROCKY SE4 144 D6
Ladywell Rd LEW SE13 144 D6
Ladywell St SRTFD E15 88 D6
Ladywell Water Tower
BROCKY SE4 * 144 C4
Ladywood Av
STMC/STPC BR5 201 K2
Ladywood Rd SURB KT6 191 H6
Lafone Av FELT TW13 154 B3
Lafone St STHWK SE1 19 J2
Lagado Ms BERM/RHTH SE16 124 A1
Lagonda Av BARK/HLT IG6 55 F2
Lagoon Rd STMC/STPC BR5 202 C2
Laidlaw Dr WCHMH N21 23 F6
Laing Cl BARK/HLT IG6 54 D2
Laing Dean NTHLT UB5 77 G6
Laings Av MTCM CR4 178 E5
Lainlock Pl HSLW TW3 135 G2
Lainson St WAND/EARL SW18 159 K2
Lairdale Cl DUL SE21 162 D3
Lairs Cl HOLWY N7 * 84 E4
Laitwood Rd BAL SW12 161 G3
Lake Av BMLY BR1 183 K2
Lake Cl BCTR RM8 91 K1
Lakedale Rd
WOOL/PLUM SE18 127 K5
Lake Dr BUSH WD23 28 C4
Lakefield Rd WDGN N22 49 H5
Lake Gdns DAGE RM10 92 C3
RCHPK/HAM TW10 156 C5
WLGTN SM6 210 B1
Lakehall Gdns THHTH CR7 196 C
Lakehall Rd THHTH CR7 196 C
Lake House Rd WAN E11 88 E
Lakehurst Rd HOR/WEW KT19 207 G
Lakeland Cl
KTN/HRWW/WS HA3 42 D
Lakenheath STHGT/OAK N14 22 D
Lake Ri ROM RM1 57 H
Lake Rd CHDH RM6 73 K
CROY/NA CR0 198 C
DAGW RM9 110 D
LEY E10 69 K
WIM/MER SW19 177 J
Lakeside BECK BR3 182 E
ENC/FH EN2 22 D
HOR/WEW KT19 207 C
WEA W13 97 J
WLGTN SM6 210 B
Lakeside Av REDBR IG4 71 H
THMD SE28 128 B
Lakeside Cl BFN/LL DA15 148 D
RSLP HA4 58 B
SNWD SE25 181 H
Lakeside Crs EBAR EN4 33 K
Lakeside Dr ESH/CLAY KT10 204 C
HAYES BR2 215
WLSDN NW10 98 E
Lakeside Rd PLMGR N13 35 F
WKENS W14 119 C
Lakeside Wy WBLY HA9 80 C
Lakes Rd HAYES BR2 215
Lakeswood Rd
STMC/STPC BR5 201
The Lake BUSH WD23 28
Lake Vw EDGW HA8 44
Lake View Est BOW E3 * 105
Lakeview Rd WELL DA16 148
WNWD SE27 180
Lake View Ter UED N18 * 36
Lakis Cl HAMP NW3 83
Laleham Av MLHL NW7 31
Laleham Ct SUT SM1 * 209
Laleham Rd CAT SE6 165
Lalor St FUL/PGN SW6 139
Lambarde Av ELTH/MOT SE9 167
Lamb Cl NTHLT UB5 95
Lamberhurst Cl
STMC/STPC BR5 202
Lamberhurst Rd BCTR RM8 74
WNWD SE27 162
Lambert Av RCH/KEW TW9 137
Lambert Jones Ms
BARB EC2Y * 12
Lambert Rd
BRXS/STRHM SW2 141
CAN/RD E16 107
NFNCH/WDSPK N12 47
Lambert's Pl CROY/NA CR0 196
Lambert's Rd BRYLDS KT5 191
Lambert St IS N1 85
Lambert Wy
NFNCH/WDSPK N12 47
Lambeth Br WEST SW1P 17
Lambeth High St STHWK SE1 17
Lambeth Hl BLKFR EC4V 12
Lambeth Palace Rd
STHWK SE1 17
Lambeth Rd CROY/NA CR0 196
STHWK SE1 17
Lambeth Wk LBTH SE11 17
PECK SE15 143
Lambkins Ms WALTH E17 70
Lamb La HACK E8 86
Lamble St KTTN NW5 84
Lambley Rd DAGW RM9 91
Lambolle Pl HAMP NW3 83
Lambolle Rd HAMP NW3 83
Lambourn Cl HNWL W7 116
KTTN NW5 * 84
SAND/SEL CR2 21
Lambourne Av
WIM/MER SW19 159
Lambourne Gdns BARK IG11 91
CHING E4 37
EN EN1 2
Lambourne Gv
BERM/RHTH SE16 12
KUT/HW KT1 17
Lambourne Pl BKHTH/KID SE3 14
Lambourne Rd BARK IG11 9
GDMY/SEVK IG3 7
WAN E11 7
Lambourn Rd VX/NE SW8 14

Lambrook Ter FUL/PGN SW6 139 H2
Lambs Cl ED N9 36 C4
Lamb's Conduit Pas
FSBYW WC1X 11 G1
Lamb's Conduit St
BMSBY WC1N 5 G7
Lambscroft Av ELTH/MOT SE9 166 B5
Lambs Meadow WFD IG8 53 H5
Lambs Ms IS N1 6 A1
Lamb's Pas STLK EC1Y 6 E7
Lambs Ter ED N9 * 35 K4
Lamb St WCHPL E1 13 J1
Lambs Wk ENC/FH EN2 23 J3
Lambton Pl NTGHL W11 * 100 D6
Lambton Rd ARCH N19 66 E5
RYNPK SW20 177 F4
Lamb Wk STHWK SE1 19 G3
Lamerock Rd BMLY BR1 165 J6
Lamerton Rd BARK/HLT IG6 54 B5
Lamerton St DEPT SE8 124 D6
Lamford Cl TOTM N17 49 K3
Lamington St HMSMTH W6 118 E4
Lamlash St LBTH SE11 18 A6
Lammas Av MTCM CR4 179 F5
Lammas La ESH/CLAY KT10 204 A2
Lammas Park Gdns EA W5 116 D1
Lammas Rd HOM E9 87 F5
LEY E10 69 G6
RCHPK/HAM TW10 156 D6
Lammermoor Rd BAL SW12 * 161 G2
Lamont Rd WBPTN SW10 120 C6
Lamont Road Pas
WBPTN SW10 * 120 C6
Lamorbey Cl BFN/LL DA15 168 A4
Lamorbey Pk BFN/LL DA15 * 168 C3
amorna Cl ORP BR6 202 B4
WALTH E17 52 A5
Lamorna Gv STAN HA7 43 K4
Lampard Gv STNW/STAM N16 68 B5
ampern Sq BETH E2 * 104 C2
ampeter Sq HMSMTH W6 119 H6
amplighter Cl WCHPL E1 104 E3
ampmead Rd
LEE/GVPK SE12 145 H6
amport Cl WOOL/PLUM SE18 126 E4
ampton Av HSLW TW3 135 F2
ampton House Cl
WIM/MER SW19 159 G6
ampton Park Rd HSLW TW3 135 G3
ampton Rd HEST TW5 135 G2
HSLW TW3 135 G3
amson Rd RAIN RM13 111 H3
anacre Av EDGW HA8 45 F4
anadron Cl ISLW TW7 136 A3
anark Cl EA W5 97 J4
anark Pl MV/WKIL W9 101 G3
anark Rd KIL/WHAMP NW6 101 F1
anbury Rd PECK SE15 144 A5
ancashire Ct
MYFR/PKLN W1K 9 J5
ancaster Av BARK IG11 90 E5
EBAR EN4 21 H1
MTCM CR4 195 K1
WAN E11 71 F1
WIM/MER SW19 177 G1
WNWD SE27 162 C4
ancaster Cl ASHF TW15 152 B6
CDALE/KGS NW9 45 H3
HAYES BR2 199 J1
STWL/WRAY TW19 152 B1
TOTM N17 * 50 C3
WPK KT4 192 E4
ncaster Dr HAMP NW3 83 J4
HCH RM12 93 K3
POP/IOD E14 125 F1
ncaster Garde BMLY BR1 200 D2
ncaster Gdn
KUTN/CMB KT2 174 E1
ncaster Gdns
KUTN/CMB KT2 175 F1
WIM/MER SW19 177 H1
ncaster Ga BAY/PAD W2 101 G6
ncaster Gv HAMP NW3 83 J4
ncaster House
WOOL/PLUM SE18 * 146 D1
ncaster Ms BAY/PAD W2 * 101 G6
RCHPK/HAM TW10 157 F1
WAND/EARL SW18 * 140 A6
ncaster Pk
RCHPK/HAM TW10 137 F6
ncaster Pl COVGDN WC2E 11 G6
TPL/STR WC2R 11 G5
TWK TW1 156 B1
WIM/MER SW19 177 G1
caster Rd EBAR EN4 21 H5
ENC/FH EN2 23 K2
FBAR/BDGN N11 48 D2
FSBYPK N4 67 G4
FSTGT E7 88 E5
NKENS W10 100 B5
NTHLT UB5 78 C4
RYLN/HDSTN HA2 60 A2
SNWD SE25 181 G5
STHL UB1 95 J6
UED N18 50 B1
WALTH E17 51 F5
WAN E11 70 C6
WIM/MER SW19 177 G1
WLSDN NW10 81 H3
caster Stables
HAMP NW3 * 83 J4
caster St STHWK SE1 18 A3
caster Ter BAY/PAD W2 8 A5
caster Wk HYS/HAR UB3 94 A5
caster Wy WPK KT4 193 F4
caster West NTGHL W11 * 100 C5
castrian Rd WLGTN SM6 210 E5
cefield St NKENS W10 100 D2
cell St STNW/STAM N16 68 A6
celot Av ALP/SUD HA0 79 K2
celot Crs ALP/SUD HA0 79 K2
celot Gdns EBAR EN4 34 A2
celot Pde ALP/SUD HA0 * 80 A3
celot Pl SKENS SW7 14 E3
celot Rd ALP/SUD HA0 79 K2
ARK/HLT IG6 54 E2
ELL DA16 148 B5
e Rd HRW HA1 60 C4
er Sq KENS W8 * 120 A2
ey Cl CHARL SE7 126 C4

Lanchester Rd HGT N6 65 K2
Lanchester Wy NWCR SE14 143 K2
Lancing Gdns ED N9 36 B3
Lancing Rd CROY/NA CR0 196 A3
FELT TW13 153 J4
GNTH/NBYPK IG2 72 D3
ORP BR6 202 C6
WEA W13 97 H6
Lancing St CAMTN NW1 4 C5
Landau Ter HAYES BR2 215 J2
Landau Wy ERITH DA8 131 G5
Landcroft Rd EDUL SE22 163 G1
Landells Rd EDUL SE22 163 G1
Landford Rd PUT/ROE SW15 139 F4
Landgrove Rd
WIM/MER SW19 177 K1
Landleys Flds HOLWY N7 * 84 D3
Landmann Wy NWCR SE14 124 A6
Landon Pl KTBR SW1X 14 E4
Landons Cl POP/IOD E14 125 F1
Landor Rd BRXN/ST SW9 141 K4
Landor Wk SHB W12 118 D2
Landra Gdns WCHMH N21 35 H1
Landridge Dr EN EN1 24 D1
Landridge Rd FUL/PGN SW6 139 H3
Landrock Rd CEND/HSY/T N8 66 E3
Landscape Rd WFD IG8 53 F3
Landseer Av MNPK E12 90 A3
Landseer Cl EDGW HA8 44 C5
EMPK RM11 75 K5
WIM/MER SW19 178 B4
Landseer Rd ARCH N19 84 E1
EN EN1 24 C6
NWMAL KT3 192 A4
SUT SM1 208 E4
Lands' End BORE WD6 29 K1
Landstead Rd
WOOL/PLUM SE18 147 J1
The Landway STMC/STPC BR5 186 D6
Lane Ap MLHL NW7 * 46 C1
Lane Cl CRICK NW2 81 K1
Lane Gdns BUSH WD23 28 E3
ESH/CLAY KT10 205 F5
Lane Ms MNPK E12 89 K1
Lanercost Gdns
STHGT/OAK N14 34 E1
Lanercost Rd
BRXS/STRHM SW2 162 B4
Laneside CHST BR7 185 G1
EDGW HA8 44 E1
Laneside Av BCTR RM8 74 B4
The Lane STJWD NW8 101 G1
Laneway PUT/ROE SW15 138 E6
Lanfranc Rd BOW E3 105 G1
Lanfrey Pl WKENS W14 119 J5
Langbourne Av HGT N6 66 A6
Langbourne Wy
ESH/CLAY KT10 205 F4
Langbrook Rd
BKHTH/KID SE3 146 C4
Langcroft Cl CAR SM5 209 K1
Langdale Av MTCM CR4 178 D6
Langdale Cl BCTR RM8 73 J5
MORT/ESHN SW14 137 J5
ORP BR6 216 B1
Langdale Dr YEAD UB4 94 C1
Langdale Gdns HCH RM12 93 J5
Langdale Pde MTCM CR4 * 178 E5
Langdale Rd GNWCH SE10 145 F1
THHTH CR7 196 B1
Langdale St WCHPL E1 * 104 D5
Langdon Ct WLSDN NW10 81 G6
Langdon Crs EHAM E6 108 A1
Langdon Dr CDALE/KGS NW9 62 E5
Langdon House
WOOL/PLUM SE18 * 146 D1
Langdon Pk TEDD TW11 174 D3
Langdon Park Rd HGT N6 66 B4
Langdon Pl
MORT/ESHN SW14 137 K4
Langdon Rd EHAM E6 90 A6
HAYES BR2 184 A6
MRDN SM4 194 B2
Langdon Shaw SCUP DA14 186 A1
Langdon Wk MRDN SM4 194 B2
Langdon Wy STHWK SE1 123 H4
Langford Cl HACK E8 86 C3
SEVS/STOTM N15 68 A3
STJWD NW8 101 G1
Langford Crs EBAR EN4 21 K5
Langford Gn CMBW SE5 143 F4
Langford Pl SCUP DA14 168 B5
STJWD NW8 101 G1
Langford Rd EBAR EN4 21 K5
FUL/PGN SW6 140 A3
WFD IG8 53 G2
Langfords BKHH IG9 39 H4
Langham Ct RSLP HA4 * 77 F3
Langham Dr GDMY/SEVK IG3 73 H3
Langham Gdns ALP/SUD HA0 61 J6
EDGW HA8 44 E3
RCHPK/HAM TW10 156 D6
WCHMH N21 23 G6
WEA W13 97 H6
Langham House Cl
RCHPK/HAM TW10 156 E6
Langham Pde
SEVS/STOTM N15 * 49 H6
Langham Park Pl HAYES BR2 199 J1
Langham Pl CHSWK W4 118 B6
REGST W1B 9 K2
SEVS/STOTM N15 49 H6
Langham Rd EDGW HA8 44 E2
RYNPK SW20 177 F4
SEVS/STOTM N15 67 J1
TEDD TW11 174 C1
Langham St GTPST W1W 10 A2
REGST W1B 9 K2
Langhedge Cl UED N18 50 B2
Langhedge La UED N18 50 B1
Langholm Cl BAL SW12 161 J2
Langholme BUSH WD23 28 C3
Langhorn Dr WHTN TW2 155 K2
Langhorne Rd DAGE RM10 92 C5
Langland Ct NTHWD HA6 40 A3
Langland Crs STAN HA7 43 K5
Langland Dr PIN HA5 41 J3
Langland Gdns CROY/NA CR0 198 C6
HAMP NW3 83 F3
Langler Rd WLSDN NW10 100 A1

Langley Av RSLP HA4 59 F6
SURB KT6 190 E5
WPK KT4 193 G6
Langley Ct BECK BR3 * 198 E1
COVGDN WC2E 10 E5
Langley Crs DAGW RM9 91 J5
EDGW HA8 30 E5
HYS/HAR UB3 133 J1
WAN E11 71 F4
Langley Dr ACT W3 117 J2
WAN E11 71 F4
Langley Gdns DAGW RM9 91 K5
STMC/STPC BR5 201 G3
Langley Gv NWMAL KT3 176 A5
Langley La VX/NE SW8 121 K6
Langley Pk MLHL NW7 45 G2
Langley Park Rd BELMT SM2 209 G4
Langley Pl WPK KT4 193 G6
Langley Rd BECK BR3 198 A1
ISLW TW7 136 A3
SAND/SEL CR2 213 F6
SURB KT6 191 F4
WIM/MER SW19 177 J4
Langley Rw BAR EN5 20 D2
Langley St LSQ/SEVD WC2H 10 E4
Langley Wy WWKM BR4 199 G5
Langley Wd BECK BR3 * 199 H2
Langmead Dr BUSH WD23 28 D3
Langmead St WNWD SE27 162 C6
Langport Ct WOT/HER KT12 188 B5
Langridge Ms HPTN TW12 172 E2
Langroyd Rd TOOT SW17 160 E4
Langside Av PUT/ROE SW15 138 D5
Langside Crs STHGT/OAK N14 34 D5
Langston Hughes Cl
HNHL SE24 * 142 C5
Lang St WCHPL E1 104 E3
Langthorn Ct LOTH EC2R * 13 F3
Langthorne Rd WAN E11 88 B1
Langthorne St FUL/PGN SW6 139 G2
Langton Av EHAM E6 108 A2
TRDG/WHET N20 33 G2
Langton Cl FSBYW WC1X 5 H5
Langton Gv NTHWD HA6 40 A1
Langton Ri EDUL SE22 163 J2
Langton Rd BRXN/ST SW9 142 C1
CRICK NW2 82 A1
E/WMO/HCT KT8 189 H2
KTN/HRWW/WS HA3 42 C3
Langton St WBPTN SW10 120 B6
Langton Vls TOTM N17 * 50 C4
Langton Wy CROY/NA CR0 212 A2
Langtry Rd NTHLT UB5 95 H1
STJWD NW8 83 F6
Langtry Wk STJWD NW8 83 G6
Langwood Cha TEDD TW11 174 D2
Langworth Dr YEAD UB4 95 F5
Lanhill Rd MV/WKIL W9 100 E3
Lanier Rd LEW SE13 165 F1
Lanigan Dr HSLW TW3 135 G6
Lankaster Gdns EFNCH N2 47 H4
Lankers Dr RYLN/HDSTN HA2 59 K3
Lankton Cl BECK BR3 183 F4
Lannock Rd HYS/HAR UB3 113 J1
Lannoy Rd ELTH/MOT SE9 167 H3
Lanrick Rd POP/IOD E14 106 B4
Lanridge Rd ABYW SE2 128 E3
Lansbury Av BARK IG11 91 G5
CHDH RM6 74 A2
EBED/NFELT TW14 154 A1
UED N18 49 K1
Lansbury Cl WLSDN NW10 80 E3
Lansbury Dr YEAD UB4 94 D4
Lansbury Gdns
POP/IOD E14 * 106 B5
Lansbury Rd PEND EN3 25 F2
Lansbury Wy UED N18 50 A1
Lanscombe Wk VX/NE SW8 * 141 K1
Lansdell Rd MTCM CR4 179 F5
Lansdown Cl WOT/HER KT12 188 B5
Lansdowne Av BXLYHN DA7 148 D1
ORP BR6 201 G5
Lansdowne Cl BRYLDS KT5 191 J6
TWK TW1 156 A3
Lansdowne Copse WPK KT4 * 192 D6
Lansdowne Ct WPK KT4 192 D6
Lansdowne Crs NTGHL W11 100 C6
Lansdowne Dr HACK E8 86 C5
Lansdowne Gdns VX/NE SW8 141 K2
Lansdowne Gn VX/NE SW8 141 K1
Lansdowne Gv WLSDN NW10 81 G2
Lansdowne Hl WNWD SE27 162 C5
Lansdowne La CHARL SE7 126 C5
Lansdowne Ms CHARL SE7 126 C5
NTGHL W11 119 J1
Lansdowne Pl NRWD SE19 181 G3
STHWK SE1 19 F4
Lansdowne Ri NTGHL W11 100 C6
Lansdowne Rd BMLY BR1 183 K3
CHING E4 37 J4
CROY/NA CR0 196 E5
FNCH N3 46 D3
GDMY/SEVK IG3 73 F5
HACK E8 86 C4
HOR/WEW KT19 206 E5
HSLW TW3 135 G4
MUSWH N10 48 C5
NTGHL W11 100 C6
RYNPK SW20 177 F3
STAN HA7 43 J2
SWFD E18 52 E6
TOTM N17 50 C4
WALTH E17 69 J3
WAN E11 70 D6
Lansdowne Ter BMSBY WC1N 5 F7
Lansdowne Wk NTGHL W11 119 H1
Lansdowne Wy VX/NE SW8 141 K2
Lansdowne Wood Cl
WNWD SE27 162 C5
Lansdown Rd FSTGT E7 89 G5
SCUP DA14 168 C5
Lansfield Av UED N18 36 C6
Lantern Cl ALP/SUD HA0 79 K3
ORP BR6 216 B2
PUT/ROE SW15 138 D5
Lanterns Ct POP/IOD E14 124 D3
Lantern Wy WDR/YW UB7 112 B2
Lant St STHWK SE1 18 C2
Lanvanor Rd PECK SE15 143 K3
Lapford Cl MV/WKIL W9 * 100 D3

Lapse Wood Wk FSTH SE23 163 J3
Lapstone Gdns
KTN/HRWW/WS HA3 61 J3
Lapwing Cl ERITH DA8 * 150 E1
Lapwing Ter FSTGT E7 89 H3
Lapwing Wy YEAD UB4 95 H5
Lapworth Cl ORP BR6 202 D6
Lapworth Ct BAY/PAD W2 101 F4
Lara Cl CHSGTN KT9 206 A5
LEW SE13 165 F1
Larbert Rd STRHM/NOR SW16 179 H4
Larch Av ACT W3 118 B1
Larch Cl BAL SW12 161 G4
DEPT SE8 124 C6
FBAR/BDGN N11 48 A3
Larch Crs HOR/WEW KT19 206 D4
YEAD UB4 95 G3
Larch Dene ORP BR6 201 F6
Larch Dr CHSWK W4 * 117 H5
Larches Av MORT/ESHN SW14 138 A5
The Larches PLMGR N13 35 J5
Larch Gv BFN/LL DA15 168 A3
Larch Rd CRICK NW2 82 A2
LEY E10 69 J6
Larch Tree Wy CROY/NA CR0 213 J1
Larch Wy HAYES BR2 201 F4
Larchwood Av CRW RM5 56 D2
Larchwood Cl CRW RM5 56 E2
Larchwood Rd ELTH/MOT SE9 167 G4
Larcombe Cl CROY/NA CR0 212 B2
Larcom St WALW SE17 18 D7
Larden Rd ACT W3 118 B2
Largewood Av SURB KT6 191 H6
Larissa St WALW SE17 * 122 E5
Larkbere Rd SYD SE26 164 B6
Larken Cl BUSH WD23 28 C3
Larken Dr BUSH WD23 28 C3
Larkfield Av
KTN/HRWW/WS HA3 43 H6
Larkfield Rd RCH/KEW TW9 137 F5
SCUP DA14 168 A5
Larkhall La CLAP SW4 141 J3
Larkhall Ri CLAP SW4 141 H4
Larkham Cl FELT TW13 153 H5
Larkhill Ter
WOOL/PLUM SE18 * 147 F1
Lark Rw BETH E2 86 E6
Larksfield Gv EN EN1 24 D2
Larks Gv BARK IG11 90 E5
Larkshall Crs CHING E4 38 A6
Larkshall Rd CHING E4 52 A1
Larkspur Cl CDALE/KGS NW9 62 D2
ORP BR6 202 D6
TOTM N17 49 K3
Larkspur Gv EDGW HA8 30 E6
Larkspur Wy HOR/WEW KT19 206 E3
Larkswood Ri PIN HA5 59 G1
Larkswood Rd CHING E4 37 J6
Lark Wy CAR SM5 194 D4
Larkway Cl CDALE/KGS NW9 63 F1
Larnach Rd HMSMTH W6 119 G6
Larne Rd RSLP HA4 58 D4
Larner Rd ERITH DA8 150 B1
Larpent Av PUT/ROE SW15 139 F6
Larwood Cl GFD/PVL UB6 78 D3
Lascelles Av HRW HA1 60 D4
Lascelles Cl WAN E11 70 B6
Lascott's Rd WDGN N22 49 F2
Lassa Rd ELTH/MOT SE9 146 D6
Lassell St GNWCH SE10 125 G5
Lasseter Pl BKHTH/KID SE3 125 H6
Latchett Rd SWFD E18 53 F4
Latchingdon Gdns WFD IG8 53 J2
Latchmere Cl
RCHPK/HAM TW10 175 F1
Latchmere La KUTN/CMB KT2 175 G2
Latchmere Rd BTSEA SW11 140 E3
KUTN/CMB KT2 175 F2
Latchmere St BTSEA SW11 140 E3
Lateward Rd BTFD TW8 116 E6
Latham Cl EHAM E6 107 J5
Latham Rd TWK TW1 156 A2
Latham's Wy CROY/NA CR0 196 A5
Lathkill Cl EN EN1 36 C2
Lathom Rd EHAM E6 89 K5
Latimer Av EHAM E6 89 K6
Latimer Cl PIN HA5 41 G4
WATW WD18 26 C2
WPK KT4 207 K2
Latimer Gdns PIN HA5 41 G4
Latimer Pl NKENS W10 100 A5
Latimer Rd BAR EN5 21 F4
CROY/NA CR0 * 211 H1
FSTGT E7 89 F2
NKENS W10 100 A4
SEVS/STOTM N15 68 A3
TEDD TW11 174 A1
WIM/MER SW19 178 A2
Latona Rd PECK SE15 123 H6
La Tourne Gdns ORP BR6 216 C1
Lattimer Pl CHSWK W4 138 B1
Latton Cl ESH/CLAY KT10 204 B2
WOT/HER KT12 188 E4
Latymer Gdns FNCH N3 * 46 C5
Latymer Rd ED N9 36 B4
Latymer Wy ED N9 35 K4
Laubin Cl TWK TW1 136 C5
Lauder Cl NTHLT UB5 95 H1
Lauderdale Dr
RCHPK/HAM TW10 156 E5
Lauderdale Pde
MV/WKIL W9 * 101 F2
Lauderdale Pl BARB EC2Y * 12 D2
Lauderdale Rd MV/WKIL W9 101 F2
Laud St CROY/NA CR0 211 J1
LBTH SE11 122 A5
Laughton Rd NTHLT UB5 95 H1
Launcelot St STHWK SE1 17 J3
Launceston Gdns
GFD/PVL UB6 79 J6
Launceston Pl KENS W8 120 B3
Launceston Rd GFD/PVL UB6 79 J6
Launch St POP/IOD E14 125 F3
Launders Ga ACT W3 * 117 J2
Laundress La
STNW/STAM N16 86 C1
Laundry Ms FSTH SE23 164 A2
Laundry Rd HMSMTH W6 119 H6
Laura Cl EN EN1 24 A6
WAN E11 71 G2

Lauradale Rd EFNCH N2 65 K1
Laura Pl CLPT E5 86 E2
Laura Ter FSBYPK N4 * 67 H6
Laurel Av TWK TW1 156 A3
Laurel Bank
NFNCH/WDSPK N12 * 33 G6
Laurel Bank Gdns
FUL/PGN SW6 139 J3
Laurel Bank Rd ENC/FH EN2 23 J2
Laurel Cl BARK/HLT IG6 54 C2
BFN/LL DA15 168 B5
OXHEY WD19 27 H2
TOOT SW17 178 D1
Laurel Crs CROY/NA CR0 213 J1
ROMW/RG RM7 75 G5
Laurel Dr WCHMH N21 35 G2
Laurel Gdns BMLY BR1 200 D1
CHING E4 37 K2
HNWL W7 115 K1
HSLWW TW4 134 D5
MLHL NW7 31 F5
Laurel Gv PGE/AN SE20 181 J3
SYD SE26 182 A1
Laurel La WDR/YW UB7 112 B4
Laurel Pk
KTN/HRWW/WS HA3 43 F3
Laurel Rd BARN SW13 138 D3
HPTN TW12 173 J1
RYNPK SW20 176 E4
The Laurels BRXN/ST SW9 * 142 C1
BUSH WD23 * 28 E4
RDART DA2 * 171 F5
Laurel St HACK E8 86 B4
Laurel Vw
NFNCH/WDSPK N12 33 F5
TRDG/WHET N20 33 F5
Laurel Vls HNWL W7 * 115 K2
Laurel Wy SWFD E18 70 D1
TRDG/WHET N20 32 E5
Laurence Ms SHB W12 118 D2
Laurence Pountney Hl
CANST EC4R 12 E5
Laurence Pountney La
CANST EC4R 12 E5
Laurie Gv NWCR SE14 144 B2
Laurie Rd HNWL W7 96 E4
Laurier Rd CROY/NA CR0 197 G4
KTTN NW5 84 B1
Laurimel Cl STAN HA7 43 H2
Laurino Pl BUSH WD23 28 C4
Lauriston Rd HOM E9 87 F5
WIM/MER SW19 177 G2
Lausanne Rd CEND/HSY/T N8 67 G1
PECK SE15 143 K2
Lavender Av CDALE/KGS NW9 62 E5
MTCM CR4 178 D4
WPK KT4 208 A1
Lavender Cl CAR SM5 210 A2
CHEL SW3 120 C6
CHING E4 37 J6
HAYES BR2 200 D3
Lavender Ct E/WMO/HCT KT8 173 G6
Lavender Gdns BTSEA SW11 140 E5
ENC/FH EN2 23 H1
KTN/HRWW/WS HA3 42 E2
Lavender Gv HACK E8 86 C5
MTCM CR4 178 D4
Lavender Hl BTSEA SW11 140 E4
ENC/FH EN2 23 G2
Lavender Pl IL IG1 90 B3
Lavender Ri WDR/YW UB7 112 D2
Lavender Rd
BERM/RHTH SE16 124 B1
BTSEA SW11 140 C4
CROY/NA CR0 196 A3
ENC/FH EN2 23 K2
HOR/WEW KT19 206 D3
SUT SM1 209 H2
WLGTN SM6 210 A3
Lavender Sweep BTSEA SW11 140 E5
Lavender Ter BTSEA SW11 * 140 D4
Lavender V WLGTN SM6 210 D4
Lavender Wk BTSEA SW11 140 E5
Lavender Wy CROY/NA CR0 198 A3
Lavengro Rd WNWD SE27 162 D4
Lavenham Rd
WAND/EARL SW18 159 J4
Lavers Rd STNW/STAM N16 86 A1
Laverstoke Gdns
PUT/ROE SW15 158 C2
Laverton Ms ECT SW5 120 A4
Laverton Pl ECT SW5 120 A4
Lavidge Rd ELTH/MOT SE9 166 D4
Lavina Gv IS N1 5 G2
Lavington Cl HOM E9 87 H4
Lavington Rd CROY/NA CR0 211 F1
WEA W13 116 C1
Lavington St STHWK SE1 18 B1
Lawdon Gdns CROY/NA CR0 211 H2
Lawford Rd CHSWK W4 137 K1
IS N1 86 A5
KTTN NW5 84 C4
Lawless St POP/IOD E14 * 105 K6
Lawley Rd STHGT/OAK N14 34 B2
Lawley St CLPT E5 86 E2
Lawn Cl BMLY BR1 184 A3
EN EN1 36 B2
NWMAL KT3 176 B5
RSLP HA4 76 D1
SWLY BR8 187 K5
Lawn Crs RCH/KEW TW9 137 H3
Lawn Farm Gv CHDH RM6 74 A1
Lawn Gdns HNWL W7 115 K1
Lawn House Cl POP/IOD E14 125 F2
Lawn La VX/NE SW8 121 K6
Lawn Rd BECK BR3 182 C3
HAMP NW3 83 K3
Lawns Ct WBLY HA9 * 62 C6
The Lawns BELMT SM2 208 C5
BKHTH/KID SE3 * 145 J4
CHING E4 51 J1
NRWD SE19 180 E4
PIN HA5 42 B3
SCUP DA14 168 C6
Lawns Wy CRW RM5 56 E3
Lawnswood BAR EN5 * 20 C6
Lawn Ter BKHTH/KID SE3 145 J4
The Lawn NWDGN UB2 115 F5
Lawn V PIN HA5 41 H5
Lawrence Av MLHL NW7 31 G6

CHING E4 51 H2
HYS/HAR UB3 94 B6
NWMAL KT3 176 A6
ORP BR6 201 G6
RSLP HA4 59 F3
SHB W12 119 F2
TRDG/WHET N20 32 C3
TWK TW1 156 A1
Limeharbour POP/IOD E14 124 E3
Limehouse POP/IOD E14 * 105 J6
Limehouse Cswy
POP/IOD E14 105 H6
Limehouse Link POP/IOD E14 105 G6
Limehouse Link (Tunnel)
POP/IOD E14 105 H6
Lime Kiln Dr CHARL SE7 126 A6
Limekiln Pl NRWD SE19 181 G3
Limerick Cl BAL SW12 161 H2
Limerston St WBPTN SW10 120 B6
Limes Av BARN SW13 138 C3
CAR SM5 194 E5
CHIG IG7 54 C1
CROY/NA CR0 211 F1
GLDGN NW11 64 C4
MLHL NW7 45 G2
NFNCH/WDSPK N12 33 G6
PGE/AN SE20 181 J3
WAN E11 71 F1
The Limes Av
FBAR/BDGN N11 48 B1
imes Cl CAR SM5 194 E6
FBAR/BDGN N11 * 48 C1
imesdale Gdns EDGW HA8 44 E5
imes Field Rd
MORT/ESHN SW14 138 B4
imesford Rd PECK SE15 144 A5
imes Gdns WAND/EARL SW18 159 K1
imes Gv LEW SE13 145 F5
imes Rd BECK BR3 182 E5
CROY/NA CR0 196 E3
imes Rw ORP BR6 216 B3
he Limes CMBW SE5 * 143 F4
WAND/EARL SW18 * 159 K1
imestone Wk ERITHM DA18 128 E2
ime St FENCHST EC3M 13 G5
WALTH E17 69 G1
ime Street Pas BANK EC3V * 13 G4
imes Wk EA W5 116 E2
PECK SE15 * 143 K5
me Tree Av ESH/CLAY KT10 189 J5
metree Cl BRXS/STRHM SW2 162 A3
me Tree Ct PIN HA5 * 42 A3
me Tree Gv CROY/NA CR0 213 H1
metree Pl MTCM CR4 179 G4
me Tree Rd HEST TW5 135 G2
me Tree Ter CAT SE6 * 164 C3
me Tree Wk BUSH WD23 28 E3
ENC/FH EN2 23 J1
WWKM BR4 214 D2
me Wk SRTFD E15 * 88 C6
mewood Cl BECK BR3 199 F2
WALTH E17 69 H1
WEA W13 97 H5
mewood Rd ERITH DA8 149 K1
mpsfield Av THHTH CR7 196 A2
WIM/MER SW19 159 G4
nacre Cl PECK SE15 143 J4
nacre Rd CRICK NW2 81 K4
nchmere Rd LEE/GVPK SE12 165 J2
ncoln Av ROMW/RG RM7 75 F5
STHGT/OAK N14 34 C5
WHTN TW2 155 H4
WIM/MER SW19 159 G5
ncoln Cl GFD/PVL UB6 78 C6
RYLN/HDSTN HA2 59 K2
ncoln Crs EN EN1 24 A6
ncoln Dr OXHEY WD19 27 G5
ncoln Est BOW E3 105 J3
coln Gdns IL IG1 71 J4
coln Green Rd
STMC/STPC BR5 202 A2
coln Ms KIL/WHAMP NW6 82 D6
SEVS/STOTM N15 67 J1
coln Pde EFNCH N2 * 47 J6
coln Rd ALP/SUD HA0 79 K4
EFNCH N2 47 J6
EN EN1 24 A5
ERITH DA8 150 C3
FELT TW13 154 E5
FSTGT E7 89 H4
MTCM CR4 195 K2
NTHWD HA6 40 D6
NWMAL KT3 175 K6
PEND EN3 24 D6
PLSTW E13 107 F3
RYLN/HDSTN HA2 59 K2
SCUP DA14 186 C1
SNWD SE25 181 J6
SWFD E18 52 D4
WPK KT4 192 E5
coln's Inn Flds LINN WC2A 11 G3
Lincolns MLHL NW7 31 H5
coln St CHEL SW3 14 E7
WAN E11 70 C6
coln Ter BELMT SM2 * 208 E5
coln Wy EN EN1 24 D6
combe Rd BMLY BR1 165 J5
al Crs ENC/FH EN2 22 E6
Lindales TOTM N17 50 C2
al Rd BROCKY SE4 144 C6
burgh Av WLGTN SM6 210 E6
en Av EN EN1 24 C2
SLW TW3 135 G6
SLP HA4 58 E5
HHTH CR7 196 C1
BLY HA9 80 B3
LSDN NW10 100 B1
en Cl ORP BR6 217 G3
SLP HA4 58 E5
TAN HA7 43 H1
THGT/OAK N14 34 C1
HDIT KT7 190 B4
en Cots WIM/MER SW19 * 177 H2
en Crs GFD/PVL UB6 79 F4
UT/HW KT1 175 G5
FD IG8 53 F2
enfield CHST BR7 185 G5
en Gdns BAY/PAD W2 100 E6
HSWK W4 118 A5
V EN1 24 C2
Linden Gv NWMAL KT3 176 B6
PECK SE15 143 J4
SYD SE26 181 K2
TEDD TW11 174 A1
Linden Lea EFNCH N2 65 G2
PIN HA5 * 41 K3
Linden Leas WWKM BR4 199 G6
Linden Ms IS N1 85 K3
NTGHL W11 * 100 E6
Linden Pl MTCM CR4 194 D1
Linden Rd FBAR/BDGN N11 33 K4
HPTN TW12 173 F4
MUSWH N10 66 B1
The Lindens CHSWK W4 137 K2
CROY/NA CR0 214 A4
NFNCH/WDSPK N12 * 47 H1
WALTH E17 * 69 K1
Linden St ROMW/RG RM7 75 F1
Linden Wk ARCH N19 * 66 C6
Linden Wy STHGT/OAK N14 34 C1
Lindfield Gdns HAMP NW3 83 G3
Lindfield Rd CROY/NA CR0 197 G3
EA W5 97 J3
Lindfield St POP/IOD E14 105 J5
Lindhill Cl PEND EN3 25 F3
Lindisfarne Md HOM E9 87 G2
Lindisfarne Rd BCTR RM8 91 J1
RYNPK SW20 176 D3
Lindley Est PECK SE15 * 143 H1
Lindley Pl RCH/KEW TW9 137 H2
Lindley Rd LEY E10 70 A6
Lindley St WCHPL E1 104 E4
Lindore Rd BTSEA SW11 140 E5
Lindores Rd CAR SM5 194 B4
Lindo St PECK SE15 143 K3
Lind Rd SUT SM1 209 G3
Lindrop St FUL/PGN SW6 140 B3
Lindsay Cl CHSGTN KT9 206 A5
STWL/WRAY TW19 132 A6
Lindsay Dr
KTN/HRWW/WS HA3 62 A3
Lindsay Rd HPTN TW12 155 G6
WPK KT4 192 E6
Lindsay Sq PIM SW1V 121 J5
Lindsell St GNWCH SE10 145 F2
Lindsey Cl BMLY BR1 184 C6
MTCM CR4 195 K1
Lindsey Gdns
EBED/NFELT TW14 * 153 G2
Lindsey Ms IS N1 85 J5
Lindsey Rd BCTR RM8 91 J1
Lindsey St FARR EC1M 12 B1
Lind St DEPT SE8 144 E3
Lindum Rd TEDD TW11 174 D3
Lindway WNWD SE27 180 C1
Linfield Cl HDN NW4 46 A6
Linford Rd WALTH E17 52 A6
Linford St VX/NE SW8 141 H2
Lingards Rd LEW SE13 145 F5
Lingey Cl BFN/LL DA15 168 A4
Lingfield Av KUT/HW KT1 191 F1
Lingfield Cl EN EN1 36 A1
NTHWD HA6 40 C3
Lingfield Ct NTHLT UB5 * 96 A1
Lingfield Crs ELTH/MOT SE9 147 J5
Lingfield Gdns ED N9 36 D2
Lingfield Rd WIM/MER SW19 177 G2
WPK KT4 208 A1
Lingham St BRXN/ST SW9 141 K3
Lingholm Wy BAR EN5 20 B6
Ling Rd CAN/RD E16 106 E4
ERITH DA8 129 K6
Lingwell Rd TOOT SW17 160 D5
Lingwood Gdns ISLW TW7 135 K1
Lingwood Rd CLPT E5 68 C4
Linhope St CAMTN NW1 2 E6
Linkfield E/WMO/HCT KT8 173 F6
Linkfield Rd ISLW TW7 136 A3
Link La WLGTN SM6 210 D4
Linklea Cl CDALE/KGS NW9 45 G3
Link Rd DAGW RM9 110 D1
EBED/NFELT TW14 153 J2
FBAR/BDGN N11 34 A6
WLGTN SM6 195 F5
Links Av GPK RM2 57 K5
MRDN SM4 193 K1
Links Dr TRDG/WHET N20 32 E3
Links Gdns STRHM/NOR SW16 180 B3
Linkside CHIG IG7 54 C1
NFNCH/WDSPK N12 46 D2
NWMAL KT3 176 B5
Linkside Cl ENC/FH EN2 23 F4
Linkside Gdns ENC/FH EN2 23 F4
Links Rd ACT W3 98 C5
CRICK NW2 63 H6
TOOT SW17 179 F2
WFD IG8 52 E1
WWKM BR4 199 F5
Links Side ENC/FH EN2 23 F4
The Links WALTH E17 69 G1
Link St HOM E9 86 E4
Links Vw FNCH N3 46 D3
Links View Cl STAN HA7 43 G2
Linksview Ct HPTN TW12 * 155 J6
Links View Rd CROY/NA CR0 213 J1
HPTN TW12 173 H1
Links Wy NTHWD HA6 40 A4
BECK BR3 198 D3
Linksway HDN NW4 46 B5
NTHWD HA6 40 B4
Links Yd WCHPL E1 13 K1
The Link ACT W3 98 D5
ALP/SUD HA0 61 J5
CRICK NW2 63 J5
NTHLT UB5 * 77 K3
PEND EN3 25 G2
PIN HA5 59 G3
TEDD TW11 174 A2
Linkway RYNPK SW20 176 E6
BCTR RM8 91 J2
FSBYPK N4 67 J4
Link Wy HAYES BR2 200 D4
Linkway NWMAL KT3 192 E1
PIN HA5 41 H4
Link Wy RCHPK/HAM TW10 156 C4
The Linkway BAR EN5 32 E1
BELMT SM2 209 G6
Linkwood Wk CAMTN NW1 84 D5
Linley Crs ROMW/RG RM7 56 D6
Linley Rd TOTM N17 50 A5
Linnell Cl GLDGN NW11 65 F3
Linnell Dr GLDGN NW11 65 F3
Linnell Rd CMBW SE5 143 F3
UED N18 50 C1
Linnet Cl BUSH WD23 28 C3
ED N9 37 F3
THMD SE28 109 J6
Linnet Ms BAL SW12 161 F2
Linnett Cl CHING E4 38 A6
Linom Rd CLAP SW4 141 K5
Linscott Rd CLPT E5 86 E2
Linsdell Rd BARK IG11 90 C6
Linsey St BERM/RHTH SE16 123 H3
Linslade Cl HSLWW TW4 134 D6
PIN HA5 41 F6
Linslade Rd ORP BR6 217 G4
Linstead St KIL/WHAMP NW6 82 E5
Linstead Wy
WAND/EARL SW18 159 H2
Lintaine Cl HMSMTH W6 * 119 H6
Linthorpe Av ALP/SUD HA0 79 J4
Linthorpe Rd EBAR EN4 21 J4
STNW/STAM N16 68 A4
Linton Cl CAR SM5 194 E4
CHARL SE7 126 B5
WELL DA16 148 B2
Linton Ct ROM RM1 57 G5
Linton Gdns EHAM E6 107 J5
Linton Gv WNWD SE27 180 C1
Linton Rd BARK IG11 90 C5
Linton St IS N1 6 D1
Lintott Ct STWL/WRAY TW19 152 A1
Linver Rd FUL/PGN SW6 139 J3
Linwood Cl CMBW SE5 143 G3
Linwood Crs EN EN1 24 C2
Linzee Rd CEND/HSY/T N8 66 E1
Lion Av TWK TW1 156 A3
Lion Cl BROCKY SE4 164 D1
Lionel Gdns ELTH/MOT SE9 146 C6
Lionel Ms NKENS W10 * 100 C4
Lionel Rd ELTH/MOT SE9 146 C6
Lionel Rd North BTFD TW8 117 F3
Lionel Rd South BTFD TW8 117 G5
Lion Gate Gdns
RCH/KEW TW9 137 G4
Lion Gate Ms
WAND/EARL SW18 159 K2
Lion Mills BETH E2 * 104 C1
Lion Park Av CHSGTN KT9 206 C2
Lion Rd CROY/NA CR0 196 D2
ED N9 36 C4
EHAM E6 107 K4
TWK TW1 156 A3
Lions Cl LEE/GVPK SE12 166 B5
Lion Wy BTFD TW8 136 E1
Lion Wharf Rd ISLW TW7 136 C4
Liphook Cl HCH RM12 93 H2
Liphook Crs FSTH SE23 163 K2
Liphook Rd OXHEY WD19 27 H6
Lipton Rd WCHPL E1 105 F5
Lisbon Av WHTN TW2 155 H4
Lisbon Cl WALTH E17 51 H5
Lisburne Rd HAMP NW3 83 K2
Lisford St PECK SE15 143 G2
Lisgar Ter WKENS W14 119 J4
Liskeard Cl CHST BR7 185 H2
Lisle Cl TOOT SW17 161 G6
Lisle St LSQ/SEVD WC2H 10 D5
Lismore WIM/MER SW19 * 177 J1
Lismore Circ KTTN NW5 83 K3
Lismore Cl ISLW TW7 136 B3
Lismore Rd SAND/SEL CR2 212 A4
TOTM N17 49 K6
Lismore Wk IS N1 85 J4
Lissant Cl SURB KT6 190 D4
Lissenden Gdns KTTN NW5 84 A2
Lisson Gv STJWD NW8 2 B6
Lisson St CAMTN NW1 8 C1
Lister Cl ACT W3 99 F4
MTCM CR4 178 D3
Lister Gdns UED N18 49 J1
Lister Rd WAN E11 70 C5
Liston Rd CLAP SW4 141 H4
TOTM N17 50 C4
Liston Wy WFD IG8 53 G3
Listowel Cl BRXN/ST SW9 142 B1
Listowel Rd DAGE RM10 92 C1
Listria Pk STNW/STAM N16 68 A6
Litchfield Av MRDN SM4 193 J4
SRTFD E15 * 88 C4
Litchfield Gdns
WLSDN NW10 81 J4
Litchfield Rd SUT SM1 209 G2
Litchfield St LSQ/SEVD WC2H 10 D5
Litchfield Wy GLDGN NW11 65 G2
Lithgow's Rd HTHAIR TW6 133 H5
Lithos Rd HAMP NW3 83 F4
Litten Cl CRW RM5 56 C2
Little Acre BECK BR3 182 D6
Little Albany St CAMTN NW1 3 K6
Little Argyll St REGST W1B * 10 A4
Little Benty WDR/YW UB7 112 A5
Little Birches BFN/LL DA15 167 K4
The Little Boltons
WBPTN SW10 120 A5
Little Bornes DUL SE21 163 F6
Little Britain STBT EC1A 12 B2
Littlebrook Cl CROY/NA CR0 198 A3
Little Brownings FSTH SE23 163 J4
Littlebury Rd CLAP SW4 * 141 J4
Little Bury St ED N9 36 A2
Little Bushey La BUSH WD23 28 D1
Little Cedars
NFNCH/WDSPK N12 33 G6
Little Chester St KTBR SW1X 15 J4
Little Cloisters WEST SW1P 16 E4
Littlecombe Cl
PUT/ROE SW15 * 159 G1
Little Common STAN HA7 29 G5
Littlecote Cl WIM/MER SW19 159 G2
Littlecote Pl PIN HA5 41 J4
Little Cottage Pl
GNWCH SE10 * 144 E1
Little Ct WWKM BR4 199 H6
Littlecroft ELTH/MOT SE9 147 F4
Littledale ABYW SE2 128 B6
Little Deans Yd WEST SW1P 16 E4
Little Dimocks BAL SW12 161 G4
Little Dorrit Ct STHWK SE1 18 D2
Little Ealing La EA W5 116 D4
Little Edward St
CAMTN NW1 * 3 K4
Little Elms HYS/HAR UB3 133 G1
Little Essex St
TPL/STR WC2R * 11 J5
Little Ferry Rd TWK TW1 * 156 C3
Littlefield Cl ARCH N19 84 C2
KUT/HW KT1 175 F5
Littlefield Rd EDGW HA8 44 E3
Little Friday Rd CHING E4 38 C4
Little Gearies BARK/HLT IG6 72 B1
Little George St WEST SW1P 16 E3
Little Green St KTTN NW5 * 84 B2
Littlegrove EBAR EN4 33 J1
Little Heath CHARL SE7 126 D6
CHDH RM6 73 H1
Littleheath Rd SAND/SEL CR2 212 D6
Little Ilford La MNPK E12 89 K2
Littlejohn Rd HNWL W7 97 F5
STMC/STPC BR5 202 B3
Little Marlborough St
REGST W1B * 10 A4
Littlemead ESH/CLAY KT10 204 D2
Littlemede ELTH/MOT SE9 166 E5
Littlemoor Rd IL IG1 90 D1
Littlemore Rd ABYW SE2 128 B2
Little Moss La PIN HA5 41 J5
Little Newport St
LSQ/SEVD WC2H 10 D5
Little New St
FLST/FETLN EC4A 11 K3
Little Orchard Cl PIN HA5 * 41 J5
Little Oxhey La OXHEY WD19 41 J1
Little Park Dr FELT TW13 154 C4
Little Park Gdns ENC/FH EN2 23 J4
Little Pluckett's Wy BKHH IG9 39 H3
Little Portland St REGST W1B 9 K3
Little Potters BUSH WD23 28 D2
Little Queens Rd TEDD TW11 174 A2
Little Redlands BMLY BR1 184 D5
Little Rd HYS/HAR UB3 113 J2
Littlers Cl WIM/MER SW19 178 C4
Little Russell St
NOXST/BSQ WC1A 10 E2
Little St James's St
WHALL SW1A 16 A1
Little St Leonards
MORT/ESHN SW14 137 K4
Little Smith St WEST SW1P 16 D4
Little Somerset St
TWRH EC3N 13 J4
Littlestone Cl BECK BR3 182 D2
Little Strd CDALE/KGS NW9 45 H5
Little Stream Cl NTHWD HA6 40 C1
Little Thrift STMC/STPC BR5 201 H1
Little Titchfield St
GTPST W1W 10 A2
Littleton Av CHING E4 38 D3
Littleton Crs HRW HA1 61 F6
Littleton Rd HRW HA1 61 F6
Littleton St WAND/EARL SW18 160 B4
Little Trinity La BLKFR EC4V 12 D5
Little Turnstile HHOL WC1V 11 G2
Littlewood LEW SE13 145 F6
Little Wood Cl
STMC/STPC BR5 186 B4
Littlewood Cl WEA W13 116 C3
Littleworth Av
ESH/CLAY KT10 204 D3
Littleworth Common Rd
ESH/CLAY KT10 204 D1
Littleworth La ESH/CLAY KT10 204 D2
Littleworth Pl ESH/CLAY KT10 204 D2
Littleworth Rd
ESH/CLAY KT10 204 D3
Livermere Rd HACK E8 86 B6
Liverpool Gv WALW SE17 122 E5
Liverpool Rd CAN/RD E16 106 C4
EA W5 116 E2
IS N1 5 K1
KUTN/CMB KT2 175 H3
LEY E10 70 A3
THHTH CR7 180 D6
Liverpool St LVPST EC2M 13 G2
Livesey Cl KUT/HW KT1 175 G6
THMD SE28 127 H3
Livesey Pl STHWK SE1 123 H6
Livingstone Rd BTSEA SW11 140 C4
HSLW TW3 135 H5
PLMGR N13 48 E2
STHL UB1 95 H6
THHTH CR7 180 E5
WALTH E17 69 K3
Lizard St FSBYE EC1V 6 D5
Lizban St BKHTH/KID SE3 146 A1
Llanelly Rd CRICK NW2 64 D6
Llanover Rd WBLY HA9 79 K1
WOOL/PLUM SE18 147 F1
Llanthony Rd MRDN SM4 194 C3
Llanvanor Rd CRICK NW2 64 D6
Llewellyn St
BERM/RHTH SE16 123 H2
Lloyd Av STRHM/NOR SW16 179 K4
Lloyd Baker St FSBYW WC1X 5 J5
Lloyd Ct PIN HA5 59 H2
Lloyd Ms PEND EN3 25 J1
Lloyd Park Av CROY/NA CR0 212 B2
Lloyd Rd DAGW RM9 92 B4
EHAM E6 89 K6
WALTH E17 69 F1
WPK KT4 208 A1
Lloyd's Av FENCHST EC3M 13 H4
Lloyd's Pl BKHTH/KID SE3 * 145 H3
Lloyd Sq FSBYW WC1X 5 J4
Lloyd's Rw CLKNW EC1R 5 K5
Lloyd St FSBYW WC1X 5 J4
Lloyds Wy BECK BR3 198 B2
Lloyd Thomas Ct WDGN N22 * 49 F3
Lloyd Vls BROCKY SE4 144 D3
Loampit Hl LEW SE13 144 D3
Loampit V LEW SE13 144 E4
Loanda Cl HACK E8 86 B6
Loats Rd BRXS/STRHM SW2 161 K1
Locarno Rd ACT W3 117 K1
GFD/PVL UB6 96 C3
Lochaber Rd LEW SE13 145 H5
Lochaline St HMSMTH W6 119 F6
Lochan Cl YEAD UB4 95 J3
Lochinvar St BAL SW12 161 G2
Lochmere Cl ERITH DA8 129 J6
Lochnagar St POP/IOD E14 106 A4
Lock Cha BKHTH/KID SE3 145 H4
Lock Cl NWDGN UB2 115 H2
Locke Cl RAIN RM13 93 H4
Lockesfield Pl POP/IOD E14 124 E4
Lockesley Dr STMC/STPC BR5 202 A3
Lockesley Sq SURB KT6 * 190 E3
Locket Rd
KTN/HRWW/WS HA3 43 F5
Locket Road Ms
KTN/HRWW/WS HA3 42 E5
Lockfield Av PEND EN3 25 G3
Lockgate Cl HOM E9 87 H3
Lockhart Cl HOLWY N7 85 F4
PEND EN3 24 D6
Lockhart St BOW E3 105 H3
Lockhurst St CLPT E5 87 F2
Lockington Rd VX/NE SW8 141 G2
Lock Keepers Cots
TOTM N17 * 68 D1
Lockmead Rd LEW SE13 145 F4
SEVS/STOTM N15 68 C3
Lock Rd RCHPK/HAM TW10 156 D5
Lock's La MTCM CR4 179 F4
Locksley Est POP/IOD E14 105 H5
Locksley St POP/IOD E14 105 H4
Locksmeade Rd
RCHPK/HAM TW10 156 C6
Lockton St NTGHL W11 * 100 B6
Lockwell Rd DAGE RM10 92 B1
Lockwood Cl EBAR EN4 21 K5
SYD SE26 164 A6
Lockwood Pl CHING E4 51 J2
Lockwood Sq
BERM/RHTH SE16 123 J3
Lockwood Wy CHSGTN KT9 206 C3
WALTH E17 51 F5
Lockyer Cl PEND EN3 25 K1
Lockyer St STHWK SE1 19 F3
Locomotive Dr
EBED/NFELT TW14 153 K2
Locton Gn BOW E3 * 87 H6
Loddiges Rd HOM E9 86 E5
Loder St PECK SE15 143 K1
Lodge Av BCTR RM8 91 H3
CROY/NA CR0 211 F1
DAGW RM9 91 G6
GPK RM2 75 J2
KTN/HRWW/WS HA3 62 A1
Lodge Cl EDGW HA8 * 44 B2
ISLW TW7 136 C2
ORP BR6 202 C5
UED N18 49 J1
WLGTN SM6 195 F5
Lodge Ct ALP/SUD HA0 * 80 A3
Lodge Crs ORP BR6 202 C5
Lodge Dr PLMGR N13 35 G6
Lodge Gdns BECK BR3 198 C2
Lodge Hl REDBR IG4 71 J1
WELL DA16 148 C1
Lodgehill Park Cl
RYLN/HDSTN HA2 60 B6
Lodge La BXLY DA5 168 E1
CROY/NA CR0 213 K5
CRW RM5 56 C2
NFNCH/WDSPK N12 47 G1
Lodge Mansions Pde
PLMGR N13 * 35 G6
Lodge Ms HBRY N5 * 85 J2
Lodge Pl SUT SM1 209 F3
Lodge Rd BMLY BR1 184 B3
CROY/NA CR0 196 C3
HDN NW4 64 A1
STJWD NW8 2 B5
SUT SM1 209 F3
WLGTN SM6 210 B3
The Lodge SHB W12 * 119 G2
Lodge Vls WFD IG8 52 D3
Lodge Wy ASHF TW15 152 B4
Lodore Gdns CDALE/KGS NW9 63 G2
Lodore St POP/IOD E14 106 A5
Lofthouse Pl CHSGTN KT9 205 J4
Loftie St BERM/RHTH SE16 123 H2
Lofting Rd IS N1 85 G5
Loftus Rd BARK IG11 90 C4
SHB W12 118 E1
Loftus Vls SHB W12 * 118 E1
Logan Cl HSLWW TW4 134 E4
PEND EN3 25 F2
Logan Ms ECT SW5 119 K4
ROM RM1 75 G2
Logan Pl ECT SW5 119 K4
Logan Rd ED N9 36 D4
WBLY HA9 62 A6
The Logans BAR EN5 * 20 B4
Logs Hl CHST BR7 184 D4
Logs Hill Cl CHST BR7 184 D4
Lolesworth Cl WCHPL E1 13 J2
Lollard St LBTH SE11 17 H6
Loman St STHWK SE1 18 B2
Lomas Cl CROY/NA CR0 214 A5
Lomas Dr HACK E8 * 86 B5
Lombard Av GDMY/SEVK IG3 72 E5
PEND EN3 24 E2
Lombard La EMB EC4Y 11 K4
Lombard Rd BTSEA SW11 140 C3
FBAR/BDGN N11 48 B1
WIM/MER SW19 178 A5
Lombard St BANK EC3V 13 F4
Lombard Vls
FBAR/BDGN N11 * 48 B1
Lombard Wall CHARL SE7 126 A3
Lombardy Cl WFD IG8 54 B3
Lombardy Pl BAY/PAD W2 101 F6
Lomond Cl ALP/SUD HA0 80 B5
SEVS/STOTM N15 68 A1
Lomond Gdns SAND/SEL CR2 213 G5
Lomond Gv CMBW SE5 142 E1
Loncroft Rd CMBW SE5 123 F6
Londesborough Rd
STNW/STAM N16 86 A2
London Br CANST EC4R 13 F6
London Bridge St STHWK SE1 19 F1
London Bridge Wk
STHWK SE1 * 13 F7
London City Airport Link
CAN/RD E16 106 D6
Londonderry Pde
ERITH DA8 * 150 A1
London Flds HACK E8 * 86 D5

London Fields East Side
HACK E8 86 D5
London Fields West Side
HACK E8 86 C5
London La BMLY BR1 183 J3
BMLY BR1 183 K3
HACK E8 86 D5
London Loop BORE WD6 30 D1
CHING E4 38 B1
ENC/FH EN2 23 J1
HAYES BR2 199 J6
ORP BR6 201 G5
SAND/SEL CR2 212 E5
STMC/STPC BR5 201 G2
WWKM BR4 214 E1
London Ms BAY/PAD W2 8 B4
London Rd ASHF TW15 152 C4
BARK IG11 90 B5
BMLY BR1 183 H2
BUSH WD23 27 K1
CHEAM SM3 193 G6
CROY/NA CR0 196 C5
ENC/FH EN2 23 K5
EW KT17 207 H6
FSTH SE23 163 K3
HRW HA1 60 E6
ISLW TW7 135 K3
KUTN/CMB KT2 175 G5
MRDN SM4 193 K2
MTCM CR4 194 D1
PLSTW E13 106 E1
ROMW/RG RM7 74 C3
STAN HA7 29 K6
STHWK SE1 18 B4
STRHM/NOR SW16 180 A5
SWLY BR8 187 K5
THHTH CR7 196 B3
TOOT SW17 178 E3
TWK TW1 156 B2
WBLY HA9 80 A3
WLGTN SM6 210 B2
London Stile CHSWK W4 117 H5
London St BAY/PAD W2 8 A3
FENCHST EC3M * 13 H5
London Ter BETH E2 * 104 C1
London Wall CITYW EC2V 12 D2
London Wall Blds
LVPST EC2M 13 F2
Lonesome Wy MTCM CR4 179 G4
Long Acre CHCR WC2N 10 E5
ORP BR6 202 E6
Long Acre Ct WEA W13 * 97 G4
Longacre Pl CAR SM5 * 210 A4
Longacre Rd WALTH E17 52 B4
Longbeach Rd BTSEA SW11 140 E4
Longboat Rw STHL UB1 95 K5
Longbridge Rd BARK IG11 90 D4
Longbridge Wy LEW SE13 145 F6
Longbury Cl STMC/STPC BR5 186 C6
Longbury Dr STMC/STPC BR5 186 C6
Longcliffe Pth OXHEY WD19 26 E5
Long Ct PUR RM19 131 K4
Longcroft ELTH/MOT SE9 167 F5
Long Cft OXHEY WD19 27 F2
Longcrofte Rd EDGW HA8 43 K3
Long Deacon Rd CHING E4 38 C3
Longdon Wd HAYES BR2 215 J2
Longdown Rd CAT SE6 164 D6
Long Dr ACT W3 99 G5
GFD/PVL UB6 78 B6
RSLP HA4 77 G2
WDR/YW UB7 * 112 B2
Long Elmes
KTN/HRWW/WS HA3 42 B4
Longfellow Rd WALTH E17 69 H3
WCHPL E1 * 105 G2
WPK KT4 192 D5
Longfellow Wy STHWK SE1 * 19 K7
Longfield BMLY BR1 183 J4
Long Fld CDALE/KGS NW9 45 G3
Longfield Av EA W5 97 J6
EMPK RM11 75 H4
MLHL NW7 45 J3
WALTH E17 69 G1
WBLY HA9 62 A5
WLGTN SM6 195 F5
Longfield Crs SYD SE26 163 K5
Longfield Dr
MORT/ESHN SW14 137 J6
MTCM CR4 178 D4
Longfield Est STHWK SE1 19 K6
Longfield Rd EA W5 97 J5
Longfield St
WAND/EARL SW18 159 K2
Longford Av
EBED/NFELT TW14 153 H1
STHL UB1 96 A6
STWL/WRAY TW19 152 B3
Longford Cl FELT TW13 154 D5
HPTN TW12 155 F6
YEAD UB4 95 H6
Longford Ct HOR/WEW KT19 206 E2
HPTN TW12 173 G2
Longford Gdns SUT SM1 209 G1
YEAD UB4 95 H6
Longford Rd WHTN TW2 155 F3
Longford St CAMTN NW1 3 K6
Longford Wy
STWL/WRAY TW19 152 B3
Longhayes Av CHDH RM6 55 K6
Longheath Gdns
CROY/NA CR0 197 K2
Longhedge St BTSEA SW11 141 F3
Longhill Rd CAT SE6 165 G4
Longhook Gdns NTHLT UB5 94 E1
Longhurst Rd CROY/NA CR0 197 J3
LEW SE13 145 H6
Longland Dr TRDG/WHET N20 33 F5
Longlands Park Crs
BFN/LL DA15 167 K5
Longlands Rd BFN/LL DA15 167 K5
BFN/LL DA15 168 A4
Long La CROY/NA CR0 197 K3
FNCH N3 47 F4
STBT EC1A 12 B1
STHWK SE1 19 F3
STWL/WRAY TW19 152 C3
Longleat Rd EN EN1 24 A6
Longleat Wy
EBED/NFELT TW14 153 F2
Longley Av ALP/SUD HA0 80 B6
Longley Rd CROY/NA CR0 196 C4
HRW HA1 60 D2
TOOT SW17 178 D2
Long Leys CHING E4 51 K2
Longley St STHWK SE1 123 H4
Longley Wy CRICK NW2 82 A1
Longmans Cl WATW WD18 26 A1
Long Mark Rd CAN/RD E16 107 H5
Longmarsh La THMD SE28 127 K1
Long Md CDALE/KGS NW9 45 H4
Longmead CHST BR7 185 F5
Longmead Dr SCUP DA14 168 E4
Long Meadow KTTN NW5 * 84 D4
Long Meadow Cl WWKM BR4 199 F4
Longmeadow Rd
BFN/LL DA15 167 K3
Longmead Rd HYS/HAR UB3 94 D6
THDIT KT7 189 K4
TOOT SW17 178 E1
Longmoore St PIM SW1V 16 A7
Longmore Av BAR EN5 33 G1
Longnor Rd WCHPL E1 105 F2
Long Pond Rd
BKHTH/KID SE3 145 H2
Longport Cl BARK/HLT IG6 55 G2
Long Reach Rd BARK IG11 109 F3
Longreach Rd ERITH DA8 150 E1
Longridge La STHL UB1 96 B6
Longridge Rd ECT SW5 119 K4
Long Rd CLAP SW4 141 H5
Longshaw Rd CHING E4 38 B5
Longshore DEPT SE8 124 C4
Longstaff Crs
WAND/EARL SW18 159 K1
Longstaff Rd
WAND/EARL SW18 159 K1
Longstone Av WLSDN NW10 81 H5
Longstone Rd TOOT SW17 179 G1
Long St BETH E2 7 J3
Longthornton Rd
STRHM/NOR SW16 179 H5
Longton Av SYD SE26 163 H6
Longton Gv SYD SE26 163 J6
Longview Wy CRW RM5 57 F4
Longville Rd LBTH SE11 18 A6
Long Wk NWMAL KT3 175 K6
STHWK SE1 19 H4
WOOL/PLUM SE18 127 G6
Longwalk Rd STKPK UB11 112 E1
Longwood Ct WPK KT4 192 D6
Longwood Dr PUT/ROE SW15 158 D1
Longwood Gdns CLAY IG5 71 K1
Longworth Cl THMD SE28 109 K5
Long Yd BMSBY WC1N 5 G7
The Loning CDALE/KGS NW9 63 H1
PEND EN3 24 E1
Lonsdale Av EHAM E6 107 H3
ROMW/RG RM7 74 E3
WBLY HA9 80 A3
Lonsdale Cl EHAM E6 107 J3
ELTH/MOT SE9 166 C5
UX/CGN UB8 94 A5
Lonsdale Crs
GNTH/NBYPK IG2 72 B3
Lonsdale Dr ENC/FH EN2 22 D5
Lonsdale Dr North
ENC/FH EN2 22 E6
Lonsdale Gdns THHTH CR7 196 A1
Lonsdale Ms NTGHL W11 100 D5
RCH/KEW TW9 * 137 H2
Lonsdale Pl IS N1 85 G5
Lonsdale Rd BARN SW13 138 C1
CHSWK W4 118 C4
KIL/WHAMP NW6 82 D6
NTGHL W11 100 D5
NWDGN UB2 114 C3
SNWD SE25 197 J1
WAN E11 70 D4
Lonsdale Sq IS N1 * 85 G5
Loobert Rd SEVS/STOTM N15 50 A6
Looe Gdns BARK/HLT IG6 54 B6
Loop Rd CHST BR7 185 H2
Lopen Rd UED N18 36 A6
Loraine Cl PEND EN3 24 E6
Loraine Cots HOLWY N7 * 85 F2
Loraine Rd CHSWK W4 117 J6
HOLWY N7 85 F2
Lord Av CLAY IG5 71 K1
Lord Chancellor Wk
KUTN/CMB KT2 175 K4
Lord Hills Rd BAY/PAD W2 101 F4
Lord Holland La
BRXN/ST SW9 * 142 B3
Lord Knyvett Cl
STWL/WRAY TW19 152 A1
Lord Knyvetts Ct
STWL/WRAY TW19 * 152 B1
Lord Napier Pl HMSMTH W6 118 D5
Lord North St WEST SW1P 16 E5
Lord Roberts Ms
FUL/PGN SW6 * 140 A1
Lords Cl DUL SE21 162 D4
FELT TW13 154 D4
Lordship Gv STNW/STAM N16 67 K6
Lordship La EDUL SE22 163 G1
WDGN N22 49 G5
Lordship Pk STNW/STAM N16 67 K6
Lordship Park Ms
STNW/STAM N16 67 J6
Lordship Pl CHEL SW3 120 D6
Lordship Rd NTHLT UB5 77 J5
STNW/STAM N16 67 K5
Lordship Ter STNW/STAM N16 67 K6
Lordsmead Rd TOTM N17 50 A4
Lord St CAN/RD E16 126 D1
Lords Vw STJWD NW8 2 C4
Lord Warwick St
WOOL/PLUM SE18 126 E3
Lorenzo St FSBYW WC1X 5 G4
Loretto Gdns
KTN/HRWW/WS HA3 62 A1
Lorian Cl NFNCH/WDSPK N12 33 F6
Loring Rd ISLW TW7 136 A3
TRDG/WHET N20 33 J4
Loris Rd HMSMTH W6 119 F3
Lorne Av CROY/NA CR0 198 A4
Lorne Cl STJWD NW8 2 D5
Lorne Gdns CROY/NA CR0 198 A4
NTGHL W11 119 G2
WAN E11 71 G1
Lorne Rd FSBYPK N4 67 F5
FSTGT E7 89 F2
KTN/HRWW/WS HA3 43 F5
RCHPK/HAM TW10 137 G6
WALTH E17 69 J2
Lorne Ter FNCH N3 * 46 D5
Lorn Rd BRXN/ST SW9 142 A3
Lorraine Pk
KTN/HRWW/WS HA3 42 E3
Lorrimore Rd WALW SE17 122 C6
Lorrimore Sq WALW SE17 122 C6
Loseberry Rd ESH/CLAY KT10 204 D3
Lothair Rd EA W5 116 E2
Lothair Rd North FSBYPK N4 67 H3
Lothair Rd South FSBYPK N4 67 G4
Lothbury LOTH EC2R 12 E3
Lothian Av YEAD UB4 95 F4
Lothian Cl ALP/SUD HA0 79 G2
Lothian Rd BRXN/ST SW9 142 C1
Lothrop St NKENS W10 100 C2
Lots Rd WBPTN SW10 140 B1
Loubet St TOOT SW17 178 E2
Loudoun Av BARK/HLT IG6 72 B2
Loudoun Rd STJWD NW8 83 G6
Loughborough Pk
BRXN/ST SW9 142 C5
Loughborough Rd
BRXN/ST SW9 142 B3
Loughborough St LBTH SE11 122 A5
Lough Rd HOLWY N7 85 F3
Loughton Wy BKHH IG9 39 H3
Louisa Cl HOM E9 86 E5
Louisa St WCHPL E1 105 F4
Louis Cl CHST BR7 166 E6
Louise Bennett Cl
HNHL SE24 * 142 C5
Louise Gdns RAIN RM13 111 G2
Louise Rd SRTFD E15 88 C4
Louisville Rd TOOT SW17 161 F5
Louvaine Rd BTSEA SW11 140 C5
Lovage Ap EHAM E6 107 J4
Lovat Cl CRICK NW2 81 H1
Lovat La FENCHST EC3M 13 G5
Lovatt Cl EDGW HA8 44 D2
Loveday Rd WEA W13 116 C1
Lovegrove St STHWK SE1 123 H5
Lovegrove Wk POP/IOD E14 125 F1
Lovekyn Cl KUTN/CMB KT2 175 F5
Lovelace Av HAYES BR2 201 F3
Lovelace Gdns BARK IG11 91 G2
SURB KT6 190 E4
Lovelace Gn ELTH/MOT SE9 146 E4
Lovelace Rd DUL SE21 162 D4
EBAR EN4 33 J2
SURB KT6 190 D4
Lovelace Vls THDIT KT7 * 190 C4
Love La BXLY DA5 169 H1
CHEAM SM3 208 C4
CITYW EC2V 12 D3
MRDN SM4 193 K4
MTCM CR4 178 D6
PIN HA5 41 J6
SNWD SE25 181 J6
SURB KT6 190 E6
TOTM N17 50 B3
WFD IG8 53 K2
WOOL/PLUM SE18 127 F4
Lovel Av WELL DA16 148 B3
Lovelinch Cl PECK SE15 123 K6
Lovell Pl BERM/RHTH SE16 124 B3
Lovell Rd RCHPK/HAM TW10 156 D5
STHL UB1 96 B5
Lovell Wk RAIN RM13 93 J4
Loveridge Ms
KIL/WHAMP NW6 82 D4
Loveridge Rd
KIL/WHAMP NW6 82 D4
Lovett Dr CAR SM5 194 B4
Lovetts Pl WAND/EARL SW18 140 B5
Lovett Wy WLSDN NW10 80 E3
Love Wk CMBW SE5 142 E3
Lovibonds Av ORP BR6 216 B1
Lowbrook Rd IL IG1 90 B2
Lowden Rd ED N9 36 D3
HNHL SE24 142 C5
STHL UB1 95 J6
Lowe Av CAN/RD E16 106 E4
Lowe Cl CHIG IG7 55 G1
Lowell St POP/IOD E14 105 G5
Lowen Rd RAIN RM13 111 F1
Lower Addiscombe Rd
CROY/NA CR0 196 E5
Lower Addison Gdns
WKENS W14 119 H2
Lower Bedfords Rd
ROM RM1 57 J2
Lower Belgrave St
BGVA SW1W 15 J5
Lower Broad St DAGE RM10 92 C6
Lower Camden CHST BR7 184 E4
Lower Church St
CROY/NA CR0 * 196 C6
Lower Clapton Rd HACK E8 86 D3
Lower Clarendon Wk
NTGHL W11 100 C5
Lower Common South
PUT/ROE SW15 138 E4
Lower Coombe St
CROY/NA CR0 211 J2
Lower Downs Rd
RYNPK SW20 177 G4
Lower Gravel Rd HAYES BR2 200 D5
Lower Green Gdns WPK KT4 192 D5
Lower Green Rd
ESH/CLAY KT10 189 G6
Lower Gn West MTCM CR4 178 D6
Lower Grosvenor Pl
BGVA SW1W 15 J4
Lower Grove Rd
RCHPK/HAM TW10 157 G1
Lower Hall La CHING E4 51 G1
Lower Hampton Rd
SUN TW16 172 C5
Lower Ham Rd
KUTN/CMB KT2 174 E2
Lower James St
SOHO/CST W1F * 10 B5
Lower John St
SOHO/CST W1F 10 B5
Lower Kenwood Av
ENC/FH EN2 22 E6
Lower Kings Rd
KUTN/CMB KT2 175 F3
Lower Lea Crossing
POP/IOD E14 106 C6
Lower Maidstone Rd
FBAR/BDGN N11 48 C2
Lower Mardyke Av
RAIN RM13 110 E1
Lower Marsh STHWK SE1 17 J3
Lower Marsh La BRYLDS KT5 191 G1
Lower Merton Ri HAMP NW3 83 J5
Lower Morden La MRDN SM4 193 F3
Lower Mortlake Rd
RCH/KEW TW9 137 F5
Lower Paddock Rd
OXHEY WD19 27 J1
Lower Park Rd BELV DA17 129 H3
FBAR/BDGN N11 48 C1
Lower Queen's Rd BKHH IG9 39 J4
Lower Richmond Rd
PUT/ROE SW15 139 F4
RCH/KEW TW9 137 H4
Lower Rd BELV DA17 129 J3
BERM/RHTH SE16 123 K2
RYLN/HDSTN HA2 60 D6
STMC/STPC BR5 202 C3
SUT SM1 209 H3
Lower Robert St CHCR WC2N 11 F6
Lower Sand Hills SURB KT6 190 D4
Lower Sloane St BGVA SW1W 15 F7
Lower Strd CDALE/KGS NW9 45 H5
Lower Sunbury Rd
E/WMO/HCT KT8 172 E5
Lower Tail OXHEY WD19 27 J5
Lower Teddington Rd
KUT/HW KT1 174 E4
Lower Ter HAMP NW3 83 G1
Lower Thames St MON EC3R 13 G6
Lower Tub BUSH WD23 28 D2
Lower Wood Rd
ESH/CLAY KT10 205 G4
Loweswater Cl WBLY HA9 61 K6
The Lowe CHIG IG7 55 G1
Lowfield Rd ACT W3 98 E5
KIL/WHAMP NW6 82 E5
Low Hall Cl CHING E4 37 J2
Low Hall La WALTH E17 69 G3
Lowick Rd HRW HA1 60 E1
Lowland Gdns
ROMW/RG RM7 74 D3
Lowlands Dr
STWL/WRAY TW19 132 A6
Lowlands Rd HRW HA1 60 E4
PIN HA5 59 G4
Lowman Rd HOLWY N7 85 F2
Lowndes Cl KTBR SW1X 15 H5
Lowndes Ct SOHO/CST W1F * 10 A4
Lowndes Ms
STRHM/NOR SW16 161 K4
Lowndes Pl KTBR SW1X * 15 G5
Lowndes Sq KTBR SW1X 15 F3
Lowndes St KTBR SW1X 15 F4
Lowood St WCHPL E1 104 D6
Lowry Cl ERITH DA8 130 A4
Lowry Crs MTCM CR4 178 D5
Lowry Rd BCTR RM8 91 H3
Lowshoe La CRW RM5 56 D4
Lowson Gv OXHEY WD19 27 J2
Lowswood Cl NTHWD HA6 40 A4
Lowther Dr ENC/FH EN2 22 E5
Lowther Hl FSTH SE23 164 B2
Lowther Man BARN SW13 * 138 D2
Lowther Rd BARN SW13 138 C2
HOLWY N7 * 85 G3
KUTN/CMB KT2 175 G4
STAN HA7 44 B6
WALTH E17 51 G5
Lowth Rd CMBW SE5 142 D3
Loxford Av EHAM E6 107 H1
Loxford La IL IG1 90 C3
Loxford Rd BARK IG11 90 B4
Loxham Rd CHING E4 51 K3
Loxham St STPAN WC1H * 5 F5
Loxley Cl SYD SE26 182 A1
Loxley Rd HPTN TW12 154 E6
WAND/EARL SW18 160 C3
Loxton Rd FSTH SE23 164 A3
Loxwood Cl
EBED/NFELT TW14 153 G3
STMC/STPC BR5 202 E6
Loxwood Rd TOTM N17 50 A6
Lubbock Rd CHST BR7 185 F4
Lubbock St NWCR SE14 143 K1
Lucan Pl CHEL SW3 14 C7
Lucan Rd BAR EN5 20 C4
Lucas Av PLSTW E13 89 F6
RYLN/HDSTN HA2 60 A6
Lucas Gdns EFNCH N2 47 G5
Lucas Rd PGE/AN SE20 181 K2
Lucas Sq GLDGN NW11 64 E3
Lucas St BROCKY SE4 144 D3
Lucerne Cl PLMGR N13 34 E5
Lucerne Gv WALTH E17 70 B1
Lucerne Rd HBRY N5 85 H2
ORP BR6 202 A5
THHTH CR7 196 C2
Lucey Rd BERM/RHTH SE16 123 H3
Lucey Wy BERM/RHTH SE16 123 H3
Lucien Rd TOOT SW17 161 F6
WIM/MER SW19 160 A4
Lucknow St
WOOL/PLUM SE18 147 K1
Lucorn Cl LEE/GVPK SE12 165 J1
Luctons Av BKHH IG9 39 G3
Ludford Cl CROY/NA CR0 211 H2
Ludgate Broadway
BLKFR EC4V * 12 B4
Ludgate Circ STP EC4M 12 A4
Ludgate Hl STP EC4M 12 A4
Ludgate Sq STP EC4M * 12 B4
Ludham Cl BARK/HLT IG6 54 C4
THMD SE28 109 J5
Ludlow Cl HAYES BR2 * 183 K6
RYLN/HDSTN HA2 77 K2
Ludlow Md OXHEY WD19 27 F5
Ludlow Rd EA W5 97 J3
FELT TW13 153 K5
Ludlow St FSBYE EC1V * 6 C6
Ludlow Wy EFNCH N2 65 G1
Ludovick Wk PUT/ROE SW15 138 B5
Luffield Rd ABYW SE2 128 C3
Luffman Rd LEE/GVPK SE12 166 A5
Lugard Rd PECK SE15 143 J3
Lugg Ap MNPK E12 90 A1
Luke St SDTCH EC2A 7 G6
Lukin Crs CHING E4 38 B5
Lukin St WCHPL E1 104 E5
Lullingstone Cl
STMC/STPC BR5 186 C3
Lullingstone Crs
STMC/STPC BR5 186 B3
Lullingstone La LEW SE13 165 G1
Lullingstone Rd BELV DA17 129 G6
Lullington Garth BMLY BR1 183 H3
NFNCH/WDSPK N12 46 D1
Lullington Rd DAGW RM9 92 A5
PGE/AN SE20 181 H3
Lulot Gdns ARCH N19 66 B6
Lulworth Av HEST TW5 135 G2
WBLY HA9 61 J4
Lulworth Cl RYLN/HDSTN HA2 77 K1
Lulworth Crs MTCM CR4 178 D5
Lulworth Dr CRW RM5 56 D1
PIN HA5 59 H4
Lulworth Gdns
RYLN/HDSTN HA2 59 J6
Lulworth Rd ELTH/MOT SE9 166 D4
PECK SE15 * 143 J3
WELL DA16 148 A3
Lulworth Waye YEAD UB4 95 F5
Lumen Rd WBLY HA9 61 K6
Lumley Cl BELV DA17 129 H6
Lumley Flats BGVA SW1W * 121 F5
Lumley Gdns CHEAM SM3 208 C3
Lumley Rd CHEAM SM3 208 C4
Lumley St OXSTW W1C 9 H4
Luna Rd THHTH CR7 180 D6
Lundin Wk OXHEY WD19 * 27 H6
Lundy Dr HYS/HAR UB3 113 H4
Lundy Wk IS N1 85 J4
Lunham Rd NRWD SE19 181 F2
Lupin Cl BRXS/STRHM SW2 162 C4
CROY/NA CR0 198 A5
ROMW/RG RM7 75 F6
WDR/YW UB7 112 A5
Lupton Cl LEE/GVPK SE12 166 A6
Lupton St KTTN NW5 84 C2
Lupus St PIM SW1V 121 G5
Lurgan Av HMSMTH W6 119 G6
Lurline Gdns BTSEA SW11 141 F2
Luscombe Wy VX/NE SW8 141 K1
Lushington Rd CAT SE6 182 E
WLSDN NW10 99 K
Lushington Ter HACK E8 * 86 C
Luther Cl EDGW HA8 30 E
Luther King Cl WALTH E17 69 G
Luther Ms TEDD TW11 174 A
Luther Rd TEDD TW11 174 A
Luton Pl GNWCH SE10 145 F
Luton Rd PLSTW E13 106 E
SCUP DA14 168 D
WALTH E17 51 G
Luton St STJWD NW8 2 B
Luttrell Av PUT/ROE SW15 138 E
Lutwyche Rd FSTH SE23 164 C
Luxborough La CHIG IG7 39 K
Luxborough St MHST W1U 9 G
Luxembourg Ms SRTFD E15 88 C
Luxemburg Gdns
HMSMTH W6 119 C
Luxfield Rd ELTH/MOT SE9 166 D
Luxford St BERM/RHTH SE16 124 A
Luxmore St BROCKY SE4 144 C
Luxor St CMBW SE5 142 D
Lyall Av DUL SE21 163
Lyall Ms KTBR SW1X 15
Lyall Ms West KTBR SW1X * 15
Lyall St KTBR SW1X 15
Lyal Rd BOW E3 105
Lycett Pl SHB W12 118
Lych Gate Rd ORP BR6 202
Lych Gate Wk HYS/HAR UB3 94
Lyconby Gdns CROY/NA CR0 198
Lydd Cl BFN/LL DA15 167
Lydden Gv WAND/EARL SW18 160
Lydden Rd WAND/EARL SW18 160
Lydeard Rd EHAM E6 89
Lydford Cl STNW/STAM N16 86
Lydford Rd CRICK NW2 82
MV/WKIL W9 100
SEVS/STOTM N15 67
Lydhurst Av
BRXS/STRHM SW2 162
Lydia Rd ERITH DA8 130
Lydney Cl WIM/MER SW19 159
Lydon Rd CLAP SW4 141
Lydstep Rd CHST BR7 167
Lyford Rd WAND/EARL SW18 160
Lyford St WOOL/PLUM SE18 126
Lygon Pl BGVA SW1W * 15
Lyham Cl BRXS/STRHM SW2 161
Lyham Rd BRXS/STRHM SW2 161
Lyle Cl MTCM CR4 195
Lyme Gv HOM E9 86
Lymer Av NRWD SE19 181
Lyme Rd WELL DA16 148
Lymescote Gdns SUT SM1 193
Lyme St CAMTN NW1 84
Lyme Ter CAMTN NW1 84
Lyminge Cl SCUP DA14 168
Lyminge Gdns
WAND/EARL SW18 160
Lymington Av WDGN N22 49
Lymington Cl
STRHM/NOR SW16 179
Lymington Dr RSLP HA4 58
Lymington Gdns
HOR/WEW KT19 207
Lymington Rd BCTR RM8 73
KIL/WHAMP NW6 * 83
Lyminster Cl YEAD UB4 95
Lympstone Gdns PECK SE15 143
Lynbridge Gdns PLMGR N13 35
Lynbrook Cl RAIN RM13 111
Lynbrook Gv PECK SE15 143
Lynchen Cl HEST TW5 133
Lyncourt BKHTH/KID SE3 * 145
Lyncroft Av PIN HA5 59

Lyncroft Gdns EW KT17 207 H6
HSLW TW3 135 H6
KIL/WHAMP NW6 82 E3
WEA W13 116 D2
Lyndale CRICK NW2 82 D1
THDIT KT7 * 189 K4
Lyndale Av CRICK NW2 82 D1
Lyndale Cl BKHTH/KID SE3 125 J6
Lyndale Hampton Court Wy
ESH/CLAY KT10 189 K4
Lynden Wy SWLY BR8 187 K6
Lyndhurst Av BRYLDS KT5 191 J5
MLHL NW7 45 G2
NFNCH/WDSPK N12 47 K2
PIN HA5 41 F4
STHL UB1 115 G1
STRHM/NOR SW16 179 J5
WHTN TW2 154 E3
Lyndhurst Cl CROY/NA CR0 212 B1
ORP BR6 216 B2
WLSDN NW10 81 F1
Lyndhurst Ct BELMT SM2 * 208 E5
Lyndhurst Dr LEY E10 70 A4
NWMAL KT3 192 B3
Lyndhurst Gdns BARK IG11 90 E4
EN EN1 24 A5
FNCH N3 46 C4
GNTH/NBYPK IG2 72 D3
HAMP NW3 83 H3
PIN HA5 41 F4
Lyndhurst Gv CMBW SE5 143 F3
Lyndhurst Leys HAYES BR2 * 183 G5
Lyndhurst Prior SNWD SE25 * 181 F6
Lyndhurst Rd CHING E4 52 A3
GFD/PVL UB6 96 B3
HAMP NW3 83 H3
THHTH CR7 196 B1
UED N18 36 C6
WDGN N22 49 G2
Lyndhurst Sq PECK SE15 143 G2
Lyndhurst Ter HAMP NW3 83 H3
Lyndhurst Wy BELMT SM2 208 E6
PECK SE15 143 G2
Lyndon Av BFN/LL DA15 148 A6
PIN HA5 41 J2
WLGTN SM6 210 A1
Lyndon Rd BELV DA17 129 H4
Lyndon Yd TOOT SW17 160 A6
Lyne Crs WALTH E17 51 H4
Lyneham Wk CLPT E5 * 87 G3
Lynette Av CLAP SW4 161 G1
Lynford Cl EDGW HA8 44 E4
Lynford Gdns EDGW HA8 30 D5
GDMY/SEVK IG3 73 F6
Lynford Ter ED N9 * 36 B3
Lynhurst Crs HGDN/ICK UB10 76 A5
Lynhurst Rd HGDN/ICK UB10 76 A5
Lynmere Rd WELL DA16 148 C3
Lyn Ms STNW/STAM N16 * 86 B2
Lynmouth Av EN EN1 36 B1
MRDN SM4 193 G4
Lynmouth Dr RSLP HA4 59 F6
Lynmouth Gdns GFD/PVL UB6 79 H6
HEST TW5 134 C2
Lynmouth Ri STMC/STPC BR5 202 C1
Lynmouth Rd EFNCH N2 47 K6
GFD/PVL UB6 79 H6
STNW/STAM N16 68 B5
WALTH E17 69 G3
Lynn Cl KTN/HRWW/WS HA3 42 D5
Lynne Cl ORP BR6 217 F4
Lynnett Rd BCTR RM8 73 K6
Lynne Wk ESH/CLAY KT10 204 C3
Lynne Wy NTHLT UB5 95 H1
Lynn Ms WAN E11 70 C6
Lynn Rd BAL SW12 161 G2
GNTH/NBYPK IG2 72 D4
WAN E11 70 C6
Lynn St ENC/FH EN2 23 K2
Lynscott Wy SAND/SEL CR2 211 H6
Lynstead Cl BMLY BR1 184 B5
Lynsted Ct BECK BR3 182 B5
Lynsted Gdns ELTH/MOT SE9 146 C5
Lynton Av CDALE/KGS NW9 63 H1
NFNCH/WDSPK N12 33 H6
ROMW/RG RM7 56 D4
STMC/STPC BR5 202 C1
WEA W13 97 G5
Lynton Cl CHSGTN KT9 206 A2
ISLW TW7 136 A5
WLSDN NW10 81 G3
Lynton Crs GNTH/NBYPK IG2 72 B3
Lynton Est STHWK SE1 19 K7
Lynton Gdns EN EN1 36 A2
FBAR/BDGN N11 48 D2
Lynton Md TRDG/WHET N20 32 E5
Lynton Rd ACT W3 98 C6
CEND/HSY/T N8 66 D2
CHING E4 51 K1
CROY/NA CR0 196 B3
KIL/WHAMP NW6 82 D6
NWMAL KT3 192 A2
RYLN/HDSTN HA2 59 J6
STHWK SE1 19 K7
Lynton Ter ACT W3 * 98 E5
Lynwood Cl CRW RM5 56 D2
RYLN/HDSTN HA2 77 J1
SWFD E18 53 G4
Lynwood Dr CRW RM5 56 D2
NTHWD HA6 40 C4
WPK KT4 192 D6
Lynwood Gdns CROY/NA CR0 211 F2
STHL UB1 95 K5
Lynwood Gv ORP BR6 201 K4
WCHMH N21 35 G3
Lynwood Rd EA W5 97 K2
THDIT KT7 190 A6
TOOT SW17 160 E5
Lynwood Ter
WIM/MER SW19 * 177 J4
Lyon Meade STAN HA7 43 J4
Lyon Park Av ALP/SUD HA0 80 A4
Lyon Rd HRW HA1 61 F3
ROM RM1 75 H4
WIM/MER SW19 178 B4
WOT/HER KT12 188 D6
Lyonsdown Av BAR EN5 33 G1
Lyonsdown Rd BAR EN5 21 G6
Lyons Pl STJWD NW8 2 A7
Lyon St IS N1 85 F5
Lyons Wk WKENS W14 119 H4
Lyon Wy GFD/PVL UB6 78 E6
Lyoth Rd STMC/STPC BR5 201 H6
Lyric Dr GFD/PVL UB6 96 B3
Lyric Ms SYD SE26 163 K6
Lyric Rd BARN SW13 138 C2
Lysander CDALE/KGS NW9 * 45 H4
Lysander Gdns SURB KT6 191 G3
Lysander Gv ARCH N19 66 D5
Lysander Ms ARCH N19 * 66 E5
Lysander Rd CROY/NA CR0 211 F4
RSLP HA4 58 B6
Lysander Wy ORP BR6 216 C1
Lysias Rd BAL SW12 161 F1
Lysia St FUL/PGN SW6 139 G1
Lysons Wk PUT/ROE SW15 * 138 D6
Lytchet Rd BMLY BR1 183 K3
Lytchet Wy PEND EN3 24 E2
Lytchgate Cl SAND/SEL CR2 212 A5
Lytcott Dr E/WMO/HCT KT8 172 E6
Lytcott Gv EDUL SE22 143 G6
Lytham Av OXHEY WD19 41 H1
Lytham Cl THMD SE28 110 A5
Lytham St WALW SE17 122 E5
Lyttelton Rd EFNCH N2 65 G2
LEY E10 87 K1
Lyttleton Cl HAMP NW3 83 J5
Lyttleton Rd
CEND/HSY/T N8 * 49 G6
Lytton Av PEND EN3 25 G1
PLMGR N13 35 G4
Lytton Cl EFNCH N2 65 H2
NTHLT UB5 77 K5
Lytton Gdns WLGTN SM6 210 D2
Lytton Gv PUT/ROE SW15 139 G6
Lytton Rd BAR EN5 21 G5
GPK RM2 75 K2
PIN HA5 41 J3
WAN E11 70 C4
Lyveden Rd BKHTH/KID SE3 146 A1
TOOT SW17 178 D2

M

Maberley Crs NRWD SE19 181 H3
Maberley Rd BECK BR3 182 A6
NRWD SE19 181 G4
Mabledon Pl CAMTN NW1 4 D5
Mablethorpe Rd
FUL/PGN SW6 139 H1
Mabley St HOM E9 87 G3
Macaret Cl TRDG/WHET N20 33 F2
Macarthur Cl FSTGT E7 88 E4
WBLY HA9 80 D4
Macarthur Ter CHARL SE7 * 126 C6
Macaulay Av ESH/CLAY KT10 189 K6
Macaulay Rd CLAP SW4 141 G4
EHAM E6 107 H1
Macbean St
WOOL/PLUM SE18 127 F3
Macbeth St HMSMTH W6 118 E5
Macclesfield Br STJWD NW8 2 D2
Macclesfield Rd FSBYE EC1V 6 C4
SNWD SE25 197 J2
Macclesfield St
SOHO/SHAV W1D * 10 D5
Macdonald Av DAGE RM10 92 D1
Macdonald Rd ARCH N19 66 C6
FBAR/BDGN N11 47 K1
FSTGT E7 88 E2
WALTH E17 52 A5
Macduff Rd BTSEA SW11 141 F2
Mace Cl WAP E1W 123 J1
Mace St BETH E2 105 F1
Macfarlane La ISLW TW7 116 A6
Macfarlane Rd SHB W12 119 F1
Mac Farren Pl CAMTN NW1 3 H7
Macgregor Rd CAN/RD E16 107 G4
Machell Rd PECK SE15 143 K4
Mackay Rd VX/NE SW8 141 G4
Mackennal St STJWD NW8 2 D3
Mackenzie Cl SHB W12 99 K6
Mackenzie Rd BECK BR3 182 A5
HOLWY N7 85 F4
Mackeson Rd HAMP NW3 * 83 K2
Mackie Rd BRXS/STRHM SW2 162 B2
Mackintosh La HOM E9 87 F3
Macklin St HOL/ALD WC2B * 11 F3
Macks Rd BERM/RHTH SE16 123 H3
Mackworth St CAMTN NW1 4 A4
Maclean Rd FSTH SE23 164 B1
Macleod House CHARL SE7 * 146 D1
Macleod Rd WCHMH N21 22 E6
Macleod St WALW SE17 122 D5
Maclise Rd WKENS W14 119 H3
Macmillan Wy TOOT SW17 161 G6
Macoma Rd
WOOL/PLUM SE18 127 J6
Macoma Ter
WOOL/PLUM SE18 127 J6
Maconochies Rd
POP/IOD E14 * 124 E5
Macquarie Wy POP/IOD E14 124 E4
Macroom Rd MV/WKIL W9 100 D2
Mada Rd ORP BR6 216 B1
Maddams St BOW E3 105 K3
Maddison Cl EFNCH N2 47 G5
TEDD TW11 174 A2
Maddocks Cl SCUP DA14 186 E2
Maddock Wy WALW SE17 122 C6
Maddox St CONDST W1S 9 K5
Madeira Av BMLY BR1 183 H4
Madeira Gv WFD IG8 53 G2
Madeira Rd MTCM CR4 194 E1
PLMGR N13 35 H6
STRHM/NOR SW16 179 K1
WAN E11 70 B5
Madeleine Ct CHDH RM6 73 J3
CHIG IG7 54 E1
Madeley Rd EA W5 97 K6
Madeline Gv IL IG1 90 D3
Madeline Rd PGE/AN SE20 181 H3
Madge Gill Wy EHAM E6 89 J6
Madge Hl HNWL W7 * 96 E6
Madinah Rd HACK E8 86 C3
Madison Cl BELMT SM2 209 H5
Madison Crs BXLYHN DA7 148 D1
Madison Gdns BXLYHN DA7 148 D1
Madras Pl HOLWY N7 85 G4
Madras Rd IL IG1 90 B2
Madrid Rd BARN SW13 138 D1
Madron St WALW SE17 123 F5
Mafeking Av BTFD TW8 117 F6
EHAM E6 107 H1
GNTH/NBYPK IG2 72 D4
Mafeking Rd CAN/RD E16 106 D3
EN EN1 24 B4
TOTM N17 50 C5
Magazine Ga BAY/PAD W2 * 8 D7
Magdala Av ARCH N19 66 C6
Magdala Rd ISLW TW7 136 B4
SAND/SEL CR2 211 K5
Magdalene Gdns EHAM E6 108 A3
Magdalen Rd
WAND/EARL SW18 160 B3
Magdalen St STHWK SE1 19 G1
Magdelan Gv ORP BR6 217 H2
Magee St LBTH SE11 122 B6
Magellan Bvd CAN/RD E16 108 C6
Magellan Pl POP/IOD E14 124 D4
Magnaville Rd BUSH WD23 28 E2
Magnet Rd WBLY HA9 61 K6
Magnin Cl HACK E8 86 C6
Magnolia Cl KUTN/CMB KT2 175 J2
LEY E10 69 J6
Magnolia Ct
KTN/HRWW/WS HA3 62 B4
Magnolia Gdns EDGW HA8 30 E6
Magnolia Pl CLAP SW4 * 141 K6
EA W5 * 97 K4
Magnolia Rd CHSWK W4 117 J6
Magnolia St WDR/YW UB7 112 A4
Magnolia Wy HOR/WEW KT19 206 E3
Magnolia Whf CHSWK W4 * 117 J6
Magpie Cl CDALE/KGS NW9 45 G5
EN EN1 24 C2
FSTGT E7 88 D3
Magpie Hall Cl HAYES BR2 200 D3
Magpie Hall La HAYES BR2 200 D4
HAYES BR2 200 E2
Magpie Hall Rd STAN HA7 28 E4
Magpie Pl NWCR SE14 * 124 B6
Magri Wk WCHPL E1 104 E4
Maguire Dr
RCHPK/HAM TW10 156 D6
Maguire St STHWK SE1 19 K2
Mahlon Av RSLP HA4 77 F3
Mahogany Cl
BERM/RHTH SE16 124 B1
Mahon Cl EN EN1 24 B2
Maida Av BAY/PAD W2 101 G4
CHING E4 37 K2
Maida Rd BELV DA17 129 H3
Maida V STJWD NW8 2 A6
Maida Wy CHING E4 37 K2
Maiden Erlegh Av BXLY DA5 169 F3
Maiden La CAMTN NW1 84 D5
COVGDN WC2E 11 F5
DART DA1 150 D4
STHWK SE1 18 D1
Maiden Rd SRTFD E15 88 C5
Maidenstone Hl GNWCH SE10 145 F2
Maidstone Av CRW RM5 56 E5
Maidstone Buildings Ms
STHWK SE1 18 D1
Maidstone Rd
FBAR/BDGN N11 48 D2
SCUP DA14 186 E2
SCUP DA14 187 G3
SWLY BR8 187 J4
Main Av EN EN1 24 B6
NTHWD HA6 26 A5
Main Barracks
WOOL/PLUM SE18 * 126 E5
Main Dr GFD/PVL UB6 * 97 G2
WBLY HA9 79 K1
Mainridge Rd CHST BR7 167 F6
Main Rd ORP BR6 * 217 J6
ROM RM1 75 H1
SCUP DA14 167 K5
STMC/STPC BR5 186 D4
STMC/STPC BR5 186 D6
SWLY BR8 203 K3
Main St FELT TW13 172 C1
Maise Webster Cl
STWL/WRAY TW19 * 152 A2
Maismore St PECK SE15 123 H6
The Maisonettes SUT SM1 * 208 D3
Maitland Cl GNWCH SE10 144 E1
HSLWW TW4 134 E4
WOT/HER KT12 188 D6
Maitland Park Rd HAMP NW3 83 K4
Maitland Park Vls HAMP NW3 83 K4
Maitland Rd PGE/AN SE20 182 A2
SRTFD E15 88 D4
Majendie Rd
WOOL/PLUM SE18 127 J5
Major Cl BRXN/ST SW9 142 C4
Major Rd BERM/RHTH SE16 * 123 H3
SRTFD E15 88 A3
Makepeace Av HGT N6 66 A6
Makepeace Rd NTHLT UB5 95 J1
WAN E11 70 E1
Makins St CHEL SW3 14 D7
Malabar St POP/IOD E14 124 D2
Malam Gdns POP/IOD E14 105 K6
Malan Sq RAIN RM13 93 K4
Malbrook Rd PUT/ROE SW15 138 E5
Malcolm Cl PGE/AN SE20 * 181 K3
Malcolm Ct STAN HA7 43 J1
Malcolm Crs HDN NW4 63 J2
Malcolm Dr SURB KT6 190 E5
Malcolm Pl BETH E2 104 E3
Malcolm Rd PGE/AN SE20 181 K3
SNWD SE25 197 H3
WCHPL E1 104 E3
WIM/MER SW19 177 H2
Malcolms Wy
STHGT/OAK N14 * 22 C6
Malcolm Wy WAN E11 70 E2
Malden Av GFD/PVL UB6 78 E4
SNWD SE25 197 J1
Malden Green Av WPK KT4 192 C5
Malden Hl NWMAL KT3 192 C1
Malden Hill Gdns NWMAL KT3 176 C6
Malden Pk NWMAL KT3 192 C3
Malden Pl KTTN NW5 84 A3
Malden Rd CHEAM SM3 208 B2
KTTN NW5 83 K3
NWMAL KT3 192 B2
Malden Wy NWMAL KT3 192 A3
Maldon Cl CMBW SE5 * 143 F4
IS N1 85 J6
Maldon Rd ACT W3 98 E6
ED N9 36 B5
ROMW/RG RM7 74 E4
WLGTN SM6 210 B3
Maldon Wk WFD IG8 53 G2
Malet St GWRST WC1E 4 C7
Maley Av WNWD SE27 162 C4
Malford Gv SWFD E18 52 D6
Malfort Rd CMBW SE5 143 F4
Malham Cl FBAR/BDGN N11 48 A2
Malham Rd FSTH SE23 164 A3
Malham Ter UED N18 * 50 D2
Mallams Ms BRXN/ST SW9 142 B4
Mallard Cl BAR EN5 * 33 H1
HNWL W7 115 K2
KIL/WHAMP NW6 100 E1
WHTN TW2 155 F2
Mallard Ct WALTH E17 * 52 B6
Mallard Pl TWK TW1 156 B5
WDGN N22 * 49 F5
Mallards Ct OXHEY WD19 27 K5
Mallards Rd BARK IG11 109 G2
WFD IG8 53 F3
Mallard Wk BECK BR3 198 A2
Mallard Wy CDALE/KGS NW9 62 E4
NTHWD HA6 40 A3
WLGTN SM6 210 C6
Mall Chambers KENS W8 * 119 K1
Mallet Dr NTHLT UB5 77 K3
Mallet Rd LEW SE13 165 G1
Malling Cl CROY/NA CR0 * 197 K3
Malling Gdns MRDN SM4 194 B3
Malling Wy HAYES BR2 199 J4
Mallinson Rd BTSEA SW11 140 D6
CROY/NA CR0 210 D1
Mallord St CHEL SW3 120 C6
Mallory Cl BROCKY SE4 144 B5
POP/IOD E14 105 K3
Mallory Ct LEE/GVPK SE12 166 A2
Mallory Gdns EBAR EN4 34 A2
Mallory St STJWD NW8 2 D7
Mallow Cl CROY/NA CR0 198 A5
Mallow Md MLHL NW7 46 C3
Mallow St FSBYE EC1V 6 E6
Mall Rd HMSMTH W6 118 E5
The Mall BTFD TW8 * 116 E6
EA W5 98 A6
EMPK RM11 75 K5
KTN/HRWW/WS HA3 62 B3
MORT/ESHN SW14 137 K6
STHGT/OAK N14 34 E5
SURB KT6 190 E2
WHALL SW1A 16 A2
Mall Vls HMSMTH W6 * 118 E5
Malmains Cl BECK BR3 199 G2
Malmains Wy BECK BR3 199 F1
Malmesbury Cl PIN HA5 58 D1
Malmesbury Rd BOW E3 105 H1
CAN/RD E16 106 C4
MRDN SM4 194 B4
SWFD E18 52 D4
Malmesbury Ter CAN/RD E16 106 D4
Malmesbury West Est
BOW E3 105 H2
Malory Cl BECK BR3 182 B5
Malpas Dr PIN HA5 59 H2
Malpas Rd BROCKY SE4 144 C3
DAGW RM9 91 K4
HACK E8 86 D4
Malta Rd LEY E10 69 J5
Malta St FSBYE EC1V 6 A6
Maltby Cl ORP BR6 202 B5
Maltby Dr EN EN1 24 D1
Maltby Rd CHSGTN KT9 206 C4
Maltby St STHWK SE1 19 J3
Malthouse Dr CHSWK W4 118 C6
FELT TW13 172 C1
Maltings Cl BOW E3 106 A2
Maltings Pl FUL/PGN SW6 140 A2
STHWK SE1 19 H2
The Maltings ORP BR6 202 A5
ROM RM1 75 H4
SNWD SE25 * 181 F6
Malting Wy ISLW TW7 136 A4
Malton Ms NKENS W10 * 100 C5
WOOL/PLUM SE18 127 K6
Malton Rd NKENS W10 100 C5
Malton St WOOL/PLUM SE18 127 K6
Maltravers St TPL/STR WC2R 11 H5
Malt St STHWK SE1 123 H6
Malva Cl WAND/EARL SW18 140 A6
Malvern Av CHING E4 52 B3
RYLN/HDSTN HA2 77 J1
Malvern Cl BUSH WD23 28 C1
MTCM CR4 179 H6
NKENS W10 100 D4
SURB KT6 191 F5
Malvern Dr FELT TW13 172 C1
GDMY/SEVK IG3 91 F2
WFD IG8 53 G1
Malvern Gdns CRICK NW2 64 C6
KTN/HRWW/WS HA3 62 A1
LOU IG10 39 K1
Malvern Ms KIL/WHAMP NW6 100 E2
Malvern Pl MV/WKIL W9 * 100 D2
Malvern Rd CEND/HSY/T N8 49 F6
EHAM E6 89 J6
HACK E8 86 C5
HPTN TW12 173 F4
HYS/HAR UB3 133 H1
KIL/WHAMP NW6 100 E2
ORP BR6 217 H2
SURB KT6 191 F6
THHTH CR7 196 B1
TOTM N17 50 C6
WAN E11 70 C6
Malvern Ter ED N9 36 B3
IS N1 85 G6
Malvern Wy WEA W13 97 H4
Malwood Rd BAL SW12 161 G1
Malyons Rd LEW SE13 144 E6
Malyons Ter LEW SE13 144 E6
Managers St POP/IOD E14 * 125 F1
Manaton Cl PECK SE15 143 J4
Manaton Crs STHL UB1 96 A5
Manbey Gv SRTFD E15 88 C4
Manbey Park Rd SRTFD E15 88 C4
Manbey Rd SRTFD E15 * 88 C4
Manbey St SRTFD E15 88 C4
Manbre Rd HMSMTH W6 119 F6
Manbrough Av EHAM E6 108 A2
Manchester Ct CAN/RD E16 107 F5
Manchester Dr NKENS W10 * 100 C3
Manchester Gv POP/IOD E14 125 F5
Manchester Ms MHST W1U 9 G2
Manchester Rd POP/IOD E14 125 F5
SEVS/STOTM N15 67 K3
THHTH CR7 180 D6
Manchester Sq MBLAR W1H 9 G3
Manchester St MHST W1U 9 G2
Manchester Wy DAGE RM10 * 92 D2
Manchuria Rd BTSEA SW11 161 F1
Manciple St STHWK SE1 19 F3
Mandalay Rd CLAP SW4 141 H6
Mandarin Wy YEAD UB4 95 H5
Mandela Cl WLSDN NW10 80 E5
Mandela Rd CAN/RD E16 106 E5
Mandela St BRXN/ST SW9 142 B1
CAMTN NW1 84 C6
Mandela Wy STHWK SE1 19 H6
Mandeville Cl WIM/MER SW19 177 H3
Mandeville Ct CHING E4 37 G6
Mandeville Dr SURB KT6 190 E5
Mandeville Pl MHST W1U 9 H3
Mandeville Rd ISLW TW7 136 B3
NTHLT UB5 77 K5
STHGT/OAK N14 34 B4
Mandeville St CLPT E5 87 G1
Mandrake Rd TOOT SW17 160 E5
Mandrake Wy SRTFD E15 * 88 C5
Mandrell Rd
BRXS/STRHM SW2 141 K6
Manette St LSQ/SEVD WC2H 10 D4
Manford Cross CHIG IG7 55 G1
Manford Wy CHIG IG7 54 E1
Manfred Rd PUT/ROE SW15 139 J6
Manger Rd HOLWY N7 84 E4
Mangold Wy ERITHM DA18 128 E3
Manilla St POP/IOD E14 124 D2
Manister Rd ABYW SE2 128 B3
Manley Ct STNW/STAM N16 86 B1
Manley St CAMTN NW1 84 A6
Mann Cl CROY/NA CR0 211 J1
Manningford Cl FSBYE EC1V * 6 A4
Manning Gdns CROY/NA CR0 197 J4
KTN/HRWW/WS HA3 61 K4
Manning Pl
RCHPK/HAM TW10 157 G1
Manning Rd DAGE RM10 92 C4
STMC/STPC BR5 202 E2
WALTH E17 69 G1
Manningtree Cl
WIM/MER SW19 159 H3
Manningtree Rd RSLP HA4 77 F2
Manningtree St WCHPL E1 104 C5
Mannin Rd CHDH RM6 73 H4
Mannock Ms SWFD E18 53 F4
Mannock Rd WDGN N22 49 H6
Mann's Cl ISLW TW7 136 A6
Manns Rd EDGW HA8 44 C2
Manoel Rd WHTN TW2 155 H4
Manor Av BROCKY SE4 144 C3
HSLWW TW4 134 C4
NTHLT UB5 77 K5
Manor Cl BAR EN5 20 C5
CDALE/KGS NW9 62 D1
DAGE RM10 93 F4
DART DA1 150 A5
MLHL NW7 * 45 F1
ROM RM1 75 J2
RSLP HA4 58 D5
THMD SE28 109 J5
WPK KT4 192 B5
Manor Cots NTHWD HA6 40 D4
Manor Cottages Ap
EFNCH N2 47 G5
Manor Ct ACT W3 * 117 H4
E/WMO/HCT KT8 * 189 F1
HRW HA1 * 61 F3
KUTN/CMB KT2 * 175 H4
WBLY HA9 * 80 A3
Manor Court Rd HNWL W7 96 E6
Manor Crs BRYLDS KT5 191 H3
Manor Cft EDGW HA8 * 44 C2
Manordene Cl THDIT KT7 190 B5
Manordene Rd THMD SE28 109 J5
Manor Dr BRYLDS KT5 191 H3
ESH/CLAY KT10 205 F1
FELT TW13 172 C1
HOR/WEW KT19 207 G4
MLHL NW7 45 F1
STHGT/OAK N14 34 B2
TRDG/WHET N20 33 J5
WBLY HA9 80 B2
Manor Dr North NWMAL KT3 192 A4
The Manor Dr WPK KT4 192 B5
Manor Est BERM/RHTH SE16 123 J4
Manor Farm Cl WPK KT4 192 B5
Manor Farm Dr CHING E4 38 C4
Manor Farm Rd ALP/SUD HA0 97 K1
STRHM/NOR SW16 180 B5
Manorfield Cl ARCH N19 84 C2
Manorfields Cl CHST BR7 186 A6
Manor Gdns ACT W3 117 H4
CLAP SW4 * 141 H3
HOLWY N7 84 E1
HPTN TW12 173 G3
RCH/KEW TW9 137 G5
RSLP HA4 77 G3
RYNPK SW20 177 J5
SAND/SEL CR2 212 B4
Manor Ga NTHLT UB5 77 J5
Manorgate Rd
KUTN/CMB KT2 175 H4
Manor Gv BECK BR3 182 E5
PECK SE15 123 K6
RCH/KEW TW9 137 H5
Manor Hall Av HDN NW4 46 A5
Manor Hall Dr HDN NW4 46 B5
Manor Hall Gdns LEY E10 69 J5
Manor House Dr
KIL/WHAMP NW6 82 B5
Manor House Wy ISLW TW7 136 C4
Manor La FELT TW13 153 K4

HYS/HAR UB3 113 G6
LEE/GVPK SE12 165 H1
SUN TW16 172 A5
SUT SM1 209 G3
Manor Lane Ter LEW SE13 145 H5
Manor Ms BROCKY SE4 144 C3
KIL/WHAMP NW6 100 E1
Manor Mt FSTH SE23 163 K3
Manor Pde HRW HA1 * 61 F3
STNW/STAM N16 * 68 B6
Manor Pk CHST BR7 185 J5
LEW SE13 145 G6
RCH/KEW TW9 137 G5
Manor Park Cl WWKM BR4 198 E5
Manor Park Crs EDGW HA8 44 C2
Manor Park Dr
RYLN/HDSTN HA2 42 B6
Manor Park Gdns EDGW HA8 44 C1
Manor Park Rd CHST BR7 185 H4
EFNCH N2 47 G6
MNPK E12 89 H2
SUT SM1 209 G3
WLSDN NW10 81 G6
WWKM BR4 198 E5
Manor Pl CHST BR7 185 J5
EBED/NFELT TW14 153 K3
MTCM CR4 179 H6
SUT SM1 209 F3
WALW SE17 122 C5
Manor Rd BAR EN5 20 C5
BARK IG11 91 F4
BECK BR3 182 D5
BELMT SM2 208 D5
BFN/LL DA15 168 A5
BXLY DA5 169 J3
CAN/RD E16 106 C4
CHDH RM6 73 K3
CHIG IG7 54 A2
DAGE RM10 92 E4
DART DA1 150 B5
E/WMO/HCT KT8 189 J1
ENC/FH EN2 23 K3
HRW HA1 61 G3
HYS/HAR UB3 94 E5
LEY E10 69 J4
LOU IG10 39 F1
MTCM CR4 179 H6
RCH/KEW TW9 137 G4
ROM RM1 75 J2
RSLP HA4 58 B5
RYNPK SW20 177 J5
SNWD SE25 197 H1
SRTFD E15 106 C2
STNW/STAM N16 68 A5
TEDD TW11 174 B1
TOTM N17 50 C4
WDGN N22 48 E2
WEA W13 97 G6
WHTN TW2 155 H4
WLGTN SM6 210 B2
WWKM BR4 198 E5
Manor Rd North
ESH/CLAY KT10 190 A6
WLGTN SM6 210 B2
Manor Rd South
ESH/CLAY KT10 204 E2
Manorside BAR EN5 20 C5
Manor Sq BCTR RM8 73 J6
Manor V BTFD TW8 116 D5
Manor Vw FNCH N3 47 F5
Manor Wy MTCM CR4 179 H6
NWDGN UB2 114 C4
RAIN RM13 111 G3
RSLP HA4 58 C4
RYLN/HDSTN HA2 60 B1
SAND/SEL CR2 212 A4
WPK KT4 192 B5
BECK BR3 182 D6
BXLY DA5 169 H3
CDALE/KGS NW9 63 G1
CHING E4 38 B6
Manorway EN EN1 36 A2
Manor Wy HAYES BR2 200 D3
STMC/STPC BR5 201 H1
Manorway WFD IG8 53 G1
The Manor Wy WLGTN SM6 210 B2
Manresa Rd CHEL SW3 120 C5
Mansard Beeches TOOT SW17 179 F1
Mansard Cl HCH RM12 75 J6
PIN HA5 41 H6
Manse Cl HYS/HAR UB3 113 G6
Mansel Gv WALTH E17 51 J4
Mansell Rd ACT W3 118 A1
GFD/PVL UB6 96 B4
Mansell St WCHPL E1 13 K4
Mansel Rd WIM/MER SW19 177 H2
Mansergh Cl CHARL SE7 146 D1
Manse Rd STNW/STAM N16 86 B1
Manser Rd RAIN RM13 111 G2
Mansfield Av EBAR EN4 33 K1
RSLP HA4 59 F5
SEVS/STOTM N15 67 K1
Mansfield Cl ED N9 36 C1
STMC/STPC BR5 202 E4
Mansfield Dr YEAD UB4 94 C3
Mansfield Hl CHING E4 37 K3
Mansfield Ms
CAVSQ/HST W1G 9 J2
Mansfield Rd ACT W3 98 D3
CHSGTN KT9 205 J3
HAMP NW3 83 K3
IL IG1 72 A6
SAND/SEL CR2 211 K4
WALTH E17 69 H1
WAN E11 71 F3
Mansfield St CAVSQ/HST W1G 9 J2
Mansford St BETH E2 104 D2
Manship Rd MTCM CR4 179 F4
Mansion Cl BRXN/ST SW9 142 B2
Mansion Gdns HAMP NW3 83 F1
Mansion House Pl
MANHO EC4N * 12 E4
Mansion House St
MANHO EC4N 12 E4
The Mansions ECT SW5 * 120 A5
Manson Ms SKENS SW7 * 120 B4
Manson Pl SKENS SW7 14 A7
Manstead Gdns CHDH RM6 73 J4
RAIN RM13 111 K5
Manston Av NWDGN UB2 115 F4
Manston Cl PGE/AN SE20 181 K4
Manstone Rd CRICK NW2 82 C3
Manston Gv KUTN/CMB KT2 174 E1
Manston Wy HCH RM12 93 K4
Manthorpe Rd
WOOL/PLUM SE18 127 H5
Mantilla Rd TOOT SW17 161 F6
Mantle Rd BROCKY SE4 144 B4
Mantlet Cl STRHM/NOR SW16 179 H3
Mantle Wy SRTFD E15 88 C5
Manton Av HNWL W7 116 A2
Manton Cl HYS/HAR UB3 94 C6
Manton Rd ABYW SE2 128 B4
PEND EN3 25 J1
Mantua St BTSEA SW11 140 C4
Mantus Cl WCHPL E1 104 E3
Mantus Rd WCHPL E1 104 E3
Manus Wy TRDG/WHET N20 33 G4
Manville Gdns TOOT SW17 161 G4
Manville Rd TOOT SW17 161 F4
Manwood Rd BROCKY SE4 144 C6
Manwood St CAN/RD E16 126 E1
Many Gates BAL SW12 161 G4
Mapesbury Ms
CDALE/KGS NW9 63 J3
Mapesbury Rd CRICK NW2 82 C4
Mapeshill Pl CRICK NW2 82 A4
Mape St BETH E2 104 D3
Maple Av ACT W3 118 B1
CHING E4 51 H2
RYLN/HDSTN HA2 60 B6
Maple Cl BARK/HLT IG6 54 E2
BKHH IG9 39 H5
CLAP SW4 161 J1
FNCH N3 46 E2
HCH RM12 93 K1
HPTN TW12 172 E2
MTCM CR4 179 G4
RSLP HA4 59 F3
STMC/STPC BR5 201 J2
STNW/STAM N16 68 C3
YEAD UB4 95 H2
Maple Ct HACK E8 * 86 C4
NWMAL KT3 176 A6
Maple Crs BFN/LL DA15 168 B1
Maplecroft Cl EHAM E6 107 H5
Mapledale Av CROY/NA CR0 212 D1
Mapledene Est HACK E8 * 86 C5
Mapledene Rd HACK E8 86 B5
Maple Gdns ASHF TW15 152 B4
EDGW HA8 45 G3
Maple Gv BTFD TW8 136 C1
CDALE/KGS NW9 62 E4
EA W5 116 E3
STHL UB1 95 K4
Maplehurst Cl KUT/HW KT1 191 F1
Maple Leaf Dr BFN/LL DA15 168 A3
Mapleleafe Gdns
BARK/HLT IG6 54 B6
Maple Leaf Sq
BERM/RHTH SE16 * 124 A2
Maple Ms KIL/WHAMP NW6 * 101 F1
STRHM/NOR SW16 180 A1
Maple Pl FITZ W1T 10 B1
TOTM N17 50 C3
WDR/YW UB7 112 B1
Maple Rd PGE/AN SE20 181 J4
SURB KT6 190 E2
WAN E11 70 C3
YEAD UB4 95 G2
Maples Pl WCHPL E1 * 104 D4
Maplestead Rd
BRXS/STRHM SW2 162 A2
DAGW RM9 91 H6
The Maples ESH/CLAY KT10 * 205 G5
KUT/HW KT1 * 174 D3
Maple St BETH E2 104 C1
FITZ W1T 10 A1
ROMW/RG RM7 74 E1
Maplethorpe Rd THHTH CR7 196 B1
Mapleton Crs PEND EN3 24 E1
WAND/EARL SW18 160 A1
Mapleton Rd CHING E4 38 A5
EN EN1 24 D3
WAND/EARL SW18 159 K1
Maple Tree Pl BKHTH/KID SE3 146 D2
Maple Wk NKENS W10 * 100 B3
Maple Wy FELT TW13 153 K5
Maplin Cl WCHMH N21 35 F1
Maplin Rd CAN/RD E16 106 E5
Maplin St BOW E3 105 H2
Mapperley Dr WFD IG8 52 C3
Marabou Cl MNPK E12 89 J3
Maran Wy ERITHM DA18 128 E3
Marathon Wy THMD SE28 128 A1
Marban Rd MV/WKIL W9 100 D2
Marble Cl ACT W3 117 J1
Marble Dr CRICK NW2 64 B4
Marble Hill Cl TWK TW1 156 C2
Marble Hill Gdns TWK TW1 156 C2
Marble Quay WAP E1W 13 K7
Marbrook Ct LEE/GVPK SE12 166 B5
Marcella Rd BRXN/ST SW9 142 B3
Marcellina Wy ORP BR6 216 E1
Marchant Cl MLHL NW7 45 G2
Marchant Rd WAN E11 70 B6
Marchant St NWCR SE14 124 B6
Marchbank Rd WKENS W14 119 J6
Marchmont Gdns
RCHPK/HAM TW10 137 F6
Marchmont Rd
RCHPK/HAM TW10 137 G6
WLGTN SM6 210 C6
Marchmont St BMSBY WC1N 4 E6
March Rd TWK TW1 156 A2
Marchside Cl HEST TW5 134 C2
Marchwood Cl CMBW SE5 143 F1
Marchwood Crs EA W5 97 J5
Marcia Rd STHWK SE1 19 H7
Marcilly Rd WAND/EARL SW18 140 C6
Marconi Pl FBAR/BDGN N11 34 B6
Marconi Rd LEY E10 69 J5
Marconi Wy STHL UB1 96 B5
Marcon Pl HACK E8 86 D4
Marco Rd HMSMTH W6 118 E3
Marcus Garvey Ms EDUL SE22 163 J1
Marcus Garvey Wy
HNHL SE24 142 B5
Marcus St SRTFD E15 88 C6
WAND/EARL SW18 160 A1
Marcus Ter WAND/EARL SW18 160 A1
Mardale Dr CDALE/KGS NW9 63 F2
Mardell Rd CROY/NA CR0 198 A2
Marden Crs CROY/NA CR0 196 A3
Marden Rd CROY/NA CR0 196 A3
ROM RM1 75 G3
TOTM N17 50 A5
Marden Sq BERM/RHTH SE16 123 J3
Marder Rd WEA W13 116 B2
Mardyke Cl RAIN RM13 110 E1
Marechal Niel Av
BFN/LL DA15 167 J5
Marechal Niel Pde
SCUP DA14 * 167 J5
Maresfield CROY/NA CR0 212 A1
Maresfield Gdns HAMP NW3 83 G3
Mare St HACK E8 86 D6
Marfield Cl WPK KT4 192 D5
Marfleet Cl CAR SM5 194 D6
Margaret Av CHING E4 37 K1
Margaret Bondfield Av
BARK IG11 91 G5
Margaret Cl GPK RM2 75 K2
Margaret Gardner Dr
ELTH/MOT SE9 166 E4
Margaret Ingram Cl
FUL/PGN SW6 * 119 J6
Margaret Lockwood Cl
KUT/HW KT1 * 191 G1
Margaret Rd BXLY DA5 168 E1
EBAR EN4 21 H5
GPK RM2 75 K2
STNW/STAM N16 * 68 B5
Margaret Rutherford Pl
BAL SW12 161 H3
Margaret St REGST W1B 9 K3
Margaretta Ter CHEL SW3 120 D6
Margaretting Rd MNPK E12 71 G6
Margaret Wy REDBR IG4 71 J3
Margate Rd
BRXS/STRHM SW2 141 K6
Margeholes OXHEY WD19 27 J4
Margery Park Rd FSTGT E7 88 E4
Margery Rd BCTR RM8 91 K1
Margery St CLKNW EC1R 5 J5
Margin Dr WIM/MER SW19 177 G1
Margravine Gdns
HMSMTH W6 119 G5
Margravine Rd HMSMTH W6 119 G6
Marguerite Vls RYNPK SW20 * 176 E3
Marham Dr CDALE/KGS NW9 45 G5
Marham Gdns MRDN SM4 194 B3
WAND/EARL SW18 160 D3
Maria Cl STHWK SE1 123 H4
Marian Cl YEAD UB4 95 H3
Marian Pl BETH E2 104 D1
Marian Rd STRHM/NOR SW16 179 H4
Marian St BETH E2 * 104 D1
Marian Wy WLSDN NW10 81 H5
Maria Ter WCHPL E1 105 F4
Maria Theresa Cl NWMAL KT3 192 A2
Maricas Av
KTN/HRWW/WS HA3 42 D4
Marie Curie CMBW SE5 * 143 F2
Marie Lloyd Wk HACK E8 * 86 C4
Mariette Wy WLGTN SM6 210 E6
Marigold Aly STHWK SE1 12 A6
Marigold Cl STHL UB1 95 J6
Marigold Rd TOTM N17 50 E3
Marigold St BERM/RHTH SE16 123 J2
Marigold Wy CROY/NA CR0 198 A5
Marina Ap YEAD UB4 95 J4
Marina Av NWMAL KT3 192 E3
Marina Dr WELL DA16 147 K3
Marina Gdns ROMW/RG RM7 74 D2
Marina Pl KUT/HW KT1 174 E4
Marina Wy TEDD TW11 174 E3
Marine Dr BARK IG11 109 G3
WOOL/PLUM SE18 126 E4
Marinefield Rd FUL/PGN SW6 140 A3
Mariner Gdns
RCHPK/HAM TW10 156 C5
Mariner Rd MNPK E12 90 A2
Mariners Ms POP/IOD E14 125 G4
Marine St BERM/RHTH SE16 123 H3
Marion Cl BARK/HLT IG6 54 D3
Marion Crs STMC/STPC BR5 202 C2
Marion Gv WFD IG8 52 C1
Marion Ms DUL SE21 162 E5
Marion Rd MLHL NW7 45 J1
THHTH CR7 196 D2
Marischal Rd LEW SE13 145 G4
Maritime Quay POP/IOD E14 124 D5
Maritime St BOW E3 105 H3
Marius Rd TOOT SW17 161 F4
Marjorie Gv BTSEA SW11 140 E5
Mark Av CHING E4 37 K1
Mark Cl HAYES BR2 215 J2
STHL UB1 115 F1
Markeston Gn OXHEY WD19 27 H6
Market Chambers
ENC/FH EN2 * 23 K4
Market Est HOLWY N7 84 E4
Market La EDGW HA8 44 E4
Market Link ROM RM1 75 G1
Market Meadow
STMC/STPC BR5 202 D1
Market Ms MYFR/PICC W1J 15 J1
Market Pde BMLY BR1 * 183 K4
EW KT17 * 207 H6
FELT TW13 * 154 D4
LEY E10 * 69 K3
SCUP DA14 * 168 B6
SNWD SE25 * 197 H1
STNW/STAM N16 * 68 C5
WALTH E17 * 51 H6
Market Pl ACT W3 117 K1
BERM/RHTH SE16 * 123 H4
BTFD TW8 136 D1
EFNCH N2 47 H6
GTPST W1W 10 A3
KUT/HW KT1 * 174 E5
ROM RM1 75 G2
Market Rd HOLWY N7 84 E4
RCH/KEW TW9 137 H4
Market Sq ED N9 36 D4
Market St EHAM E6 107 K1
WOOL/PLUM SE18 127 F4
Market Ter BTFD TW8 * 117 F6
The Market HNWL W7 * 116 A2
PECK SE15 * 143 H3
SUT SM1 * 194 B5
Market Yard Ms STHWK SE1 19 G4
Markfield Gdns CHING E4 37 K2
Markfield Rd
SEVS/STOTM N15 68 C1
Markham Pl CHEL SW3 120 E5
Markham Sq CHEL SW3 120 E5
Markham St CHEL SW3 120 D5
Markhole Cl HPTN TW12 172 E3
Markhouse Av WALTH E17 69 G3
Markhouse Rd WALTH E17 69 H3
Mark La MON EC3R 13 H5
Markmanor Av WALTH E17 69 G4
Mark Rd WDGN N22 49 H5
Marksbury Av RCH/KEW TW9 137 H4
Marks Rd ROMW/RG RM7 74 E2
Markstone Ter ORP BR6 * 202 B4
Mark St SDTCH EC2A 7 G6
SRTFD E15 88 C5
Mark Ter RYNPK SW20 * 177 F3
Markwade Cl MNPK E12 71 H5
The Markway SUN TW16 172 B5
Markwell Cl SYD SE26 163 J6
Markyate Rd BCTR RM8 91 H3
Marlands Rd CLAY IG5 53 J6
Marlborogh Rd ISLW TW7 136 C2
Marlborough Av EDGW HA8 30 D5
HACK E8 86 C6
RSLP HA4 58 A3
STHGT/OAK N14 34 C5
Marlborough Cl ORP BR6 202 A4
TRDG/WHET N20 33 K5
WALW SE17 18 B7
WIM/MER SW19 178 D2
Marlborough Ct REGST W1B * 10 A5
Marlborough Crs CHSWK W4 118 A3
HYS/HAR UB3 133 G1
Marlborough Dr CLAY IG5 53 J6
Marlborough Gdns
TRDG/WHET N20 33 K5
Marlborough Ga BAY/PAD W2 8 A6
Marlborough Gv STHWK SE1 123 H5
Marlborough Hl HRW HA1 60 E1
STJWD NW8 83 G6
Marlborough La CHARL SE7 126 B6
Marlborough Ms
BRXS/STRHM SW2 142 A5
Marlborough Pde
FSBYPK N4 * 67 J5
Marlborough Park Av
BFN/LL DA15 168 B3
Marlborough Pl STJWD NW8 101 G1
Marlborough Rd ARCH N19 66 E6
BCTR RM8 91 J2
CHING E4 51 K2
CHSWK W4 117 K5
EA W5 116 E2
ED N9 36 B3
FELT TW13 154 C4
FSTGT E7 89 G5
HAYES BR2 200 B1
HPTN TW12 173 F2
NWDGN UB2 114 B3
RCHPK/HAM TW10 157 F1
ROMW/RG RM7 74 C1
SAND/SEL CR2 211 J5
SRTFD E15 * 88 C2
SUT SM1 208 E1
SWFD E18 52 E6
WDGN N22 49 F3
WELL DA16 148 E4
WHALL SW1A 16 B1
WIM/MER SW19 178 D2
WOOL/PLUM SE18 127 G3
Marlborough St CHEL SW3 14 C7
Marlborough Yd ARCH N19 66 D6
Marler Rd FSTH SE23 164 C3
Marley Av BXLYHN DA7 128 E6
Marley Cl GFD/PVL UB6 96 A2
SEVS/STOTM N15 67 H1
Marley Rd BERM/RHTH SE16 * 124 A4
Marlingdene Cl HPTN TW12 173 F2
Marlings Cl CHST BR7 201 K1
Marlings Park Av CHST BR7 185 K6
Marlins Cl SUT SM1 * 209 G3
Marlins Meadow WATW WD18 26 B1
The Marlins NTHWD HA6 40 D2
Marloes Cl ALP/SUD HA0 79 K2
Marloes Rd KENS W8 120 A3
Marlow Av PUR RM19 131 K4
Marlow Cl PGE/AN SE20 181 J6
Marlow Ct CDALE/KGS NW9 45 H6
Marlow Crs TWK TW1 156 A1
Marlow Dr CHEAM SM3 208 B1
Marlowe Cl BARK/HLT IG6 54 C4
CHST BR7 185 J2
Marlowe Rd WALTH E17 70 A1
Marlowe Sq MTCM CR4 195 H1
The Marlowes STJWD NW8 2 A1
Marlowe Wy CROY/NA CR0 195 K6
Marlow Gdns HYS/HAR UB3 113 G3
Marlow Rd EHAM E6 107 K2
NWDGN UB2 114 E3
PGE/AN SE20 181 J6
Marlow Wy
BERM/RHTH SE16 124 A2
Marl Rd WAND/EARL SW18 140 A5
Marlton St GNWCH SE10 125 J5
Marlwood Cl BFN/LL DA15 167 K4
Marlyon Rd BARK/HLT IG6 55 H1
Marmadon Rd
WOOL/PLUM SE18 128 A4
Marmion Ap CHING E4 37 J6
Marmion Av CHING E4 37 H6
Marmion Cl CHING E4 37 H6
Marmion Ms BTSEA SW11 * 141 F4
Marmion Rd BTSEA SW11 141 F5
Marmont Rd PECK SE15 143 H2
Marmora Rd EDUL SE22 163 K1
Marmot Rd HSLWW TW4 134 C4
Marne Av FBAR/BDGN N11 34 B6
WELL DA16 148 B4
Marnell Wy HSLWW TW4 134 C4
Marne St NKENS W10 100 C2
Marney Rd BTSEA SW11 141 F5
Marnfield Crs
BRXS/STRHM SW2 162 A3
Marnham Av CRICK NW2 82 C2
Marnham Crs GFD/PVL UB6 96 B1
Marnham Cresent
GFD/PVL UB6 96 B1
Marnock Rd BROCKY SE4 144 C6
Maroon St POP/IOD E14 105 G4
Maroons Wy CAT SE6 182 D1
Marquess Rd IS N1 85 K4
Marquess Rd North IS N1 85 J4
Marquess Rd South IS N1 * 85 J4
Marquis Cl ALP/SUD HA0 80 B5
Marquis Rd CAMTN NW1 84 D4
FSBYPK N4 67 F5
WDGN N22 49 F2
Marrabon Cl BFN/LL DA15 168 B3
Marrick Cl PUT/ROE SW15 138 D5
Married Quarters
EDGW HA8 * 44 D3
Marrilyne Av PEND EN3 25 H1
Marriner Ct HYS/HAR UB3 * 94 C6
Marriot Rd MUSWH N10 47 K4
Marriott Cl EBED/NFELT TW14 153 G1
Marriott Rd BAR EN5 20 B4
FSBYPK N4 67 F5
SRTFD E15 88 C6
Marriotts Cl CDALE/KGS NW9 63 H3
Marriotts Yd BAR EN5 * 20 B4
Marryat Cl HSLWW TW4 134 E5
Marryat Pl WIM/MER SW19 159 H6
Marryat Rd WIM/MER SW19 177 G1
Marryfields Wy CAT SE6 164 E2
Marsala Rd LEW SE13 144 E5
Marsden Rd ED N9 36 D4
PECK SE15 143 G4
Marsden St KTTN NW5 84 A4
Marsden Wy ORP BR6 217 F2
Marshall Cl FBAR/BDGN N11 34 B6
HRW HA1 60 D4
HSLWW TW4 134 E6
WAND/EARL SW18 160 B1
Marshall Dr YEAD UB4 94 D4
Marshall Est MLHL NW7 * 31 J6
Marshall Rd LEY E10 87 K2
TOTM N17 49 K4
Marshalls Dr ROM RM1 57 G6
Marshalls Gv
WOOL/PLUM SE18 126 D4
Marshall's Pl
BERM/RHTH SE16 19 K5
Marshalls Rd ROMW/RG RM7 75 F1
Marshall's Rd SUT SM1 209 F2
Marshall St SOHO/CST W1F 10 B4
Marshalsea Rd STHWK SE1 18 D2
Marsham Cl CHST BR7 * 185 G1
Marsham St WEST SW1P 16 D6
Marsh Av MTCM CR4 178 E5
Marshbrook Cl
BKHTH/KID SE3 146 C4
Marsh Cl MLHL NW7 31 H5
Marsh Dr CDALE/KGS NW9 63 H3
Marsh Farm Rd WHTN TW2 156 A3
Marshfield St POP/IOD E14 125 F3
Marsh Green Rd DAGE RM10 92 C6
Marsh Hl HOM E9 87 G3
Marsh La LEY E10 69 H6
MLHL NW7 31 G5
STAN HA7 43 J1
TOTM N17 50 D3
Marsh Rd ALP/SUD HA0 97 K2
PIN HA5 59 J1
Marshside Cl ED N9 36 E3
Marsh St DART DA1 151 K5
POP/IOD E14 * 124 E4
Marsh Ter STMC/STPC BR5 * 202 E1
Marsh Wall POP/IOD E14 124 D2
Marsh Wy RAIN RM13 111 H5
Marsland Cl WALW SE17 122 C5
Marston Av CHSGTN KT9 206 A4
DAGE RM10 92 C1
Marston Cl DAGE RM10 92
KIL/WHAMP NW6 83
Marston Ct WOT/HER KT12 * 188
Marston Rd CLAY IG5 53
TEDD TW11 174
Marston Wy NRWD SE19 180
Marsworth Av PIN HA5 41
Marsworth Cl WATW WD18 * 26
YEAD UB4 95
Martaban Rd
STNW/STAM N16 68
Martara Ms WALW SE17 122
Martello St HACK E8 86
Martell Rd DUL SE21 162
Martel Pl HACK E8 86
Marten Rd WALTH E17 51
Martens Av BXLYHN DA7 149
Martham Cl BARK/HLT IG6 54
THMD SE28 109
Martha Rd SRTFD E15 88
Martha's Blds FSBYE EC1V 6
Martha St WCHPL E1 104
Marthorne Crs
KTN/HRWW/WS HA3 42
Martin Bowes Rd
ELTH/MOT SE9 146
Martin Cl ED N9 37
Martin Crs CROY/NA CR0 196
Martindale MORT/ESHN SW14 137
Martindale Av CAN/RD E16 106
ORP BR6 217
Martindale Rd BAL SW12 161
HSLWW TW4 134
Martin Dr NTHLT UB5 77
RAIN RM13 111
Martineau Cl ESH/CLAY KT10 204
Martineau Dr TWK TW1 136
Martineau Rd HBRY N5 85
Martingales Cl
RCHPK/HAM TW10 156
Martin Gdns BCTR RM8 91
Martin Gv MRDN SM4 177
Martin La CANST EC4R 13
Martin Rd BCTR RM8 91
Martins Cl STMC/STPC BR5 186
WWKM BR4 199
Martins Mt BAR EN5 20
Martins Pl THMD SE28 127
Martin's Rd HAYES BR2 183
The Martins SYD SE26 181
WBLY HA9 * 80
Martin St THMD SE28 127
Martins Wk MUSWH N10 * 48

THMD SE28 127 K1
Martin Wy MRDN SM4 177 H6
Martlet Gv NTHLT UB5 95 H2
Martlett Ct HOL/ALD WC2B 11 F4
Martley Dr GNTH/NBYPK IG2 72 B2
Martock Cl
KTN/HRWW/WS HA3 61 G1
Martock Gdns
FBAR/BDGN N11 47 K1
Marton Cl CAT SE6 164 D5
Marton Rd STNW/STAM N16 * 68 A6
Martys Yd HAMP NW3 * 83 H2
Marvell Av YEAD UB4 94 E4
Marvels Cl LEE/GVPK SE12 166 A4
Marvels La LEE/GVPK SE12 166 A4
Marville Rd FUL/PGN SW6 139 J1
Marvin St HACK E8 * 86 D4
Marwell Cl ROM RM1 75 J3
WWKM BR4 199 J6
Marwood Cl WELL DA16 148 C4
Marwood Dr MLHL NW7 46 B3
Mary Adelaide Cl
PUT/ROE SW15 158 B5
Mary Ann Blds DEPT SE8 124 D6
Maryat Sq FUL/PGN SW6 139 H2
Maryatt Av RYLN/HDSTN HA2 60 B6
Marybank WOOL/PLUM SE18 126 E4
Mary Cl KTN/HRWW/WS HA3 62 B1
Mary Datchelor Cl CMBW SE5 142 E2
Mary Gn STJWD NW8 * 83 F6
Maryland Pk SRTFD E15 88 C3
Maryland Rd MV/WKIL W9 100 E3
SRTFD E15 88 B3
THHTH CR7 180 C4
WDGN N22 49 G2
Maryland Sq SRTFD E15 88 C3
Marylands Rd MV/WKIL W9 100 E3
Maryland St SRTFD E15 88 B3
Maryland Wk IS N1 * 85 J6
Marylebone F/O BAY/PAD W2 8 C2
Marylebone High St
CAVSQ/HST W1G 9 H2
Marylebone La MHST W1U 9 H3
Marylebone Ms
CAVSQ/HST W1G 9 H2
Marylebone Pas GTPST W1W 10 B3
Marylebone Rd MBLAR W1H 8 D1
Marylebone St
CAVSQ/HST W1G 9 H2
Marylee Wy LBTH SE11 17 H7
Maryon Gv CHARL SE7 126 D4
Maryon Ms HAMP NW3 83 J2
Maryon Rd CHARL SE7 126 D4
Mary Peters Dr GFD/PVL UB6 78 D3
Mary Pl NTGHL W11 100 C6
Mary Rose Cl HPTN TW12 173 F4
Maryrose Wy
TRDG/WHET N20 33 H3
Mary Seacole Cl HACK E8 86 B6
Mary's Ter TWK TW1 156 B2
Mary St CAN/RD E16 106 D4
IS N1 6 D1
Mary Ter CAMTN NW1 4 A1
Mary Wy OXHEY WD19 27 G6
Masbro' Rd WKENS W14 119 G3
Mascalls Rd CHARL SE7 126 B6
Mascotts Cl CRICK NW2 81 K1
Masefield Av STAN HA7 43 F1
STHL UB1 96 A6
Masefield Cl ERITH DA8 150 C2
HARH RM3 57 K4
Masefield Crs STHGT/OAK N14 22 C6
Masefield Gdns EHAM E6 108 A3
Masefield La YEAD UB4 95 F3
Masefield Rd HPTN TW12 154 E6
Masefield Vw ORP BR6 216 C1
Masefield Wy
STWL/WRAY TW19 152 C3
Mashie Rd ACT W3 99 G5
Mashiters Hl ROM RM1 57 F4
Mashiters Wk ROM RM1 57 G6
Maskall Cl
BRXS/STRHM SW2 * 162 B3
Maskell Rd TOOT SW17 160 B5
Maskelyne Cl BTSEA SW11 140 D2
Mason Cl BERM/RHTH SE16 123 H5
CAN/RD E16 106 E6
HPTN TW12 172 E4
RYNPK SW20 177 G4
Mason Ct WBLY HA9 * 62 C6
Mason Rd SUT SM1 209 F3
WFD IG8 38 C6
Mason's Arms Ms
CONDST W1S * 9 K4
Masons Av
KTN/HRWW/WS HA3 42 E6
Mason's Av CITYW EC2V 12 E3
CROY/NA CR0 211 J1
Masons Ct EW KT17 * 207 J6
Masons Hl BMLY BR1 183 K6
HAYES BR2 200 A1
HAYES BR2 183 K6
WOOL/PLUM SE18 127 G4
Mason's Pl FSBYE EC1V 6 B4
MTCM CR4 178 E4
Mason St WALW SE17 19 F7
Masons Yd FSBYE EC1V 6 C6
STJS SW1Y 10 B7
Massey Cl FBAR/BDGN N11 48 B1
Massie Rd HACK E8 86 C4
Massingberd Wy TOOT SW17 161 G6
Massinger St WALW SE17 19 G7
Massingham St WCHPL E1 105 F3
Masson Av RSLP HA4 77 G4
Masterman Rd EHAM E6 107 J2
Masters Cl STRHM/NOR SW16 179 H2
Masters Dr BERM/RHTH SE16 123 J5
Master's St WCHPL E1 105 F4
Master House Ter
POP/IOD E14 * 124 D4
Masthouse Ter POP/IOD E14 124 D4
Mastmaker Rd POP/IOD E14 124 D2
Mast Quay WOOL/PLUM SE18 126 E3
Maswell Park Crs HSLW TW3 135 H5
Maswell Park Rd HSLW TW3 135 G6
Matcham Rd WAN E11 88 C1
Matchless Dr
WOOL/PLUM SE18 147 F1
Matfield Rd BELV DA17 129 H6
Matham Gv EDUL SE22 143 G5
Matham Rd E/WMO/HCT KT8 189 J2
Matheson Rd WKENS W14 119 J4
Mathews Av EHAM E6 108 A1
Mathews Park Av SRTFD E15 88 D4
Mathews Yd
LSQ/SEVD WC2H * 10 E4
Mathieson Ct STHWK SE1 18 B3
Matilda Cl NRWD SE19 180 E3
Matilda Gdns BOW E3 105 J1
Matilda St IS N1 5 H1
Matlock Cl BAR EN5 20 B6
HNHL SE24 142 D5
Matlock Crs CHEAM SM3 208 C2
OXHEY WD19 27 G5
Matlock Gdns CHEAM SM3 208 C2
Matlock Pl CHEAM SM3 208 C2
Matlock Rd LEY E10 70 A3
Matlock St POP/IOD E14 105 G5
Matlock Wy NWMAL KT3 176 A4
Matthew Cl NKENS W10 * 100 B3
Matthew Ct MTCM CR4 195 J2
Matthews Rd GFD/PVL UB6 78 D3
Matthews St BTSEA SW11 * 140 E3
Matthias Rd STNW/STAM N16 85 K3
Mattingly Wy PECK SE15 143 G1
Mattison Rd FSBYPK N4 67 G3
Mattock La WEA W13 116 C1
Maud Cashmore Wy
WOOL/PLUM SE18 126 E3
Maude Rd CMBW SE5 143 F3
WALTH E17 69 G2
Maudesville Cots HNWL W7 115 K1
Maude Ter WALTH E17 69 G1
Maud Gdns BARK IG11 109 F1
PLSTW E13 106 D1
Maudlins Gn WAP E1W * 123 H1
Maud Rd LEY E10 88 A1
PLSTW E13 106 D1
Maudslay Rd ELTH/MOT SE9 146 E4
Maud St CAN/RD E16 106 D4
Maud Wilkes Cl KTTN NW5 84 C3
Mauleverer Rd
BRXS/STRHM SW2 141 K6
Maundeby Wk
WLSDN NW10 * 81 G3
Maunder Rd HNWL W7 115 K1
Maunsel St WEST SW1P 16 C6
Maurice Av WDGN N22 49 H5
Maurice Browne Cl
MLHL NW7 46 B1
Maurice St SHB W12 99 K5
Maurice Wk GLDGN NW11 65 G1
Maurier Cl NTHLT UB5 77 G6
Mauritius Rd GNWCH SE10 125 H4
Maury Rd STNW/STAM N16 68 C6
Mauveine Gdns HSLW TW3 135 F5
Mavelstone Rd BMLY BR1 184 C4
Maverton Rd BOW E3 * 87 J6
Mavis Av HOR/WEW KT19 207 G3
Mavis Cl HOR/WEW KT19 207 G3
Mawbey Pl STHWK SE1 123 G5
Mawbey Rd STHWK SE1 123 G5
Mawbey St VX/NE SW8 141 K1
Mawney Cl ROMW/RG RM7 56 D6
Mawney Rd ROMW/RG RM7 56 D5
Mawson Cl RYNPK SW20 177 H5
Mawson La CHSWK W4 118 C6
Maxey Gdns DAGW RM9 92 A2
Maxey Rd DAGW RM9 92 A2
WOOL/PLUM SE18 127 H4
Maxfield Cl TRDG/WHET N20 33 G2
Maxilla Wk NKENS W10 100 B5
Maxim Rd WCHMH N21 35 G1
Maxted Pk HRW HA1 60 E4
Maxted Rd PECK SE15 143 G4
Maxwell Cl CROY/NA CR0 195 K5
HYS/HAR UB3 94 E6
Maxwell Gdns ORP BR6 217 F1
Maxwell Ri OXHEY WD19 27 J2
Maxwell Rd FUL/PGN SW6 140 A1
NTHWD HA6 40 B3
WDR/YW UB7 112 B4
WELL DA16 148 B5
Maxwelton Av MLHL NW7 45 F1
Maxwelton Cl MLHL NW7 45 F1
Maya Cl PECK SE15 143 J3
Mayall Cl PEND EN3 25 J1
STHWK SE1 18 D1
Mayall Rd HNHL SE24 142 C6
Maya Pl FBAR/BDGN N11 48 D3
Maya Rd EFNCH N2 65 G1
May Av STMC/STPC BR5 202 C2
Maybank Av ALP/SUD HA0 79 G3
HCH RM12 93 K3
SWFD E18 53 F5
Maybank Gdns PIN HA5 58 E2
Maybank Rd SWFD E18 53 G4
May Bate Av KUTN/CMB KT2 174 E4
Mayberry Pl BRYLDS KT5 191 G4
Maybourne Cl SYD SE26 181 J1
Maybury Cl EN EN1 24 D1
STMC/STPC BR5 201 G2
Maybury Gdns WLSDN NW10 81 J5
Maybury Ms HGT N6 66 C4
Maybury Rd BARK IG11 109 G1
PLSTW E13 107 G3
Maybury St TOOT SW17 178 D1
Maychurch Cl STAN HA7 43 K4
May Cl CHSGTN KT9 206 B4
Maycock Gv NTHWD HA6 40 D2
Maycroft PIN HA5 41 F5
Maycross Av MRDN SM4 193 J1
Mayday Gdns BKHTH/KID SE3 146 D3
Mayday Rd THHTH CR7 196 C3
Mayefield Rd THHTH CR7 196 A1
Mayerne Rd ELTH/MOT SE9 146 C6
Mayesbrook Rd BARK IG11 91 F6
Mayesford Rd CHDH RM6 73 J4
Mayes Rd WDGN N22 49 F5
Mayeswood Rd
LEE/GVPK SE12 166 B6
Mayfair Av BXLYHN DA7 148 E2
CHDH RM6 73 K3
IL IG1 71 K6
WHTN TW2 155 H2
WPK KT4 192 D5
Mayfair Cl BECK BR3 182 E4
SURB KT6 191 F5
Mayfair Ct EDGW HA8 44 B1
Mayfair Gdns TOTM N17 49 J2
WFD IG8 52 E3
Mayfair Ms CAMTN NW1 * 83 K5
Mayfair Pl MYFR/PICC W1J 9 K7
Mayfair Ter STHGT/OAK N14 34 D2
Mayfield Av CHSWK W4 118 B4
KTN/HRWW/WS HA3 61 H2
NFNCH/WDSPK N12 33 G6
ORP BR6 202 A5
STHGT/OAK N14 34 C4
WEA W13 116 C3
WFD IG8 52 E2
Mayfield Cl CLAP SW4 141 J6
HACK E8 86 B5
PGE/AN SE20 181 J4
THDIT KT7 190 C5
Mayfield Crs ED N9 36 D1
THHTH CR7 196 A1
Mayfield Dr PIN HA5 59 K1
Mayfield Gdns HDN NW4 64 B3
HNWL W7 96 D5
Mayfield Rd ACT W3 98 D6
BCTR RM8 73 J5
BELMT SM2 209 H4
BELV DA17 129 K4
BMLY BR1 200 D2
CEND/HSY/T N8 67 F3
CHING E4 38 A4
HACK E8 * 86 B5
PEND EN3 25 F3
PLSTW E13 106 D3
SAND/SEL CR2 211 K6
SHB W12 118 B2
WALTH E17 51 G5
WIM/MER SW19 177 J4
Mayfields WBLY HA9 62 C6
Mayfields Cl WBLY HA9 62 C6
Mayfield Vls SCUP DA14 * 186 D2
Mayflower Cl
BERM/RHTH SE16 124 A4
RSLP HA4 58 A3
Mayflower Rd BRXN/ST SW9 141 K4
Mayflower St
BERM/RHTH SE16 123 K2
Mayfly Cl PIN HA5 59 G4
STMC/STPC BR5 202 E1
Mayford Cl BAL SW12 160 E2
BECK BR3 182 A6
Mayford Rd BAL SW12 160 E2
May Gdns ALP/SUD HA0 97 J2
Maygood St IS N1 5 H2
Maygreen Crs EMPK RM11 75 J4
Maygrove Rd
KIL/WHAMP NW6 82 D4
Mayhew Cl CHING E4 37 J5
Mayhill Rd BAR EN5 20 C6
CHARL SE7 126 A6
Maylands Av HCH RM12 93 K2
Maylands Dr SCUP DA14 168 E5
Maylands Rd OXHEY WD19 27 G6
Maynard Cl ERITH DA8 150 C1
FUL/PGN SW6 140 A1
SEVS/STOTM N15 68 A2
Maynard Rd WALTH E17 70 A2
Maynards Quay WAP E1W * 104 E6
Maynooth Gdns CAR SM5 194 E4
Mayola Rd CLPT E5 86 E2
Mayo Rd CROY/NA CR0 196 E2
WLSDN NW10 81 G4
Mayow Rd SYD SE26 164 A6
Mayplace Av DART DA1 150 D5
Mayplace La
WOOL/PLUM SE18 127 G6
Mayplace Rd BXLYHN DA7 149 K4
Mayplace Rd East
BXLYHN DA7 149 K4
Maypole Crs BARK/HLT IG6 54 D3
ERITH DA8 131 G6
May Rd CHING E4 51 J2
PLSTW E13 106 E1
WHTN TW2 155 K3
Mayroyd Av SURB KT6 191 H6
May's Buildings Ms
GNWCH SE10 145 G1
Mays Ct CHCR WC2N 10 E6
May's Hill Rd HAYES BR2 183 H5
May's La BAR EN5 31 K2
Maysoule Rd BTSEA SW11 140 C5
Mays Rd TEDD TW11 173 J1
May St WKENS W14 119 J5
Mayswood Gdns DAGE RM10 92 E4
Maythorne Cots LEW SE13 165 G1
Mayton St HOLWY N7 85 F1
Maytree Cl EDGW HA8 30 E5
RAIN RM13 111 G1
Maytree Ct MTCM CR4 179 F6
Maytree La STAN HA7 43 F2
Maytree Wk
BRXS/STRHM SW2 * 162 B4
Mayville Est
STNW/STAM N16 * 86 A3
Mayville Rd IL IG1 90 B3
WAN E11 70 C6
Maywood Cl BECK BR3 182 E3
Maze Hl GNWCH SE10 125 H6
Mazenod Av
KIL/WHAMP NW6 82 E5
Maze Rd RCH/KEW TW9 137 H1
McAdam Dr ENC/FH EN2 23 H3
McAuley Cl ELTH/MOT SE9 147 F6
STHWK SE1 17 J4
McCall Cl CLAP SW4 141 K3
McCall Crs CHARL SE7 126 D5
McCarthy Rd FELT TW13 172 C1
McCoid Wy STHWK SE1 18 C3
McCrone Ms HAMP NW3 83 H4
McCullum Rd BOW E3 87 H6
McDermott Cl BTSEA SW11 140 D3
McDermott Rd PECK SE15 143 H4
McDonough Cl CHSGTN KT9 206 A2
McDougall Ct RCH/KEW TW9 137 H3
McDowall Cl CAN/RD E16 106 E4
McDowall Rd CMBW SE5 142 D2
McEntee Av WALTH E17 51 G4
McEwan Wy SRTFD E15 * 88 B6
McGrath Rd SRTFD E15 88 D3
McGregor Rd NTGHL W11 100 D5
McIntosh Cl ROM RM1 57 G6
WLGTN SM6 210 E5
McIntosh Rd ROM RM1 57 G6
McKay Rd RYNPK SW20 176 E3
Mc Kellar Cl BUSH WD23 28 C4
McKerrell Rd PECK SE15 143 H2
McKillop Wy SCUP DA14 186 D3
McLeod's Ms SKENS SW7 120 A3
McMillan St DEPT SE8 124 D6
McNair Rd NWDGN UB2 115 F3
McNeil Rd CMBW SE5 143 F3
McNicol Dr WLSDN NW10 98 E1
McRae La MTCM CR4 194 E4
Mead Cl CAMTN NW1 84 A5
GPK RM2 57 J5
KTN/HRWW/WS HA3 42 D4
Mead Ct CDALE/KGS NW9 62 E2
Mead Crs CHING E4 38 A6
SUT SM1 209 J2
Meadcroft Rd LBTH SE11 122 B6
Meade Cl CHSWK W4 117 H6
Meadfield EDGW HA8 30 D4
Mead Fld RYLN/HDSTN HA2 * 77 K1
Meadfoot Rd
STRHM/NOR SW16 179 H4
Meadgate Av WFD IG8 53 J1
Mead Gv CHDH RM6 55 K6
Mead House La YEAD UB4 94 B3
Meadlands Dr
RCHPK/HAM TW10 156 E4
Meadow Av CROY/NA CR0 198 A3
Meadowbank BKHTH/KID SE3 145 J4
BRYLDS KT5 191 G3
HAMP NW3 83 K5
OXHEY WD19 27 G2
WCHMH N21 35 F1
Meadowbank Cl
FUL/PGN SW6 139 F1
Meadowbank Gdns
HSLWW TW4 133 K3
Meadowbank Rd
CDALE/KGS NW9 63 F4
Meadow Cl BAR EN5 32 D1
BARK IG11 91 F5
CAT SE6 182 D1
CHING E4 37 K3
CHST BR7 185 G1
ESH/CLAY KT10 205 F1
HOM E9 87 H3
HSLWW TW4 155 F1
NTHLT UB5 96 A1
PEND EN3 25 G2
RCHPK/HAM TW10 157 F3
RSLP HA4 58 D3
RYNPK SW20 193 F1
Meadowcourt Rd
BKHTH/KID SE3 145 J5
Meadow Cft BMLY BR1 184 E6
Meadowcroft BUSH WD23 * 28 B1
Meadowcroft Cl
PLMGR N13 * 35 H4
Meadowcroft Rd PLMGR N13 35 G4
Meadow Dr HDN NW4 46 A5
MUSWH N10 48 A6
Meadowford Cl THMD SE28 109 G6
Meadow Gdns EDGW HA8 44 D2
Meadow Garth WLSDN NW10 80 E4
Meadow Hl NWMAL KT3 192 B3
Meadow La LEE/GVPK SE12 166 B5
Meadowlea Cl WDR/YW UB7 112 A6
Meadow Ms VX/NE SW8 122 A6
Meadow Pl CHSWK W4 * 138 B1
VX/NE SW8 141 K1
Meadow Rd BARK IG11 91 F5
ESH/CLAY KT10 204 E3
FELT TW13 154 D4
HAYES BR2 183 H4
PIN HA5 59 H1
ROMW/RG RM7 74 E5
STHL UB1 95 K6
SUT SM1 209 J2
VX/NE SW8 122 A6
WIM/MER SW19 178 B3
Meadow Rw STHWK SE1 18 C5
Meadows Cl LEY E10 69 J6
Meadowside BKHTH/KID SE3 146 B5
TWK TW1 156 E2
WOT/HER KT12 188 B6
Meadowside Rd BELMT SM2 208 C6
The Meadows ORP BR6 217 J4
Meadow Stile CROY/NA CR0 211 J1
Meadowsweet Cl
CAN/RD E16 107 H4
NWMAL KT3 193 F2
The Meadow CHST BR7 185 H2
Meadow Vw BFN/LL DA15 168 C1
HRW HA1 60 E5
STMC/STPC BR5 186 D6
Meadowview Rd BXLY DA5 169 F1
CAT SE6 164 D6
HOR/WEW KT19 207 G6
Meadow View Rd THHTH CR7 196 C2
YEAD UB4 94 B3
Meadow Wk DAGW RM9 92 B4
HOR/WEW KT19 207 G4
SWFD E18 70 E1
WLGTN SM6 210 B1
Meadow Wy CDALE/KGS NW9 63 F2
CHSGTN KT9 206 A3
ORP BR6 216 A1
RSLP HA4 59 F3
WBLY HA9 79 K2
Meadow Waye HEST TW5 134 D1
The Meadow Wy
KTN/HRWW/WS HA3 42 E4
Mead Pl CROY/NA CR0 196 C5
HOM E9 86 E4
Mead Plat WLSDN NW10 80 E4
Mead Rd CHST BR7 185 H2
EDGW HA8 44 C2
RCHPK/HAM TW10 156 D5
Mead Rw STHWK SE1 17 J4
Meadside Cl BECK BR3 182 B4
Meads La GDMY/SEVK IG3 73 F4
Meads Rd PEND EN3 25 G2
WDGN N22 49 H5
The Meads CHEAM SM3 208 B1
EDGW HA8 45 F2
MRDN SM4 * 194 D2
The Mead BECK BR3 183 F5
EFNCH N2 47 G5
OXHEY WD19 27 J5
WEA W13 97 H4
WLGTN SM6 210 D4
WWKM BR4 199 G5
Meadvale Rd CROY/NA CR0 197 G4
EA W5 97 H3
Mead Wy HAYES BR2 199 J3
RSLP HA4 58 B3
Meadway ASHF TW15 152 D6
BAR EN5 20 E5
BECK BR3 183 F4
BRYLDS KT5 191 K5
Mead Wy CROY/NA CR0 198 B6
Meadway ESH/CLAY KT10 204 B6
GDMY/SEVK IG3 90 E2
GLDGN NW11 65 F3
GPK RM2 57 J5
RYNPK SW20 193 F1
STHGT/OAK N14 34 D4
WFD IG8 53 G1
WHTN TW2 155 J3
Meadway Cl BAR EN5 20 E4
GLDGN NW11 65 F3
PIN HA5 42 B2
Meadway Ct EA W5 * 98 B4
Meadway Gdns RSLP HA4 58 B3
The Meadway BKHH IG9 39 H3
BKHTH/KID SE3 145 G3
ORP BR6 217 H3
Meaford Wy PGE/AN SE20 181 J3
Meanley Rd MNPK E12 89 J3
Meard St SOHO/CST W1F 10 C4
Meath Cl STMC/STPC BR5 202 C2
Meath Crs BETH E2 105 F2
Meath Rd IL IG1 90 C1
SRTFD E15 106 D1
Meath St BTSEA SW11 141 G2
Mecklenburgh Pl
BMSBY WC1N 5 G6
Mecklenburgh Sq
BMSBY WC1N 5 G6
Mecklenburgh St
BMSBY WC1N 5 G6
Medburn St CAMTN NW1 4 C2
Medcroft Gdns
MORT/ESHN SW14 137 K5
Medesenge Wy PLMGR N13 49 H2
Medfield St PUT/ROE SW15 158 D2
Medhurst Cl BOW E3 105 G1
Medhurst Dr BMLY BR1 183 H1
Median Rd CLPT E5 86 E3
Medici Cl GDMY/SEVK IG3 73 G3
Medina Av ESH/CLAY KT10 204 E1
Medina Rd HOLWY N7 85 G1
Medland Cl WLGTN SM6 195 F5
Medlar Cl NTHLT UB5 95 H1
Medlar St CMBW SE5 142 D2
Medley Rd KIL/WHAMP NW6 82 E4
Medora Rd BRXS/STRHM SW2 162 A1
ROMW/RG RM7 75 F1
Medusa Rd CAT SE6 164 E1
Medway Cl CROY/NA CR0 197 K3
IL IG1 90 C3
Medway Dr GFD/PVL UB6 97 F1
Medway Gdns ALP/SUD HA0 79 G2
Medway Pde GFD/PVL UB6 * 97 F1
Medway Rd BOW E3 105 G1
DART DA1 150 D4
Medway St WEST SW1P 16 C5
Medwin St CLAP SW4 142 A5
Meerbrook Rd
BKHTH/KID SE3 146 B4
Meeson Rd SRTFD E15 88 D5
Meeson St CLPT E5 87 G2
Meesons Whf SRTFD E15 * 106 A1
Meeting Field Pth HOM E9 * 86 E4
Meeting House Aly
WAP E1W * 123 J1
Meeting House La PECK SE15 143 J2
Mehetabel Rd HOM E9 86 E4
Meister Cl IL IG1 72 D5
Melanda Cl CHST BR7 184 E1
Melbourne Av PIN HA5 42 B6
WDGN N22 49 F2
WEA W13 116 B1
Melbourne Cl ORP BR6 201 K4
WLGTN SM6 210 C3
Melbourne Gdns CHDH RM6 74 A2
Melbourne Gv EDUL SE22 143 F5
Melbourne Ms BRXN/ST SW9 142 B2
CAT SE6 165 F2
Melbourne Pl HOL/ALD WC2B 11 H4
Melbourne Rd BUSH WD23 28 B1
EHAM E6 89 K6
IL IG1 72 B5
LEY E10 69 K4
TEDD TW11 174 D2
WALTH E17 69 G1
WIM/MER SW19 177 K4
WLGTN SM6 210 B3
Melbourne Sq BRXN/ST SW9 142 B2
Melbourne Ter EDUL SE22 * 143 F5
FUL/PGN SW6 * 140 A1
Melbourne Wy EN EN1 36 B1
Melbury Av NWDGN UB2 115 G3
Melbury Cl CHST BR7 184 E2
ESH/CLAY KT10 205 H4
Melbury Ct KENS W8 119 J3
Melbury Dr CMBW SE5 143 F1
Melbury Gdns RYNPK SW20 176 E4
Melbury Rd
KTN/HRWW/WS HA3 62 B2
WKENS W14 119 J3
Melbury Ter CAMTN NW1 2 D7
Melcombe Gdns
KTN/HRWW/WS HA3 62 B3
Melcombe Pl CAMTN NW1 8 E1
Melcombe St CAMTN NW1 3 F7
Meldex Cl MLHL NW7 46 A2
Meldon Cl FUL/PGN SW6 * 140 A2
Meldone Cl BRYLDS KT5 191 J3
Meldrum Cl STMC/STPC BR5 202 D3
Meldrum Rd GDMY/SEVK IG3 73 G6
Melfield Gdns CAT SE6 164 E6
Melford Av BARK IG11 90 E4
Melford Cl CHSGTN KT9 206 B3
Melford Rd EDUL SE22 163 H3
EHAM E6 107 K3
IL IG1 72 D6
WALTH E17 69 G1
WAN E11 70 C6
Melfort Av THHTH CR7 180 C6
Melfort Rd THHTH CR7 180 C6

Melgund Rd HBRY N5 — 85 C3
Melina Cl HYS/HAR UB3 — 94 B4
Melina Pl STJWD NW8 — 2 A5
Melina Rd SHB W12 — 118 E2
Melior Pl STHWK SE1 * — 19 G2
Melior St STHWK SE1 — 19 G2
Meliot Rd CAT SE6 — 165 G4
Meller Cl CROY/NA CR0 — 210 E1
Mellifont Cl CAR SM5 — 194 C4
 MRDN SM4 — 194 C4
Melling Dr EN EN1 — 24 C2
Melling St WOOL/PLUM SE18 — 127 K6
Mellish Gdns WFD IG8 — 52 E1
Mellish St POP/IOD E14 — 124 D3
Mellison Rd TOOT SW17 — 178 D1
Melliss Av RCH/KEW TW9 — 137 J2
Mellitus St SHB W12 — 99 H5
Mellor Cl WOT/HER KT12 — 188 E4
Mellow La East HGDN/ICK UB10 — 94 A3
Mellows Rd CLAY IG5 — 53 K6
 WLGTN SM6 —
Mells Crs ELTH/MOT SE9 — 166 E6
Mell St GNWCH SE10 — 125 H5
Melody La HBRY N5 — 85 H3
Melody Rd WAND/EARL SW18 — 140 B6
Melon Pl KENS W8 —
Melon Rd PECK SE15 — 143 H2
 WAN E11 — 88 C1
Melrose Av CRICK NW2 — 82 A3
 GFD/PVL UB6 — 96 B1
 MTCM CR4 — 179 G3
 STRHM/NOR SW16 — 180 A6
 WDGN N22 — 49 H4
 WHTN TW2 — 155 C2
 WIM/MER SW19 — 159 J4
Melrose Cl GFD/PVL UB6 — 96 B1
 YEAD UB4 — 94 C4
Melrose Crs ORP BR6 — 216 D2
Melrose Dr STHL UB1 — 115 F1
Melrose Gdns EDGW HA8 — 44 D6
 HMSMTH W6 — 119 F3
 NWMAL KT3 —
Melrose Ms NWMAL KT3 — 176 A6
Melrose Rd BARN SW13 — 138 C3
 PIN HA5 — 59 K1
 WAND/EARL SW18 — 159 J1
 WIM/MER SW19 — 177 K5
Melrose Ter HMSMTH W6 — 119 F2
Melrose Vls BER BR3 * — 182 D5
Melsa Rd MRDN SM4 — 194 B3
Melthorne Dr RSLP HA4 — 77 C1
Melthorpe Gdns BKHTH/KID SE3 — 146 C2
Melton Cl RSLP HA4 — 59 G5
Melton Flds HOR/WEW KT19 — 207 F6
Melton Gdns ROM RM1 — 75 H4
Melton Pl HOR/WEW KT19 — 207 F6
Melton St CAMTN NW1 — 4 B5
Melville Av GFD/PVL UB6 — 79 F3
 RYNPK SW20 — 176 D3
 SAND/SEL CR2 — 212 B3
Melville Cl HGDN/ICK UB10 — 76 B1
Melville Ct DEPT SE8 — 124 A4
Melville Gdns PLMGR N13 — 49 H1
Melville Pl IS N1 — 85 J5
Melville Rd BARN SW13 — 138 D2
 CRW RM5 — 56 D3
 RAIN RM13 — 111 J1
 SCUP DA14 — 168 D4
 WALTH E17 — 69 H1
 WLSDN NW10 — 81 F5
Melville Villas Rd ACT W3 * — 118 A1
Melvin Rd PGE/AN SE20 — 181 K4
Memel St STLK EC1Y — 6
Memorial Av SRTFD E15 — 106 C2
Memorial Cl HEST TW5 — 114 E6
Memorial Sq KUT/HW KT1 — 174 E5
Mendip Cl HYS/HAR UB3 — 133 C1
 SYD SE26 —
 WPK KT4 — 193 F6
Mendip Dr CRICK NW2 — 64 C6
Mendip Houses BETH E2 * — 104 E2
Mendip Rd BTSEA SW11 — 140 B4
 BUSH WD23 — 28 A1
 EMPK RM11 — 75 J4
 GNTH/NBYPK IG2 — 72 E2
Mendora Rd FUL/PGN SW6 — 139 H1
Menelik Rd CRICK NW2 — 82 C2
Menlo Gdns NRWD SE19 — 180 E3
Menon Dr ED N9 — 36 D5
Menotti St BETH E2 * — 104 C3
Mentmore Cl KTN/HRWW/WS HA3 — 61 J3
Mentmore Ter HACK E8 — 86 D5
Meon Rd ACT W3 — 117 K2
Meopham Rd MTCM CR4 — 179 H4
Mepham Crs KTN/HRWW/WS HA3 — 42 C3
Mepham Gdns KTN/HRWW/WS HA3 — 42 C3
Mepham St STHWK SE1 — 17 H1
Merantum Wy WIM/MER SW19 — 178 B4
Merbury Cl LEW SE13 — 145 F6
 THMD SE28 — 127 J1
Merbury Rd THMD SE28 — 127 J1
Merbury St WOOL/PLUM SE18 — 127 G3
Mercator Pl POP/IOD E14 — 124 D5
Mercator Rd LEW SE13 — 145 G5
Mercer Cl THDT KT7 — 190 A4
Merceron Houses BETH E2 * — 104 E2
Merceron St WCHPL E1 — 104 D3
Mercer Pl PIN HA5 — 41 G5
Mercers Cl GNWCH SE10 — 125 J4
Mercers Cots WCHPL E1 * — 105 G5
Mercers Ms ARCH N19 — 84 D1
Mercers Pl HMSMTH W6 — 119 F4
Mercers Rd ARCH N19 — 84 D1
Mercer St LSO/SEVD WC2H — 10 E4
Merchants Cl SNWD SE25 — 197 H1
Merchant St BOW E3 — 105 H2
Merchiston Rd CAT SE6 — 165 G4
Merchland Rd ELTH/MOT SE9 — 167 H3
Mercia Gv LEW SE13 — 145 F4
Mercier Rd PUT/ROE SW15 — 139 H6
Mercury Gdns ROM RM1 — 75 G1
Mercury Rd BTFD TW8 — 116 D5
Mercury Wy NWCR SE14 — 124 A6
Mercy Ter LEW SE13 — 144 E6

Merebank La WLGTN SM6 — 211 F3
Mere Cl ORP BR6 — 201 G6
 WIM/MER SW19 — 159 G2
Meredith Av CRICK NW2 — 82 A3
Meredith Cl PIN HA5 — 41 H3
Meredith Ms BROCKY SE4 — 144 C5
Meredith St CLKNW EC1R — 6 A5
 PLSTW E13 — 106 E2
Meredyth Rd BARN SW13 — 138 D3
Mere End CROY/NA CR0 — 198 A4
Mereside ORP BR6 — 201 F6
Mereside Pk ASHF TW15 * — 153 F5
Meretone Cl BROCKY SE4 — 144 B5
Merevale Crs MRDN SM4 — 194 B3
Mereway Rd WHTN TW2 — 155 J3
Merewood Cl BMLY BR1 — 185 F5
Merewood Gdns CROY/NA CR0 —
Merewood Rd BXLYHN DA7 — 149 K3
Mereworth Cl HAYES BR2 — 199 J2
Mereworth Dr WOOL/PLUM SE18 — 147 G5
Meriden Cl BARK/HLT IG6 — 54 C4
 BMLY BR1 — 184 C3
Meridian Cl MLHL NW7 — 31 F6
Meridian Ct CHARL SE7 — 146 C1
Meridian Sq SRTFD E15 — 88 B5
Meridian Wy ED N9 — 37 F5
 UED N18 — 50 E2
Merifield Rd ELTH/MOT SE9 — 146 B6
Merino Cl WAN E11 — 71 G1
Merivale Rd HRW HA1 — 60 C4
 PUT/ROE SW15 — 139 H5
Merlewood Dr CHST BR7 — 184 E4
Merley Ct CDALE/KGS NW9 — 62 E5
Merlin Cl CROY/NA CR0 — 212 A2
 CRW RM5 — 57 F2
 MTCM CR4 — 178 D6
 NTHLT UB5 — 95 G2
 WLGTN SM6 — 211 F4
Merlin Crs EDGW HA8 — 44 B4
Merlin Gdns CRW RM5 — 57 F2
Merling Cl CHSGTN KT9 — 205 K3
Merlin Gv BARK/HLT IG6 — 54 B5
 BECK BR3 — 198 C1
Merlin Rd CRW RM5 — 57 F2
 MNPK E12 — 71 H6
 WELL DA16 — 148 B5
Merlin Rd North WELL DA16 — 148 B5
Merlins Av RYLN/HDSTN HA2 — 77 K1
Merlin St FSBYW WC1X — 5 J5
Mermagen Dr RAIN RM13 — 93 K5
Mermaid Ct STHWK SE1 — 18 E2
 BRXS/STRHM SW2 — 162 A1
Merriam Av HOM E9 — 87 H4
Merriam Cl CHING E4 — 52 A1
Merrick Rd NWDGN UB2 — 114 E4
Merrick Sq STHWK SE1 — 18 D4
Merridene WCHMH N21 — 35 H1
Merrielands Crs DAGW RM9 — 110 D1
Merrilands Rd WPK KT4 — 193 F5
Merrilees Rd BFN/LL DA15 — 167 K2
Merrilyn Cl ESH/CLAY KT10 — 205 G4
Merriman Rd BKHTH/KID SE3 — 146 B2
Merrington Rd FUL/PGN SW6 — 119 K6
Merrion Av STAN HA7 — 43 K1
Merritt Gdns CHSGTN KT9 — 205 J5
Merritt Rd BROCKY SE4 — 144 C6
Merrivale N14 — 22 D1
Merrivale Av REDBR IG4 — 71 H1
Merrivale Ms WDR/YW UB7 * — 112 A1
Merrow Rd BELMT SM2 — 208 B6
Merrows Cl NTHWD HA6 — 40 A2
Merrow St WALW SE17 — 122 E5
Merrow Wy WALW SE17 — 122 E5
 CROY/NA CR0 — 214 A4
Merrydown Wy CHST BR7 — 184 D4
Merryfield BKHTH/KID SE3 — 145 J3
Merryfield Gdns STAN HA7 — 43 J1
Merryfield Wy CAT SE6 — 164 E2
Merryhill Cl CHING E4 — 37 K2
Merry Hill Mt BUSH WD23 — 28 B3
Merry Hill Rd BUSH WD23 — 28 A2
Merryhills Dr ENC/FH EN2 — 22 E5
Merryweather Ct NWMAL KT3 * — 192 B2
Mersey Rd WALTH E17 — 51 H6
Mersham Dr CDALE/KGS NW9 — 62 A4
Mersham Pl PGE/AN SE20 — 181 J4
 THHTH CR7 — 180 E5
Mersham Rd THHTH CR7 — 180 E5
Merten Rd CHDH RM6 — 74 A4
Merthyr Ter BARN SW13 — 118 E6
Merton Av CHSWK W4 — 118 C4
 NTHLT UB5 — 78 C3
Merton Gdns STMC/STPC BR5 — 201 G4
Merton Hall Gdns RYNPK SW20 — 177 H4
Merton Hall Rd WIM/MER SW19 — 177 H4
Merton High St WIM/MER SW19 — 178 B3
Merton La HGT N6 — 65 K6
Merton Rd WIM/MER SW19 * — 178 B3
 BARK IG11 — 91 F5
 ENC/FH EN2 — 23 K1
 GDMY/SEVK IG3 — 73 F4
 RYLN/HDSTN HA2 — 60 C5
 SNWD SE25 — 197 G2
 WALTH E17 — 70 A2
 WAND/EARL SW18 — 159 K3
 WIM/MER SW19 — 178 A3
Merton Wy E/WMO/HCT KT8 — 189 H1
Mertoun Ter MBLAR W1H * — 8 E3
Merttins Rd PECK SE15 — 144 A5
Meru Cl KTTN NW5 — 84 A2
Mervan Rd BRXS/STRHM SW2 — 142 B5
Mervyn Av ELTH/MOT SE9 — 167 H5
Mervyn Rd WEA W13 — 116 B3
Messaline Av ACT W3 — 98 E5
Messent Rd ELTH/MOT SE9 — 146 B6
Messeter Pl ELTH/MOT SE9 — 167 F1
Messina Av KIL/WHAMP NW6 — 82 E6
Meteor St BTSEA SW11 — 141 F5
Meteor Wy WLGTN SM6 — 210 E5
Metford Crs PEND EN3 — 25 J1
Methley St LBTH SE11 — 122 B5
Methuen Cl EDGW HA8 — 44 C3
Methuen Pk MUSWH N10 — 48 B5

Methuen Rd BELV DA17 — 129 J4
 BXLYHN DA7 — 149 F4
 EDGW HA8 — 44 C3
Methwold Rd NKENS W10 — 100 B4
Metro Centre STMC/STPC BR5 * — 202 C3
Metropolitan Cl POP/IOD E14 — 105 J4
Metropolitan Whf WAP E1W * — 123 K1
Mews North BGVA SW1W — 15 J6
Mews Pl WFD IG8 — 38 E6
Mews South PIM SW1V — 121 H5
Mews St WAP E1W — 13 K7
The Mews BECK BR3 — 182 D4
 CEND/HSY/T N8 — 67 F3
 NFNCH/WDSPK N12 * — 47 F1
 REDBR IG4 — 71 H2
 ROM RM1 — 75 G1
 SEVS/STOTM N15 — 68 A1
 TWK TW1 — 156 C1
Mexfield Rd PUT/ROE SW15 — 139 J6
Meyer Gn EN EN1 — 24 C1
Meyer Rd ERITH DA8 — 129 K6
Meynell Crs HOM E9 — 87 F5
Meynell Gdns HOM E9 — 87 F5
Meynell Rd HARH RM3 — 57 K2
 HOM E9 — 87 F5
Meyrick Rd BTSEA SW11 — 140 C4
 WLSDN NW10 — 81 J5
Mezen Cl NTHWD HA6 — 40 B1
Miah Ter WAP E1W * — 123 H1
Micawber St IS N1 — 6 D4
Michael Gaynor Cl HNWL W7 — 116 A1
Michaelmas Cl RYNPK SW20 — 177 F6
Michael Rd FUL/PGN SW6 — 140 A2
 SNWD SE25 — 181 F6
 WAN E11 — 70 C5
Michaels Cl LEW SE13 — 145 H4
Micheldever Rd LEE/GVPK SE12 — 165 H1
Michelham Gdns TWK TW1 — 156 A5
Michelsdale Dr RYNPK SW20 — 137 F5
Michel Wk WOOL/PLUM SE18 — 127 G5
Michigan Av MNPK E12 — 89 J2
Michleham Down NFNCH/WDSPK N12 — 32 D6
Mickleham Cl STMC/STPC BR5 — 186 A5
Mickleham Gdns CHEAM SM3 — 208 C4
Mickleham Rd STMC/STPC BR5 — 186 A4
Mickleham Wy CROY/NA CR0 — 214 B5
Micklethwaite Rd FUL/PGN SW6 — 119 K6
Midcroft RSLP HA4 — 58 C5
Middle Dartrey Wk WBPTN SW10 * — 140 B1
Middle Dene MLHL NW7 — 31 F5
Middlefield STJWD NW8 — 83 H6
Middlefield WEA W13 — 97 H4
Middlefields CROY/NA CR0 — 213 G6
 WEA W13 — 97 H4
Middle Green Cl BRYLDS KT5 — 191 G3
Middleham Gdns UED N18 — 50 C2
Middleham Rd UED N18 — 50 C2
Middle La CEND/HSY/T N8 — 66 E2
 TEDD TW11 — 174 A2
Middle Lane Ms CEND/HSY/T N8 — 66 E2
Middle Park Av ELTH/MOT SE9 — 166 C1
Middle Rd EBAR EN4 — 33 J1
 PLSTW E13 — 106 E1
 RYLN/HDSTN HA2 — 60 D6
 STRHM/NOR SW16 — 179 H5
Middle Rw NKENS W10 — 100 C3
Middlesborough Rd UED N18 — 50 C2
Middlesex Cl STHL UB1 — 96 B5
Middlesex Pl HOM E9 — 86 E4
Middlesex Rd MTCM CR4 — 195 K2
Middlesex St WCHPL E1 — 13 H2
Middle St CROY/NA CR0 — 196 A6
Middle St EC1A — 12 C1
Middle Temple La EMB EC4Y — 11 J4
Middleton Av CHING E4 — 37 H6
 GFD/PVL UB6 — 96 D1
 SCUP DA14 — 186 D2
Middleton Cl CHING E4 — 37 H5
Middleton Dr BERM/RHTH SE16 — 124 A2
 PIN HA5 — 40 E6
Middleton Gdns GNTH/NBYPK IG2 — 72 B3
Middleton Gv HOLWY N7 — 84 E3
Middleton Ms HOLWY N7 — 84 E3
Middleton Pl GTPST W1W — 10 A2
Middleton Rd CAR SM5 — 194 C4
 E/WMO/HCT KT8 — 188 E2
 GLDGN NW11 — 64 E4
 HACK E8 — 86 B5
 HYS/HAR UB3 — 94 B4
 MRDN SM4 — 194 A3
 NWMAL KT3 — 175 K6
Middleton St BETH E2 — 104 D2
Middleton Wy LEW SE13 — 145 G5
Middleway GLDGN NW11 — 65 F2
Middle Wy STRHM/NOR SW16 — 179 J5
The Middle Wy KTN/HRWW/WS HA3 — 43 F5
Middle Yd STHWK SE1 * — 13 F7
Midfield Av BXLYHN DA7 — 149 K4
Midfield Wy STMC/STPC BR5 — 186 C4
Midford Pl FITZ W1T * — 4 B7
Midholm GLDGN NW11 — 65 F1
 WBLY HA9 — 62 C5
Midholm Cl GLDGN NW11 — 65 F1
Midhope St STPAN WC1H — 5 F5
Midhurst Av CROY/NA CR0 — 196 B4
 MUSWH N10 — 48 A6
Midhurst Gdns HGDN/ICK UB10 — 76 A5
Midhurst Hl BXLYHN DA7 — 149 H6
Midhurst Pde MUSWH N10 * — 48 A6
Midhurst Rd WEA W13 — 116 B3
Midhurst Wy CLPT E5 — 86 C2
Midland Arches CRICK NW2 * — 63 K6
Midland Crs HAMP NW3 — 83 G3
Midland Pl POP/IOD E14 — 124 E5
Midland Rd CAMTN NW1 — 4 D3
 LEY E10 — 70 A4
Midland Ter CRICK NW2 — 82 B1
 WLSDN NW10 — 99 G3

Midlothian Rd BOW E3 — 105 H3
Midmoor Rd BAL SW12 — 161 H3
 WIM/MER SW19 — 177 G4
Midship Cl BERM/RHTH SE16 * — 124 A1
Midship Point POP/IOD E14 — 124 D2
Midstrath Rd WLSDN NW10 — 81 G2
Midsummer Av HSLWW TW4 — 134 E5
Midway CHEAM SM3 — 193 J4
 WOT/HER KT12 — 188 A6
Midwinter Cl WELL DA16 — 148 B4
Midwood Cl CRICK NW2 — 81 J1
Mighell Av REDBR IG4 — 71 H2
Milan Rd STHL UB1 — 114 E2
Milborne Gv WBPTN SW10 — 120 B5
Milborne St HOM E9 — 86 E4
Milborough Crs LEE/GVPK SE12 — 165 H1
Milbourne La ESH/CLAY KT10 — 204 C4
Milbrook ESH/CLAY KT10 — 204 C4
Milcote St STHWK SE1 — 18 A3
Mildenhall Rd CLPT E5 — 86 E2
Mildmay Av IS N1 — 85 K4
Mildmay Gv North IS N1 — 85 K3
Mildmay Gv South IS N1 — 85 K3
Mildmay Pk IS N1 — 85 K3
Mildmay Pl STNW/STAM N16 * — 86 A3
Mildmay Rd IL IG1 — 90 B1
 ROMW/RG RM7 — 74 E2
 IS N1 — 85 K4
Mildmay St IS N1 — 85 K4
Mildred Av HYS/HAR UB3 — 113 G4
 NTHLT UB5 — 78 B3
Mildred Cl DART DA1 — 171 K1
Mile End Pl WCHPL E1 * — 105 F3
Mile End Rd WCHPL E1 — 104 C4
The Mile End WALTH E17 — 51 F4
Mile Rd WLGTN SM6 — 195 F5
Milespit Hl MLHL NW7 — 31 K5
Miles Pl BRYLDS KT5 * — 191 G1
Miles Rd CEND/HSY/T N8 — 48 E6
 MTCM CR4 — 178 D6
Miles St VX/NE SW8 — 121 K6
Milestone Cl BELMT SM2 — 209 H4
 ED N9 — 36 C4
Milestone Rd NRWD SE19 — 181 G2
Miles Wy TRDG/WHET N20 — 33 J4
Milfoil St SHB W12 — 99 J6
Milford Cl ABYW SE2 — 129 F6
Milford Gdns ALP/SUD HA0 — 79 K3
 CROY/NA CR0 — 198 A5
 EDGW HA8 — 44 C3
Milford Gv SUT SM1 — 209 G2
Milford La TPL/STR WC2R — 11 J5
Milford Ms STRHM/NOR SW16 — 162 A5
Milford Rd STHL UB1 — 96 A6
 WEA W13 — 116 C1
Milk St BMLY BR1 — 184 A1
 CAN/RD E16 — 127 G1
 CITYW EC2V — 12 D3
Milkwell Gdns WFD IG8 — 53 F3
Milkwell Yd CMBW SE5 — 142 D2
Milkwood Rd HNHL SE24 — 142 C6
Milk Yd WAP E1W — 104 E6
Millais Av MNPK E12 — 90 A3
Millais Crs HOR/WEW KT19 — 207 G5
Millais Gdns EDGW HA8 — 44 C5
Millais Rd EN EN1 — 24 B6
 NWMAL KT3 — 192 B4
 WAN E11 — 88 A2
Millais Wy HOR/WEW KT19 — 206 E3
Millard Cl STNW/STAM N16 — 86 A3
Millard Rd DEPT SE8 — 124 C5
Millbank WEST SW1P — 17 F5
Millbank Est WEST SW1P * — 16 E6
Millbourne Rd FELT TW13 — 154 D6
Mill Br Barn EN5 * — 20 D6
Millbrook Av WELL DA16 — 147 J5
Millbrook Gdns CHDH RM6 — 74 A3
 GPK RM2 — 57 K6
Millbrook Rd BRXN/ST SW9 — 142 C4
 ED N9 — 36 D3
Mill Cl CAR SM5 — 195 F6
 WDR/YW UB7 — 112 A3
Mill Cnr BAR EN5 — 20 D2
Mill Ct WDR/YW UB7 — 112 A3
Millender Wk BERM/RHTH SE16 — 124 A4
Millennium Br CAN/RD E16 — 106 E5
Millennium Br POP/IOD E14 — 125 G3
Millennium Dr BETH E2 * — 104 C1
Millennium Sq STHWK SE1 — 19 J2
Millennium Wy GNWCH SE10 — 125 H2
Miller Av PEND EN3 — 25 J1
Miller Cl BMLY BR1 — 183 K1
 CRW RM5 — 56 C3
 MTCM CR4 — 194 E4
Miller Rd CROY/NA CR0 — 196 A5
 WIM/MER SW19 — 178 C2
Miller's Av HACK E8 — 86 B3
Millers Cl MLHL NW7 — 31 J6
Millers Ct CHSWK W4 — 118 C5
Millers Green Cl ENC/FH EN2 — 23 H4
Miller's Ter HACK E8 — 86 B3
Miller St CAMTN NW1 — 4 A2
Millers Yd FNCH N3 — 47 F4
Miller Wk STHWK SE1 — 17 K1
Millet Rd GFD/PVL UB6 — 96 B2
Mill Farm Cl PIN HA5 — 41 G5
Mill Farm Crs HSLWW TW4 — 154 D3
Millfield Av WALTH E17 — 51 G4
Millfield La HGT N6 — 65 K6
 HGT N6 — 66 A6
Millfield Rd EDGW HA8 — 44 E5
 HSLWW TW4 — 154 D3
Millfields Cl STMC/STPC BR5 — 202 C1
Millfields Rd CLPT E5 — 86 E2
Mill Gdns SYD SE26 — 163 J6
Mill Gn MTCM CR4 — 195 F6
Mill Green Rd MTCM CR4 — 195 F6
Millgrove St BTSEA SW11 — 141 F2
Millharbour POP/IOD E14 — 124 E3
Millhaven Cl CHDH RM6 — 73 H3
Mill Hill BARN SW13 — 138 D3
Mill Hill Gv ACT W3 * — 117 J1
Mill Hill Rd ACT W3 — 117 J2
Mill Hill Ter ACT W3 * — 117 J1

 BARN SW13 — 138 E4
Millhouse Pl WNWD SE27 — 162 C6
Millicent Rd LEY E10 — 69 H5
Milligan St POP/IOD E14 — 105 J6
Milling Rd EDGW HA8 — 45 F3
Millington Rd HYS/HAR UB3 — 113 H3
Mill La CAR SM5 — 210 A2
 CHDH RM6 — 74 A3
 CHING E4 — 25 K4
 CRICK NW2 — 82 C3
 CROY/NA CR0 — 211 G1
 EW KT17 — 207 H6
 KIL/WHAMP NW6 — 82 E5
 WFD IG8 — 52 D1
 WOOL/PLUM SE18 — 127 F5
Millman Ms BMSBY WC1N — 5 G7
Millman St BMSBY WC1N — 5 G7
Millmark Gv NWCR SE14 — 144 B3
Millmarsh La PEND EN3 — 25 G3
Mill Mead Rd TOTM N17 — 50 D6
Mill Pl CHST BR7 — 185 G4
 DART DA1 — 150 D5
 KUT/HW KT1 — 175 G6
 POP/IOD E14 — 105 G5
Mill Plat ISLW TW7 — 136 B3
Mill Plat Av ISLW TW7 — 136 B3
Mill Pond Cl VX/NE SW8 — 141 J1
Millpond Est BERM/RHTH SE16 * — 123 J2
Mill Rdg EDGW HA8 — 44 B1
Mill Rd CAN/RD E16 — 126 A1
 ESH/CLAY KT10 — 189 F6
 IL IG1 — 90 A1
 WDR/YW UB7 — 112 A3
 WHTN TW2 — 155 H4
 WIM/MER SW19 — 178 B3
Mill Rw BXLY DA5 * — 169 J2
 IS N1 — 7 H1
Mills Gv HDN NW4 — 46 B6
 POP/IOD E14 — 106 A4
Millshot Cl FUL/PGN SW6 — 139 F2
Millshott Cl WHALL SW1A * — 10 D7
Millside CAR SM5 — 194 E6
Millside Pl ISLW TW7 — 136 C3
Millson Cl TRDG/WHET N20 — 33 H4
Mills Rw CHSWK W4 — 118 A4
Millstone Cl SRTFD E15 — 88 B4
Millstream Cl PLMGR N13 — 49 G5
Millstream Rd STHWK SE1 — 19 J3
Mill St CONDST W1S — 9 K6
 KUT/HW KT1 — 175 F6
 STHWK SE1 — 19 K3
Mill V HAYES BR2 — 183 J5
Mill View Cl EW KT17 — 207 H5
Mill View Gdns CROY/NA CR0 — 213 F1
Millwall Dock Rd POP/IOD E14 — 124 D3
Mill Wy EBED/NFELT TW14 — 134 A4
 MLHL NW7 — 45 G1
Millway Gdns NTHLT UB5 — 77 K4
Millwell Crs CHIG IG7 — 54 B1
Millwood Rd HSLW TW3 — 135 H5
 STMC/STPC BR5 — 186 D5
Millwood St NKENS W10 — 100 C4
Milman Cl PIN HA5 — 41 H6
Milman Rd KIL/WHAMP NW6 — 100 C1
Milman's St WBPTN SW10 — 120 C6
Milne Fld PIN HA5 — 41 K3
Milne Gdns ELTH/MOT SE9 — 146 D5
Milner Dr WHTN TW2 — 155 J2
Milner Pl IS N1 — 85 G6
Milner Rd BCTR RM8 — 73 K5
 KUT/HW KT1 — 174 E6
 MRDN SM4 — 194 C3
 SRTFD E15 — 106 C2
 WIM/MER SW19 — 178 A3
Milner Sq IS N1 — 85 H5
Milner St CHEL SW3 — 14 E6
Milnthorpe Rd CHSWK W4 — 118 A6
Milo Rd EDUL SE22 — 143 G6
Milroy Wk STHWK SE1 — 11 K7
Milson Rd WKENS W14 — 119 G3
Milton Av BAR EN5 — 20 D6
 CDALE/KGS NW9 — 44 E6
 CROY/NA CR0 — 196 E4
 EHAM E6 — 89 H6
 HGT N6 — 66 C4
 SUT SM1 — 209 H1
 WLSDN NW10 — 80 E6
Milton Cl EFNCH N2 — 65 G2
 STHWK SE1 — 19 J5
 SUT SM1 — 209 H1
 YEAD UB4 — 94 E3
Milton Court Rd NWCR SE14 — 124 B6
Milton Gdns STWL/WRAY TW19 — 152 B2
 STNW/STAM N16 — 85 K3
Milton Pk HGT N6 — 66 C4
Milton Rd ACT W3 — 99 F6
 BELV DA17 — 129 H4
 CDALE/KGS NW9 — 45 J6
 CROY/NA CR0 — 196 E5
 HGT N6 — 66 C4
 HNHL SE24 — 142 C6
 HPTN TW12 — 173 F4
 HRW HA1 — 60 E2
 MLHL NW7 — 31 H5
 MTCM CR4 — 160 A5
 ROM RM1 — 75 H3
 SEVS/STOTM N15 — 49 K6
 SUT SM1 — 208 E2
 WALTH E17 — 69 J1
 WELL DA16 — 148 A2
 WIM/MER SW19 — 178 A2
 WLGTN SM6 — 210 C4
Milton St BARB EC2Y — 12 E1
Milton Wy WDR/YW UB7 — 112 C4
Milverton Dr HGDN/ICK UB10 — 76 B2

Milverton Gdns
GDMY/SEVK IG3 73 F6
Milverton Rd
KIL/WHAMP NW6 82 A5
Milverton St LBTH SE11 122 B5
Milverton Wy ELTH/MOT SE9 167 F6
Milward St WCHPL E1 104 D4
Mimosa Cl ORP BR6 202 D6
Mimosa Rd YEAD UB4 95 C4
Mimosa St FUL/PGN SW6 139 J2
Minard Rd CAT SE6 165 H2
Mina Rd STHWK SE1 123 F5
WIM/MER SW19 177 K4
Minchenden Crs
STHGT/OAK N14 34 D5
Mincing La MON EC3R 13 G5
Minden Rd CHEAM SM3 193 H6
PGE/AN SE20 181 J4
Minehead Rd
RYLN/HDSTN HA2 78 A1
STRHM/NOR SW16 180 A1
Mineral Cl BAR EN5 32 A1
Mineral St WOOL/PLUM SE18 127 K4
Minera Ms BGVA SW1W 15 H6
Minerva Cl BRXN/ST SW9 142 B1
SCUP DA14 167 K6
Minerva Rd CHING E4 51 K3
KUT/HW KT1 175 G5
WLSDN NW10 98 E3
Minerva St BETH E2 104 D1
Minet Av WLSDN NW10 99 G1
Minet Dr HYS/HAR UB3 113 K1
Minet Gdns HYS/HAR UB3 114 A1
WLSDN NW10 99 G1
Minet Rd BRXN/ST SW9 142 C3
Minford Gdns WKENS W14 119 G2
Ming St POP/IOD E14 * 105 J6
Minimax Cl EBED/NFELT TW14 153 K1
Ministry Wy ELTH/MOT SE9 166 E4
Mink Ct HSLWW TW4 134 B3
Minniedale BRYLDS KT5 191 G2
Minnow Wk WALW SE17 19 H7
Minories TWRH EC3N 13 J4
Minshull Pl BECK BR3 * 182 D3
Minshull St VX/NE SW8 * 141 J2
Minson Rd HOM E9 87 F6
Minstead Gdns
PUT/ROE SW15 158 C2
Minstead Wy NWMAL KT3 192 B3
Minster Av SUT SM1 193 K6
Minster Ct MON EC3R * 13 G5
Minster Dr CROY/NA CR0 212 A2
Minster Gdns
E/WMO/HCT KT8 188 E1
Minster Rd BMLY BR1 184 A3
CRICK NW2 82 C3
Minster Wk CEND/HSY/T N8 66 E1
Minstrel Gdns BRYLDS KT5 191 G1
Mintern Cl PLMGR N13 35 H5
Minterne Av NWDGN UB2 115 F4
Minterne Rd
KTN/HRWW/WS HA3 62 B2
Minterne Waye YEAD UB4 95 G5
Mintern St IS N1 7 F2
Minton Ms KIL/WHAMP NW6 83 F4
Mint Rd WLGTN SM6 210 B3
Mint St STHWK SE1 18 C2
Mint Wk CROY/NA CR0 211 J1
Mirabel Rd FUL/PGN SW6 139 J1
Miranda Cl WCHPL E1 104 E4
Miranda Rd ARCH N19 66 C5
Mirfield St CHARL SE7 126 C3
Miriam Rd WOOL/PLUM SE18 127 K5
Mirren Cl RYLN/HDSTN HA2 77 K2
issenden Cl
EBED/NFELT TW14 153 J3
issenden Gdns MRDN SM4 194 B3
ission Gv WALTH E17 69 G2
ission Pl PECK SE15 143 H2
istletoe Cl CROY/NA CR0 198 A5
isty's Fld WOT/HER KT12 188 B5
itali Pas WCHPL E1 104 C5
itcham La
STRHM/NOR SW16 179 H1
itcham Pk MTCM CR4 194 D1
itcham Rd CROY/NA CR0 195 K3
EHAM E6 107 J2
GDMY/SEVK IG3 73 F4
TOOT SW17 178 E1
itchellbrook Wy
WLSDN NW10 81 F4
tchell Cl BELV DA17 129 K3
tchell Rd ORP BR6 217 F2
PLMGR N13 49 H1
tchell St FSBYE EC1V 6 C6
tchell Wy BMLY BR1 183 K4
WLSDN NW10 80 E4
tchison Rd IS N1 85 K4
tchley Rd TOTM N17 50 C6
tford Rd ARCH N19 66 E6
tre Cl BELMT SM2 209 G5
tre Rd SRTFD E15 106 C1
STHWK SE1 17 K2
tre Sq HDTCH EC3A 13 H4
tre St HDTCH EC3A 13 H4
e Mitre POP/IOD E14 105 H6
tre Wy NKENS W10 99 K4
at Cl ORP BR6 217 F4
at Ct ELTH/MOT SE9 * 166 E1
at Crs FNCH N3 47 F6
at Cft WELL DA16 148 D4
at Dr HRW HA1 60 C1
PLSTW E13 107 G1
RSLP HA4 58 C4
at Farm Rd NTHLT UB5 77 K4
at La ERITH DA8 150 D2
at Pl ACT W3 98 D5
BRXN/ST SW9 142 A4
at Side FELT TW13 154 B6
PEND EN3 24 E5
Moat NWMAL KT3 176 B4
berly Rd CLAP SW4 161 J2
dbury Gdns KTTN NW5 84 A4
del Cots
MORT/ESHN SW14 137 K4
WEA W13 * 116 C2
del Farm Cl ELTH/MOT SE9 166 D5
elyn Ms HRW HA1 61 G2
ffat Rd PLMGR N13 48 E2
HHTH CR7 180 D5
TOOT SW17 160 D6
Mogden La ISLW TW7 136 A6
Mohmmad Khan Rd
WAN E11 * 70 D5
Moiety Rd POP/IOD E14 124 D2
Moira Cl TOTM N17 50 A5
Moira Rd ELTH/MOT SE9 146 E5
Moir Cl SAND/SEL CR2 212 C6
Molash Rd STMC/STPC BR5 202 E1
Mole Abbey Gdns
E/WMO/HCT KT8 173 F6
Mole Ct HOR/WEW KT19 206 E2
Molember Ct
E/WMO/HCT KT8 189 K2
Molember Rd
E/WMO/HCT KT8 189 K2
Molescroft ELTH/MOT SE9 167 H5
Molesey Av E/WMO/HCT KT8 188 E1
Molesey Dr CHEAM SM3 193 H6
Molesey Park Av
E/WMO/HCT KT8 189 G2
Molesey Park Cl
E/WMO/HCT KT8 189 H2
Molesey Park Rd
E/WMO/HCT KT8 189 G2
Molesey Rd WOT/HER KT12 188 D5
Molesford Rd FUL/PGN SW6 * 139 K2
Molesham Cl
E/WMO/HCT KT8 173 G6
Molesham Wy
E/WMO/HCT KT8 189 G1
Molesworth St LEW SE13 145 F4
Mollison Av PEND EN3 25 G3
Mollison Dr WLGTN SM6 210 E5
Mollison Wy EDGW HA8 44 B5
Molly Huggins Cl BAL SW12 161 H2
Molyneux Dr TOOT SW17 161 G6
Molyneux St MBLAR W1H 8 D2
Monarch Cl
EBED/NFELT TW14 153 H2
RAIN RM13 111 J1
WWKM BR4 214 D2
Monarch Dr CAN/RD E16 107 H4
Monarch Ms
STRHM/NOR SW16 180 B1
Monarch Pde MTCM CR4 * 178 E5
Monarch Pl BKHH IG9 39 G4
Monarch Rd BELV DA17 129 H3
Monarchs Wy RSLP HA4 58 C5
Monarch Wy
GNTH/NBYPK IG2 72 D3
Mona Rd PECK SE15 143 K3
Monastery Gdns ENC/FH EN2 23 K3
Mona St CAN/RD E16 106 D4
Monaveen Gdns
E/WMO/HCT KT8 173 G6
Monck's Rw
WAND/EARL SW18 * 159 J1
Monck St WEST SW1P 16 D5
Monclar Rd CMBW SE5 142 E5
Moncorvo Cl SKENS SW7 14 C3
Moncrieff Cl EHAM E6 107 J5
Moncrieff St PECK SE15 143 H3
Monday Aly STNW/STAM N16 86 B1
Mondial Wy HYS/HAR UB3 133 F1
Monega Rd FSTGT E7 89 G4
MNPK E12 89 H4
Money La WDR/YW UB7 112 A3
Monier Rd BOW E3 87 J5
Monivea Rd BECK BR3 182 C3
Monk Dr CAN/RD E16 106 E6
Monkfrith Av STHGT/OAK N14 34 B1
Monkfrith Wy
STHGT/OAK N14 34 B2
Monkham's Av WFD IG8 53 F1
Monkham's Dr WFD IG8 53 F1
Monkham's La WFD IG8 39 F6
Monkleigh Rd MRDN SM4 177 H6
Monks Av BAR EN5 33 G1
E/WMO/HCT KT8 188 E2
Monks Cl ABYW SE2 128 E4
ENC/FH EN2 23 J3
RSLP HA4 77 H2
RYLN/HDSTN HA2 * 60 A6
Monks Crs WOT/HER KT12 188 A5
Monksdene Gdns SUT SM1 209 F1
Monks Dr ACT W3 98 C4
Monks Orchard Rd BECK BR3 198 D5
Monks Pk WBLY HA9 80 D4
Monks Park Gdns WBLY HA9 80 D4
Monks Rd ENC/FH EN2 23 H3
Monk St WOOL/PLUM SE18 127 F4
Monks Wy BECK BR3 198 D3
GLDGN NW11 64 D1
STMC/STPC BR5 201 H5
Monkswood Gdns CLAY IG5 54 A6
Monk Ter FSTH SE23 164 C4
Monkton Rd WELL DA16 148 A3
Monkton St LBTH SE11 17 K6
Monkville Av GLDGN NW11 64 D1
Monkville Pde GLDGN NW11 * 64 D1
Monkwell Sq BARB EC2Y 12 D2
Monkwood Cl ROM RM1 75 J2
Monmouth Av KUT/HW KT1 174 D3
SWFD E18 71 F1
Monmouth Cl CHSWK W4 118 A3
MTCM CR4 195 K1
WELL DA16 148 B5
Monmouth Gv BTFD TW8 117 F4
Monmouth Pl BAY/PAD W2 100 E5
Monmouth Rd BAY/PAD W2 100 E5
DAGW RM9 92 B3
ED N9 36 D4
EHAM E6 107 K2
HYS/HAR UB3 113 H4
Monmouth St
LSQ/SEVD WC2H 10 E4
Monnery Rd ARCH N19 84 C1
Monnow Rd STHWK SE1 123 H5
Mono La FELT TW13 154 A4
Monoux Gv WALTH E17 51 H4
Monroe Crs EN EN1 24 D2
Monroe Dr MORT/ESHN SW14 137 J6
Monro Gdns
KTN/HRWW/WS HA3 42 E3
Monro Pl HOR/WEW KT19 206 C6
Monsell Rd FSBYPK N4 85 H1
Monson Rd NWCR SE14 144 A1
WLSDN NW10 99 J1
Mons Wy HAYES BR2 200 D3
Montacute Rd BUSH WD23 28 E2
CAT SE6 164 C2
CROY/NA CR0 214 A6
MRDN SM4 194 C3
Montagu Crs UED N18 36 D6
Montague Av BROCKY SE4 144 C5
HNWL W7 116 A1
Montague Cl BAR EN5 20 D5
STHWK SE1 12 E7
Montague Gdns EA W5 98 C6
Montague Hall Pl BUSH WD23 28 A1
Montague Pl GWRST WC1E 10 D1
Montague Rd
CEND/HSY/T N8 67 F2
CROY/NA CR0 196 C5
HACK E8 86 C3
HNWL W7 116 A2
HSLW TW3 135 G4
NWDGN UB2 114 D4
RCHPK/HAM TW10 157 F1
SEVS/STOTM N15 * 68 C1
WAN E11 70 D6
WEA W13 97 H5
WIM/MER SW19 178 A3
Montague Sq PECK SE15 143 K1
Montague St RSQ WC1B 10 E1
STBT EC1A 12 C2
Montague Ter HAYES BR2 * 199 J1
Montague Waye NWDGN UB2 114 D3
Montagu Gdns UED N18 36 D6
WLGTN SM6 210 C2
Montagu Man MHST W1U 9 F2
Montagu Ms North
MBLAR W1H 9 F2
Montagu Ms South
MBLAR W1H 9 F3
Montagu Ms West
MBLAR W1H 8 E3
Montagu Pl MBLAR W1H 8 E2
Montagu Rd ED N9 36 E5
HDN NW4 63 J3
UED N18 50 D1
Montagu Rw MHST W1U 9 F2
Montagu Sq MBLAR W1H 9 F2
Montagu St MBLAR W1H 9 F3
Montaigne Cl WEST SW1P * 16 D7
Montaigne Cl WEST SW1P 16 D7
Montalt Rd WFD IG8 52 D1
Montana Gdns SUT SM1 209 G3
SYD SE26 182 C1
Montana Rd RYNPK SW20 177 F4
TOOT SW17 161 F5
Montbelle Rd ELTH/MOT SE9 167 G5
Montbretia Cl
STMC/STPC BR5 202 D1
Montcalm Cl YEAD UB4 95 F2
Montcalm Rd CHARL SE7 146 C1
Montclare St BETH E2 7 J5
Monteagle Av BARK IG11 90 C4
Monteagle Wy PECK SE15 143 J4
Montefiore St VX/NE SW8 141 G3
Montem Rd FSTH SE23 164 C2
NWMAL KT3 192 B1
Montem St FSBYPK N4 67 F5
Montenotte Rd
CEND/HSY/T N8 66 C2
Monterey Cl BXLY DA5 169 K4
Montesole Ct PIN HA5 41 G5
Montesquieu Ter
CAN/RD E16 * 106 D5
Montford Pl LBTH SE11 122 B5
Montfort Gdns BARK/HLT IG6 54 C2
Montfort Pl WIM/MER SW19 159 G3
Montgomerie Ms FSTH SE23 163 K2
Montgomery Av
ESH/CLAY KT10 189 K6
Montgomery Cl BFN/LL DA15 147 K6
MTCM CR4 * 195 K1
Montgomery Gdns
BELMT SM2 209 H5
Montgomery Rd CHSWK W4 117 K4
EDGW HA8 44 B2
Montgomery St POP/IOD E14 124 E1
Montholme Rd BTSEA SW11 160 E1
Monthorpe Rd WCHPL E1 104 C4
Montolieu Gdns
PUT/ROE SW15 138 E6
Montpelier Av BXLY DA5 168 E2
EA W5 97 J4
Montpelier Gdns CHDH RM6 73 J4
EHAM E6 107 H2
Montpelier Gv KTTN NW5 84 C3
Montpelier Ms SKENS SW7 14 D4
Montpelier Pl SKENS SW7 14 D4
WCHPL E1 104 E5
Montpelier Ri GLDGN NW11 64 C4
WBLY HA9 61 K5
Montpelier Rd EA W5 97 K4
FNCH N3 47 G4
PECK SE15 143 J2
SUT SM1 209 G2
Montpelier Rw
BKHTH/KID SE3 145 J3
TWK TW1 156 C2
Montpelier Sq SKENS SW7 14 D4
Montpelier St SKENS SW7 14 D3
Montpelier Ter SKENS SW7 14 D3
Montpelier V
BKHTH/KID SE3 * 145 J3
Montpelier Wk SKENS SW7 14 D3
Montpelier Wy GLDGN NW11 64 C4
Montrave Rd PGE/AN SE20 181 K2
Montreal Pl HOL/ALD WC2B 11 G5
Montreal Rd IL IG1 72 C4
Montrell Rd
BRXS/STRHM SW2 161 K3
Montrose Av BFN/LL DA15 168 B2
EDGW HA8 45 F5
KIL/WHAMP NW6 100 C1
WELL DA16 147 J4
WHTN TW2 155 G2
Montrose Cl WELL DA16 148 A4
WFD IG8 38 E6
Montrose Crs ALP/SUD HA0 80 A4
NFNCH/WDSPK N12 * 47 F2
Montrose Gdns MTCM CR4 178 E6
SUT SM1 194 A6
Montrose Pl KTBR SW1X 15 H3
Montrose Rd
EBED/NFELT TW14 153 G1
KTN/HRWW/WS HA3 42 E5
Montrose Vls HMSMTH W6 * 118 D5
Montrose Wy FSTH SE23 164 A3
Montserrat Av WFD IG8 52 B3
Montserrat Cl NRWD SE19 180 E1
Montserrat Rd
PUT/ROE SW15 139 H5
Monument Wy TOTM N17 50 B6
Monza St WAP E1W 104 E6
Moodkee St
BERM/RHTH SE16 123 K3
Moody St WCHPL E1 105 F2
Moon La BAR EN5 20 D4
Moon St IS N1 85 H6
Moorcroft EDGW HA8 * 44 D4
Moorcroft Gdns HAYES BR2 200 D2
Moorcroft Rd
STRHM/NOR SW16 161 K5
Moorcroft Wy PIN HA5 59 J2
Moordown WOOL/PLUM SE18 147 F2
Moore Cl MORT/ESHN SW14 137 K4
MTCM CR4 * 179 G5
Moore Crs DAGW RM9 91 H6
Moorefield Rd TOTM N17 50 B6
Mooreland Rd BMLY BR1 183 J3
Moore Park Rd FUL/PGN SW6 140 A1
Moore Rd NRWD SE19 180 D2
Moore St CHEL SW3 14 E6
Moore Wy BELMT SM2 208 E6
Moorey Cl SRTFD E15 88 D6
Moorfield Av EA W5 97 K3
Moorfield Rd CHSGTN KT9 206 A3
ORP BR6 202 B4
PEND EN3 24 E2
Moorfields LVPST EC2M 12 E2
Moorfields Highwalk
BARB EC2Y 12 E2
Moorgate LOTH EC2R 12 E3
Moorgate Pl LOTH EC2R * 12 E3
Moorhead Wy
BKHTH/KID SE3 146 A4
Moorhouse Rd BAY/PAD W2 100 E5
KTN/HRWW/WS HA3 43 K6
The Moorings CHSWK W4 * 117 H6
Moorland Cl CRW RM5 56 D4
WHTN TW2 155 F2
Moorland Rd BRXN/ST SW9 142 C5
Moorlands Av MLHL NW7 45 K2
Moor La BARB EC2Y 12 E2
CHSGTN KT9 206 A2
Moor Lane Crossing
WATW WD18 26 A2
Moormead Dr
HOR/WEW KT19 207 G3
Moor Mead Rd TWK TW1 156 B1
Moor Park Gdns
KUTN/CMB KT2 176 B3
NTHWD HA6 * 26 A4
Moor Park Rd NTHWD HA6 40 B2
Moorside Rd BMLY BR1 165 H6
Moor St SOHO/SHAV W1D 10 D4
Moortown Rd OXHEY WD19 27 G6
Moor Vw WATW WD18 26 E2
Morant Gdns CRW RM5 56 D1
Morant St POP/IOD E14 105 J6
Mora Rd CRICK NW2 82 A2
Mora St FSBYE EC1V 6 D5
Morat St BRXN/ST SW9 142 A2
Moravian Pl WBPTN SW10 120 C6
Moravian St BETH E2 104 E1
Moray Av HYS/HAR UB3 113 J1
Moray Cl EDGW HA8 * 30 D4
ROM RM1 57 G3
Moray Ms HOLWY N7 67 F6
Moray Rd HOLWY N7 67 F6
Moray Wy ROM RM1 57 F3
Morcambe St WALW SE17 18 D7
Mordaunt Gdns DAGW RM9 92 A5
Mordaunt Rd WLSDN NW10 81 F6
Mordaunt St BRXN/ST SW9 142 A4
Morden Ct MRDN SM4 194 A1
Morden Court Pde
MRDN SM4 * 178 A6
Morden Gdns GFD/PVL UB6 79 F3
MTCM CR4 194 C1
Morden Hall Rd MRDN SM4 178 A6
Morden Hl LEW SE13 145 F3
Morden La LEW SE13 145 F3
Morden Rd CHDH RM6 74 A4
MTCM CR4 194 C1
WIM/MER SW19 178 A5
Morden St LEW SE13 144 E2
Morden Wy CHEAM SM3 193 K4
Morden Wharf Rd
GNWCH SE10 125 H3
Mordon Rd GDMY/SEVK IG3 73 F4
Mordred Rd CAT SE6 165 H4
Morecambe Cl HCH RM12 93 K3
WCHPL E1 * 105 F4
Morecambe Gdns STAN HA7 29 K6
Morecambe St POP/IOD E14 124 E5
Morecambe Ter UED N18 * 35 K6
More Cl CAN/RD E16 106 D5
WKENS W14 119 G4
Morecoombe Cl
KUTN/CMB KT2 175 J3
Moree Wy UED N18 36 C6
Moreland Cots BOW E3 * 105 J1
Moreland St FSBYE EC1V 6 B4
Moreland Wy CHING E4 37 K5
More La ESH/CLAY KT10 204 B1
Morella Rd BTSEA SW11 160 E2
More London Riverside
STHWK SE1 19 H1
Moremead Rd CAT SE6 164 C6
Morena St CAT SE6 164 E2
Moresby Av BRYLDS KT5 191 J4
Moresby Rd CLPT E5 68 D5
Mores Gdn CHEL SW3 * 120 C6
Moretaine Rd ASHF TW15 152 A5
Moreton Av ISLW TW7 135 J2
Moreton Cl CLPT E5 68 E6
MLHL NW7 46 A2
SEVS/STOTM N15 67 K3
Moreton Ct DART DA1 150 B4
Moreton Gdns WFD IG8 53 J1
Moreton Pl PIM SW1V 121 H5
Moreton Rd SAND/SEL CR2 211 K3
SEVS/STOTM N15 67 K3
WPK KT4 192 D6
Moreton St PIM SW1V 121 J5
Moreton Ter PIM SW1V 121 H5
Moreton Terrace Ms North
PIM SW1V 121 H5
Moreton Terrace Ms South
PIM SW1V * 121 H5
Morford Cl RSLP HA4 59 F4
Morford Wy RSLP HA4 59 F4
Morgan Av WALTH E17 70 B1
Morgan Cl DAGE RM10 92 C5
NTHWD HA6 40 D1
Morgan Rd BMLY BR1 183 K3
HOLWY N7 85 G3
NKENS W10 100 D4
Morgan's La HYS/HAR UB3 94 B4
Morgan St BOW E3 105 G2
CAN/RD E16 106 D4
Morgan Wy WFD IG8 53 J2
Moriarty Cl BMLY BR1 201 G1
Moriatry Cl HOLWY N7 84 E2
Morie St WAND/EARL SW18 140 A5
Morieux Rd LEY E10 69 H5
Moring Rd TOOT SW17 161 F6
Morkyns Wk DUL SE21 * 163 F5
Morland Av CROY/NA CR0 197 F5
Morland Cl GLDGN NW11 65 F5
HPTN TW12 172 E1
MTCM CR4 178 D6
Morland Est HACK E8 * 86 C5
Morland Gdns STHL UB1 115 G1
WLSDN NW10 81 F5
Morland Ms IS N1 85 G5
Morland Rd CROY/NA CR0 197 G4
DAGE RM10 92 C5
IL IG1 72 B6
KTN/HRWW/WS HA3 62 A2
PGE/AN SE20 182 A3
SUT SM1 209 G3
WALTH E17 69 F2
Morley Av CHING E4 52 B3
UED N18 36 C6
WDGN N22 49 G5
Morley Cl ORP BR6 201 G6
Morley Crs EDGW HA8 30 E4
RSLP HA4 59 G6
Morley Crs East STAN HA7 43 J6
Morley Crs West STAN HA7 43 J6
Morley Hl ENC/FH EN2 23 K1
Morley Rd BARK IG11 90 D6
CHDH RM6 74 A2
CHEAM SM3 193 J5
CHST BR7 185 H4
LEW SE13 145 F5
LEY E10 70 A5
SRTFD E15 106 D1
TWK TW1 156 E1
Morley St STHWK SE1 17 K3
Morna Rd CMBW SE5 142 D3
Morning La HOM E9 86 E4
Morningside Rd WPK KT4 192 E6
Mornington Av HAYES BR2 184 B6
IL IG1 72 A4
WKENS W14 119 J4
Mornington Crs CAMTN NW1 4 A2
HEST TW5 134 A2
Mornington Gv BOW E3 105 J2
Mornington Ms CMBW SE5 142 D2
Mornington Pl CAMTN NW1 3 K2
Mornington Rd CHING E4 38 B2
GFD/PVL UB6 96 B4
NWCR SE14 144 C1
WAN E11 70 D5
WFD IG8 38 D6
Mornington St CAMTN NW1 3 K2
Mornington Ter CAMTN NW1 3 K1
Mornington Wk
RCHPK/HAM TW10 156 D6
Morocco St STHWK SE1 19 G3
Morpeth Gv HOM E9 87 F6
Morpeth Rd HOM E9 86 E6
Morpeth St BETH E2 105 F2
Morpeth Ter WEST SW1P 16 A5
Morpeth Wk TOTM N17 * 50 D3
Morrab Gdns GDMY/SEVK IG3 91 F1
Morrel Cl BAR EN5 21 G4
Morrells Yd LBTH SE11 * 122 B5
Morris Av MNPK E12 89 K3
Morris Bishop Ter HGT N6 * 66 A3
Morris Cl CROY/NA CR0 198 B3
ORP BR6 216 E1
Morris Ct CHING E4 37 K5
Morris Gdns
WAND/EARL SW18 159 K2
Morrish Rd BRXS/STRHM SW2 161 K2
Morrison Av CHING E4 51 J2
TOTM N17 50 A6
Morrison Rd BARK IG11 110 A1
YEAD UB4 95 F2
Morrison St BTSEA SW11 141 F4
Morris Pl FSBYPK N4 67 G6
Morris Rd BCTR RM8 74 B6
HARH RM3 57 K3
ISLW TW7 136 A4
POP/IOD E14 105 K4
SRTFD E15 88 C2
Morris St WCHPL E1 104 D5
Morriston Cl OXHEY WD19 41 G1
Morse Cl PLSTW E13 106 E2
Morshead Rd MV/WKIL W9 100 E2
Morson Rd PEND EN3 37 G1
Morteyne Rd TOTM N17 49 K4
Mortham St SRTFD E15 88 C6
Mortimer Cl BUSH WD23 28 B1
CRICK NW2 82 D1
STRHM/NOR SW16 161 J4
Mortimer Crs
KIL/WHAMP NW6 83 F6
WPK KT4 207 F1
Mortimer Dr EN EN1 23 K6
Mortimer Pl KIL/WHAMP NW6 83 F6
Mortimer Rd EHAM E6 107 K2
IS N1 86 A5
MTCM CR4 178 E4
ORP BR6 202 B6
WEA W13 97 J5
WLSDN NW10 100 A2
Mortimer Sq NTGHL W11 100 B6
Mortimer St GTPST W1W 9 K3
Mortimer Ter KTTN NW5 * 84 B2
Mortlake Cl CROY/NA CR0 210 E1

Mortlake Dr *MTCM* CR4 178 D4
Mortlake High St
MORT/ESHN SW14 138 A4
Mortlake Rd *CAN/RD* E16 107 F5
IL IG1 90 C2
MORT/ESHN SW14 137 J4
RCH/KEW TW9 137 H1
Morton Cl *CLAP* SW4 161 J1
WCHPL E1 104 E5
WLGTN SM6 211 F5
Morton Crs *STHGT/OAK* N14 34 D6
Morton Gdns *WLGTN* SM6 210 C3
Morton Ms *ECT* SW5 120 A4
Morton Pl *STHWK* SE1 17 J5
Morton Rd *IS* N1 85 J5
MRDN SM4 194 C2
SRTFD E15 88 D5
Morton Wy *STHGT/OAK* N14 34 C5
Morvale Cl *BELV* DA17 129 G4
Morval Rd
BRXS/STRHM SW2 142 B6
Morven Rd *TOOT* SW17 160 E5
Morville St *BOW* E3 105 J1
Morwell St *RSQ* WC1B 10 C2
Moscow Pl *BAY/PAD* W2 * 101 F6
Moscow Rd *BAY/PAD* W2 100 E6
Moselle Av *WDGN* N22 49 G5
Moselle Cl *CEND/HSY/T* N8 49 F6
Moselle Pl *TOTM* N17 50 B3
Moselle St *TOTM* N17 50 B3
Mossborough Cl
NFNCH/WDSPK N12 47 F2
Mossbury Rd *BTSEA* SW11 140 D4
Moss Cl *PIN* HA5 41 K5
WCHPL E1 104 C4
Mossdown Cl *BELV* DA17 129 H4
Mossford Gn *BARK/HLT* IG6 54 B6
Mossford La *BARK/HLT* IG6 54 C5
Mossford St *BOW* E3 105 H3
Moss Gdns *FELT* TW13 153 K4
SAND/SEL CR2 213 F5
Moss Hall Crs
NFNCH/WDSPK N12 47 F2
Moss Hall Gv
NFNCH/WDSPK N12 47 F2
Moss La *PIN* HA5 41 J5
ROM RM1 75 H3
Mosslea Rd *HAYES* BR2 200 C2
ORP BR6 216 C1
PGE/AN SE20 181 K2
Mossop St *CHEL* SW3 14 D6
Moss Rd *DAGE* RM10 92 C5
Mossville Gdns *MRDN* SM4 177 J6
Moston Cl *HYS/HAR* UB3 113 J5
Mostyn Av *WBLY* HA9 80 B3
Mostyn Gdns *WLSDN* NW10 100 B2
Mostyn Gv *BOW* E3 105 H1
Mostyn Rd *BRXN/ST* SW9 142 B2
EDGW HA8 45 F3
WIM/MER SW19 177 J6
Mosul Wy *HAYES* BR2 200 D3
Mosyer Dr *STMC/STPC* BR5 202 E6
Motcomb St *KTBR* SW1X 15 G4
Moth Cl *WLGTN* SM6 210 E5
The Mothers Sq *CLPT* E5 * 86 D2
Moth House
WOOL/PLUM SE18 * 146 D1
Motley St *VX/NE* SW8 141 H3
Motspur Pk *NWMAL* KT3 192 C3
Mottingham Gdns
ELTH/MOT SE9 166 C3
Mottingham La
LEE/GVPK SE12 166 B3
Mottingham Rd *ED* N9 37 F1
ELTH/MOT SE9 166 D5
Mottisfont Rd *ABYW* SE2 128 B3
Moulins Rd *HOM* E9 86 F5
Moulton Av *HSLW* TW3 134 D3
Moundfield Rd
STNW/STAM N16 68 C3
Mountacre Cl *SYD* SE26 163 G6
Mount Adon Pk *EDUL* SE22 163 H2
Mountague Pl *POP/IOD* E14 106 A6
Mount Angelus Rd
PUT/ROE SW15 158 C2
Mount Ararat Rd
RCHPK/HAM TW10 137 F6
Mount Ash Rd *SYD* SE26 163 J5
Mount Av *CHING* E4 37 J5
EA W5 97 K4
STHL UB1 96 A5
Mountbatten Cl *NRWD* SE19 181 F1
WOOL/PLUM SE18 127 K6
Mountbatten Ct *BKHH* IG9 39 H4
Mountbel Rd *STAN* HA7 * 43 G5
Mount Cl *BMLY* BR1 184 D4
CAR SM5 210 A6
EA W5 * 97 J4
EBAR EN4 22 A5
Mountcombe Cl *SURB* KT6 191 F4
Mount Ct *WWKM* BR4 199 H6
Mount Culver Av *SCUP* DA14 186 E2
Mount Dr *RYLN/HDSTN* HA2 59 K2
WBLY HA9 62 E6
Mountearl Gdns
STRHM/NOR SW16 162 A5
Mount Echo Av *CHING* E4 37 K3
Mount Echo Dr *CHING* E4 37 K3
Mount Ephraim La
STRHM/NOR SW16 161 J5
Mount Ephraim Rd
STRHM/NOR SW16 161 J5
Mountfield Cl *CAT* SE6 165 G2
Mountfield Rd *EA* W5 97 K5
EHAM E6 108 A1
FNCH N3 46 E6
Mountfield Ter *CAT* SE6 165 G2
Mountfield Wy
STMC/STPC BR5 202 D1
Mountfort Crs *IS* N1 85 G5
Mountfort Ter *IS* N1 85 G5
Mount Gdns *SYD* SE26 163 J5
Mount Gv *EDGW* HA8 30 E5
Mountgrove Rd *HBRY* N5 85 J1
Mount Holme *THDIT* KT7 190 C4
Mountington Park Cl
KTN/HRWW/WS HA3 61 K3
Mountjoy Cl *ABYW* SE2 128 C2
Mount Ms *HPTN* TW12 173 G4
Mount Mills *FSBYE* EC1V 6 B5
Mount Nod Rd
STRHM/NOR SW16 162 A5
Mount Pde *EBAR* EN4 * 21 J5
Mount Pk *CAR* SM5 210 A6
Mount Park Av *HRW* HA1 60 D6
SAND/SEL CR2 211 H6
Mount Park Crs *EA* W5 97 K5
Mount Park Rd *EA* W5 97 K4
HRW HA1 60 D6
PIN HA5 58 E2
Mount Pl *ACT* W3 117 J1
Mount Pleasant
ALP/SUD HA0 80 A6
EBAR EN4 21 K5
FSBYW WC1X 5 H7
HRW HA1 * 60 E6
RSLP HA4 77 G1
WNWD SE27 162 D6
Mount Pleasant Crs
FSBYPK N4 * 67 F4
Mount Pleasant Hl *CLPT* E5 68 D6
Mount Pleasant La *CLPT* E5 68 D5
Mount Pleasant Pl
WOOL/PLUM SE18 127 J4
Mount Pleasant Rd *CRW* RM5 57 F2
EA W5 97 J3
LEW SE13 165 F1
NWMAL KT3 175 K6
TOTM N17 50 A6
WALTH E17 51 G5
WLSDN NW10 82 A5
Mount Pleasant Vls
FSBYPK N4 67 F4
Mount Ri *FSTH* SE23 163 K4
Mount Rd *BCTR* RM8 74 B5
CHSGTN KT9 206 B2
CRICK NW2 81 K1
EBAR EN4 21 J6
FELT TW13 154 D5
HDN NW4 63 J3
HYS/HAR UB3 113 K2
MTCM CR4 178 C5
NRWD SE19 * 180 E2
NWMAL KT3 176 A6
WIM/MER SW19 159 K4
Mount Rw *MYFR/PKLN* W1K 9 J6
Mountside
KTN/HRWW/WS HA3 43 F4
Mounts Pond Rd
BKHTH/KID SE3 145 G3
The Mount Sq *HAMP* NW3 * 83 G1
Mount Stewart Av
KTN/HRWW/WS HA3 61 K3
Mount St *MYFR/PKLN* W1K 9 G6
Mount Ter *WCHPL* E1 104 D4
The Mount *BMLY* BR1 * 184 D4
CLPT E5 * 68 D6
ESH/CLAY KT10 204 A4
EW KT17 207 K2
HAMP NW3 83 G2
NTHLT UB5 * 78 B3
NWMAL KT3 176 C6
TRDG/WHET N20 33 G4
WBLY HA9 62 D6
Mount Vw *NWDGN* UB2 * 114 C4
ENC/FH EN2 23 F1
Mountview *MLHL* NW7 31 F5
NTHWD HA6 40 E2
Mountview Cl *HAMP* NW3 65 G5
Mount View Rd
CDALE/KGS NW9 63 F1
CHING E4 38 A2
ESH/CLAY KT10 205 H5
FSBYPK N4 67 F4
Mountview Rd *ORP* BR6 202 B4
Mount Vls *WNWD* SE27 162 C5
Mount Wy *CAR* SM5 210 A6
Mountwood *E/WMO/HCT* KT8 173 G6
Movers La *BARK* IG11 90 D6
Mowatt Cl *ARCH* N19 66 D5
Mowbray Gdns *NTHLT* UB5 * 78 A6
Mowbray Rd *BAR* EN5 21 G5
EDGW HA8 30 C6
KIL/WHAMP NW6 82 C5
NRWD SE19 181 G4
RCHPK/HAM TW10 156 D5
Mowbrays Cl *CRW* RM5 56 E4
Mowbrays Rd *CRW* RM5 56 E5
Mowlem St *BETH* E2 104 D1
Mowll St *BRXN/ST* SW9 142 B1
Moxon Cl *PLSTW* E13 106 D1
Moxon St *BAR* EN5 20 D4
MHST W1U 9 G2
Moye Cl *BETH* E2 86 C6
Moyers Rd *LEY* E10 70 A5
Moylan Rd *HMSMTH* W6 119 H6
Moyne Pl *WLSDN* NW10 98 C2
Moynihan Dr *WCHMH* N21 22 E6
Moys Cl *CROY/NA* CR0 195 K3
Moyser Rd *STRHM/NOR* SW16 179 G1
Mozart St *NKENS* W10 100 D2
Muchelney Rd *MRDN* SM4 194 B3
Muggeridge Cl *SAND/SEL* CR2 211 K3
Muggeridge Rd *DAGE* RM10 92 D2
Muirdown Av
MORT/ESHN SW14 137 K5
Muir Dr *WAND/EARL* SW18 160 C1
Muirfield *ACT* W3 99 G5
Muirfield Cl
BERM/RHTH SE16 * 123 J5
OXHEY WD19 * 41 G1
Muirfield Crs *POP/IOD* E14 124 E3
Muirfield Gn *OXHEY* WD19 27 G6
Muirfield Rd *OXHEY* WD19 27 F6
Muirkirk Rd *CAT* SE6 165 F3
Muir Rd *CLPT* E5 86 C1
Muir St *CAN/RD* E16 126 E1
Mulberry Av
STWL/WRAY TW19 152 B3
Mulberry Cl *CEND/HSY/T* N8 66 E2
CHEL SW3 * 120 C6
CHING E4 37 J4
EBAR EN4 21 H5
GPK RM2 75 K1
HDN NW4 46 A6
NTHLT UB5 95 J1
STRHM/NOR SW16 161 H6
Mulberry Crs *BTFD* TW8 136 C1
WDR/YW UB7 112 D2
Mulberry Dr *PUR* RM19 131 J4
Mulberry La *CROY/NA* CR0 197 G5
Mulberry Ms *NWCR* SE14 144 C2
Mulberry Pde *WDR/YW* UB7 112 D3
Mulberry Pl *ELTH/MOT* SE9 146 C5
HMSMTH W6 118 D5
Mulberry Rd *HACK* E8 86 B5
Mulberry St *WCHPL* E1 104 C5
Mulberry Wk *CHEL* SW3 120 C6
Mulberry Wy *BARK/HLT* IG6 72 C1
BELV DA17 129 K2
SWFD E18 53 F5
Mulgrave Rd *BELMT* SM2 208 D5
CROY/NA CR0 211 K1
EA W5 97 K2
HRW HA1 61 G6
WKENS W14 119 J6
WLSDN NW10 81 H2
WOOL/PLUM SE18 126 E4
Mulholland Cl *MTCM* CR4 179 G5
Mulkern Rd *ARCH* N19 66 D5
Mullards Cl *MTCM* CR4 194 E5
Mullet Gdns *BETH* E2 104 C2
Mullins Pth
MORT/ESHN SW14 138 A4
Mullion Cl
KTN/HRWW/WS HA3 42 B4
Mullion Wk *OXHEY* WD19 27 H6
Mull Wk *IS* N1 85 J4
Mulready St *STJWD* NW8 2 C7
Multi Wy *ACT* W3 118 B2
Multon Rd *WAND/EARL* SW18 160 C2
Mumford Ct *CITYW* EC2V 12 D3
Mumford Mills *GNWCH* SE10 144 D1
Mumford Rd *HNHL* SE24 142 C6
Muncaster Cl *ASHF* TW15 152 D6
Muncaster Rd *CLAP* SW4 140 E5
Muncies Ms *CAT* SE6 165 F4
Mundania Rd *EDUL* SE22 163 J1
Munday Rd *CAN/RD* E16 106 E5
Munden St *WKENS* W14 119 H4
Mundesly Cl *OXHEY* WD19 27 G6
Mundford Rd *CLPT* E5 68 E6
Mundon Gdns *IL* IG1 72 D5
Mund St *WKENS* W14 119 J5
Mundy St *IS* N1 7 G4
Mungo-Park Cl *BUSH* WD23 * 28 C4
Mungo Park Rd *RAIN* RM13 93 J4
Mungo Park Wy
STMC/STPC BR5 202 D4
Munnery Wy *ORP* BR6 216 A1
Munnings Gdns *ISLW* TW7 135 J6
Munro Dr *FBAR/BDGN* N11 48 C2
Munroe Ter *WBPTN* SW10 140 C1
Munro Ms *NKENS* W10 100 C4
Munro Ter *WBPTN* SW10 120 C6
Munro Wy *CLPT* E5 86 C2
Munslow Gdns *SUT* SM1 209 G2
Munster Av *HSLWW* TW4 134 D5
Munster Ct *FUL/PGN* SW6 139 J3
Munster Gdns *PLMGR* N13 35 J6
Munster Ms *FUL/PGN* SW6 * 139 J1
Munster Rd *FUL/PGN* SW6 139 H1
TEDD TW11 174 D2
Munster Sq *CAMTN* NW1 3 K5
Munton Rd *WALW* SE17 18 D6
Murchison Av *BXLY* DA5 168 E3
Murchison Rd *LEY* E10 70 A6
Murdock Cl *CAN/RD* E16 106 D5
Murdock St *PECK* SE15 123 J6
Murfett Cl *WIM/MER* SW19 159 H4
Muriel St *IS* N1 5 H1
Murillo Rd *LEW* SE13 145 G5
Murphy St *STHWK* SE1 17 J3
Murray Av *BMLY* BR1 184 A6
HSLW TW3 135 G6
Murray Cl *THMD* SE28 127 K1
Murray Crs *PIN* HA5 41 H4
Murray Gv *IS* N1 6 E3
Murray House
WOOL/PLUM SE18 * 146 D1
Murray Ms *CAMTN* NW1 84 D5
Murray Rd *EA* W5 116 D4
NTHWD HA6 40 C4
RCHPK/HAM TW10 156 C4
STMC/STPC BR5 186 C6
WIM/MER SW19 177 G2
Murray Sq *CAN/RD* E16 106 E5
Murray St *CAMTN* NW1 84 D5
Murray Ter *HAMP* NW3 83 G2
Murtwell Dr *CHIG* IG7 54 C2
Musard Rd *HMSMTH* W6 119 H6
Musbury St *WCHPL* E1 104 E5
Muscatel Pl *CMBW* SE5 143 F2
Muschamp Rd *CAR* SM5 194 D6
PECK SE15 143 G4
Muscovy St *MON* EC3R 13 H6
Museum St *NOXST/BSQ* WC1A 10 E2
Museum Wy *ACT* W3 117 H2
Musgrave Cl *EBAR* EN4 21 G2
Musgrave Crs *FUL/PGN* SW6 139 K1
Musgrave Rd *ISLW* TW7 136 A2
Musgrove Rd *NWCR* SE14 144 A2
Musjid Rd *BTSEA* SW11 140 C3
Musquash Wy *HSLWW* TW4 134 B3
Muston Rd *CLPT* E5 68 D6
Muswell Av *MUSWH* N10 48 B5
Muswell Hl *MUSWH* N10 48 B6
Muswell Hill Broadway
MUSWH N10 48 B6
Muswell Hill Pl *MUSWH* N10 66 B1
Muswell Hill Rd *HGT* N6 66 A3
Muswell Ms *MUSWH* N10 48 B6
Muswell Rd *MUSWH* N10 48 B5
Mutrix Rd *KIL/WHAMP* NW6 82 E6
Mutter Rd *CLAP* SW4 161 J1
Mutton Pl *CAMTN* NW1 84 A4
Muybridge Rd *NWMAL* KT3 175 K5
Myatt Rd *BRXN/ST* SW9 142 C2
Myddelton Av *EN* EN1 24 A1
Myddelton Gdns
WCHMH N21 35 J2
Myddelton Pk
TRDG/WHET N20 33 H5
Myddelton Pas *CLKNW* EC1R 5 K4
Myddelton Rd
CEND/HSY/T N8 48 E6
Myddelton Sq *CLKNW* EC1R 5 K4
Myddelton St *CLKNW* EC1R 5 K5
Myddleton Av *FSBYPK* N4 67 H6
Myddleton Cl *STAN* HA7 29 G4
Myddleton Rd *WDGN* N22 48 E3
Myers La *NWCR* SE14 124 A6
Mylis Cl *SYD* SE26 163 J6
Mylne Cl *HMSMTH* W6 * 118 D5
Mylne St *IS* N1 5 J3
Myra St *ABYW* SE2 128 B5
Myrdle St *WCHPL* E1 104 C5
Myrna Cl *WIM/MER* SW19 178 D3
Myron Pl *LEW* SE13 145 F4
Myrtle Aly *WOOL/PLUM* SE18 127 F3
Myrtle Av *EBED/NFELT* TW14 133 H5
RSLP HA4 58 E4
Myrtleberry Cl *HACK* E8 * 86 B4
Myrtle Cl *EBAR* EN4 33 K3
WDR/YW UB7 112 C4
Myrtledene Rd *ABYW* SE2 128 B5
Myrtle Gdns *HNWL* W7 115 K1
Myrtle Gv *ENC/FH* EN2 23 K1
NWMAL KT3 175 K5
Myrtle Rd *ACT* W3 117 K1
CROY/NA CR0 213 J1
EHAM E6 89 J6
HPTN TW12 173 H2
HSLW TW3 135 H3
IL IG1 72 B6
PLMGR N13 35 J5
SUT SM1 209 G3
WALTH E17 69 G3
Myrtleside Cl *NTHWD* HA6 40 B3
Myrtle St *IS* N1 7 G3
Myrtle Wk *IS* N1 7 G3
Mysore Rd *BTSEA* SW11 140 E5
Myton Rd *DUL* SE21 162 E5

N

Nadine St *CHARL* SE7 126 B5
Nagle Cl *WALTH* E17 52 B5
Nag's Head La *WELL* DA16 148 C4
Nags Head Rd *PEND* EN3 24 E5
Nairne Gv *HNHL* SE24 142 E6
Nairn Gn *OXHEY* WD19 26 E5
Nairn Rd *RSLP* HA4 77 G4
Nairn St *POP/IOD* E14 106 A4
Nallhead Rd *FELT* TW13 172 B1
Namba Roy Cl
STRHM/NOR SW16 162 A6
Namton Dr *THHTH* CR7 196 A1
Nan Clark's La *MLHL* NW7 31 H4
Nancy Downs *OXHEY* WD19 27 G2
Nankin St *POP/IOD* E14 105 J5
Nansen Rd *BTSEA* SW11 141 F5
Nansen Village
NFNCH/WDSPK N12 * 33 F6
Nantes Cl *WAND/EARL* SW18 140 B5
Nant Rd *CRICK* NW2 64 D6
Nant St *BETH* E2 104 D2
Naoroji St *FSBYW* WC1X 5 J5
Napier Av *FUL/PGN* SW6 139 J4
POP/IOD E14 124 D5
Napier Cl *DEPT* SE8 144 C1
EMPK RM11 75 K5
WDR/YW UB7 112 C3
Napier Ct *LEE/GVPK* SE12 166 A4
Napier Gv *IS* N1 6 D3
Napier Pl *WKENS* W14 119 J3
Napier Rd *ALP/SUD* HA0 79 K3
BELV DA17 129 G4
EHAM E6 90 A6
HAYES BR2 184 A6
ISLW TW7 136 B5
PEND EN3 25 F6
SAND/SEL CR2 211 K5
SNWD SE25 197 J1
SRTFD E15 106 C1
TOTM N17 50 A6
WAN E11 88 C1
WKENS W14 119 J3
WLSDN NW10 99 K2
Napier Ter *IS* N1 85 H5
Napoleon Rd *CLPT* E5 86 D1
TWK TW1 * 156 C2
Napton Cl *YEAD* UB4 95 J3
Narbonne Av *CLAP* SW4 141 H6
Narboro Ct *ROM* RM1 75 J3
Narborough Cl
HGDN/ICK UB10 58 A6
Narborough St *FUL/PGN* SW6 140 A3
Narcissus Rd
KIL/WHAMP NW6 82 E3
Narford Rd *CLPT* E5 86 C1
Narrow Boat Cl *THMD* SE28 127 J2
Narrow St *ACT* W3 117 J1
POP/IOD E14 105 G6
Narrow Wy *HAYES* BR2 200 D3
Nascot St *SHB* W12 100 A5
Naseby Cl *ISLW* TW7 135 K2
KIL/WHAMP NW6 * 83 G5
Naseby Ct *WOT/HER* KT12 * 188 B6
Naseby Rd *CLAY* IG5 53 K4
DAGE RM10 92 C1
NRWD SE19 180 E2
Nash Cl *SUT* SM1 209 H1
Nash Gn *BMLY* BR1 183 K3
Nash La *HAYES* BR2 214 E4
Nash Rd *BROCKY* SE4 144 B5
CHDH RM6 73 K1
ED N9 36 E4
Nash St *CAMTN* NW1 3 K4
Nash Wy *KTN/HRWW/WS* HA3 61 H3
Nasmyth St *HMSMTH* W6 118 E3
Nassau Rd *BARN* SW13 138 C2
Nassau St *GTPST* W1W 10 A2
Nassington Rd *HAMP* NW3 83 J2
Natalie Cl *EBED/NFELT* TW14 153 G2
Natalie Ms *WHTN* TW2 155 J5
Natal Rd *FBAR/BDGN* N11 48 E1
IL IG1 90 B2
STRHM/NOR SW16 179 J2
THHTH CR7 180 E6
Nathaniel Cl *WCHPL* E1 13 K2
Nathans Rd *ALP/SUD* HA0 61 J6
Nathan Wy *ABYW* SE2 128 B2
THMD SE28 128 A3
National Ter
BERM/RHTH SE16 * 123 J2
Nation Wy *CHING* E4 38 A3
Naval Rw *POP/IOD* E14 106 A6
Navarino Gv *HACK* E8 86 C4
Navarino Rd *HACK* E8 86 C4
Navarre Gdns *CRW* RM5 56 D2
Navarre Rd *EHAM* E6 107 J1
Navarre St *BETH* E2 7 J6
Navestock Cl *CHING* E4 * 38 A5
Navestock Crs *WFD* IG8 53 G4
Navestock Ter *WFD* IG8 53 G3
Navigator Dr *NWDGN* UB2 115 H2
Navy St *CLAP* SW4 141 J4
Nayim Pl *HACK* E8 86 D4
Naylor Gv *PEND* EN3 25 F6
Naylor Rd *PECK* SE15 143 J1
TRDG/WHET N20 33 G4
Nazareth Cl *PECK* SE15 143 J3
Nazrul St *BETH* E2 7 J4
Neal Av *STHL* UB1 95 K3
Neal Cl *NTHWD* HA6 40 E4
Nealden St *BRXN/ST* SW9 142 A4
Neale Cl *EFNCH* N2 47 G6
Neal St *LSQ/SEVD* WC2H 10 E4
Neal Ter *FSTH* SE23 * 164 A3
Neal Yd *LSQ/SEVD* WC2H 10 E4
Near Acre *CDALE/KGS* NW9 45 H4
Neasden Cl *WLSDN* NW10 81 G3
Neasden La *WLSDN* NW10 81 F1
Neasham Rd *BCTR* RM8 91 H3
Neate St *CMBW* SE5 123 G6
Neath Gdns *MRDN* SM4 194 B3
Neathouse Pl *PIM* SW1V 16 A6
Neats Acre *RSLP* HA4 58 B4
Neatscourt Rd *EHAM* E6 107 H4
Neckinger *BERM/RHTH* SE16 19 K4
Neckinger Est
BERM/RHTH SE16 19 K4
Neckinger St *STHWK* SE1 19 K3
Nectarine Wy *LEW* SE13 144 E3
Needham Rd *BAY/PAD* W2 100 E5
Needleman St
BERM/RHTH SE16 124 A2
Neeld Crs *HDN* NW4 63 K2
WBLY HA9 80 C3
Neils Yd *LSQ/SEVD* WC2H * 10 E4
Nelgarde Rd *CAT* SE6 164 D2
Nella Rd *HMSMTH* W6 119 G6
Nelldale Rd *BERM/RHTH* SE16 123 J4
Nello James Gdns
WNWD SE27 162 E6
Nelson Cl *CROY/NA* CR0 196 C5
EBED/NFELT TW14 * 153 J3
KIL/WHAMP NW6 100 E2
ROMW/RG RM7 56 D4
WOT/HER KT12 188 A6
Nelson Gdns *BETH* E2 104 C
HSLW TW3 155 F
Nelson Grove Rd
WIM/MER SW19 178 A
Nelson Mandela Cl
MUSWH N10 47 K
Nelson Mandela Rd
BKHTH/KID SE3 146 E
Nelson Pl *IS* N1 6 E
Nelson Rd *BELV* DA17 129 G
CEND/HSY/T N8 67 F
CHING E4 51 K
ED N9 36 D
GNWCH SE10 125 F
HAYES BR2 200 E
HRW HA1 60 D
HTHAIR TW6 132
NWMAL KT3 192
PEND EN3 37
RAIN RM13 111
SCUP DA14 168
SEVS/STOTM N15 68
STAN HA7 43
WAN E11 70
WHTN TW2 155
WIM/MER SW19 178
Nelson Sq *STHWK* SE1 18
Nelsons Rw *CLAP* SW4 141
Nelson St *CAN/RD* E16 106
EHAM E6 90
WCHPL E1 104
Nelson Ter *FSBYE* EC1V 6
Nelson Wk *HOR/WEW* KT19 206
Nemoure Rd *ACT* W3 98
Nene Gdns *FELT* TW13 154
Nene Rd *HTHAIR* TW6 132
Nepaul Rd *BTSEA* SW11 140
Nepean St *PUT/ROE* SW15 158
Neptune Cl *RAIN* RM13 111
Neptune Rd *HRW* HA1 60
HTHAIR TW6 * 133
Neptune St *BERM/RHTH* SE16 123
Nesbit Cl *BKHTH/KID* SE3 145
Nesbit Rd *ELTH/MOT* SE9 146
Nesbitts Aly *BAR* EN5 * 20
Nesbitt Sq *NRWD* SE19 * 181
Nesham St *WAP* E1W 123
Ness Rd *ERITH* DA8 131
Ness St *BERM/RHTH* SE16 123
Nesta Rd *WFD* IG8 52
Nestle's Av *HYS/HAR* UB3 113
Nestor Av *WCHMH* N21 35
Netheravon Rd *CHSWK* W4 118
HNWL W7 116
Netheravon Rd South
CHSWK W4 118
Netherbury Rd *EA* W5 116
Netherby Gdns *ENC/FH* EN2 22
Netherby Rd *FSTH* SE23 163
Nether Cl *FNCH* N3 46
Nether Ct *MLHL* NW7 * 4
Nethercourt Av *FNCH* N3 4
Netherfield Gdns *BARK* IG11 9
Netherfield Rd
NFNCH/WDSPK N12 4
TOOT SW17 16
Netherford Rd *VX/NE* SW8 14
Netherhall Gdns *HAMP* NW3 8
Netherhall Wy *HAMP* NW3 8
Netherlands Rd *BAR* EN5 3
Netherleigh Cl *HGT* N6 6
Netherpark Dr *GPK* RM2 5
Nether St *FNCH* N3 4
Netherton Gv *WBPTN* SW10 1
Netherton Rd
SEVS/STOTM N15 6

TWK TW1 136 B6
Netherwood Pl
HMSMTH W6 * 119 G3
Netherwood Rd WKENS W14 119 G3
Netherwood St
KIL/WHAMP NW6 82 D5
Netley Cl CHEAM SM3 208 B3
CROY/NA CR0 214 A5
Netley Dr WOT/HER KT12 188 E4
Netley Gdns MRDN SM4 194 B4
Netley Rd BTFD TW8 117 F6
GNTH/NBYPK IG2 72 D2
MRDN SM4 194 B4
WALTH E17 69 H2
Netley St CAMTN NW1 4 A5
Nettlecombe Cl BELMT SM2 209 F6
Nettleden Av WBLY HA9 80 C4
Nettlefold Pl WNWD SE27 162 C5
Nettlestead Cl BECK BR3 182 C3
Nettleton Rd HTHAIR TW6 132 E2
NWCR SE14 144 A1
Nettlewood Rd
STRHM/NOR SW16 179 J3
Neuchatel Rd CAT SE6 164 C4
Nevada Cl NWMAL KT3 191 K1
Nevada St GNWCH SE10 145 F1
Nevern Pl ECT SW5 119 K4
Nevern Rd ECT SW5 119 K4
Nevern Sq ECT SW5 119 K4
Nevil Cl NTHWD HA6 40 B1
Neville Av NWMAL KT3 176 A4
Neville Cl ACT W3 117 K2
BFN/LL DA15 168 A6
CAMTN NW1 4 D3
HSLW TW3 135 F3
KIL/WHAMP NW6 100 D1
PECK SE15 143 H1
WAN E11 88 D1
Neville Dr EFNCH N2 65 G3
Neville Gdns BCTR RM8 91 K1
Neville Gill Cl
WAND/EARL SW18 159 K1
Neville Pl WDGN N22 49 F4
Neville Rd BARK/HLT IG6 54 C4
BCTR RM8 73 K6
CROY/NA CR0 196 E4
EA W5 97 K3
FSTGT E7 88 E5
KIL/WHAMP NW6 * 100 D1
KUT/HW KT1 175 H5
RCHPK/HAM TW10 156 D5
Neville St SKENS SW7 120 C5
Neville Ter SKENS SW7 * 120 C5
Neville Wk CAR SM5 194 D4
Nevill Rd STNW/STAM N16 86 A2
Nevill Wy LOU IG10 39 J1
Nevil Wk CAR SM5 * 194 D4
Nevin Dr CHING E4 37 K3
Nevinson Cl
WAND/EARL SW18 160 C1
Nevis Cl ROM RM1 57 G2
Nevis Rd TOOT SW17 161 F4
New Acres Rd THMD SE28 127 K1
Newall Rd HTHAIR TW6 133 F2
Newark Ct WOT/HER KT12 188 B5
Newark Crs WLSDN NW10 99 F2
Newark Knok EHAM E6 108 A5
Newark Rd SAND/SEL CR2 211 K4
Newark St WCHPL E1 104 D4
Newark Wy HDN NW4 45 J6
New Ash Cl EFNCH N2 47 H6
New Barn Cl WLGTN SM6 211 F4
New Barns Av MTCM CR4 195 J1
New Barn St PLSTW E13 106 E3
Newbery Rd ERITH DA8 150 C2
Newbiggin Pth OXHEY WD19 27 G6
Newbold Cots WCHPL E1 * 104 E5
Newbolt Av CHEAM SM3 208 A3
Newbolt Rd STAN HA7 43 F2
New Bond St CONDST W1S 9 K4
MYFR/PICC W1J 9 K5
Newborough Gn NWMAL KT3 192 A1
New Brent St HDN NW4 64 A2
New Bridge St EMB EC4Y 12 A4
New Broad St LVPST EC2M 13 F2
New Broadway EA W5 97 J6
Newburgh Rd ACT W3 117 K1
Newburgh St SOHO/CST W1F 10 A4
New Burlington Ms
CONDST W1S 10 A5
New Burlington Pl
CONDST W1S 10 A5
New Burlington St
CONDST W1S 10 A5
Newburn St LBTH SE11 122 A5
Newbury Cl NTHLT UB5 77 K4
Newbury Gdns
HOR/WEW KT19 207 H2
Newbury Ms KTTN NW5 84 A4
Newbury Rd CHING E4 52 A2
GNTH/NBYPK IG2 72 D3
HAYES BR2 183 K6
HTHAIR TW6 132 C2
Newbury St STBT EC1A 12 C2
Newbury Wy NTHLT UB5 77 J4
New Butt La DEPT SE8 * 144 D1
Newby Cl EN EN1 24 A3
Newby Pl POP/IOD E14 106 A6
Newby St VX/NE SW8 141 G4
Newcastle Av BARK/HLT IG6 55 G2
Newcastle Cl
FLST/FETLN EC4A 12 A3
Newcastle Pl BAY/PAD W2 8 B2
Newcastle Rw CLKNW EC1R 5 K7
New Cavendish St
CAVSQ/HST W1G 9 H2
GTPST W1W 10 A1
New Change STP EC4M 12 C4
New Charles St FSBYE EC1V 6 B4
New Church Rd CMBW SE5 142 D1
New City Rd PLSTW E13 107 G2
New Cl FELT TW13 172 D1
WIM/MER SW19 178 B6
New College Ms IS N1 * 85 G5
New College Pde
HAMP NW3 * 83 G4
Newcombe Gdns
HSLWW TW4 134 E5
Newcombe Pk ALP/SUD HA0 80 B6
MLHL NW7 45 G1
Newcombe St KENS W8 * 119 K1
Newcome Gdns
STRHM/NOR SW16 161 K6
Newcomen Rd BTSEA SW11 140 C4
WAN E11 * 88 D1
Newcomen St STHWK SE1 18 E2
New Compton St
LSQ/SEVD WC2H * 10 D4
New Ct EMB EC4Y * 11 J5
NTHLT UB5 78 B3
Newcourt St STJWD NW8 2 C3
New Crane Pl WAP E1W * 123 K1
New Crescent Yd
WLSDN NW10 * 99 H1
New Cross Rd NWCR SE14 143 K1
Newdales Cl ED N9 36 C4
Newdene Av NTHLT UB5 95 H1
Newdigate
STRHM/NOR SW16 * 162 B6
Newell St POP/IOD E14 105 H6
New End HAMP NW3 83 G2
New End Sq HAMP NW3 83 H2
Newent Cl CAR SM5 194 E5
PECK SE15 143 F1
New Era Est IS N1 7 G1
New Farm La NTHWD HA6 40 C4
New Ferry Ap
WOOL/PLUM SE18 127 F3
New Fetter La
FLST/FETLN EC4A 11 K3
Newfield Cl HPTN TW12 173 F4
Newfield Ri CRICK NW2 81 J1
New Forest La CHIG IG7 54 A2
Newgale Gdns EDGW HA8 44 B4
New Garden Dr WDR/YW UB7 112 B2
Newgate CROY/NA CR0 196 D5
Newgate Cl FELT TW13 154 D4
Newgate St CHING E4 38 C5
STBT EC1A 12 B3
New Globe Wk STHWK SE1 12 C7
New Goulston St WCHPL E1 13 J3
New Green Pl
BRXS/STRHM SW2 162 B2
NRWD SE19 181 F2
Newhall Gdns WOT/HER KT12 188 B6
Newham's Rw STHWK SE1 19 H3
Newham Wy CAN/RD E16 106 D4
EHAM E6 107 J3
Newhaven Cl HYS/HAR UB3 113 J4
Newhaven Gdns
ELTH/MOT SE9 146 C5
Newhaven La PLSTW E13 106 D4
Newhaven Rd SNWD SE25 196 E2
New Heston Rd HEST TW5 134 E1
Newhouse Av CHDH RM6 55 K6
Newhouse Cl NWMAL KT3 192 B4
Newhouse Wk MRDN SM4 194 B4
Newick Cl BXLY DA5 169 J1
Newick Rd CLPT E5 86 D1
Newing Gn BMLY BR1 184 C3
Newington Barrow Wy
HOLWY N7 85 F1
Newington Butts WALW SE17 18 B7
Newington Cswy STHWK SE1 18 C4
Newington Gn IS N1 85 K3
Newington Green Rd IS N1 85 K3
New Inn Broadway
SDTCH EC2A * 7 H6
New Inn Sq SDTCH EC2A * 7 H6
New Inn St SDTCH EC2A * 7 H6
New Inn Yd SDTCH EC2A 7 H6
New Kelvin Av TEDD TW11 173 K2
New Kent Rd WALW SE17 18 D6
New King's Rd FUL/PGN SW6 139 K2
New King St DEPT SE8 124 D6
Newland Cl PIN HA5 41 J2
Newland Ct WBLY HA9 62 C6
Newland Dr EN EN1 24 D2
Newland Gdns WEA W13 116 B2
Newland Rd CEND/HSY/T N8 48 E6
Newlands Av THDIT KT7 189 K5
Newlands Cl ALP/SUD HA0 79 J4
EDGW HA8 30 A5
NWDGN UB2 114 D5
Newlands Pk SYD SE26 181 K2
Newlands Pl BAR EN5 20 B6
Newlands Quay WAP E1W 104 E6
Newlands Rd
STRHM/NOR SW16 179 K5
WFD IG8 38 D4
The Newlands WLGTN SM6 210 C5
Newland St CAN/RD E16 126 D1
Newlands Wy CHSGTN KT9 205 J3
Newlands Woods
CROY/NA CR0 213 H6
Newling Cl EHAM E6 107 K5
Newling Est BETH E2 7 K4
New London St MON EC3R * 13 H5
New Lydenburg St CHARL SE7 126 B3
Newlyn Cl ORP BR6 217 F2
Newlyn Gdns
RYLN/HDSTN HA2 59 K4
Newlyn Rd BAR EN5 20 D5
TOTM N17 50 B4
WELL DA16 148 A3
Newman Ms WDGN N22 49 F3
Newman Rd BMLY BR1 183 K4
CROY/NA CR0 196 A4
HYS/HAR UB3 95 F6
PLSTW E13 107 F2
WALTH E17 69 F2
Newmans La SURB KT6 190 E3
Newman's Rw LINN WC2A 11 H2
Newman St FITZ W1T 10 B2
Newman's Wy EBAR EN4 21 G3
Newmarket Av NTHLT UB5 78 A3
Newmarsh Rd THMD SE28 128 A1
New Mill Rd STMC/STPC BR5 186 D4
Newminster Ct ENC/FH EN2 * 23 H3
Newminster Rd MRDN SM4 194 B3
New Mount St SRTFD E15 88 B5
Newnham Av RSLP HA4 59 G5
Newnham Cl LOU IG10 39 H1
NTHLT UB5 78 C4
THHTH CR7 180 D5
Newnham Gdns NTHLT UB5 78 C4
Newnham Gn WDGN N22 * 49 G4
Newnham Rd WDGN N22 49 F4
Newnhams Cl BMLY BR1 184 E6
Newnham Ter STHWK SE1 17 J4
Newnham Wy
KTN/HRWW/WS HA3 62 A2
New North Pl SDTCH EC2A 7 G6
New North Rd BARK/HLT IG6 54 D3
IS N1 7 F3
New North St BMSBY WC1N 11 G1
Newnton Cl FSBYPK N4 67 K4
New Oak Rd EFNCH N2 47 G5
New Oxford St
NOXST/BSQ WC1A 10 D3
New Pde ASHF TW15 * 152 C6
WDR/YW UB7 * 112 B1
New Park Av PLMGR N13 35 J5
New Park Cl NTHLT UB5 77 J4
New Park Est UED N18 50 E1
New Park Rd
BRXS/STRHM SW2 161 K2
New Place Sq
BERM/RHTH SE16 * 123 J3
New Plaistow Rd SRTFD E15 88 C6
New Pond Pde RSLP HA4 * 76 E1
Newport Av POP/IOD E14 106 B6
Newport Ct LSQ/SEVD WC2H 10 D5
Newport Md OXHEY WD19 * 27 H6
Newport Pl
SOHO/SHAV W1D * 10 D5
Newport Rd HTHAIR TW6 132 D2
ACT W3 117 K2
BARN SW13 138 D2
HTHAIR TW6 132 D2
LEY E10 70 B6
WALTH E17 * 69 G1
YEAD UB4 94 B4
Newport St LBTH SE11 17 G7
Newquay Crs
RYLN/HDSTN HA2 59 J6
Newquay Gdns OXHEY WD19 27 F4
Newquay Rd CAT SE6 164 E4
New Quebec St MBLAR W1H 9 F4
New River Av
CEND/HSY/T N8 49 F6
New River Crs PLMGR N13 35 H6
New River Wy FSBYPK N4 67 K4
New Rd ABYW SE2 128 E4
BORE WD6 29 K1
BTFD TW8 * 116 E6
CEND/HSY/T N8 66 D2
CHING E4 37 K6
DAGE RM10 110 C1
E/WMO/HCT KT8 173 F6
EBED/NFELT TW14 153 G1
ED N9 36 D4
ESH/CLAY KT10 204 C2
FELT TW13 172 D1
GDMY/SEVK IG3 72 E6
HRW HA1 79 F2
HSLW TW3 135 G5
HYS/HAR UB3 133 F1
KUTN/CMB KT2 175 H3
MLHL NW7 46 C3
MTCM CR4 195 F5
ORP BR6 202 B4
RAIN RM13 110 E2
RCHPK/HAM TW10 156 D6
TOTM N17 50 B4
UX/CGN UB8 94 A3
WCHPL E1 104 C4
WDGN N22 49 J4
WELL DA16 148 C3
New Road Hl HAYES BR2 215 J6
New Rw CHCR WC2N 10 E5
Newry Rd TWK TW1 136 B5
Newsam Av SEVS/STOTM N15 67 K2
Newsholme Dr WCHMH N21 23 F6
New Spring Gardens Wk
STHWK SE1 * 121 K5
New Sq EBED/NFELT TW14 153 F3
LINN WC2A 11 H3
Newstead Av ORP BR6 216 D1
Newstead Cl
NFNCH/WDSPK N12 47 J2
Newstead Ct NTHLT UB5 * 95 J2
Newstead Rd LEE/GVPK SE12 165 J2
Newstead Wk CAR SM5 194 B4
Newstead Wy
WIM/MER SW19 159 G6
New St LVPST EC2M 13 H2
New Street Hl BMLY BR1 184 A1
New Street Sq
FLST/FETLN EC4A 11 K3
Newton Av ACT W3 117 K2
MUSWH N10 48 A4
Newton Cl RYLN/HDSTN HA2 60 A6
WALTH E17 69 G3
Newton Gv CHSWK W4 118 B3
Newton Park Pl CHST BR7 184 E3
Newton Pl POP/IOD E14 124 D4
Newton Rd ALP/SUD HA0 80 B5
BAY/PAD W2 101 F5
CRICK NW2 82 A2
HTHAIR TW6 132 B2
ISLW TW7 136 A3
KTN/HRWW/WS HA3 42 E4
SEVS/STOTM N15 68 B2
SRTFD E15 88 B3
WELL DA16 148 B4
WIM/MER SW19 177 H3
Newtons Cl RAIN RM13 93 G5
Newton St HOL/ALD WC2B 11 F3
Newton's Yd
WAND/EARL SW18 139 K6
Newton Ter HAYES BR2 200 C3
Newton Wk EDGW HA8 44 E4
Newton Wy UED N18 49 J1
New Tower Blds WAP E1W * 123 J1
Newtown St BTSEA SW11 141 G2
New Trinity Rd EFNCH N2 47 H6
New Union Cl POP/IOD E14 125 F3
New Union St BARB EC2Y 12 E2
New Vls TOTM N17 * 50 C4
New Wanstead WAN E11 70 E3
New Way Rd CDALE/KGS NW9 63 G1
New Wharf Rd IS N1 5 F2
New Zealand Wy RAIN RM13 111 H2
Niagara Av EA W5 116 D4
Niagara Cl IS N1 6 D2
Nibthwaite Rd HRW HA1 60 E2
Nicholas Cl GFD/PVL UB6 96 B1
Nicholas Gdns EA W5 116 E1
Nicholas La MANHO EC4N 13 F5
Nicholas Rd BCTR RM8 74 B6
BORE WD6 30 B1
CROY/NA CR0 210 E2
WCHPL E1 104 E3
Nicholas Wy NTHWD HA6 40 A4
Nicholay Rd ARCH N19 66 D5
Nichol Cl STHGT/OAK N14 34 D3
Nicholes Rd HSLW TW3 135 F5
Nichol La BMLY BR1 183 K3
Nichollsfield Wk HOLWY N7 84 E3
Nicholl St BETH E2 86 C6
Nichols Cl FSBYPK N4 * 67 G5
Nichols Gn EA W5 98 A4
Nicholson Dr BUSH WD23 28 C3
Nicholson House CHARL SE7 * 146 D1
Nicholson Ms KUT/HW KT1 191 F1
Nicholson Rd CROY/NA CR0 197 G5
Nicholson St STHWK SE1 18 A1
Nickelby Cl THMD SE28 109 J5
Nickols Wk WAND/EARL SW18 140 A5
Nicola Cl KTN/HRWW/WS HA3 42 D5
SAND/SEL CR2 211 J4
Nicola Ms BARK/HLT IG6 54 B3
Nicol Cl TWK TW1 156 C1
Nicoll Pl HDN NW4 63 K3
Nicoll Rd WLSDN NW10 81 G6
Nicolson Rd STMC/STPC BR5 202 D4
Nicosia Rd WAND/EARL SW18 160 D2
Niederwald Rd SYD SE26 164 B6
Nield Rd HYS/HAR UB3 113 J2
Nigel Cl NTHLT UB5 77 J6
Nigel Fisher Wy CHSGTN KT9 205 J5
Nigel Ms IL IG1 90 B2
Nigel Playfair Av
HMSMTH W6 118 E4
Nigel Rd FSTGT E7 89 G3
PECK SE15 143 H4
Nigeria Rd CHARL SE7 146 B1
Nightingale Av CHING E4 52 C1
Nightingale Cl CAR SM5 195 F6
CHING E4 38 C6
CHSWK W4 117 K6
PIN HA5 59 G2
Nightingale Cnr
STMC/STPC BR5 * 202 E1
Nightingale Ct SUT SM1 209 G3
Nightingale Dr
HOR/WEW KT19 206 D4
Nightingale Gv LEW SE13 145 G6
Nightingale La BAL SW12 161 F1
BMLY BR1 184 B5
CEND/HSY/T N8 66 E1
RCHPK/HAM TW10 157 F2
WAN E11 71 F2
Nightingale Ms KUT/HW KT1 * 174 E6
LBTH SE11 17 K6
Nightingale Pl WBPTN SW10 120 B6
WOOL/PLUM SE18 127 F6
Nightingale Rd CAR SM5 209 K1
CLPT E5 86 D1
E/WMO/HCT KT8 189 G2
ED N9 36 E2
HNWL W7 116 A1
HPTN TW12 173 F2
STMC/STPC BR5 201 H3
WDGN N22 48 E4
WLSDN NW10 99 H1
WOT/HER KT12 * 188 B4
Nightingale Sq BAL SW12 161 F2
The Nightingales
STWL/WRAY TW19 152 C3
Nightingale V
WOOL/PLUM SE18 127 F6
Nightingale Wk BAL SW12 161 G1
Nightingale Wy EHAM E6 107 J4
Nigntingale Av HRW HA1 61 H4
Nile Cl STNW/STAM N16 86 B1
Nile Dr ED N9 36 E4
Nile Rd PLSTW E13 107 G1
Nile St IS N1 6 E4
Nile Ter PECK SE15 123 G5
Nimmo Dr BUSH WD23 28 D2
Nimrod Cl NTHLT UB5 95 H2
Nimrod Pas IS N1 86 A4
Nimrod Rd STRHM/NOR SW16 179 G2
Nina Mackay Cl SRTFD E15 * 88 C6
Nine Acres Cl HYS/HAR UB3 113 F3
MNPK E12 89 J3
Nine Elms Cl
EBED/NFELT TW14 153 J3
Nine Elms La VX/NE SW8 141 H1
Nineteenth Rd MTCM CR4 195 K1
Ninhams Wd ORP BR6 216 A2
Ninth Av HYS/HAR UB3 94 E6
Nisbett Wk SCUP DA14 168 B6
Nithdale Rd
WOOL/PLUM SE18 147 G1
Nithsdale Gv HGDN/ICK UB10 76 A1
Niton Cl BAR EN5 32 B1
Niton Rd RCH/KEW TW9 * 137 H4
Niton St FUL/PGN SW6 139 G1
No1 St WOOL/PLUM SE18 127 G3
No2 St WOOL/PLUM SE18 127 G3
Noak Hill Rd ABR/ST RM4 57 K1
Nobel Dr HYS/HAR UB3 133 H1
Nobel Rd UED N18 36 E6
Noble Cnr HEST TW5 * 135 F2
Noble St CITYW EC2V 12 C3
Noel Rd ACT W3 98 C5
EHAM E6 107 J3
IS N1 6 A2
Noel St SOHO/CST W1F 10 B4
Nolan Wy CLPT E5 86 C2
Nolton Pl EDGW HA8 44 B4
Nonsuch Cl CHIG IG7 54 B2
Nonsuch Pl CHEAM SM3 * 208 B5
Norbiton Av KUT/HW KT1 175 H5
Norbiton Common Rd
KUT/HW KT1 175 J6
Norbiton Rd POP/IOD E14 105 H5
Norbreck Pde EA W5 98 A2
Norbroke St SHB W12 99 H6
Norburn St NKENS W10 100 C4
Norbury Av HSLW TW3 135 J6
STRHM/NOR SW16 180 A4
Norbury Cl STRHM/NOR SW16 180 B4
Norbury Court Rd
STRHM/NOR SW16 179 K5
Norbury Crs
STRHM/NOR SW16 180 B5
Norbury Cross
STRHM/NOR SW16 179 K6
Norbury Gdns CHDH RM6 73 K2
Norbury Gv MLHL NW7 31 G5
Norbury Hl STRHM/NOR SW16 180 B3
Norbury Ri STRHM/NOR SW16 179 K6
Norbury Rd CHING E4 51 J1
FELT TW13 153 J5
THHTH CR7 180 D5
Norbury Vls KUT/HW KT1 * 175 G5
Norcombe Gdns
KTN/HRWW/WS HA3 61 J3
Norcott Cl YEAD UB4 95 G3
Norcott Rd STNW/STAM N16 68 C6
Norcroft Gdns EDUL SE22 163 H2
Norcutt Rd WHTN TW2 155 K3
Norfield Rd RDART DA2 169 K6
Norfolk Av PLMGR N13 49 H2
SEVS/STOTM N15 68 B3
Norfolk Cl EBAR EN4 22 A5
EFNCH N2 47 J6
PLMGR N13 49 H2
TWK TW1 * 156 C1
Norfolk Ct BAR EN5 * 20 C5
Norfolk Crs BAY/PAD W2 8 C3
BFN/LL DA15 167 K2
Norfolk House Rd
STRHM/NOR SW16 161 J5
Norfolk Ms NKENS W10 100 C4
Norfolk Pl BAY/PAD W2 8 B3
WELL DA16 148 B3
Norfolk Rd BAR EN5 20 E4
BARK IG11 90 E5
DAGE RM10 92 D3
EHAM E6 89 K6
ESH/CLAY KT10 204 E3
FELT TW13 154 B3
GDMY/SEVK IG3 72 E5
HRW HA1 60 B2
PEND EN3 24 D6
ROMW/RG RM7 74 E3
STJWD NW8 2 B1
THHTH CR7 180 D6
WALTH E17 51 F4
WIM/MER SW19 178 D3
WLSDN NW10 81 G5
Norfolk Rw STHWK SE1 17 G6
Norfolk Sq BAY/PAD W2 8 B4
Norfolk Square Ms
BAY/PAD W2 8 B4
Norfolk St FSTGT E7 88 E3
Norgrove St BAL SW12 161 F3
Norhyrst Av SNWD SE25 181 G6
Norland Pl NTGHL W11 119 H1
Norland Rd NTGHL W11 119 G1
Norlands Crs CHST BR7 185 G4
Norlands Ga CHST BR7 * 185 G4
Norland Sq NTGHL W11 119 H1
Norley V PUT/ROE SW15 158 D3
Norlington Rd LEY E10 70 A5
Norman Av FELT TW13 154 D4
STHL UB1 95 J6
TWK TW1 156 C2
WDGN N22 49 J4
Normanby Cl PUT/ROE SW15 139 J6
Normanby Rd WLSDN NW10 81 H3
Norman Cl ORP BR6 216 C1
ROMW/RG RM7 56 D5
Norman Crs HEST TW5 134 C1
PIN HA5 41 G4
Normand Gdns WKENS W14 * 119 H6
Normand Ms WKENS W14 119 H6
Normand Rd WKENS W14 119 J6
Normandy Av BAR EN5 20 D6
Normandy Cl SYD SE26 164 B5
Normandy Dr HYS/HAR UB3 94 A5
Normandy Rd BRXN/ST SW9 142 B2
Normandy Ter CAN/RD E16 107 F5
Norman Gv BOW E3 105 G1
Normanhurst Av WELL DA16 148 E2
Normanhurst Dr TWK TW1 136 C6
Normanhurst Rd
BRXS/STRHM SW2 162 A4
STMC/STPC BR5 186 C5
WOT/HER KT12 188 C6
Norman Pde SCUP DA14 * 169 F5
Norman Rd BELV DA17 129 J1
EHAM E6 107 K3
EMPK RM11 75 J4
GNWCH SE10 144 E1
IL IG1 90 B3
SEVS/STOTM N15 68 B2
SUT SM1 208 E3
THHTH CR7 196 C2
WAN E11 70 C6
WIM/MER SW19 178 B3
Normans Cl WDGN N22 * 49 J4
WLSDN NW10 81 F4
Normansfield Av
KUT/HW KT1 174 D3
Normansfield Cl BUSH WD23 28 B2
Normanshire Dr CHING E4 37 J6
Normans Md WLSDN NW10 81 F4
Norman St FSBYE EC1V 6 C5
Norman Ter
KIL/WHAMP NW6 * 82 D3
Normanton Av
WAND/EARL SW18 159 K4
Normanton Pk CHING E4 38 C5
Normanton Rd
SAND/SEL CR2 212 A4
Normanton St FSTH SE23 164 A4
Norman Wy ACT W3 98 D4
STHGT/OAK N14 34 E4
Normington Cl
STRHM/NOR SW16 180 B1
Norrice Lea EFNCH N2 65 H2
Norris St STJS SW1Y 10 C6
Norris Wy DART DA1 150 C4
Norroy Rd PUT/ROE SW15 139 G5
Norrys Cl EBAR EN4 21 K6
Norrys Rd EBAR EN4 21 K5
Norseman Cl GDMY/SEVK IG3 73 H5
Norseman Wy GFD/PVL UB6 78 B6
Norstead Pl PUT/ROE SW15 158 D4
North Access Rd WALTH E17 69 F3
North Acre CDALE/KGS NW9 45 G4
North Acton Rd WLSDN NW10 99 F1
Northall Rd BXLYHN DA7 149 K3
Northampton Gv IS N1 85 K3

Northampton Pk IS N1 85 J4
Northampton Rd
CLKNW EC1R 5 K6
CROY/NA CR0 197 H6
PEND EN3 25 G5
Northampton Rw
CLKNW EC1R * 5 K6
Northampton Sq FSBYE EC1V 6 A5
Northampton St IS N1 85 J5
Northanger Rd
STRHM/NOR SW16 179 K2
North Ap NTHWD HA6 26 A4
North Audley St
MYFR/PKLN W1K 9 G5
North Av CAR SM5 210 A5
HYS/HAR UB3 94 E6
RCH/KEW TW9 137 H2
RYLN/HDSTN HA2 60 B3
STHL UB1 95 K6
UED N18 36 C6
WEA W13 97 H5
North Bank STJWD NW8 2 C5
Northbank Rd WALTH E17 52 A5
North Birkbeck Rd WAN E11 88 B1
Northborough Rd
STRHM/NOR SW16 179 K5
Northbourne Rd CLAP SW4 141 J5
Northbrook Dr NTHWD HA6 40 C4
Northbrook Rd BAR EN5 32 C1
CROY/NA CR0 196 E2
IL IG1 72 A6
LEW SE13 145 G6
WDGN N22 48 E2
Northburgh St FSBYE EC1V 6 B7
North Carriage Dr
BAY/PAD W2 8 D5
Northchurch Rd IS N1 85 J5
WBLY HA9 80 C4
Northchurch Ter IS N1 86 A5
North Circular PLMGR N13 49 G1
WALTH E17 51 K4
North Circular Rd BARK IG11 90 A5
CHING E4 * 51 G2
EFNCH N2 47 G5
GLDGN NW11 64 C3
IL IG1 71 H3
NFNCH/WDSPK N12 47 J3
REDBR IG4 53 G6
WLSDN NW10 98 B1
Northcliffe Cl WPK KT4 207 G1
Northcliffe Dr
TRDG/WHET N20 32 D3
North Cl BAR EN5 20 A6
BXLYHS DA6 148 E5
CHIG IG7 55 G1
DAGE RM10 92 C6
EBED/NFELT TW14 153 G1
MRDN SM4 193 H1
The North Colonnade
POP/IOD E14 124 E1
North Common Rd EA W5 98 A6
Northcote Av BRYLDS KT5 191 H4
EA W5 98 A6
ISLW TW7 136 B6
STHL UB1 95 J6
Northcote Rd BTSEA SW11 140 D5
CROY/NA CR0 196 E3
NWMAL KT3 175 K6
SCUP DA14 167 K6
TWK TW1 136 B6
WALTH E17 69 G1
WLSDN NW10 81 G5
Northcott Av WDGN N22 48 E4
North Countess Rd
WALTH E17 51 H5
Northcourt FITZ W1T 10 B1
North Cray Rd BXLY DA5 169 H4
SCUP DA14 169 G5
SCUP DA14 187 F1
North Crs CAN/RD E16 106 B3
FNCH N3 46 D5
GWRST WC1E 10 C1
Northcroft Rd
HOR/WEW KT19 207 G5
WEA W13 116 C2
North Cross Rd BARK/HLT IG6 72 C1
EDUL SE22 143 G6
Northdene CHIG IG7 54 D1
North Dene HSLW TW3 135 G2
MLHL NW7 31 F5
Northdene Gdns
SEVS/STOTM N15 68 A3
Northdown Cl RSLP HA4 76 D1
Northdown Gdns
GNTH/NBYPK IG2 72 E2
Northdown Rd EMPK RM11 75 K4
WELL DA16 148 C3
Northdown St IS N1 5 G3
North Dr BECK BR3 198 E1
HSLW TW3 135 H3
ORP BR6 216 E2
RSLP HA4 58 C4
STRHM/NOR SW16 161 H6
North End BKHH IG9 39 G2
CROY/NA CR0 196 D5
HAMP NW3 65 G6
North End Av HAMP NW3 65 G6
North End Crs WKENS W14 119 J4
North End La ORP BR6 216 B6
North End Rd FUL/PGN SW6 139 K1
GLDGN NW11 64 E5
WBLY HA9 80 C1
WKENS W14 119 H4
North End Wy HAMP NW3 65 G6
Northern Av ED N9 36 B4
Northernhay Wk MRDN SM4 193 H1
Northern Perimeter Rd
HTHAIR TW6 133 F2
Northern Perimeter Road (West) HTHAIR TW6 132 B2
Northern Relief Rd BARK IG11 90 C5
North Eyot Gdns
HMSMTH W6 * 118 C5
Northey St POP/IOD E14 105 G6
North Farm LOU IG10 39 G1
Northfield Av PIN HA5 59 H1
STMC/STPC BR5 202 D3
WEA W13 116 C2
Northfield Cl BMLY BR1 184 D4
HYS/HAR UB3 113 J3
Northfield Crs CHEAM SM3 208 C2
Northfield Pde
HYS/HAR UB3 * 113 J3
Northfield Pk HYS/HAR UB3 113 H3
Northfield Recreation Gnd
EA W5 * 116 C4
Northfield Rd DAGW RM9 92 B2
EBAR EN4 21 J4
ED N9 * 24 D6
EHAM E6 89 K4
HEST TW5 114 C6
PEND EN3 36 D1
STNW/STAM N16 68 A4
WEA W13 116 C2
Northfields WAND/EARL SW18 139 K5
Northfields Rd ACT W3 98 E4
North Gdns WIM/MER SW19 178 C3
Northgate NTHWD HA6 40 A3
Northgate Dr
CDALE/KGS NW9 63 G3
North Gower St CAMTN NW1 4 A5
North Gv HGT N6 66 A4
SEVS/STOTM N15 67 K2
North Hl HGT N6 65 K3
North Hill Av HGT N6 65 K3
North Hyde Gdns
HYS/HAR UB3 113 K3
North Hyde La NWDGN UB2 114 D5
North Hyde Rd HYS/HAR UB3 113 H3
North Hyde Whf
NWDGN UB2 * 114 B4
Northiam NFNCH/WDSPK N12 32 E6
Northiam St HACK E8 86 D6
Northington St
BMSBY WC1N 11 G1
Northlands Av ORP BR6 216 E2
Northlands St CMBW SE5 142 D3
North La TEDD TW11 174 A2
North Lodge Cl
PUT/ROE SW15 * 139 G6
North Ms BMSBY WC1N 5 H7
North Mt TRDG/WHET N20 * 33 G4
Northolm EDGW HA8 31 F6
Northolme Gdns EDGW HA8 44 C4
Northolme Ri ORP BR6 201 K6
Northolme Rd HBRY N5 85 J2
Northolt Av RSLP HA4 77 F3
Northolt Gdns GFD/PVL UB6 79 F3
Northolt Rd HTHAIR TW6 132 B2
RYLN/HDSTN HA2 78 B2
Northover BMLY BR1 165 J5
North Pde CHSGTN KT9 206 B3
EDGW HA8 * 44 C5
STHL UB1 * 96 A5
North Pk ELTH/MOT SE9 166 E1
North Pas WAND/EARL SW18 139 K6
North Peckham Est
PECK SE15 143 G1
North Pl MTCM CR4 178 E3
TEDD TW11 174 A2
Northpoint Cl SUT SM1 209 G1
North Pole La HAYES BR2 214 E4
North Pole Rd SHB W12 100 A5
Northport St IS N1 7 F1
North Ri BAY/PAD W2 * 8 D4
North Rd BELV DA17 129 J3
BMLY BR1 184 A4
BTFD TW8 117 F6
CHDH RM6 74 A2
EA W5 116 E3
EBED/NFELT TW14 153 G1
ED N9 36 D3
EDGW HA8 44 D4
GDMY/SEVK IG3 72 E6
HEST TW5 114 B6
HGT N6 66 A4
HOLWY N7 84 E4
HYS/HAR UB3 94 B4
RCH/KEW TW9 137 H3
STHL UB1 96 A5
STHL UB1 96 A6
SURB KT6 190 E3
WDR/YW UB7 112 C3
WIM/MER SW19 178 B2
WOOL/PLUM SE18 127 K4
WWKM BR4 198 E5
Northrop Rd HTHAIR TW6 133 H2
North Rw MYFR/PKLN W1K 9 F5
North Several
BKHTH/KID SE3 * 145 G3
Northside Rd BMLY BR1 183 K4
North Side Wandsworth Common
WAND/EARL SW18 140 B6
Northspur Rd SUT SM1 208 E1
North Sq ED N9 36 D4
GLDGN NW11 64 E2
Northstead Rd
BRXS/STRHM SW2 162 B4
North St BARK IG11 90 B5
BMLY BR1 183 K4
CAR SM5 209 K2
CLAP SW4 141 G4
HDN NW4 64 A2
ISLW TW7 136 B4
PLSTW E13 107 F1
ROM RM1 75 F1
North Tenter St WCHPL E1 13 K4
North Ter SKENS SW7 14 C6
Northumberland Aly
FENCHST EC3M * 13 H4
Northumberland Av
CHCR WC2N 10 E7
EN EN1 24 D1
ISLW TW7 136 A2
MNPK E12 71 G5
WELL DA16 147 K5
Northumberland Cl
STWL/WRAY TW19 152 B1
Northumberland Crs
EBED/NFELT TW14 153 H1
Northumberland Gdns
BMLY BR1 201 F1
ED N9 36 B5
MTCM CR4 195 J2
Northumberland Gv
TOTM N17 50 D3
Northumberland Pk
ERITH DA8 149 K1
TOTM N17 50 C3
Northumberland Pl
BAY/PAD W2 100 E5
Northumberland Rd BAR EN5 33 G1
EHAM E6 107 J5
RYLN/HDSTN HA2 59 K2
WALTH E17 69 J4
Northumberland St
CHCR WC2N 10 E7
Northumberland Wy
ERITH DA8 149 K2
Northumbria St POP/IOD E14 105 J5
North Verbena Gdns
HMSMTH W6 * 118 D5
North Vw EA W5 97 J3
PIN HA5 59 G4
WIM/MER SW19 176 E1
Northview Crs WLSDN NW10 81 H2
Northview Dr WFD IG8 53 H5
Northview Pde HOLWY N7 * 84 E1
North View Rd
CEND/HSY/T N8 48 D6
North Vls CAMTN NW1 84 D4
North Wk CROY/NA CR0 213 K3
North Wy PIN HA5 41 G6
CDALE/KGS NW9 44 D6
ED N9 36 E4
FBAR/BDGN N11 48 C2
Northway GLDGN NW11 65 F2
MRDN SM4 177 H6
WLGTN SM6 210 C2
Northway Crs MLHL NW7 31 G6
Northway Rd CMBW SE5 142 D4
CROY/NA CR0 197 G3
Northways Pde HAMP NW3 * 83 H5
North Weald Cl HCH RM12 93 K5
North Weald La
KUTN/CMB KT2 174 D1
North Wharf Rd BAY/PAD W2 8 A2
Northwick Av
KTN/HRWW/WS HA3 61 G3
Northwick Cir
KTN/HRWW/WS HA3 61 J3
Northwick Cl STJWD NW8 2 A6
Northwick Park Rd HRW HA1 61 F3
Northwick Rd ALP/SUD HA0 79 K6
OXHEY WD19 27 G6
Northwick Ter STJWD NW8 2 A6
Northwold Dr PIN HA5 41 G6
Northwold Rd
STNW/STAM N16 68 C6
Northwood Av HCH RM12 93 J2
Northwood Gdns CLAY IG5 72 A1
GFD/PVL UB6 79 F3
NFNCH/WDSPK N12 47 H1
Northwood Pl ERITHM DA18 129 G3
Northwood Rd CAR SM5 210 A4
FSTH SE23 164 C3
HGT N6 66 B4
HTHAIR TW6 132 A2
THHTH CR7 180 D5
Northwood Wy NTHWD HA6 40 E3
North Woolwich Rd
CAN/RD E16 125 K1
CAN/RD E16 126 A1
North Worple Wy
MORT/ESHN SW14 138 A4
Norton Av BRYLDS KT5 191 J4
Norton Cl CHING E4 51 J1
Norton Folgate WCHPL E1 7 H7
Norton Gdns
STRHM/NOR SW16 179 K5
Norton Rd ALP/SUD HA0 79 K4
DAGE RM10 93 F4
LEY E10 69 H5
Norval Gn BRXN/ST SW9 * 142 B3
Norval Rd ALP/SUD HA0 61 H6
Norway Ga BERM/RHTH SE16 124 B3
Norway Pl POP/IOD E14 105 H5
Norway St GNWCH SE10 124 E6
Norwich Crs CHDH RM6 73 H2
Norwich Ms GDMY/SEVK IG3 73 G5
Norwich Rd FSTGT E7 88 E3
GFD/PVL UB6 78 B6
NTHWD HA6 40 D6
THHTH CR7 180 D6
Norwich St FLST/FETLN EC4A 11 J3
Norwich Wk EDGW HA8 44 E3
Norwood Av ALP/SUD HA0 80 B6
ROMW/RG RM7 75 F4
Norwood Cl CRICK NW2 82 C1
NWDGN UB2 115 F4
WHTN TW2 155 J4
Norwood Dr
RYLN/HDSTN HA2 59 K3
Norwood Gdns NWDGN UB2 114 E4
YEAD UB4 95 G3
Norwood Green Rd
NWDGN UB2 115 F4
Norwood High St
WNWD SE27 162 C5
Norwood Park Rd
WNWD SE27 180 D1
Norwood Rd NWDGN UB2 114 D3
WNWD SE27 162 C4
Notley St CMBW SE5 142 E1
Notson Rd SNWD SE25 197 J1
Notting Barn Rd NKENS W10 100 B3
Nottingdale Sq NTGHL W11 * 119 H1
Nottingham Av CAN/RD E16 107 G4
Nottingham Ct
LSQ/SEVD WC2H 10 E4
Nottingham Pl CAMTN NW1 3 G7
Nottingham Rd ISLW TW7 136 A3
LEY E10 70 A3
SAND/SEL CR2 211 J2
TOOT SW17 160 E3
Nottingham St MHST W1U 9 G1
Nottingham Ter CAMTN NW1 3 G7
Notting Hill Ga KENS W8 119 K1
Nova Ms CHEAM SM3 193 H4
Novar Cl ORP BR6 202 A4
Nova Rd CROY/NA CR0 196 C5
Novar Rd ELTH/MOT SE9 167 H3
Novello St FUL/PGN SW6 139 K2
Nowell Rd BARN SW13 118 D6
Nower Hl PIN HA5 59 K1
Noyna Rd TOOT SW17 160 E5
Nubia Wy BMLY BR1 165 H6
Nuding Cl LEW SE13 144 D4
Nugent Rd ARCH N19 66 E5
SNWD SE25 181 G6
Nugents Ct PIN HA5 * 41 J4
Nugent's Pk PIN HA5 41 J4
Nugent Ter STJWD NW8 101 G1
Nuneaton Rd DAGW RM9 91 K5
Nunhead Crs PECK SE15 143 J4
Nunhead Gv PECK SE15 143 J4
Nunhead La PECK SE15 143 J4
Nunnington Cl ELTH/MOT SE9 166 D5
Nunn's Rd ENC/FH EN2 23 J3
Nupton Dr BAR EN5 32 A1
Nurse Cl EDGW HA8 44 E4
Nursery Av CROY/NA CR0 198 A6
FNCH N3 47 F5
Nursery Cl BROCKY SE4 144 C3
CHDH RM6 73 K3
CROY/NA CR0 198 A6
EBED/NFELT TW14 154 A2
ORP BR6 202 A4
OXHEY WD19 27 F3
PEND EN3 25 F2
PUT/ROE SW15 139 G6
SWLY BR8 187 K5
WFD IG8 53 F1
Nursery Gdns CHST BR7 185 G2
HPTN TW12 154 E6
HSLWW TW4 134 E6
PEND EN3 25 F2
Nursery La BETH E2 7 J1
FSTGT E7 88 E4
NKENS W10 100 A4
Nurserymans Rd
FBAR/BDGN N11 34 A4
Nursery Rd BRXN/ST SW9 142 A5
EFNCH N2 47 H4
HOM E9 86 E4
MTCM CR4 178 D6
PIN HA5 41 G6
STHGT/OAK N14 34 C2
SUT SM1 209 G2
THHTH CR7 196 E1
WIM/MER SW19 177 H3
Nursery Rw BAR EN5 * 20 C4
WALW SE17 18 E7
Nursery St TOTM N17 50 B3
The Nursery ERITH DA8 150 C1
Nursery Wk HDN NW4 45 K6
ROMW/RG RM7 75 F4
Nutbourne St NKENS W10 100 C2
Nutbrook St PECK SE15 143 G4
Nutbrowne Rd DAGW RM9 92 B6
Nutcroft Rd PECK SE15 143 J1
Nutfield Cl CAR SM5 209 J1
UED N18 50 C2
Nutfield Gdns
GDMY/SEVK IG3 73 F6
NTHLT UB5 95 G1
Nutfield Rd CRICK NW2 63 J6
EDUL SE22 143 G6
SRTFD E15 88 A2
THHTH CR7 196 C1
Nutfield Wy ORP BR6 201 F6
Nutford Pl MBLAR W1H 8 D3
Nuthatch Cl
STWL/WRAY TW19 152 C3
Nuthatch Gdns THMD SE28 127 J2
Nuthurst Av
BRXS/STRHM SW2 162 A4
Nutley Ter HAMP NW3 83 H4
Nutmead Cl BXLY DA5 169 K3
Nutmeg Cl CAN/RD E16 106 C3
Nutmeg La POP/IOD E14 106 B5
Nuttall St IS N1 7 H2
Nutter La WAN E11 71 G2
Nutt Gv EDGW HA8 29 K4
Nut Tree Cl ORP BR6 217 K1
Nutt St PECK SE15 143 G1
Nutwell St TOOT SW17 178 D1
Nuxley Rd BELV DA17 129 G6
Nyanza St WOOL/PLUM SE18 127 J6
WOOL/PLUM SE18 147 J1
Nylands Av RCH/KEW TW9 137 H3
Nymans Gdns RYNPK SW20 176 E6
Nynehead St NWCR SE14 144 B1
Nyon Gv CAT SE6 164 C4
Nyssa Cl WFD IG8 53 K2
Nyton Cl ARCH N19 66 E5

O

Oak Av CEND/HSY/T N8 66 E1
CROY/NA CR0 198 D6
ENC/FH EN2 23 F2
HEST TW5 134 C1
HPTN TW12 172 D1
MUSWH N10 48 B3
TOTM N17 49 K3
WDR/YW UB7 112 D3
Oakbank CROY/NA CR0 214 A4
Oakbank Av WOT/HER KT12 188 E4
Oakbank Gv HNHL SE24 142 D5
Oakbrook Cl BMLY BR1 166 A6
Oakbury Rd FUL/PGN SW6 140 A3
Oak Cl STHGT/OAK N14 34 B2
Oakcombe Cl NWMAL KT3 176 B4
Oak Cottage Cl CAT SE6 165 H3
Oak Cots HNWL W7 * 115 K2
Oak Crs CAN/RD E16 106 C4
Oakcroft Cl PIN HA5 41 F5
Oakcroft Rd CHSGTN KT9 206 B2
LEW SE13 145 G3
Oakcroft Vls CHSGTN KT9 206 B2
Oakdale STHGT/OAK N14 34 B3
Oakdale Av
KTN/HRWW/WS HA3 62 A2
NTHWD HA6 40 E5
Oakdale Cl OXHEY WD19 27 G6
Oakdale Gdns CHING E4 52 A1
Oakdale Rd FSBYPK N4 67 J3
FSTGT E7 89 F5
HOR/WEW KT19 207 F6
OXHEY WD19 27 G5
PECK SE15 143 K4
STRHM/NOR SW16 179 K1
SWFD E18 53 F5
WAN E11 70 B6
Oakdale Wy MTCM CR4 195 F4
Oakdene WEA W13 97 H4
Oakdene Av CHST BR7 185 F1
ERITH DA8 129 K6
THDIT KT7 190 B5
Oak Dene Cl EMPK RM11 75 K3
Oakdene Cl PIN HA5 41 K3
Oakdene Dr BRYLDS KT5 191 K5
Oakdene Ms CHEAM SM3 193 J5
Oakdene Pk FNCH N3 46 D3
Oakdene Rd STMC/STPC BR5 202 B3
Oakden St LBTH SE11 17 K6
Oaken Dr ESH/CLAY KT10 205 F4
Oaken La ESH/CLAY KT10 204 E2
Oakenshaw Cl SURB KT6 191 F4
Oakeshott Av HGT N6 66 A6
Oakey La STHWK SE1 17 J4
Oakfield CHING E4 51 K1
Oakfield Av
KTN/HRWW/WS HA3 43 H6
Oakfield Cl NWMAL KT3 192 C2
RSLP HA4 58 D3
Oakfield Gdns BECK BR3 198 D2
CAR SM5 194 D5
GFD/PVL UB6 96 D3
UED N18 36 A6
Oakfield La HAYES BR2 215 G2
Oakfield Rd ASHF TW15 152 E6
CROY/NA CR0 196 D5
EHAM E6 89 J6
FNCH N3 47 F4
FSBYPK N4 67 G3
IL IG1 90 B1
PGE/AN SE20 181 J3
STHGT/OAK N14 34 E4
WALTH E17 51 G5
WIM/MER SW19 159 G5
Oakfields Rd GLDGN NW11 64 C3
Oakfield St WBPTN SW10 120 B6
Oakford Rd KTTN NW5 84 C2
Oak Gdns CROY/NA CR0 198 D6
EDGW HA8 44 E5
Oak Gv CRICK NW2 82 B2
RSLP HA4 59 F5
SUN TW16 172 A3
WWKM BR4 199 F6
Oak Grove Rd PGE/AN SE20 181 K4
Oak Hall Rd WAN E11 71 F3
Oakham Cl CAT SE6 * 164 C4
Oakhampton Rd MLHL NW7 46 B4
Oakhill ESH/CLAY KT10 205 G4
Oak Hl SURB KT6 191 F4
WFD IG8 52 B3
Oakhill Av HAMP NW3 83 F2
PIN HA5 41 J5
Oak Hill Crs SURB KT6 191 F4
WFD IG8 52 C3
Oak Hill Gdns WFD IG8 52 C4
Oak Hill Gv SURB KT6 191 F3
Oak Hill Pk HAMP NW3 83 F2
Oak Hill Park Ms HAMP NW3 83 G2
Oakhill Pl PUT/ROE SW15 139 K6
Oak Hill Rd SURB KT6 * 191 F3
Oakhill Rd BECK BR3 183 F5
ORP BR6 202 A6
PUT/ROE SW15 139 J6
STRHM/NOR SW16 179 K4
SUT SM1 209 F1
Oak Hill Wy HAMP NW3 83 F2
Oakhurst Av EBAR EN4 33 J2
Oakhurst Cl BARK/HLT IG6 54 C4
CHST BR7 184 E4
TEDD TW11 173 K1
WALTH E17 70 C1
Oakhurst Gdns CHING E4 38 D3
WALTH E17 70 C1
Oakhurst Gv EDUL SE22 143 H5
Oakhurst Rd HOR/WEW KT19 206 E4
Oakington Av HYS/HAR UB3 113 G4
RYLN/HDSTN HA2 60 A4
WBLY HA9 80 B1
Oakington Cl SUN TW16 172 B5
Oakington Dr SUN TW16 172 B5
Oakington Manor Dr
WBLY HA9 80 C3
Oakington Rd MV/WKIL W9 * 100 E3
Oakington Wy
CEND/HSY/T N8 66 E3
Oakland Pl BKHH IG9 38 E4
Oakland Rd SRTFD E15 88 C2
Oaklands WCHMH N21 35 F4
Oaklands Av BFN/LL DA15 168 A2
ED N9 36 D
ESH/CLAY KT10 189 J5
ISLW TW7 116 A6
OXHEY WD19 27 F3
ROM RM1 57 G
THHTH CR7 196 B
WWKM BR4 213 K
Oaklands Cl ALP/SUD HA0 79 K
CHSGTN KT9 205 J
STMC/STPC BR5 201 K
Oaklands Dr WHTN TW2 155 H
Oaklands Ga NTHWD HA6 40 C
Oaklands Gv SHB W12 118 D
Oaklands Ms CRICK NW2 82 B
Oaklands Park Av IL IG1 72 C
Oaklands Pl CLAP SW4 141
Oaklands Rd BMLY BR1 183 H
CRICK NW2 82 B
HNWL W7 116 A
MORT/ESHN SW14 138 A
TRDG/WHET N20 32 D
Oaklands Wy WLGTN SM6 210 C
Oakland Wy HOR/WEW KT19 207 F
Oak La EFNCH N2 47 H
FBAR/BDGN N11 48 D
ISLW TW7 135 K
POP/IOD E14 105 H
TWK TW1 156 B
WFD IG8 38 D
Oakleafe Gdns BARK/HLT IG6 54 B
Oakleigh Av EDGW HA8 44 D
SURB KT6 191 H
TRDG/WHET N20 33 H
Oakleigh Cl TRDG/WHET N20 33
Oakleigh Ct EDGW HA8 * 44
Oakleigh Crs TRDG/WHET N20 33
Oakleigh Dr
RKW/CH/CXG WD3 26
Oakleigh Gdns EDGW HA8 44

ORP BR6 216 E2
TRDG/WHET N20 33 G3
Oakleigh Ms TRDG/WHET N20 33 G4
Oakleigh Park Av CHST BR7 185 F5
Oakleigh Pk North
TRDG/WHET N20 33 H3
Oakleigh Pk South
TRDG/WHET N20 33 J3
Oakleigh Rd HGDN/ICK UB10 76 A5
PIN HA5 41 K2
Oakleigh Rd North
TRDG/WHET N20 33 H4
Oakleigh Rd South
FBAR/BDGN N11 34 A6
Oakleigh Wy MTCM CR4 179 G4
SURB KT6 191 H5
Oakley Av BARK IG11 91 F5
CROY/NA CR0 210 E2
EA W5 98 C6
Oakley Cl CHING E4 38 A5
EHAM E6 107 J5
HNWL W7 96 E6
ISLW TW7 135 J2
Oakley Ct MTCM CR4 195 F4
Oakley Crs FSBYE EC1V * 6 B3
Oakley Dr CAT SE6 165 G1
ELTH/MOT SE9 167 J3
HAYES BR2 215 J1
Oakley Gdns CEND/HSY/T N8 67 F2
CHEL SW3 120 D6
Oakley Pk BXLY DA5 168 D2
Oakley Pl STHWK SE1 123 G5
Oakley Rd HAYES BR2 215 J1
HRW HA1 60 E3
IS N1 85 K5
SNWD SE25 197 J2
Oakley Sq CAMTN NW1 4 B2
Oakley St CHEL SW3 120 D6
Oakley Yd BETH E2 * 7 K6
Oak Lodge Av CHIG IG7 54 D1
Oak Lodge Cl STAN HA7 43 J1
Oak Lodge Dr WWKM BR4 198 E4
Oaklodge Wy MLHL NW7 45 H2
Oakmeade PIN HA5 42 A2
Oakmead Gdns EDGW HA8 31 F6
Oakmead Pl MTCM CR4 178 D4
Oakmead Rd BAL SW12 161 G3
CROY/NA CR0 195 J3
Oakmere Rd ABYW SE2 128 B6
Oakmoor Wy CHIG IG7 54 E1
Oakmore Gdns
STMC/STPC BR5 202 D1
Oak Park Gdns
WIM/MER SW19 159 G3
Oakridge Dr EFNCH N2 47 H6
Oakridge La BMLY BR1 183 G1
Oakridge Rd BMLY BR1 165 H6
Oak Ri BKHH IG9 39 H5
Oak Rd EA W5 97 K6
ERITH DA8 150 D2
NWMAL KT3 176 A5
ORP BR6 217 G5
Oak Rw MTCM CR4 179 H5
Oaks Av CRW RM5 56 E5
FELT TW13 154 D4
NRWD SE19 181 F1
WPK KT4 207 K2
Oaksford Av SYD SE26 163 J5
Oaks Gv CHING E4 38 C4
Oakshade Rd BMLY BR1 165 G6
Oakshaw Rd
WAND/EARL SW18 160 A2
Oaks La CROY/NA CR0 212 E1
GNTH/NBYPK IG2 72 E1
Oaks Rd CROY/NA CR0 212 D3
STWL/WRAY TW19 132 A6
The Oaks CHSGTN KT9 205 J1
FELT TW13 * 154 D4
HAYES BR2 * 201 F3
MRDN SM4 * 193 H1
NFNCH/WDSPK N12 33 F6
OXHEY WD19 27 G3
RSLP HA4 58 B4
WFD IG8 52 C3
WOOL/PLUM SE18 127 H5
YEAD UB4 94 A1
Oak St ROMW/RG RM7 74 E2
Oaks Wy CAR SM5 209 K5
SURB KT6 190 E6
Oakthorpe Rd PLMGR N13 49 G1
Oaktree Av PLMGR N13 35 G5
Oak Tree Cl EA W5 * 97 J5
STAN HA7 43 J3
Oak Tree Ct BORE WD6 * 29 K1
Oak Tree Dell
CDALE/KGS NW9 62 E2
Oak Tree Dr TRDG/WHET N20 33 F3
Oak Tree Gdns BMLY BR1 184 A1
Oaktree Gv IL IG1 90 D3
Oak Tree Rd STJWD NW8 2 B5
Oakview Cl OXHEY WD19 27 G1
Oakview Gdns EFNCH N2 65 H1
Oakview Gv CROY/NA CR0 198 B5
Oakview Rd CAT SE6 182 E1
Oak Village HAMP NW3 84 A2
Oak Vls GLDGN NW11 * 64 D3
Oak Wy ACT W3 118 B1
STHGT/OAK N14 34 A2
CROY/NA CR0 198 A3
EBED/NFELT TW14 153 H3
Oakway HAYES BR2 183 G5
RYNPK SW20 193 F1
Oakway Cl BXLY DA5 169 F1
Oakways ELTH/MOT SE9 167 G1
Oakwood WLGTN SM6 210 B6
Oakwood Av BECK BR3 183 F5
CHSGTN KT9 206 A5
HAYES BR2 184 A6
MTCM CR4 178 C5
STHGT/OAK N14 34 D2
STHL UB1 96 A6
Oakwood Cl CHST BR7 184 E2
LEW SE13 165 G2
STHGT/OAK N14 34 C1
WFD IG8 53 J2
Oakwood Ct WKENS W14 119 J3
Oakwood Crs GFD/PVL UB6 79 G4
WCHMH N21 34 E1
Oakwood Dr BXLYHN DA7 149 K5
EDGW HA8 44 E2
NRWD SE19 180 E2
Oakwood Gdns
GDMY/SEVK IG3 73 F6
ORP BR6 201 H6
SUT SM1 193 K6
Oakwood La WKENS W14 119 J3
Oakwood Pde
STHGT/OAK N14 * 22 C6
Oakwood Park Cots
WCHMH N21 * 35 F1
Oakwood Park Rd
STHGT/OAK N14 34 E1
Oakwood Pl CROY/NA CR0 196 B3
Oakwood Rd CROY/NA CR0 196 B3
GLDGN NW11 64 E2
ORP BR6 201 H6
PIN HA5 41 F5
RYNPK SW20 176 D4
Oakworth Rd NKENS W10 100 A4
Oarsman Pl E/WMO/HCT KT8 189 K1
Oast House Wy
STMC/STPC BR5 202 C1
Oates Cl HAYES BR2 183 G6
Oates Rd CRW RM5 56 D1
Oatfield Rd ORP BR6 202 A5
Oatland Ri WALTH E17 51 G5
Oatlands Rd PEND EN3 24 E2
Oat La CITYW EC2V 12 C3
Oban Cl PLSTW E13 107 G3
Oban Rd PLSTW E13 107 G2
THHTH CR7 196 E1
Oban St POP/IOD E14 106 B5
Oberstein Rd BTSEA SW11 140 C5
Oborne Cl HNHL SE24 142 C6
Observatory Gdns KENS W8 119 K2
Observatory Rd
MORT/ESHN SW14 137 K5
SKENS SW7 14 B4
Occupation La EA W5 116 E4
WOOL/PLUM SE18 147 G2
Occupation Rd WALW SE17 122 D5
WEA W13 116 C2
Ocean Est WCHPL E1 105 F3
Ocean St WCHPL E1 105 F4
Ockendon Ms IS N1 * 85 K4
Ockendon Rd IS N1 85 K4
Ockham Dr GFD/PVL UB6 78 D5
STMC/STPC BR5 186 B3
Ockley Rd CROY/NA CR0 196 A4
STRHM/NOR SW16 161 K6
Octagon Ar LVPST EC2M * 13 G2
Octavia Cl MTCM CR4 194 D2
Octavia Ms CRICK NW2 * 81 K4
Octavia Rd ISLW TW7 136 A4
Octavia St BTSEA SW11 140 D2
Octavius St DEPT SE8 144 D1
October Pl HDN NW4 * 46 B6
Odard Rd E/WMO/HCT KT8 189 F1
Odell Cl BARK IG11 91 F5
Odell Wk LEW SE13 144 E4
Odeon Pde ELTH/MOT SE9 * 146 D5
GFD/PVL UB6 * 79 H4
HOLWY N7 * 84 E1
ISLW TW7 * 135 K3
Odessa Rd FSTGT E7 88 D2
WLSDN NW10 99 J1
Odessa St BERM/RHTH SE16 124 C3
Odger St BTSEA SW11 140 E3
Odhams Wk
LSQ/SEVD WC2H * 10 E4
Odsey Vls FSBYPK N4 * 67 G3
Offa's Md HOM E9 87 G2
Offenham Rd ELTH/MOT SE9 166 E6
Offerton Rd CLAP SW4 141 H4
Offham Slope
NFNCH/WDSPK N12 46 D1
Offley Pl ISLW TW7 135 J3
Offley Rd BRXN/ST SW9 142 B1
Offord Cl TOTM N17 50 C3
Offord Rd IS N1 85 F5
Offord St HOLWY N7 85 F5
Ogilby St WOOL/PLUM SE18 126 E4
Oglander Rd PECK SE15 143 G5
Ogle St GTPST W1W 10 A1
Oglethorpe Rd DAGE RM10 92 B1
Ohio Rd PLSTW E13 106 D3
Oil Mill La HMSMTH W6 118 D5
Okeburn Rd TOOT SW17 179 F1
Okehampton Crs WELL DA16 148 C2
Okehampton Rd
WLSDN NW10 82 A6
Olaf St NTGHL W11 100 B6
Old Bailey STP EC4M 12 B4
Old Barn Cl BELMT SM2 208 C5
Old Barn Wy BXLYHN DA7 150 A5
Old Barrack Yd KTBR SW1X 15 G2
Old Bellgate Whf
POP/IOD E14 124 D3
Oldberry Rd EDGW HA8 45 F2
Old Bethnal Green Rd
BETH E2 104 D2
Old Bond St CONDST W1S 10 A6
Oldborough Rd ALP/SUD HA0 61 J6
Old Brewery Ms HAMP NW3 83 H2
Old Bridge Cl NTHLT UB5 96 A1
Old Bridge St KUT/HW KT1 174 E5
Old Broad St OBST EC2N 13 F3
Old Bromley Rd BMLY BR1 183 G1
Old Brompton Rd ECT SW5 120 A5
Old Blds LINN WC2A 11 J3
Old Burlington St
CONDST W1S 10 A5
Oldbury Cl STMC/STPC BR5 202 E1
Oldbury Pl MHST W1U 9 H1
Oldbury Rd EN EN1 24 C3
Old Castle St WCHPL E1 13 J3
Old Cavendish St OXSTW W1C 9 J4
Old Chapel Rd SWLY BR8 203 K4
Old Chestnut Av
ESH/CLAY KT10 204 A4
Old Church Cl ORP BR6 202 C5
Old Church La
CDALE/KGS NW9 62 E6
GFD/PVL UB6 97 G2
STAN HA7 43 H2
Old Church Pth
ESH/CLAY KT10 204 B2
Oldchurch Ri ROMW/RG RM7 75 G3
Old Church Rd WCHPL E1 * 105 F5
CHING E4 37 J5
Oldchurch Rd ROMW/RG RM7 75 F4
Old Church St CHEL SW3 120 C5
Old Claygate La
ESH/CLAY KT10 205 G4
Old Compton St
SOHO/SHAV W1D 10 C5
Old Cote Dr HEST TW5 115 F6
Old Court Pl KENS W8 120 A2
The Old Ctyd BMLY BR1 184 A4
Old Dairy Ms BAL SW12 161 F3
KTTN NW5 * 84 B4
Old Deer Pk RCH/KEW TW9 * 137 G4
Old Deer Park Gdns
RCH/KEW TW9 137 F4
Old Devonshire Rd BAL SW12 161 G2
Old Dock Cl RCH/KEW TW9 117 H6
Old Farm Av BFN/LL DA15 167 J3
BFN/LL DA15 168 A4
STHGT/OAK N14 34 C2
Old Farm Cl HSLWW TW4 134 E5
Old Farm Rd EFNCH N2 47 H4
HPTN TW12 172 E2
WDR/YW UB7 112 A2
Old Farm Rd East
BFN/LL DA15 168 B4
Old Farm Rd West
BFN/LL DA15 168 A4
Oldfield Cl BMLY BR1 200 E1
GFD/PVL UB6 78 E3
STAN HA7 43 G1
Oldfield Farm Gdns
GFD/PVL UB6 78 D6
Oldfield Gv BERM/RHTH SE16 124 A4
Oldfield La North
GFD/PVL UB6 78 D6
Oldfield La South
GFD/PVL UB6 96 C2
Oldfield Ms HGT N6 66 C4
Oldfield Rd ACT W3 118 C2
BMLY BR1 200 E1
HPTN TW12 173 F4
STNW/STAM N16 86 A1
WIM/MER SW19 177 H2
WLSDN NW10 81 H5
Oldfields Circ NTHLT UB5 78 C4
Oldfields Rd SUT SM1 193 K6
Old Fish Street Hl
BLKFR EC4V * 12 C5
Old Fleet La FLST/FETLN EC4A 12 A3
Old Fold Cl BAR EN5 * 20 D2
Old Fold La BAR EN5 20 D2
Old Fold Vw BAR EN5 20 A4
Old Ford Lock BOW E3 * 87 J5
Old Ford Rd BETH E2 104 E1
BOW E3 87 G6
Old Forge Cl STAN HA7 29 G6
Old Forge Ms SHB W12 118 E2
Old Forge Rd ARCH N19 66 D6
EN EN1 24 B1
Old Forge Wy SCUP DA14 168 C6
Old Gannon Cl NTHWD HA6 26 A6
Old Gloucester St
BMSBY WC1N 11 F1
Old Hall Cl PIN HA5 41 J4
Old Hall Dr PIN HA5 41 J4
Oldham Ter ACT W3 117 K1
Old Hatch Mnr RSLP HA4 58 D4
Old Hl CHST BR7 185 F4
ORP BR6 216 E4
Oldhill St STNW/STAM N16 68 C5
Old Homesdale Rd
HAYES BR2 200 B1
Old Hospital Cl BAL SW12 * 160 E3
Old House Cl WIM/MER SW19 177 H1
Old House Gdns TWK TW1 * 156 D1
Old Howletts La RSLP HA4 58 B3
Old Jamaica Rd
BERM/RHTH SE16 123 H3
Old James St PECK SE15 143 J4
Old Jewry LOTH EC2R * 12 E4
Old Kenton La
CDALE/KGS NW9 62 D2
Old Kent Rd PECK SE15 123 J6
STHWK SE1 19 G6
Old Kingston Rd WPK KT4 206 E1
Old Lodge Wy STAN HA7 43 G1
Old London Rd
KUTN/CMB KT2 175 F5
Old Maidstone Rd SCUP DA14 187 G3
Old Malden La WPK KT4 192 B6
Old Manor Dr ISLW TW7 155 H1
Old Manor Rd NWDGN UB2 114 C4
Old Manor Wy CHST BR7 184 E1
Old Manor Yd ECT SW5 * 120 A4
Old Market Sq BETH E2 7 J4
Old Marylebone Rd
CAMTN NW1 8 D2
Old Mill Ct SWFD E18 53 G6
Old Mill Rd WOOL/PLUM SE18 127 J6
Old Mitre Ct EMB EC4Y * 11 K4
Old Montague St WCHPL E1 104 C4
Old Nichol St BETH E2 7 J6
Old North St FSBYW WC1X * 11 G1
Old Oak Common La ACT W3 99 G5
Old Oak La WLSDN NW10 99 H2
Old Oak Rd ACT W3 99 H6
Old Orch SUN TW16 172 B5
Old Orchard Cl EBAR EN4 21 H1
The Old Orch HAMP NW3 * 83 K2
Old Palace Rd CROY/NA CR0 211 J1
Old Palace Yd RCH/KEW TW9 136 D6
WHALL SW1A 16 E4
Old Paradise St LBTH SE11 17 G6
Old Park Av BAL SW12 161 F1
ENC/FH EN2 23 J5
Old Park Gv ENC/FH EN2 23 J5
Old Park La MYFR/PKLN W1K 15 H1
Old Park Ms HEST TW5 134 E1
Old Park Ridings
WCHMH N21 35 H1
Old Park Rd ABYW SE2 128 B5
ENC/FH EN2 23 H4
PLMGR N13 35 F5
Old Park Rd South
ENC/FH EN2 23 H5
Old Park Vw ENC/FH EN2 23 G4
Old Pearson St GNWCH SE10 144 E1
Old Perry St CHST BR7 185 K3
Old Post Office La
BKHTH/KID SE3 146 A4
Old Pound Cl ISLW TW7 136 B2
Old Pye St WEST SW1P 16 C4
Old Quebec St MBLAR W1H 9 F4
Old Queen St STJSPK SW1H 16 D3
Old Rectory Gdns EDGW HA8 44 C2
Old Redding
KTN/HRWW/WS HA3 42 B1
Oldridge Rd BAL SW12 161 F2
Old Rd LEW SE13 145 H5
PEND EN3 24 E2
Old Royal Free Sq IS N1 5 K1
Old Ruislip Rd NTHLT UB5 95 G1
Old's Ap WATW WD18 26 A3
Old School Cl BECK BR3 182 A5
Old School Crs FSTGT E7 88 E4
Old School Pl CROY/NA CR0 211 G2
Old Schools La EW KT17 207 H6
Old School Sq THDIT KT7 190 A3
Old School Ter CHEAM SM3 * 208 B5
Old Seacoal La STP EC4M 12 A4
Old South Cl PIN HA5 41 H4
Old South Lambeth Rd
VX/NE SW8 * 141 K1
Old Sq LINN WC2A 11 H3
Old Stable Ms HBRY N5 85 J1
Old Station Gdns
TEDD TW11 * 174 B2
Old Station Rd HYS/HAR UB3 113 J3
The Old Station Yd
WALTH E17 70 A1
Oldstead Rd BMLY BR1 165 G6
Old St FSBYE EC1V 6 C6
PLSTW E13 107 F1
Old Studio Cl CROY/NA CR0 196 E4
Old Swan Yd CAR SM5 209 K2
Old Town CLAP SW4 141 H4
CROY/NA CR0 211 H1
Old Tramyard
WOOL/PLUM SE18 127 K4
Old Woolwich Rd
GNWCH SE10 125 G6
Old York Rd
WAND/EARL SW18 140 A6
Oleander Cl ORP BR6 216 D3
O'Leary Sq WCHPL E1 104 E4
Olga St BOW E3 105 G1
Olinda Rd STNW/STAM N16 68 B3
Oliphant St NKENS W10 100 C2
Olive Gv SEVS/STOTM N15 67 J1
Oliver Av SNWD SE25 181 G6
Oliver Cl CHSWK W4 117 J6
Oliver Gdns EHAM E6 107 J4
Oliver Gv SNWD SE25 197 G1
Oliver Ms PECK SE15 143 H3
Olive Rd CRICK NW2 82 A2
EA W5 116 E3
PLSTW E13 107 G2
WIM/MER SW19 * 178 B3
Oliver Rd LEY E10 87 K1
NWMAL KT3 175 K5
RAIN RM13 93 H6
SUT SM1 209 H2
WALTH E17 70 A2
Oliver's Yd STLK EC1Y 7 F6
Olive St ROMW/RG RM7 75 F2
Ollerton Gn BOW E3 87 H6
Ollerton Rd FBAR/BDGN N11 48 D1
Olley Cl WLGTN SM6 210 E5
Ollgar Cl SHB W12 118 C1
Olliffe St POP/IOD E14 125 F3
Olmar St STHWK SE1 123 H6
Olney Rd WALW SE17 122 C6
Olron Crs BXLYHS DA6 148 E6
Olven Rd WOOL/PLUM SE18 147 H1
Olveston Wk CAR SM5 194 C3
Olwen Ms PIN HA5 41 H5
Olyffe Av WELL DA16 148 B3
Olyffe Dr BECK BR3 183 F4
Olympia Wy WKENS W14 119 H3
Olympic Wy GFD/PVL UB6 78 B6
WBLY HA9 80 C1
Olympus Gv WDGN N22 49 G4
Olympus Sq CLPT E5 86 D1
Oman Av CRICK NW2 82 A3
O'Meara St STHWK SE1 18 D1
Omega Pl IS N1 * 5 F3
Omega St NWCR SE14 144 C2
Ommaney Rd NWCR SE14 144 A2
Omnibus Wy WALTH E17 51 J5
Ondine Rd PECK SE15 143 G5
Onega Ga BERM/RHTH SE16 124 B3
One Tree Cl FSTH SE23 163 K1
Ongar Cl CHDH RM6 73 J2
Ongar Rd FUL/PGN SW6 119 K6
Ongar Wy RAIN RM13 93 G6
Onra Rd WALTH E17 69 J4
Onslow Av RCHPK/HAM TW10 137 F6
Onslow Cl CHING E4 38 B4
NKENS W10 100 D2
Onslow Crs CHST BR7 185 G4
SKENS SW7 14 B7
Onslow Dr SCUP DA14 168 E5
Onslow Gdns MUSWH N10 66 B2
SKENS SW7 14 A7
SWFD E18 53 F6
THDIT KT7 189 K5
WCHMH N21 23 G6
WLGTN SM6 210 C5
Onslow Ms East SKENS SW7 14 A7
Onslow Ms West SKENS SW7 14 A7
Onslow Pde
STHGT/OAK N14 * 34 B3
Onslow Rd CROY/NA CR0 196 B4
NWMAL KT3 192 D1
RCHPK/HAM TW10 157 F1
Onslow Sq SKENS SW7 14 A7
Onslow St CLKNW EC1R 5 K7
Onslow Wy THDIT KT7 189 K5
Ontario St STHWK SE1 18 B5
Ontario Wy POP/IOD E14 105 J6
On The Hl OXHEY WD19 27 J4
Onyx Ms SRTFD E15 88 C4
Opal Cl CAN/RD E16 107 H5
Opal Ms KIL/WHAMP NW6 82 D6
Opal St LBTH SE11 18 A7
Openshaw Rd ABYW SE2 128 C4
Openview WAND/EARL SW18 160 B3
Ophir Ter PECK SE15 143 H2
Opossum Wy HSLWW TW4 134 B4
Oppenheim Rd LEW SE13 145 F3
Oppidans Rd HAMP NW3 83 K5
Optima Pk DART DA1 * 150 D4
Orange Court La ORP BR6 216 A6
Orange Gv CHIG IG7 54 C2
WAN E11 88 C1
Orange Hill Rd EDGW HA8 44 E3
Orange Pl BERM/RHTH SE16 123 K3
Orangery La ELTH/MOT SE9 146 E6
The Orangery
RCHPK/HAM TW10 156 D4
Orange St LSQ/SEVD WC2H 10 D6
WAP E1W 123 H1
Orange Tree Hl ABR/ST RM4 57 F1
Oransay Rd IS N1 85 J4
Oratory La CHEL SW3 * 120 C5
Orbain Rd FUL/PGN SW6 139 H1
Orbel St BTSEA SW11 140 D2
Orb St WALW SE17 18 E7
Orchard Av BELV DA17 129 F6
CROY/NA CR0 198 B6
EBED/NFELT TW14 133 G6
FNCH N3 46 E6
HEST TW5 134 D1
MTCM CR4 195 F5
NWMAL KT3 176 B5
STHGT/OAK N14 34 C1
STHL UB1 114 D1
THDIT KT7 190 B5
TRDG/WHET N20 33 H4
Orchard Cl ALP/SUD HA0 80 A6
BUSH WD23 28 D3
CHING E4 37 J6
CRICK NW2 81 J1
EDGW HA8 44 A2
FSTH SE23 163 K1
HOR/WEW KT19 * 206 D4
IS N1 85 J5
NKENS W10 100 C4
RSLP HA4 58 A4
RYNPK SW20 193 F1
THDIT KT7 190 C5
WOT/HER KT12 188 A4
Orchard Cots HYS/HAR UB3 * 113 H2
KUTN/CMB KT2 * 175 H4
Orchard Ct WLGTN SM6 * 210 B3
WPK KT4 * 192 D5
Orchard Crs EDGW HA8 44 E1
EN EN1 24 B2
Orchard Dr BKHTH/KID SE3 145 H3
EDGW HA8 44 B1
Orchard Gdns CHSGTN KT9 206 A2
Orchard Ga CDALE/KGS NW9 63 G1
ESH/CLAY KT10 189 J5
GFD/PVL UB6 79 H4
Orchard Gn ORP BR6 201 K6
Orchard Gv CROY/NA CR0 198 B4
EDGW HA8 44 C4
KTN/HRWW/WS HA3 62 B2
ORP BR6 202 A6
PGE/AN SE20 181 H3
Orchard Hl LEW SE13 144 E2
Orchard La E/WMO/HCT KT8 189 J3
RYNPK SW20 176 E4
WFD IG8 39 G6
Orchardleigh Av PEND EN3 24 E3
Orchardmede WCHMH N21 35 K1
Orchard Ms IS N1 85 K5
TOOT SW17 160 B5
Orchard Pl POP/IOD E14 106 C6
STMC/STPC BR5 * 186 D6
TOTM N17 50 B3
Orchard Ri CROY/NA CR0 198 B5
KUTN/CMB KT2 175 K4
PIN HA5 40 D6
RCHPK/HAM TW10 137 J5
Orchard Ri East BFN/LL DA15 147 K6
Orchard Ri West BFN/LL DA15 147 K6
Orchard Rd BAR EN5 20 C5
BELV DA17 129 H4
BMLY BR1 184 B4
BTFD TW8 116 D6
CHSGTN KT9 206 A2
DAGE RM10 92 C6
FELT TW13 153 K3
HGT N6 66 B4
HSLWW TW4 134 E6
HYS/HAR UB3 94 E6
KUT/HW KT1 175 F5
ORP BR6 216 B3
ORP BR6 217 J6
PEND EN3 24 E6
RCH/KEW TW9 137 H4
ROMW/RG RM7 56 D5
SCUP DA14 167 K6
SUN TW16 172 A3
SUT SM1 208 E3
TWK TW1 136 B6
WELL DA16 148 C4
Orchardson St STJWD NW8 2 A7
Orchard Sq WKENS W14 * 119 J5
Orchard St MBLAR W1H 9 G4
WALTH E17 69 G1
Orchard Ter EN EN1 * 36 C1
WLSDN NW10 * 81 H2
The Orchard BKHTH/KID SE3 145 G3
CHSWK W4 118 A4
EW KT17 207 H5
GLDGN NW11 64 E2
HSLW TW3 135 H3
TRDG/WHET N20 33 F3
WCHMH N21 35 K1
Orchard Vls SCUP DA14 * 186 D2
Orchard Wy ASHF TW15 152 C4
CROY/NA CR0 198 B4
EN EN1 24 A4
ESH/CLAY KT10 204 C4
RDART DA2 171 G5
SUT SM1 209 H2
Orchid Cl CHSGTN KT9 205 J5
EHAM E6 107 J4
LEW SE13 145 G6
STHL UB1 95 J5
Orchid Gdns HSLWW TW4 134 E5
Orchid Rd STHGT/OAK N14 34 C2
Orchid St SHB W12 99 J6
Orde Hall St BMSBY WC1N * 11 G1
Ordell Rd BOW E3 105 H1
Ordnance Cl FELT TW13 153 K4
Ordnance Crs GNWCH SE10 125 H2
Ordnance Hl STJWD NW8 2 B1

Ordnance Ms STJWD NW8 2 B2
Ordnance Rd CAN/RD E16 106 D4
WOOL/PLUM SE18 127 F6
Oregano Dr POP/IOD E14 106 B5
Oregon Av MNPK E12 89 K2
Oregon Cl NWMAL KT3 191 K1
Oregon Sq ORP BR6 201 J5
Orestes Ms KIL/WHAMP NW6 82 E3
Orford Gdns TWK TW1 156 A4
Orford Rd CAT SE6 164 E5
SWFD E18 53 F6
WALTH E17 69 J2
Oriel Cl MTCM CR4 195 J1
Oriel Ct HAMP NW3 83 G2
Oriel Dr BARN SW13 119 F6
Oriel Gdns CLAY IG5 53 K6
Oriel Rd HOM E9 87 F4
Oriel Wy NTHLT UB5 78 B5
Oriental Rd CAN/RD E16 126 C1
Orient St LBTH SE11 18 A6
Orient Wy CLPT E5 87 F1
LEY E10 69 J6
Oriole Wy THMD SE28 109 H6
Orion Rd MUSWH N10 48 A2
Orion Wy NTHWD HA6 26 D6
Orissa Rd WOOL/PLUM SE18 127 K5
Orkney St BTSEA SW11 141 F3
Orlando Rd CLAP SW4 141 H4
Orleans Rd NRWD SE19 180 E2
TWK TW1 156 C2
Orleston Ms HOLWY N7 * 85 G4
Orleston Rd HOLWY N7 85 G4
Orley Farm Rd HRW HA1 78 E1
Ormanton Rd SYD SE26 163 H6
Orme Ct BAY/PAD W2 101 F6
Ormeley Rd BAL SW12 161 G2
Orme Rd KUT/HW KT1 175 J5
SUT SM1 209 F4
Ormerod Gdns MTCM CR4 179 F5
Ormesby Cl THMD SE28 109 K6
Ormesby Wy
KTN/HRWW/WS HA3 62 B3
Orme Sq BAY/PAD W2 101 F6
Orme Square Ga BAY/PAD W2 101 F6
Ormiston Gv SHB W12 118 D1
Ormond Av HPTN TW12 173 G4
Ormond Cl BMSBY WC1N 11 F1
Ormond Crs HPTN TW12 173 G3
Ormond Dr HPTN TW12 173 G3
Ormonde Av HOR/WEW KT19 207 F6
ORP BR6 201 H6
Ormonde Ct STJWD NW8 * 2 E1
Ormonde Ga CHEL SW3 * 120 E5
Ormonde Pl BGVA SW1W 15 H7
Ormonde Ri BKHH IG9 39 G3
Ormonde Rd
MORT/ESHN SW14 137 J4
NTHWD HA6 26 B6
Ormonde Ter STJWD NW8 2 E1
Ormond Rd ARCH N19 66 E5
RCHPK/HAM TW10 136 E6
Ormond Yd STJS SW1Y 10 B7
Ormsby BELMT SM2 * 209 F5
Ormsby Gdns GFD/PVL UB6 96 C1
Ormsby Pl STNW/STAM N16 86 B1
Ormsby St BETH E2 7 J2
Ormside St PECK SE15 123 K6
Ormskirk Rd OXHEY WD19 27 H6
Ornan Rd HAMP NW3 83 J3
Oronsay Wk IS N1 * 85 J4
Orpheus St CMBW SE5 142 E2
Orpington Gdns UED N18 36 A5
Orpington Rd CHST BR7 185 K6
WCHMH N21 35 G3
Orpwood Cl HPTN TW12 172 E2
Orsett Ms BAY/PAD W2 101 F5
Orsett St LBTH SE11 122 A5
Orsett Ter BAY/PAD W2 101 F5
WFD IG8 53 G4
Orsman Rd IS N1 7 G1
Orton Gv EN EN1 24 B2
Orton St WAP E1W 123 H1
Orville Rd BTSEA SW11 140 C3
Orwell Cl HYS/HAR UB3 94 C6
Orwell Rd PLSTW E13 107 G1
Osbaldeston Rd
STNW/STAM N16 68 C6
Osbert St WEST SW1P 16 C7
Osborn Cl HACK E8 86 C6
Osborne Av
STWL/WRAY TW19 152 B3
Osborne Cl BECK BR3 198 B1
EBAR EN4 21 K4
EMPK RM11 75 K3
FELT TW13 172 C1
Osborne Ct EA W5 * 98 A4
Osborne Gdns THHTH CR7 180 D5
Osborne Gv WALTH E17 69 H1
Osborne Ms WALTH E17 69 H2
Osborne Rd ACT W3 117 J2
BELV DA17 129 G5
BKHH IG9 39 F3
CRICK NW2 81 K4
EMPK RM11 75 K3
FSBYPK N4 67 G5
FSTGT E7 89 F3
HOM E9 87 H4
HSLW TW3 134 E4
KUTN/CMB KT2 175 F3
LEY E10 87 K1
PEND EN3 25 G3
PLMGR N13 35 G5
STHL UB1 96 C5
THHTH CR7 180 D5
Osborne Sq DAGW RM9 92 B2
Osborne Ter TOOT SW17 * 179 F1
Osborne Wy CHSGTN KT9 206 B3
Osborn Gdns MLHL NW7 46 B3
Osborn La FSTH SE23 164 B2
Osborn St WCHPL E1 13 K2
Osborn Ter BKHTH/KID SE3 145 J5
Osbourne Ct
RYLN/HDSTN HA2 * 60 B1
Oscar Faber Pl IS N1 * 86 A5
Oscar St BROCKY SE4 144 D3
DEPT SE8 144 D2
Oseney Crs KTTN NW5 84 C4
Osgood Av ORP BR6 217 F3
Osgood Gdns ORP BR6 217 F3
Osidge La STHGT/OAK N14 34 A3
Osier Crs MUSWH N10 47 K4
Osiers Rd WAND/EARL SW18 139 K5
Osier St WCHPL E1 104 E3
Osier Wy LEY E10 87 K1
MTCM CR4 194 D2
Oslac Rd CAT SE6 182 E1
Oslo Sq BERM/RHTH SE16 124 B3
Osman Rd ED N9 36 C5
HMSMTH W6 * 119 F3
Osmond Cl RYLN/HDSTN HA2 60 C6
Osmond Gdns WLGTN SM6 210 C3
Osmund St SHB W12 99 H5
Osnaburgh St CAMTN NW1 3 K6
Osnaburgh Ter CAMTN NW1 3 K6
Osney Wk MRDN SM4 194 C3
Osprey Cl EHAM E6 107 J4
HAYES BR2 200 D5
SUT SM1 208 D3
WALTH E17 51 G3
WAN E11 70 E1
WDR/YW UB7 112 A2
Osprey Est BERM/RHTH SE16 124 A4
Osprey Ms PEND EN3 24 D6
Ospringe Cl PGE/AN SE20 181 K3
Ospringe Rd KTTN NW5 84 C2
Osram Rd WBLY HA9 79 K1
Ossian Rd FSBYPK N4 67 F4
Ossier Ms CHSWK W4 118 C6
Ossington Blds MHST W1U * 9 G1
Ossington Cl BAY/PAD W2 * 100 E6
Ossington St BAY/PAD W2 * 101 F6
Ossory Rd STHWK SE1 123 H5
Ossulston St CAMTN NW1 4 D3
Ossulton Pl EFNCH N2 * 47 G6
Ossulton Wy EFNCH N2 65 G1
Ostade Rd BRXS/STRHM SW2 162 A2
Ostell Crs PEND EN3 25 J1
Osten Ms SKENS SW7 * 120 A3
Osterberg Rd DART DA1 151 J5
Osterley Av ISLW TW7 135 J1
Osterley Cl STMC/STPC BR5 186 B4
Osterley Crs ISLW TW7 135 K2
Osterley Gdns THHTH CR7 180 D5
Osterley La ISLW TW7 115 H4
NWDGN UB2 115 G5
Osterley Park Rd
NWDGN UB2 114 E3
Osterley Park View Rd
HNWL W7 115 K2
Osterley Rd ISLW TW7 135 K1
STNW/STAM N16 86 A2
Ostliffe Rd PLMGR N13 49 H1
Oswald Rd STHL UB1 114 D1
Oswald's Md HOM E9 87 G2
Oswald St CLPT E5 87 F1
Oswald Ter CRICK NW2 * 82 A1
Osward CROY/NA CR0 213 H6
Osward Pl ED N9 36 C4
Osward Rd BAL SW12 160 E4
Oswin St LBTH SE11 18 B6
Oswyth Rd CMBW SE5 143 F3
Otford Cl BMLY BR1 185 F6
BXLY DA5 169 J1
PGE/AN SE20 181 K4
Otford Crs BROCKY SE4 164 C1
Othello Cl LBTH SE11 122 C5
Otis St BOW E3 106 A2
Otley Ct FBAR/BDGN N11 48 A2
Otley Dr GNTH/NBYPK IG2 72 B3
Otley Rd CAN/RD E16 107 G5
Otley Ter CLPT E5 68 E6
Otley Wy OXHEY WD19 27 G5
Otlinge Rd STMC/STPC BR5 202 E1
Ottawa Gdns DAGE RM10 93 F5
Ottaway St CLPT E5 86 C1
Otterbourne Rd CHING E4 38 B5
CROY/NA CR0 196 D6
Otterburn Gdns ISLW TW7 136 B1
Otterburn St TOOT SW17 178 E2
Otter Cl SRTFD E15 88 A6
Otterden Cl ORP BR6 216 E2
Otterden St CAT SE6 164 D6
Otter Rd GFD/PVL UB6 96 C3
Otters Cl STMC/STPC BR5 202 E1
Otto Cl CAT SE6 164 C5
SYD SE26 163 J4
Otto St WALW SE17 122 C6
Otway Gdns BUSH WD23 28 E2
Oulton Cl THMD SE28 109 J5
Oulton Crs BARK IG11 91 F4
Oulton Rd SEVS/STOTM N15 67 K2
Oulton Wy OXHEY WD19 27 K6
Oundle Av BUSH WD23 28 C1
Ouseley Rd BAL SW12 160 E3
Outer Cir CAMTN NW1 2 D3
Outgate Rd WLSDN NW10 81 H5
Outram Pl IS N1 84 E6
Outram Rd CROY/NA CR0 197 G6
EHAM E6 89 J6
WDGN N22 48 D4
Outwich St HDTCH EC3A * 13 H3
Oval Ct EDGW HA8 * 44 E3
Oval Pl VX/NE SW8 142 A1
Oval Rd CAMTN NW1 84 B6
CROY/NA CR0 196 E6
Oval Rd North DAGE RM10 92 D6
Oval Rd South DAGE RM10 110 D1
The Oval BETH E2 104 D1
BFN/LL DA15 168 B2
Oval Wy LBTH SE11 122 A5
Overbrae BECK BR3 182 D2
Overbrook Wk EDGW HA8 44 C3
Overbury Av BECK BR3 182 E6
Overbury Rd FSBYPK N4 67 K3
Overbury St CLPT E5 87 F2
Overcliff Rd BROCKY SE4 144 D4
Overcourt Cl BFN/LL DA15 168 C1
Overdale Av NWMAL KT3 175 K5
Overdale Rd EA W5 116 D3
Overdown Rd CAT SE6 164 D6
Overhill Cots MTCM CR4 * 179 F5
Overhill Rd EDUL SE22 163 H2
PUR/KEN CR8 211 G6
Overhill Wy BECK BR3 199 G2
Overlea Rd CLPT E5 68 C4
Overmead ELTH/MOT SE9 167 J2
Overstand Cl BECK BR3 198 D2
Overstone Gdns
CROY/NA CR0 198 C4
Overstone Rd HMSMTH W6 119 F4
Overton Cl ISLW TW7 136 A2
WLSDN NW10 80 E4
Overton Dr CHDH RM6 73 J4
WAN E11 71 F4
Overton Rd BELMT SM2 208 E4
BRXN/ST SW9 142 B3
LEY E10 69 G5
STHGT/OAK N14 22 E6
Overton's Yd CROY/NA CR0 211 J1
Ovesdon Av
RYLN/HDSTN HA2 59 K5
Ovett Cl NRWD SE19 181 F2
Ovex Cl POP/IOD E14 125 F3
Ovington Gdns CHEL SW3 14 D5
Ovington Ms CHEL SW3 14 D5
Ovington Sq CHEL SW3 14 D5
Ovington St CHEL SW3 14 D5
Owen Cl CROY/NA CR0 196 E3
CRW RM5 56 C2
NTHLT UB5 77 J4
THMD SE28 128 D1
YEAD UB4 * 95 F2
Owen Gdns WFD IG8 53 J2
Owenite St ABYW SE2 128 C4
Owen Rd PLMGR N13 49 J1
Owens Ms WAN E11 70 C6
Owen's Rw FSBYE EC1V 6 A4
Owen St FSBYE EC1V 5 K3
Owens Wy FSTH SE23 164 B2
Owen Wk PGE/AN SE20 181 H3
Owen Wy WLSDN NW10 80 E4
Owgan Cl CMBW SE5 142 E1
Oxberry Av FUL/PGN SW6 139 H3
Oxenden Wood Rd ORP BR6 217 H4
Oxendon St
SOHO/SHAV W1D * 10 C6
Oxenford St PECK SE15 143 G4
Oxenpark Av WBLY HA9 62 A4
Oxestalls Rd DEPT SE8 124 B5
Oxford Av HEST TW5 115 F5
HYS/HAR UB3 133 J1
RYNPK SW20 177 H5
STHGT/OAK N14 34 C3
Oxford Cl ED N9 36 D4
GPK RM2 75 J2
MTCM CR4 179 H6
NTHWD HA6 26 A6
Oxford Ct MANHO EC4N 12 E5
Oxford Crs NWMAL KT3 192 A3
Oxford Dr RSLP HA4 59 G6
Oxford Gdns CHSWK W4 117 H5
NKENS W10 100 B5
TRDG/WHET N20 33 H3
WCHMH N21 35 J2
Oxford Ga HMSMTH W6 119 G4
Oxford Ms BXLY DA5 169 H3
Oxford Rd CAR SM5 209 J4
EA W5 97 K6
ED N9 36 D4
FSBYPK N4 67 G5
HRW HA1 60 C3
IL IG1 90 C2
KIL/WHAMP NW6 100 E1
KTN/HRWW/WS HA3 43 F6
NRWD SE19 180 E2
PEND EN3 24 D6
PUT/ROE SW15 139 H5
SCUP DA14 186 C1
SRTFD E15 88 B4
TEDD TW11 173 J1
WFD IG8 53 H1
WLGTN SM6 * 210 C3
Oxford Rd North CHSWK W4 117 J5
Oxford Rd South CHSWK W4 117 H5
Oxford Rw SUN TW16 * 172 B6
Oxford Sq BAY/PAD W2 8 C4
Oxford St OXSTW W1C 9 G4
SOHO/SHAV W1D 10 A3
Oxford Wk STHL UB1 114 E1
Oxford Wy FELT TW13 154 C6
Oxgate Court Pde
CRICK NW2 * 63 K6
Oxgate Gdns CRICK NW2 81 K1
Oxgate La CRICK NW2 63 K6
Oxhawth Crs HAYES BR2 201 F2
STMC/STPC BR5 201 G3
Oxhey Av OXHEY WD19 27 H2
Oxhey Dr NTHWD HA6 41 F1
OXHEY WD19 27 G5
Oxhey La OXHEY WD19 27 H2
PIN HA5 27 K6
Oxhey Ridge Cl NTHWD HA6 40 E1
Oxhey Rd OXHEY WD19 27 G2
Oxleas EHAM E6 108 B5
Oxleas Cl WELL DA16 147 J3
Oxleay Rd RYLN/HDSTN HA2 60 A5
Oxleigh Cl NWMAL KT3 192 B2
Oxley Cl STHWK SE1 123 G5
Oxleys Rd CRICK NW2 81 K1
Oxlow La DAGE RM10 92 C2
DAGW RM9 92 B2
Oxonian St EDUL SE22 143 G5
Oxted Cl MTCM CR4 178 C6
Oxtoby Wy
STRHM/NOR SW16 179 J4
Oyster Catchers Cl
CAN/RD E16 107 F5
Oyster Rw WCHPL E1 104 E5
Ozolins Wy CAN/RD E16 106 D5

P

Pablo Neruda HNHL SE24 142 C5
Paceheath Cl CRW RM5 57 F2
Pace Pl WCHPL E1 104 D5
Pacific Cl EBED/NFELT TW14 153 J3
Pacific Rd CAN/RD E16 106 E5
Packham Cl ORP BR6 217 J1
Packington Sq IS N1 6 C1
Packington St IS N1 6 B1
Packmores Rd ELTH/MOT SE9 147 J6
Padbury Cl EBED/NFELT TW14 153 G3
Padbury Ct BETH E2 7 K5
Padcroft Rd WDR/YW UB7 112 A1
Paddenswick Rd
HMSMTH W6 118 D3
Paddington Cl YEAD UB4 95 H3
Paddington Gn BAY/PAD W2 8 A2
Paddington Recreation Gnd
MV/WKIL W9 * 101 F2
Paddington St MHST W1U 9 G1
Paddock Cl NTHLT UB5 96 A1
ORP BR6 216 B2
OXHEY WD19 27 J1
SYD SE26 164 A6
WPK KT4 192 B5
Paddock Gdns NRWD SE19 181 F2
Paddock Rd CRICK NW2 81 J1
RSLP HA4 77 H1
Paddocks Cl
RYLN/HDSTN HA2 78 B2
STMC/STPC BR5 202 E6
The Paddocks EA W5 * 116 E3
EBAR EN4 21 K4
MLHL NW7 * 46 D2
WBLY HA9 62 D6
Paddock Wy CHST BR7 185 J3
PUT/ROE SW15 159 F2
Padelford La STAN HA7 29 G4
Padfield Rd BRXN/ST SW9 142 D4
Padley Cl CHSGTN KT9 206 B3
Padnall Rd CHDH RM6 55 K6
Padstow Cl ORP BR6 217 F2
Padstow Rd ENC/FH EN2 23 H3
Padstow Wk FELT TW13 153 J4
Padua Rd PGE/AN SE20 181 K4
Pagden St VX/NE SW8 141 G2
Pageant Crs
BERM/RHTH SE16 124 C1
Pageant Wk CROY/NA CR0 212 A1
Page Av WBLY HA9 80 E1
Page Cl DAGW RM9 92 A3
HPTN TW12 172 D2
KTN/HRWW/WS HA3 62 B3
Page Crs CROY/NA CR0 211 H3
Page Green Rd
SEVS/STOTM N15 * 68 C2
Page Green Ter
SEVS/STOTM N15 68 B2
Page Heath La BMLY BR1 184 C6
Page Heath Vls BMLY BR1 184 C6
Pagehurst Rd CROY/NA CR0 197 H4
Page Meadow MLHL NW7 45 J3
Page Rd EBED/NFELT TW14 153 G1
Page's Hl MUSWH N10 48 A5
Page's La MUSWH N10 48 A5
Page St MLHL NW7 45 J4
WEST SW1P 16 D6
Page's Wk STHWK SE1 19 G6
Page's Yd CHSWK W4 118 C6
Paget Av SUT SM1 209 H1
Paget Cl HPTN TW12 155 J6
Paget Gdns CHST BR7 185 G4
Paget La ISLW TW7 135 J4
Paget Pl KUTN/CMB KT2 * 175 K2
THDIT KT7 190 A5
Paget Ri WOOL/PLUM SE18 147 F1
Paget Rd HGDN/ICK UB10 94 A3
IL IG1 90 B2
STNW/STAM N16 67 K5
Paget St FSBYE EC1V 6 A4
Paget Ter WOOL/PLUM SE18 127 G6
Pagitts Gv EBAR EN4 21 F2
Pagnell St NWCR SE14 144 C1
Pagoda Av RCH/KEW TW9 137 G4
Pagoda Gdns BKHTH/KID SE3 145 G3
Pagoda Gv WNWD SE27 162 D4
Paignton Rd RSLP HA4 76 E1
SEVS/STOTM N15 68 A3
Paines Cl PIN HA5 41 J6
Paine's La PIN HA5 41 J5
Pain's Cl MTCM CR4 179 G5
Painsthorpe Rd
STNW/STAM N16 86 A1
Painters Ms
BERM/RHTH SE16 123 H4
Painters Rd GNTH/NBYPK IG2 55 G6
Paisley Rd CAR SM5 194 C5
WDGN N22 49 H4
Paisley Ter CAR SM5 194 C5
Pakeman St HOLWY N7 85 F1
Pakenham Cl BAL SW12 161 F3
Pakenham St FSBYW WC1X 5 H5
Palace Av KENS W8 120 A2
Palace Cl HOM E9 87 H4
Palace Ct BAY/PAD W2 101 F6
KTN/HRWW/WS HA3 62 A3
Palace Court Gdns
MUSWH N10 48 C6
Palace Garden Ms KENS W8 120 A1
Palace Gdns BKHH IG9 39 H3
Palace Gardens Ter KENS W8 119 K1
Palace Ga KENS W8 120 B2
Palace Gates Rd WDGN N22 48 E4
Palace Gn CROY/NA CR0 213 H5
KENS W8 120 A1
Palace Gv BMLY BR1 184 A4
NRWD SE19 181 G3
Palace Ms FUL/PGN SW6 139 J1
WALTH E17 69 H1
Palace Pde WALTH E17 * 69 H1
Palace Pl BGVA SW1W 16 A4
Palace Rd BMLY BR1 184 A4
BRXS/STRHM SW2 162 A3
CEND/HSY/T N8 66 D2
E/WMO/HCT KT8 173 H6
FBAR/BDGN N11 48 E3
KUT/HW KT1 190 E1
NRWD SE19 181 G3
RSLP HA4 77 J2
Palace Sq NRWD SE19 181 G3
Palace St WESTW SW1E 15 K4
Palace Vw BMLY BR1 184 A6
CROY/NA CR0 213 H2
Palace View Rd CHING E4 51 K1
Palamos Rd LEY E10 69 J5
Palatine Av STNW/STAM N16 86 A2
Palatine Rd STNW/STAM N16 86 A2
Palemead Cl FUL/PGN SW6 139 G2
Palermo Rd WLSDN NW10 99 J1
Palestine Gv WIM/MER SW19 178 C4
Palewell Cl STMC/STPC BR5 186 C5
Palewell Common Dr
MORT/ESHN SW14 138 A6
Palewell Pk
MORT/ESHN SW14 138 A6
Palfrey Pl VX/NE SW8 142 A1
Palgrave Av STHL UB1 96 A6
Palgrave Gdns CAMTN NW1 2 D6
Palgrave Rd SHB W12 118 C3
Palissy St BETH E2 7 J5
Pallant Wy ORP BR6 216 A1
Pallet Wy WOOL/PLUM SE18 146 D2
Palliser Dr RAIN RM13 111 J4
Palliser Rd WKENS W14 119 H5
Pall Ml STJS SW1Y 16 C1
Pall Ml East STJS SW1Y 10 C7
Pall Mall Pl STJS SW1Y 16 B1
Palmarsh Rd STMC/STPC BR5 202 E1
Palm Av SCUP DA14 186 E2
Palm Cl LEY E10 87 K1
Palmeira Rd BXLYHN DA7 148 E4
Palmer Av BUSH WD23 28 B1
CHEAM SM3 208 A2
Palmer Cl HEST TW5 135 F2
NTHLT UB5 77 J4
WWKM BR4 199 G6
Palmer Crs KUT/HW KT1 175 F6
Palmer Gdns BAR EN5 20 B6
Palmer Pl HOLWY N7 85 G3
Palmer Rd BCTR RM8 73 K5
PLSTW E13 107 F3
Palmers Gv E/WMO/HCT KT8 189 F1
Palmers La PEND EN3 24 E2
Palmers Rd BETH E2 105 F1
MORT/ESHN SW14 137 K4
STRHM/NOR SW16 180 A5
Palmer's Rd FBAR/BDGN N11 48 C1
Palmerston Ct BKHH IG9 39 G4
Palmerston Crs PLMGR N13 49 F1
WOOL/PLUM SE18 127 H6
Palmerston Gv
WIM/MER SW19 177 K3
Palmerston Rd ACT W3 117 K2
BKHH IG9 39 G
CAR SM5 209 K
CROY/NA CR0 196 E
FSTGT E7 89 F
HSLW TW3 135 H
KIL/WHAMP NW6 82 D
KTN/HRWW/WS HA3 43 F
MORT/ESHN SW14 137 K
ORP BR6 216 C
SUT SM1 209 C
WALTH E17 69 H
WDGN N22 49 F
WHTN TW2 155
WIM/MER SW19 177
Palmerston Wy VX/NE SW8 * 141
Palmer St STJSPK SW1H 16
Palmers Whf KUT/HW KT1 * 174
Palm Gv EA W5 117
Palm Rd ROMW/RG RM7 74
Pamela Ct
NFNCH/WDSPK N12 * 47
Pamela Gdns PIN HA5 59
Pampisford Rd
SAND/SEL CR2 211
Pams Wy HOR/WEW KT19 207
Pancras La MANHO EC4N 12
Pancras Rd CAMTN NW1 4
Pancras Wy BOW E3 105
Pandian Wy KTTN NW5 84
Pandora Rd KIL/WHAMP NW6 82
Panfield Ms GNTH/NBYPK IG2 72
Panfield Rd ABYW SE2 128
Pangbourne Av NKENS W10 * 100
Pangbourne Dr STAN HA7 43
Panhard Pl STHL UB1 96
Pank Av BAR EN5 21
Pankhurst Av CAN/RD E16 * 126
Pankhurst Cl ISLW TW7 136
NWCR SE14 144
Pankhurst Rd WOT/HER KT12 188
Pankridge OXHEY WD19 * 27
Panmuir Rd RYNPK SW20 176
Panmure Cl HBRY N5 85
Panmure Rd SYD SE26 163
Pansy Gdns SHB W12 99
Panther Dr WLSDN NW10 81
Pantiles Cl PLMGR N13 49
The Pantiles BMLY BR1 184
BUSH WD23 28
Panton Cl CROY/NA CR0 196
Panton St STJS SW1Y 10
Paper Blds EMB EC4Y * 11
Papermill Cl CAR SM5 210
Papworth Gdns HOLWY N7 85
Papworth Wy
BRXS/STRHM SW2 162
Parade Ms BRXS/STRHM SW2 162
Parade Ter CDALE/KGS NW9 * 63
The Parade BROCKY SE4 * 144
BTSEA SW11 * 140
CAR SM5 * 209
CROY/NA CR0 * 19
DART DA1 * 15
EA W5 * 9
EDUL SE22 * 14
ESH/CLAY KT10 20
FSBYPK N4 * 6
GFD/PVL UB6 * 7
KUT/HW KT1 * 17
OXHEY WD19 2
PGE/AN SE20 * 18
RCH/KEW TW9 * 13
SUT SM1 * 20
SYD SE26 * 16
WLGTN SM6 * 21
Paradise Pas HOLWY N7 8
Paradise Rd CLAP SW4 14
RCH/KEW TW9 13
Paradise Rw BETH E2 * 10
Paradise St BERM/RHTH SE16 12
Paradise Wk CHEL SW3 1
Paragon Cl CAN/RD E16 10
Paragon Gv BRYLDS KT5 19
Paragon Ms STHWK SE1
Paragon Pl BKHTH/KID SE3 14
Paragon Rd HACK E8 8
Parbury Ri CHSGTN KT9 20
Parbury Rd FSTH SE23 16
Parchmore Rd THHTH CR7 18
Parchmore Wy THHTH CR7 18
Pardoe Rd LEY E10
Pardoner St STHWK SE1
Pardon St FSBYE EC1V

Parfett St WCHPL E1 104 C4
Parfitt Cl HAMP NW3 65 G5
Parfrey St HMSMTH W6 119 F6
Parham Dr GNTH/NBYPK IG2 72 B3
Paris Gdn STHWK SE1 12 A7
Parish Cl HCH RM12 75 K6
Parish Gate Dr BFN/LL DA15 167 K1
Parish La PGE/AN SE20 182 A2
Parish Whf WOOL/PLUM SE18 126 D4
Park Ap BERM/RHTH SE16 * 123 K3
WELL DA16 148 C5
Park Av BARK IG11 90 C4
BMLY BR1 183 K2
CAR SM5 210 A4
CRICK NW2 81 K4
EHAM E6 90 A6
EN EN1 23 K6
FNCH N3 47 F4
GLDGN NW11 65 F5
HSLW TW3 155 G1
IL IG1 72 A5
MORT/ESHN SW14 138 A5
ORP BR6 200 E6
ORP BR6 217 G1
PLMGR N13 35 G5
RSLP HA4 58 C3
SRTFD E15 88 C4
STHL UB1 114 E2
UED N18 36 C6
WDGN N22 48 E5
WFD IG8 53 F1
WLSDN NW10 98 B2
WWKM BR4 199 F6
Park Av East EW KT17 207 J4
Park Avenue Ms MTCM CR4 179 G3
Park Av North
CEND/HSY/T N8 66 D1
WLSDN NW10 81 K3
Park Avenue Rd TOTM N17 50 D3
Park Av South
CEND/HSY/T N8 66 D1
Park Av West EW KT17 207 J4
Park Bvd GPK RM2 57 H4
Park Cha WBLY HA9 80 B2
Park Cl CAR SM5 209 K4
CRICK NW2 81 J1
HOM E9 86 E6
HPTN TW12 173 H4
HSLW TW3 135 H6
KTN/HRWW/WS HA3 42 E4
KUTN/CMB KT2 175 H4
NFNCH/WDSPK N12 * 33 H6
SKENS SW7 * 14 E3
WKENS W14 119 J3
WLSDN NW10 98 B2
Park Cots FNCH N3 * 46 D5
Park Ct DUL SE21 * 162 E5
NWMAL KT3 192 A1
SYD SE26 * 181 J2
WBLY HA9 80 A3
Park Crs EMPK RM11 75 J4
ENC/FH EN2 23 K5
ERITH DA8 129 K6
FNCH N3 47 F3
KTN/HRWW/WS HA3 42 E4
REGST W1B 3 J7
WHTN TW2 155 J3
Park Crescent Ms East
GTPST W1W 3 K7
Park Crescent Ms West
CAVSQ/HST W1G 3 J7
Park Cft EDGW HA8 44 E4
Parkcroft Rd LEE/GVPK SE12 165 J2
Parkdale Crs WPK KT4 207 F1
Parkdale Rd
WOOL/PLUM SE18 127 K5
Park Dr ACT W3 117 H3
CHARL SE7 126 D5
DAGE RM10 92 E1
GLDGN NW11 65 F5
KTN/HRWW/WS HA3 42 D2
MORT/ESHN SW14 138 A6
ROM RM1 75 F1
RYLN/HDSTN HA2 60 A4
WCHMH N21 35 J1
Park End BMLY BR1 183 J4
HAMP NW3 83 J2
Park End Rd ROM RM1 75 G1
Parker Cl CAN/RD E16 126 D1
CAR SM5 209 K4
Parker Ms HOL/ALD WC2B * 11 F3
Parke Rd BARN SW13 138 D2
Parker Rd CROY/NA CR0 211 J2
Parker's Rw STHWK SE1 19 K3
Parker St CAN/RD E16 126 D1
HOL/ALD WC2B 11 F3
Parker Ter FSTH SE23 164 C4
Parkes Rd CHIG IG7 55 F1
Park Farm Cl EFNCH N2 47 G6
PIN HA5 59 F2
Park Farm Rd BMLY BR1 184 C4
KUTN/CMB KT2 175 F3
Parkfield Av FELT TW13 153 K5
MORT/ESHN SW14 138 B5
NTHLT UB5 95 H1
RYLN/HDSTN HA2 42 C5
Parkfield Cl EDGW HA8 44 D2
NTHLT UB5 95 J1
Parkfield Crs FELT TW13 153 K5
RSLP HA4 59 J6
RYLN/HDSTN HA2 42 C5
Parkfield Dr NTHLT UB5 95 H1
Parkfield Gdns
RYLN/HDSTN HA2 42 B6
Parkfield Pde FELT TW13 * 153 K5
Parkfield Rd FELT TW13 153 K5
NTHLT UB5 95 J1
NWCR SE14 144 C2
RYLN/HDSTN HA2 78 C1
WLSDN NW10 81 J5
Parkfields CROY/NA CR0 198 C5
PUT/ROE SW15 139 F5
Parkfields Av
CDALE/KGS NW9 63 F5
RYNPK SW20 176 E4
Parkfields Cl CAR SM5 210 A2
Parkfields Rd KUTN/CMB KT2 175 G1
Parkfield St IS N1 5 K2
Parkfield Wy HAYES BR2 200 E3
Park Gdns CDALE/KGS NW9 44 D6
ERITH DA8 130 A4
KUTN/CMB KT2 175 G1
Parkgate BKHTH/KID SE3 145 J4
Park Ga EA W5 97 K4
EFNCH N2 47 H6
WCHMH N21 35 F2
Parkgate Av EBAR EN4 21 G2
Parkgate Cl KUTN/CMB KT2 175 J2
Park Gate Ct HPTN TW12 * 173 H1
Parkgate Crs EBAR EN4 21 G2
Parkgate Gdns
MORT/ESHN SW14 138 A6
Parkgate Ms HGT N6 66 C4
Parkgate Rd BTSEA SW11 140 D1
WLGTN SM6 210 A3
Park Gates
RYLN/HDSTN HA2 * 78 A2
Park Gv BMLY BR1 184 A4
EDGW HA8 44 B1
FBAR/BDGN N11 48 D3
SRTFD E15 88 E6
Park Grove Rd WAN E11 70 C6
Park Hall Rd DUL SE21 162 E4
EFNCH N2 65 J1
Parkham St BTSEA SW11 140 C2
Park Hl BMLY BR1 200 D1
CAR SM5 209 K4
CLAP SW4 141 J6
EA W5 97 K4
FSTH SE23 163 J4
RCHPK/HAM TW10 157 G1
Park Hill Cl CAR SM5 209 J3
Park Hill Ri CROY/NA CR0 197 F6
Park Hill Rd CROY/NA CR0 212 A2
HAYES BR2 183 H5
WLGTN SM6 210 B5
Parkhill Rd BFN/LL DA15 167 K5
BXLY DA5 169 G2
CHING E4 38 A2
HAMP NW3 83 K3
Park Hill Wk HAMP NW3 83 K3
Parkholme Rd HACK E8 86 C4
Park House Gdns TWK TW1 136 D6
Parkhouse St CMBW SE5 142 E1
Parkhurst Gdns BXLY DA5 169 H2
Parkhurst Rd BXLY DA5 169 H2
FBAR/BDGN N11 34 A6
HOLWY N7 84 E2
MNPK E12 90 A2
SUT SM1 209 H2
TOTM N17 50 C5
WALTH E17 * 69 G1
WDGN N22 49 F3
Parkland Av ROM RM1 57 G5
Parkland Gv ASHF TW15 152 D6
ISLW TW7 136 A2
Parkland Md BMLY BR1 185 F6
Parkland Rd ASHF TW15 152 D6
WDGN N22 49 F5
WFD IG8 53 F3
Parklands BRYLDS KT5 191 G2
BUSH WD23 * 28 C1
HGT N6 66 B4
Parklands Cl EBAR EN4 21 H1
GNTH/NBYPK IG2 72 C4
MORT/ESHN SW14 137 K6
Parklands Dr FNCH N3 46 C6
Parklands Pde HEST TW5 * 134 C3
Parklands Rd
STRHM/NOR SW16 179 G1
Parklands Wy WPK KT4 192 B6
Park La CAR SM5 210 A2
CHDH RM6 73 K3
CHEAM SM3 208 C4
CROY/NA CR0 211 K1
EMPK RM11 75 J4
HCH RM12 93 K4
HEST TW5 133 K1
OXSTW W1C 9 F5
RCH/KEW TW9 136 E5
RYLN/HDSTN HA2 78 B1
SRTFD E15 * 88 A6
STAN HA7 29 G5
TEDD TW11 174 A2
TOTM N17 50 B3
UED N18 36 B5
WBLY HA9 80 B2
YEAD UB4 94 C4
Park Lane Cl TOTM N17 50 C3
Parklea Cl CDALE/KGS NW9 45 G4
Parkleigh Rd WIM/MER SW19 178 A5
Parkleys RCHPK/HAM TW10 156 E6
Parkleys Pde
RCHPK/HAM TW10 * 156 E6
Park Lodge Av WDR/YW UB7 112 C2
Park Md BFN/LL DA15 148 B6
Parkmead PUT/ROE SW15 158 E1
Park Md RYLN/HDSTN HA2 78 B1
Parkmead Gdns MLHL NW7 45 H2
Park Ms GNWCH SE10 125 J5
NKENS W10 100 C1
RAIN RM13 93 J4
STWL/WRAY TW19 152 C2
Park Pde ACT W3 * 117 H3
HYS/HAR UB3 * 94 C5
WLSDN NW10 99 H1
Park Piazza LEW SE13 165 G1
Park Pl ACT W3 117 H4
BMLY BR1 * 184 A4
EA W5 116 E1
HPTN TW12 173 H2
IS N1 85 K6
POP/IOD E14 124 D1
WBLY HA9 80 B2
WHALL SW1A 16 A1
Park Place Vls BAY/PAD W2 101 G4
Park Ridings CEND/HSY/T N8 49 G6
Park Ri KTN/HRWW/WS HA3 42 E4
Park Rise Rd FSTH SE23 164 B3
Park Rd ALP/SUD HA0 80 A4
BAR EN5 20 D5
BECK BR3 182 C3
BMLY BR1 184 A4
BRYLDS KT5 191 G3
BUSH WD23 28 A1
CDALE/KGS NW9 63 F4
CEND/HSY/T N8 66 D2
CHEAM SM3 208 C4
CHST BR7 185 G2
CHSWK W4 118 A6
E/WMO/HCT KT8 189 H1
EBAR EN4 21 H5
EFNCH N2 47 H6
ESH/CLAY KT10 204 B2
FBAR/BDGN N11 48 D3
FELT TW13 154 C6
HDN NW4 63 K3
HNWL W7 97 F6
HPTN TW12 173 H1
HSLW TW3 135 H6
IL IG1 90 D1
ISLW TW7 136 C2
KUT/HW KT1 174 D4
LEY E10 69 J5
MNPK E12 89 H2
NWMAL KT3 192 A1
PLSTW E13 89 G6
RCHPK/HAM TW10 157 G1
SNWD SE25 197 F1
SRTFD E15 88 E6
STHGT/OAK N14 34 D2
STJWD NW8 2 D5
STMC/STPC BR5 202 D3
SUN TW16 172 A3
TEDD TW11 174 A2
TWK TW1 156 D1
UED N18 36 B6
WALTH E17 69 H2
WIM/MER SW19 178 C2
WLGTN SM6 210 B3
WLSDN NW10 * 81 G6
YEAD UB4 94 C4
Park Rd East ACT W3 117 K2
Park Rd North ACT W3 117 J2
Park Rw GNWCH SE10 125 G6
Park Royal Rd WLSDN NW10 98 E2
Parkshot RCH/KEW TW9 136 E5
Park Side BKHH IG9 39 F4
CRICK NW2 81 J1
HYS/HAR UB3 * 94 C6
Parkside BECK BR3 * 182 E5
BKHTH/KID SE3 * 145 J1
CHEAM SM3 208 C4
FNCH N3 47 F4
HPTN TW12 173 J1
MLHL NW7 45 J2
OXHEY WD19 * 27 G1
SCUP DA14 168 C4
WIM/MER SW19 177 G1
Parkside Av BMLY BR1 200 D1
BXLYHN DA7 150 A3
ROM RM1 57 F5
WIM/MER SW19 177 G1
Parkside Cl PGE/AN SE20 181 K3
Parkside Crs BRYLDS KT5 191 K3
HOLWY N7 85 G1
Parkside Dr EDGW HA8 30 C5
Parkside Est HOM E9 * 87 F6
Parkside Gdns EBAR EN4 33 K3
WIM/MER SW19 159 G6
Parkside Pde DART DA1 * 150 C3
Parkside Rd BELV DA17 129 J4
HSLW TW3 135 G6
NTHWD HA6 40 D1
Parkside St BTSEA SW11 141 F2
Parkside Ter ORP BR6 * 202 B5
UED N18 * 35 K6
Parkside Wy
RYLN/HDSTN HA2 60 B1
Park Sq East CAMTN NW1 3 J6
Park Square Ms CAMTN NW1 3 J7
Park Sq West CAMTN NW1 3 J6
Parkstead Rd PUT/ROE SW15 138 D6
Park Steps BAY/PAD W2 * 8 D5
Parkstone Av UED N18 50 B1
Parkstone Rd PECK SE15 * 143 H3
WALTH E17 52 A6
Park St CROY/NA CR0 211 J1
MYFR/PKLN W1K 9 G6
STHWK SE1 12 C7
TEDD TW11 173 K2
Park Ter CAR SM5 * 209 J1
PEND EN3 * 25 G1
WPK KT4 192 D5
The Park CAR SM5 209 K3
EA W5 116 E1
GLDGN NW11 65 F5
HGT N6 66 A4
SCUP DA14 186 A1
Parkthorne Cl
RYLN/HDSTN HA2 * 60 B3
Parkthorne Dr
RYLN/HDSTN HA2 60 A3
Parkthorne Rd BAL SW12 161 J2
Park Vw ACT W3 98 E4
NWMAL KT3 176 C6
PIN HA5 41 K4
WBLY HA9 80 D3
WCHMH N21 35 F2
Park View Cl CAR SM5 209 K5
Park View Ct
NFNCH/WDSPK N12 * 33 J6
Park View Crs
FBAR/BDGN N11 34 B6
Parkview Crs WPK KT4 193 F5
Park View Dr MTCM CR4 178 C5
Park View Est HBRY N5 * 85 J2
Parkview Gdns CLAY IG5 71 K1
Park View Gdns HDN NW4 64 A2
WDGN N22 * 49 G4
Parkview Ms RAIN RM13 111 K4
Park View Rd CRICK NW2 81 H2
Parkview Rd CROY/NA CR0 197 H5
Park View Rd EA W5 98 A4
ELTH/MOT SE9 167 G3
FNCH N3 47 F4
PIN HA5 41 F2
STHL UB1 115 F1
TOTM N17 50 C6
WELL DA16 148 D4
Park Village East
CAMTN NW1 3 J2
Park Village West
CAMTN NW1 3 J2
Park Vls TOOT SW17 * 178 D1
Parkville Rd FUL/PGN SW6 139 J1
Park Vis GNWCH SE10 125 G6
Park Vista Apartments
CAN/RD E16 106 D2
Park Wk WBPTN SW10 120 B6
Parkwat Crs SRTFD E15 88 B3
Park Wy E/WMO/HCT KT8 173 G6
EBED/NFELT TW14 154 A2
EDGW HA8 44 D4
ENC/FH EN2 23 G3
GLDGN NW11 64 C2
RSLP HA4 58 E5
TRDG/WHET N20 33 K6
Parkway CROY/NA CR0 214 A6
ERITHM DA18 129 F3
GDMY/SEVK IG3 91 F1
GPK RM2 57 H5
RAIN RM13 111 J3
RYNPK SW20 193 G1
STHGT/OAK N14 34 E4
WFD IG8 53 G1
The Parkway HEST TW5 113 K6
NTHLT UB5 95 H2
NWDGN UB2 114 A3
YEAD UB4 95 G6
Park West Pl BAY/PAD W2 8 D3
Parkwood BECK BR3 182 D3
Parkwood Av ESH/CLAY KT10 189 H5
Parkwood Ms HGT N6 66 B3
Parkwood Rd BXLY DA5 169 G2
ISLW TW7 136 A2
WIM/MER SW19 177 J1
Parliament Ct WCHPL E1 * 13 H2
Parliament Hl HAMP NW3 83 J2
Parliament Hill Flds
KTTN NW5 * 84 A1
Parliament Ms
MORT/ESHN SW14 137 K3
Parliament Sq WEST SW1P 16 E3
Parliament St WHALL SW1A 16 E2
Parma Crs BTSEA SW11 140 E5
Parmiter St BETH E2 104 D1
Parnell Cl EDGW HA8 30 D6
SHB W12 118 E3
Parnell Rd BOW E3 87 H6
Parnham Cl BMLY BR1 185 G6
Parnham St POP/IOD E14 * 105 G5
Parolles Rd ARCH N19 66 C5
Paroma Rd BELV DA17 129 H3
Parr Av EW KT17 207 K6
Parr Cl ED N9 36 D6
Parr Rd EHAM E6 89 H6
STAN HA7 43 K4
Parrs Cl SAND/SEL CR2 211 K6
Parr's Pl HPTN TW12 173 F3
Parr St IS N1 6 E2
Parry Av EHAM E6 107 K5
Parry Cl EW KT17 207 J5
Parry Pl WOOL/PLUM SE18 127 G4
Parry Rd NKENS W10 100 C2
SNWD SE25 181 F6
Parry St VX/NE SW8 121 K6
Parsifal Rd KIL/WHAMP NW6 82 E3
Parsloes Av DAGW RM9 92 A3
Parsonage Cl HYS/HAR UB3 94 D5
Parsonage Gdns ENC/FH EN2 23 J3
Parsonage La ENC/FH EN2 23 K3
SCUP DA14 169 G6
Parsonage Manorway
BELV DA17 129 H6
Parsonage St POP/IOD E14 125 F4
Parsons Crs EDGW HA8 30 C5
Parsons Gn FUL/PGN SW6 139 K2
Parsons Green La
FUL/PGN SW6 139 K2
Parsons Gv EDGW HA8 30 C5
Parsons Md E/WMO/HCT KT8 173 H6
Parson's Md CROY/NA CR0 196 C5
Parsons Rd PLSTW E13 107 G1
Parson St HDN NW4 46 A6
Parthenia Rd FUL/PGN SW6 139 K2
Partingdale La MLHL NW7 46 B1
Partington Cl ARCH N19 66 D5
Partridge Cl BAR EN5 32 A1
BUSH WD23 * 28 C3
CAN/RD E16 107 H4
STAN HA7 30 A6
Partridge Dr ORP BR6 216 C1
Partridge Gn ELTH/MOT SE9 167 F5
Partridge Rd HPTN TW12 172 E2
SCUP DA14 167 K5
Partridge Sq EHAM E6 107 J4
Partridge Wy WDGN N22 48 E4
Pasadena Cl HYS/HAR UB3 113 K2
Pascal St VX/NE SW8 141 J1
Pascoe Rd LEW SE13 145 G6
Pasley Cl WALW SE17 122 C5
Pasquier Rd WALTH E17 51 G6
Passey Pl ELTH/MOT SE9 166 E1
Passfield Dr POP/IOD E14 105 K4
Passmore Gdns
FBAR/BDGN N11 48 D2
Passmore St BGVA SW1W 15 G7
Pasteur Cl CDALE/KGS NW9 45 G5
Pasteur Gdns UED N18 49 J1
Paston Cl WLGTN SM6 210 C1
Paston Crs LEE/GVPK SE12 166 A2
Pastor St LBTH SE11 18 B6
Pasture Cl ALP/SUD HA0 79 H1
BUSH WD23 28 C2
Pasture Rd ALP/SUD HA0 61 H6
CAT SE6 165 H3
DAGW RM9 92 B3
The Pastures OXHEY WD19 27 F2
TRDG/WHET N20 32 D3
Patcham Ter VX/NE SW8 141 G2
Patching Wy YEAD UB4 95 J4
Paternoster Sq STP EC4M 12 B4
Pater St KENS W8 119 K3
Pates Manor Dr
EBED/NFELT TW14 153 G2
Pathfield Rd
STRHM/NOR SW16 179 J2
The Path WIM/MER SW19 178 A4
The Pathway OXHEY WD19 27 H3
Patience Rd BTSEA SW11 140 D3
Patio Cl CLAP SW4 161 J1
Patmore St VX/NE SW8 141 H2
Patmore Wy CRW RM5 56 D1
Patmos Rd BRXN/ST SW9 142 C1
Paton Cl BOW E3 105 J2
Patricia Ct WELL DA16 148 C1
Patricia Vls TOTM N17 * 50 D4
Patrick Rd PLSTW E13 107 G2
Patriot Sq BETH E2 104 D1
Patrol Pl CAT SE6 164 E1
Patshull Pl KTTN NW5 84 C4
Patshull Rd KTTN NW5 84 C4
Pattenden Rd CAT SE6 164 C3
Patten Rd WAND/EARL SW18 160 D2
Patterdale Cl BMLY BR1 183 H2
Patterdale Rd PECK SE15 143 K1
Patterson Rd NRWD SE19 181 G2
Pattina Wk BERM/RHTH SE16 124 B1
Pattison Rd CRICK NW2 82 E1
Paul Cl SRTFD E15 88 C5
Paulet Rd CMBW SE5 142 C3
Paulet Wy WLSDN NW10 * 81 G5
Paul Gdns CROY/NA CR0 197 G6
Paulhan Rd
KTN/HRWW/WS HA3 61 K1
Paulin Dr WCHMH N21 35 G2
Pauline Crs WHTN TW2 155 H3
Paulinus Cl STMC/STPC BR5 186 D5
Paul Julius Cl POP/IOD E14 106 B6
Paul Robeson Cl EHAM E6 108 A2
Paul St SDTCH EC2A 7 G6
SRTFD E15 88 C6
Paultons Sq CHEL SW3 120 C6
Paultons St CHEL SW3 120 C6
Pauntley St ARCH N19 66 C5
Paveley Dr BTSEA SW11 140 D1
Paveley St STJWD NW8 2 D5
Pavement Sq CROY/NA CR0 197 H5
The Pavement CLAP SW4 141 H5
EA W5 * 117 F3
TEDD TW11 * 174 C3
WAN E11 * 70 A5
WIM/MER SW19 * 177 J2
WNWD SE27 * 162 D6
Pavet Cl DAGE RM10 92 D4
Pavilion Ldg
RYLN/HDSTN HA2 * 60 D5
Pavilion Ms FNCH N3 46 E5
Pavilion Pde SHB W12 * 100 A5
Pavilion Rd IL IG1 71 K4
KTBR SW1X 15 F3
Pavilion St KTBR SW1X 15 F5
The Pavilion VX/NE SW8 * 141 J1
Pavilion Wy EDGW HA8 44 E3
RSLP HA4 59 G6
Pavillion Sq TOOT SW17 160 D5
Pavillion Ter SHB W12 * 100 A5
Pawleyne Cl PGE/AN SE20 181 K3
Pawsey Cl PLSTW E13 88 E6
Pawson's Rd THHTH CR7 196 D3
Paxford Rd ALP/SUD HA0 61 H6
Paxton Cl RCH/KEW TW9 137 G3
WOT/HER KT12 188 B4
Paxton Pl WNWD SE27 163 F6
Paxton Rd BMLY BR1 183 K3
CHSWK W4 118 B6
FSTH SE23 164 B5
TOTM N17 50 B3
Paxton Ter PIM SW1V 121 G6
Payne Cl BARK IG11 90 E5
Paynell Ct BKHTH/KID SE3 145 H4
Payne Rd BOW E3 105 K1
Paynesfield Av
MORT/ESHN SW14 138 A4
Paynesfield Rd BUSH WD23 29 F2
Payne St DEPT SE8 124 C6
Paynes Wk HMSMTH W6 119 H6
Payzes Gdns WFD IG8 * 52 D2
Peabody Av PIM SW1V * 121 G5
Peabody Cl CROY/NA CR0 197 K5
GNWCH SE10 * 144 E2
PIM SW1V 121 G5
Peabody Cots HNHL SE24 * 162 D2
Peabody Est BTSEA SW11 * 140 D5
CHEL SW3 * 120 D6
CLKNW EC1R * 5 K7
CMBW SE5 * 142 E2
HMSMTH W6 * 119 F5
HNHL SE24 162 C2
NKENS W10 * 100 A4
STHWK SE1 * 11 K7
STLK EC1Y * 6 D7
TOTM N17 * 50 A4
Peabody Hl DUL SE21 162 C3
Peabody Sq IS N1 * 85 J6
Peabody Ter CLKNW EC1R * 5 K7
Peace Cl GFD/PVL UB6 78 D6
SNWD SE25 197 F1
STHGT/OAK N14 22 B6
Peace Gv WBLY HA9 80 D1
Peace St WOOL/PLUM SE18 127 F6
Peaches Cl BELMT SM2 208 C5
Peach Gv WAN E11 88 B1
Peach Rd FELT TW13 153 K3
NKENS W10 100 B2
Peachum Rd BKHTH/KID SE3 125 J6
Peachy Cl EDGW HA8 44 C2
Peacock Av
EBED/NFELT TW14 153 G3
Peacock Cl BCTR RM8 73 J5
CHING E4 51 H3
MLHL NW7 46 C1
Peacock St WALW SE17 18 B7
Peacock Yd WALW SE17 18 B7
Peaketon Av REDBR IG4 71 H2
Peak Hl SYD SE26 163 K6
Peak Hill Av SYD SE26 163 K6
Peak Hill Gdns SYD SE26 * 163 K6
The Peak SYD SE26 163 K5
Peal Gdns WEA W13 97 G2
Peall Rd CROY/NA CR0 196 A3
Pearce Cl MTCM CR4 179 F5
Pearcefield Av FSTH SE23 163 K3
Pear Cl CDALE/KGS NW9 63 F1
NWCR SE14 144 B1
Pearcroft Rd WAN E11 70 B6
Peardon St VX/NE SW8 141 G4
Peareswood Gdns STAN HA7 43 K4
Peareswood Rd ERITH DA8 150 C2
Pearfield Rd FSTH SE23 164 B5
Pearing Cl WPK KT4 193 G6
Pearl Cl CRICK NW2 64 B4
EHAM E6 108 A5
Pearl Rd WALTH E17 51 J6
Pearl St WAP E1W 123 J1
Pearman St STHWK SE1 17 K4
Pear Pl STHWK SE1 17 J2
Pear Rd WAN E11 88 B1
Pearscroft Ct FUL/PGN SW6 140 A2

Pearscroft Rd FUL/PGN SW6 ... 140 A3
Pearse St PECK SE15 ... 123 F6
Pearson Cl BAR EN5 ... 21 F4
Pearson's NWCR SE14 ... 144 D2
Pearson's Rd NWCR SE14 * ... 144 D2
Pearson St BETH E2 ... 7 J2
Pearson Wy MTCM CR4 ... 179 F4
Pears Rd HSLW TW3 ... 135 H4
Peartree Av TOOT SW17 ... 178 E2
Pear Tree Cl CHSGTN KT9 ... 206 C3
Peartree Cl HAYES BR2 ... 200 C2
Pear Tree Cl MTCM CR4 ... 178 D5
Pear Tree Ct CLKNW EC1R ... 5 K7
Peartree Gdns BCTR RM8 ... 91 H3
ROMW/RG RM7 ... 56 D5
Peartree La WAP E1W * ... 104 E6
Peartree Rd EN EN1 ... 24 A4
Pear Tree St FSBYE EC1V ... 6 B6
Pearwood Cots STAN HA7 * ... 29 J4
Peary Pl BETH E2 ... 104 E2
Pease Cl HCH RM12 ... 93 K5
Peasmead Ter CHING E4 * ... 38 A6
Peatfield Cl BFN/LL DA15 ... 167 K5
Pebworth Rd HRW HA1 ... 61 G6
Peckarmans Wd SYD SE26 ... 163 H5
Peckett Sq HBRY N5 * ... 85 J2
Peckford Pl BRXN/ST SW9 ... 142 B3
Peckham Gv PECK SE15 ... 143 F1
Peckham High St PECK SE15 ... 143 H2
Peckham Hill St PECK SE15 ... 143 H1
Peckham Park Rd PECK SE15 ... 143 H1
Peckham Rd CMBW SE5 ... 143 F2
Peckham Rye EDUL SE22 ... 143 H5
Pecks Yd WCHPL E1 * ... 13 J1
Peckwater St KTTN NW5 ... 84 C3
Pedlars Wk HOLWY N7 * ... 84 E3
Pedley Rd BCTR RM8 ... 73 J5
Pedley St WCHPL E1 ... 7 K7
Pedro St CLPT E5 ... 87 F1
Peek Crs WIM/MER SW19 ... 177 G1
Peel Cl CHING E4 ... 37 K4
ED N9 ... 36 C5
Peel Dr CDALE/KGS NW9 ... 45 H6
CLAY IG5 ... 53 J6
Peel Gv BETH E2 ... 104 E1
Peel Pas KENS W8 ... 119 K1
Peel Pl CLAY IG5 ... 53 J5
Peel Prec KIL/WHAMP NW6 ... 100 D1
Peel Rd ALP/SUD HA0 ... 79 J1
KIL/WHAMP NW6 ... 100 E2
KTN/HRWW/WS HA3 ... 43 F6
ORP BR6 ... 216 C2
SWFD E18 ... 52 D4
Peel St KENS W8 ... 119 K1
Peerglow Est PEND EN3 * ... 24 E6
Peerless St FSBYE EC1V ... 6 E5
Pegamoid Rd UED N18 ... 36 E5
Pegasus Cl STNW/STAM N16 * ... 85 K2
Pegasus Ct BTFD TW8 ... 117 G5
Pegasus Pl FUL/PGN SW6 * ... 139 K2
LBTH SE11 * ... 122 B6
Pegasus Rd CROY/NA CR0 ... 211 G4
Pegasus Wy FBAR/BDGN N11 ... 48 B2
Pegg Rd HEST TW5 ... 134 C1
Pegwell St WOOL/PLUM SE18 ... 147 K1
Pekin St POP/IOD E14 ... 105 J5
Peldon Wk IS N1 * ... 85 H6
Pelham Av BARK IG11 ... 91 F6
Pelham Cl CMBW SE5 ... 143 F4
Pelham Cots BXLY DA5 * ... 169 J3
Pelham Crs SKENS SW7 ... 14 C7
Pelham Pl SKENS SW7 ... 14 C6
Pelham Rd IL IG1 ... 72 D6
PGE/AN SE20 ... 181 K5
SEVS/STOTM N15 ... 68 B1
SWFD E18 ... 53 F6
WDGN N22 ... 49 G5
WIM/MER SW19 ... 177 K3
Pelhams Cl ESH/CLAY KT10 ... 204 A3
Pelham St SKENS SW7 ... 14 B6
Pelhams Wk ESH/CLAY KT10 ... 204 A1
Pelier St WALW SE17 ... 122 D6
Pelinore Rd CAT SE6 ... 165 H4
Pellant Rd FUL/PGN SW6 ... 139 H1
Pellatt Gv WDGN N22 ... 49 G4
Pellatt Rd EDUL SE22 ... 143 G6
WBLY HA9 ... 62 A6
Pellerin Rd STNW/STAM N16 ... 86 A3
Pellings Cl HAYES BR2 ... 183 H6
Pelling St POP/IOD E14 ... 105 H5
Pellipar Cl PLMGR N13 ... 35 G5
Pellipar Rd WOOL/PLUM SE18 ... 126 E5
Pellow Cl BAR EN5 ... 32 D1
Pelly Rd PLSTW E13 ... 106 E1
Pelter St BETH E2 ... 7 J4
Pelton Rd GNWCH SE10 ... 125 H5
Pembar Av WALTH E17 * ... 51 G6
Pemberley Cha
HOR/WEW KT19 ... 206 D3
Pemberley Cl HOR/WEW KT19 ... 206 D3
Pember Rd WLSDN NW10 ... 100 B2
Pemberton Av GPK RM2 ... 57 K6
Pemberton Cl
STWL/WRAY TW19 ... 152 B3
Pemberton Gdns ARCH N19 ... 84 C1
CHDH RM6 ... 74 A2
Pemberton Pl ESH/CLAY KT10 ... 204 C1
HACK E8 ... 86 D5
Pemberton Rd
E/WMO/HCT KT8 ... 189 H1
FSBYPK N4 ... 67 H2
Pemberton Rw
FLST/FETLN EC4A ... 11 K3
Pemberton Ter ARCH N19 ... 84 C1
Pembridge Av WHTN TW2 ... 154 E3
Pembridge Crs NTGHL W11 ... 100 D6
Pembridge Gdns
BAY/PAD W2 * ... 100 E6
Pembridge Ms NTGHL W11 ... 100 E6
Pembridge Pl NTGHL W11 ... 100 E6
Pembridge Rd NTGHL W11 ... 100 E6
Pembridge Sq BAY/PAD W2 ... 100 E6
Pembridge Vls BAY/PAD W2 ... 100 E6
Pembroke Av BRYLDS KT5 ... 191 J2
EN EN1 ... 24 D2
IS N1 ... 84 E6
KTN/HRWW/WS HA3 ... 43 G6
PIN HA5 ... 59 H5
Pembroke Cl ERITH DA8 ... 129 K4
KTBR SW1X ... 15 H3
Pembroke Gdns DAGE RM10 ... 92 D1
KENS W8 ... 119 J3
Pembroke Gardens Cl
KENS W8 ... 119 J3
Pembroke Ldg STAN HA7 * ... 43 J2
Pembroke Ms KENS W8 ... 119 K3
MUSWH N10 ... 48 A4
Pembroke Pde ERITH DA8 * ... 129 K5
Pembroke Pl EDGW HA8 ... 44 C3
ISLW TW7 ... 135 K3
KENS W8 ... 119 K3
Pembroke Rd BMLY BR1 ... 184 B5
CEND/HSY/T N8 ... 66 E1
EHAM E6 ... 107 K4
ERITH DA8 ... 129 K5
GDMY/SEVK IG3 ... 73 F5
GFD/PVL UB6 ... 96 B3
KENS W8 ... 119 K4
MTCM CR4 ... 179 F5
MUSWH N10 ... 48 A4
NTHWD HA6 ... 26 A5
PLMGR N13 ... 35 J5
RSLP HA4 ... 58 C5
SEVS/STOTM N15 ... 68 B2
SNWD SE25 ... 197 F1
WALTH E17 ... 69 K2
WBLY HA9 ... 79 K1
Pembroke Sq KENS W8 ... 119 K3
Pembroke St IS N1 ... 84 E5
Pembroke Ter STJWD NW8 * ... 2 A1
Pembroke Vls KENS W8 ... 119 K4
Pembroke Wk KENS W8 ... 119 K4
Pembrook Ms BTSEA SW11 * ... 140 C5
Pembry Cl BRXN/ST SW9 ... 142 B2
Pembury Av WPK KT4 ... 192 D4
Pembury Cl CLPT E5 * ... 86 D3
HAYES BR2 ... 199 J4
Pembury Ct HYS/HAR UB3 ... 113 G6
Pembury Crs SCUP DA14 ... 169 F4
Pembury Rd CLPT E5 ... 86 D3
SNWD SE25 ... 197 H1
TOTM N17 ... 50 B4
Pemdevon Rd CROY/NA CR0 ... 196 B4
Pemell Cl WCHPL E1 ... 104 E3
Pemerich Cl HYS/HAR UB3 * ... 113 J5
Pempath Pl WBLY HA9 ... 61 K6
Penally Pl IS N1 ... 85 K6
Penang St WAP E1W ... 123 J1
Penard Rd NWDGN UB2 ... 115 F3
Penarth St PECK SE15 ... 123 K6
Penates ESH/CLAY KT10 ... 204 D2
Penberth Rd CAT SE6 ... 165 F3
Penbury Rd NWDGN UB2 ... 114 E5
Pencombe Ms NTGHL W11 ... 100 D6
Pencraig Wy PECK SE15 ... 123 J6
Pendall Cl EBAR EN4 ... 21 J5
Pendarves Rd RYNPK SW20 ... 177 F4
Penda's Md HOM E9 ... 87 G2
Pendell Av HYS/HAR UB3 ... 133 J1
Pendennis Rd ORP BR6 ... 202 D6
STRHM/NOR SW16 ... 161 K6
TOTM N17 ... 49 K6
Penderel Rd HSLW TW3 ... 135 F6
Penderry Ri CAT SE6 ... 165 G4
Penderyn Wy HOLWY N7 ... 84 D2
Pendlebury House
CHARL SE7 * ... 146 D1
Pendle Rd STRHM/NOR SW16 ... 179 G2
Pendlestone Rd WALTH E17 ... 69 K2
Pendlewood Cl EA W5 ... 97 J4
Pendrell Rd NWCR SE14 ... 144 B4
Pendrell St WOOL/PLUM SE18 ... 127 J6
Pendula Dr YEAD UB4 ... 95 H3
Pendulum Ms HACK E8 * ... 86 B3
Penerley Rd CAT SE6 ... 164 E3
RAIN RM13 ... 111 K4
Penfold Cl CROY/NA CR0 ... 211 G1
Penfold La BXLY DA5 ... 168 E3
Penfold Pl BAY/PAD W2 ... 8 C1
Penfold Rd ED N9 ... 37 F3
Penfold St STJWD NW8 ... 2 B7
Penford Gdns ELTH/MOT SE9 ... 146 C5
Penford St CMBW SE5 ... 142 C3
Pengarth Rd BXLY DA5 ... 148 E6
Penge La PGE/AN SE20 ... 181 K3
Penge Rd PLSTW E13 ... 89 G5
SNWD SE25 ... 181 H6
Penhale Cl ORP BR6 ... 217 G2
Penhall Rd CHARL SE7 ... 126 C4
Penhill Rd BXLY DA5 ... 168 D2
Penhurst Rd BARK/HLT IG6 ... 54 B3
Penifather La GFD/PVL UB6 ... 96 D2
Peninsular Cl
EBED/NFELT TW14 ... 153 G1
Penistone Rd
STRHM/NOR SW16 ... 179 K3
Penketh Dr HRW HA1 ... 78 D1
Penmon Rd ABYW SE2 ... 128 B3
Pennack Rd PECK SE15 ... 123 G6
Pennant Ms KENS W8 ... 120 A4
Pennant Ter WALTH E17 ... 51 H5
Pennard Rd SHB W12 ... 119 F2
The Pennards SUN TW16 ... 172 B6
Penn Cl GFD/PVL UB6 ... 96 B1
KTN/HRWW/WS HA3 ... 61 J1
Penner Cl WIM/MER SW19 ... 159 H4
Penners Gdns SURB KT6 ... 191 F4
Pennethorne Cl HOM E9 ... 86 E6
Pennethorne Rd PECK SE15 ... 143 J1
Penn Gdns CHST BR7 ... 185 G5
CRW RM5 ... 56 C3
Pennine Dr CRICK NW2 ... 64 B6
Pennine La CRICK NW2 ... 64 C6
Pennine Pde CRICK NW2 * ... 64 C6
Pennine Wy HYS/HAR UB3 ... 133 G1
Pennington Cl CRW RM5 ... 56 C2
Pennington Dr WCHMH N21 ... 22 E6
Pennington St WAP E1W ... 104 D6
Pennington Wy
LEE/GVPK SE12 ... 166 A4
Penniston Cl TOTM N17 ... 49 J5
Penniwell Cl EDGW HA8 ... 30 B6
Penn La BXLY DA5 ... 168 E1
Penn Rd HOLWY N7 ... 84 E3
Penn St IS N1 ... 7 F1
Penny Cl RAIN RM13 ... 111 K2
Pennycroft CROY/NA CR0 ... 213 G6
Pennyfields POP/IOD E14 ... 105 J6
Pennymead Pl
ESH/CLAY KT10 ... 204 A4
Penny Ms WAND/EARL SW18 ... 139 K6
Pennymoor Wk MV/WKIL W9 ... 100 D3
Penny Rd WLSDN NW10 ... 98 D2
Pennyroyal Av EHAM E6 ... 108 A5
Penpoll Rd HACK E8 ... 86 D4
Penpool La WELL DA16 ... 148 C4
Penrhyn Av WALTH E17 ... 51 J4
Penrhyn Crs
MORT/ESHN SW14 ... 137 K5
WALTH E17 ... 51 J4
Penrhyn Gdns KUT/HW KT1 ... 190 E1
Penrhyn Gv WALTH E17 ... 51 J4
Penrhyn Rd KUT/HW KT1 ... 175 F6
Penrith Cl BECK BR3 ... 182 E4
PUT/ROE SW15 ... 139 H6
Penrith Crs HCH RM12 ... 93 J3
Penrith Pl WNWD SE27 ... 162 C4
Penrith Rd BARK/HLT IG6 ... 55 F2
NWMAL KT3 ... 192 A1
SEVS/STOTM N15 ... 67 K2
THHTH CR7 ... 180 D5
Penrith St STRHM/NOR SW16 ... 179 H2
Penrose Av OXHEY WD19 ... 27 J4
Penrose Gv WALW SE17 ... 122 D5
Penrose St WALW SE17 ... 122 D5
Penryn St CAMTN NW1 ... 4 C2
Penry St STHWK SE1 ... 19 H7
Pensbury Pl VX/NE SW8 ... 141 H3
Pensbury St VX/NE SW8 ... 141 H3
Pensford Av RCH/KEW TW9 ... 137 H3
Penshurst Av BFN/LL DA15 ... 168 B1
Penshurst Gdns EDGW HA8 ... 44 D1
Penshurst Gn HAYES BR2 ... 199 J2
Penshurst Rd HOM E9 ... 87 F5
THHTH CR7 ... 196 C2
TOTM N17 ... 50 B3
Penshurst Wy BELMT SM2 ... 208 E5
STMC/STPC BR5 ... 202 D1
Pensilver Cl EBAR EN4 * ... 21 J5
Penstemon Cl FNCH N3 ... 46 E2
Pentelow Gdns
EBED/NFELT TW14 ... 153 K1
Pentire Rd WALTH E17 ... 52 B4
Pentland Av EDGW HA8 ... 30 D4
Pentland Cl ED N9 ... 36 E4
GLDGN NW11 ... 64 C6
Pentland Pl NTHLT UB5 ... 77 J6
Pentland Rd BUSH WD23 ... 28 C1
KIL/WHAMP NW6 ... 100 E2
Pentlands Cl MTCM CR4 ... 179 G6
Pentland St
WAND/EARL SW18 ... 160 B1
Pentland Wy HGDN/ICK UB10 ... 76 A1
Pentlow St PUT/ROE SW15 ... 139 F3
Pentlow Wy BKHH IG9 ... 39 J2
Pentney Rd BAL SW12 ... 161 H3
CHING E4 ... 38 B3
RYNPK SW20 ... 177 H4
Penton Gv IS N1 ... 5 J3
Penton Pl WALW SE17 ... 18 B7
Penton Ri FSBYW WC1X ... 5 H4
Penton St IS N1 ... 5 J2
Pentonville Rd IS N1 ... 5 G3
Pentrich Av EN EN1 ... 24 C1
Pentridge St PECK SE15 ... 143 G1
Pentyre Av UED N18 ... 49 K1
Penwerris Av ISLW TW7 ... 135 H1
Penwith Rd
WAND/EARL SW18 ... 160 A4
Penwortham Rd
STRHM/NOR SW16 ... 179 G2
Penylan Pl EDGW HA8 * ... 44 C4
Penywern Rd ECT SW5 ... 119 K5
Penzance Pl NTGHL W11 ... 119 H1
Penzance St NTGHL W11 ... 119 H1
Peony Gdns SHB W12 ... 99 J6
Pepler Ms CMBW SE5 ... 123 G5
Peploe Rd KIL/WHAMP NW6 ... 100 B1
Peplow Cl WDR/YW UB7 ... 112 A1
Pepper Cl EHAM E6 ... 107 K4
Peppercorn Cl THHTH CR7 ... 180 E5
Peppermead Sq LEW SE13 ... 144 D6
Peppermint Cl CROY/NA CR0 ... 195 K4
Peppermint Pl WAN E11 ... 88 C1
Pepper St POP/IOD E14 ... 124 E3
STHWK SE1 ... 18 C2
Peppie Cl STNW/STAM N16 ... 68 A6
Pepys Crs BAR EN5 ... 20 A6
CAN/RD E16 ... 125 K1
Pepys Est DEPT SE8 ... 124 B4
Pepys Park Est DEPT SE8 ... 124 C4
Pepys Ri ORP BR6 ... 202 A5
Pepys Rd NWCR SE14 ... 144 A3
RYNPK SW20 ... 177 F5
Pepys St TWRH EC3N ... 13 H5
Perceval Av HAMP NW3 ... 83 J3
Percheron Rd BORE WD6 ... 31 F1
Perch St HACK E8 ... 86 B2
Percival Ct TOTM N17 ... 50 B3
Percival Gdns CHDH RM6 ... 73 J3
Percival Rd EN EN1 ... 24 B5
FELT TW13 ... 153 J4
MORT/ESHN SW14 ... 137 K6
ORP BR6 ... 201 G6
Percival St FSBYE EC1V ... 6 A6
Percival Wy HOR/WEW KT19 ... 206 E2
Percy Bush Rd WDR/YW UB7 ... 112 C3
Percy Gdns PEND EN3 ... 25 F6
WPK KT4 ... 192 A5
YEAD UB4 ... 94 C2
Percy Ms FITZ W1T ... 10 C2
Percy Rd CAN/RD E16 ... 106 C4
GDMY/SEVK IG3 ... 73 G4
HPTN TW12 ... 173 F3
ISLW TW7 ... 136 B5
MTCM CR4 ... 195 F4
NFNCH/WDSPK N12 ... 47 G1
PGE/AN SE20 ... 182 A4
ROMW/RG RM7 ... 56 E6
SHB W12 ... 118 D2
SNWD SE25 ... 197 G2
WAN E11 ... 70 C4
WCHMH N21 ... 35 J2
WHTN TW2 ... 155 G3
Percy St FITZ W1T ... 10 C2
Percy Ter BMLY BR1 ... 185 G6
Percy Wy WHTN TW2 ... 155 H3
Peregrine Cl WLSDN NW10 ... 81 F3
Peregrine Ct WELL DA16 ... 148 A2
Peregrine Gdns CROY/NA CR0 ... 198 B6
Peregrine Rd BARK/HLT IG6 ... 55 H1
TOTM N17 ... 49 J3
Peregrine Wy
WIM/MER SW19 ... 177 F3
Perham Rd WKENS W14 ... 119 H5
Peridot St EHAM E6 ... 107 J4
Perifield DUL SE21 ... 162 D3
Perimeade Rd GFD/PVL UB6 ... 97 J1
Periton Rd ELTH/MOT SE9 ... 146 C5
Perivale Gdns WEA W13 ... 97 H3
Perivale La GFD/PVL UB6 ... 97 G2
Perivale Village
GFD/PVL UB6 * ... 97 J2
Periwood Crs GFD/PVL UB6 ... 79 G6
Perkin Cl ALP/SUD HA0 ... 79 H3
HSLW TW3 ... 135 G5
Perkin's Rents WEST SW1P ... 16 C4
Perkins Rd BARK/HLT IG6 ... 72 D2
Perkins Sq STHWK SE1 ... 12 D7
Perks Cl BKHTH/KID SE3 ... 145 H3
Perpins Rd ELTH/MOT SE9 ... 167 K1
Perran Rd BRXS/STRHM SW2 ... 162 C4
Perrers Rd HMSMTH W6 ... 118 E3
Perrin Rd ALP/SUD HA0 ... 79 G2
Perrin's Ct HAMP NW3 * ... 83 G2
Perrin's Wk HAMP NW3 ... 83 G2
Perry Av ACT W3 ... 99 F5
Perry Cl RAIN RM13 ... 111 F1
Perry Ct SEVS/STOTM N15 * ... 68 A3
Perryfield Wy
CDALE/KGS NW9 ... 63 H3
RCHPK/HAM TW10 ... 156 C4
Perry Gdns ED N9 ... 36 A5
Perry Garth NTHLT UB5 ... 77 G6
Perry Gv DART DA1 ... 151 K5
Perry Hall Cl ORP BR6 ... 202 B4
Perry Hall Rd ORP BR6 ... 202 A3
Perry Hl CAT SE6 ... 164 C4
Perry How WPK KT4 ... 192 C5
Perry Mnr CHST BR7 ... 185 K2
Perrymans Farm Rd
GNTH/NBYPK IG2 ... 72 D3
Perry Md BUSH WD23 ... 28 C1
ENC/FH EN2 ... 23 H3
Perrymead St FUL/PGN SW6 ... 139 K2
Perryn Rd ACT W3 ... 99 F6
BERM/RHTH SE16 ... 123 J3
Perry Ri FSTH SE23 ... 164 B5
Perry Rd DAGW RM9 ... 110 B4
Perry St CHST BR7 ... 185 K2
Perry V FSTH SE23 ... 163 K4
Persant Rd CAT SE6 ... 165 H5
Perseverance Pl
BRXN/ST SW9 ... 142 B1
Pershore Cl GNTH/NBYPK IG2 ... 72 B2
Pershore Gv CAR SM5 ... 194 C3
Pert Cl MUSWH N10 ... 48 B3
Perth Av CDALE/KGS NW9 ... 63 F4
YEAD UB4 ... 95 G3
Perth Cl NTHLT UB5 ... 78 A4
NWMAL KT3 ... 176 C5
Perth Rd BARK IG11 ... 108 D1
BECK BR3 ... 183 F5
FSBYPK N4 ... 67 G5
GNTH/NBYPK IG2 ... 72 B3
LEY E10 ... 69 G5
PLSTW E13 ... 107 F1
WDGN N22 ... 49 H4
Perth Ter GNTH/NBYPK IG2 ... 72 C4
Perwell Av RYLN/HDSTN HA2 ... 59 K5
Petavel Rd TEDD TW11 ... 173 K2
Peter Av WLSDN NW10 ... 81 K5
Peterboat Cl GNWCH SE10 ... 125 H4
Peterborough Ms
FUL/PGN SW6 ... 139 K3
Peterborough Rd CAR SM5 ... 194 D3
FUL/PGN SW6 ... 139 K3
HRW HA1 ... 60 E5
LEY E10 ... 70 A2
Peterborough Vls
FUL/PGN SW6 ... 140 A2
Petergate BTSEA SW11 ... 140 B5
Peters Cl BCTR RM8 ... 73 K5
STAN HA7 ... 43 K2
WELL DA16 ... 147 K3
Petersfield Cl UED N18 ... 49 J1
Petersfield Ri PUT/ROE SW15 ... 158 E3
Petersfield Rd ACT W3 ... 117 K2
Petersham Cl
RCHPK/HAM TW10 ... 156 E4
SUT SM1 ... 208 D3
Petersham Dr
STMC/STPC BR5 ... 186 A5
Petersham La SKENS SW7 * ... 120 B3
Petersham Ms SKENS SW7 ... 120 B3
Petersham Pl SKENS SW7 ... 120 B3
Petersham Rd
RCHPK/HAM TW10 ... 156 E5
Petersham Ter
CROY/NA CR0 * ... 210 E1
Peter's Hl BLKFR EC4V ... 12 C5
Peterstone Rd ABYW SE2 ... 128 C2
Peterstow Cl WIM/MER SW19 ... 159 H4
Peter St SOHO/CST W1F ... 10 C5
Peterwood Wy CROY/NA CR0 ... 196 A6
Petherton Rd HBRY N5 ... 85 J3
Petiver Cl HOM E9 * ... 86 E5
Petley Rd HMSMTH W6 ... 119 F6
Peto Pl CAMTN NW1 ... 3 K6
Peto St North CAN/RD E16 ... 106 D5
Petrie Cl CRICK NW2 * ... 82 C4
Petros Gdns
KIL/WHAMP NW6 * ... 83 F3
Petro St South CAN/RD E16 ... 106 D6
Pettacre Cl THMD SE28 ... 127 H3
Pett Cl EMPK RM11 ... 75 K6
Petten Cl STMC/STPC BR5 ... 202 E5
Petten Gv STMC/STPC BR5 ... 202 D5
Petticoat La WCHPL E1 ... 13 H2
Petticoat Sq WCHPL E1 ... 13 J3
Petticoat Tower WCHPL E1 * ... 13 J3
Pettits Bvd ROM RM1 ... 57 G5
Pettits Cl ROM RM1 ... 57 G5
Pettits La ROM RM1 ... 57 G5
Pettits La North ROM RM1 ... 57 F4
Pettit's Pl DAGE RM10 ... 92 C3
Pettit's Rd DAGE RM10 ... 92 C3
Pettiward Cl PUT/ROE SW15 ... 139 F5
Pettley Gdns ROMW/RG RM7 ... 75 F2
Pettman Crs THMD SE28 ... 127 J3
Pettsgrove Av ALP/SUD HA0 ... 79 J3
Pett's Hl NTHLT UB5 ... 78 B3
Pett St WOOL/PLUM SE18 ... 126 D4
Petts Wood Rd
STMC/STPC BR5 ... 201 J2
Petty France WESTW SW1E ... 16 B4
Petty Wales MON EC3R ... 13 H6
Petworth Cl NTHLT UB5 ... 77 K5
Petworth Gdns
HGDN/ICK UB10 ... 76 A6
RYNPK SW20 ... 176 E6
Petworth Rd
NFNCH/WDSPK N12 ... 47 J1
Petworth St BTSEA SW11 ... 140 D2
Petworth Wy HCH RM12 ... 93 H2
Petyt Pl CHEL SW3 * ... 120 D6
Petyward CHEL SW3 ... 14 D7
Pevensey Av EN EN1 ... 24 A3
FBAR/BDGN N11 ... 48 D1
Pevensey Cl ISLW TW7 ... 135 H1
Pevensey Rd FELT TW13 ... 154 D3
FSTGT E7 ... 88 E2
TOOT SW17 ... 160 C6
Peverel EHAM E6 ... 108 A5
Peveret Cl FBAR/BDGN N11 * ... 48 B1
Peveril Dr TEDD TW11 ... 173 J1
Pewsey Cl CHING E4 ... 51 J1
Peyton Pl GNWCH SE10 ... 145 F1
Pharaoh Cl MTCM CR4 ... 194 E4
Pheasant Cl CAN/RD E16 ... 107 F5
Phelp St WALW SE17 ... 122 E6
Phelps Wy HYS/HAR UB3 ... 113 J4
Phene St CHEL SW3 ... 120 D6
Philan Wy CRW RM5 ... 57 F2
Philbeach Gdns ECT SW5 ... 119 K5
Philchurch Pl WCHPL E1 ... 104 C5
Philimore Cl
WOOL/PLUM SE18 ... 127 K5
Philip Av ROMW/RG RM7 ... 75 F5
Philip Gdns CROY/NA CR0 ... 198 C6
Philip La SEVS/STOTM N15 ... 67 K1
Philippa Gdns ELTH/MOT SE9 ... 146 C6
Philip Rd RAIN RM13 ... 111 G2
Philips Cl CAR SM5 ... 195 F5
Philip St PLSTW E13 ... 106 E3
Philip Wk PECK SE15 ... 143 H4
Phillimore Gdns KENS W8 ... 119 K2
WLSDN NW10 ... 82 A6
Phillimore Gardens Cl
KENS W8 ... 119 K3
Phillimore Pl KENS W8 ... 119 K2
Phillimore Ter KENS W8 * ... 119 K3
Phillimore Wk KENS W8 ... 119 K3
Phillipp St IS N1 ... 7 H1
Philpot La FENCHST EC3M ... 13 G5
Philpot St WCHPL E1 * ... 104 D5
Phineas Pett Rd
ELTH/MOT SE9 ... 146 D4
Phipp's Bridge Rd
WIM/MER SW19 ... 178 B5
Phipps Hatch La ENC/FH EN2 ... 23 J1
Phipp's Ms BGVA SW1W ... 15 J5
Phipp St SDTCH EC2A ... 7 G6
Phoebeth Rd LEW SE13 ... 144 D6
Phoenix Cl HACK E8 * ... 86 B6
NTHWD HA6 ... 26 D6
WALTH E17 ... 51 H5
WWKM BR4 ... 199 G6
Phoenix Ct BTFD TW8 ... 117 F5
POP/IOD E14 ... 124 D4
Phoenix Dr HAYES BR2 ... 215 H
Phoenix Pk BTFD TW8 * ... 116 E5
Phoenix Pl FSBYW WC1X ... 5 H6
Phoenix Rd CAMTN NW1 ... 4 C4
PGE/AN SE20 ... 181 K
Phoenix St LSQ/SEVD WC2H ... 10 D4
Phoenix Wy HEST TW5 ... 114 C
Phoenix Wharf Rd
STHWK SE1 ... 19 K
Phyllis Av NWMAL KT3 ... 192 E
Physic Pl CHEL SW3 ... 120 E
Picardy Manorway
BELV DA17 ... 129 J
Picardy Rd BELV DA17 ... 129 H
Picardy St BELV DA17 ... 129 H
Piccadilly MYFR/PICC W1J ... 10 A
Piccadilly Ar STJS SW1Y ... 10 A
Piccadilly Circ REGST W1B ... 10 B
Pickard Cl STHGT/OAK N14 ... 34 D
Pickard St FSBYE EC1V ... 6 E
Pickering Av EHAM E6 ... 108
Pickering Gdns CROY/NA CR0 ... 197 C
FBAR/BDGN N11 ... 48
Pickering Ms BAY/PAD W2 ... 101
Pickering Pl WHALL SW1A * ... 16 E
Pickering St IS N1 ... 85
Pickets Cl BUSH WD23 ... 28
Pickets St BAL SW12 ... 161
Pickett Cft STAN HA7 ... 43
Pickett's Lock La ED N9 ... 36
Pickfords Whf IS N1 * ... 6
Pickhurst Gn HAYES BR2 ... 199
Pickhurst La WWKM BR4 ... 199
Pickhurst Md HAYES BR2 ... 199
Pickhurst Pk HAYES BR2 ... 199
Pickhurst Ri WWKM BR4 ... 199
Pickwick Cl HSLWW TW4 ... 134
Pickwick Ms UED N18 ... 50
Pickwick Pl HRW HA1 ... 60
Pickwick Rd DUL SE21 ... 162
Pickwick St STHWK SE1 ... 18
Pickwick Wy CHST BR7 ... 185
Pickworth Cl VX/NE SW8 * ... 141
Picton Pl MHST W1U ... 9
SURB KT6 ... 191
Picton St CMBW SE5 ... 142
Pied Bull Yd IS N1 ... 6
Piedmont Rd
WOOL/PLUM SE18 ... 127
Pier Head WAP E1W * ... 123
Piermont Pl BMLY BR1 ... 184
Piermont Rd EDUL SE22 ... 143
Pierrepoint Ar IS N1 * ... 6
Pierrepoint Rd ACT W3 ... 98
Pierrepoint Rw IS N1 ... 6
Pier Rd CAN/RD E16 ... 126
EBED/NFELT TW14 ... 134
ERITH DA8 ... 130
Pier St POP/IOD E14 ... 125
Pier Ter WAND/EARL SW18 ... 140

Pier Wy THMD SE28 127 J3
Pigeon La HPTN TW12 155 F6
Pigott St POP/IOD E14 105 J5
Pike Cl BMLY BR1 184 A1
Pike Rd MLHL NW7 31 F6
Pike's End PIN HA5 59 F1
Pikestone Cl YEAD UB4 * 95 J3
Pilgrimage St STHWK SE1 18 E3
Pilgrim Cl MRDN SM4 194 A4
Pilgrim Hl WNWD SE27 162 D6
Pilgrims Cl NTHLT UB5 78 C3
PLMGR N13 35 F6
Pilgrim's La HAMP NW3 83 H2
Pilgrims Ms POP/IOD E14 106 B6
Pilgrims Pl ASHF TW15 * 152 C6
Pilgrim's Ri EBAR EN4 21 J6
Pilgrim St BLKFR EC4V * 12 A4
Pilgrims Wy ARCH N19 66 D5
WBLY HA9 62 D5
Pilgrim's Wy SAND/SEL CR2 212 B4
Pilkington Rd ORP BR6 216 C1
PECK SE15 143 J3
Pilot Cl DEPT SE8 124 C6
Pilsden Cl WIM/MER SW19 * 159 G3
Piltdown Rd OXHEY WD19 27 H6
Pilton Pl WALW SE17 122 D5
Pimlico Rd BGVA SW1W 121 F5
Pinchbeck Rd ORP BR6 217 F4
Pinchin & Johnsons Yd
WCHPL E1 * 104 C6
Pinchin St WCHPL E1 104 C6
Pincott Pl BROCKY SE4 144 A4
Pincott Rd WIM/MER SW19 178 B3
Pindar St SDTCH EC2A 13 G1
Pindock Ms MV/WKIL W9 101 F3
Pine Apple Ct WESTW SW1E * 16 A4
Pine Av SRTFD E15 88 B3
WWKM BR4 198 E5
Pine Cl LEY E10 69 J6
PGE/AN SE20 181 K4
STAN HA7 29 H6
STHGT/OAK N14 34 C2
Pine Coombe CROY/NA CR0 213 F2
Pinecrest Gdns ORP BR6 216 B2
Pinecroft
KTN/HRWW/WS HA3 62 B2
WOOL/PLUM SE18 148 B1
Pinecroft Crs BAR EN5 20 C5
Pinefield Cl POP/IOD E14 * 105 J6
Pine Gdns BRYLDS KT5 191 H3
RSLP HA4 59 F5
Pine Gld ORP BR6 215 K2
Pine Gv FSBYPK N4 66 E6
TRDG/WHET N20 32 D3
WIM/MER SW19 177 J1
Pinelands Cl BKHTH/KID SE3 * 145 J1
Pinelees Ct
MORT/ESHN SW14 * 137 K5
Pinemartin Cl CRICK NW2 82 A1
Pine Rdg CAR SM5 210 A6
Pine Rd CRICK NW2 82 A2
FBAR/BDGN N11 34 A4
Pines Cl NTHWD HA6 40 C2
Pines Rd BMLY BR1 184 D5
The Pines NRWD SE19 * 180 C2
STHGT/OAK N14 22 C6
WFD IG8 38 D5
Pine St CLKNW EC1R 5 J6
Pine Tree Cl HEST TW5 134 A2
Pine Tree Wy LEW SE13 144 E4
Pine Wk BRYLDS KT5 191 H3
Pinewood Av BFN/LL DA15 167 K3
PIN HA5 42 B2
RAIN RM13 111 K3
Pinewood Cl CROY/NA CR0 213 G1
NTHWD HA6 40 E1
ORP BR6 201 J5
PIN HA5 42 B2
Pinewood Dr ORP BR6 216 E3
Pinewood Gv WEA W13 97 J5
inewood Ldg BUSH WD23 * 28 D3
Pinewood Ms
STWL/WRAY TW19 152 A1
inewood Rd ABYW SE2 128 E6
FELT TW13 154 A5
infold Rd STRHM/NOR SW16 161 K6
inglestone Cl WDR/YW UB7 132 B1
inkcoat Cl FELT TW13 154 A5
inkwell Av HYS/HAR UB3 113 G4
inkwell La HYS/HAR UB3 113 G4
inley Gdns DAGW RM9 91 H6
innata Cl ENC/FH EN2 23 J2
innell Rd ELTH/MOT SE9 146 C5
nner Ct PIN HA5 60 A1
nner Gn PIN HA5 41 G5
nner Gv PIN HA5 59 J1
nner Hl PIN HA5 41 F3
nner Hill Rd PIN HA5 41 G4
nner Park Av
RYLN/HDSTN HA2 42 C5
nner Park Gdns
RYLN/HDSTN HA2 42 C5
nner Rd HRW HA1 60 B2
NTHWD HA6 40 D4
OXHEY WD19 27 H1
PIN HA5 59 K1
nner Vw HRW HA1 60 C2
nn Wy RSLP HA4 58 B4
ntail Cl EHAM E6 107 J4
ntail Rd WFD IG8 53 F3
ntail Wy YEAD UB4 95 H4
nto Cl BORE WD6 * 31 F1
nto Wy BKHTH/KID SE3 146 A5
oneer Cl BOW E3 105 K4
SHB W12 99 K5
oneer St PECK SE15 143 H2
oneer Wy SHB W12 100 A5
WATW WD18 26 D1
per Cl HOLWY N7 85 F4
per Rd KUT/HW KT1 175 H6
pers Gdns CROY/NA CR0 198 B4
pers Gn CDALE/KGS NW9 62 E2
pers Green La STAN HA7 30 A5
per Wy IL IG1 72 D5
pewell Rd CAR SM5 194 D3
pin Cl CRICK NW2 81 J1
CROY/NA CR0 198 C5
ppins Cl WDR/YW UB7 112 A3
quet Rd PGE/AN SE20 181 K5
rbright Crs CROY/NA CR0 214 A4
Pirbright Rd
WAND/EARL SW18 159 J3
Pirie St CAN/RD E16 126 A1
Pitcairn Cl ROMW/RG RM7 74 C1
Pitcairn Rd MTCM CR4 178 E3
Pitchford St SRTFD E15 88 B5
Pitfield Crs THMD SE28 128 B1
Pitfield St IS N1 7 G4
Pitfield Wy PEND EN3 24 E2
WLSDN NW10 80 E4
Pitlake CROY/NA CR0 196 C6
Pitman St CMBW SE5 142 D1
Pitsea Pl WCHPL E1 105 F5
Pitsea St WCHPL E1 105 F5
Pitshanger La EA W5 97 H3
Pitt Crs WIM/MER SW19 160 A6
Pittman Gdns IL IG1 90 C3
Pitt Rd ORP BR6 216 C2
RYLN/HDSTN HA2 60 C6
THHTH CR7 196 D2
Pitts Head Ms
MYFR/PICC W1J 15 H1
Pitt St KENS W8 119 K2
Pittville Gdns SNWD SE25 181 H6
Pixley St POP/IOD E14 105 H5
Pixton Wy CROY/NA CR0 213 G6
Place Farm Av ORP BR6 201 J5
Plaistow Gv BMLY BR1 184 A3
SRTFD E15 88 D6
Plaistow La BMLY BR1 184 B4
BMLY BR1 183 K3
Plaistow Park Rd PLSTW E13 107 F1
Plaistow Rd SRTFD E15 88 D6
Plane St SYD SE26 163 J5
Plane Tree Crs FELT TW13 154 A5
Plantagenet Cl WPK KT4 207 F2
Plantagenet Gdns CHDH RM6 73 K4
Plantagenet Pl CHDH RM6 73 K4
Plantagenet Rd BAR EN5 21 G5
Plantain Gdns WAN E11 * 88 B1
Plantain Pl STHWK SE1 18 E2
Plantation Dr
STMC/STPC BR5 202 E5
Plantation La FENCHST EC3M 13 G5
Plantation Rd ERITH DA8 150 D2
Plashet Gv EHAM E6 89 G6
Plashet Rd PLSTW E13 88 E6
Plassy Rd CAT SE6 164 E2
Platina St SDTCH EC2A 7 F6
Plato Rd BRXS/STRHM SW2 141 K5
Platt's La HAMP NW3 82 E1
Platts Rd PEND EN3 24 E2
Platt St CAMTN NW1 4 C2
Plawsfield Rd BECK BR3 182 A4
Plaxtol Cl BMLY BR1 184 B4
Playfair St HMSMTH W6 * 119 F5
Playfield Av CRW RM5 56 E4
Playfield Crs EDUL SE22 143 F6
Playfield Rd EDGW HA8 44 E5
Playford Rd FSBYPK N4 67 F6
Playgreen Wy CAT SE6 164 D6
Playground Cl BECK BR3 182 A5
Playhouse Ct STHWK SE1 * 18 C2
Playhouse Yd BLKFR EC4V 12 A4
Plaza Pde ALP/SUD HA0 * 80 A4
Plaza Wk CDALE/KGS NW9 44 E6
Pleasance Rd PUT/ROE SW15 138 E6
STMC/STPC BR5 186 C5
The Pleasance
PUT/ROE SW15 138 E5
Pleasant Gv CROY/NA CR0 213 H1
Pleasant Pl IS N1 85 H5
Pleasant Vw ORP BR6 216 C3
Pleasant Wy ALP/SUD HA0 97 J1
Plender St CAMTN NW1 4 A1
Pleshey Rd ARCH N19 84 D2
Plesman Wy WLGTN SM6 * 210 E6
Plevna Crs SEVS/STOTM N15 68 A3
Plevna Rd ED N9 36 C5
HPTN TW12 173 G4
Plevna St POP/IOD E14 125 F3
Pleydell Av HMSMTH W6 118 C3
NRWD SE19 181 G3
Pleydell Est FSBYE EC1V * 6 D5
Pleydell Gdns NRWD SE19 * 181 G2
Pleydell St EMB EC4Y 11 K4
Plimsoll Cl POP/IOD E14 105 K5
Plimsoll Rd FSBYPK N4 85 H1
Plough Farm Cl RSLP HA4 58 B3
Plough La EDUL SE22 163 G1
PUR/KEN CR8 210 E6
TEDD TW11 174 B1
WIM/MER SW19 178 A1
WLGTN SM6 210 E3
Plough Lane Cl WLGTN SM6 210 E3
Ploughmans Cl CAMTN NW1 84 D6
Ploughmans End ISLW TW7 135 J6
Plough Pl FLST/FETLN EC4A 11 K3
Plough Rd BTSEA SW11 140 C4
HOR/WEW KT19 207 F5
Plough St WCHPL E1 * 104 C5
Plough Ter BTSEA SW11 140 C5
Plough Wy BERM/RHTH SE16 124 A4
Plough Yd SDTCH EC2A 7 H7
Plover Wy BERM/RHTH SE16 124 B3
YEAD UB4 95 H5
Plowden Blds EMB EC4Y * 11 J5
Plowman Cl UED N18 49 K1
Plowman Wy BCTR RM8 73 J5
Plumbers Rw WCHPL E1 104 C4
Plumbridge St GNWCH SE10 * 145 F2
Plum Cl FELT TW13 153 K3
Plum Garth BTFD TW8 116 E4
Plum La WOOL/PLUM SE18 147 G1
Plummer La MTCM CR4 178 E4
Plummer Rd CLAP SW4 161 J2
Plumpton Wy CAR SM5 209 J1
Plumstead Common Rd
WOOL/PLUM SE18 127 H6
Plumstead High St
WOOL/PLUM SE18 127 J4
Plumstead Rd
WOOL/PLUM SE18 127 H4
Plumtree Cl DAGE RM10 92 D4
WLGTN SM6 210 D5
Plumtree Ct FLST/FETLN EC4A 11 K3
Plymouth Rd BMLY BR1 184 A4
CAN/RD E16 106 E4
Plymouth Whf POP/IOD E14 125 G4
Plympton Av
KIL/WHAMP NW6 82 D5
Plympton Cl BELV DA17 129 F3
Plympton Pl STJWD NW8 * 2 C7
Plympton Rd
KIL/WHAMP NW6 82 D5
Plympton St STJWD NW8 2 C7
Plymstock Rd WELL DA16 148 D1
Pocklington Cl
CDALE/KGS NW9 45 G5
Pocock Av WDR/YW UB7 112 C3
Pocock St STHWK SE1 18 A2
Podmore Rd
WAND/EARL SW18 140 B5
Poets Ms HNHL SE24 142 C6
Poet's Rd HBRY N5 85 K3
Poets Wy HRW HA1 60 E1
Pointalls Cl FNCH N3 47 G5
Point Cl GNWCH SE10 145 F2
Pointer Cl THMD SE28 109 K5
Pointers Cl POP/IOD E14 124 E5
Point Hl GNWCH SE10 145 F2
Point Pl WBLY HA9 80 D5
Point Pleasant
WAND/EARL SW18 139 K5
Point Wharf La BTFD TW8 136 E1
Poland St SOHO/SHAV W1D 10 B3
Polebrook Rd BKHTH/KID SE3 146 B4
Polecroft La CAT SE6 164 C4
Pole Hill Rd CHING E4 38 A2
Polesden Gdns RYNPK SW20 176 E6
Polesworth Rd DAGW RM9 110 B1
Polish War Memorial Rbt
RSLP HA4 77 G4
Pollard Cl CAN/RD E16 106 E6
CHIG IG7 55 G1
HOLWY N7 85 F2
Pollard Rd MRDN SM4 194 C2
TRDG/WHET N20 33 J4
Pollard Rw BETH E2 104 C2
Pollards Crs
STRHM/NOR SW16 179 K6
Pollards Hl East
STRHM/NOR SW16 180 A6
Pollards Hl North
STRHM/NOR SW16 180 A6
Pollards Hl South
STRHM/NOR SW16 179 K6
Pollards Hl West
STRHM/NOR SW16 179 K6
Pollard St BETH E2 * 104 C2
Pollards Wood Rd
STRHM/NOR SW16 179 K5
Pollen St CONDST W1S 9 K4
Pollitt Dr STJWD NW8 2 A6
Polperro Cl ORP BR6 202 A3
Polperro Ms LBTH SE11 17 K6
Polsted Rd CAT SE6 164 C2
Polthorne Gv
WOOL/PLUM SE18 127 H4
Polworth Rd
STRHM/NOR SW16 179 K1
Polygon Rd CAMTN NW1 4 C3
The Polygon CLAP SW4 * 141 H5
Polytechnic St
WOOL/PLUM SE18 127 F4
Pomell Wy WCHPL E1 13 K3
Pomeroy Cl TWK TW1 136 C5
Pomeroy St NWCR SE14 143 K1
Pomfret Rd CMBW SE5 142 C4
Pomoja La ARCH N19 66 E6
Pond Cl NFNCH/WDSPK N12 47 J2
Pond Cottage La BECK BR3 198 D5
Pond Cots DUL SE21 163 F3
Ponder St HOLWY N7 * 85 F5
Pond Farm Est CLPT E5 * 86 E1
Pondfield Rd DAGE RM10 92 D3
HAYES BR2 199 H5
ORP BR6 216 B1
Pond Gn RSLP HA4 58 C6
Pond Hill Gdns CHEAM SM3 * 208 C4
Pond Lees Cl DAGE RM10 93 F5
Pond Md DUL SE21 162 E1
Pond Pl CHEL SW3 14 C7
Pond Rd SRTFD E15 106 C1
Pondside Av WPK KT4 193 F5
Pondside Cl HYS/HAR UB3 133 G1
Pond St HAMP NW3 83 J3
Pond Wy TEDD TW11 174 D2
Pondwood Ri ORP BR6 201 K4
Ponler St WCHPL E1 104 D5
Ponsard Rd WLSDN NW10 99 K2
Ponsford St HOM E9 86 E4
Ponsonby Pl WEST SW1P 121 J5
Ponsonby Rd PUT/ROE SW15 158 E2
Ponsonby Ter WEST SW1P 121 J5
Pontefract Rd BMLY BR1 183 K1
Ponton Rd VX/NE SW8 141 J1
Pont St KTBR SW1X 14 E5
Pont Street Ms KTBR SW1X 14 E5
Pool Cl BECK BR3 182 D1
E/WMO/HCT KT8 188 E2
Pool Ct CAT SE6 164 D4
Poole Cl RSLP HA4 58 C6
Poole Court Rd HSLWW TW4 134 D3
Poole Rd HOM E9 87 F4
HOR/WEW KT19 207 F4
Pooles Blds FSBYW WC1X 5 J7
Pooles La WBPTN SW10 140 B1
Pooles Pk FSBYPK N4 67 G6
Poole St IS N1 6 E1
Poole Wy YEAD UB4 * 94 C2
Pooley Dr MORT/ESHN SW14 137 K4
Poolmans St
BERM/RHTH SE16 124 A2
Pool Rd E/WMO/HCT KT8 188 E2
HRW HA1 60 D4
Poolsford Rd
CDALE/KGS NW9 63 G1
Poonah St WCHPL E1 104 E5
Pope Cl EBED/NFELT TW14 153 J3
WIM/MER SW19 * 178 C2
Pope Rd HAYES BR2 200 C2
Pope's Av WHTN TW2 155 K4
Popes Dr FNCH N3 46 E4
Popes Gv CROY/NA CR0 213 H1
Pope's Gv WHTN TW2 155 K4
Pope's La EA W5 116 E3
Pope's Rd BRXN/ST SW9 * 142 B5
Pope St STHWK SE1 19 H3
Popham Cl FELT TW13 154 D5
Popham Gdns
RCH/KEW TW9 * 137 J4
Popham Rd IS N1 85 J6
Popham St IS N1 85 J6
Popinjays Rw CHEAM SM3 * 208 B3
Poplar Av MTCM CR4 178 E4
NWDGN UB2 115 G3
ORP BR6 201 G6
Poplar Bath St POP/IOD E14 105 K6
Poplar Cl HOM E9 87 H3
PIN HA5 41 H4
Poplar Court Pde TWK TW1 * 156 D1
Poplar Crs HOR/WEW KT19 206 E4
Poplar Farm Cl
HOR/WEW KT19 206 E4
Poplar Gdns NWMAL KT3 176 A5
Poplar Gv FBAR/BDGN N11 48 A2
HMSMTH W6 119 F2
NWMAL KT3 176 A6
WBLY HA9 80 E1
Poplar High St POP/IOD E14 105 K6
Poplar La BECK BR3 198 E2
Poplar Ms SHB W12 119 F1
Poplar Mt BELV DA17 129 J4
Poplar Pl BAY/PAD W2 101 F6
HYS/HAR UB3 94 E6
THMD SE28 109 J6
Poplar Rd CHEAM SM3 193 J5
HNHL SE24 142 D5
WIM/MER SW19 177 K5
Poplar Rd South
WIM/MER SW19 177 K6
Poplars Cl RSLP HA4 58 C5
Poplars Rd WALTH E17 69 K3
The Poplars STHGT/OAK N14 22 B6
Poplar St ROMW/RG RM7 74 E1
Poplar Vw WBLY HA9 * 61 K6
Poplar Wk CROY/NA CR0 196 D6
HNHL SE24 142 D5
Poplar Wy BARK/HLT IG6 72 C1
FELT TW13 153 K5
Poppins Ct FLST/FETLN EC4A 12 A4
Poppleton Rd WAN E11 70 C3
Poppy Cl BELV DA17 129 J3
NTHLT UB5 77 K4
WLGTN SM6 195 F5
Poppy La CROY/NA CR0 197 K4
Porchester Garden Ms
BAY/PAD W2 * 101 F5
Porchester Gdns
BAY/PAD W2 101 F6
Porchester Gardens Ms
BAY/PAD W2 101 F5
Porchester Ga BAY/PAD W2 * 101 G6
Porchester Md BECK BR3 182 E2
Porchester Pl BAY/PAD W2 8 D4
Porchester Rd BAY/PAD W2 101 F5
KUT/HW KT1 175 J5
Porchester Sq BAY/PAD W2 101 F5
Porchester Square Ms
BAY/PAD W2 * 101 F5
Porchester Ter BAY/PAD W2 101 G6
Porch Wy TRDG/WHET N20 33 K5
Porcupine Cl ELTH/MOT SE9 166 D4
Porden Rd BRXS/STRHM SW2 142 A5
Porlock Av RYLN/HDSTN HA2 60 C5
Porlock Rd EN EN1 36 B2
Porlock St STHWK SE1 19 F2
Porrington Cl CHST BR7 184 E4
Portal Cl RSLP HA4 76 E2
WNWD SE27 162 B5
Portal Wy ACT W3 99 F4
Portbury Cl PECK SE15 143 H2
Portchester Cl HNHL SE24 142 D5
Portcullis Lodge Rd EN EN1 23 K4
Portelet Rd WCHPL E1 105 F2
Porten Houses WKENS W14 * 119 H3
Porten Rd WKENS W14 119 H3
Porter Rd EHAM E6 107 K5
Porters Av DAGW RM9 91 H4
Porter Sq ARCH N19 66 E5
Porter St MHST W1U 9 F1
STHWK SE1 12 D7
Porters Wk WAP E1W * 104 D6
Porters Wy WDR/YW UB7 112 C3
Porteus Rd BAY/PAD W2 101 G4
Portgate Cl MV/WKIL W9 100 D3
Porthallow Cl ORP BR6 217 F2
Porthcawe Rd SYD SE26 164 B6
Porthkerry Av WELL DA16 148 B5
Portia Wy BOW E3 105 H3
The Porticos CHEL SW3 * 120 C6
Portinscale Rd
PUT/ROE SW15 139 H6
Portland Av BFN/LL DA15 168 B1
NWMAL KT3 192 C4
STNW/STAM N16 68 B5
Portland Cl CHDH RM6 74 A2
WPK KT4 192 E4
Portland Cots CROY/NA CR0 * 195 J4
Portland Crs ELTH/MOT SE9 166 D4
FELT TW13 153 G6
GFD/PVL UB6 96 B3
STAN HA7 43 K5
Portland Crs West STAN HA7 43 K6
Portland Dr ENC/FH EN2 24 A1
Portland Gdns CHDH RM6 73 K2
FSBYPK N4 67 H3
Portland Gv VX/NE SW8 142 A2
Portland Ms SOHO/CST W1F 10 B4
Portland Pl REGST W1B 3 J7
SNWD SE25 197 H1
Portland Ri FSBYPK N4 67 H5
Portland Rd ASHF TW15 152 B5
BMLY BR1 166 B6
ELTH/MOT SE9 166 D4
KUT/HW KT1 175 F6
MTCM CR4 178 D5
NTGHL W11 100 C6
NWDGN UB2 114 E3
SEVS/STOTM N15 68 A1
SNWD SE25 197 H1
YEAD UB4 94 C2
Portland Sq WAP E1W 123 J1
Portland St WALW SE17 122 E5
Portland Ter RCH/KEW TW9 * 136 E5
Portman Av
MORT/ESHN SW14 138 A4
Portman Cl BXLYHS DA6 148 E4
MBLAR W1H 9 G3
Portman Dr WFD IG8 53 H5
Portman Gdns
CDALE/KGS NW9 45 F6
Portman Ga CAMTN NW1 2 D7
Portman Ms South
MBLAR W1H 9 G4
Portman Pl BETH E2 104 E2
Portman Rd KUT/HW KT1 175 G5
Portman Sq MBLAR W1H 9 F3
Portman St MBLAR W1H 9 G4
Portmeadow Wk ABYW SE2 128 E2
Portmeers Cl WALTH E17 * 69 H3
Portmore Gdns CRW RM5 56 C1
Portnall Rd MV/WKIL W9 100 D2
Portnoi Cl ROM RM1 57 F5
Portobello Ct NTGHL W11 * 100 D6
Portobello Ms NTGHL W11 100 E6
Portobello Rd NKENS W10 100 C4
Portpool La FSBYW WC1X 11 J1
Portree St POP/IOD E14 106 B5
Portsdown Av GLDGN NW11 64 D3
Portsdown Ms GLDGN NW11 64 D3
Portsea Ms BAY/PAD W2 * 8 D4
Portsea Pl BAY/PAD W2 8 D4
Portslade Rd VX/NE SW8 141 H3
Portsmouth Av THDIT KT7 190 B4
Portsmouth Ms CAN/RD E16 107 F6
Portsmouth Rd
ESH/CLAY KT10 204 A4
KUT/HW KT1 174 E6
PUT/ROE SW15 158 E2
THDIT KT7 190 C4
Portsmouth St LINN WC2A 11 G3
Portsoken St TWRH EC3N 13 J5
Portugal Gdns WHTN TW2 * 155 H4
Portugal St LINN WC2A 11 H4
Portway RAIN RM13 93 J6
SRTFD E15 88 E6
Portway Crs EW KT17 207 J6
Portway Gdns
WOOL/PLUM SE18 146 C2
Postern Gn ENC/FH EN2 23 G3
The Postern BARB EC2Y * 12 D2
Post La WHTN TW2 155 J3
Postmill Cl CROY/NA CR0 212 E1
Post Office Ap FSTGT E7 89 F3
Post Office Wy VX/NE SW8 141 J1
Post Rd NWDGN UB2 115 G3
Postway Ms IL IG1 90 B1
Potier St STHWK SE1 19 F5
Potter Cl MTCM CR4 * 179 G5
The Potteries BAR EN5 * 20 E6
Potterne Cl WIM/MER SW19 159 G2
Potters Cl CROY/NA CR0 198 B5
PECK SE15 * 143 F1
Potters Fld EN EN1 * 24 A5
Potters Flds STHWK SE1 19 H1
Potters Gv NWMAL KT3 191 K1
Potters Heights Cl PIN HA5 41 F3
Potter's La BAR EN5 20 E5
STRHM/NOR SW16 * 179 J2
Potters Ms BORE WD6 29 K1
Potters Rd FUL/PGN SW6 140 B3
Potter's Rd BAR EN5 21 F5
Potter St NTHWD HA6 40 E4
Potter Street Hl PIN HA5 41 F2
Pottery La NTGHL W11 119 H1
Pottery Rd BTFD TW8 117 F6
BXLY DA5 169 K4
Pottery St
BERM/RHTH SE16 * 123 J2
Pott St BETH E2 104 D2
Poulett Gdns TWK TW1 156 A4
Poulett Rd EHAM E6 107 K1
Poulter Pk MRDN SM4 * 194 D3
Poulters Wd HAYES BR2 215 H3
Poulton Av SUT SM1 209 H1
Poultry LOTH EC2R 12 E4
Pound Cl ORP BR6 201 J6
SURB KT6 190 D5
Pound Court Dr ORP BR6 201 J6
Pound Farm Cl
ESH/CLAY KT10 189 J5
Pound La WLSDN NW10 81 J4
Pound Park Rd CHARL SE7 126 C4
Pound Pl ELTH/MOT SE9 167 F1
Pound St CAR SM5 209 K3
Pountney Rd BTSEA SW11 141 F4
Poverest Rd STMC/STPC BR5 202 A2
Powder Mill La WHTN TW2 154 E3
Powell Cl EDGW HA8 44 B2
Powell Gdns DAGE RM10 92 C2
Powell Rd BKHH IG9 39 G2
CLPT E5 86 D1
Power Rd CHSWK W4 117 H4
Powers Ct TWK TW1 156 E2
Powerscroft Rd CLPT E5 86 E2
SCUP DA14 186 D2
Powis Ct BUSH WD23 * 28 D3
Powis Gdns GLDGN NW11 64 D4
NTGHL W11 100 D5
Powis Ms NTGHL W11 100 D5
Powis Pl BMSBY WC1N 5 F7
Powis Rd BOW E3 105 K2
Powis Sq NTGHL W11 100 D5
Powis St WOOL/PLUM SE18 127 F3
Powis Ter NTGHL W11 100 D5
Powlett Pl CAMTN NW1 * 84 B5
Pownall Gdns HSLW TW3 135 G5
Pownall Rd HACK E8 86 C6
HSLW TW3 135 G5
Pownsett Ter IL IG1 * 90 C3
Powster Rd BMLY BR1 183 K1
Powys Cl BXLYHN DA7 128 E6
Powys La PLMGR N13 34 E6
Poynders Rd CLAP SW4 161 H2
Poynings Cl ORP BR6 202 D6
Poynings Rd ARCH N19 84 C1
Poynings Wy
NFNCH/WDSPK N12 46 E1
Poyntell Crs CHST BR7 185 J4
Poynter Rd EN EN1 24 B6
Poynton Rd TOTM N17 50 C5
Poyntz Rd BTSEA SW11 140 E3
Poyser St BETH E2 104 D1
Praed Ms BAY/PAD W2 8 B3
Praed St BAY/PAD W2 8 B3
Pragel St PLSTW E13 107 F1
Pragnell Rd LEE/GVPK SE12 166 A4

Prague Pl BRXS/STRHM SW2...141 K6
Prah Rd FSBYPK N4...67 G6
Prairie St VX/NE SW8...141 F3
Pratt Ms CAMTN NW1 *...4 A1
Pratt St CAMTN NW1...4 A1
Pratt Wk LBTH SE11...17 H6
Prayle Gv CRICK NW2...64 B5
Prebend Gdns HMSMTH W6...118 C4
Prebend St IS N1...6 C1
Precinct Rd HYS/HAR UB3...94 E6
The Precinct IS N1 *...6 C1
Premiere Pl POP/IOD E14...105 J6
Premier Park Rd
 WLSDN NW10...98 D1
Prendergast Rd
 BKHTH/KID SE3...145 H4
Prentis Rd STRHM/NOR SW16...161 J6
Prentiss Ct CHARL SE7...126 C4
Presburg Rd NWMAL KT3...192 B2
Prescelly Pl EDGW HA8...44 B4
Prescot St WCHPL E1...13 K5
Prescott Av STMC/STPC BR5...201 G3
Prescott Cl EMPK RM11...75 K5
Prescott Pl CLAP SW4...141 J4
Presentation Ms
 BRXS/STRHM SW2...162 A4
Presidents Dr WAP E1W...123 J1
President St FSBYE EC1V *...6 C4
Prespa Cl ED N9...36 E4
Press Rd WLSDN NW10...81 F1
Prestage Wy POP/IOD E14...106 A6
Prestbury Rd FSTGT E7...89 G5
Prestbury Sq ELTH/MOT SE9...166 E6
Prested Rd BTSEA SW11...140 D5
Preston Av CHING E4...52 B2
Preston Cl STHWK SE1...19 H4
 WHTN TW2...155 K5
Preston Ct BAR EN5...21 G5
 WOT/HER KT12...188 B5
Preston Dr BXLYHN DA7...148 E2
 HOR/WEW KT19...207 G4
 WAN E11...71 G2
Preston Gdns IL IG1...71 J3
 WLSDN NW10...81 G4
Preston HI
 KTN/HRWW/WS HA3...62 A4
Preston Pl CRICK NW2...81 J4
Preston Rd
 KTN/HRWW/WS HA3...62 A4
 NRWD SE19...180 C2
 RYNPK SW20...176 D3
 WAN E11...70 C3
 WBLY HA9...62 A6
Prestons Rd WWKM BR4...214 E1
Preston's Rd POP/IOD E14...106 A6
Preston Vw KUT/HW KT1 *...175 G5
Preston Wave
 KTN/HRWW/WS HA3...61 H1
Prestwich Ter CLAP SW4 *...141 J6
Prestwick Cl NWDGN UB2...114 D5
Prestwood Cl
 KTN/HRWW/WS HA3...61 H1
 WOOL/PLUM SE18...148 B1
Prestwood Dr CRW RM5...56 E1
Prestwood Gdns
 CROY/NA CRO...196 D4
Prestwood St IS N1...6 D3
Pretoria Av WALTH E17...69 G1
Pretoria Crs CHING E4...38 A3
Pretoria Pde BROCKY SE4 *...144 D3
Pretoria Rd CAN/RD E16...106 D2
 CHING E4...38 A3
 IL IG1...90 B2
 LEY E10...70 B5
 ROMW/RG RM7...74 E1
 STRHM/NOR SW16...179 G2
 TOTM N17...50 B2
Pretoria Rd North UED N18...50 B2
Prevost Rd FBAR/BDGN N11...34 A4
Price Cl MLHL NW7...46 C2
 TOOT SW17...160 E5
Price's St STHWK SE1...18 B1
Pricklers HI BAR EN5...21 F6
Prickley Wd HAYES BR2...199 J5
Priddy's Yd CROY/NA CRO...196 D6
Prideaux Pl ACT W3...98 F6
 FSBYW WC1X...5 H4
Prideaux Rd BRXN/ST SW9...141 K4
Pridham Rd THHTH CR7...196 E1
Priestfield Rd SYD SE26...164 B5
Priestlands Park Rd
 BFN/LL DA15...168 A3
 SCUP DA14...168 A5
Priestley Cl
 STNW/STAM N16 *...68 B4
Priestley Gdns CHDH RM6...73 H3
Priestley Rd MTCM CR4...179 F5
Priestley Wy CRICK NW2...63 J5
 WALTH E17...51 F6
Priest Park Av
 RYLN/HDSTN HA2...60 A6
Priests Av ROM RM1...57 F5
Priests Br MORT/ESHN SW14...138 B4
Prima Rd BRXN/ST SW9...142 B1
Primrose Av ENC/FH EN2...23 K2
 GDMY/SEVK IG3...73 G4
Primrose Cl BOW E3...105 J1
 CAT SE6...183 F1
 FNCH N3...47 K1
 RYLN/HDSTN HA2...77 K1
 WLGTN SM6...195 G5
Primrose Dr WDR/YW UB7...112 A4
Primrose Gdns BUSH WD23...28 B2
 HAMP NW3...83 J4
 RSLP HA4...77 G5
Primrose HI EMB EC4Y...11 K4
Primrose Hill Rd HAMP NW3...83 K4
Primrose Hill Studios
 CAMTN NW1 *...84 A6
Primrose La CROY/NA CRO...197 K5
Primrose Ms CAMTN NW1 *...83 K5
Primrose Pl ISLW TW7...136 A3
Primrose Rd LEY E10...69 K5
 SWFD E18...53 F5
Primrose Sq HOM E9...86 E5

Primrose St SDTCH EC2A...13 G1
Primrose Wk EW KT17...207 H5
 NWCR SE14...144 B1
Primrose Wy ALP/SUD HA0...97 K1
Primula St SHB W12...99 J6
Prince Albert Rd STJWD NW8...2 C4
Prince Charles Dr HDN NW4...64 A4
Prince Charles Rd
 BKHTH/KID SE3...145 J2
Prince Charles Wy
 WLGTN SM6...210 B1
Prince Consort Dr CHST BR7...185 J4
Prince Consort Rd
 SKENS SW7...14 A4
Princedale Rd NTGHL W11...119 H1
Prince Edward Rd HOM E9...87 H4
Prince George Av
 STHGT/OAK N14...34 C1
Prince George Rd
 STNW/STAM N16...86 A2
Prince George's Av
 RYNPK SW20...177 F5
Prince George's Rd
 WIM/MER SW19...178 C4
Prince Henry Rd CHARL SE7...146 C1
Prince Imperial Rd CHST BR7...185 G3
 WOOL/PLUM SE18...146 E2
Prince John Rd
 ELTH/MOT SE9...146 D6
Princelet St WCHPL E1...13 K1
Prince of Orange La
 GNWCH SE10 *...145 F1
Prince of Wales Cl HDN NW4 *...63 K1
Prince of Wales Dr
 BTSEA SW11...140 D2
 VX/NE SW8...141 G1
Prince of Wales Ga
 SKENS SW7 *...14 C2
Prince of Wales Pas
 CAMTN NW1 *...4 A5
Prince of Wales Rd
 BKHTH/KID SE3...145 J2
 CAN/RD E16...107 G5
 KTTN NW5...84 A4
Prince of Wales Ter
 CHSWK W4...118 B5
 KENS W8 *...120 A2
Prince Regent La
 CAN/RD E16...107 G5
Prince Regent Ms
 CAMTN NW1 *...4 A5
Prince Regent Rd HSLW TW3...135 G4
Prince Rd SNWD SE25...197 F2
Prince Rupert Rd
 ELTH/MOT SE9...146 E5
Princes Av ACT W3...117 H6
 CAR SM5...209 K5
 CDALE/KGS NW9...62 C1
 FNCH N3...47 F4
 MUSWH N10...48 A6
 PLMGR N13...49 G1
 STMC/STPC BR5...201 K2
 SURB KT6...191 H6
 WDGN N22...48 D4
 WFD IG8...39 F6
Princes Cl CDALE/KGS NW9...62 C1
 EDGW HA8...44 C1
 FSBYPK N4...67 H5
 SCUP DA14...168 E5
Prince's Cl HPTN TW12...155 J6
Princes Ct WAP E1W...104 D6
 WBLY HA9...80 A3
Princes Dr HRW HA1...42 F4
Prince's Dr ESH/CLAY KT10...189 J4
Princes Gdns ACT W3...98 C5
 EA W5...97 J3
 SKENS SW7...14 B4
Prince's Ga SKENS SW7...14 B4
Princes Gate Ms SKENS SW7...14 B4
Princes La MUSWH N10...48 A6
Prince's Ms HMSMTH W6 *...118 E5
 HSLW TW3...135 F5
Prince's Ms BAY/PAD W2...100 E6
Princes Pde GLDGN NW11 *...64 C3
 PIN HA5 *...41 H3
Princes Park Av GLDGN NW11...64 C3
 HYS/HAR UB3...94 B6
Princes Park Cir
 HYS/HAR UB3...94 B6
Princes Park Cl HYS/HAR UB3...94 B6
Princes Park La
 HYS/HAR UB3...94 B6
Princes Park Pde
 HYS/HAR UB3...94 B6
Princes Pl NTGHL W11...119 H1
Prince's Pln HAYES BR2...200 D4
Princes Ri LEW SE13...145 F3
Princes Riverside Rd
 BERM/RHTH SE16...124 A1
Princes Rd BARK/HLT IG6...72 D1
 BUSH WD23...28 B1
 FELT TW13...153 J5
 KUTN/CMB KT2...175 H4
 PGE/AN SE20...182 A2
 RCHPK/HAM TW10...137 G6
 ROMW/RG RM1...75 J2
 TEDD TW11...155 H6
 UED N18...36 E6
 WEA W13...116 C1
Prince's Rd MORT/ESHN SW14...138 A4
 RSLP HA4...59 G4
 WIM/MER SW19...177 K2
Princess Alice Wy THMD SE28...127 J2
Princess Av WBLY HA9...62 A6
Princess Crs FSBYPK N4...67 H6
Princesses Pde DART DA1 *...150 C6
Princess La RSLP HA4...58 C5
Princess Louise Cl
 BAY/PAD W2...8 B1
Princess May Rd
 STNW/STAM N16...86 A2
Princess Ms HAMP NW3...83 H4
Princess Pde ORP BR6 *...216 A1

Princess St STHWK SE1...18 B5
Princes St REGST W1B...9 K4
 SUT SM1...209 H2
 TOTM N17...50 A2
 RCH/KEW TW9...137 F5
Prince's Ter PLSTW E13...89 F6
Prince's Yd DEPT SE8...124 C6
Princes Wy BKHH IG9...39 G4
 CROY/NA CRO...211 F3
 RSLP HA4...77 J2
 WIM/MER SW19...159 G2
 WWKM BR4...214 D2
Prince's Yd IS N1...5 H1
 NTGHL W11...119 H1
Princethorpe Rd SYD SE26...164 A6
Princeton St GINN WC1R...11 G2
Pringle Gdns
 STRHM/NOR SW16...161 H6
Printers Inn Ct
 FLST/FETLN EC4A...11 J3
Printinghouse La
 HYS/HAR UB3...113 H2
Printing House Yd BETH E2 *...7 H5
Priolo Rd CHARL SE7...126 B5
Prior Av BELMT SM2...209 J5
Prior Bolton St IS N1...85 H4
Prioress Rd WNWD SE27...162 C5
Prioress St STHWK SE1...19 F5
Prior Rd IL IG1...90 A1
Priors Cft WALTH E17...51 G5
Priors Fld NTHLT UB5...77 J4
Priorsford Av
 STMC/STPC BR5...202 B1
Priors Gdns RSLP HA4...77 G3
Priors Md EN EN1...24 A2
Prior St GNWCH SE10...145 F1
Priory Av ALP/SUD HA0...79 G1
 CEND/HSY/T N8...66 D1
 CHEAM SM3...208 B2
 CHING E4...37 H5
 CHSWK W4...118 B4
 STMC/STPC BR5...201 J3
 WALTH E17...69 J2
Priory Cl ALP/SUD HA0...79 F2
 BECK BR3...182 B6
 CHING E4...37 H5
 CHST BR7...184 E4
 FNCH N3...46 D6
 HPTN TW12...172 E4
 HYS/HAR UB3...95 F6
 RSLP HA4...58 D5
 STAN HA7...29 F5
 STHGT/OAK N14...32 D2
 SWFD E18...52 E4
 TRDG/WHET N20...32 D2
 WAN E11 *...70 C3
Priory Cots EA W5 *...98 B4
Priory Ct BLKFR EC4V *...12 B4
 VX/NE SW8...141 J2
 WALTH E17...51 H5
Priory Crs ALP/SUD HA0...79 G1
 CHEAM SM3...208 B2
 NRWD SE19...180 D3
Priory Dr ABYW SE2...128 E5
 STAN HA7...29 F5
Priory Field Dr EDGW HA8...30 D6
Priory Gdns ALP/SUD HA0...79 G2
 BARN SW13...138 C4
 CHSWK W4...118 B4
 HGT N6...66 B3
 HPTN TW12...172 E4
 SNWD SE25...197 G1
Priory Green Est IS N1...5 G2
Priory Gv VX/NE SW8...141 K2
Priory Hl ALP/SUD HA0...79 G2
Priory La E/WMO/HCT KT8...189 F1
 PUT/ROE SW15...138 C6
Priory Leas ELTH/MOT SE9...166 D3
Priory Ms BKHTH/KID SE3...145 J4
Priory Park Rd ALP/SUD HA0...79 G2
 KIL/WHAMP NW6...82 D6
Priory Rd BARK IG11...90 D5
 CEND/HSY/T N8...66 D1
 CHEAM SM3...208 B2
 CHSGTN KT9...206 A1
 CHSWK W4...118 A3
 CROY/NA CRO...196 A4
 EHAM E6...89 H6
 HPTN TW12...172 E3
 HSLW TW3...135 H6
 KIL/WHAMP NW6...83 F5
 MUSWH N10...48 A4
 RCH/KEW TW9...117 H6
Priory St BOW E3...105 K2
Priory Ter KIL/WHAMP NW6...83 F6
The Priory BKHTH/KID SE3...145 J4
 CROY/NA CRO *...211 H2
 EDGW HA8 *...30 C6
Priory Vw BUSH WD23...28 D3
Priory Vls FBAR/BDGN N11 *...47 K2
Priory Wk WBPTN SW10...120 B5
Priory Wy NWDGN UB2...114 C3
 RYLN/HDSTN HA2...60 B1
 WDR/YW UB7...112 A6
Pritchard's Rd BETH E2...104 C1
Priter Rd BERM/RHTH SE16...123 H3
Private Rd EN EN1...23 K6
Probert Rd BRXS/STRHM SW2...142 B6
Probyn Rd BRXS/STRHM SW2...162 C4
Procter St HHOL WC1V...11 G2
Proctor Cl MTCM CR4...179 F4
Proctors Cl EBED/NFELT TW14...153 K3
Progress Wy CROY/NA CRO...196 A6
 EN EN1...24 C4
 WDGN N22...49 G4
Promenade Approach Rd
 CHSWK W4...138 B2
The Promenade CHSWK W4...138 B2
 EDGW HA8 *...44 C1
Prospect Cl BELV DA17...129 H4
 BUSH WD23...28 D2
 HSLW TW3...134 E2
 RSLP HA4...59 H4
 SYD SE26...163 J6
Prospect Cots
 WAND/EARL SW18...139 K5
Prospect Crs WHTN TW2...155 H1
Prospect HI WALTH E17...69 K1

Prospect Pl CHSWK W4...118 A5
 CRICK NW2...89 F6
 CRW RM5...56 E5
 EFNCH N2...65 H1
 HAYES BR2...199 J5
 RYNPK SW20...176 E3
 WAP E1W...123 K1
Prospect Ring EFNCH N2...65 H1
Prospect Rd BAR EN5...20 E5
 CRICK NW2...64 B3
 SURB KT6...190 D3
 WFD IG8...53 G1
Prospect St BERM/RHTH SE16...123 J3
Prospect V WOOL/PLUM SE18...126 D4
Prospero Rd ARCH N19...66 D5
Protea Cl CAN/RD E16...106 D3
Prothero Gdns HDN NW4...63 K2
Prothero Rd FUL/PGN SW6...139 H1
Prout Gv WLSDN NW10...81 G2
Prout Rd CLPT E5...86 D1
Provence St IS N1...6 C2
Providence Av
 RYLN/HDSTN HA2...60 A5
Providence Ct HAM E9 *...87 F6
Providence Ct
 MYFR/PKLN W1K...9 H5
Providence La HYS/HAR UB3...133 G1
Providence Pl CRW RM5...56 B4
 IS N1...6 A1
Providence Rd WDR/YW UB7...112 B1
Providence Row BETH E2...104 D2
Providence Sq STHWK SE1...19 G2
Providence Yd BETH E2 *...104 C2
Provincial Ter PGE/AN SE20 *...182 A3
Provost Est IS N1...6 E4
Provost Rd HAMP NW3...83 K5
Provost St IS N1...6 E5
Prowse Av BUSH WD23...28 B4
Prowse Pl CAMTN NW1...84 C5
Prudence La ORP BR6...216 A2
Pruden Cl STHGT/OAK N14 *...34 C4
Prusom St WAP E1W...123 J1
Pucknells Cl SWLY BR8...187 K4
Pudding La MON EC3R...13 F5
Pudding Mill La SRTFD E15...87 K6
Puddle Dock BLKFR EC4V...12 B5
Puffin Cl BARK IG11...109 H2
 BECK BR3...198 A2
Pulborough Rd
 WAND/EARL SW18...159 J2
Pulford Rd SEVS/STOTM N15...67 K3
Pulham Av EFNCH N2...65 G1
Puller Rd BAR EN5...20 B3
Pulleyns Av EHAM E6...107 J2
Pullman Gdns PUT/ROE SW15...159 F1
Pullman Ms LEE/GVPK SE12...166 A5
Pullman Pl ELTH/MOT SE9...146 D5
Pulross Rd BRXN/ST SW9...142 A4
Pulteney Cl BOW E3...87 H6
 ISLW TW7 *...136 D4
Pulteney Rd SWFD E18...53 F6
Pulton Pl FUL/PGN SW6...139 K1
Puma Ct WCHPL E1...13 J1
Pump Al BTFD TW8...136 E1
Pump Cl NTHLT UB5...96 A1
Pump Ct EMB EC4Y...11 J4
Pump House Cl HAYES BR2...215 J5
Pump House Ms WCHPL E1 *...104 C6
Pumping Station Rd
 CHSWK W4...138 B1
Pump La HYS/HAR UB3...113 K2
 NWCR SE14...143 K1
Punchard Crs PEND EN3...25 K1
Punderson's Gdns BETH E2...104 D2
Purbeck Av NWMAL KT3...192 C3
Purbeck Dr CRICK NW2...64 B6
Purbeck Rd EMPK RM11...75 J3
Purbrook St STHWK SE1...19 H4
Purcell Crs FUL/PGN SW6...139 G1
Purcell Ms WLSDN NW10...81 G5
Purcell St IS N1...7 G2
Purchese St CAMTN NW1...4 C2
Purdy St BOW E3...105 K3
Purelake Ms LEW SE13 *...145 G4
Purkis Cl UX/CGN UB8...94 A4
Purland Cl BCTR RM8...74 B5
Purland Rd THMD SE28...128 A3
Purleigh Av WFD IG8...53 J2
Purley Av CRICK NW2...64 C6
Purley Cl CLAY IG5...54 A5
Purley Pl IS N1 *...85 H5
Purley Rd ED N9...35 K5
 SAND/SEL CR2...211 K6
Purley Wy CROY/NA CRO...196 A6
Purneys Rd ELTH/MOT SE9...146 C5
Purrett Rd WOOL/PLUM SE18...128 A5
Pursers Cross Rd
 FUL/PGN SW6...139 J2
Pursewardens Cl WEA W13...116 D1
Pursley Rd MLHL NW7...45 K3
Purves Rd WLSDN NW10...99 K2
Putney Bridge Ap
 FUL/PGN SW6...139 H4
Putney Bridge Rd
 PUT/ROE SW15...139 H5
Putney Common
 PUT/ROE SW15...139 F4
Putney Ex PUT/ROE SW15 *...139 G5
Putney Heath PUT/ROE SW15...158 E1
Putney Heath La
 PUT/ROE SW15...159 G1
Putney High St
 PUT/ROE SW15...139 G5
Putney HI PUT/ROE SW15...159 F2
Putney Park Av
 PUT/ROE SW15...138 D5
Putney Park La
 PUT/ROE SW15...139 F5
Puttenham Cl OXHEY WD19...27 G5
Pycombe Cnr
 NFNCH/WDSPK N12...32 D6
Pycroft Wy ED N9...36 C6
Pylbrook Rd SUT SM1...208 E1
Pylon Wy CROY/NA CRO...195 K5

Pym Cl EBAR EN4...21 H6
Pymers Md DUL SE21...162 D3
Pymmes Brook Trail
 EBAR EN4...33 K2
Pymmes Cl PLMGR N13...49 F1
 TOTM N17...50 D4
Pymmes Gdns North ED N9...36 B5
Pymmes Gdns South ED N9...36 B5
Pymmes Green Rd
 FBAR/BDGN N11...34 B6
Pymmes Rd PLMGR N13...48 E2
Pymms Brook Dr EBAR EN4...21 J5
Pyne Rd SURB KT6...191 H5
Pynham Cl ABYW SE2...128 B3
Pynnacles Cl STAN HA7...43 H2
Pyrland Rd HBRY N5...85 K3
 RCHPK/HAM TW10...157 G1
Pyrmont Gv WNWD SE27...162 C5
Pyrmont Rd CHSWK W4...117 H6
Pytchley Crs NRWD SE19...180 D2
Pytchley Rd EDUL SE22...143 F4

Q

The Quadrangle BAY/PAD W2...8 C3
 HNHL SE24 *...142 D6
 WBPTN SW10 *...140 B2
Quadrant Ar REGST W1B...10 B6
Quadrant Cl HDN NW4 *...63 K2
Quadrant Gv KTTN NW5...83 K3
Quadrant Rd RCH/KEW TW9...136 E6
 THHTH CR7...196 C1
Quad Rd WBLY HA9...79 K1
Quainton St WLSDN NW10...81 F1
Quaker La NWDGN UB2...115 F3
Quakers Course
 CDALE/KGS NW9...45 H4
Quakers La ISLW TW7...136 B3
Quakers Pl FSTGT E7...89 H3
Quaker St WCHPL E1...7 J7
Quakers Wk WCHMH N21...35 K1
Quality Ct LINN WC2A...11 J3
Quantock Cl HYS/HAR UB3...133 G1
Quantock Gdns CRICK NW2...64 B6
Quantock Ms PECK SE15...143 H3
Quarles Cl CRW RM5...56 C2
Quarles Park Rd CHDH RM6...73 H3
Quarrendon St FUL/PGN SW6...139 K2
Quarr Rd CAR SM5...194 C3
Quarry Ms PUR RM19...131 K4
Quarry Park Rd SUT SM1...208 D4
Quarry Ri SUT SM1...208 D4
Quarry Rd WAND/EARL SW18...160 B1
Quarter Ports CHING E4...52 B1
Quay House POP/IOD E14 *...124 D2
Quayside Ms MBLAR W1H...9 F4
Quebec Rd GNTH/NBYPK IG2...72 C4
 YEAD UB4...95 G6
Quebec Wy BERM/RHTH SE16...124 A2
Queen Adelaide Rd
 PGE/AN SE20...181 K2
Queen Anne Dr
 ESH/CLAY KT10...204 E5
Queen Anne Ga BXLYHN DA7...148 E4
Queen Anne Ms
 CAVSQ/HST W1G...9 K2
Queen Anne Rd HOM E9...87 F4
Queen Anne's Cl WHTN TW2...155 J5
Queen Anne's Gdns
 CHSWK W4...118 B3
 EA W5...117 F2
 EN EN1...36 A4
 MTCM CR4...178 E6
Queen Anne's Ga
 STJSPK SW1H...16 C5
Queen Anne's Gv CHSWK W4...118 B3
 EA W5...117 F2
 EN EN1...35 K4
Queen Anne's Pl EN EN1...36 A4
Queen Anne St
 CAVSQ/HST W1G...9 J2
Queen Anne Ter WAP E1W *...104 D6
Queen Borough Gdns
 CHST BR7...185 J2
Queenborough Gdns
 GNTH/NBYPK IG2...72 A4
Queen Caroline Est
 HMSMTH W6...119 F5
Queen Caroline St
 HMSMTH W6...119 F5
Queen Elizabeth Blds
 EMB EC4Y *...11 J5
Queen Elizabeth College
 GNWCH SE10 *...145 F1
Queen Elizabeth Gdns
 MRDN SM4...193 K1
Queen Elizabeth's Cl
 KUTN/CMB KT2...175 C1
 WALTH E17...51 G6
Queen Elizabeth's Dr
 STHGT/OAK N14...34 E2
Queen Elizabeth St
 STHWK SE1...19 H2
Queen Elizabeth's Wk
 STNW/STAM N16...67 K4
 WLGTN SM6...210 D3
Queen Elizabeth Wk
 BARN SW13...138 E2
Queenhithe BLKFR EC4V...12 D5
Queen Isabella Wy STBT EC1A...12 B2
Queen Margaret's Gv IS N1...86 A3
Queen Mary Av MRDN SM4...193 G2
Queen Mary Cl ROM RM1...75 G2
 SURB KT6...206 A2
Queen Mary Rd NRWD SE19...180 B2
Queen Mary's Av CAR SM5...209 K5

Queen Mother Ga
MYFR/PICC W1J 15 H1
Queens Acre CHEAM SM3 208 B5
Queens Av FELT TW13 154 B6
KTN/HRWW/WS HA3 43 H6
MUSWH N10 48 A6
TRDG/WHET N20 33 H4
Queen's Av FNCH N3 47 G3
GFD/PVL UB6 96 B5
WCHMH N21 35 H3
WFD IG8 53 F1
Queensberry Ms West
SKENS SW7 * 14 A6
Queensberry Pl MNPK E12 89 H3
SKENS SW7 14 A6
Queensberry Wy
SKENS SW7 * 14 A6
Queensborough Ms
BAY/PAD W2 * 101 G6
Queensborough Studios
BAY/PAD W2 * 101 F6
Queensborough Ter
BAY/PAD W2 101 F6
Queensbridge Pk ISLW TW7 155 K1
Queensbridge Rd HACK E8 7 K1
Queensbury Rd ALP/SUD HA0 98 B1
CDALE/KGS NW9 63 F4
Queensbury St IS N1 85 J5
Queens Circ VX/NE SW8 141 G1
Queens Cl ESH/CLAY KT10 * 204 B2
Queen's Cl EDGW HA8 44 C1
WLGTN SM6 210 B3
Queen's Club Gdns
WKENS W14 119 H6
Queens Club Ter
WKENS W14 * 119 J6
ueenscourt WBLY HA9 80 A2
ueens Crs
RCHPK/HAM TW10 137 G6
Queen's Crs KTTN NW5 84 A3
ueenscroft Rd
ELTH/MOT SE9 146 C6
ueensdale Crs NTGHL W11 119 G1
ueensdale Pl NTGHL W11 119 H1
ueensdale Rd NTGHL W11 119 G1
ueensdale Wk NTGHL W11 119 H1
ueens Down Rd CLPT E5 86 D2
ueens Dr BRYLDS KT5 191 H4
LEY E10 69 J4
ueen's Dr EA W5 98 B5
FSBYPK N4 67 H6
THDIT KT7 190 B3
ueen's Elm Sq WBPTN SW10 120 C5
ueens Gdns HDN NW4 64 A2
RAIN RM13 111 F1
ueen's Gdns BAY/PAD W2 101 G6
EA W5 97 J4
HEST TW5 134 D2
ueens Garth FSTH SE23 * 163 K4
ueen's Ga SKENS SW7 14 A7
ueens Gate Gdns CHST BR7 185 J4
ueensgate Gdns
PUT/ROE SW15 138 E5
ueen's Gate Gdns
SKENS SW7 120 B3
ueen's Gate Ms SKENS SW7 120 B3
ueensgate Pl
KIL/WHAMP NW6 82 E5
een's Gate Pl SKENS SW7 * 120 B3
een's Gate Place Ms
SKENS SW7 * 120 B4
een's Gate Ter
SKENS SW7 * 120 B3
een's Gv STJWD NW8 2 A1
een's Grove Rd CHING E4 38 B3
een's Head St IS N1 6 B1
eens Keep TWK TW1 * 156 D1
eensland Av UED N18 49 J2
WIM/MER SW19 178 A4
eensland Cl WALTH E17 51 H5
eensland Rd HOLWY N7 85 G2
eens La MUSWH N10 48 B6
eens Md EDGW HA8 44 B2
eensmead STJWD NW8 83 H6
een's Mead Rd HAYES BR2 183 J5
eensmere Cl
WIM/MER SW19 159 G4
eensmere Rd
WIM/MER SW19 159 G4
eensmill Rd FUL/PGN SW6 139 G1
eens Pde
CEND/HSY/T N8 * 67 H1
CRICK NW2 * 82 A4
EA W5 * 98 B5
FBAR/BDGN N11 * 47 K1
HDN NW4 * 63 K2
eens Parade Cl
FBAR/BDGN N11 47 K1
eens Park Gdns
FELT TW13 * 153 J5
en's Pl MRDN SM4 193 K1
ens Prom KUT/HW KT1 190 E1
en Sq BMSBY WC1N 5 F7
en's Ride PUT/ROE SW15 138 D5
en's Ri RCHPK/HAM TW10 157 G1
ens Rd BAR EN5 20 B4
YS/HAR UB3 94 C5
RDN SM4 193 K1
DR/YW UB7 112 C2
en's Rd BARK IG11 90 C5
ECK BR3 182 B5
KHH IG9 39 F4
MLY BR1 183 K5
HST BR7 185 G2
ROY/NA CR0 196 C3
A W5 98 A5
D N9 36 D4
N EN1 24 A5
BAR/BDGN N11 48 E3
ELT TW13 154 A3
NCH N3 47 G4
DN NW4 64 A2
PTN TW12 155 G6
SLW TW3 135 G4
UTN/CMB KT2 175 H3
ORT/ESHN SW14 138 A4
TCM CR4 178 C6
WDGN UB2 114 C2
WMAL KT3 192 C1
ECK SE15 143 K2

PLSTW E13 89 F6
RCHPK/HAM TW10 175 H1
TEDD TW11 174 A2
THDIT KT7 190 A2
TWK TW1 156 A3
WALTH E17 69 H3
WAN E11 70 C4
WELL DA16 148 C3
WIM/MER SW19 177 K2
WLGTN SM6 210 B3
Queen's Rd West PLSTW E13 106 E1
Queen's Rw WALW SE17 122 E6
Queens Ter ISLW TW7 136 B5
PLSTW E13 89 F6
THDIT KT7 * 190 B3
WCHPL E1 * 104 E3
Queen's Ter ISLW TW7 136 B5
STJWD NW8 2 A1
Queens Terrace Cots
HNWL W7 * 115 K2
Queensthorpe Ms SYD SE26 * 164 A6
Queensthorpe Rd SYD SE26 164 A6
Queenstown Gdns
RAIN RM13 111 H2
Queenstown Rd VX/NE SW8 141 G3
Queen St CROY/NA CR0 211 J2
ERITH DA8 * 130 B6
MYFR/PICC W1J 9 J7
ROMW/RG RM7 75 F3
STP EC4M 12 D4
TOTM N17 50 A2
Queen Street Pl CANST EC4R 12 D6
Queensville Rd BAL SW12 161 J2
Queens Wk ASHF TW15 152 A6
CDALE/KGS NW9 62 E6
CHING E4 38 B3
HRW HA1 60 E1
RSLP HA4 77 G1
Queen's Wk EA W5 97 J3
Queens Walk Ter RSLP HA4 * 77 G1
The Queens Wk STHWK SE1 13 H7
Queens Wy FELT TW13 154 B6
HDN NW4 64 A2
Queensway BAY/PAD W2 101 F5
CROY/NA CR0 211 F4
PEND EN3 24 E5
STMC/STPC BR5 201 H2
SUN TW16 172 A5
WWKM BR4 214 E2
Queens Well Av
TRDG/WHET N20 33 J6
Queen's Whf HMSMTH W6 119 F5
Queenswood Av HPTN TW12 173 G2
HSLW TW3 134 E3
THHTH CR7 196 B2
WALTH E17 52 A4
WLGTN SM6 210 D2
Queenswood Gdns WAN E11 70 E5
Queenswood Pk FNCH N3 46 C5
Queenswood Rd
BFN/LL DA15 148 A6
FSTH SE23 164 B5
Queen's Wood Rd HGT N6 66 B3
Queen's Yd FITZ W1T 4 B7
Queen Victoria Av
ALP/SUD HA0 79 K5
Queen Victoria St
BLKFR EC4V 12 A5
Queen Victoria Ter
WAP E1W * 104 D6
Quemerford Rd HOLWY N7 85 F3
Quentin Pl LEW SE13 145 H4
Quentin Rd LEW SE13 145 H4
Quernmore Cl BMLY BR1 183 K2
Quernmore Rd BMLY BR1 183 K2
FSBYPK N4 67 G3
Querrin St FUL/PGN SW6 140 B3
Questor DART DA1 * 171 J4
Quex Ms KIL/WHAMP NW6 82 E6
Quex Rd KIL/WHAMP NW6 82 E6
Quick Rd CHSWK W4 118 B5
Quicks Rd WIM/MER SW19 178 A3
Quick St IS N1 6 B3
Quickswood HAMP NW3 83 J5
Quiet Nook HAYES BR2 215 H1
Quill St EA W5 98 A2
FSBYPK N4 85 G1
Quilp St STHWK SE1 18 C2
Quilter Rd STMC/STPC BR5 202 E5
Quilters Pl ELTH/MOT SE9 167 H3
Quilter St BETH E2 104 C2
WOOL/PLUM SE18 128 A5
Quince Rd LEW SE13 144 E3
Quinnel Cl WOOL/PLUM SE18 128 A5
Quinnell Cl WOOL/PLUM SE18 128 A5
Quintin Av RYNPK SW20 177 H4
Quinton Cl BECK BR3 183 F6
HEST TW5 134 A1
WLGTN SM6 210 B2
Quinton Rd THDIT KT7 190 B5
Quinton St WAND/EARL SW18 160 B4
Quixley St POP/IOD E14 106 B6
Quorn Rd EDUL SE22 143 F5

R

Rabbit Rw KENS W8 * 119 K1
Rabbits Rd MNPK E12 89 J2
Rabournmead Dr NTHLT UB5 77 J3
Raby Rd NWMAL KT3 192 A1
Raby St POP/IOD E14 * 105 G5
Raccoon Wy HSLWW TW4 134 B3
Rachel Cl BARK/HLT IG6 72 D1
Rackham Cl WELL DA16 148 C3
Rackham Ms
STRHM/NOR SW16 179 H2
Racton Rd FUL/PGN SW6 119 K6
Radbourne Av EA W5 116 D4
Radbourne Cl CLPT E5 87 F2
Radbourne Ct
KTN/HRWW/WS HA3 * 61 H3
Radbourne Crs WALTH E17 52 B6
Radbourne Rd BAL SW12 161 H2
Radcliffe Av ENC/FH EN2 23 J2
WLSDN NW10 99 J1
Radcliffe Gdns CAR SM5 209 J5
Radcliffe Rd CROY/NA CR0 197 G6

KTN/HRWW/WS HA3 43 G5
STHWK SE1 19 H4
WCHMH N21 35 H3
Radcliffe Sq PUT/ROE SW15 159 G1
Radcliffe Wy NTHLT UB5 95 H2
Radcot St LBTH SE11 122 B5
Raddington Rd NKENS W10 100 C4
Radfield Wy BFN/LL DA15 167 J2
Radford Est WLSDN NW10 * 99 G2
Radford Rd LEW SE13 165 F1
Radford Wy BARK IG11 109 F2
Radipole Rd FUL/PGN SW6 139 J2
Radius Pk
EBED/NFELT TW14 * 133 J5
Radland Rd CAN/RD E16 106 E5
Radlet Av SYD SE26 163 J5
Radlett Cl FSTGT E7 88 D4
Radlett Pl STJWD NW8 2 C1
Radley Av GDMY/SEVK IG3 91 F2
Radley Cl EBED/NFELT TW14 153 J3
Radley Ct BERM/RHTH SE16 124 A2
Radley Gdns
KTN/HRWW/WS HA3 62 A1
Radley Ms KENS W8 119 K3
Radley Rd TOTM N17 50 A5
Radley's La SWFD E18 52 E5
Radleys Md DAGE RM10 92 D4
Radley Sq CLPT E5 * 68 E6
Radley Ter CAN/RD E16 106 D4
Radlix Rd LEY E10 69 J5
Radnor Av HRW HA1 60 E2
WELL DA16 148 C6
Radnor Cl CHST BR7 185 K2
MTCM CR4 195 K2
Radnor Crs REDBR IG4 71 K2
WOOL/PLUM SE18 148 B1
Radnor Gdns EN EN1 24 A2
TWK TW1 156 A4
Radnor Ms BAY/PAD W2 8 B4
Radnor Pl BAY/PAD W2 8 C4
Radnor Rd HRW HA1 60 D2
KIL/WHAMP NW6 82 C6
PECK SE15 143 H1
TWK TW1 156 A3
Radnor St FSBYE EC1V 6 D5
Radnor Ter WKENS W14 119 J4
Radnor Wk CHEL SW3 120 D5
CROY/NA CR0 198 B4
Radnor Wy WLSDN NW10 98 D3
Radstock Av
KTN/HRWW/WS HA3 43 G6
Radstock Cl FBAR/BDGN N11 48 A1
Radstock St BTSEA SW11 * 140 D1
Raeburn Av BRYLDS KT5 191 J4
Raeburn Cl GLDGN NW11 65 G3
KUT/HW KT1 174 E3
Raeburn Rd BFN/LL DA15 167 K1
EDGW HA8 44 C5
YEAD UB4 94 B1
Raeburn St BRXS/STRHM SW2 141 K5
Rafford Wy BMLY BR1 184 A5
Raggleswood CHST BR7 185 F4
Raglan Cl HSLWW TW4 134 D6
Raglan Ct SAND/SEL CR2 211 H3
Raglan Gdns OXHEY WD19 27 F3
Raglan Rd BELV DA17 129 G4
EN EN1 36 A2
HAYES BR2 200 B1
WALTH E17 70 A2
WOOL/PLUM SE18 127 H5
Raglan St KTTN NW5 84 B4
Raglan Ter
RYLN/HDSTN HA2 * 78 B2
Raglan Vls WALTH E17 * 70 A2
Raglan Wy NTHLT UB5 78 C4
Ragley Cl ACT W3 117 K2
Raider Cl ROMW/RG RM7 56 D4
Railey Ms KTTN NW5 84 C3
Railshead Rd ISLW TW7 136 C5
Railton Rd HNHL SE24 142 B6
Railway Ap FSBYPK N4 67 G3
HRW HA1 61 F1
STHWK SE1 12 E7
TWK TW1 156 B2
WLGTN SM6 * 210 B4
Railway Ar BRXN/ST SW9 * 142 B5
Railway Av BERM/RHTH SE16 123 K2
Railway Cots HMSMTH W6 * 119 F2
SRTFD E15 * 106 C1
WIM/MER SW19 * 160 A6
Railway Gv NWCR SE14 144 C1
Railway Pl BELV DA17 129 H3
Railway Ri EDUL SE22 143 F5
Railway Rd TEDD TW11 155 K6
Railway Side BARN SW13 138 B4
Railway Station Whf
LEY E10 * 69 G5
Railway St CHDH RM6 73 J5
IS N1 5 F3
Railway Ter FELT TW13 153 K3
LEW SE13 144 E6
WALTH E17 52 A4
Rainborough Cl WBLY HA9 80 E4
Rainbow Av POP/IOD E14 124 E5
Rainbow Ct OXHEY WD19 27 G1
Rainbow Quay
BERM/RHTH SE16 124 B3
Rainbow St CMBW SE5 143 F1
Raine St WAP E1W 123 J1
Rainham Cl BTSEA SW11 160 D1
ELTH/MOT SE9 167 K1
Rainham Rd RAIN RM13 111 J2
WLSDN NW10 100 A2
Rainham Rd North
DAGE RM10 74 D6
Rainham Rd South
DAGE RM10 92 E4
Rainhill Wy BOW E3 105 J2
Rainsborough Av DEPT SE8 124 B4
Rainsford Rd WLSDN NW10 98 C2
Rainsford St BAY/PAD W2 8 C3
Rainsford Wy HCH RM12 75 J5
Rainville Rd HMSMTH W6 119 F6
Raisins Hl PIN HA5 41 F6
Raith Av STHGT/OAK N14 34 D5
Raleigh Av WLGTN SM6 210 D2
YEAD UB4 95 F4
Raleigh Cl ERITH DA8 130 C6
HDN NW4 64 A2
PIN HA5 59 H4

RSLP HA4 58 D6
Raleigh Dr BRYLDS KT5 191 K5
ESH/CLAY KT10 204 D3
TRDG/WHET N20 33 J5
Raleigh Gdns
BRXS/STRHM SW2 162 A1
MTCM CR4 178 E5
Raleigh Ms IS N1 6 B1
ORP BR6 217 F3
Raleigh Rd CEND/HSY/T N8 67 G1
ENC/FH EN2 23 K5
FELT TW13 153 J4
NWDGN UB2 114 D5
PGE/AN SE20 182 A3
RCH/KEW TW9 137 G4
Raleigh St IS N1 6 B1
Raleigh Wy FELT TW13 172 B1
STHGT/OAK N14 34 D3
Ralph Perring Ct BECK BR3 198 D1
Ralston St CHEL SW3 120 E5
Ralston Wy OXHEY WD19 27 H4
Rama Cl STRHM/NOR SW16 179 K3
Ramac Wy CHARL SE7 126 A4
Rama La NRWD SE19 181 G3
Rambler Cl STRHM/NOR SW16 161 H6
Rame Cl TOOT SW17 179 F1
Ramillies Cl BRXS/STRHM SW2 161 K1
Ramillies Pl SOHO/CST W1F 10 A4
Ramillies Rd BFN/LL DA15 168 C1
CHSWK W4 118 A3
MLHL NW7 31 G4
Ramillies St SOHO/SHAV W1D 10 A4
Ramones Ter MTCM CR4 * 195 H1
Rampart St WCHPL E1 104 D5
Ram Pas KUT/HW KT1 174 E5
Rampayne St PIM SW1V 121 J5
Rampton Cl CHING E4 37 J5
Ramsay Gdns HARH RM3 57 K4
Ramsay Rd ACT W3 117 K3
FSTGT E7 88 D2
Ramscroft Cl ED N9 36 A2
Ramsdale Rd TOOT SW17 179 F1
Ramsden Cl STMC/STPC BR5 202 D5
Ramsden Dr CRW RM5 56 C3
Ramsden Ga BAL SW12 * 161 G2
Ramsden Rd BAL SW12 161 F2
FBAR/BDGN N11 47 K1
ORP BR6 202 C4
STMC/STPC BR5 202 D5
Ramsey Cl CDALE/KGS NW9 63 H3
GFD/PVL UB6 78 D3
Ramsey Rd THHTH CR7 196 A3
Ramsey St BETH E2 104 C3
Ramsey Wk IS N1 85 K4
Ramsey Wy STHGT/OAK N14 34 C2
Ramsgate Cl CAN/RD E16 126 A1
Ramsgate St HACK E8 * 86 B4
Ramsgill Ap GNTH/NBYPK IG2 73 F1
Ramsgill Dr GNTH/NBYPK IG2 73 F2
Rams Gv CHDH RM6 74 A1
Ramulis Dr YEAD UB4 95 J3
Ramus Wood Av ORP BR6 216 E3
Rancliffe Gdns ELTH/MOT SE9 146 D5
Rancliffe Rd EHAM E6 107 J1
Randall Av CRICK NW2 63 G6
Randall Cl BTSEA SW11 140 D2
ERITH DA8 129 K6
Randall Pl GNWCH SE10 145 F1
Randall Rd LBTH SE11 122 A5
Randall Rw LBTH SE11 17 G7
Randell's Rd IS N1 84 E6
Randisbourne Gdns CAT SE6 * 164 E5
Randle Rd RCHPK/HAM TW10 156 D6
Randlesdown Rd CAT SE6 164 D6
Randolf Rd HAYES BR2 200 E5
Randolph Ap CAN/RD E16 107 G5
Randolph Av MV/WKIL W9 101 F1
Randolph Cl KUTN/CMB KT2 * 175 K1
Randolph Crs MV/WKIL W9 101 G3
Randolph Gdns
KIL/WHAMP NW6 101 F1
Randolph Gv CHDH RM6 73 J2
Randolph Ms MV/WKIL W9 101 G3
Randolph Rd MV/WKIL W9 101 G3
STHL UB1 * 114 E2
WALTH E17 * 69 K2
Randon Cl RYLN/HDSTN HA2 42 B5
Ranelagh Av BARN SW13 138 D3
Ranelagh Cl EDGW HA8 30 C6
Ranelagh Dr EDGW HA8 30 C6
TWK TW1 136 C5
Ranelagh Gdns CHSWK W4 137 K1
FUL/PGN SW6 139 H4
IL IG1 72 A5
WAN E11 71 G2
Ranelagh Gv BGVA SW1W 121 F5
Ranelagh Pl NWMAL KT3 192 B2
Ranelagh Rd ALP/SUD HA0 79 K3
EA W5 116 E2
EHAM E6 90 A6
PIM SW1V 121 H5
SRTFD E15 88 C6
STHL UB1 114 C1
TOTM N17 50 A6
WAN E11 88 C2
WDGN N22 49 F4
WLSDN NW10 99 H1
Ranfurly Rd SUT SM1 193 K6
Rangefield Rd BMLY BR1 183 H1
Rangemoor Rd
SEVS/STOTM N15 68 B2
Rangers Rd BKHH IG9 38 E2
Rangeworth Pl BFN/LL DA15 168 A5
Rangoon St TWRH EC3N * 13 J4
Rankin Cl CDALE/KGS NW9 45 G6
Ranmere St BAL SW12 161 G3
Ranmoor Cl HRW HA1 60 D1
Ranmoor Gdns HRW HA1 60 D1
Ranmore Av CROY/NA CR0 212 B1
Ranmore Pth STMC/STPC BR5 202 B1
Ranmore Rd BELMT SM2 208 B6
Rannoch Cl EDGW HA8 30 D4
Rannoch Rd HMSMTH W6 119 F6
Rannock Av CDALE/KGS NW9 63 F4
Ransom Cl OXHEY WD19 27 G2
Ransom Rd CHARL SE7 * 126 B5
Ranston St CAMTN NW1 8 C1
Ranulf Rd CRICK NW2 82 D2
Ranwell Cl BOW E3 * 87 H6
Ranworth Rd ED N9 36 E4

Ranyard Cl CHSGTN KT9 206 B1
Raphael Av ROM RM1 57 H6
Raphael Cl KUT/HW KT1 190 E1
Raphael Dr THDIT KT7 190 A5
Raphael St SKENS SW7 14 E3
Rapier Cl PUR RM19 131 J4
Rasper Rd TRDG/WHET N20 33 G4
Rastell Av BRXS/STRHM SW2 161 J4
Ratcliffe Cross St WCHPL E1 * 105 F5
Ratcliffe La POP/IOD E14 105 G5
Ratcliff Rd FSTGT E7 89 G3
Rathbone Market
CAN/RD E16 * 106 D4
Rathbone Pl FITZ W1T 10 C2
Rathbone Sq CROY/NA CR0 * 211 J2
Rathbone St CAN/RD E16 106 D4
FITZ W1T 10 B2
Rathcoole Av
CEND/HSY/T N8 67 F2
Rathcoole Gdns
CEND/HSY/T N8 67 F2
Rathfern Rd CAT SE6 164 C3
Rathgar Av WEA W13 116 C1
Rathgar Cl FNCH N3 46 D5
Rathgar Rd BRXN/ST SW9 142 C4
Rathmell Dr CLAP SW4 161 J1
Rathmore Rd CHARL SE7 126 A5
Rattray Rd BRXS/STRHM SW2 142 B5
Raul Rd PECK SE15 143 H3
Raveley St KTTN NW5 84 C2
Ravencroft Crs
ELTH/MOT SE9 166 E5
Ravenet St BTSEA SW11 141 G2
Ravenfield Rd TOOT SW17 160 E5
Ravenhill Rd PLSTW E13 89 G6
Ravenna Rd PUT/ROE SW15 139 G6
Ravenoak Wy CHIG IG7 54 E1
Ravenor Park Rd
GFD/PVL UB6 96 B2
Raven Rd SWFD E18 53 G5
Raven Rw WCHPL E1 104 D4
Ravens Ait SURB KT6 * 190 E2
Ravensbourne Av HAYES BR2 183 G4
STWL/WRAY TW19 152 B3
Ravensbourne Gdns CLAY IG5 54 A4
WEA W13 97 H4
Ravensbourne Pk CAT SE6 164 D2
Ravensbourne Park Crs
CAT SE6 164 C2
Ravensbourne Pl LEW SE13 144 E3
Ravensbourne Rd BMLY BR1 183 K6
CAT SE6 164 C2
DART DA1 150 D4
TWK TW1 156 D1
Ravensbury Av MRDN SM4 194 B2
Ravensbury Gv MTCM CR4 194 C1
Ravensbury La MTCM CR4 194 C1
Ravensbury Rd
STMC/STPC BR5 202 A1
WAND/EARL SW18 160 A4
Ravensbury Ter
WAND/EARL SW18 160 A4
Ravenscar Rd BMLY BR1 165 H6
SURB KT6 191 G6
Ravens Cl CDALE/KGS NW9 45 H5
EN EN1 24 A3
HAYES BR2 183 J5
SURB KT6 190 E3
Ravenscourt Av HMSMTH W6 118 D4
Ravenscourt Cl DEN/HRF UB9 58 A4
Ravenscourt Gdns
HMSMTH W6 118 C4
Ravenscourt Pk HMSMTH W6 118 D4
Ravenscourt Pl HMSMTH W6 118 E4
Ravenscourt Rd HMSMTH W6 118 E4
STMC/STPC BR5 186 B6
Ravenscourt Sq HMSMTH W6 118 D3
Ravenscraig Rd
FBAR/BDGN N11 34 B6
Ravenscroft Av GLDGN NW11 64 D4
WBLY HA9 62 A5
Ravenscroft Cl CAN/RD E16 106 E4
Ravenscroft Cots BAR EN5 * 32 E1
Ravenscroft Pk BAR EN5 20 B4
Ravenscroft Rd BECK BR3 181 K5
CAN/RD E16 106 E4
CHSWK W4 117 K4
PGE/AN SE20 181 K5
Ravenscroft St BETH E2 7 K3
Ravensdale Av
NFNCH/WDSPK N12 33 G6
Ravensdale Gdns NRWD SE19 180 E3
Ravensdale Rd HSLWW TW4 134 D4
STNW/STAM N16 68 B4
Ravensdon St LBTH SE11 122 B5
Ravensfield DAGW RM9 91 K2
Ravensfield Gdns
HOR/WEW KT19 207 G3
Ravenshaw St
KIL/WHAMP NW6 82 D3
Ravenshill CHST BR7 185 G4
Ravenshurst Av HDN NW4 64 A1
Ravenside Cl UED N18 51 F1
Ravenslea Rd BAL SW12 160 E2
Ravensleigh Gdns BMLY BR1 183 K1
Ravensmead Rd HAYES BR2 183 G3
Ravensmede Wy CHSWK W4 118 C4
Ravenstone Rd
CDALE/KGS NW9 * 63 H3
CEND/HSY/T N8 49 F6
Ravenstone St BAL SW12 161 F3
Ravenswood BXLY DA5 169 F3
Ravenswood Av SURB KT6 191 G6
WWKM BR4 199 F5
Ravenswood Cl CRW RM5 56 D1
Ravenswood Ct
KUTN/CMB KT2 * 175 K2
Ravenswood Crs
RYLN/HDSTN HA2 59 K6
WWKM BR4 199 F5
Ravenswood Gdns ISLW TW7 135 K2
Ravenswood Pk NTHWD HA6 40 E2
Ravenswood Rd BAL SW12 161 G2
CROY/NA CR0 211 H1
WALTH E17 70 A1
Ravensworth Rd
ELTH/MOT SE9 166 E6
WLSDN NW10 * 99 K2
Ravey St SDTCH EC2A 7 G6
Ravine Gv WOOL/PLUM SE18 127 K6

Rav Pinter Cl
STNW/STAM N16 68 A4
Rawlings Cl BECK BR3 199 F2
ORP BR6 217 F3
Rawlings Crs WBLY HA9 80 D1
Rawlings St CHEL SW3 14 E6
Rawlins Cl FNCH N3 46 C6
SAND/SEL CR2 213 H5
Rawnsley Av MTCM CR4 194 C2
Rawreth Wk IS N1 * 85 J6
Rawson St BTSEA SW11 141 F2
Rawsthorne Cl CAN/RD E16 126 E1
Rawstorne Pl FSBYE EC1V * 6 A4
Rawstorne St FSBYE EC1V 6 A4
Ray Bell Ct BROCKY SE4 * 144 C3
Raydean Rd BAR EN5 20 E6
Raydons Gdns DAGW RM9 92 A2
Raydons Rd DAGW RM9 92 A3
Raydon St ARCH N19 66 B6
Rayfield Cl HAYES BR2 200 D3
Rayford Av LEE/GVPK SE12 165 J2
Ray Gdns BARK IG11 109 G1
STAN HA7 43 H1
Rayleas Cl WOOL/PLUM SE18 147 G2
Rayleigh Av TEDD TW11 173 K2
Rayleigh Cl PLMGR N13 35 K5
Rayleigh Ct KUT/HW KT1 175 H5
Rayleigh Ri SAND/SEL CR2 212 A4
Rayleigh Rd CAN/RD E16 126 A1
PLMGR N13 35 J5
WFD IG8 53 G3
WIM/MER SW19 177 J4
Ray Lodge Rd WFD IG8 53 G2
Raymead Av THHTH CR7 196 B2
Raymere Gdns
WOOL/PLUM SE18 147 J1
Raymond Av SWFD E18 52 D6
WEA W13 116 B3
Raymond Blds GINN WC1R * 11 H1
Raymond Cl SYD SE26 181 K1
Raymond Rd BECK BR3 198 B1
GNTH/NBYPK IG2 72 D4
PLSTW E13 89 G5
WIM/MER SW19 177 H2
Raymond Wy
ESH/CLAY KT10 * 205 G4
Raymouth Rd
BERM/RHTH SE16 123 J4
Rayne Ct SWFD E18 70 D1
Rayners Cl ALP/SUD HA0 79 K3
Rayners Gdns NTHLT UB5 95 F2
Rayners La PIN HA5 59 K4
RYLN/HDSTN HA2 60 A6
Rayner's Rd PUT/ROE SW15 139 H6
Raynes Av WAN E11 71 G4
Raynes Pk RYNPK SW20 177 F5
Raynham Av UED N18 50 C2
Raynham Rd HMSMTH W6 118 E4
UED N18 50 C1
Raynham Ter UED N18 50 C1
Raynor Cl STHL UB1 114 E1
Raynor Pl IS N1 85 J6
Raynton Cl RYLN/HDSTN HA2 59 J4
YEAD UB4 94 D3
Raynton Dr YEAD UB4 94 C1
Ray Rd CRW RM5 56 D1
E/WMO/HCT KT8 189 G2
Rays Av UED N18 36 E6
Rays Rd UED N18 36 E6
WWKM BR4 199 F4
Ray St CLKNW EC1R 5 K7
Ray Street Br CLKNW EC1R * 5 K7
Raywood Cl HYS/HAR UB3 133 F1
Reachview Cl CAMTN NW1 84 C5
Read Cl THDIT KT7 190 B4
Reading La HACK E8 86 D4
Reading Rd NTHLT UB5 78 B3
SUT SM1 209 G3
Reading Wy MLHL NW7 46 B1
Reads Cl IL IG1 90 B1
Reapers Cl CAMTN NW1 84 D6
Reapers Wy ISLW TW7 135 J6
Reardon Pth WAP E1W 123 J1
Reardon St WAP E1W 123 J1
Reaston St NWCR SE14 143 K1
Reckitt Rd CHSWK W4 118 B5
Record St PECK SE15 123 K6
Recovery St TOOT SW17 178 D1
Recreation Av
ROMW/RG RM7 74 E2
Recreation Rd HAYES BR2 183 J5
NWDGN UB2 114 D4
SYD SE26 164 A6
Recreation Wy MTCM CR4 179 K6
Rectar Pl ARCH N19 66 B6
Rector St IS N1 6 C1
Rectory Cl CHING E4 37 J5
FNCH N3 46 D4
RYNPK SW20 177 F5
SCUP DA14 168 C6
STAN HA7 43 H2
SURB KT6 190 D5
Rectory Field Crs CHARL SE7 146 B1
Rectory Gdns BECK BR3 * 182 D4
CEND/HSY/T N8 66 E1
CHST BR7 * 185 H4
NTHLT UB5 77 K6
Rectory Gn BECK BR3 182 C4
Rectory Gv CLAP SW4 141 H4
CROY/NA CR0 196 C6
HPTN TW12 154 E6
Rectory La BUSH WD23 28 A1
EDGW HA8 44 C2
SCUP DA14 168 C6
SCUP DA14 186 D1
STAN HA7 43 H1
SURB KT6 190 D5
TOOT SW17 179 F1
WLGTN SM6 210 C2
Rectory Orch WIM/MER SW19 159 H6
Rectory Park Av NTHLT UB5 95 K2
Rectory Pl CHST BR7 * 185 H4
WOOL/PLUM SE18 127 F4
Rectory Rd BARN SW13 138 D3
BECK BR3 182 D4
DAGE RM10 92 C4
HAYES BR2 215 H5
HSLWW TW4 134 A3
HYS/HAR UB3 94 E5
MNPK E12 89 K3
NWDGN UB2 114 E3
STNW/STAM N16 86 B1
SUT SM1 208 E1
WALTH E17 69 K1
Rectory Sq WCHPL E1 105 F4
Reculver Ms UED N18 36 C6
Reculver Rd
BERM/RHTH SE16 124 A5
Red Anchor Cl CHEL SW3 120 C6
Redan Pl BAY/PAD W2 * 101 F5
Redan St WKENS W14 119 G3
Redan Ter CMBW SE5 142 C3
Red Barracks Rd
WOOL/PLUM SE18 126 E4
Redberry Gv SYD SE26 163 K5
Redbourne Av FNCH N3 46 E4
Redbourne Dr THMD SE28 109 K5
Redbridge Gdns CMBW SE5 143 F1
Redbridge La East REDBR IG4 71 H3
Redbridge La West WAN E11 71 F3
Redburn St CHEL SW3 120 E6
Redbury Cl RAIN RM13 111 K3
Redcar Cl NTHLT UB5 78 B3
Redcar St CMBW SE5 * 142 D1
Redcastle Cl WAP E1W 104 E6
Red Cedars Rd ORP BR6 201 K4
Redchurch St BETH E2 7 J6
WCHPL E1 7 J6
Redcliffe Cl ECT SW5 120 A5
Redcliffe Gdns IL IG1 72 A5
WBPTN SW10 120 A5
Redcliffe Ms WBPTN SW10 120 A5
Redcliffe Pl WBPTN SW10 120 B6
Redcliffe Rd WBPTN SW10 120 B5
Redcliffe Sq WBPTN SW10 120 A5
Redcliffe St WBPTN SW10 * 120 A6
Redclose Av MRDN SM4 193 K2
Redclyffe Rd PLSTW E13 89 G6
Redcroft Rd STHL UB1 96 C6
Redcross Wy STHWK SE1 18 D2
Reddings Cl MLHL NW7 31 H6
The Reddings MLHL NW7 31 H5
Reddington Cl SAND/SEL CR2 211 K6
Reddins Rd PECK SE15 143 H1
Reddons Rd BECK BR3 182 B3
Reddy Rd ERITH DA8 130 C6
Rede Pl BAY/PAD W2 100 E5
Redesdale Gdns ISLW TW7 136 B1
Redesdale St CHEL SW3 120 E6
Redfern Av HSLWW TW4 155 F2
Redfern Rd CAT SE6 165 F2
WLSDN NW10 81 G5
Redfield La ECT SW5 119 K4
Redfield Ms ECT SW5 119 K4
Redford Av THHTH CR7 196 A1
WLGTN SM6 210 E4
Redford Cl FELT TW13 153 J4
Redford Wk IS N1 * 85 H6
Redgate Dr HAYES BR2 200 A6
Redgate Ter PUT/ROE SW15 159 G1
Redgrave Cl CROY/NA CR0 197 G3
Redgrave Rd PUT/ROE SW15 139 G4
Redgrave Ter BETH E2 * 104 C2
Redhall Ter EA W5 * 98 C6
Red Hl CHST BR7 185 F1
Redhill Dr EDGW HA8 44 D5
Redhill St CAMTN NW1 3 K3
Red House La BXLYHS DA6 148 E5
Red House Rd CROY/NA CR0 195 J3
Red House Sq IS N1 85 J5
Redington Gdns HAMP NW3 83 F2
Redington Rd HAMP NW3 83 F1
Redland Gdns
E/WMO/HCT KT8 * 188 E1
Redlands Rd PEND EN3 25 G2
Redlands Wy
BRXS/STRHM SW2 161 K2
Red La ESH/CLAY KT10 205 G4
Redleaf Cl BXLYHN DA7 129 H6
Redlees Cl ISLW TW7 136 B5
Red Lion Cl STMC/STPC BR5 202 D3
WALW SE17 122 E6
Red Lion Ct FLST/FETLN EC4A 11 K3
HSLW TW3 * 135 G4
Red Lion Hl EFNCH N2 47 H5
Red Lion La
WOOL/PLUM SE18 147 F2
Red Lion Pde PIN HA5 * 41 J6
Red Lion Pl
WOOL/PLUM SE18 * 147 F2
Red Lion Rd SURB KT6 191 G6
Red Lion Rw CMBW SE5 122 D6
Red Lion Sq GINN WC1R 11 G2
WAND/EARL SW18 * 139 K6
Red Lion St GINN WC1R 11 G2
RCH/KEW TW9 136 E6
Red Lion Yd
MYFR/PKLN W1K * 9 H7
Red Lodge Rd WWKM BR4 199 F5
Redman Cl NTHLT UB5 95 G1
Redman's Rd WCHPL E1 104 E4
Redmead La WAP E1W 123 H1
Redmead Rd HYS/HAR UB3 113 H4
Redmore Rd HMSMTH W6 * 118 E4
Red Oak Cl ORP BR6 201 G6
Red Pl MYFR/PKLN W1K 9 G5
Redpoll Wy ERITHM DA18 128 E3
Red Post Hl HNHL SE24 142 E6
Redriffe Rd PLSTW E13 106 D1
Redriff Rd BERM/RHTH SE16 124 B3
ROMW/RG RM7 56 D5
Redroofs Cl BECK BR3 182 E4
Redruth Cl WDGN N22 49 F3
Redruth Gdns ESH/CLAY KT10 205 F5
Redruth Rd HOM E9 86 E6
Redstart Cl EHAM E6 107 J4
NWCR SE14 * 144 B1
Redston Rd CEND/HSY/T N8 66 D1
Redvers Rd WDGN N22 49 G5
Redvers St IS N1 7 H4
Redwald Rd CLPT E5 87 F2
Redway Dr WHTN TW2 155 H2
Redwing Ct ORP BR6 202 B4
Redwing Ms CMBW SE5 142 D3
Redwing Rd WLGTN SM6 210 E5
Redwood Cl
BERM/RHTH SE16 124 B1
BFN/LL DA15 168 B3
BOW E3 105 J1
OXHEY WD19 27 G6
STHGT/OAK N14 34 D2
Redwood Gdns CHIG IG7 55 G1
CHING E4 37 K1
Redwood Gv EA W5 116 D3
Redwood Ms VX/NE SW8 141 G4
Redwood Wy BAR EN5 20 B6
Reece Ms SKENS SW7 14 A6
Reed Av ORP BR6 216 E1
Reed Cl CAN/RD E16 106 E4
Reede Rd DAGE RM10 92 C4
Reede Wy DAGE RM10 92 D4
Reedham Cl TOTM N17 68 D1
Reedham St PECK SE15 * 143 H3
Reedholm Vls
STNW/STAM N16 85 K2
Reed Pl BTSEA SW11 140 D5
CLAP SW4 141 J5
Reed Pond Wk GPK RM2 57 H5
Reed Rd TOTM N17 50 B5
Reedsfield Cl ASHF TW15 152 E5
Reedsfield Rd ASHF TW15 152 D6
Reed's Pl CAMTN NW1 84 C5
Reedworth St LBTH SE11 17 K7
Reenglass Rd STAN HA7 * 29 K6
Rees Dr STAN HA7 30 A6
Rees Gdns CROY/NA CR0 197 G3
Reesland Cl MNPK E12 90 A4
Rees St IS N1 6 D1
Reets Farm Cl
CDALE/KGS NW9 63 G3
Reeves Av CDALE/KGS NW9 63 F4
Reeves Cnr CROY/NA CR0 196 C6
Reeves Ms MYFR/PKLN W1K 9 G6
Reeves Rd BOW E3 105 K3
WOOL/PLUM SE18 127 G6
Reform Rw TOTM N17 50 B5
Reform St BTSEA SW11 140 E3
Regal Cl EA W5 97 K4
WCHPL E1 104 C4
Regal Ct MTCM CR4 178 E6
UED N18 50 B1
Regal Crs WLGTN SM6 210 B1
Regal Dr FBAR/BDGN N11 48 B1
Regal La CAMTN NW1 3 H1
Regal Rw PECK SE15 143 K2
Regal Wy
KTN/HRWW/WS HA3 62 A3
Regan Wy IS N1 7 G3
Regarder Rd CHIG IG7 55 H1
Regarth Av ROM RM1 75 G3
Regency Cl CHIG IG7 54 C1
EA W5 98 A5
HPTN TW12 172 E1
Regency Ct EN EN1 23 K6
Regency Crs HDN NW4 46 B5
Regency Dr RSLP HA4 58 C5
Regency Gdns
WOT/HER KT12 188 C5
Regency Lawn KTTN NW5 * 84 B1
Regency Ms BECK BR3 183 F4
WLSDN NW10 81 J4
Regency Pde HAMP NW3 * 83 H5
Regency Pl WEST SW1P * 16 C6
Regency St WEST SW1P 16 D7
Regency Ter HGT N6 * 65 K3
SEVS/STOTM N15 68 A2
SKENS SW7 * 120 C5
Regency Wk CROY/NA CR0 198 B3
Regency Wy BXLYHS DA6 148 E4
Regeneration Rd
BERM/RHTH SE16 124 A4
Regent Cl HSLWW TW4 134 A2
KTN/HRWW/WS HA3 62 A3
NFNCH/WDSPK N12 47 G1
Regent Gdns GDMY/SEVK IG3 73 G3
Regent Pde BELMT SM2 * 209 G4
STNW/STAM N16 * 68 B4
Regent Pl CROY/NA CR0 197 G5
WIM/MER SW19 178 B1
Regent Rd BRYLDS KT5 191 G2
HNHL SE24 162 C1
Regents Av PLMGR N13 49 G1
Regents Bridge Gdns
VX/NE SW8 121 K6
Regents Cl SAND/SEL CR2 212 A4
YEAD UB4 94 C4
Regents Dr HAYES BR2 215 H3
WFD IG8 54 A2
Regents Ms STJWD NW8 101 G1
Regent's Park Rd
CAMTN NW1 83 K6
FNCH N3 46 D6
Regent's Park Ter
CAMTN NW1 84 B6
Regents Pl LOU IG10 39 H2
Regents Plaza
KIL/WHAMP NW6 * 101 F1
Regent Sq BELV DA17 129 J4
BOW E3 105 K2
STPAN WC1H 5 F5
Regent's Rw BETH E2 86 C6
Regent St CHSWK W4 117 H5
REGST W1B 9 K3
STJS SW1Y 10 C6
WLSDN NW10 100 B2
Regents Whf IS N1 * 5 G2
Regent Whf IS N1 * 5 G2
Reginald Rd DEPT SE8 144 D1
FSTGT E7 88 E5
NTHWD HA6 40 D4
Reginald Sq DEPT SE8 144 D1
Regina Rd FSBYPK N4 67 F5
NWDGN UB2 114 D4
SNWD SE25 181 H6
WEA W13 116 B1
Regina Ter WEA W13 116 B1
Regis Rd KTTN NW5 84 B3
Regnart Blds CAMTN NW1 4 B5
Reid Cl HYS/HAR UB3 94 C5
PIN HA5 40 E6
Reidhaven Rd
WOOL/PLUM SE18 127 K4
Reigate Av SUT SM1 194 A5
Reigate Rd GDMY/SEVK IG3 73 F6
Reigate Wy WLGTN SM6 210 E3
Reighton Rd CLPT E5 86 C1
Reinckendorf Av
ELTH/MOT SE9 147 H6
Reindeer Cl PLSTW E13 88 E6
Reizel Cl STNW/STAM N16 68 B5
Relay Rd SHB W12 100 A6
Relf Rd PECK SE15 143 H4
Reliance Ar BRXN/ST SW9 * 142 B5
Relton Ms SKENS SW7 14 D4
Rembrandt Cl BGVA SW1W * 121 F5
POP/IOD E14 125 G3
Rembrandt Ct
HOR/WEW KT19 207 H4
Rembrandt Rd EDGW HA8 * 44 C5
LEW SE13 145 H5
Rembrandt Wy
WOT/HER KT12 188 A6
Remington Rd EHAM E6 107 J5
SEVS/STOTM N15 67 K3
Remington St IS N1 6 B3
Remnant St HOL/ALD WC2B 11 G3
Remus Rd BOW E3 87 J5
Renaissance Wk GNWCH SE10 125 J3
Rendle Cl CROY/NA CR0 197 G2
Rendlesham Rd CLPT E5 86 C2
ENC/FH EN2 23 H2
Renforth St
BERM/RHTH SE16 123 K2
Renfrew Cl EHAM E6 108 A6
Renfrew Rd HSLWW TW4 134 C3
KUTN/CMB KT2 175 K3
LBTH SE11 18 A6
Renmuir St TOOT SW17 178 E2
Rennell St LEW SE13 145 F4
Renness Rd WALTH E17 51 G6
Rennets Cl ELTH/MOT SE9 147 J6
Rennets Wood Rd
ELTH/MOT SE9 147 J6
Rennie Cl ASHF TW15 152 A5
Rennie Est BERM/RHTH SE16 123 J4
Rennie St STHWK SE1 12 A7
Renown Cl CROY/NA CR0 196 C5
ROMW/RG RM7 56 C4
Rensburg Rd WALTH E17 69 F2
Rensburg Vls WALTH E17 * 69 F2
Renshaw Cl BELV DA17 129 G6
Renters Av HDN NW4 64 A3
Renton Cl BRXS/STRHM SW2 * 162 A1
Renton Dr STMC/STPC BR5 202 E4
Renwick Rd BARK IG11 109 H3
Repens Wy YEAD UB4 95 H3
Rephidim St STHWK SE1 19 F5
Replingham Rd
WAND/EARL SW18 159 J3
Reporton Rd FUL/PGN SW6 139 H2
Repository Rd
WOOL/PLUM SE18 126 E6
Repton Av ALP/SUD HA0 79 J2
GPK RM2 57 J6
HYS/HAR UB3 113 G4
Repton Cl CAR SM5 209 J3
Repton Ct BECK BR3 182 E4
Repton Dr GPK RM2 75 J1
Repton Gdns GPK RM2 57 J6
Repton Gv CLAY IG5 53 K4
Repton Rd
KTN/HRWW/WS HA3 62 B1
ORP BR6 217 G2
Repton St POP/IOD E14 105 G5
Repulse Cl CRW RM5 56 D4
Reservoir Cl THHTH CR7 180 E6
Reservoir Rd BROCKY SE4 144 B3
RSLP HA4 58 A2
STHGT/OAK N14 22 C6
Resham Cl NWDGN UB2 114 B3
Resolution Wy DEPT SE8 144 D1
Restell Cl BKHTH/KID SE3 125 H6
Restmor Wy CAR SM5 195 F6
Reston Pl KENS W8 120 B2
Restons Crs ELTH/MOT SE9 167 J1
Reston Wy CAN/RD E16 107 H6
Restormel Cl HSLW TW3 135 F6
Retford St BETH E2 * 7 J4
Retingham Wy CHING E4 37 K4
Retreat Cl
KTN/HRWW/WS HA3 61 J2
Retreat Pl HOM E9 86 E4
Retreat Rd RCH/KEW TW9 136 E6
The Retreat BRYLDS KT5 191 G3
CDALE/KGS NW9 63 F2
MORT/ESHN SW14 138 B4
ORP BR6 217 H4
RYLN/HDSTN HA2 60 A4
THHTH CR7 196 E1
WPK KT4 192 E6
Reunion Rw WAP E1W * 104 D6
Reveley Sq BERM/RHTH SE16 124 B2
Revell Ri WOOL/PLUM SE18 128 A6
Revell Rd KUT/HW KT1 175 J5
SUT SM1 208 D4
Revelon Rd BROCKY SE4 144 B5
Revelstoke Rd
WIM/MER SW19 159 H6
Reventlow Rd ELTH/MOT SE9 167 H3
Reverdy Rd STHWK SE1 123 H4
Reverend Cl
RYLN/HDSTN HA2 78 B1
Revere Wy HOR/WEW KT19 207 G6
Revesby Rd CAR SM5 194 D3
Review Rd CRICK NW2 63 H6
DAGE RM10 110 D1
Rewell St FUL/PGN SW6 * 140 B1
Rewley Rd CAR SM5 194 C3
Rex Pl MYFR/PKLN W1K 9 H7
Reydon Av WAN E11 71 G3
Reynard Cl BMLY BR1 184 E6
Reynard Dr NRWD SE19 181 G3
Reynard Pl NWCR SE14 * 124 B6
Reynardson Rd TOTM N17 49 J3
Reynola Gdns CHARL SE7 126 A5
Reynolds Av CHDH RM6 73 J4
CHSGTN KT9 206 A5
MNPK E12 90 A3
Reynolds Cl CAR SM5 194 E5
GLDGN NW11 65 F4
WIM/MER SW19 178 C4
Reynolds Dr EDGW HA8 44 B6
Reynolds Pl BKHTH/KID SE3 146 A1
RCHPK/HAM TW10 157 G1
Reynolds Rd CHSWK W4 117 K3
NWMAL KT3 192 A4
PECK SE15 143 K6
YEAD UB4 95 G3
Reynolds Wy CROY/NA CR0 212 A2
Rheidol Ms IS N1 6 C2
Rheidol Ter IS N1 6 B2
Rheingold Wy WLGTN SM6 210 E6
Rheola Cl TOTM N17 50 B4
Rhoda St BETH E2 7 K6
Rhodes Av WDGN N22 48 C4
Rhodesia Rd BRXN/ST SW9 141 K3
WAN E11 70 B6
Rhodes St HOLWY N7 85 F3
Rhodeswell Rd POP/IOD E14 105 G4
Rhodrons Av CHSGTN KT9 206 A3
Rhondda Gv BOW E3 105 G2
Rhyl Rd GFD/PVL UB6 97 F1
Rhyl St KTTN NW5 84 A4
Rhys Av FBAR/BDGN N11 48 D3
Rialto Rd MTCM CR4 179 F5
Ribble Cl WFD IG8 53 G2
Ribblesdale Av
FBAR/BDGN N11 47 K2
NTHLT UB5 78 B4
Ribblesdale Rd
CEND/HSY/T N8 67 F1
STRHM/NOR SW16 179 G1
Ribbon Dance Ms CMBW SE5 142 E2
Ribchester Av GFD/PVL UB6 97 F2
Ribston Cl HAYES BR2 200 E5
Ricardo St POP/IOD E14 105 K5
Ricards Rd WIM/MER SW19 177 J1
Rice Pde STMC/STPC BR5 * 201 J2
Richard Cl WOOL/PLUM SE18 126 D4
Richard House Dr
CAN/RD E16 107 H5
Richards Av ROMW/RG RM7 74 E2
Richards Cl BUSH WD23 28 D2
HRW HA1 61 G2
HYS/HAR UB3 113 G6
Richards Cots CAR SM5 * 209 K3
Richards Fld HOR/WEW KT19 207 F6
Richardson Cl HACK E8 * 86 B6
Richardson Gdns DAGE RM10 92 D4
Richardson Rd SRTFD E15 * 106 C1
Richardson's Ms FITZ W1T 4 A7
Richards Pl WALTH E17 51 J6
Richard's Pl CHEL SW3 14 D6
Richard St WCHPL E1 104 D5
Richbell Pl FSBYW WC1X 11 G
Richborne Ter VX/NE SW8 142 A
Richborough Cl
STMC/STPC BR5 202 E
Richborough Rd CRICK NW2 82 B
Richens Cl HSLW TW3 135 J
Riches Rd IL IG1 72 C
Richfield Rd BUSH WD23 28 C
Richford Ga HMSMTH W6 * 119 F
Richford Rd SRTFD E15 88 D
Richford St HMSMTH W6 119 F
Richill Ldg WHTN TW2 * 155 F
Richlands Av EW KT17 207 J
Richmer Rd ERITH DA8 150 D
Richmond Av CHING E4 52 B
EBED/NFELT TW14 153 H
IS N1 85 F
RYNPK SW20 177 H
Richmond Br TWK TW1 136 E
Richmond Blds
SOHO/SHAV W1D 10 C
Richmond Cl WALTH E17 69 H
Richmond Crs CHING E4 52 E
ED N9 36 C
IS N1 85 F
Richmond Dr WFD IG8 54 A
Richmond Gdns HDN NW4 63
KTN/HRWW/WS HA3 43
Richmond Ga
RCHPK/HAM TW10 157 C
Richmond Gn CROY/NA CR0 210 E
Richmond Gv IS N1 85 H
Richmond Hl
RCHPK/HAM TW10 157
Richmond Ms
SOHO/SHAV W1D 10
Richmond Pde TWK TW1 * 156
Richmond Park Rd
KUTN/CMB KT2 175
MORT/ESHN SW14 137
Richmond Pl
WOOL/PLUM SE18 127
Richmond Rd BAR EN5 21
CHING E4 * 38
CROY/NA CR0 210
EA W5 117
EFNCH N2 * 47
FBAR/BDGN N11 48
FSTGT E7 89
HACK E8 86
IL IG1 90
ISLW TW7 136
KUTN/CMB KT2 174
ROM RM1 75
RYNPK SW20 176
SEVS/STOTM N15 68
THHTH CR7 196
TWK TW1 156
WAN E11 70
Richmond St PLSTW E13 106
Richmond Ter WHALL SW1A 16
Richmond Vls WALTH E17 * 51
Richmond Wy SHB W12 119
WAN E11 70
Rich St POP/IOD E14 105
Rickard Cl BRXS/STRHM SW2 162
HDN NW4 63
WDR/YW UB7 112
Rickards Cl SURB KT6 191
Rickett St FUL/PGN SW6 119
Rickman St WCHPL E1 104
Rickmansworth Rd
NTHWD HA6 40
Rick Roberts Wy SRTFD E15 88
Rickthorne Rd ARCH N19 66
Ridding La GFD/PVL UB6 79
Riddons Rd LEE/GVPK SE12 166
Rideout St WOOL/PLUM SE18 126
Rider Cl BFN/LL DA15 167
The Ride BTFD TW8 116
PEND EN3 24
Ridgdale St BOW E3 105
Ridge Av WCHMH N21 3
Ridgebrook Rd
BKHTH/KID SE3 14
Ridge Cl CDALE/KGS NW9 6

HDN NW4 46 B5
THMD SE28 127 J2
Ridge Crest ENC/FH EN2 23 F2
Ridgecroft Cl BXLY DA5 169 K3
Ridge Hl GLDGN NW11 64 C5
Ridgemead Cl
STHGT/OAK N14 34 E4
Ridgemont Gdns EDGW HA8 30 E6
Ridgemount Av
CROY/NA CR0 198 A6
Ridgemount Cl PGE/AN SE20 181 J3
Ridgemount Gdns
ENC/FH EN2 23 H4
Ridge Rd CEND/HSY/T N8 67 F3
CHEAM SM3 193 J5
CRICK NW2 82 D1
MTCM CR4 179 G3
WCHMH N21 35 K3
Ridges Yd CROY/NA CR0 211 H1
Ridge Ter WCHMH N21 * 35 J2
The Ridge BAR EN5 * 20 D6
BRYLDS KT5 191 H2
BXLY DA5 169 G2
ORP BR6 201 J6
WHTN TW2 155 J2
Ridgeview Cl BAR EN5 32 B1
Ridgeview Rd
TRDG/WHET N20 33 F5
Ridge Wy FELT TW13 154 D5
Ridgeway WFD IG8 39 G6
Ridgeway Av EBAR EN4 33 K1
Ridgeway Crs ORP BR6 216 E1
Ridgeway Crescent Gdns
ORP BR6 201 K6
Ridgeway Dr BMLY BR1 166 A6
Ridgeway East BFN/LL DA15 148 A6
Ridgeway Gdns HGT N6 66 C4
REDBR IG4 71 J2
Ridgeway Rd ISLW TW7 135 K1
Ridgeway Rd North
ISLW TW7 135 K1
The Ridgeway ACT W3 117 H3
CDALE/KGS NW9 63 F1
CHING E4 38 A3
CROY/NA CR0 211 F1
ENC/FH EN2 23 G2
FBAR/BDGN N11 33 K6
FNCH N3 47 F3
GLDGN NW11 64 D5
GPK RM2 75 J1
KTN/HRWW/WS HA3 61 J3
MLHL NW7 31 J6
RSLP HA4 58 D4
RYLN/HDSTN HA2 59 K2
STAN HA7 43 J2
STHGT/OAK N14 34 E4
Ridgeway West BFN/LL DA15 147 K6
Ridgewell Cl DAGE RM10 92 D6
IS N1 85 J6
SYD SE26 164 C6
Ridgmount Gdns
GWRST WC1E 10 C1
Ridgmount Rd
WAND/EARL SW18 140 A6
Ridgmount St GWRST WC1E 10 C1
Ridgway RCHPK/HAM TW10 * 157 F1
WIM/MER SW19 177 F3
Ridgway Gdns
WIM/MER SW19 177 G3
Ridgway Pl WIM/MER SW19 177 H2
Ridgway Rd BRXN/ST SW9 142 C4
The Ridgway BELMT SM2 209 H5
Ridgwell Rd CAN/RD E16 107 G4
Riding House St GTPST W1W 10 A2
REGST W1B 9 K3
Ridings Av WCHMH N21 23 H5
Ridings Cl HGT N6 66 C4
The Ridings BRYLDS KT5 191 H2
EA W5 98 B3
EBAR EN4 * 33 J2
EW KT17 207 H6
The Riding GLDGN NW11 64 D4
Ridler Rd EN EN1 24 A1
Ridley Av WEA W13 116 C3
Ridley Cl BARK IG11 91 F5
HARH RM3 57 K4
Ridley Rd FSTGT E7 89 G2
HACK E8 86 B3
WELL DA16 148 C2
WIM/MER SW19 178 A3
WLSDN NW10 99 J1
Ridsdale Rd PGE/AN SE20 181 J4
Riefield Rd ELTH/MOT SE9 147 H5
Riesco Dr CROY/NA CR0 212 E4
Riffel Rd CRICK NW2 82 A3
Rifle Pl NTGHL W11 119 G1
Rifle Range La HRW HA1 61 F5
Rifle St POP/IOD E14 105 K4
Rigault Rd FUL/PGN SW6 139 H3
Rigby Cl CROY/NA CR0 211 G1
Rigby La HYS/HAR UB3 113 F2
Rigby Ms IL IG1 72 A6
Rigden St POP/IOD E14 105 K5
Rigeley Rd WLSDN NW10 99 J2
Rigg Ap LEY E10 69 F5
Rigge Pl CLAP SW4 141 J5
Riggindale Rd
STRHM/NOR SW16 179 J1
Right Side STHGT/OAK N14 * 34 D3
Riley Rd PEND EN3 24 E1
STHWK SE1 19 J4
Riley St WBPTN SW10 140 C1
Rinaldo Rd BAL SW12 161 G2
Ring Cl BMLY BR1 184 A3
Ringcroft St HOLWY N7 85 G3
Ringer's Rd BMLY BR1 183 K6
Ringford Rd
WAND/EARL SW18 139 J6
Ringlet Cl CAN/RD E16 107 F4
Ringlewell Cl EN EN1 24 D3
Ringmer Av FUL/PGN SW6 139 H2
Ringmer Pl WCHMH N21 23 K6
Ringmer Wy BMLY BR1 200 E2
Ringmore Ri FSTH SE23 163 J2
Ring Rd SHB W12 119 F1
Ringshall Rd STMC/STPC BR5 186 B6
Ringslade Rd WDGN N22 49 F5
Ringstead Rd CAT SE6 164 E2
SUT SM1 209 H2
Ring Wy FBAR/BDGN N11 48 C2
Ringway NWDGN UB2 114 C5
Ringwold Cl BECK BR3 182 B3
Ringwood Av CROY/NA CR0 195 K4
EFNCH N2 47 K6
Ringwood Cl PIN HA5 * 41 G6
Ringwood Gdns
PUT/ROE SW15 158 D4
Ringwood Rd WALTH E17 69 H3
Ringwood Wy HPTN TW12 155 F6
WCHMH N21 35 H2
Ripley Cl BMLY BR1 200 E2
CROY/NA CR0 214 A4
Ripley Gdns
MORT/ESHN SW14 138 A4
Ripley Ms WAN E11 70 C3
Ripley Rd BELV DA17 129 H4
CAN/RD E16 107 G5
ENC/FH EN2 23 J2
GDMY/SEVK IG3 72 E6
HPTN TW12 173 F3
Ripleys Market DART DA1 * 171 H2
Ripley Vls EA W5 * 97 J5
Ripon Cl NTHLT UB5 78 A3
Ripon Gdns CHSGTN KT9 205 K3
IL IG1 71 J3
Ripon Rd ED N9 36 D2
TOTM N17 49 K6
WOOL/PLUM SE18 127 G6
Rippersley Rd WELL DA16 148 B2
Ripple Rd BARK IG11 90 C5
DAGW RM9 110 A1
Ripplevale Gv IS N1 85 F5
Rippolson Rd
WOOL/PLUM SE18 128 A5
Risborough Cl MUSWH N10 * 48 B6
Risborough Dr WPK KT4 192 D4
Risborough St STHWK SE1 18 B2
Risdon St BERM/RHTH SE16 123 K2
Risebridge Cha ROM RM1 57 H3
Risebridge Rd GPK RM2 57 H5
Risedale Rd BXLYHN DA7 149 J4
Riseldine Rd FSTH SE23 164 B1
Rise Park Bvd ROM RM1 57 H4
Rise Park Pde ROM RM1 57 G5
The Rise BKHH IG9 39 H3
BXLY DA5 168 D2
EDGW HA8 44 D1
GFD/PVL UB6 79 G3
MLHL NW7 45 H2
PLMGR N13 35 G6
SAND/SEL CR2 212 E6
WAN E11 70 E2
WLSDN NW10 81 F1
Rising Hill Cl NTHWD HA6 * 40 A2
Risinghill St IS N1 5 J2
Risingholme Cl BUSH WD23 28 B2
KTN/HRWW/WS HA3 42 E4
Risingholme Rd
KTN/HRWW/WS HA3 42 E5
The Risings WALTH E17 70 B1
Risley Av TOTM N17 49 J4
Rita Rd VX/NE SW8 141 K1
Ritches Rd SEVS/STOTM N15 67 J2
Ritchie Rd CROY/NA CR0 197 J3
Ritchie St IS N1 5 K2
Ritchings Av WALTH E17 69 G1
Ritherdon Rd TOOT SW17 161 F4
Ritson Rd HACK E8 86 B4
Ritter St WOOL/PLUM SE18 127 F6
Rivaz Pl HOM E9 86 E4
Rivenhall Gdns SWFD E18 70 D1
River Av PLMGR N13 35 H5
THDIT KT7 190 B4
Riverbank E/WMO/HCT KT8 173 K6
River Bank THDIT KT7 190 A2
WCHMH N21 35 J2
Riverbank Wy BTFD TW8 116 D6
River Barge Cl POP/IOD E14 125 F2
River Cl NWDGN UB2 115 H2
RAIN RM13 111 K4
RSLP HA4 58 D3
WAN E11 71 G3
Rivercourt Rd HMSMTH W6 118 E4
Riverdale Dr
WAND/EARL SW18 160 A3
Riverdale Gdns TWK TW1 136 D6
Riverdale Rd BXLY DA5 169 G2
ERITH DA8 129 J5
FELT TW13 154 D6
TWK TW1 156 D1
WOOL/PLUM SE18 128 A5
Riverdene EDGW HA8 30 E6
Riverdene Rd IL IG1 90 A1
River Front EN EN1 23 K4
River Gdns CAR SM5 195 F6
EBED/NFELT TW14 134 A6
River Grove Pk BECK BR3 182 C4
Riverhead Cl WALTH E17 51 F5
Riverholme Dr
HOR/WEW KT19 207 F6
River La RCHPK/HAM TW10 156 E3
Rivermead E/WMO/HCT KT8 173 H6
KUT/HW KT1 * 190 E2
Rivermead Cl TEDD TW11 174 C1
Rivermead Rd UED N18 * 51 F1
River Meads Av WHTN TW2 155 G5
Rivernook Cl WOT/HER KT12 188 B2
Riverpark Gdns HAYES BR2 183 G3
River Park Rd WDGN N22 49 F5
River Park Vw ORP BR6 202 C4
River Pl IS N1 85 J5
River Reach TEDD TW11 174 D2
River Rd BARK IG11 108 E2
BKHH IG9 39 J3
Riversdale Rd CRW RM5 56 D3
HBRY N5 85 H1
THDIT KT7 190 B2
Riversfield Rd EN EN1 24 A4
Riverside CHARL SE7 126 A3
HDN NW4 63 K4
RCH/KEW TW9 * 117 H6
RCH/KEW TW9 136 E6
SUN TW16 * 172 C5
TWK TW1 156 C3
Riverside Av E/WMO/HCT KT8 189 J2
Riverside Cl CLPT E5 68 E5
HNWL W7 96 E3
KUT/HW KT1 190 E1
ROMW/RG RM7 75 F1
STMC/STPC BR5 186 D5
WLGTN SM6 210 B1
Riverside Ct CHING E4 * 37 K1
Riverside Dr CHSWK W4 138 A1
ESH/CLAY KT10 204 A2
GLDGN NW11 * 64 C3
MTCM CR4 194 D2
RCHPK/HAM TW10 156 C5
Riverside Gdns ALP/SUD HA0 98 A1
ENC/FH EN2 23 J3
HMSMTH W6 118 E5
Riverside Ms CROY/NA CR0 * 210 E1
Riverside Pl
FBAR/BDGN N11 * 34 C5
STWL/WRAY TW19 152 A1
Riverside Rd IL IG1 90 B1
OXHEY WD19 27 F1
SCUP DA14 169 F5
SEVS/STOTM N15 68 C3
SRTFD E15 106 A1
STWL/WRAY TW19 132 A6
TOOT SW17 160 A6
The Riverside
E/WMO/HCT KT8 173 J6
Riverside Vls SURB KT6 * 190 D3
Riverside Wk ISLW TW7 135 K4
KUT/HW KT1 174 E5
Riverside Wy DART DA1 151 H6
Riverside Yd TOOT SW17 160 A5
Riverstone Cl
RYLN/HDSTN HA2 60 D6
River St CLKNW EC1R 5 J4
River Ter HMSMTH W6 119 F5
Riverton Cl MV/WKIL W9 * 100 D2
Riverview Gdns BARN SW13 118 E6
River View Gdns TWK TW1 156 A4
Riverview Gv CHSWK W4 117 J6
Riverview Pk CAT SE6 164 D4
Riverview Rd CHSWK W4 137 J1
HOR/WEW KT19 206 E2
River Wk SUN TW16 172 C5
River Wy WHTN TW2 155 G4
GNWCH SE10 125 J3
HOR/WEW KT19 207 F3
Riverway PLMGR N13 49 G1
River Whf BELV DA17 * 130 A2
Riverwood La CHST BR7 185 J5
Rivington Av WFD IG8 53 H5
Rivington Crs MLHL NW7 45 G3
Rivington Pl FSBYE EC1V 7 H5
Rivington St SDTCH EC2A 7 H5
Rivington Wk HACK E8 * 86 C6
Rivulet Rd TOTM N17 49 J3
Rixon St HOLWY N7 85 G1
Rixsen Rd MNPK E12 89 J3
Roach Rd BOW E3 87 J5
Roads Pl ARCH N19 66 E6
Roan St GNWCH SE10 125 F6
Robarts Cl PIN HA5 59 F2
Robb Rd STAN HA7 43 G2
Robert Adam St MHST W1U 9 G3
Roberta St BETH E2 104 C2
Robert Cl CHIG IG7 55 F1
MV/WKIL W9 101 G3
Robert Dashwood Wy
WALW SE17 18 C7
Robert Keen Cl PECK SE15 143 H2
Robert Lowe Cl NWCR SE14 144 A1
Roberton Dr BMLY BR1 184 B5
Robertsbridge Rd CAR SM5 194 B4
Roberts Cl CHEAM SM3 208 B5
DAGE RM10 92 C4
ELTH/MOT SE9 167 J3
HARH RM3 57 K4
STMC/STPC BR5 202 D2
THHTH CR7 180 E6
WDR/YW UB7 112 B1
Roberts Ct CHSGTN KT9 205 K3
PGE/AN SE20 181 K4
WLSDN NW10 81 G4
Roberts House
WOOL/PLUM SE18 * 146 D1
Roberts Ms KTBR SW1X * 15 G5
Robertson St VX/NE SW8 141 G3
Robert's Pl CLKNW EC1R * 5 K6
Robert Sq LEW SE13 145 F5
Roberts Rd BELV DA17 129 H5
MLHL NW7 46 C1
WALTH E17 51 K4
Robert St CAMTN NW1 3 K5
CHCR WC2N 11 F6
CROY/NA CR0 211 J1
WOOL/PLUM SE18 127 J4
Robeson St BOW E3 105 H4
Robina Cl BXLYHS DA6 148 E5
NTHWD HA6 40 D5
Robin Cl CRW RM5 57 F3
FELT TW13 172 D1
MLHL NW7 31 G5
Robin Gv BTFD TW8 116 D6
HGT N6 66 A6
KTN/HRWW/WS HA3 62 B3
Robin Hill Dr CHST BR7 184 D2
Robinhood Cl MTCM CR4 195 H1
Robin Hood Dr
KTN/HRWW/WS HA3 43 F3
Robin Hood Gdns
POP/IOD E14 * 106 A6
Robin Hood Gn
STMC/STPC BR5 202 B2
Robinhood La MTCM CR4 179 H6
Robin Hood La POP/IOD E14 106 A6
PUT/ROE SW15 158 B5
SUT SM1 208 E3
Robin Hood Rd
PUT/ROE SW15 158 B6
WIM/MER SW19 176 D1
Robin Hood Wy GFD/PVL UB6 79 F4
PUT/ROE SW15 158 B6
RYNPK SW20 176 C3
Robinia Cl BARK/HLT IG6 54 E2
PGE/AN SE20 181 H4
Robinia Crs LEY E10 69 K6
Robin La HDN NW4 46 B6
Robins Gv WWKM BR4 214 E1
Robinson Cl ENC/FH EN2 23 J4
HCH RM12 93 K5
WAN E11 88 C1
Robinson Crs BUSH WD23 28 C3
Robinson Rd BETH E2 104 E1
DAGE RM10 92 C2
TOOT SW17 178 D2
Robinson's Cl WEA W13 97 G4
Robinson St CHEL SW3 120 E6
Robinswood Ms HBRY N5 85 H3
Robin Wy STMC/STPC BR5 186 C6
Robinwood Pl
PUT/ROE SW15 158 A6
Rob Pascoe La DAGW RM9 110 A2
Robsart St BRXN/ST SW9 142 A3
Robson Av WLSDN NW10 81 J5
Robson Cl EHAM E6 107 J5
ENC/FH EN2 23 H3
Robson Rd WNWD SE27 162 C5
Rocastle Rd BROCKY SE4 144 B6
Roch Av EDGW HA8 44 B5
Rochdale Rd ABYW SE2 128 C4
WALTH E17 69 J4
Rochdale Wy DEPT SE8 144 D1
Rochelle Cl BTSEA SW11 140 C5
Rochelle St BETH E2 7 J5
Rochemont Wk HACK E8 * 7 K1
Roche Rd STRHM/NOR SW16 179 K4
Rochester Av BMLY BR1 184 A5
FELT TW13 153 J4
PLSTW E13 89 G6
Rochester Cl BFN/LL DA15 168 C1
EN EN1 24 A2
STRHM/NOR SW16 * 179 K3
Rochester Dr BXLY DA5 169 H1
PIN HA5 59 H2
Rochester Gdns
CROY/NA CR0 212 A1
IL IG1 71 K4
Rochester Ms CAMTN NW1 84 C5
EA W5 * 116 D4
Rochester Pde FELT TW13 * 153 K5
Rochester Pl CAMTN NW1 84 C4
Rochester Rd CAMTN NW1 84 C4
CAR SM5 209 K2
HCH RM12 93 K5
NTHWD HA6 40 D6
Rochester Rw WEST SW1P 16 B6
Rochester Sq CAMTN NW1 84 C5
Rochester St WEST SW1P 16 C5
Rochester Ter CAMTN NW1 84 C4
Rochester Wk STHWK SE1 * 12 E7
Rochester Wy BKHTH/KID SE3 146 A2
ELTH/MOT SE9 146 C4
ELTH/MOT SE9 146 E4
Rochester Way Relief Rd
ELTH/MOT SE9 146 D6
ELTH/MOT SE9 147 G5
Roche Wk CAR SM5 194 C3
Rochford Av CHDH RM6 73 J2
Rochford Cl EHAM E6 107 H1
HCH RM12 93 K4
Rochford Wk HACK E8 * 86 C5
Rochford Wy CROY/NA CR0 195 K3
Rock Av MORT/ESHN SW14 138 A4
Rockbourne Rd FSTH SE23 164 A3
Rock Cl MTCM CR4 178 C5
Rockell's Pl EDUL SE22 163 J1
Rockford Av GFD/PVL UB6 97 H1
Rock Grove Wy
BERM/RHTH SE16 123 H4
Rockhall Rd CRICK NW2 82 B2
Rockhampton Rd
SAND/SEL CR2 212 A4
STRHM/NOR SW16 162 B6
Rock Hl DUL SE21 163 G6
Rockingham Av EMPK RM11 75 K3
Rockingham Cl
PUT/ROE SW15 138 C5
Rockingham Ga BUSH WD23 28 C1
Rockingham St STHWK SE1 18 C5
Rockland Rd PUT/ROE SW15 139 H5
Rocklands Dr
KTN/HRWW/WS HA3 43 H5
Rockley Rd SHB W12 119 G2
Rockmount Rd NRWD SE19 180 E2
WOOL/PLUM SE18 128 A5
Rocks La BARN SW13 138 D4
Rock St FSBYPK N4 67 G6
Rockware Av GFD/PVL UB6 78 E6
Rockways BAR EN5 31 H1
Rockwell Gdns NRWD SE19 163 F6
Rockwell Rd DAGE RM10 92 D3
Rocliffe St IS N1 6 B3
Rocombe Crs FSTH SE23 * 163 K2
Rocque La BKHTH/KID SE3 145 J4
Rodborough Rd
GLDGN NW11 64 E5
Roden Gdns CROY/NA CR0 197 F3
Rodenhurst Rd CLAP SW4 161 H2
Roden St HOLWY N7 85 F1
IL IG1 90 A1
Roderick Rd HAMP NW3 83 K2
Rodgers Cl BORE WD6 29 K1
Roding Gdns LOU IG10 39 J1
Roding La BKHH IG9 39 J3
Roding La North WFD IG8 53 J5
Roding La South REDBR IG4 71 H1
Roding Ms WAP E1W 123 H1
Roding Rd CLPT E5 87 F2
EHAM E6 108 B4
Rodings Rw BAR EN5 * 20 C5
Roding Vw BKHH IG9 39 H3
Rodmarton St MHST W1U 9 F2
Rodmell Cl YEAD UB4 95 J3
Rodmell Slope
NFNCH/WDSPK N12 46 D1
Rodmere St GNWCH SE10 125 H5
Rodney Cl CROY/NA CR0 196 C5
NWMAL KT3 192 B2
PIN HA5 59 J4
WOT/HER KT12 * 188 B5
Rodney Gdns PIN HA5 59 F2
WWKM BR4 214 E2
Rodney Pl STHWK SE1 18 D6
WALTH E17 51 G5
WIM/MER SW19 178 B4
Rodney Rd MTCM CR4 178 D5
NWMAL KT3 192 B2
WALW SE17 18 D7
WAN E11 71 F1
WHTN TW2 155 F2
WOT/HER KT12 188 A6
Rodney St IS N1 5 H2
Rodney Wy ROMW/RG RM7 56 D4
Rodway Rd BMLY BR1 184 A4
PUT/ROE SW15 158 D2
Rodwell Cl RSLP HA4 * 59 G5
Rodwell Rd EDUL SE22 163 G1
Roebuck Cl FELT TW13 154 A6
Roebuck La BKHH IG9 39 G3
Roebuck Rd BARK/HLT IG6 55 H2
CHSGTN KT9 206 C3
Roedean Av PEND EN3 24 E2
Roedean Cl ORP BR6 217 H2
PEND EN3 24 E2
Roedean Crs PUT/ROE SW15 158 B1
Roe End CDALE/KGS NW9 62 E1
Roe Gn CDALE/KGS NW9 62 E2
Roehampton Cl
PUT/ROE SW15 138 D5
Roehampton Dr CHST BR7 185 H2
Roehampton Ga
PUT/ROE SW15 158 B1
Roehampton High St
PUT/ROE SW15 158 D2
Roehampton La
PUT/ROE SW15 158 D2
Roehampton V
PUT/ROE SW15 158 C5
Roe La CDALE/KGS NW9 62 D1
Roe Rd WLGTN SM6 210 E4
Rofant Rd NTHWD HA6 40 C2
Roffey St POP/IOD E14 125 F2
Rogers Gdns DAGE RM10 92 C3
Rogers Rd CAN/RD E16 106 D5
DAGE RM10 92 C3
TOOT SW17 160 C6
Rogers Ruff NTHWD HA6 40 A4
Roger St BMSBY WC1N 5 H7
Rogers Wk
NFNCH/WDSPK N12 33 F5
Rojack Rd FSTH SE23 164 A3
Rokeby Gdns WFD IG8 52 E4
Rokeby Pl RYNPK SW20 176 E3
Rokeby Rd BROCKY SE4 * 144 C3
Rokeby St SRTFD E15 88 C6
Rokesby Cl WELL DA16 147 J3
Rokesby Pl ALP/SUD HA0 79 K3
Rokesly Av CEND/HSY/T N8 66 E2
Roland Gdns SKENS SW7 120 B5
Roland Ms WCHPL E1 * 105 F4
Roland Rd WALTH E17 70 B1
Roland Wy SKENS SW7 120 B5
WALW SE17 122 E5
WPK KT4 192 C6
Roles Gv CHDH RM6 73 K1
Rolfe Cl EBAR EN4 21 J5
Rolinsden Wy HAYES BR2 215 H2
Rollesby Rd CHSGTN KT9 206 C4
Rollesby Wy THMD SE28 109 J6
Rolleston Av STMC/STPC BR5 201 G3
Rolleston Cl STMC/STPC BR5 201 G4
Rolleston Rd SAND/SEL CR2 211 K5
Roll Gdns GNTH/NBYPK IG2 72 A2
Rollins St PECK SE15 123 K6
Rollit Crs HSLW TW3 135 F6
Rollit St HOLWY N7 85 G3
Rolls Blds FLST/FETLN EC4A 11 J3
Rollscourt Av HNHL SE24 142 D6
Rolls Park Av CHING E4 51 J2
Rolls Park Rd CHING E4 51 K1
Rolls Rd STHWK SE1 123 G5
Rolls Royce Cl WLGTN SM6 210 E5
Rolt St DEPT SE8 124 C6
NWCR SE14 124 B6
Rolvenden Gdns BMLY BR1 184 C4
Rolvenden Pl TOTM N17 50 C4
Roman Cl ACT W3 117 J2
EBED/NFELT TW14 134 B6
RAIN RM13 111 F1
Romanfield Rd
BRXS/STRHM SW2 162 A2
Romanhurst Av HAYES BR2 199 H1
Romanhurst Gdns HAYES BR2 199 H1
Roman Rd BORE WD6 29 K1
CAR SM5 209 K6
Roman Ri NRWD SE19 180 E2
Roman Rd BETH E2 105 F1
BOW E3 87 H6
CHSWK W4 118 B4
CRICK NW2 82 A1
EHAM E6 107 H3
IL IG1 90 B4
MUSWH N10 48 B3
Roman Sq THMD SE28 128 B1
Roman Wy CROY/NA CR0 196 C6
EN EN1 24 B6
HOLWY N7 85 F4
Romany Gdns CHEAM SM3 193 K4
Romany Ri STMC/STPC BR5 201 H5
Roma Rd WALTH E17 51 G6
Romberg Rd TOOT SW17 161 F5
Romborough Gdns LEW SE13 145 F6
Romborough Wy LEW SE13 145 F6
Rom Crs ROMW/RG RM7 75 G4
Romeland BORE WD6 29 K1
Romero Cl BRXN/ST SW9 142 A4
Romero Sq BKHTH/KID SE3 146 B5
Romeyn Rd
STRHM/NOR SW16 162 A5
Romford Rd CHIG IG7 55 K2
SRTFD E15 88 D4
Romford St WCHPL E1 104 C4
Romilly Dr OXHEY WD19 27 J6
Romilly Rd FSBYPK N4 67 H6
Romilly St SOHO/SHAV W1D 10 D5
Rommany Rd WNWD SE27 162 E6
Romney Cl CHSGTN KT9 206 A2
GLDGN NW11 65 G5
NWCR SE14 143 K1
RYLN/HDSTN HA2 60 A4
TOTM N17 50 D4
Romney Dr BMLY BR1 184 C3
RYLN/HDSTN HA2 60 A4
Romney Rd GNWCH SE10 125 F6
NWMAL KT3 192 A3
WOOL/PLUM SE18 127 H3
YEAD UB4 94 B1
Romney Rw CRICK NW2 * 64 B6
Romney St WEST SW1P 16 D5
Romola Rd HNHL SE24 162 C3
Romsey Cl ORP BR6 216 C2
Romsey Rd DAGW RM9 91 K6
WEA W13 * 97 G6
Romside Pl ROMW/RG RM7 75 F1

Rom Valley Wy ROMW/RG RM7 75 G3
Ronald Av SRTFD E15 106 C2
Ronald Cl BECK BR3 198 C2
Ronalds Rd BMLY BR1 183 K4
HBRY N5 85 G3
Ronaldstone Rd BFN/LL DA15 167 K1
Rona Rd HAMP NW3 84 A2
Ronart St KTN/HRWW/WS HA3 43 F6
Rona Wk IS N1 85 K4
Rondu Rd CRICK NW2 82 C3
Ronelean Rd SURB KT6 191 G6
Roneo Cnr ROMW/RG RM7 75 H5
Roneo Link HCH RM12 75 H5
Ronfearn Av STMC/STPC BR5 202 E2
Ron Leighton Wy EHAM E6 89 J6
Ronnie La BCTR RM8 73 J6
Ron Todd Cl DAGE RM10 92 C6
Rood La FENCHST EC3M 13 G5
Rookby Ct WCHMH N21 35 H4
Rook Cl WBLY HA9 80 D1
Rookeries Cl FELT TW13 154 A5
Rookery Dr CHST BR7 185 F4
Rookery Gdns STMC/STPC BR5 202 D2
Rookery La HAYES BR2 200 C3
Rookery Rd CLAP SW4 141 H5
The Rookery STRHM/NOR SW16 * 180 A2
Rookery Wy CDALE/KGS NW9 63 H2
Rookesley Rd STMC/STPC BR5 202 E4
Rookfield Av MUSWH N10 66 C1
Rookfield Cl MUSWH N10 66 C1
Rookley Cl BELMT SM2 209 F6
Rooks Ter WDR/YW UB7 * 112 B2
Rookstone Rd TOOT SW17 178 E1
Rookwood Av NWMAL KT3 192 D1
WLGTN SM6 210 D2
Rookwood Gdns CHING E4 * 38 D4
Rookwood Rd STNW/STAM N16 68 C4
Roosevelt Wy DAGE RM10 93 F4
Rootes Dr NKENS W10 100 B3
Ropemaker Rd BERM/RHTH SE16 124 B2
Ropemaker's Flds POP/IOD E14 * 105 H6
Ropemaker St BARB EC2Y 12 E1
Roper La STHWK SE1 19 H3
Ropers Av CHING E4 52 A1
Ropers Orch CHEL SW3 * 120 D6
Roper St ELTH/MOT SE9 146 E6
Roper Wy MTCM CR4 179 F5
Ropery St BOW E3 105 H3
Rope St BERM/RHTH SE16 124 B3
Ropewalk Gdns WCHPL E1 104 C5
Ropewalk Ms HACK E8 * 86 B5
Rope Yard Rails WOOL/PLUM SE18 127 G3
Ropley St BETH E2 104 C1
Rosa Alba Ms HBRY N5 85 J2
Rosa Av ASHF TW15 152 D6
Rosaline Rd FUL/PGN SW6 139 H1
Rosaline Ter FUL/PGN SW6 * 139 H1
Rosamond St SYD SE26 163 J5
Rosamond Vls MORT/ESHN SW14 * 138 A5
Rosamund Cl SAND/SEL CR2 211 K2
Rosamun Rd NWDGN UB2 114 D4
Rosary Cl HSLW TW3 134 D3
Rosary Gdns ASHF TW15 152 E6
BUSH WD23 28 E2
SKENS SW7 120 B4
Rosary Ga BTSEA SW11 141 G1
Rosaville Rd FUL/PGN SW6 139 J1
Roscoe St STLK EC1Y 6 D7
Roscoff Cl EDGW HA8 44 D4
Roseacre Cl WEA W13 97 H4
Roseacre Rd WELL DA16 148 C4
Rose Aly LVPST EC2M 13 H2
STHWK SE1 12 D7
Roseary Cl WDR/YW UB7 112 A4
Rose Av MRDN SM4 194 B2
MTCM CR4 178 E4
SWFD E18 53 F5
Rosebank PGE/AN SE20 181 J3
Rosebank Av ALP/SUD HA0 79 F2
Rose Bank Cl NFNCH/WDSPK N12 47 J1
Rosebank Cl TEDD TW11 174 B2
Rosebank Est BOW E3 105 H1
Rosebank Gdns ACT W3 * 99 F5
BOW E3 * 105 G1
Rosebank Gv WALTH E17 51 H6
Rosebank Rd HNWL W7 115 K2
WALTH E17 69 J3
Rosebank Wk CAMTN NW1 * 84 D5
Rosebank Wy ACT W3 99 F5
Roseberry Gdns FSBYPK N4 67 H3
ORP BR6 216 E1
Roseberry Pl HACK E8 86 B4
Roseberry St BERM/RHTH SE16 123 J4
Rosebery Av BFN/LL DA15 167 K2
CLKNW EC1R 5 J7
MNPK E12 89 J4
NWMAL KT3 176 C5
RYLN/HDSTN HA2 77 J2
THHTH CR7 180 D5
TOTM N17 50 C5
Rosebery Cl MRDN SM4 193 G3
Rosebery Ct CLKNW EC1R 5 J6
Rosebery Gdns CEND/HSY/T N8 * 66 E2
SUT SM1 209 F2
WEA W13 97 G5
Rosebery Ms MUSWH N10 48 C5
Rosebery Pde EW KT17 * 207 H5
Rosebery Rd BUSH WD23 28 B3
CLAP SW4 161 K1
HSLW TW3 135 H6
KUT/HW KT1 175 J5
MUSWH N10 48 C5
SUT SM1 208 D4
Rosebine Av WHTN TW2 155 J2
Rosebriars ESH/CLAY KT10 204 C3
Rosebury Rd FUL/PGN SW6 140 A3
Rosebury Sq WFD IG8 54 A3
Rosebury V RSLP HA4 58 E6
Rose Ct WCHPL E1 13 J2
Rosecourt Rd CROY/NA CR0 196 A3
Rosecroft Av HAMP NW3 82 E1
Rosecroft Cl STMC/STPC BR5 202 D3
Rosecroft Ct NTHWD HA6 * 40 A2
Rose Croft Gdns CRICK NW2 81 J1
Rosecroft Gdns WHTN TW2 155 J3
Rosecroft Rd STHL UB1 96 A3
Rosecroft Wk ALP/SUD HA0 79 K3
PIN HA5 59 H2
Rose & Crown Yd STJS SW1Y * 16 B1
Rose Dl ORP BR6 201 G6
Rosedale Av HYS/HAR UB3 94 B4
Rosedale Cl ABYW SE2 128 C3
HNWL W7 116 A2
STAN HA7 43 H2
Rosedale Dr DAGW RM9 91 H6
Rosedale Gdns DAGW RM9 91 H5
Rosedale Pl CROY/NA CR0 198 A4
Rosedale Rd DAGW RM9 91 H5
EW KT17 207 J3
FSTGT E7 89 G3
RCH/KEW TW9 137 F5
ROM RM1 56 E6
Rosedene Av CROY/NA CR0 195 K4
GFD/PVL UB6 96 A2
MRDN SM4 193 K2
STRHM/NOR SW16 162 A5
Rosedene Gdns GNTH/NBYPK IG2 72 A1
Rosedene Ter LEY E10 69 K6
Rosedew Rd HMSMTH W6 119 G6
Rose End WPK KT4 193 G5
Rosefield POP/IOD E14 105 J6
Rosefield Cl CAR SM5 209 J3
Rosefield Gdns POP/IOD E14 105 J6
Rose Garden Cl EDGW HA8 44 A2
Rose Gdns EA W5 116 E3
FELT TW13 153 K4
STHL UB1 96 A3
STWL/WRAY TW19 152 A2
Rose Gln CDALE/KGS NW9 63 F1
ROMW/RG RM7 75 G5
Rosehart Ms NTGHL W11 100 E5
Rosehatch Av CHDH RM6 55 K6
Roseheath Rd HSLWW TW4 134 E6
Rosehill ESH/CLAY KT10 205 G4
HPTN TW12 173 F4
Rose Hl SUT SM1 194 A6
Rosehill Av SUT SM1 194 B5
Rosehill Court Pde MRDN SM4 * 194 B4
Rosehill Gdns GFD/PVL UB6 79 F3
SUT SM1 194 A6
Rose Hill Pk West SUT SM1 194 B5
Rosehill Rd WAND/EARL SW18 160 B1
Rose Joan Ms KIL/WHAMP NW6 82 E2
Roseland Cl TOTM N17 49 K3
Rose La CHDH RM6 74 A1
Rose Lawn BUSH WD23 28 C3
Roseleigh Av HBRY N5 85 H2
Roseleigh Cl TWK TW1 156 E1
Rosemary Av E/WMO/HCT KT8 173 F6
ED N9 36 D3
ENC/FH EN2 23 K2
FNCH N3 47 F5
HSLWW TW4 134 C3
ROM RM1 57 H6
Rosemary Cl CROY/NA CR0 195 K4
Rosemary Dr POP/IOD E14 106 B5
REDBR IG4 71 H2
Rosemary Gdns BCTR RM8 74 B5
CHSGTN KT9 206 A2
Rosemary La MORT/ESHN SW14 137 K4
Rosemary Rd PECK SE15 143 G1
TOOT SW17 160 B5
WELL DA16 148 A2
Rosemary St IS N1 85 K6
Rosemead CDALE/KGS NW9 63 H4
Rosemead Av FELT TW13 153 J4
MTCM CR4 179 H6
WBLY HA9 80 A3
Rose Ms UED N18 36 D6
Rosemont Av NFNCH/WDSPK N12 47 G2
Rosemont Rd ACT W3 98 D6
HAMP NW3 83 G4
NWMAL KT3 175 K6
RCHPK/HAM TW10 157 F1
Rosemoor St CHEL SW3 14 E7
Rosemount Cl WFD IG8 53 K2
Rosemount Dr BMLY BR1 200 E1
Rosemount Rd ALP/SUD HA0 80 A6
WEA W13 97 G5
Rosenau Crs BTSEA SW11 140 E2
Rosenau Rd BTSEA SW11 140 D2
Rosendale Rd DUL SE21 162 D4
Roseneath Av WCHMH N21 35 H3
Roseneath Pl STRHM/NOR SW16 162 B6
Roseneath Rd BTSEA SW11 161 F1
Roseneath Wk EN EN1 24 A5
Rosenheath Cl ORP BR6 217 H5
Rosens Wk EDGW HA8 30 D5
Rosenthal Rd CAT SE6 164 E1
Rosenthorpe Rd PECK SE15 144 A6
Rose Park Cl YEAD UB4 95 G4
Roserton St POP/IOD E14 125 F2
The Rosery CROY/NA CR0 198 A3
Rose Sq CHEL SW3 * 120 C5
The Roses WFD IG8 * 52 D3
Rose St COVGDN WC2E 10 E5
Rosethorn Cl BAL SW12 161 H2
Rosetree Pl HPTN TW12 173 F3
Rosetta Cl VX/NE SW8 141 K1
Roseveare Rd LEE/GVPK SE12 166 B6
Roseville WCHMH N21 35 G3
Roseville Av HSLW TW3 135 F6
Roseville Rd HYS/HAR UB3 113 K5
Rosevine Rd RYNPK SW20 177 F4
Rose Wk BRYLDS KT5 191 J2
WWKM BR4 199 F6
Roseway DUL SE21 162 E1
EDGW HA8 30 E6
Rosewell Cl PGE/AN SE20 181 J3
Rosewood Av GFD/PVL UB6 79 G3
HCH RM12 93 J3
Rosewood Cl SCUP DA14 168 D5
Rosewood Ct KUTN/CMB KT2 175 H3
Rosewood Gv SUT SM1 194 B6
Rosewood Ter PGE/AN SE20 * 181 K3
Rosher Cl SRTFD E15 88 B5
Rosina St HOM E9 87 F4
Roskell Rd PUT/ROE SW15 139 G4
Roslin Rd ACT W3 117 J3
Roslin Wy BMLY BR1 183 K1
Roslyn Cl MTCM CR4 178 C5
Roslyn Gdns GPK RM2 57 H5
Roslyn Ms SEVS/STOTM N15 * 68 A2
Roslyn Rd SEVS/STOTM N15 67 K2
Rosmead Rd NTGHL W11 100 C6
Rosoman Pl CLKNW EC1R 5 K6
Rosoman St CLKNW EC1R 5 K5
Rossall Cl EMPK RM11 75 J3
Rossall Crs WLSDN NW10 98 B2
Ross Av BCTR RM8 74 B6
Ross Cl HYS/HAR UB3 113 G4
KTN/HRWW/WS HA3 42 C3
NTHLT UB5 78 D2
Rossdale SUT SM1 209 J3
Rossdale Dr CDALE/KGS NW9 62 E5
ED N9 36 E1
Rossdale Rd PUT/ROE SW15 139 F5
Rosse Ms BKHTH/KID SE3 146 A2
Rossendale St CLPT E5 68 D6
Rossendale Wy CAMTN NW1 84 C6
Rossetti Ms STJWD NW8 2 A1
Rossetti Rd BERM/RHTH SE16 123 J5
Ross House CHARL SE7 * 146 D1
Rossignol Gdns CAR SM5 195 F6
Rossindel Rd HSLW TW3 135 F6
Rossington Cl EN EN1 24 D1
Rossington St CLPT E5 68 C6
Rossiter Cl NRWD SE19 180 D3
Rossiter Flds BAR EN5 32 C1
Rossiter Rd BAL SW12 161 G3
Rosslyn Av BARN SW13 138 B4
BCTR RM8 74 B4
CHING E4 38 D4
EBAR EN4 33 J1
EBED/NFELT TW14 153 K1
Rosslyn Cl HYS/HAR UB3 94 B4
WWKM BR4 214 D1
Rosslyn Crs HRW HA1 61 F1
WBLY HA9 80 A1
Rosslyn Hl HAMP NW3 83 H3
Rosslyn Park Ms HAMP NW3 83 H3
Rosslyn Rd BARK IG11 90 D5
TWK TW1 156 D1
WALTH E17 * 70 A1
Rossmore Cl CAMTN NW1 * 2 D7
PEND EN3 25 F5
Rossmore Rd CAMTN NW1 2 D6
Ross Pde WLGTN SM6 210 B4
Ross Rd SNWD SE25 181 F6
WHTN TW2 155 H3
WLGTN SM6 210 C4
Ross Wy ELTH/MOT SE9 146 D4
NTHWD HA6 26 D6
Rosswood Gdns WLGTN SM6 210 B4
Rostella Rd TOOT SW17 160 C6
Rostrever Gdns HYS/HAR UB3 113 H1
Rostrevor Av SEVS/STOTM N15 68 B3
Rostrevor Gdns NWDGN UB2 114 D5
Rostrevor Rd FUL/PGN SW6 139 J2
WIM/MER SW19 177 K1
Rotary St STHWK SE1 18 A4
Rothbury Av RAIN RM13 111 K4
Rothbury Cots GNWCH SE10 125 H4
Rothbury Gdns ISLW TW7 136 B1
Rothbury Rd HOM E9 87 H5
Rotherfield Rd CAR SM5 210 A2
Rotherfield St IS N1 85 J5
Rotherham Wk STHWK SE1 * 18 B1
Rotherhill Av STRHM/NOR SW16 179 J2
Rotherhithe New Rd BERM/RHTH SE16 123 J5
Rotherhithe Old Rd BERM/RHTH SE16 124 A4
Rotherhithe St BERM/RHTH SE16 123 J2
Rotherhithe Tnl BERM/RHTH SE16 123 K2
Rothermere Rd CROY/NA CR0 211 F3
Rotherwick Hl EA W5 98 B3
Rotherwick Rd GLDGN NW11 64 E4
Rotherwood Cl RYNPK SW20 177 H4
Rotherwood Rd PUT/ROE SW15 139 G4
Rothery St IS N1 85 H6
Rothery Ter BRXN/ST SW9 * 142 C1
Rothesay Av GFD/PVL UB6 78 D4
RCHPK/HAM TW10 137 J5
RYNPK SW20 177 H5
Rothesay Rd SNWD SE25 196 E1
Rothsay Rd FSTGT E7 89 G5
Rothsay St STHWK SE1 19 G4
Rothschild Rd CHSWK W4 117 K4
Rothschild St WNWD SE27 162 C6
Rothwell Gdns DAGW RM9 91 J5
Rothwell Rd DAGW RM9 91 J6
Rothwell St CAMTN NW1 83 K6
Rotten Rw BAY/PAD W2 14 D2
Rotterdam Dr POP/IOD E14 125 F3
Rouel Rd BERM/RHTH SE16 123 H3
Rougemont Av MRDN SM4 193 K3
The Roughs NTHWD HA6 26 C5
Roundaway Rd CLAY IG5 53 K5
Roundel Cl BROCKY SE4 144 C5
Round Gv CROY/NA CR0 198 A4
Roundhay Cl FSTH SE23 164 A4
Roundhedge Wy ENC/FH EN2 23 F1
Round Hl SYD SE26 163 J4
Roundhill Dr ENC/FH EN2 23 F5
Roundlyn Gdns STMC/STPC BR5 202 C1
Roundtree Rd ALP/SUD HA0 79 H3
Roundways RSLP HA4 76 D1
The Roundway ESH/CLAY KT10 205 F4
TOTM N17 49 J4
WATW WD18 26 D1
Roundwood CHST BR7 185 G5
Roundwood Av STKPK UB11 113 F1
Roundwood Cl RSLP HA4 * 58 B4
Roundwood Pk WLSDN NW10 * 81 J6
Roundwood Rd WLSDN NW10 81 G4
Roundwood Ter STNW/STAM N16 68 A4
Rounton Rd BOW E3 105 J3
Roupell Rd BRXS/STRHM SW2 162 A3
Roupell St STHWK SE1 17 K1
Rousden St CAMTN NW1 84 C5
Rouse Gdns DUL SE21 163 F6
Rous Rd BKHH IG9 39 J2
Routemaster Cl PLSTW E13 107 F2
Routh Ct EBED/NFELT TW14 153 G3
Routh Rd WAND/EARL SW18 160 D2
Routh St EHAM E6 107 K4
Rover Av BARK/HLT IG6 55 F2
Rowallan Rd FUL/PGN SW6 139 H1
Rowan Av CHING E4 51 H2
Rowan Cl ALP/SUD HA0 79 G1
ASHF TW15 152 A6
EA W5 117 F2
IL IG1 90 D3
NWMAL KT3 176 B5
STAN HA7 43 F2
STRHM/NOR SW16 179 H4
Rowan Crs STRHM/NOR SW16 179 H4
Rowan Dr CDALE/KGS NW9 45 J6
Rowan Gdns CROY/NA CR0 212 B1
Rowan Pl HYS/HAR UB3 94 D6
Rowan Rd BTFD TW8 136 C1
HMSMTH W6 119 G4
STRHM/NOR SW16 179 H5
WDR/YW UB7 112 A4
The Rowans PLMGR N13 35 J5
Rowan Ter HMSMTH W6 119 G4
PGE/AN SE20 * 181 H4
WIM/MER SW19 * 177 H3
Rowantree Cl WCHMH N21 35 K3
Rowantree Ms ENC/FH EN2 23 H3
Rowantree Rd ENC/FH EN2 23 H3
WCHMH N21 35 K3
Rowan Wk EFNCH N2 65 G3
HAYES BR2 215 K1
NKENS W10 * 100 C3
Rowan Wy CHDH RM6 55 J6
Rowanwood Av BFN/LL DA15 168 B3
Rowben Cl TRDG/WHET N20 33 F3
Rowberry Cl FUL/PGN SW6 139 G1
Rowcross St STHWK SE1 123 G5
Rowdell Rd NTHLT UB5 78 A6
Rowden Pde CHING E4 * 51 J2
Rowden Rd BECK BR3 182 B4
CHING E4 51 K2
HOR/WEW KT19 206 E2
Rowditch La BTSEA SW11 141 F3
Rowdon Av WLSDN NW10 81 K5
Rowdown Crs CROY/NA CR0 214 B6
Rowdowns Rd DAGW RM9 92 B6
Rowe Gdns BARK IG11 109 F1
Rowe La HOM E9 86 E3
Rowena Crs BTSEA SW11 140 D3
Rowe Wk RYLN/HDSTN HA2 78 A1
Rowfant Rd TOOT SW17 161 F4
Rowhill Rd CLPT E5 86 D2
Rowington Cl BAY/PAD W2 101 F4
Rowland Av KTN/HRWW/WS HA3 43 J6
Rowland Gv SYD SE26 163 J5
Rowland Hill Av TOTM N17 49 J3
Rowland Hill St HAMP NW3 83 J3
Rowland Pl NTHWD HA6 * 40 C3
Rowlands Av PIN HA5 42 A2
Rowlands Cl HGT N6 * 66 A3
MLHL NW7 45 J3
Rowlands Rd BCTR RM8 74 B6
Rowland Wy WIM/MER SW19 178 A4
Rowley Av BFN/LL DA15 168 C2
Rowley Cl ALP/SUD HA0 80 B5
OXHEY WD19 27 J1
Rowley Cots WKENS W14 * 119 J4
Rowley Gdns FSBYPK N4 67 J4
Rowley Rd SEVS/STOTM N15 67 J2
Rowley Wy STJWD NW8 83 G6
Rowlheys Pl WDR/YW UB7 112 B3
Rowlls Rd KUT/HW KT1 175 G6
Rowney Gdns DAGW RM9 91 J4
Rowney Rd DAGW RM9 91 H4
Rowntree Clifford Cl PLSTW E13 107 F3
Rowntree Cl KIL/WHAMP NW6 * 82 E4
Rowntree Rd WHTN TW2 155 K3
Rowse Cl SRTFD E15 88 A6
Rowsley Av HDN NW4 46 A6
Rowstock Gdns HOLWY N7 84 D4
Rowton Rd WOOL/PLUM SE18 147 H1
Roxborough Av HRW HA1 60 D4
ISLW TW7 136 A1
Roxborough Pk HRW HA1 60 E4
Roxborough Rd HRW HA1 60 D2
Roxbourne Cl NTHLT UB5 77 H4
Roxburgh Rd WNWD SE27 180 C1
Roxburn Wy RSLP HA4 76 D1
Roxby Pl FUL/PGN SW6 119 K6
Roxeth Green Av RYLN/HDSTN HA2 78 B1
Roxeth Gv RYLN/HDSTN HA2 78 B2
Roxeth Hl RYLN/HDSTN HA2 60 D6
Roxley Rd LEW SE13 164 E1
Roxton Gdns CROY/NA CR0 213 H4
Roxwell Rd BARK IG11 109 G1
SHB W12 118 D2
Roxwell Wy WFD IG8 53 G3
Roxy Av CHDH RM6 73 J4
Royal Albert Wy CAN/RD E16 107 H6
Royal Ar CONDST W1S 10 A6
Royal Arsenal West WOOL/PLUM SE18 * 127 F5
Royal Av CHEL SW3 120 E5
WPK KT4 192 B6
Royal Circ WNWD SE27 162 B5
Royal Cl DEPT SE8 124 C6
GDMY/SEVK IG3 73 G4
ORP BR6 216 B2
STNW/STAM N16 68 A5
WIM/MER SW19 159 G4
WPK KT4 192 B6
Royal College St CAMTN NW1 84 C5
Royal Ct BANK EC3V 13 F4
ELTH/MOT SE9 * 166 E3
EN EN1 * 36 A1
Royal Crs GNTH/NBYPK IG2 72 D3
NTGHL W11 119 G2
RSLP HA4 77 J2
Royal Crescent Ms NTGHL W11 119 G2
Royal Docks Rd EHAM E6 108 B4
Royal Dr FBAR/BDGN N11 48 A1
Royal Herbert Pavilions WOOL/PLUM SE18 * 146 E2
Royal Hl GNWCH SE10 145 F1
Royal Hospital Rd CHEL SW3 120 E6
Royal Ms BAL SW12 161 G2
Royal Mint Pl WCHPL E1 13 K5
Royal Mint St WCHPL E1 13 K5
Royal Naval Pl NWCR SE14 144 C1
Royal Oak Ms TEDD TW11 174 B1
Royal Oak Pl EDUL SE22 163 J1
Royal Oak Rd HACK E8 86 D4
Royal Oak Yd STHWK SE1 19 G3
Royal Opera Ar STJS SW1Y * 10 C7
Royal Orchard Cl WAND/EARL SW18 159 H2
Royal Pde BKHTH/KID SE3 145 J3
CHST BR7 185 H3
FUL/PGN SW6 * 139 H1
Royal Pl GNWCH SE10 145 F1
Royal Rd CAN/RD E16 107 H5
LBTH SE11 122 C6
SCUP DA14 168 E5
TEDD TW11 173 J1
Royal Route WBLY HA9 80 B2
Royal St STHWK SE1 17 H4
Royal Victor Pl BOW E3 105 F1
Roycraft Av BARK IG11 109 F1
Roycroft Cl BRXS/STRHM SW2 * 162 B3
SWFD E18 53 F4
Roydene Rd WOOL/PLUM SE18 127 K6
Roydon Cl LOU IG10 39 J2
Roy Gdns GNTH/NBYPK IG2 72 E1
Roy Gv HPTN TW12 173 G2
Royle Cl GPK RM2 75 K2
Royle Crs WEA W13 97 G3
Roy Rd NTHWD HA6 40 D3
Roy Sq POP/IOD E14 105 G6
Royston Av CHING E4 51 J1
SUT SM1 209 H1
WLGTN SM6 210 D2
Royston Cl HEST TW5 134 A2
Royston Gdns IL IG1 71 H3
Royston Gv PIN HA5 41 K2
Royston Park Rd PIN HA5 41 K2
Royston Rd PGE/AN SE20 182 A4
RCHPK/HAM TW10 137 F6
The Roystons BRYLDS KT5 191 J2
Royston St BETH E2 104 E1
Rozel Rd VX/NE SW8 141 H3
Rubastic Rd NWDGN UB2 11[illegible] B3
Rubens Rd NTHLT UB5 95 G1
Rubens St CAT SE6 164 C4
Ruby Ms WALTH E17 * 51 J6
Ruby Rd WALTH E17 51 J6
Ruby St PECK SE15 123 J6
WLSDN NW10 80 E5
Ruby Triangle PECK SE15 * 123 J6
Ruckholt Cl LEY E10 87 K1
Ruckholt Rd LEY E10 87 K2
Rucklidge Av WLSDN NW10 99 H1
Rudall Crs HAMP NW3 83 H2
Ruddington Cl CLPT E5 87 G2
Ruddock Cl EDGW HA8 44 E3
Ruddstreet Cl WOOL/PLUM SE18 127 G4
Rudgwick Ter STJWD NW8 * 2 D1
Rudloe Rd BAL SW12 161 H2
Rudolf Pl VX/NE SW8 121 K6
Rudolph Rd BUSH WD23 28 A1
KIL/WHAMP NW6 100 E1
PLSTW E13 106 D1
Rudyard Gv EDGW HA8 44 E2
Ruffetts Cl SAND/SEL CR2 212 D5
The Ruffetts SAND/SEL CR2 212 D5
Ruffle Cl WDR/YW UB7 112 B2
Rufford Cl KTN/HRWW/WS HA3 61 G3
Rufford St IS N1 84 E6
Rufford Street Ms IS N1 84 E5
Rufus Cl RSLP HA4 77 H
Rufus St FSBYE EC1V 7 G
Rugby Av ALP/SUD HA0 79 J
ED N9 36 B
GFD/PVL UB6 78 D
Rugby Cl HRW HA1 60 E
Rugby Gdns DAGW RM9 91 J
Rugby La BELMT SM2 208 B
Rugby Rd CDALE/KGS NW9 62 C
CHSWK W4 118 B
DAGW RM9 91 H
TWK TW1 155 K
Rugby St BMSBY WC1N 5 C
Rugg St POP/IOD E14 105
Ruislip Cl GFD/PVL UB6 96 E
Ruislip Ct RSLP HA4 * 58 D
Ruislip Rd GFD/PVL UB6 96
NTHLT UB5 77
Ruislip Rd East GFD/PVL UB6 96
Ruislip St TOOT SW17 160
Rumbold Rd FUL/PGN SW6 140
Rum Cl WAP E1W 104
Rumsey Cl HPTN TW12 172
Rumsey Rd BRXN/ST SW9 142
Runbury Cir CDALE/KGS NW9 63
Runcorn Cl TOTM N17 68
Runcorn Pl NTGHL W11 100
Rundell Crs HDN NW4 63
Runes Cl MTCM CR4 194
Runnelfield HRW HA1 78
Runnymede WIM/MER SW19 178
Runnymede Cl WHTN TW2 155
Runnymede Crs STRHM/NOR SW16 179
Runnymede Gdns GFD/PVL UB6 96
HSLW TW3 155
Runnymede Rd WHTN TW2 155
Runway Cl CDALE/KGS NW9 45

The Runway RSLP HA4 77 F3
Rupack St BERM/RHTH SE16 * 123 K2
Rupert Av WBLY HA9 80 A3
Rupert Ct E/WMO/HCT KT8 * 189 F1
SOHO/SHAV W1D 10 C5
Rupert Gdns BRXN/ST SW9 142 C3
Rupert Rd ARCH N19 84 D1
CHSWK W4 118 B3
KIL/WHAMP NW6 100 D1
Rupert St SOHO/SHAV W1D 10 C5
Rural Cl EMPK RM11 75 K5
Rural Wy STRHM/NOR SW16 179 G3
Rusbridge Cl HACK E8 86 C3
Ruscoe Rd CAN/RD E16 106 D5
Ruscombe Wy
EBED/NFELT TW14 153 J2
Rusham Rd BAL SW12 160 E1
Rushbridge Cl CROY/NA CR0 196 D3
Rushbrook Crs WALTH E17 51 H4
Rushbrook Rd ELTH/MOT SE9 167 H4
Rush Common Ms
BRXS/STRHM SW2 161 K2
Rushcroft Rd
BRXS/STRHM SW2 142 B5
CHING E4 51 K3
Rushden Cl NRWD SE19 180 E3
Rushdene Av EBAR EN4 33 J2
Rushdene Cl NTHLT UB5 95 G1
Rushdene Crs NTHLT UB5 95 F1
Rushdene Rd PIN HA5 59 G3
Rushden Gdns CLAY IG5 54 A6
MLHL NW7 46 A2
Rushdon Cl ROM RM1 75 J2
Rushet Rd STMC/STPC BR5 186 B5
Rushett Cl THDIT KT7 190 C5
Rushett Rd THDIT KT7 190 C4
Rushey Cl NWMAL KT3 192 A1
Rushey Gn CAT SE6 164 E2
Rushey Hl ENC/FH EN2 23 F5
Rushey Md BROCKY SE4 144 D6
Rushford Rd BROCKY SE4 164 C1
Rush Green Gdns
ROMW/RG RM7 74 E5
Rush Green Rd
ROMW/RG RM7 74 E5
Rushgrove Av
CDALE/KGS NW9 63 H1
Rushgrove Pde
CDALE/KGS NW9 * 63 H2
Rushgrove St
WOOL/PLUM SE18 126 E4
Rush Hill Ms BTSEA SW11 141 F4
Rush Hill Rd BTSEA SW11 141 F4
Rushley Cl HAYES BR2 215 H2
Rushmead BETH E2 104 D2
RCHPK/HAM TW10 156 C5
Rushmead Cl CROY/NA CR0 212 B2
Rushmere Ct WPK KT4 192 D6
Rushmere Pl WIM/MER SW19 177 G1
Rushmon Pl CHEAM SM3 * 208 C4
Rushmon Vls NWMAL KT3 * 192 C1
Rushmoor Cl PIN HA5 59 F1
Rushmore Cl BMLY BR1 184 D6
Rushmore Ct WATW WD18 * 26 B1
Rushmore Rd CLPT E5 86 E2
Rusholme Av DAGE RM10 92 C1
Rusholme Gv NRWD SE19 181 F1
Rusholme Rd PUT/ROE SW15 159 G1
ushout Av
KTN/HRWW/WS HA3 61 H3
ushton St IS N1 7 F2
ushworth St STHWK SE1 18 B2
ushy Meadow La CAR SM5 194 D6
uskin Av EBED/NFELT TW14 153 J2
MNPK E12 89 J4
RCH/KEW TW9 137 H1
WELL DA16 148 B4
uskin Cl GLDGN NW11 65 F3
uskin Dr ORP BR6 216 E1
WELL DA16 148 B4
WPK KT4 192 E6
uskin Gdns EA W5 97 K3
HARH RM3 57 K4
KTN/HRWW/WS HA3 62 B2
uskin Gv WELL DA16 148 B3
uskin Rd BELV DA17 129 H4
CAR SM5 210 A3
CROY/NA CR0 196 C6
ISLW TW7 136 A4
STHL UB1 95 J6
TOTM N17 50 B4
skin Wk ED N9 36 C4
HAYES BR2 200 D3
HNHL SE24 142 D6
skin Wy WIM/MER SW19 178 C5
sland Av ORP BR6 216 D1
sland Park Rd HRW HA1 60 E1
sper Cl CRICK NW2 82 A1
STAN HA7 29 J6
sper Rd DAGW RM9 91 J4
WDGN N22 49 H5
ssel Cl BECK BR3 182 E6
ssell Av WDGN N22 49 H5
ssell Cl BKHTH/KID SE3 146 B1
CHSWK W4 118 C6
DART DA1 150 D4
NTHWD HA6 40 A1
RSLP HA4 59 G6
WLSDN NW10 80 E5
ssell Ct BAR EN5 * 21 G5
WHALL SW1A 16 B1
ssell Dr STWL/WRAY TW19 152 A1
ssell Gdns GLDGN NW11 64 C3
RCHPK/HAM TW10 156 D4
TRDG/WHET N20 33 J4
WDR/YW UB7 112 D5
WKENS W14 * 119 H3
sell Gardens Ms
WKENS W14 119 H2
sell Gv BRXN/ST SW9 142 B2
MLHL NW7 45 G1
sell Kerr Cl CHSWK W4 * 137 K1
sell La TRDG/WHET N20 33 K4
sell Pde GLDGN NW11 * 64 C3
sell Pl HAMP NW3 83 J3
sell Rd BKHH IG9 39 G3
AN/RD E16 106 E5
DALE/KGS NW9 63 H3
END/HSY/T N8 66 D3
HING E4 37 H6
EN EN1 24 B1
MTCM CR4 178 D6
NTHLT UB5 78 C3
NTHWD HA6 26 A5
SEVS/STOTM N15 68 A2
TRDG/WHET N20 33 J4
WALTH E17 69 K3
WDGN N22 49 F2
WHTN TW2 156 A1
WIM/MER SW19 177 K3
WKENS W14 119 H3
Russell Sq RSQ WC1B 10 D1
Russell St HOL/ALD WC2B 11 F5
Russell Wy OXHEY WD19 27 F2
SUT SM1 209 F3
Russell Yd PUT/ROE SW15 139 H5
Russet Cl HGDN/ICK UB10 94 A3
Russet Crs HOLWY N7 * 85 F3
Russet Dr CROY/NA CR0 198 B5
Russets Cl CHING E4 38 B6
Russett Cl ORP BR6 217 H3
Russia Dock Rd
BERM/RHTH SE16 * 124 B1
Russia La BETH E2 104 E1
Russia Rw CITYW EC2V 12 D4
Rusthall Av CHSWK W4 118 A3
Rusthall Cl CROY/NA CR0 197 K3
Rustic Av STRHM/NOR SW16 179 G3
Rustic Pl ALP/SUD HA0 79 K2
Rustington Wk CHEAM SM3 193 J4
Ruston Av BRYLDS KT5 191 J4
Ruston Gdns STHGT/OAK N14 34 A1
Ruston Ms NTGHL W11 * 100 C5
Ruston Rd WOOL/PLUM SE18 126 D3
Ruston St BOW E3 87 H6
Rust Sq CMBW SE5 142 E1
Rutford Rd
STRHM/NOR SW16 179 K1
Ruth Cl STAN HA7 62 B1
Rutherford Cl BELMT SM2 209 H4
Rutherford St WEST SW1P 16 C6
Rutherford Wy BUSH WD23 28 D3
WBLY HA9 80 C1
Rutherglen Rd ABYW SE2 128 B6
Rutherwyke Cl EW KT17 207 J4
Ruthin Cl CDALE/KGS NW9 63 G3
Ruthven St HOM E9 87 F6
Rutland Av BFN/LL DA15 168 B2
Rutland Cl BXLY DA5 168 E3
CHSGTN KT9 206 B4
MORT/ESHN SW14 137 J4
WIM/MER SW19 178 D2
Rutland Ct CHST BR7 185 F4
SKENS SW7 14 D3
Rutland Dr MRDN SM4 193 K4
RCHPK/HAM TW10 156 E3
Rutland Gdns BCTR RM8 91 J3
CROY/NA CR0 212 A2
FSBYPK N4 67 H3
SKENS SW7 14 D3
WEA W13 * 97 G4
Rutland Gardens Ms
SKENS SW7 14 D3
Rutland Ga BELV DA17 129 J5
HAYES BR2 199 J1
SKENS SW7 14 C3
Rutland Gate Ms
SKENS SW7 * 14 C3
Rutland Gv HMSMTH W6 118 E5
Rutland Ms STJWD NW8 * 83 G6
Rutland Ms South
SKENS SW7 * 14 C4
Rutland Pk CAT SE6 164 C4
CRICK NW2 82 A4
Rutland Pl BUSH WD23 * 28 D3
FARR EC1M * 12 B1
Rutland Rd FSTGT E7 89 H5
HOM E9 87 F6
HRW HA1 60 C3
HYS/HAR UB3 113 G4
IL IG1 90 B2
STHL UB1 96 A3
WALTH E17 69 J3
WAN E11 71 F2
WHTN TW2 155 J4
Rutland St SKENS SW7 14 D4
Rutland Wk CAT SE6 164 C4
Rutland Wy STMC/STPC BR5 202 D3
Rutley Cl WALW SE17 122 C6
Rutlish Rd WIM/MER SW19 177 K4
Rutter Gdns MTCM CR4 194 C1
Rutters Cl WDR/YW UB7 112 D2
Rutt's Ter NWCR SE14 144 A2
The Rutts BUSH WD23 28 D3
Ruvigny Gdns PUT/ROE SW15 139 G4
Ruxley Cl HOR/WEW KT19 206 D3
SCUP DA14 186 E2
Ruxley Crs ESH/CLAY KT10 205 H5
Ruxley La HOR/WEW KT19 206 E3
Ruxley Ms HOR/WEW KT19 206 D3
Ruxley Rdg ESH/CLAY KT10 205 G5
Ruxley Towers
ESH/CLAY KT10 * 205 G5
Ryan Cl BKHTH/KID SE3 146 A5
RSLP HA4 59 F5
Ryan Ct OXHEY WD19 * 27 J2
Ryan Dr BTFD TW8 116 B6
Ryarsh Crs ORP BR6 216 E2
Rycroft Wy TOTM N17 * 50 B6
Rycullf Sq BKHTH/KID SE3 145 J3
Rydal Cl HDN NW4 46 C4
Rydal Crs GFD/PVL UB6 97 H2
Rydal Dr WWKM BR4 199 H6
Rydal Gdns CDALE/KGS NW9 63 G2
HSLW TW3 155 G1
PUT/ROE SW15 176 B1
WBLY HA9 61 J5
Rydal Mt HAYES BR2 * 199 J1
Rydal Rd STRHM/NOR SW16 179 J1
Rydal Wy PEND EN3 36 E1
RSLP HA4 77 G2
Rydens Av WOT/HER KT12 188 B6
Rydens Cl WOT/HER KT12 188 B6
Rydens Pk WOT/HER KT12 188 C6
Rydens Rd WOT/HER KT12 188 B6
Ryde Pl TWK TW1 156 D1
Ryder Cl BUSH WD23 28 B1
Ryder Dr BERM/RHTH SE16 123 J5
Ryder Gdns RAIN RM13 93 H4
Ryder St WHALL SW1A 10 A7
Ryder Yd STJS SW1Y 10 B7
Ryde Vale Rd BAL SW12 161 G4
Rydon Ms WIM/MER SW19 177 F3
Rydston Cl HOLWY N7 85 F5
Rye Cl BXLY DA5 169 J1
Ryecotes Md DUL SE21 163 F3
Rye Crs STMC/STPC BR5 202 E5
Ryecroft Av CLAY IG5 54 B5
WHTN TW2 155 G3
Ryecroft Rd LEW SE13 145 F6
STMC/STPC BR5 201 J3
STRHM/NOR SW16 180 B2
Ryecroft St FUL/PGN SW6 140 A2
Ryedale EDUL SE22 163 J1
Ryefield Av HGDN/ICK UB10 76 A6
Ryefield Crs PIN HA5 * 40 E5
Ryefield Pde NTHWD HA6 * 40 E5
Ryefield Rd NRWD SE19 180 D2
Rye Hill Pk PECK SE15 143 K5
Ryelands Crs LEE/GVPK SE12 166 B1
Rye La PECK SE15 143 H3
Rye Rd PECK SE15 144 A5
The Rye STHGT/OAK N14 34 C2
Rye Wk PUT/ROE SW15 139 G6
Rye Wy EDGW HA8 44 B2
Ryfold Rd WIM/MER SW19 159 K5
Ryhope Rd FBAR/BDGN N11 34 B6
Ryland Cl FELT TW13 153 J6
Rylandes Rd CRICK NW2 81 J1
SAND/SEL CR2 212 D6
Ryland Rd KTTN NW5 * 84 B4
Rylett Crs SHB W12 118 C3
Rylett Rd SHB W12 118 C2
Rylston Rd FUL/PGN SW6 119 J6
PLMGR N13 35 K5
Rymer Rd CROY/NA CR0 197 F4
Rymer St HNHL SE24 162 C1
Rymill St CAN/RD E16 127 F1
Rysbrack St CHEL SW3 14 E4
Rythe Cl CHSGTN KT9 205 J5
Rythe Ct THDIT KT7 190 B4
Rythe Rd ESH/CLAY KT10 204 D3
Ryves Cots MTCM CR4 * 179 F5

S

Sabbarton St CAN/RD E16 106 D5
Sabine Rd BTSEA SW11 140 E4
Sable Cl HSLWW TW4 134 B4
Sable St IS N1 85 H5
Sach Rd CLPT E5 68 D6
Sackville Cl RYLN/HDSTN HA2 78 D1
Sackville Est
STRHM/NOR SW16 161 K5
Sackville Gdns IL IG1 71 K5
Sackville Rd BELMT SM2 208 E5
Sackville St CONDST W1S 10 A6
Saddlers Cl PIN HA5 42 A1
Saddlers Ms KUT/HW KT1 174 D4
Saddlescombe Wy
NFNCH/WDSPK N12 46 E1
Sadler Cl MTCM CR4 178 E5
Sadlers Gate Ms
PUT/ROE SW15 139 F4
Sadlers Ride E/WMO/HCT KT8 173 H5
Saffron Av POP/IOD E14 106 B6
Saffron Cl CROY/NA CR0 195 K3
GLDGN NW11 64 D2
Saffron Hl HCIRC EC1N 11 K1
Saffron Rd CRW RM5 57 F5
Saffron St HCIRC EC1N 11 K1
Saffron Wy SURB KT6 190 E5
Sage Cl EHAM E6 107 K4
Sage Ms EDUL SE22 143 G6
Sage St WCHPL E1 104 E6
Sage Wy FSBYW WC1X 5 G5
Sage Yd SURB KT6 191 G5
Saigasso Cl CAN/RD E16 107 H5
Sail St LBTH SE11 17 H6
Sainfoin Rd TOOT SW17 161 F4
Sainsbury Rd NRWD SE19 181 F1
St Agatha's Dr
KUTN/CMB KT2 175 G2
St Agatha's Gv CAR SM5 194 E5
St Agnes Cl HOM E9 * 86 E6
St Agnes Pl LBTH SE11 122 C6
St Agnes Well STLK EC1Y 7 F6
St Aidan's Rd EDUL SE22 163 J1
WEA W13 116 C2
St Albans Av CHSWK W4 118 A3
FELT TW13 172 C1
St Alban's Av EHAM E6 107 K2
St Albans Crs WDGN N22 49 G4
St Albans Farm
EBED/NFELT TW14 * 134 B6
St Alban's Gdns TEDD TW11 174 B1
St Alban's Gv CAR SM5 194 D4
KENS W8 120 A3
St Albans La GLDGN NW11 64 E5
St Alban's Ms BAY/PAD W2 8 B1
St Alban's Pl IS N1 6 A1
St Albans Rd BAR EN5 20 C2
GDMY/SEVK IG3 73 F5
KUTN/CMB KT2 175 F2
SUT SM1 208 D2
St Alban's Rd KTTN NW5 84 A1
WFD IG8 52 E3
WLSDN NW10 81 G6
St Alban's St STJS SW1Y 10 C6
St Albans Ter HMSMTH W6 119 H6
St Alfege Pas GNWCH SE10 125 F6
St Alfege Rd CHARL SE7 126 C6
St Alphage Gdns BARB EC2Y 12 D2
St Alphage Highwalk
BARB EC2Y 12 D2
St Alphage Wk EDGW HA8 * 44 E5
St Alphege Rd ED N9 36 E2
St Alphonsus Rd CLAP SW4 141 H5
St Amunds Cl CAT SE6 164 D6
St Andrews Av ALP/SUD HA0 79 G2
HCH RM12 93 H3
St Andrews Cl
BERM/RHTH SE16 * 123 J5
RSLP HA4 59 H6
STAN HA7 * 43 J5
THDIT KT7 190 C5
THMD SE28 109 K5
WIM/MER SW19 178 A2
St Andrew's Cl CRICK NW2 * 81 K1
ISLW TW7 135 J2
NFNCH/WDSPK N12 * 33 G6
St Andrew's Ct
WAND/EARL SW18 160 B4
St Andrews Dr STAN HA7 43 J4
STMC/STPC BR5 202 C3
St Andrew's Gv
STNW/STAM N16 67 K5
St Andrew's Hl BLKFR EC4V 12 B4
St Andrews Ms BAL SW12 161 J3
St Andrew's Ms
STNW/STAM N16 68 A5
St Andrew's Pl CAMTN NW1 3 J6
St Andrews Rd CAR SM5 209 J1
CDALE/KGS NW9 63 F5
ED N9 36 E2
ROMW/RG RM7 75 F3
SCUP DA14 168 E5
St Andrew's Rd ACT W3 99 G5
CROY/NA CR0 211 J2
EN EN1 23 K4
GLDGN NW11 64 D3
HNWL W7 115 K2
IL IG1 71 K4
PLSTW E13 107 F2
SURB KT6 190 E3
WALTH E17 51 F5
WAN E11 70 C3
WKENS W14 119 H6
WLSDN NW10 81 K4
St Andrew's Sq NTGHL W11 * 100 C5
SURB KT6 190 E3
St Andrews Ter
OXHEY WD19 * 41 G1
St Andrew St HCIRC EC1N 11 K2
St Andrews Wy BOW E3 105 K3
St Anna Rd BAR EN5 * 20 B6
St Anne's Av
STWL/WRAY TW19 152 A2
St Annes Cl OXHEY WD19 27 G6
St Anne's Cl HGT N6 84 A1
St Annes Ct SOHO/CST W1F 10 C4
St Annes Gdns WLSDN NW10 98 B2
St Anne's Pas POP/IOD E14 * 105 H5
St Anne's Rd ALP/SUD HA0 79 K3
LEY E10 70 B6
St Anne's Rw POP/IOD E14 105 H5
St Anne St POP/IOD E14 105 H5
St Ann's BARK IG11 90 C6
St Anns Ct HDN NW4 * 45 K6
St Ann's Crs
WAND/EARL SW18 160 A1
St Ann's Gdns KTTN NW5 84 A4
St Ann's Hl WAND/EARL SW18 140 A6
St Ann's Park Rd
WAND/EARL SW18 160 B1
St Anns Rd BARN SW13 * 138 C3
St Ann's Rd BARK IG11 90 C6
ED N9 36 B4
HRW HA1 60 E3
NTGHL W11 100 B6
SEVS/STOTM N15 67 J2
St Ann's St WEST SW1P 16 D4
St Ann's Ter STJWD NW8 2 B2
St Ann's Vls NTGHL W11 119 G1
St Ann's Wy CROY/NA CR0 211 H4
St Anselms Rd HYS/HAR UB3 113 J2
St Anthony's Av WFD IG8 53 G2
St Anthonys Cl TOOT SW17 160 D4
St Anthony's Cl WAP E1W * 123 H1
St Anthony's Ct ORP BR6 201 G5
St Anthony's Wy
EBED/NFELT TW14 133 J5
St Antony's Rd FSTGT E7 89 F5
St Arvans Cl CROY/NA CR0 212 A1
St Asaph Rd BROCKY SE4 144 A4
St Aubyn's Av HSLW TW3 135 F6
WIM/MER SW19 177 J1
St Aubyns Cl ORP BR6 217 F1
St Aubyns Gdns ORP BR6 202 A6
St Aubyn's Rd NRWD SE19 181 G2
St Augustine's Av EA W5 98 A1
HAYES BR2 200 D2
SAND/SEL CR2 211 J5
WBLY HA9 80 A1
St Augustine's Rd BELV DA17 129 G4
CAMTN NW1 84 D5
St Austell Cl EDGW HA8 44 B5
St Austell Rd LEW SE13 145 F3
St Awdry's Rd BARK IG11 90 D5
St Barnabas Cl BECK BR3 183 F5
EDUL SE22 143 F5
St Barnabas' Gdns
E/WMO/HCT KT8 189 F2
St Barnabas Rd MTCM CR4 179 F3
SUT SM1 209 H3
WALTH E17 69 J3
WFD IG8 53 F4
St Barnabas St BGVA SW1W 121 F5
St Barnabas Ter HOM E9 87 F3
St Barnabas Vls VX/NE SW8 141 K2
St Bartholomew's Cl
SYD SE26 163 K6
St Bartholomew's Rd
EHAM E6 89 J6
St Benets Cl TOOT SW17 160 D4
St Benet's Gv CAR SM5 194 B4
St Benjamins Dr ORP BR6 217 J6
St Bernards CROY/NA CR0 212 A1
St Bernards Cl WNWD SE27 162 E6
St Bernard's Rd EHAM E6 89 H6
St Blaise Av BMLY BR1 184 A5
St Botolph St TWRH EC3N 13 J3
St Bride's Av EDGW HA8 44 B4
St Brides Cl ERITHM DA18 128 E2
St Bride St FLST/FETLN EC4A 12 A3
St Catherines Cl CHSGTN KT9 205 K4
TOOT SW17 * 160 D4
St Catherines Ct FELT TW13 153 K3
St Catherine's Dr NWCR SE14 144 A3
St Catherines Ms CHEL SW3 14 E6
St Catherines Rd CHING E4 37 J4
RSLP HA4 58 A2
St Chads Cl SURB KT6 190 D4
St Chad's Gdns CHDH RM6 74 A4
St Chad's Pl FSBYW WC1X 5 F4
St Chad's Rd CHDH RM6 74 A3
St Chad's St STPAN WC1H 5 F4
St Charles Pl NKENS W10 100 C4
St Charles Sq NKENS W10 100 B4
St Christopher's Cl ISLW TW7 135 K2
St Christophers Dr
HYS/HAR UB3 95 F6
St Christopher's Ms
WLGTN SM6 210 C3
St Christopher's Pl
MHST W1U 9 H4
St Clair Cl CLAY IG5 53 K5
St Clair Dr WPK KT4 207 K1
St Clair Rd PLSTW E13 107 F1
St Clair's Rd CROY/NA CR0 197 F6
St Clare St TWRH EC3N 13 J4
St Clement's La LINN WC2A 11 H4
St Clements St HOLWY N7 85 G5
St Clements Yd EDUL SE22 * 143 G6
St Cloud Rd WNWD SE27 162 D6
St Crispins Cl HAMP NW3 83 J2
St Crispin's Cl STHL UB1 95 K5
St Cross St HCIRC EC1N 11 K1
St Cuthberts Gdns PIN HA5 * 41 K3
St Cuthberts Rd PLMGR N13 49 G2
St Cuthbert's Rd CRICK NW2 82 D4
St Cyprian's St TOOT SW17 160 E6
St Davids Cl
BERM/RHTH SE16 * 123 J5
WBLY HA9 80 E1
St David's Cl WWKM BR4 198 E4
St David's Dr EDGW HA8 44 B4
St Davids Ms BOW E3 * 105 G2
St David's Pl HDN NW4 63 K4
St Davids Sq POP/IOD E14 124 E5
St Denis Rd WNWD SE27 162 D6
St Dionis Rd FUL/PGN SW6 139 J3
MNPK E12 89 J1
St Donatt's Rd NWCR SE14 144 C2
St Dunstan's Av ACT W3 99 F6
St Dunstans Cl HYS/HAR UB3 113 J4
St Dunstan's Gdns ACT W3 99 F6
St Dunstan's Hl MON EC3R * 13 G6
SUT SM1 208 C4
St Dunstan's La MON EC3R * 13 G6
St Dunstans Rd FSTGT E7 89 F4
St Dunstan's Rd FELT TW13 153 J5
HMSMTH W6 119 G5
HNWL W7 115 K2
HSLWW TW4 134 A3
SNWD SE25 197 G1
St Edmunds Av RSLP HA4 58 B3
St Edmunds Cl ERITHM DA18 128 E2
TOOT SW17 160 D4
St Edmund's Cl STJWD NW8 2 E1
St Edmunds Dr STAN HA7 43 G4
St Edmund's La WHTN TW2 155 G2
St Edmunds Rd DART DA1 151 J5
ED N9 36 C2
St Edmund's Rd IL IG1 71 K3
St Edmunds Sq BARN SW13 119 F6
St Edmund's Ter STJWD NW8 2 D1
St Edward's Cl GLDGN NW11 64 E3
St Edwards Wy ROM RM1 75 F2
St Egberts Wy CHING E4 38 A3
St Elmo Rd SHB W12 118 C2
St Elmos Rd
BERM/RHTH SE16 124 B2
St Erkenwald Ms BARK IG11 90 D6
St Erkenwald Rd BARK IG11 90 D6
St Ervans Rd NKENS W10 100 C4
St Faith's Cl ENC/FH EN2 23 J2
St Faith's Rd DUL SE21 162 C3
St Fidelis' Rd ERITH DA8 130 A4
St Fillans Rd CAT SE6 165 F3
St Francis Cl ORP BR6 201 K3
OXHEY WD19 27 F3
St Francis Rd EDUL SE22 143 F5
St Francis Wy IL IG1 90 D2
St Gabriel's Cl WAN E11 71 F5
St Gabriels Rd CRICK NW2 82 B3
St George's Av
CDALE/KGS NW9 62 E1
EA W5 116 E2
FSTGT E7 89 F5
HOLWY N7 84 D2
STHL UB1 95 K6
St George's Circ STHWK SE1 18 A3
St Georges Cl HRW HA1 79 G1
THMD SE28 109 K5
VX/NE SW8 141 H2
St George's Cl GLDGN NW11 64 D3
St George's Dr OXHEY WD19 27 J5
PIM SW1V 15 K7
St Georges Flds
BAY/PAD W2 8 D5
St George's Gdns SURB KT6 191 J6
St George's Gv TOOT SW17 160 C5
St George's Industrial Est
KUTN/CMB KT2 174 E1
St George's La MON EC3R * 13 F5
St Georges Ms CHSWK W4 * 117 K6
DEPT SE8 124 C4
St George's Ms CAMTN NW1 83 K5
St Georges Pde CAT SE6 * 164 C4
St Georges Rd BMLY BR1 184 E5
CHSWK W4 118 A2
DAGW RM9 92 A3
STMC/STPC BR5 201 J3
St George's Rd BECK BR3 182 E4
EN EN1 24 B1
FELT TW13 154 C6
FSTGT E7 89 F5
GLDGN NW11 64 D3
HNWL W7 116 A1
IL IG1 71 K4
KUTN/CMB KT2 175 G3
LEY E10 88 A1
MTCM CR4 179 G6
PLMGR N13 35 F4
RCH/KEW TW9 137 G4
SCUP DA14 186 E2
STHWK SE1 18 A5
TWK TW1 136 C6
WIM/MER SW19 177 J2
WLGTN SM6 210 B3
St Georges Rd West
BMLY BR1 184 D5
St Georges's Ct STP EC4M * 12 A3
St Georges Sq NWMAL KT3 * 176 B6
St George's Sq FSTGT E7 89 F5
PIM SW1V 121 J5

St George's Square Ms
　PIM SW1V 121 J5
St Georges Ter PECK SE15 * 143 H1
St George St CONDST W1S 9 K5
St George's Wk CROY/NA CRO.. 196 D6
St George's Wy PECK SE15 .... 123 F6
St Gerards Cl CLAP SW4 .... 141 H6
St German's Rd FSTH SE23 .... 164 B3
St Giles Av DAGE RM10 .... 92 D5
　HGDN/ICK UB10 .... 76 A2
St Giles Churchyard
　BARB EC2Y * 12 D2
St Giles Circ SOHO/SHAV W1D ... 10 D3
St Giles Cl DAGE RM10 .... 92 D5
　HEST TW5 .... 134 D1
　ORP BR6 .... 216 D3
St Giles High St
　LSO/SEVD WC2H * 10 D3
St Giles Pas LSO/SEVD WC2H 10 D4
St Giles Rd CMBW SE5 .... 143 F2
St Gothard Rd WNWD SE27 .... 162 E6
St Gregory Cl RSLP HA4 .... 77 C2
St Helena Rd
　BERM/RHTH SE16 .... 124 A4
St Helena Ter RTM FSBYW WC1X * ... 5 J5
St Helena Ter RCH/KEW TW9 * .. 136 E6
St Helens Ct RAIN RM13 .... 111 J3
St Helen's Cr
　STRHM/NOR SW16 .... 180 A4
St Helen's Gdns NKENS W10 ..... 100 B5
St Helen's Pl LEY E10 .... 69 G4
St Helen's Pl HDTCH EC3A 13 G3
St Helen's Rd ERITHM DA18 ...... 128 E2
St Helen's Rd IL IG1 .... 71 J5
　STRHM/NOR SW16 .... 180 A5
　WEA W13 .... 116 C1
St Helier Av MRDN SM4 .... 194 B4
St Helier's Av HSLWW TW4 .... 135 F6
St Helier's Rd LEY E10 .... 69 K3
St Hildas Cl
　KIL/WHAMP NW6 * 82 B6
　TOOT SW17 .... 160 D4
St Hilda's Rd BARN SW13 .... 118 E6
St Hughes Cl TOOT SW17 * 160 D4
St Hugh's Rd PGE/AN SE20 * 181 J4
St Ivians Dr GPK RM2 .... 57 J6
St James' Av SUT SM1 .... 208 E3
　TRDG/WHET N20 .... 33 J5
St James' Av WEA W13 .... 116 B1
St James Cl EBAR EN4 .... 21 K5
St James Cl
　STJWD NW8 .... 2 E2
　TRDG/WHET N20 .... 33 J5
St James' Cl NWMAL KT3 .... 192 C2
　RSLP HA4 .... 59 G6
St James Ct WESTW SW1E * 16 B4
St James Gdns CHDH RM6.......... 73 H1
St James's Cl ALSP/SUD HA0 ..... 79 K5
St James's Dr BAL SW12 .... 142 B4
St James's Gdns
　CAMTN NW1 * 4 A5
　NTGHL W11 .... 119 C1
St James's Gv BTSEA SW11 .... 140 E3
St James's La MUSWH N10 .... 66 B1
St James's Market
　STJS SW1Y * 10 C6
St James's Ms WALTH E17 .... 69 G2
St James's Pk CROY/NA CRO 196 D4
St James's Pl WHALL SW1A 16 A1
St James's Sq SURB KT6 .... 190 D4
St James's Sq
　BERM/RHTH SE16 .... 123 H5
St James's Cots
　RCH/KEW TW9 * 136 F6
St James's Ct KUT/HW K11 * 175 F6
　WESTW SW1E 16 B4

St James's Crs BRXN/ST SW9 ... 142 B4
St James's Dr BAL SW12 .... 142 B4
St James's Gdns
　CAMTN NW1 * 4 A5
　NTGHL W11 .... 119 C1
St James's Rd
　BERM/RHTH SE16 .... 123 H5
　CROY/NA CRO 196 D4
　HPTN TW12 .... 173 H1
　KUT/HW KT1 .... 174 E5
St James's Rw CHSGTN KT9 * ... 205 K4
St James's Sq STJS SW1Y 10 C7
St James's St WALTH E17 .... 69 G2
　WHALL SW1A 10 A7
St James's
　Terrace Ms STJWD NW8 .... 2 E1
St James Ter BAL SW12 * 161 F3
　ORP BR6 .... 217 J6
St James Wk CLKNW EC1R 6 A6
St James Wy SCUP DA14 .... 169 F6
St Jerome's Gv UX/CGN UB8 ...... 94 A3
St Joan's Rd ED N9 .... 36 B4
St John Cl FUL/PGN SW6 .... 139 K1
St John's Av FBAR/BDGN N11 .... 47 K1
　PUT/ROE SW15 .... 139 G6
　WLSDN NW10 .... 81 H6
St John's Church Rd
　HOM E9 * 86 E3
St Johns Cl STHGT/OAK N14 ..... 34 C1
St John's Cl FUL/PGN SW6 * 139 K1
　RAIN RM13 .... 93 J5
　TRDG/WHET N20 * 33 J4
　WBLY HA9 .... 80 A3
St Johns Cots PGE/AN SE20 * 181 K3
St Johns Ct BKHH IG9 .... 39 F3
St Johns Ct BKHH IG9 .... 39 F5
　ISLW TW7 .... 136 A3
St Johns Crs BRXN/ST SW9 .... 142 B4
St Johns Dr WOT/HER KT12 .... 188 B5
St John's Dr
　WAND/EARL SW18 .... 160 A3

St John's Gdns NTCHL W11 .... 100 C6
St John's Gv ARCH N19 .... 66 C6
　BARN SW13 * 138 C3
　RCH/KEW TW9 .... 136 E5
St John's HI BTSEA SW11 .... 140 D5
St John's Hill Gv BTSEA SW11 ... 140 C5
St John's La FARR EC1M 6 A7
St Johns Pde SCUP DA14 * 168 C6
　WEA W13 * 116 C1
St John's Pth FARR EC1M 6 A7
St Johns Rd CRW RM5 .... 56 E1
　CNTH/NBYPK IG2 .... 72 E4
　NWMAL KT3 .... 175 K6
　STMC/STPC BR5 .... 201 J3
St John's Rd BARK IG11 .... 140 D5
　BTSEA SW11 .... 140 D5
　CAR SM5 .... 209 J1
　CHING E4 .... 37 K5
　CROY/NA CRO 211 H1
　E/WMO/HCT KT8 .... 189 J1
　EHAM E6 .... 89 J6
　FELT TW13 .... 154 D6
　GLDGN NW11 .... 64 D5
　HRW HA1 .... 61 F3
　ISLW TW7 .... 136 A3
　KUT/HW K11 .... 174 D5
　NWDGN UB2 .... 114 D3
　PGE/AN SE20 .... 181 K3
　RCH/KEW TW9 .... 137 F5
　SCUP DA14 .... 168 C6
　SEVS/STOTM N15 .... 68 A3
　SUT SM1 .... 193 K6
　WALTH E17 .... 51 K5
　WBLY HA9 .... 79 K2
　WELL DA16 .... 148 C4
　WIM/MER SW19 .... 177 H3
St John's Sq FARR EC1M 6 A7
St John's Ter EN EN1 .... 24 B2
St John's Ter FSTGT E7 * 89 F4
　NKENS W10 .... 100 B3
　WOOL/PLUM SE18 .... 127 H6
St John's V BROCKY SE4 .... 144 D3
St Johns Vis KENS W8 * 120 A3
St John's Vls ARCH N19 .... 66 C6
　ARCH N19 .... 66 D5
St John's Wood High St 2 B3
St John's Wood Pk
　STJWD NW8 .... 2 A1
St John's Wood Rd
　STJWD NW8 .... 2 C2
St John's Wood Ter
　STJWD NW8 .... 2 C1
St Josephs Cl NKENS W10 .... 100 C4
　ORP BR6 .... 217 F2
St Josephs Dr STHL UB1 .... 114 D1
St Josephs Gv HDN NW4 .... 63 K1
St Joseph's St VX/NE SW8 * 141 G2
St Joseph's V BKHTH/KID SE3 ... 145 G3
St Jude's Rd BETH E2 .... 104 D1
St Jude St STNW/STAM N16 ...... 86 A3
St Julian's Cl
　STRHM/NOR SW16 * 162 B6
St Julian's Farm Rd
　WNWD SE27 .... 162 B6
St Julian's Rd
　KIL/WHAMP NW6 .... 82 D5
St Justin Ct STMC/STPC BR5 .... 186 E6
St Katharine's Prec
　CAMTN NW1 * 3 J2
St Katharine's Wy WAP E1W 13 K7
St Katherines Rd
　ERITHM DA18 .... 128 E2
St Katherines Wk
　NTGHL W11 * 100 B6
St Keverne Rd ELTH/MOT SE9 .. 166 D6
　ELTH/MOT SE9 .... 166 E2
St Kilda Rd ORP BR6 .... 202 A5
　WEA W13 .... 116 B2
St Kilda's Rd HRW HA1 .... 60 E3
　STNW/STAM N16 .... 67 K5
St Kitts Ter NRWD SE19 .... 181 F1
St Laurence Cl
　STMC/STPC BR5 .... 186 E6
St Laurence's Cl
　KIL/WHAMP NW6 .... 82 B6
St Lawrence Dr EDGW HA8 .... 44 B3
St Lawrence Cots
　POP/IOD E14 * 125 F1
St Lawrence Dr PIN HA5 .... 59 F2
St Lawrence Rd POP/IOD E14 ... 125 F1
St Lawrence Ter NKENS W10 ..... 100 C4
St Lawrence Wy
　BRXN/ST SW9 .... 142 B3
St Leonards Av CHING E4 .... 52 B2
St Leonards Cl WELL DA16 .... 148 B4
St Leonards Gdns IL IG1 .... 90 C3
St Leonards Ri ORP BR6 .... 216 D2
St Leonards Rd
　MORT/ESHN SW14 .... 137 K4
St Leonard's Rd CROY/NA CRO.. 211 H1
　ESH/CLAY KT10 .... 205 F4
　POP/IOD E14 .... 106 A5
　THDT K17 .... 190 B3
　WEA W13 .... 97 J6
　WLSDN NW10 .... 99 F3
St Leonards Sq KTTN NW5 .... 84 A4
　SURB KT6 .... 190 E2
St Leonard's St BOW E3 .... 105 K2
St Leonard's Ter CHEL SW3 .... 120 E5
St Leonard's Wk
　STRHM/NOR SW16 .... 180 A3
St Leonards Wy EMPK RM11 ...... 75 K5
St Loo Av CHEL SW3 .... 120 D6
St Louis Rd WNWD SE27 .... 162 D6
St Loy's Rd TOTM N17 .... 50 A5
St Lucia Dr SRTFD E15 .... 88 D6
St Luke's Av CLAP SW4 .... 141 J5
　ENC/FH EN2 .... 23 K1
　IL IG1 .... 90 B3
St Luke's Cl SNWD SE25 .... 197 J3
St Luke's Est FSBYE EC1V 6 E5
St Luke's Ms NTGHL W11 .... 100 D5
St Luke's Rd NTGHL W11 .... 100 D4
St Lukes Cl FSBYE EC1V * 6 D6

St Luke's Sq CAN/RD E16 .... 106 D5
St Luke's St CHEL SW3 .... 120 D5
St Lukes Yd MV/WKIL W9 * 100 D1
St Malo Av ED N9 .... 36 E5
St Margarets BARK IG11 .... 90 D6
　KUTN/CMB KT2 * 175 K1
St Margarets Av ASHF TW15 .... 152 E6
　BFN/LL DA15 .... 167 J3
　TRDG/WHET N20 .... 33 G3
St Margaret's Av CHEAM SM3 .... 208 C1
　RYLN/HDSTN HA2 .... 78 C1
　SEVS/STOTM N15 .... 67 H1
St Margarets Cl ORP BR6 .... 217 H2
St Margarets Ct
　PUT/ROE SW15 * 138 C5
St Margaret's Crs
　PUT/ROE SW15 .... 138 E6
St Margaret's Dr TWK TW1 .... 156 D6
St Margaret's Gv TWK TW1 .... 156 B1
　WAN E11 .... 88 D1
　WOOL/PLUM SE18 .... 127 H6
St Margarets La KENS W8 * 120 A3
St Margarets Ms
　KUTN/CMB KT2 * 175 K1
St Margarets Rd EDGW HA8 ...... 44 D1
　RSLP HA4 .... 58 B3
St Margaret's Rd BROCKY SE4 .. 144 C5
　HNWL W7 .... 115 K2
　KIL/WHAMP NW6 .... 82 B1
　TOTM N17 .... 50 A6
　TWK TW1 .... 136 C5
　WLSDN NW10 .... 100 A2
St Margaret's Ter
　WOOL/PLUM SE18 .... 127 H5
St Margaret St WEST SW1P 16 E3
St Mark's Cl BAR EN5 .... 21 F4
St Mark's Crs CAMTN NW1 * 84 A6
St Mark's Ga HOM E9 .... 87 H5
St Mark's Gv WBPTN SW10 * 140 A1
St Marks HI SURB KT6 .... 191 F3
St Marks Pl DAGE RM10 .... 92 C4
St Mark's Pl NTCHL W11 .... 100 C5
St Mark's Ri HACK E8 .... 86 B3
St Mark's Rd EA W5 .... 117 F1
　EN EN1 .... 24 B6
　HAYES BR2 .... 184 A6
　HNWL W7 .... 115 K2
　MTCM CR4 .... 178 E5
　NKENS W10 .... 100 B5
　SNWD SE25 .... 197 H1
　TEDD TW11 .... 174 C3
St Marks Sq CAMTN NW1 .... 3 G1
St Mark St WCHPL E1 .... 13 K4
St Martins Av EHAM E6 .... 107 H1
St Martins Cl ERITHM DA18 .... 128 E2
　OXHEY WD19 .... 27 G6
St Martins Ct CHCR WC2N 10 E5
St Martin's La BECK BR3 .... 198 E2
　CHCR WC2N 10 E5
St Martin's le Grand
　STBT EC1A 12 C3
St Martin's Pl CHCR WC2N 10 E6
St Martin's Rd BRXN/ST SW9 .... 142 A3
　ED N9 .... 36 D4
　EFNCH N2 .... 47 H4
St Martin's St
　LSO/SEVD WC2H * 10 D6
St Martin's Wy TOOT SW17 .... 160 D5
St Mary Abbot's Pl KENS W8 ...... 119 J3
St Mary Abbots Ter
　WKENS W14 .... 119 J3
St Mary At HI MON EC3R 13 G6
St Mary Av WLGTN SM6 .... 210 A1
St Mary Axe HDTCH EC3A 13 G4
St Marychurch St
　BERM/RHTH SE16 .... 123 K2
St Mary Graces Ct
　WCHPL E1 * 13 K6
St Mary Newington Cl
　WALW SE17 * 123 F5
St Mary Rd WALTH E17 .... 69 K1
St Marys BARK IG11 .... 108 D1
St Marys Ap MNPK E12 .... 89 K3
St Marys Av NWDGN UB2 .... 115 F4
St Mary's Av FNCH N3 .... 46 C5
　HAYES BR2 .... 183 H6
　STHL UB1 .... 114 E4
　TEDD TW11 .... 174 A2
　WAN E11 .... 71 F3
St Mary's Cl CHSGTN KT9 .... 206 B5
　EW KT17 .... 207 H5
　STMC/STPC BR5 .... 186 C5
　SUT SM1 .... 209 G4
St Mary's Ct HMSMTH W6 * 118 C3
　HYS/HAR UB3 .... 94 D6
　ISLW TW7 .... 135 J1
　WWKM BR4 .... 199 J6
St Mary's Crs
　EBED/NFELT TW14 .... 153 F2
St Marys Est
　BERM/RHTH SE16 .... 123 K2
St Mary's Gdns LBTH SE11 .... 17 K6
St Marys Ga KENS W8 .... 120 A3
St Mary's Gn EFNCH N2 .... 47 G6
St Mary's Gv BARN SW13 .... 138 E4
　CHSWK W4 .... 117 J6
　IS N1 .... 85 H4
　RCH/KEW TW9 .... 137 G5
St Mary's Man BAY/PAD W2 .... 101 G4
St Mary's Ms
　KIL/WHAMP NW6 .... 83 F5
St Mary's Pth IS N1 * 85 H6
St Mary's Pl EA W5 .... 116 E2
　KENS W8 * 120 A3
St Mary's Rd IL IG1 .... 72 C6
St Marys Rd BXLY DA5 .... 169 K3
　CEND/HSY/T N8 .... 66 E1
St Petersburgh Ms
　BAY/PAD W2 .... 101 F6

EA W5 .... 116 E2
　EBAR EN4 .... 33 K2
　GLDGN NW11 .... 64 C4
　HYS/HAR UB3 .... 94 D6
　LEY E10 .... 88 A1
　PECK SE15 .... 143 J3
　PLSTW E13 .... 107 F1
　SNWD SE25 .... 181 F6
　SURB KT6 .... 190 D4
　WIM/MER SW19 .... 177 H1
　WLSDN NW10 .... 81 G6
　WPK KT4 .... 192 B6
St Mary's Sq BAY/PAD W2 .... 101 G4
St Marys Sq EA W5 .... 116 E2
St Mary's Ter BORE WD6 * 29 K1
St Mary's Ter BAY/PAD W2 .... 8 A1
St Mary's Vw WOOL/PLUM SE18 .. 126 E4
St Marys Vw
　KTN/HRWW/WS HA3 .... 61 J2
St Mary's Wk HYS/HAR UB3 .... 94 D6
　LBTH SE11 .... 17 K6
St Mary Wy CHIG IG7 .... 54 A1
St Mary's Av SURB KT6 .... 191 F5
St Matthews Cl RAIN RM13 .... 93 J5
St Matthews Ct SRTFD E15 .... 88 D5
St Matthews Dr BMLY BR1 .... 184 E6
St Matthew's Rd
　BRXS/STRHM SW2 .... 142 A6
　EA W5 .... 117 F1
St Matthew's Rw BETH E2 .... 104 C2
St Matthew's St WEST SW1P 16 C4
St Matthias Cl
　CDALE/KGS NW9 .... 63 H2
St Maur Rd FUL/PGN SW6 .... 139 J2
St Meddens CHST BR7 * 185 J3
St Mellion Cl THMD SE28 .... 109 K5
St Merryn Cl
　WOOL/PLUM SE18 .... 147 J1
St Michael's Aly BANK EC3V 13 F4
St Michaels Av ED N9 .... 36 E2
St Michael's Av WBLY HA9 .... 80 C4
St Michaels Cl BMLY BR1 .... 184 D6
　CAN/RD E16 .... 107 H4
　WPK KT4 .... 192 C6
St Michael's Cl ERITHM DA18 * .. 128 E2
　FNCH N3 .... 46 D5
　NFNCH/WDSPK N12 .... 47 J1
　WED/HER KT12 .... 188 B6
St Michaels Ct GLDGN NW11 * ... 64 D4
St Michael's Crs PIN HA5 .... 59 J3
St Michaels Gdns NKENS W10 ... 100 C4
St Michaels Ms BCVA SW1W 15 G7
St Michaels Ri WELL DA16 * 148 C2
St Michael's Rd BRXN/ST SW9 ... 142 A3
　CRICK NW2 .... 82 A2
　CROY/NA CRO 196 D5
　WELL DA16 .... 148 C4
　WLGTN SM6 .... 210 C4
St Michael's St BAY/PAD W2 .... 8 B3
St Michael's Ter HGT N6 * 66 A5
St Mildred's Ct LOTH EC2R * 12 E4
St Mildreds Rd CAT SE6 .... 165 H2
St Nicholas Av HCH RM12 .... 93 J1
St Nicholas Gv BORE WD6 .... 29 K1
St Nicholas Glebe
　TOOT SW17 .... 179 F2
St Nicholas Rd SUT SM1 .... 209 F3
　THDT K17 .... 190 A3
　WOOL/PLUM SE18 .... 128 A4
St Nicholas St DEPT SE8 .... 144 C2
St Nicholas St SUT SM1 .... 209 F2
St Nicolas La CHST BR7 .... 184 D4
St Ninian's Ct
　TRDG/WHET N20 .... 33 K5
St Norbert Rd BROCKY SE4 .... 144 B5
St Olaf's Rd FUL/PGN SW6 .... 139 H1
St Olave's Rd EHAM E6 .... 90 A6
St Olave's Wk
　STRHM/NOR SW16 .... 179 H5
St Onge Pde EN EN1 * 23 K4
St Oswald's Pl LBTH SE11 .... 122 A5
St Oswald's Rd
　STRHM/NOR SW16 .... 180 C4
St Oswulf St WEST SW1P * 16 D7
St Pancras Gdns
　CAMTN NW1 * 4 D1
St Pancras Station Forecourt
　CAMTN NW1 * 4 D1
St Pancras Wy CAMTN NW1 .... 84 C5
St Paul's Av
　BERM/RHTH SE16 .... 124 A1
　CRICK NW2 .... 81 K4
　KTN/HRWW/WS HA3 .... 62 A2
St Paul's Church Yd
　STP EC4M 12 B4
St Pauls Cl EA W5 .... 117 G2
　HYS/HAR UB3 .... 113 G5
St Pauls Cl CAR SM5 .... 194 D6
　CHARL SE7 .... 126 C5
　CHSGTN KT9 .... 205 K2
　EA W5 .... 117 G2
　HSLW TW3 .... 134 D3
St Paul's Cray Rd CHST BR7 ...... 185 J4
St Pauls Crs CAMTN NW1 .... 84 D4
　HDN NW4 * 64 A1
St Paul's Dr SRTFD E15 .... 88 B3
St Paul's Pl IS N1 .... 85 K4
St Pauls Pl PLMGR N13 .... 49 H2
St Paul's Ri PLMGR N13 * 49 H2
　RCH/KEW TW9 .... 137 G4
St Paul's Rd BTFD TW8 .... 116 E6
　IS N1 .... 85 H4
　THHTH CR7 .... 180 D6
　TOTM N17 .... 50 C3
St Pauls Ter WALW SE17 * 122 C6
St Paul St IS N1 .... 6 C1
St Paul's Wy FNCH N3 .... 47 F3
　POP/IOD E14 .... 105 H4
St Peter's Av BETH E2 .... 104 C1
　WLSDN NW10 .... 70 C1
St Petersburgh Ms
　BAY/PAD W2 * 101 F6

St Petersburgh Pl
　BAY/PAD W2 .... 101 F6
St Peters Cl CHST BR7 .... 185 J3
　CNTH/NBYPK IG2 .... 72 E1
　TOOT SW17 .... 160 D4
St Peter's Ct BETH E2 .... 104 C1
　BUSH WD23 .... 28 B1
　RSLP HA4 .... 59 H6
St Peter's Ct BKHTH/KID SE3 * .. 146 A5
　E/WMO/HCT KT8 .... 189 H1
St Peter's Pl HDN NW4 .... 64 A2
St Peter's Gdns WNWD SE27 .... 162 B5
St Peter's Gv HMSMTH W6 .... 118 D4
St Peters Ms FSBYPK N4 * 67 H2
St Peters Pl MV/WKIL W9 .... 101 F3
St Peters Rd KUT/HW KT1 .... 175 H5
　CROY/NA CRO 211 H1
　E/WMO/HCT KT8 .... 189 F1
St Peter's Rd HDN NW4 * 36 D3
　HMSMTH W6 .... 118 D5
　STHL UB1 .... 96 A4
　TWK TW1 .... 136 C6
St Peter's Sq BETH E2 * 104 C1
　HMSMTH W6 .... 118 C5
St Peter's St IS N1 .... 6 B1
　SAND/SEL CR2 .... 211 K3
St Peter's Ter FUL/PGN SW6 ...... 139 H1
St Peter's Vls HMSMTH W6 .... 118 C4
St Peter's Wy HYS/HAR UB3 ...... 113 G5
St Peters Wy IS N1 * 97 K4
　IS N1 .... 86 A5
St Philip's Av WPK KT4 .... 192 E6
St Philip Sq VX/NE SW8 * 141 G3
St Philip's Rd HACK E8 .... 86 C4
　SURB KT6 .... 190 E3
St Philip St VX/NE SW8 .... 141 G3
St Philip's Wy IS N1 .... 85 J6
St Quentin Rd WELL DA16 .... 148 A4
St Quintin Av NKENS W10 .... 100 A4
St Quintin Gdns NKENS W10 ...... 100 A4
St Quintin's Cl PLSTW E13 .... 107 F2
St Raphael's Wy
　WLSDN NW10 .... 80 E3
St Regis Cl MUSWH N10 .... 48 B5
St Ronans Ct EBAR EN4 .... 21 H1
St Ronans Crs WFD IG8 .... 52 E3
St Rule St VX/NE SW8 .... 141 H3
St Saviours Ct WDGN N22 .... 48 D5
St Saviour's Est STHWK SE1 ...... 19 J4
St Saviour's Rd
　BRXS/STRHM SW2 .... 142 A6
　CROY/NA CRO 196 D3
Saints Cl WNWD SE27 .... 162 C6
Saints Dr FSTGT E7 .... 89 H3
St Silas Pl KTTN NW5 .... 84 A4
St Simon's Av PUT/ROE SW15 ... 139 F6
St Stephen's Av SHB W12 .... 118 E2
　WALTH E17 .... 70 A2
　WEA W13 .... 97 H5
St Stephens Cl KTTN NW5 .... 83 K3
　STJWD NW8 .... 2 C2
St Stephen's Cl STHL UB1 .... 96 A4
　WALTH E17 .... 69 K2
St Stephen's Crs BAY/PAD W2 ... 100 E5
　THHTH CR7 .... 180 B6
St Stephen's Gdns
　BAY/PAD W2 .... 100 E5
　TWK TW1 .... 156 D1
St Stephen's Gv LEW SE13 .... 145 F4
St Stephens Ms BAY/PAD W2 .... 100 E4
St Stephens Pde
　WHALL SW1A * 16 E2
St Stephen's Rd BAR EN5 .... 20 B6
　BOW E3 .... 87 G6
　EHAM E6 .... 89 G5
　HSLW TW5 .... 155 F1
　WALTH E17 .... 69 K2
　WDR/YW UB7 .... 112 A1
　WEA W13 .... 97 H5
St Stephen's Ter VX/NE SW8 ...... 142 A1
St Stephen's Wk SKENS SW7 * ... 120 B4
St Swithin's La MANHO EC4N 12 E5
St Swithun's Rd LEW SE13 * 145 G6
St Theresas Cl HOM E9 * 87 J3
St Theresa's Rd
　EBED/NFELT TW14 .... 133 J4
St Thomas Ct SURB KT6 .... 191 G3
St Thomas Dr PIN HA5 .... 41 J6
　STMC/STPC BR5 .... 201 J3
St Thomas Gdns IL IG1 .... 90 C3
St Thomas' Rd BELV DA17 .... 129 K4
　CAN/RD E16 .... 106 D5
　STHGT/OAK N14 .... 34 C2
St Thomas' Rd CHSWK W4 .... 137 K6
St Thomas Gdns KTTN NW5 ...... 84 B4
St Thomas's Pl HOM E9 * 86 E4
St Thomas's Rd FSBYPK N4 * 67 F6
　WLSDN NW10 .... 81 G6
St Thomas's Sq HOM E9 .... 86 D4
St Thomas's St STHWK SE1 .... 19 F1
St Thomas's Wy
　FUL/PGN SW6 .... 139 J1
St Ursula Gv PIN HA5 .... 59 J3
St Ursula Rd STHL UB1 .... 96 A5
St Vincent Cl WNWD SE27 .... 180 C1
St Vincent Rd WHTN TW2 .... 155 H1
St Vincents La MLHL NW7 .... 31 K5
St Vincent St MHST W1U 9 G2
St Wilfrid's Cl EBAR EN4 .... 21 J2
St Wilfrid's Rd EBAR EN4 * 21 J3
St Winefride's Av MNPK E12 .... 89 K3
St Winifred's Cl CHIG IG7 .... 54 D1
St Winifred's Rd TEDD TW11 ...... 174 C2
Sakura Dr WDGN N22 .... 48 E4
Salamanca Pl STHWK SE1 * 17 H7
Salamanca St STHWK SE1 .... 17 H7
Salamander Cl
　KUTN/CMB KT2 * 174 E1
Salamander Quay
　KUT/HW KT1 * 174
Salmons Rd RAIN RM13 111
Salcombe Dr CHDH RM6 73
　MRDN SM4 193
Salcombe Gdns MLHL NW7 46
Salcombe Rd ASHF TW15 152
　STNW/STAM N16 86
　WALTH E17 69
Salcombe Wy RSLP HA4 58
Salcott Rd BTSEA SW11 140

CROY/NA CR0 210 E1
Salehurst Cl
KTN/HRWW/WS HA3 62 A2
Salehurst Rd BROCKY SE4 164 C1
Salem Pl CROY/NA CR0 211 J1
Sale Pl BAY/PAD W2 8 C2
Sale St BETH E2 104 C3
Salford Rd BRXS/STRHM SW2 161 J3
Salhouse Cl THMD SE28 109 J5
Salisbury Av BARK IG11 90 D5
FNCH N3 46 D5
SUT SM1 208 D4
Salisbury Cl WALW SE17 18 E6
WPK KT4 207 H1
Salisbury Ct EMB EC4Y 11 K4
Salisbury Gdns
WIM/MER SW19 * 177 H3
Salisbury Pavement
FUL/PGN SW6 * 139 K1
Salisbury Pl BRXN/ST SW9 142 C1
MBLAR W1H 8 E1
Salisbury Prom
CEND/HSY/T N8 * 67 H2
Salisbury Rd BAR EN5 20 C4
BXLY DA5 169 H3
CAR SM5 209 K4
CHING E4 37 J5
DAGE RM10 92 D4
FELT TW13 154 B3
FSBYPK N4 67 H2
FSTGT E7 88 E4
GDMY/SEVK IG3 72 E6
GPK RM2 75 K2
HAYES BR2 200 D2
HRW HA1 60 D2
HSLWW TW4 134 B4
LEY E10 70 A6
MNPK E12 89 H3
NWDGN UB2 * 114 D4
NWMAL KT3 176 A6
PIN HA5 58 E1
RCH/KEW TW9 137 F5
SNWD SE25 197 H3
WALTH E17 70 A2
WDGN N22 49 H5
WEA W13 116 C2
WIM/MER SW19 177 H3
WPK KT4 207 F2
Salisbury Sq EMB EC4Y * 11 K4
Salisbury St ACT W3 117 K2
STJWD NW8 2 B7
Salisbury Ter PECK SE15 143 K4
Salisbury Wk ARCH N19 66 C6
Salix Cl SUN TW16 172 A3
Sally Murray Cl MNPK E12 90 A2
Salmen Rd PLSTW E13 106 D1
Salmond Cl STAN HA7 43 G2
Salmon La POP/IOD E14 105 G5
Salmon Ms
KIL/WHAMP NW6 * 82 E3
Salmon Rd BELV DA17 129 H5
Salmons Rd CHSGTN KT9 206 A4
ED N9 36 C3
Salmon St CDALE/KGS NW9 62 D5
POP/IOD E14 * 105 H5
Salomons Rd PLSTW E13 107 G4
Salop Rd WALTH E17 69 F3
Saltash Cl SUT SM1 208 D2
Saltash Rd BARK/HLT IG6 54 D3
WELL DA16 148 D2
Saltcoats Rd CHSWK W4 118 B2
Saltcroft Cl WBLY HA9 62 D5
Salter Cl RYLN/HDSTN HA2 77 K1
Salterford Rd TOOT SW17 179 F2
Salter Rd BERM/RHTH SE16 124 A1
Salters' Hall Ct
MANHO EC4N * 12 E5
Salter's Hl NRWD SE19 180 E1
Salters Rd NKENS W10 100 B3
WALTH E17 70 B1
Salters Rw IS N1 * 85 K4
Salter St POP/IOD E14 105 J6
WLSDN NW10 99 J2
Salterton Rd HOLWY N7 84 E1
Saltford Cl ERITH DA8 130 B5
Saltley Cl EHAM E6 107 J5
Saltoun Rd BRXS/STRHM SW2 142 B5
Saltram Cl SEVS/STOTM N15 68 B1
Saltram Crs MV/WKIL W9 100 D2
Saltwell St POP/IOD E14 105 J6
Saltwood Cl ORP BR6 217 J2
Saltwood Gv WALW SE17 * 122 E5
Salusbury Rd
KIL/WHAMP NW6 82 C6
Salvador TOOT SW17 178 D1
Salvia Gdns GFD/PVL UB6 97 G1
Salvin Rd PUT/ROE SW15 139 G4
Salway Cl WFD IG8 52 E3
Salway Rd SRTFD E15 88 B4
Samantha Cl WALTH E17 69 H4
Sam Bartram Cl CHARL SE7 126 B5
Samels Ct HMSMTH W6 118 D5
Samford St STJWD NW8 2 C7
Samira Cl WALTH E17 69 H3
Samos Rd PGE/AN SE20 181 J5
Sampson Av BAR EN5 20 B6
Sampson Cl BELV DA17 128 E3
Sampson St WAP E1W * 123 H1
Samson St PLSTW E13 107 G1
Samuel Cl HACK E8 86 B6
NWCR SE14 124 A6
STAN HA7 29 G4
WOOL/PLUM SE18 126 D4
Samuel Gray Gdns
KUTN/CMB KT2 174 E4
Samuel Lewis Trust Dwellings
CHEL SW3 * 120 D5
CMBW SE5 * 142 D2
HACK E8 * 86 C2
WKENS W14 * 119 H4
Samuel St WOOL/PLUM SE18 126 E4
Sancroft Cl CRICK NW2 81 K1
Sancroft Rd
KTN/HRWW/WS HA3 43 F5
Sancroft St LBTH SE11 122 B5
Sanctuary Ms HACK E8 86 B4
Sanctuary Rd HTHAIR TW6 152 D1
Sanctuary St STHWK SE1 18 D3
The Sanctuary BXLY DA5 168 E1
WEST SW1P 16 D4
Sandall Cl EA W5 98 A3
Sandall Rd EA W5 98 A3
KTTN NW5 84 C4
Sandal Rd NWMAL KT3 192 B1
UED N18 50 C1
Sandal St SRTFD E15 88 C6
Sandalwood Cl WCHPL E1 105 G3
Sandalwood Dr RSLP HA4 58 A4
Sandalwood Rd FELT TW13 154 A5
Sandbach Pl
WOOL/PLUM SE18 127 H4
Sandbourne Av
WIM/MER SW19 178 A6
Sandbourne Rd NWCR SE14 144 B3
Sandbrook Cl MLHL NW7 45 F2
Sandbrook Rd
STNW/STAM N16 86 A1
Sandby Gn ELTH/MOT SE9 146 D4
Sandcroft Cl PLMGR N13 49 H2
Sandell's Av ASHF TW15 153 F6
Sandell St STHWK SE1 17 J2
Sanders Cl HPTN TW12 173 H1
Sanders La MLHL NW7 46 A3
Sanderson Cl KTTN NW5 * 84 B2
Sanders Pde
STRHM/NOR SW16 * 179 K2
Sanderstead Av GLDGN NW11 64 C6
Sanderstead Cl BAL SW12 161 H2
Sanderstead Rd LEY E10 69 G5
SAND/SEL CR2 211 K5
STMC/STPC BR5 202 C3
Sandfield Gdns THHTH CR7 180 C6
Sandfield Pl THHTH CR7 180 D6
Sandfield Rd THHTH CR7 180 C6
Sandford Av WDGN N22 49 H4
Sandford Rd EHAM E6 107 K2
Sandford Rw WALW SE17 122 E5
Sandford St FUL/PGN SW6 140 A1
Sandgate Cl ROMW/RG RM7 74 E4
Sandgate La
WAND/EARL SW18 160 D3
Sandgate Rd WELL DA16 148 D1
Sandgate St PECK SE15 123 J6
Sandhills WLGTN SM6 210 D2
The Sandhills WBPTN SW10 * 120 B6
Sandhurst Av BRYLDS KT5 191 J4
RYLN/HDSTN HA2 60 B3
Sandhurst Cl SAND/SEL CR2 212 A6
Sandhurst Dr GDMY/SEVK IG3 91 F2
Sandhurst Market CAT SE6 * 165 F3
Sandhurst Pde CAT SE6 * 165 F3
Sandhurst Rd BFN/LL DA15 168 A5
BXLY DA5 148 E6
CAT SE6 165 G3
CDALE/KGS NW9 44 C6
ED N9 36 E1
ORP BR6 217 G1
Sandhurst Wy SAND/SEL CR2 212 A5
Sandifer Dr CRICK NW2 82 B1
Sandiford Rd CHEAM SM3 193 J6
Sandiland Crs HAYES BR2 199 J6
Sandilands CROY/NA CR0 212 C1
Sandilands Rd FUL/PGN SW6 140 A2
Sandison St PECK SE15 143 G4
Sandland St GINN WC1R 11 H2
Sandling Ri ELTH/MOT SE9 167 F5
Sandlings Cl PECK SE15 143 J3
The Sandlings WDGN N22 49 G5
Sandmartin Wy WLGTN SM6 195 F5
Sandmere Rd CLAP SW4 141 K5
Sandon Cl ESH/CLAY KT10 189 J4
Sandow Crs HYS/HAR UB3 113 J3
Sandown Av DAGE RM10 92 E4
ESH/CLAY KT10 204 C3
Sandown Cl HEST TW5 133 K2
Sandown Ct BELMT SM2 * 209 F5
DAGE RM10 92 E4
SYD SE26 * 163 J5
Sandown Dr CAR SM5 210 A6
Sandown Ga ESH/CLAY KT10 189 J6
Sandown Rd ESH/CLAY KT10 204 C2
SNWD SE25 197 J2
Sandown Wy NTHLT UB5 77 J4
Sandpiper Cl
BERM/RHTH SE16 124 C2
WALTH E17 51 F3
Sandpiper Rd SUT SM1 208 D3
Sandpiper Ter CLAY IG5 * 54 B6
Sandpiper Wy
STMC/STPC BR5 202 E1
Sandpit Pl CHARL SE7 126 D5
Sandpit Rd BMLY BR1 183 H1
DART DA1 151 F5
Sandpits Rd CROY/NA CR0 213 F2
RCHPK/HAM TW10 156 E3
Sandra Cl HSLW TW3 135 G6
WDGN N22 49 J4
Sandridge Cl HRW HA1 60 E1
Sandridge St ARCH N19 66 C6
Sandringham Av
RYNPK SW20 177 H4
Sandringham Cl EN EN1 24 A3
WIM/MER SW19 159 G3
Sandringham Crs
RYLN/HDSTN HA2 78 A1
Sandringham Dr ASHF TW15 152 A6
WELL DA16 147 K3
Sandringham Gdns
BARK/HLT IG6 54 C6
CEND/HSY/T N8 66 E3
E/WMO/HCT KT8 189 F1
HEST TW5 133 K2
NFNCH/WDSPK N12 47 H2
Sandringham Ms EA W5 97 K6
HPTN TW12 172 E4
Sandringham Rd BARK IG11 91 F4
BMLY BR1 183 K1
CRICK NW2 81 K3
FSTGT E7 89 G3
GLDGN NW11 64 C4
HACK E8 86 B3
HTHAIR TW6 132 B6
LEY E10 70 B4
NTHLT UB5 78 A5
THHTH CR7 196 D2
WDGN N22 49 J6
WPK KT4 207 J1
Sandrock Pl CROY/NA CR0 213 F2
Sandrock Rd LEW SE13 144 D4
Sands End La FUL/PGN SW6 140 A2
Sandstone La CAN/RD E16 107 F6
Sandstone Pl ARCH N19 66 B6
Sandstone Rd LEE/GVPK SE12 166 A4
Sands Wy WFD IG8 53 K2
Sandtoft Rd CHARL SE7 126 A6
Sandway Rd STMC/STPC BR5 202 D1
Sandwell Crs
KIL/WHAMP NW6 82 E4
Sandwich St STPAN WC1H 4 E5
Sandwick Cl MLHL NW7 45 J3
Sandy Bury ORP BR6 216 D1
Sandycombe Rd
EBED/NFELT TW14 153 K3
RCH/KEW TW9 137 H3
Sandycoombe Rd TWK TW1 156 D1
Sandycroft ABYW SE2 128 B6
Sandy Dr EBED/NFELT TW14 153 H3
Sandy Hill Av
WOOL/PLUM SE18 127 G5
Sandy Hill La
WOOL/PLUM SE18 127 G4
Sandyhill Rd IL IG1 90 B2
Sandy Hill Rd WLGTN SM6 210 C6
WOOL/PLUM SE18 127 G5
Sandy La BELMT SM2 208 C6
KTN/HRWW/WS HA3 62 B3
MTCM CR4 179 F4
NTHWD HA6 26 D4
ORP BR6 202 B4
RCHPK/HAM TW10 156 D4
SCUP DA14 186 E3
STMC/STPC BR5 186 E5
TEDD TW11 174 B3
WOT/HER KT12 188 A3
Sandy La North WLGTN SM6 210 D3
Sandy La South WLGTN SM6 210 C6
Sandy Ldg PIN HA5 * 42 A2
Sandy Lodge Ct
NTHWD HA6 * 40 C1
Sandy Lodge La NTHWD HA6 26 B4
Sandy Lodge Wy NTHWD HA6 40 C1
Sandy Md HOR/WEW KT19 206 C6
Sandymount Av STAN HA7 43 J1
Sandy Rdg CHST BR7 185 F2
Sandy Rd HAMP NW3 65 F6
Sandy's Rw WCHPL E1 13 H2
Sandy Wy CROY/NA CR0 213 H1
Sanford La STNW/STAM N16 68 B6
Sanford St NWCR SE14 124 B6
Sanford Ter STNW/STAM N16 86 B1
Sanger Av CHSGTN KT9 206 B3
Sangley Rd CAT SE6 164 E2
SNWD SE25 197 F1
Sangora Rd BTSEA SW11 140 C5
Sansom Rd WAN E11 * 70 D6
Sansom St CMBW SE5 142 E1
Sans Wk CLKNW EC1R 6 A6
Santley St CLAP SW4 141 K5
Santos Rd WAND/EARL SW18 139 K6
Saperton Wk LBTH SE11 17 H6
Saphora Cl ORP BR6 216 D3
Sapphire Cl BCTR RM8 73 J5
Sapphire Rd DEPT SE8 124 B4
WLSDN NW10 80 E5
Saracen Cl CROY/NA CR0 196 E3
Saracen's Head Yd
FENCHST EC3M 13 H4
Saracen St POP/IOD E14 105 J5
Saratoga Rd CLPT E5 86 E2
Sardinia St HOL/ALD WC2B 11 G4
Sarita Cl KTN/HRWW/WS HA3 42 D5
Sark Cl HEST TW5 135 F1
Sarnesfield Rd ENC/FH EN2 * 23 K5
Sarre Rd CRICK NW2 82 D3
STMC/STPC BR5 202 D2
Sarsen Av HSLW TW3 134 E3
Sarsfeld Rd BAL SW12 160 E3
Sarsfield Rd GFD/PVL UB6 97 H1
Sartor Rd PECK SE15 144 A5
Sarum Ter BOW E3 * 105 H3
Satanita Cl CAN/RD E16 107 H5
Satchell Md CDALE/KGS NW9 45 H4
Satchwell Rd BETH E2 104 C2
Sattar Ms STNW/STAM N16 * 85 K1
Sauls Gn WAN E11 88 C1
Saunders Cl IL IG1 72 D5
POP/IOD E14 * 105 H6
Saunders Ness Rd
POP/IOD E14 125 G4
Saunders Rd
WOOL/PLUM SE18 128 A5
Saunders St LBTH SE11 17 J6
Saunders Wy THMD SE28 109 H6
Saunderton Rd ALP/SUD HA0 79 H3
Saunton Av HYS/HAR UB3 133 J1
Saunton Rd HCH RM12 75 J6
Savage Gdns EHAM E6 107 K5
TWRH EC3N 13 H5
Savanah Cl PECK SE15 143 G1
Savera Cl NWDGN UB2 114 B3
Savernake Ct STAN HA7 * 43 J2
Savernake Rd ED N9 36 C1
HAMP NW3 83 K2
Savery Dr SURB KT6 190 C4
Savile Cl NWMAL KT3 192 B2
THDIT KT7 190 A5
Savile Gdns CROY/NA CR0 197 G6
Savile Rw CONDST W1S 10 A5
Saville Rd CAN/RD E16 126 D1
CHDH RM6 74 B3
CHSWK W4 118 A3
TWK TW1 156 A3
Saville Rw HAYES BR2 199 J5
PEND EN3 25 F3
Savill Gdns RYNPK SW20 176 D6
Savill Rw WFD IG8 52 D2
Savona Cl WIM/MER SW19 177 G3
Savona St VX/NE SW8 141 H1
Savoy Av HYS/HAR UB3 113 H5
Savoy Cl EDGW HA8 44 C1
SRTFD E15 88 C6
Savoy Ct TPL/STR WC2R * 11 F6
Savoy Hl TPL/STR WC2R 11 G6
Savoy Ms BRXN/ST SW9 141 K4
Savoy Pde EN EN1 * 24 A4
Savoy Pl CHCR WC2N 11 F6
Savoy Rw TPL/STR WC2R 11 G5
Savoy Steps TPL/STR WC2R * 11 G6
Savoy St TPL/STR WC2R 11 G5
Savoy Wy TPL/STR WC2R 11 G6
Sawbill Cl YEAD UB4 95 H4
Sawkins Cl WIM/MER SW19 159 G4
Sawley Rd SHB W12 118 D1
Sawtry Cl CAR SM5 194 C4
Sawyer Cl ED N9 36 C4
Sawyers Cl DAGE RM10 92 E4
Sawyer's Hl
MORT/ESHN SW14 157 K2
RCHPK/HAM TW10 157 G2
Sawyers Lawn WEA W13 97 G5
Sawyer St STHWK SE1 18 C2
Saxby Rd BRXS/STRHM SW2 161 K2
Saxham Rd BARK IG11 90 E6
Saxlingham Rd CHING E4 38 B5
Saxon Av FELT TW13 154 D4
Saxonbury Av SUN TW16 172 A6
Saxonbury Cl MTCM CR4 178 C6
Saxonbury Gdns SURB KT6 190 D5
Saxon Cl SURB KT6 190 E3
WALTH E17 69 J4
Saxon Dr ACT W3 98 D5
Saxonfield Cl
BRXS/STRHM SW2 162 A2
Saxon Rd BOW E3 105 H1
EHAM E6 107 K3
IL IG1 90 B4
KUTN/CMB KT2 175 F4
SNWD SE25 196 E2
STHL UB1 95 J6
WBLY HA9 80 E1
WDGN N22 49 H4
Saxon Wy STHGT/OAK N14 34 D1
Saxony Pde HYS/HAR UB3 94 A4
Saxton Cl LEW SE13 145 G4
Saxville Rd STMC/STPC BR5 186 C6
Sayesbury La UED N18 50 C1
Sayes Court Rd
STMC/STPC BR5 186 B6
Sayes Court St DEPT SE8 124 C5
Scadbury Gdns
STMC/STPC BR5 186 B5
Scads Hill Cl ORP BR6 202 A3
Scala St FITZ W1T 10 B1
Scales Rd TOTM N17 50 B6
Scammell Wy WATW WD18 26 D1
Scampton Rd
STWL/WRAY TW19 152 C1
Scandrett St WAP E1W * 123 J1
Scarba Wk IS N1 85 K4
Scarborough Rd ED N9 36 E2
FSBYPK N4 67 G4
HTHAIR TW6 153 F1
WAN E11 70 B5
Scarborough St WCHPL E1 13 K4
Scarbrook Rd CROY/NA CR0 211 J1
Scarle Rd ALP/SUD HA0 79 K4
Scarlet Cl STMC/STPC BR5 202 C1
Scarlet Rd CAT SE6 165 H5
Scarsbrook Rd
BKHTH/KID SE3 146 C4
Scarsdale Pl KENS W8 120 A3
Scarsdale Rd
RYLN/HDSTN HA2 78 C1
Scarsdale Vls KENS W8 119 K3
Scarth Rd BARN SW13 138 C4
Scawen Cl CAR SM5 210 A2
Scawen Rd DEPT SE8 124 B5
Scawfell St BETH E2 7 K3
Scaynes Link
NFNCH/WDSPK N12 32 E6
Sceptre Rd BETH E2 104 E2
Scholars Cl BAR EN5 20 C5
Scholars Rd BAL SW12 161 H3
CHING E4 38 A3
Scholars Wy GPK RM2 75 K2
Scholefield Rd ARCH N19 66 D6
Schonfeld Sq
STNW/STAM N16 67 K6
Schoolbank Rd GNWCH SE10 125 J4
School House La TEDD TW11 174 C3
Schoolhouse La WAP E1W * 105 F6
School La BUSH WD23 28 B3
KUT/HW KT1 174 D4
PIN HA5 * 59 J1
SURB KT6 191 G5
School Pas KUT/HW KT1 175 G5
STHL UB1 114 E1
School Rd CHST BR7 185 H4
DAGE RM10 92 C6
E/WMO/HCT KT8 189 J1
HPTN TW12 173 H2
HSLW TW3 135 H4
KUT/HW KT1 * 174 D4
MNPK E12 89 K2
WDR/YW UB7 112 A6
WLSDN NW10 99 F3
School Road Av HPTN TW12 173 H2
School Sq GNWCH SE10 125 J3
School Wy BCTR RM8 91 H1
Schoolway
NFNCH/WDSPK N12 47 H2
Schooner Cl BARK IG11 109 H2
BERM/RHTH SE16 124 A2
POP/IOD E14 125 G3
Schubert Rd BORE WD6 29 K1
PUT/ROE SW15 139 J6
Sclater St WCHPL E1 7 J6
Scoble Pl STNW/STAM N16 86 B2
Scoles Crs BRXS/STRHM SW2 162 B3
Scope Wy KUT/HW KT1 191 F1
Scoresby St STHWK SE1 18 A1
Scorton Av GFD/PVL UB6 97 G1
Scotch Common WEA W13 97 G4
Scoter Cl WFD IG8 53 F3
Scot Gv PIN HA5 41 H3
Scotia Rd BRXS/STRHM SW2 162 B2
Scotland Gn TOTM N17 50 B5
Scotland Green Rd PEND EN3 25 F6
Scotland Green Rd North
PEND EN3 25 F5
Scotland Rd BKHH IG9 39 G3
Scotney Cl ORP BR6 216 A2
Scots Cl STWL/WRAY TW19 152 A3
Scotsdale Cl CHEAM SM3 208 C5
STMC/STPC BR5 201 K1
Scotsdale Rd LEE/GVPK SE12 146 A6
Scotswood St CLKNW EC1R * 5 K6
Scotswood Wk TOTM N17 * 50 D3
Scott Av PUT/ROE SW15 159 H1
Scott Cl HOR/WEW KT19 206 E3
STRHM/NOR SW16 180 A4
WDR/YW UB7 112 C4
Scott Crs RYLN/HDSTN HA2 60 B5
Scott Ellis Gdns STJWD NW8 2 A5
Scottes La BCTR RM8 73 K5
Scott Farm Cl THDIT KT7 190 C5
Scott Gdns HEST TW5 134 C1
Scott Lidgett Crs
BERM/RHTH SE16 123 H2
Scott Rd EDGW HA8 44 D5
Scotts Av HAYES BR2 183 G5
Scotts Dr HPTN TW12 173 G3
Scotts Farm Rd
HOR/WEW KT19 206 E4
Scott's La HAYES BR2 183 G6
Scotts Pas
WOOL/PLUM SE18 * 127 G4
Scotts Rd BMLY BR1 183 K3
NWDGN UB2 114 B3
Scott's Rd LEY E10 70 A5
SHB W12 118 E2
Scott St WCHPL E1 104 D3
Scott's Yd MANHO EC4N 12 E5
Scott Trimmer Wy HSLW TW3 134 D3
Scottwell Dr CDALE/KGS NW9 63 H2
Scoulding Rd CAN/RD E16 106 D5
Scouler St POP/IOD E14 106 B6
Scout Ap WLSDN NW10 81 G2
Scout Wy MLHL NW7 31 F6
Scovell Crs STHWK SE1 * 18 C3
Scovell Rd STHWK SE1 18 C3
Scrattons Ter BARK IG11 109 K1
Scriven St HACK E8 86 B6
Scrooby St CAT SE6 164 E1
Scrubs La WLSDN NW10 99 J2
Scrutton Cl BAL SW12 161 J2
Scrutton St SDTCH EC2A 7 G7
Scutari Rd EDUL SE22 143 J6
Scylla Crs HTHAIR TW6 152 E2
Scylla Rd HTHAIR TW6 152 E1
PECK SE15 143 J4
Seabright St BETH E2 104 D2
Seabrook Dr WWKM BR4 199 H6
Seabrook Gdns
ROMW/RG RM7 74 C4
Seabrook Rd BCTR RM8 91 K1
Seaburn Cl RAIN RM13 111 G2
Seacole Cl ACT W3 99 F5
Seacourt Rd ABYW SE2 128 E2
Seacroft Gdns OXHEY WD19 27 H5
Seafield Rd FBAR/BDGN N11 34 D6
Seaford Cl RSLP HA4 58 B6
Seaford Rd EN EN1 24 A5
HTHAIR TW6 132 A6
SEVS/STOTM N15 67 K2
WALTH E17 51 K6
WEA W13 116 C1
Seaford St STPAN WC1H 5 F5
Seaforth Av NWMAL KT3 192 E2
Seaforth Cl ROM RM1 57 G3
Seaforth Crs HBRY N5 85 J3
Seaforth Gdns
HOR/WEW KT19 207 H2
WCHMH N21 35 F2
WFD IG8 53 G1
Seaforth Pl WESTW SW1E 16 B4
Seager Blds DEPT SE8 * 144 D2
Seager Pl BOW E3 105 H4
Seagrave Cl WCHPL E1 * 105 F4
Seagrave Rd FUL/PGN SW6 119 K6
Seagry Rd WAN E11 70 E3
Seagull La CAN/RD E16 106 E6
Sealand Rd HTHAIR TW6 132 D6
Seal St HACK E8 86 B2
Searles Cl BTSEA SW11 140 D1
Searles Dr EHAM E6 108 B4
Searles Rd STHWK SE1 19 F6
Sears St CMBW SE5 142 E1
Seasons Cl HNWL W7 116 A1
Seasprite Cl NTHLT UB5 95 H2
Seaton Av GDMY/SEVK IG3 90 E3
Seaton Cl LBTH SE11 122 C5
PLSTW E13 106 E3
PUT/ROE SW15 158 E2
WHTN TW2 155 J1
Seaton Dr ASHF TW15 152 B4
Seaton Gdns RSLP HA4 76 E1
Seaton Rd ALP/SUD HA0 * 98 A1
HYS/HAR UB3 113 G4
MTCM CR4 178 D5
WELL DA16 148 D1
WHTN TW2 155 H1
Seaton St UED N18 50 C1
Sebastian St FSBYE EC1V 6 B5
Sebastopol Rd ED N9 36 C6
Sebbon St IS N1 85 H5
Sebergham Gv MLHL NW7 45 J3
Sebert Rd FSTGT E7 89 F3
Sebright Rd BAR EN5 20 B3
Secker Crs
KTN/HRWW/WS HA3 42 C4
Secker St STHWK SE1 17 J1
Second Av ACT W3 118 C1
CHDH RM6 73 J2
DAGE RM10 110 D1
EN EN1 24 B6
HDN NW4 64 B1
HYS/HAR UB3 113 J1
MNPK E12 89 J2
MORT/ESHN SW14 138 B4
NKENS W10 100 C3
PLSTW E13 106 E2
UED N18 36 E6
WALTH E17 69 J2
WBLY HA9 61 K6
WOT/HER KT12 188 A3
Second Cl E/WMO/HCT KT8 189 G1
Second Cross Rd WHTN TW2 155 J4
Second Wy WBLY HA9 80 D2
Sedan Wy WALW SE17 123 F5
Sedcombe Cl SCUP DA14 168 C6
Sedcote Rd PEND EN3 24 E6
Sedding St KTBR SW1X 15 G6
Seddon Rd MRDN SM4 194 C2
Seddon St FSBYW WC1X 5 G5
Sedgebrook Rd
BKHTH/KID SE3 146 C3
Sedgecombe Av
KTN/HRWW/WS HA3 61 J2
Sedgeford Rd SHB W12 118 C1

Sedgehill Rd CAT SE6 182 D1
Sedgemere Av EFNCH N2 47 G6
Sedgemoor Dr DAGE RM10 92 C2
Sedge Rd TOTM N17 50 E3
Sedgeway CAT SE6 165 J3
Sedgewood Cl HAYES BR2 199 J4
Sedgmoor Pl CMBW SE5 143 F1
Sedgwick Rd LEY E10 70 A6
Sedgwick St HOM E9 87 F3
Sedleigh Rd
WAND/EARL SW18 159 J1
Sedlescombe Rd
FUL/PGN SW6 119 J6
Sedley Cl EN EN1 24 D1
Sedley Pl OXSTW W1C 9 J4
Sednem Ct PECK SE15 143 H3
Sedum Cl CDALE/KGS NW9 62 D2
Seeley Dr DUL SE21 163 F6
Seelig Av CDALE/KGS NW9 63 J4
Seely Rd TOOT SW17 179 F2
Seething La TWRH EC3N 13 H5
Seething Wells La SURB KT6 190 D3
Sefton Av
KTN/HRWW/WS HA3 42 D4
MLHL NW7 45 F1
Sefton Cl STMC/STPC BR5 202 A1
Sefton Ct ENC/FH EN2 * 23 H3
Sefton Rd CROY/NA CR0 197 H5
STMC/STPC BR5 202 A1
Sefton St PUT/ROE SW15 139 F3
Sekforde St CLKNW EC1R 6 A7
Sekhon Ter FELT TW13 155 F5
Selah Dr SWLY BR8 187 K4
Selan Gdns YEAD UB4 95 F4
Selbie Av WLSDN NW10 81 H3
Selborne Av BXLY DA5 169 F3
MNPK E12 90 A2
Selborne Gdns GFD/PVL UB6 97 G1
HDN NW4 63 J1
Selborne Rd CMBW SE5 142 E3
CROY/NA CR0 212 A1
IL IG1 72 A6
NWMAL KT3 176 B5
SCUP DA14 168 C6
STHGT/OAK N14 34 E5
WALTH E17 69 H2
WDGN N22 49 F4
Selbourne Av SURB KT6 191 G6
Selby Cha RSLP HA4 59 F6
Selby Cl CHSGTN KT9 206 A5
CHST BR7 185 F2
Selby Gdns STHL UB1 96 A3
Selby Gn CAR SM5 194 D4
Selby Rd CAR SM5 194 D4
EA W5 97 H3
PGE/AN SE20 181 H5
PLSTW E13 107 F4
TOTM N17 50 A2
WAN E11 88 C1
Selby St WCHPL E1 104 C3
Selden Rd PECK SE15 143 K3
Selhurst Cl WIM/MER SW19 159 G3
Selhurst New Rd SNWD SE25 197 F3
Selhurst Pl SNWD SE25 197 F3
Selhurst Rd ED N9 35 K5
SNWD SE25 197 F2
Selinas La BCTR RM8 74 A4
Selkirk Dr ERITH DA8 150 B2
Selkirk Rd TOOT SW17 160 D6
WHTN TW2 155 H4
Sellers Hall Cl FNCH N3 46 E3
Sellincourt Rd TOOT SW17 178 D1
Sellindge Cl BECK BR3 182 C3
Sellons Av WLSDN NW10 81 H6
Sellwood Dr BAR EN5 20 B6
Selsdon Av SAND/SEL CR2 211 K4
Selsdon Cl CRW RM5 56 E1
SURB KT6 191 F2
Selsdon Park Rd
SAND/SEL CR2 213 F6
Selsdon Rd CRICK NW2 63 H6
PLSTW E13 89 G6
SAND/SEL CR2 211 K4
WAN E11 70 E4
WNWD SE27 162 C5
Selsdon Wy POP/IOD E14 124 E3
Selsea Pl STNW/STAM N16 86 A3
Selsey Crs WELL DA16 148 E2
Selsey St BOW E3 105 J4
Selvage La MLHL NW7 45 F1
Selway Cl PIN HA5 59 F1
Selwood Pl SKENS SW7 120 C5
Selwood Rd CHEAM SM3 193 J5
CHSGTN KT9 205 K2
CROY/NA CR0 197 J6
Selwood Ter SKENS SW7 120 C5
Selworthy Cl WAN E11 70 E2
Selworthy Rd CAT SE6 164 C5
Selwyn Av CHING E4 52 A2
GDMY/SEVK IG3 73 F3
RCH/KEW TW9 137 G4
Selwyn Cl HSLWW TW4 134 D5
Selwyn Ct EDGW HA8 44 D3
Selwyn Crs WELL DA16 148 C4
Selwyn Rd BOW E3 105 H1
NWMAL KT3 192 A2
PLSTW E13 89 F6
WLSDN NW10 81 G5
Semley Pl BGVA SW1W 15 H7
STRHM/NOR SW16 180 A5
Semley Rd STRHM/NOR SW16 179 K5
Senate St PECK SE15 143 K3
Seneca Rd THHTH CR7 196 D1
Senga Rd WLGTN SM6 195 F5
Senhouse Rd CHEAM SM3 208 B1
Senior St BAY/PAD W2 101 F4
Senlac Rd LEE/GVPK SE12 166 A3
Sennen Rd EN EN1 36 B2
Senrab St WCHPL E1 105 F5
Sentamu Cl HNHL SE24 162 C3
Sentinel Cl NTHLT UB5 95 J3
September Wy STAN HA7 43 H2
Sequoia Cl BUSH WD23 28 D3
Sequoia Gdns ORP BR6 202 A4
Sequoia Pk PIN HA5 42 B2
Serbin Cl LEY E10 70 A4
Serenaders Rd BRXN/ST SW9 142 B3
Serjeant's Inn EMB EC4Y * 11 K4
Serle St LINN WC2A 11 H3
Sermon Dr SWLY BR8 187 K6
Sermon La BLKFR EC4V 12 C4
Serpentine Rd BAY/PAD W2 14 D1
Service Route No 1
SRTFD E15 88 B5
Service Route No 2
SRTFD E15 88 B5
Service Route No 3
SRTFD E15 88 B4
Serviden Dr BMLY BR1 184 C4
Setchell Est STHWK SE1 19 J6
Setchell Rd STHWK SE1 19 J6
Setchell Wy STHWK SE1 19 J6
Seth St BERM/RHTH SE16 123 K2
Seton Gdns DAGW RM9 91 J5
Settles St WCHPL E1 104 C5
Settrington Rd FUL/PGN SW6 140 A3
Seven Acres CAR SM5 194 D6
NTHWD HA6 40 E2
Seven Dials LSQ/SEVD WC2H 10 E4
Sevenex Pde WBLY HA9 * 80 A3
Seven Kings Rd
GDMY/SEVK IG3 72 E5
Seven Kings Wy
KUTN/CMB KT2 174 E4
Sevenoaks Rd BROCKY SE4 164 C1
ORP BR6 217 F2
ORP BR6 217 F6
ORP BR6 217 K6
Sevenoaks Wy
STMC/STPC BR5 186 C6
Seven Seas Rd HTHAIR TW6 153 F1
Seven Sisters Rd FSBYPK N4 67 H6
HOLWY N7 85 F1
SEVS/STOTM N15 67 K3
Seven Stars Yd WCHPL E1 13 K1
Seventh Av HYS/HAR UB3 113 K1
MNPK E12 89 K2
Severnake Cl POP/IOD E14 124 D4
Severn Av GPK RM2 57 K6
NKENS W10 100 C2
Severn Dr EN EN1 24 C1
ESH/CLAY KT10 190 B6
WOT/HER KT12 188 C6
Severn Wy WLSDN NW10 81 H3
Severus Rd BTSEA SW11 140 D5
Seville Ms IS N1 86 A5
Seville St KTBR SW1X 15 F3
Sevington Rd HDN NW4 63 K3
Sevington St MV/WKIL W9 101 F3
Seward Rd BECK BR3 182 A5
HNWL W7 116 B2
Sewardstone Rd BETH E2 104 E1
CHING E4 25 K5
Seward St FSBYE EC1V 6 B6
Sewdley St CLPT E5 87 F1
Sewell Rd ABYW SE2 128 B2
Sewell St PLSTW E13 106 E2
Sextant Av POP/IOD E14 125 G4
Sexton Cl RAIN RM13 93 H6
Seymer Rd ROM RM1 57 F6
Seymour Av EW KT17 207 K6
MRDN SM4 193 G4
TOTM N17 50 C5
Seymour Cl E/WMO/HCT KT8 189 H2
LOU IG10 39 J1
PIN HA5 41 K4
Seymour Dr HAYES BR2 200 E5
Seymour Gdns BROCKY SE4 144 B4
BRYLDS KT5 191 G2
FELT TW13 154 A6
IL IG1 71 K5
RSLP HA4 59 H5
TWK TW1 156 C2
Seymour Ms MBLAR W1H 9 G3
Seymour Pl MBLAR W1H 8 E2
SNWD SE25 197 J1
Seymour Rd CAR SM5 210 A3
CEND/HSY/T N8 67 H2
CHING E4 37 K3
CHSWK W4 117 K4
E/WMO/HCT KT8 189 H2
ED N9 36 D4
EHAM E6 89 H6
FNCH N3 47 F3
HPTN TW12 173 H1
KUT/HW KT1 174 E4
LEY E10 69 H5
MTCM CR4 195 F4
WAND/EARL SW18 159 J2
WIM/MER SW19 159 G5
Seymour St BAY/PAD W2 8 E4
WOOL/PLUM SE18 127 H3
Seymour Ter PGE/AN SE20 181 J4
Seymour Vls PGE/AN SE20 181 J4
Seymour Wk WBPTN SW10 120 B6
Seyssel St POP/IOD E14 125 F4
Shaa Rd ACT W3 99 F6
Shacklegate La TEDD TW11 155 K6
Shackleton Cl FSTH SE23 163 J4
Shackleton Rd STHL UB1 95 K6
Shacklewell La HACK E8 86 B2
Shacklewell Rd
STNW/STAM N16 86 B2
Shacklewell Rw HACK E8 86 B2
Shacklewell St BETH E2 7 K6
Shadbolt Av CHING E4 51 G1
Shadbolt Cl WPK KT4 192 C6
Shad Thames STHWK SE1 19 J1
Shadwell Dr NTHLT UB5 95 K2
Shadwell Gdns WCHPL E1 * 104 E6
Shadwell Pierhead WAP E1W 104 E6
Shady Bush Cl BUSH WD23 28 C2
Shaef Wy TEDD TW11 174 B3
Shafter Rd DAGE RM10 92 E4
Shaftesbury Av BAR EN5 21 G5
EBED/NFELT TW14 153 K1
KTN/HRWW/WS HA3 61 K3
LSQ/SEVD WC2H 10 E3
NWDGN UB2 115 F4
PEND EN3 25 F3
RYLN/HDSTN HA2 60 B5
SOHO/SHAV W1D 10 C5
Shaftesbury Cir
RYLN/HDSTN HA2 * 60 C5
Shaftesbury Gdns
WLSDN NW10 99 G3
Shaftesbury Ms CLAP SW4 141 H6
KENS W8 119 K3
Shaftesbury Pde
RYLN/HDSTN HA2 * 60 C5
Shaftesbury Pl BARB EC2Y * 12 C2
Shaftesbury Rd ARCH N19 66 E5
BECK BR3 182 C5
CAR SM5 194 C4
CHING E4 38 B3
FSTGT E7 89 G5
LEY E10 69 J5
RCH/KEW TW9 137 F4
ROM RM1 75 H3
UED N18 50 A2
WALTH E17 69 K2
The Shaftesburys BARK IG11 108 C1
Shaftesbury St IS N1 6 D3
Shaftesbury Ter
HMSMTH W6 * 118 C4
Shaftesbury Wy WHTN TW2 155 J5
Shaftesbury Waye YEAD UB4 95 F4
Shafteswood Ct TOOT SW17 160 E5
Shafto Ms KTBR SW1X 14 E5
Shafton Ms HOM E9 * 87 F6
Shafton Rd HOM E9 87 F6
Shakespeare Av
EBED/NFELT TW14 153 K1
FBAR/BDGN N11 48 C1
WLSDN NW10 80 E6
YEAD UB4 94 E5
Shakespeare Crs MNPK E12 89 K5
WLSDN NW10 81 F6
Shakespeare Dr
KTN/HRWW/WS HA3 62 B3
Shakespeare Gdns EFNCH N2 65 K1
Shakespeare Rd ACT W3 117 K1
DART DA1 151 K5
FNCH N3 * 46 E4
HNHL SE24 142 C6
HNWL W7 97 F6
MLHL NW7 31 J6
ROM RM1 75 H3
WALTH E17 51 F5
Shakespeare Sq
BARK/HLT IG6 54 B2
Shakespeare Ter
RCH/KEW TW9 * 137 H4
Shakespeare Wy FELT TW13 154 B6
Shakspeare Ms
STNW/STAM N16 86 A2
Shakspeare Wk
STNW/STAM N16 86 A2
Shalbourne Sq HOM E9 87 H4
Shalcomb St WBPTN SW10 120 B6
Shaldon Dr MRDN SM4 193 H2
RSLP HA4 77 G1
Shaldon Rd EDGW HA8 44 B5
Shalfleet Dr NKENS W10 100 B6
Shalford Cl ORP BR6 216 C2
Shalford Ct IS N1 * 6 A2
Shalimar Gdns ACT W3 98 E6
Shalimar Rd ACT W3 98 E6
Shallons Rd ELTH/MOT SE9 167 G6
Shalstone Rd
MORT/ESHN SW14 137 J4
Shalston Vls SURB KT6 191 G3
Shamrock Rd CROY/NA CR0 196 A3
Shamrock St CLAP SW4 141 J4
Shamrock Wy
STHGT/OAK N14 34 B3
Shandon Rd CLAP SW4 161 H1
Shand St STHWK SE1 19 H2
Shandy St WCHPL E1 105 F4
Shanklin Gdns OXHEY WD19 27 G6
Shanklin Rd CEND/HSY/T N8 66 D2
SEVS/STOTM N15 68 C1
Shannon Cl CRICK NW2 82 B1
NWDGN UB2 114 C5
Shannon Cv BRXN/ST SW9 142 A5
Shannon Pl STJWD NW8 2 D2
Shannon Wy BECK BR3 182 E2
Shap Crs CAR SM5 194 E5
Shapland Wy PLMGR N13 49 F1
Shapwick Cl FBAR/BDGN N11 47 K1
Shardcroft Av HNHL SE24 142 C6
Shardeloes Rd BROCKY SE4 * 144 C6
NWCR SE14 144 C3
Shard's Sq PECK SE15 123 H6
Sharland Cl THHTH CR7 196 B3
Sharman Ct SCUP DA14 168 B6
Sharnbrooke Cl WELL DA16 148 D4
Sharon Cl SURB KT6 190 D5
Sharon Gdns HOM E9 86 E6
Sharon Rd CHSWK W4 118 A5
PEND EN3 25 G3
Sharples Hall St CAMTN NW1 83 K5
Sharps La RSLP HA4 58 B4
Sharp Wy DART DA1 151 J4
Sharratt St PECK SE15 123 K6
Sharsted St WALW SE17 122 C5
Sharvel La YEAD UB4 76 E6
Shavers Pl MYFR/PICC W1J 10 C6
Shaw Av BARK IG11 110 A1
Shawbrooke Rd
ELTH/MOT SE9 146 C5
Shawbury Cl CDALE/KGS NW9 45 G4
Shawbury Rd EDUL SE22 143 G6
Shaw Cl BUSH WD23 28 E4
EMPK RM11 75 K5
THMD SE28 128 C1
Shaw Crs POP/IOD E14 105 G5
Shaw Dr WOT/HER KT12 188 B4
Shawfield Pk BMLY BR1 184 C5
Shawfield St CHEL SW3 120 D5
Shawford Rd HOR/WEW KT19 207 F4
Shaw Gdns BARK IG11 110 A1
Shaw Rd BMLY BR1 165 J5
EDUL SE22 143 F5
PEND EN3 25 F2
Shaw's Cots FSTH SE23 164 B5
Shaw Sq WALTH E17 51 G4
The Shaw CHST BR7 * 185 H3
Shaw Wy WLGTN SM6 210 E5
Shaxton Crs CROY/NA CR0 214 A6
Sheaf Cots THDIT KT7 * 189 K5
Shearing Dr CAR SM5 194 B4
Shearling Wy HOLWY N7 84 E4
Shearman Rd
BKHTH/KID SE3 145 J5
Shears Cl DART DA1 171 F4
Shearwater Cl BARK IG11 109 G2
Shearwater Rd SUT SM1 208 D3
Shearwater Wy YEAD UB4 95 H5
Sheaths Cots THDIT KT7 * 190 C4
Sheaveshill Av
CDALE/KGS NW9 45 G6
Sheaveshill Pde
CDALE/KGS NW9 * 63 G1
Sheen Common Dr
RCHPK/HAM TW10 137 H5
Sheen Court Rd
RCHPK/HAM TW10 137 H5
Sheendale Rd RCH/KEW TW9 137 G5
Sheenewood SYD SE26 181 J1
Sheen Ga MORT/ESHN SW14 158 A1
Sheen Gate Gdns
MORT/ESHN SW14 137 K5
Sheen Gv IS N1 85 G6
Sheen La MORT/ESHN SW14 137 K5
Sheen Pk RCH/KEW TW9 137 F5
Sheen Rd RCH/KEW TW9 137 F5
STMC/STPC BR5 202 A1
Sheen Wy WLGTN SM6 211 F3
Sheen Wd MORT/ESHN SW14 137 K6
Sheepcote Cl HEST TW5 133 K1
Sheepcote La BTSEA SW11 140 E3
STMC/STPC BR5 203 H1
Sheepcote Rd HRW HA1 61 F3
Sheepcotes Rd CHDH RM6 73 K1
Sheephouse Wy NWMAL KT3 192 A5
Sheep La HACK E8 86 D6
Sheep Walk Ms
WIM/MER SW19 177 G2
Sheerwater Rd CAN/RD E16 107 H4
Sheffield Rd HTHAIR TW6 153 F1
Sheffield St LINN WC2A * 11 G4
Sheffield Ter KENS W8 119 K2
Shefton Ri NTHWD HA6 40 E3
Sheila Rd CRW RM5 56 D3
Shelbourne Cl PIN HA5 41 K6
Shelbourne Rd TOTM N17 50 D4
Shelburne Dr HSLWW TW4 155 F1
Shelburne Rd HOLWY N7 85 F2
Shelbury Cl SCUP DA14 168 B5
Shelbury Rd EDUL SE22 143 J6
Sheldon Av CLAY IG5 54 B5
HGT N6 65 K4
Sheldon Cl LEE/GVPK SE12 146 A6
PGE/AN SE20 181 J4
Sheldon Pl BETH E2 104 C1
Sheldon Rd CRICK NW2 82 B2
DAGW RM9 92 A5
UED N18 36 A6
Sheldon Sq BAY/PAD W2 101 G4
Sheldon St CROY/NA CR0 211 J1
Sheldrake Cl CAN/RD E16 126 E1
Sheldrake Pl KENS W8 119 J2
Sheldrick Cl MTCM CR4 178 C5
Shelduck Cl SRTFD E15 88 D3
Sheldwich Ter HAYES BR2 * 200 D3
Shelford Pl STNW/STAM N16 85 K1
Shelford Ri NRWD SE19 181 F3
Shelford Rd BAR EN5 32 A1
Shelgate Rd BTSEA SW11 140 E6
Shell Cl HAYES BR2 200 D3
Shellduck Cl CDALE/KGS NW9 45 G5
Shelley Av GFD/PVL UB6 96 D2
HCH RM12 75 H6
MNPK E12 89 J4
Shelley Cl EDGW HA8 30 C6
GFD/PVL UB6 96 D2
NTHWD HA6 40 D1
ORP BR6 216 E1
PECK SE15 143 J3
YEAD UB4 94 E4
Shelley Crs HEST TW5 134 C2
STHL UB1 95 K5
Shelley Dr WELL DA16 147 K2
Shelley Gdns ALP/SUD HA0 61 J6
Shelley Rd WLSDN NW10 81 F6
Shelley Wy WIM/MER SW19 178 C2
Shellgrove Rd
STNW/STAM N16 * 86 A3
Shellness Rd CLPT E5 86 D3
Shell Rd LEW SE13 144 E4
Shellwood Rd BTSEA SW11 140 E3
Shelmerdine Cl BOW E3 105 J4
Shelson Av FELT TW13 153 J5
Shelson Pde FELT TW13 * 153 J5
Shelton Rd WIM/MER SW19 177 K4
Shelton St LSQ/SEVD WC2H * 10 E4
Shenfield Rd WFD IG8 53 F3
Shenfield St IS N1 7 H3
Shenley Av RSLP HA4 58 D6
Shenley Rd CMBW SE5 143 F2
HEST TW5 134 D2
Shepherd Cl FELT TW13 154 D6
Shepherdess Pl FSBYE EC1V 6 D4
Shepherdess Wk IS N1 6 D2
Shepherd Market
MYFR/PICC W1J 15 J1
Shepherd's Bush Gn SHB W12 119 F2
Shepherd's Bush Market
SHB W12 119 F2
Shepherd's Bush Pl
SHB W12 * 119 G2
Shepherd's Bush Rd
HMSMTH W6 119 F3
Shepherds Cl CHDH RM6 73 K2
ORP BR6 217 F1
STAN HA7 43 G1
Shepherd's Cl HGT N6 66 B3
Shepherds Gn CHST BR7 185 J3
Shepherd's Hl HGT N6 66 B3
Shepherds La THMD SE28 127 K1
Shepherd's La HOM E9 87 F3
Shepherd's Leas
ELTH/MOT SE9 * 147 J5
Shepherds Pl
MYFR/PKLN W1K 9 G5
Shepherd St MYFR/PICC W1J 15 J1
Shepherds Wk BUSH WD23 28 D4
CRICK NW2 63 J6
Shepherd's Wk HAMP NW3 83 H3
Shepherds Wy SAND/SEL CR2 213 F5
Shepiston La HYS/HAR UB3 112 E4
Shepley Cl CAR SM5 210 A1
Shepley Ms PEND EN3 25 J1
Sheppard Cl EN EN1 24 D1
KUT/HW KT1 191 F1
Sheppard Dr
BERM/RHTH SE16 123 J5
Sheppard St CAN/RD E16 106 D3
Shepperton Rd IS N1 85 K6
STMC/STPC BR5 201 H3
Sheppey Cl ERITH DA8 150 E1
Sheppey Gdns DAGW RM9 91 J5
Sheppey Rd DAGW RM9 91 H5
Sheppey Wk IS N1 * 85 J5
Shepton Houses BETH E2 * 104 E2
Sherard Rd ELTH/MOT SE9 146 D6
Sheraton St SOHO/CST W1F * 10 C4
Sherborne Av NWDGN UB2 115 F4
PEND EN3 24 E3
Sherborne Cl YEAD UB4 95 G5
Sherborne Crs CAR SM5 194 D4
Sherborne Gdns
CDALE/KGS NW9 44 C6
WEA W13 97 H5
Sherborne La MANHO EC4N 12 E5
Sherborne Pl NTHWD HA6 40 B2
Sherborne Rd CHEAM SM3 193 K6
CHSGTN KT9 206 A3
EBED/NFELT TW14 153 G2
STMC/STPC BR5 202 A2
Sherborne St IS N1 85 K6
Sherborne Vls WEA W13 * 97 H4
Sherboro Rd
SEVS/STOTM N15 68 B3
Sherbrooke Rd FUL/PGN SW6 139 H1
Sherbrooke Ter
FUL/PGN SW6 * 139 H1
Sherbrooke Wy WPK KT4 192 E4
Sherbrook Gdns WCHMH N21 35 H2
Shere Cl CHSGTN KT9 205 K3
Sheredan Rd CHING E4 52 B1
Shere Rd GNTH/NBYPK IG2 72 A2
Sherfield Cl NWMAL KT3 191 J1
Sherfield Gdns
PUT/ROE SW15 158 C1
Sheridan Cl HARH RM3 57 K3
Sheridan Ct DART DA1 151 K5
HSLWW TW4 134 D6
Sheridan Crs CHST BR7 185 G5
Sheridan Gdns
KTN/HRWW/WS HA3 61 K3
Sheridan Ms WAN E11 71 F3
Sheridan Pl BMLY BR1 184 C5
HPTN TW12 173 G4
Sheridan Rd BELV DA17 129 H4
FSTGT E7 88 D1
MNPK E12 89 J3
OXHEY WD19 27 H2
RCHPK/HAM TW10 156 D5
WIM/MER SW19 177 J4
Sheridan Ter NTHLT UB5 * 78 B3
Sheridan Wk CAR SM5 209 K3
GLDGN NW11 64 E3
Sheridan Wy BECK BR3 182 C4
Sheringham Av MNPK E12 89 K2
ROMW/RG RM7 74 E3
STHGT/OAK N14 22 D6
WHTN TW2 154 E3
Sheringham Dr BARK IG11 91 F3
Sheringham Rd HOLWY N7 85 G4
PGE/AN SE20 181 J5
Sherington Av PIN HA5 42 A3
Sherington Rd
BKHTH/KID SE3 126 A6
Sherland Rd TWK TW1 156 A3
Sherlies Av ORP BR6 201 K6
Sherlock Ms MHST W1U 9 G
Shermanbury Cl ERITH DA8 150 C
Sherman Gdns CHDH RM6 73 J
Sherman Rd BMLY BR1 183 K
Shernhall St WALTH E17 70 A
Sherrard Rd FSTGT E7 89 G
MNPK E12 89 H
Sherrards Wy BAR EN5 20 E
Sherrick Green Rd
WLSDN NW10 81 K
Sherriff Cl ESH/CLAY KT10 189
Sherriff Rd KIL/WHAMP NW6 82 E
Sherringham Av FELT TW13 153 K
TOTM N17 50 C
Sherrock Gdns HDN NW4 63 J
Sherry Ms BARK IG11 90 D
Sherwin Rd NWCR SE14 144 A
Sherwood SURB KT6 190 E
Sherwood Av GFD/PVL UB6 78 E
RSLP HA4 58 C
STRHM/NOR SW16 179
SWFD E18 53 F
YEAD UB4 95 F
Sherwood Cl BXLY DA5 168
WALTH E17 51 H
WEA W13 116
Sherwood Ct MBLAR W1H * 8
Sherwood Gdns BARK IG11 90
BERM/RHTH SE16 123
POP/IOD E14 124
Sherwood House
RYLN/HDSTN HA2 * 78
Sherwood Park Av
BFN/LL DA15 168
Sherwood Park Rd
MTCM CR4 195
SUT SM1 208
Sherwood Rd BARK/HLT IG6 72
CROY/NA CR0 197
HDN NW4 46
HPTN TW12 173
RYLN/HDSTN HA2 60
WELL DA16 147
WIM/MER SW19 177
Sherwoods Rd OXHEY WD19 27
Sherwood St SOHO/CST W1F 10
TRDG/WHET N20 33
Sherwood Ter
TRDG/WHET N20 33
Sherwood Wy WWKM BR4 199
Shetland Cl BORE WD6 31
Shetland Rd BOW E3 105
Shield Dr BTFD TW8 116
Shield Rd ASHF TW15 153
Shifford Pth FSTH SE23 164
Shillibeer Pl MBLAR W1H 8
Shillingford Cl MLHL NW7 46
Shillingford St IS N1 85
Shilling Pl HNWL W7 * 116
Shinfield St SHB W12 100
Shinners Cl SNWD SE25 197
Shipka Rd BAL SW12 161
Ship La MORT/ESHN SW14 137

Shipman Rd CAN/RD E16 107 F5
FSTH SE23 164 A4
Ship & Mermaid Rw
STHWK SE1 * 19 F2
Ship St DEPT SE8 144 D2
Ship Tavern Pas BANK EC3V 13 G5
Shipton Cl BCTR RM8 91 K1
Shipton St BETH E2 7 K4
Shipwright Rd
BERM/RHTH SE16 124 B2
Shipwright Yd STHWK SE1 * 19 G1
Shirburn Cl FSTH SE23 163 K2
Shirbutt St POP/IOD E14 105 J6
Shirebrook Rd
BKHTH/KID SE3 146 C3
Shire Ct EW KT17 207 H5
Shirehall Cl HDN NW4 64 B3
Shirehall Gdns HDN NW4 64 B3
Shirehall La HDN NW4 64 B3
Shirehall Pk HDN NW4 64 B3
Shire Horse Wy ISLW TW7 136 A4
Shire La ORP BR6 215 K5
ORP BR6 216 D4
Shire Ms WHTN TW2 155 H1
Shire Pl WAND/EARL SW18 160 B2
The Shires RCHPK/HAM TW10 157 F6
Shirland Ms MV/WKIL W9 100 D2
Shirland Rd MV/WKIL W9 100 D2
Shirley Av BXLY DA5 168 E2
CROY/NA CR0 197 K5
SUT SM1 209 J2
Shirley Church Rd
CROY/NA CR0 213 F1
Shirley Cl HSLW TW3 135 H6
WALTH E17 * 69 K2
Shirley Crs BECK BR3 198 B1
Shirley Dr HSLW TW3 135 H6
Shirley Gdns BARK IG11 90 E4
HNWL W7 116 A1
Shirley Gv BTSEA SW11 141 F4
ED N9 36 E2
Shirley Hills Rd CROY/NA CR0 213 F2
Shirley Oaks Rd CROY/NA CR0 198 A5
Shirley Park Rd CROY/NA CR0 197 J5
Shirley Rd BFN/LL DA15 167 K5
CHSWK W4 118 A2
CROY/NA CR0 197 J5
ENC/FH EN2 23 J4
SRTFD E15 88 C5
WLGTN SM6 210 C6
Shirley Rw SNWD SE25 * 181 H5
Shirley St CAN/RD E16 106 D5
Shirley Wy CROY/NA CR0 213 H1
Shirlock Rd HAMP NW3 83 K2
Shirwell Cl MLHL NW7 46 B3
Shobden Rd TOTM N17 49 K4
Shobroke Cl CRICK NW2 82 A1
Shoebury Rd EHAM E6 89 K5
Shoe La FLST/FETLN EC4A 11 K3
HCIRC EC1N 12 A2
Sholden Gdns
STMC/STPC BR5 202 D2
Shooters Av
KTN/HRWW/WS HA3 61 J1
Shooters Hill Rd
BKHTH/KID SE3 146 B1
GNWCH SE10 145 H2
Shooters Rd ENC/FH EN2 23 G2
Shoot-Up Hl CRICK NW2 82 C4
Shore Cl EBED/NFELT TW14 153 K2
HPTN TW12 172 D1
Shoreditch High St
FSBYE EC1V 7 H5
WCHPL E1 13 H1
Shore Gv FELT TW13 155 F4
Shoreham Cl CROY/NA CR0 197 K3
WAND/EARL SW18 140 A6
Shoreham Rd
STMC/STPC BR5 186 C4
Shoreham Road (East)
HTHAIR TW6 132 B6
Shoreham Road (West)
HTHAIR TW6 132 B6
Shore Pl HOM E9 86 E5
Shore Rd HOM E9 86 E5
Shore Wy BRXN/ST SW9 142 B3
Shorncliffe Rd STHWK SE1 123 G5
Shorndean St CAT SE6 165 F3
Shorne Cl BFN/LL DA15 168 C1
STMC/STPC BR5 202 E1
Shornefield Cl BMLY BR1 185 F6
Shorrolds Rd FUL/PGN SW6 139 K1
Shortcroft Rd EW KT17 207 H5
Shortcrofts Rd DAGW RM9 92 B4
Shorter St TWRH EC3N 13 J5
Shortgate
NFNCH/WDSPK N12 32 D6
Shortlands HMSMTH W6 119 G4
HYS/HAR UB3 113 G6
Shortlands Cl BELV DA17 129 G3
UED N18 35 K5
Shortlands Gdns HAYES BR2 183 H5
Shortlands Gv HAYES BR2 183 G6
Shortlands Rd HAYES BR2 183 G6
KUTN/CMB KT2 175 G3
LEY E10 69 K4
Short La STWL/WRAY TW19 152 C2
Short Rd CHSWK W4 118 B6
WAN E11 70 C6
Shorts Cft CDALE/KGS NW9 62 D1
Shorts Gdns
LSQ/SEVD WC2H * 10 E4
Shorts Rd CAR SM5 209 J2
Short St HDN NW4 64 A1
STHWK SE1 17 K2
Shortway ELTH/MOT SE9 146 D4
Short Wy NFNCH/WDSPK N12 47 J2
WHTN TW2 155 H2
Shotfield WLGTN SM6 210 B4
Shott Cl SUT SM1 209 G3
Shottendane Rd
FUL/PGN SW6 * 139 K2
Shottery Cl ELTH/MOT SE9 166 D5
Shottfield Av
MORT/ESHN SW14 138 B5
Shoulder of Mutton Aly
POP/IOD E14 105 G6
Shouldham St MBLAR W1H 8 D2
Showers Wy HYS/HAR UB3 113 K1
Shrapnel Cl WOOL/PLUM SE18 146 E1
Shrapnel Rd ELTH/MOT SE9 146 E4
Shrewsbury Av
KTN/HRWW/WS HA3 62 A1
MORT/ESHN SW14 137 K5
Shrewsbury Cl SURB KT6 191 F6
Shrewsbury Crs
WLSDN NW10 81 F6
Shrewsbury La
WOOL/PLUM SE18 147 G2
Shrewsbury Ms BAY/PAD W2 100 E5
Shrewsbury Rd BAY/PAD W2 100 E5
BECK BR3 182 B6
CAR SM5 194 D4
FBAR/BDGN N11 48 D2
FSTGT E7 89 H4
HTHAIR TW6 153 F1
Shrewsbury St NKENS W10 100 A3
Shrewton Rd TOOT SW17 * 178 E3
Shroffold Rd BMLY BR1 165 H6
Shropshire Cl MTCM CR4 195 K1
Shropshire Rd WDGN N22 49 F3
Shroton St CAMTN NW1 8 C1
The Shrubberies CHIG IG7 54 C1
SWFD E18 52 E5
Shrubbery Gdns WCHMH N21 35 H2
Shrubbery Rd ED N9 36 C5
STHL UB1 114 E1
STRHM/NOR SW16 161 K6
The Shrubbery SURB KT6 * 191 F5
Shrubland Cl
TRDG/WHET N20 * 33 H4
Shrubland Gv WPK KT4 208 A1
Shrubland Rd HACK E8 86 C6
LEY E10 69 J4
WALTH E17 69 J2
Shrublands Av CROY/NA CR0 213 J2
Shrublands Cl CHIG IG7 54 C2
SYD SE26 163 K5
TRDG/WHET N20 33 H3
Shrubsall Cl ELTH/MOT SE9 166 D3
Shubbery Cl IS N1 85 J6
Shuna Wk IS N1 * 85 K4
Shurland Av EBAR EN4 33 H1
Shurland Gdns PECK SE15 * 143 G1
Shurlock Dr ORP BR6 216 C2
Shuters Sq WKENS W14 * 119 J5
Shuttle Cl BFN/LL DA15 168 A2
Shuttlemead BXLY DA5 169 G2
Shuttle Rd DART DA1 150 D4
Shuttle St WCHPL E1 104 C3
Shuttleworth Rd BTSEA SW11 140 C3
Sibella Rd CLAP SW4 141 J3
Sibley Cl BMLY BR1 200 D2
Sibley Ct UX/CGN UB8 94 A4
Sibley Gv EHAM E6 89 J5
Sibthorpe Rd LEE/GVPK SE12 166 A2
Sibthorp Rd MTCM CR4 * 178 E5
Sibton Rd CAR SM5 194 D4
Sicilian Av NOXST/BSQ WC1A * 11 F2
Sidbury St FUL/PGN SW6 139 H2
Sidcup By-Pass Rd
SCUP DA14 167 K6
SCUP DA14 186 B2
Sidcup Hl SCUP DA14 186 C1
Sidcup Hill Gdns SCUP DA14 * 186 D1
Sidcup Pl SCUP DA14 186 B1
Sidcup Rd ELTH/MOT SE9 166 E4
ELTH/MOT SE9 167 G4
LEE/GVPK SE12 146 A6
LEE/GVPK SE12 166 B2
Siddeley Dr HSLWW TW4 134 D4
Siddons La CAMTN NW1 3 F7
Siddons Rd CROY/NA CR0 211 G1
FSTH SE23 164 B4
TOTM N17 50 C4
Side Rd WALTH E17 69 H2
Sidewood Rd ELTH/MOT SE9 167 J3
Sidford Pl STHWK SE1 17 H5
Sidings Ms HOLWY N7 85 G2
The Sidings LOU IG10 39 J1
WAN E11 70 A5
Sidmouth Av ISLW TW7 135 K3
Sidmouth Cl OXHEY WD19 27 F4
Sidmouth Dr RSLP HA4 76 E1
Sidmouth Pde CRICK NW2 * 82 A5
Sidmouth Rd CRICK NW2 82 A5
LEY E10 70 A6
PECK SE15 143 G2
STMC/STPC BR5 202 C1
WELL DA16 148 D1
Sidmouth St STPAN WC1H 5 F5
Sidney Av PLMGR N13 49 F1
Sidney Elson Wy EHAM E6 108 A1
Sidney Gdns BTFD TW8 116 E6
Sidney Gv FSBYE EC1V 6 A3
Sidney Rd BECK BR3 182 B5
BRXN/ST SW9 142 A3
FSTGT E7 88 E1
RYLN/HDSTN HA2 42 C6
SNWD SE25 197 H2
TWK TW1 156 B1
WDGN N22 49 F3
WOT/HER KT12 188 A5
Sidney Sq WCHPL E1 * 104 E4
Sidney St WCHPL E1 104 D4
Sidworth St HACK E8 86 D5
Siemens Rd
WOOL/PLUM SE18 126 C3
Sienna Cl CHSGTN KT9 205 K4
Sienna Ter CRICK NW2 * 63 J6
Sierra Dr DAGE RM10 110 D1
Sigdon Rd HACK E8 86 C3
The Sigers PIN HA5 59 F3
Signmakers Yd CAMTN NW1 * 3 K1
Sigrist Sq KUTN/CMB KT2 175 F4
Silbury Av MTCM CR4 178 D4
Silbury St IS N1 * 6 E4
Silesia Blds HACK E8 86 D5
Silex St STHWK SE1 18 B3
Silkfield Rd CDALE/KGS NW9 63 G2
Silkin Ms PECK SE15 143 H1
Silk Mill Rd OXHEY WD19 27 F2
Silk Mills Pth LEW SE13 145 F4
Silkstream Pde EDGW HA8 * 44 E4
Silkstream Rd EDGW HA8 44 E4
Silk St BARB EC2Y 12 D1
Silsoe Rd WDGN N22 49 F6
Silver Birch Av CHING E4 51 H1
Silver Birch Cl CAT SE6 164 C5
FBAR/BDGN N11 48 A2
THMD SE28 128 B1
Silver Birch Ms BARK/HLT IG6 54 C2
Silverbirch Wk HAMP NW3 * 83 K4
Silvercliffe Gdns EBAR EN4 21 J5
Silver Cl KTN/HRWW/WS HA3 42 D3
NWCR SE14 * 144 B1
Silver Crs CHSWK W4 117 J4
Silverdale ENC/FH EN2 22 E5
SYD SE26 163 K6
Silverdale Cl HNWL W7 115 K1
NTHLT UB5 77 K3
SUT SM1 208 D2
Silverdale Dr ELTH/MOT SE9 166 D4
HCH RM12 93 K3
SUN TW16 172 A5
Silverdale Gdns HYS/HAR UB3 113 K2
Silverdale Rd CHING E4 52 B2
HYS/HAR UB3 113 K2
STMC/STPC BR5 186 B6
STMC/STPC BR5 201 H1
Silverdene
NFNCH/WDSPK N12 * 47 F2
Silver Dene PUT/ROE SW15 * 139 F6
Silvergate HOR/WEW KT19 206 E3
Silverhall St ISLW TW7 136 B4
Silverholme Cl
KTN/HRWW/WS HA3 62 A4
Silver La WWKM BR4 199 G6
Silverleigh Rd THHTH CR7 196 A1
Silvermere Av CRW RM5 56 D2
Silvermere Dr UED N18 * 51 F1
Silvermere Rd CAT SE6 164 D1
Silvermere Rw SNWD SE25 * 181 H5
Silver Pl SOHO/CST W1F 10 B4
Silver Rd LEW SE13 144 E4
NKENS W10 100 B6
Silver Spring Cl ERITH DA8 129 J6
Silverston Wy STAN HA7 43 J2
Silver St EN EN1 23 K4
UED N18 35 K6
Silverthorne Rd VX/NE SW8 141 G3
Silverthorn Gdns CHING E4 37 J4
Silverton Rd HMSMTH W6 139 G1
Silvertown Wy CAN/RD E16 106 D6
Silvertree La GFD/PVL UB6 96 D2
Silver Wk BERM/RHTH SE16 124 C1
Silver Wy ROMW/RG RM7 56 D6
Silverwood Cl BECK BR3 182 D3
CROY/NA CR0 213 H6
NTHWD HA6 40 A4
Silvester Rd EDUL SE22 143 G6
Silvester St STHWK SE1 18 E3
Silwood Estate Regeneration
Area BERM/RHTH SE16 124 A5
Silwood St BERM/RHTH SE16 124 A5
Simmil Rd ESH/CLAY KT10 204 E3
Simmons Cl TRDG/WHET N20 33 J3
Simmons Dr BCTR RM8 92 A1
Simmons Ga ESH/CLAY KT10 204 C3
Simmons La CHING E4 38 B4
Simmons Rd
WOOL/PLUM SE18 127 G5
Simmons' Wy
TRDG/WHET N20 33 J4
Simms Cl CAR SM5 194 D6
Simms Gdns EFNCH N2 47 G5
Simms Rd STHWK SE1 123 H4
Simnel Rd LEE/GVPK SE12 166 A2
Simon Cl NTGHL W11 100 D6
Simonds Rd LEY E10 69 J6
Simone Cl BMLY BR1 184 C4
Simons Wk SRTFD E15 88 B3
Simpson Cl CROY/NA CR0 196 D3
WCHMH N21 23 F6
Simpson Dr ACT W3 99 F5
Simpson Rd HSLWW TW4 154 E1
RAIN RM13 93 H4
RCHPK/HAM TW10 156 D6
Simpson's Rd HAYES BR2 183 K6
POP/IOD E14 105 K6
Simpson St BTSEA SW11 140 D3
Simpson Wy SURB KT6 190 D3
Simrose Ct WAND/EARL SW18 139 K6
Sims Cl ROM RM1 75 H1
Sinclair Dr BELMT SM2 209 F6
Sinclair Gdns WKENS W14 119 G2
Sinclair Gv GLDGN NW11 64 B3
Sinclair Rd CHING E4 51 H1
WKENS W14 119 H3
Sinclare Cl EN EN1 24 B2
Singapore Rd WEA W13 116 B1
Singer St FSBYE EC1V 7 F5
Singleton Cl CROY/NA CR0 196 D4
HCH RM12 93 H2
TOOT SW17 178 E3
Singleton Rd DAGW RM9 92 B3
Singleton Scarp
NFNCH/WDSPK N12 46 E1
Sinnott Rd WALTH E17 51 F4
Sion Rd TWK TW1 156 C3
Sipson Cl WDR/YW UB7 112 D6
Sipson La WDR/YW UB7 112 E6
Sipson Rd WDR/YW UB7 132 D1
Sipson Wy WDR/YW UB7 132 D1
Sir Abraham Dawes Cots
PUT/ROE SW15 * 139 H5
Sir Alexander Cl ACT W3 118 C1
Sir Cyril Black Wy
WIM/MER SW19 177 J3
Sirdar Rd MTCM CR4 179 F2
NTGHL W11 100 B6
WDGN N22 49 H6
Sir John Kirk Cl CMBW SE5 142 D1
Sir Thomas More Est
CHEL SW3 120 C6
Sirus Rd NTHWD HA6 40 E1
Sise La MANHO EC4N * 12 E4
Sisley Rd BARK IG11 90 E6
Sispara Gdns
WAND/EARL SW18 159 J1
Sissinghurst Cl BMLY BR1 183 H1
Sissinghurst Rd CROY/NA CR0 197 H4
Sister Mabels Wy PECK SE15 * 143 H1
Sisters Av BTSEA SW11 140 E5
Sistova Rd BAL SW12 161 G3
Sisulu Pl BRXN/ST SW9 142 B4
Sittingbourne Av EN EN1 35 K1
Sitwell Gv STAN HA7 43 F1
Siverst Cl NTHLT UB5 78 B4
Siviter Wy DAGE RM10 92 D5
Siward Rd HAYES BR2 184 A6
TOOT SW17 160 B5
TOTM N17 49 K4
Sixth Av HYS/HAR UB3 113 J1
MNPK E12 89 K2
NKENS W10 100 C3
Sixth Cross Rd WHTN TW2 155 H5
Skardu Rd CRICK NW2 82 C3
Skeena Hl WAND/EARL SW18 159 H2
Skeet Hill La STMC/STPC BR5 203 G6
Skeffington Rd EHAM E6 89 K6
Skeffington St
WOOL/PLUM SE18 127 H3
Skelbrook St
WAND/EARL SW18 160 A4
Skelgill Rd PUT/ROE SW15 139 J5
Skelley Rd SRTFD E15 88 D5
Skelton Cl HACK E8 * 86 B4
Skelton Rd FSTGT E7 88 E4
Skelton's La LEY E10 69 K4
Skelwith Rd HMSMTH W6 119 F6
Skerne Rd KUTN/CMB KT2 174 E4
Skerne Wk KUTN/CMB KT2 174 E4
Sketchley Gdns
BERM/RHTH SE16 124 A5
Sketty Rd EN EN1 24 B4
Skiers St SRTFD E15 88 C6
Skiffington Cl
BRXS/STRHM SW2 162 B3
Skinner Pl BGVA SW1W * 15 G7
Skinners La BLKFR EC4V 12 D5
HEST TW5 135 G2
Skinner St CLKNW EC1R 6 A6
Skipsey Av EHAM E6 107 K2
Skipton Cl FBAR/BDGN N11 48 A2
Skipton Dr HYS/HAR UB3 113 F3
Skipworth Rd HOM E9 86 E6
Skylines POP/IOD E14 125 F2
Skylines Village
POP/IOD E14 * 125 F2
Sky Peals Rd WFD IG8 52 B3
Skyport Dr WDR/YW UB7 132 A1
Sladebrook Rd
BKHTH/KID SE3 146 C4
Sladedale Rd
WOOL/PLUM SE18 127 K5
Slade Gdns ERITH DA8 150 C2
Sladen Pl CLPT E5 86 D2
Slades Cl ENC/FH EN2 23 G4
Slades Dr CHST BR7 167 H5
ELTH/MOT SE9 167 H6
Slades Gdns ENC/FH EN2 23 G3
Slades Hl ENC/FH EN2 23 G4
Slades Ri ENC/FH EN2 23 G4
The Slade WOOL/PLUM SE18 127 K6
Slade Wk WALW SE17 122 C6
Slade Wy MTCM CR4 179 F4
Slagrove Pl LEW SE13 144 D6
Slaidburn St WBPTN SW10 120 B6
Slaithwaite Rd LEW SE13 145 F5
Slaney Pl HOLWY N7 85 G3
Slaney Rd ROM RM1 75 G2
Slattery Rd FELT TW13 154 B3
Sleaford Gn OXHEY WD19 27 H5
Sleaford St VX/NE SW8 141 H1
Sledmere Ct
EBED/NFELT TW14 153 H3
Slievemore Cl CLAP SW4 141 J4
Slingsby Pl LSQ/SEVD WC2H 10 E5
Slippers Pl BERM/RHTH SE16 123 J3
Sloane Av CHEL SW3 14 D7
Sloane Ct East CHEL SW3 121 F5
Sloane Ct West CHEL SW3 121 F5
Sloane Gdns BGVA SW1W 15 G7
ORP BR6 216 C1
Sloane Sq BGVA SW1W 15 F7
Sloane St KTBR SW1X 15 F3
Sloane Ter KTBR SW1X 15 F6
Sloane Wk CROY/NA CR0 198 C3
Slocum Cl THMD SE28 109 J6
Slough La CDALE/KGS NW9 62 E3
Sly St WCHPL E1 * 104 D5
Smaldon Cl WDR/YW UB7 112 D3
Smallberry Av ISLW TW7 136 A3
Smallbrook Ms BAY/PAD W2 8 A4
Smalley Cl STNW/STAM N16 86 B1
Smallwood Rd TOOT SW17 160 C6
Smarden Cl BELV DA17 129 H5
Smart Cl HARH RM3 57 K4
Smart's Pl NOXST/BSQ WC1A 11 F3
UED N18 50 C1
Smart St BETH E2 105 F2
Smeaton Rd
WAND/EARL SW18 159 K2
WFD IG8 53 K1
Smeaton St WAP E1W 123 J1
Smedley St VX/NE SW8 141 J3
Smeed Rd BOW E3 87 J5
Smiles Pl LEW SE13 145 F3
Smith Cl BERM/RHTH SE16 124 A1
Smithfield St STBT EC1A 12 A2
Smithies Rd ABYW SE2 128 C4
Smith's Ct SOHO/SHAV W1D * 10 C5
Smithson Rd TOTM N17 49 K4
Smith Sq WEST SW1P 16 E5
Smith St BRYLDS KT5 191 G3
CHEL SW3 120 E5
Smith's Yd CROY/NA CR0 211 J1
Smith Ter CHEL SW3 120 E5
Smithwood Cl
WIM/MER SW19 159 H3
Smithy St WCHPL E1 104 E4
Smythe Cl ED N9 36 C5
Smugglers Wy
WAND/EARL SW18 140 A5
Smyrk's Rd WALW SE17 123 F5
Smyrna Rd KIL/WHAMP NW6 82 E5
Smythe St POP/IOD E14 105 K6
Snakes La EBAR EN4 22 B4
Snakes La East WFD IG8 53 G2
Snakes La West WFD IG8 52 E2
Snakey La FELT TW13 153 K6
Snaresbrook Dr STAN HA7 29 K6
Snaresbrook Rd WALTH E17 70 C1
WAN E11 70 D1
Snarsgate St NKENS W10 100 A4
Sneath Av GLDGN NW11 64 D4
Snell's Pk UED N18 50 B2
Sneyd Rd CRICK NW2 82 A3
Snowberry Cl SRTFD E15 88 B2
Snowbury Rd FUL/PGN SW6 140 A3
Snowden Dr CDALE/KGS NW9 63 G3
Snowdon Crs HYS/HAR UB3 113 F3
Snowdon Rd HTHAIR TW6 153 F1
Snowdown Cl PGE/AN SE20 181 K4
Snowdrop Cl HPTN TW12 173 F2
Snow Hl STBT EC1A 12 A2
Snowsfields STHWK SE1 19 F2
Snowshill Rd MNPK E12 89 J3
Snowy Fielder Waye
ISLW TW7 136 C3
Soames St PECK SE15 143 G4
Soames Wk NWMAL KT3 176 B4
Soane Cl EA W5 116 E2
Soaphouse La BTFD TW8 137 F1
Soho Sq SOHO/SHAV W1D 10 C3
Soho St SOHO/SHAV W1D 10 C3
Sojourner-Truth Cl HACK E8 86 D4
Solander Gdns WCHPL E1 104 D6
Solebay St WCHPL E1 105 G3
Solent Ri PLSTW E13 106 E2
Solent Rd KIL/WHAMP NW6 82 E3
Solna Av PUT/ROE SW15 139 F6
Solna Rd WCHMH N21 35 K3
Solomon Av UED N18 36 C6
Solomon's Pas PECK SE15 143 J5
Solon New Rd CLAP SW4 141 K5
Solon Rd BRXS/STRHM SW2 141 K5
Solway Cl HACK E8 86 B4
HSLWW TW4 134 D4
Solway Rd EDUL SE22 143 H5
WDGN N22 49 H4
Somaford Gv EBAR EN4 33 H1
Somali Rd CRICK NW2 82 D2
Somerby Rd BARK IG11 90 D5
Somercoates Cl EBAR EN4 21 J4
Somerden Rd
STMC/STPC BR5 202 E4
Somerfield Rd FSBYPK N4 67 H6
Somerfield St
BERM/RHTH SE16 124 A5
Somerford Cl PIN HA5 58 E1
Somerford Gv
STNW/STAM N16 86 B2
TOTM N17 50 C3
Somerford St WCHPL E1 * 104 D3
Somerford Wy
BERM/RHTH SE16 124 B2
Somerhill Av BFN/LL DA15 168 C2
Somerhill Rd WELL DA16 148 C3
Somerleyton Rd
BRXN/ST SW9 142 B5
Somersby Gdns REDBR IG4 71 K2
Somers Cl CAMTN NW1 4 C2
Somers Crs BAY/PAD W2 8 C4
Somerset Av CHSGTN KT9 205 K2
RYNPK SW20 176 E5
WELL DA16 148 A6
Somerset Cl CHEAM SM3 208 A1
NWMAL KT3 192 B3
TOTM N17 49 K5
WFD IG8 52 E4
Somerset Gdns HGT N6 66 A4
LEW SE13 144 E3
STRHM/NOR SW16 180 A6
TEDD TW11 173 K1
TOTM N17 * 50 A3
Somerset Rd BAR EN5 21 F6
BTFD TW8 116 D6
CHSWK W4 118 A3
HDN NW4 64 A1
HRW HA1 60 C3
KUT/HW KT1 175 G5
ORP BR6 202 B4
PEND EN3 25 J1
STHL UB1 96 A4
TEDD TW11 173 K1
TOTM N17 50 B6
WALTH E17 69 J2
WEA W13 116 C1
WIM/MER SW19 159 G5
Somerset Sq WKENS W14 * 119 H3
Somerset Waye HEST TW5 114 D6
Somers Pl BRXS/STRHM SW2 162 A2
Somers Rd BRXS/STRHM SW2 162 A1
WALTH E17 69 H1
Somers Wy BUSH WD23 28 C2
Somerton Av RCH/KEW TW9 137 J4
Somerton Rd CRICK NW2 82 B1
PECK SE15 143 J5
Somertrees Av
LEE/GVPK SE12 166 A4
Somervell Rd
RYLN/HDSTN HA2 77 K3
Somerville Av BARN SW13 119 F6
Somerville Cl BRXN/ST SW9 142 A2
Somerville Rd CHDH RM6 73 J2
PGE/AN SE20 182 A3
Sonderburg Rd HOLWY N7 67 F6
Sondes St WALW SE17 122 E6
Songhurst Cl CROY/NA CR0 196 A3
Sonia Cl OXHEY WD19 27 G2
Sonia Gdns HEST TW5 135 F1
NFNCH/WDSPK N12 33 G6
WLSDN NW10 81 H2
Sonning Gdns HPTN TW12 172 D2
Sonning Rd SNWD SE25 197 H3
Soper Cl CHING E4 51 H1
FSTH SE23 164 A3
Soper Ms PEND EN3 25 J1
Sophia Cl HOLWY N7 85 F4
Sophia Rd CAN/RD E16 107 F4
LEY E10 69 K5
Sophia Sq BERM/RHTH SE16 105 G6
Sopwith Av CHSGTN KT9 206 A3
Sopwith Cl KUTN/CMB KT2 175 G1
Sopwith Rd HEST TW5 134 B1
Sopwith Wy KUTN/CMB KT2 175 F4
VX/NE SW8 141 G1
Sorrel Bank CROY/NA CR0 * 213 G6
Sorrel Cl THMD SE28 128 B1
Sorrel Gdns EHAM E6 107 J4
Sorrel La POP/IOD E14 106 B5
Sorrell Cl BRXN/ST SW9 * 142 B3
NWCR SE14 144 B1
Sorrel Wk ROM RM1 57 H6
Sorrento Rd SUT SM1 209 F1
Sotheby Rd HBRY N5 85 J2
Sotheran Cl HACK E8 86 C6
Soudan Rd BTSEA SW11 140 E2

Souldern Rd WKENS W14 * 119 G3
Sounds Ldg SWLY BR8 203 K3
South Access Rd LEY E10 69 F4
South Africa Rd SHB W12 99 K6
Southall Ct STHL UB1 * 95 K6
Southall La HEST TW5 114 A6
Southall Pl STHWK SE1 18 E3
Southampton Blds
LINN WC2A * 11 J2
Southampton Gdns
MTCM CR4 195 K2
Southampton Ms
CAN/RD E16 126 A1
Southampton Pl
NOXST/BSQ WC1A 11 F2
Southampton Rd HAMP NW3 83 K3
Southampton Rd East
HTHAIR TW6 152 C1
Southampton Rd West
HTHAIR TW6 152 C1
Southampton Rw RSQ WC1B 10 E1
Southampton St
COVGDN WC2E 11 F5
Southampton Wy CMBW SE5 142 E1
Southam St NKENS W10 100 C3
South Ap NTHWD HA6 26 B5
South Audley St
MYFR/PKLN W1K 9 H6
South Av CAR SM5 210 A5
CHING E4 37 K2
RCH/KEW TW9 * 137 H3
STHL UB1 95 K6
South Avenue Gdns
STHL UB1 95 K6
South Bank STHWK SE1 11 K6
SURB KT6 191 F3
Southbank THDIT KT7 190 C4
South Bank Ter SURB KT6 * 191 F3
South Birkbeck Rd WAN E11 88 B1
South Black Lion La
HMSMTH W6 118 D5
South Bolton Gdns
WBPTN SW10 120 A5
Southborough Cl SURB KT6 190 E5
Southborough La HAYES BR2 200 D2
HAYES BR2 201 F2
Southborough Rd BMLY BR1 184 D6
HOM E9 86 E6
SURB KT6 191 F5
Southborough Road (The Lane) SURB KT6 * 191 F5
Southbourne Av
CDALE/KGS NW9 44 E5
Southbourne Cl PIN HA5 59 J4
Southbourne Crs HDN NW4 64 C1
Southbourne Gdns IL IG1 90 C3
LEE/GVPK SE12 146 A6
RSLP HA4 59 F5
Southbridge Pl CROY/NA CR0 211 J2
Southbridge Rd
CROY/NA CR0 211 J2
Southbridge Wy NWDGN UB2 114 D2
Southbrook Rd
LEE/GVPK SE12 165 H1
STRHM/NOR SW16 179 K4
Southbury Av EN EN1 24 C5
RAIN RM13 111 K4
Southbury Rd EN EN1 24 B5
South Carriage Dr SKENS SW7 14 C3
Southchurch Rd EHAM E6 107 K1
South Cl BAR EN5 20 D4
BXLYHS DA6 148 E5
DAGE RM10 92 C6
HGT N6 66 B3
PIN HA5 59 K4
WDR/YW UB7 112 C3
WHTN TW2 155 F5
The South Colonnade
POP/IOD E14 124 D1
Southcombe St WKENS W14 119 H4
Southcote Av BRYLDS KT5 191 J4
FELT TW13 153 J4
Southcote Ri RSLP HA4 58 B4
Southcote Rd ARCH N19 84 C2
SNWD SE25 197 J2
WALTH E17 69 F2
South Countess Rd
WALTH E17 51 H6
South Crs CAN/RD E16 106 B3
Southcroft Av WELL DA16 147 K4
WWKM BR4 199 F6
Southcroft Rd ORP BR6 216 E1
TOOT SW17 179 F2
South Cross Rd BARK/HLT IG6 72 C2
South Croxted Rd DUL SE21 162 E5
Southdale CHIG IG7 54 D2
Southdean Gdns
WIM/MER SW19 159 J4
South Dene MLHL NW7 31 F5
Southdown Av HNWL W7 116 B3
Southdown Crs
GNTH/NBYPK IG2 72 E2
RYLN/HDSTN HA2 60 C5
Southdown Dr RYNPK SW20 177 G3
Southdown Rd CAR SM5 210 A6
EMPK RM11 75 K4
RYNPK SW20 177 G4
Southdown Vls
SEVS/STOTM N15 * 67 H2
South Dr ORP BR6 216 E3
RSLP HA4 58 C5
South Ealing Rd EA W5 116 E2
South Eastern Av ED N9 36 B5
South Eaton Pl BGVA SW1W 15 H6
South Eden Park Rd
BECK BR3 198 E2
South Edwardes Sq KENS W8 119 J3
South End CROY/NA CR0 211 J2
KENS W8 * 120 A3
Southend Cl ELTH/MOT SE9 167 G1
Southend Crs ELTH/MOT SE9 167 F1
Southend La SYD SE26 164 C6
Southend Rd BECK BR3 182 D4
CLAY IG5 53 J6
EHAM E6 89 K5
South End Rd HAMP NW3 83 J2
RAIN RM13 93 J6
Southend Road (North Circular) WALTH E17 52 B4
South End Rw KENS W8 120 A3
Southern Av
EBED/NFELT TW14 153 K3
SNWD SE25 181 G6
Southern Down FELT TW13 * 154 B3
Southern Dr LOU IG10 39 K1
Southerngate Wy NWCR SE14 144 B1
Southern Gv BOW E3 105 H2
Southern Perimeter Rd
HTHAIR TW6 133 F6
STWL/WRAY TW19 152 C1
Southern Rd EFNCH N2 65 K1
PLSTW E13 107 F1
Southern Rw NKENS W10 100 B3
Southern St IS N1 5 G2
Southern Wy GNWCH SE10 125 H4
ROMW/RG RM7 74 C3
Southerton Rd
HMSMTH W6 * 119 F4
South Esk Rd FSTGT E7 89 G4
Southey Rd BRXN/ST SW9 142 B2
SEVS/STOTM N15 68 A2
WIM/MER SW19 177 K3
Southey St PGE/AN SE20 182 A3
Southfield BAR EN5 32 B1
Southfield Gdns TWK TW1 156 A6
Southfield Pk
RYLN/HDSTN HA2 60 B1
Southfield Rd CHST BR7 186 A6
CHSWK W4 118 A2
PEND EN3 36 D1
Southfields E/WMO/HCT KT8 189 K3
HDN NW4 45 K6
Southfields Ms
WAND/EARL SW18 * 159 K1
Southfields Rd
WAND/EARL SW18 159 K1
Southfleet Rd ORP BR6 216 E1
South Gdns WBLY HA9 * 62 C6
WIM/MER SW19 178 C3
South Gate Av FELT TW13 153 G6
Southgate Gv IS N1 85 K5
Southgate Rd IS N1 85 K6
South Gate Rd MNPK E12 89 H1
South Gipsy Rd WELL DA16 148 E4
South Gv HGT N6 66 A5
SEVS/STOTM N15 67 K2
WALTH E17 69 H2
South Hall Dr RAIN RM13 111 K4
South Hl CHST BR7 184 E2
NTHWD HA6 * 40 C4
South Hill Av
RYLN/HDSTN HA2 78 C1
South Hill Gv HRW HA1 78 E2
South Hill Pk HAMP NW3 83 J2
South Hill Park Gdns
HAMP NW3 83 J2
South Hill Rd HAYES BR2 183 H6
Southholme Cl NRWD SE19 181 F4
Southill La PIN HA5 58 E1
Southill Rd CHST BR7 184 D3
Southill St POP/IOD E14 105 K5
South Island Pl BRXN/ST SW9 142 A1
South Kensington Station Ar
SKENS SW7 14 B6
South Lambeth Pl VX/NE SW8 122 A6
South Lambeth Rd
VX/NE SW8 141 K1
Southland Rd
WOOL/PLUM SE18 128 B6
WOOL/PLUM SE18 148 A1
Southlands Av ORP BR6 216 E2
Southlands Dr
WIM/MER SW19 159 G4
Southlands Gv BMLY BR1 184 D6
Southlands Rd HAYES BR2 200 C1
Southland Wy HSLW TW3 135 J6
South La KUT/HW KT1 174 E6
NWMAL KT3 192 A1
South La West NWMAL KT3 192 A1
South Lodge Av MTCM CR4 195 K1
South Lodge Crs ENC/FH EN2 22 D5
South Lodge Dr
STHGT/OAK N14 22 D5
South Md CDALE/KGS NW9 45 H4
HOR/WEW KT19 207 H5
Southmead Rd
WIM/MER SW19 159 H3
South Molton La
MYFR/PKLN W1K 9 J4
South Molton Rd CAN/RD E16 106 E5
South Molton St
MYFR/PKLN W1K 9 J4
Southmont Rd
ESH/CLAY KT10 189 K6
Southmoor Wy HOM E9 87 H4
South Mt TRDG/WHET N20 * 33 G4
South Norwood Hl
SNWD SE25 181 F4
South Oak Rd
STRHM/NOR SW16 162 A6
Southold Ri ELTH/MOT SE9 166 E5
Southolm St BTSEA SW11 141 G2
South Ordnance Rd
PEND EN3 25 J1
Southover BMLY BR1 183 K1
NFNCH/WDSPK N12 32 E6
South Pde CHEL SW3 120 C5
CHSWK W4 118 A4
EDGW HA8 * 44 C5
WLGTN SM6 * 210 C4
South Park Crs CAT SE6 165 H3
IL IG1 90 D1
South Park Dr
GDMY/SEVK IG3 90 E3
South Park Gv NWMAL KT3 191 K1
South Park Hill Rd
SAND/SEL CR2 211 K3
South Park Ms FUL/PGN SW6 140 A4
South Park Rd IL IG1 90 D2
WIM/MER SW19 178 A2
South Park Ter IL IG1 90 D1
South Park Wy RSLP HA4 77 G4
South Pl BRYLDS KT5 191 G4
LVPST EC2M 13 F2
PEND EN3 24 E6
South Place Ms LVPST EC2M 13 F2
Southport Rd
WOOL/PLUM SE18 127 J4
Southridge Pl RYNPK SW20 177 G3
South Ri BAY/PAD W2 * 8 D5
CAR SM5 209 J6
South Rd CHDH RM6 73 J2
EA W5 116 E4
ED N9 36 C3
EDGW HA8 44 D4
FELT TW13 172 C1
FSTH SE23 164 A4
HPTN TW12 172 D2
STHL UB1 114 E1
WDR/YW UB7 112 D3
WHTN TW2 155 J5
WIM/MER SW19 178 C2
Southsea Rd KUT/HW KT1 191 F1
South Sea St
BERM/RHTH SE16 124 C3
South Side HMSMTH W6 118 C3
SEVS/STOTM N15 * 68 B1
Southside Common
WIM/MER SW19 177 G2
Southspring BFN/LL DA15 167 J2
South Sq GINN WC1R 11 J2
GLDGN NW11 64 E3
South St BMLY BR1 183 K5
EMPK RM11 75 J3
ISLW TW7 136 B4
MYFR/PKLN W1K 9 H7
PEND EN3 25 F6
RAIN RM13 110 E1
ROM RM1 75 G3
South Tenter St WCHPL E1 13 K5
South Ter SKENS SW7 14 C6
SURB KT6 191 F3
WDGN N22 48 E5
South V HRW HA1 78 E2
NRWD SE19 181 F2
Southvale Rd BKHTH/KID SE3 145 H3
South Vale Rd SURB KT6 191 F6
South Vw BMLY BR1 184 B5
Southview Av WLSDN NW10 81 H3
South View Cl BXLY DA5 169 G1
Southview Cl TOOT SW17 179 F1
South View Ct NRWD SE19 * 180 D3
South View Crs
GNTH/NBYPK IG2 72 B3
Southview Dr SWFD E18 53 F6
Southview Gdns WLGTN SM6 210 C5
Southview Rd BMLY BR1 165 G6
South View Rd
CEND/HSY/T N8 48 D6
LOU IG10 39 K1
PIN HA5 41 F2
Southviews SAND/SEL CR2 213 F6
South Vls CAMTN NW1 84 D4
Southville VX/NE SW8 141 J2
Southville Cl
EBED/NFELT TW14 153 H2
HOR/WEW KT19 207 F6
Southville Crs
EBED/NFELT TW14 153 H3
Southville Rd
EBED/NFELT TW14 153 H3
THDIT KT7 190 B4
South Wk WWKM BR4 214 C1
Southwark Br CANST EC4R 12 D6
Southwark Bridge Rd
STHWK SE1 18 B4
Southwark Park Est
BERM/RHTH SE16 * 123 J4
Southwark Park Rd
BERM/RHTH SE16 19 K6
Southwark Pl BMLY BR1 184 E6
Southwark St STHWK SE1 12 B7
Southwater Cl BECK BR3 182 E3
POP/IOD E14 105 H5
South Wy RYLN/HDSTN HA2 60 A1
WBLY HA9 80 C3
CROY/NA CR0 213 G1
ED N9 36 E4
FBAR/BDGN N11 48 C2
Southway GLDGN NW11 65 F3
RYNPK SW20 193 G1
TRDG/WHET N20 32 E4
WLGTN SM6 210 C2
Southway Cl SHB W12 118 E2
Southwell Av NTHLT UB5 78 A4
Southwell Gdns SKENS SW7 120 B4
Southwell Grove Rd WAN E11 70 C6
Southwell Rd CMBW SE5 142 D4
CROY/NA CR0 196 B3
KTN/HRWW/WS HA3 61 K3
South Western Rd TWK TW1 156 B1
South West India Dock
Entrance POP/IOD E14 125 F2
Southwest Rd WAN E11 70 B5
South Wharf Rd BAY/PAD W2 8 A3
Southwick Ms BAY/PAD W2 8 B3
Southwick Pl BAY/PAD W2 8 C4
Southwick St BAY/PAD W2 8 C3
Southwick Yd BAY/PAD W2 * 8 D4
Southwold Dr BARK IG11 91 G3
Southwold Rd BXLY DA5 169 J1
CLPT E5 68 D6
Southwood Av HGT N6 66 B4
KUTN/CMB KT2 175 K4
Southwood Cl BMLY BR1 200 E1
WPK KT4 193 G5
Southwood Dr BRYLDS KT5 191 K4
South Woodford SWFD E18 52 E5
Southwood Gdns
ESH/CLAY KT10 205 G1
GNTH/NBYPK IG2 72 B1
Southwood La HGT N6 66 A4
Southwood Lawn Rd HGT N6 66 A4
Southwood Pk HGT N6 * 66 B4
Southwood Rd
ELTH/MOT SE9 167 G4
THMD SE28 128 C1
South Worple Wy
MORT/ESHN SW14 138 A4
Southy Ms CAN/RD E16 125 K1
Sovereign Cl EA W5 97 J4
RSLP HA4 58 C5
WAP E1W 104 D6
Sovereign Ct
E/WMO/HCT KT8 188 E1
Sovereign Crs
BERM/RHTH SE16 105 G6
Sovereign Gv ALP/SUD HA0 79 K1
Sovereign Ms BETH E2 * 7 J2
EBAR EN4 21 K4
Sovereign Pk WLSDN NW10 * 98 D3
Sovereign Pl HRW HA1 61 F2
Sovereign Rd BARK IG11 109 J2
Sowerby Cl ELTH/MOT SE9 146 E6
Sowrey Av RAIN RM13 93 H4
Space Waye
EBED/NFELT TW14 134 A6
Spafield St CLKNW EC1R 5 J6
Spa Green Est CLKNW EC1R * 5 K4
Spa Hl NRWD SE19 180 E4
Spalding Cl EDGW HA8 45 G3
Spalding Rd HDN NW4 64 A3
TOOT SW17 179 G1
Spanby Rd BOW E3 105 J3
Spaniards Cl GLDGN NW11 65 G5
Spaniards End HAMP NW3 65 G5
Spaniards Rd HAMP NW3 65 G6
Spanish Pl MHST W1U * 9 H3
Spanish Rd WAND/EARL SW18 140 B6
Sparkbridge Rd HRW HA1 60 E1
Sparkes Cl HAYES BR2 200 A1
Sparke Ter CAN/RD E16 * 106 D5
Sparkford Gdns
FBAR/BDGN N11 48 A1
Sparks Cl ACT W3 99 F5
BCTR RM8 73 K6
HPTN TW12 172 D2
Spa Rd BERM/RHTH SE16 19 J5
Sparrow Cl HPTN TW12 172 D2
Sparrow Dr STMC/STPC BR5 201 H5
Sparrow Farm Dr
EBED/NFELT TW14 154 B2
Sparrow Farm Rd EW KT17 207 J2
Sparrow Gn DAGE RM10 92 D1
Sparrows Herne BUSH WD23 28 B2
Sparrows La ELTH/MOT SE9 167 H2
Sparrows Wy BUSH WD23 * 28 C2
Sparrows Wick BUSH WD23 * 28 C3
Sparsholt Rd ARCH N19 67 F5
BARK IG11 90 E6
Spartan Cl WLGTN SM6 210 E5
Sparta St GNWCH SE10 145 F2
Speakers Ct CROY/NA CR0 * 196 E5
Spearman St
WOOL/PLUM SE18 * 127 F6
Spear Ms ECT SW5 119 K4
Spears Rd ARCH N19 66 E5
Speart La HEST TW5 134 D1
Spectrum Pl WALW SE17 122 E5
Spedan Cl HAMP NW3 83 F1
Speedwell St DEPT SE8 144 D1
Speedy Pl STPAN WC1H 4 E5
Speer Rd THDIT KT7 190 A3
Speirs Cl NWMAL KT3 192 C3
Spekehill ELTH/MOT SE9 166 E5
Speke Rd THHTH CR7 180 E5
Speldhurst Cl HAYES BR2 199 J2
Speldhurst Rd CHSWK W4 118 A3
HOM E9 87 F5
Spellbrook Wk IS N1 * 85 J6
Spelman St WCHPL E1 104 C4
Spence Cl BERM/RHTH SE16 124 C2
Spencer Av PLMGR N13 49 F2
YEAD UB4 94 E4
Spencer Cl FNCH N3 46 D5
ORP BR6 201 K6
WFD IG8 53 G1
WLSDN NW10 98 B2
Spencer Dr EFNCH N2 65 G3
Spencer Gdns
MORT/ESHN SW14 137 K6
Spencer Hl WIM/MER SW19 177 H2
Spencer Hill Rd
WIM/MER SW19 177 H3
Spencer House SURB KT6 * 191 F2
Spencer Ms CLAP SW4 141 K2
HMSMTH W6 119 H6
Spencer Pk WAND/EARL SW18 140 C6
Spencer Pl CROY/NA CR0 196 E4
IS N1 85 H5
WEST SW1P 16 B5
Spencer Ri KTTN NW5 84 B2
Spencer Rd ACT W3 117 K1
ALP/SUD HA0 61 J6
BMLY BR1 183 J3
BTSEA SW11 140 C5
CEND/HSY/T N8 67 F2
CHSWK W4 137 K1
E/WMO/HCT KT8 189 H1
EHAM E6 89 H6
FBAR/BDGN N11 34 B6
GDMY/SEVK IG3 73 F5
ISLW TW7 135 J2
KTN/HRWW/WS HA3 42 E5
MTCM CR4 194 E4
RAIN RM13 111 F2
RYNPK SW20 176 E4
SAND/SEL CR2 212 A3
TOTM N17 50 C4
WALTH E17 52 A5
WHTN TW2 155 K5
Spencer St FSBYE EC1V 6 A5
NWDGN UB2 114 C3
Spencer Wk PUT/ROE SW15 139 G5
Spencer Wy WCHPL E1 104 D5
Spenser Gv STNW/STAM N16 86 A2
Spenser Ms DUL SE21 162 E3
Spenser Rd HNHL SE24 142 C6
Spenser St WESTW SW1E 16 B4
Spensley Wk
STNW/STAM N16 85 K1
Speranza St
WOOL/PLUM SE18 128 A5
Sperling Rd TOTM N17 50 B5
Spert St POP/IOD E14 105 G6
Speyside STHGT/OAK N14 34 C1
Spey St POP/IOD E14 106 A4
Spey Wy ROM RM1 57 G3
Spezia Rd WLSDN NW10 99 J1
Spicer Cl BRXN/ST SW9 142 C3
WOT/HER KT12 188 B3
Spices Yd CROY/NA CR0 211 J2
Spielman Rd DART DA1 151 J5
Spigurnell Rd TOTM N17 49 K4
Spikes Bridge Rd STHL UB1 95 J5
Spindle Cl WOOL/PLUM SE18 126 D3
Spindlewood Gdns
CROY/NA CR0 212 A2
Spindrift Av POP/IOD E14 124 E4
Spinel Cl WOOL/PLUM SE18 128 A5
Spinnaker Cl BARK IG11 109 H2
Spinnells Rd
RYLN/HDSTN HA2 59 K5
Spinney Cl BECK BR3 198 E1
NWMAL KT3 192 B2
RAIN RM13 111 G1
WPK KT4 207 H1
Spinney Dr EBED/NFELT TW14 153 F2
Spinney Gdns DAGW RM9 92 A3
NRWD SE19 181 G1
Spinney Oak BMLY BR1 184 D5
The Spinneys BMLY BR1 184 E5
The Spinney ALP/SUD HA0 79 G1
BAR EN5 21 F3
BARN SW13 * 118 E6
CHEAM SM3 208 A2
NFNCH/WDSPK N12 * 47 G3
SCUP DA14 187 F1
STAN HA7 30 A6
STRHM/NOR SW16 161 H5
WCHMH N21 35 G2
Spirit Quay WAP E1W 123 H1
Spital Sq WCHPL E1 13 H1
Spital St WCHPL E1 104 C4
Spital Yd WCHPL E1 * 13 H1
Spitfire Est HEST TW5 * 114 B5
Spitfire House
WOOL/PLUM SE18 * 146 D1
Spitfire Rd WLGTN SM6 211 F5
Spitfire Wy HEST TW5 114 B5
Spode Wk KIL/WHAMP NW6 * 83 F3
Spondon Rd
SEVS/STOTM N15 68 C1
Spoonbill Wy YEAD UB4 95 H4
Spooner Wk WLGTN SM6 210 D3
Sportsbank St CAT SE6 165 F2
Sportsman Pl BETH E2 86 C6
Spottons Gv TOTM N17 49 J4
Spout Hl CROY/NA CR0 213 J3
Spratt Hall Rd WAN E11 70 E3
Spray St WOOL/PLUM SE18 127 G4
Spreighton Rd
E/WMO/HCT KT8 189 G1
Sprimont Pl CHEL SW3 120 E5
Springall St PECK SE15 143 J1
Springbank WCHMH N21 35 F1
Springbank Rd LEW SE13 165 H1
Springbank Wk CAMTN NW1 84 D5
Springbourne Ct BECK BR3 183 F4
Spring Bridge Rd EA W5 97 K6
Spring Cl BAR EN5 20 B6
BCTR RM8 73 K4
Springclose La CHEAM SM3 208 C4
Spring Cnr FELT TW13 * 153 K5
Spring Cots SURB KT6 * 190 E2
Spring Court Rd ENC/FH EN2 23 G1
Springcroft Av EFNCH N2 47 K6
Springdale Rd
STNW/STAM N16 85 K2
Spring Dr PIN HA5 58 E3
Springfield BUSH WD23 28 D3
CLPT E5 68 D5
Springfield Av HPTN TW12 173 G2
MUSWH N10 48 C6
RYNPK SW20 177 J6
Springfield Cl
NFNCH/WDSPK N12 47 F1
STAN HA7 29 G5
Springfield Dr
GNTH/NBYPK IG2 72 C2
Springfield Gdns BMLY BR1 200 E1
CDALE/KGS NW9 63 F2
CLPT E5 68 D5
RSLP HA4 59 F5
WFD IG8 53 G3
WWKM BR4 198 E6
Springfield Gv CHARL SE7 126 B6
Springfield La
KIL/WHAMP NW6 83 F6
Springfield Mt
CDALE/KGS NW9 63 G2
Springfield Parade Ms
PLMGR N13 35 G6
Springfield Pl NWMAL KT3 191 K
Springfield Ri SYD SE26 163 J
Springfield Rd BMLY BR1 200 E
CHING E4 38 C
EHAM E6 89 K
FBAR/BDGN N11 48 C
HNWL W7 115 K
HRW HA1 60 E
KUT/HW KT1 191 F
SEVS/STOTM N15 68 C
SRTFD E15 * 106 C
STJWD NW8 83 C
SYD SE26 181
TEDD TW11 174 B
THHTH CR7 180 D
WALTH E17 69 H
WELL DA16 148 C
WHTN TW2 155 F
WIM/MER SW19 177
WLGTN SM6 210 E
YEAD UB4 114 E
Springfield Wk
KIL/WHAMP NW6 83
Spring Gdns E/WMO/HCT KT8 189
HBRY N5 85
HCH RM12 93
ORP BR6 217
ROMW/RG RM7 74
WFD IG8 53
WHALL SW1A 10
WLGTN SM6 210
Spring Gv CHSWK W4 117
HPTN TW12 173
LOU IG10 39
MTCM CR4 179
Spring Grove Crs HSLW TW3 135
Spring Grove Rd HSLW TW3 135
RCHPK/HAM TW10 137
Spring Hl CLPT E5 68
SYD SE26 163
Springhill Cl CMBW SE5 142
Springhurst Cl CROY/NA CR0 213
Spring Lake STAN HA7 29
Spring La CLPT E5 68
MUSWH N10 48
SNWD SE25 197
Spring Ms MHST W1U * 9

Spring Park Av CROY/NA CRO.. 198 A6
Springpark Dr BECK BR3 .... 183 F6
FSBYPK N4.................................. 67 J5
Spring Park Rd CROY/NA CRO.. 198 A6
Springpoint Rd DAGW RM9 ...... 92 A3
Springrice Rd LEW SE13............ 165 F1
Spring Rd FELT TW13 .... 153 J5
Spring St BAY/PAD W2................. 8 A4
EW KT17..................................... 207 H6
Spring Tide Cl DEPT SE8 * 143 H2
Springvale Av BTFD TW8 .... 116 E5
Spring V South DART DA1 * 171 G2
Spring Ter WKENS W14 .... 119 C3
Springvale Wy
STMC/STPC BR5 .... 186 D6
Spring Villa Rd EDGW HA8......... 44 C3
Spring Vls WEA W13 *................ 116 C1
Spring Wk WCHPL E1.................. 104 C4
Springwater Cl
WOOL/PLUM SE18 * 147 F2
Springwell Av WLSDN NW10...... 81 H6
Springwell Rd HEST TW5.......... 134 C6
STRHM/NOR SW16.................. 162 A6
Springwood Cl BOW E3.............. 106 C2
Springwood Ct EDGW HA8 .... 30 E4
Springwood Wy ROM RM1........... 75 J2
Sprowston Ms FSTGT E7........... 88 E3
Sprowston Rd FSTGT E7............ 88 E3
Sprucedale Gdns
CROY/NA CRO........................ 213 F2
WLGTN SM6............................ 210 E6
Spruce Hills Rd WALTH E17....... 51 K5
Sprules Rd BROCKY SE4 .... 144 B3
Spurfield E/WMO/HCT KT8 ...... 173 G6
Spurgeon Av NRWD SE19 .... 180 E4
Spurgeon Rd NRWD SE19 .... 180 E3
Spurgeon St STHWK SE1 .... 18 E5
Spurling Rd DAGW RM9 .... 92 B4
EDUL SE22 *............................. 143 G5
Spur Rd BARK IG11 .... 108 C2
EBED/NFELT TW14 .... 134 A1
EDGW HA8 .... 30 A6
ISLW TW7.................................. 136 B1
ORP BR6................................... 202 B6
SEVS/STOTM N15 *.................. 67 K1
STHWK SE1 .... 17 J2
WHALL SW1A 16 A3
Spurstowe Rd HACK E8 .... 86 D4
Spurstowe Ter HACK E8 .... 86 D4
The Square CAR SM5................ 210 A3
HMSMTH W6............................ 119 F5
IL IG1.. 72 A4
RCH/KEW TW9 .... 137 F6
STKPK UB11............................. 113 G1
WFD IG8.................................... 52 E1
Squarey St TOOT SW17 .... 160 B5
Squire Gdns STJWD NW8 .... 2 A5
Squires Ct WIM/MER SW19 ...... 159 K6
Squires La FNCH N3................... 47 F4
Squire's Mt HAMP NW3.............. 83 H2
Squires Wood Dr CHST BR7 * ... 184 E3
Squirrel Cl HSLWW TW4............ 134 B4
Squirrel Ms WEA W13 * 97 G6
Squirrels Cl
NFNCH/WDSPK N12................. 33 G6
Squirrels Gn WPK KT4 .... 192 C6
Squirrels Heath Av GPK RM2..... 57 K6
The Squirrels BUSH WD23......... 28 D1
LEW SE13.................................. 145 G4
PIN HA5..................................... 41 G6
Squirries St BETH E2............... 104 C2
Stable Cl KUTN/CMB KT2......... 175 C2
NTHLT UB5................................ 96 A1
Stable Ms TWK TW1................... 156 A3
WNWD SE27.............................. 180 D1
Stables End ORP BR6 .... 216 C1
Stables Ms WL LBTH SE11........ 122 B5
Stable Wy NFNCH E2................. 47 H4
IS N1... 5 F2
Stacey Cl LEY E10 .... 100 A5
Stable Yard Rd WHALL SW1A ... 16 B2
Stacey St NKENS W10 .... 100 A5
Stacey Cl LEY E10...................... 70 B2
Stacey St HOLWY N7.................. 85 C1
LSQ/SEVD WC2H 110 C6
Stackhouse St KTBR SW1X........ 14 E4
Stacy Pth CMBW SE5 *.............. 143 F1
Staddon Cl BECK BR3................ 198 B3
Staddon Ct BECK BR3 *............. 198 B1
Stadium Rd HDN NW4............... 63 J3
WOOL/PLUM SE18................... 146 E1
Stadium St WBPTN SW10......... 140 B1
Stadium Wy WBLY HA9.............. 80 B2
Staffa Rd LEY E10...................... 69 C5
Stafford Av CLAY IG5................. 54 B4
Stafford Cl CHEAM SM3 .... 208 C4
KIL/WHAMP NW6...................... 100 E2
STHGT/OAK N14....................... 22 C6
WALTH E17 .... 69 H5
Stafford Cross CROY/NA CRO.. 211 F3
Stafford Gdns CROY/NA CRO.. 211 F3
Stafford PI RCH/KEW/HAM TW10. 157 G2
WESTW SW1E.......................... 16 A4
Stafford Rd BOW E3 .... 105 H1
CROY/NA CRO......................... 211 G2
FSTGT E7.................................. 89 G5
KIL/WHAMP NW6...................... 100 E2
KTN/HRWW/WS HA3................. 42 C3
NWMAL KT3............................. 175 K6
RSLP HA4.................................. 76 D2
SCUP DA14 .... 167 K6
WLGTN SM6............................. 210 C4
Staffordshire St PECK SE15..... 143 H2
Stafford St CONDST W1S........... 10 A7
Stafford Ter KENS W8................ 119 K3
Stag Cl EDGW HA8.................... 44 D5
Staggart Gn CHIG IG7 .... 55 F1
Stag La BKHH IG9....................... 39 F4
EDGW HA8 .... 44 D5
PUT/ROE SW15........................ 158 C5
Stag PI WESTW SW1E.............. 16 A4
Stags Wy ISLW TW7................... 116 A6
Stainbank Rd MTCM CR4........ 179 G6
Stainby Cl WDR/YW UB7 .... 112 B3
Stainby Rd TOTM N17 .... 50 B6

Stainer St STHWK SE1................ 19 F1
Staines Av CHEAM SM3............ 193 C6
Staines Rd EBED/NFELT TW14.. 134 C6
EBED/NFELT TW14................. 152 E5
IL IG1.. 90 D2
WHTN TW2................................ 155 C1
Staines Rd East SUN TW16...... 172 B4
Stainforth Rd
GNTH/NBYPK IG2 .... 72 D4
WALTH E17 .... 69 J1
Staining La CITYW EC2V.......... 12 D3
Stainmore Cl CHST BR7 .... 185 J4
Stainsbury St BETH E2.............. 104 E1
Stainsby Rd POP/IOD E14 *...... 105 J5
Stainsby Rd POP/IOD E14......... 105 J5
Stainton Rd CAT SE6................ 165 C2
PEND EN3.................................. 24 E2
Stalbridge St CAMTN NW1.......... 8 D1
Stalham St BERM/RHTH SE16.. 123 J3
Stalham Wy BARK/HLT IG6......... 54 B4
Stambourne Wy NRWD SE19.... 181 F5
WWKM BR4 .... 214 A1
Stambourne Woodland Wk
NRWD SE19............................. 181 F3
Stamford Brook Av
HMSMTH W6............................ 118 C3
Stamford Brook Gdns
HMSMTH W6 * 118 C3
Stamford Brook Rd
HMSMTH W6............................ 118 C3
Stamford Cl HAMP NW3 *......... 83 H2
KTN/HRWW/WS HA3 .... 42 E3
SEVS/STOTM N15.................... 68 C1
STHL UB1.................................. 96 A6
Stamford Cots
WBPTN SW10 *......................... 140 A1
Stamford Dr HAYES BR2........... 199 J1
Stamford Gdns DAGW RM9...... 91 J5
Stamford Gv East
STNW/STAM N16...................... 68 C5
Stamford Gv West
STNW/STAM N16...................... 68 B5
Stamford Hl STNW/STAM N16... 68 B5
Stamford Rd DAGW RM9........... 91 H5
EHAM E6.................................... 89 J6
IS N1... 86 A5
SEVS/STOTM N15.................... 68 C2
Stamford St STHWK SE1 *.......... 11 J7
Stamp PI BETH E2........................ 7 J3
Stanborough Cl HPTN TW12 .... 172 E2
Stanborough Pas HACK E8 .... 86 B4
Stanborough Rd HSLW TW3..... 135 J4
Stanbridge PI WCHMH N21...... 35 H4
Stanbridge Rd
PUT/ROE SW15........................ 139 F4
Stanbrook Rd ABYW SE2......... 128 C2
Stanbury Ct HAMP NW3............ 83 K4
Stanbury Rd PECK SE15........... 143 J2
Stancroft CDALE/KGS NW9 ...... 63 G1
Standale Gv RSLP HA4............... 58 A2
Standard PI SDTCH EC2A *.......... 7 H5
Standard Rd BELV DA17........... 129 H5
HSLWW TW4............................ 134 D4
PEND EN3.................................. 25 C1
WLSDN NW10........................... 98 E3
Standen Rd
WAND/EARL SW18.................. 159 K2
Standfield Rd DAGE RM10......... 92 C3
Standish Rd HMSMTH W6........ 118 D3
Stane Cl WIM/MER SW19 .... 178 A4
Stane Gv VX/NE SW8................ 141 J3
Stane Wy WOOL/PLUM SE18.... 146 C1
Stanford Cl HPTN TW12............ 172 E2
ROMW/RG RM7 .... 74 D3
RSLP HA4.................................. 58 A3
WFD IG8.................................... 53 J3
Stanford PI WALW SE17............. 19 G7
Stanford Rd FBAR/BDGN N11.. 47 K1
SKENS SW7 *........................... 120 A3
STRHM/NOR SW16.................. 179 K5
Stanford St PIM SW1V............... 16 C7
Stanford Wy
STRHM/NOR SW16.................. 179 J5
Stangate Gdns STAN HA7.......... 29 H6
Stanger Rd SNWD SE25........... 197 H1
Stanhope Av FNCH N3............... 46 D5
KTN/HRWW/WS HA3 .... 42 D4
Stanhope Cl
BERM/RHTH SE16 *.................. 124 A2
Stanhope Gdns BCTR RM8........ 92 B1
FSBYPK N4............................... 67 H3
HGT N6...................................... 66 B3
IL IG1.. 71 K5
MLHL NW7................................. 45 H1
SKENS SW7 .... 120 B4
Stanhope Ga BAY/PAD W2 .... 8 E5
MYFR/PKLN W1L...................... 15 H1
Stanhope Ms East SKENS SW7. 120 B4
Stanhope Ms South
SKENS SW7 * 120 B4
Stanhope Ms West
SKENS SW7............................. 120 B4
Stanhope Pde CAMTN NW1........ 3 K4
Stanhope Pl BAR EN5 .... 32 B1
Stanhope PI BAY/PAD W2........... 8 E4
Stanhope Rd
GFD/PVL UB6............................ 96 C3
BAR EN5.................................... 32 B1
BCTR RM8................................. 74 B6
BFN/LL DA15........................... 168 B6
CAR SM5................................. 210 A5
CROY/NA CRO......................... 212 A1
GFD/PVL UB6............................ 96 C4
HGT N6...................................... 66 C3
NFNCH/WDSPK N12................. 47 G1
RAIN RM13............................... 111 J1
WALTH E17............................... 69 K2
Stanhope Rw
MYFR/PICC W1J *..................... 15 J1
Stanhope St CAMTN NW1........... 4 A4
Stanhope Ter BAY/PAD W2 .... 8 E5
WHTN TW2 *............................. 156 A2
Stanier Cl WKENS W14............. 119 J5
Stanlake Rd SHB W12............... 119 F1
Stanlake Vls SHB W12 *............ 119 F1
Stanley Av ALP/SUD HA0........... 80 A5

GPK RM2 .... 75 J1
NWMAL KT3.............................. 192 D2
Stanley Cl ALP/SUD HA0 .... 80 A5
ELTH/MOT SE9........................ 167 H3
VX/NE SW8............................... 142 A6
Stanley Crs NTGHL W11........... 100 D6
Stanleycroft Cl ISLW TW7......... 135 K2
Stanley Gdns ACT W3............... 118 B2
CRICK NW2................................ 82 A3
MTCM CR4 *............................. 179 F2
NTGHL W11............................. 100 D6
WLGTN SM6............................ 210 C4
Stanley Gardens Rd
TEDD TW11............................... 173 K1
Stanley Gv CROY/NA CRO....... 196 B3
VX/NE SW8............................... 141 F3
Stanley Park Dr ALP/SUD HA0.. 80 B5
Stanley Park Rd CAR SM5....... 209 K5
WLGTN SM6............................ 210 B5
Stanley Pas CAMTN NW1............ 4 E3
Stanley Rd ACT W3.................... 117 J3
BELMT SM2.............................. 209 K6
CAR SM5.................................. 209 K6
CHING E4.................................... 38 B3
CROY/NA CRO......................... 196 B4
ED N9... 36 C4
EFNCH N2................................... 65 H1
EN EN1....................................... 24 A4
FBAR/BDGN N11...................... 48 D2
HAYES BR2.............................. 200 B1
HSLW TW3............................... 135 H5
IL IG1.. 72 D6
MNPK E12.................................. 89 J3
MORT/ESHN SW14.................. 137 J5
MRDN SM4............................... 193 K1
MTCM CR4............................... 179 F5
MUSWH N10.............................. 48 B3
NTHWD HA6............................... 40 E4
ORP BR6.................................. 202 A5
RYLN/HDSTN HA2..................... 60 C6
SCUP DA14.............................. 168 B5
SEVS/STOTM N15.................... 67 H1
STHL UB1................................... 95 J6
SWFD E18.................................. 52 D4
TEDD TW11.............................. 173 K1
WALTH E17 .... 69 J3
WBLY HA9.................................. 80 B4
WHTN TW2............................... 155 J5
WIM/MER SW19....................... 177 K3
Stanley Rd North RAIN RM13... 93 G6
Stanley Rd South RAIN RM13... 111 H1
Stanley Sq CAR SM5 *.............. 209 K6
Stanley St DEPT SE8................ 144 C1
Stanley Ter ARCH N19 *............ 66 E6
Stanley Wy STMC/STPC BR5 ... 202 C2
Stant Gv BTSEA SW11.............. 140 D2
Stanmore Gdns
RCH/KEW TW9........................ 137 G4
SUT SM1.................................. 209 G1
Stanmore HI STAN HA7.............. 29 H6
Stanmore Rd BELV DA17......... 129 K4
FSTGT E7.................................... 89 F4
RCH/KEW TW9........................ 137 G4
SEVS/STOTM N15.................... 68 A2
WAN E11.................................... 70 D5
Stanmore St IS N1....................... 85 F6
Stanmore Ter BECK BR3.......... 182 D5
Stanmark Av SUT SM1............. 208 C5
Stannard Rd HACK E8................ 86 C4
Stannary PI LBTH SE11............ 122 B5
Stannary St LBTH SE11............ 122 B5
Stannet Wy WLGTN SM6.......... 210 C2
Stansbury Sq NKENS W10........ 100 C2
Stansfield Rd BRXN/ST SW9.... 142 A4
HSLWW TW4............................ 134 A3
Stansgate Rd DAGE RM10......... 74 C6
Stanstead Cl HAYES BR2......... 199 J2
Stanstead Gv CAT SE6............. 164 C5
Stanstead Rd FSTH SE23.......... 164 A3
WAN E11.................................... 71 F2
Stansted Cl HCH RM12............... 93 K4
Stansted Crs BXLY DA5............. 168 E3
Stanswood Gdns CMBW SE5.... 143 F1
Stanthorpe Cl
STRHM/NOR SW16 *............... 179 K1
Stanthorpe Rd
STRHM/NOR SW16.................. 179 K1
Stanton Av TEDD TW11............ 173 K2
Stanton Cl HOR/WEW KT19.... 206 D3
WPK KT4................................. 193 G5
Stanton Rd BARN SW13........... 138 C3
CROY/NA CRO......................... 196 D4
RYNPK SW20........................... 177 G5
Stanton St PECK SE15............. 143 H2
Stanton Wy SYD SE26.............. 164 C6
Stanway Cl CHIG IG7................. 54 E1
Stanway Gdns ACT W3............. 117 H1
EDGW HA8................................. 30 E6
Stanway St IS N1.......................... 7 H2
Stanwell Cl STWL/WRAY TW19. 152 A1
Stanwell Gdns
STWL/WRAY TW19................. 152 A1
Stanwick Rd WKENS W14........ 119 J4
Stanworth St STHWK SE1 .... 19 J3
Stanwyck Gdns HARH RM3....... 57 J1
Stapenhill Rd ALP/SUD HA0...... 79 H1
Staplefield Cl
BRXS/STRHM SW2 *................ 161 K3
PIN HA5...................................... 41 J3
Stapleford Av
GNTH/NBYPK IG2 .... 72 E2
Stapleford Cl CHING E4.............. 38 A5
KUT/HW KT1............................ 175 H5
WIM/MER SW19....................... 159 H2
Stapleford Gdns CHDH RM6..... 55 J6
Stapleford Rd ALP/SUD HA0..... 79 K6
Stapleford Wy BARK IG11....... 109 H2
Staplehurst Rd CAR SM5......... 209 J5
LEW SE13................................. 145 G6
Staple Inn HHOL WC1V............. 11 J2
Staple Inn Buildings
BERM/RHTH SE16.................. 124 B1
Staples Cl BERM/RHTH SE16... 124 B1
Stapleton Crs RAIN RM13......... 93 J4
Stapleton Gdns CROY/NA CRO. 211 G3
Stapleton Hall Rd FSBYPK N4... 67 F4
Stapleton Rd ORP BR6.............. 217 F1
TOOT SW17............................. 161 F5

Stapleton Vls
STNW/STAM N16 * 86 A2
Stapley Rd BELV DA17............. 129 H5
Stapylton Rd BAR EN5 .... 20 C4
Starboard Wy POP/IOD E14.... 124 D3
Starbuck Cl ELTH/MOT SE9.... 167 F2
Starch House La
BARK/HLT IG6........................... 54 D5
Star Cl PEND EN3....................... 36 E1
Starcross St CAMTN NW1.......... 4 B6
Starfield Rd SHB W12.............. 118 D2
Star & Garter HI
RCHPK/HAM TW10.................. 157 F3
Star La CAN/RD E16.................. 106 C5
STMC/STPC BR5..................... 187 G6
Starling Cl BKHH IG9................. 39 F3
PIN HA5...................................... 41 G6
Starling Rd CROY/NA CRO....... 198 B3
Starmans Cl DAGW RM9........... 92 A6
Star PI WAP E1W....................... 13 K6
Star Rd HGDN/ICK UB10........... 94 A3
ISLW TW7................................. 135 J3
WKENS W14............................. 119 J6
Star St BAY/PAD W2..................... 8 B3
Starts Cl ORP BR6.................... 216 A1
Starts Hill Av ORP BR6............. 216 B3
Starts Hill Rd ORP BR6............. 216 B1
Starveall Cl WDR/YW UB7........ 112 C3
Star Yd LINN WC2A..................... 11 J3
State Farm Av ORP BR6........... 216 B2
Staten Gdns TWK TW1.............. 156 A3
Statham Gv STNW/STAM N16... 85 K1
UED N18..................................... 50 A1
Station Ap ALP/SUD HA0........... 80 A1
BAR EN5.................................... 21 C5
BECK BR3................................ 182 B4
BELMT SM2.............................. 208 C5
BKHH IG9................................... 39 F5
BKHTH/KID SE3....................... 146 A4
CAMTN NW1 *............................. 3 C7
CHST BR7................................ 184 D2
CHST BR7................................ 185 F4
CROY/NA CRO......................... 196 E6
ESH/CLAY KT10...................... 205 G3
FBAR/BDGN N11...................... 48 B1
FSTGT E7.................................... 89 F2
FUL/PGN SW6......................... 139 H4
GFD/PVL UB6............................ 78 C5
GLDGN NW11 *......................... 64 B4
HOR/WEW KT19...................... 207 H5
HYS/HAR UB3.......................... 113 J3
KUT/HW KT1............................ 175 H5
NFNCH/WDSPK N12................. 33 F6
NTHWD HA6............................... 40 D3
ORP BR6.................................. 202 A6
ORP BR6.................................. 217 H3
OXHEY WD19............................. 27 H5
PIN HA5...................................... 41 J6
RCH/KEW TW9........................ 137 H2
RSLP HA4................................... 58 B4
RSLP HA4................................... 77 F5
SAND/SEL CR2........................ 211 K6
STMC/STPC BR5..................... 202 C1
STRHM/NOR SW16.................. 179 J1
SURB KT6................................. 190 E4
SWFD E18 *................................ 53 F5
SYD SE26................................. 182 C1
WALTH E17................................. 69 J2
WAN E11..................................... 70 E2
WDR/YW UB7.......................... 112 B1
WELL DA16.............................. 148 A3
WFD IG8..................................... 53 G2
WLSDN NW10........................... 99 H2
Station Approach Rd
CHSWK W4.............................. 137 K1
Station Ar GTPST W1W *............. 3 K7
Station Av HOR/WEW KT19.... 207 C6
NWMAL KT3............................. 176 B6
RCH/KEW TW9........................ 137 H2
Station Chambers EA W5 *......... 98 C3
Station Cl HPTN TW12.............. 173 G4
Station Cots WDGN N22 *.......... 48 E5
Station Crs ALP/SUD HA0.......... 80 A1
ASHF TW15.............................. 152 A6
SEVS/STOTM N15.................... 68 A1
Station Est BECK BR3 *............. 198 A1
Station Estate Rd
EBED/NFELT TW14.................. 154 A3
Station Garage Ms
STRHM/NOR SW16 *............... 179 J2
Station Gdns CHSWK W4.......... 137 K1
Station Gv ALP/SUD HA0........... 80 A4
Station House Ms ED N9............ 36 C6
Station Pde ACT W3 *................. 99 G4
BAL SW12 *.............................. 161 F3
BARK IG11................................. 90 C5
BELMT SM2.............................. 209 G4
BMLY BR1 *.............................. 183 K4
CHSWK W4 *............................ 137 K1
CRICK NW2................................ 82 A4
EA W5 *...................................... 117 C1
EBAR EN4................................... 22 A5
EBED/NFELT TW14.................. 154 A2
EDGW HA8................................. 44 A3
EHAM E6.................................... 89 J5
HCH RM12.................................. 93 K2
KTN/HRWW/WS HA3 .... 43 H5
NTHLT UB5 *.............................. 78 A4
PLSTW E13 *............................. 89 C6
RCH/KEW TW9........................ 137 H2
ROM RM1 *................................ 75 C3
RSLP HA4 *................................ 58 A6
STHGT/OAK N14....................... 34 D3
WALTH E17 *............................. 51 H6
WHTN TW2................................ 155 J3
Station Pas PECK SE15............ 143 K2
SWFD E18.................................. 53 F5
Station PI FSBYPK N4................ 67 G6
Station Rd ASHF TW15............. 152 C6
BAR EN5.................................... 21 F6
BARK/HLT IG6........................... 54 D6
BARN SW13............................. 138 C3
BCTR RM8................................. 73 K5
BELV DA17............................... 129 H3

BFN/LL DA15........................... 168 B4
BMLY BR1................................ 183 K4
CAR SM5.................................. 209 K2
CHING E4.................................... 38 B3
CHSGTN KT9............................ 206 A3
CROY/NA CRO......................... 196 D5
EA W5.. 98 B5
EDGW HA8................................. 44 C2
ESH/CLAY KT10...................... 204 D3
FBAR/BDGN N11...................... 34 B2
FNCH N3..................................... 46 E4
GPK RM2.................................... 75 K1
HAYES BR2.............................. 183 H5
HDN NW4.................................... 63 J3
HNWL W7................................. 115 K1
HOLWY N7.................................. 84 C1
HPTN TW12.............................. 173 G4
HRW HA1.................................... 60 B2
HSLW TW3............................... 135 G5
HYS/HAR UB3.......................... 113 H4
IL IG1... 72 B6
KUT/HW KT1............................ 174 E4
LEW SE13................................. 145 F4
MLHL NW7................................. 45 C2
MNPK E12.................................. 89 J2
NWMAL KT3............................. 192 E2
ORP BR6.................................. 202 A6
PGE/AN SE20........................... 181 K2
RYLN/HDSTN HA2..................... 60 B2
SCUP DA14.............................. 168 B5
SNWD SE25............................. 197 G1
STMC/STPC BR5..................... 202 D1
TEDD TW11.............................. 174 B2
THDIT KT7................................ 190 A4
TOTM N17.................................. 50 C6
TWK TW1.................................. 156 A3
WALTH E17................................. 69 G3
WCHMH N21............................. 35 H3
WDGN N22................................. 48 E5
WDR/YW UB7.......................... 112 B2
WIM/MER SW19...................... 178 B4
WLSDN NW10........................... 99 H1
WWKM BR4.............................. 199 F5
Station Rd North BELV DA17... 129 J3
Station Sq STMC/STPC BR5.... 201 H2
Station St SRTFD E15................. 88 B5
Station Ter CMBW SE5............ 142 D2
WLSDN NW10........................... 100 B1
Station Vw GFD/PVL UB6.......... 78 D6
Station Wy BKHH IG9................. 39 H6
CHEAM SM3............................ 208 C4
ESH/CLAY KT10...................... 204 E4
Station Yd ASHF TW15............. 152 C6
RSLP HA4 *................................ 58 B6
STHL UB1 *............................... 114 E2
SUT SM1.................................. 209 F2
Staunton Rd KUTN/CMB KT2... 175 G3
Staunton St DEPT SE8............. 124 C6
Staveley Cl HOLWY N7 *............ 84 E2
PECK SE15 *............................ 143 K2
Staveley Gdns CHSWK W4...... 138 A2
Staveley Rd CHSWK W4.......... 117 K6
Staverton Rd CRICK NW2......... 82 A5
Stave Yard Rd
BERM/RHTH SE16................... 124 B1
Stavordale Rd CAR SM5.......... 194 B4
HBRY N5.................................... 85 H2
Stayners Rd WCHPL E1 *......... 105 F3
Stayton Rd SUT SM1................ 208 E1
Steadfast Rd KUT/HW KT1....... 174 E4
Stead St WALW SE17................. 18 E7
Steam Farm La
EBED/NFELT TW14.................. 133 J5
Stean St HACK E8....................... 86 B6
Stebbing Rd BARK IG11.......... 109 G1
Stebondale St POP/IOD E14.... 125 F4
Stedly SCUP DA14................... 168 B6
Steed Cl EMPK RM11................. 75 K6
Steedman St WALW SE17........... 18 C7
Steeds Rd MUSWH N10............. 47 K4
Steel Ap BARK IG11................. 109 H1
Steele Rd CHSWK W4............... 117 K3
ISLW TW7 *.............................. 136 B5
TOTM N17.................................. 50 A6
WAN E11..................................... 88 C2
WLSDN NW10........................... 98 E1
Steele's Ms North
HAMP NW3 *.............................. 83 K4
Steele's Ms South HAMP NW3.. 83 K4
Steele's Rd HAMP NW3.............. 83 K4
Steeles Studios HAMP NW3 *.... 83 K4
Steel's La WCHPL E1................ 104 E5
Steep Cl ORP BR6.................... 217 F4
Steep HI CROY/NA CRO........... 212 A2
STRHM/NOR SW16.................. 161 J5
Steeplands BUSH WD23............ 28 A2
Steeple Cl FUL/PGN SW6....... 139 H4
WIM/MER SW19....................... 177 H2
Steeplestone Cl UED N18........... 49 J1
Steeple Wk IS N1 *..................... 85 J6
Steerforth St
WAND/EARL SW18.................. 160 A4
Steering Cl ED N9....................... 36 E3
Steers Md MTCM CR4.............. 178 E4
Steers Wy BERM/RHTH SE16.. 124 B2
Stella Rd TOOT SW17.............. 178 E3
Stelling Rd ERITH DA8............. 150 A1
Stellman Cl CLPT E5................... 86 C1
Stembridge Rd PGE/AN SE20.. 181 J5
Stephan Cl HACK E8................... 86 C6
Stephen Av RAIN RM13............. 93 J4
Stephen Cl ORP BR6................. 217 F1
Stephendale Rd
FUL/PGN SW6.......................... 140 A3
Stephen Ms FITZ W1T.................. 10 C2
Stephen Pl CLAP SW4.............. 141 H4
Stephen Rd BXLYHN DA7......... 149 K4
Stephens Cl WELL DA16............ 148 B3
Stephenson Cl WELL DA16...... 147 K2
Stephenson Rd HNWL W7.......... 97 F5
WALTH E17................................. 69 G2
WHTN TW2............................... 155 F2
Stephenson St CAN/RD E16.... 106 C3
WLSDN NW10........................... 99 G2
Stephenson Wy CAMTN NW1..... 4 B6
Stephens Rd SRTFD E15........... 88 C6
Stephen St FITZ W1T.................. 10 C2
Stepney Cswy WCHPL E1........ 105 F5
Stepney Gn WCHPL E1............ 104 E4
Stepney High St WCHPL E1..... 105 F4
Stepney Wy MTCM CR4........... 179 F4

WCHPL E1 104 D4
Sterling Av EDGW HA8 30 B6
Sterling Cl WLSDN NW10 81 J5
Sterling Gdns NWCR SE14 124 B6
Sterling Pl EA W5 117 F4
Sterling Rd ENC/FH EN2 23 K2
Sterling St SKENS SW7 14 D3
Sterling Way (North Circular)
UED N18 49 K1
Stern Cl BARK IG11 109 J1
Sterndale Rd WKENS W14 * 119 G3
Sterne St SHB W12 119 G2
Sternhall La PECK SE15 143 H4
Sternhold Av
BRXS/STRHM SW2 161 J4
Sterry Crs DAGE RM10 92 C3
Sterry Dr HOR/WEW KT19 207 G2
THDIT KT7 189 K3
Sterry Gdns DAGE RM10 92 C4
Sterry Rd BARK IG11 91 F6
Sterry St STHWK SE1 18 E3
Steucers La FSTH SE23 164 B3
Steve Biko La CAT SE6 164 D6
Steve Biko Rd HOLWY N7 85 G1
Steve Biko Wy HSLW TW3 135 F4
Stevedale Rd WELL DA16 148 D3
Stevedore St WAP E1W 123 J1
Stevenage Rd EHAM E6 90 A4
FUL/PGN SW6 139 G2
Stevens Av HOM E9 86 E4
Stevens Cl BECK BR3 182 D2
HPTN TW12 172 E2
PIN HA5 59 G2
Stevens Gn BUSH WD23 28 C3
Stevens' La ESH/CLAY KT10 205 G5
Stevenson Cl BAR EN5 33 H1
Stevenson Crs
BERM/RHTH SE16 123 H5
Stevens Rd BCTR RM8 73 H6
Stevens St STHWK SE1 19 H4
Steventon Rd SHB W12 99 H6
Stewart Cl CDALE/KGS NW9 * 62 E3
CHST BR7 185 G1
HPTN TW12 172 D2
Stewart Quay HYS/HAR UB3 113 H2
Stewart Rd SRTFD E15 88 B2
Stewartsby Cl UED N18 49 J1
Stewart's Gv CHEL SW3 120 C5
Stewart's La VX/NE SW8 141 G1
Stewart's Rd VX/NE SW8 141 H2
Stewart St POP/IOD E14 125 F2
Stew La BLKFR EC4V 12 C5
Steyne Rd ACT W3 117 J1
Steyning Gv ELTH/MOT SE9 166 E6
Steynings Wy
NFNCH/WDSPK N12 46 E1
Steyning Wy HSLWW TW4 134 B5
Steynton Av BXLY DA5 169 F4
Stickland Rd BELV DA17 129 H4
Stickleton Cl GFD/PVL UB6 96 B2
Stilecroft Gdns ALP/SUD HA0 79 H1
Stile Hall Gdns CHSWK W4 117 H5
Stiles Cl ERITH DA8 129 J5
HAYES BR2 200 E3
Stillingfleet Rd BARN SW13 138 D1
Stillington St WEST SW1P 16 B6
Stillness Rd FSTH SE23 164 B1
Stipularis Dr YEAD UB4 95 H3
Stirling Av PIN HA5 59 H4
WLGTN SM6 210 E5
Stirling Cl RAIN RM13 111 K2
SCUP DA14 167 K6
STRHM/NOR SW16 179 H4
Stirling Dr ORP BR6 217 H3
Stirling Gv HSLW TW3 135 H3
Stirling Rd ACT W3 117 J3
BRXN/ST SW9 141 K3
HYS/HAR UB3 95 F6
KTN/HRWW/WS HA3 43 F6
PLSTW E13 107 F1
TOTM N17 50 C4
WALTH E17 51 G6
WDGN N22 49 H4
WHTN TW2 155 F2
Stirling Wk BRYLDS KT5 191 J3
Stirling Wy BORE WD6 31 F1
CROY/NA CR0 195 K4
Stiven Crs RYLN/HDSTN HA2 77 K1
St John's Est IS N1 7 F3
STHWK SE1 19 J2
St Martin-in-the-Fields
CHCR WC2N * 10 E6
Stockbury Rd CROY/NA CR0 197 K3
Stockdale Rd BCTR RM8 74 B6
Stockdove Wy GFD/PVL UB6 97 F2
Stocker Gdns DAGW RM9 91 J5
Stockfield Rd ESH/CLAY KT10 204 E3
STRHM/NOR SW16 162 A5
Stockford Av MLHL NW7 46 B3
Stockholm Rd
BERM/RHTH SE16 123 K5
Stockholm Wy WAP E1W 123 H1
Stockhurst Cl PUT/ROE SW15 139 F3
Stockingswater La PEND EN3 25 G4
Stockland Rd ROMW/RG RM7 75 F3
Stockley Cl WDR/YW UB7 112 E2
Stockley Farm Rd
WDR/YW UB7 112 E3
Stockley Rd WDR/YW UB7 112 E3
Stock Orchard Crs
HOLWY N7 * 85 F2
Stock Orchard St HOLWY N7 85 F3
Stockport Rd
STRHM/NOR SW16 179 J4
Stocksfield Rd WALTH E17 * 52 A6
Stocks Pl POP/IOD E14 105 H6
Stock St PLSTW E13 106 E1
Stockton Cl BAR EN5 21 G5
Stockton Gdns MLHL NW7 31 F5
TOTM N17 49 J3
Stockton Rd TOTM N17 49 J3
UED N18 50 C2
Stockwell Av BRXN/ST SW9 142 A4
Stockwell Cl BMLY BR1 184 A5
Stockwell Gdns
BRXN/ST SW9 142 A2
Stockwell Gn BRXN/ST SW9 142 A3
Stockwell La BRXN/ST SW9 142 A3
Stockwell Park Crs
BRXN/ST SW9 142 A3
Stockwell Park Rd
BRXN/ST SW9 142 A2
Stockwell Park Wk
BRXN/ST SW9 142 A4
Stockwell Rd BRXN/ST SW9 142 A3
Stockwell St GNWCH SE10 125 F6
Stockwell Ter BRXN/ST SW9 142 A2
Stodart Rd PGE/AN SE20 181 K4
Stofield Gdns ELTH/MOT SE9 166 C5
Stoford Cl WIM/MER SW19 159 H3
Stoke Av BARK/HLT IG6 55 G2
Stokenchurch St
FUL/PGN SW6 140 A2
Stoke Newington Church St
STNW/STAM N16 85 K1
Stoke Newington Common
STNW/STAM N16 68 B6
Stoke Newington High St
STNW/STAM N16 86 B1
Stoke Newington Rd
HACK E8 86 B3
Stoke Pl WLSDN NW10 99 H2
Stoke Rd KUTN/CMB KT2 175 K3
Stokesby Rd CHSGTN KT9 206 B4
Stokesley St SHB W12 99 H5
Stokes Rd CROY/NA CR0 198 A3
EHAM E6 107 J3
Stoll Cl CRICK NW2 82 A1
Stonard Rd BCTR RM8 91 H3
PLMGR N13 35 G5
Stonards Hl LOU IG10 39 K1
Stondon Pk FSTH SE23 164 B1
Stonebridge Pk WLSDN NW10 81 F5
Stonebridge Rd
SEVS/STOTM N15 68 A2
Stonebridge Wy WBLY HA9 80 D4
Stone Blds LINN WC2A 11 H2
Stonechat Sq EHAM E6 107 J4
Stone Cl BCTR RM8 74 B6
CLAP SW4 141 H3
WDR/YW UB7 112 C1
Stonecot Cl CHEAM SM3 193 H5
Stonecot Hl CHEAM SM3 193 H5
Stone Crs EBED/NFELT TW14 153 J2
Stonecroft Wy CROY/NA CR0 195 K4
Stonecrop Cl CDALE/KGS NW9 45 F6
Stonecutter St
FLST/FETLN EC4A 12 A3
Stonefield Cl RSLP HA4 77 J3
Stonefield St IS N1 85 G6
Stonefield Wy CHARL SE7 146 C1
RSLP HA4 77 H3
Stonegate Cl STMC/STPC BR5 186 D6
Stone Gv EDGW HA8 30 A6
Stonegrove Gdns EDGW HA8 44 A1
Stonehall Av IL IG1 71 J3
Stone Hall Gdns KENS W8 * 120 A3
Stone Hall Pl KENS W8 * 120 A3
Stone Hall Rd WCHMH N21 35 F2
Stoneham Rd
FBAR/BDGN N11 48 C1
Stonehill Cl
MORT/ESHN SW14 138 A6
Stonehill Rd CHSWK W4 117 H5
MORT/ESHN SW14 137 K6
Stonehills Ct DUL SE21 163 F5
Stonehill Woods Pk
SCUP DA14 * 187 J2
Stonehorse Rd PEND EN3 24 E6
Stone House Ct LVPST EC2M 13 H3
Stonehouse La RSEV TN14 217 K6
Stonehouse Rd RSEV TN14 217 K6
Stoneleigh Av EN EN1 24 D1
WPK KT4 207 J1
Stoneleigh Broadway
EW KT17 207 J3
Stoneleigh Crs
HOR/WEW KT19 207 J3
Stoneleigh Park Av
CROY/NA CR0 198 A3
Stoneleigh Park Rd
HOR/WEW KT19 207 H4
Stoneleigh Pl NTGHL W11 100 B6
Stoneleigh Rd BMLY BR1 185 G6
CAR SM5 194 D4
CLAY IG5 53 J6
TOTM N17 50 B5
Stoneleigh St NTGHL W11 100 B6
Stoneleigh Ter ARCH N19 66 B6
Stonell's Rd TOOT SW17 160 B5
Stonemasons Cl
SEVS/STOTM N15 * 67 K1
Stonenest St FSBYPK N4 67 F5
Stone Park Av BECK BR3 198 D1
Stone Pl WPK KT4 192 D6
Stones Cross Rd SWLY BR8 203 K2
Stones End St STHWK SE1 18 C3
Stonewall EHAM E6 108 A4
Stoney Aly WOOL/PLUM SE18 147 F3
Stoneyard La POP/IOD E14 105 K6
Stoneycroft Cl
LEE/GVPK SE12 165 J2
Stoneycroft Rd WFD IG8 53 J2
Stoneydown WALTH E17 69 G1
Stoneydown Av WALTH E17 69 G1
Stoneyfields Gdns EDGW HA8 30 E6
Stoneyfields La EDGW HA8 44 E1
Stoney La HDTCH EC3A 13 H3
NRWD SE19 181 G2
Stoney St STHWK SE1 12 E7
Stonhouse St CLAP SW4 141 H4
Stonnell's Rd BTSEA SW11 140 E6
Stonor Rd WKENS W14 119 J4
Stonycroft Cl PEND EN3 25 G3
Stopes St PECK SE15 143 G1
Stopford Rd PLSTW E13 88 E6
WALW SE17 122 C5
Store Rd CAN/RD E16 127 F2
Storers Quay POP/IOD E14 125 G4
Store St GWRST WC1E 10 C2
SRTFD E15 88 B3
Storey Rd HGT N6 65 K3
WALTH E17 69 H1
Storey's Ga STJSPK SW1H 16 D3
Stories Ms CMBW SE5 * 143 F3
Stories Rd CMBW SE5 143 F4
Stork Rd FSTGT E7 88 D4
Storksmead Rd EDGW HA8 45 G3
Storks Rd BERM/RHTH SE16 * 123 H3
Stormont Rd BTSEA SW11 141 F5
HGT N6 65 K4
Stormont Wy CHSGTN KT9 205 J3
Stormount Dr HYS/HAR UB3 113 F2
Storrington Rd CROY/NA CR0 197 G5
Story St IS N1 85 F5
Stothard St WCHPL E1 104 E3
Stott Cl WAND/EARL SW18 160 C1
Stoughton Av CHEAM SM3 208 B3
Stoughton Cl LBTH SE11 17 H7
PUT/ROE SW15 158 D3
Stour Av NWDGN UB2 115 F3
Stourcliffe St MBLAR W1H 8 E4
Stour Cl HAYES BR2 215 G2
Stourhead Cl WIM/MER SW19 159 G2
Stourhead Gdns RYNPK SW20 176 D6
Stour Rd BOW E3 87 J5
DAGE RM10 74 C6
Stourton Av FELT TW13 154 E6
Stowage DEPT SE8 124 E6
The Stowage DEPT SE8 124 D6
Stow Crs WALTH E17 51 G4
Stowe Gdns ED N9 36 B3
Stowe Rd ORP BR6 217 H2
SHB W12 118 E2
Stowting Rd ORP BR6 216 E2
Stox Md KTN/HRWW/WS HA3 42 D4
Stracey Rd WLSDN NW10 81 F6
Strachan Pl RYNPK SW20 177 F2
Stradbroke Dr CHIG IG7 54 B2
Stradbroke Gv BKHH IG9 39 H3
CLAY IG5 53 J6
Stradbroke Pk CHIG IG7 54 B2
Stradbroke Rd HBRY N5 85 J2
Stradbrook Cl
RYLN/HDSTN HA2 77 K1
Stradella Rd HNHL SE24 162 D1
Strafford Rd ACT W3 117 K2
BAR EN5 20 C4
HSLW TW3 134 E4
TWK TW1 156 B2
Strafford St POP/IOD E14 124 D2
Strahan Rd BOW E3 105 G1
Straight Rd HARH RM3 57 K1
Straightsmouth GNWCH SE10 145 F1
The Straight NWDGN UB2 114 C2
Strait Rd EHAM E6 107 J6
Straker's Rd EDUL SE22 143 J5
Strand CHCR WC2N 11 F6
Strand Dr RCH/KEW TW9 137 H1
Strandfield Cl
WOOL/PLUM SE18 127 K5
Strand-On-The-Green
CHSWK W4 117 H6
Strand Pl UED N18 36 A6
Strangways Ter WKENS W14 119 J3
Stranraer Wy IS N1 84 E5
Strasburg Rd BTSEA SW11 141 F2
Stratfield Park Cl
WCHMH N21 35 H2
Stratford Cl BARK IG11 91 G5
DAGE RM10 92 E5
Stratford Ct NWMAL KT3 192 A1
Stratford Gv PUT/ROE SW15 139 G5
Stratford House Av
BMLY BR1 184 D6
Stratford Pl OXSTW W1C 9 J4
Stratford Rd HTHAIR TW6 152 E1
KENS W8 119 K4
NWDGN UB2 114 D4
PLSTW E13 88 E6
THHTH CR7 196 B1
YEAD UB4 95 F3
Stratford Studios KENS W8 119 K3
Stratford Vls CAMTN NW1 84 C5
Strathan Cl WAND/EARL SW18 159 H1
Strathaven Rd
LEE/GVPK SE12 166 A1
Strathblaine Rd BTSEA SW11 140 C6
Strathbrook Rd
STRHM/NOR SW16 180 A3
Strathcona Rd WBLY HA9 61 K6
Strathdale STRHM/NOR SW16 180 A1
Strathdon Dr TOOT SW17 160 C5
Strathearn Av HYS/HAR UB3 133 J1
WHTN TW2 155 H3
Strathearn Cots
TRDG/WHET N20 * 32 E5
Strathearn Pl BAY/PAD W2 8 C5
Strathearn Rd SUT SM1 208 E3
WIM/MER SW19 177 K1
Strathfield Gdns BARK IG11 90 D4
Strathleven Rd
BRXS/STRHM SW2 141 K6
Strathmore Gdns EDGW HA8 44 D5
FNCH N3 47 F4
HCH RM12 75 H5
KENS W8 119 K1
Strathmore Rd CROY/NA CR0 196 D4
TEDD TW11 155 K6
WIM/MER SW19 159 K5
Strathnairn St STHWK SE1 123 H4
Strathray Gdns HAMP NW3 * 83 J4
Strath Ter BTSEA SW11 140 D5
Strathville Rd
WAND/EARL SW18 159 K4
Strathyre Av
STRHM/NOR SW16 180 B6
Stratton Av WLGTN SM6 210 D6
Stratton Cl EDGW HA8 44 B2
HSLW TW3 134 E2
WIM/MER SW19 177 J5
WOT/HER KT12 * 188 B5
Strattondale St POP/IOD E14 125 F3
Stratton Dr BARK IG11 90 E3
Stratton Gdns STHL UB1 95 K5
Stratton Rd WIM/MER SW19 177 K5
Stratton St MYFR/PICC W1J 9 K7
Strauss Rd CHSWK W4 * 118 A2
Strawberry Flds ORP BR6 216 B3
Strawberry Hill Rd TWK TW1 156 A5
Strawberry La CAR SM5 209 K1
Strawberry Ter
MUSWH N10 * 47 K4
Strawberry V EFNCH N2 47 H4
TWK TW1 156 A5
Streakes Field Rd CRICK NW2 63 J6
Streamdale ABYW SE2 128 C6
Stream La EDGW HA8 44 D2
Streamline Ms EDUL SE22 163 J3
Streamside Cl ED N9 36 B3
Stream Wy BELV DA17 129 H6
Streatfeild Av EHAM E6 89 K6
Streatfield Rd
KTN/HRWW/WS HA3 43 J6
Streatham Cl
STRHM/NOR SW16 * 161 K4
Streatham Common
STRHM/NOR SW16 * 179 J3
Streatham Common North
STRHM/NOR SW16 180 A1
Streatham Common South
STRHM/NOR SW16 179 K2
Streatham Ct
STRHM/NOR SW16 161 K5
Streatham Gn
STRHM/NOR SW16 * 161 K6
Streatham High Rd
STRHM/NOR SW16 179 K3
Streatham Hl
BRXS/STRHM SW2 161 K3
Streatham Pl
BRXS/STRHM SW2 161 K2
Streatham Rd MTCM CR4 179 F4
Streatham St
NOXST/BSQ WC1A 10 E3
Streatham V
STRHM/NOR SW16 179 H3
Streathbourne Rd
TOOT SW17 161 F4
Streatleigh Pde
STRHM/NOR SW16 * 161 K4
Streatley Pl HAMP NW3 83 H2
Streatley Rd
KIL/WHAMP NW6 82 D5
Streeters La WLGTN SM6 210 D1
Streimer Rd SRTFD E15 106 A1
Strelley Wy ACT W3 99 G6
Stretton Rd CROY/NA CR0 197 F4
RCHPK/HAM TW10 156 D4
Strickland Rw
WAND/EARL SW18 160 C2
Strickland St DEPT SE8 144 D3
Strickland Wy ORP BR6 217 F2
Stride Rd PLSTW E13 106 D1
Strimon Cl ED N9 36 E4
Stripling Wy WATW WD18 26 E1
Strode Cl MUSWH N10 48 A3
Strode Rd FSTGT E7 88 E2
FUL/PGN SW6 139 G1
TOTM N17 50 A5
WLSDN NW10 81 J4
Strond Green Gdns
CROY/NA CR0 197 K4
Strond Green Wy
CROY/NA CR0 197 K4
Strone Rd FSTGT E7 89 G4
MNPK E12 89 H4
Strone Wy YEAD UB4 95 J3
Strongbow Crs
ELTH/MOT SE9 146 E6
Strongbow Rd ELTH/MOT SE9 146 E6
Strongbridge Cl
RYLN/HDSTN HA2 60 A5
Stronsa Rd SHB W12 118 C2
Strood Av ROMW/RG RM7 75 F5
Stroud Crs PUT/ROE SW15 158 C5
Stroudes Cl WPK KT4 192 C4
Stroud Fld NTHLT UB5 77 J4
Stroud Ga RYLN/HDSTN HA2 78 B2
Stroud Green Rd FSBYPK N4 67 F5
Stroud Green Wy
CROY/NA CR0 197 J4
Stroud Rd SNWD SE25 197 H3
WIM/MER SW19 159 K5
Strouds Cl CHDH RM6 73 H2
Strout's Pl BETH E2 7 J4
Strutton Gnd STJSPK SW1H 16 C4
Strype St WCHPL E1 13 J2
Stuart Av CDALE/KGS NW9 63 J4
EA W5 117 G2
RYLN/HDSTN HA2 77 K1
WOT/HER KT12 188 B5
Stuart Cl BORE WD6 29 K1
Stuart Crs CROY/NA CR0 213 H1
HYS/HAR UB3 94 A5
WDGN N22 49 F4
Stuart Evans Cl WELL DA16 148 D4
Stuart Gv TEDD TW11 173 K1
Stuart Pl MTCM CR4 178 E4
Stuart Rd ACT W3 117 K1
BARK IG11 91 F6
EBAR EN4 33 J2
KIL/WHAMP NW6 100 E2
KTN/HRWW/WS HA3 43 F6
PECK SE15 143 K5
RCHPK/HAM TW10 156 C4
THHTH CR7 196 D1
WELL DA16 148 C2
WIM/MER SW19 159 K5
Stubbs Cl CDALE/KGS NW9 62 E2
Stubbs Dr BERM/RHTH SE16 123 J5
Stubbs Wy WIM/MER SW19 178 C4
Stucley Pl CAMTN NW1 84 B5
Stucley Rd HEST TW5 135 H1
Studdridge St FUL/PGN SW6 139 K3
Studd St IS N1 85 H6
Studholme Ct HAMP NW3 * 82 E2
Studholme St PECK SE15 143 J1
Studio Ms HDN NW4 64 A1
Studio Pl KTBR SW1X 15 F3
The Studios BUSH WD23 28 A1
Studland Cl BFN/LL DA15 168 A5
Studland Rd HNWL W7 96 D5
KUTN/CMB KT2 175 F2
SYD SE26 182 A1
Studland St HMSMTH W6 118 E4
Studley Av CHING E4 52 B3
Studley Cl CLPT E5 87 G3
Studley Ct SCUP DA14 186 C1
Studley Dr REDBR IG4 71 H3
Studley Grange Rd HNWL W7 115 K3
Studley Rd CLAP SW4 141 K2
DAGW RM9 91 K5
FSTGT E7 89 F4
Stukeley Rd FSTGT E7 89 F5
Stukeley St HOL/ALD WC2B 11 F3
Stumps Hill La BECK BR3 182 D2
Sturdy Rd PECK SE15 143 J3
Sturge Av WALTH E17 51 K4
Sturgeon Rd WALW SE17 122 D5
Sturges Fld CHST BR7 185 J2
Sturgess Av HDN NW4 63 K4
Sturge St STHWK SE1 18 C3
Sturmer Wy HOLWY N7 85 F3
Sturminster Cl YEAD UB4 95 G5
Sturrock Cl SEVS/STOTM N15 67 K1
Sturry St POP/IOD E14 105 K5
Sturt St IS N1 6 D3
Stutfield St WCHPL E1 104 C5
Styles Gdns BRXN/ST SW9 142 C4
Styles Wy BECK BR3 199 F1
Sudbourne Rd
BRXS/STRHM SW2 141 K6
Sudbrooke Rd BAL SW12 160 E1
Sudbrook Gdns
RCHPK/HAM TW10 157 F5
Sudbrook La
RCHPK/HAM TW10 157 F3
Sudbury EHAM E6 108 A5
Sudbury Av ALP/SUD HA0 79 J1
Sudbury Court Dr HRW HA1 79 G1
Sudbury Court Rd HRW HA1 79 G1
Sudbury Crs ALP/SUD HA0 79 H3
BMLY BR1 183 K1
Sudbury Cft ALP/SUD HA0 79 F2
Sudbury Gdns CROY/NA CR0 212 A2
Sudbury Heights Av
GFD/PVL UB6 79 F3
Sudbury Hl HRW HA1 79 F1
Sudbury Hill Cl ALP/SUD HA0 79 F1
Sudbury Rd BARK IG11 91 F3
Sudeley St IS N1 6 B3
Sudlow Rd WAND/EARL SW18 139 K5
Sudrey St STHWK SE1 18 C3
Suez Av GFD/PVL UB6 97 F1
Suez Rd PEND EN3 25 G5
Suffield Rd CHING E4 37 K5
PGE/AN SE20 181 K5
SEVS/STOTM N15 * 68 B2
Suffolk La CANST EC4R 12 E5
Suffolk Park Rd WALTH E17 69 G1
Suffolk Rd BARK IG11 90 D5
BARN SW13 138 C1
DAGE RM10 92 D3
GDMY/SEVK IG3 72 E3
PEND EN3 24 D6
PLSTW E13 106 D2
RYLN/HDSTN HA2 59 K3
SCUP DA14 186 D2
SEVS/STOTM N15 67 K3
SNWD SE25 197 G1
WLSDN NW10 81 G5
WPK KT4 192 C6
Suffolk St FSTGT E7 88 E
STJS SW1Y 10 D
Suffolk Vls
WAND/EARL SW18 * 159 K
Sugar House La SRTFD E15 106 A
Sugar Loaf Wk BETH E2 * 104 E
Sugden Rd BTSEA SW11 141 F
THDIT KT7 190 B
Sugden Wy BARK IG11 109 F
Sulgrave Gdns HMSMTH W6 119 F
Sulgrave Rd HMSMTH W6 119 F
Sulina Rd BRXS/STRHM SW2 161 K
Sulivan Ct FUL/PGN SW6 139 K
Sulivan Rd FUL/PGN SW6 139 K
Sullivan Av CAN/RD E16 107 H
Sullivan Cl BTSEA SW11 140 D
E/WMO/HCT KT8 173 F
YEAD UB4 95 G
Sullivan Rd LBTH SE11 17 K
Sullivan Wy BORE WD6 29
Sultan Rd WAN E11 71
Sultan St BECK BR3 182
CMBW SE5 142 D
Sumatra Rd KIL/WHAMP NW6 82
Sumburgh Rd BAL SW12 161
Summer Av E/WMO/HCT KT8 189
Summer Crossing THDIT KT7 190
Summerene Cl
STRHM/NOR SW16 179
Summerfield Av
KIL/WHAMP NW6 100
NFNCH/WDSPK N12 47
Summerfield La SURB KT6 190
Summerfield Rd EA W5 97
LOU IG10 39
Summer Gdns
E/WMO/HCT KT8 189
Summer Gv BORE WD6 29
Summer Hl CHST BR7 185
Summerhill Cl ORP BR6 216
Summerhill Gv EN EN1 36
Summerhill Rd
SEVS/STOTM N15 67
Summerhill Wy MTCM CR4 179
Summerhouse Av HEST TW5 134
Summerhouse La
WDR/YW UB7 112
Summerhouse Rd
STNW/STAM N16 68
Summerland Gdns
MUSWH N10 48
Summerlands Av ACT W3 98
Summerlee Av EFNCH N2 65
Summerlee Gdns EFNCH N2 65
Summerley St
WAND/EARL SW18 160
Summer Pl WATW WD18 * 26
Summer Rd E/WMO/HCT KT8 189
Summersby Rd HGT N6 66
Summers Cl BELMT SM2 208
WBLY HA9 62
Summerskille Cl ED N9 36
Summers La
NFNCH/WDSPK N12 4
Summers Rw
NFNCH/WDSPK N12 4
Summers St CLKNW EC1R
Summerstown TOOT SW17 16
Summerton Wy THMD SE28 10
Summer Trees SUN TW16 17
Summerville Gdns SUT SM1 20
Summerwood Rd ISLW TW7 15
Summit Av CDALE/KGS NW9 6
Summit Cl CDALE/KGS NW9 6
EDGW HA8 4
STHGT/OAK N14 3
Summit Dr WFD IG8 5

Summit Est
STNW/STAM N16 * 68 C4
Summit Rd NTHLT UB5 78 A5
WALTH E17 69 K1
Summit Wy NRWD SE19 181 F3
STHGT/OAK N14 34 B4
Sumner Av PECK SE15 * 143 G2
Sumner Cl ORP BR6 216 C2
Sumner Gdns CROY/NA CR0 196 B5
Sumner Pl SKENS SW7 14 B7
Sumner Place Ms SKENS SW7 14 B7
Sumner Rd CROY/NA CR0 196 C5
HRW HA1 60 C4
PECK SE15 143 G2
Sumner Rd South
CROY/NA CR0 196 B5
Sumner St STHWK SE1 12 C7
Sumpter Cl HAMP NW3 83 G4
Sunbeam Crs NKENS W10 100 A3
Sunbeam Rd WLSDN NW10 98 E3
Sunbury Av MLHL NW7 45 F1
MORT/ESHN SW14 138 A5
Sunbury Ct BAR EN5 * 20 C5
SUN TW16 172 C5
Sunbury Court Rd SUN TW16 172 B5
Sunbury Gdns MLHL NW7 45 F1
Sunbury La BTSEA SW11 140 C2
Sunbury Rd CHEAM SM3 208 B1
FELT TW13 153 J5
Sunbury St WOOL/PLUM SE18 126 E3
Sunbury Wy FELT TW13 172 B1
Sun Ct ERITH DA8 150 C3
Suncroft Pl SYD SE26 163 K5
Sunderland Mt FSTH SE23 * 164 A4
Sunderland Rd EA W5 116 E3
FSTH SE23 164 A3
Sunderland Ter
BAY/PAD W2 * 101 F5
Sunderland Wy MNPK E12 71 H6
Sundew Av SHB W12 99 J6
Sundew Ct ALP/SUD HA0 * 98 A1
Sundial Av SNWD SE25 181 G5
Sundorne Rd CHARL SE7 126 A5
Sundridge Av BMLY BR1 184 C3
WELL DA16 147 J3
Sundridge Pde BMLY BR1 * 184 A3
Sundridge Pl CROY/NA CR0 197 H5
Sundridge Rd CROY/NA CR0 197 G5
Sunfields Pl BKHTH/KID SE3 146 A1
Sun in Sands Rbt
BKHTH/KID SE3 146 A1
Sunken Rd CROY/NA CR0 212 E3
Sunkist Wy WLGTN SM6 210 E6
Sun La BKHTH/KID SE3 146 A1
Sunleigh Rd ALP/SUD HA0 80 A6
Sunley Gdns GFD/PVL UB6 97 G1
Sunlight Cl WIM/MER SW19 * 178 B2
Sunlight Sq BETH E2 104 D2
Sunna Gdns SUN TW16 172 A5
Sunningdale STHGT/OAK N14 48 D1
Sunningdale Av ACT W3 99 G6
BARK IG11 90 D6
FELT TW13 154 D4
RAIN RM13 111 K3
RSLP HA4 59 G5
Sunningdale Cl
BERM/RHTH SE16 * 123 J5
STAN HA7 43 G3
SURB KT6 191 F6
THMD SE28 110 A5
Sunningdale Gdns
CDALE/KGS NW9 62 E2
KENS W8 * 119 K3
Sunningdale Ldg EDGW HA8 * 44 B1
Sunningdale Rd BMLY BR1 200 D1
RAIN RM13 93 J5
SUT SM1 208 D1
Sunningfield Rd HDN NW4 45 K6
Sunningfields Crs HDN NW4 45 K5
Sunninghill Ct ACT W3 * 117 K2
Sunninghill Rd LEW SE13 144 E3
Sunny Bank SNWD SE25 181 H6
Sunny Crs WLSDN NW10 80 E5
Sunnycroft Rd HSLW TW3 135 G3
SNWD SE25 197 H1
STHL UB1 96 A4
Sunnydale ORP BR6 201 F6
Sunnydale Gdns MLHL NW7 45 F2
Sunnydale Rd LEE/GVPK SE12 146 A6
Sunnydene Av CHING E4 52 B1
RSLP HA4 58 E5
Sunnydene Gdns
ALP/SUD HA0 79 J4
Sunnydene St SYD SE26 164 B6
Sunnyfield MLHL NW7 31 H6
Sunny Gardens Rd HDN NW4 46 A6
Sunny Hl HDN NW4 45 K6
Sunnyhill Cl CLPT E5 87 G2
Sunnyhill Rd
STRHM/NOR SW16 161 K6
Sunnyhurst Cl SUT SM1 208 E1
Sunnymead Av MTCM CR4 179 J6
Sunnymead Rd
CDALE/KGS NW9 63 F4
PUT/ROE SW15 138 E6
Sunnymede Av
HOR/WEW KT19 207 G6
Sunnymede Dr BARK/HLT IG6 72 B1
Sunny Ms CRW RM5 56 E3
Sunny Nook Gdns
SAND/SEL CR2 211 K4
Sunny Pl HDN NW4 64 A1
The Sunny Rd PEND EN3 25 F2
Sunnyside CAT SE6 * 164 C2
CRICK NW2 82 D1
WOT/HER KT12 188 B2
Sunnyside Dr CHING E4 38 A2
Sunnyside Pl WIM/MER SW19 177 H2
Sunnyside Rd ARCH N19 66 D4
EA W5 116 E1
IL IG1 90 C1
LEY E10 69 J5
TEDD TW11 155 J6
Sunnyside Rd East ED N9 36 C5
Sunnyside Rd North ED N9 36 B5
Sunnyside Rd South ED N9 36 B5
Sunny Vw CDALE/KGS NW9 63 F2
Sunny Wy
NFNCH/WDSPK N12 47 J3
Sun Pas BERM/RHTH SE16 123 H3
Sunray Av BRYLDS KT5 191 J6
HAYES BR2 200 D3
HNHL SE24 142 E5
WDR/YW UB7 112 A2
Sunrise Cl FELT TW13 154 E5
Sun Rd WKENS W14 119 J5
Sunset Av CHING E4 37 K3
WFD IG8 52 E1
Sunset Dr ABR/ST RM4 57 K1
Sunset Gdns SNWD SE25 181 F5
Sunset Rd HNHL SE24 142 D5
THMD SE28 128 B1
WIM/MER SW19 176 E1
Sunset Vw BAR EN5 20 C3
Sunshine Wy MTCM CR4 178 E5
Sun St SDTCH EC2A 13 F1
Sun Street Pas LVPST EC2M 13 G2
Superior Dr ORP BR6 217 F4
Surbiton Ct SURB KT6 190 D3
Surbiton Court Ms SURB KT6 190 E3
Surbiton Crs KUT/HW KT1 191 F1
Surbiton Hall Cl KUT/HW KT1 191 F1
Surbiton Hill Pk BRYLDS KT5 191 G2
Surbiton Hill Rd SURB KT6 191 F1
Surbiton Rd KUT/HW KT1 190 E1
Surlingham Cl THMD SE28 109 K6
Surma Cl WCHPL E1 104 C3
Surmans Cl DAGW RM9 91 J6
Surrendale Pl MV/WKIL W9 100 E3
Surrey Canal Rd PECK SE15 123 K6
Surrey Cl FNCH N3 46 C6
Surrey Crs CHSWK W4 117 H5
Surrey Gdns FSBYPK N4 67 J3
Surrey Gv SUT SM1 209 H1
WALW SE17 123 F5
Surrey La BTSEA SW11 140 D2
Surrey Ms WNWD SE27 163 F6
Surrey Mt FSTH SE23 163 J3
Surrey Quays Rd
BERM/RHTH SE16 123 K3
Surrey Rd BARK IG11 90 E5
DAGE RM10 92 D3
HRW HA1 60 C3
PECK SE15 144 A6
WWKM BR4 198 E5
Surrey Rw STHWK SE1 18 A2
Surrey Sq WALW SE17 123 F5
Surrey St CROY/NA CR0 211 J1
PLSTW E13 107 F2
TPL/STR WC2R 11 H5
Surrey Ter WALW SE17 19 H7
Surrey Water Rd
BERM/RHTH SE16 124 A1
Surridge Gdns NRWD SE19 180 E2
Surr St HOLWY N7 84 E3
Sury Basin KUTN/CMB KT2 175 F4
Susan Cl ROMW/RG RM7 56 E6
Susannah St POP/IOD E14 105 K5
Susan Rd BKHTH/KID SE3 146 A3
Susan Wd CHST BR7 185 F4
Sussex Av ISLW TW7 135 K4
Sussex Cl ARCH N19 * 66 E6
NWMAL KT3 192 B1
REDBR IG4 71 K3
TWK TW1 156 C1
Sussex Crs NTHLT UB5 78 A4
Sussex Gdns BAY/PAD W2 8 B3
CHSGTN KT9 205 K4
FSBYPK N4 67 J2
HGT N6 65 K2
Sussex Ga HGT N6 65 K2
Sussex Ms East
BAY/PAD W2 * 8 B5
Sussex Ms West BAY/PAD W2 8 B5
Sussex Pl BAY/PAD W2 8 B4
CAMTN NW1 2 E6
HMSMTH W6 119 F5
NWMAL KT3 192 B1
Sussex Ring
NFNCH/WDSPK N12 46 E1
Sussex Rd CAR SM5 209 K4
EHAM E6 108 A1
HGDN/ICK UB10 76 A2
HRW HA1 60 C2
MTCM CR4 * 195 K2
NWDGN UB2 114 C3
NWMAL KT3 192 B1
SAND/SEL CR2 211 K4
SCUP DA14 186 C1
STMC/STPC BR5 202 D3
WWKM BR4 198 E5
Sussex Sq BAY/PAD W2 8 B5
Sussex St PIM SW1V 121 G5
PLSTW E13 107 F2
Sussex Ter PGE/AN SE20 * 181 K3
Sussex Wy ARCH N19 66 D5
EBAR EN4 22 B6
Sutcliffe Cl GLDGN NW11 65 F2
Sutcliffe Rd WELL DA16 148 D3
WOOL/PLUM SE18 127 K6
Sutherland Av HYS/HAR UB3 113 K4
MV/WKIL W9 100 E3
STMC/STPC BR5 202 A3
WEA W13 97 H5
WELL DA16 147 J5
WELL DA16 148 A6
Sutherland Cl BAR EN5 20 C5
Sutherland Ct
CDALE/KGS NW9 62 D1
Sutherland Dr
WIM/MER SW19 178 C4
Sutherland Gdns
MORT/ESHN SW14 138 B4
WPK KT4 192 E5
Sutherland Gv TEDD TW11 173 K1
WAND/EARL SW18 159 J2
Sutherland House
WALTH E17 * 51 G6
Sutherland Pl BAY/PAD W2 100 E5
Sutherland Rd BELV DA17 129 H3
BOW E3 105 H1
CHSWK W4 118 A6
CROY/NA CR0 196 B4
ED N9 36 C3
STHL UB1 95 K5
TOTM N17 50 C3
WEA W13 97 G5
Sutherland Rw PIM SW1V * 121 G5
Sutherland Sq WALW SE17 122 D5
Sutherland St PIM SW1V 121 G5
Sutherland Vls WEA W13 * 97 G6
Sutherland Wk WALW SE17 122 D5
Sutlej Rd CHARL SE7 146 B1
Sutterton St HOLWY N7 85 F4
Sutton Cl BECK BR3 182 E4
CHSWK W4 * 117 K6
LOU IG10 39 J2
PIN HA5 58 E2
Sutton Common Rd
CHEAM SM3 193 J4
Sutton Ct BELMT SM2 209 G5
CHSWK W4 * 117 K6
EA W5 * 117 F1
Sutton Court Rd CHSWK W4 117 K6
PLSTW E13 107 G2
SUT SM1 209 G4
Sutton Crs BAR EN5 20 B6
Sutton Dene HSLW TW3 135 G2
Sutton Dwelling Est
CHEL SW3 120 D5
Sutton Est IS N1 * 85 H5
The Sutton Est IS N1 * 85 H5
Sutton Gdns CROY/NA CR0 197 G2
Sutton Gv SUT SM1 209 H3
Sutton Hall Rd HEST TW5 135 F1
Sutton La FARR EC1M 6 B7
HSLW TW3 134 E3
Sutton La North CHSWK W4 117 K5
Sutton La South CHSWK W4 117 K6
Sutton Park Rd SUT SM1 209 F4
Sutton Pl HOM E9 86 E3
Sutton Rd BARK IG11 108 E1
HEST TW5 135 F2
MUSWH N10 48 A4
PLSTW E13 106 D3
WALTH E17 51 F4
Sutton Rw SOHO/SHAV W1D 10 C3
Sutton Sq HEST TW5 134 E2
HOM E9 * 86 E3
Sutton St WCHPL E1 104 E5
Sutton Wy HEST TW5 134 E2
NKENS W10 100 A4
STLK EC1Y 6 D7
Swaby Rd WAND/EARL SW18 160 B4
Swaffield Rd
WAND/EARL SW18 160 B2
Swain Cl STRHM/NOR SW16 179 G2
Swain Rd THHTH CR7 196 D2
Swains Cl WDR/YW UB7 112 B2
Swain's La HGT N6 84 A1
Swainson Rd ACT W3 118 C2
Swains Rd MTCM CR4 178 E3
Swain St STJWD NW8 2 B7
Swaisland Dr DART DA1 150 C6
Swaledale Cl FBAR/BDGN N11 48 A2
Swale Rd DART DA1 150 D4
Swallands Rd CAT SE6 164 D5
Swallow Cl BUSH WD23 28 B3
NWCR SE14 143 K2
Swallow Ct RSLP HA4 * 59 G5
Swallowdale SAND/SEL CR2 213 F6
Swallow Dr NTHLT UB5 96 A1
WLSDN NW10 81 F4
Swallowfield Rd CHARL SE7 126 A5
Swallowfield Wy
HYS/HAR UB3 113 G2
Swallow Gdns
STRHM/NOR SW16 179 J1
Swallow Pl REGST W1B 9 K4
Swallow St EHAM E6 107 J4
REGST W1B 10 B6
Swallowtail Cl
STMC/STPC BR5 202 E1
Swanage Rd CHING E4 52 A3
WAND/EARL SW18 160 B1
Swanage Waye YEAD UB4 95 G5
Swan Ap EHAM E6 107 J4
Swan Cl CROY/NA CR0 * 197 F4
FELT TW13 154 D6
STMC/STPC BR5 186 B6
WALTH E17 51 G4
Swandon Wy
WAND/EARL SW18 140 A5
Swan Dr CDALE/KGS NW9 45 G5
Swanfield St BETH E2 7 J5
Swan Island TWK TW1 * 156 B5
Swan La CANST EC4R 12 E6
LOU IG10 39 G2
TRDG/WHET N20 33 G5
Swanley Rd WELL DA16 148 D2
Swan Md STHWK SE1 19 G5
Swan Ms BRXN/ST SW9 142 A3
Swan Pas WCHPL E1 13 K6
Swan & Pike Rd PEND EN3 25 J1
Swan Pl BARN SW13 138 C3
Swan Rd BERM/RHTH SE16 123 K2
FELT TW13 154 D6
STHL UB1 96 B5
WDR/YW UB7 112 A2
WOOL/PLUM SE18 126 C3
Swanscombe Rd CHSWK W4 118 B5
NTGHL W11 119 G1
Swansea Cl CRW RM5 57 F3
Swansea Rd HTHAIR TW6 153 F1
PEND EN3 24 E5
Swanston Pth OXHEY WD19 27 G5
Swan St ISLW TW7 136 C4
STHWK SE1 18 D3
Swanton Gdns
WIM/MER SW19 159 G3
Swan Wk CHEL SW3 120 E6
Swan Wy PEND EN3 25 F3
Swanwick Cl PUT/ROE SW15 158 C2
Swan Yd IS N1 85 H4
Sward Rd STMC/STPC BR5 202 B3
Swaton Rd BOW E3 105 J3
Swaylands Rd BELV DA17 129 H6
Swaythling Cl UED N18 36 D6
Swedenbourg Gdns
WCHPL E1 104 C6
Sweden Ga BERM/RHTH SE16 124 B4
Sweeney Crs STHWK SE1 19 K3
Sweeps La STMC/STPC BR5 202 E2
Sweet Briar Gn ED N9 36 B5
Sweet Briar Gv ED N9 36 B5
Sweet Briar Wk UED N18 36 B6
Sweetmans Av PIN HA5 41 H6
Sweets Wy TRDG/WHET N20 33 H4
Swete St PLSTW E13 106 E1
Swift Cl HYS/HAR UB3 94 D5
RYLN/HDSTN HA2 60 B6
THMD SE28 109 H5
WALTH E17 51 G3
Swift Rd FELT TW13 154 C6
NWDGN UB2 114 E3
Swiftsden Wy BMLY BR1 183 H2
Swift St FUL/PGN SW6 139 H2
Swinbrook Rd NKENS W10 100 C4
Swinburne Crs CROY/NA CR0 197 K3
Swinburne Rd
PUT/ROE SW15 138 D5
Swinderby Rd ALP/SUD HA0 80 A4
Swindon Cl GDMY/SEVK IG3 72 E6
Swindon Rd HTHAIR TW6 133 F6
Swindon St SHB W12 * 118 E1
Swinfield Cl FELT TW13 154 D6
Swinford Gdns BRXN/ST SW9 142 C4
Swingate La
WOOL/PLUM SE18 147 K1
Swinnerton St HOM E9 87 G3
Swinton Cl WBLY HA9 62 D5
Swinton Pl FSBYW WC1X 5 G4
Swinton St FSBYW WC1X 5 G4
Swires Shaw HAYES BR2 215 H2
Swithland Gdns
ELTH/MOT SE9 166 E6
Swyncombe Av EA W5 116 C4
Swynford Gdns HDN NW4 63 J1
Sybil Ms FSBYPK N4 67 H3
Sybil Phoenix Cl DEPT SE8 124 A5
Sybourn St WALTH E17 69 H4
Sycamore Av BFN/LL DA15 168 A1
BOW E3 87 H6
EA W5 116 E3
HYS/HAR UB3 94 C6
Sycamore Cl ACT W3 118 B1
CAN/RD E16 106 C3
CAR SM5 209 K2
EBAR EN4 33 H1
ED N9 36 C6
EDGW HA8 30 E6
FELT TW13 153 K5
NTHLT UB5 77 J6
SAND/SEL CR2 212 A3
Sycamore Gdns MTCM CR4 178 C5
SHB W12 118 E2
Sycamore Gv CAT SE6 165 F1
CDALE/KGS NW9 62 E4
GPK RM2 57 J5
NWMAL KT3 176 B6
PGE/AN SE20 181 H4
Sycamore Hl FBAR/BDGN N11 48 A2
Sycamore Ms CLAP SW4 141 H4
ERITH DA8 * 130 A5
Sycamore Rd WIM/MER SW19 177 F2
Sycamore St FSBYE EC1V 6 C7
Sycamore Wk NKENS W10 100 C3
Sycamore Wy TEDD TW11 174 D2
Sydcote DUL SE21 * 162 D4
Sydenham Av SYD SE26 181 J1
Sydenham Cl ROM RM1 75 H1
Sydenham Cots
LEE/GVPK SE12 * 166 B4
Sydenham Hl FSTH SE23 163 J4
SYD SE26 163 H5
Sydenham Pk SYD SE26 163 K5
Sydenham Park Rd SYD SE26 163 K5
Sydenham Ri FSTH SE23 163 J4
Sydenham Rd CROY/NA CR0 196 D6
SYD SE26 182 A1
Sydenham Station Ap
SYD SE26 163 K6
Sydmons Ct FSTH SE23 * 163 K2
Sydner Rd STNW/STAM N16 86 B2
Sydney Chapman Wy
BAR EN5 20 D3
Sydney Cl SKENS SW7 14 B7
Sydney Gv HDN NW4 64 A2
Sydney Ms CHEL SW3 14 B7
Sydney Pl SKENS SW7 14 B7
Sydney Rd ABYW SE2 128 E3
BARK/HLT IG6 54 C5
BXLYHS DA6 148 E5
CEND/HSY/T N8 67 G1
EBED/NFELT TW14 153 K3
ENC/FH EN2 23 K5
MUSWH N10 48 B4
RCH/KEW TW9 137 F5
RYNPK SW20 177 G5
SCUP DA14 167 K6
SUT SM1 208 E2
TEDD TW11 174 A1
WAN E11 71 F3
WEA W13 116 B1
WFD IG8 38 E6
Sydney St CHEL SW3 120 D5
Sydney Ter ESH/CLAY KT10 * 205 F4
Sylvan Av CHDH RM6 74 B3
MLHL NW7 45 G2
WDGN N22 49 G3
Sylvan Gdns SURB KT6 190 E4
Sylvan Gv CRICK NW2 82 B2
PECK SE15 123 J6
Sylvan Hl NRWD SE19 181 F4
Sylvan Rd FSTGT E7 88 E4
IL IG1 72 C6
NRWD SE19 181 G4
WALTH E17 * 69 J2
WAN E11 70 E2
Sylvan Ter PECK SE15 * 143 J1
Sylvan Wk BMLY BR1 184 E6
Sylvan Wy BCTR RM8 91 H1
WWKM BR4 214 C2
Sylverdale Rd CROY/NA CR0 211 H1
Sylvester Av CHST BR7 184 E2
Sylvester Pth HACK E8 * 86 D4
Sylvester Rd ALP/SUD HA0 79 J3
EFNCH N2 47 G5
HACK E8 * 86 D4
WALTH E17 * 69 H4
Sylvia Av PIN HA5 41 K2
Sylvia Gdns WBLY HA9 80 D5
Symes Ms CAMTN NW1 4 A2
Symington Ms HOM E9 87 F3
Symister Ms IS N1 7 G5
Symons Cl PECK SE15 143 K3
Symons St CHEL SW3 15 F7
Symphony Cl EDGW HA8 44 D3
Symphony Ms NKENS W10 100 C2
Syon Gate Wy BTFD TW8 136 B1
Syon La ISLW TW7 136 B1
Syon Pk ISLW TW7 * 136 C4
Syon Park Gdns ISLW TW7 136 A1

T

Tabard Garden Est
STHWK SE1 18 E2
Tabard St STHWK SE1 18 E3
Tabernacle Av PLSTW E13 106 E3
Tabernacle St SDTCH EC2A 7 F7
Tableer Av CLAP SW4 141 H6
Tabley Rd HOLWY N7 84 E2
Tabor Gdns CHEAM SM3 208 C4
Tabor Gv WIM/MER SW19 177 H3
Tabor Rd HMSMTH W6 118 E3
Tachbrook Rd
EBED/NFELT TW14 153 J2
NWDGN UB2 114 C4
Tachbrook St PIM SW1V 16 B7
Tack Ms BROCKY SE4 144 D4
Tadema Rd WBPTN SW10 140 B1
Tadmor St SHB W12 119 G1
Tadworth Av NWMAL KT3 192 C1
Tadworth Pde HCH RM12 93 K2
Tadworth Rd CRICK NW2 63 J6
Taeping St POP/IOD E14 124 E4
Taffy's How MTCM CR4 178 D6
Tait Ct BOW E3 87 H6
Tait Rd CROY/NA CR0 197 F4
Tait St WCHPL E1 104 D5
Takeley Cl CRW RM5 57 F5
Talacre Rd KTTN NW5 84 A4
Talbot Av EFNCH N2 47 H6
OXHEY WD19 27 J2
Talbot Cl SEVS/STOTM N15 68 B1
Talbot Ct BANK EC3V 13 F5
Talbot Crs HDN NW4 63 J2
Talbot Gdns GDMY/SEVK IG3 73 G6
Talbot Pl BKHTH/KID SE3 145 H3
Talbot Rd ALP/SUD HA0 79 K3
CAR SM5 210 A3
DAGW RM9 92 B5
EDUL SE22 143 F5
EHAM E6 107 K1
FSTGT E7 88 E2
HGT N6 66 A3
ISLW TW7 136 B5
KTN/HRWW/WS HA3 43 F5
NTGHL W11 100 D5
NWDGN UB2 114 D4
SEVS/STOTM N15 68 B1
THHTH CR7 196 E1
WDGN N22 48 C5
WEA W13 * 97 G6
WHTN TW2 155 K3
Talbot Sq BAY/PAD W2 8 A4
Talbot Wk NTGHL W11 100 C5
WLSDN NW10 * 81 G4
Talbot Yd STHWK SE1 18 E1
Talcott Pth
BRXS/STRHM SW2 * 162 B3
Talehangers Cl BXLYHS DA6 148 E5
Talfourd Pl PECK SE15 143 G2
Talfourd Rd PECK SE15 143 G2
Talgarth Rd WKENS W14 119 H5
Talgarth Wk CDALE/KGS NW9 63 G2
Talisman Cl GDMY/SEVK IG3 73 H5
Talisman Sq SYD SE26 163 H6
Talisman Wy WBLY HA9 80 B1
Tallack Cl
KTN/HRWW/WS HA3 42 E3
Tallack Rd LEY E10 69 H5
Tall Elms Cl HAYES BR2 199 J2
Tallis Cl CAN/RD E16 107 F5
Tallis Gv CHARL SE7 126 A6
Tallis St EMB EC4Y 11 K5
Tallis Vw WLSDN NW10 81 F4
Tallow Cl DAGW RM9 91 K4
Tallow Rd BTFD TW8 116 D6
Tall Trees STRHM/NOR SW16 180 A6
Talma Gdns WHTN TW2 155 K2
Talmage Cl FSTH SE23 163 K2
Talman Gv STAN HA7 43 K2
Talma Rd BRXS/STRHM SW2 142 B5
Talwin St BOW E3 105 K2
Tamar Cl BOW E3 * 87 H6
Tamarind Yd WAP E1W 123 H1
Tamarisk Sq SHB W12 99 H6
Tamar St CHARL SE7 126 D4
Tamesis Gdns WPK KT4 192 B6
Tamian Wy HSLWW TW4 134 B5
Tamworth Av WFD IG8 52 C2
Tamworth La MTCM CR4 179 G6
Tamworth Pk MTCM CR4 195 G1
Tamworth Pl CROY/NA CR0 * 196 D6
Tamworth Rd CROY/NA CR0 196 D6
Tamworth St FUL/PGN SW6 119 K6
Tancred Rd FSBYPK N4 67 H3
Tandridge Dr ORP BR6 201 J5
Tanfield Av CRICK NW2 81 H2
Tanfield Rd CROY/NA CR0 211 J2
Tangier Rd RCHPK/HAM TW10 137 H5
Tangleberry Cl BMLY BR1 200 E1
Tangle Tree Cl FNCH N3 47 F5
Tanglewood Cl CROY/NA CR0 212 E1
STAN HA7 28 E4
Tanglewood Wy FELT TW13 154 A5
Tangley Gv PUT/ROE SW15 158 C2
Tangley Park Rd
HPTN TW12 * 172 E1
Tangmere Crs HCH RM12 93 K4
Tangmere Gdns NTHLT UB5 95 G1
Tangmere Gv KUTN/CMB KT2 174 E1
Tangmere Wy
CDALE/KGS NW9 45 G5
Tanhouse Fld KTTN NW5 * 84 D3
Tankerton Houses
STPAN WC1H * 5 F5
Tankerton Rd SURB KT6 191 G6
Tankerton St STPAN WC1H 5 F5
Tankerton Ter CROY/NA CR0 * 196 A4
Tankerville Rd
STRHM/NOR SW16 179 J3
Tankridge Rd CRICK NW2 63 K6
The Tanneries WCHPL E1 * 104 E3
Tanners Cl WOT/HER KT12 188 A3

Tanners End La *UED* N18 36 A6
Tanner's Hl *DEPT* SE8 144 D2
Tanners La *BARK/HLT* IG6 54 C6
Tanners Ms *DEPT* SE8 144 C2
Tanner St *BARK* IG11 90 C4
STHWK SE1 19 H3
Tannery Cl *CROY/NA* CR0 198 A2
DAGE RM10 92 D1
Tannington Ter *HBRY* N5 85 G1
Tannsfeld Rd *SYD* SE26 182 A1
Tansley Cl *HOLWY* N7 84 D3
Tanswell St *STHWK* SE1 * 17 J3
Tansy Cl *EHAM* E6 108 A5
Tantallon Rd *BAL* SW12 161 F3
Tant Av *CAN/RD* E16 106 D5
Tantony Gv *CHDH* RM6 55 K6
Tanworth Cl *NTHWD* HA6 40 A2
Tanworth Gdns *PIN* HA5 41 F5
Tan Yard La *BXLY* DA5 * 169 H2
Tanza Rd *HAMP* NW3 83 K2
Tapestry Cl *BELMT* SM2 209 F5
Taplow Ct *MTCM* CR4 194 D1
Taplow Rd *PLMGR* N13 35 J6
Taplow St *IS* N1 6 D3
Tappesfield Rd *PECK* SE15 143 K4
Tapping Cl *KUTN/CMB* KT2 * 175 H3
Tapp St *WCHPL* E1 104 D3
Tapster St *BAR* EN5 20 D4
Tara Ms *CEND/HSY/T* N8 66 E3
Taransay Wk *IS* N1 85 K4
Tara Ter *BROCKY* SE4 * 144 B4
Tarbert Rd *EDUL* SE22 143 F6
Tarbert Wk *WCHPL* E1 104 E6
Target Cl *EBED/NFELT* TW14 153 H1
Tariff Rd *UED* N18 50 C2
Tarleton Gdns *FSTH* SE23 163 J3
Tarling Cl *SCUP* DA14 168 C5
Tarling Rd *CAN/RD* E16 106 D5
EFNCH N2 47 G4
Tarling St *WCHPL* E1 104 D5
Tarnbank *ENC/FH* EN2 22 E6
Tarn St *STHWK* SE1 18 C5
Tarnwood Pk *ELTH/MOT* SE9 166 E3
Tarragon Cl *NWCR* SE14 144 B1
Tarragon Gv *SYD* SE26 182 A2
Tarrant Pl *MBLAR* W1H 8 E2
Tarriff Crs *DEPT* SE8 124 C4
Tarrington Cl
STRHM/NOR SW16 161 J6
Tarver Rd *WALW* SE17 122 C5
Tarves Wy *GNWCH* SE10 144 E1
Tash Pl *FBAR/BDGN* N11 * 48 B1
Tasker Cl *HYS/HAR* UB3 133 F1
Tasker Rd *HAMP* NW3 83 K3
Tasmania Ter *UED* N18 49 J2
Tasman Rd *BRXN/ST* SW9 141 K4
Tasso Rd *HMSMTH* W6 119 H6
Tate Gdns *BUSH* WD23 28 E2
Tate Rd *CAN/RD* E16 126 E1
SUT SM1 208 E3
Tatham Pl *STJWD* NW8 2 B2
Tatnell Rd *FSTH* SE23 164 B1
Tattersall Cl *ELTH/MOT* SE9 146 D6
Tatton Cl *CAR* SM5 195 F5
Tatton Crs *CLPT* E5 68 B4
Tatum Rd *WLSDN* NW10 80 E5
Tatum St *WALW* SE17 19 F7
Tauheed Cl *FSBYPK* N4 67 J6
Taunton Av *HSLW* TW3 135 H3
RYNPK SW20 176 E5
Taunton Cl *BARK/HLT* IG6 55 F2
BXLYHN DA7 150 A4
CHEAM SM3 193 K5
Taunton Dr *EFNCH* N2 47 G5
ENC/FH EN2 23 G4
Taunton Ms *CAMTN* NW1 2 E7
Taunton Pl *CAMTN* NW1 2 E6
Taunton Rd *GFD/PVL* UB6 78 B5
LEE/GVPK SE12 145 H6
Taunton Wy *STAN* HA7 44 A5
Tavern Cl *CAR* SM5 194 D4
Taverners Cl *NTGHL* W11 119 H1
Taverner Sq *HBRY* N5 * 85 J2
Taverners Wy *CHING* E4 38 C3
Tavistock Av *GFD/PVL* UB6 97 G1
MLHL NW7 46 B3
WALTH E17 51 F6
Tavistock Cl
STNW/STAM N16 * 86 A3
Tavistock Ct *COVGDN* WC2E * 11 F5
Tavistock Crs *MTCM* CR4 195 K1
NTGHL W11 100 D4
Tavistock Gdns
GDMY/SEVK IG3 90 E2
Tavistock Gv *CROY/NA* CR0 196 E4
Tavistock Ms *NTGHL* W11 * 100 D5
Tavistock Pl *STHGT/OAK* N14 * 34 B1
STPAN WC1H 4 D6
Tavistock Rd *CAR* SM5 194 C5
CROY/NA CR0 196 E5
EDGW HA8 44 B4
FSBYPK N4 67 K3
HAYES BR2 199 J1
HGDN/ICK UB10 76 B3
NTGHL W11 100 D4
SRTFD E15 88 D4
SWFD E18 52 E6
WDR/YW UB7 112 A1
WELL DA16 148 D2
WLSDN NW10 99 H1
Tavistock Sq *STPAN* WC1H 4 D6
Tavistock St *COVGDN* WC2E 11 F5
Tavistock Ter *ARCH* N19 84 D1
Taviton St *STPAN* WC1H 4 C6
Tavy Cl *LBTH* SE11 122 B5
Tawney Rd *THMD* SE28 109 H6
Tawny Cl *FELT* TW13 153 K5
WEA W13 116 C1
Tawny Wy *BERM/RHTH* SE16 124 A4
Tayben Av *WHTN* TW2 155 K1
Taybridge Rd *BTSEA* SW11 141 F4
Tayburn Cl *POP/IOD* E14 106 A5
Tayfield Cl *HGDN/ICK* UB10 76 A1
Taylor Av *RCH/KEW* TW9 137 J3
Taylor Cl *CRW* RM5 56 C3
DEPT SE8 124 C6
HPTN TW12 173 H1
HSLW TW3 135 H2
ORP BR6 217 F2
TOTM N17 50 C3
Taylor Rd *MTCM* CR4 178 D3
WLGTN SM6 210 B3
Taylor's Blds
WOOL/PLUM SE18 127 G4
Taylors Cl *SCUP* DA14 168 A6
Taylors Ct *FELT* TW13 153 K4
Taylor's Gn *ACT* W3 * 99 G5
Taylor's La *BAR* EN5 20 D2
SYD SE26 163 J6
WLSDN NW10 81 G5
Taylors Md *MLHL* NW7 * 45 J1
Taymount Ri *FSTH* SE23 163 K4
Tayport Cl *IS* N1 85 F5
Tayside Dr *EDGW* HA8 30 D5
Tay Wy *ROM* RM1 57 H4
Taywood Rd *NTHLT* UB5 95 J3
Teak Cl *BERM/RHTH* SE16 124 B1
Teal Av *STMC/STPC* BR5 202 E1
Teal Cl *CAN/RD* E16 107 H4
Teal Dr *NTHWD* HA6 40 A3
Teale St *BETH* E2 104 C1
Tealing Dr *HOR/WEW* KT19 207 F2
Teal Pl *SUT* SM1 208 D3
Teasel Cl *CROY/NA* CR0 198 A5
Teasel Crs *THMD* SE28 127 K1
Teasel Wy *SRTFD* E15 106 C2
Tebworth Rd *TOTM* N17 50 B3
Technology Pk
CDALE/KGS NW9 * 45 F6
Teck Cl *ISLW* TW7 136 B3
Tedder Cl *CHSGTN* KT9 205 J3
RSLP HA4 76 E3
Tedder Rd *SAND/SEL* CR2 213 F5
Teddington Pk *TEDD* TW11 174 A1
Teddington Park Rd
TEDD TW11 156 A6
Tedworth Gdns *CHEL* SW3 120 E5
Tedworth Sq *CHEL* SW3 * 120 E5
Tees Av *GFD/PVL* UB6 96 E1
Teesdale Av *ISLW* TW7 136 B2
Teesdale Cl *BETH* E2 104 C1
Teesdale Gdns *ISLW* TW7 136 B2
SNWD SE25 181 F5
Teesdale Rd *WAN* E11 70 D3
Teesdale St *BETH* E2 104 D1
Teesdale Yd *BETH* E2 * 104 D1
The Tee *ACT* W3 99 G5
Teevan Cl *CROY/NA* CR0 197 H4
Teevan Rd *CROY/NA* CR0 197 H4
Teign Ms *ELTH/MOT* SE9 166 D4
Teignmouth Cl *CLAP* SW4 141 J5
EDGW HA8 44 B5
Teignmouth Gdns
GFD/PVL UB6 97 G1
Teignmouth Rd *CRICK* NW2 82 B3
WELL DA16 148 D3
Telcote Wy *RSLP* HA4 * 59 G4
Telegraph Hl *HAMP* NW3 83 F1
Telegraph La *ESH/CLAY* KT10 205 F2
Telegraph Ms *GDMY/SEVK* IG3 73 F5
Telegraph Pas
BRXS/STRHM SW2 161 K2
Telegraph Pl *POP/IOD* E14 124 E4
Telegraph Rd *PUT/ROE* SW15 158 E2
Telegraph St *LOTH* EC2R 12 E3
Telephone Pl *WKENS* W14 * 119 J6
Telferscot Rd *BAL* SW12 161 J3
Telford Av *BRXS/STRHM* SW2 161 J3
Telford Cl *NRWD* SE19 181 G2
WALTH E17 69 G4
Telford Dr *WOT/HER* KT12 188 B4
Telford Rd *CDALE/KGS* NW9 63 H3
ELTH/MOT SE9 167 J4
NKENS W10 100 C4
STHL UB1 96 B6
WHTN TW2 155 F2
Telford Road North Circular
Rd *FBAR/BDGN* N11 48 C1
Telfords Yd *WAP* E1W * 104 C6
Telford Ter *PIM* SW1V * 121 H6
Telford Wy *ACT* W3 99 G4
YEAD UB4 95 J4
Telham Rd *EHAM* E6 108 A1
Tell Gv *EDUL* SE22 143 G5
Tellisford *ESH/CLAY* KT10 204 B2
Tellson Av *WOOL/PLUM* SE18 146 D2
Telscombe Cl *ORP* BR6 201 K6
Temeraire Pl *BTFD* TW8 117 G5
Temeraire St
BERM/RHTH SE16 123 K2
Tempelhof Av *HDN* NW4 64 A4
Temperley Rd *BAL* SW12 161 F2
Tempest Wy *RAIN* RM13 93 J4
Templar Dr *THMD* SE28 109 K5
Templar Pl *HPTN* TW12 173 F3
Templars Av *GLDGN* NW11 64 D3
Templars Ct *DART* DA1 * 151 K6
Templars Crs *FNCH* N3 46 E5
Templars Dr
KTN/HRWW/WS HA3 * 42 D2
Templar St *CMBW* SE5 142 C3
Temple Av *BCTR* RM8 74 C5
CROY/NA CR0 213 H1
EMB EC4Y 11 K5
TRDG/WHET N20 33 H2
Temple Cl *FNCH* N3 46 D5
THMD SE28 127 H3
WAN E11 70 C4
Templecombe Rd *HOM* E9 86 E6
Templecombe Wy *MRDN* SM4 193 H2
Temple Dwellings *BETH* E2 * 104 D1
Temple Fortune Hl
GLDGN NW11 64 E2
Temple Fortune La
GLDGN NW11 64 D3
Temple Gdns *BCTR* RM8 91 K1
EMB EC4Y * 11 J5
GLDGN NW11 64 D3
WCHMH N21 * 35 H4
Temple Gv *ENC/FH* EN2 23 H4
GLDGN NW11 64 E3
Temple La *EMB* EC4Y 11 K4
Templeman Rd *HNWL* W7 97 F4
Templemead Cl *ACT* W3 99 G5
Temple Mead Cl *STAN* HA7 43 H2
Temple Mills La *LEY* E10 87 K2
Temple Pde *BAR* EN5 * 33 H2
Temple Pl *TPL/STR* WC2R 11 H5
Temple Rd *CEND/HSY/T* N8 67 F1
CHSWK W4 117 K3
CRICK NW2 82 A2
CROY/NA CR0 211 K2
EA W5 116 E3
EHAM E6 89 J6
HSLW TW3 135 G5
RCH/KEW TW9 137 G3
Temple Sheen Rd
MORT/ESHN SW14 137 K5
Temple St *BETH* E2 104 D1
Temple Ter *WDGN* N22 * 49 G5
Templeton Av *CHING* E4 37 J6
Templeton Cl *NRWD* SE19 180 E4
STNW/STAM N16 * 86 A3
Templeton Pl *ECT* SW5 119 K4
Templeton Rd *FSBYPK* N4 67 K3
Temple Wy *SUT* SM1 209 H1
Templewood *WEA* W13 97 H4
Templewood Av *HAMP* NW3 83 F1
Templewood Gdns
HAMP NW3 83 F1
Temple Yd *BETH* E2 104 C2
Tempsford Cl *ENC/FH* EN2 23 J4
Temsford Cl
RYLN/HDSTN HA2 42 C5
Tenbury Cl *FSTGT* E7 89 H3
Tenbury Ct *BAL* SW12 161 J3
Tenby Av *KTN/HRWW/WS* HA3 43 H5
Tenby Cl *CHDH* RM6 74 A3
SEVS/STOTM N15 68 B1
Tenby Gdns *NTHLT* UB5 78 A4
Tenby Rd *CHDH* RM6 74 A3
EDGW HA8 44 B4
PEND EN3 24 E4
WALTH E17 69 G2
WELL DA16 148 E2
Tench St *WAP* E1W * 123 J1
Tenda Rd *STHWK* SE1 123 J4
Tendring Wy *CHDH* RM6 73 J2
Tenham Av *BRXS/STRHM* SW2 161 J4
Tenison Wy *STHWK* SE1 17 J1
Tenniel Cl *BAY/PAD* W2 101 G5
Tennison Rd *SNWD* SE25 197 G1
Tennis St *STHWK* SE1 18 E2
Tenniswood Rd *EN* EN1 24 A2
Tennyson Av *CDALE/KGS* NW9 44 E6
MNPK E12 89 J5
NWMAL KT3 192 E2
TWK TW1 156 A3
WAN E11 70 E4
Tennyson Cl
EBED/NFELT TW14 153 K1
PEND EN3 25 F6
WELL DA16 147 K2
Tennyson Rd *HNWL* W7 97 F6
HSLW TW3 135 H3
KIL/WHAMP NW6 82 D6
LEY E10 69 K5
MLHL NW7 45 H1
PGE/AN SE20 182 A3
SRTFD E15 88 C5
WALTH E17 69 H3
WIM/MER SW19 178 B2
Tennyson St *VX/NE* SW8 141 G3
Tennyson Wy *HCH* RM12 75 H5
Tensing Rd *NWDGN* UB2 115 F3
Tentelow La *NWDGN* UB2 115 G3
Tenterden Cl *ELTH/MOT* SE9 166 E6
HDN NW4 46 B6
Tenterden Dr *HDN* NW4 46 B6
Tenterden Gdns
CROY/NA CR0 197 H4
HDN NW4 46 B6
Tenterden Gv *HDN* NW4 64 A1
Tenterden Rd *BCTR* RM8 74 B6
CROY/NA CR0 197 H4
TOTM N17 50 B3
Tenterden St *CONDST* W1S 9 K4
Tenter Gnd *WCHPL* E1 13 J2
Tent Peg La *STMC/STPC* BR5 201 H2
Tent St *WCHPL* E1 104 D3
Teredo St *LEW* SE13 144 E3
Terling Cl *WAN* E11 88 D1
Terling Rd *BCTR* RM8 74 C6
Terling Wk *IS* N1 * 85 J6
Terminus Pl *BGVA* SW1W 15 K5
Terrace Gdns *BARN* SW13 138 C3
Terrace Rd *HOM* E9 87 F5
PLSTW E13 88 E6
WOT/HER KT12 188 A3
The Terrace *BARN* SW13 138 B3
BETH E2 * 104 E2
CHING E4 * 38 C5
DEPT SE8 * 124 C4
EFNCH N2 * 66 A1
FNCH N3 * 46 D5
FSTH SE23 * 164 B2
KIL/WHAMP NW6 82 E6
Terrace Vls *HMSMTH* W6 * 118 D5
Terrace Wk *DAGW* RM9 92 A3
Terrac St *RCH/KEW* TW9 137 G5
Terrapin Rd *TOOT* SW17 161 G5
Terretts Pl *IS* N1 85 H5
Terrick Rd *WDGN* N22 48 E4
Terrick St *SHB* W12 99 K5
Terrilands *PIN* HA5 41 K6
Terront Rd *SEVS/STOTM* N15 67 J2
Tessa Sanderson Wy
GFD/PVL UB6 78 D3
Testerton Rd *NTGHL* W11 * 100 B6
Testerton Wk *NTGHL* W11 * 100 B6
Tetbury Pl *IS* N1 6 A1
Tetcott Rd *WBPTN* SW10 140 B1
Tetherdown *MUSWH* N10 48 A6
Tetty Wy *BMLY* BR1 183 K5
Teversham La *VX/NE* SW8 141 K2
Teviot Cl *WELL* DA16 148 C2
Teviot St *POP/IOD* E14 106 A4
Tewkesbury Av *FSTH* SE23 163 J3
PIN HA5 59 J2
Tewkesbury Cl *LOU* IG10 39 J1
Tewkesbury Gdns
CDALE/KGS NW9 44 D6
Tewkesbury Rd *CAR* SM5 194 C5
SEVS/STOTM N15 67 K4
WEA W13 116 B1
Tewkesbury Ter
FBAR/BDGN N11 48 C2
Tewson Rd *WOOL/PLUM* SE18 127 K5
Teynham Av *EN* EN1 35 K1
Teynton Ter *TOTM* N17 49 J4
Thackeray Av *TOTM* N17 50 C5
Thackeray Cl *ISLW* TW7 136 B3
WIM/MER SW19 177 G3
Thackeray Dr *CHDH* RM6 73 H4
Thackeray Ms *HACK* E8 86 C4
Thackeray Rd *EHAM* E6 107 H1
VX/NE SW8 141 G3
Thackeray St *KENS* W8 120 A3
Thakeham Cl *SYD* SE26 181 J1
Thalia Cl *GNWCH* SE10 125 G6
Tham Cl *HNHL* SE24 142 C4
Thame Rd *BERM/RHTH* SE16 124 A2
Thames Av *DAGW* RM9 110 D3
GFD/PVL UB6 97 F1
WBPTN SW10 140 B2
WPK KT4 193 F5
Thames Bank
MORT/ESHN SW14 137 K3
Thamesbank Pl *THMD* SE28 109 J5
Thames Cir *POP/IOD* E14 124 D4
Thames Cl *HPTN* TW12 173 G5
RAIN RM13 111 K5
Thames Crs *CHSWK* W4 138 B1
Thames Down Link
BRYLDS KT5 191 K2
HOR/WEW KT19 206 C5
Thames Dr *RSLP* HA4 58 A3
Thames Eyot *TWK* TW1 * 156 B4
Thamesgate Cl
RCHPK/HAM TW10 156 C6
Thameside *TEDD* TW11 174 E3
Thames Meadow
E/WMO/HCT KT8 173 F6
Thamesmere Dr *THMD* SE28 109 G6
Thames Pth *CHARL* SE7 126 B3
ISLW TW7 136 C3
POP/IOD E14 124 D3
SUN TW16 172 D5
THDIT KT7 190 C3
TPL/STR WC2R 11 J5
TWRH EC3N 13 H7
VX/NE SW8 121 J6
WAND/EARL SW18 139 J5
WEST SW1P 17 F5
Thames Pl *PUT/ROE* SW15 139 G4
Thamespoint *TEDD* TW11 * 174 E3
Thames Quay *WBPTN* SW10 * 140 B2
Thames Reach *KUT/HW* KT1 * 174 E4
Thames Rd *BARK* IG11 109 G2
CAN/RD E16 126 C1
CHSWK W4 117 H6
DART DA1 150 D4
Thames Side *KUT/HW* KT1 174 E4
THDIT KT7 190 C3
Thames St *GNWCH* SE10 124 E6
KUT/HW KT1 174 E5
SUN TW16 172 A6
Thamesvale Cl *HSLW* TW3 135 F3
Thames Village *CHSWK* W4 137 K2
Thamley *PUR* RM19 131 K4
Thanescroft Gdns
CROY/NA CR0 212 A1
Thanet Dr *HAYES* BR2 215 H1
Thanet Pl *CROY/NA* CR0 211 J2
Thanet Rd *BXLY* DA5 169 H2
Thanet St *STPAN* WC1H 4 E5
Thane Vls *HOLWY* N7 85 F1
Thant Cl *LEY* E10 87 K1
Tharp Rd *WLGTN* SM6 210 D3
Thatcham Gdns
TRDG/WHET N20 33 G2
Thatcher Cl *WDR/YW* UB7 112 B2
Thatchers Wy *ISLW* TW7 135 J6
Thatches Gv *CHDH* RM6 56 A6
Thavies Inn *FLST/FETLN* EC4A 11 K3
Thaxted Pl *RYNPK* SW20 177 G3
Thaxted Rd *BKHH* IG9 39 J2
ELTH/MOT SE9 167 H4
Thaxton Rd *WKENS* W14 119 J6
Thayers Farm Rd *BECK* BR3 182 B4
Thayer St *MHST* W1U 9 H3
Theatre Sq *SRTFD* E15 88 B4
Theatre St *BTSEA* SW11 140 E4
Theberton St *IS* N1 85 G6
The Beverly *MRDN* SM4 193 G3
The Courtyard *HAYES* BR2 215 J4
Theed St *STHWK* SE1 17 J1
The Green *WIM/MER* SW19 177 G1
Thelma Gv *TEDD* TW11 174 B2
Theobald Crs
KTN/HRWW/WS HA3 42 B4
Theobald Rd *CROY/NA* CR0 196 C6
WALTH E17 69 H4
Theobald's Rd *GINN* WC1R 11 G1
Theobald St *STHWK* SE1 18 E5
Theodora Wy *PIN* HA5 40 D6
Theodore Rd *LEW* SE13 165 G1
Therapia La *CROY/NA* CR0 195 J4
Therapia Rd *EDUL* SE22 163 K1
Theresa Rd *HMSMTH* W6 118 D4
Theresa's Wk *SAND/SEL* CR2 211 K6
Thermopylae Ga
POP/IOD E14 124 E4
Theseus Wk *IS* N1 6 B3
Thesiger Rd *PGE/AN* SE20 182 A3
Thessaly Rd *VX/NE* SW8 141 J2
Thetford Cl *PLMGR* N13 49 H2
Thetford Rd *ASHF* TW15 152 B6
DAGW RM9 91 K5
NWMAL KT3 192 A3
Theydon Gdns *RAIN* RM13 93 G5
Theydon Gv *WFD* IG8 53 G2
Theydon Rd *CLPT* E5 68 E6
Theydon St *WALTH* E17 69 H4
Thicket Crs *SUT* SM1 209 G2
Thicket Gv *DAGW* RM9 91 J4
PGE/AN SE20 181 H3
Thicket Rd *PGE/AN* SE20 181 J3
SUT SM1 209 G2
Thicket Ter *PGE/AN* SE20 * 181 H3
Third Av *ACT* W3 118 C1
CHDH RM6 73 J3
DAGE RM10 92 D6
EN EN1 24 B6
HYS/HAR UB3 113 J1
MNPK E12 89 J2
NKENS W10 100 C2
PLSTW E13 106 E2
WALTH E17 69 J2
WBLY HA9 61 K6
Third Cl *E/WMO/HCT* KT8 189 G1
Third Cross Rd *WHTN* TW2 155 J4
Thirleby Rd *EDGW* HA8 45 F4
WEST SW1P 16 B5
Thirlmere Av *GFD/PVL* UB6 97 J2
Thirlmere Gdns *WBLY* HA9 61 J5
Thirlmere Ri *BMLY* BR1 183 J2
Thirlmere Rd *BXLYHN* DA7 149 K3
MUSWH N10 48 B4
STRHM/NOR SW16 161 J6
Thirsk Cl *NTHLT* UB5 78 A4
Thirsk Rd *BTSEA* SW11 141 F4
MTCM CR4 179 F3
SNWD SE25 196 E1
Thisilefield Cl *BXLY* DA5 168 E3
Thistlecroft Gdns *STAN* HA7 43 K4
Thistledene *THDIT* KT7 189 K3
Thistledene Av *CRW* RM5 56 D1
RYLN/HDSTN HA2 77 J1
Thistle Gv *WBPTN* SW10 * 120 B5
Thistlemead *CHST* BR7 185 G5
Thistlewaite Rd *CLPT* E5 86 D1
Thistlewood Cl *HOLWY* N7 67 F6
Thistleworth Cl *ISLW* TW7 135 J1
Thistley Cl
NFNCH/WDSPK N12 47 J2
Thomas A Beckett Cl
HRW HA1 79 F2
Thomas Baines Rd
BTSEA SW11 140 C4
Thomas Cribb Ms *EHAM* E6 107 K5
Thomas Dean Rd *SYD* SE26 * 164 C6
Thomas Dinwiddy Rd
LEE/GVPK SE12 166 A4
Thomas Doyle St *STHWK* SE1 18 A4
Thomas' La *CAT* SE6 164 E2
Thomas Moore Wy *EFNCH* N2 47 G6
Thomas More St *WAP* E1W * 104 C6
Thomas North Ter
CAN/RD E16 * 106 D4
Thomas Pl *KENS* W8 * 120 A3
Thomas Rd *POP/IOD* E14 105 H5
Thomas St *WOOL/PLUM* SE18 127 F4
Thomas Wall Cl *SUT* SM1 209 F3
Thompson Av *CMBW* SE5 142 D1
RCH/KEW TW9 137 J4
Thompson Cl *CHEAM* SM3 193 K5
IL IG1 72 C6
Thompson Rd *DAGW* RM9 92 B1
EDUL SE22 163 G1
HSLW TW3 135 G5
Thompson's Av *CMBW* SE5 * 142 D1
Thomson Crs *CROY/NA* CR0 196 B5
Thomson Rd
KTN/HRWW/WS HA3 42 E6
Thorburn Sq *STHWK* SE1 123 H4
Thorburn Wy
WIM/MER SW19 * 178 C4
Thoresby St *IS* N1 6 D4
Thorkhill Gdns *THDIT* KT7 190 B5
Thorkhill Rd *THDIT* KT7 190 C
Thornaby Gdns *UED* N18 50 C
Thorn Av *BUSH* WD23 28 C
Thornbury Av *ISLW* TW7 135 J
Thornbury Cl
STNW/STAM N16 86 A
Thornbury Rd *CLAP* SW4 161 K
ISLW TW7 135 J1
Thornbury Sq *HGT* N6 66 C
Thornby Rd *CLPT* E5 86 E
Thorncliffe Rd *CLAP* SW4 161
NWDGN UB2 114
Thorn Cl *HAYES* BR2 201
NTHLT UB5 95
Thorncombe Rd *EDUL* SE22 143
Thorn Ct *BELMT* SM2 * 209
Thorncroft *EMPK* RM11 75
Thorncroft Rd *SUT* SM1 209
Thorncroft St *VX/NE* SW8 141
Thorndean St
WAND/EARL SW18 160
Thorndene Av
TRDG/WHET N20 34
Thorndike Av *NTHLT* UB5 77
Thorndike Cl *WBPTN* SW10 140
Thorndike Rd *IS* N1 85
Thorndike St *PIM* SW1V * 16
Thorndon Cl *STMC/STPC* BR5 186
Thorndon Gdns
HOR/WEW KT19 207
Thorndon Rd *STMC/STPC* BR5 186
Thorndyke Ct *PIN* HA5 41
Thorne Cl *CAN/RD* E16 106
ERITH DA8 129
ESH/CLAY KT10 205
WAN E11 88
Thorneloe Gdns
CROY/NA CR0 211
Thorne Rd *VX/NE* SW8 141
Thorne's Cl *BECK* BR3 183
Thorne St *BARN* SW13 138
Thornet Wood Rd *BMLY* BR1 185
Thorney Crs *BTSEA* SW11 * 140
Thorneycroft Cl
WOT/HER KT12 188
Thorneycroft Dr *PEND* EN3 25
Thorney Hedge Rd
CHSWK W4 117
Thorney St *WEST* SW1P 16
Thornfield Av *MLHL* NW7 46
Thornfield Pde *MLHL* NW7 * 46
Thornfield Rd *SHB* W12 118
Thornford Rd *LEW* SE13 145
Thorngate Rd *MV/WKIL* W9 100
Thorngrove Rd *PLSTW* E13 89
Thornham Gv *SRTFD* E15 88
Thornham St *GNWCH* SE10 124
Thornhaugh St *STPAN* WC1H
Thornhill Av *SURB* KT6 19
WOOL/PLUM SE18 14
Thornhill Bridge Whf *IS* N1
Thornhill Crs *IS* N1 8
Thornhill Gdns *BARK* IG11 9
LEY E10 6
Thornhill Gv *IS* N1 8
Thornhill Rd *CROY/NA* CR0 19
IS N1 8
LEY E10 6
NTHWD HA6 2
SURB KT6 19

Thornhill Sq IS N1 85 F6
Thornlaw Rd WNWD SE27 162 B6
Thornley Cl TOTM N17 50 C3
Thornley Dr RYLN/HDSTN HA2 60 B6
Thornsbeach Rd CAT SE6 165 F3
Thornsett Pl PGE/AN SE20 181 J5
Thornsett Rd PGE/AN SE20 181 J5
WAND/EARL SW18 160 A4
Thornsett Ter PGE/AN SE20 * 181 J5
Thornton Av
BRXS/STRHM SW2 161 J3
CHSWK W4 118 B4
CROY/NA CR0 196 A3
WDR/YW UB7 112 C3
Thornton Cl WDR/YW UB7 112 C3
Thornton Dene BECK BR3 182 D5
Thornton Gdns BAL SW12 161 J3
Thornton Gv PIN HA5 42 A2
Thornton Hl WIM/MER SW19 177 H3
Thornton Pl MBLAR W1H 8 E1
Thornton Rd BAL SW12 161 J2
BAR EN5 20 C4
BELV DA17 * 129 J4
BMLY BR1 183 K1
CAR SM5 194 C5
IL IG1 90 B2
MORT/ESHN SW14 138 A4
THHTH CR7 196 B2
UED N18 36 E5
WAN E11 70 B6
WIM/MER SW19 177 G2
Thornton Rw THHTH CR7 196 B2
Thorntons Farm Av
ROMW/RG RM7 74 E6
Thornton St BRXN/ST SW9 142 B3
Thornton Wy GLDGN NW11 65 F2
Thorntree Rd CHARL SE7 126 C5
Thornville Gv MTCM CR4 178 B5
Thornville St DEPT SE8 144 D2
Thornwood Cl SWFD E18 53 F5
Thornwood Rd LEW SE13 145 H6
Thorogood Gdns SRTFD E15 88 C3
Thorogood Wy RAIN RM13 93 G6
Thorold Rd IL IG1 72 B6
WDGN N22 48 E3
Thorparch Rd VX/NE SW8 141 J2
Thorpebank Rd SHB W12 118 D1
Thorpe Cl NKENS W10 100 C5
ORP BR6 201 K6
SYD SE26 * 164 A6
Thorpe Ct TOOT SW17 160 D6
Thorpe Crs OXHEY WD19 27 F2
WALTH E17 51 H5
Thorpedale Gdns
GNTH/NBYPK IG2 72 A1
Thorpedale Rd FSBYPK N4 67 F5
Thorpe Hall Rd WALTH E17 52 A4
Thorpe Rd BARK IG11 90 D5
EHAM E6 89 K6
FSTGT E7 88 E1
KUTN/CMB KT2 175 F3
SEVS/STOTM N15 68 A3
WALTH E17 52 A5
Thorpewood Av SYD SE26 163 J4
horpland Av HGDN/ICK UB10 76 A1
horsden Wy NRWD SE19 * 181 F1
horverton Rd CRICK NW2 82 C1
hoydon Rd BOW E3 105 G1
hrale Rd STRHM/NOR SW16 179 H1
hrale St STHWK SE1 18 D1
hrasher Cl HACK E8 * 86 B6
hrawl St WCHPL E1 13 K2
hreadneedle St LOTH EC2R 13 F4
hree Colts La BETH E2 104 D3
hree Colt St POP/IOD E14 * 105 H6
hree Kings Yd
MYFR/PKLN W1K 9 J5
hree Meadows Ms
KTN/HRWW/WS HA3 43 F4
ree Mill La BOW E3 106 A2
ree Oak La STHWK SE1 19 J2
hreshers Pl NTGHL W11 100 C6
hriffwood SYD SE26 163 K5
hrigby Rd CHSGTN KT9 206 B4
hrockmorten Rd
CAN/RD E16 107 F5
hrogmorton Av OBST EC2N 13 F3
hrogmorton St OBST EC2N 13 F3
hrowley Rd SUT SM1 209 F3
hrowley Wy SUT SM1 209 F2
hrupp Cl MTCM CR4 179 G5
hrush Gn RYLN/HDSTN HA2 60 A1
rush St WALW SE17 122 D5
underer Rd DAGW RM9 110 A3
urbarn Rd CAT SE6 182 E1
urland Rd
BERM/RHTH SE16 123 H3
urlby Cl WFD IG8 53 K1
urlby Rd ALP/SUD HA0 79 K4
WNWD SE27 162 B6
urleigh Av BAL SW12 161 F1
urleigh Rd BAL SW12 160 E1
urleston Av MRDN SM4 193 H2
urlestone Av
GDMY/SEVK IG3 91 F2
NFNCH/WDSPK N12 47 K2
urlestone Rd WNWD SE27 162 B5
urloe Cl SKENS SW7 14 C6
urloe Gdns ROM RM1 75 G3
urloe Pl SKENS SW7 14 B6
urloe Place Ms
SKENS SW7 * 14 B6
urloe Sq SKENS SW7 14 B6
urloe St SKENS SW7 14 B6
urlow Cl CHING E4 51 K2
urlow Gdns ALP/SUD HA0 * 79 K3
BARK/HLT IG6 54 D2
urlow Hl DUL SE21 162 D3
urlow Park Rd DUL SE21 162 C4
urlow Rd HAMP NW3 83 H3
HNWL W7 116 B2
rlow St WALW SE17 123 F5
rlow Ter KTTN NW5 83 K3
rlow Wk WALW SE17 123 F5
rston Rd RSLP HA4 76 E1
rsland Rd SCUP DA14 187 F1
rsley Crs CROY/NA CR0 214 B5
rsley Gdns
VIM/MER SW19 159 G4
rsley Rd ELTH/MOT SE9 166 E5
Thurso St TOOT SW17 160 C6
Thurstan Rd RYNPK SW20 176 E3
Thurston Rd DEPT SE8 144 E3
STHL UB1 95 K5
Thurtle Rd BETH E2 7 K1
Thwaite Cl ERITH DA8 129 K6
Thyer Cl ORP BR6 216 C2
Thyra Gv NFNCH/WDSPK N12 * 47 F2
Tibbatt's Rd BOW E3 105 K3
Tibbenham Pl CAT SE6 164 D4
Tibberton Sq IS N1 * 85 J5
Tibbets Cl WIM/MER SW19 159 G3
Tibbet's Ride PUT/ROE SW15 159 G2
Tiber Cl BOW E3 87 J6
Tiber Gdns IS N1 5 F1
Ticehurst Cl STMC/STPC BR5 186 B3
Ticehurst Rd FSTH SE23 164 B4
Tidal Basin Rd CAN/RD E16 106 D6
Tide Cl MTCM CR4 179 F4
Tidenham Gdns
CROY/NA CR0 212 A1
Tideswell Rd CROY/NA CR0 213 J1
PUT/ROE SW15 139 F5
Tideway Cl RCHPK/HAM TW10 156 C6
Tideway Wk VX/NE SW8 * 121 H6
Tidey St BOW E3 105 J4
Tidford Rd WELL DA16 148 A3
Tidworth Rd BOW E3 105 J2
Tiepigs La WWKM BR4 199 H6
Tierney Rd BRXS/STRHM SW2 161 K3
Tierney Ter
BRXS/STRHM SW2 * 161 K3
Tiger La HAYES BR2 200 A1
Tiger Wy CLPT E5 86 D2
Tigres Cl ED N9 36 E4
Tilbrook Rd BKHTH/KID SE3 146 B4
Tilbury Cl PECK SE15 143 G1
PIN HA5 * 41 K3
STMC/STPC BR5 186 C5
Tilbury Rd EHAM E6 107 K1
LEY E10 70 A4
Tildesley Rd PUT/ROE SW15 159 F1
Tile Farm Rd ORP BR6 216 D1
Tilehurst Rd CHEAM SM3 208 C3
WAND/EARL SW18 160 C3
Tile Kiln La BXLY DA5 169 K4
HGT N6 66 B5
PLMGR N13 49 J1
Tileyard Rd HOLWY N7 84 E5
Tilford Av CROY/NA CR0 214 A5
Tilford Gdns WIM/MER SW19 159 G3
Tilia Cl SUT SM1 208 D3
Tilia Rd CLPT E5 86 D2
Tilia Wk BRXN/ST SW9 142 C5
Tiller Rd POP/IOD E14 124 D3
Tillett Cl WLSDN NW10 80 E4
Tillet Wy BETH E2 104 C2
Tilley Rd FELT TW13 153 K3
Tillingbourne Gdns FNCH N3 46 D6
Tillingbourne Gn
STMC/STPC BR5 202 B1
Tillingbourne Wy FNCH N3 64 D1
Tillingham Wy
NFNCH/WDSPK N12 32 E6
Tilling Rd CRICK NW2 63 K5
Tilling Wy WBLY HA9 * 79 K1
Tillman St WCHPL E1 104 D5
Tilloch St IS N1 * 85 F5
Tillotson Rd ED N9 36 B4
IL IG1 72 A4
KTN/HRWW/WS HA3 42 B3
Tilney Gdns IS N1 85 K4
Tilney Rd DAGW RM9 92 B4
NWDGN UB2 114 B4
Tilney St MYFR/PKLN W1K 9 H7
Tilson Cl CMBW SE5 143 F1
Tilson Gdns
BRXS/STRHM SW2 161 K2
Tilson Rd TOTM N17 50 C4
Tilston Cl WAN E11 88 D1
Tilton St FUL/PGN SW6 119 H6
The Tiltwood ACT W3 98 E6
Tilt Yard Ap ELTH/MOT SE9 166 E1
Timber Cl CHST BR7 185 F5
Timbercroft HOR/WEW KT19 207 G2
Timbercroft La
WOOL/PLUM SE18 127 K6
Timberdene Av BARK/HLT IG6 54 C4
Timberland Cl PECK SE15 * 143 H1
Timberland Rd WCHPL E1 * 104 D5
Timber Mill Wy CLAP SW4 141 J4
Timber Pond Rd
BERM/RHTH SE16 124 A2
Timberslip Dr WLGTN SM6 210 D6
The Timbers CHEAM SM3 * 208 C4
Timber St FSBYE EC1V * 6 C6
Timberwharf Rd
SEVS/STOTM N15 68 C3
Time Sq HACK E8 * 86 B3
Times Sq SUT SM1 * 209 F3
Timms Cl BMLY BR1 200 E1
Timothy Cl CLAP SW4 141 H6
Tindal St BRXN/ST SW9 142 C2
Tine Rd CHIG IG7 54 E1
Tinniswood Cl HBRY N5 85 G3
Tinsley Cl SNWD SE25 181 J6
Tinsley Rd WCHPL E1 104 E4
Tintagel Crs EDUL SE22 143 G5
Tintagel Dr STAN HA7 43 K1
Tintagel Rd ORP BR6 202 D6
Tintern Av CDALE/KGS NW9 44 D6
Tintern Cl PUT/ROE SW15 139 H6
WIM/MER SW19 178 B3
Tintern Gdns STHGT/OAK N14 34 E2
Tintern Rd CAR SM5 194 C5
WDGN N22 49 J4
Tintern St CLAP SW4 141 K5
Tintern Wy RYLN/HDSTN HA2 60 B5
Tinto Rd CAN/RD E16 106 E4
Tinworth St STHWK SE1 121 K5
Tippetts Cl ENC/FH EN2 23 J2
Tipthorpe Rd BTSEA SW11 141 F4
Tipton Dr CROY/NA CR0 212 A2
Tiptree Cl CHING E4 38 A5
Tiptree Crs CLAY IG5 54 A5
Tiptree Dr ENC/FH EN2 23 K5
Tiptree Rd RSLP HA4 77 F2
Tirlemont Rd SAND/SEL CR2 211 J5
Tirrell Rd CROY/NA CR0 196 D3
Tisbury Rd STRHM/NOR SW16 179 K5
Tisdall Pl WALW SE17 19 F7
Titan Ct BTFD TW8 117 G5
Titchborne Rw BAY/PAD W2 8 D4
Titchfield Rd CAR SM5 194 C5
STJWD NW8 2 D1
Titchfield Wk CAR SM5 194 C4
Titchwell Rd
WAND/EARL SW18 160 C2
Tite St CHEL SW3 120 E6
Tithe Barn Cl KUTN/CMB KT2 175 G4
Tithe Barn Wy NTHLT UB5 95 F1
Tithe Cl MLHL NW7 45 J4
WOT/HER KT12 188 A3
YEAD UB4 94 D4
Tithe Ct HDN NW4 * 45 J4
Tithe Farm Av
RYLN/HDSTN HA2 78 A1
Tithe Farm Cl
RYLN/HDSTN HA2 78 A1
Tithe Wk MLHL NW7 45 J4
Titian Av BUSH WD23 28 E2
Titley Cl CHING E4 51 J1
Titmus Cl UX/CGN UB8 94 A5
Titmuss Av THMD SE28 109 H6
Titmuss St SHB W12 * 118 E2
Tiverton Av CLAY IG5 54 A6
Tiverton Cl CROY/NA CR0 197 G4
Tiverton Rd ALP/SUD HA0 98 A1
EDGW HA8 44 B5
HSLW TW3 135 G3
RSLP HA4 76 E1
SEVS/STOTM N15 67 K3
UED N18 50 A1
WLSDN NW10 82 B6
Tiverton St STHWK SE1 18 C4
Tiverton Wy CHSGTN KT9 205 J3
MLHL NW7 46 B3
Tivoli Gdns WOOL/PLUM SE18 126 D4
Tivoli Rd CEND/HSY/T N8 66 D2
HSLWW TW4 134 D5
WNWD SE27 180 D1
Toad La HSLWW TW4 134 E5
Tobago St POP/IOD E14 124 D2
Tobin Cl HAMP NW3 83 J5
Toby La WCHPL E1 105 G3
Toby Wy SURB KT6 191 J6
Tokenhouse Yd LOTH EC2R 12 E3
Token Yd PUT/ROE SW15 139 H5
Tokyngton Av WBLY HA9 80 C4
Toland Sq PUT/ROE SW15 138 D6
Tolcarne Dr PIN HA5 40 E5
Toley Av KTN/HRWW/WS HA3 62 A4
Tollbridge Cl NKENS W10 100 C3
Tollesbury Gdns
BARK/HLT IG6 54 D6
Tollet St WCHPL E1 105 F3
Tollgate Dr DUL SE21 163 F4
YEAD UB4 95 H6
Tollgate Gdns
KIL/WHAMP NW6 * 100 E1
Tollgate Rd CAN/RD E16 107 G4
EHAM E6 107 J4
Tollhouse La WLGTN SM6 210 C6
Tollhouse Wy ARCH N19 66 C6
Tollington Pk FSBYPK N4 67 F6
Tollington Pl FSBYPK N4 67 F6
Tollington Rd HOLWY N7 85 F2
Tollington Wy HOLWY N7 84 E1
Tolmer's Sq CAMTN NW1 4 B6
Tolpits La WATW WD18 26 A3
Tolpuddle Av PLSTW E13 89 G6
Tolpuddle St IS N1 5 J2
Tolsford Rd HACK E8 86 D3
Tolson Rd ISLW TW7 136 B4
Tolverne Rd RYNPK SW20 177 F4
Tolworth Broadway
SURB KT6 191 H5
Tolworth Cl SURB KT6 191 J5
Tolworth Gdns CHDH RM6 73 K2
Tolworth Park Rd SURB KT6 191 G6
Tolworth Ri North
BRYLDS KT5 191 K4
Tolworth Rise North (Kingston
By-Pass) BRYLDS KT5 191 J5
Tolworth Ri South
BRYLDS KT5 191 K4
Tolworth Rd SURB KT6 191 F6
Tolworth Underpass (Kingston
By-Pass) SURB KT6 206 C1
Tom Cribb Rd THMD SE28 127 J3
WOOL/PLUM SE18 127 H3
Tom Groves Cl SRTFD E15 88 B3
Tom Hood Cl SRTFD E15 88 B3
Tom Jenkinson Rd
CAN/RD E16 125 K1
Tomlin's Gv BOW E3 105 J2
Tomlinson Cl BETH E2 7 K5
CHSWK W4 117 J5
Tomlins Orch BARK IG11 90 C6
Tomlin's Ter POP/IOD E14 105 H5
Tom Mann Cl BARK IG11 90 E6
Tom Nolan Cl SRTFD E15 106 C1
Tompion St FSBYE EC1V 6 A5
Tom Smith Cl GNWCH SE10 125 H6
Tomswood Hl BARK/HLT IG6 54 B3
Tomswood Rd CHIG IG7 54 A2
Tonbridge Crs
KTN/HRWW/WS HA3 62 A1
Tonbridge Rd
E/WMO/HCT KT8 188 D1
Tonbridge St STPAN WC1H 4 E5
Tonfield Rd CHEAM SM3 193 J5
Tonge Cl BECK BR3 198 D2
Tonsley Hl WAND/EARL SW18 140 A6
Tonsley Pl WAND/EARL SW18 140 A6
Tonsley Rd WAND/EARL SW18 140 A6
Tonsley St WAND/EARL SW18 140 A6
Tonstall Rd MTCM CR4 179 F5
Tooke Cl PIN HA5 41 J4
Tookey Cl
KTN/HRWW/WS HA3 62 B4
Took's Ct FLST/FETLN EC4A 11 J3
Tooley St STHWK SE1 19 J2
Toorack Rd
KTN/HRWW/WS HA3 42 D5
Tooting Bec Gdns
STRHM/NOR SW16 161 J6
Tooting Bec Rd TOOT SW17 161 F5
Tooting Gv TOOT SW17 178 D1
Tooting High St TOOT SW17 178 D2
Tootswood Rd HAYES BR2 199 H2
Topcliffe Dr ORP BR6 216 D2
Topham Sq TOTM N17 49 J4
Topham St CLKNW EC1R * 5 J6
Top House Ri CHING E4 38 A2
Topiary Sq RCH/KEW TW9 137 G4
Topley St ELTH/MOT SE9 146 B5
Topmast Point
POP/IOD E14 * 124 D2
Top Pk BECK BR3 199 H2
Topsfield Cl CEND/HSY/T N8 66 D2
Topsfield Pde
CEND/HSY/T N8 * 66 E2
Topsfield Rd CEND/HSY/T N8 66 E2
Topsham Rd TOOT SW17 160 E5
Torbay Rd KIL/WHAMP NW6 82 D5
RYLN/HDSTN HA2 59 J6
Torbay St CAMTN NW1 * 84 B5
Torbitt Wy GNTH/NBYPK IG2 73 F2
Torbridge Cl EDGW HA8 44 A3
Torcross Dr FSTH SE23 163 K4
Torcross Rd RSLP HA4 77 F1
Tor Gdns KENS W8 119 K2
Tor Gv THMD SE28 127 K1
Tormead Cl SUT SM1 208 E4
Tormount Rd
WOOL/PLUM SE18 127 K6
Toronto Av MNPK E12 89 K2
Toronto Rd IL IG1 72 B5
Torquay Gdns REDBR IG4 71 H1
Torquay St BAY/PAD W2 101 F4
Torrens Rd BRXS/STRHM SW2 142 A6
SRTFD E15 88 D4
Torrens Sq SRTFD E15 88 D4
Torrens St FSBYE EC1V 6 A3
Torres Sq POP/IOD E14 124 D5
Torrey Dr BRXN/ST SW9 142 B3
Torriano Av KTTN NW5 84 D3
Torriano Cots KTTN NW5 84 D3
Torriano Ms KTTN NW5 84 C3
Torridge Gdns PECK SE15 143 K5
Torridge Rd THHTH CR7 196 C2
Torridon Rd CAT SE6 165 G3
Torrington Av
NFNCH/WDSPK N12 47 H1
Torrington Cl ESH/CLAY KT10 204 E4
Torrington Dr
RYLN/HDSTN HA2 78 B2
Torrington Gdns
FBAR/BDGN N11 48 C2
GFD/PVL UB6 79 J6
Torrington Gv
NFNCH/WDSPK N12 47 J1
Torrington Pk
NFNCH/WDSPK N12 33 H6
Torrington Pl FITZ W1T 10 B1
GWRST WC1E 4 C7
WAP E1W 123 H1
Torrington Rd BCTR RM8 74 B5
ESH/CLAY KT10 204 E4
GFD/PVL UB6 79 J6
RSLP HA4 76 E1
Torrington Sq CROY/NA CR0 * 196 E4
STPAN WC1H 4 D7
Torrington Wy MRDN SM4 193 K4
Tor Rd WELL DA16 148 D2
Torr Rd PGE/AN SE20 182 A3
Torver Rd HRW HA1 60 E1
Torver Wy ORP BR6 216 D1
Torwood Rd PUT/ROE SW15 138 D6
Tothill St STJSPK SW1H 16 C3
Totnes Rd WELL DA16 148 C1
Totnes Vls FBAR/BDGN N11 * 48 C1
Totnes Wk EFNCH N2 65 H1
Tottan Ter WCHPL E1 * 105 F5
Tottenhall Rd PLMGR N13 49 G2
Tottenham Court Rd
FITZ W1T 4 B7
Tottenham Gn East
SEVS/STOTM N15 68 B1
Tottenham Green East South
Side SEVS/STOTM N15 68 B1
Tottenham La
CEND/HSY/T N8 66 E2
Tottenham Ms FITZ W1T * 10 B1
Tottenham Rd IS N1 86 A4
Tottenham St FITZ W1T 10 B2
Totterdown St TOOT SW17 160 E6
Totteridge Common
TRDG/WHET N20 31 J4
Totteridge La
TRDG/WHET N20 32 E4
Totteridge Village
TRDG/WHET N20 32 C3
Totternhoe Cl
KTN/HRWW/WS HA3 61 J2
Totton Rd THHTH CR7 180 B6
Toucan Cl WLSDN NW10 98 C2
Toulmin St STHWK SE1 18 C3
Toulon St CMBW SE5 142 D1
Tournay Rd FUL/PGN SW6 139 J1
Toussaint Wk
BERM/RHTH SE16 123 H3
Tovil Cl PGE/AN SE20 181 H5
Towcester Rd BOW E3 105 K3
Tower Br WAP E1W 13 J7
Tower Bridge Ap TWRH EC3N 13 J7
Tower Bridge Ms
ALP/SUD HA0 79 F2
Tower Bridge Rd STHWK SE1 19 G5
Tower Blds WAP E1W * 123 J1
Tower Cl CHIG IG7 54 B2
HAMP NW3 83 H3
ORP BR6 202 A6
PGE/AN SE20 181 J3
Tower Ct LSQ/SEVD WC2H * 10 E4
Tower Gdns ESH/CLAY KT10 205 G5
Tower Gardens Rd TOTM N17 49 J4
Tower Hamlets Rd FSTGT E7 88 D2
WALTH E17 51 J6
Tower Hl TWRH EC3N 13 J6
Tower Hill Ter MON EC3R 13 H6
Tower La WBLY HA9 * 79 K1
Tower Ms CLPT E5 87 G2
WALTH E17 69 J1
Tower Mill Rd CMBW SE5 * 143 F1
Tower Pl MON EC3R 13 H6
Tower Ri RCH/KEW TW9 137 F4
Tower Rd BELV DA17 129 K4
ORP BR6 202 A6
TWK TW1 156 A5
WLSDN NW10 81 J5
Tower Royal MANHO EC4N * 12 D5
Towers Av HGDN/ICK UB10 94 A2
Towers Ct HGDN/ICK UB10 * 94 A2
Towers Pl RCH/KEW TW9 137 F6
Towers Rd PIN HA5 41 J4
STHL UB1 96 A3
Tower St LSQ/SEVD WC2H 10 E4
Tower Ter WDGN N22 49 F5
Tower Vw BUSH WD23 28 E2
CROY/NA CR0 198 B5
Towfield Rd FELT TW13 154 E4
Towncourt Crs
STMC/STPC BR5 201 H2
Towncourt La
STMC/STPC BR5 201 J3
Towncourt Pth FSBYPK N4 67 J5
Town End Pde KUT/HW KT1 * 174 E6
Towney Md NTHLT UB5 95 K1
Town Farm Wy
STWL/WRAY TW19 * 152 A2
Townfield Rd HYS/HAR UB3 113 J1
Townfield Sq HYS/HAR UB3 113 J1
Town Field Wy ISLW TW7 136 B3
Town Hall Approach Rd
SEVS/STOTM N15 68 B1
Townhall Av CHSWK W4 118 A5
Town Hall Pde
BRXS/STRHM SW2 * 142 A5
Town Hall Rd BTSEA SW11 140 E4
Townholm Crs HNWL W7 116 A3
Town La STWL/WRAY TW19 152 A1
Townley Ct SRTFD E15 88 D4
Townley Rd EDUL SE22 143 F6
Townley St WALW SE17 * 122 E5
Town Meadow BTFD TW8 136 E1
Townmead Rd FUL/PGN SW6 140 A4
RCH/KEW TW9 137 J3
Town Quay BARK IG11 90 B6
Town Rd ED N9 36 D4
Townsend Av STHGT/OAK N14 34 D6
Townsend La
CDALE/KGS NW9 63 F4
Townsend Ms
WAND/EARL SW18 160 B4
Townsend Rd
SEVS/STOTM N15 68 B2
STHL UB1 114 D1
STJWD NW8 2 D2
WOOL/PLUM SE18 127 G3
Townsend St WALW SE17 19 F7
Townsend Wy NTHWD HA6 40 D3
Townsend Yd HGT N6 66 A5
Townshend Cl SCUP DA14 186 C2
Townshend Est STJWD NW8 2 C2
Townshend Rd CHST BR7 185 G1
RCH/KEW TW9 137 G5
STJWD NW8 2 C1
Townshend Ter
RCH/KEW TW9 137 G5
Townson Av NTHLT UB5 95 F1
Townson Wy NTHLT UB5 94 E1
Town Whf ISLW TW7 * 136 C4
Towpath WOT/HER KT12 * 188 A1
Towpath Rd UED N18 51 F2
Towpath Wy CROY/NA CR0 197 G3
Towton Rd WNWD SE27 162 D4
Toynbec Cl CHST BR7 167 G6
Toynbee Rd RYNPK SW20 177 H4
Toynbee St WCHPL E1 13 J2
Toyne Wy HGT N6 65 K3
Tracey Av CRICK NW2 * 82 A3
Trade Cl PLMGR N13 35 G6
Trader Rd EHAM E6 108 B5
Tradescant Rd VX/NE SW8 141 K1
Trading Estate Rd
WLSDN NW10 * 98 E3
Trafalgar Av PECK SE15 143 G2
TOTM N17 50 A2
WPK KT4 193 G5
Trafalgar Chambers
CHEL SW3 * 120 C5
Trafalgar Gdns KENS W8 * 120 A3
WCHPL E1 105 F4
Trafalgar Gv GNWCH SE10 125 G6
Trafalgar Ms HOM E9 * 87 H4
Trafalgar Pl UED N18 50 C1
WAN E11 70 E1
Trafalgar Rd GNWCH SE10 125 H5
RAIN RM13 111 H1
WHTN TW2 155 J4
WIM/MER SW19 178 A3
Trafalgar Sq STJS SW1Y * 10 D7
Trafalgar St WALW SE17 122 E5
Trafalgar Wy CROY/NA CR0 196 A6
POP/IOD E14 106 A6
Trafford Cl BARK/HLT IG6 55 F2
Trafford Rd THHTH CR7 196 A2
Trahorn Cl WCHPL E1 104 C3
Tramway Av ED N9 36 D2
Tramway Cl PGE/AN SE20 181 K4
Tramway Pth MTCM CR4 194 D1
Tranby Ms HOM E9 87 F3
Tranley Ms HAMP NW3 * 83 J2
Tranmere Rd ED N9 36 B2
WAND/EARL SW18 160 B4
WHTN TW2 155 G2
Tranquil Pas BKHTH/KID SE3 * 145 J3
Tranquil V BKHTH/KID SE3 145 H3
Transept St CAMTN NW1 8 C2
Transmere Rd
STMC/STPC BR5 201 H3
Transom Cl BERM/RHTH SE16 124 B4
Transom Sq POP/IOD E14 124 E5
Transport Av BTFD TW8 116 B5
Tranton Rd BERM/RHTH SE16 123 H3
Traps La NWMAL KT3 176 B5
Travellers Site CHING E4 * 51 H3
Travellers Wy HSLWW TW4 134 B3
Travers Cl WALTH E17 51 F4
Travers Rd HOLWY N7 85 G1
Treacy Cl BUSH WD23 28 C4
Treadgold St NTGHL W11 100 B6
Treadway St BETH E2 104 D1
Treaty St IS N1 5 G1
Trebeck St MYFR/PICC W1J 9 J7
Trebovir Rd ECT SW5 119 K5
Treby St BOW E3 105 H3
Trecastle Wy HOLWY N7 84 D2

Tredegar Rd BOW E3 105 H1
FBAR/BDGN N11 48 D3
Tredegar Sq BOW E3 105 H2
Trederwen Rd HACK E8 86 C6
Tredown Rd SYD SE26 181 K1
Tredwell Cl HAYES BR2 200 C1
Tredwell Rd WNWD SE27 162 C6
Tree Cl RCHPK/HAM TW10 156 E3
Treen Av BARN SW13 138 B4
Tree Rd CAN/RD E16 107 G5
Treeside Cl WDR/YW UB7 112 A4
Tree Top Ms DAGE RM10 93 F4
Treetops Cl ABYW SE2 129 F5
NTHWD HA6 40 B1
Treetops Vw LOU IG10 39 H1
Tree View Cl NRWD SE19 181 F4
Treewall Gdns BMLY BR1 166 A6
Trefgarne Rd DAGE RM10 74 C6
Trefoil Rd WAND/EARL SW18 140 B6
Tregaron Av CEND/HSY/T N8 66 E4
Tregaron Gdns NWMAL KT3 192 B1
Tregarvon Rd BTSEA SW11 141 F5
Tregenna Av
RYLN/HDSTN HA2 78 A2
Tregenna Cl STHGT/OAK N14 22 C6
Tregony Rd ORP BR6 217 F2
Trego Rd HOM E9 87 J5
Tregothnan Rd BRXN/ST SW9 141 K4
Tregunter Rd WBPTN SW10 120 B6
Trehearn Rd BARK/HLT IG6 54 D3
Treherne Ct BRXN/ST SW9 * 142 C2
Trehern Rd MORT/ESHN SW14 138 A4
Trehurst St CLPT E5 87 G3
Trelawney Est HOM E9 * 86 E4
Trelawney Rd BARK/HLT IG6 54 D3
Trelawn Rd BRXS/STRHM SW2 142 B6
LEY E10 88 A1
Trelawny Cl WALTH E17 69 K1
Trellis Sq BOW E3 105 H2
Treloar Gdns NRWD SE19 180 E2
Trelwney Est HOM E9 * 86 E4
Tremadoc Rd CLAP SW4 141 J5
Tremaine Cl BROCKY SE4 144 D3
Tremaine Rd PGE/AN SE20 181 J5
Trematon Pl TEDD TW11 174 D3
Tremlett Gv ARCH N19 84 C1
Tremlett Ms ARCH N19 * 84 C1
Trenance Gdns
GDMY/SEVK IG3 91 G1
Trenchard Av RSLP HA4 77 F3
Trenchard Cl CDALE/KGS NW9 45 G4
STAN HA7 43 H2
Trenchard St GNWCH SE10 125 G5
Trenchold St VX/NE SW8 * 121 K6
Trenear Cl ORP BR6 217 G2
Trenholme Rd PGE/AN SE20 181 J3
Trenholme Ter PGE/AN SE20 181 J3
Trenmar Gdns WLSDN NW10 99 K2
Trent Av EA W5 116 D3
Trentbridge Cl BARK/HLT IG6 55 F2
Trent Ct WAN E11 70 E2
Trent Gdns STHGT/OAK N14 34 B1
Trentham Dr STMC/STPC BR5 202 B1
Trentham St
WAND/EARL SW18 159 K3
Trent Pk EBAR EN4 * 22 C3
Trent Rd BKHH IG9 39 F3
BRXS/STRHM SW2 142 A6
Trent Wy WPK KT4 208 A1
YEAD UB4 94 C2
Trentwood Side ENC/FH EN2 23 F4
Treport St WAND/EARL SW18 160 A2
Tresco Cl BMLY BR1 183 H2
Trescoe Gdns CRW RM5 56 E1
RYLN/HDSTN HA2 59 J4
Tresco Gdns GDMY/SEVK IG3 73 F6
Tresco Rd PECK SE15 143 J5
Tresham Crs STJWD NW8 2 C6
Tresham Rd BARK IG11 91 F5
Tresilian Av WCHMH N21 23 F6
Tressell Cl IS N1 85 H5
Tressillian Crs BROCKY SE4 144 D4
Tressillian Rd BROCKY SE4 144 D4
Trestis Cl YEAD UB4 95 H3
Treswell Rd DAGW RM9 92 A6
Tretawn Gdns MLHL NW7 31 G6
Tretawn Pk MLHL NW7 31 G6
Trevanion Rd WKENS W14 * 119 H5
Treve Av HRW HA1 60 C4
Trevelyan Av MNPK E12 89 K2
Trevelyan Crs
KTN/HRWW/WS HA3 61 K4
Trevelyan Gdns
WLSDN NW10 * 82 A6
Trevelyan Rd SRTFD E15 88 C2
TOOT SW17 178 E2
Treveris St STHWK SE1 18 B1
Treverton St NKENS W10 100 B3
Treves Cl WCHMH N21 23 F6
Treville St PUT/ROE SW15 158 E2
Treviso Rd FSTH SE23 164 A4
Trevithick Cl
EBED/NFELT TW14 153 J3
Trevithick St DEPT SE8 124 D6
Trevone Gdns PIN HA5 59 J3
Trevor Cl EBAR EN4 33 H1
ISLW TW7 136 A6
KTN/HRWW/WS HA3 43 F3
NTHLT UB5 95 G1
Trevor Crs RSLP HA4 76 D2
Trevor Gdns EDGW HA8 45 F4
Trevor Pl SKENS SW7 14 D3
Trevor Rd EDGW HA8 45 F4
HYS/HAR UB3 113 H2
WFD IG8 52 E3
WIM/MER SW19 177 H3
Trevor Sq SKENS SW7 14 D3
Trevor St SKENS SW7 14 D3
Trevose Rd WALTH E17 52 B4
Trevose Wy OXHEY WD19 27 G5
Trewenna Dr CHSGTN KT9 205 K3
Trewince Rd RYNPK SW20 177 F4
Trewint St WAND/EARL SW18 160 B4
Trewsbury Rd SYD SE26 182 A1
Triandra Wy YEAD UB4 95 H4
Triangle Est LBTH SE11 * 122 A5
Triangle Pas EBAR EN4 * 21 G5
Triangle Pl CLAP SW4 141 J5
Triangle Rd HACK E8 86 D6
The Triangle BFN/LL DA15 * 168 B2
HACK E8 86 D6
KUT/HW KT1 175 K5
Triangle Wy ACT W3 117 H3
Trident Pl CHEL SW3 * 120 C6
Trident St BERM/RHTH SE16 124 A4
Trident Wy NWDGN UB2 114 A3
Trigon Rd VX/NE SW8 142 A1
Trilby Rd FSTH SE23 164 A4
Trim St NWCR SE14 124 C6
Trinder Rd ARCH N19 66 E5
BAR EN5 20 A6
Tring Av EA W5 117 G1
STHL UB1 95 K5
WBLY HA9 80 C4
Tring Cl GNTH/NBYPK IG2 72 C2
Trinidad Gdns DAGE RM10 93 F5
Trinidad St POP/IOD E14 105 H6
Trinity Av EFNCH N2 47 H6
EN EN1 36 B1
Trinity Buoy Whf
POP/IOD E14 * 106 B4
Trinity Church Rd BARN SW13 118 E6
Trinity Church Sq STHWK SE1 18 D4
Trinity Cl CLAP SW4 * 141 H5
HACK E8 * 86 B4
HAYES BR2 200 D5
HSLWW TW4 134 D5
LEW SE13 145 G5
NTHWD HA6 40 C2
SAND/SEL CR2 212 A6
WAN E11 70 C6
Trinity Ct ELTH/MOT SE9 167 G1
Trinity Crs TOOT SW17 160 E4
Trinity Dr UX/CGN UB8 94 A5
Trinity Est DEPT SE8 124 C5
Trinity Gdns BRXN/ST SW9 142 A5
CAN/RD E16 106 D4
Trinity Gn WCHPL E1 * 104 E4
Trinity Gv GNWCH SE10 145 F2
Trinity Ms PGE/AN SE20 181 J5
Trinity Pde HSLW TW3 * 135 G4
Trinity Pk CHING E4 * 51 H2
Trinity Ri BRXS/STRHM SW2 162 C2
Trinity Rd BARK/HLT IG6 54 C6
EFNCH N2 47 H6
RCH/KEW TW9 * 137 G4
STHL UB1 114 D1
WAND/EARL SW18 160 C1
WDGN N22 48 E3
WIM/MER SW19 177 K2
Trinity Sq TWRH EC3N 13 H6
Trinity St CAN/RD E16 106 D4
ENC/FH EN2 23 J3
STHWK SE1 18 D3
Trinity Wy ACT W3 99 G6
CHING E4 51 H2
Trio Pl STHWK SE1 18 D3
Tristan Sq BKHTH/KID SE3 145 H4
Tristram Cl WALTH E17 52 B6
Tristram Dr ED N9 36 B5
Tristram Rd BMLY BR1 165 J6
Tritton Av CROY/NA CR0 210 E2
Tritton Rd DUL SE21 162 E5
Triumph Cl HYS/HAR UB3 133 F2
Triumph Rd EHAM E6 107 K5
Trojan Wy CROY/NA CR0 211 F1
Troon Cl BERM/RHTH SE16 * 123 J5
THMD SE28 109 K5
Troon St WCHPL E1 105 G5
Trosley Rd BELV DA17 129 H6
Trossachs Rd EDUL SE22 143 F6
Trothy Rd STHWK SE1 123 H4
Trott Rd MUSWH N10 48 A3
Trott St BTSEA SW11 140 C2
Trotwood CHIG IG7 54 D1
Troughton Rd CHARL SE7 126 A5
Troutbeck Rd NWCR SE14 144 B2
Trout Rd WDR/YW UB7 112 A2
Trouville Rd CLAP SW4 161 H1
Trowbridge Rd HOM E9 87 H4
Trowlock Av TEDD TW11 174 D2
Trowlock Wy TEDD TW11 174 D2
Troy Ct KENS W8 119 K3
Troy Rd NRWD SE19 180 E2
Troy Town PECK SE15 143 H4
Trubshaw Rd NWDGN UB2 115 F3
Trueman Cl EDGW HA8 * 44 D3
Trulock Rd TOTM N17 50 C3
Truman's Rd STNW/STAM N16 86 A3
Trumpers Wy HNWL W7 116 A3
Trumpington Rd FSTGT E7 88 D2
Trump St CITYW EC2V 12 D4
Trundlers Wy BUSH WD23 28 E3
Trundle St STHWK SE1 18 C2
Trundley's Rd DEPT SE8 124 A5
Trundley's Ter DEPT SE8 124 A4
Truro Gdns IL IG1 71 J4
Truro Rd WALTH E17 69 H1
WDGN N22 48 E3
Truro St KTTN NW5 84 A4
Truro Wy YEAD UB4 94 C2
Trusedale Rd EHAM E6 107 K5
Truslove Rd WNWD SE27 180 B1
Trussley Rd HMSMTH W6 119 F3
Trustons Gdns EMPK RM11 75 J4
Tryfan Cl REDBR IG4 71 H2
Tryon Crs HOM E9 86 E6
Tryon St CHEL SW3 120 E5
Trystings Cl ESH/CLAY KT10 205 G4
Tuam Rd WOOL/PLUM SE18 127 J6
Tubbenden Cl ORP BR6 201 K6
Tubbenden Dr ORP BR6 216 D2
Tubbenden La ORP BR6 216 D2
Tubbenden La South
ORP BR6 216 D3
Tubbs Rd WLSDN NW10 99 H1
Tuck Rd RAIN RM13 93 J4
Tudor Av GPK RM2 57 J6
HPTN TW12 173 F2
WPK KT4 207 K1
Tudor Cl ASHF TW15 152 A6
BRXS/STRHM SW2 * 162 A1
CDALE/KGS NW9 62 E6
CHEAM SM3 208 B3
CHSGTN KT9 206 A3
CHST BR7 184 E4
HAMP NW3 83 J3
HGT N6 66 C4
HPTN TW12 173 H1
MLHL NW7 45 J2
PIN HA5 58 E2
WFD IG8 53 F1
WLGTN SM6 210 C5
Tudor Ct ELTH/MOT SE9 * 146 D5
SWLY BR8 203 K4
WALTH E17 69 H4
Tudor Ct North WBLY HA9 80 C3
Tudor Ct South WBLY HA9 80 C3
Tudor Crs BARK/HLT IG6 54 C2
ENC/FH EN2 23 J2
Tudor Dr GPK RM2 75 J1
KUTN/CMB KT2 175 F1
MRDN SM4 193 G3
WOT/HER KT12 188 C5
Tudor Est WLSDN NW10 * 98 D1
Tudor Gdns ACT W3 98 C5
BARN SW13 138 B4
CDALE/KGS NW9 62 E6
GPK RM2 75 J1
TWK TW1 156 A3
WWKM BR4 214 A1
Tudor Gv HOM E9 86 E5
Tudor Ms WLSDN NW10 81 J4
Tudor Pde ELTH/MOT SE9 * 146 D5
Tudor Pl MTCM CR4 178 D3
NRWD SE19 * 181 G3
Tudor Rd BAR EN5 20 E4
BARK IG11 91 F5
BECK BR3 183 F6
CHING E4 51 K2
ED N9 36 D2
HACK E8 86 D6
HPTN TW12 173 F3
HSLW TW3 135 J5
HYS/HAR UB3 94 B5
KTN/HRWW/WS HA3 42 D5
KUTN/CMB KT2 175 H3
NRWD SE19 181 G3
PIN HA5 41 G5
PLSTW E13 89 G6
SNWD SE25 197 J2
STHL UB1 95 J6
Tudor Sq HYS/HAR UB3 94 B4
Tudor St EMB EC4Y 11 K5
Tudor Wy ACT W3 117 H2
STHGT/OAK N14 34 D3
STMC/STPC BR5 201 J3
Tudor Well Cl STAN HA7 43 H1
Tudway Rd BKHTH/KID SE3 146 B5
Tufnell Park Rd HOLWY N7 84 D2
Tufter Rd CHIG IG7 55 F1
Tufton Gdns E/WMO/HCT KT8 173 G5
Tufton Rd CHING E4 37 J6
Tufton St WEST SW1P 16 E5
Tugboat St THMD SE28 127 K2
Tugela Rd CROY/NA CR0 196 E3
Tugela St CAT SE6 164 C4
Tugmutton Cl ORP BR6 216 B2
Tulip Cl CROY/NA CR0 198 A5
EHAM E6 107 J4
HPTN TW12 172 E2
NWDGN UB2 115 H2
Tulip Gdns CHING E4 * 38 B5
IL IG1 90 B4
Tulip Wy WDR/YW UB7 112 A4
Tull St CAR SM5 194 E4
Tulse Cl BECK BR3 183 F6
Tulse Hl BRXS/STRHM SW2 162 B2
Tulsemere Rd WNWD SE27 162 D4
Tummons Gdns SNWD SE25 181 F5
Tuncombe Rd UED N18 36 A6
Tunis Rd SHB W12 119 F1
Tunley Gn POP/IOD E14 105 H4
Tunley Rd TOOT SW17 161 F4
WLSDN NW10 81 G6
Tunmarsh La PLSTW E13 107 F2
Tunnan Leys EHAM E6 108 A5
Tunnel Av GNWCH SE10 125 G2
Tunnel Gdns FBAR/BDGN N11 48 C3
Tunnel Link Rd HTHAIR TW6 132 D6
Tunnel Rd BERM/RHTH SE16 123 K2
Tunnel Rd East WDR/YW UB7 132 E1
Tunnel Rd West WDR/YW UB7 132 D2
Tunstall Av BARK/HLT IG6 55 G2
Tunstall Cl ORP BR6 216 E2
Tunstall Rd BRXN/ST SW9 142 A5
CROY/NA CR0 197 F5
Tunstock Wy BELV DA17 129 F3
Tunworth Cl CDALE/KGS NW9 62 E3
Tunworth Crs PUT/ROE SW15 158 C1
Tupelo Rd LEY E10 69 K6
Tuppy St THMD SE28 127 H3
Turene Cl WAND/EARL SW18 140 B5
Turin Rd ED N9 36 E2
Turin St BETH E2 104 C2
Turkey Oak Cl NRWD SE19 181 F4
Turks Rw CHEL SW3 120 E5
Turle Rd FSBYPK N4 * 67 F6
STRHM/NOR SW16 179 K5
Turlewray Cl FSBYPK N4 67 F5
Turley Cl SRTFD E15 88 C6
Turnagain La
FLST/FETLN EC4A * 12 A3
Turnage Rd BCTR RM8 74 A5
Turnant Rd TOTM N17 49 J4
Turnberry Cl
BERM/RHTH SE16 * 123 J5
HDN NW4 46 B5
Turnberry Ct OXHEY WD19 * 27 G5
Turnberry Wy ORP BR6 201 J5
Turnbury Cl THMD SE28 109 K5
Turnchapel Ms CLAP SW4 141 G4
Turner Av MTCM CR4 178 E4
SEVS/STOTM N15 68 A1
WHTN TW2 155 H5
Turner Cl ALP/SUD HA0 79 K3
BRXN/ST SW9 142 C2
GLDGN NW11 65 F3
Turner Ct CMBW SE5 * 142 E5
Turner Crs THHTH CR7 196 D3
Turner Dr GLDGN NW11 65 F3
Turner Ms BELMT SM2 209 F5
Turner Rd EDGW HA8 44 A5
NWMAL KT3 192 A4
WALTH E17 70 A1
Turners Cl TRDG/WHET N20 33 K5
Turners Meadow Wy
BECK BR3 182 C4
Turner's Rd BOW E3 105 H4
Turner St CAN/RD E16 106 D5
WCHPL E1 104 D4
Turners Wy CROY/NA CR0 196 B6
Turner's Wd GLDGN NW11 65 G5
Turneville Rd WKENS W14 119 J6
Turney Rd DUL SE21 162 D2
Turnham Green Ter
CHSWK W4 118 B4
Turnham Rd BROCKY SE4 144 B6
Turnmill St FARR EC1M 5 K7
Turnpike Cl DEPT SE8 144 C1
Turnpike Dr ORP BR6 217 J6
Turnpike La CEND/HSY/T N8 67 G1
SUT SM1 209 G3
Turnpike Link CROY/NA CR0 197 F6
Turnpike Ms
CEND/HSY/T N8 * 49 G6
Turnpike Pde
SEVS/STOTM N15 * 49 H6
Turnpike Wy ISLW TW7 136 B2
Turnstone Cl
CDALE/KGS NW9 * 45 G5
PLSTW E13 106 E2
Turnstone Ter WEA W13 * 97 F3
Turpentine La PIM SW1V 121 G5
Turpin Av CRW RM5 56 C3
Turpin Cl WAP E1W 105 F6
Turpington Cl HAYES BR2 200 D3
Turpington La HAYES BR2 200 D2
Turpin La ERITH DA8 130 D6
Turpin Rd EBED/NFELT TW14 153 J1
Turpin's La WFD IG8 53 K1
Turpins Yd CRICK NW2 * 63 K6
GNWCH SE10 145 F1
Turpin Wy WLGTN SM6 210 B5
Turquand St WALW SE17 18 D7
Turret Gv CLAP SW4 141 H4
Turton Rd ALP/SUD HA0 80 A3
Turville St BETH E2 7 J6
Tuscan Rd WOOL/PLUM SE18 127 J5
Tuskar St GNWCH SE10 125 H5
Tweeddale Gv
HGDN/ICK UB10 76 A1
Tweeddale Rd CAR SM5 194 C5
Tweedmouth Rd PLSTW E13 107 F1
Tweed Wy ROM RM1 57 F3
Tweedy Rd BMLY BR1 183 K4
Twelvetrees Crs BOW E3 106 A3
Twentyman Cl WFD IG8 52 E1
Twickenham Br TWK TW1 136 D6
Twickenham Cl CROY/NA CR0 211 F1
Twickenham Gdns
GFD/PVL UB6 79 G3
KTN/HRWW/WS HA3 42 E3
Twickenham Rd FELT TW13 154 D6
ISLW TW7 136 A5
TEDD TW11 156 B6
WAN E11 70 B6
Twig Folly Cl BETH E2 105 F1
Twig Folly Whf BETH E2 * 105 F1
Twigg Cl ERITH DA8 150 B1
Twilley St WAND/EARL SW18 160 A2
Twine Cl BARK IG11 109 H2
Twine Ct WCHPL E1 104 E6
Twineham Gn
NFNCH/WDSPK N12 32 E6
Twine Ter BOW E3 * 105 H3
Twining Av WHTN TW2 155 H5
Twinn Rd MLHL NW7 46 C2
Twin Tumps Wy THMD SE28 109 G6
Twisden Rd KTTN NW5 84 B2
Twybridge Wy WLSDN NW10 80 E5
Twycross Ms GNWCH SE10 125 H4
Twyford Abbey Rd
WLSDN NW10 98 B2
Twyford Av ACT W3 98 C6
EFNCH N2 47 K6
Twyford Crs ACT W3 117 H1
Twyford Rd CAR SM5 194 C5
IL IG1 90 C3
RYLN/HDSTN HA2 60 B4
Twyford St IS N1 85 F6
Tyas Rd CAN/RD E16 106 D3
Tybenham Rd
WIM/MER SW19 177 K6
Tyberry Rd PEND EN3 24 D4
Tyburn La HRW HA1 60 E4
Tyburn Wy MBLAR W1H 9 F5
Tye La ORP BR6 216 C3
Tyers Ga STHWK SE1 19 G3
Tyers St LBTH SE11 122 A5
Tyers Ter LBTH SE11 122 A5
Tyeshurst Cl ABYW SE2 129 F5
Tylecroft Rd
STRHM/NOR SW16 179 K5
Tylehurst Gdns IL IG1 90 C3
Tyler Cl BETH E2 7 J2
Tylers Ga KTN/HRWW/WS HA3 62 A3
Tylers Green Rd SWLY BR8 203 K3
Tyler St GNWCH SE10 125 H5
Tylney Av NRWD SE19 181 G1
Tylney Cl CHIG IG7 55 F1
Tylney Rd BMLY BR1 184 C5
FSTGT E7 89 G2
Tynan Cl EBED/NFELT TW14 153 K3
Tyndale La IS N1 85 H5
Tyndale Ter IS N1 85 H5
Tyndall Rd LEY E10 70 A6
WELL DA16 148 A4
Tyneham Cl BTSEA SW11 * 141 F4
Tyneham Rd BTSEA SW11 141 F3
Tynemouth Cl EHAM E6 108 B5
Tynemouth Dr EN EN1 24 C1
Tynemouth Rd MTCM CR4 179 F3
SEVS/STOTM N15 68 B1
WOOL/PLUM SE18 127 K5
Tynemouth St FUL/PGN SW6 140 B3
Tynemouth Ter
SEVS/STOTM N15 * 68 B1
Tyne St WCHPL E1 13 K3
Tynsdale Rd WLSDN NW10 81 G5
Type St BETH E2 105 F1
Tyrawley Rd FUL/PGN SW6 140 A2
Tyre La CDALE/KGS NW9 * 63 G1
Tyrell Cl HRW HA1 78 E2
Tyrone Rd EHAM E6 107 K1
Tyron Wy SCUP DA14 167 K6
Tyrrell Av WELL DA16 148 B6
Tyrrell Rd EDUL SE22 143 H5
Tyrrel Wy CDALE/KGS NW9 63 H4
Tyrwhitt Rd BROCKY SE4 144 D4
Tysoe St FSBYW WC1X 5 J5
Tyson Gdns FSTH SE23 * 163 K2
Tyson Rd FSTH SE23 163 K2
Tyssen Rd STNW/STAM N16 * 86 B1
Tyssen St HACK E8 86 B4
IS N1 7 H2
Tytherton Rd ARCH N19 84 D1

U

Uamvar St POP/IOD E14 105 K4
Uckfield Gv MTCM CR4 179 F4
Udall Gdns CRW RM5 56 C2
Udall St WEST SW1P 16 B7
Udney Park Rd TEDD TW11 174 B1
Uffington Rd WLSDN NW10 81 J6
WNWD SE27 162 B6
Ufford Cl KTN/HRWW/WS HA3 42 B3
Ufford Rd
KTN/HRWW/WS HA3 42 B3
Ufford St STHWK SE1 17 K2
Ufton Rd IS N1 86 A5
Uhura Sq STNW/STAM N16 * 86 A1
Ullathorne Rd
STRHM/NOR SW16 161 H6
Ulleswater Rd
STHGT/OAK N14 34 E6
Ulleswater Vls
STHGT/OAK N14 * 34 E6
Ullin St POP/IOD E14 106 A4
Ullswater Cl BMLY BR1 183 H2
PUT/ROE SW15 * 158 A6
YEAD UB4 94 C1
Ullswater Ct
RYLN/HDSTN HA2 * 60 A4
Ullswater Crs PUT/ROE SW15 158 A6
Ullswater Rd BARN SW13 138 D1
WNWD SE27 162 C5
Ullswater Wy HCH RM12 93 J3
Ulster Gdns PLMGR N13 35 J6
Ulster Pl CAMTN NW1 3 J7
Ulundi Rd BKHTH/KID SE3 125 H6
Ulva Rd PUT/ROE SW15 139 G5
Ulverscroft Rd EDUL SE22 143 H6
Ulverston Rd WALTH E17 52 B5
Ulysses Rd KIL/WHAMP NW6 82 D3
Umberston St WCHPL E1 * 104 C5
Umbria St PUT/ROE SW15 158 D1
Umfreville Rd FSBYPK N4 67 H3
Undercliff Rd LEW SE13 144 D4
Underhill BAR EN5 20 E6
Underhill Ct BAR EN5 * 20 E6
Underhill Rd EDUL SE22 143 H6
Underhill St CAMTN NW1 3 K1
Underne Av STHGT/OAK N14 34 B4
Undershaft HDTCH EC3A 13 G4
Undershaw Rd BMLY BR1 165 H5
Underwood CROY/NA CR0 214 A4
Underwood Rd CHING E4 51 K1
WCHPL E1 104 C3
WFD IG8 53 H3
Underwood Rw IS N1 6 D4
Underwood St IS N1 6 D4
The Underwood
ELTH/MOT SE9 166 E4
Undine Rd POP/IOD E14 124 E4
Undine St TOOT SW17 178 E1
Uneeda Dr GFD/PVL UB6 78 D6
Union Cl WAN E11 88 B2
Union Ct CLAP SW4 141 K3
OBST EC2N 13 G3
Union Dr WCHPL E1 * 105 G3
Union Gv VX/NE SW8 141 J3
Union Pk GNWCH SE10 125 J5
Union Rd ALP/SUD HA0 80 A4
CLAP SW4 141 J
CROY/NA CR0 196 D
FBAR/BDGN N11 48 D
HAYES BR2 200 C
NTHLT UB5 96 A
Union Sq IS N1 6 C
Union St BAR EN5 20 C
KUT/HW KT1 174 E
STHWK SE1 18 B
Union Wk BETH E2 7 J
Unity Cl CROY/NA CR0 213 K
NRWD SE19 180 D
WLSDN NW10 81 J
Unity Ms CAMTN NW1 4 C
Unity Wy WOOL/PLUM SE18 126 C
University Cl MLHL NW7 45 H
University Gdns BXLY DA5 169 C
University Rd
WIM/MER SW19 178 C
University St FITZ W1T 4 E
University Wy CAN/RD E16 108
Unwin Av EBED/NFELT TW14 133 C
Unwin Cl PECK SE15 123 H
Unwin Rd ISLW TW7 135 H
SKENS SW7 14
Upbrook Ms BAY/PAD W2 101
Upcerne Rd WBPTN SW10 140
Upcroft Av EDGW HA8 44
Updale Rd SCUP DA14 168
Upfield CROY/NA CR0 197
Upfield Rd HNWL W7 97
Uphall Rd IL IG1 90
Upham Park Rd CHSWK W4 118
Uphill Dr CDALE/KGS NW9 62
MLHL NW7 45
Uphill Gv MLHL NW7 31
Uphill Rd MLHL NW7 31
Upland Rd BELMT SM2 209
EDUL SE22 163
PLSTW E13 106
SAND/SEL CR2 211
Uplands BECK BR3 182
Uplands Cl MORT/ESHN SW14 137
WOOL/PLUM SE18 127
Uplands Park Rd ENC/FH EN2 23
Uplands Rd CEND/HSY/T N8 67
CHDH RM6 55
EBAR EN4 34
ORP BR6 202
WFD IG8 53
The Uplands RSLP HA4 58
Uplands Wy WCHMH N21 23

Upminster Rd South
RAIN RM13 111 J3
Upney La BARK IG11 91 F5
Upnor Wy WALW SE17 123 F5
Uppark Dr GNTH/NBYPK IG2 72 C3
Upper Abbey Rd BELV DA17 129 G4
Upper Addison Gdns
WKENS W14 119 H2
Upper Bank St POP/IOD E14 124 E1
Upper Bardsey Wk IS N1 * 85 J4
Upper Belgrave St
KTBR SW1X 15 H4
Upper Berenger Wk
WBPTN SW10 * 140 C1
Upper Berkeley St
MBLAR W1H 8 E4
Upper Beulah Hl NRWD SE19 181 F4
Upper Blantyre Wk
WBPTN SW10 * 140 C1
Upper Brighton Rd SURB KT6 190 E3
Upper Brockley Rd
BROCKY SE4 144 C3
Upper Brook St
MYFR/PKLN W1K 9 G5
Upper Butts BTFD TW8 116 D6
Upper Caldy Wk IS N1 * 85 J4
Upper Camelford Wk
NTGHL W11 * 100 C5
Upper Cavendish Av
FNCH N3 46 E6
Upper Cheyne Rw CHEL SW3 120 D6
Upper Clapton Rd CLPT E5 68 D6
Upper Clarendon Wk
NTGHL W11 * 100 C5
Upper Dartrey Wk
WBPTN SW10 * 140 B1
Upper Dengie Wk IS N1 * 85 J6
Upper Elmers End Rd
BECK BR3 198 B1
Upper Farm Rd
E/WMO/HCT KT8 188 E1
Upper Gn East MTCM CR4 178 E5
Upper Gn West MTCM CR4 178 E5
Upper Grosvenor St
MYFR/PKLN W1K 9 G6
Upper Grotto Rd TWK TW1 156 A4
Upper Gnd STHWK SE1 11 J7
Upper Gv SNWD SE25 197 F1
Upper Grove Rd BELV DA17 129 G6
Upper Gulland Wk IS N1 * 85 J4
Upper Ham Rd
RCHPK/HAM TW10 156 E6
Upper Handa Wk IS N1 * 85 K4
Upper Harley St CAMTN NW1 3 H7
Upper Hawkwell Wk IS N1 * 85 J6
Upper Hitch OXHEY WD19 27 J3
Upper Holly Hill Rd
BELV DA17 129 J5
Upper John St
SOHO/CST W1F 10 B5
Upper Lismore Wk IS N1 * 85 J4
Upper Ldg KENS W8 * 120 A1
Upper Ml HMSMTH W6 118 D5
Upper Marsh STHWK SE1 17 H4
Upper Montagu St
MBLAR W1H 8 E1
Upper Mulgrave Rd
BELMT SM2 208 C5
Upper North St POP/IOD E14 105 J4
Upper Paddock Rd
OXHEY WD19 27 J1
Upper Park Rd BELV DA17 129 J4
BMLY BR1 184 A4
FBAR/BDGN N11 48 B1
HAMP NW3 83 K4
KUTN/CMB KT2 175 H2
Upper Phillimore Gdns
KENS W8 * 119 K2
Upper Rainham Rd
HCH RM12 93 H2
Upper Ramsey Wk IS N1 85 K4
Upper Rawreth Wk IS N1 * 85 J6
Upper Richmond Rd
PUT/ROE SW15 138 E5
Upper Richmond Rd West
RCHPK/HAM TW10 137 H5
Upper Rd PLSTW E13 106 E2
WLGTN SM6 210 D3
Upper St Martin's La
LSQ/SEVD WC2H 10 E4
Upper Selsdon Rd
SAND/SEL CR2 212 B6
Upper Sheppey Wk IS N1 85 J4
Upper Sheridan Rd
BELV DA17 129 H4
Upper Shirley Rd
CROY/NA CR0 212 E1
Upper Sq ISLW TW7 136 B4
Upper St IS N1 5 K2
Upper Sunbury Rd
HPTN TW12 172 E4
Upper Sutton La HEST TW5 135 F2
Upper Tachbrook St
PIM SW1V 16 A6
Upper Tail OXHEY WD19 27 J5
Upper Talbot Wk
NTGHL W11 * 100 C5
Upper Teddington Rd
KUT/HW KT1 174 D4
Upper Ter HAMP NW3 83 G1
Upper Thames St BLKFR EC4V 12 C5
Upper Tollington Pk
FSBYPK N4 67 G5
Upperton Rd SCUP DA14 186 A1
Upperton Rd East PLSTW E13 107 G2
Upperton Rd West
PLSTW E13 107 G2
Upper Tooting Pk TOOT SW17 160 E4
Upper Tooting Rd
TOOT SW17 160 E6
Upper Town Rd STHL UB1 96 B3
Upper Tulse Hl
BRXS/STRHM SW2 162 A2
Upper Vernon Rd SUT SM1 209 H3
Upper Walthamstow Rd
WALTH E17 70 B1
Upper Whistler Wk
WBPTN SW10 * 140 B1
Upper Wickham La
WELL DA16 148 C3
Upper Wimpole St
CAVSQ/HST W1G 9 H1
Upper Woburn Pl
STPAN WC1H 4 D6
Uppingham Av STAN HA7 43 J6
Upsdell Av PLMGR N13 49 G2
Upstall St CMBW SE5 142 C2
Upton Av FSTGT E7 88 E5
Upton Cl BXLY DA5 169 G1
CRICK NW2 82 C1
Upton Dene BELMT SM2 209 F5
Upton Gdns
KTN/HRWW/WS HA3 61 J3
Upton La FSTGT E7 89 F4
Upton Lodge Cl BUSH WD23 80 B5
Upton Park Rd FSTGT E7 89 F5
Upton Rd HSLW TW3 135 F4
THHTH CR7 180 E5
UED N18 50 C1
WOOL/PLUM SE18 127 H6
Upton Rd South BXLY DA5 169 G1
Upway NFNCH/WDSPK N12 47 J3
Upwood Rd
STRHM/NOR SW16 179 K4
Urban Ms FSBYPK N4 67 H4
Urlwin St CMBW SE5 122 D6
Urlwin Wk BRXN/ST SW9 142 B2
Urmston Dr WIM/MER SW19 159 H3
Ursula Ms FSBYPK N4 67 H5
Ursula St BTSEA SW11 140 D2
Urswick Gdns DAGW RM9 92 A5
Urswick Rd CLPT E5 86 E3
DAGW RM9 92 A5
Usborne Ms VX/NE SW8 142 A1
Usher Rd BOW E3 105 H1
Usk Rd BTSEA SW11 140 B5
Usk St BETH E2 105 F2
Uvedale Rd DAGE RM10 92 C1
ENC/FH EN2 23 K6
Uverdale Rd WBPTN SW10 140 B1
Uxbridge Rd EA W5 98 A6
FELT TW13 154 C4
HGDN/ICK UB10 94 A3
HNWL W7 115 K1
HPTN TW12 173 G1
KUT/HW KT1 190 E1
SHB W12 118 D1
STHL UB1 115 F1
YEAD UB4 94 E5
Uxbridge Road
(Harrow Weald)
KTN/HRWW/WS HA3 42 C3
STAN HA7 43 G1
Uxbridge Road (Hatch End)
PIN HA5 41 J4
Uxbridge Road High St
STHL UB1 114 E1
Uxbridge Road (Pinner)
PIN HA5 41 H5
Uxbridge Road (Stanmore)
STAN HA7 43 F2
Uxbridge Road The Broadway
YEAD UB4 95 H6
Uxbridge St KENS W8 119 K1
Uxendon Crs WBLY HA9 62 A5
Uxendon Hl WBLY HA9 62 B5

V

Valance Av CHING E4 38 D3
Valan Leas HAYES BR2 183 H6
Vale Cl EFNCH N2 47 K6
MV/WKIL W9 101 G2
ORP BR6 216 A2
TWK TW1 * 156 B5
Vale Cots PUT/ROE SW15 * 158 B5
Vale Ct ACT W3 * 118 C1
Vale Crs PUT/ROE SW15 158 B6
Vale Cft ESH/CLAY KT10 205 F5
PIN HA5 59 J2
Vale Dr BAR EN5 20 D5
Vale End EDUL SE22 143 G5
Vale Gv ACT W3 118 C1
FSBYPK N4 67 J4
Vale La ACT W3 98 C4
Valence Av BCTR RM8 73 K5
Valence Circ BCTR RM8 91 K1
Valence Rd ERITH DA8 150 A1
Valence Wood Rd BCTR RM8 91 K1
Valencia Rd STAN HA7 29 J6
Valency Cl NTHWD HA6 26 D6
Valentia Pl BRXN/ST SW9 142 B5
Valentine Av BXLY DA5 169 F4
Valentine Pl STHWK SE1 18 A2
Valentine Rd HOM E9 * 87 F4
RYLN/HDSTN HA2 78 B1
Valentines Rd IL IG1 72 B5
Valentines Wy
ROMW/RG RM7 75 G6
Vale of Health HAMP NW3 83 G1
Valerian Wy SRTFD E15 106 C2
Vale Ri GLDGN NW11 64 D5
Vale Rd BMLY BR1 185 F5
ESH/CLAY KT10 204 E6
FSBYPK N4 67 J4
FSTGT E7 89 F4
HOR/WEW KT19 207 H2
MTCM CR4 179 J6
SUT SM1 209 F2
Vale Rw HBRY N5 85 H1
Vale Royal HOLWY N7 84 E5
Vale St DUL SE21 162 E5
Valeswood Rd BMLY BR1 183 J1
Vale Ter FSBYPK N4 67 J3
The Vale ACT W3 118 A1
CHEL SW3 120 C6
CROY/NA CR0 198 A6
EBED/NFELT TW14 154 A1
GLDGN NW11 82 B1
HEST TW5 114 D6
MUSWH N10 48 B6
RSLP HA4 77 G2
SHB W12 118 C1
STHGT/OAK N14 34 E2
WFD IG8 52 E3
Valetta Gv PLSTW E13 106 E1
Valetta Rd ACT W3 118 B2
Valette St HACK E8 * 86 D4
Valiant Cl NTHLT UB5 95 H2
ROMW/RG RM7 56 C5
Valiant Wy EHAM E6 107 K4
Vallance Rd MUSWH N10 48 C5
WCHPL E1 104 C3
Vallentin Rd WALTH E17 70 A1
Valley Av NFNCH/WDSPK N12 33 H6
Valley Cl LOU IG10 39 K1
PIN HA5 41 F5
Valley Dr CDALE/KGS NW9 62 D2
Valleyfield Rd
STRHM/NOR SW16 180 A1
Valley Fields Crs ENC/FH EN2 23 G3
Valley Gdns ALP/SUD HA0 80 B5
WIM/MER SW19 178 C3
Valley Gv CHARL SE7 126 B5
Valley Hl LOU IG10 39 J2
Valley Pk WATW WD18 26 A2
Valley Rd ERITH DA8 129 K4
HAYES BR2 183 H5
STMC/STPC BR5 186 C4
STRHM/NOR SW16 162 A6
Valley Side CHING E4 37 J3
Valley Vw BAR EN5 32 C1
Valley Wk CROY/NA CR0 197 K6
Valliere Rd WLSDN NW10 99 J2
Valliers Wood Rd
BFN/LL DA15 167 J3
Vallis Wy CHSGTN KT9 205 K2
WEA W13 97 G4
Valmar Rd CMBW SE5 142 D2
Val McKenzie Av HOLWY N7 85 G1
Valnay St TOOT SW17 178 E1
Valognes Av WALTH E17 51 G4
Valonia Gdns
WAND/EARL SW18 159 J1
Vambery Rd
WOOL/PLUM SE18 127 H6
Vanbrough Crs NTHLT UB5 95 G1
Vanbrugh Cl WOT/HER KT12 188 B4
Vanbrugh Flds
BKHTH/KID SE3 125 J6
Vanbrugh Hl GNWCH SE10 125 H5
Vanbrugh Pk BKHTH/KID SE3 145 J1
Vanbrugh Park Rd
BKHTH/KID SE3 145 J1
Vanbrugh Park Rd West
BKHTH/KID SE3 145 J1
Vanbrugh Rd CHSWK W4 118 A3
Vanbrugh Ter BKHTH/KID SE3 145 J2
Vanburgh Cl CAN/RD E16 107 H4
ORP BR6 201 K5
Vancouver Cl ORP BR6 217 G2
Vancouver Man EDGW HA8 * 44 D4
Vancouver Rd EDGW HA8 44 D4
FSTH SE23 164 B4
RCHPK/HAM TW10 156 D6
YEAD UB4 95 F3
Vanderbilt Rd
WAND/EARL SW18 160 A3
Vanderbilt Vls SHB W12 * 119 G2
Vanderville Gdns EFNCH N2 47 G5
Vandome Cl CAN/RD E16 107 F5
Vandon St STJSPK SW1H 16 B4
Van Dyck Av NWMAL KT3 192 A4
Vandyke Cl PUT/ROE SW15 159 G1
Vandyke Cross
ELTH/MOT SE9 146 D6
Vandy St SDTCH EC2A 7 G7
Vane Cl HAMP NW3 83 H3
KTN/HRWW/WS HA3 62 B3
Vanessa Cl BELV DA17 129 H5
Van Gogh Cl ISLW TW7 136 B4
Vanguard CDALE/KGS NW9 * 45 G3
Vanguard Cl CAN/RD E16 106 E4
CROY/NA CR0 196 C5
ROMW/RG RM7 56 D5
Vanguard St DEPT SE8 144 D2
Vanguard Wy CROY/NA CR0 212 B2
HTHAIR TW6 133 H3
SAND/SEL CR2 212 C3
WLGTN SM6 210 E5
Vanneck Sq PUT/ROE SW15 * 138 D6
Vanquish Cl WHTN TW2 155 F2
Vansittart Rd FSTGT E7 88 E2
Vansittart St NWCR SE14 144 B1
Vanston Pl FUL/PGN SW6 139 K1
Vantage Pl KENS W8 119 K3
Vant Rd TOOT SW17 178 E1
Varcoe Rd BERM/RHTH SE16 123 J5
Vardens Rd BTSEA SW11 140 C5
Varden St WCHPL E1 104 D5
Vardon Cl ACT W3 99 F5
Varley Dr TWK TW1 136 C5
Varley Rd CAN/RD E16 107 F5
Varley Wy MTCM CR4 178 C5
Varna Rd FUL/PGN SW6 139 H1
HPTN TW12 * 173 G4
Varndell St CAMTN NW1 4 A4
Varsity Dr TWK TW1 135 K6
Varsity Rw MORT/ESHN SW14 137 K3
Vartry Rd SEVS/STOTM N15 68 A3
Vassall Rd BRXN/ST SW9 142 B1
Vauban Est BERM/RHTH SE16 19 K5
Vauban St BERM/RHTH SE16 19 K5
Vaughan Av HDN NW4 63 J2
HMSMTH W6 118 C4
Vaughan Est BETH E2 * 7 J4
Vaughan Gdns IL IG1 71 K4
Vaughan Rd CMBW SE5 142 D3
HRW HA1 60 C4
SRTFD E15 88 D4
THDIT KT7 190 C4
WELL DA16 148 A3
Vaughan St BERM/RHTH SE16 124 C2
Vaughan Wy WAP E1W 104 C6
Vaughan Williams Cl
DEPT SE8 144 D1
Vauxhall Br VX/NE SW8 121 K5
Vauxhall Bridge Rd
PIM SW1V 16 A5
Vauxhall Gdns SAND/SEL CR2 211 J4
Vauxhall Gv VX/NE SW8 122 A6
Vauxhall St LBTH SE11 122 A5
Vauxhall Wk LBTH SE11 122 A5
Vawdrey Cl WCHPL E1 104 E3
Veals Md MTCM CR4 178 D4
Vectis Gdns TOOT SW17 179 G2
Vectis Rd TOOT SW17 179 G2
Veda Rd LEW SE13 144 D5
Vega Crs NTHWD HA6 40 D1
Vega Rd BUSH WD23 28 C2
Veitch Cl EBED/NFELT TW14 153 J2
Veldene Wy RYLN/HDSTN HA2 77 K1
Vellum Dr CAR SM5 210 A1
Venables Cl DAGE RM10 92 D2
Venables St STJWD NW8 2 B7
Vencourt Pl HMSMTH W6 118 D4
Venetian Rd CMBW SE5 142 D3
Venetia Rd EA W5 116 E2
FSBYPK N4 67 H3
Venette Cl RAIN RM13 111 K4
Venner Rd SYD SE26 181 K2
Venners Cl BXLYHN DA7 150 B3
Venn St CLAP SW4 141 H5
Ventnor Av STAN HA7 43 H4
Ventnor Dr TRDG/WHET N20 33 F5
Ventnor Gdns BARK IG11 90 E4
Ventnor Rd BELMT SM2 209 F5
NWCR SE14 144 A1
Ventnor Ter
SEVS/STOTM N15 * 68 C1
Venture Cl BXLY DA5 169 F2
Venue St POP/IOD E14 105 K4
Venus Ms MTCM CR4 178 D6
Venus Rd WOOL/PLUM SE18 126 E3
Vera Av WCHMH N21 23 G6
Vera Ct OXHEY WD19 27 H2
Vera Lynn Cl FSTGT E7 88 E2
Vera Rd FUL/PGN SW6 139 H2
Verbena Cl CAN/RD E16 106 C3
Verbena Gdns HMSMTH W6 118 D5
Verdant La CAT SE6 165 H3
Verdayne Av CROY/NA CR0 198 A5
Verderers Rd CHIG IG7 55 G1
Verdun Rd BARN SW13 138 D1
WOOL/PLUM SE18 128 B6
Vereker Rd WKENS W14 * 119 H5
Vere St CAVSQ/HST W1G 9 J4
Vermont Cl ENC/FH EN2 23 H5
Vermont Rd NRWD SE19 180 E2
SUT SM1 209 F1
WAND/EARL SW18 160 A1
Verney Gdns DAGW RM9 92 A2
Verney Rd BERM/RHTH SE16 123 J5
DAGW RM9 92 A2
Verney St WLSDN NW10 81 F1
Verney Wy BERM/RHTH SE16 123 J5
Vernham Rd
WOOL/PLUM SE18 127 H6
Vernon Av MNPK E12 89 K2
RYNPK SW20 177 G5
WFD IG8 53 F2
Vernon Cl HOR/WEW KT19 206 E4
STMC/STPC BR5 186 C6
STWL/WRAY TW19 152 B3
Vernon Crs EBAR EN4 22 A6
Vernon Dr STAN HA7 43 G4
Vernon Pl FSBYW WC1X 11 F2
Vernon Ri FSBYW WC1X 5 H4
GFD/PVL UB6 78 D3
Vernon Rd BOW E3 105 H1
CEND/HSY/T N8 * 49 G6
CRW RM5 56 E1
FELT TW13 153 J4
GDMY/SEVK IG3 73 F5
MORT/ESHN SW14 138 A4
SRTFD E15 88 C5
SUT SM1 209 G3
WALTH E17 69 H1
WAN E11 70 C5
Vernon Sq FSBYW WC1X 5 H4
Vernon St WKENS W14 119 H4
Vernon Yd NTGHL W11 100 D6
Verona Ct CHSWK W4 118 B5
Verona Dr SURB KT6 191 F6
Veronica Gdns
STRHM/NOR SW16 179 H4
Veronica Rd TOOT SW17 161 G5
Veronique Gdns
BARK/HLT IG6 72 C2
Verran Rd BAL SW12 * 161 G2
Versailles Rd PGE/AN SE20 181 H3
Verulam Av WALTH E17 69 H3
Verulam Ct CDALE/KGS NW9 * 63 J4
Verulam Rd GFD/PVL UB6 96 A3
Verulam St FSBYW WC1X 11 J1
Verwood Dr EBAR EN4 21 K4
Verwood Rd
RYLN/HDSTN HA2 42 C5
Veryan Cl STMC/STPC BR5 202 D1
Vespan Rd SHB W12 118 D2
Vesta Rd BROCKY SE4 144 B3
Vestris Rd FSTH SE23 164 A4
Vestry Ms CMBW SE5 143 F2
Vestry Rd CMBW SE5 143 F2
WALTH E17 69 K2
Vestry St IS N1 6 E4
Vevey St CAT SE6 164 C4
Viaduct Pl BETH E2 104 D2
Viaduct St BETH E2 104 D2
The Viaduct MUSWH N10 * 66 B1
SWFD E18 52 E5
Vian St LEW SE13 144 E4
Vibart Gdns
BRXS/STRHM SW2 162 A2
Vibart Wk IS N1 * 84 E6
Vibia Cl STWL/WRAY TW19 152 A2
Vicarage Cl ERITH DA8 129 K6
NTHLT UB5 77 K6
RSLP HA4 58 B4
WPK KT4 192 B5
Vicarage Ct BECK BR3 * 182 B6
Vicarage Crs BTSEA SW11 140 C3
Vicarage Dr BARK IG11 90 C5
BECK BR3 182 D4
MORT/ESHN SW14 138 A6
Vicarage Farm Rd
HSLWW TW4 134 D3
Vicarage Flds WOT/HER KT12 188 B3
Vicarage Gdns MTCM CR4 178 D6
Vicarage Ga KENS W8 120 A2
Vicarage Gv CMBW SE5 142 E2
Vicarage La EHAM E6 107 K2
IL IG1 72 D5
SRTFD E15 88 C4
Vicarage Ms CHSWK W4 * 118 B6
Vicarage Pde
SEVS/STOTM N15 * 67 J1
Vicarage Pk
WOOL/PLUM SE18 127 H5
Vicarage Rd BXLY DA5 169 J3
CROY/NA CR0 211 G1
DAGE RM10 92 D5
HCH RM12 75 J5
HDN NW4 63 J3
KUT/HW KT1 174 D4
LEY E10 69 K4
MORT/ESHN SW14 137 K6
SRTFD E15 88 D5
SUT SM1 208 E2
TEDD TW11 174 B1
TOTM N17 50 C3
WATW WD18 26 E2
WFD IG8 53 J3
WHTN TW2 155 H1
WOOL/PLUM SE18 127 H5
Vicarage Wk BTSEA SW11 * 140 C2
Vicarage Wy
RYLN/HDSTN HA2 60 A4
WLSDN NW10 81 F1
Vicars Bridge Cl ALP/SUD HA0 98 A1
Vicar's Cl EN EN1 24 A3
HOM E9 86 E6
SRTFD E15 88 E6
Vicars Hl LEW SE13 144 E5
Vicar's Moor La WCHMH N21 35 G2
Vicars Oak Rd NRWD SE19 181 F2
Vicar's Rd KTTN NW5 84 A3
Viceroy Cl EFNCH N2 * 65 J1
Viceroy Pde EFNCH N2 * 65 J1
Viceroy Rd VX/NE SW8 141 K2
Vickers Cl WLGTN SM6 211 F5
Vickers Rd ERITH DA8 130 A5
Victor Gv ALP/SUD HA0 80 A5
Victoria Ar WESTW SW1E 15 K5
Victoria Av CRW RM5 56 D2
E/WMO/HCT KT8 173 G6
EHAM E6 89 H6
FNCH N3 46 D4
HSLW TW3 135 F6
SURB KT6 190 E3
WBLY HA9 80 D4
WLGTN SM6 210 A1
Victoria Cl E/WMO/HCT KT8 173 F6
EBAR EN4 21 H5
HRW HA1 61 F3
HYS/HAR UB3 94 B5
Victoria Cots RCH/KEW TW9 137 G2
WCHPL E1 * 104 C4
Victoria Ct WBLY HA9 80 C4
Victoria Crs NRWD SE19 181 F2
SEVS/STOTM N15 68 A2
WIM/MER SW19 * 177 J3
Victoria Dock Rd CAN/RD E16 106 D5
Victoria Dr WIM/MER SW19 159 H4
Victoria Emb TPL/STR WC2R 11 G6
WHALL SW1A 17 F3
Victoria Embankment Gdns
CHCR WC2N * 11 F6
Victoria Gdns HEST TW5 134 D2
NTGHL W11 119 K1
Victoria Ga BAY/PAD W2 8 B5
Victoria Gv KENS W8 120 B3
NFNCH/WDSPK N12 47 H1
Victoria Grove Ms
BAY/PAD W2 * 101 F6
Victoria La BAR EN5 20 D5
HYS/HAR UB3 113 G5
Victoria Ms KIL/WHAMP NW6 82 E6
WAND/EARL SW18 160 B3
Victorian Gv STNW/STAM N16 86 A1
Victorian Rd STNW/STAM N16 86 A1
Victoria Pde RCH/KEW TW9 * 137 H2
Victoria Park Rd HOM E9 86 E6
Victoria Park Sq BETH E2 104 E2
Victoria Park Studios
HOM E9 * 86 E4
Victoria Pl RCH/KEW TW9 136 E6
Victoria Ri CLAP SW4 141 G4
Victoria Rd ACT W3 99 F4
BARK IG11 90 B4
BFN/LL DA15 168 A5
BKHH IG9 39 H4
BUSH WD23 28 B3
CHING E4 38 C3
CHST BR7 185 F1
DAGE RM10 92 E3
EA W5 97 H4
EBAR EN4 21 H5
ED N9 36 B5
ERITH DA8 130 B6
FELT TW13 154 A3
FSBYPK N4 67 F4
HAYES BR2 200 C2
HDN NW4 64 A1
KENS W8 120 B3
KIL/WHAMP NW6 100 D1
KUT/HW KT1 175 G5
MLHL NW7 45 H1
MORT/ESHN SW14 138 A4
MTCM CR4 178 D3
NWDGN UB2 114 E3
PLSTW E13 106 E1
ROM RM1 75 H2
RSLP HA4 77 F2
SEVS/STOTM N15 * 68 C1
SURB KT6 190 E3
SUT SM1 209 H3
SWFD E18 53 F6
TEDD TW11 174 B2
TWK TW1 156 C2
UED N18 36 B6
WALTH E17 52 A5
WAN E11 88 B2
WDGN N22 48 D4
WIM/MER SW19 178 D3
WLSDN NW10 99 G3
Victoria Sq BGVA SW1W 15 K4
Victoria St BELV DA17 129 G5
SRTFD E15 88 C5
WESTW SW1E 15 K5
Victoria Ter EA W5 * 116 E1
FSBYPK N4 67 G5
HRW HA1 60 E5
Victoria Vls RCH/KEW TW9 137 G4
Victoria Wy CHARL SE7 126 A5
Victoria Works
STMC/STPC BR5 201 H2

Victoria Yd WCHPL E1 * 104 C5
Victor Rd PGE/AN SE20 182 A3
RYLN/HDSTN HA2 42 C6
TEDD TW11 173 K1
WLSDN NW10 99 K2
Victors Dr HPTN TW12 * 172 D2
Victors Wy BAR EN5 20 D4
Victor Vls ED N9 * 35 K5
Victory Av MRDN SM4 194 B2
Victory Cl STWL/WRAY TW19 152 B3
Victory Pk WBLY HA9 * 79 K1
Victory Pl NRWD SE19 * 181 F2
WALW SE17 18 D6
Victory Rd RAIN RM13 111 J1
WAN E11 70 E1
WIM/MER SW19 178 B3
Victory Road Ms
WIM/MER SW19 178 B3
Victory Wy BERM/RHTH SE16 124 B2
HEST TW5 114 B5
ROMW/RG RM7 56 D5
Vienna Cl WFD IG8 53 H5
View Cl CHIG IG7 54 D1
HGT N6 65 K4
HRW HA1 60 D1
View Crs CEND/HSY/T N8 66 D2
Viewfield Cl
KTN/HRWW/WS HA3 62 A4
Viewfield Rd BFN/LL DA15 168 D3
WAND/EARL SW18 159 J1
Viewland Rd
WOOL/PLUM SE18 128 A5
View Rd HGT N6 65 K4
The View ABYW SE2 129 F5
Viga Rd WCHMH N21 35 G1
Vigilant Cl SYD SE26 163 H6
Vignoles Rd ROMW/RG RM7 74 C4
Vigo St CONDST W1S 10 A6
Viking Cl BOW E3 105 G1
Viking Gdns EHAM E6 107 J4
Viking Pl LEY E10 69 H5
Viking Rd STHL UB1 95 J6
Viking Wy ERITH DA8 129 K3
Villacourt Rd
WOOL/PLUM SE18 148 B1
Village Ar CHING E4 * 38 B3
Village Cl CHING E4 52 A1
HAMP NW3 * 83 H3
Village Ms CDALE/KGS NW9 * 63 F6
Village Mt HAMP NW3 * 83 G2
Village Park Cl EN EN1 36 A1
Village Rd EN EN1 35 K1
FNCH N3 46 C5
Village Rw BELMT SM2 208 E5
The Village CHARL SE7 126 B6
HAMP NW3 * 65 G6
Village Wy ASHF TW15 152 C6
BARK/HLT IG6 54 C6
BECK BR3 182 D6
DUL SE21 162 E1
PIN HA5 59 J4
WLSDN NW10 81 F2
Village Wy East PIN HA5 59 K4
Villa Rd BRXN/ST SW9 142 B4
Villas Rd WOOL/PLUM SE18 127 H4
Villa St WALW SE17 122 E5
Villiers Av BRYLDS KT5 191 G2
WHTN TW2 154 E3
Villiers Cl BRYLDS KT5 191 G1
LEY E10 69 J6
Villiers Gv BELMT SM2 208 B6
Villiers Rd BECK BR3 182 A5
CRICK NW2 81 J4
ISLW TW7 135 K3
KUT/HW KT1 175 G6
OXHEY WD19 27 J1
STHL UB1 114 E1
Villiers St CHCR WC2N 11 F7
Vimy Cl HSLWW TW4 134 E6
Vincam Cl WHTN TW2 155 F2
Vincennes Est WNWD SE27 * 162 E6
Vincent Av BRYLDS KT5 191 J5
Vincent Cl BAR EN5 20 E4
BARK/HLT IG6 54 C2
BFN/LL DA15 167 K3
ESH/CLAY KT10 204 B1
HAYES BR2 200 A1
WDR/YW UB7 112 D6
Vincent Gdns CRICK NW2 81 H1
Vincent Pde FSBYPK N4 * 66 E5
Vincent Rd ACT W3 117 K3
ALP/SUD HA0 80 B5
CHING E4 52 B2
CROY/NA CR0 197 F4
DAGW RM9 92 A5
HSLWW TW4 134 C4
ISLW TW7 135 J2
KUT/HW KT1 175 H6
SEVS/STOTM N15 67 J1
WDGN N22 49 G5
WOOL/PLUM SE18 127 G4
Vincent Rw HPTN TW12 173 H2
Vincents Cl BERM/RHTH SE16 124 B2
Vincent Sq WDGN N22 * 49 G5
WEST SW1P 16 B6
Vincent St CAN/RD E16 106 E4
WEST SW1P 16 C6
Vincent Ter IS N1 6 A2
Vincent Vls
SEVS/STOTM N15 * 67 J1
Vince St FSBYE EC1V 7 F5
Vine Cl BRYLDS KT5 191 G3
CLPT E5 86 C2
SUT SM1 209 G1
WDR/YW UB7 112 D4
Vine Cots HNWL W7 * 115 K1
WCHPL E1 * 104 E5
Vine Ct KTN/HRWW/WS HA3 62 A3
WCHPL E1 104 C4
Vine Gdns IL IG1 90 C3
Vinegar St WAP E1W 123 J1
Vinegar Yd STHWK SE1 19 G2
Vine Hl CLKNW EC1R 5 J7
Vine La STHWK SE1 19 H1
Vine Pl HSLW TW3 135 G5
Vineries Cl WDR/YW UB7 112 D6
The Vineries CAT SE6 * 164 D3
EN EN1 24 A4
STHGT/OAK N14 34 C1
Vine Rd BARN SW13 138 C4
E/WMO/HCT KT8 189 H1
ORP BR6 217 F4
SRTFD E15 88 D5
Vine Rw RCHPK/HAM TW10 * 137 F6
Viners Cl WOT/HER KT12 188 B3
Vines Av FNCH N3 47 F4
Vine Sq WKENS W14 * 119 J5
Vine St MYFR/PICC W1J 10 B6
ROMW/RG RM7 74 E2
TWRH EC3N 13 J4
Vine Street Br FARR EC1M 5 K7
Vine Yd STHWK SE1 18 D2
Vineyard Av MLHL NW7 46 C3
Vineyard Cl CAT SE6 164 D3
KUT/HW KT1 175 G6
Vineyard Gv FNCH N3 47 F4
Vineyard Hill Rd
WIM/MER SW19 159 K6
Vineyard Ms CLKNW EC1R * 5 J6
Vineyard Pth
MORT/ESHN SW14 138 A4
Vineyard Rd FELT TW13 153 K5
Vineyard Rw KUT/HW KT1 174 D4
The Vineyard
RCHPK/HAM TW10 136 E6
Vineyard Wk CLKNW EC1R 5 J6
Viney Bank CROY/NA CR0 213 H6
Viney Rd LEW SE13 144 E4
Vining St BRXS/STRHM SW2 142 B5
Vinries Bank MLHL NW7 45 K1
Vinson Cl ORP BR6 202 B5
Vintage Ms CHING E4 37 J6
Vintry Ms WALTH E17 69 J1
Viola Av ABYW SE2 128 C4
EBED/NFELT TW14 154 B1
STWL/WRAY TW19 152 B3
Viola Sq SHB W12 99 H6
Violet Av ENC/FH EN2 23 K1
Violet Cl CAN/RD E16 106 C3
CHEAM SM3 193 H5
DEPT SE8 124 C6
WLGTN SM6 195 F5
Violet Gdns CROY/NA CR0 211 H3
Violet Hl STJWD NW8 101 G1
Violet La SAND/SEL CR2 211 H3
Violet Rd BOW E3 105 K3
SWFD E18 53 F5
WALTH E17 69 J3
Violet St BETH E2 104 D3
Virgil St STHWK SE1 17 H4
Virginia Cl CRW RM5 56 E3
HAYES BR2 183 H6
NWMAL KT3 191 K1
Virginia Gdns BARK/HLT IG6 54 D5
Virginia Rd BETH E2 7 J5
THHTH CR7 180 C4
Virginia St WCHPL E1 * 104 C6
Viscount Cl FBAR/BDGN N11 48 B1
Viscount Dr EHAM E6 107 K4
Viscount Gv NTHLT UB5 95 H2
Viscount Rd
STWL/WRAY TW19 152 A2
Viscount St BARB EC2Y 6 C7
Viscount Wy HTHAIR TW6 133 H5
Vista Av PEND EN3 25 F3
Vista Dr REDBR IG4 71 H2
The Vista CHING E4 38 B2
ELTH/MOT SE9 166 C1
Vista Wy KTN/HRWW/WS HA3 62 A3
Viveash Cl HYS/HAR UB3 113 J3
Vivian Av HDN NW4 63 K2
WBLY HA9 80 C4
Vivian Cl OXHEY WD19 26 E4
Vivian Gdns OXHEY WD19 26 E3
WBLY HA9 80 C3
Vivian Rd BOW E3 105 G1
Vivian Sq PECK SE15 143 J4
Vivian Wy EFNCH N2 65 H2
Vivien Cl CHSGTN KT9 206 A5
Vivienne Cl TWK TW1 156 E1
Vixen Ms HACK E8 * 86 B6
Voce Rd WOOL/PLUM SE18 147 J1
Voewood Cl NWMAL KT3 192 C3
Voltaire Rd CLAP SW4 141 J4
Volt Av WLSDN NW10 99 F2
Volta Wy CROY/NA CR0 196 A5
Voluntary Pl WAN E11 70 E3
Vorley Rd ARCH N19 66 C6
Voss Ct STRHM/NOR SW16 179 K2
Voss St BETH E2 104 C2
Voyagers Cl THMD SE28 109 J5
Vulcan Cl EHAM E6 108 A5
Vulcan Ga ENC/FH EN2 23 G3
Vulcan Rd BROCKY SE4 144 C3
Vulcan Ter BROCKY SE4 144 C3
Vulcan Wy HOLWY N7 85 F4
WLGTN SM6 210 E6
Vyner Rd ACT W3 99 F6
Vyner St BETH E2 104 D1
Vyse Cl BAR EN5 20 A5

W

Wadbrook St KUT/HW KT1 174 E5
Wadding St WALW SE17 18 E7
Waddington Cl EN EN1 24 A5
Waddington Rd SRTFD E15 88 B3
Waddington St SRTFD E15 88 B4
Waddington Wy NRWD SE19 180 D4
Waddon Cl CROY/NA CR0 211 G1
Waddon Court Rd
CROY/NA CR0 211 G2
Waddon Marsh Wy
CROY/NA CR0 196 A5
Waddon New Rd
CROY/NA CR0 211 H1
Waddon Park Av
CROY/NA CR0 211 G2
Waddon Rd CROY/NA CR0 211 G1
Waddon Wy CROY/NA CR0 211 G4
Wade Av STMC/STPC BR5 202 E4
Wade House STHWK SE1 * 123 H2
Wade's Gv WCHMH N21 35 G2
Wade's Hl WCHMH N21 35 G1
Wade's La TEDD TW11 174 B1
Wadeson St BETH E2 104 D1
Wade's Pl POP/IOD E14 105 K6
Wadeville Av CHDH RM6 74 A3
Wadeville Cl BELV DA17 129 H5
Wadham Av WALTH E17 51 K3
Wadham Gdns GFD/PVL UB6 78 D4
HAMP NW3 83 J5
Wadham Rd CHING E4 52 A4
PUT/ROE SW15 139 H5
WALTH E17 51 K4
Wadhurst Cl PGE/AN SE20 181 J5
Wadhurst Rd CHSWK W4 118 A3
Wadley Rd WAN E11 70 C4
Wadsworth Cl GFD/PVL UB6 97 J1
PEND EN3 25 F6
Wadsworth Rd GFD/PVL UB6 97 H1
Wager St BOW E3 105 H3
Waghorn Rd
KTN/HRWW/WS HA3 43 K6
PLSTW E13 89 G6
Waghorn St PECK SE15 143 H4
Wagner St PECK SE15 143 K1
Wagstaff Gdns DAGW RM9 91 J5
Wagtail Cl CDALE/KGS NW9 45 G5
EN EN1 24 D2
Wagtail Wk BECK BR3 199 F2
Wagtail Wy STMC/STPC BR5 202 E1
Waights Ct KUTN/CMB KT2 175 F4
Wainfleet Av CRW RM5 56 E5
Wainford Cl WIM/MER SW19 159 G3
Wainwright Gv ISLW TW7 135 J5
Waite Davies Rd
LEE/GVPK SE12 165 J2
Waite St CMBW SE5 123 G6
Waithman St STP EC4M 12 A4
Wakefield Gdns IL IG1 71 J3
NRWD SE19 181 F3
Wakefield Ms STPAN WC1H 4 E5
Wakefield Rd
FBAR/BDGN N11 48 D1
RCHPK/HAM TW10 136 E6
SEVS/STOTM N15 68 B2
Wakefield St BMSBY WC1N 5 F6
EHAM E6 89 J6
STPAN WC1H 5 F5
UED N18 50 C1
Wakehams Hl PIN HA5 41 K6
Wakeham St IS N1 85 K4
Wakehurst Rd BTSEA SW11 140 D6
Wakeling La ALP/SUD HA0 79 H1
Wakeling Rd HNWL W7 97 F4
Wakeling St WCHPL E1 * 105 G5
Wakelin Rd SRTFD E15 106 C1
Wakeman Rd WLSDN NW10 100 A2
Wakemans Hill Av
CDALE/KGS NW9 63 F2
Wakering Rd BARK IG11 90 C4
Wakerly Cl EHAM E6 107 K5
Wakley St FSBYE EC1V 6 A4
Walberswick St VX/NE SW8 141 K1
Walbrook MANHO EC4N 12 E5
Walburgh St WCHPL E1 104 D5
Walcorde Av WALW SE17 18 D7
Walcot Rd PEND EN3 25 H3
Walcot Sq LBTH SE11 17 K6
Walcott St WEST SW1P * 16 B6
Waldeck Gv WNWD SE27 162 C5
Waldeck Rd CHSWK W4 117 H6
MORT/ESHN SW14 137 K4
SEVS/STOTM N15 49 H6
WEA W13 97 H5
Waldegrave Gdns TWK TW1 156 A4
Waldegrave Pk TWK TW1 156 A6
Waldegrave Rd BCTR RM8 73 J6
BMLY BR1 200 D2
CEND/HSY/T N8 * 49 G6
EA W5 98 B6
NRWD SE19 181 G3
TWK TW1 156 A6
Waldegrove CROY/NA CR0 212 B1
Waldemar Av FUL/PGN SW6 139 H2
WEA W13 116 D1
Waldemar Rd
WIM/MER SW19 177 K1
Walden Av CHST BR7 166 E6
PLMGR N13 35 J6
RAIN RM13 111 F1
Walden Cl BELV DA17 129 G5
Walden Gdns THHTH CR7 196 A1
Waldenhurst Rd
STMC/STPC BR5 202 E4
Walden Pde CHST BR7 * 184 E2
Walden Rd CHST BR7 184 E2
TOTM N17 49 K4
Waldens Cl STMC/STPC BR5 202 E4
Waldenshaw Rd FSTH SE23 163 K3
Waldens Rd STMC/STPC BR5 203 F3
Walden St WCHPL E1 * 104 D5
Walden Wy BARK/HLT IG6 54 E3
MLHL NW7 46 B2
Waldo Cl CLAP SW4 141 H6
Waldo Pl MTCM CR4 178 D3
Waldorf Cl SAND/SEL CR2 211 H6
Waldo Rd BMLY BR1 184 B6
WLSDN NW10 99 J2
Waldram Crs FSTH SE23 163 K3
Waldram Park Rd FSTH SE23 164 A3
Waldrist Wy ERITHM DA18 129 G2
Waldron Gdns HAYES BR2 183 G6
Waldronhyrst CROY/NA CR0 211 H2
Waldron Ms CHEL SW3 120 C6
Waldron Rd RYLN/HDSTN HA2 60 E5
WAND/EARL SW18 160 B5
The Waldrons CROY/NA CR0 211 J2
Waldron's Yd
RYLN/HDSTN HA2 60 D6
Waldstock Rd THMD SE28 109 G6
Waleran Cl STAN HA7 43 F2
Walerand Rd LEW SE13 145 F3
Wales Av CAR SM5 209 J3
Wales Cl PECK SE15 143 J1
Wales Farm Rd ACT W3 99 F4
Waleton Acres WLGTN SM6 * 210 C4
Waley St WCHPL E1 * 105 F4
Walfield Av TRDG/WHET N20 33 F2
Walford Rd STNW/STAM N16 86 A2
Walfrey Gdns DAGW RM9 92 A5
Walham Green Ct
FUL/PGN SW6 * 140 A1
Walham Gv FUL/PGN SW6 139 K1
Walham Ri WIM/MER SW19 177 H2
Walham Yd FUL/PGN SW6 139 K1
Walkden Rd CHST BR7 167 F6
Walker Cl DART DA1 150 C4
EBED/NFELT TW14 153 J2
FBAR/BDGN N11 34 C6
HNWL W7 115 K1
HPTN TW12 172 E2
WOOL/PLUM SE18 127 H4
Walker's Ct SOHO/CST W1F 10 C5
Walkerscroft Md CAT SE6 164 E4
DUL SE21 162 D3
Walker's Pl PUT/ROE SW15 139 G5
The Walks EFNCH N2 47 H6
The Walk PLMGR N13 * 35 G5
Wallace Cl THMD SE28 109 K6
Wallace Crs CAR SM5 209 K3
Wallace Rd IS N1 85 J4
Wallace Wy ROM RM1 57 F3
Wallbutton Rd BROCKY SE4 144 B3
Wallcote Av CRICK NW2 64 B5
Walled Garden Cl BECK BR3 198 E1
Wall End Rd EHAM E6 90 A5
Wallenger Av GPK RM2 57 K6
Waller Dr NTHWD HA6 40 E4
Waller Rd NWCR SE14 144 A2
Wallers Cl DAGW RM9 92 A6
WFD IG8 53 K2
Wallflower St SHB W12 99 H6
Wallgrave Rd ECT SW5 120 A4
Wallingford Av NKENS W10 100 B4
Wallington Cl RSLP HA4 58 A3
Wallington Rd
GDMY/SEVK IG3 73 F4
Wallis Cl BTSEA SW11 140 C4
EMPK RM11 75 K5
Wallis Rd HOM E9 87 H4
STHL UB1 96 B5
Wallman Pl WDGN N22 49 F4
Wallorton Gdns
MORT/ESHN SW14 138 A5
Wallside BARB EC2Y * 12 D2
Wall St IS N1 85 K4
Wallwood Rd WAN E11 70 B4
Wallwood St POP/IOD E14 105 H4
Walmar Cl EBAR EN4 21 H2
Walmer Cl CHING E4 37 K4
ORP BR6 216 D2
ROMW/RG RM7 56 D5
Walmer Gdns WEA W13 116 B2
Walmer Pl MBLAR W1H * 8 E1
Walmer Rd NTGHL W11 100 C6
Walmer Ter
WOOL/PLUM SE18 127 H4
Walmgate Rd GFD/PVL UB6 79 H6
Walmington Fold
NFNCH/WDSPK N12 46 E2
Walm La CRICK NW2 82 B3
Walney Wk IS N1 * 85 J4
Walnut Av WDR/YW UB7 112 D3
Walnut Cl BARK/HLT IG6 72 C1
CAR SM5 209 K3
DEPT SE8 124 C6
HYS/HAR UB3 94 C6
Walnut Ct EA W5 * 117 F2
Walnut Gdns SRTFD E15 88 C3
Walnut Gv EN EN1 23 K6
Walnut Ms BELMT SM2 209 G5
Walnut Rd LEY E10 69 J6
Walnuts Rd ORP BR6 202 B5
Walnut Tree Av MTCM CR4 * 178 D6
Walnut Tree Cl BARN SW13 138 C2
CHST BR7 185 H4
Walnut Tree Rd BCTR RM8 73 K6
BTFD TW8 117 F6
GNWCH SE10 * 125 H5
HEST TW5 114 E6
Walnut Tree Wk LBTH SE11 17 J6
Walnut Wy BKHH IG9 39 H5
RSLP HA4 77 G4
Walpole Av RCH/KEW TW9 137 G3
Walpole Cl PIN HA5 42 A2
WEA W13 116 D2
Walpole Crs TEDD TW11 174 A1
Walpole Gdns CHSWK W4 117 K5
WHTN TW2 155 K4
Walpole Ms STJWD NW8 2 A1
Walpole Pl TEDD TW11 174 A1
Walpole Rd CROY/NA CR0 196 E6
EHAM E6 89 G5
HAYES BR2 200 C2
SURB KT6 191 F4
SWFD E18 52 D4
TEDD TW11 174 A1
TOTM N17 49 J5
WALTH E17 69 G1
WHTN TW2 155 K4
WIM/MER SW19 178 C2
Walpole St CHEL SW3 120 E5
Walrond Av WBLY HA9 80 A3
Walsham Cl STNW/STAM N16 68 C5
THMD SE28 109 K6
Walsham Rd
EBED/NFELT TW14 154 A2
NWCR SE14 144 A3
Walsingham Gdns
HOR/WEW KT19 207 G2
Walsingham Pk CHST BR7 185 J5
Walsingham Rd CLAP SW4 161 F1
CLPT E5 86 C1
ENC/FH EN2 23 K5
MTCM CR4 194 E2
STMC/STPC BR5 186 C4
WEA W13 * 116 B1
Walsingham Wk BELV DA17 129 H6
Walter Rodney Cl MNPK E12 89 K4
Walters Cl HYS/HAR UB3 113 J2
Walters Rd PEND EN3 24 E6
Walter's Rd SNWD SE25 197 F1
Walter St BETH E2 105 F2
KUTN/CMB KT2 * 175 F4
Walters Wy FSTH SE23 164 A1
Walters Yd BMLY BR1 183 K5
Walter Ter WCHPL E1 105 F5
Walterton Rd MV/WKIL W9 100 D3
Walter Wk EDGW HA8 44 E2
Waltham Av CDALE/KGS NW9 62 C3
HYS/HAR UB3 113 F3
Waltham Cl STMC/STPC BR5 202 E5
Waltham Dr EDGW HA8 44 C5
Waltham Pk WALTH E17 51 J3
Waltham Park Wy CHING E4 * 51 J3
Waltham Rd CAR SM5 194 C5
NWDGN UB2 114 D3
WFD IG8 53 J2
Walthamstow Av CHING E4 51 J3
Walthamstow Avenue (North
Circular) CHING E4 51 G1
Waltham Wy CHING E4 37 H5
Waltheof Av TOTM N17 49 K4
Waltheof Gdns TOTM N17 49 K4
Walton Av CHEAM SM3 208 D1
NWMAL KT3 192 C1
RYLN/HDSTN HA2 77 K2
WBLY HA9 80 D1
Walton Cl CRICK NW2 63 K6
HRW HA1 60 D1
VX/NE SW8 141 K1
Walton Dr HRW HA1 60 D1
WLSDN NW10 81 F4
Walton Gdns ACT W3 98 D4
FELT TW13 153 J6
WBLY HA9 62 A6
Walton Gn CROY/NA CR0 213 K6
Walton Pk WOT/HER KT12 188 C6
Walton Park La
WOT/HER KT12 188 C6
Walton Pl CHEL SW3 14 E4
Walton Rd CRW RM5 56 B3
E/WMO/HCT KT8 189 F1
HRW HA1 60 D1
MNPK E12 90 A2
PLSTW E13 107 G1
SCUP DA14 168 C5
SEVS/STOTM N15 * 68 B1
WOT/HER KT12 188 C2
Walton St CHEL SW3 14 D6
ENC/FH EN2 23 K2
Walton Vls IS N1 * 86 A5
Walton Wy ACT W3 98 D4
MTCM CR4 195 H1
Walt Whitman Cl HNHL SE24 * 142 C5
Walverns Cl OXHEY WD19 27 G1
Walworth Pl WALW SE17 122 D5
Walworth Rd STHWK SE1 18 C6
Walwyn Av BMLY BR1 184 C6
Wanborough Dr
PUT/ROE SW15 158 E3
Wanderer Dr BARK IG11 109 H2
Wandle Bank CROY/NA CR0 210 E1
WIM/MER SW19 178 C2
Wandle Ct HOR/WEW KT19 206 E2
Wandle Court Gdns
CROY/NA CR0 210 E1
Wandle Rd CROY/NA CR0 210 E1
MRDN SM4 194 C2
TOOT SW17 160 D4
WLGTN SM6 195 G6
Wandle Side WLGTN SM6 210 B1
Wandle Wy MTCM CR4 194 E2
WAND/EARL SW18 160 A3
Wandsworth Br
WAND/EARL SW18 140 B4
Wandsworth Bridge Rd
FUL/PGN SW6 140 A
Wandsworth Common West
Side WAND/EARL SW18 140 B
Wandsworth High St
WAND/EARL SW18 139 K
Wandsworth Rd VX/NE SW8 141 G
Wangey Rd CHDH RM6 73 K
Wanless Rd HNHL SE24 142 D
Wanley Rd CMBW SE5 142 E
Wanlip Rd PLSTW E13 107 F
Wannock Gdns BARK/HLT IG6 54 E
Wansbeck Rd HOM E9 87 H
Wansdown Pl FUL/PGN SW6 140 A
Wansey St WALW SE17 18 D
Wansford Rd WFD IG8 53 C
Wanstead Cl BMLY BR1 184 E
Wanstead La IL IG1 71
Wanstead Park Av MNPK E12 71 H
Wanstead Park Rd IL IG1 71
Wanstead Pl WAN E11 70
Wanstead Rd BMLY BR1 184
Wansunt Rd BXLY DA5 169
Wantage Rd LEE/GVPK SE12 145
Wantz La RAIN RM13 111
Wantz Rd DAGE RM10 92
Wapping Dock St WAP E1W * 123
Wapping High St WAP E1W 123
Wapping La WAP E1W 104
Wapping Wall WAP E1W 123
Warbank La KUTN/CMB KT2 176
Warbeck Rd SHB W12 118
Warberry Rd WDGN N22 49
Warboys Ap KUTN/CMB KT2 175
Warboys Crs CHING E4 52
Warboys Rd KUTN/CMB KT2 175
Warburton Cl IS N1 86
KTN/HRWW/WS HA3 42
Warburton Rd HACK E8 86
WHTN TW2 155
Warburton St HACK E8 86
Warburton Ter WALTH E17 51
Wardalls Gv NWCR SE14 * 143
Ward Cl ERITH DA8 130
SAND/SEL CR2 212
Wardell Cl EDGW HA8 45
Wardell Fld CDALE/KGS NW9 45
Warden Av CRW RM5 56
RYLN/HDSTN HA2 59
Warden Rd KTTN NW5 84
Wardens Gv STHWK SE1 18
Wardle St HOM E9 87
Wardley St WAND/EARL SW18 16
Wardo Av FUL/PGN SW6 13
Wardour Ms SOHO/CST W1F 1
Wardour St SOHO/CST W1F 1
Ward Rd ARCH N19 84
SRTFD E15 * 88
Wardrobe Pl BLKFR EC4V * 1
The Wardrobe
RCH/KEW TW9 * 13
Wards Rd GNTH/NBYPK IG2 7
Wards Wharf Ap CAN/RD E16 12
Wareham Cl HSLW TW3 13
Waremead Rd
GNTH/NBYPK IG2 7
Warepoint Dr THMD SE28 12
Warfield Rd
EBED/NFELT TW14 15

HPTN TW12 173 G4
WLSDN NW10 100 B2
Warfield Yd WLSDN NW10 * 100 B2
Wargrave Av
SEVS/STOTM N15 68 B3
Wargrave Rd
RYLN/HDSTN HA2 78 C1
Warham Rd FSBYPK N4 67 G2
KTN/HRWW/WS HA3 43 F5
SAND/SEL CR2 211 J3
Warham St CMBW SE5 142 C1
Waring Cl ORP BR6 217 F4
Waring Dr ORP BR6 217 F4
Waring Rd SCUP DA14 186 D2
Waring St WNWD SE27 162 D6
Warkworth Gdns ISLW TW7 136 B1
Warkworth Rd TOTM N17 49 K3
Warland Rd
WOOL/PLUM SE18 147 J1
Warley Av BCTR RM8 74 B4
YEAD UB4 94 E5
Warley Rd ED N9 36 E4
WFD IG8 53 F3
YEAD UB4 94 E5
Warley St BETH E2 105 F2
Warlingham Rd THHTH CR7 196 C1
Warlock Rd MV/WKIL W9 100 D3
Warlters Cl HOLWY N7 * 84 E2
Warlters Rd HOLWY N7 84 E2
Warltersville Rd ARCH N19 66 E4
Warming Cl CLPT E5 * 87 F1
Warmington Rd HNHL SE24 162 D1
Warmington St PLSTW E13 106 E3
Warminster Rd SNWD SE25 181 H5
Warminster Sq SNWD SE25 181 H5
Warminster Wy MTCM CR4 179 G4
Warmwell Av
CDALE/KGS NW9 45 G4
Warndon St
BERM/RHTH SE16 123 K4
Warneford Pl OXHEY WD19 27 J1
Warneford Rd
KTN/HRWW/WS HA3 43 K6
Warneford St HOM E9 86 D6
Warne Pl BFN/LL DA15 168 C1
Warner Av CHEAM SM3 193 H6
Warner Cl CDALE/KGS NW9 63 H4
EBAR EN4 21 J1
HPTN TW12 172 E1
HYS/HAR UB3 133 G1
SRTFD E15 88 C3
Warner Pl BETH E2 104 C1
Warner Rd BMLY BR1 183 J3
CEND/HSY/T N8 66 D1
CMBW SE5 142 D2
WALTH E17 69 G1
Warner St CLKNW EC1R 5 J7
Warner Ter POP/IOD E14 * 105 J4
Warner Yd CLKNW EC1R 5 J7
Warnford Rd ORP BR6 217 F3
Warnham Court Rd CAR SM5 209 K5
Warnham Rd
NFNCH/WDSPK N12 47 J1
Warple Ms ACT W3 * 118 B2
Warple Wy ACT W3 118 B2
Warren Av BMLY BR1 183 H3
ORP BR6 217 F3
RCHPK/HAM TW10 137 J5
SAND/SEL CR2 213 F5
WAN E11 * 88 B1
Warren Cl ED N9 37 F2
ESH/CLAY KT10 204 C2
WBLY HA9 61 K6
YEAD UB4 95 G4
Warren Ct CHARL SE7 126 B5
Warren Crs ED N9 36 B2
Warren Cutting
KUTN/CMB KT2 176 A3
Warrender Rd ARCH N19 84 C1
Warrender Wy RSLP HA4 58 E4
Warren Dr GFD/PVL UB6 96 B3
HCH RM12 93 J1
ORP BR6 217 H3
RSLP HA4 59 H4
Warren Dr North BRYLDS KT5 191 J5
Warren Dr South BRYLDS KT5 191 K5
The Warren Dr WAN E11 71 G4
Warren Flds STAN HA7 * 29 J6
Warren Gdns ORP BR6 217 G3
Warren La STAN HA7 29 G4
WOOL/PLUM SE18 127 G3
Warren Lane Ga
WOOL/PLUM SE18 127 G3
Warren Ms FITZ W1T 4 A7
Warren Pk KUTN/CMB KT2 175 K2
Warren Park Rd SUT SM1 209 H4
Warren Pond Rd CHING E4 38 D3
Warren Ri KUTN/CMB KT2 176 A4
Warren Rd BARK/HLT IG6 72 D2
BUSH WD23 28 C3
CHING E4 38 A4
CRICK NW2 63 H6
CROY/NA CR0 197 F5
KUTN/CMB KT2 175 K2
LEY E10 88 A1
ORP BR6 217 F3
SCUP DA14 168 D5
WAN E11 71 G3
WHTN TW2 155 J1
WIM/MER SW19 178 D2
Warrens Shawe La
EDGW HA8 30 D4
Warren St FITZ W1T 4 A7
The Warren BELMT SM2 209 H6
HEST TW5 134 E1
MNPK E12 89 J2
WPK KT4 207 F2
YEAD UB4 94 E5
Warren Wy EDGW HA8 44 D5
Warriner Dr ED N9 36 C5
Warriner Gdns BTSEA SW11 140 E2
Warrington Crs MV/WKIL W9 101 G3
Warrington Gdns
MV/WKIL W9 101 G3
Warrington Pl POP/IOD E14 * 125 F1
Warrington Rd BCTR RM8 73 K6
CROY/NA CR0 211 H1
HRW HA1 60 E2
RCHPK/HAM TW10 136 E6
Warrington Sq BCTR RM8 73 K6
Warrior Cl THMD SE28 127 K1
Warrior Sq MNPK E12 90 A2
Warsaw Cl RSLP HA4 77 F4
Warspite Rd
WOOL/PLUM SE18 126 D3
Warton Rd SRTFD E15 88 A6
Warwall EHAM E6 108 B5
Warwick Av EDGW HA8 30 D5
MV/WKIL W9 101 F3
RYLN/HDSTN HA2 77 K2
Warwick Chambers
KENS W8 * 119 K3
Warwick Cl BUSH WD23 28 E2
BXLY DA5 169 G2
EBAR EN4 21 H6
HPTN TW12 173 H3
ORP BR6 217 G1
Warwick Ct HHOL WC1V 11 H2
SURB KT6 191 F6
Warwick Crs BAY/PAD W2 101 G4
YEAD UB4 94 D3
Warwick Dene EA W5 117 F1
Warwick Dr PUT/ROE SW15 138 E4
Warwick Gdns FSBYPK N4 67 J2
IL IG1 72 B5
THDIT KT7 190 A2
THHTH CR7 * 196 B1
WKENS W14 119 J3
Warwick Gv BRYLDS KT5 191 G4
CLPT E5 68 D5
Warwick House St STJS SW1Y 10 D7
Warwick La STP EC4M 12 B3
Warwick Pde
KTN/HRWW/WS HA3 * 43 H5
Warwick Pl EA W5 116 E2
MV/WKIL W9 101 G4
THDIT KT7 * 190 B3
Warwick Pl North
PIM SW1V * 16 A7
Warwick Rd BAR EN5 21 F5
CHING E4 51 J1
EA W5 117 F1
FBAR/BDGN N11 48 D2
HSLWW TW4 134 A4
KUT/HW KT1 174 D4
MNPK E12 89 J3
NWDGN UB2 114 E3
NWMAL KT3 175 K6
PGE/AN SE20 181 J6
SCUP DA14 186 C1
SRTFD E15 88 D4
SUT SM1 209 G3
THDIT KT7 190 A2
THHTH CR7 180 B6
UED N18 36 A6
WALTH E17 51 H4
WAN E11 71 F2
WDR/YW UB7 112 B1
WELL DA16 148 D4
WHTN TW2 155 K3
WKENS W14 119 J4
Warwick Rw WESTW SW1E 16 A4
Warwick Sq PIM SW1V 16 A7
STP EC4M * 12 B3
Warwick Square Ms
PIM SW1V 16 A7
Warwick St REGST W1B 10 B5
Warwick Ter WALTH E17 * 70 B2
WOOL/PLUM SE18 127 J6
Warwick Wy PIM SW1V 16 A7
Warwick Yd STLK EC1Y * 6 D7
Washington Av MNPK E12 89 J2
Washington Cl BOW E3 105 K2
Washington Rd BARN SW13 138 D1
EHAM E6 89 G5
KUT/HW KT1 175 H5
SWFD E18 52 D5
WPK KT4 192 E6
Wastdale Rd FSTH SE23 164 A3
Watchfield Ct CHSWK W4 * 117 K5
The Watch
NFNCH/WDSPK N12 * 33 G6
Watcombe Rd SNWD SE25 197 J2
Waterbank Rd CAT SE6 164 E5
Waterbeach Rd DAGW RM9 91 J4
Water Brook La HDN NW4 64 A2
Watercress Pl IS N1 86 A5
Waterdale Rd ABYW SE2 128 B6
Waterer Ri WLGTN SM6 210 D4
Waterfall Rd FBAR/BDGN N11 34 B6
WIM/MER SW19 178 C2
Waterfall Ter TOOT SW17 178 D2
Waterfield Cl BELV DA17 129 H3
THMD SE28 128 C1
Waterfield Cots
MORT/ESHN SW14 * 137 J5
Waterfield Gdns SNWD SE25 197 F1
Waterford Rd FUL/PGN SW6 140 A1
Waterford Wy WLSDN NW10 81 K3
The Waterfront BORE WD6 * 29 H1
Water Gdns STAN HA7 43 H2
The Water Gdns BAY/PAD W2 8 C3
Watergate EMB EC4Y 12 A5
Watergate St DEPT SE8 124 D6
The Watergate OXHEY WD19 27 H4
Waterhall Av CHING E4 38 C6
Waterhall Cl WALTH E17 51 F4
Waterhead Cl ERITH DA8 150 B1
Waterhouse Cl HAMP NW3 83 H3
Wateridge Cl POP/IOD E14 124 D3
Wateringbury Cl
STMC/STPC BR5 186 C6
Water La CAMTN NW1 84 B5
ED N9 36 D3
GDMY/SEVK IG3 91 F1
KUT/HW KT1 174 E4
NWCR SE14 143 K1
SCUP DA14 169 G4
SRTFD E15 88 C4
TWK TW1 156 B3
Water Lily Cl NWDGN UB2 115 H2
Waterloo Br TPL/STR WC2R 11 G6
Waterloo Cl
EBED/NFELT TW14 153 J3
HOM E9 86 E3
Waterloo Gdns BETH E2 104 E1
ROMW/RG RM7 75 F3
Waterloo Pl CAR SM5 * 209 K1
RCH/KEW TW9 117 H6
STJS SW1Y 10 C7
Waterloo Rd BARK/HLT IG6 54 C5
CRICK NW2 63 J6
FSTGT E7 88 D3
LEY E10 69 J4
ROMW/RG RM7 75 F2
STHWK SE1 11 H7
SUT SM1 209 H3
Waterloo Ter IS N1 85 H5
Waterlow Rd ARCH N19 66 C5
Waterman Cl OXHEY WD19 27 F1
Watermans Cl
KUTN/CMB KT2 * 175 F3
Watermans Ms EA W5 * 98 A6
Waterman Sq PGE/AN SE20 181 K3
Waterman St PUT/ROE SW15 139 G4
Waterman Wy WAP E1W 123 J1
Watermead
EBED/NFELT TW14 153 H3
Watermead La CAR SM5 194 E3
Watermeadow La
FUL/PGN SW6 140 B3
Watermead Rd CAT SE6 165 F6
Watermead Wy TOTM N17 50 D4
Watermens Sq PGE/AN SE20 * 181 K3
Water Ms PECK SE15 143 K5
Watermill Cl
RCHPK/HAM TW10 156 D5
Watermill La UED N18 50 A1
Water Mill Wy FELT TW13 154 E4
Watermill Wy
WIM/MER SW19 178 B4
Watermint Cl STMC/STPC BR5 202 E1
Watermint Quay
STNW/STAM N16 68 C4
Water Rd ALP/SUD HA0 80 B6
Watersedge HOR/WEW KT19 206 E2
Water's Edge FUL/PGN SW6 * 139 G2
Watersfield Wy EDGW HA8 43 K3
Waterside WALTH E17 68 E3
Waterside Av BECK BR3 198 E2
Waterside Cl BARK IG11 91 G2
BERM/RHTH SE16 123 H2
BOW E3 87 H6
NTHLT UB5 95 K2
SURB KT6 191 F6
THMD SE28 128 A1
Waterside Ct LEW SE13 * 145 G5
Waterside Dr WOT/HER KT12 188 A2
Waterside Rd NWDGN UB2 115 F3
Waterside Wy TOOT SW17 160 B6
Watersmeet Wy THMD SE28 109 K5
Waterson St BETH E2 7 H4
Watersplash Cl KUT/HW KT1 175 F6
Watersplash La HYS/HAR UB3 113 K4
Waters Rd CAT SE6 165 H5
KUT/HW KT1 175 J5
Waters Sq KUT/HW KT1 175 J6
Water St TPL/STR WC2R 11 J5
Water Tower Hl CROY/NA CR0 211 K2
Water Tower Pl IS N1 5 K1
Waterway Av LEW SE13 144 E4
Waterworks La CLPT E5 69 F6
Waterworks Rd
BRXS/STRHM SW2 161 K1
Watery La HYS/HAR UB3 113 G5
NTHLT UB5 95 G1
RYNPK SW20 177 J5
STMC/STPC BR5 186 C2
Wates Wy MTCM CR4 194 E3
Wateville Rd TOTM N17 49 J4
Watford Cl BTSEA SW11 140 D2
Watford Heath OXHEY WD19 27 H2
Watford Heath Farm
OXHEY WD19 * 27 H2
Watford Rd BORE WD6 29 J1
CAN/RD E16 106 E4
HRW HA1 61 G6
NTHWD HA6 40 D3
Watford Wy HDN NW4 63 J1
MLHL NW7 31 F6
Watford Wy (Barnet By-Pass)
MLHL NW7 31 G6
Watkin Rd WBLY HA9 80 D1
Watkinson Rd HOLWY N7 85 F4
Watling Av EDGW HA8 44 E4
Watling Ct STP EC4M 12 D4
Watling Farm Cl BORE WD6 29 J3
Watlings Cl CROY/NA CR0 198 B3
Watling St PECK SE15 123 F6
STP EC4M 12 C4
Watlington Gv SYD SE26 182 B1
Watney Market WCHPL E1 104 D5
Watney Rd MORT/ESHN SW14 137 K4
Watneys Rd CROY/NA CR0 195 J2
Watney St WCHPL E1 104 D5
Watson Av CHEAM SM3 193 H6
EHAM E6 90 A5
Watson Cl STNW/STAM N16 85 K3
WIM/MER SW19 178 D2
Watson's Ms CAMTN NW1 8 D2
Watsons Rd WDGN N22 49 F4
Watson's St DEPT SE8 144 D1
Wattisfield Rd CLPT E5 86 E1
Watts Cl SEVS/STOTM N15 68 A2
Wattsdown Cl PLSTW E13 88 E6
Watts Gv BOW E3 105 J4
Watt's La CHST BR7 185 G4
TEDD TW11 174 B1
Watts Rd THDIT KT7 190 B4
Watts St PECK SE15 143 G2
WAP E1W 123 J1
Wat Tyler Rd GNWCH SE10 145 F3
Wauthier Cl PLMGR N13 49 H1
Wavell Dr BFN/LL DA15 167 K1
Wavel Ms KIL/WHAMP NW6 83 F5
Wavel Pl SYD SE26 163 G6
Wavendon Av CHSWK W4 118 A5
Waveney Av PECK SE15 143 J5
Waveney Cl WAP E1W 123 H1
Waverley Av BRYLDS KT5 191 J3
CHING E4 37 H6
SUT SM1 194 A6
WALTH E17 52 B6
WBLY HA9 80 B3
WHTN TW2 154 E3
Waverley Cl E/WMO/HCT KT8 189 F2
HAYES BR2 200 C2
HYS/HAR UB3 113 G4
Waverley Crs
WOOL/PLUM SE18 127 J6
Waverley Gdns BARK IG11 108 E1
BARK/HLT IG6 54 C5
EHAM E6 107 J4
NTHWD HA6 40 E4
Waverley Gv FNCH N3 46 B6
Waverley Pl FSBYPK N4 * 67 H5
STJWD NW8 2 A2
Waverley Rd CEND/HSY/T N8 66 D3
ENC/FH EN2 23 H5
EW KT17 207 K3
RAIN RM13 111 K2
RYLN/HDSTN HA2 59 J6
SNWD SE25 197 J1
STHL UB1 96 A6
SWFD E18 53 G4
TOTM N17 50 D3
WALTH E17 52 A6
WOOL/PLUM SE18 127 H5
Waverley Wy CAR SM5 209 J4
Waverton Rd
WAND/EARL SW18 160 B2
Waverton St
MYFR/PKLN W1K 9 H7
Wavertree Rd
BRXS/STRHM SW2 162 A3
SWFD E18 52 E5
Waxlow Crs STHL UB1 96 A5
Waxlow Rd WLSDN NW10 98 E1
Waxlow Wy NTHLT UB5 95 K3
Waxwell La PIN HA5 41 H6
Wayborne Gv RSLP HA4 58 A3
Waye Av HEST TW5 133 K2
Wayfarer Rd NTHLT UB5 95 J2
Wayford St BTSEA SW11 140 D3
Wayland Av HACK E8 86 C3
Waylands HYS/HAR UB3 94 B4
Waylett Pl ALP/SUD HA0 * 79 K2
WNWD SE27 162 C5
Wayne Cl ORP BR6 217 F1
Wayneflete Pl ESH/CLAY KT10 204 A1
Wayneflete Tower Av
ESH/CLAY KT10 204 A1
Waynflete Av CROY/NA CR0 211 H1
Waynflete Sq NKENS W10 100 B6
Waynflete St
WAND/EARL SW18 160 B4
Wayside CROY/NA CR0 * 213 K4
GLDGN NW11 64 C5
MORT/ESHN SW14 137 K5
Wayside Av BUSH WD23 28 D1
Wayside Cl ROM RM1 57 H6
STHGT/OAK N14 34 C1
Wayside Ct TWK TW1 156 D1
Wayside Gdns DAGE RM10 92 C3
Wayside Gv ELTH/MOT SE9 166 E6
Wayside Ms GNTH/NBYPK IG2 72 A3
Weald Cl BERM/RHTH SE16 123 J5
HAYES BR2 200 D6
Weald La KTN/HRWW/WS HA3 42 D5
Weald Ri KTN/HRWW/WS HA3 43 F3
Weald Sq CLPT E5 * 68 D6
Wealdstone Rd CHEAM SM3 193 J6
The Weald CHST BR7 184 E2
Weald Wy ROMW/RG RM7 74 D3
YEAD UB4 94 C2
Wealdwood Gdns PIN HA5 42 B2
Weale Rd CHING E4 38 B5
Weardale Gdns ENC/FH EN2 23 K2
Weardale Rd LEW SE13 145 G5
Wear Pl BETH E2 104 D2
Wearside Rd LEW SE13 144 E5
Weatherley Cl BOW E3 105 H4
Weaver Cl CROY/NA CR0 212 B2
EHAM E6 108 B6
Weavers Cl ISLW TW7 135 K5
Weaver's La STHWK SE1 19 H1
Weavers Ter FUL/PGN SW6 * 119 K6
Weaver St WCHPL E1 104 C3
Weavers Wy CAMTN NW1 84 D6
Weaver Wk WNWD SE27 162 C6
Webb Cl NKENS W10 100 A3
Webber Cl BORE WD6 29 K1
Webber Rw STHWK SE1 17 K3
Webber St STHWK SE1 17 K2
Webb Est CLPT E5 * 68 C4
Webb Pl WLSDN NW10 99 H2
Webb Rd BKHTH/KID SE3 125 J6
Webbscroft Rd DAGE RM10 92 D2
Webbs Rd YEAD UB4 94 E2
Webb's Rd BTSEA SW11 140 E6
Webb St STHWK SE1 19 G5
Webster Gdns EA W5 116 E1
Webster Rd
BERM/RHTH SE16 123 H3
WAN E11 88 A1
Wedderburn Rd BARK IG11 90 D6
HAMP NW3 83 H3
Wedgewood Cl NTHWD HA6 * 40 A3
Wedgwood Wk
KIL/WHAMP NW6 * 83 F3
Wedgwood Wy NRWD SE19 180 D3
Wedlake St NKENS W10 100 C3
Wedmore Av CLAY IG5 54 A4
Wedmore Gdns ARCH N19 66 E6
Wedmore Ms ARCH N19 84 D1
Wedmore Rd GFD/PVL UB6 96 D2
Wedmore St ARCH N19 84 D1
Weech Rd KIL/WHAMP NW6 82 E2
Weedington Rd KTTN NW5 84 A3
Weekley Sq BTSEA SW11 * 140 C4
Weighhouse St
MYFR/PKLN W1K 9 H5
Weighton Rd
KTN/HRWW/WS HA3 42 D4
PGE/AN SE20 181 J5
Weihurst Gdns SUT SM1 209 H3
Weimar St PUT/ROE SW15 139 H4
Weirdale Av TRDG/WHET N20 33 K4
Weir Hall Av UED N18 49 K2
Weir Hall Gdns UED N18 49 K1
Weir Hall Rd UED N18 49 K1
Weir Rd BAL SW12 161 H3
BXLY DA5 169 J2
WIM/MER SW19 160 A5
Weirside Gdns WDR/YW UB7 112 A1
Weirs Pas CAMTN NW1 4 D4
Weiss Rd PUT/ROE SW15 139 G4
Welbeck Av BFN/LL DA15 168 B3
YEAD UB4 95 F3
Welbeck Cl EW KT17 207 J5
NWMAL KT3 192 C2
Welbeck Rd CAR SM5 194 D4
EBAR EN4 33 H1
EHAM E6 107 H2
RYLN/HDSTN HA2 60 B5
SUT SM1 194 C6
Welbeck St CAVSQ/HST W1G 9 H2
Welbeck Vls WCHMH N21 * 35 J3
Welbeck Wy CAVSQ/HST W1G 9 J3
Welby Ct PLSTW E13 107 G1
Welby St CMBW SE5 142 C2
Welch Pl PIN HA5 * 41 G4
Weldon Cl RSLP HA4 77 F4
Weldon Dr E/WMO/HCT KT8 188 E1
Weld Pl FBAR/BDGN N11 48 B1
Welfare Rd SRTFD E15 88 C5
Welford Cl CLPT E5 87 F1
Welford Pl WIM/MER SW19 159 H6
Welham Rd TOOT SW17 179 F1
Welhouse Rd CAR SM5 194 D5
Wellacre Rd
KTN/HRWW/WS HA3 61 H3
Wellan Cl BFN/LL DA15 148 C6
Welland Gdns GFD/PVL UB6 97 F1
Welland Ms WAP E1W 123 H1
Wellands Cl BMLY BR1 184 E5
Welland St GNWCH SE10 125 F6
Well Ap BAR EN5 20 A6
Wellbrook Rd ORP BR6 216 A2
Wellby Cl ED N9 36 C3
Well Cl RSLP HA4 77 J1
STRHM/NOR SW16 162 A6
Wellclose Sq WCHPL E1 104 C6
Wellclose St WCHPL E1 104 C6
Well Cottage Cl WAN E11 71 G4
Well Ct STP EC4M 12 D4
Welldon Crs HRW HA1 60 E3
Weller Ms HAYES BR2 200 A1
Weller St STHWK SE1 18 C2
Wellesley Av HMSMTH W6 118 E3
NTHWD HA6 40 D1
Wellesley Cl CHARL SE7 * 126 B5
Wellesley Ct MV/WKIL W9 101 G2
Wellesley Court Rd
CROY/NA CR0 * 196 E6
Wellesley Crs WHTN TW2 155 K4
Wellesley Gv CROY/NA CR0 196 E6
Wellesley Pde WHTN TW2 * 155 K5
Wellesley Park Ms
ENC/FH EN2 23 H3
Wellesley Pl CAMTN NW1 * 4 C5
KTTN NW5 84 A3
Wellesley Rd BELMT SM2 209 G4
CHSWK W4 117 H5
CROY/NA CR0 196 D5
HRW HA1 60 E2
IL IG1 72 B6
KTTN NW5 84 A3
WALTH E17 69 J3
WAN E11 70 E2
WHTN TW2 155 K5
Wellesley St WCHPL E1 105 F4
Wellesley Ter IS N1 6 D4
Wellfield Av MUSWH N10 48 B6
Wellfield Gdns CAR SM5 209 J6
Wellfield Rd
STRHM/NOR SW16 161 K6
Wellfit St HNHL SE24 142 C4
Wellgarth GFD/PVL UB6 79 H4
Wellgarth Rd GLDGN NW11 65 F5
Well Gv TRDG/WHET N20 33 G3
Well Hall Pde ELTH/MOT SE9 146 E5
Well Hall Rd ELTH/MOT SE9 146 E4
Wellhouse La BAR EN5 20 A5
Wellhouse Rd BECK BR3 198 C1
Wellhurst Cl ORP BR6 217 F5
Welling High St WELL DA16 148 C4
Wellington Av BFN/LL DA15 168 B1
CHING E4 37 J4
ED N9 36 D5
HSLW TW3 135 F6
PIN HA5 41 K4
SEVS/STOTM N15 68 C3
WPK KT4 208 A1
Wellington Cl DAGE RM10 92 E5
NTGHL W11 100 E5
NWCR SE14 144 A2
OXHEY WD19 27 J5
Wellington Crs NWMAL KT3 175 K6
Wellington Dr DAGE RM10 92 E5
Wellington Gdns CHARL SE7 126 B5
WHTN TW2 155 J6
Wellington Gv GNWCH SE10 145 G1
Wellington Ms CHARL SE7 126 B6
EDUL SE22 143 H5
HOLWY N7 85 F4
STRHM/NOR SW16 161 J5
Wellington Pde
BFN/LL DA15 * 148 B6
Wellington Park Est
CRICK NW2 * 63 J6
Wellington Pas WAN E11 70 E2
Wellington Pl EFNCH N2 * 65 J2
STJWD NW8 2 B4
Wellington Rd BELV DA17 129 G5
BXLY DA5 168 E1
CROY/NA CR0 196 C4
EA W5 116 D4
EBED/NFELT TW14 133 H6
EHAM E6 89 K6
EN EN1 36 A2
FSTGT E7 88 D2
HAYES BR2 200 B1
HPTN TW12 155 J6
KTN/HRWW/WS HA3 42 E6
LEY E10 69 G5
NKENS W10 * 100 B2
PIN HA5 41 K4
STJWD NW8 2 B3
STMC/STPC BR5 202 C3
WALTH E17 51 G6
WAN E11 70 E2
WIM/MER SW19 159 K4
Wellington Rd North
HSLWW TW4 134 E4
Wellington Rd South
HSLWW TW4 134 E5
Wellington Rw BETH E2 7 K4
Wellington Sq CHEL SW3 120 E5
IS N1 * 84 E6

Wellington St COVGDN WC2E 11 F5
WOOL/PLUM SE18 127 F4
Wellington Ter BAY/PAD W2 * 100 E6
CEND/HSY/T N8 * 49 G6
HRW HA1 60 D5
WAP E1W * 123 J1
Wellington Wy BOW E3 105 J2
Welling Wy ELTH/MOT SE9 147 J4
WELL DA16 147 K4
Well La MORT/ESHN SW14 137 K6
Wellmeadow Rd CAT SE6 165 H3
HNWL W7 116 B4
Well Rd BAR EN5 20 A6
HAMP NW3 83 H1
Wells Cl NTHLT UB5 95 G2
SAND/SEL CR2 212 A3
Wells Dr CDALE/KGS NW9 63 F5
Wells Gdns IL IG1 71 J4
RAIN RM13 93 H4
Wells House Rd WLSDN NW10 99 G4
Wellside Cl BAR EN5 20 A5
Wellside Gdns
MORT/ESHN SW14 137 K5
Wells Ms FITZ W1T * 10 B2
Wellsmoor Gdns BMLY BR1 185 F6
Wells Park Rd SYD SE26 163 H5
Wells Pl CMBW SE5 143 F1
WAND/EARL SW18 160 B2
Wellspring Crs WBLY HA9 62 D6
Wells Ri STJWD NW8 2 E1
Wells Rd BMLY BR1 184 E5
SHB W12 119 F2
Wells Sq FSBYW WC1X 5 G5
Wells St GTPST W1W 10 A2
Wellstead Av ED N9 36 E2
Wellstead Rd EHAM E6 108 A1
Wells Ter FSBYPK N4 67 G6
The Wells STHGT/OAK N14 34 D3
Well St HOM E9 86 E5
SRTFD E15 88 C4
Wells Wy SKENS SW7 14 A4
WALW SE17 122 E6
Well Wk HAMP NW3 83 H1
Wellwood Rd GDMY/SEVK IG3 73 G5
Welsford St STHWK SE1 123 H5
Welsh Cl PLSTW E13 106 E2
Welshpool St HACK E8 * 86 C6
Welshside CDALE/KGS NW9 * 63 G2
Welstead Wy CHSWK W4 118 C3
Weltje Rd HMSMTH W6 118 D5
Welton Rd WOOL/PLUM SE18 147 K1
Welwyn Av
EBED/NFELT TW14 153 J1
Welwyn St BETH E2 104 E2
Welwyn Wy YEAD UB4 94 C3
Wembley Hill Rd WBLY HA9 80 B3
Wembley Park Dr WBLY HA9 80 B2
Wembley Rd HPTN TW12 173 F4
Wembley Wy WBLY HA9 80 D4
Wemborough Rd STAN HA7 43 H4
Wembury Ms HGT N6 66 B4
Wembury Rd HGT N6 66 B4
Wemyss Rd BKHTH/KID SE3 145 J3
Wendela Ct HRW HA1 78 E1
Wendell Rd SHB W12 118 C2
Wendling Rd SUT SM1 194 C5
Wendon St BOW E3 87 H6
Wendover Cl YEAD UB4 95 H3
Wendover Dr NWMAL KT3 192 C3
Wendover Rd ELTH/MOT SE9 146 C4
HAYES BR2 200 A1
WLSDN NW10 99 H1
Wendover Wy BUSH WD23 28 C1
ORP BR6 202 B3
WELL DA16 148 B6
Wendy Cl EN EN1 36 B1
Wendy Wy ALP/SUD HA0 80 A6
Wenlock Gdns HDN NW4 * 63 J1
Wenlock Rd EDGW HA8 44 D2
IS N1 6 C3
Wenlock St IS N1 6 D3
Wennington Rd BOW E3 105 F1
RAIN RM13 111 K4
Wensley Av WFD IG8 52 E3
Wensley Cl CRW RM5 56 C1
ELTH/MOT SE9 166 E1
FBAR/BDGN N11 48 A2
Wensleydale Av CLAY IG5 53 J5
Wensleydale Gdns
HPTN TW12 173 G3
Wensleydale Rd HPTN TW12 173 F4
Wensley Rd UED N18 50 D2
Wentland Cl CAT SE6 165 G4
Wentland Rd CAT SE6 165 G4
Wentworth Av FNCH N3 46 E3
Wentworth Cl ASHF TW15 152 E6
FNCH N3 47 F3
MRDN SM4 193 K4
ORP BR6 216 E3
SURB KT6 190 E6
THMD SE28 109 K5
Wentworth Crs HYS/HAR UB3 113 G3
PECK SE15 143 H1
Wentworth Dr OXHEY WD19 41 H1
PIN HA5 58 E2
Wentworth Gdns PLMGR N13 35 H5
Wentworth Hl WBLY HA9 62 B5
Wentworth Ms BOW E3 105 G3
Wentworth Pk FNCH N3 47 F3
Wentworth Pl STAN HA7 * 43 H2
Wentworth Rd BAR EN5 20 B3
CROY/NA CR0 196 B4
GLDGN NW11 64 D3
MNPK E12 89 H2
NWDGN UB2 114 B4
Wentworth St WCHPL E1 13 J3
Wentworth Wy PIN HA5 59 H1
RAIN RM13 111 K2
Wepham Cl YEAD UB4 95 H4
Wernbrook St
WOOL/PLUM SE18 127 H6
Werndee Rd SNWD SE25 197 H1
Werneth Hall Rd CLAY IG5 53 K6
Werrington St CAMTN NW1 4 B3
Werter Rd PUT/ROE SW15 139 H5
Wesleyan Pl KTTN NW5 84 B2
Wesley Av CAN/RD E16 125 K1
CAN/RD E16 126 A1
HSLW TW3 134 D3
WLSDN NW10 99 F2
Wesley Cl HOLWY N7 67 F6
LBTH SE11 122 C5
RYLN/HDSTN HA2 60 C6
STMC/STPC BR5 186 D6
WALW SE17 18 B7
Wesley Rd HYS/HAR UB3 94 E6
LEY E10 70 A4
WLSDN NW10 80 E6
Wesley Sq NTGHL W11 100 B5
Wesley St CAVSQ/HST W1G 9 H2
Wessex Av WIM/MER SW19 177 K5
Wessex Cl GDMY/SEVK IG3 72 E3
KUT/HW KT1 175 J4
THDIT KT7 190 A6
Wessex Ct BECK BR3 * 182 B4
Wessex Dr PIN HA5 41 J3
Wessex Gdns GLDGN NW11 64 C5
Wessex La GFD/PVL UB6 96 D1
Wessex St BETH E2 104 E2
Wessex Ter MTCM CR4 * 194 D2
Wessex Wy GLDGN NW11 64 C4
Wesson Md CMBW SE5 * 142 D1
Westacott YEAD UB4 94 C4
Westacott Cl ARCH N19 66 D5
West Ap STMC/STPC BR5 201 H2
West Arbour St WCHPL E1 104 E5
West Av FNCH N3 46 E2
HDN NW4 64 B2
HYS/HAR UB3 94 D6
PIN HA5 59 K3
STHL UB1 95 K6
WALTH E17 69 K2
WLGTN SM6 210 E3
West Avenue Rd WALTH E17 69 J1
West Bank BARK IG11 90 B6
ENC/FH EN2 23 J4
STNW/STAM N16 68 A4
Westbank Rd HPTN TW12 173 H2
West Barnes La NWMAL KT3 192 D2
RYNPK SW20 176 E6
Westbeech Rd WDGN N22 49 G6
Westbere Dr STAN HA7 43 K1
Westbere Rd CRICK NW2 82 C2
Westbourne Av ACT W3 99 F5
CHEAM SM3 193 H6
Westbourne Cl YEAD UB4 95 G2
Westbourne Crs BAY/PAD W2 8 A5
Westbourne Crescent Ms
BAY/PAD W2 8 A5
Westbourne Dr FSTH SE23 164 A3
Westbourne Gdns
BAY/PAD W2 101 F5
Westbourne Ga BAY/PAD W2 8 B5
Westbourne Gv BAY/PAD W2 100 E5
Westbourne Grove Ms
NTGHL W11 100 E5
Westbourne Grove Ter
BAY/PAD W2 101 F5
Westbourne Park Rd
NTGHL W11 100 D5
Westbourne Pl ED N9 36 D5
Westbourne Rd BXLYHN DA7 148 E1
CROY/NA CR0 197 G3
FELT TW13 153 J5
HOLWY N7 85 F4
SYD SE26 182 A2
Westbourne St BAY/PAD W2 8 A5
Westbourne Ter BAY/PAD W2 101 G4
Westbourne Terrace Ms
BAY/PAD W2 101 G5
Westbourne Terrace Rd
BAY/PAD W2 101 G4
Westbridge Cl SHB W12 118 D1
Westbridge Rd BTSEA SW11 140 C2
Westbrook Av HPTN TW12 172 E3
Westbrook Cl EBAR EN4 21 H4
Westbrook Crs EBAR EN4 21 H4
Westbrook Dr
STMC/STPC BR5 202 E5
Westbrooke Crs WELL DA16 148 D4
Westbrooke Rd BFN/LL DA15 167 J4
WELL DA16 148 D4
Westbrook Rd
BKHTH/KID SE3 146 A2
HEST TW5 134 E1
THHTH CR7 180 E4
Westbury Ar WDGN N22 * 49 H6
Westbury Av ALP/SUD HA0 80 A5
ESH/CLAY KT10 205 F4
SEVS/STOTM N15 49 H6
STHL UB1 96 A3
WDGN N22 49 H5
Westbury Cl RSLP HA4 58 E4
Westbury Gv
NFNCH/WDSPK N12 46 E2
Westbury La BKHH IG9 39 G4
Westbury Lodge Cl PIN HA5 41 H6
Westbury Pl BTFD TW8 116 E6
Westbury Rd ALP/SUD HA0 80 A5
BARK IG11 90 D6
BECK BR3 182 B6
BKHH IG9 39 G3
BMLY BR1 184 C4
CROY/NA CR0 196 E3
EA W5 98 A5
FBAR/BDGN N11 48 E2
FELT TW13 154 C3
FSTGT E7 89 F3
IL IG1 72 A6
NFNCH/WDSPK N12 46 E2
NTHWD HA6 26 C6
NWMAL KT3 192 A1
PGE/AN SE20 182 A4
WALTH E17 69 J1
Westbury Ter FSTGT E7 89 F4
West Carriage Dr
BAY/PAD W2 14 B2
West Central St
LSQ/SEVD WC2H 10 E3
West Chantry
KTN/HRWW/WS HA3 42 B4
Westchester Dr HDN NW4 46 B6
Westcliffe Vls KUT/HW KT1 * 175 G5
West Cl ASHF TW15 152 B6
EBAR EN4 22 A5
ED N9 36 B5
GFD/PVL UB6 96 C1
RAIN RM13 111 K3
WBLY HA9 62 B5
Westcombe Av CROY/NA CR0 195 K3
Westcombe Dr BAR EN5 20 E6
Westcombe Lodge Dr
YEAD UB4 94 B4
Westcombe Park Rd
BKHTH/KID SE3 125 H6
West Common Rd HAYES BR2 215 F2
Westcoombe Av RYNPK SW20 176 C4
Westcote Ri RSLP HA4 58 A4
Westcote Rd
STRHM/NOR SW16 179 H1
Westcott Cl BMLY BR1 200 D2
CROY/NA CR0 213 K6
SEVS/STOTM N15 68 B3
Westcott Crs HNWL W7 96 E4
Westcott House
POP/IOD E14 * 105 J6
Westcott Rd WALW SE17 122 C6
West Ct ALP/SUD HA0 61 J6
Westcroft Cl CRICK NW2 82 C2
PEND EN3 24 E1
Westcroft Gdns MRDN SM4 177 J6
Westcroft Ms HMSMTH W6 * 118 D4
Westcroft Rd CAR SM5 210 A2
Westcroft Sq HMSMTH W6 118 D4
Westcroft Wy CRICK NW2 82 C2
West Cromwell Rd ECT SW5 119 K4
West Cross Route
NTGHL W11 119 G1
West Cross Wy BTFD TW8 116 C6
Westdale Rd
WOOL/PLUM SE18 127 G6
Westdean Av LEE/GVPK SE12 166 A3
Westdean Cl
WAND/EARL SW18 160 A1
Westdown Rd CAT SE6 164 D2
SRTFD E15 88 A2
West Drayton Park Av
WDR/YW UB7 112 B3
West Drayton Rd
UX/CGN UB8 94 A4
West Dr BELMT SM2 208 B6
KTN/HRWW/WS HA3 42 D2
STRHM/NOR SW16 161 G6
West Drive Gdns
KTN/HRWW/WS HA3 42 D2
West Eaton Pl BGVA SW1W 15 G6
West Eaton Place Ms
KTBR SW1X 15 G6
West Ella Rd WLSDN NW10 81 G5
West End Av LEY E10 70 A2
PIN HA5 59 H1
West End Cl WLSDN NW10 80 E5
West End Ct PIN HA5 * 59 H1
West End Gdns NTHLT UB5 95 G1
West End La BAR EN5 20 B5
HYS/HAR UB3 133 F1
KIL/WHAMP NW6 82 E6
PIN HA5 59 H1
West End Rd NTHLT UB5 77 G5
RSLP HA4 76 D1
STHL UB1 114 D1
Westerfield Rd
SEVS/STOTM N15 * 68 B2
Westergate Rd ABYW SE2 129 F6
Westerham Av ED N9 35 K5
Westerham Dr BFN/LL DA15 168 D1
Westerham Rd HAYES BR2 215 H4
LEY E10 69 K3
Westerley Crs SYD SE26 * 182 C1
Western Av DAGE RM10 92 E4
EA W5 98 A2
GFD/PVL UB6 78 A6
GLDGN NW11 64 B3
RSLP HA4 77 F5
Western Ct FNCH N3 * 46 E2
Western Gdns EA W5 98 C6
Western Gtwy CAN/RD E16 106 E6
Western La BAL SW12 161 F2
Western Man BAR EN5 * 21 F6
Western Ms MV/WKIL W9 100 D3
Western Pde BAR EN5 20 E6
Western Pl BERM/RHTH SE16 123 K2
Western Rd BRXN/ST SW9 142 B4
EA W5 97 K6
EFNCH N2 47 K6
MTCM CR4 178 D4
NWDGN UB2 114 B4
PLSTW E13 89 F6
ROM RM1 75 G2
SUT SM1 208 E3
WALTH E17 70 A2
WDGN N22 49 F5
WLSDN NW10 98 E3
Western Ter HMSMTH W6 * 118 D5
Western Vw HYS/HAR UB3 113 J2
Westernville Gdns
GNTH/NBYPK IG2 72 C4
Western Wy BAR EN5 32 E1
THMD SE28 127 J3
Westferry Circ POP/IOD E14 124 D1
Westferry Rd POP/IOD E14 124 D3
Westfield Cl CDALE/KGS NW9 44 E6
PEND EN3 25 G4
SUT SM1 208 D2
WBPTN SW10 140 B1
Westfield Dr
KTN/HRWW/WS HA3 61 K2
Westfield Gdns CHDH RM6 73 J3
KTN/HRWW/WS HA3 61 K1
Westfield Pk PIN HA5 41 K3
Westfield Park Dr WFD IG8 53 J2
Westfield Rd BECK BR3 182 C5
CROY/NA CR0 196 C6
DAGW RM9 92 A2
MLHL NW7 31 F5
MTCM CR4 178 D5
SURB KT6 190 E2
SUT SM1 208 D2
WEA W13 116 B1
WOT/HER KT12 188 D4
Westfields BARN SW13 138 C4
Westfields Av BARN SW13 138 B4
Westfields Rd ACT W3 98 D4
Westfield St
WOOL/PLUM SE18 126 C3
Westfield Wy RSLP HA4 76 C1
WCHPL E1 105 G2
West Gdns TOOT SW17 178 D2
WAP E1W 104 D6
West Ga EA W5 98 A2
Westgate Est
EBED/NFELT TW14 * 152 E3
Westgate Rd BECK BR3 183 F4
SNWD SE25 197 J1
Westgate St HACK E8 86 D6
Westgate Ter WBPTN SW10 120 A5
Westglade Ct
KTN/HRWW/WS HA3 61 K2
West Green Pl GFD/PVL UB6 78 D6
West Green Rd
SEVS/STOTM N15 67 H1
West Gv GNWCH SE10 145 F2
WFD IG8 53 G2
Westgrove La GNWCH SE10 145 F2
West Halkin St KTBR SW1X 15 G4
West Hallowes
ELTH/MOT SE9 166 C3
West Ham La SRTFD E15 88 B5
West Hampstead Ms
KIL/WHAMP NW6 83 F4
West Harding St
FLST/FETLN EC4A * 11 K3
West Hatch Mnr RSLP HA4 58 D5
Westhay Gdns
MORT/ESHN SW14 137 J6
West Heath Av GLDGN NW11 64 E5
West Heath Cl DART DA1 * 170 C1
HAMP NW3 82 E1
West Heath Dr GLDGN NW11 64 E5
West Heath Gdns HAMP NW3 64 E6
West Heath Rd ABYW SE2 128 E6
HAMP NW3 64 E6
West Hl PUT/ROE SW15 159 H1
RYLN/HDSTN HA2 60 E6
SAND/SEL CR2 212 A6
WAND/EARL SW18 139 K6
WBLY HA9 62 B5
WIM/MER SW19 159 G2
Westhill Pk HGT N6 65 K6
West Hill Rd
WAND/EARL SW18 159 J1
West Hill Wy TRDG/WHET N20 33 F3
Westholm GLDGN NW11 65 F1
West Holme ERITH DA8 149 K2
Westholme ORP BR6 201 K4
Westholme Gdns RSLP HA4 58 E5
Westhorne Av ELTH/MOT SE9 146 C6
ELTH/MOT SE9 166 B1
Westhorpe Gdns HDN NW4 46 A6
Westhorpe Rd
PUT/ROE SW15 139 F4
West House Cl
WIM/MER SW19 159 H3
Westhurst Dr CHST BR7 185 G1
West India Av POP/IOD E14 124 D1
West India Dock Rd
POP/IOD E14 105 K6
Westlake Cl PLMGR N13 35 G5
YEAD UB4 95 J3
Westland Cl
STWL/WRAY TW19 * 152 B1
Westland Dr HAYES BR2 199 J6
Westland Pl FSBYE EC1V 6 E4
Westlands Cl HYS/HAR UB3 113 K4
Westlands Ter BAL SW12 161 H1
West La BERM/RHTH SE16 123 J2
Westlea Rd HNWL W7 116 B3
Westleigh Av PUT/ROE SW15 139 F6
Westleigh Dr BMLY BR1 184 D5
Westleigh Gdns EDGW HA8 44 C4
West Links ALP/SUD HA0 97 K2
Westlinton Cl MLHL NW7 46 C2
West Lodge Av ACT W3 117 H1
West Lodge Ct ACT W3 * 117 H1
Westmacott Dr
EBED/NFELT TW14 153 J2
West Ml KENS W8 * 119 K1
West Malling Wy HCH RM12 93 K3
West Md HOR/WEW KT19 207 G4
Westmead PUT/ROE SW15 158 E2
West Md RSLP HA4 77 G2
Westmead Rd SUT SM1 209 H2
Westmede BARK/HLT IG6 54 C2
Westmere Dr MLHL NW7 31 F5
West Mersea Cl CAN/RD E16 126 A1
West Ms PIM SW1V 15 K7
TOTM N17 * 50 D3
Westminster Av THHTH CR7 180 C5
Westminster Br WHALL SW1A 17 F3
Westminster Bridge Rd
WHALL SW1A 17 F3
Westminster Cl
EBED/NFELT TW14 153 K3
TEDD TW11 174 B1
Westminster Dr PLMGR N13 48 E1
Westminster Gdns BARK IG11 108 E1
BARK/HLT IG6 54 D5
CHING E4 38 C3
Westminster Rd ED N9 36 D3
HNWL W7 115 K1
SUT SM1 194 C6
Westmoat Cl BECK BR3 183 F3
Westmont Rd ESH/CLAY KT10 189 K6
Westmoor Gdns PEND EN3 25 F3
Westmoor Rd PEND EN3 25 F3
Westmoor St CHARL SE7 126 C4
Westmoreland Av WELL DA16 147 K4
Westmoreland Dr
BELMT SM2 209 F6
Westmoreland Pl BMLY BR1 * 183 K6
EA W5 * 97 K4
PIM SW1V * 121 G5
Westmoreland Rd
BARN SW13 138 C2
HAYES BR2 199 H2
KTN/HRWW/WS HA3 62 B1
WALW SE17 122 E6
WWKM BR4 199 H2
Westmoreland St
CAVSQ/HST W1G 9 H2
Westmoreland Ter
PGE/AN SE20 * 181 J3
PIM SW1V 121 G5
Westmorland Cl MNPK E12 71 H6
TWK TW1 156 C1
Westmorland Rd HRW HA1 60 B2
WALTH E17 69 J3
Westmorland Wy
MTCM CR4 195 J1
Westmount Ct EA W5 * 98 B4
Westmount Rd
ELTH/MOT SE9 146 E3
ELTH/MOT SE9 147 F6
West Oak BECK BR3 183 G4
Westoe Rd ED N9 36 D4
Weston Av E/WMO/HCT KT8 188 D1
THDIT KT7 189 K4
Weston Dr STAN HA7 43 H4
Weston Gdns ISLW TW7 135 J2
Weston Gn DAGW RM9 92 A2
THDIT KT7 189 K6
Weston Green Rd
ESH/CLAY KT10 189 J5
Weston Gv BMLY BR1 183 J3
Weston Pk CEND/HSY/T N8 66 E3
KUT/HW KT1 175 F5
THDIT KT7 189 K5
Weston Park Cl THDIT KT7 * 189 K5
Weston Ri FSBYW WC1X 5 H4
Weston Rd BMLY BR1 183 J4
CHSWK W4 117 K3
DAGW RM9 92 A2
ENC/FH EN2 23 K3
THDIT KT7 189 K5
Weston St STHWK SE1 19 F4
Weston Wk HACK E8 86 D5
Westover Cl BELMT SM2 209 F6
Westover Hl HAMP NW3 64 E6
Westover Rd
WAND/EARL SW18 160 B1
Westow Hl NRWD SE19 181 F2
Westow St NRWD SE19 181 F2
West Pk ELTH/MOT SE9 166 D4
West Park Av RCH/KEW TW9 137 H2
West Park Cl CHDH RM6 73 K2
HEST TW5 114 E6
West Park Rd NWDGN UB2 115 H1
RCH/KEW TW9 137 H2
West Parkside GNWCH SE10 125 H2
West Pl NWDGN UB2 * 115 G4
WIM/MER SW19 177 F1
Westpole Av EBAR EN4 22 B5
Westport Rd PLSTW E13 107 F3
Westport St WCHPL E1 105 F5
West Poultry Av FARR EC1M 12 A2
West Quarters SHB W12 99 J5
West Quay Dr YEAD UB4 95 J4
West Ridge Gdns
GFD/PVL UB6 96 C1
West Ri BAY/PAD W2 * 8 D5
West Rd CHDH RM6 74 A3
CHEL SW3 120 E6
CLAP SW4 141 J6
EA W5 98 A4
EBAR EN4 34 A3
EBED/NFELT TW14 153 G2
KUTN/CMB KT2 175 K4
ROMW/RG RM7 75 F4
SRTFD E15 88 D6
TOTM N17 50 D2
WDR/YW UB7 112 C3
West Rw NKENS W10 100 C3
Westrow Dr BARK IG11 91 F4
Westrow Gdns
GDMY/SEVK IG3 73 F6
West Sheen V RCH/KEW TW9 137 G5
Westside HDN NW4 45 K5
West Side Common
WIM/MER SW19 177 F1
West Smithfield STBT EC1A 12 A2
West Sq LBTH SE11 18 A5
West St BETH E2 104 D1
BMLY BR1 183 K4
CAR SM5 209 K1
CROY/NA CR0 211 J2
HRW HA1 60 D5
LSQ/SEVD WC2H 10 D4
SUT SM1 209 F3
WALTH E17 69 K2
WAN E11 88 C1
West Street La CAR SM5 209 K2
West Street Pl
CROY/NA CR0 * 211 J2
West Temple Sheen
MORT/ESHN SW14 137 J6
West Tenter St WCHPL E1 13 K4
West Ter BFN/LL DA15 * 167 K
West Towers PIN HA5 59 H
West Vw EBED/NFELT TW14 153 F
Westview HNWL W7 96 E
Westview Cl NKENS W10 100 A
WLSDN NW10 81 H
Westview Ct BORE WD6 29 K
Westview Crs ED N9 36 A
Westview Dr WFD IG8 53 H
West View Gdns BORE WD6 29 K
Westville Rd SHB W12 118 D
THDIT KT7 190 E
West Wk EBAR EN4 34 A
HYS/HAR UB3 113 H
Westward Rd CHING E4 51 H
Westward Wy
KTN/HRWW/WS HA3 62
West Warwick Pl PIM SW1V * 16
West Wy CROY/NA CR0 198
EDGW HA8 44
HEST TW5 134
PIN HA5 41
RSLP HA4 58
STMC/STPC BR5 201
UED N18 35
WLSDN NW10 81
WWKM BR4 199
Westway NKENS W10 100
RYNPK SW20 192
SHB W12 99
Westway Cl RYNPK SW20 176
West Way Gdns CROY/NA CR0 198
Westways HOR/WEW KT19 207
Westwell Cl STMC/STPC BR5 202
Westwell Rd
STRHM/NOR SW16 179
Westwell Road Ap
STRHM/NOR SW16 179
Westwick Gdns HMSMTH W6 119
HSLWW TW4 134
Westwood Av NRWD SE19 180
RYLN/HDSTN HA2 78
Westwood Cl BMLY BR1 184
ESH/CLAY KT10 204

Westwood Gdns BARN SW13 138 C4
Westwood Hl SYD SE26 181 H1
Westwood La WELL DA16 148 B5
Westwood Pk FSTH SE23 163 J2
Westwood Pl SYD SE26 * 181 H1
Westwood Rd BARN SW13 138 C4
GDMY/SEVK IG3 73 F5
West Woodside BXLY DA5 169 F3
Wetheral Dr STAN HA7 43 H4
Wetherby Cl NTHLT UB5 78 B4
Wetherby Gdns ECT SW5 120 B5
Wetherby Ms ECT SW5 120 A5
Wetherby Pl ECT SW5 120 B4
Wetherby Rd ENC/FH EN2 23 J2
Wetherby Wy CHSGTN KT9 206 A5
Wetherden St WALTH E17 69 H4
Wetherell Rd HOM E9 87 F6
Wetherill Rd MUSWH N10 48 A4
Wexford Rd BAL SW12 160 E2
Weybourne St
WAND/EARL SW18 160 B4
Weybridge Ct
BERM/RHTH SE16 * 123 J5
Weybridge Rd THHTH CR7 196 B1
Wey Ct HOR/WEW KT19 206 E2
Weydown Cl WIM/MER SW19 159 H3
Weyhill Rd WCHPL E1 * 104 C5
Weylond Rd BCTR RM8 92 B1
Weyman Rd BKHTH/KID SE3 146 B2
Weymouth Av EA W5 116 D3
MLHL NW7 45 G1
Weymouth Cl EHAM E6 108 B5
Weymouth Ct BELMT SM2 * 209 F5
Weymouth Ms
CAVSQ/HST W1G 9 J1
Weymouth Rd YEAD UB4 94 C2
Weymouth St
CAVSQ/HST W1G 9 H1
Weymouth Ter BETH E2 7 K2
Weymouth Vls FSBYPK N4 * 67 F6
Weymouth Wk STAN HA7 43 G2
Whadcoat St FSBYPK N4 67 G6
Whalebone Av CHDH RM6 74 B3
Whalebone Gv CHDH RM6 74 B3
Whalebone La North
CHDH RM6 74 A1
CRW RM5 56 A3
Whalebone La South
BCTR RM8 74 B4
Whales Yd SRTFD E15 * 88 C5
Wharfdale Cl
FBAR/BDGN N11 48 A2
Wharfdale Rd IS N1 5 F2
Wharfedale Gdns THHTH CR7 196 A1
Wharfedale St WBPTN SW10 120 A5
Wharf La POP/IOD E14 105 H5
TWK TW1 156 B3
Wharf Pl BETH E2 86 C6
Wharf Rd CAMTN NW1 4 D1
PEND EN3 37 G1
SRTFD E15 88 B6
Wharfside Rd POP/IOD E14 106 C5
Wharf St CAN/RD E16 106 C4
Wharf Ter PUT/ROE SW15 139 H4
Wharncliffe Dr STHL UB1 115 J1
Wharncliffe Gdns SNWD SE25 181 F5
Wharncliffe Rd SNWD SE25 180 E5
Wharton Cl WLSDN NW10 81 G4
Wharton Cots FSBYW WC1X * 5 H5
Wharton Rd BMLY BR1 184 A4
Wharton St FSBYW WC1X 5 H5
Whateley Rd EDUL SE22 143 G6
PGE/AN SE20 182 A3
Whatley Av RYNPK SW20 177 G6
Whatman Rd FSTH SE23 164 A2
Wheastone Rd NKENS W10 * 100 C4
Wheatfields PEND EN3 25 G2
Wheatfield Wy KUT/HW KT1 175 F5
Wheathill Rd PGE/AN SE20 181 J5
Wheatlands HEST TW5 115 F6
Wheatlands Rd TOOT SW17 161 F5
Wheatley Cl HDN NW4 45 J5
Wheatley Crs HYS/HAR UB3 94 E6
Wheatley Gdns ED N9 36 A4
Wheatley Rd ISLW TW7 136 A4
Wheatley St CAVSQ/HST W1G 9 H2
Wheatsheaf Cl NTHLT UB5 77 J3
Wheat Sheaf Cl POP/IOD E14 124 D4
Wheatsheaf La FUL/PGN SW6 139 F1
VX/NE SW8 141 K1
Wheatsheaf Rd ROM RM1 75 H3
Wheatsheaf Ter
FUL/PGN SW6 * 139 J1
Wheatstone Cl
WIM/MER SW19 178 C4
Wheatstone Rd NKENS W10 100 C4
Wheeler Gdns IS N1 * 84 E6
Wheeler La WCHPL E1 13 J1
Wheeler Pl HAYES BR2 200 A1
Wheelers Cross BARK IG11 108 D1
Wheelers Dr RSLP HA4 58 A3
Wheelers's St SUT SM1 208 E1
Wheel Farm Dr DAGE RM10 92 E1
Wheelright Cl BUSH WD23 28 B1
Wheelwright St HOLWY N7 85 F5
Whelan Wy WLGTN SM6 210 D1
Wheler St WCHPL E1 7 J7
Whellock Rd CHSWK W4 118 B3
Whenman Av BXLY DA5 169 K4
hetstone Cl
TRDG/WHET N20 33 H4
hetstone Pk LINN WC2A 11 G3
hetstone Rd
BKHTH/KID SE3 146 B3
hewell Rd ARCH N19 66 E6
hichcote St STHWK SE1 * 17 J1
hidborne Cl DEPT SE8 144 D3
hidborne St STPAN WC1H 5 F5
himbrel Wy YEAD UB4 95 H5
hinchat Rd THMD SE28 127 J3
hinfell Cl STRHM/NOR SW16 179 J1
hinyates Rd ELTH/MOT SE9 146 D4
nippendell Cl
STMC/STPC BR5 186 C4
nippendell Wy
STMC/STPC BR5 186 C4
nipps Cross Rd WAN E11 70 C2
hiskin St CLKNW EC1R 6 A5
nistler Gdns EDGW HA8 44 B5
nistlers Av BTSEA SW11 * 140 C1
Whistler St HBRY N5 85 H2
Whistler Wk WBPTN SW10 * 140 B1
Whiston Rd BETH E2 7 J2
Whitbread Cl TOTM N17 50 C4
Whitbread Rd BROCKY SE4 144 B5
Whitburn Rd LEW SE13 144 E6
Whitby Av WLSDN NW10 98 D2
Whitby Gdns CDALE/KGS NW9 44 C6
SUT SM1 194 C6
Whitby Pde RSLP HA4 * 59 G6
Whitby Rd RSLP HA4 59 G6
RYLN/HDSTN HA2 78 C1
SUT SM1 194 C6
WOOL/PLUM SE18 126 E4
Whitby St WCHPL E1 7 J6
Whitcher Cl NWCR SE14 124 B6
Whitcher Pl CAMTN NW1 84 C4
Whitchurch Av EDGW HA8 44 B3
Whitchurch Cl EDGW HA8 44 B2
Whitchurch Gdns EDGW HA8 44 B2
Whitchurch La EDGW HA8 44 A3
Whitchurch Pde EDGW HA8 * 44 C3
Whitchurch Rd NKENS W10 100 B6
Whitcomb St
SOHO/SHAV W1D 10 C5
Whitcome Ms RCH/KEW TW9 137 J2
Whiteadder Wy POP/IOD E14 124 E4
Whitear Wk SRTFD E15 88 B4
Whitebarn La DAGE RM10 92 C6
Whitebeam Av HAYES BR2 201 F4
Whitebeam Cl VX/NE SW8 * 142 A1
White Bear Pl HAMP NW3 * 83 H2
White Bear Yd CLKNW EC1R * 5 J7
White Bridge Av MTCM CR4 194 C1
White Bridge Cl
EBED/NFELT TW14 153 J1
White Butts Rd RSLP HA4 77 H1
Whitechapel High St
TWRH EC3N 13 K3
Whitechapel Rd WCHPL E1 104 C5
White Church La WCHPL E1 104 C5
White City Cl SHB W12 100 A6
White City Rd SHB W12 99 K6
White Conduit St IS N1 5 K2
Whitecote Rd STHL UB1 96 C5
White Craig Cl PIN HA5 42 A1
Whitecroft Cl BECK BR3 199 G1
Whitecroft Wy BECK BR3 199 F1
Whitecross St STLK EC1Y 6 D6
Whitefield Av CRICK NW2 64 A4
Whitefield Cl PUT/ROE SW15 159 H1
STMC/STPC BR5 186 D6
Whitefoot La BMLY BR1 165 G6
Whitefoot Ter BMLY BR1 165 J5
Whitefriars Av
KTN/HRWW/WS HA3 42 E5
Whitefriars Dr
KTN/HRWW/WS HA3 42 E5
Whitefriars St EMB EC4Y 11 K4
White Gdns DAGE RM10 92 C4
White Gate Gdns
KTN/HRWW/WS HA3 42 E3
White Gates THDIT KT7 190 B4
Whitehall WHALL SW1A 16 E1
Whitehall Ct WHALL SW1A 16 E1
Whitehall Crs CHSGTN KT9 205 K3
Whitehall Gdns ACT W3 117 H1
CHING E4 38 B3
CHSWK W4 117 J6
WHALL SW1A 16 E1
Whitehall La BKHH IG9 38 E4
ERITH DA8 150 C3
Whitehall Pk ARCH N19 66 C5
Whitehall Park Rd CHSWK W4 117 J6
Whitehall Pl WHALL SW1A 16 E1
WLGTN SM6 210 B2
Whitehall Rd CHING E4 38 C4
HAYES BR2 200 C2
HNWL W7 116 B2
HRW HA1 60 E4
THHTH CR7 196 B2
WFD IG8 38 E5
Whitehall St TOTM N17 50 B3
White Hart Av
WOOL/PLUM SE18 128 A3
White Hart La BARN SW13 138 B3
ROMW/RG RM7 56 C4
WDGN N22 49 G4
White Hart Rd ORP BR6 202 B4
WOOL/PLUM SE18 127 K4
White Hart St LBTH SE11 122 B5
White Hart Ter TOTM N17 * 50 B3
White Hart Yd STHWK SE1 18 E1
Whitehaven St STJWD NW8 2 C7
Whitehead Cl UED N18 49 K1
WAND/EARL SW18 160 B2
Whiteheads Gv CHEL SW3 14 D7
Whitehead's Gv CHEL SW3 120 D5
White Heart Av UX/CGN UB8 94 A4
Whiteheath Av RSLP HA4 58 A4
White Heron Ms TEDD TW11 * 174 A2
Whitehorn Pl WDR/YW UB7 112 C1
White Horse Hl CHST BR7 167 F6
Whitehorse La SNWD SE25 197 F1
White Horse La WCHPL E1 105 F3
Whitehorse Rd CROY/NA CR0 196 D4
White Horse Rd EHAM E6 107 K2
Whitehorse Rd WCHPL E1 105 G4
White Horse Rd WCHPL E1 105 G5
White Horse St
MYFR/PICC W1J 15 K1
White House Dr STAN HA7 29 J6
White House La ENC/FH EN2 23 J2
Whitehouse Wy
STHGT/OAK N14 34 B4
Whitehurst Dr UED N18 * 51 F1
White Kennett St
HDTCH EC3A 13 H3
Whitelands Crs
WAND/EARL SW18 159 H2
White Ledges WEA W13 97 J5
Whitelegg Rd PLSTW E13 106 D1
Whiteley Rd NRWD SE19 180 E1
Whiteleys Wy FELT TW13 155 F5
White Lion Ct LOTH EC2R 13 G4
PECK SE15 * 123 K6
White Lion Hl BLKFR EC4V 12 B5
White Lion St IS N1 5 J3
White Ldg NRWD SE19 180 C3
White Lodge Cl BELMT SM2 209 G5
EFNCH N2 65 H3
ISLW TW7 136 B3
The White Ldg BAR EN5 * 20 C4
White Lyon Ct STBT EC1A 12 C1
White Oak Dr BECK BR3 183 F5
White Oak Gdns BFN/LL DA15 168 A2
Whiteoaks La GFD/PVL UB6 96 D1
White Orchards STAN HA7 43 G1
TRDG/WHET N20 32 D2
White Post La HOM E9 87 H5
White Post St NWCR SE14 143 K1
White Rd SRTFD E15 88 C5
Whites Av GNTH/NBYPK IG2 72 E3
White's Grounds STHWK SE1 19 H2
Whites Grounds Est
STHWK SE1 19 H2
Whites Meadow BMLY BR1 * 201 F1
White's Rw WCHPL E1 13 J2
White's Sq CLAP SW4 141 J5
Whitestile Rd BTFD TW8 116 D5
Whitestone La HAMP NW3 83 G1
Whitestone Wk HAMP NW3 83 G1
White St STHL UB1 114 C2
Whitethorn Gdns
CROY/NA CR0 197 J6
ENC/FH EN2 23 K6
Whitethorn St BOW E3 105 J3
White Tower Wy WCHPL E1 105 G4
Whitewebbs Wy
STMC/STPC BR5 186 A4
Whitfield Ct RYNPK SW20 177 G5
Whitfield Pl FITZ W1T 4 A7
Whitfield Rd EHAM E6 89 G5
GNWCH SE10 145 G2
Whitfield St FITZ W1T 10 B1
Whitford Gdns MTCM CR4 178 E6
Whitgift Av SAND/SEL CR2 211 J3
Whitgift St CROY/NA CR0 211 J1
STHWK SE1 17 G6
Whitings Rd BAR EN5 20 A6
Whitings Wy EHAM E6 108 A4
Whitland Rd CAR SM5 194 C5
Whitley Cl STWL/WRAY TW19 152 B1
Whitley Rd TOTM N17 50 A5
Whitlock Dr WIM/MER SW19 159 H2
Whitman Rd WCHPL E1 105 G3
Whitmead Cl SAND/SEL CR2 211 K4
Whitmore Cl FBAR/BDGN N11 48 B1
Whitmore Est IS N1 7 H1
Whitmore Gdns
WLSDN NW10 100 A1
Whitmore Rd BECK BR3 182 C6
HRW HA1 60 C4
IS N1 7 G1
Whitnell Wy PUT/ROE SW15 * 139 F6
Whitney Av REDBR IG4 71 H1
Whitney Rd LEY E10 69 J4
Whitney Wk SCUP DA14 187 F2
Whitstable Cl BECK BR3 182 C4
Whitstable Pl CROY/NA CR0 211 J2
Whitstone La BECK BR3 198 E2
Whittaker Av RCH/KEW TW9 * 136 E6
Whittaker Rd CHEAM SM3 208 D1
EHAM E6 89 G5
Whittaker St BGVA SW1W 15 G7
Whitta Rd MNPK E12 89 H2
Whittell Gdns SYD SE26 163 K5
Whittingstall Rd
FUL/PGN SW6 139 J2
Whittington Av BANK EC3V 13 G4
YEAD UB4 94 D4
Whittington Ms
NFNCH/WDSPK N12 33 G6
Whittington Rd WDGN N22 48 E3
Whittington Wy PIN HA5 59 J2
Whittlebury Cl CAR SM5 209 K5
Whittle Cl STHL UB1 96 B5
WALTH E17 69 G3
Whittle Rd HEST TW5 134 B1
NWDGN UB2 115 G2
Whittlesea Rd
KTN/HRWW/WS HA3 42 C3
Whittlesey St STHWK SE1 17 K1
Whitton Av East
GFD/PVL UB6 79 F3
Whitton Av West NTHLT UB5 78 B3
Whitton Cl GFD/PVL UB6 79 H4
Whitton Dene HSLW TW3 135 G6
WHTN TW2 155 J1
Whitton Dr GFD/PVL UB6 79 G4
Whitton Manor Rd
WHTN TW2 155 H1
Whitton Rd HSLW TW3 135 G6
WHTN TW2 155 K1
Whitton Waye HSLW TW3 155 F1
Whitwell Rd PLSTW E13 106 E2
Whitworth Rd SNWD SE25 181 F6
WOOL/PLUM SE18 147 F1
Whitworth St GNWCH SE10 125 H5
Whorlton Rd PECK SE15 143 H4
Whybridge Cl RAIN RM13 93 G6
Whymark Av WDGN N22 49 G6
Whytecroft HEST TW5 134 C1
Whyteville Rd FSTGT E7 89 F4
Wichling Cl STMC/STPC BR5 202 E5
Wickersley Rd BTSEA SW11 141 F3
Wickers Oake NRWD SE19 163 G6
Wicker St WCHPL E1 * 104 C5
Wicket Rd GFD/PVL UB6 97 G2
Wickets Cl STMC/STPC BR5 202 D2
The Wickets ASHF TW15 152 B6
Wickets Wy BARK/HLT IG6 55 F2
The Wicket CROY/NA CR0 213 J3
Wickford St WCHPL E1 104 E3
Wickford Wy WALTH E17 69 F1
Wickham Av CHEAM SM3 208 A3
CROY/NA CR0 198 B6
Wickham Cha WWKM BR4 199 G4
Wickham Cl NWMAL KT3 192 C2
PEND EN3 24 D4
WCHPL E1 104 E4
Wickham Ct WWKM BR4 * 214 B2
Wickham Court Rd
WWKM BR4 199 F6
Wickham Crs WWKM BR4 199 F6
Wickham Gdns BROCKY SE4 144 C4
Wickham La ABYW SE2 128 B6
Wickham Ms BROCKY SE4 144 C3
Wickham Rd BECK BR3 182 E6
BROCKY SE4 144 C4
CHING E4 52 A3
CROY/NA CR0 197 K6
KTN/HRWW/WS HA3 42 D5
Wickham St LBTH SE11 122 A5
WELL DA16 147 K3
WELL DA16 148 B2
Wickham Wy BECK BR3 199 F2
Wick La BOW E3 105 J1
Wickliffe Av FNCH N3 46 C5
Wickliffe Gdns WBLY HA9 62 C6
Wicklow St FSBYW WC1X 5 G4
Wick Rd HOM E9 87 F4
TEDD TW11 174 C3
Wicks Cl LEE/GVPK SE12 166 C6
Wickwood St CMBW SE5 142 C3
Widdenham Rd HOLWY N7 85 F2
Widdicombe Av
RYLN/HDSTN HA2 59 J6
Widdin St SRTFD E15 88 C5
Widecombe Gdns REDBR IG4 71 J1
Widecombe Rd
ELTH/MOT SE9 166 D5
Widecombe Wy EFNCH N2 65 H2
Widegate St WCHPL E1 13 H2
Widenham Cl PIN HA5 59 G2
Wide Wy MTCM CR4 179 J6
Widgeon Cl CAN/RD E16 107 F5
Widley Rd MV/WKIL W9 100 E2
Widmore Lodge Rd
BMLY BR1 184 C5
Widmore Rd BMLY BR1 184 A5
Wieland Rd NTHWD HA6 40 E3
Wigeon Wy YEAD UB4 95 H5
Wiggins La RCHPK/HAM TW10 156 D4
Wiggins Md CDALE/KGS NW9 45 H3
Wigginton Av WBLY HA9 80 C4
Wightman Rd
CEND/HSY/T N8 67 G1
Wigley Rd FELT TW13 154 C3
Wigmore Pl MHST W1U * 9 J3
Wigmore Rd CAR SM5 194 C6
Wigmore St MHST W1U 9 H3
Wigram Rd WAN E11 71 G3
Wigram Sq WALTH E17 52 A6
Wigston Cl UED N18 50 A1
Wigston Rd PLSTW E13 107 F3
Wigton Gdns STAN HA7 44 A4
Wigton Pl LBTH SE11 122 B5
Wigton Rd WALTH E17 51 H4
Wilberforce Ms CLAP SW4 141 J5
Wilberforce Rd
CDALE/KGS NW9 63 J3
FSBYPK N4 67 H6
Wilberforce Wy
WIM/MER SW19 177 G2
Wilbraham Pl KTBR SW1X 15 G6
Wilbury Wy UED N18 49 K1
Wilby Ms NTGHL W11 100 D6
Wilcot Av OXHEY WD19 27 J2
Wilcot Cl OXHEY WD19 27 J2
Wilcox Cl VX/NE SW8 141 K1
Wilcox Rd SUT SM1 * 209 F2
TEDD TW11 155 J6
VX/NE SW8 141 K1
Wildacres NTHWD HA6 26 D6
Wild Ct HOL/ALD WC2B 11 G3
Wildcroft Gdns STAN HA7 43 K2
Wildcroft Rd PUT/ROE SW15 159 F2
Wilde Cl HACK E8 86 C6
Wilde Pl PLMGR N13 49 H2
WAND/EARL SW18 160 C2
Wilder Cl RSLP HA4 59 F5
Wilderness Ms CLAP SW4 141 G5
Wilderness Rd CHST BR7 185 G3
The Wilderness
E/WMO/HCT KT8 189 H2
HPTN TW12 * 155 G6
Wilderton Rd
STNW/STAM N16 68 A4
Wildfell Rd CAT SE6 164 E2
Wild Goose Dr NWCR SE14 143 K2
Wild Hatch GLDGN NW11 64 E3
Wild Oaks Cl NTHWD HA6 40 D2
Wild's Rents STHWK SE1 19 G4
Wild St HOL/ALD WC2B 11 F4
Wildwood NTHWD HA6 40 B2
Wildwood Cl LEE/GVPK SE12 165 J2
Wildwood Gv HAMP NW3 65 G5
Wildwood Ri GLDGN NW11 65 G5
Wildwood Rd GLDGN NW11 65 F3
Wildwood Ter HAMP NW3 65 G5
Wilford Cl ENC/FH EN2 * 23 K4
NTHWD HA6 40 B3
Wilfred Av RAIN RM13 111 J4
Wilfred Owen Cl
WIM/MER SW19 178 B2
Wilfred St WESTW SW1E 16 A4
Wilfrid Gdns ACT W3 98 E4
Wilkes Rd BTFD TW8 117 F6
Wilkes St WCHPL E1 13 K1
Wilkins Cl HYS/HAR UB3 113 J5
MTCM CR4 178 D4
Wilkinson Gdns SNWD SE25 181 F4
Wilkinson Rd CAN/RD E16 107 G5
Wilkinson St VX/NE SW8 142 A1
Wilkinson Wy CHSWK W4 118 A2
Wilkin St KTTN NW5 84 A4
Wilkin Street Ms KTTN NW5 84 A4
Wilks Gdns CROY/NA CR0 198 B5
Wilks Pl IS N1 7 H3
Willan Rd TOTM N17 49 K5
Willan Wall CAN/RD E16 106 D6
Willard St VX/NE SW8 141 G4
Willcocks Cl CHSGTN KT9 206 A1
Willcott Rd ACT W3 117 J1
Will Crooks Gdns
ELTH/MOT SE9 146 C5
Willenfield Rd WLSDN NW10 98 D1
Willenhall Av BAR EN5 33 G1
Willenhall Dr HYS/HAR UB3 94 C6
Willenhall Rd
WOOL/PLUM SE18 127 G5
Willersley Av BFN/LL DA15 168 A3
ORP BR6 216 D1
Willersley Cl BFN/LL DA15 168 A3
Willesden La
KIL/WHAMP NW6 82 B5
Willes Rd KTTN NW5 84 B4
Willett Cl NTHLT UB5 95 G2
STMC/STPC BR5 201 K3
Willett Rd THHTH CR7 196 B2
Willett Wy STMC/STPC BR5 201 J2
William Ash Cl DAGW RM9 91 H4
William Barefoot Dr
ELTH/MOT SE9 167 F4
ELTH/MOT SE9 167 F6
William Booth Rd
PGE/AN SE20 181 H4
William Carey Wy HRW HA1 60 E3
William Cl CRW RM5 56 E4
EFNCH N2 47 H5
LEW SE13 145 F4
NWDGN UB2 115 H2
William Covell Cl
ENC/FH EN2 * 23 F1
William Dr STAN HA7 43 G2
William Ellis Wy
BERM/RHTH SE16 * 123 H3
William Foster La WELL DA16 148 B3
William Gdns PUT/ROE SW15 138 E6
William Guy Gdns BOW E3 105 K2
William IV St CHCR WC2N 10 E6
William Margrie Cl
PECK SE15 * 143 H3
William Ms KTBR SW1X 15 F3
William Morley Cl EHAM E6 89 H6
William Morris Cl WALTH E17 51 H6
William Morris Wy
FUL/PGN SW6 140 B4
William Petty Wy
STMC/STPC BR5 202 D5
William Rd CAMTN NW1 4 A5
SUT SM1 209 G3
WIM/MER SW19 177 H3
Williams Av WALTH E17 51 H4
William's Blds WCHPL E1 * 104 E3
Williams Cl CEND/HSY/T N8 * 66 D3
FUL/PGN SW6 139 H1
Williams Dr HSLW TW3 135 F5
Williams Gv SURB KT6 190 D3
WDGN N22 49 G4
Williams La
MORT/ESHN SW14 137 K3
MRDN SM4 194 B3
Williamson Cl GNWCH SE10 125 J5
Williamson Rd FSBYPK N4 67 H3
Williamson St HOLWY N7 * 84 E2
Williamson Wy MLHL NW7 46 C2
William Sq BERM/RHTH SE16 124 B1
Williams Rd NWDGN UB2 114 D4
William's Rd WEA W13 * 116 B1
Williams Ter CROY/NA CR0 211 G4
William St BARK IG11 90 C5
CAR SM5 209 J1
KTBR SW1X 15 F3
LEY E10 69 K3
TOTM N17 50 B3
Willifield Wy GLDGN NW11 64 E2
Willingdon Rd WDGN N22 49 H5
Willingham Cl KTTN NW5 84 C3
Willingham Ter KTTN NW5 * 84 C3
Willingham Wy KUT/HW KT1 175 H5
Willington Rd BRXN/ST SW9 141 K4
Willis Av BELMT SM2 209 J4
Willis Rd CROY/NA CR0 196 D4
ERITH DA8 129 K4
SRTFD E15 88 D6
Willis St POP/IOD E14 105 K5
Willmore End
WIM/MER SW19 178 A4
Willoughby Av CROY/NA CR0 211 F2
Willoughby Dr RAIN RM13 93 G5
Willoughby Gv TOTM N17 50 D3
Willoughby La TOTM N17 50 D3
Willoughby Ms TOTM N17 50 D3
Willoughby Park Rd
TOTM N17 50 D3
Willoughby Rd
CEND/HSY/T N8 49 G6
HAMP NW3 83 H2
KUTN/CMB KT2 175 G4
TWK TW1 136 D6
Willoughby Wy CHARL SE7 126 A4
Willow Av BARN SW13 138 C3
BFN/LL DA15 168 B1
Willow Bank
RCHPK/HAM TW10 156 C5
Willowbay Cl BAR EN5 32 B1
Willow Bridge Rd IS N1 85 J4
Willowbrook HPTN TW12 173 G1
Willowbrook Est PECK SE15 * 143 G1
Willowbrook Rd NWDGN UB2 114 E3
PECK SE15 123 G6
STWL/WRAY TW19 152 B3
The Willow Centre
MTCM CR4 194 E2
Willow Cl BKHH IG9 39 H5
BTFD TW8 116 D6
BXLY DA5 169 G1
CAT SE6 165 J3
HAYES BR2 200 E2
HCH RM12 93 K1
STMC/STPC BR5 202 C3
Willow Ct STAN HA7 * 43 K3
Willowcourt Av
KTN/HRWW/WS HA3 61 H2
Willow Dean PIN HA5 * 41 H5
Willow Dene PIN HA5 41 H5
BUSH WD23 28 E2
Willowdene HGT N6 * 65 K4
Willowdene Cl WHTN TW2 155 H2
Willow Dr BAR EN5 20 C5
Willow End NTHWD HA6 40 E2
SURB KT6 191 F5
TRDG/WHET N20 32 E4
Willowfields Cl
WOOL/PLUM SE18 127 K5
Willow Gdns HSLW TW3 * 135 F2
RSLP HA4 58 D6
Willow Gv CHST BR7 185 F2
RSLP HA4 58 D6
Willowhayne Dr
WOT/HER KT12 188 A4
Willowhayne Gdns WPK KT4 208 A2
Willow La MTCM CR4 194 E4
WOOL/PLUM SE18 126 E4
Willowmead Cl EA W5 97 K4
Willowmere ESH/CLAY KT10 204 C2
Willow Mt CROY/NA CR0 212 A2
Willow Pl WEST SW1P 16 B6

Willow Rd CHDH RM6 74 A3
EA W5 117 F2
EN EN1 24 A3
ERITH DA8 150 D2
HAMP NW3 83 H2
NWMAL KT3 191 K1
WLGTN SM6 210 B5
Willows Av MRDN SM4 194 A2
Willows Cl PIN HA5 41 G5
Willows Ter WLSDN NW10 * 99 H1
The Willows BECK BR3 * 182 D4
EBAR EN4 * 33 J1
ESH/CLAY KT10 204 E4
OXHEY WD19 27 F2
Willow St CHING E4 38 B2
ROMW/RG RM7 74 E1
SDTCH EC2A 7 G6
Willow Ter PGE/AN SE20 * 181 J4
Willow Tree Cl NTHLT UB5 77 J4
WAND/EARL SW18 160 A3
YEAD UB4 95 G3
BOW E3 87 H1
Willowtree Cl HGDN/ICK UB10 76 A1
Willow Tree La YEAD UB4 95 G3
Willow Tree Rd YEAD UB4 95 H4
Willow Tree Wk BMLY BR1 184 A4
Willowtree Wy THHTH CR7 180 B4
Willow V CHST BR7 185 F2
SHB W12 118 D1
Willow Vw WIM/MER SW19 178 C4
Willow Wk CHEAM SM3 208 D1
DART DA1 * 151 H6
ORP BR6 216 B1
SEVS/STOTM N15 67 H1
STHWK SE1 19 H6
WALTH E17 69 H2
WCHMH N21 35 F1
Willow Wy ALP/SUD HA0 * 79 G1
FNCH N3 47 F3
HOR/WEW KT19 207 F4
NTGHL W11 100 B6
SYD SE26 163 J5
WHTN TW2 155 G4
Willow Wood Crs SNWD SE25 197 F3
Willow Wren Whf
NWDGN UB2 * 114 A4
Will Rd KTTN NW5 84 B4
Willrose Crs ABYW SE2 128 C5
Wills Crs HSLW TW3 155 G1
Wills Gv MLHL NW7 45 J1
Wilman Gv HACK E8 86 C5
Wilmar Cl YEAD UB4 94 B3
Wilmar Gdns WWKM BR4 198 E5
Wilmer Cl KUTN/CMB KT2 175 G1
Wilmer Crs KUTN/CMB KT2 175 G1
Wilmer Gdns IS N1 7 G1
Wilmer Lea Cl SRTFD E15 88 A5
Wilmer Pl STNW/STAM N16 68 B6
Wilmer Wy FBAR/BDGN N11 48 D1
Wilmington Av CHSWK W4 138 A1
ORP BR6 202 D6
Wilmington Gdns BARK IG11 90 D5
Wilmington Sq FSBYW WC1X 5 J5
Wilmington St FSBYW WC1X 5 J5
Wilmot Cl PECK SE15 * 143 H1
Wilmot Pl CAMTN NW1 84 C5
HNWL W7 115 K1
Wilmot Rd CAR SM5 * 209 K3
LEY E10 69 K6
TOTM N17 49 K6
Wilmot St BETH E2 104 D3
Wilmount St
WOOL/PLUM SE18 127 G4
Wilna Rd WAND/EARL SW18 160 B2
Wilsham St NTGHL W11 119 G1
Wilshaw Cl HDN NW4 45 J6
Wilshaw St NWCR SE14 144 D2
Wilsmere Dr
KTN/HRWW/WS HA3 42 E3
NTHLT UB5 77 J4
Wilson Av MTCM CR4 178 D3
Wilson Cl SAND/SEL CR2 211 K3
WBLY HA9 62 B4
Wilson Dr WBLY HA9 62 B4
Wilson Gdns HRW HA1 60 C4
Wilson Gv BERM/RHTH SE16 123 J2
Wilson Rd CHSGTN KT9 206 B4
CMBW SE5 142 E2
IL IG1 71 K4
PLSTW E13 107 H2
Wilson's Av TOTM N17 50 B5
Wilson's Pl POP/IOD E14 105 H5
Wilson's Rd HMSMTH W6 119 G5
Wilson St LVPST EC2M 13 F1
WALTH E17 70 A2
WCHMH N21 35 G2
Wilson Wk CHSWK W4 * 118 C4
Wilstone Cl YEAD UB4 95 J3
Wilthorne Gdns DAGE RM10 92 D5
Wilton Av CHSWK W4 118 B5
Wilton Cl WDR/YW UB7 112 A6
Wilton Crs KTBR SW1X 15 G3
WIM/MER SW19 177 J4
Wilton Dr CRW RM5 56 E3
Wilton Est HACK E8 * 86 C4
Wilton Gdns E/WMO/HCT KT8 173 F6
WOT/HER KT12 188 C5
Wilton Gv NWMAL KT3 192 C3
WIM/MER SW19 177 J3
Wilton Ms HACK E8 * 86 D4
KTBR SW1X 15 H4
Wilton Pl KTBR SW1X 15 G2
Wilton Rd EBAR EN4 21 K5
HSLWW TW4 134 C4
MUSWH N10 48 A5
PIM SW1V 15 K5
WIM/MER SW19 178 D3
Wilton Rw KTBR SW1X 15 G3
Wilton Sq IS N1 85 K6
Wilton St KTBR SW1X 15 J4
Wilton Ter KTBR SW1X 15 G4
Wilton Vls IS N1 6 E1
Wilton Wk FELT TW13 * 154 A4
Wilton Wy HACK E8 86 C4
Wiltshire Cl CHEL SW3 14 D7
MLHL NW7 * 45 H1
Wiltshire Gdns FSBYPK N4 67 J3
WHTN TW2 155 H3
Wiltshire La PIN HA5 40 D6
Wiltshire Rd BRXN/ST SW9 142 B4
ORP BR6 202 B4
THHTH CR7 180 B6
Wiltshire Rw IS N1 6 E1
Wilverley Crs NWMAL KT3 192 B3
Wimbart Rd
BRXS/STRHM SW2 * 162 A2
Wimbledon Br
WIM/MER SW19 177 J2
Wimbledon Hill Rd
WIM/MER SW19 177 H2
Wimbledon Park Rd
WIM/MER SW19 159 H5
Wimbledon Park Side
PUT/ROE SW15 158 E3
Wimbledon Rd TOOT SW17 160 B6
Wimbolt St BETH E2 104 C2
Wimborne Av NWDGN UB2 115 F4
STMC/STPC BR5 186 A6
YEAD UB4 95 F5
Wimborne Cl BKHH IG9 39 G4
LEE/GVPK SE12 145 J6
WPK KT4 193 F5
Wimborne Dr EDGW HA8 44 C6
PIN HA5 59 H4
Wimborne Gdns WEA W13 97 H5
Wimborne Rd ED N9 36 C4
TOTM N17 50 A5
Wimborne Wy BECK BR3 182 A6
Wimbourne St IS N1 6 E2
Wimpole Cl HAYES BR2 200 B1
KUT/HW KT1 175 G5
Wimpole Ms CAVSQ/HST W1G 9 J1
Wimpole Rd WDR/YW UB7 112 A1
Wimpole St CAVSQ/HST W1G 9 J2
Wimshurst Cl CROY/NA CR0 195 K5
Winans Wk BRXN/ST SW9 142 B3
Wincanton Crs NTHLT UB5 78 A3
Wincanton Gdns
BARK/HLT IG6 54 B6
Wincanton Rd
WAND/EARL SW18 159 J2
Winchcombe Rd CAR SM5 194 C6
Winchcomb Gdns
ELTH/MOT SE9 146 C4
Winchelsea Cl PUT/ROE SW15 139 G6
Winchelsea Rd FSTGT E7 88 E2
TOTM N17 50 A6
WLSDN NW10 81 F6
Winchelsey Ri SAND/SEL CR2 212 B4
Winchendon Rd
FUL/PGN SW6 139 J1
TEDD TW11 155 J6
Winchester Av
CDALE/KGS NW9 44 B6
HEST TW5 114 E6
KIL/WHAMP NW6 82 C5
Winchester Cl EN EN1 * 24 A6
ESH/CLAY KT10 204 A2
HAYES BR2 183 J6
KUTN/CMB KT2 175 J3
LBTH SE11 * 18 B7
Winchester Dr PIN HA5 59 H2
Winchester Ms WPK KT4 193 G6
Winchester Pk HAYES BR2 183 J6
Winchester Pl HACK E8 86 B3
HGT N6 66 B5
Winchester Rd BXLYHN DA7 148 E3
CHING E4 52 A3
ED N9 36 B3
FELT TW13 154 E5
HAMP NW3 83 H5
HAYES BR2 183 J6
HGT N6 66 B5
HYS/HAR UB3 133 H1
IL IG1 90 D1
KTN/HRWW/WS HA3 62 A1
ORP BR6 217 J2
TWK TW1 156 C1
Winchester Sq STHWK SE1 12 E7
Winchester St ACT W3 117 K1
PIM SW1V 121 G5
Winchester Wk STHWK SE1 12 E7
Winchfield Cl
KTN/HRWW/WS HA3 61 J3
Winchfield Rd SYD SE26 182 B1
Winchilsea Crs
E/WMO/HCT KT8 173 H5
Winchmore Hill Rd
STHGT/OAK N14 34 D3
Winchmore Vls
WCHMH N21 * 35 F2
Winckley Cl
KTN/HRWW/WS HA3 62 B2
Wincott St LBTH SE11 17 K6
Wincrofts Dr ELTH/MOT SE9 147 J5
Windall Cl NRWD SE19 181 H4
Windborough Rd CAR SM5 210 A5
Windermere Av FNCH N3 46 E5
HCH RM12 93 J3
KIL/WHAMP NW6 82 C6
RSLP HA4 59 G4
WBLY HA9 61 J5
WIM/MER SW19 178 A6
Windermere Cl
EBED/NFELT TW14 153 H3
ORP BR6 216 B1
STWL/WRAY TW19 152 A4
Windermere Gdns REDBR IG4 71 J2
Windermere Gv WBLY HA9 61 J5
Windermere Hall EDGW HA8 * 44 B1
Windermere Rd ARCH N19 * 66 C6
BXLYHN DA7 149 K3
CROY/NA CR0 197 G5
EA W5 116 D3
MUSWH N10 48 B4
PUT/ROE SW15 158 B6
STHL UB1 95 K4
STRHM/NOR SW16 179 H4
WWKM BR4 199 H6
Windermere Wy
WDR/YW UB7 112 B1
Winders Rd BTSEA SW11 140 D3
Windfield Cl SYD SE26 164 A6
Windham Rd RCH/KEW TW9 137 G4
Winding Wy BCTR RM8 91 J1
Windlass Pl DEPT SE8 124 B4
Windlesham Gv
WIM/MER SW19 159 G3
Windley Cl FSTH SE23 163 K4
Windmill Cl LEW SE13 * 145 F3
STHWK SE1 * 123 H4
SURB KT6 190 D5
Windmill Dr CLAP SW4 141 G6
CRICK NW2 82 C1
Windmill Gdns ENC/FH EN2 23 G3
Windmill Gv CROY/NA CR0 196 D4
Windmill Hl ENC/FH EN2 23 H4
HAMP NW3 * 83 G1
RSLP HA4 58 D4
Windmill La BAR EN5 31 H1
BUSH WD23 28 E3
GFD/PVL UB6 96 C4
HAYES BR2 215 G2
NWDGN UB2 115 H2
SRTFD E15 88 B4
SURB KT6 190 C4
Windmill Pas CHSWK W4 * 118 B4
Windmill Ri KUTN/CMB KT2 175 J3
Windmill Rd CHSWK W4 118 B4
CROY/NA CR0 196 D4
EA W5 116 D4
HPTN TW12 173 G1
MTCM CR4 195 H2
UED N18 35 K6
WAND/EARL SW18 160 C1
WIM/MER SW19 176 E1
Windmill Rw LBTH SE11 * 122 B5
Windmill St BUSH WD23 28 E3
FITZ W1T 10 C2
Windmill Wk STHWK SE1 * 17 K1
Windmill Wy RSLP HA4 58 D5
Windover Av CDALE/KGS NW9 63 F1
Windrose Cl
BERM/RHTH SE16 124 A2
Windrush NWMAL KT3 191 J1
Windrush Cl BTSEA SW11 * 140 C5
CHSWK W4 * 137 K1
HACK E8 86 C5
TOTM N17 50 A4
Windrush La FSTH SE23 164 A5
Windrush Rd WLSDN NW10 81 F6
Windsor Av CHEAM SM3 208 C1
E/WMO/HCT KT8 173 F6
EDGW HA8 30 D6
NWMAL KT3 191 K2
WALTH E17 51 G5
WIM/MER SW19 178 B4
Windsor Cl CHST BR7 185 G1
FNCH N3 46 C5
NTHWD HA6 40 E5
RYLN/HDSTN HA2 78 A1
WNWD SE27 162 D6
Windsor Ct NTHLT UB5 77 K3
PIN HA5 * 41 H6
STHGT/OAK N14 34 C2
Windsor Crs
RYLN/HDSTN HA2 78 A1
WBLY HA9 80 C1
Windsor Dr ASHF TW15 152 A6
EBAR EN4 33 K1
ORP BR6 217 G4
Windsor Gdns CROY/NA CR0 210 E1
HYS/HAR UB3 113 G3
MV/WKIL W9 100 E4
Windsor Gv WNWD SE27 162 D6
Windsor Ms CAT SE6 165 F5
Windsor Park Rd
HYS/HAR UB3 133 J1
Windsor Rd BAR EN5 32 B1
BCTR RM8 92 A1
CHING E4 37 K6
CRICK NW2 81 K4
EA W5 98 A6
FNCH N3 46 C5
FSTGT E7 89 F3
HOLWY N7 84 E1
HSLWW TW4 134 A3
IL IG1 90 C2
KTN/HRWW/WS HA3 42 C4
KUTN/CMB KT2 175 F3
LEY E10 69 K6
NWDGN UB2 114 E3
PLMGR N13 35 G5
RCH/KEW TW9 137 G3
TEDD TW11 173 J1
THHTH CR7 180 C5
TOTM N17 50 C5
WAN E11 70 E5
WPK KT4 192 D6
The Windsors BKHH IG9 39 J4
Windsor St IS N1 85 H6
Windsor Ter IS N1 6 D4
Windsor Wk CMBW SE5 142 E3
Windsor Wy WKENS W14 119 G4
Windspoint Dr PECK SE15 123 J6
Windstock Cl
BERM/RHTH SE16 124 C3
Windus Rd STNW/STAM N16 68 B5
Windy Rdg BMLY BR1 184 D4
Windy Ridge Cl
WIM/MER SW19 177 G1
Wine Cl WAP E1W 104 E6
Wine Office Ct
FLST/FETLN EC4A 11 K3
Winery La KUT/HW KT1 175 G6
Winey Cl CHSGTN KT9 205 J5
Winforton St GNWCH SE10 145 F2
Winfrith Rd
WAND/EARL SW18 160 B2
Wingate Crs CROY/NA CR0 195 K3
Wingate Rd HMSMTH W6 118 E3
IL IG1 90 B3
SCUP DA14 186 D1
Wingfield Ct WATW WD18 * 26 B1
Wingfield Ms PECK SE15 143 H4
Wingfield Rd KUTN/CMB KT2 175 G2
SRTFD E15 88 C3
WALTH E17 69 K2
Wingfield St PECK SE15 143 H4
Wingfield Wy RSLP HA4 77 F4
Wingford Rd
BRXS/STRHM SW2 161 K1
Wingmore Rd HNHL SE24 142 D4
Wingrave Rd HMSMTH W6 119 F6
Wingrove Rd CAT SE6 165 H4
Wings Cl SUT SM1 208 E2
Winifred Cl BAR EN5 31 H1
Winifred Pl
NFNCH/WDSPK N12 47 G1
Winifred Rd BCTR RM8 74 A6
ERITH DA8 130 B5
HPTN TW12 155 F6
WIM/MER SW19 177 K4
Winifred St CAN/RD E16 126 E1
Winifred Ter EN EN1 36 B2
PLSTW E13 106 E1
Winkfield Rd WDGN N22 49 G4
Winkley St BETH E2 104 D1
Winkworth Cots WCHPL E1 * 104 E3
Winlaton Rd BMLY BR1 165 G6
Winmill Rd BCTR RM8 92 B1
Winn Common Rd
WOOL/PLUM SE18 127 K6
Winnett St SOHO/SHAV W1D 10 C5
Winnington Cl EFNCH N2 65 H3
Winnington Rd EFNCH N2 65 H4
PEND EN3 24 E1
Winnipeg Dr ORP BR6 217 F4
Winnock Rd WDR/YW UB7 112 A1
Winns Av WALTH E17 51 H6
Winns Ms SEVS/STOTM N15 68 A1
Winns Ter WALTH E17 51 J5
Winsbeach WALTH E17 52 B6
Winscombe Crs EA W5 97 K3
Winscombe St KTTN NW5 84 B1
Winscombe Wy STAN HA7 43 G1
Winsford Rd CAT SE6 164 C5
Winsford Ter UED N18 * 49 K1
Winsham Gv BTSEA SW11 141 F6
Winslade Rd
BRXS/STRHM SW2 141 K6
Winsland Ms BAY/PAD W2 8 A3
Winsland St BAY/PAD W2 8 A3
Winsley St GTPST W1W 10 A3
Winslow Cl PIN HA5 59 F3
WLSDN NW10 81 G1
Winslow Gv CHING E4 38 C4
Winslow Rd HMSMTH W6 119 F6
Winslow Wy FELT TW13 154 C5
Winsor Ter EHAM E6 108 A4
Winstanley Rd BTSEA SW11 140 C4
Winstead Gdns DAGE RM10 92 E3
Winston Av CDALE/KGS NW9 63 G4
Winston Cl
KTN/HRWW/WS HA3 43 F2
ROMW/RG RM7 74 D1
Winston Ct
KTN/HRWW/WS HA3 42 B3
Winston House SURB KT6 * 191 F2
Winston Rd STNW/STAM N16 85 K2
Winston Wy IL IG1 90 B1
Winter Av EHAM E6 89 J6
Winterborne Av ORP BR6 216 D1
Winterbourne Rd BCTR RM8 73 J6
CAT SE6 164 C3
THHTH CR7 196 B1
Winter Box Wk
RCHPK/HAM TW10 137 G6
Winterbrook Rd HNHL SE24 162 D1
Winterburn Cl
FBAR/BDGN N11 48 A2
Winterfold Cl WIM/MER SW19 159 H4
Winters Rd THDIT KT7 190 C4
Winterstoke Rd FSTH SE23 164 C3
Winterton Pl WBPTN SW10 120 B6
Winterwell Rd
BRXS/STRHM SW2 141 K6
Winthorpe Rd PUT/ROE SW15 139 H5
Winthrope St WCHPL E1 104 D4
Winthrop St WCHPL E1 * 104 D4
Winton Av FBAR/BDGN N11 48 C3
Winton Cl ED N9 37 F2
Winton Gdns EDGW HA8 44 B3
Winton Rd ORP BR6 216 B2
The Wintons BUSH WD23 * 28 D5
Winton Wy
STRHM/NOR SW16 180 B1
Wirral Wood Cl CHST BR7 185 F2
Wisbeach Rd CROY/NA CR0 196 E2
Wisborough Rd
SAND/SEL CR2 212 B6
Wisdons Cl DAGE RM10 74 D5
Wise La MLHL NW7 45 J2
WDR/YW UB7 112 A4
Wiseman Rd LEY E10 * 69 J6
Wise Rd SRTFD E15 88 A6
Wiseton Rd TOOT SW17 160 D3
Wishart Rd BKHTH/KID SE3 146 C2
Wishaw Wk FBAR/BDGN N11 48 E2
Wisley Rd BTSEA SW11 140 E6
STMC/STPC BR5 186 B3
Wistaria Cl ORP BR6 201 G6
Wisteria Cl IL IG1 90 B3
MLHL NW7 45 H2
Wisteria Rd LEW SE13 145 G5
Witanhurst La HGT N6 66 A5
Witan St BETH E2 104 D2
Witham Cl LOU IG10 39 J1
Witham Rd DAGE RM10 92 C3
GPK RM2 75 K2
ISLW TW7 135 J2
PGE/AN SE20 181 K6
WEA W13 116 B1
Withens Cl STMC/STPC BR5 * 202 D1
Witherby Cl CROY/NA CR0 212 A3
Witherington Rd HBRY N5 * 85 G3
Withers Md CDALE/KGS NW9 45 H4
Witherston Wy
ELTH/MOT SE9 167 F4
Withycombe Rd
WIM/MER SW19 159 G2
Withy La RSLP HA4 58 A2
Withy Md CHING E4 38 B5
Witley Crs CROY/NA CR0 214 A4
Witley Gdns NWDGN UB2 114 E4
Witley Rd ARCH N19 66 C6
Witney Cl PIN HA5 41 K2
Witney Pth FSTH SE23 164 A5
Wittenham Wy CHING E4 38 B5
Wittering Cl KUTN/CMB KT2 174 E1
Wittersham Rd BMLY BR1 183 J1
Wivenhoe Cl PECK SE15 143 H4
Wivenhoe Ct HSLW TW3 134 E5
Wivenhoe Rd BARK IG11 109 G1
Wiverton Rd SYD SE26 181 K2
Wix Rd DAGW RM9 91 K6
Wix's La CLAP SW4 141 G5
Woburn WEA W13 * 97 H4
Woburn Av HCH RM12 93 J2
Woburn Cl BUSH WD23 28 C1
THMD SE28 109 K5
WIM/MER SW19 178 B2
Woburn Pl STPAN WC1H 4 E6
Woburn Rd CAR SM5 194 D5
CROY/NA CR0 196 D5
Woburn Sq STPAN WC1H 4 D7
Woburn Wk STPAN WC1H * 4 D5
Wodeham Gdns WCHPL E1 104 C4
Wodehouse Av CMBW SE5 143 G2
Wodehouse Rd DART DA1 151 K5
Woffington Cl TEDD TW11 174 D3
Woking Cl PUT/ROE SW15 138 C5
Woldham Pl HAYES BR2 200 B1
Woldham Rd HAYES BR2 200 B1
Wolds Dr ORP BR6 216 A2
Wolfe Cl YEAD UB4 95 F2
Wolfe Crs BERM/RHTH SE16 124 A2
CHARL SE7 126 C5
Wolferton Rd MNPK E12 89 K2
Wolfington Rd WNWD SE27 162 C6
Wolfram Cl LEW SE13 145 H6
Wolftencroft Cl BTSEA SW11 140 D4
Wollaston Cl STHWK SE1 18 B6
Wolmer Cl EDGW HA8 30 C6
Wolmer Gdns EDGW HA8 30 C5
Wolseley Av
WAND/EARL SW18 159 K4
Wolseley Gdns CHSWK W4 117 J6
Wolseley Rd CEND/HSY/T N8 66 D3
CHSWK W4 117 K4
FSTGT E7 89 F5
KTN/HRWW/WS HA3 42 E6
MTCM CR4 195 F4
ROMW/RG RM7 75 F4
WDGN N22 49 F4
Wolseley St STHWK SE1 19 K3
Wolsey Av EHAM E6 108 A2
THDIT KT7 190 A2
WALTH E17 51 H6
Wolsey Cl HSLW TW3 135 H5
KUTN/CMB KT2 175 J4
NWDGN UB2 115 H3
RYNPK SW20 176 E3
WPK KT4 207 J2
Wolsey Ct ELTH/MOT SE9 * 166 E1
Wolsey Crs CROY/NA CR0 214 A6
MRDN SM4 193 J4
Wolsey Dr KUTN/CMB KT2 175 F1
WOT/HER KT12 188 C5
Wolsey Gdns BARK/HLT IG6 54 B2
Wolsey Gv EDGW HA8 45 F3
ESH/CLAY KT10 204 B2
Wolsey Ms KTTN NW5 84 C4
ORP BR6 217 F3
Wolsey Rd ASHF TW15 152 B6
E/WMO/HCT KT8 189 J1
EN EN1 24 D3
ESH/CLAY KT10 204 B2
HPTN TW12 173 G2
IS N1 85 K3
NTHWD HA6 26 A4
Wolsey St WCHPL E1 104 E4
Wolsey Wy CHSGTN KT9 206 C3
Wolstonbury
NFNCH/WDSPK N12 46 E1
Wolvercote Rd ABYW SE2 128 E2
Wolverley St BETH E2 * 104 D2
Wolverton Av KUTN/CMB KT2 175 H4
Wolverton Gdns EA W5 98 B6
HMSMTH W6 119 G4
Wolverton Rd STAN HA7 43 H2
Wolverton Wy
STHGT/OAK N14 22 C6
Wolves La WDGN N22 40 G3
Womersley Rd
CEND/HSY/T N8 67 F3
Wonersh Wy BELMT SM2 208 B6
Wonford Cl KUTN/CMB KT2 176 B4
Wontner Cl IS N1 85 J5
Wontner Rd BAL SW12 160 E4
Woodall Cl CHSGTN KT9 205 J5
Woodall Rd PEND EN3 25 F6
Woodbank Rd BMLY BR1 165 J5
Woodbastwick Rd SYD SE26 182 A2
Woodberry Av
RYLN/HDSTN HA2 60 C1
WCHMH N21 35 G4
Woodberry Cl MLHL NW7 46 B3
Woodberry Crs MUSWH N10 48 B6
Woodberry Down FSBYPK N4 67 J5
Woodberry Gdns
NFNCH/WDSPK N12 47 G2
Woodberry Gv FSBYPK N4 67 J4
NFNCH/WDSPK N12 47 G2
Woodberry Wy CHING E4 38 A2
NFNCH/WDSPK N12 47 G2
Woodbine Cl WHTN TW2 155 J4
Woodbine Gv ENC/FH EN2 23 K1
PGE/AN SE20 181 J3
Woodbine La WPK KT4 207 K1
Woodbine Pl WAN E11 70 E3
Woodbine Rd BFN/LL DA15 167 K3
Woodbines Av KUT/HW KT1 174 E6
Woodbine Ter HOM E9 86 E4
Woodborough Rd
PUT/ROE SW15 138 E5
Woodbourne Av
STRHM/NOR SW16 161 J5
Woodbourne Dr
ESH/CLAY KT10 205 F4
Woodbourne Gdns
WLGTN SM6 210 B5
Woodbridge Cl HOLWY N7 67 F
Woodbridge Rd BARK IG11 91 F
Woodbridge St CLKNW EC1R 6 A
Woodbrook Rd ABYW SE2 128 B
Woodburn Cl HDN NW4 64 B
Woodbury Cl CROY/NA CR0 197 G
WAN E11 71 F
Woodbury Gdns
LEE/GVPK SE12 166 A
Woodbury Park Rd WEA W13 97 H
Woodbury Rd WALTH E17 69 K
Woodbury St TOOT SW17 178 D
Woodchester Sq
BAY/PAD W2 101 F
Woodchurch Cl SCUP DA14 167 J
Woodchurch Dr BMLY BR1 184 C
Woodchurch Rd
KIL/WHAMP NW6 82 E

Wood Cl BETH E2 104 C3
CDALE/KGS NW9 63 F4
HRW HA1 60 D4
Woodclyffe Dr CHST BR7 185 F5
Woodcock Dell Av
KTN/HRWW/WS HA3 61 J4
Woodcock Hl
KTN/HRWW/WS HA3 61 J3
Woodcocks CAN/RD E16 107 G4
Woodcombe Crs FSTH SE23 163 K3
Woodcote Cl PEND EN3 36 E1
Woodcote Av HCH RM12 93 J2
MLHL NW7 46 A2
THHTH CR7 196 C1
WLGTN SM6 210 B6
Woodcote Cl KUTN/CMB KT2 175 G1
Woodcote Dr ORP BR6 201 J4
Woodcote Gn WLGTN SM6 210 C6
Woodcote Ms LOU IG10 39 H2
WLGTN SM6 210 B4
Woodcote Pl WNWD SE27 * 180 C1
Woodcote Rd WAN E11 70 E4
WLGTN SM6 210 B4
Wood Crest BELMT SM2 * 209 G5
Woodcroft ELTH/MOT SE9 166 E5
GFD/PVL UB6 79 G4
WCHMH N21 35 F3
Woodcroft Av MLHL NW7 45 G3
STAN HA7 43 G4
Woodcroft Ms DEPT SE8 124 B4
Woodcroft Rd THHTH CR7 196 C2
Wood Dene PECK SE15 * 143 J2
Wood Dr CHST BR7 184 D2
Woodedge Cl CHING E4 38 D3
Wooden Bridge Ter
WNWD SE27 * 162 C5
Wood End HYS/HAR UB3 94 C5
Woodend ESH/CLAY KT10 189 H6
NRWD SE19 180 D2
SUT SM1 194 B6
Wood End SWLY BR8 203 K1
Wood End Av
RYLN/HDSTN HA2 78 B2
Wood End Cl NTHLT UB5 78 D3
Woodend Gdns ENC/FH EN2 22 E5
Wood End Gdns NTHLT UB5 78 C3
Wood End Gn YEAD UB4 94 D4
Wood End Green Rd
HYS/HAR UB3 94 B4
Wood End La NTHLT UB5 78 B4
Wood End Rd HRW HA1 78 D2
Woodend Rd WALTH E17 52 A5
The Wood End WLGTN SM6 210 B6
Wood End Wy NTHLT UB5 78 C3
Wooder Gdns FSTGT E7 88 D2
Wooderson Cl SNWD SE25 197 F1
Woodfall Av BAR EN5 20 D6
Woodfall Dr DART DA1 150 C5
Woodfall Rd FSBYPK N4 67 G5
Woodfall St CHEL SW3 120 E5
Woodfarrs CMBW SE5 142 E5
Wood Fld HAMP NW3 * 83 K3
Woodfield Av ALP/SUD HA0 79 J1
CAR SM5 210 A4
CDALE/KGS NW9 63 G1
EA W5 97 J3
NTHWD HA6 26 C6
STRHM/NOR SW16 161 J5
Woodfield Cl EN EN1 24 A5
NRWD SE19 180 D3
Woodfield Crs EA W5 97 K3
Woodfield Dr EBAR EN4 34 A3
GPK RM2 75 J1
Woodfield Gdns NWMAL KT3 192 C2
Woodfield Gv
STRHM/NOR SW16 161 J5
Woodfield La
STRHM/NOR SW16 161 J5
Woodfield Pl MV/WKIL W9 100 D4
Woodfield Ri BUSH WD23 28 D2
Woodfield Rd EA W5 97 J3
HSLWW TW4 134 A3
MV/WKIL W9 100 D4
THDIT KT7 190 A6
Woodfield Wy
FBAR/BDGN N11 48 D3
Woodford Av
GNTH/NBYPK IG2 71 K2
Woodford Bridge Rd
REDBR IG4 53 H6
Woodford Crs PIN HA5 41 F5
Woodford New Rd
WALTH E17 52 C6
Woodford Pl WBLY HA9 62 A5
Woodford Rd FSTGT E7 89 F2
SWFD E18 70 E1
Woodgate Av CHSGTN KT9 205 K3
Woodgate Crs NTHWD HA6 40 E2
Woodgate Dr
STRHM/NOR SW16 179 J3
Woodger Rd SHB W12 119 F2
Woodget Cl EHAM E6 107 J5
Woodgrange Av EA W5 117 G1
EN EN1 36 C1
KTN/HRWW/WS HA3 61 J2
NFNCH/WDSPK N12 47 H2
Woodgrange Cl
KTN/HRWW/WS HA3 61 K2
Woodgrange Gdns EN EN1 36 C1
Woodgrange Rd FSTGT E7 88 E3
Woodgrange Ter EN EN1 * 36 C1
Woodhall Av DUL SE21 163 G5
PIN HA5 41 J4
Woodhall Dr DUL SE21 163 G5
PIN HA5 41 H4
Woodhall Ga PIN HA5 41 H3
Woodhall La OXHEY WD19 27 H5
Woodham Ct SWFD E18 70 D1
Woodham Rd CAT SE6 165 F5
Woodhatch Cl EHAM E6 107 J4
Woodhaven Gdns
BARK/HLT IG6 72 C1
Woodhayes Rd
WIM/MER SW19 177 F2
Woodhead Dr ORP BR6 216 E1
Woodheyes Rd WLSDN NW10 81 G3
Woodhill WOOL/PLUM SE18 126 D4
Woodhill Crs
KTN/HRWW/WS HA3 61 K3
Woodhouse Av GFD/PVL UB6 97 F1
Woodhouse Cl EDUL SE22 143 H5
GFD/PVL UB6 97 F1
HYS/HAR UB3 113 H3
Woodhouse Eaves
NTHWD HA6 40 E1
Woodhouse Gv FSTGT E7 89 J4
Woodhouse Rd
NFNCH/WDSPK N12 47 G2
WAN E11 88 D1
Woodhurst Av
STMC/STPC BR5 201 H3
Woodhurst Rd ABYW SE2 128 B5
ACT W3 117 K1
Woodington Cl
ELTH/MOT SE9 167 F1
Woodknoll Dr CHST BR7 184 E4
Woodland Ap GFD/PVL UB6 79 G4
Woodland Cl CDALE/KGS NW9 62 E3
HOR/WEW KT19 * 207 G4
NRWD SE19 181 F2
WFD IG8 39 F5
Woodland Ct GLDGN NW11 * 64 C2
Woodland Crs
BERM/RHTH SE16 124 A2
GNWCH SE10 125 H6
Woodland Gdns ISLW TW7 135 K4
MUSWH N10 66 B2
Woodland Gv CROY/NA CR0 211 G5
GNWCH SE10 125 H5
Woodland Hl NRWD SE19 181 F2
Woodland Ms
STRHM/NOR SW16 161 K5
Woodland Ri GFD/PVL UB6 79 G4
MUSWH N10 66 B1
Woodland Rd CHING E4 38 A3
FBAR/BDGN N11 48 B1
NRWD SE19 181 F1
THHTH CR7 196 B1
Woodlands GLDGN NW11 64 C2
RYLN/HDSTN HA2 60 A1
RYNPK SW20 193 F1
Woodlands Av ACT W3 117 J1
BFN/LL DA15 167 K3
CHDH RM6 74 A3
FNCH N3 47 G3
NWMAL KT3 176 A4
RSLP HA4 59 G5
WAN E11 71 F5
WPK KT4 192 C6
Woodlands Cl BMLY BR1 184 E5
ESH/CLAY KT10 205 F5
GLDGN NW11 64 C2
Woodlands Dr STAN HA7 43 F2
SUN TW16 172 B5
Woodlands Gdns
WALTH E17 * 70 C1
Woodlands Gv ISLW TW7 135 K3
Woodlands Pk BXLY DA5 169 K6
Woodlands Park Rd
GNWCH SE10 125 H6
SEVS/STOTM N15 67 J2
Woodlands Rd BARN SW13 138 C4
BMLY BR1 184 E5
ED N9 36 E3
ENC/FH EN2 23 K1
HRW HA1 61 F2
IL IG1 90 C1
ISLW TW7 135 K4
ORP BR6 217 G4
ROM RM1 57 H6
STHL UB1 114 C1
SURB KT6 190 E4
WALTH E17 52 A6
WAN E11 70 C6
Woodlands St LEW SE13 165 G2
Woodlands Ter SWLY BR8 * 203 K3
The Woodlands
BRXN/ST SW9 * 142 C1
ESH/CLAY KT10 189 H6
HRW HA1 * 60 E6
ISLW TW7 136 A3
LEW SE13 165 G2
NRWD SE19 180 D3
ORP BR6 217 H4
STAN HA7 * 43 H1
STHGT/OAK N14 34 B3
WLGTN SM6 210 B6
Woodland St HACK E8 * 86 B4
Woodlands Wy
PUT/ROE SW15 139 J6
Woodland Ter CHARL SE7 126 D4
Woodland Wk HAMP NW3 83 J3
HOR/WEW KT19 206 C4
Woodland Wy ABYW SE2 128 E4
BRYLDS KT5 191 J6
CROY/NA CR0 198 B5
MLHL NW7 45 G2
MRDN SM4 193 J1
MTCM CR4 179 F3
STMC/STPC BR5 201 H1
WCHMH N21 35 G4
WFD IG8 39 F5
WWKM BR4 214 A1
Wood La BCTR RM8 74 C6
CDALE/KGS NW9 63 F4
DAGW RM9 92 A1
HCH RM12 93 J3
HGT N6 66 B3
ISLW TW7 115 K6
MUSWH N10 66 C2
RSLP HA4 58 B6
SHB W12 100 A6
STAN HA7 29 H5
WFD IG8 52 D1
Woodlawn Cl PUT/ROE SW15 139 J6
Woodlawn Crs WHTN TW2 155 G4
Woodlawn Dr FELT TW13 154 C4
Woodlawn Rd FUL/PGN SW6 139 G1
Woodlea Dr HAYES BR2 199 H2
Woodlea Gv NTHWD HA6 40 A2
Woodlea Rd STNW/STAM N16 86 A1
Woodleigh Av
NFNCH/WDSPK N12 47 J2
Woodleigh Gdns
STRHM/NOR SW16 161 K5
Woodley Cl TOOT SW17 178 E3
Woodley La SUT SM1 209 J1
Woodley Rd ORP BR6 202 D6
Wood Lodge Gdns BMLY BR1 184 D3
Wood Lodge La WWKM BR4 214 A1
Woodman Ms RCH/KEW TW9 137 J2
Woodman Pth BARK/HLT IG6 54 E1
Woodman Rd BARK/HLT IG6 54 E2
Woodmans Gv WLSDN NW10 81 H3
Woodmansterne Rd CAR SM5 209 J6
STRHM/NOR SW16 179 H3
Woodman St CAN/RD E16 127 F1
Wood Md TOTM N17 * 50 C2
Woodmere ELTH/MOT SE9 166 E2
Woodmere Av CROY/NA CR0 198 A4
Woodmere Cl BTSEA SW11 141 F4
CROY/NA CR0 198 A4
Woodmere Gdns
CROY/NA CR0 198 A4
Woodmere Wy BECK BR3 199 G2
Woodmill Rd CLPT E5 68 E6
Woodnook Rd
STRHM/NOR SW16 179 G1
Woodpecker Cl BUSH WD23 28 C3
ED N9 36 D1
KTN/HRWW/WS HA3 43 F4
Woodpecker Ms LEW SE13 145 G5
Woodpecker Mt
CROY/NA CR0 213 G6
Woodpecker Rd THMD SE28 109 J6
Woodquest Av HNHL SE24 142 C6
Wood Ride EBAR EN4 21 H2
STMC/STPC BR5 201 J1
Woodridge Cl ENC/FH EN2 * 23 G2
Woodridge Wy NTHWD HA6 40 C2
Woodridings Av PIN HA5 41 K4
Woodridings Cl PIN HA5 41 K3
Woodriffe Rd WAN E11 70 B4
Wood Ri PIN HA5 58 E2
Wood Rd WLSDN NW10 80 E5
Woodrow WOOL/PLUM SE18 126 D4
Woodrow Av YEAD UB4 94 D4
Woodrow Cl GFD/PVL UB6 79 H5
Woodrow Ct TOTM N17 50 D3
Woodrush Cl NWCR SE14 144 B1
Woodrush Wy CHDH RM6 73 K1
Woodseer St WCHPL E1 13 K1
Woodsford Sq WKENS W14 119 H2
Woodshire Rd DAGE RM10 92 D1
Woodside BKHH IG9 39 G4
GLDGN NW11 64 E2
ORP BR6 217 G3
WIM/MER SW19 177 J1
Woodside Av ALP/SUD HA0 80 A6
CHST BR7 185 H1
ESH/CLAY KT10 189 K4
HGT N6 65 K2
NFNCH/WDSPK N12 33 G6
SNWD SE25 197 J3
Woodside Cl ALP/SUD HA0 80 A6
BRYLDS KT5 191 K4
BXLYHN DA7 150 A5
RSLP HA4 58 B3
STAN HA7 43 G1
Woodside Ct EA W5 * 117 F1
Woodside Court Rd
CROY/NA CR0 197 H4
Woodside Crs BFN/LL DA15 167 K5
Woodside End ALP/SUD HA0 80 A6
Woodside Gdns CHING E4 51 K1
TOTM N17 50 B5
Woodside Grange Rd
NFNCH/WDSPK N12 33 F6
Woodside Gn SNWD SE25 197 H3
Woodside Gv
NFNCH/WDSPK N12 33 G5
Woodside La BXLY DA5 168 E1
TRDG/WHET N20 33 F5
Woodside Pde BFN/LL DA15 * 167 K5
Woodside Pk SNWD SE25 197 H3
Woodside Park Av
WALTH E17 70 B1
Woodside Park Rd
NFNCH/WDSPK N12 33 F6
Woodside Pl ALP/SUD HA0 80 A6
Woodside Rd BFN/LL DA15 167 K5
BMLY BR1 200 D2
BXLYHN DA7 150 A5
KUTN/CMB KT2 175 F3
NTHWD HA6 40 D3
NWMAL KT3 176 A5
PLSTW E13 107 G3
SNWD SE25 197 J3
SUT SM1 209 G1
WDGN N22 49 G3
WFD IG8 38 E6
Woodside Wy CROY/NA CR0 197 K3
MTCM CR4 179 G4
Wood's Ms MYFR/PKLN W1K 9 F5
Woodsome Rd KTTN NW5 84 A1
Wood's Pl STHWK SE1 19 H5
Woodspring Rd
WIM/MER SW19 159 H4
Wood's Rd PECK SE15 143 J2
Woodstead Gv EDGW HA8 44 A2
The Woods NTHWD HA6 40 E1
Woodstock Av CHEAM SM3 193 J4
GLDGN NW11 64 C4
ISLW TW7 136 B6
STHL UB1 95 K2
WEA W13 116 B3
Woodstock Cl BXLY DA5 169 G3
STAN HA7 44 A5
Woodstock Crs ED N9 36 D1
Woodstock Gdns BECK BR3 182 E4
GDMY/SEVK IG3 73 G6
YEAD UB4 94 D4
Woodstock Gra EA W5 * 117 F1
Woodstock Gv SHB W12 119 G2
Woodstock La North
SURB KT6 190 D6
Woodstock La South
ESH/CLAY KT10 205 H3
Woodstock Ms
CAVSQ/HST W1G 9 H2
Woodstock Ri CHEAM SM3 193 J5
Woodstock Rd ALP/SUD HA0 80 B5
BUSH WD23 28 E2
CAR SM5 210 A3
CHSWK W4 118 B4
CROY/NA CR0 211 K1
FSBYPK N4 67 G5
FSTGT E7 89 G5
GLDGN NW11 64 D4
WALTH E17 52 B5
Woodstock St CAN/RD E16 106 D5
OXSTW W1C 9 J4
Woodstock Ter POP/IOD E14 105 K6
Woodstock Wy MTCM CR4 179 H5
Woodstone Av EW KT17 207 J3
Wood St BAR EN5 20 A5
CAN/RD E16 107 F6
CHSWK W4 118 B5
CITYW EC2V 12 D3
KUT/HW KT1 174 E4
MTCM CR4 195 F4
WALTH E17 52 A6
Woodsyre SYD SE26 163 G6
Wood Ter CRICK NW2 * 63 H6
Woodthorpe Rd ASHF TW15 152 B6
PUT/ROE SW15 138 E5
Woodtree Cl HDN NW4 46 A5
Wood V FSTH SE23 163 J3
MUSWH N10 66 C2
Woodvale Av SNWD SE25 181 G6
Woodvale Wy GLDGN NW11 82 B1
Woodview Av CHING E4 38 A6
Woodview Cl ORP BR6 201 H6
PUT/ROE SW15 158 A6
Woodview Rd SWLY BR8 187 K5
Woodville Cl TEDD TW11 156 B6
Woodville Gdns BARK/HLT IG6 54 B6
EA W5 98 A5
RSLP HA4 58 A4
SURB KT6 * 190 E4
Woodville Gv WELL DA16 * 148 B4
Woodville Rd BAR EN5 21 F4
EA W5 98 A5
GLDGN NW11 64 C4
KIL/WHAMP NW6 * 100 D1
MRDN SM4 193 K1
RCHPK/HAM TW10 156 C5
STNW/STAM N16 86 A3
SWFD E18 53 F5
THHTH CR7 180 E6
WALTH E17 69 G1
WAN E11 70 D5
Woodville St
WOOL/PLUM SE18 126 D4
Woodward Av HDN NW4 63 J2
Woodward Cl ESH/CLAY KT10 205 F4
Woodwarde Rd EDUL SE22 163 F1
Woodward Gdns DAGW RM9 91 J5
STAN HA7 43 F3
Woodward Rd DAGW RM9 91 H5
Wood Wy ORP BR6 201 F6
Woodway Crs HRW HA1 61 G3
Woodwaye OXHEY WD19 27 G2
Woodwell St
WAND/EARL SW18 140 B6
Wood Whf GNWCH SE10 124 E6
Woodyard Cl KTTN NW5 84 A3
Woodyard La DUL SE21 163 F2
Woolacombe Rd
BKHTH/KID SE3 146 B3
Woolacombe Wy
HYS/HAR UB3 113 H4
Wooler St WALW SE17 122 E5
Woolf Cl THMD SE28 128 C1
Woolf Ms STPAN WC1H 4 E6
Woollaston Rd FSBYPK N4 67 H3
Woolmead Av
CDALE/KGS NW9 63 J4
Woolmer Gdns UED N18 50 C2
Woolmer Rd UED N18 50 C1
Woolmore St POP/IOD E14 106 A6
Woolneigh St FUL/PGN SW6 140 A4
Woolridge Cl
EBED/NFELT TW14 153 F3
Woolridge Wy HOM E9 * 86 E5
Wool Rd RYNPK SW20 176 E2
Woolstaplers Wy
BERM/RHTH SE16 123 H3
Woolston Cl WALTH E17 51 F5
Woolstone Rd FSTH SE23 164 B4
Woolwich Church St
WOOL/PLUM SE18 126 C4
Woolwich Common
WOOL/PLUM SE18 127 F6
WOOL/PLUM SE18 147 F1
Woolwich Foot Tnl
CAN/RD E16 127 F2
Woolwich High St
WOOL/PLUM SE18 127 F3
Woolwich Manor Wy
CAN/RD E16 127 G1
Woolwich Manorway
CAN/RD E16 127 G2
Woolwich Manor Wy
EHAM E6 107 K3
Woolwich New Rd
WOOL/PLUM SE18 127 F5
Woolwich Rd ABYW SE2 128 E6
BELV DA17 129 G5
CHARL SE7 126 B4
Wooster Gdns POP/IOD E14 106 B5
Wootton Gv FNCH N3 46 E4
Wootton St STHWK SE1 17 K2
Worbeck Rd PGE/AN SE20 181 J5
Worcester Av TOTM N17 50 C3
Worcester Cl CRICK NW2 81 J1
CROY/NA CR0 198 C6
MTCM CR4 179 F5
Worcester Ct WOT/HER KT12 188 B6
Worcester Crs MLHL NW7 31 G5
WFD IG8 39 G6
Worcester Dr CHSWK W4 118 B3
Worcester Gdns
GFD/PVL UB6 78 C4
IL IG1 71 J4
WPK KT4 207 G1
Worcester Ms
KIL/WHAMP NW6 83 F4
Worcester Park Rd WPK KT4 206 E1
Worcester Rd BELMT SM2 208 E5
MNPK E12 89 K1
WALTH E17 51 F5
WIM/MER SW19 177 J1
Worcesters Av EN EN1 24 C1
Wordsworth Av GFD/PVL UB6 96 D1
MNPK E12 89 J5
SWFD E18 52 D6
Wordsworth Dr CHEAM SM3 208 A2
Wordsworth Pde
CEND/HSY/T N8 * 67 H1
Wordsworth Pl HAMP NW3 83 K3
Wordsworth Rd HPTN TW12 154 E6
PGE/AN SE20 182 A3
STHWK SE1 19 J7
STNW/STAM N16 86 A2
WELL DA16 147 K2
WLGTN SM6 210 C4
Wordsworth Wk
GLDGN NW11 64 D1
Wordsworth Wy DART DA1 151 K5
WDR/YW UB7 112 B4
Worfield St BTSEA SW11 140 D1
Worgan St BERM/RHTH SE16 124 A3
LBTH SE11 122 A5
Worland Rd SRTFD E15 88 C5
Worlds End Est
WBPTN SW10 * 140 C1
Worlds End La ORP BR6 217 G5
World's End La WCHMH N21 23 F6
Worlds End Pas
WBPTN SW10 * 140 C1
Worleys Dr ORP BR6 216 D2
Worlidge St HMSMTH W6 119 F5
Worlingham Rd EDUL SE22 143 G5
Wormholt Rd SHB W12 118 D1
Wormholt Ter SHB W12 * 118 D1
Wormwood St OBST EC2N 13 G3
Wornington Rd NKENS W10 100 C4
Woronzow Rd STJWD NW8 2 B1
Worple Av ISLW TW7 136 B6
WIM/MER SW19 177 G3
Worple Cl RYLN/HDSTN HA2 59 K5
Worple Rd ISLW TW7 136 B5
RYNPK SW20 177 F5
Worple Road Ms
WIM/MER SW19 177 J2
Worple St MORT/ESHN SW14 138 A4
Worple Wy RCHPK/HAM TW10 137 F6
RYLN/HDSTN HA2 59 K5
Worship St SDTCH EC2A 7 F7
Worslade Rd TOOT SW17 160 C6
Worsley Bridge Rd SYD SE26 182 C1
Worsley Gv CLPT E5 86 C2
Worsley Rd WAN E11 88 C2
Worsopp Dr CLAP SW4 141 H6
Worth Cl ORP BR6 216 E2
Worthfield Cl HOR/WEW KT19 207 F5
Worth Gv WALW SE17 * 122 E5
Worthing Cl SRTFD E15 88 C6
Worthing Rd HEST TW5 114 E6
Worthington Cl MTCM CR4 195 G1
Worthington Rd SURB KT6 191 G5
Wortley Rd CROY/NA CR0 196 B4
EHAM E6 89 H5
Worton Gdns ISLW TW7 135 J3
Worton Rd ISLW TW7 136 A4
Worton Wy ISLW TW7 135 J3
Wotton Gn STMC/STPC BR5 202 E1
Wotton Rd CRICK NW2 82 A2
DEPT SE8 124 C6
Wouldham Rd CAN/RD E16 106 D5
Wouldham Ter
STMC/STPC BR5 * 186 C6
Wragby Rd WAN E11 * 88 C1
Wrampling Pl ED N9 36 C3
Wray Av CLAY IG5 54 A6
Wray Crs FSBYPK N4 66 E6
Wrayfield Rd CHEAM SM3 208 B1
Wray Rd BELMT SM2 208 D6
Wraysbury Cl HSLWW TW4 134 D6
Wrays Wy YEAD UB4 94 C4
Wrekin Rd WOOL/PLUM SE18 147 H1
Wren Av CRICK NW2 82 A2
NWDGN UB2 114 E4
Wren Cl CAN/RD E16 106 D5
ED N9 37 F3
STMC/STPC BR5 186 E6
Wren Crs BUSH WD23 28 C3
Wren Dr WDR/YW UB7 112 A2
Wren Gdns DAGW RM9 91 K3
HCH RM12 75 H5
Wren Ms LEW SE13 * 145 H5
Wren Rd CMBW SE5 142 E2
DAGW RM9 91 K3
SCUP DA14 168 D5
Wren St FSBYW WC1X 5 H6
Wrentham Av WLSDN NW10 100 B1
Wrenthorpe Rd BMLY BR1 165 H6
Wrenwood Wy PIN HA5 59 F1
Wrexham Rd BOW E3 105 J1
Wricklemarsh Rd
BKHTH/KID SE3 146 A3
Wrigglesworth St NWCR SE14 144 A1
Wright Cl LEW SE13 145 G5
Wright Rd HEST TW5 134 B1
Wrights Aly WIM/MER SW19 177 F2
Wrights Cl DAGE RM10 92 D2
Wright's La KENS W8 119 K2
Wrights Pl WLSDN NW10 * 80 E4
Wrights Rd SNWD SE25 181 F6
Wright's Rd BOW E3 105 H1
Wright's Rw WLGTN SM6 210 B2
Wrigley Cl CHING E4 * 52 B1
Wrotham Rd BAR EN5 20 C3
CAMTN NW1 * 84 C5
WEA W13 116 D1
WELL DA16 148 D2
Wrottesley Rd WLSDN NW10 99 J1
WOOL/PLUM SE18 127 H6
Wroughton Rd BTSEA SW11 160 E1
Wroughton Ter HDN NW4 * 63 K1
Wroxall Rd DAGW RM9 91 J4
Wroxham Gdns
FBAR/BDGN N11 48 C3
Wroxham Rd THMD SE28 109 K6
Wroxham Wy BARK/HLT IG6 54 B4
Wroxton Rd PECK SE15 143 J3
Wrythe Gn CAR SM5 209 K1
Wrythe Green Rd CAR SM5 209 K1
Wrythe La CAR SM5 194 C5
Wulfstan St SHB W12 99 H5
Wyatt Cl BUSH WD23 28 E2
FELT TW13 154 C3
YEAD UB4 94 E4
Wyatt Dr BARN SW13 118 E6
Wyatt Park Rd
BRXS/STRHM SW2 162 A4
Wyatt Rd FSTGT E7 88 E4
HBRY N5 85 J1
Wyatt's La WALTH E17 52 A6

Wybert St CAMTN NW1 3 K6
Wyborne Wy WLSDN NW10 80 E5
Wyburn Av BAR EN5 20 D4
Wychcombe Studios
HAMP NW3 * 83 K4
Wyche Gv SAND/SEL CR2 211 J5
Wych Elm Cl KUTN/CMB KT2 175 G3
Wycherley Cl BKHTH/KID SE3 145 J1
Wycherley Crs BAR EN5 33 F1
Wychwood Av EDGW HA8 43 K2
THHTH CR7 180 C6
Wychwood Cl EDGW HA8 43 K2
Wychwood End HGT N6 66 C4
Wychwood Gdns CLAY IG5 71 K1
Wychwood Wy NTHWD HA6 40 D3
Wycliffe Cl WELL DA16 148 A2
Wycliffe Rd BTSEA SW11 141 F3
WIM/MER SW19 178 A2
Wyclif St FSBYE EC1V 6 A5
Wycombe Gdns GLDGN NW11 64 D6
Wycombe Pl
WAND/EARL SW18 160 B1
Wycombe Rd ALP/SUD HA0 80 C6
GNTH/NBYPK IG2 71 K2
TOTM N17 50 C4
Wycombe Sq KENS W8 119 J1
Wydell Cl MRDN SM4 193 F3
Wydenhurst Rd
CROY/NA CR0 197 H4
Wydeville Manor Rd
LEE/GVPK SE12 166 A6
Wye Cl ASHF TW15 152 E6
ORP BR6 202 A4
RSLP HA4 58 A3
Wyemead Crs CHING E4 38 C4
Wye St BTSEA SW11 140 C4
Wyevale Cl NTHWD HA6 40 E6
Wyfields CLAY IG5 54 B4
Wyfold Rd FUL/PGN SW6 139 H2
Wyke Cl ISLW TW7 116 A6
Wyke Gdns HNWL W7 116 A3
Wykeham Av DAGW RM9 91 J4
Wykeham Cl WDR/YW UB7 112 D6
Wykeham Gn DAGW RM9 91 J4
Wykeham Hl WBLY HA9 62 B5
Wykeham Ri
TRDG/WHET N20 32 C3
Wykeham Rd HDN NW4 64 A2
KTN/HRWW/WS HA3 61 H1
Wyke Rd BOW E3 87 J5
RYNPK SW20 177 F5
Wylchin Cl PIN HA5 58 D1
Wyldes Cl GLDGN NW11 65 G5
Wyldfield Gdns ED N9 36 B4
Wyld Wy WBLY HA9 80 D4
Wyleu St FSTH SE23 164 B2
Wylie Rd NWDGN UB2 115 F3
Wyllen Cl WCHPL E1 104 E3
Wylo Dr BAR EN5 31 H1
Wymark Cl RAIN RM13 111 H1
Wymering Rd MV/WKIL W9 100 E2
Wymond St PUT/ROE SW15 139 F4
Wynan Rd POP/IOD E14 124 E5
Wynaud Ct WDGN N22 49 F2
Wyncham Av BFN/LL DA15 167 K3
Wynchgate
KTN/HRWW/WS HA3 42 E3
STHGT/OAK N14 34 E2
Wyncote Wy SAND/SEL CR2 213 F6
Wyncroft Cl BMLY BR1 184 E6
Wyndale Av CDALE/KGS NW9 62 C3
Wyndcliff Rd CHARL SE7 126 A6
Wyndcroft Cl ENC/FH EN2 23 H4
Wyndham Cl BELMT SM2 208 E5
ORP BR6 201 H5
Wyndham Crs HSLWW TW4 154 E1
KTTN NW5 84 C1
Wyndham Est CMBW SE5 142 D1
Wyndham Ms MBLAR W1H 8 E2
Wyndham Pl MBLAR W1H 8 E2
Wyndham Rd CMBW SE5 142 D1
EBAR EN4 33 K3
EHAM E6 89 H5
KUTN/CMB KT2 175 G3
WEA W13 116 C3
Wyndham St CAMTN NW1 8 E1
Wyndham Yd MBLAR W1H * 8 E2
Wyndhurst Cl SAND/SEL CR2 211 H5
Wyneham Rd HNHL SE24 142 E6
Wynell Rd FSTH SE23 164 A5
Wynford Gv STMC/STPC BR5 186 C6
Wynford Pl BELV DA17 129 H6
Wynford Rd IS N1 5 G2
Wynford Wy ELTH/MOT SE9 166 E5
Wynlie Gdns PIN HA5 41 F5
Wynn Bridge Cl WFD IG8 53 H4
Wynndale Rd SWFD E18 53 F4
Wynne Rd BRXN/ST SW9 142 B3
Wynn's Av BFN/LL DA15 148 B6
Wynnstay Gdns KENS W8 * 119 K3
Wynter St BTSEA SW11 140 B5
Wynton Gdns SNWD SE25 197 F2
Wynton Pl ACT W3 98 D5
Wynyard Ter LBTH SE11 * 122 A5
Wynyatt St FSBYE EC1V 6 A4
Wyre Gv EDGW HA8 30 D5
HYS/HAR UB3 113 K4
Wyresdale Crs GFD/PVL UB6 97 F2
Wyteleaf Cl RSLP HA4 58 A3
Wythburn Pl MBLAR W1H 8 E4
Wythenshawe Rd
DAGE RM10 92 C1
Wythes Cl BMLY BR1 184 E5
Wythes Rd CAN/RD E16 126 D1
Wythfield Rd ELTH/MOT SE9 166 E1
Wyvenhoe Rd
RYLN/HDSTN HA2 78 C1
Wyvern Cl ORP BR6 217 H1
Wyvern Est NWMAL KT3 * 176 D6
Wyvil Rd VX/NE SW8 141 K1
Wyvis St POP/IOD E14 105 K4

Y

Yabsley St POP/IOD E14 125 F1
Yalding Gv STMC/STPC BR5 202 E1
Yalding Rd BERM/RHTH SE16 123 H3
Yale Cl HSLWW TW4 134 E6
Yale Wy HCH RM12 93 J2
Yarborough Rd
WIM/MER SW19 178 C4
Yardley Cl CHING E4 25 K6
Yardley La CHING E4 25 K6
Yardley St FSBYW WC1X 5 J5
Yarmouth Crs TOTM N17 68 D2
Yarmouth Pl MYFR/PICC W1J 15 J1
Yarnton Wy ERITHM DA18 129 F2
Yarrow Crs EHAM E6 107 J4
Yateley St WOOL/PLUM SE18 126 C3
Yeading Av RYLN/HDSTN HA2 59 J6
Yeading Fk YEAD UB4 95 G4
Yeading Gdns YEAD UB4 95 F4
Yeading La YEAD UB4 95 F5
Yeames Cl WEA W13 97 G5
Yeate St IS N1 85 K5
Yeatman Rd HGT N6 65 K3
Yeats Cl HNWL W7 97 F6
LEW SE13 * 145 G3
WLSDN NW10 81 G4
Ye Cnr OXHEY WD19 27 H1
Yeend Cl E/WMO/HCT KT8 189 F1
Yeldham Rd HMSMTH W6 119 G5
Yeldham Vls HMSMTH W6 * 119 G5
Yelverton Rd BTSEA SW11 140 C3
Yenston Cl MRDN SM4 193 K3
Yeoman Cl EHAM E6 108 B6
Yeoman Dr STWL/WRAY TW19 152 B3
Yeoman Rd NTHLT UB5 77 J5
Yeomans Acre RSLP HA4 58 E3
Yeoman's Rw CHEL SW3 14 D5
Yeoman St BERM/RHTH SE16 124 B4
Yeomans Wy PEND EN3 * 24 D3
Yeoman's Yd WCHPL E1 13 K5
Yeomen Wy BARK/HLT IG6 54 C2
Yeo St BOW E3 105 K4
Yeovil Cl ORP BR6 201 K6
Yeovilton Pl KUTN/CMB KT2 174 E1
Yerbury Rd ARCH N19 84 D1
Yester Dr CHST BR7 184 D3
Yester Pk CHST BR7 184 E3
Yester Rd CHST BR7 184 E3
Yew Cl BKHH IG9 39 H4
Yewdale Cl BMLY BR1 183 H2
Yewfield Rd WLSDN NW10 81 H4
Yew Gv CRICK NW2 82 B2
The Yews ASHF TW15 * 152 E6
Yew Tree Cl WCHMH N21 35 G2
WPK KT4 192 B5
LEW SE13 145 F4
Yewtree Cl MUSWH N10 48 C4
RYLN/HDSTN HA2 60 B1
Yew Tree Cl WELL DA16 148 B2
Yew Tree Ct BORE WD6 29 K1
Yew Tree Gdns CHDH RM6 74 A2
ROMW/RG RM7 75 F2
Yew Tree Rd BECK BR3 182 C6
SHB W12 99 H6
Yew Tree Wk HSLWW TW4 134 E6
Yew Wk HRW HA1 60 E5
Yoakley Rd STNW/STAM N16 68 A6
Yoke Cl HOLWY N7 84 E4
Yolande Gdns ELTH/MOT SE9 146 D6
Yonge Pk HOLWY N7 85 G1
York Av BFN/LL DA15 167 K4
HNWL W7 115 K1
HYS/HAR UB3 94 A5
MORT/ESHN SW14 137 K6
STAN HA7 43 H4
York Br CAMTN NW1 3 G6
York Blds CHCR WC2N 11 F6
York Cl CMBW SE5 * 142 D3
EHAM E6 107 K5
HNWL W7 115 K1
MRDN SM4 194 A1
York Gdns WOT/HER KT12 188 C6
York Ga CAMTN NW1 3 H7
STHGT/OAK N14 34 E2
York Gv PECK SE15 143 K2
York Hl WNWD SE27 162 C5
York House Pl KENS W8 120 A2
Yorkland Av WELL DA16 148 A5
York Ms IL IG1 72 A6
KTTN NW5 84 B3
York Pde BTFD TW8 * 116 E5
CDALE/KGS NW9 * 63 J3
York Pl BTSEA SW11 140 B4
IL IG1 72 A6
York Ri KTTN NW5 84 B1
ORP BR6 201 K5
York Rd ACT W3 98 E5
BAR EN5 21 G6
BELMT SM2 208 E6
BTFD TW8 116 E5
BTSEA SW11 140 B5
CHING E4 51 J1
CROY/NA CR0 196 B4
EA W5 116 D3
FBAR/BDGN N11 48 D2
FSTGT E7 88 E4
HSLW TW3 135 G4
IL IG1 90 A1
KUTN/CMB KT2 175 G3
LEY E10 88 A1
NTHWD HA6 40 E5
RAIN RM13 93 F5
RCHPK/HAM TW10 137 G6
STHWK SE1 17 H2
TEDD TW11 155 K6
UED N18 50 D1
WALTH E17 69 F2
WCHMH N21 35 K2
WIM/MER SW19 178 A2
Yorkshire Cl STNW/STAM N16 86 A1
Yorkshire Gdns UED N18 50 D1
Yorkshire Grey Yd
GINN WC1R * 11 G2
Yorkshire Rd MTCM CR4 195 K2
POP/IOD E14 105 G5
York Sq POP/IOD E14 105 G5
York St MBLAR W1H 8 E2
MHST W1U 9 F1
MTCM CR4 195 F4
York Street Chambers
MHST W1U * 9 F1
York Ter ENC/FH EN2 23 J1
York Ter East CAMTN NW1 3 H7
York Ter West CAMTN NW1 3 G7
Yorkton St BETH E2 104 C1
York Wy CHSGTN KT9 205 K5
FELT TW13 154 E5
HOLWY N7 84 D4
IS N1 5 F1
TRDG/WHET N20 33 K5
York Way Ct IS N1 5 F1
York Way Est HOLWY N7 84 E4
Youngmans Cl ENC/FH EN2 23 J2
Young Rd CAN/RD E16 107 G5
Youngs Rd GNTH/NBYPK IG2 72 D2
Young St KENS W8 120 A2
Yoxley Ap GNTH/NBYPK IG2 72 C3
Yoxley Dr GNTH/NBYPK IG2 72 C3
Yukon Rd BAL SW12 161 G2
Yunus Khan Cl WALTH E17 69 J2

Z

Zambezie Dr ED N9 36 E5
Zampa Rd BERM/RHTH SE16 123 K5
Zander Ct BETH E2 104 C2
Zangwill Rd BKHTH/KID SE3 146 C2
Zealand Av WDR/YW UB7 132 A1
Zealand Rd BOW E3 105 G1
Zelah Rd STMC/STPC BR5 202 C4
Zennor Rd BAL SW12 161 H3
Zenoria St EDUL SE22 143 G5
Zermatt Rd THHTH CR7 196 D1
Zetland St POP/IOD E14 106 A4
Zion Pl THHTH CR7 196 E1
Zion Rd THHTH CR7 196 E1
Zoar St STHWK SE1 12 C7

Index - featured places

7/7 Memorial
MYFR/PKLN W1K 15 G1
2 Willow Road (NT)
HAMP NW3 83 J2
30 St Mary Axe
HDTCH EC3A 13 H4
41 Hotel
BGVA SW1W 15 K4
51 Buckingham Gate (Hotel)
WESTW SW1E 16 B4
Aarotya Medical Centre
SEVS/STOTM N15 67 J1
Abbey Business Centre
VX/NE SW8 141 H2
Abbey Christian School for the English Language
STJWD NW8 101 G1
The Abbey Clinic
BELV DA17 129 G5
Abbey College London
BAY/PAD W2 100 E5
Abbey Industrial Estate
ALP/SUD HA0 80 B6
MTCM CR4 194 E2
Abbey Lane Commercial Estate
SRTFD E15 106 B1
Abbey Medical Centre
STJWD NW8 83 F6
Abbey Mills
WIM/MER SW19 178 B4
Abbey Park Industrial Estate
BARK IG11 108 B1
Abbey Primary School
ABYW SE2 128 D3
MRDN SM4 193 K4
Abbey Road ⊖
SRTFD E15 106 B1
Abbey Road Health Centre
SRTFD E15 88 C6
Abbey Road Studios
STJWD NW8 101 G1
Abbey Sports Centre
BARK IG11 90 C6
Abbey Trading Estate
SYD SE26 182 B1
Abbey Wharf Industrial Estate
BARK IG11 108 D2
Abbey Wood ⇌
ABYW SE2 128 D3
Abbey Wood School
ABYW SE2 128 B3
Abbotsbury Primary School
MRDN SM4 193 K2
Abbs Cross School & Arts College
HCH RM12 93 K1
ABC Cinema
PUT/ROE SW15 139 H4
Abercorn Place School
CAMTN NW1 8 D1
Abercorn School
MBLAR W1H 8 E2
Aberdeen Wharf
WAP E1W 123 J1
Aberglen Industrial Estate
HYS/HAR UB3 113 G2
Abingdon House School
KENS W8 119 K3
Abney Park Cemetery
STNW/STAM N16 68 A6
Acacia Business Centre
WAN E11 88 C1
The Academy at Peckham
PECK SE15 143 G2
The Academy School
HAMP NW3 83 H2
Acland Burghley School
KTTN NW5 84 B2
Acorn Industrial Park
DART DA1 150 D6
Acorn Medical Centre
TWK TW1 156 B3
Acre Road Health Clinic
KUTN/CMB KT2 175 G3
Acton Business Centre
WLSDN NW10 99 F3
Acton Central ⊖
ACT W3 118 A1
Acton Central Industrial Estate
ACT W3 98 D6
Acton Health Centre
ACT W3 117 K1
Acton High School
ACT W3 117 H2
Acton Hospital
ACT W3 117 H2
Acton Lane Medical Centre
CHSWK W4 117 K2
Acton Main Line ⇌
ACT W3 98 E5
Acton Park Industrial Estate
ACT W3 118 A2
Acton Superbowl
ACT W3 98 C4
Acton Swimming Baths
ACT W3 117 K1
Acton Town ⊖
ACT W3 117 H2
Acton & West London College
ACT W3 117 J1
Acumen (Anglo School)
NRWD SE19 181 F4
Adams Bridge Business Centre
WBLY HA9 80 D3
Adamsrill Primary School
SYD SE26 164 B5
Adath Yisroel Cemetery
EN EN1 24 B2
Addey & Stanhope School
NWCR SE14 144 C2
Addington Court Golf Club
CROY/NA CR0 213 H6
Addington Golf Club
CROY/NA CR0 213 H2
Addington Palace Golf Club
CROY/NA CR0 213 G4
Addington Village
CROY/NA CR0 213 J4
Addiscombe
CROY/NA CR0 197 H5
Addiscombe CC
CROY/NA CR0 212 C1
Addison Primary School
WKENS W14 119 G3
Adelphi Theatre
COVGDN WC2E 11 F6
Adler Industrial Estate
HYS/HAR UB3 113 G2
Admiral Hyson Industrial Estate
STHWK SE1 123 J4
Admiralty Arch
STJS SW1Y 10 D7
The Adult College of Barking & Dagenham
BARK IG11 90 E4
Aerodrome Hotel
CROY/NA CR0 211 G4
Africa Centre
COVGDN WC2E 11 F5
Aga Khan University
CAN/RD E16 106 D4
RSQ WC1B 10 D2
Agency of Jewish Education
HDN NW4 64 B1
Agnew's
CONDST W1S 10 A7
Agora Shopping Centre
PECK SE15 143 H3
AHA International London Centre
BMSBY WC1N 11 H1
Ainslie Wood Primary School
CHING E4 51 K1
Airbase Unity Elementary School
RSLP HA4 58 A6
Airbus Coach Station
HTHAIR TW6 132 C4
Air Call Business Centre
CDALE/KGS NW9 45 F6
Airedale Physiotherapy Clinic
CHSWK W4 118 C5
Airlinks Golf Club
NWDGN UB2 114 B4
Air Links Industrial Estate
HEST TW5 114 B5
Airport Gate Business Centre
WDR/YW UB7 132 C1
Akiva School
FNCH N3 46 E5
Aksaray Sports Club
STNW/STAM N16 85 K2
Albany Centre & Theatre
DEPT SE8 144 C1
Albany Clinic
BFN/LL DA15 168 B6
WIM/MER SW19 178 A3
Albany Park ⇌
SCUP DA14 168 E4
Albany Park Canoe & Sailing Club
KUTN/CMB KT2 174 E2
Albany School (Grant Maintained)
PEND EN3 25 F1
The Albany School
HCH RM12 75 K6
Albemarle College
BAY/PAD W2 101 F6
Albemarle Primary School
WIM/MER SW19 159 H4
Albert Memorial
SKENS SW7 14 A2
Albion College
RSQ WC1B 10 E2
Albion Health Centre
WCHPL E1 104 D4
Albion J & I School
BERM/RHTH SE16 123 K2
Albion Street Health Centre
BERM/RHTH SE16 123 K2
Albright Industrial Estate
RAIN RM13 111 H4
Alchemea
IS N1 85 H6
The Alchemy Gallery
CLKNW EC1R 5 J6
Alderbrook Primary School
BAL SW12 161 G2
Aldersbrook County Secondary School
MNPK E12 71 G5
Aldersbrook Primary School
MNPK E12 71 F5
Alderwood Primary School
ELTH/MOT SE9 167 J1
Aldgate ⊖
TWRH EC3N 13 J4
Aldgate Bus Station
HDTCH EC3A 13 J3
Aldgate East ⊖
WCHPL E1 13 K3
Aldwych Theatre
HOL/ALD WC2B 11 G4
Alexander McLeod Primary School
ABYW SE2 128 C5
Alexandra Avenue Clinic
RYLN/HDSTN HA2 59 K6
Alexandra Business Centre
PEND EN3 25 F5
Alexandra Infant School
KUTN/CMB KT2 175 H3
PGE/AN SE20 182 A3
Alexandra Junior School
HSLW TW3 135 G3
SYD SE26 182 A2
Alexandra Palace
WDGN N22 48 D6
WDGN N22 48 E5
Alexandra Palace Ice Rink
WDGN N22 48 D5
Alexandra Park School
FBAR/BDGN N11 48 C3
Alexandra Primary School
WDGN N22 49 F5
Alexandra School
RYLN/HDSTN HA2 59 K6
Al Falah Boys School
CLPT E5 86 D
Alfred Salter Primary School
BERM/RHTH SE16 124 A
Alfreds Way Industrial Estate
BARK IG11 91 G
Al-Khair Primary & Secondary School
CROY/NA CR0 196 E
Allenby Primary School
STHL UB1 96 A
Allen Edwards Primary School
CLAP SW4 141 K
The All England Lawn Tennis & Croquet Club
WIM/MER SW19 159 G
Alleyns Junior School
EDUL SE22 143 F
Allfarthing JMI School
WAND/EARL SW18 160 B
All Saints ⊖
POP/IOD E14 106 A
All Saints Benhilton CE Primary School
SUT SM1 209 F
All Saints Catholic School & Technology College
BCTR RM8 74 C
All Saints CE Junior School
NRWD SE19 181 F
All Saints CE Primary School
BKHTH/KID SE3 145
CAR SM5 210
CRICK NW2 82
FUL/PGN SW6 139
PUT/ROE SW15 139
TRDG/WHET N20 33
WIM/MER SW19 178
All Souls CE Primary School
GTPST W1W 10
Allum Medical Centre
WAN E11 70

Alma Primary School
BERM/RHTH SE16 123 H4
PEND EN3 25 G6
Almeida Theatre
IS N1 85 H5
Al-Noor Primary School
GDMY/SEVK IG3 73 H5
Alperton ⊖
ALP/SUD HA0 79 K6
Alperton Cemetery
ALP/SUD HA0 79 K6
Alperton Community School
ALP/SUD HA0 80 A5
Alperton High School
ALP/SUD HA0 79 K6
Alperton Sports Ground
ALP/SUD HA0 97 K1
Alpha Business Centre
WALTH E17 69 H2
Alpha Preparatory School
HRW HA1 60 E2
Alpine Business Centre
EHAM E6 108 A4
Al-Risaala Boys Secondary School
BAL SW12 161 G3
Al Sadiq & Al-Zahra High School
KIL/WHAMP NW6 82 C6
Alscot Road Industrial Estate
STHWK SE1 19 K6
Altmore Infant School
EHAM E6 89 K5
The Alton School
PUT/ROE SW15 158 C2
Ambler Primary School
FSBYPK N4 85 H1
Ambleside Junior School
WOT/HER KT12 188 B5
Ambulance Centre
STRHM/NOR SW16 162 A5
AMC Business Centre
WLSDN NW10 98 D2
American Intercontinental University
MHST W1U 9 H2
AMF Bowling
LEW SE13 145 F4
Amida Golf
FELT TW13 155 F5
Ampere Way ●
CROY/NA CR0 196 A5
Ampthill Square Medical Centre
CAMTN NW1 4 B3
Anchorage Point Industrial Estate
CHARL SE7 126 B3
Anchor Bay Industrial Estate
ERITH DA8 150 C1
Anchor Retail Park
WCHPL E1 104 E3
Andaz Hotel
LVPST EC2M 13 G2
Andover Medical Centre
HOLWY N7 85 F1
The Andrew Ewing Primary School
HEST TW5 134 E1
Anerley ⇌ ⊖
PGE/AN SE20 181 H4
Anerley School
NRWD SE19 181 H4
Angel ⊖
IS N1 6 A2
Angel Centre
DART DA1 171 H1
Angel Road ⇌
UED N18 50 E1
Angerstein Business Park
GNWCH SE10 125 K4
Anglian Industrial Estate
BARK IG11 109 F3
Animal Cemetery
REDBR IG4 53 H6
Annemount School
EFNCH N2 65 G3
Annunciation RC Infant School
EDGW HA8 45 F4
The Annunciation RC Junior School
MLHL NW7 45 F2
Anson Primary School
CRICK NW2 82 B3
Apex Hotel
MON EC3R 13 H5
Apex Industrial Estate
WLSDN NW10 99 H3
Apex Primary School
IL IG1 72 A5
Apex Retail Park
FELT TW13 154 E5
Apollo Theatre
SOHO/SHAV W1D 10 C5
pollo Victoria Theatre
PIM SW1V 16 A5
postolic Nuncio
WIM/MER SW19 159 F5
pplegarth Primary School
CROY/NA CR0 213 K4
psley House, The Wellington Museum
KTBR SW1X 15 G2
quarius Business Park
CRICK NW2 63 J5
quarius Golf Club
EDUL SE22 143 K6
ragon Primary School
MRDN SM4 193 H4
rcadia Shopping Centre
EA W5 97 K6
rcadia University
BAY/PAD W2 101 F6
e Archbishop Lanfranc School
CROY/NA CR0 195 K3
rchbishop Sumners CE Primary School
LBTH SE11 17 K7
Archbishop Tenisons CE School
CROY/NA CR0 212 B1
Archbishop Tenison's School
VX/NE SW8 122 A6
Archdale Business Centre
RYLN/HDSTN HA2 60 C6
Archdeacon Cambridge's CE Primary School
WHTN TW2 155 K4
Arches Business Centre
NWDGN UB2 114 E2
Arches Leisure Centre
GNWCH SE10 125 G6
Archgate Business Centre
NFNCH/WDSPK N12 33 G6
Architectural Association School of Architecture
RSQ WC1B 10 C2
Archway ⊖
ARCH N19 66 C6
Archway Business Centre
ARCH N19 84 D1
Archway Leisure Centre
ARCH N19 66 C6
Arena ●
SNWD SE25 197 K2
Arena Estate
FSBYPK N4 67 H3
Argent Centre Industrial Estate
HYS/HAR UB3 113 K2
Argyle Primary School
STPAN WC1H 5 F5
Arklow Trading Estate
NWCR SE14 124 B6
Armourers & Braziers' Hall
LOTH EC2R 12 E2
Arndale Health Centre
WAND/EARL SW18 159 K1
Arnhem Wharf Primary School
POP/IOD E14 124 C3
Arnold House School
STJWD NW8 2 A2
Arnos Grove ⊖
FBAR/BDGN N11 34 C6
Arnos Pool
FBAR/BDGN N11 48 D1
Arsenal ⊖
HBRY N5 85 G1
Arsenal FC (Emirates Stadium)
HOLWY N7 85 G2
Artsdepot
NFNCH/WDSPK N12 47 G1
The Arts Educational School
CHSWK W4 118 B4
Arts Theatre
LSQ/SEVD WC2H 10 D5
Ashburnham Primary School
WBPTN SW10 140 C1
Ashburton Community School
CROY/NA CR0 197 J4
Ashburton Primary School
CROY/NA CR0 197 J3
Ashby Mill
BRXS/STRHM SW2 161 K1
Ashby Mill School
CLAP SW4 141 K6
Ashcroft Technology Academy
PUT/ROE SW15 139 J6
Ashfield Junior School
BUSH WD23 28 B2
Ashford ⇌
ASHF TW15 152 C5
Ashford Cemetery
STWL/WRAY TW19 152 C4
Ashford Clinic
ASHF TW15 152 B5
Ashford Hospital
STWL/WRAY TW19 152 B4
Ashford Industrial Estate
ASHF TW15 153 F6
Ashford Sports Club
ASHF TW15 152 A6
STWL/WRAY TW19 152 C3
Ashgrove College
WALTH E17 51 J6
Ashgrove Trading Estate
BMLY BR1 183 G2
Ashleigh Commercial Estate
CHARL SE7 126 B4
Ashmead Primary School
BROCKY SE4 144 D3
Ashmole Centre
STHGT/OAK N14 34 C3
Ashmole Primary School
VX/NE SW8 122 A6
Ashmole School
STHGT/OAK N14 34 C3
Ashmount Primary School
ARCH N19 66 D4
Ashton House School
ISLW TW7 135 J2
Ashton Playing Fields Track
WFD IG8 53 J2
Aspen House School
LBTH SE11 122 C6
Aspen House Secondary & Primary School
BRXS/STRHM SW2 161 K3
Asquith Court School
HPTN TW12 173 G4
KTN/HRWW/WS HA3 61 H3
Asquith School
PEND EN3 24 E5
Assembly Rooms
SURB KT6 191 F1
Associated Newspapers Offices
BERM/RHTH SE16 124 A3
Assunah School
TOTM N17 50 B5
Aston Clinic
NWMAL KT3 192 B1
Aston House School
EA W5 97 K5
Asylum Medical Centre
CEND/HSY/T N8 49 G6
Athelney Primary School
CAT SE6 164 D5
Athelstan House School
HPTN TW12 173 F4
Athenaeum Hotel
MYFR/PICC W1J 15 J1
Athena Medical Centre
CLPT E5 86 E2
Atherton Leisure Centre
SRTFD E15 88 D4
Athlone House Hospital
HGT N6 65 K5
Athlon Industrial Estate
ALP/SUD HA0 97 K1
Atkinson Morley Hospital
RYNPK SW20 176 E3
Atlantic House (Richmond American International University)
KENS W8 120 A3
Atlas Business Centre
CRICK NW2 63 K6
Atlas Transport Estate
BTSEA SW11 140 B3
Attlee Youth & Community Centre
WCHPL E1 13 K2
Auriol Junior School
HOR/WEW KT19 207 H2
Australia House
HOL/ALD WC2B 11 H4
Avenue House Museum
FNCH N3 46 D5
Avenue House School
WEA W13 97 H5
Avenue Industrial Estate
CHING E4 51 H2
Avenue Pre-Preparatory School
HGT N6 66 B4
Avenue Primary School
MNPK E12 89 J2
Avenue Road ●
BECK BR3 182 A5
Avery Hill Park
ELTH/MOT SE9 167 H1
Avondale Park Primary School
NTGHL W11 100 B6
Avon House School
WFD IG8 38 E6
Avon Trading Estate
WKENS W14 119 J4
Axis Business Centre
SRTFD E15 87 K6
The Aylesham Centre
PECK SE15 143 H2
Ayloff Primary School
HCH RM12 93 K2
Aylward First & Middle Schools
STAN HA7 43 K1
Azhar Academy
FSTGT E7 88 E4
B6 Sixth Form College
CLPT E5 86 D1
BAA Heathrow Visitor Centre
HTHAIR TW6 132 E2
Babington House School
CHST BR7 184 E2
BackCare Clinic
WPK KT4 192 D5
Bacon's College
BERM/RHTH SE16 124 B1
Baden Powell House
SKENS SW7 120 B4
Baglioni Hotel
KENS W8 120 B2
Bakers Hall
MON EC3R 13 H6
Baker Street ⊖
CAMTN NW1 3 F7
Balaam Leisure Centre
PLSTW E13 106 E3
Bales College
NKENS W10 100 B2
Balfour Business Centre
NWDGN UB2 114 C3
Balgowan Primary School
BECK BR3 182 B5
Balham ⇌ ⊖
BAL SW12 161 G3
Balham Girls Preparatory Secondary School
TOOT SW17 160 E5
Balham Health Centre
BAL SW12 161 G4
Balham Leisure Centre
TOOT SW17 161 F4
Balmoral Trading Estate
BARK IG11 109 F3
Baltic Exchange
HDTCH EC3A 13 H3
Bancrofts School
WFD IG8 38 E5
Bandon Hill Cemetery
WLGTN SM6 210 D3
Bandon Hill Primary School
WLGTN SM6 210 D4
Bangabandhu Primary School
BETH E2 104 E2
Bank ⊖ ⊖
LOTH EC2R 12 E4
Bank of England Extension
CITYW EC2V 12 C4
Bank of England (& Museum)
LOTH EC2R 12 E4
Bankside Gallery
STHWK SE1 12 B6
Bankside Jetty
STHWK SE1 12 C6
Bankside Park Industrial Estate
BARK IG11 109 G2
Bannister Stadium
KTN/HRWW/WS HA3 42 C2
Bannockburn Primary School
WOOL/PLUM SE18 128 A4
The Banqueting House, Whitehall
WHALL SW1A 16 E1
Barbara Speake Theatre School
ACT W3 99 G6
Barber Surgeons' Hall
BARB EC2Y 12 D2
Barbican ⊖
FARR EC1M 12 B1
Barbican Cinema
BARB EC2Y 12 C1
Barbican Exhibition Halls
BARB EC2Y 12 D1
The Barbican
BARB EC2Y 12 C1
Barbican Theatre
BARB EC2Y 12 D1
Barclay Primary School
LEY E10 70 B3
Barham Primary School
ALP/SUD HA0 79 J4
Baring Primary School
LEE/GVPK SE12 165 K2
Baring Road Medical Centre
BMLY BR1 165 K4
Barkantine Clinic
POP/IOD E14 124 D2
Barking ⇌ ⊖ ⊖
BARK IG11 90 C5
Barking Abbey Comprehensive School (Lower)
IL IG1 90 D3
Barking Abbey Comprehensive School (Upper)
BARK IG11 91 F4
Barking Abbey Industrial Estate
BARK IG11 90 B6
Barking Abbey Leisure Centre
BARK IG11 91 G4
Barking Abbey School
BARK IG11 91 F4
Barking College
ROMW/RG RM7 75 F6
Barking FC
BCTR RM8 91 H3
Barking Hospital
BARK IG11 91 F5
Barking Industrial Park
BARK IG11 91 F6
Barking RUFC
DAGW RM9 91 K6
Barkingside ⊖
BARK/HLT IG6 72 D1
Barkingside Cemetery
BARK/HLT IG6 54 B6
Barkingside FC
BARK/HLT IG6 72 D1
Barlby Primary School
NKENS W10 100 B3
Barley Lane Primary School
GDMY/SEVK IG3 73 G4
Barnabas Medical Centre
NTHLT UB5 78 C4
Barn Croft Primary School
WALTH E17 69 G3
Barnehurst ⇌
BXLYHN DA7 149 K3
Barnehurst Primary School
ERITH DA8 149 K2
Barnehurst Public Golf Club
BXLYHN DA7 150 A4
Barn Elms Athletics Track
BARN SW13 138 E3
Barn Elms Sports Centre
BARN SW13 139 F2
Barn Elms Water Sports Centre
PUT/ROE SW15 139 F3
Barnes ⇌
BARN SW13 138 D4
Barnes Bridge ⇌
BARN SW13 138 B3
Barnes Cray Primary School
DART DA1 150 D5
Barnes Hospital
MORT/ESHN SW14 138 B4
Barnes Primary School
BARN SW13 138 B4
Barnes Sports Club
BARN SW13 138 C2
Barnet College
BAR EN5 20 D5
CDALE/KGS NW9 45 H4
EBAR EN4 33 K3
FBAR/BDGN N11 33 K5
HDN NW4 63 J3
NFNCH/WDSPK N12 47 G1
Barnet Copthall Pool
HDN NW4 45 K3
Barnet Copthall Stadium
HDN NW4 46 A4
Barnet FC (Underhill)
BAR EN5 20 E6
Barnet General Hospital
BAR EN5 20 B5
Barnet Health Centre
BAR EN5 20 E6
Barnet Hill JMI School
BAR EN5 20 D6
Barnet Hospital Chest Clinic
BAR EN5 20 B5
Barnet Museum
BAR EN5 20 C5
Barnet Trading Estate
BAR EN5 20 D4
Barnfield Primary School
EDGW HA8 44 E4
Barnhill Community High School
YEAD UB4 95 F2
Barn Hotel
RSLP HA4 58 C6
Barnsbury Complex
HOLWY N7 85 G5
Barnsbury School for Girls
IS N1 85 G4
Barons Court ⊖
HMSMTH W6 119 G5
Barons Court Theatre
WKENS W14 119 H5
Barratt Industrial Park
BOW E3 106 A3
Barrett Industrial Park
STHL UB1 115 F1
Barrett Way Industrial Estate
RYLN/HDSTN HA2 42 D6
Barrington Primary School
WELL DA16 148 E3
Barrow Hedges Primary School
CAR SM5 209 J5
Barrow Hill Junior School
STJWD NW8 2 C3
Barton House Health Centre
STNW/STAM N16 85 K1
Barwell Business Park
CHSGTN KT9 205 K5
Bassett House School
NKENS W10 100 B5
Baston School
HAYES BR2 200 A6
Bath Factory Estate
HNHL SE24 162 D1
Battersea Arts Centre (BAC)
BTSEA SW11 140 E4
Battersea Business Centre
BTSEA SW11 141 F4
Battersea Dogs' Home
VX/NE SW8 141 G1
Battersea Park ⇌
BTSEA SW11 141 G1
Battersea Power Station (disused)
VX/NE SW8 121 G6
Battersea Sports Centre
BTSEA SW11 140 C4
Battersea Technology College
BTSEA SW11 140 E2
Battersea Tutorial College
TOOT SW17 161 F4
Bayswater ⊖
BAY/PAD W2 101 F6
BBC Broadcasting House
REGST W1B 9 K2
BBC Media Village
SHB W12 100 A6
BBC Studios
MV/WKIL W9 101 F3
BBC Television Centre
SHB W12 100 A6
BBC Worldwide
SHB W12 100 A5
Beal High School
REDBR IG4 53 J6
Beam Primary School
DAGE RM10 110 E1
Beatrice Tate School
BETH E2 104 D2
Beatrix Potter Primary School
WAND/EARL SW18 160 B3
Beauclerc Infant School
SUN TW16 172 B6
The Beaufort Hotel
CHEL SW3 14 E5
Beaumont Primary School
LEY E10 69 K4
Beaver College
BAY/PAD W2 100 E6
The Beavers Community Primary School
HSLWW TW4 134 B4
Beaverwood School for Girls
CHST BR7 185 K2
Beckenham Business Centre
BECK BR3 182 B2
Beckenham Crematorium
BECK BR3 181 K6
Beckenham CC
BECK BR3 182 E3
Beckenham Hill ⇌
CAT SE6 183 F1
Beckenham Hospital
BECK BR3 182 C5
Beckenham Junction ⇌ ●
BECK BR3 182 D4
Beckenham Leisure Centre
BECK BR3 182 B4
Beckenham Place Park Golf Course
BECK BR3 182 E2
Beckenham RFC
BECK BR3 198 B1
Beckenham Road ●
BECK BR3 182 A4
Beckenham School of Art
BECK BR3 198 B2
Beckenham Theatre Centre
BECK BR3 182 E5
Beckenham Town FC
BECK BR3 198 D2
Becket Sports Centre
DART DA1 171 F1
Beckford Primary School
KIL/WHAMP NW6 82 D3
Beckmead School
BECK BR3 198 D5
The Beck Theatre
HYS/HAR UB3 94 D5
Beckton ⊖
EHAM E6 108 A4
Beckton Park ⊖
EHAM E6 107 K6
Beckton Ski Centre
EHAM E6 108 A3
Beckton Triangle Retail Park
EHAM E6 108 B2
Becontree ⊖
DAGW RM9 91 J4
Becontree Day Hospital
BCTR RM8 74 A6
Becontree Primary School
BCTR RM8 91 H1
Bective House Clinic
PUT/ROE SW15 139 J5
Beddington Infants School
WLGTN SM6 210 C1

Beddington Lane ⊖ *CROY/NA* CR0 .... 195 H3
Beddington Medical Centre *CROY/NA* CR0 .... 210 E2
Beddington Park Primary School *CROY/NA* CR0 .... 210 D1
Beddington Trading Estate *CROY/NA* CR0 .... 195 K5
Bedelsford School *KUT/HW* KT1 .... 175 F6
Bedensfield Clinic *SCUP* DA14 .... 187 F1
Bedfont Cemetery *EBED/NFELT* TW14 .... 153 F3
Bedfont Health Clinic *EBED/NFELT* TW14 .... 153 H2
Bedfont Industrial Park *ASHF* TW15 .... 153 G5
Bedfont J & I School *EBED/NFELT* TW14 .... 153 H1
Bedfont Lakes Country Park *EBED/NFELT* TW14 .... 153 F4
Bedfont Lakes Office Park *EBED/NFELT* TW14 .... 153 F3
Bedford Hotel *RSQ* WC1B 11 F1
Bedington Infant School *WLGTN* SM6 .... 210 C2
Bedonwell Clinic *ABYW* SE2 .... 129 F6
Bedonwell Medical Centre *BELV* DA17 .... 129 G5
Bedonwell Primary School *BXLYHN* DA7 .... 129 F6
Beecholme Primary School *MTCM* CR4 .... 179 G4
Beechwood School *STRHM/NOR* SW16 .... 161 K5
Beehive Preparatory School *REDBR* IG4 .... 71 K1
The Beehive School *ARCH* N19 .... 66 D4
Beis Hamedrash Elyon *GLDGN* NW11 .... 64 C4
Beis Malka Girls School *STNW/STAM* N16 .... 68 B5
Beis Rochel D'Satmar Girls School *STNW/STAM* N16 .... 68 A4
Beis Yaakov Primary School *CDALE/KGS* NW9 .... 45 F6
Belgrave Walk ⊖ *MTCM* CR4 .... 194 C1
Bellamy's Wharf *BERM/RHTH* SE16 .... 124 A1
Bellenden Primary School *PECK* SE15 .... 143 H4
Bellenden Road Business Centre *PECK* SE15 .... 143 G3
Bellenden Road Retail Park *PECK* SE15 .... 143 G2
Bellerbys College *DEPT* SE8 .... 124 E6
Belleville Primary School *BTSEA* SW11 .... 140 E6
Belle Vue Cinema *WLSDN* NW10 .... 81 K5
Bell Industrial Estate *CHSWK* W4 .... 117 K4
Bellingham ⇌ *CAT* SE6 .... 164 E5
Bellingham Trading Estate *CAT* SE6 .... 164 E5
Bell Lane JMI School *HDN* NW4 .... 64 B1
Belmont Bowling Club *STRHM/NOR* SW16 .... 161 K5
Belmont First School *KTN/HRWW/WS* HA3 .... 43 F5
Belmont Infant School *TOTM* N17 .... 49 J6
Belmont (Mill Hill Preparatory School) *MLHL* NW7 .... 31 J5
Belmont Park School *LEY* E10 .... 70 A3
Belmont Primary School *CHSWK* W4 .... 118 A4; *ERITH* DA8 .... 149 H1
Belmore Primary School *YEAD* UB4 .... 95 F2
Belsize Park ⊖ *HAMP* NW3 .... 83 J3
Belvedere ⇌ *BELV* DA17 .... 129 J3
Belvedere Day Hospital *WLSDN* NW10 .... 81 J6
Belvedere Industrial Estate *BELV* DA17 .... 130 A1
Belvedere Link Business Park *ERITH* DA8 .... 129 K3
Belvedere Primary School *BELV* DA17 .... 129 J4
Belvue Business Centre *NTHLT* UB5 .... 78 B5
Belvue School *NTHLT* UB5 .... 78 A6
Benedict House Preparatory School *BFN/LL* DA15 .... 168 A6
Benedict Primary School *MTCM* CR4 .... 178 C6
Ben Jonson Primary School *WCHPL* E1 .... 105 G3
Bensham Manor School *THHTH* CR7 .... 196 D2
Benson Primary School *CROY/NA* CR0 .... 213 G1
Bentalls Shopping Centre *KUT/HW* KT1 .... 174 E5
Benthal Primary School *STNW/STAM* N16 .... 86 C1
The Bentley Kempinski Hotel *SKENS* SW7 .... 120 B4
Bentley Wood Girls School *STAN* HA7 .... 43 F1
Bentworth Primary School *SHB* W12 .... 99 K5
Ben Uri Gallery, London Jewish Museum of Art *STJWD* NW8 .... 83 F6
Beormund School *STHWK* SE1 .... 18 E3
Berger Primary School *HOM* E9 .... 87 F4
The Berkeley Hotel *KTBR* SW1X 15 G2
Berkeley Primary School *HEST* TW5 .... 114 C6
Berlitz School of Languages *HHOL* WC1V 11 H2
Bermondsey ⊖ ⊖ *BERM/RHTH* SE16 .... 123 H3
Bermondsey Town Hall *STHWK* SE1 .... 19 J5
Bermondsey Trading Estate *BERM/RHTH* SE16 .... 123 K4
Berrylands ⇌ *BRYLDS* KT5 .... 191 J1
Berrymede Infant School *ACT* W3 .... 117 J2
Berrymede Junior School *ACT* W3 .... 117 J2
Bertram House School *TOOT* SW17 .... 161 F4
Bessemer Grange J & I School *HNHL* SE24 .... 142 E6
Bessemer Park Industrial Estate *BRXN/ST* SW9 .... 142 C5
Best Western Bromley Court Hotel *BMLY* BR1 .... 183 H2
Best Western Cumberland Hotel *HRW* HA1 .... 61 F3
Best Western Lodge Hotel *PUT/ROE* SW15 .... 139 J6
Best Western Master Robert Hotel *HEST* TW5 .... 134 E2
Best Western Mostyn Hotel *MBLAR* W1H 9 F4
Bethlem Royal Hospital *BECK* BR3 .... 198 D4
Bethnal Green ⊖ *BETH* E2 .... 104 E2
Bethnal Green ⇌ *WCHPL* E1 .... 104 D3
Bethnal Green Technology College *BETH* E2 .... 7 K5
Beths Grammar School for Boys *BXLY* DA5 .... 169 H1
The Betty Layward School *STNW/STAM* N16 .... 85 K1
Beulah Infant School *THHTH* CR7 .... 180 D5
Beverley School *NWMAL* KT3 .... 192 D2
Beverley Trading Estate *MRDN* SM4 .... 193 G4
Bevington Primary School *NKENS* W10 .... 100 C4
Bexley ⇌ *BXLY* DA5 .... 169 H3
Bexley College *BELV* DA17 .... 129 K4
Bexley CC *BXLY* DA5 .... 169 H3
Bexley Grammar School *WELL* DA16 .... 148 C5
Bexleyheath ⇌ *BXLYHN* DA7 .... 149 F3
Bexleyheath Cemetery *BXLYHN* DA7 .... 149 G4
Bexleyheath Centre *BXLYHS* DA6 .... 149 F5
Bexleyheath Golf Club *BXLYHS* DA6 .... 149 F6
Bexleyheath Marriott Hotel *BXLYHS* DA6 .... 149 J5
Bexleyheath School *BXLYHN* DA7 .... 149 G4
Bexleyheath Superbowl *BXLYHS* DA6 .... 149 G5
Bexley RFC *BXLY* DA5 .... 169 H2
BFI London IMAX Cinema *STHWK* SE1 .... 17 H1
Bickerly School of Dance *HAYES* BR2 .... 200 D2
Bickley ⇌ *BMLY* BR1 .... 184 D6
Bickley Park CC *BMLY* BR1 .... 184 D5
Bickley Park Pre-Preparatory School *BMLY* BR1 .... 184 D6
Bickley Park Preparatory School *BMLY* BR1 .... 184 C6
Big Ben *WHALL* SW1A 17 F3
Bigland Green Primary School *WCHPL* E1 .... 104 D5
Billingsgate Fish Market *POP/IOD* E14 .... 124 E1
Bingham Hotel *TWK* TW1 .... 156 E1
Birchmere Business Park *THMD* SE28 .... 128 B2
Birchwood Park Golf Club *RDART* DA2 .... 187 K3
Bird College *SCUP* DA14 .... 168 B5
Birkbeck ⇌ ⊖ *BECK* BR3 .... 181 K5
Birkbeck College *GWRST* WC1E .... 4 D7; *RSQ* WC1B 10 D2
Birkbeck Primary School *SCUP* DA14 .... 168 C5
Bishop Challoner Catholic Collegiate School *WCHPL* E1 .... 104 E6
Bishop Challoner Girls School *WCHPL* E1 .... 104 C6
Bishop Challoner School *HAYES* BR2 .... 183 G5
Bishop Douglass RC School *EFNCH* N2 .... 47 G5
Bishop Gilpin Primary School *WIM/MER* SW19 .... 177 J1
Bishop John Robinson CE Primary School *THMD* SE28 .... 109 J6
Bishop Justus CE (Secondary) School *HAYES* BR2 .... 200 D4
Bishop Perrin CE Primary School *WHTN* TW2 .... 155 G2
Bishop Ramsey CE School (Upper) *RSLP* HA4 .... 58 E4
Bishop Ramsey CE School *RSLP* HA4 .... 58 D4
Bishopsgate Institute *LVPST* EC2M 13 H2
Bishop Thomas Grant School *STRHM/NOR* SW16 .... 180 A1
Bishop Winnington-Ingram CE Primary School *RSLP* HA4 .... 58 B4
Bittacy Business Centre *MLHL* NW7 .... 46 C2
Blackburn Trading Estate *STWL/WRAY* TW19 .... 152 C1
Blackfen Medical Centre *BFN/LL* DA15 .... 148 A6
Blackfen School for Girls *BFN/LL* DA15 .... 168 C1
Blackfriars ⇌ *BLKFR* EC4V 12 A6
Blackfriars Millennium Pier *EMB* EC4Y 11 K5
Blackfriars Pier *BLKFR* EC4V 12 B6
Blackheath ⇌ *BKHTH/KID* SE3 .... 145 J4
Blackheath Bluecoat School *BKHTH/KID* SE3 .... 146 A1
Blackheath Business Estate *GNWCH* SE10 .... 145 F2
The Blackheath Clinic *BKHTH/KID* SE3 .... 145 K5
Blackheath High School GDST *BKHTH/KID* SE3 .... 145 J3
Blackheath High Senior School *BKHTH/KID* SE3 .... 145 K1
Blackheath Hospital *BKHTH/KID* SE3 .... 145 J4
Blackheath Preparatory School *BKHTH/KID* SE3 .... 145 K2
Blackheath RFC (The Rectory Field) *BKHTH/KID* SE3 .... 146 A1
Blackhorse Lane ⊖ *CROY/NA* CR0 .... 197 H4
Blackhorse Road ⊖ ⊖ *WALTH* E17 .... 69 F1
Blackwall ⊖ *POP/IOD* E14 .... 106 A6
Blackwall Trading Estate *POP/IOD* E14 .... 106 B4
Blair Peach Primary School *STHL* UB1 .... 114 C1
Blake College *GTPST* W1W 10 A1
Blanche Nevile School *HGT* N6 .... 65 K3; *MUSWH* N10 .... 48 A6
Blenheim Business Centre *MTCM* CR4 .... 178 E4
Blenheim Primary School *ORP* BR6 .... 202 E6
Blenheim Shopping Centre *PGE/AN* SE20 .... 181 K3
Blessed Dominic RC Primary School *CDALE/KGS* NW9 .... 45 G5
Blessed Sacrament RC Primary School *IS* N1 .... 5 F1
Blood Transfusion Centre *EDGW* HA8 .... 44 D3
Bloomfield Clinic Guys *STHWK* SE1 .... 19 F2
Bloomsbury International *NOXST/BSQ* WC1A 11 F2
Bloomsbury Theatre *GWRST* WC1E 4 C6
Blossom House School *RYNPK* SW20 .... 177 F3
Blossoms Inn Medical Centre *BLKFR* EC4V 12 D5
Blue Gate Fields Infant School *WCHPL* E1 .... 104 E6
The Blue School *ISLW* TW7 .... 136 B4
Blyth's Wharf *POP/IOD* E14 .... 105 G6
BMI Medical Centre *CAVSQ/HST* W1G 9 H2
Bnois Jerusalem Girls School *STNW/STAM* N16 .... 67 K4
The Bob Hope Theatre *ELTH/MOT* SE9 .... 166 E1
Bodywise Natural Health Centre *BETH* E2 .... 104 E2
Boleyn Cinema *EHAM* E6 .... 107 H1
Bolingbroke Hospital *BTSEA* SW11 .... 140 D6
Bolingbroke Primary School *BTSEA* SW11 .... 140 C2
Bond First School *MTCM* CR4 .... 178 E5
Bond Primary School *MTCM* CR4 .... 178 E5
Bond Street ⊖ *OXSTW* W1C 9 H4
Bonner Primary School *BETH* E2 .... 105 F1
Bonneville Primary School *CLAP* SW4 .... 161 H1
Bonnington Hotel *RSQ* WC1B 11 F1
Bonus Pastor Catholic College *BMLY* BR1 .... 165 G6
Boomes Industrial Estate *RAIN* RM13 .... 111 H3
Booster Cushion Theatre *WDGN* N22 .... 49 F5
Borough ⊖ *STHWK* SE1 .... 18 D3
Borough Cemetery *HSLWW* TW4 .... 155 F2
Borough Market *STHWK* SE1 .... 12 E7
Borthwick Wharf *DEPT* SE8 .... 124 D5
Boston Business Park *HNWL* W7 .... 115 K3
Boston Manor ⊖ *HNWL* W7 .... 116 B4
Boston University *SKENS* SW7 .... 120 B4
Botwell RC Primary School *HYS/HAR* UB3 .... 113 J2
Boundary Business Park *MTCM* CR4 .... 178 C5
Bounds Green ⊖ *FBAR/BDGN* N11 .... 48 D3
Bounds Green Health Centre *FBAR/BDGN* N11 .... 48 D3
Bounds Green Industrial Estate *FBAR/BDGN* N11 .... 48 B2
Bounds Green Infant School *FBAR/BDGN* N11 .... 48 D3
Bourne CP School *RSLP* HA4 .... 77 G3
Bourne Hall Health Centre *EW* KT17 .... 207 H6
Bourne Hall Museum *EW* KT17 .... 207 H6
Bourne Road Industrial Park *DART* DA1 .... 150 A6
Bourneside Sports Club *STHGT/OAK* N14 .... 34 E3
Bousfield Primary School *WBPTN* SW10 .... 120 B5
Boutcher CE Primary School *STHWK* SE1 .... 19 J5
Bowater House *SKENS* SW7 .... 14 E3
Bow Church ⊖ *BOW* E3 .... 105 J2
Bowden House Clinic *HRW* HA1 .... 60 E6
Bower Park School *ROM* RM1 .... 57 G2
Bowes Park ⇌ *WDGN* N22 .... 48 E3
Bowes Primary School *FBAR/BDGN* N11 .... 48 D1
Bowes Road Clinic *FBAR/BDGN* N11 .... 48 C1
Bow Junior & Youth Centre *BOW* E3 .... 105 H4
Ealing Conservative Bowling Club *EA* W5 .... 97 J6
Bowman Trading Estate *CDALE/KGS* NW9 .... 44 C6
Bow Road ⊖ *BOW* E3 .... 105 J2
Bow Secondary School *BOW* E3 .... 105 J1
Bow Triangle Business Centre *BOW* E3 .... 105 J3
Boxgrove Primary School *ABYW* SE2 .... 128 D3
BPP Law School *HHOL* WC1V 11 G2
Brackenbury Health Centre *HMSMTH* W6 .... 118 E3
Brackenbury Primary School *HMSMTH* W6 .... 118 E3
Bracken Industrial Estate *BARK/HLT* IG6 .... 55 F3
Bracton Centre *RDART* DA2 .... 170 C4
Brady Recreation Centre *WCHPL* E1 .... 104 C4
Braeside Senior School *BKHH* IG9 .... 39 F3
Braincroft Primary School *CRICK* NW2 .... 81 H1
Braintree Road Industrial Estate *RSLP* HA4 .... 77 F2
Bramah's Tea & Coffee Museum *STHWK* SE1 .... 18 D1
Brampton College *HDN* NW4 .... 64 A1
Brampton Manor School *EHAM* E6 .... 107 H3
Brampton Primary School *BXLYHN* DA7 .... 148 E3; *EHAM* E6 .... 107 J2
Brandlehow Primary School *PUT/ROE* SW15 .... 139 J5
Branollys Health Centre *PLSTW* E13 .... 106 E3
Breakspear Crematorium *RSLP* HA4 .... 58 A2
Breaside Preparatory School *BMLY* BR1 .... 184 B4
Brecknock Primary School *HOLWY* N7 .... 84 D4
Bredinghurst School *PECK* SE15 .... 143 K5
Brent Adult College *WLSDN* NW10 .... 81 F6
Brent Arts Council *CRICK* NW2 .... 81 J1
Brent Child & Family Clinic *WLSDN* NW10 .... 81 H3
Brent Cross ⊖ *GLDGN* NW11 .... 64 B4
Brent Cross Shopping Centre *HDN* NW4 .... 64 A4
Brentfield Medical Centre *WLSDN* NW10 .... 81 F4
Brentfield Primary School *WLSDN* NW10 .... 81 F4
Brentford ⇌ *BTFD* TW8 .... 116 E6
Brentford Business Centre *BTFD* TW8 .... 136 D1
Brentford FC (Griffin Park) *BTFD* TW8 .... 116 E6
Brentford Fountain Leisure Centre *BTFD* TW8 .... 117 G5
Brentford Health Centre *BTFD* TW8 .... 116 D6
Brentford School for Girls *BTFD* TW8 .... 116 E6
Brent Knoll School *FSTH* SE23 .... 164 A5
Brent Park Industrial Estate *NWDGN* UB2 .... 114 A3
Brentside First School *HNWL* W7 .... 96 E4
Brentside High School *HNWL* W7 .... 96 E3
Brentside Primary School *HNWL* W7 .... 96 E3
Brent Trading Estate *WLSDN* NW10 .... 81 G3
Brent Valley Golf Club *HNWL* W7 .... 96 E6
Brentwaters Business Park *BTFD* TW8 .... 136 D1
Brettenham Primary School *ED* N9 .... 36 C6
Brewers' Hall *CITYW* EC2V 12 D2
Brewery Industrial Estate *IS* N1 .... 6 C3
Brewery Mews Business Centre *ISLW* TW7 .... 136 A4
The Brewery *ROMW/RG* RM7 .... 75 G3
Brick Lane Music Hall *CAN/RD* E16 .... 126 C1
Brick Lane Music House *WCHPL* E1 .... 7 K7
Bricklayer Arms Industrial Estate *STHWK* SE1 .... 19 J7
The Bridewell Theatre *EMB* EC4Y 12 A4
The Bridge Academy *BETH* E2 .... 7 J1
The Bridge Business Centre *NWDGN* UB2 .... 115 F2
Bridge Lane Theatre *BTSEA* SW11 .... 140 D2
The Bridge Leisure Centre *SYD* SE26 .... 182 C1
Bridge Park Business & Leisure Centre *WLSDN* NW10 .... 80 D5
The Bridge School *ARCH* N19 .... 66 C6; *HOLWY* N7 .... 84 D4
Brigham Young University *BAY/PAD* W2 .... 100 E6
Bright Sparks Montessori School *WKENS* W14 .... 119 G
Brigstock Medical Centre *THHTH* CR7 .... 196 C
Brimsdown ⇌ *PEND* EN3 .... 25 G
Brimsdown Industrial Estate *PEND* EN3 .... 24 E
Brimsdown Infant School *PEND* EN3 .... 25 F
Brindishe Primary School *LEE/GVPK* SE12 .... 145 J
Britain & London Visitor Centre *STJS* SW1Y .... 10 C
Britannia Business Centre *CRICK* NW2 .... 82 E
Britannia Leisure Centre *IS* N1 .... 7 F
Britannia Sports Ground *WALTH* E17 51
Britannia Village Primary School *CAN/RD* E16 126
British Airways Museum *HTHAIR* TW6 133
The British American Drama Academy *CAMTN* NW1 .... 3; *SRTFD* E15 106
British Cartoon Centre *BMSBY* WC1N 5
British College of Osteopathy *HAMP* NW3 83
British Dental Association *CAVSQ/HST* W1G 9
The British Hernia Centre *HDN* NW4 63
British Library *CAMTN* NW1 4
British Library Newspaper Library *CDALE/KGS* NW9 45
British Medical Association *STPAN* WC1H 4
British Museum *RSQ* WC1B 10
British Telecom Tower *GTPST* W1W 10
BRIT School for Performing Arts *CROY/NA* CR0 196
Brittons School Technology College *RAIN* RM13 93

Brixton ⇌ ⊖ BRXN/ST SW9 142 B5
Brixton Academy BRXN/ST SW9 142 B4
Brixton Recreation Centre BRXN/ST SW9 142 B4
Broadfields Primary School EDGW HA8 30 C4
Broadgate LVPST EC2M 13 F1
Broadgate Ice Arena LVPST EC2M 13 F2
Broadhurst School KIL/WHAMP NW6 83 G5
Broadmead J & I School CROY/NA CR0 196 E3
Broadreach College THMD SE28 128 A3
Broadwalk Shopping Centre EDGW HA8 44 C2
Broadwater Farm Primary School TOTM N17 49 K5
Broadwater Primary School TOOT SW17 160 C6
Broadway Clinic EDGW HA8 44 D4
Broadway Retail Park CRICK NW2 82 B2
Broadway Shopping Centre HMSMTH W6 119 F5
Broadway Square BXLYHS DA6 149 H5
Broadway Squash & Fitness Centre HMSMTH W6 119 G4
Brocklebank Health Centre WAND/EARL SW18 160 A2
Brocklebank Industrial Estate GNWCH SE10 125 K4
Brockley ⇌ ⊖ BROCKY SE4 144 C4
Brockley Cross Business Centre BROCKY SE4 144 B4
Brockley Primary School BROCKY SE4 144 C6
Brockwell Lido HNHL SE24 162 C1
Bromet Primary School OXHEY WD19 27 H2
Bromley by Bow ⊖ BOW E3 105 K2
Bromley Cemetery BMLY BR1 183 J3
Bromley Civic Centre BMLY BR1 184 A5
Bromley College of Further & Higher Education
BMLY BR1 183 K4
HAYES BR2 200 C3
Bromley FC HAYES BR2 200 A2
Bromley Golf Club HAYES BR2 200 D4
Bromley High School GDST BMLY BR1 201 F1
Bromley Industrial Centre BMLY BR1 184 C6
Bromley Mall Indoor Market BMLY BR1 183 K5
Bromley Museum ORP BR6 202 C4
Bromley North ⇌ BMLY BR1 183 K4
Bromley Road Infant School BECK BR3 182 E4
Bromley Road Retail Park CAT SE6 164 E4
Bromley Ski Centre STMC/STPC BR5 186 E4
Bromley South ⇌ BMLY BR1 184 A6
Bromley Tennis Centre ORP BR6 216 D1
Bromley Wendover Lawn Tennis Club HAYES BR2 200 A1
Brompton Cemetery WBPTN SW10 120 A6
Brompton Medical Centre ECT SW5 120 A5
Brompton Oratory SKENS SW7 14 C5
Bromyard Leisure Centre ACT W3 118 B1
Brondesbury ⊖ KIL/WHAMP NW6 82 D5
Brondesbury College for Boys KIL/WHAMP NW6 82 B5
Brondesbury Park ⊖ KIL/WHAMP NW6 82 C6
Brook Community Primary School HACK E8 86 C3
Brooke Trading Estate ROM RM1 75 H4
Brookfield House School WFD IG8 52 C2
Brookfield Primary School
CHEAM SM3 193 H5
HGT N6 66 B6
Brook House FC YEAD UB4 94 D2
Brook Industrial Estate YEAD UB4 114 C1
Brook Industrial Park STMC/STPC BR5 202 D1
Brookland Junior School GLDGN NW11 65 F1
Brooklands Primary School BKHTH/KID SE3 145 K4
Brook Lane Business Centre BTFD TW8 116 E5
Brookmarsh Trading Estate DEPT SE8 144 E1
Brookmead Industrial Estate CROY/NA CR0 195 H3
Brookside Primary School YEAD UB4 95 G2
Broomfield House School RCH/KEW TW9 137 G2
Broomfield School FBAR/BDGN N11 48 D1
Broomsleigh Business Park SYD SE26 182 C1
Broomwood Hall Lower School
BAL SW12 160 E1
STRHM/NOR SW16 161 J5
Brownlow Medical Centre FBAR/BDGN N11 48 E1
Brown's Hotel MYFR/PICC W1J 9 K6
Bruce Castle Museum TOTM N17 50 A4
Bruce Grove ⇌ TOTM N17 50 B5
Bruce Grove Primary School TOTM N17 50 B5
Brunei Gallery STPAN WC1H 4 D7
Brunel Engine House BERM/RHTH SE16 123 K2
Brunel University
GLDGN NW11 64 B3
ISLW TW7 135 K1
TWK TW1 136 C5
Brunel University (Osterley Campus) Track ISLW TW7 135 K1
Brunswick Health Centre FBAR/BDGN N11 34 A4
Brunswick Housing & Shopping Centre BMSBY WC1N 5 F6
Brunswick Industrial Park FBAR/BDGN N11 34 B6
Brunswick Medical Centre BMSBY WC1N 4 E6
Brunswick Park JMI School STHGT/OAK N14 34 A3
Brunswick Park Primary School CMBW SE5 142 E1
BT Centre STBT EC1A 12 C3
Buckhurst Hill ⊖ BKHH IG9 39 H4
Buckhurst Hill FC BKHH IG9 39 J3
Buckhurst Hill Primary School BKHH IG9 39 J4
Buckingham College Preparatory School PIN HA5 59 K4
Buckingham Palace WHALL SW1A 16 A3
Buckingham Primary School HPTN TW12 172 E1
Buckingham Road Cemetery IL IG1 72 D6
Building Centre GWRST WC1E 10 C2
Bullers Wood School CHST BR7 184 E4
Bullsbridge Industrial Estate NWDGN UB2 114 A4
The Bull Theatre BAR EN5 20 D5
BUPA Roding Hospital REDBR IG4 53 H6
Burbage School IS N1 7 G2
Burdett Coutts CE Primary School WEST SW1P 16 C5
Burgess Business Park CMBW SE5 142 E1
Burgess Park Tennis Centre CMBW SE5 122 D6
Burlington Danes School SHB W12 99 K5
Burlington Infant School NWMAL KT3 192 C1
Burney Street Clinic GNWCH SE10 145 F1
Burnham Trading Estate DART DA1 151 G5
Burnhill Business Centre BECK BR3 182 D5
Burnley Road Clinic WLSDN NW10 81 J3
Burns Hotel ECT SW5 120 A4
Burnside Industrial Estate BARK/HLT IG6 55 H1
Burnt Ash Primary School BMLY BR1 183 K1
Burnt Oak ⊖ EDGW HA8 44 E4
Burnt Oak Junior School BFN/LL DA15 168 B3
Burntwood School TOOT SW17 160 C4
Bursted Wood Primary School BXLYHN DA7 149 J3
Burwell Industrial Estate LEY E10 69 G5
Burwood School ORP BR6 202 E6
Bushey ⇌ ⊖ OXHEY WD19 27 H1
Bushey Golf & Country Club BUSH WD23 28 A1
Bushey Hall School BUSH WD23 27 K1
Bushey Health Centre BUSH WD23 27 K1
Bushey Heath Primary School BUSH WD23 28 D3
Bushey Museum & Art Gallery BUSH WD23 28 A1
Bush Hill Park ⇌ EN EN1 36 B1
Bush Hill Park Golf Club WCHMH N21 23 J6
Bush Hill Park Medical Centre EN EN1 36 B1
Bush Hill Park Primary School EN EN1 24 C6
BBC Bush House HOL/ALD WC2B 11 G4
Bush Industrial Estate
ARCH N19 84 C1
WLSDN NW10 99 F3
The Business Academy Bexley ERITHM DA18 129 F2
The Business Centre
CEND/HSY/T N8 48 E5
IL IG1 72 B6
The Business Design Centre IS N1 5 K1
Business Training & Solutions CDALE/KGS NW9 45 H4
Bute House Preparatory School for Girls HMSMTH W6 119 F4
Butlers Wharf STHWK SE1 19 K1
Butler's Wharf Business Centre STHWK SE1 19 K2
Butler's Wharf Pier STHWK SE1 19 K1
Butterfly Sports Club ELTH/MOT SE9 167 G1
Buxlow Preparatory School WBLY HA9 80 A1
Buzzard Creek Industrial Estate BARK IG11 109 F4
Byam Shaw School of Art ARCH N19 66 C6
Byfleet Industrial Estate WATW WD18 26 A3
Bygrove Prim School POP/IOD E14 105 K5
Byron Court Primary School ALP/SUD HA0 61 J6
Cabot Place POP/IOD E14 124 D1
The Cadogan Hotel KTBR SW1X 15 F5
Cadogan Pier CHEL SW3 120 D6
Caledonian Market STHWK SE1 19 H4
Caledonian Road ⊖ HOLWY N7 84 E3
Caledonian Road & Barnsbury ⊖ HOLWY N7 85 F5
Cally Pool IS N1 85 F6
Calverton Primary School CAN/RD E16 107 H5
Cambell Primary School DAGW RM9 91 K5
Camberwell Business Centre CMBW SE5 142 E1
Camberwell College of Arts CMBW SE5 143 F2
Camberwell Leisure Centre CMBW SE5 142 E2
Camberwell New Cemetery PECK SE15 164 A1
Camberwell Trading Estate CMBW SE5 142 C3
Cambridge Heath ⇌ BETH E2 104 D1
Cambridge Park Bowling & Sports Club TWK TW1 156 D1
Cambridge School HMSMTH W6 118 E4
Cambridge Theatre LSQ/SEVD WC2H 10 E4
Camden Arts Centre HAMP NW3 83 F3
Camden House Clinic BKHTH/KID SE3 145 H3
Camden Junior School CAR SM5 209 K2
Camden Market CAMTN NW1 84 A5
Camden Mews Day Hospital CAMTN NW1 84 C5
Camden People's Theatre CAMTN NW1 4 A5
Camden Road ⊖ CAMTN NW1 84 C5
Camden School for Girls KTTN NW5 84 C4
Camden Theatre CAMTN NW1 4 A2
Camden Town ⊖ CAMTN NW1 84 B6
Camden Town Hall & St Pancras Library CAMTN NW1 4 E4
Camelot Primary School PECK SE15 143 J1
Cameron House School CHEL SW3 120 C6
Camperdown House WCHPL E1 13 K4
Campion House College ISLW TW7 135 J1
Campsbourne School CEND/HSY/T N8 48 E6
Canada House STJS SW1Y 10 D7
Canada House Business Centre RSLP HA4 59 G5
Canada Place POP/IOD E14 124 D1
Canada Square POP/IOD E14 124 E1
Canada Water ⊖ ⊖ BERM/RHTH SE16 123 K3
Canada Water Retail Park BERM/RHTH SE16 124 A3
Canada Wharf Museum BERM/RHTH SE16 124 C1
Canal Cafe Theatre BAY/PAD W2 101 G4
Canary Riverside BERM/RHTH SE16 124 C1
Canary Wharf ⊖ POP/IOD E14 124 D1
Canary Wharf Pier POP/IOD E14 124 C1
Canberra Primary School SHB W12 99 K6
Canbury 2000 Business Park KUTN/CMB KT2 175 F4
Canbury Business Centre KUTN/CMB KT2 175 F4
Canbury Medical Centre KUTN/CMB KT2 175 G4
Canbury School KUTN/CMB KT2 175 J2
Cann Hall Primary School WAN E11 88 D1
Canning Town ⊖ ⊖ POP/IOD E14 106 C5
Cannizaro House Hotel WIM/MER SW19 177 F2
Cannon Hill Clinic STHGT/OAK N14 34 E5
Cannon Lane First School PIN HA5 59 H3
Cannon Sports Club CANST EC4R 12 D5
Cannon Street ⇌ ⊖ CANST EC4R 12 E6
Cannon Trading Estate WBLY HA9 80 D2
Cannon Wharf Business Centre DEPT SE8 124 B4
Canon Barnett Primary School WCHPL E1 13 K3
Canonbury ⊖ HBRY N5 85 J3
Canonbury Business Centre IS N1 85 J6
Canonbury Primary School IS N1 85 H4
Canon Palmer RC High School IL IG1 72 E5
Canons High School EDGW HA8 44 B5
The Canons Leisure Centre MTCM CR4 194 E1
Canons Park ⊖ EDGW HA8 44 A3
Canterbury Industrial Estate NWCR SE14 124 A6
Cantium Retail Park STHWK SE1 123 H6
Capital Business Centre
ALP/SUD HA0 97 K1
MTCM CR4 194 E2
SAND/SEL CR2 211 K4
Capital City Academy WLSDN NW10 81 K6
The Capital Hotel CHEL SW3 14 E3
Capital Industrial Estate BELV DA17 129 K1
Capital Radio LSQ/SEVD WC2H 10 D6
Capital Wharf WAP E1W 123 H1
Capitol Industrial Park CDALE/KGS NW9 44 E6
Caplan Estate MTCM CR4 179 H4
Cardiff Road Industrial Estate WATW WD18 27 F1
Cardinal Hinsley College WLSDN NW10 81 J6
Cardinal Pole RC School HOM E9 87 G4
Cardinal Pole RC Secondary Lower School HOM E9 87 F5
Cardinal Road Infant School FELT TW13 154 A3
The Cardinal Vaughan Memorial School WKENS W14 119 H2
Cardinal Wiseman RC School (Technology & Art College) GFD/PVL UB6 96 C4
Cardwell Primary School WOOL/PLUM SE18 126 E4
Carew Manor School WLGTN SM6 210 D1
Carlisle Infant School HPTN TW12 173 G2
Carlton House STJS SW1Y 16 C1
The Carlton Mitre Hotel E/WMO/HCT KT8 173 K6
Carlton Primary School KTTN NW5 84 A3
Carlton Vale Infant School MV/WKIL W9 100 D2
Carlyle's House (NT) CHEL SW3 120 D6
Carnwath Road Industrial Estate FUL/PGN SW6 140 A4
Carpenders Park ⊖ OXHEY WD19 27 H5
Carpenders Park Cemetery OXHEY WD19 27 K6
Carpenters' Hall OBST EC2N 13 F2
Carpenters Primary School SRTFD E15 88 A6
Carshalton ⇌ CAR SM5 209 J2
Carshalton AFC SUT SM1 209 J1
Carshalton Beeches ⇌ CAR SM5 209 K4
Carshalton College CAR SM5 209 K1
Carshalton High School for Boys CAR SM5 194 C6
Carshalton High School for Girls CAR SM5 209 J1
Carshalton War Memorial Hospital CAR SM5 209 K3
Carterhatch Infant School EN EN1 24 D2
The Cartoon Museum RSQ WC1B 10 E2
Caryl Thomas Clinic HRW HA1 60 E1
The Cassel Hospital RCHPK/HAM TW10 156 E6
Cassidy Medical Centre FUL/PGN SW6 139 K1
Castilion Primary School THMD SE28 109 J5
Castle Bar Park ⇌ HNWL W7 97 F4
Castlebar School HNWL W7 97 F4
Castlebar Special School WEA W13 97 G4
Castlecombe Primary School ELTH/MOT SE9 184 D1
Castle Hill Primary School CROY/NA CR0 214 A4
Castle Industrial Estate WALW SE17 18 C6
Casualty Plus Clinic BTFD TW8 116 D5
Caterham High School CLAY IG5 53 K5
Catford ⇌ CAT SE6 164 D2
Catford Bridge ⇌ CAT SE6 164 D2
Catford Cricket & Sports Club CAT SE6 164 E3
Catford Cyphers CC CAT SE6 164 C4
Catford High School CAT SE6 165 G5
Catford Trading Estate CAT SE6 164 E4
Catford Wanderers Sports Club CAT SE6 165 F6
Cathall Leisure Centre WAN E11 88 B1
The Cathedral School of St Saviour & St Mary Overy STHWK SE1 18 D2
Cator Park School for Girls BECK BR3 182 B3
Cavendish College FITZ W1T 10 C1
Cavendish Hotel STJS SW1Y 10 B7
Cavendish Primary School CHSWK W4 138 B1
Cavendish School BERM/RHTH SE16 123 K4
The Cavendish School CAMTN NW1 84 B6
Cavendish Special School HNWL W7 97 F5
Caxton Hall STJSPK SW1H 16 C4
Caxton Trading Estate HYS/HAR UB3 113 H2
Cayley Primary School WCHPL E1 105 G4
Cecil Park Clinic PIN HA5 59 J1
The Cedar School FSTGT E7 89 G4
Cedars Manor School KTN/HRWW/WS HA3 42 C4
The Cedars Primary School HEST TW5 133 K1
Cedar Way Industrial Estate CAMTN NW1 84 D5
Cenotaph WHALL SW1A 16 E2
Centaurs Business Centre ISLW TW7 116 B6
Centaurs RFC ISLW TW7 116 A6
Central Business Centre WLSDN NW10 81 G3
Centrale ⊖ CROY/NA CR0 196 D6
Centrale Shopping Centre CROY/NA CR0 196 D6
Central Foundation Boys School SDTCH EC2A 7 F6
Central Foundation Girls School (Lower) BOW E3 105 G2
Central Foundation Girls School (Upper) BOW E3 105 H2
Central Hall STJSPK SW1H 16 D3
Central Hendon Clinic HDN NW4 63 K1
Central London Golf Club TOOT SW17 160 C4
Central London Markets STBT EC1A 12 A2
Central Medical Centre MRDN SM4 194 B1
Central Middlesex Hospital WLSDN NW10 98 E2
Central Park Arena DART DA1 171 H3
Central Park Primary School EHAM E6 107 H1
Central St Martins College of Art & Design RSQ WC1B 11 G2
Central School of Ballet CLKNW EC1R 5 K7
Central School of Fashion GTPST W1W 10 A2

Central School of Speech & Drama
HAMP NW3 83 H5
Central Square Shopping Centre
WBLY HA9 80 A4
Centre Court Shopping Centre
WIM/MER SW19 177 J2
The Centre Performing Arts College
CHARL SE7 126 C3
Centre Point
LSQ/SEVD WC2H 10 D3
Chace Community School
EN EN1 24 A2
Chadwell Heath ⇌
CHDH RM6 73 K4
The Chadwell Heath Foundation School
CHDH RM6 73 H3
Chadwell Heath Industrial Park
BCTR RM8 74 A5
Chadwell Heath Leisure Centre
CHDH RM6 73 K3
Chadwell Infant & Primary School
CHDH RM6 73 J4
Chaffinch Business Park
BECK BR3 182 A6
Chailey Industrial Estate
HYS/HAR UB3 113 K2
Chalcot School
CAMTN NW1 84 B4
Chalgrove Primary School
FNCH N3 46 C6
Chalk Farm ⊖
HAMP NW3 84 A5
Chalkhill Primary School
WBLY HA9 80 D1
The Chamberlain Hotel
TWRH EC3N 13 J5
Chambers Business Park
WDR/YW UB7 112 D6
Chambers Wharf
BERM/RHTH SE16 123 H2
Chancery Court Hotel
HHOL WC1V 11 G2
Chancery Lane ⊖
FSBYW WC1X 11 J2
Chandlers Field Primary School
E/WMO/HCT KT8 189 F2
Chandos Business Centre
WLGTN SM6 210 C4
Channelsea Business Centre
SRTFD E15 106 B1
Channing School
HGT N6 66 B5
Chapel End Infant School
WALTH E17 51 K5
Chapel End Junior School
WALTH E17 51 K4
Chapman Park Industrial Estate
WLSDN NW10 81 H4
Charing Cross ⇌ ⊖
CHCR WC2N 10 E7
Charing Cross Hospital
HMSMTH W6 119 G6
Charing Cross Hotel
CHCR WC2N 10 E6
The Charles Dickens Museum
BMSBY WC1N 5 G7
Charles Dickens Primary School
STHWK SE1 18 C3
Charles Edward Brooke School (Lower School)
CMBW SE5 142 C2
Charles Edward Brooke School (Upper School)
BRXN/ST SW9 142 C2
Charlotte Sharman Primary School
LBTH SE11 18 A5
Charlotte Turner Primary School
DEPT SE8 124 D6
Charlton ⇌
CHARL SE7 126 B5
Charlton Athletic FC (The Valley)
CHARL SE7 126 B5
Charlton Cemetery
CHARL SE7 126 D6
Charlton Health & Fitness Centre
CHARL SE7 126 B5
Charlton House
CHARL SE7 126 C6
Charlton Manor Junior School
CHARL SE7 146 C1
Charlton RFC
ELTH/MOT SE9 167 G2
Charlton School
CHARL SE7 126 D6
Charrington Bowl
SURB KT6 191 J6
Charrville Primary School
YEAD UB4 94 C1
Charter Clinic
CHEL SW3 120 E5
Charterhouse
FARR EC1M 6 B7
Charteris Road Sports Centre
HAMP NW3 83 J3
KIL/WHAMP NW6 82 D6
Charter Nightingale Hospital & Counselling Centre
CAMTN NW1 8 D1
The Charter School
HNHL SE24 142 E6
Chartwell Business Centre
BMLY BR1 184 C6
Chase Bridge Primary School
WHTN TW2 155 K1
Chase Farm Hospital
ENC/FH EN2 23 G1
Chase Lane Primary School
CHING E4 37 H6
Chase Road Trading Estate
WLSDN NW10 99 F3
Chase Side Primary School
ENC/FH EN2 23 J3
Chaseville Clinic
WCHMH N21 35 F1
Chatsworth Infant School
BFN/LL DA15 168 B3
Chatsworth J & I School
HSLW TW3 135 H5
Chaucer Clinic
NWDGN UB2 115 J2
Cheam ⇌
BELMT SM2 208 D5
Cheam Common J & I School
WPK KT4 192 E6
Cheam Fields Primary School
CHEAM SM3 208 C3
Cheam High School
CHEAM SM3 208 C2
Cheam Leisure Centre
CHEAM SM3 208 B2
Cheam Park Farm Junior School
CHEAM SM3 208 C1
Cheam Sports Club
CHEAM SM3 208 C5
Chelsea Bridge Business Centre
VX/NE SW8 141 G1
Chelsea Centre & Theatre
WBPTN SW10 140 B1
Chelsea Cinema
CHEL SW3 120 D5
The Chelsea Club Leisure Centre
FUL/PGN SW6 120 A6
Chelsea College of Art & Design
CHEL SW3 120 D5
FUL/PGN SW6 140 B3
SHB W12 118 E2
WEST SW1P 121 K5
Chelsea FC (Stamford Bridge)
FUL/PGN SW6 140 A1
Chelsea Fields Industrial Estate
WIM/MER SW19 178 C4
Chelsea Group of Children
WBPTN SW10 140 B1
Chelsea Independent College
FUL/PGN SW6 140 A1
Chelsea Leisure Centre
CHEL SW3 120 D5
Chelsea Old Town Hall
CHEL SW3 120 D5
Chelsea Physic Garden
CHEL SW3 120 E6
Chelsea & Westminster Hospital
WBPTN SW10 120 B6
Chelsea Wharf
WBPTN SW10 140 C1
Chelsfield ⇌
ORP BR6 217 H3
Chennestone Community School
SUN TW16 172 A5
Cherington House Health Centre
HNWL W7 116 A1
Cherry Garden Pier
BERM/RHTH SE16 123 J2
Cherry Garden School
BERM/RHTH SE16 123 H4
Cherry Lane Primary School
WDR/YW UB7 112 C4
Cherry Orchard Primary School
CHARL SE7 146 B1
Chessington CC
CHSGTN KT9 205 J5
Chessington Community College & Sports Centre
CHSGTN KT9 205 K5
Chessington Golf Club
CHSGTN KT9 205 K5
Chessington North ⇌
CHSGTN KT9 206 A3
Chessington South ⇌
CHSGTN KT9 205 K5
The Chesterfield Mayfair Hotel
MYFR/PICC W1J 9 J7
Chesterton Primary School
BTSEA SW11 141 F2
Chestnut Grove School
BAL SW12 161 F3
Chestnuts Primary School
SEVS/STOTM N15 67 J2
Cheyne Centre
CHEL SW3 120 C6
Chicken Shed Theatre
STHGT/OAK N14 22 A6
Chigwell Golf Club
CHIG IG7 54 A1
Childeric Primary School
NWCR SE14 144 B1
Childs Hill Clinic
CRICK NW2 64 D6
Childs Hill Primary School
CRICK NW2 82 C1
Childs Welfare Clinic
BCTR RM8 91 J3
Chiltonian Industrial Estate
LEE/GVPK SE12 165 J1
Chimnocks Wharf
POP/IOD E14 105 G6
Chingford ⇌
CHING E4 38 C2
Chingford CE Infant School
CHING E4 38 B3
Chingford CE Junior School
CHING E4 38 B3
Chingford Foundation School
CHING E4 37 K3
Chingford Hall Primary School
CHING E4 51 H2
Chingford Health Centre
CHING E4 37 J6
Chingford Industrial Centre
CHING E4 51 G1
Chingford Mount Cemetery
CHING E4 37 K5
Chingford RFC
CHING E4 37 J3
Chisenhale Primary School
BOW E3 105 G1
Chislehurst ⇌
BMLY BR1 185 F5
Chislehurst Caves
CHST BR7 185 F4
Chislehurst Cemetery
CHST BR7 185 K1
Chislehurst Golf Club
CHST BR7 185 G3
Chislehurst Natural Health Centre
CHST BR7 185 G2
Chislehurst & Sidcup Grammar School
BFN/LL DA15 168 C4
Chiswick ⇌
CHSWK W4 137 K1
Chiswick & Bedford Park Preparatory School
CHSWK W4 118 B4
Chiswick Business Park
CHSWK W4 117 J4
Chiswick Community School
CHSWK W4 138 A1
Chiswick House
CHSWK W4 118 A6
Chiswick Moran Hotel
CHSWK W4 117 J5
Chiswick Park ⊖
CHSWK W4 117 K4
Chrisp Street Health Centre
POP/IOD E14 105 K5
Christ Church Bentinck CE Primary School
CAMTN NW1 8 C1
Christ Church Brondesbury CE J & I School
KIL/WHAMP NW6 82 D6
Christ Church CE Junior School
EA W5 97 K6
Christ Church CE Primary School
BAR EN5 20 B3
BRXN/ST SW9 142 B2
BRXS/STRHM SW2 162 A3
BRYLDS KT5 191 H3
BTSEA SW11 140 D4
CHEL SW3 120 E6
FSTH SE23 164 A4
WOOL/PLUM SE18 147 F2
Christchurch CE Primary School
HAMP NW3 83 H1
WCHPL E1 13 K2
Christchurch Industrial Centre
STHWK SE1 12 A7
Christ Church Malden CE Primary School
NWMAL KT3 176 B6
Christ Church Primary School
ERITH DA8 130 A6
NWMAL KT3 176 A6
Christ Church School
CAMTN NW1 3 K3
Christian Meeting Hall
BECK BR3 182 D4
Christopher Hatton Primary School
FSBYW WC1X 5 J7
Christs College Finchley
FNCH N3 47 F6
Christs College School
EFNCH N2 47 F6
Christs School
RCHPK/HAM TW10 137 G6
Christ the King RC Primary School
FSBYPK N4 67 F5
Christ the King Sixth Form College
LEW SE13 145 G4
Chrysalis Theatre
BAL SW12 161 F3
Chrysanthemum Clinic
CHSWK W4 137 K1
Chrysolyte Independent Christian School
STHWK SE1 19 F4
Church Down Adult School
LEE/GVPK SE12 165 K4
Church End Medical Centre
WLSDN NW10 81 G4
Church Farm House Museum
HDN NW4 45 K6
Church Farm Swimming Pool
EBAR EN4 33 K3
Churchfield Primary School
ED N9 36 B3
Churchfields J & I School
SWFD E18 52 E4
Churchfields Primary School
BECK BR3 182 A6
Church Hill Primary School
EBAR EN4 33 K2
Church House
WEST SW1P 16 D4
Churchill Clinic
STHWK SE1 17 K4
Churchill College
RYNPK SW20 177 F5
Churchill Gardens Primary School
PIM SW1V 121 H5
Churchill Museum & Cabinet War Rooms
STJSPK SW1H 16 D2
Churchill Theatre
BMLY BR1 183 K5
Church Stairs
BERM/RHTH SE16 123 J2
Church Street
CROY/NA CR0 196 D6
Church Trading Estate
ERITH DA8 150 D1
Cineworld
BXLYHS DA6 149 J5
CHEL SW3 120 C6
CRICK NW2 63 K5
EA W5 97 K6
EN EN1 24 C5
FELT TW13 154 A4
HMSMTH W6 118 E4
SOHO/SHAV W1D 10 C6
WBPTN SW10 120 C5
WDGN N22 49 G5
Citigroup Tower
POP/IOD E14 124 E1
City Business Centre
BERM/RHTH SE16 123 K2
City Business College
FSBYE EC1V 6 B5
City Central Estate
FSBYE EC1V 6 C5
City College of Higher Education
IS N1 7 F4
City & Guilds of London Art School
LBTH SE11 122 B5
City Health Centre
FSBYE EC1V 6 E6
City & Islington College
FSBYE EC1V 6 D5
FSBYPK N4 67 H6
HBRY N5 85 G4
HOLWY N7 84 E2
IS N1 85 J6
STLK EC1Y 6 E7
City & Islington Sixth Form College
FSBYE EC1V 6 A3
City Literary College
HHOL WC1V 11 F3
City of East London College
WCHPL E1 104 C5
The City of London Academy Islington
IS N1 6 C1
The City of London Academy
EDUL SE22 143 H6
STHWK SE1 123 H5
City of London Business College
SEVS/STOTM N15 68 A2
SEVS/STOTM N15 68 C2
City of London Cemetery
MNPK E12 71 J6
City of London Club
OBST EC2N 13 G3
City of London College
WCHPL E1 104 C5
City of London Crematorium
MNPK E12 89 J1
City of London School
BLKFR EC4V 12 B5
City of London School for Girls
BARB EC2Y 12 C1
City of London School Sports Ground
LEE/GVPK SE12 166 B4
City of Westminster Cemetery
HNWL W7 116 A1
City of Westminster College
BAY/PAD W2 8 A1
MV/WKIL W9 100 D2
MV/WKIL W9 101 F3
City of Westminster Vehicle Pound
MYFR/PKLN W1K 9 F6
City Thameslink ⇌
FLST/FETLN EC4A 12 A3
City University
CLKNW EC1R 6 A5
STBT EC1A 12 C2
City University Business School
BARB EC2Y 12 D1
Civil Service Sports Ground
CHSWK W4 138 B2
LEE/GVPK SE12 166 B1
Clapham Common ⊖
CLAP SW4 141 H5
Clapham Common Clinic
CLAP SW4 141 J5
Clapham High Street ⇌ ⊖
CLAP SW4 141 J4
Clapham Junction ⇌ ⊖
BTSEA SW11 140 D5
Clapham Manor Primary School
CLAP SW4 141 H4
Clapham Manor Street Public Baths
CLAP SW4 141 J4
Clapham North ⊖
CLAP SW4 141 K4
Clapham North Business Centre
CLAP SW4 141 J4
Clapham Picture House
CLAP SW4 141 H5
Clapham South ⊖
CLAP SW4 161 G1
Clapton ⇌
CLPT E5 68 D6
Clapton Girls Technology College
CLPT E5 86 E2
Clara Grant Primary School
BOW E3 105 J3
Clare House Primary School
BECK BR3 183 F5
Claremont Clinic
FSTGT E7 89 G3
Claremont Fan Court School
ESH/CLAY KT10 204 B4
Claremont High School
KTN/HRWW/WS HA3 62 A2
Claremont Landscape Garden (NT)
ESH/CLAY KT10 204 A5
Claremont Primary School
CRICK NW2 64 B6
Claremont Way Industrial Estate
CRICK NW2 64 A5
Clarence House
WHALL SW1A 16 B2
Clarendon Primary School
ASHF TW15 152 C5
Clarendon Special School
HPTN TW12 173 G2
Claridge's Hotel
MYFR/PKLN W1K 9 J5
Claverings Industrial Estate
ED N9 36 E4
Claygate ⇌
ESH/CLAY KT10 204 D4
Claygate Primary School
ESH/CLAY KT10 204 E5
Clayhall Clinic
CLAY IG5 53 J6
Clayponds Hospital
BTFD TW8 117 F4
Cleeve Park School
SCUP DA14 168 D5
Clementine Churchill Hospital
HRW HA1 78 E1
Cleopatra's Needle
CHCR WC2N 11 G7
Clerkenwell Heritage Centre
FARR EC1M 6 A7
Clerkenwell Parochial CE Primary School
CLKNW EC1R 5 J5
Cleveland Primary School
IL IG1 90 B2
Cleves Primary School
EHAM E6 89 H6
C & L Golf & Country Club
NTHLT UB5 77 F5
Clifton Lodge School
EA W5 97 J6
Clifton Primary School
NWDGN UB2 114 D4
Clink Exhibition
STHWK SE1 12 E7
Clissold Leisure Centre
STNW/STAM N16 85 K1
Clissold Park Natural Health Centre
STNW/STAM N16 68 A6
C & L Leisure Centre
RSLP HA4 77 F5
Clock House ⇌
BECK BR3 182 B5
Clockhouse Industrial Estate
EBED/NFELT TW14 152 E3
Clockhouse Primary School
CRW RM5 56 D2
Clock Museum
CITYW EC2V 12 D3
Cloisters Business Centre
VX/NE SW8 141 G1
Clore Gallery
WEST SW1P 16 E7
Clore Tikva School
BARK/HLT IG6 54 C
Clothworkers' Hall
FENCHST EC3M 13 H
Clouster's Green
WAP E1W 123 H
Cobbold Estate
WLSDN NW10 81 H
Cobourg Primary School
CMBW SE5 123 G
Cochrane Theatre
GINN WC1R 11 G
Cockfosters ⊖
EBAR EN4 22 A
Cockfosters Sports Ground
EBAR EN4 21 K
The Cockpit Theatre
STJWD NW8 2 C
Coldharbour Industrial Estate
CMBW SE5 142 D
Coldharbour Leisure Centre
ELTH/MOT SE9 166 E
Coldharbour Sports Ground
ELTH/MOT SE9 167 F
Colebrooke Primary School
IS N1 6
Colegrave School
SRTFD E15 88 E
Coleraine Park Primary School
TOTM N17 50
Coleridge Primary School
HGT N6 66
Colfe's Preparatory School
LEE/GVPK SE12 165
Colfe's Senior School
LEE/GVPK SE12 165
Colindale ⊖
CDALE/KGS NW9 45
Colindale Business Park
CDALE/KGS NW9 44
Colindale Hospital
CDALE/KGS NW9 45
Colindale Primary School
CDALE/KGS NW9 63
Coliseum Theatre
CHCR WC2N 10
College Fields Business Centre
WIM/MER SW19 178
College of Arms
BLKFR EC4V 12
College of Business & Technology
FSTGT E7 88
College of Central London
SDTCH EC2A 7
College of Fuel Technology
HGT N6 66
The College of Law
FITZ W1T 10
LINN WC2A 11

College of North East London
CEND/HSY/T N8 ... 67 G1
SEVS/STOTM N15 ... 68 B1
WDGN N22 ... 48 C4
College of North West London
KIL/WHAMP NW6 ... 82 E6
WBLY HA9 ... 80 C1
WLSDN NW10 ... 81 H3
College of Organists
FLST/FETLN EC4A ... 11 K2
College Park School
BAY/PAD W2 ... 101 F5
Collier Row Clinic
CRW RM5 ... 56 D4
Collier Row FC
CRW RM5 ... 56 B4
Collier's Wood ⊖
WIM/MER SW19 ... 178 C3
Collingwood Business Centre
ARCH N19 ... 84 E1
Collingwood Preparatory School
WLGTN SM6 ... 210 B3
Collins Method School
CRICK NW2 ... 82 A4
Collis Primary School
TEDD TW11 ... 174 C2
Colnbrook School
OXHEY WD19 ... 27 G4
Coloma Convent Girls School
CROY/NA CR0 ... 213 F1
Colonnades Leisure Park
CROY/NA CR0 ... 211 G4
The Colonnades Shopping Centre
BGVA SW1W ... 15 J6
Colours Sports Club
SUT SM1 ... 209 G3
Columbia Primary School
BETH E2 ... 7 K4
Colvestone Primary School
HACK E8 ... 86 B3
Colville Primary School
NTGHL W11 ... 100 D5
Colyers Lane Medical Centre
ERITH DA8 ... 150 A2
Comber Grove Primary School
CMBW SE5 ... 142 D1
Comedy Theatre
STJS SW1Y ... 10 C6
Comelle House Trading Estate
DEPT SE8 ... 124 B5
Comfort Hotel
ENC/FH EN2 ... 23 H3
Comfort Inn
HYS/HAR UB3 ... 113 H5
Commonwealth Institute
WKENS W14 ... 119 J3
Community Arts Centre
GNWCH SE10 ... 144 E1
Community Care Centre
ENC/FH EN2 ... 23 K2
Community Centre (Island History Trust)
POP/IOD E14 ... 125 F4
Community College & School
GNWCH SE10 ... 145 F1
The Community College
HACK E8 ... 86 D6
Compass Theatre
HGDN/ICK UB10 ... 76 A1
Complementary Health Centre
LEE/GVPK SE12 ... 165 H1
Compton Leisure Centre
NTHLT UB5 ... 77 J6
The Compton School
NFNCH/WDSPK N12 ... 47 J2
Compton Sports Centre
NFNCH/WDSPK N12 ... 47 J2
Concord Business Centre
ACT W3 ... 98 D4
Conductive Education Centre
MUSWH N10 ... 48 B6
Conduit House
GNWCH SE10 ... 145 G1
Coney Hill School
HAYES BR2 ... 199 J6
Connaught Business Centre
CDALE/KGS NW9 ... 63 H2
CROY/NA CR0 ... 211 F4
MTCM CR4 ... 194 E2
The Connaught Hotel
MYFR/PKLN W1K ... 9 H6
Connaught House School
BAY/PAD W2 ... 8 D4
Connaught School for Girls
WAN E11 ... 70 C5
Consort Clinic
PECK SE15 ... 143 J4
Consulate General of Monaco
SKENS SW7 ... 14 A6
Consulate of Burkina Faso
BTSEA SW11 ... 140 B4
Consulate of Chile
CAVSQ/HST W1G ... 3 J7
Consulate of Colombia
GTPST W1W ... 10 A3
Consulate of Eritrea
IS N1 ... 5 K2
Consulate of Guinea
MYFR/PKLN W1K ... 9 G6
Consulate of Panama
MYFR/PICC W1J ... 15 J1
Convent of Jesus & Mary Infant School
CRICK NW2 ... 82 A4
Convent of Jesus & Mary Language College
WLSDN NW10 ... 81 H6
Convoy's Wharf
DEPT SE8 ... 124 C5
Conway Medical Centre
WOOL/PLUM SE18 ... 127 J5
Conway Primary School
WOOL/PLUM SE18 ... 127 K4
Coombe Girls School
NWMAL KT3 ... 176 A5
Coombe Hill Golf Club
KUTN/CMB KT2 ... 176 A3
Coombe Hill J & I School
NWMAL KT3 ... 176 A4
Coombe Lane ●
CROY/NA CR0 ... 212 E3
Coombe Wood Golf Club
KUTN/CMB KT2 ... 175 J3
Coopers' Hall
LVPST EC2M ... 13 H2
Coopers Lane Primary School
LEE/GVPK SE12 ... 165 K4
Coopers Technology College
CHST BR7 ... 185 H4
Copenhagen Primary School
IS N1 ... 5 F1
Copland Specialist Science College
WBLY HA9 ... 80 B3
Coppermill Primary School
WALTH E17 ... 69 F2
Coppetts Wood Hospital
MUSWH N10 ... 47 K4
Coppetts Wood Primary School
MUSWH N10 ... 48 A4
Coppice Primary School
CHIG IG7 ... 55 G1
Copthall School
MLHL NW7 ... 45 K3
Copthorne Tara Hotel
KENS W8 ... 120 A3
Cordwainers College
HACK E8 ... 86 E5
Corinthian Casuals FC
SURB KT6 ... 206 C1
Coronet Cinema
KENS W8 ... 119 K1
SEVS/STOTM N15 ... 49 H6
Corpus Christi RC Primary School
BRXS/STRHM SW2 ... 142 A6
Corus Hotel
BAY/PAD W2 ... 8 A5
BORE WD6 ... 30 A2
Cosmopolitan College
IS N1 ... 5 G3
Coston Primary School
GFD/PVL UB6 ... 96 C2
Coteford Infant School
PIN HA5 ... 58 E2
Courtauld Institute of Art
TPL/STR WC2R ... 11 H6
Court Farm Industrial Estate
STWL/WRAY TW19 ... 152 C1
Courtfield Medical Centre
ECT SW5 ... 120 A4
Courtland JMI School
MLHL NW7 ... 31 G4
Covent Garden ⊖
COVGDN WC2E ... 10 E5
Covent Garden Flower Market
VX/NE SW8 ... 121 J6
Covent Garden Medical Centre
LSQ/SEVD WC2H ... 10 E4
Crafts Council
IS N1 ... 5 K3
Crampton Primary School
WALW SE17 ... 18 B7
Cranbrook College
IL IG1 ... 72 A6
Cranbrook Primary School
IL IG1 ... 71 K4
Crane Park Island Nature Reserve
WHTN TW2 ... 154 E4
Cranford Community College
HEST TW5 ... 114 A6
Cranford Infant School
HSLWW TW4 ... 133 K3
Cranford Junior School
HSLWW TW4 ... 134 A3
Cranford Park Junior School
HYS/HAR UB3 ... 113 J4
Cranford Park Primary School
HYS/HAR UB3 ... 113 J2
Cranleigh Gardens Industrial Estate
STHL UB1 ... 95 K4
Cranmer Primary School
MTCM CR4 ... 194 E1
The Craven Clinic
HMSMTH W6 ... 118 E4
Craven Park Medical Centre
WLSDN NW10 ... 81 F6
Crawford Primary School
CMBW SE5 ... 142 D2
Crayfield Industrial Park
STMC/STPC BR5 ... 186 D5
Crayfields Business Park
STMC/STPC BR5 ... 186 D4
Crayford ⇌
DART DA1 ... 170 B1
Crayford Commercial Centre
DART DA1 ... 150 B6
Crayford Industrial Estate
DART DA1 ... 150 C6
Crayford Leisure Centre & Greyhound Stadium
DART DA1 ... 170 B1
Crayford Medical Centre
DART DA1 ... 150 C6
Crayside Industrial Estate
DART DA1 ... 150 D4
Cray Valley Golf Club
STMC/STPC BR5 ... 187 F4
Creekmouth Industrial Estate
BARK IG11 ... 109 F3
Creek Road Health Centre
DEPT SE8 ... 124 D6
Creek Road Industrial Estate
DEPT SE8 ... 124 E6
Crescent Hotel
HRW HA1 ... 60 E3
Crewe House
MYFR/PICC W1J ... 9 J7
Cricket Green School
MTCM CR4 ... 178 D6
Cricklefield Stadium
IL IG1 ... 72 E6
Cricklewood ⇌
CRICK NW2 ... 82 B1
Cricklewood Trading Estate
CRICK NW2 ... 82 C1
Crispin Industrial Centre
UED N18 ... 50 E1
Criterion Theatre
MYFR/PICC W1J ... 10 B6
Crockenhill Primary School
SWLY BR8 ... 203 K3
Crofton Leisure Centre
BROCKY SE4 ... 164 D1
Crofton Park ⇌
BROCKY SE4 ... 144 C6
Croham Hurst Golf Club
SAND/SEL CR2 ... 212 B4
Cromer Road Primary School
BAR EN5 ... 21 F4
Cromwell Business Centre
BARK IG11 ... 108 E2
Cromwell Hospital
KENS W8 ... 120 A4
Crook Log Primary School
BXLYHS DA6 ... 148 E5
Crook Log Sports Centre
WELL DA16 ... 148 E4
Crossharbour ⊖
POP/IOD E14 ... 124 E3
Crossways Academy
BROCKY SE4 ... 144 B3
Crouch End Art School
CEND/HSY/T N8 ... 66 E2
Crouch End Health Centre
CEND/HSY/T N8 ... 66 E2
Crouch Hill ⊖
FSBYPK N4 ... 67 F4
Crouch Hill Recreation Centre
CEND/HSY/T N8 ... 66 E4
Crowland Primary School
SEVS/STOTM N15 ... 68 C2
Crowlands Primary School
ROMW/RG RM7 ... 74 E3
Crown Business Centre
WDR/YW UB7 ... 112 C1
Crown Close Business Centre
BOW E3 ... 87 J6
Crowndale Health Centre
CAMTN NW1 ... 4 B2
Crowne Plaza
CAN/RD E16 ... 106 E6
EA W5 ... 98 A2
WDR/YW UB7 ... 112 D4
Crownfield Primary School
ROMW/RG RM7 ... 56 C5
Crown Lane Clinic
STHGT/OAK N14 ... 34 C3
Crown Lane Primary School
WNWD SE27 ... 162 D6
Crown Moran Hotel
CRICK NW2 ... 82 B2
Crown Trading Centre
HYS/HAR UB3 ... 113 H2
Crown Woods School
ELTH/MOT SE9 ... 147 H6
Croydon Airport Industrial Estate
CROY/NA CR0 ... 211 G5
Croydon Bowling Club
SAND/SEL CR2 ... 211 J3
Croydon Cemetery
CROY/NA CR0 ... 196 A2
Croydon Clocktower Cinema
CROY/NA CR0 ... 211 J1
Croydon College
CROY/NA CR0 ... 196 E6
CROY/NA CR0 ... 211 K1
Croydon Crematorium
THHTH CR7 ... 195 K2
Croydon Fairfield Halls Cinema
CROY/NA CR0 ... 211 K1
Croydon FC
SNWD SE25 ... 197 K2
Croydon Road Industrial Estate
BECK BR3 ... 197 K1
Croydon Sports Arena
SNWD SE25 ... 197 K2
Crusader Industrial Estate
FSBYPK N4 ... 67 J3
Crystal Palace ⇌ ⊖
PGE/AN SE20 ... 181 H2
Crystal Palace FC (Selhurst Park)
SNWD SE25 ... 197 F1
Crystal Palace FC Soccer & Sports Centre
BRXN/ST SW9 ... 142 A4
Crystal Palace Museum
NRWD SE19 ... 181 G2
Cuaco Sports Ground
BECK BR3 ... 182 D2
Cubitt Town Infants School
POP/IOD E14 ... 125 F3
Cuddington Cemetery
WPK KT4 ... 192 E6
Cuddington CP School
WPK KT4 ... 207 H1
Cuddington Croft Primary School
BELMT SM2 ... 208 B6
Culloden Primary School
POP/IOD E14 ... 106 B5
Culvers House Primary School
MTCM CR4 ... 195 F5
Cumberland Business Park
WLSDN NW10 ... 98 D2
The Cumberland Hotel
FITZ W1T ... 10 C3
OXSTW W1C ... 9 F4
Cumberland Park Industrial Estate
WLSDN NW10 ... 99 J2
The Cumming Museum
WALW SE17 ... 18 C7
Cumnor House School
SAND/SEL CR2 ... 211 H6
Curwen Primary School
PLSTW E13 ... 106 E1
Curzon Mayfair Cinema
MYFR/PICC W1J ... 15 J1
Curzon Soho Cinema
SOHO/SHAV W1D ... 10 D5
Custom House
MON EC3R ... 13 G6
Custom House for ExCeL ⊖
CAN/RD E16 ... 107 F6
Cutlers' Hall
STP EC4M ... 12 B3
Cutty Sark ⊖
GNWCH SE10 ... 125 F6
Cutty Sark Clipper Ship
GNWCH SE10 ... 125 F6
Cygnet Clinic Beckton
EHAM E6 ... 108 B4
Cygnus Business Centre
WLSDN NW10 ... 81 H3
Cypress Infant School
SNWD SE25 ... 181 F5
Cypress Junior School
SNWD SE25 ... 181 F5
Cyprus ⊖
CAN/RD E16 ... 108 A6
Cyprus College of Art
WNWD SE27 ... 162 C6
Cyril Jackson Primary School
POP/IOD E14 ... 105 H6
Dagenham Chest Clinic
BCTR RM8 ... 92 B1
Dagenham Civic Centre
DAGE RM10 ... 74 D6
Dagenham Dock ⇌
DAGW RM9 ... 110 B1
Dagenham East ⊖
DAGE RM10 ... 92 E4
Dagenham Heathway ⊖
DAGW RM9 ... 92 B4
Dagenham Priory Comprehensive School & Performing Arts College
DAGE RM10 ... 92 D5
Dagenham & Redbridge FC
DAGE RM10 ... 92 D3
Dagenham Superbowl
DAGE RM10 ... 110 D1
Dagenham Swimming Pool
DAGE RM10 ... 74 C6
Daiglen School
BKHH IG9 ... 39 G3
Daily Telegraph Newspaper Offices
POP/IOD E14 ... 124 D3
Dairy Meadow Primary School
NWDGN UB2 ... 114 E3
D'Albiac House
HTHAIR TW6 ... 132 D3
Dali Universe
STHWK SE1 ... 17 G2
Dallington School
FSBYE EC1V ... 6 B6
Dalmain Primary School
FSTH SE23 ... 164 B3
Dalston Junction ⊖
HACK E8 ... 86 B4
Dalston Kingsland ⊖
IS N1 ... 86 A4
Damilola Taylor Centre
PECK SE15 ... 143 G1
Danegrove Primary School
EBAR EN4 ... 33 J1
Danesfield Manor School
WOT/HER KT12 ... 188 A6
Danetree School
HOR/WEW KT19 ... 206 E5
Danson House
BXLYHS DA6 ... 148 D5
Danson Primary School
WELL DA16 ... 148 C5
Danson Watersports Centre
BXLYHS DA6 ... 148 D6
Darell Primary School
RCH/KEW TW9 ... 137 H4
Darent Industrial Park
ERITH DA8 ... 131 G5
Darrick Wood Primary School
ORP BR6 ... 216 B2
Darrick Wood School
ORP BR6 ... 216 B1
Darrick Wood Sports Centre
ORP BR6 ... 216 C1
Darrick Wood Swimming Pool
ORP BR6 ... 216 B1
Dartford ⇌
DART DA1 ... 151 H6
Dartford Adult Education Centre
DART DA1 ... 171 F2
Dartford Golf Club
DART DA1 ... 170 E4
Dartford Grammar School for Boys
DART DA1 ... 171 F1
Dartford Grammar School for Girls
DART DA1 ... 171 F2
Dartford Museum & Library
DART DA1 ... 171 H2
Dartford Natural Health Centre
DART DA1 ... 171 H2
Dartford Technology College
DART DA1 ... 171 F2
Dartford West Health Centre
DART DA1 ... 171 F1
Darwin Centre
SKENS SW7 ... 14 A5
Datapoint Business Centre
BOW E3 ... 106 B3
Daubeney Primary School
CLPT E5 ... 87 G2
The David Beckham Academy
GNWCH SE10 ... 125 J2
David Livingstone Primary School
THHTH CR7 ... 180 D4
David Lloyd Leisure
BKHH IG9 ... 39 K3
NFNCH/WDSPK N12 ... 47 H3
David Lloyd Leisure Centre
KENS W8 ... 120 A4
David Lloyd Sports Centre
EN EN1 ... 24 C3
David Lloyd Tennis Centre
SCUP DA14 ... 186 D1
Davidson Primary School
CROY/NA CR0 ... 197 G4
Davies Lane Primary School
WAN E11 ... 70 D6
Davies's College
STHWK SE1 ... 18 E2
Dawlish Primary School
LEY E10 ... 70 A6
Days Hotel
BAY/PAD W2 ... 8 B4
MLHL NW7 ... 30 E4
RSLP HA4 ... 77 G3
STHWK SE1 ... 17 J5
Days Hotel London South Ruislip
RSLP HA4 ... 77 G2
Days Inn
PIM SW1V ... 121 H5
Days Lane Primary School
BFN/LL DA15 ... 168 A1
Dean College of London
HOLWY N7 ... 85 F1
Deanesfield Primary School
RSLP HA4 ... 77 H2
Deansbrook Infant School
MLHL NW7 ... 44 E2
Deansfield Primary School
ELTH/MOT SE9 ... 147 F4
De Bohun Primary School
STHGT/OAK N14 ... 22 B6
Delta Wharf
GNWCH SE10 ... 125 G2
Denmark Hill ⇌ ⊖
CMBW SE5 ... 142 E4
Denmead School
HPTN TW12 ... 173 F3
Denvale Trade Centre
STMC/STPC BR5 ... 202 C2
Denver Industrial Estate
RAIN RM13 ... 111 H5
Department for Environment, Food & Rural Affairs
CHCR WC2N ... 10 E7
Department for Transport
WEST SW1P ... 16 D6
Department of Art & Design (London Metropolitan University)
WCHPL E1 ... 13 K3
Department of Economics (London Metropolitan University)
TWRH EC3N ... 13 J4
Department of Education
STJSPK SW1H ... 16 D3
Department of Health
WHALL SW1A ... 16 E2
Department of Trade & Industry
STJSPK SW1H ... 16 D4
Deptford ⇌
DEPT SE8 ... 144 D1
Deptford Bridge ⊖
DEPT SE8 ... 144 D2
Deptford Business Centre
NWCR SE14 ... 124 A5
Deptford Green School
NWCR SE14 ... 144 C1
Deptford Park Business Centre
DEPT SE8 ... 124 B5
Deptford Park Primary School
DEPT SE8 ... 124 B5
Deptford Trading Estate
DEPT SE8 ... 124 B5
Dersingham Infant School
MNPK E12 ... 89 K3
Derwentwater Primary School
ACT W3 ... 117 K1
Design Centre Chelsea Harbour
FUL/PGN SW6 ... 140 B2
Design Museum
STHWK SE1 ... 19 K1
Deutsche Schule
RCHPK/HAM TW10 ... 156 E3
Devonshire Hospital
MHST W1U ... 9 H1
Devonshire House Preparatory School
HAMP NW3 ... 83 G3
Devonshire Primary School
BELMT SM2 ... 209 G5
Devons Road ⊖
BOW E3 ... 105 K3
Diamond College
SOHO/SHAV W1D ... 10 D3
Diana Fountain
E/WMO/HCT KT8 ... 174 A5
Diana Princess of Wales Memorial Fountain
BAY/PAD W2 ... 14 B1
Diane Matthews Clinic
ROMW/RG RM7 ... 75 F1
Dilloway Industrial Estate
NWDGN UB2 ... 114 D2
Discovery Business Park
BERM/RHTH SE16 ... 123 H3
Discovery Primary School
THMD SE28 ... 128 A1
Docklands Medical Centre
POP/IOD E14 ... 124 D4
Docklands Sailing & Watersports Centre
POP/IOD E14 ... 124 D3
Dockmaster's House
POP/IOD E14 ... 105 J6
Dock Offices
BERM/RHTH SE16 ... 123 K3
Dockwell's Industrial Estate
EBED/NFELT TW14 ... 134 A6
Dockyard Industrial Estate
WOOL/PLUM SE18 ... 126 D3

Dog Kennel Hill
Primary School
EDUL SE22 ....143 F4
Dokal Industrial Estate
NWDGN UB2 ....114 D2
Dollis Hill ↔
WLSDN NW10 ....81 J3
Dollis Infant School
MLHL NW7 ....46 A3
The Dolphin Leisure Centre
ROM RM1 ....75 H1
Dolphin School
BTSEA SW11 ....140 D6
The Dominie
BTSEA SW11 ....140 E2
Dominion Business Park
ED N9 ....37 F4
Dominion Theatre
RSQ WC1B 10 D3
Donhead (Wimbledon College
Preparatory School)
WIM/MER SW19 ....177 G3
Donmar Warehouse Theatre
LSO/SEVD WC2H 10 C4
Donnington Primary School
WLSDN NW10 ....81 K5
The Dorchester Hotel
MYFR/PKLN W1K 9 H7
Dorchester Primary School
WPK KT4 ....193 F5
Dorma Trading Park
LEY E10 ....69 F5
Dormers Wells High School
STHL UB1 ....96 A5
Dormers Wells Junior School
STHL UB1 ....96 B6
Dormers Wells Leisure Centre
STHL UB1 ....96 B5
Dormers Wells Medical Centre
STHL UB1 ....96 A5
Dorothy Barley
Primary School
BCTR RM8 ....91 H3
Dorset Road Infant School
ELTH/MOT SE9 ....166 D4
Dorset Square Hotel
CAMTN NW1 ....8 E1
Douglas Bader Foundation
PUT/ROE SW15 ....158 D1
Dovers Corner
Industrial Estate
RAIN RM13 ....111 H2
Downderry Primary School
BMLY BR1 ....165 H6
Downe Manor Primary School
NTHLT UB5 ....95 F2
Downham Health Centre
BMLY BR1 ....165 H6
Downhills Primary School
TOTM N17 ....67 K1
Downsell Primary School
SRTFD E15 ....88 B2
Downshall Primary School
GNTH/NBYPK IG2 ....72 E4
Downsview Primary School
NRWD SE19 ....180 D3
Downsview School
CLPT E5 ....86 D2
Drapers Hall
LOTH EC2R 13 F3
Drapers Sports Ground
SRTFD E15 ....88 A2
The Draycott Hotel
CHEL SW3 ....15 F6
Drayton Green ↔
HNWL W7 ....97 F6
Drayton Green
Primary School
WEA W13 ....97 G6
Drayton Manor High School
HNWL W7 ....97 F6
Drayton Park ↔
HOLWY N7 ....85 G3
Drayton Park Primary School
HBRY N5 ....85 G3
DRCA Business Centre
BTSEA SW11 ....141 F2
Drew Primary School
CAN/RD E16 ....126 D1
The Drill Hall
GWRST WC1E 10 C1
The Drizen School
EDGW HA8 ....44 C3
Dr Johnson's House
FLST/FETLN EC4A 11 K3
Dr Tripletts CE J & I School
HYS/HAR UB3 ....94 D5
Drury Way Industrial Estate
WLSDN NW10 ....81 F2
Duchess Theatre
COVGDN WC2E 11 G5
Duff Miller College
SKENS SW7 ....120 B3
Duke of York Column
STJS SW1Y 16 D1
Duke of York Theatre
CHCR WC2N 10 E6
Dukes Hotel
WHALL SW1A 16 A1
Dulverton Primary School
ELTH/MOT SE9 ....167 J4
Dulwich College
DUL SE21 ....163 F5
Dulwich College Track
DUL SE21 ....163 F4
Dulwich Hamlet FC
EDUL SE22 ....143 F5
Dulwich Hamlet Junior School
HNHL SE24 ....162 E1
Dulwich Hospital
EDUL SE22 ....143 F5
Dulwich Leisure Centre
EDUL SE22 ....143 H5
Dulwich Medical Centre
EDUL SE22 ....143 H6
Dulwich Picture Gallery
DUL SE21 ....163 F2
Dulwich & Sydenham Hill
Golf Club
DUL SE21 ....163 H4

Dulwich Village CE
Infant School
DUL SE21 ....163 F1
Dunbar Wharf
POP/IOD E14 ....105 H6
Duncombe Primary School
ARCH N19 ....66 E5
Dundee Wharf
POP/IOD E14 ....105 H6
Dundonald Primary School
WIM/MER SW19 ....177 J3
Dundonald Road ↔
WIM/MER SW19 ....177 J3
Dunningford Primary School
HCH RM12 ....93 H3
Dunraven School
STRHM/NOR SW16 .....179 K5
Duppas Junior School
CROY/NA CR0 ....211 H3
Durand Primary School
BRXN/ST SW9 ....142 A2
Durands Wharf
BERM/RHTH SE16 .....124 C2
Durants School
PEND EN3 ....24 E2
Durdans Park Primary School
STHL UB1 ....95 K4
Durston House School
EA W5 ....97 K6
Dysart School
KUTN/CMB KT2 ....156 E6
SURB KT6 ....191 F4
Dyslexia Teaching Centre
SKENS SW7 ....120 A5
Eaglesfield School
WOOL/PLUM SE18 .....147 F2
Eagle Trading Estate
MTCM CR4 ....194 E3
Ealdham Primary School
ELTH/MOT SE9 ....146 B5
Ealing Abbey
EA W5 ....97 J5
Ealing Abbey Scriptorium
WEA W13 ....97 J5
Ealing Broadway ↔ ↔
EA W5 ....97 K6
The Ealing Broadway Centre
EA W5 ....97 K6
Ealing Central Sports Ground
GFD/PVL UB6 ....97 G1
Ealing Civic Centre
EA W5 ....97 J6
Ealing College Upper School
WEA W13 ....97 H5
Ealing Common ↔
EA W5 ....117 G1
Ealing CC
EA W5 ....98 A5
Ealing Film Studios
EA W5 ....116 D1
Ealing Golf Club
GFD/PVL UB6 ....97 H2
Ealing Hammersmith & West
London College
WKENS W14 ....119 G4
Ealing Hospital
NWDGN UB2 ....115 J2
Ealing Independent College
EA W5 ....116 D1
Ealing Northern Sports Centre
GFD/PVL UB6 ....78 D2
Ealing Park Health Centre
EA W5 ....116 E5
Ealing Road Trading Estate
BTFD TW8 ....116 E5
Ealing Snooker Club
WEA W13 ....116 C1
Ealing Sports Centre
EA W5 ....98 A6
Ealing & West London College
STRHM/NOR SW16 .....116 D1
Eardley Primary School
STRHM/NOR SW16 .....179 H2
Earlham Primary School
FSTGT E7 ....88 D3
Earl's Court ↔
ECT SW5 ....119 K4
Earl's Court Exhibition Centre
FUL/PGN SW6 ....119 K5
Earlsfield ↔
WAND/EARL SW18 .....160 B3
Earlsfield Primary School
WAND/EARL SW18 .....160 B4
Earlsmead First &
Middle School
RYLN/HDSTN HA2 ......77 K2
Earlsmead Primary School
SEVS/STOTM N15 ......68 B1
Earth Galleries
SKENS SW7 ....15 J4
East Acton ↔
SHB W12 ....99 H5
East Acton Primary School
ACT W3 ....99 G6
East Barking Centre
BCTR RM8 ....91 J3
East Barnet Health Centre
EBAR EN4 ....21 H6
East Barnet School
EBAR EN4 ....21 H4
EBAR EN4 ....33 K1
East Beckton District Centre
EHAM E6 ....107 K5
Eastbrook
Comprehensive School
DAGE RM10 ....92 E2
Eastbrook End Cemetery
ROMW/RG RM7 ....93 G1
Eastbrookend Country Park
ROMW/RG RM7 ....93 G2
Eastbury
Comprehensive School
BARK IG11 ....91 F6
Eastbury Farm JMI School
NTHWD HA6 ....26 D6
Eastbury Primary School
BARK IG11 ....91 F5
Eastcote ↔
RSLP HA4 ....59 G4

Eastcote CC
PIN HA5 ....59 F2
Eastcote Health Centre
PIN HA5 ....59 G4
Eastcote Industrial Estate
RSLP HA4 ....59 G4
Eastcote Lane Cemetery
RYLN/HDSTN HA2 ......78 B1
Eastcote Primary School
WELL DA16 ....147 J4
Eastcourt
Independent School
CDMY/SEVK IG3 ....73 G5
East Croydon ↔ ↔
CROY/NA CR0 ....196 E6
East Dulwich ↔
EDUL SE22 ....143 F5
East End Computing &
Business College
WCHPL E1 ....104 D5
Eastern Business Park
HTHAIR TW6 ....133 J3
Eastfield Primary School
PEND EN3 ....25 F1
East Finchley ↔
EFNCH N2 ....65 J1
East Finchley Cemetery
EFNCH N2 ....47 F6
East Finchley Medical Centre
EFNCH N2 ....65 J1
East Finchley School
of English
EFNCH N2 ....47 J6
Eastgate Business Park
LEY E10 ....69 G5
East Greenwich Christ Church
CE Primary School
GNWCH SE10 ....125 H4
East Ham ↔
EHAM E6 ....89 J5
East Ham Industrial Estate
EHAM E6 ....107 H4
East Ham Jewish Cemetery
EHAM E6 ....107 J2
East Ham Leisure Centre
EHAM E6 ....89 K6
East Ham Memorial Hospital
EHAM E6 ....89 H5
East Ham Nature Reserve
EHAM E6 ....107 K3
East Hill Cemetery
DART DA1 ....171 K2
East India ↔
POP/IOD E14 ....106 B6
Eastlea Community Centre
CAN/RD E16 ....106 D3
Eastlea Community School
CAN/RD E16 ....106 C3
East London Business College
WAN E11 ....70 C5
East London Cemetery
PLSTW E13 ....106 D2
East London Crematorium
SRTFD E15 ....106 D2
East London RFC
EHAM E6 ....107 K4
East London RUFC
SRTFD E15 ....106 D1
Eastman Dental Hospital
FSBYW WC1X 5 G4
East Molesey CC
E/WMO/HCT KT8 ......173 H6
East Putney ↔
PUT/ROE SW15 ....139 H6
East Sheen Cemetery
RCHPK/HAM TW10 .....137 H6
East Sheen Primary School
MORT/ESHN SW14 .....138 B5
East Thamesmead
Business Park
ERITHM DA18 ....129 G2
East Wickham Primary School
WELL DA16 ....148 A2
Eaton Manor RFC
WAN E11 ....71 G2
Eaton Square
Preparatory School
BGVA SW1W 15 J6
Eaton Square School
PIM SW1V 16 A7
Ecclesbourne Primary School
THHTH CR7 ....196 D2
Eden College
STHWK SE1 ....18 B4
Edenham High School
CROY/NA CR0 ....198 B4
Eden High School
FUL/PGN SW6 ....139 J2
Eden Medical Centre
WKENS W14 ....119 J4
Eden Park ↔
BECK BR3 ....198 D2
Edenvale Child Health Clinic
MTCM CR4 ....179 F3
Eden Walk Shopping Centre
KUT/HW KT1 ....175 F5
Edes Business Park
WLGTN SM6 ....195 F6
Edgebury Primary School
CHST BR7 ....167 H6
Edge Business Centre
CRICK NW2 ....63 K6
Edgware ↔
EDGW HA8 ....44 D2
Edgwarebury Cemetery
EDGW HA8 ....30 C4
Edgware Clinic
EDGW HA8 ....44 D2
Edgware College
KIL/WHAMP NW6 ....83 G4
Edgware
Community Hospital
EDGW HA8 ....44 D3
Edgware FC & Wealdstone FC
EDGW HA8 ....44 C3
Edgware Infant School
EDGW HA8 ....44 C2
Edgware Jewish
Primary School
EDGW HA8 ....44 D1

Edgware Junior School
EDGW HA8 ....44 D2
Edgware Road ↔
BAY/PAD W2 ....8 B2
Edinburgh Primary School
WALTH E17 ....69 H2
Edith Neville Primary School
CAMTN NW1 ....4 C3
Edmonton Cemetery
WCHMH N21 ....35 K4
Edmonton Green ↔
ED N9 ....36 C4
Edmonton Green
Shopping Centre
ED N9 ....36 D4
Edmonton Leisure Centre
ED N9 ....36 C5
Edmonton Lower School
ED N9 ....36 A3
Edmonton Upper School
EN EN1 ....36 B2
Edmund Waller
Primary School
NWCR SE14 ....144 A3
Education Centre
WOOL/PLUM SE18 .....127 G5
Edward Betham CE
Primary School
GFD/PVL UB6 ....96 D2
Edward Pauling School
FELT TW13 ....153 H4
Edward Wilson
Primary School
BAY/PAD W2 ....101 F4
Edwin Lambert School
EMPK RM11 ....75 J3
Effra Road Retail Park
BRXS/STRHM SW2 .....142 B6
The Egerton House Hotel
CHEL SW3 ....14 D5
Eglinton Junior School
WOOL/PLUM SE18 .....127 G5
Eglinton Primary School
WOOL/PLUM SE18 .....147 F1
Elbourne Trading Estate
BELV DA17 ....129 J3
Eldenwall Industrial Estate
BCTR RM8 ....74 A5
Eldon Infant School
ED N9 ....36 D3
Eldon Junior School
ED N9 ....36 E3
Eleanor Palmer
Primary School
KTTN NW5 ....84 C2
Eleanor Smith Special School
PLSTW E13 ....106 E1
Electrical Trades
Union College
ESH/CLAY KT10 ......204 A2
Electric Cinema
NTGHL W11 ....100 D5
Electron Trade Centre
STMC/STPC BR5 ......202 C1
Elephant & Castle ↔ ↔
LBTH SE11 ....18 C6
Elephant & Castle
Leisure Centre
LBTH SE11 ....18 B6
Elephant & Castle
Shopping Centre
STHWK SE1 ....18 B5
Elers Clinic
HYS/HAR UB3 ....113 G4
Elfrida Primary School
CAT SE6 ....164 E6
Eliot Bank Primary School
FSTH SE23 ....163 J4
Elizabeth Garrett
Anderson Hospital
CAMTN NW1 ....4 D5
Elizabeth Selby
Infant School
BETH E2 ....104 C2
Elizabeth Trading Estate
NWCR SE14 ....124 A6
Ellen Wilkinson
Primary School
CAN/RD E16 ....107 H4
Ellen Wilkinson School
for Girls
ACT W5 ....98 B5
Ellern Mede School
TRDG/WHET N20 ....32 B3
Ellerslie Square
Industrial Estate
BRXS/STRHM SW2 .....141 K5
Ellingham Primary School
CHSGTN KT9 ....205 K5
Elmbridge Leisure Centre
WOT/HER KT12 ....188 A2
Elm Court School
SKENS SW7 ....162 C4
Elmers End ↔ ↔
BECK BR3 ....198 A1
The Elmgreen School
WNWD SE27 ....162 C4
Elmgrove Middle School
KTN/HRWW/WS HA3 .....61 G1
Elmhurst Primary School
FSTGT E7 ....89 F5
Elmhurst School
SAND/SEL CR2 ....211 K3
Elm Lea Trading Estate
TOTM N17 ....50 C3
Elm Park ↔
HCH RM12 ....93 J2
The Elms Football &
Tennis Club
STAN HA7 ....43 H1
Elmstead Woods ↔
CHST BR7 ....184 D2
Elmwood J & I School
CROY/NA CR0 ....196 C4
Elm Wood Primary School
DUL SE21 ....162 E4
Elsdale Street Health Centre
HOM E9 ....86 E5
Elsley Primary School
WBLY HA9 ....80 B4

Elsley School
BTSEA SW11 ....141 F4
Eltham ↔
ELTH/MOT SE9 ....146 E5
Eltham Bus Station
ELTH/MOT SE9 ....146 E6
Eltham CE Primary School
ELTH/MOT SE9 ....146 E6
Eltham College Junior School
ELTH/MOT SE9 ....166 C3
Eltham College
Senior School
ELTH/MOT SE9 ....166 C4
Eltham Crematorium
ELTH/MOT SE9 ....147 J5
Eltham Green School
ELTH/MOT SE9 ....166 C1
Eltham Health Clinic
ELTH/MOT SE9 ....146 D6
Eltham Health &
Fitness Centre
ELTH/MOT SE9 ....167 F1
Eltham Hill
Technology College
ELTH/MOT SE9 ....166 D1
Eltham Palace
ELTH/MOT SE9 ....166 D2
Eltham Pools
ELTH/MOT SE9 ....166 D1
Eltham Warren Golf Club
ELTH/MOT SE9 ....147 G6
Elthorne Park High School
HNWL W7 ....116 A3
Elthorne Sports Centre
HNWL W7 ....116 A3
Elverson Road ↔
LEW SE13 ....144 E3
Elystan Business Centre
YEAD UB4 ....95 G6
Emanuel School
BTSEA SW11 ....140 C6
Embankment ↔
CHCR WC2N 11 F7
Embankment Pier
CHCR WC2N 11 G7
Embassy of Afghanistan
SKENS SW7 ....14 A3
Embassy of Albania
BCVA SW1W 15 K5
Embassy of Algeria
NTGHL W11 ....119 H6
Embassy of Angola
MYFR/PKLN W1K 9 G4
Embassy of Argentina
MYFR/PKLN W1K 9 J5
Embassy of Armenia
KENS W8 ....120 A2
Embassy of Austria
KTBR SW1X 120 E3
Embassy of Bahrain
SKENS SW7 ....120 E4
Embassy of Belarus
KENS W8 ....120 A2
Embassy of Belgium
KTBR SW1X 15 H4
Embassy of Bolivia
BGVA SW1W 15 H6
Embassy of Bosnia-
Herzegovina
CAVSO/HST W1G 9 J3
Embassy of Brazil
MYFR/PKLN W1K 9 H5
Embassy of Bulgaria
SKENS SW7 ....120 B2
Embassy of Cameroon
NTGHL W11 ....119 H4
Embassy of China
CAVSO/HST W1G 9 J3
Embassy of Costa Rica
BAY/PAD W2 ....101 G5
Embassy of Cote d'Ivoire
KTBR SW1X 15 J4
Embassy of Croatia
GTPST W1W 3 K7
Embassy of Cuba
LSO/SEVD WC2H 10 E3
Embassy of Democratic
Republic of the Congo
KTBR SW1X 15 G5
Embassy of Denmark
KTBR SW1X 15 H4
Embassy of
Dominican Republic
BAY/PAD W2 ....101 G4
Embassy of Ecuador
KTBR SW1X 14 E4
Embassy of Egypt
MYFR/PICC W1J 9 K1
Embassy of Estonia
SKENS SW7 ....120 C3
Embassy of Ethiopia
SKENS SW7 ....14 A4
Embassy of Finland
KTBR SW1X 15 J4
Embassy of France
KTBR SW1X 15 H3
Embassy of Georgia
KENS W8 ....120 A1
Embassy of Germany
KTBR SW1X 15 H3
Embassy of Ghana
HGT N6 ....66 B5
Embassy of Greece
NTGHL W11 ....119 J2
Embassy of Guatemala
WBPTN SW10 ....120 C6
Embassy of Honduras
MBLAR W1H 9 G1
Embassy of Hungary
KTBR SW1X 15 J2
Embassy of Iceland
KTBR SW1X 15 J3
Embassy of Indonesia
MYFR/PKLN W1K 9 J4
Embassy of Iran
SKENS SW7 ....14 A4
Embassy of Iraq
SKENS SW7 ....14 A2
Embassy of Ireland
KTBR SW1X 15 J2

Embassy of Israel *KENS* W8 120 A2
Embassy of Italy *MYFR/PKLN* W1K 9 H5
Embassy of Japan *MYFR/PICC* W1J 15 K1
Embassy of Jordan *KENS* W8 119 K2
Embassy of Korea *WESTW* SW1E 16 B4
Embassy of Krygyzstan *MBLAR* W1H 8 E2
Embassy of Kuwait *KTBR* SW1X 15 F2
Embassy of Latvia *CAMTN* NW1 3 G7
Embassy of Lebanon *KENS* W8 120 A1
Embassy of Liberia *BAY/PAD* W2 100 E6
Embassy of Lithuania *MBLAR* W1H 8 E2
Embassy of Luxembourg *KTBR* SW1X 15 G3
Embassy of Mexico *MYFR/PICC* W1J 15 J1
Embassy of Mongolia *KENS* W8 120 A2
Embassy of Morocco *SKENS* SW7 120 B4
Embassy of Mozambique *FITZ* W1T 4 A7
Embassy of Myanmar *MYFR/PICC* W1J 9 J7
Embassy of Nepal *KENS* W8 120 A1
Embassy of Netherlands *SKENS* SW7 120 B2
Embassy of Norway *KTBR* SW1X 15 H4
Embassy of Paraguay *SKENS* SW7 120 A3
Embassy of Peru *KTBR* SW1X 15 F4
Embassy of Philippines *KENS* W8 120 A1
Embassy of Poland *CAVSQ/HST* W1G 9 J1
mbassy of Portugal *KTBR* SW1X 15 G3
mbassy of Qatar *MYFR/PKLN* W1K 9 H7
mbassy of Romania *KENS* W8 120 A2
mbassy of Russian Federation *KENS* W8 120 A1
mbassy of Saudi Arabia *MYFR/PICC* W1J 9 J7
nbassy of Senegal *CRICK* NW2 82 A5
mbassy of Slovak Republic *KENS* W8 120 A1
mbassy of Slovenia *MHST* W1U 9 J3
nbassy of Spain *KTBR* SW1X 15 H4
nbassy of Sudan *WHALL* SW1A 16 A1
nbassy of Sweden *MBLAR* W1H 8 E2
ıbassy of Switzerland *MBLAR* W1H 8 E2
nbassy of Syria *KTBR* SW1X 15 G3
ıbassy of Thailand *SKENS* SW7 120 B3
ıbassy of the Holy See *WIM/MER* SW19 159 F5
ıbassy of the Republic of Gabon *SKENS* SW7 120 B3
bassy of the United States *MYFR/PKLN* W1K 9 G5
bassy of Tunisia *SKENS* SW7 14 B3
bassy of Turkey *KTBR* SW1X 15 H3
bassy of Turkmenistan *FITZ* W1T 10 B2
bassy of Ukraine *NTGHL* W11 119 H1
bassy of United Arab Emirates *BAY/PAD* W2 14 B2
bassy of Uruguay *SKENS* SW7 14 D4
bassy of Uzbekistan *NTGHL* W11 119 J1
bassy of Venezuela *SKENS* SW7 14 B5
bassy of Yemen *SKENS* SW7 14 A6
erhurst School *SH/CLAY* KT10 189 J4
er Sports Club *SH/CLAY* KT10 189 H5
roidery World usiness Centre *FD* IG8 53 H5
Walthamstow Cinema *ALTH* E17 69 J1
ry Theatre *OP/IOD* E14 105 K5
nanuel CE Primary School *L/WHAMP* NW6 82 E3
re Cinema *Q/SEVD* WC2H 10 D5
leigh Industrial Estate *WDGN* UB2 114 D4
ld Business Centre *ND* EN3 24 E3
ld CC EN1 24 A5
ld Chace Lower School *C/FH* EN2 24 A1
d Chase ⇄ *C/FH* EN2 23 J4
ld College *ND* EN3 24 E4
Enfield County School *ENC/FH* EN2 23 K4
Enfield FC *ED* N9 36 E4
Enfield Golf Club *ENC/FH* EN2 23 H5
Enfield Grammar School (Upper) *ENC/FH* EN2 23 K4
Enfield Town ⇄ *EN* EN1 23 K5
English Martyrs RC Primary School *WALW* SE17 18 E7
WCHPL E1 13 K4
Ensham Secondary School *TOOT* SW17 178 E1
Enterprise Business Park *POP/IOD* E14 124 E2
Enterprise Industrial Estate *BERM/RHTH* SE16 123 K5
Epsom & Ewell High School *HOR/WEW* KT19 206 E4
Eric Liddell Sports Centre *ELTH/MOT* SE9 166 C4
Eridge House Preparatory School *FUL/PGN* SW6 139 J3
Erith ⇄ *ERITH* DA8 130 A5
Erith & District Hospital *ERITH* DA8 130 A6
Erith Health Centre *ERITH* DA8 130 B6
Erith Library & Museum *ERITH* DA8 130 B5
Erith Playhouse *ERITH* DA8 130 C5
Erith School *ERITH* DA8 149 K1
Erith School Community Sports Centre *ERITH* DA8 149 K1
Erith Small Business Centre *ERITH* DA8 130 C6
Erith Sports Centre *ERITH* DA8 130 B6
Erith Stadium *ERITH* DA8 130 B6
Ernest Bevin College *TOOT* SW17 160 D5
Eros *MYFR/PICC* W1J 10 C6
Esher ⇄ *ESH/CLAY* KT10 189 J6
Esher CE High School *ESH/CLAY* KT10 204 A1
Esher Church Primary School *ESH/CLAY* KT10 204 C4
Esher College *THDIT* KT7 189 K4
Esher RFC *WOT/HER* KT12 188 D6
Essendine Primary School *MV/WKIL* W9 100 E2
Essex Primary School *MNPK* E12 89 J4
Essex Road ⇄ *IS* N1 85 J5
Ethelburga GM School *BTSEA* SW11 140 D2
Euro Business Centre *SRTFD* E15 88 D6
Euro Freightliner Terminal ⇄ *WLSDN* NW10 99 G2
Eurolink Business Centre *BRXS/STRHM* SW2 142 B5
Europa Trading Estate *ERITH* DA8 130 A5
European Business Centre *CDALE/KGS* NW9 45 F6
European Business School London *CAMTN* NW1 3 G6
European College of Business Management *SDTCH* EC2A 7 G6
European School of Economics *KTBR* SW1X 15 H3
European Vocational College *HDTCH* EC3A 13 H4
Euro Way School *CEND/HSY/T* N8 49 G6
Euro Way School London *FSBYPK* N4 67 H4
Euston ⇄ ⊖ ⊖ *CAMTN* NW1 4 C5
Euston Centre University of Westminster *CAMTN* NW1 3 K6
Euston Square ⊖ *CAMTN* NW1 4 B6
Euston Tower *CAMTN* NW1 4 A6
Evans Business Centre *CRICK* NW2 81 J1
Eveline Day School *TOOT* SW17 160 E4
Eveline Lowe Primary School *PECK* SE15 123 G5
Evendine College *SOHO/SHAV* W1D 10 C3
Eversley Medical Centre *CROY/NA* CR0 196 B3
Eversley Primary School *WCHMH* N21 22 E6
Everyman Belsize Park *HAMP* NW3 83 J3
Everyman Cinema *HAMP* NW3 83 G2
Evolution House, Kew Gardens *RCH/KEW* TW9 137 F3
Ewell Athletics Track *HOR/WEW* KT19 207 F4
Ewell Castle Junior School *EW* KT17 207 H6
Ewell Castle School *EW* KT17 207 J6
Ewell Grove Infant School *EW* KT17 207 H6
Ewell West ⇄ *HOR/WEW* KT19 207 G6
ExCeL Exhibition Centre *CAN/RD* E16 107 F6
Excelsior College *UED* N18 50 A2
Exchange Square *SDTCH* EC2A 13 G1
The Exchange *IL* IG1 72 B6
Executive Medical & Occupational Health Centre *CROY/NA* CR0 211 K1
Exhibition Halls *WBLY* HA9 80 C2
Express by Holiday Inn *CAN/RD* E16 106 D5
CHING E4 51 J3
CROY/NA CR0 196 D6
GNTH/NBYPK IG2 72 D3
HMSMTH W6 118 E4
PIM SW1V 121 H5
SDTCH EC2A 7 G5
STHWK SE1 12 B7
WAND/EARL SW18 140 A5
WAP E1W 105 F6
WIM/MER SW19 178 C3
The Eye Clinic *NOXST/BSQ* WC1A 10 D3
Faculty of Engineering & Science (University of Westminster) *FITZ* W1T 10 B1
Faircharm Trading Estate *DEPT* SE8 144 E1
IS N1 6 C2
The Faircross Complementary Medical Centre *BARK* IG11 90 E4
Fairfield Clinic *BKHH* IG9 39 F3
Fairfield Pool & Leisure Centre *DART* DA1 171 H2
Fairfield Trade Park *KUT/HW* KT1 175 G6
Fairholme Primary School *EBED/NFELT* TW14 153 G3
Fairlawn Primary School *FSTH* SE23 163 K2
Fairley House School *PIM* SW1V 16 C7
Fairlop ⊖ *BARK/HLT* IG6 54 E4
Fairlop Primary School *BARK/HLT* IG6 54 C4
Fairview Industrial Centre *RAIN* RM13 111 F5
Fairview Industrial Estate *HYS/HAR* UB3 113 J2
Fairview Medical Centre *STRHM/NOR* SW16 179 K4
Fairway Primary School *MLHL* NW7 31 F4
Fairways Business Park *LEY* E10 69 G6
Falconbrook Primary School *BTSEA* SW11 140 C3
Falcon Business Centre *BTSEA* SW11 140 D5
Falcon Park Industrial Estate *WLSDN* NW10 81 G3
The Falcons Preparatory School for Boys *RCH/KEW* TW9 136 E4
The Falcons School for Girls *EA* W5 117 G1
Falconwood ⇄ *ELTH/MOT* SE9 147 J4
Falkner House School *SKENS* SW7 120 B5
Family Records Centre *FSBYW* WC1X 5 J5
Fanmakers' Hall *LVPST* EC2M 13 G2
The Fan Museum *GNWCH* SE10 145 F1
Faraday Building *BLKFR* EC4V 12 B4
Farm Lane Trading Estate *FUL/PGN* SW6 119 K6
Farnborough Primary School *ORP* BR6 216 D3
Farnell House Medical Centre *HSLW* TW3 135 G2
Farnham Green Primary School *GDMY/SEVK* IG3 73 G3
Farringdon ⇄ ⊖ *FARR* EC1M 11 K1
Farrington & Stratford House School *CHST* BR7 185 J3
Featherstone Industrial Estate *NWDGN* UB2 114 D2
Featherstone Primary School *NWDGN* UB2 114 C4
Featherstone Road Health Clinic *NWDGN* UB2 114 D3
Federation St Elpheges RC School *WLGTN* SM6 210 E4
Felnex Trading Estate *WLGTN* SM6 195 F6
Feltham ⇄ *FELT* TW13 154 A3
Feltham Airparcs Leisure Centre *FELT* TW13 154 C4
Feltham Athletics Arena *EBED/NFELT* TW14 153 K2
Felthambrook Industrial Estate *FELT* TW13 154 A5
Feltham Cemetery *FELT* TW13 153 J5
Feltham Community College *FELT* TW13 154 B4
Feltham Hill Infant School *FELT* TW13 153 J5
Feltham Hill Junior School *FELT* TW13 153 J5
Feltham & Hounslow Borough FC *EBED/NFELT* TW14 153 K2
Feltham Superbowl *FELT* TW13 154 A4
Fenchurch Street ⇄ *FENCHST* EC3M 13 H5
Fenstanton J & I School *BRXS/STRHM* SW2 162 B3
Fenton House (NT) *HAMP* NW3 83 G1
Ferrier Industrial Estate *WAND/EARL* SW18 140 A5
Ferry Island Retail Park *TOTM* N17 50 B6
Ferry Lane Industrial Estate *RAIN* RM13 111 J4
WALTH E17 50 E6
Ferry Lane Primary School *TOTM* N17 68 D1
Festival Pier *STHWK* SE1 11 H7
Field End J & I Schools *RSLP* HA4 59 H6
Fielding Primary School *WEA* W13 116 C3
Fieldway ⊖ *CROY/NA* CR0 213 K5
Film House Cinema *RCH/KEW* TW9 136 E6
Financial Times *STHWK* SE1 12 D7
Financial Times Newspaper Offices *POP/IOD* E14 106 A5
Finchley Catholic High School *NFNCH/WDSPK* N12 33 G5
Finchley Central ⊖ *FNCH* N3 46 E4
Finchley CC *FNCH* N3 47 F5
Finchley Golf Club *MLHL* NW7 46 D2
Finchley Industrial Centre *NFNCH/WDSPK* N12 33 G6
Finchley Lawn Tennis Club *FNCH* N3 46 D2
Finchley Lido Leisure Centre *NFNCH/WDSPK* N12 47 H3
Finchley Memorial Hospital *NFNCH/WDSPK* N12 47 G3
Finchley Road ⊖ *KIL/WHAMP* NW6 83 G4
Finchley Road & Frognal ⊖ *KIL/WHAMP* NW6 83 F3
Finchley Youth Theatre *EFNCH* N2 47 J6
Finsbury Circus Medical Centre *LVPST* EC2M 13 F2
Finsbury Health Centre *CLKNW* EC1R 5 J6
Finsbury Leisure Centre *FSBYE* EC1V 6 D5
Finsbury Park ⇄ ⊖ *FSBYPK* N4 67 G6
Finsbury Park Track *FSBYPK* N4 67 H4
Finton House School *TOOT* SW17 160 E4
Fircroft Primary School *TOOT* SW17 160 E4
Fire Brigade HQ *STHWK* SE1 17 G6
Fire Brigade Museum *STHWK* SE1 18 C2
Firepower Royal Artillery Museum *WOOL/PLUM* SE18 127 G3
Firs Farm Primary School *PLMGR* N13 35 K5
Fisher Athletic FC *BERM/RHTH* SE16 124 A1
Fishmonger's Hall *CANST* EC4R 12 E6
Fitness Unlimited Leisure Centre *BOW* E3 105 J1
Fitzrovia Medical Centre *FITZ* W1T 4 A7
Fitzroy Nuffield Hospital *MBLAR* W1H 8 E3
Five Bridges School *LBTH* SE11 122 A5
Five Elms Primary School *DAGW* RM9 92 B1
Five Ways Business Centre *FELT* TW13 154 A5
Flamsteed House Museum *GNWCH* SE10 145 G1
Flaxman Sports Centre *CMBW* SE5 142 D3
Fleecefield Primary School *ED* N9 36 C6
Fleet Primary School *HAMP* NW3 83 K3
Fleetway Business Park *GFD/PVL* UB6 97 H1
Fleming Lab Museum *BAY/PAD* W2 8 B3
Flora Gardens Primary School *HMSMTH* W6 118 E4
Florence Nightingale Museum *STHWK* SE1 17 G3
Flutters Leisure Centre *FUL/PGN* SW6 139 K1
Follys End Christian High School *SNWD* SE25 197 F3
Follys End Christian School *SAND/SEL* CR2 212 A2
The Foot Clinic *WIM/MER* SW19 177 H2
Fordbridge Medical Centre *ASHF* TW15 152 C6
The Ford College *CONDST* W1S 9 K4
Fordgate Business Park *BELV* DA17 129 K2
Ford Industrial Park *DAGW* RM9 110 D2
Fordview Industrial Estate *RAIN* RM13 111 F2
Foreign & Commonwealth Office *WHALL* SW1A 16 D2
Foreland Medical Centre *NTGHL* W11 100 C6
Forest Business Park *LEY* E10 69 F4
Forestdale Primary School *CROY/NA* CR0 213 G6
Foresters Primary School *WLGTN* SM6 210 D4
Forest Gate ⇄ *FSTGT* E7 88 E3
Forest Gate Community School *FSTGT* E7 88 E3
Forest Hill ⇄ ⊖ *FSTH* SE23 163 K4
Forest Hill Business Centre *FSTH* SE23 163 K4
Forest Hill Industrial Estate *FSTH* SE23 163 K4
Forest Hill Pools *SYD* SE26 163 K4
Forest Hill School *FSTH* SE23 164 A5
Forest House Business Centre *WAN* E11 70 D4
Forest Industrial Park *BARK/HLT* IG6 54 E3
Forest Park Cemetery & Crematorium *BARK/HLT* IG6 55 J1
Forest Preparatory School *WALTH* E17 70 C1
Forest Road Medical Centre *WALTH* E17 51 H6
Forest Trading Estate *WALTH* E17 51 F6
Forge Close Clinic *HAYES* BR2 199 K5
Forge Lane Primary School *FELT* TW13 172 D2
The Former Health Centre *CHARL* SE7 126 C4
Forster Park Primary School *CAT* SE6 165 H5
Fortismere School *EFNCH* N2 47 K5
Fortune Theatre *HOL/ALD* WC2B 11 F4
The Forum *EDGW* HA8 44 C2
Fossdene Primary School *CHARL* SE7 126 A5
Foster's Primary School *WELL* DA16 148 D4
Foulds School *BAR* EN5 20 B4
The Foundling Museum *BMSBY* WC1N 5 F6
The Fountain Studios *WBLY* HA9 80 C1
Fountayne Business Centre *SEVS/STOTM* N15 68 C1
Fountayne Road Health Centre *STNW/STAM* N16 68 C6
Four Seasons Hotel *BERM/RHTH* SE16 124 C1
MYFR/PKLN W1K 15 J2
Foxfield Primary School *WOOL/PLUM* SE18 127 H5
Fox Primary School *KENS* W8 119 K1
Frances Bardsley School for Girls *ROM* RM1 75 J2
Franciscan Primary School *TOOT* SW17 161 F6
Francis Holland School *BGVA* SW1W 15 H7
CAMTN NW1 2 E7
Frank Barnes Primary School *STJWD* NW8 83 H5
Franklin Industrial Estate *PGE/AN* SE20 181 K4
Frederick Bremer Secondary School *WALTH* E17 52 A5
Freehold Industrial Centre *HSLWW* TW4 134 B6
Free Trade Wharf *WAP* E1W 105 F6
Freightliners City Farm *HOLWY* N7 85 F4
The French Institute *SKENS* SW7 14 A6
Fresh Wharf Estate *BARK* IG11 90 B6
Freuchen Medical Centre *WLSDN* NW10 99 H1
Freud Museum *HAMP* NW3 83 H4
Friars Primary Foundation School *STHWK* SE1 18 A2
Friends House *CAMTN* NW1 4 C5
Friern Barnet School *FBAR/BDGN* N11 47 K1
Friern Bridge Retail Park *FBAR/BDGN* N11 48 B2
Frithwood Primary School *NTHWD* HA6 40 D2
Frogmore Industrial Estate *HBRY* N5 85 J2
HYS/HAR UB3 113 H2

WLSDN NW10 98 E2
Fryent Country Park
KTN/HRWW/WS HA3 62 C4
Fryent Medical Centre
CDALE/KGS NW9 62 E4
Fryent Primary School
CDALE/KGS NW9 62 E4
Fulham Broadway ⊖
FUL/PGN SW6 139 K1
Fulham Cemetery
FUL/PGN SW6 139 G1
Fulham Clinic
HMSMTH W6 119 H6
Fulham Cross Girls Secondary School
FUL/PGN SW6 139 G1
Fulham FC (Craven Cottage)
PUT/ROE SW15 139 F2
Fulham Medical Centre
FUL/PGN SW6 140 A1
Fulham Palace
FUL/PGN SW6 139 G3
Fulham Pools
FUL/PGN SW6 119 J6
Fulham Preparatory School
WKENS W14 119 H6
Fulham Pre-Preparatory School
FUL/PGN SW6 139 H3
Fulham Primary School
FUL/PGN SW6 119 K6
Fuller Smith & Turner Sports Club
CHSWK W4 138 B2
Fullwell Cross Health Centre
BARK/HLT IG6 54 C5
Fullwell Cross Swimming Pool & Recreation Centre
BARK/HLT IG6 54 C5
Fullwood Primary School
BARK/HLT IG6 72 C1
Fulwell ⇌
WHTN TW2 155 J6
Fulwell Golf Club
HPTN TW12 155 J6
Furness Primary School
WLSDN NW10 99 J1
Furzedown Primary School
TOOT SW17 179 G2
Furze Infant School
CHDH RM6 74 A3
Future Business College
CONDST W1S 9 K4
Gainsborough Clinic
PLMGR N13 35 F6
Gainsborough Primary School
HOM E9 87 H4
SRTFD E15 106 C2
Galliard Primary School
ED N9 36 C1
Gallions Mount Primary School
WOOL/PLUM SE18 128 A5
Gallions Primary School
EHAM E6 108 B5
Gallions Reach ⊖
EHAM E6 108 B6
Gallions Reach Shopping Park
EHAM E6 108 B4
Gants Hill ⊖
GNTH/NBYPK IG2 72 A3
Gants Hill Medical Centre
GNTH/NBYPK IG2 72 A3
Gardener Industrial Estate
SYD SE26 182 B1
Garden House School
BGVA SW1W 121 F5
Garden Primary School
MTCM CR4 179 J6
Garden Suburb Infant School
GLDGN NW11 64 D2
Garfield Primary School
FBAR/BDGN N11 48 B1
WIM/MER SW19 178 B2
Garratt Park Secondary Special School
WAND/EARL SW18 160 B5
Garrick Industrial Centre
CDALE/KGS NW9 63 H2
Garrick Theatre
LSQ/SEVD WC2H 10 E6
Garth Primary School
MRDN SM4 194 C2
The Garth Road Industrial Centre
MRDN SM4 193 F4
Gascoigne Primary School
BARK IG11 90 C6
Gate Cinema
KENS W8 119 K1
Gatehouse School
BETH E2 105 F1
The Gatehouse Theatre
HGT N6 66 A4
Gate Theatre
NTGHL W11 119 K1
Gateway
EHAM E6 108 B3
Gateway Business Centre
SYD SE26 182 B2
WOOL/PLUM SE18 127 H3
Gateway Industrial Estate
WLSDN NW10 99 H2
Gatton School
TOOT SW17 160 D6
Gayhurst Primary School
HACK E8 86 C5
Gearies Infant School
GNTH/NBYPK IG2 72 A2
Gearies Junior School
GNTH/NBYPK IG2 72 B2
Geffrye Museum
BETH E2 7 H3
Gemini Business Estate
NWCR SE14 124 A5
General Medical Clinics
WCHPL E1 13 J1
Genesis Cinema
WCHPL E1 104 E3
Geoffrey Chaucer Technology College
STHWK SE1 18 E5
The Geoffrey Lloyd Foulkes Clinic
IL IG1 72 A6
Geoffrey Whitworth Theatre
DART DA1 150 D5
George Eliot J & I School
STJWD NW8 83 G6
George Greens School
POP/IOD E14 125 F5
George Mitchell School
LEY E10 69 K5
George Spicer Primary School
EN EN1 24 B4
George Street ●
CROY/NA CR0 196 D6
George Tomlinson Primary School
WAN E11 70 C5
Germal College
FSBYPK N4 67 G5
Gibbs Green Special School
WKENS W14 119 J5
Gibson Business Centre
TOTM N17 50 B2
The Gibson Business Centre
TOTM N17 50 B3
Gidea Park ⇌
GPK RM2 75 K1
Gidea Park College
GPK RM2 57 J6
Gidea Park Primary School
GPK RM2 75 H1
The Gielgud Theatre
SOHO/CST W1F 10 C5
Giffin Business Centre
DEPT SE8 144 D1
Gifford Primary School
NTHLT UB5 95 K1
Gilbert Collection
TPL/STR WC2R 11 H5
Gilbert Colvin Primary School
CLAY IG5 54 A4
Gilbert Scott Primary School
SAND/SEL CR2 213 G5
Gillespie Primary School
HBRY N5 85 H1
Gipsy Hill ⇌
NRWD SE19 181 F1
Girdlers' Hall
CITYW EC2V 12 D2
Glade Primary School
CLAY IG5 53 K4
The Glades Shopping Centre
BMLY BR1 183 K5
Gladstone Medical Centre
CRICK NW2 81 H2
Gladstone Park Primary School
WLSDN NW10 81 J3
The Gladys Aylward School
UED N18 35 K6
Glaziers/Scientific Instrument Makers Hall
STHWK SE1 12 E7
Glebe First & Middle School
KTN/HRWW/WS HA3 61 K1
Glebe Primary School
HGDN/ICK UB10 76 B2
Glebe School
WWKM BR4 199 G5
Gleen Lecky Health Centre
PUT/ROE SW15 139 G5
Glenbrook Primary School
CLAP SW4 161 J1
Glencairn Sports Club
FBAR/BDGN N11 48 C3
Glendower Preparatory School
SKENS SW7 120 B4
Glenham College
IL IG1 72 B6
Glenlyn Medical Centre
E/WMO/HCT KT8 189 H2
Glenthorne High Specialist Arts
CHEAM SM3 193 K5
Globe Academy
STHWK SE1 18 E5
Globe Primary School
BETH E2 104 E2
Globe Wharf
BERM/RHTH SE16 105 F6
Gloucester Primary School
PECK SE15 143 F1
Gloucester Road ⊖
SKENS SW7 120 B4
Godolphin & Latymer School
HMSMTH W6 118 E4
Godwin Junior School
FSTGT E7 89 F2
Goethe Institute
SKENS SW7 14 B4
Golborne Medical Centre
NKENS W10 100 D3
Goldbeaters Primary School
EDGW HA8 45 F4
Golden Hinde Educational Trust
STHWK SE1 12 E6
Golders Green ⊖
GLDGN NW11 64 E4
Golders Green Crematorium
GLDGN NW11 64 E4
Golders Green Health Centre
GLDGN NW11 65 F5
Golders Hill Health Centre
GLDGN NW11 65 G3
Golders Hill School
GLDGN NW11 64 E4
Goldhawk Industrial Estate
SHB W12 118 E3
Goldhawk Road ⊖
SHB W12 119 F2
Goldsmiths College Sports Ground
SCUP DA14 169 G5
Goldsmiths Hall
STBT EC1A 12 C3
Goldsmiths University of London
DEPT SE8 124 D6
LEW SE13 145 H5
NWCR SE14 144 B2
Gonville Primary School
THHTH CR7 196 A2
Goodge St ⊖
FITZ W1T 10 B1
Goodinge Health Centre
HOLWY N7 84 E4
Goodmayes ⇌
GDMY/SEVK IG3 73 G5
Goodmayes Retail Park
CHDH RM6 73 H4
Goodrich J & I School
EDUL SE22 163 H1
Good Shepherd RC Primary School
BMLY BR1 165 J6
CROY/NA CR0 213 K5
The Good Shepherd RC Primary School
SHB W12 118 C2
Goodwyn School
MLHL NW7 45 J1
Goose Green Primary School
EDUL SE22 143 G5
Goose Green Trading Estate
EDUL SE22 143 H5
Gordonbrock Primary School
BROCKY SE4 144 D6
Gordon Hill ⇌
ENC/FH EN2 23 H2
Gordon Hospital
WEST SW1P 16 C7
Gordon House Health Centre
WEA W13 116 C1
Gordon Infant School
IL IG1 90 D1
Gordon Primary School
ELTH/MOT SE9 146 E5
Goresbrook Leisure Centre
DAGW RM9 91 K6
Goresbrook Sports Centre
DAGW RM9 91 K6
The Goring Hotel
BGVA SW1W 15 K4
Gorringe Park Primary School
MTCM CR4 179 F4
Gosai Cinema
WEA W13 116 C1
Gosbury Hill Health Centre
CHSGTN KT9 206 A2
Gosford Primary School
REDBR IG4 71 K2
Gospel Oak ⊖
HAMP NW3 84 A2
Gove Farm Retail Park
CHDH RM6 73 J4
Government Offices
WHALL SW1A 10 E7
Gower House School
CDALE/KGS NW9 62 E6
Grace Business Centre
MTCM CR4 194 E3
Grace Theatre at the Latchmere
BTSEA SW11 140 E3
Graduate School of Management
TOTM N17 50 B4
Grafton Primary School
BCTR RM8 74 A6
HOLWY N7 84 E1
Grahame Park Health Centre
CDALE/KGS NW9 45 G4
Grahame Park J & I School
CDALE/KGS NW9 45 G4
Granard Business Centre
MLHL NW7 45 G2
Granard Primary School
PUT/ROE SW15 158 E1
Granby Sports Club
CHST BR7 184 D1
Grand Avenue Primary School
BRYLDS KT5 191 K3
Grande Vitesse Industrial Centre
STHWK SE1 18 B1
Grand Union Industrial Estate
WLSDN NW10 98 D2
The Grange City Hotel
TWRH EC3N 13 J5
Grange First School
RYLN/HDSTN HA2 60 B5
The Grange Museum
CRICK NW2 81 H2
Grange Park ⇌
WCHMH N21 23 H6
Grange Park Clinic
YEAD UB4 94 D3
Grange Park Junior School
YEAD UB4 94 D3
Grange Park Preparatory School
WCHMH N21 35 H1
Grange Park Primary School
WCHMH N21 23 G5
Grange Primary School
CAN/RD E16 106 D3
EA W5 116 E2
STHWK SE1 19 G5
Grange Whitehall Hotel
RSQ WC1B 10 E2
Grangewood Independent School
FSTGT E7 89 H5
Grangewood School
PIN HA5 58 E2
Granton Primary School
STRHM/NOR SW16 179 H3
Granville Road Industrial Estate
CRICK NW2 64 D6
Grasmere Primary School
STNW/STAM N16 85 K2
Grasshoppers RFC
ISLW TW7 116 A6
Grassroots School
HPTN TW12 173 F4
Grasvenor Avenue Infant School
BAR EN5 32 E1
Gravel Hill ●
CROY/NA CR0 213 G5
Gravel Hill Primary School
BXLYHS DA6 149 J6
Graveney School
TOOT SW17 179 G2
Graves Yard Industrial Estate
WELL DA16 148 B3
Grays Farm Primary School
STMC/STPC BR5 186 C4
Grazebrook Primary School
STNW/STAM N16 68 A6
Great Cambridge Industrial Estate
EN EN1 24 D6
Great Chapel Street Medical Centre
SOHO/SHAV W1D 10 C3
Greater London Authority Headquarters (City Hall)
STHWK SE1 19 H1
Great Jubilee Wharf
WAP E1W 123 K1
Great Ormond Street Hospital for Children
BMSBY WC1N 5 F7
Great Portland Street ⊖
GTPST W1W 3 K7
Great Scotland Yard
WHALL SW1A 10 E7
Great Western Industrial Park
NWDGN UB2 115 G2
Great West Trading Estate
BTFD TW8 116 C6
Greek School of London
ACT W3 98 D6
Greenacres Primary School
ELTH/MOT SE9 167 F4
The Green CE Primary School
TOTM N17 50 B6
Green Dragon Primary School
BTFD TW8 117 F5
Greenfield Medical Centre
CRICK NW2 82 C1
Greenfields Junior School
SHB W12 99 H6
Greenfields Primary School
OXHEY WD19 41 G1
Greenfields Special School
MUSWH N10 47 K4
Greenford ⇌ ⊖
GFD/PVL UB6 78 D6
Greenford Avenue Medical Centre
HNWL W7 96 E4
Greenford Green Clinic
GFD/PVL UB6 78 E3
Greenford High School
STHL UB1 96 A2
Greenford Industrial Estate
GFD/PVL UB6 78 B6
Greenford Park Cemetery
Greenford Park Cemetery
GFD/PVL UB6 96 B4
Greenford Road Medical Centre
GFD/PVL UB6 96 D1
Greenford Sports Centre
STHL UB1 96 A2
Greengate Medical Centre
PLSTW E13 107 F2
Greengrove College
STHGT/OAK N14 34 E4
Greenheath Business Centre
BETH E2 104 D2
Greenhill College
HRW HA1 61 F2
Greenhill Park Medical Centre
WLSDN NW10 81 G6
Greenland Pier
BERM/RHTH SE16 124 C3
Green Lane Business Park
ELTH/MOT SE9 167 F4
Green Lane Primary School
WPK KT4 192 E4
Greenleaf Primary School
WALTH E17 51 H6
Greenmead Primary School
PUT/ROE SW15 138 E6
Green Park ⊖
MYFR/PICC W1J 15 K1
The Green School
ISLW TW7 136 B1
Greenshaw High School
SUT SM1 194 B6
Greenshields Industrial Estate
CAN/RD E16 125 K1
Greenside Primary School
SHB W12 118 D2
Greenslade Primary School
WOOL/PLUM SE18 127 J6
Green Street Green Primary School
ORP BR6 217 F4
Greenvale School
FSTH SE23 164 B5
Greenwich ⇌ ⊖
GNWCH SE10 144 E1
Greenwich Centre Business Park
DEPT SE8 144 E1
Greenwich Cinema
GNWCH SE10 145 F1
Greenwich Community College
WOOL/PLUM SE18 127 G4
Greenwich Industrial Estate
CHARL SE7 126 A4
GNWCH SE10 144 E1
Greenwich Natural Health Centre
GNWCH SE10 145 F1
Greenwich Odeon Cinema
GNWCH SE10 125 J4
Greenwich Pier
GNWCH SE10 125 F5
Greenwich School of Management
GNWCH SE10 145 F1
Greenwich Theatre & Art Gallery
GNWCH SE10 145 G1
Greenwood Primary School
NTHLT UB5 78 C3
Greenwood Theatre
STHWK SE1 19 F2
Green Wrythe Primary School
CAR SM5 194 C3
Gresham College
HCIRC EC1N 11 J2
Gresham Way Industrial Estate
WIM/MER SW19 160 A5
Grey Coat Hospital School for Girls
WEST SW1P 16 C5
The Greycoat Hospital
WEST SW1P 16 C7
Grey Court School
RCHPK/HAM TW10 156 E5
Griffen Manor School
WOOL/PLUM SE18 147 K2
Grimsdyke First & Middle School
PIN HA5 41 K2
Grims Dyke Golf Club
PIN HA5 42 A1
Grim's Dyke Hotel
KTN/HRWW/WS HA3 28 C6
Grinling Gibbons Primary School
DEPT SE8 124 C6
Grist Memorial Sports Club
E/WMO/HCT KT8 189 K2
Grocers' Hall
CITYW EC2V 12 E4
Grosvenor House Hotel
MYFR/PKLN W1K 9 G6
The Grove Health Centre
SHB W12 118 E2
Grove House (Froebel College)
PUT/ROE SW15 158 C1
Grove House Primary School for Deaf Children
WNWD SE27 162 C4
Grovelands Priory Hospital
STHGT/OAK N14 34 E
Grovelands School
WOT/HER KT12 188 A
Grove Medical Centre
DEPT SE8 124 B
The Grove Medical Centre
ARCH N19 66 D
Grove Park ⇌
BMLY BR1 165 K
Grove Park Cemetery
LEE/GVPK SE12 166 C
Grove Park Industrial Estate
CDALE/KGS NW9 63 F
Grove Park Primary School
CHSWK W4 117 K
Grove Park School
CDALE/KGS NW9 62 E
Grove Primary School
CHDH RM6 73 H
Grove Road Primary School
HSLW TW3 135 H
The Groves Medical Centre
NWMAL KT3 176 E
Grove Village Medical Centre
EBED/NFELT TW14 153 H
Guardian Angels RC Primary School
BOW E3 105
Guardian Newspapers
POP/IOD E14 124
Guards' Chapel & Museum
STJSPK SW1H 16
Gumley House Convent School
ISLW TW7 136
Gunnersbury ⇌ ⊖
CHSWK W4 117
Gunnersbury Catholic School
BTFD TW8 116
Gunnersbury Cemetery
BTFD TW8 117
Gunnersbury Park Museum
ACT W3 117
Gurnell Leisure Centre
WEA W13 97
Guru Gobind Singh Khalsa College
CHIG IG7 39
Guru Nanak Medical Centre
STHL UB1 114
Guru Nanak Sikh Primary School
YEAD UB4 114
Guru Nanak Sikh Secondary School
YEAD UB4 114
Guy's Hospital
STHWK SE1 19
Guys Kings & Thomas Medical School (Kings College London)
STHWK SE1 12
Gwyn Jones Primary School
WAN E11 70
GX Superbowl
EHAM E6 108
Gypsy Moth IV
GNWCH SE10 125
Haberdashers Askes Hatcham College
NWCR SE14 144
Haberdashers Askes Knights Academy
BMLY BR1 16
Haberdashers' Hall
STBT EC1A 1

Hackbridge ⇌ WLGTN SM6 ... 195 G6
Hackbridge Primary School WLGTN SM6 ... 195 F5
Hackney Business Centre HACK E8 ... 86 D4
Hackney Central ⊖ HACK E8 ... 86 D4
Hackney City Farm BETH E2 ... 104 C1
Hackney Community College IS N1 ... 7 G3
Hackney Downs ⇌ HACK E8 ... 86 C3
Hackney Empire Variety Theatre HACK E8 ... 86 D4
Hackney Free & Parochial CE School HOM E9 ... 86 E4
The Hackney Museum HACK E8 ... 86 D4
Hackney Sports Centre HOM E9 ... 87 J2
Hackney Wick ⊖ HOM E9 ... 87 J4
Hadley Wood ⇌ EBAR EN4 ... 21 G1
Hadley Wood Golf Club EBAR EN4 ... 21 J2
Hadley Wood Primary School EBAR EN4 ... 21 G1
The Haelan Clinic CEND/HSY/T N8 ... 66 E3
Haggerston ⊖ HACK E8 ... 86 A5
Haggerston School BETH E2 ... 7 K2
Haggerston Swimming Pool BETH E2 ... 7 K1
Hague Primary School BETH E2 ... 104 D3
Hailey Road Business Park ERITHM DA18 ... 129 H2
Haimo Primary School ELTH/MOT SE9 ... 146 C6
Hainault ⊖ BARK/HLT IG6 ... 54 D3
Hainault Business Park BARK/HLT IG6 ... 55 J1
Hainault Forest Golf Complex CHIG IG7 ... 55 K2
Hainault Forest High School & the Learning Centre BARK/HLT IG6 ... 55 G1
Hakim Qureshi Clinic NWDGN UB2 ... 114 D3
The Hale Clinic CAMTN NW1 ... 3 K7
Half Moon Theatre WCHPL E1 ... 105 F3
Haling Manor High School SAND/SEL CR2 ... 211 H5
'he Halkin Hotel KTBR SW1X ... 15 H3
Ialley Primary School POP/IOD E14 ... 105 G4
Iallfield Clinic BAY/PAD W2 ... 101 G5
Iallfield Infant School BAY/PAD W2 ... 101 F5
allmark Trading Estate WBLY HA9 ... 80 E2
all Place & Gardens BXLY DA5 ... 169 K1
he Hall Pre-Preparatory School NTHWD HA6 ... 40 B2
alls Business Centre HYS/HAR UB3 ... 113 K3
he Hall School HAMP NW3 ... 83 H4
all School Wimbledon RYNPK SW20 ... 177 G4
all School Wimbledon Junior Department PUT/ROE SW15 ... 158 D5
allsville Primary School CAN/RD E16 ... 106 E5
lstow Primary School GNWCH SE10 ... 125 J5
mbledon Clinic CMBW SE5 ... 142 E4
mbrough Primary School STHL UB1 ... 114 D1
mer Indoor Market BOW E3 ... 105 H1
m Health Clinic RCHPK/HAM TW10 ... 156 D5
m House & Garden (NT) RCHPK/HAM TW10 ... 156 D3
milton Road Industrial Estate WNWD SE27 ... 162 E6
n Lands Nature Reserve RCHPK/HAM TW10 ... 156 C6
mlet International ndustrial Estate ERITH DA8 ... 130 A5
nmersmith ⊖ HMSMTH W6 ... 119 F4
nmersmith Apollo HMSMTH W6 ... 119 F5
nmersmith Cemetery HMSMTH W6 ... 119 G5
nmersmith Hospital HB W12 ... 99 J5
nmersmith ndustrial Estate MSMTH W6 ... 119 F6
nmersmith New Cemetery CH/KEW TW9 ... 137 J3
nmersmith Physio & ports Injury Clinic MSMTH W6 ... 119 F4
nmersmith & West ondon College KENS W14 ... 119 H4
pden Gurney School BLAR W1H ... 8 D3
Ham & Petersham CC RCHPK/HAM TW10 ... 156 E6
The Hampshire School SKENS SW7 ... 14 C3
Hampstead ⊖ HAMP NW3 ... 83 G2
Hampstead Cemetery CRICK NW2 ... 82 D2
Hampstead College of Fine Art & Humanities HAMP NW3 ... 83 J4
Hampstead CC KIL/WHAMP NW6 ... 83 F4
Hampstead Golf Club GLDGN NW11 ... 65 G4
Hampstead Heath ⊖ HAMP NW3 ... 83 J2
Hampstead Medical Centre HAMP NW3 ... 83 G2
Hampstead Parochial CE School HAMP NW3 ... 83 G2
Hampstead School CRICK NW2 ... 82 C2
The Hampstead School of Art HAMP NW3 ... 82 E2
Hampstead School of English KIL/WHAMP NW6 ... 82 E2
Hampstead Theatre HAMP NW3 ... 83 H5
Hampton ⇌ HPTN TW12 ... 173 F4
Hampton Cemetery HPTN TW12 ... 173 F3
Hampton Community College HPTN TW12 ... 173 F1
Hampton Court ⇌ E/WMO/HCT KT8 ... 189 K1
Hampton Court House School E/WMO/HCT KT8 ... 173 K5
Hampton Court Palace E/WMO/HCT KT8 ... 174 A6
Hampton Court Palace Golf Club SURB KT6 ... 190 D2
Hampton Farm Industrial Estate FELT TW13 ... 154 D5
Hampton FC HPTN TW12 ... 173 G4
Hampton Hill Junior School HPTN TW12 ... 173 H1
Hampton Infant School HPTN TW12 ... 172 E3
Hampton Junior School HPTN TW12 ... 173 F4
The Hampton Medical Centre HPTN TW12 ... 173 F3
Hampton Open Air Pool HPTN TW12 ... 173 H3
Hampton Road Industrial Park CROY/NA CR0 ... 196 D3
Hampton School HPTN TW12 ... 173 F1
Hampton Wick ⇌ KUT/HW KT1 ... 174 E4
Hampton Wick Infants School TEDD TW11 ... 174 D3
Handel's House MYFR/PKLN W1K ... 9 J5
Handsworth Health Clinic CHING E4 ... 52 B2
Hanger Lane ⊖ EA W5 ... 98 B2
Hanover Primary School IS N1 ... 6 B2
Hanover Trading Estate HOLWY N7 ... 84 E3
Hanover West Industrial Estate WLSDN NW10 ... 98 E2
Hanwell ⇌ HNWL W7 ... 96 E6
Hanworth Trading Estate FELT TW13 ... 154 D5
Harbinger Primary School POP/IOD E14 ... 124 D4
Harborough School ARCH N19 ... 66 D6
Harefield Manor Hotel ROM RM1 ... 75 H1
Harenc School SCUP DA14 ... 186 D1
Hargrave Park Primary School ARCH N19 ... 66 C6
Haringey Arts Council ED N9 ... 36 C4
Haringey Community Health Clinic SEVS/STOTM N15 ... 68 B1
Haringey Sixth Form Centre TOTM N17 ... 50 B3
Harlequins RFC & Harlequins RL (The Stoop) WHTN TW2 ... 155 K2
Harlesden ⊖ ⊖ WLSDN NW10 ... 99 F1
Harlesden Primary School WLSDN NW10 ... 99 G1
Harley Medical Centre CAVSQ/HST W1G ... 9 K3
The Harley Medical Centre CANST EC4R ... 12 D5
Harley Street Clinic CAVSQ/HST W1G ... 9 J2
The Harley Street Clinic CAVSQ/HST W1G ... 9 J1
Harlington Community School HYS/HAR UB3 ... 113 G4
Harlyn Primary School PIN HA5 ... 41 F6
The Harold Macmillan Medical Centre HRW HA1 ... 60 D4
Harp Business Centre CRICK NW2 ... 63 J6
Harringay ⇌ FSBYPK N4 ... 67 G3
Harringay Green Lanes ⊖ FSBYPK N4 ... 67 H3
Harrington Hill Primary School CLPT E5 ... 68 D5
Harrington Road ⊖ SNWD SE25 ... 181 K6
Harris Academy Bermondsey STHWK SE1 ... 19 K6
Harris Academy Falconwood WELL DA16 ... 147 J5
Harris Academy Merton School STRHM/NOR SW16 ... 179 J6
Harris Academy South Norwood SNWD SE25 ... 181 G6
Harris City Academy Crystal Palace NRWD SE19 ... 181 G4
Harris Girls Academy EDUL SE22 ... 143 K6
Harrodian School BARN SW13 ... 138 C1
Harrods Store CHEL SW3 ... 14 E4
Harrovian Business Village HRW HA1 ... 60 D4
Harrow Arts Centre PIN HA5 ... 42 A3
Harrow Borough FC RYLN/HDSTN HA2 ... 78 A2
Harrow Cemetery HRW HA1 ... 60 D3
Harrow College HRW HA1 ... 60 E4
KTN/HRWW/WS HA3 ... 42 E2
Harrow CC HRW HA1 ... 78 E2
Harrow Driving Cycling & Road Safety Centre KTN/HRWW/WS HA3 ... 43 G6
Harrow Heritage Museum RYLN/HDSTN HA2 ... 42 C6
Harrow High School HRW HA1 ... 61 G3
Harrow Leisure Centre KTN/HRWW/WS HA3 ... 43 F6
Harrow-on-the-Hill ⇌ ⊖ HRW HA1 ... 60 E3
Harrow RFC STAN HA7 ... 29 H5
Harrow Road Health Centre BAY/PAD W2 ... 100 E4
Harrow School RYLN/HDSTN HA2 ... 60 E6
Harrow Town CC RYLN/HDSTN HA2 ... 60 A5
Harrow Weald Cemetery KTN/HRWW/WS HA3 ... 42 E2
Harrow & Wealdstone ⇌ ⊖ ⊖ HRW HA1 ... 60 E1
Harry Gosling Primary School WCHPL E1 ... 104 C5
Hartley Primary School EHAM E6 ... 89 J6
Hartsbourne Primary School BUSH WD23 ... 28 D4
Harvington School EA W5 ... 97 J5
Haseltine Primary School SYD SE26 ... 164 C6
Haslemere Business Centre EN EN1 ... 24 D5
Haslemere Industrial Estate EBED/NFELT TW14 ... 133 K6
WAND/EARL SW18 ... 160 A4
Haslemere Primary School MTCM CR4 ... 178 C5
Hasmonean High School Boys Site HDN NW4 ... 46 B5
Hasmonean High School Girls Site MLHL NW7 ... 45 J4
Hasmonean Primary School HDN NW4 ... 64 B2
Haste Hill Golf Club NTHWD HA6 ... 40 C5
Hastings Clinic BRXS/STRHM SW2 ... 142 A6
Hastingwood Trading Estate UED N18 ... 51 G2
Hatcham Mews Business Centre NWCR SE14 ... 144 A1
Hatch End ⊖ PIN HA5 ... 42 A3
Hatch End High School KTN/HRWW/WS HA3 ... 42 B3
Hatch End Swimming Pool PIN HA5 ... 42 A3
Hatfield Primary School MRDN SM4 ... 193 H3
Hatton Cross ⊖ HTHAIR TW6 ... 133 J5
Hatton School WFD IG8 ... 53 H6
Havelock Primary School NWDGN UB2 ... 114 E3
Haven Green Clinic EA W5 ... 97 K5
Havering College of Further & Higher Education EMPK RM11 ... 75 K4
Haverstock School HAMP NW3 ... 84 A4
Hawes Down Clinic WWKM BR4 ... 199 G6
Hawes Down Primary School WWKM BR4 ... 199 G5
The Hawker Centre KUTN/CMB KT2 ... 174 E1
Hawkesdown House School KENS W8 ... 119 K1
Hawkins Clinic PUT/ROE SW15 ... 139 G5
RYNPK SW20 ... 176 C4
Hawksmoor Primary School THMD SE28 ... 109 H6
Hawley Infant School CAMTN NW1 ... 84 B5
Haydon School PIN HA5 ... 40 E6
Haydons Road ⇌ WIM/MER SW19 ... 178 B1
Hayes ⇌ HAYES BR2 ... 199 J5
Hayes Bridge Middle School STHL UB1 ... 114 D2
Hayes Bridge Retail Park YEAD UB4 ... 95 G6
Hayes CC HYS/HAR UB3 ... 94 D5
Hayes FC HYS/HAR UB3 ... 94 D6
Hayes Grove Priory Hospital HAYES BR2 ... 199 K6
Hayes & Harlington ⇌ HYS/HAR UB3 ... 113 J3
The Hayes Manor School HYS/HAR UB3 ... 94 B5
Hayes Park J & I School YEAD UB4 ... 94 D3
Hayes Pool HYS/HAR UB3 ... 113 J1
Hayes Primary School HAYES BR2 ... 200 A5
Hayes School HAYES BR2 ... 200 A6
Hayes Social & Sports Club HYS/HAR UB3 ... 94 D6
Hayes Stadium Sports Centre HYS/HAR UB3 ... 94 B5
Hay Lane School CDALE/KGS NW9 ... 62 E1
Haymerle School PECK SE15 ... 123 H6
Hays Galleria STHWK SE1 ... 13 G7
Hayward Gallery STHWK SE1 ... 17 H1
Hazelbury Junior School ED N9 ... 36 A5
Hazeldene Medical Centre WBLY HA9 ... 80 D4
Hazelwood Infant School PLMGR N13 ... 35 H6
Hazelwood Junior School PLMGR N13 ... 35 G6
Headstart Montessori School TOOT SW17 ... 160 B5
Headstone Lane ⊖ RYLN/HDSTN HA2 ... 42 B4
Health & Vitality Osteopathic Clinic HOR/WEW KT19 ... 207 F3
The Heart Hospital CAVSQ/HST W1G ... 9 H2
The Heart of Greenwich development GNWCH SE10 ... 125 J5
Heathbrook Primary School VX/NE SW8 ... 141 H3
Heath Business Centre HSLW TW3 ... 135 H5
Heathcote School CHING E4 ... 38 C4
Heathfield College HAYES BR2 ... 215 G4
Heathfield House School CHSWK W4 ... 117 K5
Heathfield Primary School WHTN TW2 ... 155 F3
Heathfield School PIN HA5 ... 59 H4
Heath House Preparatory School BKHTH/KID SE3 ... 145 J3
The Heathland School HSLWW TW4 ... 154 E1
Heathmere Primary School PUT/ROE SW15 ... 158 D3
Heathrow Airport Central Bus & Coach Station HTHAIR TW6 ... 132 D4
Heathrow Airport Terminal 4 HTHAIR TW6 ... 132 E6
Heathrow Airport (Terminals 1 & 3) HTHAIR TW6 ... 132 E3
Heathrow Air Traffic Control Tower HTHAIR TW6 ... 132 E4
Heathrow International Trading Estate HSLWW TW4 ... 134 A4
Heathrow Medical Centre HYS/HAR UB3 ... 113 G5
Heathrow Primary School WDR/YW UB7 ... 112 C6
Heathrow Terminal 4 ⇌ ⊖ HTHAIR TW6 ... 153 F1
Heathrow Terminals 1 & 3 ⇌ ⊖ HTHAIR TW6 ... 132 E4
Heathrow Viewing Area HTHAIR TW6 ... 132 E4
Heathrow World Cargo Centre HTHAIR TW6 ... 132 C6
Heathside Preparatory School HAMP NW3 ... 83 G2
Heathside Preparatory School (Lower) HAMP NW3 ... 83 G2
Heathside Preparatory School (Upper) HAMP NW3 ... 83 G2
Heathway Industrial Estate DAGE RM10 ... 92 D2
Heathway Medical Centre DAGW RM9 ... 92 B2
Heavers Farm Primary School SNWD SE25 ... 197 G2
Heber Primary School EDUL SE22 ... 163 G1
Heckford Street Business Centre WAP E1W ... 105 F6
Hedges & Butler Estate SRTFD E15 ... 106 A1
Hedgewood School YEAD UB4 ... 94 C2
Helena Road Clinic WLSDN NW10 ... 81 K2
Heliport Industrial Estate BTSEA SW11 ... 140 C3
Helston Court Business Centre WIM/MER SW19 ... 176 E1
Henderson Hospital BELMT SM2 ... 208 E6
Hendon ⇌ HDN NW4 ... 63 J3
Hendon Cemetery MLHL NW7 ... 46 B4
Hendon Central ⊖ HDN NW4 ... 63 K2
Hendon Crematorium MLHL NW7 ... 46 B3
Hendon FC CRICK NW2 ... 64 B6
Hendon Golf Club MLHL NW7 ... 46 A3
Hendon Hall Hotel HDN NW4 ... 46 A6
Hendon Preparatory School HDN NW4 ... 46 B6
Hendon School HDN NW4 ... 64 B2
Hendon Secretarial College HDN NW4 ... 63 K2
Hendon Youth Sports Centre CRICK NW2 ... 64 B4
Henrietta Barnett School GLDGN NW11 ... 65 F2
Henry Cavendish Primary School BAL SW12 ... 161 H3
Henry Compton School FUL/PGN SW6 ... 139 G2
Henry Fawcett Primary School LBTH SE11 ... 122 B6
Henry Green Primary School BCTR RM8 ... 73 K5
Henry Maynard J & I School WALTH E17 ... 70 A2
Henwick Primary School ELTH/MOT SE9 ... 146 C4
Herbert Morrison Primary School VX/NE SW8 ... 141 K1
Hereward House School HAMP NW3 ... 83 J4
Her Majestys' Theatre STJS SW1Y ... 10 D7
Hermitage Primary School WAP E1W ... 123 H1
Herne Hill ⇌ HNHL SE24 ... 142 C6
Herne Hill School HNHL SE24 ... 142 D6
Herne Hill Stadium (Cycle Centre) HNHL SE24 ... 162 E1
Heron Industrial Estate SRTFD E15 ... 105 K1
Heron Quays ⊖ POP/IOD E14 ... 124 D1
Heronsgate Primary School THMD SE28 ... 127 J3
Heron Trading Estate ACT W3 ... 98 D4
Hersham Trading Estate WOT/HER KT12 ... 188 D6
Heston Community School HEST TW5 ... 135 F1
Heston Community Sports Hall HEST TW5 ... 135 F1
Heston Industrial Mall HEST TW5 ... 134 E1
Heston Infant School HEST TW5 ... 135 F1
Heston Junior School HEST TW5 ... 135 F1
Heston Park CC HEST TW5 ... 114 E6
Heston Swimming Baths HEST TW5 ... 114 E6
Higgs Industrial Estate HNHL SE24 ... 142 C4
Highams Lodge Business Centre WALTH E17 ... 51 F6
Highams Park ⇌ CHING E4 ... 52 A2
Highams Park Primary School CHING E4 ... 52 B2
High Barnet ⊖ BAR EN5 ... 20 E5
Highbury Fields School HBRY N5 ... 85 H2
Highbury Grove School HBRY N5 ... 85 J3
Highbury & Islington ⇌ ⊖ ⊖ IS N1 ... 85 G4
Highbury Park Clinic HBRY N5 ... 85 H1
Highbury Pool HBRY N5 ... 85 H4
Highbury Quadrant Primary School HBRY N5 ... 85 J2
Highbury Square Development HBRY N5 ... 85 H1
High Commission of Angola MHST W1U ... 9 F2
High Commission of Antigua & Barbuda MHST W1U ... 9 G3
High Commission of Bahamas MYFR/PICC W1J ... 9 H7

High Commission of Bangladesh
SKENS SW7 120 B3
High Commission of Barbados
FITZ W1T 10 C3
High Commission of Belize
CAVSQ/HST W1G 9 K3
High Commission of Botswana
OXSTW W1C 9 J4
High Commission of Brunei
KTBR SW1X 15 G4
High Commission of Canada
MYFR/PKLN W1K 9 H5
High Commission of Cyprus
MYFR/PKLN W1K 9 G5
High Commission of Dominica
ECT SW5 120 A4
High Commission of Fiji
SKENS SW7 120 B2
High Commission of Grenada
ECT SW5 120 A5
High Commission of Guyana
BAY/PAD W2 101 F6
High Commission of Jamaica
SKENS SW7 14 A3
High Commission of Kenya
CAVSQ/HST W1G 9 J1
High Commission of Lesotho
KTBR SW1X 15 G4
High Commission of Malawi
MYFR/PKLN W1K 9 J5
High Commission of Malaysia
KTBR SW1X 15 H3
High Commission of Maldives
MHST W1U 9 G1
High Commission of Malta
CONDST W1S 10 B6
High Commission of Namibia
CAVSQ/HST W1G 9 K2
High Commission of New Zealand
STJS SW1Y 10 C7
High Commission of Nigeria
CHCR WC2N 10 E7
EMB EC4Y 11 K4
High Commission of Pakistan
KTBR SW1X 15 F4
High Commission of Papua New Guinea
STJS SW1Y 10 B7
High Commission of St Lucia
KENS W8 120 A2
High Commission of Seychelles
MHST W1U 9 F1
High Commission of Sierra Leone
REGST W1B 10 A3
High Commission of Singapore
KTBR SW1X 15 F3
High Commission of South Africa
CHCR WC2N 10 E7
High Commission of Sri Lanka
BAY/PAD W2 8 B5
High Commission of Swaziland
WESTW SW1E 16 A4
High Commission of the Gambia
KENS W8 120 A2
High Commission of Tonga
MBLAR W1H 8 D2
High Commission of Trinidad & Tobago
KTBR SW1X 15 G4
High Commission of Uganda
CHCR WC2N 10 D7
High Commission of Zambia
SKENS SW7 120 B2
High Commission of Zimbabwe
CHCR WC2N 10 E6
High Cross Centre
SEVS/STOTM N15 68 C1
High Elms Country Park
ORP BR6 216 C5
High Elms Golf Club
ORP BR6 216 C5
Highfield Infant School
HAYES BR2 199 J1
Highfield Junior School
HAYES BR2 199 H1
Highfield Primary School
WCHMH N21 35 H3
Highfield School
WAND/EARL SW18 160 D2
Highgate ⊖
HGT N6 66 B3
Highgate Cemetery
HGT N6 66 A5
Highgate Golf Club
EFNCH N2 65 J3
Highgate Junior School
HGT N6 65 K4
Highgate Private Hospital
HGT N6 65 K3
Highgate School
HGT N6 65 K4
Highgate Wood School
MUSWH N10 66 C2
Highgrove Pool
RSLP HA4 58 E4
Highlands J & I School
IL IG1 71 K5
Highlands Primary School
IL IG1 71 J5
Highshore School
PECK SE15 143 G2
High Street Kensington ⊖
KENS W8 120 A3
High View Primary School
BTSEA SW11 140 C5
Highview Primary School
WLGTN SM6 210 E3
The Highway Primary School
ORP BR6 217 J3
The Highway Trading Centre
WAP E1W 105 F6
Hillbrook Primary School
TOOT SW17 160 E6
Hill Crest London School
CROY/NA CR0 197 G5
Hillcross Primary School
MRDN SM4 193 J1
Hill House International Junior School
KTBR SW1X 15 F5
Hill House Preparatory School
CHEL SW3 120 D6
Hill House School
KTBR SW1X 14 E5
Hill Mead Infant School
BRXN/ST SW9 142 C5
Hillmead Primary School
BRXN/ST SW9 142 C5
Hills Grove Primary School
WELL DA16 148 D1
Hillside Infant School
NTHWD HA6 40 E3
Hillside Primary School
STMC/STPC BR5 202 D4
Hillyfield Primary School
WALTH E17 51 G6
Hilly Fields Medical Centre
BROCKY SE4 144 D6
Hilton Docklands Pier
BERM/RHTH SE16 124 C1
The Hiltongrove Business Centre
WALTH E17 69 J1
Hinchley Wood ≠
ESH/CLAY KT10 205 F1
Hinchley Wood Primary School
ESH/CLAY KT10 190 B6
Hinchley Wood School & Sixth Form Centre
ESH/CLAY KT10 190 B6
Hinley Clinic
LBTH SE11 17 K7
Hispaniola
WHALL SW1A 17 F1
Hitherfield Primary School
STRHM/NOR SW16 162 B4
Hither Green ≠
LEW SE13 165 H1
Hither Green Cemetery
CAT SE6 165 J4
Hither Green Primary School
LEW SE13 165 G1
HM Customs & Excise
HTHAIR TW6 132 E2
HM Prison
BRXS/STRHM SW2 161 K1
HOLWY N7 84 E2
SHB W12 99 J5
THMD SE28 127 K3
WAND/EARL SW18 160 C2
HMS Belfast
STHWK SE1 13 H7
HMS President
EMB EC4Y 11 K5
HM Young Offenders Institution
FELT TW13 153 G5
Hobbayne First & Middle School
HNWL W7 97 F5
Hobbayne Primary School
HNWL W7 96 E5
Hogarth Business Park
CHSWK W4 118 B6
Hogarth Industrial Estate
WLSDN NW10 99 J3
Hogarth's House
CHSWK W4 118 A6
Holbeach Primary School
CAT SE6 164 D2
Holborn ⊖
HHOL WC1V 11 F3
Holborn College
WOOL/PLUM SE18 126 C4
Holborn College Independent School
HMSMTH W6 119 F5
Holborn Medical Centre
BMSBY WC1N 5 G7
Holborn Town Hall
HHOL WC1V 11 F3
Holiday Inn
BTFD TW8 136 D1
BXLY DA5 169 J1
CAMTN NW1 84 B5
CHSGTN KT9 205 J6
FSBYW WC1X 5 H5
HYS/HAR UB3 133 G2
SUT SM1 209 F3
WDR/YW UB7 132 D2
Holland House
WKENS W14 119 J2
Holland House School
EDGW HA8 30 C6
Holland Park ⊖
NTGHL W11 119 J1
Holland Park Pre-Preparatory School
WKENS W14 119 J3
Holland Park School
KENS W8 119 J2
Holland Park Theatre
WKENS W14 119 J2
Holland Street Clinic
KENS W8 119 K2
Hollickwood JMI School
MUSWH N10 48 B3
Holloway Road ⊖
HOLWY N7 85 F3
Holloway School
HOLWY N7 84 D3
Hollydale Primary School
PECK SE15 143 K3
The Hollyfield School
SURB KT6 191 F2
Holly House Private Hospital
BKHH IG9 39 F4
Hollymount Primary School
RYNPK SW20 177 F4
Holly Park JMI School
FBAR/BDGN N11 48 A1
Hollywood Bowl
BERM/RHTH SE16 124 A3
The Holme
CAMTN NW1 3 F5
Holmleigh Primary School
STNW/STAM N16 68 B5
Holocaust Memorial Garden
KTBR SW1X 15 F2
The Holy Cross Catholic Girls School
NWMAL KT3 192 A1
Holy Cross Preparatory School
KUTN/CMB KT2 175 K3
Holy Cross RC Primary School
CAT SE6 165 F3
Holy Family RC Primary School
BKHTH/KID SE3 146 A5
POP/IOD E14 105 J6
Holy Family Technology College
WALTH E17 69 K1
Holy Ghost RC Primary School
BAL SW12 160 E2
Holy Innocents Catholic Primary School
ORP BR6 217 F1
Holy Trinity CE Junior School
WLGTN SM6 210 C2
Holy Trinity CE Primary School
BRXS/STRHM SW2 162 A2
DART DA1 151 F6
EFNCH N2 47 H6
KIL/WHAMP NW6 83 G4
KTBR SW1X 15 G6
NTHWD HA6 40 A2
RCHPK/HAM TW10 137 H5
SYD SE26 163 K4
Holy Trinity College
BMLY BR1 184 B4
Holy Trinity in St Silas
CAMTN NW1 84 B5
Holy Trinity Lamorbey CE Primary School
BFN/LL DA15 168 B3
Holy Trinity Primary School
HACK E8 86 B4
WIM/MER SW19 177 K2
Holy Trinity School
CHEL SW3 15 F6
Holywell School
WATW WD18 26 D1
Homefield Preparatory School
SUT SM1 208 E3
Home Office
WEST SW1P 16 D5
Homerton ⊖
HOM E9 87 F4
Homerton University Hospital
HOM E9 87 F3
Homoeopathic Health Centre
PLSTW E13 106 E3
The Homoeopathic Health Centre
MLHL NW7 45 H1
Honeypot Business Centre
STAN HA7 44 A4
Honeypot Lane Centre
STAN HA7 43 K4
Honeypot Medical Centre
STAN HA7 44 A5
Honeywell Primary School
BTSEA SW11 160 E1
Honor Oak Crematorium
FSTH SE23 144 A6
Honor Oak Gallery
FSTH SE23 164 A1
Honor Oak Health Centre
BROCKY SE4 144 B5
Honor Oak Park ≠ ⊖
FSTH SE23 164 A1
Honourable Artillery Company
STLK EC1Y 6 E7
Hook Lane Primary School
WELL DA16 148 B4
Hook Rise South Industrial Park
CHSGTN KT9 206 B1
Hopewell School
BARK IG11 90 D4
Horizon Business Centre
ED N9 37 F4
Horizon Industrial Estate
PECK SE15 123 H6
Horizon School
STNW/STAM N16 86 A2
The Horniman Museum & Gardens
FSTH SE23 163 J3
Horniman Primary School
FSTH SE23 163 J3
Horn Park Primary School
LEE/GVPK SE12 166 A2
Hornsby House School
BAL SW12 161 F3
Hornsey ≠
CEND/HSY/T N8 67 F1
Hornsey Central Hospital
CEND/HSY/T N8 66 C2
Hornsey Rise Health Centre
ARCH N19 66 D4
Hornsey Secondary School for Girls
CEND/HSY/T N8 67 F2
Horn Stairs
BERM/RHTH SE16 124 C1
Horse Guards Parade
WHALL SW1A 16 D1
Horsenden Hill Golf Club
GFD/PVL UB6 79 H4
Horsenden Primary School
GFD/PVL UB6 78 E4
Horton Country Park
HOR/WEW KT19 206 C6
Horton Industrial Park
WDR/YW UB7 112 C1
Horton Park Golf & Country Club
HOR/WEW KT19 206 E5
Hortus Cemetery
NWDGN UB2 114 E2
Hospital of St John & St Elizabeth
STJWD NW8 2 A3
The Hotel Russell
RSQ WC1B 4 E7
Hotham Primary School
PUT/ROE SW15 139 G5
Hotspur Industrial Estate
TOTM N17 50 D2
Houndsfield Primary School
ED N9 36 C2
Hounslow ≠
HSLW TW3 135 H5
Hounslow Business Park
HSLW TW3 135 F5
Hounslow CC
HSLW TW3 134 E3
Hounslow Cemetery
HSLWW TW4 154 E2
Hounslow Central ⊖
HSLW TW3 135 G3
Hounslow East ⊖
HSLW TW3 135 H3
Hounslow Heath Golf Club
HSLWW TW4 134 C6
Hounslow Heath Infant School
HSLWW TW4 134 D4
Hounslow Heath Junior School
HSLWW TW4 134 D4
Hounslow Manor School
HSLW TW3 135 G4
Hounslow Manor Sports Hall
HSLW TW3 135 G4
Hounslow Town Primary School
HSLW TW3 135 H4
Hounslow West ⊖
HSLWW TW4 134 D3
House of Detention
CLKNW EC1R 5 K6
House of St Barnabus
SOHO/SHAV W1D 10 C4
Houses of Parliament
WHALL SW1A 17 F3
Houston Business Park
YEAD UB4 114 B1
Howard Primary School
SAND/SEL CR2 211 J2
Howbury Centre
ERITH DA8 150 D1
Howland Quay
BERM/RHTH SE16 124 A3
Hoxton ⊖
BETH E2 7 J3
Hoxton Hall Community Theatre
IS N1 7 G2
HQS Wellington (Master Mariners)
TPL/STR WC2R 11 J6
HSBC Sports Club
BECK BR3 182 B2
HSBC Tower
POP/IOD E14 124 E1
Hubbinet Industrial Estate
ROMW/RG RM7 56 E6
Hugh Myddelton Primary School
CLKNW EC1R 5 K5
The Humana Wellington Hospital
STJWD NW8 2 B4
Humber Trading Estate
CRICK NW2 63 K6
Hunterian Museum
LINN WC2A 11 H3
Hunters Hall Primary School
DAGE RM10 92 D3
Hunter Street Health Centre
STPAN WC1H 4 E6
Huntsman Sports Club
BKHTH/KID SE3 145 K5
Hurlingham Business Park
FUL/PGN SW6 139 K4
Hurlingham House
FUL/PGN SW6 139 K4
Hurlingham Private School
PUT/ROE SW15 139 J5
Huron University
RSQ WC1B 10 E1
Hurricane Trading Centre
CDALE/KGS NW9 45 H4
Hurstmere School
BFN/LL DA15 168 C3
Hurst Park Primary School
E/WMO/HCT KT8 173 F6
Hurst Primary School
BXLY DA5 168 E3
Hyatt Carlton Tower Hotel
KTBR SW1X 15 F5
Hyatt Regency, The Churchill
MBLAR W1H 9 F3
The Hyde Industrial Estate
CDALE/KGS NW9 63 H2
Hyde Park Corner ⊖
KTBR SW1X 15 G2
The Hyde School
CDALE/KGS NW9 63 H2
Hyland House School
WALTH E17 52 B5
Hyleford Leavers Unit School
BARK/HLT IG6 54 D5
Hythe Road Industrial Estate
WLSDN NW10 99 J3
Ian Mikardo High School
BOW E3 105 K2
Ibis Hotel
CAMTN NW1 4 B5
CAN/RD E16 107 F6
FUL/PGN SW6 119 K6
GNWCH SE10 125 F6
HYS/HAR UB3 133 H2
POP/IOD E14 106 A6
SRTFD E15 88 C4
WBLY HA9 80 C3
Ibstock Place School
PUT/ROE SW15 158 B1
ICA Cinema
STJS SW1Y 10 D7
Ickburgh School
CLPT E5 86 D1
Ickenham ⊖
HGDN/ICK UB10 76 A2
Ickenham Clinic
HGDN/ICK UB10 76 A1
Ihlara Sport FC
HBRY N5 85 J2
Ilderton Primary School
PECK SE15 123 K6
Ilford ≠
IL IG1 90 A1
Ilford County High School
BARK/HLT IG6 54 C5
Ilford Golf Club
IL IG1 71 K5
Ilford Jewish Primary School
BARK/HLT IG6 54 D6
Ilford Medical Centre
IL IG1 90 B1
Ilford Preparatory School
GDMY/SEVK IG3 73 F5
Ilford Retail Park
IL IG1 72 C6
Ilford Swimming Pool
IL IG1 72 D6
Ilford Ursuline High School
IL IG1 72 B6
Ilford Ursuline Preparatory School
IL IG1 72 B6
Iman Zakaria Academy
FSTGT E7 89 F3
Imber Court Trading Estate
E/WMO/HCT KT8 189 J3
Immanuel CE Primary School
STRHM/NOR SW16 179 K2
Immanuel College
BUSH WD23 28 E2
Immanuel School
ROM RM1 57 G2
Imperial College
PUT/ROE SW15 139 G3
SKENS SW7 14 A4
SKENS SW7 120 C5
Imperial College Athletic Ground
HYS/HAR UB3 113 F6
Imperial College of London
SKENS SW7 14 A3
Imperial College of Science
FUL/PGN SW6 119 K6
Imperial College of Science & Technology
SKENS SW7 14 B3
Imperial College School of Medicine
PIM SW1V 16 C7
Imperial War Museum
STHWK SE1 17 K5
Imperial War Museum Annexe
LBTH SE11 17 K5
Imperial Wharf ≠ ⊖
FUL/PGN SW6 140 B2
Inchbald School of Design
BGVA SW1W 15 H
PIM SW1V 16 A
Independent Industrial Estate
WDR/YW UB7 112 C
Independent Jewish School
HDN NW4 64 B
India House
HOL/ALD WC2B 11 G
Innellan House School
PIN HA5 41 J
Innholders Hall
CANST EC4R 12 E
Innkeeper's Lodge
BECK BR3 198 D
CHEAM SM3 193 K
NTHLT UB5 78 A
SAND/SEL CR2 211 J
STHGT/OAK N14 34 E
WAN E11 70 E
WFD IG8 53 K
Inns of Court & Chancery
TPL/STR WC2R 11
Inns of Court Law School
GINN WC1R 11 H
Institute of Education University of London
RSQ WC1B 4
Instituto Espanol Canada Blanch
NKENS W10 100
Intercontinental Hotel
MYFR/PICC W1J 15
International Community School
CAMTN NW1 3
International School of Business Studies (ISBS)
PIN HA5 60
International School of London
ACT W3 117
International Trading Estate
NWDGN UB2 114
Invicta Industrial Estate
SRTFD E15 106
Invicta Primary School
BKHTH/KID SE3 125
Invicta Sports Club
DART DA1 151
Inwood Business Centre
HSLW TW3 135
IQRA Independent School
BRXN/ST SW9 142
Ironmonger Row Baths
FSBYE EC1V 6

Ironmongers Hall
STBT EC1A 12 C2
Islamia Girls School
KIL/WHAMP NW6 82 C6
Islamic College for Advanced Studies
WLSDN NW10 81 K5
The Islamic Grammar School
WAND/EARL SW18 159 J2
Islamic Shaksiyah Foundation School
WALTH E17 69 G2
Island Clinic
POP/IOD E14 125 F2
Island Gardens
POP/IOD E14 125 F4
Isleworth
ISLW TW7 136 A3
Isleworth Cemetery
ISLW TW7 136 B3
Isleworth Recreation Centre
ISLW TW7 136 A5
Isleworth & Syon School for Boys
ISLW TW7 135 K1
Isleworth Town Primary School
ISLW TW7 136 A3
Islington Arts & Media School
FSBYPK N4 67 F5
Islington Business Centre
IS N1 85 J6
Islington Crematorium
MUSWH N10 47 K4
Islington Green Medical Centre
IS N1 85 H6
Islington Tennis Centre
HOLWY N7 84 E4
Islington Town Hall
IS N1 85 H5
Ismaili Centre
SKENS SW7 14 B6
Italia Conti Academy of Theatre Art
FARR EC1M 6 C7
Italia Conti Academy of Theatre Arts
BRXN/ST SW9 141 K4
Italian Hospital
PIM SW1V 16 A6
Ithaca College
SKENS SW7 120 B4
Ivybridge Primary School
TWK TW1 156 A1
Ivybridge Retail Park
ISLW TW7 136 A6
Ivydale Primary School
PECK SE15 144 A5
Jack & Jill School
HPTN TW12 173 F2
WHTN TW2 155 K4
Jack Taylor School
STJWD NW8 83 G6
Jack Tizard School
FUL/PGN SW6 139 G2
SHB W12 100 A6
Jacques Prevert School
HMSMTH W6 119 G4
Jamahiriya School
CHEL SW3 120 D6
James Allens Preparatory Girls School
HNHL SE24 142 E6
James Dixon Primary School
PGE/AN SE20 181 H4
Jamestown Mental Health Centre
HAMP NW3 83 K5
James Wolfe Primary School
GNWCH SE10 144 E1
Jamiatul Ummah School
WCHPL E1 104 D5
Janet Adegoke Leisure Centre
SHB W12 99 J6
The Japanese School
ACT W3 98 C6
Japan Green Medical Centre
ACT W3 117 J1
Jenner Health Centre
FSTH SE23 164 B3
Jenny Hammond Primary School
WAN E11 88 C2
Jermyn Street Theatre
MYFR/PICC W1J 10 B6
Jessop Primary School
HNHL SE24 142 C5
Jewel Tower
WEST SW1P 16 E4
Jewish Cemetery
GLDGN NW11 64 E3
Jewish Community Theatre
HNHL SE24 142 E4
Jewish Free School
KTN/HRWW/WS HA3 62 C3
KTTN NW5 84 D4
The Jewish Museum
CAMTN NW1 3 J1
FNCH N3 47 F5
Johanna Primary School
STHWK SE1 17 J3
John Ball Primary School
BKHTH/KID SE3 145 H3
John Betts Primary School
HMSMTH W6 118 D3
John Bramston Primary School
BARK/HLT IG6 55 G2
John Burns Primary School
BTSEA SW11 141 F3
John Chilton School
NTHLT UB5 77 J5
John Dixon Clinic
BERM/RHTH SE16 123 J3
John Donne Primary School
PECK SE15 143 J2
John F Kennedy School
CAN/RD E16 107 H4
John F Kennedy Special School
SRTFD E15 88 C6
John Keble CE Primary School
WLSDN NW10 99 H1
John Kelly Girls Technology College
CRICK NW2 81 H1
The John Loughborough School
TOTM N17 50 B5
John Lyon School
RYLN/HDSTN HA2 60 D5
John Nightingale School
E/WMO/HCT KT8 172 E6
John Orwell Sports Centre
WAP E1W 123 H1
John Paul II RC School
WIM/MER SW19 159 G2
John Perryn Primary School
ACT W3 99 G5
John Perry Primary School
DAGE RM10 93 F4
John Roan Lower School
BKHTH/KID SE3 145 J1
John Roan School
BKHTH/KID SE3 145 H1
John Ruskin College
SAND/SEL CR2 213 G5
John Ruskin Primary School
WALW SE17 122 D6
John Scott Health Centre
FSBYPK N4 67 J5
John Scurr Primary School
WCHPL E1 104 E3
John Smith House
WALW SE17 18 C7
Johnsons Industrial Estate
HYS/HAR UB3 113 K3
John Stainer Primary School
BROCKY SE4 144 B4
The Jo Richardson Community School
DAGW RM9 91 K6
Joseph Clarke Special School
CHING E4 52 B2
Joseph Hood Primary School
RYNPK SW20 177 H5
Joseph Lancaster Primary School
STHWK SE1 18 D5
Joydens Wood Infant School
RDART DA2 170 B6
Joydens Wood Junior School
BXLY DA5 170 B6
Jubilee Country Park
BMLY BR1 201 G1
Jubilee Market
COVGDN WC2E 11 F5
Jubilee Primary School
BRXS/STRHM SW2 162 B1
THMD SE28 109 J6
Jubilee Sports Ground
CHING E4 38 B6
Julians Primary School
STRHM/NOR SW16 162 B6
Jumeirah Carlton Tower Hotel
KTBR SW1X 15 F4
Jumeirah Lowndes Hotel
KTBR SW1X 15 F4
Juno Way Industrial Estate
NWCR SE14 124 A6
Jurys Clifton-Ford Hotel
MHST W1U 9 H2
Jurys Great Russell Street
RSQ WC1B 10 D3
Jurys Inn
CROY/NA CR0 196 D6
Jurys Inn Chelsea
FUL/PGN SW6 140 B2
Jurys Inn Hotel
HTHAIR TW6 133 J4
Jurys Inn Islington
IS N1 5 J3
Jurys Kensington Hotel
SKENS SW7 14 A7
JVC Business Park
CRICK NW2 63 J5
Kaizen Primary School
PLSTW E13 107 F3
Kangley Business Centre
SYD SE26 182 C1
Katella Trading Estate
BARK IG11 108 E2
Katherine Road Medical Centre
FSTGT E7 89 G4
Keats House
HAMP NW3 83 H2
Keble Preparatory School
WCHMH N21 35 G2
Keen Students Supplementary School
WCHPL E1 104 C4
Keir Hardie Primary School
CAN/RD E16 106 E4
Keith Davis Cue Sports Club
DAGW RM9 91 K5
Kelmscott Community Centre
WALTH E17 69 H3
Kelmscott Leisure Centre
WALTH E17 69 H3
Kelmscott School
WALTH E17 69 H3
Kelsey Park Sports College
BECK BR3 182 D6
Kelvin Industrial Estate
GFD/PVL UB6 78 B6
Kemnal Technology College
STMC/STPC BR5 186 C3
Kempton Park
SUN TW16 172 A3
Kempton Park Racecourse
SUN TW16 172 A3
Ken Barrington Centre
LBTH SE11 122 A6
Kender Primary School
NWCR SE14 143 K2
Kenmont Primary School
WLSDN NW10 99 J2
Kenmore Park First School
KTN/HRWW/WS HA3 43 K6
Kenneth More Theatre
IL IG1 90 C1
Kennington
LBTH SE11 122 C5
Kensal Green
WLSDN NW10 100 A2
Kensal Green Cemetery
WLSDN NW10 99 K2
Kensal Rise
WLSDN NW10 100 A1
Kensal Rise Primary School
KIL/WHAMP NW6 100 B1
Kensington & Chelsea College
NKENS W10 100 C3
Kensington Avenue Primary School
THHTH CR7 180 B4
Kensington Business Centre
SKENS SW7 14 D4
Kensington & Chelsea College
NTGHL W11 119 J2
WBPTN SW10 140 B1
Kensington & Chelsea Town Hall
KENS W8 119 K2
The Kensington Dyslexia Teaching Centre
KENS W8 120 A3
Kensington Leisure Centre
NTGHL W11 100 B6
Kensington Market
KENS W8 120 A2
Kensington (Olympia)
WKENS W14 119 H3
Kensington Palace
KENS W8 120 A1
Kensington Park School
REGST W1B 9 K1
Kensington Preparatory School
FUL/PGN SW6 139 J2
Kensington Primary School
MNPK E12 89 K4
Kensington School of Business
HCIRC EC1N 11 K1
Kensington Wharf
WBPTN SW10 140 C1
Kensit Memorial College
FNCH N3 46 C5
Kent House
BECK BR3 182 B4
Kentish Town
KTTN NW5 84 C3
Kentish Town CE Primary School
KTTN NW5 84 C3
Kentish Town Health Centre
KTTN NW5 84 C4
Kentish Town Industrial Estate
KTTN NW5 84 B3
Kentish Town Sports Centre
KTTN NW5 84 A4
Kentish Town West
KTTN NW5 84 B4
Kenton
KTN/HRWW/WS HA3 61 H3
Kenton CC
KTN/HRWW/WS HA3 61 J1
Kenton Clinic
KTN/HRWW/WS HA3 62 A2
Kent Park Industrial Estate
PECK SE15 123 J6
Kenwood House
HAMP NW3 65 J5
The Kerem School
EFNCH N2 65 H2
Keston CE Primary School
HAYES BR2 215 H3
Kew Bridge
BTFD TW8 117 G5
Kew Bridge Steam Museum
BTFD TW8 117 G5
Kew College
RCH/KEW TW9 137 H1
Kew Gardens
RCH/KEW TW9 137 H2
Kew Palace
RCH/KEW TW9 137 F1
Kew Retail Park
RCH/KEW TW9 137 J2
Kew Riverside Primary School
RCH/KEW TW9 137 J3
Keyplan & Roxburghe College
FITZ W1T 4 B7
Keys Meadow Primary School
PEND EN3 25 J1
Keyworth Primary School
WALW SE17 122 C5
Khalsa College London
HRW HA1 61 F3
Kidbrooke
BKHTH/KID SE3 146 B4
Kidbrooke Park Primary School
BKHTH/KID SE3 146 B3
Kidbrooke School
BKHTH/KID SE3 146 C3
Kilburn
CRICK NW2 82 C4
Kilburn High Road
KIL/WHAMP NW6 83 F6
Kilburn Park
KIL/WHAMP NW6 100 E1
Kilburn Park Junior School
KIL/WHAMP NW6 100 D2
Killick Street Medical Centre
IS N1 5 G2
Kilmorie Primary School
FSTH SE23 164 B4
Kimberley Industrial Estate
WALTH E17 51 H3
Kimpton Industrial Estate
CHEAM SM3 193 J6
King Alfred School
GLDGN NW11 65 F5
King Athelstan Primary School
KUT/HW KT1 175 G6
Kingdom Hall of Jehovah's Witnesses
ORP BR6 202 A6
King Edwards Road Clinic
RSLP HA4 58 B5
King Edward VII Hospital for Officers
MHST W1U 9 H1
King Fahad Academy
ACT W3 99 G6
King Fahad Academy (Girls Upper School)
EA W5 116 D4
The Kingfisher Medical Centre
DEPT SE8 124 C6
The Kingfisher Sports Centre
KUT/HW KT1 175 F5
King George Hospital
GNTH/NBYPK IG2 73 G2
King George V
CAN/RD E16 127 F1
King George VI Youth Hostel
KENS W8 119 J2
Kingham Industrial Estate
WLSDN NW10 99 F2
King Henry VIII Mound
RCHPK/HAM TW10 157 G3
King Henry's Drive
CROY/NA CR0 213 K6
King & Queen Wharf
BERM/RHTH SE16 105 F6
Kings Avenue Medical Centre
STHL UB1 96 C5
Kings Avenue School
CLAP SW4 141 K6
Kingsbury
CDALE/KGS NW9 62 C2
Kingsbury Green Primary School
CDALE/KGS NW9 62 D2
Kingsbury High School
CDALE/KGS NW9 62 D1
Kingsbury Hospital
CDALE/KGS NW9 62 C1
Kingsbury Trading Estate
CDALE/KGS NW9 62 E3
Kings College (Hampstead Campus)
HAMP NW3 82 E2
King's College Hospital
CMBW SE5 142 D4
Kings College London
HOL/ALD WC2B 11 F4
KENS W8 119 K2
STHWK SE1 12 A7
WEST SW1P 16 B6
Kings College London - Humanities
TPL/STR WC2R 11 G5
Kings College London - Law
TPL/STR WC2R 11 H5
Kings College London (Waterloo Campus)
STHWK SE1 17 J1
Kings College School
WIM/MER SW19 177 F2
Kings College School of Medicine & Dentistry
CMBW SE5 142 E3
DUL SE21 162 E1
Kings College Sports Ground
RSLP HA4 58 C3
King's Cross
CAMTN NW1 4 E3
King's Cross St Pancras
CAMTN NW1 4 E4
Kingsdale School
DUL SE21 163 F5
Kings Estate
HCH RM12 93 J2
Kingsford Community School
PLSTW E13 107 G3
Kingsgate Business Centre
KUTN/CMB KT2 175 F4
Kingsgate Primary School
KIL/WHAMP NW6 82 E5
Kings Hall Leisure Centre
CLPT E5 86 E3
Kings Head Theatre
IS N1 85 G6
Kings House School
RCHPK/HAM TW10 137 G6
Kingsland College of Business Studies
SRTFD E15 106 B1
Kingsland Health Centre
HACK E8 86 B5
Kingsland Shopping Centre
HACK E8 86 B4
Kingsley Primary School
CROY/NA CR0 196 A5
Kings Mall Shopping Centre
HMSMTH W6 119 F4
Kingsmeadow Athletics Centre
KUT/HW KT1 175 H6
Kingsmead Primary School
CLPT E5 87 G2
Kingsmead School
EN EN1 24 C4
The Kings Oak Private Hospital
ENC/FH EN2 23 G1
King Solomon High School
BARK/HLT IG6 54 D5
Kings Private Clinic
GDMY/SEVK IG3 73 F5
MHST W1U 9 G1
Kings School of English
BECK BR3 182 C5
Kings Stairs
BERM/RHTH SE16 123 J2
Kingston
KUTN/CMB KT2 175 F4
Kingston Business Centre
CHSGTN KT9 206 A1
Kingston Cemetery
KUT/HW KT1 175 G6
Kingston College of Further Education
KUT/HW KT1 175 F6
Kingston College Theatre
KUT/HW KT1 174 E6
Kingston Crematorium
KUT/HW KT1 175 H6
Kingston Grammar School
KUT/HW KT1 175 G5
Kingston Hospital
KUTN/CMB KT2 175 H4
Kingstonian FC
NWMAL KT3 175 J6
Kingston University
KUT/HW KT1 175 F6
KUT/HW KT1 191 F1
KUTN/CMB KT2 176 A3
PUT/ROE SW15 158 C4
King Street College
HMSMTH W6 119 F4
Kingsway Business Park
HPTN TW12 172 E4
Kingsway College
CAMTN NW1 4 A6
STPAN WC1H 5 G5
Kingswood Primary School
WNWD SE27 162 E6
Kisharon School
GLDGN NW11 64 D3
K+K Hotel George
ECT SW5 119 K4
KLC School of Design
WBPTN SW10 140 B2
Knightsbridge
CHEL SW3 14 D4
Knightsbridge Barracks
SKENS SW7 14 D3
Knightsbridge Medical Centre
KTBR SW1X 15 F4
Knightsbridge School
KTBR SW1X 14 E5
The Knightsbridge Under School
SKENS SW7 120 B4
Knollmead Primary School
BRYLDS KT5 191 K6
Knowledge Point School
HOLWY N7 85 F4
Kobi Nazrul Primary School
WCHPL E1 104 C5
KP Estate
RAIN RM13 111 G6
Krishna-Avanti Primary School
EDGW HA8 44 C4
Kubrick Business Estate
FSTGT E7 89 F2
Laban Centre for Movement & Dance
DEPT SE8 144 E1
Laburnum Health Centre
DAGE RM10 74 C6
Ladbroke Grove
NKENS W10 100 C5
Lady Bankes Junior School
RSLP HA4 58 E6
The Lady Eleanor Holles School
HPTN TW12 173 G1
Lady Margaret Primary School
STHL UB1 95 K4
Lady Margaret School
FUL/PGN SW6 139 K2
Ladywell
LEW SE13 144 E6
Ladywell Arena
LEW SE13 164 E1
Ladywell Cemetery
BROCKY SE4 144 C6
Ladywell Leisure Centre
LEW SE13 145 F6
Lake Business Centre
TOTM N17 50 C2
Laker Industrial Estate
BECK BR3 182 C1
Lambeth Academy
CLAP SW4 141 H6
Lambeth Cemetery
TOOT SW17 178 B1
Lambeth College
BRXS/STRHM SW2 142 A6
CLAP SW4 141 H6
STHWK SE1 19 H1
STRHM/NOR SW16 161 K4
VX/NE SW8 141 J2
Lambeth Crematorium
TOOT SW17 160 B6
Lambeth Hospital
BRXN/ST SW9 141 K4
Lambeth North
STHWK SE1 17 J4
Lambeth Palace
STHWK SE1 17 G5
Lambs Court
POP/IOD E14 105 G6
Lammas School
LEY E10 69 H5
Lamont Business Centre
CROY/NA CR0 195 K4
Lamorbey Swimming Centre
BFN/LL DA15 168 B4
Lampton School
HSLW TW3 135 F2
The Lanark Medical Centre
MV/WKIL W9 101 F2
Lancaster Gate
BAY/PAD W2 8 A5
Lancaster House
WHALL SW1A 16 A2
Lancasterian Primary School
TOTM N17 50 A4
Lancaster Road Industrial Estate
EBAR EN4 21 H6
Lancelot Medical Centre
ALP/SUD HA0 79 K3

The Landmark Hotel
CAMTN NW1 8 E1
The Lanesborough Hotel
KTBR SW1X 15 G2
Lanford Obesity Clinic
ED N9 36 D2
Langbourne Primary School
DUL SE21 163 F5
Langdon Down Centre
TEDD TW11 174 D3
Langdon Park
POP/IOD E14 105 K4
Langdon Park School
POP/IOD E14 105 K5
Langdon School
EHAM E6 108 B1
Langford Primary School
FUL/PGN SW6 140 A3
Langham Hotel
CAVSQ/HST W1G 9 K3
Langhedge Lane Industrial Estate
UED N18 50 B2
Langley Park Girls School & Sports Centre
BECK BR3 198 E2
Langley Park Golf Club
BECK BR3 199 G3
Langley Park School for Boys
BECK BR3 198 E3
Langthorne Health Centre
WAN E11 88 B1
Langthorne Hospital
WAN E11 88 B2
Lansbury Lawrence Primary School
POP/IOD E14 105 K5
Lansdowne College
BAY/PAD W2 101 F6
Lansdowne School
BRXN/ST SW9 142 A4
La Retraite RC Girls School
BAL SW12 161 H2
Lark Hall Primary School
CLAP SW4 141 J3
Larkshall Business Centre
CHING E4 38 B4
Larkswood Primary School
CHING E4 37 K6
Larmenier & Sacred Catholic Primary School
HMSMTH W6 119 G4
La Sainte Union Catholic Secondary School
HGT N6 84 A1
La Sainte Union Convent School
KTTN NW5 84 B1
La Salette RC Primary School
RAIN RM13 111 J2
Latchmere Leisure Centre
BTSEA SW11 140 E3
Latchmere Primary School
KUTN/CMB KT2 175 G2
Lathom Junior School
EHAM E6 89 J5
Latimer Road
NTGHL W11 100 B6
Latymer All Saints CE Primary School
ED N9 36 B4
The Latymer Preparatory School
HMSMTH W6 118 D5
The Latymer School
ED N9 36 A4
Latymer Upper School
HMSMTH W6 118 D4
Launcelot Primary School
BMLY BR1 165 K6
Laurance Haines School
WATW WD18 26 E1
Laurel Clinic
EA W5 116 D4
Lauriston Primary School
HOM E9 87 F6
Lavender Primary School
ENC/FH EN2 23 K1
Lawdale Junior School
BETH E2 104 C2
Lawrence Trading Estate
GNWCH SE10 125 H4
Lawrence Wharf
BERM/RHTH SE16 124 C1
Laycock Primary School
IS N1 85 G4
Lazards Sports Club
SUN TW16 172 A4
Leadenhall Market
BANK EC3V 13 G4
Lea Park Trading Estate
LEY E10 69 H4
Leaside Business Centre
PEND EN3 25 H3
Leathermarket Gardens
STHWK SE1 19 G3
Leathersellers Sports Ground
LEE/GVPK SE12 166 B2
Leathers Hall
HDTCH EC3A 13 G3
Lea Valley Primary School
TOTM N17 50 C3
Lea Valley Trading Estate
UED N18 36 E6
UED N18 51 F2
Lebanon Road
CROY/NA CR0 197 F6
L'Ecoles Des Petits School
FUL/PGN SW6 140 A3
Lee
LEE/GVPK SE12 165 K1
Lee Manor Primary School
LEW SE13 165 H1
Leeside Court
BERM/RHTH SE16 124 A1
Leeside Trading Estate
TOTM N17 50 E3
Leesons Primary School
STMC/STPC BR5 186 B6
Lee Valley Camping & Caravan Park
ED N9 37 G3
Lee Valley Campsite
CHING E4 25 K3
Lee Valley Ice Centre
LEY E10 69 F6
Lee Valley Leisure Complex, Athletics Centre & Golf Club
ED N9 37 G2
Lee Valley Watersports Centre
CHING E4 51 G2
Leicester Square
LSQ/SEVD WC2H 10 D5
Leigh Close Industrial Estate
NWMAL KT3 192 A1
Leigh Technology Academy
DART DA1 171 K3
Leighton House Museum
WKENS W14 119 J3
Lena Gardens Primary School
HMSMTH W6 119 F3
Leopold Primary School
WLSDN NW10 81 H5
Leopold Street Clinic
BOW E3 105 H4
Lesnes Abbey
BELV DA17 128 E4
Lesnes Abbey (remains of)
ABYW SE2 128 C6
Lessness Heath Primary School
BELV DA17 129 H5
The Levin Hotel
KTBR SW1X 14 E4
Lewin Mead Community Mental Health Centre
STRHM/NOR SW16 179 J2
Lewis Clinic
CAR SM5 210 A2
Lewisham
DEPT SE8 144 E3
Lewisham Bridge Primary School
LEW SE13 144 E4
Lewisham Business Centre
NWCR SE14 124 A6
Lewisham Centre
LEW SE13 145 F5
Lewisham College
BROCKY SE4 144 D3
Lewisham Crematorium
CAT SE6 165 J4
Lewisham Lions Centre
BERM/RHTH SE16 123 K5
The Leys Primary School
DAGE RM10 92 E5
Leyton
WAN E11 88 A1
Leyton Business Centre
LEY E10 69 H6
Leyton Cross
RDART DA2 170 D4
Leyton FC
LEY E10 69 H5
Leyton Industrial Village
LEY E10 69 F4
Leyton Leisure Centre
LEY E10 69 K4
Leyton Midland Road
LEY E10 70 A5
Leyton Orient FC (Matchroom Stadium)
LEY E10 87 K1
Leyton Sixth Form College
LEY E10 70 B3
Leytonstone
WAN E11 70 C5
Leytonstone High Road
WAN E11 70 C6
Leytonstone School
WAN E11 70 C3
Leyton Youth Sports Ground
LEY E10 69 K5
The Liberty City Clinic
SDTCH EC2A 7 G6
Liberty II Centre
ROM RM1 75 G1
Liberty Middle School
MTCM CR4 178 D5
The Liberty
ROM RM1 75 G2
Library & Community Centre
BTSEA SW11 140 C4
L'Ile Aux Enfants
KTTN NW5 84 A3
Lilian Baylis Technology School
LBTH SE11 122 A5
Lillian Baylis School
LBTH SE11 17 H7
VX/NE SW8 121 K6
Lillian Baylis Theatre
CLKNW EC1R 6 A4
Lillian Bishop School of English
SKENS SW7 14 A6
Limehouse
WCHPL E1 105 G5
Limehouse Hole Stairs
BERM/RHTH SE16 124 C1
Limes Farm Primary School
CHIG IG7 54 D2
Lime Trees Park Golf Club
NTHLT UB5 77 G6
Lincoln Road Clinic
EN EN1 24 C6
Lincoln's Inn
LINN WC2A 11 H3
Linden Bridge School
WPK KT4 207 G1
Linden Lodge School
WIM/MER SW19 159 H3
Lindon Bennett School
FELT TW13 172 C1
Linford Christie Stadium
SHB W12 99 J4
The Link Day Primary School
CROY/NA CR0 210 E2
The Link Secondary School
CROY/NA CR0 211 F2
Links Primary School
TOOT SW17 179 F2
Linley House School
BRYLDS KT5 191 G3
Linley Sambourne House
WKENS W14 119 J2
Linnet House Clinic
STJWD NW8 2 C3
Linton Mead Primary School
THMD SE28 109 H6
Lionel Road Primary School
BTFD TW8 117 F4
Liongate Hotel
E/WMO/HCT KT8 174 A6
Lion House School
PUT/ROE SW15 139 G5
Lismarrine Industrial Park
BORE WD6 29 H1
Lisson Grove Health Centre
STJWD NW8 2 C6
Lister Community School
PLSTW E13 107 F1
The Lister Hospital
BGVA SW1W 121 G5
Lister House Clinic
CAVSQ/HST W1G 9 J3
Little Danson Welfare Clinic
WELL DA16 148 B5
Little Davids School
CROY/NA CR0 213 K4
Little Hands Theatre
HDN NW4 64 A1
Little Heath School
CHDH RM6 73 H1
Little Ilford School
MNPK E12 89 K3
Little St Helens School
NTHWD HA6 40 C2
Little Stanmore First & Middle School
EDGW HA8 44 A4
Little Wandsworth School
TOOT SW17 161 F4
Liverpool Street
LVPST EC2M 13 G2
Livesey Museum for Children
PECK SE15 123 J6
Livingstone Hospital
DART DA1 171 J2
Livingstone Primary School
EBAR EN4 21 H4
The Livity School
BRXS/STRHM SW2 141 K6
Lloyd Park
CROY/NA CR0 212 B2
Lloyd Park Centre
WALTH E17 51 J5
Lloyd's
FENCHST EC3M 13 G4
Lloyds Register CC
DUL SE21 162 E3
Locks View Court
POP/IOD E14 105 G6
Lockwood Industrial Park
TOTM N17 50 D6
Lombard Business Centre
BTSEA SW11 140 C3
Lombard Business Park
CROY/NA CR0 196 A4
WAND/EARL SW18 160 C1
WIM/MER SW19 178 B5
Lombard Trading Estate
CHARL SE7 126 A4
Lombardy Retail Park
HYS/HAR UB3 95 F6
London Academy
EDGW HA8 30 B6
London Academy of Music & Dramatic Art
KENS W8 119 K4
London Allergy Clinic
CAVSQ/HST W1G 9 J2
London Bridge
STHWK SE1 19 F1
London Bridge City Pier
STHWK SE1 13 G7
London Bridge Hospital
STHWK SE1 13 F7
London Bridge Hotel
STHWK SE1 18 E1
London Bridge Sports Centre
CANST EC4R 12 E6
London Brookes College
HDN NW4 63 K1
London Business School
CAMTN NW1 2 E6
London Butterfly House
BTFD TW8 136 D2
The London Canal Museum
IS N1 5 F2
London Capital College
CAMTN NW1 84 B6
London Centre of Contemporary Music
STHWK SE1 18 D1
London Chest Hospital
BETH E2 104 E1
London Chinese Dance School
CAN/RD E16 106 B4
REGST W1B 9 K1
London City Airport
CAN/RD E16 126 D1
London City College (English Language Institute) & Schiller International University
STHWK SE1 17 H1
London City Mission
STHWK SE1 19 H2
The London Clinic
CAVSQ/HST W1G 3 H7
London College of Business & Computer Services
CLAP SW4 141 J5
London College of Business & Computing
BETH E2 104 D1
London College of Communication
LBTH SE11 18 B5
London College of Fashion
CAVSQ/HST W1G 9 K3
MHST W1U 9 H3
SDTCH EC2A 7 H6
London College of Further Education
LBTH SE11 18 A7
London College of Higher Education
CLAP SW4 141 G4
London College of International Business Studies
HHOL WC1V 11 F2
London College of Science & Technology
GDMY/SEVK IG3 73 G5
The London College
KENS W8 119 K1
London Commodity Exchange
WAP E1W 13 K6
London Contemporary Dance School
CAMTN NW1 4 D5
PLSTW E13 106 D2
London Cornish RFC
PUT/ROE SW15 158 C5
The London Dungeon
STHWK SE1 19 F1
London Esthetique
POP/IOD E14 106 C5
London Eye
STHWK SE1 17 G2
London Eye Clinic
CAVSQ/HST W1G 9 J2
London Fields
HACK E8 86 D5
London Fields Lido
HACK E8 86 D5
London Fields Primary School
HACK E8 86 D6
London Film Academy
FUL/PGN SW6 139 K1
London Film School
LSQ/SEVD WC2H 10 E4
London Financial Training College
FSBYPK N4 67 H2
London Foot Hospital
FITZ W1T 4 A7
London Gender Clinic
HDN NW4 63 K3
London Group Business Park
CRICK NW2 63 H5
London Heart Clinic
CAVSQ/HST W1G 9 J2
The London Industrial Estate
EHAM E6 108 A4
London Industrial Park
EHAM E6 108 B4
London International College
POP/IOD E14 106 C5
SOHO/SHAV W1D 10 B3
The London Irish Youth Theatre
HGT N6 66 B5
London Islamic School / Madrasah
WCHPL E1 104 D5
London Jewish Girls High School
HDN NW4 64 A2
London Ladies & Girls FC
CAT SE6 182 E1
London Lane Clinic
BMLY BR1 183 J3
London Lighthouse
NTGHL W11 100 C5
London Living Theatre
SYD SE26 164 A6
The London Make-up Academy
UED N18 50 D1
London Marriott Hotel
HAMP NW3 83 J5
MYFR/PKLN W1K 9 H5
OXSTW W1C 9 F5
STHWK SE1 17 G2
London Marriott West India Quay Hotel
POP/IOD E14 105 J6
London Metrocity College
BOW E3 105 J2
London Metropolitan University
HBRY N5 85 J3
HOLWY N7 85 F3
LVPST EC2M 13 F2
WCHPL E1 13 J3
WCHPL E1 104 C5
London Natural Therapy School
POP/IOD E14 106 C6
SOHO/CST W1F 10 B5
London Nautical School
STHWK SE1 11 K7
London Open College
FSBYE EC1V 6 B4
London Oratory School
FUL/PGN SW6 139 K1
London Road Medical Centre
CROY/NA CR0 196 B3
London School of Economics
CLKNW EC1R 5 K5
HHOL WC1V 10 E3
HOL/ALD WC2B 11 G4
STHWK SE1 12 C7
London School of Hygiene & Tropical Medicine
GWRST WC1E 10 D1
London School of Theology
NTHWD HA6 40 B2
London Scottish Golf Club
WIM/MER SW19 158 E5
London Silver Vaults
LINN WC2A 11 J2
London South Bank University
STHWK SE1 18 B4
London Stock Exchange
STBT EC1A 12 B3
London's Transport Museum
HOL/ALD WC2B 11 F5
The London Television Centre
STHWK SE1 11 J7
London Tourist Board & Convention Centre
BGVA SW1W 15 J4
London Toy & Model Museum
BAY/PAD W2 101 G6
London Transport Bus Depot
BXLYHN DA7 149 J4
London Underwriting Centre
MON EC3R 13 G5
London Wall
BARB EC2Y 12 C2
London Weather Centre
HCIRC EC1N 11 J1
The London Welbeck Hospital
CAVSQ/HST W1G 9 H2
London Welsh FC
RCH/KEW TW9 137 F4
London Welsh School
CRICK NW2 82 A4
London West Crematorium
WLSDN NW10 99 K3
London Wetland Centre
BARN SW13 138 E2
Lonesome Primary School
MTCM CR4 179 G5
Long Ditton Cemetery
SURB KT6 190 D6
Long Ditton County Infant School
SURB KT6 190 D5
Long Ditton St Marys CE Junior School
THDIT KT7 190 C5
Longfield Primary School
RYLN/HDSTN HA2 60 A3
Longford Community School
EBED/NFELT TW14 153 J2
Longford Industrial Estate
HPTN TW12 173 G2
Longlands Primary School
BFN/LL DA15 167 K5
Long Lane AFC
BKHTH/KID SE3 146 B3
Longmead Primary School
WDR/YW UB7 112 A4
Longshaw Primary School
CHING E4 38 B5
Lord Chancellors Department
WEST SW1P 16 D5
Lord Lister Health Centre
FSTGT E7 88 E2
Lordship Lane Clinic
TOTM N17 50 A5
Lordship Lane Primary School
WDGN N22 49 J4
Lord's Tour & MCC Museum
STJWD NW8 2 A5
Lord Williamson School
NKENS W10 100 C4
Lorimar Business Centre
RAIN RM13 111 G5
Loughborough Junction
CMBW SE5 142 C3
Loughborough Primary School
CMBW SE5 142 C3
Lovelace Primary School
CHSGTN KT9 205 J3
Lovell's Wharf
GNWCH SE10 125 G5
Lower Clapton Health Centre
CLPT E5 86 E3
Lower Place Business Centre
WLSDN NW10 98 E
Lower Sydenham
SYD SE26 182 C
Lower Sydenham Industrial Estate
SYD SE26 182 C
Lowfield Medical Centre
DART DA1 171 H
Low Hall Sports Ground
LEY E10 69 F
Lowther Primary School
BARN SW13 118 D
Loxford School of Science & Technology
IL IG1 90 D
Loyola Preparatory School
BKHH IG9 39 G
LPR Sports Club
BARK/HLT IG6 55 F
LSE Sports Club
NWMAL KT3 192
Lubavitch Boys Primary School
CLPT E5 68 E
Lubavitch House School (Senior Girls)
STNW/STAM N16 68
Lucas Vale Primary School
DEPT SE8 144
Lutomer House Business Centre
POP/IOD E14 124
Lux Cinema
IS N1 7
Lycee Francais
SKENS SW7 14
Lycee Francais Charles De Gaulle
BTSEA SW11 141
The Lyceum Theatre
COVGDN WC2E 11
Lyndean Industrial Estate
ABYW SE2 128
Lyndhurst House Preparatory School
HAMP NW3 83
Lyndhurst Primary School
CMBW SE5 142

Lyon Business Park
BARK IG11 108 E1
Lyon Park Infant School
ALP/SUD HA0 80 B5
Lyonsdown School
BAR EN5 21 G6
Lyric Theatre
SOHO/SHAV W1D 10 C5
Lyric Theatre Hammersmith
HMSMTH W6 119 F4
Mabwin
Supplementary School
ED N9 36 D4
Macaulay CE Primary School
CLAP SW4 141 G4
Madame Tussauds & the
London Auditorium
CAMTN NW1 3 F7
Madeira Grove Clinic
WFD IG8 53 F1
Madison Bowl
NTHWD HA6 40 C3
Madni Girls School
WCHPL E1 104 D5
Madrasah-E-Darue Qirat
Majidiah School
WCHPL E1 104 D6
Mahatma Gandhi
Industrial Estate
BRXN/ST SW9 142 C4
Maida Vale ⊖
MV/WKIL W9 101 F2
Maida Vale Medical Centre
MV/WKIL W9 101 F2
Malcolm Primary School
PGE/AN SE20 181 K3
The Malden Centre
NWMAL KT3 192 C1
Malden Golf Club
NWMAL KT3 176 B5
Malden Manor ⇌
NWMAL KT3 192 B4
Malden Manor Primary School
NWMAL KT3 192 B4
Malden Parochial
Primary School
WPK KT4 192 B5
Malden Road Baths
CHEAM SM3 208 B2
Malham Road
Industrial Estate
FSTH SE23 164 A3
The Mall Bexleyheath
BXLYHS DA6 149 H5
Mall Galleries
STJS SW1Y 10 D7
The Mall School
WHTN TW2 155 J5
Malmaison Charterhouse
Square Hotel
FARR EC1M 12 B1
Malmesbury Primary School
BOW E3 105 H2
MRDN SM4 194 B4
Malorees Junior School
KIL/WHAMP NW6 82 B5
Mandarin Oriental Hotel
KTBR SW1X 15 F2
The Mandeville Hotel
MHST W1U 9 H3
Mandeville Primary School
CLPT E5 87 G1
Mandeville Special School
NTHLT UB5 77 K4
Manford Industrial Estate
ERITH DA8 130 E6
Manford Primary School
CHIG IG7 55 F1
Manford Way Health Centre
BARK/HLT IG6 55 F2
Manor Brook Medical Centre
BKHTH/KID SE3 146 A3
Manor Drive Health Centre
WPK KT4 192 C5
Manorfield Primary School
POP/IOD E14 105 K4
Manor House ⊖
FSBYPK N4 67 J5
Manor Infant School
BARK IG11 91 F4
Manor Oak Primary School
STMC/STPC BR5 202 E2
Manor Park ⇌
MNPK E12 89 H2
Manor Park Cemetery
FSTGT E7 89 H2
Manor Park Crematorium
FSTGT E7 89 G2
Manor Park Methodist School
MNPK E12 89 J2
Manor Park Primary School
SUT SM1 209 G3
Manor Primary School
SRTFD E15 106 C1
The Manor Primary School
ROM RM1 75 H2
Manorside Primary School
FNCH N3 47 F4
Manor Special School
WLSDN NW10 100 B1
Manor Way Business Centre
RAIN RM13 111 F4
Mansfield Infant College
IL IG1 72 A6
Mansion House ⊖
STP EC4M 12 D4
Mapledown School
CRICK NW2 64 B4
Maple Grove
Business Centre
HSLWW TW4 134 B5
Maple House Independant
Montessori School
THHTH CR7 180 C6
Maple Industrial Estate
FELT TW13 153 K4
Maples Business Centre
… N1 85 G5
Marble Arch
MBLAR W1H 9 F5
Marble Arch ⊖
MBLAR W1H 9 F4
Marble Hill House
TWK TW1 156 D2
Maria Fidelis Convent School
CAMTN NW1 4 B5
Maria Montessori
Childrens House
HAMP NW3 83 H3
Mariner Business Centre
CROY/NA CR0 211 F3
Marion Richardson
Primary School
WCHPL E1 105 F5
Marion Vian Primary School
BECK BR3 198 A2
Maritime Greenwich College
DEPT SE8 144 D1
Maritime Industrial Estate
CHARL SE7 126 A4
Maritime Museum
GNWCH SE10 125 H4
Marjorie McClure School
CHST BR7 185 H4
The Marjory Kinnon School
EBED/NFELT TW14 133 H6
The Market
COVGDN WC2E 11 F5
Market Trading Estate
NWDGN UB2 114 A4
Marks Gate Junior School
CHDH RM6 56 A6
Marlborough CC
DUL SE21 163 H3
Marlborough Day Hospital
STJWD NW8 101 G1
Marlborough First &
Middle School
HRW HA1 60 E1
Marlborough House
STJS SW1Y 16 B1
Marlborough Primary School
CHEL SW3 14 D7
ISLW TW7 136 B2
Marlborough School
BFN/LL DA15 168 B3
Marlborough Trading Estate
RCH/KEW TW9 137 J2
Marlowe Business Centre
NWCR SE14 144 B1
Marner Primary School
BOW E3 105 K3
Marriott Hotel
ECT SW5 120 A4
HYS/HAR UB3 133 G1
KIL/WHAMP NW6 101 F1
MBLAR W1H 8 D3
Marshalls Park School
ROM RM1 57 G5
Marsh Gate Business Centre
SRTFD E15 106 A1
Marshgate Primary School
RCHPK/HAM TW10 137 G6
Marsh Green School
DAGW RM9 110 C1
Martan College
HOL/ALD WC2B 11 F3
Martinbridge Industrial Estate
EN EN1 24 C6
Martindale Industrial Estate
EN EN1 24 A6
Martin Primary School
EFNCH N2 65 J1
Marvels Lane Primary School
LEE/GVPK SE12 166 B6
Mary Boone School
WKENS W14 119 H4
Maryland ⇌
SRTFD E15 88 C3
Maryland Industrial Estate
SRTFD E15 88 C3
Maryland Primary School
SRTFD E15 88 C3
Marylebone ⇌ ⊖
CAMTN NW1 2 D7
Marylebone Health Centre
CAMTN NW1 3 H7
Marymount
International School
KUTN/CMB KT2 175 K3
Mary Wallace Theatre
TWK TW1 156 B3
Maswell Park
Health Centre
HSLW TW3 135 H6
Mathilda Marks Kennedy
Primary School
MLHL NW7 45 F1
Matrix Business Centre
DART DA1 151 H6
Maudlin's Green
WAP E1W 13 K7
The Maudsley Hospital
CMBW SE5 142 E3
Maughan Library
(Kings College)
LINN WC2A 11 J3
Mawbrey Brough
Health Centre
VX/NE SW8 141 K1
The Mawney School
ROMW/RG RM7 75 F2
Mayday University Hospital
THHTH CR7 196 C3
Mayesbrook Park Arena
BARK IG11 91 G3
Mayespark Primary School
GDMY/SEVK IG3 91 G1
Mayfield Primary School
HNWL W7 96 D5
Mayfield School
PIN HA5 41 J6
Mayflower Primary School
POP/IOD E14 105 J5
Mayplace Primary School
BXLYHN DA7 150 A5
Maypole Primary School
RDART DA2 170 B5
Maytime School
IL IG1 90 A1
Mayville J & P School
WAN E11 88 C1
Maze Hill ⇌
GNWCH SE10 125 H6
McKay Trading Estate
NKENS W10 100 C3
McMillan Clinic
HYS/HAR UB3 94 A6
MDQ Majidiah School
WCHPL E1 104 D6
The Mead Infant School
WPK KT4 207 H1
Meadlands Primary School
RCHPK/HAM TW10 156 D6
Meadowgate School
BROCKY SE4 144 A4
Meadowside Leisure Centre
BKHTH/KID SE3 146 B5
The Meadow Special School
STMC/STPC BR5 186 B3
Mead Road Infant School
CHST BR7 185 H2
Medical Express Clinic
CAVSQ/HST W1G 9 J1
Mednurs Clinic
SEVS/STOTM N15 67 K3
Megabowl
KUTN/CMB KT2 175 F5
Melcombe Primary School
HMSMTH W6 119 G6
Melia White House Hotel
CAMTN NW1 3 K6
Mellish Industrial Estate
WOOL/PLUM SE18 126 C3
Mellow Lane School
HGDN/ICK UB10 94 A3
Melrose Special School
MTCM CR4 178 D6
Memorial Hospital
WOOL/PLUM SE18 147 F3
Menorah Grammar School
EDGW HA8 44 E3
GLDGN NW11 64 C4
Menorah High School for Girls
CRICK NW2 81 H1
Menorah Primary School
GLDGN NW11 64 C4
MERC Education
WOOL/PLUM SE18 127 G3
Mercers' Hall
CITYW EC2V 12 D4
The Merchant Taylors Hall
BANK EC3V 13 F4
Merchant Taylors School
NTHWD HA6 26 C3
Mercure London City
Bankside Hotel
STHWK SE1 18 C1
Meridian Clinic
BRXN/ST SW9 142 A4
Meridian Locality Mental
Health Centre
CHARL SE7 126 B6
Meridian Primary School
GNWCH SE10 125 G5
Meridian Sports Club
CHARL SE7 146 D1
Meridian Trading Estate
CHARL SE7 126 A4
Merlin Primary School
BMLY BR1 165 K5
Merlin School
PUT/ROE SW15 139 G6
Mermaid Theatre
BLKFR EC4V 12 B5
Merrielands Retail Park
DAGW RM9 92 B6
Merry Hill Infant School
BUSH WD23 28 B2
Merryhills Clinic
ENC/FH EN2 23 F4
Merryhills Primary School
ENC/FH EN2 23 F5
Merton Abbey Primary School
WIM/MER SW19 178 A4
Merton Adult College
RYNPK SW20 177 H6
Merton College
MRDN SM4 193 J3
Merton Court
Preparatory School
SCUP DA14 168 D6
Merton Industrial Park
WIM/MER SW19 178 B4
Merton Park ⊖
WIM/MER SW19 177 K4
Merton Park Primary School
WIM/MER SW19 177 J5
Merton Road Industrial Estate
WAND/EARL SW18 159 K2
The Method Studio
FSBYW WC1X 11 G1
Metro Business Centre
SYD SE26 182 C2
The Metro Golf Centre
HDN NW4 46 A4
Metro Industrial Centre
ISLW TW7 135 K3
Metropolitan
Business Centre
IS N1 86 A5
Metropolitan Hospital
STHWK SE1 17 K4
The Metropolitan Hotel
MYFR/PKLN W1K 15 J1
Metropolitan Police FC
E/WMO/HCT KT8 189 J3
Metropolitan Police Hayes
Sports Club
HAYES BR2 199 J6
Metropolitan Police
(Hendon) Track
CDALE/KGS NW9 45 H6
Metropolitan Police Training
School, Hendon
CDALE/KGS NW9 45 H6
Metropolitan Tabernacle
STHWK SE1 18 B6
Metro Trading Centre
WBLY HA9 80 D2
Michael Faraday
Primary School
WALW SE17 122 E5
Michael Manley
Industrial Estate
VX/NE SW8 141 H2
Michael Sobell Sinai School
KTN/HRWW/WS HA3 62 C3
The Michael Tippett School
LBTH SE11 17 K7
Midas Business Centre
DAGE RM10 92 C2
Midas Industrial Estate
DAGE RM10 92 C2
Middle Park Primary School
ELTH/MOT SE9 166 C2
Middle Row Primary School
NKENS W10 100 C3
Middlesex Business Centre
NWDGN UB2 115 F2
Middlesex CCC (Lord's
Cricket Ground)
STJWD NW8 2 B4
Middlesex Hospital
Medical School
FITZ W1T 10 B1
Middlesex Hospital
Nurses Home
GTPST W1W 10 A1
Middlesex Hospital School
of Physiotherapy
FITZ W1T 10 B1
Middlesex Hospital
Sports Ground
CHST BR7 186 A1
Middlesex School of
Complementary Medicine
STAN HA7 44 A4
Middlesex University
ARCH N19 66 C5
GLDGN NW11 65 F5
PEND EN3 25 F6
WDGN N22 48 E5
Middlesex University (Cat
Hill Campus)
EBAR EN4 34 A1
Middlesex University
(Enfield Campus)
PEND EN3 24 D6
Middlesex University
(Hendon Campus)
HDN NW4 63 K1
Middlesex University (Trent
Park Campus)
EBAR EN4 22 C3
Midfield Primary School
STMC/STPC BR5 186 B3
Midway Mission Hospital
BETH E2 7 J5
Milbourne Lodge
Junior School
ESH/CLAY KT10 204 C3
Milbourne Lodge School
ESH/CLAY KT10 204 D4
Mile End ⊖
BOW E3 105 H3
Mile End & Bow
Business Centre
WCHPL E1 104 D4
Mile End Hospital
WCHPL E1 105 F2
Mile End Stadium
POP/IOD E14 105 H4
Milehams Industrial Estate
PUR RM19 131 K3
Miles Coverdale
Primary School
SHB W12 119 F2
Milestone Hotel
KENS W8 120 A2
Military Barracks
WOOL/PLUM SE18 127 F5
Millbank Millennium Pier
WEST SW1P 16 E7
Millbank Primary School
WEST SW1P 16 D7
Millbank Tower
WEST SW1P 16 E7
Millennium Arena
BTSEA SW11 141 F1
Millennium Bailey's Hotel
SKENS SW7 120 B4
Millennium Balloon
STHWK SE1 19 H1
Millennium & Copthorne
Hotels at Chelsea FC
FUL/PGN SW6 140 A1
Millennium Dance 2000
Theatre School
HAMP NW3 83 J3
Millennium
Gloucester Hotel
ECT SW5 120 A4
Millennium Harbour
POP/IOD E14 124 C2
Millennium Hotel
KTBR SW1X 15 F3
Millennium Hotel
London Mayfair
MYFR/PKLN W1K 9 H6
Millennium Primary School
GNWCH SE10 125 J3
Millennium Quay
DEPT SE8 124 E6
Millennium Wharf
POP/IOD E14 125 G3
Mill Farm Business Park
HSLWW TW4 154 D2
Millfields Primary School
CLPT E5 86 E2
Millfield Theatre
UED N18 35 K6
Mill Green Business Park
MTCM CR4 194 E4
Mill Hill Broadway ⇌
MLHL NW7 45 G2
Mill Hill Cemetery
MLHL NW7 46 A2
Mill Hill County High School
MLHL NW7 31 G4
The Mill Hill CC
MLHL NW7 32 A5
Mill Hill East ⊖
MLHL NW7 46 B3
Mill Hill Golf Club
MLHL NW7 31 G4
Mill Hill Industrial Estate
MLHL NW7 45 H2
Mill Hill School
MLHL NW7 31 K6
Mill Lane Medical Centre
KIL/WHAMP NW6 82 E3
Mill Lane Trading Estate
CROY/NA CR0 211 F1
Mill River Trading Estate
PEND EN3 25 G5
Millside Industrial Estate
DART DA1 151 G5
Mill Street Clinic
STHWK SE1 19 K2
Mill Trading Estate
WLSDN NW10 98 D1
The Mill Trading Estate
WLSDN NW10 98 E2
Millwall FC (The New Den)
BERM/RHTH SE16 123 K5
Milmead Industrial Centre
TOTM N17 50 D5
Milton Natural Health Centre
HGT N6 66 C4
Minet Clinic
HYS/HAR UB3 113 K1
Minet J & I Schools
HYS/HAR UB3 114 A1
Ministry of Defence
WHALL SW1A 16 E1
Mint Business Park
CAN/RD E16 106 E4
Mirravale Trading Estate
CHDH RM6 74 A4
Mission Grove Primary School
WALTH E17 69 H2
Mitcham ⊖
MTCM CR4 194 D1
Mitcham CC
MTCM CR4 194 D1
Mitcham Eastfields ⇌
MTCM CR4 179 F5
Mitcham Golf Club
MTCM CR4 195 F2
Mitcham Industrial Estate
MTCM CR4 179 F4
Mitcham Junction ⇌ ⊖
MTCM CR4 195 F2
Mitcham Vale High School
STRHM/NOR SW16 179 H5
Mitchell Brook
Primary School
WLSDN NW10 81 F4
Mitre Bridge Industrial Park
NKENS W10 99 K3
Mitre House Hotel
BAY/PAD W2 8 A4
Moatbridge School
ELTH/MOT SE9 166 C1
The Moat School
FUL/PGN SW6 139 H3
Moberly Sports &
Education Centre
WLSDN NW10 100 B2
Molesey Cemetery
E/WMO/HCT KT8 173 F6
Molesey Hospital
E/WMO/HCT KT8 189 F2
Mollison Drive Health Centre
WLGTN SM6 210 E5
Monega Primary School
MNPK E12 89 H3
Monken Hadley CE
Primary School
BAR EN5 20 E2
Monkfrith Primary School
EBAR EN4 34 A2
Monks Hill Sports Centre
SAND/SEL CR2 213 F5
Monks Orchard
Primary School
CROY/NA CR0 198 A2
The Montague on the
Gardens Hotel
RSQ WC1B 10 E1
Montbelle Primary School
ELTH/MOT SE9 167 F6
The Montcalm-Hotel Nikko
MBLAR W1H 9 F4
Monteagle Primary School
DAGW RM9 91 H6
Montem Primary School
HOLWY N7 85 F1
Montpelier Primary School
EA W5 97 K4
Monument ⊖
MANHO EC4N 13 F5
The Monument
CANST EC4R 13 F5
Moore Place Golf Club
ESH/CLAY KT10 204 A3
Moorfields Eye Hospital
FSBYE EC1V 6 E5
Moorgate ⇌ ⊖
BARB EC2Y 12 E2
Moor Lane Junior School
CHSGTN KT9 206 B3
Moor Park ⊖
NTHWD HA6 26 B5
Moor Park
Industrial Estate
WATW WD18 26 A2
Mora Primary School
CRICK NW2 82 A2
Morden ⊖
WIM/MER SW19 178 A6
Morden Cemetery
MRDN SM4 193 F3
Morden College Homes
BKHTH/KID SE3 145 K3
Morden First School
MRDN SM4 193 K2
Morden Hall Medical Centre
WIM/MER SW19 178 A6

Morden Hall Park (NT) MRDN SM4....194 B1
Morden Mount Primary School LEW SE13....144 E3
Morden Park Pool MRDN SM4....193 J2
Morden Road ⊖ WIM/MER SW19....178 A5
Morden Road Clinic WIM/MER SW19....178 A6
Morden South ⇌ MRDN SM4....193 K2
Moreland Primary School FSBYE EC1V....6 B4
Moriah Jewish Day School PIN HA5....59 J5
Morley College STHWK SE1....17 K4
Morningside Primary School HOM E9....86 E4
Mornington Crescent ⊖ CAMTN NW1....4 A2
Mornington Sports & Fitness Centre CAMTN NW1....84 B6
Morpeth School BETH E2....104 E3
Mortimer Road Clinic WLSDN NW10....100 A2
Mortimer School STRHM/NOR SW16....161 J4
Mortlake ⇌ MORT/ESHN SW14....137 K4
Mortlake Cemetery MORT/ESHN SW14....138 B4
Mortlake Crematorium RCH/KEW TW9....137 J3
Moselle School TOTM N17....50 A5
Moselle Special School TOTM N17....49 K5
Mosiah Foundation Supplementary School STNW/STAM N16....68 A5
Mossbourne Community Academy HACK E8....86 C2
Mossford Green Primary School BARK/HLT IG6....54 C5
Moss Hall Junior School FNCH N3....47 F2
The Mother & Baby Clinic HOM E9....86 E4
Motspur Park ⇌ NWMAL KT3....192 E2
Mottingham ⇌ ELTH/MOT SE9....166 E3
Mottingham Community Health Clinic ELTH/MOT SE9....166 D6
Mottingham Primary School ELTH/MOT SE9....166 E6
Mount Carmel RC Primary School EA W5....116 D3
Mount Carmel RC Technical College for Girls ARCH N19....66 D5
The Mount Infant School FELT TW13....154 D4
Mount Medical Centre FELT TW13....154 D4
Mount School MLHL NW7....45 K1
Mount Stewart Infant School KTN/HRWW/WS HA3....61 K5
The Muvileum of London STHWK SE1....17 G2
Mowlem Primary School BETH E2....104 E1
Mowlem Trading Estate TOTM N17....50 E3
MPR Eurotots School KIL/WHAMP NW6....82 B5
MS Business Centre PIN HA5....41 H6
MSP Business Centre WBLY HA9....80 D2
Mudchute POP/IOD E14....124 E4
Mudchute City Farm POP/IOD E14....125 F4
Mudlands Estate RAIN RM13....111 G2
Mulberry Business Centre BERM/RHTH SE16....124 A2
Mulberry House School CRICK NW2....82 C3
Mulberry Primary School TOTM N17....50 B6
Mulberry School for Girls WCHPL E1....104 D5
Mulgrave Primary School WOOL/PLUM SE18....127 F4
Munroe Centre STHWK SE1....19 F2
Murky Puddle Theatre NWMAL KT3....176 C6
Murray Business Centre STMC/STPC BR5....186 C6
Muschamp Primary School CAR SM5....194 D6
Museum in Docklands POP/IOD E14....105 J6
Museum of Domestic Design & Architecture EBAR EN4....21 K6
Museum of Fulham Palace FUL/PGN SW6....139 G3
Museum of Garden History STHWK SE1....17 F5
Museum of London BARB EC2Y....12 C2
Museum of London Archaeology IS N1....6 D1
Museum of Richmond TWK TW1....136 E6

Museum of the Artillery in the Rotunda CHARL SE7....126 D5
Museum of the Order of St John FARR EC1M....6 B7
Musical Museum BTFD TW8....117 F6
Muswell Hill Bowling Club MUSWH N10....48 A6
Muswell Hill Golf Club MUSWH N10....48 B4
Muswell Hill Primary School MUSWH N10....48 B6
Myatt Garden Primary School BROCKY SE4....144 C3
Myatts Field Clinic BRXN/ST SW9....142 C2
N1 Shopping Centre IS N1....5 K2
Nagi Business Centre ALP/SUD HA0....97 K1
Nags Head Shopping Centre HOLWY N7....84 E1
Naima Jewish Preparatory School KIL/WHAMP NW6....101 F1
Nancy Rueben Primary School HDN NW4....64 B1
Nash College of Further Education WWKM BR4....214 D1
The National Archives RCH/KEW TW9....137 H1
National Army Museum CHEL SW3....120 E6
National Film Theatre STHWK SE1....11 H7
National Gallery LSQ/SEVD WC2H....10 D2
National Hospital for Neurology & Neurosurgery RSQ WC1B....4 E7
National Maritime Museum GNWCH SE10....125 G6
National Physical Laboratory TEDD TW11....173 K2
National Portrait Gallery LSQ/SEVD WC2H....10 D6
National Sports Centre NRWD SE19....181 H2
National Temperance Hospital CAMTN NW1....4 A4
National Tennis Centre PUT/ROE SW15....138 B6
National Youth Theatre Great Britain HOLWY N7....84 E1
The Natural History Museum SKENS SW7....14 A5
Natural Therapy Clinic TOOT SW17....179 G1
Natwest Sports Club BECK BR3....182 C2
Navigation College CANST EC4R....12 D5
Neasden ⊖ WLSDN NW10....81 G3
Negus Sixth Form Centre WOOL/PLUM SE18....127 J6
Nelson Dock Museum BERM/RHTH SE16....124 C1
Nelson Hospital RYNPK SW20....177 J5
Nelson Primary School EHAM E6....108 A1
WHTN TW2....155 G1
Nelson's Column STJS SW1Y....10 D7
Nelson Trading Estate PIM/MER SW19....178 A4
Neo Clinic PIM SW1V....16 A6
The New Ambassadors Theatre LSQ/SEVD WC2H....10 D4
New Atlas Wharf POP/IOD E14....124 C3
The New Aylesbury Medical Centre WALW SE17....122 E5
New Barnet ⇌ BAR EN5....21 G6
New Beckenham ⇌ BECK BR3....182 B3
New Brentford Cemetery HSLW TW3....134 E3
Newbridge School CHDH RM6....73 H2
Newbury Park ⊖ GNTH/NBYPK IG2....72 D3
Newbury Park Health Centre GNTH/NBYPK IG2....72 D3
The New Business Centre WLSDN NW10....99 H2
New Caledonian Wharf BERM/RHTH SE16....124 C3
New Chiswick Pool CHSWK W4....138 B1
New City Primary School PLSTW E13....107 G2
New Connaught Rooms HOL/ALD WC2B....11 F4
New Covent Garden Market VX/NE SW8....141 J1
New Crane Wharf WAP E1W....123 K1
New Cross ⇌⊖ NWCR SE14....144 C1
New Cross Gate ⇌⊖ NWCR SE14....144 B1
New Cross Sports Arena NWCR SE14....144 B1
New Eltham ⇌ ELTH/MOT SE9....167 G3
New End Primary School HAMP NW3....83 G2
New End Theatre HAMP NW3....83 G1

New England Industrial Estate BARK IG11....108 C1
Newfield Primary School WLSDN NW10....81 H5
Newham City Farm CAN/RD E16....107 H5
Newham College of Further Education EHAM E6....107 K1
SRTFD E15....88 C5
Newham General Hospital PLSTW E13....107 G3
Newham Leisure Centre PLSTW E13....107 G4
Newham Medical Centre PLSTW E13....107 G1
Newham Sixth Form College PLSTW E13....107 F3
Newham Training & Education Centre SRTFD E15....88 C4
New Hope Christian School EDUL SE22....143 G5
New Horizons Computer Learning Centre FSBYE EC1V....6 E5
Newington Court Business Centre STHWK SE1....18 C5
Newington Green Primary School STNW/STAM N16....86 A3
Newington Industrial Estate WALW SE17....18 B7
New Kings Primary School FUL/PGN SW6....139 J3
Newland House School TWK TW1....156 A6
New London Theatre LSQ/SEVD WC2H....11 F3
New Malden ⇌ NWMAL KT3....176 B6
Newnham Junior School RSLP HA4....59 G5
New North Community School IS N1....85 J5
Newport School LEY E10....70 A6
New River Sports Centre WDGN N22....49 H3
New River Village CEND/HSY/T N8....49 F6
New Rush Hall School IL IG1....72 C6
New School FUL/PGN SW6....139 J4
New Scotland Yard STJSPK SW1H....16 C4
News International Offices WAP E1W....104 D6
New Southgate ⇌ FBAR/BDGN N11....48 A1
New Southgate Cemetery FBAR/BDGN N11....34 B5
New Southgate Crematorium FBAR/BDGN N11....34 B5
New Southgate Industrial Estate FBAR/BDGN N11....48 C1
New Southgate Pain Clinic & Medical Centre FBAR/BDGN N11....48 C1
New Spitalfields Market LEY E10....87 J2
Newstead Wood School for Girls ORP BR6....216 D1
Newton Farm First & Middle School RYLN/HDSTN HA2....59 K6
Newton Industrial Estate CHDH RM6....73 K1
Newton Medical Centre BAY/PAD W2....101 F5
Newton Preparatory School VX/NE SW8....141 G1
Newtons Primary School RAIN RM13....111 F1
New Victoria Hospital KUTN/CMB KT2....176 B4
New Woodlands School BMLY BR1....165 H6
N H Harrington Hall Hotel SKENS SW7....120 B4
Nightingale Clinic PLSTW E13....107 G1
Nightingale Primary School CLPT E5....86 C1
SWFD E18....71 G1
WDGN N22....49 F4
WOOL/PLUM SE18....127 G6
Nightingale School TOOT SW17....160 D4
Noam Primary School NFNCH/WDSPK N12....47 F1
Noel Coward Theatre CHCR WC2N....10 C5
Noel Park Primary School WDGN N22....49 H5
Nonsuch High School for Girls CHEAM SM3....208 B5
Nonsuch Park Hotel EW KT17....208 A3
Nonsuch Primary School EW KT17....207 K3
Noor Ul Islam Primary School LEY E10....70 A6
Norbiton ⇌ KUTN/CMB KT2....175 H4
Norbury ⇌ STRHM/NOR SW16....180 A4
Norbury Business & Enterprise College STRHM/NOR SW16....180 B4
Norbury Complementary Therapy Clinic STRHM/NOR SW16....180 A4

Norbury First & Middle School HRW HA1....60 E2
Norbury Health Centre STRHM/NOR SW16....180 A5
Norbury Manor Primary School STRHM/NOR SW16....179 K4
Norbury Trading Estate STRHM/NOR SW16....180 A5
Norland Place School NTGHL W11....119 H1
Norlington School LEY E10....70 B5
Normand Croft Community School WKENS W14....119 J6
Normandy Primary School BXLYHN DA7....150 A2
Normanhurst School CHING E4....38 B2
Norman Park Athletics Track HAYES BR2....200 A3
Norman Shaw Building (MP's Offices) WHALL SW1A....16 E2
North Acton ⊖ WLSDN NW10....99 F3
North Acton Business Park ACT W3....99 F3
North Beckton Primary School EHAM E6....107 K3
North Bridge House HAMP NW3....83 C4
North Bridge House Preparatory School CAMTN NW1....3 J1
North Bridge House School HAMP NW3....83 H4
Northbrook CE School LEE/GVPK SE12....145 H6
Northbury Primary School BARK IG11....90 B4
North Clinic BMLY BR1....183 K4
North Croydon Medical Centre THHTH CR7....196 C3
North Dulwich ⇌ HNHL SE24....142 E6
North Ealing ⊖ ACT W3....98 B5
North Ealing Primary School WEA W13....97 H3
North East Surrey Crematorium NWMAL KT3....193 F3
Northend Primary School ERITH DA8....150 C2
North End Trading Estate ERITH DA8....150 B1
North Feltham Trading Estate EBED/NFELT TW14....134 A5
Northfields ⊖ WEA W13....116 D3
Northfields Industrial Estate ALP/SUD HA0....80 C6
Northfields Prospect Business Centre PUT/ROE SW15....139 J5
Northgate Business Centre EN EN1....24 D4
Northgate Clinic CDALE/KGS NW9....63 G3
Northgate Industrial Park CRW RM5....56 B5
North Greenwich ⊖ GNWCH SE10....125 H2
North Harringay Primary School CEND/HSY/T N8....67 G1
North Harrow ⊖ RYLN/HDSTN HA2....60 A2
North Havering College of Adult Education ROM RM1....75 G1
North Kensington Video-Drama Project NKENS W10....100 C5
North London College SEVS/STOTM N15....50 B6
North London Collegiate School EDGW HA8....44 A2
The North London Hospice NFNCH/WDSPK N12....33 F5
North London International School (Diploma Centre) NFNCH/WDSPK N11....47 J1
North London International School (Lower School) NFNCH/WDSPK N12....33 F5
North London International School (Upper School) FBAR/BDGN N11....47 K1
North London Nuffield Hospital ENC/FH EN2....23 G3
North London School of Physiotherapy ARCH N19....66 C5
North London Tutorial College HDN NW4....64 A3
North Middlesex Golf Club NFNCH/WDSPK N12....33 H5
North Middlesex Hospital UED N18....50 A1
Northolt ⊖ NTHLT UB5....78 A5
Northolt Aerodrome RSLP HA4....76 E4
Northolt High School NTHLT UB5....77 K4
Northolt Park ⇌ RYLN/HDSTN HA2....78 B2
Northolt Primary School NTHLT UB5....77 H5
Northolt Road Clinic RYLN/HDSTN HA2....78 C1

Northolt Swimarama NTHLT UB5....78 A4
North Pole Depot WLSDN NW10....99 H3
North Primary School STHL UB1....95 K6
North Sheen ⇌ RCH/KEW TW9....137 H5
Northside Primary School NFNCH/WDSPK N12....47 G1
The North Street Health Centre CLAP SW4....141 H4
Northumberland Heath Medical Centre ERITH DA8....150 A1
Northumberland Heath Primary School ERITH DA8....149 J1
Northumberland Park ⇌ TOTM N17....50 D4
Northumberland Park Industrial Estate TOTM N17....50 D2
Northumberland Park School TOTM N17....50 C3
Northview Primary School WLSDN NW10....81 G2
Northway School MLHL NW7....31 F4
North Wembley ⊖ ALP/SUD HA0....79 K1
North West Kent College RDART DA2....170 E4
North West London Jewish Primary School CRICK NW2....82 C5
North West London Medical Centre MV/WKIL W9....101 G2
North Westminster Community Secondary School MV/WKIL W9....100 E3
North Weylands Industrial Estate WOT/HER KT12....188 D6
Northwick Park ⊖ KTN/HRWW/WS HA3....61 H4
Northwick Park Hospital & Clinical Research Centre HRW HA1....61 H4
Northwold Primary School CLPT E5....68 C3
Northwood ⊖ NTHWD HA6....40 C3
Northwood Cemetery NTHWD HA6....40 D5
Northwood College NTHWD HA6....40 B3
Northwood FC NTHWD HA6....40 D5
Northwood Golf Club NTHWD HA6....40 B3
Northwood Hills ⊖ NTHWD HA6....40 E4
Northwood & Pinner Community Hospital NTHWD HA6....40 E4
Northwood Preparatory School RKW/CH/CXG WD3....26 A1
Northwood Primary School ERITHM DA18....129 F3
Northwood School NTHWD HA6....40 D4
Northwood Sports Centre NTHWD HA6....41 F4
Norwegian/British Monument BAY/PAD W2....8 C7
The Norwegian School WIM/MER SW19....177 F2
Norwood Green Infant School NWDGN UB2....114 D3
Norwood Green Junior School NWDGN UB2....114 D3
Norwood Heights Shopping Centre NRWD SE19....181 G2
Norwood Junction ⇌⊖ SNWD SE25....197 H1
Norwood School NRWD SE19....180 D3
Notre Dame RC Girls School STHWK SE1....18 A4
Notre Dame RC Primary School WOOL/PLUM SE18....127 G6
Notre Dame University LSQ/SEVD WC2H....10 D2
Notting Hill & Ealing High School WEA W13....97 H2
Notting Hill Gate ⊖ BAY/PAD W2....119 K1
Novello Theatre HOL/ALD WC2B....11 G4
Novotel CAMTN NW1....4
CAN/RD E16....107
GNWCH SE10....144
STHWK SE1....17
STHWK SE1....13
TWRH EC3N....13
WDR/YW UB7....112
Novotel London West HMSMTH W6....119
Nower Hill High School PIN HA5....60
NTGB Sports Ground EHAM E6....90
Nugent Shopping Park STMC/STPC BR5....202
Number 10 Bowling ROM RM1....75
Nunhead ⇌ PECK SE15....143
NutriLife Clinic MHST W1U....9

The O2
POP/IOD E14 ... 125 G1
Oakdale Infant School
SWFD E18 ... 53 F5
Oakdale Junior School
SWFD E18 ... 53 G5
Oakfield Preparatory School
DUL SE21 ... 162 E4
Oakfield Primary School
DART DA1 ... 171 G4
Oakfield Road Industrial Estate
PGE/AN SE20 ... 181 J3
Oak Heights Independent School
HSLW TW3 ... 135 G4
Oak Hill Health Centre
SURB KT6 ... 191 F3
Oakington Manor School
WBLY HA9 ... 80 D3
Oakland CP School
EBAR EN4 ... 33 K1
Oaklands Primary School
HNWL W7 ... 116 A2
Oaklands School
ISLW TW7 ... 135 J4
Oaklands Secondary School
BETH E2 ... 104 C2
Oak Lane Cemetery
TWK TW1 ... 156 B2
Oak Lane Medical Centre
TWK TW1 ... 156 C2
Oakleigh Park
TRDG/WHET N20 ... 33 H2
Oakleigh School
TRDG/WHET N20 ... 33 J5
Oak Lodge JMI School
WWKM BR4 ... 198 E4
Oak Lodge Medical Centre
EDGW HA8 ... 44 D3
Oak Lodge School
BAL SW12 ... 160 E2
EFNCH N2 ... 47 G6
Oaks Park High School
GNTH/NBYPK IG2 ... 72 D2
Oakthorpe Primary School
UED N18 ... 49 J1
Oak Tree Medical Centre
GDMY/SEVK IG3 ... 72 E6
Oakwood
STHGT/OAK N14 ... 22 C5
Oakwood Business Park
WLSDN NW10 ... 99 F2
Oakwood Medical Centre
STHGT/OAK N14 ... 22 C6
Oakwood School
BXLYHN DA7 ... 150 A5
Oasis Sports Centre
LSQ/SEVD WC2H ... 10 E3
Odeon Cinema
BAR EN5 ... 20 E6
BAY/PAD W2 ... 8 E4
BECK BR3 ... 182 D5
BERM/RHTH SE16 ... 124 A3
CAMTN NW1 ... 84 B6
ED N9 ... 37 F2
ELTH/MOT SE9 ... 146 D5
ESH/CLAY KT10 ... 204 B2
FITZ W1T ... 10 C2
HAMP NW3 ... 83 H5
HAYES BR2 ... 183 K5
HOLWY N7 ... 84 E1
KENS W8 ... 119 K3
KUT/HW KT1 ... 175 F5
MUSWH N10 ... 66 A1
RCH/KEW TW9 ... 136 E6
ROM RM1 ... 75 H2
STJS SW1Y ... 10 C6
STRHM/NOR SW16 ... 161 K5
SWFD E18 ... 52 E5
WIM/MER SW19 ... 177 K3
Odeon Covent Garden Cinema
LSQ/SEVD WC2H ... 10 D4
Odeon Wardour Street Cinema
SOHO/SHAV W1D ... 10 C5
Odessa Infant School
FSTGT E7 ... 88 E3
Odyssey Business Park
RSLP HA4 ... 77 F3
Old Abbotstonians RFC
YEAD UB4 ... 94 B1
Old Actonians Sports Club
EA W5 ... 117 G2
Old Admiralty
STJS SW1Y ... 16 D1
Old Bancroftians FC
BKHH IG9 ... 39 H6
Old Barnes Cemetery
BARN SW13 ... 138 E3
Old Beckenhamian RFC
WWKM BR4 ... 214 B1
Old Bellgate Wharf
POP/IOD E14 ... 124 C3
Old Bexley Business Park
BXLY DA5 ... 169 J2
Old Bexley CE Primary School
BXLY DA5 ... 169 G3
Old Brockleians Sports Ground
LEE/GVPK SE12 ... 166 B1
Old Bromlians CC
HAYES BR2 ... 200 A2
Old Cemetery
EDUL SE22 ... 163 J1
Old Colfeian Sports Club
LEE/GVPK SE12 ... 145 K6
Old Curiosity Shop
LINN WC2A ... 11 G3
Old Elthamians Sports Club
CHST BR7 ... 185 K2
Oldfield House Special School
HPTN TW12 ... 172 E4
Oldfield Primary School
GFD/PVL UB6 ... 96 D1
Oldfields Trading Estate
SUT SM1 ... 208 E1
Old Fold Manor Golf Club
BAR EN5 ... 20 C2
Old Ford Primary School
BOW E3 ... 105 H1
Oldhill Medical Centre
STNW/STAM N16 ... 68 B5
Old Jamaica Business Estate
BERM/RHTH SE16 ... 19 K4
Old Lyonian Sports Ground
RYLN/HDSTN HA2 ... 60 C2
Old Millhillians Sports Ground
RYLN/HDSTN HA2 ... 42 A4
Old Oak Primary School
SHB W12 ... 99 H5
Old Operating Theatre & Herb Garret Museum
STHWK SE1 ... 18 E1
Old Owens Sports Ground
TRDG/WHET N20 ... 33 H3
Old Palace Primary School
BOW E3 ... 105 K2
Old Palace School
CROY/NA CR0 ... 211 H1
Old Royal Naval College
GNWCH SE10 ... 125 G5
Old Royal Observatory Greenwich
GNWCH SE10 ... 145 G1
Old Spitalfields Market Hall
WCHPL E1 ... 13 J1
Old Street
FSBYE EC1V ... 6 E5
Old Sun Wharf
POP/IOD E14 ... 105 G6
Old Tiffinians Sports Ground
E/WMO/HCT KT8 ... 189 K2
Old Treasury
WHALL SW1A ... 16 E2
Old Vicarage School
RCHPK/HAM TW10 ... 157 F1
Old Vic Theatre
STHWK SE1 ... 17 K2
Old War Office
WHALL SW1A ... 16 E1
Old Wilsonians Sports Club
WWKM BR4 ... 199 H5
Olga Primary School
BOW E3 ... 105 G1
Oliver Business Park
WLSDN NW10 ... 98 E1
Oliver Goldsmith Primary School
CDALE/KGS NW9 ... 63 F2
CMBW SE5 ... 143 G2
Oliver House Preparatory School
CLAP SW4 ... 161 G1
Olympia
WKENS W14 ... 119 H3
Olympia Industrial Estate
WDGN N22 ... 49 F5
Olympic Industrial Estate
WBLY HA9 ... 80 D2
Olympic Retail Park
WBLY HA9 ... 80 C2
Olympic site (under development)
SRTFD E15 ... 87 K5
Olympic Trading Estate
WBLY HA9 ... 80 D2
One Aldwych Hotel
COVGDN WC2E ... 11 G5
The One Stanley Medical Centre
ALP/SUD HA0 ... 80 A5
On Sai Clinic
ECT SW5 ... 120 A4
The Open University
FSBYW WC1X ... 5 G4
HAMP NW3 ... 82 E2
Ophaboom Theatre
WLSDN NW10 ... 99 K1
Optimax Laser Eye Clinic
HAMP NW3 ... 83 G4
Orange Tree Theatre
RCH/KEW TW9 ... 137 F5
Orchard Business Centre
BECK BR3 ... 182 C1
The Orchard Health Centre
BARK IG11 ... 108 C1
Orchard Hill College
WLGTN SM6 ... 210 B4
Orchard House School
CHSWK W4 ... 118 A4
Orchard J & I School
HOM E9 ... 86 E5
The Orchard Junior School
HSLWW TW4 ... 135 F5
Orchard Primary School
SCUP DA14 ... 186 C1
The Orchard School
BRXS/STRHM SW2 ... 162 A3
E/WMO/HCT KT8 ... 189 J2
Orchard Shopping Centre
DART DA1 ... 171 H1
The Orchard Theatre
DART DA1 ... 171 H1
Orchard Way Primary School
CROY/NA CR0 ... 198 B4
Oriel Primary School
FELT TW13 ... 154 D5
Orient Industrial Park
LEY E10 ... 69 J6
Orion Business Centre
NWCR SE14 ... 124 A5
The Orion Primary School
CDALE/KGS NW9 ... 45 G4
Orleans House Gallery
TWK TW1 ... 156 C3
Orleans Infant School
TWK TW1 ... 156 C2
Orley Farm School
HRW HA1 ... 78 D1
Orpington
ORP BR6 ... 201 K6
Orpington College of Further Education
ORP BR6 ... 202 B5
The Orpington Halls
ORP BR6 ... 202 B6
Orpington Hospital
ORP BR6 ... 217 F2
Orpington Mental Health Centre
ORP BR6 ... 217 F1
Orpington Priory
ORP BR6 ... 202 C4
Orpington Retail Park
STMC/STPC BR5 ... 202 D1
Orpington Superbowl
ORP BR6 ... 202 B5
Orpington Trade Centre
STMC/STPC BR5 ... 186 C6
Osidge JMI School
STHGT/OAK N14 ... 34 C3
Osier Industrial Estate
WAND/EARL SW18 ... 139 K5
Osmani Primary School
WCHPL E1 ... 104 C4
Osterley
ISLW TW7 ... 135 J1
Osterley Park & House (NT)
ISLW TW7 ... 115 H6
Osterley RFC
NWDGN UB2 ... 115 G3
Our Lady Immaculate RC Primary School
BRYLDS KT5 ... 191 J5
Our Lady of Dolours RC Primary School
BAY/PAD W2 ... 101 F4
Our Lady of Grace RC Junior School
CRICK NW2 ... 81 K1
Our Lady of Grace RC Primary School
CHARL SE7 ... 126 A6
Our Lady of Lourdes RC Primary School
FBAR/BDGN N11 ... 48 B1
NFNCH/WDSPK N12 ... 47 G3
WAN E11 ... 70 D3
WLSDN NW10 ... 80 E6
Our Lady of Muswell RC Primary School
MUSWH N10 ... 48 A5
Our Lady of the Rosary RC School
ELTH/MOT SE9 ... 167 K1
Our Lady of the Sacred Heart School
HOLWY N7 ... 85 F3
Our Lady of the Visitation RC Primary School
GFD/PVL UB6 ... 96 C3
Our Lady of Victories RC Primary School
PUT/ROE SW15 ... 139 G5
SKENS SW7 ... 120 B4
Our Lady Queen of Heaven RC Primary School
PUT/ROE SW15 ... 159 G2
Our Lady RC Primary School
POP/IOD E14 ... 105 H5
Our Lady & St Johns RC Primary School
BTFD TW8 ... 116 D5
Our Lady & St Joseph Primary School
IS N1 ... 86 A4
Our Lady & St Philip Neri Infants School
FSTH SE23 ... 164 A5
Our Lady & St Philip Neri RC Primary School
SYD SE26 ... 164 B6
Our Ladys Catholic Primary School
DART DA1 ... 171 G1
Our Ladys RC Primary School
CAMTN NW1 ... 84 C6
Oval
LBTH SE11 ... 122 B6
Oval Business Centre
LBTH SE11 ... 122 A5
Oval House Theatre
LBTH SE11 ... 122 B6
Oval Primary School
CROY/NA CR0 ... 197 F5
Overton Grange School
BELMT SM2 ... 209 F6
Oxford Circus
REGST W1B ... 9 K3
Oxford Gardens Primary School
NKENS W10 ... 100 B5
Oxford House College
SOHO/SHAV W1D ... 10 C3
Oxhey Park Golf Centre
OXHEY WD19 ... 27 H3
Oxhey Wood Primary School
OXHEY WD19 ... 27 G6
Oxo Tower Wharf
STHWK SE1 ... 11 K6
Paddington
BAY/PAD W2 ... 8 A3
Paddington Academy
MV/WKIL W9 ... 100 E3
Paddington Bowling & Sports Club
MV/WKIL W9 ... 101 F3
Paddington Green Primary School
BAY/PAD W2 ... 2 A7
Paddington Recreation Ground Athletics Track
MV/WKIL W9 ... 100 E2
Paddock Primary School
BTSEA SW11 ... 141 F5
Paddock School
PUT/ROE SW15 ... 138 C5
Paines Lane Cemetery
PIN HA5 ... 41 J6
Pain Relief Clinic
HDN NW4 ... 63 K3
Paint Pots Montessori School
WBPTN SW10 ... 120 B6
Pakeman Primary School
HOLWY N7 ... 85 F1
Palace Gardens Shopping Centre
ENC/FH EN2 ... 23 K4
Palace of Westminster
WHALL SW1A ... 17 F3
Palace Theatre
SOHO/SHAV W1D ... 10 D5
Palladium Theatre
SOHO/CST W1F ... 10 A4
Palmers Green
PLMGR N13 ... 35 F6
Palmers Green High School
WCHMH N21 ... 35 G4
Palmerston Business Centre
SUT SM1 ... 209 G3
Palm House, Kew Gardens
RCH/KEW TW9 ... 137 G2
Panorama Pier
STHWK SE1 ... 12 C6
Paradise Swimming Pools
MLHL NW7 ... 45 G1
Paray House School
FUL/PGN SW6 ... 139 J3
Parayhouse School
WBPTN SW10 ... 140 B1
Parchmore Medical Centre
THHTH CR7 ... 180 D6
Pardes House & Beis Yaakov School
FNCH N3 ... 46 D5
Parent Infant Clinic
HAMP NW3 ... 83 G3
Parish CE Primary School
BMLY BR1 ... 183 K3
Park Business Centre
MV/WKIL W9 ... 100 E2
Parkes Hotel
CHEL SW3 ... 14 D4
Parkfield Industrial Estate
BTSEA SW11 ... 141 F3
Parkfield JMI School
HDN NW4 ... 63 K4
Parkgate House School
CLAP SW4 ... 141 F5
Park Hall Trading Estate
WNWD SE27 ... 162 D5
Park High School
STAN HA7 ... 43 K5
Park Hill Junior School
CROY/NA CR0 ... 211 K1
Parkhill Primary School
CLAY IG5 ... 53 K6
Park Hill School
KUTN/CMB KT2 ... 175 H3
Park House Medical Centre
KIL/WHAMP NW6 ... 100 C1
Park House RFC
HAYES BR2 ... 200 B6
Parklands Primary School
ROM RM1 ... 57 F6
Park Lane Primary School
WBLY HA9 ... 80 A2
Park Medical Centre
BERM/RHTH SE16 ... 124 A4
Park Mews Small Business Centre
HNHL SE24 ... 162 D1
Park Plaza County Hall Hotel
STHWK SE1 ... 17 H2
STHWK SE1 ... 17 H2
Park Primary School
SRTFD E15 ... 88 D5
Park Road Clinic
CEND/HSY/T N8 ... 66 D2
Park Road Swimming Centre
CEND/HSY/T N8 ... 66 D2
Park Royal
EA W5 ... 98 C3
Park Royal Business Centre
WLSDN NW10 ... 99 F3
Park School for Girls
IL IG1 ... 72 A6
Parkside Business Estate
DEPT SE8 ... 124 C6
Parkside Clinic
NTGHL W11 ... 100 C5
Parkside Health
NTGHL W11 ... 100 C5
Parkside Hospital
WIM/MER SW19 ... 159 G5
Park View Academy
SEVS/STOTM N15 ... 67 J1
Park Walk Primary School
WBPTN SW10 ... 120 C6
Parkway Primary School
ERITHM DA18 ... 129 F3
Parkway Trading Estate
HEST TW5 ... 114 B6
Parkwood Primary School
FSBYPK N4 ... 67 H6
Parliament Hill Fields Athletics Track
HAMP NW3 ... 83 K2
Parliament Hill Lido
HAMP NW3 ... 84 A2
Parliament Hill School
KTTN NW5 ... 84 A2
Parmiter Industrial Centre
BETH E2 ... 104 D1
Parnells Sports Ground
KTN/HRWW/WS HA3 ... 62 B3
Parsloes Primary School
DAGW RM9 ... 92 B4
Parsons Green
FUL/PGN SW6 ... 139 K2
Parsons Green Health Clinic
FUL/PGN SW6 ... 139 K2
Pascals College
BECK BR3 ... 182 D5
Passport Language Schools
BMLY BR1 ... 184 A4
Pastoria Hotel
LSQ/SEVD WC2H ... 10 D6
Patent Office
FLST/FETLN EC4A ... 11 J2
The Patrick Doody Clinic & Health Centre
WIM/MER SW19 ... 177 K3
Pattinson Clinic
RCH/KEW TW9 ... 136 E6
The Paul Robeson Theatre
HSLW TW3 ... 135 G4
Pavilion Barclays Sports Ground
EA W5 ... 98 A4
The Pavilion Leisure Centre
BMLY BR1 ... 183 K5
Pavilion Restaurant
RCH/KEW TW9 ... 137 F3
Paxton Primary School
NRWD SE19 ... 181 G2
PCMS London
SRTFD E15 ... 106 B1
PDSA Hospital
REDBR IG4 ... 53 H6
Peace Pagoda
CHEL SW3 ... 140 E1
Peacock Estate
TOTM N17 ... 50 B2
Peacock Industrial Estate
TOTM N17 ... 50 B3
The Peacock Theatre
HOL/ALD WC2B ... 11 G4
Peall Road Industrial Estate
CROY/NA CR0 ... 196 A3
Peckham Park Primary School
PECK SE15 ... 143 H1
The Peckham Pulse Health & Leisure Centre
PECK SE15 ... 143 H2
Peckham Rye
PECK SE15 ... 143 H3
Pelham Primary School
BXLYHN DA7 ... 149 H4
WIM/MER SW19 ... 177 K3
Pembridge Hall Preparatory School for Girls
BAY/PAD W2 ... 100 E6
Pendragon School
BMLY BR1 ... 165 K5
Penge East
SYD SE26 ... 181 K2
Penge West
PGE/AN SE20 ... 181 J3
Pentavia Retail Park
MLHL NW7 ... 45 H3
Penwortham Primary School
STRHM/NOR SW16 ... 179 G2
Percival David Foundation of Chinese Art
STPAN WC1H ... 4 D6
Perivale
GFD/PVL UB6 ... 97 G1
Perivale Industrial Park
GFD/PVL UB6 ... 97 G1
Perivale New Business Centre
GFD/PVL UB6 ... 97 J1
Perivale Park Athletics Track
GFD/PVL UB6 ... 96 E2
Perivale Park Golf Course
GFD/PVL UB6 ... 96 E2
Perrin Road Clinic
ALP/SUD HA0 ... 79 H2
Perry Hall Primary School
ORP BR6 ... 202 A3
Perrymount Primary School
FSTH SE23 ... 164 A4
The Petchy Academy
HACK E8 ... 86 B3
Peterborough Primary School
FUL/PGN SW6 ... 139 K3
Peterborough & St Margaret's School
STAN HA7 ... 28 E5
Peter Hills School
BERM/RHTH SE16 ... 124 A1
Peter James Business Centre
HYS/HAR UB3 ... 113 K2
Peterley Business Centre
BETH E2 ... 104 D1
Peter Pan Statue
BAY/PAD W2 ... 8 A7
The Petersham Hotel
RCHPK/HAM TW10 ... 157 F2
Petrie Museum of Egyptian Archaeology
FITZ W1T ... 4 B7
Petts Hill Primary School
NTHLT UB5 ... 78 B3
Petts Wood
STMC/STPC BR5 ... 201 H2
Pewterers' Hall
CITYW EC2V ... 12 D2
Pheasantry Welcome Centre
TEDD TW11 ... 174 A4
Phipps Bridge
WIM/MER SW19 ... 178 B6
Phoenix Academy
ED N9 ... 36 D3
Phoenix Business Centre
POP/IOD E14 ... 105 J4
Phoenix Cinema
EFNCH N2 ... 65 J1
Phoenix College
MRDN SM4 ... 194 A2
Phoenix High School
SHB W12 ... 99 J6
Phoenix Industrial Estate
HRW HA1 ... 61 F1
Phoenix Leisure Centre
CAT SE6 ... 164 E2
Phoenix School
HAMP NW3 ... 83 H4
Phoenix Secondary & Primary School
BOW E3 ... 105 H2
Phoenix Theatre
LSQ/SEVD WC2H ... 10 D4
Phoenix Trading Estate
GFD/PVL UB6 ... 79 J6
Physical Energy Statue
BAY/PAD W2 ... 14 A1
Piccadilly Circus
MYFR/PICC W1J ... 10 C6
Piccadilly Theatre
SOHO/SHAV W1D ... 10 C5
Pickford Lane Medical Centre
BXLYHN DA7 ... 149 F2
Pickhurst Infant School
WWKM BR4 ... 199 H3

Pickhurst Junior School WWKM BR4 199 J3
Picture House Cinema SRTFD E15 88 B4
Pilgrims Way J & I School PECK SE15 123 K6
Pilot Industrial Centre WLSDN NW10 99 G3
Pilton Estate CROY/NA CR0 196 C6
Pimlico ⊖ PIM SW1V 121 J5
Pimlico Academy PIM SW1V 121 H5
Pinewood Primary School CRW RM5 56 D1
Pinkwell Primary School HYS/HAR UB3 113 F4
Pinnacles Cricket & Squash Club SUT SM1 208 E4
Pinner ⊖ PIN HA5 59 J1
Pinner Hill Golf Club PIN HA5 41 F2
Pinner Medical Centre PIN HA5 59 J1
Pinner New Cemetery PIN HA5 42 A6
Pinner Park Primary School PIN HA5 42 B6
Pinner View Medical Centre HRW HA1 60 C2
Pinner Wood School PIN HA5 41 G4
Pioneers Industrial Park CROY/NA CR0 195 K5
Pippins School ASHF TW15 152 C6
Pitshanger Manor Museum EA W5 116 D1
Plaisterers Hall STBT EC1A 12 C2
Plaistow ⊖ SRTFD E15 106 D1
Plaistow Hospital PLSTW E13 107 F1
Plaistow Primary School PLSTW E13 107 F1
Plantation House Medical Centre LOTH EC2R 13 F3
Plashet Jewish Cemetery MNPK E12 89 H4
Plashet Road Medical Centre FSTGT E7 89 F5
Plashet School EHAM E6 89 J5
Players Theatre CHCR WC2N 11 F7
Playgolf Northwick Park HRW HA1 61 G5
The Playhouse CHCR WC2N 11 F7
Plaza Business Centre PEND EN3 25 H3
Pleasance Theatre HOLWY N7 84 E4
Plumcroft Primary School WOOL/PLUM SE18 127 H6
Plumstead ⇌ WOOL/PLUM SE18 127 J4
Plumstead Cemetery ABYW SE2 148 C1
Plumstead Leisure Centre WOOL/PLUM SE18 128 A5
Plumstead Manor School WOOL/PLUM SE18 127 J5
The Pointer School BKHTH/KID SE3 145 K2
Police Cadet School WAN E11 70 E5
The Polish Institute & Sikorski Museum SKENS SW7 14 B3
Polish War Memorial RSLP HA4 77 F4
Polka Theatre for Children WIM/MER SW19 178 A2
Ponders End ⇌ PEND EN3 25 G6
Ponders End Industrial Estate PEND EN3 25 H5
Pontoon Dock ⊖ CAN/RD E16 126 B1
Pooles Park Primary School FSBYPK N4 67 F6
Pools on the Park RCH/KEW TW9 136 E5
Pope John Primary School SHB W12 99 K6
Pop In Business Centre WBLY HA9 80 D3
Poplar ⊖ POP/IOD E14 105 K6
Poplar Business Park POP/IOD E14 124 D2
Poplar Primary School WIM/MER SW19 177 K6
Pop Up Theatre CLKNW EC1R 5 K3
Porchester Leisure Centre BAY/PAD W2 101 F5
Portcullis House WHALL SW1A 17 F3
Portico City Learning Centre CLPT E5 86 E2
The Portland Hospital REGST W1B 3 K7
Portland House Medical Centre GFD/PVL UB6 96 B3
Portland Medical Centre SNWD SE25 197 J2
Portland Place School REGST W1B 9 K1
The Portman Clinic HAMP NW3 83 H4
Portobello Market NKENS W10 100 C4
Portobello Medical Centre NTGHL W11 100 C5
Portway Primary School SRTFD E15 88 E6
Pound Park Nursery School CHARL SE7 126 C5
The Pountney Clinic HSLW TW3 135 F4
Poverest Primary School STMC/STPC BR5 202 B2
Powergate Business Park WLSDN NW10 99 F2
Power Industrial Estate ERITH DA8 150 C2
Premier Cinema PECK SE15 143 H3
Prendergast Ladywell Fields College BROCKY SE4 164 D1
Prendergast School BROCKY SE4 144 D5
Preston Manor School WBLY HA9 62 B6
Preston Medical Centre WBLY HA9 80 A1
Preston Park Primary School WBLY HA9 61 K5
Preston Road ⊖ WBLY HA9 62 A5
Priestmead Middle School KTN/HRWW/WS HA3 43 H6
Primrose Hill School CAMTN NW1 84 A6
Primrose Montessori School HBRY N5 85 J1
Prince Charles Cinema LSQ/SEVD WC2H 10 D5
Prince Edward Theatre SOHO/SHAV W1D 10 C4
Prince of Wales Theatre STJS SW1Y 10 C6
Prince Regent ⊖ CAN/RD E16 107 G6
Princes College NOXST/BSQ WC1A 10 E3
Princes Court Business Centre WAP E1W 104 D6
Princes Park Stadium DART DA1 171 K3
Princes Plain Primary School HAYES BR2 200 D4
Princess Avenue School MUSWH N10 48 B6
Princess Frederica CE J & I School WLSDN NW10 99 K1
Princess Grace Hospital MHST W1U 3 G7
Princess Louise Hospital NKENS W10 100 A4
Princess May Primary School STNW/STAM N16 86 A3
Princess of Wales Conservatory RCH/KEW TW9 137 G1
The Princess Royal Distribution Centre WLSDN NW10 80 D6
The Princess Royal University Hospital ORP BR6 216 A1
Prior Weston Primary School STLK EC1Y 6 D7
Priory CE Primary School WIM/MER SW19 178 A1
The Priory Leisure Centre STMC/STPC BR5 202 D5
Priory Retail Park WIM/MER SW19 178 C3
Priory School STMC/STPC BR5 202 D5
Priory Shopping Centre DART DA1 171 G1
Priory Special School SNWD SE25 197 G1
Privy Council STJS SW1Y 16 C1
Privy Council Office WHALL SW1A 16 E1
Progress Business Park CROY/NA CR0 196 A6
Pronto Trading Estate YEAD UB4 94 C4
Prospect House School PUT/ROE SW15 159 G2
Proteus School KIL/WHAMP NW6 83 F5
Proud Gallery CHCR WC2N 10 E6
Providence Road School WDR/YW UB7 112 B1
Provident Industrial Estate HYS/HAR UB3 113 K2
PS Tattershall Castle WHALL SW1A 17 F1
Pudding Mill Lane ⊖ SRTFD E15 87 K6
Pumphouse Educational Museum BERM/RHTH SE16 124 B1
Pump Lane Industrial Estate HYS/HAR UB3 114 A2
The Purcell School HRW HA1 78 D1
Purdy Hicks Gallery STHWK SE1 12 A7
Purfleet ⇌ PUR RM19 131 K5
Purfleet Industrial Park SOCK/AV RM15 131 J1
Purfleet Primary School PUR RM19 131 K4
Purley Oaks ⇌ SAND/SEL CR2 211 K6
Purley Oaks Primary School SAND/SEL CR2 211 K5
Pursuit Centre WAP E1W 104 E6
Putney ⇌ PUT/ROE SW15 139 G5
Putney Animal Hospital PUT/ROE SW15 139 G5
Putney Arts Theatre PUT/ROE SW15 139 G5
Putney Bridge ⊖ FUL/PGN SW6 139 H4
Putney Exchange Shopping Centre PUT/ROE SW15 139 G5
Putney High School PUT/ROE SW15 139 G6
Putney Leisure Centre PUT/ROE SW15 139 F5
Putney Lower Common Cemetery BARN SW13 138 E3
Putneymead Medical Centre PUT/ROE SW15 139 F5
Putney Park School PUT/ROE SW15 138 E5
Putney School of Art PUT/ROE SW15 139 H5
Putney Town Social & Bowls Club PUT/ROE SW15 139 F3
Putney Vale Cemetery PUT/ROE SW15 158 D4
Putney Vale Crematorium PUT/ROE SW15 158 D4
Pylon Trading Estate CAN/RD E16 106 B3
Quadrant Business Park KIL/WHAMP NW6 82 C6
Quality Hotel HRW HA1 60 D3
WBLY HA9 80 C2
Quebec Industrial Estate BERM/RHTH SE16 124 B2
Queen Charlotte's & Chelsea Hospital SHB W12 99 K5
Queen Charlotte's Cottage, Kew Gardens RCH/KEW TW9 136 E3
Queen Elizabeth Conference Centre WEST SW1P 16 D3
Queen Elizabeth Hall STHWK SE1 11 G7
Queen Elizabeth Hospital WOOL/PLUM SE18 126 E6
Queen Elizabeth II School MV/WKIL W9 100 D3
Queen Elizabeth Leisure Centre BAR EN5 20 D5
Queen Elizabeth Museum CHING E4 38 D2
Queen Elizabeths Boys School BAR EN5 20 B4
Queen Elizabeths Girls School BAR EN5 20 D5
Queen Elizabeth Stadium EN EN1 24 B3
Queenhithe Stairs BLKFR EC4V 12 C6
Queen Mary College WCHPL E1 105 F3
Queen Mary's Hospital HAMP NW3 83 G1
Queen Marys Hospital SCUP DA14 186 B1
Queen Mary's Hospital for Children SUT SM1 194 B5
Queen Mary's University Hospital PUT/ROE SW15 158 D1
Queen Mary & Westfield College SWFD E18 52 E4
Queen Mother Sports Centre PIM SW1V 16 A6
Queensbridge Primary School HACK E8 86 B5
Queensbridge Sports Centre HACK E8 86 B5
Queen's Building HTHAIR TW6 132 E4
Queensbury ⊖ STAN HA7 44 B6
Queens Business & Secretarial College SKENS SW7 14 A6
The Queens CE Primary School RCH/KEW TW9 137 G1
Queen's Club WKENS W14 119 H5
Queens College London CAVSQ/HST W1G 9 J2
Queens College Preparatory School CAVSQ/HST W1G 9 J1
The Queen's Gallery BGVA SW1W 15 K3
Queens Gate School SKENS SW7 14 A6
Queens Hospital ROMW/RG RM7 75 G4
The Queens House GNWCH SE10 125 G6
Queens Ice Rink & Bowl BAY/PAD W2 101 F6
Queens Manor Primary School FUL/PGN SW6 139 F1
Queensmead School RSLP HA4 77 H2
Queensmead Sports Centre RSLP HA4 77 H3
Queens Medical Centre RCHPK/HAM TW10 137 G6
Queensmill School FUL/PGN SW6 139 K3
Queens Park ⊖ ⊖ KIL/WHAMP NW6 100 D1
Queens Park Community School WLSDN NW10 82 A6
Queens Park Health Centre NKENS W10 100 C2
Queens Park Primary School NKENS W10 100 C2
Queens Park Rangers FC (Loftus Road Stadium) SHB W12 118 E1
Queen's Road Cemetery CROY/NA CR0 196 D3
Queen's Road Peckham ⇌ ⊖ PECK SE15 143 J2
Queens Theatre SOHO/SHAV W1D 10 C5
Queenstown Road Battersea ⇌ VX/NE SW8 141 G2
Queensway ⊖ BAY/PAD W2 101 F6
Queensway Business Centre PEND EN3 24 E5
Queenswell J & I School TRDG/WHET N20 33 H4
Queen Victoria Memorial WHALL SW1A 16 A3
The Questors Theatre EA W5 97 J6
Quwwat UL Islam Girl's School FSTGT E7 88 E4
Radcliffe College SOHO/SHAV W1D 10 A4
Radisson Edwardian Berkshire Hotel OXSTW W1C 9 J4
Radisson Edwardian Grafton Hotel CAMTN NW1 4 A6
Radisson Edwardian Hampshire Hotel LSQ/SEVD WC2H 10 D6
Radisson Edwardian Hotel HYS/HAR UB3 133 F1
Radisson Edwardian Kenilworth Hotel RSQ WC1B 10 D2
Radisson Edwardian Marlborough Hotel NOXST/BSQ WC1A 10 D3
Radisson Edwardian Mayfair Hotel MYFR/PICC W1J 9 K6
Radisson Edwardian Mountbatten Hotel LSQ/SEVD WC2H 10 E4
Radisson Edwardian Vanderbilt Hotel SKENS SW7 120 B4
Radisson SAS Portman Hotel MBLAR W1H 9 F3
RAF West Ruislip (University of Maryland) HGDN/ICK UB10 58 A6
Raglan Infant School EN EN1 36 A1
Raglan Junior School EN EN1 36 A2
Raglan Primary School HAYES BR2 200 B1
Railton Road Clinic HNHL SE24 142 C6
Rainbow Industrial Estate RYNPK SW20 176 E5
Rainbow Quay BERM/RHTH SE16 124 B3
Rainbow School for Autistic Children WAND/EARL SW18 160 B4
Raines Foundation School BETH E2 104 D2
Rainham ⇌ RAIN RM13 111 H3
Rainham Hall (NT) RAIN RM13 111 J3
Rainham Marshes RSPB Reserve RAIN RM13 111 K6
Rainham Trading Estate RAIN RM13 111 G2
Rainham Village Primary School RAIN RM13 111 J3
Ramac Industrial Estate CHARL SE7 125 K5
Ramada Encore Hotel ACT W3 99 F4
Ramada Hotel BAY/PAD W2 101 F6
EA W5 98 B6
Rambert School TWK TW1 136 C6
Randal Cremer Primary School BETH E2 7 J2
Ranelagh Gardens (site of Chelsea Flower Show) CHEL SW3 121 F5
Ranelagh Primary School SRTFD E15 106 C1
Rangefield Primary School BMLY BR1 183 H1
Ransomes Dock Business Centre BTSEA SW11 140 D1
Raphael Independent School EMPK RM11 75 J3
The Rathbone Education Centre CAN/RD E16 106 D4
Rathbow Clinic BAY/PAD W2 2 B7
Rathfern Primary School FSTH SE23 164 C3
Ravenor Primary School GFD/PVL UB6 96 A2
Ravensbourne ⇌ BECK BR3 183 F3
Ravensbourne College of Design & Communication CHST BR7 185 F1
The Ravensbourne School HAYES BR2 200 A1
Ravenscourt Park ⊖ HMSMTH W6 118 D4
Ravenscourt Park Preparatory School HMSMTH W6 118 D4
Ravenscroft Medical Centre GLDGN NW11 64 D4
Ravenscroft Primary School CAN/RD E16 106 E3
Ravenscroft School TRDG/WHET N20 32 D2
Ravenside Retail Park UED N18 51 F2
Ravens Lawn Tennis Club NFNCH/WDSPK N12 33 H6
Ravensquay Business Centre STMC/STPC BR5 202 C2
Ravenstone Preparatory School SKENS SW7 120 B3
Ravenstone Primary School BAL SW12 161 F3
Ravenswood Industrial Estate WALTH E17 70 A1
Ravens Wood School HAYES BR2 215 H1
Ray Lodge Primary School WFD IG8 53 H2
Rayners Lane ⊖ RYLN/HDSTN HA2 59 K5
Raynes Park ⇌ RYNPK SW20 177 F5
Raynes Park High School RYNPK SW20 176 E6
Raynes Park Sports Ground RYNPK SW20 176 D5
Raynes Park Vale FC RYNPK SW20 193 G2
Raynham Primary School UED N18 50 C1
Reay Primary School BRXN/ST SW9 142 B1
Records Office CLKNW EC1R 5 K6
Rectory Business Centre SCUP DA14 168 C6
Rectory Road ⇌ STNW/STAM N16 86 C1
Redbridge ⊖ REDBR IG4 71 H3
Redbridge College CHDH RM6 73 H2
Redbridge Drama Centre SWFD E18 52 E4
Redbridge Museum IL IG1 90 B1
Redbridge Primary School REDBR IG4 71 J2
Redbridge Sports Centre BARK/HLT IG6 54 D4
Redburn Industrial Estate PEND EN3 37 F1
Redcliffe School WBPTN SW10 120 B6
Reddiford School PIN HA5 59 J1
Redford Lodge Psychiatric Hospital ED N9 36 C4
Red Gates School CROY/NA CR0 211 G3
Redhill Primary School CHST BR7 185 G
Red House (NT) BXLYHS DA6 149 F5
Redlands Primary School WCHPL E1 104 E
Red Lion Business Park SURB KT6 191 G6
Redriff Primary School BERM/RHTH SE16 124 B
Red Rose Trading Estate EBAR EN4 21 H6
Reeves Corner ⊖ CROY/NA CR0 196 C
Regal International College ALP/SUD HA0 80 A
Regent Business Centre HYS/HAR UB3 114 A
Regent Clinic CAVSQ/HST W1G 9 J
Regent College London PIN HA5 59 K
Regent's Park ⊖ CAMTN NW1 3
Regent's Park Barracks CAMTN NW1 3
Regent's Park Clinic CAMTN NW1 2
Regent's Park Medical Centre CAMTN NW1 3
Regent's Park Open Air Theatre CAMTN NW1 3
Regent's Park Track STJWD NW8 2
Regina Coeli RC Primary School SAND/SEL CR2 211
Renaissance Hotel HTHAIR TW6 132
Renoir Cinema BMSBY WC1N 5
Renwick Industrial Estate BARK IG11 109
Rewards Centre HSLW TW3 135
Reynard Mills Trading Estate BTFD TW8 116
Reynolds Health & Fitness RDART DA2 170
Reynolds Sports Centre ACT W3 117
Rhodes Avenue Primary School WDGN N22 48
Rhodes Farm Clinic MLHL NW7 32
Rhyl Primary School KTTN NW5 84

RIBA Library Drawings &
Manuscript Collection
MBLAR W1H............................9 F3
Ricards Lodge High School
WIM/MER SW19.............159 J6
Richard Alibon
Primary School
DAGE RM10........................92 C3
Richard Atkins
Primary School
BRXS/STRHM SW2........161 K2
Richard Cloudesley School
STLK EC1Y..............................6 C7
Richard Cobden
Primary School
CAMTN NW1..........................4 B1
Richdales Institute
ALP/SUD HA0......................79 K6
Rich Industrial Estate
STHWK SE1..........................19 H5
Richmond ⇌ ⊖ ⊕
RCH/KEW TW9..................137 F5
Richmond Adult &
Community College
RCH/KEW TW9..................136 E5
Richmond American
International University
RCHPK/HAM TW10..........157 F1
The Richmond Clinic
RCH/KEW TW9..................137 G5
Richmond
Community College
TWK TW1............................156 A3
Richmond FC
RCH/KEW TW9..................136 E5
Richmond Gate Hotel
RCHPK/HAM TW10..........157 F2
The Richmond Golf Club
RCHPK/HAM TW10..........157 F4
The Richmond Green
Medical Centre
RCH/KEW TW9..................136 E6
Richmond Hill Hotel
RCHPK/HAM TW10..........157 F2
Richmond House School
HPTN TW12........................172 E1
Richmond Park Golf Club
PUT/ROE SW15..................158 B2
Richmond Park National
Nature Reserve
RCHPK/HAM TW10..........158 B4
Richmond Road
Medical Centre
KUTN/CMB KT2................175 F3
Richmond Theatre
RCH/KEW TW9..................136 E5
Richmond upon
Thames College
WHTN TW2........................155 K2
Ridge Home Clinic
WCHMH N21........................35 K2
Ridgeway Hotel
CHING E4..............................37 K4
Ridgeway Primary School
SAND/SEL CR2.................212 A6
Rio Cinema
HACK E8..............................86 B3
Ripley Arts Centre
BMLY BR1..........................184 C4
Ripple Infant School
BARK IG11............................90 E6
Rippleside Cemetery
BARK IG11............................91 G6
Risebridge Golf Club
ROM RM1..............................57 H3
Rise Park Primary School
ROM RM1..............................57 F4
Risley Avenue Primary School
TOTM N17..............................50 A4
The Ritz Hotel
WHALL SW1A........................10 A7
Ritzy Cinema
BRXN/ST SW9...................142 B5
Riverbank Park Plaza Hotel
STHWK SE1..........................17 G7
River Brent Business Park
NWNL W7............................115 K3
River Gardens
Business Centre
EBED/NFELT TW14...........134 A5
River House
Montessori School
POP/IOD E14.......................124 D1
Riverley Primary School
LEY E10................................69 J5
River Mole Business Park
ESH/CLAY KT10...............189 F5
River Place Health Centre
IS N1.......................................85 J5
River Road Business Park
BARK IG11..........................108 E2
Riversdale Primary School
WAND/EARL SW18...........159 K3
Riverside Business Centre
WAND/EARL SW18...........160 A3
Riverside Business Park
WIM/MER SW19................178 B4
Riverside Community
Health Care
WKENS W14........................119 G3
Riverside Golf Club
THMD SE28........................110 A3
Riverside Industrial Estate
BARK IG11..........................109 G2
DART DA1...........................151 H6
Riverside Primary School
BERM/RHTH SE16.............123 H2
Riverside Quarter
WAND/EARL SW18...........139 K5
Riverside School
STMC/STPC BR5...............186 D5
Riverside Studios Cinema
HMSMTH W6......................119 F5
Riverside Swimming Centre
ERITH DA8.........................130 B5
Riverside Wandle
Trading Estate
MTCM CR4.........................194 E4
Riverston School
LEE/GVPK SE12................145 K6

Riverview C E Primary School
HOR/WEW KT19...............206 E2
The RJ Mitchell
Primary School
TWRH ECSN............................93 K4
RNLI Lifeboat Station
TWRH ECSN............................13 H7
Roan Industrial Estate
MTCM CR4.........................178 D4
Robert Blair Primary School
HOLWY N7...........................84 E4
Robert Browning
Primary School
WALW SE17........................122 E5
Robin Hood Infant School
SUT SM1.............................208 E3
Robin Hood Junior School
SUT SM1.............................209 F3
Robin Hood Lane
Health Centre
SUT SM1.............................208 E3
Robin Hood Primary School
KUTN/CMB KT2................176 A1
Robinsfield Infant School
STJWD NW8............................2 B2
The Roche School
WAND/EARL SW18...........139 K6
Rockliffe Manor
Primary School
WOOL/PLUM SE18...........128 A6
Rockmount Primary School
NRWD SE19........................180 D2
Rockware Business Centre
GFD/PVL UB6......................78 D6
The Rockwell Hotel
ECT SW5.............................120 A4
Roding Lane Cemetery
WFD IG8................................53 J4
Roding Primary School
BCTR RM8.............................91 J2
WFD IG8................................53 J3
Roding Valley ⊖
BKHH IG9...............................39 H6
Roebuck Road Trading Estate
BARK/HLT IG6.....................55 H2
Roe Green Junior School
CDALE/KGS NW9................62 D1
Roehampton Church School
PUT/ROE SW15..................158 C2
The Roehampton
Priory Hospital
PUT/ROE SW15..................138 C5
Roehampton
Recreation Centre
PUT/ROE SW15..................158 C2
Roehampton University
(Digby Stuart College)
PUT/ROE SW15..................138 C6
Roehampton University
(Froebel College)
PUT/ROE SW15..................158 C1
Roehampton University
(Southlands College)
PUT/ROE SW15..................138 C6
Roehampton University
(Whitelands College)
PUT/ROE SW15..................158 C2
Roger Ascham
Primary School
WALTH E17...........................51 H4
Roger Bannister
Sports Ground
KTN/HRWW/WS HA3..........42 C2
Rokeby School
KUTN/CMB KT2................175 K3
SRTFD E15............................88 B5
Rokesly Junior School
CEND/HSY/T N8...................66 E2
Roman Bath
TPL/STR WC2R......................11 H5
Roman Industrial Estate
CROY/NA CR0....................197 F4
Roman Road Primary School
EHAM E6.............................107 H3
Romford ⇌
ROM RM1..............................75 G3
Romford Cemetery
ROMW/RG RM7...................74 E4
Romford Clinic
ROM RM1..............................75 H1
Romford Golf Club
GPK RM2...............................57 J6
Romford Ice Arena
ROMW/RG RM7...................75 G4
Romford IT Learning Centre
ROM RM1..............................75 G2
Romford Shopping Hall
ROM RM1..............................75 G1
Ronald Rose Primary School
PUT/ROE SW15..................159 G2
Rood Lane Medical Centre
FENCHST EC3M....................13 G5
Rooks Heath College for
Business & Enterprise
RYLN/HDSTN HA2...............78 A1
Roosevelt Memorial
MYFR/PKLN W1K...................9 H5
Ropery Business Park
CHARL SE7.........................126 B4
Rosary Priory High School
BUSH WD23..........................28 E1
Rosary RC Infant School
HEST TW5...........................114 E6
Rosary RC Primary School
HAMP NW3...........................83 J5
Rosebery Industrial Park
TOTM N17..............................50 D5
Rose Bruford College
BFN/LL DA15......................168 C3
Rosedale College
HYS/HAR UB3.......................94 B5
Roselands Clinic
NWMAL KT3........................191 K1
Rose McAndrew Clinic
BRXN/ST SW9...................142 A3
Rosemead
Preparatory School
DUL SE21...........................162 D4
Rosendale Primary School
DUL SE21...........................162 D2

Rose of Kingston
(Kingston Theatre)
KUT/HW KT1......................174 E5
Rose Theatre Exhibition
STHWK SE1..........................12 C7
Rosetta Primary School
CAN/RD E16.......................107 F4
Rosewood Medical Centre
HCH RM12............................93 K5
Rosh Pinah Primary School
EDGW HA8............................30 D4
Roslyn Park RFC
PUT/ROE SW15..................138 C5
Rotherfield Primary School
IS N1......................................85 J6
Rotherhithe ⊖
BERM/RHTH SE16.............123 K2
Rotherhithe Civic Centre
BERM/RHTH SE16.............123 K2
Rotherhithe Primary School
BERM/RHTH SE16.............123 K4
The Rotunda
KUT/HW KT1......................175 F5
The Roundhouse Theatre
CAMTN NW1........................84 A5
Roundshaw J & I School
WLGTN SM6........................210 E5
Rowan Preparatory School
ESH/CLAY KT10.................205 F5
Rowans School
RYNPK SW20......................176 D3
Rowhill Grange
RDART DA2........................171 F6
Rowley Industrial Park
ACT W3...............................117 J3
Roxbourne First School
RYLN/HDSTN HA2...............59 J6
Roxbourne Medical Centre
RYLN/HDSTN HA2...............60 B6
Roxeth First & Middle School
RYLN/HDSTN HA2...............60 D6
Roxeth Mead School
RYLN/HDSTN HA2...............60 D6
Roxwell Trading Park
LEY E10................................69 G4
Royal Academy of Arts
MYFR/PICC W1J...................10 A6
Royal Academy of Dance
BTSEA SW11......................140 D2
Royal Academy of
Dramatic Art
GWRST WC1E.......................10 C1
Royal Academy of Music
CAMTN NW1..........................3 H7
Royal Air Force
Museum London
CDALE/KGS NW9................45 J5
Royal Albert ⊖
CAN/RD E16.......................107 J6
Royal Albert Hall
SKENS SW7..........................14 A3
Royal Arsenal
WOOL/PLUM SE18...........127 G3
The Royal Ballet School
RCHPK/HAM TW10...........158 A3
Royal Ballet Upper School
COVGDN WC2E....................11 G4
Royal Blackheath Golf Club
ELTH/MOT SE9..................166 E2
Royal Botanic Gardens, Kew
BTFD TW8...........................137 F1
Royal Botanic Gardens
Kew School
RCH/KEW TW9..................137 G1
Royal Brompton Hospital
CHEL SW3..........................120 C5
Royal Chace Hotel
ENC/FH EN2.........................23 F1
Royal College
of Anaesthetists
RSQ WC1B............................10 E1
Royal College of Art
SKENS SW7........................120 B3
Royal College of Art
Sculpture School
BTSEA SW11......................140 D1
Royal College of Music
SHB W12.............................118 D3
SKENS SW7..........................14 A4
Royal College of Nursing
CAMTN NW1..........................4 B6
IS N1..6 A1
Royal College of Obstetricians
& Gynaecologists
CAMTN NW1..........................2 E6
Royal College
of Ophthalmologists
CAMTN NW1..........................3 G7
Royal College of Paediatrics &
Child Health
GTPST W1W...........................9 K1
The Royal College
of Pathology
STJS SW1Y...........................16 C1
Royal College of Physicians
CAMTN NW1..........................3 J6
Royal College of Surgeons
LINN WC2A...........................11 H3
Royal College of
Veterinary Surgeons
WEST SW1P..........................16 E6
Royal Courts of Justice
LINN WC2A...........................11 H4
Royal Court Theatre
BGVA SW1W.........................15 G7
Royal Court Young
Peoples Theatre
NKENS W10........................100 C4
The Royal Docks
Community School
EHAM E6.............................107 G5
Royal Docks Medical Centre
EHAM E6.............................108 A5
Royal Epping Forest
Golf Club
CHING E4..............................38 C2
Royal Exchange
BANK EC3V...........................13 F4
Royal Festival Hall
STHWK SE1..........................17 G1

Royal Free Hospital
HAMP NW3...........................83 J3
Royal Garden Hotel
KENS W8............................120 A2
Royal Geographical Society
SKENS SW7..........................14 A3
The Royal Horseguards Hotel
WHALL SW1A........................17 F1
Royal Horticultural Society
New Hall
WEST SW1P..........................16 C5
Royal Horticultural Society
Old Hall
WEST SW1P..........................16 C6
Royal Hospital
RCH/KEW TW9..................137 F4
Royal Hospital Chelsea
CHEL SW3..........................120 C5
Royal Hospital for Neuro-
disability
PUT/ROE SW15..................159 H1
Royal Hospital & Home
PUT/ROE SW15..................158 E2
Royal Hospital Museum
CHEL SW3..........................121 F5
Royal Institute of
British Architects
REGST W1B.............................9 K1
Royal Institution's
Faraday Museum
MYFR/PICC W1J.....................9 K6
Royal Lancaster Hotel
BAY/PAD W2..........................8 B6
The Royal London Estate
TOTM N17..............................50 D3
Royal London
Homeopathic Hospital
BMSBY WC1N.......................11 F1
Royal Marsden Hospital
CHEL SW3..........................120 C5
The Royal Mews
BGVA SW1W.........................15 K4
Royal Mid-Surrey Golf Club
RCH/KEW TW9..................136 E4
Royal Military School of Music
WHTN TW2........................155 J1
Royal Mint Court
TWRH EC3N..........................13 K6
Royal National
Orthopaedic Hospital
GTPST W1W...........................3 K7
STAN HA7..............................29 H3
Royal National Theatre
STHWK SE1..........................11 J7
Royal National Throat Nose &
Ear Hospital
FSBYW WC1X.........................5 G4
Royal Oak ⊖
BAY/PAD W2......................101 F4
Royal Opera House
COVGDN WC2E....................11 F4
Royal Park Primary School
SCUP DA14.........................169 F5
Royal Russell
Preparatory School
CROY/NA CR0....................212 D4
The Royal School
HAMP NW3...........................83 H2
Royal Society of Arts
CHCR WC2N.........................11 F6
Royal Society of Medicine
CAVSO/HST W1G...................9 J3
Royal Veterinary College
CAMTN NW1..........................4 C1
Royal Victoria ⊖
CAN/RD E16.......................106 E6
Royal Victoria Docks
Watersports Centre
CAN/RD E16.......................106 E6
Royal Wimbledon Golf Club
WIM/MER SW19................176 E1
Royston Primary School
PGE/AN SE20.....................182 A4
RSPCA Animal Hospital
FSBYPK N4...........................67 F6
Rudolph Steiner Hall
CAMTN NW1..........................2 E6
Rufus Business Centre
WIM/MER SW19................160 A4
Ruislip ⊖
RSLP HA4..............................58 C6
Ruislip Gardens ⊖
RSLP HA4..............................76 E2
Ruislip Gardens
Primary School
RSLP HA4..............................76 C2
Ruislip Golf Club
HGDN/ICK UB10..................58 A6
Ruislip High School
RSLP HA4..............................76 E1
Ruislip Manor ⊖
RSLP HA4..............................58 E5
Ruislip Manor FC
RSLP HA4..............................58 D6
Ruislip RFC
RSLP HA4..............................58 C6
Ruislip Woods National
Nature Reserve
NTHWD HA6.........................40 A6
RSLP HA4..............................58 C2
Rushcroft School
CHING E4..............................51 K3
Rushey Green Primary School
CAT SE6.............................164 E3
Rush Green Primary School
ROMW/RG RM7...................75 F5
Rushmore Primary School
CLPT E5................................86 E2
Ruskin House School
HNHL SE24.........................142 D6
The Russell JMI School
RCHPK/HAM TW10...........156 E4
The Russell School
RCHPK/HAM TW10...........156 E4
Russell Square ⊖
STPAN WC1H.........................4 E7
Russet House School
EN EN1..................................24 D2
Rutlish School
RYNPK SW20.....................177 J5

Ruxley Corner
Industrial Estate
SCUP DA14.........................186 E2
Ruxley Park Centre
STMC/STPC BR5...............186 E4
Ryefield Primary School
HGDN/ICK UB10..................76 B6
Ryelands Primary School
SNWD SE25........................197 J2
Rye Oak Primary School
PECK SE15.........................143 J4
Sacred Heart Catholic
Primary School
PUT/ROE SW15..................138 D6
Sacred Heart High School
HMSMTH W6.....................119 F4
Sacred Heart
Language College
KTN/HRWW/WS HA3..........42 E5
Sacred Heart RC Infant School
BTSEA SW11......................140 D3
Sacred Heart RC JMI School
TRDG/WHET N20..................33 J4
Sacred Heart RC
Primary School
NWMAL KT3.......................192 D1
OXHEY WD19........................27 K1
RSLP HA4..............................58 C6
TEDD TW11........................174 C3
Sacred Heart RC School
CMBW SE5.........................142 D2
Sacred Heart School
HOLWY N7...........................85 F3
Saddlers Hall
CITYW EC2V........................12 D3
Sadler's Wells Theatre
CLKNW EC1R..........................5 K4
Safari Cinema
CROY/NA CR0....................196 C5
Safari Cinema & Bingo
HRW HA1..............................61 F2
Sai Medical Centre
POP/IOD E14......................106 A6
St Agathas RC Primary School
KUTN/CMB KT2................175 G2
St Agnes RC Primary School
BOW E3...............................105 J2
CRICK NW2...........................82 C1
St Aidans Primary School
FSBYPK N4...........................67 G4
St Aidans RC Primary School
IL IG1....................................72 D5
St Albans CE Primary School
HCIRC EC1N.........................11 J1
St Albans Health Clinic
HGT N6..................................84 A1
St Albans RC Aided
Primary School
E/WMO/HCT KT8...............189 G2
St Albans RC Church &
School Presbytery
HCH RM12............................93 J3
St Albans RC JMI School
HCH RM12............................93 K5
St Albans Road Infant School
DART DA1...........................171 J1
St Alfege with St Peter CE
Primary School
GNWCH SE10......................125 F5
St Aloysius College
HGT N6..................................66 C5
St Aloysius RC Infant School
CAMTN NW1..........................4 C1
St Aloysius RC Junior School
CAMTN NW1..........................4 B3
St Andrew & St Francis CE
JMI School
CRICK NW2...........................81 J4
St Andrews CE JMI School
TRDG/WHET N20..................33 D4
St Andrews CE
Primary School
EN EN1..................................23 K3
STHGT/OAK N14..................34 C2
St Andrews CE VA High School
CROY/NA CR0....................211 H1
St Andrews Greek School
CAMTN NW1..........................84 B4
St Andrews Primary School
BRXN/ST SW9...................142 A3
IS N1......................................85 F6
St Andrews School
RYLN/HDSTN HA2...............60 B2
WLSDN NW10......................81 K5
St Angelas Ursuline School
FSTGT E7..............................89 F4
St Annes Catholic High School
for Girls
ENC/FH EN2.........................23 K5
St Annes Catholic Primary School
PLMGR N13..........................35 G6
St Annes CE Primary School
WAND/EARL SW18...........140 A6
St Annes CP School
STWL/WRAY TW19...........152 B2
St Annes RC Primary School
LBTH SE11..........................122 A6
St Anne's Special School
MRDN SM4.........................193 K2
St Anne's Trading Estate
POP/IOD E14......................105 H5
St Anns CE Primary School
SEVS/STOTM N15................67 K2
St Ann's General Hospital
FSBYPK N4...........................67 J2
St Anns School
HNWL W7...........................115 K1
St Ann's Shopping Centre
HRW HA1..............................60 E3
St Anselms RC Primary School
DART DA1...........................151 J6
HRW HA1..............................60 D6
NWDGN UB2......................114 E2
TOOT SW17........................161 F5
St Anthonys Hospital
WPK KT4.............................193 G5
St Anthonys RC
Primary School
EDUL SE22.........................163 H1
PGE/AN SE20.....................181 J4

St Anthony's School (Junior House)
HAMP NW3 83 H3
St Anthony's School (Senior House)
HAMP NW3 83 G3
St Antonys RC Primary School
FSTGT E7 88 E5
WFD IG8 38 E6
St Aubyns School
WFD IG8 52 D3
St Augustines CE High School
KIL/WHAMP NW6 100 E1
St Augustines Primary School
BELV DA17 129 G3
KIL/WHAMP NW6 101 F1
St Augustines Priory School
EA W5 98 A4
St Augustines RC Infant School
GNTH/NBYPK IG2 72 B2
St Augustines RC Primary School
CAT SE6 182 E1
GNTH/NBYPK IG2 72 B2
WKENS W14 119 H6
St Barnabas & St Philip's CE Primary School
KENS W8 119 K3
St Bartholomews CE Primary School
SYD SE26 163 K6
St Bartholomews Hospital
STBT EC1A 12 B2
St Bartholomews Medical School
FARR EC1M 6 B7
St Bartholomews & Royal London School of Medicine
FARR EC1M 12 C1
St Bartholomew's the Great
STBT EC1A 12 B2
St Barts Hospital Sports Ground
CHST BR7 185 J2
St Barts & the Royal London Hospital
WCHPL E1 104 D4
St Bedes RC Infant School
BAL SW12 161 J3
St Bedes RC Primary School
CHDH RM6 73 J2
St Benedicts Junior School
EA W5 97 J4
St Benedicts School
EA W5 97 K4
St Bernadette Catholic Junior School
BAL SW12 161 H2
St Bernadettes RC Primary School
KTN/HRWW/WS HA3 62 B1
St Bonaventures School
FSTGT E7 88 E5
St Boniface RC Primary School
TOOT SW17 178 E1
St Catherines RC Girls School
BXLYHS DA6 149 J6
St Catherines RC J & I School
WDR/YW UB7 112 A2
St Catherines RC School
BAR EN5 20 D5
St Catherines School
TWK TW1 156 A4
St Cecilias CE School
WAND/EARL SW18 159 J2
St Cecilias RC Primary School
WPK KT4 193 G6
St Chads RC Primary School
SNWD SE25 197 F2
St Charles Hospital
NKENS W10 100 B4
St Charles Primary School
NKENS W10 100 B4
St Christinas RC Preparatory School
STJWD NW8 2 D2
St Christophers School
BECK BR3 183 F5
HAMP NW3 83 H3
WBLY HA9 80 B1
St Clare Business Park
HPTN TW12 173 H2
St Clement Danes CE Primary School
HOL/ALD WC2B 11 G4
St Clement & St James CE Primary School
NTGHL W11 119 G1
St Clements Hospital
BOW E3 105 H2
St Clements Primary School
EW KT17 207 H6
St Columbas RC Boys School
BXLYHS DA6 149 J6
St Cuthbert with St Mattias CE Primary School
ECT SW5 119 K5
St Cyprians Greek Orthodox Primary School
THHTH CR7 180 D5
St Davids College
WWKM BR4 198 E4
St Davids Health Centre
STWL/WRAY TW19 152 A2
St Davids School
ASHF TW15 152 C5
St Dominics RC Primary School
HAMP NW3 83 K3
HOM E9 87 G4
St Dominics Sixth Form College
HRW HA1 60 E6
St Dunstans CE Primary School
CHEAM SM3 208 C4
St Dunstans College
CAT SE6 164 C3
St Ebba's Hospital
HOR/WEW KT19 206 E6
St Edmunds RC Primary School
ED N9 36 D3
POP/IOD E14 124 D4
WHTN TW2 155 G2
St Edwards CE Comprehensive School
CHDH RM6 74 C3
St Edwards CE Primary School
ROM RM1 75 F1
St Edwards RC JMI School
STJWD NW8 2 C7
St Elizabeths RC Primary School
BETH E2 104 E1
RCHPK/HAM TW10 157 G1
St Eugene de Mazenod RC Primary School
KIL/WHAMP NW6 82 E5
St Faiths CE School
WAND/EARL SW18 140 A6
St Fidelis Catholic Primary School
ERITH DA8 129 K6
St Francesca Cabrini Primary School
FSTH SE23 163 K1
St Francis de Sales RC J & I School
TOTM N17 50 B3
St Francis of Assisi Primary School
NKENS W10 100 B6
St Francis RC Primary School
PECK SE15 123 H6
SRTFD E15 88 C3
St Francis Xavier College
BAL SW12 161 G1
St Gabriels CE Primary School
PIM SW1V 121 H5
St George's Cathedral
STHWK SE1 17 K4
St Georges CE Primary School
BMLY BR1 184 B5
CMBW SE5 143 F1
VX/NE SW8 141 H2
St Georges College
HOLWY N7 85 G1
St Georges Elizabethan Theatre
HOLWY N7 84 D2
St Georges Hanover Square CE Primary School
MYFR/PKLN W1K 9 H6
St Georges Hospital
TOOT SW17 178 D1
St Georges Industrial Estate
KUTN/CMB KT2 174 E1
PLMGR N13 49 H3
St Georges Medical Centre
HDN NW4 45 K6
St Georges RC Primary School
ENC/FH EN2 23 K3
HRW HA1 79 F1
St Georges RC School
MV/WKIL W9 101 F1
St Georges Shopping Centre & Cinema
HRW HA1 60 D3
St Georges University of London
TOOT SW17 178 C1
St George the Martyr CE Primary School
BMSBY WC1N 5 G7
St George Wharf
VX/NE SW8 121 K6
St Gildas RC Junior School
CEND/HSY/T N8 66 E4
St Giles College London Central
RSQ WC1B 11 F1
St Giles School
SAND/SEL CR2 211 H4
St Gregorys High School
KTN/HRWW/WS HA3 61 K2
St Gregorys RC Primary School
EA W5 97 J3
St Helens Catholic Infant School
WALTH E17 70 A2
St Helens RC Primary School
BRXN/ST SW9 142 B4
CAN/RD E16 106 D3
St Helens School
NTHWD HA6 40 C2
St Helier ⇌
MRDN SM4 193 K3
St Helier Hospital
CAR SM5 194 B5
St Hildas School
BUSH WD23 28 B2
St Ignatius RC Primary School
SEVS/STOTM N15 68 A3
St James CE J & I School
BERM/RHTH SE16 123 H3
St James CE Primary School
MUSWH N10 66 A1
NWCR SE14 144 B2
PEND EN3 24 E3
St James CE Junior School
FSTGT E7 88 D3
St James Independent School for Senior Boys
TWK TW1 156 B4
St James Independent School for Senior Girls
WKENS W14 119 H4
St James Independent Schools for Juniors & Girls
WKENS W14 119 H4
St James Medical Centre
CROY/NA CR0 196 E4
St James RC Primary School
HAYES BR2 201 G2
WHTN TW2 155 K5
St James St ⇌
WALTH E17 69 G2
St James's Health Centre
WALTH E17 69 G2
St James's Palace
WHALL SW1A 16 B1
St James's Park ⊖
STJSPK SW1H 16 C4
St James the Great RC Primary School
PECK SE15 143 G2
THHTH CR7 180 C5
St Joachims RC Primary School
CAN/RD E16 107 G5
St Joan of Arc RC Primary School
HBRY N5 85 H2
St John Fisher RC First & Middle School
PIN HA5 60 A1
St John Fisher RC Primary School
ERITHM DA18 129 F3
GFD/PVL UB6 97 J2
RYNPK SW20 193 F2
St John of Jerusalem CE Primary School
HOM E9 86 E5
St Johns ⇌
DEPT SE8 144 D3
St Johns & St James CE School
UED N18 50 B1
St Johns Angell Town CE Primary School
BRXN/ST SW9 142 B3
St Johns CE Primary School
BETH E2 104 E1
BKHH IG9 39 F3
CROY/NA CR0 213 F1
FBAR/BDGN N11 33 K6
KUT/HW KT1 175 F6
PGE/AN SE20 181 K3
TRDG/WHET N20 33 G4
St Johns CE School
CDALE/KGS NW9 63 G2
St John's CE Walham Green Primary School
FUL/PGN SW6 139 H2
St Johns Church of England School
STAN HA7 29 G6
St John's Concert Hall
WEST SW1P 16 E5
St Johns Highbury Vale CE Primary School
HBRY N5 85 H2
St John's Hospital Day Centre
BTSEA SW11 140 C5
St John's Lodge
CAMTN NW1 3 G4
St Johns Primary School
WEA W13 97 G6
St Johns RC Primary School
BERM/RHTH SE16 124 B2
St Johns RC Special School
WFD IG8 54 A1
St Johns & St Clements CE J & I School
PECK SE15 143 H4
St Johns School
NTHWD HA6 41 F2
St Johns Senior School
ENC/FH EN2 23 G2
St Johns Upper Holloway CE Primary School
ARCH N19 66 C6
St Johns Walworth CE Primary School
WALW SE17 18 C7
St Johns Way Medical Centre
ARCH N19 66 D5
St John's Wood ⊖
STJWD NW8 2 A2
St Johns Wood Pre-Preparatory School
STJWD NW8 2 C4
St John the Baptist CE Junior School
KUT/HW KT1 174 E3
St John the Baptist CE Primary School
BMLY BR1 165 F6
St John the Baptist VA CE Primary School
IS N1 7 G3
St John the Divine CE Primary School
CMBW SE5 142 C1
St John the Evangelist RC Primary
IS N1 6 A2
St John Vianney RC Primary School
SEVS/STOTM N15 67 H1
St Joseph's Annexe
ABYW SE2 128 D6
St Josephs Catholic Infant School
LEY E10 69 H5
St Josephs Catholic Junior School
CMBW SE5 142 D1
St Josephs Catholic Primary School
BMLY BR1 184 B3
DAGW RM9 92 B2
St Josephs College
STRHM/NOR SW16 180 C2
St Josephs Convent School
WAN E11 70 E3
St Josephs Primary School
WAND/EARL SW18 139 K6
St Joseph's RC College
MLHL NW7 31 H6
St Josephs RC First & Middle School
KTN/HRWW/WS HA3 43 G5
St Josephs RC Infant School
NRWD SE19 180 D2
St Josephs RC J & I School
HDN NW4 63 K1
St Josephs RC Junior School
LEY E10 69 J5
NRWD SE19 180 D2
WBLY HA9 80 B3
St Josephs RC Primary School
ARCH N19 66 B5
BARK IG11 90 C6
BERM/RHTH SE16 123 K3
CHEL SW3 14 E7
DART DA1 150 A5
DEPT SE8 144 D1
GNWCH SE10 125 H5
HNWL W7 115 K1
HOL/ALD WC2B 11 F3
KUT/HW KT1 175 F5
MV/WKIL W9 101 G2
OXHEY WD19 27 F5
STHWK SE1 18 D2
STHWK SE1 123 H2
WLSDN NW10 81 G5
St Judes CE Primary School
HNHL SE24 162 C1
STHWK SE1 18 A5
St Judes & St Pauls CE Primary School
IS N1 86 A3
St Katharine Pier
WAP E1W 13 K7
St Katherine
TPL/STR WC2R 11 H6
St Lawrence Business Centre
FELT TW13 154 A4
St Lawrence Catholic School
FELT TW13 154 A4
St Lawrence Junior School
E/WMO/HCT KT8 173 J6
St Lawrence University
BMSBY WC1N 5 H7
St Leonards CE Primary School
STRHM/NOR SW16 179 J1
St Leonards Hospital
IS N1 7 H2
St Luke's Catholic Sixth Form College
SCUP DA14 186 A1
St Lukes Cemetery
HAYES BR2 200 E3
St Lukes CE Primary School
CAN/RD E16 106 D5
FSBYE EC1V 6 D5
KUTN/CMB KT2 175 G4
MV/WKIL W9 100 D1
POP/IOD E14 125 G4
WNWD SE27 180 D1
St Luke's Health Centre
CAN/RD E16 106 D5
St Lukes Hospital for the Clergy
FITZ W1T 4 A7
St Lukes School
THHTH CR7 196 B1
St Lukes Woodside Hospital
MUSWH N10 66 A1
St Margaret Clitherow RC Primary
THMD SE28 128 C1
St Margaret's ⇌
TWK TW1 156 C1
St Margarets Business Centre
TWK TW1 156 B2
St Margarets CE Primary School
WOOL/PLUM SE18 127 H6
St Margarets Clitherow RC Primary
WBLY HA9 80 E1
St Margarets Primary School
BARK IG11 90 B6
St Margarets School
BUSH WD23 28 A2
HAMP NW3 83 F2
St Marks Catholic School
HSLW TW3 134 E4
St Marks CE Academy
MTCM CR4 179 G5
St Marks CE Primary School
ARCH N19 66 E6
HAYES BR2 183 K6
LBTH SE11 122 A6
SNWD SE25 197 H1
St Marks Industrial Estate
CAN/RD E16 126 C1
St Marks Primary School
HNWL W7 115 K2
MTCM CR4 178 E5
St Marthas Junior School
BAR EN5 20 C4
St Marthas Senior School
EBAR EN4 20 E2
St Martin-in-the-Fields
CHCR WC2N 10 E6
St Martin in the Fields High School
BRXS/STRHM SW2 162 C3
St Martin of Porres RC Primary School
FBAR/BDGN N11 48 C2
St Martins Hospital
MYFR/PKLN W1K 9 G5
St Martins Medical Centre
RSLP HA4 58 C4
St Martins School
MLHL NW7 45 G1
St Martins School of Art
SOHO/SHAV W1D 10 D4
St Martins Theatre
LSQ/SEVD WC2H 10 D5
St Mary Abbots CE Primary School
KENS W8 120 A2
St Mary Cray ⇌
STMC/STPC BR5 202 B1
St Mary Cray Cemetery
STMC/STPC BR5 202 E1
The St Marylebone CE School
MHST W1U 9 H1
St Marylebone Crematorium
FNCH N3 47 F6
St Mary Magdalene CE Primary School
MV/WKIL W9 101 F4
WOOL/PLUM SE18 126 E4
St Mary Magdalen RC Junior School
CRICK NW2 81 K4
St Mary Magdalens Catholic Primary School
BROCKY SE4 144 B5
St Mary Magdalens Primary School
MORT/ESHN SW14 138 A4
St Mary of the Angels RC Primary School
NTGHL W11 100 E5
St Marys Abbey
MLHL NW7 31 J5
St Mary & St Michael Primary School
WCHPL E1 104 E5
St Mary & St Peters CE Primary School
TEDD TW11 173 K1
St Marys Bryanston Square CE Primary School
MBLAR W1H 8 D1
St Marys Catholic Primary School
CHING E4 38 B3
HCH RM12 75 J5
St Marys CE Junior School
CEND/HSY/T N8 66 E1
STWL/WRAY TW19 152 B1
St Mary's Cemetery
BTSEA SW11 140 D6
St Marys CE Primary School
CHSGTN KT9 206 A4
EBAR EN4 33 J1
FNCH N3 46 D4
IS N1 85 H5
LEW SE13 144 E6
PUT/ROE SW15 139 G4
STNW/STAM N16 67 K6
TWK TW1 156 B2
WALTH E17 69 K1
WLSDN NW10 81 G4
St Mary's CE School
HDN NW4 45 K6
St Marys Greek Cathedral
WDGN N22 49 F4
St Marys High School
CROY/NA CR0 196 D5
St Marys Hospital
BAY/PAD W2 8 B3
St Marys Hospital Medical School
BAY/PAD W2 8 B3
St Marys Infant School
CAR SM5 209 J2
St Mary's Junior School
TWK TW1 156 C2
St Marys Kilburn Primary School
KIL/WHAMP NW6 82 E6
St Marys Primary School
WKENS W14 119 G3
St Marys RC Infant School
CAR SM5 209 K3
St Marys RC J & I School
CROY/NA CR0 196 E5
St Marys RC Junior School
FSBYPK N4 67 K2
WALTH E17 52 A6
St Marys RC Primary School
BECK BR3 183 F3
CHSWK W4 118 B5
CLAP SW4 141 H6
ELTH/MOT SE9 147 F6
ISLW TW7 136 B4
KIL/WHAMP NW6 100 E1
NKENS W10 100 C3
PEND EN3 25 F5
VX/NE SW8 141 G2
WIM/MER SW19 177 K3
St Marys & St Johns CE Primary School
HDN NW4 63 K2
St Marys School
CEND/HSY/T N8 67 F2
HAMP NW3 83 G3
St Mary's Western Eye Hospital
MBLAR W1H 8 E1
St Matthew Academy
LEW SE13 145 G4
St Matthews CE Primary School
PEND EN3 24 E6
RYNPK SW20 176 D4
SURB KT6 191 F4
WDR/YW UB7 112 B1
St Matthias CE Primary School
BETH E2 7 K6
STNW/STAM N16 86 A3
St Meryl JMI School
OXHEY WD19 27 J5
St Michael & All Angels CE Academy
CMBW SE5 142 C1
St Michael at Bowes Junior School
PLMGR N13 49 G2
St Michaels & St Martins RC Primary School
HSLWW TW4 134 E4
St Michaels Catholic Grammar School
NFNCH/WDSPK N12 47 F1
St Michaels CE Primary School
ENC/FH EN2 23 J2
HGT N6 66 A4
WAND/EARL SW18 159 J2
WDGN N22 49 F4
WELL DA16 148 D2
St Michaels RC Primary School
EHAM E6 107 K1

St Michaels RC Secondary School
BERM/RHTH SE16 123 H2
St Michaels Sydenham CE Primary School
SYD SE26 164 B6
The St Michael Steiner School
WAND/EARL SW18 139 K6
St Monica's RC Primary School
IS N1 7 G4
St Monicas RC Primary School
STHGT/OAK N14 34 E5
St Nicholas Centre
SUT SM1 209 F3
St Nicholas Preparatory School
SKENS SW7 14 B3
St Nicholas School
BORE WD6 30 A1
CDALE/KGS NW9 62 E6
CHST BR7 185 H3
St Olaves Grammar School
ORP BR6 217 H1
St Olaves Preparatory School
ELTH/MOT SE9 167 G4
St Pancras Hospital
CAMTN NW1 4 C1
St Pancras International ⇌ ⊖
CAMTN NW1 4 E3
St Pancras International Youth Hostel
CAMTN NW1 4 D4
St Pancras & Islington Cemetery
EFNCH N2 47 J4
St Patricks Church School
STHWK SE1 17 J1
St Patricks Infants School
WAP E1W 123 J1
St Patricks International School
SOHO/SHAV W1D 10 B3
St Patricks Primary School
KTTN NW5 84 B4
St Patricks RC JMI School
ROMW/RG RM7 56 D4
St Patricks RC Primary School
WALTH E17 69 G1
WOOL/PLUM SE18 127 J4
St Paulinus CE Primary School
DART DA1 150 B5
St Paul's ⊖
STP EC4M 12 C3
St Pauls & All Hallows Infant School
TOTM N17 50 C3
St Pauls & All Hallows Junior School
TOTM N17 50 C3
St Paul's Cathedral
STP EC4M 12 C4
St Paul's Cathedral School
STP EC4M 12 C4
St Pauls CE Primary School
BTFD TW8 116 E6
CHSGTN KT9 206 A2
FBAR/BDGN N11 48 A1
HAMP NW3 83 J5
MLHL NW7 31 K6
WALW SE17 122 C5
WCHMH N21 35 H2
WCHPL E1 104 C6
St Pauls CE Junior School
KUTN/CMB KT2 175 H3
St Pauls Cray CE Primary School
STMC/STPC BR5 186 D6
St Pauls Cray Health Clinic
STMC/STPC BR5 186 B5
St Pauls Girls School
HMSMTH W6 119 G4
St Paul's Primary School
HMSMTH W6 119 F5
St Pauls RC Primary School
THDIT KT7 189 K4
WDGN N22 49 F5
St Pauls RC School
ABYW SE2 128 B6
St Pauls Road Medical Centre
IS N1 85 H4
St Pauls School
BARN SW13 118 E5
St Pauls Steiner School
IS N1 85 K4
St Pauls Way Community School
BOW E3 105 J4
St Pauls with St Lukes CE Primary School
BOW E3 105 H4
St Pauls with St Michaels CE School
HACK E8 86 C6
St Peter Chanel RC Primary School
SCUP DA14 186 D1
St Peter & Paul RC Primary School
STMC/STPC BR5 185 K5
St Peter & St Pauls Primary School
FSBYE EC1V 6 A6
St Peters Catholic Primary School
ROM RM1 57 F6
St Peters CE Primary School
HMSMTH W6 118 D5
MV/WKIL W9 100 E3
WALW SE17 122 E5
WAP E1W 123 K1
St Peter's Church
KTBR SW1X 15 J4
St Peters Eaton Square CE Primary School
BGVA SW1W 15 J5
St Peter's Hospital
COVGDN WC2E 11 F5
St Peters Primary School
SAND/SEL CR2 211 K4
St Peters RC Primary School
DAGW RM9 92 B6
WOOL/PLUM SE18 127 G5
St Philips School
CHSGTN KT9 205 K4
SKENS SW7 120 B4
St Phillips Infant School
SYD SE26 163 J6
St Philomenas Catholic High School
CAR SM5 209 J3
St Philomenas RC Primary School
STMC/STPC BR5 202 D4
St Quintins Health Centre
NKENS W10 100 A4
St Raphaels Hospice
WPK KT4 193 G6
St Raphaels RC Primary School
NTHLT UB5 95 F1
St Raphaels Way Medical Centre
WLSDN NW10 80 E3
St Richards with St Andrews CE Primary School
RCHPK/HAM TW10 156 C5
St Robert Southwell RC Primary School
CDALE/KGS NW9 62 E3
St Saviour & St Olaves School
STHWK SE1 19 F5
St Saviours CE Primary School
HNHL SE24 142 D4
MV/WKIL W9 101 F3
POP/IOD E14 105 K4
WALTH E17 69 H4
St Saviours CE Infant School
EA W5 116 E1
St Saviours RC Primary School
LEW SE13 145 F5
St Scholasticas RC Primary School
CLPT E5 86 C1
St Stephens CE Junior School
TWK TW1 156 B1
St Stephens CE Primary School
BAY/PAD W2 100 E4
DEPT SE8 144 D3
SHB W12 118 E1
St Stephens CE School
VX/NE SW8 141 K1
St Stephens Primary School
EHAM E6 89 G5
St Stephens RC Primary School
WELL DA16 148 B4
St Swithun Wells RC Primary School
RSLP HA4 77 G1
St Teresa RC First & Middle School
KTN/HRWW/WS HA3 42 C4
St Teresa RC Primary School
BCTR RM8 91 J2
St Theresas RC Primary School
FNCH N3 46 E6
St Thomas a' Becket RC Primary School
ABYW SE2 128 B3
St Thomas Becket RC Primary School
SNWD SE25 197 H3
St Thomas CE Primary School
NKENS W10 100 C3
St Thomas' Hospital
STHWK SE1 17 G4
STHWK SE1 17 G4
St Thomas More RC Primary School
BXLYHN DA7 149 G3
ELTH/MOT SE9 146 D4
St Thomas More RC School
CHEL SW3 14 E6
ELTH/MOT SE9 167 F1
WDGN N22 49 G3
St Thomas of Canterbury
MTCM CR4 179 F6
St Thomas of Canterbury RC Primary School
FUL/PGN SW6 139 J1
St Thomas the Apostle College
PECK SE15 143 K2
St Ursulas Catholic Infant School
HARH RM3 57 K2
St Ursulas Convent School
GNWCH SE10 145 G1
St Vincent de Paul RC Primary
WEST SW1P 16 A5
St Vincents Catholic Primary School
ELTH/MOT SE9 166 D6
St Vincents Hospital
PIN HA5 40 C6
St Vincents RC Primary School
BCTR RM8 73 J6
St Vincent's RC Primary School
MHST W1U 9 G2
St Vincents RC Primary School
MLHL NW7 31 K6
St Walter & St John Sports Ground
TOOT SW17 160 D3
St William of York Primary School
FSTH SE23 164 B2
St Winefrides Catholic Primary School
MNPK E12 89 K3
St Winifreds Catholic Junior School
LEE/GVPK SE12 165 J1
St Winifreds RC Infant School
LEW SE13 145 H6
SS Andrews & Marks CE Junior School
SURB KT6 190 E2
SS Mary & Pancras CE Primary School
CAMTN NW1 4 C3
SS Peter & Paul RC Primary School
MTCM CR4 194 E1
SS Peter & Pauls RC Primary School
IL IG1 90 D1
Salcombe Preparatory School (Infants)
STHGT/OAK N14 34 B1
Salcombe Preparatory School (Juniors)
STHGT/OAK N14 34 B2
Salisbury Primary School
MNPK E12 89 H3
Salisbury School
ED N9 36 E3
Salters' Hall
BARB EC2Y 12 D2
Salusbury Primary School
KIL/WHAMP NW6 82 C6
Salvatorian College
KTN/HRWW/WS HA3 42 D5
Samuel Jones Industrial Estate
PECK SE15 143 F1
Samuel Rhodes School
IS N1 85 G6
Sanderstead ⇌
SAND/SEL CR2 211 K6
Sanderstead Junior School
SAND/SEL CR2 211 K6
Sandgate Trading Estate
BERM/RHTH SE16 123 J5
Sandhurst Primary School
CAT SE6 165 H2
Sandilands ⊖
CROY/NA CR0 197 G6
Sandown Grandstand & Exhibition Centre
ESH/CLAY KT10 204 B1
Sandown Industrial Park
ESH/CLAY KT10 189 F6
Sandown Park Racecourse
ESH/CLAY KT10 204 B1
Sandown Sports Club & Dry Ski Slope
ESH/CLAY KT10 204 B1
Sandringham Primary School
FSTGT E7 89 G4
Sandy Lodge Golf Club
NTHWD HA6 26 B4
Sapcote Trading Centre
WLSDN NW10 81 H3
Sarah Bonnell School
SRTFD E15 88 C4
Sarum Hall School
HAMP NW3 83 J5
Satmer Trust School
STNW/STAM N16 68 C6
Savoy Pier
TPL/STR WC2R 11 G6
The Savoy
TPL/STR WC2R 11 F6
Savoy Theatre
TPL/STR WC2R 11 G6
Saxon Business Centre
WIM/MER SW19 178 B5
Sayer Clinic
CROY/NA CR0 211 F2
Sayer Clinics
MBLAR W1H 9 F4
Scargill Infant School
RAIN RM13 93 J5
Scargill Junior School
RAIN RM13 93 J4
School of Oriental & African Studies
GWRST WC1E 4 D7
Schomberg House
STJS SW1Y 16 B1
School of English
GLDGN NW11 64 E5
School of Islamic Republic Iran
KIL/WHAMP NW6 100 E1
School of Oriental & African Studies
STPAN WC1H 4 D7
The School of Pharmacy
BMSBY WC1N 5 F6
The School of St David & St Katharine
CEND/HSY/T N8 66 E1
Science Museum
SKENS SW7 14 B5
Science Museum IMAX Cinema
SKENS SW7 14 A5
The Science Museum Library
SKENS SW7 14 A4
Scotts Park Primary School
BMLY BR1 184 B4
Scott Wilkie Primary School
CAN/RD E16 107 G5
Screen on Baker Street Cinema
MHST W1U 9 F1
Screen on the Green Cinema
IS N1 6 A1
Sealife London Aquarium
WHALL SW1A 17 G3
Sebright Primary School
BETH E2 104 C1
Secombe Centre
SUT SM1 209 F4
Sedgehill School
CAT SE6 182 E1
Sedgewick Centre
WCHPL E1 13 K3
Selborne Primary School
GFD/PVL UB6 97 F1
The Selfridge Hotel
MBLAR W1H 9 H4
Selhurst ⇌
SNWD SE25 197 F2
The Selhurst Medical Centre
SNWD SE25 197 F3
Sellincourt School
TOOT SW17 178 D2
Selsdon High School
SAND/SEL CR2 213 F5
Selsdon Primary School
SAND/SEL CR2 212 E6
Selsdon Road Industrial Estate
SAND/SEL CR2 211 K5
Selwyn Primary School
CHING E4 52 A3
PLSTW E13 88 E6
Sergeant Industrial Estate
WAND/EARL SW18 160 A1
Serpentine Gallery
BAY/PAD W2 14 B1
Serpentine Lido & Cafe
SKENS SW7 14 C2
Servite RC Primary School
WBPTN SW10 120 B6
Seven Islands Leisure Centre
BERM/RHTH SE16 123 K3
Seven Kings ⇌
GDMY/SEVK IG3 72 E5
Seven Kings Health Centre
GDMY/SEVK IG3 72 E5
Seven Kings High School
GNTH/NBYPK IG2 72 D4
Seven Mills Primary School
POP/IOD E14 124 D2
Sevenoaks Way Industrial Estate
STMC/STPC BR5 186 D6
Seven Sisters ⇌ ⊖
SEVS/STOTM N15 68 A2
Seven Sisters Primary School
SEVS/STOTM N15 67 K2
Seymour Gardens Medical Centre
IL IG1 71 K5
Seymour Leisure Centre
MBLAR W1H 8 E2
Shaare Zedek Medical Centre
GLDGN NW11 64 D3
Shacklewell Primary School
HACK E8 86 B2
Shadwell ⊖ ⊖
WCHPL E1 104 D5
Shadwell Dock Stairs
WAP E1W 105 F6
Shaftesbury High School
KTN/HRWW/WS HA3 42 B4
Shaftesbury Hospital
LSQ/SEVD WC2H 10 E4
Shaftesbury Medical Centre
RYLN/HDSTN HA2 60 C5
Shaftesbury Park Primary School
BTSEA SW11 141 F4
Shaftesbury Primary School
FSTGT E7 89 G5
Shaftesbury Theatre
LSQ/SEVD WC2H 10 E3
Shahjalal Medical Centre
WCHPL E1 104 C5
Shakespeare Business Centre
BRXN/ST SW9 142 C4
Shakespeare's Globe Theatre & Exhibition
STHWK SE1 12 C7
The Shamrock Sports Club
ACT W3 98 E5
Shannon Corner Retail Park
NWMAL KT3 192 D1
Shapla Primary School
WCHPL E1 104 C6
Sharp Sports Centre
EDGW HA8 44 C2
Shawcroft School
STMC/STPC BR5 203 F2
Sheen Lane Health Centre
MORT/ESHN SW14 137 K4
Sheen Lawn Tennis & Squash Club
MORT/ESHN SW14 137 K6
Sheen Mount Primary School
RCHPK/HAM TW10 137 J6
Sheen Sports Centre
MORT/ESHN SW14 138 B5
Shell Centre
STHWK SE1 17 H1
Shelley School
CLAP SW4 141 H4
Shene School
MORT/ESHN SW14 138 B5
Shenstone School
DART DA1 150 A6
Shepherd's Bush ⇌ ⊖ ⊖
SHB W12 119 G2
Shepherd's Bush CC
ACT W3 99 G6
Shepherd's Bush Empire
SHB W12 119 F2
Shepherd's Bush Market ⊖
SHB W12 119 F1
Sheraton Belgravia Hotel
KTBR SW1X 15 G5
Sheraton Business Centre
GFD/PVL UB6 97 J1
Sheraton Park Tower Hotel
KTBR SW1X 15 F2
Sheraton Skyline Hotel
HYS/HAR UB3 133 G1
Sheringdale Primary School
WAND/EARL SW18 159 J3
Sheringham Junior School
MNPK E12 89 K2
Sherington Primary School
CHARL SE7 126 A6
Sherlock Holmes Hotel
MHST W1U 9 F1
Sherlock Holmes Museum
CAMTN NW1 3 F7
Sherwood Park Primary School
BFN/LL DA15 168 C1
Sherwood Park School
WLGTN SM6 210 D1
Sherwood School
MTCM CR4 195 H1
The Shire London
BAR EN5 20 A1
Shirley Clinic
CROY/NA CR0 197 K5
Shirley High School
CROY/NA CR0 213 F1
Shirley Oaks Hospital
CROY/NA CR0 197 K4
Shirley Park Golf Club
CROY/NA CR0 197 J6
Shirley Wanderers RFC
WWKM BR4 214 A2
Shirley Windmill
CROY/NA CR0 212 E1
Shooters Hill Golf Club
WOOL/PLUM SE18 147 H2
Shooters Hill Post 16 Campus
WOOL/PLUM SE18 147 F1
Shooting Star House (Childrens Hospice)
HPTN TW12 172 E2
Shopping City
WDGN N22 49 F5
Shore Business Centre
HOM E9 86 E5
Shoreditch Comprehensive School
IS N1 7 H3
Shoreditch High Street ⊖
WCHPL E1 7 J7
Shortlands ⇌
HAYES BR2 183 H5
Shotfield Health Clinic
WLGTN SM6 210 B4
Showcase Cinema
WDGN N22 49 G5
Showcase Newham Cinema
BARK IG11 108 C2
Shrewsbury House School
SURB KT6 190 E6
Shrewsbury Road Health Centre
FSTGT E7 89 H5
Sidcup ⇌
BFN/LL DA15 168 B4
Sidcup Cemetery
BXLY DA5 168 E4
Sidcup Golf Club
BFN/LL DA15 168 B4
Sidcup Health Centre
SCUP DA14 168 B5
Sidcup Sports Club
SCUP DA14 168 A6
Sidney Russell School
DAGW RM9 92 A2
Silicon Business Centre
GFD/PVL UB6 97 J1
Silverdale Industrial Estate
HYS/HAR UB3 113 K2
Silver Industrial Estate
TOTM N17 50 B5
Silver Street ⇌
UED N18 36 B6
Silver Street Medical Centre
UED N18 36 A6
Silver Wing Industrial Estate
CROY/NA CR0 211 F4
Simon Marks Jewish Primary School
STNW/STAM N16 68 B5
Singlegate Primary School
WIM/MER SW19 178 C3
Sion College
EMB EC4Y 11 K5
Sion Manning RC Girls School
NKENS W10 100 B4
Sir Francis Drake Primary School
DEPT SE8 124 B5
Sir George Monoux College
WALTH E17 51 K5
Sir James Altham Swimming Pool
OXHEY WD19 41 J1
Sir James Barrie School
VX/NE SW8 141 H2
Sir John Cass Foundation School
HDTCH EC3A 13 H4
Sir John Cass Found/ Redcoat School
WCHPL E1 105 F4
Sir John Heron Primary School
MNPK E12 89 K2
Sir John Lillie Primary School
HMSMTH W6 119 H6
Sir John Soane's Museum
LINN WC2A 11 G3
Sir Thomas Abney Primary School
STNW/STAM N16 67 K4
Sir Thomas Lipton Memorial Hospital
STHGT/OAK N14 34 B2
Sir William Burrough Primary School
POP/IOD E14 105 G5
Six Bridges Trading Estate
STHWK SE1 123 H5
Skillion Business Park
BARK IG11 109 F2
Skinners Company Lower Girls School
CLPT E5 68 D5
Skinners Company School for Girls
STNW/STAM N16 68 A4
Slade Green ⇌
ERITH DA8 150 D2
Slade Green FC
ERITH DA8 150 E2
Slade Green Primary School
ERITH DA8 150 D1
Slade School of Fine Art
STPAN WC1H 4 D5

Sleaford Industrial Estate
VX/NE SW8 ....141 H1
Sloane Hospital
BECK BR3 ☉ 183 G4
Sloane Square ☉
BCVA SW1W 15 G7
Smallberry Green
Primary School
ISLW TW7 ....136 B5
Smallwood Primary School
TOOT SW17 ....160 C6
SMA Medical Centre
LEY E10 ....69 K4
Smithy Street School
WCHPL E1 ....104 E4
Snaresbrook ☉
WAN E11 ....70 E2
Snaresbrook College
Preparatory School
SWFD E18 ....52 E5
Snaresbrook Primary School
SWFD E18 ....70 E1
Snowsfields Primary School
STHWK SE1 ....19 G2
Sobell Leisure Centre
HOLWY N7 ....85 F1
Sobell Medical Centre
HOLWY N7 ....85 G2
Sofitel St James Hotel
STJS SW1Y 10 C7
Soho Parish CE
Primary School
SOHO/CST W1F 10 C5
Solent Road Health Centre
KIL/WHAMP NW6 ....82 E4
Somerset House
COVGDN WC2E 11 G5
Somers Town Community
Sports Centre
CAMTN NW1 ....4 B3
Sorsby Health Centre
CLPT E5 ....87 F2
South Acton ☉
ACT W3 ....117 K3
Southall ☉
STHL UB1 ....114 E2
Southall & West
London College
STHL UB1 ....114 D2
South Bank Business Centre
VX/NE SW8 ....121 J6
Southbank International
School Hampstead
HAMP NW3 ☉ 83 G4
Southbank International
School Kensington
NTGHL W11 ....100 D6
South Bank University
STHWK SE1 ....18 A4
South Bermondsey ☉
BERM/RHTH SE16 ....123 K5
Southborough
Primary School
HAYES BR2 ....201 F2
Southborough School
SURB KT6 ....206 A1
Southbury ☉
EN EN1 ....24 D5
Southbury Primary School
PEND EN3 ....24 D5
South Camden
Community School
CAMTN NW1 ....4 B2
South Chelsea College
BRXN/ST SW9 ....142 A5
South Croydon ☉
SAND/SEL CR2 ....211 K3
South Croydon
Medical Centre
SAND/SEL CR2 ....211 J5
South Croydon
Sports Club
CROY/NA CR0 ....212 A3
South Ealing ☉
EA W5 ....116 E3
South Ealing Cemetery
EA W5 ....116 E4
South Eastern University
HOLWY N7 ....85 F1
Southern Road
Primary School
PLSTW E13 ....107 F1
Southfield First &
Middle School
CHSWK W4 ....118 B2
Southfield Medical Centre
CHSWK W4 ....118 A2
Southfields ☉
WAND/EARL SW18 ....159 J3
The Southfields Clinic
WAND/EARL SW18 ....159 K1
Southfields
Community College
WAND/EARL SW18 ....159 K3
Southgate ☉
STHGT/OAK N14 ....34 D3
Southgate Cemetery
STHGT/OAK N14 ....34 C4
Southgate College
STHGT/OAK N14 ....34 C4
Southgate Compton CC
EBAR EN4 ....21 K5
Southgate Leisure Centre
STHGT/OAK N14 ....34 D2
Southgate Road
Medical Centre
IS N1 ....85 K5
Southgate School
EBAR EN4 ....22 B6
South Greenford ☉
GFD/PVL UB6 ....96 E2
South Grove Primary School
WALTH E17 ....69 G3
South Hampstead ☉
STJWD NW8 ....83 G5
South Hampstead CC
CRICK NW2 ....82 A5
South Hampstead
High School
HAMP NW3 ....83 H4

South Haringay
Infant School
FSBYPK N4 ....67 H2
South Harrow ☉
RYLN/HDSTN HA2 ....78 C1
South Herts Golf Club
TRDG/WHET N20 ....32 E3
South Kensington ☉
SKENS SW7 ....14 B6
South Kenton ☉
ALP/SUD HA0 ....61 J5
Southlake Primary School
ABYW SE2 ....128 E2
South Lewisham
Health Centre
CAT SE6 ....165 F6
South London Crematorium
MTCM CR4 ....179 H5
South London Gallery
CMBW SE5 ....143 F2
The South London Natural
Health Centre
CLAP SW4 ....141 H5
South London Tamil School
CROY/NA CR0 ....196 D4
South London Theatre
WNWD SE27 ....162 D5
Southmead Primary School
WIM/MER SW19 ....159 H3
South Merton ☉
RYNPK SW20 ....177 J6
South Norwood Country Park
SNWD SE25 ....197 K1
South Norwood Hill
Medical Centre
SNWD SE25 ....181 F5
South Norwood
Medical Centre
SNWD SE25 ....197 F1
South Norwood Pools &
Fitness Centre
SNWD SE25 ....197 H2
South Norwood
Primary School
SNWD SE25 ....197 H2
South Park Business Centre
IL IG1 ....72 E6
South Park Clinic
IL IG1 ....90 D2
South Park Hotel
SAND/SEL CR2 ....212 A2
South Park Primary School
GDMY/SEVK IG3 ....90 E1
South Quay ☉
POP/IOD E14 ....124 E2
South Quay Plaza
POP/IOD E14 ....124 E2
South Rise Primary School
WOOL/PLUM SE18 ....127 J5
South Ruislip ☉
RSLP HA4 ....77 G2
Southside Industrial Estate
VX/NE SW8 ....141 H1
Southside Shopping Centre
WAND/EARL SW18 ....160 A1
South Thames College
PUT/ROE SW15 ....139 G6
PUT/ROE SW15 ....158 C1
TOOT SW17 ....178 D1
WAND/EARL SW18 ....140 A6
South Tottenham ☉
SEVS/STOTM N15 ....68 B2
Southville Infant School
EBED/NFELT TW14 ....153 J3
Southwark ☉
STHWK SE1 ....18 A1
Southwark Bridge Stairs
BLKFR EC4V 12 C6
Southwark Cathedral
STHWK SE1 ....12 E7
Southwark College
BERM/RHTH SE16 ....123 J5
CMBW SE5 ....143 F1
STHWK SE1 ....17 K2
STHWK SE1 ....19 H4
Southwark Park
Primary School
BERM/RHTH SE16 ....123 J5
Southwark Park
Sports Centre
BERM/RHTH SE16 ....123 K4
Southwark Sports Ground
DUL SE21 ....163 G3
South West
Middlesex Crematorium
FELT TW13 ....154 D3
South Wimbledon ☉
WIM/MER SW19 ....178 A3
Southwold Primary School
CLPT E5 ....68 E6
South Woodford ☉
SWFD E18 ....52 E5
South Woodford
Health Centre
SWFD E18 ....52 E4
Southwood Hospital
HGT N6 ....66 A4
Southwood Primary School
DAGW RM9 ....92 A2
Sovereign Business Centre
PEND EN3 ....25 H4
The Space Arts
Centre Cinema
DEPT SE8 ....124 C4
Sparrow Farm Community
Junior School
EBED/NFELT TW14 ....207 K3
Sparrow Farm Infant School
EBED/NFELT TW14 ....154 B2
Sparrow Farm
Junior School
EBED/NFELT TW14 ....154 B2
Spa School
STHWK SE1 ....123 H4
Speakers Corner
BAY/PAD W2 ....9 F5
The Speech Centre
CAMTN NW1 ....4 D4
Speedway Industrial Estate
HYS/HAR UB3 ....113 G2

Speke's Monument
BAY/PAD W2 ....101 G6
Spencer House
WHALL SW1A 16 A1
The Spires Shopping Centre
BAR EN5 ....20 C4
Spitalfields Community Farm
WCHPL E1 ....104 C3
Spitalfields Health Centre
WCHPL E1 ....13 K2
Spitfire Business Park
CROY/NA CR0 ....211 G4
Splashworld
Swimming Centre
BXLYHS DA6 ....148 D5
Springfield Christian School
CAT SE6 ....164 C5
Springfield Community
Primary School
SEVS/STOTM N15 ....68 C3
Springfield Hospital
TOOT SW17 ....160 D5
Springfield Primary School
VX/NE SW8 ....141 J1
Spring Grove Primary School
ISLW TW7 ....135 J3
Springhallow School
HNWL W7 ....97 F5
Spring Park Primary School
CROY/NA CR0 ....213 J1
Springvale Retail Park
STMC/STPC BR5 ....186 D6
Springwell Infant School
HEST TW5 ....134 D1
Springwell Junior School
HEST TW5 ....134 D1
Squirrels Heath Infant School
GPK RM2 ....75 K2
Squirrels Heath Junior School
GPK RM2 ....75 K2
Squirrels Trading Estate
HYS/HAR UB3 ....113 J3
The Stables Gallery &
Art Centre
CRICK NW2 ....81 J2
Stadium Business Centre
WBLY HA9 ....80 D1
Stadium Industrial Estate
WBLY HA9 ....80 D3
Stadium Retail Park
WBLY HA9 ....80 C1
Stafford Cross Business Park
CROY/NA CR0 ....211 F3
The Stafford Hotel
WHALL SW1A 16 A1
Stag Lane First School
EDGW HA8 ....44 C5
Stag Lane Medical Centre
CDALE/KGS NW9 ....44 E6
Stamford Brook ☉
CHSWK W4 ....118 C4
Stamford Clinic
HMSMTH W6 ....118 D4
Stamford Hill ☉
SEVS/STOTM N15 ....68 A3
Stamford Hill Primary School
SEVS/STOTM N15 ....67 K3
Stanburn First School
STAN HA7 ....43 J3
Standard Industrial Estate
CAN/RD E16 ....126 C2
Stanford Primary School
STRHM/NOR SW16 ....179 J4
Stanhope Primary School
GFD/PVL UB6 ....96 C3
Stanley Infant School
TEDD TW11 ....153 K6
Stanley Park High School
CAR SM5 ....210 A4
Stanley Park
Primary School
CAR SM5 ....209 K5
Stanmore ☉
STAN HA7 ....29 K6
Stanmore College
STAN HA7 ....43 H2
Stanmore Golf Club
STAN HA7 ....43 H3
Stanton School of English
BAY/PAD W2 ....101 F5
Stanton Square
Industrial Estate
SYD SE26 ....164 C6
Staple Inn Buildings
HHOL WC1V 11 J2
Staples Corner Business Park
CRICK NW2 ....63 J5
Star Business Centre
RAIN RM13 ....111 F4
Starksfield Primary School
ED N9 ....36 A3
Star Lane ☉
CAN/RD E16 ....106 C3
Star Primary School
CAN/RD E16 ....106 C3
Stationers Hall
STP EC4M 12 B4
Stationery Office
HOL/ALD WC2B 11 G3
Stebon Primary School
POP/IOD E14 ....105 H4
Stephen Hawking Primary
Special School
POP/IOD E14 ....105 G3
Stepney Day Hospital
WCHPL E1 ....104 E5
Stepney Green ☉
WCHPL E1 ....105 F3
Stepney Greencoat CE
Primary School
POP/IOD E14 ....105 H5
Stepney Green College
WCHPL E1 ....105 H5
Sterling Industrial Estate
DAGE RM10 ....92 D2
Sterling Way Clinic
UED N18 ....50 B1
Stewart Fleming
Primary School
PGE/AN SE20 ....181 K6

Stewart Headlam
Primary School
WCHPL E1 ....104 D3
Stillness Primary School
FSTH SE23 ....164 B1
Stirling Retail Park
BORE WD6 ....31 F1
Stirling Way Industrial Estates
CROY/NA CR0 ....195 K4
Stockley Park Business Centre
STKPK UB11 ....113 F1
Stockley Park Golf Club
STKPK UB11 ....94 A6
Stockwell ☉
CLAP SW4 ....141 K3
Stockwell Park School
BRXN/ST SW9 ....142 A2
Stockwell Primary School
BRXN/ST SW9 ....142 A4
Stoke Newington ☉
STNW/STAM N16 ....68 B6
Stonebridge Park ☉
ALP/SUD HA0 ....80 C5
The Stonebridge Primary
School (London
Welsh School)
WLSDN NW10 ....80 E6
Stonebridge Shopping Centre
WLSDN NW10 ....81 F6
Stonehill Business Centre
UED N18 ....51 F2
Stonehill Business Park
UED N18 ....51 F1
Stone Lake Retail Park
CHARL SE7 ....126 B4
Stoneleigh ☉
HOR/WEW KT19 ....207 H3
Stoneleigh First School
EW KT17 ....207 K2
Stoneydown Park
Primary School
WALTH E17 ....69 G1
Stowford College
BELMT SM2 ....209 G5
Strand on the Green
J & I School
CHSWK W4 ....117 H6
Strand Palace Hotel
COVGDN WC2E 11 F5
Stratford College
SRTFD E15 ....88 C5
Stratford High Street ☉
SRTFD E15 ....88 B5
Stratford International ☉
SRTFD E15 ....88 A4
Stratford ☉
SRTFD E15 ....88 C5
Stratford School
FSTGT E7 ....88 E5
Stratford Shopping Centre
SRTFD E15 ....88 B5
Strathmore School
RCHPK/HAM TW10 ....156 E3
Strawberry Fields School
NTGHL W11 ....100 E5
Strawberry Hill ☉
WHTN TW2 ....155 K5
Strawberry Hill Golf Club
WHTN TW2 ....155 K5
Stream House
STRHM/NOR SW16 ....179 J1
Streatham Cemetery
TOOT SW17 ....160 D5
Streatham & Clapham
High School
STRHM/NOR SW16 ....161 H5
BRXS/STRHM SW2 ....162 A3
Streatham Common ☉
STRHM/NOR SW16 ....179 J2
Streatham & Croydon RFC
THHTH CR7 ....196 B2
Streatham Hill ☉
STRHM/NOR SW16 ....161 K4
Streatham Ice Rink
STRHM/NOR SW16 ....179 K1
Streatham Leisure Centre
STRHM/NOR SW16 ....161 K4
Streatham Modern School
STRHM/NOR SW16 ....179 K2
Streatham Park Cemetery
MTCM CR4 ....179 H5
Streatham Swimming Pool
STRHM/NOR SW16 ....179 K1
Streatham Vale Sports Club
STRHM/NOR SW16 ....179 H3
Streatham Wells
Primary School
BRXS/STRHM SW2 ....162 A4
Stroud Green
Primary School
FSBYPK N4 ....67 G5
Studholme Medical Centre
ASHF TW15 ....152 C6
The
Preparatory School
WIM/MER SW19 ....177 G1
The Study School
NWMAL KT3 ....192 B2
Sudbourne Primary School
BRXS/STRHM SW2 ....142 A6
Sudbury Court Sports Club
ALP/SUD HA0 ....79 J1
Sudbury Golf Club
GFD/PVL UB6 ....79 H1
Sudbury & Harrow Road ☉
ALP/SUD HA0 ....79 H1
Sudbury Hill ☉
HRW HA1 ....78 E2
Sudbury Primary School
ALP/SUD HA0 ....79 H2
Sudbury Town ☉
GFD/PVL UB6 ....79 H4
Suffolks Primary School
EN EN1 ....24 D3
Sulivan Primary School
FUL/PGN SW6 ....139 K3
Summerside JMI School
NFNCH/WDSPK N12 ....47 H2
Sunbury Court
SUN TW16 ....172 C5

Sundridge Park ☉
BMLY BR1 ....184 A3
Sundridge Park Golf Club
BMLY BR1 ....184 B2
Sun Life Trading Estate
EBED/NFELT TW14 ....133 K4
Sunnyfields Primary School
HDN NW4 ....45 K6
Sunnyhill Primary School
STRHM/NOR SW16 ....162 A4
Sunrise School
TOTM N17 ....50 C2
Sunshine House School
NTHWD HA6 ....40 B2
Surbiton ☉
SURB KT6 ....191 F5
Surbiton Business Centre
SURB KT6 ....190 E3
Surbiton Cemetery
KUT/HW KT1 ....191 H1
Surbiton Golf Club
CHSGTN KT9 ....205 H2
Surbiton High School
KUT/HW KT1 ....191 F1
Surbiton Hospital
SURB KT6 ....191 F3
Surbiton Natural
Health Centre
SURB KT6 ....191 F3
Surrey CCC (The Oval)
LBTH SE11 ....122 A6
Surrey Docks Farm
BERM/RHTH SE16 ....124 C2
Surrey Docks Health Centre
BERM/RHTH SE16 ....124 B2
Surrey Docks
Watersports Centre
BERM/RHTH SE16 ....124 B3
Surrey Quays ☉
BERM/RHTH SE16 ....124 A4
Surrey Quays Leisure Park
BERM/RHTH SE16 ....124 A3
Surrey Quays
Shopping Centre
BERM/RHTH SE16 ....124 A3
Surrey Square Primary School
WALW SE17 ....123 F5
Susi Earnshaw Theatre School
BAR EN5 ....20 D4
Sussex Hotel
OXSTW W1C 9 G4
Sussex House School
KTBR SW1X 14 E6
Sutcliffe Park Athletics Track
LEE/GVPK SE12 ....146 A4
Sutton ☉
SUT SM1 ....209 G4
Sutton Alternative
Health Centre
SUT SM1 ....209 F3
Sutton Arena
CAR SM5 ....194 C4
Sutton Bowling Club
BELMT SM2 ....208 E6
Sutton Cemetery
CHEAM SM3 ....193 J6
Sutton Civic Centre
SUT SM1 ....209 F3
Sutton College of Learning
for Adults
SUT SM1 ....209 F3
Sutton Common ☉
SUT SM1 ....193 K6
Sutton Grammar School
for Boys
SUT SM1 ....209 G4
Sutton High Junior School
SUT SM1 ....209 F4
Sutton High School for
Girls GDST
SUT SM1 ....208 E4
Sutton House
HACK E8 ....86 E3
Suttons Business Park
RAIN RM13 ....111 F2
Sutton Superbowl
SUT SM1 ....209 F3
Sutton United FC
SUT SM1 ....208 D2
Sutton West Centre
SUT SM1 ....208 E3
Swaffield Primary School
WAND/EARL SW18 ....160 B1
Swaminarayan School
WLSDN NW10 ....81 F4
Swan Business Centre
CHSWK W4 ....118 A4
Swan Business Park
DART DA1 ....151 G2
Swan Lane Pier
CANST EC4R 12 E6
Swanlea School
WCHPL E1 ....104 D3
Swansmere School
WOT/HER KT12 ....188 B5
Swedish School
BARN SW13 ....118 D6
Swiss Cottage ☉
KIL/WHAMP NW6 ....83 H5
Swiss Cottage Hotel
HAMP NW3 ....83 H5
Swiss Cottage Leisure Centre
HAMP NW3 ....83 H5
Swiss Cottage School
STJWD NW8 ....83 H6
Swissotel The Howard
TPL/STR WC2R 11 H5
Sybil Elgar School
EA W5 ....98 A6
NWDGN UB2 ....114 E3
Sybourn Infant School
LEY E10 ....69 G5
The Sybourn Junior School
WALTH E17 ....69 H4
Sydenham ☉
SYD SE26 ....181 K1
Sydenham Girls School
SYD SE26 ....163 J5
Sydenham High Junior School
SYD SE26 ....163 J6

Sydenham High School Sports Ground
CAT SE6 .... 182 D1

Sydenham High Senior School
SYD SE26 .... 181 J1

Sydenham Hill ≈
DUL SE21 .... 163 F5

The Sydney Russell School
DAGW RM9 .... 91 K3

Syon House
BTFD TW8 .... 136 D2

Syon Lane ≈
ISLW TW7 .... 136 D1

Syon Park
BTFD TW8 .... 136 D3

Syracuse University
NTGHL W11 .... 100 D6

Tabard Theatre
CHSWK W4 .... 118 B4

Tabernacle School
NTGHL W11 .... 119 C1

Taberner House
CROY/NA CR0 .... 211 J1

TA Centre
EDGW HA8 .... 44 D3
HRW HA1 .... 61 F2
NFNCH/WDSPK N12 .... 47 H4

Tait Road Industrial Estate
CROY/NA CR0 .... 197 F3

Talmud Torah School
STNW/STAM N16 .... 67 K4

Tamian Industrial Estate
HSLWW TW4 .... 134 B5

Tandem Centre
WIM/MER SW19 .... 178 C4

Tashbar of Edgware Primary School
EDGW HA8 .... 30 C6

Tate Britain
WEST SW1P 16 E7

Tate Modern
STHWK SE1 .... 12 B7

Tavistock Clinic
HAMP NW3 .... 83 H4

TAVR Centre
KUT/HW KT1 .... 190 E1

Tavy Clinic
ABYW SE2 .... 128 D2

Tawhid Boys School
STNW/STAM N16 .... 68 B6

Tayyibah Girls School
STNW/STAM N16 .... 68 C5

Teddington ≈
TEDD TW11 .... 174 B2

Teddington Business Park
TEDD TW11 .... 174 A1

Teddington Cemetery
TEDD TW11 .... 155 K6

Teddington Clinic
TEDD TW11 .... 173 K2

Teddington Memorial Hospital
TEDD TW11 .... 173 K2

Teddington Pool & Fitness Centre
TEDD TW11 .... 174 B1

Teddington School
TEDD TW11 .... 174 E2

The Teddington Theatre Club
E/WMO/HCT KT8 .... 189 J2

Telferscot Primary School
BAL SW12 .... 161 H3

Temperate House, Kew Gardens
RCH/KEW TW9 .... 137 G3

Temple Grove Hatcham School
NWCR SE14 .... 144 A1

Temple Hill Primary School
DART DA1 .... 151 K6

Temple of Bacchus
CMBW SE5 .... 142 D3

Temple of Mithras
MANHO EC4N 12 E4

Temple ⊖
TPL/STR WC2R 11 J5

Tenby Road Clinic
EDGW HA8 .... 44 B5

Tenterden Sports Ground
KTN/HRWW/WS HA3 .... 62 A4

Terence McMillan Stadium
PLSTW E13 .... 107 G3

Tetherdown Primary School
MUSWH N10 .... 66 A1

Thames Barrier
CAN/RD E16 .... 126 C2

Thames Barrier Information & Learning Centre
CHARL SE7 .... 126 C3

Thames Christian College
BTSEA SW11 .... 140 C4

Thames Ditton ≈
THDIT KT7 .... 189 K4

Thames Ditton & Esher Golf Club
ESH/CLAY KT10 .... 189 J6

Thames Ditton Infant School
THDIT KT7 .... 190 A3

Thames Ditton Junior School
THDIT KT7 .... 190 A4

Thames Gateway Park
DAGW RM9 .... 110 B2

Thames House
WEST SW1P 16 E6

Thameside Industrial Estate
CAN/RD E16 .... 126 C1

Thamesmead Leisure Centre
THMD SE28 .... 109 H6

Thames Valley University
EA W5 .... 97 J6
EA W5 .... 116 D1

Thamesview Business Centre
RAIN RM13 .... 111 G4

Thames View Clinic
BARK IG11 .... 109 F1

Thames View J & I School
BARK IG11 .... 109 G1

Thames Water Tower
NTGHL W11 .... 119 G2

Theatre de l'Ange Fou International School of Corporeal Mime
ARCH N19 .... 66 E5

Theatre for Mankind
FSBYPK N4 .... 67 F5

Theatre Museum Library & Archive
COVGDN WC2E 11 F5

Theatre of the Dispossessed
WIM/MER SW19 .... 159 G3

Theatre Royal
HOL/ALD WC2B 11 F4
SRTFD E15 .... 88 B4

Theatre Royal Haymarket
STJS SW1Y 10 D6

Theodore McLeary Primary School
EDUL SE22 .... 143 G5

Therapia Lane ⊖
CROY/NA CR0 .... 195 K4

Therapia Trading Estate
CROY/NA CR0 .... 195 J4

Thistlebrook Industrial Estate
ABYW SE2 .... 128 D3

Thistle Hotel
BGVA SW1W 15 K5
CAMTN NW1 .... 4 B5
FITZ W1T 10 B3
FSBYE EC1V 6 C5
NOXST/BSQ WC1A 10 E2
WESTW SW1E 15 K5

Thistle Hyde Park Hotel
BAY/PAD W2 .... 101 G6

Thistle Kensington Gardens Hotel
BAY/PAD W2 .... 101 G6

Thistle Marble Arch Hotel
MBLAR W1H 9 F4

Thistle Piccadilly Hotel
SOHO/SHAV W1D 10 C6

Thomas Arnold Primary School
DAGW RM9 .... 92 B5

Thomas Buxton Infant School
WCHPL E1 .... 104 C3

Thomas Fairchild Primary School
IS N1 .... 6 E2

Thomas Francis Academy
BRXN/ST SW9 .... 142 C5

Thomas Gamuel Primary School
WALTH E17 .... 69 J3

Thomas Jones Primary School
NTGHL W11 .... 100 C5

Thomas Knyvett College
ASHF TW15 .... 152 B5

Thomas London Independent Day School
KENS W8 .... 120 A3

Thomas Road Industrial Estate
POP/IOD E14 .... 105 J4

Thomas's Fulham
FUL/PGN SW6 .... 140 A4

Thomas's Preparatory School
BTSEA SW11 .... 140 C2
BTSEA SW11 .... 140 E6

Thomas Tallis School
BKHTH/KID SE3 .... 146 A4

Thornhill Primary School
IS N1 .... 85 G5

Thornton Heath ≈
THHTH CR7 .... 196 D1

Thornton Heath Health Centre
THHTH CR7 .... 196 D1

Thornton Heath Pools & Fitness Centre
THHTH CR7 .... 196 D1

Thornton Road Industrial Estate
CROY/NA CR0 .... 195 K3

Thorntree Primary School
CHARL SE7 .... 126 C5

Thorpe Hall Primary School
WALTH E17 .... 52 A4

Three Bridges Business Centre
NWDGN UB2 .... 115 H2

Three Bridges Primary School
NWDGN UB2 .... 115 G3

Three Mills Heritage Centre
BOW E3 .... 106 A2

Thurston Industrial Estate
LEW SE13 .... 144 E4

Tibetan Buddhist Centre
WALW SE17 .... 122 D5

Tidemill Primary School
DEPT SE8 .... 144 D1

Tideway Industrial Estate
VX/NE SW8 .... 121 H6

Tiffin Girls School
KUTN/CMB KT2 .... 175 F2

Tiffin School & Sports Centre
KUTN/CMB KT2 .... 175 G5

Tiller Centre (Swimming Baths)
POP/IOD E14 .... 124 D3

Tiller Leisure Centre
POP/IOD E14 .... 124 D3

Timbercroft Primary School
WOOL/PLUM SE18 .... 147 K1

Timbers Clinic
KTN/HRWW/WS HA3 .... 42 D2

Timebridge Youth & Community Centre
CROY/NA CR0 .... 213 K3

Times Square Shopping Centre
SUT SM1 .... 209 F3

Tiverton Primary School
SEVS/STOTM N15 .... 67 K3

Tobacco Dock
WAP E1W 104 D6

Tokyngton Community Centre
WBLY HA9 .... 80 D3

Toldos School
STNW/STAM N16 .... 67 K5

Tollgate
STHL UB1 .... 163 F4

Tollgate Primary School
PLSTW E13 .... 107 G3

Tolworth ≈
BRYLDS KT5 .... 191 J6

Tolworth CP School
SURB KT6 .... 191 J5

Tolworth Girls School
SURB KT6 .... 191 J5

Tolworth Recreation Centre
SURB KT6 .... 206 B1

Tom Hood School
WAN E11 .... 88 D1

Tooting ⊖
TOOT SW17 .... 178 E2

Tooting Bec ⊖
TOOT SW17 .... 161 F5

Tooting Bec Athletics Track
TOOT SW17 .... 161 G6

Tooting Broadway ⊖
TOOT SW17 .... 178 D1

Tooting Leisure Centre
TOOT SW17 .... 160 C6

Tooting & Mitcham United FC
MTCM CR4 .... 179 F4

Torah Temimah Primary School
CRICK NW2 .... 81 K2

Torah Vodaas
GLDGN NW11 .... 64 D6

Torriano Junior School
KTTN NW5 .... 84 C3

Torridon Primary School
CAT SE6 .... 165 G4

Torrington Clinic
NFNCH/WDSPK N12 .... 47 G1

Torrington Park Health Centre
NFNCH/WDSPK N12 .... 33 G6

Total Health Clinic
SHB W12 .... 118 E2

Tottenham Cemetery
TOTM N17 .... 50 A3

Tottenham Court Road ⊖
SOHO/SHAV W1D 10 C3

Tottenham Green Leisure Centre
SEVS/STOTM N15 .... 68 A1

Tottenham Hale ≈⊖
TOTM N17 .... 50 D6

Tottenham Hale Retail Park
SEVS/STOTM N15 .... 68 C1

Tottenham Hotspur FC (White Hart Lane)
TOTM N17 .... 50 B3

Tottenham Park Cemetery
ED N9 .... 36 D5

Tottenham Sports Centre
TOTM N17 .... 50 B4

Totteridge CC
TRDG/WHET N20 .... 32 E4

Totteridge & Whetstone ⊖
TRDG/WHET N20 .... 33 F4

Tower 42
OBST EC2N 13 G3

The Tower Bridge Exhibition
STHWK SE1 .... 19 J1

Tower Bridge Primary School
STHWK SE1 .... 19 J2

Tower Bridge Wharf
WAP E1W 123 H1

Tower Gateway ⊖
TWRH EC3N 13 J5

Tower Hamlets College
POP/IOD E14 .... 105 K6
WCHPL E1 .... 104 E4

Tower Hill ⊖
TWRH EC3N 13 J6

The Tower Hotel
WAP E1W 13 K7

Tower Industrial Estate
SNWD SE25 .... 197 H1

Tower Medical Centre
WCHPL E1 .... 104 C5

Tower Millennium Pier
TWRH EC3N 13 H7

Tower of London
TWRH EC3N 13 J6

Tower Retail Park
DART DA1 .... 150 C6

Towers Business Park
WBLY HA9 .... 80 D2

Tower Stairs
MON EC3R 13 G7

Town Farm Primary School
STWL/WRAY TW19 .... 152 A2

Townley Grammar School for Girls
BXLYHS DA6 .... 169 G1

Townmead Business Centre
FUL/PGN SW6 .... 140 B3

Townsend Industrial Estate
WLSDN NW10 .... 80 E6

Townsend Primary School
WALW SE17 .... 19 F6

Toynbee Hall & Curtain Theatre
WCHPL E1 .... 13 J2

Trade Union Congress
NOXST/BSQ WC1A 10 D3

Trafalgar Business Centre
BARK IG11 .... 109 F3

Trafalgar Infant & Junior School
WHTN TW2 .... 155 J4

Trafalgar Infant School
WHTN TW2 .... 155 J3

Trafalgar Square
STJS SW1Y 10 D7

Trafalgar Trading Estate
PEND EN3 .... 25 H5

Tramshed Theatre
WOOL/PLUM SE18 .... 127 G4

Trans Atlantic College
BETH E2 .... 7 H2

Transport for London Lost Property Office
CAMTN NW1 .... 3 F7

Transport House
WEST SW1P 16 E5

Travelodge
ACT W3 .... 98 C3
BTFD TW8 .... 117 F6
BTSEA SW11 .... 140 B4
CAMTN NW1 .... 4 D1
CAN/RD E16 .... 126 C1
FELT TW13 .... 153 K3
FSBYW WC1X 5 H4
HEST TW5 .... 114 B6
IL IG1 .... 90 B1
KUTN/CMB KT2 .... 175 F5
LSQ/SEVD WC2H 10 E3
POP/IOD E14 .... 106 B5
REDBR IG4 .... 71 K3
STPAN WC1H 5 G4
SURB KT6 .... 191 J5
WCHPL E1 .... 13 J3
WLSDN NW10 .... 98 C1

Travelodge Croydon Central
CROY/NA CR0 .... 196 E6

The Treaty Centre
HSLW TW3 .... 135 G4

Treehouse School
MUSWH N10 .... 66 A1

The Treehouse School
BMSBY WC1N 5 G6

Trent CE Primary School
EBAR EN4 .... 21 K5

Trent Country Park
EBAR EN4 .... 22 A3

Trent Park Cemetery
EBAR EN4 .... 22 A4

Trent Park Golf Club
STHGT/OAK N14 .... 22 C5

Trevor Roberts School
HAMP NW3 .... 83 H5

Tricycle Theatre
KIL/WHAMP NW6 .... 82 D5

Trident Business Centre
TOOT SW17 .... 178 E1

Trinity Business Centre
BERM/RHTH SE16 .... 124 C2

Trinity Catholic Lower High School
WFD IG8 .... 38 E6

Trinity College Centre
PECK SE15 .... 143 F1

Trinity College London
STHWK SE1 .... 121 K5

Trinity College of Music
GNWCH SE10 .... 125 F6
MHST W1U 9 H2

Trinity Hospital
GNWCH SE10 .... 125 G5

Trinity House
TWRH EC3N 13 H5

Trinity RC High School (Upper)
WFD IG8 .... 38 E6

Trinity St Marys Primary School
BAL SW12 .... 161 F3

Trinity School
CROY/NA CR0 .... 197 K6
DAGE RM10 .... 92 C1

Trinity School Belvedere
BELV DA17 .... 129 K4

Trinity Trading Estate
HYS/HAR UB3 .... 113 K3

Tripcock Point Development Site
THMD SE28 .... 109 F6

Triumph Trading Estate
TOTM N17 .... 50 C2

Trocadero
SOHO/SHAV W1D 10 C6

Trojan Business Centre
WLSDN NW10 .... 81 H4

Troy Industrial Estate
HRW HA1 .... 61 F2

True Buddha School
IS N1 .... 6 A2

TS Queen Mary
TPL/STR WC2R 11 G6

TTMH Belz Day School
STNW/STAM N16 .... 68 C4

Tubbenden J & I Schools
ORP BR6 .... 216 D2

Tudor Enterprise Park
KTN/HRWW/WS HA3 .... 42 D6

Tudor Lodge Health Centre
WIM/MER SW19 .... 159 G3

Tudor Lodge Hotel
PIN HA5 .... 59 F3

Tudor Primary School
FNCH N3 .... 47 G4
STHL UB1 .... 95 J6

Tufnell Park ⊖
KTTN NW5 .... 84 B2

Tufnell Park Primary School
HOLWY N7 .... 84 D2

Tulse School
PECK SE15 .... 143 J2

Tulse Hill ≈
WNWD SE27 .... 162 C4

Tunnel Avenue Trading Estate
GNWCH SE10 .... 125 G2

Turin Grove School
ED N9 .... 36 E2

Turney School
DUL SE21 .... 162 D2

Turnham Green ⊖
CHSWK W4 .... 118 B4

Turnham Primary School
BROCKY SE4 .... 144 B5

Turnpike Lane ⊖
SEVS/STOTM N15 .... 49 H6

Turtle Key Arts Centre
FUL/PGN SW6 .... 119 K6

Tutorial College of West London
STHL UB1 .... 115 F1

Tweeddale Primary School
CAR SM5 .... 194 C4

Twenty Nevern Square Hotel
ECT SW5 .... 119 K4

Twickenham ≈
TWK TW1 .... 156 B2

Twickenham Cemetery
WHTN TW2 .... 155 G3

Twickenham Park Health Centre
TWK TW1 .... 156 D1

Twickenham Preparatory School
HPTN TW12 .... 173 G4

Twickenham Stadium
ISLW TW7 .... 155 K1

Twickenham Trading Estate
TWK TW1 .... 156 A1

Two Bridges Business Park
SAND/SEL CR2 .... 211 K4

Twyford CE High School
ACT W3 .... 117 H1

Twyford Sports Centre
ACT W3 .... 117 J1

Tyburn Infant School
STJWD NW8 .... 2 B6

Tynemouth Road Health Centre
SEVS/STOTM N15 .... 68 B1

The Type Museum
BRXN/ST SW9 .... 142 A2

Tyssen Primary School
STNW/STAM N16 .... 68 C5

UCI Cinema
SUT SM1 .... 209 F3

UCI Empire Cinema
LSQ/SEVD WC2H 10 D6

UK Passport Office
PIM SW1V 15 K6

Underhill Infant School
BAR EN5 .... 20 C6

Unicorn Primary School
BECK BR3 .... 198 E2

Unicorn School
RCH/KEW TW9 .... 137 G2

Unicorn Theatre
STHWK SE1 .... 19 H2

United Medical & Dental Schools
STHWK SE1 .... 17 G4

Unity College
KTTN NW5 .... 84 B2

Unity Trading Estate
WFD IG8 .... 53 H6

University Church of Christ the King
STPAN WC1H 4 C7

University College Hospital
CAMTN NW1 .... 4 B6
HAMP NW3 .... 83 H4

University College London
FITZ W1T 10 B1
GWRST WC1E 4 C6
STPAN WC1H 4 C6

University College London, Astor College
FITZ W1T 10 B1

University College London Medical School
FITZ W1T 10 A1

University College London Obstetrics Hospital
GWRST WC1E 4 B7

University College Lewisham
LEW SE13 .... 144 E6

University Hospital Lewisham
WHALL SW1A 16 A1

University of California
WHALL SW1A 16 A1

University of East London
BARK IG11 .... 91 G2
CAN/RD E16 .... 108 A6
PLSTW E15 .... 107 F2
SRTFD E15 .... 88 B6

University of Greenwich
DART DA1 .... 171 J4
GNWCH SE10 .... 125 G5
WOOL/PLUM SE18 .... 127 F4

University of Greenwich (Mansion Site)
ELTH/MOT SE9 .... 167 H1

University of Greenwich (Southwood Site)
ELTH/MOT SE9 .... 167 H2

University of Greenwich Sports Ground
ELTH/MOT SE9 .... 146 D5
ELTH/MOT SE9 .... 167 H2

University of London
BAY/PAD W2 .... 8 A4
BMSBY WC1N 5 F7
CLKNW EC1R 5 K6
FITZ W1T 10 B1
MBLAR W1H 8 D3
STHWK SE1 .... 18 E1
STPAN WC1H 4 D6

University of London Athletics Ground
NWMAL KT3 .... 192 D2

University of the Arts London
MYFR/PKLN W1K 9 J4

University of Westminster
CAMTN NW1 .... 4 A6
CAVSQ/HST W1G 9 K3
CHSWK W4 .... 137 K2
GTPST W1W 9 K1
HRW HA1 .... 61 G4

University of Westminster, Environment
MHST W1U 9 G1

Uphall Primary School
IL IG1 .... 90 B3

Upland Primary School
BXLYHN DA7 .... 149 G4

Uplands Business Park
WALTH E17 .... 51 F5

Upney ⊖
BARK IG11 ....91 F5
Upper Holloway ⊖
ARCH N19 ....66 D6
Upper Montagu Street Clinic
CAMTN NW1 ....8 E1
Upper Tooting Independent
High School
TOOT SW17 ....160 D4
Upton Cross Primary School
PLSTW E13 ....89 F6
Upton Day Hospital
BXLYHS DA6 ....149 F5
Upton Lane Medical Centre
FSTGT E7 ....89 F4
Upton Park ⊖
PLSTW E13 ....89 G6
Upton Primary School
BXLY DA5 ....149 F6
Upton Road School
BXLYHS DA6 ....149 F6
The Urdang Academy
LSQ/SEVD WC2H 10 E4
Ursuline High School
RYNPK SW20 ....177 G3
Ursuline Preparatory School
RYNPK SW20 ....177 G3
Uxbridge College
HYS/HAR UB3 ....94 E6
Uxendon Manor JM&I School
KTN/HRWW/WS HA3 ....62 A2
Vale Farm Sports Centre
ALP/SUD HA0 ....79 H2
Vale Industrial Estate
WATW WD18 ....26 A3
The Vale Medical Centre
FSTH SE23 ....164 B4
Valence House Museum
& Library
BCTR RM8 ....73 K6
Valence Primary School
BCTR RM8 ....73 K6
Valentine High School
GNTH/NBYPK IG2 ....72 A3
Valentines High Lower School
GNTH/NBYPK IG2 ....72 B2
Vale Park Industrial
ACT W5 ....118 B2
Vale Resource Base
TOTM N17 ....50 A4
The Vale School
SKENS SW7 ....120 B3
Valley Link Business Centre
PEND EN3 ....37 G1
Valley Link Business Estate
PEND EN3 ....37 G1
Valley Primary School
HAYES BR2 ....183 J5
Valmar Trading Estate
CMBW SE5 ....142 D2
V & A Museum of
Childhood
BETH E2 ....104 E2
Vanbrugh Theatre
CWRST WC1E 4 C7
Vanguard Trading Estate
SRTFD E15 ....88 A6
Vaudeville Theatre
COVGN WC2E 11 F5
Vaughan First &
Middle School
RYLN/HDSTN HA2 ....60 C3
Vauxhall ⊖ ≋
VX/NE SW8 ....121 K6
Vauxhall Primary School
LBTH SE11 ....122 A5
Vernon House Special School
WLSDN NW10 ....80 E3
Vestry Hall
MTCM CR4 ....178 E6
Vestry House Museum
WALTH E17 ....69 K1
Vicarage Fields Health Clinic
BARK IG11 ....90 C5
The Vicarage Field
Shopping Centre
BARK IG11 ....90 C5
Vicarage Primary School
EHAM E6 ....107 K2
Vicars Green Primary School
GFD/PVL UB6 ....97 J1
V I Components
Industrial Park
ERITH DA8 ....130 B5
Victoria ⊖ ≋
PIM SW1V 15 K6
Victoria & Albert Museum
SKENS SW7 ....14 B5
Victoria Business Centre
WELL DA16 ....148 B3
Victoria Bus Station
PIM SW1V 15 K5
Victoria Chiropractic Clinic
SKENS SW7 ....14 B3
Victoria Coach Station
BGVA SW1W 15 J7
Victoria Hall
FNCH N3 ....46 D4
Victoria Industrial Estate
ACT W3 ....99 F4
Victoria Industrial Park
DART DA1 ....151 G6
Victoria Junior School
FELT TW13 ....154 A4
Victoria Medical Centre
PIM SW1V 16 B7
Victoria Palace Theatre
BGVA SW1W 15 K5
Victoria Park
Industrial Centre
HOM E9 ....87 H5
Victoria Park Plaza Hotel
PIM SW1V 16 A6
Victoria Place
Shopping Centre
BGVA SW1W 15 K6
Victoria Rail/Air Terminal
PIM SW1V 15 K6
Victoria Retail Park
RSLP HA4 ....77 H3

Victoria Wharf
POP/IOD E14 ....105 G6
Victoria Wharf
Industrial Estate
DEPT SE8 ....124 B5
Victor Seymour
Infant School
CAR SM5 ....209 K1
Victory Business Centre
ISLW TW7 ....136 A5
Victory Day School
THHTH CR7 ....196 D1
Victory Primary School
WALW SE17 ....18 D6
Viking Business Centre
ROMW/RG RM7 ....74 E4
Viking Primary School
NTHLT UB5 ....95 H2
Village Infant School
DAGE RM10 ....92 C5
The Village School
HAMP NW3 ....83 K4
Villiers High School
STHL UB1 ....115 F1
The Vine Clinic
KUTN/CMB KT2 ....175 F2
Vine Medical Centre
E/WMO/HCT KT8 ....173 H6
The Vines School
BTSEA SW11 ....141 F5
The Vineyard Primary School
RCHPK/HAM TW10 ....157 F1
Vinopolis, City of Wine
STHWK SE1 ....12 D7
Vinters' Hall
BLKFR EC4V 12 D5
V I P Trading Estate
CHARL SE7 ....126 B4
Virginia Primary School
BETH E2 ....7 J5
Virgo Fidelis Convent Schools
NRWD SE19 ....180 D2
Visage School of Hair
& Beauty
ELTH/MOT SE9 ....167 F1
Vision College of Technology
HOM E9 ....87 J4
Vita et Pax School
STHGT/OAK N14 ....22 B4
Vittoria Primary School
IS N1 ....5 H1
Voyager Business Estate
BERM/RHTH SE16 ....123 H3
Vue Cinema
ACT W3 ....98 C3
CROY/NA CR0 ....196 A6
DAGW RM9 ....92 A6
FUL/PGN SW6 ....139 K1
HAMP NW3 ....85 G4
HRW HA1 ....60 E3
LSQ/SEVD WC2H 10 D5
NFNCH/WDSPK N12 ....47 H3
ROMW/RG RM7 ....75 G2
SHB W12 ....119 G2
Vulcan Business Centre
CROY/NA CR0 ....214 C6
Waddon ≋
CROY/NA CR0 ....211 G2
Waddon Clinic
CROY/NA CR0 ....211 G3
Waddon Infant School
CROY/NA CR0 ....211 G3
Waddon Marsh ⊖
CROY/NA CR0 ....196 B6
Wadham College
Sports Centre
WALTH E17 ....51 K4
Wadsworth Business Centre
GFD/PVL UB6 ....97 J1
The Waldegrave Clinic
TEDD TW11 ....174 A1
Waldegrave Girls School
WHTN TW2 ....155 J5
Waldo Industrial Estate
BMLY BR1 ....184 B6
Waldorf School of South
West London
BAL SW12 ....161 H4
Waldron Health Centre
& Surgery
NWCR SE14 ....144 C1
Walker Primary School
STHGT/OAK N14 ....34 C1
The Wallace Collection
DEPT SE8 ....124 E6
The Wallace Collection
MHST W1U 9 G3
Wallbrook Business Centre
HSLWW TW4 ....134 A4
Wallington ≋
WLGTN SM6 ....210 B4
Wallington County
Grammar School
WLGTN SM6 ....210 B1
Wallington High School
for Girls
WLGTN SM6 ....210 B6
Walmer Road Clinic
NTGHL W11 ....100 C6
Walm Lane Clinic
CRICK NW2 ....82 B3
Walnuts Leisure Centre
ORP BR6 ....202 B5
Walnuts Shopping Centre
ORP BR6 ....202 B5
Walnut Tree Walk
Primary School
LBTH SE11 ....17 J6
Waltham Forest College
WALTH E17 ....50 E6
Waltham Forest Pool & Track
WALTH E17 ....51 K6
Waltham Forest Theatre
WALTH E17 ....51 H6
Walthamstow Academy
WALTH E17 ....51 H4
Walthamstow
Business Centre
WALTH E17 ....52 A5

Walthamstow Central ≋ ⊖
WALTH E17 ....69 J2
Walthamstow Marsh
Nature Reserve
CLPT E5 ....68 D4
Walthamstow
Queens Road ⊖
WALTH E17 ....69 J2
Walthamstow
School for Girls
WALTH E17 ....69 K1
Walton Business Centre
WOT/HER KT12 ....188 A4
Walton Casuals FC
WOT/HER KT12 ....188 A2
Walton Community Hospital
WOT/HER KT12 ....188 A6
Walton Swimming Pool
WOT/HER KT12 ....188 A5
Walworth Academy
STHWK SE1 ....123 F5
Walworth Lower
Secondary School
WALW SE17 ....122 C5
Walworth Town Hall
WALW SE17 ....18 C7
Wandle Park ⊖
CROY/NA CR0 ....196 B6
Wandle Recreation Centre
WAND/EARL SW18 ....160 A1
Wandle Trading Estate
MTCM CR4 ....194 E4
Wandle Valley School
CAR SM5 ....194 D4
Wandsworth Adult College
BTSEA SW11 ....141 F2
TOOT SW17 ....160 D4
Wandsworth Cemetery
WAND/EARL SW18 ....160 B3
Wandsworth Common ≋
TOOT SW17 ....160 D2
Wandsworth Road ≋ ⊖
VX/NE SW8 ....141 H3
Wandsworth Town ≋
WAND/EARL SW18 ....140 A5
Wandsworth Trading Estate
WAND/EARL SW18 ....160 A2
Wanstead ⊖
WAN E11 ....71 F3
Wanstead CC
WAN E11 ....71 F4
Wanstead CE Primary School
WAN E11 ....70 E2
Wanstead Golf Club
WAN E11 ....71 G4
Wanstead High School
WAN E11 ....71 G3
Wanstead Hospital
WAN E11 ....71 G3
Wanstead Leisure Centre
WAN E11 ....71 G3
Wanstead Park ≋
FSTGT E7 ....89 F2
Wapping ⊖
WAP E1W 123 K1
Wapping Wharf
WAP E1W 123 K1
War Memorial
Sports Ground
SUT SM1 ....209 J2
Warnford Industrial Estate
HYS/HAR UB3 ....113 H2
Warren
Comprehensive School
CHDH RM6 ....74 B2
Warren Dell Primary School
OXHEY WD19 ....27 G5
Warrender School
RSLP HA4 ....58 D4
Warren Junior School
CHDH RM6 ....74 B2
The Warren Medical Centre
YEAD UB4 ....95 F5
Warren Road Primary School
ORP BR6 ....217 F2
Warren Sports Centre
CHDH RM6 ....74 B2
Warren Street ⊖
CAMTN NW1 ....4 A6
Warwick Avenue ⊖
MV/WKIL W9 ....101 G3
Warwick Dubbing Theatre
SOHO/CST W1F 10 C4
Warwick Estate
BAY/PAD W2 ....101 F4
Warwick Leadlay Gallery
GNWCH SE10 ....125 F6
Warwick School for Boys
WALTH E17 ....70 A1
The Washington
Mayfair Hotel
MYFR/PICC W1J 9 K7
Waterfront Leisure Centre
WOOL/PLUM SE18 ....127 F3
Watergate School
CAT SE6 ....182 E1
LEE/GVPK SE12 ....144 E5
Waterloo ≋ ⊖
STHWK SE1 ....17 J2
Waterloo East ≋
STHWK SE1 ....17 K1
Waterloo Health Centre
STHWK SE1 ....17 J3
Waterloo School of English
NOXST/BSQ WC1A 10 E2
Watermans Arts, Cinema &
Theatre Centre
BTFD TW8 ....117 F6
The Watermans Hall
MON EC3R 13 G6
Watermeads High School
MRDN SM4 ....194 A3
Watermill Business Centre
PEND EN3 ....25 H3
Water Rats Theatre
STPAN WC1H 5 F4
Waterside Business Centre
ISLW TW7 ....136 C5
Waterside Primary School
WOOL/PLUM SE18 ....127 J5

The Waterside Trading Centre
HNWL W7 ....115 K3
Watersports Centre
STNW/STAM N16 ....67 J5
Waterways Business Centre
PEND EN3 ....25 H1
Watling Boys' Club
EDGW HA8 ....44 C3
Watling Clinic
EDGW HA8 ....45 F3
Watling Medical Centre
EDGW HA8 ....44 E4
Wavelengths Leisure Pool
& Library
DEPT SE8 ....144 D1
Waverley Industrial Estate
HRW HA1 ....42 D6
Waverley Lower
Secondary School
EDUL SE22 ....143 J6
Waverley School
PEND EN3 ....24 E6
Waxchandlers' Hall
CITYW EC2V 12 D3
Weald Middle School
KTN/HRWW/WS HA3 ....43 F3
Wealdstone Cemetery
KTN/HRWW/WS HA3 ....43 G6
Webster Graduate
Studies Center
CAMTN NW1 ....3 F6
Welbeck Clinic
CRICK NW2 ....82 E1
Welbourne Primary School
SEVS/STOTM N15 ....68 C1
Wellcome Institute
CAMTN NW1 ....4 C6
Welldon Park Middle School
RYLN/HDSTN HA2 ....78 C2
Wellesley Road ⊖
CROY/NA CR0 ....196 D6
Welling ≋
WELL DA16 ....148 B3
The Welling Clinic
WELL DA16 ....148 B3
Welling Medical Centre
WELL DA16 ....148 A5
Welling School
WELL DA16 ....148 A5
Wellington Arch
MYFR/PICC W1J 15 H2
Wellington Barracks
WESTW SW1E 16 B3
Wellington Primary School
BOW E3 ....105 J2
CHING E4 ....37 K4
HSLW TW3 ....134 E3
Welling United FC
WELL DA16 ....148 D4
Wells Primary School
WFD IG8 ....39 F6
Wembley Arena
WBLY HA9 ....80 C2
Wembley Central ≋ ⊖
WBLY HA9 ....80 A3
Wembley Commercial Centre
WBLY HA9 ....61 K6
Wembley Conference Centre
WBLY HA9 ....80 B2
Wembley FC
ALP/SUD HA0 ....79 H2
Wembley High
Technology College
ALP/SUD HA0 ....79 J1
Wembley Hospital
ALP/SUD HA0 ....79 K4
Wembley Park ⊖
WBLY HA9 ....80 C1
Wembley Park
Business Centre
WBLY HA9 ....80 D1
Wembley Primary School
WBLY HA9 ....80 A1
Wembley Stadium
WBLY HA9 ....80 C2
Wembley Stadium ≋
WBLY HA9 ....80 C2
Wembley Stadium
Industrial Estate
WBLY HA9 ....80 C2
WBLY HA9 ....80 E1
Wendell Park Primary School
SHB W12 ....118 C2
Wentworth Tutorial College
GLDGN NW11 ....64 B3
The Wernher Collection at
Ranger's House
GNWCH SE10 ....145 G2
Wesley's Chapel, House
& Museum
STLK EC1Y 6 E6
Wessex Gardens
Primary School
GLDGN NW11 ....64 C3
West 12 Shopping &
Leisure Centre
SHB W12 ....119 G2
West Acton ⊖
ACT W3 ....98 C5
West Acton Primary School
ACT W3 ....98 C5
West Beckton Health Centre
CAN/RD E16 ....107 G4
Westbourne Green
Sports Complex
BAY/PAD W2 ....100 D4
Westbourne Primary School
SUT SM1 ....208 D1
Westbridge College
BTSEA SW11 ....140 D2
West Brompton ≋ ⊖
ECT SW5 ....119 K5
Westbrooke School
WELL DA16 ....148 A4
The Westbury Hotel
CONDST W1S 9 K5
Westbury Medical Centre
WDGN N22 ....49 J5

Westcombe Park ≋
BKHTH/KID SE3 ....125 K5
Westcroft Leisure Centre
CAR SM5 ....210 A2
West Croydon ≋ ⊖ ⊖
CROY/NA CR0 ....196 D5
West Drayton ≋
WDR/YW UB7 ....112 B1
West Drayton Cemetery
WDR/YW UB7 ....112 B3
West Drayton
Primary School
WDR/YW UB7 ....112 B2
West Dulwich ≋
DUL SE21 ....162 E3
West Ealing ≋
WEA W13 ....97 H6
West Ealing Business Centre
WEA W13 ....97 G6
Western Avenue
Business Park
ACT W3 ....98 D3
Western
International Market
NWDGN UB2 ....114 A4
Western Trading Estate
WLSDN NW10 ....98 E3
West Ewell Infant School
HOR/WEW KT19 ....207 F3
Westferry ⊖
POP/IOD E14 ....105 H6
Westfield London
SHB W12 ....119 F1
Westfield Stratford City
development
SRTFD E15 ....88 A4
Westfields Primary School
BARN SW13 ....138 C3
West Finchley ⊖
FNCH N3 ....47 F2
Westgate Business Centre
NKENS W10 ....100 C3
Westgate Primary School
DART DA1 ....171 G2
West Green Primary School
SEVS/STOTM N15 ....67 J1
West Grove
Primary School
STHGT/OAK N14 ....34 D2
West Ham ≋ ⊖
SRTFD E15 ....106 C2
West Ham Church
Primary School
SRTFD E15 ....88 D6
West Ham Lane Clinic
SRTFD E15 ....88 C6
West Hampstead ≋ ⊖
KIL/WHAMP NW6 ....82 E4
West Hampstead
KIL/WHAMP NW6 ....83 F4
West Hampstead Medical Clinic
KIL/WHAMP NW6 ....82 E5
West Hampstead
Thameslink ≋
KIL/WHAMP NW6 ....82 E4
West Ham United FC
(Upton Park)
PLSTW E13 ....107 H1
West Harrow ⊖
HRW HA1 ....60 C3
West Hatch High School
WFD IG8 ....53 K1
West Hendon Clinic
CDALE/KGS NW9 ....63 H3
West Hill Primary School
DART DA1 ....171 F1
WAND/EARL SW18 ....139 K6
West India Pier
POP/IOD E14 ....124 C2
West India Quay ⊖
POP/IOD E14 ....105 J6
West India Shopping Centre
POP/IOD E14 ....124 D1
West Kensington ⊖
WKENS W14 ....119 J5
Westland Heliport
BTSEA SW11 ....140 C4
West Lea School
ED N9 ....36 A5
West Lodge Middle School
PIN HA5 ....59 H1
West Lodge Park Hotel
EBAR EN4 ....21 K1
West Lodge
Preparatory School
BFN/LL DA15 ....168 A5
West London Academy
NTHLT UB5 ....77 K1
West London
Academy Primary
NTHLT UB5 ....77 H5
West London Tamil School
NWDGN UB2 ....99 H1
West Mead Clinic
RSLP HA4 ....77 G5
West Middlesex Golf Club
STHL UB1 ....96 C6
West Middlesex
University Hospital
ISLW TW7 ....136 B3
Westminster ⊖
WHALL SW1A 17 F3
Westminster Abbey
WEST SW1P ....16 E
Westminster Abbey
Choir School
WEST SW1P ....16 E
Westminster Academy
BAY/PAD W2 ....100 E
Westminster Bridge Park
Plaza Hotel
STHWK SE1 ....17 C
Westminster
Business Square
LBTH SE11 ....122 A
Westminster Cathedral
WESTW SW1E ....16 A
Westminster Cathedral
Choir School
WEST SW1P ....16 E

Westminster Cathedral RC
Primary School
PIM SW1V 121 J5
Westminster City Hall
WESTW SW1E 16 B5
Westminster City School
WESTW SW1E 16 B5
Westminster Hall
WHALL SW1A 17 F3
Westminster Industrial Estate
WOOL/PLUM SE18 ....126 C3
Westminster
Kingsway College
CAMTN NW1 ....4 A5
WEST SW1P 16 B6
Westminster Natural
Health Centre
PIM SW1V 16 A7
Westminster Pier
WHALL SW1A 17 F3
Westminster School
WEST SW1P 16 A4
Westminster Theatre
WESTW SW1E 16 A4
Westminster Under School
WEST SW1P 16 C7
Westmoor Community Clinic
PUT/ROE SW15 ....158 D2
West Norwood ⇌ ⊖
WNWD SE27 ....162 C6
West Norwood Clinic
WNWD SE27 ....162 D4
West Norwood Crematorium
WNWD SE27 ....162 D5
West One Shopping Centre
MYFR/PKLN W1K 9 H4
Weston Green School
THDIT KT7 ....189 K5
Weston Park Clinic
CEND/HSY/T N8 ....66 E2
Weston Park Primary School
CEND/HSY/T N8 ....67 F2
Westpoint Trading Estate
ACT W3 ....98 D4
West Ramp Coach Park
HTHAIR TW6 ....132 D2
West Ruislip ⊖ ⇌
RSLP HA4 ....58 A6
West Silvertown ⊖
CAN/RD E16 ....125 K1
West Sutton ⇌
SUT SM1 ....208 E2
West Thames College
ISLW TW7 ....135 K2
West Thamesmead
Business Park
THMD SE28 ....128 A3
West Thornton
Primary School
CROY/NA CR0 ....196 A4
West Twyford Primary School
WLSDN NW10 ....98 C1
Westward Preparatory School
WOT/HER KT12 ....188 A6
Westway Business Centre
BAY/PAD W2 ....101 F4
Westway Sports Centre
NKENS W10 ....100 B5
West Wickham ⇌
WWKM BR4 ....199 F4
West Wickham
Swimming Baths
WWKM BR4 ....199 F5
West Wimbledon
Primary School
RYNPK SW20 ....176 E6
Westwood Language College
for Girls
NRWD SE19 ....180 D3
Westwood Primary School
WELL DA16 ....147 K5
Westwood School
BUSH WD23 ....
Wetherby
Preparatory School
NTGHL W11 ....100 E6
Whaddon House Clinic
CMBW SE5 ....143 F4
Whipps Cross Hospital
LEY E10 ....70 B3
Whitchurch Middle School
STAN HA7 ....43 J3
White Bridge Primary School
LOU IG10 ....39 J2
Whitechapel ⊖ ⊖
WCHPL E1 ....104 D4
Whitechapel Art Gallery
WCHPL E1 ....13 K3
Whitechapel Sports Centre
WCHPL E1 ....104 C4
White City ⊖
SHB W12 ....100 A6
Whitefield School
CRICK NW2 ....64 B4
Whitefield School &
Leisure Centre
WALTH E17 ....52 B4
Whitefriars First &
Middle School
KTN/HRWW/WS HA3 ....42 E5
Whitefriars Trading Estate
KTN/HRWW/WS HA3 ....42 D5
Whitehall Theatre
WHALL SW1A 10 D7
White Hart Lane ⇌
TOTM N17 ....50 B3
Whiteheath Junior School
RSLP HA4 ....58 A3
Whitehorse Manor
Primary School
THHTH CR7 ....196 E2
The White House
Preparatory School
BAL SW12 ....161 J3
Whiteleys Shopping Centre
BAY/PAD W2 ....101 F5
Whiterose Trading Estate
EBAR EN4 ....33 J2
Whitgift Almshouses
CROY/NA CR0 ....196 D6

Whitgift School
SAND/SEL CR2 ....211 J3
Whitgift Shopping Centre
CROY/NA CR0 ....196 D6
Whitings Hill Primary School
BAR EN5 ....20 A6
Whitmore High School
RYLN/HDSTN HA2 ....60 C5
Whitmore Primary School
IS N1 ....7 F2
Whittingham Community
Primary School
WALTH E17 ....51 G4
Whittington Hospital
ARCH N19 ....66 B6
Whitton ⇌
WHTN TW2 ....155 H2
Whitton Health Centre
WHTN TW2 ....155 H3
Whitton Health Clinic
WHTN TW2 ....155 G3
Whitton School
WHTN TW2 ....155 G3
Whitton Sports &
Fitness Centre
WHTN TW2 ....155 G4
Whybridge Infant School
RAIN RM13 ....93 J6
Whybridge Junior School
RAIN RM13 ....93 H6
Wickham Theatre
WWKM BR4 ....214 B1
Wide Way Health Clinic
MTCM CR4 ....179 J6
Widmore Centre
BMLY BR1 ....184 B5
Wigmore Hall
CAVSQ/HST W1G 9 J3
Wigram House (University
of Westminster)
WEST SW1P 16 C5
Wilberforce Primary School
NKENS W10 ....100 C2
Wilbury Primary School
UED N18 ....49 K1
Willesden Centre for Health
& Care
WLSDN NW10 ....81 J5
Willesden Green ⊖
CRICK NW2 ....82 A4
Willesden Junction ⊖ ⇌ ⊖
WLSDN NW10 ....99 H1
Willesden Medical Centre
CRICK NW2 ....81 K4
Willesden New Cemetery
WLSDN NW10 ....81 H5
Willesden Sports Centre
WLSDN NW10 ....81 K6
Willesden Sports Stadium
WLSDN NW10 ....81 K6
William Bellamy J & I School
DAGE RM10 ....74 C6
William Byrd School
HYS/HAR UB3 ....113 F6
William Davies
Primary School
FSTGT E7 ....89 H4
William Ellis School
KTTN NW5 ....84 A1
William Ellis Sports Ground
EDGW HA8 ....44 C4
William Ford CE
Junior School
DAGE RM10 ....92 C5
William Hogarth School
CHSWK W4 ....118 B6
William Morris Academy
HMSMTH W6 ....119 G5
William Morris Gallery
WALTH E17 ....51 J6
William Morris
Primary School
MTCM CR4 ....179 J6
William Morris School
WALTH E17 ....51 G4
William Patten
Primary School
STNW/STAM N16 ....68 B4
William Torbitt J & I School
GNTH/NBYPK IG2 ....72 E2
William Tyndale
Primary School
IS N1 ....85 H5
Willington School
WIM/MER SW19 ....177 J3
Willow Brook Primary
LEY E10 ....69 J5
Willow Business Centre
MTCM CR4 ....194 E2
Willow Business Park
SYD SE26 ....163 K5
Willowfield Adult
Education Centre
WALTH E17 ....51 F6
Willowfield School
WALTH E17 ....51 G6
The Willows Clinic
CHST BR7 ....185 F2
The Willows School
YEAD UB4 ....95 H3
Willow Tree Primary School
NTHLT UB5 ....77 J4
Wilmington
Entreprise College
RDART DA2 ....170 D5
Wilmington Grammar School
for Boys
RDART DA2 ....170 E4
Wilmington Grammar School
for Girls
RDART DA2 ....170 E4
Wilmington
Primary School
RDART DA2 ....170 E5
Wilson's School
WLGTN SM6 ....210 E4
Wimbledon ⇌ ⊖ ⊖
WIM/MER SW19 ....177 J2
Wimbledon Chase ⇌
RYNPK SW20 ....177 H5

Wimbledon Chase
Primary School
RYNPK SW20 ....177 H4
Wimbledon Common
Golf Club
WIM/MER SW19 ....176 E1
Wimbledon Common
Pre-Preparatory School
WIM/MER SW19 ....177 G3
Wimbledon (Gap
Road) Cemetery
WIM/MER SW19 ....160 A6
Wimbledon High School
WIM/MER SW19 ....177 H2
Wimbledon House School
WIM/MER SW19 ....177 J4
Wimbledon Lawn
Tennis Museum
WIM/MER SW19 ....159 H5
Wimbledon Park ⊖
WIM/MER SW19 ....159 K5
Wimbledon Park
Athletics Track
WIM/MER SW19 ....159 J4
Wimbledon Park Golf Club
WIM/MER SW19 ....159 J5
Wimbledon Park
Primary School
WIM/MER SW19 ....159 K4
Wimbledon Recreation Centre
WIM/MER SW19 ....178 A2
Wimbledon RFC
RYNPK SW20 ....176 C3
Wimbledon School of Art
WIM/MER SW19 ....177 H4
Wimbledon Squash &
Badminton Club
WIM/MER SW19 ....177 H3
Wimbledon Stadium
WIM/MER SW19 ....160 A6
Wimbledon Stadium
Business Centre
WIM/MER SW19 ....160 A5
Wimbledon Theatre
WIM/MER SW19 ....177 K3
Wimbledon Windmill
WIM/MER SW19 ....159 F5
Winchcombe Business Centre
PECK SE15 ....123 F6
Winchmore Hill ⇌
WCHMH N21 ....35 H2
Winchmore Hill Klinic
WCHMH N21 ....35 H5
Winchmore Hill CC
WCHMH N21 ....35 J3
Winchmore School
WCHMH N21 ....35 J4
Windmill Business Centre
NWDGN UB2 ....115 H1
Windmill Trading Estate
MTCM CR4 ....195 H2
Windrush Primary School
THMD SE28 ....128 C1
Winfield House
CAMTN NW1 ....2 D4
Wingate & Finchley FC
NFNCH/WDSPK N12 ....47 H3
Wingate Trading Estate
TOTM N17 ....50 B3
Wingfield Primary School
BKHTH/KID SE3 ....145 K4
Winns Primary School
WALTH E17 ....51 H5
Winsor Primary School
EHAM E6 ....108 A5
Winston Churchill's Britain at
War Experience
STHWK SE1 ....19 F1
Winston House
Preparatory School
SWFD E18 ....52 E4
Winston Way Primary School
IL IG1 ....90 A1
Winterbourne Infant School
THHTH CR7 ....196 B1
Winton Primary School
IS N1 ....5 G3
Witley Industrial Estate
NWDGN UB2 ....114 E4
Wolf Fields Primary School
NWDGN UB2 ....114 E4
Wolfson Hillel
Primary School
STHGT/OAK N14 ....34 D1
Wolfson Medical Centre
RYNPK SW20 ....176 D3
Wolsey Business Park
WATW WD18 ....26 B2
Wolsey Junior School
CROY/NA CR0 ....214 B5
The Women's Library
WCHPL E1 ....13 J3
The Woodberry Clinic
MUSWH N10 ....48 B6
Woodberry Down Centre
FSBYPK N4 ....67 J5
Woodberry Down
Community Primary
FSBYPK N4 ....67 J4
Woodbridge High School &
Language College
WFD IG8 ....53 F3
Woodcroft Primary School
EDGW HA8 ....45 F3
Wood End J & I Schools
GFD/PVL UB6 ....78 D3
Wood End Park Junior School
UX/CGN UB8 ....94 A6
Woodfield School
CDALE/KGS NW9 ....65 G5
Woodford ⊖
WFD IG8 ....53 F2
Woodford County High
School Girls
WFD IG8 ....52 D2
Woodford Golf Club
WFD IG8 ....52 D1
Woodford Green
Preparatory School
WFD IG8 ....52 E2

Woodford Green
Primary School
WFD IG8 ....52 D1
Woodford Trading Estate
WFD IG8 ....53 G5
Woodgrange Infant School
FSTGT E7 ....89 F2
Woodgrange Park ⇌
FSTGT E7 ....89 H3
Woodgrange Park Cemetery
MNPK E12 ....89 H3
Wood Green ⊖
WDGN N22 ....49 G5
Wood Green Health Centre
WDGN N22 ....49 F4
Wood Green Old Boys FC
WDGN N22 ....49 G3
Woodhall School
OXHEY WD19 ....27 J6
Woodhill Primary School
CHARL SE7 ....126 D4
Woodhouse College
NFNCH/WDSPK N12 ....47 H2
Woodlands First &
Middle School
KTN/HRWW/WS HA3 ....42 C3
Woodlands J & I School
IL IG1 ....90 D2
Woodlands Medical Centre
LEW SE13 ....165 G1
Wood Lane ⊖
SHB W12 ....100 A6
Wood Lane Medical Centre
RSLP HA4 ....58 C5
Wood Lane School
FUL/PGN SW6 ....140 B2
Wood Lane Sports Centre
BCTR RM8 ....74 D5
Woodmansterne
Primary School
STRHM/NOR SW16 ....179 J4
Woodridge Primary School
NFNCH/WDSPK N12 ....32 E5
Woodside ⊖
SNWD SE25 ....197 J5
Woodside Health Centre
SNWD SE25 ....197 J2
Woodside High School
WDGN N22 ....49 H3
Woodside Infant School
CROY/NA CR0 ....197 H4
Woodside Park ⊖
NFNCH/WDSPK N12 ....32 E6
Woodside Park Golf Club
NFNCH/WDSPK N12 ....32 E6
Woodside Park
International School
NFNCH/WDSPK N12 ....33 F6
Woodside Primary School
WALTH E17 ....52 A6
Woodside School
BELV DA17 ....129 H4
Wood Street ⇌
WALTH E17 ....70 B1
Wood Wharf
POP/IOD E14 ....124 E1
Wood Wharf Business Park
POP/IOD E14 ....125 F2
Woolmore Primary School
POP/IOD E14 ....106 A6
Woolwich Arsenal ⇌ ⊖
WOOL/PLUM SE18 ....127 G4
Woolwich Cemetery
WOOL/PLUM SE18 ....148 A1
Woolwich Dockyard ⇌
WOOL/PLUM SE18 ....126 E4
Woolwich Polytechnic School
THMD SE28 ....128 B1
Worcester Park ⇌
WPK KT4 ....192 D5
Worcesters Primary School
ENC/FH EN2 ....24 B1
World Business
Centre Heathrow
HTHAIR TW6 ....133 F2
World Rugby Museum
& Twickenham
Stadium Tours
WHTN TW2 ....155 K1
Worlds End Place
WBPTN SW10 ....140 B1
World Spiritual University
WLSDN NW10 ....81 J5
World University Service
STLK EC1Y 6 E7
Wormholt Park
Primary School
SHB W12 ....99 J6
Worple Primary School
ISLW TW7 ....136 B5
Worsley Bridge Junior School
BECK BR3 ....182 D3
Worton Hall
Industrial Estate
ISLW TW7 ....135 K5
Wren Academy
NFNCH/WDSPK N12 ....47 H1
Wrencote House
CROY/NA CR0 ....211 J1
Wyborne Primary School
ELTH/MOT SE9 ....167 G3
Wyke Green Golf Club
ISLW TW7 ....116 A6
Wykeham Primary School
WLSDN NW10 ....81 H1
Wyndham Grand Hotel
WBPTN SW10 ....140 B2
Wyndhams Theatre
CHCR WC2N 10 D5
Wyvil Primary School
VX/NE SW8 ....141 K1
Yale University Press
HAMP NW3 ....83 J2
Yardley Primary School
CHING E4 ....37 K1
Yeading FC
YEAD UB4 ....114 B1
Yeading Junior School
YEAD UB4 ....95 G4

Yeading Medical Centre
NTHLT UB5 ....95 G2
Yeading Primary School
YEAD UB4 ....95 G4
Yerbury Primary School
ARCH N19 ....84 D1
Yeshivo Horomo
Talmudical College
STNW/STAM N16 ....67 K5
Yesodey Hatorah Jewish
Boys School
SEVS/STOTM N15 ....68 B4
Yesodey Hatorah School
For Girls
STNW/STAM N16 ....68 B4
Yetev Lev Day School
for Boys
STNW/STAM N16 ....68 C5
Yiewsley Health Centre
WDR/YW UB7 ....112 B1
YMCA Leisure Centre
RSQ WC1B 10 D3
York Clinic
STHWK SE1 ....18 E1
York Hall
BETH E2 ....104 D1
York Road Junior School &
Language Unit
DART DA1 ....171 J2
York Water Gate
CHCR WC2N 11 F7
Young Actors Theatre
IS N1 ....5 J1
Young England RFC
VX/NE SW8 ....142 A1
Young Vic Theatre
STHWK SE1 ....17 K2
Zennor Road Industrial Estate
BAL SW12 ....161 K3
Zephyr Business Centre
SEVS/STOTM N15 ....68 A1
The Zetter Hotel
FARR EC1M 6 A7
Ziam Trading Estate
CLPT E5 ....68 E5
ZSL London Zoo
CAMTN NW1 ....3 G2

Schools address data provided by Education Direct.

Petrol station information supplied by Johnsons.

Garden centre information provided by:

Garden Centre Association Britains best garden centres

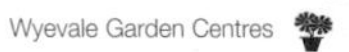

Wyevale Garden Centres

The boundary of the London Congestion Charging Zone and Low Emission Zone supplied by Transport for London

The statement on the front cover of this atlas is sourced, selected and quoted
from a reader comment and feedback form received in 2004

Camera   GPS   Congestion
Warning   Information   Charge

RoadPilot is the UK's pioneer and market leader in GPS (Global Positioning System) road safety technologies and the developer of one of the largest and most accurate databases of speed camera locations in the UK and Europe. It has provided the speed camera information in this atlas.

RoadPilot's latest speed camera location system is now available on your mobile phone. It improves road safety by alerting you to the location of accident black spots and fixed and mobile camera sites, and is completely legal.

RoadPilot **mobile** enables you to always have the very latest data of fixed and mobile sites on your mobile phone without having to connect it to your computer.

Updates are available automatically.

There is also the facility to report new data that will be shared with the RoadPilot community.

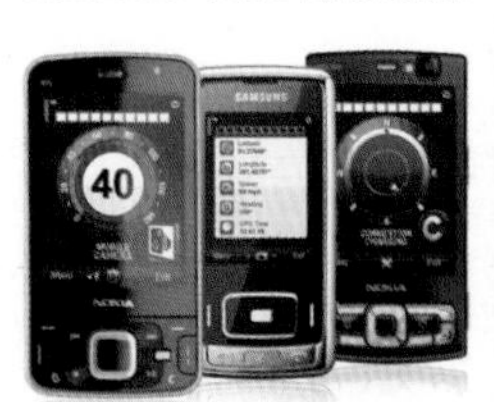

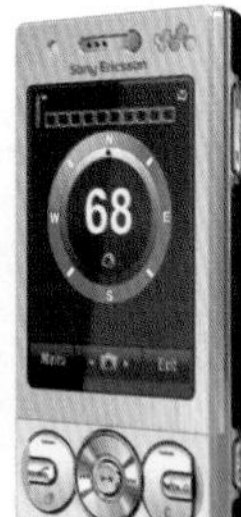

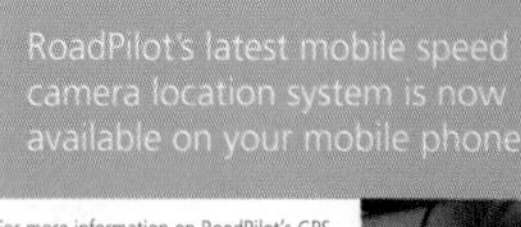

RoadPilot's latest mobile speed camera location system is now available on your mobile phone.

For more information on RoadPilot's GPS road safety products and a list of compatible phones, please visit **www.roadpilot.com** or telephone 0870 240 1701.

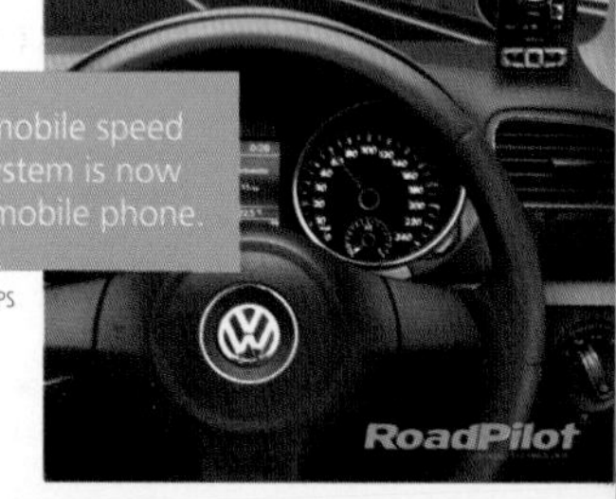

AA **Street by Street** QUESTIONNAIRE

Dear Atlas User
Your comments, opinions and recommendations are very important to us.
So please help us to improve our street atlases by taking a few minutes
to complete this simple questionnaire.

You do not need a stamp (unless posted outside the UK). If you do not want to remove
this page from your street atlas, then photocopy it or write your answers on a plain sheet
of paper.

Send to: Marketing Assistant, AA Publishing, 14th Floor Fanum House,
Freepost SCE 4598, Basingstoke RG21 4GY

ABOUT THE ATLAS...

Please state which city / town / county you bought:

_____

Where did you buy the atlas? (City, Town, County)

_____

For what purpose? (please tick all applicable)

To use in your local area ☐   **To use on business or at work** ☐

Visiting a strange place ☐   **In the car** ☐   **On foot** ☐

Other (please state)

_____

Have you ever used any street atlases other than AA Street by Street?

Yes ☐   No ☐

If so, which ones?

_____

Is there any aspect of our street atlases that could be improved?
(Please continue on a separate sheet if necessary)

_____
_____
_____

Please list the features you found most useful:

_____
_____
_____

Please list the features you found least useful:

_____
_____
_____

LOCAL KNOWLEDGE...

Local knowledge is invaluable. Whilst every attempt has been made to make the information contained in this atlas as accurate as possible, should you notice any inaccuracies, please detail them below (if necessary, use a blank piece of paper) or e-mail us at *streetbystreet@theAA.com*

_____
_____
_____

ABOUT YOU...

Name (Mr/Mrs/Ms) _____

Address _____

_____ **Postcode** _____

Daytime tel no _____

E-mail address _____

Which age group are you in?

Under 25 ☐ **25-34** ☐ **35-44** ☐ **45-54** ☐ **55-64** ☐ **65+** ☐

Are you an AA member?   YES ☐   NO ☐

Do you have Internet access?   YES ☐   NO ☐

_____

Thank you for taking the time to complete this questionnaire. Please send it to us as soon as possible, and remember, you do not need a stamp (unless posted outside the UK).

We may use information we hold about you to, telephone or email you about other products and services offered by the AA, we do NOT disclose this information to third parties.

Please tick here if you do not wish to hear about products and services from the AA. ☐